The Bedford
INTRODUCTION TO
LITERATURE

The Bedford
INTRODUCTION TO
LITERATURE

Third Edition

MICHAEL MEYER
University of Connecticut

BEDFORD BOOKS OF ST. MARTIN'S PRESS

BOSTON

For Bedford Books

Publisher: Charles H. Christensen
Associate Publisher/General Manager: Joan E. Feinberg
Managing Editor: Elizabeth M. Schaaf
Developmental Editor: Karen S. Henry
Production Editor: Tara L. Masih
Copyeditor: Dan Otis
Text Design: Sandra Rigney, The Book Department, Inc.
Cover Design: Hannus Design Associates
Cover Art: Festa del Redentore, ca. 1899, by Maurice Brazil Prendergast. Watercolor and pencil on paper, 11″ × 17″. Williams College Museum of Art, Massachusetts. Gift of Mrs. Charles Prendergast (91.18.5).

Library of Congress Catalog Card Number: 92–52518

Manufactured in the United States of America.
7 6 5 4 3
f   e   d

For information, write: St. Martin's Press, Inc.
175 Fifth Avenue, New York, NY 10010

Editorial Offices: Bedford Books of St. Martin's Press
29 Winchester Street, Boston, MA 02116

ISBN: 0–312–06546–9

Acknowledgments

FICTION

Isabel Allende. "The Judge's Wife," reprinted with the permission of Athaneum Publishers, an imprint of Macmillan Publishing Company, from *The Stories of Eva Luna* by Isabel Allende, translated from the Spanish by Margaret Sayers Peden. Copyright © 1989 by Isabel Allende. English translation copyright © 1991 by Macmillan Publishing Company.

Margaret Atwood. "Death by Landscape" from *Wilderness Tips* by Margaret Atwood. Copyright © 1991 by O. W. Toad Limited. Used by permission of Doubleday, a Division of Bantam Doubleday Dell Publishing Group, Inc., and Canadian Publishers McClelland and Stewart, Toronto.

A. L. Bader. "Nothing Happens in Modern Short Stories," excerpt from "The Structure of the Modern Story," *College English*, November 1945. Copyright © 1945 by the National Council of Teachers of English. Reprinted with permission.

Toni Cade Bambara. "The Lesson" from *Gorilla, My Love* by Toni Cade Bambara. Copyright © 1972 by Toni Cade Bambara. Reprinted by permission of Random House, Inc.

Paul Barolsky. "Gretta's Name," excerpt from *James Joyce Quarterly* (Winter 1991, pp. 519–20). Copyright © 1991 by the University of Tulsa. Reprinted by permission.

John Barth. "On Minimalist Fiction" from "A Few Words about Minimalism" by John Barth, December 28, 1986, the *New York Times.* Copyright © 1986 by the New York Times Company. Reprinted by permission.

Warren Beck. "On Frank as Savior in Eveline" from *Joyce's Dubliners: Substance, Vision, and Art* by Warren Beck. Duke University Press, Durham, 1969. Reprinted with permission of the publisher.

Mody C. Boatright. "A Typical Western Plot Formula" from "The Formula in Cowboy Fiction and Drama," *Western Folklore* 28 (April 1969). Reprinted by permission of the California Folklore Society.

Elizabeth Bowen. "The Writer's Roving Eye" from *Afterthoughts.* © Elizabeth Bowen 1962. Reproduced by permission of Curtis Brown, London.

Matthew C. Brennan. "Point of View and Plotting in Chekhov's and Oates's 'The Lady with the Pet Dog'" excerpted from "Plotting against Chekhov: Joyce Carol Oates and 'The Lady with the Pet Dog'" in *Notes on Modern American Literature* (Winter 1985). Reprinted by permission of the author.

Cleanth Brooks and Robert Penn Warren. "Point of View in 'Araby'" from *Understanding Fiction,* 3e, © 1979, pp. 127–28. Reprinted by permission of Prentice Hall, Englewood Cliffs, New Jersey.

Edgar Rice Burroughs. Excerpt from *Tarzan of the Apes* by Edgar Rice Burroughs. Copyright © 1912 by Frank A. Munsey Company, used by permission of Edgar Rice Burroughs, Inc.

Raymond Carver. "Popular Mechanics" from *What We Talk about When We Talk about Love* by Raymond Carver. Copyright © 1981 by Raymond Carver. Reprinted by permission of Alfred A. Knopf, Inc.

Anton Chekhov. "The Lady with the Pet Dog" from *The Portable Chekhov* edited by Avrahm Yarmolinsky. Copyright 1947, 1968 by Viking Penguin, Inc. Renewed copyright © 1975 by Avrahm Yarmolinsky. Used by permission of Viking Penguin, a division of Penguin Books USA Inc.

John Cheever. "Reunion" from *The Stories of John Cheever.* Copyright © 1962 by John Cheever. Reprinted by permission of Alfred A. Knopf, Inc. "John Cheever Interview (On Morals in Fiction)" from *Writers at Work, Fifth Series* edited by George

Acknowledgments and copyrights are continued at the back of the book on pages 2089–2097, which constitute an extension of the copyright page.

For My Wife
Regina Barreca

Preface for Instructors

Like its predecessors, the third edition of *The Bedford Introduction to Literature* reflects the assumptions that understanding enhances the enjoyment of literature and that reading literature offers a valuable and unique means of apprehending life in its richness and diversity. The book also reflects the hope that the selections included will encourage students to become lifelong readers of imaginative literature. Designed to accommodate a variety of teaching styles, the collection of 51 stories (17 of them new to the third edition), 414 poems (111 of them new), and 19 plays (5 of them new) represents a wide range of periods, nationalities, and voices. Each selection has been carefully chosen for its appeal to students today and for its usefulness in demonstrating the effects, significance, and pleasures of literature.

Again, like its predecessors, the third edition of *The Bedford Introduction to Literature* is designed for the introductory course as it is taught today, which varies — from school to school and from instructor to instructor — more than ever before. Even the traditional course emphasizing the elements of literature and a broad range of works from the Western canon is changing in response to important developments in literary studies and, more generally, in higher education and in American society. The course is now viewed by many teachers as a rich opportunity to supplement classics of Western literature with the work of writers previously excluded from the traditional canon. Increasingly, it now also serves as an introduction to the discipline of literary study, a challenging development which brings to the undergraduate classroom important trends in literary theory and provocative new readings of both familiar and unfamiliar texts. Finally, and perhaps most often, the introduction to literature course is now also taught as a second course in composition in which the critical thinking and writing that students do are as important as the reading that they do. The third edition of *The Bedford Introduction to Literature* responds to these developments with distinctive features that address the needs of instructors who teach a traditional course but who are also concerned about canonical issues, literary theory, and writing about literature.

Selected Major Authors Treated in Depth

The book includes for each genre chapters focusing on two or more major figures. There are four stories each by Nathaniel Hawthorne, James Joyce, and Flannery O'Connor; an extensive selection of poems by John Keats, Emily Dickinson, and Robert Frost; and two plays by Sophocles and three by Shakespeare. Substantial introductions provide useful biographical and critical information about each of these important writers. A selection of "Perspectives" — excerpts from letters, journals, and critical commentaries — follows each writer's works to provide a context for discussion and writing. In addition, "Considerations for Critical Thinking and Writing" follow both selections and "Perspectives"; these questions for discussion or writing encourage critical thinking and provide stimulating opportunities for student essays.

New to this edition are in-depth treatments of Joyce and Dickinson, chronologies summarizing important dates for the eight major writers featured, and "Two Complementary Critical Readings" on a particular work by each of the eight authors. These critical readings offer students examples of the variety of approaches they can take in reading and writing about literature. The two readings on Hawthorne, for instance, focus on feminist and psychological approaches to "The Birthmark." By reading commentaries by two critics who argue competing ideas about one text or who illuminate different aspects of that text, students can see immediately that there is no single way to read a work of literature, an important and necessary step for learning how to formulate their own critical approaches in their essays.

Albums of Contemporary and World Literature

For each genre an album of contemporary selections offers some of the most interesting and lively stories, poems, and plays published in the last ten years, including works by Margaret Atwood, Gish Jen, Fay Weldon, Amy Clampitt, Galway Kinnell, Sharon Olds, August Wilson, David Henry Hwang, and Wendy Wasserstein. Biographical information about the album authors is now included in the text in order to introduce instructors and students to these important but, perhaps, unfamiliar writers.

In addition, albums of world literature in each genre section offer students a sampling of stories, poems, and plays from other cultures, including the work of Isabel Allende (Chilean), Yukio Mishima (Japanese), Tatyana Tolstaya (Russian), Claribel Alegría (Salvadoran), Tomas Transtromer (Swedish), Muhammad al-Maghut (Syrian), and Wole Soyinka (Nigerian), among many others. Over half the stories and over a third of the poems and plays in this edition are by women and minority writers and writers from other cultures.

"Connections to Other Selections" consist of questions that link the selections in the albums of contemporary and world literature to more traditional selections in the text. For example, August Wilson's *Fences* is linked with Arthur Miller's *Death of a Salesman* and Ralph Ellison's "Battle Royal," while Wole Soyinka's play *The Strong Breed* is connected to *Oedipus the King*. These questions provide engaging writing opportunities and provocative topics for class discussion. "Connections to Other Selections" questions also appear after many of the works in the chapters on the elements of fiction, poetry, and drama.

Perspectives on Literature

This popular feature has been expanded in ways that make the third edition's "Perspectives" — journal notes, letters, classic and contemporary theoretical essays, interviews, and student responses — even more useful for class discussion and student writing. "Perspectives" are included in five different places in the text: in the chapters treating major authors in depth; in a chapter-length collection at the end of each genre section; in the three new "Critical Case Study" chapters focusing on a particular work in each genre; at the end of Chapter 35, on literary theory; and, finally, throughout the text's discussion chapters. Individual "Perspectives" in these chapters follow the works to which they refer and, in many cases, discuss a literary work in terms of the element of literature for which it serves as an illustration. Not only does the third edition significantly increase the number of "Perspectives" but, more importantly, it also integrates them throughout the book in new ways to teach students how to think critically and write effectively about literature. For example, the new "Critical Case Study" chapter in each genre section gathers four critical "Perspectives" about a single work — such as T. S. Eliot's "The Love Song of J. Alfred Prufrock" — in order to illustrate the variety of approaches available to students. The questions following these readings guide students to analyze the assumptions behind a particular approach and thus help them to think critically.

Focus on Critical Reading and Thinking

To further encourage critical reading and thinking, discussions of how to read imaginative literature appear at the beginning of each genre section. They offer practical advice about the kinds of questions active readers ask themselves as they read. In addition, Chapter 35 on "Critical Strategies for Reading" deepens the introductory discussions of active reading by focusing on the different reading strategies employed by contemporary literary theorists. This chapter, which can be assigned at any point in the course, introduces students to eight major contemporary theoretical approaches — formalist, biographical, psychological, historical, sociological (including Marxist and feminist strategies), mythological, reader-response, and deconstructionist. In brief examples the approaches are applied in analyzing Kate Chopin's "The Story of an Hour," as well as other works, so that students will have a sense of how to use these strategies in their own reading and writing. A selected bibliography for the approaches and a set of "Perspectives" by contemporary literary critics conclude this unique chapter.

Although the emphasis in this text is on critical reading and understanding rather than on critical terminology, terms such as *symbol, irony,* and *metaphor* are defined and illustrated to equip students with a basic working vocabulary for discussing and writing about literature. When first defined in the text, these terms appear in boldface type. An "Index of Terms" appears inside the back cover of the book for easy reference.

Writing about Literature

The book's concern with helping students write about literature is pervasive. The chapters treating major figures in depth, the albums of contemporary and world literature, the "Connections to Other Selections" questions, the "Perspectives," and each "Critical Case Study" all offer intriguing writing opportunities. To provoke students' interest, sharpen their thinking, and help them improve their writing skills, the number and variety of writing assignments have been increased throughout the third edition. "Considerations for Critical Thinking and Writing" (questions and suggestions useful for class discussion or writing assignments) accompany virtually every selection in the discussion chapters and all the "Perspectives." In addition to the assignments, the expanded final section of the book on "Critical Thinking and Writing" offers a practical discussion of writing about literature, including advice about how to read a work closely, take notes, and develop a topic into a thesis. A new section on "Arguing about Literature" discusses how arguments on literary topics can be generated and made persuasive. A list of questions based on the critical approaches covered in the chapter on "Critical Strategies for Reading" helps students to discover the significant issues regarding a short story, poem, or play that may be arguable. Furthermore, an annotated list of important reference sources for literary research is provided. There is also useful information on revising and editing a paper. Student examples illustrate the entire process and offer concrete models of the different types of papers usually assigned in an introductory course, including explication, analysis, and comparison-contrast. A detailed chapter on the literary research paper, with a student example, concludes the section. In short, the integrated coverage of critical reading and thinking enables students to master the critical strategies necessary for writing with confidence about literary experiences.

Connections between "Popular" and "Literary" Culture

As in previous editions, *The Bedford Introduction to Literature,* Third Edition, features introductions to each genre section that draw on carefully chosen examples from popular culture to explain the elements of the genre, inviting students to make connections between what they already know and what they will encounter in subsequent selections. Comparisons between popular culture and more canonical literary selections offer excellent writing opportunities, and suggestions are provided after each popular culture example. The examples include excerpts from a romance novel and from *Tarzan of the Apes,* greeting card verse and Tracy Chapman's "Fast Car," and scenes from a television script for *Northern Exposure.*

Resources for Teaching *The Bedford Introduction to Literature,* Third Edition

This thorough and practical instructor's manual — now nearly 500 pages long and spiral bound — discusses virtually every selection and suggests answers to the questions posed in the text, along with providing additional questions and writing assignments. The manual also offers questions and writing assignments for the selections in the collection chapter at the end of each genre section. It includes biographical information for authors whose backgrounds are not discussed in the text and offers selected bibliographies for authors treated in depth, as well as a bibliography of articles on teaching literature. Finally, the manual gives several suggestions for thematic units and provides an annotated list of videos, films, and recordings related to the works of literature in the text.

Classic and Contemporary Poems

An audiotape of poetry selections from the book is available to instructors who adopt *The Bedford Introduction to Literature.* Poems linked by "Connections to Other Selections" questions are read together to offer an added resource for class discussion. In addition, the tape features the work of poets treated in depth (Keats, Dickinson, and Frost); poems that serve as good examples of the elements of poetry discussed in the book; and, finally, a rich selection of classic and contemporary poems.

Acknowledgments

This book has benefited from the ideas, suggestions, and corrections of scores of careful readers who helped transform various stages of an evolving manuscript into a finished book and into subsequent editions. I remain grateful to those I have thanked in previous prefaces, particularly Robert Wallace of Case Western Reserve University. In addition, many instructors who used the second edition of *The Bedford Introduction to Literature* responded to a questionnaire on the book. For their valuable comments and advice I am grateful to Janet Abramson, Lansing Community College; Helen J. Aling, Northwestern College; Barbara Barnard, Hunter College, CUNY; Claudia A. Basha, Victor Valley College; Srileka Bell, University of New Haven; Stephen Benz, Barry University; Paul R. Brandt, Kent State University; Sister Anne Denise Brennan, College of Mount St. Vincent; Jon C. Burton, Northern Virginia Community College; Laura L. Bush, Ricks College; Ruth A. Cameron, Eastern Nazarene College; J. Rocky Colavito, Central Arizona College/Winkelman; Debra Conner, West Virginia University/Parkersburg; Janice Reynolds

Cooke, University of New Orleans; Joan Kuzma Costello, Inver Hills Community College; Albert C. DeCiccio, Merrimack College; Emeric DeLuca, Harrisburg Area Community College; George Dennis, Southeastern Illinois College; Brian Dillon, Eastern Montana College; Paul M. Dombrowski, Ohio University; Olivia Carr Edenfield, Georgia Southern University; David L. Elliott, Keystone Junior College; Audrey Elwood, Merritt College; James P. Erickson, Wichita State University; Irene R. Fairley, Northeastern University; Jacqueline Fuller, University of Southern Maine; Marshall Bruce Gentry, University of Indianapolis; Christopher Golden, Kennesaw State College; Rosalie Hewitt, Northern Illinois University; M. Jean Jones, Columbia State Community College; AnnLouise Keating, Eastern New Mexico University; Carolyn Kipnis, Montgomery County Community College; Bernard M. Knab, Chemeketa Community College; Robert S. Kunzinger, Tidewater Community College; Dr. Harvey Lehman, La Guardia Community College; G. T. Lenard, Stockton State College; Marcia P. Lin; Edgar J. Lovelady, Grace College; Sandra Marshburn, West Virginia State College; John J. McKenna, University of Nebraska/Omaha; Chris McKinnon, Lansing Community College; Gayle H. Miller, Western Carolina University; Scott Moncrieff, Andrews University; Janice T. Moore, Young Harris College; Dr. Michael Olendzenski, Cape Cod Community College; Richard J. Panofsky, University of Massachusetts/N. Dartmouth; Christopher M. Patterson, Iona College, Adelphi University; Richard A. Peacock, Birmingham-Southern College; Julie Pember, University of Rhode Island; Timothy K. Rice, University of Toledo; David Schelhaas, Dordt College; Allen Schwab, Washington University; Susan Seyfarth, Valdosta State College; Margaret C. Sims, Delta State University; Dennis P. Slattery, Incarnate Word College; Ernest Smith, University of Central Florida; Marianne Taylor, Fullerton College; Pamela Thoma, Colorado State University; Dr. Larry Thompson, Ricks College; Marilyn Price Voss, Western Illinois University; William B. Watterson, Lees-McRae College; Thomas A. Westerfield, University of Northern Iowa; Brett Westbrook; Isabelle White, Eastern Kentucky University; Andrew Woolf, Northern Essex Community College; and Karen Wunsch, Queensboro College.

I am also indebted to those who cheerfully answered questions and generously provided miscellaneous bits of information. What might have seemed to them like inconsequential conversations turned out to be important leads. Among these friends and colleagues are Raymond Anselment, Ann Charters, Irving Cummings, William Curtin, Herbert Goldstone, Patrick Hogan, Lee Jacobus, Greta Little, George Monteiro, William Moynihan, Brenda Murphy, Joel Myerson, Thomas Recchio, William Sheidley, Milton Stern, Kenneth Wilson, Joseph Zornado, and the dedicated reference librarians at the Homer Babbidge Library, University of Connecticut.

I continue to be grateful for what I have learned from my students as I have taught them. I am particularly grateful to Monica Casis, who provided a student paper for *The Bedford Introduction to Literature*. (The other student samples, indebted to the many student papers I have received over the years, were constructed to serve as good and accessible models of student writing.) I am also indebted to Christine Francis and Anne Phillips for their extensive work on the third edition of *Resources for Teaching the Bedford Introduction to Literature,* and to J. Michael O'Neill for writing the manual entry for *Hamlet.*

At Bedford Books, my debts once again require more time to acknowledge than the deadline allows. Charles H. Christensen and Joan Feinberg initiated this project and launched it with their intelligence, energy, and sound advice. Karen Henry tirelessly steered this as well as earlier editions through rough as well as becalmed moments; her work was as first-rate as it was essential. Kathy Retan oversaw the revision of *Resources for Teaching the Bedford Introduction to Literature* with clear-headedness and perseverance. The difficult tasks of production were skillfully managed by Tara L. Masih. (I also thank Jonathan Burns and Andrea Goldman for their assistance with these tasks.) Dan Otis provided careful copyediting, Martha Stearns did more than meticulous proofreading, and Ed Freedman cheerfully assisted her when the schedule became tight. Ellen Kuhl deftly arranged the permissions, and all the people at Bedford Books — including Laura McCready, George Scribner, Donna Lee Dennison, David Gibbs, and Kim Chabot — helped to make this enormous project a manageable one.

Finally, I am grateful to my sons Timothy and Matthew for all kinds of help, but mostly I'm just grateful they're my sons. And for making all the difference, I dedicate this book to my wife, Regina Barreca.

Brief Contents

Contents

POETRY   585

13. Reading Poetry   587

14. Word Choice, Word Order, and Tone   618

25. Perspectives on Poetry   1061

DRAMA   1079

26. Reading Drama   1081

27. A Study of Sophocles   1113

The Bedford
INTRODUCTION TO
LITERATURE

INTRODUCTION

Reading
Imaginative Literature

THE NATURE OF LITERATURE

Literature does not lend itself to a single tidy definition, because the making of it over the centuries has been as complex, unwieldy, and natural as life itself. Is literature everything that is written, from ancient prayers to graffiti? Does it include songs and stories that were not written down until many years after they were recited? Does literature include the television scripts from *The Cosby Show* as well as Shakespeare's *King Lear?* Is literature only that which has permanent value and continues to move people? Must literature be true or beautiful or moral? Should it be socially useful?

Although these kinds of questions are not conclusively answered in this book, they are implicitly raised by the stories, poems, and plays included here. No definition of literature, particularly a brief one, is likely to satisfy everyone, because definitions tend to weaken and require qualification when confronted by the uniqueness of individual works. In this context it is worth recalling Herman Melville's humorous use of a definition of a whale in *Moby-Dick* (1851). In the course of the novel Melville presents his imaginative and symbolic whale as inscrutable, but he begins with a quotation from Georges Cuvier, a French naturalist who defines a whale in his nineteenth-century study *The Animal Kingdom* this way: "The whale is a mammiferous animal without hind feet." Cuvier's description is technically correct, of course, but there is little wisdom in it. Melville understood that the reality of the whale (which he describes as the "ungraspable phantom of life") cannot be caught by isolated facts. If the full meaning of the whale is to be understood, it must be sought on the open sea of experience, where the whale itself is, rather than in exclusionary definitions. Facts and definitions are helpful; however, they do not always reveal the whole truth.

Despite Melville's reminder that a definition can be too limiting and even comical, it is useful for our purposes to describe literature as a fiction consisting of carefully arranged words designed to stir the imagination. Stories, poems, and plays are fictional. They are made up — imagined —

even when based upon actual historic events. Such imaginative writing differs from other kinds of writing because its purpose is not primarily to transmit facts or ideas. Imaginative literature is a source more of pleasure than of information, and we read it for basically the same reasons we listen to music or view a dance: enjoyment, delight, and satisfaction. Like other art forms, imaginative literature offers pleasure and usually attempts to convey a perspective, mood, feeling, or experience. Writers transform the facts the world provides — people, places, and objects — into experiences that suggest meanings.

Consider, for example, the difference between the following factual description of a snake and a poem on the same subject. Here is *Webster's Ninth New Collegiate Dictionary* definition:

> any of numerous limbless scaled reptiles (suborder Serpentes or Ophidia) with a long tapering body and with salivary glands often modified to produce venom which is injected through grooved or tubular fangs.

Contrast this matter-of-fact definition with Emily Dickinson's poetic evocation of a snake in "A narrow Fellow in the Grass":

> A narrow Fellow in the Grass
> Occasionally rides —
> You may have met Him — did you not
> His notice sudden is —
>
> The Grass divides as with a Comb — 5
> A spotted shaft is seen —
> And then it closes at your feet
> And opens further on —
>
> He likes a Boggy Acre
> A floor too cool for Corn — 10
> Yet when a Boy, and Barefoot —
> I more than once at Noon
> Have passed, I thought, a Whip lash
> Unbraiding in the Sun
> When stooping to secure it 15
> It wrinkled, and was gone —
>
> Several of Nature's People
> I know, and they know me —
> I feel for them a transport
> Of cordiality — 20
>
> But never met this Fellow
> Attended, or alone
> Without a tighter breathing
> And Zero at the Bone —

The dictionary provides a succinct, anatomical description of what a snake is, while Dickinson's poem suggests what a snake can mean. The definition offers facts; the poem offers an experience. The dictionary would probably allow someone who had never seen a snake to sketch one with reasonable accuracy. The poem also provides some vivid subjective descriptions — for example, the snake dividing the grass "as with a Comb" — yet it offers more than a picture of serpentine movements. The poem conveys the ambivalence many people have about snakes — the kind of feeling, for example, so evident on the faces of visitors viewing the snakes at a zoo. In the poem there is both a fascination with and a horror of what might be called snakehood; this combination of feelings has been coiled in most of us since Adam and Eve.

That "narrow Fellow" so cordially introduced by way of a riddle (the word *snake* is never used in the poem) is, by the final stanza, revealed as a snake in the grass. In between, Dickinson uses language expressively to convey her meaning. For instance, in the line "His notice sudden is," listen to the *s*-sound in each word and note how the verb *is* unexpectedly appears at the end, making the snake's hissing presence all the more "sudden." And anyone who has ever been surprised by a snake knows the "tighter breathing / And Zero at the Bone" that Dickinson evokes so successfully by the rhythm of her word choices and line breaks. Perhaps even more significant, Dickinson's poem allows those who have never encountered a snake to imagine such an experience.

A good deal more could be said about the numbing fear that undercuts the affection for nature at the beginning of this poem, but the point here is that imaginative literature gives us not so much the full, factual proportions of the world as some of its experiences and meanings. Instead of defining the world, literature encourages us to try it out in our imaginations.

THE VALUE OF LITERATURE

Mark Twain once shrewdly observed that a person who chooses not to read has no advantage over a person who is unable to read. In industrialized societies today, however, the question is not who reads, because nearly everyone can and does, but what is read. Why should anyone spend precious time with literature when there is so much reading material available that provides useful information about everything from the daily news to personal computers? Why should a literary artist's imagination compete for attention that could be spent on the firm realities that constitute everyday life? In fact, national best-seller lists much less often include collections of stories, poems, or plays than they do cookbooks and, not surprisingly, diet books. Although such fare may be filling, it doesn't stay with you. Most people have other appetites too.

Certainly one of the most important values of literature is that it nourishes our emotional lives. An effective literary work may seem to speak directly to us, especially if we are ripe for it. The inner life that good writers reveal in their characters often gives us glimpses of some portion of ourselves. We can be moved to laugh, cry, tremble, dream, ponder, shriek, or rage with a character by simply turning a page instead of turning our lives upside down. Although the experience itself is imagined, the emotion is real. That's why the final chapters of a good adventure novel can make a reader's heart race as much as a 100-yard dash or why the repressed love of Hester Prynne in *The Scarlet Letter* by Nathaniel Hawthorne is painful to a sympathetic reader. Human emotions speak a universal language regardless of when or where a work was written.

In addition to appealing to our emotions, literature broadens our perspectives on the world. Most of the people we meet are pretty much like ourselves, and what we can see of the world even in a lifetime is astonishingly limited. Literature allows us to move beyond the inevitable boundaries of our own lives and culture because it introduces us to people different from ourselves, places remote from our neighborhoods, and times other than our own. Reading makes us more aware of life's possibilities as well as its subtleties and ambiguities. Put simply, people who read literature experience more life and have a keener sense of a common human identity than those who do not. It is true, of course, that many people go through life without reading imaginative literature, but that is a loss rather than a gain. They may find themselves troubled by the same kinds of questions that reveal Daisy Buchanan's restless, vague discontentment in F. Scott Fitzgerald's *The Great Gatsby*: "What'll we do with ourselves this afternoon?" cried Daisy, "and the day after that, and the next thirty years?"

Sometimes students mistakenly associate literature more with school than with life. Accustomed to reading it in order to write a paper or pass an examination, students may perceive such reading as a chore instead of a pleasurable opportunity, something considerably less important than studying for the "practical" courses that prepare them for a career. The study of literature, however, is also practical, because it engages you in the kinds of problem solving important in a variety of fields, from philosophy to science and technology. The interpretation of literary texts requires you to deal with uncertainties, value judgments, and emotions; these are unavoidable aspects of life.

People who make the most significant contributions to their professions — whether in business, engineering, teaching, or some other area — tend to be challenged rather than threatened by multiple possibilities. Instead of retreating to the way things have always been done, they bring freshness and creativity to their work. F. Scott Fitzgerald once astutely described the "test of a first-rate intelligence" as "the ability to hold two opposed ideas in the mind at the same time, and still retain the ability to function." People with such intelligence know how to read situations, shape questions, interpret details, and evaluate competing points of view. Equipped with a healthy respect for facts, they also understand the value of pursuing hunches and exercising their imaginations. Reading literature encourages a suppleness of mind that is helpful in any discipline or work.

Once the requirements for your degree are completed, what ultimately matters are not the courses listed on your transcript but the sensibilities and habits of mind that you bring to your work, friends, family, and, indeed, the rest of your life. A healthy economy changes and grows with the times; people do too if they are prepared for more than simply filling a job description. The range and variety of life that literature affords can help you to interpret your own experiences and the world in which you live.

To discover the insights that literature reveals requires careful reading and sensitivity. One of the purposes of a college introduction to literature is to cultivate the analytic skills necessary for reading well. Class discussions often help establish a dialogue with a work that perhaps otherwise would not speak to you. Analytic skills can also be developed by writing about what you read. Writing is an effective means of clarifying your responses and ideas, because it requires you to account for the author's use of language as well as your own. This book is based on two premises: that reading literature is pleasurable, and that the more sensitively a work is read and understood by thinking, talking, or writing about it the more pleasurable the experience of it is.

Understanding its basic elements — such as point of view, symbol, theme, tone, irony, and so on — is a prerequisite to an informed appreciation of literature. This kind of understanding allows you to perceive more in a literary work in much the same way that a spectator at a tennis match sees more if he or she understands the rules and conventions of the game. But literature is not simply a spectator sport. The analytic skills that open up literature also have their uses when you watch a television program or film, and, more important, when you attempt to sort out the significance of the people, places, and events that constitute your own life. Literature enhances and sharpens your perceptions. What could be more lastingly practical as well as satisfying?

THE CHANGING LITERARY CANON

Perhaps the best reading is that which creates some kind of change in us: we see more clearly; we're alert to nuances; we ask questions that previously didn't occur to us. Henry Thoreau had that sort of reading in mind when he remarked in *Walden* that the books he valued most were those that caused him to date "a new era in his life from the reading." Readers are sometimes changed by literature, but it is also worth noting that the life of a literary work can also be affected by its readers. Melville's *Moby-Dick,* for example, was not valued as a classic until the 1920s, when critics rescued the novel from the obscurity of being cataloged in many libraries (including Yale's) not under fiction but under cetology, the study of whales. Indeed, many writers contemporary to Melville who were important and popular in the nineteenth century — William Cullen Bryant, Henry Wadsworth Longfellow, and James Russell Lowell, to name a few — are now mostly unread; their names appear more often on elementary schools built early in this century than in anthologies. Clearly, literary reputations and what is valued as great literature change over time and in the eyes of readers.

Such changes have accelerated during the past thirty years as the literary *canon* — those works considered by scholars, critics, and teachers to be the most important to read and study — has undergone a significant series of shifts. Writers who previously were overlooked, undervalued, neglected, or studiously ignored have been brought into focus in an effort to create a more diverse literary canon, one that recognizes the contributions of the many cultures that make up American society. Since the 1960s, for example, some critics have reassessed writings by women who had been left out of the standard literary traditions dominated by male writers. Many more female writers are now read alongside the male writers who traditionally populated literary history. Hence, a reader of Mark Twain and Stephen Crane is now just as likely to encounter Kate Chopin in a literary anthology. Until fairly recently Chopin was mostly regarded as a minor "local colorist" of Louisiana life. In the 1960s, however, the feminist movement helped to establish her present reputation as a significant voice in American literature owing to the feminist concerns so compellingly articulated by her female characters. This kind of enlargement of the canon also resulted from another reform movement of the 1960s. The civil rights movement sensitized literary critics to the political, moral, and aesthetic necessity of rediscovering African-American literature, and more recently Asian and Hispanic writers are making their way into the canon. Moreover, on a broader scale the canon is being revised and enlarged to include the works of writers from parts of the world other than the West, a development that reflects the changing values, concerns, and complexities of the past several years, when literary landscapes have shifted as dramatically as the political boundaries of Eastern Europe and what was once the Soviet Union.

No semester's reading list — or anthology — can adequately or accurately echo all the new voices competing to be heard as part of the mainstream literary canon, but recent efforts to open up the canon attempt to sensitize readers to the voices of women, minorities, and writers from all over the world. This development has not occurred without its urgent advocates or passionate dissenters. It's no surprise that issues about race, gender, and class often get people off the fence and on their feet (these controversies are discussed further in Chapter 35, "Critical Strategies for Reading"). Although what we regard as literature — whether it's called great, classic, or canonical — continues to generate debate, there is no question that such controversy will continue to reflect readers' values as well as the writers they admire.

FICTION

FICTION

1. Reading Fiction

READING FICTION RESPONSIVELY

Reading a literary work responsively can be an intensely demanding activity. Henry David Thoreau — about as intense and demanding a reader and writer as they come — insists that "books must be read as deliberately and reservedly as they were written." Thoreau is right about the necessity for a conscious, sustained involvement with a literary work. Imaginative literature does demand more from us than, say, browsing through *People* magazine in a dentist's waiting room, but Thoreau makes the process sound a little more daunting than it really is. For when we respond to the demands of responsive reading, our efforts are usually rewarded with pleasure as well as understanding. Careful, deliberate reading — the kind that engages a reader's imagination as it calls forth the writer's — is a means of exploration that can take a reader outside whatever circumstance or experience previously defined his or her world. Just as we respond moment by moment to people and situations in our lives, we also respond to literary works as we read them, though we may not be fully aware of how we are affected at each point along the way. The more conscious we are of how and why we respond to works in particular ways, the more likely we are to be imaginatively engaged in our reading.

In a very real sense both the reader and the author create the literary work. How a reader responds to a story, poem, or play will help to determine its meaning. The author arranges the various elements that constitute his or her craft — elements you will be examining in subsequent chapters on plot, character, setting, point of view, symbolism, and so on — but the author cannot completely control the reader's response any more than a person can absolutely predict how a remark or action will be received by a stranger, friend, or even family member. Few authors *tell* readers how to respond. Our sympathy, anger, confusion, laughter, sadness, or whatever the feeling might be is left up to us to experience. Writers may have the talent to evoke such feelings, but they don't have the power and authority to enforce them.

Because of the range of possible responses produced by imaginative literature, there is no single, correct, definitive response or interpretation. There can be readings that are wrongheaded or foolish, and some readings are better than others — that is, more responsive to a work's details and more persuasive — but that doesn't mean there is only one possible reading of a work (see p. 457 for Questions for Responsive Reading).

Experience tells us that different people respond differently to the same work. Consider, for example, how often you've heard Melville's *Moby-Dick* described as one of the greatest American novels. This, however, is how a reviewer in *New Monthly Magazine* described the book when it was published in 1851: it is "a huge dose of hyperbolical slang, maudlin sentimentalism and tragic-comic bubble and squeak." Melville surely did not intend or desire this response; but there it is, and neither was it a singular, isolated reaction. This reading — like any reading — was influenced by the values, assumptions, and expectations that the readers brought to the novel from both previous readings and life experiences. The reviewer's refusal to take the book seriously may have missed the boat from the perspective of many other readers of *Moby-Dick,* but it indicates that even "classics" (perhaps especially those kinds of works) can generate disparate readings.

Consider the following brief story by Kate Chopin, a writer whose fiction (like Melville's) sometimes met with indifference or hostility in her own time. As you read, keep track of your responses to the central character, Mrs. Mallard. Write down your feelings about her in a substantial paragraph when you finish the story. Think, for example, about how you respond to the emotions she expresses concerning news of her husband's death. What do you think of her feelings about marriage? Do you think you would react the way she does under similar circumstances?

KATE CHOPIN (1851–1904)
The Story of an Hour   1894

Knowing that Mrs. Mallard was afflicted with a heart trouble, great care was taken to break to her as gently as possible the news of her husband's death.

It was her sister Josephine who told her, in broken sentences; veiled hints that revealed in half concealing. Her husband's friend Richards was there, too, near her. It was he who had been in the newspaper office when intelligence of the railroad disaster was received, with Brently Mallard's name leading the list of "killed." He had only taken the time to assure himself of its truth by a second telegram, and had hastened to forestall any less careful, less tender friend in bearing the sad message.

She did not hear the story as many women have heard the same, with a paralyzed inability to accept its significance. She wept at once, with sudden, wild abandonment, in her sister's arms. When the storm of grief had spent itself she went away to her room alone. She would have no one follow her.

There stood, facing the open window, a comfortable, roomy armchair. Into this she sank, pressed down by a physical exhaustion that haunted her body and seemed to reach into her soul.

She could see in the open square before her house the tops of trees that were all aquiver with the new spring life. The delicious breath of rain was in the air. In the street below a peddler was crying his wares. The notes of a distant song which some one was singing reached her faintly, and countless sparrows were twittering in the eaves.

There were patches of blue sky showing here and there through the clouds that had met and piled one above the other in the west facing her window.

She sat with her head thrown back upon the cushion of the chair, quite motionless, except when a sob came up into her throat and shook her, as a child who has cried itself to sleep continues to sob in its dreams.

She was young, with a fair, calm face, whose lines bespoke repression and even a certain strength. But now there was a dull stare in her eyes, whose gaze was fixed away off yonder on one of those patches of blue sky. It was not a glance of reflection, but rather indicated a suspension of intelligent thought.

There was something coming to her and she was waiting for it, fearfully. What was it? She did not know; it was too subtle and elusive to name. But she felt it, creeping out of the sky, reaching toward her through the sounds, the scents, the color that filled the air.

Now her bosom rose and fell tumultuously. She was beginning to recognize this thing that was approaching to possess her, and she was striving to beat it back with her will — as powerless as her two white slender hands would have been.

When she abandoned herself a little whispered word escaped her slightly parted lips. She said it over and over under her breath: "free, free, free!" The vacant stare and the look of terror that had followed it went from her eyes. They stayed keen and bright. Her pulses beat fast, and the coursing blood warmed and relaxed every inch of her body.

She did not stop to ask if it were or were not a monstrous joy that held her. A clear and exalted perception enabled her to dismiss the suggestion as trivial.

She knew that she would weep again when she saw the kind, tender hands folded in death; the face that had never looked save with love upon her, fixed and gray and dead. But she saw beyond that bitter moment a long procession of years to come that would belong to her absolutely. And she opened and spread her arms out to them in welcome.

There would be no one to live for her during those coming years; she would live for herself. There would be no powerful will bending hers in that blind persistence with which men and women believe they have a right to impose a private will upon a fellow-creature. A kind intention or a cruel intention made the act seem no less a crime as she looked upon it in that brief moment of illumination.

And yet she had loved him — sometimes. Often she had not. What did it matter! What could love, the unsolved mystery, count for in face of this possession of self-assertion which she suddenly recognized as the strongest impulse of her being!

"Free! Body and soul free!" she kept whispering.

Josephine was kneeling before the closed door with her lips to the keyhole, imploring for admission. "Louise, open the door! I beg; open the door — you will make yourself ill. What are you doing, Louise? For heaven's sake open the door."

"Go away. I am not making myself ill." No; she was drinking in a very elixir of life through that open window.

Her fancy was running riot along those days ahead of her. Spring days, and summer days, and all sorts of days that would be her own. She breathed a quick prayer that life might be long. It was only yesterday she had thought with a shudder that life might be long.

She arose at length and opened the door to her sister's importunities. There 20 was a feverish triumph in her eyes, and she carried herself unwittingly like a goddess of Victory. She clasped her sister's waist, and together they descended the stairs. Richards stood waiting for them at the bottom.

Some one was opening the front door with a latchkey. It was Brently Mallard who entered, a little travel-stained, composedly carrying his gripsack and umbrella. He had been far from the scene of accident, and did not even know there had been one. He stood amazed at Josephine's piercing cry; at Richards' quick motion to screen him from the view of his wife.

But Richards was too late.

When the doctors came they said she had died of heart disease — of joy that kills.

Did you find Mrs. Mallard a sympathetic character? Some readers think that she is callous, selfish, and unnatural — even "monstrous" — because she ecstatically revels in her newly discovered sense of freedom so soon after learning of her husband's presumed death. Others read her as a victim of her inability to control her own life in a repressive, male-dominated society. Is it possible to hold both views simultaneously, or are they mutually exclusive? Are your views in any way influenced by your being male or female? Does your age affect your perception? What about your social and economic background? Does your nationality, race, or religion in any way shape your attitudes? Do you have particular views about the institution of marriage that inform your assessment of Mrs. Mallard's character? Have other reading experiences — perhaps a familiarity with some of Chopin's other stories — predisposed you one way or another to Mrs. Mallard?

Understanding potential influences might be useful in determining whether a particular response to Mrs. Mallard is based primarily on the story's details and their arrangement or on an overt or subtle bias that is brought to the story. If you unconsciously project your beliefs and assumptions onto a literary work, you run the risk of distorting it to accommodate your prejudice. Your feelings can be a reliable guide to interpretation, but you should be aware of what those feelings are based on.

Often specific questions about literary works cannot be answered definitively. For example, Chopin does not explain why Mrs. Mallard suffers a heart attack at the end of this story. Is the shock of seeing her "dead" husband simply too much for this woman "afflicted with a heart trouble"? Does she die of what the doctors call a "joy that kills" because she was so glad to see her husband? Is she so profoundly guilty about feeling "free" at her husband's expense that she has a heart attack? Is her death a kind of willed suicide in reaction to her loss of freedom? Your answers to these questions will depend on which details you emphasize in your interpretation of the story and the kinds of perspectives and values you bring to it. If, for example, you read the story from a feminist perspective, you would be likely to pay close attention to Chopin's comments about marriage in paragraph 14. Or if you read the story as an oblique attack on the insensitivity of physicians of the period, you might want to find out if Chopin wrote elsewhere about doctors (she did) and compare her comments with historic sources. (A number of "Critical Strategies for Reading," including feminist and historical approaches, appear in Chapter 35.)

Reading responsively makes you an active participant in the process of creating meaning in a literary work. The experience that you and the author create will most likely not be identical to another reader's encounter with the same work, but then that's true of nearly any experience you'll have, and it is part of the pleasure of reading. Indeed, talking and writing about literature is a way of sharing responses so that they can be enriched and deepened.

EXPLORATIONS AND FORMULAS

Each time we pick up a work of fiction, go to the theater, or turn on the television, we have a trace of the same magical expectation that can be heard in the voice of a child who begs, "Tell me a story." Human beings have enjoyed stories ever since they learned to speak. Whatever the motive for creating stories — even if simply to delight or instruct — the basic human impulse to tell and hear stories existed long before the development of written language. Myths about the origins of the world and legends about the heroic exploits of demigods were among the earliest forms of storytelling to develop into oral traditions, which were eventually written down. These narratives are the ancestors of the stories we read on the printed page today. Unlike the early listeners to ancient myths and legends, we read our stories silently, but the pleasure derived from the mysterious power of someone else's artfully arranged words remains largely the same. Every one of us likes a good story.

The stories that appear in anthologies for college students are generally chosen for their high literary quality. Such stories can affect us at the deepest emotional level, reveal new insights into ourselves or the world, and stretch us by exercising our imaginations. They warrant careful reading and close study to appreciate the art that has gone into creating them. The following chapters on plot, character, setting, and the other elements of literature are designed to provide the terms and concepts that can help you understand how a work of fiction achieves its effects and meanings. It is worth acknowledging, however, that many people buy and read fiction that is quite different from the stories usually anthologized in college texts. What about all those paperbacks with exciting, colorful covers near the cash registers in shopping malls and corner drugstores?

These books, known as *formula fiction*, are the adventure, western, detective, science-fiction, and romance novels that entertain millions of readers annually. What makes them so popular? What do their characters, plots, and themes offer readers that accounts for the tremendous sales of stories with titles like *Caves of Doom, Silent Scream, Colt .45,* and *Forbidden Ecstasy?* Many of the writers included in this book have enjoyed wide popularity and written best-sellers, but there are more readers of formula fiction than there are readers of Hemingway, Faulkner, or Oates, to name only a few. Formula novels do, of course, provide entertainment, but that makes them no different from serious stories, if entertainment means pleasure. Any of the stories in this or any other anthology can be read for pleasure.

Formula fiction, though, is usually characterized as escape literature. There are sensible reasons for this description. Adventure stories about soldiers of fortune are eagerly read by men who live pretty average lives doing ordinary jobs. Romance novels about attractive young women falling in love with tall, dark, handsome men are read mostly by women who dream themselves out of their familiar existences. The excitement, violence, and passion that such stories provide are a kind of reprieve from everyday experience.

And yet readers of serious fiction may also use it as a refuge, a liberation from monotony and boredom. Mark Twain's humorous stories have, for example, given countless hours of pleasurable relief to readers who would rather spend time in Twain's light and funny world than in their own. Others might prefer the terror of Edgar Allan Poe's fiction or the painful predicament of two lovers in a Joyce Carol Oates story.

Thus, to get at some of the differences between formula fiction and serious literature, it is necessary to go beyond the motives of the reader to the motives of the writer and the qualities of the work itself.

Unlike serious fiction, the books displayed next to the cash registers (and their short story equivalents on the magazine racks) are written with only one object: to be sold. They are aimed at specific consumer markets that can be counted on to buy them. This does not mean that all serious writers must live in cold garrets writing for audiences who have not yet discovered their work. No one writes to make a career of poverty. It does mean, however, that if a writer's primary purpose is to anticipate readers' generic expectations about when the next torrid love scene, bloody gunfight, or thrilling chase is due, there is little room to be original or to have something significant to say. There is little if any chance to explore seriously a character, idea, or incident if the major focus is not on the integrity of the work itself.

Although the specific elements of formula fiction differ depending on the type of story, some basic ingredients go into all westerns, mysteries, adventures, science fiction, and romances. From the very start, a reader can anticipate a happy ending for the central character, with whom he or she will identify. There may be suspense, but no matter what or how many the obstacles, complications, or near defeats, the hero or heroine succeeds and reaffirms the values and attitudes the reader brings to the story. Virtue triumphs; love conquers all; honesty is the best policy; and hard work guarantees success. Hence, the villains are corralled; the wedding vows are exchanged; the butler confesses; and gold is discovered at the last moment. The visual equivalents of such formula stories are readily available at movie theaters and in a variety of television series. Some are better than others, but all are relatively limited by the necessity to give audiences what will sell.

Although formula fiction may not offer many surprises, it provides pleasure to a wide variety of readers. College professors, for example, are just as likely to be charmed by formula stories as anyone else. Readers of serious fiction who revel in exploring more challenging imaginative worlds can also enjoy formulaic stories, which offer little more than an image of the world as a simple place in which our assumptions and desires are confirmed. The familiarity of a given formula is emotionally satisfying because we are secure in our expectations of it. We know at the start of a Sherlock Holmes story that the mystery will be solved by that famous detective's relentless scientific analysis of the clues, but we take pleasure in seeing how Holmes unravels the mystery before us. Similarly, we know that James Bond's wit, grace, charm, courage, and skill will ultimately prevail over the diabolic schemes of eccentric villains, but we volunteer for the mission anyway.

Perhaps that happens for the same reason that we climb aboard a roller coaster: no matter how steep and sharp the curves, we stay on a track that is both exciting and safe. Although excitement, adventure, mystery, and romance are major routes to escape in formula fiction, most of us make that trip only temporarily, for a little relaxation and fun. Momentary relief from our everyday concerns is as healthy and desirable as an occasional daydream or fantasy. Such reading is a form of play because we — like spectators of or participants in a game — experience a formula of excitement, tension, and then release that can fascinate us regardless of how many times the game is played.

Many publishers of formula fiction — such as romance, adventure, or detective stories — issue a set number of new novels each month. Readers can buy them in stores or subscribe to them through the mail. These same publishers send "tip sheets" upon request to authors who want to write for a particular series. The details of the formula differ from one series to another, but each tip sheet covers the basic elements that go into a story.

The following composite tip sheet summarizes the typical advice offered by publishers of romance novels. These are among the most popular titles published in the United States; it has been estimated that four out of every ten paperbacks sold are romance novels. The categories and the tone of the language in this composite tip sheet are derived from a number of publishers and provide a glimpse of how formula fiction is written and what the readers of romance novels are looking for in their escape literature.

A Composite of a Romance Tip Sheet

PLOT

The story focuses on the growing relationship between the heroine and hero. After a number of complications, they discover lasting love and make a permanent commitment to each other in marriage. The plot should move quickly. Background information about the heroine should be kept to a minimum. The hero should appear as early as possible (preferably in the first chapter and no later than the second), so that the hero's and heroine's feelings about each other are in the foreground as they cope with misperceptions that keep them apart until the final pages of the story. The more tension created by their uncertainty about each other's love, the greater the excitement and anticipation for the reader.

Love is the major interest. Do not inject murder, extortion, international intrigue, hijacking, horror, or supernatural elements into the plot. Controversial social issues and politics, if mentioned at all, should never be allowed a significant role. Once the heroine and hero meet, they should clearly be interested in each other, but that interest should be complicated by some kind of misunderstanding. He, for example, might find her too ambitious, an opportunist, cold, or flirtatious; or he might assume that she is attached to someone else. She might think he is haughty, snobbish, power hungry, indifferent, or contemptuous of her. The reader knows what they do not: that eventually these obstacles will be overcome. Interest is sustained by keeping the lovers apart until very near the end so that the reader will stay with the plot to see how they get together.

HEROINE

The heroine is a modern American woman between the ages of nineteen and twenty-eight who reflects today's concerns. The story is told in the third person from her point of view. She is attractive and nicely dressed but not glamorous; glitter and sophistication should be reserved for the other woman (the heroine's rival for the hero), who will compare unfavorably with the heroine's modesty. When the heroine does dress up, however, her beauty should be stunningly apparent. Her trim figure is appealing but not abundant; a petite healthy appearance is desirable. Both her looks and clothes should be generously detailed.

Her personality is spirited and independent without being pushy or stubborn, because she knows when to give in. Although sensitive, she doesn't cry every time she is confronted with a problem (though she might cry in private moments). Because she is on her own, away from parents (usually deceased) or other protective relationships, she is self-reliant as well as vulnerable. The story may begin with her on the verge of an important decision about her life. She is clearly competent but not entirely certain of her own qualities. She does not take her attractiveness for granted or realize how much the hero is drawn to her.

Common careers for the heroine include executive secretary, nurse, teacher, interior designer, assistant manager, department store buyer, travel agent, or struggling photographer (no menial work). Her job can be described in some detail and made exciting, but it must not dominate her life. Although she is smart, she is not intellectual or defined by her work. Often she meets the hero through work, but her major concerns center on love, marriage, home, and family. White wine is okay, but she never drinks alone — or uses drugs. She may be troubled, frustrated, threatened, and momentarily thwarted in the course of the story, but she never totally gives in to despair or desperation. She has strengths that the hero recognizes and admires.

HERO

The hero should be about ten years older than the heroine and can be foreign or American. He needn't be handsome in a traditional sense, but he must be strongly masculine. Always tall and well built (not brawny or thick) and usually dark, he looks as terrific in a three-piece suit as he does in sports clothes. His clothes reflect good taste and an affluent life-style. Very successful professionally and financially, he is a man in charge of whatever work he's engaged in (financier, doctor, publisher, architect, business executive, airline pilot, artist, etc.). His wealth is manifested in his sophistication and experience.

His past may be slightly mysterious or shrouded by some painful moment (perhaps with a woman) that he doesn't want to discuss. Whatever the circumstance — his wife's death or divorce are common — it was not his fault. Avoid chronic problems such as alcoholism, drug addiction, or sexual dysfunctions. To others he may appear moody, angry, unpredictable, and explosively passionate, but the heroine eventually comes to realize his warm, tender side. He should be attractive not only as a lover but also as a potential husband and father.

SECONDARY CHARACTERS

Because the major interest is in how the heroine will eventually get together with the hero, the other characters are used to advance the action. There are three major types:

(1) *The Other Woman:* Her vices serve to accent the virtues of the heroine; immediately beneath her glamorous sophistication is a deceptive, selfish, mean-

spirited, rapacious predator. She may seem to have the hero in her clutches, but she never wins him in the end.

(2) *The Other Man:* He usually falls into two types: (a) the decent sort who is there when the hero isn't around, and (b) the selfish sort who schemes rather than loves. Neither is a match for the hero's virtues.

(3) *Other Characters:* Like furniture, they fill in the background and are useful for positioning the hero and heroine. These characters are familiar types such as the hero's snobbish aunt, the heroine's troubled younger siblings, the loyal friend, or the office gossip. They should be realistic, but they must not be allowed to obscure the emphasis on the lovers. The hero may have children from a previous marriage, but they should rarely be seen or heard. It's usually simpler and better not to include them.

SETTING

The setting is always contemporary. Romantic, exciting places are best: New York City, London, Paris, Rio, the mountains, the ocean — wherever it is exotic and love's possibilities are the greatest. Marriage may take the heroine and hero to a pretty suburb or small town.

LOVE SCENES

The hero and heroine may make love before marriage. The choice will depend largely on the heroine's sensibilities and circumstances. She should reflect modern attitudes. If the lovers do engage in premarital sex, it should be made clear that neither is promiscuous, especially the heroine. Even if their relationship is consummated before marriage, their lovemaking should not occur until late in the story. There should be at least several passionate scenes, but complications, misunderstandings, and interruptions should keep the couple from actually making love until they have made a firm commitment to each other. Descriptions should appeal to the senses; however, detailed, graphic close-ups are unacceptable. Passion can be presented sensually but not clinically; the lovemaking should be seen through a soft romantic lens. Violence and any out of the way sexual acts should not even be hinted at. No coarse language.

WRITING

Avoid extremely complex sentences, very long paragraphs, and lengthy descriptions. Use concise, vivid details to create the heroine's world. Be sure to include full descriptions of the hero's and heroine's physical features and clothes. Allow the reader to experience the romantic mood surrounding the lovers. Show how the heroine feels; do not simply report her feelings. Dialogue should sound like ordinary conversation, and the overall writing should be contemporary English without slang, difficult foreign expressions, strange dialects, racial epithets, or obscenities ("hell," "damn," and a few other mild swears are all right).

LENGTH

55,000 to 65,000 words in ten to twelve chapters.

Considerations for Critical Thinking and Writing

1. Who is the intended audience for this type of romance? Try to describe the audience in detail: how does a romance novel provide escape for these readers?
2. Why is it best that the heroine be "attractive and nicely dressed but not glamorous"? Why do you think publishers advise writers to include detailed descriptions of her clothes? Do you find the heroine appealing? Why or why not?
3. Why should the hero be "about ten years older than the heroine"? If he is divorced, why is it significant that "it was not his fault"?
4. Why do you think the hero and heroine are kept apart by complications until the end of the story? Does the outline of the plot sound familiar to you or remind you of any other stories?
5. Why do you think restrictions are placed on the love scenes?
6. Why are "extremely complex sentences, very long paragraphs, and lengthy descriptions" discouraged?
7. Given the expectations implied by the tip sheet, what is revealed about those likely to write formula fiction? Do you think it is possible to write creatively within the demands of the formula?
8. To what extent does the tip sheet describe the strategies used in popular television soap operas? How do you account for the appeal of these shows?
9. Explain how the tip sheet confirms traditional views of male and female roles in society. Does it accommodate any broken traditions?
10. Write up a tip sheet for another kind of popular formula story, such as a western or a detective story, that you have observed in a novel, television show, or film. How is the plot patterned? How are the characters made familiar? How is the setting related to the story? What are the obligatory scenes? How is the overall style consistent? To get started, you might consider an Agatha Christie novel, an episode from a police series on television, or a *Rocky* film.
11. Try writing a scene for a formula romance, or read the excerpt from Edgar Rice Burroughs's *Tarzan of the Apes* (p. 39) and try an adventure scene.

A COMPARISON OF TWO STORIES

Each of the following contemporary pieces of fiction is about a woman who experiences deep sorrow. The first, from *A Secret Sorrow* by Karen Van Der Zee, is an excerpt from a romance by Harlequin Books, a major publisher of formula fiction that has sold well over a billion copies of its romance titles — enough for about twenty percent of the world's population. The second piece, Gail Godwin's "A Sorrowful Woman," is a complete short story that originally appeared in *Esquire;* it is not a formula story. Unlike *A Secret Sorrow,* Godwin's story does not have a standard plot pattern employing familiar character types that appear in a series of separate but similar works.

Read each selection carefully and look for evidence of formulaic writing in the chapters from *A Secret Sorrow.* Pay particular attention to the advice offered in the composite tip sheet on plotting and characterization. As you read Godwin's short story, think about how it is different from Van Der Zee's excerpt; note also any similarities. The questions that follow the stories should help you consider how the experiences of reading the two are different.

KAREN VAN DER ZEE (b. 1947)

This excerpt consists of the final two chapters of *A Secret Sorrow*. This is what has happened so far: the central character, Faye, is recuperating from the psychological effects of a serious car accident in which she received a permanent internal injury. After the accident, she quits her job and breaks her engagement to Greg. She moves into her brother Chuck's house and falls in love with Kai, a visiting Texan and good friend of her brother. At the end of Chapter 10, Kai insists upon knowing why she will not marry him and asks, "Who is Doctor Jaworski?"

From A Secret Sorrow   1981

CHAPTER ELEVEN

Faye could feel the blood drain from her face and for one horrifying moment she thought she was going to faint right in Kai's arms. The room tilted and everything swirled around in a wild madman's dance. She clutched at him for support, fighting for control, trying to focus at some point beyond his shoulder. Slowly, everything steadied.

"I . . . I don't know him," she murmured at last. "I . . . ."

He reached in the breast pocket of his shirt, took out a slip of paper, and held it out for her to see. One glance and Faye recognized it as the note from Doctor Martin with Doctor Jaworski's name scrawled on it, thickly underlined.

"How did you get that?" Her voice was a terrified whisper. She was still holding on, afraid she would fall if she let go.

"I found it on the floor in my bedroom. It must have fallen out of your 5 wallet along with everything else on Saturday morning."

Yes — oh God! Her legs were shaking so badly, she knew it was only his arms that kept her from falling.

"Who is Doctor Jaworski, Faye?" His voice was patiently persistent.

"I . . . he. . . ." Her voice broke. "Let me go, please let me go." She felt as if she were suffocating in his embrace and she struggled against him, feebly, but it was no use.

"He's a psychiatrist, isn't he?" His voice was gentle, very gentle, and she looked up at him in stunned surprise.

He knew, oh God, he knew. She closed her eyes, a helpless sense of inevitability engulfing her.

"You know," she whispered. "How do you know?"

"Simple. Two minutes on the phone to Chicago." He paused. "Doctor Martin — was he one of the doctors who treated you at the hospital?"

"Yes."

"Why did he give you Doctor Jaworski's name? Did he want you to make an appointment with him?"

"Yes." Despondency overtook her. There was no going back now. No escape from the truth. No escape from his arms. Resistance faded and she felt numbed and lifeless. It didn't matter any more. Nothing mattered.

"Did you?" Kai repeated.

"Did I what?"

"See him — Doctor Jaworski."

"No."

"Why did Doctor Martin want you to see a psychiatrist?"

"I. . . ." Faye swallowed miserably. "It's . . . it's therapy for grieving . . . mourning." She made a helpless gesture with her hand. "When people lose a . . . a wife, or husband for instance, they go through a more or less predictable pattern of emotions. . . ." She gave him a quick glance, then looked away. "Like denial, anger. . . ."

". . . depression, mourning, acceptance," Kai finished for her, and she looked back at him in surprise.

"Yes."

His mouth twisted in a little smile. "I'm not totally ignorant about subjects other than agronomy." There was a momentary pause as he scrutinized her face. "Why did you need that kind of therapy, Faye?"

And then it was back again, the resistance, the revolt against his probing questions. She stiffened in defense — her whole body growing rigid with instinctive rebellion.

"It's none of your business!"

"Oh, yes, it is. We're talking about our life together. Your life and mine."

She strained against him, hands pushing against his chest. "Let me go! Please let me go!" Panic changed into tears. She couldn't take his nearness any more, the feel of his hard body touching hers, the strength of him.

"No, Faye, no. You're going to tell me. Now. I'm not letting you go until you've told me everything. Everything, you hear?"

"I can't!" she sobbed. "I can't!"

"Faye," he said slowly, "you'll *have* to. You told me you love me, but you don't want to marry me. You have given me no satisfactory reasons, and I'll be damned if I'm going to accept your lack of explanations."

"You have no right to demand an explanation!"

"Oh, yes, I have. You're part of me, Faye. Part of my life."

"You talk as if you own me!" She was trembling, struggling to get away from him. She couldn't stand there, so close to him with all the pent-up despair inside her, the anger, the fear of what she knew not how to tell him.

His hands were warm and strong on her back, holding her steady. Then, with one hand, he tilted back her head and made her look at him. "You gave me your love — I own that," he said softly. "True loving involves commitment, vulnerability, trust. Don't you trust me, Faye?"

New tears ran silently down her cheeks. "If I told you," she blurted out, "you wouldn't . . . you wouldn't. . . ."

"I wouldn't *what?*"

"You wouldn't want me any more!" The words were wrenched from her in blind, agonizing grief. "You wouldn't *want* me any more!"

He shook his head incredulously. "What makes you think you can make that decision for me? Do you have so little trust in my love for you?"

Faye didn't answer, couldn't answer. Through a mist of tears he was nothing 40
but a blur in front of her eyes.

"What is so terrible that you can't tell me?"

She shrank inwardly, as if shriveling away in pain. "Let me go," she whispered. "Please let me go and I'll tell you."

After a moment's hesitation Kai released her. Faye backed away from him, feeling like a terrified animal. She stood with her back against the wall, glad for the support, her whole body shaking. She took a deep breath and wiped her face dry with her hand.

"I'm afraid . . . afraid to marry you."

"Afraid?" He looked perplexed. "Afraid of what? Of me? Of marriage?" 45

Faye closed her eyes, taking another deep breath. "I can't be what you want me to be. We can't have the kind of life you want." She looked at him, standing only a few feet away, anguish tearing through her. "I'm so afraid . . . you'll be disappointed," she whispered.

"Oh God, Faye," he groaned, "I love you." He came toward her and panic surged through her as he held her against the wall, his hands reaching up to catch her face between them.

"Don't," she whispered. "Please, don't touch me." But it was no use. His mouth came down on hers and he kissed her with a hard, desperate passion.

"I love you," he said huskily. "I love you."

Faye wrenched her face free from his hands. "Don't touch me! Please don't 50
touch me!" She was sobbing now, her words barely audible. Her knees gave way and her back slid down along the wall until she crumpled on to the floor, face in her hands.

Kai took a step backward and pulled her up. "Stand up, Faye. For God's sake stand up!" He held her against the wall and she looked at him, seeing every line in his dark face, the intense blue of his eyes, and knew that this was the moment, that there was no more waiting.

And Kai knew it too. His eyes held hers locked in unrelenting demand. "Why should I be disappointed, Faye? *Why?*"

Her heart was thundering in her ears and it seemed as if she couldn't breathe, as if she were going to drown.

"Because . . . because I can't give you children! Because I can't get pregnant! I can't have babies! That's why!" Her voice was an agonized cry, torn from the depths of her misery. She yanked down his arms that held her locked against the wall and moved away from him. And then she saw his face.

It was ashen, gray under his tan. He stared at her as if he had never seen 55
her before.

"Oh my God, Faye. . . ." His voice was low and hoarse. "Why didn't you tell me, why. . . ."

Faye heard no more. She ran out the door, snatching her bag off the chair as she went by. The only thought in her mind was to get away — away from Kai and what was in his eyes.

She reached for Kai's spare set of car keys in her bag, doing it instinctively, knowing she couldn't walk home alone in the dark. How she managed to get the keys in the door lock and in the ignition she never knew. Somehow, she made it home.

The phone rang as Faye opened the front door and she heard Chuck answer it in the kitchen.

"She's just got in," he said into the mouthpiece, smiling at Faye as she came into view. He listened for a moment, nodded. "Okay, fine with me."

Faye turned and walked up the stairs, taking deep breaths to calm her shattered nerves. Kai hadn't wasted any time checking up on her. She didn't care what he was telling Chuck, but she wasn't going to stand there listening to a one-sided conversation. But only a second later Chuck was behind her on the stairs.

"Kai wanted to know whether you'd arrived safely."

"I did, thank you," she said levelly, her voice surprisingly steady.

"I take it you ran out and took off with his car?"

"Did he say that?"

"No. He was *worried* about you. He wanted to make sure you went home." He sounded impatient, and she couldn't blame him. She was making life unbearable for everyone around her. Everybody worried about her. Everybody loved her. Everything should be right. Only it wasn't.

"Well, I'm home now, and I'm going to bed. Good night."

"Good night, Faye."

Faye lay in bed without any hope of sleep. Mechanically she started to sort through her thoughts and emotions, preparing mentally for the next confrontation. There would be one, she didn't doubt it for a moment. But she needed time — time to clear her head, time to look at everything in a reasonable, unemotional way.

It was a temptation to run — get in the car and keep driving, but it would be a stupid thing to do. There was no place for her to go, and Kai would find her, no matter what. If there was one thing she knew about Kai it was his stubbornness and his persistence. She had to stick it out, right here, get it over with, deal with it. Only she didn't know how.

She lay listening to the stillness, just a few sounds here and there — the house creaking, a car somewhere in the distance, a dog barking. She had to think, but her mind refused to cooperate. She *had* to think, decide what to say to Kai the next time she saw him, but she couldn't think, she *couldn't think*.

And then, as she heard the door open in the silence, the quiet footsteps coming up the stairs, she knew it was too late, that time had run out.

Without even knocking he came into her room and walked over to the bed. She could feel the mattress sag as his weight came down on it. Her heart was pounding like a sledgehammer, and then his arms came around her and he drew her against him.

"Faye," he said quietly, "please marry me."

"No," she said thickly. "No." She could feel him stiffen against her and she released herself from his arms and slid off the bed. She switched on the light and stood near the window, far from the bed, far from Kai. "I don't expect you to play the gentleman, I don't expect you to throw out a life of dreams just for the sake of chivalry. You don't have to marry me, Kai." She barely recognized her own voice. It was like the cool calm sound of a stranger, unemotional, cold. "You don't have to marry me," she repeated levelly, giving him a steady look. 75

Her words were underlined by the silence that followed, a silence loaded with a strange, vibrating energy, a force in itself, filling the room.

Kai rose to his feet, slowly, and the face that looked at her was like that of a stranger, a dangerous, angry stranger. Never before had she seen him so angry, so full of hot, fuming fury.

"Shut up," he said in a low, tight voice. "Shut up and stop playing the martyr!"

The sound of his voice and the words he said shocked Faye into silence. She stared at him open-mouthed, and then a slow, burning anger arose inside her.

"How dare you! How. . . ." 80

He strode toward her and took her upper arms and shook her. "Shut up and listen to me! What the hell are you thinking? What the hell did you expect me to do when you told me? You throw me a bomb and then walk out on me! What did you expect my reaction to be? Was I supposed to stay cool and calm and tell you it didn't matter? Would you have married me then? Well, let me tell you something! It matters! It matters to me! I am not apologizing for my reaction!" He paused, breathing hard. "You know I always wanted children, but what in God's name makes you think you're the only one who has the right to feel bad about it? I have that right too, you hear! I love you, dammit, and I want to marry you, and if we can't have children I have all the right in the world to feel bad about it!"

He stopped talking. He was still breathing hard and he looked at her with stormy blue eyes. Faye felt paralyzed by his tirade and she stared at him, incapable of speech. She couldn't move, she couldn't think.

"Why do you think I want you for my wife?" he continued on a calmer note. "Because you're some kind of baby factory? What kind of man do you think I am? I love *you*, not your procreating ability. So we have a problem. Well, we'll learn to deal with it, one way or another."

There was another silence, and still Faye didn't speak, and she realized she was crying, soundlessly, tears slowly dripping down her cheeks. She was staring at his chest, blindly, not knowing what to think, not thinking at all.

He lifted her chin, gently. "Look at me, Faye." 85

She did, but his face was only a blur.

"Faye, we're in this together — you and I. Don't you see that? It's not just *your* problem, it's *ours*."

"No," she whispered. "No!" She shook her head wildly. "You have a choice, don't you see that? You don't have to marry me. You could marry someone else and have children of your own."

"Oh, God, Faye," he groaned, "you're wrong. Don't you know? Don't you see? I *don't* have a choice. I never did have a choice, or a chance. Not since I met you and fell in love with you. I don't *want* anybody else, don't you understand that? I want you, only you."

She wanted to believe it, give in to him. Never before had she wanted anything more desperately than she wanted to give in to him now. But she couldn't, she couldn't. . . . She closed her eyes, briefly, fighting for reason, common sense.

"Kai, I . . . I can't live all my life with your regret and your disappointment. Every time we see some pregnant woman, every time we're with somebody else's children I'll feel I've failed you! I. . . ." Her voice broke and new sobs came unchecked.

He held her very tightly until she calmed down and then he put her from him a little and gave her a dark, compelling look.

"It's not *my* regret, or *my* disappointment," he said with quiet emphasis. "It's *ours*. We're not talking about *you* or *me*. We're taking about *us*. I love you, and you love me, and that's the starting point, that comes first. From then on we're in it together."

Faye moved out of his arms, away from him, but her legs wouldn't carry her and she sank into a chair. She covered her face with her hands and tried desperately to stop the crying, to stop the tears from coming and coming as if they would never end.

"How . . . how can I ever believe it?"

"Because I'm asking you to," he said quietly. He knelt in front of her, took her hands away from her wet face. "Look at me, Faye. No other woman can give me what you can — yourself, your love, your warmth, your sense of humor. All the facets of your personality that make up the final you. I've known other women, Faye, but none of them have ever stirred in me any feelings that come close to what I feel for you. You're an original, remember? There's no replacement for an original. There are only copies, and I don't want a copy. To me you're special, and you'll have to believe it, take it on faith. That's what love is all about."

He was holding her hands in his, strong brown hands, and she was looking down on them, fighting with herself, fighting with everything inside her to believe what he was saying, to accept it, to give into it.

Leaning forward, Kai kissed her gently on the mouth and smiled. "It's all been too much too soon for you, hasn't it? You never really got a chance to get over the shock, and when I fell in love with you it only made things worse." He smiled ruefully and Faye was surprised at his insight.

"Yes," she said. "It all happened too fast."

"Bad timing. If only we could have met later, after you'd sorted it all out in your mind, then it would never have been such a crisis."

She looked at him doubtfully. "It wouldn't have changed the facts."

"No, but it might have changed your perspective."

Would it have? she wondered. Could she ever feel confident and secure in her worth as a woman? Or was she at this moment too emotionally bruised to accept that possibility?

"I don't understand," he said, "why I never guessed what was wrong. Now that I know, it all seems so obvious." He looked at her thoughtfully. "Faye," he said gently, "I want you to tell me exactly what happened to you, what Doctor Martin told you."

She stared at him, surprised a little. A thought stirred in the back of her mind. Greg. He had never even asked. The why and the what had not interested him. But Kai, he wanted to know. She swallowed nervously and began the story, slowly, word for word, everything Doctor Martin had said. And he listened, quietly, not interrupting. "So you see," she said at last, "we don't have to hope for any miracles either." 105

"We'll make our own miracles," he said, and smiled. "Come here," he said then, "kiss me."

She did, shyly almost, until he took over and lifted her up and carried her to the bed. He looked down on her, eyes thoughtful. "I won't pretend I understand your feelings about this, the feelings you have about yourself as a woman, but I'll try." He paused for a moment. "Faye," he said then, speaking with slow emphasis, "don't *ever,* not for a single moment, think that you're not good enough for me. You're the best there is, Faye, the very best."

His mouth sought hers and he kissed her with gentle reassurance at first, then with rising ardor. His hands moved over her body, touching her with sensual, intimate caresses.

"You're my woman, Faye, you're mine. . . ."

Her senses reeled. She could never love anyone like she loved him. No one had ever evoked in her this depth of emotion. This was real, this was forever. Kai wanted her as much as ever. No chivalry, this, no game of pretense, she was very sure of that. And when he lifted his face and looked at her, it was all there in his eyes and the wonder of it filled her with joy. 110

"Do you believe me now?" he whispered huskily. "Do you believe I love you and want you and need you?"

She nodded wordlessly, incapable of uttering a sound.

"And do you love me?"

Again she nodded, her eyes in his.

"Okay, then." In one smooth flowing movement he got to his feet. He crossed to the closet, opened it and took out her suitcases. He put one on the end of the bed and began to pile her clothes in it, taking armfuls out of the closet. 115

Faye watched incredulously. "What are you doing?" she managed at last.

Kai kept on moving around, opening drawers, taking out her things, filling the suitcase until it could hold no more. "Get dressed. We're going home."

"Home . . . ?"

For a moment he stopped and he looked at her with a deep blue glitter in his eyes. "Yes, *home* — where you belong. With me, in my house, in my bed, in my arms."

"Oh, Kai," she said tremulously, smiling suddenly, "It's midnight!" 120

His eyes were very dark. "I've waited long enough, I'm not waiting any more. You're coming with me, now. And I'm not letting you out of my sight until we're safely married. I don't want you getting any crazy ideas about running off to save me from myself, or some such notion."

Her throat was dry. "Please, let's not rush into it! Let's think about it first!"

Calmly he zipped up the full suitcase, swung it off the bed, and put it near the door. "I'm not rushing into anything," he said levelly. "I've wanted to marry you for quite a while, remember?"

He crossed to the bed, sat down next to her, and put his arm around her. "Faye, I wish you wouldn't worry so. I'm not going to change my mind. And I haven't shelved my hopes for a family, either." There was a brief silence. "When we're ready to have kids, we'll have them. We'll adopt them. There are orphanages the world over, full of children in need of love and care. We'll do whatever it takes. We'll get them, one way or another."

Faye searched his face, faint hope flickering deep inside her. 125

"Would you want that?"

"Why not?"

"I don't know, really. I thought you . . . it isn't the same."

"No," he said levelly, "it isn't. Adoption is a different process from pregnancy and birth, but the kids will be ours just the same and we'll love them no less."

"Yes," she said, "yes." And suddenly it seemed as if a light had been turned 130 on inside her, as if suddenly she could see again, a future with Kai, a future with children.

A bronzed hand lifted her face. "Look, Faye, I'll always be sorry. I'll always be sorry not to see you pregnant, not to see you with a big stomach knowing you're carrying my child, but I'll live."

Faye lowered her eyes and tears threatened again. With both his hands he cupped her face.

"Look at me, Faye. I want you to stop thinking of yourself as a machine with a defect. You're not a damaged piece of merchandise, you hear? You're a living, breathing human being, a warm-blooded female, and I love you."

Through a haze of tears she looked at him, giving a weak smile. "I love you too." She put her arms around him and he heaved an unsteady breath.

"Faye," he said huskily, "you're my first and only choice." 135

CHAPTER TWELVE

Kai and Faye had their family, two girls and a boy. They came to them one at a time, from faraway places, with small faces and large dark eyes full of fear. In their faces Faye could read the tragedies of war and death and poverty. They were hungry for love, hungry for nourishment and care. At night they woke in terror, screaming, their memories alive in sleep.

Time passed, and in the low white ranch house under the blue skies of Texas they flourished like the crops in the fields. They grew tall and straight and healthy and the fear in the dark eyes faded. Like their father they wore jeans and boots and large-brimmed hats, and they rode horses and played the guitar. They learned to speak English with a Southern twang.

One day Kai and Faye watched them as they played in the garden, and joy and gratitude overflowed in Faye's heart. Life was good and filled with love.

"They're all ours," she said. Even now after all these years she sometimes still couldn't believe it was really so.

Kai smiled at her. His eyes, still very blue, crinkled at the corners. "Yes, and 140 you're all mine."

"They don't even look like us," she said. "Not even a tiny little bit." No blondes, no redheads.

Taking her in his arms, Kai kissed her. "They're true originals, like their mother. I wouldn't want it any other way."

There was love in his embrace and love in his words and in her heart there was no room now for doubt, no room for sorrow.

Sometimes in the night he would reach for her and she would wake to his touch, his hands on her breast, her stomach, searching. In the warm darkness of their bed she would come to him and they would hold each other close and she knew he had been dreaming.

She knew the dream. She was walking away from him, calling out that she couldn't marry him, the words echoing all around. *"I can't marry you! I can't marry you!"* And Kai was standing there watching her go, terrified, unable to move, his legs frozen to the ground. He wanted to follow her, keep her from leaving, but his legs wouldn't move. 145

Kai had told her of the dream, of the panic that clutched at him as he watched her walk out of his life. And always he would wake and search for her in the big bed, and she knew of only one way to reassure him. And in the warm afterglow of lovemaking, their bodies close together, she knew that to him she was everything, to him she was the only woman, beautiful, complete, whole.

GAIL GODWIN (b. 1937)
A Sorrowful Woman   1971

Once upon a time there was a wife and mother one too many times

One winter evening she looked at them: the husband durable, receptive, gentle; the child a tender golden three. The sight of them made her so sad and sick she did not want to see them ever again.

She told the husband these thoughts. He was attuned to her; he understood such things. He said he understood. What would she like him to do? "If you could put the boy to bed and read him the story about the monkey who ate too many bananas, I would be grateful." "Of course," he said. "Why, that's a pleasure." And he sent her off to bed.

The next night it happened again. Putting the warm dishes away in the cupboard, she turned and saw the child's gray eyes approving her movements. In the next room was the man, his chin sunk in the open collar of his favorite wool shirt. He was dozing after her good supper. The shirt was the gray of the child's trusting gaze. She began yelping without tears, retching in between. The man woke in alarm and carried her in his arms to bed. The boy followed them up the stairs, saying, "It's all right, Mommy," but this made her scream. "Mommy is sick," the father said, "go wait for me in your room."

The husband undressed her, abandoning her only long enough to root beneath the eiderdown for her flannel gown. She stood naked except for her bra, which hung by one strap down the side of her body; she had not the impetus to shrug it off. She looked down at the right nipple, shriveled with chill, and thought, How absurd, a vertical bra. "If only there were instant sleep," she said, hiccuping, and the husband bundled her into the gown and went out and came back with a sleeping draught guaranteed swift. She was to drink a little glass of cognac followed by a big glass of dark liquid and afterwards there was just time to say Thank you and could you get him a clean pair of pajamas out of the laundry, it came back today.

The next day was Sunday and the husband brought her breakfast in bed 5 and let her sleep until it grew dark again. He took the child for a walk, and when they returned, red-cheeked and boisterous, the father made supper. She heard them laughing in the kitchen. He brought her up a tray of buttered toast, celery sticks, and black bean soup. "I am the luckiest woman," she said, crying real tears. "Nonsense," he said. "You need a rest from us," and went to prepare the sleeping draught, find the child's pajamas, select the story for the night.

She got up on Monday and moved about the house till noon. The boy, delighted to have her back, pretended he was a vicious tiger and followed her from room to room, growling and scratching. Whenever she came close, he would growl and scratch at her. One of his sharp little claws ripped her flesh, just above the wrist, and together they paused to watch a thin red line materialize on the inside of her pale arm and spill over in little beads. "Go away," she said. She got herself upstairs and locked the door. She called the husband's office and said, "I've locked myself away from him. I'm afraid." The husband told her in his richest voice to lie down, take it easy, and he was already on the phone to call one of the baby-sitters they often employed. Shortly after, she heard the girl let herself in, heard the girl coaxing the frightened child to come and play.

After supper several nights later, she hit the child. She had known she was going to do it when the father would see. "I'm sorry," she said, collapsing on the floor. The weeping child had run to hide. "What has happened to me, I'm not myself anymore." The man picked her tenderly from the floor and looked at her with much concern. "Would it help if we got, you know, a girl in? We could fix the room downstairs. I want you to feel freer," he said, understanding these things. "We have the money for a girl. I want you to think about it."

And now the sleeping draught was a nightly thing, she did not have to ask. He went down to the kitchen to mix it, he set it nightly beside her bed. The little glass and the big one, amber and deep rich brown, the flannel gown and the eiderdown.

The man put out the word and found the perfect girl. She was young, dynamic, and not pretty. "Don't bother with the room, I'll fix it up myself." Laughing, she employed her thousand energies. She painted the room white, fed the child lunch, read edifying books, raced the boy to the mailbox, hung her own watercolors on the fresh-painted walls, made spinach soufflé, cleaned a spot from the mother's coat, made them all laugh, danced in stocking feet to music in the white room after reading the child to sleep. She knitted dresses for herself and played chess with the husband. She washed and set the mother's soft ash-blonde hair and gave her neck rubs, offered to.

The woman now spent her winter afternoons in the big bedroom. She made 10 a fire in the hearth and put on slacks and an old sweater she had loved at school, and sat in the big chair and stared out the window at snow-ridden branches, or went away into long novels about other people moving through other winters.

The girl brought the child in twice a day, once in the later afternoon when he would tell of his day, all of it tumbling out quickly because there was not much time, and before he went to bed. Often now, the man took his wife to dinner. He made a courtship ceremony of it, inviting her beforehand so she could get used to the idea. They dressed and were beautiful together again and went out into the frosty night. Over candlelight he would say, "I think you are better, you know." "Perhaps I am," she would murmur. "You look . . . like a cloistered queen," he said once, his voice breaking curiously.

One afternoon the girl brought the child into the bedroom. "We've been out playing in the park. He found something he wants to give you, a surprise." The little boy approached her, smiling mysteriously. He placed his cupped hands in hers and left a live dry thing that spat brown juice in her palm and leapt away. She screamed and wrung her hands to be rid of the brown juice. "Oh, it was only a grasshopper," said the girl. Nimbly she crept to the edge of the curtain, did a quick knee bend, and reclaimed the creature, led the boy competently from the room.

"The girl upsets me," said the woman to her husband. He sat frowning on the side of the bed he had not entered for so long. "I'm sorry, but there it is." The husband stroked his creased brow and said he was sorry too. He really did not know what they would do without that treasure of a girl. "Why don't you stay here with me in bed," the woman said.

Next morning she fired the girl who cried and said, "I loved the little boy, what will become of him now?" But the mother turned away her face and the girl took down the watercolors from the walls, sheathed the records she had danced to, and went away.

"I don't know what we'll do. It's all my fault, I know. I'm such a burden, I know that." 15

"Let me think. I'll think of something." (Still understanding these things.)

"I know you will. You always do," she said.

With great care he rearranged his life. He got up hours early, did the shopping, cooked the breakfast, took the boy to nursery school. "We will manage," he said, "until you're better, however long that is." He did his work, collected the boy from the school, came home and made the supper, washed the dishes, got the child to bed. He managed everything. One evening, just as she was on the verge of swallowing her draught, there was a timid knock on her door. The little boy came in wearing his pajamas. "Daddy has fallen asleep on my bed and I can't get in. There's not room."

Very sedately she left her bed and went to the child's room. Things were much changed. Books were rearranged, toys. He'd done some new drawings. She came as a visitor to her son's room, wakened the father and helped him to bed. "Ah, he shouldn't have bothered you," said the man, leaning on his wife. "I've told him not to." He dropped into his own bed and fell asleep with a moan. Meticulously she undressed him. She folded and hung his clothes. She covered his body with the bedclothes. She flicked off the light that shone in his face.

The next day she moved her things into the girl's white room. She put her 20 hairbrush on the dresser; she put a note pad and pen beside the bed. She stocked the little room with cigarettes, books, bread, and cheese. She didn't need much.

At first the husband was dismayed. But he was receptive to her needs. He understood these things. "Perhaps the best thing is for you to follow it through," he said. "I want to be big enough to contain whatever you must do."

All day long she stayed in the white room. She was a young queen, a virgin in a tower; she was the previous inhabitant, the girl with all the energies. She tried these personalities on like costumes, then discarded them. The room had a new view of streets she'd never seen that way before. The sun hit the room in late afternoon and she took to brushing her hair in the sun. One day she decided to write a poem. "Perhaps a sonnet." She took up her pen and pad and began working from words that had lately lain in her mind. She had choices for the sonnet, ABAB or ABBA for a start. She pondered these possibilities until she tottered into a larger choice: she did not have to write a sonnet. Her poem could be six, eight, ten, thirteen lines, it could be any number of lines, and it did not even have to rhyme.

She put down the pen on top of the pad.

In the evenings, very briefly, she saw the two of them. They knocked on her door, a big knock and a little, and she would call Come in, and the husband would smile though he looked a bit tired, yet somehow this tiredness suited him. He would put her sleeping draught on the bedside table and say, "The boy and I have done all right today," and the child would kiss her. One night she tasted for the first time the power of his baby spit.

"I don't think I can see him anymore," she whispered sadly to the man. 25 And the husband turned away, but recovered admirably and said, "Of course, I see."

So the husband came alone. "I have explained to the boy," he said. "And we are doing fine. We are managing." He squeezed his wife's pale arm and put the two glasses on her table. After he had gone, she sat looking at the arm.

"I'm afraid it's come to that," she said. "Just push the notes under the door; I'll read them. And don't forget to leave the draught outside."

The man sat for a long time with his head in his hands. Then he rose and went away from her. She heard him in the kitchen where he mixed the draught in batches now to last a week at a time, storing it in a corner of the cupboard. She heard him come back, leave the big glass and the little one outside on the floor.

Outside her window the snow was melting from the branches, there were more people on the streets. She brushed her hair a lot and seldom read anymore. She sat in her window and brushed her hair for hours, and saw a boy fall off his new bicycle again and again, a dog chasing a squirrel, an old woman peek slyly over her shoulder and then extract a parcel from a garbage can.

In the evening she read the notes they slipped under her door. The child 30 could not write, so he drew and sometimes painted his. The notes were painstaking at first; the man and boy offering the final strength of their day to her. But sometimes, when they seemed to have had a bad day, there were only hurried scrawls.

One night, when the husband's note had been extremely short, loving but short, and there had been nothing from the boy, she stole out of her room as she often did to get more supplies, but crept upstairs instead and stood outside their doors, listening to the regular breathing of the man and boy asleep. She hurried back to her room and drank the draught.

She woke earlier now. It was spring, there were birds. She listened for sounds of the man and the boy eating breakfast; she listened for the roar of the motor when they drove away. One beautiful noon, she went out to look at her kitchen in the daylight. Things were changed. He had bought some new dish towels. Had the old ones worn out? The canisters seemed closer to the sink. She got out flour, baking powder, salt, milk (he bought a different brand of butter), and baked a loaf of bread and left it cooling on the table.

The force of the two joyful notes slipped under her door that evening pressed her into the corner of the little room; she had hardly space to breathe. As soon as possible, she drank the draught.

Now the days were too short. She was always busy. She woke with the first bird. Worked till the sun set. No time for hair brushing. Her fingers raced the hours.

Finally, in the nick of time, it was finished one late afternoon. Her veins 35 pumped and her forehead sparkled. She went to the cupboard, took what was hers, closed herself into the little white room and brushed her hair for a while.

The man and boy came home and found: five loaves of warm bread, a roast stuffed turkey, a glazed ham, three pies of different fillings, eight molds of the boy's favorite custard, two weeks' supply of fresh-laundered sheets and shirts and towels, two hand-knitted sweaters (both of the same gray color), a sheath of marvelous watercolor beasts accompanied by mad and fanciful stories nobody could ever make up again, and a tablet full of love sonnets addressed to the man. The house smelled redolently of renewal and spring. The man ran to the little room, could not contain himself to knock, flung back the door.

"Look, Mommy is sleeping," said the boy. "She's tired from doing all our things again." He dawdled in a stream of the last sun for that day and watched his father roll tenderly back her eyelids, lay his ear softly to her breast, test the delicate bones of her wrist. The father put down his face into her fresh-washed hair.

"Can we eat the turkey for supper?" the boy asked.

Considerations for Critical Thinking and Writing

1. Describe what you found appealing in each story. Can you point to passages in both that strike you as especially well written or interesting? Was there anything in either story that did not appeal to you? Why?
2. How do the two women's attitudes toward family life differ? How does that difference constitute the problem in each story?
3. How is the woman's problem in "A Sorrowful Woman" made more complex than Faye's in A Secret Sorrow? What is the purpose of the husband and child in Godwin's story?
4. How would you describe the theme, the central point and meaning, in each story?
5. To what extent might "A Sorrowful Woman" be regarded as an unromantic sequel to A Secret Sorrow?
6. Can both stories be read a second or third time and still be interesting? Why or why not?

7. Explain how you think a romance formula writer would end "A Sorrowful Woman," or write the ending yourself.
8. Contrast what marriage means in the two stories.
9. Discuss your feelings about the woman in "A Sorrowful Woman." How does she remain a sympathetic character in spite of her refusal to be a traditional wife and mother? (It may take more than one reading of the story to see that Godwin does sympathize with her.)
10. The happy ending of *A Secret Sorrow* may seem like that of a fairy tale, but it is realistically presented, because there is nothing strange, mysterious, or fabulous that tests our ability to believe it could happen. In contrast, "A Sorrowful Woman" begins with an epigraph *("Once upon a time . . .")* that causes us to expect a fairy-tale ending, but that story is clearly a fairy tale gone wrong. Consider the two stories as fairy tales. How might "A Sorrowful Woman" be read as a dark version of "Sleeping Beauty"?
11. Read the section on feminist criticism in Chapter 35, "Critical Strategies for Reading." Based on that discussion, what do you think a feminist critic might have to say about these two stories?

PERSPECTIVE

TANIA MODLESKI (b. 1949)
The Popularity of Romance Novels   1982

In Harlequin Romances, the need of women to find meaning and pleasure in activities which are not wholly male-centered such as work or artistic creation is generally scoffed at. Soap operas also undercut, though in subtler fashion, the idea that a woman might obtain satisfaction from these activities. A soap-opera woman might very well be engaged in important work like law or medicine, but even on the job she is likely to be obsessed with her love-life or perhaps actually carrying on her love-life, simultaneously weeping over and operating on the weak heart of her intended. Thus, while popular feminine texts provide outlets for women's dissatisfaction with male-female relationships, they never question the primacy of these relationships. Nor do they overtly question the myth of male superiority or the institutions of marriage and the family. Indeed, patriarchal myths and institutions are, on the manifest level, wholeheartedly embraced, although the anxieties and tensions they give rise to may be said to provoke the need for the texts in the first place.

It is useless to deplore the texts for their omissions, distortions, and conservative affirmations. It is crucial to understand them: to let their very omissions and distortions speak, informing us of the contradictions they are meant to conceal and, equally importantly, of the fears that lie behind them. For the texts often do speak profoundly to us, even those of us who like to think we have shed our "false consciousness" and are actively engaged in challenging patriarchal authority. We cannot rest content with theories which would attribute the texts' popularity to the successful conspiracy of a group of patriarchal capitalists plotting to keep women so happy at home that they remain unwilling to make demands which would greatly restructure the work place and the family. Such changes are frightening to *most* of us, for they involve an entire reorganization not just of our social lives, but of our psychic lives as well. Given the radical nature of the feminist task, it is no wonder that college students occasionally cut their women's studies classes to find out what is going on in their favorite soap opera.

From *Loving with a Vengeance: Mass-Produced Fantasies for Women*

Considerations for Critical Thinking and Writing

1. Does the excerpt from the Harlequin Romance, *A Secret Sorrow* (p. 22), reflect what Modleski characterizes as a "myth of male superiority"? Explain how evidence from the text supports or refutes Modleski's assertion that romances contain "omissions, distortions, and conservative affirmations."

2. Explain why you agree or disagree that "anxieties and tensions" account for the popularity of Harlequin romances. From your perspective what does account for their enormous popularity?

3. Write an essay in which you consider a book, film, or television program that appeals to male fantasies, and explore some of the similarities and differences between male and female popular tastes.

2. Plot

Created by a writer's imagination, a work of fiction need not be factual or historically accurate. Although actual people, places, and events may be included in fiction, what is primarily important are not facts so much as the writer's use of them. We can learn much about Russian life in the early part of the nineteenth century from Leo Tolstoy's *War and Peace,* but that historical information is incidental to Tolstoy's exploration of human nature. Tolstoy, like most successful writers, makes us accept as real the world in his novel no matter how foreign it may be to our own reality. One of the ways a writer achieves this acceptance and engagement — and one of a writer's few obligations — is to interest us in what is happening in the story. We are carried into the writer's fictional world by the plot.

Plot is the author's arrangement of incidents in a story. It is the organizing principle that controls the order of events. This structure is, in a sense, what remains after a writer edits out what is irrelevant to the story being told. We don't need to know, for example, what happens to Rip Van Winkle's faithful dog, Wolf, while his amiable master takes his twenty-year nap in the Catskill Mountains in order to be enchanted by Washington Irving's story of a henpecked husband. Instead, what is told takes on meaning as it is brought into focus by a skillful writer who selects and orders the events that constitute the story's plot.

Events can be presented in a variety of orders. A chronological arrangement begins with what happens first, then second, and so on, until the last incident is related. That is how "Rip Van Winkle" is told. The events in William Faulkner's "A Rose for Emily," however, are not arranged in chronological order because that would give away the story's surprise ending; instead, Faulkner moves back and forth between the past and present to provide information that leads up to the final startling moment (which won't be given away here either; the story begins on p. 47).

Some stories begin at the end and then lead up to why or how events worked out as they did. If you read the first paragraph of Yukio Mishima's "Patriotism" (p. 506), you'll find an example of this arrangement that will make it difficult for you to stop reading. Stories can also begin in the middle of things (the Latin term for this common plot strategy is *in medias res*). In this kind of plot we enter the story on the verge of some important moment. John Updike's "A & P" (p. 485) begins with the narrator, a teenager working at a checkout counter in a supermarket, telling us: "In walks these three girls in nothing but bathing suits." Right away we are brought into the middle of a situation that will ultimately create the conflict in the story.

Another common strategy is the *flashback*, a device that informs us about events that happened before the opening scene of a work. Nearly all of Ralph Ellison's "Battle Royal" (p. 187) takes the form of a flashback as the narrator recounts how his identity as a black man was shaped by the circumstances that attended a high-school graduation speech he delivered twenty years earlier in a hotel ballroom before a gathering of the town's leading white citizens, most of whom were "quite tipsy." Whatever the plot arrangement, you should be aware of how the writer's conscious ordering of events affects your responses to the action.

EDGAR RICE BURROUGHS (1875–1950)

A great many stories share a standard plot pattern. The following excerpt from Edgar Rice Burroughs's novel *Tarzan of the Apes* provides a conventional plot pattern in which the *character,* an imagined person in the story, is confronted with a problem leading to a climactic struggle that is followed by a resolution of the problem. The elements of a conventional plot are easily recognizable to readers familiar with fast-paced, action-packed mysteries, spy thrillers, westerns, or adventure stories. These page-turners are carefully plotted so that the reader is swept up by the action. More serious writers sometimes use similar strategies, but they do so with greater subtlety and for some purpose that goes beyond providing a thrill a minute. The writer of serious fiction is usually less concerned with what happens next to the central character than with why it happens. In Burroughs's adventure story, however, the emphasis is clearly upon action. *Tarzan of the Apes* may add little or nothing to our understanding of life, but it is useful for delineating some important elements of plot. Moreover, it is great fun.

Burroughs's novel, published in 1914 and the first of a series of enormously popular Tarzan books and films, charts the growth to manhood of a child raised in the African jungle by great apes. (See Gore Vidal's discussion of the popularity of Tarzan books in the Perspective on p. 45.) Tarzan struggles to survive his primitive beginnings and to reconcile what he has learned in the jungle with his equally powerful instincts to be a civilized human being. One of the more exciting moments in Tarzan's development is his final confrontation with his old enemy, Terkoz, a huge tyrannical ape that has kidnapped Jane, a pretty nineteen-year-old from Baltimore, Maryland, who has accompanied her father on an expedition to the jungle.

In the chapter preceding this excerpt, Tarzan falls in love with Jane and writes this pointed, if not eloquent, note to her: "I am Tarzan of the Apes. I want you. I am yours. You are mine." Just as he finishes the note, he hears "the agonized screams of a woman" and rushes to their source to find Esmeralda, Jane's maid, hysterical with fear and grief. She reports that Jane, the fair and gentle embodiment of civilization in the story, has been carried off by a gorilla. Here is the first half of the next chapter, which illustrates how Burroughs plots the sequence of events so that the emphasis is on physical action.

From Tarzan of the Apes   1914

From the time Tarzan left the tribe of great anthropoids in which he had been raised, it was torn by continual strife and discord. Terkoz proved a cruel and capricious king, so that, one by one, many of the older and weaker apes, upon whom he was particularly prone to vent his brutish nature, took their families and sought the quiet and safety of the far interior.

But at last those who remained were driven to desperation by the continued truculence of Terkoz, and it so happened that one of them recalled the parting admonition of Tarzan:

"If you have a chief who is cruel, do not do as the other apes do, and attempt, any one of you, to pit yourself against him alone. But, instead, let two or three or four of you attack him together. Then, if you will do this, no chief will dare to be other than he should be, for four of you can kill any chief who may ever be over you."

And the ape who recalled this wise counsel repeated it to several of his fellows, so that when Terkoz returned to the tribe that day he found a warm reception awaiting him.

There were no formalities. As Terkoz reached the group, five huge, hairy 5 beasts sprang upon him.

At heart he was an arrant coward, which is the way with bullies among apes as well as among men; so he did not remain to fight and die, but tore himself away from them as quickly as he could and fled into the sheltering boughs of the forest.

Two more attempts he made to rejoin the tribe, but on each occasion he was set upon and driven away. At last he gave it up, and turned, foaming with rage and hatred, into the jungle.

For several days he wandered aimlessly, nursing his spite and looking for some weak thing on which to vent his pent anger.

It was in this state of mind that the horrible, manlike beast, swinging from tree to tree, came suddenly upon two women in the jungle.

He was right above them when he discovered them. The first intimation 10 Jane Porter had of his presence was when the great hairy body dropped to the earth beside her, and she saw the awful face and the snarling, hideous mouth thrust within a foot of her.

One piercing scream escaped her lips as the brute hand clutched her arm. Then she was dragged toward those awful fangs which yawned at her throat. But ere they touched that fair skin another mood claimed the anthropoid.

The tribe had kept his women. He must find others to replace them. This hairless white ape would be the first of his new household, and so he threw her roughly across his broad, hairy shoulders and leaped back into the trees, bearing Jane away.

Esmeralda's scream of terror had mingled once with that of Jane, and then, as was Esmeralda's manner under stress of emergency which required presence of mind, she swooned.

But Jane did not once lose consciousness. It is true that that awful face, pressing close to hers, and the stench of the foul breath beating upon her nostrils, paralyzed her with terror; but her brain was clear, and she comprehended all that transpired.

With what seemed to her marvelous rapidity the brute bore her through 15 the forest, but still she did not cry out or struggle. The sudden advent of the ape had confused her to such an extent that she thought now that he was bearing her toward the beach.

For this reason she conserved her energies and her voice until she could see that they had approached near enough to the camp to attract the succor she craved.

She could not have known it, but she was being borne farther and farther into the impenetrable jungle.

The scream that had brought Clayton and the two older men stumbling through the undergrowth had led Tarzan of the Apes straight to where Esmeralda lay, but it was not Esmeralda in whom his interest centered, though pausing over her he saw that she was unhurt.

For a moment he scrutinized the ground below and the trees above, until the ape that was in him by virtue of training and environment, combined with the intelligence that was his by right of birth, told his wondrous woodcraft the whole story as plainly as though he had seen the thing happen with his own eyes.

And then he was gone again into the swaying trees, following the high-flung 20 spoor which no other human eye could have detected, much less translated.

At boughs' ends, where the anthropoid swings from one tree to another, there is most to mark the trail, but least to point the direction of the quarry; for there the pressure is downward always, toward the small end of the branch, whether the ape be leaving or entering a tree. Nearer the center of the tree, where the signs of passage are fainter, the direction is plainly marked.

Here, on this branch, a caterpillar has been crushed by the fugitive's great foot, and Tarzan knows instinctively where that same foot would touch in the next stride. Here he looks to find a tiny particle of the demolished larva, ofttimes not more than a speck of moisture.

Again, a minute bit of bark has been upturned by the scraping hand, and the direction of the break indicates the direction of the passage. Or some great limb, or the stem of the tree itself has been brushed by the hairy body, and a tiny shred of hair tells him by the direction from which it is wedged beneath the bark that he is on the right trail.

Nor does he need to check his speed to catch these seemingly faint records of the fleeing beast.

To Tarzan they stand out boldly against all the myriad other scars and 25 bruises and signs upon the leafy way. But strongest of all is the scent, for Tarzan is pursuing up the wind, and his trained nostrils are as sensitive as a hound's.

There are those who believe that the lower orders are specially endowed by nature with better olfactory nerves than man, but it is merely a matter of development.

Man's survival does not hinge so greatly upon the perfection of his senses. His power to reason has relieved them of many of their duties, and so they have, to some extent, atrophied, as have the muscles which move the ears and scalp, merely from disuse.

The muscles are there, about the ears and beneath the scalp, and so are the nerves which transmit sensations to the brain, but they are underdeveloped because they are not needed.

Not so with Tarzan of the Apes. From early infancy his survival had depended upon acuteness of eyesight, hearing, smell, touch, and taste far more than upon the more slowly developed organ of reason.

The least developed of all in Tarzan was the sense of taste, for he could eat 30 luscious fruits, or raw flesh, long buried with almost equal appreciation; but in that he differed but slightly from more civilized epicures.

Almost silently the ape-man sped on in the track of Terkoz and his prey, but the sound of his approach reached the ears of the fleeing beast and spurred it on to greater speed.

Three miles were covered before Tarzan overtook them, and then Terkoz, seeing that further flight was futile, dropped to the ground in a small open glade, that he might turn and fight for his prize or be free to escape unhampered if he saw that the pursuer was more than a match for him.

He still grasped Jane in one great arm as Tarzan bounded like a leopard into the arena which nature had provided for this primeval-like battle.

When Terkoz saw that it was Tarzan who pursued him, he jumped to the conclusion that this was Tarzan's woman, since they were of the same kind — white and hairless — and so he rejoiced at this opportunity for double revenge upon his hated enemy.

To Jane the strange apparition of this godlike man was as wine to sick 35 nerves.

From the description which Clayton and her father and Mr. Philander had given her, she knew that it must be the same wonderful creature who had saved them, and she saw in him only a protector and a friend.

But as Terkoz pushed her roughly aside to meet Tarzan's charge, and she saw the great proportions of the ape and the mighty muscles and the fierce fangs, her heart quailed. How could any vanquish such a mighty antagonist?

Like two charging bulls they came together, and like two wolves sought each other's throat. Against the long canines of the ape was pitted the thin blade of the man's knife.

Jane — her lithe, young form flattened against the trunk of a great tree, her hands tight pressed against her rising and falling bosom, and her eyes wide with mingled horror, fascination, fear, and admiration — watched the primordial ape battle with the primeval man for possession of a woman — for her.

As the great muscles of the man's back and shoulders knotted beneath the tension of his efforts, and the huge biceps and forearm held at bay those mighty tusks, the veil of centuries of civilization and culture were swept from the blurred vision of the Baltimore girl. 40

When the long knife drank deep a dozen times of Terkoz' heart's blood, and the great carcass rolled lifeless upon the ground, it was a primeval woman who sprang forward with outstretched arms toward the primeval man who had fought for her and won.

And Tarzan?

He did what no red-blooded man needs lessons in doing. He took his woman in his arms and smothered her upturned, panting lips with kisses.

For a moment Jane lay there with half-closed eyes. For a moment — the first in her young life — she knew the meaning of love.

But as suddenly as the veil had been withdrawn it dropped again, and an outraged conscience suffused her face with its scarlet mantle, and a mortified woman thrust Tarzan of the Apes from her and buried her face in her hands. 45

Tarzan had been surprised when he had found the girl he had learned to love after a vague and abstract manner a willing prisoner in his arms. Now he was surprised that she repulsed him.

He came close to her once more and took hold of her arm. She turned upon him like a tigress, striking his great breast with her tiny hands.

Tarzan could not understand it.

A moment ago, and it had been his intention to hasten Jane back to her people, but that little moment was lost now in the dim and distant past of things which were but can never be again, and with it the good intention had gone to join the impossible.

Since then Tarzan of the Apes had felt a warm, lithe form close pressed to his. Hot, sweet breath against his cheek and mouth had fanned a new flame to life within his breast, and perfect lips had clung to his in burning kisses that had seared a deep brand into his soul — a brand which marked a new Tarzan. 50

Again he laid his hand upon her arm. Again she repulsed him. And then Tarzan of the Apes did just what his first ancestor would have done.

He took his woman in his arms and carried her into the jungle.

This episode begins with *exposition,* the background information the reader needs to make sense of the situation in which the characters are placed. The first eight paragraphs let us know that Terkoz has been overthrown as leader of the ape tribe and that he is roaming the jungle "looking for some weak thing on which to vent his pent anger." This exposition is in the form of a flashback. (Recall that the previous chapter ended with Esmeralda's report of the kidnapping; now we will see what happened.)

Once this information supplies a context for the characters, the plot gains momentum with the *rising action,* a complication that intensifies the situation: Terkoz, looking for a victim, discovers the vulnerable Esmeralda and Jane. His first impulse is to kill Jane, but his "mood" changes when he remembers that he has no woman of his own after having been forced to leave the tribe (more exposition). Hence, there is a further complication in the rising action when he decides to carry her off. Just when it seems that the situation could not get any worse, it does. The reader is invited to shudder even more than if Terkoz had made a meal of Jane, because she may have to endure the "awful face," "foul breath," and lust of this beast.

At this point we are brought up to the action that ended the preceding chapter. Tarzan races to the rescue by unerringly following the trail from the place where Jane was kidnapped. He relentlessly tracks Terkoz. Unfortunately, Burroughs slows down the pursuit here by including several paragraphs that abstractly consider the evolutionary development of humans relying on reason more than on their senses for survival. This discussion offers a rationale for Tarzan's remarkable ability to track Jane, but it is an interruption in the chase.

When Tarzan finally catches up to Terkoz, the *conflict* of this episode fully emerges. Tarzan must save the woman he loves by defeating his long-standing enemy. For Terkoz seeks to achieve a "double revenge" by killing Tarzan and taking his woman. Terkoz's assumption that Jane is Tarzan's woman is a *foreshadowing,* a suggestion of what is yet to come. In this conflict Tarzan is the *protagonist* or *hero,* the central character who engages our interest and empathy. *Protagonist* is often a more useful term than hero or *heroine,* however, because the central character of a story can be despicable as well as heroic. In Edgar Allan Poe's "The Tell-Tale Heart," for example, the central character is a madman and murderer. Terkoz is the *antagonist,* the force that opposes the protagonist.

The battle between Tarzan and Terkoz creates *suspense,* because the reader is made anxious about what is going to happen. Burroughs makes certain that the reader will worry about the outcome by having Jane wonder, "How could any vanquish such a mighty antagonist?" If we are caught up in the moment, we watch the battle, as Jane does, with "mingled horror, fascination, fear, and admiration" to see what will happen next. The moment of greatest emotional tension, the *climax,* occurs when Tarzan kills Terkoz. Tarzan's victory is the *resolution* of the conflict, also known as the *dénouement* (a French word meaning the "untying of the knot"). This could have been the conclusion to the episode except that Jane and Tarzan simultaneously discover their "primeval" selves sexually drawn to each other. Burroughs resolves one conflict — the battle with Terkoz — but then immediately creates another — by raising the question of what a respectable professor's daughter from Baltimore is doing in the sweaty arms of a panting, half-naked man.

For a brief moment the cycle of conflict, suspense, and resolution begins again as Jane passionately kisses Tarzan; then her "outraged conscience" causes her to regain her sense of propriety and she pushes him away. Although Tarzan succeeds in the encounter with Terkoz, he is not successful with Jane. However, Burroughs creates suspense for a third time at the very end of the episode, when the "new Tarzan," having been transformed by this sexual awakening, "took his woman in his arms and carried her into the jungle." What will he do next? Despite the novel's implausibility (beginning with the premise that apes could raise a human child) and its heavy use of coincidences (not the least of which is Tarzan's donning a loincloth for the first time only four pages before he meets Jane), the story is difficult to put down. The plot swings us swiftly and smoothly from incident to incident, even if there is an occasional interruption, such as Burroughs's discussion of evolution, in the flow of the action.

Although this pattern of exposition, rising action, conflict, suspense, climax, and resolution provides a useful outline of many plots that emphasize physical action, a greater value of this pattern is that it helps us to see how innovative artists move beyond formula fiction by manipulating and changing the pattern for their own purposes. At the furthest extreme are those modern storytellers who reject traditional plotting techniques in favor of experimental approaches. Instead of including characters who wrestle with conflicts, experimental fiction frequently may concern the writer's own efforts to create a story. Rather than ordering experience, such writers disrupt it by insisting that meanings in fiction are as elusive — or nonexistent — as meanings in life; they are likely to reject both traditional values and traditional forms of writing. Most writers, however, use conflicts in their plots to reveal characters and convey meanings. The nature of those conflicts can help determine how important physical action is to the plot.

The primary conflict that Tarzan experiences in his battle with Terkoz is external. External conflict is popular in adventure stories because the protagonist's physical struggles with a formidable foe or the ever-present dangers of a dense jungle echoing wild screams provide plenty of excitement. External conflicts may place the protagonist in opposition to another individual, nature, or society. Tarzan's battle with societal values begins the moment he instinctively takes Jane in his arms to carry her off into the jungle. He will learn that an individual's conflict with society can be as frustrating as it is complex, which is why so many plots in serious fiction focus on this conflict. It can be seen, to cite only two examples, in a mysterious stranger's alienation from a materialistic culture in Herman Melville's "Bartleby, the Scrivener" (p. 83) and in a young black man's struggle with racism in Ralph Ellison's "Battle Royal" (p. 187).

Conflict may also be internal; in such a case some moral or psychological issue must be resolved within the protagonist. Inner conflicts frequently accompany external ones, as in Godwin's "A Sorrowful Woman" (p. 31). Godwin's story is quiet and almost uneventful compared with *Tarzan of the Apes*. The conflict, though puzzling, is more significant in "A Sorrowful Woman," because that story subtly explores some troubling issues that cannot be resolved simply by "huge biceps" or a "lithe, young form." The protagonist struggles with both internal and external forces. We are not told why she withdraws from her considerate husband and beautiful son. There is no exposition to explain why she is hopelessly "sad and sick" of them. There is no readily identifiable antagonist in her way, but there are several possibilities. Her antagonist is some part of herself that cannot find satisfaction in playing the roles of wife and mother, yet her husband and child also seem to bear some of the responsibility, as does the domestic environment that defines her.

Godwin creates questions for the reader rather than suspense. We are compelled to keep asking why the protagonist in her story is so unhappy instead of what is going to happen next. The story ends with her flurry of domestic activity and her death, but we do not feel as if we have come to a resolution. "A Sorrowful Woman" will not let us go because we keep coming back to what causes the protagonist's rejection of her role. Has she gone mad? Are the husband and child not what they seem to be? Is her domestic life stifling rather than nourishing? Does her family destroy rather than support her? Who or what is to blame? No one is able to rescue the sorrowful woman from her conflict, nor does the design of Godwin's plot relieve the reader of the questions the story raises. The meaning of the action is not self-evident as it is in *Tarzan of the Apes*. It must be drawn from a careful reading of the interrelated details and dialogues that constitute this story's action.

Although Burroughs makes enormous demands on Tarzan to survive the perils of the jungle, the author makes few demands on the reader. In part, that's why *Tarzan of the Apes* is so much fun: we sit back while Tarzan does all the work, struggling heroically through all the conflicts Burroughs planted along his jungle paths. Godwin's story, in contrast, illustrates that there are other kinds of plots, less dependent on action but equally full of conflict. This kind of reading is more demanding, but ultimately more satisfying, because as we confront conflicts in serious fiction we read not only absorbing stories but also ourselves. We are invited not to escape life but to look long and hard at it. Although serious fiction can be as diverting and pleasurable as most standard action-packed plots, serious fiction offers an additional important element: a perspective on experience that reflects rather than deflects life.

PERSPECTIVE

GORE VIDAL (b. 1925)
The Popularity of the Tarzan Books   1963

These books are clearly for men. I have yet to meet a woman who found Tarzan interesting: no identification, as they say in series land.

Though Burroughs is innocent of literature . . . he does have a gift very few writers of any kind possess: he can describe action vividly. I give away no trade secrets when I say that this is as difficult for a Tolstoi as it is for a Burroughs (even William). Because it is so hard, the draftier contemporary novelists usually prefer to tell their stories in the first person, which is simply writing dialogue. In character, as it were, the writer settles for an impression of what happened rather than creating the sense of a happening. Tarzan *in action* is excellent.

There is something basic in the appeal of the 1914 Tarzan which makes me think that he can still hold his own as a daydream figure, despite the sophisticated challenge for his two contemporary competitors, Ian Fleming and Mickey Spillane. For most adults, Tarzan (and John Carter of Mars) can hardly compete with the conspicuous consumer consumption of James Bond or the sickly violence of Mike Hammer, but for children and adolescents, the old appeal continues. All of us need the idea of a world alternative to this one. From Plato's *Republic* to Opar to Bondland, at every level, the human imagination has tried to imagine something better for itself than the existing society. Man left Eden when we got up off all fours, endowing most of his descendants with nostalgia as well as chronic backache. In its naïve way, the Tarzan legend returns us to that Eden where, free of clothes and the inhibitions of an oppressive society, a man can achieve in reverie his continuing need, which is, as William Faulkner put it in his high Confederate style, to prevail as well as endure. . . . The individual's desire to dominate his environment is not a desirable trait in a society which every day grows more and more confining. Since there are few legitimate releases for the average man, he must take to daydreaming. James Bond, Mike Hammer, and Tarzan are all dream-selves, and the aim of each is to establish personal primacy in a world which in reality diminishes the individual. Among adults, increasing popularity of these lively inferior fictions strikes me as a most significant (and unbearably sad) phenomenon.

From "Tarzan Revisited" in *Esquire*

Considerations for Critical Thinking and Writing

1. What does Vidal see as the lasting appeal of the Tarzan books? Is this true of most popular literature?
2. Explain why you agree or disagree with Vidal's view that "these books are clearly for men" rather than for women.
3. Vidal praises Burroughs's writing when he says, "Tarzan *in action* is excellent." Do you think the excerpt from *Tarzan of the Apes* (p. 39) supports this view? Explain why or why not.

Connections to Other Selections

1. How might the excerpts from *Tarzan of the Apes* (p. 39) and *A Secret Sorrow* (p. 22) be regarded as stories that return us to what Vidal calls a kind of "Eden"? What constitutes "Eden" in each story? How does each author's gender help to explain the difference in their versions of an ideal existence?
2. Write an essay exploring the differences between how Burroughs writes about action in the Tarzan excerpt and how Tim O'Brien handles action in the plot of "How to Tell a True War Story" (p. 552).

The following two stories, William Faulkner's "A Rose for Emily" and Andre Dubus's "Killings," are remarkable for the different kinds of tension produced in each by a subtle use of plot.

WILLIAM FAULKNER (1897–1962)

Born into an old Mississippi family that had lost its influence and wealth during the Civil War, William Faulkner lived nearly all his life in the South writing about Yoknapatawpha County, an imagined Mississippi county similar to his home in Oxford. Among his novels based on this fictional location are *The Sound and the Fury* (1929), *As I Lay Dying* (1930), *Light in August* (1932), and *Absalom, Absalom!* (1936). Although his writings are regional in their emphasis on local social history, his concerns are broader. In his 1950 acceptance speech for the Nobel Prize, he insisted that the "problems of the human heart in conflict with itself . . . alone can make good writing because only that is worth writing about, worth the agony and the sweat." This commitment is evident in his novels and in *The Collected Stories of William Faulkner* (1950). "A Rose for Emily," about the mysterious life of Emily Grierson, presents a personal conflict rooted in her southern identity. It also contains a grim surprise.

A Rose for Emily   1931

I

When Miss Emily Grierson died, our whole town went to her funeral: the men through a sort of respectful affection for a fallen monument, the women mostly out of curiosity to see the inside of her house, which no one save an old manservant — a combined gardener and cook — had seen in at least ten years.

It was a big, squarish frame house that had once been white, decorated with cupolas and spires and scrolled balconies in the heavily lightsome style of the seventies, set on what had once been our most select street. But garages and cotton gins had encroached and obliterated even the august names of that neighborhood; only Miss Emily's house was left, lifting its stubborn and coquettish decay above the cotton wagons and the gasoline pumps — an eyesore among eyesores. And now Miss Emily had gone to join the representatives of those august names where they lay in the cedar-bemused cemetery among the ranked and anonymous graves of Union and Confederate soldiers who fell at the battle of Jefferson.

Alive, Miss Emily had been a tradition, a duty, and a care; a sort of hereditary obligation upon the town, dating from that day in 1894 when Colonel Sartoris, the mayor — he who fathered the edict that no Negro woman should appear on the streets without an apron — remitted her taxes, the dispensation dating from the death of her father on into perpetuity. Not that Miss Emily would have accepted charity. Colonel Sartoris invented an involved tale to the effect that Miss Emily's father had loaned money to the town, which the town, as a matter of business, preferred this way of repaying. Only a man of Colonel Sartoris' generation and thought could have invented it, and only a woman could have believed it.

When the next generation, with its more modern ideas, became mayors and aldermen, this arrangement created some little dissatisfaction. On the first of the year they mailed her a tax notice. February came, and there was no reply. They wrote her a formal letter, asking her to call at the sheriff's office at her convenience. A week later the mayor wrote her himself, offering to call or to send his car for her, and received in reply a note on paper of an archaic shape, in a thin, flowing calligraphy in faded ink, to the effect that she no longer went out at all. The tax notice was also enclosed, without comment.

They called a special meeting of the Board of Aldermen. A deputation waited 5 upon her, knocked at the door through which no visitor had passed since she ceased giving china-painting lessons eight or ten years earlier. They were admitted by the old Negro into a dim hall from which a stairway mounted into still more shadow. It smelled of dust and disuse — a close, dank smell. The Negro led them into the parlor. It was furnished in heavy, leather-covered furniture. When the Negro opened the blinds of one window, they could see that the leather was cracked; and when they sat down, a faint dust rose sluggishly about their thighs, spinning with slow motes in the single sun-ray. On a tarnished gilt easel before the fireplace stood a crayon portrait of Miss Emily's father.

They rose when she entered — a small, fat woman in black, with a thin gold chain descending to her waist and vanishing into her belt, leaning on an ebony cane with a tarnished gold head. Her skeleton was small and spare; perhaps that was why what would have been merely plumpness in another was obesity in her. She looked bloated, like a body long submerged in motionless water, and of that pallid hue. Her eyes, lost in the fatty ridges of her face, looked like two small pieces of coal pressed into a lump of dough as they moved from one face to another while the visitors stated their errand.

She did not ask them to sit. She just stood in the door and listened quietly until the spokesman came to a stumbling halt. Then they could hear the invisible watch ticking at the end of the gold chain.

Her voice was dry and cold. "I have no taxes in Jefferson. Colonel Sartoris explained it to me. Perhaps one of you can gain access to the city records and satisfy yourselves."

"But we have. We are the city authorities, Miss Emily. Didn't you get a notice from the sheriff, signed by him?"

"I received a paper, yes," Miss Emily said. "Perhaps he considers himself 10 the sheriff . . . I have no taxes in Jefferson."

"But there is nothing on the books to show that, you see. We must go by the — "

"See Colonel Sartoris. I have no taxes in Jefferson."

"But, Miss Emily — "

"See Colonel Sartoris." (Colonel Sartoris had been dead almost ten years.) "I have no taxes in Jefferson. Tobe!" The Negro appeared. "Show these gentlemen out."

So she vanquished them, horse and foot, just as she had vanquished their 15
fathers thirty years before about the smell. That was two years after her father's
death and a short time after her sweetheart — the one we believed would marry
her — had deserted her. After her father's death she went out very little; after
her sweetheart went away, people hardly saw her at all. A few of the ladies had
the temerity to call, but were not received, and the only sign of life about the
place was the Negro man — a young man then — going in and out with a market
basket.

"Just as if a man — any man — could keep a kitchen properly," the ladies
said; so they were not surprised when the smell developed. It was another link
between the gross, teeming world and the high and mighty Griersons.

A neighbor, a woman, complained to the mayor, Judge Stevens, eighty years
old.

"But what will you have me do about it, madam?" he said.

"Why, send her word to stop it," the woman said. "Isn't there a law?"

"I'm sure that won't be necessary," Judge Stevens said. "It's probably just a 20
snake or a rat that nigger of hers killed in the yard. I'll speak to him about it."

The next day he received two more complaints, one from a man who came
in diffident deprecation. "We really must do something about it, Judge. I'd be
the last one in the world to bother Miss Emily, but we've got to do something."
That night the Board of Aldermen met — three graybeards and one younger
man, a member of the rising generation.

"It's simple enough," he said. "Send her word to have her place cleaned
up. Give her a certain time to do it in, and if she don't . . ."

"Dammit, sir," Judge Stevens said, "will you accuse a lady to her face of
smelling bad?"

So the next night, after midnight, four men crossed Miss Emily's lawn and
slunk about the house like burglars, sniffing along the base of the brickwork
and at the cellar openings while one of them performed a regular sowing motion
with his hand out of a sack slung from his shoulder. They broke open the cellar
door and sprinkled lime there, and in all the outbuildings. As they recrossed the
lawn, a window that had been dark was lighted and Miss Emily sat in it, the light
behind her, and her upright torso motionless as that of an idol. They crept
quietly across the lawn and into the shadow of the locusts that lined the street.
After a week or two the smell went away.

That was when people had begun to feel really sorry for her. People in our 25
town, remembering how old lady Wyatt, her great-aunt, had gone completely
crazy at last, believed that the Griersons held themselves a little too high for
what they really were. None of the young men were quite good enough for Miss
Emily and such. We had long thought of them as a tableau, Miss Emily a
slender figure in white in the background, her father a spraddled silhouette in
the foreground, his back to her and clutching a horsewhip, the two of them
framed by the back-flung front door. So when she got to be thirty and was still
single, we were not pleased exactly, but vindicated; even with insanity in the family
she wouldn't have turned down all of her chances if they had really materialized.

When her father died, it got about that the house was all that was left to
her; and in a way, people were glad. At last they could pity Miss Emily. Being

left alone, and a pauper, she had become humanized. Now she too would know the old thrill and the old despair of a penny more or less.

The day after his death all the ladies prepared to call at the house and offer condolence and aid, as is our custom. Miss Emily met them at the door, dressed as usual and with no trace of grief on her face. She told them that her father was not dead. She did that for three days, with the ministers calling on her, and the doctors, trying to persuade her to let them dispose of the body. Just as they were about to resort to law and force, she broke down, and they buried her father quickly.

We did not say she was crazy then. We believed she had to do that. We remembered all the young men her father had driven away, and we knew that with nothing left, she would have to cling to that which had robbed her, as people will.

III

She was sick for a long time. When we saw her again, her hair was cut short, making her look like a girl, with a vague resemblance to those angels in colored church windows — sort of tragic and serene.

The town had just let the contracts for paving the sidewalks, and in the summer after her father's death they began the work. The construction company came with niggers and mules and machinery, and a foreman named Homer Barron, a Yankee — a big, dark, ready man, with a big voice and eyes lighter than his face. The little boys would follow in groups to hear him cuss the niggers, and the niggers singing in time to the rise and fall of picks. Pretty soon he knew everybody in town. Whenever you heard a lot of laughing anywhere about the square, Homer Barron would be in the center of the group. Presently we began to see him and Miss Emily on Sunday afternoons driving in the yellow-wheeled buggy and the matched team of bays from the livery stable.

At first we were glad that Miss Emily would have an interest, because the ladies all said, "Of course a Grierson would not think seriously of a Northerner, a day laborer." But there were still others, older people, who said that even grief could not cause a real lady to forget *noblesse oblige*° — without calling it *noblesse oblige*. They just said, "Poor Emily. Her kinsfolk should come to her." She had some kin in Alabama; but years ago her father had fallen out with them over the estate of old lady Wyatt, the crazy woman, and there was no communication between the two families. They had not even been represented at the funeral.

And as soon as the old people said, "Poor Emily," the whispering began. "Do you suppose it's really so?" they said to one another. "Of course it is. What else could . . ." This behind their hands; rustling of craned silk and satin behind jalousies closed upon the sun of Sunday afternoon as the thin, swift clop-clop-clop of the matched team passed: "Poor Emily."

---

noblesse oblige: The obligation of people of high social position.

She carried her head high enough — even when we believed that she was fallen. It was as if she demanded more than ever the recognition of her dignity as the last Grierson; as if it had wanted that touch of earthiness to reaffirm her imperviousness. Like when she bought the rat poison, the arsenic. That was over a year after they had begun to say "Poor Emily," and while the two female cousins were visiting her.

"I want some poison," she said to the druggist. She was over thirty then, still a slight woman, though thinner than usual, with cold, haughty black eyes in a face the flesh of which was strained across the temples and about the eye-sockets as you imagine a lighthouse-keeper's face ought to look. "I want some poison," she said.

"Yes, Miss Emily. What kind? For rats and such? I'd recom — " 35

"I want the best you have. I don't care what kind."

The druggist named several. "They'll kill anything up to an elephant. But what you want is — "

"Arsenic," Miss Emily said. "Is that a good one?"

"Is . . . arsenic? Yes, ma'am. But what you want — "

"I want arsenic." 40

The druggist looked down at her. She looked back at him, erect, her face like a strained flag. "Why, of course," the druggist said. "If that's what you want. But the law requires you to tell what you are going to use it for."

Miss Emily just stared at him, her head tilted back in order to look him eye for eye, until he looked away and went and got the arsenic and wrapped it up. The Negro delivery boy brought her the package; the druggist didn't come back. When she opened the package at home there was written on the box, under the skull and bones: "For rats."

IV

So the next day we all said, "She will kill herself"; and we said it would be the best thing. When she had first begun to be seen with Homer Barron, we had said, "She will marry him." Then we said, "She will persuade him yet," because Homer himself had remarked — he liked men, and it was known that he drank with the younger men in the Elks' Club — that he was not a marrying man. Later we said, "Poor Emily" behind the jalousies as they passed on Sunday afternoon in the glittering buggy, Miss Emily with her head high and Homer Barron with his hat cocked and a cigar in his teeth, reins and whip in a yellow glove.

Then some of the ladies began to say that it was a disgrace to the town and a bad example to the young people. The men did not want to interfere, but at last the ladies forced the Baptist minister — Miss Emily's people were Episcopal — to call upon her. He would never divulge what happened during that interview, but he refused to go back again. The next Sunday they again drove about the streets, and the following day the minister's wife wrote to Miss Emily's relations in Alabama.

So she had blood-kin under her roof again and we sat back to watch 45 developments. At first nothing happened. Then we were sure that they were to be married. We learned that Miss Emily had been to the jeweler's and ordered a man's toilet set in silver, with the letters H. B. on each piece. Two days later we learned that she had bought a complete outfit of men's clothing, including a nightshirt, and we said, "They are married." We were really glad. We were glad because the two female cousins were even more Grierson than Miss Emily had ever been.

So we were not surprised when Homer Barron — the streets had been finished some time since — was gone. We were a little disappointed that there was not a public blowing-off, but we believed that he had gone on to prepare for Miss Emily's coming, or to give her a chance to get rid of the cousins. (By that time it was a cabal, and we were all Miss Emily's allies to help circumvent the cousins.) Sure enough, after another week they departed. And, as we had expected all along, within three days Homer Barron was back in town. A neighbor saw the Negro man admit him at the kitchen door at dusk one evening.

And that was the last we saw of Homer Barron. And of Miss Emily for some time. The Negro man went in and out with the market basket, but the front door remained closed. Now and then we would see her at a window for a moment, as the men did that night when they sprinkled the lime, but for almost six months she did not appear on the streets. Then we knew that this was to be expected too; as if that quality of her father which had thwarted her woman's life so many times had been too virulent and too furious to die.

When we next saw Miss Emily, she had grown fat and her hair was turning gray. During the next few years it grew grayer and grayer until it attained an even pepper-and-salt iron-gray, when it ceased turning. Up to the day of her death at seventy-four it was still that vigorous iron-gray, like the hair of an active man.

From that time on her front door remained closed, save for a period of six or seven years, when she was about forty, during which she gave lessons in china-painting. She fitted up a studio in one of the downstairs rooms, where the daughters and granddaughters of Colonel Sartoris' contemporaries were sent to her with the same regularity and in the same spirit that they were sent to church on Sundays with a twenty-five-cent piece for the collection plate. Meanwhile her taxes had been remitted.

Then the newer generation became the backbone and the spirit of the town, 50 and the painting pupils grew up and fell away and did not send their children to her with boxes of color and tedious brushes and pictures cut from the ladies' magazines. The front door closed upon the last one and remained closed for good. When the town got free postal delivery, Miss Emily alone refused to let them fasten the metal numbers above her door and attach a mailbox to it. She would not listen to them.

Daily, monthly, yearly we watched the Negro grow grayer and more stooped, going in and out with the market basket. Each December we sent her a tax notice, which would be returned by the post office a week later, unclaimed. Now and then we would see her in one of the downstairs windows — she had evidently shut up the top floor of the house — like the carven torso of an idol in a niche, looking or not looking at us, we could never tell which. Thus she passed from generation to generation — dear, inescapable, impervious, tranquil, and perverse.

And so she died. Fell ill in the house filled with dust and shadows, with only a doddering Negro man to wait on her. We did not even know she was sick; we had long since given up trying to get information from the Negro. He talked to no one, probably not even to her, for his voice had grown harsh and rusty, as if from disuse.

She died in one of the downstairs rooms, in a heavy walnut bed with a curtain, her gray head propped on a pillow yellow and moldy with age and lack of sunlight.

V

The Negro met the first of the ladies at the front door and let them in, with their hushed, sibilant voices and their quick, curious glances, and then he disappeared. He walked right through the house and out the back and was not seen again.

The two female cousins came at once. They held the funeral on the second 55 day, with the town coming to look at Miss Emily beneath a mass of bought flowers, with the crayon face of her father musing profoundly above the bier and the ladies sibilant and macabre; and the very old men — some in their brushed Confederate uniforms — on the porch and the lawn, talking of Miss Emily as if she had been a contemporary of theirs, believing that they had danced with her and courted her perhaps, confusing time with its mathematical progression, as the old do, to whom all the past is not a diminishing road but, instead, a huge meadow which no winter ever quite touches, divided from them now by the narrow bottle-neck of the most recent decade of years.

Already we knew that there was one room in that region above stairs which no one had seen in forty years, and which would have to be forced. They waited until Miss Emily was decently in the ground before they opened it.

The violence of breaking down the door seemed to fill this room with pervading dust. A thin, acrid pall as of the tomb seemed to lie everywhere upon this room decked and furnished as for a bridal: upon the valance curtains of faded rose color, upon the rose-shaded lights, upon the dressing table, upon the delicate array of crystal and the man's toilet things backed with tarnished silver, silver so tarnished that the monogram was obscured. Among them lay a collar and tie, as if they had just been removed, which, lifted, left upon the surface a pale crescent in the dust. Upon a chair hung the suit, carefully folded; beneath it the two mute shoes and the discarded socks.

The man himself lay in the bed.

For a long while we just stood there, looking down at the profound and fleshless grin. The body had apparently once lain in the attitude of an embrace, but now the long sleep that outlasts love, that conquers even the grimace of love, had cuckolded him. What was left of him, rotted beneath what was left of the nightshirt, had become inextricable from the bed in which he lay; and upon him and upon the pillow beside him lay that even coating of the patient and biding dust.

Then we noticed that in the second pillow was the indentation of a head. 60 One of us lifted something from it, and leaning forward, that faint and invisible dust dry and acrid in the nostrils, we saw a long strand of iron-gray hair.

Considerations for Critical Thinking and Writing

1. What is the effect of the final paragraph of the story? How does it contribute to your understanding of Emily? Why is it important that we get this information last rather than at the beginning of the story?
2. What details foreshadow the conclusion of the story? Did you anticipate the ending?
3. Contrast the order of events as they happen in the story with the order in which they are told. How does this plotting create interest and suspense?
4. Faulkner uses a number of gothic elements in this plot: the imposing decrepit house, the decayed corpse, and the mysterious secret horrors connected with Emily's life. How do these elements forward the plot and establish the atmosphere?
5. How does the information provided by the exposition indicate the nature of the conflict in the story? What does Emily's southern heritage contribute to the story?
6. Who or what is the antagonist of the story? Why is it significant that Homer Barron is a construction foreman and a northerner?
7. In what sense does the narrator's telling of the story serve as "A Rose for Emily"? Why do you think the narrator uses *we* rather than *I*?
8. Explain how Emily's reasons for murdering Homer are related to her personal history and to the way she handled previous conflicts.
9. Discuss how Faulkner's treatment of the North and South contributes to the meaning of the story.
10. Provide an alternative title and explain how the emphasis in your title is reflected in the story.
11. Describe how this story could be rewritten as a piece of formula fiction and comment on the differences between Faulkner's story and your imagined formulaic version.

Connections to Another Selection

1. Contrast Faulkner's ordering of events with Yukio Mishima's strategy in "Patriotism" (p. 506). How does each author's arrangement of incidents create different effects on the reader?
2. To what extent do concepts of honor and tradition influence the action in "A Rose for Emily" and "Patriotism"?
3. Compare and contrast Faulkner's and Mishima's uses of death as a means of resolving conflicts having to do with love.

PERSPECTIVES ON FAULKNER

WILLIAM FAULKNER (1897–1962)
On "A Rose for Emily"   1959

Q. What is the meaning of the title "A Rose for Emily"?

A. Oh, it's simply the poor woman had had no life at all. Her father had kept her more or less locked up and then she had a lover who was about to quit her, she had to murder him. It was just "A Rose for Emily" — that's all.

Q. . . . What ever inspired you to write this story?

A. That to me was another sad and tragic manifestation of man's condition in which he dreams and hopes, in which he is in conflict with himself or with his environment or with others. In this case there was the young girl with a young girl's normal aspirations to find love and then a husband and a family, who was brow-beaten and kept down by her father, a selfish man who didn't want her to leave home because he wanted a housekeeper, and it was a natural instinct of — repressed which — you can't repress it — you can mash it down but it comes up somewhere else and very likely in a tragic form, and that was simply another manifestation of man's injustice to man, of the poor tragic human being struggling with its own heart, with others, with its environment, for the simple things which all human beings want. In that case it was a young girl that just wanted to be loved and to love and to have a husband and a family.

Q. And that purely came from your imagination?

A. Well, the story did but the condition is there. It exists. I didn't invent that condition, I didn't invent the fact that young girls dream of someone to love and children and a home, but the story of what her own particular tragedy was was invented, yes. . . .

Q. Sir, it has been argued that "A Rose for Emily" is a criticism of the North, and others have argued saying that it is a criticism of the South. Now, could this story, shall we say, be more properly classified as a criticism of the times?

A. Now that I don't know, because I was simply trying to write about people. The writer uses environment — what he knows — and if there's a symbolism in which the lover represented the North and the woman who murdered him represents the South, I don't say that's not valid and not there, but it was no intention of the writer to say, Now let's see, I'm going to write a piece in which I will use a symbolism for the North and another symbol for the South, that he was simply writing about people, a story which he thought was tragic and true, because it came out of the human heart, the human aspiration, the human — the conflict of conscience with glands, with the Old Adam. It was a conflict not between North and the South so much as between, well you might say, God and Satan.

Q. Sir, just a little more on that thing. You say it's a conflict between God and Satan. Well, I don't quite understand what you mean. Who is — did one represent the ——

A. The conflict was in Miss Emily, that she knew that you do not murder people. She had been trained that you do not take a lover. You marry, you don't take a lover. She had broken all the laws of her tradition, her background, and she had finally broken the law of God too, which says you do not take human life. And she knew she was doing wrong, and that's why her own life was wrecked. Instead of murdering one lover, and then to go and take another and when she used him up to murder him, she was expiating her crime.

Q. Was the "Rose for Emily" an idea or a character? Just how did you go about it?

A. That came from a picture of the strand of hair on the pillow. It was a ghost story. Simply a picture of a strand of hair on the pillow in the abandoned house.

From Frederick Gwynn and Joseph Blotner, eds., *Faulkner in the University*

Considerations for Critical Thinking and Writing

1. Discuss whether you think Faulkner's explanation of the conflict between "God and Satan" limits or expands the meaning of the story for you.
2. In what sense is "A Rose for Emily" a "ghost story"?
3. Compare Faulkner's account of how he conceived "A Rose for Emily" with Flannery O'Connor's description of "Good Country People" (p. 379). To what extent are their attitudes about symbolism similar?

SALLY R. PAGE (b. 1938)
The Hostile Community in "A Rose for Emily" 1972

Miss Emily is denied normal participation in the life of the community because she represents a traditional aristocracy of a higher social class than the norm. This situation, created by her ancestry and a father who refused to allow her a normal social life as a girl from the fear that she might marry beneath herself, is perpetuated by the community, which denies Miss Emily's humanity by thinking of her as their symbol of the past. Miss Emily is "a tradition, a duty, and a care"; the town prefers that she remain intact within her old mansion, an idol, "dear, inescapable, impervious, tranquil, and perverse." Jefferson is smugly pleased at possessing a relic of a dead but honorable time; when Miss Emily dies, she becomes their "fallen monument."

Miss Emily is the source of mystery and intrigue for the community. Though she makes little or no effort during her adult life to become a part of the community, it is apparent that the people of Jefferson prefer that she remain a separated object, for upon her they can vent their feelings of hostility and inferiority, and at her expense they can enjoy their feelings of self-righteousness and success. The community experiences a self-comforting and self-vindicating pity when Emily reaches thirty and is still unmarried and when her buggy rides with Homer Barron convince them that she is a fallen woman. . . .

Emily [and other Faulkner women] lead tragic lives because they are unable to assume the procreative role set aside for woman by the natural processes of life. Alienated from the forces of life, they are idle, useless women doomed to death and to sterility, the sign of death in life. Their tragedies are in part the product of a society which encourages sexual repression. [They] are cold and perverse women who reject the normal reproductive process of life. Likewise, because of their traditions of restrictive sexual mores, the communities of which [they] are a part limit the woman's freedom to escape the bonds of death. Yet, these women are the rejected victims of the general social power, thrust into complete aloneness and isolation from the rest of humanity, because they have failed to serve woman's "appointed ends."

To compensate for their failure in real life, these women indulge in fantasy and make-believe in order to create for themselves a world in which their natures can be fulfilled. Such a denial of reality, however, is disastrous, for thereby the women give up all hope of entry into the real world and the assumption of a normal role within it. As a result these women emerge as fragile, child-like figures, incapable of accepting or comprehending reality, and as figures in black who are pallid and bloated with decay and death. With these women characters Faulkner creates superbly an outward appearance which is parallel to and symbolic of the psychological and spiritual condition of their lives. Despite their failure and their decay, Faulkner is able to portray them sympathetically.

From *Faulkner's Women: Characterization and Meaning*

Considerations for Critical Thinking and Writing

1. Why does Page characterize Jefferson as repressive and hostile? Do you think it's possible to see the community as sympathetic and deferential rather than oppressive? Explain why or why not.
2. According to Page what is the effect on Emily of Jefferson's treatment of her?
3. Write an essay that discusses Emily's and Abner Snope's (from Faulkner's "Barn Burning," p. 436) relationships to their respective communities. Consider whether or not they are at all treated differently owing to their class and sex.

ANDRE DUBUS (b. 1936)

Though a native of Louisiana, where he attended the Christian Brothers School and McNeese State College, Andre Dubus has lived much of his life in Massachusetts; many of his stories are set in the Merrimack Valley north of Boston. After college Dubus served as an officer for five years in the Marine Corps. He then took an M.F.A. at the University of Iowa in 1966 and began teaching at Bradford College in Massachusetts. His fiction has earned him numerous awards, and he has been both a Guggenheim and a MacArthur Fellow. Among his collections of fiction are *Separate Flights* (1975), *Adultery and Other Choices* (1977), *Finding a Girl in America* (1980), from which "Killings" is taken, *The Last Worthless Evening* (1986), and *Collected Stories* (1988). His fictions are often tense with violence, anger, tenderness, and guilt; they are populated by characters who struggle to understand and survive their experiences, painful with failure and the weight of imperfect relationships. In "Killings" Dubus offers a powerful blend of intimate domestic life and shocking violence.

Killings   1979

On the August morning when Matt Fowler buried his youngest son, Frank, who had lived for twenty-one years, eight months, and four days, Matt's older son, Steve, turned to him as the family left the grave and walked between their friends, and said: "I should kill him." He was twenty-eight, his brown hair starting to thin in front where he used to have a cowlick. He bit his lower lip, wiped his eyes, then said it again. Ruth's arm, linked with Matt's tightened; he looked at her. Beneath her eyes there was swelling from the three days she had suffered. At the limousine Matt stopped and looked back at the grave, the casket, and the Congregationalist minister who he thought had probably had a difficult job with the eulogy though he hadn't seemed to, and the old funeral director who was saying something to the six young pallbearers. The grave was on a hill and overlooked the Merrimack, which he could not see from where he stood; he looked at the opposite bank, at the apple orchard with its symmetrically planted trees going up a hill.

Next day Steve drove with his wife back to Baltimore where he managed the branch office of a bank, and Cathleen, the middle child, drove with her husband back to Syracuse. They had left the grandchildren with friends. A month after the funeral Matt played poker at Willis Trottier's because Ruth, who knew this was the second time he had been invited, told him to go, he couldn't sit home with her for the rest of her life, she was all right. After the game Willis went outside to tell everyone good night and, when the others had driven away, he walked with Matt to his car. Willis was a short, silver-haired man who had opened a diner after World War II, his trade then mostly very early breakfast, which he cooked, and then lunch for the men who worked at the leather and shoe factories. He now owned a large restaurant.

"He walks the Goddamn streets," Matt said.

"I know. He was in my place last night, at the bar. With a girl."

"I don't see him. I'm in the store all the time. Ruth sees him. She sees him 5 too much. She was at Sunnyhurst today getting cigarettes and aspirin, and there he was. She can't even go out for cigarettes and aspirin. It's killing her."

"Come back in for a drink."

Matt looked at his watch. Ruth would be asleep. He walked with Willis back into the house, pausing at the steps to look at the starlit sky. It was a cool summer night; he thought vaguely of the Red Sox, did not even know if they were at home tonight; since it happened he had not been able to think about any of the small pleasures he believed he had earned, as he had earned also what was shattered now forever: the quietly harried and quietly pleasurable days of fatherhood. They went inside. Willis's wife, Martha, had gone to bed hours ago, in the rear of the large house which was rigged with burglar and fire alarms. They went downstairs to the game room: the television set suspended from the ceiling, the pool table, the poker table with beer cans, cards, chips, filled ashtrays, and the six chairs where Matt and his friends had sat, the friends picking up the old banter as though he had only been away on vacation; but he could see the affection and courtesy in their eyes. Willis went behind the bar and mixed them each a Scotch and soda; he stayed behind the bar and looked at Matt sitting on the stool.

"How often have you thought about it?" Willis said.

"Every day since he got out. I didn't think about bail. I thought I wouldn't have to worry about him for years. She sees him all the time. It makes her cry."

"He was in my place a long time last night. He'll be back." 10

"Maybe he won't."

"The band. He likes the band."

"What's he doing now?"

"He's tending bar up to Hampton Beach. For a friend. Ever notice even the worst bastard always has friends? He couldn't get work in town. It's just tourists and kids up to Hampton. Nobody knows him. If they do, they don't care. They drink what he mixes."

"Nobody tells me about him." 15

"I hate him, Matt. My boys went to school with him. He was the same then. Know what he'll do? Five at the most. Remember that woman about seven years ago? Shot her husband and dropped him off the bridge in the Merrimack with a hundred-pound sack of cement and said all the way through it that nobody helped her. Know where she is now? She's in Lawrence now, a secretary. And whoever helped her, where the hell is he?"

"I've got a .38 I've had for years, I take it to the store now. I tell Ruth it's for the night deposits. I tell her things have changed: we got junkies here now too. Lots of people without jobs. She knows though."

"What does she know?"

"She knows I started carrying it after the first time she saw him in town. She knows it's in case I see him, and there's some kind of a situation — "

He stopped, looked at Willis, and finished his drink. Willis mixed him 20 another.

"What kind of situation?"

"Where he did something to me. Where I could get away with it."

"How does Ruth feel about that?"

"She doesn't know."

"You said she does, she's got it figured out." 25

He thought of her that afternoon: when she went into Sunnyhurst, Strout was waiting at the counter while the clerk bagged the things he had bought; she turned down an aisle and looked at soup cans until he left.

"Ruth would shoot him herself, if she thought she could hit him."

"You got a permit?"

"No."

"I do. You could get a year for that." 30

"Maybe I'll get one. Or maybe I won't. Maybe I'll just stop bringing it to the store."

Richard Strout was twenty-six years old, a high school athlete, football scholarship to the University of Massachusetts where he lasted for almost two semesters before quitting in advance of the final grades that would have forced him not to return. People then said: Dickie can do the work; he just doesn't want to. He came home and did construction work for his father but refused his father's offer to learn the business; his two older brothers had learned it, so that Strout and Sons trucks going about town, and signs on construction sites, now slashed wounds into Matt Fowler's life. Then Richard married a young girl and became a bartender, his salary and tips augmented and perhaps sometimes matched by his father, who also posted his bond. So his friends, his enemies (he had those: fist fights or, more often, boys and then young men who had not fought him when they thought they should have), and those who simply knew him by face and name, had a series of images of him which they recalled when they heard of the killing: the high school running back, the young drunk in bars, the oblivious hard-hatted young man eating lunch at a counter, the bartender who could perhaps be called courteous but not more than that: as he tended bar, his dark eyes and dark, wide-jawed face appeared less sullen, near blank.

One night he beat Frank. Frank was living at home and waiting for September, for graduate school in economics, and working as a lifeguard at Salisbury Beach, where he met Mary Ann Strout, in her first month of separation. She spent most days at the beach with her two sons. Before ten o'clock one night Frank came home; he had driven to the hospital first, and he walked into the living room with stitches over his right eye and both lips bright and swollen.

"I'm all right," he said, when Matt and Ruth stood up, and Matt turned off the television, letting Ruth get to him first: the tall, muscled but slender suntanned boy. Frank tried to smile at them but couldn't because of his lips.

"It was her husband, wasn't it?" Ruth said. 35

"Ex," Frank said. "He dropped in."

Matt gently held Frank's jaw and turned his face to the light, looked at the stitches, the blood under the white of the eye, the bruised flesh.

"Press charges," Matt said.

"No."

"What's to stop him from doing it again? Did you hit him at all? Enough so 40 he won't want to next time?"

"I don't think I touched him."

"So what are you going to do?"

"Take karate," Frank said, and tried again to smile.

"That's not the problem," Ruth said.

"You know you like her," Frank said. 45

"I like a lot of people. What about the boys? Did they see it?"

"They were asleep."

"Did you leave her alone with him?"

"He left first. She was yelling at him. I believe she had a skillet in her hand."

"Oh for God's sake," Ruth said. 50

Matt had been dealing with that too: at the dinner table on evenings when Frank wasn't home, was eating with Mary Ann; or, on the other nights — and Frank was with her every night — he talked with Ruth while they watched television, or lay in bed with the windows open and he smelled the night air and imagined, with both pride and muted sorrow, Frank in Mary Ann's arms. Ruth didn't like it because Mary Ann was in the process of divorce, because she had two children, because she was four years older than Frank, and finally — she told this in bed, where she had during all of their marriage told him of her deepest feelings: of love, of passion, of fears about one of the children, of pain Matt had caused her or she had caused him — she was against it because of what she had heard: that the marriage had gone bad early, and for most of it Richard and Mary Ann had both played around.

"That can't be true," Matt said. "Strout wouldn't have stood for it."

"Maybe he loves her."

"He's too hot-tempered. He couldn't have taken that."

But Matt knew Strout had taken it, for he had heard the stories too. He 55 wondered who had told them to Ruth; and he felt vaguely annoyed and isolated:

living with her for thirty-one years and still not knowing what she talked about with her friends. On these summer nights he did not so much argue with her as try to comfort her, but finally there was no difference between the two: she had concrete objections, which he tried to overcome. And in his attempt to do this, he neglected his own objections, which were the same as hers, so that as he spoke to her he felt as disembodied as he sometimes did in the store when he helped a man choose a blouse or dress or piece of costume jewelry for his wife.

"The divorce doesn't mean anything," he said. "She was young and maybe she liked his looks and then after a while she realized she was living with a bastard. I see it as a positive thing."

"She's not divorced yet."

"It's the same thing. Massachusetts has crazy laws, that's all. Her age is no problem. What's it matter when she was born? And that other business: even if it's true, which it probably isn't, it's got nothing to do with Frank, and it's in the past. And the kids are no problem. She's been married six years; she ought to have kids. Frank likes them. He plays with them. And he's not going to marry her anyway, so it's not a problem of money."

"Then what's he doing with her?"

"She probably loves him, Ruth. Girls always have. Why can't we just leave 60 it at that?"

"He got home at six o'clock Tuesday morning."

"I didn't know you knew. I've already talked to him about it."

Which he had: since he believed almost nothing he told Ruth, he went to Frank with what he believed. The night before, he had followed Frank to the car after dinner.

"You wouldn't make much of a burglar," he said.

"How's that?" 65

Matt was looking up at him; Frank was six feet tall, an inch and a half taller than Matt, who had been proud when Frank at seventeen outgrew him; he had only felt uncomfortable when he had to reprimand or caution him. He touched Frank's bicep, thought of the young taut passionate body, believed he could sense the desire, and again he felt the pride and sorrow and envy too, not knowing whether he was envious of Frank or Mary Ann.

"When you came in yesterday morning, I woke up. One of these mornings your mother will. And I'm the one who'll have to talk to her. She won't interfere with you. Okay? I know it means — " But he stopped, thinking: I know it means getting up and leaving that suntanned girl and going sleepy to the car, I know —

"Okay," Frank said, and touched Matt's shoulder and got into the car.

There had been other talks, but the only long one was their first one: a night driving to Fenway Park, Matt having ordered the tickets so they could talk, and knowing when Frank said yes, he would go, that he knew the talk was coming too. It took them forty minutes to get to Boston, and they talked about Mary Ann until they joined the city traffic along the Charles River, blue in the late sun. Frank told him all the things that Matt would later pretend to believe when he told them to Ruth.

"It seems like a lot for a young guy to take on," Matt finally said. 70

"Sometimes it is. But she's worth it."

"Are you thinking about getting married?"

"We haven't talked about it. She can't for over a year. I've got school."

"I *do* like her," Matt said.

He did. Some evenings, when the long summer sun was still low in the sky, Frank brought her home; they came into the house smelling of suntan lotion and the sea, and Matt gave them gin and tonics and started the charcoal in the backyard, and looked at Mary Ann in the lawn chair: long and very light brown hair (Matt thinking that twenty years ago she would have dyed it blonde), and the long brown legs he loved to look at; her face was pretty; she had probably never in her adult life gone unnoticed into a public place. It was in her wide brown eyes that she looked older than Frank; after a few drinks Matt thought what he saw in her eyes was something erotic, testament to the rumors about her; but he knew it wasn't that, or all that: she had, very young, been through a sort of pain that his children, and he and Ruth, had been spared. In the moments of his recognizing that pain, he wanted to tenderly touch her hair, wanted with some gesture to give her solace and hope. And he would glance at Frank, and hope they would love each other, hope Frank would soothe that pain in her heart, take it from her eyes; and her divorce, her age, and her children did not matter at all. On the first two evenings she did not bring her boys, and then Ruth asked her to bring them the next time. In bed that night Ruth said, "She hasn't brought them because she's embarrassed. She shouldn't feel embarrassed."

Richard Strout shot Frank in front of the boys. They were sitting on the living room floor watching television, Frank sitting on the couch, and Mary Ann just returning from the kitchen with a tray of sandwiches. Strout came in the front door and shot Frank twice in the chest and once in the face with a 9 mm. automatic. Then he looked at the boys and Mary Ann, and went home to wait for the police.

It seemed to Matt that from the time Mary Ann called weeping to tell him until now, a Saturday night in September, sitting in the car with Willis, parked beside Strout's car, waiting for the bar to close, that he had not so much moved through his life as wandered through it, his spirits like a dazed body bumping into furniture and corners. He had always been a fearful father: when his children were young, at the start of each summer he thought of them drowning in a pond or the sea, and he was relieved when he came home in the evenings and they were there; usually that relief was his only acknowledgment of his fear, which he never spoke of, and which he controlled within his heart. As he had when they were very young and all of them in turn, Cathleen too, were drawn to the high oak in the backyard, and had to climb it. Smiling, he watched them, imagining the fall: and he was poised to catch the small body before it hit the earth. Or his legs were poised; his hands were in his pockets or his arms were folded and, for the child looking down, he appeared relaxed and confident while his heart beat with the two words he wanted to call out but did not: *Don't fall.* In winter he was less afraid: he made sure the ice would hold him before they skated, and he brought or sent them to places where they could sled without ending in the street. So he and his children had survived their childhood, and he only worried about them when he knew they were driving a long distance, and then he lost Frank in a way no father expected to lose his son, and he felt that all the fears he had borne while they were growing up, and all the grief he had been afraid of, had backed up like a huge wave and struck him on the beach and swept him out to sea. Each day he felt the same and when he was able to forget how he felt, when he was able to force himself not to feel that way, the eyes of his clerks and customers defeated him. He wished those eyes were oblivious, even cold; he felt he was withering in their tenderness. And beneath his listless wandering, every day in his soul he shot Richard Strout in the face; while Ruth, going about town on errands, kept seeing him. And at nights in bed she would hold Matt and cry, or sometimes she was silent and Matt would touch her tightening arm, her clenched fist.

As his own right fist was now, squeezing the butt of the revolver, the last of the drinkers having left the bar, talking to each other, going to their separate cars which were in the lot in front of the bar, out of Matt's vision. He heard their voices, their cars, and then the ocean again, across the street. The tide was in and sometimes it smacked the sea wall. Through the windshield he looked at the dark red side wall of the bar, and then to his left, past Willis, at Strout's car, and through its windows he could see the now-emptied parking lot, the road, the sea wall. He could smell the sea.

The front door of the bar opened and closed again and Willis looked at Matt then at the corner of the building; when Strout came around it alone Matt got out of the car, giving up the hope he had kept all night (and for the past week) that Strout would come out with friends, and Willis would simply drive away; thinking: *All right then. All right;* and he went around the front of Willis's car, and at Strout's he stopped and aimed over the hood at Strout's blue shirt ten feet away. Willis was aiming too, crouched on Matt's left, his elbow resting on the hood.

"Mr. Fowler," Strout said. He looked at each of them, and at the guns. "Mr. 80 Trottier."

Then Matt, watching the parking lot and the road, walked quickly between the car and the building and stood behind Strout. He took one leather glove from his pocket and put it on his left hand.

"Don't talk. Unlock the front and back and get in."

Strout unlocked the front door, reached in and unlocked the back, then got in, and Matt slid into the back seat, closed the door with his gloved hand, and touched Strout's head once with the muzzle.

"It's cocked. Drive to your house."

When Strout looked over his shoulder to back the car, Matt aimed at his 85 temple and did not look at his eyes.

"Drive slowly," he said. "Don't try to get stopped."

They drove across the empty front lot and onto the road, Willis's headlights shining into the car; then back through town, the sea wall on the left hiding the beach, though far out Matt could see the ocean; he uncocked the revolver; on the right were the places, most with their neon signs off, that did so much business in summer: the lounges and cafés and pizza houses, the street itself empty of traffic, the way he and Willis had known it would be when they decided to take Strout at the bar rather than knock on his door at two o'clock one morning and risk that one insomniac neighbor. Matt had not told Willis he was afraid he could not be alone with Strout for very long, smell his smells, feel the presence of his flesh, hear his voice, and then shoot him. They left the beach town and then were on the high bridge over the channel: to the left the smacking curling white at the breakwater and beyond that the dark sea and the full moon, and down to his right the small fishing boats bobbing at anchor in the cove. When they left the bridge, the sea was blocked by abandoned beach cottages, and Matt's left hand was sweating in the glove. Out here in the dark in the car he believed Ruth knew. Willis had come to his house at eleven and asked if he wanted a nightcap; Matt went to the bedroom for his wallet, put the gloves in one trouser pocket and the .38 in the other and went back to the living room, his hand in his pocket covering the bulge of the cool cylinder pressed against his fingers, the butt against his palm. When Ruth said good night she looked at his face, and he felt she could see in his eyes the gun, and the night he was going to. But he knew he couldn't trust what he saw. Willis's wife had taken her sleeping pill, which gave her eight hours — the reason, Willis had told Matt, he had the alarms installed, for nights when he was late at the restaurant — and when it was all done and Willis got home he would leave ice and a trace of Scotch and soda in two glasses in the game room and tell Martha in the morning that he had left the restaurant early and brought Matt home for a drink.

"He was making it with my wife." Strout's voice was careful, not pleading.

Matt pressed the muzzle against Strout's head, pressed it harder than he wanted to, feeling through the gun Strout's head flinching and moving forward; then he lowered the gun to his lap.

"Don't talk," he said.

90

Strout did not speak again. They turned west, drove past the Dairy Queen closed until spring, and the two lobster restaurants that faced each other and were crowded all summer and were now also closed, onto the short bridge crossing the tidal stream, and over the engine Matt could hear through his open window the water rushing inland under the bridge; looking to his left he saw its swift moonlit current going back into the marsh which, leaving the bridge, they entered: the salt marsh stretching out on both sides, the grass tall in patches but mostly low and leaning earthward as though windblown, a large dark rock sitting as though it rested on nothing but itself, and shallow pools reflecting the bright moon.

Beyond the marsh they drove through woods, Matt thinking now of the hole he and Willis had dug last Sunday afternoon after telling their wives they were going to Fenway Park. They listened to the game on a transistor radio, but heard none of it as they dug into the soft earth on the knoll they had chosen because elms and maples sheltered it. Already some leaves had fallen. When the hole was deep enough they covered it and the piled earth with dead branches, then cleaned their shoes and pants and went to a restaurant farther up in New Hampshire where they ate sandwiches and drank beer and watched the rest of the game on television. Looking at the back of Strout's head he thought of Frank's grave; he had not been back to it; but he would go before winter, and its second burial of snow.

He thought of Frank sitting on the couch and perhaps talking to the children as they watched television, imagined him feeling young and strong, still warmed from the sun at the beach, and feeling loved, hearing Mary Ann moving about in the kitchen, hearing her walking into the living room; maybe he looked up at her and maybe she said something, looking at him over the tray of sandwiches, smiling at him, saying something the way women do when they offer food as a gift, then the front door opening and this son of a bitch coming in and Frank seeing that he meant the gun in his hand, this son of a bitch and his gun the last person and thing Frank saw on earth.

When they drove into town the streets were nearly empty: a few slow cars, a policeman walking his beat past the darkened fronts of stores. Strout and Matt both glanced at him as they drove by. They were on the main street, and all the stoplights were blinking yellow. Willis and Matt had talked about that too: the lights changed at midnight, so there would be no place Strout had to stop and where he might try to run. Strout turned down the block where he lived and Willis's headlights were no longer with Matt in the back seat. They had planned that too, had decided it was best for just the one car to go to the house, and again Matt had said nothing about his fear of being alone with Strout, especially in his house: a duplex, dark as all the houses on the street were, the street itself lit at the corner of each block. As Strout turned into the driveway Matt thought of the one insomniac neighbor, thought of some man or woman sitting alone in the dark living room, watching the all-night channel from Boston. When Strout stopped the car near the front of the house, Matt said: "Drive it to the back."

He touched Strout's head with the muzzle.   95

"You wouldn't have it cocked, would you? For when I put on the brakes."

Matt cocked it, and said: "It is now."

Strout waited a moment; then he eased the car forward, the engine doing little more than idling, and as they approached the garage he gently braked. Matt opened the door, then took off the glove and put it in his pocket. He stepped out and shut the door with his hip and said: "All right."

Strout looked at the gun, then got out, and Matt followed him across the grass, and as Strout unlocked the door Matt looked quickly at the row of small backyards on either side, and scattered tall trees, some evergreens, others not, and he thought of the red and yellow leaves on the trees over the hole, saw them falling soon, probably in two weeks, dropping slowly, covering. Strout stepped into the kitchen.

"Turn on the light."   100

Strout reached to the wall switch, and in the light Matt looked at his wide back, the dark blue shirt, the white belt, the red plaid pants.

"Where's your suitcase?"

"My suitcase?"

"Where is it?"

"In the bedroom closet."   105

"That's where we're going then. When we get to a door you stop and turn on the light."

They crossed the kitchen, Matt glancing at the sink and stove and refrigerator: no dishes in the sink or even the dish rack beside it, no grease splashings on the stove, the refrigerator door clean and white. He did not want to look at any more but he looked quickly at all he could see: in the living room magazines and newspapers in a wicker basket, clean ashtrays, a record player, the records shelved next to it, then down the hall where, near the bedroom door, hung a color photograph of Mary Ann and the two boys sitting on a lawn — there was no house in the picture — Mary Ann smiling at the camera or Strout or whoever held the camera, smiling as she had on Matt's lawn this summer while he waited for the charcoal and they all talked and he looked at her brown legs and at Frank touching her arm, her shoulder, her hair; he moved down the hall with her smile in his mind, wondering: was that when they were both playing around and she was smiling like that at him and they were happy, even sometimes, making it worth it? He recalled her eyes, the pain in them, and he was conscious of the circles of love he was touching with the hand that held the revolver so tightly now as Strout stopped at the door at the end of the hall.

"There's no wall switch."

"Where's the light?"

"By the bed." 110

"Let's go."

Matt stayed a pace behind, then Strout leaned over and the room was lighted: the bed, a double one, was neatly made; the ashtray on the bedside table clean, the bureau top dustless, and no photographs; probably so the girl — who *was* she? — would not have to see Mary Ann in the bedroom she believed was theirs. But because Matt was a father and a husband, though never an ex-husband, he knew (and did not want to know) that this bedroom had never been theirs alone. Strout turned around; Matt looked at his lips, his wide jaw, and thought of Frank's doomed and fearful eyes looking up from the couch.

"Where's Mr. Trottier?"

"He's waiting. Pack clothes for warm weather."

"What's going on?" 115

"You're jumping bail."

"Mr. Fowler — "

He pointed the cocked revolver at Strout's face. The barrel trembled but not much, not as much as he had expected. Strout went to the closet and got the suitcase from the floor and opened it on the bed. As he went to the bureau, he said: "He was making it with my wife. I'd go pick up my kids and he'd be there. Sometimes he spent the night. My boys told me."

He did not look at Matt as he spoke. He opened the top drawer and Matt stepped closer so he could see Strout's hands: underwear and socks, the socks rolled, the underwear folded and stacked. He took them back to the bed, arranged them neatly in the suitcase, then from the closet he was taking shirts and trousers and a jacket; he laid them on the bed and Matt followed him to the bathroom and watched from the door while he packed those things a person accumulated and that became part of him so that at times in the store Matt felt he was selling more than clothes.

"I wanted to try to get together with her again." He was bent over the 120 suitcase. "I couldn't even talk to her. He was always with her. I'm going to jail for it; if I ever get out I'll be an old man. Isn't that enough?"

"You're not going to jail."

Strout closed the suitcase and faced Matt, looking at the gun. Matt went to his rear, so Strout was between him and the lighted hall; then using his handkerchief he turned off the lamp and said: "Let's go."

They went down the hall, Matt looking again at the photograph, and through the living room and kitchen, Matt turning off the lights and talking, frightened that he was talking, that he was telling this lie he had not planned: "It's the trial. We can't go through that, my wife and me. So you're leaving. We've got you a ticket, and a job. A friend of Mr. Trottier's. Out west. My wife keeps seeing you. We can't have that anymore."

Matt turned out the kitchen light and put the handkerchief in his pocket, and they went down the two brick steps and across the lawn. Strout put the suitcase on the floor of the back seat, then got into the front seat and Matt got in the back and put on his glove and shut the door.

"They'll catch me. They'll check passenger lists." 125

"We didn't use your name."

"They'll figure that out too. You think I wouldn't have done it myself if it was that easy?"

He backed into the street, Matt looking down the gun barrel but not at the profiled face beyond it.

"You were alone," Matt said. "We've got it worked out."

"There's no planes this time of night, Mr. Fowler." 130

"Go back through town. Then north on 125."

They came to the corner and turned, and now Willis's headlights were in the car with Matt.

"Why north, Mr. Fowler?"

"Somebody's going to keep you for a while. They'll take you to the airport." He uncocked the hammer and lowered the revolver to his lap and said wearily: "No more talking."

As they drove back through town, Matt's body sagged, going limp with his 135 spirit and its new and false bond with Strout, the hope his lie had given Strout. He had grown up in this town whose streets had become places of apprehension and pain for Ruth as she drove and walked, doing what she had to do; and for him too, if only in his mind as he worked and chatted six days a week in his store; he wondered now if his lie would have worked, if sending Strout away would have been enough; but then he knew that just thinking of Strout in Montana or whatever place lay at the end of the lie he had told, thinking of him walking the streets there, loving a girl there (who *was* she?) would be enough to slowly rot the rest of his days. And Ruth's. Again he was certain that she knew, that she was waiting for him.

They were in New Hampshire now, on the narrow highway, passing the shopping center at the state line, and then houses and small stores and sandwich shops. There were few cars on the road. After ten minutes he raised his trembling hand, touched Strout's neck with the gun, and said: "Turn in up here. At the dirt road."

Strout flicked on the indicator and slowed.

"Mr. Fowler?"

"They're waiting here."

Strout turned very slowly, easing his neck away from the gun. In the 140 moonlight the road was light brown, lighter and yellowed where the headlights shone; weeds and a few trees grew on either side of it, and ahead of them were the woods.

"There's nothing back here, Mr. Fowler."

"It's for your car. You don't think we'd leave it at the airport, do you?"

He watched Strout's large, big-knuckled hands tighten on the wheel, saw Frank's face that night: not the stitches and bruised eye and swollen lips, but his own hand gently touching Frank's jaw, turning his wounds to the light. They rounded a bend in the road and were out of sight of the highway: tall trees all around them now, hiding the moon. When they reached the abandoned gravel pit on the left, the bare flat earth and steep pale embankment behind it, and the black crowns of trees at its top, Matt said: "Stop here."

Strout stopped but did not turn off the engine. Matt pressed the gun hard against his neck, and he straightened in the seat and looked in the rearview mirror, Matt's eyes meeting his in the glass for an instant before looking at the hair at the end of the gun barrel.

"Turn it off."   145

Strout did, then held the wheel with two hands, and looked in the mirror.

"I'll do twenty years, Mr. Fowler; at least. I'll be forty-six years old."

"That's nine years younger than I am," Matt said, and got out and took off the glove and kicked the door shut. He aimed at Strout's ear and pulled back the hammer. Willis's headlights were off and Matt heard him walking on the soft thin layer of dust, the hard earth beneath it. Strout opened the door, sat for a moment in the interior light, then stepped out onto the road. Now his face was pleading. Matt did not look at his eyes, but he could see it in the lips.

"Just get the suitcase. They're right up the road."

Willis was beside him now, to his left. Strout looked at both guns. Then he 150
opened the back door, leaned in, and with a jerk brought the suitcase out. He was turning to face them when Matt said: "Just walk up the road. Just ahead."

Strout turned to walk, the suitcase in his right hand, and Matt and Willis followed; as Strout cleared the front of his car he dropped the suitcase and, ducking, took one step that was the beginning of a sprint to his right. The gun kicked in Matt's hand, and the explosion of the shot surrounded him, isolated him in a nimbus of sound that cut him off from all his time, all his history, isolated him standing absolutely still on the dirt road with the gun in his hand, looking down at Richard Strout squirming on his belly, kicking one leg behind him, pushing himself forward, toward the woods. Then Matt went to him and shot him once in the back of the head.

Driving south to Boston, wearing both gloves now, staying in the middle lane and looking often in the rearview mirror at Willis's headlights, he relived the suitcase dropping, the quick dip and turn of Strout's back, and the kick of the gun, the sound of the shot. When he walked to Strout, he still existed within the first shot, still trembled and breathed with it. The second shot and the burial seemed to be happening to someone else, someone he was watching. He and Willis each held an arm and pulled Strout face-down off the road and into the woods, his bouncing sliding belt white under the trees where it was so dark that when they stopped at the top of the knoll, panting and sweating, Matt could not see where Strout's blue shirt ended and the earth began. They pulled off the branches then dragged Strout to the edge of the hole and went behind him and lifted his legs and pushed him in. They stood still for a moment. The woods were quiet save for their breathing, and Matt remembered hearing the movements of birds and small animals after the first shot. Or maybe he had not heard them. Willis went down to the road. Matt could see him clearly out on the tan dirt, could see the glint of Strout's car and, beyond the road, the gravel pit. Willis came back up the knoll with the suitcase. He dropped it in the hole and took off his gloves and they went down to his car for the spades. They worked quietly. Sometimes they paused to listen to the woods. When they were finished Willis turned on his flashlight and they covered the earth with leaves and branches and then went down to the spot in front of the car, and while Matt held the light Willis crouched and sprinkled dust on the blood, backing up till he reached the grass and leaves, then he used leaves until they had worked up to the grave again. They did not stop. They walked around the grave and through the woods, using the light on the ground, looking up through the trees to where they ended at the lake. Neither of them spoke above the sounds of their heavy and clumsy strides through low brush and over fallen branches. Then they reached it: wide and dark, lapping softly at the bank, pine needles smooth under Matt's feet, moonlight on the lake, a small island near its middle, with black, tall evergreens. He took out the gun and threw for the island: taking two steps back on the pine needles, striding with the throw and going to one knee as he followed through, looking up to see the dark shapeless object arcing downward, splashing.

They left Strout's car in Boston, in front of an apartment building on Commonwealth Avenue. When they got back to town Willis drove slowly over the bridge and Matt threw the keys into the Merrimack. The sky was turning light. Willis let him out a block from his house, and walking home he listened for sounds from the houses he passed. They were quiet. A light was on in his living room. He turned it off and undressed in there, and went softly toward the bedroom; in the hall he smelled the smoke, and he stood in the bedroom doorway and looked at the orange of her cigarette in the dark. The curtains were closed. He went to the closet and put his shoes on the floor and felt for a hanger.

"Did you do it?" she said.

He went down the hall to the bathroom and in the dark he washed his 155 hands and face. Then he went to her, lay on his back, and pulled the sheet up to his throat.

"Are you all right?" she said.

"I think so."

Now she touched him, lying on her side, her hand on his belly, his thigh.

"Tell me," she said.

He started from the beginning, in the parking lot at the bar; but soon with 160 his eyes closed and Ruth petting him, he spoke of Strout's house: the order, the woman presence, the picture on the wall.

"The way she was smiling," he said.

"What about it?"

"I don't know. Did you ever see Strout's girl? When you saw him in town?"

"No."

"I wonder who she was." 165

Then he thought: *not was: is. Sleeping now she is his girl.* He opened his eyes, then closed them again. There was more light beyond the curtains. With Ruth now he left Strout's house and told again his lie to Strout, gave him again that hope that Strout must have for a while believed, else he would have to believe only the gun pointed at him for the last two hours of his life. And with

Ruth he saw again the dropping suitcase, the darting move to the right: and he told of the first shot, feeling her hand on him but his heart isolated still, beating on the road still in that explosion like thunder. He told her the rest, but the words had no images for him, he did not see himself doing what the words said he had done; he only saw himself on that road.

"We can't tell the other kids," she said. "It'll hurt them, thinking he got away. But we mustn't."

"No."

She was holding him, wanting him, and he wished he could make love with her but he could not. He saw Frank and Mary Ann making love in her bed, their eyes closed, their bodies brown and smelling of the sea; the other girl was faceless, bodiless, but he felt her sleeping now; and he saw Frank and Strout, their faces alive; he saw red and yellow leaves falling on the earth, then snow: falling and freezing and falling; and holding Ruth, his cheek touching her breast, he shuddered with a sob that he kept silent in his heart.

Considerations for Critical Thinking and Writing

1. Discuss the significance of the title. Why is "Killings" a more appropriate title than "Killers"?
2. What are the effects of Dubus's ordering of events in the story? How would the effects be different if the story were told in a chronological order?
3. Describe the Fowler family before Frank's murder. How does the murder affect Matt?
4. What is learned about Richard from the flashback in paragraphs 32 to 76? How does this information affect your attitude toward him?
5. What is the effect of the description of Richard shooting Frank in paragraph 76?
6. How well planned is Matt's revenge? Why does he lie to Richard about sending him out west?
7. How do the details of the killing and the disposal of Richard's body reveal Matt's emotions? What is he thinking and feeling as he performs these actions? How did you feel reading about them?
8. Describe Matt at the end of the story when he tells his wife about the killing. How do you think this revenge killing will affect the Fowler family?
9. How might "Killings" be considered a love story as well as a murder story?

Connections to Other Selections

1. Compare and contrast Matt's motivation for murder with Emily's in "A Rose for Emily." Which character made you feel more empathy and sympathy for his or her actions? Why?
2. Explore the father-son relationships in "Killings" and Faulkner's "Barn Burning" (p. 436). Read the section on psychological criticism in Chapter 35, "Critical Strategies for Reading." How do you think a psychological critic would interpret these relationships in each story?
3. In an essay discuss the respective treatments of family life in "Killings" and Gish Jen's "In the American Society" (p. 541). Do these very different stories have anything in common?

3. Character

Character is essential to plot. Without characters Burroughs's *Tarzan of the Apes* would be a travelogue through the jungle and Faulkner's "A Rose for Emily" little more than a faded history of a sleepy town in the South. If stories were depopulated, the plots would disappear because stories and plots are interrelated. A dangerous jungle is important only because we care what effect it has on a character. Characters are influenced by events just as events are shaped by characters. Tarzan's physical strength is the result of his growing up in the jungle, and his strength, along with his inherited intelligence, allows him to be master there.

The methods by which a writer creates people in a story so that they seem actually to exist are called ***characterization***. Huck Finn never lived, yet those who have read Mark Twain's novel about his adventures along the Mississippi River feel as if they know him. A good writer gives us the illusion that a character is real, but we should also remember that a character is not an actual person but instead has been created by the author. Though we might walk out of a room in which Huck Finn's Pap talks racist nonsense, we would not throw away the book in a similar fit of anger. This illusion of reality is the magic that allows us to move beyond the circumstances of our own lives into a writer's fictional world, where we can encounter everyone from royalty to paupers, murderers, lovers, cheaters, martyrs, artists, destroyers, and, nearly always, some part of ourselves. The life that a writer breathes into a character adds to our own experiences and enlarges our view of the world.

A character is usually but not always a person. In Jack London's *Call of the Wild,* the protagonist is a devoted sled dog; in Herman Melville's *Moby-Dick,* the antagonist is an unfathomable whale. Perhaps the only possible qualification to be placed on character is that whatever it is — whether an animal or even an inanimate object, such as a robot — it must have some recognizable human qualities. The action of the plot interests us primarily because we care about what happens to people and what they do. We may identify with a character's desires and aspirations, or we may be disgusted by his or her viciousness and selfishness. To understand our response to a story, we should be able to recognize the methods of characterization the author uses.

CHARLES DICKENS (1812–1870)

Charles Dickens is well known for creating characters who have stepped off the pages of his fictions into the imaginations and memories of his readers. His characters are successful not because readers might have encountered such people in their own lives, but because his characterizations are vivid and convincing. He manages to make strange and eccentric people appear familiar. The following excerpt from *Hard Times* is the novel's entire first chapter. In it Dickens introduces and characterizes a school principal addressing a classroom full of children.

From *Hard Times*   1854

"Now, what I want is, Facts. Teach these boys and girls nothing but Facts. Facts alone are wanted in life. Plant nothing else, and root out everything else. You can only form the minds of reasoning animals upon Facts: nothing else will ever be of any service to them. This is the principle on which I bring up my own children, and this is the principle on which I bring up these children. Stick to Facts, sir!"

The scene was a plain, bare, monotonous vault of a schoolroom, and the speaker's square forefinger emphasized his observations by underscoring every sentence with a line on the schoolmaster's sleeve. The emphasis was helped by the speaker's square wall of a forehead, which had his eyebrows for its base, while his eyes found commodious cellarage in two dark caves, overshadowed by the wall. The emphasis was helped by the speaker's mouth, which was wide, thin, and hard set. The emphasis was helped by the speaker's voice, which was inflexible, dry, and dictatorial. The emphasis was helped by the speaker's hair, which bristled on the skirts of his bald head, a plantation of firs to keep the wind from its shining surface, all covered with knobs, like the crust of a plum pie, as if the head had scarcely warehouse-room for the hard facts stored inside. The speaker's obstinate carriage, square coat, square legs, square shoulders — nay, his very neckcloth, trained to take him by the throat with an unaccommodating grasp, like a stubborn fact, as it was — all helped the emphasis.

"In this life, we want nothing but Facts, sir; nothing but Facts!"

The speaker, and the schoolmaster, and the third grown person present, all backed a little, and swept with their eyes the inclined plane of little vessels then and there arranged in order, ready to have imperial gallons of facts poured into them until they were full to the brim.

Dickens withholds his character's name until the beginning of the second chapter; he calls this fact-bound educator Mr. Gradgrind. Authors sometimes put as much time and effort into naming their characters as parents invest in naming their children. Names can be used to indicate qualities that the writer associates with the characters. Mr. Gradgrind is precisely what his name suggests. The "schoolmaster" employed by Gradgrind is Mr. M'Choakumchild. Pronounce this name aloud and you have the essence of this teacher's educational philosophy. In Nathaniel Hawthorne's *Scarlet Letter,* Chillingworth is cold and relentless in his single-minded quest for revenge. The innocent and youthful protagonist in Herman Melville's *Billy Budd* is nipped in the bud by the evil Claggart, whose name simply sounds unpleasant.

Names are also used in films to suggest a character's nature. One example that is destined to be a classic is the infamous villain Darth Vader, whose name identifies his role as an invader allied with the dark and death. On the heroic side, it makes sense that Marion Morrison decided to change his box-office name to John Wayne in order to play tough, masculine roles because both the first and last of his chosen names are unambiguously male and to the point, while his given name is androgynous. There may also be some significance to the lack of a specific identity. In Godwin's "A Sorrowful Woman" (p. 31) the woman, man, boy, and girl are reduced to a set of domestic functions, and their not being named emphasizes their roles as opposed to their individual identities. Of course, not every name is suggestive of the qualities a character may embody, but it is frequently worth determining what is in a name.

The only way to tell whether a name reveals character is to look at the other information the author supplies about the character. We evaluate fictional characters in much the same way we understand people in our own lives. By piecing together bits of information, we create a context that allows us to interpret their behavior. We can predict, for instance, that an acquaintance who is a chronic complainer is not likely to have anything good to say about a roommate. We interpret words and actions in the light of what we already know about someone, and that is why keeping track of what characters say (and how they say it) along with what they do (and don't do) is important.

Authors reveal characters by other means too. Physical descriptions can indicate important inner qualities; disheveled clothing, a crafty smile, or a blush might communicate as much as or more than what a character says. Characters can also be revealed by the words and actions of others who respond to them. In literature, moreover, we have one great advantage that life cannot offer; a work of fiction can give us access to a person's thoughts. Although in Herman Melville's "Bartleby, the Scrivener" (p. 83) we learn about Bartleby primarily through descriptive details, words, actions, and his relationships with the other characters, Melville allows us to enter the lawyer's consciousness.

Authors have two major methods of presenting characters: *showing* and *telling*. Characters shown in dramatic situations reveal themselves indirectly by what they say and do. In the first paragraph of the excerpt from *Hard Times*, Dickens shows us some of Gradgrind's utilitarian educational principles by having him speak. We can infer the kind of person he is from his reference to boys and girls as "reasoning animals," but we are not told what to think of him until the second paragraph. It would be impossible to admire Gradgrind after reading the physical description of him and the school that he oversees. The adjectives in the second paragraph make the author's evaluation of Gradgrind's values and personality clear: everything about him is rigidly "square"; his mouth is "thin and hard set"; his voice is "inflexible, dry, and dictatorial"; and he presides over a "plain, bare, monotonous vault of a schoolroom." Dickens directly lets us know how to feel about Gradgrind, but he does so artistically. Instead of simply being presented with a statement that Gradgrind is destructively practical, we get a detailed and amusing description.

We can contrast Dickens's direct presentation in this paragraph with the indirect showing that Gail Godwin uses in "A Sorrowful Woman" (p. 30). Godwin avoids telling us how we should think about the characters. Their story includes little description and no evaluations or interpretations by the author. To determine the significance of the events, the reader must pay close attention to what the characters say and do. Like Godwin, many twentieth-century authors favor showing over telling, because showing allows readers to discover the meanings, which modern authors are often reluctant to impose on an audience for whom fixed meanings and values are not as strong as they once were. However, most writers continue to reveal characters by telling as well as showing when the technique suits their purposes — when, for example, a minor character must be sketched economically or when a long time has elapsed, causing changes in a major character. Telling and showing complement each other.

Characters can be convincing whether they are presented by telling or showing, provided their actions are *motivated*. There must be reasons for how they behave and what they say. If adequate motivation is offered, we can understand and find *plausible* their actions no matter how bizarre. In "A Rose for Emily" (p. 47), Faulkner makes Emily Grierson's intimacy with a corpse credible by preparing us with information about her father's death along with her inability to leave the past and live in the present. Emily turns out to be *consistent*. Although we are surprised by the ending of the story, the behavior it reveals is compatible with her temperament.

Some kinds of fiction consciously break away from our expectations of traditional realistic stories. Consistency, plausibility, and motivation are not very useful concepts for understanding and evaluating characterizations in modern *absurdist literature*, for instance, in which characters are often alienated from themselves and their environment in an irrational world. In this world there is no possibility for traditional heroic action; instead we find an *antihero* who has little control over events. Yossarian from Joseph

Heller's *Catch-22* is an example of a protagonist who is thwarted by the absurd terms on which life offers itself to many twentieth-century characters.

In most stories we expect characters to act plausibly and in ways consistent with their personalities, but that does not mean that characters cannot develop and change. A *dynamic* character undergoes some kind of change because of the action of the plot. Huck Finn's view of Jim, the runaway slave in Mark Twain's novel, develops during their experiences on the raft. Huck discovers Jim's humanity and, therefore, cannot betray him, because Huck no longer sees his companion as merely the property of a white owner. On the other hand, Huck's friend, Tom Sawyer, is a *static* character because he does not change. He remains interested only in high adventure, even at the risk of Jim's life. As static characters often do, Tom serves as a foil to Huck; his frivolous concerns are contrasted with Huck's serious development. A *foil* helps to reveal by contrast the distinctive qualities of another character.

The protagonist in a story is usually a dynamic character who experiences some conflict that makes an impact on his or her life. Less commonly, static characters can also be protagonists. Rip Van Winkle wakes up from his twenty-year sleep in Washington Irving's story to discover his family dramatically changed and his country no longer a British colony, but none of these important events has an impact on his character; he continues to be the same shiftless and idle man that he was before he fell asleep. The protagonist in Faulkner's "A Rose for Emily" is also a static character; indeed, she rejects all change. Our understanding of her changes, but she does not. Ordinarily, however, a plot contains one or two dynamic characters with any number of static characters in supporting roles. This is especially true of short stories, in which brevity limits the possibilities of character development.

The extent to which a character is developed is another means by which character can be analyzed. The novelist E. M. Forster coined the terms *flat* and *round* to distinguish degrees of character development. A *flat character* embodies one or two qualities, ideas, or traits that can be readily described in a brief summary. For instance, Mr. M'Choakumchild in Dickens's *Hard Times* stifles students instead of encouraging them to grow. Flat characters tend to be one-dimensional. They are readily accessible because their characteristics are few and simple; they are not created to be psychologically complex.

Some flat characters are immediately recognizable as *stock characters.* These stereotypes are particularly popular in formula fiction, television programs, and drive-in movies. Stock characters are types rather than individuals. The poor but dedicated writer falls in love with a hard-working understudy who gets nowhere because the corrupt producer favors his boozy, pampered mistress for the leading role. Characters such as these — the loyal servant, the mean stepfather, the henpecked husband, the dumb blonde, the sadistic army officer, the dotty grandmother — are prepackaged; they lack individuality because their authors have, in a sense, not imaginatively created them but simply summoned them from a warehouse of clichés and social prejudices. Stock characters can become fresh if a good writer makes them vivid, interesting, or memorable, but too often a writer's use of these stereotypes is simply weak characterization.

Round characters are more complex than flat or stock characters. Round characters have more depth and require more attention. They may surprise us or puzzle us. Although they are more fully developed, round characters are also more difficult to summarize, because we are aware of competing ideas, values, and possibilities in their lives. As a flat character, Huck Finn's alcoholic, bigoted father is clear to us; we know that Pap is the embodiment of racism and irrationality. But Huck is considerably less predictable, because he struggles with what Twain calls a "sound heart and a deformed conscience."

In making distinctions between flat and round characters, you must understand that an author's use of a flat character — even as a protagonist — does not necessarily represent an artistic flaw. Moreover, both flat and round characters can be either dynamic or static. Each plot can be made most effective by its own special kind of characterization. Terms such as *round* and *flat* are helpful tools to determine what we know about a character, but they should not be used as an infallible measurement for the quality of a story.

The next two stories — Bharati Mukherjee's "Fathering" and Herman Melville's "Bartleby, the Scrivener" — offer character studies worthy of close analysis. As you read them, notice the methods of characterization used to bring each to life.

BHARATI MUKHERJEE (b. 1940)

Born in Calcutta, India, Bharati Mukherjee lived in London as a young girl but returned to India at the age of eleven, where she was subsequently educated at the universities of Calcutta and Baroda. After winning a scholarship to the University of Iowa Writer's Workshop, she moved to the United States and married novelist Clark Blaise in the early sixties. Though she lived in Canada for a decade and returned to India for a year, she now lives in the United States, where she teaches and writes. Mukherjee's fiction includes three novels — *The Tiger's Daughter* (1971), *Wife* (1972), and *Jasmine* (1989) — and two collections of short stories, *Darkness* (1985) and *The Middleman and Other Stories* (1988). Much of her work examines the stress and confusion immigrants experience as they struggle to secure identities and find a place in foreign cultures that tend to render them invisible or cast them as ethnic stereotypes. In "Fathering," taken from *The Middleman,*

Mukherjee explores the painful legacy of the Vietnam war as it manifests itself in the relationship between a father and a newly rediscovered daughter.

Fathering

1988

Eng stands just inside our bedroom door, her fidgety fist on the doorknob which Sharon, in a sulk, polished to a gleam yesterday afternoon.

"I'm starved," she says.

I know a sick little girl when I see one. I brought the twins up without much help ten years ago. Eng's got a high fever. Brownish stains stiffen the nap of her terry robe. Sour smells fill the bedroom.

"For God's sake leave us alone," Sharon mutters under the quilt. She turns away from me. We bought the quilt at a garage sale in Rock Springs the Sunday two years ago when she moved in. "Talk to her."

Sharon works on this near-marriage of ours. I'll hand it to her, she really 5 does. I knead her shoulders, and I say, "Easy, easy," though I really hate it when she treats Eng like a deaf-mute. "My girl speaks English, remember?"

Eng can outcuss any freckle-faced kid on the block. Someone in the killing fields must have taught her. Maybe her mama, the honeyest-skinned bar girl with the tiniest feet in Saigon. I was an errand boy with the Combined Military Intelligence. I did the whole war on Dexedrine. Vietnam didn't happen, and I'd put it behind me in marriage and fatherhood and teaching high school. Ten years later came the screw-ups with the marriage, the job, women, the works. Until Eng popped up in my life, I really believed it didn't happen.

"Come here, sweetheart," I beg my daughter. I sidle closer to Sharon, so there'll be room under the quilt for Eng.

"I'm starved," she complains from the doorway. She doesn't budge. The robe and hair are smelling something fierce. She doesn't show any desire to cuddle. She must be sick. She must have thrown up all night. Sharon throws the quilt back. "Then go raid the refrigerator like a normal kid," she snaps.

Once upon a time Sharon used to be a cheerful, accommodating woman. It isn't as if Eng was dumped on us out of the blue. She knew I was tracking my kid. Coming to terms with the past was Sharon's idea. I don't know what happened to *that* Sharon. "For all you know, Jason," she'd said, "the baby died of malaria or something." She said, "Go on, find out and deal with it." She said she could handle being a stepmother — better a fresh chance with some orphan off the streets of Saigon than with my twins from Rochester. My twins are being raised in some organic-farming lesbo commune. Their mother breeds Nubian goats for a living. "Come get in bed with us, baby. Let Dad feel your forehead. You burning up with fever?"

"She isn't hungry, I think she's sick," I tell Sharon, but she's already tugging 10 her sleeping mask back on. "I think she's just letting us know she hurts."

I hold my arms out wide for Eng to run into. If I could, I'd suck the virus right out of her. In the jungle, VC mamas used to do that. Some nights we's steal right up to a hootch — just a few of us intense sons of bitches on some special mission — and the women would be at their mumbo jumbo. They'd be sticking coins and amulets into napalm burns.

"I'm hungry, Dad." It comes out as a moan. Okay, she doesn't run into my arms, but at least she's come as far as the foot of our bed. "Dad, let's go down to the kitchen. Just you and me."

I am about to let that pass though I can feel Sharon's body go into weird little jerks and twitches when my baby adds with emphatic viciousness, "Not her, Dad. We don't want her with us in the kitchen."

"She loves you," I protest. Love — not spite — makes Eng so territorial; that's what I want to explain to Sharon. She's a sick, frightened, foreign kid, for Chrissake. "Don't you, Sharon? Sharon's concerned about you."

But Sharon turns over on her stomach. "You know what's wrong with you,   15 Jase? You can't admit you're being manipulated. You can't cut through the 'frightened-foreign-kid' shit."

Eng moves closer. She comes up to the side of my bed, but doesn't touch the hand I'm holding out. She's a fighter.

"I feel fire-hot, Dad. My bones feel pain."

"Sharon?" I want to deserve this woman. "Sharon, I'm so sorry." It isn't anybody's fault. You need uppers to get through peace times, too.

"Dad. Let's go. Chop-chop."

"You're too sick to keep food down, baby. Curl up in here. Just for a bit?"   20

"I'd throw up, Dad."

"I'll carry you back to your room. I'll read you a story, okay?"

Eng watches me real close as I pull the quilt off. "You got any scars you haven't shown me yet? My mom had a big scar on one leg. Shrapnel. Boom boom. I got scars. See? I got lots of bruises."

I scoop up my poor girl and rush her, terry robe flapping, to her room which Sharon fixed up with white girlish furniture in less complicated days. Waiting for Eng was good. Sharon herself said it was good for our relationship. "Could you bring us some juice and aspirin?" I shout from the hallway.

"Aspirin isn't going to cure Eng," I hear Sharon yell. "I'm going to call Dr.   25 Kearns."

Downstairs I hear Sharon on the phone. She isn't talking flu viruses. She's talking social workers and shrinks. My girl isn't crazy; she's picked up a bug in school as might anyone else.

"The child's arms are covered with bruises," Sharon is saying. "Nothing major. They look like . . . well, they're sort of tiny circles and welts." There's nothing for a while. Then she says, "Christ! no, Jason can't do enough for her! That's not what I'm saying! What's happening to this country? You think we're perverts? What I'm saying is the girl's doing it to herself."

"Who are you talking to?" I ask from the top of the stairs. "What happened to the aspirin?"

I lean as far forward over the railing as I dare so I can see what Sharon's up to. She's getting into her coat and boots. She's having trouble with buttons and snaps. In the bluish light of the foyer's broken chandelier, she looks old, harrowed, depressed. What have I done to her?

"What's going on?" I plead. "You deserting me?"   30

"Don't be so fucking melodramatic. I'm going to the mall to buy some aspirin."

"How come we don't have any in the house?"

"Why are you always picking on me?"

"Who was that on the phone?"

"So now you want me to account for every call and every trip?" She ties an angry knot into her scarf. But she tells me. "I was talking to Meg Kearns. She says Dr. Kearns has gone hunting for the day."

"Great!"

"She says he has his beeper on him."

I hear the back door stick and Sharon swear. She's having trouble with the latch. "Jiggle it gently," I shout, taking the stairs two at a time. But before I can come down, her Nissan backs out of the parking apron.

Back upstairs I catch Eng in the middle of a dream or delirium. "They got Grandma!" she screams. She goes very rigid in bed. It's a four-poster with canopy and ruffles and stuff that Sharon put on her MasterCard. The twins slept on bunk beds. With the twins it was different, totally different. Dr. Spock can't be point man for Eng, for us.

"She bring me food," Eng's screaming. "She bring me food from the forest. They shoot Grandma! Bastards!"

"Eng?" I don't dare touch her. I don't know how.

"You shoot my grandmother?" She whacks the air with her bony arms. Now I see the bruises, the small welts all along the insides of her arms. Some have to be weeks old, they're that yellow. The twins' scrapes and cuts never turned that ochre. I can't help wondering if maybe Asian skin bruises differently from ours, even though I want to say skin is skin; especially hers is skin like mine.

"I want to be with Grandma. Grandma loves me. I want to be ghost. I don't want to get better."

I read to her. I read to her because good parents are supposed to read to their kids laid up sick in bed. I want to do it right. I want to be a good father. I read from a sci-fi novel that Sharon must have picked up. She works in a camera store in the mall, right next to a B. Dalton. I read three pages out loud, then I read four chapters to myself because Eng's stopped up her ears. Aliens have taken over small towns all over the country. Idaho, Nebraska: no state is safe from aliens.

Some time after two, the phone rings. Since Sharon doesn't answer it on the second ring, I know she isn't back. She carries a cordless phone everywhere around the house. In the movies, when cops have bad news to deliver, they lean on your doorbell; they don't call. Sharon will come back when she's ready. We'll make up. Things will get back to normal.

"Jason?"

I know Dr. Kearns's voice. He saw the twins through the usual immunizations.

"I have Sharon here. She'll need a ride home. Can you drive over?"

"God! What's happened?"

"Nothing to panic about. Nothing physical. She came for a consultation."

"Give me a half-hour. I have to wrap Eng real warm so I can drag her out in this miserable weather."

"Take your time. This way I can take a look at Eng, too."

"What's wrong with Sharon?"

"She's a little exercised about a situation. I gave her a sedative. See you in a half-hour."

I ease delirious Eng out of the overdecorated four-poster, prop her against 55
my body while I wrap a blanket around her. She's a tiny thing, but she feels stiff and heavy, a sleepwalking mummy. Her eyes are dry-bright, strange.

It's a sunny winter day, and the evergreens in the front yard are glossy with frost. I press Eng against my chest as I negotiate the front steps. Where the gutter leaks, the steps feel spongy. The shrubs and bushes my ex-wife planted clog the front path. I've put twenty years into this house. The steps, the path, the house all have a right to fall apart.

I'm thirty-eight. I've let a lot of people down already.

The inside of the van is deadly cold. Mid-January ice mottles the windshield. I lay the bundled-up child on the long seat behind me and wait for the engine to warm up. It feels good with the radio going and the heat coming on. I don't want the ice on the windshield to melt. Eng and I are safest in the van.

In the rear-view mirror, Eng's wrinkled lips begin to move. "Dad, can I have a quarter?"

"May I, kiddo," I joke. 60

There's all sorts of junk in the pockets of my parka. Buckshot, dimes and quarters for the vending machine, a Blistex.

"What do you need it for, sweetheart?"

Eng's quick. Like the street kids in Saigon who dove for cigarettes and sticks of gum. She's loosened the blanket folds around her. I watch her tuck the quarter inside her wool mitt. She grins. "Thanks, soldier."

At Dr. Kearns's, Sharon is lying unnaturally slack-bodied on the lone vinyl sofa. Her coat's neatly balled up under her neck, like a bolster. Right now she looks amiable, docile. I don't think she exactly recognizes me, although later she'll say she did. All that stuff about Kearns going hunting must have been a lie. Even the stuff about having to buy aspirins in the mall. She was planning all along to get here.

"What's wrong?" 65

"It's none of my business, Jason, but you and Sharon might try an honest-to-goodness heart-to-heart." Then he makes a sign to me to lay Eng on the examining table. "We don't look so bad," he says to my daughter. Then he excuses himself and goes into a glass-walled cubicle.

Sharon heaves herself into a sitting position of sorts on the sofa. "Everything was fine until she got here. Send her back, Jase. If you love me, send her back." She's slouched so far forward, her pointed, sweatered breasts nearly touch her corduroy pants. She looks helpless, pathetic. I've brought her to this state. Guilt, not love, is what I feel.

I want to comfort Sharon, but my daughter with the wild, grieving pygmy face won't let go of my hand. "She's bad, Dad. Send *her* back."

Dr. Kearns comes out of the cubicle balancing a sample bottle of pills or caplets on a flattened palm. He has a boxer's tough, squarish hands. "Miraculous stuff, this," he laughs. "But first we'll stick our tongue out and say *ahh*. Come on, open wide."

Eng opens her mouth real wide, then brings her teeth together, hard, on 70 Dr. Kearns's hand. She leaps erect on the examining table, tearing the disposable paper sheet with her toes. Her tiny, funny toes are doing a frantic dance. "Don't let him touch me, Grandma!"

"He's going to make you all better, baby." I can't pull my alien child down, I can't comfort her. The twins had diseases with easy names, diseases we knew what to do with. The thing is, I never felt for them what I feel for her.

"Don't let him touch me, Grandma!" Eng's screaming now. She's hopping on the table and screaming. "Kill him, Grandma! Get me out of here, Grandma!"

"Baby, it's all right."

But she looks through me and the country doctor as though we aren't here, as though we aren't pulling at her to make her lie down.

"Lie back like a good girl," Dr. Kearns commands. 75

But Eng is listening to other voices. She pulls her mitts off with her teeth, chucks the blanket, the robe, the pajamas to the floor; then, naked, hysterical, she presses the quarter I gave her deep into the soft flesh of her arm. She presses and presses that coin, turning it in nasty half-circles until blood starts to pool under the skin.

"Jason, grab her at the knees. Get her back down on the table."

From the sofa, Sharon moans. "See, I told you the child was crazy. She hates me. She's possessive about Jason."

The doctor comes at us with his syringe. He's sedated Sharon; now he wants to knock out my kid with his cures.

"Get the hell out, you bastard!" Eng yells. "*Vamos!* Bang bang!" She's pointing 80 her arm like a semiautomatic, taking out Sharon, then the doctor. My Rambo. "Old way is good way. Money cure is good cure. When they shoot my grandma, you think pills do her any good? You Yankees, please go home." She looks straight at me. "Scram, Yankee bastard!"

Dr. Kearns has Eng by the wrist now. He has flung the quarter I gave her on the floor. Something incurable is happening to my women.

Then, as in fairy tales, I know what has to be done. "Coming, pardner!" I whisper. "I got no end of coins." I jiggle the change in my pocket. I jerk her away from our enemies. My Saigon kid and me: we're a team. In five minutes we'll be safely away in the cold chariot of our van.

Considerations for Critical Thinking and Writing

1. What do we learn from the story's exposition that helps us to understand Eng's character? How does her behavior reveal her character?
2. The first words that Eng speaks are "I'm starved." Why is this line (repeated in para. 8) particularly significant given the rest of the story?
3. What do we learn about Jason's past? What sort of man is he?
4. Why did Sharon urge Jason to find out what had happened to Eng? How does Sharon feel about Eng now compared to how she felt when she and Jason were searching for her? Why does she feel differently now?
5. Explain why you think Sharon can or cannot be cast as a stock version of a bad stepmother. Discuss whether or not she is a flat or round character.

6. What does Jason think of his marriage? How does that marriage help to characterize him?
7. Jason's wife is briefly described in paragraph 9. How effectively is she characterized? How does that characterization affect your attitude toward Jason?
8. How does Jason treat Sharon? Explain why you think he is considerate or inconsiderate of her.
9. Jason says of his twins, "I never felt for them what I feel for Eng." Why does he feel that way? What do you think about him for feeling more for Eng than the twins?
10. What is the significance of the title? How does it affect your reading of the story?
11. Who is the central character? Explain your choice.
12. In the final paragraph Jason describes his taking Eng "away from our enemies," as if his actions were the happy conclusion to a fairy tale. Is the ending convincing to you? Is there a resolution to the conflict? Where do you think they'll go from here? Write an essay that considers their future and cite supporting evidence from the story to explain your response.

Connections to Other Selections

1. Compare and contrast Jason's "fathering" in Mukherjee's story with Abner's in William Faulkner's "Barn Burning" (p. 436). Write an essay that discusses how each author's characterization of the father results in differing themes.
2. Compare the use of exposition to reveal character in "Fathering" and Raymond Carver's "Popular Mechanics" (p. 235). How does exposition (or its relative absence) affect your understanding and response to the characters in each story?
3. Read the section on psychological criticism in Chapter 35, "Critical Strategies for Reading." How do you think a psychological critic would make sense of the triangular relationship of Eng, Jason, and Sharon?

HERMAN MELVILLE (1819–1891)

Hoping to improve his distressed financial situation, Herman Melville left New York and went to sea as a young common sailor. He returned to become an uncommon writer. His experiences at sea became the basis for his early novels: *Typee* (1846), *Omoo* (1847), *Mardi* (1849), *Redburn* (1849), and *White-Jacket* (1850). Ironically, with the publication of his masterpiece, *Moby-Dick* (1851), Melville lost the popular success he had enjoyed with his earlier books, because his readers were not ready for its philosophical complexity. Although he wrote more, Melville's works were read less and slipped into obscurity. His final short novel, *Billy Budd*, was not published until the 1920s, when critics rediscovered him. In "Bartleby, the Scrivener," Melville presents a quiet clerk in a law office whose baffling "passive resistance" disrupts the life of his employer, a man who attempts to make sense of Bartleby's refusal to behave reasonably.

Bartleby, the Scrivener

A STORY OF WALL STREET

I am a rather elderly man. The nature of my avocations, for the last thirty years, has brought me into more than ordinary contact with what would seem an interesting and somewhat singular set of men, of whom, as yet, nothing, that I know of, has ever been written — I mean, the law-copyists, or scriveners. I have known very many of them, professionally and privately, and, if I pleased, could relate divers histories, at which good-natured gentlemen might smile, and sentimental souls might weep. But I waive the biographies of all other scriveners, for a few passages in the life of Bartleby, who was a scrivener, the strangest I ever saw, or heard of. While, of other law-copyists, I might write the complete life, of Bartleby nothing of that sort can be done. I believe that no materials exist, for a full and satisfactory biography of this man. It is an irreparable loss to literature. Bartleby was one of those beings of whom nothing is ascertainable, except from the original sources, and, in his case, those are very small. What my own astonished eyes saw of Bartleby, *that* is all I know of him, except, indeed, one vague report, which will appear in the sequel.

Ere introducing the scrivener, as he first appeared to me, it is fit I make some mention of myself, my *employés,* my business, my chambers, and general surroundings, because some such description is indispensable to an adequate understanding of the chief character about to be presented. Imprimis:° I am a man who, from his youth upwards, has been filled with a profound conviction that the easiest way of life is the best. Hence, though I belong to a profession proverbially energetic and nervous, even to turbulence, at times, yet nothing of that sort have I ever suffered to invade my peace. I am one of those unambitious lawyers who never address a jury, or in any way draw down public applause; but, in the cool tranquillity of a snug retreat, do a snug business among rich men's bonds, and mortgages, and title-deeds. All who know me, consider me an eminently *safe* man. The late John Jacob Astor,° a personage little given to poetic enthusiasm, had no hesitation in pronouncing my first grand point to be prudence; my next, method. I do not speak it in vanity, but simply record the fact, that I was not unemployed in my profession by the late John Jacob Astor; a name which, I admit, I love to repeat; for it hath a rounded and orbicular sound to it, and rings like unto bullion. I will freely add, that I was not insensible to the late John Jacob Astor's good opinion.

Some time prior to the period at which this little history begins, my avocations had been largely increased. The good old office, now extinct in the State of New York, of a Master in Chancery, had been conferred upon me. It was not a very arduous office, but very pleasantly remunerative. I seldom lose my temper; much more seldom indulge in dangerous indignation at wrongs and outrages; but I must be permitted to be rash here and declare, that I consider the sudden and violent abrogation of the office of Master in Chancery, by the new Constitution, as a —— premature act; inasmuch as I had counted upon a life-lease of

Imprimis: In the first place.
John Jacob Astor (1763–1848): An enormously wealthy American capitalist.

Melville / Bartleby, the Scrivener **83**

the profits, whereas I only received those of a few short years. But this is by the way.

My chambers were up stairs, at No. — Wall Street. At one end, they looked upon the white wall of the interior of a spacious skylight shaft, penetrating the building from top to bottom.

This view might have been considered rather tame than otherwise, deficient 5 in what landscape painters call "life." But, if so, the view from the other end of my chambers offered, at least, a contrast, if nothing more. In that direction, my windows commanded an unobstructed view of a lofty brick wall, black by age and everlasting shade; which wall required no spyglass to bring out its lurking beauties, but, for the benefit of all near-sighted spectators, was pushed up to within ten feet of my window-panes. Owing to the great height of the surrounding buildings, and my chambers being on the second floor, the interval between this wall and mine not a little resembled a huge square cistern.

At the period just preceding the advent of Bartleby, I had two persons as copyists in my employment, and a promising lad as an office-boy. First, Turkey; second, Nippers; third, Ginger Nut. These may seem names, the like of which are not usually found in the Directory. In truth, they were nicknames, mutually conferred upon each other by my three clerks, and were deemed expressive of their respective persons or characters. Turkey was a short, pursy Englishman, of about my own age — that is, somewhere not far from sixty. In the morning, one might say, his face was of a fine florid hue, but after twelve o'clock, meridian — his dinner hour — it blazed like a grate full of Christmas coals; and continued blazing — but, as it were, with a gradual wane — till six o'clock, P.M., or there-abouts; after which, I saw no more of the proprietor of the face, which, gaining its meridian with the sun, seemed to set with it, to rise, culminate, and decline the following day, with the like regularity and undiminished glory. There are many singular coincidences I have known in the course of my life, not the least among which was the fact, that, exactly when Turkey displayed his fullest beams from his red and radiant countenance, just then, too, at that critical moment, began the daily period when I considered his business capacities as seriously disturbed for the remainder of the twenty-four hours. Not that he was absolutely idle, or averse to business then; far from it. The difficulty was, he was apt to be altogether too energetic. There was a strange, inflamed, flurried, flighty reck-lessness of activity about him. He would be incautious in dipping his pen into his inkstand. All his blots upon my documents were dropped there after twelve o'clock, meridian. Indeed, not only would he be reckless, and sadly given to making blots in the afternoon, but, some days, he went further, and was rather noisy. At such times, too, his face flamed with augmented blazonry, as if cannel coal had been heaped on anthracite. He made an unpleasant racket with his chair; spilled his sand-box; in mending his pens, impatiently split them all to pieces, and threw them on the floor in a sudden passion; stood up, and leaned over his table, boxing his papers about in a most indecorous manner, very sad to behold in an elderly man like him. Nevertheless, as he was in many ways a most valuable person to me, and all the time before twelve o'clock, meridian, was the quickest, steadiest creature, too, accomplishing a great deal of work in a style not easily to be matched — for these reasons, I was willing to overlook his eccentricities, though, indeed, occasionally, I remonstrated with him. I did this very gently, however, because, though the civilest, nay, the blandest and most reverential of men in the morning, yet, in the afternoon, he was disposed, upon provocation, to be slightly rash with his tongue — in fact, insolent. Now, valuing his morning services as I did, and resolved not to lose them — yet, at the same time, made uncomfortable by his inflamed ways after twelve o'clock — and being a man of peace, unwilling by my admonitions to call forth unseemly retorts from him, I took upon me, one Saturday noon (he was always worse on Saturdays) to hint to him, very kindly, that, perhaps, now that he was growing old, it might be well to abridge his labors; in short, he need not come to my chambers after twelve o'clock, but, dinner over, had best go home to his lodgings, and rest himself till tea-time. But no; he insisted upon his afternoon devotions. His countenance became intolerably fervid, as he oratorically assured me — gesti- culating with a long ruler at the other end of the room — that if his services in the morning were useful, how indispensable, then, in the afternoon?

"With submission, sir," said Turkey, on this occasion, "I consider myself your right-hand man. In the morning I but marshal and deploy my columns; but in the afternoon I put myself at their head, and gallantly charge the foe, thus" — and he made a violent thrust with the ruler.

"But the blots, Turkey," intimated I.

"True; but, with submission, sir, behold these hairs! I am getting old. Surely, sir, a blot or two of a warm afternoon is not to be severely urged against gray hairs. Old age — even if it blot the page — is honorable. With submission, sir, we *both* are getting old."

This appeal to my fellow-feeling was hardly to be resisted. At all events, I 10 saw that go he would not. So, I made up my mind to let him stay, resolving, nevertheless, to see to it that, during the afternoon, he had to do with my less important papers.

Nippers, the second on my list, was a whiskered, sallow, and, upon the whole, rather piratical-looking young man, of about five-and-twenty. I always deemed him the victim of two evil powers — ambition and indigestion. The ambition was evinced by a certain impatience of the duties of a mere copyist, an unwarrantable usurpation of strictly professional affairs such as the original drawing up of legal documents. The indigestion seemed betokened in an occa- sional nervous testiness and grinning irritability, causing the teeth to audibly grind together over mistakes committed in copying; unnecessary maledictions, hissed, rather than spoken, in the heat of business; and especially by a continual discontent with the height of the table where he worked. Though of a very ingenious mechanical turn, Nippers could never get this table to suit him. He put chips under it, blocks of various sorts, bits of pasteboard, and at last went so far as to attempt an exquisite adjustment, by final pieces of folded blotting- paper. But no invention would answer. If, for the sake of easing his back, he brought the table-lid at a sharp angle well up towards his chin, and wrote there like a man using the steep roof of a Dutch house for his desk, then he declared that it stopped the circulation in his arms. If now he lowered the table to his waistbands, and stooped over it in writing, then there was a sore aching in his back. In short, the truth of the matter was, Nippers knew not what he wanted. Or, if he wanted anything, it was to be rid of a scrivener's table altogether. Among the manifestations of his diseased ambition was a fondness he had for receiving visits from certain ambiguous-looking fellows in seedy coats, whom he called his clients. Indeed, I was aware that not only was he, at times, considerable of a ward-politician, but he occasionally did a little business at the justices' courts, and was not unknown on the steps of the Tombs.° I have good reason to believe, however, that one individual who called upon him at my chambers, and who, with a grand air, he insisted was his client, was no other than a dun, and the alleged title-deed, a bill. But, with all his failings, and the annoyances he caused me, Nippers, like his compatriot Turkey, was a very useful man to me; wrote a neat, swift hand; and, when he chose, was not deficient in a gentlemanly sort of deportment. Added to this, he always dressed in a gentlemanly sort of way; and so, incidentally, reflected credit upon my chambers. Whereas, with respect to Turkey, I had much ado to keep him from being a reproach to me. His clothes were apt to look oily, a smell of eating-houses. He wore his pantaloons very loose and baggy in summer. His coats were execrable, his hat not to be handled. But while the hat was a thing of indifference to me, inasmuch as his natural civility and deference, as a dependent Englishman, always led him to doff it the moment he entered the room, yet his coat was another matter. Concerning his coats, I reasoned with him; but with no effect. The truth was, I suppose, that a man with so small an income could not afford to sport such a lustrous face and a lustrous coat at one and the same time. As Nippers once observed, Turkey's money went chiefly for red ink. One winter day, I presented Turkey with a highly respectable-looking coat of my own — a padded gray coat, of a most comfortable warmth, and which buttoned straight up from the knee to the neck. I thought Turkey would appreciate the favor, and abate his rashness and obstreperousness of afternoons. But no; I verily believe that buttoning himself up in so downy and blanket-like a coat had a pernicious effect upon him — upon the same principle that too much oats are bad for horses. In fact, precisely as a rash, restive horse is said to feel his oats, so Turkey felt his coat. It made him insolent. He was a man whom prosperity harmed.

Though, concerning the self-indulgent habits of Turkey, I had my own private surmises, yet, touching Nippers, I was well persuaded that, whatever might be his faults in other respects, he was, at least, a temperate young man. But indeed, nature herself seemed to have been his vintner, and, at his birth, charged him so thoroughly with an irritable, brandy-like disposition, that all subsequent potations were needless. When I consider how, amid the stillness of my chambers, Nippers would sometimes impatiently rise from his seat, and stooping over his table, spread his arms wide apart, seize the whole desk, and move it, and jerk it, with a grim, grinding motion on the floor, as if the table were a perverse voluntary agent, intent on thwarting and vexing him, I plainly perceive that, for Nippers, brandy-and-water were altogether superfluous.

It was fortunate for me that, owing to its peculiar cause — indigestion — the irritability and consequent nervousness of Nippers were mainly observable in the morning, while in the afternoon he was comparatively mild. So that, Turkey's paroxysms only coming on about twelve o'clock, I never had to do with their eccentricities at one time. Their fits relieved each other, like guards. When

the Tombs: A jail in New York City.

Nippers' was on, Turkey's was off; and *vice versa*. This was a good natural arrangement, under the circumstances.

Ginger Nut, the third on my list, was a lad, some twelve years old. His father was a carman, ambitious of seeing his son on the bench instead of a cart, before he died. So he sent him to my office, as student at law, errand-boy, cleaner, and sweeper, at the rate of one dollar a week. He had a little desk to himself, but he did not use it much. Upon inspection, the drawer exhibited a great array of the shells of various sorts of nuts. Indeed, to this quick-witted youth, the whole noble science of the law was contained in a nutshell. Not the least among the employments of Ginger Nut, as well as one which he dischaged with the most alacrity, was his duty as cake and apple purveyor for Turkey and Nippers. Copying lawpapers being proverbially a dry, husky sort of business, my two scriveners were fain to moisten their mouths very often with Spitzenbergs, to be had at the numerous stalls nigh the Custom House and Post Office. Also, they sent Ginger Nut very frequently for that peculiar cake — small, flat, round, and very spicy — after which he had been named by them. Of a cold morning, when business was but dull, Turkey would gobble up scores of these cakes, as if they were mere wafers — indeed, they sell them at the rate of six or eight for a penny — the scrape of his pen blending with the crunching of the crisp particles in his mouth. Of all the fiery afternoon blunders and flurried rashness of Turkey, was his once moistening a ginger-cake between his lips, and clapping it on to a mortgage, for a seal. I came within an ace of dismissing him then. But he mollified me by making an oriental bow, and saying —

"With submission, sir, it was generous of me to find you in stationery on my own account." 15

Now my original business — that of a conveyancer and title hunter, and drawer-up of recondite documents of all sorts — was considerably increased by receiving the Master's office. There was now great work for scriveners. Not only must I push the clerks already with me, but I must have additional help.

In answer to my advertisement, a motionless young man one morning stood upon my office threshold, the door being open, for it was summer. I can see that figure now — pallidly neat, pitiably respectable, incurably forlorn! It was Bartleby.

After a few words touching his qualifications, I engaged him, glad to have among my corps of copyists a man of so singularly sedate an aspect, which I thought might operate beneficially upon the flighty temper of Turkey, and the fiery one of Nippers.

I should have stated before that ground-glass folding-doors divided my premises into two parts, one of which was occupied by my scriveners, the other by myself. According to my humor, I threw open these doors, or closed them. I resolved to assign Bartleby a corner by the folding-doors, but on my side of them, so as to have this quiet man within easy call, in case any trifling thing was to be done. I placed his desk close up to a small side-window in that part of the room, a window which originally had afforded a lateral view of certain grimy brickyards and bricks, but which, owing to subsequent erections, commanded at present no view at all, though it gave some light. Within three feet of the panes was a wall, and the light came down from far above, between two lofty buildings, as from a very small opening in a dome. Still further to a satisfactory arrangement, I procured a high green folding screen, which might entirely isolate Bartleby from my sight, though not remove him from my voice. And thus, in a manner, privacy and society were conjoined.

At first, Bartleby did an extraordinary quantity of writing. As if long famishing 20 for something to copy, he seemed to gorge himself on my documents. There was no pause for digestion. He ran a day and night line, copying by sunlight and by candle-light. I should have been quite delighted with his application, had he been cheerfully industrious. But he wrote on silently, palely, mechanically.

It is, of course, an indispensable part of a scrivener's business to verify the accuracy of his copy, word by word. Where there are two or more scriveners in an office, they assist each other in this examination, one reading from the copy, the other holding the original. It is a very dull, wearisome, and lethargic affair. I can readily imagine that, to some sanguine temperaments, it would be altogether intolerable. For example, I cannot credit that the mettlesome poet, Byron, would have contentedly sat down with Bartleby to examine a law document of, say five hundred pages, closely written in a crimpy hand.

Now and then, in the haste of business, it had been my habit to assist in comparing some brief document myself, calling Turkey or Nippers for this purpose. One object I had, in placing Bartleby so handy to me behind the screen, was, to avail myself of his services on such trivial occasions. It was on the third day, I think, of his being with me, and before any necessity had arisen for having his own writing examined, that, being much hurried to complete a small affair I had in hand, I abruptly called to Bartleby. In my haste and natural expectancy of instant compliance, I sat with my head bent over the original on my desk, and my right hand sideways, and somewhat nervously extended with the copy, so that, immediately upon emerging from his retreat, Bartleby might snatch it and proceed to business without the least delay.

In this very attitude did I sit when I called to him, rapidly stating what it was I wanted him to do — namely, to examine a small paper with me. Imagine my surprise, nay, my consternation, when, without moving from his privacy, Bartleby, in a singularly mild, firm voice, replied, "I would prefer not to."

I sat awhile in perfect silence, rallying my stunned faculties. Immediately it occurred to me that my ears had deceived me, or Bartleby had entirely misunderstood my meaning. I repeated my request in the clearest tone I could assume; but in quite as clear a one came the previous reply, "I would prefer not to."

"Prefer not to," echoed I, rising in high excitement, and crossing the room 25 with a stride. "What do you mean? Are you moonstruck? I want you to help me compare this sheet here — take it," and I thrust it towards him.

"I would prefer not to," said he.

I looked at him steadfastly. His face was leanly composed; his gray eye dimly calm. Not a wrinkle of agitation rippled him. Had there been the least uneasiness, anger, impatience, or impertinence in his manner; in other words, had there been anything ordinarily human about him, doubtless I should have violently dismissed him from the premises. But as it was, I should have as soon thought of turning my pale plaster-of-paris bust of Cicero out of doors. I stood gazing at him awhile, as he went on with his own writing, and then reseated myself at my desk. This is very strange, thought I. What had one best do? But my business hurried me. I concluded to forget the matter for the present, reserving it for my future leisure. So, calling Nippers from the other room, the paper was speedily examined.

A few days after this, Bartleby concluded four lengthy documents, being quadruplicates of a week's testimony taken before me in my High Court of Chancery. It became necessary to examine them. It was an important suit, and great accuracy was imperative. Having all things arranged, I called Turkey, Nippers, and Ginger Nut, from the next room, meaning to place the four copies in the hands of my four clerks, while I should read from the original. Accordingly, Turkey, Nippers, and Ginger Nut had taken their seats in a row, each with his document in his hand, when I called to Bartleby to join this interesting group.

"Bartleby! quick, I am waiting."

I heard a slow scrape of his chair legs on the uncarpeted floor, and soon 30 he appeared standing at the entrance of his hermitage.

"What is wanted?" said he, mildly.

"The copies, the copies," said I, hurriedly. "We are going to examine them. There" — and I held towards him the fourth quadruplicate.

"I would prefer not to," he said, and gently disappeared behind the screen.

For a few moments I was turned into a pillar of salt, standing at the head of my seated column of clerks. Recovering myself, I advanced towards the screen, and demanded the reason for such extraordinary conduct.

"*Why* do you refuse?"   35

"I would prefer not to."

With any other man I should have flown outright into a dreadful passion, scorned all further words, and thrust him ignominiously from my presence. But there was something about Bartleby that not only strangely disarmed me, but, in a wonderful manner, touched and disconcerted me. I began to reason with him.

"These are your own copies we are about to examine. It is labor saving to you, because one examination will answer for your four papers. It is common usage. Every copyist is bound to help examine his copy. Is it not so? Will you not speak? Answer!"

"I prefer not to," he replied in a flute-like tone. It seemed to me that, while I had been addressing him, he carefully revolved every statement that I made; fully comprehended the meaning; could not gainsay the irresistible conclusion; but, at the same time, some paramount consideration prevailed with him to reply as he did.

"You are decided, then, not to comply with my request — a request made 40 according to common usage and common sense?"

He briefly gave me to understand, that on that point my judgment was sound. Yes: his decision was irreversible.

It is not seldom the case that, when a man is browbeaten in some unprecedented and violently unreasonable way, he begins to stagger in his own plainest faith. He begins, as it were, vaguely to surmise that, wonderful as it may be, all the justice and all the reason is on the other side. Accordingly, if any disinterested persons are present, he turns to them for some reinforcement for his own faltering mind.

"Turkey," said I, "what do you think of this? Am I not right?"

"With submission, sir," said Turkey, in his blandest tone, "I think that you are."

"Nippers," said I, "what do *you* think of it?"

"I think I should kick him out of the office."

(The reader of nice perceptions will have perceived that, it being morning, Turkey's answer is couched in polite and tranquil terms, but Nippers replies in ill-tempered ones. Or, to repeat a previous sentence, Nippers' ugly mood was on duty, and Turkey's off.)

"Ginger Nut," said I, willing to enlist the smallest suffrage in my behalf, "what do *you* think of it?"

"I think, sir, he's a little *luny*," replied Ginger Nut, with a grin.

"You hear what they say," said I, turning towards the screen, "come forth 50 and do your duty."

But he vouchsafed no reply. I pondered a moment in sore perplexity. But once more business hurried me. I determined again to postpone the consideration of this dilemma to my future leisure. With a little trouble we made out to examine the papers without Bartleby, though at every page or two Turkey deferentially dropped his opinion, that this proceeding was quite out of the common; while Nippers, twitching in his chair with a dyspeptic nervousness, ground out, between his set teeth, occasional hissing maledictions against the stubborn oaf behind the screen. And for his (Nippers') part, this was the first and the last time he would do another man's business without pay.

Meanwhile Bartleby sat in his hermitage, oblivious to everything but his own peculiar business there.

Some days passed, the scrivener being employed upon another lengthy work. His late remarkable conduct led me to regard his ways narrowly. I observed that he never went to dinner; indeed, that he never went anywhere. As yet I had never, of my personal knowledge, known him to be outside of my office. He was a perpetual sentry in the corner. At about eleven o'clock though, in the morning, I noticed that Ginger Nut would advance toward the opening in Bartleby's screen, as if silently beckoned thither by a gesture invisible to me where I sat. The boy would then leave the office, jingling a few pence, and reappear with a handful of ginger-nuts, which he delivered in the hermitage, receiving two of the cakes for his trouble.

He lives, then, on ginger-nuts, thought I; never eats a dinner, properly speaking; he must be a vegetarian, then, but no; he never eats even vegetables, he eats nothing but ginger-nuts. My mind then ran on in reveries concerning the probable effects upon the human constitution of living entirely on ginger-nuts. Ginger-nuts are so called, because they contain ginger as one of their peculiar constituents, and the final flavoring one. Now, what was ginger? A hot, spicy thing. Was Bartleby hot and spicy? Not at all. Ginger, then, had no effect upon Bartleby. Probably he preferred it should have none.

Nothing so aggravates an earnest person as a passive resistance. If the 55 individual so resisted be of a not inhumane temper, and the resisting one perfectly harmless in his passivity, then, in the better moods of the former, he will endeavor charitably to construe to his imagination what proves impossible to be solved by his judgment. Even so, for the most part, I regarded Bartleby and his ways. Poor fellow! thought I, he means no mischief; it is plain he intends no insolence; his aspect sufficiently evinces that his eccentricities are involuntary. He is useful to me. I can get along with him. If I turn him away, the chances are he will fall in with some less indulgent employer, and then he will be rudely treated, and perhaps driven forth miserably to starve. Yes. Here I can cheaply purchase a delicious self-approval. To befriend Bartleby; to humor him in his strange wilfulness, will cost me little or nothing, while I lay up in my soul what will eventually prove a sweet morsel for my conscience. But this mood was not invariable with me. The passiveness of Bartleby sometimes irritated me. I felt strangely goaded on to encounter him in new opposition — to elicit some angry spark from him answerable to my own. But, indeed, I might as well have essayed to strike fire with my knuckles against a bit of Windsor soap. But one afternoon the evil impulse in me mastered me, and the following little scene ensued:

"Bartleby," said I, "when those papers are all copied, I will compare them with you."

"I would prefer not to."

"How? Surely you do not mean to persist in that mulish vagary?"

No answer.

I threw open the folding-doors nearby, and turning upon Turkey and Nip- 60
pers, exclaimed:

"Bartleby a second time says, he won't examine his papers. What do you think of it, Turkey?"

It was afternoon, be it remembered. Turkey sat glowing like a brass boiler; his bald head steaming; his hands reeling among his blotted papers.

"Think of it?" roared Turkey. "I think I'll just step behind his screen, and black his eyes for him!"

So saying, Turkey rose to his feet and threw his arms into a pugilistic position. He was hurrying away to make good his promise, when I detained him, alarmed at the effect of incautiously rousing Turkey's combativeness after dinner.

"Sit down, Turkey," said I, "and hear what Nippers has to say. What do you 65
think of it, Nippers? Would I not be justified in immediately dismissing Bartleby?"

"Excuse me, that is for you to decide, sir. I think his conduct quite unusual, and, indeed, unjust, as regards Turkey and myself. But it may only be a passing whim."

"Ah," exclaimed I, "you have strangely changed your mind, then — you speak very gently of him now."

"All beer," cried Turkey; "gentleness is effects of beer — Nippers and I dined together to-day. You see how gentle *I* am, sir. Shall I go and black his eyes?"

"You refer to Bartleby, I suppose. No, not to-day, Turkey," I replied; "pray, put up your fists."

I closed the doors, and again advanced towards Bartleby. I felt additional 70
incentives tempting me to my fate. I burned to be rebelled against again. I remembered that Bartleby never left the office.

"Bartleby," said I, "Ginger Nut is away; just step around to the Post Office, won't you?" (it was but a three minutes' walk) "and see if there is anything for me."

"I would prefer not to."

"You *will* not?"

"I *prefer* not."

I staggered to my desk, and sat there in a deep study. My blind inveteracy 75
returned. Was there any other thing in which I could procure myself to be

ignominiously repulsed by this lean, penniless wight? — my hired clerk? What added thing is there, perfectly reasonable, that he will be sure to refuse to do?

"Bartleby!"

No answer.

"Bartleby," in a louder tone.

No answer.

"Bartleby," I roared.

Like a very ghost, agreeably to the laws of magical invocation, at the third summons, he appeared at the entrance of his hermitage.

"Go to the next room, and tell Nippers to come to me."

"I prefer not to," he respectfully and slowly said, and mildly disappeared.

"Very good, Bartleby," said I, in a quiet sort of serenely-severe self-possessed tone, intimating the unalterable purpose of some terrible retribution very close at hand. At the moment I half intended something of the kind. But upon the whole, as it was drawing towards my dinner-hour, I thought it best to put on my hat and walk home for the day, suffering much from perplexity and distress of mind.

Shall I acknowledge it? The conclusion of this whole business was, that it soon became a fixed fact of my chambers, that a pale young scrivener, by the name of Bartleby, had a desk there; that he copied for me at the usual rate of four cents a folio (one hundred words); but he was permanently exempt from examining the work done by him, that duty being transferred to Turkey and Nippers, out of compliment, doubtless, to their superior acuteness; moreover, said Bartleby was never, on any account, to be dispatched on the most trivial errand of any sort; and that even if entreated to take upon him such a matter, it was generally understood that he would "prefer not to" — in other words, that he would refuse point-blank.

As days passed on, I became considerably reconciled to Bartleby. His steadiness, his freedom from all dissipation, his incessant industry (except when he chose to throw himself into a standing revery behind his screen), his great stillness, his unalterableness of demeanor under all circumstances, made him a valuable acquisition. One prime thing was this — *he was always there* — first in the morning, continually through the day, and the last at night. I had a singular confidence in his honesty. I felt my most precious papers perfectly safe in his hands. Sometimes, to be sure, I could not, for the very soul of me, avoid falling into sudden spasmodic passions with him. For it was exceeding difficult to bear in mind all the time those strange peculiarities, privileges, and unheard-of exemptions, forming the tacit stipulations on Bartleby's part under which he remained in my office. Now and then, in the eagerness of dispatching pressing business, I would inadvertently summon Bartleby, in a short, rapid tone, to put his finger, say, on the incipient tie of a bit of red tape with which I was about compressing some papers. Of course, from behind the screen the usual answer, "I prefer not to," was sure to come; and then, how could a human creature, with the common infirmities of our nature, refrain from bitterly exclaiming upon such perverseness — such unreasonableness? However, every added repulse of this sort which I received only tended to lessen the probability of my repeating the inadvertence.

Here it must be said, that, according to the custom of most legal gentlemen occupying chambers in densely populated law buildings, there were several keys to my door. One was kept by a woman residing in the attic, which person weekly scrubbed and daily swept and dusted my apartments. Another was kept by Turkey for convenience sake. The third I sometimes carried in my own pocket. The fourth I knew not who had.

Now, one Sunday morning I happened to go to Trinity Church, to hear a celebrated preacher, and finding myself rather early on the ground I thought I would walk round to my chambers for a while. Luckily I had my key with me; but upon applying it to the lock, I found it resisted by something inserted from the inside. Quite surprised, I called out; when to my consternation a key was turned from within; and thrusting his lean visage at me, and holding the door ajar, the apparition of Bartleby appeared, in his shirt-sleeves, and otherwise in a strangely tattered *deshabille,* saying quietly that he was sorry, but he was deeply engaged just then, and — preferred not admitting me at present. In a brief word or two, he moreover added, that perhaps I had better walk round the block two or three times, and by that time he would probably have concluded his affairs.

Now, the utterly unsurmised appearance of Bartleby, tenanting my law-chambers of a Sunday morning, with his cadaverously gentlemanly *nonchalance,* yet withal firm and self-possessed, had such a strange effect upon me, that incontinently I slunk away from my own door, and did as desired. But not without sundry twinges of impotent rebellion against the mild effrontery of this unaccountable scrivener. Indeed, it was his wonderful mildness chiefly, which not only disarmed me, but unmanned me, as it were. For I consider that one, for the time, is sort of unmanned when he tranquilly permits his hired clerk to dictate to him, and order him away from his own premises. Furthermore, I was full of uneasiness as to what Bartleby could possibly be doing in my office in his shirt-sleeves, and in an otherwise dismantled condition of a Sunday morning. Was anything amiss going on? Nay, that was out of the question. It was not to be thought of for a moment that Bartleby was an immoral person. But what could he be doing there? — copying? Nay again, whatever might be his eccentricities, Bartleby was an eminently decorous person. He would be the last man to sit down to his desk in any state approaching to nudity. Besides, it was Sunday; and there was something about Bartleby that forbade the supposition that he would by any secular occupation violate the proprieties of the day.

Nevertheless, my mind was not pacified; and full of a restless curiosity, at 90 last I returned to the door. Without hindrance I inserted my key, opened it, and entered. Bartleby was not to be seen. I looked round anxiously, peeped behind his screen; but it was very plain that he was gone. Upon more closely examining the place, I surmised that for an indefinite period Bartleby must have ate, dressed, and slept in my office, and that too without plate, mirror, or bed. The cushioned seat of a rickety old sofa in one corner bore the faint impress of a lean, reclining form. Rolled away under his desk, I found a blanket; under the empty grate, a blacking box and brush; on a chair, a tin basin, with soap and a ragged towel; in a newspaper a few crumbs of ginger-nuts and a morsel of cheese. Yes, thought I, it is evident enough that Bartleby has been making his home here, keeping bachelor's hall all by himself. Immediately then the thought came sweeping across me, what miserable friendlessness and loneliness are here revealed! His poverty is great; but his solitude, how horrible! Think of it. Of a Sunday, Wall

Street is deserted as Petra;° and every night of every day it is an emptiness. This building, too, which of week-days hums with industry and life, at nightfall echoes with sheer vacancy, and all through Sunday is forlorn. And here Bartleby makes his home; sole spectator of a solitude which he has seen all populous — a sort of innocent and transformed Marius brooding among the ruins of Carthage?°

For the first time in my life a feeling of overpowering stinging melancholy seized me. Before, I had never experienced aught but a not unpleasing sadness. The bond of a common humanity now drew me irresistibly to gloom. A fraternal melancholy! For both I and Bartleby were sons of Adam. I remembered the bright silks and sparkling faces I had seen that day, in gala trim, swan-like sailing down the Mississippi of Broadway; and I contrasted them with the pallid copyist, and thought to myself, Ah, happiness courts the light, so we deem the world is gay; but misery hides aloof, so we deem that misery there is none. These sad fancyings — chimeras, doubtless, of a sick and silly brain — led on to other and more special thoughts, concerning the eccentricities of Bartleby. Presentiments of strange discoveries hovered round me. The scrivener's pale form appeared to me laid out, among uncaring strangers, in its shivering winding-sheet.

Suddenly I was attracted by Bartleby's closed desk, the key in open sight left in the lock.

I mean no mischief, seek the gratification of no heartless curiosity, thought I; besides, the desk is mine, and its contents, too, so I will make bold to look within. Everything was methodically arranged, the papers smoothly placed. The pigeon-holes were deep, and removing the files of documents, I groped into their recesses. Presently I felt something there, and dragged it out. It was an old bandanna handkerchief, heavy and knotted. I opened it, and saw it was a saving's bank.

I now recalled all the quiet mysteries which I had noted in the man. I remembered that he never spoke but to answer; that, though at intervals he had considerable time to himself, yet I had never seen him reading — no, not even a newspaper; that for long periods he would stand looking out, at his pale window behind the screen, upon the dead brick wall; I was quite sure he never visited any refectory or eating-house; while his pale face clearly indicated that he never drank beer like Turkey; or tea and coffee even, like other men; that he never went anywhere in particular that I could learn; never went out for a walk, unless, indeed, that was the case at present; that he had declined telling who he was, or whence he came, or whether he had any relatives in the world; that though so thin and pale, he never complained of ill-health. And more than all, I remembered a certain unconscious air of pallid — how shall I call it? — of pallid haughtiness, say, or rather an austere reserve about him, which had positively awed me into my tame compliance with his eccentricities, when I had feared to ask him to do the slightest incidental thing for me, even though I might know, from his long-continued motionlessness, that behind his screen he must be standing in one of those dead-wall reveries of his.

Revolving all these things, and coupling them with the recently discovered 95

Petra: An ancient Arabian city abandoned for many centuries.
Marius: Gaius Marius (157–86 B.C.), an exiled Roman general who sought refuge in *Carthage,* a city destroyed by the Romans.

fact, that he made my office his constant abiding place and home, and not forgetful of his morbid moodiness; revolving all these things, a prudential feeling began to steal over me. My first emotions had been those of pure melancholy and sincerest pity; but just in proportion as the forlornness of Bartleby grew and grew to my imagination, did that same melancholy merge into fear, that pity into repulsion. So true it is, and so terrible, too, that up to a certain point the thought or sight of misery enlists our best affections; but, in certain special cases, beyond that point it does not. They err who would assert that invariably this is owing to the inherent selfishness of the human heart. It rather proceeds from a certain hopelessness of remedying excessive and organic ill. To a sensitive being, pity is not seldom pain. And when at last it is perceived that such pity cannot lead to effectual succor, common sense bids the soul be rid of it. What I saw that morning persuaded me that the scrivener was the victim of innate and incurable disorder. I might give alms to his body; but his body did not pain him; it was his soul that suffered, and his soul I could not reach.

I did not accomplish the purpose of going to Trinity Church that morning. Somehow, the things I had seen disqualified me for the time from church-going. I walked homeward, thinking what I would do with Bartleby. Finally, I resolved upon this — I would put certain calm questions to him the next morning, touching his history, etc., and if he declined to answer them openly and unre-servedly (and I supposed he would prefer not), then to give him a twenty dollar bill over and above whatever I might owe him, and tell him his services were no longer required; but that if in any other way I could assist him, I would be happy to do so, especially if he desired to return to his native place, wherever that might be, I would willingly help to defray the expenses. Moreover, if, after reaching home, he found himself at any time in want of aid, a letter from him would be sure of a reply.

The next morning came.

"Bartleby," said I, gently calling to him behind his screen.

No reply.

"Bartleby," said I, in a still gentler tone, "come here; I am not going to ask 100
you to do anything you would prefer not to do — I simply wish to speak to you."

Upon this he noiselessly slid into view.

"Will you tell me, Bartleby, where you were born?"

"I would prefer not to."

"Will you tell me *anything* about yourself?"

"I would prefer not to." 105

"But what reasonable objection can you have to speak to me? I feel friendly towards you."

He did not look at me while I spoke, but kept his glance fixed upon my bust of Cicero, which, as I then sat, was directly behind me, some six inches above my head.

"What is your answer, Bartleby?" said I, after waiting a considerable time for a reply, during which his countenance remained immovable, only there was the faintest conceivable tremor of the white attenuated mouth.

"At present I prefer to give no answer," he said, and retired into his hermitage.

It was rather weak in me I confess, but his manner, on this occasion, nettled 110 me. Not only did there seem to lurk in it a certain calm disdain, but his perverseness seemed ungrateful, considering the undeniable good usage and indulgence he had received from me.

Again I sat ruminating what I should do. Mortified as I was at his behavior, and resolved as I had been to dismiss him when I entered my office, nevertheless I strangely felt something superstitious knocking at my heart, and forbidding me to carry out my purpose, and denouncing me for a villain if I dared to breathe one bitter word against this forlornest of mankind. At last, familiarly drawing my chair behind his screen, I sat down and said: "Bartleby, never mind, then, about revealing your history; but let me entreat you, as a friend, to comply as far as may be with the usages of this office. Say now, you will help to examine papers tomorrow or next day: in short, say now, that in a day or two you will begin to be a little reasonable: — say so, Bartleby."

"At present I would prefer not to be a little reasonable," was his mildly cadaverous reply.

Just then the folding-doors opened, and Nippers approached. He seemed suffering from an unusually bad night's rest, induced by severer indigestion than common. He overhead those final words of Bartleby.

"Prefer not, eh?" gritted Nippers — "I'd *prefer* him, if I were you, sir," addressing me — "I'd *prefer* him; I'd give him preferences, the stubborn mule! What is it, sir, pray, that he *prefers* not to do now?"

Bartleby moved not a limb.   115

"Mr. Nippers," said I, "I'd prefer that you would withdraw for the present."

Somehow, of late, I had got into the way of involuntarily using this word "prefer" upon all sorts of not exactly suitable occasions. And I trembled to think that my contact with the scrivener had already and seriously affected me in a mental way. And what further and deeper aberration might it not yet produce? This apprehension had not been without efficacy in determining me to summary measures.

As Nippers, looking very sour and sulky, was departing, Turkey blandly and deferentially approached.

"With submission, sir," said he, "yesterday I was thinking about Bartleby here, and I think that if he would but prefer to take a quart of good ale every day, it would do much towards mending him, and enabling him to assist in examining his papers."

"So you have got the word, too," said I, slightly excited.   120

"With submission, what word, sir?" asked Turkey, respectfully crowding himself into the contracted space behind the screen, and by so doing, making me jostle the scrivener. "What word, sir?"

"I would prefer to be left alone here," said Bartleby, as if offended at being mobbed in his privacy.

"That's the word, Turkey," said I — *"that's* it."

"Oh, *prefer?* oh yes — queer word. I never use it myself. But, sir, as I was saying, if he would but prefer — "

"Turkey," interrupted I, "you will please withdraw."   125

"Oh certainly, sir, if you prefer that I should."

As he opened the folding-door to retire, Nippers at his desk caught a glimpse of me, and asked whether I would prefer to have a certain paper copied on blue paper or white. He did not in the least roguishly accent the word "prefer." It was plain that it involuntarily rolled from his tongue. I thought to myself, surely I must get rid of a demented man, who already has in some degree turned the tongues, if not the heads of myself and clerks. But I thought it prudent not to break the dismission at once.

The next day I noticed that Bartleby did nothing but stand at his window in his dead-wall revery. Upon asking him why he did not write, he said that he had decided upon doing no more writing.

"Why, how now? what next?" exclaimed I, "do no more writing?"

"No more."   130

"And what is the reason?"

"Do you not see the reason for yourself?" he indifferently replied.

I looked steadfastly at him, and perceived that his eyes looked dull and glazed. Instantly it occurred to me, that his unexampled diligence in copying by his dim window for the first few weeks of his stay with me might have temporarily impaired his vision.

I was touched. I said something in condolence with him. I hinted that of course he did wisely in abstaining from writing for a while; and urged him to embrace that opportunity of taking wholesome exercise in the open air. This, however, he did not do. A few days after this, my other clerks being absent, and being in a great hurry to dispatch certain letters by the mail, I thought that, having nothing else earthly to do, Bartleby would surely be less inflexible than usual, and carry these letters to the Post Office. But he blankly declined. So, much to my inconvenience, I went myself.

Still added days went by. Whether Bartleby's eyes improved or not, I could   135
not say. To all appearance, I thought they did. But when I asked him if they did, he vouchsafed no answer. At all events, he would do no copying. At last, in replying to my urgings, he informed me that he had permanently given up copying.

"What!" exclaimed I; "suppose your eyes should get entirely well — better than ever before — would you not copy then?"

"I have given up copying," he answered, and slid aside.

He remained as ever, a fixture in my chamber. Nay — if that were possible — he became still more of a fixture than before. What was to be done? He would do nothing in the office; why should he stay there? In plain fact, he had now become a millstone to me, not only useless as a necklace, but afflictive to bear. Yet I was sorry for him. I speak less than truth when I say that, on his own account, he occasioned me uneasiness. If he would but have named a single relative or friend, I would instantly have written, and urged their taking the poor fellow away to some convenient retreat. But he seemed alone, absolutely alone in the universe. A bit of wreck in the mid-Atlantic. At length, necessities connected with my business tyrannized over all other considerations. Decently as I could, I told Bartleby that in six days' time he must unconditionally leave the office. I warned him to take measures, in the interval, for procuring some other abode. I offered to assist him in this endeavor, if he himself would but take the first step towards a removal. "And when you finally quit me, Bartleby," added I, "I shall see that you go not away entirely unprovided. Six days from this hour, remember."

At the expiration of that period, I peeped behind the screen, and lo! Bartleby was there.

I buttoned up my coat, balanced myself; advanced slowly towards him, 140 touched his shoulder, and said, "The time has come; you must quit this place; I am sorry for you; here is money; but you must go."

"I would prefer not," he replied, with his back still towards me.

"You *must*."

He remained silent.

Now I had an unbounded confidence in this man's common honesty. He had frequently restored to me sixpences and shillings carelessly dropped upon the floor, for I am apt to be very reckless in such shirt-button affairs. The proceeding, then, which followed will not be deemed extraordinary.

"Bartleby," said I, "I owe you twelve dollars on account; here are thirty-two, 145 the odd twenty are yours — Will you take it?" and I handed the bills towards him.

But he made no motion.

"I will leave them here, then," putting them under a weight on the table. Then taking my hat and cane and going to the door, I tranquilly turned and added — "After you have removed your things from these offices, Bartleby, you will of course lock the door — since every one is now gone for the day but you — and if you please, slip your key underneath the mat, so that I may have it in the morning. I shall not see you again; so good-bye to you. If, hereafter, in your new place of abode, I can be of any service to you, do not fail to advise me by letter. Good-bye, Bartleby, and fare you well."

But he answered not a word; like the last column of some ruined temple, he remained standing mute and solitary in the middle of the otherwise deserted room.

As I walked home in a pensive mood, my vanity got the better of my pity. I could not but highly plume myself on my masterly management in getting rid of Bartleby. Masterly I call it, and such it must appear to any dispassionate thinker. The beauty of my procedure seemed to consist in its perfect quietness. There was no vulgar bullying, no bravado of any sort, no choleric hectoring, and striding to and fro across the apartment, jerking out vehement commands for Bartleby to bundle himself off with his beggarly traps. Nothing of the kind. Without loudly bidding Bartleby depart — as an inferior genius might have done — I *assumed* the ground that depart he must; and upon that assumption built all I had to say. The more I thought over my procedure, the more I was charmed with it. Nevertheless, next morning, upon awakening, I had my doubts — I had somehow slept off the fumes of vanity. One of the coolest and wisest hours a man has, is just after he awakes in the morning. My procedure seemed as sagacious as ever — but only in theory. How it would prove in practice — there was the rub. It was truly a beautiful thought to have assumed Bartleby's departure; but, after all, that assumption was simply my own, and none of Bartleby's. The great point was, not whether I had assumed that he would quit me, but whether he would prefer to do so. He was more a man of preferences than assumptions.

After breakfast, I walked down town, arguing the probabilities *pro* and *con*. 150 One moment I thought it would prove a miserable failure, and Bartleby would be found all alive at my office as usual; the next moment it seemed certain that

I should find his chair empty. And so I kept veering about. At the corner of Broadway and Canal Street, I saw quite an excited group of people standing in earnest conversation.

"I'll take odds he doesn't," said a voice as I passed.

"Doesn't go? — done!" said I, "put up your money."

I was instinctively putting my hand in my pocket to produce my own, when I remembered that this was an election day. The words I had overheard bore no reference to Bartleby, but to the success or non-success of some candidate for the mayoralty. In my intent frame of mind, I had, as it were, imagined that all Broadway shared in my excitement, and were debating the same question with me. I passed on, very thankful that the uproar of the street screened my momentary absent-mindedness.

As I had intended, I was earlier than usual at my office door. I stood listening for a moment. All was still. He must be gone. I tried the knob. The door was locked. Yes, my procedure had worked to a charm; he indeed must be vanished. Yet a certain melancholy mixed with this: I was almost sorry for my brilliant success. I was fumbling under the door mat for the key, which Bartleby was to have left there for me, when accidentally my knee knocked against a panel, producing a summoning sound, and in response a voice came to me from within — "Not yet; I am occupied."

It was Bartleby. 155

I was thunderstruck. For an instant I stood like the man who, pipe in mouth, was killed one cloudless afternoon long ago in Virginia, by summer lightning; at his own warm open window he was killed, and remained leaning out there upon the dreamy afternoon, till some one touched him, when he fell.

"Not gone!" I murmured at last. But again obeying that wondrous ascendancy which the inscrutable scrivener had over me, and from which ascendancy, for all my chafing, I could not completely escape, I slowly went down stairs and out into the street, and while walking round the block, considered what I should next do in this unheard-of perplexity. Turn the man out by an actual thrusting I could not; to drive him away by calling him hard names would not do; calling in the police was an unpleasant idea; and yet, permit him to enjoy his cadaverous triumph over me — this, too, I could not think of. What was to be done? or, if nothing could be done, was there anything further that I could *assume* in the matter? Yes, as before I had prospectively assumed that Bartleby would depart, so now I might retrospectively assume that departed he was. In the legitimate carrying out of this assumption, I might enter my office in a great hurry, and pretending not to see Bartleby at all, walk straight against him as if he were air. Such a proceeding would in a singular degree have the appearance of a home-thrust. It was hardly possible that Bartleby could withstand such an application of the doctrine of assumption. But upon second thoughts the success of the plan seemed rather dubious. I resolved to argue the matter over with him again.

"Bartleby," said I, entering the office, with a quietly severe expression, "I am seriously displeased. I am pained, Bartleby. I had thought better of you. I had imagined you of such a gentlemanly organization, that in any delicate dilemma a slight hint would suffice — in short, an assumption. But it appears I am deceived. Why," I added, unaffectedly starting, "you have not even touched that money yet," pointing to it, just where I had left it the evening previous.

He answered nothing.

"Will you, or will you not, quit me?" I now demanded in a sudden passion, 160 advancing close to him.

"I would prefer *not* to quit you," he replied, gently emphasizing the *not.*

"What earthly right have you to stay here? Do you pay any rent? Do you pay my taxes? Or is this property yours?"

He answered nothing.

"Are you ready to go on and write now? Are your eyes recovered? Could you copy a small paper for me this morning? or help examine a few lines? or step round to the Post Office? In a word, will you do anything at all, to give a coloring to your refusal to depart the premises?"

He silently retired into his hermitage. 165

I was now in such a state of nervous resentment that I thought it but prudent to check myself at present from further demonstrations. Bartleby and I were alone. I remembered the tragedy of the unfortunate Adams and the still more unfortunate Colt° in the solitary office of the latter; and how poor Colt, being dreadfully incensed by Adams, and imprudently permitting himself to get wildly excited, was at unawares hurried into his fatal act — an act which certainly no man could possibly deplore more than the actor himself. Often it had occurred to me in my ponderings upon the subject that had that altercation taken place in the public street, or at a private residence, it would not have terminated as it did. It was the circumstance of being alone in a solitary office, up stairs, of a building entirely unhallowed by humanizing domestic associations — an uncarpeted office, doubtless, of a dusty, haggard sort of appearance — this it must have been, which greatly helped to enhance the irritable desperation of the hapless Colt.

But when this old Adam of resentment rose in me and tempted me concerning Bartleby, I grappled him and threw him. How? Why, simply by recalling the divine injunction: "A new commandment give I unto you, that ye love one another." Yes, this it was that saved me. Aside from higher considerations, charity often operates as a vastly wise and prudent principle — a great safeguard to its possessor. Men have committed murder for jealousy's sake, and anger's sake, and hatred's sake, and selfishness' sake, and spiritual pride's sake; but no man, that ever I heard of, ever committed a diabolical murder for sweet charity's sake. Mere self-interest, then, if no better motive can be enlisted, should, especially with high-tempered men, prompt all beings to charity and philanthropy. At any rate, upon the occasion in question, I strove to drown my exasperated feelings towards the scrivener by benevolently construing his conduct. Poor fellow, poor fellow! thought I, he don't mean anything; and besides, he has seen hard times, and ought to be indulged.

I endeavored, also, immediately to occupy myself, and at the same time to comfort my despondency. I tried to fancy, that in the course of the morning, at such time as might prove agreeable to him, Bartleby, of his own free accord, would emerge from his hermitage and take up some decided line of march in the direction of the door. But no. Half-past twelve o'clock came; Turkey began to glow in the face, overturn his inkstand, and become generally obstreperous;

John C. Colt: Brother of the gun maker. Killed *Samuel Adams* during a quarrel in 1842, leading to a sensational court case. Colt committed suicide just before he was to be hanged.

Nippers abated down into quietude and courtesy; Ginger Nut munched his noon apple; and Bartleby remained standing at his window in one of his profoundest dead-wall reveries. Will it be credited? Ought I to acknowledge it? That afternoon I left the office without saying one further word to him.

Some days now passed, during which, at leisure intervals I looked a little into "Edwards on the Will," and "Priestley on Necessity."° Under the circumstances, those books induced a salutary feeling. Gradually I slid into the persuasion that these troubles of mine, touching the scrivener, had been all predestined from eternity, and Bartleby was billeted upon me for some mysterious purpose of an all-wise Providence, which it was not for a mere mortal like me to fathom. Yes, Bartleby, stay there behind your screen, thought I; I shall persecute you no more; you are harmless and noiseless as any of these old chairs; in short, I never feel so private as when I know you are here. At last I see it, I feel it; I penetrate to the predestined purpose of my life. I am content. Others may have loftier parts to enact; but my mission in this world, Bartleby, is to furnish you with office-room for such period as you may see fit to remain.

I believe that this wise and blessed frame of mind would have continued 170 with me, had it not been for the unsolicited and uncharitable remarks obtruded upon me by my professional friends who visited the rooms. But thus it often is, that the constant friction of illiberal minds wears out at last the best resolves of the more generous. Though to be sure, when I reflected upon it, it was not strange that people entering my office should be struck by the peculiar aspect of the unaccountable Bartleby, and so be tempted to throw out some sinister observations concerning him. Sometimes an attorney, having business with me, and calling at my office, and finding no one but the scrivener there, would undertake to obtain some sort of precise information from him touching my whereabouts; but without heeding his idle talk, Bartleby would remain standing immovable in the middle of the room. So after contemplating him in that position for a time, the attorney would depart, no wiser than he came.

Also, when a reference was going on, and the room full of lawyers and witnesses, and business driving fast, some deeply-occupied legal gentleman present, seeing Bartleby wholly unemployed, would request him to run round to his (the legal gentleman's) office and fetch some papers for him. Thereupon, Bartleby would tranquilly decline, and yet remain idle as before. Then the lawyer would give a great stare, and turn to me. And what could I say? At last I was made aware that all through the circle of my professional acquaintance, a whisper of wonder was running round, having reference to the strange creature I kept at my office. This worried me very much. And as the idea came upon me of his possibly turning out a long-lived man, and keeping occupying my chambers, and denying my authority; and perplexing my visitors; and scandalizing my professional reputation; and casting a general gloom over the premises; keeping soul and body together to the last upon his savings (for doubtless he spent but half a dime a day), and in the end perhaps outlive me, and claim possession of my office by right of his perpetual occupancy: as all these dark anticipations crowded upon me more and more, and my friends continually intruded their relentless remarks upon the apparition in my room; a great change was wrought in me. I

Jonathan Edwards, Freedom of the Will (1754), *Joseph Priestley,* Doctrine of Philosophical Necessity (1777): Argued that human beings do not have free will.

resolved to gather all my faculties together, and forever rid me of this intolerable incubus.

Ere revolving any complicated project, however, adapted to this end, I first simply suggested to Bartleby the propriety of his permanent departure. In a calm and serious tone, I commended the idea to his careful and mature consideration. But, having taken three days to meditate upon it, he apprised me, that his original determination remained the same; in short, that he still preferred to abide with me.

What shall I do? I now said to myself, buttoning up my coat to the last button. What shall I do? what ought I to do? what does conscience say I *should* do with this man, or, rather, ghost. Rid myself of him, I must; go, he shall. But how? You will not thrust him, the poor, pale, passive mortal — you will not thrust such a helpless creature out of your door? you will not dishonor yourself by such cruelty? No, I will not, I cannot do that. Rather would I let him live and die here, and then mason up his remains in the wall. What, then, will you do? For all your coaxing, he will not budge. Bribes he leaves under your own paper-weight on your table; in short, it is quite plain that he prefers to cling to you.

Then something severe, something unusual must be done. What! surely you will not have him collared by a constable, and commit his innocent pallor to the common jail? And upon what ground could you procure such a thing to be done? — a vagrant, is he? What! he a vagrant, a wanderer, who refuses to budge? It is because he will *not* be a vagrant, then, that you seek to count him *as* a vagrant. That is too absurd. No visible means of support: there I have him. Wrong again: for indubitably he *does* support himself, and that is the only unanswerable proof that any man can show of his possessing the means so to do. No more, then. Since he will not quit me, I must quit him. I will change my offices; I will move elsewhere, and give him fair notice, that if I find him on my new premises I will then proceed against him as a common trespasser.

Acting accordingly, next day I thus addressed him: "I find these chambers 175 too far from the City Hall; the air is unwholesome. In a word, I propose to remove my offices next week, and shall no longer require your services. I tell you this now, in order that you may seek another place."

He made no reply, and nothing more was said.

On the appointed day I engaged carts and men, proceeded to my chambers, and having but little furniture, everything was removed in a few hours. Through-out, the scrivener remained standing behind the screen, which I directed to be removed the last thing. It was withdrawn; and, being folded up like a huge folio, left him the motionless occupant of a naked room. I stood in the entry watching him a moment, while something from within me upbraided me.

I re-entered, with my hand in my pocket — and — and my heart in my mouth.

"Good-bye, Bartleby; I am going — good-bye, and God some way bless you; and take that," slipping something in his hand. But it dropped upon the floor, and then — strange to say — I tore myself from him whom I had so longed to be rid of.

Established in my new quarters, for a day or two I kept the door locked, 180 and started at every footfall in the passages. When I returned to my rooms, after any little absence, I would pause at the threshold for an instant, and attentively listen, ere applying my key. But these fears were needless. Bartleby never came nigh me.

I thought all was going well, when a perturbed-looking stranger visited me, inquiring whether I was the person who had recently occupied rooms at No. — Wall Street.

Full of forebodings, I replied that I was.

"Then, sir," said the stranger, who proved a lawyer, "you are responsible for the man you left there. He refuses to do any copying; he refuses to do anything; he says he prefers not to; and he refuses to quit the premises."

"I am very sorry, sir," said I, with assumed tranquillity, but an inward tremor, "but, really, the man you allude to is nothing to me — he is no relation or apprentice of mine, that you should hold me responsible for him."

"In mercy's name, who is he?" 185

"I certainly cannot inform you. I know nothing about him. Formerly I employed him as a copyist; but he has done nothing for me now for some time past."

"I shall settle him, then — good morning, sir."

Several days passed, and I heard nothing more; and, though I often felt a charitable prompting to call at the place and see poor Bartleby, yet a certain squeamishness, of I know not what, withheld me.

All is over with him, by this time, thought I, at last, when, through another week, no further intelligence reached me. But, coming to my room the day after, I found several persons waiting at my door in a high state of nervous excitement.

"That's the man — here he comes," cried the foremost one, whom I rec- 190 ognized as the lawyer who had previously called upon me alone.

"You must take him away, sir, at once," cried a portly person among them, advancing upon me, and whom I knew to be the landlord of No. — Wall Street. "These gentlemen, my tenants, cannot stand it any longer; Mr. B——," pointing to the lawyer, "has turned him out of his room, and he now persists in haunting the building generally, sitting upon the banisters of the stairs by day, and sleeping in the entry by night. Everybody is concerned; clients are leaving the offices; some fears are entertained of a mob; something you must do, and that without delay."

Aghast at this torrent, I fell back before it, and would fain have locked myself in my new quarters. In vain I persisted that Bartleby was nothing to me — no more than to any one else. In vain — I was the last person known to have anything to do with him, and they held me to the terrible account. Fearful, then, of being exposed in the papers (as one person present obscurely threatened), I considered the matter, and, at length, said, that if the lawyer would give me a confidential interview with the scrivener, in his (the lawyer's) own room, I would, that afternoon, strive my best to rid them of the nuisance they complained of.

Going up stairs to my old haunt, there was Bartleby silently sitting upon the banister at the landing.

"What are you doing here, Bartleby?" said I.

"Sitting upon the banister," he mildly replied. 195

I motioned him into the lawyer's room, who then left us.

"Bartleby," said I, "are you aware that you are the cause of great tribulation to me, by persisting in occupying the entry after being dismissed from the office?"

No answer.

"Now one of two things must take place. Either you must do something, or something must be done to you. Now what sort of business would you like to engage in? Would you like to re-engage in copying for some one?"

"No; I would prefer not to make any change."   200

"Would you like a clerkship in a dry-goods store?"

"There is too much confinement about that. No, I would not like a clerkship; but I am not particular."

"Too much confinement," I cried, "why, you keep yourself confined all the time!"

"I would prefer not to take a clerkship," he rejoined, as if to settle that little item at once.

"How would a bar-tender's business suit you? There is no trying of the eye-   205
sight in that."

"I would not like it at all; though, as I said before, I am not particular."

His unwonted wordiness inspirited me. I returned to the charge.

"Well, then, would you like to travel through the country collecting bills for the merchants? That would improve your health."

"No, I would prefer to be doing something else."

"How, then, would going as a companion to Europe, to entertain some   210
young gentleman with your conversation — how would that suit you?"

"Not at all. It does not strike me that there is anything definite about that. I like to be stationary. But I am not particular."

"Stationary you shall be, then," I cried, now losing all patience, and, for the first time in all my exasperating connection with him, fairly flying into a passion. "If you do not go away from these premises before night, I shall feel bound — indeed, I *am* bound — to — to quit the premises myself!" I rather absurdly concluded, knowing not with what possible threat to try to frighten his immobility into compliance. Despairing of all further efforts, I was precipitately leaving him, when a final thought occurred to me — one which had not been wholly unin-dulged before.

"Bartleby," said I, in the kindest tone I could assume under such exciting circumstances, "will you go home with me now — not to my office, but my dwelling — and remain there till we can conclude upon some convenient ar-rangement for you at our leisure? Come, let us start now, right away."

"No: at present I would prefer not to make any change at all."

I answered nothing; but, effectually dodging every one by the sudden-   215
ness and rapidity of my flight, rushed from the building, ran up Wall Street towards Broadway, and, jumping into the first omnibus, was soon removed from pursuit. As soon as tranquillity returned, I distinctly perceived that I had now done all that I possibly could, both in respect to the demands of the landlord and his tenants, and with regard to my own desire and sense of duty, to benefit Bartleby, and shield him from rude persecution. I now strove to be entirely care-free and quiescent; and my conscience justified me in the attempt; though, indeed, it was not so successful as I could have wished. So fearful was I of being again hunted out by the incensed landlord and his exasperated tenants, that, surrendering my business to Nippers, for a few days, I drove about the upper part of the town and through the suburbs, in my rockaway; crossed over to Jersey City and Hoboken, and paid

fugitive visits to Manhattanville and Astoria. In fact, I almost lived in my rockaway for the time.

When again I entered my office, lo, a note from the landlord lay upon the desk. I opened it with trembling hands. It informed me that the writer had sent to the police, and had Bartleby removed to the Tombs as a vagrant. Moreover, since I knew more about him than any one else, he wished me to appear at that place, and make a suitable statement of the facts. These tidings had a conflicting effect upon me. At first I was indignant; but, at last, almost approved. The landlord's energetic, summary disposition, had led him to adopt a procedure which I do not think I would have decided upon myself; and yet, as a last resort, under such peculiar circumstances, it seemed the only plan.

As I afterwards learned, the poor scrivener, when told that he must be conducted to the Tombs, offered not the slightest obstacle, but, in his pale, unmoving way, silently acquiesced.

Some of the compassionate and curious by-standers joined the party; and headed by one of the constables arm-in-arm with Bartleby, the silent procession filed its way through all the noise, and heat, and joy of the roaring thoroughfares at noon.

The same day I received the note, I went to the Tombs, or, to speak more properly, the Halls of Justice. Seeking the right officer, I stated the purpose of my call, and was informed that the individual I described was, indeed, within. I then assured the functionary that Bartleby was a perfectly honest man, and greatly to be compassionated, however unaccountably eccentric. I narrated all I knew, and closed by suggesting the idea of letting him remain in as indulgent confine-ment as possible, till something less harsh might be done — though, indeed, I hardly knew what. At all events, if nothing else could be decided upon, the alms-house must receive him. I then begged to have an interview.

Being under no disgraceful charge, and quite serene and harmless in all 220 his ways, they had permitted him freely to wander about the prison, and, espe-cially, in the inclosed grass-platted yards thereof. And so I found him there, standing all alone in the quietest of the yards, his face towards a high wall, while all around, from the narrow slits of the jail windows, I thought I saw peering out upon him the eyes of murderers and thieves.

"Bartleby!"

"I know you," he said, without looking round — "and I want nothing to say to you."

"It was not I that brought you here, Bartleby," said I, keenly pained at his implied suspicion. "And to you, this should not be so vile a place. Nothing reproachful attaches to you by being here. And see, it is not so sad a place as one might think. Look, there is the sky, and here is the grass."

"I know where I am," he replied, but would say nothing more, and so I left him.

As I entered the corridor again, a broad meat-like man, in an apron, accosted 225 me, and, jerking his thumb over his shoulder, said — "Is that your friend?"

"Yes."

"Does he want to starve? If he does, let him live on the prison fare, that's all."

"Who are you?" asked I, not knowing what to make of such an unofficially speaking person in such a place.

"I am the grub-man. Such gentlemen as have friends here, hire me to provide them with something good to eat."

"Is this so?" said I, turning the turnkey.   230

He said it was.

"Well, then," said I, slipping some silver into the grub-man's hands (for so they called him), "I want you to give particular attention to my friend there; let him have the best dinner you can get. And you must be as polite to him as possible."

"Introduce me, will you?" said the grub-man, looking at me with an expression which seemed to say he was all impatience for an opportunity to give a specimen of his breeding.

Thinking it would prove of benefit to the scrivener, I acquiesced; and, asking the grub-man his name, went up with him to Bartleby.

"Bartleby, this is a friend; you will find him very useful to you."   235

"Your sarvant, sir, your sarvant," said the grub-man, making a low salutation behind his apron. "Hope you find it pleasant here, sir; nice grounds — cool apartments — hope you'll stay with us some time — try to make it agreeable. What will you have for dinner to-day?"

"I prefer not to dine to-day," said Bartleby, turning away. "It would disagree with me; I am unused to dinners." So saying, he slowly moved to the other side of the inclosure, and took up a position fronting the deadwall.

"How's this?" said the grub-man, addressing me with a stare of astonishment. "He's odd, ain't he?"

"I think he is a little deranged," said I, sadly.

"Deranged? deranged is it? Well, now, upon my word, I thought that friend   240
of yourn was a gentleman forger; they are always pale and genteel-like, them forgers. I can't help pity 'em — can't help it, sir. Did you know Monroe Edwards?" he added, touchingly, and paused. Then, laying his hand piteously on my shoulder, sighed, "he died of consumption at Sing-Sing. So you weren't acquainted with Monroe?"

"No, I was never socially acquainted with any forgers. But I cannot stop longer. Look to my friend yonder. You will not lose by it. I will see you again."

Some few days after this, I again obtained admission to the Tombs, and went through the corridors in quest of Bartleby; but without finding him.

"I saw him coming from his cell not long ago," said a turnkey, "may be he's gone to loiter in the yards."

So I went in that direction.

"Are you looking for the silent man?" said another turnkey, passing me.   245
"Yonder he lies — sleeping in the yard there. 'Tis not twenty minutes since I saw him lie down."

The yard was entirely quiet. It was not accessible to the common prisoners. The surrounding walls, of amazing thickness, kept off all sounds behind them. The Egyptian character of the masonry weighed upon me with its gloom. But a soft imprisoned turf grew under foot. The heart of the eternal pyramids, it seemed, wherein, by some strange magic, through the clefts, grass-seed, dropped by birds, had sprung.

Strangely huddled at the base of the wall, his knees drawn up, and lying on his side, his head touching the cold stones, I saw the wasted Bartleby. But nothing stirred. I paused; then went close up to him; stooped over, and saw that his dim eyes were open; otherwise he seemed profoundly sleeping. Something prompted me to touch him. I felt his hand, when a tingling shiver ran up my arm and down my spine to my feet.

The round face of the grub-man peered upon me now. "His dinner is ready. Won't he dine to-day, either? Or does he live without dining?"

"Lives without dining," said I, and closed the eyes.

"Eh! — He's asleep, ain't he?"

"With kings and counselors,"° murmured I.   250

There would seem little need for proceeding further in this history. Imagination will readily supply the meagre recital of poor Bartleby's interment. But, ere parting with the reader, let me say, that if this little narrative has sufficiently interested him, to awaken curiosity as to who Bartleby was, and what manner of life he led prior to the present narrator's making his acquaintance, I can only reply, that in such curiosity I fully share, but am wholly unable to gratify it. Yet here I hardly know whether I should divulge one little item of rumor, which came to my ear a few months after the scrivener's decease. Upon what basis it rested, I could never ascertain; and hence, how true it is I cannot now tell. But, inasmuch as this vague report has not been without a certain suggestive interest to me, however sad, it may prove the same with some others; and so I will briefly mention it. The report was this: that Bartleby had been a subordinate clerk in the Dead Letter Office at Washington, from which he had been suddenly removed by a change in the administration. When I think over this rumor, hardly can I express the emotions which seize me. Dead letters! does it not sound like dead men? Conceive a man by nature and misfortune prone to a pallid hopelessness, can any business seem more fitted to heighten it than that of continually handling these dead letters, and assorting them for the flames? For by the cartload they are annually burned. Sometimes from out the folded paper the pale clerk takes a ring — the finger it was meant for, perhaps, moulders in the grave; a bank-note sent in swiftest charity — he whom it would relieve, nor eats nor hungers any more; pardon for those who died despairing; hope for those who died unhoping; good tidings for those who died stifled by unrelieved calamities. On errands of life, these letters speed to death.

Ah, Bartleby! Ah, humanity!

Considerations for Critical Thinking and Writing

1. How does the lawyer's description of himself serve to characterize him? Why is it significant that he is a lawyer? Are his understandings and judgments about Bartleby and himself always sound?
2. Why do you think Turkey, Nippers, and Ginger Nut are introduced to the reader before Bartleby?
3. Describe Bartleby's physical characteristics. How is his physical description a foreshadowing of what happens to him?
4. How does Bartleby's "I would prefer not to" affect the routine of the lawyer and his employees?

°*With kings and counselors*: From Job 3:13–14: "then had I been at rest, / With kings and counsellors of the earth, / which built desolate places for themselves."

5. What is the significance of the subtitle: "A Story of Wall Street"?
6. Who is the protagonist? Whose story is it?
7. Does the lawyer change during the story? Does Bartleby? Who is the antagonist?
8. What motivates Bartleby's behavior? Why do you think Melville withholds the information about the Dead Letter Office until the end of the story? Does this background adequately explain Bartleby?
9. Does Bartleby have any lasting impact on the lawyer?
10. Do you think Melville sympathizes more with Bartleby or with the lawyer?
11. Describe the lawyer's changing attitudes toward Bartleby.
12. Consider how this story could be regarded as a kind of protest with nonnegotiable demands.
13. Discuss the story's humor and how it affects your response to Bartleby.
14. Trace your emotional reaction to Bartleby as he is revealed in the story.

Connections to Other Selections

1. Compare Bartleby's withdrawal from life with that of the protagonist in Godwin's "A Sorrowful Woman" (p. 30). Why does each character choose death?
2. How is Melville's use of Bartleby's experience in the Dead Letter Office similar to Nathaniel Hawthorne's use of Brown's forest encounter with the devil in "Young Goodman Brown" (p. 242)? Why is each experience crucial to an understanding of what informs the behavior of these characters?
3. Discuss the significant parallels between "Bartleby, the Scrivener" and Franz Kafka's "A Hunger Artist" (p. 462), both stories about self-denial and isolation. Explain whether you think Bartleby's and the hunger artist's responses to their environments are similar or different.

PERSPECTIVES ON MELVILLE

NATHANIEL HAWTHORNE (1804–1864)
On Herman Melville's Philosophic Stance   1856

[Melville] stayed with us from Tuesday till Thursday; and, on the intervening day, we took a pretty long walk together, and sat down in a hollow among the sand hills (sheltering ourselves from the high, cool wind) and smoked a cigar. Melville, as he always does, began to reason of Providence and futurity, and of everything that lies beyond human ken, and informed me that he had "pretty much made up his mind to be annihilated"; but still he does not seem to rest in that anticipation; and, I think, will never rest until he gets hold of a definite belief. It is strange how he persists — and has persisted ever since I knew him, and probably long before — in wandering to-and-fro over these deserts, as dismal and monotonous as the sand hills amid which we were sitting. He can neither believe, nor be comfortable in his unbelief; and he is too honest and courageous not to try to do one or the other. If he were a religious man, he would be one of the most truly religious and reverential; he has a very high and noble nature, and better worth immortality than most of us.

From *The American Notebooks*

Considerations for Critical Thinking and Writing

1. How does this description of Melville shed light on the central concerns of "Bartleby, the Scrivener"?
2. Which side does Hawthorne seem to be on — "belief" or "unbelief"? Why?
3. Compare Hawthorne's description with Melville's view of Hawthorne (p. 296). What attitudes about life do they share?
4. Write an essay about the issue of "belief" and "unbelief" in "Bartleby, the Scrivener" and Ernest Hemingway's "Soldier's Home" (p. 125).

DAN McCALL (b. 1940)
On the Lawyer's Character in "Bartleby, the Scrivener" 1989

The overwhelming majority of the Bartleby Industry reads the narrator of the story in a way that is not only different from mine but quite incompatible with mine. Every virtue I see in the man, they see as a vice; where I see his strength, they see his weakness; what I see as his genuine responsiveness, they see as his cold self-absorption. Some critics read the story as I do, but we are in a distinct minority. There are several reasons this should be so, and I think I understand at least some of them, but first I should like to present as fairly as I can the majority opinion.

Robert Weisbuch, who has said the Lawyer is Charles Dickens, refers to the Lawyer as "unnatural," "anti-natural," "lifeless," "self-satisfied," "pompous," and "rationalizing." The Lawyer "investigates Bartleby but refuses authentic emotional commitment in so doing," and "Bartleby rightly refuses to credit the Lawyer's false commitment." The Lawyer is guilty of "toadyism" and his final heartbroken outburst, "Ah, Bartleby! Ah, humanity!" is no more than "a someways hollow and unfeeling exclamation."[1] Another critic calls the Lawyer a "smug fool" who is "terribly unkind to a very sick man."[2] I had always thought of the Lawyer as a kind of stand-in for us, a figure we could identify with as we struggled to understand Bartleby. On the contrary, the narrator is "deficient in humanity and quite obtuse towards human beings." I must have had it backwards, for "surely this was Melville's intention: to have his reader *not* sympathize with the Lawyer, *not* to identify with him, *not* to put himself in the Lawyer's place" (*his* italics, not mine).[3] Another critic says, "The narrator attains new heights of vague sentimentality rather than a peak of awareness in his climactic and highly re-

[1]Robert Weisbuch, "Melville's 'Bartleby' and the Dead Letter of Charles Dickens," *Atlantic Double-Cross: American Literature and British Influence in the Age of Emerson* (Chicago: University of Chicago Press, 1986), pp. 44, 45–47.
[2]David Shusterman, "The 'Reader Fallacy' and 'Bartleby, The Scrivener,'" *New England Quarterly*, 45 (March, 1972), 118–24, pp. 122–23.
[3]Ibid., p. 121.

vealing sigh: 'Ah, Bartleby! Ah, humanity!'" This reader provides dismissive certainty in answering the question

> Who then is Melville's narrator? He is that sort of man one tends to find in high places: the snug man whose worldly success has convinced him that this is the "best of all possible worlds," and whose virtues cluster around a "prudential" concern for maintaining his own situation. The narrator can never fully understand or truly befriend Bartleby because the narrator is simply too complacent, both philosophically and morally, to sympathize with human dissatisfaction and despair.[4]

Still another reader tells us the Lawyer's commentary "rings with blasphemy" and demonstrates "grotesque manifestations of diseased conscience."[5]

Authority is the enemy here. In the extended quotation just above it is taken for granted that the "sort of man one tends to find in high places" is superficial and selfish. Worldly success is bad for the character. The Lawyer has to be bad, or he wouldn't be in an office on Wall Street. Hershel Parker tells us that "our ultimate opinion" of the Lawyer "is not contempt so much as bleak astonishment at his secure blindness. With a bitterer irony than the narrator is capable of, we murmur something like 'Ah, narrator! Ah, humanity!' In his self-consciously eloquent sequel, after all, the lawyer has merely made his last cheap purchase of a 'delicious self-approval.'" Parker maintains that when "this easy-conscienced" man speaks of kings and counselors, "he is experiencing a comfortable, self-indulgent variety of melancholy"; when he quotes words from the Book of Job he does so "with prideful aptness," and "characteristically perverts them from profound lament to sonorous urbanity."[6]

This last feature of Parker's argument is interesting to me because it reminds me of the first time I read the story, at eighteen. I was overwhelmed by the discovery that Bartleby had died, and I didn't know that "With kings and counselors" was a quotation from the Book of Job. The phrase "With kings and counselors" seemed to me majestic and solemn and final. That "murmured I" put a deep hush around it. But it never occurred to me that the man who said those words was "easy-conscienced" or "self-indulgent" or the sort of man who "characteristically perverts" a "profound lament to sonorous urbanity." The figure of Bartleby seemed so weird and funny and painful, his death at once inevitable and shocking, that I did not see it as an occasion for the man who was telling me about it to make a "last cheap purchase" of "delicious self-approval." I trusted that Lawyer.

Thirty years later, I still do. He seems to me extremely intelligent, whimsical and ironic, generous, self-aware, passionate, and thoroughly competent.

From *The Silence of Bartleby*

[4]Allan Emery, "The Alternatives of Melville's 'Bartleby,'" *Nineteenth-Century Fiction*, 31 (1976), 170–87, pp. 186–87.
[5]William Bysshe Stein, "Bartleby: The Christian Conscience," in *Melville Annual 1965, A Symposium: "Bartleby, the Scrivener,"* ed. Howard P. Vincent (Kent, Ohio: Kent State University Press, 1966), p. 107.
[6]Hershel Parker, "The Sequel in 'Bartleby,'" in *Bartleby the Inscrutable: A Collection of Commentary on Herman Melville's Tale "Bartleby, the Scrivener,"* ed. M. Thomas Inge (Hamden, Conn.: Archon Books, 1979), 159–65, pp. 163–64.

Considerations for Critical Thinking and Writing

1. How does McCall characterize the "majority opinion" on the lawyer's character? What is his opinion of the lawyer?
2. How does McCall's opinion of the lawyer compare with Hawthorne's opinion of Herman Melville in the preceding Perspective (p. 108)?
3. Write an essay explaining whether you find the "majority opinion" or McCall's view of the lawyer more convincing.

4. Setting

Setting is the context in which the action of a story occurs. The major elements of setting are the time, place, and social environment that frame the characters. These elements establish the world in which the characters act. In most stories they also serve as more than backgrounds and furnishings. If we are sensitive to the contexts provided by setting, we are better able to understand the behavior of the characters and the significance of their actions. It may be tempting to read quickly through a writer's descriptions and ignore the details of the setting once a geographic location and a historic period are established. But if you read a story so impatiently, the significance of the setting may slip by you. That kind of reading is similar to traveling on interstate highways: a lot of ground gets covered but very little is seen along the way.

Settings can be used to evoke a mood or atmosphere that will prepare the reader for what is to come. In "Young Goodman Brown" (p. 242), Nathaniel Hawthorne has his pious protagonist leave his wife and village one night to keep an appointment in a New England forest near the site of the seventeenth-century witch trials. This is Hawthorne's description of Brown entering the forest:

> He had taken a dreary road, darkened by all the gloomiest trees of the forest, which barely stood aside to let the narrow path creep through, and closed immediately behind. It was all lonely as could be; and there is this peculiarity in such a solitude, that the traveler knows not who may be concealed by the innumerable trunks and the thick boughs overhead; so that with lonely footsteps he may yet be passing through an unseen multitude.

The atmosphere established in this descriptive setting is somber and threatening. Careful reading reveals that the forest is not simply the woods; it is a moral wilderness, where anything can happen.

If we ask why a writer chooses to include certain details in a work, then we are likely to make connections that relate the details to some larger purpose, such as the story's meaning. The final scene in Godwin's "A Sorrowful Woman" (p. 30) occurs in the spring, an ironic time for the action to be set because instead of rebirth for the protagonist there is only death. There is usually a reason for placing a story in a particular time or location. Katherine Mansfield has the protagonist in "Miss Brill" (p. 211) discover her loneliness and old age in a French vacation town, a lively atmosphere that serves as a cruel contrast to an elderly (and foreign) lady's painful realization.

Melville's "Bartleby, the Scrivener" (p. 83) takes on meaning as Bartleby's "dead-wall reveries" begin to reflect his shattered vision of life. He is surrounded by walls. A folding screen separates him from others in the office; he is isolated. The office window faces walls; there is no view to relieve the deadening work. Bartleby faces a wall at the prison where he dies; the final wall is death. As the subtitle indicates, this is "A Story of Wall Street." Unless the geographic location or the physical details of a story are used merely as necessary props, they frequently shed light on character and action. All offices have walls, but Melville transforms the walls into an antagonist that represents the limitations Bartleby sees and feels all around him but does not speak of.

Time, location, and the physical features of a setting can all be relevant to the overall purpose of a story. So too is the social environment in which the characters are developed. In Faulkner's "A Rose for Emily" (p. 47) the changes in her southern town serve as a foil for Emily's tenacious hold on a lost past. She is regarded as a "fallen monument," as old-fashioned and peculiar as the "stubborn and coquettish decay" of her house. Neither she nor her house fits into the modern changes that are paving and transforming the town. Without the social context, this story would be mostly an account of a bizarre murder rather than an exploration of the conflicts Faulkner associated with the changing South. Setting enlarges the meaning of Emily's actions.

Some settings have traditional associations that are closely related to the action of a story. Adventure and romance, for example, flourish in the fertile soil of most exotic settings: the film version of Isak Dinesen's novel *Out of Africa* is a lush visual demonstration of how a jungle setting can play a significant role in generating the audience's expectations of love and excitement.

Sometimes, writers reverse traditional expectations. When a tranquil garden is the scene for a horrendously bloody murder, we are as much taken by surprise as the victim is. In John Updike's "A & P" (p. 485) there seems to be little possibility for heroic action in so mundane a place as a supermarket, but the setting turns out to be appropriate for the important, unexpected decision the protagonist makes about life. Traditional associations are also disrupted in "A Sorrowful Woman" (p. 30), in which Godwin disassociates home from the safety, security, and comfort usually connected with it by presenting the protagonist's home as a deadly trap. By drawing on traditional associations, a writer can fulfill or disrupt a reader's expectations about a setting in order to complement the elements of the story.

Not every story uses setting as a means of revealing mood, idea, meaning, or characters' actions. Some stories have no particularly significant setting. It is entirely possible to envision a story in which two characters speak to each other about a conflict between them and little or no mention is made of the time or place they inhabit. If, however, a shift in setting would make a serious difference to our understanding of a story, then the setting is probably an important element in the work. Consider how different "Bartleby, the Scrivener" (p. 83) would be if it were set in a relaxed, pleasant, sunny town in the South rather than in the grinding, limiting, materialism of Wall Street. Bartleby's withdrawal from life would be less comprehensible and meaningful in such a setting. The setting is integral to that story.

The following three stories — Eudora Welty's "Livvie," Ernest Hemingway's "Soldier's Home," and Louise Erdrich's "I'm a Mad Dog Biting Myself for Sympathy" — include settings that serve to shape their meanings.

EUDORA WELTY (b. 1909)

Eudora Welty has spent almost her entire life in Jackson, Mississippi, where she was born in 1909. She began her undergraduate education at Mississippi State College for Women and then graduated from the University of Wisconsin in 1929. After studying advertising at the Columbia University School of Business, she returned to the South for a variety of jobs and to write fiction. Since the 1930s she has published short stories; many of these were brought together in *The Collected Stories of Eudora Welty* (1980). She has also published a number of novels, including *The Optimist's Daughter*, which was awarded the Pulitzer Prize in 1972. Her collection of essays and reviews, *The Eye of the Story* (1977), and *One Writer's Beginnings* (1984) offer insights into her responses to other writers' work as well as her own. Welty's stories are solidly grounded in Mississippi soil. "Livvie" appeared originally in *The Wide Net and Other Stories* (1943), a collection based on the history and geography of the Natchez Trace, an early nineteenth-century road that followed an old Indian trail from Natchez, Mississippi, to Nashville, Tennessee. Like so much of Welty's fiction, "Livvie" focuses on the protagonist's mysterious inner life, which is revealed by the suggestive details of Livvie's outer life.

Solomon carried Livvie twenty-one miles away from her home when he married her. He carried her away up on the Old Natchez Trace into the deep country to live in his house. She was sixteen — only a girl, then. Once people said he thought nobody would ever come along there. He told her himself that it had been a long time, and a day she did not know about, since that road was a traveled road with *people* coming and going. He was good to her, but he kept her in the house. She had not thought that she could not get back. Where she came from, people said an old man did not want anybody in the world to ever find his wife, for fear they would steal her back from him. Solomon asked her before he took her, would she be happy? — very dignified, for he was a colored man that owned his land and had it written down in the courthouse; and she said, "Yes, sir," since he was an old man and she was young and just listened and answered. He asked her, if she was choosing winter, would she pine for spring, and she said, "No indeed." Whatever she said, always, was because he was an old man . . . while nine years went by. All the time, he got older, and he got so old he gave out. At last he slept the whole day in bed, and she was young still.

It was a nice house, inside and outside both. In the first place, it had three rooms. The front room was papered in holly paper, with green palmettos from the swamp spaced at careful intervals over the walls. There was fresh newspaper cut with fancy borders on the mantel-shelf, on which were propped photographs of old or very young men printed in faint yellow — Solomon's people. Solomon had a houseful of furniture. There was a double settee, a tall scrolled rocker and an organ in the front room, all around a three-legged table with a pink marble top, on which was set a lamp with three gold feet, besides a jelly glass with pretty hen feathers in it. Behind the front room, the other room had the bright iron bed with the polished knobs like a throne, in which Solomon slept all day. There were snow-white curtains of wiry lace at the window, and a lace bedspread belonged on the bed. But what old Solomon slept so sound under was a big feather-stitched piece-quilt in the pattern "Trip Around the World," which had twenty-one different colors, four hundred and forty pieces, and a thousand yards of thread, and that was what Solomon's mother made in her life and old age. There was a table holding the Bible, and a trunk with a key. On the wall were two calendars, and a diploma from somewhere in Solomon's family, and under that, Livvie's one possession was nailed, a picture of the little white baby of the family she worked for, back in Natchez before she was married. Going through that room and on to the kitchen, there was a big wood stove and a big round table always with a wet top and with the knives and forks in one jelly glass and the spoons in another, and a cut-glass vinegar bottle between, and going out from those, many shallow dishes of pickled peaches, fig preserves, watermelon pickles and blackberry jam always sitting there. The churn sat in the sun, the doors of the safe were always both shut, and there were four baited mousetraps in the kitchen, one in every corner.

The outside of Solomon's house looked nice. It was not painted, but across the porch was an even balance. On each side there was one easy chair with high springs, looking out, and a fern basket hanging over it from the ceiling, and a dishpan of zinnia seedlings growing at its foot on the floor. By the door was a plow-wheel, just a pretty iron circle, nailed up on one wall, and a square mirror on the other, a turquoise-blue comb stuck up in the frame, with the wash stand beneath it. On the door was a wooden knob with a pearl in the end, and Solomon's black hat hung on that, if he was in the house.

Out front was a clean dirt yard with every vestige of grass patiently uprooted and the ground scarred in deep whorls from the strike of Livvie's broom. Rose bushes with tiny blood-red roses blooming every month grew in threes on either side of the steps. On one side was a peach tree, on the other a pomegranate. Then coming around up the path from the deep cut of the Natchez Trace below was a line of bare crape-myrtle trees with every branch of them ending in a colored bottle, green or blue. There was no word that fell from Solomon's lips to say what they were for, but Livvie knew that there could be a spell put in trees, and she was familiar from the time she was born with the way bottle trees kept evil spirits from coming into the house — by luring them inside the colored bottles, where they cannot get out again. Solomon had made the bottle trees with his own hands over the nine years, in labor amounting to about a tree a year, and without a sign that he had any uneasiness in his heart, for he took as much pride in his precautions against spirits coming in the house as he took in the house, and sometimes in the sun the bottle trees looked prettier than the house did.

It was a nice house. It was in a place where the days would go by and surprise anyone that they were over. The lamplight and the firelight would shine out the door after dark, over the still and breathing country, lighting the roses and the bottle trees, and all was quiet there. 5

But there was nobody, nobody at all, not even a white person. And if there had been anybody, Solomon would not have let Livvie look at them, just as he would not let her look at a field hand, or a field hand look at her. There was no house near, except for the cabins of the tenants that were forbidden to her, and there was no house as far as she had been, stealing away down the still, deep Trace. She felt as if she waded a river when she went, for the dead leaves on the ground reached as high as her knees, and when she was all scratched and bleeding she said it was not like a road that went anywhere. One day, climbing up the high bank, she had found a graveyard without a church, with ribbon-grass growing about the foot of an angel (she had climbed up because she thought she saw angel wings), and in the sun, trees shining like burning flames through the great caterpillar nets which enclosed them. Scarey thistles stood looking like the prophets in the Bible in Solomon's house. Indian paint brushes grew over her head, and the mourning dove made the only sound in the world. Oh, for a stirring of the leaves, and a breaking of the nets! But not by a ghost, prayed Livvie, jumping down the bank. After Solomon took to his bed, she never went out, except one more time.

Livvie knew she made a nice girl to wait on anybody. She fixed things to eat on a tray like a surprise. She could keep from singing when she ironed, and to sit by a bed and fan away the flies, she could be so still she could not hear herself breathe. She could clean up the house and never drop a thing, and wash the dishes without a sound, and she would step outside to churn, for churning sounded too sad to her, like sobbing, and if it made her homesick and not Solomon, she did not think of that.

But Solomon scarcely opened his eyes to see her, and scarcely tasted his food. He was not sick or paralyzed or in any pain that he mentioned, but he was surely wearing out in the body, and no matter what nice hot thing Livvie would bring him to taste, he would only look at it now, as if he were past seeing how he could add anything more to himself. Before she could beg him, he would go fast asleep. She could not surprise him any more, if he would not taste, and she was afraid that he was never in the world going to taste another thing she brought him — and so how could he last?

But one morning it was breakfast time and she cooked his eggs and grits, carried them in on a tray, and called his name. He was sound asleep. He lay in a dignified way with his watch beside him, on his back in the middle of the bed. One hand drew the quilt up high, though it was the first day of spring. Through the white lace curtains a little puffy wind was blowing as if it came from round cheeks. All night the frogs had sung out in the swamp, like a commotion in the room, and he had not stirred, though she lay wide awake and saying "Shh, frogs!" for fear he would mind them.

He looked as if he would like to sleep a little longer, and so she put back 10 the tray and waited. When she tiptoed and stayed so quiet, she surrounded herself with a little reverie, and sometimes it seemed to her when she was so stealthy that the quiet she kept was for a sleeping baby, and that she had a baby and was its mother. When she stood at Solomon's bed and looked down at him, she would be thinking, "He sleeps so well," and she would hate to wake him up. And in some other way, too, she was afraid to wake him up because even in his sleep he seemed to be such a strict man.

Of course, nailed to the wall over the bed — only she would forget who it was — there was a picture of him when he was young. Then he had a fan of hair over his forehead like a king's crown. Now his hair lay down on his head, the spring had gone out of it. Solomon had a lightish face, with eyebrows scattered but rugged, the way privet grows, strong eyes, with second sight, a strict mouth, and a little gold smile. This was the way he looked in his clothes, but in bed in the daytime he looked a different and smaller man, even when he was wide awake, and holding the Bible. He looked like somebody kin to himself. And then sometimes when he lay in sleep and she stood fanning the flies away, and the light came in, his face was like new, so smooth and clear that it was like a glass of jelly held to the window, and she could almost look through his forehead and see what he thought.

She fanned him and at length he opened his eyes and spoke her name, but he would not taste the nice eggs she had kept warm under a pan.

Back in the kitchen she ate heartily, his breakfast and hers, and looked out the open door at what went on. The whole day, and the whole night before, she had felt the stir of spring close to her. It was as present in the house as a young man would be. The moon was in the last quarter and outside they were turning the sod and planting peas and beans. Up and down the red fields, over which smoke from the brush-burning hung showing like a little skirt of sky, a white horse and a white mule pulled the plow. At intervals hoarse shouts came through the air and roused her as if she dozed neglectfully in the shade, and they were telling her, "Jump up!" She could see how over each ribbon of field were moving men and girls, on foot and mounted on mules, with hats set on their heads and bright with tall hoes and forks as if they carried streamers on them and were going to some place on a journey — and how as if at a signal now and then they would all start at once shouting, hollering, cajoling, calling and answering back, running, being leaped on and breaking away, flinging to earth with a shout and lying motionless in the trance of twelve o'clock. The old women came out of the cabins and brought them the food they had ready for them, and then all worked together, spread evenly out. The little children came too, like a bouncing stream overflowing the fields, and set upon the men, the women, the dogs, the rushing birds, and the wave-like rows of earth, their little voices almost too high to be heard. In the middle distance like some white and gold towers were the haystacks, with black cows coming around to eat their edges. High above every-thing, the wheel of fields, house, and cabins, and the deep road surrounding like a moat to keep them in, was the turning sky, blue with long, far-flung white mare's-tail clouds, serene and still as high flames. And sound asleep while all this went around him that was his, Solomon was like a little still spot in the middle.

Even in the house the earth was sweet to breathe. Solomon had never let Livvie go any farther than the chicken house and the well. But what if she would walk now into the heart of the fields and take a hoe and work until she fell stretched out and drenched with her efforts, like other girls, and laid her cheek against the laid-open earth, and shamed the old man with her humbleness and delight? To shame him! A cruel wish could come in uninvited and so fast while she looked out the back door. She washed the dishes and scrubbed the table. She could hear the cries of the little lambs. Her mother, that she had not seen since her wedding day, had said one time, "I rather a man be anything, than a woman be mean."

So all morning she kept tasting the chicken broth on the stove, and when it was right she poured off a nice cupful. She carried it in to Solomon, and there he lay having a dream. Now what did he dream about? For she saw him sigh gently as if not to disturb some whole thing he held round in his mind, like a fresh egg. So even an old man dreamed about something pretty. Did he dream of her, while his eyes were shut and sunken, and his small hand with the wedding ring curled close in sleep around the quilt? He might be dreaming of what time it was, for even through his sleep he kept track of it like a clock, and knew how much of it went by, and waked up knowing where the hands were even before he consulted the silver watch that he never let go. He would sleep with the watch in his palm, and even holding it to his cheek like a child that loves a plaything. Or he might dream of journeys and travels on a steamboat to Natchez. Yet she thought he dreamed of her; but even while she scrutinized him, the rods of the foot of the bed seemed to rise up like a rail fence between them, and she could see that people never could be sure of anything as long as one of them was asleep and the other awake. To look at him dreaming of her when he might be going to die frightened her a little, as if he might carry her with him that way, and she wanted to run out of the room. She took hold of the bed and held on, and Solomon opened his eyes and called her name, but he did not want anything. He would not taste the good broth.

Just a little after that, as she was taking up the ashes in the front room for the last time in the year, she heard a sound. It was somebody coming. She pulled the curtains together and looked through the slit.

Coming up the path under the bottle trees was a white lady. At first she looked young, but then she looked old. Marvelous to see, a little car stood steaming like a kettle out in the field-track — it had come without a road.

Livvie stood listening to the long, repeated knockings at the door, and after a while she opened it just a little. The lady came in through the crack, though she was more than middle-sized and wore a big hat.

"My name is Miss Baby Marie," she said.

Livvie gazed respectfully at the lady and at the little suitcase she was holding 20 close to her by the handle until the proper moment. The lady's eyes were running over the room, from palmetto to palmetto, but she was saying, "I live at home . . . out from Natchez . . . and get out and show these pretty cosmetic things to the white people and the colored people both . . . all around . . . years and years. . . . Both shades of powder and rouge . . . . It's the kind of work a girl can do and not go clear 'way from home. . . ." And the harder she looked, the more she talked. Suddenly she turned up her nose and said, "It is not Christian or sanitary to put feathers in a vase," and then she took a gold key out of the front of her dress and began unlocking the locks on her suitcase. Her face drew the light, the way it was covered with intense white and red, with a little patty-cake of white between the wrinkles by her upper lip. Little red tassels of hair bobbed under the rusty wires of her picture-hat, as with an air of triumph and secrecy she now drew open her little suitcase and brought out bottle after bottle and jar after jar, which she put down on the table, the mantel-piece, the settee, and the organ.

"Did you ever see so many cosmetics in your life?" cried Miss Baby Marie.

"No'm" Livvie tried to say, but the cat had her tongue.

"Have you ever applied cosmetics?" asked Miss Baby Marie next.

"No'm," Livvie tried to say.

"Then look!" she said, and pulling out the last thing of all, "Try this!" she 25 said. And in her hand was unclenched a golden lipstick which popped open like magic. A fragrance came out of it like incense, and Livvie cried out suddenly, "Chinaberry flowers!"

Her hand took the lipstick, and in an instant she was carried away in the air through the spring, and looking down with a half-drowsy smile from a purple cloud she saw from above a chinaberry tree, dark and smooth and neatly leaved, neat as a guinea hen in the dooryard, and there was her home that she had left. On one side of the tree was her mama holding up her heavy apron, and she could see it was loaded with ripe figs, and on the other side was her papa holding a fish-pole over the pond, and she could see it transparently, the little clear fishes swimming up to the brim.

"Oh, no, not chinaberry flowers — secret ingredients," said Miss Baby Marie. "My cosmetics have secret ingredients — not chinaberry flowers."

"It's purple," Livvie breathed, and Miss Baby Marie said, "Use it freely. Rub it on."

Livvie tiptoed out to the wash stand on the front porch and before the mirror put the paint on her mouth. In the wavery surface her face danced before her like a flame. Miss Baby Marie followed her out, took a look at what she had done, and said, "That's it."

Livvie tried to say "Thank you" without moving her parted lips where the paint lay so new.

By now Miss Baby Marie stood behind Livvie and looked in the mirror over her shoulder, twisting up the tassels of her hair. "The lipstick I can let you have for only two dollars," she said, close to her neck.

"Lady, but I don't have no money, never did have," said Livvie.

"Oh, but you don't pay the first time. I make another trip, that's the way I do. I come back again — later."

"Oh," said Livvie, pretending she understood everything so as to please the lady.

"But if you don't take it now, this may be the last time I'll call at your house," said Miss Baby Marie sharply. "It's far away from anywhere, I'll tell you that. You don't live close to anywhere."

"Yes'm. My husband, he keep the *money,*" said Livvie, trembling. "He is strict as he can be. He don't know *you* walk in here — Miss Baby Marie!"

"Where is he?"

"Right now, he in yonder sound asleep, an old man. I wouldn't ever ask him for anything."

Miss Baby Marie took back the lipstick and packed it up. She gathered up the jars for both black and white and got them all inside the suitcase, with the same little fuss of triumph with which she had brought them out. She started away.

"Good-bye," she said, making herself look grand from the back, but at the last minute she turned around in the door. Her old hat wobbled as she whispered, "Let me see your husband."

Livvie obediently went on tiptoe and opened the door to the other room. Miss Baby Marie came behind her and rose on her toes and looked in.

"My, what a little tiny old, old man!" she whispered, clasping her hands and shaking her head over them. "What a beautiful quilt! What a tiny old, old man!"

"He can sleep like that all day," whispered Livvie proudly.

They looked at him awhile so fast asleep, and then all at once they looked at each other. Somehow that was as if they had a secret, for he had never stirred. Livvie then politely, but all at once, closed the door.

"Well! I'd certainly like to leave you with a lipstick!" said Miss Baby Marie vivaciously. She smiled in the door.

"Lady, but I told you I don't have no money, and never did have."

"And never will?" In the air and all around, like a bright halo around the white lady's nodding head, it was a true spring day.

"Would you take eggs, lady?" asked Livvie softly.

"No, I have plenty of eggs — plenty," said Miss Baby Marie.

"I still don't have no money," said Livvie, and Miss Baby Marie took her suitcase and went on somewhere else.

Livvie stood watching her go, and all the time she felt her heart beating in her left side. She touched the place with her hand. It seemed as if her heart beat and her whole face flamed from the pulsing color of her lips. She went to sit by Solomon and when he opened his eyes he could not see a change in her. "He's fixin' to die," she said inside. That was the secret. That was when she went out of the house for a little breath of air.

She went down the path and down the Natchez Trace a way, and she did not know how far she had gone, but it was not far, when she saw a sight. It was a man, looking like a vision — she standing on one side of the Old Natchez Trace and he standing on the other.

As soon as this man caught sight of her, he began to look himself over. Starting at the bottom with his pointed shoes, he began to look up, lifting his peg-top pants the higher to see fully his bright socks. His coat long and wide and leaf-green he opened like doors to see his high-up tawny pants and his pants he smoothed downward from the points of his collar, and he wore a luminous baby-pink satin shirt. At the end, he reached gently above his wide platter-shaped round hat, the color of a plum, and one finger touched at the feather, emerald green, blowing in the spring winds.

No matter how she looked, she could never look so fine as he did, and she was not sorry for that, she was pleased.

He took three jumps, one down and two up, and was by her side.   55

"My name is Cash," he said.

He had a guinea pig in his pocket. They began to walk along. She stared on and on at him, as if he were doing some daring spectacular thing, instead of just walking beside her. It was not simply the city way he was dressed that made her look at him and see hope in its insolence looking back. It was not only the way he moved along kicking the flowers as if he could break through everything in the way and destroy anything in the world, that made her eyes grow bright. It might be, if he had not appeared *that day* she would never have looked so closely at him, but the time people come makes a difference.

They walked through the still leaves of the Natchez Trace, the light and the shade falling through trees about them, the white irises shining like candles on the banks and the new ferns shining like green stars up in the oak branches. They came out at Solomon's house, bottle trees and all. Livvie stopped and hung her head.

Cash began whistling a little tune. She did not know what it was, but she had heard it before from a distance, and she had a revelation. Cash was a field hand. He was a transformed field hand. Cash belonged to Solomon. But he had stepped out of his overalls into this. There in front of Solomon's house he laughed. He had a round head, a round face, all of him was young, and he flung his head up, rolled it against the mare's-tail sky in his round hat, and he could laugh just to see Solomon's house sitting there. Livvie looked at it, and there was Solomon's black hat hanging on the peg on the front door, the blackest thing in the world.

"I been to Natchez," Cash said, wagging his head around against the sky. "*I*   60 taken a trip, I ready for Easter!"

How was it possible to look so fine before the harvest? Cash must have stolen the money, stolen it from Solomon. He stood in the path and lifted his spread hand high and brought it down again and again in his laughter. He kicked up his heels. A little chill went through her. It was as if Cash was bringing that strong hand down to beat a drum or to rain blows upon a man, such an abandon and menace were in his laugh. Frowning, she went closer to him and his swinging arm drew her in at once and the fright was crushed from her body, as a little match-flame might be smothered out by what it lighted. She gathered the folds of his coat behind him and fastened her red lips to his mouth, and she was dazzled at herself then, the way he had been dazzled at himself to begin with.

In that instant she felt something that could not be told — that Solomon's death was at hand, that he was the same to her as if he were dead now. She cried out, and uttering little cries turned and ran for the house.

At once Cash was coming, following after, he was running behind her. He came close, and half-way up the path he laughed and passed her. He even picked up a stone and sailed it into the bottle trees. She put her hands over her head, and sounds clattered through the bottle trees like cries of outrage. Cash stamped and plunged zigzag up the front steps and in at the door.

When she got there, he had stuck his hands in his pockets and was turning slowly about in the front room. The little guinea pig peeped out. Around Cash, the pinned-up palmettos looked as if a lazy green monkey had walked up and down and around the walls leaving green prints of his hands and feet.

She got through the room and his hands were still in his pockets, and she 65 fell upon the closed door to the other room and pushed it open. She ran to Solomon's bed, calling "Solomon! Solomon!" The little shape of the old man never moved at all, wrapped under the quilt as if it were winter still.

"Solomon!" She pulled the quilt away, but there was another one under that, and she fell on her knees beside him. He made no sound except a sigh, and then she could hear in the silence the light springy steps of Cash walking and walking in the front room, and the ticking of Solomon's silver watch, which came from the bed. Old Solomon was far away in his sleep, his face looked small, relentless, and devout, as if he were walking somewhere where she could imagine the snow falling.

Then there was a noise like a hoof pawing the floor, and the door gave a creak, and Cash appeared beside her. When she looked up, Cash's face was so black it was bright, and so bright and bare of pity that it looked sweet to her. She stood up and held up her head. Cash was so powerful that his presence gave her strength even when she did not need any.

Under their eyes Solomon slept. People's faces tell of things and places not known to the one who looks at them while they sleep, and while Solomon slept under the eyes of Livvie and Cash his face told them like a mythical story that all his life he had built, little scrap by little scrap, respect. A beetle could not have been more laborious or more ingenious in the task of its destiny. When Solomon was young, as he was in his picture overhead, it was the infinite thing with him, and he could see no end to the respect he would contrive and keep in a house. He had built a lonely house, the way he would make a cage, but it grew to be the same with him as a great monumental pyramid and sometimes in his absorption of getting it erected he was like the builder-slaves of Egypt who forgot or never knew the origin and meaning of the thing to which they gave all the strength of their bodies and used up all their days. Livvie and Cash could see that as a man might rest from a life-labor he lay in his bed, and they could hear how, wrapped in his quilt, he sighed to himself comfortably in sleep, while in his dreams he might have been an ant, a beetle, a bird, an Egyptian, assembling and carrying on his back and building with his hands, or he might have been an old man of India or a swaddled baby, about to smile and brush all away.

Then without warning old Solomon's eyes flew wide open under the hedge-like brows. He was wide awake.

And instantly Cash raised his quick arm. A radiant sweat stood on his temples. But he did not bring his arm down — it stayed in the air, as if something might have taken hold.

It was not Livvie — she did not move. As if something said "Wait," she stood waiting. Even while her eyes burned under motionless lids, her lips parted in a stiff grimace, and with her arms stiff at her sides she stood above the prone old man and the panting young one, erect and apart.

Movement when it came came in Solomon's face. It was an old and strict face, a frail face, but behind it, like a covered light, came an animation that could play hide and seek, that would dart and escape, had always escaped. The mystery flickered in him, and invited from his eyes. It was that very mystery that Cash with his quick arm would have to strike, and that Livvie could not weep for. But Cash only stood holding his arm in the air, when the gentlest flick of his great strength, almost a puff of his breath, would have been enough, if he had known how to give it, to send the old man over the obstruction that kept him away from death.

"Young ones can't wait," said Solomon.

Livvie shuddered violently, and then in a gush of tears she stooped for a glass of water and handed it to him, but he did not see her.

"So here come the young man Livvie wait for. Was no prevention. No prevention. Now I lay eyes on young man and it come to be somebody I know all the time, and been knowing since he were born in a cotton patch, and watched grow up year to year, Cash McCord, growed to size, growed up to come in my house in the end — ragged and barefoot."

Solomon gave a cough of distaste. Then he shut his eyes vigorously, and his lips began to move like a chanter's.

"When Livvie married, her husband were already somebody. He had paid great cost for his land. He spread sycamore leaves over the ground from wagon to door, day he brought her home, so her foot would not have to touch ground. He carried her through his door. Then he growed old and could not lift her, and she were still young."

Livvie's sobs followed his words like a soft melody repeating each thing as he stated it. His lips moved for a little without sound, or she cried too fervently, and unheard he might have been telling his whole life, and then he said, "God forgive Solomon for sins great and small. God forgive Solomon for carrying away too young girl for wife and keeping her away from her people and from all the young people would clamor for her back."

Then he lifted up his right hand toward Livvie where she stood by the bed and offered her his silver watch. He dangled it before her eyes, and she hushed crying; her tears stopped. For a moment the watch could be heard ticking as it always did, precisely in his proud hand. She lifted it away. Then he took hold of the quilt; then he was dead.

Livvie left Solomon dead and went out of the room. Stealthily, nearly without noise, Cash went beside her. He was like a shadow, but his shiny shoes moved over the floor in spangles, and the green downy feather shone like a light in his hat. As they reached the front room, he seized her deftly as a long black cat and dragged her hanging by the waist round and round him, while he turned in a circle, his face bent down to hers. The first moment, she kept one arm and its hand stiff and still, the one that held Solomon's watch. Then the fingers softly let go, all of her was limp, and the watch fell somewhere on the floor. It ticked away in the still room, and all at once there began outside the full song of a bird.

They moved around and around the room and into the brightness of the open door, then he stopped and shook her once. She rested in silence in his trembling arms, unprotesting as a bird on a nest. Outside the redbirds were flying and criss-crossing, the sun was in all the bottles on the prisoned trees, and the young peach was shining in the middle of them with the bursting light of spring.

Considerations for Critical Thinking and Writing

1. Describe Solomon's temperament. How does he live his life? What details about his house and yard reveal his character?
2. How do Livvie's attitudes and actions concerning the way she and Solomon live serve to characterize her?
3. What is Miss Baby Marie's function in the story? How is the lipstick she attempts to sell related to the plot?
4. Explain how Cash is a foil to Solomon.
5. What is the significance of Livvie's name? Do the names of the other three characters suggest any meanings?
6. What is the central conflict? How is it resolved?
7. Why do you think Welty sets the story at the beginning of spring? How are conventional associations with spring used to enhance the story's meaning?
8. How is Solomon's watch used symbolically? Why does he give Livvie the watch just before he dies? Explain the significance of her letting it drop to the floor. What other objects and actions are used to convey meanings in the story?
9. Choose a richly detailed paragraph and write an explication that relates the paragraph's details to the rest of the story.
10. Explore how time is an important element in the conflicts in "Livvie."

Connections to Other Selections

1. Discuss the significance of the settings in "Livvie" and Faulkner's "A Rose for Emily" (p. 47). Explain how the South is used as a means of characterizing the protagonist in each story.
2. How is the meaning of "home" essential to the meanings of "Livvie" and Ernest Hemingway's "Soldier's Home" (p. 125)?
3. Write an essay on the significance for the protagonists of the deaths of their husbands in "Livvie" and Chopin's "The Story of an Hour" (p. 12).

ERNEST HEMINGWAY (1899–1961)

In 1918, a year after graduating from high school in Oak Park, Illinois, Ernest Hemingway volunteered as an ambulance driver in World War I. At the Italian front, he was seriously wounded. This experience haunted him and many of the characters in his short stories and novels. *In Our Time* (1925) is a collection of short stories, including "Soldier's Home," that reflect some of Hemingway's own attempts to readjust to life back home after the war. *The Sun Also Rises* (1926), *A Farewell to Arms* (1929), and *For Whom the Bell Tolls* (1940) are also about war and its impact on people's lives. Hemingway courted violence all his life in war, the bullring, the boxing ring, and big game hunting. When he was sixty-two years old and terminally ill with cancer, he committed suicide by shooting himself with a shotgun. "Soldier's Home" takes place in a small town in Oklahoma; the war, however, is never distant from the protagonist's mind as he struggles to come home again.

Soldier's Home   1925

Krebs went to the war from a Methodist college in Kansas. There is a picture which shows him among his fraternity brothers, all of them wearing exactly the same height and style collar. He enlisted in the Marines in 1917 and did not return to the United States until the second division returned from the Rhine in the summer of 1919.

There is a picture which shows him on the Rhine with two German girls and another corporal. Krebs and the corporal look too big for their uniforms. The German girls are not beautiful. The Rhine does not show in the picture.

By the time Krebs returned to his home town in Oklahoma the greeting of heroes was over. He came back much too late. The men from the town who had been drafted had all been welcomed elaborately on their return. There had been a great deal of hysteria. Now the reaction had set in. People seemed to think it was rather ridiculous for Krebs to be getting back so late, years after the war was over.

At first Krebs, who had been at Belleau Wood, Soissons, the Champagne, St. Mihiel, and in the Argonne° did not want to talk about the war at all. Later he felt the need to talk but no one wanted to hear about it. His town had heard too many atrocity stories to be thrilled by actualities. Krebs found that to be listened to at all he had to lie, and after he had done this twice he, too, had a reaction against the war and against talking about it. A distaste for everything

---

Belleau Wood . . . Argonne: Sites of battles in World War I in which American troops were instrumental in pushing back the Germans.

that had happened to him in the war set in because of the lies he had told. All of the times that had been able to make him feel cool and clear inside himself when he thought of them; the times so long back when he had done the one thing, the only thing for a man to do, easily and naturally, when he might have done something else, now lost their cool, valuable quality and then were lost themselves.

His lies were quite unimportant lies and consisted in attributing to himself 5 things other men had seen, done, or heard of, and stating as facts certain apocryphal incidents familiar to all soldiers. Even his lies were not sensational at the pool room. His acquaintances, who had heard detailed accounts of German women found chained to machine guns in the Argonne forest and who could not comprehend, or were barred by their patriotism from interest in, any German machine gunners who were not chained, were not thrilled by his stories.

Krebs acquired the nausea in regard to experience that is the result of untruth or exaggeration, and when he occasionally met another man who had really been a soldier and they talked a few minutes in the dressing room at a dance he fell into the easy pose of the old soldier among other soldiers: that he had been badly, sickeningly frightened all the time. In this way he lost everything.

During this time, it was late summer, he was sleeping late in bed, getting up to walk down town to the library to get a book, eating lunch at home, reading on the front porch until he became bored, and then walking down through the town to spend the hottest hours of the day in the cool dark of the pool room. He loved to play pool.

In the evening he practiced on his clarinet, strolled down town, read, and went to bed. He was still a hero to his two young sisters. His mother would have given him breakfast in bed if he had wanted it. She often came in when he was in bed and asked him to tell her about the war, but her attention always wandered. His father was noncommittal.

Before Krebs went away to the war he had never been allowed to drive the family motor car. His father was in the real estate business and always wanted the car to be at his command when he required it to take clients out into the country to show them a piece of farm property. The car always stood outside the First National Bank building where his father had an office on the second floor. Now, after the war, it was still the same car.

Nothing was changed in the town except that the young girls had grown 10 up. But they lived in such a complicated world of already defined alliances and shifting feuds that Krebs did not feel the energy or the courage to break into it. He liked to look at them, though. There were so many good-looking young girls. Most of them had their hair cut short. When he went away only little girls wore their hair like that or girls that were fast. They all wore sweaters and shirt waists with round Dutch collars. It was a pattern. He liked to look at them from the front porch as they walked on the other side of the street. He liked to watch them walking under the shade of the trees. He liked the round Dutch collars above their sweaters. He liked their silk stockings and flat shoes. He liked their bobbed hair and the way they walked.

When he was in town their appeal to him was not very strong. He did not like them when he saw them in the Greek's ice cream parlor. He did not want them themselves really. They were too complicated. There was something else.

Vaguely he wanted a girl but he did not want to have to work to get her. He would have liked to have a girl but he did not want to have to spend a long time getting her. He did not want to get into the intrigue and the politics. He did not want to have to do any courting. He did not want to tell any more lies. It wasn't worth it.

He did not want any consequences. He did not want any consequences ever again. He wanted to live along without consequences. Besides he did not really need a girl. The army had taught him that. It was all right to pose as though you had to have a girl. Nearly everybody did that. But it wasn't true. You did not need a girl. That was the funny thing. First a fellow boasted how girls mean nothing to him, that he never thought of them, that they could not touch him. Then a fellow boasted that he could not get along without girls, that he had to have them all the time, that he could not go to sleep without them.

That was all a lie. It was all a lie both ways. You did not need a girl unless you thought about them. He learned that in the army. Then sooner or later you always got one. When you were really ripe for a girl you always got one. You did not have to think about it. Sooner or later it would come. He had learned that in the army.

Now he would have liked a girl if she had come to him and not wanted to talk. But here at home it was all too complicated. He knew he could never get through it all again. It was not worth the trouble. That was the thing about French girls and German girls. There was not all this talking. You couldn't talk much and you did not need to talk. It was simple and you were friends. He thought about France and then he began to think about Germany. On the whole he had liked Germany better. He did not want to leave Germany. He did not want to come home. Still, he had come home. He sat on the front porch.

He liked the girls that were walking along the other side of the street. He 15 liked the look of them much better than the French girls or the German girls. But the world they were in was not the world he was in. He would like to have one of them. But it was not worth it. They were such a nice pattern. He liked the pattern. It was exciting. But he would not go through all the talking. He did not want one badly enough. He liked to look at them all, though. It was not worth it. Not now when things were getting good again.

He sat there on the porch reading a book on the war. It was a history and he was reading about all the engagements he had been in. It was the most interesting reading he had ever done. He wished there were more maps. He looked forward with a good feeling to reading all the really good histories when they would come out with good detail maps. Now he was really learning about the war. He had been a good soldier. That made a difference.

One morning after he had been home about a month his mother came into his bedroom and sat on the bed. She smoothed her apron.

"I had a talk with your father last night, Harold," she said, "and he is willing for you to take the car out in the evenings."

"Yeah?" said Krebs, who was not fully awake. "Take the car out? Yeah?"

"Yes. Your father has felt for some time that you should be able to take the 20 car out in the evenings whenever you wished but we only talked it over last night."

"I'll bet you made him," Krebs said.

"No. It was your father's suggestion that we talk the matter over."

"Yeah. I'll bet you made him," Krebs sat up in bed.

"Will you come down to breakfast, Harold?" his mother said.

"As soon as I get my clothes on," Krebs said.   25

His mother went out of the room and he could hear her frying something downstairs while he washed, shaved, and dressed to go down into the dining-room for breakfast. While he was eating breakfast his sister brought in the mail.

"Well, Hare," she said. "You old sleepyhead. What do you ever get up for?"

Krebs looked at her. He liked her. She was his best sister.

"Have you got the paper?" he asked.

She handed him the Kansas City *Star* and he shucked off its brown wrapper   30
and opened it to the sporting page. He folded the *Star* open and propped it against the water pitcher with his cereal dish to steady it, so he could read while he ate.

"Harold," his mother stood in the kitchen doorway, "Harold, please don't muss up the paper. Your father can't read his *Star* if it's been mussed."

"I won't muss it," Krebs said.

His sister sat down at the table and watched him while he read.

"We're playing indoor over at school this afternoon," she said. "I'm going to pitch."

"Good," said Krebs. "How's the old wing?"   35

"I can pitch better than lots of the boys. I tell them all you taught me. The other girls aren't much good."

"Yeah?" said Krebs.

"I tell them all you're my beau. Aren't you my beau, Hare?"

"You bet."

"Couldn't your brother really be your beau just because he's your brother?"   40

"I don't know."

"Sure you know. Couldn't you be my beau, Hare, if I was old enough and if you wanted to?"

"Sure. You're my girl now."

"Am I really your girl?"

"Sure."   45

"Do you love me?"

"Uh, huh."

"Will you love me always?"

"Sure."

"Will you come over and watch me play indoor?"   50

"Maybe."

"Aw, Hare, you don't love me. If you loved me, you'd want to come over and watch me play indoor."

Krebs's mother came into the dining-room from the kitchen. She carried a plate with two fried eggs and some crisp bacon on it and a plate of buckwheat cakes.

"You run along, Helen," she said. "I want to talk to Harold."

She put the eggs and bacon down in front of him and brought in a jug of   55
maple syrup for the buckwheat cakes. Then she sat down across the table from Krebs.

"I wish you'd put down the paper a minute, Harold," she said.

Krebs took down the paper and folded it.

"Have you decided what you are going to do yet, Harold?" his mother said, taking off her glasses.

"No," said Krebs.

"Don't you think it's about time?" His mother did not say this in a mean 60
way. She seemed worried.

"I hadn't thought about it," Krebs said.

"God has some work for everyone to do," his mother said. "There can be no idle hands in His Kingdom."

"I'm not in His Kingdom," Krebs said.

"We are all of us in His Kingdom."

Krebs felt embarrassed and resentful as always. 65

"I've worried about you so much, Harold," his mother went on. "I know the temptations you must have been exposed to. I know how weak men are. I know what your own dear grandfather, my own father, told us about the Civil War and I have prayed for you. I pray for you all day long, Harold."

Krebs looked at the bacon fat hardening on his plate.

"Your father is worried, too," his mother went on. "He thinks you have lost your ambition, that you haven't got a definite aim in life. Charley Simmons, who is just your age, has a good job and is going to be married. The boys are all settling down; they're all determined to get somewhere; you can see that boys like Charley Simmons are on their way to being really a credit to the community."

Krebs said nothing.

"Don't look that way, Harold," his mother said. "You know we love you and 70
I want to tell you for your own good how matters stand. Your father does not want to hamper your freedom. He thinks you should be allowed to drive the car. If you want to take some of the nice girls out riding with you, we are only too pleased. We want you to enjoy yourself. But you are going to have to settle down to work, Harold. Your father doesn't care what you start in at. All work is honorable as he says. But you've got to make a start at something. He asked me to speak to you this morning and then you can stop in and see him at his office."

"Is that all?" Krebs said.

"Yes. Don't you love your mother, dear boy?"

"No," Krebs said.

His mother looked at him across the table. Her eyes were shiny. She started crying.

"I don't love anybody," Krebs said. 75

It wasn't any good. He couldn't tell her, he couldn't make her see it. It was silly to have said it. He had only hurt her. He went over and took hold of her arm. She was crying with her head in her hands.

"I didn't mean it," he said. "I was just angry at something. I didn't mean I didn't love you."

His mother went on crying. Krebs put his arm on her shoulder.

"Can't you believe me, mother?"

His mother shook her head. 80

"Please, please, mother. Please believe me."

"All right," his mother said chokily. She looked up at him. "I believe you, Harold."

Krebs kissed her hair. She put her face up to him.

"I'm your mother," she said. "I held you next to my heart when you were a tiny baby."

Krebs felt sick and vaguely nauseated.

"I know, Mummy," he said. "I'll try and be a good boy for you."

"Would you kneel and pray with me, Harold?" his mother asked.

They knelt down beside the dining-room table and Krebs's mother prayed.

"Now, you pray, Harold," she said.

"I can't," Krebs said.

"Try, Harold."

"I can't."

"Do you want me to pray for you?"

"Yes."

So his mother prayed for him and then they stood up and Krebs kissed his mother and went out of the house. He had tried so to keep his life from being complicated. Still, none of it had touched him. He had felt sorry for his mother and she had made him lie. He would go to Kansas City and get a job and she would feel all right about it. There would be one more scene maybe before he got away. He would not go down to his father's office. He would miss that one. He wanted his life to go smoothly. It had just gotten going that way. Well, that was all over now, anyway. He would go over to the schoolyard and watch Helen play indoor baseball.

Considerations for Critical Thinking and Writing

1. What does the photograph of Krebs, the corporal, and the German girls reveal?
2. Belleau Wood, Soissons, the Champagne, St. Mihiel, and the Argonne were the sites of fierce and bloody fighting. What effect have these battles had on Krebs? Why do you think he won't talk about them to the people at home?
3. Why does Krebs avoid complications and consequences? How has the war changed his attitudes toward work and women? How is his hometown different from Germany and France? What is the conflict in the story?
4. Why do you think Hemingway refers to the protagonist as Krebs rather than Harold? What is the significance of his sister calling him "Hare"?
5. Describe Krebs's home. How does Hemingway use the reader's traditional associations with home in this story? What is there about the routine at home that alienates Krebs? Why does the war seem more real to him?
6. How does Krebs's mother embody the community's values? What does Krebs think of those values?
7. Why can't Krebs pray with his mother?
8. What is the resolution to Krebs's conflict?
9. Comment on the appropriateness of the story's title.
10. Explain how Krebs's war experiences are present throughout the story even though we get no details about them.
11. Perhaps, after having been away from home for a time, you have returned to find yourself feeling alienated from your family or friends. Describe your experience. What caused the change?

Connections to Other Selections

1. Contrast the attitudes toward patriotism implicit in this story with those in Yukio Mishima's "Patriotism" (p. 506). How do the stories' settings help to account for the differences between them?

2. How might Krebs's rejection of his community's values be related to Sammy's relationship to his supermarket job in John Updike's "A & P" (p. 485)? What details does Updike use to make the setting in "A & P" a comic, though none-theless serious, version of Krebs's hometown?
3. Explain how the violent details that Tim O'Brien uses to establish the setting in "How to Tell a True War Story" (p. 552) can be considered representative of the kinds of horrors that haunt Krebs after he returns home.

PERSPECTIVE

e. e. cummings (1894–1962)
my sweet old etcetera   1926

my sweet old etcetera
aunt lucy during the recent

war could and what
is more did tell you just
what everybody was fighting   5

for,
my sister

isabel created hundreds
(and
hundreds) of socks not to   10
mention shirts fleaproof earwarmers

etcetera wristers etcetera, my

mother hoped that

i would die etcetera
bravely of course my father used   15
to become hoarse talking about how it was
a privilege and if only he
could meanwhile my

self etcetera lay quietly
in the deep mud et   20

cetera
(dreaming,

etcetera, of
Your smile
eyes knees and of your Etcetera)   25

Considerations for Critical Thinking and Writing

1. Compare and contrast the narrator's view of the home front with Krebs's in "Soldier's Home." To what extent does he sound like Krebs? Are there any signif-icant differences between the narrator's voice and Krebs's?

2. Write an essay on images of home in "my sweet old etcetera" and "Soldier's Home." Consider how the setting is used in each work to suggest the nature of the conflict.

LOUISE ERDRICH (b. 1954)

Louise Erdrich is of Chippewa Indian and German heritage. Born in 1954 in Little Falls, Minnesota, she grew up as part of the Turtle Mountain Band of Chippewa in Wahpeton, North Dakota. After graduating from Dartmouth College (where her poetry and fiction won several awards, including the American Academy of Poets Prize), she moved back to North Dakota to teach in the Poetry in the Schools Program. Her first novel, *Love Medicine,* winner of the 1984 National Book Critics Circle Award, is part of an interlocking series of novels concerning Native American life in North Dakota. She is presently at work on the next of these books, having published *The Beet Queen* in 1986 and *Tracks* in 1988. She enjoys a very close professional relationship with her husband, Michael Dorris. The two worked together on Dorris's *The Broken Cord: A Family's Ongoing Struggle with Fetal Alcohol Syndrome* (1989) and on a novel called *The Crown of Columbus,* (1991) which concerns a Native American woman who discovers Christopher Columbus. In the following story Erdrich uses the setting to establish the circumstances of her narrator's desperate tumbling life.

I'm a Mad Dog Biting Myself for Sympathy   1990

Who I am is just the habit of what I always was, and who I'll be is the result. This comes clear to me at the wrong time. I am standing in a line, almost rehabilitated. Walgreens is the store in downtown Fargo. I have my purchase in my arms, and I am listening to canned carols on the loudspeaker. I plan to buy this huge stuffed parrot with purple wings and a yellow beak. Really, it is a toucan, I get told this later in the tank.

You think you know everything about yourself — how much money it would take, for instance, to make you take it. How you would react when caught. But then you find yourself walking out the door with a stuffed toucan, just to see if shit happens, if do-do occurs. And it does, though no one stops me right at first.

My motive is my girlfriend's Christmas present. And it is strange because I do have the money to pay for a present, though nothing very big or elaborate. I think of Dawn the minute I see the bird, and wish I'd won it for her at a county fair, though we never went to a fair. I see myself throwing a half-dozen softballs and hitting every wooden milk jug, or maybe tossing rings. But those things are weighted or loaded wrong and that's another reason. I never could have won this toucan for Dawn, because the whole thing's a cheat in general. So what the hell, I think, and lift the bird.

Outside in the street it is one of my favorite kind of days, right there in the drag middle of winter when the snow is a few hard gray clumps and a dusty grass shows on the boulevards. I like the smell in the air, the dry dirt, the patches of water shrinking and the threat of snow, too, in the gloom of the sky.

The usual rubber-neck turns to look at me. This bird is really huge and 5 furry, with green underneath its floppy wings and fat stuffed orange feet. I don't know why they'd have a strange thing like this in Walgreens. Maybe a big promotion, maybe some kind of come-on for the holiday season. And then the manager yells at me from the door. I am half-way down the street when I hear him. "Come back here!" Probably pointing at me, too, though there is no reason, as I stick out plenty and still more when I run.

First I put the bird underneath my arm. But it throws off my balance. So I clutch it to my chest; that is no better. Thinking back now I should have ditched it, and slipped off through the alleys and disappeared. Of course, I didn't— otherwise none of all that happened would have happened. I sit the bird on my shoulders and hold the lumpy feet under my chin and then I bear down, like going for the distance or the gold, let my legs churn beneath me. I leap curbs, dodge among old men in long gray coats and babies in strollers, shoot up and over car hoods until I come to the railroad depot and, like it is some sort of destination, though it isn't, I slip in the door and look out the window.

A gathering crowd follows with the manager. There is a policewoman, a few local mall-sitters, passers-by. They are stumbling and talking together and making big circles of their arms, to illustrate the toucan, and closing in.

That's when my stroke of luck, good or bad is no telling, occurs. The car drives into the parking lot, a solid plastic luggage rack strapped on its roof. A man and a woman jump out, late for a connection, and they leave the car running in neutral. I walk out of the depot and stand before the car. At that moment, it seems as though events are taking me somewhere. I open up the hinges on the plastic rack, stuff in the bird. No one seems to notice me. En- couraged, I get in. I put my hands on the wheel. I take the car out of neutral and we start to roll, back out of the lot. I change gears, then turn at the crossroads, and look both ways.

I don't know what you'd do in this situation. I'll ask you. There you are in a car. It isn't yours but for the time being that doesn't matter. You look up the street one way. It's clear. You look down the other, and a clump of people still are arguing and trying to describe you with their hands. Either way, the road will take you straight out of town. The clear way is north, where you don't know anyone. South, what's there?

I let the car idle. 10

My parents. It's not like I hate them or anything. I just can't see them. I can close my eyes and form my sister's face behind my eyelids, but not my parents' faces. Where their eyes should meet mine, nothing. That's all. I shouldn't show up at the farm, not with the toucan. Much less the car. I think a few seconds longer. The bird on the roof. It is for Dawn. You could say she got me into this, so Dawn should get me out. But she doesn't live in Fargo anymore, she lives south. She lives in Colorado, which complicates everything later for it means crossing state lines and all just to bring her that bird, and then another complexity, although at the time I don't realize, occurs when the woman at the depot, the one who has left the car, appears very suddenly in the rearview mirror.

I have just started moving south when I hear a thump from behind. It is so surprising. Just imagine. She is there on the trunk, hanging on as though by magnetics. She reaches up and grabs the hitches on the roof-top luggage rack, gets a better grip, and sprawls across the back window. She is a little woman. Through the side-view, I see her blue heels in the air, the edge of a black coat. I hear her shrieking in an inhuman desperate way that horrifies me so much I floor the gas.

We must go by everyone fast, but the effect is dreamlike, so slow. I see the faces of the clump of people, their mouths falling open, arms stretching and grasping as I turn the corner and the woman rolls over and over like a seal in water. Then she flies off the trunk and bowls them before in her rush so they heap on the ground. She is in their arms. They put her down as though she is a live torpedo and keep running after me.

"Scandinavians," I think, because my grandmother's one, "they don't give up the ghost." I just want to yell out, tell them. "OK, so it's stolen. It's gone! It's a cheap stuffed bird anyhow and I will *park* the car. I promise."

I start talking to myself. "I'll check the oil in Sioux Falls. No sweat." Then 15 the worst thing comes about, and all of a sudden I understand the woman with her eyes rearing back in her skull, her little heels pointed in the air. I understand the faces of the people in the group, their blurting voices, "b . . . b . . . baby".

As from the back seat, it wails.

I have my first reaction, disbelief. I have taken the scenic route at a fast clip, but I know the view anyway. I am down near the river and have decided from there I will take 30 and avoid the Interstate, always so well patrolled. I park and turn around in a frantic whirl. I revolve twice in my seat. And I still can't see the baby. I am behind on the new equipment. He sits in something round and firm, shaped like a big football, strapped down the chest and over the waist, held tight by a padded cushion. Above his face there is a little diamond attachment made of plastic, a bunch of keys and plastic balls that dangle out of reach.

I have never seen a child this little before, so small that it is not a child yet. Its face is tiny and dark, almost reddish, or copper, and its fingers, splayed out against its cheeks, are the feet of a sparrow. There is a bottle of milk in a bag beside it. I put the end in its mouth and it sucks. But it will not hold the bottle. I keep putting the end in its hand, and it won't grasp.

"Oh screw it," I finally say, and gun right out of there. Its cry begins again and I wish I knew how to stop it. I have to slow down to get through some traffic. Sirens rush ahead on their way to the Interstate, passing in a squeal which surprises me. This car, this pack on top, I am so obvious. I think I'll maybe park at the old King Leo's, get out, and run. But then I pass it. I think it will be better if I get down south around the South Dakota border, or in the sandhills, where I can hide out in cow shelters. So I do go south. Over me the sky is bearing down and bearing down, so I think now maybe snow will fall. A White Christmas like the music in the drugstore. I know how to drive in snow and this car has decent tires, I can feel them. They never lose grip or plane above the road. They just keep rolling, humming, below me, all four in this unified direction, so dull that after some time it all seems right again.

The baby drops off, stops crying. It shouldn't have been there, should it. I 20 have to realize the situation. There is no use in thinking back, in saying to myself, well you shouldn't have stole the damn bird in the first place, because I did do that and then, well as you see, it is like I went along with the arrangement of things as they happened.

Of course, around halfway down there is a smokey waiting, which I knew would happen, but not whether it would be before or behind me. So now my answer comes. The officer's car turns off a dirt road and starts flashing, starts coming at me from the rear. I take it up to eighty and we move, *move,* so the frozen water standing in the fields flashes by like scarves and the silver snow whirls out of nowhere, to either side of us, and what rushes up before us is a heat of road and earth.

I am not all that afraid. I never am and that's my problem. I feel sure they will not use their weapons. I keep driving and then, as we take a turn, as we come to a railroad crossing, I hear the plastic roof rack snap open. I look through the rearview by reflex, and see the bird as it dives out of the sky, big and plush, a purple blur that plunges its yellow beak through the windshield and throws the state police off course so that they skid, roll over once, come back with such force the car righted itself. They sit there in shock.

I keep on going. The pack blows off and I reason that now the car is less obvious. I should have thought about that in the first place, but then the bird would not have hatched out and demolished the police car. Just about this time, however, being as the toucan is gone, I begin to feel perhaps there is no reason to go on traveling this way. I begin to think I will just stop at the nearest farm, leave the car and the baby, and keep hitching south. I begin to think if I show up at Dawn's, even with nothing, on a Christmas Eve, she will not throw me out. She will have to take me, let me stay there, on the couch. She lives with someone now, a guy ten years older than me, five years older than her. By now he has probably taken her places, shown her restaurants and zoos, gone camping in the wilderness, skied. She will know things and I will still be the same person that I was the year before. And I am glad about the toucan, then, which would have made me look ridiculous. Showing up there like a kid in junior high school with a stuffed animal, when her tastes have broadened. I should have sent her chocolates, a little red and green box. I was wishing I had. And then I look past the road in front of me and realize it is snowing.

It isn't just like ordinary snow even from the first. It is like that rhyme or story in the second grade, the sky falling and let's go and tell the king. It comes down. I think to myself, *well, let it come down.* And I keep driving. I know you'll say it, you'll wonder, you'll think what about the child in back of him, that baby, only three weeks old, little Mason Joseph Andrews? Because he does have a name and all, but what could I know of that?

I talk to it. I am good at driving in the snow but I need to talk while I'm 25 driving. I'll tell this now, it doesn't matter. I say, "You little bastard you, what are you doing here!" It is my state of mind. I put the window open. Snow whites out the windshield and I can't see the road in front of us. I watch the margin, try to follow the yellow line which is obscured by a twisting blanket. I am good at this though I need my concentration, which vanishes when he bawled. My ears are full. He roars and I hear the sound as wind, as sounds that came out of its mother. I hit the plastic egg and feel the straps give, feel the car give on the road. I swerve into another car's ruts, weave along the dotted yellow, and then under me is snow and still I keep going at a steady pace although the ground feels all hollow and uncertain. The tracks narrow into one, and then widen, so I suddenly realize this: I have followed a snowmobile trail and now I am somewhere off the road. Immediately, just like in a cartoon, like Dumbo flying and he realizes that he isn't supposed to be up in the air, I panic and get stuck.

So now I am in awful shape, out there in a field, in a storm that could go on for three more minutes or three more days. I sit there thinking until the baby gets discouraged and falls asleep. And get this. It is a white car. Harder to see than ever. And not a bit of this did I ever think or plan for. I can't remember what they say in the papers every fall, the advice about what to do when a blizzard hits. Whether to stay on the road, with the car, or set out walking for help. There is the baby. It is helpless, but does not seem so helpless. I know now that I should have left the car run, the heater, but at the time I don't think. Except I do rip that dangle of toys off its seat and tie it on the aerial when I go out, and I do leave its blankets in there, never take any. I just wrap my arms around my chest and start walking south.

By not stopping for a minute I live through the storm, though I am easy to catch after it lets up, and I freeze an ear. All right, you know that baby wasn't hurt anyway. You heard. Cold, yes, but it lived. They ask me in court why I didn't take it along with me, bundled in my jacket, and I say, well it lived, didn't it? Proving I did right. But I know better sometimes, now that I've spent time alone here in Mandan, more time running than I knew I had available.

I think about that boy. He'll grow up, but already I am more to him than his own father because I taught him what I know about the cold. It sinks in, there to stay, doesn't it? And people. They will leave you, no matter what you say there's no return. There's just the emptiness all around, and you in it, like singing up from the bottom of a well, like nothing else, until you harm yourself, until you are a mad dog just biting yourself for sympathy, because there is no relenting, and there is no hand that falls, and there is no woman come home to take you in her arms.

I know I taught that boy something in those hours I was walking south. I know I'll always be inside him, cold and black, about the size of a coin, maybe, something he touches against and skids. And he'll say, *what is this,* and the thing is he won't know it is a piece of thin ice I have put there, the same as I have in me.

Considerations for Critical Thinking and Writing

1. Consider the first sentence of the story as a statement that summarizes the narrator's life. How accurate is this self-assessment of his character?
2. What do you learn about his past? How much control does he have over his life?
3. Why is it significant that the narrator's name is never mentioned?
4. Why does the narrator steal the toucan instead of paying for it? How does this reveal his attitude toward life?
5. Describe the various settings that the narrator moves through. Do they have any qualities in common?

6. Consider the significance of some of the story's details. Why, for example, do you think the story begins in Fargo at a Walgreens? What is the significance of the present for Dawn being a toucan rather than just a stuffed parrot? Why do you think his girlfriend's name is "Dawn"?

7. When the narrator finds the car idling at the railroad depot, he calls it a "stroke of luck." What role does "luck" play in the plot? What would be a more accurate term to describe how and why events occur?

8. Explain why you do or don't sympathize with the narrator.

9. Try to recall your first reading of the story. Before reading the final three paragraphs, how did you think the story would end when you reached the end of paragraph 26?

10. Discuss the significance of the title.

11. What has the narrator taught the baby boy he inadvertently kidnapped and abandoned in the car? Why do you think the story ends with this information?

Connections to Other Selections

1. How does the narrator's voice compare with that of the narrator in Sandra Cisneros's "Barbie-Q" (p. 182). How does the manner in which each protagonist tells his or her story affect your response to the narrator?

2. Compare the narrator's motivation for his actions with Bartleby's in Herman Melville's story (p. 83). Why do they behave as they do?

3. Write an essay that explores how the settings of Erdrich's story and Eudora Welty's "Livvie" affect the lives of their respective antagonists.

4. To what extent is the narrator's life fated? Compare the circumstances that inform his life with those of the Judge's wife in Isabel Allende's story (p. 495).

5. Point of View

Because one of the pleasures of reading fiction consists of seeing the world through someone else's eyes, it is easy to overlook the eyes that control our view of the plot, characters, and setting. *Point of view* refers to who tells us the story and how it is told. What we know and how we feel about the events in a story are shaped by the author's choice of a point of view. The teller of a story, the *narrator,* inevitably affects our understanding of the characters' actions by filtering what is told through his or her own perspective. The narrator should not be confused with the author who has created the narrative voice, because the two are usually distinct (more on this point later).

If the narrative voice is changed, the story will change. Consider, for example, how different "Bartleby, the Scrivener" (p. 83) would be if Melville had chosen to tell the story from Bartleby's point of view instead of the lawyer's. With Bartleby as narrator, much of the mystery concerning his behavior would be lost. The peculiar force of his saying "I would prefer not to" would be lessened amid all the other things he would have to say as narrator. Moreover, the lawyer's reaction — puzzled, upset, outraged, and finally sympathetic to Bartleby — would be lost too. It would be entirely possible, of course, to write a story from Bartleby's point of view, but it would not be the story Melville wrote.

The possible ways of telling a story are many, and more than one point of view can be worked into a single story. However, the various points of view that storytellers draw upon can be conveniently grouped into two broad categories: (1) the third-person narrator, and (2) the first-person narrator. The third-person narrator uses *he, she,* or *they* to tell the story and does not participate in the action. The first-person narrator uses *I* and is a major or minor participant in the action. A second-person narrator, *you,* is possible but rarely used because of the awkwardness in thrusting the reader into the story, as in "You are minding your own business on a park bench when a drunk steps out of the bushes and demands your lunch bag."

Let's look now at the most important and most often used variations within first- and third-person narrations.

THIRD-PERSON NARRATOR (nonparticipant)

1. Omniscient (the narrator takes us inside the character[s])
2. Limited omniscient (the narrator takes us inside one or two characters)
3. Objective (the narrator is outside the characters)

FIRST-PERSON NARRATOR (participant)

1. Major character
2. Minor character

No type of third-person narrator appears as a character in a story. The *omniscient narrator* is all-knowing. From this point of view, the narrator can move from place to place and pass back and forth through time, slipping into and out of characters as no human being possibly could in real life. This narrator can report the characters' thoughts and feelings as well as what they say and do. In the excerpt from *Tarzan of the Apes* (p. 39), Burroughs's narrator tells us about events concerning Terkoz in another part of the jungle that long preceded the battle between Terkoz and Tarzan. We also learn Tarzan's and Jane's inner thoughts and emotions during the episode. And Burroughs's narrator describes Terkoz as "an arrant coward" and a bully, thereby evaluating the character for the reader. This kind of intrusion is called *editorial omniscience.* In contrast, narration that allows characters' actions and thoughts to speak for themselves is known as *neutral omniscience.* Most modern writers use neutral omniscience so that readers can reach their own conclusions.

The *limited omniscient narrator* is much more confined than the omniscient narrator. With limited omniscience the author very often restricts the narrator to the single perspective of either a major or a minor character. Sometimes a narrator can see into more than one character, particularly in a longer work that focuses, for example, on two characters alternately from one chapter to the next. Short stories, however, frequently are restricted by length to a single character's point of view. The way people, places, and events appear to that character is the way they appear to the reader. The reader has access to the thoughts and feelings of the characters revealed by the narrator, but neither the reader nor the character has access to the inner lives of any of the other characters in the story. The events in Katherine Mansfield's "Miss Brill" (p. 211) are viewed entirely through the protagonist's eyes; we see a French vacation town as an elderly woman does. Miss

Brill represents the central consciousness of the story. She unifies the story by being present through all the action. We are not told of anything that happens away from the character because the narration is based on her perception of things.

The most intense use of a central consciousness in narration can be seen in the **stream of consciousness technique** developed by modern writers such as James Joyce, Virginia Woolf, and William Faulkner. This technique takes a reader inside a character's mind to reveal perceptions, thoughts, and feelings on a conscious or unconscious level. A stream of consciousness suggests the flow of thought as well as its content; hence, complete sentences may give way to fragments as the character's mind makes rapid associations free of conventional logic or transitions.

The following passage is from Joyce's *Ulysses,* a novel famous for its extended use of this technique. In this paragraph the narrator describes a funeral.

> Coffin now. Got here before us, dead as he is. Horse looking round at it with his plume skeowways [askew]. Dull eye: collar tight on his neck, pressing on a bloodvessel or something. Do they know what they cart out of here every day? Must be twenty or thirty funerals every day. Then Mount Jerome for the protestants. Funerals all over the world everywhere every minute. Shovelling them under by the cartload doublequick. Thousands every hour. Too many in the world.

The narrator's thoughts range from specific observations to speculations about death. Joyce creates the illusion that we are reading the narrator's thoughts as they occur. The stream of consciousness technique provides an intimate perspective on a character's thoughts.

In contrast, the **objective point of view** employs a narrator who does not see into the mind of any character. From this detached and impersonal perspective, the narrator reports action and dialogue without telling us directly what characters feel and think. We observe the characters in much the same way we would perceive events in a film or play: we supply the meanings; no analysis or interpretation is provided by a narrator. This point of view places a heavy premium on dialogue, actions, and details to reveal character.

In Hemingway's "Soldier's Home" (p. 125), a limited omniscient narration is the predominant point of view. Krebs's thoughts and reaction to being home from the war are made available to the reader by the narrator, who tells us that Krebs "felt embarrassed and resentful" or "sick and vaguely nauseated" by the small-town life he has reentered. Occasionally, however, Hemingway uses an objective point of view when he dramatizes particularly tense moments between Krebs and his mother. In the following excerpt, Hemingway's narrator shows us Krebs's feelings instead of telling us what they are. Krebs's response to his mother's concerns is presented without comment. The external details of the scene reveal his inner feelings.

"I've worried about you so much, Harold," his mother went on. "I know the temptations you must have been exposed to. I know how weak men are. I know what your own dear grandfather, my own father, told us about the Civil War and I have prayed for you. I pray for you all day long, Harold."

Krebs looked at the bacon fat hardening on his plate.

"Your father is worried, too," his mother went on. "He thinks you have lost your ambition, that you haven't got a definite aim in life. Charley Simmons, who is just your age, has a good job and is going to be married. The boys are all settling down; they're all determined to get somewhere; you can see that boys like Charley Simmons are on their way to being really a credit to the community."

Krebs said nothing.

"Don't look that way, Harold. . . ."

When Krebs looks at the bacon fat we can see him cooling and hardening too. Hemingway did not describe the expression on Krebs's face, yet we know it is a look that disturbed his mother as she "went on" about what she thinks she knows. Krebs and his mother are clearly tense and upset; the details, action, and dialogue reveal that without the narrator telling the reader how each character feels.

With a *first-person narrator,* the *I* presents the point of view of only one character's consciousness. The reader is restricted to the perceptions, thoughts, and feelings of that single character. This is Melville's technique with the lawyer in "Bartleby, the Scrivener" (p. 83). Everything learned about the characters, action, and plot comes from the unnamed lawyer. Bartleby remains a mystery because we are limited to what the lawyer knows and reports. The lawyer cannot explain what Bartleby means because he does not entirely know himself. Melville's use of the first person encourages us to identify with the lawyer's confused reaction to Bartleby so that we pay attention not only to the scrivener but also to the lawyer's response to him. We are as perplexed as the lawyer and share his effort to make sense of Bartleby.

The lawyer is a major character in Melville's story; indeed, many readers take him to be the protagonist. A first-person narrator can, however, also be a minor character (imagine how different the story would be if it were told by, say, Ginger Nut or by an observer who has little or nothing to do with the action). Faulkner uses an observer in "A Rose for Emily" (p. 47). His *we,* though plural and representative of the town's view of Emily, is nonetheless a first-person narrator.

One of the primary reasons for identifying the point of view in a story is to determine where the author stands in relation to the story. Behind the narrative voice of any story is the author, manipulating events and providing or withholding information. It is a mistake to assume that the narrative voice of a story is the author. The narrator, whether a first-person participant or a third-person nonparticipant, is a creation of the writer. A narrator's perceptions may be accepted, rejected, or modified by an author, depending on how the narrative voice is articulated.

Faulkner seems to have shared the fascination, sympathy, and horror of the narrator in "A Rose for Emily," but Melville must not be so readily identified with the lawyer in "Bartleby, the Scrivener." The lawyer's description of himself as "an eminently *safe* man," convinced "that the easiest way of life is the best," raises the question of how well equipped he is to fathom Bartleby's protest. To make sense of Bartleby, it is also necessary to understand the lawyer's point of view. Until the conclusion of the story, this *"safe* man" is too self-serving, defensive, and obtuse to comprehend the despair embodied in Bartleby and the deadening meaninglessness of Wall Street life.

The lawyer is an **unreliable narrator**, whose interpretation of events is different from the author's. We cannot entirely accept the lawyer's assessment of Bartleby because we see that the lawyer's perceptions are not totally to be trusted. Melville does not expect us, for example, to agree with the lawyer's suggestion that the solution to Bartleby's situation might be to "entertain some young gentleman with your conversation" on a trip to Europe. Given Bartleby's awful silences, this absurd suggestion reveals the lawyer's superficial understanding. The lawyer's perceptions frequently do not coincide with those Melville expects his readers to share. Hence, the lawyer's unreliability preserves Bartleby's mysterious nature while revealing the lawyer's sensibilities. The point of view is artistically appropriate for Melville's purposes, because the eyes through which we perceive the plot, characters, and setting are also the subject of the story.

Narrators can be unreliable for a variety of reasons: they might lack self-knowledge, like Melville's lawyer, or they might be innocent and inexperienced, like Ralph Ellison's young narrator in "Battle Royal" (p. 187). Youthful innocence frequently characterizes a **naive narrator** such as Mark Twain's Huck Finn or Holden Caufield, J. D. Salinger's twentieth-century version of Huck in *The Catcher in the Rye*. These narrators lack the sophistication to interpret accurately what they see; they are unreliable because the reader must go beyond their understanding of events to comprehend the situations described. Huck and Holden describe their respective social environments, but the reader, with more experience, supplies the critical perspective that each boy lacks. In "Battle Royal" that perspective is supplemented by Ellison dividing the narration between the young man who experiences events and the mature man who reflects back on those events.

Few generalizations can be made about the advantages or disadvantages of using a specific point of view. What can be said with confidence, however, is that writers choose a point of view to achieve particular effects, because point of view determines what we know about the characters and events in a story. We should, therefore, be aware of who is telling the story and whether the narrator sees things clearly and reliably.

The next three works warrant a careful examination of their points of view. In Toni Cade Bambara's "The Lesson," we hear the voice of a streetwise young black girl who resists instruction. In Anton Chekhov's and Joyce Carol Oates's versions of "The Lady with the Pet Dog," we are presented with similar stories told from two different perspectives that make for intriguing comparisons and contrasts.

TONI CADE BAMBARA (b. 1939)

Raised in New York City's Harlem and Bedford-Stuyvesant communities, Toni Cade Bambara graduated from Queens College in 1959, studied in Florence and Paris, and earned her M.A. at City College of New York in 1964. She has also studied dance, linguistics, and film-making and has worked a variety of jobs in welfare, recreation, and community housing, in addition to teaching at various schools, including Rutgers University and Spelman College. She describes her writing as "straight-up fiction . . . 'cause I value my family and friends, and mostly 'cause I lie a lot anyway." Her fiction has been collected in *Gorilla, My Love* (1972) and *The Sea Birds Are Still Alive* (1977), and in 1980 she published her first novel, *Salt Eaters*. A number of her screenplays have been produced, including "Epitaph for Willie" and "Tar Baby." In the following story a serious lesson is prescribed with a healthy dose of humor.

The Lesson 1972

Back in the days when everyone was old and stupid or young and foolish and me and Sugar were the only ones just right, this lady moved on our block with nappy hair and proper speech and no makeup. And quite naturally we laughed at her, laughed the way we did at the junk man who went about his business like he was some big-time president and his sorry-ass horse his secretary. And we kinda hated her too, hated the way we did the winos who cluttered up our parks and pissed on our handball walls and stank up our hallways and stairs so you couldn't halfway play hide-and-seek without a goddamn gas mask. Miss Moore was her name. The only woman on the block with no first name. And she was black as hell, cept for her feet, which were fish-white and spooky. And she was always planning these boring-ass things for us to do, us being my cousin, mostly, who lived on the block cause we all moved North the same time and to the same apartment then spread out gradual to breathe. And our parents would yank our heads into some kinda shape and crisp up our clothes so we'd be presentable for travel with Miss Moore, who always looked like she was going to church, though she never did. Which is just one of the things the grownups talked about when they talked behind her back like a dog. But when she came calling with some sachet she'd sewed up or some gingerbread she'd made or some book, why then they'd all be too embarrassed to turn her down and we'd get handed over all spruced up. She'd been to college and said it was only right that she should take responsibility for the young ones' education, and she not even related by marriage or blood. So they'd go for it. Specially Aunt Gretchen. She was the main gofer in the family. You got some ole dumb shit foolishness you want somebody to go for, you send for Aunt Gretchen. She been screwed into the go-along for so long, it's a blood-deep natural thing with her. Which is how she got saddled with me and Sugar and Junior in the first place while our mothers were in a la-de-da apartment up the block having a good ole time.

So this one day Miss Moore rounds us all up at the mailbox and it's puredee hot and she's knockin herself out about arithmetic. And school suppose to let up in summer I heard, but she don't never let up. And the starch in my pinafore scratching the shit outta me and I'm really hating this nappy-head bitch and her goddamn college degree. I'd much rather go to the pool or to the show where it's cool. So me and Sugar leaning on the mailbox being surly, which is a Miss Moore word. And Flyboy checking out what everybody brought for lunch. And Fat Butt already wasting his peanut-butter-and-jelly sandwich like the pig he is. And Junebug punchin on Q.T.'s arm for potato chips. And Rosie Giraffe shifting from one hip to the other waiting for somebody to step on her foot or ask her if she from Georgia so she can kick ass, preferably Mercedes'. And Miss Moore asking us do we know what money is, like we a bunch of retards. I mean real money, she say, like it's only poker chips or monopoly papers we lay on the grocer. So right away I'm tired of this and say so. And would much rather snatch Sugar and go to the Sunset and terrorize the West Indian kids and take their hair ribbons and their money too. And Miss Moore files that remark away for next week's lesson on brotherhood, I can tell. And finally I say we oughta get to the subway cause it's cooler and besides we might meet some cute boys. Sugar done swiped her mama's lipstick, so we ready.

So we heading down the street and she's boring us silly about what things cost and what our parents make and how much goes for rent and how money ain't divided up right in this country. And then she gets to the part about we all poor and live in the slums, which I don't feature. And I'm ready to speak on that, but she steps out in the street and hails two cabs just like that. Then she hustles half the crew in with her and hands me a five-dollar bill and tells me to calculate 10 percent tip for the driver. And we're off. Me and Sugar and Junebug and Flyboy hangin out the window and hollering to everybody, putting lipstick on each other cause Flyboy a faggot anyway, and making farts with our sweaty armpits. But I'm mostly trying to figure how to spend this money. But they all fascinated with the meter ticking and Junebug starts laying bets as to how much it'll read when Flyboy can't hold his breath no more. Then Sugar lays bets as to how much it'll be when we get there. So I'm stuck. Don't nobody want to go for my plan, which is to jump out at the next light and run off to the first bar-b-que we can find. Then the driver tells us to get the hell out cause we there already. And the meter reads eighty-five cents. And I'm stalling to figure out the tip and Sugar say give him a dime. And I decide he don't need it bad as I do, so later for him. But then he tries to take off with Junebug foot still in the door so we talk about his mama something ferocious. Then we check out that we on Fifth Avenue and everybody dressed up in stockings. One lady in a fur coat, hot as it is. White folks crazy.

"This is the place," Miss Moore say, presenting it to us in the voice she uses at the museum. "Let's look in the windows before we go in."

"Can we steal?" Sugar asks very serious like she's getting the ground rules 5 squared away before she plays. "I beg your pardon," say Miss Moore, and we fall out. So she leads us around the windows of the toy store and me and Sugar screamin, "This is mine, that's mine, I gotta have that, that was made for me, I was born for that," till Big Butt drowns us out.

"Hey, I'm goin to buy that there."

"That there? You don't even know what it is, stupid."

"I do so," he say punchin on Rosie Giraffe. "It's a microscope."

"Whatcha gonna do with a microscope, fool?"

"Look at things." 10

"Like what, Ronald?" ask Miss Moore. And Big Butt ain't got the first notion. So here go Miss Moore gabbing about the thousands of bacteria in a drop of water and the somethinorother in a speck of blood and the million and one living things in the air around us is invisible to the naked eye. And what she say that for? Junebug go to town on that "naked" and we rolling. Then Miss Moore ask what it cost. So we all jam into the window smudgin it up and the price tag say $300. So then she ask how long'd take for Big Butt and Junebug to save up their allowances. "Too long," I say. "Yeh," adds Sugar, "outgrown it by that time." And Miss Moore say no, you never outgrow learning instruments. "Why, even medical students and interns and," blah, blah, blah. And we ready to choke Big Butt for bringing it up in the first damn place.

"This here costs four hundred eighty dollars," says Rosie Giraffe. So we pile up all over her to see what she pointin out. My eyes tell me it's a chunk of glass cracked with something heavy, and different-color inks dripped into the splits, then the whole thing put into a oven or something. But for $480 it don't make sense.

"That's a paperweight made of semi-precious stones fused together under tremendous pressure," she explains slowly, with her hands doing the mining and all the factory work.

"So what's a paperweight?" asks Rosie Giraffe.

"To weigh paper with, dumbbell," say Flyboy, the wise man from the East. 15

"Not exactly," say Miss Moore, which is what she say when you warm or way off too. "It's to weigh paper down so it won't scatter and make your desk untidy." So right away me and Sugar curtsy to each other and then to Mercedes who is more the tidy type.

"We don't keep paper on top of the desk in my class," say Junebug, figuring Miss Moore crazy or lyin one.

"At home, then," she say. "Don't you have a calendar and pencil case and a blotter and a letter-opener on your desk at home where you do your homework?" And she know damn well what our homes look like cause she nosys around in them every chance she gets.

"I don't even have a desk," say Junebug. "Do we?"

"No. And I don't get no homework neither," says Big Butt. 20

"And I don't even have a home," say Flyboy like he do at school to keep the white folks off his back and sorry for him. Send this poor kid to camp posters, is his specialty.

"I do," says Mercedes. "I have a box of stationery on my desk and a picture of my cat. My godmother bought the stationery and the desk. There's a big rose on each sheet and the envelopes smell like roses."

"Who wants to know about your smelly-ass stationery," say Rosie Giraffe fore I can get my two cents in.

"It's important to have a work area all your own so that . . ."

"Will you look at this sailboat, please," say Flyboy, cuttin her off and pointin 25 to the thing like it was his. So once again we tumble all over each other to gaze at this magnificent thing in the toy store which is just big enough to maybe sail two kittens across the pond if you strap them to the posts tight. We all start reciting the price tag like we in assembly. "Handcrafted sailboat of fiberglass at one thousand one hundred ninety-five dollars."

"Unbelievable," I hear myself say and am really stunned. I read it again for myself just in case the group recitation put me in a trance. Same thing. For some reason this pisses me off. We look at Miss Moore and she lookin at us, waiting for I dunno what.

"Who'd pay all that when you can buy a sailboat set for a quarter at Pop's, a tube of glue for a dime, and a ball of string for eight cents? It must have a motor and a whole lot else besides," I say. "My sailboat cost me about fifty cents."

"But will it take water?" say Mercedes with her smart ass.

"Took mine to Alley Pond Park once," say Flyboy. "String broke. Lost it. Pity."

"Sailed mine in Central Park and it keeled over and sank. Had to ask my 30 father for another dollar."

"And you got the strap," laugh Big Butt. "The jerk didn't even have a string on it. My old man wailed on his behind."

Little Q.T. was staring hard at the sailboat and you could see he wanted it bad. But he too little and somebody'd just take it from him. So what the hell. "This boat for kids, Miss Moore?"

"Parents silly to buy something like that just to get all broke up," say Rosie Giraffe.

"That much money it should last forever," I figure.

"My father'd buy it for me if I wanted it." 35

"Your father, my ass," say Rosie Giraffe getting a chance to finally push Mercedes.

"Must be rich people shop here," say Q.T.

"You are a very bright boy," say Flyboy. "What was your first clue?" And he rap him on the head with the back of his knuckles, since Q.T. the only one he could get away with. Though Q.T. liable to come up behind you years later and get his licks in when you half expect it.

"What I want to know is," I says to Miss Moore though I never talk to her, I wouldn't give the bitch that satisfaction, "is how much a real boat costs? I figure a thousand'd get you a yacht any day."

"Why don't you check that out," she says, "and report back to the group?" 40 Which really pains my ass. If you gonna mess up a perfectly good swim day least you could do is have some answers. "Let's go in," she say like she got something up her sleeve. Only she don't lead the way. So me and Sugar turn the corner to where the entrance is, but when we get there I kinda hang back. Not that I'm scared, what's there to be afraid of, just a toy store. But I feel funny, shame. But what I got to be shamed about? Got as much right to go in as anybody. But somehow I can't seem to get hold of the door, so I step away from Sugar to lead. But she hangs back too. And I look at her and she looks at me and this is ridiculous. I mean, damn, I have never ever been shy about doing nothing or going nowhere. But then Mercedes steps up and then Rosie Giraffe and Big Butt crowd in behind and shove, and next thing we all stuffed into the doorway with only Mercedes squeezing past us, smoothing out her jumper and walking right down the aisle. Then the rest of us tumble in like a glued-together jigsaw done all wrong. And people lookin at us. And it's like the time me and Sugar crashed into the Catholic church on a dare. But once we got in there and everything so hushed and holy and the candles and the bowin and the handkerchiefs on all the drooping heads, I just couldn't go through with the plan. Which was for me to run up to the altar and do a tap dance while Sugar played the nose flute and messed around in the holy water. And Sugar kept givin me the elbow. Then later teased me so bad I tied her up in the shower and turned it on and locked her in. And she'd be there till this day if Aunt Gretchen hadn't finally figured I was lyin about the boarder takin a shower.

Same thing in the store. We all walkin on tiptoe and hardly touchin the games and puzzles and things. And I watched Miss Moore who is steady watchin us like she waitin for a sign. Like Mama Drewery watches the sky and sniffs the air and takes note of just how much slant is in the bird formation. Then me and Sugar bump smack into each other, so busy gazing at the toys, specially the sailboat. But we don't laugh and go into our fat-lady bump-stomach routine. We just stare at that price tag. Then Sugar run a finger over the whole boat. And I'm jealous and want to hit her. Maybe not her, but I sure want to punch somebody in the mouth.

"Watcha bring us here for, Miss Moore?"

"You sound angry, Sylvia. Are you mad about something?" Givin me one of them grins like she tellin a grown-up joke that never turns out to be funny. And she's lookin very closely at me like maybe she planning to do my portrait from memory. I'm mad, but I won't giver her that satisfaction. So I slouch around the store bein very bored and say, "Let's go."

Me and Sugar at the back of the train watchin the tracks whizzin by large then small then getting gobbled up in the dark. I'm thinkin about this tricky toy I saw in the store. A clown that somersaults on a bar then does chin-ups just cause you yank lightly at his leg. Cost $35. I could see me askin my mother for a $35 birthday clown. "You wanna who that costs what?" she'd say, cocking her head to the side to get a better view of the hole in my head. Thirty-five dollars could buy new bunk beds for Junior and Gretchen's boy. Thirty-five dollars and the whole household could go visit Granddaddy Nelson in the country. Thirty-five dollars would pay for the rent and the piano bill too. Who are these people that spend that much for performing clowns and $1000 for toy sailboats? What kinda work they do and how they live and how come we ain't in on it? Where we are is who we are, Miss Moore always pointin out. But it don't necessarily have to be that way, she always adds then waits for somebody to say that poor people have to wake up and demand their share of the pie and don't none of us know what kind of pie she talking about in the first damn place. But she ain't so smart cause I still got her four dollars from the taxi and she sure ain't gettin it. Messin up my day with this shit. Sugar nudges me in my pocket and winks.

Miss Moore lines us up in front of the mailbox where we started from, seem like years ago, and I got a headache for thinkin so hard. And we lean all over each other so we can hold up under the draggy-ass lecture she always finishes us off with at the end before we thank her for borin us to tears. But she just looks at us like she readin tea leaves. Finally she say, "Well, what did you think of F. A. O. Schwarz?"

Rosie Giraffe mumbles, "White folks crazy."

"I'd like to go there again when I get my birthday money," says Mercedes, and we shove her out the pack so she has to lean on the mailbox by herself.

"I'd like a shower. Tiring day," say Flyboy.

Then Sugar surprises me by sayin, "You know, Miss Moore, I don't think all of us here put together eat in a year what that sailboat costs." And Miss Moore lights up like somebody goosed her. "And?" she say, urging Sugar on. Only I'm standin on her foot so she don't continue.

"Imagine for a minute what kind of society it is in which some people can spend on a toy what it would cost to feed a family of six or seven. What do you think?"

"I think," say Sugar pushing me off her feet like she never done before, cause I whip her ass in a minute, "that this is not much of a democracy if you ask me. Equal chance to pursue happiness means an equal crack at the dough, don't it?" Miss Moore is beside herself and I am disgusted with Sugar's treachery. So I stand on her foot one more time to see if she'll shove me. She shuts up, and Miss Moore looks at me, sorrowfully I'm thinkin. And somethin weird is goin on, I can feel it in my chest.

"Anybody else learn anything today?" lookin dead at me. I walk away and Sugar has to run to catch up and don't even seem to notice when I shrug her arm off my shoulder.

"Well, we got four dollars anyway," she says.

"Uh hunh."

"We could go to Hascombs and get half a chocolate layer and then go to the Sunset and still have plenty money for potato chips and ice cream sodas."

"Un hunh."

"Race you to Hascombs," she say.

We start down the block and she gets ahead which is O.K. by me cause I'm going to the West End and then over to the Drive to think this day through. She can run if she want to and even run faster. But ain't nobody gonna beat me at nuthin.

Considerations for Critical Thinking and Writing

1. What is the lesson Miss Moore tries to teach Sylvia? Is she successful? Invent an alternative title that captures for you the central meaning of the story.
2. What is the conflict in this story? Is there more than one? How are these conflicts resolved?
3. Write a paragraph characterizing Miss Moore's point of view about herself. Then write a descriptive paragraph of Miss Moore from Sylvia's point of view. Try to capture their voices in your descriptions.

4. The story begins with an adult narrator recalling her youth: "Back in the days when. . . ." Although that adult perspective is quickly replaced by the young girl's point of view, what do you think the adult narrator thinks of herself as a young girl?
5. Explain why the use of an editorial omniscient point of view in this story would be inappropriate.
6. How does Sylvia's use of language serve to characterize her?
7. How do you feel about Miss Moore at the end of the story compared with your feelings about her at the beginning? Why?
8. How do Sylvia and Sugar get along? What does this relationship reveal about Sylvia?
9. What do you think the last line of the story means? Does Sylvia think Sugar is smarter than she is because Sugar knew the answer to Miss Moore's question and she didn't? Who else could the "nobody" in that line refer to besides Sugar?
10. How does Bambara include serious social commentary in the story without sounding preachy?

Connections to Other Selections

1. Compare the treatment of youth and age in "The Lesson" with the treatment in Katherine Mansfield's "Miss Brill" (p. 211).
2. Discuss Bambara's characterization of children with Flannery O'Connor's in "A Good Man Is Hard to Find" (p. 368). Which author's treatment of children seems more convincing to you? Why?
3. Write an essay comparing the lessons learned by the protagonists in "The Lesson" and in Ralph Ellison's "Battle Royal" (p. 187).

ANTON CHEKHOV (1860–1904)

Born in a small town in Russia, Anton Chekhov gave up the career his medical degree prepared him for in order to devote himself to writing. His concentration on realistic detail in the hundreds of short stories he published has had an important influence on fiction writing. Modern drama has also been strengthened by his plays, among them these classics: *The Seagull* (1896), *Uncle Vanya* (1899), *The Three Sisters* (1901), and *The Cherry Orchard* (1904). Chekhov was a close observer of people in ordinary situations who struggle to live their lives as best they can. They are not very often completely successful. Chekhov's compassion, however, makes their failures less significant than their humanity. In "The Lady with the Pet Dog," love is at the heart of a struggle that begins in Yalta, a resort town on the Black Sea.

The Lady with the Pet Dog

1899

TRANSLATED BY AVRAHM YARMOLINSKY

I

A new person, it was said, had appeared on the esplanade: a lady with a pet dog. Dmitry Dmitrich Gurov, who had spent a fortnight at Yalta and had got used to the place, had also begun to take an interest in new arrivals. As he sat in Vernet's confectionery shop, he saw, walking on the esplanade, a fair-haired young woman of medium height, wearing a beret; a white Pomeranian was trotting behind her.

And afterwards he met her in the public garden and in the square several times a day. She walked alone, always wearing the same beret and always with the white dog; no one knew who she was and everyone called her simply "the lady with the pet dog."

"If she is here alone without husband or friends," Gurov reflected, "it wouldn't be a bad thing to make her acquaintance."

He was under forty, but he already had a daughter twelve years old, and two sons at school. They had found a wife for him when he was very young, a student in his second year, and by now she seemed half as old again as he. She was a tall, erect woman with dark eyebrows, stately and dignified and, as she said of herself, intellectual. She read a great deal, used simplified spelling in her letters, called her husband, not Dmitry, but Dimitry, while he privately considered her of limited intelligence, narrow-minded, dowdy, was afraid of her, and did not like to be at home. He had begun being unfaithful to her long ago — had been unfaithful to her often and, probably for that reason, almost always spoke ill of women, and when they were talked of in his presence used to call them "the inferior race."

It seemed to him that he had been sufficiently tutored by bitter experience to call them what he pleased, and yet he could not have lived without "the inferior race" for two days together. In the company of men he was bored and ill at ease, he was chilly and uncommunicative with them; but when he was among women he felt free, and knew what to speak to them about and how to comport himself; and even to be silent with them was no strain on him. In his appearance, in his character, in his whole makeup there was something attractive and elusive that disposed women in his favor and allured them. He knew that, and some force seemed to draw him to them, too.

Oft-repeated and really bitter experience had taught him long ago that with decent people — particularly Moscow people — who are irresolute and slow to move, every affair which at first seems a light and charming adventure inevitably grows into a whole problem of extreme complexity, and in the end a painful situation is created. But at every new meeting with an interesting woman this lesson of experience seemed to slip from his memory, and he was eager for life, and everything seemed so simple and diverting.

One evening while he was dining in the public garden the lady in the beret walked up without haste to take the next table. Her expression, her gait, her dress, and the way she did her hair told him that she belonged to the upper class, that she was married, that she was in Yalta for the first time and alone, and that she was bored there. The stories told of the immorality in Yalta are to a great extent untrue; he despised them, and knew that such stories were made up for the most part by persons who would have been glad to sin themselves if they had had the chance; but when the lady sat down at the next table three paces from him, he recalled these stories of easy conquests, of trips to the mountains, and the tempting thought of swift, fleeting liaison, a romance with an unknown woman of whose very name he was ignorant suddenly took hold of him.

He beckoned invitingly to the Pomeranian, and when the dog approached him, shook his finger at it. The Pomeranian growled; Gurov threatened it again.

The lady glanced at him and at once dropped her eyes.

"He doesn't bite," she said and blushed. 10

"May I give him a bone?" he asked; and when she nodded he inquired affably, "Have you been in Yalta long?"

"About five days."

"And I am dragging out the second week here."

There was a short silence.

"Time passes quickly, and yet it is so dull here!" she said, not looking at 15 him.

"It's only the fashion to say it's dull here. A provincial will live in Belyov or Zhizdra and not be bored, but when he comes here it's 'Oh, the dullness! Oh, the dust!' One would think he came from Granada."

She laughed. Then both continued eating in silence, like strangers, but after dinner they walked together and there sprang up between them the light banter of people who are free and contented, to whom it does not matter where they go or what they talk about. They walked and talked of the strange light on the sea: the water was a soft, warm, lilac color, and there was a golden band of moonlight upon it. They talked of how sultry it was after a hot day. Gurov told her that he was a native of Moscow, that he had studied languages and literature at the university, but had a post in a bank; that at one time he had trained to become an opera singer but had given it up, that he owned two houses in Moscow. And he learned from her that she had grown up in Petersburg, but had lived in S —— since her marriage two years previously, that she was going to stay in Yalta for about another month, and that her husband, who needed a rest, too, might perhaps come to fetch her. She was not certain whether her husband was a member of a Government Board or served on a Zemstvo Council,° and this amused her. And Gurov learned too that her name was Anna Sergeyevna.

Afterwards in his room at the hotel he thought about her — and was certain that he would meet her the next day. It was bound to happen. Getting into bed he recalled that she had been a schoolgirl only recently, doing lessons like his own daughter; he thought how much timidity and angularity there was still in her laugh and her manner of talking with a stranger. It must have been the first time in her life that she was alone in a setting in which she was followed, looked

Zemstvo Council: A district council.

at, and spoken to for one secret purpose alone, which she could hardly fail to guess. He thought of her slim, delicate throat, her lovely gray eyes.

"There's something pathetic about her, though," he thought, and dropped off.

II

A week had passed since they had struck up an acquaintance. It was a 20 holiday. It was close indoors, while in the street the wind whirled the dust about and blew people's hats off. One was thirsty all day, and Gurov often went into the restaurant and offered Anna Sergeyevna a soft drink or ice cream. One did not know what to do with oneself.

In the evening when the wind had abated they went out on the pier to watch the steamer come in. There were a great many people walking about the dock; they had come to welcome someone and they were carrying bunches of flowers. And two peculiarities of a festive Yalta crowd stood out: the elderly ladies were dressed like young ones and there were many generals.

Owing to the choppy sea, the steamer arrived late, after sunset, and it was a long time tacking about before it put in at the pier. Anna Sergeyevna peered at the steamer and the passengers through her lorgnette as though looking for acquaintances, and whenever she turned to Gurov her eyes were shining. She talked a great deal and asked questions jerkily, forgetting the next moment what she had asked; then she lost her lorgnette in the crush.

The festive crowd began to disperse; it was now too dark to see people's faces; there was no wind any more, but Gurov and Anna Sergeyevna still stood as though waiting to see someone else come off the steamer. Anna Sergeyevna was silent now, and sniffed her flowers without looking at Gurov.

"The weather has improved this evening," he said. "Where shall we go now? Shall we drive somewhere?"

She did not reply. 25

Then he looked at her intently, and suddenly embraced her and kissed her on the lips, and the moist fragrance of her flowers enveloped him; and at once he looked round him anxiously, wondering if anyone had seen them.

"Let us go to your place," he said softly. And they walked off together rapidly.

The air in her room was close and there was the smell of the perfume she had bought at the Japanese shop. Looking at her, Gurov thought: "What encounters life offers!" From the past he preserved the memory of carefree, good-natured women whom love made gay and who were grateful to him for the happiness he gave them, however brief it might be; and of women like his wife who loved without sincerity, with too many words, affectedly, hysterically, with an expression that it was not love or passion that engaged them but something more significant; and of two or three others, very beautiful, frigid women, across whose faces would suddenly flit a rapacious expression — an obstinate desire to take from life more than it could give, and these were women no longer young, capricious, unreflecting, domineering, unintelligent, and when Gurov grew cold to them their beauty aroused his hatred, and the lace on their lingerie seemed to him to resemble scales.

But here there was the timidity, the angularity of inexperienced youth, a feeling of awkwardness; and there was a sense of embarrassment, as though someone had suddenly knocked at the door. Anna Sergeyevna, "the lady with the pet dog," treated what had happened in a peculiar way, very seriously, as though it were her fall — so it seemed, and this was odd and inappropriate. Her features drooped and faded, and her long hair hung down sadly on either side of her face; she grew pensive and her dejected pose was that of a Magdalene in a picture by an old master.

"It's not right," she said. "You don't respect me now, you first of all." 30

There was a watermelon on the table. Gurov cut himself a slice and began eating it without haste. They were silent for at least half an hour.

There was something touching about Anna Sergeyevna; she had the purity of a well-bred, naive woman who has seen little of life. The single candle burning on the table barely illumined her face, yet it was clear that she was unhappy.

"Why should I stop respecting you, darling?" asked Gurov. "You don't know what you're saying."

"God forgive me," she said, and her eyes filled with tears. "It's terrible."

"It's as though you were trying to exonerate yourself." 35

"How can I exonerate myself? No. I am a bad, low woman; I despise myself and I have no thought of exonerating myself. It's not my husband but myself I have deceived. And not only just now; I have been deceiving myself for a long time. My husband may be a good, honest man, but he is a flunkey! I don't know what he does, what his work is, but I know he is a flunkey! I was twenty when I married him. I was tormented by curiosity; I wanted something better. 'There must be a different sort of life,' I said to myself. I wanted to live! To live, to live! Curiosity kept eating at me — you don't understand it, but I swear to God I could no longer control myself; something was going on in me: I could not be held back. I told my husband I was ill, and came here. And here I have been walking about as though in a daze, as though I were mad; and now I have become a vulgar, vile woman whom anyone may despise."

Gurov was already bored with her; he was irritated by her naive tone, by her repentance, so unexpected and so out of place; but for the tears in her eyes he might have thought she was joking or play-acting.

"I don't understand, my dear," he said softly. "What do you want?"

She hid her face on his breast and pressed close to him.

"Believe me, believe me, I beg you," she said, "I love honesty and purity, 40 and sin is loathsome to me; I don't know what I'm doing. Simple people say, 'The Evil One has led me astray.' And I may say of myself now that the Evil One has led me astray."

"Quiet, quiet," he murmured.

He looked into her fixed, frightened eyes, kissed her, spoke to her softly and affectionately, and by degrees she calmed down, and her gaiety returned; both began laughing.

Afterwards when they went out there was not a soul on the esplanade. The town with its cypresses looked quite dead, but the sea was still sounding as it broke upon the beach; a single launch was rocking on the waves and on it a lantern was blinking sleepily.

They found a cab and drove to Oreanda.

"I found out your surname in the hall just now: it was written on the board — von Dideritz," said Gurov. "Is your husband German?" 45

"No; I believe his grandfather was German, but he is Greek Orthodox himself."

At Oreanda they sat on a bench not far from the church, looked down at the sea, and were silent. Yalta was barely visible through the morning mist; white clouds rested motionlessly on the mountaintops. The leaves did not stir on the trees, cicadas twanged, and the monotonous muffled sound of the sea that rose from below spoke of the peace, the eternal sleep awaiting us. So it rumbled below when there was no Yalta, no Oreanda here; so it rumbles now, and it will rumble as indifferently and as hollowly when we are no more. And in this constancy, in this complete indifference to the life and death of each of us, there lies, perhaps, a pledge of our eternal salvation, of the unceasing advance of life upon earth, of unceasing movement towards perfection. Sitting beside a young woman who in the dawn seemed so lovely, Gurov, soothed and spellbound by these magical surroundings — the sea, the mountains, the clouds, the wide sky — thought how everything is really beautiful in this world when one reflects: everything except what we think or do ourselves when we forget the higher aims of life and our own human dignity.

A man strolled up to them — probably a guard — looked at them and walked away. And this detail, too, seemed so mysterious and beautiful. They saw a steamer arrive from Feodosia, its lights extinguished in the glow of dawn.

"There is dew on the grass," said Anna Sergeyevna, after a silence.

"Yes, it's time to go home." 50

They returned to the city.

Then they met every day at twelve o'clock on the esplanade, lunched and dined together, took walks, admired the sea. She complained that she slept badly, that she had palpitations, asked the same questions, troubled now by jealousy and now by the fear that he did not respect her sufficiently. And often in the square or the public garden, when there was no one near them, he suddenly drew her to him and kissed her passionately. Complete idleness, these kisses in broad daylight exchanged furtively in dread of someone's seeing them, the heat, the smell of the sea, and the continual flitting before his eyes of idle, well-dressed, well-fed people, worked a complete change in him; he kept telling Anna Sergeyevna how beautiful she was, how seductive, was urgently passionate; he would not move a step away from her, while she was often pensive and continually pressed him to confess that he did not respect her, did not love her in the least, and saw in her nothing but a common woman. Almost every evening rather late they drove somewhere out of town, to Oreanda or to the waterfall; and the excursion was always a success, the scenery invariably impressed them as beautiful and magnificent.

They were expecting her husband, but a letter came from him saying that he had eye-trouble, and begging his wife to return home as soon as possible. Anna Sergeyevna made haste to go.

"It's a good thing I am leaving," she said to Gurov. "It's the hand of Fate!"

She took a carriage to the railway station, and he went with her. They were 55 driving the whole day. When she had taken her place in the express, and when the second bell had rung, she said, "Let me look at you once more — let me look at you again. Like this."

She was not crying but was so sad that she seemed ill, and her face was quivering.

"I shall be thinking of you — remembering you," she said. "God bless you; be happy. Don't remember evil against me. We are parting forever — it has to be, for we ought never to have met. Well, God bless you."

The train moved off rapidly, its lights soon vanished, and a minute later there was no sound of it, as though everything had conspired to end as quickly as possible that sweet trance, that madness. Left alone on the platform, and gazing into the dark distance, Gurov listened to the twang of the grasshoppers and the hum of the telegraph wires, feeling as though he had just waked up. And he reflected, musing, that there had now been another episode or adventure in his life, and it, too, was at an end, and nothing was left of it but a memory. He was moved, sad, and slightly remorseful: this young woman whom he would never meet again had not been happy with him; he had been warm and affectionate with her, but yet in his manner, his tone, and his caresses there had been a shade of light irony, the slightly coarse arrogance of a happy male who was, besides, almost twice her age. She had constantly called him kind, exceptional, high-minded; obviously he had seemed to her different from what he really was, so he had involuntarily deceived her.

Here at the station there was already a scent of autumn in the air; it was a chilly evening.

"It is time for me to go north, too," thought Gurov as he left the platform. 60 "High time!"

III

At home in Moscow the winter routine was already established: the stoves were heated, and in the morning it was still dark when the children were having breakfast and getting ready for school, and the nurse would light the lamp for a short time. There were frosts already. When the first snow falls, on the first day the sleighs are out, it is pleasant to see the white earth, the white roofs; one draws easy, delicious breaths, and the season brings back the days of one's youth. The old limes and birches, white with hoar-frost, have a good-natured look; they are closer to one's heart than cypresses and palms, and near them one no longer wants to think of mountains and the sea.

Gurov, a native of Moscow, arrived there on a fine frosty day, and when he put on his fur coat and warm gloves and took a walk along Petrovka, and when on Saturday night he heard the bells ringing, his recent trip and the places he had visited lost all charm for him. Little by little he became immersed in Moscow life, greedily read three newspapers a day, and declared that he did not read the Moscow papers on principle. He already felt a longing for restaurants, clubs, formal dinners, anniversary celebrations, and it flattered him to entertain distinguished lawyers and actors, and to play cards with a professor at the physicians' club. He could eat a whole portion of meat stewed with pickled cabbage and served in a pan, Moscow style.

A month or so would pass and the image of Anna Sergeyevna, it seemed to him, would become misty in his memory, and only from time to time he would dream of her with her touching smile as he dreamed of others. But more than a month went by, winter came into its own, and everything was still clear in his memory as though he had parted from Anna Sergeyevna only yesterday. And his memories glowed more and more vividly. When in the evening stillness the voices of his children preparing their lessons reached his study, or when he listened to a song or to an organ playing in a restaurant, or when the storm howled in the chimney, suddenly everything would rise up in his memory: what had happened on the pier and the early morning with the mist on the mountains, and the steamer coming from Feodosia, and the kisses. He would pace about his room a long time, remembering and smiling; then his memories passed into reveries, and in his imagination the past would mingle with what was to come. He did not dream of Anna Sergeyevna, but she followed him about everywhere and watched him. When he shut his eyes he saw her before him as though she were there in the flesh; and she seemed to him lovelier, younger, tenderer than she had been, and he imagined himself a finer man than he had been in Yalta. Of evenings she peered out at him from the bookcase, from the fireplace, from the corner — he heard her breathing, the caressing rustle of her clothes. In the street he followed the women with his eyes, looking for someone who resembled her.

Already he was tormented by a strong desire to share his memories with someone. But in his home it was impossible to talk of his love, and he had no one to talk to outside; certainly he could not confide in his tenants or in anyone at the bank. And what was there to talk about? He hadn't loved her then, had he? Had there been anything beautiful, poetical, edifying, or simply interesting in his relations with Anna Sergeyevna? And he was forced to talk vaguely of love, of women, and no one guessed what he meant; only his wife would twitch her black eyebrows and say, "The part of a philanderer does not suit you at all, Dimitry."

One evening, coming out of the physicians' club with an official with whom 65 he had been playing cards, he could not resist saying:

"If you only knew what a fascinating woman I became acquainted with at Yalta!"

The official got into his sledge and was driving away, but turned suddenly and shouted: "Dmitry Dmitrich!"

"What is it?"

"You were right this evening: the sturgeon was a bit high."

These words, so commonplace, for some reason moved Gurov to indigna- 70 tion, and struck him as degrading and unclean. What savage manners, what mugs! What stupid nights, what dull, humdrum days! Frenzied gambling, gluttony, drunkenness, continual talk always about the same things! Futile pursuits and conversations always about the same topics take up the better part of one's time, the better part of one's strength, and in the end there is left a life clipped and wingless, an absurd mess, and there is no escaping or getting away from it — just as though one were in a madhouse or a prison.

Gurov, boiling with indignation, did not sleep all night. And he had a headache all the next day. And the following nights too he slept badly; he sat up in bed, thinking, or paced up and down his room. He was fed up with his children, fed up with the bank; he had no desire to go anywhere or to talk of anything.

In December during the holidays he prepared to take a trip and told his wife he was going to Petersburg to do what he could for a young friend — and he set off for S——. What for? He did not know, himself. He wanted to see Anna Sergeyevna and talk with her, to arrange a rendezvous if possible.

He arrived at S—— in the morning, and at the hotel took the best room, in which the floor was covered with gray army cloth, and on the table there was an inkstand, gray with dust and topped by a figure on horseback, its hat in its raised hand and its head broken off. The porter gave him the necessary information: von Dideritz lived in a house of his own on Staro-Goncharnaya Street, not far from the hotel: he was rich and lived well and kept his own horses; everyone in the town knew him. The porter pronounced the name: "Dridiritz."

Without haste Gurov made his way to Staro-Goncharnaya Street and found the house. Directly opposite the house stretched a long gray fence studded with nails.

"A fence like that would make one run away," thought Gurov, looking now 75 at the fence, now at the windows of the house.

He reflected: this was a holiday, and the husband was apt to be at home. And in any case, it would be tactless to go into the house and disturb her. If he were to send her a note, it might fall into her husband's hands, and that might spoil everything. The best thing was to rely on chance. And he kept walking up and down the street and along the fence, waiting for the chance. He saw a beggar go in at the gate and heard the dogs attack him; then an hour later he heard a piano, and the sound came to him faintly and indistinctly. Probably it was Anna Sergeyevna playing. The front door opened suddenly, and an old woman came out, followed by the familiar white Pomeranian. Gurov was on the point of calling to the dog, but his heart began beating violently, and in his excitement he could not remember the Pomeranian's name.

He kept walking up and down, and hated the gray fence more and more, and by now he thought irritably that Anna Sergeyevna had forgotten him, and was perhaps already diverting herself with another man, and that that was very natural in a young woman who from morning till night had to look at that damn fence. He went back to his hotel room and sat on the couch for a long while, not knowing what to do, then he had dinner and a long nap.

"How stupid and annoying all this is!" he thought when he woke and looked at the dark windows: it was already evening. "Here I've had a good sleep for some reason. What am I going to do at night?"

He sat on the bed, which was covered with a cheap gray blanket of the kind seen in hospitals, and he twitted himself in his vexation:

"So there's your lady with the pet dog. There's your adventure. A nice place 80 to cool your heels in."

That morning at the station a playbill in large letters had caught his eye. *The Geisha* was to be given for the first time. He thought of this and drove to the theater.

"It's quite possible that she goes to first nights," he thought.

The theater was full. As in all provincial theaters, there was a haze above the chandelier, the gallery was noisy and restless; in the front row, before the beginning of the performance the local dandies were standing with their hands clasped behind their backs; in the Governor's box the Governor's daughter, wearing a boa, occupied the front seat, while the Governor himself hid modestly behind the portiere and only his hands were visible; the curtain swayed; the orchestra was a long time tuning up. While the audience were coming in and taking their seats, Gurov scanned the faces eagerly.

Anna Sergeyevna, too, came in. She sat down in the third row, and when Gurov looked at her his heart contracted, and he understood clearly that in the whole world there was no human being so near, so precious, and so important to him; she, this little, undistinguished woman, lost in a provincial crowd, with a vulgar lorgnette in her hand, filled his whole life now, was his sorrow and his joy, the only happiness that he now desired for himself, and to the sounds of the bad orchestra, of the miserable local violins, he thought how lovely she was. He thought and dreamed.

A young man with small side-whiskers, very tall and stooped, came in with Anna Sergeyevna and sat down beside her; he nodded his head at every step and seemed to be bowing continually. Probably this was the husband whom at Yalta, in an access of bitter feeling, she had called a flunkey. And there really was in his lanky figure, his side-whiskers, his small bald patch, something of a flunkey's retiring manner; his smile was mawkish, and in his buttonhole there was an academic badge like a waiter's number. 85

During the first intermission the husband went out to have a smoke; she remained in her seat. Gurov, who was also sitting in the orchestra, went up to her and said in a shaky voice, with a forced smile:

"Good evening!"

She glanced at him and turned pale, then looked at him again in horror, unable to believe her eyes, and gripped the fan and the lorgnette tightly together in her hands, evidently trying to keep herself from fainting. Both were silent. She was sitting, he was standing, frightened by her distress and not daring to take a seat beside her. The violins and the flute that were being tuned up sang out. He suddenly felt frightened: it seemed as if all the people in the boxes were looking at them. She got up and went hurriedly to the exit; he followed her, and both of them walked blindly along the corridors and up and down stairs, and figures in the uniforms prescribed for magistrates, teachers, and officials of the Department of Crown Lands, all wearing badges, flitted before their eyes, as did also ladies, and fur coats on hangers; they were conscious of drafts and the smell of stale tobacco. And Gurov, whose heart was beating violently, thought:

"Oh, Lord! Why are these people here and this orchestra!"

And at that instant he suddenly recalled how when he had seen Anna 90 Sergeyevna off at the station he had said to himself that all was over between them and that they would never meet again. But how distant the end still was!

On the narrow, gloomy staircase over which it said "To the Amphitheatre," she stopped.

"How you frightened me!" she said, breathing hard, still pale and stunned. "Oh, how you frightened me! I am barely alive. Why did you come? Why?"

"But do understand, Anna, do understand — " he said hurriedly, under his breath. "I implore you, do understand — "

She looked at him with fear, with entreaty, with love; she looked at him intently, to keep his features more distinctly in her memory.

"I suffer so," she went on, not listening to him. "All this time I have been 95 thinking of nothing but you; I live only by the thought of you. And I wanted to forget, to forget; but why, oh, why have you come?"

On the landing above them two high school boys were looking down and smoking, but it was all the same to Gurov; he drew Anna Sergeyevna to him and began kissing her face and her hands.

"What are you doing, what are you doing!" she was saying in horror, pushing him away. "We have lost our senses. Go away today; go away at once — I conjure you by all that is sacred, I implore you — People are coming this way!"

Someone was walking up the stairs.

"You must leave," Anna Sergeyevna went on in a whisper. "Do you hear, Dmitry Dmitrich? I will come and see you in Moscow. I have never been happy; I am unhappy now, and I never, never shall be happy, never! So don't make me suffer still more! I swear I'll come to Moscow. But now let us part. My dear, good, precious one, let us part!"

She pressed his hand and walked rapidly downstairs, turning to look round 100 at him, and from her eyes he could see that she really was unhappy. Gurov stood for a while, listening, then when all grew quiet, he found his coat and left the theater.

IV

And Anna Sergeyevna began coming to see him in Moscow. Once every two or three months she left S——, telling her husband that she was going to consult a doctor about a woman's ailment from which she was suffering — and her husband did and did not believe her. When she arrived in Moscow she would stop at the Slavyansky Bazar Hotel, and at once send a man in a red cap to Gurov. Gurov came to see her, and no one in Moscow knew of it.

Once he was going to see her in this way on a winter morning (the messenger had come the evening before and not found him in). With him walked his daughter, whom he wanted to take to school: it was on the way. Snow was coming down in big wet flakes.

"It's three degrees above zero,° and yet it's snowing," Gurov was saying to his daughter. "But this temperature prevails only on the surface of the earth; in the upper layers of the atmosphere there is quite a different temperature."

"And why doesn't it thunder in winter, papa?"

He explained that, too. He talked, thinking all the while that he was on his 105 way to a rendezvous, and no living soul knew of it, and probably no one would ever know. He had two lives: an open one, seen and known by all who needed to know it, full of conventional truth and conventional falsehood, exactly like the lives of his friends and acquaintances; and another life that went on in secret. And through some strange, perhaps accidental, combination of circumstances, everything that was of interest and importance to him, everything that was essential to him, everything about which he felt sincerely and did not deceive

three degrees above zero: On the Celsius scale; about thirty-eight degrees Fahrenheit.

himself, everything that constituted the core of his life, was going on concealed from others; while all that was false, the shell in which he hid to cover the truth — his work at the bank, for instance, his discussions at the club, his references to the "inferior race," his appearances at anniversary celebrations with his wife — all that went on in the open. Judging others by himself, he did not believe what he saw, and always fancied that every man led his real, most interesting life under cover of secrecy as under cover of night. The personal life of every individual is based on secrecy, and perhaps it is partly for that reason that civilized man is so nervously anxious that personal privacy should be respected.

Having taken his daughter to school, Gurov went on to the Slavyansky Bazar Hotel. He took off his fur coat in the lobby, went upstairs, and knocked gently at the door. Anna Sergeyevna, wearing his favorite gray dress, exhausted by the journey and by waiting, had been expecting him since the previous evening. She was pale, and looked at him without a smile, and he had hardly entered when she flung herself on his breast. Their kiss was a long, lingering one, as though they had not seen one another for two years.

"Well, darling, how are you getting on there?" he asked. "What news?"

"Wait; I'll tell you in a moment — I can't speak."

She could not speak; she was crying. She turned away from him, and pressed her handkerchief to her eyes.

"Let her have her cry; meanwhile I'll sit down," he thought, and he seated   110
himself in an armchair.

Then he rang and ordered tea, and while he was having his tea she remained standing at the window with her back to him. She was crying out of sheer agitation, in the sorrowful consciousness that their life was so sad; that they could only see each other in secret and had to hide from people like thieves! Was it not a broken life?

"Come, stop now, dear!" he said.

It was plain to him that this love of theirs would not be over soon, that the end of it was not in sight. Anna Sergeyevna was growing more and more attached to him. She adored him, and it was unthinkable to tell her that their love was bound to come to an end some day; besides, she would not have believed it!

He went up to her and took her by the shoulders, to fondle her and say something diverting, and at that moment he caught sight of himself in the mirror.

His hair was already beginning to turn gray. And it seemed odd to him that   115
he had grown so much older in the last few years, and lost his looks. The shoulders on which his hands rested were warm and heaving. He felt compassion for this life, still so warm and lovely, but probably already about to begin to fade and wither like his own. Why did she love him so much? He always seemed to women different from what he was, and they loved in him not himself, but the man whom their imagination created and whom they had been eagerly seeking all their lives; and afterwards, when they saw their mistake, they loved him nevertheless. And not one of them had been happy with him. In the past he had met women, come together with them, parted from them, but he had never once loved; it was anything you please, but not love. And only now when his head was gray he had fallen in love, really, truly — for the first time in his life.

Anna Sergeyevna and he loved each other as people do who are very close and intimate, like man and wife, like tender friends; it seemed to them that Fate itself had meant them for one another, and they could not understand why he had a wife and she a husband; and it was as though they were a pair of migratory birds, male and female, caught and forced to live in different cages. They forgave each other what they were ashamed of in their past, they forgave everything in the present, and felt that this love of theirs had altered them both.

Formerly in moments of sadness he had soothed himself with whatever logical arguments came into his head, but now he no longer cared for logic; he felt profound compassion, he wanted to be sincere and tender.

"Give it up now, my darling," he said. "You've had your cry; that's enough. Let us have a talk now, we'll think up something."

Then they spent a long time taking counsel together, they talked of how to avoid the necessity for secrecy, for deception, for living in different cities, and not seeing one another for long stretches of time. How could they free themselves from these intolerable fetters?

"How? How?" he asked, clutching his head. "How?"   120

And it seemed as though in a little while the solution would be found, and then a new and glorious life would begin; and it was clear to both of them that the end was still far off, and that what was to be most complicated and difficult for them was only just beginning.

Considerations for Critical Thinking and Writing

1. Why is it significant that the setting of this story is a resort town? How does the vacation atmosphere affect the action?
2. What does Gurov's view of women reveal about him? Why does he regard them as an "inferior race"?
3. What do we learn about Gurov's wife and Anna's husband? Why do you think Chekhov includes this exposition? How does it affect our view of the lovers?
4. When and why do Gurov's feelings about Anna begin to change? Is he really in love with her?
5. Who or what is the antagonist in this story? What is the nature of the conflict?
6. What is the effect of Gurov being the central consciousness? How would the story be different if it were told from Anna's perspective?
7. Why do you think Chekhov does not report what ultimately becomes of the lovers? Is there a resolution to the conflict? Is the ending of the story effective?
8. Discuss the validity of Gurov's belief that people lead their real lives in private rather than in public: "The personal life of every individual is based on secrecy, and perhaps it is partly for that reason that civilized man is so nervously anxious that personal privacy should be respected."
9. Describe your response to Gurov in Parts I and II, and discuss how your judgment of him changes in the last two parts of the story.
10. Based on your understanding of the characterizations of Gurov and Anna, consider the final paragraph of the story and summarize what you think will happen to them.
11. Consider the following assessment of the story: "No excuses can be made for the lovers' adulterous affair. They behave selfishly and irresponsibly. They are immoral — and so is the story." Explain what you think Chekhov's response to this view would be, given his treatment of the lovers.

ANTON CHEKHOV (1860–1904)
On Morality in Fiction
1890

You abuse me for objectivity, calling it indifference to good and evil, lack of ideals and ideas, and so on. You would have me, when I describe horse-thieves, say: "Stealing horses is an evil." But that has been known for ages without my saying so. Let the jury judge them; it's my job simply to show what sort of people they are. I write: You are dealing with horse-thieves, so let me tell you that they are not beggars but well-fed people, that they are people of a special cult, and that horse-stealing is not simply theft but a passion. Of course it would be pleasant to combine art with a sermon, but for me personally it is extremely difficult and almost impossible, owing to the conditions of technique. You see, to depict horse-thieves in seven hundred lines I must all the time speak and think in their tone and feel in their spirit, otherwise, if I introduce subjectivity, the image becomes blurred and the story will not be as compact as all short stories ought to be. When I write, I reckon entirely upon the reader to add for himself the subjective elements that are lacking in the story.

From a letter to Aleksey S. Suvorin in *Letters on the Short Story, the Drama, and Other Literary Topics* by Anton Chekhov

Considerations for Critical Thinking and Writing

1. Why does Chekhov reject sermonizing in his fiction?
2. How does his "objectivity" affect your reading of "The Lady with the Pet Dog"?
3. Compare and contrast Chekhov's views with Thomas Jefferson's belief that fiction should offer "sound morality" (p. 568).

JOYCE CAROL OATES (b. 1938)

Raised in upstate New York, Joyce Carol Oates earned degrees at Syracuse University and the University of Wisconsin. Both the range and volume of her writing are extensive. A writer of novels, plays, short stories, poetry, and literary criticism, she has published some eighty books. Oates has described the subject matter of her fiction as "real people in a real society," but her method of expression ranges from the realistic to the experimental. Her novels include *them* (1969), *Do with Me What You Will* (1973), *Childwold* (1976), *Bellefleur* (1980), *A Bloodsmoor Romance* (1982), *Marya: A Life* (1986), and *You Must Remember This* (1987). Among her collections of short stories are *Marriages and Infidelities* (1972), which includes "The Lady with the Pet Dog," *Raven's Wing* (1986), *The Assignation* (1988), and *Heat* (1991). This story is her modern version of the Chekhov story of the same name, this time told from the woman's perspective.

The Lady with the Pet Dog   1972

I

Strangers parted as if to make way for him.

There he stood. He was there in the aisle, a few yards away, watching her.

She leaned forward at once in her seat, her hand jerked up to her face as if to ward off a blow — but then the crowd in the aisle hid him, he was gone. She pressed both hands against her cheeks. He was not here, she had imagined him.

"My God," she whispered.

She was alone. Her husband had gone out to the foyer to make a telephone call; it was intermission at the concert, a Thursday evening.

Now she saw him again, clearly. He was standing there. He was staring at her. Her blood rocked in her body, draining out of her head . . . she was going to faint . . . They stared at each other. They gave no sign of recognition. Only when he took a step forward did she shake her head *no — no — keep away.* It was not possible.

When her husband returned, she was staring at the place in the aisle where her lover had been standing. Her husband leaned forward to interrupt that stare.

"What's wrong?" he said. "Are you sick?"

Panic rose in her in long shuddering waves. She tried to get to her feet, panicked at the thought of fainting here, and her husband took hold of her. She stood like an aged woman, clutching the seat before her.

At home he helped her up the stairs and she lay down. Her head was like a large piece of crockery that had to be held still, it was so heavy. She was still panicked. She felt it in the shallows of her face, behind her knees, in the pit of her stomach. It sickened her, it made her think of mucus, of something thick and gray congested inside her, stuck to her, that was herself and yet not herself — a poison.

She lay with her knees drawn up toward her chest, her eyes hotly open, while her husband spoke to her. She imagined that other man saying, *Why did you run away from me?* Her husband was saying other words. She tried to listen to them. He was going to call the doctor, he said, and she tried to sit up. "No, I'm all right now," she said quickly. The panic was like lead inside her, so thickly congested. How slow love was to drain out of her, how fluid and sticky it was inside her head!

Her husband believed her. No doctor. No threat. Grateful, she drew her husband down to her. They embraced, not comfortably. For years now they had not been comfortable together, in their intimacy and at a distance, and now they struggled gently as if the paces of this dance were too rigorous for them. It was something they might have known once, but had now outgrown. The panic in her thickened at this double betrayal: she drew her husband to her, she caressed him wildly, she shut her eyes to think about that other man.

A crowd of men and women parting, unexpectedly, and there he stood — there he stood — she kept seeing him, and yet her vision blotched at the memory. It had been finished between them, six months before, but he had come out here . . . and she had escaped him, now she was lying in her husband's arms, in his embrace, her face pressed against his. It was a kind of sleep, this love-making. She felt herself falling asleep, her body falling from her. Her eyes shut.

"I love you," her husband said fiercely, angrily.

She shut her eyes and thought of that other man, as if betraying him would 15 give her life a center.

"Did I hurt you? Are you — ?" Her husband whispered.

Always this hot flashing of shame between them, the shame of her husband's near failure, the clumsiness of his love —

"You didn't hurt me," she said.

II

They had said good-by six months before. He drove her from Nantucket, where they had met, to Albany, New York, where she visited her sister. The hours of intimacy in the car had sealed something between them, a vow of silence and impersonality: she recalled the movement of the highways, the passing of other cars, the natural rhythms of the day hypnotizing her toward sleep while he drove. She trusted him, she could sleep in his presence. Yet she could not really fall asleep in spite of her exhaustion, and she kept jerking awake, frightened, to discover that nothing had changed — still the stranger who was driving her to Albany, still the highway, the sky, the antiseptic odor of the rented car, the sense of a rhythm behind the rhythm of the air that might unleash itself at any second. Everywhere on this highway, at this moment, there were men and women driving together, bonded together — what did that mean, to be together? What did it mean to enter into a bond with another person?

No, she did not really trust him; she did not really trust men. He would 20 glance at her with his small cautious smile and she felt a declaration of shame between them.

Shame.

In her head she rehearsed conversations. She said bitterly, "You'll be relieved when we get to Albany. Relieved to get rid of me." They had spent so many days talking, confessing too much, driven to a pitch of childish excitement, laughing together on the beach, breaking into that pose of laughter that seems to eradicate the soul, so many days of this that the silence of the trip was like the silence of a hospital — all these surface noises, these rattles and hums, but an interior silence, a befuddlement. She said to him in her imagination, "One of us should die." Then she leaned over to touch him. She caressed the back of his neck. She said, aloud, "Would you like me to drive for a while?"

They stopped at a picnic area where other cars were stopped — couples, families — and walked together, smiling at their good luck. He put his arm around her shoulders and she sensed how they were in a posture together, a man and a woman forming a posture, a figure, that someone might sketch and show to them. She said slowly, "I don't want to go back. . . ."

Silence. She looked up at him. His face was heavy with her words, as if she had pulled at his skin with her fingers. Children ran nearby and distracted him — yes, he was a father too, his children ran like that, they tugged at his skin with their light, busy fingers.

"Are you so unhappy?" he said.   25

"I'm not unhappy, back there. I'm nothing. There's nothing to me," she said.

They stared at each other. The sensation between them was intense, exhausting. She thought that this man was her savior, that he had come to her at a time in her life when her life demanded completion, an end, a permanent fixing of all that was troubled and shifting and deadly. And yet it was absurd to think this. No person could save another. So she drew back from him and released him.

A few hours later they stopped at a gas station in a small city. She went to the women's rest room, having to ask the attendant for a key, and when she came back her eye jumped nervously onto the rented car — why? did she think he might have driven off without her? — onto the man, her friend, standing in conversation with the young attendant. Her friend was as old as her husband, over forty, with lanky, sloping shoulders, a full body, his hair thick, a dark, burnished brown, a festive color that made her eye twitch a little — and his hands were always moving, always those rapid conversational circles, going nowhere, gestures that were at once a little aggressive and apologetic.

She put her hand on his arm, a claim. He turned to her and smiled and she felt that she loved him, that everything in her life had forced her to this moment and that she had no choice about it.

They sat in the car for two hours, in Albany, in the parking lot of a Howard 30
Johnson's restaurant, talking, trying to figure out their past. There was no future. They concentrated on the past, the several days behind them, lit up with a hot, dazzling August sun, like explosions that already belonged to other people, to strangers. Her face was faintly reflected in the green-tinted curve of the windshield, but she could not have recognized that face. She began to cry; she told herself: *I am not here, this will pass, this is nothing.* Still, she could not stop crying. The muscles of her face were springy, like a child's, unpredictable muscles. He stroked her arms, her shoulders, trying to comfort her. "This is so hard . . . this is impossible . . ." he said. She felt panic for the world outside this car, all that was not herself and this man, and at the same time she understood that she was free of him, as people are free of other people, she would leave him soon, safely, and within a few days he would have fallen into the past, the impersonal past. . . .

"I'm so ashamed of myself!" she said finally.

She returned to her husband and saw that another woman, a shadow-woman, had taken her place — noiseless and convincing, like a dancer performing certain difficult steps. Her husband folded her in his arms and talked to her of his own loneliness, his worries about his business, his health, his mother, kept tranquilized and mute in a nursing home, and her spirit detached itself from her and drifted about the rooms of the large house she lived in with her husband, a shadow-woman delicate and imprecise. There was no boundary to her, no edge. Alone, she took hot baths and sat exhausted in the steaming water, wondering at her perpetual exhaustion. All that winter she noticed the limp, languid weight of her arms, her veins bulging slightly with the pressure of her extreme weariness. *This is fate,* she thought, to be here and not there, to be one person and not another, a certain man's wife and not the wife of another man. The long, slow pain of this certainty rose in her, but it never became clear, it was baffling and imprecise. She could not be serious about it; she kept congratulating herself on her own good luck, to have escaped so easily, to have freed herself. So much love had gone into the first several years of her marriage that there wasn't much left, now, for another man. . . . She was certain of that. But the bath water made her dizzy, all that perpetual heat, and one day in January she drew a razor blade lightly across the inside of her arm, near the elbow, to see what would happen.

Afterward she wrapped a small towel around it, to stop the bleeding. The towel soaked through. She wrapped a bath towel around that and walked through the empty rooms of her home, lightheaded, hardly aware of the stubborn seeping of blood. There was no boundary to her in this house, no precise limit. She could flow out like her own blood and come to no end.

She sat for a while on a blue love seat, her mind empty. Her husband telephoned her when he would be staying late at the plant. He talked to her always about his plans, his problems, his business friends, his future. It was obvious that he had a future. As he spoke she nodded to encourage him, and her heartbeat quickened with the memory of her own, personal shame, the shame of this man's particular, private wife. One evening at dinner he leaned forward and put his head in his arms and fell asleep, like a child. She sat at the table with him for a while, watching him. His hair had gone gray, almost white, at the temples — no one would guess that he was so quick, so careful a man, still fairly young about the eyes. She put her hand on his head, lightly, as if to prove to herself that he was real. He slept, exhausted.

One evening they went to a concert and she looked up to see her lover 35 there, in the crowded aisle, in this city, watching her. He was standing there, with his overcoat on, watching her. She went cold. That morning the telephone had rung while her husband was still home, and she had heard him answer it, heard him hang up — it must have been a wrong number — and when the telephone rang again, at 9:30, she had been afraid to answer it. She had left home to be out of the range of that ringing, but now, in this public place, in this busy auditorium, she found herself staring at that man, unable to make any sign to him, any gesture of recognition. . . .

He would have come to her but she shook her head. *No. Stay away.*

Her husband helped her out of the row of seats, saying, "Excuse us, please. Excuse us," so that strangers got to their feet, quickly, alarmed, to let them pass. Was that woman about to faint? What was wrong?

At home she felt the blood drain slowly back into her head. Her husband embraced her hips, pressing his face against her, in that silence that belonged to the earliest days of their marriage. She thought, *He will drive it out of me.* He made love to her and she was back in the auditorium again, sitting alone, now that the concert was over. The stage was empty; the heavy velvet curtains had not been drawn; the musicians' chairs were empty, everything was silent and expectant; in the aisle her lover stood and smiled at her — Her husband was impatient. He was apart from her, working on her, operating on her; and then, stricken, he whispered, "Did I hurt you?"

The telephone rang the next morning. Dully, sluggishly, she answered it. She recognized his voice at once — that "Anna?" with its lifting of the second syllable, questioning and apologetic and making its claim — "Yes, what do you want?" she said.

"Just to see you. Please — "   40

"I can't."

"Anna, I'm sorry, I didn't mean to upset you — "

"I can't see you."

"Just for a few minutes — I have to talk to you — "

"But why, why now? Why now?" she said.   45

She heard her voice rising, but she could not stop it. He began to talk again, drowning her out. She remembered his rapid conversation. She remembered his gestures, the witty energetic circling of his hands.

"Please don't hang up!" he cried.

"I can't — I don't want to go through it again — "

"I'm not going to hurt you. Just tell me how you are."

"Everything is the same."   50

"Everything is the same with me."

She looked up at the ceiling, shyly. "Your wife? Your children?"

"The same."

"Your son?"

"He's fine — "   55

"I'm so glad to hear that. I — "

"Is it still the same with you, your marriage? Tell me what you feel. What are you thinking?"

"I don't know. . . ."

She remembered his intense, eager words, the movement of his hands, that impatient precise fixing of the air by his hands, the jabbing of his fingers.

"Do you love me?" he said.   60

She could not answer.

"I'll come over to see you," he said.

"No," she said.

What will come next, what will happen?

Flesh hardening on his body, aging. Shrinking. He will grow old, but not 65
soft like her husband. They are two different types: he is nervous, lean, energetic, wise. She will grow thinner, as the tension radiates out from her backbone, wearing down her flesh. Her collarbones will jut out of her skin. Her husband, caressing her in their bed, will discover that she is another woman — she is not there with him — instead she is rising in an elevator in a downtown hotel, carrying a book as a prop, or walking quickly away from that hotel, her head bent and filled with secrets. Love, what to do with it? . . . Useless as moths' wings, as moths' fluttering. . . . She feels the flutterings of silky, crazy wings in her chest.

He flew out to visit her every several weeks, staying at a different hotel each time. He telephoned her, and she drove down to park in an underground garage at the very center of the city.

She lay in his arms while her husband talked to her, miles away, one body fading into another. He will grow old, his body will change, she thought, pressing her cheek against the back of one of these men. If it was her lover, they were in a hotel room: always the propped-up little booklet describing the hotel's many services, with color photographs of its cocktail lounge and dining room and coffee shop. Grow old, leave me, die, go back to your neurotic wife and your sad, ordinary children, she thought, but still her eyes closed gratefully against his skin and she felt how complete their silence was, how they had come to rest in each other.

"Tell me about your life here. The people who love you," he said, as he always did.

One afternoon they lay together for four hours. It was her birthday and she was intoxicated with her good fortune, this prize of the afternoon, this man in her arms! She was a little giddy, she talked too much. She told him about her parents, about her husband. . . . "They were all people I believed in, but it turned out wrong. Now, I believe in you. . . ." He laughed as if shocked by her words. She did not understand. Then she understood. "But I believe truly in you. I can't think of myself without you," she said. . . . He spoke of his wife, her ambitions, her intelligence, her use of the children against him, her use of his younger son's blindness, all of his words gentle and hypnotic and convincing in the late afternoon peace of this hotel room . . . and she felt the terror of laughter, threatening laughter. Their words, like their bodies, were aging.

She dressed quickly in the bathroom, drawing her long hair up around the back of her head, fixing it as always, anxious that everything be the same. Her face was slightly raw, from his face. The rubbing of his skin. Her eyes were too bright, wearily bright. Her hair was blond but not so blond as it had been that summer in the white Nantucket air.

She ran water and splashed it on her face. She blinked at the water. Blind. Drowning. She thought with satisfaction that soon, soon, he would be back home, in that house on Long Island she had never seen, with that woman she had never seen, sitting on the edge of another bed, putting on his shoes. She wanted nothing except to be free of him. Why not be free? *Oh*, she thought suddenly, *I will follow you back and kill you. You and her and the little boy. What is there to stop me?*

She left him. Everyone on the street pitied her, that look of absolute zero.

III

A man and a child, approaching her. The sharp acrid smell of fish. The crashing of waves. Anna pretended not to notice the father with his son — there was something strange about them. That frank, silent intimacy, too gentle, the man's bare feet in the water and the boy a few feet away, leaning away from his father. He was about nine years old and still his father held his hand.

A small yipping dog, a golden dog, bounded near them.

Anna turned shyly back to her reading; she did not want to have to speak 75
to these neighbors. She saw the man's shadow falling over her legs, then over
the pages of her book, and she had the idea that he wanted to see what she was
reading. The dog nuzzled her; the man called him away.

She watched them walk down the beach. She was relieved that the man
had not spoken to her.

She saw them in town later that day, the two of them brown-haired and
patient, now wearing sandals, walking with that same look of care. The man's
white shorts were soiled and a little baggy. His pullover shirt was a faded green.
His face was broad, the cheekbones wide, spaced widely apart, the eyes stark in
their sockets, as if they fastened onto objects for no reason, ponderous and edgy.
The little boy's face was pale and sharp; his lips were perpetually parted.

Anna realized that the child was blind.

The next morning, early, she caught sight of them again. For some reason
she went to the back door of her cottage. She faced the sea breeze eagerly. Her
heart hammered. . . . She had been here, in her family's old house, for three
days, alone, bitterly satisfied at being alone, and now it was a puzzle to her how
her soul strained to fly outward, to meet with another person. She watched the
man with his son, his cautious, rather stooped shoulders above the child's small
shoulders.

The man was carrying something, it looked like a notebook. He sat on the 80
sand, not far from Anna's spot of the day before, and the dog rushed up to them.
The child approached the edge of the ocean, timidly. He moved in short jerky
steps, his legs stiff. The dog ran around him. Anna heard the child crying out a
word that sounded like "Ty" — it must have been the dog's name — and then
the man joined in, his voice heavy and firm.

"Ty —"

Anna tied her hair back with a yellow scarf and went down to the beach.

The man glanced around at her. He smiled. She stared past him at the
waves. To talk to him or not to talk — she had the freedom of that choice. For
a moment she felt that she had made a mistake, that the child and the dog
would not protect her, that behind this man's ordinary, friendly face there was
a certain arrogant maleness — then she relented, she smiled shyly.

"A nice house you've got there," the man said.

She nodded her thanks. 85

The man pushed his sunglasses up on his forehead. Yes, she recognized
the eyes of the day before — intelligent and nervous, the sockets pale, untanned.

"Is that your telephone ringing?" he said.

She did not bother to listen. "It's a wrong number," she said.

Her husband calling: she had left home for a few days, to be alone.

But the man, settling himself on the sand, seemed to misinterpret this. He 90
smiled in surprise, one corner of his mouth higher than the other. He said
nothing. Anna wondered: *What is he thinking?* The dog was leaping about her,
panting against her legs, and she laughed in embarrassment. She bent to pet it,
grateful for its busyness. "Don't let him jump up on you," the man said. "He's a
nuisance."

The dog was a small golden retriever, a young dog. The blind child, standing
now in the water, turned to call the dog to him. His voice was shrill and impatient.

"Our house is the third one down — the white one," the man said.

She turned, startled. "Oh, did you buy it from Dr. Patrick? Did he die?"

"Yes, finally. . . ."

Her eyes wandered nervously over the child and the dog. She felt the 95
nervous beat of her heart out to the very tips of her fingers, the fleshy tips of
her fingers: little hearts were there, pulsing. *What is he thinking?* The man had
opened his notebook. He had a piece of charcoal and he began to sketch
something.

Anna looked down at him. She saw the top of his head, his thick brown
hair, the freckles on his shoulders, the quick, deft movement of his hand. Upside
down, Anna herself being drawn. She smiled in surprise.

"Let me draw you. Sit down," he said.

She knelt awkwardly a few yards away. He turned the page of the sketch
pad. The dog ran to her and she sat, straightening out her skirt beneath her,
flinching from the dog's tongue. "Ty!" cried the child. Anna sat, and slowly the
pleasure of the moment began to glow in her; her skin flushed with gratitude.

She sat there for nearly an hour. The man did not talk much. Back and
forth the dog bounded, shaking itself. The child came to sit near them, in silence.
Anna felt that she was drifting into a kind of trance while the man sketched her,
half a dozen rapid sketches, the surface of her face given up to him. "Where are
you from?" the man asked.

"Ohio. My husband lives in Ohio." 100

She wore no wedding band.

"Your wife — " Anna began.

"Yes?"

"Is she here?"

"Not right now." 105

She was silent, ashamed. She had asked an improper question. But the man
did not seem to notice. He continued drawing her, bent over the sketch pad.
When Anna said she had to go, he showed her the drawings — one after another
of her, Anna, recognizably Anna, a woman in her early thirties, her hair smooth
and flat across the top of her head, tied behind by a scarf. "Take the one you
like best," he said, and she picked one of her with the dog in her lap, sitting
very straight, her brows and eyes clearly defined, her lips girlishly pursed, the
dog and her dress suggested by a few quick irregular lines.

"Lady with pet dog," the man said.

She spent the rest of that day reading, nearer her cottage. It was not really
a cottage — it was a two-story house, large and ungainly and weathered. It was
mixed up in her mind with her family, her own childhood, and she glanced up
from her book, perplexed, as if waiting for one of her parents or her sister to
come up to her. Then she thought of that man, the man with the blind child,
the man with the dog, and she could not concentrate on her reading. Someone —
probably her father — had marked a passage that must be important, but
she kept reading and rereading it: *We try to discover in things, endeared to
us on that account, the spiritual glamour which we ourselves have cast upon
them; we are disillusioned, and learn that they are in themselves barren and
devoid of the charm that they owed, in our minds, to the association of certain
ideas. . . .*

She thought again of the man on the beach. She lay the book aside and
thought of him: his eyes, his aloneness, his drawings of her.

They began seeing each other after that. He came to her front door in the 110
evening, without the child; he drove her into town for dinner. She was shy and
extremely pleased. The darkness of the expensive restaurant released her; she
heard herself chatter; she leaned forward and seemed to be offering her face up
to him, listening to him. He talked about his work on a Long Island newspaper
and she seemed to be listening to him, as she stared at his face, arranging her
own face into the expression she had seen in that charcoal drawing. Did he see
her like that, then? — girlish and withdrawn and patrician? She felt the weight
of his interest in her, a force that fell upon her like a blow. A repeated blow. Of
course he was married, he had children — of course she was married, permanently married. This flight from her husband was not important. She had left
him before, to be alone, it was not important. Everything in her was slender and
delicate and not important.

They walked for hours after dinner, looking at the other strollers, the
weekend visitors, the tourists, the couples like themselves. Surely they were
mistaken for a couple, a married couple. *This is the hour in which everything is
decided,* Anna thought. They had both had several drinks and they talked a great
deal. Anna found herself saying too much, stopping and starting giddily. She put
her hand to her forehead, feeling faint.

"It's from the sun — you've had too much sun — " he said.

At the door to her cottage, on the front porch, she heard herself asking
him if he would like to come in. She allowed him to lead her inside, to close
the door. *This is not important,* she thought clearly, *he doesn't mean it, he
doesn't love me, nothing will come of it.* She was frightened, yet it seemed
to her necessary to give in; she had to leave Nantucket with that act completed,
an act of adultery, an accomplishment she would take back to Ohio and to her
marriage.

Later, incredibly, she heard herself asking: "Do you . . . do you love me?"

"You're so beautiful!" he said, amazed.   115

She felt this beauty, shy and glowing and centered in her eyes. He stared
at her. In this large, drafty house, alone together, they were like accomplices,
conspirators. She could not think: how old was she? which year was this? They
had done something unforgivable together, and the knowledge of it was tugging
at their faces. A cloud seemed to pass over her. She felt herself smiling shrilly.

Afterward, a peculiar raspiness, a dryness of breath. He was silent. She felt
a strange, idle fear, a sense of the danger outside this room and this old
comfortable bed — a danger that would not recognize her as the lady in that
drawing, the lady with the pet dog. There was nothing to say to this man, this
stranger. She felt the beauty draining out of her face, her eyes fading.

"I've got to be alone," she told him.

He left, and she understood that she would not see him again. She stood
by the window of the room, watching the ocean. A sense of shame overpowered
her: it was smeared everywhere on her body, the smell of it, the richness of it.
She tried to recall him, and his face was confused in her memory: she would
have to shout to him across a jumbled space, she would have to wave her arms
wildly. *You love me! You must love me!* But she knew he did not love her, and
she did not love him; he was a man who drew everything up into himself, like
all men, walking away, free to walk away, free to have his own thoughts, free to
envision her body, all the secrets of her body. . . . And she lay down again in

the bed, feeling how heavy this body had become, her insides heavy with shame, the very backs of her eyelids coated with shame.

"This is the end of one part of my life," she thought. 120

But in the morning the telephone rang. She answered it. It was her lover: they talked brightly and happily. She could hear the eagerness in his voice, the love in his voice, that same still, sad amazement — she understood how simple life was, there were no problems.

They spent most of their time on the beach, with the child and the dog. He joked and was serious at the same time. He said, once, "You have defined my soul for me," and she laughed to hide her alarm. In a few days it was time for her to leave. He got a sitter for the boy and took the ferry with her to the mainland, then rented a car to drive her up to Albany. She kept thinking: *Now something will happen. It will come to an end.* But most of the drive was silent and hypnotic. She wanted him to joke with her, to say again that she had defined his soul for him, but he drove fast, he was serious, she distrusted the hawkish look of his profile — she did not know him at all. At a gas station she splashed her face with cold water. Alone in the grubby little rest room, shaky and very much alone. In such places are women totally alone with their bodies. The body grows heavier, more evil, in such silence. . . . On the beach everything had been noisy with sunlight and gulls and waves; here, as if run to earth, everything was cramped and silent and dead.

She went outside, squinting. There he was, talking with the station attendant. She could not think as she returned to him whether she wanted to live or not.

She stayed in Albany for a few days, then flew home to her husband. He met her at the airport, near the luggage counter, where her three pieces of pale-brown luggage were brought to him on a conveyer belt, to be claimed by him. He kissed her on the cheek. They shook hands, a little embarrassed. She had come home again.

"How will I live out the rest of my life?" she wondered. 125

In January her lover spied on her: she glanced up and saw him, in a public place, in the DeRoy Symphony Hall. She was paralyzed with fear. She nearly fainted. In this faint she felt her husband's body, loving her, working its love upon her, and she shut her eyes harder to keep out the certainty of his love — sometimes he failed at loving her, sometimes he succeeded, it had nothing to do with her or her pity or her ten years of love for him, it had nothing to do with a woman at all. It was a private act accomplished by a man, a husband, or a lover, in communion with his own soul, his manhood.

Her husband was forty-two years old now, growing slowly into middle age, getting heavier, softer. Her lover was about the same age, narrower in the shoulders, with a full, solid chest, yet lean, nervous. She thought, in her paralysis, of men and how they love freely and eagerly so long as their bodies are capable of love, love for a woman; and then, as love fades in their bodies, it fades from their souls and they become immune and immortal and ready to die.

Her husband was a little rough with her, as if impatient with himself. "I love you," he said fiercely, angrily. And then, ashamed, he said, "Did I hurt you? . . ."

"You didn't hurt me," she said.

Her voice was too shrill for their embrace. 130

While he was in the bathroom she went to her closet and took out that drawing of the summer before. There she was, on the beach at Nantucket, a lady with a pet dog, her eyes large and defined, the dog in her lap hardly more than a few snarls, a few coarse soft lines of charcoal . . . her dress smeared, her arms oddly limp . . . her hands not well drawn at all. . . . She tried to think: did she love the man who had drawn this? did he love her? The fever in her husband's body had touched her and driven her temperature up, and now she stared at the drawing with a kind of lust, fearful of seeing an ugly soul in that woman's face, fearful of seeing the face suddenly through her lover's eyes. She breathed quickly and harshly, staring at the drawing.

And so, the next day, she went to him at his hotel. She wept, pressing against him, demanding of him, "What do you want? Why are you here? Why don't you let me alone?" He told her that he wanted nothing. He expected nothing. He would not cause trouble.

"I want to talk about last August," he said.

"Don't — " she said.

She was hypotized by his gesturing hands, his nervousness, his obvious 135 agitation. He kept saying, "I understand. I'm making no claims upon you."

They became lovers again.

He called room service for something to drink and they sat side by side on his bed, looking through a copy of *The New Yorker,* laughing at the cartoons. It was so peaceful in this room, so complete. They were on a holiday. It was a secret holiday. Four-thirty in the afternoon, on a Friday, an ordinary Friday: a secret holiday.

"I won't bother you again," he said.

He flew back to see her again in March, and in late April. He telephoned her from his hotel — a different hotel each time — and she came down to him at once. She rose to him in various elevators, she knocked on the doors of various rooms, she stepped into his embrace, breathless and guilty and already angry with him, pleading with him. One morning in May, when he telephoned, she pressed her forehead against the doorframe and could not speak. He kept saying, "What's wrong? Can't you talk? Aren't you alone?" She felt that she was going insane. Her head would burst. Why, why did he love her, why did he pursue her? Why did he want her to die?

She went to him in the hotel room. A familiar room: had they been here 140 before? "Everything is repeating itself. Everything is stuck," she said. He framed her face in his hands and said that she looked thinner — was she sick? — what was wrong? She shook herself free. He, her lover, looked about the same. There was a small, angry pimple on his neck. He stared at her, eagerly and suspiciously. Did she bring bad news?

"So you love me? You love me?" she asked.

"Why are you so angry?"

"I want to be free of you. The two of us free of each other."

"That isn't true — you don't want that — "

He embraced her. She was wild with that old, familiar passion for him, her 145 body clinging to his, her arms not strong enough to hold him. Ah, what despair! — what bitter hatred she felt! — she needed this man for her salvation, he was all she had to live for, and yet she could not believe in him. He embraced her thighs, her hips, kissing her, pressing his warm face against her, and yet she could not believe in him, not really. She needed him in order to live, but he was not worth her love, he was not worth her dying. . . . She promised herself this: when she got back home, when she was alone, she would draw the razor more deeply across her arm.

The telephone rang and he answered it: a wrong number.

"Jesus," he said.

They lay together, still. She imagined their posture like this, the two of them one figure, one substance; and outside this room and this bed there was a universe of disjointed, separate things, blank things, that had nothing to do with them. She would not be Anna out there, the lady in the drawing. He would not be her lover.

"I love you so much . . ." She whispered.

"Please don't cry! We have only a few hours, please. . . ."   150

It was absurd, their clinging together like this. She saw them as a single figure in a drawing, their arms and legs entwined, their heads pressing mutely together. Helpless substance, so heavy and warm and doomed. It was absurd that any human being should be so important to another human being. She wanted to laugh: a laugh might free them both.

She could not laugh.

Sometime later he said, as if they had been arguing, "Look. It's you. You're the one who doesn't want to get married. You lie to me — "

"Lie to you?"

"You love me but you won't marry me, because you want something left 155
over — Something not finished — All your life you can attribute your misery to me, to our not being married — you are using me — "

"Stop it! You'll make me hate you!" she cried.

"You can say to yourself that you're miserable because of *me*. We will never be married, you will never be happy, neither one of us will ever be happy — "

"I don't want to hear this!" she said.

She pressed her hands flatly against her face.

She went to the bathroom to get dressed. She washed her face and part of 160
her body, quickly. The fever was in her, in the pit of her belly. She would rush home and strike a razor across the inside of her arm and free that pressure, that fever.

The impatient bulging of the veins: an ordeal over.

The demand of the telephone's ringing: that ordeal over.

The nuisance of getting the car and driving home in all that five o'clock traffic: an ordeal too much for a woman.

The movement of this stranger's body in hers: over, finished.

Now, dressed, a little calmer, they held hands and talked. They had to talk 165
swiftly, to get all their news in: he did not trust the people who worked for him, he had faith in no one, his wife had moved to a textbook publishing company and was doing well, she had inherited a Ben Shahn painting from her father and wanted to "touch it up a little" — she was crazy! — his blind son was at another school, doing fairly well, in fact his children were all doing fairly well in spite of the stupid mistake of their parents' marriage — and what about her? what about her life? She told him in a rush the one thing he wanted to hear: that she

lived with her husband lovelessly, the two of them polite strangers, sharing a bed, lying side by side in the night in that bed, bodies out of which souls had fled. There was no longer even any shame between them.

"And what about me? Do you feel shame with me still?" he asked.

She did not answer. She moved away from him and prepared to leave.

Then, a minute later, she happened to catch sight of his reflection in the bureau mirror — he was glancing down at himself, checking himself mechanically, impersonally, preparing also to leave. He too would leave this room: he too was headed somewhere else.

She stared at him. It seemed to her that in this instant he was breaking from her, the image of her lover fell free of her, breaking from her . . . and she realized that he existed in a dimension quite apart from her, a mysterious being. And suddenly, joyfully, she felt a miraculous calm. This man was her husband, truly — they were truly married, here in this room — they had been married haphazardly and accidentally for a long time. In another part of the city she had another husband, a "husband," but she had not betrayed that man, not really. This man, whom she loved above any other person in the world, above even her own self-pitying sorrow and her own life, was her truest lover, her destiny. And she did not hate him, she did not hate herself any longer; she did not wish to die; she was flooded with a strange certainty, a sense of gratitude, of pure selfless energy. It was obvious to her that she had, all along, been behaving correctly; out of instinct.

What triumph, to love like this in any room, anywhere, risking even the 170 craziest of accidents!

"Why are you so happy? What's wrong?" he asked, startled. He stared at her. She felt the abrupt concentration in him, the focusing of his vision on her, almost a bitterness in his face, as if he feared her. What, was it beginning all over again? Their love beginning again, in spite of them? "How can you look so happy?" he asked. "We don't have any right to it. Is it because . . . ?"

"Yes," she said.

Considerations for Critical Thinking and Writing

1. How would this story be different if it were told only in chronological order as it is in Part III? What do Parts I and II contribute to the details and information provided in Part III?
2. Why are Anna and her lover drawn to each other? What do we learn about their spouses that helps explain their attraction? Are there any other explanations?
3. Why is Anna so unhappy after the affair on Nantucket begins? Why does she think of suicide?
4. What is Anna's attitude toward men? Does it change during the story?
5. What details in the story make the narration particularly convincing from a woman's perspective? How might a man tell the story differently?
6. "What triumph, to love like this in any room, anywhere, risking even the craziest of accidents!" Explain this reflection of Anna's (at the end of Part III) and relate it to her character.
7. How does Oates's arrangement of incidents validate Anna's feeling that "everything is repeating itself. Everything is stuck"?

8. Consider whether Anna reaches any kind of resolution to her problems by the end of the story. Is she merely "repeating" herself, or do you think she develops?
9. At the end of the first paragraph of Part II, Oates has Anna ask herself the question "What did it mean to enter into a bond with another person?" Write an essay explaining how the story answers that question.

Connections to Another Selection

1. What similarities in setting, plot, and character are there between Oates's version and Chekhov's story? Are there any significant differences?
2. Is it necessary to be familiar with Chekhov's story to appreciate Oates's? What's the point of retelling the story?
3. Describe how a familiarity with Chekhov's story affected your reading and expectations of Oates's version. Choose one version of the story and write an essay explaining why you prefer it over the other.

PERSPECTIVE

MATTHEW C. BRENNAN (b. 1955)
Point of View and Plotting in Chekhov's and Oates's "The Lady with the Pet Dog"
1985

Oates . . . retains Chekhov's third-person point of view. But unlike Chekhov, who focuses on the male lover, Gurov, Oates makes Anna S., the female lover, the center of consciousness. Because Chekhov privileges Gurov, he represents Anna's feelings only when she speaks to Gurov. In fact, when Anna S. expresses her shame to Gurov, Chekhov says, "The solitary candle on the table scarcely lit up her face"; and rather than reveal her inner thoughts he merely tells us, "it was obvious that her heart was heavy." So, by subordinating Anna S. to Gurov, Chekhov gives readers no way to understand the feminine side of a masculine story. In contrast, Oates presents what Chekhov leaves out — the female's experience — and so relegates the male lover (who in her version is nameless) to the limited status Chekhov relegates Anna S.: Oates privileges the point of view of Anna. Furthermore, because Anna S. says she feels "like a madwoman," Oates fragments Chekhov's traditionally chronological plot, which becomes a subtext against which Oates can foreground Anna's confusion, doubt, and struggle to find an identity. . . .

Chekhov develops a conventional, sequential plot. He spreads the five-step plot through the four formal divisions of his story. Part I consists of the exposition, during which Gurov and Anna S. meet at the resort, Yalta. Part II continues the exposition, as the characters become lovers, and it also introduces the rising action as they separate at the train station, Anna S. returning to her home in the town of S——, Gurov to his in Moscow. Then, in part III, the action continues to rise as Gurov misses Anna and eventually goes to the town of S——. Here, at a concert, the two climactically meet again, and, as part III ends, Anna

S. agrees to come to Moscow. Finally, in part IV, the action falls as Chekhov describes their affair and dramatizes it in a scene that forms the resolution, through which Gurov realizes, after looking in a mirror, that he is in love for the first time: he and Anna S. really are "as husband and wife" though separated by law.

Oates borrows all these events for her plot, but if Chekhov's is linear, hers is circular. Oates breaks her story into three parts. Part I depicts the climax, immediately giving her version the intensity that the high-strung center of consciousness, Anna, is experiencing. We are with her at the concert hall, where her lover appears and she faints, and then with her back home, where her husband clumsily makes love to her while she thinks of her lover. Part II opens with a flashback to the rising action — when the lover drives Anna to Albany where they separate, just as Chekhov's lovers separate at the train station; next, part II both repeats the climax (at the concert and in the bedroom) and relates, for the first time, the falling action in which the lovers continue the affair. Part I, then, presents only the climax, and part II widens the plot to record not just the center, the climax, but also the rising and falling actions that surround it. Part III, however, widens the circular plot still further. Expanding outward from the climactic center, first the plot regresses to embrace the exposition (in which the lovers meet and make love at the resort, in this version Nantucket); then it moves inward again, retracing chronologically the rising action, climax, and falling action; and finally, as part III concludes, the plot introduces the resolution, rounding out its pattern.

Before the resolution, however, as we witness the falling action (the resumption of the affair) for the second time, Oates stresses the lack of development: Anna says, "'Everything is repeating itself. Everything is stuck.'" By having the plot repeat itself, and so fail to progress toward resolution, Oates conveys Anna's lack of identity: Anna is trapped between two relationships, two "husbands," and hence wavers throughout this version between feeling like "nothing" in her legal husband's house where "there was no boundary to her," "no precise limit," and feeling defined — as "recognizably Anna" — by her illicit lover, her true "husband," who has sketched her portrait, to which she continually refers as if grasping for a rope.

Here, then, with the climax repeated three times and the rising and falling actions twice, the plot finally progresses from this impasse to its resolution. And, appropriately, as the plot finally achieves its completion, so too does Anna, discovering as she symbolically looks into the mirror,

> this man was her husband, truly — they were truly married, here in this room — they had been married haphazardly and accidentally for a long time. In another part of the city she had another husband, a "husband," but she had not betrayed that man, not really. This man, whom she loved above any other person in the world . . . was her truest lover, her destiny.

Oates allows the plot to progress sequentially to the resolution — to integrity — only as Anna's consciousness discovers its true identity, its integration.

From *Notes on Modern American Literature*

Considerations for Critical Thinking and Writing

1. What does Brennan mean by characterizing Chekhov's story as "masculine" and Oates's as "feminine"? How is each writer's use of point of view related to this question?
2. Brennan describes Chekhov's plot as "linear" and Oates's as "circular." How is this contrast influenced by the writer's use of point of view?
3. Brennan asserts that in Oates's story, "Anna's consciousness discovers its true identity, its integration." Write an essay explaining whether you agree or disagree with this assessment. In your response, consider how Oates's use of point of view affects your reading of Anna's character.

6. Symbolism

A *symbol* is a person, object, or event that suggests more than its literal meaning. This basic definition is simple enough, but the use of symbol in literature makes some students slightly nervous because they tend to regard it as a booby trap, a hidden device that can go off during a seemingly harmless class discussion. "I didn't see that when I was reading the story" is a frequently heard comment. This sort of surprise and recognition is both natural and common. Most readers go through a story for the first time getting their bearings, figuring out what is happening to whom and so on. Patterns and significant details often require a second or third reading before they become evident — before a symbol sheds light on a story. Then the details of a work may suddenly fit together and its meaning may be reinforced, clarified, or enlarged by the symbol. Symbolic meanings are usually embedded in the texture of a story, but they are not "hidden"; instead, they are carefully placed. Reading between the lines (where there is only space) is unnecessary. What is needed is a careful consideration of the elements of the story, a sensitivity to its language, and some common sense.

Common sense is a good place to begin. Symbols appear all around us; anything can be given symbolic significance. Without symbols our lives would be curiously stark and vacant. Awareness of a writer's use of symbols is not all that different from the kinds of perceptions and interpretations that allow us to make sense of our daily lives. We know, for example, that a ring used in a wedding is more than just a piece of jewelry because it suggests the unity and intimacy of a closed circle. The bride's gown may be white because we associate innocence and purity with that color. Or consider the meaning of a small alligator sewn on a shirt or some other article of clothing. What started out as a company trademark has gathered around it a range of meanings suggesting everything from quality and money to preppiness and silliness. The ring, the white gown, and the alligator trademark are symbolic because each has meanings that go beyond its specific qualities and functions.

Symbols such as these that are widely recognized by a society or culture are called *conventional symbols*. The Christian cross, the Star of

David, a swastika, or a nation's flag all have meanings understood by large groups of people. Certain kinds of experiences also have traditional meanings in Western cultures. Winter, the setting sun, and the color black suggest death, while spring, the rising sun, and the color green evoke images of youth and new beginnings. (It is worth noting, however, that individual cultures sometimes have their own conventions; some Oriental countries associate white rather than black with death and mourning. And obviously the alligator trademark would mean nothing to anyone totally unfamiliar with American culture.) These broadly shared symbolic meanings are second nature to us.

Writers use conventional symbols to reinforce meanings. Kate Chopin, for example, emphasizes the spring setting in "The Story of an Hour" (p. 12) as a way of suggesting the renewed sense of life that Mrs. Mallard feels when she thinks herself free from her husband.

A *literary symbol* can include traditional, conventional, or public meanings, but it may also be established internally by the total context of the work in which it appears. In "Soldier's Home" (p. 125), Hemingway does not use Krebs's family home as a conventional symbol of safety, comfort, and refuge from the war. Instead, Krebs's home becomes symbolic of provincial, erroneous presuppositions compounded by blind innocence, sentimentality, and smug middle-class respectability. The symbolic meaning of his home reveals that Krebs no longer shares his family's and town's view of the world. Their notions of love, the value of a respectable job, and a belief in God seem to him petty, complicated, and meaningless. The significance of Krebs's home is determined by the events within the story, which reverse and subvert the traditional associations readers might bring to it. Krebs's interactions with his family and the people in town reveal what home has come to mean to him.

A literary symbol can be a setting, character, action, object, name, or anything else in a work that maintains its literal significance while suggesting other meanings. Symbols cannot be restricted to a single meaning; they are suggestive rather than definitive. Their evocation of multiple meanings allows a writer to say more with less. Symbols are economical devices for evoking complex ideas without having to resort to painstaking explanations that would make a story more like an essay than an experience. The many walls in Melville's "Bartleby, the Scrivener" (p. 83) cannot be reduced to one idea. They have multiple meanings that unify the story. The walls are symbols of the deadening, dehumanizing, restrictive repetitiveness of the office routine, as well as of the confining, materialistic sensibilities of Wall Street. They suggest whatever limits and thwarts human aspirations, including death itself. We don't know precisely what shatters Bartleby's will to live, but the walls in the story, through their symbolic suggestiveness, indicate the nature of the limitations that cause the scrivener to slip into hopelessness and his "dead-wall reveries."

When a character, object, or incident indicates a single, fixed meaning, the writer is using *allegory* rather than symbol. Unlike with symbols, which have literal functions as well as multiple meanings, the primary focus in allegory is on the abstract idea called forth by the concrete object. John Bunyan's *Pilgrim's Progress,* published during the seventeenth century, is a classic example of allegory, because the characters, action, and setting have no existence beyond their abstract meanings. Bunyan's purpose is to teach his readers the exemplary way to salvation and heaven. The protagonist, named Christian, flees the City of Destruction in search of the Celestial City. Along the way he encounters characters who either help or hinder his spiritual journey. Among them are Mr. Worldly Wiseman, Faithful, Prudence, Piety, and a host of others named after the virtues or vices they display. These characters, places, and actions exist solely to illustrate religious doctrine. Allegory tends to be definitive rather than suggestive. It drives meaning into a corner and keeps it there. Most modern writers prefer the exploratory nature of symbol to the reductive nature of pure allegory.

Stories often include symbols that you may or may not perceive on a first reading. Their subtle use is a sign of a writer's skill in weaving symbols into the fabric of the characters' lives. Symbols may sometimes escape you, but that is probably better than finding symbols where only literal meanings are intended. Allow the text to help you determine if a symbolic reading is appropriate. Once you are clear about what literally happens, read carefully and notice the placement of details that are emphasized. The pervasive references to time in Faulkner's "A Rose for Emily" (p. 47) and the many kinds of walls that appear throughout "Bartleby, the Scrivener" call attention to themselves and warrant symbolic readings. A symbol, however, need not be repeated to have an important purpose in a story. In Welty's "Livvie" (p. 115), the simple application of lipstick helps to reinforce symbolically Livvie's eventual movement away from the repressive Solomon to the compelling freedom associated with Cash.

By keeping track of the total context of the story, you should be able to decide if your reading is reasonable and consistent with the other facts; plenty of lemons in literature yield no symbolic meaning even if they are squeezed. Be sensitive to the meanings that the author associates with people, places, objects, and actions. You may not associate home with provincial innocence as Hemingway does in "Soldier's Home," but a close reading of the story will permit you to see how and why he constructs that symbolic meaning. If you treat stories like people — with tact and care — they ordinarily are accessible and enjoyable.

The next three stories — Sandra Cisneros's "Barbie-Q," Colette's "The Hand," and Ralph Ellison's "Battle Royal" — rely on symbols to convey meanings that go far beyond the specific incidents described in their plots.

SANDRA CISNEROS (b. 1954)

Born to a Mexican father and a Mexican-American mother, Sandra Cisneros grew up in Chicago along with her six brothers. Before teaching as a writer-in-residence at California State University at Chico, the University of California at Berkeley and at Irvine, and the University of Michigan, she taught high school, served as a college admissions officer, and worked as an arts administrator. Her poetry and fiction have earned her two National Endowment for the Arts fellowships. She is the author of two collections of fiction: *The House on Mango Street* (1989), about growing up in the Hispanic section of Chicago, and *Woman Hollering Creek* (1991), from which "Barbie-Q" is taken. Cisneros's fiction explores the difficulties of living in poor neighborhoods where issues of race, class, and gender complicate her characters' lives. In "Barbie-Q" a young girl's description of her dolls suggests significant parallels to her own life.

Barbie-Q   1991

Yours is the one with mean eyes and a ponytail. Striped swimsuit, stilettos, sunglasses, and gold hoop earrings. Mine is the one with bubble hair. Red swimsuit, stilettos, pearl earrings, and a wire stand. But that's all we can afford, besides one extra outfit apiece. Yours, "Red Flair," sophisticated A-line coatdress with a Jackie Kennedy pillbox hat, white gloves, handbag, and heels included. Mine, "Solo in the Spotlight," evening elegance in black glitter strapless gown with a puffy skirt at the bottom like a mermaid tail, formal-length gloves, pink chiffon scarf, and mike included. From so much dressing and undressing, the black glitter wears off where her titties stick out. This and a dress invented from an old sock when we cut holes here and here and here, the cuff rolled over for the glamorous, fancy-free, off-the-shoulder look.

Every time the same story. Your Barbie is roommates with my Barbie, and my Barbie's boyfriend comes over and your Barbie steals him, okay? Kiss kiss kiss. Then the two Barbies fight. You dumbbell! He's mine. Oh no he's not, you stinky! Only Ken's invisible, right? Because we don't have money for a stupid-looking boy doll when we'd both rather ask for a new Barbie outfit next Christmas. We have to make do with your mean-eyed Barbie and my bubblehead Barbie and our one outfit apiece not including the sock dress.

Until next Sunday when we are walking through the flea market on Maxwell Street and *there!* Lying on the street next to some tool bits, and platform shoes with the heels all squashed, and a fluorescent green wicker wastebasket, and aluminum foil, and hubcaps, and a pink shag rug, and windshield wiper blades, and dusty mason jars, and a coffee can full of rusty nails. *There!* Where? Two Mattel boxes. One with the "Career Gal" ensemble, snappy black-and-white business suit, three-quarter-length sleeve jacket with kick-pleat skirt, red sleeveless shell, gloves, pumps, and matching hat included. The other, "Sweet Dreams," dreamy pink-and-white plaid nightgown and matching robe, lace-trimmed slippers, hairbrush and hand mirror included. How much? Please, please, please, please, please, please, please, until they say okay.

On the outside you and me skipping and humming but inside we are doing loopity-loops and pirouetting. Until at the next vendor's stand, next to boxed pies, and bright orange toilet brushes, and rubber gloves, and wrench sets, and bouquets of feather flowers, and glass towel racks, and steel wool, and Alvin and the Chipmunks records, *there!* And *there!* And *there!* And *there!* and *there!* and *there!* and *there!* Bendable Legs Barbie with her new page-boy hairdo. Midge, Barbie's best friend. Ken, Barbie's boyfriend. Skipper, Barbie's little sister. Tutti and Todd, Barbie and Skipper's tiny twin sister and brother. Skipper's friends, Scooter and Ricky. Alan, Ken's buddy. And Francie, Barbie's MOD'ern cousin.

Everybody today selling toys, all of them damaged with water and smelling 5 of smoke. Because a big toy warehouse on Halsted Street burned down yesterday — see there? — the smoke still rising and drifting across the Dan Ryan expressway. And now there is a big fire sale at Maxwell Street, today only.

So what if we didn't get our new Bendable Legs Barbie and Midge and Ken and Skipper and Tutti and Todd and Scooter and Ricky and Alan and Francie in nice clean boxes and had to buy them on Maxwell Street, all water-soaked and sooty. So what if our Barbies smell like smoke when you hold them up to your nose even after you wash and wash and wash them. And if the prettiest doll, Barbie's MOD'ern cousin Francie with real eyelashes, eyelash brush included, has a left foot that's melted a little — so? If you dress her in her new "Prom Pinks" outfit, satin splendor with matching coat, gold belt, clutch, and hair bow included, so long as you don't lift her dress, right? — who's to know.

Considerations for Critical Thinking and Writing

1. What kinds of values, assumptions, and life-styles do Barbie dolls evoke for you? Why do the dolls play so central a role in this story?
2. Describe the protagonist. How does the protagonist's language reveal her character?
3. What is the significance of the "same story" the girls play all the time?
4. What sort of place is Maxwell Street? How important is the story's setting?
5. Is there a conflict in this story? Is there a resolution?
6. What, if any, social commentary is there in the story?
7. Discuss the significance of the title.
8. What emotions does the story inspire in you? How do you think the protagonist feels at the end when she says "who's to know"?

Connections to Other Selections

1. Compare and contrast the symbolic purpose of the dolls in "Barbie-Q" with that of the dancer described as "a circus kewpie doll" in Ralph Ellison's "Battle Royal" (p. 187, paras. 7–9).
2. "Barbie-Q" and Raymond Carver's "Popular Mechanics" (p. 235) are very brief short stories. Which one is — for you — the more effective story? Explain why.
3. Write an essay that considers the ending of "Barbie-Q" and Colette's "The Hand" (p. 184). Is either conclusion a "happy ending"?

COLETTE
[SIDONIE-GABRIELLE COLETTE] (1873–1954)

Born in Burgundy, France, Sidonie-Gabrielle Colette lived a long and remarkably diverse life. At various points during her career she supported herself as a novelist, music-hall performer, and journalist. Her professional life and three marriages helped to shape her keen insights into modern love and women's lives. She is regarded as a significant feminist voice in the twentieth century, and her reputation is firmly fixed by her having been the first woman admitted to the Goncourt Academy and by the continued popularity of her work among readers internationally. Her best-known works include *Mitsou, or, How Girls Grow Wise* (1919), *Chéri* (1920), *Claudine's House* (1922), and *Gigi* (1944). "The Hand" signals a telling moment in the life of a young bride.

The Hand   1924

He had fallen asleep on his young wife's shoulder, and she proudly bore the weight of the man's head, blond, ruddy-complexioned, eyes closed. He had slipped his big arm under the small of her slim, adolescent back, and his strong hand lay on the sheet next to the young woman's right elbow. She smiled to see the man's hand emerging there, all by itself and far away from its owner. Then she let her eyes wander over the half-lit room. A veiled conch shed a light across the bed the color of periwinkle.

"Too happy to sleep," she thought.

Too excited also, and often surprised by her new state. It had been only two weeks since she had begun to live the scandalous life of a newlywed who tastes the joys of living with someone unknown and with whom she is in love. To meet a handsome, blond young man, recently widowed, good at tennis and rowing, to marry him a month later: her conjugal adventure had been little more than a kidnapping. So that whenever she lay awake beside her husband, like tonight, she still kept her eyes closed for a long time, then opened them again in order to savor, with astonishment, the blue of the brand-new curtains, instead of the apricot-pink through which the first light of day filtered into the room where she had slept as a little girl.

A quiver ran through the sleeping body lying next to her, and she tightened her left arm around her husband's neck with the charming authority exercised by weak creatures. He did not wake up.

"His eyelashes are so long," she said to herself.   5

To herself she also praised his mouth, full and likable, his skin the color of pink brick, and even his forehead, neither noble nor broad, but still smooth and unwrinkled.

Her husband's right hand, lying beside her, quivered in turn, and beneath the curve of her back she felt the right arm, on which her whole weight was resting, come to life.

"I'm so heavy . . . I wish I could get up and turn the light off. But he's sleeping so well . . ."

The arm twisted again, feebly, and she arched her back to make herself lighter.

"It's as if I were lying on some animal," she thought.   10

She turned her head a little on the pillow and looked at the hand lying there next to her.

"It's so big! It really is bigger than my whole head."

The light, flowing out from under the edge of a parasol of bluish crystal, spilled up against the hand, and made every contour of the skin apparent, exaggerating the powerful knuckles and the veins engorged by the pressure on the arm. A few red hairs, at the base of the fingers, all curved in the same direction, like ears of wheat in the wind, and the flat nails, whose ridges the nail buffer had not smoothed out, gleamed, coated with pink varnish.

"I'll tell him not to varnish his nails," thought the young wife. "Varnish and pink polish don't go with a hand so . . . a hand that's so . . ."

An electric jolt ran through the hand and spared the young woman from   15
having to find the right adjective. The thumb stiffened itself out, horribly long and spatulate, and pressed tightly against the index finger, so that the hand suddenly took on a vile, apelike appearance.

"Oh!" whispered the young woman, as though faced with something slightly indecent.

The sound of a passing car pierced the silence with a shrillness that seemed luminous. The sleeping man did not wake, but the hand, offended, reared back and tensed up in the shape of a crab and waited, ready for battle. The screeching sound died down and the hand, relaxing gradually, lowered its claws, and became a pliant beast, awkwardly bent, shaken by faint jerks which resembled some sort of agony. The flat, cruel nail of the overlong thumb glistened. A curve in the little finger, which the young woman had never noticed, appeared, and the wallowing hand revealed its fleshy palm like a red belly.

"And I've kissed that hand! . . . How horrible! Haven't I ever looked at it?"

The hand, disturbed by a bad dream, appeared to respond to this startling discovery, this disgust. It regrouped its forces, opened wide, and splayed its tendons, lumps, and red fur like battle dress, then slowly drawing itself in again, grabbed a fistful of the sheet, dug into it with its curved fingers, and squeezed, squeezed with the methodical pleasure of a strangler.

"Oh!" cried the young woman.   20

The hand disappeared and a moment later the big arm, relieved of its burden, became a protective belt, a warm bulwark against all the terrors of night. But the next morning, when it was time for breakfast in bed — hot chocolate and toast — she saw the hand again, with its red hair and red skin, and the ghastly thumb curving out over the handle of a knife.

"Do you want this slice, darling? I'll butter it for you."

She shuddered and felt her skin crawl on the back of her arms and down her back.

"Oh, no . . . no . . ."

Then she concealed her fear, bravely subdued herself, and, beginning her 25
life of duplicity, of resignation, and of a lowly, delicate diplomacy, she leaned
over and humbly kissed the monstrous hand.

Considerations for Critical Thinking and Writing

1. How well did the young woman know her husband before she married him?
   What attracted her to him?
2. How does the wife regard the hand at the very beginning of the story? At what
   point does she begin to change her attitude?
3. Explain how the wife's description of the hand affects your own response to it.
   What prompts her "Oh!" in paragraphs 16 and 20? What do you suppose the wife
   is thinking at these moments?
4. What powerful feelings does the hand evoke in the wife? How do her descriptions
   of the hand suggest symbolic readings of it?
5. Describe the conflict in the story. Explain whether there is a resolution to this
   conflict.
6. Do you think the story is more about the husband or about the wife? Who is the
   central character? Explain your choice. Consider also whether the characters are
   static or dynamic.
7. Why do you think the narrator mentions that the husband was "recently widowed"?
8. How significant is the setting of the story?
9. Why do you think the wife kisses her husband's hand in the final paragraph?
   Write an essay explaining how the kiss symbolizes the nature of their relationship.
10. Describe the point of view in the story. Why do you suppose Colette doesn't use
    a first-person perspective that would reveal more intimately the wife's perceptions
    and concerns?

Connections to Other Selections

1. In "The Birthmark" (p. 261) Nathaniel Hawthorne also uses a hand for symbolic
   purposes. Compare the meanings he associates with the hand in his story with
   Colette's. How does each writer invest meanings in a central symbol? What are
   the significant similarities and differences in meanings? Write an essay explaining
   why you find one story more effective than the other.
2. Compare the use of settings in "The Hand" and in John Updike's "A & P" (p.
   485). To what extent does each story attach meaning to its setting?
3. How might Godwin's "A Sorrowful Woman" (p. 30) be read as a kind of sequel
   to "The Hand"?

RALPH ELLISON (b. 1914)

Born in Oklahoma and educated at the Tuskegee Institute in Alabama,
where he studied music, Ralph Ellison gained his reputation as a writer on
the strength of his only published novel, *Invisible Man* (1952). He has also

published some scattered short stories and two collections of essays, *Shadow and Act* (1964) and *Going to the Territory* (1986). Although his writing has not been extensive, it is important because Ellison writes about race relations in the context of universal human concerns. *Invisible Man* is the story of a young black man who moves from the South to the North and discovers what it means to be black in America. "Battle Royal," published in 1947 as a short story, became the first chapter of *Invisible Man*. It concerns the beginning of the protagonist's long struggle for an adult identity in a world made corrupt by racial prejudice.

Battle Royal   1947

It goes a long way back, some twenty years. All my life I had been looking for something, and everywhere I turned someone tried to tell me what it was. I accepted their answers too, though they were often in contradiction and even self-contradictory. I was naïve. I was looking for myself and asking everyone except myself questions which I, and only I, could answer. It took me a long time and much painful boomeranging of my expectations to achieve a realization everyone else appears to have been born with: That I am nobody but myself. But first I had to discover that I am an invisible man!

And yet I am no freak of nature, nor of history. I was in the cards, other things having been equal (or unequal) eighty-five years ago. I am not ashamed of my grandparents for having been slaves. I am only ashamed of myself for having at one time been ashamed. About eighty-five years ago they were told that they were free, united with others of our country in everything pertaining to the common good, and, in everything social, separate like the fingers of the hand. And they believed it. They exulted in it. They stayed in their place, worked hard, and brought up my father to do the same. But my grandfather is the one. He was an odd old guy, my grandfather, and I am told I take after him. It was he who caused the trouble. On his deathbed he called my father to him and said, "Son, after I'm gone I want you to keep up the good fight. I never told you, but our life is a war and I have been a traitor all my born days, a spy in the enemy's country ever since I give up my gun back in the Reconstruction. Live with your head in the lion's mouth. I want you to overcome 'em with yeses, undermine 'em with grins, agree 'em to death and destruction, let 'em swoller you till they vomit or bust wide open." They thought the old man had gone out of his mind. He had been the meekest of men. The younger children were rushed from the room, the shades drawn and the flame of the lamp turned so low that it sputtered on the wick like the old man's breathing. "Learn it to the younguns," he whispered fiercely; then he died.

But my folks were more alarmed over his last words than over his dying. It was as though he had not died at all, his words caused so much anxiety. I was warned emphatically to forget what he had said and, indeed, this is the first time it has been mentioned outside the family circle. It had a tremendous effect upon me, however. I could never be sure of what he meant. Grandfather had been a quiet old man who never made any trouble, yet on his deathbed he had called himself a traitor and a spy, and he had spoken of his meekness as a dangerous activity. It became a constant puzzle which lay unanswered in the back of my mind. And whenever things went well for me I remembered my grandfather and felt guilty and uncomfortable. It was as though I was carrying out his advice in spite of myself. And to make it worse, everyone loved me for it. I was praised by the most lily-white men of the town. I was considered an example of desirable conduct — just as my grandfather had been. And what puzzled me was that the old man had defined it as *treachery*. When I was praised for my conduct I felt a guilt that in some way I was doing something that was really against the wishes of the white folks, that if they had understood they would have desired me to act just the opposite, that I should have been sulky and mean, and that that really would have been what they wanted, even though they were fooled and thought they wanted me to act as I did. It made me afraid that some day they would look upon me as a traitor and I would be lost. Still I was more afraid to act any other way because they didn't like that at all. The old man's words were like a curse. On my graduation day I delivered an oration in which I showed that humility was the secret, indeed, the very essence of progress. (Not that I believed this — how could I, remembering my grandfather? — I only believed that it worked.) It was a great success. Everyone praised me and I was invited to give the speech at a gathering of the town's leading white citizens. It was a triumph for our whole community.

It was in the main ballroom of the leading hotel. When I got there I discovered that it was on the occasion of a smoker, and I was told that since I was to be there anyway I might as well take part in the battle royal to be fought by some of my schoolmates as part of the entertainment. The battle royal came first.

All of the town's big shots were there in their tuxedoes, wolfing down the buffet foods, drinking beer and whiskey and smoking black cigars. It was a large room with a high ceiling. Chairs were arranged in neat rows around three sides of a portable boxing ring. The fourth side was clear, revealing a gleaming space of polished floor. I had some misgivings over the battle royal, by the way. Not from a distaste for fighting, but because I didn't care too much for the other fellows who were to take part. They were tough guys who seemed to have no grandfather's curse worrying their minds. No one could mistake their toughness. And besides, I suspected that fighting a battle royal might detract from the dignity of my speech. In those pre-invisible days I visualized myself as a potential Booker T. Washington. But the other fellows didn't care too much for me either, and there were nine of them. I felt superior to them in my way, and I didn't like the manner in which we were all crowded together into the servants' elevator. Nor did they like my being there. In fact, as the warmly lighted floors flashed past the elevator we had words over the fact that I, by taking part in the fight, had knocked one of their friends out of a night's work.

We were led out of the elevator through a rococo hall into an anteroom and told to get into our fighting togs. Each of us was issued a pair of boxing gloves and ushered out into the big mirrored hall, which we entered looking cautiously about us and whispering, lest we might accidentally be heard above the noise of the room. It was foggy with cigar smoke. And already the whiskey was taking effect. I was shocked to see some of the most important men of the town quite tipsy. They were all there — bankers, lawyers, judges, doctors, fire chiefs, teachers, merchants. Even one of the more fashionable pastors. Something we could not see was going on up front. A clarinet was vibrating sensuously and the men were standing up and moving eagerly forward. We were a small tight group, clustered together, our bare upper bodies touching and shining with anticipatory sweat; while up front the big shots were becoming increasingly excited over something we still could not see. Suddenly I heard the school superintendent, who had told me to come, yell, "Bring up the shines, gentlemen! Bring up the little shines!"

We were rushed up to the front of the ballroom, where it smelled even more strongly of tobacco and whiskey. Then we were pushed into place. I almost wet my pants. A sea of faces, some hostile, some amused, ringed around us, and in the center, facing us, stood a magnificent blonde — stark naked. There was dead silence. I felt a blast of cold air chill me. I tried to back away, but they were behind me and around me. Some of the boys stood with lowered heads, trembling. I felt a wave of irrational guilt and fear. My teeth chattered, my skin turned to goose flesh, my knees knocked. Yet I was strongly attracted and looked in spite of myself. Had the price of looking been blindness, I would have looked. The hair was yellow like that of a circus kewpie doll, the face heavily powdered and rouged, as though to form an abstract mask, the eyes hollow and smeared a cool blue, the color of a baboon's butt. I felt a desire to spit upon her as my eyes brushed slowly over her body. Her breasts were firm and round as the domes of East Indian temples, and I stood so close as to see the fine skin texture and beads of pearly perspiration glistening like dew around the pink and erected buds of her nipples. I wanted at one and the same time to run from the room, to sink through the floor, or go to her and cover her from my eyes and the eyes of the others with my body; to feel the soft thighs, to caress her and destroy her, to love her and murder her, to hide from her, and yet to stroke where below the small American flag tattooed upon her belly her thighs formed a capital V. I had a notion that of all in the room she saw only me with her impersonal eyes.

And then she began to dance, a slow sensuous movement; the smoke of a hundred cigars clinging to her like the thinnest of veils. She seemed like a fair bird-girl girdled in veils calling to me from the angry surface of some gray and threatening sea. I was transported. Then I became aware of the clarinet playing and the big shots yelling at us. Some threatened us if we looked and others if we did not. On my right I saw one boy faint. And now a man grabbed a silver pitcher from a table and stepped close as he dashed ice water upon him and stood him up and forced two of us to support him as his head hung and moans issued from his thick bluish lips. Another boy began to plead to go home. He was the largest of the group, wearing dark red fighting trunks much too small to conceal the erection which projected from him as though in answer to the insinuating low-registered moaning of the clarinet. He tried to hide himself with his boxing gloves.

And all the while the blonde continued dancing, smiling faintly at the big shots who watched her with fascination, and faintly smiling at our fear. I noticed a certain merchant who followed her hungrily, his lips loose and drooling. He was a large man who wore diamond studs in a shirtfront which swelled with the ample paunch underneath, and each time the blonde swayed her undulating hips he ran his hand through the thin hair of his bald head and, with his arms upheld, his posture clumsy like that of an intoxicated panda, wound his belly in a slow and obscene grind. This creature was completely hypnotized. The music had quickened. As the dancer flung herself about with a detached expression on her face, the men began reaching out to touch her. I could see their beefy fingers sink into the soft flesh. Some of the others tried to stop them as she began to move around the floor in graceful circles, as they gave chase, slipping and sliding over the polished floor. It was mad. Chairs went crashing, drinks were spilt, as they ran laughing and howling after her. They caught her just as she reached a door, raised her from the floor, and tossed her as college boys are tossed at a hazing, and above her red, fixed-smiling lips I saw the terror and disgust in her eyes, almost like my own terror and that which I saw in some of the other boys. As I watched, they tossed her twice and her soft breasts seemed to flatten against the air and her legs flung wildly as she spun. Some of the more sober ones helped her to escape. And I started off the floor, heading for the anteroom with the rest of the boys.

Some were still crying in hysteria. But as we tried to leave we were stopped 10 and ordered to get into the ring. There was nothing to do but what we were told. All ten of us climbed under the ropes and allowed ourselves to be blind-folded with broad bands of white cloth. One of the men seemed to feel a bit sympathetic and tried to cheer us up as we stood with our backs against the ropes. Some of us tried to grin. "See that boy over there?" one of the men said. "I want you to run across at the bell and give it to him right in the belly. If you don't get him, I'm going to get you. I don't like his looks." Each of us was told the same. The blindfolds were put on. Yet even then I had been going over my speech. In my mind each word was as bright as flame. I felt the cloth pressed into place, and frowned so that it would be loosened when I relaxed.

But now I felt a sudden fit of blind terror. I was unused to darkness. It was as though I had suddenly found myself in a dark room filled with poisonous cottonmouths. I could hear the bleary voices yelling insistently for the battle royal to begin.

"Get going in there!"

"Let me at that big nigger!"

I strained to pick up the school superintendent's voice, as though to squeeze some security out of that slightly more familiar sound.

"Let me at those black sonsabitches!" someone yelled. 15

"No, Jackson, no!" another voice yelled. "Here, somebody, help me hold Jack."

"I want to get at that ginger-colored nigger. Tear him limb from limb," the first voice yelled.

I stood against the ropes trembling. For in those days I was what they called ginger-colored, and he sounded as though he might crunch me between his teeth like a crisp ginger cookie.

Quite a struggle was going on. Chairs were being kicked about and I could hear voices grunting as with a terrific effort. I wanted to see, to see more desperately than ever before. But the blindfold was tight as a thick skin-puckering scab and when I raised my gloved hands to push the layers of white aside a voice yelled, "Oh, no you don't, black bastard! Leave that alone!"

"Ring the bell before Jackson kills him a coon!" someone boomed in the ²⁰ sudden silence. And I heard the bell clang and the sound of the feet scuffling forward.

A glove smacked against my head. I pivoted, striking out stiffly as some-one went past, and felt the jar ripple along the length of my arm to my shoulder. Then it seemed as though all nine of the boys had turned upon me at once. Blows pounded me from all sides while I struck out as best I could. So many blows landed upon me that I wondered if I were not the only blindfolded fighter in the ring, or if the man called Jackson hadn't succeeded in getting me after all.

Blindfolded, I could no longer control my motions. I had no dignity. I stumbled about like a baby or a drunken man. The smoke had become thicker and with each new blow it seemed to sear and further restrict my lungs. My saliva became like hot bitter glue. A glove connected with my head, filling my mouth with warm blood. It was everywhere. I could not tell if the moisture I felt upon my body was sweat or blood. A blow landed hard against the nape of my neck. I felt myself going over, my head hitting the floor. Streaks of blue light filled the black world behind the blindfold. I lay prone, pretending that I was knocked out, but felt myself seized by hands and yanked to my feet. "Get going, black boy! Mix it up!" My arms were like lead, my head smarting from blows. I managed to feel my way to the ropes and held on, trying to catch my breath. A glove landed in my mid-section and I went over again, feeling as though the smoke had become a knife jabbed into my guts. Pushed this way and that by the legs milling around me, I finally pulled erect and discovered that I could see the black, sweat-washed forms weaving in the smoky-blue atmosphere like drunken dancers weaving to the rapid drumlike thuds of blows.

Everyone fought hysterically. It was complete anarchy. Everybody fought everybody else. No group fought together for long. Two, three, four, fought one, then turned to fight each other, were themselves attacked. Blows landed below the belt and in the kidney, with the gloves open as well as closed, and with my eye partly opened now there was not so much terror. I moved carefully, avoiding blows, although not too many to attract attention, fighting from group to group. The boys groped about like blind, cautious crabs crouching to protect their mid-sections, their heads pulled in short against their shoulders, their arms stretched nervously before them, with their fists testing the smoke-filled air like the knobbed feelers of hypersensitive snails. In one corner I glimpsed a boy violently punching the air and heard him scream in pain as he smashed his hand against a ring post. For a second I saw him bent over holding his hand, then going down as a blow caught his unprotected head. I played one group against the other, slipping in and throwing a punch then stepping out of range while pushing the others into the melee to take the blows blindly aimed at me. The smoke was agonizing and there were no rounds, no bells at three minute intervals to relieve our exhaustion. The room spun round me, a swirl of lights, smoke, sweating bodies surrounded by tense white faces. I bled from both nose and mouth, the blood spattering upon my chest.

The men kept yelling, "Slug him, black boy! Knock his guts out!"

"Uppercut him! Kill him! Kill that big boy!" ²⁵

Taking a fake fall, I saw a boy going down heavily beside me as though we were felled by a single blow, saw a sneaker-clad foot shoot into his groin as the two who had knocked him down stumbled upon him. I rolled out of range, feeling a twinge of nausea.

The harder we fought the more threatening the men became. And yet, I had begun to worry about my speech again. How would it go? Would they recognize my ability? What would they give me?

I was fighting automatically when suddenly I noticed that one after another of the boys was leaving the ring. I was surprised, filled with panic, as though I had been left alone with an unknown danger. Then I understood. The boys had arranged it among themselves. It was the custom for the two men left in the ring to slug it out for the winner's prize. I discovered this too late. When the bell sounded two men in tuxedoes leaped into the ring and removed the blindfold. I found myself facing Tatlock, the biggest of the gang. I felt sick at my stomach. Hardly had the bell stopped ringing in my ears than it clanged again and I saw him moving swiftly toward me. Thinking of nothing else to do I hit him smash on the nose. He kept coming, bringing the rank sharp violence of stale sweat. His face was a black blank of a face, only his eyes alive — with hate of me and aglow with a feverish terror from what had happened to us all. I became anxious. I wanted to deliver my speech and he came at me as though he meant to beat it out of me. I smashed him again and again, taking his blows as they came. Then on a sudden impulse I struck him lightly and as we clinched, I whispered, "Fake like I knocked you out, you can have the prize."

"I'll break your behind," he whispered hoarsely.

"For *them?*"

"For *me,* sonofabitch!"

They were yelling for us to break it up and Tatlock spun me half around with a blow, and as a joggled camera sweeps in a reeling scene, I saw the howling red faces crouching tense beneath the cloud of blue-gray smoke. For a moment the world wavered, unraveled, flowed, then my head cleared and Tatlock bounced before me. That fluttering shadow before my eyes was his jabbing left hand. Then falling forward, my head against his damp shoulder, I whispered,

"I'll make it five dollars more."

"Go to hell!"

But his muscles relaxed a trifle beneath my pressure and I breathed, "Seven?"

"Give it to your ma," he said, ripping me beneath the heart.

And while I still held him I butted him and moved away. I felt myself bombarded with punches. I fought back with hopeless desperation. I wanted to deliver my speech more than anything else in the world, because I felt that only these men could judge truly my ability, and now this stupid clown was ruining my chances. I began fighting carefully now, moving in to punch him and out again with my greater speed. A lucky blow to his chin and I had him going too — until I heard a loud voice yell, "I got my money on the big boy."

Hearing this, I almost dropped my guard. I was confused: Should I try to win against the voice out there? Would not this go against my speech, and was not this a moment for humility, for nonresistance? A blow to my head as I danced about sent my right eye popping like a jack-in-the-box and settled my dilemma. The room went red as I fell. It was a dream fall, my body languid and fastidious as to where to land, until the floor became impatient and smashed up to meet me. A moment later I came to. An hypnotic voice said FIVE emphatically. And I lay there, hazily watching a dark red spot of my own blood shaping itself into a butterfly, glistening and soaking into the soiled gray world of the canvas.

When the voice drawled TEN I was lifted up and dragged to a chair. I sat dazed. My eye pained and swelled with each throb of my pounding heart and I wondered if now I would be allowed to speak. I was wringing wet, my mouth still bleeding. We were grouped along the wall now. The other boys ignored me as they congratulated Tatlock and speculated as to how much they would be paid. One boy whimpered over his smashed hand. Looking up front, I saw attendants in white jackets rolling the portable ring away and placing a small square rug in the vacant space surrounded by chairs. Perhaps, I thought, I will stand on the rug to deliver my speech.

Then the M.C. called to us, "Come on up here boys and get your money." 40 We ran forward to where the men laughed and talked in their chairs, waiting. Everyone seemed friendly now.

"There it is on the rug," the man said. I saw the rug covered with coins of all dimensions and a few crumpled bills. But what excited me, scattered here and there, were the gold pieces.

"Boys, it's all yours," the man said. "You get all you grab."

"That's right, Sambo," a blond man said, winking at me confidentially.

I trembled with excitement, forgetting my pain. I would get the gold and the bills, I thought. I would use both hands. I would throw my body against the boys nearest me to block them from the gold.

"Get down around the rug now," the man commanded, "and don't anyone 45 touch it until I give the signal."

"This ought to be good," I heard.

As told, we got around the square rug on our knees. Slowly the man raised his freckled hand as we followed it upward with our eyes.

I heard, "These niggers look like they're about to pray!"

Then, "Ready," the man said. "Go!"

I lunged for a yellow coin lying on the blue design of the carpet, touching 50 it and sending a surprised shriek to join those rising around me. I tried frantically to remove my hand but could not let go. A hot, violent force tore through my body, shaking me like a wet rat. The rug was electrified. The hair bristled up on my head as I shook myself free. My muscles jumped, my nerves jangled, writhed. But I saw that this was not stopping the other boys. Laughing in fear and embarrassment, some were holding back and scooping up the coins knocked off by the painful contortions of the others. The men roared above us as we struggled.

"Pick it up, goddamnit, pick it up!" someone called like a bass-voiced parrot. "Go on, get it!"

I crawled rapidly around the floor, picking up the coins, trying to avoid the coppers and to get greenbacks and the gold. Ignoring the shock by laughing, as I brushed the coins off quickly, I discovered that I could contain the electricity — a contradiction, but it works. Then the men began to push us onto the rug. Laughing embarrassedly, we struggled out of their hands and kept after the coins. We were all wet and slippery and hard to hold. Suddenly I saw a boy lifted into the air, glistening with sweat like a circus seal, and dropped, his wet back landing flush upon the charged rug, heard him yell and saw him literally dance upon his back, his elbows beating a frenzied tattoo upon the floor, his muscles twitching like the flesh of a horse stung by many flies. When he finally rolled off, his face was gray and no one stopped him when he ran from the floor amid booming laughter.

"Get the money," the M.C. called. "That's good hard American cash!"

And we snatched and grabbed, snatched and grabbed. I was careful not to come too close to the rug now, and when I felt the hot whiskey breath descend upon me like a cloud of foul air I reached out and grabbed the leg of a chair. It was occupied and I held on desperately.

"Leggo, nigger! Leggo!"   55

The huge face wavered down to mine as he tried to push me free. But my body was slippery and he was too drunk. It was Mr. Colcord, who owned a chain of movie houses and "entertainment palaces." Each time he grabbed me I slipped out of his hands. It became a real struggle. I feared the rug more than I did the drunk, so I held on, surprising myself for a moment by trying to topple *him* upon the rug. It was such an enormous idea that I found myself actually carrying it out. I tried not to be obvious, yet when I grabbed his leg, trying to tumble him out of the chair, he raised up roaring with laughter, and, looking at me with soberness dead in the eye, kicked me viciously in the chest. The chair leg flew out of my hand and I felt myself going and rolled. It was as though I had rolled through a bed of hot coals. It seemed a whole century would pass before I would roll free, a century in which I was seared through the deepest levels of my body to the fearful breath within me and the breath seared and heated to the point of explosion. It'll all be over in a flash, I thought as I rolled clear. It'll all be over in a flash.

But not yet, the men on the other side were waiting, red faces swollen as though from apoplexy as they bent forward in their chairs. Seeing their fingers coming toward me I rolled away as a fumbled football rolls off the receiver's fingertips, back into the coals. That time I luckily sent the rug sliding out of place and heard the coins ringing against the floor and the boys scuffling to pick them up and the M.C. calling, "All right, boys, that's all. Go get dressed and get your money."

I was limp as a dish rag. My back felt as though it had been beaten with wires.

When we had dressed the M.C. came in and gave us each five dollars, except Tatlock, who got ten for being last in the ring. Then he told us to leave. I was not to get a chance to deliver my speech, I thought. I was going out into the dim alley in despair when I was stopped and told to go back. I returned to the ballroom, where the men were pushing back their chairs and gathering in groups to talk.

The M.C. knocked on a table for quiet. "Gentlemen," he said, "we almost   60 forgot an important part of the program. A most serious part, gentlemen. This boy was brought here to deliver a speech which he made at his graduation yesterday . . ."

"Bravo!"

"I'm told that he is the smartest boy we've got out there in Greenwood. I'm told that he knows more big words than a pocket-sized dictionary."

Much applause and laughter.

"So now, gentlemen, I want you to give him your attention."

There was still laughter as I faced them, my mouth dry, my eye throbbing. 65
I began slowly, but evidently my throat was tense, because they began shouting,
"Louder! Louder!"

"We of the younger generation extol the wisdom of that great leader and
educator," I shouted, "who first spoke these flaming words of wisdom: 'A ship
lost at sea for many days suddenly sighted a friendly vessel. From the mast of
the unfortunate vessel was seen a signal: "Water, water; we die of thirst!" The
answer from the friendly vessel came back: "Cast down your bucket where you
are." The captain of the distressed vessel, at last heeding the injunction, cast
down his bucket, and it came up full of fresh sparkling water from the mouth
of the Amazon River.' And like him I say, and in his words, 'To those of my race
who depend upon bettering their condition in a foreign land, or who underestimate the importance of cultivating friendly relations with the Southern white
man, who is his next-door neighbor, I would say: "Cast down your bucket where
you are" — cast it down in making friends in every manly way of the people of
all races by whom we are surrounded . . .'"

I spoke automatically and with such fervor that I did not realize that the
men were still talking and laughing until my dry mouth, filling up with blood
from the cut, almost strangled me. I coughed, wanting to stop and go to one of
the tall brass, sand-filled spittoons to relieve myself, but a few of the men,
especially the superintendent, were listening and I was afraid. So I gulped it
down, blood, saliva, and all, and continued. (What powers of endurance I had
during those days! What enthusiasm! What a belief in the rightness of things!) I
spoke even louder in spite of the pain. But still they talked and still they laughed,
as though deaf with cotton in dirty ears. So I spoke with greater emotional
emphasis. I closed my ears and swallowed blood until I was nauseated. The
speech seemed a hundred times as long as before, but I could not leave out a
single word. All had to be said, each memorized nuance considered, rendered.
Nor was that all. Whenever I uttered a word of three or more syllables a group
of voices would yell for me to repeat it. I used the phrase "social responsibility"
and they yelled:

"What's that word you say, boy?"

"Social responsibility," I said.

"What?"

"Social . . ." 70

"Louder."

". . . responsibility."

"More!"

"Respon — " 75

"Repeat!"

" — sibility."

The room filled with the uproar of laughter until, no doubt, distracted by
having to gulp down my blood, I made a mistake and yelled a phrase I had often
seen denounced in newspaper editorials, heard debated in private.

"Social . . ."

"What?" they yelled. 80

". . . equality —"

The laughter hung smokelike in the sudden stillness. I opened my eyes, puzzled. Sounds of displeasure filled the room. The M.C. rushed forward. They shouted hostile phrases at me. But I did not understand.

A small dry mustached man in the front row blared out, "Say that slowly, son!"

"What, sir?"

"What you just said!"

"Social responsibility, sir," I said. 85

"You weren't being smart, were you, boy?" he said, not unkindly.

"No, sir!"

"You sure that about 'equality' was a mistake?"

"Oh, yes, sir," I said. "I was swallowing blood." — *literally & symbolically* 90

"Well, you had better speak more slowly so we can understand. We mean to do right by you, but you've got to know your place at all times. All right, now, go on with your speech."

I was afraid. I wanted to leave but I wanted also to speak and I was afraid they'd snatch me down.

"Thank you, sir," I said, beginning where I had left off, and having them ignore me as before.

Yet when I finished there was a thunderous applause. I was surprised to see the superintendent come forth with a package wrapped in white tissue paper, and, gesturing for quiet, address the men.

"Gentlemen, you see that I did not overpraise this boy. He makes a good 95 speech and some day he'll lead his people in the proper paths. And I don't have to tell you that that is important in these days and times. This is a good, smart boy, and so to encourage him in the right direction, in the name of the Board of Education I wish to present him a prize in the form of this . . ."

He paused, removing the tissue paper and revealing a gleaming calfskin brief case.

". . . in the form of this first-class article from Shad Whitmore's shop."

"Boy," he said, addressing me, "take this prize and keep it well. Consider it a badge of office. Prize it. Keep developing as you are and some day it will be filled with important papers that will help shape the destiny of your people."

I was so moved that I could hardly express my thanks. A rope of bloody saliva forming a shape like an undiscovered continent drooled upon the leather and I wiped it quickly away. I felt an importance that I had never dreamed.

"Open it and see what's inside," I was told. 100

My fingers a-tremble, I complied, smelling the fresh leather and finding an official-looking document inside. It was a scholarship to the state college for Negroes. My eyes filled with tears and I ran awkwardly off the floor.

I was overjoyed; I did not even mind when I discovered that the gold pieces I had scrambled for were brass pocket tokens advertising a certain make of automobile.

When I reached home everyone was excited. Next day the neighbors came to congratulate me. I even felt safe from grandfather, whose deathbed curse usually spoiled my triumphs. I stood beneath his photograph with my brief case in hand and smiled triumphantly into his stolid black peasant's face. It was a face that fascinated me. The eyes seemed to follow everywhere I went.

That night I dreamed I was at a circus with him and that he refused to laugh at the clowns no matter what they did. Then later he told me to open my brief case and read what was inside and I did, finding an official envelope stamped with the state seal; and inside the envelope I found another and another, endlessly, and I thought I would fall of weariness. "Them's years," he said. "Now open that one." And I did and in it I found an engraved document containing a short message in letters of gold. "Read it," my grandfather said. "Out loud!"

"To Whom It May Concern," I intoned. "Keep This Nigger-Boy Running." 105
I awoke with the old man's laughter ringing in my ears.

(It was a dream I was to remember and dream again for many years after. But at that time I had no insight into its meaning. First I had to attend college.)

Considerations for Critical Thinking and Writing

1. How does the first paragraph of the story sum up the conflict that the narrator confronts? In what sense is he "invisible"?
2. Why do his grandfather's last words cause so much anxiety in the family? What does his grandfather mean when he says, "I want you to overcome 'em with yeses, undermine 'em with grins, agree 'em to death"?
3. What is the symbolic significance of the naked blonde? What details reveal that she represents more than a sexual tease in the story?
4. How does the battle in the boxing ring and the scramble for money afterward suggest the kind of control whites have over blacks in the story?
5. Why is it significant that the town is named Greenwood and that the briefcase award comes from Shad Whitmore's shop? Can you find any other details that serve to reinforce the meaning of the story?
6. What is the narrator's perspective as an educated adult telling the story, in contrast to his assumptions and beliefs as a recent high-school graduate? How is this contrast especially evident in the speech before the "leading white citizens" of the town?
7. How can the dream at the end of the story be related to the major incidents that precede it?
8. Discuss how the young black man's expectations are similar to what has come to be known as the American dream, that assumes that ambition, hard work, perseverance, intelligence, and virtue always lead to success.
9. Given the grandfather's advice, explain how "meekness" can be a "dangerous activity" and a weapon against oppression.
10. Imagine the story as told from a third-person point of view. How would this change the story? Do you think the story would be more or less effective told from a third-person point of view? Explain your answer.

Connections to Other Selections

1. Compare and contrast Ellison's view of the South with Faulkner's in "A Rose for Emily" (p. 47).
2. Write an essay comparing and contrasting "Battle Royal" and James Joyce's "Araby" (p. 310) as symbolic stories that focus on their respective protagonists' illusions and disillusions about life.
3. Compare and contrast this story with M. Carl Holman's poem "Mr. Z" (p. 962).

RALPH ELLISON (b. 1914)
On Fiction as an Oblique Process   1974

[John] Hersey [Interviewer]: Do you have in mind an image of some actualized reader to whom you are communicating as you write?

Ellison: There is no *specific* person there, but there is a sort of ideal reader, or informed persona, who has some immediate sense of the material that I'm working with. Beyond that there is my sense of the rhetorical levers within American society, and these attach to all kinds of experiences and values. I don't want to be a behaviorist here, but I'm referring to the systems of values, the beliefs and customs and sense of the past, and that hope for the future, which have evolved through the history of the republic. These do provide a medium of communication.

For instance, the old underdog pattern. It turns up in many guises, and it allows the writer to communicate with the public over and beyond whatever the immediate issues of his fiction happen to be. That is, deep down we believe in the underdog, even though we give him hell; and this provides a rhetoric through which the writer can communicate with a reader beyond any questions of their disagreements over class values, race, or anything else. But the writer must be aware that that is what is there. On the other hand, I do not think he can manipulate his readers too directly; it must be an oblique process, if for no other reason than that to do it too directly throws you into propaganda, as against that brooding, questioning stance that is necessary for fiction.

From "A Talk with Ralph Ellison" in *Ralph Ellison: A Collection of Essays*

Considerations for Critical Thinking and Writing

1. What "rhetorical levers" does Ellison pull in "Battle Royal" to "provide a medium of communication" with his readers? What values do you think Ellison attributes to his readers?
2. How does Ellison's use of symbols in "Battle Royal" contribute to the "oblique process" he says is "necessary for fiction"?
3. Explain how "the old underdog pattern" functions in "Battle Royal" and how it affects your response to the narrator.
4. To what extent is the "underdog pattern" applicable to Isabel Allende's "The Judge's Wife" (p. 495)?

7. Theme

Theme is the central idea or meaning of a story. It provides a unifying point around which the plot, characters, setting, point of view, symbols, and other elements of a story are organized. In some works the theme is explicitly stated. Nathaniel Hawthorne's "Wakefield," for example, begins with the author telling the reader that the point of his story is "done up neatly, and condensed into the final sentence." Most modern writers, however, present their themes implicitly (as Hawthorne does in the majority of his stories), so determining the underlying meaning of a work often requires more effort than it does from the reader of "Wakefield." One reason for the difficulty is that the theme is fused into the elements of the story, and these must be carefully examined in relation to one another as well as to the work as a whole. But then that's the value of determining the theme, for it requires a close analysis of all the elements of a work. This close reading often results in sharper insights into this overlooked character or that seemingly unrelated incident. Accounting for the details and seeing how they fit together result in greater understanding of the story. Such familiarity creates pleasure in much the same way that a musical piece heard more than once becomes a rich experience rather than simply a repetitive one.

Themes are not always easy to express, but some principles can aid you in articulating the central meaning of a work. First distinguish between the theme of a story and its subject. They are not equivalents. Many stories share identical subjects, such as fate, death, innocence, youth, loneliness, racial prejudice, and disillusionment. Yet each story usually makes its own statement about the subject and expresses some view of life. Hemingway's "Soldier's Home" (p. 125) and Faulkner's "Barn Burning" (p. 436) both describe young men who are unhappy at home and decide that they must leave, but the meaning of each story is quite different. A thematic generalization about "Soldier's Home" could be something like this: "The brutal experience of war can alienate a person from those who are innocent of war's actualities — even family and friends." The theme of Faulkner's story could be stated this way: "No matter how much one might love one's father, there comes a time when family loyalties must be left behind in order to be true to one's self."

These two statements of theme do not definitively sum up each story — there is no single, absolute way of expressing a work's theme — but they do describe a central idea in each. Furthermore, the emphasis in each of these themes could be modified or expanded, because interpretations of interesting, complex works are always subject to revision. People have different responses to life, and so it is hardly surprising that responses to literature are not identical. A consideration of theme usually expands the possibilities for meaning rather than reducing them to categories such as "right" or "wrong."

Although readers may differ in their interpretations of a story, that does not mean that *any* interpretation is valid. If we were to assert that the soldier's dissatisfactions in Hemingway's story could be readily eliminated by his settling down to marriage and a decent job (his mother's solution), we would have missed Hemingway's purposes in writing the story; we would have failed to see how Krebs's war experiences have caused him to re-examine the assumptions and beliefs that previously nurtured him but now seem unreal to him. We would have to ignore much in the story in order to arrive at such a reading. To be valid, the statement of the theme should be responsive to the details of the story. It must be based on evidence within the story rather than solely on experiences, attitudes, or values the reader brings to the work — such as personally knowing a war veteran who successfully adjusted to civilian life after getting a good job and marrying. Familiarity with the subject matter of a story can certainly be an aid to interpretation, but it should not get in the way of seeing the author's perspective.

Sometimes readers too hastily conclude that a story's theme always consists of a moral, some kind of lesson that is dramatized by the various elements of the work. There are stories that do this — Hawthorne's "Wakefield," for example. Here are the final sentences in his story about a middle-aged man who drops out of life for twenty years:

> He has left us much food for thought, a portion of which shall lend its wisdom to a moral, and be shaped into a figure. Amid the seeming confusion of our mysterious world, individuals are so nicely adjusted to a system, and systems to one another and to a whole, that, by stepping aside for a moment, a man exposes himself to a fearful risk of losing his place forever. Like Wakefield, he may become, as it were, the Outcast of the Universe.

Most stories, however, do not include such direct caveats about the conduct of life. A tendency to look for a lesson in a story can produce a reductive and inaccurate formulation of its theme. Consider the damage done to Colette's "The Hand" (p. 184) if its theme is described as this: "Adolescents are too young to cope with the responsibilities of marriage."

Colette's focus in this story is on the young woman's response to her husband's powerful sexuality and dominance rather than on her inability to be a good wife.

In fact, a good many stories go beyond traditional moral values to explore human behavior instead of condemning or endorsing it. Chekhov's treatment of the adulterous affair between Gurov and Anna in "The Lady with the Pet Dog" (p. 150) portrays a love that is valuable and true despite the conventional moral codes it violates. That is not to say that the reader must agree with Chekhov's attitude that such love has a validity of its own. We are obligated to see that Chekhov is sympathetic to the lovers, but that does not necessitate our approval. All that is required is our willingness to explore with the author the issues set before us. The themes we encounter in literature may challenge as well as reassure us.

Determining the theme of a story can be a difficult task, because all the story's elements may contribute to its central idea. Indeed, you may discover that finding the theme is more challenging than coming to grips with the author's values as they are revealed in the story. There is no precise formula that can take you to the center of a story's meaning and help you to articulate it. However, several strategies are practical and useful once you have read the story. Apply these pointers during a second or third reading.

1. Pay attention to the title of the story; it will often provide a lead to a major symbol (Faulkner's "Barn Burning," p. 436) or focus on the subject around which the theme develops (Godwin's "A Sorrowful Woman," p. 30).

2. Look for details in the story that have potential for symbolic meanings. Careful consideration of names, places, objects, minor characters, and incidents can lead you to the central meaning — for example, think of the stripper in Ellison's "Battle Royal" (p. 187). Be especially attentive to elements you did not understand on the first reading.

3. Decide if the protagonist changes or develops some important insight as a result of the action. Carefully examine any generalizations the protagonist or narrator makes about the events in the story.

4. When you formulate the theme of the story in your own words, write it down in a complete sentence or two that make some point about the subject matter. Revenge may be the subject of a story, but its theme should make a statement about revenge: "Instead of providing satisfaction, revenge defeats the best in one's self" is one possibility.

5. Be certain that your expression of the theme is a generalized statement rather than a specific description of particular people, places, and incidents in the story. Contrast the preceding statement of a theme on revenge with this too-specific one: "In Nathaniel Hawthorne's *The Scarlet Letter*, Roger Chillingworth loses his humanity owing to his single-minded attempts to punish Arthur Dimmesdale for having an affair with Chillingworth's wife, Hester." Hawthorne's theme is not

restricted to a single fictional character named Chillingworth but to anyone whose life is ruined by revenge. Be certain that your statement of theme does not focus on only part of the story. The theme just cited for *The Scarlet Letter,* for example, relegates Hester to the status of a minor character. What it says about Chillingworth is true, but the statement is incomplete as a generalization about the novel.

6. Be wary of using clichés as a way of stating theme. They tend to short-circuit ideas instead of generating them. It may be tempting to resort to something like "Love conquers all" as a statement of the theme of Chekhov's "The Lady with the Pet Dog" (p. 150); however, even the slightest second thought reveals how much more ambiguous the ending of that story is.

7. Be aware that some stories emphasize theme less than others. Stories that have as their major purpose adventure, humor, mystery, or terror may have little or no theme. In Edgar Allan Poe's "The Pit and the Pendulum," for example, the protagonist is not used to condemn torture; instead, he becomes a sensitive gauge to measure the pain and horror he endures at the hands of his captors.

What is most valuable about articulating the theme of a work is not a brief summary statement but the process by which the theme is determined. Ultimately, the theme is expressed by the story itself and is inseparable from the experience of reading the story. Tim O'Brien's explanation about "How to Tell a True War Story" (p. 552) is probably true of most kinds of stories: "In a true war story, if there's a moral [or theme] at all, it's like the thread that makes the cloth. You can't tease it out. You can't extract the meaning without unraveling the deeper meaning." Describing the theme should not be a way to consume a story, to be done with it. It is a means of clarifying our thinking about what we've read and probably felt intuitively.

Stephen Crane's "The Bride Comes to Yellow Sky" and Katherine Mansfield's "Miss Brill" are two stories whose respective themes emerge from the authors' skillful use of plot, character, setting, and symbol.

STEPHEN CRANE (1871–1900)

Born in Newark, New Jersey, Stephen Crane attended Lafayette College and Syracuse University and then worked as a free-lance journalist in New York City. He wrote newspaper pieces, short stories, poems, and novels for his entire, brief adult life. His first book, *Maggie: A Girl of the Streets* (1893), is a story about New York slum life and prostitution. His most famous novel, *The Red Badge of Courage* (1895), gives readers a vivid, convincing re-creation of Civil War battles, even though Crane had never been to war. However, Crane was personally familiar with the American West, where he traveled as a reporter. "The Bride Comes to Yellow Sky" includes some of the ingredients of a typical popular western — a confrontation between a marshal and a drunk who shoots up the town — but the story's theme is less predictable and more serious than the plot seems to suggest.

The Bride Comes to Yellow Sky   1898

I

The great Pullman was whirling onward with such dignity of motion that a glance from the window seemed simply to prove that the plains of Texas were pouring eastward. Vast flats of green grass, dull-hued spaces of mesquit and cactus, little groups of frame houses, woods of light and tender trees, all were sweeping into the east, sweeping over the horizon, a precipice.

A newly married pair had boarded this coach at San Antonio. The man's face was reddened from many days in the wind and sun, and a direct result of his new black clothes was that his brick-colored hands were constantly performing in a most conscious fashion. From time to time he looked down respectfully at his attire. He sat with a hand on each knee, like a man waiting in a barber's shop. The glances he devoted to other passengers were furtive and shy.

The bride was not pretty, nor was she very young. She wore a dress of blue cashmere, with small reservations of velvet here and there, and with steel buttons abounding. She continually twisted her head to regard her puff sleeves, very stiff, straight, and high. They embarrassed her. It was quite apparent that she had cooked, and that she expected to cook, dutifully. The blushes caused by the careless scrutiny of some passengers as she had entered the car were strange to see upon this plain, under-class countenance, which was drawn in placid, almost emotionless lines.

They were evidently very happy. "Ever been in a parlor-car before?" he asked, smiling with delight.

"No," she answered; "I never was. It's fine, ain't it?"   5

"Great! And then after a while we'll go forward to the diner, and get a big lay-out. Finest meal in the world. Charge a dollar."

"Oh, do they?" cried the bride. "Charge a dollar? Why, that's too much — for us — ain't it, Jack?"

"Not this trip, anyhow," he answered bravely. "We're going to go the whole thing."

Later he explained to her about the trains. "You see, it's a thousand miles from one end of Texas to the other; and this train runs right across it, and never stops but four times." He had the pride of an owner. He pointed out to her the dazzling fittings of the coach; and in truth her eyes opened wider as she contemplated the sea-green figured velvet, the shining brass, silver, and glass, the wood that gleamed as darkly brilliant as the surface of a pool of oil. At one end a bronze figure sturdily held a support for a separated chamber, and at convenient places on the ceiling were frescos in olive and silver.

To the minds of the pair, their surroundings reflected the glory of their marriage that morning in San Antonio; this was the environment of their new estate; and the man's face in particular beamed with an elation that made him appear ridiculous to the negro porter. This individual at times surveyed them from afar with an amused and superior grin. On other occasions he bullied them with skill in ways that did not make it exactly plain to them that they were being bullied. He subtly used all the manners of the most unconquerable kind of snobbery. He oppressed them; but of this oppression they had small knowledge, and they speedily forgot that infrequently a number of travellers covered them with stares of derisive enjoyment. Historically there was supposed to be something infinitely humorous in their situation.

"We are due in Yellow Sky at 3:42," he said, looking tenderly into her eyes.

"Oh, are we?" she said, as if she had not been aware of it. To evince surprise at her husband's statement was part of her wifely amiability. She took from a pocket a little silver watch; and as she held it before her, and stared at it with a frown of attention, the new husband's face shone.

"I bought it in San Anton' from a friend of mine," he told her gleefully.

"It's seventeen minutes past twelve," she said, looking up at him with a kind of shy and clumsy coquetry. A passenger, noting this play, grew excessively sardonic, and winked at himself in one of the numerous mirrors.

At last they went to the dining-car. Two rows of negro waiters, in glowing white suits, surveyed their entrance with the interest, and also the equanimity, of men who had been forewarned. The pair fell to the lot of a waiter who happened to feel pleasure in steering them through their meal. He viewed them with the manner of a fatherly pilot, his countenance radiant with benevolence. The patronage, entwined with the ordinary deference, was not plain to them. And yet, as they returned to their coach, they showed in their faces a sense of escape.

To the left, miles down a long purple slope, was a little ribbon of mist where moved the keening Rio Grande. The train was approaching it at an angle, and the apex was Yellow Sky. Presently it was apparent that, as the distance from Yellow Sky grew shorter, the husband became commensurately restless. His brick-red hands were more insistent in their prominence. Occasionally he was even rather absent-minded and far-away when the bride leaned forward and addressed him.

As a matter of truth, Jack Potter was beginning to find the shadow of a deed weigh upon him like a leaden slab. He, the town marshal of Yellow Sky, a man known, liked, and feared in his corner, a prominent person, had gone to San Antonio to meet a girl he believed he loved, and there, after the usual prayers, had actually induced her to marry him, without consulting Yellow Sky for any part of the transaction. He was now bringing his bride before an innocent and unsuspecting community.

Of course people in Yellow Sky married as it pleased them in accordance with a general custom; but such was Potter's thought of his duty to his friends, or of their idea of his duty, or of an unspoken form which does not control men in these matters, that he felt he was heinous. He had committed an extraordinary crime. Face to face with this girl in San Antonio, and spurred by his sharp impulse, he had gone headlong over all the social hedges. At San Antonio he was like a man hidden in the dark. A knife to sever any friendly duty, any form, was easy to his hand in that remote city. But the hour of Yellow Sky — the hour of daylight — was approaching.

He knew full well that his marriage was an important thing to his town. It could only be exceeded by the burning of the new hotel. His friends could not forgive him. Frequently he had reflected on the advisability of telling them by telegraph, but a new cowardice had been upon him. He feared to do it. And now the train was hurrying him toward a scene of amazement, glee, and reproach. He glanced out of the window at the line of haze swinging slowly in toward the train.

Yellow Sky had a kind of brass band, which played painfully, to the delight 20 of the populace. He laughed without heart as he thought of it. If the citizens could dream of his prospective arrival with his bride, they would parade the band at the station and escort them, amid cheers and laughing congratulations, to his adobe home.

He resolved that he would use all the devices of speed and plainscraft in making the journey from the station to his house. Once within that safe citadel, he could issue some sort of vocal bulletin, and then not go among the citizens until they had time to wear off a little of their enthusiasm.

The bride looked anxiously at him. "What's worrying you, Jack?"

He laughed again. "I'm not worrying, girl; I'm only thinking of Yellow Sky."

She flushed in comprehension.

A sense of mutual guilt invaded their minds and developed a finer tender- 25 ness. They looked at each other with eyes softly aglow. But Potter often laughed the same nervous laugh; the flush upon the bride's face seemed quite permanent.

The traitor to the feelings of Yellow Sky narrowly watched the speeding landscape. "We're nearly there," he said.

Presently the porter came and announced the proximity of Potter's home. He held a brush in his hand, and, with all his airy superiority gone, he brushed Potter's new clothes as the latter slowly turned this way and that way. Potter fumbled out a coin and gave it to the porter, as he had seen others do. It was a heavy and muscle-bound business, as that of a man shoeing his first horse.

The porter took their bag, and as the train began to slow they moved forward to the hooded platform of the car. Presently the two engines and their long string of coaches rushed into the station of Yellow Sky.

"They have to take water here," said Potter, from a constricted throat and in mournful cadence, as one announcing death. Before the train stopped his eye had swept the length of the platform, and he was glad and astonished to see there was none upon it but the station-agent, who, with a slightly hurried and anxious air, was walking toward the water-tanks. When the train had halted, the porter alighted first, and placed in position a little temporary step.

"Come on, girl," said Potter, hoarsely. As he helped her down they each 30 laughed on a false note. He took the bag from the negro, and bade his wife cling to his arm. As they slunk rapidly away, his hang-dog glance perceived that they were unloading the two trunks, and also that the station-agent, far ahead near the baggage-car, had turned and was running toward him, making gestures. He laughed, and groaned as he laughed, when he noted the first effect of his marital bliss upon Yellow Sky. He gripped his wife's arm firmly to his side, and they fled. Behind them the porter stood, chuckling fatuously.

II

The California express on the Southern Railway was due at Yellow Sky in twenty-one minutes. There were six men at the bar of the Weary Gentleman saloon. One was a drummer who talked a great deal and rapidly; three were Texans who did not care to talk at that time; and two were Mexican sheep-herders, who did not talk as a general practice in the Weary Gentleman saloon. The barkeeper's dog lay on the board walk that crossed in front of the door. His head was on his paws, and he glanced drowsily here and there with the constant vigilance of a dog that is kicked on occasion. Across the sandy street were some vivid green grass-plots, so wonderful in appearance, amid the sands that burned near them in a blazing sun, that they caused a doubt in the mind. They exactly resembled the grass mats used to represent lawns on the stage. At the cooler end of the railway station, a man without a coat sat in a tilted chair and smoked his pipe. The fresh-cut bank of the Rio Grande circled near the town, and there could be seen beyond it a great plum-colored plain of mesquit.

Save for the busy drummer and his companions in the saloon, Yellow Sky was dozing. The new-comer leaned gracefully upon the bar, and recited many tales with the confidence of a bard who has come upon a new field.

" — and at the moment that the old man fell downstairs with the bureau in his arms, the old woman was coming up with two scuttles of coal, and of course — "

The drummer's tale was interrupted by a young man who suddenly appeared in the open door. He cried: "Scratchy Wilson's drunk, and has turned loose with both hands." The two Mexicans at once set down their glasses and faded out of the rear entrance of the saloon.

The drummer, innocent and jocular, answered: "All right, old man. S'pose ³⁵ he has? Come in and have a drink, anyhow."

But the information had made such an obvious cleft in every skull in the room that the drummer was obliged to see its importance. All had become instantly solemn. "Say," said he, mystified, "what is this?" His three companions made the introductory gesture of eloquent speech; but the young man at the door forestalled them.

"It means, my friend," he answered, as he came into the saloon, "that for the next two hours this town won't be a health resort."

The barkeeper went to the door, and locked and barred it; reaching out of the window, he pulled in heavy wooden shutters, and barred them. Immediately a solemn, chapel-like gloom was upon the place. The drummer was looking from one to another.

"But, say," he cried, "what is this, anyhow? You don't mean there is going to be a gun-fight?"

"Don't know whether there'll be a fight or not," answered one man, grimly; ⁴⁰ "but there'll be some shootin' — some good shootin'."

The young man who had warned them waved his hand. "Oh, there'll be a fight fast enough, if any one wants it. Anybody can get a fight out there in the street. There's a fight just waiting."

The drummer seemed to be swayed between the interest of a foreigner and a perception of personal danger.

"What did you say his name was?" he asked.

"Scratchy Wilson," they answered in chorus.

"And will he kill anybody? What are you going to do? Does this happen often? Does he rampage around like this once a week or so? Can he break in that door?"

"No; he can't break down that door," replied the barkeeper. "He's tried it three times. But when he comes you'd better lay down on the floor, stranger. He's dead sure to shoot at it, and a bullet may come through."

Thereafter the drummer kept a strict eye upon the door. The time had not yet called for him to hug the floor, but, as a minor precaution, he sidled near the wall. "Will he kill anybody?" he said again.

The men laughed low and scornfully at the question.

"He's out to shoot, and he's out for trouble. Don't see any good in experimentin' with him."

"But what do you do in a case like this? What do you do?"

A man responded: "Why, he and Jack Potter — "

"But," in chorus the other men interrupted, "Jack Potter's in San Anton'."

"Well, who is he? What's he got to do with it?"

"Oh, he's the town marshal. He goes out and fights Scratchy when he gets on one of these tears."

"Wow!" said the drummer, mopping his brow. "Nice job he's got."

The voices had toned away to mere whisperings. The drummer wished to ask further questions, which were born of an increasing anxiety and bewilderment; but when he attempted them, the men merely looked at him in irritation and motioned him to remain silent. A tense waiting hush was upon them. In the deep shadows of the room their eyes shone as they listened for sounds from the street. One man made three gestures at the barkeeper; and the latter, moving like a ghost, handed him a glass and a bottle. The man poured a full glass of whisky, and set down the bottle noiselessly. He gulped the whisky in a swallow, and turned again toward the door in immovable silence. The drummer saw that the barkeeper, without a sound, had taken a Winchester from beneath the bar. Later he saw this individual beckoning to him, so he tiptoed across the room.

"You better come with me back of the bar."

"No thanks," said the drummer, perspiring; "I'd rather be where I can make a break for the back door."

Whereupon the man of bottles made a kindly but peremptory gesture. The drummer obeyed it, and, finding himself seated on a box with his head below the level of the bar, balm was laid upon his soul at sight of various zinc and copper fittings that bore a resemblance to armor-plate. The barkeeper took a seat comfortably upon an adjacent box.

"You see," he whispered, "this here Scratchy Wilson is a wonder with a gun — a perfect wonder; and when he goes on the war-trail, we hunt our holes — naturally. He's about the last one of the old gang that used to hang out along the river here. He's a terror when he's drunk. When he's sober he's all right — kind of simple — wouldn't hurt a fly — nicest fellow in town. But when he's drunk — whoo!"

There were periods of stillness. "I wish Jack Potter was back from San Anton'," said the barkeeper. "He shot Wilson up once — in the leg — and he would sail in and pull out the kinks in this thing."

Presently they heard from a distance the sound of a shot, followed by three wild yowls. It instantly removed a bond from the men in the darkened saloon. There was a shuffling of feet. They looked at each other. "Here he comes," they said.

III

A man in a maroon-colored flannel shirt, which had been purchased for purposes of decoration, and made principally by some Jewish women on the East Side of New York, rounded a corner and walked into the middle of the main street of Yellow Sky. In either hand the man held a long, heavy, blue-black revolver. Often he yelled, and these cries rang through a semblance of a deserted village, shrilly flying over the roofs in a volume that seemed to have no relation to the ordinary vocal strength of a man. It was as if the surrounding stillness formed the arch of a tomb over him. These cries of ferocious challenge rang against walls of silence. And his boots had red tops with gilded imprints, of the kind beloved in winter by little sledding boys on the hillsides of New England.

The man's face flamed in a rage begot of whisky. His eyes, rolling, and yet keen for ambush, hunted the still doorways and windows. He walked with the creeping movement of the midnight cat. As it occurred to him, he roared menacing information. The long revolvers in his hands were as easy as straws; they were removed with an electric swiftness. The little fingers of each hand played sometimes in a musician's way. Plain from the low collar of the shirt, the cords of his neck straightened and sank, straightened and sank, as passion moved him. The only sounds were his terrible invitations. The calm adobes preserved their demeanor at the passing of this small thing in the middle of the street.

There was no offer of fight — no offer of fight. The man called to the sky. 65 There were no attractions. He bellowed and fumed and swayed his revolvers here and everywhere.

The dog of the barkeeper of the Weary Gentleman saloon had not appreciated the advance of events. He yet lay dozing in front of his master's door. At sight of the dog, the man paused and raised his revolver humorously. At sight of the man, the dog sprang up and walked diagonally away, with a sullen head, and growling. The man yelled, and the dog broke into a gallop. As it was about to enter the alley, there was a loud noise, a whistling, and something spat the ground directly before it. The dog screamed, and, wheeling in terror, galloped headlong in a new direction. Again there was a noise, a whistling, and sand was kicked viciously before it. Fear-stricken, the dog turned and flurried like an animal in a pen. The man stood laughing, his weapons at his hips.

Ultimately the man was attracted by the closed door of the Weary Gentleman saloon. He went to it and, hammering with a revolver, demanded drink.

The door remaining imperturbable, he picked a bit of paper from the walk, and nailed it to the framework with a knife. He then turned his back contemptuously upon this popular resort and, walking to the opposite side of the street and spinning there on his heel quickly and lithely, fired at the bit of paper. He missed it by a half inch. He swore at himself, and went away. Later he comfortably fusilladed the windows of his most intimate friend. The man was playing with this town; it was a toy for him.

But still there was no offer of fight. The name of Jack Potter, his ancient antagonist, entered his mind, and he concluded that it would be a glad thing if he should go to Potter's house, and by bombardment induce him to come out and fight. He moved in the direction of his desire, chanting Apache scalp-music.

When he arrived at it, Potter's house presented the same still front as had the other adobes. Taking up a strategic position, the man howled a challenge. But this house regarded him as might a great stone god. It gave no sign. After a decent wait, the man howled further challenges, mingling with them wonderful epithets. 70

Presently there came the spectacle of a man churning himself into deepest rage over the immobility of a house. He fumed at it as the winter wind attacks a prairie cabin in the North. To the distance there should have gone the sound of a tumult like the fighting of two hundred Mexicans. As necessity bade him, he paused for breath or to reload his revolvers.

IV

Potter and his bride walked sheepishly and with speed. Sometimes they laughed together shamefacedly and low.

"Next corner, dear," he said finally.

They put forth the efforts of a pair walking bowed against a strong wind. Potter was about to raise a finger to point the first appearance of the new home when, as they circled the corner, they came face to face with a man in a maroon-colored shirt, who was feverishly pushing cartridges into a large revolver. Upon the instant the man dropped his revolver to the ground and, like lightning, whipped another from its holster. The second weapon was aimed at the bride-groom's chest.

There was a silence. Potter's mouth seemed to be merely a grave for his tongue. He exhibited an instinct to at once loosen his arm from the woman's grip, and he dropped the bag to the sand. As for the bride, her face had gone as yellow as old cloth. She was a slave to hideous rites, gazing at the apparitional snake. 75

The two men faced each other at a distance of three paces. He of the revolver smiled with a new and quiet ferocity.

"Tried to sneak up on me," he said. "Tried to sneak up on me!" His eyes grew more baleful. As Potter made a slight movement, the man thrust his revolver venomously forward. "No, don't you do it, Jack Potter. Don't you move a finger toward a gun just yet. Don't you move an eyelash. The time has come for me to settle with you and I'm goin' to do it my own way, and loaf along with no interferin'. So if you don't want a gun bent on you, just mind what I tell you."

Potter looked at his enemy. "I ain't got a gun on me, Scratchy," he said. "Honest, I ain't." He was stiffening and steadying, but yet somewhere at the back of his mind a vision of the Pullman floated: the sea-green figured velvet, the shining brass, silver, and glass, the wood that gleamed as darkly brilliant as the surface of a pool of oil — all the glory of marriage, the environment of the new estate. "You know I fight when it comes to fighting, Scratchy Wilson; but I ain't got a gun on me. You'll have to do all the shootin' yourself."

His enemy's face went livid. He stepped forward, and lashed his weapon to and fro before Potter's chest. "Don't you tell me you ain't got no gun on you, you whelp. Don't tell me no lie like that. There ain't a man in Texas ever seen you without no gun. Don't take me for no kid." His eyes blazed with light, and his throat worked like a pump.

"I ain't takin' you for no kid," answered Potter. His heels had not moved an 80 inch backward. "I'm takin' you for a damn fool. I tell you I ain't got a gun, and I ain't. If you're goin' to shoot me up, you better begin now; you'll never get a chance like this again."

So much enforced reasoning had told on Wilson's rage; he was calmer. "If you ain't got a gun, why ain't you got a gun?" he sneered. "Been to Sunday-school?"

"I ain't got a gun because I've just come from San Anton' with my wife. I'm married," said Potter. "And if I'd thought there was going to be any galoots like you prowling around when I brought my wife home, I'd had a gun, and don't you forget it."

"Married!" said Scratchy, not at all comprehending.

"Yes, married. I'm married," said Potter, distinctly.

"Married?" said Scratchy. Seemingly for the first time, he saw the drooping, 85 drowning woman at the other man's side. "No!" he said. He was like a creature allowed a glimpse of another world. He moved a pace backward, and his arm, with the revolver, dropped to his side. "Is this the lady?" he asked.

"Yes; this is the lady," answered Potter.

There was another period of silence.

"Well," said Wilson at last, slowly, "I s'pose it's all off now."

"It's all off if you say so, Scratchy. You know I didn't make the trouble." Potter lifted his valise.

"Well, I 'low it's off, Jack," said Wilson. He was looking at the ground. 90 "Married!" He was not a student of chivalry; it was merely that in the presence of this foreign condition he was a simple child of the earlier plains. He picked up his starboard revolver, and, placing both weapons in their holsters, he went away. His feet made funnel-shaped tracks in the heavy sand.

Considerations for Critical Thinking and Writing

1. What is the nature of the conflict Marshal Potter feels on the train in Part I? Why does he feel like a "traitor" bringing a bride home to Yellow Sky?
2. What is the function of the "drummer," the traveling salesman, in Part II?
3. How do Mrs. Potter and Scratchy Wilson serve as foils for each other? What does each represent in the story?
4. What is the significance of the setting?
5. How does Crane create suspense about what will happen when Marshal Potter meets Scratchy Wilson? Is suspense the major point of the story?
6. Is Scratchy Wilson too drunk, comical, and ineffective to be a sympathetic character? What is the meaning of his conceding that "I s'pose it's all off now" at the end of Part IV? Is he a dynamic or a static character?

7. How do the title and first paragraph suggest the theme of the story? How does the theme differ from those of typical western stories you have read or seen?
8. What details seem to support the story's theme? Consider, for example, the descriptions of the bride's clothes and Scratchy Wilson's shirt and boots.
9. Explain why the heroes in western stories are rarely married and why Crane's use of marriage is central to his theme.
10. Compare and contrast the setting, characters, action, and theme in this story with the same elements in another western you have read or seen.

Connections to Other Selections

1. Although Scratchy Wilson and Katherine Mansfield's "Miss Brill" (below) are radically different kinds of people, they share a painful recognition at the end of their stories. What does each of them learn? Discuss whether you think what each of them learns is of equal importance in changing his or her life.
2. Write an essay comparing Crane's use of suspense with William Faulkner's in "A Rose for Emily" (p. 47).

KATHERINE MANSFIELD (1888–1923)

Born in New Zealand, Katherine Mansfield moved to London when she was a young woman and began writing short stories. Her first collection, *In a German Pension,* appeared in 1911. Subsequent publications, which include *Bliss and Other Stories* (1920) and *The Garden Party* (1922), secured her reputation as an important writer. The full range of her short stories is available in *The Collected Short Stories of Katherine Mansfield* (1945). Mansfield tends to focus her stories on intelligent, sensitive protagonists who undergo subtle but important changes in their lives. In "Miss Brill," an aging Englishwoman spends the afternoon in a park located in an unnamed French vacation town watching the activities of the people around her. Through those observations, Mansfield characterizes Miss Brill and permits us to see her experience a moment that changes her view of the world as well as of herself.

Miss Brill   1922

Although it was so brilliantly fine — the blue sky powdered with gold and great spots of light like white wine splashed over the Jardins Publiques — Miss Brill was glad that she had decided on her fur. The air was motionless, but when you opened your mouth there was just a faint chill, like a chill from a glass of iced water before you sip, and now and again a leaf came drifting — from nowhere, from the sky. Miss Brill put up her hand and touched her fur. Dear little thing! It was nice to feel it again. She had taken it out of its box that afternoon, shaken out the moth-powder, given it a good brush, and rubbed the life back into the dim little eyes. "What has been happening to me?" said the sad little eyes. Oh, how sweet it was to see them snap at her again from the red eiderdown! . . . But the nose, which was of some black composition, wasn't at all firm. It must have had a knock, somehow. Never mind — a little dab of black sealing-wax when the time came — when it was absolutely necessary. . . . Little rogue! Yes, she really felt like that about it. Little rogue biting its tail just by her left ear. She could have taken it off and laid it on her lap and stroked it. She felt a tingling in her hands and arms, but that came from walking, she supposed. And when she breathed, something light and sad — no, not sad, exactly — something gentle seemed to move in her bosom.

There were a number of people out this afternoon, far more than last Sunday. And the band sounded louder and gayer. That was because the Season had begun. For although the band played all the year round on Sundays, out of season it was never the same. It was like some one playing with only the family to listen; it didn't care how it played if there weren't any strangers present. Wasn't the conductor wearing a new coat, too? She was sure it was new. He scraped with his foot and flapped his arms like a rooster about to crow, and the bandsmen sitting in the green rotunda blew out their cheeks and glared at the music. Now there came a little "flutey" bit — very pretty! — a little chain of bright drops. She was sure it would be repeated. It was; she lifted her head and smiled.

Only two people shared her "special" seat: a fine old man in a velvet coat, his hands clasped over a huge carved walking-stick, and a big old woman, sitting upright, with a roll of knitting on her embroidered apron. They did not speak. This was disappointing, for Miss Brill always looked forward to the conversation. She had become really quite expert, she thought, at listening as though she didn't listen, at sitting in other people's lives just for a minute while they talked around her.

She glanced, sideways, at the old couple. Perhaps they would go soon. Last Sunday, too, hadn't been as interesting as usual. An Englishman and his wife, he wearing a dreadful Panama hat and she button boots. And she'd gone on the whole time about how she ought to wear spectacles; she knew she needed them; but that it was no good getting any; they'd be sure to break and they'd never keep on. And he'd been so patient. He'd suggested everything — gold rims, the kind that curved round your ears, little pads inside the bridge. No, nothing would please her. "They'll always be sliding down my nose!" Miss Brill had wanted to shake her.

The old people sat on the bench, still as statues. Never mind, there was always the crowd to watch. To and fro, in front of the flower-beds and the band rotunda, the couples and groups paraded, stopped to talk, to greet, to buy a handful of flowers from the old beggar who had his tray fixed to the railings. Little children ran among them, swooping and laughing; little boys with big white silk bows under their chins, little girls, little French dolls, dressed up in velvet and lace. And sometimes a tiny staggerer came suddenly rocking into the open from under the trees, stopped, stared, as suddenly sat down "flop," until its small high-stepping mother, like a young hen, rushed scolding to its rescue. Other people sat on the benches and green chairs, but they were nearly always the same, Sunday after Sunday, and — Miss Brill had often noticed — there was something funny about nearly all of them. They were odd, silent, nearly all old, and from the way they stared they looked as though they'd just come from dark little rooms or even — even cupboards!

Behind the rotunda the slender trees with yellow leaves down drooping, and through them just a line of sea, and beyond the blue sky with gold-veined clouds.

Tum-tum-tum tiddle-um! tiddle-um! tum tiddley-um tum ta! blew the band.

Two young girls in red came by and two young soldiers in blue met them, and they laughed and paired and went off arm-in-arm. Two peasant women with funny straw hats passed, gravely, leading beautiful smoke-colored donkeys. A cold, pale nun hurried by. A beautiful woman came along and dropped her bunch of violets, and a little boy ran after to hand them to her, and she took them and threw them away as if they'd been poisoned. Dear me! Miss Brill didn't know whether to admire that or not! And now an ermine toque and a gentleman in grey met just in front of her. He was tall, stiff, dignified, and she was wearing the ermine toque she'd bought when her hair was yellow. Now everything, her hair, her face, even her eyes, was the same color as the shabby ermine, and her hand, in its cleaned glove, lifted to dab her lips, was a tiny yellowish paw. Oh, she was so pleased to see him — delighted! She rather thought they were going to meet that afternoon. She described where she'd been — everywhere, here, there, along by the sea. The day was so charming — didn't he agree? And wouldn't he, perhaps? . . . . But he shook his head, lighted a cigarette, slowly breathed a great deep puff into her face, and, even while she was still talking and laughing, flicked the match away and walked on. The ermine toque was alone; she smiled more brightly than ever. But even the band seemed to know what she was feeling and played more softly, played tenderly, and the drum beat, "The Brute! The Brute!" over and over. What would she do? What was going to happen now? But as Miss Brill wondered, the ermine toque turned, raised her hand as though she'd seen some one else, much nicer, just over there, and pattered away. And the band changed again and played more quickly, more gaily than ever, and the old couple on Miss Brill's seat got up and marched away, and such a funny old man with long whiskers hobbled along in time to the music and was nearly knocked over by four girls walking abreast.

Oh, how fascinating it was! How she enjoyed it! How she loved sitting here, watching it all! It was like a play. It was exactly like a play. Who could believe the sky at the back wasn't painted? But it wasn't till a little brown dog trotted on solemn and then slowly trotted off, like a little "theatre" dog, a little dog that had been drugged, that Miss Brill discovered what it was that made it so exciting. They were all on the stage. They weren't only the audience, not only looking on; they were acting. Even she had a part and came every Sunday. No doubt somebody would have noticed if she hadn't been there; she was part of the performance after all. How strange she'd never thought of it like that before! And yet it explained why she made such a point of starting from home at just the same time each week — so as not to be late for the performance — and it also explained why she had quite a queer, shy feeling at telling her English pupils how she spent her Sunday afternoons. No wonder! Miss Brill nearly laughed out loud. She was on the stage. She thought of the old invalid gentleman to whom she read the newspaper four afternoons a week while he slept in the garden. She had got quite used to the frail head on the cotton pillow, the hollowed eyes, the open mouth, and the high pinched nose. If he'd been dead she mightn't have noticed for weeks; she wouldn't have minded. But suddenly he knew he was having the paper read to him by an actress! "An actress!" The old head lifted; two points of light quivered in the old eyes. "An actress — are ye?" And Miss Brill smoothed the newspaper as though it were the manuscript of her part and said gently: "Yes, I have been an actress for a long time."

The band had been having a rest. Now they started again. And what they played was warm, sunny, yet there was just a faint chill — a something, what was it? — not sadness — no, not sadness — a something that made you want to sing. The tune lifted, lifted, the light shone; and it seemed to Miss Brill that in another moment all of them, all the whole company, would begin singing. The young ones, the laughing ones who were moving together, they would begin, and the men's voices, very resolute and brave, would join them. And then she too, she too, and the others on the benches — they would come in with a kind of accompaniment — something low, that scarcely rose or fell, something so beautiful — moving. . . . And Miss Brill's eyes filled with tears and she looked smiling at all the other members of the company. Yes, we understand, we understand, she thought — though what they understood she didn't know. 10

Just at that moment a boy and a girl came and sat down where the old couple had been. They were beautifully dressed; they were in love. The hero and heroine, of course, just arrived from his father's yacht. And still soundlessly singing, still with that trembling smile, Miss Brill prepared to listen.

"No, not now," said the girl. "Not here, I can't."

"But why? Because of that stupid old thing at the end there?" asked the boy. "Why does she come here at all — who wants her? Why doesn't she keep her silly old mug at home?"

"It's her fu-fur which is so funny," giggled the girl. "It's exactly like a fried whiting."

"Ah, be off with you!" said the boy in an angry whisper. Then: "Tell me, ma petite chère ——" 15

"No, not here," said the girl. "Not *yet.*"

On her way home she usually bought a slice of honey-cake at the baker's. It was her Sunday treat. Sometimes there was an almond in her slice, sometimes not. It made a great difference. If there was an almond it was like carrying home a tiny present — a surprise — something that might very well not have been there. She hurried on the almond Sundays and struck the match for the kettle in quite a dashing way.

But today she passed the baker's by, climbed the stairs, went into the little dark room — her room like a cupboard — and sat down on the red eiderdown. She sat there for a long time. The box that the fur came out of was on the bed. She unclasped the necklet quickly; quickly, without looking, laid it inside. But when she put the lid on she thought she heard something crying.

Considerations for Critical Thinking and Writing

1. How does the calculated omission of Miss Brill's first name contribute to her characterization?
2. What details make Miss Brill more than a stock characterization of a frail old lady?
3. What do Miss Brill's observations about the people she encounters reveal about her?
4. What is the conflict in the story? Who or what is the antagonist?
5. Locate the climax of the story. How is it resolved?
6. What is the purpose of the fur piece? What is the source of the crying in the final sentence of the story?
7. Is Miss Brill a static or a dynamic character?
8. Describe Miss Brill's sense of herself at the end of the story.
9. Discuss the function of the minor characters mentioned in the story. Analyze how Mansfield used them to reveal Miss Brill's character.
10. There is almost no physical description of Miss Brill in the story. Develop a detailed description that you think would be consistent with her behavior.

Connections to Other Selections

1. Compare Miss Brill's recognition with that of the narrator in Fay Weldon's "IND AFF, or Out of Love in Sarajevo" (p. 562).
2. Write an essay comparing the themes in "Miss Brill" and James Joyce's "Eveline" (p. 315).

PERSPECTIVE

EUDORA WELTY (b. 1909)
On the Plots of "The Bride Comes to Yellow Sky" and "Miss Brill"

1949

Stephen Crane's "The Bride Comes to Yellow Sky" tells a story of situation; it is a playful story, using two situations, like counters.

Jack Potter, the town marshal of Yellow Sky, has gone to San Anton' and gotten married and is bringing his bride home in a Pullman — the whole errand to be a complete surprise to the town of Yellow Sky. "He knew full well that his marriage was an important thing to his town. It could only be exceeded by the burning of the new hotel."

And in Yellow Sky another situation is building up in matching tempo with the running wheels. A messenger appears in the door of the Weary Gentleman saloon crying "Scratchy Wilson's drunk and has turned loose with both hands." "Immediately a solemn, chapel-like gloom was upon the place. . . . 'Scratchy Wilson is a wonder with a gun, a perfect wonder, and when he goes on the war-trail, we hunt our holes — naturally.' " Scratchy enters town, pistols in both hands.

His "cries of ferocious challenge rang against walls of silence. And his boots had red tops with gilded imprints, of the kind beloved in winter by little sledding boys on the hillsides of New England. . . . He walked with the creeping movement of the midnight cat. As it occurred to him, he roared menacing information. . . . The little fingers of each hand played sometimes in a musician's way. . . . The only sounds were his terrible invitations."

All this is delightful to us not only for itself but for its function of play, of assuring our anticipation; the more ferocious Scratchy is, the more we are charmed. Our sense of the fairness, the proportion of things is gratified when he "comfortably fusilladed the windows of his most intimate friend. The man was playing with this town; it was a toy for him." This plot of situation gives us a kind of kinetic pleasure; just as being on a seesaw is pleasant not only for where we are but for where the other person is.

The train arrives, Jack Potter and bride get off, and Jack's emotion-charged meeting with Yellow Sky is due; and Scratchy Wilson turns out to be its protagonist. They come face to face, and Potter, who says, "I ain't got a gun on me, Scratchy," takes only a minute to make up his mind to be shot on his wedding day.

"'If you ain't got a gun, why ain't you got a gun?' Scratchy sneers at the marshal. And Potter says, 'I ain't got a gun because I've just come from San Anton' with my wife. I'm married.' 'Married?' asks Scratchy — he has to ask it several times, uncomprehending. 'Married?'

"Seemingly for the first time, he saw the drooping, drowning woman at the other man's side. 'No!' he said. He was like a creature allowed a glimpse of another world. . . . 'Is this the lady?'

"'Yes; this is the lady,' answered Potter.

"'Well,' said Wilson at last, slowly, 'I s'pose it's all off now.'

". . . He was not a student of chivalry; it was merely that in the presence of this foreign condition he was a simple child of the earlier plains. He picked up his starboard revolver, and, placing both weapons in their holsters, he went away. His feet made funnel-shaped tracks in the heavy sand."

So, in Crane's story, two situations, two forces, gather, meet — or rather are magnetized toward one another, almost — and collide. One is vanquished — the unexpected one — with neatness and absurdity, and the vanquished one exists; all equivalents of comedy.

In Katherine Mansfield's "Miss Brill," there are only one character and only one situation. The narrative is simple, Miss Brill's action consists nearly altogether in sitting down; she does nothing but go and sit in the park, return home, and sit on her bed in her little room. Yet considerably more of a story is attempted by this lesser to-do than Crane attempted in "Yellow Sky"; its plot is all implication.

"Miss Brill" is set on a stage of delight. "Although it was so brilliantly fine — the blue sky powdered with gold, and great spots of light like white wine splashed over the Jardins Publiques — Miss Brill was glad that she had decided on her fur. . . . [She] put up her hand and touched her fur. Dear little thing!" We see right off that for Miss Brill delight is a kind of coziness. She sits listening to the band, her Sunday habit, and "Now there came a little flutely bit — very pretty! —

a little chain of bright drops. She was sure it would be repeated. It was; she lifted her head and smiled."

Miss Brill has confidence in her world — anticipation: what will happen next? Ah, but she knows. She's delighted but safe. She sees the others from her little perch, her distance — the gay ones and then those on benches: "Miss Brill had often noticed there was something funny about nearly all of *them*. They were odd, silent, nearly all old, and from the way they stared they looked as though they'd just come from dark little rooms or even — even cupboards!" For she hasn't identified herself at all.

The drama is slight in this story. There is no collision. Rather the forces meeting in the Jardins Publiques have, at the story's end, passed through each other and come out the other side; there has not been a collision, but a change — something much more significant. This is because, though there is one small situation going on, a very large and complex one is implied — the outside world, in fact.

One of the forces in the story is life itself, corresponding to the part of Scratchy Wilson, so to speak. Not violent life — life in the setting of a park on Sunday afternoon in Paris. All it usually does for Miss Brill is promenade stylishly while the band plays, form little tableaux, separate momently into minor, rather darker encounters, and keep in general motion with bright colors and light touches — there are no waving pistols at all, to storm and threaten.

Yet, being life, it does threaten. In what way, at last? Well, how much more deadly to Miss Brill than a flourished pistol is an overheard remark — about *her*. Miss Brill's vision — a vision of love — is brought abruptly face to face with another, ruder vision of love. The boy and girl in love sit down on her bench, but they cannot go on with what they have been saying because of her, though "still soundlessly singing, still with that trembling smile, Miss Brill prepared to listen.

" 'No, not now,' said the girl. 'Not here, I can't.'

" 'But why? Because of that stupid old thing at the end there? . . . Why does she come here at all — who wants her? Why doesn't she keep her silly old mug at home?'

" 'It's her fur which is so funny,' giggled the girl. 'It's exactly like a fried whiting.'

" 'Ah, be off with you!' said the boy in an angry whisper."

So Miss Brill, she who could spare even pity for this world, in her innocence — pity, the spectator's emotion — is defeated. She had allowed herself occasional glimpses of lives not too happy, here in the park, which had moved her to little flutters of sadness. But that too had been coziness — coziness, a remedy visitors seek to take the chill off a strange place with. She hadn't known it wasn't good enough. All through the story she has sat in her "special seat" — another little prop to endurance — and all unknown to her she sat in mortal danger. This is the story. The danger nears, a word is spoken, the blow falls — and Miss Brill retires, ridiculously easy to mow down, as the man with the pistols was easy to stare down in "Yellow Sky," for comedy's sake. But Miss Brill was from the first defenseless and on the losing side, and her defeat is the deeper for it, and one feels sure it is for ever.

From "The Reading and Writing of Short Stories" in the *Atlantic Monthly*

Considerations for Critical Thinking and Writing

1. What does Welty see as the essential difference between the plots of these two stories? Why does she describe Mansfield in "Miss Brill" as attempting "considerably more of a story" than "Yellow Sky"?
2. Write an essay that compares and contrasts the plots of Faulkner's "A Rose for Emily" (p. 47) and Cisneros's "Barbie-Q" (p. 182). Which is "considerably more of a story" in the sense that Welty uses this phrase? Do you agree with her assessment of what makes a good story?

PERSPECTIVE

KATHERINE MANSFIELD (1888–1923)
On the Style of "Miss Brill" 1921

It's a very queer thing how *craft* comes into writing. I mean down to details. *Par example*. In *Miss Brill* I choose not only the length of every sentence, but even the sound of every sentence. I choose the rise and fall of every paragraph to fit her, and to fit her on that day at that very moment. After I'd written it I read it aloud — numbers of times — just as one would *play over* a musical composition — trying to get it nearer and nearer to the expression of Miss Brill — until it fitted her.

Don't think I'm vain about the little sketch. It's only the method I wanted to explain. I often wonder whether other writers do the same — If a thing has really come off it seems to me there mustn't be one single word out of place, or one word that could be taken out. That's how I AIM at writing. It will take some time to get anywhere near there.

From a letter to Richard Murry, January 17, 1921,
in *The Letters of Katherine Mansfield*

Considerations for Critical Thinking and Writing

1. How does the style of "Miss Brill" "fit" the character of the protagonist?
2. Choose any other story from this anthology and explain how its style is "fitted" to its protagonist.

8. Style, Tone, and Irony

STYLE

Style is a concept that everyone understands on some level because in its broadest sense it refers to the particular way in which anything is made or done. Style is everywhere around us. The world is saturated with styles in cars, clothing, buildings, teaching, dancing, music, politics — in anything that reflects a distinctive manner of expression or design. Consider, for example, how a tune sung by the Beatles differs from the same tune performed by a string orchestra. There's no mistaking the two styles.

Authors also have different characteristic styles. *Style* refers to the distinctive manner in which a writer arranges words to achieve particular effects. That arrangement includes individual word choices and matters such as the length of sentences, their structure, tone, and the use of irony.

Diction refers to a writer's choice of words. Because different words evoke different associations in a reader's mind, the writer's choice of words is crucial in controlling a reader's response. The diction must be appropriate for the characters and the situations in which the author places them. Consider how inappropriate it would have been if Melville had had Bartleby respond to the lawyer's requests with "Hell no!" instead of "I would prefer not to." The word *prefer* and the tentativeness of *would* help reinforce the scrivener's mildness, his dignity, and even his seeming reasonableness — all of which frustrate the lawyer's efforts to get rid of him. Bartleby, despite his passivity, seems to be in control of the situation. If he were to shout "Hell no!" he would appear angry, aggressive, desperate, and too informal, none of which would fit with his solemn, conscious decision to die. Melville makes the lawyer the desperate party by carefully choosing Bartleby's words.

Sentence structure is another element of a writer's style. Hemingway's terse, economical sentences are frequently noted and readily perceived. Here are the concluding sentences of Hemingway's "Soldier's Home" (p. 125), in which Krebs decides to leave home:

He had tried so to keep his life from being complicated. Still, none of it had touched him. He had felt sorry for his mother and she had made him lie. He would go to Kansas City and get a job and she would feel all right about it. There would be one more scene maybe before he got away. He would not go down to his father's office. He would miss that one. He wanted his life to go smoothly. It had just gotten going that way. Well, that was all over now, anyway. He would go over to the schoolyard and watch Helen play indoor baseball.

Hemingway expresses Krebs's thought the way Krebs thinks. The style avoids any "complicated" sentence structures. Seven of the eleven sentences begin with the word *He*. There are no abstractions or qualifications. We feel as if we are listening not only to *what* Krebs thinks but to *how* he thinks. The style reflects his firm determination to make, one step at a time, a clean, unobstructed break from his family and the entangling complications they would impose on him.

Contrast this straightforward style with Vladimir Nabokov's description of a woman in his short story "The Vane Sisters." The sophisticated narrator teaches French literature at a women's college and is as observant as he is icily critical of the woman he describes in this passage.

Her fingernails were gaudily painted, but badly bitten and not clean. Her lovers were a silent young photographer with a sudden laugh and two older men, brothers, who owned a small printing establishment across the street. I wondered at their tastes whenever I glimpsed, with a secret shudder, the higgledy-piggledy striation of black hairs that showed all along her pale shins through the nylon of her stockings with the scientific distinctness of a preparation flattened under glass; or when I felt, at her every movement, the dullish, stalish, not particularly conspicuous but all-pervading and depressing emanation that her seldom bathed flesh spread from under weary perfumes and creams.

This portrait — etched with a razor blade — is restrained but devastating. The woman's fingernails are "gaudily painted." She has no taste in men either. One of her lovers is "silent" except for a "sudden laugh," a telling detail that suggests a strikingly odd personality. Her other lovers, the two brothers (!), run a "small" business. We are invited to "shudder" along with the narrator as he vividly describes the "striation of black hairs" on her legs; we see the woman as if she were displayed under a microscope, an appropriate perspective given the narrator's close inspection. His scrutiny is relentless, and its object smells as awful as it looks (notice the difference in the language between this blunt description and the narrator's elegant distaste). He finds the woman "depressing" because the weight of her unpleasantness oppresses him.

The narrator reveals nearly as much about himself as about the woman, but Nabokov leaves the reader with the task of assessing the narrator's fastidious reactions. The formal style of this description is appropriately that of an educated, highly critical, close observer of life who knows how to convey the "dullish, stalish" essence of this woman. But, you might ask, what about the curious informality of *higgledy-piggledy?* Does that fit the formal professorial voice? Given Nabokov's well-known fascination with wit and, more important, the narrator's obvious relish for verbally slicing this woman into a slide specimen, the term is revealed as appropriately chosen once the reader sees the subtle, if brutal, pun on *piggledy.*

Hemingway's and Nabokov's uses of language are very different, yet each style successfully fuses what is said with how it is said. We could write summaries of both passages, but our summaries, owing to their styles, would not have the same effect as the originals. And that makes all the difference.

TONE

Style reveals *tone,* the author's implicit attitude toward the people, places, and events in a story. When we speak, tone is conveyed by our voice inflections, our wink of an eye, or some other gesture. A professor who says "You're going to fail the next exam" may be indicating concern, frustration, sympathy, alarm, humor, or indifference, depending on the tone of voice. In a literary work that spoken voice is unavailable; instead we must rely on the context in which a statement appears to interpret it correctly.

In Chopin's "Story of an Hour" (p. 12), for example, we can determine that the author sympathizes with Mrs. Mallard despite the fact that her grief over her husband's assumed death is mixed with joy. Though she thinks she's lost her husband, she experiences relief because she feels liberated from an oppressive male-dominated life. That's why she collapses when she sees her husband alive at the end of the story. Chopin makes clear by the tone of the final line ("When the doctors came they said she had died of heart disease — of joy that kills.") that the men misinterpret both her grief and joy, for in the larger context of Mrs. Mallard's emotions we see, unlike the doctors, that her death is caused not by a shock of joy but by an overwhelming recognition of her lost freedom.

If we are sensitive to tone, we can get behind a character and see him or her from the author's perspective. In Melville's "Bartleby, the Scrivener" (p. 83) everything is told from the lawyer's point of view, but the tone of his remarks often separates him from the author's values and attitudes. When the lawyer characterizes himself at the beginning of the story, his use of language effectively allows us to see Melville disapproving of what the lawyer takes pride in.

> The late John Jacob Astor, a personage little given to poetic enthusiasm, had no hesitation in pronouncing my first grand point to be prudence; my next, method. I do not speak it in vanity.

But, of course, he is vain and a name-dropper as well. He likes the "rounded and orbicular sound" of Astor's name, because it "rings like unto bullion."

Tone, here, helps to characterize the lawyer. Melville doesn't tell us that the lawyer is status conscious and materialistic; instead, we discover that through the tone. This stylistic technique is frequently an important element for interpreting a story. An insensitivity to tone can lead a reader astray in determining the theme of a work. Regardless of who is speaking in a story, it is wise to listen for the author's voice too.

IRONY

One of the enduring themes in literature is that things are not always what they seem to be. What we see — or think we see — is not always what we get. The unexpected complexity that often surprises us in life — what Herman Melville in *Moby-Dick* called the "universal thump" — is fertile ground for writers of imaginative literature. They cultivate that ground through the use of *irony,* a device that reveals a reality different from what appears to be true.

Verbal irony consists of a person saying one thing but meaning the opposite. If a student driver smashes into a parked car and the angry instructor turns to say "You sure did well today," the statement is an example of verbal irony. What is meant is not what is said. Verbal irony that is calculated to hurt someone by false praise is commonly known as **sarcasm.** In literature, however, verbal irony is usually not so openly aggressive; instead, it is more subtle and restrained though no less intense.

In Godwin's "A Sorrowful Woman" (p. 31), a mother and wife retreats from her family because she cannot live in the traditional role that her husband and son expect of her. When the husband tries to be sympathetic about her withdrawal from family life, the narrator tells us three times that "he understood such things," and that in "understanding these things" he tried to be patient by "[s]till understanding these things." The narrator's repetition of these phrases constitutes verbal irony because they call attention to the fact that the husband doesn't understand his wife at all. His "understanding" is really only a form of condescension that represents part of her problem rather than a solution.

Situational irony exists when there is an incongruity between what is expected to happen and what actually happens. For instance, at the climactic showdown between Marshal Potter and Scratchy Wilson in Crane's "The Bride Comes to Yellow Sky" (p. 203), there are no gunshots, only talk — and what subdues Wilson is not Potter's strength and heroism but the fact that the marshal is now married. To take one more example, the protagonist in Godwin's "A Sorrowful Woman" seems, by traditional societal standards, to have all that a wife and mother could desire in a family, but, given her needs, that turns out not to be enough to sustain even her life, let alone her happiness. In each of these instances the ironic situation creates a distinction between appearances and realities and brings the reader closer to the central meaning of the story.

Another form of irony occurs when an author allows the reader to know more about a situation than a character knows. *Dramatic irony* creates a discrepancy between what a character believes or says and what the reader understands to be true. In Flannery O'Connor's "Revelation" (p. 394) the insecure Mrs. Turpin, as a member of "the home-and-land owner" class, believes herself to be superior to "niggers," "white-trash," and mere "home-owners." She takes pride in her position in the community and in what she perceives to be her privileged position in relation to God. The reader, however, knows that her remarks underscore her failings rather than any superiority. Dramatic irony can be an effective way for an author to have a character unwittingly reveal himself or herself.

As you read Gabriel García Márquez's "A Very Old Man with Enormous Wings," Tillie Olsen's "I Stand Here Ironing," and Raymond Carver's "Popular Mechanics," pay attention to the authors' artful use of style, tone, and irony to convey meanings.

GABRIEL GARCÍA MÁRQUEZ (b. 1928)

Born in Aracataca, Colombia, Gabriel García Márquez worked for many years as a journalist, film critic, and screenwriter. His fiction is characterized by a compelling combination of magic and realism that results in a mystical lyricism that is nonetheless grounded in common experience. His first book was *Leaf Storm and Other Stories* (1955), which includes "A Very Old Man with Enormous Wings." *One Hundred Years of Solitude* (1967) is generally regarded as his masterpiece. Other novels include *The Autumn of the Patriarch* (1976), *Chronicle of a Death Foretold* (1982), and *Love in the Time of Cholera* (1988). His stories are gathered in *The Collected Stories of Gabriel García Márquez* (1984). In 1982 he was awarded the Nobel Prize for literature. In "A Very Old Man with Enormous Wings" a stranger mystifies a community by his enigmatic presence.

A Very Old Man with Enormous Wings   1955
TRANSLATED BY GREGORY RABASSA

On the third day of rain they had killed so many crabs inside the house that Pelayo had to cross his drenched courtyard and throw them into the sea, because the newborn child had a temperature all night and they thought it was due to the stench. The world had been sad since Tuesday. Sea and sky were a single ash-gray thing and the sands of the beach, which on March nights glimmered like powdered light, had become a stew of mud and rotten shell-fish. The light was so weak at noon that when Pelayo was coming back to the house after throwing away the crabs, it was hard for him to see what it was that was moving and groaning in the rear of the courtyard. He had to go very close to see that it was an old man, a very old man, lying face down in the mud, who, in spite of his tremendous efforts, couldn't get up, impeded by his enormous wings.

Frightened by that nightmare, Pelayo ran to get Elisenda, his wife, who was putting compresses on the sick child, and he took her to the rear of the courtyard. They both looked at the fallen body with mute stupor. He was dressed like a ragpicker. There were only a few faded hairs left on his bald skull and very few teeth in his mouth, and his pitiful condition of a drenched great-grandfather had taken away any sense of grandeur he might have had. His huge buzzard wings, dirty and half-plucked, were forever entangled in the mud. They looked at him so long and so closely that Pelayo and Elisenda very soon overcame their surprise and in the end found him familiar. Then they dared speak to him, and he answered in an incomprehensible dialect with a strong sailor's voice. That was how they skipped over the inconvenience of the wings and quite intelligently concluded that he was a lonely castaway from some foreign ship wrecked by the storm. And yet, they called in a neighbor woman who knew everything about life and death to see him, and all she needed was one look to show them their mistake.

"He's an angel," she told them. "He must have been coming for the child, but the poor fellow is so old that the rain knocked him down."

On the following day everyone knew that a flesh-and-blood angel was held captive in Pelayo's house. Against the judgment of the wise neighbor woman, for whom angels in those times were the fugitive survivors of a celestial con-spiracy, they did not have the heart to club him to death. Pelayo watched over him all afternoon from the kitchen, armed with his bailiff's club, and before going to bed he dragged him out of the mud and locked him up with the hens in the wire chicken coop. In the middle of the night, when the rain stopped, Pelayo and Elisenda were still killing crabs. A short time afterward the child woke up without a fever and with a desire to eat. Then they felt magnanimous and decided to put the angel on a raft with fresh water and provisions for three days and leave him to his fate on the high seas. But when they went out into the courtyard with the first light of dawn, they found the whole neighborhood in front of the chicken coop having fun with the angel, without the slightest reverence, tossing him things to eat through the openings in the wire as if he weren't a supernatural creature but a circus animal.

Father Gonzaga arrived before seven o'clock, alarmed at the strange news. By that time onlookers less frivolous than those at dawn had already arrived and they were making all kinds of conjectures concerning the captive's future. The simplest among them thought that he should be named mayor of the world. Others of sterner mind felt that he should be promoted to the rank of five-star general in order to win all wars. Some visionaries hoped that he could be put to stud in order to implant on earth a race of winged wise men who could take charge of the universe. But Father Gonzaga, before becoming a priest, had been a robust woodcutter. Standing by the wire, he reviewed his catechism in an instant and asked them to open the door so that he could take a close look at that pitiful man who looked more like a huge decrepit hen among the fascinated chickens. He was lying in a corner drying his open wings in the sunlight among the fruit peels and breakfast leftovers that the early risers had thrown him. Alien to the impertinences of the world, he only lifted his antiquarian eyes and murmured something in his dialect when Father Gonzaga went into the chicken coop and said good morning to him in Latin. The parish priest had his first suspicion of an impostor when he saw that he did not understand the language of God or know how to greet His ministers. Then he noticed that seen close up he was much too human: he had an unbearable smell of the outdoors, the back side of his wings were strewn with parasites and his main feathers had been mistreated by terrestrial winds, and nothing about him measured up to the proud dignity of angels. Then he came out of the chicken coop and in a brief sermon warned the curious against the risks of being ingenuous. He reminded them that the devil had the bad habit of making use of carnival tricks in order to confuse the unwary. He argued that if wings were not the essential element in determining the difference between a hawk and an airplane, they were even less so in the recognition of angels. Nevertheless, he promised to write a letter to his bishop so that the latter would write to his primate so that the latter would write to the Supreme Pontiff in order to get the final verdict from the highest courts.

His prudence fell on sterile hearts. The news of the captive angel spread with such rapidity that after a few hours the courtyard had the bustle of a marketplace and they had to call in troops with fixed bayonets to disperse the mob that was about to knock the house down. Elisenda, her spine all twisted from sweeping up so much marketplace trash, then got the idea of fencing in the yard and charging five cents admission to see the angel.

The curious came from far away. A traveling carnival arrived with a flying acrobat who buzzed over the crowd several times, but no one paid any attention to him because his wings were not those of an angel but, rather, those of a sidereal° bat. The most unfortunate invalids on earth came in search of health: a poor woman who since childhood had been counting her heartbeats and had run out of numbers; a Portuguese man who couldn't sleep because the noise of the stars disturbed him; a sleepwalker who got up at night to undo the things he had done while awake; and many others with less serious ailments. In the midst of that shipwreck disorder that made the earth tremble, Pelayo and Elisenda were happy with fatigue, for in less than a week they had crammed their rooms with money and the line of pilgrims waiting their turn to enter still reached beyond the horizon.

The angel was the only one who took no part in his own act. He spent his time trying to get comfortable in his borrowed nest, befuddled by the hellish heat of the oil lamps and sacramental candles that had been placed along the wire. At first they tried to make him eat some mothballs, which, according to the wisdom of the wise neighbor woman, were the food prescribed for angels. But he turned them down, just as he turned down the papal lunches that the

sidereal: Coming from the stars.

penitents brought him, and they never found out whether it was because he was an angel or because he was an old man that in the end ate nothing but eggplant mush. His only supernatural virtue seemed to be patience. Especially during the first days, when the hens pecked at him, searching for the stellar parasites that proliferated in his wings, and the cripples pulled out feathers to touch their defective parts with, and even the most merciful threw stones at him, trying to get him to rise so they could see him standing. The only time they succeeded in arousing him was when they burned his side with an iron for branding steers, for he had been motionless for so many hours that they thought he was dead. He awoke with a start, ranting in his hermetic language and with tears in his eyes, and he flapped his wings a couple of times, which brought on a whirlwind of chicken dung and lunar dust and a gale of panic that did not seem to be of this world. Although many thought that his reaction had been one not of rage but of pain, from then on they were careful not to annoy him, because the majority understood that his passivity was not that of a hero taking his ease but that of a cataclysm in repose.

Father Gonzaga held back the crowd's frivolity with formulas of maidservant inspiration while awaiting the arrival of a final judgment on the nature of the captive. But the mail from Rome showed no sense of urgency. They spent their time finding out if the prisoner had a navel, if his dialect had any connection with Aramaic, how many times he could fit on the head of a pin,° or whether he wasn't just a Norwegian with wings. Those meager letters might have come and gone until the end of time if a providential event had not put an end to the priest's tribulations.

It so happened that during those days, among so many other carnival 10 attractions, there arrived in town the traveling show of the woman who had been changed into a spider for having disobeyed her parents. The admission to see her was not only less than the admission to see the angel, but people were permitted to ask her all manner of questions about her absurd state and to examine her up and down so that no one would ever doubt the truth of her horror. She was a frightful tarantula the size of a ram and with the head of a sad maiden. What was most heart-rending, however, was not her outlandish shape but the sincere affliction with which she recounted the details of her misfortune. While still practically a child she had sneaked out of her parents' house to go to a dance, and while she was coming back through the woods after having danced all night without permission, a fearful thunderclap rent the sky in two and through the crack came the lightning bolt of brimstone that changed her into a spider. Her only nourishment came from the meatballs that charitable souls chose to toss into her mouth. A spectacle like that, full of so much human truth and with such a fearful lesson, was bound to defeat without even trying that of a haughty angel who scarcely deigned to look at mortals. Besides, the few miracles attributed to the angel showed a certain mental disorder, like the blind man who didn't recover his sight but grew three new teeth, or the paralytic who didn't get to walk but almost won the lottery, and the leper whose sores sprouted sunflowers. Those consolation miracles, which were more like mocking fun, had already ruined the angel's reputation when the woman who had been changed

---

fit on the head of a pin: An allusion to the medieval theological debate over how many angels could fit on the head of a pin.

into a spider finally crushed him completely. That was how Father Gonzaga was cured forever of his insomnia and Pelayo's courtyard went back to being as empty as during the time it had rained for three days and crabs walked through the bedrooms.

The owners of the house had no reason to lament. With the money they saved they built a two-story mansion with balconies and gardens and high netting so that crabs wouldn't get in during the winter, and with iron bars on the windows so that angels wouldn't get in. Pelayo also set up a rabbit warren close to town and gave up his job as bailiff for good, and Elisenda bought some satin pumps with high heels and many dresses of iridescent silk, the kind worn on Sunday by the most desirable women in those times. The chicken coop was the only thing that didn't receive any attention. If they washed it down with Creolin° and burned tears of myrrh inside it every so often, it was not in homage to the angel but to drive away the dungheap stench that still hung everywhere like a ghost and was turning the new house into an old one. At first, when the child learned to walk, they were careful that he not get too close to the chicken coop. But then they began to lose their fears and got used to the smell, and before the child got his second teeth he'd gone inside the chicken coop to play, where the wires were falling apart. The angel was no less standoffish with him than with other mortals, but he tolerated the most ingenious infamies with the patience of a dog who had no illusions. They both came down with chicken pox at the same time. The doctor who took care of the child couldn't resist the temptation to listen to the angel's heart, and he found so much whistling in the heart and so many sounds in his kidneys that it seemed impossible for him to be alive. What surprised him most, however, was the logic of his wings. They seemed so natural on that completely human organism that he couldn't understand why other men didn't have them too.

When the child began school it had been some time since the sun and rain had caused the collapse of the chicken coop. The angel went dragging himself about here and there like a stray dying man. They would drive him out of the bedroom with a broom and a moment later find him in the kitchen. He seemed to be in so many places at the same time that they grew to think that he'd been duplicated, that he was reproducing himself all through the house, and the exasperated and unhinged Elisenda shouted that it was awful living in that hell full of angels. He could scarcely eat and his antiquarian eyes had also become so foggy that he went about bumping into posts. All he had left were the bare cannulae° of his last feathers. Pelayo threw a blanket over him and extended him the charity of letting him sleep in the shed, and only then did they notice that he had a temperature at night, and was delirious with the tongue twisters of an old Norwegian. That was one of the few times they became alarmed, for they thought he was going to die and not even the wise neighbor woman had been able to tell them what to do with dead angels.

And yet he not only survived his worst winter, but seemed improved with the first sunny days. He remained motionless for several days in the farthest corner of the courtyard, where no one would see him, and at the beginning of December some large, stiff feathers began to grow on his wings, the feathers of

Creolin: Trade name for a cleaning product.
cannulae: The tubular pieces by which feathers are attached to a body.

a scarecrow, which looked more like another misfortune of decrepitude. But he must have known the reason for those changes, for he was quite careful that no one should notice them, that no one should hear the sea chanteys that he sometimes sang under the stars. One morning Elisenda was cutting some bunches of onions for lunch when a wind that seemed to come from the high seas blew into the kitchen. Then she went to the window and caught the angel in his first attempts at flight. They were so clumsy that his fingernails opened a furrow in the vegetable patch and he was on the point of knocking the shed down with the ungainly flapping that slipped on the light and couldn't get a grip on the air. But he did manage to gain altitude. Elisenda let out a sigh of relief, for herself and for him, when she saw him pass over the last houses, holding himself up in some way with the risky flapping of a senile vulture. She kept watching him even when she was through cutting the onions and she kept on watching until it was no longer possible for her to see him, because then he was no longer an annoyance in her life but an imaginary dot on the horizon of the sea.

Considerations for Critical Thinking and Writing

1. What is the impact of the story's first sentence and the last phrase of the first paragraph? How do they affect your expectations about the rest of the story?
2. In what sort of world is the story set?
3. Pelayo and Elisenda are described as looking at the old man "so long and so closely" that "very soon [they] overcame their surprise and in the end found him familiar." To what extent is your experience as a reader similar to their response to the old man? How does the author's style contribute to this creating of familiarity?
4. Characterize Pelayo and Elisenda. Are they merely crass exploiters?
5. What is Father Gonzaga's assessment of the angel? How do the crowds of people who pay admission to see the angel regard the old man?
6. How does the presence of the spider woman affect the angel's reputation as a curiosity? Why does the crowd prefer one over the other?
7. How does the angel manage to leave? Why does he do so?
8. How successfully have people in the town defined the angel? How do you explain him?
9. Locate instances of humor in the story. What kind of tone is established by the humor?

Connections to Other Selections

1. Compare García Márquez's mysterious angel and Melville's inscrutable Bartleby, the scrivener (p. 83). How is each made to seem like a plausible character despite his bizarre qualities?
2. Consider the public's reactions to the angel and to Franz Kafka's hunger artist (p. 462). Write an essay that explores what each of these extraordinary characters reveals about his public.
3. Compare García Márquez's angel with Kafka's hunger artist. How might the experiences of each character be read as a commentary on the decline of religion in the modern world?

TILLIE OLSEN (b. 1913)

Born in Omaha, Nebraska, Tillie Olsen lived through the struggles of working-class poverty that she described in her first novel, *Yonnondio,* begun in the early 1930s but not published until 1974. Her writing all but ended in the mid-1930s as she raised four children while working full-time, first in a factory and then as a secretary. During the 1950s she began writing again and published four stories in *Tell Me a Riddle* (1961), from which "I Stand Here Ironing" is excerpted. *Silences* (1978) is a collection of essays on the difficulties writers, particularly women, have in continuing to remain creative and productive. "I Stand Here Ironing," written during the early 1950s, concerns a mother who reflects on raising her oldest daughter.

I Stand Here Ironing   1961

I stand here ironing, and what you asked me moves tormented back and forth with the iron.

"I wish you would manage the time to come in and talk with me about your daughter. I'm sure you can help me understand her. She's a youngster who needs help and whom I'm deeply interested in helping."

"Who needs help." . . . Even if I came, what good would it do? You think because I am her mother I have a key, or that in some way you could use me as a key? She has lived for nineteen years. There is all that life that has happened outside of me, beyond me.

And when is there time to remember, to sift, to weigh, to estimate, to total? I will start and there will be an interruption and I will have to gather it all together again. Or I will become engulfed with all I did or did not do, with what should have been and what cannot be helped.

She was a beautiful baby. The first and only one of our five that was beautiful   5 at birth. You do not guess how new and uneasy her tenancy in her now-loveliness. You did not know her all those years she was thought homely, or see her poring over her baby pictures, making me tell her over and over how beautiful she had been — and would be, I would tell her — and was now, to the seeing eye. But the seeing eyes were few or nonexistent. Including mine.

I nursed her. They feel that's important nowadays. I nursed all the children, but with her, with all the fierce rigidity of first motherhood, I did like the books then said. Though her cries battered me to trembling and my breasts ached with swollenness, I waited till the clock decreed.

Why do I put that first? I do not even know if it matters, or if it explains anything.

She was a beautiful baby. She blew shining bubbles of sound. She loved motion, loved light, loved color and music and textures. She would lie on the floor in her blue overalls patting the surface so hard in ecstasy her hands and feet would blur. She was a miracle to me, but when she was eight months old I had to leave her daytimes with the woman downstairs to whom she was no miracle at all, for I worked or looked for work and for Emily's father, who "could no longer endure" (he wrote in his good-bye note) "sharing want with us."

I was nineteen. It was the pre-relief, pre-WPA world of the depression. I would start running as soon as I got off the streetcar, running up the stairs, the place smelling sour, and awake or asleep to startle awake, when she saw me she would break into a clogged weeping that could not be comforted, a weeping I can hear yet.

After a while I found a job hashing at night so I could be with her days, 10 and it was better. But it came to where I had to bring her to his family and leave her.

It took a long time to raise the money for her fare back. Then she got chicken pox and I had to wait longer. When she finally came, I hardly knew her, walking quick and nervous like her father, looking like her father, thin, and dressed in a shoddy red that yellowed her skin and glared at the pockmarks. All the baby loveliness gone.

She was two. Old enough for nursery school they said, and I did not know then what I know now — the fatigue of the long day, and the lacerations of group life in the kinds of nurseries that are only parking places for children.

Except that it would have made no difference if I had known. It was the only place there was. It was the only way we could be together, the only way I could hold a job.

And even without knowing, I knew. I knew the teacher that was evil because all these years it has curdled into my memory, the little boy hunched in the corner, her rasp, "why aren't you outside, because Alvin hits you? that's no reason, go out, scaredy." I knew Emily hated it even if she did not clutch and implore "don't go Mommy" like the other children, mornings.

She always had a reason why we should stay home. Momma, you look sick. 15 Momma, I feel sick. Momma, the teachers aren't here today, they're sick. Momma, we can't go, there was a fire there last night. Momma, it's a holiday today, no school, they told me.

But never a direct protest, never rebellion. I think of our others in their three-, four-year-oldness — the explosions, tempers, the denunciations, the demands — and I feel suddenly ill. I put the iron down. What in me demanded that goodness in her? And what was the cost, the cost to her of such goodness?

The old man living in the back once said in his gentle way: "You should smile at Emily more when you look at her." What *was* in my face when I looked at her? I loved her. There were all the acts of love.

It was only with the others I remembered what he said, and it was the face of joy, and not of care or tightness or worry I turned to them — too late for Emily. She does not smile easily, let alone almost always as her brothers and sisters do. Her face is closed and sombre, but when she wants, how fluid. You must have seen it in her pantomimes, you spoke of her rare gift for comedy on the stage that rouses laughter out of the audience so dear they applaud and applaud and do not want to let her go.

Where does it come from, that comedy? There was none of it in her when she came back to me that second time, after I had to send her away again. She had a new daddy now to learn to love, and I think perhaps it was a better time.

Except when we left her alone nights, telling ourselves she was old enough. 20
"Can't you go some other time, Mommy, like tomorrow?" she would ask. "Will it be just a little while you'll be gone? Do you promise?"

The time we came back, the front door open, the clock on the floor in the hall. She rigid awake. "It wasn't just a little while. I didn't cry. Three times I called you, just three times, and then I ran downstairs to open the door so you could come faster. The clock talked loud. I threw it away, it scared me what it talked."

She said the clock talked loud again that night I went to the hospital to have Susan. She was delirious with the fever that comes before red measles, but she was fully conscious all the week I was gone and the week after we were home when she could not come near the new baby or me.

She did not get well. She stayed skeleton thin, not wanting to eat, and night after night she had nightmares. She would call for me, and I would rouse from exhaustion to sleepily call back: "You're all right, darling, go to sleep, it's just a dream," and if she still called, in a sterner voice, "now to go sleep, Emily, there's nothing to hurt you." Twice, only twice, when I had to get up for Susan anyhow, I went in to sit with her.

Now when it is too late (as if she would let me hold and comfort her like 25 I do the others) I get up and go to her at once at her moan or restless stirring. "Are you awake, Emily? Can I get you something?" And the answer is always the same: "No, I'm all right, go back to sleep, Mother."

They persuaded me at the clinic to send her away to a convalescent home in the country where "she can have the kind of food and care you can't manage for her, and you'll be free to concentrate on the new baby." They still send children to that place. I see pictures on the society page of sleek young women planning affairs to raise money for it, or dancing at the affairs, or decorating Easter eggs or filling Christmas stockings for the children.

They never have a picture of the children so I do not know if the girls still wear those gigantic red bows and the ravaged looks on the every other Sunday when parents can come to visit "unless otherwise notified" — as we were notified the first six weeks.

Oh it is a handsome place, green lawns and tall trees and fluted flower beds. High up on the balconies of each cottage the children stand, the girls in their red bows and white dresses, the boys in white suits and giant red ties. The parents stand below shrieking up to be heard and the children shriek down to be heard, and between them the invisible wall "Not To Be Contaminated by Parental Germs or Physical Affection."

There was a tiny girl who always stood hand in hand with Emily. Her parents never came. One visit she was gone. "They moved her to Rose Cottage" Emily shouted in explanation. "They don't like you to love anybody here."

She wrote once a week, the labored writing of a seven-year-old. "I am fine. 30 How is the baby. If I write my leter nicly I will have a star. Love." There never was a star. We wrote every other day, letters she could never hold or keep but only hear read — once. "We simply do not have room for children to keep any personal possessions," they patiently explained when we pieced one Sunday's shrieking together to plead how much it would mean to Emily, who loved so to keep things, to be allowed to keep her letters and cards.

Each visit she looked frailer. "She isn't eating," they told us.

(They had runny eggs for breakfast or mush with lumps, Emily said later, I'd hold it in my mouth and not swallow. Nothing ever tasted good, just when they had chicken.)

It took us eight months to get her released home, and only the fact that she gained back so little of her seven lost pounds convinced the social worker.

I used to try to hold and love her after she came back, but her body would stay stiff, and after a while she'd push away. She ate little. Food sickened her, and I think much of life too. Oh she had physical lightness and brightness, twinkling by on skates, bouncing like a ball up and down up and down over the jump rope, skimming over the hill; but these were momentary.

She fretted about her appearance, thin and dark and foreign-looking at a 35 time when every little girl was supposed to look or thought she should look a chubby blonde replica of Shirley Temple. The doorbell sometimes rang for her, but no one seemed to come and play in the house or be a best friend. Maybe because we moved so much.

There was a boy she loved painfully through two school semesters. Months later she told me how she had taken pennies from my purse to buy him candy. "Licorice was his favorite and I brought him some every day, but he still liked Jennifer better'n me. Why, Mommy?" The kind of question for which there is no answer.

School was a worry to her. She was not glib or quick in a world where glibness and quickness were easily confused with ability to learn. To her over-worked and exasperated teachers she was an overconscientious "slow learner" who kept trying to catch up and was absent entirely too often.

I let her be absent, though sometimes the illness was imaginary. How different from my now-strictness about attendance with the others. I wasn't working. We had a new baby, I was home anyhow. Sometimes, after Susan grew old enough, I would keep her home from school, too, to have them all together.

Mostly Emily had asthma, and her breathing, harsh and labored, would fill the house with a curiously tranquil sound. I would bring the two old dresser mirrors and her boxes of collections to her bed. She would select beads and single earrings, bottle tops and shells, dried flowers and pebbles, old postcards and scraps, all sorts of oddments; then she and Susan would play Kingdom, setting up landscapes and furniture, peopling them with action.

Those were the only times of peaceful companionship between her and 40 Susan. I have edged away from it, that poisonous feeling between them, that terrible balancing of hurts and needs I had to do between the two, and did so badly, those earlier years.

Oh there are conflicts between the others too, each one human, needing, demanding, hurting, taking — but only between Emily and Susan, no, Emily toward Susan that corroding resentment. It seems so obvious on the surface, yet it is not obvious. Susan, the second child, Susan, golden- and curly-haired and chubby, quick and articulate and assured, everything in appearance and manner Emily was not; Susan, not able to resist Emily's precious things, losing or some-times clumsily breaking them; Susan telling jokes and riddles to company for applause while Emily sat silent (to say to me later: that was *my* riddle, Mother, I told it to Susan); Susan, who for all the five years' difference in age was just a year behind Emily in developing physically.

I am glad for that slow physical development that widened the difference between her and her contemporaries, though she suffered over it. She was too vulnerable for that terrible world of youthful competition, of preening and parading, of constant measuring of yourself against every other, of envy, "If I had that copper hair," "If I had that skin. . . ." She tormented herself enough about not looking like the others, there was enough of the unsureness, the having to be conscious of words before you speak, the constant caring—what are they thinking of me? without having it all magnified by the merciless physical drives.

Ronnie is calling. He is wet and I change him. It is rare there is such a cry now. That time of motherhood is almost behind me when the ear is not one's own but must always be racked and listening for the child cry, the child call. We sit for a while and I hold him, looking out over the city spread in charcoal with its soft aisles of light. *"Shoogily,"* he breathes and curls closer. I carry him back to bed, asleep. *Shoogily.* A funny word, a family word, inherited from Emily, invented by her to say: *comfort.*

In this and other ways she leaves her seal, I say aloud. And startle at my saying it. What do I mean? What did I start to gather together, to try and make coherent? I was at the terrible, growing years. War years. I do not remember them well. I was working, there were four smaller ones now, there was not time for her. She had to help be a mother, and housekeeper, and shopper. She had to set her seal. Mornings of crisis and near hysteria trying to get lunches packed, hair combed, coats and shoes found, everyone to school or Child Care on time, the baby ready for transportation. And always the paper scribbled on by a smaller one, the book looked at by Susan then mislaid, the homework not done. Running out to that huge school where she was one, she was lost, she was a drop; suffering over the unpreparedness, stammering and unsure in her classes.

There was so little time left at night after the kids were bedded down. She 45 would struggle over books, always eating (it was in those years she developed her enormous appetite that is legendary in our family) and I would be ironing, or preparing food for the next day, or writing V-mail to Bill, or tending the baby. Sometimes, to make me laugh, or out of her despair, she would imitate happenings or types at school.

I think I said once: "Why don't you do something like this in the school amateur show?" One morning she phoned me at work, hardly understandable through the weeping: "Mother, I did it. I won, I won; they gave me first prize; they clapped and clapped and wouldn't let me go."

Now suddenly she was Somebody, and as imprisoned in her difference as she had been in anonymity.

She began to be asked to perform at other high schools, even in colleges, then at city and statewide affairs. The first one we went to, I only recognized her that first moment when thin, shy, she almost drowned herself into the curtains. Then: Was this Emily? The control, the command, the convulsing and deadly clowning, the spell, then the roaring, stamping audience, unwilling to let this rare and precious laughter out of their lives.

Afterwards: You ought to do something about her with a gift like that— but without money or knowing how, what does one do? We have left it all to her, and the gift has as often eddied inside, clogged and clotted, as been used and growing.

She is coming. She runs up the stairs two at a time with her light graceful 50 step, and I know she is happy tonight. Whatever it was that occasioned your call did not happen today.

"Aren't you ever going to finish the ironing, Mother? Whistler painted his mother in a rocker. I'd have to paint mine standing over an ironing board." This is one of her communicative nights and she tells me everything and nothing as she fixes herself a plate of food out of the icebox.

She is so lovely. Why did you want me to come in at all? Why were you concerned? She will find her way.

She starts up the stairs to bed. "Don't get me up with the rest in the morning." "But I thought you were having midterms." "Oh, those," she comes back in, kisses me, and says quite lightly, "in a couple of years when we'll all be atom-dead they won't matter a bit."

She has said it before. She *believes* it. But because I have been dredging the past, and all that compounds a human being is so heavy and meaningful in me, I cannot endure it tonight.

I will never total it all. I will never come in to say: She was a child seldom 55 smiled at. Her father left me before she was a year old. I had to work her first six years when there was work, or I sent her home and to his relatives. There were years she had care she hated. She was dark and thin and foreign-looking in a world where the prestige went to blondeness and curly hair and dimples, she was slow where glibness was prized. She was a child of anxious, not proud, love. We were poor and could not afford for her the soil of easy growth. I was a young mother, I was a distracted mother. There were other children pushing up, demanding. Her younger sister seemed all that she was not. There were years she did not want me to touch her. She kept too much in herself, her life was such she had to keep too much in herself. My wisdom came too late. She has much to her and probably little will come of it. She is a child of her age, of depression, of war, of fear.

Let her be. So all that is in her will not bloom — but in how many does it? There is still enough left to live by. Only help her to know — help make it so there is cause for her to know — that she is more than this dress on the ironing board, helpless before the iron.

Considerations for Critical Thinking and Writing

1. Who is speaking in the second paragraph of this story? Is it possible to be specific?
2. Is this story primarily about the mother or about Emily? What does the point of view reveal?
3. How and why has the mother treated Emily differently from the other children?
4. What sort of mother is the narrator? Does your view of her change as you learn more about her?
5. What is the author's attitude toward the mother?
6. Why is it ironic that Emily is a talented comedienne?
7. Does the mother's ironing have any symbolic significance?
8. How is the summary in the next to last paragraph different in style and tone from the rest of the mother's account of Emily? What is the effect of this paragraph on your understanding of the mother's relationship with Emily?

9. Comment on Emily's reason for not worrying about her midterm exams: "in a couple of years when we'll all be atom-dead they won't matter a bit."
10. Describe what the mother's account of her daughter's experience reveals to her about her own life.

Connections to Other Selections

1. Contrast the narrator in this story with the mother in Godwin's "A Sorrowful Woman" (p. 30).
2. Contrast the tone of the mother's narration in this story with that of the teenager Sammy in John Updike's "A & P" (p. 485). How does each author achieve a convincing voice for the first-person narrator?

RAYMOND CARVER (1938–1988)

Born in 1938 in Clatskanie, Oregon, to working-class parents, Carver grew up in Yakima, Washington, was educated at Humboldt State College in California, and did graduate work at the University of Iowa. He married at age nineteen and during his college years worked at a series of low-paying jobs to help support his family. These difficult years eventually ended in divorce. He taught at a number of universities, among them the University of California at Berkeley, the University of Iowa, the University of Texas at El Paso, and Syracuse University. Carver's collections of stories include *Will You Please Be Quiet, Please?* (1976), *What We Talk About When We Talk About Love* (1981), from which "Popular Mechanics" is taken, *Cathedral* (1984), and *Where I'm Calling From: New and Selected Stories* (1988). Though extremely brief, "Popular Mechanics" describes a stark domestic situation with a startling conclusion.

Popular Mechanics 1981

Early that day the weather turned and the snow was melting into dirty water. Streaks of it ran down from the little shoulder-high window that faced the backyard. Cars slushed by on the street outside, where it was getting dark. But it was getting dark on the inside too.

He was in the bedroom pushing clothes into a suitcase when she came to the door.

I'm glad you're leaving! I'm glad you're leaving! she said. Do you hear?

He kept on putting his things into the suitcase.

Son of a bitch! I'm so glad you're leaving! She began to cry. You can't even 5 look me in the face, can you?

Then she noticed the baby's picture on the bed and picked it up.

He looked at her and she wiped her eyes and stared at him before turning and going back to the living room.

Bring that back, he said.

Just get your things and get out, she said.

He did not answer. He fastened the suitcase, put on his coat, looked around 10 the bedroom before turning off the light. Then he went out to the living room.

She stood in the doorway of the little kitchen, holding the baby.

I want the baby, he said.

Are you crazy?

No, but I want the baby. I'll get someone to come by for his things.

You're not touching this baby, she said. 15

The baby had begun to cry and she uncovered the blanket from around his head.

Oh, oh, she said, looking at the baby.

He moved toward her.

For God's sake! she said. She took a step back into the kitchen.

I want the baby. 20

Get out of here!

She turned and tried to hold the baby over in a corner behind the stove.

But he came up. He reached across the stove and tightened his hands on the baby.

Let go of him, he said.

Get away, get away! she cried. 25

The baby was red-faced and screaming. In the scuffle they knocked down a flowerpot that hung behind the stove.

He crowded her into the wall then, trying to break her grip. He held on to the baby and pushed with all his weight.

Let go of him, he said.

Don't, she said. You're hurting the baby, she said.

I'm not hurting the baby, he said. 30

The kitchen window gave no light. In the near-dark he worked on her fisted fingers with one hand and with the other hand he gripped the screaming baby up under an arm near the shoulder.

She felt her fingers being forced open. She felt the baby going from her.

No! she screamed just as her hands came loose.

She would have it, this baby. She grabbed for the baby's other arm. She caught the baby around the wrist and leaned back.

But he would not let go. He felt the baby slipping out of his hands and he 35 pulled back very hard.

In this manner, the issue was decided. *In this manner, they decided the issue*

They didn't

Make the decision the issue did

Considerations for Critical Thinking and Writing

1. Though there is little description of the setting in this story, how do the few details that are provided help to establish the tone?
2. How do small actions take on larger significance in the story? Consider the woman picking up the baby's picture and the knocked-down flowerpot.
3. Why is this couple splitting up? Do we know? Does it matter? Explain your response.

4. Discuss the title of the story. The original title was "Mine." Which do you think is more effective?
5. What is the conflict? How is it resolved?
6. Discuss the last line. What is the "issue" that is "decided"?
7. Read I Kings 3 in the Bible for the story of Solomon. How might "Popular Mechanics" be read as a retelling of this story? What significant differences do you find in the endings of each?
8. Explain how Carver uses irony to convey theme.

Connections to Other Selections

1. Compare Carver's style with Ernest Hemingway's in "Soldier's Home" (p. 125).
2. How is the ending of "Popular Mechanics" similar to the ending of Nathaniel Hawthorne's "The Birthmark" (p. 261)?

9. A Study of Three Authors: Nathaniel Hawthorne, James Joyce, and Flannery O'Connor

This chapter includes a number of short stories by Nathaniel Hawthorne, Flannery O'Connor, and James Joyce in order to provide an opportunity to study three major fiction writers in some depth. Getting to know an author's work is similar to developing a friendship with someone: the more encounters, the more intimate the relationship becomes. Familiarity with a writer's concerns and methods in one story can help to illuminate another story. As we become accustomed to someone's voice — a friend's or a writer's — we become attuned to nuances in tone and meaning.

The nuances in Hawthorne's, Joyce's, and O'Connor's fiction warrant close analysis. Each of the following works is a unique and absorbing story that rewards additional readings. Although none of the groupings is wholly representative of the writer's work, each offers enough stories to suggest some of the techniques and concerns that characterize their work. Each grouping provides a useful context for reading individual stories. Moreover, the works of all three authors invite comparisons and contrasts in their styles and themes. Following each set of stories are some brief commentaries by and about Hawthorne, Joyce, and O'Connor that establish additional contexts for understanding their fiction.

NATHANIEL HAWTHORNE (1804–1864)

Nathaniel Hawthorne once described himself as "the obscurest man of letters in America." During the early years of his career, this self-assessment was mostly accurate, but the publication of *The Scarlet Letter* in 1850 marked the beginning of Hawthorne's reputation as a major American writer. His novels and short stories have entertained and challenged generations of readers; they have wide appeal because they can be read on many levels. Hawthorne skillfully creates an atmosphere of complexity and ambiguity that makes it difficult to reduce his stories to a simple view of life. The moral and psychological issues that he examines through the conflicts his characters experience are often intricate and mysterious. Readers are frequently made to feel that in exploring Hawthorne's characters they are also encountering some part of themselves.

Hawthorne achieved success as a writer only after a steady and intense struggle. His personal history was hardly conducive to producing a professional writer. Born in Salem, Massachusetts, Hawthorne came from a Puritan family of declining fortunes that prided itself on an energetic pursuit of practical matters such as law and commerce. He never knew his father, a sea captain who died in Dutch Guiana when Hawthorne was only four years old, but he did have a strong imaginative sense of an early ancestor, who as a Puritan judge persecuted Quakers, and of a later ancestor, who was a judge during the Salem witchcraft trials. His forebears seemed to haunt Hawthorne, so that in some ways he felt more involved in the past than in the present.

In "The Custom-House," the introduction to *The Scarlet Letter,* Hawthorne considers himself in relation to his severe Puritan ancestors.

> No aim, that I have ever cherished, would they recognize as laudable; no success of mine . . . would they deem otherwise than worthless, if not positively disgraceful. "What is he?" murmurs one gray shadow of my forefathers to the other. "A writer of story-books! What kind of a business in life, — what mode of glorifying God, or being serviceable to mankind in his day and generation, — may that be? Why, the degenerate fellow might as well have been a fiddler!" Such are the compliments bandied between my great-grandsires and myself, across the gulf of time! And yet, let them scorn me as they will, strong traits of their nature have intertwined with mine.

Hawthorne's sense of what his forebears might think of his work caused him to worry that the utilitarian world was more real and important than his imaginative creations. This issue became a recurring theme in his work.

Despite the Puritan strain in Hawthorne's sensibilities and his own deep suspicion that a literary vocation was not serious or productive work, Hawthorne was determined to become a writer. He found encouragement at Bowdoin College in Maine and graduated in 1825 with a class that included the poet Henry Wadsworth Longfellow and Franklin Pierce, who would be elected president of the United States in the early 1850s. After graduation Hawthorne returned to his mother's house in Salem, where for the next twelve years he read New England history as well as writers such as John Milton, William Shakespeare, and John Bunyan. During this time he lived a relatively withdrawn life devoted to developing his literary art. Hawthorne wrote and revised stories as he sought a style that would express his creative energies. Many of these early efforts were destroyed when they did not meet his high standards. His first novel, *Fanshawe,* was published anonymously in 1828; it concerns a solitary young man who fails to realize his potential and dies young. Hawthorne very nearly succeeded in reclaiming and destroying all the published copies of this work. It was not attributed to the author until after his death; not even his wife was aware that he had written it. The stories eventually published as *Twice-Told Tales* (1837) represent work that was carefully revised and survived Hawthorne's critical judgments.

Writing did not provide an adequate income, so like nearly all nineteenth-century American writers, Hawthorne had to take on other employment. He worked in the Boston Custom House from 1839 through 1840 to save money to marry Sophia Peabody, but he lost that politically appointed job when administrations changed. In 1841 he lived at Brook Farm, a utopian community founded by idealists who hoped to combine manual labor with art and philosophy. Finding that monotonous physical labor left little time for thinking and writing, Hawthorne departed after seven months. The experience failed to improve his financial situation, but it did eventually serve as the basis for a novel, *The Blithedale Romance* (1852).

Married in the summer of 1842, Hawthorne and his wife moved to the Old Manse in Concord, Massachusetts, where their neighbors included Ralph Waldo Emerson, Henry David Thoreau, Amos Bronson Alcott, and other writers and thinkers who contributed to the lively literary environment of that small town. Although Hawthorne was on friendly terms with these men, his skepticism concerning human nature prevented him from sharing either their optimism or their faith in radical reform of individuals or society. Hawthorne's view of life was chastened by a sense of what he called in "Wakefield" the "iron tissue of necessity." His sensibilities were more akin to Herman Melville's. When Melville and Hawthorne met while Hawthorne was living in the Berkshires of western Massachusetts, they responded to each other intensely. Melville admired the "power of blackness" he discovered in Hawthorne's writings and dedicated *Moby-Dick* to him.

During the several years he lived in the Old Manse, Hawthorne published a second collection of *Twice-Told Tales* (1842) and additional stories in *Mosses from an Old Manse* (1846). To keep afloat financially, he worked in the Salem Custom House from 1846 until 1849, when he again lost his job through a change in administrations. This time, however, he discovered that by leaving the oppressive materialism of the Custom House he found more energy to write: "So little adapted is the atmosphere of a Custom House to the delicate harvest of fancy and sensibility, that, had I remained there through ten Presidencies yet to come, I doubt whether the tale of 'The Scarlet Letter' would ever have been brought before the public. My imagination was a tarnished mirror" there. Free of the Custom House, Hawthorne was at the height of his creativity and productivity during the early 1850s. In addition to *The Scarlet Letter* and *The Blithedale Romance*, he wrote *The House of the Seven Gables* (1851); *The Snow-Image, and Other Twice-Told Tales* (1852); a campaign biography of his Bowdoin classmate, *The Life of Franklin Pierce* (1852); and two collections of stories for children, *A Wonder Book* (1852) and *Tanglewood Tales* (1853).

Hawthorne's financial situation improved during the final decade of his life. In 1853 his friend President Pierce appointed him to the U.S. consulship in Liverpool, where he remained for the next four years. Following a tour of Europe from 1858 to 1860, Hawthorne and his family returned to Concord, and he published *The Marble Faun* (1860), his final completed work of fiction. He died while traveling through New Hampshire with ex-President Pierce.

Hawthorne's stories are much more complex than the melodramatic but usually optimistic fiction published in many magazines contemporary to him. Instead of cheerfully confirming public values and attitudes, his work tends to be dark and brooding. Modern readers remain responsive to Hawthorne's work — despite the fact that his nineteenth-century style takes some getting used to — because his psychological themes are as fascinating as they are disturbing. The range of his themes is not broad, but their treatment is remarkable for its insights.

Hawthorne wrote about individuals who suffer from inner conflicts caused by sin, pride, untested innocence, hidden guilt, perverse secrecy, cold intellectuality, and isolation. His characters are often consumed by their own passions, whether those passions are motivated by an obsession with goodness or evil. He looks inside his characters and reveals to us that portion of their hearts, minds, and souls which they keep from the world and even from themselves. This emphasis accounts for the private, interior, and sometimes gloomy atmosphere in Hawthorne's works. His stories rarely end on a happy note, because the questions his characters raise are almost never completely answered. Rather than positing solutions to the problems and issues his characters encounter, Hawthorne leaves us with ambiguities suggesting that experience cannot always be fully understood and controlled. Beneath the surface appearances in his stories lurk ironies and shifting meanings that point to many complex truths instead of a single simple moral.

The following four Hawthorne stories provide an opportunity to study this writer in some depth. These stories are not intended to be entirely representative of the 120 or so that Hawthorne wrote, but they do offer some sense of the range of his techniques and themes. Hawthorne's fictional world of mysterious incidents and sometimes bizarre characters increases in meaning the more his stories are read in the context of one another.

Chronology

1804   Born on July 4 in Salem, Massachusetts.

1808   Hawthorne's father, a sea captain, dies in Surinam, Dutch Guiana, leaving the family dependent on relatives.

1821–25 Attends Bowdoin College in Maine. Franklin Pierce (later to become president) and Henry Wadsworth Longfellow are classmates. Graduates eighteenth in a class of thirty-eight.

1828	Publishes *Fanshawe: A Tale* anonymously at his own expense.
1830–37	Publishes numerous stories in periodicals anonymously or pseudonymously, collected in *Twice-Told Tales*.
1838	Becomes engaged to Sophia Peabody.
1839–40	Works in Boston Custom House.
1841	From April, lives at the utopian Brook Farm Community, but leaves in November.
1842–45	Marries (eventually has three children) and lives at the Old Manse in Concord, Massachusetts, where he meets Ralph Waldo Emerson and Henry David Thoreau.
1844	Publishes his second collection of stories, *Mosses from an Old Manse*.
1846–49	Works as a surveyor in the Salem Custom House.
1850	Publishes *The Scarlet Letter;* becomes a friend of Herman Melville.
1851	Publishes *The House of the Seven Gables; The Snow-Image, and Other Twice-Told Tales;* and *True Stories from History and Biography*.
1852	Publishes *The Blithedale Romance; A Wonder Book for Girls and Boys;* and *The Life of Franklin Pierce,* a campaign biography.
1853–57	Appointed by President Pierce, Hawthorne serves as United States Consul at Liverpool.
1857–59	Lives in Rome and Florence.
1860	Publishes *The Marble Faun;* returns to Concord.
1863	Publishes *Our Old Home: A Series of English Sketches*.
1864	Dies on May 19 at Plymouth, New Hampshire.

Young Goodman Brown   1835

Young Goodman Brown came forth at sunset into the street at Salem village; but put his head back, after crossing the threshold, to exchange a parting kiss with his young wife. And Faith, as the wife was aptly named, thrust her own pretty head into the street, letting the wind play with the pink ribbons of her cap while she called to Goodman Brown.

"Dearest heart," whispered she, softly and rather sadly, when her lips were close to his ear, "prithee put off your journey until sunrise and sleep in your own bed tonight. A lone woman is troubled with such dreams and such thoughts that she's afeared of herself sometimes. Pray tarry with me this night, dear husband, of all nights in the year."

"My love and my Faith," replied young Goodman Brown, "of all nights in the year, this one night must I tarry away from thee. My journey, as thou callest it, forth and back again, must needs be done 'twixt now and sunrise. What, my sweet, pretty wife, dost thou doubt me already, and we but three months married?"

"Then God bless you!" said Faith, with the pink ribbons; "and may you find all well when you come back."

"Amen!" cried Goodman Brown. "Say thy prayers, dear Faith, and go to bed ₅ at dusk, and no harm will come to thee."

So they parted; and the young man pursued his way until, being about to turn the corner by the meeting-house, he looked back and saw the head of Faith still peeping after him with a melancholy air, in spite of her pink ribbons.

"Poor little Faith!" thought he, for his heart smote him. "What a wretch am I to leave her on such an errand! She talks of dreams, too. Methought as she spoke there was trouble in her face, as if a dream had warned her what work is to be done tonight. But no, no; 't would kill her to think it. Well, she's a blessed angel on earth; and after this one night I'll cling to her skirts and follow her to heaven."

With this excellent resolve for the future, Goodman Brown felt himself justified in making more haste on his present evil purpose. He had taken a dreary road, darkened by all the gloomiest trees of the forest, which barely stood aside to let the narrow path creep through, and closed immediately behind. It was all as lonely as could be; and there is this peculiarity in such a solitude, that the traveler knows not who may be concealed by the innumerable trunks and the thick boughs overhead; so that with lonely footsteps he may yet be passing through an unseen multitude.

"There may be a devilish Indian behind every tree," said Goodman Brown to himself; and he glanced fearfully behind him as he added, "What if the devil himself should be at my very elbow!"

His head being turned back, he passed a crook of the road, and, looking ₁₀ forward again, beheld the figure of a man, in grave and decent attire, seated at the foot of an old tree. He arose at Goodman Brown's approach and walked onward side by side with him.

"You are late, Goodman Brown," said he. "The clock of the Old South was striking as I came through Boston, and that is full fifteen minutes agone."

"Faith kept me back a while," replied the young man, with a tremor in his voice, caused by the sudden appearance of his companion, though not wholly unexpected.

It was now deep dusk in the forest, and deepest in that part of it where these two were journeying. As nearly as could be discerned, the second traveler was about fifty years old, apparently in the same rank of life as Goodman Brown, and bearing a considerable resemblance to him, though perhaps more in expression than features. Still they might have been taken for father and son. And yet, though the elder person was as simply clad as the younger, and as simple in manner too, he had an indescribable air of one who knew the world, and who would not have felt abashed at the governor's dinner table or in King William's court, were it possible that his affairs should call him thither. But the only thing about him that could be fixed upon as remarkable was his staff, which bore the likeness of a great black snake, so curiously wrought that it might almost be seen to twist and wriggle itself like a living serpent. This, of course, must have been an ocular deception, assisted by the uncertain light.

"Come, Goodman Brown," cried his fellow-traveler, "this is a dull pace for the beginning of a journey. Take my staff, if you are so soon weary."

"Friend," said the other, exchanging his slow pace for a full stop, "having kept covenant by meeting thee here, it is my purpose now to return whence I came. I have scruples touching the matter thou wot'st of." 15

"Sayest thou so?" replied he of the serpent, smiling apart. "Let us walk on, nevertheless, reasoning as we go; and if I convince thee not thou shalt turn back. We are but a little way in the forest yet."

"Too far! too far!" exclaimed the goodman, unconsciously resuming his walk. "My father never went into the woods on such an errand, nor his father before him. We have been a race of honest men and good Christians since the days of the martyrs; and shall I be the first of the name of Brown that ever took this path and kept" —

"Such company, thou wouldst say," observed the elder person, interpreting his pause. "Well said, Goodman Brown! I have been as well acquainted with your family as with ever a one among the Puritans; and that's no trifle to say. I helped your grandfather, the constable, when he lashed the Quaker woman so smartly through the streets of Salem; and it was I that brought your father a pitch-pine knot, kindled at my own hearth, to set fire to an Indian village, in King Philip's war. They were my good friends, both; and many a pleasant walk have we had along this path, and returned merrily after midnight. I would fain be friends with you for their sake."

"If it be as thou sayest," replied Goodman Brown, "I marvel they never spoke of these matters; or, verily, I marvel not, seeing that the least rumor of the sort would have driven them from New England. We are a people of prayer, and good works to boot, and abide no such wickedness."

"Wickedness or not," said the traveler with the twisted staff, "I have a very general acquaintance here in New England. The deacons of many a church have drunk the communion wine with me; the selectmen of divers towns make me their chairman; and a majority of the Great and General Court are firm supporters of my interest. The governor and I, too — But these are state secrets." 20

"Can this be so?" cried Goodman Brown, with a stare of amazement at his undisturbed companion. "Howbeit, I have nothing to do with the governor and council; they have their own ways, and are no rule for a simple husbandman like me. But, were I to go on with thee, how should I meet the eye of that good old man, our minister, at Salem village? Oh, his voice would make me tremble both Sabbath day and lecture day."

Thus far the elder traveler had listened with due gravity; but now burst into a fit of irrepressible mirth, shaking himself so violently that his snakelike staff actually seemed to wriggle in sympathy.

"Ha! ha! ha!" shouted he again and again; then composing himself, "Well, go on, Goodman Brown, go on; but, prithee, don't kill me with laughing."

"Well, then, to end the matter at once," said Goodman Brown, considerably nettled, "there is my wife, Faith. It would break her dear little heart; and I'd rather break my own."

"Nay, if that be the case," answered the other, "e'en go thy ways, Goodman 25
Brown. I would not for twenty old women like the one hobbling before us that
Faith should come to any harm."

As he spoke he pointed his staff at a female figure on the path, in whom
Goodman Brown recognized a very pious and exemplary dame, who had taught
him his catechism in youth, and was still his moral and spiritual adviser, jointly
with the minister and Deacon Gookin.

"A marvel, truly that Goody Cloyse should be so far in the wilderness at
nightfall," said he. "But with your leave, friend, I shall take a cut through the
woods until we have left this Christian woman behind. Being a stranger to you,
she might ask whom I was consorting with and whither I was going."

"Be it so," said his fellow-traveler. "Betake you to the woods, and let me
keep the path."

Accordingly the young man turned aside, but took care to watch his companion, who advanced softly along the road until he had come within a staff's
length of the old dame. She, meanwhile, was making the best of her way, with
singular speed for so aged a woman, and mumbling some indistinct words — a
prayer, doubtless — as she went. The traveler put forth his staff and touched her
withered neck with what seemed the serpent's tail.

"The devil!" screamed the pious old lady.   30

"Then Goody Cloyse knows her old friend?" observed the traveler, confronting her and leaning on his writhing stick.

"Ah, forsooth, and is it your worship indeed?" cried the good dame. "Yea,
truly is it, and in the very image of my old gossip, Goodman Brown, the
grandfather of the silly fellow that now is. But — would your worship believe
it? — my broomstick hath strangely disappeared, stolen, as I suspect, by that
unhanged witch, Goody Cory, and that, too, when I was all anointed with the
juice of smallage, and cinquefoil, and wolfsbane" —

"Mingled with fine wheat and the fat of a newborn babe," said the shape of
old Goodman Brown.

"Ah, your worship knows the recipe," cried the old lady, cackling aloud.
"So, as I was saying, being all ready for the meeting, and no horse to ride on, I
made up my mind to foot it; for they tell me there is a nice young man to be
taken into communion tonight. But now your good worship will lend me your
arm, and we shall be there in a twinkling."

"That can hardly be," answered her friend. "I may not spare you my arm, 35
Goody Cloyse; but here is my staff, if you will."

So saying, he threw it down at her feet, where, perhaps, it assumed life,
being one of the rods which its owner had formerly lent to the Egyptian magi.
Of this fact, however, Goodman Brown could not take cognizance. He had cast
up his eyes in astonishment, and, looking down again, beheld neither Goody
Cloyse nor the serpentine staff, but his fellow-traveler alone, who waited for him
as calmly as if nothing had happened.

"That old woman taught me my catechism," said the young man; and there
was a world of meaning in this simple comment.

They continued to walk onward, while the elder traveler exhorted his
companion to make good speed and persevere in the path, discoursing so aptly
that his arguments seemed rather to spring up in the bosom of his auditor than
to be suggested by himself. As they went, he plucked a branch of maple to serve

for a walking stick, and began to strip it of the twigs and little boughs, which were wet with evening dew. The moment his fingers touched them they became strangely withered and dried up as with a week's sunshine. Thus the pair proceeded, at a good free pace, until suddenly, in a gloomy hollow of the road, Goodman Brown sat himself down on the stump of a tree and refused to go any farther.

"Friend," he said, stubbornly, "my mind is made up. Not another step will I budge on this errand. What if a wretched old woman do choose to go to the devil when I thought she was going to heaven: is that any reason why I should quit my dear Faith and go after her?"

"You will think better of this by and by," said his acquaintance, composedly. 40 "Sit here and rest yourself a while; and when you feel like moving again, there is my staff to help you along."

Without more words, he threw his companion the maple stick, and was as speedily out of sight as if he had vanished into the deepening gloom. The young man sat a few moments by the roadside, applauding himself greatly, and thinking with how clear a conscience he should meet the minister in his morning walk, nor shrink from the eye of good old Deacon Gookin. And what calm sleep would be his that very night, which was to have been spent so wickedly, but so purely and sweetly now, in the arms of Faith! Amidst these pleasant and praise-worthy meditations, Goodman Brown heard the tramp of horses along the road, and deemed it advisable to conceal himself within the verge of the forest, conscious of the guilty purpose that had brought him thither, though now so happily turned from it.

On came the hoof trams and the voices of the riders, two grave old voices, conversing soberly as they drew near. These mingled sounds appeared to pass along the road, within a few yards of the young man's hiding-place; but, owing doubtless to the depth of the gloom at that particular spot, neither the travelers nor their steeds were visible. Though their figures brushed the small boughs by the wayside, it could not be seen that they intercepted, even for a moment, the faint gleam from the strip of bright sky athwart which they must have passed. Goodman Brown alternately crouched and stood on tiptoe, pulling aside the branches and thrusting forth his head as far as he durst without discerning so much as a shadow. It vexed him the more, because he could have sworn, were such a thing possible, that he recognized the voices of the minister and Deacon Gookin, jogging along quietly, as they were wont to do, when bound to some ordination or ecclesiastical council. While yet within hearing, one of the riders stopped to pluck a switch.

"Of the two, reverend sir," said the voice like the deacon's, "I had rather miss an ordination dinner than tonight's meeting. They tell me that some of our community are to be here from Falmouth and beyond, and others from Con-necticut and Rhode Island, besides several of the Indian powwows, who, after their fashion, know almost as much deviltry as the best of us. Moreover, there is a goodly young woman to be taken into communion."

"Mighty well, Deacon Gookin!" replied the solemn old tones of the minister. "Spur up, or we shall be late. Nothing can be done, you know, until I get on the ground."

The hoofs clattered again; and the voices, talking so strangely in the empty 45 air, passed on through the forest, where no church had ever been gathered or solitary Christian prayed. Whither, then, could these holy men be journeying so deep into the heathen wilderness? Young Goodman Brown caught hold of a tree for support, being ready to sink down on the ground, faint and overburdened with the heavy sickness of his heart. He looked up to the sky, doubting whether there really was a heaven above him. Yet there was the blue arch, and the stars brightening in it.

"With heaven above and Faith below, I will yet stand firm against the devil!" cried Goodman Brown.

While he still gazed upward into the deep arch of the firmament and had lifted his hands to pray, a cloud, though no wind was stirring, hurried across the zenith and hid the brightening stars. The blue sky was still visible, except directly overhead, where this black mass of cloud was sweeping swiftly northward. Aloft in the air, as if from the depths of the cloud, came a confused and doubtful sound of voices. Once the listener fancied that he could distinguish the accents of townspeople of his own, men and women, both pious and ungodly, many of whom he had met at the communion table, and had seen others rioting at the tavern. The next moment, so indistinct were the sounds, he doubted whether he had heard aught but the murmur of the old forest, whispering without a wind. Then came a stronger swell of those familiar tones, heard daily in the sunshine at Salem village, but never until now from a cloud of night. There was one voice, of a young woman, uttering lamentations, yet with an uncertain sorrow, and entreating for some favor, which, perhaps, it would grieve her to obtain; and all the unseen multitude, both saints and sinners, seemed to encourage her onward.

"Faith!" shouted Goodman Brown, in a voice of agony and desperation; and the echoes of the forest mocked him, crying, "Faith! Faith!" as if bewildered wretches were seeking her all through the wilderness.

The cry of grief, rage, and terror was yet piercing the night, when the unhappy husband held his breath for a response. There was a scream, drowned immediately in a louder murmur of voices, fading into far-off laughter, as the dark cloud swept away, leaving the clear and silent sky above Goodman Brown. But something fluttered lightly down through the air and caught on the branch of a tree. The young man seized it, and beheld a pink ribbon.

"My Faith is gone!" cried he after one stupefied moment. "There is no good 50 on earth; and sin is but a name. Come, devil; for to thee is this world given."

And, maddened with despair, so that he laughed loud and long, did Goodman Brown grasp his staff and set forth again, at such a rate that he seemed to fly along the forest path rather than to walk or run. The road grew wilder and drearier and more faintly traced, and vanished at length, leaving him in the heart of the dark wilderness, still rushing onward with the instinct that guides mortal man to evil. The whole forest was peopled with frightful sounds — the creaking of the trees, the howling of wild beasts, and the yell of Indians; while sometimes the wind tolled like a distant church bell, and sometimes gave a broad roar around the traveler, as if all Nature were laughing him to scorn. But he was himself the chief horror of the scene, and shrank not from its other horrors.

"Ha! ha! ha!" roared Goodman Brown when the wind laughed at him. "Let us hear which will laugh loudest. Think not to frighten me with your deviltry.

Come witch, come wizard, come Indian powwow, come devil himself, and here comes Goodman Brown. You may as well fear him as he fear you."

In truth, all through the haunted forest there could be nothing more frightful than the figure of Goodman Brown. On he flew among the black pines, brandishing his staff with frenzied gestures, now giving vent to an inspiration of horrid blasphemy, and now shouting forth such laughter as set all the echoes of the forest laughing like demons around him. The fiend in his own shape is less hideous than when he rages in the breast of man. Thus sped the demoniac on his course, until, quivering among the trees, he saw a red light before him, as when the felled trunks and branches of a clearing have been set on fire, and throw up their lurid blaze against the sky, at the hour of midnight. He paused, in a lull of the tempest that had driven him onward, and heard the swell of what seemed a hymn, rolling solemnly from a distance with the weight of many voices. He knew the tune; it was a familiar one in the choir of the village meeting-house. The verse died heavily away, and was lengthened by a chorus, not of human voices, but of all the sounds of the benighted wilderness pealing in awful harmony together. Goodman Brown cried out, and his cry was lost to his own ear by its unison with the cry of the desert.

In the interval of silence he stole forward until the light glared full upon his eyes. At one extremity of an open space, hemmed in by the dark wall of the forest, arose a rock, bearing some rude, natural resemblance either to an altar or a pulpit, and surrounded by four blazing pines, their tops aflame, their stems untouched, like candles at an evening meeting. The mass of foliage that had overgrown the summit of the rock was all on fire, blazing high into the night and fitfully illuminating the whole field. Each pendent twig and leafy festoon was in a blaze. As the red light arose and fell, a numerous congregation alternately shone forth, then disappeared in shadow, and again grew, as it were, out of the darkness, peopling the heart of the solitary woods at once.

"A grave and dark-clad company," quoth Goodman Brown. 55

In truth they were such. Among them, quivering to and fro between gloom and splendor, appeared faces that would be seen next day at the council board of the province, and others which, Sabbath after Sabbath, looked devoutly heavenward, and benignantly over the crowded pews, from the holiest pulpits in the land. Some affirm that the lady of the governor was there. At least there were high dames well known to her, and wives of honored husbands, and widows, a great multitude, and ancient maidens, all of excellent repute, and fair young girls, who trembled lest their mothers should espy them. Either the sudden gleams of light flashing over the obscure field bedazzled Goodman Brown, or he recognized a score of the church members of Salem village famous for their especial sanctity. Good old Deacon Gookin had arrived, and waited at the skirts of that venerable saint, his revered pastor. But, irreverently consorting with these grave, reputable, and pious people, these elders of the church, these chaste dames and dewy virgins, there were men of dissolute lives and women of spotted fame, wretches given over to all mean and filthy vice, and suspected even of horrid crimes. It was strange to see that the good shrank not from the wicked, nor were the sinners abashed by the saints. Scattered also among their pale-faced enemies were the Indian priests, or powwows, who had often scared their native forest with more hideous incantations than any known to English witchcraft.

"But where is Faith?" thought Goodman Brown; and, as hope came into his heart, he trembled.

Another verse of the hymn arose, a slow and mournful strain, such as the pious love, but joined to words which expressed all that our nature can conceive of sin, and darkly hinted at far more. Unfathomable to mere mortals is the lore of fiends. Verse after verse was sung; and still the chorus of the desert swelled between like the deepest tone of a mighty organ; and with the final peal of that dreadful anthem there came a sound, as if the roaring wind, the rushing streams, the howling beasts, and every other voice of the unconcerted wilderness were mingling and according with the voice of guilty man in homage to the prince of all. The four blazing pines threw up a loftier flame, and obscurely discovered shapes and visages of horror on the smoke wreaths above the impious assembly. At the same moment the fire on the rock shot redly forth and formed a glowing arch above its base, where now appeared a figure. With reverence be it spoken, the figure bore no slight similitude, both in garb and manner, to some grave divine of the New England churches.

"Bring forth the converts!" cried a voice that echoed through the field and rolled into the forest.

At the word, Goodman Brown stepped forth from the shadow of the trees 60 and approached the congregation, with whom he felt a loathful brotherhood by the sympathy of all that was wicked in his heart. He could have well-nigh sworn that the shape of his own dead father beckoned him to advance, looking downward from a smoke wreath, while a woman, with dim features of despair, threw out her hand to warn him back. Was it his mother? But he had no power to retreat one step, nor to resist, even in thought, when the minister and good old Deacon Gookin seized his arms and led him to the blazing rock. Thither came also the slender form of a veiled female, led between Goody Cloyse, that pious teacher of the catechism, and Martha Carrier, who had received the devil's promise to be queen of hell. A rampant hag was she. And there stood the proselytes beneath the canopy of fire.

"Welcome, my children," said the dark figure, "to the communion of your race. Ye have found thus young your nature and your destiny. My children, look behind you!"

They turned; and flashing forth, as it were, in a sheet of flame, the fiend worshipers were seen; the smile of welcome gleamed darkly on every visage.

"There," resumed the sable form, "are all whom ye have reverenced from youth. Ye deemed them holier than yourselves and shrank from your own sin, contrasting it with their lives of righteousness and prayerful aspirations heavenward. Yet here are they all in my worshiping assembly. This night it shall be granted you to know their secret deeds: how hoary-bearded elders of the church have whispered wanton words to the young maids of their households; how many a woman, eager for widows' weeds, has given her husband a drink at bedtime and let him sleep his last sleep in her bosom; how beardless youths have made haste to inherit their fathers' wealth; and how fair damsels — blush not, sweet ones — have dug little graves in the garden, and bidden me, the sole guest, to an infant's funeral. By the sympathy of your human hearts for sin ye shall scent out all the places — whether in church, bedchamber, street, field, or forest — where crime has been committed, and shall exult to behold the whole earth one stain of guilt, one mighty blood spot. Far more than this. It shall be yours to penetrate, in every bosom, the deep mystery of sin, the fountain of all wicked arts, and which inexhaustibly supplies more evil impulses than human power — than my power at its utmost — can make manifest in deeds. And now, my children, look upon each other."

They did so; and, by the blaze of the hell-kindled torches, the wretched man beheld his Faith, and the wife her husband, trembling before that unhallowed altar.

"Lo, there ye stand, my children," said the figure, in a deep and solemn 65 tone, almost sad with its despairing awfulness, as if his once angelic nature could yet mourn for our miserable race. "Depending upon one another's hearts, ye had still hoped that virtue were not all a dream. Now are ye undeceived. Evil is the nature of mankind. Evil must be your only happiness. Welcome again, my children, to the communion of your race."

"Welcome," repeated the fiend worshipers; in one cry of despair and triumph.

And there they stood, the only pair, as it seemed, who were yet hesitating on the verge of wickedness in this dark world. A basin was hollowed, naturally, in the rock. Did it contain water, reddened by the lurid light? or was it blood? or, perchance, a liquid flame? Herein did the shape of evil dip his hand and prepare to lay the mark of baptism upon their foreheads, that they might be partakers of the mystery of sin, more conscious of the secret guilt of others, both in deed and thought, than they could now be of their own. The husband cast one look at his pale wife, and Faith at him. What polluted wretches would the next glance show them to each other, shuddering alike at what they disclosed and what they saw!

"Faith! Faith!" cried the husband, "look up to heaven, and resist the wicked one."

Whether Faith obeyed he knew not. Hardly had he spoken when he found himself amid calm night and solitude, listening to a roar of the wind which died heavily away through the forest. He staggered against the rock, and felt it chill and damp; while a hanging twig, that had been all on fire, besprinkled his cheek with the coldest dew.

The next morning young Goodman Brown came slowly into the street of 70 Salem village, staring around him like a bewildered man. The good old minister was taking a walk along the graveyard to get an appetite for breakfast and meditate his sermon, and bestowed a blessing, as he passed, on Goodman Brown. He shrank from the venerable saint as if to avoid an anathema. Old Deacon Gookin was at domestic worship, and the holy words of his prayer were heard through the open window. "What God doth the wizard pray to?" quoth Goodman Brown. Goody Cloyse, that excellent old Christian, stood in the early sunshine at her own lattice, catechizing a little girl who had brought her a pint of morning's milk. Goodman Brown snatched away the child as from the grasp of the fiend himself. Turning the corner by the meeting-house, he spied the head of Faith, with the pink ribbons, gazing anxiously forth, and bursting into such joy at sight of him that she skipped along the street and almost kissed her husband before the whole village. But Goodman Brown looked sternly and sadly into her face, and passed on without a greeting.

Had Goodman Brown fallen asleep in the forest and only dreamed a wild dream of a witch-meeting?

Be it so if you will; but, alas! it was a dream of evil omen for young Goodman Brown. A stern, a sad, a darkly meditative, a distrustful, if not a desperate man did he become from the night of that fearful dream. On the Sabbath day, when the congregation were singing a holy psalm, he could not listen because an anthem of sin rushed loudly upon his ear and drowned all the blessed strain. When the minister spoke from the pulpit with power and fervid eloquence, and, with his hand on the open Bible, of the sacred truths of our religion, and of saintlike lives and triumphant deaths, and of future bliss or misery unutterable, then did Goodman Brown turn pale, dreading lest the roof should thunder down upon the gray blasphemer and his hearers. Often, awaking suddenly at midnight, he shrank from the bosom of Faith; and at morning or eventide, when the family knelt down at prayer, he scowled and muttered to himself, and gazed sternly at his wife, and turned away. And when he had lived long, and was borne to his grave a hoary corpse, followed by Faith, an aged woman, and children and grandchildren, a goodly procession, besides neighbors not a few, they carved no hopeful verse upon his tombstone, for his dying hour was gloom.

Considerations for Critical Thinking and Writing

1. What is the significance of Young Goodman Brown's name?
2. What is the symbolic value of the forest in this story? How are the descriptions of the forest contrasted with those of Salem village?
3. Characterize Young Goodman Brown at the beginning of the story. Why does he go into the forest? What does he mean when he says "Faith kept me back a while"?
4. What function do Faith's ribbons have in the story?
5. What foreshadows Young Goodman Brown's meeting with his "fellow-traveler"? Who is he? How do we know that Brown is keeping an appointment with a supernatural being?
6. The narrator describes the fellow-traveler's staff wriggling like a snake, but then says, "This, of course, must have been an ocular deception, assisted by the uncertain light." What is the effect of this and other instances of ambiguity in the story?
7. What does Young Goodman Brown discover in the forest? What does he come to think of his ancestors, the church and state, Goody Cloyse, and even his wife?
8. Is Salem populated by hypocrites who cover hideous crimes with a veneer of piety and respectability? Do Faith and the other characters Brown sees when he returns from the forest appear corrupt to you?
9. Near the end of the story the narrator asks, "Had Goodman Brown fallen asleep in the forest and only dreamed a wild dream of a witch-meeting?" Was it a dream or did the meeting actually happen? How does the answer to this question affect your reading of the story? Write an essay giving an answer to the narrator's question.
10. How is Young Goodman Brown changed by his experience in the forest? Does the narrator endorse Brown's unwillingness to trust anyone?
11. Discuss this story as an inward, psychological journey in which Young Goodman Brown discovers the power of blackness in himself but refuses to acknowledge that dimension of his personality.
12. Consider the story as a criticism of the village's hypocrisy.
13. Explain why it is difficult to summarize "Young Goodman Brown" with a tidy moral.

Connections to Other Selections

1. Compare and contrast Young Goodman Brown's reasons for withdrawal with those of Melville's Bartleby, the scrivener (p. 83). Do you find yourself more sympathetic with one character than the other? Explain.
2. To what extent is Hawthorne's use of dreams crucial in this story and in "The Birthmark" (p. 261)? Explain how Hawthorne uses dreams as a means to complicate our view of his characters.
3. What does Young Goodman Brown's pursuit of sin have in common with Aylmer's quest for perfection in "The Birthmark" (p. 261)? How do these pursuits reveal the characters' personalities and shed light on the theme of each story?

The Minister's Black Veil   1836

A PARABLE°

The sexton stood in the porch of Milford meeting-house, pulling lustily at the bell-rope. The old people of the village came stooping along the street. Children, with bright faces, tript merrily beside their parents, or mimicked a graver gait, in the conscious dignity of their Sunday clothes. Spruce bachelors looked sidelong at the pretty maidens, and fancied that the Sabbath sunshine made them prettier than on weekdays. When the throng had mostly streamed into the porch, the sexton began to toll the bell, keeping his eye on the Reverend Mr. Hooper's door. The first glimpse of the clergyman's figure was the signal for the bell to cease its summons.

"But what has good Parson Hooper got upon his face?" cried the sexton in astonishment.

All within hearing immediately turned about, and beheld the semblance of Mr. Hooper, pacing slowly his meditative way towards the meeting-house. With one accord they started, expressing more wonder than if some strange minister were coming to dust the cushions of Mr. Hooper's pulpit.

"Are you sure it is our parson?" inquired Goodman Gray of the sexton.

"Of a certainty it is good Mr. Hooper," replied the sexton. "He was to have 5 exchanged pulpits with Parson Shute of Westbury; but Parson Shute sent to excuse himself yesterday, being to preach a funeral sermon."

The cause of so much amazement may appear sufficiently slight. Mr. Hooper, a gentlemanly person of about thirty, though still a bachelor, was dressed with due clerical neatness, as if a careful wife had starched his band, and brushed the weekly dust from his Sunday's garb. There was but one thing remarkable in his appearance. Swathed about his forehead, and hanging down over his face, so low as to be shaken by his breath, Mr. Hooper had on a black veil. On a nearer

Another clergyman in New England, Mr. Joseph Moody, of York, Maine, who died about eighty years since, made himself remarkable by the same eccentricity that is here related of the Reverend Mr. Hooper. In his case, however, the symbol had a different import. In early life he had accidentally killed a beloved friend; and from that day till the hour of his own death, he hid his face from men. [Hawthorne's note.]

view, it seemed to consist of two folds of crape, which entirely concealed his features, except the mouth and chin, but probably did not intercept his sight, farther than to give a darkened aspect to all living and inanimate things. With this gloomy shade before him, good Mr. Hooper walked onward, at a slow and quiet pace, stooping somewhat and looking on the ground, as is customary with abstracted men, yet nodding kindly to those of his parishioners who still waited on the meeting-house steps. But so wonder-struck were they, that his greeting hardly met with a return.

"I can't really feel as if good Mr. Hooper's face was behind that piece of crape," said the sexton.

"I don't like it," muttered an old woman, as she hobbled into the meeting-house. "He has changed himself into something awful, only by hiding his face."

"Our parson has gone mad!" cried Goodman Gray, following him across the threshold.

A rumor of some unaccountable phenomenon had preceded Mr. Hooper 10 into the meeting-house, and set all the congregation astir. Few could refrain from twisting their heads towards the door; many stood upright, and turned directly about; while several little boys clambered upon the seats, and came down again with a terrible racket. There was a general bustle, a rustling of the women's gowns and shuffling of the men's feet, greatly at variance with that hushed repose which should attend the entrance of the minister. But Mr. Hooper appeared not to notice the perturbation of his people. He entered with an almost noiseless step, bent his head mildly to the pews on each side, and bowed as he passed his oldest parishioner, a white-haired great-grandsire, who occupied an arm-chair in the center of the aisle. It was strange to observe, how slowly this venerable man became conscious of something singular in the appearance of his pastor. He seemed not fully to partake of the prevailing wonder, till Mr. Hooper had ascended the stairs, and showed himself in the pulpit, face to face with his congregation, except for the black veil. That mysterious emblem was never once withdrawn. It shook with his measured breath as he gave out the psalm; it threw its obscurity between him and the holy page, as he read the Scriptures; and while he prayed, the veil lay heavily on his uplifted countenance. Did he seek to hide it from the dread Being whom he was addressing?

Such was the effect of this simple piece of crape, that more than one woman of delicate nerves was forced to leave the meeting-house. Yet perhaps the pale-faced congregation was almost as fearful a sight to the minister, as his black veil to them.

Mr. Hooper had the reputation of a good preacher, but not an energetic one: he strove to win his people heavenward, by mild persuasive influences, rather than to drive them thither, by the thunders of the Word. The sermon which he now delivered, was marked by the same characteristics of style and manner, as the general series of his pulpit oratory. But there was something, either in the sentiment of the discourse itself, or in the imagination of the auditors, which made it greatly the most powerful effort that they had ever heard from their pastor's lips. It was tinged, rather more darkly than usual, with the gentle gloom of Mr. Hooper's temperament. The subject had reference to secret sin, and those sad mysteries which we hide from our nearest and dearest, and would fain conceal from our own consciousness, even forgetting that the

Omniscient can detect them. A subtle power was breathed into his words. Each member of the congregation, the most innocent girl, and the man of hardened breast, felt as if the preacher had crept upon them, behind his awful veil, and discovered their hoarded iniquity of deed or thought. Many spread their clasped hands on their bosoms. There was nothing terrible in what Mr. Hooper said; at least, no violence; and yet, with every tremor of his melancholy voice, the hearers quaked. An unsought pathos came hand in hand with awe. So sensible were the audience of some unwonted attribute in their minister, that they longed for a breath of wind to blow aside the veil, almost believing that a stranger's visage would be discovered, though the form, gesture, and voice were those of Mr. Hooper.

At the close of the services, the people hurried out with indecorous confusion, eager to communicate their pent-up amazement, and conscious of lighter spirits, the moment they lost sight of the black veil. Some gathered in little circles, huddled closely together, with their mouths all whispering in the center; some went homeward alone, wrapt in silent meditation; some talked loudly, and profaned the Sabbath-day with ostentatious laughter. A few shook their sagacious heads, intimating that they could penetrate the mystery; while one or two affirmed that there was no mystery at all, but only that Mr. Hooper's eyes were so weakened by the midnight lamp, as to require a shade. After a brief interval, forth came good Mr. Hooper also, in the rear of his flock. Turning his veiled face from one group to another, he paid due reverence to the hoary heads, saluted the middle-aged with kind dignity, as their friend and spiritual guide, greeted the young with mingled authority and love, and laid his hands on the little children's heads to bless them. Such was always his custom on the Sabbath-day. Strange and bewildered looks repaid him for his courtesy. None, as on former occasions, aspired to the honor of walking by their pastor's side. Old Squire Saunders, doubtless by an accidental lapse of memory, neglected to invite Mr. Hooper to his table, where the good clergyman had been wont to bless the food, almost every Sunday since his settlement. He returned, therefore, to the parsonage, and, at the moment of closing the door, was observed to look back upon the people, all of whom had their eyes fixed upon the minister. A sad smile gleamed faintly from beneath the black veil, and flickered about his mouth, glimmering as he disappeared.

"How strange," said a lady, "that a simple black veil, such as any woman might wear on her bonnet, should become such a terrible thing on Mr. Hooper's face!"

"Something must surely be amiss with Mr. Hooper's intellects," observed 15 her husband, the physician of the village. "But the strangest part of the affair is the effect of this vagary, even on a sober-minded man like myself. The black veil, though it covers only our pastor's face, throws its influence over his whole person, and makes him ghost-like from head to foot. Do you not feel it so?"

"Truly do I," replied the lady; "and I would not be alone with him for the world. I wonder he is not afraid to be alone with himself!"

"Men sometimes are so," said her husband.

That afternoon service was attended with similar circumstances. At its conclusion, the bell tolled for the funeral of a young lady. The relatives and friends were assembled in the house, and the more distant acquaintances stood about the door, speaking of the good qualities of the deceased, when their talk was interrupted by the appearance of Mr. Hooper, still covered with his black veil. It was now an appropriate emblem. The clergyman stepped into the room where the corpse was laid, and bent over the coffin, to take a last farewell of his deceased parishioner. As he stooped, the veil hung straight down from his forehead, so that, if her eye-lids had not been closed for ever, the dead maiden might have seen his face. Could Mr. Hooper be fearful of her glance, that he so hastily caught back the black veil? A person, who watched the interview between the dead and living, scrupled not to affirm, that, at the instant when the clergyman's features were disclosed, the corpse had slightly shuddered, rustling the shroud and muslin cap, though the countenance retained the composure of death. A superstitious old woman was the only witness of this prodigy. From the coffin, Mr. Hooper passed into the chamber of the mourners, and thence to the head of the staircase, to make the funeral prayer. It was a tender and heart-dissolving prayer, full of sorrow, yet so imbued with celestial hopes, that the music of a heavenly harp, swept by the fingers of the dead, seemed faintly to be heard among the saddest accents of the minister. The people trembled, though they but darkly understood him, when he prayed that they, and himself, and all of mortal race, might be ready, as he trusted this young maiden had been, for the dreadful hour that should snatch the veil from their faces. The bearers went heavily forth, and the mourners followed, saddening all the street, with the dead before them, and Mr. Hooper in his black veil behind.

"Why do you look back?" said one in the procession to his partner.

"I had a fancy," replied she, "that the minister and the maiden's spirit were 20 walking hand in hand."

"And so had I, at the same moment," said the other.

That night, the handsomest couple in Milford village were to be joined in wedlock. Though reckoned a melancholy man, Mr. Hooper had a placid cheerfulness for such occasions, which often excited a sympathetic smile, where livelier merriment would have been thrown away. There was no quality of his disposition which made him more beloved than this. The company at the wedding awaited his arrival with impatience, trusting that the strange awe, which had gathered over him throughout the day, would now be dispelled. But such was not the result. When Mr. Hooper came, the first thing that their eyes rested on was the same horrible black veil, which had added deeper gloom to the funeral, and could portend nothing but evil to the wedding. Such was its immediate effect on the guests, that a cloud seemed to have rolled duskily from beneath the black crape, and dimmed the light of the candles. The bridal pair stood up before the minister. But the bride's cold fingers quivered in the tremulous hand of the bridegroom, and her death-like paleness caused a whisper, that the maiden who had been buried a few hours before, was come from her grave to be married. If ever another wedding were so dismal, it was that famous one, where they tolled the wedding-knell. After performing the ceremony, Mr. Hooper raised a glass of wine to his lips, wishing happiness to the new-married couple, in a strain of mild pleasantry that ought to have brightened the features of the guests, like a cheerful gleam from the hearth. At that instant, catching a glimpse of his figure in the looking-glass, the black veil involved his own spirit in the horror with which it overwhelmed all others. His frame shuddered — his lips grew white — he spilt the untasted wine upon the carpet — and rushed forth into the darkness. For the Earth, too, had on her Black Veil.

The next day, the whole village of Milford talked of little else than Parson Hooper's black veil. That, and the mystery concealed behind it, supplied a topic for discussion between acquaintances meeting in the street, and good women gossiping at their open windows. It was the first item of news that the tavern-keeper told to his guests. The children babbled of it on their way to school. One imitative little imp covered his face with an old black handkerchief, thereby so affrighting his playmates, that the panic seized himself, and he well nigh lost his wits by his own waggery.

It was remarkable, that, of all the busy-bodies and impertinent people in the parish, not one ventured to put the plain question to Mr. Hooper, wherefore he did this thing. Hitherto, whenever there appeared the slightest call for such interference, he had never lacked advisers, nor shown himself averse to be guided by their judgment. If he erred at all, it was by so painful a degree of self-distrust, that even the mildest censure would lead him to consider an indifferent action as a crime. Yet, though so well acquainted with this amiable weakness, no individual among his parishioners chose to make the black veil a subject of friendly remonstrance. There was a feeling of dread, neither plainly confessed nor carefully concealed, which caused each to shift the responsibility upon another, till at length it was found expedient to send a deputation of the church, in order to deal with Mr. Hooper about the mystery, before it should grow into a scandal. Never did an embassy so ill discharge its duties. The minister received them with friendly courtesy, but became silent, after they were seated, leaving to his visitors the whole burthen of introducing their important business. The topic, it might be supposed, was obvious enough. There was the black veil, swathed round Mr. Hooper's forehead, and concealing every feature above his placid mouth, on which, at times, they could perceive the glimmering of a melancholy smile. But that piece of crape, to their imagination, seemed to hang down before his heart, the symbol of a fearful secret between him and them. Were the veil but cast aside, they might speak freely of it, but not till then. Thus they sat a considerable time, speechless, confused, and shrinking uneasily from Mr. Hooper's eye, which they felt to be fixed upon them with an invisible glance. Finally, the deputies returned abashed to their constituents, pronouncing the matter too weighty to be handled, except by a council of the churches, if, indeed, it might not require a general synod.

But there was one person in the village, unappalled by the awe with which 25 the black veil had impressed all beside herself. When the deputies returned without an explanation, or even venturing to demand one, she, with the calm energy of her character, determined to chase away the strange cloud that appeared to be settling round Mr. Hooper, every moment more darkly than before. As his plighted wife, it should be her privilege to know what the black veil concealed. At the minister's first visit, therefore, she entered upon the subject, with a direct simplicity, which made the task easier both for him and her. After he had seated himself, she fixed her eyes steadfastly upon the veil, but could discern nothing of the dreadful gloom that had so overawed the multitude: it was but a double fold of crape, hanging down from his forehead to his mouth, and slightly stirring with his breath.

"No," said she aloud, and smiling, "there is nothing terrible in this piece of crape, except that it hides a face which I am always glad to look upon. Come, good sir, let the sun shine from behind the cloud. First lay aside your black veil: then tell me why you put it on."

Mr. Hooper's smile glimmered faintly.

"There is an hour to come," said he, "when all of us shall cast aside our veils. Take it not amiss, beloved friend, if I wear this piece of crape till then."

"Your words are a mystery too," returned the young lady. "Take away the veil for them, at least."

"Elizabeth, I will," said he, "so far as my vow may suffer me. Know, then, 30 this veil is a type and a symbol, and I am bound to wear it ever, both in light and darkness, in solitude and before the gaze of multitudes, and as with strangers, so with my familiar friends. No mortal eye will see it withdrawn. This dismal shade must separate me from the world: even you, Elizabeth, can never come behind it!"

"What grievous affliction hath befallen you," she earnestly inquired, "that you should thus darken your eyes for ever?"

"If it be a sign of mourning," replied Mr. Hooper, "I, perhaps, like most other mortals, have sorrows dark enough to be typified by a black veil."

"But what if the world will not believe that it is the type of an innocent sorrow?" urged Elizabeth. "Beloved and respected as you are, there may be whispers, that you hide your face under the consciousness of secret sin. For the sake of your holy office, do away this scandal!"

The color rose into her cheeks, as she intimated the nature of the rumors that were already abroad in the village. But Mr. Hooper's mildness did not forsake him. He even smiled again — that same sad smile, which always appeared like a faint glimmering of light, proceeding from the obscurity beneath the veil.

"If I hide my face for sorrow, there is cause enough," he merely replied; 35 "and if I cover it for secret sin, what mortal might not do the same?"

And with this gentle, but unconquerable obstinacy, did he resist all her entreaties. At length Elizabeth sat silent. For a few moments she appeared lost in thought, considering, probably, what new methods might be tried, to withdraw her lover from so dark a fantasy, which, if it had no other meaning, was perhaps a symptom of mental disease. Though of a firmer character than his own, the tears rolled down her cheeks. But, in an instant, as it were, a new feeling took the place of sorrow: her eyes were fixed insensibly on the black veil, when, like a sudden twilight in the air, its terrors fell around her. She arose, and stood trembling before him.

"And do you feel it then at last?" said he mournfully.

She made no reply, but covered her eyes with her hand, and turned to leave the room. He rushed forward and caught her arm.

"Have patience with me, Elizabeth!" cried he passionately. "Do not desert me, though this veil must be between us here on earth. Be mine, and hereafter there shall be no veil over my face, no darkness between our souls! It is but a mortal veil — it is not for eternity! Oh! you know not how lonely I am, and how frightened to be alone behind my black veil. Do not leave me in this miserable obscurity for ever!"

"Lift the veil but once, and look me in the face," said she. 40

"Never! It cannot be!" replied Mr. Hooper.

"Then, farewell!" said Elizabeth.

She withdrew her arm from his grasp, and slowly departed, pausing at the door, to give one long, shuddering gaze, that seemed almost to penetrate the mystery of the black veil. But, even amid his grief, Mr. Hooper smiled to think that only a material emblem had separated him from happiness, though the horrors which it shadowed forth, must be drawn darkly between the fondest of lovers.

From that time no attempts were made to remove Mr. Hooper's black veil, or, by a direct appeal, to discover the secret which it was supposed to hide. By persons who claimed a superiority to popular prejudice, it was reckoned merely an eccentric whim, such as often mingles with the sober actions of men otherwise rational, and tinges them all with its own semblance of insanity. But with the multitude, good Mr. Hooper was irreparably a bugbear. He could not walk the streets with any peace of mind, so conscious was he that the gentle and timid would turn aside to avoid him, and that others would make it a point of hardihood to throw themselves in his way. The impertinence of the latter class compelled him to give up his customary walk, at sunset, to the burial ground, for when he leaned pensively over the gate, there would always be faces behind the grave-stones, peeping at his black veil. A fable went the rounds that the stare of the dead people drove him thence. It grieved him, to the very depth of his kind heart, to observe how the children fled from his approach, breaking up their merriest sports, while his melancholy figure was yet afar off. Their instinctive dread caused him to feel, more strongly than aught else, that a preternatural horror was interwoven with the threads of the black crape. In truth, his own antipathy to the veil was known to be so great, that he never willingly passed before a mirror, nor stooped to drink at a still fountain, lest, in its peaceful bosom, he should be affrighted by himself. This was what gave plausibility to the whispers, that Mr. Hooper's conscience tortured him for some great crime, too horrible to be entirely concealed, or otherwise than so obscurely intimated. Thus, from beneath the black veil, there rolled a cloud into the sunshine, an ambiguity of sin or sorrow, which enveloped the poor minister, so that love or sympathy could never reach him. It was said, that ghost and fiend consorted with him there. With self-shudderings and outward terrors, he walked continually in its shadow, groping darkly within his own soul, or gazing through a medium that saddened the whole world. Even the lawless wind, it was believed, respected his dreadful secret, and never blew aside the veil. But still good Mr. Hooper sadly smiled, at the pale visages of the worldly throng as he passed by.

Among all its bad influences, the black veil had the one desirable effect, of 45 making its wearer a very efficient clergyman. By the aid of his mysterious emblem — for there was no other apparent cause — he became a man of awful power, over souls that were in agony for sin. His converts always regarded him with a dread peculiar to themselves, affirming, though but figuratively, that, before he brought them to celestial light, they had been with him behind the black veil. Its gloom, indeed, enabled him to sympathize with all dark affections. Dying sinners cried aloud for Mr. Hooper, and would not yield their breath till he appeared; though ever, as he stooped to whisper consolation, they shuddered at the veiled face so near their own. Such were the terrors of the black veil, even when Death had bared his visage! Strangers came long distances to attend service at his church, with the mere idle purpose of gazing at his figure, because it was forbidden them to behold his face. But many were made to quake ere they departed! Once, during Governor Belcher's administration, Mr. Hooper was appointed to preach the election sermon. Covered with his black veil, he stood before the chief magistrate, the council, and the representatives, and wrought so deep an impression, that the legislative measures of that year, were characterized by all the gloom and piety of our earliest ancestral sway.

In this manner Mr. Hooper spent a long life, irreproachable in outward act, yet shrouded in dismal suspicions; kind and loving, though unloved, and dimly feared; a man apart from men, shunned in their health and joy, but ever summoned to their aid in mortal anguish. As years wore on, shedding their snows above his sable veil, he acquired a name throughout the New-England churches, and they called him Father Hooper. Nearly all his parishioners, who were of mature age when he was settled, had been borne away by many a funeral: he had one congregation in the church, and a more crowded one in the church-yard; and having wrought so late into the evening, and done his work so well, it was now good Father Hooper's turn to rest.

Several persons were visible by the shaded candlelight, in the death-chamber of the old clergyman. Natural connections he had none. But there was the decorously grave, though unmoved physician, seeking only to mitigate the last pangs of the patient whom he could not save. There were the deacons, and other eminently pious members of his church. There, also, was the Reverend Mr. Clark, of Westbury, a young and zealous divine, who had ridden in haste to pray by the bedside of the expiring minister. There was the nurse, no hired handmaiden of death, but one whose calm affection had endured thus long, in secrecy, in solitude, amid the chill of age, and would not perish, even at the dying hour. Who, but Elizabeth! And there lay the hoary head of good Father Hooper upon the death-pillow, with the black veil still swathed about his brow and reaching down over his face, so that each more difficult gasp of his faint breath caused it to stir. All through life that piece of crape had hung between him and the world: it had separated him from cheerful brotherhood and woman's love, and kept him in that saddest of all prisons, his own heart; and still it lay upon his face, as if to deepen the gloom of his darksome chamber, and shade him from the sunshine of eternity.

For some time previous, his mind had been confused, wavering doubtfully between the past and the present, and hovering forward, as it were, at intervals, into the indistinctness of the world to come. There had been feverish turns, which tossed him from side to side, and wore away what little strength he had. But in his most convulsive struggles, and in the wildest vagaries of his intellect, when no other thought retained its sober influence, he still showed an awful solicitude lest the black veil should slip aside. Even if his bewildered soul could have forgotten, there was a faithful woman at his pillow, who, with averted eyes, would have covered that aged face, which she had last beheld in the comeliness of manhood. At length the death-stricken old man lay quietly in the torpor of mental and bodily exhaustion, with an imperceptible pulse, and breath that grew fainter and fainter, except when a long, deep, and irregular inspiration seemed to prelude the flight of his spirit.

The minister of Westbury approached the bedside.

"Venerable Father Hooper," said he, "the moment of your release is at hand. 50 Are you ready for the lifting of the veil, that shuts in time from eternity?"

Father Hooper at first replied merely by a feeble motion of his head; then, apprehensive, perhaps, that his meaning might be doubtful, he exerted himself to speak.

"Yea," said he, in faint accents, "my soul hath a patient weariness until that veil be lifted."

"And is it fitting," resumed the Reverend Mr. Clark, "that a man so given to prayer, of such a blameless example, holy in deed and thought, so far as mortal judgment may pronounce; is it fitting that a father in the church should leave a shadow on his memory, that may seem to blacken a life so pure? I pray you, my venerable brother, let not this thing be! Suffer us to be gladdened by your triumphant aspect, as you go to your reward. Before the veil of eternity be lifted, let me cast aside this black veil from your face!"

And thus speaking, the Reverend Mr. Clark bent forward to reveal the mystery of so many years. But, exerting a sudden energy, that made all the beholders stand aghast, Father Hooper snatched both his hands from beneath the bed-clothes, and pressed them strongly on the black veil, resolute to struggle, if the minister of Westbury would contend with a dying man.

"Never!" cried the veiled clergyman. "On earth, never!" 55

"Dark old man!" exclaimed the affrighted minister, "with what horrible crime upon your soul are you now passing to the judgment?"

Father Hooper's breath heaved; it rattled in his throat; but, with a mighty effort, grasping forward with his hands, he caught hold of life, and held it back till he should speak. He even raised himself in bed; and there he sat, shivering with the arms of death around him, while the black veil hung down, awful, at that last moment, in the gathered terrors of a life-time. And yet the faint, sad smile, so often there, now seemed to glimmer from its obscurity, and linger on Father Hooper's lips.

"Why do you tremble at me alone?" cried he, turning his veiled face round the circle of pale spectators. "Tremble also at each other! Have men avoided me, and women shown no pity, and children screamed and fled, only for my black veil? What, but the mystery which it obscurely typifies, has made this piece of crape so awful? When the friend shows his inmost heart to his friend; the lover to his best-beloved; when man does not vainly shrink from the eye of his Creator, loathsomely treasuring up the secret of his sin; then deem me a monster, for the symbol beneath which I have lived, and die! I look around me, and, lo! on every visage a Black Veil!"

While his auditors shrank from one another, in mutual affright, Father Hooper fell back upon his pillow, a veiled corpse, with a faint smile lingering on the lips. Still veiled, they laid him in his coffin, and a veiled corpse they bore him to the grave. The grass of many years has sprung up and withered on that grave, the burial-stone is moss-grown, and good Mr. Hooper's face is dust; but awful is still the thought, that it moldered beneath the Black Veil!

Considerations for Critical Thinking and Writing

1. Describe the veil Hooper wears. How does it affect his vision?
2. Characterize the townspeople. How does the community react to the veil?
3. What is Hooper's explanation for why he wears the veil? Is he more or less effective as a minister because he wears it?
4. What is the one feature of Hooper's face that we see? What does that feature reveal about him?
5. Describe what happens at the funeral and wedding ceremonies at which Hooper officiates. How are the incidents at these events organized around the veil?
6. Why does Elizabeth think "it should be her privilege to know what the black veil concealed"? Why doesn't Hooper remove it at her request?
7. How does Elizabeth react to Hooper's refusal to take off the veil? Why is her response especially significant?
8. How do others in town explain why Hooper wears the veil? Do these explanations seem adequate to you? Why or why not?
9. Why is Hooper buried with the veil? Of what significance is it that grass "withered" on his grave?
10. Describe the story's point of view. How would a first-person narrative change the story dramatically?
11. Why do you think Hooper wears the veil? Explain whether you think Hooper was right or wrong to wear it.

Connections to Other Selections

1. How might this story be regarded as a sequel to "Young Goodman Brown"? How are the themes similar?
2. Explain how Faith in "Young Goodman Brown," Georgiana in "The Birthmark," (below), and Elizabeth in "The Minister's Black Veil" are used to reveal the central male characters in each story. Describe the similarities that you see among these women characters.
3. Compare Hawthorne's use of symbol in "The Minister's Black Veil" and "The Birthmark." Write an essay explaining which symbol you think works more effectively to evoke the theme of its story.

The Birthmark   1843

In the latter part of the last century there lived a man of science, an eminent proficient in every branch of natural philosophy, who not long before our story opens had made experience of a spiritual affinity more attractive than any chemical one. He had left his laboratory to the care of an assistant, cleared his fine countenance from the furnace smoke, washed the stain of acids from his fingers, and persuaded a beautiful woman to become his wife. In those days when the comparatively recent discovery of electricity and other kindred mysteries of Nature seemed to open paths into the region of miracle, it was not unusual for the love of science to rival the love of woman in its depth and absorbing energy. The higher intellect, the imagination, the spirit, and even the heart might all find their congenial ailment in pursuits which, as some of their ardent votaries believed, would ascend from one step of powerful intelligence to another, until the philosopher should lay his hand on the secret of creative force and perhaps make new worlds for himself. We know not whether Aylmer possessed this degree of faith in man's ultimate control over Nature. He had devoted himself, however, too unreservedly to scientific studies ever to be weaned from them by any second passion. His love for his young wife might prove the stronger of the two; but it could only be by intertwining itself with his love of science, and uniting the strength of the latter to his own.

Such a union accordingly took place, and was attended with truly remarkable consequences and a deeply impressive moral. One day, very soon after their marriage, Aylmer sat gazing at his wife with a trouble in his countenance that grew stronger until he spoke.

"Georgiana," said he, "has it never occurred to you that the mark upon your cheek might be removed?"

"No, indeed," said she, smiling; but perceiving the seriousness of his manner, she blushed deeply. "To tell you the truth it has been so often called a charm that I was simple enough to imagine it might be so."

"Ah, upon another face perhaps it might," replied her husband; "but never 5 on yours. No, dearest Georgiana, you came so nearly perfect from the hand of Nature that this slightest possible defect, which we hesitate whether to term a defect or a beauty, shocks me, as being the visible mark of earthly imperfection."

"Shocks you, my husband!" cried Georgiana, deeply hurt; at first reddening with momentary anger, but then bursting into tears. "Then why did you take me from my mother's side? You cannot love what shocks you!"

To explain this conversation it must be mentioned that in the center of Georgiana's left cheek there was a singular mark, deeply interwoven, as it were, with the texture and substance of her face. In the usual state of her complexion — a healthy though delicate bloom — the mark wore a tint of deeper crimson, which imperfectly defined its shape amid the surrounding rosiness. When she blushed it gradually became more indistinct, and finally vanished amid the triumphant rush of blood that bathed the whole cheek with its brilliant glow. But if any shifting motion caused her to turn pale, there was the mark again, a crimson stain upon the snow, in what Aylmer sometimes deemed an almost fearful distinctness. Its shape bore not a little similarity to the human hand, though of the smallest pygmy size. Georgiana's lovers were wont to say that some fairy at her birth hour had laid her tiny hand upon the infant's cheek, and left this impress there in token of the magic endowments that were to give her such sway over all hearts. Many a desperate swain would have risked life for the privilege of pressing his lips to the mysterious hand. It must not be concealed, however, that the impression wrought by this fairy sign manual varied exceedingly, according to the difference of temperament in the beholders. Some fastidious persons — but they were exclusively of her own sex — affirmed that the bloody hand, as they chose to call it, quite destroyed the effect of Georgiana's beauty, and rendered her countenance even hideous. But it would be as reasonable to say that one of those small blue stains which sometimes occur in the purest statuary marble would convert the Eve of Powers to a monster. Masculine observers, if the birthmark did not heighten their admiration, contented themselves with wishing it away, that the world might possess one living specimen of ideal loveliness without the semblance of a flaw. After his marriage, — for he thought little or nothing of the matter before, — Aylmer discovered that this was the case with himself.

Had she been less beautiful, — if Envy's self could have found aught else to sneer at, — he might have felt his affection heightened by the prettiness of this mimic hand, now vaguely portrayed, now lost, now stealing forth again and glimmering to and fro with every pulse of emotion that throbbed within her heart; but seeing her otherwise so perfect, he found this one defect grow more and more intolerable with every moment of their united lives. It was the fatal flaw of humanity which Nature, in one shape or another, stamps ineffaceably on all her productions, either to imply that they are temporary and finite, or that their perfection must be wrought by toil and pain. The crimson hand expressed the ineludible gripe in which mortality clutches the highest and purest of earthly mold, degrading them into kindred with the lowest, and even with the very brutes, like whom their visible frames return to dust. In this manner, selecting it as the symbol of his wife's liability to sin, sorrow, decay, and death, Aylmer's somber imagination was not long in rendering the birthmark a frightful object, causing him more trouble and horror than ever Georgiana's beauty, whether of soul or sense, had given him delight.

At all the seasons which should have been their happiest, he invariably and without intending it, nay, in spite of a purpose to the contrary, reverted to this one disastrous topic. Trifling as it at first appeared, it so connected itself with innumerable trains of thought and modes of feeling that it became the central point of all. With the morning twilight Aylmer opened his eyes upon his wife's face and recognized the symbol of imperfection; and when they sat together at the evening hearth his eyes wandered stealthily to her cheek, and beheld, flickering with the blaze of the wood fire, the spectral hand that wrote mortality where he would fain have worshiped. Georgiana soon learned to shudder at his gaze. It needed but a glance with the peculiar expression that his face often wore to change the roses of her cheek into a deathlike paleness, amid which the crimson hand was brought strongly out, like a bas-relief of ruby on the whitest marble.

Late one night when the lights were growing dim, so as hardly to betray 10 the stain on the poor wife's cheek, she herself, for the first time, voluntarily took up the subject.

"Do you remember, my dear Aylmer," said she, with a feeble attempt at a smile, "have you any recollection of a dream last night about this odious hand?"

"None! none whatever!" replied Aylmer, starting; but then he added, in a dry, cold tone, affected for the sake of concealing the real depth of his emotion, "I might well dream of it; for before I fell asleep it had taken a pretty firm hold of my fancy."

"And you did dream of it?" continued Georgiana hastily, for she dreaded lest a gush of tears should interrupt what she had to say. "A terrible dream! I wonder that you can forget it. Is it possible to forget this one expression? — 'It is in her heart now; we must have it out!' Reflect, my husband; for by all means I would have you recall that dream."

The mind is in a sad state when Sleep, the all-involving, cannot confine her specters within the dim region of her sway, but suffers them to break forth, affrighting this actual life with secrets that perchance belong to a deeper one.

Aylmer now remembered his dream. He had fancied himself with his servant Aminadab, attempting an operation for the removal of the birthmark; but the deeper went the knife, the deeper sank the hand, until at length its tiny grasp appeared to have caught hold of Georgiana's heart; whence, however, her husband was inexorably resolved to cut or wrench it away.

When the dream had shaped itself perfectly in his memory, Aylmer sat in 15 his wife's presence with a guilty feeling. Truth often finds its way to the mind close muffled in robes of sleep, and then speaks with uncompromising directness of matters in regard to which we practice an unconscious self-deception during our waking moments. Until now he had not been aware of the tyrannizing influence acquired by one idea over his mind, and of the lengths which he might find in his heart to go for the sake of giving himself peace.

"Aylmer," resumed Georgiana solemnly, "I know not what may be the cost to both of us to rid me of this fatal birthmark. Perhaps its removal may cause cureless deformity; or it may be the stain goes as deep as life itself. Again: do we know that there is a possibility, on any terms, of unclasping the firm grip of this little hand which was laid upon me before I came into the world?"

"Dearest Georgiana, I have spent much thought upon the subject," hastily interrupted Aylmer. "I am convinced of the perfect practicability of its removal."

"If there be the remotest possibility of it," continued Georgiana, "let the attempt be made at whatever risk. Danger is nothing to me; for life, while this hateful mark makes me the object of your horror and disgust, — life is a burden which I would fling down with joy. Either remove this dreadful hand, or take my wretched life! You have deep science. All the world bears witness of it. You have achieved great wonders. Cannot you remove this little, little mark, which I cover with the tips of two small fingers? Is this beyond your power, for the sake of your own peace, and to save your poor wife from madness?"

"Noblest, dearest, tenderest wife," cried Aylmer rapturously, "doubt not my power. I have already given this matter the deepest thought — thought which might almost have enlightened me to create a being less perfect than yourself. Georgiana, you have led me deeper than ever into the heart of science. I feel myself fully competent to render this dear cheek as faultless as its fellow; and then, most beloved, what will be my triumph when I shall have corrected what Nature left imperfect in her fairest work! Even Pygmalion, when his sculptured woman assumed life, felt not greater ecstasy than mine will be."

"It is resolved, then," said Georgiana, faintly smiling. "And, Aylmer, spare 20 me not, though you should find the birthmark take refuge in my heart at last."

Her husband tenderly kissed her cheek — her right cheek — not that which bore the impress of the crimson hand.

The next day Aylmer apprised his wife of a plan that he had formed whereby he might have opportunity for the intense thought and constant watchfulness which the proposed operation would require; while Georgiana, likewise, would enjoy the perfect repose essential to its success. They were to seclude themselves in the extensive apartments occupied by Aylmer as a laboratory, and where, during his toilsome youth, he had made discoveries in the elemental powers of Nature that had roused the admiration of all the learned societies in Europe. Seated calmly in this laboratory, the pale philosopher had investigated the secrets of the highest cloud region and of the profoundest mines; he had satisfied himself of the causes that kindled and kept alive the fires of the volcano; and had explained the mystery of fountains, and how it is that they gush forth, some so bright and pure, and others with such rich medicinal virtues, from the dark bosom of the earth. Here, too, at an earlier period, he had studied the wonders of the human frame, and attempted to fathom the very process by which Nature assimilates all her precious influences from earth and air, and from the spiritual world, to create and foster man, her masterpiece. The latter pursuit, however, Aylmer had long laid aside in unwilling recognition of the truth — against which all seekers sooner or later stumble — that our great creative Mother, while she amuses us with apparently working in the broadest sunshine, is yet severely careful to keep her own secrets, and, in spite of her pretended openness, shows us nothing but results. She permits us, indeed, to mar, but seldom to mend, and, like a jealous patentee, on no account to make. Now, however, Aylmer resumed these half-forgotten investigations, — not, of course, with such hopes or wishes as first suggested them, but because they involved much physiological truth and lay in the path of his proposed scheme for the treatment of Georgiana.

As he led her over the threshold of the laboratory, Georgiana was cold and tremulous. Aylmer looked cheerfully into her face, with intent to reassure her, but was so startled with the intense glow of the birthmark upon the whiteness of her cheek that he could not restrain a strong convulsive shudder. His wife fainted.

"Aminadab! Aminadab!" shouted Aylmer, stamping violently on the floor.

Forthwith there issued from an inner apartment a man of low stature, but 25 bulky frame, with shaggy hair hanging about his visage, which was grimed with the vapors of the furnace. This personage had been Aylmer's underworker during his whole scientific career, and was admirably fitted for that office by his great mechanical readiness, and the skill with which, while incapable of comprehending a single principle, he executed all the details of his master's experiments. With his vast strength, his shaggy hair, his smoky aspect, and the indescribable earthiness that encrusted him, he seemed to represent man's physical nature; while Aylmer's slender figure, and pale, intellectual face, were no less apt a type of the spiritual element.

"Throw open the door of the boudoir, Aminadab," said Aylmer, "and burn a pastille."

"Yes, master," answered Aminadab, looking intently at the lifeless form of Georgiana; and then he muttered to himself, "If she were my wife, I'd never part with that birthmark."

When Georgiana recovered consciousness she found herself breathing an atmosphere of penetrating fragrance, the gentle potency of which had recalled her from her deathlike faintness. The scene around her looked like enchantment. Aylmer had converted those smoky, dingy, somber rooms, where he had spent his brightest years in recondite pursuits, into a series of beautiful apartments not unfit to be the secluded abode of a lovely woman. The walls were hung with gorgeous curtains, which imparted the combination of grandeur and grace that no other species of adornment can achieve; and as they fell from the ceiling to the floor, their rich and ponderous folds, concealing all angles and straight lines, appeared to shut in the scene from infinite space. For aught Georgiana knew, it might be a pavilion among the clouds. And Aylmer, excluding the sunshine, which would have interfered with his chemical processes, had supplied its place with perfumed lamps, emitting flames of various hue, but all uniting in a soft, empurpled radiance. He now knelt by his wife's side, watching her earnestly, but without alarm; for he was confident in his science, and felt that he could draw a magic circle round her within which no evil might intrude.

"Where am I? Ah, I remember," said Georgiana faintly; and she placed her hand over her cheek to hide the terrible mark from her husband's eyes.

"Fear not, dearest!" exclaimed he. "Do not shrink from me! Believe me, 30 Georgiana, I even rejoice in this single imperfection, since it will be such a rapture to remove it."

"Oh, spare me!" sadly replied his wife. "Pray do not look at it again. I never can forget that convulsive shudder."

In order to soothe Georgiana, and, as it were, to release her mind from the burden of actual things, Aylmer now put in practice some of the light and playful secrets which science had taught him among its profounder lore. Airy figures, absolutely bodiless ideas, and forms of unsubstantial beauty came and danced before her, imprinting their momentary footsteps on beams of light. Though she had some indistinct idea of the method of these optical phenomena, still the illusion was almost perfect enough to warrant the belief that her husband possessed sway over the spiritual world. Then again, when she felt a wish to look forth from her seclusion, immediately, as if her thoughts were answered, the procession of external existence flitted across a screen. The scenery and the figures of actual life were perfectly represented, but with that bewitching, yet indescribable difference which always makes a picture, an image, or a shadow so much more attractive than the original. When wearied of this, Aylmer bade her cast her eyes upon a vessel containing a quantity of earth. She did so, with little interest at first; but was soon startled to perceive the germ of a plant shooting upward from the soil. Then came the slender stalk; the leaves gradually unfolded themselves; and amid them was a perfect and lovely flower.

"It is magical!" cried Georgiana. "I dare not touch it."

"Nay, pluck it," answered Aylmer: "pluck it, and inhale its brief perfume while you may. The flower will wither in a few moments and leave nothing save its brown seed vessels; but thence may be perpetuated a race as ephemeral as itself."

But Georgiana had no sooner touched the flower than the whole plant 35 suffered a blight, its leaves turning coal-black as if by the agency of fire.

"There was too powerful a stimulus," said Aylmer thoughtfully.

To make up for this abortive experiment, he proposed to take her portrait by a scientific process of his own invention. It was to be effected by rays of light striking upon a polished plate of metal. Georgiana assented; but, on looking at the result, was affrighted to find the features of the portrait blurred and indefinable; while the minute figure of a hand appeared where the cheek should have been. Aylmer snatched the metallic plate and threw it into a jar of corrosive acid.

Soon, however, he forgot these mortifying failures. In the intervals of study and chemical experiment he came to her flushed and exhausted, but seemed invigorated by her presence, and spoke in glowing language of the resources of his art. He gave a history of the long dynasty of the alchemists, who spent so many ages in quest of the universal solvent by which the golden principle might be elicited from all things vile and base. Aylmer appeared to believe that, by the

plainest scientific logic, it was altogether within the limits of possibility to discover this long-sought medium; "but," he added, "a philosopher who should go
deep enough to acquire the power would attain too lofty a wisdom to stoop to
the exercise of it." Not less singular were his opinions in regard to the elixir
vitae. He more than intimated that it was at his option to concoct a liquid that
should prolong life for years, perhaps interminably; but that it would produce a
discord in Nature which all the world, and chiefly the quaffer of the immortal
nostrum, would find cause to curse.

"Aylmer, are you in earnest?" asked Georgiana, looking at him with amazement and fear. "It is terrible to possess such power, or even to dream of
possessing it."

"Oh, do not tremble, my love," said her husband. "I would not wrong either   40
you or myself by working such inharmonious effects upon our lives; but I would
have you consider how trifling, in comparison, is the skill requisite to remove
this little hand."

At the mention of the birthmark, Georgiana, as usual, shrank as if a red-hot
iron had touched her cheek.

Again Aylmer applied himself to his labors. She could hear his voice in the
distant furnace-room giving directions to Aminadab, whose harsh, uncouth, misshapen tones were audible in response, more like the grunt or growl of a brute
than human speech. After hours of absence, Aylmer reappeared and proposed
that she should now examine his cabinet of chemical products and natural
treasures of the earth. Among the former he showed her a small vial, in which,
he remarked, was contained a gentle yet most powerful fragrance, capable of
impregnating all the breezes that blow across a kingdom. They were of inestimable value, the contents of that little vial; and, as he said so, he threw some of
the perfume into the air and filled the room with piercing and invigorating
delight.

"And what is this?" asked Georgiana, pointing to a small crystal globe
containing a gold-colored liquid. "It is so beautiful to the eye that I could imagine
it the elixir of life."

"In one sense it is," replied Aylmer; "or rather, the elixir of immortality. It
is the most precious poison that ever was concocted in this world. By its aid I
could apportion the lifetime of any mortal at whom you might point your finger.
The strength of the dose would determine whether he were to linger out years,
or drop dead in the midst of a breath. No king on his guarded throne could
keep his life if I, in my private station, should deem that the welfare of millions
justified me in depriving him of it."

"Why do you keep such a terrific drug?" inquired Georgiana in horror.   45

"Do not mistrust me, dearest," said her husband, smiling; "its virtuous
potency is yet greater than its harmful one. But see! here is a powerful cosmetic.
With a few drops of this in a vase of water, freckles may be washed away as
easily as the hands are cleansed. A stronger infusion would take the blood out
of the cheek, and leave the rosiest beauty a pale ghost."

"Is it with this lotion that you intend to bathe my cheek?" asked Georgiana,
anxiously.

"Oh, no," hastily replied her husband; "this is merely superficial. Your case
demands a remedy that shall go deeper."

In his interviews with Georgiana, Aylmer generally made minute inquiries as to her sensations and whether the confinement of the rooms and the temperature of the atmosphere agreed with her. These questions had such a particular drift that Georgiana began to conjecture that she was already subjected to certain physical influences, either breathed in with the fragrant air or taken with her food. She fancied likewise, but it might be altogether fancy, that there was a stirring up of her system — a strange, indefinite sensation creeping through her veins, and tingling, half painfully, half pleasurably, at her heart. Still, whenever she dared to look into the mirror, there she beheld herself pale as a white rose and with the crimson birthmark stamped upon her cheek. Not even Aylmer now hated it so much as she.

To dispel the tedium of the hours which her husband found it necessary to devote to the processes of combination and analysis, Georgiana turned over the volumes of his scientific library. In many dark old tomes she met with chapters full of romance and poetry. They were the works of the philosophers of the middle ages, such as Albertus Magnus, Cornelius Agrippa, Paracelsus, and the famous friar who created the prophetic Brazen Head. All these antique naturalists stood in advance of their centuries, yet were imbued with some of their credulity, and therefore were believed, and perhaps imagined themselves to have acquired from the investigation of Nature a power above Nature, and from physics a sway over the spiritual world. Hardly less curious and imaginative were the early volumes of the Transactions of the Royal Society, in which the members, knowing little of the limits of natural possibility, were continually recording wonders or proposing methods whereby wonders might be wrought.

But to Georgiana the most engrossing volume was a large folio from her husband's own hand, in which he had recorded every experiment of his scientific career, its original aim, the methods adopted for its development, and its final success or failure, with the circumstances to which either event was attributable. The book, in truth, was both the history and emblem of his ardent, ambitious, imaginative, yet practical and laborious life. He handled physical details as if there were nothing beyond them; yet spiritualized them all, and redeemed himself from materialism by his strong and eager aspiration towards the infinite. In his grasp the veriest clod of earth assumed a soul. Georgiana, as she read, reverenced Aylmer and loved him more profoundly than ever, but with a less entire dependence on his judgment than heretofore. Much as he had accomplished, she could not but observe that his most splendid successes were almost invariably failures, if compared with the ideal at which he aimed. His brightest diamonds were the merest pebbles, and felt to be so by himself, in comparison with the inestimable gems which lay hidden beyond his reach. The volume, rich with achievements that had won renown for its author, was yet as melancholy a record as ever mortal hand had penned. It was the sad confession and continual exemplification of the shortcomings of the composite man, the spirit burdened with clay and working in matter, and of the despair that assails the higher nature at finding itself so miserably thwarted by the earthly part. Perhaps every man of genius in whatever sphere might recognize the image of his own experience in Aylmer's journal.

So deeply did these reflections affect Georgiana that she laid her face upon the open volume and burst into tears. In this situation she was found by her husband.

"It is dangerous to read in a sorcerer's books," said he with a smile, though his countenance was uneasy and displeased. "Georgiana, there are pages in that volume which I can scarcely glance over and keep my senses. Take heed lest it prove as detrimental to you."

"It has made me worship you more than ever," said she.

"Ah, wait for this one success," rejoined he, "then worship me if you will. 55 I shall deem myself hardly unworthy of it. But come, I have sought you for the luxury of your voice. Sing to me, dearest."

So she poured out the liquid music of her voice to quench the thirst of his spirit. He then took his leave with a boyish exuberance of gaiety, assuring her that her seclusion would endure but a little longer, and that the result was already certain. Scarcely had he departed when Georgiana felt irresistibly impelled to follow him. She had forgotten to inform Aylmer of a symptom which for two or three hours past had begun to excite her attention. It was a sensation in the fatal birthmark, not painful, but which induced a restlessness throughout her system. Hastening after her husband, she intruded for the first time into the laboratory.

The first thing that struck her eye was the furnace, that hot and feverish worker, with the intense glow of its fire, which by the quantities of soot clustered above it seemed to have been burning for ages. There was a distilling apparatus in full operation. Around the room were retorts, tubes, cylinders, crucibles, and other apparatus of chemical research. An electrical machine stood ready for immediate use. The atmosphere felt oppressively close, and was tainted with gaseous odors which had been tormented forth by the processes of science. The severe and homely simplicity of the apartment, with its naked walls and brick pavement, looked strange, accustomed as Georgiana had become to the fantastic elegance of her boudoir. But what chiefly, indeed almost solely, drew her attention, was the aspect of Aylmer himself.

He was pale as death, anxious and absorbed, and hung over the furnace as if it depended upon his utmost watchfulness whether the liquid which it was distilling should be the draught of immortal happiness or misery. How different from the sanguine and joyous mien that he had assumed for Georgiana's encouragement!

"Carefully now, Aminadab; carefully, thou human machine; carefully, thou man of clay!" muttered Aylmer, more to himself than his assistant. "Now, if there be a thought too much or too little, it is all over."

"Ho! ho!" mumbled Aminadab. "Look, master! look!" 60

Aylmer raised his eyes hastily, and at first reddened, then grew paler than ever, on beholding Georgiana. He rushed towards her and seized her arm with a gripe that left the print of his fingers upon it.

"Why do you come hither? Have you no trust in your husband?" cried he impetuously. "Would you throw the blight of that fatal birthmark over my labors? It is not well done. Go, prying woman, go!"

"Nay, Aylmer," said Georgiana with the firmness of which she possessed no stinted endowment, "it is not you that have a right to complain. You mistrust your wife; you have concealed the anxiety with which you watch the development of this experiment. Think not so unworthily of me, my husband. Tell me all the risk we run, and fear not that I shall shrink; for my share in it is far less than your own."

"No, no, Georgiana!" said Aylmer impatiently; "it must not be."

"I submit," replied she calmly. "And, Aylmer, I shall quaff whatever draught 65 you bring me; but it will be on the same principle that would induce me to take a dose of poison if offered by your hand."

"My noble wife," said Aylmer, deeply moved, "I knew not the height and depth of your nature until now. Nothing shall be concealed. Know, then, that this crimson hand, superficial as it seems, has clutched its grasp into your being with a strength of which I had no previous conception. I have already administered agents powerful enough to do aught except to change your entire physical system. Only one thing remains to be tried. If that fail us we are ruined."

"Why did you hesitate to tell me this?" asked she.

"Because, Georgiana," said Aylmer in a low voice, "there is danger."

"Danger? There is but one danger — that this horrible stigma shall be left upon my cheek!" cried Georgiana. "Remove it, remove it, whatever be the cost, or we shall both go mad!"

"Heaven knows your words are too true," said Aylmer sadly. "And now, 70 dearest, return to your boudoir. In a little while all will be tested."

He conducted her back and took leave of her with a solemn tenderness which spoke far more than his words how much was now at stake. After his departure Georgiana became rapt in musings. She considered the character of Aylmer, and did it completer justice than at any previous moment. Her heart exulted, while it trembled, at his honorable love — so pure and lofty that it would accept nothing less than perfection nor miserably make itself contented with an earthlier nature than he had dreamed of. She felt how much more precious was such a sentiment than that meaner kind which would have borne with the imperfection for her sake, and have been guilty of treason to holy love by degrading its perfect idea to the level of the actual; and with her whole spirit she prayed that, for a single moment, she might satisfy his highest and deepest conception. Longer than one moment she well knew it could not be; for his spirit was ever on the march, ever ascending, and each instant required something that was beyond the scope of the instant before.

The sound of her husband's footsteps aroused her. He bore a crystal goblet containing a liquor colorless as water, but bright enough to be the draught of immortality. Aylmer was pale; but it seemed rather the consequence of a highly wrought state of mind and tension of spirit than of fear or doubt.

"The concoction of the draught has been perfect," said he, in answer to Georgiana's look. "Unless all my science have deceived me, it cannot fail."

"Save on your account, my dearest Aylmer," observed his wife, "I might wish to put off this birthmark of mortality by relinquishing mortality itself in preference to any other mode. Life is but a sad possession to those who have attained precisely the degree of moral advancement at which I stand. Were I weaker and blinder it might be happiness. Were I stronger, it might be endured hopefully. But, being what I find myself, methinks I am of all mortals the most fit to die."

"You are fit for heaven without tasting death!" replied her husband. "But 75 why do we speak of dying? The draught cannot fail. Behold its effect upon this plant."

On the window seat there stood a geranium diseased with yellow blotches, which had overspread all its leaves. Aylmer poured a small quantity of the liquid upon the soil in which it grew. In a little time, when the roots of the plant had taken up the moisture, the unsightly blotches began to be extinguished in a living verdure.

"There needed no proof," said Georgiana quietly. "Give me the goblet. I joyfully stake all upon your word."

"Drink, then, thou lofty creature!" exclaimed Aylmer, with fervid admiration. "There is no taint of imperfection on thy spirit. Thy sensible frame, too, shall soon be all perfect."

She quaffed the liquid and returned the goblet to his hand.

"It is grateful," said she, with a placid smile. "Methinks it is like water from a heavenly fountain; for it contains I know not what of unobtrusive fragrance and deliciousness. It allays a feverish thirst that had parched me for many days. Now, dearest, let me sleep. My earthly senses are closing over my spirit like the leaves around the heart of a rose at sunset." 80

She spoke the last words with a gentle reluctance, as if it required almost more energy than she could command to pronounce the faint and lingering syllables. Scarcely had they loitered through her lips ere she was lost in slumber. Aylmer sat by her side, watching her aspect with the emotions proper to a man the whole value of whose existence was involved in the process now to be tested. Mingled with this mood, however, was the philosophic investigation characteristic of the man of science. Not the minutest symptom escaped him. A heightened flush of the cheek, a slight irregularity of breath, a quiver of the eyelid, a hardly perceptible tremor through the frame, — such were the details which, as the moments passed, he wrote down in his folio volume. Intense thought had set its stamp upon every previous page of that volume, but the thoughts of years were all concentrated upon the last.

While thus employed, he failed not to gaze often at the fatal hand, and not without a shudder. Yet once, by a strange and unaccountable impulse, he pressed it with his lips. His spirit recoiled, however, in the very act; and Georgiana, out of the midst of her deep sleep, moved uneasily and murmured as if in remonstrance. Again Aylmer resumed his watch. Nor was it without avail. The crimson hand, which at first had been strongly visible upon the marble paleness of Georgiana's cheek, now grew more faintly outlined. She remained not less pale than ever; but the birthmark, with every breath that came and went, lost somewhat of its former distinctness. Its presence had been awful; its departure was more awful still. Watch the stain of the rainbow fading out of the sky, and you will know how that mysterious symbol passed away.

"By Heaven! it is well-nigh gone!" said Aylmer to himself, in almost irrepressible ecstasy. "I can scarcely trace it now. Success! success! And now it is like the faintest rose color. The lightest flush of blood across her cheek would overcome it. But she is so pale!"

He drew aside the window curtain and suffered the light of natural day to fall into the room and rest upon her cheek. At the same time he heard a gross, hoarse chuckle, which he had long known as his servant Aminadab's expression of delight.

"Ah, clod! ah, earthly mass!" cried Aylmer, laughing in a sort of frenzy, "you have served me well! Matter and spirit — earth and heaven — have both done their part in this! Laugh, thing of the senses! You have earned the right to laugh." 85

These exclamations broke Georgiana's sleep. She slowly unclosed her eyes and gazed into the mirror which her husband had arranged for that purpose. A faint smile flitted over her lips when she recognized how barely perceptible was now that crimson hand which had once blazed forth with such disastrous brilliancy as to scare away all their happiness. But then her eyes sought Aylmer's face with a trouble and anxiety that he could by no means account for.

"My poor Aylmer!" murmured she.

"Poor? Nay, richest, happiest, most favored!" exclaimed he. "My peerless bride, it is successful! You are perfect!"

"My poor Aylmer," she repeated, with a more than human tenderness, "you have aimed loftily; you have done nobly. Do not repent that with so high and pure a feeling, you have rejected the best the earth could offer. Aylmer, dearest Aylmer, I am dying!"

Alas! it was too true! The fatal hand had grappled with the mystery of life, and was the bond by which an angelic spirit kept itself in union with a mortal frame. As the last crimson tint of the birthmark — that sole token of human imperfection — faded from her cheek, the parting breath of the now perfect woman passed into the atmosphere, and her soul, lingering a moment near her husband, took its heavenward flight. Then a hoarse, chuckling laugh was heard again! Thus ever does the gross fatality of earth exult in its invariable triumph over the immortal essence which, in this dim sphere of half development, demands the completeness of a higher state. Yet, had Aylmer reached a profounder wisdom, he need not thus have flung away the happiness which would have woven his mortal life of the selfsame texture with the celestial. The momentary circumstance was too strong for him; he failed to look beyond the shadowy scope of time, and, living once for all in eternity, to find the perfect future in the present.

Considerations for Critical Thinking and Writing

1. Is Aylmer evil? Is he simply a stock version of a mad scientist? In what sense might he be regarded as an idealist?
2. What does the birthmark symbolize? How does Aylmer's view of it differ from the other perspectives provided in the story? What is the significance of its handlike shape?
3. Does Aylmer love Georgiana? Why does she allow him to risk her life to remove the birthmark?
4. In what sense can Aylmer be characterized as guilty of the sin of pride?
5. How is Aminadab a foil for Aylmer?
6. What is the significance of the descriptions of Aylmer's laboratory?
7. What do Aylmer's other experiments reveal about the nature of his work? How do they constitute foreshadowings of what will happen to Georgiana?
8. What is the theme of the story? What point is made about what it means to be a human being?
9. Despite the risks to Georgiana, Aylmer conducts his experiments in the hope and expectation of achieving a higher good. He devotes his life to science and yet he is an egotist. Explain.
10. Write an essay exploring this story as an early version of our modern obsession with physical perfection.
11. Discuss the extent to which Georgiana is responsible for her own death.

Connections to Other Selections

1. Compare Aylmer's unwillingness to accept things as they are with Young Goodman Brown's refusal to be a part of a community he regards as fallen.
2. Consider the devotion Georgiana expresses toward Aylmer along with Reiko's commitment to her soldier-husband in Yukio Mishima's "Patriotism" (p. 506). How might a feminist critic (see the brief discussion concerning this type of approach in Chapter 35) assess these relationships? Do Georgiana and Reiko have more or less in common as devoted, self-sacrificing wives?
3. What similarities do you see in Aylmer's growing feelings about the "crimson hand" on Georgiana's cheek and the young wife's feelings about her husband's hand in Colette's "The Hand" (p. 184)? How do Aylmer and the young wife cope with these feelings? How do you account for the differences between them?

Rappaccini's Daughter   1844

A young man, named Giovanni Guasconti, came, very long ago, from the more southern region of Italy, to pursue his studies at the University of Padua. Giovanni, who had but a scanty supply of gold ducats in his pocket, took lodgings in a high and gloomy chamber of an old edifice, which looked not unworthy to have been the palace of a Paduan noble, and which, in fact, exhibited over its entrance the armorial bearings of a family long since extinct. The young stranger, who was not unstudied in the great poem of his country, recollected that one of the ancestors of this family, and perhaps an occupant of this very mansion, had been pictured by Dante as a partaker of the immortal agonies of his Inferno. These reminiscences and associations, together with the tendency to heartbreak natural to a young man for the first time out of his native sphere, caused Giovanni to sigh heavily, as he looked around the desolate and ill-furnished apartment.

"Holy Virgin, signor," cried old dame Lisabetta, who, won by the youth's remarkable beauty of person, was kindly endeavoring to give the chamber a habitable air, "what a sigh was that to come out of a young man's heart! Do you find this old mansion gloomy? For the love of heaven, then, put your head out of the window, and you will see as bright sunshine as you have left in Naples."

Guasconti mechanically did as the old woman advised, but could not quite agree with her that the Lombard sunshine was as cheerful as that of southern Italy. Such as it was, however, it fell upon a garden beneath the window, and expended its fostering influences on a variety of plants, which seemed to have been cultivated with exceeding care.

"Does this garden belong to the house?" asked Giovanni.

"Heaven forbid, signor! — unless it were fruitful of better pot-herbs than   5 any that grow there now," answered old Lisabetta. "No: that garden is cultivated by the own hands of Signor Giacomo Rappaccini, the famous Doctor, who, I warrant him, has been heard of as far as Naples. It is said he distils these plants into medicines that are as potent as a charm. Oftentimes you may see the signor Doctor at work, and perchance the signora his daughter, too, gathering the strange flowers that grow in the garden."

The old woman had now done what she could for the aspect of the chamber, and, commending the young man to the protection of the saints, took her departure.

Giovanni still found no better occupation than to look down into the garden beneath his window. From its appearance, he judged it to be one of those botanic gardens, which were of earlier date in Padua than elsewhere in Italy, or in the world. Or, not improbably, it might once have been the pleasure-place of an opulent family; for there was the ruin of a marble fountain in the centre, sculptured with rare art, but so woefully shattered that it was impossible to trace the original design from the chaos of remaining fragments. The water, however, continued to gush and sparkle into the sunbeams as cheerfully as ever. A little gurgling sound ascended to the young man's window, and made him feel as if the fountain were an immortal spirit, that sung its song unceasingly, and without heeding the vicissitudes around it; while one century embodied it in marble, and another scattered the garniture on the soil. All about the pool into which the water subsided, grew various plants, that seemed to require a plentiful supply of moisture for the nourishment of gigantic leaves, and, in some instances, flowers gorgeously magnificent. There was one shrub in particular, set in a marble vase in the midst of the pool, that bore a profusion of purple blossoms, each of which had the lustre and richness of a gem; and the whole together made a show so resplendent that it seemed enough to illuminate the garden, even had there been no sunshine. Every portion of the soil was peopled with plants and herbs, which, if less beautiful, still bore tokens of assiduous care; as if all had their individual virtues, known to the scientific mind that fostered them. Some were placed in urns, rich with old carving, and others in common garden-pots; some crept serpent-like along the ground, or climbed on high, using whatever means of ascent was offered them. One plant had wreathed itself round a statue of Vertumnus,° which was thus quite veiled and shrouded in a drapery of hanging foliage, so happily arranged that it might have served a sculptor for a study.

While Giovanni stood at the window, he heard a rustling behind a screen of leaves, and became aware that a person was at work in the garden. His figure soon emerged into view, and showed itself to be that of no common laborer, but a tall, emaciated, sallow, and sickly-looking man, dressed in a scholar's garb of black. He was beyond the middle term of life, with gray hair, a thin gray beard, and a face singularly marked with intellect and cultivation, but which could never, even in his more youthful days, have expressed much warmth of heart.

Nothing could exceed the intentness with which this scientific gardener examined every shrub which grew in his path; it seemed as if he was looking into their inmost nature, making observations in regard to their creative essence, and discovering why one leaf grew in this shape, and another in that, and wherefore such and such flowers differed among themselves in hue and perfume. Nevertheless, in spite of the deep intelligence on his part, there was no approach to intimacy between himself and these vegetable existences. On the contrary, he avoided their actual touch, or the direct inhaling of their odors, with a caution that impressed Giovanni most disagreeably; for the man's demeanor was that of one walking among malignant influences, such as savage beasts, or deadly snakes,

---

Vertumnus: The Roman god of the seasons and the vegetation produced during the changing seasons.

or evil spirits, which, should he allow them one moment of license, would wreak upon him some terrible fatality. It was strangely frightful to the young man's imagination, to see this air of insecurity in a person cultivating a garden, that most simple and innocent of human toils, and which had been alike the joy and labor of the unfallen parents of the race. Was this garden, then, the Eden of the present world? — and this man, with such a perception of harm in what his own hands caused to grow, was he the Adam?

The distrustful gardener, while plucking away the dead leaves or pruning 10 the too luxuriant growth of the shrubs, defended his hands with a pair of thick gloves. Nor were these his only armor. When, in his walk through the garden, he came to the magnificent plant that hung its purple gems beside the marble fountain, he placed a kind of mask over his mouth and nostrils, as if all this beauty did but conceal a deadlier malice. But finding his task still too dangerous, he drew back, removed the mask, and called loudly, but in the infirm voice of a person affected with inward disease:

"Beatrice! — Beatrice!"

"Here am I, my father! What would you?" cried a rich and youthful voice from the window of the opposite house; a voice as rich as a tropical sunset, and which made Giovanni, though he knew not why, think of deep hues of purple or crimson, and of perfumes heavily delectable. — "Are you in the garden?"

"Yes, Beatrice," answered the gardener, "and I need your help."

Soon there emerged from under a sculptured portal the figure of a young girl, arrayed with as much richness of taste as the most splendid of the flowers, beautiful as the day, and with a bloom so deep and vivid that one shade more would have been too much. She looked redundant with life, health, and energy; all of which attributes were bound down and compressed, as it were, and girdled tensely, in their luxuriance, by her virgin zone.° Yet Giovanni's fancy must have grown morbid, while he looked down into the garden; for the impression which the fair stranger made upon him was as if here were another flower, the human sister of those vegetable ones, as beautiful as they — more beautiful than the richest of them — but still to be touched only with a glove, nor to be approached without a mask. As Beatrice came down the garden path, it was observable that she handled and inhaled the odor of several of the plants, which her father had most sedulously avoided.

"Here, Beatrice," said the latter, — "see how many needful offices require 15 to be done to our chief treasure. Yet, shattered as I am, my life might pay the penalty of approaching it so closely as circumstances demand. Henceforth, I fear, this plant must be consigned to your sole charge."

"And gladly will I undertake it," cried again the rich tones of the young lady, as she bent towards the magnificent plant, and opened her arms as if to embrace it. "Yes, my sister, my splendor, it shall be Beatrice's task to nurse and serve thee; and thou shalt reward her with thy kisses and perfumed breath, which to her is as the breath of life!"

Then, with all the tenderness in her manner that was so strikingly expressed in her words, she busied herself with such attentions as the plant seemed to require; and Giovanni, at his lofty window, rubbed his eyes, and almost doubted whether it were a girl tending her favorite flower, or one sister performing the

virgin zone: A wide belt worn by an unmarried woman.

duties of affection to another. The scene soon terminated. Whether Doctor Rappaccini had finished his labors in the garden, or that his watchful eye had caught the stranger's face, he now took his daughter's arm and retired. Night was already closing in; oppressive exhalations seemed to proceed from the plants, and steal upward past the open window; and Giovanni, closing the lattice, went to his couch, and dreamed of a rich flower and beautiful girl. Flower and maiden were different and yet the same, and fraught with some strange peril in either shape.

But there is an influence in the light of morning that tends to rectify whatever errors of fancy, or even of judgment, we may have incurred during the sun's decline, or among the shadows of the night, or in the less wholesome glow of moonshine. Giovanni's first movement on starting from sleep, was to throw open the window, and gaze down into the garden which his dreams had made so fertile of mysteries. He was surprised, and a little ashamed, to find how real and matter-of-fact an affair it proved to be, in the first rays of the sun, which gilded the dew-drops that hung upon leaf and blossom, and, while giving a brighter beauty to each rare flower, brought everything within the limits of ordinary experience. The young man rejoiced, that, in the heart of the barren city, he had the privilege of overlooking this spot of lovely and luxuriant vegetation. It would serve, he said to himself, as a symbolic language, to keep him in communion with nature. Neither the sickly and thought-worn Doctor Giacomo Rappaccini, it is true, nor his brilliant daughter were now visible; so that Giovanni could not determine how much of the singularity which he attributed to both, was due to their own qualities, and how much to his wonder-working fancy. But he was inclined to take a most rational view of the whole matter.

In the course of the day, he paid his respects to Signor Pietro Baglioni, professor of medicine in the University, a physician of eminent repute, to whom Giovanni had brought a letter of introduction. The professor was an elderly personage, apparently of genial nature, and habits that might almost be called jovial; he kept the young man to dinner, and made himself very agreeable by the freedom and liveliness of his conversation, especially when warmed by a flask or two of Tuscan wine. Giovanni, conceiving that men of science, inhabitants of the same city, must needs be on familiar terms with one another, took an opportunity to mention the name of Dr. Rappaccini. But the professor did not respond with so much cordiality as he had anticipated.

"Ill would it become a teacher of the divine art of medicine," said Professor Pietro Baglioni, in answer to a question of Giovanni, "to withhold due and well-considered praise of a physician so eminently skilled as Rappaccini. But, on the other hand, I should answer it but scantily to my conscience, were I to permit a worthy youth like yourself, Signor Giovanni, the son of an ancient friend, to imbibe erroneous ideas respecting a man who might hereafter chance to hold your life and death in his hands. The truth is, our worshipful Doctor Rappaccini has as much science as any member of the faculty — with perhaps one single exception — in Padua, or all Italy. But there are certain grave objections to his professional character."

"And what are they?" asked the young man.

"Has my friend Giovanni any disease of body or heart, that he is so inquisitive about physicians?" said the Professor, with a smile. "But as for Rappaccini, it is said of him — and I, who know the man well, can answer for its truth — that he cares infinitely more for science than for mankind. His patients are interesting to him only as subjects for some new experiment. He would sacrifice human life, his own among the rest, or whatever else was dearest to him, for the sake of adding so much as a grain of mustard-seed to the great heap of his accumulated knowledge."

"Methinks he is an awful man, indeed," remarked Guasconti, mentally recalling the cold and purely intellectual aspect of Rappaccini. "And yet, worshipful Professor, is it not a noble spirit? Are there many men capable of so spiritual a love of science?"

"God forbid," answered the Professor, somewhat testily — "at least, unless they take sounder views of the healing art than those adopted by Rappaccini. It is his theory, that all medicinal virtues are comprised within those substances which we term vegetable poisons. These he cultivates with his own hands, and is said even to have produced new varieties of poison, more horribly deleterious than Nature, without the assistance of this learned person, would ever have plagued the world with. That the signor Doctor does less mischief than might be expected, with such dangerous substances, is undeniable. Now and then, it must be owned, he has effected — or seemed to effect — a marvellous cure. But, to tell you my private mind, Signor Giovanni, he should receive little credit for such instances of success — they being probably the work of chance — but should be held strictly accountable for his failures, which may justly be considered his own work."

The youth might have taken Baglioni's opinions with many grains of allowance, had he known that there was a professional warfare of long continuance between him and Doctor Rappaccini, in which the latter was generally thought to have gained the advantage. If the reader be inclined to judge for himself, we refer him to certain black-letter tracts on both sides, preserved in the medical department of the University of Padua.

"I know not, most learned Professor," returned Giovanni, after musing on what had been said of Rappaccini's exclusive zeal for science — "I know not how dearly this physician may love his art; but surely there is one object more dear to him. He has a daughter."

"Aha!" cries the Professor with a laugh. "So now our friend Giovanni's secret is out. You have heard of his daughter, whom all the young men in Padua are wild about, though not half a dozen have ever had the good hap to see her face. I know little of the Signora Beatrice, save that Rappaccini is said to have instructed her deeply in his science, and that, young and beautiful as fame reports her, she is already qualified to fill a professor's chair. Perchance her father destines her for mine! Other absurd rumors there be, not worth talking about, or listening to. So now, Signor Giovanni, drink of your glass of Lacryma."°

Guasconti returned to his lodgings somewhat heated with the wine he had quaffed, and which caused his brain to swim with strange fantasies in reference to Doctor Rappaccini and the beautiful Beatrice. On his way, happening to pass by a florist's, he bought a fresh bouquet of flowers.

Ascending to his chamber, he seated himself near the window, but within

25

Lacryma: An Italian wine.

the shadow thrown by the depth of the wall, so that he could look down into the garden with little risk of being discovered. All beneath his eye was a solitude. The strange plants were basking in the sunshine, and now and then nodding gently to one another, as if in acknowledgment of sympathy and kindred. In the midst, by the shattered fountain, grew the magnificent shrub, with its purple gems clustering all over it; they glowed in the air, and gleamed back again out of the depths of the pool, which thus seemed to overflow with colored radiance from the rich reflection that was steeped in it. At first, as we have said, the garden was a solitude. Soon, however, — as Giovanni had half-hoped, half-feared, would be the case, — a figure appeared beneath the antique sculptured portal, and came down between the rows of plants, inhaling their various perfumes, as if she were one of those beings of old classic fable, that lived upon sweet odors. On again beholding Beatrice, the young man was even startled to perceive how much her beauty exceeded his recollection of it; so brilliant, so vivid in its character, that she glowed amid the sunlight, and, as Giovanni whispered to himself, positively illuminated the more shadowy intervals of the garden path. Her face being now more revealed than on the former occasion, he was struck by its expression of simplicity and sweetness; qualities that had not entered into his idea of her character, and which made him ask anew, what manner of mortal she might be. Nor did he fail again to observe, or imagine, an analogy between the beautiful girl and the gorgeous shrub that hung its gem-like flowers over the fountain; a resemblance which Beatrice seemed to have indulged a fantastic humor in heightening, both by the arrangement of her dress and the selection of its hues.

Approaching the shrub, she threw upon her arms, as with a passionate 30 ardor, and drew its branches into an intimate embrace; so intimate, that her features were hidden in its leafy bosom, and her glistening ringlets all intermingled with the flowers.

"Give me thy breath, my sister," exclaimed Beatrice; "for I am faint with common air! And give me this flower of thine, which I separate with gentlest fingers from the stem, and place it close beside my heart."

With these words, the beautiful daughter of Rappaccini plucked one of the richest blossoms of the shrub, and was about to fasten it in her bosom. But now, unless Giovanni's draughts of wine had bewildered his senses, a singular incident occurred. A small orange-colored reptile of the lizard or chameleon species, chanced to be creeping along the path, just at the feet of Beatrice. It appeared to Giovanni — but, at the distance from which he gazed, he could scarcely have seen anything so minute — it appeared to him, however, that a drop or two of moisture from the broken stem of the flower descended upon the lizard's head. For an instant, the reptile contorted itself violently, and then lay motionless in the sunshine. Beatrice observed this remarkable phenomenon, and crossed herself, sadly, but without surprise; nor did she therefore hesitate to arrange the fatal flower in her bosom. There it blushed, and almost glimmered with the dazzling effect of a precious stone, adding to her dress and aspect the one appropriate charm, which nothing else in the world could have supplied. But Giovanni, out of the shadow of his window bent forward and shrank back, and murmured and trembled.

"Am I awake? Have I my senses?" said he to himself. "What is this being? — beautiful, shall I call her? — or inexpressibly terrible?"

Beatrice now strayed carelessly through the garden, approaching closer beneath Giovanni's window, so that he was compelled to thrust his head quite out of its concealment in order to gratify the intense and painful curiosity which she excited. At this moment, there came a beautiful insect over the garden wall; it had perhaps wandered through the city and found no flowers nor verdure among those antique haunts of men, until the heavy perfumes of Doctor Rappaccini's shrubs had lured it from afar. Without alighting on the flowers, this winged brightness seemed to be attracted by Beatrice, and lingered in the air and fluttered about her head. Now here it could not be but that Giovanni Guasconti's eyes deceived him. Be that as it might, he fancied that while Beatrice was gazing at the insect with childish delight, it grew faint and fell at her feet! — its bright wings shivered! it was dead! — from no cause that he could discern, unless it were the atmosphere of her breath. Again Beatrice crossed herself and sighed heavily, as she bent over the dead insect.

An impulsive movement of Giovanni drew her eyes to the window. There 35 she beheld the beautiful head of the young man — rather a Grecian than an Italian head, with fair, regular features, and a glistening of gold among his ringlets — gazing down upon her like a being that hovered in mid-air. Scarcely knowing what he did, Giovanni threw down the bouquet which he had hitherto held in his hand.

"Signora," said he, "there are pure and healthful flowers. Wear them for the sake of Giovanni Guasconti!"

"Thanks, Signor," replied Beatrice, with her rich voice, that came forth as it were like a gush of music; and with a mirthful expression half childish and half woman-like. "I accept your gift, and would fain recompense it with this precious purple flower; but if I toss it into the air, it will not reach you. So Signor Guasconti must even content himself with my thanks."

She lifted the bouquet from the ground, and then as if inwardly ashamed at having stepped aside from her maidenly reserve to respond to a stranger's greeting, passed swiftly homeward through the garden. But, few as the moments were, it seemed to Giovanni when she was on the point of vanishing beneath the sculptured portal, that his beautiful bouquet was already beginning to wither in her grasp. It was an idle thought; there could be no possibility of distinguishing a faded flower from a fresh one at so great a distance.

For many days after the incident, the young man avoided the window that looked into Doctor Rappaccini's garden, as if something ugly and monstrous would have blasted his eye-sight, had he been betrayed into a glance. He felt conscious of having put himself, to a certain extent, within the influence of an unintelligible power, by the communication which he had opened with Beatrice. The wisest course would have been, if his heart were in any real danger, to quit his lodgings and Padua itself, at once; the next wiser, to have accustomed himself, as far as possible, to the familiar and daylight view of Beatrice; thus bringing her rigidly and systematically within the limits of ordinary experience. Least of all, while avoiding her sight, should Giovanni have remained so near this extraordinary being, that the proximity and possibility even of intercourse, should give a kind of substance and reality to the wild vagaries which his imagination ran riot continually in producing. Guasconti had not a deep heart — or at all events, its depths were not sounded now — but he had a quick fancy, and an ardent southern temperament, which rose every instant to a higher fever-pitch. Whether or no Beatrice possessed those terrible attributes — that fatal breath — the affinity with those so beautiful and deadly flowers — which were indicated by what Giovanni had witnessed, she had at least instilled a fierce and subtle poison into his system. It was not love, although her rich beauty was a madness to him; nor horror, even while he fancied her spirit to be imbued with the same baneful essence that seemed to pervade her physical frame; but a wild offspring of both love and horror that had each parent in it, and burned like one and shivered like the other. Giovanni knew not what to dread; still less did he know what to hope; *hope* and *dread* kept a continual warfare in his breast, alternately vanquishing one another and starting up afresh to renew the contest. Blessed are all simple emotions, be they dark or bright! It is the lurid intermixture of the two that produces the illuminating blaze of the infernal regions.

Sometimes he endeavored to assuage the fever of his spirit by a rapid walk 40 through the streets of Padua, or beyond its gates; his footsteps kept time with the throbbings of his brain, so that the walk was apt to accelerate itself to a race. One day, he found himself arrested; his arm was seized by a portly personage who had turned back on recognizing the young man, and expended much breath in overtaking him.

"Signor Giovanni! — stay, my young friend!" cried he. "Have you forgotten me? That might well be the case, if I were as much altered as yourself."

It was Baglioni, whom Giovanni had avoided, ever since their first meeting, from a doubt that the professor's sagacity would look too deeply into his secrets. Endeavoring to recover himself, he stared forth wildly from his inner world into the outer one, and spoke like a man in a dream:

"Yes; I am Giovanni Guasconti. You are Professor Pietro Baglioni. Now let me pass!"

"Not yet — not yet, Signor Giovanni Guasconti," said the Professor, smiling, but at the same time scrutinizing the youth with an earnest glance. — "What; did I grow up side by side with your father, and shall his son pass me like a stranger, in these old streets of Padua? Stand still, Signor Giovanni; for we must have a word or two, before we part."

"Speedily, then, most worshipful Professor, speedily!" said Giovanni, with 45 feverish impatience. "Does not your worship see that I am in haste?"

Now, while he was speaking, there came a man in black along the street, stooping and moving feebly, like a person in inferior health. His face was all overspread with a most sickly and sallow hue, but yet so pervaded with an expression of piercing and active intellect, that an observer might easily have overlooked the merely physical attributes, and have seen only this wonderful energy. As he passed, this person exchanged a cold and distant salutation with Baglioni, but fixed his eyes upon Giovanni with an intentness that seemed to bring out whatever was within him worthy of notice. Nevertheless, there was a peculiar quietness in the look, as if taking merely a speculative, not a human interest, in the young man.

"It is Doctor Rappaccini!" whispered the Professor, when the stranger had passed. — "Has he ever seen your face before?"

"Not that I know," answered Giovanni, starting at the name.

"He *has* seen you! — he must have seen you!" said Baglioni, hastily. "For some purpose or other, this man of science is making a study of you. I know that look of his! It is the same that coldly illuminates his face, as he bends over a bird, a mouse, or a butterfly, which, in pursuance of some experiment, he has killed by the perfume of a flower; — a look as deep as nature itself, but without nature's warmth of love. Signor Giovanni, I will stake my life upon it, you are the subject of one of Rappaccini's experiments!"

"Will you make a fool of me?" cried Giovanni, passionately. "*That,* Signor Professor, were an untoward experiment." 50

"Patience, patience!" replied the imperturbable Professor. — "I tell thee, my poor Giovanni, that Rappaccini has a scientific interest in thee. Thou hast fallen into fearful hands! And the Signora Beatrice? What part does she act in this mystery?"

But Guasconti, finding Baglioni's pertinacity intolerable, here broke away, and was gone before the Professor could again seize his arm. He looked after the young man intently, and shook his head.

"This must not be," said Baglioni to himself. "The youth is the son of my old friend, and should not come to any harm from which the arcana of medical science can preserve him. Besides, it is too insufferable an impertinence in Rappaccini, thus to snatch the bud out of my own hands, as I may say, and make use of him for his infernal experiments. This daughter of his! It shall be looked to. Perchance, most learned Rappaccini, I may foil you where you little dream of it!"

Meanwhile, Giovanni had pursued a circuitous route, and at length found himself at the door of his lodgings. As he crossed the threshold, he was met by old Lisabetta, who smirked and smiled, and was evidently desirous to attract his attention; vainly, however, as the ebullition of his feelings had momentarily subsided into a cold and dull vacuity. He turned his eyes full upon the withered face that was puckering itself into a smile, but seemed to behold it not. The old dame, therefore, laid her grasp upon his cloak.

"Signor! — Signor!" whispered she, still with a smile over the whole breadth 55 of her visage, so that it looked not unlike a grotesque carving in wood, darkened by centuries — "Listen, Signor! There is a private entrance into the garden!"

"What do you say?" exclaimed Giovanni, turning quickly about, as if an inanimate thing should start into feverish life. — "A private entrance into Doctor Rappaccini's garden!"

"Hush! hush! — not so loud!" whispered Lisabetta, putting her hand over his mouth. "Yes; into the worshipful Doctor's garden, where you may see all his fine shrubbery. Many a young man in Padua would give gold to be admitted among those flowers."

Giovanni put a piece of gold into her hand.

"Show me the way," said he.

A surmise, probably excited by his conversation with Baglioni crossed his 60 mind, that this interposition of old Lisabetta might perchance be connected with the intrigue, whatever were its nature, in which the Professor seemed to suppose that Doctor Rappaccini was involving him. But such a suspicion, though it disturbed Giovanni, was inadequate to restrain him. The instant he was aware of the possibility of approaching Beatrice, it seemed an absolute necessity of his existence to do so. It mattered not whether she were angel or demon; he was irrevocably within her sphere, and must obey the law that whirled him onward, in ever lessening circles, towards a result which he did not attempt to foreshadow. And yet, strange to say, there came across him a sudden doubt, whether this intense interest on his part were not delusory — whether it were really of so deep and positive a nature as to justify him in now thrusting himself into an incalculable position — whether it were not merely the fantasy of a young man's brain, only slightly, or not at all, connected with his heart!

He paused — hesitated — turned half about — but again went on. His withered guide led him along several obscure passages, and finally undid a door, through which, as it was opened, there came the sight and sound of rustling leaves, with the broken sunshine glimmering among them. Giovanni stepped forth, and forcing himself through the entanglement of a shrub that wreathed its tendrils over the hidden entrance, he stood beneath his own window, in the open area of Doctor Rappaccini's garden.

How often is it the case, that, when impossibilities have come to pass, and dreams have condensed their misty substance into tangible realities, we find ourselves calm, and even coldly self-possessed, amid circumstances which it would have been a delirium of joy or agony to anticipate! Fate delights to thwart us thus. Passion will choose his own time to rush upon the scene, and lingers sluggishly behind, when an appropriate adjustment of events would seem to summon his appearance. So was it now with Giovanni. Day after day, his pulses had throbbed with feverish blood, at the improbable idea of an interview with Beatrice, and of standing with her, face to face, in this very garden, basking in the oriental sunshine of her beauty, and snatching from her full gaze the mystery which he deemed the riddle of his own existence. But now there was a singular and untimely equanimity within his breast. He threw a glance around the garden to discover if Beatrice or her father were present, and perceiving that he was alone, began a critical observation of the plants.

The aspect of one and all of them dissatisfied him; their gorgeousness seemed fierce, passionate, and even unnatural. There was hardly an individual shrub which a wanderer, straying by himself through a forest, would not have been startled to find growing wild, as if an unearthly face had glared at him out of the thicket. Several, also, would have shocked a delicate instinct by an appearance of artificialness, indicating that there had been such commixture, and, as it were, adultery of various vegetable species, that the production was no longer of God's making, but the monstrous offspring of man's depraved fancy, glowing with only an evil mockery of beauty. They were probably the result of experiment, which, in one or two cases, had succeeded in mingling plants individually lovely into a compound possessing the questionable and ominous character that distinguished the whole growth of the garden. In fine, Giovanni recognized but two or three plants in the collection, and those of a kind that he well knew to be poisonous. While busy with these contemplations, he heard the rustling of a silken garment, and turning, beheld Beatrice emerging from beneath the sculptured portal.

Giovanni had not considered with himself what should be his deportment; whether he should apologize for his intrusion into the garden, or assume that he was there with the privity, at least, if not the desire of Doctor Rappaccini or his daughter. But Beatrice's manner placed him at his ease, though leaving him still in doubt by what agency he had gained admittance. She came lightly along the path, and met him near the broken fountain. There was surprise in her face, but brightened by a simple and kind expression of pleasure.

"You are a connoisseur in flowers, Signor," said Beatrice with a smile, 65 alluding to the bouquet which he had flung her from the window. "It is no marvel, therefore, if the sight of my father's rare collection has tempted you to take a nearer view. If he were here, he could tell you many strange and interesting facts as to the nature and habits of these shrubs, for he has spent a life-time in such studies, and this garden is his world."

"And yourself, lady" — observed Giovanni — "if fame says true — you, likewise, are deeply skilled in the virtues indicated by these rich blossoms, and these spicy perfumes. Would you deign to be my instructress, I should prove an apter scholar than under Signor Rappaccini himself."

"Are there such idle rumors?" asked Beatrice, with the music of a pleasant laugh. "Do people say that I am skilled in my father's science of plants? What a jest is there! No; though I have grown up among these flowers, I know no more of them than their hues and perfume; and sometimes, methinks I would fain rid myself of even that small knowledge. There are many flowers here, and those not the least brilliant, that shock and offend me, when they meet my eye. But, pray, Signor, do not believe these stories about my science. Believe nothing of me save what you see with your own eyes."

"And must I believe all that I have seen with my own eyes?" asked Giovanni pointedly, while the recollection of former scenes made him shrink. "No, Signora, you demand too little of me. Bid me believe nothing, save what comes from your own lips."

It would appear that Beatrice understood him. There came a deep flush to her cheek; but she looked full into Giovanni's eyes, and responded to his gaze of uneasy suspicion with a queen-like haughtiness.

"I do so bid you, Signor!" she replied. "Forget whatever you may have 70 fancied in regard to me. If true to the outward senses, still it may be false in its essence. But the words of Beatrice Rappaccini's lips are true from the heart outward. Those you may believe!"

A fervor glowed in her whole aspect, and beamed upon Giovanni's consciousness like the light of truth itself. But while she spoke, there was a fragrance in the atmosphere around her, rich and delightful, though evanescent, yet which the young man, from an indefinable reluctance, scarcely dared to draw into his lungs. It might be the odor of the flowers. Could it be Beatrice's breath, which thus embalmed her words with a strange richness, as if by steeping them in her heart? A faintness passed like a shadow over Giovanni, and flitted away; he seemed to gaze through the beautiful girl's eyes into her transparent soul, and felt no more doubt or fear.

The tinge of passion that had colored Beatrice's manner vanished; she became gay, and appeared to derive a pure delight from her communion with the youth, not unlike what the maiden of a lonely island might have felt, conversing with a voyager from the civilized world. Evidently her experience of life had been confined within the limits of that garden. She talked now about matters as simple as the day-light or summer-clouds, and now asked questions in reference to the city, or Giovanni's distant home, his friends, his mother, and his sisters; questions indicating such seclusion, and such lack of familiarity with modes and forms, that Giovanni responded as if to an infant. Her spirit gushed out before him like a fresh rill, that was just catching its first glimpse of the sunlight, and wondering at the reflections of earth and sky which were flung into its bosom. There came thoughts, too, from a deep source, and fantasies of a gem-like brilliancy, as if diamonds and rubies sparkled upward among the bubbles of the fountain. Ever and anon, there gleamed across the young man's mind a sense of wonder, that he should be walking side by side with the being who had so wrought upon his imagination — whom he had idealized in such hues of terror — in whom he had positively witnessed such manifestations of dreadful attributes — that he should be conversing with Beatrice like a brother, and should find her so human and so maiden-like. But such reflections were only momentary; the effect of her character was too real, not to make itself familiar at once.

In this free intercourse, they had strayed through the garden, and now, after many turns among its avenues, were come to the shattered fountain, beside which grew the magnificent shrub with its treasury of glowing blossoms. A fragrance was diffused from it, which Giovanni recognized as identical with that which he had attributed to Beatrice's breath, but incomparably more powerful. As her eyes fell upon it, Giovanni beheld her press her hand to her bosom, as if her heart were throbbing suddenly and painfully.

"For the first time in my life," murmured she, addressing the shrub, "I had forgotten thee!"

"I remember, Signora," said Giovanni, "that you once promised to reward 75 me with one of these living gems for the bouquet, which I had the happy boldness to fling to your feet. Permit me now to pluck it as a memorial of this interview."

He made a step towards the shrub, with extended hand. But Beatrice darted forward, uttering a shriek that went through his heart like a dagger. She caught his hand, and drew it back with the whole force of her slender figure. Giovanni felt her touch thrilling through his fibers.

"Touch it not!" exclaimed she, in a voice of agony. "Not for thy life! It is fatal!"

Then, hiding her face, she fled from him, and vanished beneath the sculptured portal. As Giovanni followed her with his eyes, he beheld the emaciated figure and pale intelligence of Doctor Rappaccini, who had been watching the scene, he knew not how long, within the shadow of the entrance.

No sooner was Guasconti alone in his chamber, than the image of Beatrice came back to his passionate musings, invested with all the witchery that had been gathering around it ever since his first glimpse of her, and now likewise imbued with a tender warmth of girlish womanhood. She was human: her nature was endowed with all gentle and feminine qualities; she was worthiest to be worshipped; she was capable, surely, on her part, of the height and heroism of love. Those tokens, which he had hitherto considered as proofs of a frightful peculiarity in her physical and moral system, were now either forgotten, or, by the subtle sophistry of passion, transmuted into a golden crown of enchantment, rendering Beatrice the more admirable, by so much as she was the more unique. Whatever had looked ugly, was now beautiful; or, if incapable of such a change, it stole away and hid itself among those shapeless half-ideas, which throng the dim region beyond the day-light of our perfect consciousness. Thus did Giovanni spend the night, nor fell asleep, until the dawn had begun to awake the slumbering flowers in Doctor Rappaccini's garden, whither his dreams doubtless led him. Up rose the sun in his due season, and flinging his beams upon the young man's eyelids, awoke him to a sense of pain. When thoroughly aroused, he became sensible of a burning and tingling agony in his hand — in his right hand — the very hand which Beatrice had grasped in her own, when he was on the point of plucking one of the gem-like flowers. On the back of that hand there was now a purple print, like that of four small fingers, and the likeness of a slender thumb upon his wrist.

Oh, how stubbornly does love — or even that cunning semblance of love 80 which flourishes in the imagination, but strikes no depth of root into the heart — how stubbornly does it hold its faith, until the moment come, when it is doomed to vanish into thin mist! Giovanni wrapt a handkerchief about his head, and wondered what evil thing had stung him, and soon forgot his pain in a reverie of Beatrice.

After the first interview, a second was in the inevitable course of what we call fate. A third; a fourth; and a meeting with Beatrice in the garden was no longer an incident in Giovanni's daily life, but the whole space in which he might be said to live; for the anticipation and memory of that ecstatic hour made up the remainder. Nor was it otherwise with the daughter of Rappaccini. She watched for the youth's appearance, and flew to his side with confidence as unreserved as if they had been playmates from early infancy — as if they were such playmates still. If, by any unwonted chance, he failed to come at the appointed moment, she stood beneath the window, and sent up the rich sweetness of her tones to float around him in his chamber, and echo and reverberate throughout his heart — "Giovanni! Giovanni! Why tarriest thou? Come down!" — And down he hastened into that Eden of poisonous flowers.

But, with all this intimate familiarity, there was still a reserve in Beatrice's demeanor, so rigidly and invariably sustained, that the idea of infringing it scarcely occurred to his imagination. By all appreciable signs, they loved; they had looked love, with eyes that conveyed the holy secret from the depths of one soul into the depths of the other, as if it were too sacred to be whispered by the way; they had even spoken love, in those gushes of passion when their spirits darted forth in articulated breath, like tongues of long-hidden flame; and yet there had been no seal of lips, no clasp of hands, nor any slightest caress, such as love claims and hallows. He had never touched one of the gleaming ringlets of her hair; her garment — so marked was the physical barrier between them — had never been waved against him by a breeze. On the few occasions when Giovanni had seemed tempted to overstep the limit, Beatrice grew so sad, so stern, and withal wore such a look of desolate separation, shuddering at itself, that not a spoken word was requisite to repel him. At such times, he was startled at the horrible suspicions that rose, monster-like, out of the caverns of his heart, and stared him in the face; his love grew thin and faint as the morning-mist; his doubts alone had substance. But when Beatrice's face brightened again, after the momentary shadow, she was transformed at once from the mysterious, questionable being, whom he had watched with so much awe and horror; she was now the beautiful and unsophisticated girl, whom he felt that his spirit knew with a certainty beyond all other knowledge.

A considerable time had now passed since Giovanni's last meeting with

Baglioni. One morning, however, he was disagreeably surprised by a visit from the Professor, whom he had scarcely thought of for whole weeks, and would willingly have forgotten still longer. Given up, as he had long been, to a pervading excitement, he could tolerate no companions, except upon condition of their perfect sympathy with his present state of feeling. Such sympathy was not to be expected from Professor Baglioni.

The visitor chatted carelessly, for a few moments, about the gossip of the city and the University, and then took up another topic.

"I have been reading an old classic author lately," said he, "and met with a 85 story that strangely interested me. Possibly you may remember it. It is of an Indian prince, who sent a beautiful woman as a present to Alexander the Great. She was as lovely as the dawn, and gorgeous as the sunset; but what especially distinguished her was a certain rich perfume in her breath — richer than a garden of Persian roses. Alexander, as was natural to a youthful conqueror, fell in love at first sight with this magnificent stranger. But a certain sage physician, happening to be present, discovered a terrible secret in regard to her."

"And what was that?" asked Giovanni, turning his eyes downward to avoid those of the Professor.

"That this lovely woman," continued Baglioni, with emphasis, "had been nourished with poisons from her birth upward, until her whole nature was so imbued with them, that she herself had become the deadliest poison in existence. Poison was her element of life. With that rich perfume of her breath, she blasted the very air. Her love would have been poison! — her embrace death! Is not this a marvellous tale?"

"A childish fable," answered Giovanni, nervously starting from his chair. "I marvel how your worship finds time to read such nonsense, among your graver studies."

"By the by," said the Professor, looking uneasily about him, "what singular fragrance is this in your apartment? Is it the perfume of your gloves? It is faint, but delicious, and yet, after all, by no means agreeable. Were I to breathe it long, methinks it would make me ill. It is like the breath of a flower — but I see no flowers in the chamber."

"Nor are there any," replied Giovanni, who had turned pale as the Professor 90 spoke; "nor, I think, is there any fragrance, except in your worship's imagination. Odors, being a sort of element combined of the sensual and the spiritual, are apt to deceive us in this manner. The recollection of a perfume — the bare idea of it — may easily be mistaken for a present reality."

"Aye; but my sober imagination does not often play such tricks," said Baglioni; "and were I to fancy any kind of odor, it would be that of some vile apothecary drug, wherewith my fingers are likely enough to be imbued. Our worshipful friend Rappaccini, as I have heard, tinctures his medicaments with odors richer than those of Araby. Doubtless, likewise, the fair and learned Signora Beatrice would minister to her patients with draughts as sweet as a maiden's breath. But woe to him that sips them!"

Giovanni's face evinced many contending emotions. The tone in which the Professor alluded to the pure and lovely daughter of Rappaccini was a torture to his soul; and yet, the intimation of a view of her character, opposite to his own, gave instantaneous distinctness to a thousand dim suspicions, which now grinned at him like so many demons. But he strove hard to quell them, and to respond to Baglioni with a true lover's perfect faith.

"Signor Professor," said he, "you were my father's friend — perchance, too, it is your purpose to act a friendly part towards his son. I would fain feel nothing towards you, save respect and deference. But I pray you to observe, Signor, that there is one subject on which we must not speak. You know not the Signora Beatrice. You cannot, therefore, estimate the wrong — the blasphemy, I may even say — that is offered to her character by a light or injurious word."

"Giovanni! — my poor Giovanni!" answered the Professor, with a calm expression of pity, "I know this wretched girl far better than yourself. You shall hear the truth in respect to the poisoner Rappaccini, and his poisonous daughter. Yes; poisonous as she is beautiful! Listen; for even should you do violence to my gray hairs, it shall not silence me. That old fable of the Indian woman has become a truth, by the deep and deadly science of Rappaccini, and in the person of the lovely Beatrice!"

Giovanni groaned and hid his face.   95

"Her father," continued Baglioni, "was not restrained by natural affection from offering up his child, in this horrible manner, as the victim of his insane zeal for science. For — let us do him justice — he is as true a man of science as ever distilled his own heart in an alembic. What, then, will be your fate? Beyond a doubt, you are selected as the material of some new experiment. Perhaps the result is to be death — perhaps a fate more awful still! Rappaccini, with what he calls the interest of science before his eyes, will hesitate at nothing."

"It is a dream!" muttered Giovanni to himself, "surely it is a dream!"

"But," resumed the professor, "be of good cheer, son of my friend! It is not yet too late for the rescue. Possibly, we may even succeed in bringing back this miserable child within the limits of ordinary nature, from which her father's madness has estranged her. Behold this little silver vase! It was wrought by the hands of the renowned Benvenuto Cellini,° and is well worthy to be a love-gift to the fairest dame in Italy. But its contents are invaluable. One little sip of this antidote would have rendered the most virulent poisons of the Borgias° innocuous. Doubt not that it will be as efficacious against those of Rappaccini. Bestow the vase, and the precious liquid within it, on your Beatrice, and hopefully await the result."

Baglioni laid a small, exquisitely wrought silver phial on the table, and withdrew, leaving what he had said to produce its effect upon the young man's mind.

"We will thwart Rappaccini yet!" thought he, chuckling to himself, as he   100 descended the stairs. "But, let us confess the truth of him, he is a wonderful man! — a wonderful man indeed! A vile empiric, however, in his practice, and therefore not to be tolerated by those who respect the good old rules of the medical profession!"

Throughout Giovanni's whole acquaintance with Beatrice, he had occasionally, as we have said, been haunted by dark surmises as to her character. Yet, so

---

Benvenuto Cellini (1500–1571): A famous Italian goldsmith and sculptor.
Borgias: A Renaissance Italian family notorious for corruption and cruelty.

thoroughly had she made herself felt by him as a simple, natural, most affection-ate and guileless creature, that the image now held up by Professor Baglioni, looked as strange and incredible, as if it were not in accordance with his own original conception. True, there were ugly recollections connected with his first glimpses of the beautiful girl; he could not quite forget the bouquet that withered in her grasp, and the insect that perished amid the sunny air, by no ostensible agency, save the fragrance of her breath. These incidents, however, dissolving in the pure light of her character, had no longer the efficacy of facts, but were acknowledged as mistaken fantasies, by whatever testimony of the senses they might appear to be substantiated. There is something truer and more real, than what we can see with the eyes, and touch with the finger. On such better evidence, had Giovanni founded his confidence in Beatrice, though rather by the necessary force of her high attributes, than by any deep and generous faith, on his part. But, now, his spirit was incapable of sustaining itself at the height to which the early enthusiasm of passion had exalted it; he fell down, grovelling among earthly doubts, and defiled therewith the pure whiteness of Beatrice's image. Not that he gave her up; he did but distrust. He resolved to institute some decisive test that should satisfy him, once for all, whether there were those dreadful peculiarities in her physical nature, which could not be supposed to exist without some corresponding monstrosity of soul. His eyes, gazing down afar, might have deceived him as to the lizard, the insect, and the flowers. But if he could witness, at the distance of a few paces, the sudden blight of one fresh and healthful flower in Beatrice's hand, there would be room for no further question. With this idea, he hastened to the florist's, and purchased a bouquet that was still gemmed with the morning dew-drops.

It was now the customary hour of his daily interview with Beatrice. Before descending into the garden, Giovanni failed not to look at his figure in the mirror; a vanity to be expected in a beautiful young man, yet, as displaying itself at that troubled and feverish moment, the token of a certain shallowness of feeling and insincerity of character. He did gaze, however, and said to himself, that his features had never before possessed so rich a grace, nor his eyes such vivacity, nor his cheeks so warm a hue of superabundant life.

"At least," thought he, "her poison has not yet insinuated itself into my system. I am no flower to perish in her grasp!"

With that thought, he turned his eyes on the bouquet, which he had never once laid aside from his hand. A thrill of indefinable horror shot through his frame, on perceiving that those dewy flowers were already beginning to droop; they wore the aspect of things that had been fresh and lovely, yesterday. Giovanni grew white as marble, and stood motionless before the mirror, staring at his own reflection there, as at the likeness of something frightful. He remembered Baglioni's remark about the fragrance that seemed to pervade the chamber. It must have been the poison in his breath! Then he shuddered — shuddered at himself! Recovering from his stupor, he began to watch, with curious eye, a spider that was busily at work, hanging its web from the antique cornice of the apartment, crossing and re-crossing the artful system of interwoven lines, as vigorous and active a spider as ever dangled from an old ceiling. Giovanni bent towards the insect, and emitted a deep, long breath. The spider suddenly ceased its toil; the web vibrated with a tremor originating in the body of the small artizan. Again Giovanni sent forth a breath, deeper, longer, and imbued with a venomous feeling out of his heart; he knew not whether he were wicked or only desperate. The spider made a convulsive gripe with his limbs, and hung dead across the window.

"Accursed! Accursed!" muttered Giovanni, addressing himself. "Hast thou grown so poisonous, that this deadly insect perishes by thy breath?" 105

At that moment, a rich, sweet voice came floating up from the garden: —

"Giovanni! Giovanni! It is past the hour! Why tarriest thou! Come down!"

"Yes," muttered Giovanni again. "She is the only being whom my breath may not slay! Would that it might!"

He rushed down, and in an instant, was standing before the bright and loving eyes of Beatrice. A moment ago, his wrath and despair had been so fierce that he could have desired nothing so much as to wither her by a glance. But, with her actual presence, there came influences which had too real an existence to be at once shaken off; recollections of the delicate and benign power of her feminine nature, which had so often enveloped him in a religious calm; recollections of many a holy and passionate outgush of her heart, when the pure fountain had been unsealed from its depths, and made visible in its transparency to his mental eye; recollections which, had Giovanni known how to estimate them, would have assured him that all this ugly mystery was but an earthly illusion, and that, whatever mist of evil might seem to have gathered over her, the real Beatrice was a heavenly angel. Incapable as he was of such high faith, still her presence had not utterly lost its magic. Giovanni's rage was quelled into an aspect of sullen insensibility. Beatrice, with a quick spiritual sense, immediately felt that there was a gulf of blackness between them, which neither he nor she could pass. They walked on together, sad and silent, and came thus to the marble fountain, and to its pool of water on the ground, in the midst of which grew the shrub that bore gem-like blossoms. Giovanni was affrighted at the eager enjoyment — the appetite, as it were — with which he found himself inhaling the fragrance of the flowers.

"Beatrice," asked he abruptly, "whence came this shrub?" 110

"My father created it," answered she, with simplicity.

"Created it! created it!" repeated Giovanni. "What mean you, Beatrice?"

"He is a man fearfully acquainted with the secrets of nature," replied Beatrice; "and, at the hour when I first drew breath, this plant sprang from the soil, the offspring of his science, of his intellect, while I was but his earthly child." "Approach it not!" continued she, observing with terror that Giovanni was drawing nearer to the shrub. "It has qualities that you little dream of. But I, dearest Giovanni, — I grew up and blossomed with the plant, and was nourished with its breath. It was my sister, and I loved it with a human affection: for — alas! hast thou not suspected it? there was an awful doom."

Here Giovanni frowned so darkly upon her that Beatrice paused and trembled. But her faith in his tenderness re-assured her, and made her blush that she had doubted for an instant.

"There was an awful doom," she continued, — "the effect of my father's fatal love of science — which estranged me from all society of any kind. Until Heaven sent thee, dearest Giovanni, Oh! how lonely was thy poor Beatrice!" 115

"Was it a hard doom?" asked Giovanni, fixing his eyes upon her.

"Only of late have I known how hard it was," answered she tenderly. "Oh, yes; but my heart was torpid, and therefore quiet."

Giovanni's rage broke forth from his sullen gloom like a lightning-flash out of a dark cloud.

"Accursed one!" cried he, with venomous scorn and anger. "And finding thy solitude wearisome, thou hast severed me, likewise, from all the warmth of life, and enticed me into thy region of unspeakable horror!"

"Giovanni!" exclaimed Beatrice, turning her large bright eyes upon his face. 120 The force of his words had not found its way into her mind; she was merely wonder-struck.

"Yes, poisonous thing!" repeated Giovanni, beside himself with passion. "Thou has done it! Thou has blasted me! Thou hast filled my veins with poison! Thou hast made me as hateful, as ugly, as loathsome and deadly a creature as thyself, — a world's wonder of hideous monstrosity! Now — if our breath be happily as fatal to ourselves as to all others — let us join our lips in one kiss of unutterable hatred, and so die!"

"What has befallen me?" murmured Beatrice, with a low moan out of her heart. "Holy Virgin pity me, a poor heart-broken child!"

"Thou! Dost thou pray?" cried Giovanni, still with the same fiendish scorn. "Thy very prayers, as they come from thy lips, taint the atmosphere with death. Yes, yes; let us pray! Let us to church, and dip our fingers in the holy water at the portal! They that come after us will perish as by a pestilence. Let us sign crosses in the air! It will be scattering curses abroad in the likeness of holy symbols!"

"Giovanni," said Beatrice calmly, for her grief was beyond passion, "why dost thou join thyself with me thus in those terrible words? I, it is true, am the horrible thing thou namest me. But thou! — what hast thou to do, save with one other shudder at my hideous misery, to go forth out of the garden and mingle with thy race, and forget that there ever crawled on earth such a monster as poor Beatrice?"

"Dost thou pretend ignorance?" asked Giovanni, scowling upon her. "Be- 125 hold! This power have I gained from the pure daughter of Rappaccini!"

There was a swarm of summer-insects flitting through the air, in search of the food promised by the flower-odors of the fatal garden. They circled round Giovanni's head, and were evidently attracted towards him by the same influence which had drawn them, for an instant, within the sphere of several of the shrubs. He sent forth a breath among them, and smiled bitterly at Beatrice, as at least a score of insects fell dead upon the ground.

"I see it! I see it!" shrieked Beatrice. "It is my father's fatal science? No, no, Giovanni; it was not I! Never, never! I dreamed only to love thee, and be with thee a little time, and so to let thee pass away, leaving but thine image in mine heart. For, Giovanni — believe it — though my body be nourished with poison, my spirit is God's creature, and craves love as its daily food. But my father! — he has united us in this fearful sympathy. Yes; spurn me! — tread upon me! — kill me! Oh, what is death, after such words as thine? But it was not I! Not for a world of bliss would I have done it!"

Giovanni's passion had exhausted itself in its outburst from his lips. There now came across a sense, mournful, and not without tenderness, of the intimate and peculiar relationship between Beatrice and himself. They stood, as if were, in an utter solitude, which would be made none the less solitary by the densest throng of human life. Ought not, then, the desert of humanity around them to press this insulated pair close together? If they should be cruel to one another, who was there to be kind to them? Besides, thought Giovanni, might there not still be a hope of his returning within the limits of ordinary nature, and leading Beatrice — the redeemed Beatrice — by the hand? Oh, weak, and selfish, and unworthy spirit, that could dream of an earthly union and earthly happiness as possible, after such deep love had been so bitterly wronged as was Beatrice's love by Giovanni's blighting words! No, no; there could be no such hope. She must pass heavily, with that broken heart, across the borders — she must bathe her hurts in some fount of Paradise, and forget her grief in the light of immortality — and *there* be well!

But Giovanni did not know it.

"Dear Beatrice," said he, approaching her, while she shrank away, as always 130 at his approach, but now with a different impulse — "dearest Beatrice, our fate is not yet so desperate. Behold! There is a medicine, potent, as a wise physician has assured me, and almost divine in its efficacy. It is composed of ingredients the most opposite to those by which thy awful father has brought this calamity upon thee and me. It is distilled of blessed herbs. Shall we not quaff it together, and thus be purified from evil?"

"Give it me!" said Beatrice, extending her hand to receive the little silver phial which Giovanni took from his bosom. She added, with a peculiar emphasis; "I will drink — but do thou await the result."

She put Baglioni's antidote to her lips; and, at the same moment the figure of Rappaccini emerged from the portal, and came slowly towards the marble fountain. As he drew near, the pale man of science seemed to gaze with a triumphant expression at the beautiful youth and maiden, as might an artist who should spend his life in achieving a picture or a group of statuary, and finally be satisfied with his success. He paused — his bent form grew erect with conscious power, he spread out his hand over them, in the attitude of a father imploring a blessing upon his children. But those were the same hands that had thrown poison into the stream of their lives! Giovanni trembled. Beatrice shuddered nervously, and pressed her hand upon her heart.

"My daughter," said Rappaccini, "thou are no longer lonely in the world! Pluck one of those precious gems from thy sister shrub, and bid thy bridegroom wear it in his bosom. It will not harm him now! My science, and the sympathy between thee and him, have so wrought within his system, that he now stands apart from common men, as thou dost, daughter of my pride and triumph, from ordinary women. Pass on, then, through the world, most dear to one another, and dreadful to all besides!"

"My father," said Beatrice, feebly — and still, as she spoke, she kept her hand upon her heart — "wherefore didst thou inflict this miserable doom upon thy child?"

"Miserable!" exclaimed Rappaccini. "What mean you, foolish girl? Dost thou 135 deem it misery to be endowed with marvellous gifts, against which no power nor strength could avail an enemy? Misery, to be able to quell the mightiest with a breath? Misery, to be as terrible as thou art beautiful? Wouldst thou, then, have preferred the condition of a weak woman, exposed to all evil, and capable of none?".

"I would fain have been loved, not feared," murmured Beatrice, sinking down upon the ground. — "But now it matters not; I am going, father, where the evil, which thou hast striven to mingle with my being, will pass away like a dream — like the fragrance of these poisonous flowers, which will no longer taint my breath among the flowers of Eden. Farewell, Giovanni! Thy words of hatred are like lead within my heart — but they, too, will fall away as I ascend. Oh, was there not, from the first, more poison in thy nature than in mine?"

To Beatrice — so radically had her earthly part been wrought upon by Rappaccini's skill — as poison had been life, so the powerful antidote was death. And thus the poor victim of man's ingenuity and of thwarted nature, and of the fatality that attends all such efforts of perverted wisdom, perished there, at the feet of her father and Giovanni. Just at that moment, Professor Pietro Baglioni looked forth from the window, and called loudly, in a tone of triumph mixed with horror, to the thunder-stricken man of science:

"Rappaccini! Rappaccini! And is *this* the upshot of your experiment?"

Considerations for Critical Thinking and Writing

1. Why is Padua, Italy, a particularly appropriate setting for this story? How does Padua differ from Giovanni's Naples? Why wouldn't Young Goodman Brown's Salem be equally appropriate?
2. Is Giovanni a sympathetic character? Explain why you think he does or doesn't love Beatrice.
3. Why does Rappaccini poison Beatrice? How does he justify his actions?
4. How does Pietro Baglioni serve as a foil to Rappaccini? What kind of professional relationship do they have?
5. How does the narrator's description of the garden — and particularly of the purple flower — connect the garden with Beatrice? What is the significance of the similarities?
6. Write an essay that responds to the question Giovanni raises in paragraph 9 about Rappaccini's garden: "Was this garden, then, the Eden of the present world? — and this man [Rappaccini], with such a perception of harm in what his own hands caused to grow, was he the Adam?" How do the allusions to Adam, Eve, and the Garden of Eden amplify the meanings of the story?
7. How does the narrator cast doubts upon Giovanni's accounts of the death of the lizard and insect and the withering of the bouquet he gives Beatrice? What is the effect of these doubts? Why do you think Hawthorne includes them in the story?
8. What is the purpose of Baglioni's description of the "old classic" he summarizes for Giovanni in paragraphs 85–88?
9. How do you answer Beatrice's final question to Giovanni: "Oh, was there not, from the first, more poison in thy nature than in mine?" In what ways is Giovanni poisoned? What do you think is the most deadly "poison" in the story?
10. Why do you suppose Hawthorne gives Baglioni the story's last words?
11. Write an essay explaining what you think happens to Giovanni after the final scene.

Connections to Other Selections

1. Compare Rappaccini's devotion to science with Alymer's in "The Birthmark." Explain the similarities and differences in the plots.
2. Write an essay comparing the themes of isolation in "Rappaccini's Daughter" and "The Minister's Black Veil." Are there any positive effects produced by isolation in each story?
3. In an essay explore ideas about innocence and guilt in "Rappaccini's Daughter" and Margaret Atwood's "Death by Landscape" (p. 529).

PERSPECTIVES ON HAWTHORNE

Hawthorne on Solitude 1837

Dear Sir,

Not to burthen you with my correspondence, I have delayed a rejoinder to your very kind and cordial letter, until now. It gratifies me to find that you have occasionally felt an interest in my situation. . . . You would have been nearer the truth if you had pictured me as dwelling in an owl's nest; for mine is about as dismal; and, like the owl I seldom venture abroad till after dark. By some witchcraft or other — for I really cannot assign any reasonable why and wherefore — I have been carried apart from the main current of life, and find it impossible to get back again. Since we last met . . . I have secluded myself from society; and yet I never meant any such thing, nor dreamed what sort of life I was going to lead. I have made a captive of myself and put me into a dungeon, and now I cannot find the key to let myself out — and if the door were open, I should be almost afraid to come out. You tell me that you have met with troubles and changes. I know not what they may have been; but I can assure you that trouble is the next best thing to enjoyment, and that there is no fate in this world so horrible as to have no share in either its joys or sorrows. For the last ten years, I have not lived, but only dreamed about living. It may be true that there have been some unsubstantial pleasures here in the shade, which I should have missed in the sunshine, but you cannot conceive how utterly devoid of satisfaction all my retrospects are. I have laid up no treasure of pleasant remembrances, against old age; but there is some comfort in thinking that my future years can hardly fail to be more varied, and therefore more tolerable, than the past.

You give me more credit than I deserve, in supposing that I have led a studious life. I have, indeed, turned over a good many books, but in so desultory a way that it cannot be called study, nor has it left me the fruits of study. As to my literary efforts, I do not think much of them — neither is it worth while to be ashamed of them. They would have been better, I trust, if written under more favorable circumstances. I have had no external excitement — no consciousness that the public would like what I wrote, nor much hope nor a very passionate desire that they should do so. Nevertheless, having nothing else to be ambitious of, I have felt considerably interested in literature; and if my writings had made any decided impression, I should probably have been stimulated to greater exertions; but there has been no warmth of approbation, so that I have always written with benumbed fingers. I have another great difficulty, in the lack of materials; for I have seen so little of the world, that I have nothing but thin air to concoct my stories of, and it is not easy to give a lifelike semblance to such shadowy stuff. Sometimes, through a peep-hole, I have caught a glimpse of the real world; and the two or three articles, in which I have portrayed such glimpses, please me better than the others. I have now, or shall soon have, one sharp spur to exertion, which I lacked at an earlier period; for I see little prospect but that I must scribble for a living. But this troubles me much less than you would suppose. I can turn my pen to all sorts of drudgery, such as children's books, etc., and by and by, I shall get some editorship that will answer my purpose. Frank Pierce, who was with us at college, offered me his influence to obtain an office in the Exploring Expedition; but I believe that he was mistaken in supposing that a vacancy existed. If such a post were attainable, I should certainly accept it; for, though fixed so long to one spot, I have always had a desire to run around the world.

The copy of my Tales was sent to Mr. Owen's, the bookseller's in Cambridge. I am glad to find that you had read and liked some of the stories. To be sure, you could not well help flattering me a little; but I value your praise too highly not to have faith in its sincerity. When I last heard from the publisher — which was not very recently — the book was doing pretty well. Six or seven hundred copies had been sold. I suppose, however, these awful times have now stopped the sale.

I intend in a week or two to come out of my owl's nest, and not return to it till late in the summer — employing the interval in making a tour somewhere in New England. You, who have the dust of distant countries on your "sandal-shoon," cannot imagine how much enjoyment I shall have in this little excursion. Whenever I get abroad, I feel just as young as I did, ten years ago. What a letter I am inflicting on you! I trust you will answer it.

Yours sincerely,
Nath. Hawthorne.
From a letter to Henry Wadsworth Longfellow, June 4, 1837

Considerations for Critical Thinking and Writing

1. How does Hawthorne regard his solitude? How does he feel it has affected his life and writing?
2. Hawthorne explains to Longfellow, one of his Bowdoin classmates, that "there is no fate in this world so horrible as to have no share in either its joys or sorrows." Explain how this idea is worked into "Young Goodman Brown."
3. Does Hawthorne indicate any positive results for having lived in his "owl's nest"? Consider how "The Minister's Black Veil" and this letter shed light on each other.

Hawthorne on the Power of the Writer's Imagination   1850

. . . Moonlight, in a familiar room, falling so white upon the carpet, and showing all its figures so distinctly — making every object so minutely visible, yet so unlike a morning or noontide visibility — is a medium the most suitable for a romance-writer° to get acquainted with his illusive guests. There is the little domestic scenery of the well-known apartment; the chairs, with each its separate individuality; the center-table, sustaining a work-basket, a volume or two, and an extinguished lamp; the sofa; the book-case; the picture on the wall — all these details, so completely seen, are so spiritualized by the unusual light, that they seem to lose their actual substance, and become things of intellect. Nothing is too small or too trifling to undergo this change, and acquire dignity thereby. A child's shoe; the doll, seated in her little wicker carriage; the hobbyhorse — whatever, in a word, has been used or played with, during the day, is now invested with a quality of strangeness and remoteness, though still almost as vividly present as by daylight. Thus, therefore, the floor of our familiar room has become a neutral territory, somewhere between the real world and fairyland, where the Actual and the Imaginary may meet, and each imbue itself with the nature of the other. Ghosts might enter here, without affrighting us. It would be too much in keeping with the scene to excite surprise, were we to look about us and discover a form, beloved, but gone hence, now sitting quietly in a streak of this magic moonshine, with an aspect that would make us doubt whether it had returned from afar, or had never once stirred from our fireside.

The somewhat dim coal-fire has an essential influence in producing the effect which I would describe. It throws its unobtrusive tinge throughout the room, with a faint ruddiness upon the walls and ceiling, and a reflected gleam from the polish of the furniture. This warmer light mingles itself with the cold spirituality of the moonbeams, and communicates, as it were, a heart and sensibilities of human tenderness to the forms which fancy summons up. It converts them from snow-images into men and women. Glancing at the looking-glass, we behold — deep within its haunted verge — the smouldering glow of the half-extinguished anthracite, the white moonbeams on the floor, and a repetition of all the gleam and shadow of the picture, with one remove farther from the actual, and nearer to the imaginative. Then, at such an hour, and with this scene before him, if a man, sitting all alone, cannot dream strange things, and make them look like truth, he need never try to write romances.

From *The Scarlet Letter*

Considerations for Critical Thinking and Writing

1. Explain how Hawthorne uses light as a means of invoking the transforming powers of the imagination.
2. How do Hawthorne's stories fulfill his definition of romance writing? Why can't they be regarded as realistic?
3. Choose one story and discuss it as an attempt to evoke "the truth of the human heart."

---

romance-writer: Hawthorne distinguished romance writing from novel writing. In the preface to *The House of the Seven Gables* he writes: "The latter form of composition is presumed to aim at a very minute fidelity, not merely to the possible, but to the probable and ordinary course of man's experience. The former — while, as a work of art, it must rigidly subject itself to laws, and while it sins unpardonably so far as it may swerve aside from the truth of the human heart — has fairly a right to present that truth under circumstances, to a great extent, of the writer's own choosing or creation."

[These stories] have the pale tint of flowers that blossomed in too retired a shade — the coolness of a meditative habit, which diffuses itself through the feeling and observation of every sketch. Instead of passion there is sentiment; and, even in what purport to be pictures of actual life, we have allegory, not always warmly dressed in its habiliments of flesh and blood as to be taken into the reader's mind without a shiver. Whether from lack of power, or an unconquerable reserve, the Author's touches have often an effect of tameness; the merriest man can hardly contrive to laugh at his broadest humor; the tenderest woman, one would suppose, will hardly shed warm tears at his deepest pathos. The book, if you would see anything in it, requires to be read in the clear brown, twilight atmosphere in which it was written; if opened in the sunshine, it is apt to look exceedingly like a volume of blank pages.

From the preface to the 1851 edition of *Twice-Told Tales*

Considerations for Critical Thinking and Writing

1. How does Hawthorne characterize his stories? Does his assessment accurately describe the stories you've read?
2. Why is a "twilight atmosphere" more conducive to an appreciation of Hawthorne's art than "sunshine"?
3. Write a one-page description of Hawthorne's stories in which you generalize about his characteristic approach to one of these elements: plot, character, setting, symbol, theme, tone.

HERMAN MELVILLE (1819–1891)
On Nathaniel Hawthorne's Tragic Vision 1851

There is a certain tragic phase of humanity which, in our opinion, was never more powerfully embodied than by Hawthorne. We mean the tragicalness of human thought in its own unbiased, native, and profounder workings. We think that in no recorded mind has the intense feeling of the visable truth ever entered more deeply than into this man's. By visable truth, we mean the apprehension of the absolute condition of present things as they strike the eye of the man who fears them not, though they do their worst to him — the man who, like Russia or the British Empire, declares himself a sovereign nature (in himself) amid the powers of heaven, hell, and earth. He may perish; but so long as he exists he insists upon treating with all Powers upon an equal basis. If any of those other Powers choose to withhold certain secrets, let them; that does not impair my sovereignty in myself; that does not make me tributary. And perhaps, after all, there is *no* secret. We incline to think that the Problem of the Universe is like the Freemason's° mighty secret, so terrible to all children. It turns out, at

---

Freemason's: A member of the secret fraternity of Freemasonry.

last, to consist in a triangle, a mallet, and an apron — nothing more! . . . There is the grand truth about Nathaniel Hawthorne. He says NO! in thunder; but the Devil himself cannot make him say *yes*. For all men who say *yes*, lie; and all men who say *no* — why, they are in the happy condition of judicious, unincumbered travellers in Europe; they cross the frontiers into Eternity with nothing but a carpet-bag — that is to say, the Ego. Whereas those *yes*-gentry, they travel with heaps of baggage, and, damn them! they will never get through the Custom House. What's the reason, Mr. Hawthorne, that in the last stages of metaphysics a fellow always falls to *swearing* so? I could rip an hour.

From a letter to Hawthorne, April 16(?), 1851

Considerations for Critical Thinking and Writing

1. What qualities in Hawthorne does Melville admire?
2. Explain how these qualities are embodied in one of the Hawthorne stories.
3. How might Melville's lawyer in "Bartleby, the Scrivener" (p. 83) be characterized as one of "those *yes*-gentry"?

HYATT H. WAGGONER (b. 1913)
Hawthorne's Style   1962

If the first thing we should notice about Hawthorne is his "modernity," his immediate relevance to us and our concerns, the second thing, if we are to avoid the distortion of seeing in him only our own image, is the way in which he is *not* one of us. It has been said that he was an eighteenth-century gentleman living in the nineteenth century, and the remark has enough truth in it to be useful to us at this point.

His style, for instance, though at its best a wonderfully effective instrument for the expression of sensibility, is likely to strike us as not nearly so modern as Thoreau's.° It was slightly old-fashioned even when he wrote it. It is very deliberate, with measured rhythms, marked by formal decorum. It is a public style and, as we might say, a "rhetorical" one — though of course all styles are rhetorical in one sense or another. It often prefers the abstract or generalized to the concrete or specific word. Compared to what the writers of handbooks, under the influence of modernist literature, have taught us to prefer — the private, informal, concrete, colloquial, imagistic, — Hawthorne's style can only be called premodern.

From *Nathaniel Hawthorne*

Considerations for Critical Thinking and Writing

1. In what ways can Hawthorne's fiction be seen as having an "immediate relevance to us and our concerns"? How do his themes continue to speak to us?
2. Choose a paragraph from a Hawthorne story that fits Waggoner's description of

Thoreau's: Henry David Thoreau (1817–1862), author of *Walden* and the equally famous essay "Civil Disobedience."

Hawthorne's characteristic style and contrast its style to a paragraph from Hemingway's "Soldier's Home" (p. 125), or John Updike's "A & P" (p. 485).

3. Take a paragraph from any twentieth-century story included in this anthology and try rewriting it in Hawthorne's style.

E. EARLE STIBITZ (b. 1909)
Irony in "The Minister's Black Veil"   1962

Because Hawthorne is always very much the same and yet also surprisingly varied, one way of understanding "The Minister's Black Veil," as with any Hawthorne tale, is to read it not only as the unique work of art that it is, but as a tale comparable to others by Hawthorne, viewing it in the context of his essentially consistent thought and art as a whole. Such a reading of "The Minister's Black Veil" yields an unambiguous meaning. Hawthorne, with his usual assumption of the reality of personal evil, presents on one level his fundamental belief in man's proneness to hide or rationalize his most private thoughts or guilt. This is the "parable" . . . that the Reverend Mr. Hooper seeks to preach with his wearing of the veil. On another level, Hawthorne reaffirms his equally constant belief that man is often guilty of pridefully and harmfully exalting one idea, frequently a valid truth in itself, to the status of an absolute. This is the sin Hooper commits by his self-righteous and self-deceptive insistence upon wearing the veil.

The second level grows out of the first and remains dependent upon it, a structural pattern repeated in varying ways in each major division of the story. Furthermore, this organic relationship of the two levels is ironic. Hooper in his stubborn use of the veil parable of one sin is unconsciously guilty of a greater one — that of egotistically warping the total meaning of life. This irony is compounded in that Hooper's sin is a hidden one — hidden not only from his fellows but from himself. He thus unintentionally dramatizes the very sin of secrecy that he intentionally sets out to symbolize. The central symbol of the veil keeps pace with this added irony: in addition to standing for man's concealment or hypocrisy and for Hooper's own sin of pride with its isolating effects, it stands also for the hidden quality of the second sin. All told, "The Minister's Black Veil" is less ambiguous and more unified because it is more ironic than has usually been recognized.

From American Literature

Considerations for Critical Thinking and Writing

1. How does Stibitz resolve the ambiguity of the story? Explain whether you find his argument convincing. Why or why not?

2. Write an essay that compares the use of irony in "The Minister's Black Veil" and one of the other Hawthorne stories in this collection. How crucial is irony to the theme of each story? Why do you think an author like Hawthorne finds irony to be a particularly useful strategy?

STEVEN MAILLOUX (b. 1950)
Gauging the Reader's Response to Giovanni 1982

The discourse encourages the reader to examine the motivation of actions toward others. Baglioni constantly points out Rappaccini's motives and designs, while the narrator continually emphasizes Giovanni's "depth" of love and Beatrice's innocence as motives for their acts. From the judgment of external facts and internal motivation, the discourse pressures the reader to move toward a judgment of moral responsibility. The points at which the discourse applies this pressure provide moments in the response structure that prepare the reader to answer the question suggested by the final line: who is really responsible for Beatrice's death?

The narrator warns the reader in the first paragraph that Giovanni has "the tendency to heartbreak natural to a young man for the first time out of his native sphere." The discourse amplifies this hint of shallowness a bit later in the story, when the narrator describes Giovanni's infatuation with Beatrice: "Guasconti had not a deep heart — or at all events, its depths were not sounded now — but he had a quick fancy, and an ardent southern temperament, which rose every instant to a higher fever-pitch." Soon the reader discovers that Giovanni questions his own motivation along these same lines (though only for a moment): "there came across him a sudden doubt, whether this intense interest on his part were not delusory . . . whether it were not merely the fantasy of a young man's brain, only slightly, or not at all, connected with his heart!" The narrator later suggests that Giovanni possesses "that cunning *semblance* of love which flourishes in the imagination, but strikes no depth of root into the heart" (emphasis added). In this and the following judgment of Giovanni's motives, we again find that play on the appearance/reality opposition that characterizes the whole discourse: "By all appreciable signs, they loved." The reader, prepared by the cumulative effect of the questions about Giovanni's motives, automatically translates this sentence into another suggestion that Giovanni only *appears* to love but is really incapable of such depth of feeling.

All that seems good in the relationship is actually a measure of Beatrice's nature, not Giovanni's. The narrator tells the reader that Giovanni's confidence in Beatrice results from "the necessary force of her high attributes" rather than "any deep and generous faith, on his part." Here the focus of the discourse begins shifting from a neutral description of motives to a moral judgment of character. The tale quickly provides the reader with a more damaging evaluation of Giovanni. About to test for himself whether Beatrice is poisonous, "Giovanni failed not to look at his figure in the mirror; a vanity to be expected in a beautiful young man, yet, as displaying itself at that troubled and feverish moment, the token of a certain shallowness of feeling and insincerity of character." Then, after becoming convinced of her poisonous physical nature, Giovanni shows no trust in Beatrice and forgets all the evidence of her innocent and pure spiritual nature. The narrator gives the reader a clear condemnation of Giovanni in one more variation on the appearance/reality opposition: Giovanni has "recollections which, had Giovanni known how to estimate them, would have assured him that all this ugly mystery was but an earthly illusion, and that, whatever mist of evil might seem to have gathered over her, the real Beatrice was a heavenly angel." But Giovanni was "incapable . . . of such high faith." Beatrice bestows the final judgment (before the reader's) when she says to Giovanni: "Oh, was there not, from the first, more poison in thy nature than in mine?"

The discourse provides this build-up of judgments in order to prepare the reader for the concluding sentence. By this final moment in the structure of response, the reader has learned that Giovanni believes and doubts, acts and does not act, for all the wrong reasons. He is blind to Beatrice's physical poison because of his delusory infatuation, and later the shallowness of these same feelings makes him blind to her true spiritual goodness. Shallowness, vanity, insensitivity, selfishness — these characteristics of Giovanni have been brought out in the text of judgment. When the reader responds to the question posed by the last sentence of the discourse — who is really responsible for Beatrice's death? — he should include Giovanni Guasconti in his answer.

From *Interpretive Conventions:*
The Reader in the Study of American Fiction

Considerations for Critical Thinking and Writing

1. According to Mailloux, how does Hawthorne complicate the reader's response to Giovanni? How did you feel about Giovanni? Did your response to him change as you read?
2. What is Mailloux's final assessment about Giovanni's character? Explain whether you agree or disagree.
3. Read the section on reader-response strategies in "Critical Strategies for Reading." Write an essay that interprets Giovanni's character as you think a feminist reader would describe him (feminist readings are discussed in the same chapter on p. 2009).

MICHAEL TRITT (b. 1950)
"Young Goodman Brown" and the
Psychology of Projection   1986

A recent bibliography of Hawthorne criticism suggests that the four hundred or so articles written about "Young Goodman Brown" "cover an intimidating array of responses that pursue every possible interpretive nuance, from esoteric theological dogma to technically precise but scientifically complex psychoanalytic themes."[1] Despite this wealth of illuminating comment, however, there is still much contention about the meaning of the tale. The psychology underlying Goodman Brown's reaction to his forest experience, for example, still remains puzzling. How exactly does Brown regard his devilish behavior in the forest?

The most common reading of the tale asserts Brown's loss of faith, in himself

---

[1]Lea Newman, *A Reader's Guide to the Short Stories of Nathaniel Hawthorne* (Boston: G. K. Hall, 1979).

and in his fellows. Critics argue that, as a result of his nighttime experience. Brown comes to believe all men corrupt and inevitably evil. Yet there is another possibility. In my view, Brown's bewilderment, and subsequent withdrawal, results from his conviction (however misguided) that he yet remains unfallen. In an attempt to *escape* his guilt-consciousness and the concomitant moral anxiety, Brown projects his guilt onto those around him. While many readers of the tale have acknowledged the extent to which Brown's feeling of his own duplicity colors his nighttime vision and subsequent sense of those around him, none has adequately examined this phenomenon of coloring (projection) as it is defined by psychology.

Readers typically assert that the horrors of Brown's dream vision and his criticism of others derive from the projection of Brown's subconscious guilt. Nevertheless, these same readers still conceive of Brown as *self-consciously* guilt-ridden, and thus desperate, at the tale's end. Yet the process of projection classically functions to "defend" the individual from his anxiety. The result is that while guilt persists, it persists only at the *subconscious* level. Brown's desperation at the end of the story is not primarily, then, the result of a guilt-consciousness, but rather originates with a guilt he is unable to recognize and admit. Conceiving of himself as unscathed, Brown obsessively locates the source of his anxieties in those around him. . . .

Brown consistently focuses his attention outwards. There is loathing, but it is manifestly not self-loathing. The congregation, from which *he* is clearly withdrawn, sings an anthem of sin, while it is the minister, speaking from the pulpit, who is the "gray blasphemer." Unlike Hooper, in "The Minister's Black Veil," Brown never glimpses his own image as something fearful and iniquitous.

Brown's focus outward suggests a psychological design, though as Hawthorne describes elsewhere [in *The House of the Seven Gables*], it is "only . . . such instinctive design as gives no account of itself to the intellect." Brown's compulsive condemnation of others, along with his consistent denial of his own culpability, illustrates a classically defined case of projection.

> A person is projecting when he ascribes to another person a trait or desire of his own that would be painful for his ego to admit. Since the act of projecting is an *unconscious mechanism,* it is not communicated to others *nor is it even recognized* as a projection by the person himself. Projection in the Freudian sense, therefore, represents a misperception or a false perception. The fault or the unsavory desire or trait is still in the person's unconscious; it is not in the person or object on whom the projection is made.[2]

The "misperception" or "false perception" is manifest in two respects. First, Brown locates his own evil in others. Second, and of greater significance to my argument, Brown believes himself to be without guilt, even though in fact, "the unsavory desire or trait is still in . . . [his] subconscious." Although Brown's lifetime obsession with the guilt of others functions, then, as a "mechanism of

[2]Harold H. Anderson and Gladys L. Anders, Eds., *An Introduction to Projective Techniques and Other Devices for Understanding the Dynamics of Human Behavior* (Englewood Cliffs: Prentice-Hall, 1951), p. 3. (Italics mine.)

defense . . . keeping off dangers" ". . . at all costs,"[3] *inevitably,* the original anxiety remains festering within.

The type of devilish behavior Brown exhibits in the forest would be sinister enough to shake most anyone's moral self-confidence, but for Brown, the Puritan, such devilishness presents an irreparable shock. Reeling from his self-revelation, he "inadvertently . . . create[s] for himself . . . the distorted and fantastic people"[4] who become his neighbors. "Then did Goodman Brown turn pale, dreading, lest the roof should thunder down. . . ." Freud suggests that "not infrequently . . . the ego . . . has paid too high a price for the services which these [defense] mechanisms render."[5] Such is the unfortunate example of Goodman Brown, who inevitably pays with a terrible isolation, becoming a "stern, a sad, a darkly meditative, a distrustful . . . man. . . ."

From *Studies in Short Fiction*

[3]Sigmund Freud, "Analysis Terminable and Interminable," *The Complete Works of Sigmund Freud* (London: The Hogarth Press, 1974), Vol. 23, p. 237.
[4]Henry P. Laughlin, *The Ego and Its Defenses* (New York: Appleton-Century-Crofts, 1970), p. 233.
[5]Freud, p. 237.

Considerations for Critical Thinking and Writing

1. How does Tritt's interpretation differ from those of the other critics he cites? How does Tritt's use of the idea of psychological projection affect his reading of Brown at the end of the story?
2. Despite Tritt's noting that Hooper, in "The Minister's Black Veil," "glimpses his own image as something fearful and iniquitous," how might Hooper's response to his community also be seen as a form of projection?
3. In the Perspective on p. 297, Melville describes Hawthorne as someone who "says NO! in thunder; but the Devil himself cannot make him say *yes*." In an essay consider whether Melville's description of Hawthorne can be accurately applied to Brown. Is a heroic view of Brown compatible with Tritt's psychological reading of his character?

TWO COMPLEMENTARY CRITICAL READINGS

JUDITH FETTERLEY (b. 1938)
A Feminist Reading of "The Birthmark"   1978

It is testimony at once to Hawthorne's ambivalence, his seeking to cover with one hand what he uncovers with the other; and to the pervasive sexism of our culture that most readers would describe "The Birthmark" as a story of failure rather than as the success story it really is — the demonstration of how to murder your wife and get away with it. It is, of course, possible to read "The Birthmark" as a story of misguided idealism, a tale of the unhappy consequences of man's nevertheless worthy passion for perfecting and transcending nature; and this is the reading usually given it. This reading, however, ignores the significance of the form idealism takes in the story. It is not irrelevant that "The Birthmark" is about a man's desire to perfect his wife, nor is it accidental that the consequence of this idealism is the wife's death. In fact, "The Birthmark" provides a brilliant analysis of the sexual politics of idealization and a brilliant exposure of the mechanisms whereby hatred can be disguised as love, neurosis can be disguised as science, murder can be disguised as idealization, and success can be disguised as failure. Thus, Hawthorne's insistence in his story on the metaphor of disguise serves as both warning and clue to a feminist reading. . . .

One cannot imagine this story in reverse — that is, a woman's discovering an obsessive need to perfect her husband and deciding to perform experiments on him — nor can one imagine the story being about a man's conceiving such an obsession for another man. It is woman, and specifically woman as wife, who elicits the obsession with imperfection and the compulsion to achieve perfection, just as it is man, and specifically man as husband, who is thus obsessed and compelled. In addition, it is clear from the summary that the imagined perfection is purely physical. Aylmer is not concerned with the quality of Georgiana's character or with the state of her soul, for he considers her "fit for heaven without tasting death." Rather, he is absorbed in her physical appearance, and perfection for him is equivalent to physical beauty. Georgiana is an exemplum of woman as beautiful object, reduced to and defined by her body. . . . "The Birthmark" demonstrates the fact that the idealization of women has its source in a profound hostility toward women and that it is at once a disguise for this hostility and the fullest expression of it. . . .

. . . Unable to accept himself for what he is, Aylmer constructs a mythology of science and adopts the character of a scientist to disguise his true nature and to hide his real motives, from himself as well as others. As a consequence, he acquires a way of acting out these motives without in fact having to be aware of them. One might describe "The Birthmark" as an exposé of science because it demonstrates the ease with which science can be invoked to conceal highly subjective motives. "The Birthmark" is an exposure of the realities that underlie the scientist's posture of objectivity and rationality and the claims of science to operate in an amoral and value-free world. Pale Aylmer, the intellectual scientist, is a mask for the brutish, earthy, soot-smeared Aminadab, just as the mythology of scientific research and objectivity finally masks murder, disguising Georgiana's death as just one more experiment that failed. . . .

The implicit feminism in "The Birthmark" is considerable. On one level the story is a study of sexual politics, of the powerlessness of women and of the psychology which results from that powerlessness. Hawthorne dramatizes the fact that woman's identity is a product of men's responses to her: "It must not be concealed, however, that the impression wrought by this fairy sign manual varied exceedingly, according to the difference of temperament in the beholders." To those who love Georgiana, her birthmark is evidence of her beauty; to those who envy or hate her, it is an object of disgust. It is Aylmer's repugnance for the birthmark that makes Georgiana blanch, thus causing the mark to emerge as a sharply-defined blemish against the whiteness of her cheek. Clearly, the birthmark takes on its character from the eye of the beholder. And just as clearly Georgiana's attitude toward her birthmark varies in response to different observers and definers. Her self-image derives from internalizing the attitudes toward her of the man or men around her. Since what surrounds Georgiana is an obsessional attraction expressed as a total revulsion, the result is not surprising: continual self-consciousness that leads to a pervasive sense of shame and a self-hatred that terminates in an utter readiness to be killed. "The Birthmark" demonstrates the consequences to women of being trapped in the laboratory of man's mind, the object of unrelenting scrutiny, examination, and experimentation.

From *The Resisting Reader:*
A Feminist Approach to American Fiction

Considerations for Critical Thinking and Writing

1. In what sense does Fetterley regard "The Birthmark" as a "success story"? How does her feminist perspective inform this view?
2. Why do you think Fetterley argues that it is impossible to imagine reversing the male-female roles in this story?
3. How does Fetterley make a case for reading the story as an "exposé of science"? Explain why science is described as an essentially male activity.
4. Although Fetterley does not include "The Minister's Black Veil" in her discussion, might it not be argued that it too harbors an "implicit feminism"? Write an analysis of the Reverend Mr. Hooper from a feminist perspective.

JAMES QUINN (b. 1937) AND
ROSS BALDESSARINI (b. 1937)
A Psychological Reading of "The Birthmark"   1981

Hawthorne's art in the creation of character in many ways anticipates modern psychoanalytic psychology. As a literary psychologist, he excels at revealing unconscious sources of obsessed behavior. In "The Birthmark," Aylmer, a scientist whose ambition may be to control nature, provides an exceptionally good example of an obsessive character. He is obsessed with imperfection in human nature and is unable to achieve a mature human relationship. . . .

. . . What has happened to make Aylmer feel this way? What indeed ails him? The question is a natural one, but useless. Hawthorne does not supply an answer and by this omission seems to suggest that insights into human behavior are likely to be subjective, imperfect, unsatisfying. What is important is not the cause of obsessive thought or compulsive behavior but the effects.

The dramatic situation here is that Aylmer, by marrying Georgiana, is forced to deal with a conflict between his earlier, somewhat distant view of her as an intellectualized feminine ideal and her present tangible reality. Clearly one meaning of the red hand is a mark of her accessibility to touch, that is, of her sexuality. It also includes conflict between personal idealization and reality — a classical and ubiquitous obsessional neurotic conflict. While Aylmer's struggle is virtually universal, his fixation on Georgiana's blemish approaches a symptom that is considered characteristic of obsessive-compulsive neurosis in modern-day psychopathological terms.[1] The function of such neurotic symptoms in the psychic economy is to inhibit intolerable anxiety by focusing on an isolated and somewhat concrete representation so as to avoid a larger emotional conflict.

The psychoanalytic theorist Fenichel has written, "Many compulsive neurotics have to worry very much about small and apparently insignificant things. In analysis, these small things turn out to be substitutes for important ones."[2] And further: "Compulsive neurotics try to use external objects for the solution or relief of their inner conflicts" (p. 293). As "the compulsive neurotic tends . . . to extend the range of his symptoms . . ." (p. 294), so Aylmer's reaction to the birthmark grew "more and more intolerable with every moment of their . . . lives," presumably as a result of Georgiana's unavoidable presence. What at first seemed a trifling matter "so connected itself with innumerable trains of thought and modes of feeling that it became the *central point of all*" [stress added]. Like Parson Hooper [in "The Minister's Black Veil"], Aylmer is another Hawthornian victim of morbid forces, largely internal, beyond his control. Surely Aylmer's aversion owes its intensity and its obsessive character precisely to the fact that it is not accessible to conscious examination.[3] . . .

He draws distinct lines between good and bad as does . . . Young Goodman Brown, who must see Faith, indeed all women, as Madonna or whore and who therefore remains immature and uncommitted. Aylmer, too, is like an adolescent, unable to find a point of equilibrium between two poles of thought, not realizing that "to be is to be imperfect, that the price of human existence is imperfection."[4]

An ironic aspect of such obsessed and morbid behavior so often seen in Hawthorne's works is that the more one struggles to attain perfection or to retain an unreasonable fixed idea, the more one is caught up in dealing with its opposite — imperfection and destruction. . . .

Up to this point we have been concerned with Hawthorne's presentation of Aylmer as one more neurotic and troubled obsessional soul. More important, however, is Aylmer's dramatically exaggerated representation of a more general

[1]Most of the characteristics of the illness can be found in the official definition of obsessive-compulsive disorder stated in the third edition of the American Psychiatric Association's (1980) *Diagnostic and Statistical Manual of Mental Disorders* (DSM-III):

The essential features are recurrent obsessions and/or compulsions. Obsessions are defined as recurrent, persistent ideas, thoughts, images or impulses which are ego-alien; that is, they are not experienced as voluntarily produced, but rather as ideas that invade the field of consciousness. Attempts are made to ignore or suppress them. Compulsions are behaviors which are not experienced as the outcome of the individual's own volition, but are accompanied by both a sense of subjective compulsion and a desire to resist (at least initially). (p. 234)

[2]Otto Fenichel, *The Psychoanalytic Theory of Neurosis* (New York, 1945), p. 290.

[3]In Freudian theory, certain ideas heavily charged or invested with affect or emotion constantly press toward conscious recognition or awareness, and certain impulses toward overt satisfaction or fulfillment. What we note in this tale is something close to "isolation of affect" or suppression and limitation or restriction of a highly charged emotion. The feeling and its source seem to be a form of anxiety, fear of being harmed through intimacy — metaphorically a problem in the category of castration anxiety or fear of being found wanting (already castrated). The idea that the birthmark is a castration symbol has already been suggested by Simon Lesser, *Fiction and the Unconscious*, p. 88.

[4]Terence Martin, *Nathaniel Hawthorne* (New Haven, 1965), p. 70.

struggle to adjust the ideal and the real. Likewise the birthmark can be viewed on more than one level. It is a mark of Georgiana's accessibility to touch, of her sexuality. It is suggestive of the scarlet letter — another public sign of secret and lustful sin, of "putting hands upon" in a sexual sense, of being touched, tainted, having sexuality and womanly characteristics. And, within the Judeo-Christian tradition . . . it seems to Hawthorne to symbolize the fallen and sinful nature of man. In an even wider application, it symbolizes the mortality of all mankind.

We miss the point, however, if we connect the birthmark solely with neurotic conflicts of atypical individuals or even with the hold death has on everyone, for the mark is also connected with sexuality and new life, indeed with aspiration to beauty and achievement and with the joy and energy for living. The importance of Hawthorne's psychological symbol is not the susceptibility of man to sin and death, but the special manner in which the marked woman suffers her fate: it is Aylmer who kills her. When the inward life concentrates narcissistically on self, demonic violence flares up in the lust to control and possess another person. Yet the first to be destroyed is Aylmer himself, who steps out of the procession of life, suffering from an incapacity to accept and integrate human emotions.

From *University of Hartford Studies in Literature:*
A Journal of Interdisciplinary Criticism

Considerations for Critical Thinking and Writing

1. According to Quinn and Baldessarini, why isn't it fruitful to inquire into the causes of Aylmer's obsession? Explain why you agree or disagree with their assessment.
2. How might Aylmer, Reverend Hooper, and Young Goodman Brown all be regarded as exhibiting obsessive behavior?
3. Write an essay that discusses how and why this psychoanalytic reading leads to a focus on Aylmer while Judith Fetterley's feminist reading (p. 302) leads to an emphasis on Georgiana. For a discussion of psychological and feminist readings see Chapter 35, "Critical Strategies for Reading."
4. Explain what you think a psychological reading of Georgiana would make of her character.

JAMES JOYCE (1882–1941)

James Joyce was born in Dublin, Ireland, during a time of political upheaval. The country had endured nearly a century of economic depression and terrible famine, and continued to suffer under what many Irish regarded as British oppression. Irish nationalism and independence movements attempted to counter British economic exploitation and cultural arrogance; Joyce believed the Irish were also unable to free themselves from the Catholic Church's compromises and their own political ineptitude. Joyce grew up in a climate in which ecclesiastical privilege and governmental authority were at once powerful and suspect. Change was in the air but Ireland was slow to be moved by the currents already astir on the continent.

Modernism, as it was developing on the continent, challenged traditional attitudes about God, humanity, and society. Scientific and industrial advances created not only material progress but also tremendous upheaval, which sometimes produced a sense of discontinuity, fragmentation, alienation, and despair. Firm certainties gave way to anxious doubts, and the past was considered more as something to be overcome than as something to revere. Heroic action seemed remote and theatrical to a writer like Joyce, who rejected the use of remarkable historic events in his fiction, preferring instead to focus on the everyday lives of ordinary people trying to make sense of themselves.

Joyce himself came from a middle-class family of more than a dozen children. The family was clearly in decline, and his father's drinking eventually reduced them to poverty. Nevertheless, Joyce received a fine classical education at Jesuit schools, including University College, Dublin. His strict early education was strongly traditional in its Catholicism, but when he entered University College, he rejected both his religion and his national heritage. By the time he took his undergraduate degree in 1902, he was more comfortable casting himself as an alienated writer than as a typical citizen of Dublin, who he thought lived a life of mediocrity, sentimentality, and self-deception. While at college he studied modern languages and taught himself Norwegian so he could read the plays of Henrik Ibsen in their original language (see p. 1517 for Ibsen's *A Doll House*). Joyce responded deeply to Ibsen's dramatizations of troubled individuals who repudiate public morality and social values in their efforts to create lives of integrity amid stifling families, institutions, and cultures.

After graduation Joyce left Dublin for Paris to study medicine, but that career soon ended when he dropped out of the single course for which he had registered. Instead, he wrote poetry, which was eventually published in 1907 as *Chamber Music*. In 1903 he returned to Dublin to be with his mother, then dying of cancer. The next summer he met Nora Barnacle, while she was working in a Dublin boardinghouse. He lived with Nora his entire life, having two children, but he did not marry her until 1931. After leaving Dublin in 1904 to return to the continent, he visited his native city only a few times (the final visit was in 1912), and he lived the rest of his life in Europe. From 1920 until shortly before his death, Joyce settled in Paris, where he enjoyed the stimulation of living amid writers and artists.

Joyce tried earning a living by teaching at a Berlitz school, tutoring, and working in a bank, but mostly he gathered impressions of the world around him — whether in Trieste, Zurich, Rome, or Paris — that he would incorporate into his literary work. His writings, however, were always about life in Ireland rather than the European cities in which he lived. Fortunately, Joyce's talents attracted several patrons who subsidized his income and helped him to publish. Given the publication history of some of his books, he needed financial help.

Joyce's first major publication in fiction was the collection of stories he titled *Dubliners*. An early version of the *Dubliners* manuscript was accepted by a publisher in 1906, but controversies surrounding the book delayed its publication for almost a decade. Because printers as well as publishers at that time were legally responsible for any libelous writings, Joyce's publisher was wary of printing a book that seemed even obliquely sexually suggestive; he described, for example, "a woman changing the position of her legs often." In addition, there was concern that Joyce would offend the British royal family — he described King Edward VII as "a bit of a knockabout" and a heavy drinker. Another worry was that some citizens of Dublin might recognize themselves in the stories and sue for libel. From the perspective of the graphic explicitness of the late twentieth century, these fears seem unwarranted, if not quaint, but they were nonetheless serious and forced Joyce to defend his work repeatedly. He did not regard his stories as offensive, because he believed that they reflected the true details of Irish life. After years of frustrating delays, *Dubliners* was finally published in 1914.

Two years later Joyce published *A Portrait of the Artist as a Young Man,* a novel. Joyce strongly identified with the protagonist, who, like Joyce, rejected custom and tradition. If the price of independence from deadening sensibilities, crass materialism, and a circumscribed life was alienation, then so be it. Joyce believed that if the artist was to see clearly and report what he saw freshly, it was necessary to stand outside the commonplace responses to experience derived from family, church, or country. Although Joyce had problems finding a publisher for his novel, he secured publication in less than two years thanks to help from the poet Ezra Pound.

His next novel, *Ulysses* (1922), ran into serious difficulties. Regarded by many readers as Joyce's masterpiece, this remarkably innovative novel is an account of one day in the life of an Irish Jew named Leopold Bloom, who, despite his small circle of life in Dublin, represents a microcosm of all human experience. *Ulysses* is a literary, historical, philosophical, and psychological odyssey into the world of its characters — and into their minds as well. Joyce's use of a stream-of-consciousness technique revealed the characters' thoughts as they experienced them (see p. 140 for a discussion of this technique). These uninhibited thoughts did not get past censors in the United States until 1933, after a judge ruled in a celebrated court case that the book was not obscene.

Though *Ulysses* is Joyce's most famous book, *Finnegans Wake* (1939) is his most challenging. Even more unconventional and experimental than *Ulysses,* it endlessly plays with language within a fluid dream world in which the characters' experiences evolve into continuously expanding meanings produced through complex allusions and elaborate puns in multiple languages. The novel's plot defies summation but its language warrants exploration, which is perhaps best begun by hearing a recording of Joyce reading aloud from the book. His stylistic innovations had as great an influence on literature as the automobile and the radio did on people's daily lives, when people started covering more ground and hearing many more voices than ever before.

Dubliners is Joyce's quarrel with his native city, and his homage to it. Written between 1904 and 1907, it is the most accessible of Joyce's works. It consists of a series of fifteen stories about characters who struggle with oppressive morality, plodding routines, somber shadows, self-conscious decency, restless desires, and frail gestures toward freedom. These stories contain no conventional high drama or action-filled episodes; instead, they are made up of small, quiet moments that turn out to be important in their characters' lives. Most of the characters are on the brink of discovering something, such as loss, shame, failure, or death. Typically, the protagonist suddenly experiences a deep realization about himself or herself, a truth which is grasped in an ordinary rather than melodramatic moment. Joyce called such a moment — when a character is overcome by a flash of recognition — an *epiphany* and defined it as "a sudden spiritual manifestation, whether in the vulgarity of speech or gesture or in a memorable phase of the mind itself." Hence, even the most commonplace experience might yield a spontaneous insight into the essential nature of a person or situation. Joyce's characters may live ordinary lives cluttered with mundane details, but that is not to say that they live lives of no significance. Indeed, they seem to stumble onto significance when they least expect it.

Joyce weaves his characters' dreams and longings into the texture of Dublin life, a social fabric that appears to limit his characters' options. He once explained to his publisher that his intention in *Dubliners* "was to write a chapter of the moral history of my country," and he focused upon Dublin because that city seemed to him "the center of paralysis." The major causes of his characters' paralysis are transmitted by their family life, Catholicism, economic situations, and their vulnerability to political forces. His characters have lives consisting largely of self-denial and drab duties, but they also have an irrepressible desire for something more — whether it's a young man's longing for an enchanted bazaar ("Araby," p. 310), a dutiful daughter's efforts to run away with her lover ("Eveline," p. 315), an anxious bachelor's uncertainty about an impending marriage ("The Boarding House," p. 319), or a husband's desire for a wife whose past complicates their present life ("The Dead," p. 324). Whatever individual issues and conflicts a protagonist might confront, there is also the city of Dublin, in either the foreground or background, serving as an implicit antagonist.

The next four stories, though independent of one another, reverberate meanings among each other when they are read together. Like the shadows that we see fall in Hawthorne's fiction or the unpredictable southern rhythms that we experience in O'Connor's, Joyce's seemingly uneventful stories startle readers into new, unexpected perceptions.

Chronology

1882   Born on February 2 in Dublin, Ireland.

1888–98 Studies at Jesuit schools in preparation for university.

1898–02 Attends University College, Dublin, another Jesuit school, and graduates with a degree in modern languages.

1902   Studies medicine in Paris but soon abandons it for writing.

1903   Returns to be at his mother's deathbed in Dublin.

1904   Meets Nora Barnacle, with whom he will have two children and live his entire life.

1905   Moves to the Continent to teach at the Berlitz school in Trieste and write.

1907   After working in a bank for a year in Rome, he returns to Trieste; publishes *Chamber Music,* a volume of poems.

1914   Publishes *Dubliners* after eight years of censorship battles.

1916   Publishes *A Portrait of the Artist as a Young Man.*

1917   Has the first of a series of eye operations.

1918   Publishes *Exiles,* a play.

1920   Settles in Paris with his family.

1922   Publishes *Ulysses* amid controversy concerning its alleged obscenity.

1927   Publishes *Pomes Penyeach.*

1931   Marries Nora Barnacle.

1934   Publishes *Colleted Poems.*

1939   Publishes *Finnegans Wake.*

1940   After the German occupation of Paris, the Joyces move to Zurich.

1941   Dies of a perforated ulcer on January 13 at Zurich.

Araby   1914

North Richmond Street, being blind,° was a quiet street except at the hour when the Christian Brothers' School set the boys free. An uninhabited house of two stories stood at the blind end, detached from its neighbors in a square

blind: A dead-end street.

ground. The other houses of the street, conscious of decent lives within them, gazed at one another with brown imperturbable faces.

The former tenant of our house, a priest, had died in the back drawing room. Air, musty from having long been enclosed, hung in all the rooms, and the waste room behind the kitchen was littered with old useless papers. Among these I found a few paper-covered books, the pages of which were curled and damp: *The Abbot,*° by Walter Scott, *The Devout Communicant,*° and *The Memoirs of Vidocq.*° I liked the last best because its leaves were yellow. The wild garden behind the house contained a central apple-tree and a few straggling bushes under one of which I found the late tenant's rusty bicycle pump. He had been a very charitable priest; in his will he had left all his money to institutions and the furniture of his house to his sister.

When the short days of winter came dusk fell before we had well eaten our dinners. When we met in the street the houses had grown somber. The space of sky above us was the color of ever-changing violet and towards it the lamps of the street lifted their feeble lanterns. The cold air stung us and we played till our bodies glowed. Our shouts echoed in the silent street. The career of our play brought us through the dark muddy lanes behind the houses where we ran the gantlet of the rough tribes from the cottages, to the back doors of the dark dripping gardens where odors arose from the ashpits, to the dark odorous stables where a coachman smoothed and combed the horse or shook music from the buckled harness. When we returned to the street light from the kitchen windows had filled the areas. If my uncle was seen turning the corner we hid in the shadow until we had seen him safely housed. Or if Mangan's sister came out on the doorstep to call her brother in to his tea we watched her from our shadow peer up and down the street. We waited to see whether she would remain or go in and, if she remained, we left our shadow and walked up to Mangan's steps resignedly. She was waiting for us, her figure defined by the light from the half-opened door. Her brother always teased her before he obeyed and I stood by the railings looking at her. Her dress swung as she moved her body and the soft rope of her hair tossed from side to side.

Every morning I lay on the floor in the front parlor watching her door. The blind was pulled down within an inch of the sash so that I could not be seen. When she came out on the doorstep my heart leaped. I ran to the hall, seized my books, and followed her. I kept her brown figure always in my eye and, when we came near the point at which our ways diverged, I quickened my pace and passed her. This happened morning after morning. I had never spoken to her, except for a few casual words, and yet her name was like a summons to all my foolish blood.

Her image accompanied me even in places the most hostile to romance. 5 On Saturday evenings when my aunt went marketing I had to go to carry some of the parcels. We walked through the flaring streets, jostled by drunken men and bargaining women, amid the curses of laborers, the shrill litanies of shop-boys who stood on guard by the barrels of pigs' cheeks, the nasal chanting of

The Abbot: A popular historical romance.
The Devout Communicant: Meditations by Pacifus Baker, published in 1873.
The Memoirs of Vidocq: A story based on François Vidocq, chief detective of the Paris police.

street singers, who sang a *come-all-you* about O'Donovan Rossa,° or a ballad about the troubles in our native land. These noises converged in a single sensation of life for me: I imagined that I bore my chalice safely through the throng of foes. Her name sprang to my lips at moments in strange prayers and praises which I myself did not understand. My eyes were often full of tears (I could not tell why) and at times a flood from my heart seemed to pour itself out into my bosom. I thought little of the future. I did not know whether I would ever speak to her or not or, if I spoke to her, how I could tell her of my confused adoration. But my body was like a harp and her words and gestures were like fingers running upon the wires.

One evening I went into the back drawing room in which the priest had died. It was a dark rainy evening and there was no sound in the house. Through one of the broken panes I heard the rain impinge upon the earth, the fine incessant needles of water playing in the sodden beds. Some distant lamp or lighted window gleamed below me. I was thankful that I could see so little. All my senses seemed to desire to veil themselves and, feeling that I was about to slip from them, I pressed the palms of my hands together until they trembled, murmuring: *O love! O love!* many times.

At last she spoke to me. When she addressed the first words to me I was so confused that I did not know what to answer. She asked me was I going to *Araby*. I forget whether I answered yes or no. It would be a splendid bazaar, she said; she would love to go.

— And why can't you? I asked.

While she spoke she turned a silver bracelet round and round her wrist. She could not go, she said, because there would be a retreat that week in her convent. Her brother and two other boys were fighting for their caps and I was alone at the railings. She held one of the spikes, bowing her head towards me. The light from the lamp opposite our door caught the white curve of her neck, lit up her hair that rested there, and, falling, lit up the hand upon the railing. It fell over one side of her dress and caught the white border of a petticoat, just visible as she stood at ease.

— It's well for you, she said. 10

— If I go, I said, I will bring you something.

What innumerable follies laid waste my waking and sleeping thoughts after that evening! I wished to annihilate the tedious intervening days. I chafed against the work of school. At night in my bedroom and by day in the classroom her image came between me and the page I strove to read. The syllables of the word *Araby* were called to me through the silence in which my soul luxuriated and cast an Eastern enchantment over me. I asked for leave to go to the bazaar on Saturday night. My aunt was surprised and hoped it was not some Freemason affair. I answered few questions in class. I watched my master's face pass from amiability to sternness; he hoped I was not beginning to idle. I could not call my wandering thoughts together. I had hardly any patience with the serious work of life which, now that it stood between me and my desire, seemed to me child's play, ugly monotonous child's play.

O'Donovan Rossa (1831–1915): One of the leaders of the Fenian Brotherhood, a secret society devoted to making Ireland free of British rule.

On Saturday morning I reminded my uncle that I wished to go to the bazaar in the evening. He was fussing at the hallstand, looking for the hat-brush, and answered me curtly:

— Yes, boy, I know.

As he was in the hall I could not go into the front parlor and lie at the window. I left the house in bad humor and walked slowly towards the school. The air was pitilessly raw and already my heart misgave me.

When I came home to dinner my uncle had not yet been home. Still it was early. I sat staring at the clock for some time and, when its ticking began to irritate me, I left the room. I mounted the staircase and gained the upper part of the house. The high cold empty gloomy rooms liberated me and I went from room to room singing. From the front window I saw my companions playing below in the street. Their cries reached me weakened and indistinct and, leaning my forehead against the cool glass, I looked over at the dark house where she lived. I may have stood there for an hour, seeing nothing but the brown-clad figure cast by my imagination, touched discreetly by the lamplight at the curved neck, at the hand upon the railings, and at the border below the dress.

When I came downstairs again I found Mrs. Mercer sitting at the fire. She was an old garrulous woman, a pawnbroker's widow, who collected used stamps for some pious purpose. I had to endure the gossip of the tea-table. The meal was prolonged beyond an hour and still my uncle did not come. Mrs. Mercer stood up to go: she was sorry she couldn't wait any longer, but it was after eight o'clock and she did not like to be out late, as the night air was bad for her. When she had gone I began to walk up and down the room, clenching my fists. My aunt said:

— I'm afraid you may put off your bazaar for this night of Our Lord.

At nine o'clock I heard my uncle's latchkey in the hall door. I heard him talking to himself and heard the hallstand rocking when it had received the weight of his overcoat. I could interpret these signs. When he was midway through his dinner I asked him to give me the money to go to the bazaar. He had forgotten.

— The people are in bed and after their first sleep now, he said.

I did not smile. My aunt said to him energetically:

— Can't you give him the money and let him go? You've kept him late enough as it is.

My uncle said he was very sorry he had forgotten. He said he believed in the old saying: *All work and no play makes Jack a dull boy.* He asked me where I was going and, when I had told him a second time he asked me did I know *The Arab's Farewell to His Steed.* When I left the kitchen he was about to recite the opening lines of the piece to my aunt.

I held a florin tightly in my hand as I strode down Buckingham Street towards the station. The sight of the streets thronged with buyers and glaring with gas recalled to me the purpose of my journey. I took my seat in a third-class carriage of a deserted train. After an intolerable delay the train moved out of the station slowly. It crept onward among ruinous houses and over the twinkling river. At Westland Row Station a crowd of people pressed to the carriage doors; but the porters moved them back saying it was a special train for the bazaar. I remained alone in the bare carriage. In a few minutes the train drew up beside an improvised wooden platform. I passed out on to the road and saw by the lighted dial of a clock that it was ten minutes to ten. In front of me was a large building which displayed the magical name.

I could not find any sixpenny entrance and, fearing that the bazaar would 25 be closed, I passed in quickly through a turnstile, handing a shilling to a weary-looking man. I found myself in a big hall girdled at half its height by a gallery. Nearly all the stalls were closed and the greater part of the hall was in darkness. I recognized a silence like that which pervades a church after a service. I walked into the center of the bazaar timidly. A few people were gathered about the stalls which were still open. Before a curtain, over which the words *Café Chantant*° were written in colored lamps, two men were counting money on a salver. I listened to the fall of the coins.

Remembering with difficulty why I had come I went over to one of the stalls and examined porcelain vases and flowered tea-sets. At the door of the stall a young lady was talking and laughing with two young gentlemen. I remarked their English accents and listened vaguely to their conversation.

— O, I never said such a thing!

— O, but you did!

— O, but I didn't!

— Didn't she say that? 30

— Yes. I heard her.

— O, there's a . . . . fib!

Observing me the young lady came over and asked me did I wish to buy anything. The tone of her voice was not encouraging; she seemed to have spoken to me out of a sense of duty. I looked humbly at the great jars that stood like eastern guards at either side of the dark entrance to the stall and murmured:

— No, thank you.

The young lady changed the position of one of the vases and went back to 35 the two young men. They began to talk of the same subject. Once or twice the young lady glanced at me over her shoulder.

I lingered before her stall, though I knew my stay was useless, to make my interest in her wares seem the more real. Then I turned away slowly and walked down the middle of the bazaar. I allowed the two pennies to fall against the sixpence in my pocket. I heard a voice call from one end of the gallery that the light was out. The upper part of the hall was now completely dark.

Gazing into the darkness I saw myself as a creature driven and derided by vanity; and my eyes burned with anguish and anger.

Considerations for Critical Thinking and Writing

1. What tone is established in the first few paragraphs by the description of the narrator's house on North Richmond Street?
2. What are the narrator's feelings about life in Dublin? How do they compare with his feelings about the bazaar? How significant are the story's settings?
3. How does the narrator feel about Mangan's sister? What do these feelings reveal about the narrator's character?
4. How do the religious images in the story contribute to an understanding of the narrator?

Café Chantant: A combination coffeehouse and music hall.

5. What is the conflict? Is it resolved?
6. What is the symbolic significance of Araby? How does this symbol contribute to the theme?
7. Consider the story's point of view. Is there any irony in the way the narrator's story is told?
8. Examine the diction used by the narrator. How does the narrator's choice of words indicate how he sees his life?
9. Why does the narrator feel "anguish and anger" at the end of the story? What has he learned about himself?
10. Why do you think Joyce has the narrator notice that the young lady and two young gentlemen who converse in the bazaar stall have "English accents" (para. 26)?

Connections to Other Selections

1. Write an essay that compares what the protagonists learn about themselves in "Araby" and John Updike's "A & P" (p. 485).
2. Compare the points of view used in "Araby" and Ralph Ellison's "Battle Royal" (p. 187). In an essay discuss how point of view is central to the themes in each story.

Eveline   1914

   She sat at the window watching the evening invade the avenue. Her head was leaned against the window curtains and in her nostrils was the odor of dusty cretonne. She was tired.

   Few people passed. The man out of the last house passed on his way home; she heard his footsteps clacking along the concrete pavement and afterwards crunching on the cinder path before the new red houses. One time there used to be a field there in which they used to play every evening with other people's children. Then a man from Belfast bought the field and built houses in it — not like their little brown houses but bright brick houses with shining roofs. The children of the avenue used to play together in that field — the Devines, the Waters, the Dunns, little Keogh the cripple, she and her brothers and sisters. Ernest, however, never played: he was too grown up. Her father used often to hunt them in out of the field with his blackthorn stick; but usually little Keogh used to keep *nix* and call out when he saw her father coming. Still they seemed to have been rather happy then. Her father was not so bad then; and besides, her mother was alive. That was a long time ago; she and her brothers and sisters were all grown up; her mother was dead. Tizzie Dunn was dead, too, and the Waters had gone back to England. Everything changes. Now she was going to go away like the others, to leave her home.

   Home! She looked round the room, reviewing all its familiar objects which she had dusted once a week for so many years, wondering where on earth all the dust came from. Perhaps she would never see again those familiar objects from which she had never dreamed of being divided. And yet during all those years she had never found out the name of the priest whose yellowing photograph hung on the wall above the broken harmonium beside the colored print of the promises made to Blessed Margaret Mary Alacoque. He had been a school friend of her father. Whenever he showed the photograph to a visitor her father used to pass it with a casual word:

— He is in Melbourne now.

She had consented to go away, to leave her home. Was that wise? She tried ₅ to weigh each side of the question. In her home anyway she had shelter and food; she had those whom she had known all her life about her. Of course she had to work hard both in the house and at business. What would they say of her in the Stores when they found out that she had run away with a fellow? Say she was a fool, perhaps; and her place would be filled up by advertisement. Miss Gavan would be glad. She had always had an edge on her, especially whenever there were people listening.

— Miss Hill, don't you see these ladies are waiting?

— Look lively, Miss Hill, please.

She would not cry many tears at leaving the Stores.

But in her new home, in a distant unknown country, it would not be like that. Then she would be married — she, Eveline. People would treat her with respect then. She would not be treated as her mother had been. Even now, though she was over nineteen, she sometimes felt herself in danger of her father's violence. She knew it was that that had given her the palpitations. When they were growing up he had never gone for her, like he used to go for Harry and Ernest, because she was a girl; but latterly he had begun to threaten her and say what he would do to her only for her dead mother's sake. And now she had nobody to protect her. Ernest was dead and Harry, who was in the church decorating business, was nearly always down somewhere in the country. Besides, the invariable squabble for money on Saturday nights had begun to weary her unspeakably. She always gave her entire wages — seven shillings — and Harry always sent up what he could but the trouble was to get any money from her father. He said she used to squander the money, that she had no head, that he wasn't going to give her his hard-earned money to throw about the streets, and much more, for he was usually fairly bad of a Saturday night. In the end he would give her the money and ask her had she any intention of buying Sunday's dinner. Then she had to rush out as quickly as she could and do her marketing, holding her black leather purse tightly in her hand as she elbowed her way through the crowds and returning home late under her load of provisions. She had hard work to keep the house together and to see that the two young children who had been left to her charge went to school regularly and got their meals regularly. It was hard work — a hard life — but now that she was about to leave it she did not find it a wholly undesirable life.

She was about to explore another life with Frank. Frank was very kind, ₁₀ manly, open-hearted. She was to go away with him by the night-boat to be his wife and to live with him in Buenos Aires where he had a home waiting for her. How well she remembered the first time she had seen him; he was lodging in a house on the main road where she used to visit. It seemed a few weeks ago. He was standing at the gate, his peaked cap pushed back on his head and his hair tumbled forward over a face of bronze. Then they had come to know each other. He used to meet her outside the Stores every evening and see her home. He took her to see *The Bohemian Girl* and she felt elated as she sat in an unaccustomed part of the theater with him. He was awfully fond of music and sang a little. People knew that they were courting and, when he sang about the lass that loves a sailor, she always felt pleasantly confused. He used to call her Poppens out of fun. First of all it had been an excitement for her to have a fellow and then she had begun to like him. He had tales of distant countries. He had started as a deck boy at a pound a month on a ship of the Allan Line going out to Canada. He told her the names of the ships he had been on and the names of the different services. He had sailed through the Straits of Magellan and he told her stories of the terrible Patagonians. He had fallen on his feet in Buenos Aires, he said, and had come over to the old country just for a holiday. Of course, her father had found out the affair and had forbidden her to have anything to say to him.

— I know these sailor chaps, he said.

One day he had quarreled with Frank and after that she had to meet her lover secretly.

The evening deepened in the avenue. The white of two letters in her lap grew indistinct. One was to Harry; the other was to her father. Ernest had been her favorite but she liked Harry too. Her father was becoming old lately, she noticed; he would miss her. Sometimes he could be very nice. Not long before, when she had been laid up for a day, he had read her out a ghost story and made toast for her at the fire. Another day, when their mother was alive, they had all gone for a picnic to the Hill of Howth. She remembered her father putting on her mother's bonnet to make the children laugh.

Her time was running out but she continued to sit by the window, leaning her head against the window curtain, inhaling the odor of dusty cretonne. Down far in the avenue she could hear a street organ playing. She knew the air. Strange that it should come that very night to remind her of the promise to her mother, her promise to keep the home together as long as she could. She remembered the last night of her mother's illness; she was again in the close dark room at the other side of the hall and outside she heard a melancholy air of Italy. The organ-player had been ordered to go away and given sixpence. She remembered her father strutting back into the sickroom saying:

— Damned Italians! coming over here!   15

As she mused the pitiful vision of her mother's life laid its spell on the very quick of her being — that life of commonplace sacrifices closing in final craziness. She trembled as she heard again her mother's voice saying constantly with foolish insistence:

— Derevaun Seraun! Derevaun Seraun!°

She stood up in a sudden impulse of terror. Escape! She must escape! Frank would save her. He would give her life, perhaps love, too. But she wanted to live. Why should she be unhappy? She had a right to happiness. Frank would take her in his arms, fold her in his arms. He would save her.

She stood among the swaying crowd in the station at the North Wall. He held her hand and she knew that he was speaking to her, saying something about the passage over and over again. The station was full of soldiers with brown baggages. Through the wide doors of the sheds she caught a glimpse of the

---

Derevaun Seraun!: "The end of pleasure is pain!" (Gaelic).

black mass of the boat, lying in beside the quay wall, with illumined portholes. She answered nothing. She felt her cheek pale and cold and, out of a maze of distress, she prayed to God to direct her, to show her what was her duty. The boat blew a long mournful whistle into the mist. If she went, tomorrow she would be on the sea with Frank, steaming toward Buenos Aires. Their passage had been booked. Could she still draw back after all he had done for her? Her distress awoke a nausea in her body and she kept moving her lips in silent fervent prayer.

A bell clanged upon her heart. She felt him seize her hand: 20
— Come!

All the seas of the world tumbled about her heart. He was drawing her into them: he would drown her. She gripped with both hands at the iron railing.
— Come!

No! No! No! It was impossible. Her hands clutched the iron in frenzy. Amid the seas she sent a cry of anguish!
— Eveline! Evvy!   25

He rushed beyond the barrier and called to her to follow. He was shouted at to go on but he still called to her. She set her white face to him, passive, like a helpless animal. Her eyes gave him no sign of love or farewell or recognition.

Considerations for Critical Thinking and Writing

1. Describe the character of Eveline. What do you think she looks like? Though there are no physical details about her in the story, write a one-page description of her as you think she would appear at the beginning of the story looking out the window.
2. Describe the physical setting of Eveline's home. How does she feel about living at home?
3. What sort of relationship does Eveline have with her father? Describe the range of her feelings toward him.
4. How is Frank characterized? Why does Eveline's father forbid them to see each other?
5. Why does thinking of her mother make Eveline want to "escape"?
6. Before she meets him at the dock, how does Eveline expect Frank to change her life?
7. Why doesn't she go with Frank to Buenos Aires?
8. What associations do you have about Buenos Aires? What symbolic value does this Argentine city have in the story?
9. Read carefully the water imagery in the final paragraphs of the story. How does this imagery help to suggest Eveline's reasons for not leaving with Frank?
10. Explain why you agree or disagree with Eveline's decision.
11. Write a one-page physical description of Eveline as you think she would be thirty years after her decision to remain at home.

Connections to Other Selections

1. How does Eveline's response to her life at home compare with that of the narrator in "Araby" (p. 310)? Write an essay that explores the similarities and differences in their efforts to escape to something better.
2. Write an essay about the meaning of "home" to the protagonists in "Eveline" and Ernest Hemingway's "Soldier's Home" (p. 125).

Mrs. Mooney was a butcher's daughter. She was a woman who was quite able to keep things to herself: a determined woman. She had married her father's foreman and opened a butcher's shop near Spring Gardens. But as soon as his father-in-law was dead Mr. Mooney began to go to the devil. He drank, plundered the till, ran headlong into debt. It was no use making him take the pledge: he was sure to break out again a few days after. By fighting his wife in the presence of customers and by buying bad meat he ruined his business. One night he went for his wife with the cleaver and she had to sleep in a neighbor's house.

After that they lived apart. She went to the priest and got a separation from him with care of the children. She would give him neither money nor food nor house-room; and so he was obliged to enlist himself as a sheriff's man. He was a shabby stooped little drunkard with a white face and a white moustache and white eyebrows, penciled above his little eyes, which were pink-veined and raw; and all day long he sat in the bailiff's room, waiting to be put on a job. Mrs. Mooney, who had taken what remained of her money out of the butcher business and set up a boarding house in Hardwicke Street, was a big imposing woman. Her house had a floating population made up of tourists from Liverpool and the Isle of Man and, occasionally, *artistes* from the music halls. Its resident population was made up of clerks from the city. She governed her house cunningly and firmly, knew when to give credit, when to be stern, and when to let things pass. All the resident young men spoke of her as *The Madam*.

Mrs. Mooney's young men paid fifteen shillings a week for board and lodgings (beer or stout at dinner excluded). They shared in common tastes and occupations and for this reason they were very chummy with one another. They discussed with one another the chances of favorites and outsiders. Jack Mooney, the Madam's son, who was clerk to a commission agent in Fleet Street, had the reputation of being a hard case. He was fond of using soldier's obscenities: usually he came home in the small hours. When he met his friends he had always a good one to tell them and he was always sure to be on to a good thing — that is to say, a likely horse or a likely *artiste*. He was also handy with the mits and sang comic songs. On Sunday nights there would often be a reunion in Mrs. Mooney's front drawing room. The music-hall *artistes* would oblige; and Sheridan played waltzes and polkas and vamped accompaniments. Polly Mooney, the Madam's daughter, would also sing. She sang:

> *I'm a . . . naughty girl.*
> *You needn't sham:*
> *You know who I am.*

Polly was a slim girl of nineteen, she had light soft hair and a small full mouth. Her eyes, which were gray with a shade of green through them, had a habit of glancing upwards when she spoke with anyone, which made her look like a little perverse madonna. Mrs. Mooney had first sent her daughter to be a typist in a corn-factor's office but, as a disreputable sheriff's man used to come every other day to the office, asking to be allowed to say a word to his daughter, she had taken her daughter home again and set her to do housework. As Polly was very lively the intention was to give her the run of the young men. Besides, young men like to feel that there is a young woman not very far away. Polly, of course, flirted with the young men but Mrs. Mooney, who was a shrewd judge, knew that the young men were only passing the time away: none of them meant business. Things went on so for a long time and Mrs. Mooney began to think of sending Polly back to typewriting when she noticed that something was going on between Polly and one of the young men. She watched the pair and kept her own counsel.

Polly knew that she was being watched, but still her mother's persistent 5 silence could not be misunderstood. There had been no open complicity between mother and daughter, no open understanding but, though people in the house began to talk of the affair, still Mrs. Mooney did not intervene. Polly began to grow a little strange in her manner and the young man was evidently perturbed. At last, when she judged it to be the right moment, Mrs. Mooney intervened. She dealt with moral problems as a cleaver deals with meat: and in this case she had made up her mind.

It was a bright Sunday morning of early summer, promising heat, but with a fresh breeze blowing. All the windows of the boarding house were open and the lace curtains ballooned gently towards the street beneath the raised sashes. The belfry of George's Church sent out constant peals and worshippers, singly or in groups, traversed the little circus before the church, revealing their purpose by their self-contained demeanor no less than by the little volumes in their gloved hands. Breakfast was over in the boarding house and the table of the breakfast room was covered with plates on which lay yellow streaks of eggs with morsels of bacon fat and bacon rind. Mrs. Mooney sat in the straw armchair and watched the servant Mary remove the breakfast things. She made Mary collect the crusts and pieces of broken bread to help to make Tuesday's bread pudding. When the table was cleared, the broken bread collected, the sugar and butter safe under lock and key, she began to reconstruct the interview which she had had the night before with Polly. Things were as she had suspected: she had been frank in her questions and Polly had been frank in her answers. Both had been somewhat awkward, of course. She had been made awkward by her not wishing to receive the news in too cavalier a fashion or to seem to have connived and Polly had been made awkward not merely because allusions of that kind always made her awkward but also because she did not wish it to be thought that in her wise innocence she had divined the intention behind her mother's tolerance.

Mrs. Mooney glanced instinctively at the little gilt clock on the mantelpiece as soon as she had become aware through her revery that the bells of George's Church had stopped ringing. It was seventeen minutes past eleven: she would have lots of time to have the matter out with Mr. Doran and then catch short twelve at Marlborough Street. She was sure she would win. To begin with she had all the weight of social opinion on her side: she was an outraged mother. She had allowed him to live beneath her roof, assuming that he was a man of honor, and he had simply abused her hospitality. He was thirty-four or thirty-five years of age, so that youth could not be pleaded as his excuse; nor could ignorance be his excuse since he was a man who had seen something of the world. He had simply taken advantage of Polly's youth and inexperience: that was evident. The question was: what reparation would he make?

There must be reparation made in such cases. It is all very well for the man: he can go his ways as if nothing had happened, having had his moment of pleasure, but the girl has to bear the brunt. Some others would be content to patch up such an affair for a sum of money; she had known cases of it. But she would not do so. For her only one reparation could make up for the loss of her daughter's honor: marriage.

She counted all her cards again before sending Mary up to Mr. Doran's room to say that she wished to speak with him. She felt sure she would win. He was a serious young man, not rakish or loud-voiced like the others. If it had been Mr. Sheridan or Mr. Meade or Bantam Lyons her task would have been much harder. She did not think he would face publicity. All the lodgers in the house knew something of the affair; details had been invented by some. Besides, he had been employed for thirteen years in a great Catholic wine-merchant's office and publicity would mean for him, perhaps, the loss of his sit.° Whereas if he agreed all might be well. She knew he had a good screw° for one thing and she suspected he had a bit of stuff put by.

Nearly the half-hour! She stood up and surveyed herself in the pier-glass.   10 The decisive expression of her great florid face satisfied her and she thought of some mothers she knew who could not get their daughters off their hands.

Mr. Doran was very anxious indeed this Sunday morning. He had made two attempts to shave but his hand had been so unsteady that he had been obliged to desist. Three days' reddish beard fringed his jaws and every two or three minutes a mist gathered on his glasses so that he had to take them off and polish them with his pocket handkerchief. The recollection of his confession of the night before was a cause of acute pain to him; the priest had drawn out every ridiculous detail of the affair and in the end had so magnified his sin that he was almost thankful at being afforded a loophole of reparation. The harm was done. What could he do now but marry her or run away? He could not brazen it out. The affair would be sure to be talked of and his employer would be certain to hear of it. Dublin is such a small city: everyone knows everyone else's business. He felt his heart leap warmly in his throat as he heard in his excited imagination old Mr. Leonard calling out in his rasping voice: *Send Mr. Doran here, please.*

All his long years of service gone for nothing! All his industry and diligence thrown away! As a young man he had sown his wild oats, of course; he had boasted of his free-thinking and denied the existence of God to his companions in public houses. But that was all passed and done with . . . nearly. He still bought a copy of *Reynold's Newspaper* every week but he attended his religious duties and for nine-tenths of the year lived a regular life. He had money enough to settle down on; it was not that. But the family would look down on her. First of all there was her disreputable father and then her mother's boarding house was beginning to get a certain fame. He had a notion that he was being had. He could imagine his friends talking of the affair and laughing. She *was* a little vulgar; sometimes she said *I seen* and *If I had've known*. But what would grammar matter if he really loved her? He could not make up his mind whether to like her or despise her for what she had done. Of course, he had done it too.

sit: Situation, slang for job.
screw: Slang for salary.

His instinct urged him to remain free, not to marry. Once you are married you are done for, it said.

While he was sitting helplessly on the side of the bed in shirt and trousers she tapped lightly at his door and entered. She told him all, that she had made a clean breast of it to her mother and that her mother would speak with him that morning. She cried and threw her arms round his neck, saying:

— O, Bob! Bob! What am I to do? What am I to do at all?

She would put an end to herself, she said.   15

He comforted her feebly, telling her not to cry, that it would be all right, never fear. He felt against his shirt the agitation of her bosom.

It was not altogether his fault that it had happened. He remembered well, with the curious patient memory of the celibate, the first casual caresses her dress, her breath, her fingers had given him. Then late one night as he was undressing for bed she had tapped at his door, timidly. She wanted to relight her candle at his for hers had been blown out by a gust. It was her bath night. She wore a loose open combing-jacket of printed flannel. Her white instep shone in the opening of her furry slippers and the blood glowed warmly behind her perfumed skin. From her hands and wrists too as she lit and steadied her candle a faint perfume arose.

On nights when he came in very late it was she who warmed up his dinner. He scarcely knew what he was eating, feeling her beside him alone, at night, in the sleeping house. And her thoughtfulness! If the night was anyway cold or wet or windy there was sure to be a little tumbler of punch ready for him. Perhaps they could be happy together. . . .

They used to go upstairs together on tiptoe, each with a candle, and on the third landing exchange reluctant good-nights. They used to kiss. He remembered well her eyes, the touch of her hand and his delirium. . . .

But delirium passes. He echoed her phrase, applying it to himself: *What* 20 *am I to do?* The instinct of the celibate warned him to hold back. But the sin was there; even his sense of honor told him that reparation must be made for such a sin.

While he was sitting with her on the side of the bed Mary came to the door and said that the missus wanted to see him in the parlor. He stood up to put on his coat and waistcoat, more helpless then ever. When he was dressed he went over to her to comfort her. It would be all right, never fear. He left her crying on the bed and moaning softly: *O my God!*

Going down the stairs his glasses became so dimmed with moisture that he had to take them off and polish them. He longed to ascend through the roof and fly away to another country where he would never hear again of his trouble, and yet a force pushed him downstairs step by step. The implacable faces of his employer and of the Madam stared upon his discomfiture. On the last flight of stairs he passed Jack Mooney who was coming up from the pantry nursing two bottles of *Bass.* They saluted coldly; and the lover's eyes rested for a second or two on a thick bulldog face and a pair of thick short arms. When he reached the foot of the staircase he glanced up and saw Jack regarding him from the door of the return room.

Suddenly he remembered the night when one of the music-hall *artistes,* a little blond Londoner, had made a rather free allusion to Polly. The reunion had been almost broken up on account of Jack's violence. Everyone tried to quiet him. The music-hall *artiste,* a little paler than usual, kept smiling and saying that there was no harm meant: but Jack kept shouting at him that if any fellow tried that sort of a game on with *his* sister he'd bloody well put his teeth down his throat, so he would.

Polly sat for a little time on the side of the bed, crying. Then she dried her eyes and went over to the looking-glass. She dipped the end of the towel in the water jug and refreshed her eyes with the cool water. She looked at herself in profile and readjusted a hairpin above her ear. Then she went back to the bed again and sat at the foot. She regarded the pillows for a long time and the sight of them awakened in her mind secret amiable memories. She rested the nape of her neck against the cool iron bed-rail and fell into a revery. There was no longer any perturbation visible on her face.

She waited on patiently, almost cheerfully, without alarm, her memories 25 gradually giving place to hopes and visions of the future. Her hopes and visions were so intricate that she no longer saw the white pillows on which her gaze was fixed or remembered that she was waiting for anything.

At last she heard her mother calling. She started to her feet and ran to the banisters.

— Polly! Polly!

— Yes, mamma?

— Come down, dear. Mr. Doran wants to speak to you.

Then she remembered what she had been waiting for. 30

Considerations for Critical Thinking and Writing

1. Describe Mrs. Mooney. In what ways does her running of the boarding house reflect her character?
2. Describe the relationship between Polly and her mother. In what sense are they "complicit" in their behavior toward Mr. Doran?
3. What sort of man is Mr. Doran? How is he different from when he was younger?
4. Why does Mrs. Mooney believe that Mr. Doran should marry her daughter?
5. What is the priest's attitude toward Mr. Doran's marrying Polly? How important is the priest's view to Mr. Doran?
6. Why doesn't Mr. Doran want to marry Polly?
7. How does Mr. Doran respond to seeing Jack Mooney on the stairs as Mr. Doran descends to talk with Mrs. Mooney?
8. What is the effect of the final paragraphs' focus on Polly's waiting in the bedroom rather than on the conversation between Mrs. Mooney and Mr. Doran?
9. Write a one-page version of the missing scene in which Mrs. Mooney confronts Mr. Doran.
10. Do you think Mr. Doran says yes or no to marrying Polly? Explain your answer.
11. Assuming that Mr. Doran marries Polly, consider whether his reasons are a significant cause of marriages in the 1990s.
12. Do you think Polly — as well as Mr. Doran — can be seen as a victim of Mrs. Mooney's conniving?

Connections to Other Selections

1. Consider in an essay how alcohol abuse by fathers affects family relationships in Joyce's "The Boarding House," "Eveline" (p. 315), and John Cheever's "Reunion" (p. 460).

2. How is Mr. Doran's decision to marry Polly in "The Boarding House" similar to the protagonist's decision not to marry Frank in "Eveline"?

3. Write an essay that discusses attitudes toward marriage in "The Boarding House" and Kate Chopin's "The Story of an Hour" (p. 12).

The Dead   1914

Lily, the caretaker's daughter, was literally run off her feet. Hardly had she brought one gentleman into the little pantry behind the office on the ground floor and helped him off with his overcoat than the wheezy hall-door bell clanged again and she had to scamper along the bare hallway to let in another guest. It was well for her she had not to attend to the ladies also. But Miss Kate and Miss Julia had thought of that and had converted the bathroom upstairs into a ladies' dressing-room. Miss Kate and Miss Julia were there, gossiping and laughing and fussing, walking after each other to the head of the stairs, peering down over the banisters and calling down to Lily to ask her who had come.

It was always a great affair, the Misses Morkan's annual dance. Everybody who knew them came to it, members of the family, old friends of the family, the members of Julia's choir, any of Kate's pupils that were grown up enough, and even some of Mary Jane's pupils too. Never once had it fallen flat. For years and years it had gone off in splendid style as long as anyone could remember; ever since Kate and Julia, after the death of their brother Pat, had left the house in Stoney Batter and taken Mary Jane, their only niece, to live with them in the dark gaunt house on Usher's Island, the upper part of which they had rented from Mr. Fulham, the cornfactor° on the ground floor. That was a good thirty years ago if it was a day. Mary Jane, who was then a little girl in short clothes, was now the main prop of the household for she had the organ in Haddington Road. She had been through the Academy and gave a pupils' concert every year in the upper room of the Antient Concert Rooms. Many of her pupils belonged to better-class families on the Kingstown and Dalkey line. Old as they were, her aunts also did their share. Julia, though she was quite gray, was still the leading soprano in Adam and Eve's,° and Kate, being too feeble to go about much, gave music lessons to beginners on the old square piano in the back room. Lily, the caretaker's daughter, did housemaid's work for them. Though their life was modest they believed in eating well; the best of everything: diamond-bone sirloins, three-shilling tea, and the best bottled stout. But Lily seldom made a mistake in the orders so that she got on well with her three mistresses. They were fussy, that was all. But the only thing they would not stand was back answers.

Of course they had good reason to be fussy on such a night. And then it was long after ten o'clock and yet there was no sign of Gabriel and his wife.

---

cornfactor: A grain merchant.
Adam and Eve's: A Dublin church.

Besides they were dreadfully afraid that Freddy Malins might turn up screwed.° They would not wish for worlds that any of Mary Jane's pupils should see him under the influence; and when he was like that it was sometimes very hard to manage him. Freddy Malins always came late but they wondered what could be keeping Gabriel: and that was what brought them every two minutes to the banisters to ask Lily had Gabriel or Freddy come.

— O, Mr. Conroy, said Lily to Gabriel when she opened the door for him, Miss Kate and Miss Julia thought you were never coming. Good-night, Mrs. Conroy.

— I'll engage they did, said Gabriel, but they forget that my wife here takes   5
three mortal hours to dress herself.

He stood on the mat, scraping the snow from his goloshes, while Lily led his wife to the foot of the stairs and called out:

— Miss Kate, here's Mrs. Conroy.

Kate and Julia came toddling down the dark stairs at once. Both of them kissed Gabriel's wife, said she must be perished alive, and asked was Gabriel with her.

— Here I am as right as the mail, Aunt Kate! Go on up. I'll follow, called out Gabriel from the dark.

He continued scraping his feet vigorously while the three women went   10
upstairs, laughing, to the ladies' dressing-room. A light fringe of snow lay like a cape on the shoulders of his overcoat and like toecaps on the toes of his goloshes; and, as the buttons of his overcoat slipped with a squeaking noise through the snow-stiffened frieze, a cold fragrant air from out-of-doors escaped from crevices and folds.

— Is it snowing again, Mr. Conroy? asked Lily.

She had preceded him into the pantry to help him off with his overcoat. Gabriel smiled at the three syllables she had given his surname and glanced at her. She was a slim, growing girl, pale in complexion and with hay-colored hair. The gas in the pantry made her look still paler. Gabriel had known her when she was a child and used to sit on the lowest step nursing a rag doll.

— Yes, Lily, he answered, and I think we're in for a night of it.

He looked up at the pantry ceiling, which was shaking with the stamping and shuffling of feet on the floor above, listened for a moment to the piano, and then glanced at the girl, who was folding his overcoat carefully at the end of a shelf.

— Tell me, Lily, he said in a friendly tone, do you still go to school?   15

— O no, sir, she answered. I'm done schooling this year and more.

— O, then, said Gabriel gaily, I suppose we'll be going to your wedding one of these fine days with your young man, eh?

The girl glanced back at him over her shoulder and said with great bitterness:

— The men that is now is only all palaver and what they can get out of you.

Gabriel colored as if he felt he had made a mistake and, without looking   20
at her, kicked off his goloshes and flicked actively with his muffler at his patent-leather shoes.

screwed: Drunk.

He was a stout tallish young man. The high color of his cheeks pushed upwards even to his forehead where it scattered itself in a few formless patches of pale red; and on his hairless face there scintillated restlessly the polished lenses and the bright gilt rims of the glasses which screened his delicate and restless eyes. His glossy black hair was parted in the middle and brushed in a long curve behind his ears where it curled slightly beneath the groove left by his hat.

When he had flicked luster into his shoes he stood up and pulled his waistcoat down more tightly on his plump body. Then he took a coin rapidly from his pocket.

— O Lily, he said, thrusting it into her hands, it's Christmas-time, isn't it? Just . . . here's a little. . . .

He walked rapidly towards the door.

— O no, sir! cried the girl, following him. Really, sir, I wouldn't take it.　25

— Christmas-time! Christmas-time! said Gabriel, almost trotting to the stairs and waving his hand to her in deprecation.

The girl, seeing that he had gained the stairs, called out after him:

— Well, thank you, sir.

He waited outside the drawing-room door until the waltz should finish, listening to the skirts that swept against it and to the shuffling of feet. He was still discomposed by the girl's bitter and sudden retort. It had cast a gloom over him which he tried to dispel by arranging his cuffs and the bows of his tie. Then he took from his waistcoat pocket a little paper and glanced at the headings he had made for his speech. He was undecided about the lines from Robert Browning for he feared they would be above the heads of his hearers. Some quotation that they could recognize from Shakespeare or from the Melodies° would be better. The indelicate clacking of the men's heels and the shuffling of their soles reminded him that their grade of culture differed from his. He would only make himself ridiculous by quoting poetry to them which they could not understand. They would think that he was airing his superior education. He would fail with them just as he had failed with the girl in the pantry. He had taken up a wrong tone. His whole speech was a mistake from first to last, an utter failure.

Just then his aunts and his wife came out of the ladies' dressing room. His　30 aunts were two small plainly dressed old women. Aunt Julia was an inch or so the taller. Her hair, drawn low over the tops of her ears, was gray; and gray also, with darker shadows, was her large flaccid face. Though she was stout in build and stood erect her slow eyes and parted lips gave her the appearance of a woman who did not know where she was or where she was going. Aunt Kate was more vivacious. Her face, healthier than her sister's, was all puckers and creases, like a shriveled red apple, and her hair, braided in the same old-fashioned way, had not lost its ripe nut color.

They both kissed Gabriel frankly. He was their favorite nephew, the son of their dead elder sister, Ellen, who had married T. J. Conroy of the Port and Docks.

— Gretta tells me you're not going to take a cab back to Monkstown tonight, Gabriel, said Aunt Kate.

— No, said Gabriel, turning to his wife, we had quite enough of that last

Melodies: Irish Melodies, lyrics by the poet Thomas Moore (1779–1852).

year, hadn't we? Don't you remember, Aunt Kate, what a cold Gretta got out of it? Cab windows rattling all the way, and the east wind blowing in after we passed Merrion. Very jolly it was. Gretta caught a dreadful cold.

Aunt Kate frowned severely and nodded her head at every word.

— Quite right, Gabriel, quite right, she said. You can't be too careful.   35

— But as for Gretta there, said Gabriel, she'd walk home in the snow if she were let.

Mrs. Conroy laughed.

— Don't mind him, Aunt Kate, she said. He's really an awful bother, what with green shades for Tom's eyes at night and making him do the dumbbells, and forcing Eva to eat the stirabout.° The poor child! And she simply hates the sight of it! . . . O, but you'll never guess what he makes me wear now!

She broke out into a peal of laughter and glanced at her husband, whose admiring and happy eyes had been wandering from her dress to her face and hair. The two aunts laughed heartily too, for Gabriel's solicitude was a standing joke with them.

— Galoshes! said Mrs Conroy. That's the latest. Whenever it's wet underfoot   40 I must put on my goloshes. Tonight even he wanted me to put them on, but I wouldn't. The next thing he'll buy me will be a diving suit.

Gabriel laughed nervously and patted his tie reassuringly while Aunt Kate nearly doubled herself, so heartily did she enjoy the joke. The smile soon faded from Aunt Julia's face and her mirthless eyes were directed towards her nephew's face. After a pause she asked:

— And what are galoshes, Gabriel?

— Galoshes, Julia! exclaimed her sister. Goodness me, don't you know what galoshes are? You wear them over your . . . over your boots, Gretta, isn't it?

— Yes, said Mrs Conroy. Guttapercha° things. We both have a pair now. Gabriel says everyone wears them on the continent.

— O, on the continent, murmured Aunt Julia, nodding her head slowly.   45

Gabriel knitted his brows and said, as if he were slightly angered:

— It's nothing very wonderful but Gretta thinks it very funny because she says the word reminds her of Christy Minstrels.°

— But tell me, Gabriel, said Aunt Kate, with brisk tact. Of course, you've seen about the room. Gretta was saying . . .

— O, the room is all right, replied Gabriel. I've taken one in the Gresham.

— To be sure, said Aunt Kate, by far the best thing to do. And the children,   50 Gretta, you're not anxious about them?

— O, for one night, said Mrs. Conroy. Besides, Bessie will look after them.

— To be sure, said Aunt Kate again. What a comfort it is to have a girl like that, one you can depend on! There's that Lily, I'm sure I don't know what has come over her lately. She's not the girl she was at all.

Gabriel was about to ask his aunt some questions on this point but she broke off suddenly to gaze after her sister who had wandered down the stairs and was craning her neck over the banisters.

---

stirabout: Porridge.
Guttapercha: A rubberlike material.
Christy Minstrels: A troupe of minstrels formed around 1845 by Edwin P. Christy.

— Now, I ask you, she said, almost testily, where is Julia going? Julia! Julia! Where are you going?

Julia, who had gone halfway down one flight, came back and announced 55 blandly:

— Here's Freddy.

At the same moment a clapping of hands and a final flourish of the pianist told that the waltz had ended. The drawing-room door was opened from within and some couples came out. Aunt Kate drew Gabriel aside hurriedly and whispered into his ear:

— Slip down, Gabriel, like a good fellow and see if he's all right, and don't let him up if he's screwed. I'm sure he's screwed. I'm sure he is.

Gabriel went to the stairs and listened over the banisters. He could hear two persons talking in the pantry. Then he recognized Freddy Malins' laugh. He went down the stairs noisily.

— It's such a relief, said Aunt Kate to Mrs. Conroy, that Gabriel is here. I 60 always feel easier in my mind when he's here.... Julia, there's Miss Daly and Miss Power will take some refreshment. Thanks for your beautiful waltz, Miss Daly. It made lovely time.

A tall wizen-faced man, with a stiff grizzled moustache and swarthy skin, who was passing out with his partner said:

— And may we have some refreshment, too, Miss Morkan?

— Julia, said Aunt Kate summarily, and here's Mr. Browne and Miss Furlong. Take them in, Julia, with Miss Daly and Miss Power.

— I'm the man for the ladies, said Mr. Browne, pursing his lips until his moustache bristled and smiling in all his wrinkles. You know, Miss Morkan, the reason they are so fond of me is —

He did not finish his sentence, but, seeing that Aunt Kate was out of earshot, 65 at once led the three young ladies into the back room. The middle of the room was occupied by two square tables placed end to end, and on these Aunt Julia and the caretaker were straightening and smoothing a large cloth. On the sideboard were arrayed dishes and plates, and glasses and bundles of knives and forks and spoons. The top of the closed square piano served also as a sideboard for viands and sweets. At a smaller sideboard in one corner two young men were standing, drinking hop-bitters.

Mr. Browne led his charges thither and invited them all, in jest, to some ladies' punch, hot, strong and sweet. As they said they never took anything strong he opened three bottles of lemonade for them. Then he asked one of the young men to move aside, and, taking hold of the decanter, filled out for himself a goodly measure of whisky. The young men eyed him respectfully while he took a trial sip.

— God help me, he said, smiling, it's the doctor's orders.

His wizened face broke into a broader smile, and the three young ladies laughed in musical echo to his pleasantry, swaying their bodies to and fro, with nervous jerks of their shoulders. The boldest said:

— O, now, Mr. Browne, I'm sure the doctor never ordered anything of the kind.

Mr. Browne took another sip of his whisky and said, with sidling mimicry: 70

— Well, you see, I'm like the famous Mrs. Cassidy, who is reported to have said: *Now, Mary Grimes, if I don't take it, make me take it, for I feel I want it.*

His hot face had leaned forward a little too confidentially and he had assumed a very low Dublin accent so that the young ladies, with one instinct, received his speech in silence. Miss Furlong, who was one of Mary Jane's pupils, asked Miss Daly what was the name of the pretty waltz she had played; and Mr. Browne, seeing that he was ignored, turned promptly to the two young men who were more appreciative.

A red-faced young woman, dressed in pansy, came into the room, excitedly clapping her hands and crying:

— Quadrilles! Quadrilles!°

Close on her heels came Aunt Kate, crying: 75

— Two gentlemen and three ladies, Mary Jane!

— O, here's Mr. Bergin and Mr. Kerrigan, said Mary Jane. Mr. Kerrigan, will you take Miss Power? Miss Furlong, may I get you a partner, Mr. Bergin. O, that'll just do now.

— Three ladies, Mary Jane, said Aunt Kate.

The two young gentlemen asked the ladies if they might have the pleasure, and Mary Jane turned to Miss Daly.

— O, Miss Daly, you're really awfully good, after playing for the last two   80
dances, but really we're so short of ladies tonight.

— I don't mind in the least, Miss Morkan.

— But I've a nice partner for you, Mr. Bartell D'Arcy, the tenor. I'll get him to sing later on. All Dublin is raving about him.

— Lovely voice, lovely voice! said Aunt Kate.

As the piano had twice begun the prelude to the first figure Mary Jane led her recruits quickly from the room. They had hardly gone when Aunt Julia wandered slowly into the room, looking behind her at something.

— What is the matter, Julia? asked Aunt Kate anxiously. Who is it?   85

Julia, who was carrying in a column of table napkins, turned to her sister and said, simply, as if the question had surprised her:

— It's only Freddy, Kate, and Gabriel with him.

In fact right behind her Gabriel could be seen piloting Freddy Malins across the landing. The latter, a young man of about forty, was of Gabriel's size and build, with very round shoulders. His face was fleshy and pallid, touched with color only at the thick hanging lobes of his ears and at the wide wings of his nose. He had coarse features, a blunt nose, a convex and receding brow, tumid and protruded lips. His heavy-lidded eyes and the disorder of his scanty hair made him look sleepy. He was laughing heartily in a high key at a story which he had been telling Gabriel on the stairs and at the same time rubbing the knuckles of his left fist backwards and forwards into his left eye.

— Good evening, Freddy, said Aunt Julia.

Freddy Malins bade the Misses Morkan good evening in what seemed an   90
offhand fashion by reason of the habitual catch in his voice and then, seeing that Mr. Browne was grinning at him from the sideboard, crossed the room on rather shaky legs and began to repeat in an undertone the story he had just told to Gabriel.

— He's not so bad, is he? said Aunt Kate to Gabriel.

Quadrilles: A dance with four couples.

Gabriel's brows were dark but he raised them quickly and answered:

— O no, hardly noticeable.

— Now, isn't he a terrible fellow! she said. And his poor mother made him take the pledge° on New Year's Eve. But come on, Gabriel, into the drawing room.

Before leaving the room with Gabriel she signaled to Mr. Browne by 95 frowning and shaking her forefinger in warning to and fro. Mr. Browne nodded in answer and, when she had gone, said to Freddy Malins:

— Now, then, Teddy, I'm going to fill you out a good glass of lemonade just to buck you up.

Freddy Malins, who was nearing the climax of his story, waved the offer aside impatiently but Mr. Browne, having first called Freddy Malins' attention to a disarray in his dress, filled out and handed him a full glass of lemonade. Freddy Malins's left hand accepted the glass mechanically, his right hand being engaged in the mechanical readjustment of his dress. Mr. Browne, whose face was once more wrinkling with mirth, poured out for himself a glass of whisky while Freddy Malins exploded, before he had well reached the climax of his story, in a kink of high-pitched bronchitic laughter and, setting down his untasted and overflowing glass, began to rub the knuckles of his left fist backwards and forwards into his left eye, repeating words of his last phrase as well as his fit of laughter would allow him.

Gabriel could not listen while Mary Jane was playing her Academy piece, full of runs and difficult passages, to the hushed drawing room. He liked music but the piece she was playing had no melody for him and he doubted whether it had any melody for the other listeners, though they had begged Mary Jane to play something. Four young men, who had come from the refreshment room to stand in the doorway at the sound of the piano, had gone away quietly in couples after a few minutes. The only persons who seemed to follow the music were Mary Jane herself, her hands racing along the keyboard or lifted from it at the pauses like those of a priestess in momentary imprecation, and Aunt Kate standing at her elbow to turn the page.

Gabriel's eyes, irritated by the floor, which glittered with beeswax under the heavy chandelier, wandered to the wall above the piano. A picture of the balcony scene in *Romeo and Juliet* hung there and beside it was a picture of the two murdered princes in the Tower° which Aunt Julia had worked in red, blue, and brown wools when she was a girl. Probably in the school they had gone to as girls that kind of work had been taught, for one year his mother had worked for him as a birthday present a waist coat of purple tabinet, with little foxes' heads upon it, lined with brown satin and having round mulberry buttons. It was strange that his mother had had no musical talent though Aunt Kate used to call her the brains carrier of the Morkan family. Both she and Julia had always seemed a little proud of their serious and matronly sister. Her photograph stood

---

pledge: A promise not to drink.

Tower: The Prince of Wales and the Duke of York were imprisoned in the Tower of London and allegedly put to death on the order of Richard III.

before the pierglass.° She held an open book on her knees and was pointing out something in it to Constantine who, dressed in a man-o'-war suit, lay at her feet. It was she who had chosen the names for her sons for she was very sensible of the dignity of family life. Thanks to her, Constantine was now senior curate in Balbriggan and, thanks to her, Gabriel himself had taken his degree in the Royal University. A shadow passed over his face as he remembered her sullen opposition to his marriage. Some slighting phrases she had used still rankled in his memory; she had once spoken of Gretta as being country cute and that was not true of Gretta at all. It was Gretta who had nursed her during all her last long illness in their house at Monkstown.

He knew that Mary Jane must be near the end of her piece for she was 100 playing again the opening melody with runs of scales after every bar and while he waited for the end the resentment died down in his heart. The piece ended with a trill of octaves in the treble and a final deep octave in the bass. Great applause greeted Mary Jane as, blushing and rolling up her music nervously, she escaped from the room. The most vigorous clapping came from the four young men in the doorway who had gone away to the refreshment room at the beginning of the piece but had come back when the piano had stopped.

Lancers° were arranged. Gabriel found himself partnered with Miss Ivors. She was a frank-mannered talkative young lady, with a freckled face and prominent brown eyes. She did not wear a low-cut bodice and the large brooch which was fixed in the front of her collar bore on it an Irish device.

When they had taken their places she said abruptly:

— I have a crow to pluck with you.

— With me? said Gabriel.

She nodded her head gravely.   105

— What is it? asked Gabriel, smiling at her solemn manner.

— Who is G.C.? answered Miss Ivors, turning her eyes upon him.

Gabriel colored and was about to knit his brows, as if he did not understand, when she said bluntly:

— O, innocent Amy! I have found out that you write for *The Daily Express.* Now, aren't you ashamed of yourself?

— Why should I be ashamed of myself? asked Gabriel, blinking his eyes 110 and trying to smile.

— Well, I'm ashamed of you, said Miss Ivors frankly. To say you'd write for a rag like that. I didn't think you were a West Briton.°

A look of perplexity appeared on Gabriel's face. It was true that he wrote a literary column every Wednesday in *The Daily Express,* for which he was paid fifteen shillings. But that did not make him a West Briton surely. The books he received for review were almost more welcome than the paltry cheque. He loved to feel the covers and turn over the pages of newly printed books. Nearly every day when his teaching in the college was ended he used to wander down the quays to the second-hand booksellers, to Hickey's on Bachelor's Walk, to Webb's or Massey's on Aston's Quay, or to O'Clohissey's in the by-street. He did not know how to meet her charge. He wanted to say that literature was above

pierglass: Mirror.
Lancers: A kind of square dance.
West Briton: A derogatory term used for Irish people more loyal to England than Ireland.

politics. But they were friends of many years' standing and their careers had been parallel, first at the University and then as teachers: he could not risk a grandiose phrase with her. He continued blinking his eyes and trying to smile and murmured lamely that he saw nothing political in writing reviews of books.

When their turn to cross had come he was still perplexed and inattentive. Miss Ivors promptly took his hand in a warm grasp and said in a soft friendly tone:

— Of course, I was only joking. Come, we cross now.

When they were together again she spoke of the University question° and Gabriel felt more at ease. A friend of hers had shown her his review of Browning's poems. That was how she had found out the secret: but she liked the review immensely. Then she said suddenly:

— O, Mr. Conroy, will you come for an excursion to the Aran Isles this summer? We're going to stay there a whole month. It will be splendid out in the Atlantic. You ought to come. Mr. Clancy is coming, and Mr. Kilkelly and Kathleen Kearney. It would be splendid for Gretta too if she'd come. She's from Connacht, isn't she?

— Her people are, said Gabriel shortly.

— But you will come, won't you? said Miss Ivors, laying her warm hand eagerly on his arm.

— The fact is, said Gabriel, I have already arranged to go —

— Go where? asked Miss Ivors.

— Well, you know, every year I go for a cycling tour with some fellows and so —

— But where? asked Miss Ivors.

— Well, we usually go to France or Belgium or perhaps Germany, said Gabriel awkwardly.

— And why do you go to France and Belgium, said Miss Ivors, instead of visiting your own land?

— Well, said Gabriel, it's partly to keep in touch with the languages and partly for a change.

— And haven't you your own language to keep in touch with — Irish? asked Miss Ivors.

— Well, said Gabriel, if it comes to that, you know, Irish is not my language.

Their neighbors had turned to listen to the cross-examination. Gabriel glanced right and left nervously and tried to keep his good humor under the ordeal which was making a blush invade his forehead.

— And haven't you your own land to visit, continued Miss Ivors, that you know nothing of, your own people, and your own country?

— O, to tell you the truth, retorted Gabriel suddenly, I'm sick of my own country, sick of it!

— Why? asked Miss Ivors.

Gabriel did not answer for his retort had heated him.

— Why? repeated Miss Ivors.

They had to go visiting together and, as he had not answered her, Miss Ivors said warmly:

— Of course, you've no answer.

University question: An issue having to do with educational opportunities for Catholics and Protestants.

Gabriel tried to cover his agitation by taking part in the dance with great energy. He avoided her eyes for he had seen a sour expression on her face. But when they met in the long chain he was surprised to feel his hand firmly pressed. She looked at him from under her brows for a moment quizzically until he smiled. Then, just as the chain was about to start again, she stood on tiptoe and whispered into his ear:

— West Briton!

When the lancers were over Gabriel went away to a remote corner of the room where Freddy Malins's mother was sitting. She was a stout feeble old woman with white hair. Her voice had a catch in it like her son's and she stuttered slightly. She had been told that Freddy had come and that he was nearly all right. Gabriel asked her whether she had had a good crossing. She lived with her married daughter in Glasgow and came to Dublin on a visit once a year. She answered placidly that she had had a beautiful crossing and that the captain had been most attentive to her. She spoke also of the beautiful house her daughter kept in Glasgow, and of all the nice friends they had there. While her tongue rambled on Gabriel tried to banish from his mind all memory of the unpleasant incident with Miss Ivors. Of course the girl or woman, or whatever she was, was an enthusiast but there was a time for all things. Perhaps he ought not to have answered her like that. But she had no right to call him a West Briton before people, even in joke. She had tried to make him ridiculous before people, heckling him and staring at him with her rabbit's eyes.

He saw his wife making her way towards him through the waltzing couples. When she reached him she said into his ear:

— Gabriel, Aunt Kate wants to know won't you carve the goose as usual.   140
Miss Daly will carve the ham and I'll do the pudding.

— All right, said Gabriel.

— She's sending in the younger ones first as soon as this waltz is over so that we'll have the tables to ourselves.

— Were you dancing? asked Gabriel.

— Of course I was. Didn't you see me? What words had you with Molly Ivors?

— No words. why? Did she say so?   145

— Something like that. I'm trying to get that Mr. D'Arcy to sing. He's full of conceit, I think.

— There were no words, said Gabriel moodily, only she wanted me to go for a trip to the west of Ireland and I said I wouldn't.

His wife clasped her hands excitedly and gave a little jump.

— O, do go, Gabriel, she cried. I'd love to see Galway again.

— You can go if you like, said Gabriel coldly.   150

She looked at him for a moment, then turned to Mrs. Malins and said:

— There's a nice husband for you, Mrs. Malins.

While she was threading her way back across the room Mrs. Malins, without adverting to the interruption, went on to tell Gabriel what beautiful places there were in Scotland and beautiful scenery. Her son-in-law brought them every year to the lakes and they used to go fishing. Her son-in-law was a splendid fisher. One day he caught a fish, a beautiful big big fish, and the man in the hotel boiled it for their dinner.

Gabriel hardly heard what she said. Now that supper was coming near he began to think again about his speech and about the quotation. When he saw Freddy Malins coming across the room to visit his mother Gabriel left the chair free for him and retired into the embrasure of the window. The room had already cleared and from the back room came the clatter of plates and knives. Those who still remained in the drawing room seemed tired of dancing and were conversing quietly in little groups. Gabriel's warm trembling fingers tapped the cold pane of the window. How cool it must be outside! How pleasant it would be to walk out alone, first along by the river and then through the park! The snow would be lying on the branches of the trees and forming a bright cap on the top of the Wellington Monument. How much more pleasant it would be there than at the supper table!

He ran over the headings of his speech: Irish hospitality, sad memories, the Three Graces, Paris,° the quotation from Browning. He repeated to himself a phrase he had written in his review: *One feels that one is listening to a thought-tormented music.* Miss Ivors had praised the review. Was she sincere? Had she really any life of her own behind all her propagandism? There had never been any ill-feeling between them until that night. It unnerved him to think that she would be at the supper table, looking up at him while he spoke with her critical quizzing eyes. Perhaps she would not be sorry to see him fail in his speech. An idea came into his mind and gave him courage. He would say, alluding to Aunt Kate and Aunt Julia: *Ladies and Gentlemen, the generation which is now on the wane among us may have had its faults but for my part I think it had certain qualities of hospitality, of humor, of humanity, which the new and very serious and hypereducated generation that is growing up around us seems to me to lack.* Very good: that was one for Miss Ivors. What did he care that his aunts were only two ignorant old women?

A murmur in the room attracted his attention. Mr. Browne was advancing from the door, gallantly escorting Aunt Julia, who leaned upon his arm, smiling and hanging her head. An irregular musketry of applause escorted her also as far as the piano and then, as Mary Jane seated herself on the stool, and Aunt Julia, no longer smiling, half turned so as to pitch her voice fairly into the room, gradually ceased. Gabriel recognized the prelude. It was that of an old song of Aunt Julia's — *Arrayed for the Bridal.* Her voice, strong and clear in tone, attacked with great spirit the runs which embellish the air and though she sang very rapidly she did not miss even the smallest of the grace notes. To follow the voice, without looking at the singer's face, was to feel and share the excitement of swift and secure flight. Gabriel applauded loudly with all the others at the close of the song and loud applause was borne in from the invisible supper table. It sounded so genuine that a little color struggled into Aunt Julia's face as she bent to replace in the music stand the old leather-bound songbook that had her initials on the cover. Freddy Malins, who had listened with his head perched sideways to hear her better, was still applauding when everyone else had ceased and talking animatedly to his mother who nodded her head gravely and slowly in acquiescence. At last, when he could clap no more, he stood up suddenly and hurried across the room to Aunt Julia whose hand he seized and held in both

Three Graces, Paris: The Three Graces were goddesses in Greek mythology who dispensed beauty, charm, and grace; Paris was another mythological figure.

his hands, shaking it when words failed him or the catch in his voice proved too much for him.

— I was just telling my mother, he said, I never heard you sing so well, never. No, I never heard your voice so good as it is tonight. Now! Would you believe that now? That's the truth. Upon my word and honor that's the truth. I never heard your voice sound so fresh and so ... so clear and fresh, never.

Aunt Julia smiled broadly and murmured something about compliments as she released her hand from his grasp. Mr Browne extended his open hand towards her and said to those who were near him in the manner of a showman introducing a prodigy to an audience:

— Miss Julia Morkan, my latest discovery!

He was laughing very heartily at this himself when Freddy Malins turned to   160
him and said:

— Well, Browne, if you're serious you might make a worse discovery. All I can say is I never heard her sing half so well as long as I am coming here. And that's the honest truth.

— Neither did I, said Mr. Browne. I think her voice has greatly improved.

Aunt Julia shrugged her shoulders and said with meek pride:

— Thirty years ago I hadn't a bad voice as voices go.

— I often told Julia, said Aunt Kate emphatically, that she was simply thrown   165
away in that choir. But she never would be said by me.

She turned as if to appeal to the good sense of the others against a refractory child while Aunt Julia gazed in front of her, a vague smile of reminiscence playing on her face.

— No, continued Aunt Kate, she wouldn't be said or led by anyone, slaving there in that choir night and day, night and day. Six o'clock on Christmas morning! And all for what?

— Well, isn't it for the honor of God, Aunt Kate? asked Mary Jane, twisting round on the piano-stool and smiling.

Aunt Kate turned fiercely on her niece and said:

— I know all about the honor of God, Mary Jane, but I think it's not at all   170
honorable for the pope to turn out the women out of the choirs that have slaved there all their lives and put little whipper-snappers of boys over their heads. I suppose it is for the good of the Church if the pope does it. But it's not just, Mary Jane, and it's not right.

She had worked herself into a passion and would have continued in defence of her sister for it was a sore subject with her but Mary Jane, seeing that all the dancers had come back, intervened pacifically:

— Now, Aunt Kate, you're giving scandal to Mr. Browne who is of the other persuasion.

Aunt Kate turned to Mr. Browne, who was grinning at this allusion to his religion, and said hastily:

— O, I don't question the pope's being right. I'm only a stupid old woman and I wouldn't presume to do such a thing. But there's such a thing as common everyday politeness and gratitude. And if I were in Julia's place I'd tell that Father Healy straight up to his face. . . .

— And besides, Aunt Kate, said Mary Jane, we really are all hungry and   175
when we are hungry we are all very quarrelsome.

— And when we are thirsty we are also quarrelsome, added Mr. Browne.

— So that we had better go to supper, said Mary Jane, and finish the discussion afterwards.

On the landing outside the drawing room Gabriel found his wife and Mary Jane trying to persuade Miss Ivors to stay for supper. But Miss Ivors, who had put on her hat and was buttoning her cloak, would not stay. She did not feel in the least hungry and she had already overstayed her time.

— But only for ten minutes, Molly, said Mrs. Conroy. That won't delay you.

— To take a pick itself, said Mary Jane, after all your dancing.   180

— I really couldn't, said Miss Ivors.

— I am afraid you didn't enjoy yourself at all, said Mary Jane hopelessly.

— Ever so much, I assure you, said Miss Ivors, but you really must let me run off now.

— But how can you get home? asked Mrs. Conroy.

— O, it's only two steps up the quay.   185

Gabriel hesitated a moment and said:

— If you will allow me, Miss Ivors, I'll see you home if you really are obliged to go.

But Miss Ivors broke away from them.

— I won't hear of it, she cried. For goodness sake go in to your suppers and don't mind me. I'm quite well able to take care of myself.

— Well, you're the comical girl, Molly, said Mrs Conroy frankly.   190

— *Beannacht libh,*° cried Miss Ivors, with a laugh, as she ran down the staircase.

Mary Jane gazed after her, a moody puzzled expression on her face, while Mrs. Conroy leaned over the banisters to listen for the hall door. Gabriel asked himself was he the cause of her abrupt departure. But she did not seem to be in ill humor: she had gone away laughing. He stared blankly down the staircase.

At that moment Aunt Kate came toddling out of the supper room, almost wringing her hands in despair.

— Where is Gabriel? she cried. Where on earth is Gabriel? There's everyone waiting in there, stage to let, and nobody to carve the goose!

— Here I am, Aunt Kate! cried Gabriel, with sudden animation, ready to   195 carve a flock of geese, if necessary.

A fat brown goose lay at one end of the table and at the other end, on a bed of creased paper strewn with sprigs of parsley, lay a great ham, stripped of its outer skin and peppered over with crust crumbs, a meat paper frill round its shin and beside this was a round of spiced beef. Between these two rival ends ran parallel lines of side dishes: two little minsters of jelly, red and yellow, a shallow dish full of blocks of blancmange and red jam, a large green leaf-shaped dish with a stalk-shaped handle, on which lay bunches of purple raisins and peeled almonds, a companion dish on which lay a solid rectangle of Smyrna figs, a dish of custard topped with grated nutmeg, a small bowl full of chocolates and sweets wrapped in gold and silver papers, and a glass vase in which stood some tall celery stalks. In the center of the table there stood, as sentries to a

---

Beannacht libh: "Good-by," used as a blessing (Gaelic).

fruit stand which upheld a pyramid of oranges and American apples, two squat old-fashioned decanters of cut glass, one containing port and the other dark sherry. On the closed square piano a pudding in a huge yellow dish lay in waiting and behind it were three squads of bottles of stout and ale and minerals, drawn up according to the colors of their uniforms, the first two black, with brown and red labels, the third and smallest squad white, with transverse green sashes.

Gabriel took his seat boldly at the head of the table and, having looked to the edge of the carver, plunged his fork firmly into the goose. He felt quite at ease now for he was an expert carver and liked nothing better than to find himself at the head of a well-laden table.

— Miss Furlong, what shall I send you? he asked. A wing or a slice of the breast?

— Just a small slice of the breast.

— Miss Higgins, what for you?   200

— O, anything at all, Mr. Conroy.

While Gabriel and Miss Daly exchanged plates of goose and plates of ham and spiced beef Lily went from guest to guest with a dish of hot floury potatoes wrapped in a white napkin. This was Mary Jane's idea and she had also suggested apple sauce for the goose but Aunt Kate had said that plain roast goose without apple sauce had always been good enough for her and she hoped she might never eat worse. Mary Jane waited on her pupils and saw that they got the best slices and Aunt Kate and Aunt Julia opened and carried across from the piano bottles of stout and ale for the gentlemen and bottles of minerals for the ladies. There was a great deal of confusion and laughter and noise, the noise of orders and counter-orders, of knives and forks, of corks and glass-stoppers. Gabriel began to carve second helpings as soon as he had finished the first round without serving himself. Everyone protested loudly so that he compromised by taking a long draught of stout for he had found the carving hot work. Mary Jane settled down quietly to her supper but Aunt Kate and Aunt Julia were still toddling round the table, walking on each other's heels, getting in each other's way, and giving each other unheeded orders. Mr. Browne begged of them to sit down and eat their suppers and so did Gabriel but they said there was time enough so that, at last, Freddy Malins stood up and, capturing Aunt Kate, plumped her down on her chair amid general laughter.

When everyone had been well served Gabriel said, smiling:

— Now, if anyone wants a little more of what vulgar people call stuffing let him or her speak.

A chorus of voices invited him to begin his own supper and Lily came 205 forward with three potatoes which she had reserved for him.

— Very well, said Gabriel amiably, as he took another preparatory draught, kindly forget my existence, ladies and gentlemen, for a few minutes.

He set to his supper and took no part in the conversation with which the table covered Lily's removal of the plates. The subject of talk was the opera company which was then at the Theatre Royal. Mr. Bartell D'Arcy, the tenor, a dark-complexioned young man with a smart moustache, praised very highly the leading contralto of the company but Miss Furlong thought she had a rather vulgar style of production. Freddy Malins said there was a negro chieftain singing in the second part of the Gaiety pantomime who had one of the finest tenor voices he had ever heard.

— Have you heard him? he asked Mr. Bartell D'Arcy across the table.

— No, answered Mr. Bartell D'Arcy carelessly.

— Because, Freddy Malins explained, now I'd be curious to hear your 210 opinion of him. I think he has a grand voice.

— It takes Teddy to find out the really good things, said Mr. Browne familiarly to the table.

— And why couldn't he have a voice too? asked Freddy Malins sharply. Is it because he's only a black?

Nobody answered this question and Mary Jane led the table back to the legitimate opera. One of her pupils had given her a pass for *Mignon.* Of course it was very fine, she said, but it made her think of poor Georgina Burns. Mr. Browne could go back farther still, to the old Italian companies that used to come to Dublin — Tietjens, Ilma de Murzka, Campanini, the great Trebelli, Giuglini, Ravelli, Aramburo. Those were the days, he said, when there was something like singing to be heard in Dublin. He told too of how the top gallery of the old Royal used to be packed night after night, of how one night an Italian tenor had sung five encores to *Let Me Like a Soldier Fall,* introducing a high C every time, and of how the gallery boys would sometimes in their enthusiasm unyoke the horses from the carriage of some great *prima donna* and pull her themselves through the streets to her hotel. Why did they never play the grand old operas now, he asked, *Dinorah, Lucrezia Borgia?* Because they could not get the voices to sing them: that was why.

— O, well, said Mr. Bartell D'Arcy, I presume there are as good singers today as there were then.

— Where are they? asked Mr. Browne defiantly. 215

— In London, Paris, Milan, said Mr. Bartell D'Arcy warmly. I suppose Caruso, for example, is quite as good, if not better than any of the men you have mentioned.

— Maybe so, said Mr. Browne. But I may tell you I doubt it strongly.

— O, I'd give anything to hear Caruso sing, said Mary Jane.

— For me, said Aunt Kate, who had been picking a bone, there was only one tenor. To please me, I mean. But I suppose none of you ever heard of him.

— Who was he, Miss Morkan? asked Mr. Bartell D'Arcy politely. 220

— His name, said Aunt Kate, was Parkinson. I heard him when he was in his prime and I think he had then the purest tenor voice that was ever put into a man's throat.

— Strange, said Mr. Bartell D'Arcy. I never even heard of him.

— Yes, yes, Miss Morkan is right, said Mr. Browne. I remember hearing of old Parkinson but he's too far back for me.

— A beautiful pure sweet mellow English tenor, said Aunt Kate with enthusiasm.

Gabriel having finished, the huge pudding was transferred to the table. The 225 clatter of forks and spoons began again. Gabriel's wife served out spoonfuls of the pudding and passed the plates down the table. Midway down they were held up by Mary Jane, who replenished them with raspberry or orange jelly or with blancmange and jam. The pudding was of Aunt Julia's making and she received praises for it from all quarters. She herself said that it was not quite brown enough.

—Well, I hope, Miss Morkan, said Mr. Browne, that I'm brown enough for you because, you know, I'm all brown.

All the gentlemen, except Gabriel, ate some of the pudding out of compliment to Aunt Julia. As Gabriel never ate sweets the celery had been left for him. Freddy Malins also took a stalk of celery and ate it with his pudding. He had been told that celery was a capital thing for the blood and he was just then under the doctor's care. Mrs. Malins, who had been silent all through the supper, said that her son was going down to Mount Melleray in a week or so. The table then spoke of Mount Melleray, how bracing the air was down there, how hospitable the monks were and how they never asked for a penny-piece from their guests.

—And do you mean to say, asked Mr. Browne incredulously, that a chap can go down there and put up there as if it were a hotel and live on the fat of the land and then come away without paying a farthing?

—O, most people give some donation to the monastery when they leave, said Mary Jane.

—I wish we had an institution like that in our Church, said Mr. Browne 230 candidly.

He was astonished to hear that the monks never spoke, got up at two in the morning, and slept in their coffins. He asked what they did it for.

—That's the rule of the order, said Aunt Kate firmly.

—Yes, but why? asked Mr. Browne.

Aunt Kate repeated that it was the rule, that was all. Mr. Browne still seemed not to understand. Freddy Malins explained to him, as best he could, that the monks were trying to make up for the sins committed by all the sinners in the outside world. The explanation was not very clear for Mr. Browne grinned and said:

—I like that idea very much but wouldn't a comfortable spring bed do 235 them as well as a coffin?

—The coffin, said Mary Jane, is to remind them of their last end.

As the subject had grown lugubrious it was buried in a silence of the table during which Mrs. Malins could be heard saying to her neighbor in an indistinct undertone:

—They are very good men, the monks, very pious men.

The raisins and almonds and figs and apples and oranges and chocolates and sweets were now passed about the table and Aunt Julia invited all the guests to have either port or sherry. At first Mr. Bartell D'Arcy refused to take either but one of his neighbours nudged him and whispered something to him upon which he allowed his glass to be filled. Gradually as the last glasses were being filled the conversation ceased. A pause followed, broken only by the noise of the wine and by unsettlings of chairs. The Misses Morkan, all three, looked down at the tablecloth. Someone coughed once or twice and then a few gentlemen patted the table gently as a signal for silence. The silence came and Gabriel pushed back his chair and stood up.

The patting at once grew louder in encouragement and then ceased alto- 240 gether. Gabriel leaned his ten trembling fingers on the tablecloth and smiled nervously at the company. Meeting a row of upturned faces he raised his eyes to the chandelier. The piano was playing a waltz tune and he could hear the skirts sweeping against the drawing-room door. People, perhaps, were standing in the snow on the quay outside, gazing up at the lighted windows and listening to the waltz music. The air was pure there. In the distance lay the park where the trees were weighted with snow. The Wellington Monument wore a gleaming cap of snow that flashed westward over the white field of Fifteen Acres.

He began:

— Ladies and Gentlemen.

— It has fallen to my lot this evening, as in years past, to perform a very pleasing task but a task for which I am afraid my poor powers as a speaker are all too inadequate.

— No, no! said Mr. Browne.

— But, however that may be, I can only ask you to-night to take the will for 245 the deed and to lend me your attention for a few moments while I endeavor to express to you in words what my feelings are on this occasion.

— Ladies and Gentlemen. It is not the first time that we have gathered together under this hospitable roof, around this hospitable board. It is not the first time that we have been the recipients — or perhaps, I had better say, the victims — of the hospitality of certain good ladies.

He made a circle in the air with his arm and paused. Everyone laughed or smiled at Aunt Kate and Aunt Julia and Mary Jane who all turned crimson with pleasure. Gabriel went on more boldly:

— I feel more strongly with every recurring year that our country has no tradition which does it so much honor and which it should guard so jealously as that of its hospitality. It is a tradition that is unique as far as my experience goes (and I have visited not a few places abroad) among the modern nations. Some would say, perhaps, that with us it is rather a failing than anything to be boasted of. But granted even that, it is, to my mind, a princely failing, and one that I trust will long be cultivated among us. Of one thing, at least, I am sure. As long as this one roof shelters the good ladies aforesaid — and I wish from my heart it may do so for many and many a long year to come — the tradition of genuine warm-hearted courteous Irish hospitality, which our forefathers have handed down to us and which we in turn must hand down to our descendants, is still alive among us.

A hearty murmur of assent ran round the table. It shot through Gabriel's mind that Miss Ivors was not there and that she had gone away discourteously: and he said with confidence in himself:

— Ladies and Gentlemen. 250

— A new generation is growing up in our midst, a generation actuated by new ideas and new principles. It is serious and enthusiastic for these new ideas and its enthusiasm, even when it is misdirected, is, I believe, in the main sincere. But we are living in a sceptical and, if I may use the phrase, a thought-tormented age: and sometimes I fear that this new generation, educated or hypereducated as it is, will lack those qualities of humanity, of hospitality, of kindly humor which belonged to an older day. Listening tonight to the names of all those great singers of the past it seemed to me, I must confess, that we were living in a less spacious age. Those days might, without exaggeration, be called spacious days: and if they are gone beyond recall let us hope, at least, that in gatherings such as this we shall still speak of them with pride and affection, still cherish in our hearts the memory of those dead and gone great ones whose fame the world will not willingly let die.

— Hear, hear! said Mr. Browne loudly.

— But yet, continued Gabriel, his voice falling into a softer inflection, there are always in gatherings such as this sadder thoughts that will recur to our minds: thoughts of the past, of youth, of changes, of absent faces that we miss here tonight. Our path through life is strewn with many such sad memories: and were we to brood upon them always we could not find the heart to go on bravely with our work among the living. We have all of us living duties and living affections which claim, and rightly claim, our strenuous endeavors.

— Therefore, I will not linger on the past. I will not let any gloomy moralizing intrude upon us here tonight. Here we are gathered together for a brief moment from the bustle and rush of our everyday routine. We are met here as friends, in the spirit of good fellowship, as colleagues, also to a certain extent, in the true spirit of *camaraderie,* and as the guests of — what shall I call them? — the Three Graces of the Dublin musical world.

The table burst into applause and laughter at this sally. Aunt Julia vainly 255 asked each of her neighbors in turn to tell her what Gabriel had said.

— He says we are the Three Graces, Aunt Julia, said Mary Jane.

Aunt Julia did not understand but she looked up, smiling, at Gabriel, who continued in the same vein:

— Ladies and Gentlemen.

— I will not attempt to play tonight the part that Paris played on another occasion. I will not attempt to choose between them. The task would be an invidious one and one beyond my poor powers. For when I view them in turn, whether it be our chief hostess herself, whose good heart, whose too good heart, has become a byword with all who knew her, or her sister, who seems to be gifted with perennial youth and whose singing must have been a surprise and a revelation to us all tonight, or, last but not least, when I consider our youngest hostess, talented, cheerful, hard-working, and the best of nieces, I confess, Ladies and Gentlemen, that I do not know to which of them I should award the prize.

Gabriel glanced down at his aunts and, seeing the large smile on Aunt 260 Julia's face and the tears which had risen to Aunt Kate's eyes, hastened to close. He raised his glass of port gallantly, while every member of the company fingered a glass expectantly, and said loudly:

— Let us toast them all three together. Let us drink to their health, wealth, long life, happiness and prosperity and may they long continue to hold the proud and self-won position which they hold in their profession and the position of honor and affection which they hold in our hearts.

All the guests stood up, glass in hand, and, turning towards the three seated ladies, sang in unison, with Mr. Browne as leader:

For they are jolly gay fellows,
For they are jolly gay fellows,
For they are jolly gay fellows,
Which nobody can deny.

Aunt Kate was making frank use of her handkerchief and even Aunt Julia seemed moved. Freddy Malins beat time with his pudding fork and the singers turned towards one another, as if in melodious conference, while they sang, with emphasis:

Unless he tells a lie,
Unless he tells a lie.

Then, turning once more towards their hostesses, they sang:

For they are jolly gay fellows,
For they are jolly gay fellows,
For they are jolly gay fellows,
Which nobody can deny.

The acclamation which followed was taken up beyond the door of the 265 supper room by many of the other guests and renewed time after time, Freddy Malins acting as officer with his fork on high.

The piercing morning air came into the hall where they were standing so that Aunt Kate said:
— Close the door, somebody. Mrs. Malins will get her death of cold.
— Browne is out there, Aunt Kate, said Mary Jane.
— Browne is everywhere, said Aunt Kate, lowering her voice.
Mary Jane laughed at her tone. 270
— Really, she said archly, he is very attentive.
— He has been laid on here like the gas, said Aunt Kate in the same tone, all during the Christmas.
She laughed herself this time good-humoredly and then added quickly:
— But tell him to come in, Mary Jane, and close the door. I hope to goodness he didn't hear me.
At that moment the hall door was opened and Mr. Browne came in from 275 the doorstep, laughing as if his heart would break. He was dressed in a long green overcoat with mock astrakhan cuffs and collar and wore on his head an oval fur cap. He pointed down the snow-covered quay from where the sound of shrill prolonged whistling was borne in.
— Teddy will have all the cabs in Dublin out, he said.
Gabriel advanced from the little pantry behind the office, struggling into his overcoat and, looking round the hall, said:
— Gretta not down yet?
— She's getting on her things, Gabriel, said Aunt Kate.
— Who's playing up there? asked Gabriel. 280
— Nobody. They're all gone.
— O no, Aunt Kate, said Mary Jane. Bartell D'Arcy and Miss O'Callaghan aren't gone yet.
— Someone is strumming at the piano, anyhow, said Gabriel.
Mary Jane glanced at Gabriel and Mr. Browne and said with a shiver:
— It makes me feel cold to look at you two gentlemen muffled up like that. 285 I wouldn't like to face your journey home at this hour.
— I'd like nothing better this minute, said Mr. Browne stoutly, than a rattling

fine walk in the country or a fast drive with a good spanking goer between the shafts.

—We used to have a very good horse and trap at home, said Aunt Julia sadly.

—The never-to-be-forgotten Johnny, said Mary Jane, laughing.

Aunt Kate and Gabriel laughed too.

—Why, what was wonderful about Johnny? asked Mr. Browne.   290

—The late lamented Patrick Morkan, our grandfather, that is, explained Gabriel, commonly known in his later years as the old gentleman, was a glue-boiler.

—O, now, Gabriel, said Aunt Kate, laughing, he had a starch mill.

—Well, glue or starch, said Gabriel, the old gentleman had a horse by the name of Johnny. And Johnny used to work in the old gentleman's mill, walking round and round in order to drive the mill. That was all very well; but now comes the tragic part about Johnny. One fine day the old gentleman thought he'd like to drive out with the quality to a military review in the park.

—The Lord have mercy on his soul, said Aunt Kate compassionately.

—Amen, said Gabriel. So the old gentleman, as I said, harnessed Johnny 295 and put on his very best tall hat and his very best stock collar and drove out in grand style from his ancestral mansion somewhere near Back Lane, I think.

Everyone laughed, even Mrs. Malins, at Gabriel's manner and Aunt Kate said:

—O now, Gabriel, he didn't live in Back Lane, really. Only the mill was there.

—Out from the mansion of his forefathers, continued Gabriel, he drove with Johnny. And everything went on beautifully until Johnny came in sight of King Billy's statue: and whether he fell in love with the horse King Billy sits on or whether he thought he was back again in the mill, anyhow he began to walk round the statue.

Gabriel paced in a circle round the hall in his galoshes amid the laughter of the others.

—Round and round he went, said Gabriel, and the old gentleman, who 300 was a very pompous old gentleman, was highly indignant. *Go on, sir! What do you mean, sir? Johnny! Johnny! Most extraordinary conduct! Can't understand the horse!*

The peals of laughter which followed Gabriel's imitation of the incident were interrupted by a resounding knock at the hall door. Mary Jane ran to open it and let in Freddy Malins. Freddy Malins, with his hat well back on his head and his shoulders humped with cold, was puffing and steaming after his exertions.

—I could only get one cab, he said.

—O, we'll find another along the quay, said Gabriel.

—Yes, said Aunt Kate. Better not keep Mrs. Malins standing in the draught.

Mrs. Malins was helped down the front steps by her son and Mr. Browne 305 and, after many maneuvers, hoisted into the cab. Freddy Malins clambered in after her and spent a long time settling her on the seat, Mr. Browne helping him with advice. At last she was settled comfortably and Freddy Malins invited Mr. Browne into the cab. There was a good deal of confused talk, and then Mr.

Browne got into the cab. The cabman settled his rug over his knees, and bent down for the address. The confusion grew greater and the cabman was directed differently by Freddy Malins and Mr. Browne, each of whom had his head out through a window of the cab. The difficulty was to know where to drop Mr. Browne along the route and Aunt Kate, Aunt Julia, and Mary Jane helped the discussion from the doorstep with cross-directions and contradictions and abundance of laughter. As for Freddy Malins he was speechless with laughter. He popped his head in and out of the window every moment, to the great danger of his hat, and told his mother how the discussion was progressing till at last Mr. Browne shouted to the bewildered cabman above the din of everybody's laughter:

— Do you know Trinity College?

— Yes, sir, said the cabman.

— Well, drive bang up against Trinity College gates, said Mr. Browne, and then we'll tell you where to go. You understand now?

— Yes, sir, said the cabman.

— Make like a bird for Trinity college.   310

— Right, sir, cried the cabman.

The horse was whipped up and the cab rattled off along the quay amid a chorus of laughter and adieus.

Gabriel had not gone to the door with the others. He was in a dark part of the hall gazing up the staircase. A woman was standing near the top of the first flight, in the shadow also. He could not see her face but he could see the terracotta and salmon-pink panels of her skirt which the shadow made appear black and white. It was his wife. She was leaning on the banisters, listening to something. Gabriel was surprised at her stillness and strained his ear to listen also. But he could hear little save the noise of laughter and dispute on the front steps, a few chords struck on the piano, and a few notes of a man's voice singing.

He stood still in the gloom of the hall, trying to catch the air that the voice was singing and gazing up at his wife. There was grace and mystery in her attitude as if she were a symbol of something. He asked himself what is a woman standing on the stairs in the shadow, listening to distant music, a symbol of. If he were a painter he would paint her in that attitude. Her blue felt hat would show off the bronze of her hair against the darkness and the dark panels of her skirt would show off the light ones. *Distant Music* he would call the picture if he were a painter.

The hall door closed; and Aunt Kate, Aunt Julia, and Mary Jane came down 315
the hall, still laughing.

— Well, isn't Freddy terrible? said Mary Jane. He's really terrible.

Gabriel said nothing but pointed up the stairs towards where his wife was standing. Now that the hall door was closed the voice and the piano could be heard more clearly. Gabriel held up his hand for them to be silent. The song seemed to be in the old Irish tonality and the singer seemed uncertain both of his words and of his voice. The voice, made plaintive by distance and by the singer's hoarseness, faintly illuminated the cadence of the air with words expressing grief:

O, the rain falls on my heavy locks
And the dew wets my skin,
My babe lies cold . . .

— O, exclaimed Mary Jane. It's Bartell D'Arcy singing and he wouldn't sing all the night. O, I'll get him to sing a song before he goes.

— O do, Mary Jane, said Aunt Kate.

Mary Jane brushed past the others and ran to the staircase but before she reached it the singing stopped and the piano was closed abruptly.

— O, what a pity! she cried. Is he coming down, Gretta?

Gabriel heard his wife answer yes and saw her come down towards them. A few steps behind her were Mr. Bartell D'Arcy and Miss O'Callaghan.

— O, Mr. D'Arcy, cried Mary Jane, it's downright mean of you to break off like that when we were all in raptures listening to you.

— I have been at him all the evening, said Miss O'Callaghan, and Mrs. Conroy too and he told us he had a dreadful cold and couldn't sing.

— O, Mr. D'Arcy, said Aunt Kate, now that was a great fib to tell.

— Can't you see that I'm as hoarse as a crow? said Mr. D'Arcy roughly.

He went into the pantry hastily and put on his overcoat. The others, taken aback by his rude speech, could find nothing to say. Aunt Kate wrinkled her brows and made signs to the others to drop the subject. Mr. D'Arcy stood swathing his neck carefully and frowning.

— It's the weather, said Aunt Julia, after a pause.

— Yes, everybody has colds, said Aunt Kate readily, everybody.

— They say, said Mary Jane, we haven't had snow like it for thirty years; and I read this morning in the newspapers that the snow is general all over Ireland.

— I love the look of snow, said Aunt Julia sadly.

— So do I, said Miss O'Callaghan. I think Christmas is never really Christmas unless we have the snow on the ground.

— But poor Mr. D'Arcy doesn't like the snow, said Aunt Kate, smiling.

Mr. D'Arcy came from the pantry, fully swathed and buttoned, and in a repentant tone told them the history of the cold. Everyone gave him advice and said it was a great pity and urged him to be very careful of his throat in the night air. Gabriel watched his wife who did not join in the conversation. She was standing right under the dusty fanlight and the flame of the gas lit up the rich bronze of her hair which he had seen her drying at the fire a few days before. She was in the same attitude and seemed unaware of the talk about her. At last she turned towards them and Gabriel saw that there was color on her cheeks and that her eyes were shining. A sudden tide of joy went leaping out of his heart.

— Mr. D'Arcy, she said, what is the name of that song you were singing?

— It's called *The Lass of Aughrim,* said Mr. D'Arcy, but I couldn't remember it properly. Why? Do you know it?

— *The Lass of Aughrim,* she repeated. I couldn't think of the name.

— It's a very nice air, said Mary Jane. I'm sorry you were not in voice tonight.

— Now, Mary Jane, said Aunt Kate, don't annoy Mr. D'Arcy. I won't have him annoyed.

Seeing that all were ready to start she shepherded them to the door where good-night was said:

— Well, good-night, Aunt Kate, and thanks for the pleasant evening.

— Good-night, Gabriel. Good-night, Gretta!

— Good-night, Aunt Kate, and thanks ever so much. Good-night, Aunt Julia.

— O, good-night, Gretta, I didn't see you.

— Good-night, Mr. D'Arcy. Good-night, Miss O'Callaghan.

— Good-night, Miss Morkan.

— Good-night, again.

— Good-night, all. Safe home.

— Good-night. Good-night.

The morning was still dark. A dull yellow light brooded over the houses 350 and the river; and the sky seemed to be descending. It was slushy underfoot; and only streaks and patches of snow lay on the roofs, on the parapets of the quay, and on the area railings. The lamps were still burning redly in the murky air and, across the river, the palace of the Four Courts stood out menacingly against the heavy sky.

She was walking on before him with Mr. Bartell D'Arcy, her shoes in a brown parcel tucked under one arm and her hands holding her skirt up from the slush. She had no longer any grace of attitude but Gabriel's eyes were still bright with happiness. The blood went bounding along his veins; and the thoughts were rioting through his brain, proud, joyful, tender, valorous.

She was walking on before him so lightly and so erect that he longed to run after her noiselessly, catch her by the shoulders, and say something foolish and affectionate into her ear. She seemed to him so frail that he longed to defend her against something and then to be alone with her. Moments of their secret life together burst like stars upon his memory. A heliotrope envelope was lying beside his breakfast cup and he was caressing it with his hand. Birds were twittering in the ivy and the sunny web of the curtain was shimmering along the floor: he could not eat for happiness. They were standing on the crowded platform and he was placing a ticket inside the warm palm of her glove. He was standing with her in the cold, looking in through a grated window at a man making bottles in a roaring furnace. It was very cold. Her face, fragrant in the cold air, was quite close to his; and suddenly she called out to the man at the furnace:

— Is the fire hot, sir?

But the man could not hear her with the noise of the furnace. It was just as well. He might have answered rudely.

A wave of yet more tender joy escaped from his heart and went coursing 355 in warm flood along his arteries. Like the tender fires of stars moments of their life together, that no one knew of or would ever know of, broke upon and illumined his memory. He longed to recall to her those moments, to make her forget the years of their dull existence together and remember only their moments of ecstasy. For the years, he felt, had not quenched his soul or hers. Their children, his writing, her household cares had not quenched all their souls' tender fire. In one letter that he had written to her then he had said: *Why is it that words like these seem to me so dull and cold? Is it because there is no word tender enough to be your name?*

Like distant music these words that he had written years before were borne towards him from the past. He longed to be alone with her. When the others had gone away, when he and she were in their room in the hotel, then they would be alone together. He would call her softly:

— Gretta!

Perhaps she would not hear at once: she would be undressing. Then something in his voice would strike her. She would turn and look at him. . . .

At the corner of Winetavern Street they met a cab. He was glad of its rattling noise as it saved him from conversation. She was looking out of the window and seemed tired. The others spoke only a few words, pointing out some building or street. The horse galloped along wearily under the murky morning sky, dragging his old rattling box after his heels, and Gabriel was again in a cab with her, galloping to catch the boat, galloping to their honeymoon.

As the cab drove across O'Connell Bridge Miss O'Callaghan said: 360

— They say you never cross O'Connell Bridge without seeing a white horse.

— I see a white man this time, said Gabriel.

— Where? asked Mr. Bartell D'Arcy.

Gabriel pointed to the statue, on which lay patches of snow. Then he nodded familiarly to it and waved his hand.

— Good-night, Dan, he said gaily.   365

When the cab drew up before the hotel Gabriel jumped out and, in spite of Mr. Bartell D'Arcy's protest, paid the driver. He gave the man a shilling over his fare. The man saluted and said:

— A prosperous New Year to you, sir.

— The same to you, said Gabriel cordially.

She leaned for a moment on his arm in getting out of the cab and while standing at the curbstone, bidding the others good-night. She leaned lightly on his arm, as lightly as when she had danced with him a few hours before. He had felt proud and happy then, happy that she was his, proud of her grace and wifely carriage. But now, after the kindling again of so many memories, the first touch of her body, musical and strange and perfumed, sent through him a keen pang of lust. Under cover of her silence he pressed her arm closely to his side; and, as they stood at the hotel door, he felt that they had escaped from their lives and duties, escaped from home and friends and run away together with wild and radiant hearts to a new adventure.

An old man was dozing in a great hooded chair in the hall. He lit a candle 370 in the office and went before them to the stairs. They followed him in silence, their feet falling in soft thuds on the thickly carpeted stairs. She mounted the stairs behind the porter, her head bowed in the ascent, her frail shoulders curved as with a burden, her skirt girt tightly about her. He could have flung his arms about her hips and held her still for his arms were trembling with desire to seize her and only the stress of his nails against the palms of his hands held the wild impulse of his body in check. The porter halted on the stairs to settle his guttering candle. They halted too on the steps below him. In the silence Gabriel could hear the falling of the molten wax into the tray and the thumping of his own heart against his ribs.

The porter led them along a corridor and opened a door. Then he set his unstable candle down on a toilet table and asked at what hour they were to be called in the morning.

— Eight, said Gabriel.

The porter pointed to the tap of the electric light and began a muttered apology but Gabriel cut him short.

— We don't want any light. We have enough light from the street. And I say, he added, pointing to the candle, you might remove that handsome article, like a good man.

The porter took up his candle again, but slowly for he was surprised by 375 such a novel idea. Then he mumbled good-night and went out. Gabriel shot the lock to.

A ghostly light from the street lamp lay in a long shaft from one window to the door. Gabriel threw his overcoat and hat on a couch and crossed the room towards the window. He looked down into the street in order that his emotion might calm a little. Then he turned and leaned against a chest of drawers with his back to the light. She had taken off her hat and cloak and was standing before a large swinging mirror, unhooking her waist. Gabriel paused for a few moments, watching her, and then said:

— Gretta!

She turned away from the mirror slowly and walked along the shaft of light towards him. Her face looked so serious and weary that the words would not pass Gabriel's lips. No, it was not the moment yet.

— You look tired, he said.

— I am a little, she answered.   380

— You don't feel ill or weak?

— No, tired: that's all.

She went on to the window and stood there, looking out. Gabriel waited again and then, fearing that diffidence was about to conquer him, he said abruptly:

— By the way, Gretta!

— What is it?   385

— You know that poor fellow Malins? he said quickly.

— Yes. What about him?

— Well, poor fellow, he's a decent sort of chap after all, continued Gabriel in a false voice. He gave me back that sovereign I lent him and I didn't expect it really. It's a pity he wouldn't keep away from that Browne, because he's not a bad fellow at heart.

He was trembling now with annoyance. Why did she seem so abstracted? He did not know how he could begin. Was she annoyed, too, about something? If she would only turn to him or come to him of her own accord! To take her as she was would be brutal. No, he must see some ardor in her eyes first. He longed to be master of her strange mood.

— When did you lend him the pound? she asked, after a pause.   390

Gabriel strove to restrain himself from breaking out into brutal language about the sottish Malins and his pound. He longed to cry to her from his soul, to crush her body against his, to overmaster her. But he said:

— O, at Christmas, when he opened that little Christmas-card shop in Henry Street.

He was in such a fever of rage and desire that he did not hear her come from the window. She stood before him for an instant, looking at him strangely. Then, suddenly raising herself on tiptoe and resting her hands lightly on his shoulders, she kissed him.

— You are a very generous person, Gabriel, she said.

Gabriel, trembling with delight at her sudden kiss and at the quaintness of 395 her phrase, put his hands on her hair and began smoothing it back, scarcely touching it with his fingers. The washing had made it fine and brilliant. His heart was brimming over with happiness. Just when he was wishing for it she had come to him of her own accord. Perhaps her thoughts had been running with his. Perhaps she had felt the impetuous desire that was in him and then the yielding mood had come upon her. Now that she had fallen to him so easily he wondered why he had been so diffident.

He stood, holding her head between his hands. Then, slipping one arm swiftly about her body and drawing her towards him, he said softly:

— Gretta dear, what are you thinking about?

She did not answer nor yield wholly to his arm. He said again, softly:

— Tell me what it is, Gretta. I think I know what is the matter. Do I know?

She did not answer at once. Then she said in an outburst of tears: 400

— O, I am thinking about that song, *The Lass of Aughrim*.

She broke loose from him and ran to the bed and, throwing her arms across the bed rail, hid her face. Gabriel stood stock still for a moment in astonishment and then followed her. As he passed in the way of the cheval-glass he caught sight of himself in full length, his broad, well-filled shirtfront, the face whose expression always puzzled him when he saw it in a mirror, and his glimmering gilt-rimmed eyeglasses. He halted a few paces from her and said:

— What about the song? Why does that make you cry?

She raised her head from her arms and dried her eyes with the back of her hand like a child. A kinder note than he had intended went into his voice.

— Why, Gretta? he asked.   405

— I am thinking about a person long ago who used to sing that song.

— And who was the person long ago? asked Gabriel, smiling.

— It was a person I used to know in Galway when I was living with my grandmother, she said.

The smile passed away from Gabriel's face. A dull anger began to gather again at the back of his mind and the dull fires of his lust began to glow angrily in his veins.

— Someone you were in love with? he asked ironically.   410

— It was a young boy I used to know, she answered, named Michael Furey. He used to sing that song, *The Lass of Aughrim*. He was very delicate.

Gabriel was silent. He did not wish her to think that he was interested in this delicate boy.

— I can see him so plainly, she said after a moment. Such eyes as he had: big dark eyes! And such an expression in them — an expression!

— O, then, you were in love with him? said Gabriel.

— I used to go out walking with him, she said, when I was in Galway.   415

A thought flew across Gabriel's mind.

— Perhaps that was why you wanted to go to Galway with that Ivors girl? he said coldly.

She looked at him and asked in surprise:

— What for?

Her eyes made Gabriel feel awkward. He shrugged his shoulders and said: 420

— How do I know? To see him perhaps.

She looked away from him along the shaft of light towards the window in silence.

— He is dead, she said at length. He died when he was only seventeen. Isn't that a terrible thing to die so young as that?

—What was he? asked Gabriel, still ironically.

—He was in the gasworks, she said. 425

Gabriel felt humiliated by the failure of his irony and by the evocation of this figure from the dead, a boy in the gasworks. While he had been full of memories of their secret life together, full of tenderness and joy and desire, she had been comparing him in her mind with another. A shameful consciousness of his own person assailed him. He saw himself as a ludicrous figure, acting as a pennyboy° for his aunts, a nervous well-meaning sentimentalist, orating to vulgarians and idealizing his own clownish lusts, the pitiable fatuous fellow he had caught a glimpse of in the mirror. Instinctively he turned his back more to the light lest she might see the shame that burned upon his forehead.

He tried to keep up his tone of cold interrogation but his voice when he spoke was humble and indifferent.

—I suppose you were in love with this Michael Furey, Gretta, he said.

—I was great with him at that time, she said.

Her voice was veiled and sad. Gabriel, feeling now how vain it would be 430
to try to lead her whither he had purposed, caressed one of her hands and said, also sadly:

—And what did he die of so young, Gretta? Consumption, was it?

—I think he died for me, she answered.

A vague terror seized Gabriel at this answer as if, at that hour when he had hoped to triumph, some impalpable and vindictive being was coming against him, gathering forces against him in its vague world. But he shook himself free of it with an effort of reason and continued to caress her hand. He did not question her again for he felt that she would tell him of herself. Her hand was warm and moist: it did not respond to his touch but he continued to caress it just as he had caressed her first letter to him that spring morning.

—It was in the winter, she said, about the beginning of the winter when I was going to leave my grandmother's and come up here to the convent. And he was ill at the time in his lodgings in Galway and wouldn't be let out and his people in Oughterard were written to. He was in decline, they said, or something like that. I never knew rightly.

She paused for a moment and sighed. 435

—Poor fellow, she said. He was very fond of me and he was such a gentle boy. We used to go out together, walking, you know, Gabriel, like the way they do in the country. He was going to study singing only for his health. He had a very good voice, poor Michael Furey.

—Well; and then? asked Gabriel.

—And then when it came to the time for me to leave Galway and come up to the convent he was much worse and I wouldn't be let see him so I wrote a letter saying I was going up to Dublin and would be back in the summer and hoping he would be better then.

She paused for a moment to get her voice under control and then went on:

—Then the night before I left I was in my grandmother's house in Nuns' 440
Island, packing up, and I heard gravel thrown up against the window. The window

---

pennyboy: Errand boy.

was so wet I couldn't see so I ran downstairs as I was and slipped out the back into the garden and there was the poor fellow at the end of the garden, shivering.

—And did you not tell him to go back? asked Gabriel.

—I implored him to go home at once and told him he would get his death in the rain. But he said he did not want to live. I can see his eyes as well as well! He was standing at the end of the wall where there was a tree.

—And did he go home? asked Gabriel.

—Yes, he went home. And when I was only a week in the convent he died and he was buried in Oughterard where his people came from. O, the day I heard that, that he was dead!

She stopped, choking with sobs, and, overcome by emotion, flung herself 445 face downward on the bed, sobbing in the quilt. Gabriel held her hand for a moment longer, irresolutely, and then, shy of intruding on her grief, let it fall gently and walked quietly to the window.

She was fast asleep.

Gabriel, leaning on his elbow, looked for a few moments unresentfully on her tangled hair and half-open mouth, listening to her deep-drawn breath. So she had had that romance in her life: a man had died for her sake. It hardly pained him now to think how poor a part he, her husband, had played in her life. He watched her while she slept as though he and she had never lived together as man and wife. His curious eyes rested long upon her face and on her hair: and, as he thought of what she must have been then, in that time of her first girlish beauty, a strange friendly pity for her entered his soul. He did not like to say even to himself that her face was no longer beautiful but he knew that it was no longer the face for which Michael Furey had braved death.

Perhaps she had not told him all the story. His eyes moved to the chair over which she had thrown some of her clothes. A petticoat string dangled to the floor. One boot stood upright, its limp upper fallen down: the fellow of it lay upon its side. He wondered at his riot of emotions of an hour before. From what had it proceeded? From his aunt's supper, from his own foolish speech, from the wine and dancing, the merry-making when saying good-night in the hall, the pleasure of the walk along the river in the snow. Poor Aunt Julia! She, too, would soon be a shade with the shade of Patrick Morkan and his horse. He had caught that haggard look upon her face for a moment when she was singing *Arrayed for the Bridal*. Soon, perhaps, he would be sitting in that same drawing room, dressed in black, his silk hat on his knees. The blinds would be drawn down and Aunt Kate would be sitting beside him, crying and blowing her nose and telling him how Julia had died. He would cast about his mind for some words that might console her, and would find only lame and useless ones. Yes, yes: that would happen very soon.

The air of the room chilled his shoulders. He stretched himself cautiously along under the sheets and lay down beside his wife. One by one they were all becoming shades. Better pass boldly into that other world, in the full glory of some passion, than fade and wither dismally with age. He thought of how she who lay beside him had locked in her heart for so many years that image of her lover's eyes when he had told her that he did not wish to live.

Generous tears filled Gabriel's eyes. He had never felt like that himself 450 towards any woman but he knew that such a feeling must be love. The tears gathered more thickly in his eyes and in the partial darkness he imagined he saw the form of a young man standing under a dripping tree. Other forms were near. His soul had approached that region where dwell the vast hosts of the dead. He was conscious of, but could not apprehend, their wayward and flickering existence. His own identity was fading out into a gray impalpable world: the solid world itself which these dead had one time reared and lived in was dissolving and dwindling.

A few light taps upon the pane made him turn to the window. It had begun to snow again. He watched sleepily the flakes, silver and dark, falling obliquely against the lamplight. The time had come for him to set out on his journey westward. Yes, the newspapers were right: snow was general all over Ireland. It was falling on every part of the dark central plain, on the treeless hills, falling softly upon the Bog of Allen and, farther westward, softly falling into the dark mutinous Shannon waves. It was falling, too, upon every part of the lonely churchyard on the hill where Michael Furey lay buried. It lay thickly drifted on the crooked crosses and headstones, on the spears of the little gate, on the barren thorns. His soul swooned slowly as he heard the snow falling faintly through the universe and faintly falling, like the descent of their last end, upon all the living and the dead.

Considerations for Critical Thinking and Writing

1. Describe the Misses Morkans' annual dance. What conflicting moods and emotions are apparent among the people who attend it?
2. How does Gabriel feel about the party? What role does he seem to be expected to play?
3. What does Gabriel's concern about galoshes suggest about him?
4. What is the conflict between Miss Ivors and Gabriel?
5. How does the conversation at the dinner table relate to subsequent events in the story?
6. How does Gabriel feel about Ireland? Why are these feelings important? How do they help you to understand him?
7. Compare Gretta's feelings as she listens to D'Arcy with Gabriel's as he watches her.
8. Are Gretta and Gabriel well matched? Are they very much alike or significantly different from each other?
9. How does learning that Michael Furey is dead affect Gabriel?
10. How does Gabriel feel about his relationship with Gretta in the last section of the story? How does this make him feel about life in general?
11. Discuss the imagery in the final paragraph. How do the images create a tone that helps to characterize Gabriel's sense of himself?
12. Comment on the appropriateness of the title.

Connections to Other Selections

1. Consider the themes of "The Dead" and Virginia Woolf's "Lappin and Lapinova" (p. 489) in an essay that pays particular attention to the conclusion of each story.
2. Write an essay that compares the function of the Irish setting in "The Dead" with

the New England setting in Nathaniel Hawthorne's "Young Goodman Brown" (p. 242).

3. In an essay discuss the nature of what each protagonist learns in "The Dead" and in Flannery O'Connor's "Revelation" (p. 394). Consider how these recognitions transform their lives.

4. Write an essay comparing the nature of the conflict in "The Dead" and in Robert Frost's "Home Burial" (p. 876). In your response pay particular attention to the author's characterization of the wives in each work.

PERSPECTIVES ON JOYCE

An Unsigned Review of Dubliners   1914

Dubliners is a collection of short stories, the scene of which is laid in Dublin. Too comprehensive for the theme, the title is nevertheless typical of a book which purports, we assume, to describe life as it is and yet regards it from one aspect only. The author, Mr. James Joyce, is not concerned with all Dubliners, but almost exclusively with those of them who would be submerged if the tide of material difficulties were to rise a little higher. It is not so much money they lack as the adaptability which attains some measure of success by accepting the world as it is. It is in so far that they are failures that his characters interest Mr. Joyce. One of them — a capable washerwoman — falls an easy prey to a rogue in a tramcar and is cozened out of the little present she was taking to her family. Another — a trusted cashier — has so ordered a blameless life that he drives to drink and suicide the only person in the world with whom he was in sympathy. A third — an amiable man of letters — learns at the moment he feels most drawn to his wife that her heart was given once and for all to a boy long dead.

Dubliners may be recommended to the large class of readers to whom the drab makes an appeal, for it is admirably written. Mr. Joyce avoids exaggeration. He leaves the conviction that his people are as he describes them. Shunning the emphatic, Mr. Joyce is less concerned with the episode than with the mood which it suggests. Perhaps for this reason he is more successful with his shorter stories. When he writes at greater length the issue seems trivial, and the connecting thread becomes so tenuous as to be scarcely perceptible. The reader's difficulty will be enhanced if he is ignorant of Dublin customs; if he does not know, for instance, that "a curate" is a man who brings strong waters.

From *The Times Literary Supplement,* June 18, 1914

Considerations for Critical Thinking and Writing

1. Describe the tone of this review. Explain why you think it is mostly positive or negative.

2. What kind of attitude is expressed in the review about the city of Dublin and its inhabitants?

3. Choose a Joyce story in this anthology and write an essay discussing the assertion that "Mr. Joyce is less concerned with the episode than with the mood which it suggests."

CLEANTH BROOKS, JR. (b. 1906) AND ROBERT PENN WARREN (1905–1989)

Point of View in "Araby"   1943

Is this a sentimental story? It is about an adolescent love affair, about "calf love," a subject which usually is not to be taken seriously and is often the cause of amusement. The boy of the story is obviously investing casual incidents with a meaning which they do not deserve; and himself admits, in the end, that he has fallen into self-deception. How does the author avoid the charge that he has taken the matter over-seriously?

The answer to this question would involve a consideration of the point of view from which the story is told. It is told by the hero himself, but after a long lapse of time, after he has reached maturity. This fact, it is true, is not stated in the story, but the style itself is not that of an adolescent boy. It is a formal and complicated style, rich, as has already been observed, in subtle implications. In other words, the man is looking back upon the boy, detachedly and judicially. For instance, the boy, in the throes of the experience, would never have said of himself: "I had never spoken to her, except for a few casual words, and yet her name was like a summons to all my foolish blood." The man knows, as it were, that the behavior of the boy was, in a sense, foolish. The emotions of the boy are confused, but the person telling the story, the boy grown up, is not confused. He has unraveled the confusion long after, knows that it existed and why it existed.

If the man has unraveled the confusions of the boy, why is the event still significant to him? Is he merely dwelling on the pathos of adolescent experience? It seems, rather, that he sees in the event, as he looks back on it, a kind of parable of a problem which has run through later experience. The discrepancy between the real and the ideal scarcely exists for the child, but it is a constant problem, in all sorts of terms, for the adult. This story is about a boy's first confrontation of that problem — that is, about his growing up. The man may have made adjustments to this problem, and may have worked out certain provisional solutions, but looking back, he still recognizes it as a problem, and an important one. The sense of isolation and disillusion which, in the boy's experience, may seem to spring from a trivial situation, becomes not less, but more aggravated and fundamental in the adult's experience. So, the story is not merely an account of a stage in the process of growing up — it does not merely represent a clinical interest in the psychology of growing up — but is a symbolic rendering of a central conflict in mature experience.

From *Understanding Fiction*

Considerations for Critical Thinking and Writing

1. According to Brooks and Warren, what point of view is used in "Araby" to tell the story?
2. How does Joyce's use of point of view avoid sentimentality?

3. In an essay discuss how the points of view used in "Araby" and "Eveline" contribute to the stories' themes.

FLORENCE L. WALZL (b. 1909)
On the Ending of "The Dead"

1966

Gabriel's vision . . . is the final stage of a development that has carried Gabriel from a selfish preoccupation with self to sympathy with Gretta, pity for his relatives, and love for all men. His illumination takes place when he realizes he is part of common humanity and shares its mutable state of being. At this moment of enlightenment he loses even the sense of his own identity, and his soul approaches "that region where dwell the vast hosts of the dead." As he watches the snow fall, he reflects that the "time had come for him to set out on his journey westward." Because of the earlier ambiguities, Joyce has made it possible for this strange statement to be either a life or a death suggestion. It is the keynote symbol of the vision, and its significance is all-important, since the meaning of the rest of the vision depends on the interpretation of this image. If it is read as a death symbol, all successive images take a like coloration. If it is read as a life symbol, the succeeding images all suggest rebirth. It signals the opening of one of the most remarkable ambiguities in literature, a conclusion that offers almost opposite meanings, each of which can be logically argued.

For the reader who has come to this conclusion by way of the fourteen preceding stories of disillusioned children, frustrated youths, sterile adults, and paralyzed social groups in *Dubliners,* the cosmic vision of "The Dead" seems the last stage in a moribund process. The final fate of the *Dubliners* everyman is a death in life, and Gabriel Conroy's illumination is that he is dead. In this interpretation the vision is a final statement of the death themes of the book. The snow that covers all Ireland images the deadly inertia of the nation. The lonely churchyard where Michael Furey lies buried pictures the end of individual hope and love. The crooked crosses on which the snow drifts represent the defective and spiritually dead Irish Church. The spears and barren thorns suggest the futility of Christ's sacrifice for a people so insensible. To the hero it is an irrevocable last judgment. Such an interpretation is a powerful and symbolically logical conclusion for *Dubliners.*

This is not the conclusion that the reader who knows only "The Dead" draws. Interpreting the journey westward as a start toward a new life of greater reality, he sees a succession of rebirth images. The snow, though it is general over Ireland, is quickly swallowed in the Shannon waves — its static iciness melting in the great waters of life. The melting snow is seen as subtly paralleling the change in the hero, whose cold conceit has disappeared with his warming humanitarianism. The snow melting is thus a baptismal symbol, and as such offers renewed life not only to Gabriel, but also all the dead who lie here. The lonely churchyard where Michael Furey is buried serves only as a reminder that the grave has already yielded up its dead. For Michael lives vibrantly in the memory of a vibrant act. The recollections of Christ's passion in the spears and thorns are reminders that sacrifice of self is the condition of revival. The judgment that Michael brings is a salvation, and Gabriel's swoon is a symbolic death from which he will rise revivified. Gabriel is rightly named: he is a figure of annunciation and new life.

Joyce thus resolved the problem in logic which arose from his changed viewpoints by composing a conclusion for "The Dead" and *Dubliners* that employed a pattern of ambivalent symbols and a great final ambiguity.

From *James Joyce Quarterly*

Considerations for Critical Thinking and Writing

1. What ambiguities does Walzl see in the conclusion of "The Dead"? How does her reading compare with your own assessment of Gabriel's character?
2. How does your reading of Joyce's "Araby" (p. 310), "Eveline" (p. 315), and "The Boarding House" (p. 319) affect your interpretation of "The Dead"? What similarities are there between Gabriel and the protagonists of these other stories?
3. Write an essay that discusses how the protagonists regard themselves at the end of "The Dead" and Flannery O'Connor's "Parker's Back" (p. 409).

LIONEL TRILLING (1905–1975)
On Personal Identity in "The Dead"   1967

Joyce writes of his own nation and city with passionate particularity. But when we consider the very high place that "The Dead" has been given in the canon of modern literature, and the admiration it has won from readers of the most diverse backgrounds, we must say that Joyce has written a chapter in the moral history not only of his own country but of the whole modern western world. Gabriel Conroy's plight, his sense that he has been overtaken by death-in-life, is shared by many in our time: it is one of the characteristics of modern society that an ever-growing number of people are not content to live by habit and routine and by the unquestioning acceptance of the circumstances into which they have been born. They believe they have the right to claim for themselves pleasure, or power, or dignity, or fullness of experience, a prerogative which in former times was exercised by relatively few people, usually members of the privileged classes, and which now seems available to many people regardless of class. Yet almost in the degree that modern man feels free to assert the personal claims which are the expression of a heightened sense of individuality, he seems to fall prey to that peculiarly modern disorder so often remarked by novelists, psychologists, and sociologists — an uncertainty about who the person is who makes the claims, a diminished sense of his personal identity.

From *The Experience of Literature*

Considerations for Critical Thinking and Writing

1. According to Trilling how can a "heightened sense of individuality" create problems for a person? How does it create problems for Gabriel?
2. How might Trilling's description of Gabriel also apply to the protagonists of "Araby" (p. 310), "Eveline" (p. 315), or "The Boarding House" (p. 319)?
3. Trilling restricts his remarks about individuality to "the whole modern *western* world" (italics added). Why do you suppose he offered this qualification? Explain why you agree or disagree with his exclusion of nonwestern cultures.

WARREN BECK (b. 1918)
On Frank as Savior in "Eveline"
1969

She believes . . . that a way to life and rightful happiness is open — "Frank would save her." He is Irish, but is in Dublin "just for a holiday" in "the old country," from which he had shipped out as a deck boy, to Canada; since then he has seen the world and reports himself "fallen on his feet" in Buenos Aires, where a "home" awaits Eveline if she will go with him. This bronze-faced sailor had been attentive, he would meet her outside the Stores every evening to see her home, and he took her to *The Bohemian Girl.* At first for her there was the excitement of having "a fellow," and "then she had begun to like him." Primarily, though, he is a refuge and her salvation. She believes he "would give her life, perhaps love, too" but certainly "would . . . fold her in his arms . . . would save her."

Such details allow a supposition that Eveline's father might not have been all wrong in forbidding her to see Frank, though the reasons were mean — a stereotyped distrust of "sailor chaps" and an unrelenting claim upon his domestic drudge. As Eveline sees Frank, he is not only spirited but "very kind, manly, open-hearted." Yet it is not quite as one reader puts it: "Marriage and flight across the sea promise life and 'perhaps love too.'"[1] For her to be a bride before the flight would require, if not a secret marriage in Dublin, an immediate ceremony in the captain's cabin — a most unlikely thing in the Catholic context of this story, and one which, had it been pending, surely would have entered into Eveline's reverie. Instead this inexperienced nineteen-year-old about to "run away with a fellow" thinks simply that she "was to go away with him by the night-boat to be his wife" and believes that "tomorrow she would be on the sea with Frank, steaming towards Buenos Aires." However, "the night-boat" from the North Wall is probably the regular one to Liverpool, and while passengers might sail to Buenos Aires from there, Liverpool could be the sordid end of this journey for Eveline; or she could reach South America still unmarried and find Frank's promises false.

Joyce has given no further or more substantial grounds for suspecting Frank besides these slight implications in the details and phrasing. If the inference is made, it merely stresses the pathos of Eveline's situation; and to leave it at that

[1]W. Y. Tindall, *A Reader's Guide to James Joyce* (New York: Noonday Press, 1959), p. 21.

would accord with the narrative's tone and intent. For Frank to have given Eveline more precise assurance or for the hint of possible betrayal to have been stronger would have made it another story, or an infringement upon the integrity of this one. It is one of its many delicate balancings, both in Eveline's mind and in the total effect itself, that Joyce makes it a matter of "perhaps love, too" but allows some uncertainty as to just what kind of escape is open to Eveline. There is a great deal of such selective economy and particular focusing in all the *Dubliners* stories, and in this technique they are still quite modern, sixty years after their composition.

From *Joyce's* Dubliners: *Substance, Vision, and Art*

Considerations for Critical Thinking and Writing

1. How convincing do you find Beck's suggestions about the possibility that Frank might disappoint Eveline?
2. Explain how Beck's reading of Frank affects your reading of the story.
3. Write an essay comparing the functions of Frank in "Eveline" and Mangan's sister in "Araby."

MARIE BARRETT (b. 1967)
From a Student's Critical Reading
of Images in "Eveline"   1986

Eveline cannot decide whether she would prefer a dull life of security in Dublin or a new life with Frank, and this indecision is reflected in many images of passage throughout the story. Windows and gates are two of the most significant images of transition. Eveline is on the verge of going from one life to another; while she thinks about this change she "lean[s] against a window curtain." Frank, by virtue of being a visitor in Dublin, is also between two lives; when she meets him he is "standing at the gate." The story takes place in the evening, a transition between day and night. A final image of transition between the present and future for Eveline is the "wide doors of the sheds [through which] she caught a glimpse of the black mass of the boat, lying in beside the quay wall, with illumined portholes." The doors and the boat offer escape from Dublin, and the illuminated portholes provide a tantalizing glimpse into the possibility of a new life. However, there is a major obstacle: the quay wall, as well as the North Wall mentioned earlier in the passage, suggests that she cannot go. These walls are barriers, rather than passages, and they are not the only things preventing her from leaving. She clings to an iron railing, which suggests the stability of Dublin life as her lover "rush[es] beyond the barrier."

Considerations for Critical Thinking and Writing

1. How do the images discussed in this passage relate to the story's action?
2. What other images can you find in "Eveline" that are used to convey thematic significance?

3. In an essay discuss Joyce's use of images in "Araby" (p. 310) or "The Boarding House" (p. 319). How do the images reinforce the themes?

FRITZ SENN (b. 1928)
"The Boarding House" Seen as a Tale of Misdirection   1986

[In "The Boarding House"] misdirection involves readers by leaving them largely out of the main events. We realize how we are cut off from the crucial events, both of them; we are detained by moments in between; the actions are off stage. We are never informed what actually happened between Mr. Doran and Polly Mooney. We learn about the enticing beginning of the affair but not its completion. We may guess, of course, and we may think we know enough. Still, the overall narrative agency and all three main characters are in harmonious collusion in withholding the facts from us. We are not even told anything concrete about the interview between mother and daughter of the night before in which, we read, "a clean breast" had been made "of it"; nor about Mr. Doran's confession. Nothing specific is passed on to us. Whenever we come close to that recent "sin" as the cause of it all, the narrative drifts into vagueness, generalities, "his delirium . . ." or "secret amiable memories . . . a revery"; we are not let into the secret of "every ridiculous detail." The ellipsis after "delirium," Joyce's, needs to be filled, and filled it will be, by a few readers with more certainty than the facts may warrant. The sin is one for which "only one reparation can be made" (there is tacit agreement on this between Mrs. Mooney and Mr. Doran's priest, who both use the word independently, which in turn tells us that the case is a standard one, not unique), but still small enough to allow of being "magnified" by a priest. The one chief witness and victim remembers an exchange of "reluctant good-nights" on the third landing. All things known considered, Mr. Doran might have to pay for much less than what we almost automatically charge him with: this would make the reparation more cruel, less contingent on deed than on mere social attitudes, "honor," or reputation, hearsay and gossip. Anyway, we were not there, and this gap is paralleled by the one in the present, the decisive interview when Mrs. Mooney will be "hav[ing] the matter out with Mr. Doran." There is no need for us to be on the spot (nor is Polly's presence required). The issue has been predetermined by a determined woman in full charge, and by Mr. Doran's known "discomfiture." Like a general before a battle, Mrs. Mooney has marshaled her forces, her arguments, even their phrasing. We may well stay with Polly and the vaguest of her memories, waiting, alone. We can fill *this* narrative vacuum easily, though we were somewhere else, apart.

From *James Joyce Quarterly*

Considerations for Critical Thinking and Writing

1. How do the misdirections and gaps that Senn describes affect your reading of "The Boarding House"? If it isn't possible to determine what has actually happened in the missing scenes, is it possible to come up with a valid interpretation of the story?
2. Consider whether there are any misdirections and gaps in "Araby" or "Eveline."

Choose one story and discuss how information left out of the story is important to your interpretation of it.

3. Apply Senn's observations about the importance of what is left out of a story to a reading of Hawthorne's "The Minister's Black Veil" (p. 252). Write an essay that explores the significance of the "misdirections" in the story.

BARBARA McLEAN (b. 1949)
"The (Boar)ding House":
Mrs. Mooney as Circe and Sow   1991

Critics tend to agree that "The Boarding House" represents a bawdy house, where Bob Doran is trapped into a marriage he does not want by Mrs. Mooney, who is aptly termed *"The Madam."* His specific inability to save himself is directly related to the paralysis theme which pervades the entire collection of stories. There have also been a number of articles written on the religious connotations of the story, including Rosenberg's convincing argument that "Bob Doran, like Jesus of Nazareth, is being crucified," that Polly represents Mary Magdalene, and Mrs. Mooney, Pontius Pilate.[1] I intend to take a slightly different approach and look at Mrs. Mooney as Joyce's representation of Ireland, referred to by Stephen Dedalus as "the old sow that eats her farrow."

Mrs. Mooney, in her plan to get her daughter off her hands, shows little regard for Polly's future. Rather, she consumes her, swallows her up into the continuing pattern of failure that Joyce ascribes to most of his fictional families. She is typical of the mother characters Florence Walzl describes who "so influence or manipulate their daughters that, in effect, the young women relive their mothers' lives . . . at worst mothers destroy their daughters; at best they maim them."[2] Polly and Bob Doran both become victims of Mrs. Mooney, and, as we can see from *Ulysses,* their futures are not bright.

The bordello aspects of the boarding house recall the Circe book of Homer's *Odyssey,* and while I would not suggest that *Dubliners* is a recapitulation of that work, I cannot help but notice the similarities between these episodes. Like Circe, Mrs. Mooney attracts men to her house, and symbolically she turns them into pigs. Her husband, although he seemed to be reliable before the wedding, "began to go to the devil" shortly after Mrs. Mooney married him, and he is described as having a porcine "white face and a white moustache and white eyebrows . . . above his little eyes, which were pink-veined and raw." Bob Doran (a stranger like the men who encounter Circe in the *Odyssey*) becomes too anxious to shave, and his face begins to show swinish bristles in the form of the "reddish beard fring[ing] his jaws." Unlike Odysseus, who has Hermes to guide him through his encounter with Circe, Doran's god will not protect him, and therefore Mrs. Mooney, like Circe, can easily rob him of his courage.

There is certainly pig imagery in the story. Mrs. Mooney is depicted as an

[1]Bruce A. Rosenberg, "The Crucifixion in 'The Boarding House,'" *Studies in Short Fiction,* 5 (Fall 1967), 50.
[2]Florence L. Walzl, *"Dubliners:* Women in Irish Society," in *Women in Joyce,* ed. Suzette Henke and Elaine Unkeless (Urbana: Univ. of Illinois Press, 1982), p. 47.

old sow with her "great florid face" and her "big imposing" body. In spite of the fact that she "was a butcher's daughter" and "opened a butcher's shop" and could be expected to be familiar with all sorts of meat, all we see in "The Boarding House" is pork: "bacon fat and bacon rind." The "little gilt clock" she keeps on the mantelpiece can be seen as a symbol for Polly. Not only is the clock encased in a deceptive covering, but the term gilt, which of course in one sense refers to covering with a thin layer of gold, is also the term used for a young female pig up to the time she first farrows. Polly is not only young and (possibly) pregnant; she also appears to be better than she is. Her "soft hair" and gray-green eyes, her "white instep" and glowing "perfumed skin" overlay her basic lack of respectability. Behind the gilded shining exterior, Polly has a tarnished "disreputable father," a mother whose "boarding house was beginning to get a certain fame," and she "*was* a little vulgar."

The swine images in "The Boarding House" reflect the *Odyssey*, as the men who come in contact with *The Madam* acquire "pigs' heads and bristles."[3] Joyce then extends the imagery to depict Polly as both gilded and gilt. Mrs. Mooney seems to be concerned with disposing of her daughter, and although she does save Polly from the clutches of her estranged father by removing her from a typing job, her reasons may very well be vengeance on Mr. Mooney. Her lack of concern for her child, her brash determination, and her consuming manner all suggest that she metaphorically epitomizes the sow Stephen Dedalus had in mind.   From *James Joyce Quarterly*

[3]*Odyssey*, trans. E. V. Rieu (Harmondsworth: Penguin, 1946), p. 162.

Considerations for Critical Thinking and Writing

1. How does McLean make a case for her reading of Mrs. Mooney? What kind of evidence does she use? How does she organize it? Explain whether you find her argument convincing.
2. Does McLean's reading enhance your understanding and appreciation of the story? Explain why or why not.
3. In an essay compare the images used to describe Mrs. Mooney with the images that characterize Mangan's sister in "Araby." In your discussion consider how these two characters represent polarities in Joyce's treatment of women.

PAUL BAROLSKY (b. 1941)
Gretta's Name   1991

Few writers of English have pondered as deeply as Joyce the meaning of words, indeed of names, and Kenneth Burke tentatively suggested that in "The Dead" Gretta's name is resonant with "great." I would like to add, however, that it can be no accident, in a book essentially about regret, that a character who crystallizes this emotion in the conclusion should have a name that resonates with "regret." No matter that Gretta is a form of Margaret, that Margaret means "pearl" in the original Greek, for it is not the etymology of her name that is significant here but the resonance in her name of the word charged with the dominant emotion of Joyce's book.

In story after story of *Dubliners* we encounter regret — the sense of loss, of disappointment, of sorrow shading into deep grief: the sadness of a child who loses a friend to death; the disappointment of boys who go on an adventure that ends badly; the bitter self-recrimination of a child who suddenly recognizes the vanity of his desires; the regret of those who envy the successes of their friends or acquaintances; tales of the thwarted ambitions, missed opportunities, or wasted lives of both men and women; sad memories of a dead hero or of better days. This regret, expressed through the "mournful music" of Joyce's prose, laden with melancholy memories, is the profound sadness of loss. All of his stories, which are intertwined, point toward "The Dead," a deeply poignant story, in which the powerful sense of regret that permeates the book is condensed. The story and the book build to the climax in which Gretta, stirred by music, is overcome by emotion, painfully remembering the young man who once loved her: "he died for me." Gretta's regret precipitates the final, dolorous reflections of the story, which resolve in harmony all the sad memories of *Dubliners*. The tears that fill Gretta's husband's eyes, as he contemplates the flickering existence of all the dead, are the tears of regret — that emotion echoed again and again in the memory-laden, bittersweet sonority of Joyce's language, not least in the haunting refrain of regret in Gretta's very name. *Nomina sunt consequentia rerum* — names are the consequences of things.

From *James Joyce Quarterly*

Considerations for Critical Thinking and Writing

1. Barolsky discusses only Gretta's name in "The Dead." Consider Gabriel's and Michael's names too. In what sense might their names also be described as "the consequences of things"?
2. Write an essay about regret in "The Dead" and one other Joyce story in this anthology.

TWO COMPLEMENTARY CRITICAL READINGS

C. H. PEAKE
On Fear in "Eveline"
1977

The irony of the story is rather obvious and "literary," perhaps because it plays, not without pity, round the traditional and particularly Victorian theme of a girl torn between love and duty who finally makes the heroic sacrifice of happiness at the call of home and religion. But Joyce conscientiously demolishes sentimentality. Eveline is hardly a girl in love: marriage for her means that "people would treat her with respect then," and her affection for Frank is far from passionate: "First of all it had been an excitement for her to have a fellow and then she had begun to like him." The love is casually tacked on as a secondary condition in her vision of their future ("He would give her life, perhaps love, too") and, when finally he goes, "her eyes gave him no sign of love or farewell or recognition." She seems as incapable of love as of movement, and, as no overpowering passion is drawing her away, so the dutifulness which holds her back is drab and halfhearted. Her life is spent between the job she would not be sorry to leave and keeping house for a father who frightens her with his threats of violence and who will give her little money for housekeeping. Nevertheless, she persuades herself that her father will miss her, and recalls two trivial occasions when he had been "very nice." Even the memory of her promise to her mother "to keep the home together as long as she could" is marred by the vision of the mother's pitiful life and final craziness. For all her prayers "to God to direct her, to show her what was her duty," there is no real fight between love and duty inside Eveline: these are merely the conventional disguises for a feebler struggle between conflicting fears.

From *James Joyce: The Citizen and the Artist*

Considerations for Critical Thinking and Writing

1. Write an alternate final paragraph for the story that would substitute a sentimental Victorian ending for Joyce's.
2. According to Peake, how does Joyce subvert a sentimental reading of Eveline's decision to remain at home?
3. How does Peake's explanation of Eveline's fears affect your view of her character? Explain why you think he would agree or disagree with Parrinder's discussion (below).
4. Apply Peake's concept of "conventional disguises" to another story by Joyce in this anthology. Discuss to what extent the concept sheds light on the protagonist's way of coping with conflict.

PATRICK PARRINDER (b. 1944)
On Self-Restraint in "Eveline"   1984

At her moment of crisis she "prayed to God to direct her, to show her what was her duty." There is more to this than the circularity of escapism followed by penitence. Eveline is a young girl, facing the first great challenge of adulthood. She is trying to defy the will of her father, but her defeat comes, not in a direct confrontation with parental authority, but through an inner struggle resolved by her prayer. What Joyce shows repeatedly in *Dubliners* is not just the direct workings of repression — parental, sexual, religious — but its reproduction and internalization. Eveline is stopped, not by external restraints, but because she has learnt a self-restraint which cuts off her capacity for action and wipes out the adult personality she was struggling to establish.

From *James Joyce*

Considerations for Critical Thinking and Writing

1. Who and what teaches Eveline "self-restraint"? Why are these internal restraints even more insidious than external parental, sexual, and religious pressures?
2. In an essay compare Parrinder's and Peake's analyses of Eveline's refusal to leave

home. Do you think one or the other critic is more sympathetic to her? Explain why or why not.

3. In an essay, compare Eveline's internal struggle with that of Hawthorne's "Young Goodman Brown" (p. 242). Pay particular attention to each character's acts of self-denial.

4. Explain to what extent self-restraint informs Mr. Doran's responses to moments of crisis in "The Boarding House" (p. 319).

FLANNERY O'CONNOR (1925–1964)

When Flannery O'Connor died of lupus before her fortieth birthday, her work was cruelly cut short. Nevertheless, she had completed two novels, *Wise Blood* (1952) and *The Violent Bear It Away* (1960), as well as thirty-one short stories. Despite her short life and relatively modest output, her work is regarded as among the most distinguished American fiction of the mid-twentieth century. Her two collections of short stories, *A Good Man Is Hard to Find* (1955) and *Everything That Rises Must Converge* (1965), were included in *The Complete Stories of Flannery O'Connor* (1971), which won the National Book Award.

O'Connor's fiction is related to living a spiritual life in a secular world. Although this major concern is worked into each of her stories, she takes a broad approach to spiritual issues by providing moral, social, and psychological contexts that offer a wealth of insights and passion that her readers have found both startling and absorbing. Her stories are challenging because her characters, who initially seem radically different from people we know, turn out to be, by the end of each story, somehow familiar — somehow connected to us.

O'Connor inhabited simultaneously two radically different worlds. The world she created in her stories is populated with bratty children, malcontents, incompetents, pious frauds, bewildered intellectuals, deformed cynics, rednecks, hucksters, racists, perverts, and murderers who experience dramatically intense moments that surprise and shock readers. Her personal life, however, was largely uneventful. She humorously acknowledged its quiet nature in 1958 when she claimed that "there won't be any biographies of me because, for only one reason, lives spent between the house and the chicken yard do not make exciting copy."

A broad outline of O'Connor's life may not offer very much "exciting copy," but it does provide clues about why she wrote such powerful fiction. The only child of Catholic parents, O'Connor was born in Savannah, Georgia, where she attended a parochial grammar school and high school. When she was thirteen, her father became ill with disseminated lupus, a rare, incurable blood disease, and had to abandon his real estate business. The family moved to Milledgeville in central Georgia, where her mother's family had lived for generations. Because there were no Catholic schools in Milledgeville, O'Connor attended a public high school. In 1942, the year after her father died of lupus, O'Connor graduated from high school and enrolled in Georgia State College for Women. There she wrote for the literary magazine until receiving her diploma in 1945. Her stories earned her a fellowship to the Writers' Workshop at the University of Iowa, and for two years she learned to write steadily and seriously. She sold her first story to *Accent* in 1946 and earned her master of fine arts degree in 1947. She wrote stories about life in the rural South, and this subject matter, along with her devout Catholic perspective, became central to her fiction.

With her formal education behind her, O'Connor was ready to begin her professional career at the age of twenty-two. Equipped with determination ("No one can convince me that I shouldn't rewrite as much as I do") and offered the opportunity to be around other practicing writers, she moved to New York, where she worked on her first novel, *Wise Blood*. In 1950, however, she was diagnosed as having lupus, and, returning to Georgia for treatment, she took up permanent residence on her mother's farm in Milledgeville. There she lived a severely restricted but productive life, writing stories and raising peacocks.

With the exception of O'Connor's early years in Iowa and New York and some short lecture trips to other states, she traveled little. Although she made a pilgrimage to Lourdes (apparently more for her mother's sake than for her own) and then to Rome for an audience with the pope, her life was centered in the South. Like those of William Faulkner and many other southern writers, O'Connor's stories evoke the rhythms of rural southern speech and manners in insulated settings where widely diverse characters mingle. Also like Faulkner, she created works whose meanings go beyond their settings. She did not want her fiction to be seen in the context of narrowly defined regionalism: she complained that "in almost every hamlet you'll find at least one old lady writing epics in Negro dialect and probably two or three old gentlemen who have impossible historical novels on the way." Refusing to be caricatured, she knew that "the woods are full of regional writers, and it is the great horror of every serious Southern writer that he will become one of them." O'Connor's stories are rooted in rural southern culture, but in a larger sense they are set within the psychological and spiritual landscapes of the human soul. This interior setting universalizes local materials in much the same way that Nathaniel Hawthorne's New England stories do. Indeed, O'Connor once described herself as "one of his descendants": "I feel more of a kinship with him than any other American."

O'Connor's deep spiritual convictions coincide with the traditional emphasis on religion in the South, where, she said, there is still the belief "that man has fallen and that he is only perfectible by God's grace, not by his own unaided efforts." Although O'Connor's Catholicism differs from the prevailing Protestant Fundamentalism of the South, the religious ethos so pervasive even in rural southern areas provided fertile ground for the spiritual crises her characters experience. In a posthumous collection of her articles, essays, and reviews aptly titled *Mystery and Manners* (1969), she summarized her basic religious convictions:

> I am no disbeliever in spiritual purpose and no vague believer. I see from the standpoint of Christian orthodoxy. This means that for me the meaning of life is centered in our Redemption by Christ and what I see in the world I see in its relation to that. I don't think that this is a position that can be taken halfway or one that is particularly easy in these times to make transparent in fiction.

O'Connor realized that she was writing against the grain of the readers who discovered her stories in the *Partisan Review, Sewanee Review, Mademoiselle,* or *Harper's Bazaar.* Many readers thought that Christian dogma would make her writing doctrinaire, but she insisted that the perspective of Christianity allowed her to interpret the details of life and guaranteed her "respect for [life's] mystery." O'Connor's stories contain no prepackaged prescriptions for living, no catechisms that lay out all the answers. Instead, her characters struggle with spiritual questions in bizarre, incongruous situations. Their lives are grotesque — even comic — precisely because they do not understand their own spiritual natures. Their actions are extreme and abnormal. O'Connor explains the reasons for this in *Mystery and Manners;* she says she sought to expose the "distortions" of "modern life" that appear "normal" to her audience. Hence, she used "violent means" to convey her vision to a "hostile audience." "When you can assume that your audience holds the same beliefs you do, you can relax a little and use more normal means of talking to it." But when the audience holds different values, "you have to make your vision apparent by shock — to the hard of hearing you shout, and for the almost-blind you draw large and startling figures." O'Connor's characters lose or find their soul-saving grace in painful, chaotic circumstances that bear little or no resemblance to the slow but sure progress to the Celestial City of repentant pilgrims in traditional religious stories.

Because her characters are powerful creations who live convincing, even if ugly, lives, O'Connor's religious beliefs never supersede her storytelling. One need not be either Christian or Catholic to appreciate her concerns about human failure and degradation and her artistic ability to render fictional lives that are alternately absurdly comic and tragic. The ironies that abound in her work leave plenty of room for readers of all persuasions. O'Connor's work is narrow in the sense that her concerns are emphatically spiritual, but her compassion and her belief in human possibilities — even among the most unlikely characters — afford her fictions a capacity for wonder that is exhilarating. Her precise, deft use of language always reveals more than it seems to tell.

Like Hawthorne's fiction, O'Connor's stories present complex experiences that cannot be tidily summarized; it takes the entire story to suggest the meanings. Read the following four stories for the pleasure of entering the remarkable world O'Connor creates. You're in for some surprises.

Chronology

1925   Born on March 25 in Savannah, Georgia.

1938   Moves with family to Milledgeville, Georgia; enters the public Peabody High School.

1941   Father dies of lupus.

1942   Graduates from Peabody High School; enters Georgia State College for Women.

1943–45 Writes stories and poems for college literary magazine; graduates from Georgia State with an undergraduate degree in English.

1945–47 Enters writing program at the University of Iowa and earns a Master of Fine Arts degree in creative writing.

1948–49 Attends Yaddo artists' colony near Saratoga Springs, New York, for several months; lives in New York and Connecticut.

1950   After an illness, returns to Milledgeville and is diagnosed as suffering from lupus, an incurable disease. Lives on her family's dairy farm the rest of her life.

1952   *Wise Blood* receives mixed reviews and upsets some Milledgeville residents.

1955   *A Good Man Is Hard to Find and Other Stories* receives critical praise; the Guggenheim foundation rejects her fellowship application for a second time.

1956   A degenerating hip forces her to use crutches; the first telephone is installed on the farm.

1957   Lectures at several universities; dislikes a television version of the short story "The Life You Save May Be Your Own"; receives a grant from the National Institute of Arts and letters.

1958   Visits Lourdes and Rome.

1960   Publishes *The Violent Bear It Away.*

1962–63 Receives honorary doctorate from Saint Mary's women's college of the University of Notre Dame; speaks at a number of colleges in the south about her writing.

1964   Dies on August 3, 1964.

1965   *Everything That Rises Must Converge* published posthumously.

The dragon is by the side of the road, watching those who pass. Beware lest he devour you. We go to the Father of Souls, but it is necessary to pass by the dragon.
                                                    – St. Cyril of Jerusalem°

The grandmother didn't want to go to Florida. She wanted to visit some of her connections in east Tennessee and she was seizing at every chance to change Bailey's mind. Bailey was the son she lived with, her only boy. He was sitting on the edge of his chair at the table, bent over the orange sports section of the *Journal.* "Now look here, Bailey," she said, "see here, read this," and she stood with one hand on her thin hip and the other rattling the newspaper at his bald head. "Here this fellow that calls himself The Misfit is aloose from the Federal Pen and headed toward Florida and you read here what it says he did to these people. Just you read it. I wouldn't take my children in any direction with a criminal like that aloose in it. I couldn't answer to my conscience if I did."

Bailey didn't look up from his reading so she wheeled around then and faced the children's mother, a young woman in slacks, whose face was as broad and innocent as a cabbage and was tied around with a green headkerchief that had two points on the top like a rabbit's ears. She was sitting on the sofa, feeding the baby his apricots out of a jar. "The children have been to Florida before," the old lady said. "You all ought to take them somewhere else for a change so they would see different parts of the world and be broad. They never have been to east Tennessee."

The children's mother didn't seem to hear her but the eight-year-old boy, John Wesley, a stocky child with glasses, said, "If you don't want to go to Florida, why dontcha stay at home?" He and the little girl, June Star, were reading the funny papers on the floor.

"She wouldn't stay at home to be queen for a day," June Star said without raising her yellow head.

"Yes and what would you do if this fellow, The Misfit, caught you?" the grandmother asked.

"I'd smack his face," John Wesley said.

"She wouldn't stay at home for a million bucks," June Star said. "Afraid she'd miss something. She has to go everywhere we go."

"All right, Miss," the grandmother said. "Just remember that the next time you want me to curl your hair."

June Star said her hair was naturally curly.

The next morning the grandmother was the first one in the car, ready to go. She had her big black valise that looked like the head of a hippopotamus in one corner, and underneath it she was hiding a basket with Pitty Sing, the cat, in it. She didn't intend for the cat to be left alone in the house for three days because he would miss her too much and she was afraid he might brush against one of the gas burners and accidentally asphyxiate himself. Her son, Bailey, didn't like to arrive at a motel with a cat.

St. Cyril of Jerusalem (315?–386): Roman Catholic ecclesiastic and bishop of Jerusalem.

She sat in the middle of the back seat with John Wesley and June Star on either side of her. Bailey and the children's mother and the baby sat in front and they left Atlanta at eight forty-five with the mileage on the car at 55890. The grandmother wrote this down because she thought it would be interesting to say how many miles they had been when they got back. It took them twenty minutes to reach the outskirts of the city.

The old lady settled herself comfortably, removing her white cotton gloves and putting them up with her purse on the shelf in front of the back window. The children's mother still had on slacks and still had her head tied up in a green kerchief, but the grandmother had on a navy blue straw sailor hat with a bunch of white violets on the brim and a navy blue dress with a small white dot in the print. Her collars and cuffs were white organdy trimmed with lace and at her neckline she had pinned a purple spray of cloth violets containing a sachet. In case of an accident, anyone seeing her dead on the highway would know at once that she was a lady.

She said she thought it was going to be a good day for driving, neither too hot nor too cold, and she cautioned Bailey that the speed limit was fifty-five miles an hour and that the patrolmen hid themselves behind billboards and small clumps of trees and sped out after you before you had a chance to slow down. She pointed out interesting details of the scenery: Stone Mountain; the blue granite that in some places came up to both sides of the highway; the brilliant red clay banks slightly streaked with purple; and the various crops that made rows of green lace-work on the ground. The trees were full of silver-white sunlight and the meanest of them sparkled. The children were reading comic magazines and their mother had gone back to sleep.

"Let's go through Georgia fast so we won't have to look at it much," John Wesley said.

"If I were a little boy," said the grandmother, "I wouldn't talk about my 15 native state that way. Tennessee has the mountains and Georgia has the hills."

"Tennessee is just a hillbilly dumping ground," John Wesley said, "and Georgia is a lousy state too."

"You said it," June Star said.

"In my time," said the grandmother, folding her thin veined fingers, "children were more respectful of their native states and their parents and everything else. People did right then. Oh look at the cute little pickaninny!" she said and pointed to a Negro child standing in the door of a shack. "Wouldn't that make a picture, now?" she asked and they all turned and looked at the little Negro out of the back window. He waved.

"He didn't have any britches on," June Star said.

"He probably didn't have any," the grandmother explained. "Little niggers 20 in the country don't have things like we do. If I could paint, I'd paint that picture," she said.

The children exchanged comic books.

The grandmother offered to hold the baby and the children's mother passed him over the front seat to her. She set him on her knee and bounced him and told him about the things they were passing. She rolled her eyes and screwed up her mouth and stuck her leathery thin face into his smooth bland one. Occasionally he gave her a faraway smile. They passed a large cotton field with five or six graves fenced in the middle of it, like a small island. "Look at the graveyard!" the grandmother said, pointing it out. "That was the old family burying ground. That belonged to the plantation."

"Where's the plantation?" John Wesley asked.

"Gone with the Wind," said the grandmother. "Ha. Ha."

When the children finished all the comic books they had brought, they opened the lunch and ate it. The grandmother ate a peanut butter sandwich and an olive and would not let the children throw the box and the paper napkins out the window. When there was nothing else to do they played a game by choosing a cloud and making the other two guess what shape it suggested. John Wesley took one the shape of a cow and June Star guessed a cow and John Wesley said, no, an automobile, and June Star said he didn't play fair, and they began to slap each other over the grandmother.

The grandmother said she would tell them a story if they would keep quiet. When she told a story, she rolled her eyes and waved her head and was very dramatic. She said once when she was a maiden lady she had been courted by a Mr. Edgar Atkins Teagarden from Jasper, Georgia. She said he was a very good-looking man and a gentleman and that he brought her a watermelon every Saturday afternoon with his initials cut in it, E. A. T. Well, one Saturday, she said, Mr. Teagarden brought the watermelon and there was nobody at home and he left it on the front porch and returned in his buggy to Jasper, but she never got the watermelon, she said, because a nigger boy ate it when he saw the initials, E. A. T.! This story tickled John Wesley's funny bone and he giggled and giggled but June Star didn't think it was any good. She said she wouldn't marry a man that just brought her a watermelon on Saturday. The grandmother said she would have done well to marry Mr. Teagarden because he was a gentleman and had bought Coca-Cola stock when it first came out and that he had died only a few years ago, a very wealthy man.

They stopped at The Tower for barbecued sandwiches. The Tower was a part stucco and part wood filling station and dance hall set in a clearing outside of Timothy. A fat man named Red Sammy Butts ran it and there were signs stuck here and there on the building and for miles up and down the highway saying, TRY RED SAMMY'S FAMOUS BARBECUE. NONE LIKE FAMOUS RED SAMMY'S! RED SAM! THE FAT BOY WITH THE HAPPY LAUGH. A VETERAN! RED SAMMY'S YOUR MAN!

Red Sammy was lying on the bare ground outside The Tower with his head under a truck while a gray monkey about a foot high, chained to a small chinaberry tree, chattered nearby. The monkey sprang back into the tree and got on the highest limb as soon as he saw the children jump out of the car and run toward him.

Inside, The Tower was a long dark room with a counter at one end and tables at the other and dancing space in the middle. They all sat down at a board table next to the nickelodeon and Red Sam's wife, a tall burnt-brown woman with hair and eyes lighter than her skin, came and took their order. The children's mother put a dime in the machine and played "The Tennessee Waltz," and the grandmother said that tune always made her want to dance. She asked Bailey if he would like to dance but he only glared at her. He didn't have a naturally sunny disposition like she did and trips made him nervous. The grandmother's brown eyes were very bright. She swayed her head from side to side and pretended she was dancing in her chair. June Star said play something she could tap to so the children's mother put in another dime and played a fast number and June Star stepped out onto the dance floor and did her tap routine.

"Ain't she cute?" Red Sam's wife said, leaning over the counter. "Would you like to come be my little girl?"

"No I certainly wouldn't," June Star said. "I wouldn't live in a broken-down place like this for a million bucks!" and she ran back to the table.

"Ain't she cute?" the woman repeated, stretching her mouth politely.

"Aren't you ashamed?" hissed the grandmother.

Red Sam came in and told his wife to quit lounging on the counter and hurry up with these people's order. His khaki trousers reached just to his hip bones and his stomach hung over them like a sack of meal swaying under his shirt. He came over and sat down at a table nearby and let out a combination sigh and yodel. "You can't win," he said. "You can't win," and he wiped his sweating red face off with a gray handkerchief. "These days you don't know who to trust," he said. "Ain't that the truth?"

"People are certainly not nice like they used to be," said the grandmother.

"Two fellers come in here last week," Red Sammy said, "driving a Chrysler. It was a old beat-up car but it was a good one and these boys looked all right to me. Said they worked at the mill and you know I let them fellers charge the gas they bought? Now why did I do that?"

"Because you're a good man!" the grandmother said at once.

"Yes'm, I suppose so," Red Sam said as if he were struck with this answer.

His wife brought the orders, carrying the five plates all at once without a tray, two in each hand and one balanced on her arm. "It isn't a soul in this green world of God's that you can trust," she said. "And I don't count nobody out of that, not nobody," she repeated, looking at Red Sammy.

"Did you read about that criminal, The Misfit, that's escaped?" asked the grandmother.

"I wouldn't be a bit surprised if he didn't attact this place right here," said the woman. "If he hears about it being here, I wouldn't be none surprised to see him. If he hears it's two cent in the cash register, I wouldn't be a tall surprised if he. . . ."

"That'll do," Red Sam said. "Go bring these people their Co'-Colas," and the woman went off to get the rest of the order.

"A good man is hard to find," Red Sammy said. "Everything is getting terrible. I remember the day you could go off and leave your screen door unlatched. Not no more."

He and the grandmother discussed better times. The old lady said that in her opinion Europe was entirely to blame for the way things were now. She said the way Europe acted you would think we were made of money and Red Sam said it was no use talking about it, she was exactly right. The children ran outside into the white sunlight and looked at the monkey in the lacy chinaberry tree. He was busy catching fleas on himself and biting each one carefully between his teeth as if it were a delicacy.

They drove off again into the hot afternoon. The grandmother took cat naps and woke up every few minutes with her own snoring. Outside of Toombsboro she woke up and recalled an old plantation that she had visited in this neighborhood once when she was a young lady. She said the house had six white columns across the front and that there was an avenue of oaks leading up to it and two little wooden trellis arbors on either side in front where you sat down with your suitor after a stroll in the garden. She recalled exactly which road to turn off to get to it. She knew that Bailey would not be willing to lose any time looking at an old house, but the more she talked about it, the more she wanted to see it once again and find out if the little twin arbors were still standing. "There was a secret panel in this house," she said craftily, not telling the truth but wishing that she were, "and the story went that all the family silver was hidden in it when Sherman° came through but it was never found. . . ."

"Hey!" John Wesley said. "Let's go see it! We'll find it! We'll poke all the woodwork and find it! Who lives there? Where do you turn off at? Hey Pop, can't we turn off there?"

"We never have seen a house with a secret panel!" June Star shrieked. "Let's go to the house with the secret panel! Hey Pop, can't we go see the house with the secret panel!"

"It's not far from here, I know," the grandmother said. "It won't take over twenty minutes."

Bailey was looking straight ahead. His jaw was as rigid as a horseshoe. "No," he said.

The children began to yell and scream that they wanted to see the house 50 with the secret panel. John Wesley kicked the back of the front seat and June Star hung over her mother's shoulder and whined desperately into her ear that they never had any fun even on their vacation, that they could never do what THEY wanted to do. The baby began to scream and John Wesley kicked the back of the seat so hard that his father could feel the blows in his kidney.

"All right!" he shouted and drew the car to a stop at the side of the road. "Will you all shut up? Will you all just shut up for one second? If you don't shut up, we won't go anywhere."

"It would be very educational for them," the grandmother murmured.

"All right," Bailey said, "but get this: this is the only time we're going to stop for anything like this. This is the one and only time."

"The dirt road that you have to turn down is about a mile back," the grandmother directed. "I marked it when we passed."

"A dirt road," Bailey groaned. 55

After they had turned around and were headed toward the dirt road, the grandmother recalled other points about the house, the beautiful glass over the front doorway and the candle-lamp in the hall. John Wesley said that the secret panel was probably in the fireplace.

"You can't go inside this house," Bailey said. "You don't know who lives there."

"While you all talk to the people in front, I'll run around behind and get in a window," John Wesley suggested.

"We'll all stay in the car," his mother said.

Sherman: William Tecumseh Sherman (1820–1891), Union Army commander who led infamous marches through the South during the Civil War.

They turned onto the dirt road and the car raced roughly along in a swirl 60
of pink dust. The grandmother recalled the times when there were no paved
roads and thirty miles was a day's journey. The dirt road was hilly and there
were sudden washes in it and sharp curves on dangerous embankments. All at
once they would be on a hill, looking down over the blue tops of trees for miles
around, then the next minute, they would be in a red depression with the dust-
coated trees looking down on them.

"This place had better turn up in a minute," Bailey said, "or I'm going to
turn around."

The road looked as if no one had traveled on it for months.

"It's not much farther," the grandmother said and just as she said it, a
horrible thought came to her. The thought was so embarrassing that she turned
red in the face and her eyes dilated and her feet jumped up, upsetting her valise
in the corner. The instant the valise moved, the newspaper top she had over the
basket under it rose with a snarl and Pitty Sing, the cat, sprang onto Bailey's
shoulder.

The children were thrown to the floor and their mother, clutching the baby,
was thrown out the door onto the ground; the old lady was thrown into the
front seat. The car turned over once and landed right-side-up in a gulch off the
side of the road. Bailey remained in the driver's seat with the cat — gray-striped
with a broad white face and an orange nose — clinging to his neck like a
caterpillar.

As soon as the children saw they could move their arms and legs, they 65
scrambled out of the car, shouting, "We've had an ACCIDENT!" The grandmother
was curled up under the dashboard, hoping she was injured so that Bailey's
wrath would not come down on her all at once. The horrible thought she had
before the accident was that the house she had remembered so vividly was not
in Georgia but in Tennessee.

Bailey removed the cat from his neck with both hands and flung it out the
window against the side of a pine tree. Then he got out of the car and started
looking for the children's mother. She was sitting against the side of the red
gutted ditch, holding the screaming baby, but she only had a cut down her face
and a broken shoulder. "We've had an ACCIDENT!" the children screamed in a
frenzy of delight.

"But nobody's killed," June Star said with disappointment as the grandmother limped out of the car, her hat still pinned to her head but the broken
front brim standing up at a jaunty angle and the violet spray hanging off the side.
They all sat down in the ditch, except the children, to recover from the shock.
They were all shaking.

"Maybe a car will come along," said the children's mother hoarsely.

"I believe I have injured an organ," said the grandmother, pressing her side,
but no one answered her. Bailey's teeth were clattering. He had on a yellow
sport shirt with bright blue parrots designed in it and his face was as yellow as
the shirt. The grandmother decided that she would not mention that the house
was in Tennessee.

The road was about ten feet above and they could see only the tops of the 70
trees on the other side of it. Behind the ditch they were sitting in there were
more woods, tall and dark and deep. In a few minutes they saw a car some

distance away on top of a hill, coming slowly as if the occupants were watching them. The grandmother stood up and waved both arms dramatically to attract their attention. The car continued to come on slowly, disappeared around a bend and appeared again, moving even slower, on top of the hill they had gone over. It was a big black battered hearse-like automobile. There were three men in it.

It came to a stop just over them and for some minutes, the driver looked down with a steady expressionless gaze to where they were sitting, and didn't speak. Then he turned his head and muttered something to the other two and they got out. One was a fat boy in black trousers and a red sweat shirt with a silver stallion embossed on the front of it. He moved around on the right side of them and stood staring, his mouth partly open in a kind of loose grin. The other had on khaki pants and a blue striped coat and a gray hat pulled down very low, hiding most of his face. He came around slowly on the left side. Neither spoke.

The driver got out of the car and stood by the side of it, looking down at them. He was an older man than the other two. His hair was just beginning to gray and he wore silver-rimmed spectacles that gave him a scholarly look. He had a long creased face and didn't have on any shirt or undershirt. He had on blue jeans that were too tight for him and was holding a black hat and a gun. The two boys also had guns.

"We've had an ACCIDENT!" the children screamed.

The grandmother had the peculiar feeling that the bespectacled man was someone she knew. His face was as familiar to her as if she had known him all her life but she could not recall who he was. He moved away from the car and began to come down the embankment, placing his feet carefully so that he wouldn't slip. He had on tan and white shoes and no socks, and his ankles were red and thin. "Good afternoon," he said. "I see you all had you a little spill."

"We turned over twice!" said the grandmother.   75

"Oncet," he corrected. "We seen it happen. Try their car and see will it run, Hiram," he said quietly to the boy with the gray hat.

"What you got that gun for?" John Wesley asked. "Whatcha gonna do with that gun?"

"Lady," the man said to the children's mother, "would you mind calling them children to sit down by you? Children make me nervous. I want all you all to sit down right together there where you're at."

"What are you telling US what to do for?" June Star asked.

Behind them the line of woods gaped like a dark open mouth. "Come   80
here," said their mother.

"Look here now," Bailey said suddenly, "we're in a predicament! We're in. . . ."

The grandmother shrieked. She scrambled to her feet and stood staring. "You're The Misfit!" she said. "I recognized you at once!"

"Yes'm," the man said, smiling slightly as if he were pleased in spite of himself to be known, "but it would have been better for all of you, lady, if you hadn't of reckernized me."

Bailey turned his head sharply and said something to his mother that shocked even the children. The old lady began to cry and The Misfit reddened.

"Lady," he said, "don't you get upset. Sometimes a man says things he don't 85
mean. I don't reckon he meant to talk to you thataway."

"You wouldn't shoot a lady, would you?" the grandmother said and removed
a clean handkerchief from her cuff and began to slap at her eyes with it.

The Misfit pointed the toe of his shoe into the ground and made a little
hole and then covered it up again. "I would hate to have to," he said.

"Listen," the grandmother almost screamed, "I know you're a good man.
You don't look a bit like you have common blood. I know you must come from
nice people!"

"Yes mam," he said, "finest people in the world." When he smiled he showed
a row of strong white teeth. "God never made a finer woman than my mother
and my daddy's heart was pure gold," he said. The boy with the red sweat shirt
had come around behind them and was standing with his gun at his hip. The
Misfit squatted down on the ground. "Watch them children, Bobby Lee," he said.
"You know they make me nervous." He looked at the six of them huddled
together in front of him and he seemed to be embarrassed as if he couldn't
think of anything to say. "Ain't a cloud in the sky," he remarked, looking up at
it. "Don't see no sun but don't see no cloud neither."

"Yes, it's a beautiful day," said the grandmother. "Listen," she said, "you 90
shouldn't call yourself The Misfit because I know you're a good man at heart. I
can just look at you and tell."

"Hush!" Bailey yelled. "Hush! Everybody shut up and let me handle this!"
He was squatting in the position of a runner about to sprint forward but he
didn't move.

"I pre-chate that, lady," The Misfit said and drew a little circle in the ground
with the butt of his gun.

"It'll take a half a hour to fix this here car," Hiram called, looking over the
raised hood of it.

"Well, first you and Bobby Lee get him and that little boy to step over
yonder with you," The Misfit said, pointing to Bailey and John Wesley. "The boys
want to ast you something," he said to Bailey. "Would you mind stepping back
in them woods there with them?"

"Listen," Bailey began, "we're in a terrible predicament! Nobody realizes 95
what this is," and his voice cracked. His eyes were as blue and intense as the
parrots in his shirt and he remained perfectly still.

The grandmother reached up to adjust her hat brim as if she were going
to the woods with him but it came off in her hand. She stood staring at it and
after a second she let it fall to the ground. Hiram pulled Bailey up by the arm
as if he were assisting an old man. John Wesley caught hold of his father's hand
and Bobby Lee followed. They went off toward the woods and just as they
reached the dark edge, Bailey turned and supporting himself against a gray
naked pine trunk, he shouted, "I'll be back in a minute, Mamma, wait on me!"

"Come back this instant!" his mother shrilled but they all disappeared into
the woods.

"Bailey Boy!" the grandmother called in a tragic voice but she found she
was looking at The Misfit squatting on the ground in front of her. "I just know
you're a good man," she said desperately. "You're not a bit common!"

"Nome, I ain't a good man," The Misfit said after a second as if he had considered her statement carefully, "but I ain't the worst in the world neither. My daddy said I was a different breed of dog from my brothers and sisters. 'You know,' Daddy said, 'it's some that can live their whole life out without asking about it and it's others has to know why it is, and this boy is one of the latters. He's going to be into everything!'" He put on his black hat and looked up suddenly and then away deep into the woods as if he were embarrassed again. "I'm sorry I don't have on a shirt before you ladies," he said, hunching his shoulders slightly. "We buried our clothes that we had on when we escaped and we're just making do until we can get better. We borrowed these from some folks we met," he explained.

"That's perfectly all right," the grandmother said. "Maybe Bailey has an extra   100
shirt in his suitcase."

"I'll look and see terrectly," The Misfit said.

"Where are they taking him?" the children's mother screamed.

"Daddy was a card himself," The Misfit said. "You couldn't put anything over on him. He never got in trouble with the Authorities though. Just had the knack of handling them."

"You could be honest too if you'd only try," said the grandmother. "Think how wonderful it would be to settle down and live a comfortable life and not have to think about somebody chasing you all the time."

The Misfit kept scratching in the ground with the butt of his gun as if he   105
were thinking about it. "Yes'm, somebody is always after you," he murmured.

The grandmother noticed how thin his shoulder blades were just behind his hat because she was standing up looking down on him. "Do you ever pray?" she asked.

He shook his head. All she saw was the black hat wiggle between his shoulder blades. "Nome," he said.

There was a pistol shot from the woods, followed closely by another. Then silence. The old lady's head jerked around. She could hear the wind move through the tree tops like a long satisfied insuck of breath. "Bailey Boy!" she called.

"I was a gospel singer for a while," The Misfit said. "I been most everything. Been in the arm service, both land and sea, at home and abroad, been twict married, been an undertaker, been with the railroads, plowed Mother Earth, been in a tornado, seen a man burnt alive oncet," and he looked up at the children's mother and the little girl who were sitting close together, their faces white and their eyes glassy; "I even seen a woman flogged," he said.

"Pray, pray," the grandmother began, "pray, pray. . . ."   110

"I never was a bad boy that I remember of," The Misfit said in an almost dreamy voice, "but somewheres along the line I done something wrong and got sent to the penitentiary. I was buried alive," and he looked up and held her attention to him by a steady stare.

"That's when you should have started to pray," she said. "What did you do to get sent to the penitentiary that first time?"

"Turn to the right, it was a wall," The Misfit said, looking up again at the cloudless sky. "Turn to the left, it was a wall. Look up it was a ceiling, look down it was a floor. I forget what I done, lady. I set there and set there, trying to remember what it was I done and I ain't recalled it to this day. Oncet in a while, I would think it was coming to me, but it never come."

"Maybe they put you in by mistake," the old lady said vaguely.

"Nome," he said. "It wasn't no mistake. They had the papers on me." 115

"You must have stolen something," she said.

The Misfit sneered slightly. "Nobody had nothing I wanted," he said. "It was a head-doctor at the penitentiary said what I had done was kill my daddy but I known that for a lie. My daddy died in nineteen ought nineteen of the epidemic flu and I never had a thing to do with it. He was buried in the Mount Hopewell Baptist churchyard and you can see for yourself."

"If you would pray," the old lady said, "Jesus would help you."

"That's right," The Misfit said.

"Well then, why don't you pray?" she asked trembling with delight sud- 120 denly.

"I don't want no hep," he said. "I'm doing all right by myself."

Bobby Lee and Hiram came ambling back from the woods. Bobby Lee was dragging a yellow shirt with bright blue parrots in it.

"Throw me that shirt, Bobby Lee," The Misfit said. The shirt came flying at him and landed on his shoulder and he put it on. The grandmother couldn't name what the shirt reminded her of. "No, lady," The Misfit said while he was buttoning it up, "I found out the crime don't matter. You can do one thing or you can do another, kill a man or take a tire off his car, because sooner or later you're going to forget what it was you done and just be punished for it."

The children's mother had begun to make heaving noises as if she couldn't get her breath. "Lady," he asked, "would you and that little girl like to step off yonder with Bobby Lee and Hiram and join your husband?"

"Yes, thank you," the mother said faintly. Her left arm dangled helplessly 125 and she was holding the baby, who had gone to sleep, in the other. "Hep that lady up, Hiram," The Misfit said as she struggled to climb out of the ditch, "and Bobby Lee, you hold onto that little girl's hand."

"I don't want to hold hands with him," June Star said. "He reminds me of a pig."

The fat boy blushed and laughed and caught her by the arm and pulled her off into the woods after Hiram and her mother.

Alone with The Misfit, the grandmother found that she had lost her voice. There was not a cloud in the sky nor any sun. There was nothing around her but woods. She wanted to tell him that he must pray. She opened and closed her mouth several times before anything came out. Finally she found herself saying, "Jesus, Jesus," meaning Jesus will help you, but the way she was saying it, it sounded as if she might be cursing.

"Yes'm," The Misfit said as if he agreed. "Jesus thown everything off bal- ance. It was the same case with Him as with me except He hadn't committed any crime and they could prove I had committed one because they had the papers on me. Of course," he said, "they never shown me my papers. That's why I sign myself now. I said long ago, you get your signature and sign everything you do and keep a copy of it. Then you'll know what you done and you can hold up the crime to the punishment and see do they match and in the end you'll have something to prove you ain't been treated right. I call myself The Misfit," he said, "because I can't make what all I done wrong fit what all I gone through in punishment."

There was a piercing scream from the woods, followed closely by a pistol 130 report. "Does it seem right to you, lady, that one is punished a heap and another ain't punished at all?"

"Jesus!" the old lady cried. "You've got good blood! I know you wouldn't shoot a lady! I know you come from nice people! Pray! Jesus, you ought not to shoot a lady. I'll give you all the money I've got!"

"Lady," The Misfit said, looking beyond her far into the woods, "there never was a body that give the undertaker a tip."

There were two more pistol reports and the grandmother raised her head like a parched old turkey hen crying for water and called, "Bailey Boy, Bailey Boy!" as if her heart would break.

"Jesus was the only One that ever raised the dead," The Misfit continued, "and He shouldn't have done it. He thown everything off balance. If He did what He said, then it's nothing for you to do but throw away everything and follow Him, and if He didn't, then it's nothing for you to do but enjoy the few minutes you got left the best way you can — by killing somebody or burning down his house or doing some other meanness to him. No pleasure but meanness," he said and his voice had become almost a snarl.

"Maybe He didn't raise the dead," the old lady mumbled, not knowing what 135 she was saying and feeling so dizzy that she sank down in the ditch with her legs twisted under her.

"I wasn't there so I can't say He didn't," The Misfit said. "I wisht I had of been there," he said, hitting the ground with his fist. "It ain't right I wasn't there because if I had of been there I would of known. Listen lady," he said in a high voice, "if I had of been there I would of known and I wouldn't be like I am now." His voice seemed about to crack and the grandmother's head cleared for an instant. She saw the man's face twisted close to her own as if he were going to cry and she murmured, "Why you're one of my babies. You're one of my own children!" She reached out and touched him on the shoulder. The Misfit sprang back as if a snake had bitten him and shot her three times through the chest. Then he put his gun down on the ground and took off his glasses and began to clean them.

Hiram and Bobby Lee returned from the woods and stood over the ditch, looking down at the grandmother who half sat and half lay in a puddle of blood with her legs crossed under her like a child's and her face smiling up at the cloudless sky.

Without his glasses, The Misfit's eyes were red-rimmed and pale and defenseless-looking. "Take her off and throw her where you thrown the others," he said, picking up the cat that was rubbing itself against his leg.

"She was a talker, wasn't she?" Bobby Lee said, sliding down the ditch with a yodel.

"She would of been a good woman," The Misfit said, "if it had been 140 somebody there to shoot her every minute of her life."

"Some fun!" Bobby Lee said.

"Shut up, Bobby Lee," The Misfit said. "It's no real pleasure in life."

Considerations for Critical Thinking and Writing

1. How do the grandmother's concerns about the trip to Florida foreshadow events in the story?
2. Describe the grandmother. How does O'Connor make her the central character?
3. How does O'Connor portray the family? What is comic about them? What qualities about them are we to take seriously? Do you think they are responsible for what happens to them? Does your attitude toward them remain constant during the course of the story?
4. What is Red Sammy's purpose in the story? Relate his view of life to the story's conflicts.
5. Characterize the Misfit. What makes him so? Can he be written off as simply insane? How does the grandmother respond to him?
6. Why does the Misfit say that "Jesus thown everything off balance"? What does religion have to do with the brutal action of this story?
7. What does the Misfit mean when he says about the grandmother "She would of been a good woman . . . if it had been somebody there to shoot her every minute of her life"?
8. Describe the story's tone. Is it consistent? What is the effect of O'Connor's use of tone?
9. How is coincidence used to advance the plot? How do coincidences lead to ironies in the story?
10. Explain how the title points to the story's theme.

Connections to Other Selections

1. Compare and contrast the realistic detail and bizarre events in this story with García Márquez's use of the supernatural and realism in "A Very Old Man with Enormous Wings" (p. 223). What makes each story so difficult to interpret in contrast, say, to reading Hawthorne's "The Birthmark" (p. 261)?
2. How does this family compare with the Snopeses in Faulkner's "Barn Burning" (p. 436)? Which family are you more sympathetic to?
3. Consider the criminal behavior of the Misfit and Abner Snopes. What motivates each character? Explain the significant similarities and differences between them.

Good Country People   1955

Besides the neutral expression that she wore when she was alone, Mrs. Freeman had two others, forward and reverse, that she used for all her human dealings. Her forward expression was steady and driving like the advance of a heavy truck. Her eyes never swerved to left or right but turned as the story turned as if they followed a yellow line down the center of it. She seldom used the other expression because it was not often necessary for her to retract a statement, but when she did, her face came to a complete stop, there was an almost imperceptible movement of her black eyes, during which they seemed to be receding, and then the observer would see that Mrs. Freeman, though she might stand there as real as several grain sacks thrown on top of each other, was no longer there in spirit. As for getting anything across to her when this was the case, Mrs. Hopewell had given it up. She might talk her head off. Mrs. Freeman could never be brought to admit herself wrong on any point. She would stand there and if she could be brought to say anything, it was something like, "Well, I wouldn't of said it was and I wouldn't of said it wasn't," or letting her gaze range over the top kitchen shelf where there was an assortment of dusty bottles, she might remark, "I see you ain't ate many of them figs you put up last summer."

They carried on their most important business in the kitchen at breakfast. Every morning Mrs. Hopewell got up at seven o'clock and lit her gas heater and Joy's. Joy was her daughter, a large blonde girl who had an artificial leg. Mrs. Hopewell thought of her as a child though she was thirty-two years old and highly educated. Joy would get up while her mother was eating and lumber into the bathroom and slam the door, and before long, Mrs. Freeman would arrive at the back door. Joy would hear her mother call, "Come on in," and then they would talk for a while in low voices that were indistinguishable in the bathroom. By the time Joy came in, they had usually finished the weather report and were on one or the other of Mrs. Freeman's daughters, Glynese or Carramae, Joy called them Glycerin and Caramel. Glynese, a redhead, was eighteen and had many admirers; Carramae, a blonde, was only fifteen but already married and pregnant. She could not keep anything on her stomach. Every morning Mrs. Freeman told Mrs. Hopewell how many times she had vomited since the last report.

Mrs. Hopewell liked to tell people that Glynese and Carramae were two of the finest girls she knew and that Mrs. Freeman was a *lady* and that she was never ashamed to take her anywhere or introduce her to anybody they might meet. Then she would tell how she had happened to hire the Freemans in the first place and how they were a godsend to her and how she had had them four years. The reason for her keeping them so long was that they were not trash. They were good country people. She had telephoned the man whose name they had given as a reference and he had told her that Mr. Freeman was a good farmer but that his wife was the nosiest woman ever to walk the earth. "She's got to be into everything," the man said. "If she don't get there before the dust settles, you can bet she's dead, that's all. She'll want to know all your business. I can stand him real good," he had said, "but me nor my wife neither could have stood that woman one more minute on this place." That had put Mrs. Hopewell off for a few days.

She had hired them in the end because there were no other applicants but she had made up her mind beforehand exactly how she would handle the woman. Since she was the type who had to be into everything, then, Mrs. Hopewell decided, she would not only let her be into everything, she would *see to it* that she was into everything — she would give her the responsibility of everything, she would put her in charge. Mrs. Hopewell had no bad qualities of her own but she was able to use other people's in such a constructive way that she never felt the lack. She had hired the Freemans and she had kept them four years.

Nothing is perfect. This was one of Mrs. Hopewell's favorite sayings. Another was: that is life! And still another, the most important, was: well, other people have their opinions too. She would make these statements, usually at the table, in a tone of gentle insistence as if no one held them but her, and the large hulking Joy, whose constant outrage had obliterated every expression from her face, would stare just a little to the side of her, her eyes icy blue, with the look of someone who has achieved blindness by an act of will and means to keep it.

When Mrs. Hopewell said to Mrs. Freeman that life was like that, Mrs. Freeman would say, "I always said so myself." Nothing had been arrived at by anyone that had not first been arrived at by her. She was quicker than Mr. Freeman. When Mrs. Hopewell said to her after they had been on the place a while, "You know, you're the wheel behind the wheel," and winked, Mrs. Freeman had said, "I know it. I've always been quick. It's some that are quicker than others."

"Everybody is different," Mrs. Hopewell said.

"Yes, most people is," Mrs. Freeman said.

"It takes all kinds to make the world."

"I always said it did myself." 10

The girl was used to this kind of dialogue for breakfast and more of it for dinner; sometimes they had it for supper too. When they had no guest they ate in the kitchen because that was easier. Mrs. Freeman always managed to arrive at some point during the meal and to watch them finish it. She would stand in the doorway if it were summer but in the winter she would stand with one elbow on top of the refrigerator and look down on them, or she would stand by the gas heater, lifting the back of her skirt slightly. Occasionally she would stand against the wall and roll her head from side to side. At no time was she in any hurry to leave. All this was very trying on Mrs. Hopewell but she was a woman of great patience. She realized that nothing is perfect and that in the Freemans she had good country people and that if, in this day and age, you get good country people, you had better hang onto them.

She had had plenty of experience with trash. Before the Freemans she had averaged one tenant family a year. The wives of these farmers were not the kind you would want to be around you for very long. Mrs. Hopewell, who had divorced her husband long ago, needed someone to walk over the fields with her; and when Joy had to be impressed for these services, her remarks were usually so ugly and her face so glum that Mrs. Hopewell would say, "If you can't come pleasantly, I don't want you at all," to which the girl, standing square and rigid-shouldered with her neck thrust slightly forward, would reply, "If you want me, here I am — LIKE I AM."

Mrs. Hopewell excused this attitude because of the leg (which had been shot off in a hunting accident when Joy was ten). It was hard for Mrs. Hopewell to realize that her child was thirty-two now and that for more than twenty years she had had only one leg. She thought of her still as a child because it tore her heart to think instead of the poor stout girl in her thirties who had never danced a step or had any *normal* good times. Her name was really Joy but as soon as she was twenty-one and away from home, she had had it legally changed. Mrs. Hopewell was certain that she had thought and thought until she had hit upon the ugliest name in any language. Then she had gone and had the beautiful name, Joy, changed without telling her mother until after she had done it. Her legal name was Hulga.

When Mrs. Hopewell thought the name, Hulga, she thought of the broad blank hull of a battleship. She would not use it. She continued to call her Joy to which the girl responded but in a purely mechanical way.

Hulga had learned to tolerate Mrs. Freeman who saved her from taking walks with her mother. Even Glynese and Carramae were useful when they occupied attention that might otherwise have been directed at her. At first she had thought she could not stand Mrs. Freeman for she had found that it was not possible to be rude to her. Mrs. Freeman would take on strange resentments and for days together she would be sullen but the source of her displeasure was always obscure; a direct attack, a positive leer, blatant ugliness to her face — these never touched her. And without warning one day, she began calling her Hulga.

She did not call her that in front of Mrs. Hopewell who would have been incensed but when she and the girl happened to be out of the house together, she would say something and add the name Hulga to the end of it, and the big spectacled Joy-Hulga would scowl and redden as if her privacy had been intruded upon. She considered the name her personal affair. She had arrived at it first purely on the basis of its ugly sound and then the full genius of its fitness had struck her. She had a vision of the name working like the ugly sweating Vulcan° who stayed in the furnace and to whom, presumably, the goddess had to come when called. She saw it as the name of her highest creative act. One of her major triumphs was that her mother had not been able to turn her dust into Joy, but the greater one was that she had been able to turn it herself into Hulga. However, Mrs. Freeman's relish for using the name only irritated her. It was as if Mrs. Freeman's beady steel-pointed eyes had penetrated far enough behind her face to reach some secret fact. Something about her seemed to fascinate Mrs. Freeman and then one day Hulga realized that it was the artificial leg. Mrs. Freeman had a special fondness for the details of secret infections, hidden deformities, assaults upon children. Of diseases, she preferred the lingering or incurable. Hulga had heard Mrs. Hopewell give her the details of the hunting accident, how the leg had been literally blasted off, how she had never lost consciousness. Mrs. Freeman could listen to it any time as if it had happened an hour ago.

When Hulga stumped into the kitchen in the morning (she could walk without making the awful noise but she made it — Mrs. Hopewell was certain — because it was ugly-sounding), she glanced at them and did not speak. Mrs. Hopewell would be in her red kimono with her hair tied around her head in rags. She would be sitting at the table, finishing her breakfast and Mrs. Freeman would be hanging by her elbow outward from the refrigerator, looking down at the table. Hulga always put her eggs on the stove to boil and then stood over them with her arms folded, and Mrs. Hopewell would look at her — a kind of indirect gaze divided between her and Mrs. Freeman — and would think that if she would only keep herself up a little, she wouldn't be so bad looking. There was nothing wrong with her face that a pleasant expression wouldn't help. Mrs. Hopewell said that people who looked on the bright side of things would be beautiful even if they were not.

Whenever she looked at Joy this way, she could not help but feel that it would have been better if the child had not taken the Ph.D. It had certainly not brought her out any and now that she had it, there was no more excuse for her to go to school again. Mrs. Hopewell thought it was nice for girls to go to school

Vulcan: Roman god of fire.

to have a good time but Joy had "gone through." Anyhow, she would not have been strong enough to go again. The doctors had told Mrs. Hopewell that with the best of care, Joy might see forty-five. She had a weak heart. Joy had made it plain that if it had not been for this condition, she would be far from these red hills and good country people. She would be in a university lecturing to people who knew what she was talking about. And Mrs. Hopewell could very well picture her there, looking like a scarecrow and lecturing to more of the same. Here she went about all day in a six-year-old skirt and a yellow sweat shirt with a faded cowboy on a horse embossed on it. She thought this was funny; Mrs. Hopewell thought it was idiotic and showed simply that she was still a child. She was brilliant but she didn't have a grain of sense. It seemed to Mrs. Hopewell that every year she grew less like other people and more like herself — bloated, rude, and squint-eyed. And she said such strange things! To her own mother she had said — without warning, without excuse, standing up in the middle of a meal with her face purple and her mouth half full — "Woman! do you ever look inside? Do you ever look inside and see what you are *not?* God!" she had cried sinking down again and staring at her plate, "Malebranche° was right: we are not our own light. We are not our own light!" Mrs. Hopewell had no idea to this day what brought that on. She had only made the remark, hoping Joy would take it in, that a smile never hurt anyone.

The girl had taken the Ph.D. in philosophy and this left Mrs. Hopewell at a complete loss. You could say, "My daughter is a nurse," or "My daughter is a schoolteacher," or even, "My daughter is a chemical engineer." You could not say, "My daughter is a philosopher." That was something that had ended with the Greeks and Romans. All day Joy sat on her neck in a deep chair, reading. Sometimes she went for walks but she didn't like dogs or cats or birds or flowers or nature or nice young men. She looked at nice young men as if she could smell their stupidity.

One day Mrs. Hopewell had picked up one of the books the girl had just 20 put down and opening it at random, she read, "Science, on the other hand, has to assert its soberness and seriousness afresh and declare that it is concerned solely with what-is. Nothing — how can it be for science anything but a horror and a phantasm? If science is right, then one thing stands firm: science wishes to know nothing of nothing. Such is after all the strictly scientific approach to Nothing. We know it by wishing to know nothing of Nothing." These words had been underlined with a blue pencil and they worked on Mrs. Hopewell like some evil incantation in gibberish. She shut the book quickly and went out of the room as if she were having a chill.

This morning when the girl came in, Mrs. Freeman was on Carramae. "She thrown up four times after supper," she said, "and was up twict in the night after three o'clock. Yesterday she didn't do nothing but ramble in the bureau drawer. All she did. Stand up there and see what she could run up on."

"She's got to eat," Mrs. Hopewell muttered, sipping her coffee, while she watched Joy's back at the stove. She was wondering what the child had said to the Bible salesman. She could not imagine what kind of a conversation she could possibly have had with him.

Nicolas Malebranche (1638–1715): French philosopher.

He was a tall gaunt hatless youth who had called yesterday to sell them a Bible. He had appeared at the door, carrying a large black suitcase that weighted him so heavily on one side that he had to brace himself against the door facing. He seemed on the point of collapse but he said in a cheerful voice, "Good morning, Mrs. Cedars!" and set the suitcase down on the mat. He was not a bad-looking young man though he had on a bright blue suit and yellow socks that were not pulled up far enough. He had prominent face bones and a streak of sticky-looking brown hair falling across his forehead.

"I'm Mrs. Hopewell," she said.

"Oh!" he said, pretending to look puzzled but with his eyes sparkling, "I 25 saw it said 'The Cedars' on the mailbox so I thought you was Mrs. Cedars!" and he burst out in a pleasant laugh. He picked up the satchel and under cover of a pant, he fell forward into her hall. It was rather as if the suitcase had moved first, jerking him after it. "Mrs. Hopewell!" he said and grabbed her hand. "I hope you are well!" and he laughed again and then all at once his face sobered completely. He paused and gave her a straight earnest look and said, "Lady, I've come to speak of serious things."

"Well, come in," she muttered, none too pleased because her dinner was almost ready. He came into the parlor and sat down on the edge of a straight chair and put the suitcase between his feet and glanced around the room as if he were sizing her up by it. Her silver gleamed on the two sideboards; she decided he had never been in a room as elegant as this.

"Mrs. Hopewell," he began, using her name in a way that sounded almost intimate, "I know you believe in Chrustian service."

"Well yes," she murmured.

"I know," he said and paused, looking very wise with his head cocked on one side, "that you're a good woman. Friends have told me."

Mrs. Hopewell never liked to be taken for a fool. "What are you selling?" 30 she asked.

"Bibles," the young man said and his eye raced around the room before he added, "I see you have no family Bible in your parlor, I see that is the one lack you got!"

Mrs. Hopewell could not say, "My daughter is an atheist and won't let me keep the Bible in the parlor." She said, stiffening slightly, "I keep my Bible by my bedside." This was not the truth. It was in the attic somewhere.

"Lady," he said, "the word of God ought to be in the parlor."

"Well, I think that's a matter of taste," she began. "I think . . ."

"Lady," he said, "for a Chrustian, the word of God ought to be in every 35 room in the house besides in his heart. I know you're a Chrustian because I can see it in every line of your face."

She stood up and said, "Well, young man, I don't want to buy a Bible and I smell my dinner burning."

He didn't get up. He began to twist his hands and looking down at them, he said softly. "Well lady, I'll tell you the truth — not many people want to buy one nowadays and besides, I know I'm real simple. I don't know how to say a thing but to say it. I'm just a country boy." He glanced up into her unfriendly face. "People like you don't like to fool with country people like me!"

"Why!" she cried, "good country people are the salt of the earth! Besides, we all have different ways of doing, it takes all kinds to make the world go 'round. That's life!"

"You said a mouthful," he said.

"Why, I think there aren't enough good people in the world!" she said, stirred. "I think that's what's wrong with it!"

His face had brightened. "I didn't introduce myself," he said. "I'm Manley Pointer from out in the country around Willohobie, not even from a place, just from near a place."

"You wait a minute," she said. "I have to see about my dinner." She went out to the kitchen and found Joy standing near the door where she had been listening.

"Get rid of the salt of the earth," she said, "and let's eat."

Mrs. Hopewell gave her a pained look and turned the heat down under the vegetables. "*I* can't be rude to anybody," she murmured and went back into the parlor.

He had opened the suitcase and was sitting with a Bible on each knee.

"You might as well put those up," she told him. "I don't want one."

"I appreciate your honesty," he said. "You don't see any more real honest people unless you go way out in the country."

"I know," she said, "real genuine folks!" Through the crack in the door she heard a groan.

"I guess a lot of boys come telling you they're working their way through college," he said, "but I'm not going to tell you that. Somehow," he said, "I don't want to go to college. I want to devote my life to Chrustian service. See," he said, lowering his voice, "I got this heart condition. I may not live long. When you know it's something wrong with you and you may not live long, well then, lady . . ." He paused, with his mouth open, and stared at her.

He and Joy had the same condition! She knew that her eyes were filling with tears but she collected herself quickly and murmured, "Won't you stay for dinner? We'd love to have you!" and was sorry the instant she heard herself say it.

"Yes mam," he said in an abashed voice, "I would sher love to do that!"

Joy had given him one look on being introduced to him and then throughout the meal had not glanced at him again. He had addressed several remarks to her, which she had pretended not to hear. Mrs. Hopewell could not understand deliberate rudeness, although she lived with it, and she felt she had always to overflow with hospitality to make up for Joy's lack of courtesy. She urged him to talk about himself and he did. He said he was the seventh child of twelve and that his father had been crushed under a tree when he himself was eight years old. He had been crushed very badly, in fact, almost cut in two and was practically not recognizable. His mother had got along the best she could by hard working and she had always seen that her children went to Sunday School and that they read the Bible every evening. He was now nineteen years old and he had been selling Bibles for four months. In that time he had sold seventy-seven Bibles and had the promise of two more sales. He wanted to become a missionary because he thought that was the way you could do most for people. "He who losest his life shall find it," he said simply and he was so sincere, so genuine and earnest that Mrs. Hopewell would not for the world have smiled.

He prevented his peas from sliding onto the table by blocking them with a piece of bread which he later cleaned his plate with. She could see Joy observing sidewise how he handled his knife and fork and she saw too that every few minutes, the boy would dart a keen appraising glance at the girl as if he were trying to attract her attention.

After dinner Joy cleared the dishes off the table and disappeared and Mrs. Hopewell was left to talk with him. He told her again about his childhood and his father's accident and about various things that had happened to him. Every five minutes or so she would stifle a yawn. He sat for two hours until finally she told him she must go because she had an appointment in town. He packed his Bibles and thanked her and prepared to leave, but in the doorway he stopped and wrung her hand and said that not on any of his trips had he met a lady as nice as her and he asked if he could come again. She had said she would always be happy to see him.

Joy had been standing in the road, apparently looking at something in the distance, when he came down the steps toward her, bent to the side with his heavy valise. He stopped where she was standing and confronted her directly. Mrs. Hopewell could not hear what he said but she trembled to think what Joy would say to him. She could see that after a minute Joy said something and that then the boy began to speak again, making an excited gesture with his free hand. After a minute Joy said something else at which the boy began to speak once more. Then to her amazement, Mrs. Hopewell saw the two of them walk off together, toward the gate. Joy had walked all the way to the gate with him and Mrs. Hopewell could not imagine what they had said to each other, and she had not yet dared to ask.

Mrs. Freeman was insisting upon her attention. She had moved from the 55 refrigerator to the heater so that Mrs. Hopewell had to turn and face her in order to seem to be listening. "Glynese gone out with Harvey Hill again last night," she said. "She had this sty."

"Hill," Mrs. Hopewell said absently, "is the one who works in the garage?"

"Nome, he's the one that goes to chiropracter school," Mrs. Freeman said. "She had this sty. Been had it two days. So she says when he brought her in the other night he says, 'Lemme get rid of that sty for you,' and she says, 'How?' and he says, 'You just lay yourself down acrost the seat of that car and I'll show you.' So she done it and he popped her neck. Kept on a-popping it several times until she made him quit. This morning," Mrs. Freeman said, "she ain't got no sty. She ain't got no traces of a sty."

"I never heard of that before," Mrs. Hopewell said.

"He ast her to marry him before the Ordinary,"° Mrs. Freeman went on, "and she told him she wasn't going to be married in no *office*."

"Well, Glynese is a fine girl," Mrs. Hopewell said. "Glynese and Carramae 60 are both fine girls."

"Carramae said when her and Lyman was married Lyman said it sure felt sacred to him. She said he said he wouldn't take five hundred dollars for being married by a preacher."

Ordinary: Justice of the peace.

"How much would he take?" the girl asked from the stove.

"He said he wouldn't take five hundred dollars," Mrs. Freeman repeated.

"Well we all have work to do," Mrs. Hopewell said.

"Lyman said it just felt more sacred to him," Mrs. Freeman said. "The doctor 65 wants Carramae to eat prunes. Says instead of medicine. Says them cramps is coming from pressure. You know where I think it is?"

"She'll be better in a few weeks," Mrs. Hopewell said.

"In the tube," Mrs. Freeman said. "Else she wouldn't be as sick as she is."

Hulga had cracked her two eggs into a saucer and was bringing them to the table along with a cup of coffee that she had filled too full. She sat down carefully and began to eat, meaning to keep Mrs. Freeman there by questions if for any reason she showed an inclination to leave. She could perceive her mother's eye on her. The first round-about question would be about the Bible salesman and she did not wish to bring it on. "How did he pop her neck?" she asked.

Mrs. Freeman went into a description of how he had popped her neck. She said he owned a '55 Mercury but that Glynese said she would rather marry a man with only a '36 Plymouth who would be married by a preacher. The girl asked what if he had a '32 Plymouth and Mrs. Freeman said what Glynese had said was a '36 Plymouth.

Mrs. Hopewell said there were not many girls with Glynese's common sense. 70 She said what she admired in those girls was their common sense. She said that reminded her that they had had a nice visitor yesterday, a young man selling Bibles. "Lord," she said, "he bored me to death but he was so sincere and genuine I couldn't be rude to him. He was just good country people, you know," she said, " — just the salt of the earth."

"I seen him walk up," Mrs. Freeman said, "and then later — I seen him walk off," and Hulga could feel the slight shift in her voice, the slight insinuation, that he had not walked off alone, had he? Her face remained expressionless but the color rose into her neck and she seemed to swallow it down with the next spoonful of egg. Mrs. Freeman was looking at her as if they had a secret together.

"Well, it takes all kinds of people to make the world go 'round," Mrs. Hopewell said. "It's very good we aren't all alike."

"Some people are more alike than others," Mrs. Freeman said.

Hulga got up and stumped, with about twice the noise that was necessary, into her room and locked the door. She was to meet the Bible salesman at ten o'clock at the gate. She had thought about it half the night. She had started thinking of it as a great joke and then she had begun to see profound implications in it. She had lain in bed imagining dialogues for them that were insane on the surface but that reached below to depths that no Bible salesman would be aware of. Their conversation yesterday had been of this kind.

He had stopped in front of her and had simply stood there. His face was 75 bony and sweaty and bright, with a little pointed nose in the center of it, and his look was different from what it had been at the dinner table. He was gazing at her with open curiosity, with fascination, like a child watching a new fantastic animal at the zoo, and he was breathing as if he had run a great distance to reach her. His gaze seemed somehow familiar but she could not think where she had been regarded with it before. For almost a minute he didn't say anything.

Then on what seemed an insuck of breath, he whispered, "You ever ate a chicken that was two days old?"

The girl looked at him stonily. He might have just put this question up for consideration at the meeting of a philosophical association. "Yes," she presently replied as if she had considered it from all angles.

"It must have been mighty small!" he said triumphantly and shook all over with little nervous giggles, getting very red in the face, and subsiding finally into his gaze of complete admiration, while the girl's expression remained exactly the same.

"How old are you?" he asked softly.

She waited some time before she answered. Then in a flat voice she said, "Seventeen."

His smiles came in succession like waves breaking on the surface of a little 80 lake. "I see you got a wooden leg," he said. "I think you're brave. I think you're real sweet."

The girl stood blank and solid and silent.

"Walk to the gate with me," he said. "You're a brave sweet little thing and I liked you the minute I seen you walk in the door."

Hulga began to move forward.

"What's your name?" he asked, smiling down on the top of her head.

"Hulga," she said. 85

"Hulga," he murmured, "Hulga. Hulga. I never heard of anybody name Hulga before. You're shy, aren't you, Hulga?" he asked.

She nodded, watching his large red hand on the handle of the giant valise.

"I like girls that wear glasses," he said. "I think a lot. I'm not like these people that a serious thought don't ever enter their heads. It's because I may die."

"I may die too," she said suddenly and looked up at him. His eyes were very small and brown, glittering feverishly.

"Listen," he said, "don't you think some people was meant to meet on 90 account of what all they got in common and all? Like they both think serious thoughts and all?" He shifted the valise to his other hand so that the hand nearest her was free. He caught hold of her elbow and shook it a little. "I don't work on Saturday," he said. "I like to walk in the woods and see what Mother Nature is wearing. O'er the hills and far away. Pic-nics and things. Couldn't we go on a pic-nic tomorrow? Say yes, Hulga," he said and gave her a dying look as if he felt his insides about to drop out of him. He had even seemed to sway slightly toward her.

During the night she had imagined that she seduced him. She imagined that the two of them walked on the place until they came to the storage barn beyond the two back fields and there, she imagined, that things came to such a pass that she very easily seduced him and that then, of course, she had to reckon with his remorse. True genius can get an idea across even to an inferior mind. She imagined that she took his remorse in hand and changed it into a deeper understanding of life. She took all his shame away and turned it into something useful.

She set off for the gate at exactly ten o'clock, escaping without drawing Mrs. Hopewell's attention. She didn't take anything to eat, forgetting that food is usually taken on a picnic. She wore a pair of slacks and a dirty white shirt, and as an afterthought, she had put some Vapex° on the collar of it since she did not own any perfume. When she reached the gate no one was there.

She looked up and down the empty highway and had the furious feeling that she had been tricked, that he had only meant to make her walk to the gate after the idea of him. Then suddenly he stood up, very tall, from behind a bush on the opposite embankment. Smiling, he lifted his hat which was new and wide-brimmed. He had not worn it yesterday and she wondered if he had bought it for the occasion. It was toast-colored with a red and white band around it and was slightly too large for him. He stepped from behind the bush still carrying the black valise. He had on the same suit and the same yellow socks sucked down in his shoes from walking. He crossed the highway and said, "I knew you'd come!"

The girl wondered acidly how he had known this. She pointed to the valise and asked, "Why did you bring your Bibles?"

He took her elbow, smiling down on her as if he could not stop. "You can never tell when you'll need the word of God, Hulga," he said. She had a moment in which she doubted that this was actually happening and then they began to climb the embankment. They went down into the pasture toward the woods. The boy walked lightly by her side, bouncing on his toes. The valise did not seem to be heavy today; he even swung it. They crossed half the pasture without saying anything and then, putting his hand easily on the small of her back, he asked softly, "Where does your wooden leg join on?"

She turned an ugly red and glared at him and for an instant the boy looked abashed. "I didn't mean you no harm," he said. "I only meant you're so brave and all. I guess God takes care of you."

"No," she said, looking forward and walking fast, "I don't even believe in God."

At this he stopped and whistled. "No!" he exclaimed as if he were too astonished to say anything else.

She walked on and in a second he was bouncing at her side, fanning with his hat. "That's very unusual for a girl," he remarked, watching her out of the corner of his eye. When they reached the edge of the wood, he put his hand on her back again and drew her against him without a word and kissed her heavily.

The kiss, which had more pressure than feeling behind it, produced that extra surge of adrenaline in the girl that enables one to carry a packed trunk out of a burning house, but in her, the power went at once to the brain. Even before he released her, her mind, clear and detached and ironic anyway, was regarding him from a great distance, with amusement but with pity. She had never been kissed before and she was pleased to discover that it was an unexceptional experience and all a matter of the mind's control. Some people might enjoy drain water if they were told it was vodka. When the boy, looking expectant but uncertain, pushed her gently away, she turned and walked on, saying nothing as if such business, for her, were common enough.

He came along panting at her side, trying to help her when he saw a root that she might trip over. He caught and held back the long swaying blades of

Vapex: Trade name for a nasal spray.

thorn vine until she had passed beyond them. She led the way and he came breathing heavily behind her. Then they came out on a sunlit hillside, sloping softly into another one a little smaller. Beyond, they could see the rusted top of the old barn where the extra hay was stored.

The hill was sprinkled with small pink weeds. "Then you ain't saved?" he asked suddenly, stopping.

The girl smiled. It was the first time she had smiled at him at all. "In my economy," she said, "I'm saved and you are damned but I told you I didn't believe in God."

Nothing seemed to destroy the boy's look of admiration. He gazed at her now as if the fantastic animal at the zoo had put its paw through the bars and given him a loving poke. She thought he looked as if he wanted to kiss her again and she walked on before he had the chance.

"Ain't there somewhere we can sit down sometime?" he murmured, his 105 voice softening toward the end of the sentence.

"In that barn," she said.

They made for it rapidly as if it might slide away like a train. It was a large two-story barn, cool and dark inside. The boy pointed up the ladder that led into the loft and said, "It's too bad we can't go up there."

"Why can't we?" she asked.

"Yer leg," he said reverently.

The girl gave him a contemptuous look and putting both hands on the 110 ladder, she climbed it while he stood below, apparently awestruck. She pulled herself expertly through the opening and then looked down at him and said, "Well, come on if you're coming," and he began to climb the ladder, awkwardly bringing the suitcase with him.

"We won't need the Bible," she observed.

"You never can tell," he said, panting. After he had got into the loft, he was a few seconds catching his breath. She had sat down in a pile of straw. A wide sheath of sunlight, filled with dust particles, slanted over her. She lay back against a bale, her face turned away, looking out the front opening of the barn where hay was thrown from a wagon into the loft. The two pink-speckled hillsides lay back against a dark ridge of woods. The sky was cloudless and cold blue. The boy dropped down by her side and put one arm under her and the other over her and began methodically kissing her face, making little noises like a fish. He did not remove his hat but it was pushed far enough back not to interfere. When her glasses got in his way, he took them off of her and slipped them into his pocket.

The girl at first did not return any of the kisses but presently she began to and after she had put several on his cheek, she reached his lips and remained there, kissing him again and again as if she were trying to draw all the breath out of him. His breath was clear and sweet like a child's and the kisses were sticky like a child's. He mumbled about loving her and about knowing when he first seen her that he loved her, but the mumbling was like the sleepy fretting of a child being put to sleep by his mother. Her mind, throughout this, never stopped or lost itself for a second to her feelings. "You ain't said you loved me none," he whispered finally, pulling back from her. "You got to say that."

She looked away from him off into the hollow sky and then down at a black ridge and then down farther into what appeared to be two green swelling lakes.

She didn't realize he had taken her glasses but this landscape could not seem exceptional to her for she seldom paid any close attention to her surroundings.

"You got to say it," he repeated. "You got to say you love me." 115

She was always careful how she committed herself. "In a sense," she began, "if you use the word loosely, you might say that. But it's not a word I use. I don't have illusions. I'm one of those people who see *through* to nothing."

The boy was frowning. "You got to say it. I said it and you got to say it," he said.

The girl looked at him almost tenderly. "You poor baby," she murmured. "It's just as well you don't understand," and she pulled him by the neck, face-down, against her. "We are all damned," she said, "but some of us have taken off our blindfolds and see that there's nothing to see. It's a kind of salvation."

The boy's astonished eyes looked blankly through the ends of her hair. "Okay," he almost whined, "but do you love me or don'tcher?"

"Yes," she said and added, "in a sense. But I must tell you something. There 120 mustn't be anything dishonest between us." She lifted his head and looked him in the eye. "I am thirty years old," she said. "I have a number of degrees."

The boy's look was irritated but dogged. "I don't care," he said. "I don't care a thing about what all you done. I just want to know if you love me or don'tcher?" and he caught her to him and wildly planted her face with kisses until she said, "Yes, yes."

"Okay then," he said, letting her go. "Prove it."

She smiled, looking dreamily out on the shifty landscape. She had seduced him without even making up her mind to try. "How?" she asked, feeling that he should be delayed a little.

He leaned over and put his lips to her ear. "Show me where your wooden leg joins on," he whispered.

The girl uttered a sharp little cry and her face instantly drained of color. 125 The obscenity of the suggestion was not what shocked her. As a child she had sometimes been subject to feelings of shame but education had removed the last traces of that as a good surgeon scrapes for cancer; she would no more have felt it over what he was asking than she would have believed in his Bible. But she was as sensitive about the artificial leg as a peacock about his tail. No one ever touched it but her. She took care of it as someone else would his soul, in private and almost with her own eyes turned away. "No," she said.

"I known it," he muttered, sitting up. "You're just playing me for a sucker."

"Oh no no!" she cried. "It joins on at the knee. Only at the knee. Why do you want to see it?"

The boy gave her a long penetrating look. "Because," he said, "it's what makes you different. You ain't like anybody else."

She sat staring at him. There was nothing about her face or her round freezing-blue eyes to indicate that this had moved her; but she felt as if her heart had stopped and left her mind to pump her blood. She decided that for the first time in her life she was face to face with real innocence. This boy, with an instinct that came from beyond wisdom, had touched the truth about her. When after a minute, she said in a hoarse high voice, "All right," it was like surrendering to him completely. It was like losing her own life and finding it again, miraculously, in his.

Very gently he began to roll the slack leg up. The artificial limb, in a white 130 sock and brown flat shoe, was bound in a heavy material like canvas and ended in an ugly jointure where it was attached to the stump. The boy's face and his voice were entirely reverent as he uncovered it and said, "Now show me how to take it off and on."

She took it off for him and put it back on again and then he took it off himself, handling it as tenderly as if it were a real one. "See!" he said with a delighted child's face. "Now I can do it myself!"

"Put it back on," she said. She was thinking that she would run away with him and that every night he would take the leg off and every morning put it back on again. "Put it back on," she said.

"Not yet," he murmured, setting it on its foot out of her reach. "Leave it off for a while. You got me instead."

She gave a little cry of alarm but he pushed her down and began to kiss her again. Without the leg she felt entirely dependent on him. Her brain seemed to have stopped thinking altogether and to be about some other function that it was not very good at. Different expressions raced back and forth over her face. Every now and then the boy, his eyes like two steel spikes, would glance behind him where the leg stood. Finally she pushed him off and said, "Put it back on me now."

"Wait," he said. He leaned the other way and pulled the valise toward him 135 and opened it. It had a pale blue spotted lining and there were only two Bibles in it. He took one of these out and opened the cover of it. It was hollow and contained a pocket flask of whiskey, a pack of cards, and a small blue box with printing on it. He laid these out in front of her one at a time in an evenly-spaced row, like one presenting offerings at the shrine of a goddess. He put the blue box in her hand. THIS PRODUCT TO BE USED ONLY FOR THE PREVENTION OF DISEASE, she read, and dropped it. The boy was unscrewing the top of the flask. He stopped and pointed, with a smile, to the deck of cards. It was not an ordinary deck but one with an obscene picture on the back of each card. "Take a swig," he said, offering her the bottle first. He held it in front of her, but like one mesmerized, she did not move.

Her voice when she spoke had an almost pleading sound. "Aren't you," she murmured, "aren't you just good country people?"

The boy cocked his head. He looked as if he were just beginning to understand that she might be trying to insult him. "Yeah," he said, curling his lip slightly, "but it ain't held me back none. I'm as good as you any day in the week."

"Give me my leg," she said.

He pushed it farther away with his foot. "Come on now, let's begin to have us a good time," he said coaxingly. "We ain't got to know one another good yet."

"Give me my leg!" she screamed and tried to lunge for it but he pushed 140 her down easily.

"What's the matter with you all of a sudden?" he asked, frowning as he screwed the top on the flask and put it quickly back inside the Bible. "You just a while ago said you didn't believe in nothing. I thought you was some girl!"

Her face was almost purple. "You're a Christian!" she hissed. "You're a fine Christian! You're just like them all — say one thing and do another. You're a perfect Christian, you're . . ."

The boy's mouth was set angrily. "I hope you don't think," he said in a lofty indignant tone, "that I believe in that crap! I may sell Bibles but I know which end is up and I wasn't born yesterday and I know where I'm going!"

"Give me my leg!" she screeched. He jumped up so quickly that she barely saw him sweep the cards and the blue box into the Bible and throw the Bible into his valise. She saw him grab the leg and then she saw it for an instant slanted forlornly across the inside of the suitcase with a Bible at either side of its opposite ends. He slammed the lid shut and snatched up the valise and swung it down the hole and then stepped through himself.

When all of him had passed but his head, he turned and regarded her with 145 a look that no longer had any admiration in it. "I've gotten a lot of interesting things," he said. "One time I got a woman's glass eye this way. And you needn't to think you'll catch me because Pointer ain't really my name. I use a different name at every house I call at and don't stay nowhere long. And I'll tell you another thing, Hulga," he said, using the name as if he didn't think much of it, "you ain't so smart. I been believing in nothing ever since I was born!" and then the toast-colored hat disappeared down the hole and the girl was left, sitting on the straw in the dusty sunlight. When she turned her churning face toward the opening, she saw his blue figure struggling successfully over the green speckled lake.

Mrs. Hopewell and Mrs. Freeman, who were in the back pasture, digging up onions, saw him emerge a little later from the woods and head across the meadow toward the highway. "Why, that looks like that nice dull young man that tried to sell me a Bible yesterday," Mrs. Hopewell said, squinting. "He must have been selling them to the Negroes back in there. He was so simple," she said, "but I guess the world would be better off if we were all that simple."

Mrs. Freeman's gaze drove forward and just touched him before he disappeared under the hill. Then she returned her attention to the evil-smelling onion shoot she was lifting from the ground. "Some can't be that simple," she said. "I know I never could."

Considerations for Critical Thinking and Writing

1. Why is it significant that Mrs. Hopewell's daughter has two names? How do the other characters' names serve to characterize them?
2. Why do you think Mrs. Freeman and Mrs. Hopewell are introduced before Hulga? What do they contribute to Hulga's story?
3. Identify the conflict in this story. How is it resolved?
4. Hulga and the Bible salesman play a series of jokes on each other. How are these deceptions related to the theme?
5. What is the effect of O'Connor's use of the phrase "good country people" throughout the story? Why is it an appropriate title?
6. The Bible salesman's final words to Hulga are "you ain't so smart. I been believing in nothing ever since I was born!" What religious values are expressed in the story?
7. After the Bible salesman leaves Hulga at the end of the story, O'Connor adds two more paragraphs concerning Mrs. Hopewell and Mrs. Freeman. What is the purpose of these final paragraphs?

8. Hulga's perspective on life is ironic, but she is also the subject of O'Connor's irony. Explain how O'Connor uses irony to reveal Hulga's character.
9. This story would be different if told from Hulga's point of view. Describe how the use of a limited omniscient narrator contributes to the story's effects.
10. Comment on Hulga's conviction that intelligence and education are incompatible with religious faith.

Connections to Other Selections

1. Compare the Bible salesman's function in this story with the role Mary Grace plays in "Revelation" (below).
2. How do Mrs. Hopewell's assumptions about life compare with those of Krebs's mother in Hemingway's "Soldier's Home" (p. 125)? Explain how the conflict in each story is related to what the mothers come to represent in the eyes of the central characters.

Revelation   1964

The doctor's waiting room, which was very small, was almost full when the Turpins entered and Mrs. Turpin, who was very large, made it look even smaller by her presence. She stood looming at the head of the magazine table set in the center of it, a living demonstration that the room was inadequate and ridiculous. Her little bright black eyes took in all the patients as she sized up the seating situation. There was one vacant chair and a place on the sofa occupied by a blond child in a dirty blue romper who should have been told to move over and make room for the lady. He was five or six, but Mrs. Turpin saw at once that no one was going to tell him to move over. He was slumped down in the seat, his arms idle at his sides and his eyes idle in his head; his nose ran unchecked.

Mrs. Turpin put a firm hand on Claud's shoulder and said in a voice that included anyone who wanted to listen, "Claud, you sit in that chair there," and gave him a push down into the vacant one. Claud was florid and bald and sturdy, somewhat shorter than Mrs. Turpin, but he sat down as if he were accustomed to doing what she told him to.

Mrs. Turpin remained standing. The only man in the room besides Claud was a lean stringy old fellow with a rusty hand spread out on each knee, whose eyes were closed as if he were asleep or dead or pretending to be so as not to get up and offer her his seat. Her gaze settled agreeably on a well-dressed gray-haired lady whose eyes met hers and whose expression said: if that child belonged to me, he would have some manners and move over — there's plenty of room there for you and him too.

Claud looked up with a sigh and made as if to rise.

"Sit down," Mrs. Turpin said. "You know you're not supposed to stand on 5 that leg. He has an ulcer on his leg," she explained.

Claud lifted his foot onto the magazine table and rolled his trouser leg up to reveal a purple swelling on a plump marble-white calf.

"My!" the pleasant lady said. "How did you do that?"

"A cow kicked him," Mrs. Turpin said.

"Goodness!" said the lady.

Claud rolled his trouser leg down.   10

"Maybe the little boy would move over," the lady suggested, but the child did not stir.

"Somebody will be leaving in a minute," Mrs. Turpin said. She could not understand why a doctor — with as much money as they made charging five dollars a day to just stick their head in the hospital door and look at you — couldn't afford a decent-sized waiting room. This one was hardly bigger than a garage. The table was cluttered with limp-looking magazines and at one end of it there was a big green glass ash tray full of cigarette butts and cotton wads with little blood spots on them. If she had had anything to do with the running of the place, that would have been emptied every so often. There were no chairs against the wall at the head of the room. It had a rectangular-shaped panel in it that permitted a view of the office where the nurse came and went and the secretary listened to the radio. A plastic fern in a gold pot sat in the opening and trailed its fronds down almost to the floor. The radio was softly playing gospel music.

Just then the inner door opened and a nurse with the highest stack of yellow hair Mrs. Turpin had ever seen put her face in the crack and called for the next patient. The woman sitting beside Claud grasped the two arms of her chair and hoisted herself up; she pulled her dress free from her legs and lumbered through the door where the nurse had disappeared.

Mrs. Turpin eased into the vacant chair, which held her tight as a corset. "I wish I could reduce," she said, and rolled her eyes and gave a comic sigh.

"Oh, *you* aren't fat," the stylish lady said.   15

"Ooooo I am too," Mrs. Turpin said. "Claud he eats all he wants to and never weighs over one hundred and seventy-five pounds, but me I just look at something good to eat and I gain some weight," and her stomach and shoulders shook with laughter. "You can eat all you want to, can't you, Claud?" she asked, turning to him.

Claud only grinned.

"Well, as long as you have such a good disposition," the stylish lady said, "I don't think it makes a bit of difference what size you are. You just can't beat a good disposition."

Next to her was a fat girl of eighteen or nineteen, scowling into a thick blue book which Mrs. Turpin saw was entitled *Human Development.* The girl raised her head and directed her scowl at Mrs. Turpin as if she did not like her looks. She appeared annoyed that anyone should speak while she tried to read. The poor girl's face was blue with acne and Mrs. Turpin thought how pitiful it was to have a face like that at that age. She gave the girl a friendly smile but the girl only scowled the harder. Mrs. Turpin herself was fat but she had always had good skin, and though she was forty-seven years old, there was not a wrinkle in her face except around her eyes from laughing too much.

Next to the ugly girl was the child, still in exactly the same position, and 20 next to him was a thin leathery old woman in a cotton print dress. She and Claud had three sacks of chicken feed in their pump house that was in the same print. She had seen from the first that the child belonged with the old woman.

She could tell by the way they sat — kind of vacant and white-trashy, as if they would sit there until Doomsday if nobody called and told them to get up. And at right angles but next to the well-dressed pleasant lady was a lank-faced woman who was certainly the child's mother. She had on a yellow sweat shirt and wine-colored slacks, both gritty-looking, and the rims of her lips were stained with snuff. Her dirty yellow hair was tied behind with a little piece of red paper ribbon. Worse than niggers any day, Mrs. Turpin thought.

The gospel hymn playing was, "When I looked up and He looked down," and Mrs. Turpin, who knew it, supplied the last line mentally, "And wona these days I know I'll we-eara crown."

Without appearing to, Mrs. Turpin always noticed people's feet. The well-dressed lady had on red and gray suede shoes to match her dress. Mrs. Turpin had on her good black patent leather pumps. The ugly girl had on Girl Scout shoes and heavy socks. The old woman had on tennis shoes and the white-trashy mother had on what appeared to be bedroom slippers, black straw with gold braid threaded through them — exactly what you would have expected her to have on.

Sometimes at night when she couldn't go to sleep, Mrs. Turpin would occupy herself with the question of who she would have chosen to be if she couldn't have been herself. If Jesus had said to her before he made her, "There's only two places available for you. You can either be a nigger or white-trash," what would she have said? "Please, Jesus, please," she would have said, "just let me wait until there's another place available," and he would have said, "No, you have to go right now and I have only those two places so make up your mind." She would have wiggled and squirmed and begged and pleaded but it would have been no use and finally she would have said, "All right, make me a nigger then — but that don't mean a trashy one." And he would have made her a neat clean respectable Negro woman, herself but black.

Next to the child's mother was a red-headed youngish woman, reading one of the magazines and working a piece of chewing gum, hell for leather, as Claud would say. Mrs. Turpin could not see the woman's feet. She was not white-trash, just common. Sometimes Mrs. Turpin occupied herself at night naming the classes of people. On the bottom of the heap were most colored people, not the kind she would have been if she had been one, but most of them; then next to them — not above, just away from — were the white-trash; then above them were the home-owners, and above them the home-and-land owners, to which she and Claud belonged. Above she and Claud were people with a lot of money and much bigger houses and much more land. But here the complexity of it would begin to bear in on her, for some of the people with a lot of money were common and ought to be below she and Claud and some of the people who had good blood had lost their money and had to rent and then there were colored people who owned their homes and land as well. There was a colored dentist in town who had two red Lincolns and a swimming pool and a farm with registered white-face cattle on it. Usually by the time she had fallen asleep all the classes of people were moiling and roiling around in her head, and she would dream they were all crammed in together in a box car, being ridden off to be put in a gas oven.

"That's a beautiful clock," she said and nodded to her right. It was a big 25 wall clock, the face encased in a brass sunburst.

"Yes, it's very pretty," the stylish lady said agreeably. "And right on the dot too," she added, glancing at her watch.

The ugly girl beside her cast an eye upward at the clock, smirked, then looked directly at Mrs. Turpin and smirked again. Then she returned her eyes to her book. She was obviously the lady's daughter because, although they didn't look anything alike as to disposition, they both had the same shape of face and the same blue eyes. On the lady they sparkled pleasantly but in the girl's seared face they appeared alternately to smolder and to blaze.

What if Jesus had said, "All right, you can be white-trash or a nigger or ugly"!

Mrs. Turpin felt an awful pity for the girl, though she thought it was one thing to be ugly and another to act ugly.

The woman with the snuff-stained lips turned around in her chair and ^{30} looked up at the clock. Then she turned back and appeared to look a little to the side of Mrs. Turpin. There was a cast in one of her eyes. "You want to know wher you can get you one of themther clocks?" she asked in a loud voice.

"No, I already have a nice clock," Mrs. Turpin said. Once somebody like her got a leg in the conversation, she would be all over it.

"You can get you one with green stamps," the woman said. "That's most likely wher he got hisn. Save you up enough, you can get you most anythang. I got me some joo'ry."

Ought to have got you a wash rag and some soap, Mrs. Turpin thought.

"I get contour sheets with mine," the pleasant lady said.

The daughter slammed her book shut. She looked straight in front of her, ^{35} directly through Mrs. Turpin and on through the yellow curtain and the plate glass window which made the wall behind her. The girl's eyes seemed lit all of a sudden with a peculiar light, an unnatural light like night road signs give. Mrs. Turpin turned her head to see if there was anything going on outside that she should see, but she could not see anything. Figures passing cast only a pale shadow through the curtain. There was no reason the girl should single her out for her ugly looks.

"Miss Finley," the nurse said, cracking the door. The gum-chewing woman got up and passed in front of her and Claud and went into the office. She had on red high-heeled shoes.

Directly across the table, the ugly girl's eyes were fixed on Mrs. Turpin as if she had some very special reason for disliking her.

"This is wonderful weather, isn't it?" the girl's mother said.

"It's good weather for cotton if you can get the niggers to pick it," Mrs. Turpin said, "but niggers don't want to pick cotton any more. You can't get the white folks to pick it and now you can't get the niggers — because they got to be right up there with the white folks."

"They gonna *try* anyways," the white-trash woman said, leaning forward. ^{40}

"Do you have one of the cotton-picking machines?" the pleasant lady asked.

"No," Mrs. Turpin said, "they leave half the cotton in the field. We don't have much cotton anyway. If you want to make it farming now, you have to have a little of everything. We got a couple of acres of cotton and a few hogs and chickens and just enough white-face that Claud can look after them himself."

"One thang I don't want," the white-trash woman said, wiping her mouth with the back of her hand. "Hogs. Nasty stinking things, a-gruntin and a-rootin all over the place."

Mrs. Turpin gave her the merest edge of her attention. "Our hogs are not dirty and they don't stink," she said. "They're cleaner than some children I've seen. Their feet never touch the ground. We have a pig parlor — that's where you raise them on concrete," she explained to the pleasant lady, "and Claud scoots them down with the hose every afternoon and washes off the floor." Cleaner by far than that child right there, she thought. Poor nasty little thing. He had not moved except to put the thumb of his dirty hand into his mouth.

The woman turned her face away from Mrs. Turpin. "I know I wouldn't 45 scoot down no hog with no hose," she said to the wall.

You wouldn't have no hog to scoot down, Mrs. Turpin said to herself.

"A-gruntin and a-rootin and a-groanin," the woman muttered.

"We got a little of everything," Mrs. Turpin said to the pleasant lady. "It's no use in having more than you can handle yourself with help like it is. We found enough niggers to pick our cotton this year but Claud he has to go after them and take them home again in the evening. They can't walk that half a mile. No they can't, I tell you," she said and laughed merrily, "I sure am tired of buttering up niggers, but you got to love em if you want em to work for you. When they come in the morning, I run out and I say, 'Hi yawl this morning?' and when Claud drives them off to the field I just wave to beat the band and they just wave back." And she waved her hand rapidly to illustrate.

"Like you read out of the same book," the lady said, showing she understood perfectly.

"Child, yes," Mrs. Turpin said. "And when they come in from the field, I run 50 out with a bucket of icewater. That's the way it's going to be from now on," she said. "You may as well face it."

"One thang I know," the white-trash woman said. "Two thangs I ain't going to do: love no niggers or scoot down no hog with no hose." And she let out a bark of contempt.

The look that Mrs. Turpin and the pleasant lady exchanged indicated they both understood that you had to *have* certain things before you could *know* certain things. But every time Mrs. Turpin exchanged a look with the lady, she was aware that the ugly girl's peculiar eyes were still on her, and she had trouble bringing her attention back to the conversation.

"When you got something," she said, "you got to look after it." And when you ain't got a thing but breath and britches, she added to herself, you can afford to come to town every morning and just sit on the Court House coping and spit.

A grotesque revolving shadow passed across the curtain behind her and was thrown palely on the opposite wall. Then a bicycle clattered down against the outside of the building. The door opened and a colored boy glided in with a tray from the drugstore. It had two large red and white paper cups on it with tops on them. He was a tall, very black boy in discolored white pants and a green nylon shirt. He was chewing gum slowly, as if to music. He set the tray down in the office opening next to the fern and stuck his head through to look for the secretary. She was not in there. He rested his arms on the ledge and waited, his narrow bottom stuck out, swaying to the left and right. He raised a hand over his head and scratched the base of his skull.

"You see that button there, boy?" Mrs. Turpin said. "You can punch that and ⁵⁵ she'll come. She's probably in the back somewhere."

"Is that right?" the boy said agreeably, as if he had never seen the button before. He leaned to the right and put his finger on it. "She sometime out," he said and twisted around to face his audience, his elbows behind him on the counter. The nurse appeared and he twisted back again. She handed him a dollar and he rooted in his pocket and made the change and counted it out to her. She gave him fifteen cents for a tip and he went out with the empty tray. The heavy door swung to slowly and closed at length with the sound of suction. For a moment no one spoke.

"They ought to send all them niggers back to Africa," the white-trash woman said. "That's wher they come from in the first place."

"Oh, I couldn't do without my good colored friends," the pleasant lady said.

"There's a heap of things worse than a nigger," Mrs. Turpin agreed. "It's all kinds of them just like it's all kinds of us."

"Yes, and it takes all kinds to make the world go round," the lady said in ⁶⁰ her musical voice.

As she said it, the raw-complexioned girl snapped her teeth together. Her lower lip turned downwards and inside out, revealing the pale pink inside of her mouth. After a second it rolled back up. It was the ugliest face Mrs. Turpin had ever seen anyone make and for a moment she was certain that the girl had made it at her. She was looking at her as if she had known and disliked her all her life — all of Mrs. Turpin's life, it seemed too, not just all the girl's life. Why, girl, I don't even know you, Mrs. Turpin said silently.

She forced her attention back to the discussion. "It wouldn't be practical to send them back to Africa," she said. "They wouldn't want to go. They got it too good here."

"Wouldn't be what they wanted — if I had anythang to do with it," the woman said.

"It wouldn't be a way in the world you could get all the niggers back over there," Mrs. Turpin said. "They'd be hiding out and lying down and turning sick on you and wailing and hollering and raring and pitching. It wouldn't be a way in the world to get them over there."

"They got over here," the trashy woman said. "Get back like they got over." ⁶⁵

"It wasn't so many of them then," Mrs. Turpin explained.

The woman looked at Mrs. Turpin as if here was an idiot indeed but Mrs. Turpin was not bothered by the look, considering where it came from.

"Nooo," she said, "they're going to stay here where they can go to New York and marry white folks and improve their color. That's what they all want to do, every one of them, improve their color."

"You know what comes of that, don't you?" Claud asked.

"No, Claud, what?" Mrs. Turpin said. ⁷⁰

Claud's eyes twinkled. "White-faced niggers," he said with never a smile.

Everybody in the office laughed except the white-trash and the ugly girl. The girl gripped the book in her lap with white fingers. The trashy woman looked around her from face to face as if she thought they were all idiots. The old woman in the feed sack dress continued to gaze expressionless across the floor at the high-top shoes of the man opposite her, the one who had been pretending to be asleep when the Turpins came in. He was laughing heartily, his hands still spread out on his knees. The child had fallen to the side and was lying now almost face down in the old woman's lap.

While they recovered from their laughter, the nasal chorus on the radio kept the room from silence.

"You go to blank blank
And I'll go to mine
But we'll all blank along
To-geth-ther,
And all along the blank
We'll hep each other out
Smile-ling in any kind of
Weath-ther!"

Mrs. Turpin didn't catch every word but she caught enough to agree with the spirit of the song and it turned her thoughts sober. To help anybody out that needed it was her philosophy of life. She never spared herself when she found somebody in need, whether they were white or black, trash or decent. And of all she had to be thankful for, she was most thankful that this was so. If Jesus had said, "You can be high society and have all the money you want and be thin and svelte-like, but you can't be a good woman with it," she would have had to say, "Well don't make me that then. Make me a good woman and it don't matter what else, how fat or how ugly or how poor!" Her heart rose. He had not made her a nigger or white-trash or ugly! He had made her herself and given her a little of everything. Jesus, thank you! she said. Thank you thank you thank you! Whenever she counted her blessings she felt as buoyant as if she weighed one hundred and twenty-five pounds instead of one hundred and eighty.

"What's wrong with your little boy?" the pleasant lady asked the white-trashy 75 woman.

"He has a ulcer," the woman said proudly. "He ain't give me a minute's peace since he was born. Him and her are just alike," she said, nodding at the old woman, who was running her leathery fingers through the child's pale hair. "Look like I can't get nothing down them two but Co' Cola and candy."

That's all you try to get down em, Mrs. Turpin said to herself. Too lazy to light the fire. There was nothing you could tell her about people like them that she didn't know already. And it was not just that they didn't have anything. Because if you gave them everything, in two weeks it would all be broken or filthy or they would have chopped it up for lightwood. She knew all this from her own experience. Help them you must, but help them you couldn't.

All at once the ugly girl turned her lips inside out again. Her eyes fixed like two drills on Mrs. Turpin. This time there was no mistaking that there was something urgent behind them.

Girl, Mrs. Turpin exclaimed silently, I haven't done a thing to you! The girl might be confusing her with somebody else. There was no need to sit by and let herself be intimidated. "You must be in college," she said boldly, looking directly at the girl. "I see you reading a book there."

The girl continued to stare and pointedly did not answer. 80

Her mother blushed at this rudeness. "The lady asked you a question, Mary Grace," she said under her breath.

"I have ears," Mary Grace said.

The poor mother blushed again. "Mary Grace goes to Wellesley College," she explained. She twisted one of the buttons on her dress. "In Massachusetts," she added with a grimace. "And in the summer she just keeps right on studying. Just reads all the time, a real book worm. She's done real well at Wellesley; she's taking English and Math and History and Psychology and Social Studies," she rattled on, "and I think it's too much. I think she ought to get out and have fun."

The girl looked as if she would like to hurl them all through the plate glass window.

"Way up north," Mrs. Turpin murmured and thought, well, it hasn't done much for her manners. 85

"I'd almost rather to have him sick," the white-trash woman said, wrenching the attention back to herself. "He's so mean when he ain't. Look like some children just take natural to meanness. It's some gets bad when they get sick but he was the opposite. Took sick and turned good. He don't give me no trouble now. It's me waitin to see the doctor," she said.

If I was going to send anybody back to Africa, Mrs. Turpin thought, it would be your kind, woman. "Yes, indeed," she said aloud, but looking up at the ceiling, "it's a heap of things worse than a nigger." And dirtier than a hog, she added to herself.

"I think people with bad dispositions are more to be pitied than anyone on earth," the pleasant lady said in a voice that was decidedly thin.

"I thank the Lord he has blessed me with a good one," Mrs. Turpin said. "The day has never dawned that I couldn't find something to laugh at."

"Not since she married me anyways," Claud said with a comical straight face. 90

Everybody laughed except the girl and the white-trash.

Mrs. Turpin's stomach shook. "He's such a caution," she said, "that I can't help but laugh at him."

The girl made a loud ugly noise through her teeth.

Her mother's mouth grew thin and tight. "I think the worst thing in the world," she said, "is an ungrateful person. To have everything and not appreciate it. I know a girl," she said, "who has parents who would give her anything, a little brother who loves her dearly, who is getting a good education, who wears the best clothes, but who can never say a kind word to anyone, who never smiles, who just criticizes and complains all day long."

"Is she too old to paddle?" Claud asked. 95

The girl's face was almost purple.

"Yes," the lady said, "I'm afraid there's nothing to do but leave her to her folly. Some day she'll wake up and it'll be too late."

"It never hurt anyone to smile," Mrs. Turpin said. "It just makes you feel better all over."

"Of course," the lady said sadly, "but there are just some people you can't tell anything to. They can't take criticism."

"If it's one thing I am," Mrs. Turpin said with feeling, "it's grateful. When I 100 think who all I could have been besides myself and what all I got, a little of everything, and a good disposition besides, I just feel like shouting, 'Thank you, Jesus, for making everything the way it is!' It could have been different!" For one thing, somebody else could have got Claud. At the thought of this, she was flooded with gratitude and a terrible pang of joy ran through her. "Oh thank you, Jesus, Jesus, thank you!" she cried aloud.

The book struck her directly over her left eye. It struck almost at the same instant that she realized the girl was about to hurl it. Before she could utter a sound, the raw face came crashing across the table toward her, howling. The girl's fingers sank like clamps into the soft flesh of her neck. She heard the mother cry out and Claud shout, "Whoa!" There was an instant when she was certain that she was about to be in an earthquake.

All at once her vision narrowed and she saw everything as if it were happening in a small room far away, or as if she were looking at it through the wrong end of a telescope. Claud's face crumpled and fell out of sight. The nurse ran in, then out, then in again. Then the gangling figure of the doctor rushed out of the inner door. Magazines flew this way and that as the table turned over. The girl fell with a thud and Mrs. Turpin's vision suddenly reversed itself and she saw everything large instead of small. The eyes of the white-trashy woman were staring hugely at the floor. There the girl, held down on one side by the nurse and on the other by her mother, was wrenching and turning in their grasp. The doctor was kneeling astride her, trying to hold her arm down. He managed after a second to sink a long needle into it.

Mrs. Turpin felt entirely hollow except for her heart which swung from side to side as if it were agitated in a great empty drum of flesh.

"Somebody that's not busy call for the ambulance," the doctor said in the off-hand voice young doctors adopt for terrible occasions.

Mrs. Turpin could not have moved a finger. The old man who had been 105 sitting next to her skipped nimbly into the office and made the call, for the secretary still seemed to be gone.

"Claud!" Mrs. Turpin called.

He was not in his chair. She knew she must jump up and find him but she felt like some one trying to catch a train in a dream, when everything moves in slow motion and the faster you try to run the slower you go.

"Here I am," a suffocated voice, very unlike Claud's, said.

He was doubled up in the corner on the floor, pale as paper, holding his leg. She wanted to get up and go to him but she could not move. Instead, her gaze was drawn slowly downward to the churning face on the floor, which she could see over the doctor's shoulder.

The girl's eyes stopped rolling and focused on her. They seemed a much 110 lighter blue than before, as if a door that had been tightly closed behind them was now open to admit light and air.

Mrs. Turpin's head cleared and her power of motion returned. She leaned forward until she was looking directly into the fierce brilliant eyes. There was no doubt in her mind that the girl did know her, knew her in some intense and personal way, beyond time and place and condition. "What you got to say to me?" she asked hoarsely and held her breath, waiting, as for a revelation.

The girl raised her head. Her gaze locked with Mrs. Turpin's. "Go back to hell where you came from, you old wart hog," she whispered. Her voice was low but clear. Her eyes burned for a moment as if she saw with pleasure that her message had struck its target.

Mrs. Turpin sank back in her chair.

After a moment the girl's eyes closed and she turned her head wearily to the side.

The doctor rose and handed the nurse the empty syringe. He leaned over 115 and put both hands for a moment on the mother's shoulders, which were shaking. She was sitting on the floor, her lips pressed together, holding Mary Grace's hand in her lap. The girl's fingers were gripped like a baby's around her thumb. "Go on to the hospital," he said. "I'll call and make the arrangements."

"Now let's see that neck," he said in a jovial voice to Mrs. Turpin. He began to inspect her neck with his first two fingers. Two little moon-shaped lines like pink fish bones were indented over her windpipe. There was the beginning of an angry red swelling above her eye. His fingers passed over this also.

"Lea' me be," she said thickly and shook him off. "See about Claud. She kicked him."

"I'll see about him in a minute," he said and felt her pulse. He was a thin gray-haired man, given to pleasantries. "Go home and have yourself a vacation the rest of the day," he said and patted her on the shoulder.

Quit your pattin me, Mrs. Turpin growled to herself.

"And put an ice pack over that eye," he said. Then he went and squatted 120 down beside Claud and looked at his leg. After a moment he pulled him up and Claud limped after him into the office.

Until the ambulance came, the only sounds in the room were the tremulous moans of the girl's mother, who continued to sit on the floor. The white-trash woman did not take her eyes off the girl. Mrs. Turpin looked straight ahead at nothing. Presently the ambulance drew up, a long dark shadow, behind the curtain. The attendants came in and set the stretcher down beside the girl and lifted her expertly onto it and carried her out. The nurse helped the mother gather up her things. The shadow of the ambulance moved silently away and the nurse came back in the office.

"That ther girl is going to be a lunatic, ain't she?" the white-trash woman asked the nurse, but the nurse kept on to the back and never answered her.

"Yes, she's going to be a lunatic," the white-trash woman said to the rest of them.

"Po' critter," the old woman murmured. The child's face was still in her lap. His eyes looked idly out over her knees. He had not moved during the disturbance except to draw one leg up under him.

"I thank Gawd," the white-trash woman said fervently, "I ain't a lunatic." 125

Claud came limping out and the Turpins went home.

As their pick-up truck turned into their own dirt road and made the crest of the hill, Mrs. Turpin gripped the window ledge and looked out suspiciously. The land sloped gracefully down through a field dotted with lavender weeds and at the start of the rise their small yellow frame house, with its little flower beds spread out around it like a fancy apron, sat primly in its accustomed place between two giant hickory trees. She would not have been startled to see a burnt wound between two blackened chimneys.

Neither of them felt like eating so they put on their house clothes and lowered the shade in the bedroom and lay down, Claud with his leg on a pillow and herself with a damp washcloth over her eye. The instant she was flat on her back, the image of a razor-backed hog with warts on its face and horns coming out behind its ears snorted into her head. She moaned, a low quiet moan.

"I am not," she said tearfully, "a wart hog. From hell." But the denial had no force. The girl's eyes and her words, even the tone of her voice, low but clear, directed only to her, brooked no repudiation. She had been singled out for the message, though there was trash in the room to whom it might justly have been applied. The full force of this fact struck her only now. There was a woman there who was neglecting her own child but she had been overlooked. The message had been given to Ruby Turpin, a respectable, hard-working, church-going woman. The tears dried. Her eyes began to burn instead with wrath.

She rose on her elbow and the washcloth fell into her hand. Claud was 130 lying on his back, snoring. She wanted to tell him what the girl had said. At the same time, she did not wish to put the image of herself as a wart hog from hell into his mind.

"Hey, Claud," she muttered and pushed his shoulder.

Claud opened one pale baby blue eye.

She looked into it warily. He did not think about anything. He just went his way.

"Wha, whasit?" he said and closed the eye again.

"Nothing," she said. "Does your leg pain you?" 135

"Hurts like hell," Claud said.

"It'll quit terreckly," she said and lay back down. In a moment Claud was snoring again. For the rest of the afternoon they lay there. Claud slept. She scowled at the ceiling. Occasionally she raised her fist and made a small stabbing motion over her chest as if she was defending her innocence to invisible guests who were like the comforters of Job, reasonable-seeming but wrong.

About five-thirty Claud stirred. "Got to go after those niggers," he sighed, not moving.

She was looking straight up as if there were unintelligible handwriting on the ceiling. The protuberance over her eye had turned a greenish-blue. "Listen here," she said.

"What?" 140

"Kiss me."

Claud leaned over and kissed her loudly on the mouth. He pinched her side and their hands interlocked. Her expression of ferocious concentration did not change. Claud got up, groaning and growling, and limped off. She continued to study the ceiling.

She did not get up until she heard the pick-up truck coming back with the Negroes. Then she rose and thrust her feet in her brown oxfords, which she did not bother to lace, and stumped out onto the back porch and got her red plastic bucket. She emptied a tray of ice cubes into it and filled it half full of water and went out into the back yard. Every afternoon after Claud brought the hands in, one of the boys helped him put out hay and the rest waited in the back of the truck until he was ready to take them home. The truck was parked in the shade under one of the hickory trees.

"Hi yawl this morning?" Mrs. Turpin asked grimly, appearing with the bucket and the dipper. There were three women and a boy in the truck.

"Us doin nicely," the oldest woman said. "Hi you doin?" and her gaze struck 145 immediately on the dark lump on Mrs. Turpin's forehead. "You done fell down, ain't you?" she asked in a solicitous voice. The old woman was dark and almost toothless. She had on an old felt hat of Claud's set back on her head. The other two women were younger and lighter and they both had new bright green sunhats. One of them had hers on her head; the other had taken hers off and the boy was grinning beneath it.

Mrs. Turpin set the bucket down on the floor of the truck. "Yawl hep yourselves," she said. She looked around to make sure Claud had gone. "No, I didn't fall down," she said, folding her arms. "It was something worse than that."

"Ain't nothing bad happen to you!" the old woman said. She said it as if they all knew that Mrs. Turpin was protected in some special way by Divine Providence. "You just had you a little fall."

"We were in town at the doctor's office for where the cow kicked Mr. Turpin," Mrs. Turpin said in a flat tone that indicated they could leave off their foolishness. "And there was this girl there. A big fat girl with her face all broke out. I could look at that girl and tell she was peculiar but I couldn't tell how. And me and her mama was just talking and going along and all of a sudden WHAM! She throws this big book she was reading at me and . . ."

"Naw!" the old woman cried out.

"And then she jumps over the table and commences to choke me." 150

"Naw!" they all exclaimed, "naw!"

"Hi come she do that?" the old woman asked. "What ail her?"

Mrs. Turpin only glared in front of her.

"Somethin ail her," the old woman said.

"They carried her off in an ambulance," Mrs. Turpin continued, "but before 155 she went she was rolling on the floor and they were trying to hold her down to give her a shot and she said something to me." She paused. "You know what she said to me?"

"What she say?" they asked.

"She said," Mrs. Turpin began, and stopped, her face very dark and heavy. The sun was getting whiter and whiter, blanching the sky overhead so that the leaves of the hickory tree were black in the face of it. She could not bring forth the words. "Something real ugly," she muttered.

"She sho shouldn't said nothin ugly to you," the old woman said. "You so sweet. You the sweetest lady I know."

"She pretty too," the one with the hat on said.

"And stout," the other one said. "I never knowed no sweeter white lady." 160

"That's the truth befo' Jesus," the old woman said. "Amen! You des as sweet and pretty as you can be."

Mrs. Turpin knew exactly how much Negro flattery was worth and it added to her rage. "She said," she began again and finished this time with a fierce rush of breath, "that I was an old wart hog from hell."

There was an astounded silence.

"Where she at?" the youngest woman cried in a piercing voice.

"Lemme see her. I'll kill her!" 165

"I'll kill her with you!" the other one cried.

"She b'long in the sylum," the old woman said emphatically. "You the sweetest white lady I know."

"She pretty too," the other two said. "Stout as she can be and sweet. Jesus satisfied with her!"

"Deed he is," the woman declared.

Idiots! Mrs. Turpin growled to herself. You could never say anything intelligent to a nigger. You could talk at them but not with them. "Yawl ain't drunk your water," she said shortly. "Leave the bucket in the truck when you're finished with it. I got more to do than just stand around and pass the time of day," and she moved off and into the house.

She stood for a moment in the middle of the kitchen. The dark protuberance over her eye looked like a miniature tornado cloud which might any moment sweep across the horizon of her brow. Her lower lip protruded dangerously. She squared her massive shoulders. Then she marched into the front of the house and out the side door and started down the road to the pig parlor. She had the look of a woman going single-handed, weaponless, into battle.

The sun was deep yellow now like a harvest moon and was riding westward very fast over the far tree line as if it meant to reach the hogs before she did. The road was rutted and she kicked several good-sized stones out of her path as she strode along. The pig parlor was on a little knoll at the end of a lane that ran off from the side of the barn. It was a square of concrete as large as a small room, with a board fence about four feet high around it. The concrete floor sloped slightly so that the hog wash could drain off into a trench where it was carried to the field for fertilizer. Claud was standing on the outside, on the edge of the concrete, hanging onto the top board, hosing down the floor inside. The hose was connected to the faucet of a water trough nearby.

Mrs. Turpin climbed up beside him and glowered down at the hogs inside. There were seven long-snouted bristly shoats in it — tan with liver-colored spots — and an old sow a few weeks off from farrowing. She was lying on her side grunting. The shoats were running about shaking themselves like idiot children, their little slit pig eyes searching the floor for anything left. She had read that pigs were the most intelligent animal. She doubted it. They were supposed to be smarter than dogs. There had even been a pig astronaut. He had performed his assignment perfectly but died of a heart attack afterwards because they left him in his electric suit, sitting upright throughout his examination when naturally a hog should be on all fours.

A-gruntin and a-rootin and a-groanin.

"Gimme that hose," she said, yanking it away from Claud. "Go on and carry them niggers home and then get off that leg."

"You look like you might have swallowed a mad dog," Claud observed, but he got down and limped off. He paid no attention to her humors.

Until he was out of earshot, Mrs. Turpin stood on the side of the pen, holding the hose and pointing the stream of water at the hind quarters of any shoat that looked as if it might try to lie down. When he had had time to get over the hill, she turned her head slightly and her wrathful eyes scanned the path. He was nowhere in sight. She turned back again and seemed to gather herself up. Her shoulders rose and she drew in her breath.

"What do you send me a message like that for?" she said in a low fierce voice, barely above a whisper but with the force of a shout in its concentrated fury. "How am I a hog and me both? How am I saved and from hell too?" Her free fist was knotted and with the other she gripped the hose, blindly pointing the stream of water in and out of the eye of the old sow whose outraged squeal she did not hear.

The pig parlor commanded a view of the back pasture where their twenty beef cows were gathered around the hay-bales Claud and the boy had put out. The freshly cut pasture sloped down to the highway. Across it was their cotton field and beyond that a dark green dusty wood which they owned as well. The sun was behind the wood, very red, looking over the paling of the trees like a farmer inspecting his own hogs.

"Why me?" she rumbled. "It's no trash around here, black or white, that I haven't given to. And break my back to the bone every day working. And do for the church."

She appeared to be the right size woman to command the arena before her. "How am I a hog?" she demanded. "Exactly how am I like them?" and she jabbed the stream of water at the shoats. "There was plenty of trash there. It didn't have to be me.

"If you like trash better, go get yourself some trash then," she railed. "You could have made me trash. Or a nigger. If trash is what you wanted why didn't you make me trash?" She shook her fist with the hose in it and a watery snake appeared momentarily in the air. "I could quit working and take it easy and be filthy," she growled. "Lounge about the sidewalks all day drinking root beer. Dip snuff and spit in every puddle and have it all over my face. I could be nasty.

"Or you could have made me a nigger. It's too late for me to be a nigger," she said with deep sarcasm, "but I could act like one. Lay down in the middle of the road and stop traffic. Roll on the ground."

In the deepening light everything was taking on a mysterious hue. The pasture was growing a peculiar glassy green and the streak of highway had turned lavender. She braced herself for a final assault and this time her voice rolled out over the pasture. "Go on," she yelled, "call me a hog! Call me a hog again. From hell. Call me a wart hog from hell. Put that bottom rail on top. There'll still be a top and bottom!"

A garbled echo returned to her.

A final surge of fury shook her and she roared, "Who do you think you are?"

The color of everything, field and crimson sky, burned for a moment with a transparent intensity. The question carried over the pasture and across the highway and the cotton field and returned to her clearly like an answer from beyond the wood.

She opened her mouth but no sound came out of it.

A tiny truck, Claud's, appeared on the highway, heading rapidly out of sight. Its gears scraped thinly. It looked like a child's toy. At any moment a bigger truck might smash into it and scatter Claud's and the niggers' brains all over the road.

Mrs. Turpin stood there, her gaze fixed on the highway, all her muscles rigid, until in five or six minutes the truck reappeared, returning. She waited until it had had time to turn into their own road. Then like a monumental statue coming to life, she bent her head slowly and gazed, as if through the very heart of mystery, down into the pig parlor at the hogs. They had settled all in one corner around the old sow who was grunting softly. A red glow suffused them. They appeared to pant with a secret life.

Until the sun slipped finally behind the tree line, Mrs. Turpin remained there with her gaze bent to them as if she were absorbing some abysmal life-giving knowledge. At last she lifted her head. There was only a purple streak in the sky, cutting through a field of crimson and leading, like an extension of the highway, into the descending dusk. She raised her hands from the side of the pen in a gesture hieratic and profound. A visionary light settled in her eyes. She saw the streak as a vast swinging bridge extending upward from the earth through a field of living fire. Upon it a vast horde of souls were rumbling toward heaven. There were whole companies of white-trash, clean for the first time in their lives, and bands of black niggers in white robes, and battalions of freaks and lunatics shouting and clapping and leaping like frogs. And bringing up the end of the procession was a tribe of people whom she recognized at once as those who, like herself and Claud, had always had a little of everything and the God-given wit to use it right. She leaned forward to observe them closer. They were marching behind the others with great dignity, accountable as they had always been for good order and common sense and respectable behavior. They alone were on key. Yet she could see by their shocked and altered faces that even their virtues were being burned away. She lowered her hands and gripped the rail of the hog pen, her eyes small but fixed unblinkingly on what lay ahead. In a moment the vision faded but she remained where she was, immobile.

At length she got down and turned off the faucet and made her slow way on the darkening path to the house. In the woods around her the invisible cricket choruses had struck up, but what she heard were the voices of the souls climbing upward into the starry field and shouting hallelujah.

Considerations for Critical Thinking and Writing

1. Why is it appropriate that the two major settings for the action in this story are a doctor's waiting room and a "pig parlor"?
2. How does Mrs. Turpin's treatment of her husband help to characterize her?
3. Mrs. Turpin notices people's shoes. What does this and her thoughts about "classes of people" reveal about her? How does she see herself in relation to other people?
4. Why does Mary Grace attack Mrs. Turpin?
5. Why is it significant that the book Mary Grace reads is *Human Development?* What is the significance of her name?
6. What does the background music played on the radio contribute to the story?
7. To whom does Mrs. Turpin address this anguished question: "What do you send me a message [Mary Grace's whispered words telling her "Go back to hell where you came from, you old wart hog"] like that for?" Why is Mrs. Turpin so angry and bewildered?
8. What is the "abysmal life-giving knowledge" that Mrs. Turpin discovers in the next to the last paragraph? Why is it "abysmal"? How is it "life-giving"?
9. Does your attitude toward Mrs. Turpin change or remain the same during the story? Explain why.
10. Given the serious theme, consider whether the story's humor is appropriate.
11. When Mrs. Turpin returns home bruised, a hired black woman tells her that nothing really "bad" happened: "You just had you a little fall." Pay particular attention to the suggestive language of this sentence, and discuss its significance in relation to the rest of the story.

Connections to Other Selections

1. Compare and contrast Mary Grace with Hulga of "Good Country People."
2. Explain how "Revelation" could be used as a title for any of the O'Connor stories you have read.
3. Discuss Mrs. Turpin's prideful hypocrisy in connection with the racial attitudes expressed by the white men at the "smoker" in Ralph Ellison's "Battle Royal" (p. 187). How do pride and personal illusions inform these characters' racial attitudes?
4. Explore the nature of the "revelation" in O'Connor's story and in John Updike's "A & P" (p. 485).

Parker's Back   1965

Parker's wife was sitting on the front porch floor, snapping beans. Parker was sitting on the step, some distance away, watching her sullenly. She was plain, plain. The skin on her face was thin and drawn as tight as the skin on an onion and her eyes were gray and sharp like the points of two icepicks. Parker understood why he had married her — he couldn't have got her any other way — but he couldn't understand why he stayed with her now. She was pregnant and pregnant women were not his favorite kind. Nonetheless, he stayed as if she had him conjured. He was puzzled and ashamed of himself.

The house they rented sat alone save for a single tall pecan tree on a high embankment overlooking a highway. At intervals a car would shoot past below and his wife's eyes would swerve suspiciously after the sound of it and then come back to rest on the newspaper full of beans in her lap. One of the things she did not approve of was automobiles. In addition to her other bad qualities, she was forever sniffing up sin. She did not smoke or dip, drink whiskey, use bad language, or paint her face, and God knew some paint would have improved it, Parker thought. Her being against color, it was the more remarkable that she had married him. Sometimes he supposed that she had married him because she meant to save him. At other times he had a suspicion that she actually liked everything she said she didn't. He could account for her one way or another; it was himself he could not understand.

She turned her head in his direction and said, "It's no reason you can't work for a man. It don't have to be a woman."

"Aw shut your mouth for a change," Parker muttered.

If he had been certain she was jealous of the woman he worked for he 5 would have been pleased but more likely she was concerned with the sin that would result if he and the woman took a liking to each other. He had told her that the woman was a hefty young blonde; in fact she was nearly seventy years old and too dried up to have an interest in anything except getting as much work out of him as she could. Not that an old woman didn't sometimes get an interest in a young man, particularly if he was as attractive as Parker felt he was, but this old woman looked at him the same way she looked at her old tractor — as if she had to put up with it because it was all she had. The tractor had broken down the second day Parker was on it and she had set him at once to cutting bushes, saying out of the side of her mouth to the nigger, "Everything he touches, he breaks." She also asked him to wear his shirt when he worked; Parker had removed it even though the day was not sultry; he put it back on reluctantly.

This ugly woman Parker married was his first wife. He had had other women but he had planned never to get himself tied up legally. He had first seen her one morning when his truck broke down on the highway. He had managed to pull it off the road into a neatly swept yard on which sat a peeling two-room house. He got out and opened the hood of the truck and began to study the motor. Parker had an extra sense that told him when there was a woman nearby watching him. After he had leaned over the motor a few minutes, his neck began to prickle. He cast his eye over the empty yard and porch of the house. A woman he could not see was either nearby beyond a clump of honeysuckle or in the house, watching him out the window.

Suddenly Parker began to jump up and down and fling his hand about as if he had mashed it in the machinery. He doubled over and held his hand close to his chest. "God dammit!" he hollered, "Jesus Christ in hell! Jesus God Almighty damm! God dammit to hell!" he went on, flinging out the same few oaths over and over as loud as he could.

Without warning a terrible bristly claw slammed the side of his face and he fell backwards on the hood of the truck. "You don't talk no filth here!" a voice close to him shrilled.

Parker's vision was so blurred that for an instant he thought he had been attacked by some creature from above, a giant hawk-eyed angel wielding a hoary weapon. As his sight cleared, he saw before him a tall raw-boned girl with a broom.

"I hurt my hand," he said. "I HURT my hand." He was so incensed that he 10 forgot that he hadn't hurt his hand. "My hand may be broke," he growled although his voice was still unsteady.

"Lemme see it," the girl demanded.

Parker stuck out his hand and she came closer and looked at it. There was no mark on the palm and she took the hand and turned it over. Her own hand was dry and hot and rough and Parker felt himself jolted back to life by her touch. He looked more closely at her. I don't want nothing to do with this one, he thought.

The girl's sharp eyes peered at the back of the stubby reddish hand she held. There emblazoned in red and blue was a tattooed eagle perched on a cannon. Parker's sleeve was rolled to the elbow. Above the eagle a serpent was coiled about a shield and in the spaces between the eagle and the serpent there were hearts, some with arrows through them. Above the serpent there was a spread hand of cards. Every space on the skin of Parker's arm, from wrist to elbow, was covered in some loud design. The girl gazed at this with an almost stupefied smile of shock, as if she had accidentally grasped a poisonous snake; she dropped the hand.

"I got most of my other ones in foreign parts," Parker said. "These here I mostly got in the United States. I got my first one when I was only fifteen year old."

"Don't tell me," the girl said, "I don't like it. I ain't got any use for it." 15

"You ought to see to ones you can't see," Parker said and winked.

Two circles of red appeared like apples on the girl's cheeks and softened her appearance. Parker was intrigued. He did not for a minute think that she didn't like the tattoos. He had never yet met a woman who was not attracted to them.

Parker was fourteen when he saw a man in a fair, tattooed from head to foot. Except for his loins which were girded with a panther hide, the man's skin was patterned in what seemed from Parker's distance — he was near the back of the tent, standing on a bench — a single intricate design of brilliant color. The man, who was small and sturdy, moved about on the platform, flexing his muscles so that the arabesque of men and beasts and flowers on his skin appeared to have a subtle motion of its own. Parker was filled with emotion, lifted up as some people are when the flag passes. He was a boy whose mouth habitually hung open. He was heavy and earnest, as ordinary as a loaf of bread. When the show was over, he had remained standing on the bench, staring where the tattooed man had been, until the tent was almost empty.

Parker had never before felt the least motion of wonder in himself. Until he saw the man at the fair, it did not enter his head that there was anything out of the ordinary about the fact that he existed. Even then it did not enter his head, but a peculiar unease settled in him. It was as if a blind boy had been turned so gently in a different direction that he did not know his destination had been changed.

He had his first tattoo some time after — the eagle perched on the cannon. 20 It was done by a local artist. It hurt very little, just enough to make it appear to Parker to be worth doing. This was peculiar too for before he had thought that only what did not hurt was worth doing. The next year he quit school because he was sixteen and could. He went to the trade school for a while, then he quit the trade school and worked for six months in a garage. The only reason he worked at all was to pay for more tattoos. His mother worked in a laundry and could support him, but she would not pay for any tattoo except her name on a heart, which he had put on, grumbling. However, her name was Betty Jean and nobody had to know it was his mother. He found out that the tattoos were attractive to the kind of girls he liked but who had never liked him before. He began to drink beer and get in fights. His mother wept over what was becoming of him. One night she dragged him off to a revival with her, not telling him where they were going. When he saw the big lighted church, he jerked out of her grasp and ran. The next day he lied about his age and joined the navy.

Parker was large for the tight sailor's pants but the silly white cap, sitting low on his forehead, made his face by contrast look thoughtful and almost intense. After a month or two in the navy, his mouth ceased to hang open. His features hardened into the features of a man. He stayed in the navy five years and seemed a natural part of the gray mechanical ship, except for his eyes, which were the same pale slate-color as the ocean and reflected the immense spaces around him as if they were a microcosm of the mysterious sea. In port Parker wandered about comparing the run-down places he was in to Birmingham, Alabama. Everywhere he went he picked up more tatoos.

He had stopped having lifeless ones like anchors and crossed rifles. He had a tiger and a panther on each shoulder, a cobra coiled about a torch on his chest, hawks on his thighs, Elizabeth II and Philip over where his stomach and liver were respectively. He did not care much what the subject was so long as it was colorful; on his abdomen he had a few obscenities but only because that seemed the proper place for them. Parker would be satisfied with each tattoo about a month, then something about it that had attracted him would wear off. Whenever a decent-sized mirror was available, he would get in front of it and study his overall look. The effect was not of one intricate arabesque of colors but of something haphazard and botched. A huge dissatisfaction would come over him and he would go off and find another tattooist and have another space filled up. The front of Parker was almost completely covered but there were no tattoos on his back. He had no desire for one anywhere he could not readily see it himself. As the space on the front of him for tattoos decreased, his dissatisfaction grew and became general.

After one of his furloughs, he didn't go back to the navy but remained away without official leave, drunk, in a rooming house in a city he did not know. His dissatisfaction, from being chronic and latent, had suddenly become acute and raged in him. It was as if the panther and the lion and the serpents and the eagles and the hawks had penetrated his skin and lived inside him in a raging warfare. The navy caught up with him, put him in the brig for nine months and then gave him a dishonorable discharge.

After that Parker decided that country air was the only kind fit to breathe. He rented the shack on the embankment and bought the old truck and took various jobs which he kept as long as it suited him. At the time he met his future wife, he was buying apples by the bushel and selling them for the same price by the pound to isolated homesteaders on back country roads.

"All that there," the woman said, pointing to his arm, "is no better than what a fool Indian would do. It's a heap of vanity." She seemed to have found the word she wanted. "Vanity of vanities," she said. 25

Well what the hell do I care what she thinks of it? Parker asked himself, but he was plainly bewildered. "I reckon you like one of these better than another anyway," he said, dallying until he thought of something that would impress her. He thrust the arm back at her. "Which you like best?"

"None of them," she said, "but the chicken is not as bad as the rest."

"What chicken?" Parker almost yelled.

She pointed to the eagle.

"That's an eagle," Parker said. "What fool would waste their time having a chicken put on themself?" 30

"What fool would have any of it?" the girl said and turned away. She went slowly back to the house and left him there to get going. Parker remained for almost five minutes, looking agape at the dark door she had entered.

The next day he returned with a bushel of apples. He was not one to be outdone by anything that looked like her. He liked women with meat on them, so you didn't feel their muscles, much less their bones. When he arrived, she was sitting on the top step and the yard was full of children, all as thin and poor as herself; Parker remembered it was Saturday. He hated to be making up to a woman when there were children around, but it was fortunate he had brought the bushel of apples off the truck. As the children approached him to see what he carried, he gave each child an apple and told it to get lost; in that way he cleared out the whole crowd.

The girl did nothing to acknowledge his presence. He might have been a stray pig or goat that had wandered into the yard and she too tired to take up the broom and send it off. He set the bushel of apples down next to her on the step. He sat down on a lower step.

"Hep yourself," he said, nodding at the basket; then he lapsed into silence.

She took an apple quickly as if the basket might disappear if she didn't make haste. Hungry people made Parker nervous. He had always had plenty to eat himself. He grew very uncomfortable. He reasoned he had nothing to say so why should he say it? He could not think now why he had come or why he didn't go before he wasted another bushel of apples on the crowd of children. He supposed they were her brothers and sisters.

She chewed the apple slowly but with a kind of relish of concentration, bent slightly but looking out ahead. The view from the porch stretched off across a long incline studded with ironweed and across the highway to a vast vista of hills and one small mountain. Long views depressed Parker. You look out into space like that and you begin to feel as if someone were after you, the navy or the government or religion.

"Who them children belong to, you?" he said at length.

"I ain't married yet," she said. "They belong to momma." She said it as if it were only a matter of time before she would be married.

Who in God's name would marry her? Parker thought.

A large barefooted woman with a wide gap-toothed face appeared in the door behind Parker. She had apparently been there for several minutes.

"Good evening," Parker said.

The woman crossed the porch and picked up what was left of the bushel of apples. "We thank you," she said and returned with it into the house.

"That your old woman?" Parker muttered.

The girl nodded. Parker knew a lot of sharp things he could have said like "You got my sympathy," but he was gloomily silent. He just sat there, looking at the view. He thought he must be coming down with something.

"If I pick up some peaches tomorrow I'll bring you some," he said.

"I'll be much obliged to you," the girl said.

Parker had no intention of taking any basket of peaches back there but the next day he found himself doing it. He and the girl had almost nothing to say to each other. One thing he did say was "I ain't got any tattoo on my back."

"What you got on it?" the girl said.

"My shirt," Parker said. "Haw."

"Haw, Haw," the girl said politely.

Parker thought he was losing his mind. He could not believe for a minute that he was attracted to a woman like this. She showed not the least interest in anything but what he brought until he appeared the third time with two cantaloupes. "What's your name?" she asked.

"O. E. Parker," he said.

"What does the O. E. stand for?"

"You can just call me O. E.," Parker said. "Or Parker. Don't nobody call me by my name."

"What's it stand for?" she persisted.

"Never mind," Parker said. "What's yours?"

"I'll tell you when you tell me what them letters are the short of," she said.

There was just a hint of flirtatiousness in her tone and it went rapidly to Parker's head. He had never revealed the name to any man or woman, only to the files of the navy and the government, and it was on his baptismal record which he got at the age of a month; his mother was a Methodist. When the name leaked out of the navy files, Parker narrowly missed killing the man who used it.

"You'll go blab it around," he said.

"I'll swear I'll never tell nobody," she said. "On God's holy word I swear it."

Parker sat for a few minutes in silence. Then he reached for the girl's neck, drew her ear close to his mouth and revealed the name in a low voice. 60

"Obadiah," she whispered. Her face slowly brightened as if the name came as a sign to her. "Obadiah," she said.

The name still stank in Parker's estimation.

"Obadiah Elihue," she said in a reverent voice.

"If you call me that aloud, I'll bust your head open," Parker said. "What's yours?"

"Sarah Ruth Cates," she said. 65

"Glad to meet you, Sarah Ruth," Parker said.

Sarah Ruth's father was a Straight Gospel preacher but he was away, spreading it in Florida. Her mother did not seem to mind his attention to the girl so long as he brought a basket of something with him when he came. As for Sarah Ruth herself, it was plain to Parker after he had visited three times that she was crazy about him. She liked him even though she insisted that pictures on the skin were vanity of vanities and even after hearing him curse, and even after she had asked him if he was saved and he had replied that he didn't see it was anything in particular to save him from. After that, inspired, Parker had said, "I'd be saved enough if you was to kiss me."

She scowled. "That ain't being saved," she said.

Not long after that she agreed to take a ride in his truck. Parker parked it on a deserted road and suggested to her that they lie down together in the back of it.

"Not until after we're married," she said — just like that. 70

"Oh, that ain't necessary," Parker said and as he reached for her, she thrust him away with such force that the door of the truck came off and he found himself flat on his back on the ground. He made up his mind then and there to have nothing further to do with her.

They were married in the County Ordinary's° office because Sarah Ruth thought churches were idolatrous. Parker had no opinion about that one way or the other. The Ordinary's office was lined with cardboard file boxes and record books with dusty yellow slips of paper hanging on out of them. The Ordinary was an old woman with red hair who had held office for forty years and looked as dusty as her books. She married them from behind the iron-grill of a stand-up desk and when she finished, she said with a flourish, "Three dollars and fifty cents and till death do you part!" and yanked some forms out of a machine.

Marriage did not change Sarah Ruth a jot and it made Parker gloomier than ever. Every morning he decided he had had enough and would not return that night; every night he returned. Whenever Parker couldn't stand the way he felt,

Ordinary: Justice of the peace.

he would have another tattoo, but the only surface left on him now was his back. To see a tattoo on his own back he would have to get two mirrors and stand between them in just the correct position and this seemed to Parker a good way to make an idiot of himself. Sarah Ruth who, if she had had better sense, could have enjoyed a tattoo on his back, would not even look at the ones he had elsewhere. When he attempted to point out especial details of them, she would shut her eyes tight and turn her back as well. Except in total darkness, she preferred Parker dressed and with his sleeves rolled down.

"At the judgment seat of God, Jesus is going to say to you, 'What you been doing all your life besides have pictures drawn all over you?'" she said.

"You don't fool me none," Parker said, "you're just afraid that hefty girl 75 I work for'll like me so much she'll say, 'Come on, Mr. Parker, let's you and me . . .'"

"You're tempting sin," she said, "and at the judgment seat of God you'll have to answer for that too. You ought to go back to selling the fruits of the earth."

Parker did nothing much when he was at home but listen to what the judgment seat of God would be like for him if he didn't change his ways. When he could, he broke in with tales of the hefty girl he worked for. "'Mr. Parker,'" he said she said, "'I hired you for your brains.'" (She had added, "So why don't you use them?")

"And you should have seen her face the first time she saw me without my shirt," he said. "'Mr. Parker,' she said, 'you're a walking panner-rammer!'" This had, in fact, been her remark but it had been delivered out of one side of her mouth.

Dissatisfaction began to grow so great in Parker that there was no containing it outside of a tattoo. It had to be his back. There was no help for it. A dim half-formed inspiration began to work in his mind. He visualized having a tattoo put there that Sarah Ruth would not be able to resist — a religious subject. He thought of an open book with HOLY BIBLE tattooed under it and an actual verse printed on the page. This seemed just the thing for a while; then he began to hear her say, "Ain't I already got a real Bible? What you think I want to read the same verse over and over for when I can read it all?" He needed something better even than the Bible! He thought about it so much that he began to lose sleep. He was already losing flesh — Sarah Ruth just threw food in the pot and let it boil. Not knowing for certain why he continued to stay with a woman who was both ugly and pregnant and no cook made him generally nervous and irritable, and he developed a little tic in the side of his face.

Once or twice he found himself turning around abruptly as if someone 80 were trailing him. He had had a granddaddy who had ended in the state mental hospital, although not until he was seventy-five, but as urgent as it might be for him to get a tattoo, it was just as urgent that he get exactly the right one to bring Sarah Ruth to heel. As he continued to worry over it, his eyes took on a hollow preoccupied expression. The old woman he worked for told him that if he couldn't keep his mind on what he was doing, she knew where she could find a fourteen-year-old colored boy who could. Parker was too preoccupied even to be offended. At any time previous, he would have left her then and there, saying drily, "Well, you go ahead on and get him then."

Two or three mornings later he was baling hay with the old woman's sorry baler and her broken-down tractor in a large field, cleared save for one enormous old tree standing in the middle of it. The old woman was the kind who would not cut down a large old tree because it was a large old tree. She had pointed it out to Parker as if he didn't have eyes and told him to be careful not to hit it as the machine picked up hay near it. Parker began at the outside of the field and made circles inward toward it. He had to get off the tractor every now and then and untangle the baling cord or kick a rock out of the way. The old woman had told him to carry the rocks to the edge of the field, which he did when she was there watching. When he thought he could make it, he ran over them. As he circled the field his mind was on a suitable design for his back. The sun, the size of a golf ball, began to switch regularly from in front to behind him, but he appeared to see it both places as if he had eyes in the back of his head. All at once he saw the tree reaching out to grasp him. A ferocious thud propelled him into the air, and he heard himself yelling in an unbelievably loud voice, "GOD ABOVE!"

He landed on his back while the tractor crashed upside-down into the tree and burst into flame. The first thing Parker saw were his shoes, quickly being eaten by the fire; one was caught under the tractor, the other was some distance away, burning by itself. He was not in them. He could feel the hot breath of the burning tree on his face. He scrambled backwards, still sitting, his eyes cavernous, and if he had known how to cross himself he would have done it.

His truck was on a dirt road at the edge of the field. He moved toward it, still sitting, still backwards, but faster and faster; halfway to it he got up and began a kind of forward-bent run from which he collapsed on his knees twice. His legs felt like two old rusted rain gutters. He reached the truck finally and took off in it, zigzagging up the road. He drove past his house on the embankment and straight for the city, fifty miles distant.

Parker did not allow himself to think on the way to the city. He only knew that there had been a great change in his life, a leap forward into a worse unknown, and that there was nothing he could do about it. It was for all intents accomplished.

The artist had two large cluttered rooms over a chiropodist's office on a 85 back street. Parker, still barefooted, burst silently in on him at a little after three in the afternoon. The artist, who was about Parker's own age — twenty-eight — but thin and bald, was behind a small drawing table, tracing a design in green ink. He looked up with an annoyed glance and did not seem to recognize Parker in the hollow-eyed creature before him.

"Let me see the book you got with all the pictures of God in it," Parker said breathlessly. "The religious one."

The artist continued to look at him with his intellectual, superior stare. "I don't put tattoos on drunks," he said.

"You know me!" Parker cried indignantly. "I'm O. E. Parker! You done work for me before and I always paid!"

The artist looked at him another moment as if he were not altogether sure. "You've fallen off some," he said. "You must have been in jail."

"Married," Parker said. 90

"Oh," said the artist. With the aid of mirrors the artist had tattooed on the top of his head a miniature owl, perfect in every detail. It was about the size of a half-dollar and served him as a show piece. There were cheaper artists in town but Parker had never wanted anything but the best. The artist went over to a cabinet at the back of the room and began to look over some art books. "Who are you interested in?" he said, "saints, angels, Christs or what?"

"God," Parker said.

"Father, Son, or Spirit?"

"Just God," Parker said impatiently. "Christ. I don't care. Just so it's God."

The artist returned with a book. He moved some papers off another table 95 and put the book down on it and told Parker to sit down and see what he liked. "The up-to-date ones are in the back," he said.

Parker sat down with the book and with his thumb. He began to go through it, beginning at the back where the up-to-date pictures were. Some of them he recognized — The Good Shepherd, Forbid Them Not, The Smiling Jesus, Jesus the Physician's Friend, but he kept turning rapidly backwards and the pictures became less and less reassuring. One showed a gaunt green dead face streaked with blood. One was yellow with sagging purple eyes. Parker's heart began to beat faster and faster until it appeared to be roaring inside him like a great generator. He flipped the pages quickly, feeling that when he reached the one ordained, a sign would come. He continued to flip through until he had almost reached the front of the book. On one of the pages a pair of eyes glanced at him swiftly. Parker sped on, then stopped. His heart too appeared to cut off; there was absolute silence. It said as plainly as if silence were a language itself, GO BACK.

Parker returned to the picture — the haloed head of a flat stern Byzantine Christ with all-demanding eyes. He sat there trembling; his heart began slowly to beat again as if it were being brought to life by a subtle power.

"You found what you want?" the artist asked.

Parker's throat was too dry to speak. He got up and thrust the book at the artist, opened at the picture.

"That'll cost you plenty," the artist said. "You don't want all those little blocks 100 though, just the outline and some better features."

"Just like it is," Parker said, "just like it is or nothing."

"It's your funeral," the artist said, "but I don't do that kind of work for nothing."

"How much?" Parker asked.

"It'll take maybe two days work."

"How much?" Parker said. 105

"On time or cash?" the artist asked. Parker's other jobs had been on time, but he had paid.

"Ten down and ten for every day it takes," the artist said.

Parker drew ten dollar bills out of his wallet; he had three left in.

"You come back in the morning," the artist said, putting the money in his own pocket. "First I'll have to trace that out of the book."

"No, no!" Parker said. "Trace it now or gimme my money back," and his 110 eyes blared as if he were ready for a fight.

The artist agreed. Anyone stupid enough to want a Christ on his back, he reasoned, would be just as likely as not to change his mind the next minute, but once the work was begun he could hardly do so.

While he worked on the tracing, he told Parker to go wash his back at the sink with the special soap he used there. Parker did it and returned to pace back and forth across the room, nervously flexing his shoulders. He wanted to go look at the picture again but at the same time he did not want to. The artist got up finally and had Parker lie down on the table. He swabbed his back with ethyl chloride and then began to outline the head on it with his iodine pencil. Another hour passed before he took up his electric instrument. Parker felt no particular pain. In Japan he had had a tattoo of the Buddha done on his upper arm with ivory needles; in Burma, a little brown root of a man had made a peacock on each of his knees using thin pointed sticks, two feet long; amateurs had worked on him with pins and soot. Parker was usually so relaxed and easy under the hand of the artist that he often went to sleep, but this time he remained awake, every muscle taut.

At midnight the artist said he was ready to quit. He propped one mirror, four feet square, on a table by the wall and took a smaller mirror off the lavatory wall and put it in Parker's hands. Parker stood with his back to the one on the table and moved the other until he saw a flashing burst of color reflected from his back. It was almost completely covered with little red and blue and ivory and saffron squares; from them he made out the lineaments of the face — a mouth, the beginning of heavy brows, a straight nose, but the face was empty; the eyes had not yet been put in. The impression for the moment was almost as if the artist had tricked him and done the Physician's Friend.

"It don't have eyes," Parker cried out.

"That'll come," the artist said, "in due time. We have another day to go on 115 it yet."

Parker spent the night on a cot at the Haven of Light Christian Mission. He found these the best places to stay in the city because they were free and included a meal of sorts. He got the last available cot and because he was still barefooted, he accepted a pair of second-hand shoes which, in his confusion, he put on to go to bed; he was still shocked from all that had happened to him. All night he lay awake in the long dormitory of cots with lumpy figures on them. The only light was from a phosphorescent cross glowing at the end of the room. The tree reached out to grasp him again, then burst into flame; the shoe burned quietly by itself; the eyes in the book said to him distinctly GO BACK and at the same time did not utter a sound. He wished that he were not in this city, not in this Haven of Light Mission, not in a bed by himself. He longed miserably for Sarah Ruth. Her sharp tongue and icepick eyes were the only comfort he could bring to mind. He decided he was losing it. Her eyes appeared soft and dilatory compared with the eyes in the book, for even though he could not summon up the exact look of those eyes, he could still feel their penetration. He felt as though, under their gaze, he was as transparent as the wing of a fly.

The tattooist had told him not to come until ten in the morning, but when he arrived at that hour, Parker was sitting in the dark hallway on the floor, waiting for him. He had decided upon getting up that, once the tattoo was on him, he would not look at it, that all his sensations of the day and night before were those of a crazy man and that he would return to doing things according to his own sound judgment.

The artist began where he left off. "One thing I want to know," he said presently as he worked over Parker's back, "why do you want this on you? Have you gone and got religion? Are you saved?" he asked in a mocking voice.

Parker's throat felt salty and dry. "Naw," he said, "I ain't got no use for none of that. A man can't save his self from whatever it is he don't deserve none of my sympathy." These words seemed to leave his mouth like wraiths and to evaporate at once as if he had never uttered them.

"Then why . . ."   120

"I married this woman that's saved," Parker said. "I never should have done it. I ought to leave her. She's done gone and got pregnant."

"That's too bad," the artist said. "Then it's her making you have this tattoo."

"Naw," Parker said, "she don't know nothing about it. It's a surprise for her."

"You think she'll like it and lay off you a while?"

"She can't help herself," Parker said. "She can't say she don't like the looks   125
of God." He decided he had told the artist enough of his business. Artists were all right in their place but he didn't like them poking their noses into the affairs of regular people. "I didn't get no sleep last night," he said. "I think I'll get some now."

That closed the mouth of the artist but it did not bring him any sleep. He lay there, imagining how Sarah Ruth would be struck speechless by the face on his back and every now and then this would be interrupted by a vision of the tree of fire and his empty shoe burning beneath it.

The artist worked steadily until nearly four o'clock, not stopping to have lunch, hardly pausing with the electric instrument except to wipe the dripping dye off Parker's back as he went along. Finally he finished. "You can get up and look at it now," he said.

Parker sat up but he remained on the edge of the table.

The artist was pleased with his work and wanted Parker to look at it at once. Instead Parker continued to sit on the edge of the table, bent forward slightly but with a vacant look. "What ails you?" the artist said. "Go look at it."

"Ain't nothing ail me," Parker said in a sudden belligerent voice. "That tattoo   130
ain't going nowhere. It'll be there when I get there." He reached for his shirt and began gingerly to put it on.

The artist took him roughly by the arm and propelled him between the two mirrors. "Now *look*," he said, angry at having his work ignored.

Parker looked, turned white, and moved away. The eyes in the reflected face continued to look at him — still, straight, all-demanding, enclosed in silence.

"It was your idea, remember," the artist said. "I would have advised something else."

Parker said nothing. He put on his shirt and went out the door while the artist shouted, "I'll expect all of my money!"

Parker headed toward a package shop on the corner. He bought a pint of   135
whiskey and took it into a nearby alley and drank it all in five minutes. Then he moved on to a pool hall nearby which he frequented when he came to the city. It was a well-lighted barnlike place with a bar up one side and gambling machines on the other and pool tables in the back. As soon as Parker entered, a large man in a red and black checkered shirt hailed him by slapping him on the back and yelling, "Yeyyyyyy boy! O. E. Parker!"

Parker was not yet ready to be struck on the back. "Lay off," he said, "I got a fresh tattoo there."

"What you got this time?" the man asked and then yelled to a few at the machines. "O. E.'s got him another tattoo."

"Nothing special this time," Parker said and slunk over to a machine that was not being used.

"Come on," the big man said, "let's have a look at O. E.'s tattoo," and while Parker squirmed in their hands, they pulled up his shirt. Parker felt all the hands drop away instantly and his shirt fell again like a veil over the face. There was a silence in the pool room which seemed to Parker to grow from the circle around him until it extended to the foundations under the building and upward through the beams of the roof.

Finally some one said, "Christ!" Then they all broke into noise at once. 140 Parker turned around, an uncertain grin on his face.

"Leave it to O. E.!" the man in the checkered shirt said, "That boy's a real card!"

"Maybe he's gone and got religion," some one yelled.

"Not on your life," Parker said.

"O. E.'s got religion and is witnessing for Jesus, ain't you, O. E.?" a little man with a piece of cigar in his mouth said wryly. "An o-riginal way to do it if I ever saw one."

"Leave it to Parker to think of a new one!" the fat man said. 145

"Yyeeeeeeyyyyyyy boy!" someone yelled and they all began to whistle and curse in compliment until Parker said, "Aaa shut up."

"What'd you do it for?" somebody asked.

"For laughs," Parker said. "What's it to you?"

"Why ain't you laughing then?" somebody yelled. Parker lunged into the midst of them and like a whirlwind on a summer's day there began a fight that raged amid overturned tables and swinging fists until two of them grabbed him and ran to the door with him and threw him out. Then a calm descended on the pool hall as nerve shattering as if the long barnlike room were the ship from which Jonah had been cast into the sea.

Parker sat for a long time on the ground in the alley behind the pool hall, 150 examining his soul. He saw it as a spider web of facts and lies that was not at all important to him but which appeared to be necessary in spite of his opinion. The eyes that were now forever on his back were eyes to be obeyed. He was as certain of it as he had ever been of anything. Throughout his life, grumbling and sometimes cursing, often afraid, once in rapture, Parker had obeyed whatever instinct of this kind had come to him — in rapture when his spirit had lifted at the sight of the tattooed man at the fair, afraid when he had joined the navy, grumbling when he had married Sarah Ruth.

The thought of her brought him slowly to his feet. She would know what he had to do. She would clear up the rest of it, and she would at least be pleased. It seemed to him that, all along, that was what he wanted, to please her. His truck was still parked in front of the building where the artist had his place, but it was not far away. He got in it and drove out of the city and into the country night. His head was almost clear of liquor and he observed that his dissatisfaction was gone, but he felt not quite like himself. It was as if he were himself but a stranger to himself, driving into a new country though everything he saw was familiar to him, even at night.

He arrived finally at the house on the embankment, pulled the truck under the pecan tree, and got out. He made as much noise as possible to assert that he was still in charge here, that his leaving her for a night without word meant nothing except it was the way he did things. He slammed the car door, stamped up the two steps and across the porch and rattled the door knob. It did not respond to his touch. "Sarah Ruth!" he yelled, "let me in."

There was no lock on the door and she had evidently placed the back of a chair against the knob. He began to beat on the door and rattle the knob at the same time.

He heard the bed springs screak and bent down and put his head to the keyhole, but it was stopped up with paper. "Let me in!" he hollered, bamming on the door again. "What you got me locked out for?"

A sharp voice close to the door said, "Who's there?"   155

"Me," Parker said, "O. E."

He waited a moment.

"Me," he said impatiently, "O. E."

Still no sound from inside.

He tried once more. "O. E.," he said, bamming the door two or three more   160
times. "O. E. Parker. You know me."

There was a silence. Then the voice said slowly, "I don't know no O. E."

"Quit fooling," Parker pleaded. "You ain't got any business doing me this way. It's me, old O. E., I'm back. You ain't afraid of me."

"Who's there?" the same unfeeling voice said.

Parker turned his head as if he expected someone behind him to give him the answer. The sky had lightened slightly and there were two or three streaks of yellow floating above the horizon. Then as he stood there, a tree of light burst over the skyline.

Parker fell back against the door as if he had been pinned there by a lance.   165

"Who's there?" the voice from inside said and there was a quality about it now that seemed final. The knob rattled and the voice said peremptorily, "Who's there, I ast you?"

Parker bent down and put his mouth near the stuffed keyhole. "Obadiah," he whispered and all at once he felt the light pouring through him, turning his spider web soul into a perfect arabesque of colors, a garden of trees and birds and beasts.

"Obadiah Elihue!" he whispered.

The door opened and he stumbled in. Sarah Ruth loomed there, hands on her hips. She began at once, "That was no hefty blonde woman you was working for and you'll have to pay her every penny on her tractor you busted up. She don't keep insurance on it. She came here and her and me had us a long talk and I . . ."

Trembling, Parker set about lighting the kerosene lamp.   170

"What's the matter with you, wasting that keresene this near daylight?" she demanded. "I ain't got to look at you."

A yellow glow enveloped them. Parker put the match down and began to unbutton his shirt.

"And you ain't going to have none of me this near morning," she said.

"Shut your mouth," he said quietly. "Look at this and then I don't want to hear no more out of you." He removed the shirt and turned his back to her.

"Another picture," Sarah Ruth growled. "I might have known you was off 175
after putting some more trash on yourself."

Parker's knees went hollow under him. He wheeled around and cried, "Look at it! Don't just say that! *Look* at it!"

"I done looked," she said.

"Don't you know who it is?" he cried in anguish.

"No, who is it?" Sarah Ruth said. "It ain't anybody I know."

"It's him," Parker said.   180

"Him who?"

"God!" Parker cried.

"God? God don't look like that!"

"What do you know how he looks?" Parker moaned. "You aint' seen him."

"He don't *look*," Sarah Ruth said. "He's a spirit. No man shall see his face." 185

"Aw listen," Parker groaned, "this is just a picture of him."

"Idolatry!" Sarah Ruth screamed. "Idolatry! Enflaming yourself with idiots under every green tree! I can put up with lies and vanity but I don't want no idolator in this house!" and she grabbed up the broom and began to thrash him across the shoulders with it.

Parker was too stunned to resist. He sat there and let her beat him until she had nearly knocked him senseless and large welts had formed on the face of the tattooed Christ. Then he staggered up and made for the door.

She stamped the broom two or three times on the floor and went to the window and shook it out to get the taint of him off it. Still gripping it, she looked toward the pecan tree and her eyes hardened still more. There he was — who called himself Obadiah Elihue — leaning against the tree, crying like a baby.

Considerations for Critical Thinking and Writing

1. Would you ever consider getting a tattoo for yourself? Why or why not?
2. How was Parker affected as a boy by seeing the tattooed man at the fair? Why does he continue to have himself tattooed?
3. How does Parker's wife regard his tattoos?
4. Why did Parker marry his wife? Why did she marry him? What keeps them together in the marriage? Which one of them seems more powerful in the relationship?
5. What is Parker's view of his wife "forever sniffing up sin"?
6. What is Parker's attitude toward the navy, the government, and religion?
7. Why and how is Parker changed by crashing the tractor into the tree? Why does he subsequently decide to get a tattoo on his back?
8. How is Parker affected by the tattoo on his back? How does he think his wife will respond? How does she actually react to it?
9. What is the significance of Parker calling himself Obadiah Elihue when he returns home to his wife?
10. Why does Obadiah Elihue cry like a baby in the final scene?
11. Discuss the significance of the title.
12. How does humor contribute to the characterization of Parker? Do you think humor is appropriate for this story?

Connections to Other Selections

1. Compare the protagonists' attitudes toward religion in "Parker's Back" and Hawthorne's "Young Goodman Brown" (p. 242).
2. Compare the symbolic value of Parker's tattoo with the crimson hand in Hawthorne's "The Birthmark" (p. 261).
3. Write an essay that compares the themes of "Parker's Back" and "Revelation" (p. 394).

PERSPECTIVES ON O'CONNOR

O'Connor on Faith   1955

I write the way I do because (not though) I am a Catholic. This is a fact and nothing covers it like the bald statement. However, I am a Catholic peculiarly possessed of the modern consciousness, the thing Jung° describes as unhistorical, solitary, and guilty. To possess this within the Church is to bear a burden, the necessary burden for the conscious Catholic. It's to feel the contemporary situation at the ultimate level. I think that the Church is the only thing that is going to make the terrible world we are coming to endurable; the only thing that makes the Church endurable is that it is somehow the body of Christ and that on this we are fed. It seems to be a fact that you suffer as much from the Church as for it but if you believe in the divinity of Christ, you have to cherish the world at the same time that you struggle to endure it. This may explain the lack of bitterness in the stories.

From a letter to "A," July 20, 1955, in *The Habit of Being*

Jung: Carl Jung (1875–1961), a Swiss psychiatrist.

Considerations for Critical Thinking and Writing

1. Consider how O'Connor's fiction expresses her belief that "you have to cherish the world at the same time that you struggle to endure it."
2. Do you agree that "bitterness" is absent from O'Connor's stories? Explain why or why not.

O'Connor on the Materials of Fiction   1969

The beginning of human knowledge is through the senses, and the fiction writer begins where human perception begins. He appeals through the senses, and you cannot appeal to the senses with abstractions. It is a good deal easier for most people to state an abstract idea than to describe and thus re-create some object that they actually see. But the world of the fiction writer is full of matter, and this is what the beginning fiction writers are very loath to create.

They are concerned primarily with unfleshed ideas and emotions. They are apt to be reformers and to want to write because they are possessed not by a story but by the bare bones of some abstract notion. They are conscious of problems, not of people, of questions and issues, not of the texture of existence, of case histories and of everything that has a sociological smack, instead of with all those concrete details of life that make actual the mystery of our position on earth. . . .

One of the most common and saddest spectacles is that of a person of really fine sensibility and acute psychological perception trying to write fiction by using these [abstract] qualities alone. This type of writer will put down one intensely emotional or keenly perceptive sentence after the other, and the result will be complete dullness. The fact is that the materials of the fiction writer are the humblest. Fiction is about everything human and we are made out of dust, and if you scorn getting yourself dusty, then you shouldn't try to write fiction. It's not a grand enough job for you.

From "The Nature and Aim of Fiction" in *Mystery and Manners*

Considerations for Critical Thinking and Writing

1. Explain O'Connor's idea that "the materials of the fiction writer are the humblest" by reference to the materials and details of her stories.
2. Choose a substantial paragraph from an O'Connor story and describe how it "appeals through the senses."
3. Write an essay in which you agree or disagree with the following statement: Hawthorne's fiction is a good example of the kinds of mistakes that O'Connor attributes to a beginning fiction writer.

O'Connor on the Use of Exaggeration and Distortion   1969

When I write a novel in which the central action is a baptism, I am very well aware that for a majority of my readers, baptism is a meaningless rite, and so in my novel I have to see that this baptism carries enough awe and mystery to jar the reader into some kind of emotional recognition of its significance. To this end I have to bend the whole novel — its language, its structure, its action. I have to make the reader feel, in his bones if nowhere else, that something is going on here that counts. Distortion in this case is an instrument; exaggeration has a purpose, and the whole structure of the story or novel has been made what it is because of belief. This is not the kind of distortion that destroys; it is the kind that reveals, or should reveal.

From "Novelist and Believer" in *Mystery and Manners*

Considerations for Critical Thinking and Writing

1. It has been observed that in many of O'Connor's works the central action takes the form of some kind of "baptism" that initiates, tests, or purifies a character. Select a story that illustrates this generalization and explain how the conflict results in a kind of baptism.
2. O'Connor says that exaggeration and distortion reveal something in her stories.

What is the effect of such exaggeration and distortion? Typically, what is revealed by it? Focus your comments on a single story to illustrate your points.

3. Do you think that O'Connor's stories have anything to offer a reader who has no religious faith? Explain why or why not.

O'Connor on Theme and Symbol 1969

When you can state the theme of a story, when you can separate it from the story itself, then you can be sure the story is not a very good one. The meaning of a story has to be embodied in it, has to be made concrete in it. A story is a way to say something that can't be said any other way, and it takes every word in the story to say what the meaning is. You tell a story because a statement would be inadequate. When anybody asks what a story is about, the only proper thing is to tell him to read the story. The meaning of fiction is not abstract meaning but experienced meaning, and the purpose of making statements about the meaning of a story is only to help you to experience that meaning more fully.

The peculiar problem of the short-story writer is how to make the action he describes reveal as much of the mystery of existence as possible. He has only a short space to do it in and he can't do it by statement. He has to do it by showing, not by saying, and by showing the concrete — so that his problem is really how to make the concrete work double time for him.

In good fiction, certain of the details will tend to accumulate meaning from the action of the story itself, and when this happens they become symbolic in the way they work. I once wrote a story called "Good Country People," in which a lady Ph.D. has her wooden leg stolen by a Bible salesman whom she has tried to seduce. Now I'll admit that, paraphrased in this way, the situation is simply a low joke. The average reader is pleased to observe anybody's wooden leg being stolen. But without ceasing to appeal to him and without making any statements of high intention, this story does manage to operate at another level of experience, by letting the wooden leg accumulate meaning. Early in the story, we're presented with the fact that the Ph.D. is spiritually as well as physically crippled. She believes in nothing but her own belief in nothing, and we perceive that there is a wooden part of her soul that corresponds to her wooden leg. Now of course this is never stated. The fiction writer states as little as possible. The reader makes this connection from things he is shown. He may not even know that he makes the connection, but the connection is there nevertheless and it has its effect on him. As the story goes on, the wooden leg continues to accumulate meaning. The reader learns how the girl feels about her leg, how her mother feels about it, and how the country woman on the place feels about it; and finally, by the time the Bible salesman comes along, the leg has accumulated so much meaning that it is, as the saying goes, loaded. And when the Bible salesman steals it, the reader realizes that he has taken away part of the girl's personality and has revealed her deeper affliction to her for the first time.

If you want to say that the wooden leg is a symbol, you can say that. But it is a wooden leg first, and as a wooden leg it is absolutely necessary to the story. It has its place on the literal level of the story, but it operates in depth as well as on the surface. It increases the story in every direction, and this is essentially the way a story escapes being short.

Now a little might be said about the way in which this happens. I wouldn't want you to think that in that story I sat down and said, "I am now going to write a story about a Ph.D. with a wooden leg, using the wooden leg as a symbol for another kind of affliction." I doubt myself if many writers know what they are going to do when they start out. When I started writing that story, I didn't know there was going to be a Ph.D. with a wooden leg in it. I merely found myself one morning writing a description of two women that I knew something about, and before I realized it, I had equipped one of them with a daughter with a wooden leg. As the story progressed, I brought in the Bible salesman, but I had no idea what I was going to do with him. I didn't know he was going to steal that wooden leg until ten or twelve lines before he did it, but when I found out that this was what was going to happen, I realized that it was inevitable. This is a story that produces a shock for the reader, and I think one reason for this is that it produced a shock for the writer.

Now despite the fact that this story came about in this seemingly mindless fashion, it is a story that almost no rewriting was done on. It is a story that was under control throughout the writing of it, and it might be asked how this kind of control comes about, since it is not entirely conscious.

From "Writing Short Stories" in *Mystery and Manners*

Considerations for Critical Thinking and Writing

1. Why is a "statement" inadequate to convey the meaning of a story?
2. O'Connor describes how the wooden leg "continues to accumulate meaning" in "Good Country People." Choose another story by O'Connor and explain how something specific and concrete is invested with symbolic meaning.

JOSEPHINE HENDIN (b. 1946)
On O'Connor's Refusal to "Do Pretty"   1970

There is, in the memory of one Milledgeville matron, the image of O'Connor at nineteen or twenty who, when invited to a wedding shower for an old family friend, remained standing, her back pressed against the wall, scowling at the group of women who had sat down to lunch. Neither the devil nor her mother could make her say yes to this fiercely gracious female society, but Flannery O'Connor could not say no even in a whisper. She could not refuse the invitation but she would not accept it either. She did not exactly "fuss" but neither did she "do pretty."

From *The World of Flannery O'Connor*

Considerations for Critical Thinking and Writing

1. How is O'Connor's personality revealed in this anecdote about her ambivalent response to society? Allow the description to be suggestive for you, and flesh out a brief portrait of her.
2. Consider how this personality makes itself apparent in any one of O'Connor's stories you have read. How does the anecdote help to characterize the narrator's voice in the story?
3. To what extent do you think biographical details such as this — assuming the Milledgeville matron's memory to be accurate — can shed light on a writer's works?

CLAIRE KAHANE (b. 1935)
The Function of Violence in O'Connor's Fiction 1974

From the moment the reader enters O'Connor's backwoods, he is poised on the edge of a pervasive violence. Characters barely contain their rage; images reflect a hostile nature; and even the Christ to whom the characters are ultimately driven is a threatening figure . . . full of the apocalyptic wrath of the Old Testament.

O'Connor's conscious purpose is evident enough . . . .: to reveal the need for grace in a world grotesque without a transcendent context. "I have found that my subject in fiction is the action of grace in territory largely held by the devil," she wrote [in *Mystery and Manners*], and she was not vague about what the devil is: "an evil intelligence determined on its own supremacy." It would seem that for O'Connor, given the fact of original Sin, any intelligence determined on its own supremacy was intrinsically evil. For in each work, it is the impulse toward secular autonomy, the smug confidence that human nature is perfectible by its own efforts, that she sets out to destroy, through an act of violence so intense that the character is rendered helpless, a passive victim of a superior power. Again and again she creates a fiction in which a character attempts to live autonomously, to define himself and his values, only to be jarred back to what she calls "reality" — the recognition of helplessness in the face of contingency, and the need for absolute submission to the power of Christ.

From "Flannery O'Connor's Rage of Vision" in *American Literature*

Considerations for Critical Thinking and Writing

1. Choose an O'Connor story and explain how grace — the divine influence from God that redeems a person — is used in it to transform a character.
2. Which O'Connor characters can be accurately described as having an "evil intelligence determined on its own supremacy"? Choose one character and write an essay explaining how this description is central to the conflict of the story.
3. Compare an O'Connor story with one of Hawthorne's in which a character

"attempts to live autonomously, to define himself and his values, only to be jarred back to . . . 'reality' — the recognition of helplessness in the face of contingency. . . ."

DOROTHY T. McFARLAND (b. 1938)
A Formalist Reading of "Revelation"   1976

Mrs. Turpin, the protagonist of "Revelation," is convinced of her own goodness. Mrs. Turpin is a good Christian woman who looks after the poor, works for the church, and thanks Jesus effusively for making her what she is — and not "a nigger or white-trash or ugly." Mrs. Turpin's failure of charity, despite her works of charity, is obvious as she sums up the other patients in the doctor's waiting room in which the story opens. Sizing up a "stylish lady" as one of her own kind and striking up a conversation with her, Mrs. Turpin reveals, through her words and thoughts, her interior judgments on the others present. Her veiled racism and social snobbery, her cheerful complacency, and her unabashed pride in her good disposition are too much for the stylish lady's daughter, a fat, scowling girl who has obviously had to suffer much of the same sort of thing from her mother. The girl responds to Mrs. Turpin's remarks with ugly looks until finally, provoked beyond endurance, she flings a book at Mrs. Turpin's head and lunges at her throat. "Go back to hell where you came from, you old wart hog," the girl whispers to her fiercely.

Hog imagery has already been introduced in the conversation between Mrs. Turpin and the stylish lady. Mrs. Turpin mentioned the hogs she raises in a concrete-floored pig parlor. Responding to an unwelcome interruption by a "white-trash woman," who declares hogs to be "Nasty stinking things, a-gruntin and a-rootin all over the place," Mrs. Turpin coldly replied that her hogs are washed down every day with a hose and are "cleaner than some children I've seen." ("Cleaner by far than that child right there" [the "white-trash" woman's child], she added to herself.)

O'Connor uses hogs in this story (and elsewhere) as symbols of unredeemed human nature. As no amount of external cleanliness can fundamentally change hog nature, so no amount of external goodness can fundamentally change human nature, which, in O'Connor's view, is contaminated with evil — whether it be . . . consciously chosen evil . . . or the more subtle evil of pride and self-righteousness displayed by . . . Mrs. Turpin.

Evil seems a strong word to apply to a character like Mrs. Turpin, who, for all her pride and complacency, is surely not a "bad" woman. Yet O'Connor obviously felt that Mrs. Turpin's belief in her own goodness was, if anything, more of an obstacle to the salvation of her soul than an outright commitment to evil. Thomas Merton reflects on this paradox: "Truly the great problem is the salvation of those who, being good, think they have no further need to be saved and imagine their task is to make others 'good' like themselves."[9]

Mrs. Turpin is at first shocked and indignant at the injustice of what has

---

Thomas Merton (1915–1968): American Roman Catholic monastic and writer; author of *Conjectures of a Guilty Bystander* (Garden City, NY: Doubleday, 1968), 170.

happened to her. Why should she, a hard-working, respectable, church-going woman, be singled out for such a message when there was "trash in the room to whom it might justly have been applied"? At the same time, however, Mrs. Turpin senses that the girl "knew her in some intense and personal way, beyond time and place and condition," and the message, unpleasant as it is, has for her the force of divine revelation.

After pondering the girl's words with increasing wrath and indignation all afternoon, Mrs. Turpin marches down to the pig parlor on her farm and contemplates her hogs. "What do you send me a message like that for?" she demands of God. "How am I a hog and me both? How am I saved and from hell too?" She rails at God with increasing sarcasm until, with a final surge of fury, she roars, "Who do you think you are?" An echo of her own words comes back to her, like an answer, out of the silence.

Who does she think she is? The imagery surrounding this scene suggests that Mrs. Turpin considers herself the equal of God. The sun, that perennial symbol of God in O'Connor's fiction, seems comically obedient to Mrs. Turpin's presumption, and hangs over the tree line in an attitude almost exactly imitative of her own position on the fence of the pig parlor: "The sun was behind the wood, very red, looking over the paling of trees like a farmer inspecting his own hogs." While this image embodies Mrs. Turpin's assumption of the equality between her and God, it also suggests that the true relation between them is that God is the farmer, the world is His farm, and Mrs. Turpin is one of the "hogs" — humanity — at which He is gazing. His gaze — His light, symbolically the infusion of His grace into the world — is transforming; in the light of the setting sun the pigs are suffused with a red glow, and appear to "pant with a secret life." Mrs. Turpin, too, is touched by this transforming light, and life flows into her. "Like a monumental statue coming to life," she bends her head and gazes, "as if through the very heart of mystery, down into the pig parlor at the hogs."

The mystery of humanity, as O'Connor saw it, is that it is rooted in earth, yet bathed in God's light that fills it with secret life, the life of grace that is in no way dependent on worthiness or on the scale of human values Mrs. Turpin cherishes. The irrelevance of social values in the sphere of grace is manifested in the vision that is given to her as she lifts her eyes from the pigs and gazes at the purple streak in the sky left like a trail by the setting sun:

> She saw the streak as a vast swinging bridge extending upward from the earth through a field of living fire. Upon it a vast horde of souls were rumbling toward heaven. There were whole companies of white-trash, clean for the first time in their lives, and bands of black niggers in white robes, and battalions of freaks and lunatics shouting and clapping and leaping like frogs. And bringing up the end of the procession was a tribe of people whom she recognized at once as those who, like herself and Claud [her husband], had always had a little of everything and the God-given wit to use it right. . . . They were marching behind the others with great dignity, accountable as they had always been for good order and common sense and respectable behavior. They alone were on key. Yet she could see by their shocked and altered faces that even their virtues were being burned away.

For her to rise, to follow even at the end of the heaven-bound procession, it is necessary for her virtues to be burned away, for her to see herself as not more worthy of God's grace than the Negroes and white trash and freaks and lunatics she habitually looks down upon. Good works, in O'Connor's view, do not redeem; they only prevent Mrs. Turpin from seeing that she shares in the poverty and limitation and evil proclivities common to all humanity. She is not capable of lifting herself out of this condition by her own efforts; indeed, her efforts to do so only compound evil by making her think herself superior to others and thus reinforcing social inequality, pride, and complacency. "Rising" comes about by grace, and by Mrs. Turpin's response of openness to it. Appropriately enough, the instrument of grace — the ugly girl who hurled a book at Mrs. Turpin's head and declared that lady's kinship with hogs and hell — is named Mary Grace.

From Flannery O'Connor

Considerations for Critical Thinking and Writing

1. According to McFarland, what is the symbolic meaning of the hogs in "Revelation"?
2. How does McFarland's discussion of the story's imagery support her reading of the hogs' significance? What other images support this view?
3. Extend McFarland's discussion by writing an analysis of the images associated with Mary Grace that explain her function in the story.

EDWARD KESSLER (b. 1927)
On O'Connor's Use of History   1986

In company with other Southern writers . . . who aspire to embrace a lost tradition and look on history as a repository of value, Flannery O'Connor seems a curious anomaly. She wrote of herself: "I am a Catholic peculiarly possessed of the modern consciousness . . . unhistorical, solitary, and guilty." Likewise her characters comprise a gallery of misfits isolated in a present and sentenced to a lifetime of exile from the human community. In O'Connor's fiction, the past neither justifies nor even explains what is happening. If she believed, for example, in the importance of the past accident that maimed Joy in "Good Country People," she could have demonstrated how the event predetermined her present rejection of both human and external nature; but Joy's past is parenthetical: "Mrs. Hopewell excused this attitude because of the leg (which had been shot off in a hunting accident when Joy was ten)." Believing that humankind is fundamentally flawed, O'Connor spends very little time constructing a past for her characters. The cure is neither behind us nor before us but within us; therefore, the past — even historical time itself — supplies only a limited base for self-discovery.

From Flannery O'Connor and the Language of Apocalypse

Considerations for Critical Thinking and Writing

1. Consider how O'Connor uses history in any one of her stories in this anthology and compare that "unhistorical" vision with Hawthorne's in "Young Goodman Brown" (p. 242) or "The Minister's Black Veil" (p. 252).

2. Write an essay in which you discuss Kessler's assertion that for O'Connor the "past is parenthetical," in contrast to most Southern writers, who "embrace a lost tradition and look on history as a repository of value." For your point of comparison choose either Eudora Welty's "Livvie" (p. 115) or a story by William Faulkner: "A Rose for Emily" (p. 47) or "Barn Burning" (p. 436).

MILES ORVELL (b. 1944)

On the Humor in "Good Country People" 1992

With dispassionate irony and a detached, finely controlled comic sense, O'Connor reveals in "Good Country People" the world as it is — without vision, without grace, without knowledge. And, what is relatively rare in her fiction, she stops short of describing in Hulga any final recognition of her self or the world. So that we are left to ourselves to construe the meaning of the experience by looking back and again looking back at the various implications of the action. It is a ribald moral fable — harsh, cold, and funny.

From *Flannery O'Connor: An Introduction*

Considerations for Critical Thinking and Writing

1. Write an essay explaining how "Good Country People" is a fable that is "moral" as well as "ribald, . . . harsh, cold, and funny."
2. Compare and contrast the tone of O'Connor's humor in "Good Country People" with either "A Good Man Is Hard to Find" or "Parker's Back."

TWO COMPLEMENTARY CRITICAL READINGS

A. R. COULTHARD (b. 1940)

On the Visionary Ending of "Revelation" 1983

The second part of the story does not keep pace with its rollicking opening, but its psychological realism gives Mrs. Turpin's ultimate redemption a hard-edged credibility. When the protagonist returns home, her first impulse is, quite naturally, to resist the message of grace brought by the girl: "'I am not,' she said tearfully, 'a wart hog. From hell.' But the denial had no force." Unable to reject the charge, Mrs. Turpin turns to resentment: "The message had been given to Ruby Turpin, a respectable, hard-working, church-going woman. The tears dried. Her eyes began to burn instead with wrath." Next she attempts to exorcise the girl's demonic words by confessing them to her black fieldhands:

> "She said," she began again and finished this time with a fierce rush of breath, "that I was an old wart hog from hell."
> There was an astounded silence.
> "Where she at?" the youngest woman cried in a piercing voice.
> "Lemme see her. I'll kill her!"

"I'll kill her with you!" the other one cried.

"She b'long in the sylum," the old woman said emphatically. "You the sweetest white lady I know."

"She pretty too," the other two said. "Stout as she can be and sweet. Jesus satisfied with her!"

"Deed he is," the old woman declared.

Idiots! Mrs. Turpin growled to herself.

This little scene is both funny and thematically significant. Mrs. Turpin's refusal to accept the phony image of herself as a good woman offered by the blacks is a step toward facing the truth.

Mrs. Turpin's next step is literal. She climbs the hill to the hogpen, apparently considering it the appropriate place to reason out the meaning of being called a wart hog from hell. Once there, Ruby gets right down to business: "What do you send me a message like that for?" she demands. "How am I a hog and me both?" Then she yells, "Go on, call me a hog! Call me a hog again. From hell. Call me a wart hog from hell." She ends her harangue by hilariously roaring at God, "Who do you think you are?" In this scene, Ruby begins to grow into a sympathetic, even lovable, character. As O'Connor said, "You got to be a very big woman to shout at the Lord across a hogpen." You also got to believe.

God answers Mrs. Turpin by sending her an epiphany which is so unobtrusively presented that at first it seems to be only description: "A tiny truck, Claud's, appeared on the highway, heading rapidly out of sight. Its gears scraped thinly. It looked like a child's toy. At any moment a bigger truck might smash into it and scatter Claud's and the niggers' brains all over the road." The answer to Ruby's question is that God is omnipotent and that Ruby, like all mortals, is an insignificant, vulnerable creature whose life can end at any moment. Her response to this new knowledge is immediate: "Then like a monumental statue coming to life, she bent her head slowly and gazed, as if through the very heart of mystery, down into the pig parlor at the hogs."

The story originally ended at this point, but O'Connor decided that "something else was needed." Fortunately, what she added is not a concluding mini-sermon but a supernatural vision which is perfectly in keeping with the serio-comic tone of the story:

A visionary light settled in her eyes . . . a vast horde of souls were rumbling toward heaven. There were whole companies of white-trash, clean for the first time in their lives, and bands of black niggers in white robes, and battalions of freaks and lunatics shouting and clapping and leaping like frogs. And bringing up the end of the procession was a tribe of people whom she recognized at once as those . . . like herself and Claud. . . . They were marching behind the others with great dignity. . . . They alone were on key. Yet she could see by their shocked and altered faces that even their virtues were being burned away.

This vision demolishes Ruby's earlier neat ranking of people, and its concluding sentence, which could have quotation marks around "virtues," completes her education by telling her that no one deserves grace and that we receive it only because of God's mysterious mercy. The epiphany takes, and the story ends with Ruby, "her eyes small but fixed unblinkingly on what lay ahead," prepared to face a humbler and more demanding life.

Though at least one reader whom O'Connor respected found "Revelation" pessimistic and considered the protagonist evil, O'Connor's main worry was that the story would "be taken to be one designed to make fun of Ruby," probably because her weaknesses are so vividly shown. But the great achievement of the protagonist's characterization is that Ruby Turpin retains her humanity to the end and does not, upon receiving grace, turn into an inspirational symbol. At the same time, O'Connor has made her conversion believable by dramatizing it in action and dialogue consistent with both Mrs. Turpin's humorous traits and her serious role in the story. "Revelation" is not only a delightful comedy but a profound dramatization of redemption as well.

From *American Literature*

Considerations for Critical Thinking and Writing

1. According to Coulthard how does O'Connor avoid turning the end of the story into a "mini-sermon"?
2. How would your response to the story be different if it ended as O'Connor first intended it to — without the concluding paragraph? How would you regard Mrs. Turpin if this paragraph did not appear in the story?
3. Write an essay in response to this judgment of "Revelation": "Religion and comedy don't mix; therefore the comic tone of 'Revelation' is inappropriate to the serious religious epiphany at the end."

MARSHALL BRUCE GENTRY (b. 1953)
On the Revised Ending of "Revelation"   1986

The precise significance of Mrs. Turpin's vision of hordes on a fiery bridge is not altogether a matter of critical agreement. And O'Connor's letters show her to have been inconsistent in her opinion of "Revelation" while she was writing it. It was the ending of the story that most troubled her, and the sequence of versions shows O'Connor trying to make clear that Ruby is not entirely corrupt. In a letter dated 25 December 1963, O'Connor mentioned that a friend who had read a draft of "Revelation" had called Mrs. Turpin "evil" and had suggested that O'Connor omit the final vision, which the friend considered to be a confirmation of Mrs. Turpin's evilness. O'Connor's reaction was, "I am not going to leave it out. I am going to deepen it so that there'll be no mistaking Ruby is not just an evil Glad Annie." As she finished revising the story, O'Connor made the final vision less obviously of Mrs. Turpin's making. One late draft, for example, contains the statement that the Turpins, "marching behind the others" toward heaven "with great dignity," were "driving them, in fact, ahead of themselves, still responsible as they had always been for good order and common sense and respectable behavior." In the published text, the Turpins are still at the end of the procession, but there is no mention of them "driving" the others on, and they are "accountable" rather than "still responsible." Another significant difference between the draft and the published text is the addition in the final version of the fact that Mrs. Turpin sees that her "virtues" are "being burned away." In both these revisions there is less emphasis on Mrs. Turpin's smug perspective, more emphasis on what shocks her.

The final version makes the vision more clearly redemptive, and one apparent implication of the revisions is that Mrs. Turpin's revelation is supernatural in origin. This implication is misleading, however; there is still much in Mrs. Turpin's vision to suggest that she produces it, and the primary effect of O'Connor's revisions is to make Mrs. Turpin's unconscious more clearly responsible for her vision of entry into a heavenly community. This view may seem peculiar when one considers Mrs. Turpin's bigotry and banality, but one's impression of that bigotry and banality is the result of the narrator's emphasis in describing Mrs. Turpin. The narrator emphasizes the ridiculous aspects of Mrs. Turpin rather than making fully apparent the tracks she has laid to carry herself to the oven in which individuality is renounced and the ideal of heavenly community achieved.

From *Flannery O'Connor's Religion of the Grotesque*

Considerations for Critical Thinking and Writing

1. What reservations, according to Gentry, did O'Connor have about the story's ending? For what purpose did O'Connor revise the manuscript?
2. How does Gentry's reading of the ending compare with Coulthard's? Which reading do you find closer to your own? Why?
3. Write an essay that considers Gentry's charge that Mrs. Turpin appears "ridiculous" at the end of the story in contrast to Coulthard's assessment that she is both "delightful" and "profound."

10. Critical Case Study: William Faulkner's "Barn Burning"

This chapter offers several critical approaches to a well-known short story by William Faulkner. Though there are many possible critical approaches to any given work (see Chapter 35, "Critical Strategies for Reading," for a discussion of a variety of methods), and there are numerous studies of Faulkner from formalist, biographical, historical, mythological, psychological, sociological, and other perspectives, it is worth noting that each reading of a work or writer is predicated on accepting certain assumptions about literature and life. Those assumptions or premises may be complementary or mutually exclusive, and they may appeal to you or appall you. What is interesting, however, is how various approaches reveal the text (as well as its readers and critics) by calling attention to certain elements or leaving others out. The following critical excerpts suggest only a portion of the range of possibilities, but even a small representation of approaches can help you to raise new questions, develop insights, recognize problems, and suggest additional ways of reading the text.

WILLIAM FAULKNER (1897–1962)

A biographical note for William Faulkner appears on page 47, before his story "A Rose for Emily." In "Barn Burning" Faulkner portrays a young boy's love and revulsion for his father, a frightening man who lives by a "ferocious conviction in the rightness of his own actions."

The store in which the Justice of the Peace's court was sitting smelled of cheese. The boy, crouched on his nail keg at the back of the crowded room, knew he smelled cheese, and more: from where he sat he could see the ranked shelves close-packed with the solid, squat, dynamic shapes of tin cans whose labels his stomach read, not from the lettering which meant nothing to his mind but from the scarlet devils and the silver curve of fish — this, the cheese which he knew he smelled and the hermetic meat which his intestines believed he smelled coming in intermittent gusts momentary and brief between the other constant one, the smell and sense just a little of fear because mostly of despair and grief, the old fierce pull of blood. He could not see the table where the Justice sat and before which his father and his father's enemy (*our enemy* he thought in that despair; *ourn! mine and hisn both! He's my father!*) stood, but he could hear them, the two of them that is, because his father had said no word yet:

"But what proof have you, Mr. Harris?"

"I told you. The hog got into my corn. I caught it up and sent it back to him. He had no fence that would hold it. I told him so, warned him. The next time I put the hog in my pen. When he came to get it I gave him enough wire to patch up his pen. The next time I put the hog up and kept it. I rode down to his house and saw the wire I gave him still rolled on to the spool in his yard. I told him he could have the hog when he paid me a dollar pound fee. That evening a nigger came with the dollar and got the hog. He was a strange nigger. He said, 'He say to tell you wood and hay kin burn.' I said, 'What?' 'That whut he say to tell you,' the nigger said. 'Wood and hay kin burn.' That night my barn burned. I got the stock out but I lost the barn."

"Where is the nigger? Have you got him?"

"He was a strange nigger, I tell you. I don't know what became of him." 5

"But that's not proof. Don't you see that's not proof?"

"Get that boy up here. He knows." For a moment the boy thought too that the man meant his older brother until Harris said, "Not him. The little one. The boy," and, crouching, small for his age, small and wiry like his father, in patched and faded jeans even too small for him, with straight, uncombed, brown hair and eyes gray and wild as storm scud, he saw the men between himself and the table part and become a lane of grim faces, at the end of which he saw the Justice, a shabby, collarless, graying man in spectacles, beckoning him. He felt no floor under his bare feet; he seemed to walk beneath the palpable weight of the grim turning faces. His father, stiff in his black Sunday coat donned not for the trial but for the moving, did not even look at him. *He aims for me to lie,* he thought, again with that frantic grief and despair. *And I will have to do hit.*

"What's your name, boy?" the Justice said.

"Colonel Sartoris Snopes," the boy whispered.

"Hey?" the Justice said. "Talk louder. Colonel Sartoris? I reckon anybody 10 named for Colonel Sartoris in this country can't help but tell the truth, can they?" The boy said nothing. *Enemy! Enemy!* he thought; for a moment he could not even see, could not see that the Justice's face was kindly nor discern that his voice was troubled when he spoke to the man named Harris: "Do you want me to question this boy?" But he could hear, and during those subsequent long seconds while there was absolutely no sound in the crowded little room save that of quiet and intent breathing it was as if he had swung outward at the end of a grape vine, over a ravine, and at the top of the swing had been caught in a prolonged instant of mesmerized gravity, weightless in time.

"No!" Harris said violently, explosively. "Damnation! Send him out of here!" Now time, the fluid world, rushed beneath him again, the voices coming to him again through the smell of cheese and sealed meat, the fear and despair and the old grief of blood:

"This case is closed. I can't find against you, Snopes, but I can give you advice. Leave this country and don't come back to it."

His father spoke for the first time, his voice cold and harsh, level, without emphasis: "I aim to. I don't figure to stay in a country among people who . . ." he said something unprintable and vile, addressed to no one.

"That'll do," the Justice said. "Take your wagon and get out of this country before dark. Case dismissed."

His father turned, and he followed the stiff black coat, the wiry figure 15 walking a little stiffly from where a Confederate provost's man's musket ball had taken him in the heel on a stolen horse thirty years ago, followed the two backs now, since his older brother had appeared from somewhere in the crowd, no taller than the father but thicker, chewing tobacco steadily, between the two lines of grim-faced men and out of the store and across the worn gallery and down the sagging steps and among the dogs and half-grown boys in the mild May dust, where as he passed a voice hissed:

"Barn burner!"

Again he could not see, whirling; there was a face in a red haze, moonlike, bigger than the full moon, the owner of it half again his size, he leaping in the red haze toward the face, feeling no blow, feeling no shock when his head struck the earth, scrabbling up and leaping again, feeling no blow this time either and tasting no blood, scrabbling up to see the other boy in full flight and himself already leaping into pursuit as his father's hand jerked him back, the harsh, cold voice speaking above him: "Go get in the wagon."

It stood in a grove of locusts and mulberries across the road. His two hulking sisters in their Sunday dresses and his mother and her sister in calico and sunbonnets were already in it, sitting on or among the sorry residue of the dozen and more movings which even the boy could remember — the battered stove, the broken beds and chairs, the clock inlaid with mother-of-pearl, which would not run, stopped at some fourteen minutes past two o'clock of a dead and forgotten day and time, which had been his mother's dowry. She was crying, though when she saw him she drew her sleeve across her face and began to descend from the wagon. "Get back," the father said.

"He's hurt. I got to get some water and wash his . . ."

"Get back in the wagon," his father said. He got in too, over the tail-gate. 20 His father mounted to the seat where the older brother already sat and struck the gaunt mules two savage blows with the peeled willow, but without heat. It was not even sadistic; it was exactly that same quality which in later years would cause his descendants to over-run the engine before putting a motor car in motion, striking and reining back in the same movement. The wagon went on, the store with its quiet crowd of grimly watching men dropped behind; a curve in the road hid it. *Forever* he thought. *Maybe he's done satisfied now, now that he has* . . . stopping himself, not to say it aloud even to himself. His mother's hand touched his shoulder.

"Does hit hurt?" she said.

"Naw," he said. "Hit don't hurt. Lemme be."

"Can't you wipe some of the blood off before hit dries?"

"I'll wash to-night," he said. "Lemme be, I tell you."

The wagon went on. He did not know where they were going. None of them ever did or ever asked, because it was always somewhere, always a house of sorts waiting for them a day or two days or even three days away. Likely his father had already arranged to make a crop on another farm before he . . . Again he had to stop himself. He (the father) always did. There was something about his wolflike independence and even courage when the advantage was at least neutral which impressed strangers, as if they got from his latent ravening ferocity not so much a sense of dependability as a feeling that his ferocious conviction in the rightness of his own actions would be of advantage to all whose interest lay with his. 25

That night they camped, in a grove of oaks and beeches where a spring ran. The nights were still cool and they had a fire against it, of a rail lifted from a nearby fence and cut into lengths — a small fire, neat, niggard almost, a shrewd fire; such fires were his father's habit and custom always, even in freezing weather. Older, the boy might have remarked this and wondered why not a big one; why should not a man who had not only seen the waste and extravagance of war, but who had in his blood an inherent voracious prodigality with material not his own, have burned everything in sight? Then he might have gone a step farther and thought that that was the reason: that niggard blaze was the living fruit of nights passed during those four years in the woods hiding from all men, blue or gray, with his strings of horses (captured horses, he called them). And older still, he might have divined the true reason: that the element of fire spoke to some deep mainspring of his father's being, as the element of steel or of powder spoke to other men, as the one weapon for the preservation of integrity, else breath were not worth the breathing, and hence to be regarded with respect and used with discretion.

But he did not think this now and he had seen those same niggard blazes all his life. He merely ate his supper beside it and was already half asleep over his iron plate when his father called him, and once more he followed the stiff back, the stiff and ruthless limp, up the slope and on to the starlit road where, turning, he could see his father against the stars but without face or depth — a shape black, flat, and bloodless as though cut from tin in the iron folds of the frockcoat which had not been made for him, the voice harsh like tin and without heat like tin:

"You were fixing to tell them. You would have told him."

He didn't answer. His father struck him with the flat of his hand on the side of the head, hard but without heat, exactly as he had struck the two mules at the store, exactly as he would strike either of them with any stick in order to kill a horse fly, his voice still without heat or anger. "You're getting to be a man. You got to learn. You got to learn to stick to your own blood or you ain't going to have any blood to stick to you. Do you think either of them, any man there this morning, would? Don't you know all they wanted was a chance to get at me because they knew I had them beat? Eh?" Later, twenty years later, he was to tell himself, "If I had said they wanted only truth, justice, he would have hit me again." But now he said nothing. He was not crying. He just stood there. "Answer me," his father said.

"Yes," he whispered. His father turned.   30

"Get on to bed. We'll be there tomorrow."

Tomorrow they were there. In the early afternoon the wagon stopped before a paintless two-room house identical almost with the dozen others it had stopped before even in the boy's ten years, and again, as on the other dozen occasions, his mother and aunt got down and began to unload the wagon, although his two sisters and his father and brother had not moved.

"Likely hit ain't fitten for hawgs," one of the sisters said.

"Nevertheless, fit it will and you'll hog it and like it," his father said. "Get out of them chairs and help your Ma unload."

The two sisters got down, big, bovine, in a flutter of cheap ribbons; one of 35 them drew from the jumbled wagon bed a battered lantern, the other a worn broom. His father handed the reins to the older son and began to climb stiffly over the wheel. "When they get unloaded, take the team to the barn and feed them." Then he said, and at first the boy thought he was still speaking to his brother. "Come with me."

"Me?" he said.

"Yes," his father said. "You."

"Abner," his mother said. His father paused and looked back — the harsh level stare beneath the shaggy, graying, irascible brows.

"I reckon I'll have a word with the man that aims to begin tomorrow owning me body and soul for the next eight months."

They went back up the road. A week ago — or before last night, that is — 40 he would have asked where they were going, but not now. His father had struck him before last night but never before had he paused afterward to explain why; it was as if the blow and the following calm, outrageous voice still rang, repercussed, divulging nothing to him save the terrible handicap of being young, the light weight of his few years, just heavy enough to prevent his soaring free of the world as it seemed to be ordered but not heavy enough to keep him footed solid in it, to resist it and try to change the course of events.

Presently he could see the grove of oaks and cedars and the other flowering trees and shrubs where the house would be, though not the house yet. They walked beside a fence massed with honeysuckle and Cherokee roses and came to a gate swinging open between two brick pillars, and now, beyond a sweep of drive, he saw the house for the first time and at that instant he forgot his father and the terror and despair both, and even when he remembered his father again (who had not stopped) the terror and despair did not return. Because, for all the twelve movings, they had sojourned until now in a poor country, a land of small farms and fields and houses, and he had never seen a house like this before. *Hit's big as a courthouse* he thought quietly, with a surge of peace and joy whose reason he could not have thought into words, being too young for that: *They are safe from him. People whose lives are a part of this peace and dignity are beyond his touch, he no more to them than a buzzing wasp: capable of stinging for a little moment but that's all; the spell of this peace and dignity rendering even the barns and stable and cribs which belong to it impervious to the puny flames he might contrive* . . . . this, the peace and joy, ebbing for an instant as he looked again at the stiff black back, the stiff and implacable limp of the figure which was not dwarfed by the house, for the reason that it had never looked big anywhere and which now, against the serene columned backdrop, had more than ever that impervious quality of something cut ruthlessly from tin, depthless, as though, sidewise to the sun, it would cast no shadow. Watching him, the boy remarked the absolutely undeviating course which his father held and saw the stiff foot come squarely down in a pile of fresh droppings where a horse had stood in the drive and which his father could have avoided by a simple change of stride. But it ebbed only for a moment, though he could not have thought this into words either, walking on in the spell of the house, which he could even want but without envy, without sorrow, certainly never with that ravening and jealous rage which unknown to him walked in the ironlike black coat before him: *Maybe he will feel it too. Maybe it will even change him now from what maybe he couldn't help but be.*

They crossed the portico. Now he could hear his father's stiff foot as it came down on the boards with clocklike finality, a sound out of all proportion to the displacement of the body it bore and which was not dwarfed either by the white door before it, as though it had attained to a sort of vicious and ravening minimum not to be dwarfed by anything — the flat, wide, black hat, the formal coat of broadcloth which had once been black but which had now that friction-glazed greenish cast of the bodies of old house flies, the lifted sleeve which was too large, the lifted hand like a curled claw. The door opened so promptly that the boy knew the Negro must have been watching them all the time, an old man with neat grizzled hair, in a linen jacket, who stood barring the door with his body, saying, "Wipe yo foots, white man, fo you come in here. Major ain't home nohow."

"Get out of my way, nigger," his father said, without heat too, flinging the door back and the Negro also and entering, his hat still on his head. And now the boy saw the prints of the stiff foot on the doorjamb and saw them appear on the pale rug behind the machinelike deliberation of the foot which seemed to bear (or transmit) twice the weight which the body compassed. The Negro was shouting "Miss Lula! Miss Lula!" somewhere behind them, then the boy, deluged as though by a warm wave by a suave turn of the carpeted stair and a pendant glitter of chandeliers and a mute gleam of gold frames, heard the swift feet and saw her too, a lady — perhaps he had never seen her like before either — in a gray, smooth gown with lace at the throat and an apron tied at the waist and the sleeves turned back, wiping cake or biscuit dough from her hands with a towel as she came up the hall, looking not at his father at all but at the tracks on the blond rug with an expression of incredulous amazement.

"I tried," the Negro cried. "I tole him to . . . ."

"Will you please go away?" she said in a shaking voice. "Major de Spain is 45 not at home. Will you please go away?"

His father had not spoken again. He did not speak again. He did not even look at her. He just stood stiff in the center of the rug, in his hat, the shaggy iron-gray brows twitching slightly above the pebble-colored eyes as he appeared to examine the house with brief deliberation. Then with the same deliberation he turned; the boy watched him pivot on the good leg and saw the stiff foot drag round the arc of the turning, leaving a final long and fading smear. His father never looked at it, he never once looked down at the rug. The Negro held the door. It closed behind them, upon the hysteric and indistinguishable woman-wail. His father stopped at the top of the steps and scraped his boot clean on the edge of it. At the gate he stopped again. He stood for a moment, planted stiffly on the stiff foot, looking back at the house. "Pretty and white, ain't it?" he said. "That's sweat. Nigger sweat. Maybe it ain't white enought yet to suit him. Maybe he wants to mix some white sweat with it."

Two hours later the boy was chopping wood behind the house within which his mother and aunt and the two sisters (the mother and aunt, not the two girls, he knew that; even at this distance and muffled by walls the flat loud voices of the two girls emanated an incorrigible idle inertia) were setting up the stove to prepare a meal; when he heard the hooves and saw the linen-clad man on a fine sorrel mare, whom he recognized even before he saw the rolled rug in front of the Negro youth following on a fat bay carriage horse — a suffused, angry face vanishing, still at full gallop, beyond the corner of the house where his father and brother were sitting in the two tilted chairs; and a moment later, almost before he could have put the axe down, he heard the hooves again and watched the sorrel mare go back out of the yard, already galloping again. Then his father began to shout one of the sisters' names, who presently emerged backward from the kitchen door dragging the rolled rug along the ground by one end while the other sister walked behind it.

"If you ain't going to tote, go on and set up the wash pot," the first said.

"You, Sarty!" the second shouted. "Set up the wash pot!" His father appeared at the door, framed against that shabbiness, as he had been against that other bland perfection, impervious to either, the mother's anxious face at his shoulder.

"Go on," the father said. "Pick it up." The two sisters stopped, broad, lethargic; stooping, they presented an incredible expanse of pale cloth and a flutter of tawdry ribbons.

"If I thought enough of a rug to have to git hit all the way from France I wouldn't keep hit where folks coming in would have to tromp on hit," the first said. They raised the rug.

"Abner," the mother said. "Let me do it."

"You go back and git dinner," his father said. "I'll tend to this."

From the woodpile through the rest of the afternoon the boy watched them, the rug spread flat in the dust beside the bubbling wash pot, the two sisters stooping over it with that profound and lethargic reluctance, while the father stood over them in turn, implacable and grim, driving them though never raising his voice again. He could smell the harsh homemade lye they were using; he saw his mother come to the door once and look toward them with an expression not anxious now but very like despair; he saw his father turn, and he fell to with the axe and saw from the corner of his eye his father raise from the ground a flattish fragment of field stone and examine it and return to the pot, and this time his mother actually spoke: "Abner. Abner. Please don't. Please, Abner."

Then he was done too. It was dusk; the whippoorwills had already begun. He could smell coffee from the room where they would presently eat the cold food remaining from the midafternoon meal, though when he entered the house he realized they were having coffee again probably because there was a fire on the hearth, before which the rug now lay spread over the backs of the two chairs. The tracks of his father's foot were gone. Where they had been were now long, water-cloudy scoriations resembling the sporadic course of a lilliputian mowing machine.

It still hung there while they ate the cold food and then went to bed, scattered without order or claim up and down the two rooms, his mother in one bed, where his father would later lie, the older brother in the other, himself, the aunt, and the two sisters on pallets on the floor. But his father was not in bed yet. The last thing the boy remembered was the depthless, harsh silhouette of the hat and coat bending over the rug and it seemed to him that he had not even closed his eyes when the silhouette was standing over him, the fire almost dead behind it, the stiff foot prodding him awake. "Catch up the mule," his father said.

When he returned with the mule his father was standing in the black door, the rolled rug over his shoulder. "Ain't you going to ride?" he said.

"No. Give me your foot."

He bent his knee into his father's hand, the wiry, surprising power flowed smoothly, rising, he rising with it, on to the mule's bare back (they had owned a saddle once; the boy could remember it though not when or where) and with the same effortlessness his father swung the rug up in front of him. Now in the starlight they retraced the afternoon's path, up the dusty road rife with honeysuckle, through the gate and up the black tunnel of the drive to the lightless house, where he sat on the mule and felt the rough warp of the rug drag across his thighs and vanish.

"Don't you want me to help?" he whispered. His father did not answer and 60 now he heard again that stiff foot striking the hollow portico with that wooden and clocklike deliberation, that outrageous overstatement of the weight it carried. The rug, hunched, not flung (the boy could tell that even in the darkness) from his father's shoulder struck the angle of wall and floor with a sound unbelievably loud, thunderous, then the foot again, unhurried and enormous; a light came on in the house and the boy sat, tense, breathing steadily and quietly and just a little fast, though the foot itself did not increase its beat at all, descending the steps now; now the boy could see him.

"Don't you want to ride now?" he whispered. "We kin both ride now," the light within the house altering now, flaring up and sinking. *He's coming down the stairs now,* he thought. He had already ridden the mule up beside the horse block; presently his father was up behind him and he doubled the reins over and slashed the mule across the neck, but before the animal could begin to trot the hard, thin arm came around him, the hard, knotted hand jerking the mule back to a walk.

In the first red rays of the sun they were in the lot, putting plow gear on the mules. This time the sorrel mare was in the lot before he heard it at all, the rider collarless and even bareheaded, trembling, speaking in a shaking voice as the woman in the house had done, his father merely looking up once before stooping again to the hame he was buckling, so that the man on the mare spoke to his stooping back:

"You must realize you have ruined that rug. Wasn't there anybody here, any of your women . . ." he ceased, shaking, the boy watching him, the older brother leaning now in the stable door, chewing, blinking slowly and steadily at nothing apparently. "It cost a hundred dollars. But you never had a hundred dollars. You never will. So I'm going to charge you twenty bushels of corn against your crop. I'll add it in your contract and when you come to the commissary you can sign it. That won't keep Mrs. de Spain quiet but maybe it will teach you to wipe your feet before you enter her house again."

Then he was gone. The boy looked at his father, who still had not spoken or even looked up again, who was now adjusting the logger-head in the hame.

"Pap," he said. His father looked at him — the inscrutable face, the shaggy 65 brows beneath which the gray eyes glinted coldly. Suddenly the boy went toward him, fast, stopping as suddenly. "You done the best you could!" he cried. "If he wanted hit done different why didn't he wait and tell you how? He won't git no twenty bushels! He won't git none! We'll gether hit and hide hit! I kin watch . . ."

"Did you put the cutter back in that straight stock like I told you?"

"No, sir," he said.

"Then go do it."

That was Wednesday. During the rest of that week he worked steadily, at what was within his scope and some which was beyond it, with an industry that did not need to be driven nor even commanded twice; he had this from his mother, with the difference that some at least of what he did he liked to do, such as splitting wood with the half-size axe which his mother and aunt had earned, or saved money somehow, to present him with at Christmas. In company with the two older women (and on one afternoon, even one of the sisters), he built pens for the shoat and the cow which were part of his father's contract with the landlord, and one afternoon, his father being absent, gone somewhere on one of the mules, he went to the field.

They were running a middle buster now, his brother holding the plow 70 straight while he handled the reins, and walking beside the straining mule, the rich black soil shearing cool and damp against his bare ankles, he thought *Maybe this is the end of it. Maybe even that twenty bushels that seems hard to have to pay for just a rug will be a cheap price for him to stop forever and always from being what he used to be;* thinking, dreaming now, so that his brother had to speak sharply to him to mind the mule: *Maybe he even won't collect the twenty bushels. Maybe it will all add up and balance and vanish — corn, rug, fire; the terror and grief; the being pulled two ways like between two teams of horses — gone, done with for ever and ever.*

Then it was Saturday; he looked up from beneath the mule he was harnessing and saw his father in the black coat and hat. "Not that," his father said. "The wagon gear." And then, two hours later, sitting in the wagon bed behind his father and brother on the seat, the wagon accomplished a final curve, and he saw the weathered paintless store with its tattered tobacco- and patent-medicine posters and the tethered wagons and saddle animals below the gallery. He mounted the gnawed steps behind his father and brother, and there again was the lane of quiet, watching faces for the three of them to walk through. He saw the man in spectacles sitting at the plank table and he did not need to be told this was a Justice of the Peace; he sent one glare of fierce, exultant, partisan defiance at the man in collar and cravat now, whom he had seen but twice before in his life, and that on a galloping horse, who now wore on his face an expression not of rage but of amazed unbelief which the boy could not have known was at the incredible circumstance of being sued by one of his own tenants, and came and stood against his father and cried at the Justice: "He ain't done it! He aint' burnt . . ."

"Go back to the wagon," his father said.

"Burnt?" the Justice said. "Do I understand this rug was burned too?"

"Does anybody here claim it was?" his father said. "Go back to the wagon." But he did not, he merely retreated to the rear of the room, crowded as that other had been, but not to sit down this time, instead, to stand pressing among the motionless bodies, listening to the voices:

"And you claim twenty bushels of corn is too high for the damage you did 75 to the rug?"

"He brought the rug to me and said he wanted the tracks washed out of it. I washed the tracks out and took the rug back to him."

"But you didn't carry the rug back to him in the same condition it was in before you made the tracks on it."

His father did not answer, and now for perhaps half a minute there was no sound at all save that of breathing, the faint, steady suspiration of complete and intent listening.

"You decline to answer that, Mr. Snopes?" Again his father did not answer. "I'm going to find against you, Mr. Snopes. I'm going to find that you were responsible for the injury to Major de Spain's rug and hold you liable for it. But twenty bushels of corn seems a little high for a man in your circumstances to have to pay. Major de Spain claims it cost a hundred dollars. October corn will be worth about fifty cents. I figure that if Major de Spain can stand a ninety-five dollar loss on something he paid cash for, you can stand a five-dollar loss you haven't earned yet. I hold you in damages to Major de Spain to the amount of ten bushels of corn over and above your contract with him, to be paid to him out of your crop at gathering time. Court adjourned."

It had taken no time hardly, the morning was but half begun. He thought 80 they would return home and perhaps back to the field, since they were late, far behind all other farmers. But instead his father passed on behind the wagon, merely indicating with his hand for the older brother to follow with it, and crossed the road toward the blacksmith shop opposite, pressing on after his father, overtaking him, speaking, whispering up at the harsh, calm face beneath the weathered hat: "He won't git no ten bushels neither. He won't git one. We'll . . ." until his father glanced for an instant down at him, the face absolutely calm, the grizzled eyebrows tangled above the cold eyes, the voice almost pleasant, almost gentle:

"You think so? Well, we'll wait till October anyway."

The matter of the wagon — the setting of a spoke or two and the tightening of the tires — did not take long either, the business of the tires accomplished by driving the wagon into the spring branch behind the shop and letting it stand there, the mules nuzzling into the water from time to time, and the boy on the seat with the idle reins, looking up the slope and through the sooty tunnel of the shed where the slow hammer rang and where his father sat on an upended cypress bolt, easily, either talking or listening, still sitting there when the boy brought the dripping wagon up out of the branch and halted it before the door.

"Take them on to the shade and hitch," his father said. He did so and returned. His father and the smith and a third man squatting on his heels inside the door were talking, about crops and animals; the boy, squatting too in the ammoniac dust and hoof-parings and scales of rust, heard his father tell a long and unhurried story out of the time before the birth of the older brother even when he had been a professional horsetrader. And then his father came up beside him where he stood before a tattered last year's circus poster on the other side of the store, gazing rapt and quiet at the scarlet horses, the incredible poisings and convolutions of tulle and tights and the painted leers of comedians, and said, "It's time to eat."

But not at home. Squatting beside his brother against the front wall, he watched his father emerge from the store and produce from a paper sack a segment of cheese and divide it carefully and deliberately into three with his pocket knife and produce crackers from the same sack. They all three squatted on the gallery and ate, slowly, without talking; then in the store again, they drank from a tin dipper tepid water smelling of the cedar bucket and of living beech trees. And still they did not go home. It was a horse lot this time, a tall rail fence upon and along which men stood and sat and out of which one by one horses were led, to be walked and trotted and then cantered back and forth along the road while the slow swapping and buying went on and the sun began to slant westward, they — the three of them — watching and listening, the older brother with his muddy eyes and his steady, inevitable tobacco, the father commenting now and then on certain of the animals, to no one in particular.

It was after sundown when they reached home. They ate supper by lamp- 85 light, then, sitting on the doorstep, the boy watched the night fully accomplish, listening to the whippoorwills and the frogs, when he heard his mother's voice: "Abner! No! No! Oh, God. Oh, God. Abner!" and he rose, whirled, and saw the altered light through the door where a candle stub now burned in a bottle neck on the table and his father, still in the hat and coat, at once formal and burlesque as though dressed carefully for some shabby and ceremonial violence, emptying the reservoir of the lamp back into the five-gallon kerosene can from which it had been filled, while the mother tugged at his arm until he shifted the lamp to the other hand and flung her back, not savagely or viciously, just hard, into the wall, her hands flung out against the wall for balance, her mouth open and in her face the same quality of hopeless despair as had been in her voice. Then his father saw him standing in the door.

"Go to the barn and get that can of oil we were oiling the wagon with," he said. The boy did not move. Then he could speak.

"What . . ." he cried. "What are you . . ."

"Go get that oil," his father said. "Go."

Then he was moving, running, outside the house, toward the stable: this the old habit, the old blood which he had not been permitted to choose for himself, which had been bequeathed him willy nilly and which had run for so long (and who knew where, battening on what of outrage and savagery and lust) before it came to him. *I could keep on*, he thought. *I could run on and on and never look back, never need to see his face again. Only I can't. I can't,* the rusted can in his hand now, the liquid sploshing in it as he ran back to the house and into it, into the sound of his mother's weeping in the next room, and handed the can to his father.

"Ain't you going to even send a nigger?" he cried. "At least you sent a nigger 90 before!"

This time his father didn't strike him. The hand came even faster than the blow had, the same hand which had set the can on the table with almost excruciating care flashing from the can toward him too quick for him to follow it, gripping him by the back of his shirt and on to tiptoe before he had seen it quit the can, the face stooping at him in breathless and frozen ferocity, the cold, dead voice speaking over him to the older brother who leaned against the table, chewing with that steady, curious, sidewise motion of cows:

"Empty the can into the big one and go on. I'll catch up with you."

"Better tie him up to the bedpost," the brother said.

"Do like I told you," the father said. Then the boy was moving, his bunched shirt and the hard, bony hand between his shoulder-blades, his toes just touching the floor, across the room and into the other one, past the sisters sitting with spread heavy thighs in the two chairs over the cold hearth, and to where his mother and aunt sat side by side on the bed, the aunt's arms about his mother's shoulders.

"Hold him," the father said. The aunt made a startled movement. "Not you," 95 the father said. "Lennie. Take hold of him. I want to see you do it." His mother took him by the wrist. "You'll hold him better than that. If he gets loose don't you know what he is going to do? He will go up yonder." He jerked his head toward the road. "Maybe I'd better tie him."

"I'll hold him," his mother whispered.

"See you do then." Then his father was gone, the stiff foot heavy and measured upon the boards, ceasing at last.

Then he began to struggle. His mother caught him in both arms, he jerking and wrenching at them. He would be stronger in the end, he knew that. But he had no time to wait for it. "Lemme go!" he cried. "I don't want to have to hit you!"

"Let him go!" the aunt said. "If he don't go, before God, I am going up there myself!"

"Don't you see I can't?" his mother cried. "Sarty! Sarty! No! No! Help me, 100 Lizzie!"

Then he was free. His aunt grasped at him but it was too late. He whirled, running, his mother stumbled forward on to her knees behind him, crying to the nearer sister. "Catch him, Net! Catch him!" But that was too late too, the sister (the sisters were twins, born at the same time, yet either of them now gave the impression of being, encompassing as much living meat and volume and weight as any other two of the family) not yet having begun to rise from the chair, her head, face, alone merely turned, presenting to him in the flying instant an astonishing expanse of young female features untroubled by any surprise even, wearing only an expression of bovine interest. Then he was out of the room, out of the house, in the mild dust of the starlit road and the heavy rifeness of honeysuckle, the pale ribbon unspooling with terrific slowness under his running feet, reaching the gate at last and turning in, running, his heart and lungs drumming, on up the drive toward the lighted house, the lighted door. He did not knock, he burst in, sobbing for breath, incapable for the moment of speech; he saw the astonished face of the Negro in the linen jacket without knowing when the Negro had appeared.

"De Spain!" he cried, panted. "Where's . . ." then he saw the white man too emerging from a white door down the hall. "Barn!" he cried. "Barn!"

"What?" the white man said. "Barn?"

"Yes!" the boy cried. "Barn!"

"Catch him!" the white man shouted. 105

But it was too late this time too. The Negro grasped his shirt, but the entire sleeve, rotten with washing, carried away, and he was out that door too and in the drive again, and had actually never ceased to run even while he was screaming into the white man's face.

Behind him the white man was shouting, "My horse! Fetch my horse!" and he thought for an instant of cutting across the park and climbing the fence into the road, but he did not know the park nor how high the vine-massed fence might be and he dared not risk it. So he ran on down the drive, blood and breath roaring; presently he was in the road again though he could not see it. He could not hear either: the galloping mare was almost upon him before he heard her, and even then he held his course, as if the very urgency of his wild grief and need must in a moment more find him wings, waiting until the ultimate instant to hurl himself aside and into the weed-choked roadside ditch as the horse thundered past and on, for an instant in furious silhouette against the stars, the tranquil early summer night sky which, even before the shape of the horse and rider vanished, strained abruptly and violently upward: a long, swirling roar incredible and soundless, blotting the stars, and he springing up and into the road again, running again, knowing it was too late yet still running even after he heard the shot and, an instant later, two shots, pausing now without knowing he had ceased to run, crying "Pap! Pap!," running again before he knew he had begun to run, stumbling, tripping over something and scrabbling up again without ceasing to run, looking backward over his shoulder at the glare as he got up, running on among the invisible trees, panting, sobbing, "Father! Father!"

At midnight he was sitting on the crest of a hill. He did not know it was midnight and he did not know how far he had come. But there was no glare behind him now and he sat now, his back toward what he had called home for four days anyhow, his face toward the dark woods which he would enter when breath was strong again, small, shaking steadily in the chill darkness, hugging himself into the remainder of his thin, rotten shirt, the grief and despair now no longer terror and fear but just grief and despair. *Father. My father,* he thought. "He was brave!" he cried suddenly, aloud but not loud, no more than a whisper: "He was! He was in the war! He was in Colonel Sartoris' cav'ry!" not knowing that his father had gone to that war a private in the fine old European sense, wearing no uniform, admitting the authority of and giving fidelity to no man or army or flag, going to war as Malbrouck° himself did: for booty — it meant nothing and less than nothing to him if it were enemy booty or his own.

Malbrouck: John Churchill, duke of Marlborough (1650–1722), English military commander who led the armies of England and Holland in the War of Spanish Succession.

The slow constellations wheeled on. It would be dawn and then sun-up after a while and he would be hungry. But that would be tomorrow and now he was only cold, and walking would cure that. His breathing was easier now and he decided to get up and go on, and then he found that he had been asleep because he knew it was almost dawn, the night almost over. He could tell that from the whippoorwills. They were everywhere now among the dark trees below him, constant and inflectioned and ceaseless, so that, as the instant for giving over to the day birds drew nearer and nearer, there was no interval at all between them. He got up. He was a little stiff, but walking would cure that too as it would the cold, and soon there would be the sun. He went on down the hill, toward the dark woods within which the liquid silver voices of the birds called unceasing — the rapid and urgent beating of the urgent and quiring heart of the late spring night. He did not look back.

Considerations for Critical Thinking and Writing

1. Explain why Sarty is a dynamic or a static character. Which term best describes his father? Why?
2. Who is the central character in this story? Explain your choice.
3. How are Sarty's emotions revealed in the story's opening paragraphs? What seems to be the function of the italicized passages there and elsewhere?
4. What do we learn from the story's exposition that helps us understand Abner's character? How does his behavior reveal his character? What do other people say about him?
5. How does Faulkner's physical description of Abner further our understanding of his personality?
6. Explain how the justice of the peace, Mr. Harris, and Major de Spain serve as foils to Abner. Discuss whether you think they are round or flat characters.
7. Who are the story's stock characters? What is their purpose?
8. Explain how the description of Major de Spain's house helps to frame the main conflicts that Sarty experiences in his efforts to remain loyal to his father.
9. Write an essay describing Sarty's attitudes toward his father as they develop and change throughout the story.
10. What do you think happens to Sarty's father and brother at the end of the story? How does your response to this question affect your reading of the last paragraph?
11. How does the language of the final paragraph suggest a kind of resolution to the conflicts Sarty has experienced?

Connections to Other Selections

1. Compare and contrast Faulkner's characterizations of Abner Snopes in this story and Miss Emily in "A Rose for Emily" (p. 47). How does the author generate sympathy for each character even though both are guilty of terrible crimes? Which character do you find more sympathetic? Explain why.
2. How does Abner Snopes's motivation for revenge compare with Matt Fowler's in Andre Dubus's "Killings" (p. 57). How do the victims of each character's revenge differ and thereby help to shape the meanings of each story?
3. Read the section on mythological criticism in Chapter 35, "Critical Strategies for Reading." How do you think a mythological critic would make sense of Sarty Snopes and Matt Fowler?

JANE HILES (b. 1951)

Hiles uses a biographical approach (see p. 2001 of "Critical Strategies for Reading") to try to determine Faulkner's intentions in his characterization of how Sarty responds to the conflicts he feels about his father.

Blood Ties in "Barn Burning"   1985

"'You're getting to be a man. . . . You got to learn to stick to your own blood or you ain't going to have any blood to stick to you'": Abner Snopes's admonition to his son, Colonel Sartoris (or "Sarty"), introduces a central issue in Faulkner's "Barn Burning" — the kinship bond, which the story's narrator calls the "old fierce pull of blood." The interpretive crux of the work is a conflict between determinism, represented by the blood tie that binds Sarty to his clan, and free will, dramatized by the boy's ultimate repudiation of family ties and his decampment. Dissonances between the structure and the imagery of the work develop and amplify Sarty's conflict: viewed in the light of the narrator's deterministic assumptions, the story's denouement is a red herring which only appears to resolve the complexities created by evocative language. Sarty's seeming interruption of the antisocial pattern established by his father is actually a continuation of it, and the ostensible resolution of his moral dilemma actually no resolution at all. . . .

In an interview in Japan sixteen years after the publication of "Barn Burning," Faulkner delivered an appraisal of the phenomenon of clannishness that bears considerable relevance to Abner Snopes's defensive posture in "Barn Burning":

> Yes, we are country people and we have never had too much in material possessions because 60 or 70 years ago we were invaded and we were con- quered. So we have been thrown back on our selves not only for entertain- ment but certain [sic] amount of defense. We have to be clannish just like the people in the Scottish highlands, each springing to defend his own blood whether it be right or wrong. Just a matter of custom and habit, we have to do it; interrelated that way, and usually there is hereditary head [sic] of the whole lot, as usually, the oldest son of the oldest son and each looked upon as chief of his own particular clan. That is the tone they live by. But I am sure it is because only a comparatively short time ago we were invaded by our own people — speaking in our own language which is always a pretty savage sort of warfare.

In Faulkner's estimation, the old pull of blood transcends considerations of caste, class, and occupation:

. . . [I]t is regional. It is through what we call the "South." It doesn't matter what the people do. They can be land people, farmers, and industrialists, but there still exists the feeling of blood, of clan, blood for blood. It is pretty general through all the classes.[1]

Faulkner's explanation of the phenomenon of Southern clannishness touches upon a number of the issues that arise in "Barn Burning." In each case, alienation from the politically and economically dominant group leads to dependence upon an alternative source of security. Just as beleaguered Southerners, Faulkner suggests, have had to look to themselves for "defense" since the South was defeated, so Ab Snopes must turn to his kin for defense not only from Union troops but also from the landed Southern aristocrat who, in what Ab perceives as a failure of paternalism, "aims to begin . . . owning [him] body and soul." The clan's identifying characteristic, then, is its orientation to survival. Perhaps most interestingly, the comments made in the interview impinge upon the central issue of the morality of Sarty's choice. Faulkner's recognition here of a private code of honor suggests that Sarty's conduct is somewhat more questionable than is generally recognized, and his articulation in the interview of a necessity for clannishness suggests at least a modicum of sympathy for the "custom and habit" of "each springing to defend his own blood whether it be right or wrong."

From *Mississippi Quarterly: The Journal of Southern Culture*

[1]James B. Meriwether and Michael Millgate, eds., *Lion in the Garden* (New York: Random House, 1968), p. 191.

Considerations for Critical Thinking and Writing

1. To what extent does Faulkner's description of clannishness in the South affect your understanding of whether Sarty resolves his dilemma at the end of the story?
2. Do you agree with Hiles that "Sarty's conduct is somewhat more questionable than is generally recognized"?

BENJAMIN DeMOTT (b. 1924)

DeMott pays close attention to matters of culture, race, class, and power that affect Abner Snopes, and from those perspectives Abner is seen as more than simply malevolent.

Abner Snopes as a Victim of Class   1988

We know that Ab Snopes is harsh to his wife, his sons, and his daughters, and that he is particularly cruel to his stock. We know that his hatred of the planters with whom he enters into sharecropping agreements repeatedly issues in acts of wanton destruction. We know that he's ridden with suspicion of his own closest kin, expecting them to betray him. And we know that — worse than any of this — he often behaves with fearful coldness to those who try desperately to communicate the loving respect they feel for him.

Given such a combination of racism, destructiveness, and blank insensitivity, it's tempting to imagine Ab as a figure in whom ignorance and brutality obliterate every sympathetic impulse, every normative response to peace, dignity, or beauty. Major de Spain seems to reach something close to that conclusion after the rug-laundering episode ("Wasn't there anybody here, any of your women . . ."). And although Ab's son is intensely loyal to his father and indignant at the injustice of the Major's twenty-bushel "charge" for the destruction of the rug, Sarty clearly has a conviction that "peace and dignity" are somehow *beyond his [father's] touch, he no more to them than a buzzing wasp.*" Is there anything to be made of Ab Snopes except a person whose raging malevolence has badly stunted if not crippled his humanity?

Denying the force of the malevolence is impossible — but tracing it solely to ignorance and insensitivity falsifies Ab's nature. Uneducated, probably illiterate, schooled in none of the revolutionary traditions which, in urban settings, were shaping popular protests against "economic injustice" when this story was written in the late 1930s, Ab nevertheless has managed, through the exercise of his own primitive intelligence, to make sense of his world, to arrive at a vision of the relations between labor, money, and the beautiful. It's a vision that's miles away from transforming itself into a broadly historical account of capital accumulation. Ab Snopes can't frame a theory to himself about, say, proletarian enslavement; he has no language in which to imagine a class solidarity leading to political action aimed at securing justice and truth. Indeed, he would explode at the notion that considerations of truth and justice have any pertinence either to the interests of the authorities opposing him or to his own interests in defying them. ("Later, twenty years later, [Sarty] was to tell himself, 'If I had said they wanted only truth, justice, he would have hit me again.'") For Ab Snopes the only principle lending significance to his war with the de Spains of this world is that of blood loyalty — determination to beat your personal enemy if you can and keep faith, at all costs, with your clan.

Yet despite all this, Ab does see that part of the power of the beautiful and the orderly to command our respect depends upon our refusal to remind ourselves that they have been brought into existence by other people's labor — by effort that often in history has been slave labor and has seldom been fairly recompensed. Sarty Snopes, grown up, presumably arrives finally at an understanding both that his father's situation was one of economic oppression and that the oppressors, when sitting in a court of law, are capable of attempting to reach beyond selfishness to a decent distribution of justice. But his father had, at the time, no grip on any of this.

Yet Ab is not a fool, and brutality and insensitivity are not the only features of character that we can make out in him. What we need also to summon is the terrible frustration of an undeveloped mind — aware of the weight of an immense unfairness, aware of the habit of the weak perpetually to behave as though the elegance, grace, beauty, and order found often in the neighborhoods of the rich somehow were traceable exclusively to the superior nature of the rich —

and yet unable to move forward from either awareness to anything approaching rational protest. His rage cannot become a force leading toward any positive principle; it has no way to express itself except in viciousness to those closest at hand. It can't begin to make a serious bid for admiration, because whatever inclination we might have to admire it is instantly crossed by repugnance at the cruelty inherent in it.

But it remains true that, together with the ignorance and brutality in Ab Snopes, there is a ferocious, primitive undeceivedness in his reading of the terms of the relationship between rich and poor, lucky and unlucky, advantaged and disadvantaged. Ab Snopes has seen a portion of the truth of the world that many on his level, and most who are luckier, never see. We can damn him for allowing that truth to wreck his humanity, but when we fully bring him to life as a character, it's impossible not to include with our indictment a sense of pity.

From *Close Imagining: An Introduction to Literature*

Considerations for Critical Thinking and Writing

1. DeMott acknowledges Abner's ignorance and brutality, but he also presents him as a man who suffers injustices. What are those injustices? Discuss whether you think they warrant a more balanced assessment of Abner's character.
2. Why doesn't Abner protest his "oppression"? Given DeMott's perspective on him, how might Abner — in another story — have been the hero rather than a terrible source of conflict?
3. To what extent can DeMott's approach to Abner's circumstances be described as a Marxist perspective? (For a discussion of Marxist critics see p. 2008.)

GAYLE EDWARD WILSON (b. 1931)

The following analysis combines psychology and myth as a means of understanding the conflicts in "Barn Burning." The "Apollonian man" alluded to in the discussion refers to the myth of Apollo and implies a person who values order, community, balance, and self-knowledge to establish true relations between the individual and his world.

Conflict in "Barn Burning"   1990

Ruth Benedict's descriptions of two major patterns of culture provide an advantageous starting point for a discussion of the way in which Faulkner develops the content of "Barn Burning." The Paranoid way of life, she comments, has "no political organization. In a strict sense it has no legality."[1] As a conse-

[1]*Patterns of Culture* (New York, 1959), p. 122.

quence of the Paranoid man's adherence to this life-style, he is "lawless," and is feared as a warrior who will hesitate "at no treachery" (p. 121). In such a culture, "every man's hand is against every other man," and as a result each man relies upon blood ties to form social alliances and to sanction his actions (pp. 122–123). The Apollonian man, on the other hand, "keeps to the middle of the road, stays within the known map," and strives to fulfill his civic role in terms of the expectations of the community at large (p. 70). Men in such a society, although the blood tie is relatively important as a bond, turn to the community and its collected wisdom, as it is embodied in the law, for the approval of their actions and for their security. Thus the sanction for a man's "acts comes from the formal structure, not the individual" (p. 99) — from the community, not the blood kin. In "Barn Burning" Faulkner develops the ideas contained in these descriptions of dissimilar life-styles in a way which creates the central tension in the story and keeps it constantly before the reader. The reader is thus made aware of the pervasiveness of Sarty's *"terror and the grief, the being pulled two ways like between two teams of horses."*

The tension is made evident by the presence of effects which follow from actions taken in accord with the dominant characteristic of each life-style. Abner's "wolflike independence . . . his latent ravening ferocity . . . [and] conviction in the rightness of his own actions," which have frequently manifested themselves in acts of destruction against the property of an established community, clearly mark him as a follower of the Paranoid way. As such, his actions inevitably, and repeatedly, alienate him from each settled society into which he moves. His disregard for a "formal structure" of any kind is indicated by such a minor detail as that which occurs when Abner fuels his fire with "a rail lifted from a nearby fence and cut into lengths," an act which is symbolic of his rejection of any societally imposed limits. It is by burning barns, however, that Abner's Paranoid life-style and its consequences are most forcefully dramatized. At Abner's trial for barn burning, Sarty sees the men "between himself and the table part and become a lane of grim faces." Abner and Sarty then walk between the "two lines of grim-faced men" and they leave a "quiet crowd of grimly watching men." This separation of the Snopes family from the larger society as a consequence of acts motivated by Abner's "ravening ferocity" is underscored by the Justice's command to Abner: "Take your wagon and get out of this country before dark." The Snopes's wagon, containing "the sorry residue of the dozen and more movings," becomes, therefore, a symbol of the transient and nomadic way of life which the Snopes family is forced to adopt because of Abner's adherence to the Paranoid way. The de Spain tenant house and the manner in which the Snopes family lives in it are also effects of a life-style which is not concerned with permanence or order or boundaries or limits. The house is a "paintless two-room" structure "identical almost with the dozen others" in which the family has lived as a result of its nomadic existence, and the members of the family are found "scattered without order or claim up and down the two rooms."

On the other hand, the Harris and de Spain barns represent productivity and fertility, permanence and continuity, because they house the equipment, stock, and seed by which a society produces the goods to sustain and perpetuate itself. A barn and its contents are the effects of a society which is built upon the willingness of men to subordinate their unfettered desires to a communal consensus in order to develop a permanent community. The importance of a barn to the Apollonian way is illustrated by Sarty's thoughts when he sees the effect brought about by what a barn symbolizes. When he comes upon the de Spain house for the first time, he feels that *"the spell"* of *"peace and dignity"* cast by the magnificent house will render *"even the barns and stable and cribs which belong to it impervious to the puny flames he* [Abner] *might contrive."* The sight of this apotheosis of the Apollonian way has a profound effect on Sarty: he "at that instant . . . forgot his father. . . ." It is most revealing that Sartoris should compare this house which symbolizes the *"peace and dignity"* of the Apollonian way with another kind of building which, because of what it represents, embodies the very essence of an ordered society: *"Hit's big as a courthouse* he thought quietly, with a surge of peace and joy."

Essentially, it is the concept of law, as symbolized by the de Spain house, that gives Sarty his sense of "peace and joy," for it is the law that provides man with the peace necessary to develop the "formal structure" of a communal, stable society. Without law, as Hobbes tells us, "there is no place for Industry; because the fruit thereof is uncertain: and consequently no Culture of the Earth; . . . no commodius Building; . . . no Society; and which is worst of all, continuall feare, and danger of violent death; And the life of man, solitary, poore, nasty, brutish, and short."[2] At its best, the law is moderate, even, and impartial. It protects as well as punishes; it is an elaborately worked out system designed to join men together in a common purpose, to insure the presumption of innocence until guilt is proved, and to make the punishment commensurate with the crime. In "Barn Burning" the primacy of the law in an Apollonian society is made quite evident. It is represented in a minor way by the contract in which Snopes engages with de Spain to work for eight months in return for a share of the crop. It is developed in a major way in the two trials which take place. In the first trial, the law protects Abner from unwarranted conclusions. Concerning the charge that Abner burned Harris's barn, the Justice asks Harris, "But what proof have you, Mr. Harris?" Harris tells of the Negro who appeared and gave him the cryptic message, "'wood and hay kin burn,'" to which the Justice replies, "But that's not proof. Don't you see that's not proof?" In the second trial, de Spain's unreasonable assessment of twenty bushels of corn in payment for the rug Abner ruined is not allowed. Abner is fined ten bushels, not twenty, as de Spain had wanted. For the men in "Barn Burning," . . . then, the law and its equitable application to all men is the *sine qua non* of the Apollonian way. . . . It is this belief in the law and its extensions of "justice" and "civilization" which guides and controls the behavior of the Apollonian man. This is the same realization that young Sarty is only able to articulate "twenty years" after Abner strikes him for not being willing to lie in his defense at the trial. "'If I had said they only wanted truth, justice, he would have hit me again.'"

From *Mississippi Quarterly*

[2]Chapter XIII, *"Of the* NATURAL CONDITION *of Mankind, as concerning their Felicity, and Misery,"* *Leviathan* . . . (1651) in *Seventeenth-Century Verse and Prose*, ed. Helen White, Ruth Wallerstein, and Ricardo Quintana (New York, 1967), I, 223.

Considerations for Critical Thinking and Writing

1. What distinctions are drawn between the "Paranoid man" and the "Apollonian man?" How do these two different types serve to frame the conflicts in "Barn Burning"?
2. How is the Snopes's wagon an appropriate symbol of the "Paranoid man," and how are the Harris and de Spain barns fitting symbols of the "Apollonian way"?
3. In an essay explain why you think Sarty chooses one way of life over the other at the end of the story.
4. Compare Wilson's description of the story's conflicts with Hiles's and DeMott's.

JAMES FERGUSON (b. 1928)

Ferguson's formalist approach (see p. 1999 of "Critical Strategies for Reading") relates Faulkner's use of point of view to his thematic concerns in the story.

Narrative Strategy in "Barn Burning"   1991

The point of view is largely limited to the consciousness of Sarty Snopes, but in spite of his sensitivity and his intuitive sense of right and wrong, the little boy is far too young to understand his father and the complexities of the moral choice he must make. To enhance the pathos of his situation and the drama of Sarty's initiation into life, Faulkner felt the need for the occasional intrusion of an authorial voice giving the reader insights far beyond the capabilities of the youthful protagonist. A passage, for example, about the fires Abner Snopes builds affords us a sense of the rationale for the man's actions, of his strangely perverse integrity, which could not be supplied to us by the consciousness of his son:

> The nights were still cool and they had a fire against it, of a rail lifted from a nearby fence and cut into lengths — a small fire, neat, niggard almost, a shrewd fire; such fires were his father's habit and custom always, even in freezing weather. Older, the boy might have remarked this and wondered why not a big one; why should not a man who had not only seen the waste and extravagance of war, but who had in his blood an inherent voracious prodigality with material not his own, have burned everything in sight? Then he might have gone a step farther and thought that that was the reason: that niggard blaze was the living fruit of nights passed during those four years in the woods hiding from all men, blue or gray, with his strings of horses (captured horses, he called them). And older still, he might have divined the true reason: that the element of fire spoke to some deep mainspring of his father's being, as the element of steel or of powder spoke to other men, as the one weapon for the preservation of integrity, else breath were not worth the breathing, and hence to be regarded with respect and used with discretion.

Again, near the end of the story, after Sarty has betrayed his father, there is another brief shift away from the consciousness of the protagonist:

> "He was brave!" he cried suddenly, aloud but not loud, no more than a whisper: "He was! He was in the war! He was in Colonel Sartoris' cav'ry!" not knowing that his father had gone to that war a private in the fine old European sense, wearing no uniform, admitting the authority of and giving fidelity to no man or army or flag, going to war as Malbrouck himself did: for booty — it meant nothing and less than nothing to him if it were enemy booty or his own.

"Barn Burning" is incomparably richer than it would have been without such additions not only because they supply us with ironies otherwise unavailable to us but also because these manipulations of point of view dramatize *on the level of technique* the thematic matter of the story. The tensions between the awareness of the boy and the information supplied us by the authorial voice undergird and emphasize the conflicts between youth and age, innocence and sophistication, intuition and abstraction, decency and corruption, all of which lie at the core of the work.

From Faulkner's Short Fiction

Considerations for Critical Thinking and Writing

1. In the first passage quoted by Ferguson how does the narrator's analysis of Abner Snopes become progressively sophisticated in explaining his reasons for building a small fire?
2. What other examples of shifts away from the consciousness of Sarty to a more informed point of view can you find in the story? Choose what you judge to be a significant example and write an essay about how Faulkner's use of point of view contributes to the story's themes.

11. A Collection of Stories

The sixteen short stories in this chapter represent a broad variety of styles and themes. They are written by men and women from a number of countries whose lives collectively span from the nineteenth century to the present. The four stories in "An Album of World Literature," by writers from Japan, Chile, Botswana, and Russia, introduce themes and styles from traditions that might differ quite a bit from your own. The four stories in "An Album of Contemporary Stories" — each written within the past six years — offer a sustained opportunity to explore the fiction being produced today. Inevitably, you will find some of the following stories more appealing than others, but every one of them is worth a careful reading, the kind of reading rewarded by pleasure and understanding.

QUESTIONS FOR RESPONSIVE READING

The following questions can help you consider important elements of fiction that reveal your responses to a story's effects and meanings. The questions are general, so they will not always be relevant to a particular story. Many of them, however, should prove useful for thinking, talking, and writing about a work of fiction. If you are uncertain about the meaning of a term used in a question, consult the Index of Terms on the inside back cover of this book for the pages that discuss the term. You should also find useful the discussion of various critical approaches to literature in Chapter 35, "Critical Strategies for Reading."

Plot

1. Does the plot conform to a formula? Is it like those of any other stories you have read? Did you find it predictable?
2. What is the source and nature of the conflict for the protagonist? Was your major interest in the story based on what happens next

or on some other concern? What does the title reveal now that you've finished the story?

3. Is the story told chronologically? If not, in what order is it told, and what is the effect of that order on your response to the action?
4. What does the exposition reveal? Are flashbacks used? Did you see any foreshadowings? Where is the climax?
5. Is the conflict resolved at the end? Would you characterize the ending as happy, unhappy, or somewhere in between?
6. Is the plot unified? Is each incident somehow related to some other element in the story?

Character

7. Do you identify with the protagonist? Who (or what) is the antagonist?
8. Does your response to any characters change as you read? What do you think caused the change? Do any characters change and develop in the course of the story? How?
9. Are round, flat, or stock characters used? Is their behavior motivated and plausible?
10. How does the author reveal characters? Are they directly described or indirectly presented? Are the characters' names used to convey something about them?
11. What is the purpose of the minor characters? Are they individualized, or do they primarily represent ideas or attitudes?

Setting

12. Is the setting important in shaping your response? If it were changed, would your response to the story's action and meaning be significantly different?
13. Is the setting used symbolically? Are the time, place, and atmosphere related to the theme?
14. Is the setting used as an antagonist?

Point of View

15. Who tells the story? Is it a first-person or third-person narrator? Is it a major or minor character or one who does not participate in the action at all? How much does the narrator know? Does the point of view change at all in the course of the story?
16. Is the narrator reliable and objective? Does the narrator appear too innocent, emotional, or self-deluded to be trusted?
17. Does the author directly comment on the action?
18. If told from a different point of view, how would your response to the story change? Would anything be lost?

Symbolism

19. Did you notice any symbols in the story? Are they actions, characters, settings, objects, or words?
20. How do the symbols contribute to your understanding of the story?

Theme

21. Did you find a theme? If so, what is it?
22. Is the theme stated directly, or is it developed implicitly through the plot, characters, or some other element?
23. Is the theme a confirmation of your values, or does it challenge them?

Style, Tone, and Irony

24. Do you think the style is consistent and appropriate throughout the story? Do all the characters use the same kind of language, or did you hear different voices?
25. Would you describe the level of diction as formal or informal? Are the sentences short and simple, long and complex, or some combination?
26. How does the author's use of language contribute to the tone of the story? Did it seem, for example, intense, relaxed, sentimental, nostalgic, humorous, angry, sad, or remote?
27. Do you think the story is worth reading more than once? Does the author's use of language bear close scrutiny so that you feel and experience more with each reading?

Critical Strategies

28. Is there a particular critical approach that seems especially appropriate for this story? (See the discussion of "Critical Strategies for Reading" beginning on p. 1995.)
29. How might biographical information about the author help to determine the central concerns of the story?
30. How might historical information about the story provide a useful context for interpretation?
31. What kinds of evidence from the story are you focusing on to support your interpretation? Does your interpretation leave out any important elements that might undercut or qualify your interpretation?
32. To what extent do your own experiences, values, beliefs, and assumptions inform your interpretation?
33. Given that there are a variety of ways to interpret the story, which one seems the most useful to you?

JOHN CHEEVER (1912–1982)
Reunion 1962

The last time I saw my father was in Grand Central Station. I was going from my grandmother's in the Adirondacks to a cottage on the Cape that my mother had rented, and I wrote my father that I would be in New York between trains for an hour and a half and asked if we could have lunch together. His secretary wrote to say that he would meet me at the information booth at noon, and at twelve o'clock sharp I saw him coming through the crowd. He was a stranger to me — my mother divorced him three years ago, and I hadn't been with him since — but as soon as I saw him I felt that he was my father, my flesh and blood, my future and my doom. I knew that when I was grown I would be something like him; I would have to plan my campaigns within his limitations. He was a big, good-looking man, and I was terribly happy to see him again. He struck me on the back and shook my hand. "Hi, Charlie," he said. "Hi, boy. I'd like to take you up to my club, but it's in the Sixties, and if you have to catch an early train I guess we'd better get something to eat around here." He put his arm around me, and I smelled my father the way my mother sniffs a rose. It was a rich compound of whiskey, after-shave lotion, shoe polish, woolens, and the rankness of a mature male. I hoped that someone would see us together. I wished that we could be photographed. I wanted some record of our having been together.

We went out of the station and up a side street to a restaurant. It was still early, and the place was empty. The bartender was quarreling with a delivery boy, and there was one very old waiter in a red coat down by the kitchen door. We sat down, and my father hailed the waiter in a loud voice. *"Kellner!"* he shouted. *"Garçon! Cameriere!° You!"* His boisterousness in the empty restaurant seemed out of place. "Could we have a little service here!" he shouted. "Chop-chop." Then he clapped his hands. This caught the waiter's attention, and he shuffled over to our table.

"Were you clapping your hands at me?" he asked.

"Calm down, calm down, *sommelier,"°* my father said. "If it isn't too much to ask of you — if it wouldn't be too much above and beyond the call of duty, we would like a couple of Beefeater Gibsons."

"I don't like to be clapped at," the waiter said. 5

"I should have brought my whistle," my father said. "I have a whistle that is audible only to the ears of old waiters. Now, take out your little pad and your little pencil and see if you can get this straight: two Beefeater Gibsons. Repeat after me: two Beefeater Gibsons."

"I think you'd better go somewhere else," the waiter said quietly.

"That," said my father, "is one of the most brilliant suggestions I have ever heard. Come on, Charlie, let's get the hell out of here."

I followed my father out of that restaurant into another. He was not so boisterous this time. Our drinks came, and he cross-questioned me about the

---

Kellner! . . . Garçon! Cameriere!: German, French, and Italian respectively for "Waiter!"
sommelier: Wine waiter (French).

baseball season. He then struck the edge of his empty glass with his knife and began shouting again. *"Garçon! Kellner! You!* Could we trouble you to bring us two more of the same."

"How old is the boy?" the waiter asked.   10

"That," my father said, "is none of your goddamned business."

"I'm sorry, sir," the waiter said, "but I won't serve the boy another drink."

"Well, I have some news for you," my father said. "I have some very interesting news for you. This doesn't happen to be the only restaurant in New York. They've opened another on the corner. Come on, Charlie."

He paid the bill, and I followed him out of that restaurant into another. Here the waiters wore pink jackets like hunting coats, and there was a lot of horse tack on the walls. We sat down, and my father began to shout again. "Master of the hounds! Tallyhoo and all that sort of thing. We'd like a little something in the way of a stirrup cup. Namely, two Bibson Greefeaters."

"Two Bibson Greefeaters?" the waiter asked, smiling.   15

"You know damned well what I want," my father said angrily. "I want two Beefeater Gibsons, and make it snappy. Things have changed in jolly old England. So my friend the duke tells me. Let's see what England can produce in the way of a cocktail."

"This isn't England," the waiter said.

"Don't argue with me," my father said. "Just do as you're told."

"I just thought you might like to know where you are," the waiter said.

"If there is one thing I cannot tolerate," my father said, "it is an impudent   20 domestic. Come on, Charlie."

The fourth place we went to was Italian. *"Buon giorno,"* my father said *"Per favore, possiamo avere due cocktail americani, forti, forti. Molto gin, poco vermut."°*

"I don't understand Italian," the waiter said.

"Oh, come off it," my father said. "You understand Italian, and you know damned well you do. *Vogliamo due cocktail americani. Subito."°*

The waiter left us and spoke with the captain, who came over to our table and said, "I'm sorry, sir, but this table is reserved."

"All right," my father said. "Get us another table."   25

"All the tables are reserved," the captain said.

"I get it," my father said. "You don't desire our patronage. Is that it? Well, the hell with you. *Vada all' inferno.°* Let's go, Charlie."

"I have to get my train," I said.

"I'm sorry, sonny," my father said. "I'm terribly sorry." He put his arm around me and pressed me against him. "I'll walk you back to the station. If there had only been time to go up to my club."

"That's all right, Daddy," I said.   30

"I'll get you a paper," he said. "I'll get you a paper to read on the train."

Then he went up to a newsstand and said, "Kind sir, will you be good enough to favor me with one of your goddamned, no-good, ten-cent afternoon

---

Buon giorno . . . Per favore . . . : "Good morning . . . Please, may we have two American cocktails, strong ones. Much gin, little vermouth" (Italian).
Vogliamo due cocktail . . . : "We want two American cocktails. Immediately" (Italian).
Vada all' inferno: "Go to hell" (Italian).

papers?" The clerk turned away from him and stared at a magazine cover. "Is it asking too much, kind sir," my father said, "is it asking too much for you to sell me one of your disgusting specimens of yellow journalism?"

"I have to go, Daddy," I said. "It's late."

"Now, just wait a second, sonny," he said. "Just wait a second. I want to get a rise out of this chap."

"Goodbye, Daddy," I said, and I went down the stairs and got my train, and that was the last time I saw my father. 35

FRANZ KAFKA (1883–1924)
A Hunger Artist   1924
TRANSLATED BY EDWIN AND WILLA MUIR

During these last decades the interest in professional fasting has markedly diminished. It used to pay very well to stage such great performances under one's own management, but today that is quite impossible. We live in a different world now. At one time the whole town took a lively interest in the hunger artist; from day to day of his fast the excitement mounted; everybody wanted to see him at least once a day; there were people who bought season tickets for the last few days and sat from morning till night in front of his small barred cage; even in the nighttime there were visiting hours, when the whole effect was heightened by torch flares; on fine days the cage was set out in the open air, and then it was the children's special treat to see the hunger artist; for their elders he was often just a joke that happened to be in fashion, but the children stood open-mouthed, holding each other's hands for greater security, marveling at him as he sat there pallid in black tights, with his ribs sticking out so prominently, not even on a seat but down among straw on the ground, sometimes giving a courteous nod, answering questions with a constrained smile, or perhaps stretching an arm through the bars so that one might feel how thin it was, and then again withdrawing deep into himself, paying no attention to anyone or anything, not even to the all-important striking of the clock that was the only piece of furniture in his cage, but merely staring into vacancy with half shut eyes, now and then taking a sip from a tiny glass of water to moisten his lips.

Besides casual onlookers there were also relays of permanent watchers selected by the public, usually butchers, strangely enough, and it was their task to watch the hunger artist day and night, three of them at a time, in case he should have some secret recourse to nourishment. This was nothing but a formality, instituted to reassure the masses, for the initiates knew well enough that during his fast the artist would never in any circumstances, not even under forcible compulsion, swallow the smallest morsel of food; the honor of his profession forbade it. Not every watcher, of course, was capable of understanding this; there were often groups of night watchers who were very lax in carrying out their duties and deliberately huddled together in a retired corner to play cards with great absorption, obviously intending to give the hunger artist the chance of a little refreshment, which they supposed he could draw from some private hoard. Nothing annoyed the artist more than such watchers; they made him miserable; they made his fast seem unendurable; sometimes he mastered his feebleness sufficiently to sing during their watch for as long as he could keep going, to show them how unjust their suspicions were. But that was of little use; they only wondered at his cleverness in being able to fill his mouth even while singing. Much more to his taste were the watchers who sat close up to the bars, who were not content with the dim night lighting of the hall but focused him in the full glare of the electric pocket torch given them by the impresario. The harsh light did not trouble him at all, in any case he could never sleep properly, and he could always drowse a little, whatever the light, at any hour, even when the hall was thronged with noisy onlookers. He was quite happy at the prospect of spending a sleepless night with such watchers; he was ready to exchange jokes with them, to tell them stories out of his nomadic life, anything at all to keep them awake and demonstrate to them again that he had no eatables in his cage and that he was fasting as not one of them could fast. But his happiest moment was when the morning came and an enormous breakfast was brought them, at his expense, on which they flung themselves with the keen appetite of healthy men after a weary night of wakefulness. Of course there were people who argued that this breakfast was an unfair attempt to bribe the watchers, but that was going rather too far, and when they were invited to take on a night's vigil without a breakfast, merely for the sake of the cause, they made themselves scarce, although they stuck stubbornly to their suspicions.

Such suspicions, anyhow, were a necessary accompaniment to the profession of fasting. No one could possibly watch the hunger artist continuously, day and night, and so no one could produce first-hand evidence that the fast had really been rigorous and continuous; only the artist himself could know that, he was therefore bound to be the sole completely satisfied spectator of his own fast. Yet for other reasons he was never satisfied; it was not perhaps mere fasting that had brought him to such skeleton thinness that many people had regretfully to keep away from his exhibitions, because the sight of him was too much for them, perhaps it was dissatisfaction with himself that had worn him down. For he alone knew, what no other initiate knew, how easy it was to fast. It was the easiest thing in the world. He made no secret of this, yet people did not believe him, at the best they set him down as modest; most of them, however, thought he was out for publicity or else was some kind of cheat who found it easy to fast because he had discovered a way of making it easy, and then had the impudence to admit the fact, more or less. He had to put up with all that, and in the course of time had got used to it, but his inner dissatisfaction always rankled, and never yet, after any term of fasting — this must be granted to his credit — had he left the cage of his own free will. The longest period of fasting was fixed by his impresario at forty days, beyond that term he was not allowed to go, not even in great cities, and there was good reason for it, too. Experience had proved that for about forty days the interest of the public could be stimulated by a steadily increasing pressure of advertisement, but after that the town began to lose interest, sympathetic support began notably to fall off; there were of course local variations as between one town and another or one country and another, but as a general rule forty days marked the limit. So on the fortieth day the flower bedecked cage was opened, enthusiastic spectators filled the hall, a military band played, two doctors entered the cage to measure the results of the fast, which were announced through a megaphone, and finally two young ladies appeared, blissful at having been selected for the honor, to help the hunger artist down the few steps leading to a small table on which was spread a carefully chosen invalid repast. And at this very moment the artist always turned stubborn. True, he would entrust his bony arms to the outstretched helping hands of the ladies bending over him, but stand up he would not. Why stop fasting at this particular moment, after forty days of it? He had held out for a long time, an illimitably long time; why stop now, when he was in his best fasting form, or rather, not yet quite in his best fasting form? Why should he be cheated of the fame he would get for fasting longer, for being not only the record hunger artist of all time, which presumably he was already, but for beating his own record by a performance beyond human imagination, since he felt that there were no limits to his capacity for fasting? His public pretended to admire him so much, why should it have so little patience with him; if he could endure fasting longer, why shouldn't the public endure it? Besides, he was tired, he was comfortable sitting in the straw, and now he was supposed to lift himself to his full height and go down to a meal the very thought of which gave him a nausea that only the presence of the ladies kept him from betraying, and even that with an effort. And he looked up into the eyes of the ladies who were apparently so friendly and in reality so cruel, and shook his head, which felt too heavy on its strengthless neck. But then there happened yet again what always happened. The impresario came forward, without a word — for the band made speech impossible — lifted his arms in the air above the artist, as if inviting Heaven to look down upon its creature here in the straw, this suffering martyr, which indeed he was, although in quite another sense; grasped him round the emaciated waist, with exaggerated caution, so that the frail condition he was in might be appreciated; and committed him to the care of the blenching ladies, not without secretly giving him a shaking so that his legs and body tottered and swayed. The artist now submitted completely; his head lolled on his breast as if it had landed there by chance; his body was hollowed out; his legs in a spasm of self-preservation clung close to each other at the knees, yet scraped on the ground as if it were not really solid ground, as if they were only trying to find solid ground; and the whole weight of his body, a feather-weight after all, relapsed onto one of the ladies, who, looking round for help and panting a little — this post of honor was not at all what she had expected it to be — first stretched her neck as far as she could to keep her face at least free from contact with the artist, when finding this impossible, and her more fortunate companion not coming to her aid but merely holding extended on her own trembling hand the little bunch of knucklebones that was the artist's, to the great delight of the spectators burst into tears and had to be replaced by an attendant who had long been stationed in readiness. Then came the food, a little of which the impresario managed to get between the artist's lips, while he sat in a kind of half-fainting trance, to the accompaniment of cheerful patter designed to distract the public's attention from the artist's condition; after that a toast was drunk to the public, supposedly prompted by a whisper from the artist in the impresario's ear; the band confirmed it with a mighty flourish, the spectators melted away, and no one had any cause to be dissatisfied with the proceedings, no one except the hunger artist himself, he only, as always.

So he lived for many years, with small regular intervals of recuperation, in visible glory, honored by the world, yet in spite of that troubled in spirit, and all the more troubled because no one would take his trouble seriously. What comfort could he possibly need? What more could he possibly wish for? And if some good-natured person, feeling sorry for him, tried to console him by pointing out that his melancholy was probably caused by fasting; it could happen, especially when he had been fasting for some time, that he reacted with an outburst of fury and to the general alarm began to shake the bars of his cage like a wild animal. Yet the impresario had a way of punishing these outbreaks which he rather enjoyed putting into operation. He would apologize publicly for the artist's behavior, which was only to be excused, he admitted, because of the irritability caused by fasting; a condition hardly to be understood by well-fed people; then by natural transition he went on to mention the artist's equally incomprehensible boast that he could fast for much longer than he was doing; he praised the high ambition, the good will, the great self-denial undoubtedly implicit in such a statement; and then quite simply countered it by bringing out photographs, which were also on sale to the public, showing the artist on the fortieth day of a fast lying in bed almost dead from exhaustion. This perversion of the truth, familiar to the artist though it was, always unnerved him afresh and proved too much for him. What was a consequence of the premature ending of his fast was here presented as the cause of it! To fight against this lack of under-standing, against a whole world of nonunderstanding, was impossible. Time and again in good faith he stood by the bars listening to the impresario, but as soon as the photographs appeared he always let go and sank with a groan back on to his straw, and the reassured public could once more come close and gaze at him.

A few years later when the witnesses of such scenes called them to mind, 5
they often failed to understand themselves at all. For meanwhile the aforemen-tioned change in public interest had set in; it seemed to happen almost overnight; there may have been profound causes for it, but who was going to bother about that; at any rate the pampered hunger artist suddenly found himself deserted one fine day by the amusement seekers, who were streaming past him to other more favored attractions. For the last time the impresario hurried him over half Europe to discover whether the old interest might still survive here and there; all in vain; everywhere, as if by secret agreement, a positive revulsion from professional fasting was in evidence. Of course it could not really have sprung up so suddenly as all that, and many premonitory symptoms which had not been sufficiently remarked or suppressed during the rush and glitter of success now came retrospectively to mind, but it was now too late to take any countermea-sures. Fasting would surely come into fashion again at some future date, yet that was no comfort for those living in the present. What, then, was the hunger artist to do? He had been applauded by thousands in his time and could hardly come down to showing himself in a street booth at village fairs, and as for adopting another profession, he was not only too old for that but too frantically devoted to fasting. So he took leave of the impresario, his partner in an unparalleled career, and hired himself to a large circus; in order to spare his own feelings he avoided reading the conditions of his contract.

A large circus with its enormous traffic in replacing and recruiting men, animals, and apparatus can always find a use for people at any time, even for a hunger artist, provided of course that he does not ask too much, and in this particular case anyhow it was not only the artist who was taken on but his famous and long-known name as well, indeed considering the peculiar nature of his performance, which was not impaired by advancing age, it could not be objected that there was an artist past his prime, no longer at the height of his professional skill, seeking a refuge in some quiet corner of a circus; on the contrary, the hunger artist averred that he could fast as well as ever, which was entirely credible; he even alleged that if he were allowed to fast as he liked, and this was at once promised him without more ado, he could astound the world by establishing a record never yet achieved, a statement which certainly provoked a smile among the other professionals, since it left out of account the change in public opinion, which the hunger artist in his zeal conveniently forgot.

He had not, however, actually lost his sense of the real situation and took it as a matter of course that he and his cage should be stationed, not in the middle of the ring as a main attraction, but outside, near the animal cages, on a site that was after all easily accessible. Large and gaily painted placards made a frame for the cage and announced what was to be seen inside it. When the public came thronging out in the intervals to see the animals, they could hardly avoid passing the hunger artist's cage and stopping there for a moment; perhaps they might even have stayed longer had not those pressing behind them in the narrow gangway, who did not understand why they should be held up on their way toward the excitements of the menagerie, made it impossible for anyone to stand gazing quietly for any length of time. And that was the reason why the hunger artist, who had of course been looking forward to these visiting hours as the main achievement of his life, began instead to shrink from them. At first he could hardly wait for the intervals; it was exhilarating to watch the crowds come streaming his way, until only too soon — not even the most obstinate self-deception, clung to almost consciously, could hold out against the fact — the conviction was borne in upon him that these people, most of them, to judge from their actions, again and again, without exception, were all on their way to the menagerie. And the first sight of them from the distance remained the best. For when they reached his cage he was at once deafened by the storm of shouting and abuse that arose from the two contending factions, which renewed themselves continuously, of those who wanted to stop and stare at him — he soon began to dislike them more than the others — not out of real interest but only out of obstinate self-assertiveness, and those who wanted to go straight on to the animals. When the first great rush was past, the stragglers came along, and these, whom nothing could have prevented from stopping to look at him as long as they had breath, raced past with long strides, hardly even glancing at him, in their haste to get to the menagerie in time. And all too rarely did it happen that he had a stroke of luck, when some father of a family fetched up before him with his children, pointed a finger at the hunger artist, and explained at length what the phenomenon meant, telling stories of earlier years when he himself had watched similar but much more thrilling performances, and the children, still rather uncomprehending, since neither inside nor outside school had they been sufficiently prepared for this lesson — what did they care about fasting? —

yet showed by the brightness of their intent eyes that new and better times might be coming. Perhaps, said the hunger artist to himself many a time, things would be a little better if his cage were set not quite so near the menagerie. That made it too easy for people to make their choice, to say nothing of what he suffered from the stench of the menagerie, the animals' restlessness by night, the carrying past of raw lumps of flesh for the beasts of prey, the roaring at feeding times, which depressed him continually. But he did not dare to lodge a complaint with the management; after all, he had the animals to thank for the troops of people who passed his cage, among whom there might always be one here and there to take an interest in him, and who could tell where they might seclude him if he called attention to his existence and thereby to the fact that, strictly speaking, he was only an impediment on the way to the menagerie.

A small impediment, to be sure, one that grew steadily less. People grew familiar with the strange idea that they could be expected, in times like these, to take an interest in a hunger artist, and with this familiarity the verdict went out against him. He might fast as much as he could, and he did so; but nothing could save him now, people passed him by. Just try to explain to anyone the art of fasting! Anyone who has no feeling for it cannot be made to understand it. The fine placards grew dirty and illegible, they were torn down; the little notice board telling the number of fast days achieved, which at first was changed carefully every day, had long stayed at the same figure, for after the first few weeks even this small task seemed pointless to the staff; and so the artist simply fasted on and on, as he had once dreamed of doing, and it was no trouble to him, just as he had always foretold, but no one counted the days, no one, not even the artist himself, knew what records he was already breaking, and his heart grew heavy. And when once in a time some leisurely passerby stopped, made merry over the old figure on the board, and spoke of swindling, that was in its way the stupidest lie ever invented by indifference and inborn malice, since it was not the hunger artist who was cheating; he was working honestly, but the world was cheating him of his reward.

Many more days went by, however, and that too came to an end. An overseer's eye fell on the cage one day and asked the attendants why this perfectly good cage should be left standing there unused with dirty straw inside it; nobody knew, until one man, helped out by the notice board, remembered about the hunger artist. They poked into the straw with sticks and found him in it. "Are you still fasting?" asked the overseer. "When on earth do you mean to stop?" "Forgive me, everybody," whispered the hunger artist; only the overseer, who had his ear to the bars, understood him. "Of course," said the overseer, and tapped his forehead with a finger to let the attendants know what state the man was in, "we forgive you." "I always wanted you to admire my fasting," said the hunger artist. "We do admire it," said the overseer, affably. "But you shouldn't admire it," said the hunger artist. "Well, then we don't admire it," said the overseer, "but why shouldn't we admire it?" "Because I have to fast, I can't help it," said the hunger artist. "What a fellow you are," said the overseer, "and why can't you help it?" "Because," said the hunger artist, lifting his head a little and speaking, with his lips pursed, as if for a kiss, right into the overseer's ear, so that no syllable might be lost, "because I couldn't find the food I liked. If I had found it, believe me, I should have made no fuss and stuffed myself like you or anyone else." These were his last words, but in his dimming eyes remained the firm though no longer proud persuasion that he was still continuing to fast.

"Well, clear this out now!" said the overseer, and they buried the hunger artist, straw and all. Into the cage they put a young panther. Even the most insensitive felt it refreshing to see this wild creature leaping around the cage that had so long been dreary. The panther was all right. The food he liked was brought him without hesitation by the attendants; he seemed not even to miss his freedom; his noble body, furnished almost to the bursting point with all that it needed, seemed to carry freedom around with it too; somewhere in his jaws it seemed to lurk; and the joy of life streamed with such ardent passion from his throat that for the onlookers it was not easy to stand the shock of it. But they braced themselves, crowded round the cage, and did not want ever to move away.

JAMAICA KINCAID (b. 1949)
Girl   1978

Wash the white clothes on Monday and put them on the stone heap; wash the color clothes on Tuesday and put them on the clothesline to dry; don't walk barehead in the hot sun; cook pumpkin fritters in very hot sweet oil; soak your little cloths right after you take them off; when buying cotton to make yourself a nice blouse, be sure that it doesn't have gum on it, because that way it won't hold up well after a wash; soak salt fish overnight before you cook it; is it true that you sing benna° in Sunday school?; always eat your food in such a way that it won't turn someone else's stomach; on Sundays try to walk like a lady and not like the slut you are so bent on becoming; don't sing benna in Sunday school; you mustn't speak to wharf-rat boys, not even to give directions; don't eat fruits on the street — flies will follow you; *but I don't sing benna on Sundays at all and never in Sunday school;* this is how to sew on a button; this is how to make a buttonhole for the button you have just sewed on; this is how to hem a dress when you see the hem coming down and so to prevent yourself from looking like the slut I know you are so bent on becoming; this is how you iron your father's khaki shirt so that it doesn't have a crease; this is how you iron your father's khaki pants so that they don't have a crease; this is how you grow okra — far from the house, because okra tree harbors red ants; when you are growing dasheen, make sure it gets plenty of water or else it makes your throat itch when you are eating it; this is how you sweep a corner; this is how you sweep a whole house; this is how you sweep a yard; this is how you smile to someone you don't like too much; this is how you smile to someone you don't like at all; this is how you smile to someone you like completely; this is how you set a table for tea; this is how you set a table for dinner; this is how you set a table for dinner with an important guest; this is how you set a table for lunch; this is how you set a table for breakfast; this is how to behave in the

___

benna: Calypso music.

presence of men who don't know you very well, and this way they won't recognize immediately the slut I have warned you against becoming; be sure to wash every day, even if it is with your own spit; don't squat down to play marbles — you are not a boy, you know; don't pick people's flowers — you might catch something; don't throw stones at blackbirds, because it might not be a blackbird at all; this is how to make a bread pudding; this is how to make doukona;° this is how to make pepper pot; this is how to make a good medicine for a cold; this is how to make a good medicine to throw away a child before it even becomes a child; this is how to catch a fish; this is how to throw back a fish you don't like, and that way something bad won't fall on you; this is how to bully a man; this is how a man bullies you; this is how to love a man, and if this doesn't work there are other ways, and if they don't work don't feel too bad about giving up; this is how to spit up in the air if you feel like it, and this is how to move quick so that it doesn't fall on you; this is how to make ends meet; always squeeze bread to make sure it's fresh; *but what if the baker won't let me feel the bread?;* you mean to say that after all you are really going to be the kind of woman who the baker won't let near the bread?

D. H. LAWRENCE (1885–1930)
The Horse Dealer's Daughter   1922

"Well, Mabel, and what are you going to do with yourself?" asked Joe, with foolish flippancy. He felt quite safe himself. Without listening for an answer, he turned aside, worked a grain of tobacco to the tip of his tongue, and spat it out. He did not care about anything, since he felt safe himself.

The three brothers and the sister sat round the desolate breakfast-table, attempting some sort of desultory consultation. The morning's post had given the final tap to the family fortunes, and all was over. The dreary dining-room itself, with its heavy mahogany furniture, looked as if it were waiting to be done away with.

But the consultation amounted to nothing. There was a strange air of ineffectuality about the three men, as they sprawled at table, smoking and reflecting vaguely on their own condition. The girl was alone, a rather short, sullen-looking young woman of twenty-seven. She did not share the same life as her brothers. She would have been good-looking, save for the impressive fixity of her face, "bull-dog," as her brothers called it.

There was a confused tramping of horses' feet outside. The three men all sprawled round in their chairs to watch. Beyond the dark holly bushes that separated the strip of lawn from the high-road, they could see a cavalcade of shire horses swinging out of their own yard, being taken for exercise. This was the last time. These were the last horses that would go through their hands. The young men watched with critical, callous look. They were all frightened at the collapse of their lives, and the sense of disaster in which they were involved left them no inner freedom.

doukona: A spicy plantain pudding.

Yet they were three fine, well-set fellows enough. Joe, the eldest, was a man ₅ of thirty-three, broad and handsome in a hot, flushed way. His face was red, he twisted his black mustache over a thick finger, his eyes were shallow and restless. He had a sensual way of uncovering his teeth when he laughed, and his bearing was stupid. Now he watched the horses with a glazed look of helplessness in his eyes, a certain stupor of downfall.

The great draft-horses swung past. They were tied head to tail, four of them, and they heaved along to where a lane branched off from the high-road, planting their great hoofs floutingly in the fine black mud, swinging their great rounded haunches sumptuously, and trotting a few sudden steps as they were led into the lane, round the corner. Every movement showed a massive, slumbrous strength, and a stupidity which held them in subjection. The groom at the head looked back, jerking the leading rope. And the cavalcade moved out of sight up the lane, the tail of the last horse, bobbed up tight and stiff, held out taut from the swinging great haunches as they rocked behind the hedges in a motionlike sleep.

Joe watched with glazed hopeless eyes. The horses were almost like his own body to him. He felt he was done for now. Luckily he was engaged to a woman as old as himself, and therefore her father, who was steward of a neighboring estate, would provide him with a job. He would marry and go into harness. His life was over, he would be a subject animal now.

He turned uneasily aside, the retreating steps of the horses echoing in his ears. Then, with foolish restlessness, he reached for the scraps of bacon-rind from the plates, and making a faint whistling sound, flung them to the terrier that lay against the fender. He watched the dog swallow them, and waited till the creature looked into his eyes. Then a faint grin came on his face, and in a high, foolish voice he said:

"You won't get much more bacon, shall you, you little b——?"

The dog faintly and dismally wagged its tail, then lowered its haunches, ₁₀ circled round, and lay down again.

There was another helpless silence at the table. Joe sprawled uneasily in his seat, not willing to go till the family conclave was dissolved. Fred Henry, the second brother, was erect, clean-limbed, alert. He had watched the passing of the horses with more *sang-froid*.° If he was an animal, like Joe, he was an animal which controls, not one which is controlled. He was master of any horse, and he carried himself with a well-tempered air of mastery. But he was not master of the situations of life. He pushed his coarse brown mustache upwards, off his lip, and glanced irritably at his sister, who sat impassive and inscrutable.

"You'll go and stop with Lucy for a bit, shan't you?" he asked. The girl did not answer.

"I don't see what else you can do," persisted Fred Henry.

"Go as a skivvy,"° Joe interpolated laconically.

The girl did not move a muscle. ₁₅

"If I was her, I should go in for training for a nurse," said Malcolm, the

sang-froid: Coolness, composure.
skivvy: Domestic worker.

youngest of them all. He was the baby of the family, a young man of twenty-two, with a fresh, jaunty *museau*.°

But Mabel did not take any notice of him. They had talked at her and round her for so many years, that she hardly heard them at all.

The marble clock on the mantelpiece softly chimed the half-hour, the dog rose uneasily from the hearth-rug and looked at the party at the breakfast-table. But still they sat on in ineffectual conclave.

"Oh, all right," said Joe suddenly, apropos of nothing. "I'll get a move on."

He pushed back his chair, straddled his knees with a downward jerk, to get them free, in horsey fashion, and went to the fire. Still he did not go out of the room; he was curious to know what the others would do or say. He began to charge his pipe, looking down at the dog and saying in a high, affected voice: 20

"Going wi' me? Going wi' me are ter? Tha'rt goin' further than tha counts on just now, dost hear?"

The dog faintly wagged its tail, the man stuck out his jaw and covered his pipe with his hands, and puffed intently, losing himself in the tobacco, looking down all the while at the dog with an absent brown eye. The dog looked up at him in mournful distrust. Joe stood with his knees stuck out, in real horsey fashion.

"Have you had a letter from Lucy?" Fred Henry asked of his sister.

"Last week," came the neutral reply.

"And what does she say?" 25

There was no answer.

"Does she *ask* you to go and stop there?" persisted Fred Henry.

"She says I can if I like."

"Well, then, you'd better. Tell her you'll come on Monday."

This was received in silence. 30

"That's what you'll do then, is it?" said Fred Henry, in some exasperation.

But she made no answer. There was a silence of futility and irritation in the room. Malcolm grinned fatuously.

"You'll have to make up your mind between now and next Wednesday," said Joe loudly, "or else find yourself lodgings on the curbstone."

The face of the young woman darkened, but she sat on immutable.

"Here's Jack Fergusson!" exclaimed Malcolm, who was looking aimlessly 35 out of the window.

"Where?" exclaimed Joe loudly.

"Just gone past."

"Coming in?"

Malcolm craned his neck to see the gate.

"Yes," he said. 40

There was a silence. Mabel sat on like one condemned, at the head of the table. Then a whistle was heard from the kitchen. The dog got up and barked sharply. Joe opened the door and shouted:

"Come on."

After a moment a young man entered. He was muffled up in overcoat and a purple woolen scarf, and his tweed cap, which he did not remove, was pulled

---

museau: Slang for face.

down on his head. He was of medium height, his face was rather long and pale, his eyes looked tired.

"Hello, Jack! Well, Jack!" exclaimed Malcolm and Joe. Fred Henry merely said: "Jack."

"What's doing?" asked the newcomer, evidently addressing Fred Henry.   45

"Same. We've got to be out by Wednesday. Got a cold?"

"I have — got it bad, too."

"Why don't you stop in?"

"*Me* stop in? When I can't stand on my legs, perhaps I shall have a chance." the young man spoke huskily. He had a slight Scotch accent.

"It's a knock-out, isn't it," said Joe, boisterously, "if a doctor goes round   50 croaking with a cold. Looks bad for the patients, doesn't it?"

The young doctor looked at him slowly.

"Anything the matter with *you,* then?" he asked sarcastically.

"Not as I know of. Damn your eyes, hope not. Why?"

"I thought you were very concerned about the patients, wondered if you might be one yourself."

"Damn it, no, I've never been patient to no flaming doctor, and hope I   55 never shall be," returned Joe.

At this point Mabel rose from the table, and they all seemed to become aware of her existence. She began putting the dishes together. The young doctor looked at her, but did not address her. He had not greeted her. She went out of the room with the tray, her face impassive and unchanged.

"When are you off then, all of you?" asked the doctor.

"I'm catching the eleven-forty," replied Malcolm. "Are you goin' down wi' th' trap,° Joe?"

"Yes, I've told you I'm going down wi' th' trap, haven't I?"

"We'd better be getting her in then. So long, Jack, if I don't see you before   60 I go," said Malcolm, shaking hands.

He went out, followed by Joe, who seemed to have his tail between his legs.

"Well, this is the devil's own," exclaimed the doctor, when he was left alone with Fred Henry. "Going before Wednesday, are you?"

"That's the orders," replied the other.

"Where, to Northampton?"

"That's it."   65

"The devil!" exclaimed Fergusson, with quiet chagrin.

And there was silence between the two.

"All settled up, are you?" asked Fergusson.

"About."

There was another pause.   70

"Well, I shall miss yer, Freddy, boy," said the young doctor.

"And I shall miss thee, Jack," returned the other.

"Miss you like hell," mused the doctor.

Fred Henry turned aside. There was nothing to say. Mabel came in again, to finish clearing the table.

trap: A light two-wheeled carriage.

"What are *you* going to do, then, Miss Pervin?" asked Fergusson. "Going to your sister's, are you?"

Mabel looked at him with her steady, dangerous eyes, that always made him uncomfortable, unsettling his superficial ease.

"No," she said.

"Well, what in the name of fortune *are* you going to do? Say what you mean to do," cried Fred Henry, with futile intensity.

But she only averted her head, and continued her work. She folded the white table-cloth, and put on the chenille cloth.

"The sulkiest bitch that ever trod!" muttered her brother.

But she finished her task with perfectly impassive face, the young doctor watching her interestedly all the while. Then she went out.

Fred Henry stared after her, clenching his lips, his blue eyes fixing in sharp antagonism, as he made a grimace of sour exasperation.

"You could bray her into bits, and that's all you'd get out of her," he said, in a small, narrowed tone.

The doctor smiled faintly.

"What's she *going* to do, then?" he asked.

"Strike me if *I* know!" returned the other.

There was a pause. Then the doctor stirred.

"I'll be seeing you tonight, shall I?" he said to his friend.

"Ay — where's it to be? Are we going over to Jessdale?"

"I don't know. I've got such a cold on me. I'll come round to the 'Moon and Stars,' anyway."

"Let Lizzie and May miss their night for once, eh?"

"That's it — if I feel as I do now."

"All's one—— "

The two young men went through the passage and down to the back door together. The house was large, but it was servantless now, and desolate. At the back was a small bricked houseyard and beyond that a big square, graveled fine and red, and having stables on two sides. Sloping, dank, winter-dark fields stretched away on the open sides.

But the stables were empty. Joseph Pervin, the father of the family, had been a man of no education, who had become a fairly large horse dealer. The stables had been full of horses, there was a great turmoil and come-and-go of horses and of dealers and grooms. Then the kitchen was full of servants. But of late things had declined. The old man had married a second time, to retrieve his fortunes. Now he was dead and everything was gone to the dogs, there was nothing but debt and threatening.

For months, Mabel had been servantless in the big house, keeping the home together in penury for her ineffectual brothers. She had kept house for ten years. But previously it was with unstinted means. Then, however brutal and coarse everything was, the sense of money had kept her proud, confident. The men might be foul-mouthed, the women in the kitchen might have bad reputations, her brothers might have illegitimate children. But so long as there was money, the girl felt herself established, and brutally proud, reserved.

No company came to the house, save dealers and coarse men. Mabel had no associates of her own sex, after her sister went away. But she did not mind.

She went regularly to church, she attended to her father. And she lived in the memory of her mother, who had died when she was fourteen, and whom she had loved. She had loved her father, too, in a different way, depending upon him, and feeling secure in him, until at the age of fifty-four he married again. And then she had set hard against him. Now he had died and left them all hopelessly in debt.

She had suffered badly during the period of poverty. Nothing, however, could shake the curious, sullen, animal pride that dominated each member of the family. Now, for Mabel, the end had come. Still she would not cast about her. She would follow her own way just the same. She would always hold the keys of her own situation. Mindless and persistent, she endured from day to day. Why should she think? Why should she answer anybody? It was enough that this was the end, and there was no way out. She need not pass any more darkly along the main street of the small town, avoiding every eye. She need not demean herself any more, going into the shops and buying the cheapest food. This was at an end. She thought of nobody, not even of herself. Mindless and persistent, she seemed in a sort of ecstasy to be coming nearer to her fulfillment, her own glorification, approaching her dead mother, who was glorified.

In the afternoon she took a little bag, with shears and sponge and a small scrubbing-brush, and went out. It was a gray, wintry day, with saddened, dark green fields and an atmosphere blackened by the smoke of foundries not far off. She went quickly, darkly along the causeway, heeding nobody, through the town to the churchyard.

There she always felt secure, as if no one could see her, although as a matter of fact she was exposed to the stare of everyone who passed along under the churchyard wall. Nevertheless, once under the shadow of the great looming church, among the graves, she felt immune from the world, reserved within the thick churchyard wall as in another country.

Carefully she clipped the grass from the grave, and arranged the pinky white, small chrysanthemums in the tin cross. When this was done, she took an empty jar from a neighboring grave, brought water, and carefully, most scrupulously sponged the marble headstone and the coping-stone.

It gave her sincere satisfaction to do this. She felt in immediate contact with the world of her mother. She took minute pains, went through the park in a state bordering on pure happiness, as if in performing this task she came into a subtle, intimate connection with her mother. For the life she followed here in the world was far less real than the world of death she inherited from her mother.

The doctor's house was just by the church. Fergusson, being a mere hired assistant, was slave to the countryside. As he hurried now to attend to the out-patients in the surgery, glancing across the graveyard with his quick eye, he saw the girl at her task at the grave. She seemed so intent and remote, it was like looking into another world. Some mystical element was touched in him. He slowed down as he walked, watching her as if spellbound.

She lifted her eyes, feeling him looking. Their eyes met. And each looked again at once, each feeling, in some way, found out by the other. He lifted his cap and passed on down the road. There remained distinct in his consciousness, like a vision, the memory of her face, lifted from the tombstone in the churchyard, and looking at him with slow, large, portentous eyes. It *was* portentous, her face.

It seemed to mesmerize him. There was a heavy power in her eyes which laid hold of his whole being, as if he had drunk some powerful drug. He had been feeling weak and done before. Now the life came back into him, he felt delivered from his own fretted, daily self.

He finished his duties at the surgery as quickly as might be, hastily filling 105 up the bottles of the waiting people with cheap drugs. Then, in perpetual haste, he set off again to visit several cases in another part of his round, before tea-time. At all times he preferred to walk if he could, but particularly when he was not well. He fancied the motion restored him.

The afternoon was falling. It was gray, deadened, and wintry, with a slow, moist, heavy coldness sinking in and deadening all the faculties. But why should he think or notice? He hastily climbed the hill and turned across the dark green fields, following the black cinder-track. In the distance, across a shallow dip in the country, the small town was clustered like smoldering ash, a tower, a spire, a heap of low, raw, extinct houses. And on the nearest fringe of the town, sloping into the dip, was Oldmeadow, the Pervins' house. He could see the stables and the outbuildings distinctly, as they lay towards him on the slope. Well, he would not go there many more times! Another resource would be lost to him, another place gone: the only company he cared for in the alien, ugly little town he was losing. Nothing but work, drudgery, constant hastening from dwelling to dwelling among the colliers and the iron-workers. It wore him out, but at the same time he had a craving for it. It was a stimulant to him to be in the homes of the working people, moving, as it were, through the innermost body of their life. His nerves were excited and gratified. He could come so near, into the very lives of the rough, inarticulate, powerful emotional men and women: He grumbled, he said he hated the hellish hole. But as a matter of fact it excited him, the contact with the rough, strongly-feeling people was a stimulant applied direct to his nerves.

Below Oldmeadow, in the green, shallow, soddened hollow of fields, lay a square, deep pond. Roving across the landscape, the doctor's quick eye detected a figure in black passing through the gate of the field, down towards the pond. He looked again. It would be Mabel Pervin. His mind suddenly became alive and attentive.

Why was she going down there? He pulled up on the path on the slope above, and stood staring. He could just make sure of the small black figure moving in the hollow of the failing day. He seemed to see her in the midst of such obscurity, that he was like a clairvoyant, seeing rather with the mind's eye than with ordinary sight. Yet he could see her positively enough, whilst he kept his eye attentive. He felt, if he looked away from her, in the thick, ugly falling dusk, he would lose her altogether.

He followed her minutely as she moved, direct and intent, like something transmitted rather than stirring in voluntary activity, straight down from the field towards the pond. There she stood on the bank for a moment. She never raised her head. Then she waded slowly into the water.

He stood motionless as the small black figure walked slowly and deliberately 110 towards the center of the pond, very slowly, gradually moving deeper into the motionless water, and still moving forward as the water got up to her breast. Then he could see her no more in the dusk of the dead afternoon.

"There!" he exclaimed. "Would you believe it?"

And he hastened straight down, running over the wet, soddened fields, pushing through the hedges, down into the depression of callous wintry obscurity. It took him several minutes to come to the pond. He stood on the bank, breathing heavily. He could see nothing. His eyes seemed to penetrate the dead water. Yes, perhaps that was the dark shadow of her black clothing beneath the surface of the water.

He slowly ventured into the pond. The bottom was deep, soft clay, he sank in, and the water clasped dead cold round his legs. As he stirred he could smell the cold, rotten clay that fouled up into the water. It was objectionable in his lungs. Still, repelled and yet not heeding, he moved deeper into the pond. The cold water rose over his thighs, over his loins, upon his abdomen. The lower part of his body was all sunk in the hideous cold element. And the bottom was so deeply soft and uncertain, he was afraid of pitching with his mouth underneath. He could not swim, and was afraid.

He crouched a little, spreading his hands under the water and moving them round, trying to feel for her. The dead cold pond swayed upon his chest. He moved again, a little deeper, and again, with his hands underneath, he felt all around under the water. And he touched her clothing. But it evaded his fingers. He made a desperate effort to grasp it.

And so doing he lost his balance and went under, horribly, suffocating in the foul earthy water, struggling madly for a few moments. At last, after what seemed an eternity, he got his footing, rose again into the air, and looked around. He gasped, and knew he was in the world. Then he looked at the water. She had risen near him. He grasped her clothing, and drawing her nearer, turned to take his way to land again.

He went very slowly, carefully, absorbed in the slow progress. He rose higher, climbing out of the pond. The water was now only about his legs; he was thankful, full of relief to be out of the clutches of the pond. He lifted her and staggered on to the bank, out of the horror of wet, gray clay.

He laid her down on the bank. She was quite unconscious and running with water. He made the water come from her mouth, he worked to restore her. He did not have to work very long before he could feel the breathing begin again in her; she was breathing naturally. He worked a little longer. He could feel her live beneath his hands; she was coming back. He wiped her face, wrapped her in his overcoat, looked round into the dim, dark gray world, then lifted her and staggered down the bank and across the fields.

It seemed an unthinkably long way, and his burden so heavy he felt he would never get to the house. But at last he was in the stable-yard, and then in the house-yard. He opened the door and went into the house. In the kitchen he laid her down on the hearth-rug and called. The house was empty. But the fire was burning in the grate.

Then again he kneeled to attend to her. She was breathing regularly, her eyes were wide open and as if conscious, but there seemed something missing in her look. She was conscious in herself, but unconscious of her surroundings.

He ran upstairs, took blankets from a bed, and put them before the fire to warm. Then he removed her saturated, earthy-smelling clothing, rubbed her dry with a towel, and wrapped her naked in the blankets. Then he went into the dining-room, to look for spirits. There was a little whiskey. He drank a gulp himself, and put some into her mouth.

The effect was instantaneous. She looked full into his face, as if she had been seeing him for some time, and yet had only just become conscious of him.

"Dr. Fergusson?" she said.

"What?" he answered.

He was divesting himself of his coat, intending to find some dry clothing upstairs. He could not bear the smell of the dead, clayey water, and he was mortally afraid for his own health.

"What did I do?" she asked.

"Walked into the pond," he replied. He had begun to shudder like one sick, and could hardly attend to her. Her eyes remained full on him, he seemed to be going dark in his mind, looking back at her helplessly. The shuddering became quieter in him, his life came back to him, dark and unknowing, but strong again.

"Was I out of my mind?" she asked, while her eyes were fixed on him all the time.

"Maybe, for the moment," he replied. He felt quiet, because his strength had come back. The strange fretful strain had left him.

"Am I out of my mind now?" she asked.

"Are you?" he reflected a moment. "No," he answered truthfully, "I don't see that you are." He turned his face aside. He was afraid now, because he felt dazed, and felt dimly that her power was stronger than his, in this issue. And she continued to look at him fixedly all the time. "Can you tell me where I shall find some dry things to put on?" he asked.

"Did you dive into the pond for me?" she asked.

"No," he answered. "I walked in. But I went in overhead as well."

There was silence for a moment. He hesitated. He very much wanted to go upstairs to get into dry clothing. But there was another desire in him. And she seemed to hold him. His will seemed to have gone to sleep, and left him, standing there slack before her. But he felt warm inside himself. He did not shudder at all, though his clothes were sodden on him.

"Why did you?" she asked.

"Because I didn't want you to do such a foolish thing," he said.

"It wasn't foolish," she said, still gazing at him as she lay on the floor, with a sofa cushion under her head. "It was the right thing to do. *I* knew best, then."

"I'll go and shift these wet things," he said. But still he had not the power to move out of her presence, until she sent him. It was as if she had the life of his body in her hands, and he could not extricate himself. Or perhaps he did not want to.

Suddenly she sat up. Then she became aware of her own immediate condition. She felt the blankets about her, she knew her own limbs. For a moment it seemed as if her reason were going. She looked round, with wild eye, as if seeking something. He stood still with fear. She saw her clothing lying scattered.

"Who undressed me?" she asked, her eyes resting full and inevitable on his face.

"I did," he replied, "to bring you round."

For some moments she sat and gazed at him, awfully, her lips parted.

"Do you love me, then?" she asked.

He only stood and stared at her, fascinated. His soul seemed to melt.

She shuffled forward on her knees, and put her arms round him, round his legs, as he stood there, pressing her breasts against his knees and thighs, clutching him with strange, convulsive certainty, pressing his thighs against her, drawing him to her face, her throat, as she looked up at him with flaring, humble eyes of transfiguration, triumphant in first possession.

"You love me," she murmured, in strange transport, yearning and trium- 145 phant and confident. "You love me. I know you love me, I know."

And she was passionately kissing his knees, through the wet clothing, passionately and indiscriminately kissing his knees, his legs, as if unaware of everything.

He looked down at the tangled wet hair, the wild, bare, animal shoulders. He was amazed, bewildered, and afraid. He had never thought of loving her. He had never wanted to love her. When he rescued her and restored her, he was a doctor, and she was a patient. He had had no single personal thought of her. Nay, this introduction of the personal element was very distasteful to him, a violation of his professional honor. It was horrible to have her there embracing his knees. It was horrible. He revolted from it, violently. And yet — and yet — he had not the power to break away.

She looked at him again, with the same supplication of powerful love, and that same transcendent, frightening light of triumph. In view of the delicate flame which seemed to come from her face like a light, he was powerless. And yet he had never intended to love her. He had never intended. And something stubborn in him could not give way.

"You love me," she repeated, in a murmur of deep, rhapsodic assurance. "You love me."

Her hands were drawing him, drawing him down to her. He was afraid, 150 even a little horrified. For he had, really, no intention of loving her. Yet her hands were drawing him towards her. He put out his hand quickly to steady himself, and grasped her bare shoulder. A flame seemed to burn the hand that grasped her soft shoulder. He had no intention of loving her: his whole will was against his yielding. It was horrible. And yet wonderful was the touch of her shoulders, beautiful the shining of her face. Was she perhaps mad? He had a horror of yielding to her. Yet something in him ached also.

He had been staring away at the door, away from her. But his hand remained on her shoulder. She had gone suddenly very still. He looked down at her. Her eyes were now wide with fear, with doubt, the light was dying from her face, a shadow of terrible grayness was returning. He could not bear the touch of her eyes' question upon him, and the look of death behind the question.

With an inward groan he gave way, and let his heart yield towards her. A sudden gentle smile came on his face. And her eyes, which never left his face, slowly, slowly filled with tears. He watched the strange water rise in her eyes, like some slow fountain coming up. And his heart seemed to burn and melt away in his breast.

He could not bear to look at her any more. He dropped on his knees and caught her head with his arms and pressed her face against his throat. She was very still. His heart, which seemed to have broken, was burning with a kind of agony in his breast. And he felt her slow, hot tears wetting his throat. But he could not move.

He felt the hot tears wet his neck and the hollows of his neck, and he remained motionless, suspended through one of man's eternities. Only now it had become indispensable to him to have her face pressed close to him; he could never let her go again. He could never let her head go away from the close clutch of his arm. He wanted to remain like that for ever, with his heart hurting him in a pain that was also life to him. Without knowing, he was looking down on her damp, soft brown hair.

Then, as it were suddenly, he smelt the horrid stagnant smell of that water. 155 And at the same moment she drew away from him and looked at him. Her eyes were wistful and unfathomable. He was afraid of them, and he fell to kissing her, not knowing what he was doing. He wanted her eyes not to have that terrible, wistful, unfathomable look.

When she turned her face to him again, a faint delicate flush was glowing, and there was again dawning that terrible shining of joy in her eyes, which really terrified him, and yet which he now wanted to see, because he feared the look of doubt still more.

"You love me?" she said, rather faltering.

"Yes." The word cost him a painful effort. Not because it wasn't true. But because it was too newly true, the *saying* seemed to tear open again his newly-torn heart. And he hardly wanted it to be true, even now.

She lifted her face to him, and he bent forward and kissed her on the mouth, gently, with the one kiss that is an eternal pledge. And as he kissed her his heart strained again in his breast. He never intended to love her. But now it was over. He had crossed over the gulf to her, and all that he had left behind had shriveled and become void.

After the kiss, her eyes again slowly filled with tears. She sat still, away from 160 him, with her face drooped aside, and her hands folded in her lap. The tears fell very slowly. There was complete silence. He too sat there motionless and silent on the hearth-rug. The strange pain of his heart that was broken seemed to consume him. That he should love her? That this was love! That he should be ripped open in this way! Him, a doctor! How they would all jeer if they knew! It was agony to him to think they might know.

In the curious naked pain of the thought he looked again to her. She was still sitting there drooped into a muse. He saw a tear fall, and his heart flared hot. He saw for the first time that one of her shoulders was quite uncovered, one arm bare, he could see one of her small breasts; dimly, because it had become almost dark in the room.

"Why are you crying?" he asked, in an altered voice.

She looked up at him, and behind her tears the consciousness of her situation for the first time brought a dark look of shame to her eyes.

"I'm not crying, really," she said, watching him, half frightened.

He reached his hand, and softly closed it on her bare arm. 165

"I love you! I love you!" he said in a soft, low vibrating voice, unlike himself.

She shrank, and dropped her head. The soft, penetrating grip of his hand on her arm distressed her. She looked up at him.

"I want to go," she said. "I want to go and get you some dry things."

"Why?" he said. "I'm all right."

"But I want to go," she said. "And I want you to change your things." 170

He released her arm, and she wrapped herself in the blanket, looking at him rather frightened. And still she did not rise.

"Kiss me," she said wistfully.

He kissed her, but briefly, half in anger.

Then, after a second, she rose nervously, all mixed up in the blanket. He watched her in her confusion as she tried to extricate herself and wrap herself up so that she could walk. He watched her relentlessly, as she knew. And as she went, the blanket trailing, and as he saw a glimpse of her feet and her white leg, he tried to remember her as she was when he had wrapped her in the blanket. But then he didn't want to remember, because she had been nothing to him then, and his nature revolted from remembering her as she was when she was nothing to him.

A tumbling, muffled noise from within the dark house startled him. Then he heard her voice: "There are clothes." He rose and went to the foot of the stairs, and gathered up the garments she had thrown down. Then he came back to the fire, to rub himself down and dress. He grinned at his own appearance when he had finished.

The fire was sinking, so he put on coal. The house was now quite dark, save for the light of a street-lamp that shone in faintly from beyond the holly trees. He lit the gas with matches he found on the mantelpiece. Then he emptied the pockets of his own clothes, and threw all his wet things in a heap into the scullery. After which he gathered up her sodden clothes, gently, and put them in a separate heap on the copper-top in the scullery.

It was six o'clock on the clock. His own watch had stopped. He ought to go back to the surgery. He waited, and still she did not come down. So he went to the foot of the stairs and called:

"I shall have to go."

Almost immediately he heard her coming down. She had on her best dress of black voile, and her hair was tidy, but still damp. She looked at him — and in spite of herself, smiled.

"I don't like you in those clothes," she said.

"Do I look a sight?" he answered.

They were shy of one another.

"I'll make you some tea," she said.

"No, I must go."

"Must you?" And she looked at him again with the wide, strained, doubtful eyes. And again, from the pain of his breast, he knew how he loved her. He went and bent to kiss her, gently, passionately, with his heart's painful kiss.

"And my hair smells so horrible," she murmured in distraction. "And I'm so awful, I'm so awful! Oh, no, I'm too awful." And she broke into bitter, heart-broken sobbing. "You can't want to love me, I'm horrible."

"Don't be silly, don't be silly," he said, trying to comfort her, kissing her, holding her in his arms. "I want you, I want to marry you, we're going to be married, quickly, quickly — tomorrow if I can."

But she only sobbed terribly, and cried:

"I feel awful. I feel awful. I feel I'm horrible to you."

"No, I want you, I want you," was all he answered, blindly, with that terrible intonation which frightened her almost more than her horror lest he should *not* want her.

175

180

185

190

GRACE PALEY (b. 1922)
Samuel   1968

Some boys are very tough. They're afraid of nothing. They are the ones who climb a wall and take a bow at the top. Not only are they brave on the roof, but they make a lot of noise in the darkest part of the cellar where even the super hates to go. They also jiggle and hop on the platform between the locked doors of the subway cars.

Four boys are jiggling on the swaying platform. Their names are Alfred, Calvin, Samuel, and Tom. The men and the women in the cars on either side watch them. They don't like them to jiggle or jump but don't want to interfere. Of course some of the men in the cars were once brave boys like these. One of them had ridden the tail of a speeding truck from New York to Rockaway Beach without getting off, without his sore fingers losing hold. Nothing happened to him then or later. He had made a compact with other boys who preferred to watch: starting at Eighth Avenue and Fifteenth Street, he would get to some specified place, maybe Twenty-third and the river, by hopping the tops of the moving trucks. This was hard to do when one truck turned a corner in the wrong direction and the nearest truck was a couple of feet too high. He made three or four starts before succeeding. He had gotten this idea from a film at school called *The Romance of Logging*. He had finished high school, married a good friend, was in a responsible job and going to night school.

These two men and others looked at the four boys jumping and jiggling on the platform and thought, It must be fun to ride that way, especially now the weather is nice and we're out of the tunnel and way high over the Bronx. Then they thought, These kids do seem to be acting sort of stupid. They *are* little. Then they thought of some of the brave things they had done when they were boys and jiggling didn't seem so risky.

The ladies in the car became very angry when they looked at the four boys. Most of them brought their brows together and hoped the boys could see their extreme disapproval. One of the ladies wanted to get up and say, be careful you dumb kids, get off that platform or I'll call a cop. But three of the boys were Negroes and the fourth was something else she couldn't tell for sure. She was afraid they'd be fresh and laugh at her and embarrass her. She wasn't afraid they'd hit her, but she was afraid of embarrassment. Another lady thought, their mothers never know where they are. It wasn't true in this particular case. Their mothers all knew that they had gone to see the missile exhibit on Fourteenth Street.

Out on the platform, whenever the train accelerated, the boys would raise 5 their hands and point them up to the sky to act like rockets going off, then they rat-tat-tatted the shatterproof glass pane like machine guns, although no machine guns had been exhibited.

For some reason known only to the motorman, the train began a sudden slowdown. The lady who was afraid of embarrassment saw the boys jerk forward and backward and grab the swinging guard chains. She had her own boy at home. She stood up with determination and went to the door. She slid it open and said, "You boys will be hurt. You'll be killed. I'm going to call the conductor if you don't just go into the next car and sit down and be quiet."

Two of the boys said, "Yes'm," and acted as though they were about to go. Two of them blinked their eyes a couple of times and pressed their lips together. The train resumed its speed. The door slid shut, parting the lady and the boys. She leaned against the side door because she had to get off at the next stop.

The boys opened their eyes wide at each other and laughed. The lady blushed. The boys looked at her and laughed harder. They began to pound each other's back. Samuel laughed the hardest and pounded Alfred's back until Alfred coughed and the tears came. Alfred held tight to the chain hook. Samuel pounded him even harder when he saw the tears. He said, "Why you bawling? You a baby, huh?" and laughed. One of the men whose boyhood had been more watchful than brave became angry. He stood up straight and looked at the boys for a couple of seconds. Then he walked in a citizenly way to the end of the car, where he pulled the emergency cord. Almost at once, with a terrible hiss, the pressure of air abandoned the brakes and the wheels were caught and held.

People standing in the most secure places fell forward, then backward. Samuel had let go of his hold on the chain so he could pound Tom as well as Alfred. All the passengers in the cars whipped back and forth, but he pitched only forward and fell head first to be crushed and killed between the cars.

The train had stopped hard, halfway into the station, and the conductor called at once for the trainmen who knew about this kind of death and how to take the body from the wheels and brakes. There was silence except for passengers from other cars who asked, What happened! What happened! The ladies waited around wondering if he might be an only child. The men recalled other afternoons with very bad endings. The little boys stayed close to each other, leaning and touching shoulders and arms and legs.

When the policeman knocked at the door and told her about it, Samuel's mother began to scream. She screamed all day and moaned all night, though the doctors tried to quiet her with pills.

Oh, oh, she hopelessly cried. She did not know how she could ever find another boy like that one. However, she was a young woman and she became pregnant. Then for a few months she was hopeful. The child born to her was a boy. They brought him to be seen and nursed. She smiled. But immediately she saw that this baby wasn't Samuel. She and her husband together have had other children, but never again will a boy exactly like Samuel be known.

MARK TWAIN (1835–1910)
The Story of the Bad Little Boy   1865

Once there was a bad little boy whose name was Jim — though, if you will notice, you will find that bad little boys are nearly always called James in your Sunday-school books. It was strange, but still it was true, that this one was called Jim.

He didn't have any sick mother, either — a sick mother who was pious and had the consumption, and would be glad to lie down in the grave and be at rest but for the strong love she bore her boy, and the anxiety she felt that the world might be harsh and cold toward him when she was gone. Most bad boys in the Sunday books are named James, and have sick mothers, who teach them to say, "Now, I lay me down," etc., and sing them to sleep with sweet, plaintive voices, and then kiss them good-night, and kneel down by the bedside and weep. But it was different with this fellow. He was named Jim, and there wasn't anything the matter with his mother — no consumption, nor anything of that kind. She was rather stout than otherwise, and she was not pious; moreover, she was not anxious on Jim's account. She said if he were to break his neck it wouldn't be much loss. She always spanked Jim to sleep, and she never kissed him good-night; on the contrary, she boxed his ears when she was ready to leave him.

Once this little bad boy stole the key of the pantry, and slipped in there and helped himself to some jam, and filled up the vessel with tar, so that his mother would never know the difference; but all at once a terrible feeling didn't come over him, and something didn't seem to whisper to him, "Is it right to disobey my mother? Isn't it sinful to do this? Where do bad little boys go who gobble up their good kind mother's jam?" and then he didn't kneel down all alone and promise never to be wicked any more, and rise up with a light, happy heart, and go and tell his mother all about it, and beg her forgiveness, and be blessed by her with tears of pride and thankfulness in her eyes. No; that is the way with all other bad boys in the books; but it happened otherwise with this Jim, strangely enough. He ate that jam, and said it was bully, in his sinful, vulgar way; and he put in the tar, and said that was bully also, and laughed, and observed "that the old woman would get up and snort" when she found it out; and when she did find it out, he denied knowing anything about it, and she whipped him severely, and he did the crying himself. Everything about this boy was curious — everything turned out differently with him from the way it does to the bad Jameses in the books.

Once he climbed up in Farmer Acorn's apple tree to steal apples, and the limb didn't break, and he didn't fall and break his arm, and get torn by the farmer's great dog, and then languish on a sickbed for weeks, and repent and become good. Oh, no; he stole as many apples as he wanted and came down all right; and he was all ready for the dog, too, and knocked him endways with a brick when he came to tear him. It was very strange — nothing like it ever happened in those mild little books with marbled backs, and with pictures in them of men with swallow-tailed coats and bell-crowned hats, and pantaloons that are short in the legs, and women with the waists of their dresses under their arms, and no hoops on. Nothing like it in any of the Sunday-school books.

Once he stole the teacher's penknife, and, when he was afraid it would be found out and he would get whipped, he slipped it into George Wilson's cap — poor Widow Wilson's son, the moral boy, the good little boy of the village, who always obeyed his mother, and never told an untruth, and was fond of his lessons, and infatuated with Sunday school. And when the knife dropped from the cap, and poor George hung his head and blushed, as if in conscious guilt, and the grieved teacher charged the theft upon him, and was just in the very act of bringing the switch down upon his trembling shoulders, a white-haired, improbable justice of the peace did not suddenly appear in their midst, and strike an attitude and say, "Spare this noble boy — there stands the cowering culprit! I was passing the school door at recess, and, unseen myself, I saw the theft committed!" And then Jim didn't get whaled, and the venerable justice didn't read the tearful school a homily, and take George by the hand and say such a boy deserved to be exalted, and then tell him to come and make his home with him, and sweep out the office, and make fires, and run errands, and chop wood, and study law, and help his wife do household labors, and have all the balance of the time to play, and get forty cents a month, and be happy. No; it would have happened that way in the books, but it didn't happen that way to Jim. No meddling old clam of a justice dropped in to make trouble, and so the model boy George got thrashed, and Jim was glad of it because, you know, Jim hated moral boys. Jim said he was "down on them milksops." Such was the coarse language of this bad, neglected boy.

But the strangest thing that ever happened to Jim was the time he went boating on Sunday, and didn't get drowned, and that other time that he got caught out in the storm when he was fishing on Sunday, and didn't get struck by lightning. Why, you might look, and look, all through the Sunday-school books from now till next Christmas, and you would never come across anything like this. Oh, no; you would find that all the bad boys who go boating on Sunday invariably get drowned; and all the bad boys who get caught out in storms when they are fishing on Sunday infallibly get struck by lightning. Boats with bad boys in them always upset on Sunday, and it always storms when bad boys go fishing on the Sabbath. How this Jim ever escaped is a mystery to me.

This Jim bore a charmed life — that must have been the way of it. Nothing could hurt him. He even gave the elephant in the menagerie a plug of tobacco, and the elephant didn't knock the top of his head off with his trunk. He browsed around the cupboard after essence of peppermint, and didn't make a mistake and drink *aqua fortis.*° He stole his father's gun and went hunting on the Sabbath, and didn't shoot three or four of his fingers off. He struck his little sister on the temple with his fist when he was angry, and she didn't linger in pain through long summer days, and die with sweet words of forgiveness upon her lips that redoubled the anguish of his breaking heart. No; she got over it. He ran off and went to sea at last, and didn't come back and find himself sad and alone in the world, his loved ones sleeping in the quiet churchyard, and the vine-embowered home of his boyhood tumbled down and gone to decay. Ah, no; he came home as drunk as a piper, and got into the station-house the first thing.

And he grew up and married, and raised a large family, and brained them all with an ax one night, and got wealthy by all manner of cheating and rascality; and now he is the infernalest wickedest scoundrel in his native village, and is universally respected, and belongs to the legislature.

So you see there never was a bad James in the Sunday-school books that had such a streak of luck as this sinful Jim with the charmed life.

aqua fortis: Nitric acid.

JOHN UPDIKE (b. 1932)

A & P 1961

In walks these three girls in nothing but bathing suits. I'm in the third checkout slot, with my back to the door, so I don't see them until they're over by the bread. The one that caught my eye first was the one in the plaid green two-piece. She was a chunky kid, with a good tan and a sweet broad soft-looking can with those two crescents of white just under it, where the sun never seems to hit, at the top of the backs of her legs. I stood there with my hand on a box of HiHo crackers trying to remember if I rang it up or not. I ring it up again and the customer starts giving me hell. She's one of these cash-register-watchers, a witch about fifty with rouge on her cheekbones and no eyebrows, and I know it made her day to trip me up. She'd been watching cash registers for fifty years and probably never seen a mistake before.

By the time I got her feathers smoothed and her goodies into a bag — she gives me a little snort in passing, if she'd been born at the right time they would have burned her over in Salem — by the time I get her on her way the girls had circled around the bread and were coming back, without a pushcart, back my way along the counters, in the aisle between the checkouts and the Special bins. They didn't even have shoes on. There was this chunky one, with the two-piece — it was bright green and the seams on the bra were still sharp and her belly was still pretty pale so I guessed she just got it (the suit) — there was this one, with one of those chubby berry-faces, the lips all bunched together under her nose, this one, and a tall one, with black hair that hadn't quite frizzed right, and one of these sunburns right across under the eyes, and a chin that was too long — you know, the kind of girl other girls think is very "striking" and "attractive" but never quite makes it, as they very well know, which is why they like her so much — and then the third one, that wasn't quite so tall. She was the queen. She kind of led them, the other two peeking around and making their shoulders round. She didn't look around, not this queen, she just walked straight on slowly, on these long white prima-donna legs. She came down a little hard on her heels, as if she didn't walk in her bare feet that much, putting down her heels and then letting the weight move along to her toes as if she was testing the floor with every step, putting a little deliberate extra action into it. You never know for sure how girls' minds work (do you really think it's a mind in there or just a little buzz like a bee in a glass jar?) but you got the idea she had talked the other two into coming in here with her, and now she was showing them how to do it, walk slow and hold yourself straight.

She had on a kind of dirty-pink — beige maybe, I don't know — bathing suit with a little nubble all over it and, what got me, the straps were down. They were off her shoulders looped loose around the cool tops of her arms, and I guess as a result the suit had slipped a little on her, so all around the top of the cloth there was this shining rim. If it hadn't been there you wouldn't have known there could have been anything whiter than those shoulders. With the straps pushed off, there was nothing between the top of the suit and the top of her head except just *her,* this clean bare plane of the top of her chest down from the shoulder bones like a dented sheet of metal tilted in the light. I mean, it was more than pretty.

She had sort of oaky hair that the sun and salt had bleached, done up in a bun that was unraveling, and a kind of prim face. Walking into the A & P with your straps down, I suppose it's the only kind of face you *can* have. She held her head so high her neck, coming up out of those white shoulders, looked kind of stretched, but I didn't mind. The longer her neck was, the more of her there was.

She must have felt in the corner of her eye me and over my shoulder 5 Stokesie in the second slot watching, but she didn't tip. Not this queen. She kept her eyes moving across the racks, and stopped, and turned so slow it made my stomach rub the inside of my apron, and buzzed to the other two, who kind of huddled against her for relief, and then they all three of them went up the cat-and-dog-food-breakfast-cereal-macaroni-rice-raisins-seasonings-spreads-spaghetti-soft-drinks-crackers-and-cookies aisle. From the third slot I look straight up this aisle to the meat counter, and I watched them all the way. The fat one with the tan sort of fumbled with the cookies, but on second thought she put the package back. The sheep pushing their carts down the aisle — the girls were walking against the usual traffic (not that we have one-way signs or anything) — were pretty hilarious. You could see them, when Queenie's white shoulders dawned on them, kind of jerk, or hop, or hiccup, but their eyes snapped back to their own baskets and on they pushed. I bet you could set off dynamite in an A & P and the people would by and large keep reaching and checking oatmeal off their lists and muttering "Let me see, there was a third thing, began with A, asparagus, no, ah, yes, applesauce!" or whatever it is they do mutter. But there was no doubt, this jiggled them. A few houseslaves in pin curlers even looked around after pushing their carts past to make sure what they had seen was correct.

You know, it's one thing to have a girl in a bathing suit down on the beach, where what with the glare nobody can look at each other much anyway, and another thing in the cool of the A & P, under the fluorescent lights, against all those stacked packages, with her feet paddling along naked over our checker-board green-and-cream rubber-tile floor.

"Oh Daddy," Stokesie said beside me. "I feel so faint."

"Darling," I said. "Hold me tight." Stokesie's married, with two babies chalked up on his fuselage already, but as far as I can tell that's the only difference. He's twenty-two, and I was nineteen this April.

"Is it done?" he asks, the responsible married man finding his voice. I forgot to say he thinks he's going to be manager some sunny day, maybe in 1990 when it's called the Great Alexandrov and Petrooshki Tea Company or something.

What he meant was, our town is five miles from a beach, with a big summer 10 colony out on the Point, but we're right in the middle of town, and the women generally put on a shirt or shorts or something before they get out of the car into the street. And anyway these are usually women with six children and varicose veins mapping their legs and nobody, including them, could care less. As I say, we're right in the middle of town, and if you stand at our front doors you can see two banks and the Congregational church and the newspaper store and three real-estate offices and about twenty-seven old freeloaders tearing up Central Street because the sewer broke again. It's not as if we're on the Cape, we're north of Boston and there's people in this town haven't seen the ocean for twenty years.

The girls had reached the meat counter and were asking McMahon something. He pointed, they pointed, and they shuffled out of sight behind a pyramid of Diet Delight peaches. All that was left for us to see was old McMahon patting his mouth and looking after them sizing up their joints. Poor kids, I began to feel sorry for them, they couldn't help it.

Now here comes the sad part of the story, at least my family says it's sad, but I don't think it's so sad myself. The store's pretty empty, it being Thursday afternoon, so there was nothing much to do except lean on the register and wait for the girls to show up again. The whole store was like a pinball machine and I didn't know which tunnel they'd come out of. After a while they come around out of the far aisle, around the light bulbs, records at discount of the Caribbean Six or Tony Martin Sings or some such gunk you wonder they waste the wax on, sixpacks of candy bars, and plastic toys done up in cellophane that fall apart when a kid looks at them anyway. Around they come, Queenie still leading the way, and holding a little gray jar in her hands. Slots Three through Seven are unmanned and I could see her wondering between Stokes and me, but Stokesie with his usual luck draws an old party in baggy gray pants who stumbles up with four giant cans of pineapple juice (what do these bums *do* with all that pineapple juice? I've often asked myself). So the girls come to me. Queenie puts down the jar and I take it into my fingers icy cold. Kingfish Fancy Herring Snacks in Pure Sour Cream: 49¢. Now her hands are empty, not a ring or a bracelet, bare as God made them, and I wonder where the money's coming from. Still with that prim look she lifts a folded dollar bill out of the hollow at the center of her nubbled pink top. The jar went heavy in my hand. Really, I thought that was so cute.

Then everybody's luck begins to run out. Lengel comes in from haggling with a truck full of cabbages on the lot and is about to scuttle into that door marked MANAGER behind which he hides all day when the girls touch his eye. Lengel's pretty dreary, teaches Sunday school and the rest, but he doesn't miss that much. He comes over and says, "Girls, this isn't the beach."

Queenie blushes, though maybe it's just a brush of sunburn I was noticing for the first time, now that she was so close. "My mother asked me to pick up a jar of herring snacks." Her voice kind of startled me, the way voices do when you see the people first, coming out so flat and dumb yet kind of tony, too, the way it ticked over "pick up" and "snacks." All of a sudden I slid right down her voice into the living room. Her father and the other men were standing around in ice-cream coats and bow ties and the women were in sandals picking up herring snacks on toothpicks off a big glass plate and they were all holding drinks the color of water with olives and sprigs of mint in them. When my parents have somebody over they get lemonade and if it's a real racy affair Schlitz in tall glasses with "They'll Do It Every Time" cartoons stenciled on.

"That's all right," Lengel said. "But this isn't the beach." His repeating this struck me as funny, as if it had just occurred to him, and he had been thinking all these years the A & P was a great big dune and he was the head lifeguard. He didn't like my smiling — as I say he doesn't miss much — but he concentrates on giving the girls that sad Sunday-school-superintendent stare. 15

Queenie's blush is no sunburn now, and the plump one in plaid, that I liked better from the back — a really sweet can — pipes up, "We weren't doing any shopping. We just came in for the one thing."

"That makes no difference," Lengel tells her, and I could see from the way his eyes went that he hadn't noticed she was wearing a two-piece before. "We want you decently dressed when you come in here."

"We *are* decent," Queenie says suddenly, her lower lip pushing, getting sore now that she remembers her place, a place from which the crowd that runs the A & P must look pretty crummy. Fancy Herring Snacks flashed in her very blue eyes.

"Girls, I don't want to argue with you. After this come in here with your shoulders covered. It's our policy." He turns his back. That's policy for you. Policy is what the kingpins want. What the others want is juvenile delinquency.

All this while, the customers had been showing up with their carts but, you know, sheep, seeing a scene, they had all bunched up on Stokesie, who shook open a paper bag as gently as peeling a peach, not wanting to miss a word. I could feel in the silence everybody getting nervous, most of all Lengel, who asks me, "Sammy, have you rung up their purchase?"

I thought and said "No" but it wasn't about that I was thinking. I go through the punches, 4, 9, GROC. TOT — it's more complicated than you think, and after you do it often enough, it begins to make a little song, that you hear words to, in my case "Hello *(bing)* there, you *(gung)* hap-py *pee*-pul *(splat)!"* — the *splat* being the drawer flying out. I uncrease the bill, tenderly as you may imagine, it just having come from between the two smoothest scoops of vanilla I had ever known were there, and pass a half and a penny into her narrow pink palm, and nestle the herrings in a bag and twist its neck and hand it over, all the time thinking.

The girls, and who'd blame them, are in a hurry to get out, so I say "I quit" to Lengel quick enough for them to hear, hoping they'll stop and watch me, their unsuspected hero. They keep right on going, into the electric eye; the door flies open and they flicker across the lot to their car, Queenie and Plaid and Big Tall Goony-Goony (not that as raw material she was so bad), leaving me with Lengel and a kink in his eyebrow.

"Did you say something, Sammy?"

"I said I quit."

"I thought you did."

"You didn't have to embarrass them."

"It was they who were embarrassing us."

I started to say something that came out "Fiddle-de-doo." It's a saying of my grandmother's, and I know she would have been pleased.

"I don't think you know what you're saying," Lengel said.

"I know you don't," I said. "But I do." I pull the bow at the back of my apron and start shrugging it off my shoulders. A couple customers that had been heading for my slot begin to knock against each other, like scared pigs in a chute.

Lengel sighs and begins to look very patient and old and gray. He's been a friend of my parents for years. "Sammy, you don't want to do this to your Mom and Dad," he tells me. It's true, I don't. But it seems to me that once you begin

20

25

30

a gesture it's fatal not to go through with it. I fold the apron, "Sammy" stitched in red on the pocket, and put it on the counter, and drop the bow tie on top of it. The bow tie is theirs, if you've ever wondered. "You'll feel this for the rest of your life," Lengel says, and I know that's true, too, but remembering how he made the pretty girl blush makes me so scrunchy inside I punch the No Sale tab and the machine whirs "pee-pul" and the drawer splats out. One advantage to this scene taking place in summer, I can follow this up with a clean exit, there's no fumbling around getting your coat and galoshes, I just saunter into the electric eye in my white shirt that my mother ironed the night before, and the door heaves itself open, and outside the sunshine is skating around on the asphalt.

I look around for my girls, but they're gone, of course. There wasn't anybody but some young married screaming with her children about some candy they didn't get by the door of a powder-blue Falcon station wagon. Looking back in the big windows, over the bags of peat moss and aluminum lawn furniture stacked on the pavement, I could see Lengel in my place in the slot, checking the sheep through. His face was dark gray and his back stiff, as if he'd just had an injection of iron, and my stomach kind of fell as I felt how hard the world was going to be to me hereafter.

VIRGINIA WOOLF (1882–1941)
Lappin and Lapinova°

1939

They were married. The wedding march pealed out. The pigeons fluttered. Small boys in Eton jackets threw rice; a fox terrier sauntered across the path; and Ernest Thorburn led his bride to the car through that small inquisitive crowd of complete strangers which always collects in London to enjoy other people's happiness or unhappiness. Certainly he looked handsome and she looked shy. More rice was thrown, and the car moved off.

That was on Tuesday. Now it was Saturday. Rosalind had still to get used to the fact that she was Mrs. Ernest Thorburn. Perhaps she never would get used to the fact that she was Mrs. Ernest Anybody, she thought, as she sat in the bow window of the hotel looking over the lake to the mountains, and waited for her husband to come down to breakfast. Ernest was a difficult name to get used to. It was not the name she would have chosen. She would have preferred Timothy, Antony, or Peter. He did not look like Ernest either. The name suggested the Albert Memorial, mahogany sideboards, steel engravings of the Prince Consort with his family — her mother-in-law's dining room in Porchester Terrace in short.

But here he was. Thank goodness he did not look like Ernest — no. But what did he look like? She glanced at him sideways. Well, when he was eating toast he looked like a rabbit. Not that anyone else would have seen a likeness

Lappin and Lapinova: Lapin is French for rabbit.

to a creature so diminutive and timid in this spruce, muscular young man with the straight nose, the blue eyes, and the very firm mouth. But that made it all the more amusing. His nose twitched very slightly when he ate. So did her pet rabbit's. She kept watching his nose twitch; and then she had to explain, when he caught her looking at him, why she laughed.

"It's because you're like a rabbit, Ernest," she said. "Like a wild rabbit," she added, looking at him. "A hunting rabbit; a King Rabbit; a rabbit that makes laws for all the other rabbits."

Ernest had no objection to being that kind of rabbit, and since it amused   5 her to see him twitch his nose — he had never known that his nose twitched — he twitched it on purpose. And she laughed and laughed; and he laughed too, so that the maiden ladies and the fishing man and the Swiss waiter in his greasy black jacket all guessed right; they were very happy. But how long does such happiness last? they asked themselves; and each answered according to his own circumstances.

At lunch time, seated on a clump of heather beside the lake, "Lettuce, rabbit?" said Rosalind, holding out the lettuce that had been provided to eat with the hard-boiled eggs. "Come and take it out of my hand," she added, and he stretched out and nibbled the lettuce and twitched his nose.

"Good rabbit, nice rabbit," she said, patting him, as she used to pat her tame rabbit at home. But that was absurd. He was not a tame rabbit, whatever he was. She turned it into French. "Lapin," she called him. But whatever he was, he was not a French rabbit. He was simply and solely English — born at Porchester Terrace, educated at Rugby; now a clerk in His Majesty's Civil Service. So she tried "Bunny" next; but that was worse. "Bunny" was someone plump and soft and comic; he was thin and hard and serious. Still, his nose twitched. "Lappin," she exclaimed suddenly; and gave a little cry as if she had found the very word she looked for.

"Lappin, Lappin, King Lappin," she repeated. It seemed to suit him exactly; he was not Ernest, he was King Lappin. Why? She did not know.

When there was nothing new to talk about on their long solitary walks — and it rained, as everyone had warned them that it would rain; or when they were sitting over the fire in the evening, for it was cold, and the maiden ladies had gone and the fishing man, and the waiter only came if you rang the bell for him, she let her fancy play with the story of the Lappin tribe. Under her hands — she was sewing; he was reading — they became very real, very vivid, very amusing. Ernest put down the paper and helped her. There were the black rabbits and the red; there were the enemy rabbits and the friendly. There were the wood in which they lived and the outlying prairies and the swamp. Above all there was King Lappin, who, far from having only the one trick — that he twitched his nose — became as the days passed an animal of the greatest character; Rosalind was always finding new qualities in him. But above all he was a great hunter.

"And what," said Rosalind, on the last day of the honeymoon, "did the King   10 do today?"

In fact they had been climbing all day; and she had worn a blister on her heel; but she did not mean that.

"Today," said Ernest, twitching his nose as he bit the end off his cigar, "he chased a hare." He paused; struck a match, and twitched again.

"A woman hare," he added.

"A white hare!" Rosalind exclaimed, as if she had been expecting this. "Rather a small hare; silver gray; with big bright eyes?"

"Yes," said Ernest, looking at her as she had looked at him, "a smallish 15 animal; with eyes popping out of her head, and two little front paws dangling." It was exactly how she sat, with her sewing dangling in her hands; and her eyes, that were so big and bright, were certainly a little prominent.

"Ah, Lapinova," Rosalind murmured.

"Is that what she's called?" said Ernest — "the real Rosalind?" He looked at her. He felt very much in love with her.

"Yes; that's what she's called," said Rosalind. "Lapinova." And before they went to bed that night it was all settled. He was King Lappin; she was Queen Lapinova. They were the opposite of each other; he was bold and determined; she wary and undependable. He ruled over the busy world of rabbits; her world was a desolate, mysterious place, which she ranged mostly by moonlight. All the same, their territories touched; they were King and Queen.

Thus when they came back from their honeymoon they possessed a private world, inhabited, save for the one white hare, entirely by rabbits. No one guessed that there was such a place, and that of course made it all the more amusing. It made them feel, more even than most young married couples, in league together against the rest of the world. Often they looked slyly at each other when people talked about rabbits and woods and traps and shooting. Or they winked furtively across the table when Aunt Mary said that she could never bear to see a hare in a dish — it looked so like a baby: or when John, Ernest's sporting brother, told him what price rabbits were fetching that autumn in Wiltshire, skins and all. Sometimes when they wanted a gamekeeper, or a poacher, or a Lord of the Manor, they amused themselves by distributing the parts among their friends. Ernest's mother, Mrs. Reginald Thorburn, for example, fitted the part of the Squire to perfection. But it was all secret — that was the point of it; nobody save themselves knew that such a world existed.

Without that world, how, Rosalind wondered, that winter could she have 20 lived at all? For instance, there was the golden-wedding party, when all the Thorburns assembled at Porchester Terrace to celebrate the fiftieth anniversary of that union which had been so blessed — had it not produced Ernest Thorburn? — and so fruitful — had it not produced nine other sons and daughters into the bargain, many themselves married and also fruitful? She dreaded that party. But it was inevitable. As she walked upstairs she felt bitterly that she was an only child and an orphan at that; a mere drop among all those Thorburns assembled in the great drawing room with the shiny satin wallpaper and the lustrous family portraits. The living Thorburns much resembled the painted; save that instead of painted lips they had real lips; out of which came jokes; jokes about schoolrooms, and how they had pulled the chair from under the governess; jokes about frogs and how they had put them between the virgin sheets of maiden ladies. As for herself, she had never even made an apple-pie bed. Holding her present in her hand she advanced toward her mother-in-law sumptuous in yellow satin; and toward her father-in-law decorated with a rich yellow carnation. All round them on tables and chairs there were golden tributes, some nestling in cotton wool; others branching resplendent — candlesticks; cigar boxes; chains; each stamped with the goldsmith's proof that it was solid gold, hallmarked, authentic. But her present was only a little pinchbeck box pierced with holes; an old sand caster, an eighteenth-century relic, once used to sprinkle sand over wet ink. Rather a senseless present she felt — in an age of blotting paper; and as she proffered it, she saw in front of her the stubby black handwriting in which her mother-in-law when they were engaged had expressed the hope that "My son will make you happy." No, she was not happy. Not at all happy. She looked at Ernest, straight as a ramrod with a nose like all the noses in the family portraits; a nose that never twitched at all.

Then they went down to dinner. She was half hidden by the great chrysanthemums that curled their red and gold petals into large tight balls. Everything was gold. A gold-edged card with gold initials intertwined recited the list of all the dishes that would be set one after another before them. She dipped her spoon in a plate of clear golden fluid. The raw white fog outside had been turned by the lamps into a golden mesh that blurred the edges of the plates and gave the pineapples a rough golden skin. Only she herself in her white wedding dress peering ahead of her with her prominent eyes seemed insoluble as an icicle.

As the dinner wore on, however, the room grew steamy with heat. Beads of perspiration stood out on the men's foreheads. She felt that her icicle was being turned to water. She was being melted; dispersed; dissolved into nothingness; and would soon faint. Then through the surge in her head and the din in her ears she heard a woman's voice exclaim, "But they breed so!"

The Thorburns — yes; they breed so, she echoed; looking at all the round red faces that seemed doubled in the giddiness that overcame her; and magnified in the gold mist that enhaloed them. "They breed so." Then John bawled:

"Little devils! . . . Shoot 'em! Jump on 'em with big boots! That's the only way to deal with 'em . . . rabbits!"

At that word, that magic word, she revived. Peeping between the chrysanthemums she saw Ernest's nose twitch. It rippled, it ran with successive twitches. And at that a mysterious catastrophe befell the Thorburns. The golden table became a moor with the gorse in full bloom; the din of voices turned to one peal of lark's laughter ringing down from the sky. It was a blue sky — clouds passed slowly. And they all been changed — the Thorburns. She looked at her father-in-law, a furtive little man with dyed moustaches. His foible was collecting things — seals, enamel boxes, trifles from eighteenth-century dressing tables which he hid in the drawers of his study from his wife. Now she saw him as he was — a poacher, stealing off with his coat bulging with pheasants and partridges to drop them stealthily into a three-legged pot in his smoky little cottage. That was her real father-in-law — a poacher. And Celia, the unmarried daughter, who always nosed out other people's secrets, the little things they wished to hide — she was a white ferret with pink eyes, and a nose clotted with earth from her horrid underground nosings and pokings. Slung round men's shoulders, in a net, and thrust down a hole — it was a pitiable life — Celia's; it was none of her fault. So she saw Celia. And then she looked at her mother-in-law — whom they dubbed The Squire. Flushed, coarse, a bully — she was all that, as she stood returning thanks, but now that Rosalind — that is Lapinova — saw her, she saw behind her the decayed family mansion, the plaster peeling off the walls, and heard her, with a sob in her voice, giving thanks to her children (who hated her) for a world that had ceased to exist. There was a sudden silence. They all stood with their glasses raised; they all drank; then it was over.

"Oh, King Lappin!" she cried as they went home together in the fog, "if your nose hadn't twitched just at that moment, I should have been trapped!"

"But you're safe," said King Lappin, pressing her paw.

"Quite safe," she answered.

And they drove back through the Park, King and Queen of the marsh, of the mist, and of the gorse-scented moor.

Thus time passed; one year; two years of time. And on a winter's night, 30 which happened by a coincidence to be the anniversary of the golden-wedding party — but Mrs. Reginald Thorburn was dead; the house was to let; and there was only a caretaker in residence — Ernest came home from the office. They had a nice little home; half a house above a saddler's shop in South Kensington, not far from the Tube station. It was cold, with fog in the air, and Rosalind was sitting over the fire, sewing.

"What d'you think happened to me today?" she began as soon as he had settled himself down with his legs stretched to the blaze. "I was crossing the stream when — "

"What stream?" Ernest interrupted her.

"The stream at the bottom, where our wood meets the black wood," she explained.

Ernest looked completely blank for a moment.

"What the deuce are you talking about?" he asked.   35

"My dear Ernest!" she cried in dismay. "King Lappin," she added, dangling her little front paws in the firelight. But his nose did not twitch. Her hands — they turned to hands — clutched the stuff she was holding; her eyes popped half out of her head. It took him five minutes at least to change from Ernest Thorburn to King Lappin; and while she waited she felt a load on the back of her neck, as if somebody were about to wring it. At last he changed to King Lappin; his nose twitched; and they spent the evening roaming the woods much as usual.

But she slept badly. In the middle of the night she woke, feeling as if something strange had happened to her. She was stiff and cold. At last she turned on the light and looked at Ernest lying beside her. He was sound asleep. He snored. But even though he snored, his nose remained perfectly still. It looked as if it had never twitched at all. Was it possible that he was really Ernest; and that she was really married to Ernest? A vision of her mother-in-law's dining room came before her; and there they sat, she and Ernest, grown old, under the engravings, in front of the sideboard. . . . It was their golden-wedding day. She could not bear it.

"Lappin, King Lappin!" she whispered, and for a moment his nose seemed to twitch of its own accord. But he still slept. "Wake up, Lappin, wake up!" she cried.

Ernest woke; and seeing her sitting bolt upright beside him he asked:

"What's the matter?"   40

"I thought my rabbit was dead!" she whimpered. Ernest was angry.

"Don't talk such rubbish, Rosalind," he said. "Lie down and go to sleep."

He turned over. In another moment he was sound asleep and snoring.

But she could not sleep. She lay curled up on her side of the bed, like a hare in its form. She had turned out the light, but the street lamp lit the ceiling faintly, and the trees outside made a lacy network over it as if there were a shadowy grove on the ceiling in which she wandered, turning, twisting, in and out, round and round, hunting, being hunted, hearing the bay of hounds and horns; flying, escaping . . . until the maid drew the blinds and brought their early tea.

Next day she could settle to nothing. She seemed to have lost something. 45 She felt as if her body had shrunk; it had grown small, and black, and hard. Her joints seemed stiff too, and when she looked in the glass, which she did several times as she wandered about the flat, her eyes seemed to burst out of her head, like currants in a bun. The rooms also seemed to have shrunk. Large pieces of furniture jutted out at odd angles and she found herself knocking against them. At last she put on her hat and went out. She walked along the Cromwell Road; and every room she passed and peered into seemed to be a dining room where people sat eating under steel engravings, with thick yellow lace curtains, and mahogany sideboards. At last she reached the Natural History Museum; she used to like it when she was a child. But the first thing she saw when she went in was a stuffed hare standing on sham snow with pink glass eyes. Somehow it made her shiver all over. Perhaps it would be better when dusk fell. She went home and sat over the fire, without a light, and tried to imagine that she was out alone on a moor; and there was a stream rushing; and beyond the stream a dark wood. But she could get no further than the stream. At last she squatted down on the bank on the wet grass, and sat crouched in her chair, with her hands dangling empty, and her eyes glazed, like glass eyes, in the firelight. Then there was the crack of a gun. . . . She started as if she had been shot. It was only Ernest, turning his key in the door. She waited, trembling. He came in and switched on the light. There he stood tall, handsome, rubbing his hands that were red with cold.

"Sitting in the dark?" he said.

"Oh, Ernest, Ernest!" she cried, starting up in her chair.

"Well, what's up, now?" he asked briskly, warming his hands at the fire.

"It's Lapinova . . ." she faltered, glancing wildly at him out of her great startled eyes. "She's gone, Ernest. I've lost her!"

Ernest frowned. He pressed his lips tight together. "Oh, that's what's up, is 50 it?" he said, smiling rather grimly at his wife. For ten seconds he stood there, silent; and she waited, feeling hands tightening at the back of her neck.

"Yes," he said at length. "Poor Lapinova . . ." He straightened his tie at the looking-glass over the mantelpiece.

"Caught in a trap," he said, "killed," and sat down and read the newspaper.

So that was the end of that marriage.

AN ALBUM OF WORLD LITERATURE

ISABEL ALLENDE (Chilean/b. 1942)

Isabel Allende was born in Chile to an intensely political family. Her father suddenly and mysteriously disappeared when she was very young. After high school she worked as a secretary in the Department of Information of the United Nations Food and Agriculture organization. She subsequently developed a weekly television program and wrote for magazines. In 1973 her father's first cousin Salvadore Allende, the president of Chile, was assassinated. To escape the repressive political climate, she moved to Venezuela in 1975, where she worked as a journalist, taught school, and began writing her first novel based on her exile. An English translation of *House of Spirits* appeared in 1985 and made her one of the most internationally popular women writers from Latin America. Her two other translated novels, *Of Love and Shadows* (1987) and *Eva Luna* (1989), also center upon the political instability in Latin America. Though her characters are often faced with terrible choices generated by repressive social conditions, she creates strong characters — particularly women — who take courageous risks.

The Judge's Wife   1989
TRANSLATED BY NICK CAISTOR

Nicolas Vidal always knew he would lose his head over a woman. So it was foretold on the day of his birth, and later confirmed by the Turkish woman in the corner shop the one time he allowed her to read his fortune in the coffee grounds. Little did he imagine though that it would be on account of Casilda, Judge Hidalgo's wife. It was on her wedding day that he first glimpsed her. He was not impressed, preferring his women dark-haired and brazen. This ethereal slip of a girl in her wedding gown, eyes filled with wonder, and fingers obviously unskilled in the art of rousing a man to pleasure, seemed to him almost ugly. Mindful of his destiny, he had always been wary of any emotional contact with women, hardening his heart and restricting himself to the briefest of encounters whenever the demands of manhood needed satisfying. Casilda, however, appeared so insubstantial, so distant, that he cast aside all precaution and, when the fateful moment arrived, forgot the prediction that usually weighed in all his decisions. From the roof of the bank, where he was crouching with two of his men, Nicolas Vidal peered down at this young lady from the capital. She had a dozen equally pale and dainty relatives with her, who spent the whole of the ceremony fanning themselves with an air of utter bewilderment, then departed straight away, never to return. Along with everyone else in the town, Vidal was convinced the young bride would not withstand the climate, and that within a few months the old women would be dressing her up again, this time for her funeral. Even if she did survive the heat and the dust that filtered in through every pore to lodge itself in the soul, she would be bound to succumb to the fussy habits of her confirmed bachelor of a husband. Judge Hidalgo was twice her age, and had slept alone for so many years he didn't have the slightest notion of how to go about pleasing a woman. The severity and stubbornness with which he executed the law even at the expense of justice had made him feared throughout the province. He refused to apply any common sense in the exercise of his profession, and was equally harsh in his condemnation of the theft of a chicken as of a premeditated murder. He dressed formally in black, and, despite the all-pervading dust in this godforsaken town, his boots always shone with beeswax. A man such as he was never meant to be a husband, and yet not only did the gloomy wedding-day prophecies remain unfulfilled, but Casilda emerged happy and smiling from three pregnancies in rapid succession. Every Sunday at noon she would go to mass with her husband, cool and collected beneath her Spanish mantilla, seemingly untouched by our pitiless summer, as wan and frail-looking as on the day of her arrival: a perfect example of delicacy and refinement. Her loudest words were a soft-spoken greeting; her most expressive gesture was a graceful nod of the head. She was such an airy, diaphanous creature that a moment's carelessness might mean she disappeared altogether. So slight an impression did she make that the changes noticeable in the Judge were all the more remarkable. Though outwardly he remained the same — he still dressed as black as a crow and was as stiff-necked and brusque as ever — his judgments in court altered dramatically. To general amazement, he found the youngster who robbed the Turkish shopkeeper innocent, on the grounds that she had been selling him short for years, and the money he had taken could therefore be seen as compensation. He also refused to punish an adulterous wife, arguing that since her husband himself kept a mistress he did not have the moral authority to demand fidelity. Word in the town had it that the Judge was transformed the minute he crossed the threshold at home: that he flung off his gloomy apparel, rollicked with his children, chuckled as he sat Casilda on his lap. Though no one ever succeeded in confirming these rumors, his wife got the credit for his newfound kindness, and her reputation grew accordingly. None of this was of the slightest interest to Nicolas Vidal, who as a wanted man was sure there would be no mercy shown him the day he was brought in chains before the Judge. He paid no heed to the talk about Doña Casilda, and the rare occasions he glimpsed her from afar only confirmed his first impression of her as a lifeless ghost.

Born thirty years earlier in a windowless room in the town's only brothel, Vidal was the son of Juana the Forlorn and an unknown father. The world had no place for him. His mother knew it, and so tried to wrench him from her womb with sprigs of parsley, candle butts, douches of ashes, and other violent purgatives, but the child clung to life. Once, years later, Juana was looking at her mysterious son and realized that, while all her infallible methods of aborting might have failed to dislodge him, they had none the less tempered his soul to the hardness of iron. As soon as he came into the world, he was lifted in the air by the midwife who examined him by the light of an oil lamp. She saw he had four nipples.

"Poor creature: he'll lose his head over a woman," she predicted, drawing on her wealth of experience.

Her words rested on the boy like a deformity. Perhaps a woman's love would have made his existence less wretched. To atone for all her attempts to kill him before birth, his mother chose him a beautiful first name, and an imposing family name picked at random. But the lofty name of Nicolas Vidal was no protection against the fateful cast of his destiny. His face was scarred from knife fights before he reached his teens, so it came as no surprise to decent folk that he ended up a bandit. By the age of twenty, he had become the leader of a band of desperadoes. The habit of violence toughened his sinews. The solitude he was condemned to for fear of falling prey to a woman lent his face a doleful expression. As soon as they saw him, everyone in the town knew from his eyes, clouded by tears he would never allow to fall, that he was the son of Juana the Forlorn. Whenever there was an outcry after a crime had been committed in the region, the police set out with dogs to track him down, but after scouring the hills invariably returned empty-handed. In all honesty they preferred it that way, because they could never have fought him. His gang gained such a fearsome reputation that the surrounding villages and estates paid to keep them away. This money would have been plenty for his men, but Nicolas Vidal kept them constantly on horseback in a whirlwind of death and destruction so they would not lose their taste for battle. Nobody dared take them on. More than once, Judge Hidalgo had asked the government to send troops to reinforce the police, but after several useless forays the soldiers returned to their barracks and Nicolas Vidal's gang to their exploits. On one occasion only did Vidal come close to falling into the hands of justice, and then he was saved by his hardened heart.

Weary of seeing the laws flouted, Judge Hidalgo resolved to forget his 5 scruples and set a trap for the outlaw. He realized that to defend justice he was committing an injustice, but chose the lesser of two evils. The only bait he could find was Juana the Forlorn, as she was Vidal's sole known relative. He had her dragged from the brothel where by now, since no clients were willing to pay for her exhausted charms, she scrubbed floors and cleaned out the lavatories. He put her in a specially made cage which was set up in the middle of the Plaza de Armas, with only a jug of water to meet her needs.

"As soon as the water's finished, she'll start to squawk. Then her son will come running, and I'll be waiting for him with the soldiers," Judge Hidalgo said.

News of this torture, unheard of since the days of slavery, reached Nicolas Vidal's ears shortly before his mother drank the last of the water. His men watched as he received the report in silence, without so much as a flicker of emotion on his blank lone wolf's face, or a pause in the sharpening of his dagger blade on a leather strap. Though for many years he had had no contact with Juana, and retained few happy childhood memories, this was a question of honor. No man can accept such an insult, his gang reasoned as they got guns and horses ready to rush into the ambush and, if need be, lay down their lives. Their chief showed no sign of being in a hurry. As the hours went by tension mounted in the camp. The perspiring, impatient men stared at each other, not daring to speak. Fretful, they caressed the butts of their revolvers and their horses' manes, or busied themselves coiling their lassos. Night fell. Nicolas Vidal was the only one in the camp who slept. At dawn, opinions were divided. Some of the men reckoned he was even more heartless than they had ever imagined, while others maintained their leader was planning a spectacular ruse to free his mother. The one thing that never crossed any of their minds was that his courage might have failed him, for he had always proved he had more than enough to spare. By noon, they could bear the suspense no longer, and went to ask him what he planned to do.

"I'm not going to fall into his trap like an idiot," he said.

"What about your mother?"

"We'll see who's got more balls, the Judge or me," Nicolas Vidal coolly 10 replied.

By the third day, Juana the Forlorn's cries for water had ceased. She lay curled on the cage floor, with wildly staring eyes and swollen lips, moaning softly whenever she regained consciousness, and the rest of the time dreaming she was in hell. Four armed guards stood watch to make sure nobody brought her water. Her groans penetrated the entire town, filtering through closed shutters or being carried by the wind through the cracks in doors. They got stuck in corners, where dogs worried at them, and passed them on in their howls to the newly born, so that whoever heard them was driven to distraction. The Judge couldn't prevent a steady stream of people filing through the square to show their sympathy for the old woman, and was powerless to stop the prostitutes going on a sympathy strike just as the miners' fortnight holiday was beginning. That Saturday, the streets were thronged with lusty workmen desperate to unload their savings, who now found nothing in town apart from the spectacle of the cage and this universal wailing carried mouth to mouth down from the river to the coast road. The priest headed a group of Catholic ladies to plead with Judge Hidalgo for Christian mercy and to beg him to spare the poor old innocent woman such a frightful death, but the man of the law bolted his door and refused to listen to them. It was then they decided to turn to Doña Casilda.

The Judge's wife received them in her shady living room. She listened to their pleas looking, as always, bashfully down at the floor. Her husband had not been home for three days, having locked himself in his office to wait for Nicolas Vidal to fall into his trap. Without so much as glancing out of the window, she was aware of what was going on, for Juana's long-drawn-out agony had forced its way even into the vast rooms of her residence. Doña Casilda waited until her visitors had left, dressed her children in their Sunday best, tied a black ribbon round their arms as a token of mourning, then strode out with them in the direction of the square. She carried a food hamper and a bottle of fresh water for Juana the Forlorn. When the guards spotted her turning the corner, they realized what she was up to, but they had strict orders, and barred her way with their rifles. When, watched now by a small crowd, she persisted, they grabbed her by the arms. Her children began to cry.

Judge Hidalgo sat in his office overlooking the square. He was the only person in the town who had not stuffed wax in his ears, because his mind was intent on the ambush and he was straining to catch the sound of horses' hoofs, the signal for action. For three long days and nights he put up with Juana's groans and the insults of the townspeople gathered outside the courtroom, but when he heard his own children start to wail he knew he had reached the bounds of his endurance. Vanquished, he walked out of the office with his three days' beard, his eyes bloodshot from keeping watch, and the weight of a thousand years on his back. He crossed the street, turned into the square and came face to face with his wife. They gazed at each other sadly. In seven years, this was the first time she had gone against him, and she had chosen to do so in front of the whole town. Easing the hamper and the bottle from Casilda's grasp, Judge Hidalgo himself opened the cage to release the prisoner.

"Didn't I tell you he wouldn't have the balls?" laughed Nicolas Vidal when the news reached him.

His laughter turned sour the next day, when he heard that Juana the Forlorn 15 had hanged herself from the chandelier in the brothel where she had spent her life, overwhelmed by the shame of her only son leaving her to fester in a cage in the middle of the Plaza de Armas.

"That Judge's hour has come," said Vidal.

He planned to take the Judge by surprise, put him to a horrible death, then dump him in the accursed cage for all to see. The Turkish shopkeeper sent him word that the Hidalgo family had left that same night for a seaside resort to rid themselves of the bitter taste of defeat.

The Judge learned he was being pursued when he stopped to rest at a wayside inn. There was little protection for him there until an army patrol could arrive, but he had a few hours' start, and his motor car could outrun the gang's horses. He calculated he could make it to the next town and summon help there. He ordered his wife and children into the car, put his foot down on the accelerator, and sped off along the road. He ought to have arrived with time to spare, but it had been ordained that Nicolas Vidal was that day to meet the woman who would lead him to his doom.

Overburdened by the sleepless nights, the townspeople's hostility, the blow to his pride, and the stress of this race to save his family, Judge Hidalgo's heart gave a massive jolt, then split like a pomegranate. The car ran out of control, turned several somersaults and finally came to a halt in the ditch. It took Doña Casilda some minutes to work out what had happened. Her husband's advancing years had often led her to think what it would be like to be left a widow, yet she had never imagined he would leave her at the mercy of his enemies. She wasted little time dwelling on her situation, knowing she must act at once to get her children to safety. When she gazed around her, she almost burst into tears. There was no sign of life in the vast plain baked by a scorching sun, only barren cliffs beneath an unbounded sky bleached colorless by the fierce light. A second look revealed the dark shadow of a passage or cave on a distant slope, so she ran towards it with two children in her arms and the third clutching her skirts.

One by one she carried her children up the cliff. The cave was a natural 20 one, typical of many in the region. She peered inside to be certain it wasn't the den of some wild animal, sat her children against its back wall, then, dry-eyed, kissed them good-bye.

"The troops will come to find you a few hours from now. Until then, don't for any reason whatsoever come out of here, even if you hear me screaming — do you understand?"

Their mother gave one final glance at the terrified children clinging to each other, then clambered back down to the road. She reached the car, closed her husband's eyes, smoothed back her hair and settled down to wait. She had no idea how many men were in Nicolas Vidal's gang, but prayed there were a lot of them so it would take them all the more time to have their way with her. She gathered strength pondering on how long it would take her to die if she determined to do it as slowly as possible. She willed herself to be desirable, luscious, to create more work for them and thus gain time for her children.

Casilda did not have long to wait. She soon saw a cloud of dust on the horizon and heard the gallop of horses' hoofs. She clenched her teeth. Then, to her astonishment, she saw there was only one rider, who stopped a few yards from her, gun at the ready. By the scar on his face she recognized Nicolas Vidal, who had set out all alone in pursuit of Judge Hidalgo, as this was a private matter between the two men. The Judge's wife understood she was going to have to endure something far worse than a lingering death.

A quick glance at her husband was enough to convince Vidal that the Judge was safely out of his reach in the peaceful sleep of death. But there was his wife, a shimmering presence in the plain's glare. He leapt from his horse and strode over to her. She did not flinch or lower her gaze, and to his amazement he realized that for the first time in his life another person was facing him without fear. For several seconds that stretched to eternity, they sized each other up, trying to gauge the other's strength, and their own powers of resistance. It gradually dawned on both of them that they were up against a formidable opponent. He lowered his gun. She smiled.

Casilda won each moment of the ensuing hours. To all the wiles of seduction 25 known since the beginning of time she added new ones born of necessity to bring this man to the heights of rapture. Not only did she work on his body like an artist, stimulating his every fiber to pleasure, but she brought all the delicacy of her spirit into play on her side. Both knew their lives were at stake, and this added a new and terrifying dimension to their meeting. Nicolas Vidal had fled from love since birth, and knew nothing of intimacy, tenderness, secret laughter, the riot of the senses, the joy of shared passion. Each minute brought the detachment of troops and the noose that much nearer, but he gladly accepted this in return for her prodigious gifts. Casilda was a passive, demure, timid woman who had been married to an austere old man in front of whom she had never even dared appear naked. Not once during that unforgettable afternoon did she forget that her aim was to win time for her children, and yet at some point, marvelling at her own possibilities, she gave herself completely, and felt something akin to gratitude towards him. That was why, when she heard the soldiers in the distance, she begged him to flee to the hills. Instead, Nicolas Vidal chose to fold her in a last embrace, thus fulfilling the prophecy that had sealed his fate from the start.

Connections to Other Selections

1. How plausible is the plot of "The Judge's Wife"? Compare the plot with that of Flannery O'Connor's "A Good Man Is Hard to Find" (p. 368) or "A Very Old Man with Enormous Wings" (p. 223) by Gabriel García Márquez. Consider whether the characters and events are believable and how that affects your reading of the stories.

2. Discuss Allende's treatment of justice with that of Andre Dubus in "Killings" (p. 57).
3. Write an essay comparing Allende's use of irony with Mark Twain's in "The Story of the Bad Little Boy" (p. 482).

BESSIE HEAD (Botswanan/1937–1986)

Born in Pietermaritzburg, South Africa, Bessie Head was the daughter of a black father and a white mother. After growing up in a foster home and orphanage, she taught grammar school and wrote fiction for a local paper. In her twenties she moved to a farm commune in Botswana to avoid the apartheid of her homeland. Her first novel, *When Rain Clouds Gather,* was published in 1969. Her collection of stories *The Collector of Treasurers and Other Botswana Village Tales* (1977) was followed by two other novels, *Serowe: Village of the Rain Wind* (1981) and *A Bewitched Crossroad* (1984). Head's familiarity with oppression and the daily difficulties endured by its victims produced in her work a heightened sensitivity to the necessity for human decency. In "The Prisoner Who Wore Glasses," oppression and decency turn out to be complex matters.

The Prisoner Who Wore Glasses   1974

Scarcely a breath of wind disturbed the stillness of the day and the long rows of cabbages were bright green in the sunlight. Large white clouds drifted slowly across the deep blue sky. Now and then they obscured the sun and caused a chill on the backs of the prisoners who had to work all day long in the cabbage field. This trick the clouds were playing with the sun eventually caused one of the prisoners who wore glasses to stop work, straighten up, and peer shortsightedly at them. He was a thin little fellow with a hollowed-out chest and comic knobbly knees. He also had a lot of fanciful ideas because he smiled at the clouds.

"Perhaps they want me to send a message to the children," he thought, tenderly, noting that the clouds were drifting in the direction of his home some hundred miles away. But before he could frame the message, the warder in charge of his work span° shouted: "Hey, what you tink you're doing, Brille?"

The prisoner swung round, blinking rapidly, yet at the same time sizing up the enemy. He was a new warder, named Jacobus Stephanus Hannetjie. His eyes were the color of the sky but they were frightening. A simple, primitive, brutal soul gazed out of them. The prisoner bent down quickly and a message was quietly passed down the line: "We're in for trouble this time, comrades."

"Why?" rippled back up the line.

span: Squad.

"Because he's not human," the reply rippled down and yet only the crunch- 5
ing of the spades as they turned over the earth disturbed the stillness.

This particular work span was known as Span One. It was composed of ten
men and they were all political prisoners. They were grouped together for
convenience as it was one of the prison regulations that no black warder should
be in charge of a political prisoner lest this prisoner convert him to his views.
It never seemed to occur to the authorities that this very reasoning was the
strength of Span One and a clue to the strange terror they aroused in the
warders. As political prisoners they were unlike the other prisoners in the sense
that they felt no guilt nor were they outcasts of society. All guilty men instinctively
cower, which was why it was the kind of prison where men got knocked out
cold with a blow at the back of the head from an iron bar. Up until the arrival
of Warder Hannetjie, no warder had dared beat any member of Span One
and no warder had lasted more than a week with them. The battle was entirely psychological. Span One was assertive and it was beyond the scope of
white warders to handle assertive black men. Thus, Span One had got out of
control. They were the best thieves and liars in the camp. They lived all day
on raw cabbages. They chatted and smoked tobacco. And since they moved,
thought, and acted as one, they had perfected every technique of group concealment.

Trouble began that very day between Span One and Warder Hannetjie. It
was because of the shortsightedness of Brille. That was the nickname he was
given in prison and is the Afrikaans word for someone who wears glasses. Brille
could never judge the approach of the prison gates and on several previous
occasions he had munched on cabbages and dropped them almost at the feet
of the warder and all previous warders had overlooked this. Not so Warder
Hannetjie.

"Who dropped that cabbage?" he thundered.

Brille stepped out of line.

"I did," he said meekly.   10

"Alright," said Hannetjie. "The whole Span goes three meals off."

"But I told you I did it," Brille protested.

The blood rushed to Warder Hannetjie's face.

"Look 'ere," he said. "I don't take orders from a kaffir.° I don't know what
kind of kaffir you tink you are. Why don't you say Baas? I'm your Baas. Why don't
you say Baas, hey?"

Brille blinked his eyes rapidly but by contrast his voice was strangely calm.   15

"I'm twenty years older than you," he said. It was the first thing that came
to mind but the comrades seemed to think it a huge joke. A titter swept up the
line. The next thing Warder Hannetjie whipped out a knobkerrie° and gave Brille
several blows about the head. What surprised his comrades was the speed with
which Brille had removed his glasses or else they would have been smashed to
pieces on the ground.

That evening in the cell Brille was very apologetic.

"I'm sorry, comrades," he said. "I've put you into a hell of a mess."

knobkerrie: A club.
kaffir: A black South African; often used as a disparaging term.

"Never mind, brother," they said. "What happens to one of us, happens to all."

"I'll try to make up for it, comrades," he said. "I'll steal something so that 20 you don't go hungry."

Privately, Brille was very philosophical about his head wounds. It was the first time an act of violence had been perpetrated against him but he had long been a witness of extreme, almost unbelievable human brutality. He had twelve children and his mind traveled back that evening through the sixteen years of bedlam in which he had lived. It had all happened in a small drab little three-bedroomed house in a small drab little street in the Eastern Cape and the children kept coming year after year because neither he nor Martha ever managed the contraceptives the right way and a teacher's salary never allowed moving to a bigger house and he was always taking exams to improve his salary only to have it all eaten up by hungry mouths. Everything was pretty horrible, especially the way the children fought. They'd get hold of each other's heads and give them a good bashing against the wall. Martha gave up somewhere along the line so they worked out a thing between them. The bashings, biting, and blood were to operate in full swing until he came home. He was to be the bogey-man and when it worked he never failed to have a sense of godhead at the way in which his presence could change savages into fairly reasonable human beings.

Yet somehow it was this chaos and mismanagement at the center of his life that drove him into politics. It was really an ordered beautiful world with just a few basic slogans to learn along with the rights of mankind. At one stage, before things became very bad, there were conferences to attend, all very far away from home.

"Let's face it," he thought ruefully. "I'm only learning right now what it means to be a politician. All this while I've been running away from Martha and the kids."

And the pain in his head brought a hard lump to his throat. That was what the children did to each other daily and Martha wasn't managing and if Warder Hannetjie had not interrupted him that morning he would have sent the following message: "Be good comrades, my children. Cooperate, then life will run smoothly."

The next day Warder Hannetjie caught this old man of twelve children 25 stealing grapes from the farm shed. They were an enormous quantity of grapes in a ten-gallon tin and for this misdeed the old man spent a week in the isolation cell. In fact, Span One as a whole was in constant trouble. Warder Hannetjie seemed to have eyes at the back of his head. He uncovered the trick about the cabbages, how they were split in two with the spade and immediately covered with earth and then unearthed again and eaten with split-second timing. He found out how tobacco smoke was beaten into the ground and he found out how conversations were whispered down the wind.

For about two weeks Span One lived in acute misery. The cabbages, tobacco, and conversations had been the pivot of jail life to them. Then one evening they noticed that their good old comrade who wore the glasses was looking rather pleased with himself. He pulled out a four-ounce packet of tobacco by way of explanation and the comrades fell upon it with great greed. Brille merely smiled. After all, he was the father of many children. But when the last shred had disappeared, it occurred to the comrades that they ought to be puzzled. Someone said: "I say, brother. We're watched like hawks these days. Where did you get the tobacco?"

"Hannetjie gave it to me," said Brille.

There was a long silence. Into it dropped a quiet bombshell.

"I saw Hannetjie in the shed today," and the failing eyesight blinked rapidly. "I caught him in the act of stealing five bags of fertilizer and he bribed me to keep my mouth shut."

There was another long silence. 30

"Prison is an evil life," Brille continued, apparently discussing some irrelevant matter. "It makes a man contemplate all kinds of evil deeds."

He held out his hand and closed it.

"You know, comrades," he said. "I've got Hannetjie. I'll betray him tomorrow."

Everyone began talking at once.

"Forget it, brother. You'll get shot." 35

Brille laughed.

"I won't," he said. "That is what I mean about evil. I am a father of children and I saw today that Hannetjie is just a child and stupidly truthful. I'm going to punish him severely because we need a good warder."

The following day, with Brille as witness, Hannetjie confessed to the theft of the fertilizer and was fined a large sum of money. From then on Span One did very much as they pleased while Warder Hannetjie stood by and said nothing. But it was Brille who carried this to extremes. One day, at the close of work Warder Hannetjie said: "Brille, pick up my jacket and carry it back to the camp."

"But nothing in the regulations say I'm your servant, Hannetjie," Brille replied coolly.

"I've told you not to call me Hannetjie. You must say, 'Baas,'" but Warder 40 Hannetjie's voice lacked conviction. In turn, Brille squinted up at him.

"I'll tell you something about this Baas business, Hannetjie," he said. "One of these days we are going to run the country. You are going to clean my car. Now I have a fifteen-year-old son and I'd die of shame if you had to tell him that I ever called you Baas."

Warder Hannetjie went red in the face and picked up his coat.

On another occasion Brille was seen to be walking about the prison yard, openly smoking tobacco. On being taken before the prison commander he claimed to have received the tobacco from Warder Hannetjie. All throughout the tirade from his chief, Warder Hannetjie failed to defend himself but his nerve broke completely. He called Brille to one side.

"Brille," he said. "This thing between you and me must end. You may not know it but I have a wife and children and you're driving me to suicide."

"Why don't you like your own medicine, Hannetjie?" Brille asked quietly. 45

"I can give you anything you want," Warder Hannetjie said in desperation.

"It's not only me but the whole of Span One," said Brille, cunningly. "The whole of Span One wants something from you."

Warder Hannetjie brightened with relief.

"I tink I can manage if it's tobacco you want," he said.

Brille looked at him, for the first time struck with pity, and guilt. 50

He wondered if he had carried the whole business too far. The man was really a child.

"It's not tobacco we want, but you," he said. "We want you on our side. We want a good warder because without a good warder we won't be able to manage the long stretch ahead."

Warder Hannetjie interpreted this request in his own fashion and his interpretation of what was good and human often left the prisoners of Span One speechless with surprise. He had a way of slipping off his revolver and picking up a spade and digging alongside Span One. He had a way of producing unheard-of luxuries like boiled eggs from his farm nearby and things like cigarettes, and Span One responded nobly and got the reputation of being the best work span in the camp. And it wasn't only take from their side. They were awfully good at stealing certain commodities like fertilizer which were needed on the farm of Warder Hannetjie.

Connections to Other Selections

1. Discuss how the issue of race relations is presented in "The Prisoner Who Wore Glasses" and Ralph Ellison's "Battle Royal" (p. 187). Compare Brille's strategy of dealing with racial issues with the strategy suggested by the last words from the grandfather in "Battle Royal" (para. 2).
2. Compare Brille's character with Abner Snopes's in William Faulkner's "Barn Burning" (p. 436). How does each character cope with oppression?
3. Write an essay about the effect of the final sentence in Head's story and in Isabel Allende's "The Judge's Wife" (p. 495). How does the last sentence of each story affect your response to what has come before it?

YUKIO MISHIMA (Japanese/1925–1970)

Yukio Mishima is the pseudonym of Kimitake Hiraoka. He was born in Tokyo and educated at an elite private school and Tokyo Imperial University. Because he failed an army physical, he did not serve in World War II. After the war, he attended law school and worked for a short time at the Finance Ministry. *Confessions of a Mask*, his first novel, was published in 1949. He wrote poetry, stories, plays, novels, travel books, articles, and he translated a number of *No* dramas. Some of his best-known works in English translation are *Temple of the Golden Pavilion* (1956), *The Sailor Who Fell from Grace with the Sea* (1963), *The Sea of Fertility* (1975), and *Acts of Worship* (1989). In addition to writing, acting, singing, and modeling, he also became an expert in martial arts. Indeed, he formed his own private army. In 1970 he took over an army headquarters because he felt Japan was drifting too far from its classic samurai traditions. When his ultra-conservative demands were unmet by the government, he committed ritual suicide, *seppuku*. In "Patriotism" Mishima's devotion to ancient traditions and honor are strikingly evident.

Patriotism

TRANSLATED BY GEOFFREY W. SARGENT

I

On the twenty-eighth of February, 1936 (on the third day, that is, of the February 26 Incident°), Lieutenant Shinji Takeyama of the Konoe Transport Battalion — profoundly disturbed by the knowledge that his closest colleagues had been with the mutineers from the beginning, and indignant at the imminent prospect of Imperial troops attacking Imperial troops — took his officer's sword and ceremoniously disemboweled himself in the eight-mat room of his private residence in the sixth block of Aoba-chō, in Yotsuya Ward. His wife, Reiko, followed him, stabbing herself to death. The lieutenant's farewell note consisted of one sentence: "Long live the Imperial Forces." His wife's, after apologies for her unfilial conduct in thus preceding her parents to the grave, concluded: "The day which, for a soldier's wife, had to come, has come. . . ." The last moments of this heroic and dedicated couple were such as to make the gods themselves weep. The lieutenant's age, it should be noted, was thirty-one, his wife's twenty-three; and it was not half a year since the celebration of their marriage.

II

Those who saw the bride and bridegroom in the commemorative photograph — perhaps no less than those actually present at the lieutenant's wedding — had exclaimed in wonder at the bearing of this handsome couple. The lieutenant, majestic in military uniform, stood protectively beside his bride, his right hand resting upon his sword, his officer's cap held at his left side. His expression was severe, and his dark brows and wide-gazing eyes well conveyed the clear integrity of youth. For the beauty of the bride in her white over-robe no comparisons were adequate. In the eyes, round beneath soft brows, in the slender, finely shaped nose, and in the full lips, there was both sensuousness and refinement. One hand, emerging shyly from a sleeve of the over-robe, held a fan, and the tips of the fingers, clustering delicately, were like the bud of a moonflower.

After the suicide, people would take out this photograph and examine it, and sadly reflect that too often there was a curse on these seemingly flawless unions. Perhaps it was no more than imagination, but looking at the picture after the tragedy it almost seemed as if the two young people before the gold-lacquered screen were gazing, each with equal clarity, at the deaths which lay before them.

Thanks to the good offices of their go-between, Lieutenant General Ozeki, they had been able to set themselves up in a new home at Aoba-chō in Yotsuya. "New home" is perhaps misleading. It was an old three-room rented house backing onto a small garden. As neither the six- nor the four-and-a-half-mat room

Incident: When right-wing officers killed several moderate officials in an effort to establish a more militant Japan.

downstairs was favored by the sun, they used the upstairs eight-mat room as both bedroom and guest room. There was no maid, so Reiko was left alone to guard the house in her husband's absence.

The honeymoon trip was dispensed with on the grounds that these were 5 times of national emergency. The two of them had spent the first night of their marriage at this house. Before going to bed, Shinji, sitting erect on the floor with his sword laid before him, had bestowed upon his wife a soldierly lecture. A woman who had become the wife of a soldier should know and resolutely accept that her husband's death might come at any moment. It could be tomorrow. It could be the day after. But, no matter when it came — he asked — was she steadfast in her resolve to accept it? Reiko rose to her feet, pulled open a drawer of the cabinet, and took out what was the most prized of her new possessions, the dagger her mother had given her. Returning to her place, she laid the dagger without a word on the mat before her, just as her husband had laid his sword. A silent understanding was achieved at once, and the lieutenant never again sought to test his wife's resolve.

In the first few months of her marriage Reiko's beauty grew daily more radiant, shining serene like the moon after rain.

As both were possessed of young, vigorous bodies, their relationship was passionate. Nor was this merely a matter of the night. On more than one occasion, returning home straight from maneuvers, and begrudging even the time it took to remove his mud-splashed uniform, the lieutenant had pushed his wife to the floor almost as soon as he had entered the house. Reiko was equally ardent in her response. For a little more or a little less than a month, from the first night of their marriage Reiko knew happiness, and the lieutenant, seeing this, was happy too.

Reiko's body was white and pure, and her swelling breasts conveyed a firm and chaste refusal; but, upon consent, those breasts were lavish with their intimate, welcoming warmth. Even in bed these two were frighteningly and awesomely serious. In the very midst of wild, intoxicating passions, their hearts were sober and serious.

By day the lieutenant would think of his wife in the brief rest periods between training; and all day long, at home, Reiko would recall the image of her husband. Even when apart, however, they had only to look at the wedding photograph for their happiness to be once more confirmed. Reiko felt not the slightest surprise that a man who had been a complete stranger until a few months ago should now have become the sun about which her whole world revolved.

All these things had a moral basis, and were in accordance with the Edu- 10 cation Rescript's injunction that "husband and wife should be harmonious." Not once did Reiko contradict her husband, nor did the lieutenant ever find reason to scold his wife. On the god shelf below the stairway, alongside the tablet from the Great Ise Shrine, were set photographs of their Imperial Majesties, and regularly every morning, before leaving for duty, the lieutenant would stand with his wife at this hallowed place and together they would bow their heads low. The offering water was renewed each morning, and the sacred sprig of *sasaki* was always green and fresh. Their lives were lived beneath the solemn protection of the gods and were filled with an intense happiness, which set every fiber in their bodies trembling.

Although Lord Privy Seal Saitō's house was in their neighborhood, neither of them heard any noise of gunfire on the morning of February 26. It was a bugle, sounding muster in the dim, snowy dawn, when the ten-minute tragedy had already ended, which first disrupted the lieutenant's slumbers. Leaping at once from his bed, and without speaking a word, the lieutenant donned his uniform, buckled on the sword held ready for him by his wife, and hurried swiftly out into the snow-covered streets of the still darkened morning. He did not return until the evening of the twenty-eighth.

Later, from the radio news, Reiko learned the full extent of this sudden eruption of violence. Her life throughout the subsequent two days was lived alone, in complete tranquillity, and behind locked doors.

In the lieutenant's face, as he hurried silently out into the snowy morning, Reiko had read the determination to die. If her husband did not return, her own decision was made: she too would die. Quietly she attended to the disposition of her personal possessions. She chose her sets of visiting kimonos as keepsakes for friends of her schooldays, and she wrote a name and address on the stiff paper wrapping in which each was folded. Constantly admonished by her husband never to think of the morrow, Reiko had not even kept a diary and was now denied the pleasure of assiduously rereading her record of the happiness of the past few months and consigning each page to the fire as she did so. Ranged across the top of the radio were a small china dog, a rabbit, a squirrel, a bear, and a fox. There were also a small vase and a water pitcher. These comprised Reiko's one and only collection. But it would hardly do, she imagined, to give such things as keepsakes. Nor again would it be quite proper to ask specifically for them to be included in the coffin. It seemed to Reiko, as these thoughts passed through her mind, that the expression on the small animals' faces grew even more lost and forlorn.

Reiko took the squirrel in her hand and looked at it. And then, her thoughts turning to a realm far beyond these childlike affections, she gazed up into the distance at the great sunlike principle which her husband embodied. She was ready, and happy, to be hurtled along to her destruction in that gleaming sun chariot — but now, for these few moments of solitude, she allowed herself to luxuriate in this innocent attachment to trifles. The time when she had genuinely loved these things, however, was long past. Now she merely loved the memory of having once loved them, and their place in her heart had been filled by more intense passions, by a more frenzied happiness. . . . For Reiko had never, even to herself, thought of those soaring joys of the flesh as a mere pleasure. The February cold, and the icy touch of the china squirrel, had numbed Reiko's slender fingers; yet, even so, in her lower limbs, beneath the ordered repetition of the pattern which crossed the skirt of her trim *meisen* kimono, she could feel now, as she thought of the lieutenant's powerful arms reaching out toward her, a hot moistness of the flesh which defied the snows.

She was not in the least afraid of the death hovering in her mind. Waiting alone at home, Reiko firmly believed that everything her husband was feeling or thinking now, his anguish and distress, was leading her — just as surely as the power in his flesh — to a welcome death. She felt as if her body could melt away with ease and be transformed to the merest fraction of her husband's thought.

Listening to the frequent announcements on the radio, she heard the names of several of her husband's colleagues mentioned among those of the insurgents. This was news of death. She followed the developments closely, wondering anxiously, as the situation became daily more irrevocable, why no Imperial ordinance was sent down, and watching what had at first been taken as a movement to restore the nation's honor come gradually to be branded with the infamous name of mutiny. There was no communication from the regiment. At any moment, it seemed, fighting might commence in the city streets, where the remains of the snow still lay.

Toward sundown on the twenty-eighth Reiko was startled by a furious pounding on the front door. She hurried downstairs. As she pulled with fumbling fingers at the bolt, the shape dimly outlined beyond the frosted-glass panel made no sound, but she knew it was her husband. Reiko had never known the bolt on the sliding door to be so stiff. Still it resisted. The door just would not open.

In a moment, almost before she knew she had succeeded, the lieutenant was standing before her on the cement floor inside the porch, muffled in a khaki greatcoat, his top boots heavy with slush from the street. Closing the door behind him, he returned the bolt once more to its socket. With what significance, Reiko did not understand.

"Welcome home."

Reiko bowed deeply, but her husband made no response. As he had already 20 unfastened his sword and was about to remove his greatcoat, Reiko moved around behind to assist. The coat, which was cold and damp and had lost the odor of horse dung it normally exuded when exposed to the sun, weighed heavily upon her arm. Draping it across a hanger, and cradling the sword and leather belt in her sleeves, she waited while her husband removed his top boots and then followed behind him into the "living room." This was the six-mat room downstairs.

Seen in the clear light from the lamp, her husband's face, covered with a heavy growth of bristle, was almost unrecognizably wasted and thin. The cheeks were hollow, their luster and resilience gone. In his normal good spirits he would have changed into old clothes as soon as he was home and have pressed her to get supper at once, but now he sat before the table still in his uniform, his head drooping dejectedly. Reiko refrained from asking whether she should prepare the supper.

After an interval the lieutenant spoke.

"I knew nothing. They hadn't asked me to join. Perhaps out of consideration, because I was newly married. Kanō, and Homma too, and Yamaguchi."

Reiko recalled momentarily the faces of high-spirited young officers, friends of her husband, who had come to the house occasionally as guests.

"There may be an Imperial ordinance sent down tomorrow. They'll be 25 posted as rebels, I imagine. I shall be in command of a unit with orders to attack them. . . . I can't do it. It's impossible to do a thing like that."

He spoke again.

"They've taken me off guard duty, and I have permission to return home for one night. Tomorrow morning, without question, I must leave to join the attack. I can't do it, Reiko."

Reiko sat erect with lowered eyes. She understood clearly that her husband had spoken of his death. The lieutenant was resolved. Each word, being rooted in death, emerged sharply and with powerful significance against this dark, unmovable background. Although the lieutenant was speaking of his dilemma, already there was no room in his mind for vacillation.

However, there was a clarity, like the clarity of a stream fed from melting snows, in the silence which rested between them. Sitting in his own home after the long two-day ordeal, and looking across at the face of his beautiful wife, the lieutenant was for the first time experiencing true peace of mind. For he had at once known, though she said nothing, that his wife divined the resolve which lay beneath his words.

"Well, then . . ." The lieutenant's eyes opened wide. Despite his exhaustion ₃₀ they were strong and clear, and now for the first time they looked straight into the eyes of his wife. "Tonight I shall cut my stomach."

Reiko did not flinch.

Her round eyes showed tension, as taut as the clang of a bell.

"I am ready," she said. "I ask permission to accompany you."

The lieutenant felt almost mesmerized by the strength of those eyes. His words flowed swiftly and easily, like the utterances of a man in delirium, and it was beyond his understanding how permission in a matter of such weight could be expressed so casually.

"Good. We'll go together. But I want you as a witness, first, for my own ₃₅ suicide. Agreed?"

When this was said a sudden release of abundant happiness welled up in both their hearts. Reiko was deeply affected by the greatness of her husband's trust in her. It was vital for the lieutenant, whatever else might happen, that there should be no irregularity in his death. For that reason there had to be a witness. The fact that he had chosen his wife for this was the first mark of his trust. The second, and even greater mark, was that though he had pledged that they should die together he did not intend to kill his wife first — he had deferred her death to a time when he would no longer be there to verify it. If the lieutenant had been a suspicious husband, he would doubtless, as in the usual suicide pact, have chosen to kill his wife first.

When Reiko said, "I ask permission to accompany you," the lieutenant felt these words to be the final fruit of the education which he had himself given his wife, starting on the first night of their marriage, and which had schooled her, when the moment came, to say what had to be said without a shadow of hesitation. This flattered the lieutenant's opinion of himself as a self-reliant man. He was not so romantic or conceited as to imagine that the words were spoken spontaneously, out of love for her husband.

With happiness welling almost too abundantly in their hearts, they could not help smiling at each other. Reiko felt as if she had returned to her wedding night.

Before her eyes was neither pain nor death. She seemed to see only a free and limitless expanse opening out into vast distances.

"The water is hot. Will you take your bath now?"   ₄₀

"Ah yes, of course."

"And supper . . . ?"

The words were delivered in such level, domestic tones that the lieutenant came near to thinking, for the fraction of a second, that everything had been a hallucination.

"I don't think we'll need supper. But perhaps you could warm some sake?"

"As you wish." 45

As Reiko rose and took a *tanzen* gown from the cabinet for after the bath, she purposely directed her husband's attention to the opened drawer. The lieutenant rose, crossed to the cabinet, and looked inside. From the ordered array of paper wrappings he read, one by one, the addresses of the keepsakes. There was no grief in the lieutenant's response to this demonstration of heroic resolve. His heart was filled with tenderness. Like a husband who is proudly shown the childish purchases of a young wife, the lieutenant, overwhelmed by affection, lovingly embraced his wife from behind and implanted a kiss upon her neck.

Reiko felt the roughness of the lieutenant's unshaven skin against her neck. This sensation, more than being just a thing of this world, was for Reiko almost the world itself, but now — with the feeling that it was soon to be lost forever — it had freshness beyond all her experience. Each moment had its own vital strength, and the senses in every corner of her body were reawakened. Accepting her husband's caresses from behind, Reiko raised herself on the tips of her toes, letting the vitality seep through her entire body.

"First the bath, and then, after some sake . . . lay out the bedding upstairs, will you?"

The lieutenant whispered the words into his wife's ear. Reiko silently nodded.

Flinging off his uniform, the lieutenant went to the bath. To faint background 50 noises of slopping water Reiko tended the charcoal brazier in the living room and began the preparations for warming the sake.

Taking the *tanzen,* a sash, and some underclothes, she went to the bathroom to ask how the water was. In the midst of a coiling cloud of steam the lieutenant was sitting cross-legged on the floor, shaving, and she could dimly discern the rippling movements of the muscles on his damp, powerful back as they responded to the movement of his arms.

There was nothing to suggest a time of any special significance. Reiko, going busily about her tasks, was preparing side dishes from odds and ends in stock. Her hands did not tremble. If anything, she managed even more efficiently and smoothly than usual. From time to time, it is true, there was a strange throbbing deep within her breast. Like distant lightning, it had a moment of sharp intensity and then vanished without trace. Apart from that, nothing was in any way out of the ordinary.

The lieutenant, shaving in the bathroom, felt his warmed body miraculously healed at last of the desperate tiredness of the days of indecision and filled — in spite of the death which lay ahead — with pleasurable anticipation. The sound of his wife going about her work came to him faintly. A healthy physical craving, submerged for two days, reasserted itself.

The lieutenant was confident there had been no impurity in that joy they had experienced when resolving upon death. They had both sensed at that moment — though not, of course, in any clear and conscious way — that those permissible pleasures which they shared in private were once more beneath the protection of Righteousness and Divine Power, and of a complete and unassailable morality. On looking into each other's eyes and discovering there an honorable death, they had felt themselves safe once more behind steel walls which none could destroy, encased in an impenetrable armor of Beauty and Truth. Thus, so far from seeing any inconsistency or conflict between the urges of his flesh and the sincerity of his patriotism, the lieutenant was even able to regard the two as parts of the same thing.

Thrusting his face close to the dark, cracked, misted wall mirror, the lieu- 55 tenant shaved himself with great care. This would be his death face. There must be no unsightly blemishes. The clean-shaven face gleamed once more with a youthful luster, seeming to brighten the darkness of the mirror. There was a certain elegance, he even felt, in the association of death with this radiantly healthy face.

Just as it looked now, this would become his death face! Already, in fact, it had half departed from the lieutenant's personal possession and had become the bust above a dead soldier's memorial. As an experiment he closed his eyes tight. Everything was wrapped in blackness, and he was no longer a living, seeing creature.

Returning from the bath, the traces of the shave glowing faintly blue beneath his smooth cheeks, he seated himself beside the now well-kindled charcoal brazier. Busy though Reiko was, he noticed, she had found time lightly to touch up her face. Her cheeks were gay and her lips moist. There was no shadow of sadness to be seen. Truly, the lieutenant felt, as he saw this mark of his young wife's passionate nature, he had chosen the wife he ought to have chosen.

As soon as the lieutenant had drained his sake cup he offered it to Reiko. Reiko had never before tasted sake, but she accepted without hesitation and sipped timidly.

"Come here," the lieutenant said.

Reiko moved to her husband's side and was embraced as she leaned back- 60 ward across his lap. Her breast was in violent commotion, as if sadness, joy, and the potent sake were mingling and reacting within her. The lieutenant looked down into his wife's face. It was the last face he would see in this world, the last face he would see of his wife. The lieutenant scrutinized the face minutely, with the eyes of a traveler bidding farewell to splendid vistas which he will never revisit. It was a face he could not tire of looking at — the features regular yet not cold, the lips lightly closed with a soft strength. The lieutenant kissed those lips, unthinkingly. And suddenly, though there was not the slightest distortion of the face into the unsightliness of sobbing, he noticed that tears were welling slowly from beneath the long lashes of the closed eyes and brimming over into the glistening stream.

When, a little later, the lieutenant urged that they should move to the upstairs bedroom, his wife replied that she would follow after taking a bath. Climbing the stairs alone to the bedroom, where the air was already warmed by the gas heater, the lieutenant lay down on the bedding with arms outstretched and legs apart. Even the time at which he lay waiting for his wife to join him was no later and no earlier than usual.

He folded his hands beneath his head and gazed at the dark boards of the ceiling in the dimness beyond the range of the standard lamp. Was it death he was now waiting for? Or a wild ecstasy of the senses? The two seemed to over-lap, almost as if the object of this bodily desire was death itself. But, however that might be, it was certain that never before had the lieutenant tasted such total freedom.

There was the sound of a car outside the window. He could hear the screech of its tires skidding in the snow piled at the side of the street. The sound of its horn reechoed from nearby walls. . . . Listening to these noises he had the feeling that the house rose like a solitary island in the ocean of a society going as restlessly about its business as ever. All around, vastly and untidily, stretched the country for which he grieved. He was to give his life for it. But would that great country, with which he was prepared to remonstrate to the extent of destroying himself, take the slightest heed of his death? He did not know; and it did not matter. His was a battlefield without glory, a battlefield where none could display deeds of valor: it was the front line of the spirit.

Reiko's footsteps sounded on the stairway. The steep stairs in this old house creaked badly. There were fond memories in that creaking, and many a time, while waiting in bed, the lieutenant had listened to its welcome sound. At the thought that he would hear it no more he listened with intense concentration, striving for every corner of every moment of this precious time to be filled with the sound of those soft footfalls on the creaking stairway. The moments seemed transformed to jewels, sparkling with inner light.

Reiko wore a Nagoya sash about the waist of her *yukata,* but as the lieutenant 65 reached toward it, its redness sobered by the dimness of the light, Reiko's hand moved to his assistance and the sash fell away, slithering swiftly to the floor. As she stood before him, still in her *yukata,* the lieutenant inserted his hands through the side slits beneath each sleeve, intending to embrace her as she was; but at the touch of his finger tips upon the warm naked flesh, and as the armpits closed gently about his hands, his whole body was suddenly aflame.

In a few moments the two lay naked before the glowing gas heater.

Neither spoke the thought, but their hearts, their bodies, and their pounding breasts blazed with the knowledge that this was the very last time. It was as if the words "The Last Time" were spelled out, in invisible brushstrokes, across every inch of their bodies.

The lieutenant drew his wife close and kissed her vehemently. As their tongues explored each other's mouths, reaching out into the smooth, moist interior, they felt as if the still-unknown agonies of death had tempered their senses to the keenness of red-hot steel. The agonies they could not yet feel, the distant pains of death, had refined their awareness of pleasure.

"This is the last time I shall see your body," said the lieutenant. "Let me look at it closely." And, tilting the shade on the lampstand to one side, he directed the rays along the full length of Reiko's outstretched form.

Reiko lay still with her eyes closed. The light from the low lamp clearly 70 revealed the majestic sweep of her white flesh. The lieutenant, not without a touch of egocentricity, rejoiced that he would never see this beauty crumble in death.

At his leisure, the lieutenant allowed the unforgettable spectacle to engrave itself upon his mind. With one hand he fondled the hair, with the other he softly stroked the magnificent face, implanting kisses here and there where his eyes lingered. The quiet coldness of the high, tapering forehead, the closed eyes with their long lashes beneath faintly etched brows, the set of the finely shaped nose, the gleam of teeth glimpsed between full, regular lips, the soft cheeks and the small, wise chin . . . these things conjured up in the lieutenant's mind the vision of a truly radiant death face, and again and again he pressed his lips tight against the white throat — where Reiko's own hand was soon to strike — and the throat reddened faintly beneath his kisses. Returning to the mouth he laid his lips against it with the gentlest of pressures, and moved them rhythmically over Reiko's with the light rolling motion of a small boat. If he closed his eyes, the world became a rocking cradle.

Wherever the lieutenant's eyes moved his lips faithfully followed. The high, swelling breasts, surmounted by nipples like the buds of a wild cherry, hardened as the lieutenant's lips closed about them. The arms flowed smoothly downward from each side of the breast, tapering toward the wrists, yet losing nothing of their roundness or symmetry, and at their tips were those delicate fingers which had held the fan at the wedding ceremony. One by one, as the lieutenant kissed them, the fingers withdrew behind their neighbor as if in shame. . . . The natural hollow curving between the bosom and the stomach carried in its lines a suggestion not only of softness but of resilient strength, and while it gave forewarning of the rich curves spreading outward from here to the hips it had, in itself, an appearance only of restraint and proper discipline. The whiteness and richness of the stomach and hips was like milk brimming in a great bowl, and the sharply shadowed dip of the navel could have been the fresh impress of a raindrop, fallen there that very moment. Where the shadows gathered more thickly, hair clustered, gentle and sensitive, and as the agitation mounted in the now no longer passive body there hung over this region a scent like the smoldering of fragrant blossoms, growing steadily more pervasive.

At length, in a tremendous voice, Reiko spoke.

"Show me. . . . Let me look too, for the last time."

Never before had he heard from his wife's lips so strong and unequivocal a request. It was as if something which her modesty had wished to keep hidden to the end had suddenly burst its bonds of constraint. The lieutenant obediently lay back and surrendered himself to his wife. Lithely she raised her white, trembling body, and — burning with an innocent desire to return to her husband what he had done for her — placed two white fingers on the lieutenant's eyes, which gazed fixedly up at her, and gently stroked them shut.

Suddenly overwhelmed by tenderness, her cheeks flushed by a dizzying uprush of emotion, Reiko threw her arms about the lieutenant's close-cropped head. The bristly hairs rubbed painfully against her breast, the prominent nose was cold as it dug into her flesh, and his breath was hot. Relaxing her embrace, she gazed down at her husband's masculine face. The severe brows, the closed eyes, the splendid bridge of the nose, the shapely lips drawn firmly together . . . the blue, clean-shaven cheeks reflecting the light and gleaming smoothly. Reiko kissed each of these. She kissed the broad nape of the neck, the strong, erect shoulders, the powerful chest with its twin circles like shields and its russet nipples. In the armpits, deeply shadowed by the ample flesh of the shoulders and chest, a sweet and melancholy odor emanated from the growth of hair, and in the sweetness of this odor was contained, somehow, the essence of young death. The lieutenant's naked skin glowed like a field of barley, and everywhere the muscles showed in sharp relief, converging on the lower abdomen about the small, unassuming navel. Gazing at the youthful, firm stomach, modestly covered by a vigorous growth of hair, Reiko thought of it as it was soon to be, cruelly cut by the sword, and she laid her head upon it, sobbing in pity, and bathed it with kisses.

At the touch of his wife's tears upon his stomach the lieutenant felt ready to endure with courage the cruelest agonies of his suicide.

What ecstasies they experienced after these tender exchanges may well be imagined. The lieutenant raised himself and enfolded his wife in a powerful embrace, her body now limp with exhaustion after her grief and tears. Passionately they held their faces close, rubbing cheek against cheek. Reiko's body was trembling. Their breasts, moist with sweat, were tightly joined, and every inch of the young and beautiful bodies had become so much one with the other that it seemed impossible there should ever again be a separation. Reiko cried out. From the heights they plunged into the abyss, and from the abyss they took wing and soared once more to dizzying heights. The lieutenant panted like the regimental standard-bearer on a route march. . . . As one cycle ended, almost immediately a new wave of passion would be generated, and together — with no trace of fatigue — they would climb again in a single breathless movement to the very summit.

IV

When the lieutenant at last turned away, it was not from weariness. For one thing, he was anxious not to undermine the considerable strength he would need in carrying out his suicide. For another, he would have been sorry to mar the sweetness of these last memories by overindulgence.

Since the lieutenant had clearly desisted, Reiko too, with her usual compliance, followed his example. The two lay naked on their backs, with fingers interlaced, staring fixedly at the dark ceiling. The room was warm from the heater, and even when the sweat had ceased to pour from their bodies they felt no cold. Outside, in the hushed night, the sounds of passing traffic had ceased. Even the noises of the trains and streetcars around Yotsuya station did not penetrate this far. After echoing through the region bounded by the moat, they were lost in the heavily wooded park fronting the broad driveway before Akasaka Palace. It was hard to believe in the tension gripping this whole quarter, where the two factions of the bitterly divided Imperial Army now confronted each other, poised for battle.

Savoring the warmth glowing within themselves, they lay still and recalled the ecstasies they had just known. Each moment of the experience was relived. They remembered the taste of kisses which had never wearied, the touch of naked flesh, episode after episode of dizzying bliss. But already, from the dark boards of the ceiling, the face of death was peering down. These joys had been final, and their bodies would never know them again. Not that joy of this intensity — and the same thought had occurred to them both — was ever likely to be reexperienced, even if they should live on to old age.

The feel of their fingers intertwined — this too would soon be lost. Even the wood-grain patterns they now gazed at on the dark ceiling boards would be taken from them. They could feel death edging in, nearer and nearer. There could be no hesitation now. They must have the courage to reach out to death themselves, and to seize it.

"Well, let's make our preparations," said the lieutenant. The note of determination in the words was unmistakable, but at the same time Reiko had never heard her husband's voice so warm and tender.

After they had risen, a variety of tasks awaited them.

The lieutenant, who had never once before helped with the bedding, now 85 cheerfully slid back the door of the closet, lifted the mattress across the room by himself, and stowed it away inside.

Reiko turned off the gas heater and put away the lamp standard. During the lieutenant's absence she had arranged this room carefully, sweeping and dusting it to a fresh cleanness, and now — if one overlooked the rosewood table drawn into one corner — the eight-mat room gave all the appearance of a reception room ready to welcome an important guest.

"We've seen some drinking here, haven't we? With Kanō and Homma and Noguchi . . ."

"Yes, they were great drinkers, all of them."

"We'll be meeting them before long, in the other world. They'll tease us, I imagine, when they find I've brought you with me."

Descending the stairs, the lieutenant turned to look back into this calm, 90 clean room, now brightly illuminated by the ceiling lamp. There floated across his mind the faces of the young officers who had drunk there, and laughed, and innocently bragged. He had never dreamed then that he would one day cut open his stomach in this room.

In the two rooms downstairs husband and wife busied themselves smoothly and serenely with their respective preparations. The lieutenant went to the toilet, and then to the bathroom to wash. Meanwhile Reiko folded away her husband's padded robe, placed his uniform tunic, his trousers, and a newly cut bleached loincloth in the bathroom, and set out sheets of paper on the living-room table for the farewell notes. Then she removed the lid from the writing box and began rubbing ink from the ink tablet. She had already decided upon the wording of her own note.

Reiko's fingers pressed hard upon the cold gilt letters of the ink tablet, and the water in the shallow well at once darkened, as if a black cloud had spread across it. She stopped thinking that this repeated action, this pressure from her fingers, this rise and fall of faint sound, was all and solely for death. It was a routine domestic task, a simple paring away of time until death should finally stand before her. But somehow, in the increasingly smooth motion of the tablet rubbing on the stone, and in the scent from the thickening ink, there was unspeakable darkness.

Neat in his uniform, which he now wore next to his skin, the lieutenant emerged from the bathroom. Without a word he seated himself at the table, bolt upright, took a brush in his hand, and stared undecidedly at the paper before him.

Reiko took a white silk kimono with her and entered the bathroom. When she reappeared in the living room, clad in the white kimono and with her face lightly made up, the farewell note lay completed on the table beneath the lamp. The thick black brushstrokes said simply:

"Long Live the Imperial Forces — Army Lieutenant Takeyama Shinji." 95

While Reiko sat opposite him writing her own note, the lieutenant gazed in silence, intensely serious, at the controlled movement of his wife's pale fingers as they manipulated the brush.

With their respective notes in their hands — the lieutenant's sword strapped to his side, Reiko's small dagger thrust into the sash of her white kimono — the two of them stood before the god shelf and silently prayed. Then they put out all the downstairs lights. As he mounted the stairs the lieutenant turned his head and gazed back at the striking, white-clad figure of his wife, climbing behind him, with lowered eyes, from the darkness beneath.

The farewell notes were laid side by side in the alcove of the upstairs room. They wondered whether they ought not to remove the hanging scroll, but since it had been written by their go-between, Lieutenant General Ozeki, and consisted, moreover, of two Chinese characters signifying "Sincerity," they left it where it was. Even if it were to become stained with splashes of blood, they felt that the lieutenant general would understand.

The lieutenant, sitting erect with his back to the alcove, laid his sword on the floor before him.

Reiko sat facing him, a mat's width away. With the rest of her so severely 100 white the touch of rouge on her lips seemed remarkably seductive.

Across the dividing mat they gazed intently into each other's eyes. The lieutenant's sword lay before his knees. Seeing it, Reiko recalled their first night and was overwhelmed with sadness. The lieutenant spoke, in a hoarse voice:

"As I have no second to help me I shall cut deep. It may look unpleasant, but please do not panic. Death of any sort is a fearful thing to watch. You must not be discouraged by what you see. Is that all right?"

"Yes."

Reiko nodded deeply.

Looking at the slender white figure of his wife the lieutenant experienced 105 a bizarre excitement. What he was about to perform was an act in his public capacity as a soldier, something he had never previously shown his wife. It called for a resolution equal to the courage to enter battle; it was a death of no less degree and quality than death in the front line. It was his conduct on the battlefield that he was now to display.

Momentarily the thought led the lieutenant to a strange fantasy. A lonely death on the battlefield, a death beneath the eyes of his beautiful wife . . . in the sensation that he was now to die in these two dimensions, realizing an impossible union of them both, there was sweetness beyond words. This must be the very pinnacle of good fortune, he thought. To have every moment of his death observed by those beautiful eyes — it was like being borne to death on a gentle, fragrant breeze. There was some special favor here. He did not understand precisely what it was, but it was a domain unknown to others: a dispensation granted to no one else had been permitted to himself. In the radiant, bridelike figure of his white-robed wife the lieutenant seemed to see a vision of all those things he had loved and for which he was to lay down his life — the Imperial Household, the Nation, the Army Flag. All these, no less than the wife who sat before him, were presences observing him closely with clear and never-faltering eyes.

Reiko too was gazing intently at her husband, so soon to die, and she thought that never in this world had she seen anything so beautiful. The lieutenant always looked well in uniform, but now, as he contemplated death with severe brows and firmly closed lips, he revealed what was perhaps masculine beauty at its most superb.

"It's time to go," the lieutenant said at last.

Reiko bent her body low to the mat in a deep bow. She could not raise her face. She did not wish to spoil her makeup with tears, but the tears could not be held back.

When at length she looked up she saw hazily through the tears that her 110 husband had wound a white bandage around the blade of his now unsheathed sword, leaving five or six inches of naked steel showing at the point.

Resting the sword in its cloth wrapping on the mat before him, the lieutenant rose from his knees, resettled himself cross-legged, and unfastened the hooks of his uniform collar. His eyes no longer saw his wife. Slowly, one by one, he undid the flat brass buttons. The dusky brown chest was revealed, and then the stomach. He unclasped his belt and undid the buttons of his trousers. The pure whiteness of the thickly coiled loincloth showed itself. The lieutenant pushed the cloth down with both hands, further to ease his stomach, and then reached for the white-bandaged blade of his sword. With his left hand he massaged his abdomen, glancing downward as he did so.

To reassure himself on the sharpness of his sword's cutting edge the lieutenant folded back the left trouser flap, exposing a little of his thigh, and lightly drew the blade across the skin. Blood welled up in the wound at once, and several streaks of red trickled downward, glistening in the strong light.

It was the first time Reiko had ever seen her husband's blood, and she felt a violent throbbing in her chest. She looked at her husband's face. The lieutenant was looking at the blood with calm appraisal. For a moment — though thinking at the same time that it was hollow comfort — Reiko experienced a sense of relief.

The lieutenant's eyes fixed his wife with an intense, hawklike stare. Moving the sword around to his front, he raised himself slightly on his hips and let the upper half of his body lean over the sword point. That he was mustering his whole strength was apparent from the angry tension of the uniform at his shoulders. The lieutenant aimed to strike deep into the left of his stomach. His sharp eye pierced the silence of the room.

Despite the effort he had himself put into the blow, the lieutenant had the 115 impression that someone else had struck the side of his stomach agonizingly with a thick rod of iron. For a second or so his head reeled and he had no idea what had happened. The five or six inches of naked point had vanished completely into his flesh, and the white bandage, gripped in his clenched fist, pressed directly against his stomach.

He returned to consciousness. The blade had certainly pierced the wall of the stomach, he thought. His breathing was difficult, his chest thumped violently, and in some far deep region, which he could hardly believe was a part of himself, a fearful and excruciating pain came welling up as if the ground had split open to disgorge a boiling stream of molten rock. The pain came suddenly nearer, with terrifying speed. The lieutenant bit his lower lip and stifled an instinctive moan.

Was this *seppuku?* — he was thinking. It was a sensation of utter chaos, as if the sky had fallen on his head and the world was reeling drunkenly. His will power and courage, which had seemed so robust before he made the incision, had now dwindled to something like a single hairlike thread of steel, and he was assailed by the uneasy feeling that he must advance along this thread, clinging to it with desperation. His clenched fist had grown moist. Looking down, he saw that both his hand and the cloth about the blade were drenched in blood. His loincloth too was dyed a deep red. It struck him as incredible that, amidst this terrible agony, things which could be seen could still be seen, and existing things existed still.

The moment the lieutenant thrust the sword into his left side and she saw the deathly pallor fall across his face, like an abruptly lowered curtain, Reiko had to struggle to prevent herself from rushing to his side. Whatever happened, she must watch. She must be a witness. That was the duty her husband had laid upon her. Opposite her, a mat's space away, she could clearly see her husband biting his lip to stifle the pain. The pain was there, with absolute certainty, before her eyes. And Reiko had no means of rescuing him from it.

The sweat glistened on her husband's forehead. The lieutenant closed his eyes, and then opened them again, as if experimenting. The eyes had lost their luster, and seemed innocent and empty like the eyes of a small animal.

The agony before Reiko's eyes burned as strong as the summer sun, utterly 120 remote from the grief which seemed to be tearing herself apart within. The pain grew steadily in stature, stretching upward. Reiko felt that her husband had already become a man in a separate world, a man whose whole being had been resolved into pain, a prisoner in a cage of pain where no hand could reach out to him. But Reiko felt no pain at all. Her grief was not pain. As she thought about this, Reiko began to feel as if someone had raised a cruel wall of glass high between herself and her husband.

Ever since her marriage her husband's existence had been her own existence, and every breath of his had been a breath drawn by herself. But now, while her husband's existence in pain was a vivid reality, Reiko could find in this grief of hers no certain proof at all of her own existence.

With only his right hand on the sword the lieutenant began to cut sideways across his stomach. But as the blade became entangled with the entrails it was pushed constantly outward by their soft resilience; and the lieutenant realized that it would be necessary, as he cut, to use both hands to keep the point pressed deep into his stomach. He pulled the blade across. It did not cut as easily as he had expected. He directed the strength of his whole body into his right hand and pulled again. There was a cut of three or four inches.

The pain spread slowly outward from the inner depths until the whole stomach reverberated. It was like the wild clanging of a bell. Or like a thousand bells which jangled simultaneously at every breath he breathed and every throb of his pulse, rocking his whole being. The lieutenant could no longer stop himself from moaning. But by now the blade had cut its way through to below the navel, and when he noticed this he felt a sense of satisfaction, and a renewal of courage.

The volume of blood had steadily increased, and now it spurted from the wound as if propelled by the beat of the pulse. The mat before the lieutenant was drenched red with splattered blood, and more blood overflowed onto it from pools which gathered in the folds of the lieutenant's khaki trousers. A spot, like a bird, came flying across to Reiko and settled on the lap of her white kimono.

By the time the lieutenant had at last drawn the sword across to the right 125 side of his stomach, the blade was already cutting shallow and had revealed its naked tip, slippery with blood and grease. But, suddenly stricken by a fit of vomiting, the lieutenant cried out hoarsely. The vomiting made the fierce pain fiercer still, and the stomach, which had thus far remained firm and compact, now abruptly heaved, opening wide its wound, and the entrails burst through, as if the wound too were vomiting. Seemingly ignorant of their master's suffering, the entrails gave an impression of robust health and almost disagreeable vitality as they slipped smoothly out and spilled over into the crotch. The lieutenant's head drooped, his shoulders heaved, his eyes opened to narrow slits, and a thin trickle of saliva dribbled from his mouth. The gold markings on his epaulets caught the light and glinted.

Blood was scattered everywhere. The lieutenant was soaked in it to his knees, and he sat now in a crumpled and listless posture, one hand on the floor. A raw smell filled the room. The lieutenant, his head drooping, retched repeatedly, and the movement showed vividly in his shoulders. The blade of the sword, now pushed back by the entrails and exposed to its tip, was still in the lieutenant's right hand.

It would be difficult to imagine a more heroic sight than that of the lieutenant at this moment, as he mustered his strength and flung back his head. The movement was performed with sudden violence, and the back of his head struck with a sharp crack against the alcove pillar. Reiko had been sitting until now with her face lowered, gazing in fascination at the tide of blood advancing toward her knees, but the sound took her by surprise and she looked up.

The lieutenant's face was not the face of a living man. The eyes were hollow, the skin parched, the once so lustrous cheeks and lips the color of dried mud. The right hand alone was moving. Laboriously gripping the sword, it hovered shakily in the air like the hand of a marionette and strove to direct the point at the base of the lieutenant's throat. Reiko watched her husband make this last, most heartrending, futile exertion. Glistening with blood and grease, the point was thrust at the throat again and again. And each time it missed its aim. The strength to guide it was no longer there. The straying point struck the collar and the collar badges. Although its hooks had been unfastened, the stiff military collar had closed together again and was protecting the throat.

Reiko could bear the sight no longer. She tried to go to her husband's help, but she could not stand. She moved through the blood on her knees, and her white skirts grew deep red. Moving to the rear of her husband, she helped no more than by loosening the collar. The quivering blade at last contacted the naked flesh of the throat. At that moment Reiko's impression was that she herself had propelled her husband forward; but that was not the case. It was a movement planned by the lieutenant himself, his last exertion of strength. Abruptly he threw his body at the blade, and the blade pierced his neck, emerging at the nape. There was a tremendous spurt of blood and the lieutenant lay still, cold blue-tinged steel protruding from his neck at the back.

Slowly, her socks slippery with blood, Reiko descended the stairway. The 130
upstairs room was now completely still.

Switching on the ground-floor lights, she checked the gas jet and the main
gas plug and poured water over the smoldering, half-buried charcoal in the
brazier. She stood before the upright mirror in the four-and-a-half mat room
and held up her skirts. The bloodstains made it seem as if a bold, vivid pattern
was printed across the lower half of her white kimono. When she sat down
before the mirror, she was conscious of the dampness and coldness of her
husband's blood in the region of her thighs, and she shivered. Then, for a long
while, she lingered over her toilet preparations. She applied the rouge generously to her cheeks, and her lips too she painted heavily. This was no longer
makeup to please her husband. It was makeup for the world which she would
leave behind, and there was a touch of the magnificent and the spectacular in
her brushwork. When she rose, the mat before the mirror was wet with blood.
Reiko was not concerned about this.

Returning from the toilet, Reiko stood finally on the cement floor of the
porchway. When her husband had bolted the door here last night it had been
in preparation for death. For a while she stood immersed in the consideration
of a simple problem. Should she now leave the bolt drawn? If she were to lock
the door, it could be that the neighbors might not notice their suicide for several
days. Reiko did not relish the thought of their two corpses putrefying before
discovery. After all, it seemed, it would be best to leave it open. . . . She released
the bolt, and also drew open the frosted-glass door a fraction. . . . At once a
chill wind blew in. There was no sign of anyone in the midnight streets, and
stars glittered ice-cold through the trees in the large house opposite.

Leaving the door as it was, Reiko mounted the stairs. She had walked here
and there for some time and her socks were no longer slippery. About halfway
up, her nostrils were already assailed by a peculiar smell.

The lieutenant was lying on his face in a sea of blood. The point protruding
from his neck seemed to have grown even more prominent than before. Reiko
walked heedlessly across the blood. Sitting beside the lieutenant's corpse, she
stared intently at the face, which lay on one cheek on the mat. The eyes were
opened wide, as if the lieutenant's attention had been attracted by something.
She raised the head, folding it in her sleeve, wiped the blood from the lips, and
bestowed a last kiss.

Then she rose and took from the closet a new white blanket and a waist 135
cord. To prevent any derangement of her skirts, she wrapped the blanket about
her waist and bound it there firmly with the cord.

Reiko sat herself on a spot about one foot distant from the lieutenant's
body. Drawing the dagger from her sash, she examined its dully gleaming blade
intently, and held it to her tongue. The taste of the polished steel was slightly
sweet.

Reiko did not linger. When she thought how the pain which had previously
opened such a gulf between herself and her dying husband was now to become
a part of her own experience, she saw before her only the joy of herself entering
a realm her husband had already made his own. In her husband's agonized face
there had been something inexplicable which she was seeing for the first time.

Now she would solve that riddle. Reiko sensed that at last she too would be able to taste the true bitterness and sweetness of that great moral principle in which her husband believed. What had until now been tasted only faintly through her husband's example she was about to savor directly with her own tongue.

Reiko rested the point of the blade against the base of her throat. She thrust hard. The wound was only shallow. Her head blazed, and her hands shook uncontrollably. She gave the blade a strong pull sideways. A warm substance flooded into her mouth, and everything before her eyes reddened, in a vision of spouting blood. She gathered her strength and plunged the point of the blade deep into her throat.

Connections to Other Selections

1. Contrast Reiko's response to her husband's death in this story with Mrs. Mallard's in Chopin's "The Story of an Hour" (p. 12). How do the differences indicate different sensibilities in the culture of each story?
2. Compare and contrast Mishima's description of the couple's suicides with Tim O'Brien's descriptions of a soldier being blown up and a water buffalo being shot in "How to Tell a True War Story" (p. 552). How do these descriptions of violent actions support the theme of each story?
3. How does Reiko's suicide provide meaning to her life in contrast to Mabel's suicide attempt in Lawrence's "The Horse Dealer's Daughter" (p. 469)? How is human passion a central concern in both stories?

TATYANA TOLSTAYA (Russian/b. 1951)

Born in Leningrad, Tatyana Tolstaya graduated from Leningrad University in 1974 and now lives in New Jersey. Though she is the great-grandniece of Leo Tolstoy, Tolstaya's enthusiastic reception in Russia is firmly based on her remarkable talents rather than on her ancestry. Her stories often appear in Russian literary journals, but she is not a prolific writer. Her collection of short stories, *On the Golden Porch,* immediately sold out when it was first published in Moscow in 1987, and the English translation established her as an important voice when it was published in the United States in 1989. Instead of focusing on social and political issues, her sensuous style explores the inner lives of her characters, who are defined by their perceptions and emotions rather than by national borders. Her writing is characterized by the kind of metaphoric intensity found more typically in poetry than in prose. The following story is a deft and delicate evocation of childhood memories that attentive readers will find to be familiar rather than foreign.

On the Golden Porch   1989

TRANSLATED BY ANTONINA W. BOUIS

FOR MY SISTER, SHURA

On the golden porch sat:
Tsar, tsarevich, king, prince,
Cobbler, tailor.
Who are you?
Tell me fast, don't hold us up.
  – Children's counting rhyme

In the beginning was the garden. Childhood was a garden. Without end or limit, without borders and fences, in noises and rustling, golden in the sun, pale green in the shade, a thousand layers thick — from heather to the crowns of the pines: to the south, the well with toads, to the north, white roses and mushrooms, to the west, the mosquitoed raspberry patch, to the east, the huckleberry patch, wasps, the cliff, the lake, the bridges. They say that early in the morning they saw a *completely* naked man at the lake. Honest. Don't tell Mother. Do you know who it was? — It can't be. — Honest, it was. He thought he was alone. We were in the bushes. — What did you see? — *Everything.*

Now, that was luck. That happens once every hundred years. Because the only available naked man — in the anatomy textbook — isn't real. Having torn off his skin for the occasion, brazen, meaty, and red, he shows off his clavicular-sternum-nipple muscles (all dirty words!) to the students of the eighth grade. When we're promoted (in a hundred years) to the eighth grade, he'll show us all that too.

The old woman, Anna Ilyinichna, feeds her tabby cat, Memeka, with red meat like that. Memeka was born after the war and she has no respect for food. Digging her four paws into the pine tree trunk, high above the ground, Memeka is frozen in immobile despair.

"Memeka, meat, meat!"

The old woman shakes the dish of steaks, lifts it higher for the cat to see 5 better.

"Just look at that meat!"

The cat and the old woman regard each other drearily. "Take it away," thinks Memeka.

"*Meat,* Memeka."

In the suffocating undergrowths of Persian red lilac, the cat mauls sparrows. We found a sparrow like that. Someone had scalped its toy head. A naked fragile skull like a gooseberry. A martyred sparrow face. We made it a cap of lace scraps, made it a white shroud, and buried it in a chocolate box. Life is eternal. Only birds die.

Four carefree dachas stood without fences — go wherever you want. The 10 fifth was a privately owned house. The black log framework spread sideways from beneath the damp overhang of maples and larches and growing brighter, multiplying its windows, thinning out into sun porches, pushing aside nasturtiums, jostling lilacs, avoiding hundred-year-old firs, it ran out laughing onto the southern side and stopped above the smooth strawberry-dahlia slope *down-*

down-down where warm air trembles and the sun breaks up on the open glass lids of magical boxes filled with cucumber babies inside rosettes of orange flowers.

By the house (and what was inside?), having flung open all the windows of the July-pierced veranda, Veronika Vikentievna, a huge white beauty, weighs strawberries: for jam and for sale to neighbors. Luxurious, golden, applelike beauty! White hens cluck at her heavy feet, turkey-cocks stick their indecent faces out of the burdock, a red-and-green rooster cocks his head and looks at us: what do you want, girls? "We'd like some strawberries." The beautiful merchant's wife's fingers in berry blood. Burdock, scales, basket.

Tsaritsa! The greediest woman in the world:

They pour foreign wines for her,
She eats iced gingerbread,
Terrifying guards surround her. . . .

Once she came out of the dark shed with red hands like that, smiling. "I killed a calf . . ."

Axes over their shoulders. . . .

Aargh! Let's get out of here, run, it's horrible — an icy horror — shed, damp, death. . . .

And Uncle Pasha is the husband of this scary woman. Uncle Pasha is small, meek, henpecked. An old man: he's fifty. He works as an accountant in Leningrad; he gets up at five in the morning and runs over hill and dale to make the commuter train. Seven kilometers at a run, ninety minutes on the train, ten minutes on the trolley, then put on black cuff protectors and sit down on a hard yellow chair. Oilcloth-covered doors, a smoky half-basement, weak light, safes, overhead costs — that's Uncle Pasha's job. And when the cheerful light blue day has rushed past, its noise done, Uncle Pasha climbs out of the basement and runs back: the postwar clatter of trolleys, the smoky rush-hour station, coal smells, fences, beggars, baskets; the wind chases crumpled paper along the emptied platform. Wearing sandals in summer and patched felt boots in winter, Uncle Pasha hurries to his Garden, his Paradise, where evening peace comes from the lake, to the House where the huge, golden-haired Tsaritsa lies waiting on a bed with four glass legs. But we didn't see the glass legs until later. Veronika Vikentievna had been feuding a long time with Mother.

The thing was that one summer she sold Mother an egg. There was an ironclad condition: the egg had to be boiled and eaten immediately. But light-hearted Mother gave the egg to the dacha's owner. The crime was revealed. The consequences could have been monstrous: the landlady could have let her hen sit on the egg, and in its chicken ignorance it could have incubated a copy of the unique breed of chicken that ran in Veronika Vikentievna's yard. It's a good thing nothing happened. The egg was eaten. But Veronika Vikentievna could not forgive Mother's treachery. She stopped selling us strawberries and milk, and Uncle Pasha smiled guiltily as he ran past. The neighbors shut themselves in; they reinforced the wire fence on metal posts, sprinkled broken glass in strategic points, stretched barbed wire and got a scary yellow dog. Of course, that wasn't enough.

After all, couldn't Mother still climb over the fence in the dead of night, kill the dog, crawl over the glass, her stomach shredded by barbed wire and bleeding, and with weakening hands steal a runner from the rare variety of strawberries in order to graft it onto her puny ones? After all, couldn't she still run to the fence with her booty and with her last ounce of strength, groaning and gasping, toss the strawberry runner to Father hiding in the bushes, his round eyeglasses glinting in the moonlight?

From May to September, Veronika Vikentievna, who suffered from insomnia, came out into the garden at night, stood in her long white nightgown holding a pitchfork like Neptune, listening to the nocturnal birds, breathing jasmine. Of late her hearing had grown more acute: Veronika Vikentievna could hear Mother and Father three hundred yards away in our dacha, with the camel's hair blanket over their heads, plotting in a whisper to get Veronika Vikentievna: they would dig a tunnel to the greenhouse with her early parsley.

The night moved on, and the house loomed black behind her. Somewhere in the dark warmth, deep in the house, lost in the bowels on their connubial bed, little Uncle Pasha lay still as a mouse. High above his head swam the oak ceiling, and even higher swam the garrets, trunks of expensive black coats sleeping in mothballs, even higher the attic with pitchforks, clumps of hay, and old magazines, and even higher the roof, the chimney, the weather vane, the moon — across the garden, through dreams, they swam, swaying, carrying Uncle Pasha into the land of lost youth, the land of hopes come true, and the chilled Veronika Vikentievna, white and heavy, would return, stepping on his small warm feet.

Hey, wake up, Uncle Pasha! Veronika is going to die soon.   20

You will wander around the empty house, not a thought in your head, and then you will straighten, blossom, look around, remember, push away memories and desire, and bring — to help with the housekeeping — Veronika's younger sister, Margarita, just as pale, large, and beautiful. And in June she'll be laughing in the bright window, bending over the rain barrel, passing among the maples on the sunny lake.

Oh, in our declining years. . . .

But we didn't even notice, we forgot Veronika, we had spent a winter, a whole winter, a winter of mumps and measles, flooding and warts and a Christmas tree blazing with tangerines, and they made a fur coat for me, and a lady in the yard touched it and said: "Mouton."°

In the winter the yardmen glued golden stars onto the black sky, sprinkled ground diamonds into the connecting courtyards of the Petrograd side of town and, clambering up the frosty air ladders to our windows, prepared morning surprises: with fine brushes they painted the silver tails of firebirds.

And when everyone got sick of winter, they took it out of town in trucks, shoving the skinny snowbanks into underground passages protected by gratings, and smeared perfumed mush with yellow seedlings around the parks. And for several days the city was pink, stone, and noisy.

And from over there, beyond the distant horizon, laughing and rumbling,   25 waving a motley flag, the green summer came running with ants and daisies.

Uncle Pasha got rid of the yellow dog — he put it in a trunk and sprinkled

---

Mouton: Sheep (French).

it with mothballs; he let summer renters onto the second floor — a strange, dark woman and her fat granddaughter; and he invited kids into the house and fed them jam.

We hung on the fence and watched the strange grandmother fling open the second-story windows every hour and, illuminated by the harlequin rhomboids of the ancient panes, call out:

"Want milkandcookies?"

"No."

"Want potty?" 30

"No."

We hopped on one leg, healed scrapes with spit, buried treasures, cut worms in half with scissors, watched the old woman wash pink underpants in the lake, and found a photograph under the owner's buffet: a surprised, big-eared family with the caption, "Don't forget us. 1908."

Let's go to Uncle Pasha's. You go first. No, you. Careful, watch the sill. I can't see in the dark. Hold on to me. Will he show us *the room*. He will, but first we have to have tea.

Ornate spoons, ornate crystal holders. Cherry jam. Silly Margarita laughs in the orange light of the lamp shade. Hurry up and drink! Uncle Pasha knows, he's waiting, holding open the sacred door to Aladdin's cave. O room! O children's dreams! O Uncle Pasha, you are King Solomon! You hold the Horn of Plenty in your mighty arms. A caravan of camels passed with spectral tread through your house and dropped its Baghdad wares in the summer twilight. A waterfall of velvet, ostrich feathers of lace, a shower of porcelain, golden columns of frames, precious tables on bent legs, locked glass cases of mounds where fragile yellow glasses are entwined by black grapes, where Negroes in golden skirts hide in the deep darkness, where something bends, transparent, silvery . . . Look, a precious clock with foreign numbers and snakelike hands. And this one, with forget-me-nots. Ah, but look, look at that one! There's a glass room over the face and in it a golden Chevalier seated at a golden table, a golden sandwich in his hand. And next to him, a Lady with a goblet: and when the clock strikes, she strikes the goblet on the table — *six, seven, eight.* . . . The lilacs are jealous, they peek through the window, and Uncle Pasha sits down at the piano and plays the *Moonlight* Sonata. Who are you, Uncle Pasha?

There it is, the bed on glass legs. Semitransparent in the twilight, invisible 35 and powerful, they raise on high the tangle of lace, the Babylon towers of pillows, the moonlit, lilac scent of the divine music. Uncle Pasha's noble white head is thrown back, a Mona Lisa smile on Margarita's golden face as she appears silently in the doorway, the lace curtains sway, the lilacs sway, the waves of dahlias sway on the slope right to the horizon, to the evening lake, to the beam of moonlight.

Play, play, Uncle Pasha! Caliph for an hour, enchanted prince, starry youth, who gave you this power over us, to enchant us, who gave you those white winds on your back, who carried your silvery head to the evening skies, crowned you with roses, illuminated you with mountain light, surrounded you with lunar wind?

O Milky Way, light brother
Of Canaan's milky rivers,
Should we swim through the starry fall

> *To the fogs, where entwined*
> *The bodies of lovers fly?*

. . . Well, enough. Time to go home. It doesn't seem right to use the ordinary word "Thanks" with Uncle Pasha. Have to be more ornamental: "I am grateful." "It's not worthy of gratitude."

"Did you notice they have only one bed in the house?"

"Where does Margarita sleep, then? In the attic?"

"Maybe. But that's where the renters are." 40

"Well, then she must sleep on the porch, on a bench."

"What if they sleep in the same bed, head to foot?"

"Stupid. They're strangers."

"You're stupid. What if they're lovers?"

"But they only have lovers in France." 45

She's right, of course. I forgot.

. . . Life changed the slides ever faster in the magic lantern. With Mother's help we penetrated into the mirrored corners of the grownups' atelier, where the bald tubby tailor took our embarrassing measurements, muttering *excuse me's*; we envied girls in nylon stockings, with pierced ears, we drew in our textbooks: glasses on Pushkin, a mustache on Mayakovsky, a large white chest on Chekhov, who was otherwise normally endowed. And we were recognized immediately and welcomed joyfully by the patient and defective nude model from the anatomy course generously offering his numbered innards; but the poor fellow no longer excited anyone. And, looking back once, with unbelieving fingers we felt the smoked glass behind which our garden waved a hankie before going down for the last time. But we didn't feel the loss yet.

Autumn came into Uncle Pasha's house and struck him on the face. Autumn, what do you want? Wait; are you kidding? . . . The leaves fell, the days grew dark, Margarita grew stooped. The white chickens died, the turkey flew off to warmer climes, the yellow dog climbed out of the trunk and, embracing Uncle Pasha, listened to the north wind howl at night. Girls, someone, bring Uncle Pasha some India tea. How you've grown. How old you've gotten, Uncle Pasha. Your hands are spotted, your knees bent. Why do you wheeze like that? I know, I can guess: in the daytime, vaguely, and at night, clearly, you hear the clang of metal locks. The chain is wearing out.

What are you bustling about for? You want to show me your treasures? Well, all right, I have five minutes for you. It's so long since I was here! I'm getting old. So that's it, *that's* what enchanted us? All this secondhand rubbish, these chipped painted night tables, these tacky oilcloth paintings, these brocade curtains, the worn plush velvet, the darned lace, the clumsy fakes from the peasant market, the cheap beads? This sang and glittered, burned and beckoned? What mean jokes you play, life! Dust, ashes, rot. Surfacing from the magical bottom of childhood, from the warm, radiant depths, we open our chilled fist in the cold wind — and what have we brought up with us besides sand? But just a quarter century ago Uncle Pasha wound the golden clock with trembling hands. Above the face, in the glass room, the little inhabitants huddle — the Lady and the Chevalier, masters of Time. The Lady strikes the table with her goblet, and the thin ringing sound tries to break through the shell of decades. *Eight, nine, ten.* No. Excuse me, Uncle Pasha. I have to go.

. . . Uncle Pasha froze to death on the porch. He could not reach the metal 50
ring of the door and fell face down in the snow. White snow daisies grew
between his stiff fingers. The yellow dog gently closed his eyes and left through
the snowflakes up the starry ladder to the black heights, carrying away the
trembling living flame.

The new owner — Margarita's elderly daughter — poured Uncle Pasha's
ashes into a metal can and set it on a shelf in the empty chicken house; it was
too much trouble to bury him.

Bent in half by the years, her face turned to the ground, Margarita wanders
through the chilled, drafty garden, as if seeking lost footsteps on the silent paths.

"You're cruel! Bury him!"

But her daughter smokes indifferently on the porch. The nights are cold.
Let's turn on the lights early. And the golden Lady of Time, drinking bottoms up
from the goblet of life, will strike a final midnight on the table for Uncle Pasha.

Connections to Other Selections

1. Write an essay comparing the narrator's attitudes toward childhood and adulthood
   in "On the Golden Porch" with the narrator's attitudes in Margaret Atwood's "Death
   by Landscape" (p. 529).
2. Compare the tone of the narrative voice in Tolstaya's story with the voice in James
   Joyce's "Araby" (p. 310). How do you characterize each voice? Explain whether
   you find them similar to or different from each other.
3. Discuss the symbolic significance of Tolstaya's naked man in the anatomy textbook
   and the naked dancer in Ralph Ellison's "Battle Royal" (p. 187). How do these
   symbols help to reveal the narrator's consciousness in each story?

AN ALBUM OF CONTEMPORARY STORIES

MARGARET ATWOOD (b. 1939)

Born in Ottawa, Ontario, Margaret Atwood was educated at the University of Toronto and Harvard University. She has been writing fiction and
poetry since she was a child; along the way she has worked odd jobs and
been a film writer and a teacher. Her latest collection of short stories,
Wilderness Tips (1991), from which "Death by Landscape" is taken, was
preceded by six novels, including *Surfacing* (1972), *The Handmaid's Tale*
(1986), and *Cat's Eye* (1989). She has also written twelve books of poetry.
Atwood has enhanced the appreciation of Canadian literature through her
editing of *The New Oxford Book of Canadian Verse in English* (1982) and
The Oxford Book of Canadian Short Stories in English (1986). Her own
work closely examines the weight of the complex human relationships that
complicate her characters' lives.

Now that the boys are grown up and Rob is dead, Lois has moved to a condominium apartment in one of the newer waterfront developments. She is relieved not to have to worry about the lawn, or about the ivy pushing its muscular little suckers into the brickwork, or the squirrels gnawing their way into the attic and eating the insulation off the wiring, or about strange noises. This building has a security system, and the only plant life is in pots in the solarium.

Lois is glad she's been able to find an apartment big enough for her pictures. They are more crowded together than they were in the house, but this arrangement gives the walls a European look: blocks of pictures, above and beside one another, rather than one over the chesterfield, one over the fireplace, one in the front hall, in the old acceptable manner of sprinkling art around so it does not get too intrusive. This way has more of an impact. You know it's not supposed to be furniture.

None of the pictures is very large, which doesn't mean they aren't valuable. They are paintings, or sketches and drawings, by artists who were not nearly as well known when Lois began to buy them as they are now. Their work later turned up on stamps, or as silk-screen reproductions hung in the principals' offices of high schools, or as jigsaw puzzles, or on beautifully printed calendars sent out by corporations as Christmas gifts, to their less important clients. These artists painted mostly in the twenties and thirties and forties; they painted landscapes. Lois has two Tom Thomsons, three A. Y. Jacksons, a Lawren Harris. She has an Arthur Lismer, she has a J. E. H. MacDonald. She has a David Milne. They are pictures of convoluted tree trunks on an island of pink wave-smoothed stone, with more islands behind: of a lake with rough, bright, sparsely wooded cliffs; of a vivid river shore with a tangle of bush and two beached canoes, one red, one gray; of a yellow autumn woods with the ice-blue gleam of a pond half-seen through the interlaced branches.

It was Lois who'd chosen them. Rob had no interest in art, although he could see the necessity of having something on the walls. He left all the decorating decisions to her, while providing the money, of course. Because of this collection of hers, Lois's friends — especially the men — have given her the reputation of having a good nose for art investments.

But this is not why she bought the pictures, way back then. She bought   5
them because she wanted them. She wanted something that was in them, although she could not have said at the time what it was. It was not peace: she does not find them peaceful in the least. Looking at them fills her with a wordless unease. Despite the fact that there are no people in them or even animals, it's as if there is something, or someone, looking back out.

When she was thirteen, Lois went on a canoe trip. She'd only been on overnights before. This was to be a long one, into the trackless wilderness, as Cappie put it. It was Lois's first canoe trip, and her last.

Cappie was the head of the summer camp to which Lois had been sent ever since she was nine. Camp Manitou, it was called; it was one of the better ones, for girls, though not the best. Girls of her age whose parents could afford it were routinely packed off to such camps, which bore a generic resemblance to one another. They favored Indian names and had hearty, energetic leaders, who were called Cappie or Skip or Scottie. At these camps you learned to swim well and sail, and paddle a canoe, and perhaps ride a horse or play tennis. When you weren't doing these things you could do Arts and Crafts and turn out dingy, lumpish clay ashtrays for your mother — mothers smoked more, then — or bracelets made of colored braided string.

Cheerfulness was required at all times, even at breakfast. Loud shouting and the banging of spoons on the tables were allowed, and even encouraged, at ritual intervals. Chocolate bars were rationed, to control tooth decay and pimples. At night, after supper, in the dining hall or outside around a mosquito-infested campfire ring for special treats, there were singsongs. Lois can still remember all the words to "My Darling Clementine," and to "My Bonnie Lies over the Ocean," with acting-out gestures: a rippling of the hands for "the ocean," two hands together under the cheek for "lies." She will never be able to forget them, which is a sad thought.

Lois thinks she can recognize women who went to these camps, and were good at it. They have a hardness to their handshakes, even now; a way of standing, legs planted firmly and farther apart than usual; a way of sizing you up, to see if you'd be any good in a canoe — the front, not the back. They themselves would be in the back. They would call it the stern.

She knows that such camps still exist, although Camp Manitou does not. 10 They are one of the few things that haven't changed much. They now offer copper enameling, and functionless pieces of stained glass baked in electric ovens, though judging from the productions of her friends' grandchildren the artistic standards have not improved.

To Lois, encountering it in the first year after the war, Camp Manitou seemed ancient. Its log-sided buildings with the white cement in between the half-logs, its flagpole ringed with whitewashed stones, its weathered gray dock jutting out into Lake Prospect, with its woven rope bumpers and its rusty rings for tying up, its prim round flowerbed of petunias near the office door, must surely have been there always. In truth it dated only from the first decade of the century; it had been founded by Cappie's parents, who'd thought of camping as bracing to the character, like cold showers, and had been passed along to her as an inheritance, and an obligation.

Lois realized, later, that it must have been a struggle for Cappie to keep Camp Manitou going, during the Depression and then the war, when money did not flow freely. If it had been a camp for the very rich, instead of the merely well off, there would have been fewer problems. But there must have been enough Old Girls, ones with daughters, to keep the thing in operation, though not entirely shipshape: furniture was battered, painted trim was peeling, roofs leaked. There were dim photographs of these Old Girls dotted around the dining hall, wearing ample woolen bathing suits and showing their fat, dimpled legs, or standing, arms twined, in odd tennis outfits with baggy skirts.

In the dining hall, over the stone fireplace that was never used, there was a huge molting stuffed moose head, which looked somehow carnivorous. It was a sort of mascot; its name was Monty Manitou. The older campers spread the story that it was haunted, and came to life in the dark, when the feeble and undependable lights had been turned off or, due to yet another generator failure, had gone out. Lois was afraid of it at first, but not after she got used to it.

Cappie was the same: you had to get used to her. Possibly she was forty, or thirty-five, or fifty. She had fawn-colored hair that looked as if it was cut with a bowl. Her head jutted forward, jigging like a chicken's as she strode around the camp, clutching notebooks and checking things off in them. She was like their minister in church: both of them smiled a lot and were anxious because they wanted things to go well; they both had the same overwashed skins and stringy necks. But all this disappeared when Cappie was leading a singsong, or otherwise leading. Then she was happy, sure of herself, her plain face almost luminous. She wanted to cause joy. At these times she was loved, at others merely trusted.

There were many things Lois didn't like about Camp Manitou, at first. She 15 hated the noisy chaos and spoon-banging of the dining hall, the rowdy singsongs at which you were expected to yell in order to show that you were enjoying yourself. Hers was not a household that encouraged yelling. She hated the necessity of having to write dutiful letters to her parents claiming she was having fun. She could not complain, because camp cost so much money.

She didn't much like having to undress in a roomful of other girls, even in the dim light, although nobody paid any attention, or sleeping in a cabin with seven other girls, some of whom snored because they had adenoids or colds, some of whom had nightmares, or wet their beds and cried about it. Bottom bunks made her feel closed in, and she was afraid of falling out of top ones; she was afraid of heights. She got homesick, and suspected her parents of having a better time when she wasn't there than when she was, although her mother wrote to her every week saying how much they missed her. All this was when she was nine. By the time she was thirteen she liked it. She was an old hand by then.

Lucy was her best friend at camp. Lois had other friends in winter, when there was school and itchy woolen clothing and darkness in the afternoons, but Lucy was her summer friend.

She turned up the second year, when Lois was ten, and a Bluejay. (Chickadees, Bluejays, Ravens, and Kingfishers — these were the names Camp Manitou assigned to the different age groups, a sort of totemic clan system. In those days, thinks Lois, it was birds for girls, animals for boys: wolves, and so forth. Though some animals and birds were suitable and some were not. Never vultures, for instance; never skunks, or rats.)

Lois helped Lucy to unpack her tin trunk and place the folded clothes on the wooden shelves, and to make up her bed. She put her in the top bunk right above her, where she could keep an eye on her. Already she knew that Lucy was an exception, to a good many rules; already she felt proprietorial.

Lucy was from the United States, where the comic books came from, and 20 the movies. She wasn't from New York or Hollywood or Buffalo, the only American cities Lois knew the names of, but from Chicago. Her house was on the lake shore and had gates to it, and grounds. They had a maid, all of the time. Lois's family only had a cleaning lady twice a week.

The only reason Lucy was being sent to *this* camp (she cast a look of minor scorn around the cabin, diminishing it and also offending Lois, while at the same time daunting her) was that her mother had been a camper here. Her mother had been a Canadian once, but had married her father, who had a patch over one eye, like a pirate. She showed Lois the picture of him in her wallet. He got the patch in the war. "Shrapnel," said Lucy. Lois, who was unsure about shrapnel, was so impressed she could only grunt. Her own two-eyed, unwounded father was tame by comparison.

"My father plays golf," she ventured at last.

"*Everyone* plays golf," said Lucy. "My *mother* plays golf."

Lois's mother did not. Lois took Lucy to see the outhouses and the swimming dock and the dining hall with Monty Manitou's baleful head, knowing in advance they would not measure up.

This was a bad beginning; but Lucy was good-natured, and accepted Camp Manitou with the same casual shrug with which she seemed to accept everything. She would make the best of it, without letting Lois forget that this was what she was doing.

However, there were things Lois knew that Lucy did not. Lucy scratched the tops off all her mosquito bites and had to be taken to the infirmary to be daubed with Ozonol. She took her T-shirt off while sailing, and although the counselor spotted her after a while and made her put it back on, she burnt spectacularly, bright red, with the X of her bathing-suit straps standing out in alarming white; she let Lois peel the sheets of whispery-thin burned skin off her shoulders. When they sang "Alouette" around the campfire, she did not know any of the French words. The difference was that Lucy did not care about the things she didn't know, whereas Lois did.

During the next winter, and subsequent winters, Lucy and Lois wrote to each other. They were both only children, at a time when this was thought to be a disadvantage, so in their letters they pretended to be sisters, or even twins. Lois had to strain a little over this, because Lucy was so blond, with translucent skin and large blue eyes like a doll's, and Lois was nothing out of the ordinary — just a tallish, thinnish, brownish person with freckles. They signed their letters LL, with the L's entwined together like the monograms on a towel. (Lois and Lucy, thinks Lois. How our names date us. Lois Lane, Superman's girlfriend, enterprising female reporter; "I Love Lucy." Now we are obsolete, and it's little Jennifers, little Emilys, little Alexandras, and Carolines and Tiffanys.)

They were more effusive in their letters than they ever were in person. They bordered their pages with X's and O's, but when they met again in the summers it was always a shock. They had changed so much, or Lucy had. It was like watching someone grow up in jolts. At first it would be hard to think up things to say.

But Lucy always had a surprise or two, something to show, some marvel to reveal. The first year she had a picture of herself in a tutu, her hair in a ballerina's knot on the top of her head; she pirouetted around the swimming dock, to show Lois how it was done, and almost fell off. The next year she had given that up and was taking horseback riding. (Camp Manitou did not have horses.) The next year her mother and father had been divorced, and she had a new stepfather, one with both eyes, and a new house, although the maid was the same. The next year, when they had graduated from Bluejays and entered Ravens, she got her period, right in the first week of camp. The two of them snitched some matches from their counselor, who smoked illegally, and made a small fire out behind the farthest outhouse, at dusk, using their flashlights. They could set all kinds of fires by now; they had learned how in Campcraft. On this fire they burned one of Lucy's used sanitary napkins. Lois is not sure why they did this, or whose idea it was. But she can remember the feeling of deep satisfaction it gave her as the white fluff singed and the blood sizzled, as if some wordless ritual had been fulfilled.

They did not get caught, but then they rarely got caught at any of their ₃₀ camp transgressions. Lucy had such large eyes, and was such an accomplished liar.

This year Lucy is different again: slower, more languorous. She is no longer interested in sneaking around after dark, purloining cigarettes from the counselor, dealing in black-market candy bars. She is pensive, and hard to wake in the mornings. She doesn't like her stepfather, but she doesn't want to live with her real father either, who has a new wife. She thinks her mother may be having a love affair with a doctor; she doesn't know for sure, but she's seen them smooching in his car, out on the driveway, when her stepfather wasn't there. It serves him right. She hates her private school. She has a boyfriend, who is sixteen and works as a gardener's assistant. This is how she met him: in the garden. She describes to Lois what it is like when he kisses her — rubbery at first, but then your knees go limp. She has been forbidden to see him, and threatened with boarding school. She wants to run away from home.

Lois has little to offer in return. Her own life is placid and satisfactory, but there is nothing much that can be said about happiness. "You're so lucky," Lucy tells her, a little smugly. She might as well say *boring* because this is how it makes Lois feel.

Lucy is apathetic about the canoe trip, so Lois has to disguise her own excitement. The evening before they are to leave, she slouches into the campfire ring as if coerced, and sits down with a sigh of endurance, just as Lucy does.

Every canoe trip that went out of camp was given a special send-off by Cappie and the section leader and counselors, with the whole section in attendance. Cappie painted three streaks of red across each of her cheeks with a lipstick. They looked like three-fingered claw marks. She put a blue circle on her forehead with fountain-pen ink, and tied a twisted bandanna around her head and stuck a row of frazzle-ended feathers around it, and wrapped herself in a red-and-black Hudson's Bay blanket. The counselors, also in blankets but with only two streaks of red, beat on tom-toms made of round wooden cheese boxes with leather stretched over the top and nailed in place. Cappie was Chief Cappeosota. They all had to say "How!" when she walked into the circle and stood there with one hand raised.

Looking back on this, Lois finds it disquieting. She knows too much about ₃₅ Indians: this is why. She knows, for instance, that they should not even be called Indians, and that they have enough worries without other people taking their names and dressing up as them. It has all been a form of stealing.

But she remembers, too, that she was once ignorant of this. Once she loved the campfire, the flickering of light on the ring of faces, the sound of the fake tom-toms, heavy and fast like a scared heartbeat; she loved Cappie in a red blanket and feathers, solemn, as a chief should be, raising her hand and saying, "Greetings, my Ravens." It was not funny, it was not making fun. She wanted to be an Indian. She wanted to be adventurous and pure, and aboriginal.

"You go on big water," says Cappie. This is her idea — all their ideas — of how Indians talk. "You go where no man has ever trod. You go many moons." This is not true. They are only going for a week, not many moons. The canoe route is clearly marked, they have gone over it on a map, and there are prepared campsites with names which are used year after year. But when Cappie says this — and despite the way Lucy rolls up her eyes — Lois can feel the water stretching out, with the shores twisting away on either side, immense and a little frightening.

"You bring back much wampum," says Cappie. "Do good in war, my braves, and capture many scalps." This is another of her pretenses: that they are boys, and bloodthirsty. But such a game cannot be played by substituting the word "squaw." It would not work at all.

Each of them has to stand up and step forward and have a red line drawn across her cheeks by Cappie. She tells them they must follow in the paths of their ancestors (who most certainly, thinks Lois, looking out the window of her apartment and remembering the family stash of daguerreotypes and sepia-colored portraits on her mother's dressing table, the stiff-shirted, black-coated, grim-faced men and the beflounced women with their severe hair and their corseted respectability, would never have considered heading off onto an open lake, in a canoe, just for fun).

At the end of the ceremony they all stood and held hands around the circle, 40 and sang taps. This did not sound very Indian, thinks Lois. It sounded like a bugle call at a military post, in a movie. But Cappie was never one to be much concerned with consistency, or with archeology.

After breakfast the next morning they set out from the main dock, in four canoes, three in each. The lipstick stripes have not come off completely, and still show faintly pink, like healing burns. They wear their white denim sailing hats, because of the sun, and thin-striped T-shirts, and pale baggy shorts with the cuffs rolled up. The middle one kneels, propping her rear end against the rolled sleeping bags. The counselors going with them are Pat and Kip. Kip is no-nonsense; Pat is easier to wheedle, or fool.

There are white puffy clouds and a small breeze. Glints come from the little waves. Lois is in the bow of Kip's canoe. She still can't do a J-stroke very well, and she will have to be in the bow or the middle for the whole trip. Lucy is behind her; her own J-stroke is even worse. She splashes Lois with her paddle, quite a big splash.

"I'll get you back," says Lois.

"There was a stable fly on your shoulder," Lucy says.

Lois turns to look at her, to see if she's grinning. They're in the habit of 45 splashing each other. Back there, the camp has vanished behind the first long point of rock and rough trees. Lois feels as if an invisible rope has broken. They're floating free, on their own, cut loose. Beneath the canoe the lake goes down, deeper and colder than it was a minute before.

"No horsing around in the canoe," says Kip. She's rolled her T-shirt sleeves up to the shoulder; her arms are brown and sinewy, her jaw determined, her stroke perfect. She looks as if she knows exactly what she is doing.

The four canoes keep close together. They sing, raucously and with defiance; they sing "The Quartermaster's Store," and "Clementine," and "Alouette." It is more like bellowing than singing.

After that the wind grows stronger, blowing slantwise against the bows, and they have to put all their energy into shoving themselves through the water.

Was there anything important, anything that would provide some sort of reason or clue to what happened next? Lois can remember everything, every detail; but it does her no good.

They stopped at noon for a swim and lunch, and went on in the afternoon. 50 At last they reached Little Birch, which was the first campsite for overnight. Lois and Lucy made the fire, while the others pitched the heavy canvas tents. The fireplace was already there, flat stones piled into a U. A burned tin can and a beer bottle had been left in it. Their fire went out, and they had to restart it. "Hustle your bustle," said Kip. "We're starving."

The sun went down, and in the pink sunset light they brushed their teeth and spat the toothpaste froth into the lake. Kip and Pat put all the food that wasn't in cans into a packsack and slung it into a tree, in case of bears.

Lois and Lucy weren't sleeping in a tent. They'd begged to be allowed to sleep out; that way they could talk without the others hearing. If it rained, they told Kip, they promised not to crawl dripping into the tent over everyone's legs: they would get under the canoes. So they were out on the point.

Lois tried to get comfortable inside her sleeping bag, which smelled of musty storage and of earlier campers, a stale salty sweetness. She curled herself up, with her sweater rolled up under her head for a pillow and her flashlight inside her sleeping bag so it wouldn't roll away. The muscles of her sore arms were making small pings, like rubber bands breaking.

Beside her Lucy was rustling around. Lois could see the glimmering oval of her white face.

"I've got a rock poking into my back," said Lucy.   55

"So do I," said Lois. "You want to go into the tent?" She herself didn't, but it was right to ask.

"No," said Lucy. She subsided into her sleeping bag. After a moment she said, "It would be nice not to go back."

"To camp?" said Lois.

"To Chicago," said Lucy. "I hate it there."

"What about your boyfriend?" said Lois. Lucy didn't answer. She was either 60 asleep or pretending to be.

There was a moon, and a movement of the trees. In the sky there were stars, layers of stars that went down and down. Kip said that when the stars were bright like that instead of hazy it meant bad weather later on. Out on the lake there were two loons, calling to each other in their insane, mournful voices. At the time it did not sound like grief. It was just background.

The lake in the morning was flat calm. They skimmed along over the glassy surface, leaving V-shaped trails behind them; it felt like flying. As the sun rose higher it got hot, almost too hot. There were stable flies in the canoes, landing on a bare arm or leg for a quick sting. Lois hoped for wind.

They stopped for lunch at the next of the named campsites, Lookout Point. It was called this because, although the site itself was down near the water on a flat shelf of rock, there was a sheer cliff nearby and a trail that led up to the top. The top was the lookout, although what you were supposed to see from there was not clear. Kip said it was just a view.

Lois and Lucy decided to make the climb anyway. They didn't want to hang around waiting for lunch. It wasn't their turn to cook, though they hadn't avoided much by not doing it, because cooking lunch was no big deal, it was just unwrapping the cheese and getting out the bread and peanut butter, but Pat and Kip always had to do their woodsy act and boil up a billy tin for their own tea.

They told Kip where they were going. You had to tell Kip where you were 65 going, even if it was only a little way into the woods to get dry twigs for kindling. You could never go anywhere without a buddy.

"Sure," said Kip, who was crouching over the fire, feeding driftwood into it. "Fifteen minutes to lunch."

"Where are they off to?" said Pat. She was bringing their billy tin of water from the lake.

"Lookout," said Kip.

"Be careful," said Pat. She said it as an afterthought, because it was what she always said.

"They're old hands," Kip said. 70

Lois looks at her watch: it's ten to twelve. She is the watch-minder; Lucy is careless of time. They walk up the path, which is dry earth and rocks, big rounded pinky-gray boulders or split-open ones with jagged edges. Spindly balsam and spruce trees grow to either side, the lake is blue fragments to the left. The sun is right overhead; there are no shadows anywhere. The heat comes up at them as well as down. The forest is dry and crackly.

It isn't far, but it's a steep climb and they're sweating when they reach the top. They wipe their faces with their bare arms, sit gingerly down on a scorching-hot rock, five feet from the edge but too close for Lois. It's a lookout all right, a sheer drop to the lake and a long view over the water, back the way they've come. It's amazing to Lois that they've traveled so far, over all that water, with nothing to propel them but their own arms. It makes her feel strong. There are all kinds of things she is capable of doing.

"It would be quite a dive off here," says Lucy.

"You'd have to be nuts," says Lois.

"Why?" says Lucy. "It's really deep. It goes straight down." She stands up 75 and takes a step nearer the edge. Lois gets a stab in her midriff, the kind she gets when a car goes too fast over a bump. "Don't," she says.

"Don't what?" says Lucy, glancing around at her mischievously. She knows how Lois feels about heights. But she turns back. "I really have to pee," she says.

"You have toilet paper?" says Lois, who is never without it. She digs in her shorts pocket.

"Thanks," says Lucy.

They are both adept at peeing in the woods: doing it fast so the mosquitoes don't get you, the underwear pulled up between the knees, the squat with the feet apart so you don't wet your legs, facing downhill. The exposed feeling of your bum, as if someone is looking at you from behind. The etiquette when you're with someone else is not to look. Lois stands up and starts to walk back down the path, to be out of sight.

"Wait for me?" says Lucy. 80

Lois climbed down, over and around the boulders, until she could not see Lucy; she waited. She could hear the voices of the others, talking and laughing, down near the shore. One voice was yelling, "Ants! Ants!" Someone must have sat on an ant hill. Off to the side, in the woods, a raven was croaking, a hoarse single note.

She looked at her watch: it was noon. This is when she heard the shout.

She has gone over and over it in her mind since, so many times that the first, real shout has been obliterated, like a footprint trampled by other footprints. But she is sure (she is almost positive, she is nearly certain) that it was not a shout of fear. Not a scream. More like a cry of surprise, cut off too soon. Short, like a dog's bark.

"Lucy?" Lois said. Then she called "Lucy!" By now she was clambering back up, over the stones of the path. Lucy was not up there. Or she was not in sight.

"Stop fooling around," Lois said. "It's lunchtime." But Lucy did not rise from 85 behind a rock or step out, smiling, from behind a tree. The sunlight was all around; the rocks looked white. "This isn't funny!" Lois said, and it wasn't, panic was rising in her, the panic of a small child who does not know where the bigger ones are hidden. She could hear her own heart. She looked quickly around; she lay down on the ground and looked over the edge of the cliff. It made her feel cold. There was nothing.

She went back down the path, stumbling; she was breathing too quickly; she was too frightened to cry. She felt terrible — guilty and dismayed, as if she had done something very bad, by mistake. Something that could never be repaired. "Lucy's gone," she told Kip.

Kip looked up from her fire, annoyed. The water in the billy can was boiling. "What do you mean, gone?" she said. "Where did she go?"

"I don't know," said Lois. "She's just gone."

No one had heard the shout, but then no one heard Lois calling, either. They had been talking among themselves, by the water.

Kip and Pat went up to the lookout and searched and called, and blew their 90 whistles. Nothing answered.

Then they came back down, and Lois had to tell exactly what had happened. The other girls all sat in a circle and listened to her. Nobody said anything. They all looked frightened, especially Pat and Kip. They were the leaders. You did not just lose a camper like this, for no reason at all.

"Why did you leave her alone?" said Kip.

"I was just down the path," said Lois. "I told you. She had to go to the bathroom." She did not say *pee* in front of people older than herself.

Kip looked disgusted.

"Maybe she just walked off into the woods and got turned around," said 95 one of the girls.

"Maybe she's doing it on purpose," said another.

Nobody believed either of these theories.

They took the canoes and searched around the base of the cliff, and peered down into the water. But there had been no sound of falling rock; there had been no splash. There was no clue, nothing at all. Lucy had simply vanished.

That was the end of the canoe trip. It took them the same two days to go back that it had taken coming in, even though they were short a paddler. They did not sing.

After that, the police went in a motorboat, with dogs; they were the Mounties 100 and the dogs were German shepherds, trained to follow trails in the woods. But it had rained since, and they could find nothing.

Lois is sitting in Cappie's office. Her face is bloated with crying, she's seen that in the mirror. By now she feels numbed; she feels as if she has drowned. She can't stay here. It has been too much of a shock. Tomorrow her parents are coming to take her away. Several of the other girls who were on the canoe trip are also being collected. The others will have to stay, because their parents are in Europe, or cannot be reached.

Cappie is grim. They've tried to hush it up, but of course everyone in camp knows. Soon the papers will know too. You can't keep it quiet, but what can be said? What can be said that makes any sense? "Girl vanishes in broad daylight, without a trace." It can't be believed. Other things, worse things, will be suspected. Negligence, at the very least. But they have always taken such care. Bad luck will gather around Camp Manitou like a fog; parents will avoid it, in favor of other, luckier places. Lois can see Cappie thinking all this, even through her numbness. It's what anyone would think.

Lois sits on the hard wooden chair in Cappie's office, beside the old wooden desk, over which hangs the thumbtacked bulletin board of normal camp routine, and gazes at Cappie through her puffy eyelids. Cappie is now smiling what is supposed to be a reassuring smile. Her manner is too casual: she's after something. Lois has seen this look on Cappie's face when she's been sniffing out contraband chocolate bars, hunting down those rumored to have snuck out of their cabins at night.

"Tell me again," says Cappie, "from the beginning."

Lois has told her story so many times by now, to Pat and Kip, to Cappie, to 105 the police, that she knows it word for word. She knows it, but she no longer believes it. It has become a story. "I told you," she said. "She wanted to go to the bathroom. I gave her my toilet paper. I went down the path, I waited for her. I heard this kind of shout . . ."

"Yes," says Cappie, smiling confidingly, "but before that. What did you say to one another?"

Lois thinks. Nobody has asked her this before. "She said you could dive off there. She said it went straight down."

"And what did you say?"

"I said you'd have to be nuts."

"Were you mad at Lucy?" says Cappie, in an encouraging voice. 110

"No," says Lois. "Why would I be mad at Lucy? I wasn't ever mad at Lucy." She feels like crying again. The times when she has in fact been mad at Lucy have been erased already. Lucy was always perfect.

"Sometimes we're angry when we don't know we're angry," says Cappie, as if to herself. "Sometimes we get really mad and we don't even know it. Sometimes we might do a thing without meaning to, or without knowing what will happen. We lose our tempers."

Lois is only thirteen, but it doesn't take her long to figure out that Cappie is not including herself in any of this. By *we* she means Lois. She is accusing Lois of pushing Lucy off the cliff. The unfairness of this hits her like a slap. "I didn't!" she says.

"Didn't what?" says Cappie softly. "Didn't what, Lois?"

Lois does the worst thing, she begins to cry. Cappie gives her a look like a pounce. She's got what she wanted. 115

Later, when she was grown up, Lois was able to understand what this interview had been about. She could see Cappie's desperation, her need for a story, a real story with a reason in it; anything but the senseless vacancy Lucy had left for her to deal with. Cappie wanted Lois to supply the reason, to be the reason. It wasn't even for the newspapers or the parents, because she could never make such an accusation without proof. It was for herself: something to explain the loss of Camp Manitou and of all she had worked for, the years of entertaining spoiled children and buttering up parents and making a fool of herself with feathers stuck in her hair. Camp Manitou was in fact lost. It did not survive.

Lois worked all this out, twenty years later. But it was far too late. It was too late even ten minutes afterwards, when she'd left Cappie's office and was walking slowly back to her cabin to pack. Lucy's clothes were still there, folded on the shelves, as if waiting. She felt the other girls in the cabin watching her with speculation in their eyes. *Could she have done it? She must have done it.* For the rest of her life, she has caught people watching her in this way.

Maybe they weren't thinking this. Maybe they were merely sorry for her. But she felt she had been tried and sentenced, and this is what has stayed with her: the knowledge that she had been singled out, condemned for something that was not her fault.

Lois sits in the living room of her apartment, drinking a cup of tea. Through the knee-to-ceiling window she has a wide view of Lake Ontario, with its skin of wrinkled blue-gray light, and of the willows of Centre Island shaken by a wind, which is silent at this distance, and on this side of the glass. When there isn't too much pollution she can see the far shore, the foreign shore; though today it is obscured.

Possibly she could go out, go downstairs, do some shopping; there isn't much in the refrigerator. The boys say she doesn't get out enough. But she isn't hungry, and moving, stirring from this space, is increasingly an effort. 120

She can hardly remember, now, having her two boys in the hospital, nursing them as babies; she can hardly remember getting married, or what Rob looked like. Even at the time she never felt she was paying full attention. She was tired a lot, as if she was living not one life but two: her own, and another, shadowy life that hovered around her and would not let itself be realized — the life of what would have happened if Lucy had not stepped sideways, and disappeared from time.

She would never go up north, to Rob's family cottage or to any place with wild lakes and wild trees and the calls of loons. She would never go anywhere near. Still, it was as if she was always listening for another voice, the voice of a person who should have been there but was not. An echo.

While Rob was alive, while the boys were growing up, she could pretend she didn't hear it, this empty space in sound. But now there is nothing much left to distract her.

She turns away from the window and looks at her pictures. There is the pinkish island, in the lake, with the intertwisted trees. It's the same landscape they paddled through, that distant summer. She's seen travelogues of this country, aerial photographs; it looks different from above, bigger, more hopeless: lake after lake, random blue puddles in dark green bush, the trees like bristles.

How could you ever find anything there, once it was lost? Maybe if they cut 125 it all down, drained it all away, they might find Lucy's bones, some time, wherever they are hidden. A few bones, some buttons, the buckle from her shorts.

But a dead person is a body; a body occupies space, it exists somewhere. You can see it; you put it in a box and bury it in the ground, and then it's in a box in the ground. But Lucy is not in a box, or in the ground. Because she is nowhere definite, she could be anywhere.

And these paintings are not landscape paintings. Because there aren't any landscapes up there, not in the old, tidy European sense, with a gentle hill, a curving river, a cottage, a mountain in the background, a golden evening sky. Instead there's a tangle, a receding maze, in which you can become lost almost as soon as you step off the path. There are no backgrounds in any of these paintings, no vistas; only a great deal of foreground that goes back and back, endlessly, involving you in its twists and turns of tree and branch and rock. No matter how far back in you go, there will be more. And the trees themselves are hardly trees; they are currents of energy, charged with violent color.

Who knows how many trees there were on the cliff just before Lucy disappeared? Who counted? Maybe there was one more, afterwards.

Lois sits in her chair and does not move. Her hand with the cup is raised halfway to her mouth. She hears something, almost hears it: a shout of recognition, or of joy.

She looks at the paintings, she looks into them. Every one of them is a 130 picture of Lucy. You can't see her exactly, but she's there, in behind the pink stone island or the one behind that. In the picture of the cliff she is hidden by the clutch of fallen rocks towards the bottom, in the one of the river shore she is crouching beneath the overturned canoe. In the yellow autumn woods she's behind the tree that cannot be seen because of the other trees, over beside the blue silver of pond; but if you walked into the picture and found the tree, it would be the wrong one, because the right one would be further on.

Everyone has to be somewhere, and this is where Lucy is. She is in Lois's apartment, in the holes that open inwards on the wall, not like windows but like doors. She is here. She is entirely alive.

Connections to Other Selections

1. Compare how the main character in "Death by Landscape" and the narrator of Tim O'Brien's "How to Tell a True War Story" (p. 552) are affected by the deaths of friends. How might each be described as a ghost story?

2. How do the descriptions of the landscapes in "Death by Landscape" and Hawthorne's "Young Goodman Brown" (p. 242) contribute to the themes of each story?
3. Write an essay that compares how Atwood creates suspense with Faulkner's strategies in "A Rose for Emily" (p. 47).

GISH JEN (b. 1956)

The daughter of Chinese immigrants, Gish Jen grew up in Yonkers and Scarsdale, New York, and was educated at Harvard, Stanford, and the Iowa Writer's Workshop. A fellowship at Radcliffe's Bunting Institute led to her first novel, *Typical American* (1991), which describes how Chinese immigrants in the United States are transformed by their efforts to pursue the American dream. Of her own family's experience as immigrants she says "my parents were born into a culture that puts society first," but "I was born into a culture that puts the individual first. This forced me to carve out a balance for myself." Jen's concern about her characters' identities is close to her own heart: her real name is Lillian but in high school she adopted Gish — after the actress Lillian Gish — because that "was part of becoming a writer" rather than "becoming the person I was supposed to be." Jen's fiction enlarges her readers' sense of what constitutes a "typical American." "In the American Society," which first appeared in the *Sewanee Review,* explores both the difficulties and humor associated with her characters' struggles with their identities.

In the American Society 1991

I. HIS OWN SOCIETY

When my father took over the pancake house, it was to send my little sister Mona and me to college. We were only in junior high at the time, but my father believed in getting a jump on things. "Those Americans always saying it," he told us. "Smart guys thinking in advance." My mother elaborated, explaining that businesses took bringing up, like children. They could take years to get going, she said, years.

In this case, though, we got rich right away. At two months we were breaking even, and at four, those same hotcakes that could barely withstand the weight of butter and syrup were supporting our family with ease. My mother bought a station wagon with air conditioning, my father an oversized, red vinyl recliner for the back room; and as time went on and the business continued to thrive, my father started to talk about his grandfather and the village he had reigned over in China — things my father had never talked about when he worked for other people. He told us about the bags of rice his family would give out to the poor at New Year's, and about the people who came to beg, on their hands and knees, for his grandfather to intercede for the more wayward of their relatives. "Like that Godfather in the movie," he would tell us as, his feet up, he distributed paychecks. Sometimes an employee would get two green envelopes instead of one, which meant that Jimmy needed a tooth pulled, say, or that Tiffany's husband was in the clinker again.

"It's nothing, nothing," he would insist, sinking back into his chair. "Who else is going to take care of you people?"

My mother would mostly just sigh about it. "Your father thinks this is China," she would say, and then she would go back to her mending. Once in a while, though, when my father had given away a particularly large sum, she would exclaim, outraged, "But this here is the U — S — of — A!" — this apparently having been what she used to tell immigrant stock boys when they came in late.

She didn't work at the supermarket anymore; but she had made it to the rank of manager before she left, and this had given her not only new words and phrases, but new ideas about herself, and about America, and about what was what in general. She had opinions, now, on how downtown should be zoned; she could pump her own gas and check her own oil; and for all she used to chide Mona and me for being "copycats," she herself was now interested in espadrilles, and wallpaper, and most recently, the town country club.

"So join already," said Mona, flicking a fly off her knee.

My mother enumerated the problems as she sliced up a quarter round of watermelon: There was the cost. There was the waiting list. There was the fact that no one in our family played either tennis or golf.

"So what?" said Mona.

"It would be waste," said my mother.

"Me and Callie can swim in the pool."

"Plus you need that recommendation letter from a member."

"Come *on,*" said Mona. "Annie's mom'd write you a letter in a *sec.*"

My mother's knife glinted in the early summer sun. I spread some more newspaper on the picnic table.

"*Plus* you have to eat there twice a month. You know what that means." My mother cut another, enormous slice of fruit.

"No, I *don't* know what that means," said Mona.

"It means Dad would have to wear a jacket, dummy," I said.

"Oh! Oh! Oh!" said Mona, clasping her hand to her breast. "Oh! Oh! Oh! Oh! Oh!"

We all laughed: my father had no use for nice clothes, and would wear only ten-year-old shirts, with grease-spotted pants, to show how little he cared what anyone thought.

"Your father doesn't believe in joining the American society," said my mother. "He wants to have his own society."

"So go to dinner without him." Mona shot her seeds out in long arcs over the lawn. "Who cares what he thinks?"

But of course we all did care, and knew my mother could not simply up and do as she pleased. For in my father's mind, a family owed its head a degree of loyalty that left no room for dissent. To embrace what he embraced was to love; and to embrace something else was to betray him.

He demanded a similar sort of loyalty of his workers, whom he treated more like servants than employees. Not in the beginning, of course. In the beginning all he wanted was for them to keep on doing what they used to do, and to that end he concentrated mostly on leaving them alone. As the months passed, though, he expected more and more of them, with the result that for all his largesse, he began to have trouble keeping help. The cooks and busboys complained that he asked them to fix radiators and trim hedges, not only at the restaurant, but at our house; the waitresses that he sent them on errands and made them chauffeur him around. Our head waitress, Gertrude, claimed that he once even asked her to scratch his back.

"It's not just the blacks don't believe in slavery," she said when she quit.

My father never quite registered her complaint, though, nor those of the others who left. Even after Eleanor quit, then Tiffany, then Gerald, and Jimmy, and even his best cook, Eureka Andy, for whom he had bought new glasses, he remained mostly convinced that the fault lay with them.

"All they understand is that assembly line," he lamented. "Robots, they are. 25 They want to be robots."

There *were* occasions when the clear running truth seemed to eddy, when he would pinch the vinyl of his chair up into little peaks and wonder if he was doing things right. But with time he would always smooth the peaks back down; and when business started to slide in the spring, he kept on like a horse in his ways.

By the summer our dishboy was overwhelmed with scraping. It was no longer just the hashbrowns that people were leaving for trash, and the service was as bad as the food. The waitresses served up French pancakes instead of German, apple juice instead of orange, spilt things on laps, on coats. On the Fourth of July some greenhorn sent an entire side of fries slaloming down a lady's *massif centrale*. Meanwhile in the back room, my father labored through articles on the economy.

"What is housing starts?" he puzzled. "What is GNP?"

Mona and I did what we could, filling in as busgirls and bookkeepers and, one afternoon, stuffing the comments box that hung by the cashier's desk. That was Mona's idea. We rustled up a variety of pens and pencils, checked boxes for an hour, smeared the cards up with coffee and grease, and waited. It took a few days for my father to notice that the box was full, and he didn't say anything about it for a few days more. Finally, though, he started to complain of fatigue; and then he began to complain that the staff was not what it could be. We encouraged him in this — pointing out, for instance, how many dishes got chipped — but in the end all that happened was that, for the first time since we took over the restaurant, my father got it into his head to fire someone. Skip, a skinny busboy who was saving up for a sportscar, said nothing as my father mumbled on about the price of dishes. My father's hands shook as he wrote out the severance check; and he spent the rest of the day napping in his chair once it was over.

As it was going on midsummer, Skip wasn't easy to replace. We hung a sign 30 in the window and advertised in the paper, but no one called the first week, and the person who called the second didn't show up for his interview. The third week, my father phoned Skip to see if he would come back, but a friend of his had already sold him a Corvette for cheap.

Finally a Chinese guy named Booker turned up. He couldn't have been more than thirty, and was wearing a lighthearted seersucker suit, but he looked as though life had him pinned: his eyes were bloodshot and his chest sunken, and the muscles of his neck seemed to strain with the effort of holding his head up. In a single dry breath he told us that he had never bussed tables but was wiling to learn, and that he was on the lam from the deportation authorities.

"I do not want to lie to you," he kept saying. He had come to the United States on a student visa, had run out of money, and was now in a bind. He was loath to go back to Taiwan, as it happened — he looked up at this point, to be sure my father wasn't pro-KMT — but all he had was a phony social security card and a willingness to absorb all blame, should anything untoward come to pass.

"I do not think, anyway, that it is against law to hire me, only to be me," he said, smiling faintly.

Anyone else would have examined him on this, but my father conceived of laws as speed bumps rather than curbs. He wiped the counter with his sleeve, and told Booker to report the next morning.

"I will be good worker," said Booker.   35

"Good," said my father.

"Anything you want me to do, I will do."

My father nodded.

Booker seemed to sink into himself for a moment. "Thank you," he said finally. "I am appreciate your help. I am very, very appreciate for everything." He reached out to shake my father's hand.

My father looked at him. "Did you eat today?" he asked in Mandarin.   40

Booker pulled at the hem of his jacket.

"Sit down," said my father. "Please, have a seat."

My father didn't tell my mother about Booker, and my mother didn't tell my father about the country club. She would never have applied, except that Mona, while over at Annie's, had let it drop that our mother wanted to join. Mrs. Lardner came by the very next day.

"Why, I'd be honored and delighted to write you people a letter," she said. Her skirt billowed around her.

"Thank you so much," said my mother. "But it's too much trouble for you,   45 and also my husband is . . ."

"Oh, it's no trouble at all, no trouble at all. I tell you." She leaned forward so that her chest freckles showed. "I know just how it is. It's a secret of course, but you know, my natural father was Jewish. Can you see it? Just look at my skin."

"My husband," said my mother.

"I'd be honored and delighted," said Mrs. Lardner with a little wave of her hands. "Just honored and delighted."

Mona was triumphant. "See, Mom," she said, waltzing around the kitchen when Mrs. Lardner left. "What did I tell you? 'I'm just honored and delighted, just honored and delighted.'" She waved her hands in the air.

"You know, the Chinese have a saying," said my mother. "To do nothing is   50 better than to overdo. You mean well, but you tell me now what will happen."

"I'll talk Dad into it," said Mona, still waltzing. "Or I bet Callie can. He'll do anything Callie says."

"I can try, anyway," I said.

"Did you hear what I said?" said my mother. Mona bumped into the broom closet door. "You're not going to talk anything; you've already made enough trouble." She started on the dishes with a clatter.

Mona poked diffidently at a mop.

I sponged off the counter. "Anyway," I ventured, "I bet our name'll never 55 even come up."

"That's if we're lucky," said my mother.

"There's all these people waiting," I said.

"Good," she said. She started on a pot.

I looked over at Mona, who was still cowering in the broom closet. "In fact, there's some black family's been waiting so long, they're going to sue," I said.

My mother turned off the water. "Where'd you hear that?"   60

"Patty told me."

She turned the water back on, started to wash a dish, then put it back down and shut the faucet.

"I'm sorry," said Mona.

"Forget it," said my mother. "Just forget it."

Booker turned out to be a model worker, whose boundless gratitude trans- 65 lated into a willingness to do anything. As he also learned quickly, he soon knew not only how to bus, but how to cook, and how to wait table, and how to keep the books. He fixed the walk-in door so that it stayed shut, reupholstered the torn seats in the dining room, and devised a system for tracking inventory. The only stone in the rice was that he tended to be sickly; but, reliable even in illness, he would always send a friend to take his place. In this way we got to know Ronald, Lynn, Dirk, and Cedric, all of whom, like Booker, had problems with their legal status and were anxious to please. They weren't all as capable as Booker, though, with the exception of Cedric, whom my father often hired even when Booker was well. A round wag of a man who called Mona and me *shou hou* — skinny monkeys — he was a professed nonsmoker who was never-theless always begging drags off of other people's cigarettes. This last habit drove our head cook, Fernando, crazy, especially since, when refused a hit, Cedric would occasionally snitch one. Winking impishly at Mona and me, he would steal up to an ashtray, take a quick puff, and then break out laughing so that the smoke came rolling out of his mouth in a great incriminatory cloud. Fernando accused him of stealing fresh cigarettes too, even whole packs.

"Why else do you think he's weaseling around in the back of the store all the time," he said. His face was blotchy with anger. "The man is a frigging thief."

Other members of the staff supported him in this contention and joined in on an "Operation Identification," which involved numbering and initialing their cigarettes — even though what they seemed to fear for wasn't so much their cigarettes as their jobs. Then one of the cooks quit; and rather than promote someone, my father hired Cedric for the position. Rumors flew that he was taking only half the normal salary, that Alex had been pressured to resign, and that my father was looking for a position with which to placate Booker, who had been bypassed because of his health.

The result was that Fernando categorically refused to work with Cedric.

"The only way I'll cook with that piece of slime," he said, shaking his huge tattooed fist, "is if it's his ass frying on the grill."

My father cajoled and cajoled, to no avail, and in the end was simply forced 70
to put them on different schedules.

The next week Fernando got caught stealing a carton of minute steaks. My
father would not tell even Mona and me how he knew to be standing by the
back door when Fernando was on his way out, but everyone suspected Booker.
Everyone but Fernando, that is, who was sure Cedric had been the tip-off. My
father held a staff meeting in which he tried to reassure everyone that Alex had
left on his own, and that he had no intention of firing anyone. But though he
was careful not to mention Fernando, everyone was so amazed that he was being
allowed to stay that Fernando was incensed nonetheless.

"Don't you all be putting your bug eyes on me," he said. "*He's* the frigging
crook." He grabbed Cedric by the collar.

Cedric raised an eyebrow. "Cook, you mean," he said.

At this Fernando punched Cedric in the mouth; and the words he had just
uttered notwithstanding, my father fired him on the spot.

With everything that was happening, Mona and I were ready to be getting 75
out of the restaurant. It was almost time: the days were still stuffy with summer,
but our window shade had started flapping in the evening as if gearing up to go
out. That year the breezes were full of salt, as they sometimes were when they
came in from the East, and they blew anchors and docks through my mind like
so many tumbleweeds, filling my dreams with wherries and lobsters and grainy-
faced men who squinted, day in and day out, at the sky.

It was time for a change, you could feel it; and yet the pancake house was
the same as ever. The day before school started my father came home with bad
news.

"Fernando called police," he said, wiping his hand on his pant leg.

My mother naturally wanted to know what police; and so with much coughing and hawing, the long story began, the latest installment of which had the
police calling immigration, and immigration sending an investigator. My mother
sat stiff as whalebone as my father described how the man summarily refused
lunch on the house and how my father had admitted, under pressure, that he
knew there were "things" about his workers.

"So now what happens?"

My father didn't know. "Booker and Cedric went with him to the jail," he 80
said. "But me, here I am." He laughed uncomfortably.

The next day my father posted bail for "his boys" and waited apprehensively
for something to happen. The day after that he waited again, and the day after
that he called our neighbor's law student son, who suggested my father call the
immigration department under an alias. My father took his advice; and it was
thus that he discovered that Booker was right: it was illegal for aliens to work,
but it wasn't to hire them.

In the happy interval that ensued, my father apologized to my mother, who
in turn confessed about the country club, for which my father had no choice
but to forgive her. Then he turned his attention back to "his boys."

My mother didn't see that there was anything to do.

"I like to talking to the judge," said my father.

"This is not China," said my mother. 85

"I'm only talking to him. I'm not give him money unless he wants it."

"You're going to land up in jail."

"So what else I should do?" My father threw up his hands. "Those are my boys."

"Your boys!" exploded my mother. "What about your family? What about your wife?"

My father took a long sip of tea. "You know," he said finally, "in the war my father sent our cook to the soldiers to use. He always said it — the province comes before the town, the town comes before the family."

"A restaurant is not a town," said my mother.

My father sipped at his tea again. "You know, when I first come to the United States, I also had to hide-and-seek with those deportation guys. If people did not helping me, I'm not here today."

My mother scrutinized her hem.

After a minute I volunteered that before seeing a judge, he might try a lawyer.

He turned. "Since when did you become so afraid like your mother?"

I started to say that it wasn't a matter of fear, but he cut me off.

"What I need today," he said, "is a son."

My father and I spent the better part of the next day standing in lines at the immigration office. He did not get to speak to a judge, but with much persistence he managed to speak to a judge's clerk, who tried to persuade him that it was not her place to extend him advice. My father, though, shamelessly plied her with compliments and offers of free pancakes until she finally conceded that she personally doubted anything would happen to either Cedric or Booker.

"Especially if they're 'needed workers.'" she said, rubbing at the red marks her glasses left on her nose. She yawned. "Have you thought about sponsoring them to become permanent residents?"

Could he do that? My father was overjoyed. And what if he saw to it right away? Would she perhaps put in a good word with the judge?

She yawned again, her nostrils flaring. "Don't worry," she said. "They'll get a fair hearing."

My father returned jubilant. Booker and Cedric hailed him as their savior, their Buddha incarnate. He was like a father to them, they said; and laughing and clapping, they made him tell the story over and over, sorting over the details like jewels. And how old was the assistant judge? And what did she say?

That evening my father tipped the paperboy a dollar and bought a pot of mums for my mother, who suffered them to be placed on the dining room table. The next night he took us all out to dinner. Then on Saturday, Mona found a letter on my father's chair at the restaurant.

Dear Mr. Chang,
You are the grat boss. But, we do not like to trial, so will runing away now. Plese to excus us. People saying the law in America is fears like dragon. Here is only $140. We hope some day we can pay back the rest bale. You will getting intrest, as you diserving, so grat a boss you are. Thank you for every thing. In next life you will be burn in rich family, with no more pancaks.

Yours truley,
Booker + Cedric

In the weeks that followed my father went to the pancake house for crises, but otherwise hung around our house, fiddling idly with the sump pump and boiler in an effort, he said, to get ready for winter. It was as though he had gone into retirement, except that instead of moving South, he had moved to the basement. He even took to showering my mother with little attentions, and to calling her "old girl," and when we finally heard that the club had entertained all the applications it could for the year, he was so sympathetic that he seemed more disappointed than my mother.

II. IN THE AMERICAN SOCIETY

Mrs. Lardner tempered the bad news with an invitation to a bon voyage 105 "bash" she was throwing for a friend of hers who was going to Greece for six months.

"Do come," she urged. "You'll meet everyone, and then, you know, if things open up in the spring . . ." She waved her hands.

My mother wondered if it would be appropriate to show up at a party for someone they didn't know, but "the honest truth" was that this was an annual affair. "If it's not Greece, it's Antibes," sighed Mrs. Lardner. "We really just do it because his wife left him and his daughter doesn't speak to him, and poor Jeremy just feels so *unloved*."

She also invited Mona and me to the goings on, as "*demi*-guests" to keep Annie out of the champagne. I wasn't too keen on the idea, but before I could say anything, she had already thanked us for so generously agreeing to honor her with our presence.

"A pair of little princesses, you are!" she told us. "A pair of princesses!"

The party was that Sunday. On Saturday, my mother took my father out 110 shopping for a suit. As it was the end of September, she insisted that he buy a worsted rather than a seersucker, even though it was only ten, rather than fifty percent off. My father protested that it was as hot out as ever, which was true — a thick Indian summer had cozied murderously up to us — but to no avail. Summer clothes, said my mother, were not properly worn after Labor Day.

The suit was unfortunately as extravagant in length as it was in price, which posed an additional quandary, since the tailor wouldn't be in until Monday. The salesgirl, though, found a way of tacking it up temporarily.

"Maybe this suit not fit me," fretted my father.

"Just don't take your jacket off," said the salesgirl.

He gave her a tip before they left, but when he got home refused to remove the price tag.

"I like to asking the tailor about the size," he insisted. 115

"You mean you're going to *wear* it and then return it?" Mona rolled her eyes.

"I didn't say I'm return it," said my father stiffly. "I like to asking the tailor, that's all."

The party started off swimmingly, except that most people were wearing bermudas or wrap skirts. Still, my parents carried on, sharing with great feeling the complaints about the heat. Of course my father tried to eat a cracker full of shallots and burnt himself in an attempt to help Mr. Lardner turn the coals of the barbecue; but on the whole he seemed to be doing all right. Not nearly so well as my mother, though, who had accepted an entire cupful of Mrs. Lardner's magic punch, and seemed indeed to be under some spell. As Mona and Annie skirmished over whether some boy in their class inhaled when he smoked, I watched my mother take off her shoes, laughing and laughing as a man with a beard regaled her with navy stories by the pool. Apparently he had been stationed in the Orient and remembered a few words of Chinese, which made my mother laugh still more. My father excused himself to go to the men's room then drifted back and "dropped" anchor at the hors d'oeuvre table, while my mother sailed on to a group of women, who tinkled at length over the clarity of her complexion. I dug out a book I had brought.

Just when I'd cracked the spine, though, Mrs. Lardner came by to bewail her shortage of servers. Her caterers were criminals, I agreed; and the next thing I knew I was handing out bits of marine life, making the rounds as amicably as I could.

"Here you go, Dad," I said when I got to the hors d'oeuvre table.   120

"Everything is fine," he said.

I hesitated to leave him alone; but then the man with the beard zeroed in on him, and though he talked of nothing but my mother, I thought it would be okay to get back to work. Just that moment, though, Jeremy Brothers lurched our way, an empty, albeit corked, wine bottle in hand. He was a slim, well-proportioned man, with a Roman nose and small eyes and a nice manly jaw that he allowed to hang agape.

"Hello," he said drunkenly. "Pleased to meet you."

"Pleased to meeting you," said my father.

"Right," said Jeremy. "Right. Listen. I have this bottle here, this most recal- 125 citrant bottle. You see that it refuses to do my bidding. I bid it open sesame, please, and it does nothing." He pulled the cork out with his teeth, then turned the bottle upside down.

My father nodded.

"Would you have a word with it please?" said Jeremy. The man with the beard excused himself. "Would you please have a god-damned word with it?"

My father laughed uncomfortably.

"Ah!" Jeremy bowed a little. "Excuse me, excuse me, excuse me. You are not my man, not my man at all." He bowed again and started to leave, but then circled back. "Viticulture is not your forte, yes I can see that, see that plainly. But may I trouble you on another matter? Forget the damned bottle." He threw it into the pool, and winked at the people he splashed. "I have another matter. Do you speak Chinese?"

My father said he did not, but Jeremy pulled out a handkerchief with some 130 characters on it anyway, saying that his daughter had sent it from Hong Kong and that he thought the characters might be some secret message.

"Long life," said my father.

"But you haven't looked at it yet."

"I know what it says without looking." My father winked at me.

"You do?"

"Yes, I do."

"You're making fun of me, aren't you?"

"No, no, no," said my father, winking again.

"Who are you anyway?" said Jeremy.

His smile fading, my father shrugged.

"Who are you?"

My father shrugged again.

Jeremy began to roar. "This is my party, *my party,* and I've never seen you before in my life." My father backed up as Jeremy came toward him. *"Who are you? WHO ARE YOU?"*

Just as my father was going to step back into the pool, Mrs. Lardner came running up. Jeremy informed her that there was a man crashing his party.

"Nonsense," said Mrs. Lardner. "This is Ralph Chang, who I invited extra especially so he could meet you." She straightened the collar of Jeremy's peach-colored polo shirt for him.

"Yes, well we've had a chance to chat," said Jeremy.

She whispered in his ear; he mumbled something; she whispered something more.

"I do apologize," he said finally.

My father didn't say anything.

"I do." Jeremy seemed genuinely contrite. "Doubtless you've seen drunks before, haven't you? You must have them in China."

"Okay," said my father.

As Mrs. Lardner glided off, Jeremy clapped his arm over my father's shoulders. "You know, I really am quite sorry, quite sorry."

My father nodded.

"What can I do, how can I make it up to you?"

"No thank you."

"No, tell me, tell me," wheedled Jeremy. "Tickets to casino night?" My father shook his head. "You don't gamble. Dinner at Bartholomew's?" My father shook his head again. "You don't eat." Jeremy scratched his chin. "You know, my wife was like you. Old Annabelle could never let me make things up — never, never, never, never, never."

My father wriggled out from under his arm.

"How about sport clothes? You are rather overdressed, you know, excuse me for saying so. But here." He took off his polo shirt and folded it up. "You can have this with my most profound apologies." He ruffled his chest hairs with his free hand.

"No thank you," said my father.

"No, take it, take it. Accept my apologies." He thrust the shirt into my father's arms. "I'm so very sorry, so very sorry. Please, try it on."

Helplessly holding the shirt, my father searched the crowd for my mother.

"Here, I'll help you off with your coat."

My father froze.

Jeremy reached over and took his jacket off. "Milton's, one hundred twenty-five dollars reduced to one hundred twelve-fifty," he read. "What a bargain, what a bargain!"

"Please give it back," pleaded my father. "Please."

"Now for your shirt," ordered Jeremy. 165

Heads began to turn.

"Take off your shirt."

"I do not take orders like a servant," announced my father.

"Take off your shirt, or I'm going to throw this jacket right into the pool, just right into this little pool here." Jeremy held it over the water.

"Go ahead." 170

"One hundred twelve-fifty," taunted Jeremy. "One hundred twelve . . ."

My father flung the polo shirt into the water with such force that part of it bounced back up into the air like a fluorescent fountain. Then it settled into a soft heap on top of the water. My mother hurried up.

"You're a sport!" said Jeremy, suddenly breaking into a smile and slapping my father on the back. "You're a sport! I like that. A man with spirit, that's what you are. A man with panache. Allow me to return to you your jacket." He handed it back to my father. "Good value you got on that, good value."

My father hurled the coat into the pool too. "We're leaving," he said grimly. "Leaving!"

"Now, Ralphie," said Mrs. Lardner, bustling up; but my father was already 175 stomping off.

"Get your sister," he told me. To my mother: "Get your shoes."

"That was *great*, Dad," said Mona as we walked down to the car. "You were *stupendous*."

"Way to show 'em," I said.

"What?" said my father offhandedly.

Although it was only just dusk, we were in a gulch, which made it hard to 180 see anything except the gleam of his white shirt moving up the hill ahead of us.

"It was all my fault," began my mother.

"Forget it," said my father grandly. Then he said, "The only trouble is I left those keys in my jacket pocket."

"Oh *no*," said Mona.

"Oh no is right," said my mother.

"So we'll walk home," I said. 185

"But how're we going to get into the *house*," said Mona.

The noise of the party churned through the silence.

"Someone has to going back," said my father.

"Let's go to the pancake house first," suggested my mother. "We can wait there until the party is finished, and then call Mrs. Lardner."

Having all agreed that that was a good plan, we started walking again. 190

"God, just think," said Mona. "We're going to have to *dive* for them."

My father stopped a moment. We waited.

"You girls are good swimmers," he said finally. "Not like me."

Then his shirt started moving again, and we trooped up the hill after it, into the dark.

Connections to Other Selections

1. Discuss the role of cultural tradition in Jen's story and Mishima's "Patriotism" (p. 506).
2. Compare the purpose of the humor in Jen's story with that of O'Connor in "A Good Man Is Hard to Find" (p. 368).
3. Write an essay on the role of fathers in Jen's story, Hemingway's "Soldier's Home" (p. 125), and Cheever's "Reunion" (p. 460).

TIM O'BRIEN (b. 1946)

Born in Austin, Minnesota, Tim O'Brien was educated at Macalester College and Harvard University. He was drafted to serve in the Vietnam War and received a Purple Heart. His work is heavily influenced by his service in the war. His first book, *If I Die in a Combat Zone, Box Me Up and Ship Me Home* (1973), is a blend of fiction and actual experiences during his tour of duty. *Going After Cacciato*, judged by many critics to be the best work of American fiction about the Vietnam War, won the National Book Award in 1978. He has also published two other novels, *Northern Lights* (1974) and *The Nuclear Age* (1985). "How to Tell a True War Story" is from a collection of interrelated stories titled *The Things They Carried* (1990). Originally published in *Esquire*, this story is at once grotesque and beautiful in its attempt to be true to experience.

How to Tell a True War Story   1987

This is true.

I had a buddy in Vietnam. His name was Bob Kiley, but everybody called him Rat.

A friend of his gets killed, so about a week later Rat sits down and writes a letter to the guy's sister. Rat tells her what a great brother she had, how strack° the guy was, a number one pal and comrade. A real soldier's soldier, Rat says. Then he tells a few stories to make the point, how her brother would always volunteer for stuff nobody else would volunteer for in a million years, dangerous stuff, like doing recon° or going out on these really badass night patrols. Stainless steel balls, Rat tells her. The guy was a little crazy, for sure, but crazy in a good way, a real daredevil, because he liked the challenge of it, he liked testing himself, just man against gook. A great, great guy, Rat says.

Anyway, it's a terrific letter, very personal and touching. Rat almost bawls

---

strack: A strict military appearance.
doing recon: Reconnaissance, or exploratory survey of enemy territory.

writing it. He gets all teary telling about the good times they had together, how her brother made the war seem almost fun, always raising hell and lighting up villes° and bringing smoke to bear every which way. A great sense of humor, too. Like the time at this river when he went fishing with a whole damn crate of hand grenades. Probably the funniest thing in world history, Rat says, all that gore, about twenty zillion dead gook fish. Her brother, he had the right attitude. He knew how to have a good time. On Halloween, this real hot spooky night, the dude paints up his body all different colors and puts on this weird mask and goes out on ambush almost stark naked, just boots and balls and an M-16. A tremendous human being, Rat says. Pretty nutso sometimes, but you could trust him with your life.

And then the letter gets very sad and serious. Rat pours his heart out. He 5 says he loved the guy. He says the guy was his best friend in the world. They were like soul mates, he says, like twins or something, they had a whole lot in common. He tells the guy's sister he'll look her up when the war's over.

So what happens?

Rat mails the letter. He waits two months. The dumb cooze never writes back.

A true war story is never moral. It does not instruct, nor encourage virtue, nor suggest models of proper human behavior, nor restrain men from doing the things they have always done. If a story seems moral, do not believe it. If at the end of a war story you feel uplifted, or if you feel that some small bit of rectitude has been salvaged from the larger waste, then you have been made the victim of a very old and terrible lie. There is no rectitude whatsover. There is no virtue. As a first rule of thumb, therefore, you can tell a true war story by its absolute and uncompromising allegiance to obscenity and evil. Listen to Rat Kiley. *Cooze,* he says. He does not say *bitch.* He certainly does not say *woman,* or *girl.* He says *cooze.* Then he spits and stares. He's nineteen years old — it's too much for him — so he looks at you with those big gentle killer eyes and says *cooze,* because his friend is dead, and because it's so incredibly sad and true: she never wrote back.

You can tell a true war story if it embarrasses you. If you don't care for obscenity, you don't care for the truth; if you don't care for the truth, watch how you vote. Send guys to war, they come home talking dirty.

Listen to Rat: "Jesus Christ, man, I write this beautiful fucking letter, I slave 10 over it, and what happens? The dumb cooze never writes back."

The dead guy's name was Curt Lemon. What happened was, we crossed a muddy river and marched west into the mountains, and on the third day we took a break along a trail junction in deep jungle. Right away, Lemon and Rat Kiley started goofing off. They didn't understand about the spookiness. They were kids; they just didn't know. A nature hike, they thought, not even a war, so they went off into the shade of some giant trees — quadruple canopy, no sunlight at all — and they were giggling and calling each other motherfucker and playing a silly game they'd invented. The game involved smoke grenades, which were harmless unless you did stupid things, and what they did was pull out the pin

---

villes: Villages.

and stand a few feet apart and play catch under the shade of those huge trees. Whoever chickened out was a motherfucker. And if nobody chickened out, the grenade would make a light popping sound and they'd be covered with smoke and they'd laugh and dance around and then do it again.

It's all exactly true.

It happened nearly twenty years ago, but I still remember that trail junction and the giant trees and a soft dripping sound somewhere beyond the trees. I remember the smell of moss. Up in the canopy there were tiny white blossoms, but no sunlight at all, and I remember the shadows spreading out under the trees where Lemon and Rat Kiley were playing catch with smoke grenades. Mitchell Sanders sat flipping his yo-yo. Norman Bowker and Kiowa and Dave Jensen were dozing, or half-dozing, and all around us were those ragged green mountains.

Except for the laughter things were quiet.

At one point, I remember, Mitchell Sanders turned and looked at me, not 15 quite nodding, then after a while he rolled up his yo-yo and moved away.

It's hard to tell what happened next.

They were just goofing. There was a noise, I suppose, which must've been the detonator, so I glanced behind me and watched Lemon step from the shade into bright sunlight. His face was suddenly brown and shining. A handsome kid, really. Sharp gray eyes, lean and narrow-waisted, and when he died it was almost beautiful, the way the sunlight came around him and lifted him up and sucked him high into a tree full of moss and vines and white blossoms.

In any war story, but especially a true one, it's difficult to separate what happened from what seemed to happen. What seems to happen becomes its own happening and has to be told that way. The angles of vision are skewed. When a booby trap explodes, you close your eyes and duck and float outside yourself. When a guy dies, like Lemon, you look away and then look back for a moment and then look away again. The pictures get jumbled; you tend to miss a lot. And then afterward, when you go to tell about it, there is always that surreal seemingness, which makes the story seem untrue, but which in fact represents the hard and exact truth as it seemed.

In many cases a true war story cannot be believed. If you believe it, be skeptical. It's a question of credibility. Often the crazy stuff is true and the normal stuff isn't because the normal stuff is necessary to make you believe the truly incredible craziness.

In other cases you can't even tell a true war story. Sometimes it's just beyond 20 telling.

I heard this one, for example, from Mitchell Sanders. It was near dusk and we were sitting at my foxhole along a wide, muddy river north of Quang Ngai. I remember how peaceful the twilight was. A deep pinkish red spilled out on the river, which moved without sound, and in the morning we would cross the river and march west into the mountains. The occasion was right for a good story.

"God's truth," Mitchell Sanders said. "A six-man patrol goes up into the mountains on a basic listening-post operation. The idea's to spend a week up there, just lie low and listen for enemy movement. They've got a radio along, so if they hear anything suspicious — anything — they're supposed to call in artillery or gunships, whatever it takes. Otherwise they keep strict field discipline. Absolute silence. They just listen."

He glanced at me to make sure I had the scenario. He was playing with his yo-yo, making it dance with short, tight little strokes of the wrist.

His face was blank in the dusk.

"We're talking hardass LP. These six guys, they don't say boo for a solid 25 week. They don't got tongues. *All* ears."

"Right," I said.

"Understand me?"

"Invisible."

Sanders nodded.

"Affirm," he said. "Invisible. So what happens is, these guys get themselves 30 deep in the bush, all camouflaged up, and they lie down and wait and that's all they do, nothing else, they lie there for seven straight days and just listen. And man, I'll tell you — it's spooky. This is mountains. You don't *know* spooky till you been there. Jungle, sort of, except it's way up in the clouds and there's always this fog — like rain, except it's not raining — everything's all wet and swirly and tangled up and you can't see jack, you can't find your own pecker to piss with. Like you don't even have a body. Serious spooky. You just go with the vapors — the fog sort of takes you in. . . . And the sounds, man. The sounds carry forever. You hear shit nobody should *ever* hear."

Sanders was quiet for a second, just working the yo-yo, then he smiled at me. "So, after a couple days the guys start hearing this real soft, kind of wacked-out music. Weird echoes and stuff. Like a radio or something, but it's not a radio, it's this strange gook music that comes right out of the rocks. Faraway, sort of, but right up close, too. They try to ignore it. But it's a listening post, right? So they listen. And every night they keep hearing this crazyass gook concert. All kinds of chimes and xylophones. I mean, this is wilderness — no way, it can't be real — but there it *is,* like the mountains are tuned in to Radio Fucking Hanoi. Naturally they get nervous. One guy sticks Juicy Fruit in his ears. Another guy almost flips. Thing is, though, they can't report music. They can't get on the horn and call back to base and say, 'Hey, listen, we need some firepower, we got to blow away this weirdo gook rock band.' They can't do that. It wouldn't go down. So they lie there in the fog and keep their mouths shut. And what makes it extra bad, see, is the poor dudes can't horse around like normal. Can't joke it away. Can't even talk to each other except maybe in whispers, all hush-hush, and that just revs up the willies. All they do is listen."

Again there was some silence as Mitchell Sanders looked out on the river. The dark was coming on hard now, and off to the west I could see the mountains rising in silhouette, all the mysteries and unknowns.

"This next part," Sanders said quietly, "you won't believe."

"Probably not," I said.

"You won't. And you know why?" 35

"Why?"

He gave me a tired smile. "Because it happened. Because every word is absolutely dead-on true."

Sanders made a little sound in his throat, like a sigh, as if to say he didn't care if I believed it or not. But he did care. He wanted me to believe, I could tell. He seemed sad, in a way.

"These six guys, they're pretty fried out by now, and one night they start hearing voices. Like at a cocktail party. That's what it sounds like, this big swank gook cocktail party somewhere out there in the fog. Music and chitchat and stuff. It's crazy, I know, but they hear the champagne corks. They hear the actual martini glasses. Real hoity-toity, all very civilized, except this isn't civilization. This is Nam.

"Anyway, the guys try to be cool. They just lie there and groove, but after a while they start hearing — you won't believe this — they hear chamber music. They hear violins and shit. They hear this terrific mama-san soprano. Then after a while they hear gook opera and a glee club and the Haiphong Boys Choir and a barbershop quartet and all kinds of weird chanting and Buddha-Buddha stuff. The whole time, in the background, there's still that cocktail party going on. All these different voices. Not human voices, though. Because it's the mountains. Follow me? The rock — it's *talking*. And the fog, too, and the grass and the goddamn mongooses. Everything talks. The trees talk politics, the monkeys talk religion. The whole country. Vietnam, the place talks.

"The guys can't cope. They lose it. They get on the radio and report enemy movement — a whole army, they say — and they order up the firepower. They get arty° and gunships. They call in air strikes. And I'll tell you, they fuckin' crash that cocktail party. All night long, they just smoke those mountains. They make jungle juice. They blow away trees and glee clubs and whatever else there is to blow away. Scorch time. They walk napalm up and down the ridges. They bring in the Cobras and F-4s, they use Willie Peter and HE° and incendiaries. It's all fire. They make those mountains burn.

"Around dawn things finally get quiet. Like you never even *heard* quiet before. One of those real thick, real misty days — just clouds and fog, they're off in this special zone — and the mountains are absolutely dead-flat silent. Like Brigadoon° — pure vapor, you know? Everything's all sucked up inside the fog. Not a single sound, except they still *hear* it.

"So they pack up and start humping. They head down the mountain, back to base camp, and when they get there they don't say diddly. They don't talk. Not a word, like they're deaf and dumb. Later on this fat bird colonel comes up and asks what the hell happened out there. What'd they hear? Why all the ordnance? The man's ragged out, he gets down tight on their case. I mean, they spent six trillion dollars on firepower, and this fatass colonel wants answers, he wants to know what the fuckin' story is.

"But the guys don't say zip. They just look at him for a while, sort of funnylike, sort of amazed, and the whole war is right there in that stare. It says everything you can't ever say. It says, man, you got *wax* in your ears. It says, poor bastard, you'll never know — wrong frequency — you don't *even* want to hear this. Then they salute the fucker and walk away, because certain stories you don't ever tell."

arty: Artillery.
Willie Peter: White phosphorus, an incendiary substance; *HE:* High explosives.
Brigadoon: A fictional village in Scotland that only appears once every one hundred years; subject of a popular American musical (1947).

You can tell a true war story by the way it never seems to end. Not then, 45 not ever. Not when Mitchell Sanders stood up and moved off into the dark.

It all happened.

Even now I remember that yo-yo. In a way, I suppose, you had to be there, you had to hear it, but I could tell how desperately Sanders wanted me to believe him, his frustration at not quite getting the details right, not quite pinning down the final and definitive truth.

And I remember sitting at my foxhole that night, watching the shadows of Quang Ngai, thinking about the coming day and how we would cross the river and march west into the mountains, all the ways I might die, all the things I did not understand.

Late in the night Mitchell Sanders touched my shoulder.

"Just came to me," he whispered. "The moral, I mean. Nobody listens. 50 Nobody hears nothing. Like that fatass colonel. The politicians, all the civilian types, what they need is to go out on LP. The vapors, man. Trees and rocks— you got to *listen* to your enemy."

And then again, in the morning, Sanders came up to me. The platoon was preparing to move out, checking weapons, going through all the little rituals that preceded a day's march. Already the lead squad had crossed the river and was filing off toward the west.

"I got a confession to make," Sanders said. "Last night, man, I had to make up a few things."

"I know that."

"The glee club. There wasn't any glee club."

"Right." 55

"No opera."

"Forget it, I understand."

"Yeah, but listen, it's still true. Those six guys, they heard wicked sound out there. They heard sound you just plain won't believe."

Sanders pulled on his rucksack, closed his eyes for a moment, then almost smiled at me.

I knew what was coming but I beat him to it. 60

"All right," I said, "what's the moral?"

"Forget it."

"No, go ahead."

For a long while he was quiet, looking away, and the silence kept stretching out until it was almost embarrassing. Then he shrugged and gave me a stare that lasted all day.

"Hear that quiet, man?" he said. "There's your moral." 65

In a true war story, if there's a moral at all, it's like the thread that makes the cloth. You can't tease it out. You can't extract the meaning without unraveling the deeper meaning. And in the end, really, there's nothing much to say about a true war story, except maybe "Oh."

True war stories do not generalize. They do not indulge in abstraction or analysis.

For example: War is hell. As a moral declaration the old truism seems perfectly true, and yet because it abstracts, because it generalizes, I can't believe it with my stomach. Nothing turns inside.

It comes down to gut instinct. A true war story, if truly told, makes the stomach believe.

This one does it for me. I've told it before — many times, many versions — 70 but here's what actually happened.

We crossed the river and marched west into the mountains. On the third day, Curt Lemon stepped on a booby-trapped 105 round. He was playing catch with Rat Kiley, laughing, and then he was dead. The trees were thick; it took nearly an hour to cut an LZ for the dustoff.°

Later, higher in the mountains, we came across a baby VC° water buffalo. What it was doing there I don't know — no farms or paddies — but we chased it down and got a rope around it and led it along to a deserted village where we set for the night. After supper Rat Kiley went over and stroked its nose.

He opened up a can of C rations, pork and beans, but the baby buffalo wasn't interested.

Rat shrugged.

He stepped back and shot it through the right front knee. The animal did 75 not make a sound. It went down hard, then got up again, and Rat took careful aim and shot off an ear. He shot it in the hindquarters and in the little hump at its back. He shot it twice in the flanks. It wasn't to kill; it was just to hurt. He put the rifle muzzle up against the mouth and shot the mouth away. Nobody said much. The whole platoon stood there watching, feeling all kinds of things, but there wasn't a great deal of pity for the baby water buffalo. Lemon was dead. Rat Kiley had lost his best friend in the world. Later in the week he would write a long personal letter to the guy's sister, who would not write back, but for now it was a question of pain. He shot off the tail. He shot away chunks of meat below the ribs. All around us there was the smell of smoke and filth, and deep greenery, and the evening was humid and very hot. Rat went to automatic. He shot randomly, almost casually, quick little spurts in the belly and butt. Then he reloaded, squatted down, and shot it in the left front knee. Again the animal fell hard and tried to get up, but this time it couldn't quite make it. It wobbled and went down sideways. Rat shot it in the nose. He bent forward and whispered something, as if talking to a pet, then he shot it in the throat. All the while the baby buffalo was silent, or almost silent, just a light bubbling sound where the nose had been. It lay very still. Nothing moved except the eyes, which were enormous, the pupils shiny black and dumb.

Rat Kiley was crying. He tried to say something, but then cradled his rifle and went off by himself.

The rest of us stood in a ragged circle around the baby buffalo. For a time no one spoke. We had witnessed something essential, something brand-new and profound, a piece of the world so startling there was not yet a name for it.

Somebody kicked the baby buffalo.

It was still alive, though just barely, just in the eyes.

"Amazing," Dave Jensen said. "My whole life, I never seen anything like it." 80

LZ: Landing zone; *dustoff*: Helicopter evacuation of a casualty.
VC: Vietcong (North Vietnamese).

"Never?"

"Not hardly. Not once."

Kiowa and Mitchell Sanders picked up the baby buffalo. They hauled it across the open square, hoisted it up, and dumped it in the village well.

Afterward, we sat waiting for Rat to get himself together.

"Amazing," Dave Jensen kept saying.

"For sure."

"A new wrinkle. I never seen it before."

Mitchell Sanders took out his yo-yo.

"Well, that's Nam," he said. "Garden of Evil. Over here, man, every sin's real fresh and original."

How do you generalize?

War is hell, but that's not the half of it, because war is also mystery and terror and adventure and courage and discovery and holiness and pity and despair and longing and love. War is nasty; war is fun. War is thrilling; war is drudgery. War makes you a man; war makes you dead.

The truths are contradictory. It can be argued, for instance, that war is grotesque. But in truth war is also beauty. For all its horror, you can't help but gape at the awful majesty of combat. You stare out at tracer rounds unwinding through the dark like brilliant red ribbons. You crouch in ambush as a cool, impassive moon rises over the nighttime paddies. You admire the fluid symmetries of troops on the move, the harmonies of sound and shape and proportion, the great sheets of metal-fire streaming down from a gunship, the illumination rounds, the white phosphorous, the purply black glow of napalm, the rocket's red glare. It's not pretty, exactly. It's astonishing. It fills the eye. It commands you. You hate it, yes, but your eyes do not. Like a killer forest fire, like cancer under a microscope, any battle or bombing raid or artillery barrage has the aesthetic purity of absolute moral indifference — a powerful, implacable beauty — and a true war story will tell the truth about this, though the truth is ugly.

To generalize about war is like generalizing about peace. Almost everything is true. Almost nothing is true. At its core, perhaps, war is just another name for death, and yet any soldier will tell you, if he tells the truth, that proximity to death brings with it a corresponding proximity to life. After a fire fight, there is always the immense pleasure of aliveness. The trees are alive. The grass, the soil — everything. All around you things are purely living, and you among them, and the aliveness makes you tremble. You feel an intense, out-of-the-skin awareness of your living self — your truest self, the human being you want to be and then become by the force of wanting it. In the midst of evil you want to be a good man. You want decency. You want justice and courtesy and human concord, things you never knew you wanted. There is a kind of largeness to it; a kind of godliness. Though it's odd, you're never more alive than when you're almost dead. You recognize what's valuable. Freshly, as if for the first time, you love what's best in yourself and in the world, all that might be lost. At the hour of dusk you sit at your foxhole and look out on a wide river turning pinkish red, and at the mountains beyond, and although in the morning you must cross the river and go into the mountains and do terrible things and maybe die, even so, you find yourself studying the fine colors on the river, you feel wonder and awe at the setting of the sun, and you are filled with a hard, aching love for how the world could be and always should be, but now is not.

Mitchell Sanders was right. For the common soldier, at least, war has the feel — the spiritual texture — of a great ghostly fog, thick and permanent. There is no clarity. Everything swirls. The old rules are no longer binding, the old truths no longer true. Right spills over into wrong. Order blends into chaos, love into hate, ugliness into beauty, law into anarchy, civility into savagery. The vapors suck you in. You can't tell where you are, or why you're there, and the only certainty is absolute ambiguity.

In war you lose your sense of the definite, hence your sense of truth itself, 95 and therefore it's safe to say that in a true war story nothing much is ever very true.

Often in a true war story there is not even a point, or else the point doesn't hit you until twenty years later, in your sleep, and you wake up and shake your wife and start telling the story to her, except when you get to the end you've forgotten the point again. And then for a long time you lie there watching the story happen in your head. You listen to your wife's breathing. The war's over. You close your eyes. You smile and think, Christ, what's the *point?*

This one wakes me up.

In the mountains that day, I watched Lemon turn sideways. He laughed and said something to Rat Kiley. Then he took a peculiar half step, moving from shade into bright sunlight, and the booby-trapped 105 round blew him into a tree. The parts were just hanging there, so Norman Bowker and I were ordered to shinny up and peel him off. I remember the white bone of an arm. I remember pieces of skin and something wet and yellow that must've been the intestines. The gore was horrible, and stays with me, but what wakes me up twenty years later is Norman Bowker singing "Lemon Tree" as we threw down the parts.

You can tell a true war story by the questions you ask. Somebody tells a story, let's say, and afterward you ask, "Is it true?" and if the answer matters, you've got your answer.

For example, we've all heard this one. Four guys go down a trail. A grenade 100 sails out. One guy jumps on it and takes the blast and saves his three buddies.

Is it true?

The answer matters.

You'd feel cheated if it never happened. Without the grounding reality, it's just a trite bit of puffery, pure Hollywood, untrue in the way all such stories are untrue. Yet even if it did happen — and maybe it did, anything's possible — even then you know it can't be true, because a true war story does not depend upon that kind of truth. Happeningness is irrelevant. A thing may happen and be a total lie; another thing may not happen and be truer than the truth. For example: Four guys go down a trail. A grenade sails out. One guy jumps on it and takes the blast, but it's a killer grenade and everybody dies anyway. Before they die, though, one of the dead guys says, "The fuck you do *that* for?" and the jumper says, "Story of my life, man," and the other guy starts to smile but he's dead.

That's a true story that never happened.

Twenty years later, I can still see the sunlight on Lemon's face. I can see him turning, looking back at Rat Kiley, then he laughed and took that curious half step from shade into sunlight, his face suddenly brown and shining, and when his foot touched down, in that instant, he must've thought it was the sunlight that was killing him. It was not the sunlight. It was a rigged 105 round. But if I could ever get the story right, how the sun seemed to gather around him and pick him up and lift him into a tree, if I could somehow recreate the fatal whiteness of that light, the quick glare, the obvious cause and effect, then you would believe the last thing Lemon believed, which for him must've been the final truth.

Now and then, when I tell this story, someone will come up to me afterward and say she liked it. It's always a woman. Usually it's an older woman of kindly temperament and humane politics. She'll explain that as a rule she hates war stories, she can't understand why people want to wallow in blood and gore. But this one she liked. Sometimes, even, there are little tears. What I should do, she'll say, is put it all behind me. Find new stories to tell.

I won't say it but I'll think it.

I'll picture Rat Kiley's face, his grief, and I'll think, *You dumb cooze.*

Because she wasn't listening.

It wasn't a war story. It was a love story. It was a ghost story.

But you can't say that. All you can do is tell it one more time, patiently, adding and subtracting, making up a few things to get at the real truth. No Mitchell Sanders, you tell her. No Lemon, no Rat Kiley. And it didn't happen in the mountains, it happened in this little village on the Batangan Peninsula, and it was raining like crazy, and one night a guy named Stink Harris woke up screaming with a leech on his tongue. You can tell a true war story if you just keep on telling it.

In the end, of course, a true war story is never about war. It's about the special way that dawn spreads out on a river when you know you must cross the river and march into the mountains and do things you are afraid to do. It's about love and memory. It's about sorrow. It's about sisters who never write back and people who never listen.

Connections to Other Selections

1. Imagine Krebs from Hemingway's "Soldier's Home" (p. 125) writing a letter home recommending "How to Tell a True War Story" to his parents. Write that letter from Krebs's point of view.
2. Compare and contrast the "sister" Rat Kiley writes to with Krebs's sister. What purpose does each sister serve?
3. How does the treatment of violence in O'Brien's story compare with that in Mishima's "Patriotism" (p. 506)? Write an essay that points to specific descriptions and explains the function of the violence in each story.

FAY WELDON (b. 1933)

Born in England and raised in New Zealand, Fay Weldon graduated from St. Andrew's University in Scotland. She wrote advertising copy for various companies and was a propaganda writer for the British Foreign Office before turning to fiction. She has written novels, short stories, plays, and radio scripts. In 1971 her script for an episode of "Upstairs, Downstairs" won an award from the Society of Film and Television Arts. She has written nearly a score of novels, including *The Fat Woman's Joke* (1967), *Down Among the Women* (1971), *Praxis* (1978), *The Life and Loves of a She-Devil* (1983), and *Life Force* (1991), and an equal number of plays and scripts. Weldon often uses ironic humor to portray carefully drawn female characters coming to terms with the facts of their lives.

IND AFF

1988

OR OUT OF LOVE IN SARAJEVO

This is a sad story. It has to be. It rained in Sarajevo, and we had expected fine weather.

The rain filled up Sarajevo's pride, two footprints set into a pavement which mark the spot where the young assassin Princip stood to shoot the Archduke Franz Ferdinand and his wife. (Don't forget his wife: everyone forgets his wife, the archduchess.) That was in the summer of 1914. Sarajevo is a pretty town, Balkan style, mountain-rimmed. A broad, swift, shallow river runs through its center, carrying the mountain snow away, arched by many bridges. The one nearest the two footprints has been named the Princip Bridge. The young man is a hero in these parts. Not only does he bring in the tourists — look, look, the spot, the very spot! — but by his action, as everyone knows, he lit a spark which fired the timber which caused World War I which crumbled the Austro-Hungarian Empire, the crumbling of which made modern Yugoslavia possible. Forty million dead (or was it thirty?) but who cares? So long as he loved his country.

The river, they say, can run so shallow in the summer it's known derisively as "the wet road." Today, from what I could see through the sheets of falling rain, it seemed full enough. Yugoslavian streets are always busy — no one stays home if they can help it (thus can an indecent shortage of housing space create a sociable nation) and it seemed as if by common consent a shield of bobbing umbrellas had been erected two meters high to keep the rain off the streets. It just hadn't worked around Princip's corner.

"Come all this way," said Peter, who was a professor of classical history, "and you can't even see the footprints properly, just two undistinguished puddles." Ah, but I loved him. I shivered for his disappointment. He was supervising my thesis on varying concepts of morality and duty in the early Greek States as evidenced in their poetry and drama. I was dependent upon him for my academic future. He said I had a good mind but not a first-class mind and somehow I didn't take it as an insult. I had a feeling first-class minds weren't all that good in bed.

Sarajevo is in Bosnia, in the center of Yugoslavia, that grouping of unlikely 5 states, that distillation of languages into the phonetic reasonableness of Serbo-Croatian. We'd sheltered from the rain in an ancient mosque in Serbian Belgrade; done the same in a monastery in Croatia; now we spent a wet couple of days in Sarajevo beneath other people's umbrellas. We planned to go on to Montenegro, on the coast, where the fish and the artists come from, to swim and lie in the sun, and recover from the exhaustion caused by the sexual and moral torments of the last year. It couldn't possibly go on raining forever. Could it? Satellite pictures showed black clouds swishing gently all over Europe, over the Balkans, into Asia — practically all the way from Moscow to London, in fact. It wasn't that Peter and myself were being singled out. No. It was raining on his wife, too, back in Cambridge.

Peter was trying to decide, as he had been for the past year, between his wife and myself as his permanent life partner. To this end we had gone away, off the beaten track, for a holiday; if not with his wife's blessing, at least with her knowledge. Were we really, truly suited? We had to be sure, you see, that this was more than just any old professor-student romance; that it was the Real Thing, because the longer the indecision went on the longer Mrs. Piper would be left dangling in uncertainty and distress. They had been married for twenty-four years; they had stopped loving each other a long time ago, of course — but there would be a fearful personal and practical upheaval entailed if he decided to leave permanently and shack up, as he put it, with me. Which I certainly wanted him to do. I loved him. And so far I was winning hands down. It didn't seem much of a contest at all, in fact. I'd been cool and thin and informed on the seat next to him in a Zagreb theater (Mrs. Piper was sweaty and only liked telly); was now eager and anxious for social and political instruction in Sarajevo (Mrs. Piper spat in the face of knowledge, he'd once told me); and planned to be lissome (and I thought topless but I hadn't quite decided: this might be the area where the age difference showed) while I splashed and shrieked like a bathing belle in the shallows of the Montenegrin coast. (Mrs. Piper was a swimming coach: I imagined she smelt permanently of chlorine.)

In fact so far as I could see, it was no contest at all between his wife and myself. But Peter liked to luxuriate in guilt and indecision. And I loved him with an inordinate affection.

Princip's prints are a meter apart, placed as a modern cop on a training shoot-out would place his feet — the left in front at a slight outward angle, the right behind, facing forward. There seemed great energy focused here. Both hands on the gun, run, stop, plant the feet, aim, fire! I could see the footprints well enough, in spite of Peter's complaint. They were clear enough to me.

We went to a restaurant for lunch, since it was too wet to do what we loved to do: that is, buy bread, cheese, sausage, wine, and go off somewhere in our hired car, into the woods or the hills, and picnic and make love. It was a private restaurant — Yugoslavia went over to a mixed capitalist-communist economy years back, so you get either the best or worst of both systems, depending on your mood — that is to say, we knew we would pay more but be given a choice. We chose the wild boar.

"Probably ordinary pork soaked in red cabbage water to darken it," said 10 Peter. He was not in a good mood.

Cucumber salad was served first.

"Everything in this country comes with cucumber salad," complained Peter. I noticed I had become used to his complaining. I supposed that when you had been married a little you simply wouldn't hear it. He was forty-six and I was twenty-five.

"They grow a lot of cucumber," I said.

"If they can grow cucumbers," Peter then asked, "why can't they grow *mange-tout?*"° It seemed a why-can't-they-eat-cake sort of argument to me, but not knowing enough about horticulture not to be outflanked if I debated the point, I moved the subject on to safer ground.

"I suppose Princip's action couldn't really have started World War I," I 15 remarked. "Otherwise, what a thing to have on your conscience! One little shot and the deaths of thirty million."

"Forty," he corrected me. Though how they reckon these things and get them right I can't imagine. "Of course he didn't start the war. That's just a simple tale to keep the children quiet. It takes more than an assassination to start a war. What happened was that the buildup of political and economic tensions in the Balkans was such that it had to find some release."

"So it was merely the shot that lit the spark that fired the timber that started the war, et cetera?"

"Quite," he said. "World War I would have had to have started sooner or later."

"A bit later or a bit sooner," I said, "might have made the difference of a million or so; if it was you on the battlefield in the mud and the rain you'd notice; exactly when they fired the starting-pistol; exactly when they blew the final whistle. Is that what they do when a war ends; blow a whistle? So that everyone just comes in from the trenches."

But he wasn't listening. He was parting the flesh of the soft collapsed 20 orangey-red pepper which sat in the middle of his cucumber salad; he was carefully extracting the pips. His nan had once told him they could never be digested, would stick inside and do terrible damage. I loved him for his dexterity and patience with his knife and fork. I'd finished my salad yonks ago, pips and all. I was hungry. I wanted my wild boar.

Peter might be forty-six, but he was six foot two and grizzled and muscled with it, in a dark-eyed, intelligent, broad-jawed kind of way. I adored him. I loved to be seen with him. "Muscular academic, not weedy academic" as my younger sister Clare once said. "Muscular academic is just a generally superior human being: everything works well from the brain to the toes. Weedy academic is when there isn't enough vital energy in the person, and the brain drains all the strength from the other parts." Well, Clare should know. Clare is only twenty-three, but of the superior human variety kind herself, vividly pretty, bright and competent — somewhere behind a heavy curtain of vibrant red hair, which

mange-tout: A sugar pea or bean (French).

she only parts for effect. She had her first degree at twenty. Now she's married to a Harvard professor of economics seconded to the United Nations. She can even cook. I gave up competing yonks ago. Though she too is capable of self-deception. I would say her husband was definitely of the weedy academic rather than the muscular academic type. And they have to live in Brussels.

The archduke's chauffeur had lost his way, and was parked on the corner trying to recover his nerve when Princip came running out of a café, planted his feet, aimed, and fired. Princip was nineteen — too young to hang. But they sent him to prison for life and, since he had TB to begin with, he only lasted three years. He died in 1918, in an Austrian prison. Or perhaps it was more than TB: perhaps they gave him a hard time, not learning till later, when the Austro-Hungarian Empire collapsed, that he was a hero. Poor Princip, too young to die — like so many other millions. Dying for love of a country.

"I love you," I said to Peter, my living man, progenitor already of three children by his chlorinated, swimming-coach wife.

"How much do you love me?"

"Inordinately! I love you with inordinate affection." It was a joke between 25 us. Ind Aff!

"Inordinate affection is a sin," he'd told me. "According to the Wesleyans. John Wesley° himself worried about it to such a degree he ended up abbreviating it in his diaries, Ind Aff. He maintained that what he felt for young Sophy, the eighteen-year-old in his congregation, was not Ind Aff, which bears the spirit away from God towards the flesh: he insisted that what he felt was a pure and spiritual, if passionate, concern for her soul."

Peter said now, as we waited for our wild boar, and he picked over his pepper, "Your Ind Aff is my wife's sorrow, that's the trouble." He wanted, I knew, one of the long half-wrangles, half soul-sharings that we could keep going for hours, and led to piercing pains in the heart which could only be made better in bed. But our bedroom at the Hotel Europa was small and dark and looked out into the well of the building — a punishment room if ever there was one. (Reception staff did sometimes take against us.) When Peter had tried to change it in his quasi-Serbo-Croatian, they'd shrugged their Bosnian shoulders and pretended not to understand, so we'd decided to put up with it. I did not fancy pushing hard single beds together — it seemed easier not to have the pain in the heart in the first place. "Look," I said, "this holiday is supposed to be just the two of us, not Mrs. Piper as well. Shall we talk about something else?"

Do not think that the archduke's chauffeur was merely careless, an inefficient chauffeur, when he took the wrong turning. He was, I imagine, in a state of shock, fright, and confusion. There had been two previous attempts on the archduke's life since the cavalcade had entered town. The first was a bomb which got the car in front and killed its driver. The second was a shot fired by none other than young Princip, which had missed. Princip had vanished into the crowd and gone to sit down in a corner café and ordered coffee to calm his nerves. I expect his hand trembled at the best of times — he did have TB. (Not the best choice of assassin, but no doubt those who arrange these things have to make do with what they can get.) The archduke's chauffeur panicked, took the wrong

John Wesley (1703–1791): English religious leader and founder of Methodism.

road, realized what he'd done, and stopped to await rescue and instructions just outside the café where Princip sat drinking his coffee.

"What shall we talk about?" asked Peter, in even less of a good mood.

"The collapse of the Austro-Hungarian Empire?" I suggested. "How does an empire collapse? Is there no money to pay the military or the police, so everyone goes home? Or what?" He liked to be asked questions.

"The Hungro-Austrarian Empire," said Peter to me, "didn't so much collapse as fail to exist any more. War destroys social organizations. The same thing happened after World War II. There being no organized bodies left between Moscow and London — and for London read Washington, then as now — it was left to these two to put in their own puppet governments. Yalta, 1944. It's taken the best part of forty-five years for nations of West and East Europe to remember who they are."

"Austro-Hungarian," I said, "not Hungro-Austrarian."

"I didn't say Hungro-Austrarian," he said.

"You did," I said.

"Didn't," he said. "What the hell are they doing about our wild boar? Are they out in the hills shooting it?"

My sister Clare had been surprisingly understanding about Peter. When I worried about him being older, she pooh-poohed it; when I worried about him being married, she said, "Just go for it, sister. If you can unhinge a marriage, it's ripe for unhinging, it would happen sooner or later, it might as well be you. See a catch, go ahead and catch! Go for it!"

Princip saw the archduke's car parked outside, and went for it. Second chances are rare in life: they must be responded to. Except perhaps his second chance was missing in the first place? Should he have taken his cue from fate, and just sat and finished his coffee, and gone home to his mother? But what's a man to do when he loves his country? Fate delivered the archduke into his hands: how could he resist it? A parked car, a uniformed and medaled chest, the persecutor of his country — how could Princip not, believing God to be on his side, but see this as His intervention, push his coffee aside and leap to his feet?

Two waiters stood idly by and watched us waiting for our wild boar. One was young and handsome in a mountainous Bosnian way — flashing eyes, hooked nose, luxuriant black hair, sensuous mouth. He was about my age. He smiled. His teeth were even and white. I smiled back, and instead of the pain in the heart I'd become accustomed to as an erotic sensation, now felt, quite violently, an associated yet different pang which got my lower stomach. The true, the real pain of Ind Aff!

"Fancy him?" asked Peter.

"No," I said. "I just thought if I smiled the wild boar might come quicker."

The other waiter was older and gentler: his eyes were soft and kind. I thought he looked at me reproachfully. I could see why. In a world which for once, after centuries of savagery, was finally full of young men, unslaughtered, what was I doing with this man with thinning hair?

"What are you thinking of?" Professor Piper asked me. He liked to be in my head.

"How much I love you," I said automatically, and was finally aware how much I lied. "And about the archduke's assassination," I went on, to cover the kind of tremble in my head as I came to my senses, "and let's not forget his wife, she died too — how can you say World War I would have happened anyway. If Princip hadn't shot the archduke, something else, some undisclosed, unsuspected variable, might have come along and defused the whole political/military situation, and neither World War I nor II ever happened. We'll just never know, will we?"

I had my passport and my travelers' checks with me. (Peter felt it was less confusing if we each paid our own way.) I stood up, and took my raincoat from the peg.

"Where are you going?" he asked, startled.   45

"Home," I said. I kissed the top of his head, where it was balding. It smelt gently of chlorine, which may have come from thinking about his wife so much, but might merely have been that he'd taken a shower that morning. ("The water all over Yugoslavia, though safe to drink, is unusually chlorinated": Guide Book.) As I left to catch a taxi to the airport the younger of the two waiters emerged from the kitchen with two piled plates of roasted wild boar, potatoes duchesse, and stewed peppers. ("Yugoslavian diet is unusually rich in proteins and fats": Guide Book.) I could tell from the glisten of oil that the food was no longer hot, and I was not tempted to stay, hungry though I was. Thus fate — or was it Bosnian willfulness? — confirmed the wisdom of my intent.

And that was how I fell out of love with my professor, in Sarajevo, a city to which I am grateful to this day, though I never got to see very much of it, because of the rain.

It was a silly sad thing to do, in the first place, to confuse mere passing academic ambition with love: to try and outdo my sister Clare. (Professor Piper was spiteful, as it happened, and did his best to have my thesis refused, but I went to appeal, which he never thought I'd dare, and won. I had a first-class mind after all.) A silly sad episode, which I regret. As silly and sad as Princip, poor young man, with his feverish mind, his bright tubercular cheeks, and his inordinate affection for his country, pushing aside his cup of coffee, leaping to his feet, taking his gun in both hands, planting his feet, aiming, and firing — one, two, three shots — and starting World War I. The first one missed, the second got the wife (never forget the wife), and the third got the archduke and a whole generation, and their children, and their children's children, and on and on forever. If he'd just hung on a bit, there in Sarajevo, that June day, he might have come to his senses. People do, sometimes quite quickly.

Connections to Other Selections

1. Compare and contrast "IND AFF" and Oates's "The Lady with the Pet Dog" (p. 163) as love stories. Do you think that the stories end happily, or the way you would want them to end? Are the endings problematic?
2. Explain how Weldon's concept of "Ind Aff" — "inordinate affection" — can be used to make sense of the relationship between Georgiana and Aylmer in Hawthorne's "The Birthmark" (p. 261).
3. How does passion figure in "IND AFF" and in Lawrence's "The Horse Dealer's Daughter" (p. 469)? Explain how Weldon's and Lawrence's perspectives on passion suggest differing views of love and human relationships.

12. Perspectives on Fiction

This chapter offers a variety of observations about fiction and individual stories. Some of these comments by writers and critics are general, while others make references to particular works. The assessments are wide-ranging: consider, for example, the difference between Thomas Jefferson's warning that reading fiction can act as a "poison [that] infects the mind" and E. L. Doctorow's celebration of storytelling a century and a half later as an "instrument of survival" for humankind. The following perspectives include Ernest Hemingway on what every writer needs to be an effective artist, William Faulkner on the demands of writing short stories, and John Cheever on morality in fiction. These and other commentaries raise a number of issues related to fiction that should help to stimulate your reading, thinking, and writing.

THOMAS JEFFERSON (1743–1826)
On the Dangers of Reading Fiction   1818

A great obstacle to good education is the inordinate passion prevalent for novels, and the time lost in that reading which should be instructively employed. When this poison infects the mind, it destroys its tone and revolts it against wholesome reading. Reason and fact, plain and unadorned, are rejected. Nothing can engage attention unless dressed in all the figments of fancy, and nothing so bedecked comes amiss. The result is a bloated imagination, sickly judgment, and disgust towards all the real businesses of life. This mass of trash, however, is not without some distinction; some few modeling their narratives, although fictitious, on the incidents of real life, have been able to make them interesting and useful vehicles of a sound morality. . . . For a like reason, too, much poetry should not be indulged. Some is useful for forming style and taste. Pope, Dryden,

Thompson, Shakespeare, and of the French, Molière, Racine, the Corneilles, may be read with pleasure and improvement.

Letter to Nathaniel Burwell, March 14, 1818, in *The Writings of Thomas Jefferson*

Considerations for Critical Thinking and Writing

1. Jefferson voices several common objections to fiction. What, according to him, are the changes associated with reading fiction? Are these concerns still expressed today? Why or why not? To what extent are Jefferson's arguments similar to twentieth-century objections to watching television?
2. Explain why you agree or disagree that works of fiction should serve as "useful vehicles of a sound morality."
3. Compare and contrast the values about art stated in this paragraph with those expressed in E. L. Doctorow's "The Importance of Fiction" (p. 576).

MARK TWAIN (1835–1910)
The Art of Authorship   1890

Your inquiry has set me thinking, but, so far, my thought fails to materialize. I mean that, upon consideration, I am not sure that I have methods in composition. I do suppose I have — I suppose I must have — but they somehow refuse to take shape in my mind; their details refuse to separate and submit to classification and description; they remain a jumble — visible, like the fragments of glass when you look in at the wrong end of a kaleidoscope, but still a jumble. If I could turn the whole thing around and look in at the other end, why then the figures would flash into form out of the chaos, and I shouldn't have any more trouble. But my head isn't right for that today, apparently. It might have been, maybe, if I had slept last night.

However, let us try guessing. Let us guess that whenever we read a sentence and like it, we unconsciously store it away in our model-chamber; and it goes with a myriad of its fellows to the building, brick, by brick, of the eventual edifice which we call our style. And let us guess that whenever we run across other forms — bricks — whose color, or some other defect, offends us, we unconsciously reject these, and so one never finds them in our edifice.

If I have subjected myself to any training processes, and no doubt I have, it must have been in this unconscious or half-conscious fashion. I think it unlikely that deliberate and consciously methodical training is usual with the craft. I think it likely that the training most in use is of this unconscious sort, and is guided and governed and made by-and-by unconsciously systematic, by an automatically-working taste — a taste which selects and rejects without asking you for any help, and patiently and steadily improves itself without troubling you to approve or applaud. Yes, and likely enough when the structure is at last pretty well up, and attracts attention, YOU feel complimented, whereas you didn't build it, and didn't even consciously superintend.

Yes; one notices, for instance, that long, involved sentences confuse him, and that he is obliged to re-read them to get the sense. Unconsciously, then, he rejects that brick. Unconsciously he accustoms himself to writing short sentences as a rule. At times he may indulge himself with a long one, but he will make sure that there are no folds in it, no vaguenesses, no parenthetical interruptions of its view as a whole; when he is done with it, it won't be a sea-serpent, with half its arches under the water, it will be a torchlight procession.

Well, also he will notice in the course of time, as his reading goes on, that the difference between the almost right word and the right word is really a large matter — 'tis the difference between the lightning-bug and the lightning. After that, of course, that exceedingly important brick, the exact word — however, this is running into an essay, and I beg pardon. So I seemed to have arrived at this: doubtless I have methods, but they begot themselves, in which case I am only their proprietor, not their father.

From *The Art of Authorship*

Considerations for Critical Thinking and Writing

1. This response to a letter describes Twain's methods of composition. Why does he "think it unlikely that deliberate and consciously methodical training is usual with the craft"? How does this compare with your own views on writing?
2. Does "The Story of the Bad Little Boy" (p. 482) reflect the heavy emphasis on individual words ("the difference between the almost right word and the right word") that Twain notes in this essay? Why or why not?
3. Write an essay that describes your own writing style and explains how you developed it. Is your method of composition similar to or different from Twain's?

F. SCOTT FITZGERALD (1896–1940)
On the Continuity of a Writer's Works   1933

I am thirty-six years old. For eighteen years, save for a short space during the war, writing has been my chief interest in life, and I am in every sense a professional.

Yet even now when, at the recurrent cry of "Baby needs shoes," I sit down facing my sharpened pencils and block of legal-sized paper, I have a feeling of utter helplessness. I may write my story in three days or, as is more frequently the case, it may be six weeks before I have assembled anything worthy to be sent out. I can open a volume from a criminal-law library and find a thousand plots. I can go into highway and byway, parlor and kitchen, and listen to personal revelations that, at the hands of other writers, might endure forever. But all that is nothing — not even enough for a false start. . . .

Mostly, we authors must repeat ourselves — that's the truth. We have two or three great and moving experiences in our lives — experiences so great and moving that it doesn't seem at the time that anyone else has been so caught up and pounded and dazzled and astonished and beaten and broken and rescued and illuminated and rewarded and humbled in just that way ever before.

Then we learn our trade, well or less well, and we tell our two or three stories — each time in a new disguise — maybe ten times, maybe a hundred, as long as people will listen.

If this were otherwise, one would have to confess to having no individuality at all. And each time I honestly believe that, because I have found a new background and a novel twist, I have really got away from the two or three fundamental tales I have to tell. But it is rather like Ed Wynn's famous anecdote about the painter of boats who was begged to paint some ancestors for a client. The bargain was arranged, but with the painter's final warning that the ancestors would all turn out to look like boats.

When I face the fact that all my stories are going to have a certain family resemblance, I am taking a step toward avoiding false starts. If a friend says he's got a story for me and launches into a tale of being robbed by Brazilian pirates in a swaying straw hut on the edge of a smoking volcano in the Andes, with his fiancée bound and gagged on the roof, I can well believe there were various human emotions involved; but having successfully avoided pirates, volcanoes, and fiancées who get themselves bound and gagged on roofs, I can't feel them. Whether it's something that happened twenty years ago or only yesterday, I must start out with an emotion — one that's close to me and that I can understand.

From "One Hundred False Starts" in *Afternoon of an Author*

Considerations for Critical Thinking and Writing

1. Why does Fitzgerald believe that it is inevitable for writers to repeat themselves?
2. Consider the stories in Chapter 9 by Nathaniel Hawthorne, James Joyce, and Flannery O'Connor. To what extent do each of these writer's stories share "a certain family resemblance"?

A. L. BADER (b. 1902)
Nothing Happens in Modern Short Stories   1945

Any teacher who has ever confronted a class with representative modern short stories will remember the disappointment, the puzzled "so-what" attitude, of certain members of the group. "Nothing happens in some of these stories," "They just end," or "They're not real stories" are frequent criticisms. . . . Sometimes the phrase "Nothing happens" seems to mean that nothing significant happens, but in a great many cases it means that the modern short story is charged with a lack of narrative structure. Readers and critics accustomed to an older type of story are baffled by a newer type. They sense the underlying and unifying design of the one, but they find nothing equivalent to it in the other. Hence they maintain that the modern short story is plotless, static, fragmentary, amorphous — frequently a mere character sketch or vignette, or a mere reporting of a transient moment, or the capturing of a mood or nuance — everything, in fact, except a story.

From "The Structure of the Modern Story" in *College English*

Considerations for Critical Thinking and Writing

1. What is the basic objection to the "newer type" of short story? How does it differ from the "older type"?
2. Consider any one of the stories from the Album of Contemporary Stories (p. 528) as an example of the newer type. Does anything "happen" in the story? How does it differ from the excerpt from Edgar Rice Burroughs's *Tarzan of the Apes* (p. 39)?
3. Read a recent story published in *The New Yorker* or the *Atlantic* and compare its narrative structure with that of Hemingway's "Soldier's Home" (p. 125) or Ellison's "Battle Royal" (p. 187).

ELIZABETH BOWEN (1899–1973)
The Writer's Roving Eye   1952

The writer, unlike his nonwriting adult friend, has no predisposed outlook; he seldom observes deliberately. He sees what he did not intend to see; he remembers what does not seem wholly possible. Inattentive learner in the schoolroom of life, he keeps some faculty free to veer and wander. His is the roving eye.

By that roving eye is his subject found. The glance, at first only vaguely caught, goes on to concentrate, deepen; becomes the vision. Just what *has* he seen, and why should it mean so much? The one face standing out of the crowd, the figure in the distance crossing the street, the glare or shade significant on a building, the episode playing out at the next table, the image springing out of a phrase of talk, the disproportionate impact of some one phrase of poetry, the reverberation after a street accident or tiny subjective echo of a huge world event, the flare-up of visual memory or of sensuous memory for which can be traced no reason at all — why should this or that be of such importance as to bring all else to a momentous stop? Fate has worked, as in a falling in love — the writer, in fact, first knows he has found his subject by finding himself already obsessed by it. The outcome of obsession is, that he writes — rationalization begins with his search for language. He must (like the child who cannot keep silent) share, make known, communicate what he has seen, or knows. The urgency of what is real to him demands that it should be realized by other people.

From *Seven Winters and Afterthoughts*

Considerations for Critical Thinking and Writing

1. According to Bowen, how does a writer's response to the world differ from a nonwriter's?
2. Choose a story that strikes you as especially rich in observed details and analyze a paragraph or two for what those details reveal about a character, action, setting, symbol, or theme.

ERNEST HEMINGWAY (1899–1961)
On What Every Writer Needs

The most essential gift for a good writer is a built-in, shock-proof, shit detector. This is the writer's radar and all great writers have had it.

From *Writers at Work: The Paris Review Interviews* (Second Series)

Considerations for Critical Thinking and Writing

1. Hemingway is typically forthright here, but it is tempting to dismiss his point as simply humorous. Take him seriously. What does he insist a good writer must be able to do?
2. How might Krebs in Hemingway's "Soldier's Home" (p. 125) be seen as having a similar kind of "shit detector" and "radar"?
3. Try writing a pithy, quotable statement that makes an observation about reading or writing.

WILLIAM FAULKNER (1897–1962)
On the Demands of Writing Short Stories

Q. Mr. Faulkner, you spoke about *The Sound and the Fury* as starting out to write a short story and it kept growing. Well now, do you think that it's easier to write a novel than a short story?

A. Yes sir. You can be more careless, you can put more trash in it and be excused for it. In a short story that's next to the poem, almost every word has got to be almost exactly right. In the novel you can be careless but in the short story you can't. I mean by that the good short stories like Chekhov wrote. That's why I rate that second — it's because it demands a nearer absolute exactitude. You have less room to be slovenly and careless. There's less room in it for trash. In poetry, of course, there's no room at all for trash. It's got to be absolutely impeccable, absolutely perfect.

From Frederick Gwynn and Joseph Blotner, eds., *Faulkner in the University*

Considerations for Critical Thinking and Writing

1. Why does short story writing place more demands on an author than novel writing? What does a short story have in common with poetry? Do you agree with Faulkner that a writer can afford to be more careless in a novel than in a short story or poem? Why or why not?
2. Which do you find more satisfying to read, a short story or a novel? Explain why.

MORDECAI MARCUS (b. 1925)
What Is an Initiation Story?

1960

An initiation story may be said to show its young protagonist experiencing a significant change of knowledge about the world or himself, or a change of character, or of both, and this change must point or lead him toward an adult world. It may or may not contain some form of ritual, but it should give some evidence that the change is at least likely to have permanent effects.

Initiation stories obviously center on a variety of experiences and the initiations vary in effect. It will be useful, therefore, to divide initiations into types according to their power and effect. First, some initiations lead only to the threshold of maturity and understanding but do not definitely cross it. Such stories emphasize the shocking effect of experience, and their protagonists tend to be distinctly young. Second, some initiations take their protagonists across a threshold of maturity and understanding but leave them enmeshed in a struggle for certainty. These initiations sometimes involve self-discovery. Third, the most decisive initiations carry their protagonists firmly into maturity and understanding, or at least show them decisively embarked toward maturity. These initiations usually center on self-discovery. For convenience, I will call these types tentative, uncompleted, and decisive initiations.

From "What Is an Initiation Story?" in *The Journal of Aesthetics and Art Criticism*

Considerations for Critical Thinking and Writing

1. For a work to be classified as an initiation story, why should it "give some evidence that the change [in the protagonist] is at least likely to have permanent effects"?
2. Marcus divides initiations into three broad types: tentative, uncompleted, and decisive. Explain how you would categorize the initiations in the following stories: Ellison's "Battle Royal" (p. 187), Hawthorne's "Young Goodman Brown" (p. 242), O'Connor's "Good Country People" (p. 379), and Updike's "A & P" (p. 485).

MODY C. BOATRIGHT (1896–1970)
A Typical Western Plot Formula

1969

The hero is going on in the even tenor of his way when something occurs, either in the community where he lives or in some place he happens to be, apparently by accident, that morally compels him to act in behalf of others. . . .

A. The hero encounters:
   1. someone in distress — often a woman or child — in the desert without water, sick in an isolated cabin, or wounded.
   2. a community being oppressed — the crooks are in control, or a cattle baron is running out the small ranchers and farmers.

3. a crime being planned — the bank is to be robbed, or the sheriff murdered.
   B. The action involves sacrifice and risk on the part of the hero:
   1. he may be a fugitive, and succor means surrender to the law.
   2. he may be a traveler passing through who must abandon, at least temporarily, the important mission of his journey.
   3. he may be a local resident who appears to be no match for his antagonist.
   C. The hero is successful; this may involve:
   1. the use of firearms, perhaps killing.
   2. a battle of wits.
   3. a show of overwhelming force (the cavalry arrives and declares marshall [sic] law).

   From "The Formula in Cowboy Fiction and Drama" in *Western Folklore*

Considerations for Critical Thinking and Writing

1. Try writing an outline similar to Boatright's for some other form of popular fiction, such as a detective or adventure story. Or try writing an outline for a favorite television program that employs a formula.
2. How does Crane's "The Bride Comes to Yellow Sky" (p. 203) use elements of Boatright's formula? How is Crane's story significantly different from the formula?

JOHN CHEEVER (1912–1982)
On Morals in Fiction 1976

Interviewer: Do you think that fiction should give lessons?

Cheever: No. Fiction is meant to illuminate, to explode, to refresh. I don't think there's any consecutive moral philosophy in fiction beyond excellence. Acuteness of feeling and velocity have always seemed to me terribly important. People look for morals in fiction because there has always been a confusion between fiction and philosophy.

Interviewer: How do you know when a story is right? Does it hit you right the first time, or are you critical as you go along?

Cheever: I think there is a certain heft in fiction. For example, my latest story isn't right. I have to do the ending over again. It's a question, I guess, of trying to get it to correspond to a vision. There is a shape, a proportion, and one knows when something that happens is wrong.

Interviewer: By instinct?

Cheever: I suppose that anyone who has written for as long as I have, it's probably what you'd call instinct. When a line falls wrong, it simply isn't right.

From *Writers at Work: The Paris Review Interviews* (Fifth Series)

Considerations for Critical Thinking and Writing

1. How does Cheever distinguish between "instinct" and "philosophy"? Why does he object to people looking for "morals" in stories?
2. Is there a moral to be found in Cheever's "Reunion" (p. 460)?
3. How do you think Cheever would respond to Hawthorne's "The Birthmark" (p. 261)? Why?

JOHN UPDIKE (b. 1932)
Fiction's Subtlety   1985

Fiction is nothing less than the subtlest instrument for self-examination and self-display that mankind has invented yet. Psychology and X-rays bring up some portentous shadows, and demographics and stroboscopic photography do some fine breakdowns, but for the full *parfum* and effluvia of being human, for feathery ambiguity and rank facticity, for the air and iron, fire and spit of our daily mortal adventure there is nothing like fiction: it makes sociology look priggish, history problematical, the film media two-dimensional, and the *National Enquirer* as silly as last week's cereal box.

From "The Importance of Fiction" in *Esquire*

Considerations for Critical Thinking and Writing

1. How do you interpret Updike's assertion that fiction is the "subtlest instrument" for understanding what it means to be human? Explain why you agree or disagree.
2. Consider Updike's claim that fiction makes film seem "two-dimensional" by comparison. What, in your view, does literature do better than film? What does film achieve more effectively than literature?
3. Using Updike's "A & P" (p. 485) as the basis for your discussion, write an essay that explains why a sociological analysis of Sammy's character would necessarily leave out significant aspects of his personality as Updike presents him. Consider also what a sociological description might add to our understanding of him. Choose either the fictional or the sociological approach, and explain why it captures your interests more.

E. L. DOCTOROW (b. 1931)
The Importance of Fiction   1986

When I was a boy everyone in my family was a good storyteller, my mother and father, my brother, my aunts and uncles and grandparents; all of them were people to whom interesting things seemed to happen. The events they spoke of were of a daily, ordinary sort, but when narrated or acted out they took on great importance and excitement as I listened.

Of course, when you bring love to the person you are listening to, the story has to be interesting, and in one sense the task of a professional writer who publishes books is to overcome the terrible loss of not being someone the reader knows and loves.

But apart from that, the people whose stories I heard as a child must have had a very firm view of themselves in the world. They must have been strong enough as presences in their own minds to trust that people would listen to them when they spoke.

I know now that everyone in the world tells stories. Relatively few people are given to mathematics or physics, but narrative seems to be within everyone's grasp, perhaps because it comes of the nature of language itself.

The moment you have nouns and verbs and prepositions, the moment you have subjects and objects, you have stories.

For the longest time there would have been nothing but stories, and no sharper distinction between what was real and what was made up than between what was spoken and what was sung. Religious arousal and scientific discourse, simple urgent communication and poetry, all burned together in the intense perception of a metaphor — that, for instance, the sun was a god's chariot driven across the heavens.

Stories were as important to survival as a spear or a hoe. They were the memory of the knowledge of the dead. They gave counsel. They connected the visible to the invisible. They distributed the suffering so that it could be borne.

In our era, even as we separate the functions of language, knowing when we speak scientifically we are not speaking poetically, and when we speak theologically we are not speaking the way we do to each other in our houses, and even as our surveys demand statistics, and our courts demand evidence, and our hypotheses demand proof — our minds are still structured for storytelling.

What we call fiction is the ancient way of knowing, the total discourse that antedates all the special vocabularies of modern intelligence.

The professional writer of fiction is a conservative who cherishes the ultimate structures of the human mind. He cultivates within himself the universal disposition to think in terms of conflict and its resolution, and in terms of character undergoing events, and of the outcome of events being not at all sure, and therefore suspenseful — the whole thing done, moreover, from a confidence of narrative that is grounded in our brains as surely as the innate talent to construe the world grammatically.

The fiction writer, looking around him, understands the homage a modern up-to-date world of nonfiction specialists pays to his craft — even as it isolates him and tells him he is a liar. Newsweeklies present the events of the world as installments in a serial melodrama. Weather reports on television are constructed with exact attention to conflict (high-pressure areas clashing with lows), suspense (the climax of tomorrow's prediction coming after the commercial), and the consistency of voice (the personality of the weathercaster). The marketing and advertising of product-facts is unquestionably a fictional enterprise. As is every government's representations of its activities. And modern psychology, with its concepts of *sublimation, repression, identity crisis, complex,* and so on, proposes the interchangeable parts for the stories of all of us; in this sense it is the industrialization of storytelling.

But nothing is as good at fiction as fiction. It is the most ancient way of knowing but also the most modern, managing when it's done right to burn all the functions of language back together into powerful fused revelation. Because it is total discourse it is ultimate discourse. It excludes nothing. It will express from the depth and range of its sources truths that no sermon or experiment or news report can begin to apprehend. It will tell you without shame what people do with their bodies and think with their minds. It will deal evenhandedly with their microbes or their intuitions. It will know their nightmares and blinding moments of moral crisis. You will experience love, if it so chooses, or starvation or drowning or dropping through space or holding a hot pistol in your hand with the police pounding on the door. This is the way it is, it will say, this is what it feels like.

Fiction is democratic, it reasserts the authority of the single mind to make and remake the world. By its independence from all institutions, from the family to the government, and with no responsibility to defend their hypocrisy or murderousness, it is a valuable resource and instrument of survival.

Fiction gives counsel. It connects the present with the past, and the visible with the invisible. It distributes the suffering. It says we must compose ourselves in our stories in order to exist. It says if we don't do it, someone else will do it for us.

From "Ultimate Discourse" in *Esquire*

Considerations for Critical Thinking and Writing

1. What does Doctorow mean when he describes fiction as the "ultimate discourse"? What is the relationship of fiction to theology, history, and science? How is fiction an "ancient way of knowing"?
2. Why is fiction a "valuable resource and instrument of survival"? Explain why you agree or disagree with this assessment of storytelling.

KENT THOMPSON (b. 1936)
A Short Short Story: "Unreeling" 1986

Helen has left me and moved back to 1930. She is singing in a log-cabin Roadhouse out on old Highway 42. Almost nobody travels out that way anymore. She wears an ivory-colored evening gown and has marcelled her hair. Her lover is the owner who sometimes gives ballroom-dancing exhibitions with her. The patrons are kids who stare in wonder — not, as Helen and her lover believe, at the grace of the old ballroom dances or the sweetness of the lachrymose songs — but at the audacity of the two of them, daring to live outside their allotted time. I sometimes go there and contribute to the decor by sitting at a table wearing a fedora. But I think I am slipping out of her memory, and will disappear as soon as I am forgotten.

From *Open Windows: Canadian Short Short Stories*

Considerations for Critical Thinking and Writing

1. This complete story appears in a collection of very brief stories known in Canada as "postcard fiction" or "quick fiction." Does it satisfy your sense of what a short story is? Explain.
2. Try applying the Questions for Responsive Reading (p. 457) to this story. Which questions seem most relevant to you? Do they make the story seem more or less of an achievement?
3. Write your own postcard story — one that attempts to offer an open window on some aspect of life.

URSULA K. LE GUIN (b. 1929)
On Conflict in Fiction

1987

From looking at manuals used in college writing courses, and from listening to participants in writing workshops, I gather that it is a generally received idea that a story is the relation of a conflict, that without conflict there is no plot, that narrative and conflict are inseparable.

Now, that something or other has to happen in a story, I agree (in very general, broad terms; there are, after all, excellent stories in which everything has happened, or is about to happen). But that what happens in a story can be defined as, limited to, conflict, I doubt. And that to assert the dependence of narrative on conflict is to uphold Social Darwinism in all its glory, I sadly suspect.

Existence as struggle, life as a battle, everything in terms of defeat and victory: Man versus Nature, Man versus Woman, Black versus White, Good versus Evil, God versus Devil — a sort of apartheid view of existence, and of literature. What a pitiful impoverishment of the complexity of both!

In E. M. Forster's famous definition (in *Aspects of the Novel*), this is a story:

> The King died and then the Queen died.

And this is a plot:

> The King died and then the Queen died of grief.

In that charming and extremely useful example, where is the "conflict"? Who is pitted against what? Who wins?

Is the first book of *Genesis* a story? Where is the "conflict"?

Has *War and Peace* a plot? Can that plot be in any useful or meaningful way reduced to "conflict," or a series of "conflicts"?

People are cross-grained, aggressive, and full of trouble, the storytellers tell us; people fight themselves and one another, and their stories are full of their struggles. But to say that that *is* the story is to use one aspect of existence, conflict, to include and submerge other aspects which it does not include and does not comprehend.

Romeo and Juliet is a story of the conflict between two families, and its plot involves the conflict of two individuals with those families. Is that all it involves? Isn't *Romeo and Juliet* about something else, and isn't it the something else that makes the otherwise trivial tale of a feud into a tragedy?

I for one will be glad when this gladiatorial view of fiction has run its course.

From *Dancing at the Edge of the World:*
Thoughts on Words, Women, Places

Considerations for Critical Thinking and Writing

1. What do you think is Le Guin's major objection to discussions of fiction that insist "narrative and conflict are inseparable"? Explain why you agree or disagree with her.
2. In a brief essay try to answer Le Guin's questions about "The King died and then the Queen died of grief." Can you identify a conflict in this "plot"?
3. Consider how practitioners of the various "Critical Strategies for Reading" in Chapter 35 (formalist, biographical, psychological, historical, Marxist, feminist, mythological, reader-response, and deconstructionist) find different kinds of conflicts in stories. Choose a story in this anthology and describe how any three of these approaches emphasize different conflicts in the story. Which approach do you find most revealing and helpful for making sense of the story?

JOHN BARTH (b. 1930)
On Minimalist Fiction   1987

Minimalism (of one sort or another) is the principle (one of the principles, anyhow) underlying (what I and many another interested observer consider to be perhaps) the most impressive phenomenon on the current (North American, especially the United States) literary scene (the gringo equivalent of *el boom* in the Latin American novel): I mean the new flowering of the (North) American short story (in particular the kind of terse, oblique, realistic or hyperrealistic, slightly plotted, extrospective, cool-surfaced fiction associated in the last five or ten years with such excellent writers as Frederick Barthelme, Ann Beattie, Raymond Carver, Bobbie Ann Mason, James Robison, Mary Robison, and Tobias Wolff, and both praised and damned under such labels as "K-Mart realism," "hick chic," "Diet-Pepsi minimalism" and "post-Vietnam, post-literary, postmodernist blue-collar neo-early-Hemingwayism"). . . .

The genre of the short story, as Poe distinguished it from the traditional tale in his 1842 review of Hawthorne's first collection of stories, is an early manifesto of modern narrative minimalism: "In the whole composition there should be no word written, of which the tendency . . . is not to the pre-established design. . . . Undue length is . . . to be avoided." Poe's codification informs such later nineteenth-century masters of terseness, selectivity, and implicitness (as opposed to leisurely once-upon-a-timelessness, luxuriant abundance, explicit and extended analysis) as Guy de Maupassant and Anton Chekhov. Show, don't tell, said Henry James in effect and at length in his prefaces to the 1908 New York edition of his novels. And don't tell a word more than you absolutely need to, added young Ernest Hemingway, who thus described his "new theory" in the early 1920's: "You could omit anything if you knew that you omitted, and the omitted part would strengthen the story and make people feel something more than they understood." . . .

Old or new, fiction can be minimalist in any or all of several ways. There are minimalisms of unit, form, and scale: short words, short sentences and paragraphs, [and] super-short stories. . . . There are minimalisms of style: a stripped-down vocabulary; a stripped-down syntax that avoids periodic sentences, serial predications, and complex subordinating constructions; a stripped-down rhetoric that may eschew figurative language altogether; a stripped-down, non-emotive tone. And there are minimalisms of material: minimal characters, minimal exposition ("all that David Copperfield kind of crap," says J. D. Salinger's catcher in the rye), minimal *mises en scène,* minimal action, minimal plot.

From *Weber Studies*

Considerations for Critical Thinking and Writing

1. To what extent do Ernest Hemingway's "Soldier's Home" (p. 125) and Raymond Carver's "Popular Mechanics" (p. 235) fulfill Barth's description of minimalist fiction? How does each story suggest that less is more?
2. Write an essay explaining why one of the short stories in this anthology by Nathaniel Hawthorne, James Joyce, or Flannery O'Connor is not a minimalist story.
3. Discuss Kent Thompson's story "Unreeling" (p. 578) as a version of minimalist fiction.

THOMAS McCORMACK (b. 1932)
On the Problem of Teaching Theme   1988

Let's start calmly: Samples of the way "theme" is taught should be sent to Atlanta so the Centers for Disease Control can get on it; the NIH° should be called in, and a "Just Say No to 'Theme'" campaign should be promulgated among the youth of America. . . .

In flat: the way "theme" is currently taught is actively harmful.

I seriously pursue this crusade here, albeit in condensed, almost outline, form, because I believe that what's being done in classrooms stunts, and even kills, the ability and appetite of many of the best students. This deprives our globe of much talent that would otherwise find itself in writing, teaching, [and] reading. . . .

[The] teaching of "theme" is harmful because of what it leads *to,* and what it leads *away from.*

In the student's mood and attitude, it leads to confusion, discouragement, and alienation.

In his knowledge it leads to error about what authors are trying to do, and about what is cherishable in fiction generally, and stories and novels individually.

It leads the student away from enjoyment, sanguine expectation, and trust

NIH: National Institutes of Health.

in literature. It actually *reduces* the possibility of his focusing where the reward is.

It does this by forcibly thrusting on the student a concept that is fuzzy, arbitrary, trivializing, irrelevant, distracting, and ultimately deadening. . . .

The goal of getting the reader to pay closer attention is a good one. The assumption of the professors is that, by compelling the student to crawl back over the narrative in the effort to ensure that all the "major details" are "accounted for" by the theme, one forces the student to focus on each scene, each character, every element in the book. But . . . because during this crawl his focus is kept on the thin, flat, ideational plane, he's likely to miss the essential lovable things, like a chemist analyzing the molecular structure of different ice creams. It calls to mind the old days when history teachers figured that they'd do the job by compelling students to memorize a thousand names and dates.

But at least the chemist and historian inculcate some facts that may ultimately have some narrow use. The English professor in the end abandons that claim. He knows that themes like "People deceive themselves" and "Jealousy exacts a terrible cost" are indefensibly meager payoffs.

Never, despite their brief, abortive invocation of "significance", *do [the text-books] show any correlation whatever between the quality of theme and the quality of the story.* . . .

But if there is no such correlation, if — as the textbook writers frequently admit — trite themes can beget great art, and great themes can beget trite art, and no theme at all can beget Poe, then the student has the right to ask: What earthly use is this vivisecting hunt for theme?

There must be ten thousand stories that, to a professor, would yield the theme "People deceive themselves." Ninety-nine percent of those stories are justifiably forgotten. But if theme is the significance of the story, why aren't all these stories equally significant? Because the professors are wrong in their teaching: the significance, the purpose, the meaning, the reason for being of a story does *not* lie in its "theme" but in something else.

Now, having dismissed theme as an end and also as a pedagogic means, it would seem meet for me to suggest an alternative technique. The technique should serve to get the student to pay the closer attention I approve of, but also to ensure that the focus is brought to bear where the true reward is.

The approach I'd recommend is based on . . . an intuition of an effect-wanted — followed by imagination's conjuring of narrative to produce that effect, and then by sensibility's judgments on those conjurings. This maintains that the aim of the artist is to produce an effect on the reader's head, heart, or gut.

[M]y own experience [is] that the most rewarding critics for me, over the years, have been those who often do no more than *point.* When Cowley° says to me, just go back and read the list of people who attended Gatsby's party, just savor how Fitzgerald describes them, it'll be worth it — he does me a profound service. If a great appreciator like Cowley tells me it will be worth it, just for itself, and not because it's necessary as step #7 in the derivation of an abstract generality, the very freedom from ulterior function enhances vision. To see the true color of the painting, do not wear glasses tinted with other intent. . . .

But then I must back down a bit and concede this teaching can't be done solely with the index finger.

Cowley: Malcolm Cowley (1898–1989), American writer, editor, poet, and critic.

What I recommend, then, is approaching the work of fiction with a program of questions devised to focus the reader on the effect achieved, and how the author achieved it.

For example, each character has a certain impact on us, the readers. To clarify how that impact is achieved, certainly notice what he says and does, what we're told about him; even ask crafty questions: What does he want or promise? What does he do to get it? What result does he cause? Why do we like or dislike him?

Move on to circuitry: How does he braid or conflict with others in the cast?

Then, really to clarify the appreciation of effects on us, and how the author is causing them, the gifted instructor, as rare teachers through the ages have when they were not fouled in the lines of theme, might bid his most gifted students to ask: *How would the story and our response be different if such-and-such were different?*

The instructor might help students to imagine a character different, or missing entirely. What happens to the circuitry? Imagine what would be the story-effect of a new character: Hamlet's sister.

Examine each scene. First ask: Do we like it? Then ask: Why? The answer to this question always takes the form, ultimately, of simply pointing at things and taking a stand: I love this sentence; I love what she says, what he does; I think this description is great.

Sometimes crafty, gridlike questions about the scene help us push below the general pleasure to the specific credit in the narrative. How does the scene reveal or change character, circuitry, or circumstance? Are things different at the end of the scene from how they were at the beginning? How much of the vital feeling stems from this advancement, from our observation that something is really *going on,* things are *happening?* Always the aim is to notice the effect on us, the readers, as we contemplate each element of the narrative. . . . (How different would we feel if this tease, hint, threat, possibility were never introduced?)

From *The Fiction Editor, the Novel, and the Novelist*

Considerations for Critical Thinking and Writing

1. According to McCormack, what does abstracting and generalizing about the theme do to a reader's response to a story?
2. Pick up McCormack's suggestion and imagine a new character for any story in this anthology and explain how the imagined character affects the story.
3. To what extent does McCormack's advice correspond with the reading strategies offered by reader-response critics (see Chapter 35)? Describe any significant differences.

POETRY

13. Reading Poetry

READING POETRY RESPONSIVELY

Perhaps the best way to begin reading poetry responsively is not to allow yourself to be intimidated by it. Come to it, initially at least, the way you might listen to a song on the radio. You probably listen to a song several times before you hear it all, before you have a sense of how it works, where it's going, and how it gets there. You don't worry about analyzing a song when you listen to it, even though after repeated experiences with it you know and anticipate a favorite part and know, on some level, why it works for you. Give yourself a chance to respond to poetry. The hardest work has already been done by the poet, so all you need to do at the start is listen for the pleasure produced by the poet's arrangement of words.

Try reading the following poem aloud. Read it aloud before you read it silently. You may stumble once or twice, but you'll make sense of it if you pay attention to its punctuation and don't stop at the end of every line where there is no punctuation. The title gives you an initial sense of what the poem is about.

MARGE PIERCY (b. 1936)
The Secretary Chant   1973

My hips are a desk.
From my ears hang
chains of paper clips.
Rubber bands form my hair.
My breasts are wells of mimeograph ink.   5
My feet bear casters.
Buzz. Click.
My head is a badly organized file.

My head is a switchboard
where crossed lines crackle.   10
Press my fingers
and in my eyes appear
credit and debit.
Zing. Tinkle.
My navel is a reject button.   15
From my mouth issue canceled reams.
Swollen, heavy, rectangular
I am about to be delivered
of a baby
Xerox machine.   20
File me under W
because I wonce
was
a woman.

What is your response to this secretary's chant? The point is simple
enough — she feels dehumanized by her office functions — but the pleasures are manifold. Piercy makes the speaker's voice sound mechanical by
using short bursts of sound and by having her make repetitive, flat, matter-
of-fact statements ("My breasts . . . My feet . . . My head . . . My navel").
"The Secretary Chant" makes a serious statement about how such women
are reduced to functionaries. The point is made, however, with humor since
we are asked to visualize the misappropriation of the secretary's body — her
identity — as it is transformed into little more than a piece of office equipment, which seems to be breaking down in the final lines, when we learn
that she "wonce / was / a woman." Is there the slightest hint of something
subversive in this misspelling of "wonce"? Maybe so, but the humor is clear
enough, particularly if you try to make a drawing of what this dehumanized
secretary has become.

The next poem creates a different kind of mood. Think about the title,
"Those Winter Sundays," before you begin reading the poem. What associations do you have with winter Sundays? What emotions does the phrase
evoke in you?

ROBERT HAYDEN (1913–1980)
Those Winter Sundays   1962

Sundays too my father got up early
and put his clothes on in the blueblack cold,
then with cracked hands that ached
from labor in the weekday weather made
banked fires blaze. No one ever thanked him.   5

I'd wake and hear the cold splintering, breaking,
When the rooms were warm, he'd call,
and slowly I would rise and dress,
fearing the chronic angers of that house,

Speaking indifferently to him,   10
who had driven out the cold
and polished my good shoes as well.
What did I know, what did I know
of love's austere and lonely offices?

Did the poem match the feelings you have about winter Sundays? Either way your response can be useful in reading the poem. For most of us Sundays are days at home; they might be cozy and pleasant experiences or they might be dull and depressing. Whatever they are, Sundays are more evocative than, say, Tuesdays. Hayden uses that response to call forth a sense of missed opportunity in the poem. The person who reflects on those winter Sundays didn't know until much later how much he had to thank his father for "love's austere and lonely offices." This is a poem about a cold past and a present reverence for his father — elements brought together by the phrase "Winter Sundays." *His* father? You may have noticed that the poem doesn't use a masculine pronoun; hence the voice could be a woman's. Does the sex of the voice make any difference to your reading? Would it make any difference about which details are included or what language is used?

What is most important about your initial readings of a poem is that you ask questions. If you read responsively, you'll find yourself asking all kinds of questions about the words, descriptions, sounds, and structures of a poem. The specifics of those questions will be generated by the particular poem. We don't, for example, ask how humor is achieved in "Those Winter Sundays" because there is none, but it is worth asking what kind of tone is established by the description of "the chronic angers of that house." The remaining chapters in this part will help you to formulate and answer questions about a variety of specific elements in poetry, such as speaker, image, metaphor, symbol, rhyme, and rhythm. For the moment, however, read the following poem several times and note your response at different points in the poem. Then write down a half dozen questions or so about what produces your response to the poem. In order to answer questions it's best to know first what the questions are, and that's what the rest of this chapter is about.

JOHN UPDIKE (b. 1932)
Dog's Death 1969

She must have been kicked unseen or brushed by a car.
Too young to know much, she was beginning to learn
To use the newspapers spread on the kitchen floor
And to win, wetting there, the words, "Good dog! Good dog!"

We thought her shy malaise was a shot reaction. 5
The autopsy disclosed a rupture in her liver.
As we teased her with play, blood was filling her skin
And her heart was learning to lie down forever.

Monday morning, as the children were noisily fed
And sent to school, she crawled beneath the youngest's bed. 10
We found her twisted and limp but still alive.
In the car to the vet's, on my lap, she tried

To bite my hand and died. I stroked her warm fur
And my wife called in a voice imperious with tears.
Though surrounded by love that would have upheld her, 15
Nevertheless she sank and, stiffening, disappeared.

Back home, we found that in the night her frame,
Drawing near to dissolution, had endured the shame
Of diarrhoea and had dragged across the floor
To a newspaper carelessly left there. *Good dog.* 20

Here's a simple question to get started with your own questions: what would its effect have been if Updike had titled the poem "Good Dog" instead of "Dog's Death"?

THE PLEASURE OF WORDS

The impulse to create and appreciate poetry is as basic to human experience as language itself. Although no one can point to the precise origins of poetry, it is one of the most ancient of the arts, because it has existed ever since human beings discovered pleasure in language. The tribal ceremonies of peoples without written language suggest evidence that the earliest primitive cultures incorporated rhythmic patterns of words into their rituals. These chants, very likely accompanied by the music of a simple beat and the dance of a measured step, expressed what people regarded as significant and memorable in their lives. They echoed the concerns of the chanters and the listeners by chronicling acts of bravery, fearsome foes, natural disasters, mysterious events, births, deaths, and whatever else brought people pain or pleasure, bewilderment or revelation. Later cultures, such as the ancient Greeks, made poetry an integral part of religion.

Thus, from its very beginnings, poetry has been associated with what has mattered most to people. These concerns — whether natural or supernatural — can, of course, be expressed without vivid images, rhythmic patterns, and pleasing sounds, but human beings have always sensed a magic in words that goes beyond rational, logical understanding. Poetry is not simply a method of communication; it is a unique kind of experience in itself.

What is special about poetry? What makes it valuable? Why should we read it? How is reading it different from reading prose? To begin with, poetry pervades our world in a variety of forms, ranging from advertising jingles to song lyrics. These may seem to be a long way from the chants heard around a primitive camp fire, but they serve some of the same purposes. Like poems printed in a magazine or book, primitive chants, catchy jingles, and popular songs attempt to stir the imagination through the carefully measured use of words.

Although reading poetry usually makes more demands than does the kind of reading used to skim a magazine or newspaper, the appreciation of poetry comes naturally enough to anyone who enjoys playing with words. Play is an important element of poetry. Consider, for example, how the following words appeal to the children who gleefully chant them in playgrounds.

> I scream, you scream
> We all scream
> For ice cream.

These lines are an exuberant evocation of the joy of ice cream. Indeed, chanting the words turns out to be as pleasurable as eating ice cream. In poetry, the expression of the idea is as important as the idea expressed.

But is "I scream . . ." poetry? Some poets and literary critics would say that it certainly is one kind of poem, because the children who chant it experience some of the pleasures of poetry in its measured beat and repeated sounds. However, other poets and critics would define poetry more narrowly and insist, for a variety of reasons (some of which are included among the definitions in Chapter 25), that this isn't true poetry but merely *doggerel,* a term used for lines whose subject matter is trite and whose rhythm and sounds are monotonously heavy-handed.

Although probably no one would argue that "I scream . . ." is a great poem, it does contain some poetic elements that appeal, at the very least, to children. Does that make it poetry? The answer depends on one's definition, but poetry has a way of breaking loose from definitions. Because there are nearly as many definitions of poetry as there are poets, Edwin Arlington Robinson's succinct observations are useful: "poetry has two outstanding characteristics. One is that it is undefinable. The other is that it is eventually unmistakable."

This comment places more emphasis on how a poem affects a reader than on how a poem is defined. By characterizing poetry as "undefinable," Robinson acknowledges that it can include many different purposes, subjects, emotions, styles, and forms. What effect does the following poem have on you?

WILLIAM HATHAWAY (b. 1944)
Oh, Oh   1982

My girl and I amble a country lane,
moo cows chomping daisies, our own
sweet saliva green with grass stems.
"Look, look," she says at the crossing,
"the choo-choo's light is on." And sure   5
enough, right smack dab in the middle
of maple dappled summer sunlight
is the lit headlight — so funny.
An arm waves to us from the black window.
We wave gaily to the arm. "When I hear   10
trains at night I dream of being president,"
I say dreamily. "And me first lady," she
says loyally. So when the last boxcars,
named after wonderful, faraway places,
and the caboose chuckle by we look   15
eagerly to the road ahead. And there,
poised and growling, are fifty Hell's Angels.

Hathaway's poem serves as a convenient reminder that poetry can be full of surprises. Even on a first reading there is no mistaking the emotional reversal created by the last few words of this poem. With the exception of the final line, the poem's language conjures up an idyllic picture of a young couple taking a pleasant walk down a country lane. Contented as "moo cows," they taste the sweetness of the grass, hear peaceful country sounds, and are dazzled by "dappled summer sunlight." Their future together seems to be all optimism as they anticipate "wonderful, faraway places" and the "road ahead." Full of confidence, this couple, like the reader, is unprepared for the shock to come. When we see those "fifty Hell's Angels," we are confronted with something like a bucket of cold water in the face.

But even though our expectations are abruptly and powerfully reversed, we are finally invited to view the entire episode from a safe distance — the distance provided by the delightful humor in this poem. After all, how seriously can we take a poem that is titled "Oh, Oh"? The poet has his way with us, but we are brought in on the joke too. The terror takes on comic proportions as the innocent couple is confronted by no fewer than *fifty* Hell's Angels. This is the kind of raucous overkill that informs a short animated film produced some years ago titled *Bambi Meets Godzilla:* you might not have seen it, but you know how it ends. The poem's good humor comes through when we realize how pathetically inadequate the response of "Oh, Oh" is to the circumstances.

As you can see, reading a description of what happens in a poem is not the same as experiencing a poem. The exuberance of "I scream . . ." and the surprise of Hathaway's "Oh, Oh" are in the hearing or reading rather than in the retelling. A *paraphrase* is a prose restatement of the central ideas of a poem in your own language. Consider the difference between the following poem and the paraphrase that follows it. What is missing from the paraphrase?

ROBERT FRANCIS (1901–1987)
Catch   1950

Two boys uncoached are tossing a poem together,
Overhand, underhand, backhand, sleight of hand, every hand,
Teasing with attitudes, latitudes, interludes, altitudes,
High, make him fly off the ground for it, low, make him stoop,
Make him scoop it up, make him as-almost-as-possible miss it,   5
Fast, let him sting from it, now, now fool him slowly,
Anything, everything tricky, risky, nonchalant,
Anything under the sun to outwit the prosy,
Over the tree and the long sweet cadence down,
Over his head, make him scramble to pick up the meaning,   10
And now, like a posy, a pretty one plump in his hands.

Paraphrase: A poet's relationship to a reader is similar to a game of catch. The poem, like a ball, should be pitched in a variety of ways to challenge and create interest. Boredom and predictability must be avoided if the game is to be engaging and satisfying.

A paraphrase can help us achieve a clearer understanding of a poem, but, unlike a poem, it misses all the sport and fun. It is the poem that "outwit[s] the prosy," because the poem serves as an example of what it suggests poetry should be. Moreover, the two players — the poet and the reader — are "uncoached." They know how the game is played, but their expectations do not preclude spontaneity and creativity or their ability to surprise and be surprised. The solid pleasure of the workout — of reading poetry — is the satisfaction derived from exercising your imagination and intellect.

That pleasure is worth emphasizing. Poetry uses language to move and delight even when it includes a cast of fifty Hell's Angels. The pleasure is in having the poem work its spell on us. For that to happen, it is best to relax and enjoy poetry rather than worrying about definitions of it. Pay attention to what the poet throws you. We read poems for emotional and intellectual discovery — to feel and experience something about the world and ourselves. The ideas in poetry — what can be paraphrased in prose — are important, but the real value of a poem consists in the words that work their magic by allowing us to feel, see, and be more than we were before. Perhaps the best way to approach a poem is similar to what Francis's "Catch" implies: expect to be surprised; stay on your toes; and concentrate on the delivery.

Write a paraphrase of this next poem. How does your prose statement differ from the effects produced by the language in the poem? Which descriptions seem particularly vivid?

X. J. KENNEDY (b. 1929)
First Confession   1961

Blood thudded in my ears. I scuffed,
    Steps stubborn, to the telltale booth
Beyond whose curtained portal coughed
    The robed repositor of truth.

The slat shot back. The universe   5
    Bowed down his cratered dome to hear
Enumerated my each curse,
    The sip snitched from my old man's beer,

My sloth pride envy lechery,
    The dime held back from Peter's Pence°   *Catholic offering*   10
With which I'd bribed my girl to pee
    That I might spy her instruments.

Hovering scale-pans when I'd done
    Settled their balance slow as silt
While in the restless dark I burned   15
    Bright as a brimstone in my guilt

Until as one feeds birds he doled
    Seven Our Fathers and a Hail
Which I to double-scrub my soul
    Intoned twice at the altar rail   20

Where Sunday in seraphic light
    I knelt, as full of grace as most,
And stuck my tongue out at the priest:
    A fresh roost for the Holy Ghost.

Innocence, piety, anxiety, humor, and irreverence tumble out of this confession booth, along with the boy's conscience and not entirely repentant attitude. Kennedy's description of the boy's first confession reveals the boy as well as redeems him.

Poets often remind us that beauty can be found in unexpected places. What is it that Elizabeth Bishop finds so beautiful about the "battered" fish she describes in the following poem?

ELIZABETH BISHOP (1911–1979)
The Fish   1946

I caught a tremendous fish
and held him beside the boat
half out of water, with my hook
fast in a corner of his mouth.
He didn't fight.   5
He hadn't fought at all.
He hung a grunting weight,
battered and venerable
and homely. Here and there
his brown skin hung in strips   10
like ancient wall-paper,
and its pattern of darker brown
was like wall-paper:
shapes like full-blown roses
stained and lost through age.   15
He was speckled with barnacles,
fine rosettes of lime,
and infested
with tiny white sea-lice,
and underneath two or three   20
rags of green weed hung down.
While his gills were breathing in
the terrible oxygen
— the frightening gills,
fresh and crisp with blood,   25
that can cut so badly —
I thought of the coarse white flesh
packed in like feathers,
the big bones and the little bones,
the dramatic reds and blacks   30
of his shiny entrails,
and the pink swim-bladder
like a big peony.
I looked into his eyes

which were far larger than mine   35
but shallower, and yellowed,
the irises backed and packed
with tarnished tinfoil
seen through the lenses
of old scratched isinglass.   40
They shifted a little, but not
to return my stare.
— It was more like the tipping
of an object toward the light.
I admired his sullen face,   45
the mechanism of his jaw,
and then I saw
that from his lower lip
— if you could call it a lip —
grim, wet, and weapon-like,   50
hung five old pieces of fish-line,
or four and a wire leader
with the swivel still attached,
with all their five big hooks
grown firmly in his mouth.   55
A green line, frayed at the end
where he broke it, two heavier lines,
and a fine black thread
still crimped from the strain and snap
when it broke and he got away.   60
Like medals with their ribbons
frayed and wavering,
a five-haired beard of wisdom
trailing from his aching jaw.
I stared and stared   65
and victory filled up
the little rented boat,
from the pool of bilge
where oil had spread a rainbow
around the rusted engine   70
to the bailer rusted orange,
the sun-cracked thwarts,
the oarlocks on their strings,
the gunnels — until everything
was rainbow, rainbow, rainbow!   75
And I let the fish go.

Considerations for Critical Thinking and Writing

1. Which lines in this poem provide especially vivid details of the fish? What makes
   these descriptions effective?
2. How is the fish characterized? Is it simply a weak victim because it "didn't fight"?

3. Comment on lines 65–76. In what sense has "victory filled up" the boat, given that the speaker finally lets the fish go?

The speaker in Bishop's "The Fish" ends on a triumphantly joyful note. The *speaker* is the voice used by the author in the poem; like the narrator in a work of fiction, the speaker is often a created identity rather than the author's actual self. The two should not automatically be equated. Contrast the attitude toward life of the speaker in "The Fish" with that of the speaker in the following poem.

PHILIP LARKIN (1922–1985)
A Study of Reading Habits   1964

When getting my nose in a book
Cured most things short of school,
It was worth ruining my eyes
To know I could still keep cool,
And deal out the old right hook   5
To dirty dogs twice my size.

Later, with inch-thick specs,
Evil was just my lark:
Me and my cloak and fangs
Had ripping times in the dark.   10
The women I clubbed with sex!
I broke them up like meringues.

Don't read much now: the dude
Who lets the girl down before
The hero arrives, the chap   15
Who's yellow and keeps the store,
Seem far too familiar. Get stewed:
Books are a load of crap.

What the speaker sees and describes in "The Fish" is close if not identical to Bishop's own vision and voice. The joyful response to the fish is clearly shared by the speaker and the poet, between whom there is little or no distance. In "A Study of Reading Habits," however, Larkin distances himself from a speaker whose sensibilities he does not wholly share. The poet — and many readers — might identify with the reading habits described by the speaker in the first twelve lines, but Larkin uses the last six lines to criticize the speaker's attitude toward life as well as reading. The speaker recalls in lines 1–6 how as a schoolboy he identified with the hero, whose virtuous strength always triumphed over "dirty dogs," and in lines 7–12 he recounts how his schoolboy fantasies were transformed by adolescence into a fascination with violence and sex. This description of early reading habits is pleasantly amusing, because most readers of popular fiction will probably recall having moved through similar stages, but at the end of the poem the speaker provides more information about himself than he intends to.

As an adult the speaker has lost interest in reading, because it is no longer an escape from his own disappointed life. Instead of identifying with heroes or villains, he finds himself identifying with minor characters who are irresponsible and cowardly. Reading is now a reminder of his failures, so he turns to alcohol. His solution, to "Get stewed," because "Books are a load of crap," is obviously self-destructive. The speaker is ultimately exposed by Larkin as someone who never grew beyond fantasies. Getting drunk is consistent with the speaker's immature reading habits. Unlike the speaker, the poet understands that life is often distorted by escapist fantasies, whether through a steady diet of popular fiction or through alcohol. The speaker in this poem, then, is not Larkin but a created identity whose voice is filled with disillusionment and delusion.

The problem with Larkin's speaker is that he misreads books as well as his own life. Reading means nothing to him unless it serves as an escape from himself. It is not surprising that Larkin has him read fiction rather than poetry, because poetry places an especially heavy emphasis upon language. Fiction, indeed any kind of writing, including essays and drama, relies upon carefully chosen and arranged words, but poetry does so to an even greater extent. Notice, for example, how Larkin's deft use of trite expressions and slang characterizes the speaker so that his language reveals nearly as much about his dreary life as what he says. Larkin's speaker would have no use for poetry.

What is "unmistakable" in poetry (to use Robinson's term again) is its intense, concentrated use of language — its emphasis on individual words to convey meanings, experiences, emotions, and effects. Poets never simply process words; they savor them. Words in poems frequently create their own tastes, textures, scents, sounds, and shapes. They often seem more sensuous than ordinary language, and readers usually sense that a word has been hefted before making its way into a poem. Although poems are crafted differently from the ways a painting, sculpture, or musical composition is created, in each form of art the creator delights in the medium. Poetry is carefully orchestrated so that the words work together as elements in a structure to sustain close, repeated readings. The words are chosen to interact with one another in order to create the maximum desired effect, whether the purpose is to capture a mood or feeling, create a vivid experience, express a point of view, narrate a story, or portray a character.

Here is a poem that looks quite different from most *verse,* a term used for lines composed in a measured rhythmical pattern, which are often, but not necessarily, rhymed.

ROBERT MORGAN (b. 1944)
Mountain Graveyard

1979

for the author of "Slow Owls"

Spore Prose

stone	notes
slate	tales
sacred	cedars
heart	earth
asleep	please
hated	death

Though unconventional in its appearance, this is unmistakably poetry because of its concentrated use of language. The poem demonstrates how serious play with words can lead to some remarkable discoveries. At first glance "Mountain Graveyard" may seem intimidating. What, after all, does this list of words add up to? How is it in any sense a poetic use of language? But if the words are examined closely, it is not difficult to see how they work. The wordplay here is literally in the form of a game. Morgan uses a series of *anagrams* (words made from the letters of other words, such as *read* and *dare*) to evoke feelings about death. "Mountain Graveyard" is one of several poems that Morgan has called "Spore Prose" (another anagram) because he finds in individual words the seeds of poetry. He wrote the poem in honor of the fiftieth birthday of another poet, Jonathan Williams, the author of "Slow Owls," whose title is also an anagram.

The title, "Mountain Graveyard," indicates the poem's setting, which is also the context in which the individual words in the poem interact to provide a larger meaning. Morgan's discovery of the words on the stones of a graveyard is more than just clever. The observations he makes among the silent graves go beyond the curious pleasure a reader experiences in finding the words *sacred cedars,* referring to evergreens common in cemeteries, to consist of the same letters. The surprise and delight of realizing the connection between heart and earth is tempered by the more sober recognition that everyone's story ultimately ends in the ground. The hope that the dead are merely asleep is expressed with a plea that is answered grimly by a hatred of death's finality.

Little is told in this poem. There is no way of knowing who is buried or who is looking at the graves, but the emotions of sadness, hope, and rage are unmistakable — and are conveyed in fewer than half the words of this sentence. Morgan takes words that initially appear to be a dead, prosaic list and energizes their meanings through imaginative juxtapositions.

The following poem also involves a startling discovery about words.

The Pleasure of Words 599

With the peculiar title "l(a," the poem cannot be read aloud, so there is no sound, but is there sense, a *theme*, a central idea or meaning, in the poem?

e. e. cummings (1894–1962)
l(a   1958

l(a

le
af
fa

ll

s)
one
l

iness

Considerations for Critical Thinking and Writing

1. Discuss the connection between what appears inside and outside the parentheses in this poem.
2. What does cummings draw attention to by breaking up the words? How do this strategy and the poem's overall shape contribute to its theme?
3. Which seems more important in this poem — what is expressed, or the way it is expressed?

Although "Mountain Graveyard" and "l(a" do not resemble the kind of verse that readers might recognize immediately as poetry on a page, both are actually a very common type of poem, called the *lyric*, usually a brief poem that expresses the personal emotions and thoughts of a single speaker. Lyrics are often written in the first person but sometimes — as in "Spore Prose" and "l(a" — no speaker is specified. Lyrics present a subjective mood, emotion, or idea. Very often they are about love or death, but almost any subject or experience that evokes some intense emotional response can be found in lyrics. In addition to brevity and emotional intensity, lyrics are also frequently characterized by their musical qualities. The word *lyric* derives from the Greek word *lyre,* meaning a musical instrument that originally accompanied the singing of a lyric. Lyric poems can be organized in a variety of ways, such as the sonnet, elegy, and ode (see Chapter 20), but it is enough to point out here that lyrics are an extremely popular kind of poetry with writers and readers.

The following anonymous lyric was found in a sixteenth-century manuscript.

ANONYMOUS
Western Wind

Western wind, when wilt thou blow,
The small rain down can rain?
Christ, if my love were in my arms,
And I in my bed again!

This speaker's intense longing for his lover is characteristic of lyric poetry. He impatiently addresses the western wind that brings spring to England and could make it possible for him to be reunited with the woman he loves. We do not know the details of these lovers' lives, because this poem focuses on the speaker's emotion. We do not learn why the lovers are apart or if they will be together again. We don't even know if the speaker is a man. But those issues are not really important. The poetry gives us a feeling rather than a story.

A poem that tells a story is called a *narrative poem.* Narrative poetry may be short or very long. An *epic,* for example, is a long narrative poem on a serious subject chronicling heroic deeds and important events. Among the most famous epics are Homer's *Iliad* and *Odyssey,* the Old English *Beowulf,* Dante's *Divine Comedy,* and John Milton's *Paradise Lost.* More typically, however, narrative poems are considerably shorter, such as the following poem, which tells the story of a child's memory of her father.

REGINA BARRECA (b. 1957)
Nighttime Fires

1986

When I was five in Louisville
we drove to see nighttime fires. Piled seven of us,
all pajamas and running noses, into the Olds,
drove fast toward smoke. It was after my father
lost his job, so not getting up in the morning   5
gave him time: awake past midnight, he read old newspapers
with no news, tried crosswords until he split the pencil
between his teeth, mad. When he heard
the wolf whine of the siren, he woke my mother,
and she pushed and shoved   10
us all into waking. Once roused we longed for burnt wood
and a smell of flames high into the pines. My old man liked
driving to rich neighborhoods best, swearing in a good mood
as he followed fire engines that snaked like dragons
and split the silent streets. It was festival, carnival.   15

If there were a Cadillac or any car

The Pleasure of Words **601**

in a curved driveway, my father smiled a smile
from a secret, brittle heart.
His face lit up in the heat given off by destruction
like something was being made, or was being set right.   20
I bent my head back to see where sparks
ate up the sky. My father who never held us
would take my hand and point to falling cinders that
covered the ground like snow, or, excited, show us
the swollen collapse of a staircase. My mother   25
watched my father, not the house. She was happy
only when we were ready to go, when it was finally over
and nothing else could burn.
Driving home, she would sleep in the front seat
as we huddled behind. I could see his quiet face in the   30
rearview mirror, eyes like hallways filled with smoke.

This narrative poem could have been a short story if the poet had wanted to say more about the "brittle heart" of this unemployed man whose daughter so vividly remembers the desperate pleasure he took in watching fire consume other people's property. Indeed, a reading of Faulkner's short story "Barn Burning" (p. 436) suggests how such a character can be further developed and how his child responds to him. The similarities between Faulkner's angry character and the poem's father, whose "eyes [are] like hallways filled with smoke," are coincidental, but the characters' sense of "something . . . being set right" by flames is worth comparing. Although we do not know everything about this man and his family, we have a much firmer sense of their story than we do of the story of the couple in "Western Wind."

Although narrative poetry is still written, short stories and novels have largely replaced the long narrative poem. Lyric poems tend to be the predominant type of poetry today. Regardless of whether a poem is a narrative or a lyric, however, the strategies for reading it are somewhat different from those for reading prose. Try these suggestions for approaching poetry.

SUGGESTIONS FOR APPROACHING POETRY

1. Assume that it will be necessary to read a poem more than once. Give yourself a chance to become familiar with what the poem has to offer. Like a piece of music, a poem becomes more pleasurable with each encounter.

2. Do pay attention to the title; it will often provide a helpful context for the poem and serve as an introduction to it. Larkin's "A Study of Reading Habits" is precisely what its title describes.

3. As you read the poem for the first time, avoid becoming entangled

in words or lines that you don't understand. Instead, give yourself a chance to take in the entire poem before attempting to resolve problems encountered along the way.

4. On a second reading, identify any words or passages that you don't understand. Look up words you don't know; these might include names, places, historical and mythical references, or anything else that is unfamiliar to you.

5. Read the poem aloud (or perhaps have a friend read it to you). You'll probably discover that some puzzling passages suddenly fall into place when you hear them. You'll find that nothing helps, though, if the poem is read in an artificial, exaggerated manner. Read in as natural a voice as possible, with slight pauses at line breaks. Silent reading is preferable to imposing a te-tumpty-te-tum reading on a good poem.

6. Read the punctuation. Poems use punctuation marks — in addition to the space on the page — as signals for readers. Be especially careful not to assume that the end of a line marks the end of a sentence, unless it is concluded by punctuation. Consider, for example, the opening lines of Hathaway's "Oh, Oh."

> My girl and I amble a country lane,
> moo cows chomping daisies, our own
> sweet saliva green with grass stems.

Line 2 makes little or no sense if a reader stops after "own." Keeping track of the subjects and verbs will help you find your way among the sentences.

7. Paraphrase the poem to determine whether you understand what happens in it. As you work through each line of the poem, a paraphrase will help you to see which words or passages need further attention.

8. Try to get a sense of who is speaking and what the setting or situation is. Don't assume that the speaker is the author; often it is a created character.

9. Assume that each element in the poem has a purpose. Try to explain how the elements of the poem work together.

10. Be generous. Be willing to entertain perspectives, values, experiences, and subjects that you might not agree with or approve. Even if you loathe baseball, you should be able to comprehend its imaginative use in Francis's "Catch."

11. Try developing a coherent approach to the poem that helps you to shape a discussion of the text. See Chapter 35, Critical Strategies for Reading (p. 1995), to review formalist, biographical, historical, psychological, feminist, and other possible critical approaches.

12. Don't expect to produce a definitive reading. Many poems do not

resolve all the ideas, issues, or tensions in them, and so it is not always possible to drive their meaning into an absolute corner. Your reading will explore rather than define the poem. Poems are not trophies to be stuffed and mounted. They're usually more elusive. And don't be afraid that a close reading will damage the poem. Poems aren't hurt when we analyze them; instead, they come alive as we experience them and put into words what we discover through them.

A list of more specific questions employing the literary terms and concepts discussed in the following chapters begins on page 918. That list, like the suggestions just made, raises issues and questions that can help you to read just about any poem closely. These strategies should be a useful means for getting inside poems to understand how they work. Furthermore, because reading poetry inevitably increases sensitivity to language, you're likely to find yourself a better reader of words in any form — whether in a novel, a newspaper editorial, an advertisement, a political speech, or a conversation — after having studied poetry. In short, many of the reading skills that make poetry accessible also open up the world you inhabit.

You'll probably find some poems amusing or sad, some fierce or tender, and some fascinating or dull. You may find, too, some poems that will get inside you. Their kinds of insights — the poet's and yours — are what Emily Dickinson had in mind when she defined poetry this way: "If I read a book and it makes my whole body so cold no fire can ever warm me, I know that it is poetry. If I feel physically as if the top of my head were taken off, I know that it is poetry." Dickinson's response may be more intense than most — poetry was, after all, at the center of her life — but you too might find yourself moved by poems in unexpected ways. In any case, as Edwin Arlington Robinson knew, poetry is, to an alert and sensitive reader, "eventually unmistakable."

POETRY IN POPULAR FORMS

Before you try out these strategies for reading on a few more poems, it is worth acknowledging that the verse which enjoys the widest readership appears not in collections, magazines, or even anthologies for students, but in greeting cards. A significant amount of the personal daily mail delivered in the United States consists of greeting cards. That represents millions of lines of verse going by us on the street and in planes over our heads. These verses share some similarities with the poetry included in this anthology, but there are also important differences that indicate the need for reading serious poetry closely rather than casually.

The popularity of greeting cards is easy to explain: just as many of us have neither the time nor the talent to make gifts for birthdays, weddings, anniversaries, graduations, Valentine's Day, Mother's Day, and other holidays, we are unlikely to write personal messages when cards conveniently say them for us. Though impersonal, cards are efficient and convey an important message no matter what the occasion for them: I care. These greetings are rarely serious poetry; they are not written to be. Nevertheless, they demonstrate the impulse in our culture to generate and receive poetry.

In a handbook for greeting-card free-lancers, a writer and past editor of such verse began with this advice:

> Once you determine what you want to say — and in this regard it is best to stick to one basic idea — you must choose your words to do several things at the same time:
>
> 1. Your idea must be expressed as a complete idea; it must have a beginning, a middle, and an end.
> 2. There must be coherence in your verse. Every line must be linked logically and smoothly with its neighbors.
> 3. Your expressions . . . must be conversational. High-flown language rarely comes off successfully in greeting card writing.
> 4. You must write with emphasis — and something else: enthusiasm. It's necessary to create interest in that all-important first line. From that point on, writing your verse is a matter of developing your idea and bringing it to a peak of emphasis in the last line. Occasionally you will find that you have shot your wad too early in the verse, and whatever you say after that point sounds like an afterthought.
> 5. You must do all of the above and at the same time make everything come out right in the meter-and-rhyme department.[1]

[handwritten marginal note: GENERIC, bracketing items 1–5]

This advice is followed by a list of approximately fifty of the most frequently used rhyme sounds accompanied by rhyming words, such as *love, of, above* for the sound *uv*. The point of these prescriptions is that the verse must be written so that it is immediately accessible — consumable — by both the buyer and the recipient. Writers of these cards are expected to avoid any complexity.

Compare the following greeting-card verse with the poem that comes after it. "Magic of Love," by Helen Farries, has been a longtime favorite in a major greeting-card company's "wedding line"; with different endings it has been used also in valentines and friendship cards.

---

[1]Chris Fitzgerald, "Conventional Verse: The Sentimental Favorite," *The Greeting Card Writer's Handbook,* ed. H. Joseph Chadwick (Cincinnati: Writer's Digest, 1975): 13, 17.

HELEN FARRIES
Magic of Love

date unknown

There's a wonderful gift that can give you a lift,
It's a blessing from heaven above!
It can comfort and bless, it can bring happiness —
It's the wonderful MAGIC OF LOVE!

Like a star in the night, it can keep your faith bright,   5
Like the sun, it can warm your hearts, too —
It's a gift you can give every day that you live,
And when given, it comes back to you!

When love lights the way, there is joy in the day
And all troubles are lighter to bear,   10
Love is gentle and kind, and through love you will find
There's an answer to your every prayer!

May it never depart from your two loving hearts,
May you treasure this gift from above —
You will find if you do, all your dreams will come true,   15
In the wonderful MAGIC OF LOVE!

JOHN FREDERICK NIMS (b. 1913)
Love Poem

1947

My clumsiest dear, whose hands shipwreck vases,
At whose quick touch all glasses chip and ring,
Whose palms are bulls in china, burs in linen,
And have no cunning with any soft thing

Except all ill-at-ease fidgeting people: 5
The refugee uncertain at the door
You make at home; deftly you steady
The drunk clambering on his undulant floor.

Unpredictable dear, the taxi drivers' terror,
Shrinking from far headlights pale as a dime   10
Yet leaping before red apoplectic streetcars —
Misfit in any space. And never on time.

A wrench in clocks and the solar system. Only
With words and people and love you move at ease.
In traffic of wit expertly maneuver   15
And keep us, all devotion, at your knees.

Forgetting your coffee spreading on our flannel,
Your lipstick grinning on our coat,

So gaily in love's unbreakable heaven
Our souls on glory of spilt bourbon float.   20

Be with me, darling, early and late. Smash glasses —
I will study wry music for your sake.
For should your hands drop white and empty
All the toys of the world would break.

Considerations for Critical Thinking and Writing

1. Read these two works aloud. Characterize their differences.
2. To what extent does the advice to would-be greeting-card writers apply to each work?
3. Compare the two speakers. Which do you find more appealing? Why?
4. How does Nims's description of love differ from Farries's?

In contrast to poetry, which transfigures and expresses an emotion or experience through an original use of language, the verse in "Magic of Love" relies upon *clichés*, ideas or expressions that have become tired and trite from overuse, such as describing love as "a blessing from heaven above." Clichés anesthetize readers instead of alerting them to the possibility of fresh perceptions. They are used to draw out **stock responses**, predictable, conventional reactions to language, characters, symbols, or situations; God, heaven, the flag, motherhood, hearts, puppies, and peace are some often-used objects of stock responses. Advertisers manufacture careers from this sort of business.

Clichés and stock responses are two of the major ingredients of sentimentality in literature. *Sentimentality* exploits the reader by inducing emotional responses that exceed what the situation warrants. This pejorative term should not be confused with *sentiment,* which is synonymous with *emotion* or *feeling.* Sentimentality cons readers into falling for the mass murderer who is devoted to stray cats, and it requires that we not think twice about what we're feeling, because those tears shed for the little old lady, the rage aimed at the vicious enemy soldier, and the longing for the simple virtues of poverty might disappear under the slightest scrutiny. The experience of sentimentality is not unlike biting into a swirl of cotton candy; it's momentarily sweet but wholly insubstantial.

Clichés, stock responses, and sentimentality are generally the hallmarks of weak writing. Poetry — the kind that is unmistakable — achieves freshness, vitality, and genuine emotion that sharpen our perceptions of life.

Although the most widely read verse is found in greeting cards, the most widely *heard* poetry appears in song lyrics. Not all songs are poetic, but a good many share the same effects and qualities as poems. Consider these lyrics by Tracy Chapman.

TRACY CHAPMAN (b. 1964)
Fast Car

1987

You got a fast car
I want a ticket to anywhere
Maybe we make a deal
Maybe together we can get somewhere
Anyplace is better   5
Starting from zero got nothing to lose
Maybe we'll make something
But me myself I got nothing to prove

You got a fast car
And I got a plan to get us out of here   10
I been working at the convenience store
Managed to save just a little bit of money
We won't have to drive too far
Just 'cross the border and into the city
You and I can both get jobs   15
And finally see what it means to be living

You see my old man's got a problem
He live with the bottle that's the way it is
He says his body's too old for working
I say his body's too young to look like his   20
My mama went off and left him
She wanted more from life than he could give
I said somebody's got to take care of him
So I quit school and that's what I did

You got a fast car   25
But is it fast enough so we can fly away
We gotta make a decision
We leave tonight or live and die this way

I remember we were driving driving in your car
The speed so fast I felt like I was drunk   30
City lights lay out before us
And your arm felt nice wrapped 'round my shoulder
And I had a feeling that I belonged
And I had feeling I could be someone, be someone, be someone

You got a fast car   35
And we go cruising to entertain ourselves
You still ain't got a job
And I work in a market as a checkout girl
I know things will get better
You'll find work and I'll get promoted   40
We'll move out of the shelter
Buy a big house and live in the suburbs

You got a fast car
And I got a job that pays all our bills
You stay out drinking late at the bar   45
See more of your friends than you do of your kids
I'd always hoped for better
Thought maybe together you and me would find it
I got no plans I ain't going nowhere
So take your fast car and keep on driving   50

You got a fast car
But is it fast enough so you can fly away
You gotta make a decision
You leave tonight or live and die this way

Considerations for Critical Thinking and Writing

1. Characterize the speaker in this song lyric. What sort of life does she live? How does she want to change it?
2. What is the effect of the repetition of "You got a fast car"? Describe the man in the song. What does his "fast car" come to represent to the speaker?
3. Why isn't punctuation necessary to read these lyrics?
4. Explain whether you think this song can be accurately called a narrative poem.

PERSPECTIVE

ROBERT FRANCIS (1901–1987)
On "Hard" Poetry   1965

When Robert Frost said he liked poems hard he could scarcely have meant he liked them difficult. If he had meant difficult he would have said he didn't like them easy. What he said was that he didn't like them soft.

Poems can be soft in several ways. They can be soft in form (invertebrate). They can be soft in thought and feeling (sentimental). They can be soft with excess verbiage. Frost used to advise one to squeeze the water out of a poem. He liked poems dry. What is dry tends to be hard, and what is hard is always dry, except perhaps on the outside.

Yet though hardness here does not mean difficulty, some difficulty naturally goes with hardness. A hard poem may not be hard to read but is hard to write. Not too hard, preferably. Not so hard to write that there is no flow in the writer. But hard enough for the growing poem to meet with some healthy resistance. Frost often found this healthy resistance in a tight rhyme scheme and strict meter. There are other ways of getting good resistance, of course.

And in the reader too, a hard poem will bring some difficulty. Preferably not too much. Not enough difficulty to completely baffle him. Ideally a hard poem should not be too hard to make sense of, but hard to exhaust its meaning and its beauty.

"What I care about is the hardness of the poems. I don't like them soft, I want them to be little pebbles, but placed where they won't dislodge easily. And I'd like them to be little pebbles of precious stone — precious, or semiprecious" (interview with John Ciardi, *Saturday Review,* March 21, 1959).

Here is hard prose talking about hard poetry. Frost was never shrewder or more illuminating. Here, as well as in anything else he ever said, is his flavor.

What contemporary of his can you imagine saying this or anything like it?

In 1843 Emerson jotted in his journal: "Hard clouds and hard expressions, and hard manners, I love."

From The Satirical Rogue on Poetry

Considerations for Critical Thinking and Writing

1. What is the distinction between "hard" and "soft" poetry?
2. Given Francis's brief essay and his poem "Catch" (p. 593), write a review of Helen Farries's "Magic of Love" (p. 606) as you think Francis would.
3. Explain whether you would characterize Chapman's "Fast Car" as hard or soft.

POEMS FOR FURTHER STUDY

ALBERTO RÍOS (b. 1952)
Seniors

1985

William cut a hole in his Levi's pocket
so he could flop himself out in class
behind the girls so the other guys
could see and shit what guts we all said.
All Konga wanted to do over and over   5
was the rubber band trick, but he showed
everyone how, so nobody wanted to see
anymore and one day he cried, just cried
until his parents took him away forever.
Maya had a Hotpoint refrigerator standing   10
in his living room, just for his family to show
anybody who came that they could afford it.

Me, I got a French kiss, finally, in the catholic
darkness, my tongue's farthest half vacationing
loudly in another mouth like a man in Bermudas,   15
and my body jumped against a flagstone wall,
I could feel it through her thin, almost
nonexistent body: I had, at that moment, that moment,
a hot girl on a summer night, the best of all
the things we tried to do. Well, she   20
let me kiss her, anyway, all over.

Or it was just a flagstone wall
with a flaw in the stone, an understanding cavity

for burning young men with smooth dreams —
the true circumstance is gone, the true   25
circumstances about us all then
are gone. But when I kissed her, all water,
she would close her eyes, and they into somewhere
would disappear. Whether she was there
or not, I remember her, clearly, and she moves   30
around the room, sometimes, until I sleep.

I have lain on the desert in watch
low in the back of a pick-up truck
for nothing in particular, for stars, for
the things behind stars, and nothing comes   35
more than the moment: always now, here in a truck,
the moment again to dream of making love and sweat,
this time to a woman, or even to all of them
in some allowable way, to those boys, then,
who couldn't cry, to the girls before they were   40
women, to friends, me on my back, the sky over me
pressing its simple weight into her body
on me, into the bodies of them all, on me.

Considerations for Critical Thinking and Writing

1. Comment on the use of slang in the poem. How does it serve to characterize the speaker?
2. How does language of the final stanza differ from that of the first stanza? To what purpose?
3. Write an essay that discusses the speaker's attitudes toward sex and life. How are they related?

Connections to Other Selections

1. Compare the treatment of sex in this poem with that in Olds's "Sex without Love" (p. 1056).
2. Think about "Seniors" as a kind of love poem and compare the speaker's voice here with the one in Eliot's "The Love Song of J. Alfred Prufrock" (p. 906). How are these two voices used to evoke different cultures? Of what value is love in these cultures?

TED KOOSER (b. 1939)
Selecting a Reader   1974

First, I would have her be beautiful,
and walking carefully up on my poetry
at the loneliest moment of an afternoon,
her hair still damp at the neck
from washing it. She should be wearing   5

a raincoat, an old one, dirty
from not having money enough for the cleaners.
She will take out her glasses, and there
in the bookstore, she will thumb
over my poems, then put the book back   10
up on its shelf. She will say to herself,
"For that kind of money, I can get
my raincoat cleaned." And she will.

Considerations for Critical Thinking and Writing

1. What do the descriptive details in this poem reveal about the kind of reader the
   poet desires?
2. Based on this description of the poet's desired reader, write a one-paragraph
   description of the poem's speaker. Try to include some imaginative details that
   suggest his personality.

JOHN DONNE (1572–1631)
The Sun Rising   c. 1633

              Busy old fool, unruly sun,
                Why dost thou thus,
Through windows, and through curtains, call on us?
Must to thy motions lovers' seasons run?
              Saucy pedantic wretch, go chide   5
              Late schoolboys, and sour prentices,
        Go tell court-huntsmen that the king will ride,
        Call country ants° to harvest offices;   *farm workers*
Love, all alike, no season knows, nor clime,
Nor hours, days, months, which are the rags of time.   10

              Thy beams, so reverend and strong
                Why shouldst thou think?
I could eclipse and cloud them with a wink,
But that I would not lose her sight so long:
              If her eyes have not blinded thine,   15
              Look, and tomorrow late, tell me
        Whether both the Indias° of spice and mine   *East and West Indies*
        Be where thou left'st them, or lie here with me.
Ask for those kings whom thou saw'st yesterday,
And thou shalt hear, all here in one bed lay.   20

              She is all states, and all princes I,
                Nothing else is.
Princes do but play us; compared to this,
All honor's mimic, all wealth alchemy.
              Thou, sun, art half as happy as we,   25
              In that the world's contracted thus;

Thine age asks ease, and since thy duties be
To warm the world, that's done in warming us.
Shine here to us, and thou art every where;
This bed thy center° is, these walls thy sphere.   *of orbit*   30

Considerations for Critical Thinking

1. What is the situation in this poem? Why is the speaker angry with the sun? What does he urge the sun to do in the first stanza?
2. What claims does the speaker make about the power of love in stanzas 2 and 3? What does he mean when he says, "Shine here to us, and thou art every where"?
3. Are any of the speaker's exaggerations in any sense true? How?

Connection to Another Selection

1. Compare this lyric poem with Richard Wilbur's "A Late Aubade" (p. 634). What similarities do you find in the ideas and emotions expressed in each?

NIKKI GIOVANNI (b. 1943)

Nikki-Rosa   1968

childhood remembrances are always a drag
if you're Black
you always remember things like living in Woodlawn
with no inside toilet
and if you become famous or something   5
they never talk about how happy you were to have your mother
all to yourself and
how good the water felt when you got your bath from one of those
big tubs that folk in chicago barbecue in
and somehow when you talk about home   10
it never gets across how much you
understood their feelings
as the whole family attended meetings about Hollydale
and even though you remember
your biographers never understand   15
your father's pain as he sells his stock
and another dream goes
and though you're poor it isn't poverty that
concerns you
and though they fought a lot   20
it isn't your father's drinking that makes any difference
but only that everybody is together and you
and your sister have happy birthdays and very good christmasses
and I really hope no white person ever has cause to write about me
because they never understand Black love is Black wealth and they'll   25
probably talk about my hard childhood and never understand that
all the while I was quite happy

Considerations for Critical Thinking and Writing

1. How does reading this poem aloud help to convey its meaning and characterize the speaker? How does the lack of punctuation contribute to our image of the speaker?
2. Is this poem addressed primarily to whites, blacks, or both? Why?
3. Does the speaker describe his or her childhood as positive or negative?
4. Is this a sentimental treatment of childhood memories? Why or why not?

Connections to Other Selections

1. Compare the feelings evoked by the "childhood remembrances" in Giovanni's poem with those in Barreca's "Nighttime Fires" (p. 601).
2. Write an essay contrasting the attitude toward the past expressed in "Nikki-Rosa" with the black man's attitude in M. Carl Holman's "Mr. Z" (p. 962).

LOUIS SIMPSON (b. 1923)
American Poetry   1963

Whatever it is, it must have
A stomach that can digest
Rubber, coal, uranium, moons, poems.

Like the shark, it contains a shoe.
It must swim for miles through the desert
Uttering cries that are almost human.

Considerations for Critical Thinking and Writing

1. According to Simpson, what kind of appetite should American poetry have for life?
2. Consider whether you think any limits should be placed on the subject matter of poetry. Explain why or why not.

MAXINE KUMIN (b. 1925)
Morning Swim   1965

Into my empty head there come
a cotton beach, a dock wherefrom

I set out, oily and nude
through mist, in chilly solitude.

There was no line, no roof or floor   5
to tell the water from the air.

Night fog thick as terry cloth
closed me in its fuzzy growth.

I hung my bathrobe on two pegs.
I took the lake between my legs.   10

Invaded and invader, I
went overhand on that flat sky.

Fish twitched beneath me, quick and tame.
In their green zone they sang my name

and in the rhythm of the swim   15
I hummed a two-four-time slow hymn.

I hummed *Abide with Me*. The beat
rose in the fine thrash of my feet,

rose in the bubbles I put out
slantwise, trailing through my mouth.   20

My bones drank water; water fell
through all my doors. I was the well

that fed the lake that met my sea
in which I sang *Abide with Me*.

Considerations for Critical Thinking and Writing

1. How does the description of swimming reveal the speaker's feelings about the morning swim?
2. What is the significance of the hymn's title, "Abide with Me"? How is it related to the central point of the poem?

LI HO (791–817)
A Beautiful Girl Combs Her Hair
TRANSLATED BY DAVID YOUNG

Awake at dawn
she's dreaming
by cool silk curtains

fragrance of spilling hair
half sandalwood, half aloes   5

windlass creaking at the well
singing jade

the lotus blossom wakes, refreshed

her mirror
two phoenixes   10
a pool of autumn light

standing on the ivory bed
loosening her hair
watching the mirror

one long coil, aromatic silk   15
a cloud down to the floor

drop the jade comb — no sound

delicate fingers
pushing the coils into place
color of raven feathers   20

shining blue-black stuff
the jewelled comb will hardly hold it

spring wind makes me restless
her slovenly beauty upsets me

eighteen and her hair's so thick   25
she wears herself out fixing it!

she's finished now
the whole arrangement in place

in a cloud-patterned skirt
she walks with even steps   30
a wild goose on the sand

turns away without a word
where is she off to?

down the steps to break a spray of
        cherry blossoms   35

Considerations for Critical Thinking and Writing

1. How does the speaker use sensuous language to create a vivid picture of the girl?
2. What are the speaker's feelings toward the girl? Do they remain the same throughout the poem?
3. Why would it be difficult to capture the essence of this poem in a paraphrase?

Connections to Other Selections

1. Compare the description of hair in this poem with that in Cathy Song's "The White Porch" (p. 1057). What significant similarities do you find?
2. Write an essay that explores the differing portraits in this poem and in Roethke's "I Knew a Woman" (p. 993). Which portrait is more interesting to you? Explain why.

14. Word Choice, Word Order, and Tone

DICTION

Like all good writers, poets are keenly aware of *diction,* their choice of words. Poets, however, choose words especially carefully, because the words in poems call attention to themselves. Characters, actions, settings, and symbols may appear in a poem, but in the foreground, before all else, is the poem's language. Also, poems are usually briefer than other forms of writing. A few inappropriate words in a two-hundred-page novel (which would have about 100,000 words) create fewer problems than they would in a 100-word poem. Functioning in a compressed atmosphere, the words in a poem must convey meanings gracefully and economically. Readers therefore have to be alert to the ways in which those meanings are released.

Although poetic language is often more intensely charged than ordinary speech, the words used in poetry are not necessarily different from everyday speech. Inexperienced readers may sometimes assume that language must be high-flown and out of date to be included in a poem: instead of reading about a boy "enjoying a swim," they expect to read about a boy "disporting with pliant arm o'er a glassy wave." During the eighteenth century this kind of *poetic diction* — the use of elevated language over ordinary language — was highly valued in English poetry, but since the nineteenth century poets have generally overridden the distinctions that were once made between words used in everyday speech and those used in poetry. Today all levels of diction can be found in poetry.

A poet, like any writer, has several levels of diction from which to choose; they range from formal to middle to informal. *Formal diction* consists of a dignified, impersonal, and elevated use of language. Notice, for example, the formality of Thomas Hardy's description of the sunken luxury liner *Titanic* in this stanza from "The Convergence of the Twain" (the entire poem appears on p. 636):

In a solitude of the sea
    Deep from human vanity,
And the Pride of Life that planned her, stilly couches she.

There is nothing casual or relaxed about these lines. Hardy's use of *stilly*, meaning "quietly" or "calmly," is purely literary; the word rarely, if ever, turns up in everyday English.

The language used in Richard Wilbur's "A Late Aubade" (p. 634) represents a less formal level of diction; the speaker uses a *middle diction* spoken by most educated people. Consider how Wilbur's speaker tells his lover what she might be doing instead of being with him.

You could be sitting now in a carrel
Turning some liver-spotted page,
Or rising in an elevator-cage
Toward Ladies' Apparel.

The speaker elegantly enumerates his lover's unattractive alternatives to being with him — reading old books in a library or shopping in a department store — but the wit of his description lessens its formality.

Informal diction is evident in Larkin's "A Study of Reading Habits" (p. 597). The speaker's account of his early reading is presented *colloquially*, in a conversational manner that in this instance includes slang expressions not used by the culture at large.

When getting my nose in a book
Cured most things short of school,
It was worth ruining my eyes
To know I could still keep cool,
And deal out the old right hook
To dirty dogs twice my size.

This level of diction is clearly not that of Hardy's or Wilbur's speakers.

Poets may also draw on another form of informal diction, called *dialect*. Dialects are spoken by definable groups of people from a particular geographic region, economic group, or social class. New England dialects are often heard in Robert Frost's poems, for example. Gwendolyn Brooks employs a black dialect in "We Real Cool" (p. 638) to characterize a group of pool players. Another form of diction related to particular groups is *jargon*, a category of language defined by a trade or profession. Sociologists, photographers, carpenters, baseball players, and dentists, for example, all use words that are specific to their fields. e. e. cummings manages to get quite a lot of mileage out of automobile jargon in "she being Brand" (p. 623).

Many levels of diction are available to poets. The variety of diction to be found in poetry is enormous, and that is how it should be. No language is foreign to poetry, because it is possible to imagine any human voice as the speaker of a poem. When we say a poem is formal, informal, or somewhere in between, we are making a descriptive statement rather than an evaluative one. What matters in a poem is not only which words are used but how they are used.

DENOTATIONS AND CONNOTATIONS

One important way that the meaning of a word is communicated in a poem is through sound: snakes *hiss,* saws *buzz.* This and other matters related to sound are discussed in Chapter 18. Individual words also convey meanings through denotations and connotations. *Denotations* are the literal, dictionary meanings of a word. For example, *bird* denotes a feathered animal with wings (other denotations for the same word include a shuttlecock, an airplane, or an odd person), but in addition to its denotative meanings *bird* also carries *connotations,* associations and implications that go beyond a word's literal meanings. Connotations derive from how the word has been used and the associations people make with it. Therefore, the connotations of *bird* might include fragility, vulnerability, altitude, the sky, or freedom, depending on the context in which the word is used. Consider also how different the connotations are for the following types of birds: hawk, dove, penguin, pigeon, chicken, peacock, duck, crow, turkey, gull, owl, goose, coot, and vulture. These words have long been used to refer to types of people as well as birds. They are rich in connotative meanings.

Connotations derive their resonance from a person's experiences with a word. Those experiences may not always be the same, especially when the people having them are in different times and places. *Theater,* for instance, was once associated with depravity, disease, and sin, while today the word usually evokes some sense of high culture and perhaps visions of elegant opulence. In several ethnic communities in the United States many people would find *squid* appetizing, but elsewhere the word is likely to produce negative connotations. Readers must recognize, then, that words written in other times and places may have unexpected connotations. Annotations usually help in these matters, which is why it makes sense to pay attention to them when they are available.

Ordinarily, though, the language of poetry is accessible, even when the circumstances of the reader and the poet are different. Although connotative language may be used subtly, it mostly draws on associations experienced by many people. Poets rely on widely shared associations rather than the idiosyncratic response that an individual might have to a word. Someone who has received a severe burn from a fireplace accident may associate the word *hearth* with intense pain instead of home and family life, but that reader must not allow a personal experience to undermine the response the poet intends to evoke. Connotative meanings are usually public meanings.

Perhaps this can be seen most clearly in advertising, where language is also used primarily to convey moods and feelings rather than information. For instance, our recent efforts to get in shape have created a collective consciousness that advertisers have capitalized on successfully. Knowing that we want to be slender or lean or slim (not spare or scrawny and certainly not gaunt), advertisers have created a new word to describe beers, wines, sodas, cheeses, canned fruits, and other products that tend to overload what used to be called sweatclothes and sneakers. The word is *lite*. The assumed denotative meaning of *lite* is low in calories, but as close readers of ingredient labels know, some *lites* are heavier than regularly prepared products. There can be no doubt about the connotative meaning of *lite,* however. Whatever is *lite* cannot hurt you; less is more. Even the word is lighter than *light;* there is no unnecessary droopy *g* or plump *h*. *Lite* is a brilliantly manufactured use of connotation.

Connotative meanings are valuable to poets because they allow them to be economical and suggestive simultaneously. In this way emotions and attitudes are carefully woven into the texture of the poem's language. Read the following poem and pay close attention to the connotative meanings of its words.

RANDALL JARRELL (1914–1965)
The Death of the Ball Turret Gunner 1945

From my mother's sleep I fell into the State
And I hunched in its belly till my wet fur froze.
Six miles from earth, loosed from its dream of life,
I woke to black flack and the nightmare fighters.
When I died they washed me out of the turret with a hose.

The title of this poem establishes the setting and the speaker's situation. Like the setting of a short story, the setting of a poem is important when the time and place influence what happens. "The Death of the Ball Turret Gunner" is set in the midst of a war and, more specifically, in a ball turret — a Plexiglas sphere housing machine guns on the underside of a bomber. The speaker's situation obviously places him in extreme danger; indeed, his fate is announced in the title.

Although the poem is written in the first-person singular, its speaker is clearly not the poet. Jarrell employs a *persona,* a speaker created by the poet. In this poem the persona is a disembodied voice that makes the gunner's story all the more powerful. What is his story? A paraphrase might read something like this:

After I was born, I grew up to find myself at war, cramped into the turret of a bomber's belly some 31,000 feet above the ground. Below me were exploding shells from antiaircraft guns and attacking fighter planes. I was killed, but the bomber returned to base, where my remains were cleaned out of the turret so the next man could take my place.

This paraphrase is accurate, but its language is much less suggestive than the poem's. The first line of the poem has the speaker emerge from his "mother's sleep," the anesthetized sleep of her giving birth. The phrase also suggests the comfort, warmth, and security he knew as a child. This safety was left behind when he "fell," a verb that evokes the danger and involuntary movement associated with his subsequent "State" (*fell* also echoes, perhaps, the fall from innocence to experience related in the Bible).

Several dictionary definitions appear for the noun *state;* it can denote a territorial unit, the power and authority of a government, a person's social status, or a person's emotional or physical condition. The context provided by the rest of the poem makes clear that "State" has several denotative meanings here: Because it is capitalized it certainly refers to the violent world of a government at war, but it also refers to the gunner's vulnerable status as well as his physical and emotional condition. By having "State" carry more than one meaning, Jarrell has created an intentional ambiguity. **Ambiguity** allows for two or more simultaneous interpretations of a word, phrase, action, or situation, all of which can be supported by the context of a work. Through his ambiguous use of "State," Jarrell connects the horrors of war not just to bombers and gunners but to the governments that control them.

Related to this ambiguity is the connotative meaning of "State" in the poem. The context demands that the word be read with a negative charge. The word is not used with patriotic pride but to suggest an anonymous, impersonal "State" that kills rather than nurtures the life in its "belly." The state's "belly" is a bomber, and the gunner is "hunched" like a fetus in the cramped turret, where, in contrast to the warmth of his mother's womb, everything is frozen, even the "wet fur" of his flight jacket (newborn infants have wet fur too). The gunner is not just 31,000 feet from the ground but "six miles from earth." *Six miles* has roughly the same denotative meaning as 31,000 feet, but Jarrell knew that the connotative meaning of *six miles* makes the speaker's position seem even more remote and frightening.

When the gunner is born into the violent world of war, he finds himself waking up to a "nightmare" that is all too real. The poem's final line is grimly understated, but it hits the reader with the force of an exploding shell: what the State-bomber-turret gives birth to is a gruesome death that is merely one of an endless series. It may be tempting to reduce the theme of this poem to the idea that "war is hell"; but Jarrell's target is more specific. He implicates the "State," which routinely executes such violence, and he does so without preaching or hysterical denunciations. Instead, his use of language conveys his theme subtly and powerfully. Consider how this next poem uses connotative meanings to express its theme.

e. e. cummings (1894–1962)

she being Brand

she being Brand

-new;and you
know consequently a
little stiff i was
careful of her and(having   5

thoroughly oiled the universal
joint tested my gas felt of
her radiator made sure her springs were O.

K.)i went right to it flooded-the-carburetor cranked her

up,slipped the   10
clutch(and then somehow got into reverse she
kicked what
the hell)next
minute i was back in neutral tried and

again slo-wly;bare,ly nudg.   ing (my   15

lev-er Right-
oh and her gears being in
A 1 shape passed
from low through
second-in-to-high like   20
greasedlightning) just as we turned the corner of Divinity

avenue i touched the accelerator and give

her the juice,good

                    (it

was the first ride and believe i we was   25
happy to see how nice she acted right up to
the last minute coming back down by the Public
Gardens i slammed on

the
internalexpanding   30
&
externalcontracting
brakes Bothatonce and

brought allofher tremB
-ling
to a:dead.   35

stand-
;Still)

Considerations for Critical Thinking and Writing

1. How does cummings's arrangement of the words on the page help you to read this poem aloud? What does the poem describe?
2. What ambiguities in language does the poem ride on? At what point were you first aware of these double meanings?
3. Explain why you think the poem is primarily serious or humorous.
4. Find some advertisements for convertibles or sports cars in magazines and read them closely. What similarities do you find in the use of connotative language in them and in cummings's poem? Write a brief essay explaining how language is used to convey the theme of one of the advertisements and the poem.

WORD ORDER

Meanings in poems are conveyed not only by denotations and connotations but also by the poet's arrangement of words into phrases, clauses, and sentences to achieve particular effects. The ordering of words into meaningful verbal patterns is called *syntax*. A poet can manipulate the syntax of a line to place emphasis on a word; this is especially apparent when a poet varies normal word order. In Dickinson's "A narrow Fellow in the Grass" (p. 4), for example, the speaker says about the snake that "His notice sudden is." Ordinarily, that would be expressed as "his notice is sudden." By placing the verb *is* unexpectedly at the end of the line, Dickinson creates the sense of surprise we feel when we suddenly come upon a snake. Dickinson's inversion of the standard word order also makes the final sound of the line a hissing *is*.

Cummings uses one long sentence in "she being Brand" to take the reader on a ride that begins with a false start but accelerates quickly before coming to a halt. The jargon creates an exuberantly humorous mood that is helped along by the poem's syntax. How do cummings's ordering of words and sentence structure reinforce the meaning of the lines?

TONE

Tone is the writer's attitude toward the subject, the mood created by all the elements in the poem. Writing, like speech, may be characterized as serious or light, sad or happy, private or public, angry or affectionate, bitter or nostalgic, or any other attitudes and feelings that human beings experience. In Jarrell's "The Death of the Ball Turret Gunner," the tone is clearly serious; the voice in the poem even sounds dead. Listen again to the persona's final words: "When I died they washed me out of the turret with a hose." The brutal, restrained matter-of-factness of this line is effective because the reader is called on to supply the appropriate anger and despair, a strategy that makes those emotions all the more convincing.

Consider how tone is used to convey meaning in the next poem, inspired by the poet's contemplating Chinese silk shoes in a museum.

RUTH FAINLIGHT (b. 1931)
Flower Feet

1989

(SILK SHOES IN THE WHITWORTH ART GALLERY,
MANCHESTER, ENGLAND)

Real women's feet wore these objects
that look like toys or spectacle cases stitched
from bands of coral, jade, and apricot silk
embroidered with twined sprays of flowers.
Those hearts, tongues, crescents, and disks, leather   5
shapes an inch across, are the soles of shoes
no wider or longer than the span of my ankle.

If the feet had been cut off and the raw stumps
thrust inside the openings, surely
it could not hurt more than broken toes, twisted   10
back and bandaged tight. An old woman,
leaning on a cane outside her door
in a Chinese village, smiled to tell how
she fought and cried, how when she stood on points
of pain that gnawed like fire, nurse and mother   15
praised her tottering walk on flower feet.
Her friends nodded, glad the times had changed.
Otherwise, they would have crippled their daughters.

Considerations for Critical Thinking and Writing

1. Why did the Chinese bind feet?
2. How is the speaker's description of the process of binding feet in lines 8–16 different from the description of the shoes in lines 1–7?
3. Describe the poem's tone. Does it remain the same throughout the poem, or does it change? Explain your response.

Connections to Other Selections

1. How is the speaker's perspective on tradition and custom in this poem similar to that in Frost's "Mending Wall" (p. 874)?
2. The final line of this poem is startling. Why? How is it similar in its strategy to James Merrill's "Casual Wear" (p. 699)?
3. Compare the view of change in this poem with that in Clampitt's "Nothing Stays Put" (p. 1040).

The next work is a *dramatic monologue,* a type of poem in which a character — the speaker — addresses a silent audience in such a way as to reveal unintentionally some aspect of his or her temperament or personality. What tone is created by Machan's use of a persona?

KATHARYN HOWD MACHAN (b. 1952)
Hazel Tells LaVerne   1976

last night
im cleanin out my
howard johnsons ladies room
when all of a sudden
up pops this frog   5
musta come from the sewer
swimmin aroun an tryin ta
climb up the sida the bowl
so i goes ta flushm down
but sohelpmegod he starts talkin   10
bout a golden ball
an how i can be a princess
me a princess
well my mouth drops
all the way to the floor   15
an he says
kiss me just kiss me
once on the nose
well i screams
ya little green pervert   20
an i hitsm with my mop
an has ta flush
the toilet down three times
me
a princess   25

Considerations for Critical Thinking and Writing

1. What do you imagine the situation and setting are for this poem?
2. What creates the poem's humor? How does Hazel's use of language reveal her personality? Is her treatment of the frog consistent with her character?
3. Although it has no punctuation, this poem is easy to follow. How does the arrangement of the lines organize Hazel's speech for clarity and emphasis?
4. What is the theme? Is it conveyed through denotative or connotative language?
5. Write what you think might be LaVerne's reply to Hazel. First, write LaVerne's response as a series of ordinary sentences, and then try editing and organizing them into poetic lines.

Connection to Another Selection

1. Although Robert Browning's "My Last Duchess" (p. 702) is a more complex poem than Machan's, both use dramatic monologues to reveal character. How are the strategies in each poem similar?

WILLIAM TROWBRIDGE (b. 1941)
Enter Dark Stranger   1985

In "Shane," when Jack Palance first appears,
a stray cur takes one look and slinks away
on tiptoes, able, we understand, to recognize
something truly dark. So it seems when we
appear, crunching through the woods. A robin   5
cocks her head, then hops off,
ready to fly like hell and leave us the worm.
A chipmunk, peering out from his hole beneath
a maple root, crash dives when he hears
our step. The alarm sounds everywhere. Squirrels,   10
finches, butterflies flee for their lives. Imagine
a snail picking up the hems of his shell
and hauling ass for cover. He's studied carnivores,
seen the menu, noticed the escargots.

But forget Palance, who would have murdered Alabama   15
just for fun. Think of Karloff's monster,
full of lonely love but too hideous
to bear; or Kong, bereft with Fay Wray
shrieking in his hand: the flies buzz our heads
like angry biplanes, and the ants hoist pitchforks   20
to march on our ankles as we watch the burgher's daughter
bob downstream in a ring of daisies.

Considerations for Critical Thinking and Writing

1. How does a human's presence change the tone of nature in the first stanza?
2. How does the shift from Jack Palance in the first stanza to Boris Karloff and King Kong in the second stanza reflect a different tone in the speaker's assessment of humankind in nature?
3. How do the references to popular films affect the overall tone of the poem?

Connections to Other Selections

1. Write an essay that considers the relationship between humankind and nature in Trowbridge's poem and in William Stafford's "Traveling through the Dark" (p. 694).
2. Compare the speaker's tone in "Enter Dark Stranger" with the speaker's tone in

"Hazel Tells LaVerne" (p. 626). How does the humor in each poem affect your sense of its meaning?

How do the speaker's attitude and tone change during the course of this next poem?

MAXINE KUMIN (b. 1925)
Woodchucks
1972

Gassing the woodchucks didn't turn out right.
The knockout bomb from the Feed and Grain Exchange
was featured as merciful, quick at the bone
and the case we had against them was airtight,
both exits shoehorned shut with puddingstone,°   5
but they had a sub-sub-basement out of range.

Next morning they turned up again, no worse
for the cyanide than we for our cigarettes
and state-store Scotch, all of us up to scratch.
They brought down the marigolds as a matter of course   10
and then took over the vegetable patch
nipping the broccoli shoots, beheading the carrots.

The food from our mouths, I said, righteously thrilling
to the feel of the .22, the bullets' neat noses.
I, a lapsed pacifist fallen from grace   15
puffed with Darwinian° pieties for killing,
now drew a bead on the littlest woodchuck's face.
He died down in the everbearing roses.

Ten minutes later I dropped the mother. She
flipflopped in the air and fell, her needle teeth   20
still hooked in a leaf of early Swiss chard.
Another baby next. O one-two-three
the murderer inside me rose up hard,
the hawkeye killer came on stage forthwith.

There's one chuck left. Old wily fellow, he keeps   25
me cocked and ready day after day after day.
All night I hunt his humped-up form. I dream
I sight along the barrel in my sleep.
If only they'd all consented to die unseen
gassed underground the quiet Nazi way.   30

5 *puddingstone:* Pebbles cemented together.   16 *Darwinian:* Charles Darwin (1809–1882), an English naturalist associated with the ideas of evolution and natural selection.

Considerations for Critical Thinking and Writing

1. How does the word *airtight* help create the tone of the first stanza?
2. How does the speaker's attitude toward the woodchucks change in the second stanza? How does that affect the tone in lines 13–24?
3. What competing emotions are present in the speaker's descriptions of the woodchucks' activities and the descriptions of killing them?
4. Given that "Gassing" begins the poem, why does the speaker withhold the description of the woodchucks being "gassed underground the quiet Nazi way" until the final line?
5. Explain how line 15 suggests, along with the final stanza, the theme of the poem.

DICTION AND TONE IN FOUR LOVE POEMS

The first three of these love poems share the same basic situation and theme: a male speaker addresses a female (in the first poem it is a type of female) urging that love should not be delayed because time is short. This theme is as familiar in poetry as it is in life. In Latin this tradition is known as *carpe diem,* for "seize the day." Notice how the poets' diction helps create a distinctive tone in each poem, even though the subject matter and central ideas are similar (though not identical) in all three.

ROBERT HERRICK (1591–1674)
To the Virgins, to Make Much of Time   1648

Gather ye rose-buds while ye may,
   Old Time is still a-flying;
And this same flower that smiles today,
   Tomorrow will be dying.

The glorious lamp of heaven, the sun,   5
   The higher he's a-getting,
The sooner will his race be run,
   And nearer he's to setting.

That age is best which is the first,
   When youth and blood are warmer;   10
But being spent, the worse, and worst
   Times still succeed the former.

Then be not coy, but use your time,
   And while ye may, go marry;
For having lost but once your prime,   15
   You may for ever tarry.

Considerations for Critical Thinking and Writing

1. Would there be any change in meaning if the title of this poem were "To Young Women, to Make Much of Time"? Do you think the poem can apply to young men too?
2. What do the virgins have in common with the flowers (lines 1–4) and the course of the day (5–8)?
3. How does the speaker develop his argument? What will happen to the virgins if they don't "marry"? Paraphrase the poem.
4. What is the tone of the speaker's advice?

The next poem was also written in the seventeenth century, but it includes some words that have changed in usage and meaning over the past three hundred years. The title of Marvell's "To His Coy Mistress" requires some explanation. *Mistress* does not refer to a married man's illicit lover but to a woman who is loved and courted — a sweetheart. Marvell uses *coy* to describe a woman who is reserved and shy rather than coquettish or flirtatious. Often such shifts in meanings over time are explained in the notes that accompany reprintings of poems. You should keep in mind, however, that it is helpful to have a reasonably thick dictionary available when you are reading poetry. The most thorough is the *Oxford English Dictionary* (*OED*), which provides histories of words. The *OED* is a multivolume leviathan, but there are other useful unabridged dictionaries as well as desk dictionaries.

Knowing its original meaning can also enrich your understanding of why a contemporary poet chooses a particular word. Elizabeth Bishop begins "The Fish" this way: "I caught a tremendous fish." We know immediately in this context that *tremendous* means very large. In addition, given that the speaker clearly admires the fish in the lines that follow, we might even understand *tremendous* in the colloquial sense of wonderful and extraordinary. But a dictionary gives us some further relevant insights. Because, by the end of the poem, we see the speaker thoroughly moved as a result of the encounter with the fish ("everything/was rainbow, rainbow, rainbow!"), the dictionary's additional information about the history of *tremendous* shows why it is the perfect adjective to introduce the fish. The word comes from the Latin *tremere* (to tremble) and therefore once meant "such as to make one tremble." That is precisely how the speaker is at the end of the poem: deeply affected and trembling. Knowing the origin of *tremendous* gives us the full heft of the poet's word choice.

Although some of the language in "To His Coy Mistress" requires annotations for the modern reader, this poem continues to serve as a powerful reminder that time is a formidable foe, even for lovers.

ANDREW MARVELL (1621–1678)

To His Coy Mistress

1681

Had we but world enough, and time,
This coyness, lady, were no crime.
We would sit down, and think which way
To walk, and pass our long love's day.
Thou by the Indian Ganges'° side   5
Shouldst rubies find; I by the tide
Of Humber° would complain.° I would   *write love songs*
Love you ten years before the Flood,
And you should, if you please, refuse
Till the conversion of the Jews.   10
My vegetable love should grow°
Vaster than empires, and more slow;
An hundred years should go to praise
Thine eyes and on thy forehead gaze,
Two hundred to adore each breast,   15
But thirty thousand to the rest:
An age at least to every part,
And the last age should show your heart.
For, lady, you deserve this state,
Nor would I love at lower rate.   20
   But at my back I always hear
Time's wingèd chariot hurrying near;
And yonder all before us lie
Deserts of vast eternity.
Thy beauty shall no more be found,   25
Nor in thy marble vault shall sound
My echoing song; then worms shall try
That long preserved virginity,
And your quaint honor turn to dust,
And into ashes all my lust.   30
The grave's a fine and private place,
But none, I think, do there embrace.
   Now, therefore, while the youthful hue
Sits on thy skin like morning dew,
And while thy willing soul transpires°   *breathes forth* 35
At every pore with instant fires,
Now let us sport us while we may,
And now, like amorous birds of prey,
Rather at once our time devour
Than languish in his slow-chapped° power.   *slow-jawed*   40

---

5 *Ganges:* A river in India sacred to the Hindus.   7 *Humber:* A river that flows through Marvell's native town, Hull.   11 *My vegetable love . . . grow:* A slow, unconscious growth.

Let us roll all our strength and all
Our sweetness up into one ball,
And tear our pleasures with rough strife
Thorough° the iron gates of life.   *through*
Thus, though we cannot make our sun   45
Stand still, yet we will make him run.

Considerations for Critical Thinking and Writing

1. This poem is divided into a three-part argument. Briefly summarize each section:
   if (lines 1–20), but (21–32), therefore (33–46).
2. What is the speaker's tone in lines 1–20? How much time would he spend adoring
   his mistress? Is he sincere? How does he expect his mistress to respond to these
   lines?
3. How does the speaker's tone change beginning with line 21? What is his view of
   time in lines 21–32? What does this description do to the lush and leisurely sense
   of time in lines 1–20? How do you think his mistress would react to lines 21–32?
4. In the final lines of Herrick's "To the Virgins, to Make Much of Time," the speaker
   urges the virgins to "go marry." What does Marvell's speaker urge in lines 33–46?
   How is the pace of these lines (notice the verbs) different from that of the first
   twenty lines of the poem?
5. This poem is sometimes read as a vigorous but simple celebration of flesh. Is
   there more to the theme than that?

PERSPECTIVE

BERNARD DUYFHUIZEN (b. 1953)
"To His Coy Mistress": On How a Female
Might Respond   1988

Clearly a female reader of "To His Coy Mistress" might have trouble identifying with the poem's speaker; therefore, her first response would be to identify
with the listener-in-the-poem, the eternally silent Coy Mistress. In such a reading
she is likely to recognize that she has heard this kind of line before although
maybe not with the same intensity and insistence. Moreover, she is likely to
(re)experience the unsettling emotions that such an egoistic assault on her
virginal autonomy would provoke. She will also see differently, even by contemporary standards, the plot beyond closure, the possible consequences—both
physical and social—that the Mistress will encounter. Lastly, she is likely to be
angered by this poem, by her marginalization in an argument that seeks to
overpower the core of her being.

From "Textual Harassment of Marvell's Coy Mistress:
The Institutionalization of Masculine Criticism,"
College English, April 1988

Considerations for Critical Thinking and Writing

1. Explain whether you find convincing Duyfhuizen's description of a female's potential response to the poem. How does his description compare with your own response?
2. Characterize the silent mistress of the poem. How do you think the speaker treats her? What do his language and tone suggest about his relationship to her?
3. Does the fact that this description of a female response is written by a man make any difference in your assessment of it? Explain why or why not.

The third in this series of *carpe diem* poems is a twentieth-century work. The language of Wilbur's "A Late Aubade" is more immediately accessible than that of Marvell's "To His Coy Mistress"; a dictionary will quickly identify any words unfamiliar to a reader, including the allusion to Arnold Schoenberg, the composer, in line 11. An *allusion* is a brief reference to a person, place, thing, event, or idea in history or literature. Allusive words, like connotative words, are both suggestive and economical; poets use allusions to conjure up biblical authority, scenes from Shakespeare's plays, historic figures, wars, great love stories, and anything else that might serve to deepen and enrich their own work. The speaker in "A Late Aubade" makes an allusion that an ordinary dictionary won't explain. He tells his lover: "I need not rehearse/The rosebuds-theme of centuries of verse." True to his word, he says no more about this for her or the reader. The lines refer, of course, to the *carpe diem* theme as found familiarly in Herrick's "To the Virgins, to Make Much of Time." Wilbur assumes that his reader will understand the allusion.

Allusions imply reading and cultural experiences shared by the poet and reader. Literate audiences once had more in common than they do today because more people had similar economic, social, and educational backgrounds. But a judicious use of specialized dictionaries, encyclopedias, and other reference tools can help you decipher allusions that grow out of this body of experience. See page 2070 for a list of useful reference works for students of literature. As you read more, you'll be able to make connections based on your own experiences with literature. In a sense, allusions make available what other human beings have deemed worth remembering, and that is certainly an economical way of supplementing and enhancing your own experience.

Wilbur's version of the *carpe diem* theme is on the next page. What strikes you as particularly modern about it?

RICHARD WILBUR (b. 1921)

A Late Aubade   1968

You could be sitting now in a carrel
Turning some liver-spotted page,
Or rising in an elevator-cage
Toward Ladies' Apparel.

You could be planting a raucous bed   5
Of salvia, in rubber gloves,
Or lunching through a screed of someone's loves
With pitying head,

Or making some unhappy setter
Heel, or listening to a bleak   10
Lecture on Schoenberg's serial technique.
Isn't this better?

Think of all the time you are not
Wasting, and would not care to waste,
Such things, thank God, not being to your taste.   15
Think what a lot

Of time, by woman's reckoning,
You've saved, and so may spend on this,
You who had rather lie in bed and kiss
Than anything.   20

It's almost noon, you say? If so,
Time flies, and I need not rehearse
The rosebuds-theme of centuries of verse.
If you *must* go,

Wait for a while, then slip downstairs   25
And bring us up some chilled white wine,
And some blue cheese, and crackers, and some fine
Ruddy-skinned pears.

Considerations for Critical Thinking and Writing

1. An *aubade* is a song about lovers parting at dawn, but in this "late aubade," "It's almost noon." Is there another way of reading the adjective *late* in the title?
2. How does the speaker's diction characterize both him and his lover? What sort of lives do they live? What does the casual allusion to Herrick's poem (line 23) reveal about them?
3. What is the effect of using "liver-spotted page," "elevator-cage," "raucous bed," "screed," "unhappy setter," and "bleak Lecture" to describe the woman's activities?

1. How does the man's argument in "A Late Aubade" differ from the speakers' in Herrick's and Marvell's poems? Which of the three arguments do you find most convincing?
2. Explain how the tone of each poem is suited to its theme.

This fourth love poem is by a woman. Listen to the speaker's voice. Does it sound different from the way the men speak in the previous three poems?

EDNA ST. VINCENT MILLAY (1892–1950)
Never May the Fruit Be Plucked   1923

Never, never may the fruit be plucked from the bough
And gathered into barrels.
He that would eat of love must eat it where it hangs.
Though the branches bend like reeds,
Though the ripe fruit splash in the grass or wrinkle on the tree,   5
He that would eat of love may bear away with him
Only what his belly can hold,
Nothing in the apron,
Nothing in the pockets.
Never, never may the fruit be gathered from the bough   10
And harvested in barrels.
The winter of love is a cellar of empty bins,
In an orchard soft with rot.

Considerations for Critical Thinking and Writing

1. Compare the meaning of the fruit in this poem with that of the rosebuds in Herrick's "To the Virgins, to Make Much of Time."
2. Explain the consequences of "eat[ing] of love" in lines 3–5.
3. Why can't love be gathered or harvested into barrels? Is this a *carpe diem* poem? Why or why not?
4. Explain why you think this poem is addressed to men, women, or both.
5. Discuss the tone of the final two lines. Do you think this poem is closer in tone to "To the Virgins, to Make Much of Time," Marvell's "To His Coy Mistress," or Wilbur's "A Late Aubade"? Why?

Connections to Other Selections

1. Write an essay comparing Millay's view of love with that of e. e. cummings in "since feeling is first" (p. 947).
2. Discuss how the idea of passionate abandon is central to Millay's poem and Emily

Dickinson's "Wild Nights—Wild Nights!" (p. 841). Consider whether the tones of these poems are similar or different.

3. Contrast the ideal of love presented by Millay with that offered by John Keats in "Ode on a Grecian Urn" (p. 813).

POEMS FOR FURTHER STUDY

THOMAS HARDY (1840–1928)
The Convergence of the Twain   1912

Lines on the Loss of the "Titanic"°

I

        In a solitude of the sea
        Deep from human vanity,
And the Pride of Life that planned her, stilly couches she.

II

        Steel chambers, late the pyres
        Of her salamandrine fires,°   5
Cold currents thrid,° and turn to rhythmic tidal lyres.   *thread*

III

        Over the mirrors meant
        To glass the opulent
The sea-worm crawls—grotesque, slimed, dumb, indifferent.

IV

        Jewels in joy designed   10
        To ravish the sensuous mind
Lie lightless, all their sparkles bleared and black and blind.

V

        Dim moon-eyed fishes near
        Gaze at the gilded gear
And query: "What does this vaingloriousness down here?"   15

VI

        Well: while was fashioning
        This creature of cleaving wing,
The Immanent Will that stirs and urges everything

VII

        Prepared a sinister mate
        For her—so gaily great—   20
A Shape of Ice, for the time far and dissociate.

Titanic: A luxurious ocean liner, reputed to be unsinkable, which sank after hitting an iceberg on its maiden voyage in 1912. Only a third of the 2,200 passengers survived. 5 *salamandrine fires:* Salamanders were, according to legend, able to survive fire; hence, the ship's fires burned even though under water.

VIII
        And as the smart ship grew
         In stature, grace, and hue,
In shadowy silent distance grew the Iceberg too.

IX
        Alien they seemed to be: 25
         No mortal eye could see
The intimate welding of their later history,

X
        Or sign that they were bent
         By paths coincident
On being anon twin halves of one august event,   30

XI
        Till the Spinner of the Years
         Said "Now!" And each one hears,
And consummation comes, and jars two hemispheres.

Considerations for Critical Thinking and Writing

1. How do the words used to describe the ship in this poem reveal the speaker's attitude toward the *Titanic?*
2. The diction of the poem suggests that the *Titanic* and the iceberg participate in something like an arranged marriage. What specific words imply this?
3. Who or what causes the disaster? Does the speaker assign responsibility?

DAVID R. SLAVITT (b. 1935)
Titanic
1983

Who does not love the *Titanic?*
If they sold passage tomorrow for that same crossing,
who would not buy?

To go down . . . We all go down, mostly
alone. But with crowds of people, friends, servants,   5
well fed, with music, with lights! Ah!

And the world, shocked, mourns, as it ought to do
and almost never does. There will be the books and movies
to remind our grandchildren who we were
and how we died, and give them a good cry.   10

Not so bad, after all. The cold
water is anesthetic and very quick.
The cries on all sides must be a comfort.

We all go: only a few, first-class.

Considerations for Critical Thinking and Writing

1. What, according to the speaker in this poem, is so compelling about the *Titanic?*
2. Discuss the speaker's tone. Why would it be inaccurate to describe it as solemn and mournful?
3. What is the effect of the poem's final line? What emotions does it produce in you?

Connections to Another Selection

1. How does "Titanic" differ in its attitude toward opulence from "The Convergence of the Twain"?
2. Which poem is more emotionally satisfying to you? Explain why.
3. Compare the speakers' tones in "Titanic" and "The Convergence of the Twain."
4. Hardy wrote his poem in 1912, the year the *Titanic* went down, but Slavitt wrote his more than seventy years later. How do you think Slavitt's poem would have been received if it had been published in 1912? Write an essay explaining why you think what you do.

GWENDOLYN BROOKS (b. 1917)
We Real Cool   1960

The Pool Players.
Seven at the Golden Shovel.

We real cool. We
Left school. We

Lurk late. We   5
Strike straight. We

Sing sin. We
Thin gin. We

Jazz June. We
Die soon.   10

Considerations for Critical Thinking and Writing

1. How does the speech of the pool players in this poem help to characterize them? What is the effect of the pronouns coming at the ends of the lines? How would the poem sound if the pronouns came at the beginnings of lines?
2. What is the author's attitude toward the players? Is there a change in tone in the last line?
3. How is the pool hall's name related to the rest of the poem and its theme?

MARGE PIERCY (b. 1936)

A Work of Artifice

1973

The bonsai tree
in the attractive pot
could have grown eighty feet tall
on the side of a mountain
till split by lightning.   5
But a gardener
carefully pruned it.
It is nine inches high.
Every day as he
whittles back the branches   10
the gardener croons,
It is your nature
to be small and cozy,
domestic and weak;
how lucky, little tree,   15
to have a pot to grow in.
With living creatures
one must begin very early
to dwarf their growth:
the bound feet,   20
the crippled brain,
the hair in curlers,
the hands you
love to touch.

Considerations for Critical Thinking and Writing

1. What is a bonsai tree? How is it likened to a woman in this poem? At what point
   in the poem does the comparison become apparent?
2. What attitudes are revealed by the language of the gardener's song? Which words
   have especially strong connotative values?
3. The final two lines ("the hands you/love to touch") allude to a soap commercial.
   Explain the effect this allusion has on your understanding of the poem's theme.

Connections to Other Selections

1. Write an essay comparing the tone of this poem with that of Stevie Smith's
   "Valuable" (p. 640).
2. How does Piercy's theme compare with Henrik Ibsen's treatment of domesticity
   in his play *A Doll House* (p. 1517)?
3. Contrast the attitudes expressed about women in Piercy's poem with those in
   Mishima's short story "Patriotism" (p. 506). How do you account for the differences
   between the two?

STEVIE SMITH (1902–1971)
Valuable

1962

After reading two paragraphs in a newspaper.

All these illegitimate babies . . .
Oh girls, girls,
Silly little cheap things,
Why do you not put some value on yourselves,
Learn to say, No?   5
Did nobody teach you?
Nobody teaches anybody to say No nowadays,
People should teach people to say No.

Oh poor panther,
Oh you poor black animal,   10
At large for a few moments in a school for young children in Paris,
Now in your cage again,
How your great eyes bulge with bewilderment,
There is something there that accuses us,
In your angry and innocent eyes,   15
Something that says:
I am too valuable to be kept in a cage.

Oh these illegitimate babies!
Oh girls, girls,
Silly little valuable things,   20
You should have said, No, I am valuable,
And again, It is because I am valuable
I say, No.

Nobody teaches anybody they are valuable nowadays.

Girls, you are valuable,   25
And you, Panther, you are valuable,
But the girls say: I shall be alone
If I say 'I am valuable' and other people do not say it of me,
I shall be alone, there is no comfort there.
No, it is not comforting but it is valuable,   30
And if everybody says it in the end
It will be comforting. And for the panther too,
If everybody says he is valuable
It will be comforting for him.

Considerations for Critical Thinking and Writing

1. Which words are repeated in the poem? What is the effect of these repetitions?
2. What relationship does the speaker establish between the girls and the panther?
3. Describe the speaker's voice. How does it produce the poem's overall tone?

640 Word Choice, Word Order, and Tone

DIANE ACKERMAN (b. 1948)

A Fine, A Private Place _ Marvell

[handwritten: she is sure of herself not coy.]

1983

He took her one day
under the blue horizon
where long sea fingers
parted like beads
hitched in the doorway   5
of an opium den,
and canyons mazed the deep
reef with hollows,
cul-de-sacs, and narrow boudoirs,
and had to ask twice   10
before she understood
his stroking her arm
with a marine feather
slobbery as aloe pulp
was wooing, or saw the octopus   15
in his swimsuit
stretch one tentacle
and ripple its silky bag.

While bubbles rose
like globs of mercury,   20
they made love
mask to mask, floating
with oceans of air between them,
she his sea-geisha
in an orange kimono   25
of belts and vests,
her lacquered hair waving,
as Indigo Hamlets
tattooed the vista,
and sunlight   30
cut through the water,
twisting its knives
into corridors of light.

His sandy hair
and sea-blue eyes,   35
his kelp-thin waist
and chest ribbed wider
than a sandbar
where muscles domed
clear and taut as shells   40
(freckled cowries,
flat, brawny scallops
the color of dawn),

his sea-battered hands
gripping her thighs   45
like tawny starfish
and drawing her close
as a pirate vessel
to let her board:
who was this she loved?   50

Overhead, sponges
sweating raw color
jutted from a coral arch,
Clown Wrasses°   *brightly colored tropical fish*
hovered like fireworks,   55
and somewhere an abalone opened
its silver wings.
Part of a lusty dream
under aspic, her hips rolled
like a Spanish galleon,   60
her eyes swam
and chest began to heave.
Gasps melted on the tide.
Knowing she would soon be
breathless as her tank,   65
he pumped his brine
deep within her,
letting sea water drive it
through petals
delicate as anemone veils   70
to the dark purpose
of a conch-shaped womb.
An ear to her loins
would have heard the sea roar.

When panting ebbed,   75
and he signaled *Okay?*
as lovers have asked,
land or waterbound
since time heaved ho,
he led her to safety: 80
shallower realms,
heading back toward
the boat's even keel,
though ocean still petted her
cell by cell, murmuring   85
along her legs and neck,
caressing her
with pale, endless arms.

Later, she thought often
of that blue boudoir, — OCEAN   90

642 Word Choice, Word Order, and Tone

pillow-soft and filled
with cascading light,
where together
they'd made a bell
that dumbly clanged   95
beneath the waves
and minutes lurched
like mountain goats.
She could still see
the quilted mosaics   100
that were fish
twitching spangles overhead,
still feel the ocean
inside and out, turning her
evolution around.   105

She thought of it miles
and fathoms away, often,
at odd moments: watching
the minnow snowflakes
dip against the windowframe,   110
holding a sponge
idly under tap-gush,
sinking her teeth
into the cleft
of a voluptuous peach.   115

Considerations for Critical Thinking and Writing

1. Read Andrew Marvell's "To His Coy Mistress" (p. 631). To what does Ackerman's
   title allude in Marvell's poem? Explain how the allusion to Marvell is crucial to
   understanding Ackerman's poem.
2. Comment on the descriptive passages of "A Fine, A Private Place." Which images
   seem especially vivid to you? How do they contribute to the poem's meanings?
3. What are the speaker's reflections upon her experience in lines 106–115? What
   echoes of Marvell do you hear in these lines?

Connections to Another Selection

1. Write an essay comparing the tone of Ackerman's poem with that of Marvell's "To
   His Coy Mistress." To what extent are the central ideas in the poems similar?
2. Compare the speaker's voice in Ackerman's poem with the voice you imagine for
   the coy mistress in Marvell's poem.

MARTÍN ESPADA (b. 1958)
Tiburón

1987

East 116th
and a long red car
stalled with the hood up
roaring salsa
like a prize shark   5
mouth yanked open
and down into the stomach
the radio
of the last fisherman
still tuned   10
to his lucky station

Considerations for Critical Thinking and Writing

1. East 116th Street is in Spanish Harlem. How does this information about the
   setting affect your reading of the poem?
2. Describe the tone of this poem.

15. Images

POETRY'S APPEAL TO THE SENSES

A poet, to borrow a phrase from Henry James, is one of those on whom nothing is lost. Poets take in the world and give us impressions of what they experience through images. An *image* is language that addresses the senses. The most common images in poetry are visual; they provide verbal pictures of the poets' encounters — real or imagined — with the world. But poets also create images that appeal to our other senses. Wilbur arouses several senses when he has the speaker in "A Late Aubade" gently urge his lover to linger in bed with him instead of getting on with her daily routines and obligations.

> Wait for a while, then slip downstairs
> And bring us up some chilled white wine,
> And some blue cheese, and crackers, and some fine
> Ruddy-skinned pears.

These images are simultaneously tempting and satisfying. We don't have to literally touch that cold, clear glass of wine (or will it come in a green bottle beaded with moisture?) or smell the cheese or taste the crackers to appreciate this vivid blend of colors, textures, tastes, and fragrances.

Images give us the physical world to experience in our imaginations. Some poems, like the following one, are written to do just that; they make no comment about what they describe.

WILLIAM CARLOS WILLIAMS (1883–1963)
Poem 1934

As the cat
climbed over
the top of

the jamcloset
first the right   5
forefoot

carefully
then the hind
stepped down

into the pit of   10
the empty
flowerpot

This poem defies paraphrase because it is all an image of agile movement. No statement is made about the movement; the title, "Poem" — really no title — signals Williams's refusal to comment on the movements. To impose a meaning on the poem, we'd probably have to knock over the flowerpot.

We experience the image in Williams's "Poem" more clearly because of how the sentence is organized into lines and groups of lines, or stanzas. Consider how differently the sentence is read if it is arranged as prose.

> As the cat climbed over the top of the jamcloset, first the right forefoot carefully then the hind stepped down into the pit of the empty flowerpot.

The poem's line and stanza division transforms what is essentially an awkward prose sentence into a rhythmic verbal picture. Especially when the poem is read aloud, this line and stanza division allows us to feel the image we see. Even the lack of a period at the end suggests that the cat is only pausing.

Images frequently do more than offer only sensory impressions, however. They also convey emotions and moods, as in the following lyric.

BONNIE JACOBSON (b. 1933)
On Being Served Apples 1989

Apples in a deep blue dish
        are the shadows of nuns

Apples in a basket
        are warm red moons on Indian women

Apples in a white bowl
        are virgins waiting in snow

Beware of apples on an orange plate:
        they are the anger of wives

The four images of apples in this poem suggest a range of emotions. How would you describe these emotions? How does the meaning of the apples change depending upon the context in which they are served? In this poem we are given more than just images of the world selected by the poet; we are also given her feelings about them.

What mood is established in this next poem's view of Civil War troops moving across a river?

WALT WHITMAN (1819–1892)
Cavalry Crossing a Ford   1865

A line in long array where they wind betwixt green islands,
They take a serpentine course, their arms flash in the sun — hark to the musical clank,
Behold the silvery river, in it the splashing horses loitering stop to drink,
Behold the brown-faced men, each group, each person, a picture, the negligent rest on the saddles,
Some emerge on the opposite bank, others are just entering the ford — while,
Scarlet and blue and snowy white,
The guidon flags flutter gaily in the wind.

Considerations for Critical Thinking and Writing

1. What effect do the colors and sounds have in establishing the mood of this poem?
2. How would the poem's mood have been changed if Whitman had used *look* or *see* instead of *behold* (lines 3, 4)?
3. Where is the speaker as he observes this troop movement?
4. Does *serpentine* in line 2 have an evil connotation in this poem? Explain your answer.

Whitman seems to capture momentarily all the troop's actions, and through carefully chosen, suggestive details — really very few — he succeeds in making "each group, each person, a picture." Specific details, even when few are provided, give us the impression that we see the entire picture; it is as if those are the details we would remember if we had viewed the scene ourselves. Notice too that the movement of the "line in long array" is emphasized by the continuous winding syntax of the poem's lengthy lines.

Poets choose details the way they choose the words to present those details: only telling ones will do. Consider the images Theodore Roethke uses in "Root Cellar."

THEODORE ROETHKE (1908–1963)
Root Cellar 1948

Nothing would sleep in that cellar, dank as a ditch,
Bulbs broke out of boxes hunting for chinks in the dark,
Shoots dangled and drooped,
Lolling obscenely from mildewed crates,
Hung down long yellow evil necks, like tropical snakes.   5
And what a congress of stinks!
Roots ripe as old bait,
Pulpy stems, rank, silo-rich,
Leaf-mold, manure, lime, piled against slippery planks.
Nothing would give up life: — ~~seething of life~~   10
Even the dirt kept breathing a small breath.

Considerations for Critical Thinking and Writing

1. What senses are engaged by the images in this poem? Is the poem simply a series of sensations, or do the detailed images make some kind of point about the root cellar?
2. What controls the choice of details in the poem? Why isn't there, for example, a rusty shovel leaning against a dirt wall or a worn gardener's glove atop one of the crates?
3. Look up *congress* in a dictionary for its denotative meanings. Explain why "congress of stinks" is especially appropriate given the nature of the rest of the poem's imagery.
4. What single line in the poem suggests a theme?

The tone of the images and mood of the speaker are consistent in Roethke's "Root Cellar." In Matthew Arnold's "Dover Beach," however, they shift as the theme is developed.

MATTHEW ARNOLD (1822–1888)
Dover Beach 1867

The sea is calm tonight.
The tide is full, the moon lies fair
Upon the straits;— on the French coast the light
Gleams and is gone; the cliffs of England stand,
Glimmering and vast, out in the tranquil bay.   5
Come to the window, sweet is the night-air!
Only, from the long line of spray
Where the sea meets the moon-blanched land,
Listen! you hear the grating roar
Of pebbles which the waves draw back, and fling,   10

At their return, up the high strand,
Begin, and cease, and then again begin,
With tremulous cadence slow, and bring
The eternal note of sadness in.

Sophocles long ago   15
Heard it on the Aegean, and it brought
Into his mind the turbid ebb and flow
Of human misery;° we
Find also in the sound a thought,
Hearing it by this distant northern sea.   20

The Sea of Faith
Was once, too, at the full, and round earth's shore
Lay like the folds of a bright girdle furled.
But now I only hear
Its melancholy, long, withdrawing roar,   25
Retreating, to the breath
Of the night-wind, down the vast edges drear
And naked shingles° of the world.   pebble beaches

Ah, love, let us be true
To one another! for the world, which seems   30
To lie before us like a land of dreams,
So various, so beautiful, so new,
Hath really neither joy, nor love, nor light,
Nor certitude, nor peace, nor help for pain;
And we are here as on a darkling plain   35
Swept with confused alarms of struggle and flight,
Where ignorant armies clash by night.

15–18 *Sophocles long ago . . . misery:* In *Antigone,* lines 557–66, Sophocles likens the disasters that
beset the house of Oedipus to a "mounting tide."

Considerations for Critical Thinking and Writing

1. Contrast the images in lines 4–8 and 9–13. How do they reveal the speaker's
   mood? To whom is he speaking?
2. What is the cause of the "sadness" in line 14? What is the speaker's response to
   the ebbing "Sea of Faith"? Is there anything to replace his sense of loss?
3. What details of the beach seem related to the ideas in the poem? How is the sea
   used differently in lines 1–14 and lines 21–28?
4. Describe the differences in tone between lines 1–8 and 35–37. What has caused
   the change?

Connections to Other Selections

1. Explain how the images in Wilfred Owen's "Dulce et Decorum Est" (p. 653)
   develop further the ideas and sentiments suggested by Arnold's final line concerning "ignorant armies clash[ing] by night."

2. Write an essay comparing Arnold's reflections on faith with Thomas Hardy's in "The Oxen" (p. 726).
3. Contrast Arnold's images with those of Anthony Hecht in his parody "The Dover Bitch" (p. 960). How do Hecht's images create a very different mood from that of "Dover Beach"?

POEMS FOR FURTHER STUDY

EAMON GRENNAN (b. 1941)
Bat   1991

With no warning and only the slightest whishing sound
it was in the room with me, trapped and flying
wall to wall, a wild heart out of its element: flat
black leather wings that never stop, body
bunched as a baby's fist, the tiny head peering   5
blindly, out of its mouth a piercing
inaudible pulse-scream that sets its course
and keeps it beating, barely grazing the painted
walls, the wardrobe, desk, chest of drawers (all
smelling of outdoors, I suppose — walnut, maple,   10
oak — and sending it, surely, round the bend)
while I try to keep track of its dodgy swerves,
ducking when it flutters at me, springing after
with my eyes. All this is happening
in a fathomless silence that binds us   15
to one another for a hypnotized little while,
making me feel as the creature circles and circles
as if I'd been kissed repeatedly in sleep, lips
lightly brushing, gone. In the end, by
luck, it seems, not navigation, it goes   20
through the window I've scrambled open, leaving
me in another kind of silence
to watch its stuttering flight over bright green grass —
by light afflicted, desperate for the dark. I keep
to myself that other, unseamed silence   25
in which it went about its woeful task, trying
to find a way to friendly shade, its own
crepuscular and insect-humming haven, those
jinking missions in the homely dark, its own
heartbeat keeping it one with an everyday world   30
of intoxicating scents and glimmers, almost infinite
possibilities. Gone for good. It's the sheer
stoic silence (to my ears) of the whole operation
that stays with me, teaching me how to behave
in a tight corner: hold your tongue, keep moving, try   35

everything more than once, steer by brief kisses and
the fleeting grace of dark advances, quick retreats,
until you find lying in your way the window, open.

doesn't want commitment

Considerations for Critical Thinking and Writing

1. Explain which images are particularly effective in capturing the desperation of the trapped bat.
2. How does the speaker's description of the bat serve to characterize the speaker?
3. In the final seven lines what does the speaker report learning from the bat's movements?
4. Given that this poem is about more than just a bat, why do you think it's entitled "Bat"? What alternative titles would appropriately sum up the poem?

Connections to Other Selections

1. Compare the description of images of flight in this poem with Emily Dickinson's "A Bird came down the Walk — " (p. 712).
2. Write an essay discussing the use of images to express confinement and freedom in this poem and in Rainer Maria Rilke's "The Panther" (p. 658).

H. D.
[HILDA DOOLITTLE] (1886–1961)
Heat   1916

O wind, rend open the heat,
cut apart the heat,
rend it to tatters.

Fruit cannot drop
through this thick air —   5
fruit cannot fall into heat
that presses up and blunts
the points of pears
and rounds the grapes.

Cut the heat —   10
plough through it,
turning it on either side
of your path.

Considerations for Critical Thinking and Writing

1. What physical properties are associated with heat in this poem?
2. Explain the effect of the description of fruit in lines 4–9.
3. Why is the image of the cutting plow especially effective in lines 10–13?

WILLIAM BLAKE (1757–1827)

London

1794

I wander through each chartered° street,   *defined by law*
Near where the chartered Thames does flow,
And mark in every face I meet
Marks of weakness, marks of woe.

In every cry of every man,   5
In every Infant's cry of fear,
In every voice, in every ban,
The mind-forged manacles I hear.

How the Chimney-sweeper's cry
Every black'ning Church appalls;   10
And the hapless Soldier's sigh
Runs in blood down Palace walls.

But most through midnight streets I hear
How the youthful Harlot's curse
Blasts the new-born Infant's tear,   15
And blights with plagues the Marriage hearse.

Considerations for Critical Thinking and Writing

1. How do the visual images in this poem suggest a feeling of being trapped?
2. What is the predominant sound heard in the poem?
3. What is the meaning of line 8? What is the cause of the problems that the speaker sees and hears in London? Does the speaker suggest additional causes?
4. The image in lines 11–12 cannot be read literally. Comment on its effectiveness.
5. How does Blake's use of denotative and connotative language enrich this poem's meaning?
6. An earlier version of Blake's last stanza appeared this way:

> But most the midnight harlot's curse
> From every dismal street I hear,
> Weaves around the marriage hearse
> And blasts the new-born infant's tear.

Examine carefully the differences between the two versions. How do Blake's revisions affect his picture of London life? Which version do you think is more effective? Why?

WILFRED OWEN (1893–1918)

Dulce et Decorum Est

1920

Bent double, like old beggars under sacks,
Knock-kneed, coughing like hags, we cursed through sludge,
Till on the haunting flares we turned our backs,

And towards our distant rest began to trudge.
Men marched asleep. Many had lost their boots,   5
But limped on, blood-shod. All went lame, all blind;
Drunk with fatigue; deaf even to the hoots
Of gas-shells dropping softly behind.

Gas! GAS! Quick, boys! — An ecstasy of fumbling,
Fitting the clumsy helmets just in time,   10
But someone still was yelling out and stumbling
And flound'ring like a man in fire or lime. —
Dim through the misty panes and thick green light,
As under a green sea, I saw him drowning.

In all my dreams before my helpless sight   15
He plunges at me, guttering, choking, drowning.

If in some smothering dreams, you too could pace
Behind the wagon that we flung him in,
And watch the white eyes writhing in his face,
His hanging face, like a devil's sick of sin,   20
If you could hear, at every jolt, the blood
Come gargling from the froth-corrupted lungs
Bitter as the cud
Of vile, incurable sores on innocent tongues, —
My friend, you would not tell with such high zest   25
To children ardent for some desperate glory,
The old lie: *Dulce et decorum est*
Pro patria mori.

Considerations for Critical Thinking and Writing

1. The Latin quotation in lines 27–28 is from Horace: "It is sweet and fitting to die
   for one's country." Owen served as a British soldier during World War I and was
   killed. Is this poem unpatriotic? What is its purpose?
2. Which images in the poem are most vivid? To which senses do they speak?
3. Describe the speaker's tone. What is his relationship to his audience?
4. How are the images of the soldiers in this poem different from the images that
   typically appear in recruiting posters?

ELIZABETH BARRETT BROWNING (1806–1861)
Grief   1844

I tell you, hopeless grief is passionless;
That only men incredulous of despair,
Half-taught in anguish, through the midnight air

Beat upward to God's throne in loud access
Of shrieking and reproach. Full desertness,   5
In souls as countries, lieth silent-bare
Under the blanching, vertical eye-glare
Of the absolute Heavens. Deep-hearted man, express
Grief for thy Dead in silence like to death —
Most like a monumental statue set   10
In everlasting watch and moveless woe
Till itself crumble to the dust beneath.
Touch it; the marble eyelids are not wet.
If it could weep, it could arise and go.

Considerations for Critical Thinking and Writing

1. What images does Browning use to describe grief?
2. What is the effect of the poem's first words, "I tell you"? How do they serve to characterize the speaker?
3. Describe the emotional tone of this poem.

ROBERT LOWELL (1917–1977)
Skunk Hour   1959

For Elizabeth Bishop

Nautilus Island's hermit
heiress still lives through winters in her Spartan cottage;
her sheep still graze above the sea.
Her son's a bishop. Her farmer
is first selectman in our village;   5
she's in her dotage.

Thirsting for
the hierarchic privacy
of Queen Victoria's century,
she buys up all   10
the eyesores facing her shore,
and lets them fall.

The season's ill —
we've lost our summer millionaire,
who seemed to leap from an L. L. Bean°   15
catalogue. His nine-knot yawl
was auctioned off to lobstermen.
A red fox stain covers Blue Hill.

And now our fairy
decorator brightens his shop for fall;   20

15 *L. L. Bean:* A famous Maine mail-order store specializing in outdoor clothes and equipment.

his fishnet's filled with orange cork,
orange, his cobbler's bench and awl;
there is no money in his work,
he'd rather marry.

One dark night,   25
my Tudor Ford climbed the hill's skull;
I watched for love-cars. Lights turned down,
they lay together, hull to hull,
where the graveyard shelves on the town. . . .
My mind's not right.   30

A car radio bleats,
"Love, O careless Love. . . ." I hear
my ill-spirit sob in each blood cell,
as if my hand were at its throat. . . .
I myself am hell;   35
nobody's here —

only skunks, that search
in the moonlight for a bite to eat.
They march on their soles up Main Street:
white stripes, moonstruck eyes' red fire   40
under the chalk-dry and spar spire
of the Trinitarian Church.

I stand on top
of our back steps and breathe the rich air —
a mother skunk with her column of kittens swills the garbage pail. 45
She jabs her wedge-head in a cup
of sour cream, drops her ostrich tail,
and will not scare.

Considerations for Critical Thinking and Writing

1. How does the speaker in this poem characterize life in this Maine coastal town? Which images suggest his attitude toward the town?
2. What is the significance of the title? How is it related to the description of the town?
3. Comment on lines 32–35. What is the speaker's state of mind? How is it reflected throughout the poem?
4. What is the effect of the skunks' appearance at the end of the poem? What does the speaker's attitude toward them reveal about the speaker?
5. Work up a series of a dozen or so images that capture your impressions of a town or city with which you are familiar. Then summarize in a few sentences the overall tone the images evoke.

JOHN REPP (b. 1953)

Cursing the Hole in the Screen, Wondering at the Romance Some Find in Summer
                                                                        1986

Interminable as a slug inching up
the mildewed wall of a chicken coop
left to fall down or be wrecked some
wrung-out night by boys marking the new
swell in their balls with ruin —   5
summer shambles on, its random tiny horrors
hatch, sting, copulate, die, all
in these rooms. Kitchen? Midges throng
to every orifice. Bathroom? Wasps lumber
down from the sill. Bedroom? Mosquitoes   10
sing like autistic children.
     Run out
to the pond with no clothes on and bob
in the tepid wet, a hellish middle C
penetrating everything. And bellicose   15
frogs feasting in chorus so dissonant
it puts to shame all the postmodernist°
harumping of hoarse tubas and hubcaps
loved by believers in naturalism
and the culturally symptomatic.   20
      Night wrings
its filthy washcloth as the first coil
of heat unwinds, the few dewdrops steam away,
here dust on the marigolds, there a cat sprawled
in the willow's crackling shade, no Artemis,°   25
no Mark Twain Mississippi River, no veranda,
just the *pop* of a billion eggs falling open.

17 *postmodernist:* A term that refers to the interest in contemporary arts in experimental forms.
25 *Artemis:* A Greek goddess of hunting, healing, and fertility.

Considerations for Critical Thinking and Writing

1. What feelings do you associate with summer? How does this poem make you feel about summer? Do the poem's images confirm or challenge your associations with summer?
2. Describe the poem's speaker. How does the voice of lines 1–8 compare with that of lines 15–20? What do the diction and allusions tell you about the speaker?
3. Comment on the appropriateness of the poem's title. Explain whether you think it is helpful or intrusive.
4. Select an image from the poem and expand on it by writing a brief essay developing further what the image mentions.

Connections to Other Selections

1. Explain which image of heat you find more effective, Repp's or H. D.'s in "Hea
   (p. 651).
2. Write a response to William Shakespeare's "Shall I compare thee to a summer's
   day?" (p. 757) from the point of view of Repp's speaker. Try to capture the speaker's
   vivid use of images.

RICHMOND LATTIMORE (b. 1906)

The Crabs   1972

There was a bucket full of them. They spilled,
crawled, climbed, clawed: slowly tossed
and fell: precision made: cold iodine color of their own
world of sand and occasional brown weed, round stone
chilled clean in the chopping waters of their coast.   5
One fell out. The marine thing on the grass
tried to trundle off, barbarian and immaculate and to be killed
with his kin. We lit water: dumped the living mass
in: contemplated tomatoes and corn: and with the good cheer of civilized man,
cigarettes, that is, and cold beer, and chatter,   10
waited out and lived down the ten-foot-away clatter
of crabs as they died for us inside their boiling can.

Considerations for Critical Thinking and Writing

1. How is the reader's initial attitude toward the crabs in this poem controlled by
   references to them as "precision made," "marine thing[s]," and "barbarian"?
2. How do the later images of the crabs as a "living mass" and their "clatter" as they
   are boiled compete with the images of them in lines 1–8?
3. What is the effect of the images describing the humans? How do you feel about
   these people?
4. The diction of this poem is informal and chatty, but it conveys a dark theme. Do
   you think the level of diction is appropriate for the theme?
5. Write a short essay that develops some point about the "chatter" of "civilized
   man" and the "clatter" of the crabs.

RAINER MARIA RILKE (1875–1926)

The Panther   1927

TRANSLATED BY STEPHEN MITCHELL

His vision, from the constantly passing bars,
has grown so weary that it cannot hold
anything else. It seems to him there are
a thousand bars; and behind the bars, no world.

As he paces in cramped circles, over and over,   5
the movement of his powerful soft strides
is like a ritual dance around a center
in which a mighty will stands paralyzed.

Only at times, the curtain of the pupils
lifts, quietly —. An image enters in,   10
rushes down through the tensed, arrested muscles,
plunges into the heart and is gone.

Considerations for Critical Thinking and Writing

1. What kind of "image enters in" the heart of the panther in the final stanza?
2. How are images of confinement achieved in the poem? Why doesn't Rilke describe
   the final image in lines 10–12?

Connections to Other Selections

1. Write an essay explaining how a sense of movement is achieved by the images
   and rhythms in this poem and in Dickinson's "A Bird came down the Walk—"
   (p. 712).
2. Discuss the idea of confinement in "The Panther" and Eamon Grennan's "Bat"
   (p. 650).

MARGARET HOLLEY (b. 1944)
The Fireflies   1991

Sparks from a bonfire,
desire's half-hidden furnace,
drift in the black meadow,

pulsing shrimps,
their candles flaring,
each comma carrying its own lantern.   5

You remain indoors
reading by lamplight, glowworm,
larva whose labor is to eat,

molt,   10
and feverishly expand before
the newly secreted chitin hardens.

This is the fire in between
the first awareness
of desire   15

and its denouement,
the time of craving unfulfilled,
a bright transparency

of the verb "to want"
in all its conjugations.   20
For now, your cocoon of pages

keeps you as quiet
as the pupa, the doll,
that seems to just hang around

doing nothing,   25
while under the exoskeleton
a major transformation occurs.

What can I say to you,
except that out here at night
the body becomes an intermittent torch   30

finally consenting to burn,
consenting to know what it is
one wants

and may or may not have,
to walk in the dark by one's own light,   35
ablaze, transparent,

and as transient
as these, their minute lamps
making a silent firework of praise.

Considerations for Critical Thinking and Writing

1. What does this poem say about desire?
2. How does the speaker describe the reader who remains indoors? Does the speaker
   offer advice or simply make an observation?
3. How might this poem's images be regarded as a "firework of praise"?

SALLY CROFT (b. 1935)
Home-Baked Bread   1981

*Nothing gives a household a greater sense of stability and common comfort than the
aroma of cooling bread. Begin, if you like, with a loaf of whole wheat, which requires
neither sifting nor kneading, and go on from there to more cunning triumphs.*
                                                        — The Joy of Cooking

What is it she is not saying?
Cunning triumphs. It rings
of insinuation. Step into my kitchen,
I have prepared a cunning triumph

for you. Spices and herbs   5
sealed in this porcelain jar,

a treasure of my great-aunt
who sat up past midnight
in her Massachusetts bedroom
when the moon was dark. Come,   10
rest your feet. I'll make
you tea with honey and slices

of warm bread spread with peach butter.
I picked the fruit this morning
still fresh with dew. The fragrance   15
is seductive? I hoped you would say that.
See how the heat rises
when the bread opens. Come,

we'll eat together, the small flakes
have scarcely any flavor. What cunning   20
triumphs we can discover in my upstairs room
where peach trees breathe their sweetness
beside the open window and
sun lies like honey on the floor.

Considerations for Critical Thinking and Writing

1. Why does the speaker in this poem seize upon the phrase "cunning triumphs" from *The Joy of Cooking* excerpt?
2. Distinguish between the voice we hear in lines 1–3 and the second voice in lines 3–24. Who is the "you" in the poem?
3. Why is "insinuation" an especially appropriate word choice in line 3?
4. How do the images in lines 20–24 bring together all the senses evoked in the preceding lines?
5. Write a paragraph that describes the sensuous (and perhaps sensual) qualities of a food you enjoy.

CAROLYN KIZER (b. 1925)
Food for Love   1984

> *Eating is touch carried to the bitter end.*
> – Samuel Butler II

I'm going to murder you with love;
I'm going to suffocate you with embraces;
I'm going to hug you, bone by bone,
Till you're dead all over.
Then I will dine on your delectable marrow.   5

You will become my personal Sahara;
I'll sun myself in you, then with one swallow
Drain your remaining brackish well.
With my female blade I'll carve my name
In your most aspiring palm   10
Before I chop it down.
Then I'll inhale your last oasis whole.

But in the total desert you become
You'll see me stretch, horizon to horizon,
Opulent mirage!   15
Wisteria balconies dripping cyclamen.
Vistas ablaze with crystal, laced in gold.

So you will summon each dry grain of sand
And move towards me in undulating dunes
Till you arrive at sudden ultramarine: 20
A Mediterranean to stroke your dusty shores;
Obstinate verdure, creeping inland, fast renudes
Your barrens; succulents spring up everywhere,
Surprising life! And I will be that green.

When you are fed and watered, flourishing   25
With shoots entwining trellis, dome and spire,
Till you are resurrected field in bloom,
I will devour you, my natural food,
My host, my final supper on the earth,
And you'll begin to die again.   30

Considerations for Critical Thinking and Writing

1. What's going on here? Is this a love poem? Explain why or why not.
2. What does the epigraph from Samuel Butler contribute to your understanding of the poem?
3. Contrast the speaker's relationship with her "personal Sahara" in lines 1–12 and in lines 13–30.

Connections to Other Selections

1. Write a reply to this poem—in poetry or prose—as you think the speaker of Andrew Marvell's "To His Coy Mistress" (p. 631) would respond.
2. Discuss the relationship between food and love in Kizer's poem and "Home-Baked Bread" (p. 660).
3. Write an essay comparing the tone of "Food for Love" and Elaine Magarrell's "The Joy of Cooking" (p. 682).

SAPPHO (c. 612–c. 580 B.C.)
With his venom
TRANSLATED BY MARY BARNARD

With his venom

Irresistible
and bittersweet

that loosener
of limbs, Love

reptile-like
strikes me down

Considerations for Critical Thinking and Writing

1. In what sense is love both "Irresistible and bittersweet" in this poem?
2. Consider the sounds in this poem. How are they related to their meanings?
3. Does it make sense to use a snakebite as an image of love? Explain why or why not.

Connections to Other Selections

1. How does your response to the images of love in this poem compare with the response evoked by the images in Cathy Song's "The White Porch" (p. 1057).
2. Discuss the attitudes toward love expressed by Sappho and by Millay in "I Too beneath Your Moon, Almighty Sex" (p. 978).

EZRA POUND (1885–1972)
In a Station of the Metro°
1913

The apparition of these faces in the crowd;
Petals on a wet, black bough.

Metro: Underground railroad in Paris.

Considerations for Critical Thinking and Writing

1. What kind of mood does the image in the second line convey?
2. Why is "apparition" a better word choice than, say, "appearance" or "sight"?

T. E. HULME (1883–1917)
On the Differences between Poetry and Prose 1924

In prose as in algebra concrete things are embodied in signs or counters which are moved about according to rules, without being visualized at all in the process. There are in prose certain type situations and arrangements of words, which move as automatically into certain other arrangements as do functions in algebra. One only changes the *X*'s and the *Y*'s back into physical things at the end of the process. Poetry, in one aspect at any rate, may be considered as an effort to avoid this characteristic of prose. It is not a counter language, but a visual concrete one. It is a compromise for a language of intuition which would hand over sensations bodily. It always endeavors to arrest you, and to make you continuously see a physical thing, to prevent you gliding through an abstract process. It chooses fresh epithets and fresh metaphors, not so much because they are new, and we are tired of the old, but because the old cease to convey a physical thing and become abstract counters. A poet says a ship "coursed the seas" to get a physical image, instead of the counter word "sailed." Visual meanings can only be transferred by the new bowl of metaphor; prose is an old pot that lets them leak out. Images in verse are not mere decoration, but the very essence of an intuitive language. Verse is a pedestrian taking you over the ground, prose—a train which delivers you at a destination.

From "Romanticism and Classicism," in *Speculations,*
edited by Herbert Read

Considerations for Critical Thinking and Writing

1. What distinctions does Hulme make between poetry and prose? Which seems to be the most important difference?
2. Write an essay that discusses Hulme's claim that poetry "is a compromise for a language of intuition which would hand over sensations bodily."

16. Figures of Speech

Figures of speech are broadly defined as a way of saying one thing in terms of something else. An overeager funeral director might, for example, be described as a vulture. Although figures of speech are indirect, they are designed to clarify, not obscure, our understanding of what they describe. Poets frequently use them because, as Emily Dickinson said, the poet's work is to "Tell all the truth but tell it slant" in order to capture the reader's interest and imagination. But figures of speech are not limited to poetry. Hearing them, reading them, or using them is as natural as using language itself.

Suppose that in the middle of a class discussion concerning the economic causes of World War II your history instructor introduces a series of statistics by saying, "Let's get down to brass tacks." Would anyone be likely to expect a display of brass tacks for students to examine? Of course not. To interpret the statement literally would be to wholly misunderstand the instructor's point that the time has come for a close look at the economic circumstances leading to the war. A literal response transforms the statement into the sort of hilariously bizarre material often found in a sketch by Woody Allen.

The class does not look for brass tacks, because, to put it in a nutshell, they understand that the instructor is speaking figuratively. They would understand, too, that in the preceding sentence *in a nutshell* refers to brevity and conciseness rather than to the covering of a kernel of a nut. Figurative language makes its way into our everyday speech and writing as well as into literature because it is a means of achieving color, vividness, and intensity.

Consider the difference, for example, between these two statements.

Literal: The diner strongly expressed anger at the waiter.
Figurative: The diner reared from his table and roared at the waiter.

The second statement is more vivid because it creates a picture of ferocious anger by likening the diner to some kind of wild animal, such as a lion or tiger. By comparison, "strongly expressed anger" is neither especially strong nor especially expressive; it is flat. Not all figurative language avoids this kind of flatness, however. Figures of speech such as "getting down to brass tacks" and "in a nutshell" are clichés because they lack originality and freshness. Still, they suggest how these devices are commonly used to give language some color, even if that color is sometimes a bit faded.

There is nothing weak about William Shakespeare's use of figurative language in the following passage from *Macbeth*. Macbeth has just learned that his wife is dead, and he laments her loss as well as the course of his own life.

WILLIAM SHAKESPEARE (1564–1616)
From *Macbeth (Act V, Scene v)* 1605–06

Tomorrow, and tomorrow, and tomorrow
Creeps in this petty pace from day to day
To the last syllable of recorded time;
And all our yesterdays have lighted fools
The way to dusty death. Out, out, brief candle!
Life's but a walking shadow, a poor player,
That struts and frets his hour upon the stage,
And then is heard no more. It is a tale
Told by an idiot, full of sound and fury,
Signifying nothing.

This passage might be summarized as "life has no meaning," but such a brief paraphrase does not take into account the figurative language that reveals the depth of Macbeth's despair and his view of the absolute meaninglessness of life. By comparing life to a "brief candle," Macbeth emphasizes the darkness and death that surround human beings. The light of life is too brief and unpredictable to be of any comfort. Indeed, life for Macbeth is a "walking shadow," futilely playing a role that is more farcical than dramatic, because life is, ultimately, a desperate story filled with pain and devoid of significance. What the figurative language provides, then, is the emotional force of Macbeth's assertion; his comparisons are disturbing because they are so apt.

The remainder of this chapter discusses some of the most important figures of speech used in poetry. A familiarity with them will help you to understand how poetry achieves its effects.

SIMILE AND METAPHOR

The two most common figures of speech are simile and metaphor. Both compare things that are ordinarily considered unlike each other. A *simile* makes an explicit comparison between two things by using words such as *like, as, than, appears,* or *seems:* "A sip of Mrs. Cook's coffee is like a punch in the stomach." The force of the simile is created by the differences between the two things compared. There would be no simile if the comparison were stated this way: "Mrs. Cook's coffee is as strong as the cafeteria's coffee." This is a literal comparison because Mrs. Cook's coffee is compared with something like it, another kind of coffee. Consider how simile is used in this poem.

MARGARET ATWOOD (b. 1939)
you fit into me   1971

you fit into me
like a hook into an eye

a fish hook
an open eye

If you blinked on a second reading, you got the point of this poem, because you recognized that the simile "like a hook into an eye" gives way to a play on words in the final two lines. There the hook and eye, no longer a pleasant domestic image of fitting closely together, become a literal, sharp fishhook and a human eye. The wordplay qualifies the simile and drastically alters the tone of this poem by creating a strong and unpleasant surprise.

A *metaphor,* like a simile, makes a comparison between two unlike things, but it does so implicitly, without words such as *like* or *as:* "Mrs. Cook's coffee is a punch in the stomach." Metaphor asserts the identity of dissimilar things. Macbeth tells us that life *is* a "brief candle," life *is* a "walking shadow," life *is* a "poor player," life *is* a "tale / Told by an idiot." Metaphor transforms people, places, objects, and ideas into whatever the poet imagines them to be, and if metaphors are effective, the reader's experience, understanding, and appreciation of what is described are enhanced. Metaphors are frequently more demanding than similes because they are not signaled by particular words. They are both subtle and powerful.

Here is a poem about presentiment, a foreboding that something terrible is about to happen.

EMILY DICKINSON (1830–1886)
Presentiment — is that long Shadow —
on the lawn —   c. 1863

Presentiment — is that long Shadow — on the lawn —
Indicative that Suns go down —

The notice to the startled Grass
That Darkness — is about to pass —

The metaphors in this poem define the abstraction *presentiment.* The sense
of foreboding that Dickinson expresses is identified with a particular moment, the moment when darkness is just about to envelop an otherwise
tranquil ordinary scene. The speaker projects that fear onto the "startled
Grass" so that it seems any life must be frightened by the approaching
"Shadow" and "Darkness" — two richly connotative words associated with
death. The metaphors obliquely tell us ("tell it slant" was Dickinson's motto,
remember) that presentiment is related to a fear of death, and, more important, the metaphors convey the feelings which attend that idea.

Some metaphors are more subtle than others, because their comparison
of terms is less explicit. Notice the difference between the following two
metaphors, both of which describe a shaggy derelict refusing to leave the
warmth of a hotel lobby. "He was a mule standing his ground" is a quite
explicit comparison. The man is a mule; X is Y. But this metaphor is much
more covert: "He brayed his refusal to leave." This second version is an
implied metaphor, because it does not explicitly identify the man with a
mule. Instead, it hints at or alludes to the mule. Braying is associated with
mules and is especially appropriate in this context because of those animals'
reputation for stubbornness. Implied metaphors can slip by readers, but they
offer the alert reader the energy and resonance of carefully chosen, highly
concentrated language.

Some poets write extended comparisons in which part or all of the
poem consists of a series of related metaphors or similes. Extended metaphors are more common than extended similes. In "Catch" (p. 593), Francis
creates an *extended metaphor* that compares poetry to a game of catch.
The entire poem is organized around this comparison, just as all of the
elements in Cummings's "she being Brand" (p. 623) are clustered around
the extended comparison of a car and a woman. Because these comparisons
are at work throughout the entire poem, they are called *controlling metaphors.* Extended comparisons can serve as a poem's organizing principle;
they are also a reminder that in good poems metaphor and simile are not
merely decorative but inseparable from what is expressed.

Notice the controlling metaphor in this poem, written by a woman
whose contemporaries identified her more as a wife and mother than as a
poet. Bradstreet's first volume of poetry, *The Tenth Muse,* was published by
her brother-in-law in 1650 without her prior knowledge.

ANNE BRADSTREET (c. 1612–1672)

The Author to Her Book

1678

Thou ill-formed offspring of my feeble brain,
Who after birth did'st by my side remain,
Till snatched from thence by friends, less wise than true,
Who thee abroad exposed to public view;
Made thee in rags, halting, to the press to trudge,   5
Where errors were not lessened, all may judge.
At thy return my blushing was not small,
My rambling brat (in print) should mother call;
I cast thee by as one unfit for light,
Thy visage was so irksome in my sight;   10
Yet being mine own, at length affection would
Thy blemishes amend, if so I could:
I washed thy face, but more defects I saw,
And rubbing off a spot, still made a flaw.
I stretched thy joints to make thee even feet,   15
Yet still thou run'st more hobbling than is meet;
In better dress to trim thee was my mind,
But nought save homespun cloth in the house I find.
In this array, 'mongst vulgars may'st thou roam;
In critics' hands beware thou dost not come;   20
And take thy way where yet thou are not known.
If for thy Father asked, say thou had'st none;
And for thy Mother, she alas is poor,
Which caused her thus to send thee out of door.

The extended metaphor likening her book to a child came naturally to Bradstreet and allowed her to regard her work both critically and affectionately. Her conception of the book as her child creates just the right tone of amusement, self-deprecation, and concern.

OTHER FIGURES

Perhaps the humblest figure of speech — if not one of the most familiar — is the pun. A *pun* is a play on words that relies on a word having more than one meaning or sounding like another word. For example, "A fad is in one era and out the other" is the sort of pun that produces obligatory groans. But most of us find pleasant and interesting surprises in puns. Here's one that has a slight edge to its humor.

EDMUND CONTI (b. 1929)

Pragmatist

1985

Apocalypse soon
Coming our way
Ground zero at noon
Halve a nice day.

Grimly practical under the circumstances, the pragmatist divides the familiar cheerful cliché by half. As simple as this poem is, its tone is mixed because it makes us laugh and wince at the same time.

Puns can be used to achieve serious effects as well as humorous ones. Although we may have learned to underrate puns as figures of speech, it is a mistake to underestimate their power and the frequency with which they appear in poetry. A close examination, for example, of Henry Reed's "Naming of Parts" (p. 700), Robert Frost's "Design" (p. 887), or almost any lengthy passage from a Shakespeare play will confirm the value of puns.

Synecdoche is a figure of speech in which part of something is used to signify the whole: a neighbor is a "wagging tongue" (a gossip); a criminal is placed "behind bars" (in prison). Less typically, synecdoche refers to the whole used to signify the part: "Germany invaded Poland"; "Princeton won the fencing match." Clearly, certain individuals participated in these activities, not all of Germany or Princeton. Another related figure of speech is *meto-nymy*, in which something closely associated with a subject is substituted for it: "She preferred the silver screen [motion pictures] to reading." "At precisely ten o'clock the paper shufflers [office workers] stopped for coffee."

Synecdoche and metonymy may overlap and are therefore sometimes difficult to distinguish. Consider this description of a disapproving minister entering a noisy tavern: "As those pursed lips came through the swinging door, the atmosphere was suddenly soured." The pursed lips signal the presence of the minister and are therefore a synecdoche, but they additionally suggest an inhibiting sense of sin and guilt that makes the bar patrons feel uncomfortable. Hence, the pursed lips are also a metonymy, since they are in this context so closely connected with religion. Although the distinction between synecdoche and metonymy can be useful, when a figure of speech overlaps categories, it is usually labeled a metonymy.

Knowing the precise term for a figure of speech is, finally, less important than responding to its use in a poem. Consider how metonymy and synecdoche convey the tone and meaning of the following poem.

DYLAN THOMAS (1914–1953)

The Hand That Signed the Paper   1936

The hand that signed the paper felled a city;
Five sovereign fingers taxed the breath,
Doubled the globe of dead and halved a country;
These five kings did a king to death.

The mighty hand leads to a sloping shoulder,   5
The finger joints are cramped with chalk;
A goose's quill has put an end to murder
That put an end to talk.

The hand that signed the treaty bred a fever,
And famine grew, and locusts came;   10
Great is the hand that holds dominion over
Man by a scribbled name.

The five kings count the dead but do not soften
The crusted wound nor stroke the brow;
A hand rules pity as a hand rules heaven;   15
Hands have no tears to flow.

 The "hand" in this poem is a synecdoche for a powerful ruler, because
it is a part of someone used to signify the entire person. The "goose's quill"
is a metonymy that also refers to the power associated with the ruler's hand.
By using these figures of speech, Thomas depersonalizes and ultimately
dehumanizes the ruler. The final synecdoche tells us that "Hands have no
tears to flow." It makes us see the political power behind the hand as remote
and inhuman. How is the meaning of the poem enlarged when the speaker
says, "A hand rules pity as a hand rules heaven"?

 One of the ways writers energize the abstractions, ideas, objects, and
animals that constitute their created worlds is through *personification,* the
attribution of human characteristics to nonhuman things: temptation pursues
the innocent; trees scream in the raging wind; mice conspire in the cupboard.
We are not explicitly told that these things are people; instead, we are invited
to see that they behave like people. Perhaps it is human vanity that makes
personification a frequently used figure of speech. Whatever the reason,
personification, a form of metaphor that connects the nonhuman with the
human, makes the world understandable in human terms. Consider this
concise example from William Blake's *The Marriage of Heaven and Hell,* a
long poem that takes delight in attacking conventional morality: "Prudence
is a rich ugly old maid courted by Incapacity." By personifying prudence,
Blake transforms what is usually considered a virtue into a comic figure
hardly worth emulating.

 Often related to personification is another rhetorical figure called *apostrophe,* an address either to someone who is absent and therefore cannot
hear the speaker or to something nonhuman that cannot comprehend. Apos-

trophe provides an opportunity for the speaker of a poem to think aloud, and often the thoughts expressed are in a formal tone. John Keats, for example, begins "Ode on a Grecian Urn" (p. 813) this way: "Thou still unravished bride of quietness." Apostrophe is frequently accompanied by intense emotion that is signaled by phrasing such as "O Life." In the right hands — such as Keats's — apostrophe can provide an intense and immediate voice in a poem, but when it is overdone or extravagant it can be ludicrous. Modern poets are more wary of apostrophe than their predecessors, because apostrophizing strikes many self-conscious twentieth-century sensibilities as too theatrical. Thus modern poets tend to avoid exaggerated situations in favor of less charged though equally meditative moments, as in this next poem, with its amusing, half-serious cosmic twist.

JANICE TOWNLEY MOORE (b. 1939)
To a Wasp   1984

You must have chortled
finding that tiny hole
in the kitchen screen. Right
into my cheese cake batter
you dived,   5
no chance to swim ashore,
no saving spoon,
the mixer whirring
your legs, wings, stinger,
churning you into such   10
delicious death.
Never mind the bright April day.
Did you not see
rising out of cumulus clouds
That fist aimed at both of us?   15

Moore's apostrophe "To a Wasp" is based on the simplest of domestic circumstances; there is almost nothing theatrical or exaggerated in the poem's tone until "That fist" in the last line, when exaggeration takes center stage. As a figure of speech exaggeration is known as **overstatement** or **hyperbole** and adds emphasis without intending to be literally true: "The teenage boy ate everything in the house." Notice how the speaker of Marvell's "To His Coy Mistress" (p. 631) exaggerates his devotion in the following overstatement.

> An hundred years should go to praise
> Thine eyes and on thy forehead gaze,
> Two hundred to adore each breast,
> But thirty thousand to the rest:

That comes to 30,500 years. What is expressed here is heightened emotion, not deception.

The speaker also uses the opposite figure of speech, **understatement,** which says less than is intended. In the next section he sums up why he cannot take 30,500 years to express his love.

> The grave's a fine and private place,
> But none, I think, do there embrace.

The speaker is correct, of course, but by deliberately understating — saying "I think" when he is actually certain — he makes his point that death will overtake their love all the more emphatic. Another powerful example of understatement appears in the final line of Randall Jarrell's "The Death of the Ball Turret Gunner" (p. 621), when the disembodied voice of the machine-gunner describes his death in a bomber: "When I died they washed me out of the turret with a hose."

Paradox is a statement that initially appears to be self-contradictory but that, on closer inspection, turns out to make sense: "The pen is mightier than the sword." In a fencing match, anyone would prefer the sword, but if the goal is to win the hearts and minds of people, the art of persuasion can be more compelling than swordplay. To resolve the paradox, it is necessary to discover the sense that underlies the statement. If we see that "pen" and "sword" are used as metonymies for writing and violence, then the paradox rings true. *Oxymoron* is a condensed form of paradox in which two contradictory words are used together. Combinations such as "sweet sorrow," "silent scream," "sad joy," and "cold fire" indicate the kinds of startling effects that oxymorons can produce. Paradox is useful in poetry because it arrests a reader's attention by its seemingly stubborn refusal to make sense, and once a reader has penetrated the paradox, it is difficult to resist a perception so well earned. Good paradoxes are knotty pleasures. Here is a simple but effective one.

MICHAEL CADNUM (b. 1949)

Cat Spy   1985

He closes both eyes
and watches.

Anyone familiar with feline behavior knows the truth of this apparent contradiction.

The following poems are rich in figurative language. As you read and study them, notice how their figures of speech vivify situations, clarify ideas, intensify emotions, and engage your imagination. Although the terms for the various figures discussed in this chapter are useful for labeling the particular devices used in poetry, they should not be allowed to get in the way of your response to a poem. Don't worry about rounding up examples of figurative language. First relax and let the figures work their effects on you. Use the terms as a means of taking you further into poetry, and they will serve your reading well.

POEMS FOR FURTHER STUDY

ERNEST SLYMAN (b. 1946)
Lightning Bugs   1988

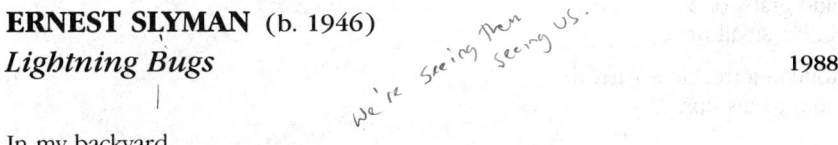
We're seeing them seeing us.

In my backyard,
They burn peepholes in the night
And take snapshots of my house.

Considerations for Critical Thinking and Writing

1. Explain why the title is essential to this poem.
2. What makes the description of the lightning bugs effective? How do the second and third lines complement each other?
3. As Slyman has done, take a simple, common fact of nature and make it vivid by using a figure of speech to describe it.

MARK IRWIN (b. 1953)
Icicles   1987

Slender beards of light
hang from the railing.

My son shows me
their array of sizes:

one oddly shaped,   5
its queer curve

a clear walrus tooth,
illumined, tinseled.

We watch crystal cones
against blue sky.   10

Suddenly some break loose,
an echo of piano notes.

The sun argues
ice to liquid.

Tiny buds of water
pendent on dropper tips   15

push to pear shapes,
prisms that shiver silver

in a slight wind
before falling.   20

alliteration

Look, he says laughing,
a pinocchio nose,

and grabs one
in his small hand,

touching the clear carrot,   25
cold to his lips.

Considerations for Critical Thinking and Writing

1. What role does the son serve in this poem?
2. Identify the metaphors in this poem. How do the metaphors help to create the
   tone?

SYLVIA PLATH (1932–1963)
Mirror   1963

I am silver and exact. I have no preconceptions.
Whatever I see I swallow immediately
Just as it is, unmisted by love or dislike.
I am not cruel, only truthful —
The eye of a little god, four-cornered.   5
Most of the time I meditate on the opposite wall.
It is pink, with speckles. I have looked at it so long
I think it is a part of my heart. But it flickers.
Faces and darkness separate us over and over.

Now I am a lake. A woman bends over me,   10
Searching my reaches for what she really is.
Then she turns to those liars, the candles or the moon.
I see her back, and reflect it faithfully.
She rewards me with tears and an agitation of hands.
I am important to her. She comes and goes.   15
Each morning it is her face that replaces the darkness.
In me she has drowned a young girl, and in me an old woman
Rises toward her day after day, like a terrible fish.

Considerations for Critical Thinking and Writing

1. What is the effect of the personification in this poem? How would our view of the aging woman be different if she, rather than the mirror, told her story?
2. What is the mythical allusion in "Now I am a lake" (line 10)?
3. In what sense can "candles or the moon" be regarded as "liars"? Explain this metaphor.
4. Discuss the effectiveness of the simile in the final line of the poem.

WILLIAM WORDSWORTH (1770–1850)
London, 1802

1802

Milton!° thou should'st be living at this hour:
England hath need of thee: she is a fen
Of stagnant waters: altar, sword, and pen,
Fireside, the heroic wealth of hall and bower,
Have forfeited their ancient English dower   5
Of inward happiness. We are selfish men;
Oh! raise us up, return to us again;
And give us manners, virtue, freedom, power.
Thy soul was like a star, and dwelt apart:
Thou hadst a voice whose sound was like the sea: 10
Pure as the naked heavens, majestic, free,
So didst thou travel on life's common way,
In cheerful godliness; and yet thy heart
The lowliest duties on herself did lay.

1 *Milton:* John Milton (1608–1674), poet, famous especially for his religious epic *Paradise Lost* and his defense of political freedom.

Considerations for Critical Thinking and Writing

1. Explain the metonymies in lines 3–6 of this poem. What is the speaker's assessment of England?
2. How would the effect of the poem be different if it were in the form of an address to Wordsworth's contemporaries rather than an apostrophe to Milton? What qualities does Wordsworth attribute to Milton by the use of figurative language?

JIM STEVENS (b. 1922)
Schizophrenia

1992

It was the house that suffered most.

It had begun with slamming doors, angry feet scuffing the carpets,
dishes slammed onto the table,
greasy stains spreading on the cloth.

Certain doors were locked at night,   5
feet stood for hours outside them,
dishes were left unwashed, the cloth
disappeared under a hardened crust.

The house came to miss the shouting voices,
the threats, the half-apologies, noisy   10
reconciliations, the sobbing that followed.

Then lines were drawn, borders established,
some rooms declared their loyalties,
keeping to themselves, keeping out the other.
The house divided against itself.   15

Seeing cracking paint, broken windows,
the front door banging in the wind,
the roof tiles flying off, one by one,
the neighbors said it was a madhouse.

It was the house that suffered most.   20

Considerations for Critical Thinking and Writing

1. What is the effect of the personification in this poem?
2. How are the people characterized who live in the house? What does their behavior reveal about them? How does the house respond to them?
3. Comment on the title. If the title were missing what, if anything, would be missing from the poem? Explain your answer.

WALT WHITMAN (1819–1892)
A Noiseless Patient Spider   1868

A noiseless patient spider,
I mark'd where on a little promontory it stood isolated,
Mark'd how to explore the vacant vast surrounding,
It launch'd forth filament, filament, filament, out of itself,
Ever unreeling them, ever tirelessly speeding them.   5

And you O my soul where you stand,
Surrounded, detached, in measureless oceans of space,
Ceaselessly musing, venturing, throwing, seeking the spheres to connect them,
Till the bridge you will need be form'd, till the ductile anchor hold,
Till the gossamer thread you fling catch somewhere, O my soul.   10

Considerations for Critical Thinking and Writing

1. Spiders are not usually regarded as pleasant creatures. Why does the speaker in this poem liken his soul to one? What similarities are there in the poem between spider and soul? Are there any significant differences?

2. How do the images of space relate to the connections made between the speaker's soul and the spider?

Connection to Another Selection

1. Read the early version of "A Noiseless Patient Spider" printed below. Which version is more unified by its metaphors? Which do you prefer? Why? Write an essay about the change of focus from the early version to the final one.

WALT WHITMAN (1819–1892)
The Soul, reaching, throwing out for love   c. 1862

The Soul, reaching, throwing out for love,
As the spider, from some little promontory, throwing out filament after filament,
    tirelessly out of itself, that one at least may catch and form a link, a bridge,
    a connection
O I saw one passing along, saying hardly a word — yet full of love I detected
    him, by certain signs
O eyes wishfully turning! O silent eyes!
For then I thought of you o'er the world,
O latent oceans, fathomless oceans of love!
O waiting oceans of love! yearning and fervid! and of you sweet souls perhaps
    in the future, delicious and long:
But Death, unknown on the earth — ungiven, dark here, unspoken, never born:
You fathomless latent souls of love — you pent and unknown oceans of love!

JOHN DONNE (1572–1631)
A Valediction: Forbidding Mourning   1611

As virtuous men pass mildly away,
    And whisper to their souls to go,
While some of their sad friends do say,
    The breath goes now, and some say, no:

So let us melt, and make no noise,   5
    No tear-floods, nor sigh-tempests move;
'Twere profanation of our joys
    To tell the laity our love.

Moving of th' earth° brings harms and fears,   *earthquakes*
    Men reckon what it did and meant,   10
But trepidation of the spheres,°
    Though greater far, is innocent.

---

11 *trepidation of the spheres:* According to Ptolemaic astronomy, the planets sometimes moved violently, like earthquakes, but these movements were not felt by people on earth.

Dull sublunary° lovers' love
    (Whose soul is sense) cannot admit
Absence, because it doth remove   15
    Those things which elemented° it.   *composed*

But we by a love so much refined,
    That ourselves know not what it is,
Inter-assured of the mind,
    Care less, eyes, lips, and hands to miss.   20

Our two souls therefore, which are one,
    Though I must go, endure not yet
A breach, but an expansion,
    Like gold to airy thinness beat.

If they be two, they are two so   25
    As stiff twin compasses are two;
Thy soul the fixed foot, makes no show
    To move, but doth, if th' other do.

And though it in the center sit,
    Yet when the other far doth roam,   30
It leans, and hearkens after it,
    And grows erect, as that comes home.

Such wilt thou be to me, who must
    Like th' other foot, obliquely run;
Thy firmness makes my circle just,°   35
    And makes me end, where I begun.

13 *sublunary:* Under the moon; hence mortal and subject to change.   35 *circle just:* The circle is a traditional symbol of perfection.

Considerations for Critical Thinking and Writing

1. A valediction is a farewell. Donne wrote this poem for his wife before leaving on a trip to France. What kind of "mourning" is the speaker forbidding?
2. Explain how the simile in lines 1–4 is related to the couple in lines 5–8. Who is described as dying?
3. How does the speaker contrast the couple's love to "sublunary lovers' love" (line 13)?
4. Explain the similes in lines 24 and 25–36.

ABRAHAM COWLEY (1618–1667)
Drinking   1656

The thirsty earth soaks up the rain,
And drinks, and gapes for drink again.
The plants suck in the earth, and are
With constant drinking fresh and fair;
The sea itself — which one would think   5
Should have but little need of drink —
Drinks ten thousand rivers up,
So filled that they o'erflow the cup.
The busy sun — and one would guess
By's drunken fiery face no less —   10
Drinks up the sea, and when he's done,
The moon and stars drink up the sun:
They drink and dance by their own light;
They drink and revel all the night.
Nothing in nature's sober found,   15
But an eternal health goes round.
Fill up the bowl then, fill it high,
Fill up the glasses there; for why
Should every creature drink but I;
Why, man of morals, tell me why?   20

Considerations for Critical Thinking and Writing

1. What is the purpose of the poet's survey of nature's drinking?
2. Consider the nature of the speaker. Explain whether you think his argument should be taken seriously or lightly.

MAY SWENSON (b. 1927)
The Secret in the Cat   1964

I took my cat apart
to see what made him purr.
Like an electric clock
or like the snore

of a warming kettle,   5
something fizzed and sizzled in him.
Was he a soft car,
the engine bubbling sound?

Was there a wire beneath his fur,
or humming throttle?   10

I undid his throat.
Within was no stir.

I opened up his chest
as though it were a door:
no whisk or rattle there.   15
I lifted off his skull:

no hiss or murmur.
I halved his little belly
but found no gear,
no cause for static.   20

So I replaced his lid,
laced his little gut.
His heart into his vest I slid
and buttoned up his throat.

His tail rose to a rod   25
and beckoned to the air.
Some voltage made him vibrate
warmer than before.

Whiskers and a tail:
perhaps they caught   30
some radar code
emitted as a pip, a dot-and-dash

of woolen sound.
My cat a kind of tuning fork? —
amplifier? — telegraph? —   35
doing secret signal work?

His eyes elliptic tubes:
there's a message in his stare.
I stroke him
but cannot find the dial.   40

Considerations for Critical Thinking and Writing

1. What is the secret in the cat? Does the poem answer this question? Explain why
   or why not.
2. What kinds of things is the cat compared to? What do they have in common? Why
   are they appropriate comparisons?

Connection to Another Selection

1. Write an essay comparing Swenson's response to her cat with Updike's treatment
   in "Dog's Death" (p. 590). How does each writer manage to evoke what is essential
   about the nature of the animal described in the poem?

LINDA PASTAN (b. 1932)
Marks
1978

My husband gives me an A
for last night's supper,
an incomplete for my ironing,
a B plus in bed.
My son says I am average,   5
an average mother, but if
I put my mind to it
I could improve.
My daughter believes
in Pass/Fail and tells me   10
I pass. Wait 'til they learn
I'm dropping out.

Considerations for Critical Thinking and Writing

1. Explain the appropriateness of the controlling metaphor in this poem. How does
   it reveal the woman's relationship to her family?
2. Discuss the meaning of the title.
3. How does the last line serve as both the climax of the woman's story and the
   controlling metaphor of the poem?

Connection to Another Selection

1. Compare the tone of this poem with that of Godwin's short story "A Sorrowful
   Woman" (p. 30).

LUCILLE CLIFTON (b. 1936)
come home from the movies
1974

come home from the movies, ~ *fantasy* *Unrealistic*
black girls and boys,
the picture be over and the screen
be cold as our neighborhood.
come home from the show,   **DIDACTIC**   5
don't be the show.
take off some flowers and plant them,
pick us some papers and read them,
stop making some babies and raise them.
come home from the movies   10

black girls and boys,
show our fathers how to walk like men,
they already know how to dance.

Considerations for Critical Thinking and Writing

1. What are the "movies" a metaphor for?
2. What advice does the speaker urge upon "black girls and boys"?
3. Explain the final two lines. Why do they come last?

ELAINE MAGARRELL (b. 1928)
The Joy of Cooking   1988

I have prepared my sister's tongue,
scrubbed and skinned it,
trimmed the roots, small bones, and gristle.
Carved through the hump it slices thin and neat.
Best with horseradish   5
and economical — it probably will grow back.
Next time perhaps a creole sauce
or mold of aspic?

I will have my brother's heart,
which is firm and rather dry,   10
slow cooked. It resembles muscle
more than organ meat
and needs an apple-onion stuffing
to make it interesting at all.
Although beef heart serves six   15
my brother's heart barely feeds two.
I could also have it braised
and served in sour sauce.

Considerations for Critical Thinking and Writing

1. How are the tongue and heart used to characterize the sister and brother in this poem?
2. Describe the speaker's tone. What effect does the title have on your determining the tone?

Connection to Another Selection

1. Write an essay that explains how cooking becomes a way of talking about something else in this poem and in Croft's "Home-Baked Bread" (p. 660).

TRUMBULL STICKNEY (1874–1904)
Sir, say no more
1904

Sir, say no more,
Within me 'tis as if
The green and climbing eyesight of a cat
Crawled near my mind's poor birds.

Considerations for Critical Thinking and Writing

1. What kind of experience does the speaker describe in this poem?
2. Why is this poem especially difficult to paraphrase?

PERSPECTIVE

JOHN R. SEARLE (b. 1932)
Figuring Out Metaphors
1979

If you hear somebody say, "Sally is a block of ice," or, "Sam is a pig," you are likely to assume that the speaker does not mean what he says literally, but that he is speaking metaphorically. Furthermore, you are not likely to have very much trouble figuring out what he means. If he says, "Sally is a prime number between 17 and 23," or "Bill is a barn door," you might still assume he is speaking metaphorically, but it is much harder to figure out what he means. The existence of such utterances — utterances in which the speaker means metaphorically something different from what the sentence means literally — poses a series of questions for any theory of language and communication: What is metaphor, and how does it differ from both literal and other forms of figurative utterances? Why do we use expressions metaphorically instead of saying exactly and literally what we mean? How do metaphorical utterances work, that is, how is it possible for speakers to communicate to hearers when speaking metaphorically inasmuch as they do not say what they mean? And why do some metaphors work and others do not?

From *Expression and Meaning*

Considerations for Critical Thinking and Writing

1. Searle poses a series of important questions. Write an essay that explores one of these questions, basing your discussion on the poems in this chapter.
2. Try writing a brief poem that provides a context for the line "Sally is a prime number between 17 and 23" or the line "Bill is a barn door." Your task is to create a context so that either one of these metaphoric statements is as readily understandable as "Sally is a block of ice" or "Sam is a pig." Share your poem with your classmates and explain how the line generated the poem you built around it.

17. Symbol, Allegory, and Irony

SYMBOL

A *symbol* is something that represents something else. An object, person, place, event, or action can suggest more than its literal meaning. A handshake between two world leaders might be simply a greeting, but if it is done ceremoniously before cameras it could be a symbolic gesture signifying unity, issues resolved, and joint policies that will be followed. We live surrounded by symbols. When a seventy-thousand-dollar Mercedes-Benz comes roaring by in the fast lane, we get a quick glimpse of not only an expensive car but an entire life-style that suggests opulence, broad lawns, executive offices, and power. One of the reasons some buyers are willing to spend roughly the cost of five Chevrolets for a single Mercedes-Benz is that they are aware of the car's symbolic value. A symbol is a vehicle for two things at once: it functions as itself and it implies meanings beyond itself.

The meanings suggested by a symbol are determined by the context in which they appear. The Mercedes could symbolize very different things depending upon where it was parked. Would an American political candidate be likely to appear in a Detroit blue-collar neighborhood with such a car? Probably not. Although a candidate might be able to afford the car, it would be an inappropriate symbol for someone seeking votes from all the people. As a symbol, the German-built Mercedes would backfire if voters perceived it as representing an entity partially responsible for layoffs of automobile workers or, worse, as a sign of decadence and corruption. Similarly, a huge statue of Lenin conveys different meanings to residents of Moscow than it would to farmers in Prairie Center, Illinois. Because symbols depend on contexts for their meaning, literary artists provide those contexts so that the reader has enough information to determine the probable range of meanings suggested by a symbol.

In the following poem the speaker describes walking at night. How is the night used symbolically?

ROBERT FROST (1874–1963)

Acquainted with the Night   1928

I have been one acquainted with the night.
I have walked out in rain — and back in rain.
I have outwalked the furthest city light.

I have looked down the saddest city lane.
I have passed by the watchman on his beat   5
And dropped my eyes, unwilling to explain.

I have stood still and stopped the sound of feet
When far away an interrupted cry
Came over houses from another street,

But not to call me back or say good-by;   10
And further still at an unearthly height
One luminary clock against the sky

Proclaimed the time was neither wrong nor right.
I have been one acquainted with the night.

In approaching this or any poem, you should read for literal meanings first, and then allow the elements of the poem to invite you to symbolic readings, if they are appropriate. Here the somber tone suggests that the lines have symbolic meaning too. The flat matter-of-factness created by the repetition of "I have" (lines 1–5, 7, 14) understates the symbolic subject matter of the poem, which is, finally, more about the "night" located in the speaker's mind or soul than it is about walking away from a city and back again. The speaker is "acquainted with the night." The importance of this phrase is emphasized by Frost's title and by the fact that he begins and ends the poem with it. Poets frequently use this kind of repetition to alert readers to details that carry more than literal meanings.

The speaker in this poem has personal knowledge of the night but does not indicate specifically what the night means. To arrive at the potential meanings of the night in this context, it is necessary to look closely at its connotations, along with the images provided in the poem. The connotative meanings of night suggest, for example, darkness, death, and grief. By drawing upon these connotations, Frost uses a ***conventional symbol,*** something that is recognized by many people to represent certain ideas. Roses conventionally symbolize love or beauty; laurels, fame; spring, growth; the moon, romance. Poets often use conventional symbols to convey tone and meaning.

Frost uses the night as a conventional symbol, but he also develops it into a ***literary*** or ***contextual symbol,*** which goes beyond traditional, public meanings. A literary symbol cannot be summarized in a word or two. It tends to be as elusive as experience itself. The night cannot be reduced or equated with darkness or death or grief, but it evokes those associations and more. Frost took what perhaps initially appears to be an overworked, conventional symbol and prevented it from becoming a cliché by deepening and extending its meaning.

The images in "Acquainted with the Night" lead to the poem's symbolic meaning. Unwilling, and perhaps unable, to explain explicitly to the watchman (and to the reader) what the night means, the speaker nevertheless conveys feelings about it. The brief images of darkness, rain, sad city lanes, the necessity for guards, the eerie sound of a distressing cry coming over rooftops, and the "luminary clock against the sky" proclaiming "the time was neither wrong nor right" all help to create a sense of anxiety in this tight-lipped speaker. Although we cannot know what unnamed personal experiences have acquainted the speaker with the night, the images suggest that whatever the night means, it is somehow associated with insomnia, loneliness, isolation, coldness, darkness, death, fear, and a sense of alienation from humanity and even time. Daylight — ordinary daytime thoughts and life itself — seems remote and unavailable in this poem. The night is literally the period from sunset to sunrise, but, more important, it is an internal state of being felt by the speaker and revealed through the images.

Frost used symbols rather than an expository essay that would explain the conditions which cause these feelings, because most readers can provide their own list of sorrows and terrors that evoke similar emotions. Through symbol, the speaker's experience is compressed and simultaneously expanded by the personal darkness that each reader brings to the poem. The suggestive nature of symbols makes them valuable for poets and evocative for readers.

ALLEGORY

Unlike expansive, suggestive symbols, *allegory* is a narration or description usually restricted to a single meaning because its events, actions, characters, settings, and objects represent specific abstractions or ideas. Although the elements in an allegory may be interesting in themselves, the emphasis tends to be on what they ultimately mean. Characters may be given names such as Hope, Pride, Youth, and Charity; they have few if any personal qualities beyond their abstract meanings. These personifications are a form of extended metaphor, but their meanings are severely restricted. They are not symbols because, for instance, the meaning of a character named Charity is precisely that virtue.

There is little or no room for broad speculation and exploration in allegories. If Frost had written "Acquainted with the Night" as an allegory, he might have named his speaker Loneliness and had him leave the City of Despair to walk the Streets of Emptiness, where Crime, Poverty, Fear, and other characters would define the nature of city life. The literal elements in an allegory tend to be deemphasized in favor of the message. Symbols, however, function both literally and symbolically, so that "Acquainted with the Night" is about both a walk and a sense that something is terribly wrong.

Allegory especially lends itself to *didactic poetry,* which is designed to teach an ethical, moral, or religious lesson. Many stories, poems, and plays are concerned with values, but didactic literature is specifically created to convey a message. "Acquainted with the Night" does not impart advice or offer guidance. If the poem argued that city life is self-destructive or sinful, it would be didactic; instead, it is a lyric poem that expresses the emotions and thoughts of a single speaker.

Although allegory is often enlisted in didactic causes because it can so readily communicate abstract ideas through physical representations, not all allegories teach a lesson. Here is a poem describing a haunted palace while also establishing a consistent pattern that reveals another meaning.

EDGAR ALLAN POE (1809–1849)
The Haunted Palace   1839

I
In the greenest of our valleys,
    By good angels tenanted,
Once a fair and stately palace —
    Radiant palace — reared its head.
In the monarch Thought's dominion —   5
    It stood there!
Never seraph spread a pinion
    Over fabric half so fair.

II
Banners yellow, glorious, golden,
    On its roof did float and flow;   10
(This — all this — was in the olden
    Time long ago)
And every gentle air that dallied,
    In that sweet day,
Along the ramparts plumed and pallid,   15
    A winged odor went away.

III
Wanderers in that happy valley
    Through two luminous windows saw
Spirits moving musically

To a lute's well-tunèd law,   20
Round about a throne, where sitting
   (Porphyrogene!)°   *born to purple, royal*
In state his glory well befitting,
   The ruler of the realm was seen.

IV
And all with pearl and ruby glowing   25
   Was the fair palace door,
Through which came flowing, flowing, flowing
   And sparkling evermore,
A troop of Echoes whose sweet duty
   Was but to sing,   30
In voices of surpassing beauty,
   The wit and wisdom of their king.

V
But evil things, in robes of sorrow,
   Assailed the monarch's high estate;
(Ah, let us mourn, for never morrow   35
   Shall dawn upon him, desolate!)
And, round about his home, the glory
   That blushed and bloomed
Is but a dim-remembered story
   Of the old time entombed.   40

VI
And travelers now within that valley,
   Through the red-litten windows see
Vast forms that move fantastically
   To a discordant melody;
While, like a rapid ghastly river,   45
   Through the pale door,
A hideous throng rush out forever,
   And laugh — but smile no more.

   On one level this poem describes how a once happy palace is desolated
by "evil things." If the reader pays close attention to the diction, however,
an allegorical meaning becomes apparent on a second reading. A systematic
pattern develops in the choice of words used to describe the palace, so that
it comes to stand for a human mind. The palace, banners, windows, door,
echoes, and throng are equated with a person's head, hair, eyes, mouth,
voice, and laughter. That mind, once harmoniously ordered, is overthrown
by evil, haunting thoughts that lead to the mad laughter in the poem's final
lines. Once the general pattern is seen, the rest of the details fall neatly into
place to strengthen the parallels between the surface description of a palace
and the allegorical representation of a disordered mind.
   Modern writers generally prefer symbol over allegory because they tend
to be more interested in opening up the potential meanings of an experience

instead of transforming it into a closed pattern of meaning. Perhaps the major difference is that while allegory may delight a reader's imagination, symbol challenges and enriches it.

IRONY

Another important resource writers use to take readers beyond literal meanings is *irony,* a technique that reveals a discrepancy between what appears to be and what is actually true. Here is a classic example in which appearances give way to the underlying reality.

EDWIN ARLINGTON ROBINSON (1869–1935)
Richard Cory   1897

Whenever Richard Cory went down town,
We people on the pavement looked at him:
He was a gentleman from sole to crown,
Clean favored, and imperially slim.

And he was always quietly arrayed,   5
And he was always human when he talked;
But still he fluttered pulses when he said,
"Good-morning," and he glittered when he walked.

And he was rich — yes, richer than a king —
And admirably schooled in every grace: 10
In fine, we thought that he was everything
To make us wish that we were in his place.

So on we worked, and waited for the light,
And went without the meat, and cursed the bread;
And Richard Cory, one calm summer night,   15
Went home and put a bullet through his head.

Richard Cory seems to have it all. Those less fortunate, "the people on the pavement," regard him as well bred, handsome, tasteful, and richly endowed with both money and grace. Until the final line of the poem, the reader, like the speaker, is charmed by Cory's good fortune, so quietly expressed in his decent, easy manner. That final, shocking line, however, shatters the appearances of Cory's life and reveals him to have been a desperately unhappy man. While everyone else assumes that Cory represented "everything" to which they aspire, the reality is that he could escape his miserable life only as a suicide. This discrepancy between what appears to be true and what actually exists is known as *situational irony:* what happens is entirely different from what is expected. We are not told why

Cory shoots himself; instead, the irony in the poem shocks us into the recognition that appearances do not always reflect realities.

Words are also sometimes intended to be taken at other than face value. *Verbal irony* is saying something different from what is meant. After reading "Richard Cory," to say "That rich gentleman sure was happy" is ironic. The tone of voice would indicate that just the opposite was meant; hence, verbal irony is usually easy to detect in spoken language. In literature, however, a reader can sometimes take literally what a writer intends ironically. The remedy for this kind of misreading is to pay close attention to the poem's context. There is no formula that can detect verbal irony, but contradictory actions and statements as well as the use of understatement and overstatement can often be signals that verbal irony is present.

Consider how verbal irony is used in this poem.

KENNETH FEARING (1902–1961)
AD 1938

Wanted: Men;
Millions of men are *wanted at once* in a big new field;
New, tremendous, thrilling, great.
If you've ever been a figure in the chamber of horrors,
If you've ever escaped from a psychiatric ward,   5
If you thrill at the thought of throwing poison into wells, have heavenly visions
    of people, by the thousands, dying in flames —

You are the very man we want
We mean business and our business is *you*
Wanted: A race of brand-new men.

Apply: Middle Europe;   10
No skill needed;
No ambition required; no brains wanted and no character allowed;

Take a permanent job in the coming profession
Wages: *Death.*

This poem was written as Nazi troops stormed across Europe at the start of World War II. The advertisement suggests on the surface that killing is just an ordinary job, but the speaker indicates through understatement that there is nothing ordinary about the "business" of this "*coming profession.*" Fearing uses verbal irony to indicate how casually and mindlessly people are prepared to accept the horrors of war.

"AD" is a *satire,* an example of the literary art of ridiculing a folly or vice in an effort to expose or correct it. The object of satire is usually some human frailty; people, institutions, ideas, and things are all fair game for satirists. Fearing satirizes the insanity of a world mobilizing itself for war:

his irony reveals the speaker's knowledge that there is nothing *"New, tremendous, thrilling,* [or] *great"* about going off to kill and be killed. The implication of the poem is that no one should respond to advertisements for war. The poem serves as a satiric corrective to those who would troop off armed with unrealistic expectations; wage war and the wages consist of death.

Dramatic irony is used when a writer allows a reader to know more about a situation than a character does. This creates a discrepancy between what a character says or thinks and what the reader knows to be true. Dramatic irony is often used to reveal character. In the following poem the speaker delivers a public speech that ironically tells us more about him than it does about the patriotic holiday he is commemorating.

e. e. cummings (1894–1962)
next to of course god america i   1926

"next to of course god america i
love you land of the pilgrims' and so forth oh
say can you see by the dawn's early my
country 'tis of centuries come and go
and are no more what of it we should worry   5
in every language even deafanddumb
thy sons acclaim your glorious name by gorry
by jingo by gee by gosh by gum
why talk of beauty what could be more beautiful than these heroic happy dead   10
who rushed like lions to the roaring slaughter
they did not stop to think they died instead
then shall the voice of liberty be mute?"

He spoke. And drank rapidly a glass of water

This verbal debauch of chauvinistic clichés (notice the run-on phrases and lines) reveals that the speaker's relationship to God and country is not, as he claims, one of love. His public address suggests a hearty mindlessness that leads to "roaring slaughter" rather than to reverence or patriotism. Cummings allows the reader to see through the speaker's words to their dangerous emptiness. What the speaker means and what Cummings means are entirely different. Like Fearing's "AD," this poem is a satire that invites the reader's laughter and contempt in order to deflate the benighted attitudes expressed in it.

When a writer uses God, destiny, or fate to dash the hopes and expectations of a character or humankind in general, it is called *cosmic irony.* In "The Convergence of the Twain" (p. 636), for example, Hardy describes how "The Immanent Will" brought together the *Titanic* and a deadly iceberg. Technology and pride are no match for "the Spinner of the Years." Here's a painfully terse version of cosmic irony.

STEPHEN CRANE (1871–1900)
A Man Said to the Universe   1899

A man said to the universe:
"Sir, I exist!"
"However," replied the universe,
"The fact has not created in me
A sense of obligation."

Unlike in "The Convergence of the Twain," there is the slightest bit of humor in Crane's poem, but the joke is on us.

    Irony is an important technique that allows a writer to distinguish between appearances and realities. In situational irony a discrepancy exists between what we expect to happen and what actually happens; in verbal irony a discrepancy exists between what is said and what is meant; in dramatic irony a discrepancy exists between what a character believes and what the reader knows to be true; and in cosmic irony a discrepancy exists between what a character aspires to and what universal forces provide. With each of these forms of irony, we are invited to move beyond surface appearances and sentimental assumptions to see the complexity of experience. Irony is often used in literature to reveal a writer's perspective on matters that previously seemed settled.

POEMS FOR FURTHER STUDY

CONRAD HILBERRY (b. 1928)
The Frying Pan   1978

My mark is my confusion.
If I believe it, I am
another long-necked girl
with the same face.
I am emptiness reflected   5
in a looking glass, a head

kept by a collar and leash,
a round belly with something
knocking to get in.

But cross the handle   10
with a short stroke
and I am Venus, the old
beauty. I am both the egg
and the pan it cooks in,
the slow heat, the miraculous   15
sun rising.

Considerations for Critical Thinking and Writing

1. Discuss the meanings of the "mark" in the first stanza. Can you think of any potential readings of it not mentioned by the speaker?
2. How is the pan transformed into an entirely different kind of symbol in the second stanza? How do the images of lines 13–16 create powerful symbolic values?
3. Discuss the significance of the poem's title.
4. The speaker of this poem is a woman, but the author is a man. Write an essay explaining whether knowing this makes any difference in your appreciation or understanding of the poem.

WILLIAM BLAKE (1757–1827)
The Sick Rose   1794

O Rose, thou art sick!
The invisible worm
That flies in the night,
In the howling storm,

Has found out thy bed
Of crimson joy,
And his dark secret love
Does thy life destroy.

Considerations for Critical Thinking and Writing

1. How does the use of personification in this poem indicate that the speaker laments the fate of more than a rose?
2. Discuss some of the possible meanings of the rose. How does the description of the worm help to explain the rose?
3. Is this poem to be read allegorically or symbolically? Can it be read literally?

PAUL LAURENCE DUNBAR (1872–1906)

We Wear the Mask

1896

We wear the mask that grins and lies,
It hides our cheeks and shades our eyes, —
This debt we pay to human guile;
With torn and bleeding hearts we smile,
And mouth with myriad subtleties.   5

Why should the world be overwise,
In counting all our tears and sighs?
Nay, let them only see us, while
   We wear the mask.

We smile, but, O great Christ, our cries   10
To thee from tortured souls arise.
We sing, but oh the clay is vile
Beneath our feet, and long the mile;
But let the world dream otherwise,
   We wear the mask!   15

Considerations for Critical Thinking and Writing

1. What does the mask symbolize? What kind of behavior does it represent?
2. Dunbar was a black man. Does awareness of that fact affect your reading of the poem? Explain why or why not.

Connections to Other Selections

1. How might the first line of this poem be used to describe the theme of Ralph Ellison's "Battle Royal" (p. 187)?
2. Write an essay on oppression as explored in "We Wear the Mask" and William Blake's "The Chimney Sweeper" (p. 703).

WILLIAM STAFFORD (b. 1914)

Traveling through the Dark

1962

Traveling through the dark I found a deer
dead on the edge of the Wilson River road.
It is usually best to roll them into the canyon:
that road is narrow; to swerve might make more dead.

By glow of the tail-light I stumbled back of the car   5
and stood by the heap, a doe, a recent killing;
she had stiffened already, almost cold.
I dragged her off; she was large in the belly.

My fingers touching her side brought me the reason —

her side was warm; her fawn lay there waiting,   10
alive, still, never to be born.
Beside that mountain road I hesitated.

The car aimed ahead its lowered parking lights;
under the hood purred the steady engine.
I stood in the glare of the warm exhaust turning red;   15
around our group I could hear the wilderness listen.

I thought hard for us all — my only swerving —
then pushed her over the edge into the river.

Considerations for Critical Thinking and Writing

1. Notice the description of the car in this poem: the "glow of the tail-light," the "lowered parking lights," and how the engine "purred." How do these and other details suggest symbolic meanings for the car and the "recent killing"?
2. Discuss the speaker's tone. Does the speaker seem, for example, tough, callous, kind, sentimental, confused, or confident?
3. What is the effect of the last stanza's having only two lines rather than the established four lines of the previous stanzas?
4. Discuss the appropriateness of this poem's title. In what sense has the speaker "thought hard for us all"? What are those thoughts?
5. Is this a didactic poem?

RICHARD EBERHART (b. 1904)

The Groundhog   1936

In June, amid the golden fields,
I saw a groundhog lying dead.
Dead lay he; my senses shook,
And mind outshot our naked frailty.
There lowly in the vigorous summer   5
His form began its senseless change,
And made my senses waver dim
Seeing nature ferocious in him.
Inspecting close his maggots' might
And seething caldron of his being,   10
Half with loathing, half with a strange love,
I poked him with an angry stick.
The fever arose, became a flame
And Vigor circumscribed the skies,
Immense energy in the sun,   15
And through my frame a sunless trembling.
My stick had done nor good nor harm.
Then stood I silent in the day
Watching the object, as before;

And kept my reverence for knowledge   20
Trying for control, to be still,
To quell the passion of the blood;
Until I had bent down on my knees
Praying for joy in the sight of decay.
And so I left; and I returned   25
In Autumn strict of eye, to see
The sap gone out of the groundhog,
But the bony sodden hulk remained.
But the year had lost its meaning,
And in intellectual chains   30
I lost both love and loathing,
Mured° up in the wall of wisdom.   *walled*
Another summer took the fields again
Massive and burning, full of life,
But when I chanced upon the spot   35
There was only a little hair left,
And bones bleaching in the sunlight
Beautiful as architecture;
I watched them like a geometer,
And cut a walking stick from a birch.   40
It has been three years, now.
There is no sign of the groundhog.
I stood there in the whirling summer,
My hand capped a withered heart,
And thought of China and of Greece,   45
Of Alexander° in his tent;
Of Montaigne° in his tower,
Of Saint Theresa° in her wild lament.

46 *Alexander:* Alexander the Great (356–323 B.C.), Macedonian king famous for conquering much of the world.   47 *Montaigne:* Michel de Montaigne (1533–1592), French essayist who commented on human affairs.   48 *Saint Theresa:* Saint Theresa of Avila (1515–1582), a mystic who founded a religious order.

Considerations for Critical Thinking and Writing

1. The speaker in this poem makes several visits to view the groundhog. Describe his changing feelings about the dead animal. What does the groundhog mean to the speaker?
2. How are the final four lines related to the speaker's response to the groundhog?
3. Why is a groundhog — rather than, say, a raccoon — an especially appropriate animal for the thematic purposes of this poem?
4. Explain whether you think this is an optimistic or pessimistic poem. Or is it somewhere in between?

Connections to Other Selections

1. Both "The Groundhog" and Stafford's "Traveling through the Dark" (p. 694) have as their subjects the death of an animal. Discuss how that death affects the speaker in each poem.

2. Write an essay that compares the symbolic meanings of the images of decay in "The Groundhog" and Roethke's "Root Cellar." (p. 648).
3. Compare and contrast the views of nature presented in "The Groundhog," "Traveling through the Dark," and D. H. Lawrence's "Snake" (below). How does each poem represent an effort to understand the nature of nature? Which view of nature do you find most convincing? Why?

D. H. LAWRENCE (1885–1930)
Snake   1923

A snake came to my water-trough
On a hot, hot day, and I in pajamas for the heat,
To drink there.

In the deep, strange-scented shade of the great dark carob-tree
I came down the steps with my pitcher   5
And must wait, must stand and wait, for there he was at the trough before me.

He reached down from a fissure in the earth-wall in the gloom
And trailed his yellow-brown slackness soft-bellied down, over the edge of the
    stone trough
And rested his throat upon the stone bottom,
And where the water had dripped from the tap, in a small clearness,   10
He sipped with his straight mouth,
Softly drank through his straight gums, into his slack long body,
Silently.

Someone was before me at my water-trough,
And I, like a second comer, waiting.   15

He lifted his head from his drinking, as cattle do,
And looked at me vaguely, as drinking cattle do,
And flickered his two-forked tongue from his lips, and mused a moment,
And stooped and drank a little more,
Being earth-brown, earth-golden from the burning bowels of the earth   20
On the day of Sicilian July, with Etna° smoking.   *a volcano*
The voice of my education said to me
He must be killed,
For in Sicily the black, black snakes are innocent, the gold are venomous.

And voices in me said, If you were a man   25
You would take a stick and break him now, and finish him off.

But must I confess how I liked him,
How glad I was he had come like a guest in quiet, to drink at my water-trough
And depart peaceful, pacified, and thankless,
Into the burning bowels of this earth?   30

Was it cowardice, that I dared not kill him?
Was it perversity, that I longed to talk to him?
Was it humility, to feel so honored?

I felt so honored.

And yet those voices: 35
If you were not afraid, you would kill him!

And truly I was afraid, I was most afraid,
But even so, honored still more
That he should seek my hospitality
From out the dark door of the secret earth.   40

He drank enough
And lifted his head, dreamily, as one who has drunken,
And flickered his tongue like a forked night on the air, so black,
Seeming to lick his lips,
And looked around like a god, unseeing, into the air,   45
And slowly turned his head,
And slowly, very slowly, as if thrice adream,
Proceeded to draw his slow length curving round
And climb again the broken bank of my wall-face.

And as he put his head into that dreadful hole,   50
And as he slowly drew up, snake-easing his shoulders, and entered farther,
A sort of horror, a sort of protest against his withdrawing into that horrid black
     hole,
Deliberately going into the blackness, and slowly drawing himself after,
Overcame me now his back was turned.

I looked round, I put down my pitcher,   55
I picked up a clumsy log
And threw it at the water-trough with a clatter.

I think it did not hit him,
But suddenly that part of him that was left behind convulsed in undignified
     haste.
Writhed like lightning, and was gone   60
Into the black hole, the earth-lipped fissure in the wall-front,
At which, in the intense still noon, I stared with fascination.

And immediately I regretted it.
I thought how paltry, how vulgar, what a mean act!
I despised myself and the voices of my accursed human education.   65

And I thought of the albatross,
And I wished he would come back, my snake.

For he seemed to me again like a king,
Like a king in exile, uncrowned in the underworld,
Now due to be crowned again.   70

And so, I missed my chance with one of the lords
Of life.
And I have something to expiate;
A pettiness.

Considerations for Critical Thinking and Writing

1. Do you think Lawrence uses the snake in this poem as a conventional symbol of evil, or does he go beyond the traditional meanings associated with snakes? Consider the images used to describe the snake.
2. What is the "voice of my education" (line 22)? What is the conflict the speaker feels about the snake?
3. Identify the allusion to the albatross (line 66).
4. Explain why the speaker wishes the snake would return (lines 67–70). Why do you think the snake is described as "one of the lords / Of life" (71–72)?

JAMES MERRILL (b. 1926)
Casual Wear   1984

Your average tourist: Fifty. 2.3
Times married. Dressed, this year, in Ferdi Plinthbower
Originals. Odds 1 to 9
Against her strolling past the Embassy

Today at noon. Your average terrorist: 5
Twenty-five. Celibate. No use for trends,
At least in clothing. Mark, though, where it ends.
People have come forth made of colored mist

Unsmiling on one hundred million screens
To tell of his prompt phone call to the station,   10
"Claiming responsibility" — devastation
Signed with a flourish, like the dead wife's jeans.

Considerations for Critical Thinking and Writing

1. What is the effect of the statistics in this poem?
2. Describe the speaker's tone. Is it appropriate for the subject matter? Explain why or why not.
3. Comment on the ironies that emerge from the final two lines. How are the tourist and terrorist linked by the speaker's description? Explain why you think the speaker sympathizes more with the tourist or terrorist — or with neither.

Connections to Other Selections

1. Compare the satire in this poem with that in Meinke's "The ABC of Aerobics" (p. 1055). What is satirized in each poem? Which satire is more pointed from your perspective?
2. Write an essay comparing this poem's profiles of the "average tourist" and "terrorist" with either Auden's "The Unknown Citizen" (p. 931) or Nemerov's "Life Cycle of Common Man" (p. 981). How are these profiles made convincing?

HENRY REED (1914–1986)

Naming of Parts   1946

Today we have naming of parts. Yesterday,
We had daily cleaning. And tomorrow morning,
We shall have what to do after firing. But today,
Today we have naming of parts. Japonica
Glistens like coral in all of the neighboring gardens,   5
        And today we have naming of parts.

This is the lower sling swivel. And this
Is the upper sling swivel, whose use you will see,
When you are given your slings. And this is the piling swivel,
Which in your case you have not got. The branches   10
Hold in the gardens their silent, eloquent gestures,
        Which in our case we have not got.

This is the safety-catch, which is always released
With an easy flick of the thumb. And please do not let me
See anyone using his finger. You can do it quite easy   15
If you have any strength in your thumb. The blossoms
Are fragile and motionless, never letting anyone see
        Any of them using their finger.

And this you can see is the bolt. The purpose of this
Is to open the breech, as you see. We can slide it   20
Rapidly backwards and forwards: we call this
Easing the spring. And rapidly backwards and forwards
The early bees are assaulting and fumbling the flowers:
        They call it easing the Spring.

They call it easing the Spring: it is perfectly easy   25
If you have any strength in your thumb: like the bolt,
And the breech, and the cocking-piece, and the point of balance,
Which in our case we have not got; and the almond-blossom
Silent in all of the gardens and the bees going backwards and forwards,
        For today we have naming of parts.   30

Considerations for Critical Thinking and Writing

1. Characterize the two speakers in this poem. Identify the lines spoken by each. How do their respective lines differ in tone?
2. What is the effect of the last line of each stanza?
3. How do ambiguities and puns contribute to the poem's meaning?
4. What symbolic contrast is made between the rifle instruction and the gardens? How is this contrast ironic?

JOHN CIARDI (1916–1986)

Suburban

1978

Yesterday Mrs. Friar phoned. "Mr. Ciardi,
　　how do you do?" she said. "I am sorry to say
this isn't exactly a social call. The fact is
　　your dog has just deposited — forgive me —
a large repulsive object in my petunias." 　　　　　　　5

I thought to ask, "Have you checked the rectal grooving
　　for a positive I.D.?" My dog, as it happened,
was in Vermont with my son, who had gone fishing —
　　if that's what one does with a girl, two cases of beer,
and a borrowed camper. I guessed I'd get no trout. 　　　10

But why lose out on organic gold for a wise crack?
　　"Yes, Mrs. Friar," I said, "I understand."
"Most kind of you," she said. "Not at all," I said.
　　I went with a spade. She pointed, looking away.
"I always have loved dogs," she said, "but really!" 　　　15

I scooped it up and bowed. "The animal of it.
　　I hope this hasn't upset you, Mrs. Friar."
"Not really," she said, "but really!" I bore the turd
　　across the line to my own petunias
and buried it till the glorious resurrection 　　　　　20

when even these suburbs shall give up their dead.

Considerations for Critical Thinking and Writing

1. How does the speaker transform Mrs. Friar into a symbolic figure of the suburbs?
2. Why do you suppose Ciardi focuses on this particular incident to make a comment upon the suburbs? What is the speaker's attitude toward suburban life?
3. Write a one-paragraph physical description of Mrs. Friar that captures her character for you.

Connection to Another Selection

1. Compare the speaker's voices in "Suburban" and in John Updike's "Dog's Death" (p. 590).

ROBERT BROWNING (1812–1889)

My Last Duchess   1842

Ferrara°

That's my last Duchess painted on the wall,
Looking as if she were alive. I call
That piece a wonder, now: Frà Pandolf's° hands
Worked busily a day, and there she stands.
Will't please you sit and look at her? I said   5
"Frà Pandolf" by design, for never read
Strangers like you that pictured countenance,
The depth and passion of its earnest glance,
But to myself they turned (since none puts by
The curtain I have drawn for you, but I)   10
And seemed as they would ask me, if they durst,
How such a glance came there; so, not the first
Are you to turn and ask thus. Sir, 'twas not
Her husband's presence only, called that spot
Of joy into the Duchess' cheek: perhaps   15
Frà Pandolf chanced to say "Her mantle laps
Over my lady's wrist too much," or "Paint
Must never hope to reproduce the faint
Half-flush that dies along her throat": such stuff
Was courtesy, she thought, and cause enough   20
For calling up that spot of joy. She had
A heart — how shall I say? — too soon made glad,
Too easily impressed; she liked whate'er
She looked on, and her looks went everywhere.
Sir, 'twas all one! My favor at her breast,   25
The dropping of the daylight in the West,
The bough of cherries some officious fool
Broke in the orchard for her, the white mule
She rode with round the terrace — all and each
Would draw from her alike the approving speech,   30
Or blush, at least. She thanked men, — good! but thanked
Somehow — I know not how — as if she ranked
My gift of a nine-hundred-years-old name
With anybody's gift. Who'd stoop to blame
This sort of trifling? Even had you skill   35
In speech — which I have not — to make your will
Quite clear to such an one, and say, "Just this
Or that in you disgusts me; here you miss,
Or there exceed the mark" — and if she let
Herself be lessoned so, nor plainly set   40

Ferrara: In the sixteenth century, the duke of this Italian city arranged to marry a second time after
the mysterious death of his very young first wife.   3 *Frà Pandolf:* A fictitious artist.

Her wits to yours, forsooth, and made excuse,
— E'en then would be some stooping; and I choose
Never to stoop. Oh sir, she smiled, no doubt,
Whene'er I passed her; but who passed without
Much the same smile? This grew; I gave commands;   45
Then all smiles stopped together. There she stands
As if alive. Will't please you rise? We'll meet
The company below, then. I repeat,
The Count your master's known munificence
Is ample warrant that no just pretense   50
Of mine for dowry will be disallowed;
Though his fair daughter's self, as I avowed
At starting, is my object. Nay, we'll go
Together down, sir. Notice Neptune, though,
Taming a sea-horse, thought a rarity,   55
Which Claus of Innsbruck° cast in bronze for me!

56 *Claus of Innsbruck:* Also a fictitious artist.

Considerations for Critical Thinking and Writing

1. To whom is the duke addressing his remarks about the duchess in this poem?
   What is ironic about the situation?
2. Why was the duke unhappy with his first wife? What does this reveal about the
   duke? What does the poem's title suggest about his attitude toward women in
   general?
3. What seems to be the visitor's response (lines 53–54) to the duke's account of his
   first wife?
4. What do you think happened to the Duchess?

Connection to Another Selection

1. Write an essay describing the ways in which the speakers of "My Last Duchess"
   and "Hazel Tells LaVerne" (p. 626) by Katharyn Howd Machan inadvertently reveal
   themselves.

WILLIAM BLAKE (1757–1827)
The Chimney Sweeper   1789

When my mother died I was very young,
And my father sold me while yet my tongue
Could scarcely cry " 'weep! 'weep! 'weep! 'weep!"
So your chimneys I sweep, and in soot I sleep.

There's little Tom Dacre, who cried when his head,   5
That curled like a lamb's back, was shaved: so I said

"Hush, Tom! never mind it, for when your head's bare
You know that the soot cannot spoil your white hair."

And so he was quiet, and that very night,
As Tom was a-sleeping, he had such a sight!   10
That thousands of sweepers, Dick, Joe, Ned, and Jack,
Were all of them locked up in coffins of black.

And by came an Angel who had a bright key,
And he opened the coffins and set them all free;
Then down a green plain leaping, laughing, they run,   15
And wash in a river, and shine in the sun.

Then naked and white, all their bags left behind,
They rise upon clouds and sport in the wind;
And the Angel told Tom, if he'd be a good boy,
He'd have God for his father, and never want joy.   20

And so Tom awoke; and we rose in the dark,
And got with our bags and our brushes to work.
Though the morning was cold, Tom was happy and warm;
So if all do their duty they need not fear harm.

Considerations for Critical Thinking and Writing

1. Characterize the speaker in this poem, and describe his tone. Is his tone the same
   as the poet's? Consider especially lines 7–8 and 24.
2. What is the symbolic value of the dream in lines 11–20?
3. Why is irony central to the meaning of this poem?
4. Discuss the validity of this statement: " 'The Chimney Sweeper' is a sentimental
   poem about a shameful eighteenth-century social problem; such a treatment of
   child abuse cannot be taken seriously."

TESS GALLAGHER (b. 1932)
Black Silk   1984

She was cleaning — there is always
that to do — when she found,
at the top of the closet, his old
silk vest. She called me
to look at it, unrolling it carefully   5
like something live
might fall out. Then we spread it
on the kitchen table and smoothed
the wrinkles down, making our hands
heavy until its shape against Formica   10
came back and the little tips
that would have pointed to his pockets

lay flat. The buttons were all there.
I held my arms out and she
looped the wide armholes over   15
them. "That's one thing I never
wanted to be," she said, "a man."
I went into the bathroom to see
how I looked in the sheen and
sadness. Wind chimes   20
off-key in the alcove. Then her
crying so I stood back in the sink-light
where the porcelain had been staring. Time
to go to her, I thought, with that
other mind, and stood still.   25

Considerations for Critical Thinking and Writing

1. Why is "Black Silk" an appropriate title?
2. Explain whether you think this poem is sentimental. Why or why not?
3. How are the speaker's emotions revealed? What is she feeling as she observes the other woman?

Connection to Another Selection

1. Write an essay comparing "Black Silk" with Emily Dickinson's "The Bustle in a House" (p. 851).

HOWARD NEMEROV (1920–1991)
The Fourth of July   1958

Because I am drunk, this Independence Night,
I watch the fireworks from far away,
From a high hill, across the moony green
Of lakes and other hills to the town harbor,
Where stately illuminations are flung aloft,   5
One light shattering in a hundred lights
Minute by minute. The reason I am crying,
Aside from only being country drunk,
That is, may be that I have just remembered
The sparklers, rockets, roman candles, and   10
So on, we used to be allowed to buy
When I was a boy, and set off by ourselves
At some peril to life and property.
Our freedom to abuse our freedom thus
Has since, I understand, been remedied   15
By legislation. Now the authorities
Arrange a perfectly safe public display

To be watched at a distance; and now also
The contribution of all the taxpayers
Together makes a more spectacular   20
Result than any could achieve alone
(A few pale pinwheels, or a firecracker
Fused at the dog's tail). It is, indeed, splendid:
Showers of roses in the sky, fountains
Of emeralds, and those profusely scattered zircons   25
Falling and falling, flowering as they fall
And followed distantly by a noise of thunder.
My eyes are half-afloat in happy tears.
God bless our Nation on a night like this,
And bless the careful and secure officials   30
Who celebrate our independence now.

Considerations for Critical Thinking and Writing

1. What is the central irony of this poem?
2. Why do you think Nemerov makes the speaker drunk? How are the speaker's
   reflections affected by his drinking?
3. Write an essay on the idea of freedom expressed in this poem.

Connections to Other Selections

1. Discuss the speakers in "The Fourth of July" and in John Ciardi's "Suburban"
   (p. 701). How do the poets ensure that readers will be sympathetic to the two
   speakers?
2. Write an essay that compares the "careful and secure officials" in Nemerov's poem
   with the public official in e. e. cummings's "next to of course god america i"
   (p. 691). What is the poet's attitude toward officialdom in each work?

PERSPECTIVE

EZRA POUND (1885–1972)
On Symbols   1912

I believe that the proper and perfect symbol is the natural object, that if a
man use "symbols" he must so use them that their symbolic function does not
obtrude; so that *a* sense, and the poetic quality of the passage, is not lost to
those who do not understand the symbol as such, to whom, for instance a hawk
is a hawk.

From "Prolegomena," *Poetry Review,* February 1912

Considerations for Critical Thinking and Writing

1. Discuss whether you agree with Pound that the "perfect symbol" is a "natural object" that does not insist on being read as a symbol.
2. Write an essay in which you discuss Eamon Grennan's "Bat" (p. 650) as an example of the "perfect symbol" Pound proposes.
3. Do you think the poems by Pound in this anthology (see the index) fit his requirements for the way a symbol should function in a poem? Explain why or why not.

18. Sounds

Poems yearn to be read aloud. Much of their energy, charm, and beauty comes to life only when they are heard. Poets choose and arrange words for their sounds as well as for their meanings. Most poetry is best read with your lips, teeth, and tongue, because they serve to articulate the effects that sound may have in a poem. When a voice is breathed into a good poem, there is pleasure in the reading, the saying, and the hearing.

LISTENING TO POETRY

The earliest poetry — before writing and painting — was chanted or sung. The rhythmic quality of such oral performances served two purposes: it helped the chanting bard remember the lines, and it entertained audiences with patterned sounds of language, which were sometimes accompanied by musical instruments. Poetry has always been closely related to music. Indeed, as the word suggests, lyric poetry evolved from songs. "Western Wind" (p. 601), an anonymous Middle English lyric, survived as song long before it was written down. Had Robert Frost lived in a nonliterate society, he probably would have sung some version — a very different version to be sure — of "Acquainted with the Night" (p. 685) instead of writing it down. Even though Frost creates a speaking rather than a singing voice, the speaker's anxious tone is distinctly heard in any careful reading of the poem.

Like lyrics, early narrative poems were originally part of an anonymous oral folk tradition. A *ballad* such as "Bonny Barbara Allan" (p. 922) told a story that was sung from one generation to the next until it was finally transcribed. Since the eighteenth century, this narrative form has sometimes been imitated by poets who write *literary ballads.* John Keats's "La Belle Dame sans Merci" (p. 807) is, for example, a more complex and sophisticated nineteenth-century reflection of the original ballad traditions that developed in the fifteenth century and earlier. In considering poetry as sound, we should not forget that poetry traces its beginnings to song.

These next lines exemplify poetry's continuing relation to song. What poetic elements can you find in this well-known song?

LEONARD COHEN (b. 1934)
Suzanne
1966

Suzanne takes you down
to her place near the river,
you can hear the boats go by
you can stay the night beside her.
And you know that she's half crazy   5
but that's why you want to be there
and she feeds you tea and oranges
that come all the way from China.
Just when you mean to tell her
that you have no gifts to give her,   10
she gets you on her wave-length
and she lets the river answer
that you've always been her lover.
   And you want to travel with her,
   you want to travel blind   15
   and you know that she can trust you
   because you've touched her perfect body
   with your mind.

Jesus was a sailor
when he walked upon the water   20
and he spent a long time watching
from a lonely wooden tower
and when he knew for certain
only drowning men could see him
he said All men will be sailors then   25
until the sea shall free them,
but he himself was broken
long before the sky would open,
forsaken, almost human,
he sank beneath your wisdom like a stone.   30
   And you want to travel with him,
   you want to travel blind
   and you think maybe you'll trust him
   because he touched your perfect body
   with his mind.   35

Now Suzanne takes your hand
and she leads you to the river,
she is wearing rags and feathers
from Salvation Army counters,
and the sun pours down like honey   40
on our lady of the harbour,
and she shows you where to look
among the garbage and the flowers.
There are heroes in the seaweed,
there are children in the morning,   45
they are leaning out for love
and they will lean that way forever
while Suzanne holds the mirror.
    And you want to travel with her,
    you want to travel blind   50
    and you know that you can trust her
    because she's touched your perfect body
    with her mind.

Considerations for Critical Thinking and Writing

1. What parallels are drawn between Jesus and Suzanne in this song? What do the
   images reveal about each of them? Which images are used metaphorically?
2. Who is the "you" of the song?
3. What is indicated by the changing pronouns in lines 17–18, 34–35, and 51–52?
4. What is the tone of this song?
5. Choose a contemporary song that you especially like and examine the lyrics. Write
   an essay explaining whether or not you consider the lyrics poetic.

Of course reading Cohen's "Suzanne" is not the same as hearing it. Like the
lyrics of a song, many poems must be heard — or at least read with listening
eyes — before they can be fully understood and enjoyed. The sounds of
words are a universal source of music for human beings. This has been so
from ancient tribes to bards to the two-year-old child in a bakery gleefully
chanting "Cuppitycake, cuppitycake!"

    Listen to the sound of this poem as you read it aloud. How do the words
provide, in a sense, their own musical accompaniment?

JOHN UPDIKE (b. 1932)
Player Piano   1958

My stick fingers click with a snicker
And, chuckling, they knuckle the keys;
Light-footed, my steel feelers flicker
And pluck from these keys melodies.

My paper can caper; abandon   5
Is broadcast by dint of my din,
And no man or band has a hand in
The tones I turn on from within.

At times I'm a jumble of rumbles,
At others I'm light like the moon,   10
But never my numb plunker fumbles,
Misstrums me, or tries a new tune.

The speaker in this poem is a piano that can play automatically by means of
a mechanism that depresses keys in response to signals on a perforated roll.
Notice how the speaker's voice approximates the sounds of a piano. In each
stanza a predominant sound emerges from the carefully chosen words. How
is the sound of each stanza tuned to its sense?

    Like Updike's "Player Piano," this next poem is also primarily about
sounds.

MAY SWENSON (b. 1919)

A Nosty Fright   1984

The roldengod and the soneyhuckle,
the sack eyed blusan and the wistle theed
are all tangled with the oison pivy,
the fallen nine peedles and the wumbleteed.

A mipchunk caught in a wobceb tried   5
to hip and skide in a dandy sune
but a stobler put up a EEP KOFF sign.
Then the unfucky lellow met a phytoon

and was sept out to swea. He difted for drays
till a hassgropper flying happened to spot   10
the boolish feast all debraggled and wet,
covered with snears and tot.

Loonmight shone through the winey poods
where rushmooms grew among risted twoots.
Back blats flew betreen the twees   15
and orned howls hounded their soots.

A kumkpin stood with tooked creeth
on the sindow will of a house
where a icked wold itch lived all alone
except for her stoombrick, a mitten and a kouse.   20

"Here we part," said hassgropper.
"Pere we hart," said mipchunk, too.

They purried away on opposite haths,
both scared of some "Bat!" or "Scoo!"

October was ending on a nosty fright   25
with scroans and greeches and chanking clains,
with oblins and gelfs, coaths and urses,
skinning grulls and stoodblains.

Will it ever be morning, Nofember virst,
skue bly and the snappy hun, our friend?   30
With light breaves of wall by the fayside?
I sope ho, so that this oem can pend.

At just the right moments Swenson transposes letters to create amusing
sound effects and wild wordplays. Although there is a story lurking in "A
Nosty Fright," any serious attempt to interpret its meaning is confronted with
"a EEP KOFF sign." Instead, we are invited to enjoy the delicious sounds the
poet has cooked up.

Few poems revel in sound so completely. More typically, the sounds of
a poem contribute to its meaning rather than become its meaning. Consider
how sound is used in this next poem.

EMILY DICKINSON (1830–1886)
A Bird came down the Walk —   c. 1862

A Bird came down the Walk —
He did not know I saw —
He bit an Angleworm in halves
And ate the fellow, raw,

And then he drank a Dew   5
From a convenient Grass —
And then hopped sidewise to the Wall
To let a Beetle pass —

He glanced with rapid eyes
That hurried all around —   10
They looked like frightened Beads, I thought —
He stirred his Velvet Head

Like one in danger, Cautious,
I offered him a Crumb
And he unrolled his feathers   15
And rowed him softer home —

Than Oars divide the Ocean,
Too silver for a seam —

Or Butterflies, off Banks of Noon
Leap, plashless as they swim.   20

    This description of a bird offers a close look at how differently a bird moves when it hops on the ground than when it flies in the air. On the ground the bird moves quickly, awkwardly, and irregularly as it plucks up a worm, washes it down with dew, and then hops aside to avoid a passing beetle. The speaker recounts the bird's rapid, abrupt actions from a some-what superior, amused perspective. By describing the bird in human terms (as if, for example, it chose to eat the worm "raw"), the speaker is almost condescending. But when the attempt to offer a crumb fails and the fright-ened bird flies off, the speaker is left looking up instead of down at the bird.

    With that shift in perspective the tone shifts from amusement to awe in response to the bird's graceful flight. The jerky movements of lines 1–13 give way to the smooth motion of lines 15–20. The pace of the first three stanzas is fast and discontinuous. We tend to pause at the end of each line, and this reinforces a sense of disconnected movements. In contrast, the final six lines are to be read as a single sentence in one flowing movement, lubricated by various sounds.

    Read again the description of the bird flying away. Several o-sounds contribute to the image of the serene, expansive, confident flight, just as the s-sounds serve as smooth transitions from one line to the next. Notice how these sounds are grouped in the following vertical columns:

unrolled	softer	too	his	Ocean	Banks
rowed	Oars	Noon	feathers	silver	plashless
home	Or		softer	seam	as
Ocean	off		Oars	Butterflies	swim

This blending of sounds (notice how "Leap, plashless" brings together the p- and l-sounds without a ripple) helps convey the bird's smooth grace in the air. Like a feathered oar, the bird moves seamlessly in its element.

    The repetition of sounds in poetry is similar to the function of the tones and melodies that are repeated, with variations, in music. Just as the patterned sounds in music unify a work, so do the words in poems, which have been carefully chosen for the combinations of sounds they create. These sounds are produced in a number of ways.

    The most direct way in which the sound of a word suggests its meaning is through *onomatopoeia,* which is the use of a word that resembles the sound it denotes: *quack, buzz, rattle, bang, squeak, bowwow, burp, choo-choo, ding-a-ling, sizzle.* The sound and sense of these words are closely related, but they represent a very small percentage of the words available to us. Poets usually employ more subtle means for echoing meanings.

    Onomatopoeia can consist of more than just single words. In its broadest meaning the term refers to lines or passages in which sounds help to convey meanings, as in these lines from Updike's "Player Piano."

My stick fingers click with a snicker
And, chuckling, they knuckle the keys.

The sharp crisp sounds of these two lines approximate the sounds of a piano; the syllables seem to "click" against one another. Contrast Updike's rendition with the following lines:

My long fingers play with abandon
And, laughing, they cover the keys.

The original version is more interesting and alive, because the sounds of the words are pleasurable and reinforce the meaning through a careful blending of consonants and vowels.

Alliteration is the repetition of the same consonant sounds at the beginnings of nearby words: "*d*escending *d*ewdrops"; "*l*uscious *l*emons." Sometimes the term is also used to describe the consonant sounds within words: "tres*p*asser's re*p*roach"; "we*dd*ed la*d*y." Alliteration is based on sound rather than spelling. "*K*ean" and "*c*ar" alliterate, but "*c*ar" does not alliterate with "*c*ite." Rarely is heavy-handed alliteration effective. Used too self-consciously, it can be distracting instead of strengthening meaning or emphasizing a relation between words. Consider the relentless *h*'s in this line: "*H*orrendous *h*orrors *h*aunted *H*elen's *h*appiness." Those *h*'s certainly suggest that Helen is being pursued, but they have a more comic than serious effect because they are overdone.

Assonance is the repetition of the same vowel sound in nearby words: "asl*ee*p under a tr*ee*"; "t*i*me and t*i*de"; "h*au*nt" and "*aw*esome"; "*ea*ch *e*vening." Both alliteration and assonance help to establish relations among words in a line or a series of lines. Whether the effect is *euphony* — lines that are musically pleasant to the ear and smooth, like the final lines of Dickinson's "A Bird came down the Walk — " — or the effect is *cacophony* — lines that are discordant and difficult to pronounce, like the claim that "never my numb plunker fumbles" in Updike's "Player Piano" — the sounds of words in poetry can be as significant as the words' denotative or connotative meanings.

This next poem provides a feast of sounds. Read the poem aloud and try to determine the effects of its sounds.

GALWAY KINNELL (b. 1927)

Blackberry Eating   1980

I love to go out in late September
among the fat, overripe, icy, black blackberries
to eat blackberries for breakfast,
the stalks very prickly, a penalty
they earn for knowing the black art   5

of blackberry-making; and as I stand among them
lifting the stalks to my mouth, the ripest berries
fall almost unbidden to my tongue,
as words sometimes do, certain peculiar words
like *strengths* or *squinched,*   10
many-lettered, one-syllabled lumps,
which I squeeze, squinch open, and splurge well
in the silent, startled, icy, black language
of blackberry-eating in late September.

Considerations for Critical Thinking and Writing

1. Underline the alliteration and circle the assonance throughout this poem. What is
   the effect of these sounds?
2. How do lines 4–6 fit into the poem? What does this prickly image add to the
   poem?
3. Explain what you think the poem's theme is.
4. Write an essay that considers the speaker's love of blackberry eating along with
   the speaker's appetite for words. How are the two blended in the poem?

RHYME

Like alliteration and assonance, *rhyme* is a way of creating sound patterns. Rhyme, broadly defined, consists of two or more words or phrases
that repeat the same sounds: *happy* and *snappy.* Rhyme words often have
similar spellings, but that is not a requirement of rhyme; what matters is that
the words sound alike: *vain* rhymes with *reign* as well as *rain.* Moreover,
words may look alike but not rhyme at all. In *eye rhyme* the spellings are
similar but the pronunciations are not, as with *bough* and *cough,* or *brow*
and *blow.*

Not all poems employ rhyme. Many great poems have no rhymes, and
many weak verses use rhyme as a substitute for poetry. These are especially
apparent in commercial messages and greeting-card lines. At its worst, rhyme
is merely a distracting decoration that can lead to dullness and predictability.
But used skillfully, rhyme creates lines that are memorable and musical.

Following is a poem using rhyme that you might remember the next
time you are in a restaurant.

RICHARD ARMOUR (1906–1989)
Going to Extremes   1954

Shake and shake
   The catsup bottle
None'll come —
   And then a lot'll.

     The experience recounted in Armour's poem is common enough, but
the rhyme's humor is special. The final line clicks the poem shut, an effect
that is often achieved by the use of rhyme. That click provides a sense of a
satisfying and fulfilled form. Rhymes have a number of uses: they can emphasize words, direct a reader's attention to relations between words, and
provide an overall structure for a poem.
     Rhyme is used in the following poem to imitate the sound of cascading
water.

ROBERT SOUTHEY (1774–1843)
From *The Cataract of Lodore*   1820

    "How does the water
    Come down at Lodore?"
. . . .
   From its sources which well
   In the tarn on the fell;
     From its fountains   5
     In the mountains,
   Its rills and its gills;
Through moss and through brake,
    It runs and it creeps
    For awhile, till it sleeps   10
    In its own little lake.
   And thence at departing,
   Awakening and starting,
   It runs through the reeds
    And away it proceeds,   15
  Through meadow and glade,
    In sun and in shade,
And through the wood-shelter,
  Among crags in its flurry,
    Helter-skelter,   20
    Hurry-scurry.

Here it comes sparkling,
And there it lies darkling;
Now smoking and frothing
Its tumult and wrath in,   25
Till in this rapid race
    On which it is bent,
It reaches the place
    Of its steep descent.

The cataract strong   30
Then plunges along,
Striking and raging
As if a war waging
Its caverns and rocks among:
    Rising and leaping,   35
Sinking and creeping,
Swelling and sweeping,
Showering and springing,
    Flying and flinging,
Writhing and ringing,   40
Eddying and whisking,
Spouting and frisking,
Turning and twisting,
    Around and around
With endless rebound!   45
Smiting and fighting,
    A sight to delight in;
Confounding, astounding,
Dizzying and deafening the ear with its sound.
. . . .

Dividing and gliding and sliding,   50
And falling and brawling and spawling,
And driving and riving and striving,
And sprinkling and twinkling and wrinkling,
And sounding and bounding and rounding,
And bubbling and troubling and doubling,   55
And grumbling and rumbling and tumbling,
And clattering and battering and shattering;
Retreating and beating and meeting and sheeting,
Delaying and straying and playing and spraying,
Advancing and prancing and glancing and dancing,   60
Recoiling, turmoiling and toiling and boiling,
And gleaming and streaming and steaming and beaming,
And rushing and flushing and brushing and gushing,
And flapping and rapping and clapping and slapping,
And curling and whirling and purling and twirling,   65
And thumping and plumping and bumping and jumping,
And dashing and flashing and splashing and clashing;

And so never ending, but always descending,
Sounds and motions forever and ever are blending,
All at once and all o'er, with a mighty uproar;   70
And this way the water comes down at Lodore.

This deluge of rhymes consists of "Sounds and motions forever and ever . . . blending" (line 69). The pace quickens as the water creeps from its mountain source and then descends in rushing cataracts. As the speed of the water increases, so do the number of rhymes, until they run in fours: "dashing and flashing and splashing and clashing." Most rhymes meander through poems instead of flooding them; nevertheless, Southey's use of rhyme suggests how sounds can flow with meanings. "The Cataract of Lodore" has been criticized, however, for overusing onomatopoeia. Some readers find the poem silly; others regard it as a brilliant example of sound effects. What do you think?

A variety of types of rhyme is available to poets. The most common form, **end rhyme,** comes at the ends of lines.

It runs through the reeds
    And away it proceeds,
Through meadow and glade,
    In sun and in shade.

Internal rhyme places at least one of the rhymed words within the line, as in "Dividing and gliding and sliding" or, more subtly, in the fourth and final words of "In mist or cloud, on mast or shroud."

The rhyming of single-syllable words such as *grade* and *shade* is known as **masculine rhyme.**

Loveliest of trees, the cherry now
Is hung with bloom along the bough.
                    –A. E. Housman

Rhymes using words of more than one syllable are also called masculine when the same sound occurs in a final stressed syllable, as in *defend, contend; betray, away.* A *feminine rhyme* consists of a rhymed stressed syllable followed by one or more rhymed unstressed syllables, as in *butter, clutter; gratitude, attitude; quivering, shivering.*

Lord confound this surly sister,
Blight her brow and blotch and blister.
                    –John Millington Synge

All the examples so far have been **exact rhymes,** because they share the same stressed vowel sounds as well as any sounds that follow the vowel. In **near rhyme** (also called *off rhyme, slant rhyme,* and *approximate rhyme*), the sounds are almost but not exactly alike. There are several kinds of near rhyme. One of the most common is **consonance,** an identical consonant sound preceded by a different vowel sound: *home, same; worth,* *breath; trophy, daffy.* Near rhyme can also be achieved by using different vowel sounds with identical consonant sounds: *sound, sand; kind, conned; fellow, fallow.* The dissonance of *blade* and *blood* in the following lines helps to reinforce their grim tone.

> Let the boy try along this bayonet-blade
> How cold steel is, and keen with hunger of blood.
> –Wilfred Owen

Near rhymes greatly broaden the possibility for musical effects in English, a language that, compared with Spanish or Italian, contains few exact rhymes. Do not assume, however, that a near rhyme represents a failed attempt at exact rhyme. Near rhymes allow a musical subtlety and variety, and can avoid the sometimes overpowering jingling effects that exact rhymes may create.

These basic terms hardly exhaust the ways in which the sound in poems can be labeled and discussed, but the terms can help you to describe how poets manipulate sounds for effect. Read "God's Grandeur" (p. 720) aloud and try to determine how the sounds of the lines contribute to their sense.

PERSPECTIVE

DAVID LENSON (b. 1945)
On the Contemporary Use of Rhyme   1988

One impediment to a respectable return to rhyme is the popular survival of "functional" verse; greeting cards, pedagogical and mnemonic devices ("Thirty days hath September"), nursery rhymes, advertising jingles, and of course song lyrics. Pentameters, irregular rhymes, and free verse aren't much use in songwriting, where the meter has to be governed by the time signature of the music.

Far from universities, there has been a revival of rhymed couplets in Rap music, in which, to the accompaniment of synthesizers, vocalists deliver lengthy first-person narratives in tetrameter. While most writing teachers would dismiss such lyrics as doggerel, the aim of the songs is really not so far from that of Alexander Pope: to use rhyme to sharpen social insight, in the hope that the world may be reordered.

From *The Chronicle of Higher Education,* February 24, 1988

Considerations for Critical Thinking and Writing

1. Read some contemporary song lyrics from a wide range of groups or vocalists. Is Lenson correct in his assessment that irregular rhyme is not much use in songwriting?

2. Examine the rhymed couplets of some rap music. Discuss whether they are used "to sharpen social insight." What is the effect of using rhymes in rap music?
3. What is your own response to rhymed poetry? Do you like yours with or without? What do you think informs your preference?

SOUND AND MEANING

GERARD MANLEY HOPKINS (1844–1889)
God's Grandeur   1877

The world is charged with the grandeur of God
    It will flame out, like shining from shook foil;°   *shaken gold foil*
    It gathers to a greatness, like the ooze of oil
Crushed.° Why do men then now not reck his rod?°
Generations have trod, have trod, have trod;   5
    And all is seared with trade; bleared, smeared with toil;
    And wears man's smudge and shares man's smell: the soil
Is bare now, nor can foot feel, being shod.

And for all this, nature is never spent;
    There lives the dearest freshness deep down things;   10
And though the last lights off the black West went
    Oh, morning, at the brown brink eastward, springs —
Because the Holy Ghost over the bent
    World broods with warm breast and with ah! bright wings.

4 *Crushed:* Olives crushed in their oil; *reck his rod:* Obey God.

    The subject of this poem is announced in the title and the first line: "The world is charged with the grandeur of God." The poem is a celebration of the power and greatness of God's presence in the world, but the speaker is also perplexed and dismayed by people who refuse to recognize God's authority and grandeur as they are manifested in the creation. Instead of glorifying God, "men" have degraded the earth through meaningless toil and cut themselves off from the spiritual renewal inherent in the beauty of nature. The relentless demands of commerce and industry have blinded people to the earth's natural and spiritual resources. In spite of this abuse and insensitivity to God's grandeur, however, "nature is never spent"; the morning light that "springs" in the east redeems the "black West" of the night and is a sign that the spirit of the Holy Ghost is ever present in the world. This summary of the poem sketches some of the thematic significance of the lines, but it does not do justice to how they are organized around the use of sound. Hopkins's poem, unlike Southey's "The Cataract of Lodore," employs sounds in a subtle and complex way.
    In the opening line Hopkins uses alliteration — a device apparent in

almost every line of the poem — to connect "Go*d*" to the "worl*d*," which is "charge*d*" with his "gran*d*eur." These consonants unify the line as well. The alliteration in lines 2–3 suggests a harmony in the creation: the *f*'s in "*f*lame" and "*f*oil," the *sh*'s in "*sh*ining" and "*sh*ook," the *g*'s in "*g*athers" and "*g*reatness," and the visual (not alliterative) similarities of "*ooze of oil*" emphasize a world that is held together by God's will.

That harmony is abruptly interrupted by the speaker's angry question in line 4: "Why do men then now not reck his rod?" The question is as painful to the speaker as it is difficult to pronounce. The arrangement of the alliteration ("*n*ow," "*n*ot"; "*r*eck," "*r*od"), the assonance ("n*o*t," "r*o*d"; "m*e*n," "th*e*n," "r*e*ck"), and the internal rhyme ("m*en*," "th*en*") contribute to the difficulty in saying the line, a difficulty associated with human behavior. That behavior is introduced in line 5 by the repetition of "have trod" to emphasize the repeated mistakes — sins — committed by human beings. The tone is dirgelike because humanity persists in its mistaken path rather than progressing. The speaker's horror at humanity is evident in the cacophonous sounds of lines 6–8. Here the alliteration of "*sm*eared," "*sm*udge," and "*sm*ell" along with the internal rhymes of "s*eared*," "bl*eared*," and "sm*eared*" echo the disgust with which the speaker views human's "toil" with the "soil," an end rhyme that calls attention to our mistaken equation of nature with production rather than with spirituality.

In contrast to this cacophony, the final six lines build toward the joyful recognition of the new possibilities that accompany the rising sun. This recognition leads to the euphonic description of the "H*o*ly Gh*o*st *o*ver" (notice the reassuring consistency of the assonance) the world. Traditionally represented as a dove, the Holy Ghost brings love and peace to the "*w*orld," and "*b*roods *w*ith *w*arm *br*east and *w*ith ah! *br*ight *w*ings." The effect of this alliteration is mellifluous: the sound bespeaks the harmony that prevails at the end of the poem resulting from the speaker's recognition that nature can "never [be] spent" because God loves and protects the world.

The sounds of "God's Grandeur" enhance the poem's theme; more can be said about its sounds, but it is enough to point out here that for this poem the sound strongly echoes the theme in nearly every line. Here are some more poems in which sound plays a significant role.

POEMS FOR FURTHER STUDY

ALICE WALKER (b. 1944)
Revolutionary Petunias 1972

Sammy Lou of Rue
sent to his reward
the exact creature who

murdered her husband,
using a cultivator's hoe   5
with verve and skill;
and laughed fit to kill
in disbelief
at the angry, militant
pictures of herself   10
the Sonneteers quickly drew:
not any of them people that
she knew.
A backwoods woman
her house was papered with   15
funeral home calendars and
faces appropriate for a Mississippi
Sunday School. She raised a George,
a Martha, a Jackie and a Kennedy. Also
a John Wesley° Junior.   20
"Always respect the word of God,"
she said on her way to she didn't
know where, except it would be by
electric chair, and she continued
"Don't yall forget to *water*   25
my purple petunias."

20 *John Wesley* (1730–1791): The British founder of Methodism.

Considerations for Critical Thinking and Writing

1. Identify the kinds of rhyme that appear in the poem.
2. How do the rhymes contribute to the poem's effect? How would your reading of
   the poem be different if all the rhymed words were replaced by words that did
   not rhyme?
3. Describe what you take to be the themes of the poem. How is the title related to
   the themes?

LEWIS CARROLL
[CHARLES LUTWIDGE DODGSON] (1832–1898)
Jabberwocky   1871

'Twas brillig, and the slithy toves
    Did gyre and gimble in the wabe:
All mimsy were the borogoves,
    And the mome raths outgrabe.

"Beware the Jabberwock, my son!   5
    The jaws that bite, the claws that catch!

Beware the Jubjub bird, and shun
    The frumious Bandersnatch!"

He took his vorpal sword in hand;
    Long time the manxome foe he sought —   10
So rested he by the Tumtum tree,
    And stood awhile in thought.

And, as in uffish thought he stood,
    The Jabberwock, with eyes of flame,
Came whiffling through the tulgey wood,   15
    And burbled as it came!

One, two! One, two! And through and through
    The vorpal blade went snicker-snack!
He left it dead, and with its head
    He went galumphing back.   20

"And hast thou slain the Jabberwock?
    Come to my arms, my beamish boy!
O frabjous day! Callooh, Callay!"
    He chortled in his joy.

'Twas brillig, and the slithy toves   25
    Did gyre and gimble in the wabe:
All mimsy were the borogoves,
    And the mome raths outgrabe.

Considerations for Critical Thinking and Writing

1. What happens in this poem? Does it have any meaning?
2. Not all the words used in this poem appear in dictionaries. In *Through the Looking Glass*, Humpty Dumpty explains to Alice that " 'slithy' means 'lithe and slimy.' 'Lithe' is the same as 'active.' You see it's like a portmanteau — there are two meanings packed up into one word." Are there any other portmanteau words in the poem?
3. Which words in the poem sound especially meaningful, even if they are devoid of any denotative meanings?

Connections to Other Selections

1. Compare Carroll's strategies for creating sound and meaning with those used by Swenson in "A Nosty Fright" (p. 711).
2. Write an essay comparing what Robert Francis says about the words of a poem in "Glass" (p. 1066) with Carroll's use of words. Discuss whether you think the two poets more or less agree or disagree in their respective approaches to writing poetry.
3. Read Marcus's "What Is an Initiation Story?" (p. 574). Consider whether the theme of "Jabberwocky" can (and should) be discussed in terms of an initiation story.

JEAN TOOMER (1894–1967)
Reapers

1923

Black reapers with the sound of steel on stones
Are sharpening scythes. I see them place the hones
In their hip-pockets as a thing that's done,
And start their silent swinging, one by one.
Black horses drive a mower through the weeds,
And there, a field rat, startled, squealing bleeds,
His belly close to ground. I see the blade,
Blood-stained, continue cutting weeds and shade.

Considerations for Critical Thinking and Writing

1. Is this poem primarily about harvesting, or does it suggest something else? Are there any symbols?
2. What is the poem's tone?
3. The reapers' work is described alliteratively as "silent swinging." How are the alliteration and assonance of lines 1–2 and 6 related to their meaning?
4. Why is Toomer's version of line 6 more effective than this one: "And there a startled, squealing field rat bleeds"?

JOHN DONNE (1572–1631)
Song

1633

Go and catch a falling star
   Get with child a mandrake root,°
Tell me where all past years are,
   Or who cleft the Devil's foot,
Teach me to hear mermaids singing,   5
   Or to keep off envy's stinging,
        And find
        What wind
Serves to advance an honest mind.

If thou be'st borne to strange sights,   10
   Things invisible to see,
Ride ten thousand days and nights,
   Till age snow white hairs on thee,
Thou, when thou return'st, wilt tell me
   All strange wonders that befell thee,   15
        And swear
        Nowhere
Lives a woman true, and fair.

2 *mandrake root:* This V-shaped root resembles the lower half of the human body.

If thou findst one, let me know,
    Such a pilgrimage were sweet —
Yet do not, I would not go,
    Though at next door we might meet;
Though she were true, when you met her,
    And last, till you write your letter,
        Yet she
        Will be
False, ere I come, to two or three.

20

25

Considerations for Critical Thinking and Writing

1. What is the speaker's tone in this poem? What is his view of a woman's love? What does the speaker's use of hyperbole reveal about his emotional state?
2. Do you think Donne wants the speaker's argument to be taken seriously? Is there any humor in the poem?
3. Most of these lines end with masculine rhymes. What other kinds of rhymes are used for end rhymes?

JUDY GRAHN (b. 1940)
She Who bears it

1972

She Who bears it
bear down, breathe
bear down, bear down, breathe
bear down, bear down, bear down, breathe

She Who lies down in the darkness and bears it   5
She Who lies down in the lightness and bears it
the labor of She Who carries and bears is the first labor

all over the world
the waters are breaking everywhere
everywhere the waters are breaking   10
the labor of She Who carries and bears
and raises and rears is the first labor,
there is no other first labor.

Considerations for Critical Thinking and Writing

1. How do the sounds of this poem contribute to its sense of urgency?
2. What is the effect of the repeated words and phrases? How is that repetition related to what happens in the poem?
3. What do you think is the meaning of the phrase "the first labor" in line 7? How does the phrase take on additional meanings in lines 12 and 13?

THOMAS HARDY (1840–1928)

The Oxen 1915

Christmas Eve, and twelve of the clock.
    "Now they are all on their knees,"
An elder said as we sat in a flock
    By the embers in hearthside ease.

We pictured the meek mild creatures where   5
    They dwelt in their strawy pen,
Nor did it occur to one of us there
    To doubt they were kneeling then.

So fair a fancy few would weave
    In these years! Yet, I feel,   10
If someone said on Christmas Eve,
    "Come; see the oxen kneel

"In the lonely barton° by yonder coomb°   *farmyard; ravine*
    Our childhood used to know,"
I should go with him in the gloom,   15
    Hoping it might be so.

Considerations for Critical Thinking and Writing

1. Traditionally, European peasants believed that animals worship God on Christmas Eve. How does the speaker feel about this belief? What is the difference between the speaker's attitude as a child and, "In these years," as an adult?
2. The speaker seems to feel nostalgic about his lost childhood. Does he feel the loss of anything more than that?
3. How do the sounds in the final stanza reinforce the tone and theme of the poem?

ALEXANDER POPE (1688–1774)

From *An Essay on Criticism* 1711

    But most by numbers° judge a poet's song;   *versification*
And smooth or rough, with them, is right or wrong;
In the bright muse though thousand charms conspire,
Her voice is all these tuneful fools admire;
Who haunt Parnassus° but to please their ear,   5
Not mend their minds; as some to church repair,
Not for the doctrine, but the music there.
These equal syllables alone require,
Though oft the ear the open vowels tire;

5 *Parnassus:* A Greek mountain sacred to the Muses.

While expletives° their feeble aid do join; 10
And ten low words oft creep in one dull line;
While they ring round the same unvaried chimes,
With sure returns of still expected rhymes;
Where'er you find "the cooling western breeze,"
In the next line, it "whispers through the trees": 15
If crystal streams "with pleasing murmurs creep,"
The reader's threatened (not in vain) with "sleep":
Then, at the last and only couplet fraught
With some unmeaning thing they call a thought,
A needless Alexandrine° ends the song, 20
That, like a wounded snake, drags its slow length along.
Leave such to tune their own dull rhymes, and know
What's roundly smooth, or languishingly slow;
And praise the easy vigor of a line,
Where Denham's strength, and Waller's° sweetness join. 25
True ease in writing comes from art, not chance,
As those move easiest who have learned to dance.
'Tis not enough no harshness gives offense,
The sound must seem an echo to the sense:
Soft is the strain when Zephyr° gently blows,   *the west wind*   30
And the smooth stream in smoother numbers flows;
But when loud surges lash the sounding shore,
The hoarse, rough verse should like the torrent roar:
When Ajax° strives some rock's vast weight to throw,
The line too labors, and the words move slow; 35
Not so, when swift Camilla° scours the plain,
Flies o'er th' unbending corn, and skims along the main.

10 *expletives:* Unnecessary words used to fill a line, as the *do* in this line.   20 *Alexandrine:* A twelve-syllable line, as line 21.   25 *Denham's, Waller's:* Sir John Denham (1615–1669), Edmund Waller (1606–1687) were poets who used heroic couplets.   34 *Ajax:* A Greek warrior famous for his strength in the Trojan War.   36 *Camilla:* A goddess famous for her delicate speed.

Considerations for Critical Thinking and Writing

1. These lines make a case for sound as an important element in poetry. In them Pope describes some faults he finds in poems and illustrates those faults within the lines that describe them. How do lines 4, 9, 10, 11, and 21 illustrate what they describe?

2. What is the objection to the "expected rhymes" in lines 12–17? How do they differ from Pope's end rhymes?

3. Some lines discuss how to write successful poetry. How do lines 23, 24, 32–33, 35, and 36–37 illustrate what they describe?

4. Do you agree that in a good poem "The sound must [always] seem an echo to the sense"?

RICHARD WILBUR (b. 1921)

Year's End   1950

Now winter downs the dying of the year,
And night is all a settlement of snow;
From the soft street the rooms of houses show
A gathered light, a shapen atmosphere,
Like frozen-over lakes whose ice is thin   5
And still allows some stirring down within.

I've known the wind by water banks to shake
The late leaves down, which frozen where they fell
And held in ice as dancers in a spell
Fluttered all winter long into a lake;   10
Graved on the dark in gestures of descent,
They seemed their own most perfect monument.

There was perfection in the death of ferns
Which laid their fragile cheeks against the stone
A million years. Great mammoths overthrown   15
Composedly have made their long sojourns,
Like palaces of patience, in the gray
And changeless lands of ice. And at Pompeii°

The little dog lay curled and did not rise
But slept the deeper as the ashes rose   20
And found the people incomplete, and froze
The random hands, the loose unready eyes
Of men expecting yet another sun
To do the shapely thing they had not done.

These sudden ends of time must give us pause.   25
We fray into the future, rarely wrought
Save in the tapestries of afterthought.
More time, more time. Barrages of applause
Come muffled from a buried radio.
The New-year bells are wrangling with the snow.   30

18 *Pompeii:* A Roman city buried by the eruption of Mount Vesuvius (79 A.D.).

Considerations for Critical Thinking and Writing

1. Identify the internal rhymes in the poem. How do they affect your reading of the lines in which they appear?
2. How does Wilbur's use of such rhyme reinforce meaning?
3. Explain why the tone of this poem is appropriate to the subject.
4. How is the speaker's sense of time woven into the poem? How does it compare with your own sense of time?

MARIANNE MOORE (1887–1972)

The Fish   1924

wade
through black jade.
   Of the crow-blue mussel shells, one keeps
   adjusting the ash heaps;
      opening and shutting itself like   5

an
injured fan.
   The branches which encrust the side
   of the wave, cannot hide
      there for the submerged shafts of the   10

sun,
split like spun
   glass, move themselves with spotlight swiftness
   into the crevices —
      in and out, illuminating   15

the
torquoise sea
   of bodies. The water drives a wedge
   of iron through the iron edge
      of the cliff; whereupon the stars,   20

pink
rice-grains, ink-
   bespattered jellyfish, crabs like green
   lilies, and submarine
      toadstools, slide each on the other.   25

All
external
   marks of abuse are present on this
   defiant edifice —
      all the physical features of   30

ac-
cident — lack
   of cornice, dynamite grooves, burns, and
   hatchet strokes, these things stand
      out on it; the chasm side is   35

dead.
Repeated
   evidence has proved that it can live
   on what can not revive
      its youth. The sea grows old in it.   40

Considerations for Critical Thinking and Writing

1. This poem is not conventionally shaped the way, for example, Thomas Hardy's "The Oxen" (p. 726) looks on a page. It does, however, have a symmetrical shape. How would you describe that shape?
2. How do the sounds in each stanza help to convey the stanzas' meanings?
3. Describe the poem's tone.
4. Comment on the appropriateness of the title. What alternative titles would suggest the poem's themes?

Connection to Another Selection

1. Write an essay that compares the themes of this poem and Elizabeth Bishop's "The Fish" (p. 595).

PAUL HUMPHREY (b. 1915)
Blow   1983

Her skirt was lofted by the gale;
When I, with gesture deft,
Essayed to stay her frisky sail
She luffed, and laughed, and left.

Considerations for Critical Thinking and Writing

1. Point out instances of alliteration and assonance in this poem, and explain how they contribute to its euphonic effects.
2. What is the poem's controlling metaphor? Why is it especially appropriate?
3. Explain the ambiguity of the title.

ROBERT FRANCIS (1901–1987)
The Pitcher   1953

His art is eccentricity, his aim
How not to hit the mark he seems to aim at,

His passion how to avoid the obvious,
His technique how to vary the avoidance.

The others throw to be comprehended. He   5
Throws to be a moment misunderstood.

Yet not too much. Not errant, arrant, wild,
But every seeming aberration willed.

Not to, yet still, still to communicate
Making the batter understand too late.   10

Considerations for Critical Thinking and Writing

1. Explain how each pair of lines in this poem describes the pitcher's art.
2. Consider how the poem itself works the way a good pitcher does. Which lines illustrate what they describe?
3. Comment on the effects of the poem's rhymes. How are the final two lines different in their rhyme from the previous lines? How does sound echo sense in lines 9–10?
4. Write an essay that considers "The Pitcher" as an extended metaphor for talking about poetry. How well does the poem characterize strategies for writing poetry as well as pitching?
5. Write an essay that develops an extended comparison between writing or reading poetry and playing or watching another sport.

Connections to Other Selections

1. Compare this poem with Robert Wallace's "The Double-Play" (p. 1010), another poem that explores the relation of baseball to poetry.
2. Write an essay comparing "The Pitcher" with Francis's "Glass" (p. 1066). One poem defines poetry implicitly, the other defines it explicitly. Which poem do you prefer? Why?

HELEN CHASIN (b. 1938)
The Word Plum
1968

The word *plum* is delicious

pout and push, luxury of
self-love, and savoring murmur

full in the mouth and falling
like fruit   5

taut skin
pierced, bitten, provoked into
juice, and tart flesh

question
and reply, lip and tongue   10
of pleasure.

Considerations for Critical Thinking and Writing

1. Underline the alliteration and circle the assonance throughout the poem. What is the effect of these repetitions?
2. Which sounds in the poem are like the sounds one makes while eating a plum?
3. Discuss the title. Explain whether you think this poem is more about the word *plum* or about the plum itself. Consider whether the two can be separated in the poem.

Connection to Another Selection

1. How is Kinnell's "Blackberry Eating" (p. 714) similar in technique to Chasin's poem? Try writing such a poem yourself: choose a food to describe that allows you to evoke its sensuousness in sounds.

RUTH PORRITT (b. 1957)

Read This Poem from the Bottom Up

This simple cathedral of praise.
How you made, from the bottom up,
Is for you to remember
Of Andromeda.° What remains

Until you meet the ancient light   5
With your sight you can keep ascending
Its final transformation into space.
And uphold

The horizon's urge to sculpt the sky
Puts into relief   10
Your family's mountain land
Upon the rising air. In the distance

A windward falcon is open high and steady
Far above the tallest tree
Just beyond your height.   15
You see a young pine lifting its green spire

By raising your eyes
Out onto the roof deck.
You pass through sliding glass doors
And up to where the stairway ends.   20

To the top of the penultimate stanza
Past the second story,
But now you're going the other way,
Line by line, to the bottom of the page.

A force that usually pulls you down,   25
Of moving against the gravity of habit,
While trying not to notice the effort
And feel what it's like to climb stairs

4 *Andromeda:* A constellation named after the daughter of Cepheus and Cassiopeia in Greek mythology who was saved from a sea monster by Perseus, her future husband. After her death, she was placed among the stars.

Considerations for Critical Thinking and Writing

1. Write this poem from the last line to the first — from the bottom up. How do the two versions complement each other? Describe the physical movement in the poems.
2. Read each version aloud. How do they sound different? Explain why.
3. Comment on the purpose and theme of the poem.
4. How important is the title?

19. Patterns of Rhythm

The rhythms of everyday life surround us in regularly recurring movements and sounds. As you read these words, your heart pulsates while somewhere else a clock ticks, a cradle rocks, a drum beats, a dancer sways, a foghorn blasts, a wave recedes, or a child skips. We may tend to overlook rhythm since it is so tightly woven into the fabric of our experience, but it is there nonetheless, one of the conditions of life. Rhythm is also one of the conditions of speech, because the voice alternately rises and falls as words are stressed or unstressed and as the pace quickens or slackens. In poetry *rhythm* refers to the recurrence of stressed and unstressed sounds. Depending upon how the sounds are arranged, this can result in a pace that is fast or slow, choppy or smooth.

SOME PRINCIPLES OF METER

Poets use rhythm to create pleasurable sound patterns and to reinforce meanings. "Rhythm," Edith Sitwell once observed, "might be described as, to the world of sound, what light is to the world of sight. It shapes and gives new meaning." Prose can use rhythm effectively too, but prose that does so tends to be more of an exception. The following exceptional lines are from a speech by Winston Churchill to the House of Commons after Allied forces lost a great battle to German forces at Dunkirk during World War II.

> We shall not flag or fail. We shall go on to the end. We shall fight in France, we shall fight on the seas and oceans, we shall fight with growing confidence and growing strength in the air, we shall defend our island, whatever the cost may be, we shall fight on the beaches, we shall fight on the landing grounds, we shall fight in the fields and in the streets, we shall fight in the hills; we shall never surrender.

The stressed repetition of "we shall" bespeaks the resolute singleness of purpose that Churchill had to convey to the British people if they were to win the war. Repetition is also one of the devices used in poetry to create rhythmic effects. In the following excerpt from "Song of the Open Road," Walt Whitman urges the pleasures of limitless freedom upon his reader.

> Allons!° the road is before us! *Let's go!*
> It is safe — I have tried it — my own feet have tried it well — be not de-
>   tain'd!
> Let the paper remain on the desk unwritten, and the book on the shelf
>   unopen'd!
> Let the tools remain in the workshop! Let the money remain unearn'd!
> Let the school stand! mind not the cry of the teacher! 5
> Let the preacher preach in his pulpit! Let the lawyer plead in the court,
>   and the judge expound the law.
>
> Camerado,° I give you my hand! *friend*
> I give you my love more precious than money,
> I give you myself before preaching or law;
> Will you give me yourself? will you come travel with me? 10
> Shall we stick by each other as long as we live?

These rhythmic lines quickly move away from conventional values to the open road of shared experiences. Their recurring sounds are not created by rhyme or alliteration and assonance (see Chapter 18) but by the repetition of words and phrases.

Although the repetition of words and phrases can be an effective means of creating rhythm in poetry, the more typical method consists of patterns of accented or unaccented syllables. Words contain syllables that are either stressed or unstressed. A **stress** (or **accent**) places more emphasis on one syllable than on another. We say "*syl*lable" not "syl*la*ble," "*em*phasis" not "em*pha*sis." We routinely stress syllables when we speak: "*Is* she con*tent* with the *con*tents of the *yel*low *pack*age?" To distinguish between two people we might say "Is *she* con*tent*. . . ." In this way stress can be used to emphasize a particular word in a sentence. Poets often arrange words so that the desired meaning is suggested by the rhythm; hence, emphasis is controlled by the poet rather than left entirely to the reader.

When a rhythmic pattern of stresses recurs in a poem, the result is **meter**. **Scansion** consists of measuring the stresses in a line to determine its metrical pattern. Several methods can be used to mark lines. One widely used system employs ´ for a stressed syllable and ˘ for an unstressed sylla-ble. In a sense, the stress mark represents the equivalent of tapping one's foot to a beat.

> Híckŏrў, díckŏrў, dóck,
> Thĕ móuse răn úp thĕ clóck.
> Thĕ clóck strŭck óne,
> Ănd dówn hĕ rún,
> Híckŏrў, díckŏrў, dóck.

In the first two lines and the final line of this familiar nursery rhyme we hear three stressed syllables. In lines 3 and 4, where the meter changes for variety, we hear just two stressed syllables. The combination of stresses provides the pleasure of the rhythm we hear.

To hear the rhythms of "Hickory, dickory, dock" does not require a formal study of meter. Nevertheless, an awareness of the basic kinds of meter that appear in English poetry can enhance your understanding of how a poem achieves its effects. Understanding the sound effects of a poem and having a vocabulary with which to discuss those effects can intensify your pleasure in poetry. Although the study of meter can be extremely technical, the terms used to describe the basic meters of English poetry are relatively easy to comprehend.

The *foot* is the metrical unit by which a line of poetry is measured. A foot usually consists of one stressed and one or two unstressed syllables. A vertical line is used to separate the feet: "The clóck | strŭck óne" consists of two feet. A foot of poetry can be arranged in a variety of patterns; here are five of the chief ones.

Foot	Pattern	Example
iamb	˘ ´	awăy
trochee	´ ˘	Lóvelў
anapest	˘ ˘ ´	understánd
dactyl	´ ˘ ˘	despĕrătĕ
spondee	´ ´	déad sét

The most common lines in English poetry contain meters based on iambic feet. However, even lines that are predominantly iambic will often include variations to create particular effects. Other important patterns include trochaic, anapestic, and dactylic feet. The spondee is not a sustained meter but occurs for variety or emphasis.

Iambic

What képt | hĭs eýes | frŏm gív | ĭng báck | thĕ gáze

Trochaic

Hé wăs | loúder | thán thĕ | préacher

Anapestic

Ĭ am cálled | tŏ thĕ frónt | ŏf thĕ roóm

Dactylic

Síng ĭt ăll | mérrĭlў

These meters have different rhythms and can create different effects. Iambic and anapestic are known as *rising meters* because they move from unstressed to stressed sounds, while trochaic and dactylic are known as *falling meters.* Anapests and dactyls tend to move more lightly and rapidly than iambs or trochees. Although no single kind of meter can be considered always better than another for a given subject, it is possible to determine whether the meter of a specific poem is appropriate for its subject. A serious poem about a tragic death would most likely not be well served by lilting rhythms. Keep in mind too that though one or another of these four basic meters might constitute the predominant rhythm of a poem, variations can occur within lines to change the pace or call attention to a particular word.

A *line* is measured by the number of feet it contains. Here, for example, is an iambic line with three feet: "If she | should write | a note." These are the names for line lengths.

monometer: one foot   pentameter: five feet
dimeter: two feet   hexameter: six feet
trimeter: three feet   heptameter: seven feet
tetrameter: four feet   octameter: eight feet

By combining the name of a line length with the name of a foot, we can describe the metrical qualities of a line concisely. Consider, for example, the pattern of feet and length of this line.

I didn't want the boy to hit the dog.

The iambic rhythm of this line falls into five feet; hence it is called *iambic pentameter.* Iambic is the most common pattern in English poetry because its rhythm appears so naturally in English speech and writing. Unrhymed iambic pentameter is called *blank verse;* Shakespeare's plays are built upon such lines.

Less common than the iamb, trochee, anapest, or dactyl is the *spondee,* a two-syllable foot in which both syllables are stressed (´ ´). Note the effect of the spondaic foot at the beginning of this line.

Dead set | against | the plan | he went | away.

Spondees can slow a rhythm and provide variety and emphasis, particularly in iambic and trochaic lines.

The effects of these English meters are easily seen in the following lines by Samuel Taylor Coleridge, in which the rhythm of each line illustrates the meter described in it.

Trochee trips from long to short;
From long to long in solemn sort
Slow Spondee stalks; strong foot yet ill able
Ever to come up with Dactylic trisyllable.
Iambics march from short to long —
With a leap and a bound the swift Anapests throng.

The speed of a line is also affected by the number of pauses in it. A pause within a line is called a *caesura* and is indicated by a double vertical line (‖). A caesura can occur anywhere within a line and need not be indicated by punctuation.

> Camerado, ‖ I give you my hand!
> I give you my love ‖ more precious than money.

A slight pause occurs within each of these lines and at its end. Both kinds of pauses contribute to the lines' rhythm.

When a line has a pause at its end, it is called an **end-stopped line.** Such pauses reflect normal speech patterns and are often marked by punctuation. A line that ends without a pause and continues into the next line for its meaning is called a **run-on line.** Running over from one line to another is also called **enjambment.** The first and eighth lines of the following poem are run-on lines; the rest are end-stopped.

WILLIAM WORDSWORTH (1770–1850)

My Heart Leaps Up   1807

My heart leaps up when I behold
   A rainbow in the sky:
So was it when my life began;
So is it now I am a man;
So be it when I shall grow old,
   Or let me die!
The child is father of the Man;
And I could wish my days to be
Bound each to each by natural piety.

Run-on lines have a different rhythm from end-stopped lines. Lines 3–4 and 8–9 are both iambic, but the effect of their rhythms is very different when we read these lines aloud. The enjambment of lines 8 and 9 reinforces their meaning; just as the "days" are bound together, so are the lines.

The rhythm of a poem can be affected by several devices: the kind and number of stresses within lines, the length of lines, and the kinds of pauses that appear within lines or at their ends. In addition, as we saw in Chapter 18, the sound of a poem is affected by alliteration, assonance, rhyme, and consonance. These sounds help to create rhythms by controlling our pronunciations, as in the following lines by Alexander Pope.

> Soft is the strain when Zephyr gently blows,
> And the smooth stream in smoother numbers flows;
> But when loud surges lash the sounding shore,
> The hoarse, rough verse should like the torrent roar.

These lines are effective because their rhythm and sound work with their meaning.

SUGGESTIONS FOR SCANNING A POEM

These suggestions should help you in talking about a poem's meter.

1. After reading the poem through, read it aloud and mark the stressed syllables in each line. Then mark the unstressed syllables.
2. From your markings, identify what kind of foot is dominant (iambic, trochaic, dactylic, or anapestic) and divide the lines into feet, keeping in mind that the vertical line marking a foot may come in the middle of a word as well as at its beginning or end.
3. Determine the number of feet in each line. Remember that there may be variations; some lines may be shorter or longer than the predominant meter. What is important is the overall pattern. Do not assume that variations represent the poet's inability to fulfill the overall pattern. Notice the effects of variations and whether they emphasize words and phrases or disrupt your expectation for some other purpose.
4. Listen for pauses within lines and mark the caesuras; many times there will be no punctuation to indicate them.
5. Recognize that scansion does not always yield a definitive measurement of a line. Even experienced readers may differ over the scansion of a given line. What is important is not a precise description of the line but an awareness of how a poem's rhythms contribute to its effects.

The following poem demonstrates how you can use an understanding of meter and rhythm to gain a greater appreciation for what a poem is saying.

TIMOTHY STEELE (b. 1948)
Waiting for the Storm 1986

Bréeze sént | ă wrínk | lĭng dárk | nĕss
Ăcróss | thĕ báy. || Ĭ knélt
Bĕnéath | ăn úp | turnĕd bóat,
Ănd, mó | mĕnt bў mó | mĕnt, félt

Thĕ sánd | ăt mў féet | grŏw cóld | ĕr,
Thĕ damp | áir chíll | ănd spréad.
Thĕn thĕ | fírst ráin | drŏps sóund | ĕd
Ŏn thĕ húll | ăbóve | mў héad.

The predominant meter of this poem is iambic trimeter, but there is plenty of variation as the storm rapidly approaches and finally begins to pelt the sheltered speaker. The emphatic spondee ("Breeze sent") pushes the darkness quickly across the bay while the caesura at the end of the sentence in line 2 creates a pause that sets up a feeling of suspense and expectation that is measured in the ticking rhythm of line 4, a run-on line that brings us into the chilly sand and air of the second stanza. Perhaps the most impressive sound effect used in the poem appears in the second syllable of "sounded" in line 7. That "*ed*" precedes the sound of the poem's final word "head" just as if it were the first drop of rain hitting the hull above the speaker. The visual, tactile, and auditory images make "Waiting for the Storm" an intense sensory experience.

This next poem also reinforces meanings through its use of meter and rhythm.

WILLIAM BUTLER YEATS (1865–1939)
That the Night Come   1912

She lived | in storm | and strife,
Her soul | had such | desire
For what | proud death | may bring
That it | could not | endure
The com | mon good | of life,   5
But lived | as 'twere | a king
That packed | his mar | riage day
With ban | neret | and pennon,
Trumpet | and kett | ledrum,
And the | outrag | eous cannon,   10
To bun | dle time | away
That the | night come.

Scansion reveals that the predominant meter here is iambic trimeter. Each line contains three stressed and unstressed syllables that form a regular, predictable rhythm through line 7. That rhythm is disrupted, however, when the speaker compares the woman's longing for what death brings to a king's eager anticipation of his wedding night. The king packs the day with noisy fanfares and celebrations to fill up time and distract himself. Unable to accept "The common good of life," the woman fills her days with "storm and strife."

In a determined effort to "bundle time away," she, like the king, impatiently awaits the night.

Lines 8–10 break the regular pattern established in the first seven lines. The extra unstressed syllable in lines 8 and 10 along with the trochaic feet in lines 9 *(trúmpĕt)* and 10 *(Ánd thĕ)* interrupt the basic iambic trimeter and parallel the woman's and the king's frenetic activity. These lines thus echo the inability of the woman and king to "endure" regular or normal time. The last line is the most irregular in the poem. The final two accented syllables sound like the deep resonant beats of a kettledrum or a cannon firing. The words "night come" dramatically remind us that what the woman anticipates is not a lover but the mysterious finality of death. The meter serves, then, in both its regularity and variations to reinforce the poem's meaning and tone.

The following poems are especially rich in their rhythms and sounds. As you read and study them, notice how patterns of rhythm and the sounds of words reinforce meanings and contribute to the poems' effects. And, perhaps most importantly, read the poems aloud so that you can hear them.

POEMS FOR FURTHER STUDY

WALTER SAVAGE LANDOR (1775–1864)
Death of the Day   1858

My pictures blacken in their frames
    As night comes on,
And youthful maids and wrinkled dames
    Are now all one.

Death of the day! a sterner Death
    Did worse before;
The fairest form, the sweetest breath,
    Away he bore.

Considerations for Critical Thinking and Writing

1. What does a scansion of this poem reveal about the rhythm of its lines?
2. Discuss the use of personification in the poem.
3. Describe the effect of the caesura in line 5.

Connection to Another Selection

1. Write an essay comparing the images and tone of "Death of the Day" and Robert Herrick's "To the Virgins, to Make Much of Time" (p. 629).

A. E. HOUSMAN (1859–1936)
When I was one-and-twenty   1896

When I was one-and-twenty
   I heard a wise man say,
"Give crowns and pounds and guineas
   But not your heart away;
Give pearls away and rubies   5
   But keep your fancy free."
But I was one-and-twenty,
   No use to talk to me.

When I was one-and-twenty
   I heard him say again,   10
"The heart out of the bosom
   Was never given in vain;
'Tis paid with sighs a plenty
   And sold for endless rue."
And I am two-and-twenty,   15
   And oh, 'tis true, 'tis true.

Considerations for Critical Thinking and Writing

1. Scan this poem. What is the basic metrical pattern?
2. How do lines 1–8 parallel lines 9–16 in their use of rhyme and metaphor? Are there any significant differences between the stanzas?
3. What do you think has happened to change the speaker's attitude toward love?
4. Explain why you agree or disagree with the advice given by the "wise man."
5. What is the effect of the repetition in line 16?

ROBERT FRANCIS (1901–1987)
Excellence   1941

Excellence is millimeters and not miles.
From poor to good is great. From good to best is small.
From almost best to best sometimes not measurable.
The man who leaps the highest leaps perhaps an inch
Above the runner-up. How glorious that inch
And that split-second longer in the air before the fall.

Considerations for Critical Thinking and Writing

1. How does alliteration help to support the meaning of this poem's first line?
2. Francis does not use iambic pentameter, the most common metrical line in English. What does he use? Why is it a more appropriate choice?

3. What is the effect of the caesura in line 2?
4. Why is Francis's version of line 6 better than this one: "And that split-second in the air before the fall"?

ROBERT HERRICK (1591–1674)
Delight in Disorder   1648

A sweet disorder in the dress
Kindles in clothes a wantonness.
A lawn° about the shoulders thrown   *linen scarf*
Into a fine distraction;
An erring lace, which here and there   5
Enthralls the crimson stomacher,
A cuff neglectful, and thereby
Ribbons to flow confusedly;
A winning wave, deserving note,
In the tempestuous petticoat;   10
A careless shoestring, in whose tie
I see a wild civility;
Do more bewitch me than when art
Is too precise in every part.

Considerations for Critical Thinking and Writing

1. Why does the speaker in this poem value "disorder" so highly?
2. What is the principal rhythmic order of the poem? Is it "precise in every part"? How does the poem's organization relate to its theme?
3. Which words in the poem indicate disorder? Which words indicate the speaker's response to that disorder? What are the connotative meanings of each set of words? Why are they appropriate? What do they suggest about the woman and the speaker?
4. Write a short essay in which you agree or disagree with the speaker's views on dress.

BEN JONSON (1573–1637)
Still to Be Neat   1609

Still° to be neat, still to be dressed,   *continually*
As you were going to a feast;
Still to be powdered, still perfumed;
Lady, it is to be presumed,
Though art's hid causes are not found,   5
All is not sweet, all is not sound.

Give me a look, give me a face
That makes simplicity a grace;
Robes loosely flowing, hair as free;
Such sweet neglect more taketh me   10
Then all th' adulteries of art.
They strike mine eyes, but not my heart.

Considerations for Critical Thinking and Writing

1. What are the speaker's reservations about the lady in the first stanza? What do you
   think "sweet" means in line 6?
2. What does the speaker want from the lady in the second stanza? How has the
   meaning of "sweet" shifted from line 6 to line 10? What other words in the poem
   are especially charged with connotative meanings?
3. How do the rhythms of Jonson's lines help to reinforce meanings? Pay particular
   attention to lines 6 and 12.

Connections to Another Selection

1. Write an essay comparing the themes of "Still to Be Neat" and Herrick's "Delight
   in Disorder." How do the speakers make similar points but from different
   perspectives?
2. How does the rhythm of "Still to Be Neat" compare with that of "Delight in
   Disorder"? Which do you find more effective? Explain why.

ANNE SEXTON (1928–1974)
Her Kind   1960

I have gone out, a possessed witch,
haunting the black air, braver at night;
dreaming evil, I have done my hitch
over the plain houses, light by light:
lonely thing, twelve-fingered, out of mind.   5
A woman like that is not a woman, quite.
I have been her kind.

I have found the warm caves in the woods,
filled them with skillets, carvings, shelves,
closets, silks, innumerable goods;   10
fixed the suppers for the worms and the elves:
whining, rearranging the disaligned.
A woman like that is misunderstood.
I have been her kind.

I have ridden in your cart, driver,   15
waved my nude arms at villages going by,
learning the last bright routes, survivor
where your flames still bite my thigh

and my ribs crack where your wheels wind.
A woman like that is not ashamed to die.   20
I have been her kind.

Considerations for Critical Thinking and Writing

1. What kind of women does the speaker describe?
2. What is the predominant meter of the poem? Describe its rhythm.
3. How does Sexton use caesura and enjambment to create the poem's rhythm?

WILLIAM BLAKE (1757–1827)
The Lamb   1789

    Little Lamb, who made thee?
    Dost thou know who made thee?
Gave thee life, and bid thee feed
By the stream and o'er the mead;
Gave thee clothing of delight,   5
Softest clothing, wooly, bright;
Gave thee such a tender voice,
Making all the vales rejoice?
    Little Lamb, who made thee?
    Dost thou know who made thee?   10

    Little Lamb, I'll tell thee,
    Little Lamb, I'll tell thee:
He is callèd by thy name,
For he calls himself a Lamb.
He is meek, and he is mild;   15
He became a little child.
I a child, and thou a lamb,
We are callèd by his name.
    Little Lamb, God bless thee!
    Little Lamb, God bless thee!   20

Considerations for Critical Thinking and Writing

1. This poem is from Blake's *Songs of Innocence*. Describe its tone. How do the
   meter, rhyme, and repetition help to characterize the speaker's voice?
2. Why is it significant that the animal addressed by the speaker is a lamb? What
   symbolic value would be lost if the animal were, for example, a doe?
3. How does the second stanza answer the question raised in the first? What is the
   speaker's view of the creation?

WILLIAM BLAKE (1757–1827)
The Tyger 1794

Tyger! Tyger! burning bright
In the forests of the night,
What immortal hand or eye
Could frame thy fearful symmetry?

In what distant deeps or skies   5
Burnt the fire of thine eyes?
On what wings dare he aspire?
What the hand dare seize the fire?

And what shoulder, and what art,
Could twist the sinews of thy heart?   10
And when thy heart began to beat,
What dread hand? and what dread feet?

What the hammer? what the chain?
In what furnace was thy brain?
What the anvil? what dread grasp   15
Dare its deadly terrors clasp?

When the stars threw down their spears,
And watered heaven with their tears,
Did he smile his work to see?
Did he who made the Lamb make thee?   20

Tyger! Tyger! burning bright
In the forests of the night,
What immortal hand or eye
Dare frame thy fearful symmetry?

Considerations for Critical Thinking and Writing

1. This poem is from Blake's *Songs of Experience* and is often paired with "The Lamb." Describe the poem's tone. Is the speaker's voice the same here as in "The Lamb"? Which words are repeated, and how do they contribute to the tone?
2. What is revealed about the nature of the tiger by the words used to describe its creation? What do you think the tiger symbolizes?
3. Unlike in "The Lamb," more than one question is raised in "The Tyger." What are these questions? Are they answered?
4. Compare the rhythms in "The Lamb" and "The Tyger." Each basically uses a seven-syllable line, but the effects are very different. Why?
5. Using these two poems as the basis of your discussion, describe what distinguishes innocence from experience.

DOROTHY PARKER (1893–1967)
One Perfect Rose   1926

A single flow'r he sent me, since we met.
    All tenderly his messenger he chose;
Deep-hearted, pure, with scented dew still wet —
    One perfect rose.

I knew the language of the floweret;   5
    "My fragile leaves," it said, "his heart enclose."
Love long has taken for his amulet
    One perfect rose.

Why is it no one ever sent me yet
    One perfect limousine, do you suppose?   10
Ah no, it's always just my luck to get
    One perfect rose.

Considerations for Critical Thinking and Writing

1. Describe the tone of the first two stanzas. How do rhyme and meter help to establish the tone?
2. How does the meaning of "One perfect rose" in line 12 compare with the way you read it in lines 4 and 8?
3. Describe the speaker. What sort of woman is she? How do you respond to her?

ALFRED, LORD TENNYSON (1809–1892)
Break, Break, Break   1842

Break, break, break,
    On thy cold gray stones, O Sea!
And I would that my tongue could utter
    The thoughts that arise in me.

O, well for the fisherman's boy,   5
    That he shouts with his sister at play!
O, well for the sailor lad,
    That he sings in his boat on the bay!

And the stately ships go on
    To their haven under the hill;   10
But O for the touch of a vanished hand,
    And the sound of a voice that is still!

Break, break, break
    At the foot of thy crags, O Sea!
But the tender grace of a day that is dead   15
    Will never come back to me.

Considerations for Critical Thinking and Writing

1. How do lines 1 and 13 differ from the predominant meter of this poem? How do these two lines control the poem's tone?
2. What is the effect of the repetition? What does "break" refer to in addition to the waves?

THEODORE ROETHKE (1908–1963)
My Papa's Waltz   1948

The whiskey on your breath
Could make a small boy dizzy;
But I hung on like death:
Such waltzing was not easy.

We romped until the pans   5
Slid from the kitchen shelf;
My mother's countenance
Could not unfrown itself.

The hand that held my wrist
Was battered on one knuckle;   10
At every step you missed
My right ear scraped a buckle.

You beat time on my head
With a palm caked hard by dirt,
Then waltzed me off to bed   15
Still clinging to your shirt.

Considerations for Critical Thinking and Writing

1. What details characterize the father in this poem? How does the speaker's choice of words reveal his feeling about his father? Is the remembering speaker still a boy?
2. Characterize the rhythm of the poem. Does it move "like death," or is it more like a waltz? Is the rhythm regular throughout the poem? What is its effect?
3. Comment on the appropriateness of the title. Why do you suppose Roethke didn't use "My Father's Waltz"?

MILLER WILLIAMS (b. 1930)

Ruby Tells All

1985

When I was told, as Delta children were,
that crops don't grow unless you sweat at night,
I thought that it was my own sweat they meant.
I have never felt as important again
as on those early mornings, waking up,   5
my body slick, the moon full on the fields.
That was before air conditioning.
Farm girls sleep cool now and wake up dry,
but still the cotton overflows the fields.
We lose everything that's grand and foolish;   10
it all becomes something else. One by one,
butterflies turn into caterpillars
and we grow up, or more or less we do,
and, Lord, we do lie then. We lie so much
the truth has a false ring and it's hard to tell.   15
I wouldn't take crap off anybody
if I just knew that I was getting crap
in time not to take it. I could have won
a small one now and then if I was smarter,
but I've poured coffee here too many years   20
for men who rolled in in Peterbilts,
and I have gotten into bed with some
if they could talk and seemed to be in pain.
I never asked for anything myself;
giving is more blessed and leaves you free.   25
There was a man, married and fond of whiskey.
Given the limitations of men, he loved me.
Lord, we laid concern upon our bodies
but then he left. Everything has its time.
We used to dance. He made me feel the way   30
a human wants to feel and fears to.
He was a slow man and didn't expect.
I would get off work and find him waiting.
We'd have a drink or two and kiss awhile.
Then a bird-loud morning late one April   35
we woke up naked. We had made a child.
She's grown up now and gone though god knows where.
She ought to write, for I do love her dearly
who raised her carefully and dressed her well.

Everything has its time. For thirty years   40
I never had a thought about time.
Now, turning through newspapers, I pause
to see if anyone who passed away

was younger than I am. If one was
I feel hollow for a little while 45
but then it passes. Nothing matters enough
to stay bent down about. You have to see
that some things matter slightly and some don't.
Dying matters a little. So does pain.
So does being old. Men do not. 50
Men live by negatives, like don't give up,
don't be a coward, don't call me a liar,
don't ever tell me don't. If I could live
two hundred years and had to be a man
I'd take my grave. What's a man but a match, 55
a little stick to start a fire with?
My daughter knows this, if she's alive.
What could I tell her now, to bring her close,
something she doesn't know, if we met somewhere?
Maybe that I think about her father, 60
maybe that my fingers hurt at night,
maybe that against appearances
there is love, constancy, and kindness,
that I have dresses I have never worn.

Considerations for Critical Thinking and Writing

1. What is the predominant meter of this poem? How does it affect the tone of Ruby's monologue?
2. Describe Ruby's attitude toward life. What does she think of men? Of herself?
3. Using the details provided in the poem write an essay that characterizes Ruby's life. Which details are especially revealing?

Connections to Other Selections

1. Write an essay that compares the speakers in "Ruby Tells All" and Katharyn Howd Machan's "Hazel Tells LaVerne" (p. 626).
2. Discuss the attitudes expressed toward men in this poem and in Sharon Olds's "Rite of Passage" (p. 783).

EDWARD HIRSCH (b. 1950)
Fast Break 1985

(In Memory of Dennis Turner, 1946–1984)

A hook shot kisses the rim and
hangs there, helplessly, but doesn't drop

and for once our gangly starting center
boxes out his man and times his jump

perfectly, gathering the orange leather   5
from the air like a cherished possession

and spinning around to throw a strike
to the outlet who is already shoveling

an underhand pass toward the other guard
scissoring past a flat-footed defender   10

who looks stunned and nailed to the floor
in the wrong direction, turning to catch sight

of a high, gliding dribble and a man
letting the play develop in front of him

in slow motion, almost exactly   15
like a coach's drawing on the blackboard,

both forwards racing down the court
the way that forwards should, fanning out

and filling the lanes in tandem, moving
together as brothers passing the ball   20

between them without a dribble, without
a single bounce hitting the hardwood

until the guard finally lunges out
and commits to the wrong man

while the power-forward explodes past them   25
in a fury, taking the ball into the air

by himself now and laying it gently
against the glass for a layup,

but losing his balance in the process,
inexplicably falling, hitting the floor   30

with a wild, headlong motion
for the game he loved like a country

and swiveling back to see an orange blur
floating perfectly through the net.

Considerations for Critical Thinking and Writing

1. Why are run-on lines especially appropriate for this poem? How do they affect its sound and sense? What is the effect of the poem being one long sentence? Do the lines have a regular meter?
2. In addition to describing accurately a fast break, this poem is a tribute to a dead friend. How are the two purposes related in the poem?
3. How might this poem — to borrow a phrase from Robert Frost — represent a "momentary stay against confusion"?

LOUISE BOGAN (1897–1970)
On Formal Poetry 1953

What is formal poetry? It is poetry written in form. And what is *form?* The elements of form, so far as poetry is concerned, are meter and rhyme. Are these elements merely mold and ornaments that have been impressed upon poetry from without? Are they indeed restrictions which blind and fetter language and the thought and emotion behind, under, within language in a repressive way? Are they arbitrary rules which have lost all validity since they have been broken to good purpose by "experimental poets," ancient and modern? Does the breaking up of form, or its total elimination, always result in an increase of power and of effect; and is any return to form a sort of relinquishment of freedom, or retreat to old fogeyism?

From *A Poet's Alphabet*

Considerations for Critical Thinking and Writing

1. Choose one of the questions Bogan raises and write an essay in response to it using two or three poems from this chapter to illustrate your answer.
2. Try writing a poem in meter and rhyme. Does the experience make your writing feel limited or not?

20. Poetic Forms

Poems come in a variety of shapes. Although the best poems always have their own unique qualities, many of them also conform to traditional patterns. Frequently the *form* of a poem — its overall structure or shape — follows an already established design. A poem that can be categorized by the patterns of its lines, meter, rhymes, and stanzas is considered a *fixed form*, because it follows a prescribed model such as a sonnet. However, poems written in a fixed form do not always fit models precisely; writers sometimes work variations on traditional forms to create innovative effects.

Not all poets are content with variations on traditional forms. Some prefer to create their own structures and shapes. Poems that do not conform to established patterns of meter, rhyme, and stanza are called *free verse* or *open form* poetry. (See Chapter 21 for further discussion of open forms.) This kind of poetry creates its own ordering principles through the careful arrangement of words and phrases in line lengths that embody rhythms appropriate to the meaning. Modern and contemporary poets in particular have learned to use the blank space on the page as a significant functional element [for a striking example see cummings's "l(a," p. 600]. Good poetry of this kind is structured in ways that can be as demanding, interesting, and satisfying as fixed forms. Open and fixed forms represent different poetic styles, but they are identical in the sense that both use language in concentrated ways to convey meanings, experiences, emotions, and effects.

SOME COMMON POETIC FORMS

A familiarity with some of the most frequently used fixed forms of poetry is useful, because it allows for a better understanding of how a poem works. Classifying patterns allows us to talk about the effects of established rhythm and rhyme and recognize how significant variations from them affect the pace and meaning of the lines. An awareness of form also allows us to anticipate how a poem is likely to proceed. As we shall see, a sonnet creates a different set of expectations in a reader from those of, say, a limerick. A reader isn't likely to find in limericks the kind of serious themes that often make their way into sonnets. The discussion that follows identifies some of the important poetic forms frequently encountered in English poetry.

The shape of a fixed form poem is often determined by the way in which the lines are organized into stanzas. A *stanza* consists of a grouping of lines, set off by a space, which usually has a set pattern of meter and rhyme. This pattern is ordinarily repeated in other stanzas throughout the poem. What is usual is not obligatory, however; some poems may use a different pattern for each stanza, somewhat like paragraphs in prose.

Traditionally, though, stanzas do share a common *rhyme scheme*, the pattern of end rhymes. We can map out rhyme schemes by noting patterns of rhyme with small letters: the first rhyme sound is designated *a*, the second becomes *b*, the third *c*, and so on. Using this system, we can describe the rhyme scheme in the following poem this way: *aabb, ccdd, eeff.*

A. E. HOUSMAN (1859–1936)
Loveliest of trees, the cherry now   1896

Loveliest of trees, the cherry now	*a*
Is hung with bloom along the bough,	*a*
And stands about the woodland ride	*b*
Wearing white for Eastertide.	*b*
Now, of my threescore years and ten,	*c*
Twenty will not come again,	*c*
And take from seventy springs a score,	*d*
It only leaves me fifty more.	*d*
And since to look at things in bloom	*e*
Fifty springs are little room,	*e*
About the woodlands I will go	*f*
To see the cherry hung with snow.	*f*

5

10

Considerations for Critical Thinking and Writing

1. What is the speaker's attitude in this poem toward time and life?
2. Why is spring an appropriate season for the setting rather than, say, winter?
3. Paraphrase each stanza. How do the images in each reinforce the poem's themes?
4. Lines 1 and 12 are not intended to rhyme, but they are close. What is the effect of the near rhyme of "now" and "snow"? How does the rhyme enhance the theme?

Poets often create their own stanzaic patterns; hence there is an infinite number of kinds of stanzas. One way of talking about stanzaic forms is to describe a given stanza by how many lines it contains.

A *couplet* consists of two lines that usually rhyme and have the same meter; couplets are frequently not separated from each other by space on the page. A *heroic couplet* consists of rhymed iambic pentameter. Here is an example from Pope's "An Essay on Criticism."

One science only will one genius fit;	*a*
So vast is art, so narrow human wit:	*a*
Not only bounded to peculiar arts,	*b*
But oft in those confined to single parts.	*b*

A *tercet* is a three-line stanza. When all three lines rhyme they are called a *triplet.* Two triplets make up this captivating poem.

ROBERT HERRICK (1591–1674)
Upon Julia's Clothes 1648

Whenas in silks my Julia goes,	*a*
Then, then, methinks, how sweetly flows	*a*
That liquefaction of her clothes.	*a*
Next, when I cast mine eyes, and see	*b*
That brave vibration, each way free,	*b*
O, how that glittering taketh me!	*b*

Considerations for Critical Thinking and Writing

1. Underline the alliteration in this poem. What purpose does it serve?
2. Comment on the effect of the meter. How is it related to the speaker's description of Julia's clothes?
3. Look up the word *brave* in the *Oxford English Dictionary.* Which of its meanings are appropriate to describe Julia's movement? Some readers interpret lines 4–6 to mean that Julia has no clothes on. What do you think?

Connection to Another Selection

1. Compare the tone of this poem with that of Humphrey's "Blow" (p. 730). Are the situations and speakers similar? Is there any difference in tone between these two poems?

Terza rima consists of an interlocking three-line rhyme scheme: *aba, bcb, cdc, ded,* and so on. Dante's *The Divine Comedy* uses this pattern, as does Frost's "Acquainted with the Night" (p. 685) and Percy Bysshe Shelley's "Ode to the West Wind" (p. 768).

A *quatrain,* or four-line stanza, is the most common stanzaic form in the English language and can have various meters and rhyme schemes (if any). The most common rhyme schemes are *aabb, abba, aaba,* and *abcb.* This last pattern is especially characteristic of the popular *ballad stanza,* which consists of alternating eight- and six-syllable lines. Samuel Taylor

Coleridge adopted this pattern in "The Rime of the Ancient Mariner"; here is one representative stanza.

> All in a hot and copper sky
> The bloody Sun, at noon,
> Right up above the mast did stand,
> No bigger than the Moon.

There are a number of longer stanzaic forms and the list of types of stanzas could be extended considerably, but knowing these three most basic patterns should prove helpful to you in talking about the form of a great many poems. In addition to stanzaic forms, there are fixed forms that characterize entire poems. Lyric poems can be, for example, sonnets, villanelles, sestinas, or epigrams.

Sonnet

The *sonnet* has been a popular literary form in English since the sixteenth century, when it was adopted from the Italian *sonnetto,* meaning "little song." A sonnet consists of fourteen lines, usually written in iambic pentameter. Because the sonnet has been such a favorite form, writers have experimented with many variations on its essential structure. Nevertheless, there are two basic types of sonnets: the Italian and the English.

The *Italian sonnet* (also known as the *Petrarchan sonnet,* from the fourteenth-century Italian poet Petrarch) divides into two parts. The first eight lines (the *octave*) typically rhyme *abbaabba.* The final six lines (the *sestet*) may vary; common patterns are *cdecde, cdcdcd,* and *cdccdc.* Very often the octave presents a situation, attitude, or problem that the sestet comments upon or resolves, as in John Keats's "On First Looking into Chapman's Homer" (p. 791).

This pattern is also used in the next sonnet, but notice that the thematic break between octave and sestet comes within line 9 rather than between lines 8 and 9. This unconventional break helps to reinforce the speaker's impatience with the conventional attitudes he describes.

WILLIAM WORDSWORTH (1770–1850)
The World Is Too Much with Us   1807

The world is too much with us; late and soon,
Getting and spending, we lay waste our powers;
Little we see in Nature that is ours;
We have given our hearts away, a sordid boon!
This Sea that bares her bosom to the moon;   5
The winds that will be howling at all hours,
And are up-gathered now like sleeping flowers;
For this, for everything, we are out of tune;

It moves us not. — Great God! I'd rather be
A Pagan suckled in a creed outworn;   10
So might I, standing on this pleasant lea,
Have glimpses that would make me less forlorn;
Have sight of Proteus rising from the sea;
Or hear old Triton blow his wreathèd horn.

Considerations for Critical Thinking and Writing

1. What is the speaker's complaint in this sonnet? How do the conditions described affect him?
2. Look up "Proteus" and "Triton." What do these mythological allusions contribute to the sonnet's tone?
3. What is the effect of the personification of the sea and wind in the octave?

Connections to Other Selections

1. Compare the theme of this sonnet with that of Hopkins's "God's Grandeur" (p. 720).
2. Write an essay that explores Amy Clampitt's "Nothing Stays Put" (p. 1040) as a modern urban version of Wordsworth's poem.

The *English sonnet,* more commonly known as the *Shakespearean sonnet,* is organized into three quatrains and a couplet, which typically rhyme *abab cdcd efef gg.* This rhyme scheme is more suited to English poetry because English has fewer rhyming words than Italian. English sonnets, because of their four-part organization, also have more flexibility about where thematic breaks can occur. Frequently, however, the most pronounced break or turn comes with the concluding couplet.

In the following Shakespearean sonnet, the three quatrains compare the speaker's loved one to a summer's day and explain why the loved one is even more lovely. The couplet bestows eternal beauty and love upon both the loved one and the sonnet.

WILLIAM SHAKESPEARE (1564–1616)
Shall I compare thee to a summer's day?   1609

Shall I compare thee to a summer's day?
Thou art more lovely and more temperate:
Rough winds do shake the darling buds of May,
And summer's lease hath all too short a date.
Sometime too hot the eye of heaven shines,   5
And often is his gold complexion dimmed;
And every fair from fair sometime declines,
By chance, or nature's changing course, untrimmed.

But thy eternal summer shall not fade,
Nor lose possession of that fair thou ow'st°   *possesses*   10
Nor shall death brag thou wand'rest in his shade,
When in eternal lines to time thou grow'st.
    So long as men can breathe or eyes can see,
    So long lives this, and this gives life to thee.

Considerations for Critical Thinking and Writing

1. Why is the speaker's loved one more lovely than a summer's day? What qualities does he admire in the loved one?
2. Describe the shift in tone and subject matter that begins in line 9.
3. What does the couplet say about the relation between art and love?
4. Which syllables are stressed in the final line? How do these syllables relate to the meaning of the line?

Sonnets have been the vehicles for all kinds of subjects, including love, death, politics, and cosmic questions. Although most sonnets tend to treat their subjects seriously, this fixed form does not mean a fixed expression; humor is also possible in it. Compare this next Shakespearean sonnet with "Shall I compare thee to a summer's day?" They are, finally, both love poems, but their tones are markedly different.

WILLIAM SHAKESPEARE (1564–1616)
My mistress' eyes are nothing like the sun   1609

My mistress' eyes are nothing like the sun;
Coral is far more red than her lips' red;
If snow be white, why then her breasts are dun;
If hairs be wires, black wires grow on her head.
I have seen roses damasked red and white,   5
But no such roses see I in her cheeks;
And in some perfumes is there more delight
Than in the breath that from my mistress reeks.
I love to hear her speak, yet well I know
That music hath a far more pleasing sound;   10
I grant I never saw a goddess go:
My mistress, when she walks, treads on the ground.
    And yet, by heaven, I think my love as rare
    As any she,° belied with false compare.   *lady*

Considerations for Critical Thinking and Writing

1. What does "mistress" mean in this sonnet?
2. Write a description of the mistress based on the images used in the sonnet.
3. What sort of person is the speaker? Does he truly love the woman he describes?
4. In what sense are this sonnet and "Shall I compare thee" about poetry as well as love?

EDNA ST. VINCENT MILLAY (1892–1950)
I will put Chaos into fourteen lines   1954

I will put Chaos into fourteen lines
And keep him there; and let him thence escape
If he be lucky; let him twist, and ape
Flood, fire, and demon — his adroit designs
Will strain to nothing in the strict confines   5
Of this sweet Order, where, in pious rape,
I hold his essence and amorphous shape,
Till he with Order mingles and combines.
Past are the hours, the years, of our duress,
His arrogance, our awful servitude: 10
I have him. He is nothing more nor less
Than something simple not yet understood;
I shall not even force him to confess;
Or answer. I will only make him good.

Considerations for Critical Thinking and Writing

1. What properties of a sonnet does this poem possess? How does the poem contain "Chaos"?
2. What do you think is meant by the phrase "pious rape" in line 6?
3. What is the effect of the personification in the poem?

Connections to Other Selections

1. Compare the theme of this poem with that of Robert Frost's "Design" (p. 887).
2. Write an essay comparing this poem with Donald Justice's "Order in the Streets" (p. 787). In your opinion which poem creates more order out of chaos?

DONALD JUSTICE (b. 1925)
The Snowfall   1959

The classic landscapes of dreams are not
More pathless, though footprints leading nowhere
Would seem to prove that a people once
Survived for a little even here.

Fragments of a pathetic culture   5
Remain, the lost mittens of children,
And a single, bright, detasseled snow-cap,
Evidence of some frantic migration.

The landmarks are gone. Nevertheless
There is something familiar about this country.   10
Slowly now we begin to recall

The terrible whispers of our elders
Falling softly about our ears
In childhood, never believed till now.

Considerations for Critical Thinking and Writing

1. What is dreamlike about what the speaker describes?
2. What does the speaker believe at the end of the poem that the speaker did not believe earlier?
3. How is tone related to theme in this poem?
4. What properties of a sonnet does this poem possess? How does it differ from a sonnet? Pay particular attention to the poem's meter and use of rhyme.

Connections to Other Selections

1. Discuss the snow imagery in "The Snowfall" and Robert Frost's "Stopping by Woods on a Snowy Evening" (p. 884).
2. In an essay compare the themes of "The Snowfall" and Mark Strand's "The Continuous Life" (p. 1006).

Villanelle

The *villanelle* is a fixed form consisting of nineteen lines of any length divided into six stanzas: five tercets and a concluding quatrain. The first and third lines of the initial tercet rhyme; these rhymes are repeated in each subsequent tercet *(aba)* and in the final two lines of the quatrain *(abaa)*. Moreover, line 1 appears in its entirety as lines 6, 12, and 18, while line 3 appears as lines 9, 15, and 19. This form may seem to risk monotony, but in competent hands a villanelle can create haunting echoes, as in Dylan Thomas's "Do not go gentle into that good night."

DYLAN THOMAS (1914–1953)
Do not go gentle into that good night

1952

Do not go gentle into that good night,
Old age should burn and rave at close of day;
Rage, rage against the dying of the light.

Though wise men at their end know dark is right,
Because their words had forked no lightning they   5
Do not go gentle into that good night.

Good men, the last wave by, crying how bright
Their frail deeds might have danced in a green bay,
Rage, rage against the dying of the light.

Wild men who caught and sang the sun in flight,   10

And learn, too late, they grieved it on its way,
Do not go gentle into that good night.

Grave men, near death, who see with blinding sight
Blind eyes could blaze like meteors and be gay,
Rage, rage against the dying of the light.   15

And you, my father, there on the sad height,
Curse, bless, me now with your fierce tears, I pray.
Do not go gentle into that good night.
Rage, rage against the dying of the light.

Considerations for Critical Thinking and Writing

1. Thomas's father was close to death when this poem was written. How does the tone contribute to the poem's theme?
2. How is "good" used in line 1?
3. Characterize the men who are "wise" (line 4), "Good" (7), "Wild" (10), and "Grave" (13).
4. What do figures of speech contribute to this poem?
5. Discuss this villanelle's sound effects.

Connections to Other Selections

1. Write an essay comparing Thomas's treatment of death with John Donne's in "Death Be Not Proud" (p. 949).
2. In Thomas's poem we experience "rage against the dying of the light." Contrast this with the rage you find in Sylvia Plath's "Daddy" (p. 986). What produces the emotion in Plath's poem?

Sestina

Although the *sestina* usually does not rhyme, it is perhaps an even more demanding fixed form than the villanelle. A sestina consists of thirty-nine lines of any length divided into six six-line stanzas and a three-line concluding stanza called an *envoy*. The difficulty is in repeating the six words at the ends of the first stanza's lines at the ends of the lines in the other five six-line stanzas as well. Those words must also appear in the final three lines, where they often resonate important themes. The sestina originated in the Middle Ages, but contemporary poets continue to find it a fascinating and challenging form.

ELIZABETH BISHOP (1911–1979)
Sestina   1965

September rain falls on the house.
In the failing light, the old grandmother
sits in the kitchen with the child

beside the Little Marvel Stove,
reading the jokes from the almanac,
laughing and talking to hide her tears.

She thinks that her equinoctial tears
and the rain that beats on the roof of the house
were both foretold by the almanac,
but only known to a grandmother.
The iron kettle sings on the stove.
She cuts some bread and says to the child,

It's time for tea now; but the child
is watching the teakettle's small hard tears
dance like mad on the hot black stove,
the way the rain must dance on the house.
Tidying up, the old grandmother
hangs up the clever almanac

on its string. Birdlike, the almanac
hovers half open above the child,
hovers above the old grandmother
and her teacup full of dark brown tears.
She shivers and says she thinks the house
feels chilly, and puts more wood in the stove.

It was to be, says the Marvel Stove.
I know what I know, says the almanac.
With crayons the child draws a rigid house
and a winding pathway. Then the child
puts in a man with buttons like tears
and shows it proudly to the grandmother.

But secretly, while the grandmother
busies herself about the stove,
the little moons fall down like tears
from between the pages of the almanac
into the flower bed the child
has carefully placed in the front of the house.

Time to plant tears, says the almanac.
The grandmother sings to the marvelous stove
and the child draws another inscrutable house.

Considerations for Critical Thinking and Writing

1. Number the end words of the first stanza 1, 2, 3, 4, 5, and 6, and then use those numbers for the corresponding end words in the remaining five stanzas to see how the pattern of the line-end words is worked out in this sestina. Also locate the six end words in the envoy.
2. What happens in this sestina? Why is the grandmother "laughing and talking to hide her tears"?

3. Underline the images that seem especially vivid to you. What effects do they create? What is the tone of the sestina?
4. How are the six end words — "house," "grandmother," "child," "stove," "almanac," and "tears" — central to the sestina's meaning?
5. How is the almanac used symbolically? Does Bishop use any other symbols to convey meanings?
6. Write a brief essay explaining why you think a poet might derive pleasure from writing in a fixed form such as a villanelle or sestina. Can you think of similar activities outside the field of writing in which discipline and restraint give pleasure?

Epigram

An *epigram* is a brief, pointed, and witty poem. Although most rhyme and often are written in couplets, epigrams take no prescribed form. Instead, they are typically polished bits of compressed irony, satire, or paradox. Here is an epigram that defines itself.

SAMUEL TAYLOR COLERIDGE (1772–1834)
What Is an Epigram? 1802

What is an epigram? A dwarfish whole;
Its body brevity, and wit its soul.

These additional examples by A. R. Ammons, David McCord, and Paul Laurence Dunbar satisfy Coleridge's definition.

A. R. AMMONS (b. 1926)
Coward 1975

Bravery runs in my family.

DAVID McCORD (b. 1897)
Epitaph on a Waiter

By and by
God caught his eye.

PAUL LAURENCE DUNBAR (1872–1906)

Theology
1896

There is a heaven, for ever, day by day,
The upward longing of my soul doth tell me so.
There is a hell, I'm quite as sure; for pray,
If there were not, where would my neighbors go?

Considerations for Critical Thinking and Writing

1. In what sense is each of these epigrams, as Coleridge puts it, a "dwarfish whole"?
2. Explain which of these epigrams, in addition to being witty, make a serious point?
3. Try writing a few epigrams that say something memorable about whatever you choose to focus upon.

Limerick

The *limerick* is always light and humorous. Its usual form consists of five predominantly anapestic lines rhyming *aabba;* lines 1, 2, and 5 contain three feet, while lines 3 and 4 contain two. Limericks have delighted everyone from schoolchildren to sophisticated adults, and they range in subject matter from the simply innocent and silly to the satiric or obscene. The sexual humor helps to explain why so many limericks are written anonymously. Here is one that is anonymous but more concerned with physics than physiology.

There was a young lady named Bright,
Who traveled much faster than light,
    She started one day
    In a relative way,
And returned on the previous night.

This next one is a particularly clever definition of a limerick.

LAURENCE PERRINE (b. 1915)

The limerick's never averse
1982

The limerick's never averse
To expressing itself in a terse
    Economical style,
    And yet, all the while,
The limerick's *always* a verse.

Considerations for Critical Thinking and Writing

1. Scan Perrine's limerick. How do the lines measure up to the traditional fixed metrical pattern?
2. Try writing a limerick. Use the following basic pattern.

⌣ ⌣ ⁄   ⌣ ⌣ ⁄   ⌣ ⌣ ⁄
⌣ ⌣ ⁄   ⌣ ⌣ ⁄   ⌣ ⌣ ⁄
          ⌣ ⌣ ⁄   ⌣ ⌣ ⁄
          ⌣ ⌣ ⁄   ⌣ ⌣ ⁄
⌣ ⌣ ⁄   ⌣ ⌣ ⁄   ⌣ ⌣ ⁄

You might begin with a friend's name or the name of your school or town. Your instructor is, of course, fair game, too, provided your tact matches your wit.

Clerihew

The *clerihew* is another humorous fixed form that, although not as popular as the limerick, has enjoyed a modest reputation ever since Edmund Clerihew Bentley created it. The clerihew usually consists of four irregular lines rhyming *aabb* that comment on a famous person who is named in the first line. Here is an example of the form by the creator himself.

EDMUND CLERIHEW BENTLEY (1875–1956)
John Stuart Mill   date unknown

John Stuart Mill
By a mighty effort of will
Overcame his natural bonhomie
And wrote *Principles of Political Economy.*

Haiku

Another brief fixed poetic form, borrowed from the Japanese, is the *haiku.* A haiku is usually described as consisting of seventeen syllables organized into three unrhymed lines of five, seven, and five syllables. Owing to language difference, however, English translations of haiku are often only approximated, because a Japanese haiku exists in time (Japanese syllables have duration). The number of syllables in our sense is not as significant as the duration. These poems typically present an intense emotion or vivid image of nature, which, in the Japanese, are also designed to lead to a spiritual insight.

MATSUO BASHŌ (1644–1694)
Under cherry trees
date unknown

Under cherry trees
Soup, the salad, fish and all . . .
Seasoned with petals.

The implied metaphor in the next haiku offers a striking comparison between a piece of land jutting out into the water and a bull charging a matador.

RICHARD WILBUR (b. 1921)
Sleepless at Crown Point
1976

All night, this headland
Lunges into the rumpling
Capework of the wind.

ETHERIDGE KNIGHT (b. 1931)
Eastern Guard Tower
1968

Eastern guard tower
glints in sunset; convicts rest
like lizards on rocks.

Considerations for Critical Thinking and Writing

1. What different emotions do these three haiku evoke?
2. What differences and similarities are there between the effects of a haiku and those of an epigram?
3. Compose a haiku; try to make it as allusive and suggestive as possible.

Elegy

An elegy in classical Greek and Roman literature was written in alternating hexameter and pentameter lines. Since the seventeenth century, however, the term *elegy* has been used to describe a lyric poem written to commemorate someone who is dead. The word is also used to refer to a serious meditative poem produced to express the speaker's melancholy thoughts. Elegies no longer conform to a fixed pattern of lines and stanzas, but their characteristic subject is related to death and their tone is mournfully contemplative.

SEAMUS HEANEY (b. 1939)

Mid-term Break

1966

I sat all morning in the college sick bay
Counting bells knelling classes to a close.
At two o'clock our neighbors drove me home.

In the porch I met my father crying —
He had always taken funerals in his stride — 5
And Big Jim Evans saying it was a hard blow.

The baby cooed and laughed and rocked the pram
When I came in, and I was embarrassed
By old men standing up to shake my hand

And tell me they were "sorry for my trouble," 10
Whispers informed strangers I was the eldest,
Away at school, as my mother held my hand

In hers and coughed out angry tearless sighs.
At ten o'clock the ambulance arrived
With the corpse, stanched and bandaged by the nurses. 15

Next morning I went up into the room. Snowdrops
And candles soothed the bedside; I saw him
For the first time in six weeks. Paler now,

Wearing a poppy bruise on his left temple,
He lay in the four foot box as in his cot. 20
No gaudy scars, the bumper knocked him clear.

A four foot box, a foot for every year.

Considerations for Critical Thinking and Writing

1. How do simple details contribute to the effects of this elegy?
2. Does this elegy use any kind of formal pattern for its structure? What is the effect of the last line standing by itself?
3. Another spelling for *stanched* (line 15) is *staunched*. Usage is about evenly divided between the two in the United States. What is the effect of Heaney choosing the former spelling rather than the latter?
4. Comment on the elegy's title.

Connections to Other Selections

1. Compare Heaney's elegy with A. E. Housman's "To an Athlete Dying Young" (p. 967). Which do you find more moving? Explain why.
2. Write an essay comparing this story of a boy's death with Updike's "Dog's Death" (p. 590). Do you think either of the poems is sentimental? Explain why or why not.

Ode

An *ode* is characterized by a serious topic and formal tone, but no prescribed formal pattern describes all odes. In some odes the pattern of each stanza is repeated throughout, while in others each stanza introduces a new pattern. Odes are lengthy lyrics that often include lofty emotions conveyed by a dignified style. Typical topics include truth, art, freedom, justice, and the meaning of life. Frequently such lyrics tend to be more public than private, and their speakers often employ apostrophe.

PERCY BYSSHE SHELLEY (1792–1822)

Ode to the West Wind   1820

I

O wild West Wind, thou breath of Autumn's being,
Thou, from whose unseen presence the leaves dead
Are driven, like ghosts from an enchanter fleeing,

Yellow, and black, and pale, and hectic red,
Pestilence-stricken multitudes: O thou,   5
Who chariotest to their dark wintry bed

The wingèd seeds, where they lie cold and low,
Each like a corpse within its grave, until
Thine azure sister of the Spring shall blow

Her clarion o'er the dreaming earth, and fill   10
(Driving sweet buds like flocks to feed in air)
With living hues and odors plain and hill:

Wild Spirit, which art moving everywhere;
Destroyer and preserver; hear, oh, hear!

II

Thou on whose stream, mid the steep sky's commotion,   15
Loose clouds like earth's decaying leaves are shed,
Shook from the tangled boughs of Heaven and Ocean,

Angels° of rain and lightning: there are spread   *messengers*
On the blue surface of thine airy surge,
Like the bright hair uplifted from the head   20

Of some fierce Maenad,° even from the dim verge
Of the horizon to the zenith's height,
The locks of the approaching storm. Thou dirge

Of the dying year, to which this closing night

---

21 *Maenad:* In Greek mythology a frenzied worshiper of Dionysus, god of wine and fertility.

Will be the dome of a vast sepulcher,   25
Vaulted with all thy congregated might

Of vapors, from whose solid atmosphere
Black rain, and fire, and hail will burst: oh, hear!

III

Thou who didst waken from his summer dreams
The blue Mediterranean, where he lay,   30
Lulled by the coil of his crystálline streams,

Beside a pumice isle in Baiae's bay,°
And saw in sleep old palaces and towers
Quivering within the wave's intenser day,

All overgrown with azure moss and flowers   35
So sweet, the sense faints picturing them! Thou
For whose path the Atlantic's level powers

Cleave themselves into chasms, while far below
The sea-blooms and the oozy woods which wear
The sapless foliage of the ocean, know   40

Thy voice, and suddenly grow gray with fear,
And tremble and despoil themselves: oh, hear!

IV

If I were a dead leaf thou mightest bear;
If I were a swift cloud to fly with thee;
A wave to pant beneath thy power, and share   45

The impulse of thy strength, only less free
Than thou, O uncontrollable! If even
I were as in my boyhood, and could be

The comrade by thy wanderings over Heaven,
As then, when to outstrip thy skyey speed   50
Scarce seemed a vision; I would ne'er have striven

As thus with thee in prayer in my sore need.
Oh, lift me as a wave, a leaf, a cloud!
I fall upon the thorns of life! I bleed!

A heavy weight of hours has chained and bowed   55
One too like thee: tameless, and swift, and proud.

V

Make me thy lyre,° even as the forest is:
What if my leaves are falling like its own!
The tumult of thy mighty harmonies

Will take from both a deep, autumnal tone,   60
Sweet though in sadness. Be thou, Spirit fierce,

---

32 *Baiae's bay:* A bay in the Mediterranean Sea.   57 *Make me thy lyre:* Sound is produced on an
Aeolian lyre, or wind harp, by wind blowing across its strings.

My spirit! Be thou me, impetuous one!

Drive my dead thoughts over the universe
Like withered leaves to quicken a new birth!
And, by the incantation of this verse,   65

Scatter, as from an unextinguished hearth
Ashes and sparks, my words among mankind!
Be through my lips to unawakened earth

The trumpet of a prophecy! O Wind,
If Winter comes, can Spring be far behind?   70

Considerations for Critical Thinking and Writing

1. Write a summary of each of this ode's five sections.
2. What is the speaker's situation? What is his "sore need"? What does the speaker ask of the wind in lines 57–70?
3. What does the wind signify in this ode? How is it used symbolically?
4. Determine the meter and rhyme of the first five stanzas. How do these elements contribute to the ode's movement? Is this pattern continued in the other four sections?

Picture Poem

By arranging lines into particular shapes, poets can sometimes organize typography into *picture poems* of what they describe. Here is an example.

GEORGE HERBERT (1593–1633)
Easter Wings   1633

Lord, who createdst man in wealth and store,
Though foolishly he lost the same,
Decaying more and more,
Till he became
Most poor:
With thee
O let me rise
As larks, harmoniously,
And sing this day thy victories:
Then shall the fall further the flight in me.

My tender age in sorrow did begin:
And still with sicknesses and shame
Thou didst so punish sin,
That I became
Most thin.
With thee
Let me combine,
And feel this day thy victory;
For, if I imp my wing on thine,
Affliction shall advance the flight in me.

Considerations for Critical Thinking and Writing

1. How is the shape of the poem connected to its theme?
2. How is the content of each line related to its length?
3. Why is the speaker's situation compared to that of larks? How do the poem's images convey the idea of humanity's fall and resurrection?

Words have been arranged into all kinds of shapes, from apples to light bulbs. Notice how the shape of this next contemporary poem embodies its meaning.

MICHAEL McFEE (b. 1954)
In Medias Res°   1985

His waist
like the plot
thickens, wedding
pants now breathtaking,
belt no longer the cinch   5
it once was, belly's cambium
expanding to match each birthday,
his body a wad of anonymous tissue
swung in the same centrifuge of years
that separates a house from its foundation,   10
undermining sidewalks grim with joggers
and loose-filled graves and families
and stars collapsing on themselves,
no preservation society capable
of plugging entropy's dike,   15
under his zipper's sneer
a belly hibernation-
soft, ready for
the kill.

In Medias Res: A Latin term for a story that begins "in the middle of things."

Considerations for Critical Thinking and Writing

1. Explain how the title is related to this poem's shape.
2. Identify the puns. How do they work in the poem?
3. What is "cambium"? Why is the phrase "belly's cambium" especially appropriate?
4. What is the tone of this poem? Is it consistent throughout?

Parody

A *parody* is a humorous imitation of another, usually serious, work. It can take any fixed or open form because parodists imitate the tone, language, and shape of the original. While a parody may be teasingly close to a work's style, it typically deflates the subject matter to make the original seem absurd. Parody can be used as a kind of literary criticism to expose the defects in a work, but it is also very often an affectionate acknowledgment that a well-known work has become both institutionalized in our culture and fair game for some fun. Read Andrew Marvell's "To His Coy Mistress" (p. 631) and then study this parody.

PETER DE VRIES (b. 1910)
To His Importunate Mistress   1986

Andrew Marvell Updated

Had we but world enough, and time,
My coyness, lady, were a crime,
But at my back I always hear
Time's wingèd chariot, striking fear
The hour is nigh when creditors   5
Will prove to be my predators.
As wages of our picaresque,
Bag lunches bolted at my desk
Must stand as fealty to you
For each expensive rendezvous.   10
Obeisance at your marble feet
Deserves the best-appointed suite,
And would have, lacked I not the pelf
To pleasure also thus myself;
But aptly sumptuous amorous scenes   15
Rule out the rake of modest means.

Since mistress presupposes wife,
It means a doubly costly life;
For fools by second passion fired
A second income is required,   20
The earning which consumes the hours
They'd hoped to spend in rented bowers.
To hostelries the worst of fates
That weekly raise their daily rates!
I gather, lady, from your scoffing   25
A bloke more solvent in the offing.
So revels thus to rivals go
For want of monetary flow.

How vexing that inconstant cash
The constant suitor must abash,   30
Who with excuses vainly pled
Must rue the undisheveled bed,
And that for paltry reasons given
His conscience may remain unriven.

Considerations for Critical Thinking and Writing

1. How is De Vries's use of the term *mistress* different from Marvell's (p. 631)? How does the speaker's complaint in this poem differ from that in "To His Coy Mistress"?
2. Explain how "picaresque" is used in line 7.
3. To what extent does this poem duplicate Marvell's style?
4. Choose a poet whose work you know reasonably well or would like to know better and determine what is characteristic about his or her style. Then choose a poem to parody. It's probably best to attempt a short poem or a section of a long work. If you have difficulty selecting an author, you might consider Herrick, Blake, Keats, Dickinson, Whitman, or Frost, since a number of their works are included in this book.

Connection to Another Selection

1. Read Anthony Hecht's "Dover Bitch" (p. 960), a parody of Arnold's "Dover Beach" (p. 648). Write an essay comparing the effectiveness of Hecht's parody with that of De Vries's "To His Importunate Mistress." Which parody do you prefer? Explain why.

PERSPECTIVE

ROBERT MORGAN (b. 1944)
On the Shape of a Poem   1983

In the body of the poem, lineation is part flesh and part skeleton, as form is the towpath along which the burden of content, floating on the formless, is pulled. All language is both mental and sacramental, is not "real" but is the working of lip and tongue to subvert the "real." Poems empearl irritating facts until they become opalescent spheres of moment, not so much résumés of history as of human faculties working with pain. Every poem is necessarily a fragment empowered by its implicitness. We sing to charm the snake in our spines, to make it sway with the pulse of the world, balancing the weight of consciousness on the topmost vertebra.

From *Epoch,* Fall–Winter 1983

Considerations for Critical Thinking and Writing

1. Explain Morgan's metaphors for describing lineation and form in a poem. Why are these metaphors useful?
2. Choose one of the poems in this chapter that makes use of a particular form and explain how it is "a fragment empowered by its implicitness."

21. Open Form

Many poems, especially those written in the twentieth century, are composed of lines that cannot be scanned for a fixed or predominant meter. Moreover, very often these poems do not rhyme. Known as *free verse* (from the French, *vers libre*), such lines can derive their rhythmic qualities from the repetition of words, phrases, or grammatical structures; the arrangement of words on the printed page; or some other means. In recent years the term *open form* has been used in place of *free verse* to avoid the erroneous suggestion that this kind of poetry lacks all discipline and shape.

Although the following two poems do not use measurable meters, they do have rhythm.

e. e. cummings (1894–1962)
in Just-   1923

in Just-
spring   when the world is mud-
luscious the little
lame balloonman

whistles   far   and wee   5

and eddieandbill come
running from marbles and
piracies and it's
spring

when the world is puddle-wonderful   10

the queer
old balloonman whistles
far   and   wee
and bettyandisbel come dancing

from hop-scotch and jump-rope and   15

it's
spring
and
   the

     goat-footed   20

balloonMan   whistles
far
and
wee

Considerations for Critical Thinking and Writing

1. What is the effect of this poem's arrangement of words and the use of space on the page?
2. What is the effect of cummings combining the names "eddieandbill" and "bettyandisbel"?
3. The allusion in line 20 refers to Pan, a Greek god associated with nature. How does this allusion add to the meaning of the poem?

WALT WHITMAN (1819–1892)
From *I Sing the Body Electric*   1855

O my body! I dare not desert the likes of you in other men and women, nor the likes of the parts of you,
I believe the likes of you are to stand or fall with the likes of the soul, (and that they are the soul,)
I believe the likes of you shall stand or fall with my poems, and that they are my poems.
Man's, woman's, child's, youth's, wife's, husband's, mother's, father's, young man's, young woman's poems.
Head, neck, hair, ears, drop and tympan of the ears.   5
Eyes, eye-fringes, iris of the eye, eyebrows, and the waking or sleeping of the lids,
Mouth, tongue, lips, teeth, roof of the mouth, jaws, and the jaw-hinges,
Nose, nostrils of the nose, and the partition,
Cheeks, temples, forehead, chin, throat, back of the neck, neck-slue,
Strong shoulders, manly beard, scapula, hind-shoulders, and the ample side-round of the chest,   10
Upper-arm, armpit, elbow-socket, lower-arm, arm-sinews, arm-bones,
Wrist and wrist-joints, hand, palm, knuckles, thumb, forefinger, finger-joints, finger-nails,
Broad breast-front, curling hair of the breast, breast-bone, breast-side,
Ribs, belly, backbone, joints of the backbone,
Hips, hip-sockets, hip-strength, inward and outward round, man-balls, man-root,   15

Strong set of thighs, well carrying the trunk above,
Leg-fibers, knee, knee-pan, upper-leg, under-leg,
Ankles, instep, foot-ball, toes, toe-joints, the heel;
All attitudes, all the shapeliness, all the belongings of my or your body or of any
    one's body, male or female,
The lung-sponges, the stomach-sac, the bowels sweet and clean,   20
The brain in its folds inside the skull-frame,
Sympathies, heart-valves, palate-valves, sexuality, maternity,
Womanhood, and all that is a woman, and the man that comes from woman,
The womb, the teats, nipples, breast-milk, tears, laughter, weeping, love-looks,
    love-perturbations and risings,
The voice, articulation, language, whispering, shouting aloud,   25
Food, drink, pulse, digestion, sweat, sleep, walking, swimming,
Poise on the hips, leaping, reclining, embracing, arm-curving and tightening,
The continual changes of the flex of the mouth, and around the eyes,
The skin, the sunburnt shade, freckles, hair,
The curious sympathy one feels when feeling with the hand the naked meat of
    the body,   30
The circling rivers the breath, and breathing it in and out,
The beauty of the waist, and thence of the hips, and thence downward toward
    the knees,
The thin red jellies within you or within me, the bones and the marrow in the
    bones,
The exquisite realization of health;
O I say these are not the parts and poems of the body only, but of the soul, 35
O I say now these are the soul!

Considerations for Critical Thinking and Writing

1. What informs the speaker's attitude toward the human body in this poem?
2. Read the poem aloud. Is it simply a tedious enumeration of body parts, or do the
   lines achieve some kind of rhythmic cadence?

PERSPECTIVE

WALT WHITMAN (1819–1892)
On Rhyme and Meter   1855

The poetic quality is not marshaled in rhyme or uniformity or abstract
addresses to things nor in melancholy complaints or good precepts, but is the
life of these and much else and is in the soul. The profit of rhyme is that it drops
seeds of a sweeter and more luxuriant rhyme, and of uniformity that it conveys
itself into its own roots in the ground out of sight. The rhyme and uniformity of
perfect poems show the free growth of metrical laws and bud from them as
unnerringly and loosely as lilacs or roses on a bush, and take shapes as compact
as the shapes of chestnuts and oranges and melons and pears, and shed the

perfume impalpable to form. The fluency and ornaments of the finest poems or music or orations or recitations are not independent but dependent. All beauty comes from beautiful blood and a beautiful brain. If the greatnesses are in conjunction in a man or woman it is enough . . . . the fact will prevail through the universe . . . but the gaggery and gilt of a million years will not prevail. Who troubles himself about his ornaments or fluency is lost.

From the preface to the 1855 edition of *Leaves of Grass*

Considerations for Critical Thinking and Writing

1. According to Whitman, what determines the shape of a poem?
2. Why does Whitman prefer open forms over fixed forms such as the sonnet?
3. Is Whitman's poetry devoid of any structure or shape? Choose one of his poems (listed in the index) to illustrate your answer.

Open form poetry is sometimes regarded as formless because it is unlike the strict fixed forms of a sonnet, villanelle, or sestina. But even though open form poems may not employ traditional meters and rhymes, they still rely on an intense use of language to establish rhythms and relations between meaning and form. Open form poems use the arrangement of words and phrases on the printed page, pauses, line lengths, and other means to create unique forms that express their particular meaning and tone.

Cummings's "in Just-" and the excerpt from Whitman's "I Sing the Body Electric" demonstrate how the white space on a page and rhythmic cadences can be aligned with meaning, but there is one kind of open form poetry that doesn't even look like poetry on a page. A *prose poem* is printed as prose and represents, perhaps, the most clear opposite of fixed forms. Here is a brief example.

GEORGE STARBUCK (b. 1931)
Japanese Fish   1985

Have you ever eaten a luchu? It's poisonous like fugu, but it's cheaper and you cook it yourself.

You cut it into little squares as fast as possible but without touching the poison-gland. But first, you get all the thrill you can out of the fact that you're going to do it. You sit around for hours with your closest friends, drinking and telling long nostalgicky stories. You make toasts. You pick up your knives and sing a little song entitled "We who are about to dice a luchu." And then you begin.

1. What is the effect of this prose poem? Does it have a theme?
2. What, if anything, is poetic in this work?
3. Arrange the lines so that they look like poetry on a page. What determines where you break the lines?

Much of the poetry published today is written in open form; however, many poets continue to take pleasure in the requirements imposed by fixed forms. Some write both fixed form and open form poetry. Each kind offers rewards to careful readers as well. Here are several more open form poems that establish their own unique patterns.

WILLIAM CARLOS WILLIAMS (1883–1963)
The Red Wheelbarrow   1923

so much depends
upon

a red wheel
barrow

glazed with rain
water

beside the white
chickens.

Considerations for Critical Thinking and Writing

1. What is the effect of these images? Do they have a particular meaning? What "depends upon" the things mentioned in the poem?
2. Do these lines have any kind of rhythm?
3. How does this poem resemble a haiku? How is it different?

ALLEN GINSBERG (b. 1926)
A Supermarket in California   1956

What thoughts I have of you tonight, Walt Whitman, for I walked down the sidestreets under the trees with a headache self-conscious looking at the full moon.

In my hungry fatigue, and shopping for images, I went into the neon fruit supermarket, dreaming of your enumerations!°

What peaches and what penumbras! Whole families shopping at night! Aisles full of husbands! Wives in the avocados, babies in the tomatoes — and you, Garcia Lorca,° what were you doing down by the watermelons?

I saw you, Walt Whitman, childless, lonely old grubber, poking among the meats in the refrigerator and eyeing the grocery boys.

I heard you asking questions of each: Who killed the pork chops? What price bananas? Are you my Angel?   5

I wandered in and out of the brilliant stacks of cans following you, and followed in my imagination by the store detective.

We strode down the open corridors together in our solitary fancy tasting artichokes, possessing every frozen delicacy, and never passing the cashier.

Where are we going, Walt Whitman? The doors close in an hour. Which way does your beard point tonight?

(I touch your book and dream of our odyssey in the supermarket and feel absurd.)

Will we walk all night through solitary streets? The trees add shade to shade, lights out in the houses, we'll both be lonely.   10

Will we stroll dreaming of the lost America of love past blue automobiles in driveways, home to our silent cottage?

Ah, dear father, graybeard, lonely old courage-teacher, what America did you have when Charon quit poling his ferry and you got out on a smoking bank and stood watching the boat disappear on the black waters of Lethe?°

Berkeley 1955

---

2 *enumerations:* See the "enumerations" (the catalog of details), a typical poetic device of Whitman's, in "I Sing the Body Electric" (p. 776).   3 *Garcia Lorca:* Federico García Lorca (1898–1936), a Spanish poet whose nonrealistic techniques Ginsberg admired.   12 *When Charon quit poling . . . Lethe:* In Greek mythology Charon ferries the dead into Hades. Lethe is one of the rivers in Hades and is associated with forgetfulness, because a drink from it causes the dead to forget those they have left behind.

Considerations for Critical Thinking and Writing

1. How is the setting used symbolically in this poem?
2. What kinds of thoughts does the speaker have about Whitman?
3. What does the speaker think about America? About himself?

Connections to Other Selections

1. How are Ginsberg's techniques similar to Whitman's in "I Sing the Body Electric" (p. 776)?
2. How is Ginsberg's America different from the description Whitman provides in "Song of the Open Road" (p. 735)? In what sense is Ginsberg "shopping for images"?
3. Write an essay contrasting the tone of this poem with that of "Song of the Open Road."

NAZIK AL-MALA'IKA (b. 1923)

I Am   1949

TRANSLATED BY KAMAL BOULLATA

The night asks me who I am
   Its impenetrable black, its unquiet secret
                 I am
   Its lull rebellious.
   I veil myself with silence   5
   Wrapping my heart with doubt
   Solemnly, I gaze
   While ages ask me
      who I am.

The wind asks me who I am   10
   Its bedevilled spirit I am
   Denied by Time, going nowhere
   I journey on and on
   Passing without a pause
   And when reaching an edge   15
   I think it may be the end
   Of suffering, but then:
      the void.

Time asks me who I am
   A giant enfolding centuries I am   20
   Later to give new births
   I have created the dim past
   From the bliss of unbound hope
   I push it back into its grave
   To make a new yesterday, its tomorrow   25
   is ice.

The self asks me who I am
   Baffled, I stare into the dark
   Nothing brings me peace
   I ask, but the answer   30
   Remains hooded in mirage
   I keep thinking it is near
   Upon reaching it, it dissolves.

Considerations for Critical Thinking and Writing

1. How does the manner in which the lines are spaced on the page structure this poem?
2. What kind of self-identity does the speaker describe? Is this person hopeful or pessimistic about finding a true self?
3. Why do you suppose the poem is titled "I Am" rather than "Who Am I"?

1. Write an essay on conceptions of the self in "I Am" and Emily Dickinson's "I'm Nobody! Who are you?" (p. 840).

DENISE LEVERTOV (b. 1923)

O Taste and See   1962

The world is
not with us enough.
O taste and see

the subway Bible poster said,
meaning The Lord, meaning   5
if anything all that lives
to the imagination's tongue,

grief, mercy, language,
tangerine, weather, to
breathe them, bite,   10
savor, chew, swallow, transform

into our flesh our
deaths, crossing the street, plum, quince,
living in the orchard and being

hungry, and plucking   15
the fruit.

Considerations for Critical Thinking and Writing

1. How does the speaker in this poem want people to respond to the world?
2. Are lines 8–11 simply a list of random words? How do they relate to one another and to the poem's theme?
3. Why are the lines arranged in stanzas? Would the experience of reading the poem be any different if it were all one stanza?

Connection to Another Selection

1. Write a short essay comparing and contrasting this poem in form and content with Wordsworth's "The World Is Too Much with Us" (p. 756).

CAROLYN FORCHÉ (b. 1950)

The Colonel

What you have heard is true. I was in his house. His wife carried
a tray of coffee and sugar. His daughter filed her nails, his son went
out for the night. There were daily papers, pet dogs, a pistol on the
cushion beside him. The moon swung bare on its black cord over
the house. On the television was a cop show. It was in English.   5
Broken bottles were embedded in the walls around the house to
scoop the kneecaps from a man's legs or cut his hands to lace. On
the windows there were gratings like those in liquor stores. We had
dinner, rack of lamb, good wine, a gold bell was on the table for
calling the maid. The maid brought green mangoes, salt, a type of   10
bread. I was asked how I enjoyed the country. There was a brief
commercial in Spanish. His wife took everything away. There was
some talk then of how difficult it had become to govern. The parrot
said hello on the terrace. The colonel told it to shut up, and pushed
himself from the table. My friend said to me with his eyes: say   15
nothing. The colonel returned with a sack used to bring groceries
home. He spilled many human ears on the table. They were like
dried peach halves. There is no other way to say this. He took one
of them in his hands, shook it in our faces, dropped it into a water
glass. It came alive there. I am tired of fooling around he said. As   20
for the rights of anyone, tell your people they can go fuck themselves. He swept the ears to the floor with his arm and held the last
of his wine in the air. Something for your poetry, no? he said. Some
of the ears on the floor caught this scrap of his voice. Some of the
ears on the floor were pressed to the ground.   25

Considerations for Critical Thinking and Writing

1. What kind of horror is described in this prose poem? Characterize the colonel.
2. What makes this prose poem not a typical prose passage? How is it organized differently?
3. What poetic elements can you find in it?
4. What is the tone of the final two sentences?

SHARON OLDS (b. 1942)

Rite of Passage

1983

As the guests arrive at my son's party
they gather in the living room —
short men, men in first grade
with smooth jaws and chins.
Hands in pockets, they stand around   5
jostling, jockeying for place, small fights

breaking out and calming. One says to another
How old are you? Six. I'm seven. So?
They eye each other, seeing themselves
tiny in the other's pupils. They clear their   10
throats a lot, a room of small bankers,
they fold their arms and frown. *I could beat you
up,* a seven says to a six,
the dark cake, round and heavy as a
turret, behind them on the table. My son,   15
freckles like specks of nutmeg on his cheeks,
chest narrow as the balsa keel of a
model boat, long hands
cool and thin as the day they guided him
out of me, speaks up as a host   20
for the sake of the group.
We could easily kill a two-year-old,
he says in his clear voice. The other
men agree, they clear their throats
like Generals, they relax and get down to   25
playing war, celebrating my son's life.

Considerations for Critical Thinking and Writing

1. In what sense is this birthday party a "Rite of Passage"?
2. How does the speaker transform these six- and seven-year-old boys into men?
   What is the point of doing so?
3. Comment on the appropriateness of the image of the cake in lines 14–15.
4. Why does the son's claim that "We could easily kill a two-year-old" come as such
   a shock at that point in the poem?

Connections to Other Selections

1. In an essay discuss the treatment of violence in "Rite of Passage" and Carolyn
   Forché's "The Colonel" (p. 783). To what extent might the colonel be regarded
   as an adult version of the generals in Olds's' poem?
2. Discuss the use of irony in "Rite of Passage" and Wilfred Owen's "Dulce et
   Decorum Est" (p. 652). Which do you think is a more effective antiwar poem?
   Explain why.

ANONYMOUS
The Frog   date unknown

What a wonderful bird the frog are!
When he stand he sit almost;
When he hop he fly almost.
He ain't got no sense hardly;
He ain't got no tail hardly either.
When he sit, he sit on what he ain't got almost.

Considerations for Critical Thinking and Writing

1. Though this poem is ungrammatical, it does have a patterned structure. How does the pattern of sentences create a formal structure?
2. How is the poem a description of the speaker as well as of a frog?

TATO LAVIERA (b. 1951)
AmeRícan
1985

we gave birth to a new generation,
AmeRícan, broader than lost gold
never touched, hidden inside the
puerto rican mountains.

we gave birth to a new generation,   5
AmeRícan, it includes everything
imaginable you-name-it-we-got-it
society.

we gave birth to a new generation,
AmeRícan salutes all folklores,   10
european, indian, black, spanish,
and anything else compatible:

AmeRícan,   singing to composer pedro flores'° palm
            trees high up in the universal sky!

AmeRícan,   sweet soft spanish danzas gypsies   15
            moving lyrics la *española*° cascabelling   *Spanish*
            presence always singing at our side!

AmeRícan,   beating jíbaro° modern troubadours
            crying guitars romantic continental
            bolero love songs!   20

AmeRícan,   across forth and across back
            back across and forth back
            forth across and back and forth
            our trips are walking bridges!

            it all dissolved into itself, the attempt   25
            was truly made, the attempt was truly
            absorbed, digested, we spit out
            the poison, we spit out the malice,
            we stand, affirmative in action,
            to reproduce a broader answer to the   30
            marginality that gobbled us up abruptly!

13 *Pedro Flores:* Puerto Rican composer of popular romantic songs.   18 *jíbaro:* A particular style of music played by Puerto Rican mountain farmers.

AmeRícan,	walking plena- rhythms° in new york,	
	strutting beautifully alert, alive,	
	many turning eyes wondering,	
	admiring!	35

AmeRícan,	defining myself my own way any way many
	ways Am e Rícan, with the big R and the
	accent on the í!

AmeRícan,	like the soul gliding talk of gospel	
	boogie music!	40

AmeRícan, speaking new words in spanglish tenements,
fast tongue moving street corner *"que
corta"*° talk being invented at the insistence   *that cuts*
of a smile!

AmeRícan, abounding inside so many ethnic english   45
people, and out of humanity, we blend
and mix all that is good!

AmeRícan, integrating in new york and defining our
own *destino,*° our own way of life,   *destiny*

AmeRícan, defining the new america, humane america,   50
admired america, loved america, harmonious
america, the world in peace, our energies
collectively invested to find other civilizations, to touch God, further and further,
to dwell in the spirit of divinity!   55

AmeRícan, yes, for now, for i love this, my second
land, and i dream to take the accent from
the altercation, and be proud to call
myself american, in the u.s. sense of the
word, AmeRícan, America!   60

32 *plena- rhythms:* African–Puerto Rican folklore, music, and dance.

Considerations for Critical Thinking and Writing

1. How does the arrangement of lines communicate a sense of energy and vitality?
2. How does the speaker portray Puerto Ricans living in the United States?
3. How does the poet describe the United States?

Connection to Another Selection

1. In an essay consider the themes, styles, and tones of "AmeRícan" and Allen
   Ginsberg's "America" (p. 952).

Found Poem

This next poem is a *found poem,* an unintentional poem discovered in a nonpoetic context, such as a conversation, news story, or advertisement. Found poems are playful reminders that the words in poems are very often the language we use every day. Whether such found language should be regarded as a poem is an issue left for you to consider.

DONALD JUSTICE (b. 1925)
Order in the Streets   1969

(From instructions printed on a child's toy, Christmas 1968, as reported in the New York Times*)*

1. 2. 3.
Switch on.

Jeep rushes
to the scene
of riot   5

Jeep goes
in all directions
by mystery action.

Jeep stops periodically
to turn hood over   10

machine gun appears
with realistic
shooting noise.

After putting down riot,
jeep goes   15
back to the headquarters.

Considerations for Critical Thinking and Writing

1. What is the effect of arranging these instructions in lines? How are the language and meaning enhanced by this arrangement?
2. Look for phrases or sentences in ads, textbooks, labels, or directions — in anything that might inadvertently contain provocative material that would be revealed by arranging the words in lines. You may even discover some patterns of rhyme and rhythm. After arranging the lines, explain why you organized them as you did.

22. A Study of Three Poets: John Keats, Emily Dickinson, and Robert Frost

This chapter includes a number of poems by John Keats, Emily Dickinson, and Robert Frost in order to provide an opportunity to study three major poets in some depth. None of the collections is wholly representative of the poet's work, but each offers enough poems to suggest some of the techniques and concerns that characterize the poet's writings. The poems within each group speak not only to readers but to one another. That's natural enough: the more familiar you are with a writer's work, the easier it is to perceive and enjoy the strategies and themes he or she employs.

JOHN KEATS (1795–1821)

The stone marking the grave of John Keats bears an epitaph composed by him shortly before his death: "Here lies one whose name was writ in water." This assessment of his own achievement and fame is informed by the disappointment and anguish that characterized much of his life, but the inscription does not — because it could not — take into account the remarkable reputation that posterity has bestowed on Keats's poetry. His name, as it turns out, is written not only in stone rather than water but also in the minds of readers who have come to appreciate his literary art.

Keats's literary career had barely started when he died at the age of twenty-five. He did not begin writing poetry until he was eighteen, and critics generally agree that this early verse was not very promising. In 1816, however, he wrote the first of his greatest poems, a sonnet entitled "On First Looking into Chapman's Homer"; as he turned twenty-one he was also turning into a genuine poet.

His first volume, *Poems,* appeared in 1817 and was largely ignored; it was followed the next year by *Endymion,* a single poem of more than 4,000 lines about a quest for ideal beauty and happiness. Keats's most productive year was 1819, when he wrote nearly all the poems that have earned him a reputation as a major poet. His third and final volume of poetry, *Lamia, Isabella, The Eve of St. Agnes, and Other Poems,* was published in 1820.

During the final year of his life Keats could not write poetry because of the tuberculosis that was overtaking him. He traveled to Rome with the hope of regaining his health but wrote to a friend that he had "an habitual feeling of my life having past, and that I am leading a posthumous existence." He knew his illness was fatal and died three months later, in February of 1821. Almost incredibly, Keats's life as a writer spanned little more than the time required by most undergraduates to earn a bachelor's degree; and, more important, within those few years he outgrew his early sentimental and derivative verse to emerge as a powerful poet.

Keats's literary life moved toward greatness as he matured, but his personal life presented a series of abrupt dislocations and unfulfilled expectations. As a young boy he was exposed to the frailty and unpredictability of life. His father, manager of a livery stable in London, was killed by falling off a horse when Keats was only eight years old, and when the poet was fourteen his mother died of tuberculosis. The next year Keats's guardian withdrew him from school and apprenticed him to a five-year course in medicine at a London hospital.

While he studied medicine, Keats pursued his interest in literary studies, and upon completion of his surgical training he gave up medicine for poetry, a decision influenced by several literary friends who encouraged his efforts to become a writer. In 1818, however, this decision was severely tested by two reviews of *Endymion* that were so brutal as to foster the legend that they were the cause of Keats's early death.

But it was tuberculosis that killed Keats and that had caused his brother's death in 1818. Keats faithfully nursed his brother and therefore had a long hard look at the disease of which he was beginning to show symptoms. During this year Keats also lost another brother, who emigrated to America. But despite all these blows, Keats's spirits were high when he fell in love with Fanny Brawne. Unfortunately, his commitment to poetry as well as his financial situation and health prohibited their marriage and made his passionate love agonizing until his death. Keats's brief life seems hopelessly sad — his letters especially convey the sense of a remarkable sensibility overcome by a "world of circumstances."

Keats took a great risk by rejecting a medical career, but his interests were elsewhere. Perhaps his choice of profession was foreshadowed by the flowers that he sketched in the margins of his anatomy notes. Keats seems always to have been more concerned with beauty in life. In a sense, beauty was life to him. In life's transient materiality he found a constant that transcends space, time, and matter. He described this perception in these famous euphonic lines from *Endymion.*

A thing of beauty is a joy for ever:
Its loveliness increases; it will never
Pass into nothingness; but still will keep
A bower quiet for us, and a sleep
Full of sweet dreams, and health, and quiet breathing.
Therefore, on every morrow, are we wreathing
A flowery band to bind us to the earth,
Spite of despondence, of the inhuman dearth
Of noble natures, of the gloomy days,
Of all the unhealthy and o'er-darkened ways
Made for our searching: yes, in spite of all,
Some shape of beauty moves away the pall
From our dark spirits.

Keats preferred a direct, spontaneous response to life over the logical, rational abstractions that informed the intellectual tenor of his times. Putting his faith in an imaginative rather than a scientific approach to existence, he believed that literary imagination requires what he called a "Negative Capability," the ability to be "in uncertainties, mysteries, doubts, without any irritable reaching after fact and reason." Keats believed that the poetic imagination can tolerate ambiguities, and though it might not have all the answers, it has a greater capacity for asking questions than the sort of mind that demands "fact and reason." Truth was infinitely complex and problematic for Keats, and he found that he could not create beauty without being alert to the ugliness of evil. His ideal of "Negative Capability" represented, however, a positive creative power for the poet, because it demanded an openness to and sympathy with the possibilities of life and thought.

Although Keats created an imaginative world in his poems, he did not abandon "fact." Indeed, one of the major characteristics of his poetry is his use of detailed sensuous description. He builds a world by invoking the reader's senses of touch, smell, taste, hearing, and seeing so that experience is richly savored. His imagery is detailed and strong. Using diction that is both precise and opulent, Keats creates images that are not unlike a holograph. His melodic lines give us more of experience than a flat objective description could possibly offer.

Sonnets, odes, and narrative poems are the three poetic forms on which Keats's reputation rests. The typical subjects of his poems are familiar ones; he writes about love, death, fame, failure, poetry, art, and nature. The common thread running through these subjects is his keen awareness that everything is subject to change. Sometimes Keats attempts to transcend this changing world by pursuing a visionary imagination, but at other points he comes to understand that an acceptance of the transient nature of existence can be a way to appreciate its beauty. This conflict leads him into a series of tensions in which he celebrates sensations but simultaneously expresses a sadness that they cannot last. For Keats, pleasure and pain, love and death, dream and reality are the breathing out and breathing in of poetic imagination. He does not resolve these conflicts so much as articulate them.

"On First Looking into Chapman's Homer" is a fitting introduction to Keats's poetry, because it is about his own sense of discovery. At the age of twenty-one, Keats was introduced by a friend to George Chapman's poetic Elizabethan translation of Homer's *Iliad* and *Odyssey.* Before his reading in Chapman, Keats had known only eighteenth-century translations, which were stilted and pedestrian, but with Chapman's version he suddenly realized the power and energy of Homer's poetry. Immediately after reading Chapman, Keats spent the night writing the following sonnet.

On First Looking into Chapman's Homer   1816

Much have I traveled in the realms of gold,
   And many goodly states and kingdoms seen;
   Round many western islands have I been
Which bards in fealty to Apollo° hold.
Oft of one wide expanse had I been told   5
   That deep-browed Homer ruled as his demesne;
   Yet did I never breathe its pure serene°   *atmosphere*
Till I heard Chapman speak out loud and bold:
Then felt I like some watcher of the skies
   When a new planet swims into his ken;   10
Or like stout Cortez° when with eagle eyes
   He stared at the Pacific — and all his men
Looked at each other with a wild surmise —
   Silent, upon a peak in Darien.

4 *Apollo:* Greek god of poetry.   11 *Cortez:* Vasco Núñez de Balboa, not Hernando Cortés, was the first European to sight the Pacific from Darien, a peak in Panama.

This is one of those rare poems in which we can accurately identify the speaker with the poet. Even so, it is less a fragment of autobiography than an evocation of excitement and wonder. This sonnet is not only about Keats's discovery of Chapman's Homer, because that personal experience serves as a symbol for any discovery. One way to state the theme is to say that reading can be a source of imaginative discovery as significant as the discovery of a planet or ocean. To express this theme, Keats uses a controlling metaphor built around a comparison of reading with traveling and exploration, an especially apt metaphor given the many journeys that appear in Homer. Keats shapes this metaphor into an Italian sonnet, which is often enough a traditional form for love poetry to suggest Keats's own passion for poetry.

In the octave, the speaker tells us that he has "traveled in the realms of gold" and seen many "goodly states and kingdoms." Given the context of the rest of the poem, we know that the speaker is referring to his wide reading in the literature of Western civilization ("western islands"). The diction of the octave is formal and dignified ("goodly states," "bards in fealty," "demesne," "serene"), fitting the respectful, if dispassionate, assessment of what the speaker has experienced in his reading. A shift occurs, however, between the octave and sestet, when the speaker moves to the impact that reading Chapman's Homer has had on him. Images of exploration give way to images of discovery, and the tone changes from elevated description to intense feelings of wonder.

Two similes in the sestet convey the speaker's wonder. First, he compares his excitement to that of an astronomer, a purposeful "watcher of the skies" who suddenly sees a new planet through a telescope. That discovery of a new world is brought down to earth in the second simile, when the speaker likens himself to Cortés, who (Keats mistakenly believed) inadvertently discovered the Pacific Ocean. Although the second simile brings us down to earth, it soars even higher than the first in its effect. The discovery of the ocean is more startling because it comes as a complete surprise. Cortés had no idea that the Pacific Ocean would be on the other side of the mountains.

The speaker's excitement is also evident in the change of rhythm in the sestet. A calm and measured movement can be heard in the octave, but the sestet's lines are less regular. This deviation from the predominant iambic pentameter is accompanied by run-on lines and dashes that convey the speaker's heightened emotions, which reach a climax in the final line. Here the trochaic "Silent," along with the comma that follows it, slows down the line, preparing us for the concluding image of awe.

The final allusive image of "stout Cortez" (notice how the heavy accents on these syllables emphasize the explorer's power) is a visual representation of the emotional intensity experienced by the speaker. This also completes the speaker's imagining himself as an explorer. We leave both the speaker and the explorer contemplating the beginning of further explorations and discoveries in worlds previously not even imagined. The sense of awe and expectation created in this poem serves as an appropriate first encounter with Keats's poetry, because it evokes some of the remarkable discoveries that readers have made in these poems.

Chronology

1795   Born on October 31 in London.

1803   Enters Clarke School.

1804   Father dies unexpectedly.

1810   Mother dies from tuberculosis.

1811	Leaves school to be apprenticed to an apothecary-surgeon; completes a prose translation of the *Aeneid*.
1814	Actively writing poetry.
1815	Continues medical education at Guy's Hospital, London.
1816	"To Solitude," a sonnet, becomes his first publication; earns his Apothecaries' Certificate but abandons further interest in medicine.
1817	*Poems,* his first book, is published.
1818	*Endymion* is published; takes a walking tour of northern England, Scotland, and Ireland; declares his love for Fanny Brawne.
1819	Writes many of his major odes as well as *Lamia* and *The Fall of Hyperion*; dogged by ill health, poverty, and frustration over not being able to marry Fanny Brawne.
1820	*Lamia; Isabella; The Eve of St. Agnes, and Other Poems* is published. Travels to Naples, Italy, in an attempt to restore his declining health.
1821	Dies on February 23 in Rome.

On the Grasshopper and the Cricket   1816

The poetry of earth is never dead:
When all the birds are faint with the hot sun,
And hide in cooling trees, a voice will run
From hedge to hedge about the new-mown mead;
That is the grasshopper's — he takes the lead   5
In summer luxury — he has never done
With his delights; for when tired out with fun
He rests at ease beneath some pleasant weed.
The poetry of earth is ceasing never:
On a lone winter evening, when the frost   10
Has wrought a silence, from the stove there shrills
The cricket's song, in warmth increasing ever,
And seems to one in drowsiness half lost,
The grasshopper's among some grassy hills.

Considerations for Critical Thinking and Writing

1. How are two seasons contrasted in the octave and sestet of this sonnet?
2. What does the speaker mean by "The poetry of earth"? What is the view of nature in the sonnet?
3. How does the imagery contribute to the sonnet's effect?

To One Who Has Been Long in City Pent

1816

To one who has been long in city pent,
    'Tis very sweet to look into the fair
    And open face of heaven, — to breathe a prayer
Full in the smile of the blue firmament.
Who is more happy, when, with heart's content,   5
    Fatigued he sinks into some pleasant lair
    Of wavy grass, and reads a debonair
And gentle tale of love and languishment?

Returning home at evening, with an ear
    Catching the notes of Philomel,° — an eye   10
Watching the sailing cloudlet's bright career,
    He mourns that day so soon has glided by:
E'en like the passage of an angel's tear
    That falls through the clear ether silently.

10 *Philomel:* A nightingale.

Considerations for Critical Thinking and Writing

1. Although the city is not described in the sonnet, how does Keats make you feel about it?
2. What values is the countryside associated with here? How does this sonnet's evocation of nature compare with that of "On the Grasshopper and the Cricket"?
3. Do you think this sonnet is more about a sense of loss or a celebration of nature?

Written in Disgust of Vulgar Superstition

1816

The church bells toll a melancholy round,
    Calling the people to some other prayers,
    Some other gloominess, more dreadful cares,
More hearkening to the sermon's horrid sound.
Surely the mind of man is closely bound   5
    In some black spell; seeing that each one tears
    Himself from fireside joys, and Lydian airs,
And converse high of those with glory crown'd.
Still, still they toll, and I should feel a damp —
    A chill as from a tomb, did I not know   10
That they are going like an outburnt lamp;
    That 'tis their sighing, wailing ere they go
    Into oblivion; — that fresh flowers will grow,
And many glories of immortal stamp.

Considerations for Critical Thinking and Writing

1. What is Keat's view of religion in this poem?
2. Use the library to explain the allusion to "Lydian airs." What does it add to the poem?
3. Discuss the bells and flowers as opposing symbols.

Connection to Another Selection

1. In an essay compare attitudes toward religion in this poem and in Emily Dickinson's "Some keep the Sabbath going to Church — " (p. 837).

On Seeing the Elgin Marbles°   1817

My spirit is too weak; mortality
    Weighs heavily on me like unwilling sleep,
    And each imagined pinnacle and steep
Of godlike hardship tells me I must die
Like a sick eagle looking at the sky.   5
    Yet 'tis a gentle luxury to weep,
    That I have not the cloudy winds to keep
Fresh for the opening of the morning's eye.
Such dim-conceived glories of the brain
    Bring round the heart an indescribable feud;   10
So do these wonders a most dizzy pain,
    That mingles Grecian grandeur with the rude
Wasting of old Time — with a billowy main,
    A sun, a shadow of a magnitude.

Elgin Marbles: The remains of ancient figures and friezes from the Athenian Parthenon, acquired by Lord Elgin for the British Museum.

Considerations for Critical Thinking and Writing

1. Why is the speaker in this sonnet "weak"? What causes the "dizzy pain" he feels in line 11?
2. What is the relationship between time and art in this sonnet?

When I have fears that I may cease to be   1818

When I have fears that I may cease to be
    Before my pen has gleaned my teeming brain,
Before high-piled books, in charactery,°   *print*
    Hold like rich garners the full ripened grain;

When I behold, upon the night's starred face,   5
    Huge cloudy symbols of a high romance,
And think that I may never live to trace
    Their shadows, with the magic hand of chance;
And when I feel, fair creature of an hour,
    That I shall never look upon thee more,   10
Never have relish in the faery° power   *magic*
    Of unreflecting love; — then on the shore
Of the wide world I stand alone, and think
Till love and fame to nothingness do sink.

Considerations for Critical Thinking and Writing

1. Describe the speaker's fear in each of the three quatrains of this sonnet. Is there any kind of progression?
2. What impact does the fear of death have on "love and fame" in the concluding couplet?

Connection to Another Selection

1. Compare the view of death in this poem with the attitude expressed in Robert Frost's "Provide, Provide" (p. 888).

The Eve of St. Agnes°   1819

I

    St. Agnes' Eve — Ah, bitter chill it was!
    The owl, for all his feathers, was a-cold;
    The hare limped trembling through the frozen grass,
    And silent was the flock in woolly fold:
    Numb were the Beadsman's° fingers, while he told   5
    His rosary, and while his frosted breath,
    Like pious incense from a censer old,
    Seemed taking flight for heaven, without a death,
Past the sweet Virgin's picture, while his prayer he saith.

II

    His prayer he saith, this patient, holy man;   10
    Then takes his lamp, and riseth from his knees,
    And back returneth, meager, barefoot, wan,
    Along the chapel aisle by slow degrees:
    The sculptured dead, on each side, seem to freeze,

Eve of St. Agnes: January 20, supposed to be the coldest night of the year. St. Agnes, martyred in the fourth century, is the patroness of virgins. According to folk legend, a girl who performed certain rituals on St. Agnes's Eve would have a vision of her future husband.   5 *Beadsman:* A person hired to pray for someone.

      Imprisoned in black, purgatorial rails: 15
      Knights, ladies, praying in dumb orat'ries,°   *chapels*
      He passeth by; and his weak spirit fails
To think how they may ache in icy hoods and mails.

III

      Northward he turneth through a little door,
      And scarce three steps, ere Music's golden tongue   20
      Flattered to tears this aged man and poor;
      But no — already had his deathbell rung:
      The joys of all his life were said and sung:
      His was harsh penance on St. Agnes' eve:
      Another way he went, and soon among   25
      Rough ashes sat he for his soul's reprieve,
And all night kept awake, for sinner's sake to grieve.

IV

      That ancient Beadsman heard the prelude soft;
      And so it chanced, for many a door was wide,
      From hurry to and fro. Soon, up aloft,   30
      The silver, snarling trumpets 'gan to chide:
      The level chambers, ready with their pride,
      Were glowing to receive a thousand guests:
      The carvèd angels, ever eager-eyed,
      Stared, where upon their heads the cornice rests,   35
With hair blown back, and wings put crosswise on their breasts.

V

      At length burst in the argent revelry,
      With plume, tiara, and all rich array,
      Numerous as shadows haunting faerily°   *magically*
      The brain, new stuffed, in youth, with triumphs gay   40
      Of old romance. These let us wish away,
      And turn, sole-thoughted, to one Lady there,
      Whose heart had brooded, all that wintry day,
      On love, and winged St. Agnes' saintly care,
As she had heard old dames full many times declare.   .45

VI

      They told her how, upon St. Agnes' Eve,
      Young virgins might have visions of delight,
      And soft adorings from their loves receive
      Upon the honeyed middle of the night,
      If ceremonies due they did aright;   50
      As, supperless to bed they must retire,
      And couch supine their beauties, lily white;
      Nor look behind, nor sideways, but require
Of heaven with upward eyes for all that they desire.

VII

      Full of this whim was thoughtful Madeline: 55
      The music, yearning like a God in pain,

> She scarcely heard: her maiden eyes divine,
> Fixed on the floor, saw many a sweeping train
> Pass by — she heeded not at all: in vain
> Came many a tiptoe, amorous cavalier,   60
> And back retired; not cooled by high disdain;
> But she saw not: her heart was otherwhere:
> She sighed for Agnes' dreams, the sweetest of the year.

VIII

> She danced along with vague, regardless eyes,
> Anxious her lips, her breathing quick and short: 65
> The hallowed hour was near at hand: she sighs
> Amid the timbrels, and the thronged resort
> Of whisperers in anger, or in sport;
> 'Mid looks of love, defiance, hate, and scorn,
> Hoodwinked with faery fancy: all amort,°   *as if dead* 70
> Save to St. Agnes and her lambs unshorn,
> And all the bliss to be before tomorrow morn.

IX

> So, purposing each moment to retire,
> She lingered still. Meantime, across the moors,
> Had come young Porphyro, with heart on fire   75
> For Madeline. Beside the portal doors,
> Buttressed from moonlight,° stands he, and implores   *in shadows*
> All saints to give him sight of Madeline,
> But for one moment in the tedious hours,
> That he might gaze and worship all unseen;   80
> Perchance speak, kneel, touch, kiss — in sooth such things have been.

X

> He ventures in: let no buzzed whisper tell:
> All eyes be muffled, or a hundred swords
> Will storm his heart, Love's fev'rous citadel:
> For him, those chambers held barbarian hordes,   85
> Hyena foeman, and hot-blooded lords,
> Whose very dogs would execrations howl
> Against his lineage: not one breast affords
> Him any mercy, in that mansion foul,
> Save one old beldame, weak in body and in soul.   90

XI

> Ah, happy chance! the aged creature came,
> Shuffling along with ivory-headed wand,
> To where he stood, hid from the torch's flame,
> Behind a broad hall-pillar, far beyond
> The sound of merriment and chorus bland:°   *soft* 95
> He startled her; but soon she knew his face,
> And grasped his fingers in her palsied hand,
> Saying, "Mercy, Porphyro! hie thee from this place;
> They are all here tonight, the whole bloodthirsty race!

XII

"Get hence! get hence! there's dwarfish Hildebrand;   100
He had a fever late, and in the fit
He cursed thee and thine, both house and land:
Then there's that old Lord Maurice, not a whit
More tame for his gray hairs — Alas me! flit!
Flit like a ghost away." — "Ah, Gossip° dear,   *friend*   105
We're safe enough; here in this armchair sit,
And tell me how" — "Good Saints! not here, not here;
Follow me, child, or else these stones will be thy bier."

XIII

He followed through a lowly arched way,
Brushing the cobwebs with his lofty plume,   110
And as she muttered "Well-a — well-a-day!"
He found him in a little moonlight room,
Pale, latticed, chill, and silent as a tomb.
"Now tell me where is Madeline," said he,
"O tell me, Angela, by the holy loom   115
Which none but secret sisterhood may see,
When they St. Agnes' wool are weaving piously."

XIV

"St. Agnes! Ah! it is St. Agnes' Eve —
Yet men will murder upon holy days:
Thou must hold water in a witch's sieve,   120
And be liege-lord of all the Elves and Fays,
To venture so: it fills me with amaze
To see thee, Porphyro! — St. Agnes' Eve!
God's help! my lady fair the conjuror plays
This very night: good angels her deceive!   125
But let me laugh awhile, I've mickle° time to grieve."   *much*

XV

Feebly she laugheth in the languid moon,
While Porphyro upon her face doth look,
Like puzzled urchin on an aged crone
Who keepeth closed a wondrous riddle-book,   130
As spectacled she sits in chimney nook.
But soon his eyes grew brilliant, when she told
His lady's purpose; and he scarce could brook°   *hold back*
Tears, at the thought of those enchantments cold,
And Madeline asleep in lap of legends old.   135

XVI

Sudden a thought came like a full-blown rose,
Flushing his brow, and in his pained heart
Made purple riot: then doth he propose
A stratagem, that makes the beldame start:
"A cruel man and impious thou art: 140
Sweet lady, let her pray, and sleep, and dream

Alone with her good angels, far apart
From wicked men like thee. Go, go! — I deem
Thou canst not surely be the same that thou didst seem."

XVII

"I will not harm her, by all saints I swear,"   145
Quoth Porphyro: "O may I ne'er find grace
When my weak voice shall whisper its last prayer,
If one of her soft ringlets I displace,
Or look with ruffian passion in her face:
Good Angela, believe me by these tears;   150
Or I will, even in a moment's space,
Awake, with horrid shout, my foeman's ears,
And beard them, though they be more fanged than wolves and bears."

XVIII

"Ah! why wilt thou affright a feeble soul?
A poor, weak, palsy-stricken, churchyard thing,   155
Whose passing bell° may ere the midnight toll;   *death knell*
Whose prayers for thee, each morn and evening,
Were never missed" — Thus plaining,° doth she bring   *complaining*
A gentler speech from burning Porphyro;
So woeful, and of such deep sorrowing,   160
That Angela gives promise she will do
Whatever he shall wish, betide her weal or woe.

XIX

Which was, to lead him, in close secrecy,
Even to Madeline's chamber, and there hide
Him in a closet, of such privacy   165
That he might see her beauty unespied,
And win perhaps that night a peerless bride,
While legioned faeries paced the coverlet,
And pale enchantment held her sleepy-eyed.
Never on such a night have lovers met,   170
Since Merlin paid his Demon all the monstrous debt.°

XX

"It shall be as thou wishest," said the Dame:
"All cates° and dainties shall be stored there   *delicacies*
Quickly on this feast night: by the tambour frame
Her own lute thou wilt see: no time to spare,   175
For I am slow and feeble, and scarce dare
On such a catering trust my dizzy head.
Wait here, my child, with patience; kneel in prayer
The while: Ah! thou must needs the lady wed,
Or may I never leave my grave among the dead."   180

171 *Since Merlin paid . . . debt:* Merlin, the great magician of Arthurian legend, was duped by a crafty woman who turned one of his spells against him, causing his death.

XXI

So saying, she hobbled off with busy fear.
The lover's endless minutes slowly passed;
The dame returned, and whispered in his ear
To follow her; with aged eyes aghast
From fright of dim espial. Safe at last,   185
Through many a dusky gallery, they gain
The maiden's chamber, silken, hushed, and chaste;
Where Porphyro took covert, pleased amain.°   *greatly*
His poor guide hurried back with agues in her brain.

XXII

Her falt'ring hand upon the balustrade,   190
Old Angela was feeling for the stair,
When Madeline, St. Agnes' charmed maid,
Rose, like a missioned spirit, unaware:
With silver taper's light, and pious care,
She turned, and down the aged gossip led   195
To a safe level matting. Now prepare,
Young Porphyro, for gazing on that bed;
She comes, she comes again, like ring-dove frayed° and fled.   *frightened*

XXIII

Out went the taper as she hurried in;
Its little smoke, in pallid moonshine, died: 200
She closed the door, she panted, all akin
To spirits of the air, and visions wide:
No uttered syllable, or, woe betide!
But to her heart, her heart was voluble,
Paining with eloquence her balmy side;   205
As though a tongueless nightingale should swell
Her throat in vain, and die, heart-stifled, in her dell.

XXIV

A casement high and triple-arched there was,
All garlanded with carven imag'ries
Of fruits, and flowers and bunches of knotgrass,   210
And diamonded with panes of quaint device,
Innumerable of stains and splendid dyes,
As are the tiger-moth's deep-damasked wings;
And in the midst, 'mong thousand heraldries,
And twilight saints, and dim emblazonings,   215
A shielded scutcheon° blushed with blood of queens and kings. *coat of arms*

XXV

Full on this casement shone the wintry moon,
And threw warm gules on Madeline's fair breast,
As down she knelt for heaven's grace and boon;
Rose-bloom fell on her hands, together pressed,   220
And on her silver cross soft amethyst,
And on her hair a glory, like a saint:

She seemed a splendid angel, newly dressed,
  Save wings, for heaven: — Porphyro grew faint:
She knelt, so pure a thing, so free from mortal taint.   225

XXVI

Anon his heart revives: her vespers done,
  Of all its wreathed pearls her hair she frees;
  Unclasps her warmed jewels one by one;
  Loosens her fragrant bodice; by degrees
  Her rich attire creeps rustling to her knees: 230
  Half-hidden, like a mermaid in sea-weed,
  Pensive awhile she dreams awake, and sees,
    In fancy, fair St. Agnes in her bed,
But dares not look behind, or all the charm is fled.

XXVII

Soon, trembling in her soft and chilly nest,   235
  In sort of wakeful swoon, perplexed she lay,
  Until the poppied warmth of sleep oppressed
  Her soothed limbs, and soul fatigued away;
  Flown, like a thought, until the morrow-day;
  Blissfully havened both from joy and pain;   240
  Clasped like a missal where swart Paynims° pray;   *dark-skinned pagans*
    Blinded alike from sunshine and from rain,
As though a rose should shut, and be a bud again.

XXVIII

Stolen to this paradise, and so entranced,
  Porphyro gazed upon her empty dress,   245
  And listened to her breathing, if it chanced
  To wake into a slumberous tenderness;
  Which when he heard, that minute did he bless,
  And breathed himself: then from the closet crept,
  Noiseless as fear in a wide wilderness,   250
    And over the hushed carpet, silent, stepped,
And tween the curtains peeped, where, lo! — how fast she slept.

XXIX

Then by the bedside, where the faded moon
  Made a dim, silver twilight, soft he set
  A table, and, half anguished, threw thereon   255
  A cloth of woven crimson, gold, and jet —
  O for some drowsy Morphean amulet!°
  The boisterous, midnight, festive clarion,
  The kettledrum, and far-heard clarinet,
    Affray his ears, though but in dying tone —   260
The hall door shuts again, and all the noise is gone.

257 *Morphean amulet:* A charm used to induce sleep.

XXX

And still she slept an azure-lidded sleep,
In blanchèd linen, smooth, and lavendered,
While he from forth the closet brought a heap
Of candied apple, quince, and plum, and gourd;   265
With jellies soother° than the creamy curd,   *sweeter*
And lucent syrups, tinct with cinnamon;
Manna and dates, in argosy transferred
From Fez; and spicèd dainties, every one,
From silken Samarcand to cedared Lebanon.   270

XXXI

These delicates he heaped with glowing hand
On golden dishes and in baskets bright
Of wreathèd silver: sumptuous they stand
In the retired quiet of the night,
Filling the chilly room with perfume light. —   275
"And now, my love, my seraph fair, awake!
Thou art my heaven, and I thine eremite:
Open thine eyes, for meek St. Agnes' sake,
Or I shall drowse beside thee, so my soul doth ache."

XXXII

Thus whispering, his warm, unnerved arm   280
Sank in her pillow. Shaded was her dream
By the dusk curtains: 'twas a midnight charm
Impossible to melt as icèd stream:
The lustrous salvers in the moonlight gleam;
Broad golden fringe upon the carpet lies: 285
It seemed he never, never could redeem
From such a stedfast spell his lady's eyes;
So mused awhile, entoiled in woofèd° phantasies.   *woven*

XXXIII

Awakening up, he took her hollow lute —
Tumultuous — and, in chords that tenderest be,   290
He played an ancient ditty, long since mute,
In Provence called, "La belle dame sans mercy":
Close to her ear touching the melody;
Wherewith disturbed, she uttered a soft moan:
He ceased — she panted quick — and suddenly   295
Her blue affrayed eyes wide open shone:
Upon his knees he sank, pale as smooth-sculptured stone.

XXXIV

Her eyes were open, but she still beheld,
Now wide awake, the vision of her sleep:
There was a painful change, that nigh expelled   300
The blisses of her dream so pure and deep,
At which fair Madeline began to weep,
And moan forth witless words with many a sigh;

While still her gaze on Porphyro would keep,
Who knelt, with joined hands and piteous eye,   305
Fearing to move or speak, she looked so dreamingly.

XXXV

"Ah, Porphyro!" said she, "but even now
Thy voice was at sweet tremble in mine ear,
Made tunable with every sweetest vow;
And those sad eyes were spiritual and clear: 310
How changed thou art! how pallid, chill, and drear!
Give me that voice again, my Porphyro,
Those looks immortal, those complainings dear!
Oh leave me not in this eternal woe,
For if thou diest, my Love, I know not where to go."   315

XXXVI

Beyond a mortal man impassioned far
At these voluptuous accents, he arose,
Ethereal, flushed, and like a throbbing star
Seen mid the sapphire heaven's deep repose;
Into her dream he melted, as the rose   320
Blendeth its odor with the violet —
Solution sweet: meantime the frost-wind blows
Like Love's alarum pattering the sharp sleet
Against the windowpanes; St. Agnes' moon hath set.

XXXVII

'Tis dark: quick pattereth the flaw-blown° sleet: *gusting*   325
"This is no dream, my bride, my Madeline!"
'Tis dark: the iced gusts still rave and beat:
"No dream, alas! alas! and woe is mine!
Porphyro will leave me here to fade and pine. —
Cruel! what traitor could thee hither bring?   330
I curse not, for my heart is lost in thine,
Though thou forsakest a deceivèd thing; —
A dove forlorn and lost with sick unprunèd wing."

XXXVIII

"My Madeline! sweet dreamer! lovely bride!
Say, may I be for aye° thy vassal blest?   *forever*   335
Thy beauty's shield, heart-shaped and vermeil dyed?
Ah, silver shrine, here will I take my rest
After so many hours of toil and quest,
A famished pilgrim — saved by miracle.
Though I have found, I will not rob thy nest   340
Saving of thy sweet self; if thou think'st well
To trust, fair Madeline, to no rude infidel.

XXXIX

"Hark! 'tis an elfin-storm from faery land,
Of haggard° seeming, but a boon indeed: *wild*
Arise — arise! the morning is at hand; —   345

The bloated wassailers will never heed: —
Let us away, my love, with happy speed;
There are no ears to hear, or eyes to see —
Drowned all in Rhenish and the sleepy mead:°
Awake! arise! my love, and fearless be,   350
For o'er the southern moors I have a home for thee."

XL
        She hurried at his words, beset with fears,
        For there were sleeping dragons all around,
        At glaring watch, perhaps, with ready spears —
        Down the wide stairs a darkling way they found. —   355
        In all the house was heard no human sound.
        A chain-drooped lamp was flickering by each door;
        The arras, rich with horseman, hawk, and hound,
        Fluttered in the besieging wind's uproar;
And the long carpets rose along the gusty floor.   360

XLI
        They glide, like phantoms, into the wide hall;
        Like phantoms, to the iron porch, they glide;
        Where lay the Porter, in uneasy sprawl,
        With a huge empty flaggon by his side:
        The wakeful bloodhound rose, and shook his hide,   365
        But his sagacious eye an inmate owns:
        By one, and one, the bolts full easy slide: —
        The chains lie silent on the footworn stones; —
The key turns, and the door upon its hinges groans.

XLII
        And they are gone: ay, ages long ago   370
        These lovers fled away into the storm.
        That night the Baron dreamt of many a woe,
        And all his warrior-guests, with shade and form
        Of witch, and demon, and large coffin-worm,
        Were long be-nightmared. Angela the old   375
        Died palsy-twitched, with meager face deform;
        The Beadsman, after thousand aves° told,   *prayers*
For aye unsought for slept among his ashes cold.

349 *Rhenish:* Rhine wine; *mead:* A fermented drink made with honey.

Considerations for Critical Thinking and Writing

1. Summarize the story told in this poem.
2. What is the setting? Contrast the interior and exterior settings. How do the descriptions of the setting help establish the poem's mood?
3. What roles do the Beadsman, Angela, and the revelers play in the story?
4. Are Madeline and Porphyro individualized characters as well as recognizable types? How are they individuals, and how are they types?
5. What do the contrasting images of sensuality and spirituality contribute to the

poem's meaning? How does Keats build on contrasts of youth and age, love and hate, opulence and austerity, life and death, and heaven and hell? Use specific examples to explain how these contrasts relate to one another and to the poem's theme.

6. What sound effects in the poem seem especially effective? Why?
7. Select a stanza and analyze it in terms of sound and meter.

Bright star! would I were steadfast as thou art — 1819

Bright star, would I were steadfast as thou art —
    Not in lone splendor hung aloft the night
And watching, with eternal lids apart,
    Like nature's patient, sleepless Eremite,
The moving waters at their priestlike task   5
    Of pure ablution round earth's human shores,
Or gazing on the new soft fallen mask
    Of snow upon the mountains and the moors —
No — yet still steadfast, still unchangeable,
    Pillowed upon my fair love's ripening breast,   10
To feel forever its soft fall and swell,
    Awake forever in a sweet unrest,
Still, still to hear her tender-taken breath,
And so live ever — or else swoon to death.

Considerations for Critical Thinking and Writing

1. What does the speaker in this sonnet admire about the star? What qualities of the star does he reject?
2. What kind of sonnet is this? How does its structure help to shape its meaning?
3. How do the sound effects, particularly assonance and consonance, contribute to the meaning?
4. How does Keats vary the iambic pentameter here? What is the effect of these variations?
5. Is the theme of this sonnet similar to or different from that of "To Autumn" (p. 816)?

Why did I laugh to-night? 1819

Why did I laugh to-night? No voice will tell:
    No God, no Demon of severe response,
Deigns to reply from Heaven or from Hell.
    Then to my human heart I turn at once.
Heart! Thou and I are here sad and alone;   5
    I say, why did I laugh? O mortal pain!

O Darkness! Darkness! ever must I moan,
    To question Heaven and Hell and Heart in vain.
Why did I laugh? I know this Being's lease,
    My fancy to its utmost blisses spreads;   10
Yet would I on this very midnight cease,
    And the world's gaudy ensigns see in shreds;
Verse, Fame, and Beauty are intense indeed,
But Death intenser — Death is Life's high meed.

Considerations for Critical Thinking and Writing

1. What is the speaker's answer to the question posed in this sonnet?
2. Describe the sonnet's tone.
3. Write an essay considering the idea that "Death is Life's high meed" is a characteristic Keatsian sentiment.

La Belle Dame sans Merci°   1819

O what can ail thee, knight-at-arms,
    Alone and palely loitering?
The sedge has withered from the lake,
    And no birds sing.

O what can ail thee, knight-at-arms,   5
    So haggard and so woe-begone?
The squirrel's granary is full,
    And the harvest's done.

I see a lily on thy brow,
    With anguish moist and fever dew,   10
And on thy cheeks a fading rose
    Fast withereth too.

I met a lady in the meads,
    Full beautiful — a faery's child,
Her hair was long, her foot was light,   15
    And her eyes were wild.

I made a garland for her head,
    And bracelets too, and fragrant zone;°   belt
She looked at me as she did love,
    And made sweet moan.   20

I set her on my pacing steed,
    And nothing else saw all day long,
For sidelong would she bend, and sing
    A faery's song.

La Belle Dame sans Merci: This title is borrowed from a medieval poem and means "The Beautiful Lady without Mercy."

John Keats 807

She found me roots of relish sweet, 25
 And honey wild, and manna dew,
And sure in language strange she said,
 "I love thee true."

She took me to her elfin grot,
 And there she wept, and sighed full sore,   30
And there I shut her wild wild eyes
 With kisses four.

And there she lullèd me asleep,
 And there I dreamed — Ah! woe betide!
The latest° dream I ever dreamed   *last* 35
 On the cold hill side.

I saw pale kings and princes too,
 Pale warriors, death-pale were they all;
They cried — "La Belle Dame sans Merci
 Hath thee in thrall!"   40

I saw their starved lips in the gloam,
 With horrid warning gapèd wide,
And I awoke and found me here,
 On the cold hill's side.

And this is why I soujourn here,   45
 Alone and palely loitering,
Though the sedge has withered from the lake,
 And no birds sing.

Considerations for Critical Thinking and Writing

1. How do the first three stanzas of this ballad serve to characterize the knight who describes his experience with the lady?
2. The lady is a familiar character in literature, a "femme fatale." Characterize her. Have you encountered other versions of her in literature or film?
3. What is the effect of the shortened final line in each stanza of this ballad?

Ode to Psyche°   1819

O Goddess! hear these tuneless numbers, wrung
 By sweet enforcement and remembrance dear,
And pardon that thy secrets should be sung
 Even into thine own soft-conchèd° ear;   *soft like a shell*

Psyche: In Greek, *psyche* means soul or mind, but Psyche was not one of the original Greek gods. Apuleius, a second-century Latin author, told the story of Cupid's love for Psyche and their eventual immortality together.

Surely I dreamt today, or did I see   5
    The winged Psyche with awakened eyes?
I wandered in a forest thoughtlessly,
    And, on the sudden, fainting with surprise,
Saw two fair creatures, couched side by side
    In deepest grass, beneath the whisp'ring roof   10
    Of leaves and trembled blossoms, where there ran
        A brooklet, scarce espied:

'Mid hushed, cool-rooted flowers, fragrant-eyed,
    Blue, silver-white, and budded Tyrian,°
They lay calm-breathing on the bedded grass;   15
    Their arms embraced, and their pinions° too;   *wings*
    Their lips touched not, but had not bade adieu,
As if disjoined by soft-handed slumber,
And ready still past kisses to outnumber
    At tender eye-dawn of aurorean love: 20
        The winged boy I knew;
    But who wast thou, O happy, happy dove?
        His Psyche true!

O latest born and loveliest vision far
    Of all Olympus' faded hierarchy!°   25
Fairer than Phoebe's° sapphire-regioned star,   *Diana, the moon*
    Or Vesper;° amorous glowworm of the sky;   *evening star*
Fairer than these, though temple thou hast none,
    Nor altar heaped with flowers;
Nor virgin choir to make delicious moan   30
    Upon the midnight hours;
    No voice, no lute, no pipe, no incense sweet
        From chain-swung censer teeming;
    No shrine, no grove, no oracle, no heat
        Of pale mouthed prophet dreaming.   35

O brightest! though too late for antique vows,
    Too, too late for the fond believing lyre,
When holy were the haunted forest boughs,
    Holy the air, the water, and the fire;
Yet even in these days so far retired   40
    From happy pieties, thy lucent fans,°   *translucent wings*
    Fluttering among the faint Olympians,
I see, and sing, by my own eyes inspired.
So let me be thy choir, and make a moan
        Upon the midnight hours;   45
Thy voice, thy lute, thy pipe, thy incense sweet
    From swinged censer teeming;
Thy shrine, thy grove, thy oracle, thy heat
    Of pale-mouthed prophet dreaming.

14 *budded Tyrian:* Purple dye produced in ancient Tyre.   25 *Of all Olympus'* . . . *hierarchy:* Psyche
was not regarded as a goddess before Apuleius wrote of her.

Yes, I will be thy priest, and build a fane   50
 In some untrodden region of my mind,
Where branched thoughts, new grown with pleasant pain,
 Instead of pines shall murmur in the wind:
Far, far around shall those dark-clustered trees
 Fledge the wild-ridged mountains steep by steep;   55
And there by zephyrs, streams, and birds, and bees,
 The moss-lain Dryads° shall be lulled to sleep;   *wood nymphs*
And in the midst of this wide quietness
A rosy sanctuary will I dress
With the wreathed trellis of a working brain,   60
 With buds, and bells, and stars without a name,
With all the gardener Fancy e'er could feign,
 Who breeding flowers, will never breed the same:
And there shall be for thee all soft delight
 That shadowy thought can win,   65
A bright torch, and a casement ope at night,
 To let the warm Love° in!   *Cupid*

Considerations for Critical Thinking and Writing

1. What does the ideal love of Psyche and Cupid represent to the speaker in this ode?
2. What does the speaker lament in lines 36–39? What kind of loss is experienced here?
3. How will the speaker be a "priest, and build a fane / In some untrodden region of my mind" (lines 50–51)?
4. In what sense might it be said that this ode is about poetic imagination?

To Sleep   1819

O soft embalmer of the still midnight,
 Shutting, with careful fingers and benign,
Our gloom-pleased eyes, embowered from the light,
 Enshaded in forgetfulness divine:
O soothest Sleep! if so it please thee, close,   5
 In midst of this thine hymn, my willing eyes,
Or wait the Amen, ere thy poppy throws
 Around my bed its lulling charities.
Then save me, or the passed day will shine
 Upon my pillow, breeding many woes: 10
Save me from curious conscience, that still hoards
 Its strength for darkness, burrowing like the mole;
Turn the key deftly in the oiled wards,
 And seal the hushed casket of my soul.

Considerations for Critical Thinking and Writing

1. How is sleep personified? What sort of "person" is it?
2. What does the speaker want to be saved from?
3. What extended metaphor is used? What purpose does it serve?

Connection to Another Selection

1. In an essay compare Keats's treatment of sleep with Robert Bly's "Waking from Sleep" (p. 937).

Ode to a Nightingale   1819

I

My heart aches, and a drowsy numbness pains
   My sense, as though of hemlock° I had drunk,   *a poison*
Or emptied some dull opiate to the drains
   One minute past, and Lethe-wards° had sunk:
'Tis not through envy of thy happy lot,   5
   But being too happy in thine happiness —
      That thou, light-wingèd Dryad° of the trees,   *wood nymph*
        In some melodious plot
   Of beechen green, and shadows numberless,
      Singest of summer in full-throated ease.   10

II

O, for a draught of vintage! that hath been
   Cooled a long age in the deep-delvèd earth,
Tasting of Flora° and the country green,   *goddess of flowers*
   Dance, and Provençal song,° and sunburnt mirth!
O for a beaker full of the warm South,   15
   Full of the true, the blushful Hippocrene,°
      With beaded bubbles winking at the brim,
        And purple-stainèd mouth;
   That I might drink, and leave the world unseen,
      And with thee fade away into the forest dim: 20

III

Fade far away, dissolve, and quite forget
   What thou among the leaves hast never known,
The weariness, the fever, and the fret
   Here, where men sit and hear each other groan;
Where palsy shakes a few, sad, last gray hairs,   25
   Where youth grows pale, and specter-thin, and dies,

---

4 *Lethe-wards:* Toward Lethe, the river of forgetfulness in the Hades of Greek mythology.
14 *Provençal song:* The medieval troubadours of Provence, France, were known for their singing.
16 *Hippocrene:* The fountain of the Muses in Greek mythology.

Where but to think is to be full of sorrow
    And leaden-eyed despairs,
Where Beauty cannot keep her lustrous eyes;
    Or new Love pine at them beyond tomorrow.   30

IV

Away! away! for I will fly to thee,
    Not charioted by Bacchus and his pards,°
But on the viewless wings of Poesy,
    Though the dull brain perplexes and retards:
Already with thee! tender is the night,   35
    And haply the Queen-Moon is on her throne,
        Clustered around by all her starry Fays;
            But here there is no light,
    Save what from heaven is with the breezes blown
        Through verdurous glooms and winding mossy ways.   40

V

I cannot see what flowers are at my feet,
    Nor what soft incense hangs upon the boughs,
But, in embalmèd° darkness, guess each sweet   *perfumed*
    Wherewith the seasonable month endows
The grass, the thicket, and the fruit-tree wild;   45
    White hawthorn, and the pastoral eglantine;
        Fast fading violets covered up in leaves;
            And mid-May's eldest child,
    The coming musk-rose, full of dewy wine,
        The murmurous haunt of flies on summer eves.   50

VI

Darkling° I listen; and for many a time   *in the dark*
    I have been half in love with easeful Death,
Called him soft names in many a musèd rhyme,
    To take into the air my quiet breath;
Now more than ever seems it rich to die,   55
    To cease upon the midnight with no pain,
        While thou art pouring forth thy soul abroad
            In such an ecstasy!
    Still wouldst thou sing, and I have ears in vain —
        To thy high requiem become a sod.   60

VII

Thou wast not born for death, immortal Bird!
    No hungry generations tread thee down;
The voice I hear this passing night was heard
    In ancient days by emperor and clown:
Perhaps the selfsame song that found a path   65

---

32 *Bacchus and his pards:* The Greek god of wine traveled in a chariot drawn by leopards.

Through the sad heart of Ruth,° when, sick for home,
    She stood in tears amid the alien corn:
        The same that oft-times hath
Charmed magic casements, opening on the foam
    Of perilous seas, in faery lands forlorn.   70

VIII
Forlorn! the very word is like a bell
    To toll me back from thee to my sole self!
Adieu! the fancy cannot cheat so well
    As she is famed to do, deceiving elf.
Adieu! adieu! thy plaintive anthem fades   75
    Past the near meadows, over the still stream,
        Up the hill side; and now 'tis buried deep
           In the next valley-glades:
Was it a vision, or a waking dream?
        Fled is that music: — Do I wake or sleep?   80

66 *Ruth:* A young widow in the Bible (see the Book of Ruth).

Considerations for Critical Thinking and Writing

1. Why does the speaker in this ode want to leave his world for the nightingale's? What does the nightingale symbolize?
2. How does the speaker attempt to escape his world? Is he successful?
3. What changes the speaker's view of death at the end of stanza VI?
4. What does the allusion to Ruth (line 66) contribute to the ode's meaning?
5. In which lines is the imagery especially sensuous? How does this effect add to the conflict presented?
6. What calls the speaker back to himself at the end of stanza VII and the beginning of stanza VIII?
7. Choose a stanza and explain how sound is related to its meaning.
8. How regular is the stanza form of this ode?

Ode on a Grecian Urn   1819

I
Thou still unravished bride of quietness,
    Thou foster-child of silence and slow time,
Sylvan° historian, who canst thus express
    A flowery tale more sweetly than our rhyme:
What leaf-fringed legend haunts about thy shape   5
        Of deities or mortals, or of both,
           In Tempe or the dales of Arcady?°

3 *Sylvan:* Rustic. The urn is decorated with a forest scene.   7 *Tempe, Arcady:* Beautiful rural valleys in Greece.

What men or gods are these? What maidens loath?
    What mad pursuit? What struggle to escape?
        What pipes and timbrels? What wild ecstasy?   10

II

Heard melodies are sweet, but those unheard
    Are sweeter; therefore, ye soft pipes, play on;
Not to the sensual ear, but, more endeared,
    Pipe to the spirit ditties of no tone:
Fair youth, beneath the trees, thou canst not leave   15
    Thy song, nor ever can those trees be bare;
        Bold Lover, never, never canst thou kiss,
Though winning near the goal — yet, do not grieve;
    She cannot fade, though thou hast not thy bliss,
        For ever wilt thou love, and she be fair!   20

III

Ah, happy, happy boughs! that cannot shed
    Your leaves, nor ever bid the Spring adieu;
And, happy melodist, unwearièd,
    For ever piping songs for ever new;
More happy love! more happy, happy love!   25
    For ever warm and still to be enjoyed,
        For ever panting, and for ever young;
All breathing human passion far above,
    That leaves a heart high-sorrowful and cloyed,
        A burning forehead, and a parching tongue.   30

IV

Who are these coming to the sacrifice?
    To what green altar, O mysterious priest,
Lead'st thou that heifer lowing at the skies,
    And all her silken flanks with garlands drest?
What little town by river or sea shore,   35
    Or mountain-built with peaceful citadel,
        Is emptied of this folk, this pious morn?
And, little town, thy streets for evermore
    Will silent be; and not a soul to tell
        Why thou art desolate, can e'er return.   40

V

O Attic° shape! Fair attitude! with brede°
    Of marble men and maidens overwrought,
With forest branches and the trodden weed;
    Thou, silent form, dost tease us out of thought
As doth eternity: Cold Pastoral!   45
    When old age shall this generation waste,
        Thou shalt remain, in midst of other woe

41 *Attic:* Possessing classic Athenian simplicity; *brede:* Design.

Than ours, a friend to man, to whom thou say'st,
   Beauty is truth, truth beauty — that is all
      Ye know on earth, and all ye need to know.   50

Considerations for Critical Thinking and Writing

1. What is the speaker's attitude toward the urn in this ode? Does his view develop or change?
2. How is the happiness in stanza III related to the assertion in lines 11–12 that "Heard melodies are sweet, but those unheard / Are sweeter"?
3. What is the difference between the world depicted on the urn and the speaker's world?
4. What do lines 49–50 suggest about the relation of art to life? Why is the urn described as a "Cold Pastoral" (line 45)?
5. Which world does the speaker seem to prefer, the urn's or his own?

Connections to Other Selections

1. Write an essay comparing the view of time in this ode with that in Marvell's "To His Coy Mistress" (p. 631).
2. Discuss the treatment and meaning of love in this ode and in Richard Wilbur's "Love Calls Us to the Things of This World" (p. 1013).
3. Compare the tone and attitude toward life in this ode with those in Keats's "To Autumn" (p. 816).

Ode on Melancholy   1819

I

No, no! go not to Lethe,° neither twist
   Wolfsbane,° tight-rooted, for its poisonous wine;
Nor suffer thy pale forehead to be kissed
   By nightshade,° ruby grape of Proserpine;°   *Queen of Hades*
Make not your rosary of yew-berries,°   5
   Nor let the beetle, nor the death-moth be
      Your mournful Psyche,° nor the downy owl
A partner in your sorrow's mysteries;
   For shade to shade will come too drowsily,
      And drown the wakeful anguish of the soul.   10

II

But when the melancholy fit shall fall
   Sudden from heaven like a weeping cloud,

---

1 *Lethe:* In Greek mythology, the river of forgetfulness, which the dead cross to enter Hades.
2 *Wolfsbane:* A poisonous plant.   4 *nightshade:* Also a poisonous plant.   5 *yew-berries:* Associated with death, as are the beetle, moth, and owl in this stanza.   6–7 *nor let the death-moth be. . . Psyche:* The soul was depicted as a butterfly in Greek mythology. *Psyche* means soul or mind in Greek.

That fosters the droop-headed flowers all,
    And hides the green hill in an April shroud;
Then glut thy sorrow on a morning rose,   15
    Or on the rainbow of the salt sand-wave,
        Or on the wealth of globed peonies;
Or if thy mistress some rich anger shows,
    Imprison her soft hand, and let her rave,
        And feed deep, deep upon her peerless eyes.   20

III
She dwells with Beauty — Beauty that must die;
    And Joy, whose hand is ever at his lips
Bidding adieu; and aching Pleasure nigh,
    Turning to Poison while the bee-mouth sips:
Aye, in the very temple of Delight   25
    Veiled Melancholy has her sovereign shrine,
        Though seen of none save him whose strenuous tongue
    Can burst Joy's grape against his palate fine;
His soul shall taste the sadness of her might,
    And be among her cloudy trophies hung.   30

Considerations for Critical Thinking and Writing

1. What is melancholy? According to the speaker of this ode (lines 27–30), what produces the most intense melancholy? Is it good or bad, a strength or a weakness, to suffer from melancholy?
2. What do the images in this ode reveal about the relation between beauty and time? Between pleasure and pain?
3. Is this a sentimental poem? Explain why or why not.

To Autumn   1819

I
Season of mists and mellow fruitfulness,
    Close bosom-friend of the maturing sun;
Conspiring with him how to load and bless
    With fruit the vines that round the thatch-eves run;
To bend with apples the mossed cottage-trees,   5
    And fill all fruit with ripeness to the core;
        To swell the gourd, and plump the hazel shells
    With a sweet kernel; to set budding more,
And still more, later flowers for the bees,
Until they think warm days will never cease,   10
    For summer has o'er-brimmed their clammy cells.

II
Who hath not seen thee oft amid thy store?
    Sometimes whoever seeks abroad may find

Thee sitting careless on a granary floor,
   Thy hair soft-lifted by the winnowing wind;   15
Or on a half-reaped furrow sound asleep,
   Drowsed with the fume of poppies, while thy hook°   *scythe*
      Spares the next swath and all its twinèd flowers:
And sometimes like a gleaner thou dost keep
   Steady thy laden head across a brook;   20
   Or by a cider-press, with patient look,
      Thou watchest the last oozings hours by hours.

III
Where are the songs of spring? Ay, where are they?
   Think not of them, thou hast thy music too, —
While barred clouds bloom the soft-dying day,   25
   And touch the stubble-plains with rosy hue;
Then in a wailful choir the small gnats mourn
   Among the river swallows,° borne aloft   *willows*
      Or sinking as the light wind lives or dies;
And full-grown lambs loud bleat from hilly bourn;°   *territory* 30
   Hedge-crickets sing; and now with treble soft
   The redbreast whistles from a garden-croft,
      And gathering swallows twitter in the skies.

Considerations for Critical Thinking and Writing

1. How is autumn personified in each stanza of this ode?
2. Which senses are most emphasized in each stanza?
3. How is the progression of time expressed in the ode?
4. How does the imagery convey tone? Which words have particularly strong connotative values?
5. What is the speaker's view of death?

Connections to Other Selections

1. Compare this poem's tone and its perspective on death with those of Robert Frost's "After Apple-Picking" (p. 879).
2. Write an essay comparing the significance of the images of "mellow fruitfulness" in "To Autumn" with that of the images of ripeness in Roethke's "Root Cellar" (p. 648). Explain how the images in each poem lead to very different feelings about the same phenomenon.

PERSPECTIVES ON KEATS

Keats on the Truth of the Imagination   1817

    I am certain of nothing but of the holiness of the Heart's affections and the truth of Imagination — What the imagination seizes as Beauty must be truth — whether it existed before or not — for I have the same Idea of all our Passions as of Love they are all in their sublime, creative of essential Beauty. . . . The

Imagination may be compared to Adam's dream° — he awoke and found it truth. I am the more zealous in this affair, because I have never yet been able to perceive how any thing can be known for truth by consequitive reasoning — and yet it must be — Can it be that even the greatest Philosopher ever ~~when~~° arrived at his goal without putting aside numerous objections — However it may be, O for a Life of Sensations rather than of Thoughts! It is "a Vision in the form of Youth" a Shadow of reality to come — and this consideration has further conv[i]nced me for it has come as auxiliary to another favorite Speculation of mine, that we shall enjoy ourselves here after by having what we called happiness on Earth repeated in a finer tone and so repeated — And yet such a fate can only befall those who delight in sensation rather than hunger as you do after Truth — Adam's dream will do here and seems to be a conviction that Imagination and its empyreal reflection is the same as human Life and its spiritual repetition. But as I was saying — The simple imaginative Mind may have its rewards in the repeti[ti]on of its own silent Working coming continually on the spirit with a fine suddenness — to compare great things with small — have you never by being surprised with an old Melody — in a delicious place — by a delicious voice, fe[l]t over again your very speculations and surmises at the time it first operated on your soul — do you not remember forming to yourself the singer's face more beautiful that [*for* than] it was possible and yet with the elevation of the Moment you did not think so — even then you were mounted on the Wings of Imagination so high — that the Prototype must be here after — that delicious face you will see — What a time! I am continually running away from the subject — sure this cannot be exactly the case with a complex Mind — one that is imaginative and at the same time careful of its fruits — who would exist partly on sensation partly on thought — to whom it is necessary that years should bring the philosophic Mind — such an one I consider your's and therefore it is necessary to your eternal Happiness that you not only ~~have~~ drink this old Wine of Heaven which I shall call the redigestion of our most ethereal Musings on Earth; but also increase in knowledge and know all things.

From a letter to Benjamin Bailey, November 22, 1817

Considerations for Critical Thinking and Writing

1. "O for a life of Sensations rather than of Thoughts!" What do you think Keats means by this? Is this an antiintellectual statement?
2. Consider this passage from a letter to a friend, C. W. Dilke (September 22, 1819), in which Keats "Talking of pleasure" writes, "this moment I was writing with one hand, and with the other holding to my mouth a Nectarine — good God how fine. It went down soft, slushy, oozy — all its delicious embonpoint [plumpness] melted down my throat like a beatified Strawberry." Why is "delight in sensation," as Keats puts it in his letter to Bailey, so important to Keats's view of life and poetry?
3. How does Keats's description of the relation between beauty and truth in this letter compare with what he says in "Ode on a Grecian Urn" (p. 813)?

Adam's dream: In John Milton's *Paradise Lost* (Book VIII, 460–90), Adam dreams of Eve's creation and wakes up to find that she exists.   *when:* Excerpts from Keats's letters in this section are reprinted from Hyder E. Rollins's edition of *The Letters of John Keats* (Cambridge, Mass.: Harvard University Press, 1970), which reproduces the letters as Keats wrote them, including the crossed-out words. Rollins's comments are in brackets.

We hate poetry that has a palpable design upon us — and if we do not agree, seems to put its hand in its breeches pocket. Poetry should be great & unobtrusive, a thing which enters into one's soul, and does not startle it or amaze it with itself but with its subject. — How beautiful are the retired flowers! how would they lose their beauty were they to throng into the highway crying out, "admire me I am a violet! dote upon me I am a primrose!"

From a letter to J. H. Reynolds, February 3, 1818

Considerations for Critical Thinking and Writing

1. Does Keats's poetry have a "palpable design" upon the reader? How do you think Keats would regard didactic poetry such as the excerpt from Pope's "An Essay on Criticism" (p. 726)?
2. In another letter to Reynolds (on April 9, 1819), Keats wrote, "I never wrote one single Line of Poetry with the least Shadow of public thought." With reference to specific poems, explain why Keats's poetry is more personal than public and more concerned with feelings than teachings.

Keats on His Poetic Principles   1818

In Poetry I have a few Axioms, and you will see how far I am from their Centre. 1st I think Poetry should surprise by a fine excess and not by Singularity — it should strike the Reader as a wording of his own highest thoughts, and appear almost a Remembrance — 2nd Its touches of Beauty should never be half way therby making the reader breathless instead of content: the rise, the progress, the setting of imagery should like the Sun come natural natural too him — shine over him and set soberly although in magnificence leaving him in the Luxury of twilight — but it is easier to think what Poetry should be than to write it — and this leads me on to another axiom. That if Poetry comes not as naturally as the Leaves to a tree it had better not come at all.

From a Letter to John Taylor, February 27, 1818

Considerations for Critical Thinking and Writing

1. The phrase *fine excess* appears to be a contradiction in terms. How does Keats's poetry resolve this seeming contradiction?
2. Given that Keats wrote in fixed poetic forms, such as the sonnet and ode, in what sense can his poetry be regarded as coming "naturally as the Leaves to a tree"?
3. Based on your reading of Keats's poems, create another axiom that serves as a useful generalization about his poetry.

The common cognomen of this world among the misguided and superstitious is "a vale of tears" from which we are to be redeemed by a certain arbitrary interposition of God and taken to Heaven — What a little circumscribe[d] straightened notion! Call the world if you Please "The vale of Soul-making" Then you will find out the use of the world (I am speaking now in the highest terms for human nature admitting it to be immortal which I will here take for granted for the purpose of showing a thought which has struck me concerning it) I say *"Soul making"* Soul as distinguished from an Intelligence — There may be intelligences or sparks of the divinity in millions — but they are not Souls the till they acquire identities, till each one is personally itself. I[n]telligences are atoms of perception — they know and they see and they are pure, in short they are God — how then are Souls to be made? How then are these sparks which are God to have identity given them — so as ever to possess a bliss peculiar to each ones individual existence? How, but by the medium of a world like this? This point I sincerely wish to consider because I think it a grander system of salvation than the chrystean religion — or rather it is a system of Spirit-creation — This is effected by three grand materials acting the one upon the other for a series of years — These three Materials are the *Intelligence* — the *human heart* (as distinguished from intelligence or Mind) and the *World* or *Elemental space* suited for the proper action of *Mind and Heart* on each other for the purpose of forming the *Soul* or *Intelligence destined to possess the sense of Identity.* I can scarcely express what I but dimly perceive — and yet I think I perceive it — that you may judge the more clearly I will put it in the most homely form possible — I will call the *world* a School instituted for the purpose of teaching little children to read — I will call the *human heart* the *horn Book* used in that School — and I will call the *Child able to read, the Soul* made from that *school* and its *hornbook.* Do you not see how necessary a World of Pains and troubles is to school an Intelligence and make it a soul? A Place where the heart must feel and suffer in a thousand diverse ways! Not merely is the Heart a Hornbook, It is the Minds Bible, it is the Minds experience, it is the teat from which the Mind or intelligence sucks its identity — As various as the Lives of Men are — so various become their souls, and thus does God make individual beings, Souls, identical Souls of the sparks of his own essence — This appears to me a faint sketch of a system of Salvation which does not affront our reason and humanity.

From a letter to George and Georgiana Keats, February 14–May 3, 1819

Considerations for Critical Thinking and Writing

1. How does Keats's perception of pain and suffering contrast with what he takes to be the traditional Christian view that life is "a vale of tears" that tests the soul? How are "Souls to be made"?
2. How is Keats's emphasis on a "World of Pains and troubles . . . to school an Intelligence and make it a soul" demonstrated in his poetry? What is the function of pain and suffering in his poetry? How are they related to the process of *"Soul Making"*?

3. Research Keats's personal life, particularly his illness. How does the biographical information you have found shed light on the characteristic tone and subject matter of his poetry?

F. SCOTT FITZGERALD (1896–1940)
On the "Extraordinary Genius" of Keats   1940

Poetry is either something that lives like fire inside you — like music to the musician or Marxism to the Communist — or else it is nothing, an empty, formalized bore, around which pedants can endlessly drone their notes and explanations. *The Grecian Urn* is unbearably beautiful, with every syllable as inevitable as the notes in Beethoven's *Ninth Symphony,* or it's just something you don't understand. It is what it is because an extraordinary genius paused at that point in history and touched it. I suppose I've read it a hundred times. About the tenth time I began to know what it was about, and caught the chime in it and the exquisite inner mechanics. Likewise with the *Nightingale,* which I can never read through without tears in my eyes; . . . and *The Eve of Saint Agnes,* which has the richest, most sensuous imagery in English, not excepting Shakespeare. And finally his three or four great sonnets: *Bright Star* and the others. . . .

Knowing those things very young and granted an ear, one could scarcely ever afterwards be unable to distinguish between gold and dross in what one read. In themselves those eight poems are a scale of workmanship for anybody who wants to know truly about words, their most utter value for evocation, persuasion, or charm. For awhile after you quit Keats all other poetry seems to be only whistling or humming.

From *The Crack-Up*

Considerations for Critical Thinking and Writing

1. What qualities does Fitzgerald particularly value in Keats's poetry?
2. Which of his comments about the poems he cites is the most specific? Explain whether you agree with it, and why.
3. Perhaps you have already read Fitzgerald's *The Great Gatsby.* Based on that novel or other information you can find in the library about his life, why do you think Fitzgerald was especially attracted to Keats's poetry?

HAROLD BLOOM (b. 1930)
On "Bright star! would I were steadfast as thou art —" 1961

Bright star, the best of Keats's sonnets, left by him unpublished, written on a blank page in Shakespeare's Poems, facing *A Lover's Complaint,* is a direct analogue to the ode *To Autumn,* for it also is a poem beyond argument, though not also calm in mind, for passion informs it throughout. The octet is one of the major expressions of Keats's humanism; the sestet one of the most piercing of his longings after the world of Beulah land, the breathing garden of repose beyond bounds. The unity of the poem is constituted by its total freedom from Keats's characteristic conflicts. The octet shares in the resolution of *To Autumn,* giving us an anagoge of poetic eternity, without contraries. The sestet, as a Beulah poem, is set in that state of being where, according to Blake, "all contraries are equally true."

The initial line is a prayer. The next seven lines *describe* the steadfastness of the star, after making it clear that Keats wants to be as steadfast as the star, but not in the star's way of steadfastness. The sestet describes Keats's mode of desired being, and finally declares for an eternity of this being, or an immediate swoon to death. This tight structure confines a remarkable contrast, between the state of Eden and the state of Beulah, Blake would have said, but Keats, by his own choice, clearly opts for the lower paradise as his own.

The Miltonic bright star is not God's hermit but nature's patient, sleepless eremite. Never sleeping, its "eternal lids apart," like Milton's Eyelids of the Morning, it watches:

> The moving waters at their priestlike task
> Of pure ablution round earth's human shores

"Human shores" is powerfully Blakean; the contrast here is between the star as motionless, solitary hermit, and the waters as moving, companionable priest, the one watching, the other cleansing man. We miss the force of this if we do not see it as humanistic, not Christian, in its religious emphasis. The oceans themselves, as a part of unfallen nature, perform their task of *pure* ablution, and the shores of earth are themselves *human.* That last is more than similitude, i.e., metaphor; it is identity, anagogical typology. As Blake saw the physical universe as having itself an ultimately human form, so here also Keats sees the shores of earth as being "men seen afar." As in *To Autumn,* nature alone is sufficient for purifying herself and ourselves, insofar as we can still be hers. Nature's own grace, akin to Keats's poetry, reveals the human countenance of earth:

> Or gazing on the new soft fallen mask
> Of snow upon the mountains and the moors —

The snow is a mask because it covers the human features of earth — that is, mountains and moors. Keats does not ask for himself the priestlike work of the moving waters. . . . Here, at the furthest reach of his poetry, he prays instead for the hermit star's eminence and function, to watch, benevolently, nature's work of humanizing herself. But in his own place; "not in lone splendour hung aloft the night," but in his own Gardens of Adonis, where, still steadfast, still unchangeable (though how, there, can he expect that?) he will be able:

> Pillow'd upon my fair love's ripening breast,
> To feel for ever its soft fall and swell,
> Awake for ever in a sweet unrest,
> Still, still to hear her tender-taken breath
> And so live ever —

Her breast would be forever ripening, never ripe; keeping its sleeping rhythm forever while Keats, awake forever in his sweet unrest, could hear always that recurrence of her breath. This poem can help explain Keats's life; his life cannot explain the poem. Alternatively, the poem can help explain certain contemporary psychological reductions of human desire, but *they* cannot explain *it*.

From *The Visionary Company: A Reading of English Romantic Poetry*

Considerations for Critical Thinking and Writing

1. Explain how Bloom distinguishes between the poem's octet and sestet.
2. How do Bloom's allusions to Blake and Milton help explain his points?
3. What attitudes concerning psychological criticism does Bloom reveal in his final comments? Explain whether you agree or not.

JACK STILLINGER (b. 1931)
On "The Eve of St. Agnes"   1961

The commonest response to *The Eve of St. Agnes* has been the celebration of its "heady and perfumed loveliness." The poem has been called "a monody of dreamy richness," "one long sensuous utterance," "an expression of lyrical emotion," "a great affirmation of love," "a great choral hymn," an expression of "unquestioning rapture," and many things else. Remarks like these tend to confirm one's uneasy feeling that what is sometimes called "the most perfect" of Keats's longer poems is a mere fairy-tale romance, unhappily short on meaning. For many readers, as for Douglas Bush, the poem is "no more than a romantic tapestry of unique richness of color"; one is "moved less by the experience of the characters than . . . by the incidental and innumerable beauties of descriptive phrase and rhythm."

To be sure, not all critics have merely praised Keats's pictures. After all, the poem opens on a note of "bitter chill," and progresses through images of cold and death before the action gets under way. When young Porphyro comes from across the moors to claim his bride, he enters a hostile castle, where Madeline's kinsmen will murder even upon holy days; and in the face of this danger he proceeds to Madeline's bedchamber. With the sexual consummation of their love, a storm comes up, and they must escape the castle, past "sleeping dragons," porter, and bloodhound, out into the night. The ending reverts to the opening notes of bitter chill and death: Madeline's kinsmen are benightmared, the old Beadsman and Madeline's nurse Angela are grotesquely dispatched into the next world. Some obvious contrasts are made in the poem: the lovers' youth and vitality are set against the old age and death associated with Angela and the Beadsman; the warmth and security of Madeline's chamber are contrasted with the coldness and hostility of the rest of the castle and the icy storm outside; the innocence and purity of young love are played off against the sensuousness of the revelers elsewhere in the castle; and so on. Through these contrasts, says one critic [R. H. Fogle], Keats created a tale of young love "not by forgetting what everyday existence is like, but by using the mean, sordid, and commonplace as a foundation upon which to build a high romance"; the result is no mere fairy tale, but a poem that "has a rounded fulness, a complexity and seriousness, a balance which remove it from the realm of mere magnificent tour de force."

From "The Hoodwinking of Madeline: Skepticism in
'The Eve of St. Agnes,'" *Studies in Philology*, 1961.

Considerations for Critical Thinking and Writing

1. What is it about "The Eve of St. Agnes" that has drawn praise for "Keats's pictures"? Identify and discuss several passages that seem especially beautiful in their "descriptive phrase and rhythm."
2. What other contrasts do you find paired in the poem besides the "obvious" one cited by Stillinger?
3. Discuss whether you agree or disagree with the claim that "The Eve of St. Agnes" is "a mere fairy-tale romance, unhappily short on meaning."

TWO COMPLEMENTARY CRITICAL READINGS

CLEANTH BROOKS (b. 1906)
History in "Ode on a Grecian Urn" 1944

The marble men and maidens of the urn will not age as flesh-and-blood men and women will: "When old age shall this generation waste." (The word "generation," by the way, is very rich. It means on one level "that which is generated" — that which springs from human loins — Adam's breed; and yet, so intimately is death wedded to men, the word "generation" itself has become, as here, a measure of time.) The marble men and women lie outside time. The urn which they adorn will remain. The "Sylvan historian" will recite its history to other generations.

What will it say to them? Presumably, what it says to the poet now: that "formed experience," imaginative insight, embodies the basic and fundamental perception of man and nature. The urn is beautiful, and yet its beauty is based — what else is the poem concerned with? — on an imaginative perception of essentials. Such a vision is beautiful but it is also true. The sylvan historian presents us with beautiful histories, but they are true histories, and it is a good historian.

Moreover, the "truth" which the sylvan historian gives is the only kind of truth which we are likely to get on this earth, and, furthermore, it is the only kind that we *have* to have. The names, dates, and special circumstances, the wealth of data — these the sylvan historian quietly ignores. But we shall never get all the facts anyway — there is no end to the accumulation of facts. Moreover, mere accumulations of facts — a point our own generation is only beginning to realize — are meaningless. The sylvan historian does better than that: it takes a few details and so orders them that we have not only beauty but insight into essential truth. Its "history," in short, is a history without footnotes. It has the validity of myth — not myth as a pretty but irrelevant make-belief, an idle fancy, but myth as a valid perception into reality. . . .

And now, what of the objection that the final lines break the tone of the poem with a display of misplaced sententiousness? One can summarize the answer already implied thus: throughout the poem the poet has stressed the paradox of the speaking urn. First, the urn itself can tell a story, can give a history. Then, the various figures depicted upon the urn play music, or speak or sing. If we have been alive to these items, we shall not, perhaps, be too much surprised to have the urn speak once more, not in the sense in which it tells a story — a metaphor which is rather easy to accept — but, to have it speak on a higher level, to have it make a commentary on its own nature. If the urn has been properly dramatized, if we have followed the development of the metaphors, if we have been alive to the paradoxes which work throughout the poem, perhaps then, we shall be prepared for the enigmatic, final paradox which the "silent form" utters. But in that case, we shall not feel that the generalization, unqualified and to be taken literally, is meant to march out of its context to compete with the scientific and philosophical generalizations which dominate our world. . . . .

To conclude thus may seem to weight the principle of dramatic propriety with more than it can bear. This would not be fair to the complexity of the problem of truth in art nor fair to Keats's little parable. Granted; and yet the principle of dramatic propriety may take us further than would first appear. Respect for it may at least insure our dealing with the problem of truth at the level on which it is really relevant to literature. If we can see that the assertions made in a poem are to be taken as part of an organic context, if we can resist the temptation to deal with them in isolation, then we may be willing to go on to deal with the world-view, or "philosophy," or "truth" of the *poem as a whole* in terms of its dramatic wholeness: that is, we shall not neglect the maturity of attitude, the dramatic tension, the emotional *and* intellectual coherence in favor of some statement of theme abstracted from it by paraphrase. Perhaps, best of all, we might learn to distrust our ability to represent any poem adequately by paraphrase. Such a distrust is healthy. Keats's sylvan historian, who is not above "teasing" us, exhibits such a distrust, and perhaps the point of what the sylvan historian "says" is to confirm us in our distrust.

From The Sewanee Review 52 (1944)

Considerations for Critical Thinking and Writing

1. According to Brooks, what sort of "history" does the urn present us with in the poem?
2. How does Brooks defend the final lines from the charge of "sententiousness"?
3. What does Brooks see as one of the dangers of paraphrase?

M. H. ABRAMS (b. 1912)
The Speakers in "Ode on a Grecian Urn" 1958

"Beauty is truth, truth beauty" is not asserted by Keats, either as a statement or as a pseudo statement. The Grecian Urn, after remaining obdurately mute under a hail of questions, unexpectedly gives voice to this proposition near the end of the poem. . . .

There is also a second and more important speaker in the poem. The whole of the "Ode on a Grecian Urn," in fact, consists of the utterance of this unnamed character, whose situation and actions we follow as he attends first to the whole, then to the sculptured parts, and again to the whole of the Urn; and who expresses in the process not only his perceptions, but his thoughts and feelings, and thereby discovers to us a determinate temperament. By a standard poetic device we accept without disbelief, he attributes to the Urn a statement about beauty and truth which is actually a thought that the Urn evokes in him. How we are to take the statement, therefore, depends not only on its status as an utterance, in that place, by the particular Urn, but beyond that as the penultimate stage, dramatically rendered, in the meditation of the lyric speaker himself.

Obviously the earlier part of the "Ode" by no means gives the Urn a character that would warrant either its profundity or its reliability as a moral philosopher. In the mixed attitudes of the lyric speaker toward the Urn the playfulness and the pity, which are no less evident than the envy and the admiration, imply a position of superior understanding:

> Bold lover, never, never canst thou kiss,
> Though winning near the goal — yet, do not grieve;
> She cannot fade, though thou hast not thy bliss. . . .

The perfection represented on the Urn is the perdurability of the specious present, which escapes the "woe" of our mutable world only by surrendering any possibility of consummation and by trading grieving flesh for marble. The Urn, then, speaks from the limited perspective of a work in Grecian art; and it is from the larger viewpoint of this life, with its possibilities and its sorrows, that the lyric speaker has the last word, addressed to the figures on the Urn:

> That is all
> Ye know on earth, and all ye need to know.

The Urn has said, "Only the beautiful exists, and all that exists is beautiful" — but not, the speaker replies, in life, only in that sculptured Grecian world of noble simplicity where much that humanly matters is sacrificed for an enduring Now.

I entirely agree, then, with Professor Brooks in his explication of the "Ode," that "Beauty is truth" is not meant "to compete with . . . scientific and philosophical generalizations," but is to be considered as a speech "in character" and "dramatically appropriate" to the Urn. I am uneasy, however, about his final reference to "the world-view, or 'philosophy,' or 'truth' of the poem as a whole." For the poem as a whole is equally an utterance by a dramatically presented speaker, and none of its statements is proffered for our endorsement as a philosophical generalization of unlimited scope. They are all, therefore, to be apprehended as histrionic elements which are "in character" and "dramatically appropriate," for their inherent interest as stages in the evolution of an artistically ordered, hence all the more emotionally effective, experience of a credible human being.

From *Literature and Belief: English Institute Essays*

Considerations for Critical Thinking and Writing

1. Who is the second speaker in the poem, according to Abrams?
2. What distinction does Abrams make between the sculptured Grecian world and the speaker's world?
3. Explain how Abrams's view of the poem compares with Brooks's.

EMILY DICKINSON (1830–1886)

Emily Dickinson grew up in a prominent and prosperous household in Amherst, Massachusetts. Along with her younger sister Lavinia and older brother Austin, she experienced a quiet and reserved family life headed by her father Edward Dickinson, a strict orthodox Protestant. In a letter to Austin at law school, she once described the atmosphere in her father's house as "pretty much all sobriety." Her mother, Emily Norcross Dickinson, was not as powerful a presence in her life; she seems not to have been as emotionally accessible as Dickinson would have liked. Her daughter is said to have characterized her as not the sort of mother "to whom you hurry when you are troubled." Both parents raised Dickinson to be a cultured Christian woman who would one day be responsible for a family of her own. Her father attempted to protect her from reading books that might "joggle" her mind, particularly her religious faith, but Dickinson's individualistic instincts and irreverent sensibilities created conflicts that did not allow her to fall into step with the conventional piety, domesticity, and social duty prescribed by her father.

The Dickinsons were well known in Massachusetts. Her father was a lawyer and served as the treasurer of Amherst College (a position Austin eventually took up as well), and her grandfather was one of the college's founders. Although nineteenth-century politics, economics, and social issues do not appear in the foreground of her poetry, Dickinson lived in a family environment that was steeped in them: her father was an active town official and served in the General Court of Massachusetts, the State Senate, and the United States House of Representatives.

Dickinson, however, withdrew not only from her father's public world but also from almost all social life in Amherst. She refused to see most people, and aside from a single year at South Hadley Female Seminary (now

Mount Holyoke College), one excursion to Philadelphia and Washington, and several brief trips to Boston to see a doctor about eye problems, she lived all her life in her father's house. She dressed only in white and developed a reputation as a reclusive eccentric. Dickinson selected her own society carefully and frugally. Like her poetry, her relationship to the world was intensely reticent. Indeed, during the last twenty years of her life she rarely left the house.

Though Dickinson never married, she had significant relationships with several men who were friends, confidantes, and mentors. She also enjoyed an intimate relationship with her friend Susan Huntington Gilbert, who became her sister-in-law by marrying Austin. Susan and her husband lived next door and were extremely close with Dickinson. Biographers have attempted to find in a number of her relationships the source for the passion of some of her love poems and letters. Several possibilities have been put forward as the person she addressed in three letters as "Dear Master": Benjamin Newton, a clerk in her father's office who talked about books with her; Samuel Bowles, editor of the *Springfield Republican* and friend of the family; the Reverend Charles Wadsworth, a Presbyterian preacher with a reputation for powerful sermons; and an old friend and widower, Judge Otis P. Lord. Despite these speculations, no biographer has been able to identify definitively the object of Dickinson's love. What matters, of course, is not with whom she was in love — if, in fact, there was any single person — but that she wrote about such passions so intensely and convincingly in her poetry.

Choosing to live life internally within the confines of her home, Dickinson brought her life into sharp focus. For she also chose to live within the limitless expanses of her imagination, a choice she was keenly aware of and which she described in one of her poems this way: "I dwell in Possibility" (p. 844). Her small circle of domestic life did not impinge upon her creative sensibilities. Like Henry David Thoreau, she simplified her life so that doing without was a means of being within. In a sense she redefined the meaning of deprivation because being denied something — whether it was faith, love, literary recognition, or some other desire — provided a sharper, more intense understanding than she would have experienced had she achieved what she wanted: "'Heaven,'" she wrote, "is what I cannot reach!" This poem (p. 838), along with many others, such as "Water, is taught by thirst" (p. 834) and "Success is counted sweetest / By those who ne'er succeed" (p. 833), suggest just how persistently she saw deprivation as a way of sensitizing herself to the value of what she was missing. For Dickinson hopeful expectation was always more satisfying than achieving a golden moment. Perhaps that's one reason she was so attracted to John Keats's poetry (see, for example, his "Ode on a Grecian Urn," p. 813).

Dickinson enjoyed reading Keats as well as Emily and Charlotte Brönte; Robert and Elizabeth Barrett Browning; Alfred, Lord Tennyson; and George Eliot. Even so, these writers had little or no effect upon the style of her writing. In her own work she was original and innovative, but she did draw upon her knowledge of the Bible, classical myths, and Shakespeare for allusions and references in her poetry. She also used contemporary popular church hymns, transforming their standard rhythms into free-form hymn meters. Among American writers she appreciated Ralph Waldo Emerson and Thoreau, but she apparently felt Walt Whitman was better left unread. She once mentioned to Thomas Wentworth Higginson, a leading critic with whom she corresponded about her poetry, that as for Whitman "I never read his Book — but was told that he was disgraceful" (for the kind of Whitman poetry she had been warned against see his "I Sing the Body Electric," p. 776). Nathaniel Hawthorne, however, intrigued her with his faith in the imagination and his dark themes: "Hawthorne appals — entices," a remark that might be used to describe her own themes and techniques.

Today, Dickinson is regarded as one of America's greatest poets, but when she died at the age of fifty-six after devoting most of her life to writing poetry, her nearly 2,000 poems — only a dozen of which were published anonymously during her lifetime — were unknown except to a small number of friends and relatives. Dickinson was not recognized as a major poet until the twentieth century, when modern readers ranked her as a major new voice whose literary innovations were unmatched by any other nineteenth-century poet in the United States.

Dickinson neither completed many poems nor prepared them for publication. She wrote her drafts on scraps of paper, grocery lists, and the backs of recipes and used envelopes. Early editors of her poems took the liberty of making them more accessible to nineteenth-century readers when several volumes of selected poems were published in the 1890s. The poems were made to appear like traditional nineteenth-century verse by assigning them titles, rearranging their syntax, normalizing their grammar, and regularizing their capitalizations. Instead of dashes editors used standard punctuation; instead of the highly elliptical telegraphic lines so characteristic of her poems editors added articles, conjunctions, and prepositions to make them more readable and in line with conventional expectations. In addition, the poems were made more predictable by organizing them into categories such as friendship, nature, love, and death. Not until 1955, when Thomas Johnson published Dickinson's complete works in a form that attempted to be true to her manuscript versions, did readers have an opportunity to see the full range of her style and themes.

Like that of Robert Frost, Dickinson's popular reputation has sometimes relegated her to the role of a New England regionalist who writes quaint uplifting verses that touch the heart. In 1971 that image was mailed first class all over the country by the United States Postal Service. In addition to issuing a commemorative stamp featuring a portrait of Dickinson, the Postal Service affixed the stamp to a first-day-of-issue envelope that included an engraved rose and one of her poems. Here's the poem chosen from among the nearly 2,000 she wrote:

If I can stop one Heart from breaking   c. 1864

If I can stop one Heart from breaking
I shall not live in vain
If I can ease one Life the Aching
or cool one Pain

Or help one fainting Robin
Unto his Nest again
I shall not live in Vain.

This is typical not only of many nineteenth-century popular poems, but of the kind of verse that can be found in contemporary greeting cards. The speaker tells us what we imagine we should think about and makes the point simply with a sentimental image of a "fainting Robin." To point out that robins don't faint or that altruism isn't necessarily the only rule of conduct by which one should live one's life is to make trouble for this poem. Moreover, its use of language is unexceptional; the metaphors used, like that Robin, are a bit weary. If this poem were characteristic of Dickinson's poetry, the Postal Service probably would not have been urged to issue a stamp in her honor nor would you be reading her poems in this anthology or many others. Here's another poem by Dickinson that is more typical of her writing:

If I shouldn't be alive   c. 1860

If I shouldn't be alive
When the Robins come,
Give the one in Red Cravat,
A Memorial crumb.

If I couldn't thank you,
Being fast asleep,
You will know I'm trying
With my Granite lip!

This poem is more representative of Dickinson's sensibilities and techniques. Although the first stanza sets up a rather mild concern that the speaker might not survive the winter (a not uncommon fear for those who fell prey to pneumonia, for example, during Dickinson's time), the concern can't be taken too seriously — a gentle humor lightens the poem when we realize that all robins have red cravats and are therefore the speaker's favorite. Furthermore, the euphemism that describes the speaker "Being fast asleep" in line 6 makes death seem not so threatening after all. But the sentimental expectations of the first six lines — lines that could have been written by any number of popular nineteenth-century writers — are dashed by the penultimate word of the last line. "Granite" is the perfect word here because it forces us to reread the poem and to recognize that it's not about feeding robins or offering a cosmetic treatment of death; rather it's a bone-chilling description of a corpse's lip that evokes the cold, hard texture and grayish color of tombstones. These lips will never say "Thank you" or anything else.

Instead of the predictable rhymes and sentiments of "If I can stop one Heart from breaking," this poem is unnervingly precise in its use of language and tidily points out how much emphasis Dickinson places on an individual word. Her use of near rhyme with "asleep" and "lip" brilliantly mocks a euphemistic approach to death by its jarring dissonance. This is a better poem, not because it's grim or about death, but because it demonstrates Dickinson's skillful use of language to produce a shocking irony.

Dickinson found irony, ambiguity, and paradox lurking in the simplest and commonest experiences. The materials and subject matter of her poetry are quite conventional. Her poems are filled with robins, bees, winter light, household items, and domestic duties. These materials represent the range of what she experienced in and around her father's house. She used them because they constituted so much of her life and, more importantly, because she found meanings latent in them. Though her world was simple, it was also complex in its beauties and its terrors. Her lyric poems capture impressions of particular moments, scenes, or moods, and she characteristically focuses upon topics such as nature, love, immorality, death, faith, doubt, pain, and the self.

Though her materials were conventional, her treatment of them was innovative, because she was willing to break whatever poetic conventions stood in the way of the intensity of her thought and images. Her conciseness, brevity, and wit are tightly packed. Typically she offers her observations via one or two images that reveal her thought in a powerful manner. She once characterized her literary art by writing "My business is circumference." Her method is to reveal the inadequacy of declarative statements by evoking qualifications and questions with images that complicate firm assertions and affirmations. In one of her poems she describes her strategies this way: "Tell all the Truth but tell it slant — / Success in Circuit lies." This might well stand as a working definition of Dickinson's aesthetics and is embodied in the following poem:

The Thought beneath so slight a film —   c. 1860

The Thought beneath so slight a film —
Is more distinctly seen —
As laces just reveal the surge —
Or Mists — The Apennine°   *Italian mountain range*

Paradoxically, "thought" is more clearly understood precisely because a slight "film" — in this case language — covers it. Language, like lace, enhances what it covers and reveals it all the more — just as a mountain range is more engaging to the imagination if it is covered in mists rather than starkly presenting itself. Poetry for Dickinson intensifies, clarifies, and organizes experience.

Dickinson's poetry is challenging because it is radical and original in its rejection of most traditional nineteenth-century themes and techniques. Her poems require active engagement from the reader, because she seems to leave out so much with her elliptical style and remarkable contracting metaphors. But these apparent gaps are filled with meaning if we are sensitive to her use of devices such as personification, allusion, symbolism, and startling syntax and grammar. Since her use of dashes is sometimes puzzling, it helps to read her poems aloud to hear how carefully the words are arranged. What might initially seem intimidating on a silent page can surprise the reader with meaning when heard. It's also worth keeping in mind that Dickinson was not always consistent in her views and that they can change from poem to poem, depending upon how she felt at a given moment. For example, her definition of religious belief in "'Faith' is a fine invention" (p. 836) reflects an ironically detached wariness in contrast to the faith embraced in "I never saw a Moor —" (p. 852). Dickinson was less interested in absolute answers to questions than she was in examining and exploring their "circumference."

Because Dickinson's poems are all relatively brief (none is longer than fifty lines), they invite browsing and sampling, but perhaps a useful way into their highly metaphoric and witty world is this "how to" poem that reads almost like a recipe:

To make a prairie
it takes a clover and one bee   date unknown

To make a prairie it takes a clover and one bee,
One clover, and a bee,
And revery.
The revery alone will do,
If bees are few.

This quiet but infinite claim for a writer's imagination brings together the range of ingredients in Dickinson's world of domestic and ordinary natural details. Not surprisingly, she deletes rather than adds to the recipe, because the one essential ingredient is the writer's creative imagination. *Bon appétit.*

Chronology

1830   Born December 10 in Amherst, Massachusetts.

1840   Starts her first year at Amherst Academy.

1847–48 Graduates from Amherst Academy and enters South Hadley Female Seminary (now Mount Holyoke College).

1855   Visits Philadelphia and Washington, D.C.

1857   Emerson lectures in Amherst.

1862   Starts corresponding with Thomas Wentworth Higginson, asking for advice about her poems.

1864   Visits Boston for eye treatments.

1870   Higginson visits her in Amherst.

1873   Higginson visits for a second and final time.

1874   Her father dies in Boston.

1875   Her mother suffers from paralysis.

1882   Her mother dies.

1886   Dies on May 15 in Amherst, Massachusetts.

1890   First edition of her poetry, edited by Mabel Loomis Todd and Thomas Wentworth Higginson, is published.

1955   Thomas H. Johnson publishes *The Poems of Emily Dickinson* in three volumes, thereby making available her poetry known to that date.

Success is counted sweetest

c. 1859

Success is counted sweetest
By those who ne'er succeed.
To comprehend a nectar
Requires sorest need.

Not one of all the purple Host   5
Who took the Flag today
Can tell the definition
So clear of Victory

As he defeated — dying —
On whose forbidden ear   10
The distant strains of triumph
Burst agonized and clear!

Considerations for Critical Thinking and Writing

1. How is success defined in this poem? To what extent does that definition agree with your own understanding of the word?
2. What do you think is meant by the use of "comprehend" in line 3? How can a nectar be comprehended?
3. Why do the defeated understand victory better than the victorious?
4. Discuss the effect of the poem's final line.

Connections to Other Selections

1. In an essay compare the themes of this poem with those of John Keats's "Ode on a Grecian Urn" (p. 813).
2. How might this poem be used as a commentary on Aylmer's character in Hawthorne's short story "The Birthmark" (p. 261)?

Water, is taught by thirst   c. 1859

Water, is taught by thirst.
Land — by the Oceans passed.
Transport — by throe —
Peace — by its battles told —
Love, by Memorial Mold —
Birds, by the Snow.

Considerations for Critical Thinking and Writing

1. How is the paradox of each line of the poem resolved? How is the first word of each line "taught" by the phrase that follows it?
2. Which image do you find most powerful? Explain why.
3. Try your hand at writing similar lines in which something is "taught."

Connections to Other Selections

1. What does this poem have in common with the preceding poem, "Success is counted sweetest"? Which poem do you think is more effective? Explain why.
2. How is the crucial point of this poem related to "I like a look of Agony," (p. 839)?

Safe in their Alabaster Chambers —   1859 version

Safe in their Alabaster Chambers —
Untouched by Morning
And untouched by Noon —
Sleep the meek members of the Resurrection —
Rafter of satin,   5
And Roof of stone.

Light laughs the breeze
In her Castle above them —
Babbles the Bee in a stolid Ear,
Pipe the Sweet Birds in ignorant cadence —   10
Ah, what sagacity perished here!

Safe in their Alabaster Chambers —   1861 version

Safe in their Alabaster Chambers —
Untouched by Morning —
And untouched by Noon —
Lie the meek members of the Resurrection —
Rafter of Satin — and Roof of Stone!   5

Grand go the Years — in the Crescent — above them —
Worlds scoop their Arcs —
And Firmaments — row —
Diadems — drop — and Doges° — surrender —
Soundless as dots — on a Disc of Snow —   10

9 *Doges:* Chief magistrates of Venice from the twelfth to the sixteenth centuries.

Considerations for Critical Thinking and Writing

1. Dickinson permitted the 1859 version of this poem, entitled "The Sleeping," to be printed in *The Springfield Republican.* The second version she sent privately to Thomas W. Higginson. Why do you suppose she would agree to publish the first but not the second version?
2. Are there any significant changes in the first stanzas of the two versions? If you answered yes, explain the significance of the changes.
3. Describe the different kinds of images used in the two second stanzas. How do those images affect the tones and meanings of those stanzas?
4. Discuss why you prefer one version of the poem over the other.

Connections to Other Selections

1. Compare the theme in the 1861 version with the theme of Robert Frost's "Design" (p. 887).
2. In an essay discuss the attitude toward death in the version of 1859 and in "Apparently with no surprise" (p. 854).

"Faith" is a fine invention

c. 1860

"Faith" is a fine invention
When Gentlemen can *see* —
But *Microscopes* are prudent
In an Emergency.

Considerations for Critical Thinking and Writing

1. What affects the speaker's attitude toward faith?
2. Describe the tone. Why can't this poem be accurately described as reverent?
3. Discuss the use of diction and its effects.

Connections to Other Selections

1. Write an essay comparing the view of faith in this poem with that expressed in "I never saw a Moor — " (p. 852).
2. Consider "I know that He exists" (p. 846) as an "Emergency" of the kind cited in this poem. How are the two poems related?
3. Compare the use of the word "fine" here with its use in the next poem, "Portraits are to daily faces."

Portraits are to daily faces

c. 1860

Portraits are to daily faces
As an Evening West,
To a fine, pedantic sunshine —
In a satin Vest!

Considerations for Critical Thinking and Writing

1. How is the basic strategy of this poem similar to the following statement: "Door-knob is to door as button is to sweater"?
2. Identify the four metonymies in the poem. Pay close attention to their connotative meanings.
3. If you don't know the meaning of *pedantic*, look it up in a dictionary. How does its meaning affect your reading of the word *fine*?
4. Dickinson once described herself as a literary artist this way: "My business is circumference." Discuss how this poem explains and expresses this characterization of her poetry.

Connections to Other Selections

1. Compare Dickinson's view of poetry in this poem with Francis's perspective in "Catch" (p. 593). What important similarities and differences do you find?
2. Write an essay describing Robert Frost's strategy in "Mending Wall" (p. 874) or "Birches" (p. 880) as the business of circumference.
3. How is the theme of this poem related to the central idea in "The Thought beneath so slight a film — " (p. 831)?

Some keep the Sabbath going to Church —   c. 1860

Some keep the Sabbath going to Church —
I keep it, staying at Home —
With a Bobolink for a Chorister —
And an Orchard, for a Dome —

Some keep the Sabbath in Surplice° —   *holy robes*   5
I just wear my Wings —
And instead of tolling the Bell, for Church,
Our little Sexton — sings.

God preaches, a noted Clergyman —
And the sermon is never long,   10
So instead of getting to Heaven, at last —
I'm going, all along.

Considerations for Critical Thinking and Writing

1. What is the effect of referring to "Some" people?
2. Characterize the speaker's tone.
3. How does the speaker distinguish himself or herself from those who go to church?
4. How might "Surplice" be read as a pun?
5. According to the speaker, how should the Sabbath be observed?

Connections to Other Selections

1. Discuss the attitude toward formal religion in this poem and in John Keats's "Written in Disgust of Vulgar Superstition" (p. 794).
2. Write an essay that discusses nature in this poem and in Walt Whitman's "When I Heard the Learned Astronomer" (p. 1063).

I taste a liquor never brewed —   1861

I taste a liquor never brewed —
From Tankards scooped in Pearl —
Not all the Vats upon the Rhine
Yield such an Alcohol!

Inebriate of Air — am I —   5
And Debauchee of Dew —
Reeling — thro endless summer days —
From inns of Molten Blue —

When "Landlords" turn the drunken Bee
Out of the Foxglove's door —   10
When Butterflies — renounce their "drams" —
I shall but drink the more!

Till Seraphs° swing their snowy Hats —   *angels*
And Saints — to windows run —
To see the little Tippler   15
Leaning against the — Sun —

Considerations for Critical Thinking and Writing

1. What is the poem's central metaphor? How is it developed in each stanza?
2. Which images suggest the causes of the speaker's intoxication?
3. Characterize the speaker's relationship to nature.

Connections to Other Selections

1. In an essay compare this speaker's relationship with nature to that of "A narrow Fellow in the Grass" (p. 4).
2. Discuss the tone created by the images in this poem and in Galway Kinnell's "Blackberry Eating" (p. 714).

"Heaven" — is what I cannot reach!   c. 1861

"Heaven" — is what I cannot reach!
The Apple on the Tree —
Provided it do hopeless — hang —
That — "Heaven" is — to Me!

The Color, on the Cruising Cloud —   5
The interdicted Land —
Behind the Hill — the House behind —
There — Paradise — is found!

Her teasing Purples — Afternoons —
The credulous — decoy —   10
Enamored — of the Conjuror —
That spurned us — Yesterday!

Considerations for Critical Thinking and Writing

1. Look up the myth of Tantalus and explain the allusion in line 3.
2. How does the speaker define heaven? How does that definition compare with conventional views of heaven?
3. Given the speaker's definition of heaven, how do you think the speaker would describe hell?

Connections to Other Selections

1. Write an essay that discusses desire in this poem and in "Water, is taught by thirst" (p. 834).
2. Discuss the speakers' attitudes toward pleasure in this poem and in Diane Ackerman's "A Fine, A Private Place" (p. 641).

"Hope" is the thing with feathers —

c. 1861

"Hope" is the thing with feathers —
That perches in the soul —
And sings the tune without the words —
And never stops — at all —

And sweetest — in the Gale — is heard —   5
And sore must be the storm —
That could abash the little Bird
That kept so many warm —

I've heard it in the chillest land —
And on the strangest Sea —   10
Yet, never, in Extremity,
It asked a crumb — of Me.

Considerations for Critical Thinking and Writing

1. Why do you think the speaker defines hope in terms of a bird? Why is this metaphor more appropriate than, say, a dog?
2. Discuss the effects of the rhymes in each stanza.
3. What is the central point of the poem?

Connections to Other Selections

1. Compare the tone of this definition of hope with that of "'Faith' is a fine invention" (p. 836). How is "Extremity" handled differently from the "Emergency" in the latter poem?
2. Compare the strategies used to define hope in this poem and heaven in the preceding poem, "Heaven — is what I cannot reach!" Which poem, in your opinion, creates a more successful definition? In an essay explain why.

I like a look of Agony,

c. 1861

I like a look of Agony,
Because I know it's true —
Men do not sham Convulsion,
Nor simulate, a Throe —

The Eyes glaze once — and that is Death —
Impossible to feign
The Beads upon the Forehead
By homely Anguish strung.

Considerations for Critical Thinking and Writing

1. Why does the speaker "like a look of Agony"?
2. Discuss the image of "The Eyes glaze once — ." Why is that a particularly effective metaphor for death?
3. Characterize the speaker. One critic once described the voice in this poem as "almost a hysterical shriek." Explain why you agree or disagree.

Connections to Other Selections

1. Write an essay on Dickinson's attitudes toward pain and deprivation, using this poem, "'Heaven' — is what I cannot reach!" (p. 838), and "Success is counted sweetest" (p. 833) as the basis for your discussion.
2. Consider how death is treated here and in "I've seen a Dying Eye" (p. 845).

I'm Nobody! Who are you? c. 1861

I'm Nobody! Who are you?
Are you — Nobody — too?
Then there's a pair of us!
Don't tell! they'd advertise — you know!

How dreary — to be — Somebody!
How public — like a Frog —
To tell your name — the livelong June —
To an admiring Bog!

Considerations for Critical Thinking and Writing

1. What does the speaker wish to have in common with the reader? Explain whether you feel it is better to be "Nobody" or "Somebody."
2. Explain why it is "dreary — to be — Somebody!"
3. Discuss the simile in line 6. Why does it work so well?
4. What does the speaker think of most people?

Connections to Other Selections

1. What significant similarities in theme and technique does this poem share with e. e. cummings's "anyone lived in a pretty how town" (p. 946)?
2. Contrast the sense of self in this poem and Walt Whitman's "One's-Self I Sing" (p. 1012).

The Robin's my Criterion for Tune c. 1861

The Robin's my Criterion for Tune —
Because I grow — where Robins do —
But, were I Cuckoo born —

I'd swear by him —
The ode familiar — rules the Noon —   5
The Buttercup's, my Whim for Bloom —
Because, we're Orchard sprung —
But, were I Britain born,
I'd Daisies spurn —
None but the Nut — October fit —   10
Because, through dropping it,
The Seasons flit — I'm taught —
Without the Snow's Tableau
Winter, were lie — to me —
Because I see — New Englandly —   15
The Queen, discerns like me —
Provincially —

Considerations for Critical Thinking and Writing

1. Why are robins crucial to the speaker?
2. How would the speaker's "Tune" be affected if she were "Britain born"?
3. How does the speaker "see — New Englandly" in this poem? Why do you suppose she transforms New England into an adverb?

Connections to Other Selections

1. Discuss Dickinson's use of robins here and in "If I can stop one Heart from breaking" and "If I shouldn't be alive" (p. 830). How are robins used in each poem to convey meanings?
2. Choose a poem by Robert Frost and explain in an essay how he too sees "New Englandly."

Wild Nights — Wild Nights!   c. 1861

Wild Nights — Wild Nights!
Were I with thee
Wild Nights should be
Our luxury!

Futile — the Winds —   5
To a Heart in port —
Done with the Compass —
Done with the Chart!

Rowing in Eden —
Ah, the Sea!   10
Might I but moor — Tonight —
In Thee!

Emily Dickinson 841

Considerations for Critical Thinking and Writing

1. Look up the meaning of "luxury" in a dictionary. Why does this word work especially well here?
2. Given the imagery of the final stanza, do you think the speaker is a man or woman? Explain why.
3. T. W. Higginson, Dickinson's mentor, once said he was afraid that some "malignant" readers might "read into [a poem like this] more than that virgin recluse ever dreamed of putting there." What do you think?

Connections to Other Selections

1. Write an essay that compares the voice, figures of speech, and theme of this poem with those of Margaret Atwood's "you fit into me" (p. 666).
2. Discuss the treatment of passion in this poem and in Sappho's "With his venom" (p. 662).

What Soft — Cherubic Creatures —   1862

What Soft — Cherubic Creatures —
These Gentlewomen are —
One would as soon assault a Plush —
Or violate a Star —

Such Dimity° Convictions —   *cotton fabric*   5
A Horror so refined
Of freckled Human Nature —
Of Deity — ashamed —

It's such a common — Glory —
A Fisherman's — Degree —   10
Redemption — Brittle Lady —
Be so — ashamed of Thee —

Considerations for Critical Thinking and Writing

1. Characterize the "Gentlewomen" in this poem.
2. How do the sounds produced in the first line help to reinforce their meaning?
3. What are "Dimity convictions," and what do they make of "freckled Human Nature"?
4. Discuss the irony in the final stanza.

Connections to Other Selections

1. In an essay discuss the theme of this poem and Flannery O'Connor's short story "Revelation" (p. 394).
2. How are the "Gentlewomen" in this poem similar to the "Gentlemen" in "'Faith' is a fine invention" (p. 836)?

The Soul selects her own Society —

c. 1862

The Soul selects her own Society —
Then — shuts the Door —
To her divine Majority —
Present no more —

Unmoved — she notes the Chariots — pausing —
At her low Gate —
Unmoved — an Emperor be kneeling
Upon her Mat —

I've known her — from an ample nation —
Choose One —
Then — close the Valves of her attention —
Like Stone —

5

10

Considerations for Critical Thinking and Writing

1. What images reveal the speaker to be self-reliant and self-sufficient?
2. Why do you suppose the "Soul" in this poem is female? Would it make any
   difference if it were male?
3. Discuss the effect of the images in the final two lines. Pay particular attention to
   the meanings of "Valves" in line 11.

Connections to Other Selections

1. Though this poem takes up a different subject matter from "Shall I take thee, the
   Poet said" (p. 853), consider the process of selection in each poem and what it
   reveals about the speakers' sensibilities.
2. Discuss, in essay, the speaker's character in this poem and the protagonist's in
   William Faulkner's short story "A Rose for Emily" (p. 47).

Much Madness is divinest Sense —

c. 1862

Much Madness is divinest Sense —
To a discerning Eye —
Much Sense — the starkest Madness —
'Tis the Majority
In this, as All, prevail —
Assent — and you are sane —
Demur — you're straightway dangerous —
And handled with a Chain —

Considerations for Critical Thinking and Writing

1. Discuss the conflict between the individual and society in this poem. Which images
   are used to describe each? How do these images affect your attitudes about them?
2. Comment on the effectiveness of the poem's final line.

3. T. W. Higginson's wife once referred to Dickinson as the "partially cracked poetess of Amherst." Assuming that Dickinson had some idea of how she was regarded by the "Majority," how might this poem be seen as an insight into her life?

Connections to Other Selections

1. How does this poem serve as a commentary on Gail Godwin's short story, "A Sorrowful Woman" (p. 30)?
2. Discuss the theme of self-reliance in this poem and the preceding one, "The Soul selects her own Society."

I dwell in Possibility —

c. 1862

I dwell in Possibility —
A fairer House than Prose —
More numerous of Windows —
Superior — for Doors —

Of Chambers as the Cedars —   5
Impregnable of Eye —
And for an Everlasting Roof
The Gambrels° of the Sky —   *angled roofs*

Of Visiters — the fairest —
For Occupation — This —   10
The spreading wide my narrow Hands
To gather Paradise —

Considerations for Critical Thinking and Writing

1. What distinction is made between poetry and prose in this poem? Explain why you agree or disagree with the speaker's distinctions.
2. What is the poem's central metaphor in the second and third stanzas?
3. How does the use of metaphor in this poem become a means for the speaker to envision and create a world beyond the circumstances of the speaker's actual life?

Connections to Other Selections

1. Compare what this poem says about poetry and prose with T. E. Hulme's comments in the perspective "On the Differences between Poetry and Prose" (p. 663).
2. How can the speaker's sense of expansiveness in this poem be reconciled with the speaker's insistence upon contraction in "The Soul selects her own Society — " (p. 843). Are these poems contradictory? Explain why or why not.

I've seen a Dying Eye

I've seen a Dying Eye
Run round and round a Room —
In search of Something — as it seemed —
Then Cloudier become —
And then — obscure with Fog —
And then — be soldered down
Without disclosing what it be
'Twere blessed to have seen —

Considerations for Critical Thinking and Writing

1. Characterize the emotional state of the person dying.
2. What is the "Something" the eye searches for?
3. Discuss the progression described in lines 4–6.
4. Discuss the wordplay at work in the speaker's use of "soldered" and "disclosing."

Connections to Other Selections

1. Discuss the similarities in theme in this poem and "If I shouldn't be alive" (p. 830).
2. In an essay explain how the images in this poem and in "I heard a Fly buzz — when I died — " (p. 847) constitute a visual and auditory evocation of death.

The Brain — is wider than the Sky —

The Brain — is wider than the Sky —
For — put them side by side —
The one the other will contain
With ease — and You — beside —

The Brain is deeper than the sea —   5
For — hold them — Blue to Blue —
The one the other will absorb —
As Sponges — Buckets — do —

The Brain is just the weight of God —
For — Heft them — Pound for Pound —   10
And they will differ — if they do —
As Syllable from Sound —

Considerations for Critical Thinking and Writing

1. What does the speaker say is the relationship between one's "Brain" and physical reality?
2. In the final stanza how do "Brain" and "God," "Syllable" and "Sound" "differ"?
3. How does this poem validate Dickinson's claim that "My business is circumference"?

Connections to Other Selections

1. Discuss the treatment in this poem and in "To make a prairie it takes a clover and one bee" (p. 832).
2. In an essay compare the sense of human possibility here with that found in "I dwell in Possibility — " (p. 844).

I know that He exists

c. 1862

I know that He exists.
Somewhere — in Silence —
He has hid his rare life
From our gross eyes.

'Tis an instant's play.   5
'Tis a fond Ambush —
Just to make Bliss
Earn her own surprise!

But — should the play
Prove piercing earnest —   10
Should the glee-glaze —
In Death's — stiff — stare —

Would not the fun
Look too expensive!
Would not the jest —   15
Have crawled too far!

Considerations for Critical Thinking and Writing

1. Identify the "He" in the first line of this poem.
2. What is the poem's controlling metaphor?
3. What does the speaker contemplate in lines 9–12?
4. How does the speaker's tone change from beginning to end? Where does it start to change?
5. Comment on the appropriateness of "crawled" (line 16). Is there an allusion here?

Connections to Other Selections

1. Discuss the theme of this poem and Robert Frost's "Provide, Provide" (p. 888).
2. Write an essay on attitudes about God in "I know that He exists" and Gerard Manley Hopkins's "God's Grandeur" (p. 720).

After great pain, a formal feeling comes —

c. 1862

After great pain, a formal feeling comes —
The Nerves sit ceremonious, like Tombs —
The stiff Heart questions was it He, that bore,
And Yesterday, or Centuries before?

The Feet, mechanical, go round —   5
Of Ground, or Air, or Ought —
A Wooden way
Regardless grown,
A Quartz contentment, like a stone —

This is the Hour of Lead —   10
Remembered, if outlived,
As Freezing persons, recollect the Snow —
First — Chill — then Stupor — then the letting go —

Considerations for Critical Thinking and Writing

1. What is the cause of the speaker's pain?
2. How does the rhythm of the lines create a slow, somber pace?
3. Discuss why "the Hour of Lead" (line 10) could serve as a useful title for this poem.

Connections to Other Selections

1. How might this poem be read as a kind of sequel to "I've seen a Dying Eye" (p. 845).
2. Write an essay that discusses this poem in relation to Robert Frost's "Home Burial" (p. 876).

I heard a Fly buzz — when I died —

c. 1862

I heard a Fly buzz — when I died —
The Stillness in the Room
Was like the Stillness in the Air —
Between the Heaves of Storm —

The Eyes around — had wrung them dry —   5
And Breaths were gathering firm
For that last Onset — when the King
Be witnessed — in the Room —

I willed my Keepsakes — Signed away
What portion of me be   10
Assignable — and then it was
There interposed a Fly —

With Blue — uncertain stumbling Buzz —
Between the light — and me —
And then the Windows failed — and then   15
I could not see to see —

Considerations for Critical Thinking and Writing

1. What was expected to happen "when the King" was "witnessed"? What happened instead?
2. Why do you think Dickinson chooses a fly rather than perhaps a bee or gnat?
3. What is the effect of the last line? Why not end the poem with "I could not see" instead of the additional "to see"?
4. Discuss three sounds in the poem. Are there any instances of onomatopoeia?

Connections to Other Selections

1. Discuss the final lines of this poem and "I've seen a Dying Eye" (p. 845). Are the themes similar or are there significant differences?
2. Contrast the symbolic significance of the fly with the spider in Walt Whitman's "A Noiseless Patient Spider" (p. 676).
3. Consider the meaning of "light" in this poem and in "There's a certain Slant of Light" (p. 2053).

It dropped so low — in my Regard —   c. 1863

It dropped so low — in my Regard —
I heard it hit the Ground —
And go to pieces on the Stones
At bottom of my Mind —

Yet blamed the Fate that flung it — *less*
Than I denounced Myself,
For entertaining Plated Wares
Upon My Silver Shelf —

Considerations for Critical Thinking and Writing

1. What does "It" refer to? Is it possible to be specific? What in the first stanza limits the meaning of "It"?
2. Why does the speaker denounce himself or herself?
3. What is the difference between "Plated Wares" and silver? Why is this crucial to an understanding of the poem?

Connections to Other Selections

1. Describe the difference in sensibility between this speaker and the "Gentlewomen" in "What Soft — Cherubic Creatures — " (p. 842).
2. In an essay compare how the mind is presented in this poem with how it is presented in "The Brain — is wider than the Sky — " (p. 845).

Because I could not stop for Death —

c. 1863

Because I could not stop for Death —
He kindly stopped for me —
The Carriage held but just Ourselves —
And Immortality.

We slowly drove — He knew no haste   5
And I had put away
My labor and my leisure too,
For His Civility —

We passed the School, where Children strove
At Recess — in the Ring —   10
We passed the Fields of Gazing Grain —
We passed the Setting Sun —

Or rather — He passed Us —
The Dews drew quivering and chill —
For only Gossamer, my Gown —   15
My Tippet° — only Tulle —   *shawl*

We paused before a House that seemed
A Swelling of the Ground —
The Roof was scarcely visible —
The Cornice — in the Ground —   20

Since then — 'tis Centuries — and yet
Feels shorter than the Day
I first surmised the Horses' Heads
Were toward Eternity —

Considerations for Critical Thinking and Writing

1. Why couldn't the speaker stop for death?
2. How is Death personified in this poem? How does the speaker respond to him? Why are they accompanied by Immortality?
3. What is the significance of the things they "passed" in the third stanza?
4. What is the "House" in lines 17–20?
5. Discuss the rhythm of the lines. How, for example, is the rhythm of line 14 related to its meaning?

Connections to Other Selections

1. Compare the tone of this poem with that of Dickinson's "I heard a Fly buzz — when I died — " (p. 847).
2. Write an essay comparing Dickinson's view of death in this poem and in "If I shouldn't be alive" (p. 830). Which poem is more powerful for you? Explain why.

My Life had stood — a Loaded Gun —

c. 1863

My Life had stood — a Loaded Gun —
In Corners — till a Day
The Owner passed — identified —
And carried Me away —

And now We roam in Sovereign Woods —   5
And now We hunt the Doe —
And every time I speak for Him —
The Mountains straight reply —

And do I smile, such cordial light
Upon the Valley glow —   10
It is as a Vesuvian face°
Had let its pleasure through —

And when at Night — Our good Day done —
I guard My Master's Head —
'Tis better than the Eider-Duck's   15
Deep Pillow — to have shared —

To foe of His — I'm deadly foe —
None stir the second time —
On whom I lay a Yellow Eye —
Or an emphatic Thumb —   20

Though I than He — may longer live
He longer must — than I —
For I have but the power to kill,
Without — the power to die —

11 *Vesuvian face:* A face that could erupt like the volcano Mt. Vesuvius.

Considerations for Critical Thinking and Writing

1. What metaphor does the speaker use to characterize herself? Why is this a surprising but appropriate metaphor?
2. What is the relationship between the speaker and the hunter?
3. To what extent can this poem be regarded as a ballad?

Connections to Other Selections

1. Compare the emotional tension in this poem with that in "Wild Nights — Wild Nights!" (p. 841).
2. Compare the theme here with the theme in "Heaven' — is what I cannot reach!" (p. 838).

The Bustle in a House

c. 1866

The Bustle in a House
The Morning after Death
Is solemnest of industries
Enacted upon Earth —

The Sweeping up the Heart
And putting Love away
We shall not want to use again
Until Eternity.

Considerations for Critical Thinking and Writing

1. What is the relationship between love and death in this poem?
2. Why do you think mourning (notice the pun in line 2) is described as an industry?
3. Discuss the tone of the ending of the poem. Consider whether you think it is hopeful, sad, resigned, or some other mood.

Connections to Other Selections

1. Compare this poem with "After great pain, a formal feeling comes — " (p. 847). Which poem is, for you, a more powerful treatment of mourning?
2. How does this poem qualify "I like a look of Agony," (p. 839)? Does it contradict the latter poem? Explain why or why not.

Tell all the Truth but tell it slant —

c. 1868

Tell all the Truth but tell it slant —
Success in Circuit lies
Too bright for our infirm Delight
The Truth's superb surprise

As Lightning to the Children eased
With explanation kind
The Truth must dazzle gradually
Or every man be blind —

Considerations for Critical Thinking and Writing

1. Why should truth be told "slant" and circuitously?
2. How does the second stanza explain the first?
3. How is this poem an example of its own theme?

Connections to Other Selections

1. How does the first stanza of "I know that He exists" (p. 846) suggest a similar idea to this poem? Why do you think the last eight lines of the former aren't similar in theme to this poem?

2. Write an essay on Dickinson's attitudes about the purpose and strategies of poetry by considering this poem as well as "The Thought beneath so slight a film — " (p. 831) and "Portraits are to daily faces" (p. 836).

From all the Jails the Boys and Girls   c. 1881

From all the Jails the Boys and Girls
Ecstatically leap —
Beloved only Afternoon
That Prison doesn't keep

They storm the Earth and stun the Air,
A Mob of solid Bliss —
Alas — that Frowns should lie in wait
For such a Foe as this —

Considerations for Critical Thinking and Writing

1. What are the "jails"?
2. Comment on the effectiveness of the description in lines 5 and 6.
3. How might "Frowns" be read symbolically?

Connections to Other Selections

1. Compare the theme of this poem with that of William Blake's "The Garden of Love" (p. 935).
2. In an essay discuss the treatment of childhood in this poem and in Robert Frost's "Out, Out — " (p. 883).

I never saw a Moor —   c. 1865

I never saw a Moor —
I never saw the Sea —
Yet know I how the Heather looks
And what a Billow be.

I never spoke with God
Nor visited in Heaven —
Yet certain am I of the spot
As if the Checks were given —

Considerations for Critical Thinking and Writing

1. How does the first stanza serve as a premise for the second stanza?
2. Comment on the poem's images. Are they effective, in your opinion?

Connections to Other Selections

1. In an essay compare this poem with Paul Laurence Dunbar's "Theology" (p. 764). How might each poem be read as a statement of faith? How are the poems different in tone?
2. Compare the themes of this poem and "I know that He exists" (p. 846).

Lightly stepped a yellow star
date unknown

Lightly stepped a yellow star
To its lofty place —
Loosed the moon her silver hat
From her lustral Face —
All of Evening softly lit
As an Astral Hall —
Father, I observed to Heaven,
You are punctual.

Considerations for Critical Thinking and Writing

1. Given the description in lines 1–7, why does the last line of this poem come as a surprise? What sort of sentiment did you expect? How does the speaker disrupt that expectation?
2. Describe the speaker's relationship to the "Father." What tone does the speaker adopt? How does the personification of the star contribute to the tone?

Connections to Other Selections

1. Write an essay comparing the theme and techniques of Dickinson's poem with those of Gerard Manley Hopkins's "God's Grandeur" (p. 720).
2. Discuss the views of God offered by Dickinson in this poem and in "I know that He exists" (p. 846). How does the tone contribute to the ways God is presented in each poem?

Shall I take thee, the Poet said
c. 1868

Shall I take thee, the Poet said
To the propounded word?
Be stationed with the Candidates
Till I have finer tried —

The Poet searched Philology   5
And when about to ring
For the suspended Candidate
There came unsummoned in —

That portion of the Vision
The World applied to fill
Not unto nomination
The Cherubim reveal —

Considerations for Critical Thinking and Writing

1. What metaphor is used to describe the poet?
2. What does it mean to search philology?
3. How does the poet wind up getting the right word?

Connection to Another Selection

1. Choose a Dickinson poem that you think is especially rich in its word choice, and discuss how substitutes wouldn't (or would) do for the "propounded word."

Apparently with no surprise   c. 1884

Apparently with no surprise
To any happy Flower
The Frost beheads it at its play —
In accidental power —
The blond Assassin passes on —
The Sun proceeds unmoved
To measure off another Day
For an Approving God.

Considerations for Critical Thinking and Writing

1. Describe the speaker's tone.
2. How is nature presented in this poem?
3. Who is the "blonde Assassin?" Explain this metaphor.
4. What does the final line suggest about the nature of God?

Connections to Other Selections

1. Compare this glimpse of nature with "A Bird came down the Walk — " (p. 712). In an essay discuss the significant differences you see in each poem's treatment of nature.
2. Discuss the theme of this poem along with that of Stephen Crane's "A Man Said to the Universe" (p. 692).

Dickinson's Description of Herself   1862

Mr Higginson,

    Your kindness claimed earlier gratitude — but I was ill — and write today, from my pillow.

    Thank you for the surgery — it was not so painful as I supposed. I bring you others° — as you ask — though they might not differ —

    While my thought is undressed — I can make the distinction, but when I put them in the Gown — they look alike, and numb.

    You asked how old I was? I made no verse — but one or two° — until this winter — Sir —

    I had a terror — since September — I could tell to none — and so I sing, as the Boy does by the Burying Ground — because I am afraid — You inquire my Books — For Poets — I have Keats — and Mr and Mrs Browning. For Prose — Mr Ruskin — Sir Thomas Browne — and the Revelations. I went to school — but in your manner of the phrase — had no education. When a little Girl, I had a friend, who taught me Immortality — but venturing too near, himself — he never returned — Soon after, my Tutor, died — and for several years, my Lexicon — was my only companion — Then I found one more — but he was not contented I be his scholar — so he left the Land.

    You ask of my Companions Hills — Sir — and the Sundown — and a Dog — large as myself, that my Father bought me — They are better than Beings — because they know — but do not tell — and the noise in the Pool, at Noon — excels my Piano. I have a Brother and Sister — My Mother does not care for thought — and Father, too busy with his Briefs — to notice what we do — He buys me many Books — but begs me not to read them — because he fears they joggle the Mind. They are religious — except me — and address an Eclipse, every morning — whom they call their "Father." But I fear my story fatigues you — I would like to learn — Could you tell me how to grow — or is it unconveyed — like Melody — or Witchcraft?

From a letter to Thomas Wentworth Higginson, April 25, 1862

Others: Dickinson had sent poems to Higginson for his opinions and enclosed more with this letter. *one or two:* Actually she had written almost 300 poems.

Considerations for Critical Thinking and Writing

1. What impressions does this letter give you of Dickinson?
2. What kinds of thoughts are in the foreground of her thinking?
3. To what extent is the style of her letter writing like her poetry?

THOMAS WENTWORTH HIGGINSON (1823–1911)
On Meeting Dickinson for the First Time   1870

A large county lawyer's house, brown brick, with great trees & a garden —
I sent up my card. A parlor dark & cool & stiffish, a few books & engravings &
an open piano. . . .

A step like a pattering child's in entry & in glided a little plain woman with
two smooth bands of reddish hair & a face a little like Belle Dove's; not plainer —
with no good feature — in a very plain & exquisitely clean white pique & a blue
net worsted shawl. She came to me with two day lilies which she put in a sort
of childlike way into my hand & said "These are my introduction" in a soft
frightened breathless childlike voice — & added under her breath Forgive me if
I am frightened; I never see strangers & hardly know what I say — but she talked
soon & thenceforward continuously — & deferentially — sometimes stopping to
ask me to talk instead of her — but readily recommencing . . . thoroughly
ingenuous & simple . . . & saying many things which you would have thought
foolish & I wise — & some things you wd. hv. liked. I add a few over the
page. . . .

"Women talk; men are silent; that is why I dread women.

"My father only reads on Sunday — he reads *lonely* & *rigorous* books."

"If I read a book [and] it makes my whole body so cold no fire ever can
warm me I know *that* is poetry. If I feel physically as if the top of my head were
taken off, I know *that* is poetry. These are the only way I know it. Is there any
other way."

"How do most people live without any thoughts. There are many people
in the world (you must have noticed them in the street) How do they live. How
do they get strength to put on their clothes in the morning"

"When I lost the use of my Eyes it was a comfort to think there were so
few real *books* that I could easily find some one to read me all of them"

"Truth is such a *rare* thing it is delightful to tell it."

"I find ecstasy in living — the mere sense of living is joy enough"

I asked if she never felt want of employment, never going off the place &
never seeing any visitor "I never thought of conceiving that I could ever have
the slightest approach to such a want in all future time" (& added) "I feel that I
have not expressed myself strongly enough."

From a letter for his wife, August 16, 1870

Considerations for Critical Thinking and Writing

1. How old is Dickinson when Higginson meets her? Does this description seem
   commensurate with her age? Explain why or why not.
2. Choose one of the quotations from Dickinson that Higginson includes and write
   an essay about what it reveals about her.

MABEL LOOMIS TODD (1856–1932)
The Character *of Amherst*   1881

I must tell you about the *character* of Amherst. It is a lady whom the people call the *Myth*. She is a sister of Mr. Dickinson, & seems to be the climax of all the family oddity. She has not been outside of her own house in fifteen years, except once to see a new church, when she crept out at night, & viewed it by moonlight. No one who calls upon her mother & sister ever see her, but she allows little children once in a great while, & one at a time, to come in, when she gives them cake or candy, or some nicety, for she is very fond of little ones. But more often she lets down the sweetmeat by a string, out of a window, to them. She dresses wholly in white, & her mind is said to be perfectly wonderful. She writes finely, but no one *ever* sees her. Her sister, who was at Mrs. Dickinson's party, invited me to come & sing to her mother sometime. . . . People tell me the *myth* will hear every note — she will be near, but unseen. . . . Isn't that like a book? So interesting.

From a letter to her parents, November 6, 1881

Considerations for Critical Thinking and Writing

1. Todd, who in the 1890s would edit Dickinson's poems and letters, had known her for only two months when she wrote this letter. How does Todd characterize Dickinson?
2. Does this description seem positive or negative to you? Explain your answer.
3. A few of Dickinson's poems, such as "Much Madness is divinest Sense — ," suggest that she was aware of this perception of her. Refer to her poems in discussing Dickinson's response to this perception.

RICHARD WILBUR (b. 1921)
On Dickinson's Sense of Privation   1960

What did Emily Dickinson do, as a poet, with her sense of privation? One thing she quite often did was to pose as the laureate and attorney of the empty-handed, and question God about the economy of His creation. Why, she asked, is a fatherly God so sparing of His presence? Why is there never a sign that prayers are heard? Why does Nature tell us no comforting news of its Maker? Why do some receive a whole loaf, while others must starve on a crumb? Where is the benevolence in shipwreck and earthquake? By asking such questions as these, she turned complaint into critique, and used her own sufferings as experiential evidence about the nature of the deity. The God who emerges from these poems is a God who does not answer, an unrevealed God whom one cannot confidently approach through Nature or through doctrine.

But there was another way in which Emily Dickinson dealt with her sentiment of lack — another emotional strategy which was both more frequent and
more fruitful. I refer to her repeated assertion of the paradox that privation is
more plentiful than plenty; that to renounce is to possess the more; that "The
Banquet of abstemiousness / Defaces that of wine." We all know how the poet
illustrated this ascetic paradox in her behavior — how in her latter years she
chose to live in relative retirement, keeping the world, even in its dearest aspects,
at a physical remove. She would write her friends, telling them how she missed
them, then flee upstairs when they came to see her; afterward, she might send
a note of apology, offering the odd explanation that "We shun because we prize."
Any reader of Dickinson biographies can furnish other examples, dramatic or
homely, of this prizing and shunning, this yearning and renouncing: in my own
mind's eye is a picture of Emily Dickinson watching a gay circus caravan from
the distance of her chamber window.

> From "Sumptuous Destination" in *Emily Dickinson: Three Views,*
> by Richard Wilbur, Louise Bogan, and Archibald MacLeish

Considerations for Critical Thinking and Writing

1. Which poems by Dickinson reprinted in this anthology suggest that she was "the
   laureate and attorney of the empty-handed"?
2. Which poems suggest that "privation is more plentiful"?
3. Of these two types of poems, which do you prefer? Write an essay that explains
   your preference.

JOHN B. PICKARD (b. 1928)
On "I heard a Fly buzz — when I died — "   1967

Some of her best lyrics on death considered the sensations of the dying
person, the physical experiences as the soul leaves the body. In all these poems
tension is established by contrasting the inertness of the dead person with the
movement of the living and the external growth of nature. "I heard a Fly buzz —
when I died — " contrasts the expectations of death with its realistic occurrence.
The traditional Christian belief that death leads to eternal happiness is undercut
by the appearance of an insignificant, distracting fly. . . .

. . . The opening lines jolt as the buzz of a fly ludicrously interrupts the
awesome approach of death. After this initial shock the poet describes the
atmosphere of the sick room. The moment is tense; the soul is poised, ready to
depart; and the stillness in the room is like the deceptively calm center of a
hurricane. The second stanza considers the dry-eyed and expectant onlookers,
as they crowd closer to view the last dying movements. The scene appears
morbid to modern readers; yet it was common practice in Emily Dickinson's
time to observe the dying. For those with a religious faith, the moment of death
meant that a soul left its body to enter paradise. Thus the dying person's final
actions were carefully scrutinized for an indication of immortality's approach.

Even Emily Dickinson avidly hoped that the last words or gestures before death would ease some of her own doubts about immortality. The final death struggle of soul and body is termed an "Onset," as the king sweeps majestically in with the treasures of paradise. Like disciples giving testimony to the grandeur of God, the onlookers expect to witness this sublime ceremony.

The last two stanzas [see pp. 847–848] bring the climax. . . . The final acts of the dying person are presented with a crisp detachment. In its careful preparation for Death's entrance, the soul rigidly controls the final moments. The pun in "Signed" and "Assignable" ironically illustrates death's supreme power, for only worthless documents, empty phrases, curious mementos, and a corrupting body can be left behind. The irony increases as the soul precisely arranges everything and waits confidently for death. Now the grand moment is at hand, but unfortunately a fly interrupts the ceremony.

Like so much of life's experience the fly comes at the wrong time, as a petty irritant which distracts from the magnificent approach of death. What the dying person fails to realize is that the fly signalizes death's presence. Its stumbling blue buzz, an apt synesthetic image that conveys the confusion of the dying mind, imitates the pattern of life, where moments of beauty and confidence are juxtaposed with ugliness and uncertainty. The fly comes between the light and the dying person, not just blocking physical sight but obscuring the radiance of immortality as well. The final line captures the desperate intensity of the person's struggle for life. Instead of the calm assurance of the earlier stanzas, the person now fails to recognize death's arrival and fights to prevent subjection. Pathetically the person claims that the windows fail, not his eyesight. "I could not see to see" is the last effort at self-control. In these few seconds the soul says that it could not will its eyes open for a final view. One of the deepest ironies here is the soul's confidence that it still controls the body. Only the reader knows the hopelessness of these attempts and how aptly the fly symbolizes life and death, since its buzz is associated with daily household activities, while its food often consists of carrion. The whole poem satirizes the traditional view of death as a peaceful release from life's pressures and a glorious entrance into immortality. Emily Dickinson sees only disappointment, a buzzing fly, and the terrible attempts of a soul to prolong life.

From *Emily Dickinson: An Introduction and Interpretation*

Considerations for Critical Thinking and Writing

1. According to Pickard what is the symbolic value of the fly? How does this symbol work with the rest of the poem?
2. Does Pickard leave out any significant elements of the poem in his analysis? Explain why or why not.
3. Choose a Dickinson poem and write a detailed analysis that attempts to account for all its major elements.

ROBERT WEISBUCH (b. 1946)
On Dickinson's Use of Analogy

1975

Dickinson is a difficult poet but she becomes incomprehensible only when we neglect to raise the questions necessary for an understanding of any poet. In what ways does this poetry create meaning from language? For what kinds of meaning should we look?

We can begin to answer these questions by considering the kind of obscurity which worried Dickinson herself. "While my thought is undressed — I can make the distinction, but when I put them in the Gown — they look alike, and numb," she complains in [a] letter to Higginson. She fears that the demands of poetic composition — rhyme, meter, all the elements of decorum, and especially, per- haps, the popular idea of poetry as a comment on a particular aspect of life, a footnote to existence — will limit the scope and obscure the outline of an individual thought. But the apparently humble note to Higginson, which takes up the clothing imagery he himself had employed in an advisory article to young writers, may have been written more as a hint toward proper appreciation than as self-criticism. For by the time she wrote the letter in 1862, Dickinson had discovered a poetic method which does not dress but illustrates, thus *is,* the pattern of her thought.

The essence of the method is analogy, and analogy becomes a way of poetic life. As "I dwell in Possibility — " develops, Dickinson reveals, with characteristic wit, that her House of Possibility is a non-house: it is all of phenomenal nature, with "The Gambrels of the Sky" affording "an Everlasting Roof." She concludes by defining more precisely her activity within that "house":

> For Occupation — This —
> The spreading wide my narrow Hands
> To gather Paradise —

Translated into the language of logic, this hand-spreading becomes a method for expanding analogical relations into inclusive visions. Dickinson's typical poem enacts a hypothesis about the world by patterning a parallel, analogical world. This is the linguistic basis for Dickinson's revolt against a mentality unwilling to look deeply into things: to make words mean as much as they can, to take them out of the dull round of cliché, to renew them by realizing their connotative and etymological potential, and to reorbit them in analogical combination. At each stage of this process in Dickinson's best poems, the persona serves to make the word flesh, to register the human consequences of the transformed meanings. Thus the very creator of a poetic world will respond to it, often with Frankenstein- like shock and always with surprise. Dickinson's visionary and confessional strains merge perfectly in the rhetorical grain of such poems.

From Emily Dickinson's Poetry

Considerations for Critical Thinking and Writing

1. According to Weisbuch why is analogy essential to Dickinson's poetry?
2. How does her use of analogy "make words mean as much as they can"?
3. Choose a Dickinson poem and explain how her use of analogy unravels what is otherwise seemingly obscure or incomprehensible.

SANDRA M. GILBERT (b. 1936) AND
SUSAN GUBAR (b. 1944)
On Dickinson's White Dress
1979

Today a dress that the Amherst Historical Society assures us is *the* white dress Dickinson wore — or at least one of her "Uniforms of Snow" — hangs in a drycleaner's plastic bag in the closet of the Dickinson homestead. Perfectly preserved, beautifully flounced and tucked, it is larger than most readers would have expected this self-consciously small poet's dress to be, and thus reminds visiting scholars of the enduring enigma of Dickinson's central metaphor, even while it draws gasps from more practical visitors, who reflect with awe upon the difficulties of maintaining such a costume. But what exactly did the literal and figurative whiteness of this costume represent? What rewards did it offer that would cause an intelligent woman to overlook those practical difficulties? Comparing Dickinson's obsession with whiteness to Melville's, William R. Sherwood suggests that "it reflected in her case the Christian mystery and not a Christian enigma . . . a decision to announce . . . the assumption of a worldly death that paradoxically involved regeneration." This, he adds, her gown — "a typically slant demonstration of truth" — should have revealed "to anyone with the wit to catch on."[1]

We might reasonably wonder, however, if Dickinson herself consciously intended her wardrobe to convey any one message. The range of associations her white poems imply suggests, on the contrary, that for her, as for Melville, white is the ultimate symbol of enigma, paradox, and irony, "not so much a color as the visible absence of color, and at the same time the concrete of all colors." Melville's question [in *Moby-Dick*] might, therefore, also be hers: "is it for these reasons that there is such a dumb blankness, full of meaning, in a wide landscape of snows — a colorless, all-color of atheism from which we shrink?" And his concluding speculation might be hers too, his remark "that the mystical cosmetic which produces every one of [Nature's] hues, the great principle of light, for ever remains white or colorless in itself, and if operating without medium upon matter, would touch all objects . . . with its own blank tinge." For white, in Dickinson's poetry, frequently represents both the energy (the white heat) of Romantic creativity, and the loneliness (the polar cold) of the renuncia-

---

[1] *Circumference and Circumstance: Stages in the Mind and Art of Emily Dickinson* (New York: Columbia UP, 1968) 152, 231.

tion or tribulation Romantic creativity may demand, both the white radiance of eternity — or Revelation — and the white terror of a shroud.

From *The Madwoman in the Attic: The Woman Writer and the Nineteenth-Century Literary Imagination*

Considerations for Critical Thinking and Writing

1. What meanings do Gilbert and Gubar attribute to Dickinson's white dress?
2. Discuss the meaning of the implicit whiteness in "Safe in their Alabaster Chambers — " (pp. 834–835) and "After great pain, a formal feeling comes — " (p. 847). To what extent do these poems incorporate the meanings of whiteness that Gilbert and Gubar suggest?
3. What other possible reasons can you think of that would account for Dickinson's wearing only white?

KARL KELLER (b. 1933)
Robert Frost on Dickinson
1979

Frost lived in Amherst for quite a number of years — 1917–20, 1923–25, 1926–38, and then intermittently in the late 1940s and throughout the 1950s when he taught regularly at Amherst College. He often recited her poems from memory, and he conversed with students, friends, and townspeople about her poetry; his concern was almost always over her ability to contain/limit an open-ended universe. He felt this was "what Emily Dickinson surely intends," as he put it, "when she contends: 'In insecurity to lie / Is Joy's insuring quality.'"

It appears that Frost had a one-track mind about Emily Dickinson — her doggedness. For him she was an example of the poet "whose 'state,'" as he put it himself, "never gets sidetracked."

> Since she wrote without thought of publication and was not under the necessity of revamping and polishing, it was easy for her to go right to the point and say precisely what she thought and felt. Her technical irregularities give her poems strength as if she were saying, "Look out, Rhyme and Meter, here I come."

Frost apparently liked this willfulness, this unmanageability of the thought by the poetic form, and yet he thought she arrived at it a little too easily and that it was therefore sometimes indistinguishable from carelessness. He felt she had given up the technical struggle too easily. For Frost, to use a general statement of his about poetic rhythm, she was a little too "easy in [her] harness."[1]

Emily Dickinson succeeded, Frost was forced to admit, by flouting poetic systems, by playing freely with the form.

> I try to make good sentences fit the meter. That is important. Good grammar. I don't like to twist the order around in order to fit a form. I try to keep to regular structure and good rhymes. Though I admit that Emily Dickinson, for

[1]Robert Francis, *Frost: A Time to Talk* (Amherst, 1972) 53–54.

one, didn't do this always. When she started a poem, it was "Here I come!" and she came plunging through. The meter and rhyme often had to take care of itself.[2]

Though envious of this carefree energy, Frost was also critical of her when she did not achieve regular forms.

> Emily Dickinson didn't study technique. But she should have been more careful. She was more interested in getting the poem down and writing a new one. I feel that she left some to be revised later, and she never revised them. And those two ladies at Amherst printed a lot of her slipshod work which she might not have liked to see printed. She has all kinds of off rhymes. Some that do not rhyme. Her meter does not always go together.[3]

She was therefore substantially different from him; her ability to be conscious of poetic conventions and yet to rise above them surprised him. He generously yielded her his highest admiration for the heresy.

> One of the great things in life is being true within the conventions. I deny in a good poem or a good life that there is compromise. When there is, it is an attempt to so flex the lines that no suspicion can be cast upon what the poet does. Emily Dickinson's poems are examples of this. When the rhyme begins to bother, she says, "Here I come with my truth. Let the rhyme take care of itself." This makes me feel her strength.[4]

For him the large strain of poetry was "a little shifted from the straight-out, a little curved from the straight." Emily Dickinson's poems were, for him, the best examples of this liberty, this flawing. "Can you imagine some people taking that? Can't you imagine some people not accepting that kind of play at all?"[5] It was this factor of play in Emily Dickinson's poetry that consistently attracted Frost. "Rime reminds you that poetry is play," he said on one occasion, after reciting a Dickinson poem ("The Mountains — grow unnoticed") and calling it "particularly fine," "and that is one of its chief importances. You shouldn't be too sincere to play or you'll be a fraud."[6] Her mischief with poetic form was an indication to him that she was serious about what she was saying and would bend conventions to get it said, and also that she was having a good time trying to say it, but more important than that, that with her poetry (and her ideas) she was *at play*. He appears to have marveled at that in her. "Poetry," Frost used to exclaim to his friends, "is fooling"[7]

From *The Only Kangaroo Among the Beauty: Emily Dickinson in America*

Considerations for Critical Thinking and Writing

1. According to Keller, how did Frost respond to Dickinson's "poetic systems" of rhyme and meter?
2. Explain why you agree or disagree with Frost's assessment of Dickinson's poetry being "slipshod."
3. Choose a poem from each poet and demonstrate how both are versions of "play."

[2]Daniel Smythe, *Robert Frost Speaks* (NY, np, 1964) 140.
[3]Smythe, 140.
[4]Reginald Lansing Cook, *The Dimensions of Robert Frost* (NY: Barnes and Noble, 1968) 57–58.
[5]Cook, 99.
[6]Cook, 180.
[7]Cook, 181.

JANE DONAHUE EBERWEIN (b. 1943)
On Making Do with Dickinson 1984

Like any Yankee girl trained from childhood in habits of thrift, Dickinson instinctively conserved her resources rather than trying to extend them, and she applied to sisterhood the same practical prudence with which she learned to "Use it up, wear it out, / Make it do, or do without." In a family whose prosperous and socially prominent mother devoted herself to mending her student son's shirts, Emily Dickinson cultivated a pride in thrift which would have extraordinary influence on the poetry she wrote and the attitude she took toward herself as a writer. She would be resourceful, careful, shrewd. She would make do with what she had or do without whatever she lacked.

This Yankee parsimony distances Dickinson from many modern admirers who wish she had been a more assertive woman and a more conscious representative of her sex. We who live in a twentieth-century middle-class economy of abundance unconsciously apply our own fiscal metaphors to social and artistic issues, and we raise questions about Dickinson's strategies in accordance with cultural assumptions which she never shared. For us, who imagined until recently that the world's resources might be infinite, it makes no sense to make do with little or do without; those who find themselves deprived should demand more. Improvement, for us, tends to be associated with expansion. Success is measured in terms of profit and celebrity. Responsibility involves identification with other people, especially those who share similar deprivations, and it requires social solidarity for the common good. Given such assumptions it is no wonder that we find Emily Dickinson so mysterious, even at times so alienating. That she, the greatest woman poet in nineteenth-century America and quite possibly the most brilliant female artist this country has yet produced, should never have earned money for her poems, never have seen her name in print except for winning a baking prize, never exerted her influence to assist her artistically deprived sisters seems to us a waste of ability. Assuming that she wanted the opportunities modern women have learned to demand, we tend to think of Emily Dickinson as a victim of cultural limitations, especially of those restrictions her society placed on gently-bred young women. We regard her as a silent and generally ineffective rebel against social conventions, writing secretly like some Soviet dissident with no assurance of ever reaching an audience. We take it for granted that she needed to break out of the limitations her culture placed around her and that she, and we, would have benefited from greater freedom.

From "Doing Without: Dickinson as Yankee Woman Poet"
in *Critical Essays on Emily Dickinson*, ed. Paul J. Ferlazzo

Considerations for Critical Thinking and Writing

1. How do you think Dickinson's "pride in thrift" is related to her style?
2. According to Eberwein, why do some readers find Dickinson "alienating"? Explain why you agree or disagree.

3. In an essay consider whether or not Dickinson's poetry "would have benefited from [her having] greater freedom."

CYNTHIA GRIFFIN WOLFF (b. 1935)
On the Many Voices in Dickinson's Poetry   1986

There were many "Voices." This fact has sometimes puzzled Dickinson's readers. One poem may be delivered in a child's Voice; another in the Voice of a young woman scrutinizing nature and the society in which she makes her place. Sometimes the Voice is that of a woman self-confidently addressing her lover in a language of passion and sexual desire. At still other times, the Voice of the verse seems so precariously balanced at the edge of hysteria that even its calmest observations grate like the shriek of dementia. There is the Voice of the housewife and the Voice that has recourse to the occasionally agonizing, occasionally regal language of the conversion experience of latter-day New England Puritanism. In some poems the Voice is distinctive principally because it speaks in the aftermath of wounding and can comprehend extremities of pain. Moreover, these Voices are not always entirely distinct from one another: the child's Voice that opens a poem may yield to the Voice of a young woman speaking the idiom of ardent love; in a different poem, the speaker may fall into a mood of almost religious contemplation in an attempt to analyze or define such abstract entities as loneliness or madness or eternity; the diction of the housewife may be conflated with the sovereign language of the New Jerusalem, and taken together, they may render some aspect of the wordsmith's labor. No manageable set of discrete categories suffices to capture the diversity of discourse, and any attempt to simplify Dickinson's methods does violence to the verse.

Yet there is a paradox here. This is, by no stretch of the imagination, a body of poetry that might be construed as a series of lyrics spoken by many different people. Disparate as these many Voices are, somehow they all appear to issue from the same "self." . . . It is the enigmatic "Emily Dickinson" readers suppose themselves to have found in this poetry, even in the extreme case when Dickinson's supposed speaker is male. One explanation for this sense of intrinsic unity in the midst of diversity is the persistence with which Dickinson addresses the same set of problems, using a remarkably durable repertoire of linguistic modes. Evocations of injury and wounding — threats to the coherence of the self — appear in the earliest poems and continue until the end; ways of rendering face-to-face encounters change, but this preoccupation with "interview" is sustained by metaphors of "confrontation" that weave throughout. The summoning of one or another Voice in a given poem, then, is not an unselfconscious emotive reflection of Emily Dickinson's mood at the moment of creation. Rather, each different Voice is a calculated tactic, an attempt to touch her readers and engage them intimately with the poetry. Each Voice had its unique advantages; each its limitations. A poet self-conscious in her craft, she calculated this element as carefully as every other.

From *Emily Dickinson*

Considerations for Critical Thinking and Writing

1. Try adding to the list of voices Wolff cites from the poems in this anthology.
2. Despite the many voices in Dickinson's poetry, why, according to Wolff, is there still a "sense of intrinsic unity" in her poetry?
3. Choose a Dickinson poem and describe how the choice of voice is a "calculated tactic."

TWO COMPLEMENTARY CRITICAL READINGS

CHARLES R. ANDERSON (b. 1902)
Eroticism in "Wild Nights — Wild Nights!" 1960

The frank eroticism of this poem might puzzle the biographer of a spinster, but the critic can only be concerned with its effectiveness as a poem. Unless one insists on taking the "I" to mean Emily Dickinson, there is not even any reversal of the lovers' roles (which has been charged, curiously enough, as a fault in this poem). The opening declaration — "Wild Nights should be / Our Luxury!" — sets the key of her song, for *luxuria* included the meaning of lust as well as lavishness of sensuous enjoyment, as she was Latinist enough to know. This is echoed at the end in "Eden," her recurring image, in letters and poems, for the paradise of earthly love. The theme here is that of sexual passion which is lawless, outside the rule of "Chart" and "Compass." But it lives by a law of its own, the law of Eden, which protects it from mundane wind and wave.

This is what gives the magic to her climactic vision, "Rowing in Eden," sheltered luxuriously in those paradisiac waters while the wild storms of this world break about them. Such love was only possible before the Fall. Since then the bower of bliss is frugal of her leases, limiting each occupant to "an instant" she says in another poem, for "Adam taught her Thrift / Bankrupt once through his excesses." In the present poem she limits her yearning to the mortal term, just "Tonight." But this echoes the surge of ecstasy that initiated her song and gives the reiterated "Wild Nights!" a double reference, to the passionate experience in Eden as well as to the tumult of the world shut out by it. So she avoids the chief pitfall of the love lyric, the tendency to exploit emotion for its own sake. Instead she generates out of the conflicting aspects of love, its ecstasy and its brevity, the symbol that contains the poem's meaning.

From Emily Dickinson's Poetry: Stairway of Surprise

Considerations for Critical Thinking and Writing

1. According to Anderson what is the theme of "Wild Nights — Wild Nights!"?
2. How does Anderson discuss the "frank eroticism" of the poem? How detailed is his discussion?
3. If there is a "reversal of the lovers' roles" in this poem, do you think it represents, as some critics have charged, "a fault in this poem"? Explain why or why not.

4. Compare Anderson's treatment of this poem with David S. Reynolds's reading below. Discuss which one you find more useful, and explain why.

DAVID S. REYNOLDS (b. 1949)
Popular Literature and "Wild Nights — Wild Nights!" 1988

It is not known whether Dickinson had read any of the erotic literature of the day or if she knew of the stereotype of the sensual woman. Given her fascination with sensational journalism and with popular literature in general, it is hard to believe she would not have had at least some exposure to erotic literature. At any rate, her treatment of the daring theme of woman's sexual fantasy in this deservedly famous poem bears comparison with erotic themes as they appeared in popular sensational writings. The first stanza of the poem provides an uplifting or purification of sexual fantasy not distant from the effect of Whitman's cleansing rhetoric, which, as we have seen, was consciously designed to counteract the prurience of the popular "love plot." Dickinson's repeated phrase "Wild Nights" is a simple but dazzling metaphor that communicates wild passion — even lust — but simultaneously lifts sexual desire out of the scabrous by fusing it with the natural image of the night. The second verse introduces a second nature image, the turbulent sea and the contrasting quiet port, which at once universalizes the passion and purifies it further by distancing it through a more abstract metaphor. Also, the second verse makes clear that this is not a poem of sexual consummation but rather of pure fantasy and sexual impossibility. Unlike popular erotic literature, the poem portrays neither a consummated seduction nor the heartless deception that it involves. There is instead a pure, fervent fantasy whose frustration is figured forth in the contrasting images of the ocean (the longed-for-but-never-achieved consummation) and the port (the reality of the poet's isolation). The third verse begins with an image, "Rowing in Eden," that further uplifts sexual passion by yoking it with a religious archetype. Here as elsewhere, Dickinson capitalizes nicely on the new religious style, which made possible such fusions of the divine and the earthly. The persona's concluding wish to "moor" in the sea expresses the sustained intense sexual longing and the simultaneous frustration of that longing. In the course of the poem, Dickinson has communicated great erotic passion, and yet, by effectively projecting this passion through unusual nature and religious images, has rid it of even the tiniest residue of sensationalism.

From *Beneath the American Renaissance:*
The Subversive Imagination in the Age of Emerson and Melville

Considerations for Critical Thinking and Writing

1. According to Reynolds, how do Dickinson's images provide a "cleansing" effect in the poem?
2. Explain whether you agree that the poem portrays a "pure, fervent fantasy" or something else.

3. Does Reynolds's reading of the poem compete with Anderson's, or complement it? Explain your answer.
4. Given the types of critical strategies described in Chapter 35, how would you characterize Anderson's and Reynolds's approaches?

ROBERT FROST (1874–1963)

Few poets have enjoyed the popular success that Robert Frost achieved during his lifetime, and no twentieth-century American poet has had his or her work as widely read and honored. Frost is as much associated with New England as the stone walls that help define its landscape; his reputation, however, transcends regional boundaries. Although he was named poet laureate of Vermont only two years before his death, he was for many years the nation's unofficial poet laureate. Frost collected honors the way some people pick up burrs on country walks. Among his awards were four Pulitzer Prizes, the Bollingen Prize, a Congressional Medal, and dozens of honorary degrees. Perhaps his most moving appearance was his recitation of "The Gift Outright" for millions of Americans at the inauguration of John F. Kennedy in 1961.

Frost's recognition as a poet is especially remarkable because his career as a writer did not attract any significant attention until he was nearly forty years old. He taught himself to write while he labored at odd jobs, taught school, or farmed.

Frost's early identity seems very remote from the New England soil. Although his parents were descended from generations of New Englanders, he was born in San Francisco and was named Robert Lee Frost after the Confederate general. After his father died in 1885, his mother moved the family back to Massachusetts to live with relatives. Frost graduated from high school sharing valedictorian honors with the classmate who would become his wife three years later. Between high school and marriage, he attended Dartmouth College for a few months and then taught. His teaching prompted him to enroll in Harvard in 1897, but after less than two years he withdrew without a degree (though Harvard would eventually award him an honorary doctorate in 1937, four years after Dartmouth conferred its honorary degree upon him). For the next decade, Frost read and wrote poems when he was not chicken farming or teaching. In 1912, he sold his farm and moved his family to England, where he hoped to find the audience that his poetry did not have in America.

Three years in England made it possible for Frost to return home as a poet. His first two volumes of poetry, *A Boy's Will* (1913) and *North of Boston* (1914), were published in England. During the next twenty years, honors and awards were conferred on collections such as *Mountain Interval* (1916),

New Hampshire (1923), *West-Running Brook* (1928), and *A Further Range* (1936). These are the volumes on which most of Frost's popular and critical reputation rests. Later collections include *A Witness Tree* (1942), *A Masque of Reason* (1945), *Steeple Bush* (1947), *A Masque of Mercy* (1947), *Complete Poems* (1949), and *In the Clearing* (1962). In addition to publishing his works, Frost endeared himself to audiences throughout the country by presenting his poetry almost as conversations. He also taught at a number of schools, including Amherst College, the University of Michigan, Harvard University, Dartmouth College, and Middlebury College.

Frost's countless poetry readings generated wide audiences eager to claim him as their poet. The image he cultivated resembled closely what the public likes to think a poet should be. Frost was seen as a lovable, wise old man; his simple wisdom and cracker-barrel sayings appeared comforting and homey. From this Yankee rustic, audiences learned that "There's a lot yet that isn't understood" or "We love the things we love for what they are" or "Good fences make good neighbors."

In a sense, Frost packaged himself for public consumption. "I am . . . my own salesman," he said. When asked direct questions about the meanings of his poems, he often winked or scratched his head to give the impression that the customer was always right. To be sure, there is a simplicity in Frost's language, but that simplicity does not fully reflect the depth of the man, the complexity of his themes, or the richness of his art.

The folksy optimist behind the public lectern did not reveal his private troubles to his audiences, although he did address those problems at his writing desk. Frost suffered from professional jealousies, anger, and depression. His family life was especially painful. Three of his four children died: a son at the age of four, a daughter in her late twenties from tuberculosis, and another son who was a suicide. His marriage was filled with tension. Although Frost's work is landscaped with sunlight, snow, birches, birds, blueberries, and squirrels, it is important to recognize that he was also intimately "acquainted with the night," a phrase that serves as the haunting title of one of his poems (see p. 685).

As a corrective to Frost's popular reputation, one critic, Lionel Trilling, described the world Frost creates in his poems as a "terrifying universe," characterized by loneliness, anguish, frustration, doubts, disappointment, and despair (see p. 896 for an excerpt from this essay). To point this out is not to annihilate the pleasantness and even good-natured cheerfulness that can be enjoyed in Frost's poetry, but it is to say that Frost is not so one-dimensional as he is sometimes assumed to be. Frost's poetry requires readers who are alert and willing to penetrate the simplicity of its language to see the elusive and ambiguous meanings that lie below the surface.

Frost's treatment of nature helps to explain the various levels of meaning in his poetry. The familiar natural world his poems evoke is sharply detailed. We hear icy branches clicking against themselves, we see the snow-white trunks of birches, we feel the smarting pain of a twig lashing across a face. The aspects of the natural world Frost describes are designed to give plea-sure, but they are also frequently calculated to provoke thought. His use of nature tends to be symbolic. Complex meanings are derived from simple facts, such as a spider killing a moth or a tiny mite on a sheet of paper (see "Design," p. 887, and "A Considerable Speck," p. 889). Although Frost's strategy is to talk about particular events and individual experiences, his poems evoke universal issues.

Frost's poetry has strong regional roots and is "versed in country things," but it flourishes in any receptive imagination because, in the final analysis, it is concerned with human beings. Frost's New England landscapes are the occasion rather than the ultimate focus of his poems. Like the rural voices he creates in his poems, Frost typically approaches his themes indirectly. He explained the reason for this in a talk titled "Education by Poetry."

> Poetry provides the one permissible way of saying one thing and meaning another. People say, "why don't you say what you mean?" We never do that, do we, being all of us too much poets. We like to talk in parables and in hints and in indirections — whether from diffidence or some other instinct.

The result is that the settings, characters, and situations that make up the subject matter of Frost's poems are vehicles for his perceptions about life.

In "Stopping by Woods on a Snowy Evening" (p. 884), for example, Frost uses the kind of familiar New England details that constitute his poetry for more than descriptive purposes. He shapes them into a meditation on the tension we sometimes feel between life's responsibilities and the "lovely, dark, and deep" attraction that death offers. When the speaker's horse "gives his harness bells a shake," we are reminded that we are confronting a universal theme as well as a quiet moment of natural beauty.

Among the major concerns that appear in Frost's poetry are the fragility of life, the consequences of rejecting or accepting the conditions of one's life, the passion of inconsolable grief, the difficulty of sustaining intimacy, the fear of loneliness and isolation, the inevitability of change, the tensions between the individual and society, and the place of tradition and custom.

Whatever theme is encountered in a poem by Frost, a reader is likely to agree with him that "the initial delight is in the surprise of remembering something I didn't know." To achieve that fresh sense of discovery, Frost allowed himself to follow his instincts; his poetry

> inclines to the impulse, it assumes direction with the first line laid down, it runs a course of lucky events, and ends in a clarification of life — not necessarily a great clarification, such as sects and cults are founded on, but in a momentary stay against confusion.

This description from "The Figure a Poem Makes" (see p. 893 for the complete essay), Frost's brief introduction to *Complete Poems,* may sound as if his poetry is formless and merely "lucky," but his poems tend to be more conventional than experimental: "The artist in me," as he put the matter in one of his poems, "cries out for design."

From Frost's perspective, "free verse is like playing tennis with the net down." He exercised his own freedom in meeting the challenges of rhyme and meter. His use of fixed forms such as couplets, tercets, quatrains, blank verse, and sonnets was not slavish, because he enjoyed working them into the natural English speech patterns — especially the rhythms, idioms, and tones of speakers living north of Boston — that give voice to his themes. Frost often liked to use "Stopping by Woods on a Snowy Evening" as an example of his graceful way of making conventions appear natural and inevitable. He explored "the old ways to be new."

Frost's eye for strong, telling details was matched by his ear for natural speech rhythms. His flexible use of what he called "iambic and loose iambic" enabled him to create moving lyric poems that reveal the personal thoughts of a speaker and dramatic poems that convincingly characterize people caught in intense emotional situations. The language in his poems appears to be little more than a transcription of casual and even rambling speech, but it is in actuality Frost's poetic creation, carefully crafted to reveal the joys and sorrows that are woven into people's daily lives. What is missing from Frost's poems is artificiality, not art. Consider this poem.

The Road Not Taken   1916

Two roads diverged in a yellow wood,
And sorry I could not travel both
And be one traveler, long I stood
And looked down one as far as I could
To where it bent in the undergrowth;   5

Then took the other, as just as fair,
And having perhaps the better claim,
Because it was grassy and wanted wear;
Though as for that the passing there
Had worn them really about the same,   10

And both that morning equally lay
In leaves no step had trodden black.
Oh, I kept the first for another day!
Yet knowing how way leads on to way,
I doubted if I should ever come back.   15

I shall be telling this with a sigh
Somewhere ages and ages hence:

Two roads diverged in a wood, and I —
I took the one less traveled by,
And that has made all the difference.   20

This poem intrigues readers because it is at once so simple and so deeply resonant. Recalling a walk in the woods, the speaker describes how he came upon a fork in the road, which forced him to choose one path over another. Though "sorry" that he "could not travel both," he made a choice after carefully weighing his two options. This, essentially, is what happens in the poem; there is no other action. However, the incident is charged with symbolic significance by the speaker's reflections on the necessity and consequences of his decision.

The final stanza indicates that the choice concerns more than simply walking down a road, for the speaker says that his chosen path has affected his entire life — "that [it] has made all the difference." Frost draws on a familiar enough metaphor when he compares life to a journey, but he is also calling attention to a less commonly noted problem: despite our expectations, aspirations, appetites, hopes, and desires, we can't have it all. Making one choice precludes another. It is impossible to determine what particular decision the speaker refers to: perhaps he had to choose a college, a career, a spouse; perhaps he was confronted with mutually exclusive ideas, beliefs, or values. There is no way to know, because Frost wisely creates a symbolic choice and implicitly invites us to supply our own circumstances.

The speaker's reflections about his choice are as central to an understanding of the poem as the choice itself; indeed, they may be more central. He describes the road taken as "having perhaps the better claim, / Because it was grassy and wanted wear"; he prefers the "less traveled" path. This seems to be an expression of individualism, which would account for "the difference" his choice made in his life. But Frost complicates matters by having the speaker also acknowledge that there was no significant difference between the two roads: one was "just as fair" as the other; each was "worn . . . really about the same"; and "both that morning equally lay / In leaves no step had trodden black."

The speaker imagines that in the future, "ages and ages hence," he will recount his choice with "a sigh" that will satisfactorily explain the course of his life, but Frost seems to be having a little fun here by showing us how the speaker will embellish his past decision to make it appear more dramatic. What we hear is someone trying to convince himself that the choice he made significantly changed his life. When he recalls what happened in the "yellow wood," a color that gives a glow to that irretrievable moment when his life seemed to be on verge of a momentous change, he appears more concerned with the path he did not choose than with the one he took. Frost shrewdly titles the poem to suggest the speaker's sense of loss at not being able to "travel both" roads. When the speaker's reflections about his choice are examined, the poem reveals his nostalgia instead of affirming his decision to travel a self-reliant path in life.

The rhymed stanzas of "The Road Not Taken" follow a pattern established in the first five lines *(abaab)*. This rhyme scheme reflects, perhaps, the speaker's efforts to shape his life into a pleasing and coherent form. The natural speech rhythms Frost uses allow him to integrate the rhymes unobtrusively, but there is a slight shift in lines 19–20, when the speaker asserts self-consciously that the "less traveled" road — which we already know to be basically the same as the other road — "made all the difference." Unlike all the other rhymes in the poem, "difference" does not rhyme precisely with "hence." The emphasis that must be placed on "differ*ence*" to make it rhyme perfectly with "hence" may suggest that the speaker is trying just a little too hard to pattern his life on his earlier choice in the woods.

Perhaps the best way to begin reading Frost's poetry is to accept the invitation he placed at the beginning of many volumes of his poems. "The Pasture" means what it says of course; it is about taking care of some farm chores, but it is also a means of "saying one thing in terms of another."

The Pasture   1913

I'm going out to clean the pasture spring;
I'll only stop to rake the leaves away
(And wait to watch the water clear, I may):
I shan't be gone long. — You come too.

I'm going out to fetch the little calf
That's standing by the mother. It's so young
It totters when she licks it with her tongue.
I shan't be gone long. — You come too.

"The Pasture" is a simple but irresistible songlike invitation to the pleasure of looking at the world through the eyes of a poet.

Chronology

1874   Born on March 26 in San Francisco, California.

1885   Father dies and family moves to Lawrence, Massachusetts.

1892   Graduates from Lawrence High School.

1893–94 Studies at Dartmouth College.

1895   Marries his high school sweetheart, Elinor White.

1897–99 Studies at Harvard College.

1900	Moves to a farm in West Derry, New Hampshire.
1912	Moves to England where he farms and writes.
1913	*A Boy's Will* is published in London.
1914	*North of Boston* is published in London.
1915	Moves to a farm near Franconia, New Hampshire.
1916	Elected to National Institute of Letters.
1917–20	Teaches at Amherst College.
1919	Moves to South Shaftsberry, Vermont.
1921–23	Teaches at University of Michigan.
1923	*Selected Poems* and *New Hampshire* are published; the latter is awarded a Pulitzer Prize.
1928	*West-Running Brook* is published.
1930	*Collected Poems* is published.
1936	*A Further Range* is published; teaches at Harvard.
1938	Wife dies.
1939–42	Teaches at Harvard.
1942	*A Witness Tree* is published, which is awarded a Pulitzer Prize.
1943–49	Teaches at Dartmouth.
1945	*A Masque of Reason* is published.
1947	*Steeple Bush* and *A Masque of Mercy* are published.
1949	*Complete Poems* (enlarged) is published.
1961	Reads "The Gift Outright" at President John F. Kennedy's inauguration.
1963	Dies on January 29 in Boston.

Mending Wall   1914

Something there is that doesn't love a wall,
That sends the frozen-ground-swell under it,
And spills the upper boulders in the sun;
And makes gaps even two can pass abreast.
The work of hunters is another thing: 5
I have come after them and made repair

Where they have left not one stone on a stone,
But they would have the rabbit out of hiding,
To please the yelping dogs. The gaps I mean,
No one has seen them made or heard them made, 10
But at spring mending-time we find them there.
I let my neighbor know beyond the hill;
And on a day we meet to walk the line
And set the wall between us once again.
We keep the wall between us as we go. 15
To each the boulders that have fallen to each.
And some are loaves and some so nearly balls
We have to use a spell to make them balance:
"Stay where you are until our backs are turned!"
We wear our fingers rough with handling them. 20
Oh, just another kind of outdoor game,
One on a side. It comes to little more:
There where it is we do not need the wall:
He is all pine and I am apple orchard.
My apple trees will never get across 25
And eat the cones under his pines, I tell him.
He only says, "Good fences make good neighbors."
Spring is the mischief in me, and I wonder
If I could put a notion in his head:
"*Why* do they make good neighbors? Isn't it 30
Where there are cows? But here there are no cows.
Before I built a wall I'd ask to know
What I was walling in or walling out,
And to whom I was like to give offense.
Something there is that doesn't love a wall, 35
That wants it down." I could say "Elves" to him,
But it's not elves exactly, and I'd rather
He said it for himself. I see him there
Bringing a stone grasped firmly by the top
In each hand, like an old-stone savage armed. 40
He moves in darkness as it seems to me,
Not of woods only and the shade of trees.
He will not go behind his father's saying,
And he likes having thought of it so well
He says again, "Good fences make good neighbors." 45

Considerations for Critical Thinking and Writing

1. How do the speaker and his neighbor in this poem differ in sensibilities? What is suggested about the neighbor in lines 41–42?
2. What might the "Something" be that "doesn't love a wall"? Why does the speaker remind his neighbor each spring that the wall needs to be repaired? Is it ironic that the *speaker* initiates the mending? Is there anything good about the wall?
3. The neighbor likes the saying "Good fences make good neighbors" so well that he repeats it. Does the speaker also say something twice? What else suggests that the speaker's attitude toward the wall is not necessarily Frost's?

4. Although the speaker's language is colloquial, what is poetic about the sounds and rhythms he uses?
5. This poem was first published in 1914; Frost read it to an audience when he visited Russia in 1962. What do these facts suggest about the symbolic value of "Mending Wall"?

Connections to Other Selections

1. How do you think the neighbor in this poem would respond to Dickinson's idea of imagination in "To make a prairie it takes a clover and one bee" (p. 832)?
2. What similarities and differences does the neighbor have with the people Frost describes in "Neither Out Far nor In Deep" (p. 887)?
3. Write an essay discussing the function of walls in this poem and in Melville's story "Bartleby, the Scrivener" (p. 83).

Home Burial   1914

He saw her from the bottom of the stairs
Before she saw him. She was starting down,
Looking back over her shoulder at some fear.
She took a doubtful step and then undid it
To raise herself and look again. He spoke   5
Advancing toward her: "What is it you see
From up there always — for I want to know."
She turned and sank upon her skirts at that,
And her face changed from terrified to dull.
He said to gain time: "What is it you see,"   10
Mounting until she cowered under him.
"I will find out now — you must tell me, dear."
She, in her place, refused him any help
With the least stiffening of her neck and silence.
She let him look, sure that he wouldn't see,   15
Blind creature; and awhile he didn't see.
But at last he murmured, "Oh," and again, "Oh."

"What is it — what?" she said.

                    "Just that I see."

"You don't," she challenged. "Tell me what it is."   20

"The wonder is I didn't see at once.
I never noticed it from here before.
I must be wonted to it — that's the reason.
The little graveyard where my people are!
So small the window frames the whole of it.   25
Not so much larger than a bedroom, is it?
There are three stones of slate and one of marble,
Broad-shouldered little slabs there in the sunlight
On the sidehill. We haven't to mind *those*.

But I understand: it is not the stones,
But the child's mound — "   30

                    "Don't, don't, don't, don't," she cried.

She withdrew, shrinking from beneath his arm
That rested on the banister, and slid downstairs;
And turned on him with such a daunting look,
He said twice over before he knew himself: 35
"Can't a man speak of his own child he's lost?"

"Not you! — Oh, where's my hat? Oh, I don't need it!
I must get out of here. I must get air.
I don't know rightly whether any man can."   40

"Amy! Don't go to someone else this time.
Listen to me. I won't come down the stairs."
He sat and fixed his chin between his fists.
"There's something I should like to ask you, dear."

"You don't know how to ask it."   45

                              "Help me, then."
Her fingers moved the latch for all reply.

"My words are nearly always an offense.
I don't know how to speak of anything
So as to please you. But I might be taught,   50
I should suppose. I can't say I see how.
A man must partly give up being a man
With women-folk. We could have some arrangement
By which I'd bind myself to keep hands off
Anything special you're a-mind to name.   55
Though I don't like such things 'twixt those that love.
Two that don't love can't live together without them.
But two that do can't live together with them."
She moved the latch a little. "Don't — don't go.
Don't carry it to someone else this time.   60
Tell me about it if it's something human.
Let me into your grief. I'm not so much
Unlike other folks as your standing there
Apart would make me out. Give me my chance.
I do think, though, you overdo it a little.   65
What was it brought you up to think it the thing
To take your mother-loss of a first child
So inconsolably — in the face of love.
You'd think his memory might be satisfied — "

"There you go sneering now!"   70

                        "I'm not, I'm not!
You make me angry. I'll come down to you.
God, what a woman! And it's come to this,
A man can't speak of his own child that's dead."

"You can't because you don't know how to speak.
If you had any feelings, you that dug
With your own hand — how could you? — his little grave;
I saw you from that very window there,
Making the gravel leap and leap in air,
Leap up, like that, like that, and land so lightly
And roll back down the mound beside the hole.
I thought, Who is that man? I didn't know you.
And I crept down the stairs and up the stairs
To look again, and still your spade kept lifting.
Then you came in. I heard your rumbling voice
Out in the kitchen, and I don't know why,
But I went near to see with my own eyes.
You could sit there with the stains on your shoes
Of the fresh earth from your own baby's grave
And talk about your everyday concerns.
You had stood the spade up against the wall
Outside there in the entry, for I saw it."

"I shall laugh the worst laugh I ever laughed.
I'm cursed. God, if I don't believe I'm cursed."

"I can repeat the very words you were saying.
'Three foggy mornings and one rainy day
Will rot the best birch fence a man can build.'
Think of it, talk like that at such a time!
What had how long it takes a birch to rot
To do with what was in the darkened parlor.
You *couldn't* care! The nearest friends can go
With anyone to death, comes so far short
They might as well not try to go at all.
No, from the time when one is sick to death,
One is alone, and he dies more alone.
Friends make pretense of following to the grave.
But before one is in it, their minds are turned
And making the best of their way back to life
And living people, and things they understand.
But the world's evil. I won't have grief so
If I can change it. Oh, I won't, I won't!"

"There, you have said it all and you feel better.
You won't go now. You're crying. Close the door.
The heart's gone out of it: why keep it up.
Amy! There's someone coming down the road!"

"*You* — oh, you think the talk is all. I must go —
Somewhere out of this house. How can I make you — "

"If — you — do!" She was opening the door wider.
"Where do you mean to go? First tell me that.
I'll follow and bring you back by force. I *will!* — "

Considerations for Critical Thinking and Writing

1. How has the burial of the child within sight of the stairway window affected the relationship of the couple in this poem? Is the child's grave a symptom or a cause of the conflict between them?
2. Is the husband insensitive and indifferent to his wife's grief? Characterize the wife. Has Frost invited us to sympathize with one character more than with the other?
3. What is the effect of splitting the iambic pentameter pattern in lines 18–19, 31–32, 45–46, and 70–71?
4. Is the conflict resolved at the conclusion of the poem? Do you think the husband and wife will overcome their differences?

After Apple-Picking   1914

My long two-pointed ladder's sticking through a tree
Toward heaven still,
And there's a barrel that I didn't fill
Beside it, and there may be two or three
Apples I didn't pick upon some bough.   5
But I am done with apple-picking now.
Essence of winter sleep is on the night,
The scent of apples: I am drowsing off.
I cannot rub the strangeness from my sight
I got from looking through a pane of glass   10
I skimmed this morning from the drinking trough
And held against the world of hoary grass.
It melted, and I let it fall and break.
But I was well
Upon my way to sleep before it fell,   15
And I could tell
What form my dreaming was about to take.
Magnified apples appear and disappear,
Stem end and blossom end,
And every fleck of russet showing clear.   20
My instep arch not only keeps the ache,
It keeps the pressure of a ladder-round.
I feel the ladder sway as the boughs bend.
And I keep hearing from the cellar bin
The rumbling sound   25
Of load on load of apples coming in.
For I have had too much
Of apple-picking: I am overtired
Of the great harvest I myself desired.
There were ten thousand thousand fruit to touch,   30
Cherish in hand, lift down, and not let fall.
For all
That struck the earth,

No matter if not bruised or spiked with stubble,
Went surely to the cider-apple heap   35
As of no worth.
One can see what will trouble
This sleep of mine, whatever sleep it is.
Were he not gone,
The woodchuck could say whether it's like his   40
Long sleep, as I describe its coming on,
Or just some human sleep.

Considerations for Critical Thinking and Writing

1. How does this poem illustrate Frost's view that "Poetry provides the one permissible way of saying one thing and meaning another"? When do you first sense that the detailed description of apple picking is being used that way?
2. What comes after apple picking? What does the speaker worry about in the dream beginning in line 18?
3. Why do you suppose Frost uses apples rather than, say, pears or squash?

Birches   1916

When I see birches bend to left and right
Across the lines of straighter darker trees,
I like to think some boy's been swinging them.
But swinging doesn't bend them down to stay
As ice-storms do. Often you must have seen them   5
Loaded with ice a sunny winter morning
After a rain. They click upon themselves
As the breeze rises, and turn many-colored
As the stir cracks and crazes their enamel.
Soon the sun's warmth makes them shed crystal shells   10
Shattering and avalanching on the snow-crust —
Such heaps of broken glass to sweep away
You'd think the inner dome of heaven had fallen.
They are dragged to the withered bracken by the load,
And they seem not to break; though once they are bowed   15
So low for long, they never right themselves:
You may see their trunks arching in the woods
Years afterwards, trailing their leaves on the ground
Like girls on hands and knees that throw their hair
Before them over their heads to dry in the sun.   20
But I was going to say when Truth broke in
With all her matter-of-fact about the ice-storm,
I should prefer to have some boy bend them
As he went out and in to fetch the cows —
Some boy too far from town to learn baseball,   25
Whose only play was what he found himself,

Summer or winter, and could play alone.
One by one he subdued his father's trees
By riding them down over and over again
Until he took the stiffness out of them,   30
And not one but hung limp, not one was left
For him to conquer. He learned all there was
To learn about not launching out too soon
And so not carrying the tree away
Clear to the ground. He always kept his poise   35
To the top branches, climbing carefully
With the same pains you use to fill a cup
Up to the brim, and even above the brim.
Then he flung outward, feet first, with a swish,
Kicking his way down through the air to the ground.   40
So was I once myself a swinger of birches.
And so I dream of going back to be.
It's when I'm weary of considerations,
And life is too much like a pathless wood
Where your face burns and tickles with the cobwebs   45
Broken across it, and one eye is weeping
From a twig's having lashed across it open.
I'd like to get away from earth awhile
And then come back to it and begin over.
May no fate willfully misunderstand me   50
And half grant what I wish and snatch me away
Not to return. Earth's the right place for love:
I don't know where it's likely to go better.
I'd like to go by climbing a birch tree,
And climb black branches up a snow-white trunk,   55
Toward heaven, till the tree could bear no more,
But dipped its top and set me down again.
That would be good both going and coming back.
One could do worse than be a swinger of birches.

Considerations for Critical Thinking and Writing

1. Why does the speaker in this poem prefer the birches to have been bent by boys instead of ice storms?
2. What does the swinging of birches symbolize?
3. How is "earth" described in the poem? Why does the speaker choose it over "heaven"?
4. How might the effect of this poem be changed if it were written in heroic couplets instead of blank verse?

All out-of-doors looked darkly in at him
Through the thin frost, almost in separate stars,
That gathers on the pane in empty rooms.
What kept his eyes from giving back the gaze
Was the lamp tilted near them in his hand.   5
What kept him from remembering what it was
That brought him to that creaking room was age.
He stood with barrels round him — at a loss.
And having scared the cellar under him
In clomping here, he scared it once again   10
In clomping off — and scared the outer night,
Which has its sounds, familiar, like the roar
Of trees and crack of branches, common things,
But nothing so like beating on a box.
A light he was to no one but himself   15
Where now he sat, concerned with he knew what,
A quiet light, and then not even that.
He consigned to the moon, such as she was,
So late-arising, to the broken moon
As better than the sun in any case   20
For such a charge, his snow upon the roof,
His icicles along the wall to keep;
And slept. The log that shifted with a jolt
Once in the stove, disturbed him and he shifted,
And eased his heavy breathing, but still slept.   25
One aged man — one man — can't keep a house,
A farm, a countryside, or if he can,
It's thus he does it of a winter night.

Considerations for Critical Thinking and Writing

1. Describe the tone of this poem. Which images are especially effective in evoking the old man, the winter, and night?
2. What emotions do you feel for the old man? Is this a sentimental poem?
3. Comment on the sounds described in the poem. What effects do they create?

Connections to Other Selections

1. Compare the speaker in "The Road Not Taken" (p. 871) with the old man in this poem. Are they essentially similar or different? Explain your response in an essay.
2. Discuss images of winter and night in "An Old Man's Winter Night" and "Stopping by Woods on a Snowy Evening" (p. 884).

"Out, Out—"°   1916

The buzz-saw snarled and rattled in the yard
And made dust and dropped stove-length sticks of wood,
Sweet-scented stuff when the breeze drew across it.
And from there those that lifted eyes could count
Five mountain ranges one behind the other   5
Under the sunset far into Vermont.
And the saw snarled and rattled, snarled and rattled,
As it ran light, or had to bear a load.
And nothing happened: day was all but done.
Call it a day, I wish they might have said   10
To please the boy by giving him the half hour
That a boy counts so much when saved from work.
His sister stood beside them in her apron
To tell them "Supper." At the word, the saw,
As if to prove saws knew what supper meant,   15
Leaped out at the boy's hand, or seemed to leap —
He must have given the hand. However it was,
Neither refused the meeting. But the hand!
The boy's first outcry was a rueful laugh,
As he swung toward them holding up the hand   20
Half in appeal, but half as if to keep
The life from spilling. Then the boy saw all —
Since he was old enough to know, big boy
Doing a man's work, though a child at heart —
He saw all spoiled. "Don't let him cut my hand off —   25
The doctor, when he comes. Don't let him, sister!"
So. But the hand was gone already.
The doctor put him in the dark of ether.
He lay and puffed his lips out with his breath.
And then — the watcher at his pulse took fright.   30
No one believed. They listened at his heart.
Little — less — nothing! — and that ended it.
No more to build on there. And they, since they
Were not the one dead, turned to their affairs.

"*Out, Out —* ": From Act V, Scene v, of Shakespeare's *Macbeth*. The passage appears on page 665.

Considerations for Critical Thinking and Writing

1. How does Frost's allusion to *Macbeth* contribute to the meaning of this poem? Does the speaker seem to agree with the view of life expressed in Macbeth's lines?
2. This narrative poem is about the accidental death of a Vermont boy. What is the purpose of the story? Some readers have argued that the final lines reveal the speaker's callousness and indifference. What do you think?

Connections to Other Selections

1. What are the similarities and differences in theme between this poem and Frost's "Nothing Gold Can Stay" (p. 885)?
2. Write an essay comparing how grief is handled by the boy's family in this poem and the couple in "Home Burial" (p. 876).
3. Compare the tone and theme of "Out, Out —" and those of Crane's "A Man Said to the Universe" (p. 692).

Fire and Ice   1923

Some say the world will end in fire,
Some say in ice.
From what I've tasted of desire
I hold with those who favor fire.
But if it had to perish twice,
I think I know enough of hate
To say that for destruction ice
Is also great
And would suffice.

Considerations for Critical Thinking and Writing

1. What theories about the end of the world are alluded to in lines 1 and 2?
2. What characteristics of human behavior does the speaker associate with fire and ice?
3. How does the speaker's use of understatement and rhyme affect the tone of this poem?

Stopping by Woods on a Snowy Evening   1923

Whose woods these are I think I know.
His house is in the village, though;
He will not see me stopping here
To watch his woods fill up with snow.

My little horse must think it queer   5
To stop without a farmhouse near
Between the woods and frozen lake
The darkest evening of the year.

He gives his harness bells a shake
To ask if there is some mistake.   10
The only other sound's the sweep
Of easy wind and downy flake.

The woods are lovely, dark and deep,

But I have promises to keep,
And miles to go before I sleep,   15
And miles to go before I sleep.

Considerations for Critical Thinking and Writing

1. What is the significance of the setting in this poem? How is tone conveyed by the images?
2. What does the speaker find appealing about the woods? What is the purpose of the horse in the poem?
3. Although the last two lines are identical, they are not read at the same speed. Why the difference? What is achieved by the repetition?
4. What is the rhyme scheme of this poem? What is the effect of the rhyme in the final stanza?

Nothing Gold Can Stay   1923

Nature's first green is gold,
Her hardest hue to hold.
Her early leaf's a flower;
But only so an hour.
Then leaf subsides to leaf.
So Eden sank to grief.
So dawn goes down to day.
Nothing gold can stay.

Considerations for Critical Thinking and Writing

1. What is meant by "gold" in the poem? Why can't it "stay"?
2. What do the leaf, humanity, and a day have in common?

Connection to Another Selection

1. Write an essay comparing the tone and theme of "Nothing Gold Can Stay" with Robert Herrick's "To the Virgins, to Make Much of Time" (p. 629).

For Once, Then, Something   1923

Others taunt me with having knelt at well-curbs
Always wrong to the light, so never seeing
Deeper down in the well than where the water
Gives me back in a shining surface picture
Me myself in the summer heaven, godlike,   5
Looking out of a wreath of fern and cloud puffs.
Once, when trying with chin against a well-curb,
I discerned, as I thought, beyond the picture,

Through the picture, a something white, uncertain,
Something more of the depths — and then I lost it.   10
Water came to rebuke the too clear water.
One drop fell from a fern, and lo, a ripple
Shook whatever it was lay there at bottom,
Blurred it, blotted it out. What was that whiteness?
Truth? A pebble of quartz? For once, then, something.   15

Considerations for Critical Thinking and Writing

1. How does this poem play on the Greek proverb that "truth lies at the bottom of wells"?
2. How do others view the speaker's way of looking in wells?
3. What is the symbolic value of the "something white" in line 9?
4. What does the poem suggest to you about humanity's search for ultimate truths?

Connections to Other Selections

1. Compare this speaker's search for truth with that of the people described in "Neither Out Far nor In Deep" (p. 887).
2. In an essay discuss "whiteness" in this poem and in "Design" (p. 887).

Desert Places   1936

Snow falling and night falling fast, oh, fast
In a field I looked into going past,
And the ground almost covered smooth in snow,
But a few weeds and stubble showing last.

The woods around it have it — it is theirs.   5
All animals are smothered in their lairs.
I am too absent-spirited to count;
The loneliness includes me unawares.

And lonely as it is, that loneliness
Will be more lonely ere it will be less —   10
A blanker whiteness of benighted snow
With no expression, nothing to express.

They cannot scare me with their empty spaces
Between stars — on stars where no human race is.
I have it in me so much nearer home   15
To scare myself with my own desert places.

Considerations for Critical Thinking and Writing

1. What kind of desert places does the speaker in this poem describe?
2. How does the speaker view the snow? Is this the same perspective as the one in "Stopping by Woods on a Snowy Evening" (p. 884)?
3. Who are "They" in line 13? Why is it that the speaker cannot be scared by them?

Design

I found a dimpled spider, fat and white,
On a white heal-all,° holding up a moth
Like a white piece of rigid satin cloth —
Assorted characters of death and blight
Mixed ready to begin the morning right,   5
Like the ingredients of a witches' broth —
A snow-drop spider, a flower like a froth,
And dead wings carried like a paper kite.

What had the flower to do with being white,
The wayside blue and innocent heal-all?   10
What brought the kindred spider to that height,
Then steered the white moth thither in the night?
What but design of darkness to appall? —
If design govern in a thing so small.

2 *heal-all:* A common flower, usually blue, once used for medicinal purposes.

Considerations for Critical Thinking and Writing

1. How does the division of the octave and sestet in this sonnet serve to organize the speaker's thoughts and feelings? What is the predominant rhyme? How does that rhyme relate to the poem's meaning?
2. Which words seem especially rich in connotative meanings? Explain how they function in the sonnet.
3. What kinds of speculations are raised in the final two lines? Consider the meaning of the title. Is there more than one way to read it?

Connections to Other Selections

1. Compare the ironic tone of "Design" with the tone of Hathaway's "Oh, Oh" (p. 592). What would you have to change in Hathaway's poem to make it more like Frost's?
2. In an essay discuss Frost's view of God in this poem and Dickinson's perspective in "I know that He exists" (p. 846).
3. Compare "Design" with "In White," Frost's early version of it (p. 891).

Neither Out Far nor In Deep

The people along the sand
All turn and look one way.
They turn their back on the land.
They look at the sea all day.

As long as it takes to pass   5
A ship keeps raising its hull;
The wetter ground like glass
Reflects a standing gull.

The land may vary more;
But wherever the truth may be —   10
The water comes ashore,
And the people look at the sea.

They cannot look out far.
They cannot look in deep.
But when was that ever a bar   15
To any watch they keep?

Considerations for Critical Thinking and Writing

1. Frost built this poem around a simple observation that raises some questions.
   Why do people at the beach almost always face the ocean? What feelings and
   thoughts are evoked by looking at the ocean?
2. Notice how the verb *look* takes on added meaning as the poem progresses. What
   are the people looking for?
3. How does the final stanza extend the poem's significance?
4. Does the speaker identify with the people described, or does he ironically distance
   himself from them?

Provide, Provide   1936

The witch that came (the withered hag)
To wash the steps with pail and rag,
Was once the beauty Abishag,°

The picture pride of Hollywood.
Too many fall from great and good   5
For you to doubt the likelihood.

Die early and avoid the fate.
Or if predestined to die late,
Make up your mind to die in state.

Make the whole stock exchange your own!   10
If need be occupy a throne,
Where nobody can call *you* crone.

Some have relied on what they knew;
Others on being simply true.
What worked for them might work for you.   15

3 *Abishag:* A beautiful young woman who comforted King David in his old age (1 Kings 1:1–4).

No memory of having starred
Atones for later disregard,
Or keeps the end from being hard.

Better to go down dignified
With boughten friendship at your side   20
Than none at all. Provide, provide!

Considerations for Critical Thinking and Writing

1. Do you agree or disagree with the sentiments expressed in lines 19–21 of this poem?
2. Does the speaker offer serious advice or satirize the values described here? Is this poem didactic or ironic?
3. What is the effect of the rhymes? Is this much rhyme characteristic of Frost's work?

The Silken Tent   1942

She is as in a field a silken tent
At midday when a sunny summer breeze
Has dried the dew and all its ropes relent,
So that in guys° it gently sways at ease,   ropes that steady a tent
And its supporting central cedar pole,   5
That is its pinnacle to heavenward
And signifies the sureness of the soul,
Seems to owe naught to any single cord,
But strictly held by none, is loosely bound
By countless silken ties of love and thought   10
To everything on earth the compass round,
And only by one's going slightly taut
In the capriciousness of summer air
Is of the slightest bondage made aware.

Considerations for Critical Thinking and Writing

1. What is being compared in this sonnet? How does the detail accurately describe both elements of the comparison?
2. How does the form of this one-sentence sonnet help to express its theme? Pay particular attention to the final three lines.
3. How do the sonnet's sounds contribute to its meaning?

A Considerable Speck   1942

(Microscopic)

A speck that would have been beneath my sight
On any but a paper sheet so white
Set off across what I had written there.

And I had idly poised my pen in air
To stop it with a period of ink   5
When something strange about it made me think.
This was no dust speck by my breathing blown,
But unmistakably a living mite
With inclinations it could call its own.
It paused as with suspicion of my pen,   10
And then came racing wildly on again
To where my manuscript was not yet dry;
Then paused again and either drank or smelt —
With loathing, for again it turned to fly.
Plainly with an intelligence I dealt.   15
It seemed too tiny to have room for feet,
Yet must have had a set of them complete
To express how much it didn't want to die.
It ran with terror and with cunning crept.
It faltered: I could see it hesitate;   20
Then in the middle of the open sheet
Cower down in desperation to accept
Whatever I accorded it of fate.
I have none of the tenderer-than-thou
Collectivistic regimenting love   25
With which the modern world is being swept
But this poor microscopic item now!
Since it was nothing I knew evil of
I let it lie there till I hope it slept.
I have a mind myself and recognize   30
Mind when I meet with it in any guise.
No one can know how glad I am to find
On any sheet the least display of mind.

Considerations for Critical Thinking and Writing

1. Describe the speaker's sense of humor. How does it help to characterize the speaker?
2. Given lines 24–26, why does the speaker spare the mite?
3. How do the final two lines sum up the point of this observation on a speck?
4. How is the tone of the speaker's voice created through rhyme, meter, and diction?

The Gift Outright   1942

The land was ours before we were the land's.
She was our land more than a hundred years
Before we were her people. She was ours
In Massachusetts, in Virginia,
But we were England's, still colonials,   5
Possessing what we still were unpossessed by,

Possessed by what we now no more possessed.
Something we were withholding made us weak
Until we found out that it was ourselves
We were withholding from our land of living,   10
And forthwith found salvation in surrender.
Such as we were we gave ourselves outright
(The deed of gift was many deeds of war)
To the land vaguely realizing westward,
But still unstoried, artless, unenhanced,   15
Such as she was, such as she would become.

Considerations for Critical Thinking and Writing

1. Frost once described this poem as "a history of the United States in sixteen lines."
   Is it? What events in American history does the poem focus on? What does it leave
   out?
2. This poem is built on several paradoxes. How are the paradoxes in lines 1, 6, 7,
   and 11 resolved?

Connections to Other Selections

1. Compare and contrast the theme and tone of this poem with those of cummings's
   "next to of course god america i" (p. 691).
2. Write an essay comparing Frost's view of America with the view offered by Allen
   Ginsberg in "America" (p. 952).

PERSPECTIVES ON FROST

In White: Frost's Early Version of *Design*   1912

A dented spider like a snow drop white
On a white Heal-all, holding up a moth
Like a white piece of lifeless satin cloth —
Saw ever curious eye so strange a sight? —
Portent in little, assorted death and blight   5
Like the ingredients of a witches' broth? —
The beady spider, the flower like a froth,
And the moth carried like a paper kite.

What had that flower to do with being white,
The blue prunella every child's delight.   10
What brought the kindred spider to that height?
(Make we no thesis of the miller's° plight.)   *miller moth*
What but design of darkness and of night?
Design, design! Do I use the word aright?

Considerations for Critical Thinking and Writing

1. Read "In White" and "Design" (p. 887) aloud. Which version sounds better to you? Why?
2. Compare these versions line for line, paying particular attention to word choice. List the differences, and try to explain why you think Frost revised the lines.
3. How does the change in titles reflect a shift in emphasis in the poem?

Frost on the Living Part of a Poem   1914

The living part of a poem is the intonation entangled somehow in the syntax, idiom, and meaning of a sentence. It is only there for those who have heard it previously in conversation. . . . It is the most volatile and at the same time important part of poetry. It goes and the language becomes dead language, the poetry dead poetry. With it go the accents, the stresses, the delays that are not the property of vowels and syllables but that are shifted at will with the sense. Vowels have length there is no denying. But the accent of sense supersedes all other accent, overrides it and sweeps it away. I will find you the word *come* variously used in various passages, a whole, half, third, fourth, fifth, and sixth note. It is as long as the sense makes it. When men no longer know the intonations on which we string our words they will fall back on what I may call the absolute length of our syllables, which is the length we would give them in passages that meant nothing. . . . I say you can't read a single good sentence with the salt in it unless you have previously heard it spoken. Neither can you with the help of all the characters and diacritical marks pronounce a single word unless you have previously heard it actually pronounced. Words exist in the mouth not books.

From a letter to Sidney Cox in *A Swinger of Birches: A Portrait of Robert Frost*

Considerations for Critical Thinking and Writing

1. Why does Frost place so much emphasis on hearing poetry spoken?
2. Choose a passage from "Home Burial" (p. 876) or "After Apple-Picking" (p. 879) and read it aloud. How does Frost's description of his emphasis on intonation help explain the effects he achieves in the passage you have selected?
3. Do you think it is true that all poetry must be heard? Do "Words exist in the mouth not books"?

AMY LOWELL (1874–1925)
On Frost's Realistic Technique   1915

I have said that Mr. Frost's work is almost photographic. The qualification was unnecessary, it is photographic. The pictures, the characters, are reproduced directly from life, they are burnt into his mind as though it were a sensitive plate. He gives out what has been put in unchanged by any personal mental process. His imagination is bounded by what he has seen, he is confined within the limits of his experience (or at least what might have been his experience) and bent all one way like the windblown trees of New England hillsides.

From a review of *North of Boston, The New Republic,* February 20, 1915

Considerations for Critical Thinking and Writing

1. Consider the "photographic" qualities of Frost's poetry by discussing particular passages that strike you as having been "reproduced directly from life."
2. Write an essay that supports or refutes Lowell's assertion that "He gives out what has been put in unchanged by any personal mental process."

Frost on the Figure a Poem Makes   1939

Abstraction is an old story with the philosophers, but it has been like a new toy in the hands of the artists of our day. Why can't we have any one quality of poetry we choose by itself? We can have in thought. Then it will go hard if we can't in practice. Our lives for it.

Granted no one but a humanist much cares how sound a poem is if it is only *a* sound. The sound is the gold in the ore. Then we will have the sound out alone and dispense with the inessential. We do till we make the discovery that the object in writing poetry is to make all poems sound as different as possible from each other, and the resources for that of vowels, consonants, punctuation, syntax, words, sentences, meter are not enough. We need the help of context — meaning — subject matter. That is the greatest help towards variety. All that can be done with words is soon told. So also with meters — particularly in our language where there are virtually but two, strict iambic and loose iambic. The ancients with many were still poor if they depended on meters for all tune. It is painful to watch our sprung-rhythmists straining at the point of omitting one short from a foot for relief from monotony. The possibilities for tune from the dramatic tones of meaning struck across the rigidity of a limited meter are endless. And we are back in poetry as merely one more art of having something to say, sound or unsound. Probably better if sound, because deeper and from wider experience.

Then there is this wildness whereof it is spoken. Granted again that it has an equal claim with sound to being a poem's better half. If it is a wild tune, it is a poem. Our problem then is, as modern abstractionists, to have the wildness pure; to be wild with nothing to be wild about. We bring up as aberrationists, giving way to undirected associations and kicking ourselves from one chance suggestion to another in all directions as of a hot afternoon in the life of a grasshopper. Theme alone can steady us down. Just as the first mystery was how a poem could have a tune in such a straightness as meter, so the second mystery is how a poem can have wildness and at the same time a subject that shall be fulfilled.

It should be of the pleasure of a poem itself to tell how it can. The figure a poem makes. It begins in delight and ends in wisdom. The figure is the same as for love. No one can really hold that the ecstasy should be static and stand still in one place. It begins in delight, it inclines to the impulse, it assumes direction with the first line laid down, it runs a course of lucky events, and ends in a clarification of life — not necessarily a great clarification, such as sects and cults are founded on, but in a momentary stay against confusion. It has denouement. It has an outcome that though unforeseen was predestined from the first image of the original mood — and indeed from the very mood. It is but a trick poem and no poem at all if the best of it was thought of first and saved for the last. It finds its own name as it goes and discovers the best waiting for it in some final phrase at once wise and sad — the happy-sad blend of the drinking song.

No tears in the writer, no tears in the reader. No surprise for the writer, no surprise for the reader. For me the initial delight is in the surprise of remembering something I didn't know I knew. I am in a place, in a situation, as if I had materialized from cloud or risen out of the ground. There is a glad recognition of the long lost and the rest follows. Step by step the wonder of unexpected supply keeps growing. The impressions most useful to my purpose seem always those I was unaware of and so made no note of at the time when taken, and the conclusion is come to that like giants we are always hurling experience ahead of us to pave the future with against the day when we may want to strike a line of purpose across it for somewhere. The line will have the more charm for not being mechanically straight. We enjoy the straight crookedness of a good walking stick. Modern instruments of precision are being used to make things crooked as if by eye and hand in the old days.

I tell how there may be a better wildness of logic than of inconsequence. But the logic is backward, in retrospect, after the act. It must be more felt than seen ahead like prophecy. It must be a revelation, or a series of revelations, as much for the poet as for the reader. For it to be that there must have been the greatest freedom of the material to move about in it and to establish relations in it regardless of time and space, previous relation, and everything but affinity. We prate of freedom. We call our schools free because we are not free to stay away from them till we are sixteen years of age. I have given up my democratic prejudices and now willingly set the lower classes free to be completely taken care of by the upper classes. Political freedom is nothing to me. I bestow it right and left. All I would keep for myself is the freedom of my material — the condition of body and mind now and then to summons aptly from the vast chaos of all I have lived through.

Scholars and artists thrown together are often annoyed at the puzzle of where they differ. Both work for knowledge; but I suspect they differ most importantly in the way their knowledge is come by. Scholars get theirs with conscientious thoroughness along projected lines of logic; poets theirs cavalierly and as it happens in and out of books. They stick to nothing deliberately, but let what will stick to them like burrs where they walk in the fields. No acquirement is on assignment, or even self-assignment. Knowledge of the second kind is much more available in the wild free ways of wit and art. A school boy may be defined as one who can tell you what he knows in the order in which he learned it. The artist must value himself as he snatches a thing from some previous order in time and space into a new order with not so much as a ligature clinging to it of the old place where it was organic.

More than once I should have lost my soul to radicalism if it had been the originality it was mistaken for by its young converts. Originality and initiative are what I ask for my country. For myself the originality need be no more than the freshness of a poem run in the way I have described: from delight to wisdom. The figure is the same as for love. Like a piece of ice on a hot stove the poem must ride on its own melting. A poem may be worked over once it is in being, but may not be worried into being. Its most precious quality will remain its having run itself and carried away the poet with it. Read it a hundred times: it will forever keep its freshness as a metal keeps its fragrance. It can never lose its sense of a meaning that once unfolded by surprise as it went.

From *Complete Poems of Robert Frost*

Considerations for Critical Thinking and Writing

1. Frost places a high premium on sound in his poetry, because it "is the gold in the ore." Choose one of Frost's poems in this book and explain the effects of its sounds and how they contribute to its meaning.
2. Discuss Frost's explanation of how his poems are written. In what sense is the process both spontaneous and "predestined"?
3. What do you think Frost means when he says he's given up his "democratic prejudices"? Why is "political freedom" nothing to him?
4. Write an essay that examines in more detail the ways scholars and artists "come by" knowledge.
5. Explain what you think Frost means when he writes that "Like a piece of ice on a hot stove the poem must ride on its own melting."

Frost on the Way to Read a Poem   1951

The way to read a poem in prose or verse is in the light of all the other poems ever written. We may begin anywhere. We *duff* into our first. We read that imperfectly (thoroughness with it would be fatal), but the better to read the second. We read the second the better to read the third, the third the better to read the fourth, the fourth the better to read the fifth, the fifth the better to read the first again, or the second if it so happens. For poems are not meant to be read in course any more than they are to be made a study of. I once made a resolve never to put any book to any use it wasn't intended for by its author. Improvement will not be a progression but a widening circulation. Our instinct is to settle down like a revolving dog and make ourselves at home among the poems, completely at our ease as to how they should be taken. The same people will be apt to take poems right as know how to take a hint when there is one and not to take a hint when none is intended. Theirs is the ultimate refinement.

From "Poetry and School," *Atlantic Monthly,* June 1951

Considerations for Critical Thinking and Writing

1. Given your own experience, how good is Frost's advice about reading in general and his poems in particular?
2. In what sense is a good reader like a "revolving dog" and a person who knows "how to take a hint"?
3. Frost elsewhere in this piece writes that "One of the dangers of college to anyone who wants to stay a human reader (that is to say a humanist) is that he will become a specialist and lose his sensitive fear of landing on the lovely too hard. (With beak and talon.)" Write an essay in response to this concern. Do you agree with Frost's distinction between a "human reader" and a "specialist"?

LIONEL TRILLING (1905–1975)
On Frost as a Terrifying Poet   1959

I have to say that my Frost — *my Frost:* what airs we give ourselves when once we believe that we have come into possession of a poet! — I have to say that my Frost is not the Frost I seem to perceive existing in the minds of so many of his admirers. He is not the Frost who confounds the characteristically modern practice of poetry by his notable democratic simplicity of utterance: on the contrary. He is not the Frost who controverts the bitter modern astonishment at the nature of human life: the opposite is so. He is not the Frost who reassures us by his affirmation of old virtues, simplicities, pieties, and ways of feeling: anything but. I will not go so far as to say that my Frost is not essentially an American poet at all: I believe that he is quite as American as everyone thinks he is, but not in the way that everyone thinks he is.

In the matter of the Americanism of American literature one of my chief guides is that very remarkable critic, D. H. Lawrence. Here are the opening sentences of Lawrence's great outrageous book about classic American literature. "We like to think of the old fashioned American classics as children's books. Just childishness on our part. The old American art speech contains an alien quality which belongs to the American continent and to nowhere else." And this unique alien quality, Lawrence goes on to say, the world has missed. "It is hard to hear a new voice," he says, "as hard as to listen to an unknown language. . . . Why? Out of fear. The world fears a new experience more than it fears anything. It can pigeonhole any idea. But it can't pigeonhole a real new experience. It can only dodge. The world is a great dodger, and the Americans the greatest. Because they dodge their own very selves." I should like to pick up a few more of Lawrence's sentences, feeling the freer to do so because they have an affinity to Mr. Frost's prose manner and substance: "An artist is usually a damned liar, but his art, if it be art, will tell you the truth of his day. And that is all that matters. Away with eternal truth. Truth lives from day to day. . . . The old American artists were hopeless liars. . . . Never trust the artist. Trust the tale. The proper function of the critic is to save the tale from the artist who created it. . . . Now listen to me, don't listen to him. He'll tell you the lie you expect, which is partly your fault for expecting it."

Now in point of fact Robert Frost is *not* a liar. I would not hesitate to say that he was if I thought he was. But no, he is not. In certain of his poems — I shall mention one or two in a moment — he makes it perfectly plain what he is doing; and if we are not aware of what he is doing in other of his poems, where he is not quite so plain, that is not his fault but our own. It is not from him that the tale needs to be saved.

I conceive that Robert Frost is doing in his poems what Lawrence says the great writers of the classic American tradition did. That enterprise of theirs was of an ultimate radicalism. It consisted, Lawrence says, of two things: a disintegration and sloughing off of the old consciousness, by which Lawrence means the old European consciousness, and the forming of a new consciousness underneath.

So radical a work, I need scarcely say, is not carried out by reassurance, nor by the affirmation of old virtues and pieties. It is carried out by the representation of the terrible actualities of life in a new way. I think of Robert Frost as a terrifying poet. Call him, if it makes things any easier, a tragic poet, but it might be useful every now and then to come out from under the shelter of that literary word. The universe that he conceives is a terrifying universe. Read the poem called "Design" and see if you sleep the better for it. Read "Neither Out Far nor In Deep," which often seems to me the most perfect poem of our time, and see if you are warmed by anything in it except the energy with which emptiness is perceived.

But the *people,* it will be objected, the *people* who inhabit this possibly terrifying universe! About them there is nothing that can terrify; surely the people in Mr. Frost's poems can only reassure us by their integrity and solidity. Perhaps so. But I cannot make the disjunction. It may well be that ultimately they reassure us in some sense, but first they terrify us, or should. We must not be misled about them by the curious tenderness with which they are represented, a tenderness which extends to a recognition of the tenderness which they themselves can often give. But when ever have people been so isolated, so lightning-blasted, so tried down and calcined by life, so reduced, each in his own way, to some last irreducible core of being. Talk of the disintegration and sloughing off of the old consciousness! The people of Robert Frost's poems have done that with a vengeance. Lawrence says that what the Americans refused to accept was "the post-Renaissance humanism of Europe," "the old European spontaneity," "the flowing easy humor of Europe" and that seems to me a good way to describe the people who inhabit Robert Frost's America. In the interests of what great other thing these people have made this rejection we cannot know for certain. But we can guess that it was in the interest of truth, of some truth of the self. This is what they all affirm by their humor (which is so *not* "the easy flowing humor of Europe"), by their irony, by their separateness and isolateness. They affirm *this* of themselves: that they are what they are, that this is their truth, and that if the truth be bare, as truth often is, it is far better than a lie. For me the process by which they arrive at that truth is always terrifying. The manifest America of Mr. Frost's poems may be pastoral; the actual America is tragic.

From "A Speech on Robert Frost: A Cultural Episode,"
Partisan Review, Summer 1959

Considerations for Critical Thinking and Writing

1. How does Trilling distinguish *"my Frost"* from other readers'?
2. Read the section on biographical criticism in Chapter 35 (p. 2001) and familiarize yourself with Frost's life. How does a knowledge of Frost's biography influence your reading of his poems?
3. Write an essay indicating whether you agree or disagree with Trilling's assessment of Frost "as a terrifying poet." Use evidence from the poems to support your view.

GALWAY KINNELL (b. 1927)
From *For Robert Frost°*   1965

    I saw you once on the TV,
Unsteady at the lectern,
The flimsy white leaf
Of hair standing straight up
In the wind, among top hats,   5
Old farmer and son
Of worse winters than this,
Stopped in the first dazzle

Of the District of Columbia,
Suddenly having to pay   10
For the cheap onionskin,
The worn-out ribbon, the eyes
Wrecked from writing poems
For us — stopped,
Lonely before millions,   15
The paper jumping in your grip,

And as the Presidents
Also on the platform
Began flashing nervously

Their Presidential smiles   20
For the harmless old guy,
And poets watching on the TV
Started thinking, Well that's
The end of *that* tradition,

And the managers of the event   25
Said, Boys this is it,
This sonofabitch poet
Is gonna croak,
Putting the paper aside

This tribute to Frost recalls his reciting "The Gift Outright" at the inauguration of John F. Kennedy in 1961. Frost originally planned to read the poem but was prevented from doing so by the glaring sun.

You drew forth From your great faithful heart
The poem.

Considerations for Critical Thinking and Writing

1. Describe the difference in attitude expressed by the "Presidents" (line 16), the "poets" (22), and the "managers" (25) and that expressed by Kinnell in this excerpt. Why does Kinnell include the others in the poem?
2. Frost is said here to represent "The end of *that* tradition." What kind of tradition does he represent?
3. Research Frost's reputation. Why was he so popular with the American public?

HERBERT R. COURSEN, JR. (b. 1932)
A Reading of "Stopping by Woods on a Snowy Evening"

1962

Much ink has spilled on many pages in exegesis of this little poem. Actually, critical jottings have only obscured what has lain beneath critical noses all these years. To say that the poem means merely that a man stops one night to observe a snowfall, or that the poem contrasts the mundane desire for creature comfort with the sweep of aesthetic appreciation, or that it renders worldly responsibilities paramount, or that it reveals the speaker's latent death-wish is to miss the point rather badly. Lacking has been that mind simple enough to see what is *really* there. . . .

The "darkest evening of the year" in New England is December 21st, a date near that on which the western world celebrates Christmas. It may be that December 21st *is* the date of the poem, or (and with poets this seems more likely) that this is the closest the poet can come to Christmas without giving it all away. Who has "promises to keep" at or near this date, and who must traverse much territory to fulfill these promises? Yes, and who but St. Nick would know the location of *each* home? Only he would know who had "just settled down for a long winter's nap" (the poem's third line — "He will not see me stopping here" — is clearly a veiled allusion) and would not be out inspecting his acreage this night. The unusual phrase "fill up with snow," in the poem's fourth line, is a transfer of Santa's occupational preoccupation to the countryside; he is mulling the filling of countless stockings hung above countless fireplaces by countless careful children. "Harness bells," of course, allude to "Sleighing Song," a popular Christmas tune of the time the poem was written in which the refrain "Jingle Bells! Jingle Bells!" appears; thus again are we put on the Christmas track. The "little horse," like the date is another attempt at poetic obfuscation. Although the "rein-reindeer" ambiguity has been eliminated from the poem's final version,[1]

[1]The original draft contained the following line: "That bid me give the reins a shake" (Stageberg-Anderson, *Poetry as Experience* [New York, 1952], p. 457). [Coursen's note]

Robert Frost 899

probably because too obvious, we may speculate that the animal is really a reindeer disguised as a horse by the poet's desire for obscurity, a desire which we must concede has been fulfilled up to now.

The animal is clearly concerned, like the faithful Rudolph — another possible allusion (post facto, hence unconscious) — lest his master fail to complete his mission. Seeing no farmhouse in the second quatrain, but pulling a load of presents, no wonder the little beast wonders! It takes him a full two quatrains to rouse his driver to remember all the empty stockings which hang ahead. And Santa does so reluctantly at that, poor soul, as he ponders the myriad farmhouses and villages which spread between him and his own "winter's nap." The modern St. Nick, lonely and overworked, tosses no "Happy Christmas to all and to all a good night!" into the precipitation. He merely shrugs his shoulders and resignedly plods away.

From "The Ghost of Christmas Past: 'Stopping by Woods on a Snowy Evening,'"
College English, December 1962

Considerations for Critical Thinking and Writing

1. Is this critical spoof at all credible? Does the interpretation hold any water? Is the evidence reasonable? Why or why not? Which of the poem's details are accounted for and which are ignored?
2. Choose a Frost poem and try writing a parodic interpretation of it.
3. What criteria do you use to distinguish between a sensible interpretation of a poem and an absurd one?

ROBERT H. SWENNES
Fear in "Home Burial"   1970

In "Home Burial" the decay of the marriage unit is placed in a setting which is harshly realistic and material. The conversations between husband and wife and their actions are filled with overtones of sexual aggression and withdrawal. For instance, the wife first appears poised near the top of the stairs, an emblem of womanhood to her husband who stands below. Yet this portrait is at once crushed as the husband ascends the stairs, demanding to know what his wife has been watching. Her face registers terror and then dullness as he continues "mounting until she cowered under him." The reader senses the antipathy which she feels toward her husband, even before she explains what he has done that so offended her. She is sickened by reality and is sure that "the world's evil." Her husband is a workaday farmer who cannot understand her growing morbidity since the death of their child. He tries to speak to her, to force the problem out into the open, but he overplays his hand. He reveals his own deep-seated sense of male superiority. He regrets, "A man must partly give up being a man / With women-folk." She interprets this as his regret of their courtship and marriage. The wife does not believe that any man can understand a woman's loss of her child. She shuns every hesitant attempt he makes to reach her. Her only comfort lies in self-pity.

The controlling emotion in the dramatic dialogue is fear. Since the awful sight of her husband burying her child behind the house, the wife has regarded him as a stranger, someone she really never knew before. She would rather leave the house than talk to this man who, together with all the world, now seems so brutal and evil to her. . . . The farmer no less than his wife is moved by fear, though it outwardly appears in both of them as anger. She threatens his personal dignity with her wild charges against him, and he reacts toward her in kind. Frost, as his biographer Lawrance Thompson explains, was himself a man who masked his fears with outward displays of anger. . . . "Home Burial" illustrates the existential fear, and sometimes even madness, which comes from the breakup of a once happy marital relationship. The farmer and his wife are being dragged down by the barriers she has raised between them. He is not adept and patient enough to minimize the conflict. The woman no longer conceives of herself as a wife, her husband's lover, or the mother of his future family. Not only has her domestic personality collapsed, but her psychological identity as well. She can relate to no one about her. With rare perception she recognizes, "from the time when one is sick to death, / One is alone." Isolated by her own hypersensitivity and refusal to talk, she wants nothing more to do with life. She waits to follow her child to the grave.

In "Home Burial" . . . the weakening of personal identity and self-assurance, the breakdown of person-to-person communication, and the death of the spiritual will to struggle and survive work to draw apart those who love. Once cast adrift, they find life to be a chaotic void.

From "Man and Wife: The Dialogue of Contraries in Robert Frost's Poetry," *American Literature,* November 1970

Considerations for Critical Thinking and Writing

1. Explain why you agree or disagree that the "controlling emotion" in the poem "is fear." What are the wife and husband afraid of and why can't they communicate adequately?
2. Discuss whether Swennes sympathizes more with the wife or husband.
3. Which character do you feel more sympathetic toward? Do you think Frost sides with one or the other? Explain your responses.

BLANCHE FARLEY (b. 1937)
The Lover Not Taken 1984

Committed to one, she wanted both
And, mulling it over, long she stood,
Alone on the road, loath
To leave, wanting to hide in the undergrowth.
This new guy, smooth as a yellow wood 5

Really turned her on. She liked his hair,
His smile. But the other, Jack, had a claim
On her already and she had to admit, he did wear

Well. In fact, to be perfectly fair,
He understood her. His long, lithe frame   10

Beside hers in the evening tenderly lay.
Still, if this blond guy dropped by someday,
Couldn't way just lead on to way?
No. For if way led on and Jack
Found out, she doubted if he would ever come back.   15

Oh, she turned with a sigh.
Somewhere ages and ages hence,
She might be telling this. "And I — "
She would say, "stood faithfully by."
But by then who would know the difference?   20

With that in mind, she took the fast way home,
The road by the pond, and phoned the blond.

Considerations for Critical Thinking and Writing

1. Which Frost poem is the object of this parody?
2. Describe how the stylistic elements mirror Frost's poem.
3. Does this parody seem successful to you? Explain what makes a successful parody.
4. Choose a Frost poem — or a portion of one if it is long — and try writing a parody of it.

TWO COMPLEMENTARY CRITICAL READINGS

REUBEN A. BROWER (1908–1975)
On the "Essence of Winter Sleep"
in "After Apple-Picking"   1963

Everything said throughout the poem comes to the reader through sentences filled with incantatory repetitions and rhymes and in waves of sound linked by likeness of pattern. From the opening lines, apparently matter-of-fact talk falls into curious chainlike sentences, rich in end-rhymes and echoes of many sorts. . . .

The meaning implied by the self-hypnosis and dreamy confusion of rhythm is finely suggested in the image of "the world of hoary grass," the blurred seeing of morning that anticipates the night vision. This blurring of experience focuses in the central metaphor of the poem, "essence of winter sleep." "Essence" is both the abstract "ultimate nature" of sleep and the physical smell, "the scent of apples" — a metaphysical image in T. S. Eliot's sense of the term. Fragrance and sleep blend, as sight and touch merge in "I cannot rub the strangeness from my sight . . ." The metaphor is renewed in many other expressions, for example, in "Magnified apples," which are apples seen against the sky with daylight accuracy, and also great dreamlike spheres. Other similarly precise details are blurred through the over-and-over way of recalling and describing them: "stem end and blossom end," "load on load," "ten thousand thousand." The closing metaphor of the poem, the woodchuck's "long sleep," adds to the strangeness of "winter sleep" by bringing in the nonhuman deathlike sleep of hibernation. We are finally quite uncertain of what *is* happening, and that is what the poem is about:

> One can see what will trouble
> This sleep of mine, whatever sleep it is.

In these two lines tone and rhythm work together beautifully, implying a great deal in relation to Frost's metaphor. The slight elevation of "One can see" recalls the more mysterious seeing of the morning, just as the almost banal lyricism of "This sleep of mine" sustains the rhythm of dream-confusion. The rest of the second line, barely iambic, barely rhyming, casual and rough, assures us that the speaker has at least one toe in reality. The contrasts of tone and rhythm, fitting the puzzlement of the sleeper's state, look ahead to the woodchuck's sleep and back to the initial balance of tones in "*sticking* through a tree / *Toward heaven* still." The poem is absorbed with "states-between," not only of winter sleep, but of all similar areas where real and unreal appear and disappear.

From *The Poetry of Robert Frost: Constellations of Intention*

Considerations for Critical Thinking and Writing

1. Discuss the sounds and images that contribute to what Brower describes as the speaker's "self-hypnosis and dreamy confusion."
2. Brower suggests that the central metaphor of the poem is "essence of winter sleep." Aside from the examples he provides, can you find other instances of this metaphor at work?
3. Write an essay that explores the idea that this poem is "absorbed with 'states-between.'"
4. Compare Brower's reading of "After Apple-Picking" with Greiner's below. Which reading do you think offers the more interesting interpretation of the poem? In your response be sure to define "interesting."

DONALD J. GREINER (b. 1940)
On What Comes "After Apple-Picking"   1982

"After Apple-Picking" was first published in *North of Boston* (1914), and it is my nomination for Frost's greatest poem. In the letter to John Cournos (27 July 1914), Frost explains that "After Apple-Picking" is the only poem in his second book that "will intone." Although he does not elaborate, he means that the rest of the poems sound like human speech whereas "After Apple-Picking" is a lyrical meditation on the tension between a job well done and the uncertainties accompanying the end of something significant. Note that the first word in the title is "After." Frost's refusal to specify what has ended, other than apple picking, is one of the glories of the poem.

The other glories are the examples of technical brilliance. The rhymes alone are worth the reading. Every one of the forty-two lines is rhymed, but Frost eschews the tradition of rhyme scheme altogether. The result is a beautiful, even haunting, rendering of the natural progression of a person's meditation as he uneasily ponders the ambiguities which suddenly well up before him now that his job is done. Similarly, the brilliant use of irregular iambic pentameter . . . to suggest the uncertain balance between the poet figure's need to maintain form in the face of confusion and the threat to his effort cast in the form of truncated lines illustrates the union of technique and theme when Frost is at his best. Although the poem begins with its longest line, the iambic heptameter "My long two-pointed ladder's sticking through a tree," and includes a line as short as "For all," the meter invariably returns to the predominant rhythm of iambic pentameter as the meditator struggles to keep his balance in uncertainty as he has kept it on the ladder of his life.

Nuances of aspiration, satisfaction, completion, rest, and death echo throughout "After Apple-Picking" beginning with the title. Like the speaker, the reader never knows how far to pursue the mythical associations between apples and man's expulsion from Eden. If such associations are to be dismissed, then the speaker has safely and satisfactorily completed his task — whatever it literally is — of harvesting the "ten thousand thousand fruit." The phrase "after apple-picking" thus suggests rest. But the genius of the poem is that the speaker is never sure. If the associations between apples and Eden are not to be dismissed, then the poet figure has finished his life's work only to be confronted with an overwhelming uncertainty about what awaits him now. "After Apple-Picking" thus suggests death.

The imagery of hazy speculation is precise. The phrase "toward heaven" indicates the speaker's ultimate aspiration, and the line "Essence of winter sleep is on the night" reverberates with suggestions of termination and the question of rebirth. The point is that the poet figure needs answers to questions he will not pose, and he can only see as through a glass darkly:

> I cannot rub the strangeness from my sight
> I got from looking through a pane of glass
> I skimmed this morning from the drinking trough. . . .

The woodchuck, so unthinkingly confident of rebirth from its winter hibernation, cannot help him. "After Apple-Picking" is a poem of encroaching fear because it is a poem of uncertainty. Although the religious connotations are never obtrusive, this great poem is another of Frost's explorations of what he considered to be man's greatest terror: that our best may not be good enough in Heaven's sight.

From "The Indispensable Robert Frost," in *Critical Essays on Robert Frost,* edited by Philip L. Gerber

Considerations for Critical Thinking and Writing

1. How far do you think "the mythical associations between apples and man's expulsion from Eden" should be pursued by readers of this poem?
2. Greiner cites several examples of the poem's "technical brilliance." What other examples can you find?
3. Write an essay that explores as the theme of the poem Greiner's idea "that our best may not be good enough in Heaven's sight."

23. Critical Case Study: T. S. Eliot's "The Love Song of J. Alfred Prufrock"

The chapter provides several critical approaches to a challenging but highly rewarding poem by T. S. Eliot. After studying this poem, you're likely to find yourself quoting bits of its striking imagery. At the very least, you'll recognize the lines when you hear other people fold them into their own conversations. There have been numerous critical approaches to this poem because it raises so many issues relating to matters such as history and biography as well as imagery, symbolism, irony, and myth. The following critical excerpts offer a small and partial sample of the possible formalist, biographical, historical, mythological, psychological, sociological, and other perspectives that have attempted to shed light on the poem (see Chapter 35, "Critical Strategies for Reading," for a discussion of a variety of critical methods). They should help you to enjoy the poem more by raising questions, providing insights, and inviting you further into the text.

T. S. ELIOT (1888–1965)

Born into a prominent New England family that had moved to St. Louis, Missouri, Thomas Stearns Eliot was a major voice in English Literature between the two world wars. He studied literature and philosophy at Harvard and on the Continent, subsequently choosing to live in England for most of his life and becoming a citizen there in 1927. His allusive and challenging poetry had a powerful influence on other writers, particularly his treatment of postwar life in *The Waste Land* (1922) and his exploration of religious questions in *The Four Quartets* (1943). In addition, he wrote plays, including *Murder in the Cathedral* (1935) and *The Cocktail Party* (1950). He was awarded the Nobel Prize for Literature in 1948. In "The Love Song of J. Alfred Prufrock," Eliot presents a comic but serious figure who expresses through

a series of fragmented images the futility, boredom, and meaninglessness
associated with much of modern life.

The Love Song of J. Alfred Prufrock

1917

S'io credessi che mia risposta fosse
A persona che mai tornasse al mondo,
Questa fiamma staria senza più scosse.
Ma perciocchè giammai di questo fondo
Non tornò vivo alcun, s'i'odo il vero,
Senza tema d'infamia ti rispondo.°

    Let us go then, you and I,
When the evening is spread out against the sky
Like a patient etherized upon a table;
Let us go, through certain half-deserted streets,
The muttering retreats   5
Of restless nights in one-night cheap hotels
And sawdust restaurants with oyster-shells:
Streets that follow like a tedious argument
Of insidious intent
To lead you to an overwhelming question . . .   10

Oh, do not ask, "What is it?"
Let us go and make our visit.

In the room the women come and go
Talking of Michelangelo.

    The yellow fog that rubs its back upon the window panes,   15
The yellow smoke that rubs its muzzle on the window panes
Licked its tongue into the corners of the evening,
Lingered upon the pools that stand in drains,
Let fall upon its back the soot that falls from chimneys,
Slipped by the terrace, made a sudden leap,   20
And seeing that it was a soft October night,
Curled once about the house, and fell asleep.

    And indeed there will be time°
For the yellow smoke that slides along the street,
Rubbing its back upon the window panes;   25

Epigraph: *S'io credesse . . . rispondo:* Dante's *Inferno,* XXVII, 58–63. In the Eighth Chasm of the
Inferno, Dante and Virgil meet Guido da Montefeltro, one of the False Counselors, who is punished
by being enveloped in an eternal flame. When Dante asks Guido to tell his life story, the spirit replies:
"If I thought that my answer were to one who might ever return to the world, this flame would shake
no more; but since from this depth none ever returned alive, if what I hear is true, I answer you
without fear of infamy."   23 *there will be time:* An allusion to Ecclesiastes 3:1–8: "To everything
there is a season, and a time to every purpose under heaven. . . ."

There will be time, there will be time
To prepare a face to meet the faces that you meet;
There will be time to murder and create,
And time for all the works and days° of hands
That lift and drop a question on your plate: 30
Time for you and time for me,
And time yet for a hundred indecisions,
And for a hundred visions and revisions,
Before the taking of a toast and tea.

In the room the women come and go   35
Talking of Michelangelo.

   And indeed there will be time
To wonder, "Do I dare?" and, "Do I dare?" —
Time to turn back and descend the stair,
With a bald spot in the middle of my hair —   40
(They will say: "How his hair is growing thin!")
My morning coat, my collar mounting firmly to the chin,
My necktie rich and modest, but asserted by a simple pin —
(They will say: "But how his arms and legs are thin!")
Do I dare   45
Disturb the universe?
In a minute there is time
For decisions and revisions which a minute will reverse.

   For I have known them already, known them all:
Have known the evenings, mornings, afternoons,   50
I have measured out my life with coffee spoons;
I know the voices dying with a dying fall
Beneath the music from a farther room.
   So how should I presume?

   And I have known the eyes already, known them all —   55
The eyes that fix you in a formulated phrase.
And when I am formulated, sprawling on a pin,
When I am pinned and wriggling on the wall,
Then how should I begin
To spit out all the butt-ends of my days and ways?   60
     And how should I presume?

   And I have known the arms already, known them all —
Arms that are braceleted and white and bare
(But in the lamplight, downed with light brown hair!)
   Is it perfume from a dress   65
   That makes me so digress?
Arms that lie along a table, or wrap about a shawl.
   And should I then presume?
     And how should I begin?

29 *works and days:* Hesiod's eighth century B.C. poem *Works and Days* gave practical advice on how
to conduct one's life in accordance with the seasons.

Shall I say, I have gone at dusk through narrow streets,   70
And watched the smoke that rises from the pipes
Of lonely men in shirtsleeves, leaning out of windows? . . .

I should have been a pair of ragged claws
Scuttling across the floors of silent seas.

          . . . . .

    And the afternoon, the evening, sleeps so peacefully!   75
Smoothed by long fingers,
Asleep . . . tired . . . or it malingers,
Stretched on the floor, here beside you and me.
Should I, after tea and cakes and ices,
Have the strength to force the moment to its crisis?   80
But though I have wept and fasted, wept and prayed,
Though I have seen my head (grown slightly bald) brought in upon a platter,°
I am no prophet — and here's no great matter;
I have seen the moment of my greatness flicker,
And I have seen the eternal Footman hold my coat, and snicker,   85
      And in short, I was afraid.

    And would it have been worth it, after all,
After the cups, the marmalade, the tea,
Among the porcelain, among some talk of you and me,
Would it have been worth while   90
To have bitten off the matter with a smile,
To have squeezed the universe into a ball°
To roll it toward some overwhelming question,
To say: "I am Lazarus,° come from the dead,
Come back to tell you all, I shall tell you all" —   95
If one, settling a pillow by her head,
    Should say: "That is not what I meant at all;
      That is not it, at all."

    And would it have been worth it, after all,
Would it have been worth while,   100
After the sunsets and the dooryards and the sprinkled streets,
After the novels, after the teacups, after the skirts that trail along the floor —
And this, and so much more? —
It is impossible to say just what I mean!
But as if a magic lantern threw the nerves in patterns on a screen: 105
Would it have been worth while
If one, settling a pillow or throwing off a shawl,

---

82 *head . . . upon a platter:* At Salome's request, Herod had John the Baptist decapitated and had
the severed head delivered to her on a platter (see Matt. 14:1–12 and Mark 6:17–29).   92 *squeezed
the universe into a ball:* See Marvell's "To His Coy Mistress" (p. 631), lines 41–42: "Let us roll all our
strength and all / Our sweetness up into one ball."   94 *Lazarus:* The brother of Mary and Martha
who was raised from the dead by Jesus (John 11:1–44). In Luke 16:19–31, a rich man asks that another
Lazarus return from the dead to warn the living about their treatment of the poor.

And turning toward the window, should say: "That is not it at all,
That is not what I meant, at all."   110
. . . . .

    No! I am not Prince Hamlet, nor was meant to be;
Am an attendant lord,° one that will do
To swell a progress,° start a scene or two   *state procession*
Advise the prince: withal, an easy tool,
Deferential, glad to be of use,   115
Politic, cautious, and meticulous;
Full of high sentence, but a bit obtuse;
At times, indeed, almost ridiculous —
Almost, at times, the Fool.

I grow old . . . I grow old . . .   120
I shall wear the bottoms of my trowsers rolled.

    Shall I part my hair behind? Do I dare to eat a peach?
I shall wear white flannel trowsers, and walk upon the beach.
I have heard the mermaids singing, each to each.
I do not think that they will sing to me.   125

I have seen them riding seaward on the waves,
Combing the white hair of the waves blown back
When the wind blows the water white and black.

We have lingered in the chambers of the sea
By seagirls wreathed with seaweed red and brown,   130
Till human voices wake us, and we drown.

112 *attendant lord:* Like Polonius in Shakespeare's *Hamlet.*

Considerations for Critical Thinking and Writing

1. What does J. Alfred Prufrock's name connote? How would you characterize him?
2. What do you think is the purpose of the epigraph from Dante's *Inferno*?
3. What is it that Prufrock wants to do? How does he behave? What does he think of himself? Which parts of the poem answer these questions?
4. Who is the "you" of line 1 and the "we" in the final lines?
5. Discuss the imagery in the poem. How does the imagery reveal Prufrock's character? Which images seem especially striking to you?

Connections to Other Selections

1. "No! I am not Prince Hamlet" says Prufrock. Despite this disclaimer, do you think it is possible to see some significant similarities between them? In an essay, acknowledge the differences between Prufrock and Hamlet (the play begins on p. 1281), and then explore what they have in common.
2. For a different side of Eliot's poetry read "Macavity: The Mystery Cat" (p. 951). How does Macavity's character serve to highlight everything that Prufrock is not? Write an essay that discusses them as character foils.

ELISABETH SCHNEIDER (1897–1984)

Schneider uses a biographical approach to the poem to suggest that part of what went into the characterization of Prufrock were some of Eliot's own sensibilities.

Hints of Eliot in Prufrock   1952

Perhaps never again did Eliot find an epigraph quite so happily suited to his use as the passage from the *Inferno* which sets the underlying serious tone for *Prufrock* and conveys more than one level of its meaning: "S'io credesse che mia risposta . . . ," lines in which Guido da Montefeltro consents to tell his story to Dante only because he believes that none ever returns to the world of the living from his depth. One in Hell can bear to expose his shame only to another of the damned; Prufrock speaks to, will be understood only by, other Prufrocks (the "you and I" of the opening, perhaps), and, I imagine the epigraph also hints, Eliot himself is speaking to those who know this kind of hell. The poem, I need hardly say, is not in a literal sense autobiographical: for one thing, though it is clear that Prufrock will never marry, the poem was published in the year of Eliot's own first marriage. Nevertheless, friends who knew the young Eliot almost all describe him, retrospectively but convincingly, in Prufrockian terms; and Eliot himself once said of dramatic monologue in general that what we normally hear in it "is the voice of the poet, who has put on the costume and make-up either of some historical character, or of one out of fiction." . . . I suppose it to be one of the many indirect clues to his own poetry planted with evident deliberation throughout his prose. "What every poet starts from," he also once said, "is his own emotions," and, writing of Dante, he asserted that the *Vita nuova* "could only have been written around a personal experience," a statement that, under the circumstances, must be equally applicable to Prufrock; Prufrock was Eliot, though Eliot was much more than Prufrock. We miss the whole tone of the poem, however, if we read it as social satire only. Eliot was not either the dedicated apostle in theory, or the great exemplar in practice, of complete "depersonalization" in poetry that one influential early essay of his for a time led readers to suppose.

From "Prufrock and After: The Theme of Change," *PMLA*, October 1952

Considerations for Critical Thinking and Writing

1. Though Schneider concedes that the poem is not literally autobiographical, she does assert that "Prufrock was Eliot." How does she argue this point? Explain why you find her argument convincing or unconvincing.
2. Find information in the library about Eliot's early career when he was writing this poem. To what extent does the poem reveal his circumstances and concerns at that point in his life?

ROBERT G. COOK (b. 1932)

This source study makes a case for Eliot's indebtedness to Ralph Waldo Emerson's 1841 essay, "Self-Reliance," as a historical influence on his characterization of Prufrock.

The Influence of Emerson's "Self-Reliance" on Prufrock   1970

It is likely that Prufrock . . . was affected by Eliot's reading of "Self-Reliance," for in that essay there are a striking number of passages that virtually define Prufrock's character . . . For example, we read:

> Let a man then know his worth, and keep things under his feet. Let him not peep or steal, or skulk up and down with the air of a charity-boy, a bastard, or an interloper in the world which exists for him. But the man in the street, finding no worth in himself which corresponds to the force which built a tower or sculptured a marble god, feels poor when he looks on these. To him a palace, a statue, or a costly book have an alien and forbidding air, much like a gay equipage, and seem to say like that, "Who are you, Sir?"

One of the main purposes of Emerson's essay is to overcome, in this fashion, the intimidations of "the man in the street." Eliot's Prufrock may be seen as a caricature of this man, an antitype to Emerson's self-reliant man, a totally un-self-reliant man. Prufrock constantly feels that he is being asked: "Who are you, Sir?"

Early in the essay Emerson points to the "nonchalance of boys who are sure of a dinner" as an example of natural self-trust and lack of self-consciousness. In contrast,

> the man is as it were clapped into jail by his consciousness. As soon as he has once acted or spoken with *éclat* he is a committed person, watched by the sympathy or the hatred of hundreds, whose affections must now enter into his account. There is no Lethe for this. Ah, that he could pass again into his neutrality! Who can thus avoid all pledges and, having observed, observe again from the same unaffected, unbiased, unbribable unaffrightened innocence, — must always be formidable. He would utter opinions on all passing affairs, which being seen to be not private but necessary, would sink like darts into the ear of men and put them in fear.

Prufrock, clapped into jail by his consciousness, has an *excessive* fear of expressing himself ("Shall I say, I have gone at dusk through narrow streets . . . ?"). For him there is no Lethe which would free him from abnormal concern for the opinions of others; he desires an even stronger Lethe, total inconspicuousness and oblivion ("I should have been a pair of ragged claws / Scuttling across the floors of silent seas"). At the same time, he longs, like a self-reliant man, to utter opinions which would sink like darts into the ear of men and put them in fear ("I am Lazarus, come from the dead . . .").

Where Emerson teaches "What I must do is all that concerns me, not what the people think," Prufrock is paralyzed by his fears of what people think. Where Emerson teaches that "the great man is he who in the midst of the crowd keeps with perfect sweetness the independence of solitude," Prufrock is "pinned and wriggling on the wall." Prufrock is incapable of regarding the faces he has known with Emerson's equanimity: "the sour faces of the multitude, like their sweet faces, have no deep cause, but are put on and off as the wind blows and a newspaper directs."

One reason Prufrock does not speak out is his fear of being misunderstood: "Would it have been worthwhile . . ." In this too, Prufrock has not profited from the teaching of Emerson: "Is it so bad then to be misunderstood? Pythagoras was misunderstood, and Socrates, and Jesus, and Luther, and Copernicus, and Galileo, and Newton, and every pure and wise spirit that ever took flesh. To be great is to be misunderstood."

One of the symptoms of Prufrock's paranoia is his lack of a sense of proportion, his inability to distinguish between great and small, with the result that everything takes on exaggerated importance. In the timorous formula "Do I dare?" eating a peach becomes tantamount to disturbing the universe. The phrase "eternal Footman" expresses his undifferentiated fear of an ordinary servant and the eternal God. Emerson's self-reliant man goes to the opposite extreme and fears nobody, not even the great: "Let us never bow and apologize more. A great man is coming to eat at my house. I do not wish to please him; I wish that he should wish to please me." As far as God is concerned, the self-reliant man need not fear Him, for in fact He is present within the self-reliant man:

> Let us affront and reprimand the smooth mediocrity and squalid contentment
> of the times, and hurl in the face of custom and trade and office, the fact
> which is the upshot of all history, that there is a great responsible Thinker
> and Actor working wherever a man works; that a true man belongs to no
> other time or place, but is the centre of things. Where he is, there is nature.
> He measures you and all men and all events.

On all these counts, basic both to Emerson's essay and to Eliot's portrayal, it is clear that Prufrock is the very opposite of the man Emerson envisions. In fact, he is remarkably like the man Emerson is preaching against: "The sinew and heart of man seem to be drawn out, and we are become timorous, desponding whimperers. We are afraid of truth, afraid of fortune, afraid of death, and afraid of each other." "Fear" is also the key word for Prufrock: "And in short, I was afraid."

From "Emerson's 'Self-Reliance,' Sweeney, and Prufrock,"
American Literature, May 1970

Considerations for Critical Thinking and Writing

1. Describe how "Self-Reliance" "virtually define[s] Prufrock's character."
2. How does this negative definition shed light on Prufrock for you? How does knowing about Emerson's essay produce better understanding of Prufrock?
3. Cook concludes his essay by noting that Prufrock's character flaws are "Eliot's realistic responses to Emerson's idealistic proposals." How does Prufrock serve to measure the distance between nineteenth- and twentieth-century views of the self?

MICHAEL L. BAUMANN (b. 1926)

Baumann takes a close look at the poem's images in his formalist efforts to make a point about Prufrock's character.

The "Overwhelming Question" for Prufrock   1981

Most critics . . . have seen the overwhelming question related to sex. . . . They have implicitly assumed — and given their readers to understand — that Prufrock's is the male's basic question: Can I?

Delmore Schwartz once said that "J. Alfred Prufrock is unable to make love to women of his own class and kind because of shyness, self-consciousness, and fear of rejection."[1] This is undoubtedly true, but Prufrock's inability to *feel* love has something to do with his inability to *make* love, too. . . . A simple desire, lust, is more than honest Prufrock can cope with as he mounts the stairs.

But Prufrock is coping with another, less simple desire as well. . . . If birth, copulation, and death is all there is, then, once we are born, once we have copulated, only death remains (for the male of the species, at least). Prufrock, having "known them all already, known them all," having "known the evenings, mornings, afternoons," having "measured out" his life "with coffee spoons," desires death. The "overwhelming question" that assails him would no longer be the romantic's rhetorical "Is life worth living?" (to which the answer is obviously No), but the more immediate shocker: "Should one commit suicide?" which is to say: "Should I?" . . .

. . . The poem makes clear that Prufrock wants more than the "entire destruction of consciousness as we understand it," a notion Prufrock expresses by wishing he were "a pair of ragged claws, / Scuttling across the floors of silent seas." Prufrock wants death itself, physical death, and the poem, I believe, is explicit about this desire.

Not only does Prufrock seem to be tired of time — "time yet for a hundred indecisions" — a tiredness that goes far beyond the acedia Prufrock is generally credited with feeling, if only because "there will be time to murder and create," time, in other words (in one sense at least) to copulate, but Prufrock is also tired of his own endless vanities, from feeling he must "prepare a face to meet the faces that you meet," to having to summon up those ironies with which to contemplate his own thin arms and legs, and, indeed, to asking if, in the rather tedious enterprise of preparing for copulation, the moment is worth "forcing to its crisis." No wonder Prufrock compares himself to John the Baptist and, in conjuring up this first concrete image of his own death, sees his head brought in upon a platter. That would be the easy way out. He had, after all, "wept and

---

[1]"T. S. Eliot as the International Hero," *Partisan Review*, 12 (1945), 202; rpt. in *T. S. Eliot: A Selected Critique*, ed. Leonard Unger (New York: Rinehart & Company, Inc., 1948), 46.

fasted, wept and prayed," but he realizes he is no prophet — and no Salome will burst into passion, will ignite for him. When the eternal Footman, Death, who holds his coat, snickers, he does so because Prufrock has let "the moment" of his "greatness" flicker, because Prufrock was unable to comply with the one imperative greatness would have thrust upon him: to kill himself. Prufrock explains: "I was afraid." Yet the achievement of his vision at the end of the poem, his being able to linger "in the chambers of the sea / By sea-girls wreathed with seaweed red and brown," is an act of the imagination that only physical death can complete, unless Prufrock wants human voices to wake him, and drown him. His romantic vision demands the voluntary act: suicide. It is to be expected that he will fail in this too, as he has failed in everything else.

From "Let Us Ask 'What Is It,'" Arizona Quarterly, Spring 1981

Considerations for Critical Thinking and Writing

1. Describe the evidence used by Baumann to argue that Prufrock contemplates suicide.
2. Explain in an essay why you do or do not find Baumann's argument convincing.
3. Later in his essay Baumann connects Prufrock's insistence that "No, I am not Prince Hamlet" with Hamlet's "To be or not to be" speech. How do you think this reference might be used to support Baumann's argument?

FREDERIK L. RUSCH (b. 1938)

Rusch makes use of the insights developed by Erich Fromm, a social psychologist who believed "psychic forces [are] a process of constant interaction between man's needs and the social and historical reality in which he participates."

Society and Character in "The Love Song of J. Alfred Prufrock" 1984

In looking at fiction, drama, and poetry from the Frommian point of view, the critic understands literature to be social portrayal as well as character portrayal or personal statement. Society and character are inextricably joined. The Frommian approach opens up the study of literary work, giving a social context to its characters, which suggests why those characters behave as they do. The Frommian approach recognizes human beings for what they are — basically gregarious individuals who are interdependent upon each other, in need of each other, and thus, to a certain degree, products of their social environments, although those environments may be inimical to their mental well-being. That is, as stated earlier, the individual's needs and drives have a social component and are not purely biological. The Frommian approach to literature assumes that a writer is — at least by implication — analyzing society and its setting as well as character. . . .

In T. S. Eliot's "The Love Song of J. Alfred Prufrock," Prufrock is talking to himself, expressing a fantasy or daydream. In his monologue, Prufrock, as noted by Grover Smith, "is addressing, as if looking into a mirror, his whole public personality."[1] Throughout the poem, Prufrock is extremely self-conscious, believing that the people in his imaginary drawing room will examine him as a specimen insect, "sprawling on a pin, / . . . pinned and wriggling on the wall. . . ." Of course, self-consciousness — being conscious of one's self — is not necessarily neurotic. Indeed, it is part of being a human being. It is only when self-consciousness, which has always led man to feel a separation from nature, becomes obsessive that we have a problem. Prufrock is certainly obsessed with his self-consciousness, convinced that everyone notices his balding head, his clothes (his prudent frocks), his thin arms and legs.

On one level, however, Prufrock is merely expressing the pain that all human beings must feel. Although his problem is extreme, he is quite representative of the human race:

> Self-awareness, reason, and imagination have disrupted the "harmony" that characterizes animal existence. Their emergence has made man into an anomaly, the freak of the universe. He is part of nature, subject to her physical laws and unable to change them, yet he transcends nature. He is set apart while being a part; he is homeless, yet chained to the home he shares with all creatures. . . . Being aware of himself, he realizes his powerlessness and the limitations of his existence. He is never free from the dichotomy of his existence: he cannot rid himself of his mind, even if he would want to; he cannot rid himself of his body as long as he is alive — and his body makes him want to be alive.[2]

This is the predicament of the human being. His self-awareness has made him feel separate from nature. This causes pain and sorrow. What, then, is the solution to the predicament? Fromm believed that mankind filled the void of alienation from nature with the creation of a culture, a society: "Man's existential, and hence unavoidable disequilibrium can be relatively stable when he has found, with the support of his culture, a more or less adequate way of coping with his existential problems" (*Destructiveness*, 225). But, unfortunately for Prufrock, his culture and society do not allow him to overcome his existential predicament. The fact is, he is bored by his modern, urban society.

In image after image, Prufrock's mind projects boredom:

> For I have known them all already, known them all:
> Have known the evenings, mornings, afternoons,
> I have measured out my life with coffee spoons. . . .

[1]Grover Smith, *T. S. Eliot's Poetry and Plays: A Study in Sources and Meaning* (Chicago: U of Chicago P, 1962), 16.
[2]Erich Fromm, *The Anatomy of Human Destructiveness* (New York: Holt, Rinehart & Winston, 1973), 225.

....

And I have known the eyes already, known them all — . . .
Then how should I begin
To spit out all the butt-ends of my days and ways?

....

And I have known the arms already, known them all — . . . .

Prufrock is completely unstimulated by his social environment, to the point of near death. The evening in which he proposes to himself to make a social visit is "etherised upon a table." The fog, as a cat, falls asleep; it is "tired . . . or it malingers, / Stretched on the floor. . . ."

Prufrock, living in a city of "half-deserted streets, / . . . one-night cheap hotels / And sawdust restaurants with oyster-shells," gets no comfort, no nurturing from his environment. He is, in the words of Erich Fromm, a "modern mass man . . . isolated and lonely" (*Destructiveness*, 107). He lives in a destructive environment. Instead of providing communion with fellow human beings, it alienates him through boredom. Such boredom leads to "a state of chronic depression" that can cause the pathology of "insufficient inner productivity" in the individual (*Destructiveness*, 243). Such a lack of productivity is voiced by Prufrock when he confesses that he is neither Hamlet nor John the Baptist.

An interesting tension in "The Love Song of J. Alfred Prufrock" is caused by the reader's knowledge that Prufrock understands his own predicament quite well. Although he calls himself a fool, he has wisdom about himself and his predicament. This, however, only reinforces his depression and frustration. In his daydream, he is able to reveal truths about himself that, while they lead to self-understanding, apparently cannot alleviate his problems in his waking life. The poem suggests no positive movement out of the predicament. Prufrock is like a patient cited by Fromm, who under hypnosis envisioned "a black barren place with many masks," and when asked what the vision meant said "that everything was dull, dull, dull; that the masks represent the different roles he takes to fool people into thinking he is feeling well" (*Destructiveness*, 246). Likewise, Prufrock understands that "There will be time, there will be time / To prepare a face to meet the faces that you meet. . . ." But despite his understanding of the nature of his existence, he cannot attain a more productive life.

It was Fromm's belief that with boredom "the decisive conditions are to be found in the overall environmental situation. . . . It is highly probable that even cases of severe depression-boredom would be less frequent and less intense . . . in a society where a mood of hope and love of life predominated. But in recent decades the opposite is increasingly the case, and thus a fertile soil for the development of individual depressive states is provided" (*Destructiveness*, 251). There is no "mood of hope and love of life" in Prufrock's society. Prufrock is a lonely man, as lonely as "the lonely men in shirt-sleeves, leaning out of windows" of his fantasy. His only solution is to return to the animal state that his race was in before evolving into human beings.

Animals are one with nature, not alienated from their environments. They *are* nature, unselfconscious. Prufrock would return to a preconscious existence in the extreme: "I should have been a pair of ragged claws / Scuttling across the floors of silent seas." Claws *without a head* surely would not be alienated, bored, or depressed. They would seek and would need no psychological nurturing from their environment. And in the end Prufrock's fantasy of becoming claws is definitely more positive for him than his life as a human being. He completes his monologue with depressing irony, to say the least: it is with human voices waking us, bringing us back to human society, that we drown.

From "Approaching Literature Through the Social Psychology of Erich Fromm," in *Psychological Perspectives on Literature: Freudian Dissidents and Non-Freudians*, ed. Joseph Natoli

Considerations for Critical Thinking and Writing

1. According to Rusch, why is Fromm's approach useful for understanding Prufrock's character as well as his social context?
2. In what ways is Prufrock "representative of the human race"? Is he like any other characters you have read about in this anthology? Explain your response.
3. In an essay consider how Rusch's analysis of Prufrock might be used to support Baumann's argument that Prufrock's "overwhelming question" is whether or not he should kill himself (p. 913).
4. Discuss the difference between Fromm's description of humanity's self-awareness and Emerson's insistence upon self-reliance (p. 911) for humanity. How do both perspectives help to account for Prufrock's characterization?

24. A Collection of Poems

QUESTIONS FOR RESPONSIVE READING

The following questions can help you respond to important elements that reveal a poem's effects and meanings. The questions are general, so not all of them will necessarily be relevant to a particular poem. Many, however, should prove useful for thinking, talking, and writing about each poem in this collection. If you are uncertain about the meaning of a term used in a question, consult the Index of Terms, which lists pages that discuss the terms and is located on the inside back cover.

Before addressing these questions, read the poem you are studying in its entirety. Don't worry about interpretation on a first reading; allow yourself the pleasure of enjoying whatever makes itself apparent to you. Then on subsequent readings, use the questions to understand and appreciate how the poem works.

1. Who is the speaker? Is it possible to determine the speaker's age, sex, sensibilities, level of awareness, and values?
2. Is the speaker addressing anyone in particular?
3. How do you respond to the speaker? favorably? negatively? What is the situation? Are there any special circumstances that inform what the speaker says?
4. Is there a specific setting of time and place?
5. Does reading the poem aloud help you to understand it?
6. Does a paraphrase reveal the basic purpose of the poem?
7. What does the title emphasize?
8. Is the theme presented directly or indirectly?
9. Do any allusions enrich the poem's meaning?
10. How does the diction reveal meaning? Are any words repeated? Do any carry evocative connotative meanings? Are there any puns or other forms of verbal wit?

11. Are figures of speech used? How does the figurative language contribute to the poem's vividness and meaning?
12. Do any objects, persons, places, events, or actions have allegorical or symbolic meanings? What other details in the poem support your interpretation?
13. Is irony used? Are there any examples of situational irony, verbal irony, or dramatic irony? Is understatement or paradox used?
14. What is the tone of the poem? Is the tone consistent?
15. Does the poem use onomatopoeia, assonance, consonance, or alliteration? How do these sounds affect you?
16. What sounds are repeated? If there are rhymes, what is their effect? Do they seem forced or natural? Is there a rhyme scheme? Do the rhymes contribute to the poem's meaning?
17. Do the lines have a regular meter? What is the predominant meter? Are there significant variations? Does the rhythm seem appropriate for the tone of the poem?
18. Does the poem's form — its overall structure — follow an established pattern? Do you think the form is a suitable vehicle for the poem's meaning and effects?
19. Is the language of the poem intense and concentrated? Do you think it warrants more than one or two close readings?
20. Did you enjoy the poem? What, specifically, pleased or displeased you about what was expressed and how it was expressed?
21. Is there a particular critical approach that seems especially appropriate for this poem? (See the discussion of "Critical Strategies for Reading" beginning on page 1995.)
22. How might biographical information about the author help to determine the central concerns of the poem?
23. How might historical information about the poem provide a useful context for interpretation?
24. To what extent do your own experiences, values, beliefs, and assumptions inform your interpretation?
25. What kinds of evidence from the poem are you focusing on to support your interpretation? Does your interpretation leave out any important elements that might undercut or qualify your interpretation?
26. Given that there are a variety of ways to interpret the poem, which one seems the most useful to you?

PAULA GUNN ALLEN (b. 1939)

Pocahontas to Her English Husband,
John Rolfe°

1988

In a way, then, Pocahontas was a kind of traitor to her people. . . . Perhaps I am being a little too hard on her. The crucial point, it seems to me, is to remember that Pocahontas was a hostage. Would she have converted freely to Christianity if she had not been in captivity? There is no easy answer to this question other than to note that once she was free to do what she wanted, she avoided her own people like the plague. . . .

Pocahontas was a white dream — a dream of cultural superiority.

–Charles Larson, American Indian Fiction

Had I not cradled you in my arms
oh beloved perfidious one,
you would have died.
And how many times did I pluck you
from certain death in the wilderness —   5
my world through which you stumbled
as though blind?
Had I not set you tasks
your masters far across the sea
would have abandoned you —   10
did abandon you, as many times
they left you
to reap the harvest of their lies.
Still you survived, oh my fair husband,
and brought them gold   15
wrung from a harvest I taught you
to plant. Tobacco.
It is not without irony that by this crop
your descendants die, for other
powers than you know   20
take part in this and all things.
And indeed I did rescue you —
not once but a thousand thousand times
and in my arms you slept, a foolish child,
and under my protecting gaze you played,   25
chattering nonsense about a God
you had not wit to name. I'm sure

Pocahontas . . . Rolfe: In 1614 Pocahontas (1595?–1617), a princess of the Wampanoag Indians, married Rolfe (1585–1622), an English colonist and founder of Jamestown, Virginia. Legend has it that she saved the life of Captain John Smith (1580–1631), another English colonist, by holding his head in her arms so that Wampanoag warriors could not club him to death.

you wondered at my silence, saying I was
a simple wanton, a savage maid,
dusky daughter of heathen sires   30
who cartwheeled naked through the muddy towns
who would learn the ways of grace only
by your firm guidance, through
your husbandly rule:
no doubt, no doubt.   35
I spoke little, you said.
And you listened less,
but played with your gaudy dreams
and sent ponderous missives to the throne
striving thereby to curry favor   40
with your king.
I saw you well. I
understood your ploys and still
protected you, going so far as to die
in your keeping — a wasting,   45
putrefying Christian death° — and you,
deceiver, whiteman, father of my son,
survived, reaping wealth greater
than any you had ever dreamed
from what I taught you and   50
from the wasting of my bones.

46 *death:* Pochahontas is supposed to have died from tuberculosis.

MAYA ANGELOU (b. 1928)
My Arkansas   1978

There is a deep brooding
in Arkansas.
Old crimes like moss pend
from poplar trees.
The sullen earth   5
is much too
red for comfort.

Sunrise seems to hesitate
and in that second
lose its
incandescent aim, and   10
dusk no more shadows
than the noon.
The past is brighter yet.

Old hates and
ante-bellum° lace, are rent   15
but not discarded.
Today is yet to come
in Arkansas.
It writhes. It writhes in awful   20
waves of brooding.

16 *ante-bellum:* Before the Civil War.

ANONYMOUS (traditional Scottish ballad)
Bonny Barbara Allan

It was in and about the Martinmas° time,
　　When the green leaves were afalling,
That Sir John Graeme, in the West Country,
　　Fell in love with Barbara Allan.

He sent his men down through the town,   5
　　To the place where she was dwelling:
"O haste and come to my master dear,
　　Gin° ye be Barbara Allan."   *if*

O hooly,° hooly rose she up,   *slowly*
　　To the place where he was lying,   10
And when she drew the curtain by:
　　"Young man, I think you're dying."

"O it's I'm sick, and very, very sick,
　　And 'tis a' for Barbara Allan." —
"O the better for me ye's never be,   15
　　Tho your heart's blood were aspilling.

"O dinna ye mind,° young man," said she,   *don't you remember*
　　"When ye was in the tavern adrinking,
That ye made the health° gae round and round,   *toasts*
　　And slighted Barbara Allan?"   20

He turned his face unto the wall,
　　And death was with him dealing:
"Adieu, adieu, my dear friends all,
　　And be kind to Barbara Allan."

And slowly, slowly raise she up,   25
　　And slowly, slowly left him,
And sighing said she could not stay,
　　Since death of life had reft him.

1 *Martinmas:* St. Martin's Day, November 11.

She had not gane a mile but twa,
    When she heard the dead-bell ringing,   30
And every jow° that the dead-bell geid,   *stroke*
    It cried, "Woe to Barbara Allan!"

"O mother, mother, make my bed!
    O make it saft and narrow!
Since my love died for me today,   35
    I'll die for him tomorrow."

ANONYMOUS

Lord Randal   1500s

"Oh, where have you been, Lord Randal, my son?
Oh, where have you been, my handsome young man?"
"Oh, I've been to the wildwood; mother, make my bed soon,
I'm weary of hunting and I fain° would lie down."   *gladly*

"And whom did you meet there, Lord Randal, my son?   5
And whom did you meet there, my handsome young man?"
"Oh, I met with my true love; mother, make my bed soon,
I'm weary of hunting and I fain would lie down."

"What got you for supper, Lord Randal, my son?
What got you for supper, my handsome young man?"   10
"I got eels boiled in broth; mother, make my bed soon,
I'm weary of hunting and I fain would lie down."

"And who got your leavings, Lord Randal, my son?
And who got your leavings, my handsome young man?"
"I gave them to my dogs; mother, make my bed soon,   15
I'm weary of hunting and I fain would lie down."

"And what did your dogs do, Lord Randal, my son?
And what did your dogs do, my handsome young man?"
"Oh, they stretched out and died; mother, make my bed soon,
I'm weary of hunting and I fain would lie down."   20

"Oh, I fear you are poisoned, Lord Randal, my son,
Oh, I fear you are poisoned, my handsome young man."
"Oh, yes, I am poisoned; mother, make my bed soon,
For I'm sick at my heart and I fain would lie down."

"What will you leave your mother, Lord Randal, my son?   25
What will you leave your mother, my handsome young man?"
"My house and my lands; mother, make my bed soon,
For I'm sick at my heart and I fain would lie down."

"What will you leave your sister, Lord Randal, my son?
What will you leave your sister, my handsome young man?"   30
"My gold and my silver; mother, make my bed soon,
For I'm sick at my heart and I fain would lie down."

"What will you leave your brother, Lord Randal, my son?
What will you leave your brother, my handsome young man?"
"My horse and my saddle; mother, make my bed soon,   35
For I'm sick at my heart and I fain would lie down."

"What will you leave your true-love, Lord Randal, my son?
What will you leave your true-love, my handsome young man?"
"A halter to hang her; mother, make my bed soon,
For I'm sick at my heart and I want to lie down."   40

ANONYMOUS

Frankie and Johnny   date unknown

Frankie and Johnny were lovers,
    Lordy, how they could love,
Swore to be true to each other,
    True as the stars up above,
        He was her man, but he done her wrong.   5

Frankie went down to the corner,
    To buy her a bucket of beer,
Frankie says "Mister Bartender,
    Has my lovin' Johnny been here?
        He is my man, but he's doing me wrong."   10

"I don't want to cause you no trouble
    Don't want to tell you no lie,
I saw your Johnny half-an-hour ago
    Making love to Nelly Bly.
        He is your man, but he's doing you wrong."   15

Frankie went down to the hotel
    Looked over the transom so high,
There she saw her lovin' Johnny
    Making love to Nelly Bly.
        He was her man; he was doing her wrong.   20

Frankie threw back her kimono,
    Pulled out her big forty-four;
Rooty-toot-toot: three times she shot
    Right through that hotel door,
        She shot her man, who was doing her wrong.   25

"Roll me over gently,
    Roll me over slow,
Roll me over on my right side,
    'Cause these bullets hurt me so,
        I was your man, but I done you wrong."   30

Bring all your rubber-tired hearses
    Bring all your rubber-tired hacks,
They're carrying poor Johnny to the burying ground
    And they ain't gonna bring him back,
        He was her man, but he done her wrong.   35

Frankie says to the sheriff,
    "What are they going to do?"
The sheriff he said to Frankie,
    "It's the 'lectric chair for you.
        He was your man, and he done you wrong."   40

"Put me in that dungeon,
    Put me in that cell,
Put me where the northeast wind
    Blows from the southeast corner of hell,
        I shot my man, 'cause he done me wrong."   45

ANONYMOUS
Scarborough Fair
date uknown

Where are you going? To Scarborough Fair?
Parsley, sage, rosemary, and thyme,
Remember me to a bonny lass there,
For once she was a true lover of mine.

Tell her to make me a cambric shirt,   5
Parsley, sage, rosemary, and thyme,
Without any needle or thread work'd in it,
And she shall be a true lover of mine.

Tell her to wash it in yonder well,
Parsley, sage, rosemary, and thyme,   10
Where water ne'er sprung nor a drop of rain fell,
And she shall be a true lover of mine.

Tell her to plough me an acre of land,
Parsley, sage, rosemary, and thyme,
Between the sea and the salt sea strand,   15
And she shall be a true lover of mine.

Tell her to plough it with one ram's horn,
Parsley, sage, rosemary, and thyme,
And sow it all over with one peppercorn,
And she shall be a true lover of mine.   20

Tell her to reap it with a sickle of leather,
Parsley, sage, rosemary, and thyme,

And tie it all up with a tom tit's feather,
And she shall be a true lover of mine.

Tell her to gather it all in a sack,   25
Parsley, sage, rosemary, and thyme,
And carry it home on a butterfly's back,
And then she shall be a true lover of mine.

ANONYMOUS
Scottsboro°   1936°

Paper come out — done strewed de news
Seven po' chillun moan deat' house blues,
Seven po' chillun moanin' deat' house blues.
Seven nappy heads wit' big shiny eye
All boun' in jail and framed to die,   5
All boun' in jail and framed to die.

Messin' white woman — snake lyin' tale
Hang and burn and jail wit' no bail.
Dat hang and burn and jail wit' no bail.
Worse ol' crime in white folks' lan'   10
Black skin coverin' po' workin' man,
Black skin coverin' po' workin' man.

Judge and jury — all in de stan'
Lawd, biggety name for same lynchin' ban'
Lawd, biggety name for same lynchin' ban'.   15
White folks and nigger in great co't house
Like cat down cellar wit' nohole mouse.
Like cat down cellar wit' nohole mouse.

Scottsboro: This blues song refers to the 1931 arrest of nine black youths in Scottsboro, Alabama, who were charged with raping two white women. All nine were acquitted after several trials, but a few of them had already been sentenced to death when this song was written.

ANONYMOUS (traditional Scottish ballad)
The Twa Corbies°   date unknown

As I was walking all alane,
I heard twa corbies making a mane;°   *lament*

The Twa Corbies: The two ravens.

The tane° unto the t' other say,   *one*
"Where sall we gang° and dine to-day?"   *shall we go*

"In behint yon auld fail dyke,°   *old turf wall*   5
I wot° there lies a new-slain knight;   *know*
And naebody kens that he lies there,
But his hawk, his hound, and lady fair.

"His hound is to the hunting gane,
His hawk, to fetch the wild-fowl hame,   10
His lady's ta'en another mate,
So we may mak our dinner sweet.

"Ye'll sit on his white hause-bane,°   *neck bone*
And I'll pike out his bonny blue een.°   *eyes*
Wi' ae° lock o' his gowden° hair   *with one; golden*   15
We'll theek° our nest when it grows bare.   *thatch*

"Mony a one for him makes mane,
But nane sall ken whare he is gane;
O'er his white banes, when they are bare,
The wind sall blaw for evermair."   20

JOHN ASHBERY (b. 1927)
Paradoxes and Oxymorons   1981

This poem is concerned with language on a very plain level.
Look at it talking to you. You look out a window
Or pretend to fidget. You have it but you don't have it.
You miss it, it misses you. You miss each other.

The poem is sad because it wants to be yours, and cannot.   5
What's a plain level? It is that and other things,
Bringing a system of them into play. Play?
Well, actually, yes, but I consider play to be

A deeper outside thing, a dreamed role-pattern,
As in the division of grace these long August days   10
Without proof. Open-ended. And before you know
It gets lost in the steam and chatter of typewriters.

It has been played once more. I think you exist only
To tease me into doing it, on your level, and then you aren't there
Or have adopted a different attitude. And the poem   15
Has set me softly down beside you. The poem is you.

W. H. AUDEN (1907–1973)
As I Walked Out One Evening 1940

As I walked out one evening,
    Walking down Bristol Street,
The crowds upon the pavement
    Were fields of harvest wheat.

And down by the brimming river 5
    I heard a lover sing
Under an arch of the railway:
    "Love has no ending.

"I'll love you, dear, I'll love you
    Till China and Africa meet, 10
And the river jumps over the mountain
    And the salmon sing in the street,

"I'll love you till the ocean
    Is folded and hung up to dry
And the seven stars go squawking 15
    Like geese about the sky.

"The years shall run like rabbits,
    For in my arms I hold
The Flower of the Ages,
    And the first love of the world." 20

But all the clocks in the city
    Began to whirr and chime:
"O let not Time deceive you,
    You cannot conquer Time.

"In the burrows of the Nightmare 25
    Where Justice naked is,
Time watches from the shadow
    And coughs when you would kiss.

"In headaches and in worry
    Vaguely life leaks away, 30
And Time will have his fancy
    Tomorrow or today.

"Into many a green valley
    Drifts the appalling snow;
Time breaks the threaded dances 35
    And the diver's brilliant bow.

"O plunge your hands in water,
    Plunge them in up to the wrist;
Stare, stare in the basin
    And wonder what you've missed. 40

"The glacier knocks in the cupboard,
    The desert sighs in the bed,
And the crack in the teacup opens
    A lane to the land of the dead.

"Where the beggars raffle the banknotes   45
    And the Giant is enchanting to Jack,
And the Lily-white Boy is a Roarer,
    And Jill goes down on her back.

"O look, look in the mirror,
    O look in your distress;   50
Life remains a blessing
    Although you cannot bless.

"O stand, stand at the window
    As the tears scald and start;
You shall love your crooked neighbor   55
    With your crooked heart."

It was late, late in the evening,
    The lovers they were gone;
The clocks had ceased their chiming,
    And the deep river ran on.   60

W. H. AUDEN (1907–1973)
Lay Your Sleeping Head, My Love   1940

Lay your sleeping head, my love,
Human on my faithless arm;
Time and fevers burn away
Individual beauty from

Thoughtful children, and the grave   5
Proves the child ephemeral:
But in my arms till break of day
Let the living creature lie,
Mortal, guilty, but to me
The entirely beautiful.   10

Soul and body have no bounds:
To lovers as they lie upon
Her tolerant enchanted slope
In their ordinary swoon,
Grave the vision Venus sends   15
Of supernatural sympathy,
Universal love and hope;
While an abstract insight wakes
Among the glaciers and the rocks
The hermit's sensual ecstasy.   20

Certainty, fidelity
On the stroke of midnight pass
Like vibrations of a bell,
And fashionable madmen raise
Their pedantic boring cry: 25
Every farthing of the cost,
All the dreaded cards foretell,
Shall be paid, but from this night
Not a whisper, not a thought,
Not a kiss nor look be lost.   30

Beauty, midnight, vision dies:
Let the winds of dawn that blow
Softly round your dreaming head
Such a day of sweetness show
Eye and knocking heart may bless,   35
Find the mortal world enough;
Noons of dryness see you fed
By the involuntary powers,
Nights of insult let you pass
Watched by every human love.   40

W. H. AUDEN (1907–1973)
Musée des Beaux Arts°   1938

About suffering they were never wrong,
The Old Masters: how well they understood
Its human position; how it takes place
While someone else is eating or opening a window or just walking dully
    along;
How, when the aged are reverently, passionately waiting   5
For the miraculous birth, there always must be
Children who did not specially want it to happen, skating
On a pond at the edge of the wood:
They never forgot
That even the dreadful martyrdom must run its course   10
Anyhow in a corner, some untidy spot
Where the dogs go on with their doggy life and the torturer's horse
Scratches its innocent behind on a tree.

In Brueghel's *Icarus,*° for instance: how everything turns away
Quite leisurely from the disaster; the plowman may   15
Have heard the splash, the forsaken cry,

Musée des Beaux Arts: Museum of Fine Arts, in Brussels.   14 *Brueghel's* Icarus: *Landscape with the Fall of Icarus,* painting by Pieter Brueghel the Elder (c. 1525–1569), in the Brussels Museum.

But for him it was not an important failure; the sun shone
As it had to on the white legs disappearing into the green
Water; and the expensive delicate ship that must have seen
Something amazing, a boy falling out of the sky,   20
Had somewhere to get to and sailed calmly on.

W. H. AUDEN (1907–1973)
The Unknown Citizen   1940

(To JS/07/M/378
This Marble Monument
Is Erected by the State)

He was found by the Bureau of Statistics to be
One against whom there was no official complaint,
And all the reports on his conduct agree
That, in the modern sense of an old-fashioned word, he was a saint,
For in everything he did he served the Greater Community.   5
Except for the War till the day he retired
He worked in a factory and never got fired,
But satisfied his employers, Fudge Motors Inc.
Yet he wasn't a scab or odd in his views,
For his Union reports that he paid his dues,   10
(Our report on his Union shows it was sound)
And our Social Psychology workers found
That he was popular with his mates and liked a drink.
The Press are convinced that he bought a paper every day
And that his reactions to advertisements were normal in every way.   15
Policies taken out in his name prove that he was fully insured,
And his Health-card shows he was once in hospital but left it cured.
Both Producers Research and High-Grade Living declare
He was fully sensible to the advantages of the Installment Plan
And had everything necessary to the Modern Man,   20
A phonograph, radio, a car and a frigidaire.
Our researchers into Public Opinion are content
That he held the proper opinions for the time of year;
When there was peace, he was for peace; when there was war, he went.
He was married and added five children to the population,   25
Which our Eugenist says was the right number for a parent of his
        generation,
And our teachers report that he never interfered with their education.
Was he free? Was he happy? The question is absurd:
Had anything been wrong, we should certainly have heard.

APHRA BEHN (1640–1689)
Love Armed

1665

Love in Fantastic Triumph sat,
Whilst Bleeding Hearts around him flowed,
For whom Fresh pains he did Create,
And strange Tyrannic power he showed;
From thy Bright Eyes he took his fire,   5
Which round about, in sport he hurled;
But 'twas from mine he took desire,
Enough to undo the Amorous World

From me he took his sighs and tears,
From thee his Pride and Cruelty;   10
From me his Languishments and Fears,
And every Killing Dart from thee;
Thus thou and I, the God° have armed,   *Cupid, god of love*
And set him up a Deity;
But my poor Heart alone is harmed,   15
Whilst thine the Victor is, and free.

JOHN BERRYMAN (1914–1972)
Dream Song 14

1964

Life, friends, is boring. We must not say so.
After all, the sky flashes, the great sea yearns,
we ourselves flash and yearn,
and moreover my mother told me as a boy
(repeatedly) "Ever to confess you're bored   5
means you have no

Inner Resources." I conclude now I have no
inner resources, because I am heavy bored.
Peoples bore me,
literature bores me, especially great literature,   10
Henry bores me, with his plights & gripes
as bad as achilles,°

Who loves people and valiant art, which bores me.
And the tranquil hills, & gin, look like a drag
and somehow a dog   15
has taken itself & its tail considerably away
into mountains or sea or sky, leaving
behind: me, wag.

12 *Achilles:* Greek hero who fought in the Trojan War.

MEI-MEI BERSSENBRUGGE (b. 1947)

Jealousy

1989

Attention was commanded through a simple, unadorned,
    unexplained, often decentered presence,
up to now, a margin of empty space like water, its surface
    contracting, then melting
along buried pipelines, where gulls gather in euphoric buoyancy.   5
    Now,
the growth of size is vital, the significance of contraction by a moat,
    a flowerbed, or
a fenced path around the reservoir, its ability to induce the mind's
    growing experience of the breadth   10
and depth of physical association, which turns out to be both vital
    and insufficient, because
nature never provides a border for us, of infinite elements irregularly
    but flexibly integrated,
like the rhythm between fatigue and relief of accommodation, or   15
    like a large apartment. Now,
the construction is not the structure of your making love to me.
    The size of your body on mine
does not equal your weight or buoyancy, like fireworks on a tele-
    vision screen, or the way   20
an absent double expresses inaccuracy between what exists and does
    not exist in the room,
of particular shape, volume, etc., minute areas and inferred lines we
    are talking about.
You have made a vow to a woman not to sleep with me. For me,   25
    it seemed enough
that love was a spiritual exercise in physical form and what was
    seen is what it was,
looking down from the twelflth floor, our arms resting on pillows
    on the windowsill. It is midnight.   30
Fireworks reflected in the reservoir burst simultaneously on the
    south and the north shores.
so we keep turning our heads quickly for both of the starry spheres,
instead of a tangible, and an intangible event that does not reflect.
    Certain   35
definite brightness contains spaciousness. A starry night, like a fully
    reflecting surface,
claims no particular status in space, or being of its own.

ELIZABETH BISHOP (1911–1979)

Manners

1965

for a Child of 1918

My grandfather said to me
as we sat on the wagon seat,
"Be sure to remember to always
speak to everyone you meet."

We met a stranger on foot.   5
My grandfather's whip tapped his hat.
"Good day, sir. Good day. A fine day."
And I said it and bowed where I sat.

Then we overtook a boy we knew
with his big pet crow on his shoulder.   10
"Always offer everyone a ride;
don't forget that when you get older,"

my grandfather said. So Willy
climbed up with us, but the crow
gave a "Caw!" and flew off. I was worried.   15
How would he know where to go?

But he flew a little way at a time
from fence post to fence post, ahead;
and when Willy whistled he answered.
"A fine bird," my grandfather said,   20

"and he's well brought up. See, he answers
nicely when he's spoken to.
Man or beast, that's good manners.
Be sure that you both always do."

When automobiles went by,   25
the dust hid the people's faces,
but we shouted "Good day! Good day!
Fine day!" at the top of our voices.

When we came to Hustler Hill,
he said that the mare was tired,   30
so we all got down and walked,
as our good manners required.

ELIZABETH BISHOP (1911–1979)
The Shampoo 1955

The still explosions on the rocks,
the lichens, grow
by spreading, gray, concentric shocks.
They have arranged
to meet the rings around the moon, although   5
within our memories they have not changed.

And since the heavens will attend
as long on us,
you've been, dear friend,
precipitate and pragmatical;   10
and look what happens. For Time is
nothing if not amenable.

The shooting stars in your black hair
in bright formation
are flocking where,   15
so straight, so soon?
— Come, let me wash it in this big tin basin,
battered and shiny like the moon.

WILLIAM BLAKE (1757–1827)
The Garden of Love 1794

I went to the Garden of Love,
And saw what I never had seen:
A Chapel was built in the midst,
Where I used to play on the green.

And the gates of this Chapel were shut,   5
And "Thou shalt not" writ over the door;
So I turned to the Garden of Love
That so many sweet flowers bore;

And I saw it was filled with graves,
And tomb-stones where flowers should be;   10
And Priests in black gowns were walking their rounds,
And binding with briars my joys and desires.

WILLIAM BLAKE (1757–1827)
The Little Black Boy
1789

Illuminated printing: Blake etched his poems and designs in relief, with acid on copper. Each printed page was then colored by hand. The design and the text work together to express Blake's vision.

WILLIAM BLAKE (1757–1827)
A Poison Tree
1794

I was angry with my friend:
I told my wrath, my wrath did end.
I was angry with my foe:
I told it not, my wrath did grow.

And I water'd it in fears,
Night & morning with my tears;
And I sunnéd it with smiles,
And with soft deceitful wiles.

5

And it grew both day and night,
Till it bore an apple bright.　　　　　　　　　　　　　　　10
And my foe beheld it shine,
And he knew that it was mine,

And into my garden stole,
When the night had veild the pole;
In the morning glad I see　　　　　　　　　　　　　　　15
My foe outstretched beneath the tree.

ROBERT BLY (b. 1926)
Waking from Sleep　　　　　　　　　　　　　　　1962

Inside the veins there are navies setting forth,
Tiny explosions at the water lines,
And seagulls weaving in the wind of the salty blood.

It is the morning. The country has slept the whole winter.
Window seats were covered with fur skins, the yard was full　　　5
Of stiff dogs, and hands that clumsily held heavy books.

Now we wake, and rise from bed, and eat breakfast! —
Shouts rise from the harbor of the blood,
Mist, and masts rising, the knock of wooden tackle in the sunlight.

Now we sing, and do tiny dances on the kitchen floor.　　　　　10
Our whole body is like a harbor at dawn;
We know that our master has left us for the day.

LOUISE BOGAN (1897–1970)
Single Sonnet　　　　　　　　　　　　　　　1930

Now, you great stanza, you heroic mould,
Bend to my will, for I must give you love:
The weight in the heart that breathes, but cannot move,
Which to endure flesh only makes so bold.

Take up, take up, as it were lead or gold　　　　　　　　　　5
The burden; test the dreadful mass thereof.
No stone, slate, metal under or above
Earth, is so ponderous, so dull, so cold.

Too long as ocean bed bears up the ocean,
As earth's core bears the earth, have I borne this;　　　　　　10

Too long have lovers, bending for their kiss,
Felt bitter force cohering without motion.

Staunch meter, great song, it is yours, at length,
To prove how stronger you are than my strength.

ANNE BRADSTREET (c. 1612–1672)
Before the Birth of One of Her Children   1678

All things within this fading world hath end,
Adversity doth still our joys attend;
No ties so strong, no friends so dear and sweet,
But with death's parting blow is sure to meet.
The sentence past is most irrevocable,   5
A common thing, yet oh, inevitable.
How soon, my Dear, death may my steps attend,
How soon't may be thy lot to lose thy friend,
We both are ignorant, yet love bids me
These farewell lines to recommend to thee,   10
That when that knot's untied that made us one,
I may seem thine, who in effect am none.
And if I see not half my days that's due,
What nature would, God grant to yours and you;
The many faults that well you know I have   15
Let be interred in my oblivious grave;
If any worth or virtue were in me,
Let that live freshly in thy memory
And when thou feel'st no grief, as I no harms,
Yet love thy dead, who long lay in thine arms,   20
And when thy loss shall be repaid with gains
Look to my little babes, my dear remains.
And if thou love thyself, or loved'st me,
These O protected from stepdame's° injury.   stepmother's
And if chance to thine eyes shall bring this verse,   25
With some sad sighs honor my absent hearse;
And kiss this paper for thy love's dear sake,
Who with salt tears this last farewell did take.

RUPERT BROOKE (1887–1915)

The Soldier   1915

If I should die, think only this of me:
    That there's some corner of a foreign field
That is for ever England. There shall be
    In that rich earth a richer dust concealed;
A dust whom England bore, shaped, made aware,   5
    Gave, once, her flowers to love, her ways to roam,
A body of England's, breathing English air,
    Washed by the rivers, blest by suns of home.

And think, this heart, all evil shed away,
    A pulse in the eternal mind, no less   10
        Gives somewhere back the thoughts by England given;
Her sights and sounds; dreams happy as her day;
    And laughter, learnt of friends; and gentleness,
        In hearts at peace, under an English heaven.

GWENDOLYN BROOKS (b. 1917)

The Bean Eaters   1959

They eat beans mostly, this old yellow pair.
Dinner is a casual affair.
Plain chipware on a plain and creaking wood,
Tin flatware.

Two who are Mostly Good.   5
Two who have lived their day,
But keep on putting on their clothes
And putting things away.

And remembering . . .
Remembering, with twinklings and twinges,   10
As they lean over the beans in their rented back room
    that is full of beads and receipts and dolls and cloths,
    tobacco crumbs, vases and fringes.

GWENDOLYN BROOKS (b. 1917)

The Mother   1945

Abortions will not let you forget.
You remember the children you got that you did not get,
The damp small pulps with a little or with no hair,
The singers and workers that never handled the air.
You will never neglect or beat   5
Them, or silence or buy with a sweet.
You will never wind up the sucking-thumb
Or scuttle off ghosts that come.
You will never leave them, controlling your luscious sigh,
Return for a snack of them, with gobbling mother-eye.   10

I have heard in the voices of the wind the voices of my dim
        killed children.
I have contracted. I have eased
My dim dears at the breasts they could never suck.
I have said, Sweets, if I sinned, if I seized
Your luck   15
And your lives from your unfinished reach,
If I stole your births and your names,
Your straight baby tears and your games,
Your stilted or lovely loves, your tumults, your marriages, aches,
        and your deaths,
If I poisoned the beginnings of your breaths,   20
Believe' that even in my deliberateness I was not deliberate.
Though why should I whine,
Whine that the crime was other than mine? —
Since anyhow you are dead.
Or rather, or instead,   25
You were never made.

But that too, I am afraid,
Is faulty: oh, what shall I say, how is the truth to be said?
You were born, you had body, you died.
It is just that you never giggled or planned or cried.   30

Believe me, I loved you all.
Believe me, I knew you, though faintly, and I loved, I loved you
All.

ROBERT BROWNING (1812–1889)
Meeting at Night   1845

The gray sea and the long black land;
And the yellow half-moon large and low;
And the startled little waves that leap
In fiery ringlets from their sleep,
As I gain the cove with pushing prow,   5
And quench its speed i' the slushy sand.

Then a mile of warm sea-scented beach;
Three fields to cross till a farm appears;
A tap at the pane, the quick sharp scratch
And blue spurt of a lighted match,   10
And a voice less loud, through its joys and fears,
Than the two hearts beating each to each!

ROBERT BROWNING (1812–1889)
Parting at Morning   1845

Round the cape of a sudden came the sea,
And the sun looked over the mountain's rim:
And straight was a path of gold for him,
And the need of a world of men for me.

ROBERT BURNS (1759–1796)
John Anderson My Jo   1790

John Anderson my jo,° John,   *dear*
    When we were first acquent,
Your locks were like the raven,
    Your bonnie brow was brent;°   *smooth*
But now your brow is beld, John,   5
    Your locks are like the snaw,
But blessings on your frosty pow,°   *head*
    John Anderson my jo!

John Anderson my jo, John,
    We clamb the hill thegither,   10
And monie a cantie° day, John   *happy*
    We've had wi' ane anither:
Now we maun° totter down, John,   *must*

And hand in hand we'll go,
And sleep thegither at the foot,   15
    John Anderson my jo!

GEORGE GORDON, LORD BYRON (1788–1824)

She Walks in Beauty   1814

FROM HEBREW MELODIES

I
She walks in Beauty, like the night
    Of cloudless climes and starry skies;
And all that's best of dark and bright
    Meet in her aspect and her eyes:
Thus mellowed to that tender light   5
    Which Heaven to gaudy day denies.

II
One shade the more, one ray the less,
    Had half impaired the nameless grace
Which waves in every raven tress,
    Or softly lightens o'er her face;   10
Where thoughts serenely sweet express,
    How pure, how dear their dwelling-place.

III
And on that cheek, and o'er that brow,
    So soft, so calm, yet eloquent,
The smiles that win, the tints that glow,   15
    But tell of days in goodness spent,
A mind at peace with all below,
    A heart whose love is innocent!

THOMAS CAMPION (1567–1620)

There is a garden in her face   1617

There is a garden in her face
Where roses and white lilies grow;
    A heav'nly paradise is that place
Wherein all pleasant fruits do flow.
    There cherries grow which none may buy   5
    Till "Cherry-ripe"° themselves do cry.

6 *"Cherry-ripe"*: Street cry of London fruit peddlers.

Those cherries fairly do enclose
Of orient pearl a double row,
    Which when her lovely laughter shows,
They look like rose-buds filled with snow;   10
    Yet them nor° peer nor prince can buy,   *neither*
    Till "Cherry-ripe" themselves do cry.

    Her eyes like angels watch them still;
Her brows like bended bows do stand,
    Threat'ning with piercing frowns to kill   15
All that attempt, with eye or hand
    Those sacred cherries to come nigh
    Till "Cherry-ripe" themselves do cry.

LUCILLE CLIFTON (b. 1936)
For de Lawd   1969

people say they have a hard time
understanding how I
go on about my business
playing my Ray Charles
hollering at the kids —   5
seem like my Afro
cut off in some old image
would show I got a long memory
and I come from a line
of black and going on women   10
who got used to making it through murdered sons
and who grief kept on pushing
who fried chicken
ironed
swept off the back steps   15
who grief kept
for their still alive sons
for their sons coming
for their sons gone
just pushing   20
in the inner city
or
like we call it
home
we think a lot about uptown   25
and the silent nights
and the houses straight as
dead men

and the pastel lights
and we hang on to our no place   30
happy to be alive
and in the inner city
or
like we call it
home   35

SAMUEL TAYLOR COLERIDGE (1772–1834)
Kubla Khan: or, a Vision in a Dream°   1798

In Xanadu did Kubla Khan°
   A stately pleasure-dome decree:
Where Alph, the sacred river, ran
Through caverns measureless to man
   Down to a sunless sea.   5
So twice five miles of fertile ground
With walls and towers were girdled round:
And here were gardens bright with sinuous rills
Where blossomed many an incense-bearing tree;
And there were forests ancient as the hills,   10
Enfolding sunny spots of greenery.

But oh! that deep romantic chasm which slanted
Down the green hill athwart a cedarn cover!°
A savage place! as holy and enchanted
As e'er beneath a waning moon was haunted   15
By woman wailing for her demon-lover!
And from this chasm, with ceaseless turmoil seething,
As if this earth in fast thick pants were breathing,
A mighty fountain momently was forced,
Amid whose swift half-intermitted burst   20
Huge fragments vaulted like rebounding hail,
Or chaffy grain beneath the thresher's flail:
And 'mid these dancing rocks at once and ever
It flung up momently the sacred river.
Five miles meandering with a mazy motion   25
Through wood and dale the sacred river ran,
Then reached the caverns measureless to man,
And sank in tumult to a lifeless ocean:
And 'mid this tumult Kubla heard from far
Ancestral voices prophesying war!   30

Vision in a Dream: This poem came to Coleridge in an opium-induced dream, but he was interrupted
while writing it down by a visitor. He was later unable to remember the rest of the poem.   1 *Kubla
Khan:* The historical Kublai Khan (1216–1294, grandson of Genghis Khan) was the founder of the
Mongol dynasty in China.   13 *athwart . . . cover:* Spanning a grove of cedar trees.

The shadow of the dome of pleasure
Floated midway on the waves;
Where was heard the mingled measure
From the fountain and the caves.
It was a miracle of rare device,   35
A sunny pleasure-dome with caves of ice!

    A damsel with a dulcimer
    In a vision once I saw:
    It was an Abyssinian maid,
    And on her dulcimer she played,   40
    Singing of Mount Abora.
    Could I revive within me
    Her symphony and song,
    To such a deep delight 'twould win me,
That with music loud and long,   45
I would build that dome in air,
That sunny dome! those caves of ice!
And all who heard should see them there,
And all should cry, Beware! Beware!
His flashing eyes, his floating hair!   50
Weave a circle round him thrice,
And close your eyes with holy dread,
For he on honey-dew hath fed,
And drunk the milk of Paradise.

COUNTEE CULLEN (1903–1946)
For a Lady I Know   1925

She even thinks that up in heaven
Her class lies late and snores,
While poor black cherubs rise at seven
To do celestial chores.

COUNTEE CULLEN (1903–1946)
Saturday's Child°   1925

Some are teethed on a silver spoon,
With the stars strung for a rattle;
I cut my teeth as the black raccoon ——
For implements of battle.

Saturday's Child: Reference to the nursery rhyme: Monday's child is fair of face . . . / Saturday's child
must work hard for a living. . . .

Some are swaddled in silk and down,   5
And heralded by a star;
They swathed my limbs in a sackcloth gown
On a night that was black as tar.

For some, godfather and goddame
The opulent fairies be;   10
Dame Poverty gave me my name,
And Pain godfathered me.

For I was born on Saturday ———
"Bad time for planting a seed,"
Was all my father had to say,   15
And, "One mouth more to feed."

Death cut the strings that gave me life,
And handed me to Sorrow,
The only kind of middle wife
My folks could beg or borrow.   20

e. e. cummings (1894–1962)
anyone lived in a pretty how town   1940

anyone lived in a pretty how town
(with up so floating many bells down)
spring summer autumn winter
he sang his didn't he danced his did.

Women and men (both little and small)   5
cared for anyone not at all
they sowed their isn't they reaped their same
sun moon stars rain

children guessed (but only a few
and down they forgot as up they grew   10
autumn winter spring summer)
that noone loved him more by more

when by now and tree by leaf
she laughed his joy she cried his grief
bird by snow and stir by still   15
anyone's any was all to her

someones married their everyones
laughed their cryings and did their dance
(sleep wake hope and then) they
said their nevers they slept their dream   20

stars rain sun moon
(and only the snow can begin to explain

how children are apt to forget to remember
with up so floating many bells down)

one day anyone died i guess   25
(and noone stooped to kiss his face)
busy folk buried them side by side
little by little and was by was

all by all and deep by deep
and more by more they dream their sleep   30
noone and anyone earth by april
wish by spirit and if by yes.

Women and men (both dong and ding)
summer autumn winter spring
reaped their sowing and went their came   35
sun moon stars rain

e. e. cummings (1894–1962)
Buffalo Bill 's°   1923

Buffalo Bill 's
defunct
          who used to
          ride a watersmooth-silver
                                        stallion   5
and break onetwothreefourfive pigeonsjustlikethat
                                        Jesus

he was a handsome man
                    and what i want to know is
how do you like your blueeyed boy   10
Mister Death

Buffalo Bill: William Frederick Cody (1846–1917). An American frontier scout and Indian killer turned
international circus showman with his Wild West show, which employed Sitting Bull and Annie
Oakley.

e. e. cummings (1894–1962)
since feeling is first   1926

since feeling is first
who pays any attention
to the syntax of things ———— sin taxes – tax on sin – alcohol, tobacco
will never wholly kiss you;

wholly to be a fool
while Spring is in the world   5

my blood approves,
and kisses are a better fate
than wisdom
lady i swear by all flowers. Don't cry   10
— the best gesture of my brain is less than
your eyelids' flutter which says

we are for each other: then
laugh, leaning back in my arms
for life's not a paragraph   15

And death i think is no parenthesis

JOHN DONNE (1572–1631)
The Apparition   c. 1600

When by thy scorn, O murderess, I am dead,
      And that thou thinkst thee free
From all solicitation from me,
Then shall my ghost come to thy bed,
And thee, feigned vestal, in worse arms shall see;   5
Then thy sick taper° will begin to wink,   *candle*
And he, whose thou art then, being tired before,
Will, if thou stir, or pinch to wake him, think
      Thou call'st for more,
And in false sleep will from thee shrink.   10
And then, poor aspen wretch, neglected, thou,
Bathed in a cold quicksilver sweat, wilt lie
      A verier° ghost than I.   *truer*
What I will say, I will not tell thee now,
Lest that preserve thee; and since my love is spent,   15
I had rather thou shouldst painfully repent,
Than by my threatenings rest still innocent.

JOHN DONNE (1572–1631)
Batter My Heart   **1610**

Batter my heart, three-personed God; for You
As yet but knock, breathe, shine, and seek to mend;
That I may rise and stand, o'erthrow me, and bend
Your force, to break, blow, burn, and make me new.
I, like an usurped town, to another due,   5

Labor to admit You, but Oh, to no end!
Reason, Your viceroy in me, me should defend,
But is captived, and proves weak or untrue.
Yet dearly I love You, and would be loved fain.
But am betrothed unto Your enemy: 10
Divorce me, untie, or break that knot again,
Take me to You, imprison me, for I,
Except You enthrall me, never shall be free,
Nor ever chaste, except You ravish me.

JOHN DONNE (1572–1631)
Death Be Not Proud   1611

Death be not proud, though some have calléd thee
Mighty and dreadful, for thou art not so;
For those whom thou think'st thou dost overthrow
Die not, poor Death, nor yet canst thou kill me.
From rest and sleep, which but thy pictures° be,   *images*   5
Much pleasure; then from thee much more must flow,
And soonest our best men with thee do go,
Rest of their bones, and soul's delivery.°   *deliverance*
Thou art slave to Fate, Chance, kings, and desperate men,
And dost with Poison, War, and Sickness dwell;   10
And poppy or charms can make us sleep as well,
And better than thy stroke; why swell'st° thou then?   *swell with pride*
One short sleep past, we wake eternally
And death shall be no more; Death, thou shalt die.

JOHN DONNE (1572–1631)
The Flea   1633

Mark but this flea, and mark in this°
How little that which thou deny'st me is;
It sucked me first, and now sucks thee,
And in this flea our two bloods mingled be;
Thou know'st that this cannot be said   5
A sin, nor shame, nor loss of maidenhead,
    Yet this enjoys before it woo,
    And pampered swells with one blood made of two,
    And this, alas, is more than we would do.°

1 *mark in this:* Take note of the moral lesson in this object.   9 *more than we would do:* I.e., if we
do not join our blood in conceiving a child.

Oh stay, three lives in one flea spare,   10
Where we almost, yea more than, married are.
This flea is you and I, and this
Our marriage bed, and marriage temple is;
Though parents grudge, and you, we're met
And cloistered in these living walls of jet.   15
    Though use° make you apt to kill me,   *habit*
    Let not to that, self-murder added be,
    And sacrilege, three sins in killing three.

Cruel and sudden, hast thou since
Purpled thy nail in blood of innocence?   20
Wherein could this flea guilty be,
Except in that drop which it sucked from thee?
Yet thou triumph'st, and say'st that thou
Find'st not thyself, nor me, the weaker now;
    'Tis true; then learn how false, fears be;   25
    Just so much honor, when thou yield'st to me,
    Will waste, as this flea's death took life from thee.

JOHN DONNE (1572–1631)
Hymn to God, My God, in My Sickness   1635

Since I am coming to that holy room
    Where, with thy choir of saints for evermore,
I shall be made thy music, as I come
    I tune the instrument here at the door,
    And what I must do then, think now before.   5

Whilst my physicians by their love are grown
    Cosmographers, and I their map, who lie
Flat on this bed, that by them may be shown
    That this is my southwest discovery,
    Per fretum febris,° by these straits to die,   *through the* 10
                                                                    strait of fever

I joy that in these straits I see my west;
    For though those currents yield return to none,
What shall my west hurt me? As west and east
    In all flat maps (and I am one) are one,
    So death doth touch the resurrectiön.   15

Is the Pacific Sea my home? Or are
    The eastern riches? Is Jerusalem?
Anyan° and Magellan and Gibraltar,   *Bering Strait*
    All straits, and none but straits, are ways to them,
    Whether where Japhet dwelt, or Cham, or Shem.°   20

20 *Japhet . . . Cham . . . Shem:* The three sons of Noah, who after the flood became the progenitors
of the northern, southern, and Semitic peoples respectively (see Gen. 9:18–27).

We think that Paradise and Calvary,
    Christ's cross and Adam's tree, stood in one place;
Look, Lord, and find both Adams met in me;
    As the first Adam's sweat surrounds my face,
    May the last Adam's blood my soul embrace.   25

So, in his purple wrapped receive me, Lord;
    By these his thorns give me his other crown;
And as to others' souls I preached thy word,
    Be this my text, my sermon to mine own:
    Therefore that he may raise, the Lord throws down.   30

MICHAEL DRAYTON (1563–1631)
Since There's No Help   1619

Since there's no help, come let us kiss and part;
Nay, I have done, you get no more of me,
And I am glad, yea glad with all my heart
That thus so cleanly I myself can free;
Shake hands for ever, cancel all our vows,   5
And when we meet at any time again,
Be it not seen in either of our brows
That we one jot of former love retain.
Now at the last gasp of Love's latest breath,
When, his pulse failing, Passion speechless lies,   10
When Faith is kneeling by his bed of death,
And Innocence is closing up his eyes,
    Now if thou wouldst, when all have given him over,
    From death to life thou mightst him yet recover.

T. S. ELIOT (1888–1965)
Macavity: The Mystery Cat   1939

Macavity's a Mystery Cat: he's called the Hidden Paw —
For he's the master criminal who can defy the Law.
He's the bafflement of Scotland Yard, the Flying Squad's despair:
For when they reach the scene of the crime — *Macavity's not there!*

    Macavity, Macavity, there's no one like Macavity,   5
He's broken every human law, he breaks the law of gravity.
His powers of levitation would make a fakir stare,
And when you reach the scene of crime — *Macavity's not there!*
You may seek him in the basement, you may look up in the air —
But I tell you once and once again, *Macavity's not there!*   10

Macavity's a ginger cat, he's very tall and thin;
You would know him if you saw him, for his eyes are sunken in.
His brow is deeply lined with thought, his head is highly domed;
His coat is dusty from neglect, his whiskers are uncombed.
He sways his head from side to side, with movements like a snake;   15
And when you think he's half asleep, he's always wide awake.

    Macavity, Macavity, there's no one like Macavity,
For he's a fiend in feline shape, a monster of depravity.
You may meet him in a by-street, you may see him in the square —
But when a crime's discovered, then *Macavity's not there!*   20

    He's outwardly respectable. (They say he cheats at cards.)
And his footprints are not found in any file of Scotland Yard's.
And when the larder's looted, or the jewel-case is rifled,
Or when the milk is missing, or another Peke's been stifled,°
Or the greenhouse glass is broken, and the trellis past repair —   25
Ay, there's the wonder of the thing! *Macavity's not there!*

    And when the Foreign Office find a Treaty's gone astray,
Or the Admiralty lose some plans and drawings by the way,
There may be a scrap of paper in the hall or on the stair —
But it's useless to investigate — *Macavity's not there!*   30
And when the loss has been disclosed, the Secret Service say:
"It *must* have been Macavity!" — but he's a mile away.
You'll be sure to find him resting, or a-licking of his thumbs,
Or engaging in doing complicated long division sums.

    Macavity, Macavity, there's no one like Macavity,   35
There never was a Cat of such deceitfulness and suavity.
He always has an alibi, and one or two to spare:
At whatever time the deed took place — MACAVITY WASN'T THERE!
And they say that all the Cats whose wicked deeds are widely known
(I might mention Mungojerrie, I might mention Griddlebone)   40
Are nothing more than agents for the Cat who all the time
Just controls their operations: the Napoleon of Crime!

24 *stifled:* A Pekinese dog is killed.

ALLEN GINSBERG (b. 1926)
America   1956

America I've given you all and now I'm nothing.
America two dollars and twentyseven cents January 17, 1956.
I can't stand my own mind.
America when will we end the human war?
Go fuck yourself with your atom bomb.   5

I don't feel good don't bother me.
I won't write my poem till I'm in my right mind.
America when will you be angelic?
When will you take off your clothes?
When will you look at yourself through the grave?   10
When will you be worthy of your million Trotskyites?°   *American communists*
America why are your libraries full of tears?
America when will you send your eggs to India?
I'm sick of your insane demands.
When can I go into the supermarket and buy what I need with my good
    looks?   15
America after all it is you and I who are perfect not the next world.
Your machinery is too much for me.
You made me want to be a saint.
There must be some other way to settle this argument.
Burroughs° is in Tangiers I don't think he'll come back it's sinister.   20
Are you being sinister or is this some form of practical joke?
I'm trying to come to the point.
I refuse to give up my obsession.
America stop pushing I know what I'm doing.
America the plum blossoms are falling.   25
I haven't read the newspapers for months, everyday somebody goes on trial
    for murder.
America I feel sentimental about the Wobblies.°
America I used to be a communist when I was a kid I'm not sorry.
I smoke marijuana every chance I get.
I sit in my house for days on end and stare at the roses in the closet.   30
When I go to Chinatown I get drunk and never get laid.
My mind is made up there's going to be trouble.
You should have seen me reading Marx.
My psychoanalyst thinks I'm perfectly right.
I won't say the Lord's Prayer.   35
I have mystical visions and cosmic vibrations.
America I still haven't told you what you did to Uncle Max after he came
    over from Russia.

I'm addressing you.
Are you going to let your emotional life be run by Time Magazine?
I'm obsessed by Time Magazine.   40
I read it every week.
Its cover stares at me every time I slink past the corner candystore.
I read it in the basement of the Berkeley Public Library.
It's always telling me about responsibility. Businessmen are serious. Movie
    producers are serious. Everybody's serious but me.
It occurs to me that I am America.   45
I am talking to myself again.

20 *Burroughs:* William Burroughs (b. 1914), author of *Naked Lunch* (1959), who traveled to Tangiers
to avoid prosecution on drug charges.   27 *Wobblies:* Members of the Industrial Workers of the
World (I.W.W.), a militant labor organization.

Asia is rising against me.
I haven't got a chinaman's chance.
I'd better consider my national resources.
My national resources consist of two joints of marijuana millions of genitals
      an unpublishable private literature that goes 1400 miles an hour and
      twentyfive-thousand mental institutions.   50
I say nothing about my prisons nor the millions of underprivileged who
      live in my flowerpots under the light of five hundred suns.
I have abolished the whorehouses of France, Tangiers is the next to go.
My ambition is to be President despite the fact that I'm a Catholic.

America how can I write a holy litany in your silly mood?
I will continue like Henry Ford my strophes are as individual as his auto-
      mobiles more so they're all different sexes.   55
America I will sell you strophes $2500 apiece $500 down on your old strophe
America free Tom Mooney°
America save the Spanish Loyalists°
America Sacco & Vanzetti° must not die
America I am the Scottsboro boys.°   60
America when I was seven momma took me to Communist Cell meet-
      ings they sold us garbanzos a handful per ticket a ticket costs a nickel
      and the speeches were free everybody was angelic and sentimental
      about the workers it was all so sincere you have no idea what a good
      thing the party was in 1835 Scott Nearing was a grand old man a real
      mensch Mother Bloor made me cry I once saw Israel Amter plain.
      Everybody must have been a spy.°
America you don't really want to go to war.
America it's them bad Russians.
Them Russians them Russians and them Chinamen. And them Russians.
The Russia wants to eat us alive. The Russia's power mad. She wants to take
      our cars from out our garages.   65
Her wants to grab Chicago. Her needs a Red Readers' Digest. Her wants
      our auto plants in Siberia. Him big bureaucracy running our filling
      stations.
That no good. Ugh. Him make Indians learn read. Him need big black
      niggers. Hah. Her make us all work sixteen hours a day. Help.
America this is quite serious.
America this is the impression I get from looking in the television set.
America is this correct?   70

---

57 *Tom Mooney*: (1882–1942) A labor organizer convicted of setting off a bomb in a San Francisco crowd; many believed in his innocence. He was released from prison after serving more than twenty years.   58 *Spanish Loyalists*:   Resistance fighters who opposed the fascist regime of Francisco Franco.   59 *Sacco & Vanzetti*: Nicola Sacco (1891–1927) and Bartolomeo Vanzetti (1888–1927), anarchists and labor agitators convicted of a payroll robbery and murder for which they were executed. They were widely viewed as victims and political martyrs rather than criminals.   60 *Scottsboro boys*: Another famous court case involving nine blacks falsely accused of raping two white girls in Scottsboro, Alabama.   61 *Everybody . . . spy*: Nearing, Bloor, and Amter were all associated with the Communist party.

I'd better get right down to the job.
It's true I don't want to join the Army or turn lathes in precision parts
    factories, I'm nearsighted and psychopathic anyway.
America I'm putting my queer shoulder to the wheel.

DONALD HALL (b. 1928)
My Son, My Executioner   1955

My son, my executioner,
    I take you in my arms,
Quiet and small and just astir,
    And whom my body warms.

Sweet death, small son, our instrument   5
    Of immortality,
Your cries and hungers document
    Our bodily decay.

We twenty-five and twenty-two,
    Who seemed to live forever,   10
Observe enduring life in you
    And start to die together.

DONALD HALL (b. 1928)
To a Waterfowl   1974

Women with hats like the rear ends of pink ducks
applauded you, my poems.
These are the women whose husbands I meet on airplanes,
who close their briefcases and ask, "What are *you* in?"
I look in their eyes, I tell them I am in poetry,   5

and their eyes fill with anxiety, and with little tears.
"Oh, yeah?" they say, developing an interest in clouds.
"My wife, she likes that sort of thing? Hah-hah?"
I guess maybe I'd better watch my grammar, huh?"
I leave them in airports, watching their grammar,   10

and take a limousine to the Women's Goodness Club
where I drink Harvey's Bristol Cream with their wives,
and eat chicken salad with capers, with little tomato wedges
and I read them "The Erotic Crocodile," and "Eating You."
Ah, when I have concluded the disbursement of sonorities,   15

crooning, "High on thy thigh I cry, Hi!" — and so forth —
they spank their wide hands, they smile like Jell-O,

and they say, "Hah-hah? My goodness, Mr. Hall,
but you certainly do have an imagination, huh?"
"Thank you, indeed," I say; "it brings in the bacon."   20

But now, my poems, now I have returned to the motel,
returned to *l'éternel retour°* of the Holiday Inn,   *endless sameness*
naked, lying on the bed, watching *Godzilla Sucks Mt. Fuji,*
addressing my poems, feeling superior, and drinking bourbon
from a flask disguised to look like a transistor radio.   25

Ah, my poems, it is true,
that with the deepest gratitude and most serene pleasure,
and with hints that I am a sexual Thomas Alva Edison,
and not without collecting an exorbitant fee,
I have accepted the approbation of feathers.   30

And what about you? You, laughing? You, in the bluejeans,
laughing at your mother who wears hats, and at your father
who rides airplanes with a briefcase watching his grammar?
Will you ever be old and dumb, like your creepy parents?
Not you, not you, not you, not you, not you, not you.   35

THOMAS HARDY (1840–1928)
Channel Firing°   April 1914

That night your great guns, unawares,
Shook all our coffins as we lay,
And broke the chancel window squares,°
We thought it was the Judgment-day°

And sat upright. While drearisome   5
Arose the howl of wakened hounds:
The mouse let fall the altar-crumb,°
The worms drew back into the mounds,

The glebe cow° drooled. Till God called, "No;
It's gunnery practice out at sea   10
Just as before you went below;
The world is as it used to be:

"All nations striving strong to make
Red war yet redder. Mad as hatters
They do no more for Christés sake   15
Than you who are helpless in such matters.

Channel Firing: The navy practiced firing guns on the English Channel in the summer of 1914, just
before World War I began.   3 *chancel window squares:* A church's altar window.   4 *Judgment-
day:* In Christian tradition, the day the dead are awakened for judgment.   7 *altar-crumb:* Particle
from the wafer used in the celebration of the Eucharist.   9 *glebe cow:* Parish cow pastured on
church land.

"That this is not the judgment-hour
For some of them's a blessed thing,
For if it were they'd have to scour
Hell's floor for so much threatening . . .   20

"Ha, ha. It will be warmer when
I blow the trumpet (if indeed
I ever do; for you are men,
And rest eternal sorely need)."

So down we lay again. "I wonder,   25
Will the world ever saner be,"
Said one, "than when He sent us under
In our indifferent century!"

And many a skeleton shook his head.
"Instead of preaching forty year,"   30
My neighbor Parson Thirdly said,
"I wish I had stuck to pipes and beer."

Again the guns disturbed the hour,
Roaring their readiness to avenge.
As far inland as Stourton Tower,°   35
And Camelot,° and starlit Stonehenge.°

35 *Stourton Tower:* Eighteenth-century commemoration of King Alfred's ninth-century victory over the Danes in Stourhead Park, Wiltshire.   36 *Camelot:* The legendary castle that housed King Arthur's court, probably located in Cornwall; *Stonehenge:* A circular formation of great stones or monoliths erected about 1800 B.C., associated with religious rituals and perhaps with astronomical calculations, and located on Salisbury Plain, Wiltshire.

THOMAS HARDY (1840–1928)
During Wind and Rain   1917

They sing their dearest songs —
He, she, all of them — yea,
Treble and tenor and bass,
    And one to play;
With the candles mooning each face. . . .   5
    Ah, no; the years O!
How the sick leaves reel down in throngs!

They clear the creeping moss —
Elders and juniors — aye,
Making the pathways neat   10
    And the garden gay;
And they build a shady seat. . . .
    Ah, no; the years, the years;
See, the white storm-birds wing across!

They are blithely breakfasting all — 15
Men and maidens — yea,
Under the summer tree,
    With a glimpse of the bay,
While pet fowl come to the knee. . . .
    Ah, no! the years O! 20
And the rotten rose is ripped from the wall.

They change to a high new house,
He, she, all of them — aye,
Clocks and carpets and chairs
    On the lawn all day, 25
And brightest things that are theirs. . . .
    Ah, no; the years, the years;
Down their carved names the raindrop plows.

THOMAS HARDY (1840–1928)
Hap 1866

If but some vengeful god would call to me
From up the sky, and laugh: "Thou suffering thing,
Know that thy sorrow is my ecstasy,
That thy love's loss is my hate's profiting!"

Then would I bear it, clench myself, and die, 5
Steeled by the sense of ire unmerited;
Half-eased in that a Powerfuller than I
Had willed and meted me the tears I shed.

But not so. How arrives it joy lies slain,
And why unblooms the best hope ever sown? 10
— Crass Casualty obstructs the sun and rain,
And dicing Time for gladness casts a moan. . . .
These purblind Doomsters had as readily strown
Blisses about my pilgrimage as pain.

THOMAS HARDY (1840–1928)
The Man He Killed 1902

    Had he and I but met
    By some old ancient inn,
We should have sat us down to wet
    Right many a nipperkin!° *half-pint cup*

    But ranged as infantry, 5
    And staring face to face,

I shot at him as he at me,
    And killed him in his place.

    I shot him dead because —
    Because he was my foe,
Just so: my foe of course he was;
    That's clear enough; although   10

    He thought he'd 'list, perhaps,
    Off-hand-like — just as I —
Was out of work — had sold his traps —   15
    No other reason why.

    Yes; quaint and curious war is!
    You shoot a fellow down
You'd treat, if met where any bar is,
    Or help to half-a-crown.   20

SEAMUS HEANEY (b. 1939)
Digging   1966

Between my finger and my thumb
The squat pen rests; snug as a gun.

Under my window, a clean rasping sound
When the spade sinks into gravelly ground:
My father, digging. I look down   5

Till his straining rump among the flowerbeds
Bends low, comes up twenty years away
Stooping in rhythm through potato drills
Where he was digging.

The coarse boot nestled on the lug, the shaft   10
Against the inside knee was levered firmly.
He rooted out tall tops, buried the bright edge deep
To scatter new potatoes that we picked
Loving their cool hardness in our hands.

By God, the old man could handle a spade.   15
Just like his old man.

My grandfather cut more turf in a day
Than any other man on Toner's bog.
Once I carried him milk in a bottle
Corked sloppily with paper. He straightened up   20
To drink it, then fell to right away

Nicking and slicing neatly, heaving sods
Over his shoulder, going down and down
For the good turf. Digging.

The cold smell of potato mould, the squelch and slap   25
Of soggy peat, the curt cuts of an edge
Through living roots awaken in my head.
But I've no spade to follow men like them.

Between my finger and my thumb
The squat pen rests.   30
I'll dig with it.

ANTHONY HECHT (b. 1923)
The Dover Bitch°   1968

A Criticism of Life

So there stood Matthew Arnold and this girl
With the cliffs of England crumbling away behind them,
And he said to her, "Try to be true to me,
And I'll do the same for you, for things are bad
All over, etc., etc."   5
Well now, I knew this girl. It's true she had read
Sophocles in a fairly good translation
And caught that bitter allusion to the sea,°
But all the time he was talking she had in mind
The notion of what his whiskers would feel like   10
On the back of her neck. She told me later on
That after a while she got to looking out
At the lights across the channel, and really felt sad,
Thinking of all the wine and enormous beds
And blandishments in French and the perfumes.   15
And then she got really angry. To have been brought
All the way down from London, and then be addressed
As a sort of mournful cosmic last resort
Is really tough on a girl, and she was pretty.
Anyway, she watched him pace the room   20
And finger his watch-chain and seem to sweat a bit,
And then she said one or two unprintable things.
But you mustn't judge her by that. What I mean to say is,
She's really all right. I still see her once in a while
And she always treats me right. We have a drink   25
And I give her a good time, and perhaps it's a year
Before I see her again, but there she is,
Running to fat, but dependable as they come.
And sometimes I bring her a bottle of *Nuit d'Amour.*

The Dover Bitch: A parody of Arnold's poem "Dover Beach" (see page 648).   8 *allusion to the sea:*
Lines 9–18 in "Dover Beach" refer to Sophocles' *Antigone,* lines 583–591.

GEORGE HERBERT (1593–1633)

The Collar

1633

I struck the board° and cried, "No more;   *table*
      I will abroad!
What? shall I ever sigh and pine?
My lines and life are free, free as the road,
    Loose as the wind, as large as store.°   5
        Shall I be still in suit?°   *serving another*
    Have I no harvest but a thorn
    To let me blood, and not restore
What I have lost with cordial° fruit?   *restorative*
        Sure there was wine   10
    Before my sighs did dry it; there was corn
      Before my tears did drown it.
    Is the year only lost to me?
      Have I no bays° to crown it,   *triumphal wreaths*
No flowers, no garlands gay? All blasted?   15
      All wasted?
    Not so, my heart; but there is fruit,
      And thou hast hands.
    Recover all thy sigh-blown age
On double pleasures: leave thy cold dispute   20
Of what is fit, and not. Forsake thy cage,
      Thy rope of sands,
Which petty thoughts have made, and made to thee
    Good cable, to enforce and draw,
        And be thy law,   25
    While thou didst wink and wouldst not see.
        Away! take heed;
        I will abroad.
Call in thy death's-head° there; tie up thy fears.
      He that forbears   30
    To suit and serve his need,
    Deserves his load."
But as I raved and grew more fierce and wild
    At every word,
Methought I heard one calling, *Child!*   35
    And I replied, *My Lord.*

---

5 *store:* A storehouse or warehouse.   29 *death's-head:* A skull, reminder of mortality.

M. CARL HOLMAN (1919–1988)

Mr. Z   1967

Taught early that his mother's skin was the sign of error,
He dressed and spoke the perfect part of honor;
Won scholarships, attended the best schools,
Disclaimed kinship with jazz and spirituals;
Chose prudent, raceless views for each situation,   5
Or when he could not cleanly skirt dissension,
Faced up to the dilemma, firmly seized
Whatever ground was Anglo-Saxonized.

In diet, too, his practice was exemplary:
Of pork in its profane forms he was wary;   10
Expert in vintage wines, sauces and salads,
His palate shrank from cornbread, yams and collards.

He was as careful whom he chose to kiss:
His bride had somewhere lost her Jewishness,
But kept her blue eyes; an Episcopalian   15
Prelate proclaimed them matched chameleon.
Choosing the right addresses, here, abroad,
They shunned those places where they might be barred;
Even less anxious to be asked to dine
Where hosts catered to kosher accent or exotic skin.   20

And so he climbed, unclogged by ethnic weights,
An airborne plant, flourishing without roots.
Not one false note was struck — until he died:
His subtly grieving widow could have flayed
The obit writers, ringing crude changes on a clumsy phrase: 25
"One of the most distinguished members of his race."

GERARD MANLEY HOPKINS (1844–1889)

Pied Beauty   1877

Glory be to God for dappled things —
     For skies of couple-color as a brinded cow;
          For rose-moles all in stipple upon trout that swim;
Fresh-firecoal chestnut-falls;° finches' wings;   *fallen chestnut*
     Landscape plotted and pieced — fold, fallow, and plow;   5
          And all trades, their gear and tackle and trim.

All things counter, original, spare, strange;
     Whatever is fickle, freckled (who knows how?)

With swift, slow; sweet, sour; adazzle, dim;
He fathers-forth whose beauty is past change: 10
                    Praise him.

GERARD MANLEY HOPKINS (1844–1889)
Spring and Fall   1880

To a Young Child

Márgarét áre you gríeving
Over Goldengrove unleaving?
Leáves, like the things of man, you
With your fresh thoughts care for, can you?
Áh! ás the heart grows older   5
It will come to such sights colder
By and by, nor spare a sigh
Though worlds of wanwood° leafmeal° lie;
And yet you wíll weep and know why.
Now no matter, child, the name: 10
Sórrow's spríngs áre the same.
Nor mouth had, no nor mind, expressed
What heart heard of, ghost° guessed: *soul*
It ís the blight man was born for,
it is Margaret you mourn for.   15

8 *wanwood:* Gloomy woods; *leafmeal:* Leaves broken up piecemeal.

GERARD MANLEY HOPKINS (1844–1889)
The Windhover°   1877

To Christ Our Lord

I caught this morning morning's minion,° king-   *favorite*
    dom of daylight's dauphin, dapple-dawn-drawn Falcon, in his riding
    Of the rolling level underneath him steady air, and striding
High there, how he rung upon the rein of a wimpling wing
In his ecstasy! then off, off forth on swing,   5
    As a skate's heel sweeps smooth on a bow-bend: the hurl and gliding
    Rebuffed the big wind. My heart in hiding
Stirred for a bird, — the achieve of, the mastery of the thing!

The Windhover: "A name for the kestrel [a kind of small hawk], from its habit of hovering or hanging with its head to the wind" [OED].

Brute beauty and valour and act, oh, air, pride, plume, here
    Buckle!° AND the fire that breaks from thee then, a billion   10
Times told lovelier, more dangerous, O my chevalier!

    No wonder of it: shéer plód makes plough down sillion°   *furrow*
Shine, and blue-bleak embers, ah my dear,
    Fall, gall themselves, and gash gold-vermilion.

10 *Buckle:* To join, to equip for battle, to crumple.

A. E. HOUSMAN (1859–1936)
Is my team ploughing   1896

"Is my team ploughing,
    That I was used to drive
And hear the harness jingle
    When I was man alive?"

Ay, the horses trample,   5
    The harness jingles now;
No change though you lie under
    The land you used to plough.

"Is football playing
    Along the river shore,   10
With lads to chase the leather,
    Now I stand up no more?"

Ay, the ball is flying,
    The lads play heart and soul;
The goal stands up, the keeper   15
    Stands up to keep the goal.

"Is my girl happy,
    That I thought hard to leave,
And has she tired of weeping
    As she lies down at eve?"   20

Ay, she lies down lightly,
    She lies not down to weep:
Your girl is well contented.
    Be still, my lad, and sleep.

"Is my friend hearty,   25
    Now I am thin and pine,
And has he found to sleep in
    A better bed than mine?"

Yes, lad, I lie easy,
    I lie as lads would choose;   30
I cheer a dead man's sweetheart,
    Never ask me whose.

A. E. HOUSMAN (1859–1936)
Terence,° this is stupid stuff   1896

"Terence, this is stupid stuff:
You eat your victuals fast enough;
There can't be much amiss, 'tis clear,
To see the rate you drink your beer.
But oh, good Lord, the verse you make,   5
It gives a chap the belly-ache.
The cow, the old cow, she is dead;
It sleeps well, the hornéd head:
We poor lads, 'tis our turn now
To hear such tunes as killed the cow.   10
Pretty friendship 'tis to rhyme
Your friends to death before their time
Moping melancholy mad:
Come, pipe a tune to dance to, lad."

Why, if 'tis dancing you would be,   15
There's brisker pipes than poetry.
Say, for what were hop-yards meant,
Or why was Burton built on Trent?°
Oh many a peer of England brews
Livelier liquor than the Muse,   20
And malt does more than Milton can
To justify God's ways to man.°
Ale, man, ale's the stuff to drink
For fellows whom it hurts to think:
Look into the pewter pot   25
To see the world as the world's not.
And faith, 'tis pleasant till 'tis past:
The mischief is that 'twill not last.
Oh I have been to Ludlow fair
And left my necktie God knows where,   30
And carried halfway home, or near,
Pints and quarts of Ludlow beer:
Then the world seemed none so bad,
And I myself a sterling lad;

Terence: Housman's name for himself.   18 *Trent:* Burton-on-Trent, an English city famous for its breweries.   22 *To . . . man:* John Milton's (1608–1674) announced purpose in *Paradise Lost.*

And down in lovely muck I've lain,   35
Happy till I woke again.
Then I saw the morning sky:
Heigho, the tale was all a lie;
The world, it was the old world yet,
I was I, my things were wet,   40
And nothing now remained to do
But begin the game anew.

    Therefore, since the world has still
Much good, but much less good than ill,
And while the sun and moon endure   45
Luck's a chance, but trouble's sure,
I'd face it as a wise man would,
And train for ill and not for good.
'Tis true, the stuff I bring for sale
Is not so brisk a brew as ale: 50
Out of a stem that scored the hand
I wrung it in a weary land.
But take it: if the smack is sour,
The better for the embittered hour;
It should do good to heart and head   55
When your soul is in my soul's stead;
And I will friend you, if I may,
In the dark and cloudy day.

    There was a king reigned in the East:
There, when kings will sit to feast,   60
They get their fill before they think
With poisoned meat and poisoned drink.
He gathered all that springs to birth
From the many-venomed earth;
First a little, thence to more,   65
He sampled all her killing store;
And easy, smiling, seasoned sound,
Sate the king when healths° went round.   *toasts*
They put arsenic in his meat
And stared aghast to watch him eat;   70
They poured strychnine in his cup
And shook to see him drink it up:
They shook, they stared as white's their shirt:
Them it was their poison hurt.
—I tell the tale that I heard told.   75
Mithridates,° he died old.

76 *Mithridates:* King of Pontus in the first century B.C., who took gradually increasing doses of poison in order to develop a tolerance for them.

A. E. HOUSMAN (1859–1936)

To an Athlete Dying Young 1896

The time you won your town the race
We chaired° you through the marketplace;
Man and boy stood cheering by,
And home we brought you shoulder-high.

Today, the road all runners come, 5
Shoulder-high we bring you home,
And set you at your threshold down,
Townsman of a stiller town.

Smart lad, to slip betimes away
From fields where glory does not stay, 10
And early though the laurel° grows
It withers quicker than the rose.

Eyes the shady night has shut
Cannot see the record cut,
And silence sounds no worse than cheers 15
After earth has stopped the ears:

Now you will not swell the rout
Of lads that wore their honors out,
Runners whom renown outran
And the name died before the man. 20

So set, before its echoes fade,
The fleet foot on the sill of shade,
And hold to the low lintel up
The still-defended challenge-cup.

And round that early-laureled head 25
Will flock to gaze the strengthless dead,
And find unwithered on its curls
The garland briefer than a girl's.

2 *chaired:* Carried on the shoulders in triumphal parade.　11 *laurel:* Flowering shrub traditionally used to fashion wreaths of honor.

LANGSTON HUGHES (1902–1967)

Ballad of the Landlord   1951

Landlord, landlord,
My roof has sprung a leak.
Don't you 'member I told you about it
Way last week?

Landlord, landlord,   5
These steps is broken down.
When you come up yourself
It's a wonder you don't fall down.

Ten Bucks you say I owe you?
Ten Bucks you say is due?   10
Well, that's Ten Bucks more'n I'll pay you
Till you fix this house up new.

What? You gonna get eviction orders?
You gonna cut off my heat?
You gonna take my furniture and   15
Throw it in the street?

Um-huh! You talking high and mighty.
Talk on — till you get through.
You ain't gonna be able to say a word
If I land my fist on you.   20

Police! Police!
Come and get this man!
He's trying to ruin the government
And overturn the land!

Copper's whistle!   25
Patrol bell!
Arrest.

Precinct Station.
Iron cell.
Headlines in press: 30

MAN THREATENS LANDLORD
TENANT HELD NO BAIL
JUDGE GIVES NEGRO 90 DAYS IN COUNTY JAIL

RANDALL JARRELL (1914–1965)

Next Day

1965

Moving from Cheer to Joy, from Joy to All,
I take a box
And add it to my wild rice, my Cornish game hens.
The slacked or shorted, basketed, identical
Food-gathering flocks   5
Are selves I overlook. Wisdom, said William James,°

Is learning what to overlook. And I am wise
If that is wisdom
Yet somehow, as I buy All from these shelves
And the boy takes it to my station wagon,   10
What I've become
Troubles me even if I shut my eyes.

When I was young and miserable and pretty
And poor, I'd wish
What all girls wish: to have a husband,   15
A house and children. Now that I'm old, my wish
Is womanish:
That the boy putting groceries in my car

See me. It bewilders me he doesn't see me.
For so many years   20
I was good enough to eat: the world looked at me
And its mouth watered. How often they have undressed me,
The eyes of strangers!
And, holding their flesh within my flesh, their vile

Imaginings within my imagining,   25
I too have taken
The chance of life. Now the boy pats my dog
And we start home. Now I am good.
The last mistaken,
Ecstatic, accidental bliss, the blind   30

Happiness that, bursting, leaves upon the palm
Some soap and water —
It was so long ago, back in some Gay
Twenties, Nineties, I don't know . . . Today I miss
My lovely daughter   35
Away at school, my sons away at school,

---

6 *William James* (1842–1910): A psychologist and philosopher, author of *Principles of Psychology* (1890).

My husband away at work — I wish for them.
The dog, the maid,
And I go through the sure unvarying days
At home in them. As I look at my life,   40
I am afraid
Only that it will change, as I am changing:

I am afraid, this morning, of my face.
It looks at me
From the rear-view mirror, with the eyes I hate,   45
The smile I hate. Its plain, lined look
Of gray discovery
Repeats to me: "You're old." That's all, I'm old.

And yet I'm afraid, as I was at the funeral
I went to yesterday.   50
My friend's cold made-up face, granite among its flowers,
Her undressed, operated-on, dressed body
Were my face and body.
As I think of her I hear her telling me

How young I seem: I *am* exceptional;   55
I think of all I have.
But really no one is exceptional,
No one has anything, I'm anybody,
I stand beside my grave
Confused with my life, that is commonplace and solitary.   60

BEN JONSON (1573–1637)
On My First Son   1603

Farewell, thou child of my right hand,° and joy.
My sin was too much hope of thee, loved boy;
Seven years thou wert lent to me, and I thee pay,
Exacted by thy fate, on the just day.°   *his birthday*
Oh, could I lose all father° now. For why   *fatherhood* 5
Will man lament the state he should envy? —
To have so soon 'scaped world's and flesh's rage,
And, if no other misery, yet age.
Rest in soft peace, and asked, say, "Here doth lie
Ben Jonson his best piece of poetry,"   10
For whose sake henceforth all his vows be such
As what he loves may never like too much.

1 *child of my right hand:* This phrase translates the Hebrew name "Benjamin," Jonson's son.

X. J. KENNEDY (b. 1929)

In a Prominent Bar in Secaucus One Day   1961

*To the tune of "The Old Orange Flute" or
the tune of "Sweet Betsy from Pike"*

In a prominent bar in Secaucus one day
Rose a lady in skunk with a topheavy sway,
Raised a knobby red finger — all turned from their beer —
While with eyes bright as snowcrust she sang high and clear:

"Now who of you'd think from an eyeload of me   5
That I once was a lady as proud as could be?
Oh I'd never sit down by a tumbledown drunk
If it wasn't, my dears, for the high cost of junk.

"All the gents used to swear that the white of my calf
Beat the down of a swan by a length and a half.   10
In the kerchief of linen I caught to my nose
Ah, there never fell snot, but a little gold rose.

"I had seven gold teeth and a toothpick of gold,
My Virginia cheroot was a leaf of it rolled
And I'd light it each time with a thousand in cash —   15
Why the bums used to fight if I flicked them an ash.

"Once the toast of the Biltmore, the belle of the Taft,
I would drink bottle beer at the Drake, never draft,
And dine at the Astor° on Salisbury steak
With a clean tablecloth for each bite I did take.   20

"In a car like the Roxy° I'd roll to the track,
A steel-guitar trio, a bar in the back,
And the wheels made no noise, they turned over so fast,
Still it took you ten minutes to see me go past.

"When the horses bowed down to me that I might choose,   25
I bet on them all, for I hated to lose.
Now I'm saddled each night for my butter and eggs
And the broken threads race down the backs of my legs.

"Let you hold in mind, girls, that your beauty must pass
Like a lovely white clover that rusts with its grass.   30
Keep your bottoms off barstools and marry you young
Or be left — an old barrel with many a bung.

"For when time takes you out for a spin in his car
You'll be hard-pressed to stop him from going too far
And be left by the roadside, for all your good deeds,   35
Two toadstools for tits and a face full of weeds."

17–19 *Biltmore . . . Astor:* The Biltmore, Taft, Drake, and Astor were elegant hotels in New York City.   21 *Roxy:* A lush New York theater.

All the house raised a cheer, but the man at the bar
Made a phonecall and up pulled a red patrol car
And she blew us a kiss as they copped her away
From that prominent bar in Secaucus, N.J.   40

ETHERIDGE KNIGHT (b. 1931)
A Watts Mother Mourns While Boiling Beans   1973

The blooming flower of my life is roaming
in the night, and I think surely
that never since he was born
have I been free from fright.
My boy is bold, and his blood   5
grows quickly hot/ even now
he could be crawling in the street
bleeding out his life, likely as not.
Come home, my bold and restless son. — Stop
my heart's yearning! But I must quit   10
this thinking — my husband is coming
and the beans are burning.

TED KOOSER (b. 1939)
The Blind Always Come as Such a Surprise   1980

The blind always come as such a surprise,
suddenly filling an elevator
with a great white porcupine of canes,
or coming down upon us in a noisy crowd
like the eye of a hurricane.   5
The dashboards of cars stopped at crosswalks
and the shoes of commuters on trains
are covered with sentences
struck down in mid-flight by the canes of the blind.
Each of them changes our lives,   10
tapping across the bright circles of our ambitions
like cracks traversing the favorite china.

PHILIP LARKIN (1922–1985)
Home Is So Sad

1964

Home is so sad. It stays as it was left,
Shaped to the comfort of the last to go
As if to win them back. Instead, bereft
Of anyone to please, it withers so,
Having no heart to put aside the theft   5

And turn again to what it started as,
A joyous shot at how things ought to be,
Long fallen wide. You can see how it was:
Look at the pictures and the cutlery.
The music in the piano stool. That vase.   10

DENISE LEVERTOV (b. 1923)
News Items

1975

i   America the Bountiful

After the welfare hotel
crumbled suddenly (after repeated warnings)
into the street,

Seventh Day Adventists brought supplies
of clothing to the survivors.   5
" 'Look at this,' exclaimed
Loretta Rollock, 48 years old,
as she held up a green dress
and lingerie. 'I've never worn
such nice clothes. I feel like   10
when I was a kid and my mom
brought me something.' Then
she began to cry."

ii   In the Rubble

For some the hotel's collapse meant
life would have to be started   15
all over again.

Sixty-year-old Charles, on welfare
like so many of the others, who said,
"We are the rootless people," and
"I have no home, no place that I can say I   20
really live in," and,
"I had become used to it here,"
also said:
"I lost

all I ever had, 25
in the rubble.
I lost my clothes,
I lost the picture of my parents
and I lost my television."

AUDRE LORDE (1934–1992)
Hanging Fire 1978

I am fourteen
and my skin has betrayed me
the boy I cannot live without
still sucks his thumb
in secret 5
how come my knees are
always so ashy
what if I die
before morning
and momma's in the bedroom 10
with the door closed.

I have to learn how to dance
in time for the next party
my room is too small for me
suppose I die before graduation 15
they will sing sad melodies
but finally
tell the truth about me
There is nothing I want to do
and too much 20
that has to be done
and momma's in the bedroom
with the door closed.

Nobody even stops to think
about my side of it 25
I should have been on Math Team
my marks were better than his
why do I have to be
the one
wearing braces 30
I have nothing to wear tomorrow
will I live long enough
to grow up
and momma's in the bedroom
with the door closed. 35

CLAUDE McKAY (1889–1948)
The Harlem Dancer   1917

Applauding youths laughed with young prostitutes
And watched her perfect, half-clothed body sway;
Her voice was like the sound of blended flutes
Blown by black players upon a picnic day.
She sang and danced on gracefully and calm,   5
The light gauze hanging loose about her form;
To me she seemed a proudly-swaying palm
Grown lovelier for passing through a storm.
Upon her swarthy neck black shiny curls
Luxuriant fell; and tossing coins in praise,   10
The wine-flushed, bold-eyed boys, and even the girls,
Devoured her shape with eager, passionate gaze;
But looking at her falsely-smiling face,
I knew her self was not in that strange place.

CHRISTOPHER MARLOWE (1564–1593)
The Passionate Shepherd to His Love   1599?

Come live with me and be my love,
And we will all the pleasures prove
That valleys, groves, hills, and fields,
Woods, or steepy mountain yields.

And we will sit upon the rocks,   5
Seeing the shepherds feed their flocks,
By shallow rivers to whose falls
Melodious birds sing madrigals.

And I will make thee beds of roses
And a thousand fragrant posies,   10
A cap of flowers, and a kirtle
Embroidered all with leaves of myrtle;

A gown made of the finest wool
Which from our pretty lambs we pull;
Fair lined slippers for the cold,   15
With buckles of the purest gold;

A belt of straw and ivy buds,
With coral clasps and amber studs:
And if these pleasures may thee move,
Come live with me, and be my love.   20

The shepherd swains shall dance and sing
For thy delight each May morning:
If these delights thy mind may move,
Then live with me and be my love.

ANDREW MARVELL (1621–1678)
The Garden   1681

How vainly men themselves amaze°   *become frenzied*
To win the palm, the oak, or bays;°   *awards*
And their incessant labors see
Crowned from some single herb, or tree,
Whose short and narrow-vergèd° shade   *trimmed*   5
Does prudently their toils upbraid;
While all flowers and all trees do close
To weave the garlands of repose!

Fair Quiet, have I found thee here,
And Innocence, thy sister dear!   10
Mistaken long, I sought you then
In busy companies of men.
Your sacred plants, if here below,
Only among the plants will grow;
Society is all but rude   15
To this delicious solitude.

No white nor red was ever seen
So amorous as this lovely green.
Fond lovers, cruel as their flame,
Cut in these trees their mistress' name: 20
Little, alas! they know or heed
How far these beauties hers exceed!
Fair trees! wheres'e'er your barks I wound
No name shall but your own be found.

When we have run our passion's heat,   25
Love hither makes his best retreat.
The gods, that mortal beauty chase,
Still in a tree did end their race;
Apollo hunted Daphne so,
Only that she might laurel grow;   30
And Pan did after Syrinx speed,
Not as a nymph, but for a reed.°

29–32 *Apollo . . . reed:* In Ovid's *Metamorphoses*, Apollo chases Daphne who is turned into a laurel,
and Pan chases Syrinx who is turned into a reed.

What wondrous life is this I lead!
Ripe apples drop about my head;
The luscious clusters of the vine   35
Upon my mouth do crush their wine;
The nectarine, and curious° peach,   *exquisite*
Into my hands themselves do reach;
Stumbling on melons, as I pass,
Ensnar'd with flowers, I fall on grass.   40

Meanwhile, the mind, from pleasure less,
Withdraws into its happiness:
The mind, that ocean where each kind
Does straight its own resemblance find;
Yet it creates, transcending these,   45
Far other worlds, and other seas;
Annihilating all that's made
To a green thought in a green shade.

Here at the fountain's sliding foot,
Or at some fruit-tree's mossy root,   50
Casting the body's vest aside,
My soul into the boughs does glide:
There like a bird it sits, and sings,
Then whets° and combs its silver wings;   *grooms*
And, till prepared for longer flight,   55
Waves in its plumes the various light.

Such was that happy garden-state,
While man there walked without a mate:
After a place so pure and sweet,
What other help could yet be meet?°   *appropriate*   60
But 'twas beyond a mortal's share
To wander solitary there:
Two paradises 'twere in one,
To live in paradise alone.

How well the skillful gardener drew   65
Of flowers, and herbs, this dial new;
Where, from above, the milder sun
Does through a fragrant zodiac run;
And, as it works, the industrious bee
Computes its time as well as we.   70
How could such sweet and wholesome hours
Be reckoned but with herbs and flowers!

EDNA ST. VINCENT MILLAY (1892–1950)
I Too beneath Your Moon, Almighty Sex   1939

I too beneath your moon, almighty Sex,
Go forth at nightfall crying like a cat,
Leaving the lofty tower I laboured at
For birds to foul and boys and girls to vex
With tittering chalk; and you, and the long necks   5
Of neighbours sitting where their mothers sat
Are well aware of shadowy this and that
In me, that's neither noble nor complex.
Such as I am, however, I have brought
To what it is, this tower; it is my own;   10
Though it was reared To Beauty, it was wrought
From what I had to build with: honest bone
Is there, and anguish; pride; and burning thought;
And lust is there, and nights not spent alone.

EDNA ST. VINCENT MILLAY (1892–1950)
What Lips My Lips Have Kissed   1923

What lips my lips have kissed, and where, and why,
I have forgotten, and what arms have lain
Under my head till morning; but the rain
Is full of ghosts tonight, that tap and sigh
Upon the glass and listen for reply,   5
And in my heart there stirs a quiet pain
For unremembered lads that not again
Will turn to me at midnight with a cry.
Thus in the winter stands the lonely tree,
Nor knows what birds have vanished one by one,   10
Yet knows its boughs more silent than before:
I cannot say what loves have come and gone,
I only know that summer sang in me
A little while, that in me sings no more.

JOHN MILTON (1608–1674)
On the Late Massacre in Piedmont°   1655

Avenge, O Lord, thy slaughtered saints, whose bones
   Lie scattered on the Alpine mountains cold;

On the Late Massacre . . . . : Milton's protest against the treatment of the Waldenses, members of a
Puritan sect living in Piedmont, was not limited to this sonnet. It is thought that he wrote Cromwell's
appeals to the duke of Savoy and to others to end the persecution.

Even them who kept thy truth so pure of old,
When all our fathers worshiped stocks and stones,°
Forget not: in thy book record their groans   5
    Who were thy sheep, and in their ancient fold
    Slain by the bloody Piedmontese, that rolled
Mother with infant down the rocks.° Their moans
The vales redoubled to the hills, and they
    To heaven. Their martyred blood and ashes sow   10
O'er all the Italian fields, where still doth sway
    The triple Tyrant;° that from these may grow
    A hundredfold, who, having learnt thy way,
Early may fly the Babylonian woe.°

4 *When . . . stones:* In Milton's Protestant view, English Catholics had worshipped their stone and
wooden statues in the twelfth century, when the Waldensian sect was formed.   5–8 *in thy book . . .
rocks:* On Easter Day, 1655, 1,700 members of the Waldensian sect were massacred in Piedmont by
the duke of Savoy's forces.   12 *triple Tyrant:* The Pope, with his three-crowned tiara, has authority
on earth and in Heaven and Hell.   14 *Babylonian woe:* The destruction of Babylon, symbol of vice
and corruption, at the end of the world (see Rev. 17–18). Protestants interpreted the "Whore of
Babylon" as the Roman Catholic Church.

JOHN MILTON (1608–1674)
When I consider how my light is spent   c. 1655

When I consider how my light is spent,°
    Ere half my days in this dark world and wide,
    And that one talent° which is death to hide
Lodged with me useless, though my soul more bent
To serve therewith my Maker, and present   5
    My true account, lest He returning chide;
    "Doth God exact day-labor, light denied?"
I fondly° ask. But Patience, to prevent   *foolishly*
That murmur, soon replies, "God doth not need
    Either man's work or His own gifts. Who best   10
    Bear His mild yoke, they serve Him best. His state
Is kingly: thousands at His bidding speed,
    And post o'er land and ocean without rest;
    They also serve who only stand and wait."

1 *how my light is spent:* Milton had been totally blind since 1651.   3 *that one talent:* Refers to
Jesus's parable of the talents (units of money), in which a servant entrusted with a talent buries it
rather than invests it, and is punished upon his master's return (Matt. 25:14–30).

MARIANNE MOORE (1887–1972)

Poetry

1921

I, too, dislike it: there are things that are important beyond all this fiddle.
    Reading it, however, with a perfect contempt for it, one discovers in it
    after all, a place for the genuine.
        Hands that can grasp, eyes
          that can dilate, hair that can rise   5
            if it must, these things are important not because a

high-sounding interpretation can be put upon them but because they are
    useful. When they become so derivative as to become unintelligible,
    the same thing may be said for all of us, that we
        do not admire what   10
        we cannot understand: the bat
            holding on upside down or in quest of something to

eat, elephants pushing, a wild horse taking a roll, a tireless wolf under
    a tree, the immovable critic twitching his skin like a horse that feels a
        flea, the base-
    ball fan, the statistician —   15
        nor is it valid
            to discriminate against "business documents and

school-books"; all these phenomena are important. One must make a
    distinction
    however: when dragged into prominence by half poets, the result is not
        poetry,
    nor till the poets among us can be   20
        "literalists of
        the imagination" — above
            insolence and triviality and can present

for inspection, "imaginary gardens with real toads in them," shall we have
    it. In the meantime, if you demand on the one hand,   25
    the raw material of poetry in
        all its rawness and
        that which is on the other hand
            genuine, you are interested in poetry.

JON MUKAND (b. 1959)
Lullaby

Each morning I finish my coffee,
And climb the stairs to the charts,
Hoping yours will be filed away.
But you can't hear me,
You can't see yourself clamped   5
Between this hard plastic binder:
Lab reports and nurses' notes, a sample
In a test tube. I keep reading
These terse comments: stable as before,
Urine output still poor, respiration normal.   10
And you keep on poisoning
Yourself, your kidneys more useless
Than seawings drenched in an oil spill.
I find my way to your room
And lean over the bedrails   15
As though I can understand
Your wheezed-out fragments.
What can I do but check
Your tubes, feel your pulse, listen
To your heartbeat insistent   20
As a spoiled child who goes on begging?

Old man, listen to me:
Let me take you in a wheelchair
To the back room of the records office,
Let me lift you in my arms   25
And lay you down in the cradle
Of a clean manila folder.

HOWARD NEMEROV (1920–1991)
Life Cycle of Common Man

Roughly figured, this man of moderate habits,
This average consumer of the middle class,
Consumed in the course of his average life span
Just under half a million cigarettes,
Four thousand fifths of gin and about   5
A quarter as much vermouth; he drank
Maybe a hundred thousand cups of coffee,
And counting his parents' share it cost
Something like half a million dollars
To put him through life. How many beasts   10

A Collection of Poems **981**

Died to provide him with meat, belt and shoes
Cannot be certainly said.
                    But anyhow,
It is in this way that a man travels through time,
Leaving behind him a lengthening trail   15
Of empty bottles and bones, of broken shoes,
Frayed collars and worn out or outgrown
Diapers and dinnerjackets, silk ties and slickers.

Given the energy and security thus achieved,
He did . . . ? What? The usual things, of course,   20
The eating, dreaming, drinking and begetting,
And he worked for the money which was to pay
For the eating, et cetera, which were necessary
If he were to go on working for the money, et cetera,
But chiefly he talked. As the bottles and bones   25
Accumulated behind him, the words proceeded
Steadily from the front of his face as he
Advanced into the silence and made it verbal.
Who can tally the tale of his words? A lifetime
Would barely suffice for their repetition;   30
If you merely printed all his commas the result
Would be a very large volume, and the number of times
He said "thank you" or "very little sugar, please,"
Would stagger the imagination. There were also
Witticisms, platitudes, and statements beginning   35
"It seems to me" or "As I always say."

Consider the courage in all that, and behold the man
Walking into deep silence, with the ectoplastic
Cartoon's balloon of speech proceeding
Steadily out of the front of his face, the words   40
Borne along on the breath which is his spirit
Telling the numberless tale of his untold Word°
Which makes the world his apple, and forces him to eat.

42 *Word:* Logos, the controlling principle of the universe.

FRANK O'HARA (1926–1966)
Ave Maria°

Mothers of America
            let your kids go to the movies!
get them out of the house so they won't know what you're up to
it's true that fresh air is good for the body
                             but what about the soul   5
that grows in darkness, embossed by silvery images
and when you grow old as grow old you must
                             they won't hate you
they won't criticize you they won't know
                    they'll be in some glamorous country   10
they first saw on a Saturday afternoon or playing hookey

they may even be grateful to you
                    for their first sexual experience
which only cost you a quarter
                  and didn't upset the peaceful home   15
they will know where candy bars come from
                    and gratuitous bags of popcorn
as gratuitous as leaving the movie before it's over
with a pleasant stranger whose apartment is in the Heaven on Earth Bldg
near the Williamsburg Bridge°   20
                  oh mothers you will have made the little tykes
so happy because if nobody does pick them up in the movies
they won't know the difference
                  and if somebody does it'll be sheer gravy
and they'll have been truly entertained either way   25
instead of hanging around the yard
                 or up in their room
                     hating you
prematurely since you won't have done anything horribly mean yet
except keeping them from the darker joys   30
                  it's unforgivable the latter
so don't blame me if you won't take this advice
                  and the family breaks up
and your children grow old and blind in front of a TV set
                     seeing   35
movies you wouldn't let them see when they were young

Ave Maria: The Catholic prayer Hail Mary, here referred to ironically.   20 *Williamsburg Bridge:* Links lower Manhattan and Brooklyn, New York.

A Collection of Poems **983**

SIMON J. ORTIZ (b. 1941)

My Father's Song

1976

Wanting to say things,
I miss my father tonight.
His voice, the slight catch,
the depth from his thin chest,
the tremble of emotion   5
in something he has just said
to his son, his song:

> We planted corn one Spring at Acu —
> we planted several times
> but this one particular time   10
> I remember the soft damp sand
> in my hand.

> My father had stopped at one point
> to show me an overturned furrow;
> the plowshare had unearthed   15
> the burrow nest of a mouse
> in the soft moist sand.

> Very gently, he scooped tiny pink animals
> into the palm of his hand
> and told me to touch them.   20
> We took them to the edge
> of the field and put them in the shade
> of a sand moist clod.

> I remember the very softness
> of cool and warm sand and tiny alive mice   25
> and my father saying things.

WILFRED OWEN (1893–1918)

Anthem for Doomed Youth

1917

What passing-bells for these who die as cattle?
Only the monstrous anger of the guns.
Only the stuttering rifles' rapid rattle
Can patter out their hasty orisons.
No mockeries now for them; no prayers nor bells,   5
Nor any voice of mourning save the choirs, —
The shrill, demented choirs of wailing shells;
And bugles calling for them from sad shires.
What candles may be held to speed them all?
Not in the hands of boys, but in their eyes   10
Shall shine the holy glimmers of good-byes.

The pallor of girls' brows shall be their pall;
Their flowers the tenderness of patient minds,
And each slow dusk a drawing-down of blinds.

LINDA PASTAN (b. 1932)
after minor surgery   1982

this is the dress rehearsal
when the body
like a constant lover
flirts for the first time
with faithlessness   5

when the body
like a passenger on a long journey
hears the conductor call out
the name
of the first stop   10

when the body
in all its fear and cunning
makes promises to me
it knows
it cannot keep   15

MARGE PIERCY (b. 1936)
Barbie Doll   1969

This girlchild was born as usual
and presented dolls that did pee-pee
and miniature GE stoves and irons
and wee lipsticks the color of cherry candy.
Then in the magic of puberty, a classmate said: 5
You have a great big nose and fat legs.

She was healthy, tested intelligent,
possessed strong arms and back,
abundant sexual drive and manual dexterity.
She went to and fro apologizing.   10
Everyone saw a fat nose on thick legs.

She was advised to play coy,
exhorted to come on hearty,
exercise, diet, smile and wheedle.
Her good nature wore out   15
like a fan belt.

So she cut off her nose and her legs
and offered them up.
In the casket displayed on satin she lay
with the undertaker's cosmetics painted on,   20
a turned-up putty nose,
dressed in a pink and white nightie.
Doesn't she look pretty? everyone said.
Consummation at last.
To every woman a happy ending.   25

SYLVIA PLATH (1932–1963)

Daddy   1962

You do not do, you do not do
Any more, black shoe
In which I have lived like a foot
For thirty years, poor and white,
Barely daring to breathe or Achoo.   5

Daddy, I have had to kill you.
You died before I had time ——
Marble-heavy, a bag full of God,
Ghastly statue with one gray toe
Big as a Frisco seal   10

And a head in the freakish Atlantic
Where it pours bean green over blue
In the waters off beautiful Nauset.°   *Cape Cod inlet*
I used to pray to recover you.
Ach, du.°   *Oh, you*   15

In the German tongue, in the Polish Town°
Scraped flat by the roller
Of wars, wars, wars.
But the name of the town is common.
My Polack friend   20

Says there are a dozen or two.
So I never could tell where you
Put your foot, your root,
I never could talk to you.
The tongue stuck in my jaw.   25

It stuck in a barb wire snare.
Ich, ich, ich, ich,°   *I, I, I, I*

16 *Polish Town:* Refers to Otto Plath's birthplace, Granbow.

I could hardly speak.
I thought every German was you.
And the language obscene   30

An engine, an engine
Chuffing me off like a Jew.
A Jew to Dachau, Auschwitz, Belsen.°
I began to talk like a Jew.
I think I may well be a Jew.   35

The snows of the Tyrol, the clear beer of Vienna
Are not very pure or true.
With my gypsy-ancestress and my weird luck
And my Taroc° pack and my Taroc pack
I may be a bit of a Jew.   40

I have always been scared of *you,*
With your Luftwaffe,° your gobbledygoo.
And your neat mustache
And your Aryan eye, bright blue.
Panzer-man, panzer-man,° O You —   45

Not God but a swastika
So black no sky could squeak through.
Every woman adores a Fascist,
The boot in the face, the brute
Brute heart of a brute like you.   50

You stand at the blackboard, daddy,
In the picture I have of you,
A cleft in your chin instead of your foot
But no less a devil for that, no not
Any less the black man who   55

Bit my pretty red heart in two.
I was ten when they buried you.
At twenty I tried to die
And get back, back, back to you.
I thought even the bones would do.   60

But they pulled me out of the sack,
And they stuck me together with glue.
And then I knew what to do.
I made a model of you,
A man in black with a Meinkampf° look   65

---

33 *Dachau . . . Belsen:* Nazi death camps in World War II.   39 *Taroc:* Or *Tarot,* a pack of cards used to tell fortunes. It is said to have originated among the early Jewish Cabalists, and to have been transmitted to European Gypsies during the Middle Ages.   42 *Luftwaffe:* World War II German air force.   45 *panzer-man:* A member of the panzer division of the German army in World War II, which used armored vehicles and was organized for rapid attack.   65 *Meinkampf:* An allusion to Hitler's autobiography *(My Struggle).*

And a love of the rack and the screw.
And I said I do, I do.
So daddy, I'm finally through.
The black telephone's off at the root,
The voices just can't worm through.   70

If I've killed one man, I've killed two ——
The vampire who said he was you
And drank my blood for a year,
Seven years, if you want to know.
Daddy, you can lie back now.   75

There's a stake in your fat black heart
And the villagers never liked you.
They are dancing and stamping on you.
They always *knew* it was you.
Daddy, daddy, you bastard, I'm through.   80

SYLVIA PLATH (1932–1963)
Metaphors   1960

I'm a riddle in nine syllables,
An elephant, a ponderous house,
A melon strolling on two tendrils.
O red fruit, ivory, fine timbers!
This loaf's big with its yeasty rising.
Money's new-minted in this fat purse.
I'm a means, a stage, a cow in calf.
I've eaten a bag of green apples,
Boarded the train there's no getting off.

EZRA POUND (1885–1972)
The Garden   1913

En robe de parade.
    –Samain°

Like a skein of loose silk blown against a wall
She walks by the railing of a path in Kensington Gardens,
And she is dying piece-meal
    of a sort of emotional anæmia.

En . . . Samain: "Dressed for an outing." From the French *Au Jardin de l'Infante* (1893) by Albert
Samain (1858–1900).

And round about there is a rabble   5
Of the filthy, sturdy, unkillable infants of the very poor.
They shall inherit the earth.

In her is the end of breeding.
Her boredom is exquisite and excessive.
She would like some one to speak to her,   10
And is almost afraid that I
    will commit that indiscretion.

EZRA POUND (1885–1972)
The River-Merchant's Wife: A Letter°   1915

While my hair was still cut straight across my forehead
I played about the front gate, pulling flowers.
You came by on bamboo stilts, playing horse,
You walked about my seat, playing with blue plums.
And we went on living in the village of Chokan: 5
Two small people, without dislike or suspicion.
At fourteen I married My Lord you.
I never laughed, being bashful.
Lowering my head, I looked at the wall.
Called to, a thousand times, I never looked back.   10

At fifteen I stopped scowling,
I desired my dust to be mingled with yours
Forever and forever and forever.
Why should I climb the lookout?

At sixteen you departed,   15
You went into far Ku-to-yen, by the river of swirling eddies,
And you have been gone five months.
The monkeys make sorrowful noise overhead.

You dragged your feet when you went out.
By the gate now, the moss is grown, the different mosses,   20
Too deep to clear them away!
The leaves fall early this autumn, in wind.
The paired butterflies are already yellow with August
Over the grass in the West garden;
They hurt me. I grow older.   25
If you are coming down through the narrows of the river Kiang,
Please let me know before hand,
And I will come out to meet you
    As far as Cho-fu-sa.

The River-Merchant's Wife: A Letter: A free translation of a poem by Li Po (Chinese, 701–762).

SIR WALTER RALEIGH (1554–1618)

The Nymph's Reply to the Shepherd   1600

If all the world and love were young,
And truth in every shepherd's tongue,
These pretty pleasures might me move
To live with thee and be thy love.

Time drives the flocks from field to fold,   5
When rivers rage, and rocks grow cold,
And Philomel° becometh dumb;
The rest complain of cares to come.

The flowers do fade, and wanton fields
To wayward winter reckoning yields: 10
A honey tongue, a heart of gall,
Is fancy's spring, but sorrow's fall.

Thy gowns, thy shoes, thy beds of roses,
Thy cap, thy kirtle, and thy posies
Soon break, soon wither, soon forgotten;   15
In folly ripe, in reason rotten.

Thy belt of straw and ivy buds,
Thy coral clasps and amber studs,
All these in me no means can move
To come to thee and be thy love.   20

But could youth last, and love still breed,
Had joys no date, nor age no need,
Then these delights my mind might move
To live with thee and be thy love.

7 *Philomel:* In Greek mythology, a Greek princess who was changed to a nightingale.

DUDLEY RANDALL (b. 1914)

Ballad of Birmingham   1969

(On the bombing of a church in Birmingham, Alabama, 1963)

"Mother dear, may I go downtown
Instead of out to play,
And march the streets of Birmingham
In a Freedom March today?"

"No, baby, no, you may not go,   5
For the dogs are fierce and wild,
And clubs and hoses, guns and jails
Aren't good for a little child."

"But, mother, I won't be alone.
Other children will go with me,   10
And march the streets of Birmingham
To make our country free."

"No, baby, no, you may not go,
For I fear those guns will fire.
But you may go to church instead   15
And sing in the children's choir."

She has combed and brushed her night-dark hair,
And bathed rose petal sweet.
And drawn white gloves on her small brown hands,
And white shoes on her feet.   20

The mother smiled to know her child
Was in the sacred place,
But that smile was the last smile
To come upon her face.

For when she heard the explosion,   25
Her eyes grew wet and wild.
She raced through the streets of Birmingham
Calling for her child.

She clawed through bits of glass and brick,
Then lifted out a shoe.   30
"Oh, here's the shoe my baby wore,
But, baby, where are you?"

ADRIENNE RICH (b. 1929)
Living in Sin   1955

She had thought the studio would keep itself,
no dust upon the furniture of love.
Half heresy, to wish the taps less vocal,
the panes relieved of grime. A plate of pears,
a piano with a Persian shawl, a cat   5
stalking the picturesque amusing mouse
had risen at his urging.
Not that at five each separate stair would writhe
under the milkman's tramp; that morning light
so coldly would delineate the scraps   10
of last night's cheese and three sepulchral bottles;
that on the kitchen shelf among the saucers
a pair of beetle-eyes would fix her own —
envoy from some black village in the mouldings . . .
Meanwhile, he, with a yawn,   15
sounded a dozen notes upon the keyboard,

declared it out of tune, shrugged at the mirror,
rubbed at his beard, went out for cigarettes;
while she, jeered by the minor demons,
pulled back the sheets and made the bed and found   20
a towel to dust the table-top,
and let the coffee-pot boil over on the stove.
By evening she was back in love again,
though not so wholly but throughout the night
she woke sometimes to feel the daylight coming   25
like a relentless milkman up the stairs.

EDWIN ARLINGTON ROBINSON (1869–1935)

Mr. Flood's Party   1921

Old Eben Flood, climbing alone one night
Over the hill between the town below
And the forsaken upland hermitage
That held as much as he should ever know
On earth again of home, paused warily.   5
The road was his and not a native near;
And Eben, having leisure, said aloud,
For no man else in Tilbury Town to hear:

"Well, Mr. Flood, we have the harvest moon
Again, and we may not have many more;   10
The bird is on the wing, the poet says,°
And you and I have said it here before.
Drink to the bird." He raised up to the light
The jug that he had gone so far to fill,
And answered huskily: "Well, Mr. Flood,   15
Since you propose it, I believe I will."

Alone, as if enduring to the end
A valiant armor of scarred hopes outworn,
He stood there in the middle of the road
Like Roland's ghost winding a silent horn.°   20
Below him, in the town among the trees,
Where friends of other days had honored him,
A phantom salutation of the dead
Rang thinly till old Eben's eyes were dim.

11 *The bird* . . . *says:* Edward Fitzgerald says this of the "Bird of Time" in "The Rubáiyát of Omar
Khayyám."   20 *Like Roland's* . . . *horn:* Roland, hero of French romance, blew his ivory horn to
warn his allies of impending attack.

Then, as a mother lays her sleeping child   25
Down tenderly, fearing it may awake,
He set the jug down slowly at his feet
With trembling care, knowing that most things break;
And only when assured that on firm earth
It stood, as the uncertain lives of men   30
Assuredly did not, he paced away,
And with his hand extended paused again:

"Well, Mr. Flood, we have not met like this
In a long time; and many a change has come
To both of us, I fear, since last it was   35
We had a drop together. Welcome home!"
Convivially returning with himself,
Again he raised the jug up to the light;
And with an acquiescent quaver said:
"Well, Mr. Flood, if you insist, I might.   40

"Only a very little, Mr. Flood —
For auld lang syne. No more, sir; that will do."
So, for the time, apparently it did,
And Eben evidently thought so too;
For soon amid the silver loneliness   45
Of night he lifted up his voice and sang,
Secure, with only two moons listening,
Until the whole harmonious landscape rang —

"For auld lang syne." The weary throat gave out,
The last word wavered, and the song being done.   50
He raised again the jug regretfully
And shook his head, and was again alone.
There was not much that was ahead of him,
And there was nothing in the town below —
Where strangers would have shut the many doors   55
That many friends had opened long ago.

THEODORE ROETHKE (1908–1963)

I Knew a Woman   1958

I knew a woman, lovely in her bones,
When small birds sighed, she would sigh back at them;
Ah, when she moved, she moved more ways than one:
The shapes a bright container can contain!
Of her choice virtues only gods should speak,   5
Or English poets who grew up on Greek
(I'd have them sing in chorus, cheek to cheek).

How well her wishes went! She stroked my chin,
She taught me Turn, and Counter-turn, and Stand;°
She taught me Touch, that undulant white skin; 10
I nibbled meekly from her proffered hand;
She was the sickle; I, poor I, the rake,
Coming behind her for her pretty sake
(But what prodigious mowing we did make).

Love likes a gander, and adores a goose: 15
Her full lips pursed, the errant note to seize;
She played it quick, she played it light and loose;
My eyes, they dazzled at her flowing knees;
Her several parts could keep a pure repose,
Or one hip quiver with a mobile nose 20
(She moved in circles, and those circles moved).

Let seed be grass, and grass turn into hay:
I'm martyr to a motion not my own;
What's freedom for? To know eternity.
I swear she cast a shadow white as stone. 25
But who would count eternity in days?
These old bones live to learn her wanton ways:
(I measure time by how a body sways).

9 *Turn . . . Stand:* Parts of a Pindaric ode.

CHRISTINA ROSSETTI (1830–1894)
Uphill   1861

Does the road wind uphill all the way?
    Yes, to the very end.
Will the day's journey take the whole long day?
    From morn to night, my friend.

But is there for the night a resting place? 5
    A roof for when the slow dark hours begin.
May not the darkness hide it from my face?
    You cannot miss that inn.

Shall I meet other wayfarers at night?
    Those who have gone before. 10
Then must I knock, or call when just in sight?
    They will not keep you standing at that door.

Shall I find comfort, travel-sore and weak?
    Of labor you shall find the sum.
Will there be beds for me and all who seek? 15
    Yea, beds for all who come.

ANNE SEXTON (1928–1974)
Lobster

1976

A shoe with legs,
a stone dropped from heaven,
he does his mournful work alone,
he is like the old prospector for gold,
with secret dreams of God-heads and fish heads.   5
Until suddenly a cradle fastens round him
and he is trapped as the U.S.A. sleeps.
Somewhere far off a woman lights a cigarette;
somewhere far off a car goes over a bridge;
somewhere far off a bank is held up.   10
This is the world the lobster knows not of.
He is the old hunting dog of the sea
who in the morning will rise from it
and be undrowned
and they will take his perfect green body   15
and paint it red.

WILLIAM SHAKESPEARE (1564–1616)
Not marble, nor the gilded monuments

1609

Not marble, nor the gilded monuments
Of princes, shall outlive this powerful rhyme;
But you shall shine more bright in these conténts
Than unswept stone, besmeared with sluttish time.
When wasteful war shall statues overturn,   5
And broils root out the work of masonry,
Nor Mars his° sword nor war's quick fire shall burn   *possessive of Mars*
The living record of your memory.
'Gainst death and all-oblivious enmity
Shall you pace forth; your praise shall still find room   10
Even in the eyes of all posterity
That wear this world out to the ending doom.
    So, till the judgment that yourself arise,
    You live in this, and dwell in lovers' eyes.

WILLIAM SHAKESPEARE (1564–1616)
Spring°

c. 1595

When daisies pied and violets blue
    And ladysmocks all silver-white
And cuckoobuds of yellow hue
    Do paint the meadows with delight,
The cuckoo then, on every tree,   5
Mocks married men;° for thus sings he,
           Cuckoo;
Cuckoo, cuckoo: Oh word of fear,
Unpleasing to a married ear!

When shepherds pipe on oaten straws,   10
    And merry larks are plowmen's clocks,
When turtles tread,° and rooks, and daws,
    And maidens bleach their summer smocks,
The cuckoo then, on every tree,
Mocks married men; for thus sings he,   15
           Cuckoo;
Cuckoo, cuckoo: Oh word of fear,
Unpleasing to a married ear!

Spring: Song from *Love's Labour's Lost,* V. ii.   6 *Mocks married men:* By singing "cuckoo," which sounds like "cuckold."   12 *turtles tread:* Turtledoves copulate.

WILLIAM SHAKESPEARE (1564–1616)
That time of year thou mayst in me behold

1609

That time of year thou mayst in me behold
When yellow leaves, or none, or few, do hang
Upon those boughs which shake against the cold,
Bare ruined choirs, where late the sweet birds sang.
In me thou see'st the twilight of such day   5
As after sunset fadeth in the west;
Which by and by black night doth take away,
Death's second self,° that seals up all in rest.   *sleep*
In me thou see'st the glowing of such fire,
That on the ashes of his youth doth lie,   10
As the deathbed whereon it must expire,
Consumed with that which it was nourished by.
    This thou perceiv'st, which makes thy love more strong,
    To love that well which thou must leave ere long.

WILLIAM SHAKESPEARE (1564–1616)
When forty winters shall besiege thy brow   1609

When forty winters shall besiege thy brow
And dig deep trenches in thy beauty's field,
Thy youth's proud livery, so gazed on now,
Will be a tattered weed,° of small worth held.   *garment*
Then being asked where all thy beauty lies,   5
Where all the treasure of thy lusty days,
To say within thine own deep-sunken eyes
Were an all-eating shame and thriftless praise.
How much more praise deserved thy beauty's use
If thou couldst answer, "This fair child of mine   10
Shall sum my count and make my old excuse,"
Proving his beauty by succession thine.
    This were to be new made when thou art old,
    And see thy blood warm when thou feel'st it cold.

WILLIAM SHAKESPEARE (1564–1616)
When, in disgrace with Fortune and men's eyes   1609

When, in disgrace with Fortune and men's eyes,
I all alone beweep my outcast state,
And trouble deaf heaven with my bootless cries,
And look upon myself and curse my fate,
Wishing me like to one more rich in hope,   5
Featured like him, like him with friends possessed,
Desiring this man's art, and that man's scope,
With what I most enjoy contented least,
Yet in these thoughts myself almost despising,
Haply I think on thee, and then my state,   10
Like to the lark at break of day arising
From sullen earth, sings hymns at heaven's gate;
    For thy sweet love remembered such wealth brings
    That then I scorn to change my state with kings.

WILLIAM SHAKESPEARE (1564–1616)
Winter°

When icicles hang by the wall
    And Dick the shepherd blows his nail,°
And Tom bears logs into the hall,
    And milk comes frozen home in pail.
When blood is nipped and ways be foul,   5
Then nightly sings the staring owl,
          Tu-who;
Tu-whit, tu-who: a merry note,
While greasy Joan doth keel the pot.°

When all aloud the wind doth blow,   10
    And coughing drowns the parson's saw,°   *maxim*
And birds sit brooding in the snow,
    And Marian's nose looks red and raw,
When roasted crabs° hiss in the bowl,   *crabapples*
Then nightly sings the staring owl,   15
          Tu-who;
Tu-whit, tu-who: a merry note
While greasy Joan doth keel the pot.

Winter: Song from *Love's Labour's Lost,* V. ii.   *2 blows his nail:* Blows on his hands for warmth.
9 keel the pot: Cool the contents of the pot by stirring.

PERCY BYSSHE SHELLEY (1792–1822)
Ozymandias°

I met a traveler from an antique land
Who said: Two vast and trunkless legs of stone
Stand in the desert. . . . Near them, on the sand,
Half sunk, a shattered visage lies, whose frown,
And wrinkled lip, and sneer of cold command,   5
Tell that its sculptor well those passions read
Which yet survive, stamped on these lifeless things,
The hand that mocked them, and the heart that fed:
And on the pedestal these words appear:
"My name is Ozymandias, King of Kings: 10

Ozymandias: Greek name for Ramses II, pharaoh of Egypt for sixty-seven years during the 13th century B.C. His colossal statue lies prostrate in the sands of Luxor. Napoleon's soldiers measured it (56 feet long, ear 3½ feet long, weight 1,000 tons). Its inscription, according to the Greek historian Diodorus Siculus, was "I am Ozymandias, King of Kings; if anyone wishes to know what I am and where I lie, let him surpass me in some of my exploits."

Look on my works, ye Mighty, and despair!"
Nothing beside remains. Round the decay
Of that colossal wreck, boundless and bare
The lone and level sands stretch far away.

SIR PHILIP SIDNEY (1554–1586)
Loving in Truth, and Fain in Verse
My Love to Show   1591

Loving in truth, and fain in verse my love to show,
That she, dear she, might take some pleasure of my pain,
Pleasure might cause her read, reading might make her know,
Knowledge might pity win, and pity grace obtain,
I sought fit words to pain the blackest face of woe,   5
Studying inventions fine, her wits to entertain,
Oft turning others' leaves, to see if thence would flow
Some fresh and fruitful showers upon my sunburnt brain.
But words came halting forth, wanting Invention's stay;
Invention, Nature's child, fled step-dame° Study's blows;   *stepmother* 10
And others' feet still seemed but strangers in my way.
Thus great with child to speak, and helpless in my throes,
Biting my truant pen, beating myself for spite:
"Fool," said my Muse to me, "look in thy heart and write."

LESLIE MARMON SILKO (b. 1948)
Where Mountain Lion Lay Down with Deer   1981

I climb the black rock mountain
  stepping from day to day
                silently.
I smell the wind for my ancestors
      pale blue leaves   5
      crushed wild mountain smell.
Returning
  up the gray stone cliff
  where I descended
                a thousand years ago   10
Returning to faded black stone
where mountain lion lay down with deer.
It is better to stay up here
            watching wind's reflection
            in tall yellow flowers.   15

The old ones who remember me are gone
        the old songs are all forgotten
and the story of my birth.

How I danced in snow-frost moonlight
        distant stars to the end of the Earth,   20
How I swam away
              in freezing mountain water
              narrow mossy canyon tumbling down
                    out of the mountain
                    out of deep canyon stone   25
          down
              the memory
                    spilling out
                    into the world.

W. D. SNODGRASS (b. 1926)
April Inventory   1959

The green catalpa tree has turned
All white; the cherry blooms once more.
In one whole year I haven't learned
A blessed thing they pay you for.
The blossoms snow down in my hair;   5
The trees and I will soon be bare.

The trees have more than I to spare.
The sleek, expensive girls I teach,
Younger and pinker every year,
Bloom gradually out of reach.   10
The pear tree lets its petals drop
Like dandruff on a tabletop.

The girls have grown so young by now
I have to nudge myself to stare.
This year they smile and mind me how   15
My teeth are falling with my hair.
In thirty years I may not get
Younger, shrewder, or out of debt.

The tenth time, just a year ago,
I made myself a little list   20
Of all the things I'd ought to know,
Then told my parents, analyst,
And everyone who's trusted me
I'd be substantial, presently.

I haven't read one book about   25
A book or memorized one plot.

Or found a mind I did not doubt.
I learned one date. And then forgot.
And one by one the solid scholars
Get the degrees, the jobs, the dollars.   30

And smile above their starchy collars.
I taught my classes Whitehead's° notions;
One lovely girl, a song of Mahler's.°
Lacking a source-book or promotions,
I showed one child the colors of   35
A luna moth and how to love.

I taught myself to name my name,
To bark back, loosen love and crying;
To ease my woman so she came,
To ease an old man who was dying.   40
I have not learned how often I
Can win, can love, but choose to die.

I have not learned there is a lie
Love shall be blonder, slimmer, younger;
That my equivocating eye   45
Loves only by my body's hunger;
That I have forces, true to feel,
Or that the lovely world is real.

While scholars speak authority
And wear their ulcers on their sleeves,   50
My eyes in spectacles shall see
These trees procure and spend their leaves.
There is a value underneath
The gold and silver in my teeth.

Though trees turn bare and girls turn wives,   55
We shall afford our costly seasons;
There is a gentleness survives
That will outspeak and has its reasons.
There is a loveliness exists,
Preserves us, not for specialists.   60

32 *Whitehead:* Alfred North Whitehead (1861–1947), English mathematician and philosopher.
33 *Mahler:* Gustav Mahler (1860–1911), Austrian Post-Romantic composer, known for his songs and
symphonies.

GARY SNYDER (b. 1930)
After weeks of watching the roof leak

1967

After weeks of watching the roof leak
      I fixed it tonight
by moving a single board

WALLACE STEVENS (1879–1955)
The Emperor of Ice-Cream

1923

Call the roller of big cigars,
The muscular one, and bid him whip
In kitchen cups concupiscent curds.°
Let the wenches dawdle in such dress
As they are used to wear, and let the boys   5
Bring flowers in last month's newspapers.
Let be be finale of seem.°
The only emperor is the emperor of ice-cream.

Take from the dresser of deal,
Lacking the three glass knobs, that sheet   10
On which she embroidered fantails once
And spread it so as to cover her face.
If her horny feet protrude, they come
To show how cold she is, and dumb.
Let the lamp affix its beam.   15
The only emperor is the emperor of ice-cream.

---

3 *concupiscent curds:* "The words 'concupiscent curds' have no genealogy; they are merely expressive: at least, I hope they are expressive. They express the concupiscence of life, but, by contrast with the things in relation in the poem, they express or accentuate life's destitution, and it is this that gives them something more than a cheap lustre" (Wallace Stevens, *Letters* [New York: Knopf, 1960], p. 500).   7 *Let . . . seem:* "The true sense of 'Let be be the finale of seem' is let being become the conclusion or denouement of appearing to be: in short, ice cream is an absolute good. The poem is obviously not about ice cream, but about being as distinguished from seeming to be" (*Letters,* p. 341).

WALLACE STEVENS (1879–1955)
Sunday Morning   1915

I
Complacencies of the peignoir, and late
Coffee and oranges in a sunny chair,
And the green freedom of a cockatoo
Upon a rug mingle to dissipate
The holy hush of ancient sacrifice.   5
She dreams a little, and she feels the dark
Encroachment of that old catastrophe,°   *the Crucifixion*
As a calm darkens among water-lights.
The pungent oranges and bright, green wings
Seem things in some procession of the dead,   10
Winding across wide water, without sound.
The day is like wide water, without sound,
Stilled for the passing of her dreaming feet
Over the seas, to silent Palestine,
Dominion of the blood and sepulcher.   15

II
Why should she give her bounty to the dead?
What is divinity if it can come
Only in silent shadows and in dreams?
Shall she not find in comforts of the sun,
In pungent fruit and bright, green wings, or else   20
In any balm or beauty of the earth,
Things to be cherished like the thought of heaven?
Divinity must live within herself:
Passions of rain, or moods in falling snow;
Grievings in loneliness, or unsubdued   25
Elations when the forest blooms; gusty
Emotions on wet roads on autumn nights;
All pleasures and all pains, remembering
The bough of summer and the winter branch.
These are the measures destined for her soul.   30

III
Jove° in the clouds had his inhuman birth.
No mother suckled him, no sweet land gave
Large-mannered motions to his mythy mind
He moved among us, as a muttering king,
Magnificent, would move among his hinds,°   *peasant subjects* 35
Until our blood, commingling, virginal,
With heaven, brought such requital to desire
The very hinds discerned it, in a star,°   *of Bethlehem*
Shall our blood fail? Or shall it come to be

31 *Jove:* Jupiter, the supreme Roman god.

The blood of paradise? And shall the earth   40
Seem all of paradise that we shall know?
The sky will be much friendlier then than now,
A part of labor and a part of pain,
And next in glory to enduring love,
Not this dividing and indifferent blue.   45

IV
She says, "I am content when wakened birds,
Before they fly, test the reality
Of misty fields, by their sweet questionings;
But when the birds are gone, and their warm fields
Return no more, where, then, is paradise?"   50
There is not any haunt of prophecy,
Nor any old chimera of the grave,
Neither the golden underground, nor isle
Melodious, where spirits gat° them home,   *got*
Nor visionary south, nor cloudy palm   55
Remote on heaven's hill, that has endured
As April's green endures, or will endure
Like her remembrance of awakened birds,
Or her desire for June and evening, tipped
By the consummation of the swallow's wings.   60

V
She says, "But in contentment I still feel
The need of some imperishable bliss."
Death is the mother of beauty; hence from her,
Alone, shall come fulfillment to our dreams
And our desires. Although she strews the leaves   65
Of sure obliteration on our paths,
The path sick sorrow took, the many paths
Where triumph rang its brassy phrase, or love
Whispered a little out of tenderness,
She makes the willow shiver in the sun   70
For maidens who were wont to sit and gaze
Upon the grass, relinquished to their feet.
She causes boys to pile new plums and pears
On disregarded plate. The maidens taste
And stray impassioned in the littering leaves.   75

VI
Is there no change of death in paradise?
Does ripe fruit never fall? Or do the boughs
Hang always heavy in that perfect sky,
Unchanging, yet so like our perishing earth,
With rivers like our own that seek for seas   80
They never find, the same receding shores
That never touch with inarticulate pang?
Why set the pear upon those river-banks
Or spice the shores with odors of the plum?

Alas, that they should wear our colors there,   85
The silken weavings of our afternoons,
And pick the strings of our insipid lutes!
Death is the mother of beauty, mystical,
Within whose burning bosom we devise
Our earthly mothers waiting, sleeplessly.   90

VII

Supple and turbulent, a ring of men
Shall chant in orgy° on a summer morn   *ritual revelry*
Their boisterous devotion to the sun,
Not as a god, but as a god might be,
Naked among them, like a savage source.   95
Their chant shall be a chant of paradise,
Out of their blood, returning to the sky;
And in their chant shall enter, voice by voice,
The windy lake wherein their lord delights,
The trees, like serafin,° and echoing hills,   100
That choir among themselves long afterward.
They shall know well the heavenly fellowship
Of men that perish and of summer morn.
And whence they came and whither they shall go
The dew upon their feet shall manifest.   105

VIII

She hears, upon that water without sound,
A voice that cries, "The tomb in Palestine
Is not the porch of spirits lingering.
It is the grave of Jesus, where he lay."
We live in an old chaos of the sun,   110
Or old dependency of day and night,
Or island solitude, unsponsored, free,
Of that wide water, inescapable.
Deer walk upon our mountains, and the quail
Whistle about us their spontaneous cries;   115
Sweet berries ripen in the wilderness;
And, in the isolation of the sky,
At evening, casual flocks of pigeons make
Ambiguous undulations as they sink,
Downward to darkness, on extended wings.   120

100 *serafin:* Seraphim, angels having three sets of wings; the highest of the nine orders of angels.

MARK STRAND (b. 1934)

The Continuous Life

1989

What of the neighborhood homes awash
In a silver light, of children hunched in the bushes,
Watching the grownups for signs of surrender,
Signs the irregular pleasures of moving
From day to day, of being adrift on the swell of duty   5
Have run their course? O parents, confess
To your little ones the night is a long way off
And your taste for the mundane grows; tell them
Your worship of household chores has barely begun;
Describe the beauty of shovels and rakes, brooms and mops;   10
Say there will always be cooking and cleaning to do,
That one thing leads to another, which leads to another;
Explain that you live between two great darks, the first
With an ending, the second without one, that the luckiest
Thing is having been born, that you live in a blur   15
Of hours and days, months and years, and believe
It has meaning, despite the occasional fear
You are slipping away with nothing completed, nothing
To prove you existed. Tell the children to come inside,
That your search goes on for something you lost: a name,   20
A book of the family that fell from its own small matter
Into another, a piece of the dark that might have been yours —
You don't really know. Say that each of you tries
To keep busy, learning to lean down close and hear
The careless breathing of earth and feel its available   25
Languor come over you, wave after wave, sending
Small tremors of love through your brief,
Undeniable selves, into your days, and beyond.

ALFRED, LORD TENNYSON (1809–1892)

Crossing the Bar

1889

Sunset and evening star,
    And one clear call for me!
And may there be no moaning of the bar
    When I put out to sea.

But such a tide as moving seems asleep,   5
    Too full for sound and foam,
When that which drew from out the boundless deep
    Turns again home.

Twilight and evening bell,
    And after that the dark!
And may there be no sadness of farewell
    When I embark;

For though from out our bourne of Time and Place
    The flood may bear me far,
I hope to see my Pilot face to face
    When I have crossed the bar.

10

15

ALFRED, LORD TENNYSON (1809–1892)
Ulysses°

1833

    It little profits that an idle king,
By this still hearth, among these barren crags,
Matched with an agéd wife,° I mete and dole   *Penelope*
Unequal laws unto a savage race,
That hoard, and sleep, and feed, and know not me.   5
    I cannot rest from travel; I will drink
Life to the lees. All times I have enjoyed
Greatly, have suffered greatly, both with those
That loved me, and alone; on shore, and when
Through scudding drifts the rainy Hyades°   10
Vexed the dim sea. I am become a name;
For always roaming with a hungry heart
Much have I seen and known — cities of men
And manners, climates, councils, governments,
Myself not least, but honored of them all —   15
And drunk delight of battle with my peers,
Far on the ringing plains of windy Troy.
I am a part of all that I have met;
Yet all experience is an arch wherethrough
Gleams that untraveled world, whose margin fades   20
For ever and for ever when I move.
How dull it is to pause, to make an end,
To rust unburnished, not to shine in use!
As though to breathe were life. Life piled on life
Were all too little, and of one to me   25
Little remains; but every hour is saved
From that eternal silence, something more,
A bringer of new things; and vile it were
For some three suns to store and hoard myself,
And this gray spirit yearning in desire   30

Ulysses: Ulysses, the hero of Homer's epic poem the *Odyssey,* is presented by Dante in *The Inferno,*
XXVI, as restless after his return to Ithaca, and eager for new adventures.   10 *Hyades:* Five stars in
the constellation Taurus, supposed by the ancients to predict rain when they rose with the sun.

To follow knowledge like a sinking star,
Beyond the utmost bound of human thought.

    This is my son, mine own Telemachus,
To whom I leave the scepter and the isle —
Well-loved of me, discerning to fulfill   35
This labor by slow prudence to make mild
A rugged people, and through soft degrees
Subdue them to the useful and the good.
Most blameless is he, centered in the sphere
Of common duties, decent not to fail   40
In offices of tenderness, and pay
Meet adoration to my household gods,
When I am gone. He works his work, I mine.

    There lies the port; the vessel puffs her sail:
There gloom the dark, broad seas. My mariners,   45
Souls that have toiled, and wrought, and thought with me —
That ever with a frolic welcome took
The thunder and the sunshine, and opposed
Free hearts, free foreheads — you and I are old;
Old age hath yet his honor and his toil.   50
Death closes all; but something ere the end,
Some work of noble note, may yet be done,
Not unbecoming men that strove with Gods.
The lights begin to twinkle from the rocks;
The long day wanes; the slow moon climbs; the deep   55
Moans round with many voices. Come, my friends.
'Tis not too late to seek a newer world.
Push off, and sitting well in order smite
The sounding furrows; for my purpose holds
To sail beyond the sunset, and the baths   60
Of all the western stars, until I die.
It may be that the gulfs will wash us down;
It may be we shall touch the Happy Isles,°
And see the great Achilles,° whom we knew.
Though much is taken, much abides; and though   65
We are not now that strength which in old days
Moved earth and heaven, that which we are, we are:
One equal temper of heroic hearts,
Made weak by time and fate, but strong in will
To strive, to seek, to find, and not to yield.   70

---

63 *Happy Isles:* Elysium, the home after death of heroes and others favored by the gods. It was thought
by the ancients to lie beyond the sunset in the uncharted Atlantic.   64 *Achilles:* The hero of Homer's
Iliad.

DYLAN THOMAS (1914–1953)

Fern Hill

1946

Now as I was young and easy under the apple boughs
About the lilting house and happy as the grass was green,
   The night above the dingle starry,
     Time let me hail and climb
    Golden in the heydays of his eyes, 5
And honored among wagons I was prince of the apple towns
And once below a time I lordly had the trees and leaves
     Trail with daisies and barley
    Down the rivers of the windfall light.

And as I was green and carefree, famous among the barns 10
About the happy yard and singing as the farm was home,
   In the sun that is young once only,
     Time let me play and be
    Golden in the mercy of his means,
And green and golden I was huntsman and herdsman, the calves 15
Sang to my horn, the foxes on the hills barked clear and cold,
     And the sabbath rang slowly
    In the pebbles of the holy streams.

All the sun long it was running, it was lovely, the hay
Fields high as the house, the tunes from the chimneys, it was air 20
   And playing, lovely and watery
     And fire green as grass.
    And nightly under the simple stars
As I rode to sleep the owls were bearing the farm away,
All the moon long I heard, blessed among stables, the nightjars 25
   Flying with the ricks, and the horses
     Flashing into the dark.

And then to awake, and the farm, like a wanderer white
With the dew, come back, the cock on his shoulder; it was all
   Shining, it was Adam and maiden, 30
     The sky gathered again
    And the sun grew round that very day.
So it must have been after the birth of the simple light
In the first, spinning place, the spellbound horses walking warm
   Out of the whinnying green stable 35
    On to the fields of praise.

And honored among foxes and pheasants by the gay house
Under the new made clouds and happy as the heart was long,
   In the sun born over and over,
    I ran my heedless ways, 40
   My wishes raced through the house-high hay
And nothing I cared, at my sky-blue trades, that time allows
In all his tuneful turning so few and such morning songs

Before the children green and golden
    Follow him out of grace,   45

Nothing I cared, in the lamb white days, that time would take me
Up to the swallow-thronged loft by the shadow of my hand,
    In the moon that is always rising,
        Nor that riding to sleep
    I should hear him fly with the high fields   50
And wake to the farm forever fled from the childless land.
Oh as I was young and easy in the mercy of his means,
        Time held me green and dying
    Though I sang in my chains like the sea.

ROBERT WALLACE (b. 1932)
The Double-Play   1961

In his sea lit
distance, the pitcher winding
like a clock about to chime comes down with

the ball, hit
sharply, under the artificial   5
banks of arc-lights, bounds like a vanishing string

over the green
to the shortstop magically
scoops to his right whirling above his invisible

shadows   10
in the dust redirects
its flight to the running poised second baseman

pirouettes
leaping, above the slide, to throw
from mid-air, across the colored tightened interval,   15

to the leaning-
out first baseman ends the dance
drawing it disappearing into his long brown glove

stretches. What
is too swift for deception   20
is final, lost, among the loosened figures

jogging off the field
(the pitcher walks), casual
in the space where the poem has happened.

EDMUND WALLER (1606–1687)
Go, Lovely Rose

1645

    Go, lovely rose,
Tell her that wastes her time and me
    That now she knows,
When I resemble° her to thee,   *compare*
How sweet and fair she seems to be.   5

    Tell her that's young
And shuns to have her graces spied,
    That hadst thou sprung
In deserts where no men abide,
Thou must have uncommended died.   10

    Small is the worth
Of beauty from the light retired:
    Bid her come forth,
Suffer herself to be desired,
And not blush so to be admired.   15

    Then die, that she
The common fate of all things rare
    May read in thee,
How small a part of time they share
That are so wondrous sweet and fair.   20

WALT WHITMAN (1819–1892)
The Dalliance of the Eagles

1880

Skirting the river road, (my forenoon walk, my rest,)
Skyward in air a sudden muffled sound, the dalliance of the eagles,
The rushing amorous contact high in space together,
The clinching interlocking claws, a living, fierce, gyrating wheel,
Four beating wings, two beaks, a swirling mass tight grappling,   5
In tumbling turning clustering loops, straight downward falling,
Till o'er the river poised, the twain yet one, a moment's lull,
A motionless still balance in the air, then parting, talons loosing,
Upward again on slow-firm pinions slanting, their separate diverse flight,
She hers, he his, pursuing.   10

WALT WHITMAN (1819–1892)
One's-Self I Sing   1867

One's-Self I sing, a simple separate person,
Yet utter the word Democratic, the word En-Masse.

Of physiology from top to toe I sing,
Not physiognomy alone nor brain alone is worthy for the Muse, I say the Form
    complete is worthier far,
The Female equally with the Male I sing.

Of Life immense in passion, pulse, and power,
Cheerful, for freest action formed under the laws divine,
The Modern Man I sing.

WALT WHITMAN (1819–1892)
There Was a Child Went Forth   1855

There was a child went forth every day,
And the first object he looked upon, that object he became,
And that object became part of him for the day or a certain part of the day,
Or for many years or stretching cycles of years.

The early lilacs became part of this child,   5
And grass and white and red morning-glories, and white and red clover,
    and the song of the phoebe-bird,
And the Third-month° lambs and the sow's pink-faint litter, and the mare's
    foal and the cow's calf,
And the noisy brood of the barnyard or by the mire of the pond-side,
And the fish suspending themselves so curiously below there, and the
    beautiful curious liquid,
And the water-plants with their graceful flat heads, all became part of him.   10

The field-sprouts of Fourth-month and Fifth-month became part of him,
Winter-grain sprouts and those of the light-yellow corn, and the esculent
    roots of the garden,
And the apple-trees covered with blossoms and the fruit afterward, and
    wood-berries, and the commonest weeds by the road,
And the old drunkard staggering home from the outhouse of the tavern
    whence he had lately risen,
And the schoolmistress that passed on her way to the school,   15
And the friendly boys that passed, and the quarrelsome boys,
And the tidy and fresh-cheeked girls, and the barefoot negro boy and girl,
And all the changes of city and country wherever he went.

---

7 *Third-month:* March; Whitman is following the Quaker practice of naming the months by their
number in the year's sequence.

His own parents, he that had fathered him and she that had conceived him
  in her womb and birthed him,
They gave this child more of themselves than that,   20
They gave him afterward every day, they became part of him.

The mother at home quietly placing the dishes on the supper-table,
The mother with mild words, clean her cap and gown, a wholesome odor
  falling off her person and clothes as she walks by,
The father, strong, self-sufficient, manly, mean, angered, unjust,
The blow, the quick loud word, the tight bargain, the crafty lure,   25
The family usages, the language, the company, the furniture, the yearning
  and swelling heart,
Affection that will not be gainsayed, the sense of what is real, the thought if
  after all it should prove unreal,
The doubts of day-time and the doubts of night-time, the curious whether
  and how,
Whether that which appears so is so, or is it all flashes and specks?
Men and women crowding fast in the streets, if they are not flashes and
  specks what are they?   30
The streets themselves and the facades of houses, and goods in the windows,
Vehicles, teams, the heavy-planked wharves, the huge crossing at the ferries,
The village on the highland seen from afar at sunset, the river between,
Shadows, aureola and mist, the light falling on roofs and gables of white or
  brown two miles off,
The schooner near by sleepily dropping down the tide, the little boat slack-
  towed astern,   35
The hurrying tumbling waves, quick-broken crests, slapping,
The strata of colored clouds, the long bar of maroon-tint away solitary by
  itself, the spread of purity it lies motionless in,
The horizon's edge, the flying sea-crow, the fragrance of salt marsh and
  shore mud,
These became part of that child who went forth every day, and who now
  goes, and will always go forth every day.

RICHARD WILBUR (b. 1921)
Love Calls Us to the Things of This World°   1956

　　The eyes open to a cry of pulleys,°
And spirited from sleep, the astounded soul
Hangs for a moment bodiless and simple
As false dawn.
　　　　　　Outside the open window   5
The morning air is all awash with angels.

Love Calls Us . . . : From St. Augustine's *Commentary on the Psalms.*   1 *pulleys:* Grooved wheels at
each end of a laundry line; clothes are hung on the line and advance as the line is moved.

Some are in bed-sheets, some are in blouses,
Some are in smocks: but truly there they are.
Now they are rising together in calm swells
Of halcyon feeling, filling whatever they wear   10
With the deep joy of their impersonal breathing;
Now they are flying in place, conveying
The terrible speed of their omnipresence, moving
And staying like white water; and now of a sudden
They swoon down into so rapt a quiet   15
That nobody seems to be there.
                              The soul shrinks

                From all that it is about to remember,
From the punctual rape of every blessèd day,
And cries,   20
            "Oh, let there be nothing on earth but laundry,
Nothing but rosy hands in the rising steam
And clear dances done in the sight of heaven."

Yet, as the sun acknowledges
With a warm look the world's hunks and colors,   25
The soul descends once more in bitter love
To accept the waking body, saying now
In a changed voice as the man yawns and rises,

"Bring them down from their ruddy gallows;
Let there be clean linen for the backs of thieves; 30
Let lovers go fresh and sweet to be undone,
And the heaviest nuns walk in a pure floating
Of dark habits,
              keeping their difficult balance."

RICHARD WILBUR (b. 1921)
The Writer   1976

In her room at the prow of the house
Where light breaks, and the windows are tossed with linden,
My daughter is writing a story.

I pause in the stairwell, hearing
From her shut door a commotion of typewriter-keys 5
Like a chain hauled over a gunwale.

Young as she is, the stuff
Of her life is a great cargo, and some of it heavy:
I wish her a lucky passage.

But now it is she who pauses,
As if to reject my thought and its easy figure.
A stillness greatens, in which   10

The whole house seems to be thinking,
And then she is at it again with a bunched clamor
Of strokes, and again is silent.   15

I remember the dazed starling
Which was trapped in that very room, two years ago;
How we stole in, lifted a sash

And retreated, not to affright it;
And how for a helpless hour, through the crack of the door,   20
We watched the sleek, wild, dark

And iridescent creature
Batter against the brilliance, drop like a glove
To the hard floor, or the desk-top,

And wait then, humped and bloody,   25
For the wits to try it again; and how our spirits
Rose when, suddenly sure,

If lifted off from a chair-back,
Beating a smooth course for the right window
And clearing the sill of the world.   30

It is always a matter, my darling,
Of life or death, as I had forgotten. I wish
What I wished you before, but harder.

MILLER WILLIAMS (b. 1930)
After a Brubeck Concert   1986

Six hundred years ago, more or less,
something more than eight million couples
coupled to have me here at last, at last.
Had not each fondling, fighting, or fumbling pair
conjoined at the exquisitely right time,   5
thirty-four million times, I would be an unborn,
one of the quiet ones who are less than air.
But I will be also, when six hundred years have passed,
one of seventeen million who made love
aiming without aiming to at one   10
barely imaginable, who may then be doing
something no one I know has ever done
or thought of doing, on some distant world
we did not know about when we were here.
Or maybe sitting in a room like this,   15

eating a cheese sandwich and drinking beer,
a small lamp not quite taking the room from the dark,
with someone sitting nearby, humming something
while two dogs, one far away, answer bark for bark.

WILLIAM CARLOS WILLIAMS (1883–1963)
Spring and All 1923

By the road to the contagious hospital
under the surge of the blue
mottled clouds driven from the
northeast — a cold wind. Beyond, the
waste of broad, muddy fields   5
brown with dried weeds, standing and fallen

patches of standing water
and scattering of tall trees

All along the road the reddish
purplish, forked, upstanding, twiggy   10
stuff of bushes and small trees
with dead, brown leaves under them
leafless vines —

Lifeless in appearance, sluggish
dazed spring approaches —   15

They enter the new world naked,
cold, uncertain of all
save that they enter. All about them
the cold, familiar wind —

Now the grass, tomorrow   20
the stiff curl of wildcarrot leaf
One by one objects are defined —
It quickens: clarity, outline of leaf

But now the stark dignity of
entrance — Still, the profound change   25
has come upon them: rooted, they
grip down and begin to awaken

WILLIAM CARLOS WILLIAMS (1883–1963)
This Is Just to Say
1934

I have eaten
the plums
that were in
the icebox

and which   5
you were probably
saving
for breakfast

Forgive me
they were delicious   10
so sweet
and so cold

WILLIAM WORDSWORTH (1770–1850)
I Wandered Lonely as a Cloud
1807

I wandered lonely as a cloud
That floats on high o'er vales and hills,
When all at once I saw a crowd,
A host, of golden daffodils,
Beside the lake, beneath the trees,   5
Fluttering and dancing in the breeze.

Continuous as the stars that shine
And twinkle on the milky way,
They stretched in never-ending line
Along the margin of a bay;   10
Ten thousand saw I at a glance,
Tossing their heads in sprightly dance.

The waves beside them danced, but they
Outdid the sparkling waves in glee;
A poet could not but be gay,   15
In such a jocund company;
I gazed — and gazed — but little thought
What wealth the show to me had brought:

For oft, when on my couch I lie
In vacant or in pensive mood,   20
They flash upon that inward eye
Which is the bliss of solitude;
And then my heart with pleasure fills,
And dances with the daffodils.

WILLIAM WORDSWORTH (1770–1850)
She Dwelt among the Untrodden Ways   1800

She dwelt among the untrodden ways
    Beside the springs of Dove,°
A Maid whom there were none to praise
    And very few to love:

A violet by a mossy stone   5
    Half hidden from the eye!
— Fair as a star, when only one
    Is shining in the sky.

She lived unknown, and few could know
    When Lucy ceased to be;   10
But she is in her grave, and, oh,
    The difference to me!

2 *Dove:* A stream near Wordsworth's home in the Lake District of England.

WILLIAM WORDSWORTH (1770–1850)
A Slumber Did My Spirit Seal   1800

A slumber did my spirit seal;
    I had no human fears —
She seemed a thing that could not feel
    The touch of earthly years.

No motion has she now, no force;
    She neither hears nor sees;
Rolled round in earth's diurnal course.
    With rocks, and stones, and trees.

WILLIAM WORDSWORTH (1770–1850)
The Solitary Reaper°   1807

Behold her, single in the field,
Yon solitary Highland lass!
Reaping and singing by herself;

The Solitary Reaper: Dorothy Wordsworth (William's sister) writes that the poem was suggested by this sentence in Thomas Wilkinson's *Tour of Scotland:* "Passed a female who was reaping alone; she sung in Erse, as she bended over her sickle; the sweetest human voice I ever heard: her strains were tenderly melancholy, and felt delicious, long after they were heard no more."

Stop here, or gently pass!
Alone she cuts and binds the grain,   5
And sings a melancholy strain;
O listen! for the vale profound
Is overflowing with the sound.

No nightingale did ever chaunt
More welcome notes to weary bands   10
Of travelers in some shady haunt
Among Arabian sands.
A voice so thrilling ne'er was heard
In springtime from the cuckoo-bird,
Breaking the silence of the seas   15
Among the farthest Hebrides.

Will no one tell me what she sings? —
Perhaps the plaintive numbers flow
For old, unhappy, far-off things,
And battles long ago.   20
Or is it some more humble lay,
Familiar matter of today?
Some natural sorrow, loss, or pain,
That has been, and may be again?

Whate'er the theme, the maiden sang   25
As if her song could have no ending;
I saw her singing at her work,
And o'er the sickle bending —
I listened, motionless and still;
And, as I mounted up the hill,   30
The music in my heart I bore
Long after it was heard no more.

JAMES WRIGHT (1927–1980)
Lying in a Hammock at William Duffy's Farm
in Pine Island, Minnesota   1961

Over my head, I see the bronze butterfly,
Asleep on the black trunk,
Blowing like a leaf in green shadow.
Down the ravine behind the empty house,
The cowbells follow one another   5
Into the distances of the afternoon.
To my right,
In a field of sunlight between two pines,
The droppings of last year's horses
Blaze up into golden stones.   10

I lean back, as the evening darkens and comes on.
A chicken hawk floats over, looking for home.
I have wasted my life.

SIR THOMAS WYATT (1503–1542)
They Flee from Me   1557

They flee from me that sometime did me seek
With naked foot stalking in my chamber.
I have seen them gentle, tame, and meek
That now are wild and do not remember
That sometime they put themselves in danger   5
To take bread at my hand; and now they range
Busily seeking with a continual change.

Thankèd be Fortune, it hath been otherwise
Twenty times better; but once in special,
In thin array after a pleasant guise,   10
When her loose gown from her shoulders did fall,
And she me caught in her arms long and small;°   *narrow*
And therewithall sweetly did me kiss,
And softly said, "Dear heart, how like you this?"

It was no dream; I lay broad waking.   15
But all is turned thorough° my gentleness   *through*
Into a strange fashion of forsaking;
And I have leave to go of her goodness,
And she also to use newfangleness.
But since that I so kindely° am served,   *kindly (ironic)* 20
I fain would know what she hath deserved.

WILLIAM BUTLER YEATS (1865–1939)
Adam's Curse°   1903

We sat together at one summer's end,
That beautiful mild woman, your close friend,
And you and I, and talked of poetry.
I said, "A line will take us hours maybe;
Yet if it does not seem a moment's thought,   5
Our stitching and unstitching has been naught.
Better go down upon your marrow-bones
And scrub a kitchen pavement, or break stones

Adam's Curse: After his fall from grace and eviction from Eden, Adam was cursed with hard work, pain, and death.

Like an old pauper, in all kinds of weather;
For to articulate sweet sounds together
Is to work harder than all these, and yet   10
Be thought an idler by the noisy set
Of bankers, schoolmasters, and clergymen
The martyrs call the world."
                              And thereupon
That beautiful mild woman for whose sake   15
There's many a one shall find out all heartache
On finding that her voice is sweet and low
Replied, "To be born woman is to know—
Although they do not talk of it at school—
That we must labor to be beautiful."   20

I said, "It's certain there is no fine thing
Since Adam's fall but needs much laboring.
There have been lovers who thought love should be
So much compounded of high courtesy
That they would sigh and quote with learned looks   25
Precedents out of beautiful old books;
Yet now it seems an idle trade enough."

We sat grown quiet at the name of love;
We saw the last embers of daylight die,
And in the trembling blue-green of the sky   30
A moon, worn as if it had been a shell
Washed by time's waters as they rose and fell
About the stars and broke in days and years.

I had a thought for no one's but your ears:
That you were beautiful, and that I strove   35
To love you in the old high way of love;
That it had all seemed happy, and yet we'd grown
As weary-hearted as that hollow moon.

WILLIAM BUTLER YEATS (1865–1939)
Crazy Jane Talks with the Bishop   1933

I met the Bishop on the road
And much said he and I.
"Those breasts are flat and fallen now,
Those veins must soon be dry;
Live in a heavenly mansion,   5
Not in some foul sty."

"Fair and foul are near of kin,
And fair needs foul," I cried.
"My friends are gone, but that's a truth

Nor grave nor bed denied,   10
Learned in bodily lowliness
And in the heart's pride.

"A woman can be proud and stiff
When on love intent;
But Love has pitched his mansion in   15
The place of excrement;
For nothing can be sole or whole
That has not been rent."

WILLIAM BUTLER YEATS (1865–1939)
The Lake Isle of Innisfree°   1892

I will arise and go now, and go to Innisfree,
And a small cabin build there, of clay and wattles made:
Nine bean-rows will I have there, a hive for the honey-bee,
And live alone in the bee-loud glade.

And I shall have some peace there, for peace comes dropping slow,   5
Dropping from the veils of the morning to where the cricket sings;
There midnight's all a glimmer, and noon a purple glow,
And evening full of the linnet's wings.

I will arise and go now, for always night and day
I hear lake water lapping with low sounds by the shore: 10
While I stand on the roadway, or on the pavements grey,
I hear it in the deep heart's core.

The Lake Isle of Innisfree: An island in Lough (or Lake) Gill, in western Ireland.

WILLIAM BUTLER YEATS (1865–1939)
Leda and the Swan°   1924

A sudden blow: the great wings beating still
Above the staggering girl, her thighs caressed
By the dark webs, her nape caught in his bill,
He holds her helpless breast upon his breast.

How can those terrified vague fingers push   5
The feathered glory from her loosening thighs?
And how can body, laid in that white rush,
But feel the strange heart beating where it lies?

Leda and the Swan: In Greek myth, Zeus in the form of a swan seduced Leda and fathered Helen of
Troy (whose abduction started the Trojan War) and Clytemnestra, Agamemnon's wife and murderer.
Yeats thought of Zeus's appearance to Leda as a type of annunciation, like the angel appearing to
Mary.

A shudder in the loins engenders there
The broken wall, the burning roof and tower   10
And Agamemnon dead.

                    Being so caught up,
So mastered by the brute blood of the air,
Did she put on his knowledge with his power
Before the indifferent beak could let her drop?

WILLIAM BUTLER YEATS (1865–1939)
Sailing to Byzantium°   1927

I
That is no country for old men.° The young
In one another's arms, birds in the trees
— Those dying generations — at their song,
The salmon-falls, the mackerel-crowded seas
Fish, flesh, or fowl, commend all summer long   5
Whatever is begotten, born and dies.
Caught in that sensual music all neglect
Monuments of unaging intellect.

II
An aged man is but a paltry thing,
A tattered coat upon a stick, unless   10
Soul clap its hands and sing, and louder sing
For every tatter in its mortal dress,
Nor is there singing school but studying
Monuments of its own magnificence;
And therefore I have sailed the seas and come   15
To the holy city of Byzantium.

III
O sages standing in God's holy fire
As in the gold mosaic of a wall,
Come from the holy fire, perne in a gyre,°
And be the singing-masters of my soul.   20
Consume my heart away; sick with desire
And fastened to a dying animal
It knows not what it is; and gather me
Into the artifice of eternity.

Byzantium: Old name for the modern city of Istanbul, capital of the Eastern Roman Empire, ancient artistic and intellectual center. Yeats uses Byzantium as a symbol for "artificial" (and therefore deathless) art and beauty, as opposed to the beauty of the natural world, which is bound to time and death.   1 *That . . . men:* Ireland, part of the time-bound world.   19 *perne in a gyre:* Bobbin making a spiral pattern.

IV

Once out of nature I shall never take   25
My bodily form from any natural thing,
But such a form as Grecian goldsmiths make
Of hammered gold and gold enameling
To keep a drowsy Emperor awake;°
Or set upon a golden bough° to sing   30
To lords and ladies of Byzantium
Of what is past, or passing, or to come.

27–29 *such . . . awake:* "I have read somewhere that in the Emperor's palace at Byzantium was a tree made of gold and silver, and artificial birds that sang" (Yeats's note).   30 *golden bough:* In Greek legend, Aeneas had to pluck a golden bough from a tree in order to descend into Hades. As soon as the bough was plucked, another grew in its place.

WILLIAM BUTLER YEATS (1865–1939)
The Second Coming°   1921

Turning and turning in the widening gyre°
The falcon cannot hear the falconer;
Things fall apart; the center cannot hold;
Mere anarchy is loosed upon the world,
The blood-dimmed tide is loosed, and everywhere   5
The ceremony of innocence is drowned;
The best lack all conviction, while the worst
Are full of passionate intensity.

Surely some revelation is at hand;
Surely the Second Coming is at hand.   10
The Second Coming! Hardly are those words out
When a vast image out of *Spiritus Mundi*°   *Soul of the world*
Troubles my sight: somewhere in sands of the desert
A shape with lion body and the head of a man,
A gaze blank and pitiless as the sun,   15
Is moving its slow thighs, while all about it
Reel shadows of the indignant desert birds.
The darkness drops again; but now I know
That twenty centuries of stony sleep
Were vexed to nightmare by a rocking cradle,   20
And what rough beast, its hour come round at last,
Slouches towards Bethlehem to be born?

The Second Coming: According to Matthew 24:29–44, Christ will return to earth after a time of tribulation to reward the righteous and establish the Millennium of Heaven on earth. Yeats saw his troubled time as the end of the Christian era, and feared the portents of the new cycle.   1 *gyre:* Widening spiral of a falcon's flight, used by Yeats to describe the cycling of history.

CLARIBEL ALEGRÍA (Salvadoran/b. 1924)

Born in Estelí, Nicaragua, Claribel Alegría moved with her family to El Salvador within a year of her birth. A 1948 graduate of George Washington University, she considers herself a Salvadoran, and much of her writing reflects the political upheaval of recent Latin American history. In 1978 she was awarded the Casa de las Americas prize for her book *I Survive*. A bilingual edition of her major works, *Flowers from the Volcano,* was published in 1982.

I Am Mirror
TRANSLATED BY ELECTA ARENAL AND MARSHA GABRIELA DREYER

Water sparkles
on my skin
and I don't feel it
water streams
down my back   5
I don't feel it
I rub myself with a towel
I pinch myself in the arm
I don't feel
frightened I look at myself in the mirror   10
she also pricks herself
I begin to get dressed
stumbling
from the corners
shouts like lightning bolts   15
tortured eyes
scurrying rats
and teeth shoot forth
although I feel nothing
I wander through the streets: 20
children with dirty faces
ask me for charity
child prostitutes
who are not yet fifteen
the streets are paved with pain   25
tanks that approach
raised bayonets

bodies that fall
weeping
finally I feel my arm   30
I am no longer a phantom
I hurt
therefore I exist
I return to watch the scene:
children who run   35
bleeding
women with panic
in their faces
this time it hurts me less
I pinch myself again   40
and already I feel nothing
I simply reflect
what happens at my side
the tanks
are not tanks   45
nor are the shouts
shouts
I am a blank mirror
that nothing penetrates
my surface   50
is hard
is brilliant
is polished
I became a mirror
and I am fleshless   55
scarcely preserving
a vague memory
of pain.

Connections to Other Selections

1. Compare the ways Alegría uses mirror images to reflect life in El Salvador with
   Plath's concerns in "Mirror" (p. 674).
2. Write an essay comparing the speaker's voice in this poem and that in Blake's
   "London" (p. 652). How do the speakers evoke emotional responses to what they
   describe?

KATERINA ANGHELÁKI-ROOKE (Greek/b. 1939)

Born in Athens, Katerina Angheláki-Rooke graduated from the University
of Geneva in 1962. She has been awarded Ford Foundation and Fulbright
grants and has taught at the universities of Iowa and Utah as well as San

Francisco State University and Harvard University. Her works include *Wolves and Clouds* (1963), *Magdalene the Vast Mammal* (1974), and *Counter Love* (1982), which was reprinted as *Being and Things on Their Own*.

Tourism   1975

TRANSLATED BY PHILIP RAMP

My land appeared to me
one morning
like a chunk of bread
tossed in the street
with its doughy crust   5
covered with ants,
countless, black with sunglasses
fidgeting
with their hands and feet.
Loaded with supplies   10
they climb the pine planted hills
the breeze of time blows
withered
while thyme barely breathes
and tightens itself   15
around into empty bottles
and the columns.
Hastily, without passion
they move their hats, antennae
touching whatever fancy   20
they fancy
the post cards, me,
the brown donkey.
Deserted morning
a haze around the keels   25
a mute thoughtful
cleaning fish . . .
Nobody else
empty, me
the ant flocks   30
strolled, shopped . . .
Then empty again.
A far away typewriter
as if from the sea
somebody was dictating   35
the end of the island.
Ant humans
behaving more and more touristically

towards life
they caress without ever   40
reaching the kernel
insects
they enjoy the luminous intervals
of skin,
but the land is swelling   45
dropsical
the owl is crippled
while West and East
both blind
poor things   50
in a ravine
with crows above
excreting on them.
Two old codgers in the countryside
St. Augustine and St. Athanasios°   55
stammer exorcism, recipes,
their holes draughty with lies
as they tremble from cold.
The consoling lines were broken
the images were transliterated   60
and were left without glow.

"Strange days down here,"
the foreign girl said,
"no matter how much you suffer
you rejoice with what you see.   65
The animals emerge from the soil
no hand guides them
they loaf about
they graze colors
and as they stand thoughtful   70
they are politely swallowed
by night."

55 *St. Augustine and St. Athanasios:* The former (354–430) was a Catholic theologian; the latter (293–373) was a Greek patriarch and defender of Catholic teachings.

Connections to Other Selections

1. Discuss the treatment of tourists in this poem and in James Merrill's "Casual Wear" (p. 699).
2. Compare the tone of "Tourism" with that of John Ciardi's "Suburban" (p. 701). How does the speaker of each poem reveal his or her emotions?

ELISABETH EYBERS (South African/b. 1915)

Born in Klerksdorp, South Africa, Elisabeth Eybers grew up speaking Afrikaans but learned English and graduated from the Anglophonic University of the Witwatersrand in 1937. In the early 1960s Eybers left South Africa to live in Holland to protest the political and racial policies of apartheid. She has won several awards, including the Herzog Prize for poetry in 1943 and the Central News Agency Prize for literature in 1973 and 1978. Among her works are *Balance* (1962), *Shelter* (1968), and *Cross of Coin* (1973).

Emily Dickinson   1989
TRANSLATED BY ELISABETH EYBERS

Essential oils are wrung:
The attar from the rose
Is not expressed by suns alone,
It is the gift of screws
             —EMILY DICKINSON

That knowledge which the ruthless screws distil
she could not weigh against the easy truth
that's cheap and readily negotiable:
as time went on, her days grew more aloof.

The years proved meager as they came and went;   5
her narrow, ardent love, commodity
that found no market, still remained unspent:
yearning, forsakenness and ecstasy.

She climbed the scaffolding of loneliness
not to escape from living, but to gain   10
a perilous glimpse into the universe;
and tunneled down into the mind's dark mine,
through tortuous shafts descending to obtain
its flawless fragments, glittering, crystalline.

Connections to Other Selections

1. How is Dickinson's rejection of what Eybers describes as "easy truth" manifested in "I like a look of Agony," (p. 839) and "Tell all the Truth but tell it slant — " (p. 851).
2. Compare this tribute to Dickinson with Galway Kinnell's tribute to Robert Frost on p. 898. Which tribute, in your opinion, is more successful in capturing the essence of its subject? Explain your response in an essay.

FAIZ AHMED FAIZ (Pakistani/1911–1984)

Born in Pakistan, Faiz Ahmed Faiz served in the British Indian Army during World War II. After the war he became a spokesman for Pakistani and Indian rights by editing the *Pakistani Times* and writing poetry in Urdu. Faiz served several jail sentences for his political activism, spending a considerable amount of time in solitary confinement. His poetry is widely known in India and the subcontinent; a translation of some is available as *The True Subject: Selected Poems of Faiz Ahmed Faiz* (1988).

Prison Daybreak   1952

TRANSLATED BY NAOMI LAZARD

Though it was still night
the moon stood beside my pillow and said:
           "Wake up,
the wine of sleep that was your portion
is finished. The wineglass is empty.   5
Morning is here."
           I said good-bye to my beloved's image
in the black satin waters of the night
that hung still and stagnant on the world.
           Here and there   10
moonlight whirled, the lotus dance commenced;
silver nebulas of stars dropped from the moon's white hand.
They went under, rose again to float, faded and opened.
For a long time night and daybreak swayed,
locked together in each other's arms.   15

           In the prison yard
my comrades' faces, incandescent as candlelight,
flickered through the gloom. Sleep had washed them
with its dew, turned them into gold.
           For that moment   20
these faces were rinsed clean of grief for our people,
absolved from the pain of separation from their dear ones.
In the distance a gong struck the hour;
wretched footsteps stumbled forward on their rounds,
wasted by near starvation, *maestros* of the morning shuffle,   25
lockstepped, arm in arm with their own terrible laments.
Mutilated voices, broken on the rack, awakened.

           Somewhere a door opened,
another one closed; a chain muttered, grumbled,
shrieked out loud. Somewhere a knife plunged   30

into the gizzard of a lock; a window went mad
and began to beat its own head.

This is the way the enemies of life,
shaken from sleep, showed themselves.
These daemons, hacked from stone and steel,   35
use their great hands to grind down the spirit,
slim as a feather now, of my useless days and nights.
They make it cry out in despair.
                                        The prisoners,
all of us, keep watch for our savior   40
who is on his way in the form of a storybook prince,
arrows of hope burning in his quiver,
                        ready to let them fly.

Connections to Other Selections

1. Write an essay on the meaning of sleep in Faiz's poem and in Robert Bly's "Waking
   from Sleep" (p. 937). Pay particular attention to the images that describe sleep in
   each poem.
2. Compare Faiz's treatment of prison life with Bessie Head's in her short story "The
   Prisoner Who Wore Glasses" (p. 501). How does each work manage to avoid a
   despairing tone?

MUHAMMAD AL-MAGHUT (Syrian/b. 1934)

Born in Syria, Muhammad al-Maghut is a playwright and poet. Two of
his plays, *The Clown* and *Hunchback Sparrow*, were published in 1973 and
performed in many Arab countries. His work reveals an abiding concern for
justice in the Arab world. His writings include *Sorrow in Moonlight* (1960),
A Room with a Million Walls (1973), and *Joy Is Not My Profession* (1973).

An Arab Traveler in a Space Ship   1987
TRANSLATED BY MAY JAYYUSI AND JOHN HEATH-STUBBS

Scientists and Technicians!
Give me a ticket to space
I've been sent by my sad country
In the name of its widows, its children and its aged
To ask for a free ticket to the sky   5
I don't bear money in my hands . . . but tears

No place for me?
Put me at the rear of the ship
Outside on top

I'm a peasant, used to all that   10
I shall not hurt a single star
Nor offend a single cloud
All that I want is to reach God
In the quickest possible way
To put a whip in His hand   15
That he may arouse us to revolt!

Connections to Other Selections

1. Discuss the theme of this poem and Langston Hughes's "Harlem (A Dream Deferred)" (p. 1780).
2. In an essay compare the irony of al-Maghut's poem and James Merrill's "Casual
   Wear" (p. 699).

VINÍCIUS DE MORAES (Brazilian/1913–1980)

Born in Brazil, Vinícius de Morales read law at the University of Brazil
and English Literature at Oxford University in England. In addition to serving
as a diplomat in Montevideo, Paris, and New York he was popular as a song
lyricist and wrote the film script for Marcel Camus's *Black Orpheus*. His
books include *My Country* (1949), *Book of Sonnets* (1957), and *Selected
Poems* (1960).

Sonnet of Intimacy   1971

Farm afternoons, there's much too much blue air.
I go out sometimes, follow the pasture track,
Chewing a blade of sticky grass, chest bare,
In threadbare pajamas of three summers back,

To the little rivulets in the riverbed   5
For a drink of water, cold and musical,
And if I spot in the brush a glow of red,
A raspberry, spit its blood at the corral.

The smell of cow manure is delicious.
The cattle look at me unenviously   10
And when there comes a sudden stream and hiss

Accompanied by a look not unmalicious,
All of us, animals, unemotionally
Partake together of a pleasant piss.

Connections to Other Selections

1. Compare the effects of the meter and rhyme scheme in "Sonnet of Intimacy" and Robert Frost's "The Pasture" (p. 873).
2. In an essay discuss the themes of "Sonnet of Intimacy" and William Stafford's "Traveling through the Dark" (p. 694). How is each speaker's relationship to nature established?

PABLO NERUDA (Chilean/1904–1973)

Born in Chile, Pablo Neruda insisted all his life on the connection between poetry and politics. He was an activist and a Chilean diplomat in a number of countries during the 1920s and 1930s and remained politically active until his death. Neruda was regarded as a great and influential poet (he was awarded the Nobel Prize in 1971) whose poetry ranged from specific political issues to the yearnings of romantic love. Among his many works are *Twenty Love Poems and a Song of Despair* (1924), *Residence on Earth* (three series, 1925–45), *Spain in the Heart* (1937), *The Captain's Verses* (1952), and *Memorial of Isla Negra* (1964).

Sweetness, Always   1958

TRANSLATED BY ALASTAIR REID

Why such harsh machinery?
Why, to write down the stuff
and people of every day,
must poems be dressed up in gold,
in old and fearful stone?   5

I want verses of felt or feather
which scarcely weigh, mild verses
with the intimacy of beds
where people have loved and dreamed.
I want poems stained   10
by hands and everydayness.

Verses of pastry which melt
into milk and sugar in the mouth,
air and water to drink,
the bites and kisses of love.   15
I long for eatable sonnets,
poems of honey and flour.

Vanity keeps prodding us
to lift ourselves skyward
or to make deep and useless   20
tunnels underground.
So we forget the joyous
love-needs of our bodies.
We forget about pastries.
We are not feeding the world.   25

In Madras a long time since,
I saw a sugary pyramid,
a tower of confectionery —
one level after another,
and in the construction, rubies,   30
and other blushing delights,
medieval and yellow.

Someone dirtied his hands
to cook up so much sweetness.

Brother poets from here   35
and there, from earth and sky,
from Medellín, from Veracruz,
Abyssinia, Antofagasta,
do you know the recipe for honeycombs?

Let's forget all about that stone.   40

Let your poetry fill up
the equinoctial pastry shop
our mouths long to devour —
all the children's mouths
and the poor adults' also.   45
Don't go on without seeing,
relishing, understanding
all these hearts of sugar.

Don't be afraid of sweetness.

With us or without us,   50
sweetness will go on living
and is infinitely alive,
forever being revived,
for it's in a man's mouth,
whether he's eating or singing,   55
that sweetness has its place.

Connections to Other Selections

1. Compare the view of life offered in this poem with that in Frost's "Provide, Provide"
   (p. 888).
2. Write an essay that discusses Kinnell's "Blackberry Eating" (p. 714) and Chasin's
   "The Word *Plum*" (p. 731) as the sort of "eatable" poetry the speaker calls for in
   this poem.

OCTAVIO PAZ (Mexican/b. 1914)

Born in Mexico City, Octavio Paz studied at the National Autonomous University and in 1943 helped found one of Mexico's most important literary reviews, *The Prodigal Son*. He served in the Mexican diplomatic corps in Paris, New Delhi, and New York. Widely traveled, Paz's poetry reflects Hispanic traditions and European modernism as well as Buddhism. In 1990 he won the Nobel Prize for literature. Paz's major poetic works include *Sun Stone* (1958), *The Violent Season* (1958), *Salamander* (1962), *Blanco* (1966), *Eastern Rampart* (1968), and *Renga* (1971).

The Street

A long silent street.
I walk in blackness and I stumble and fall
and rise, and I walk blind, my feet
stepping on silent stones and dry leaves.
Someone behind me also stepping on stones, leaves: 5
if I slow down, he slows;
if I run, he runs. I turn: nobody.
Everything dark and doorless.
Turning and turning among these corners
which lead forever to the street   10
where nobody waits for, nobody follows me,
where I pursue a man who stumbles
and rises and says when he sees me: nobody.

Connections to Other Selections

1. How does the speaker's anxiety in this poem compare with that in Frost's "Acquainted with the Night" (p. 685)?
2. Write an essay comparing the tone of this poem and that of Wright's "Lying in a Hammock at William Duffy's Farm in Pine Island, Minnesota" (p. 1019). Pay particular attention to how you read the final lines of each poem.

WOLE SOYINKA (Nigerian/b. 1934)

A biographical note for Wole Soyinka appears on page 1846, before his play *The Strong Breed*.

Future Plans

The meeting is called
To odium: Forgers, framers
Fabricators Inter-
national. Chairman,
A dark horse, a circus nag turned blinkered sprinter   5

Mach Three°
We rate him — one for the Knife°
Two for 'iavelli,° Three —
Breaking speed
Of the truth barrier by a swooping detention decree   10
Projects in view:
Mao Tse Tung° in league
With Chiang Kai. Nkrumah°
Makes a secret
Pact with Verwood,° sworn by Hastings Banda.°   15
Proven: Arafat°
In flagrante cum
Golda Meir. Castro° drunk
With Richard Nixon°
Contraceptives stacked beneath the papal bunk . . .   20
                    . . . *and more to come*

6 *Mach Three:* An air speed of three times the speed of sound.   7 *Knife:* Mack the Knife, an unsavory character from *Threepenny Opera* (1933), by Bertolt Brecht and Kurt Weill.   8 *'iavelli:* Niccolò Machiavelli (1469–1527), an Italian political theorist who described ruthless strategies for gaining power in *The Prince* (1532).   12 *Mao Tse Tung* (1893–1975): Chinese Communist leader. 13 *Chiang Kai, Nkrumah:* Chiang Kai-shek (1887–1975), Nationalist Chinese political leader exiled in Taiwan by Mao Tse Tung; Kwame Nkrumah (1909–1972), first president of Ghana.   15 *Verwood:* Hendrick Verwoerd (1901–1966), former prime minister of South Africa, assassinated in 1966; *Hastings Banda* (b. 1905): African political leader and first president of Malawi.   16 *Arafat:* Yasir Arafat (b. 1929), Palestinian leader.   18 *Golda Meir. Castro:* Golda Meir (1898–1978), former prime minister of Israel; Fidel Castro (b. 1927), Cuban premier since 1959.   19 *Richard Nixon* (b. 1913): Former U.S. president forced to resign in 1974 due to political scandal.

Connections to Other Selections

1. Discuss the political satire in "Future Plans" and in Kenneth Fearing's "AD" (p. 690).
2. Write an essay on whether the leaders alluded to in "Future Plans" are manifestations of the type of leader described in Dylan Thomas's "The Hand That Signed the Paper" (p. 670).

WISLAWA SZYMBORSKA (Polish/b. 1923)

Born in Poland, Wislawa Szymborska has lived in Cracow since the age of eight. She steadfastly refuses to reveal biographical details of her life, insisting that her poems should speak for themselves. With the exception of *Sounds, Feelings, Thoughts: Seventy Poems by Wislawa Szymborska* (1981), translated and introduced by Magnus J. Krynski and Robert A. Maguire, only about a score of Szymborska's poems have been translated into English. Two of her later poetry collections — as yet untranslated — are *There But for the Grace* (1972) and *A Great Number* (1976).

The Joy of Writing   1981

TRANSLATED BY MAGNUS J. KRYNSKI AND ROBERT A. MAGUIRE

Where through the written forest runs that written doe?
Is it to drink from the written water,
which will copy her gentle mouth like carbon paper?
Why does she raise her head, is it something she hears?
Poised on four fragile legs borrowed from truth   5
she pricks up her ears under my fingers.
Stillness — this word also rustles across the paper
and parts
the branches brought forth by the word "forest."

Above the blank page lurking, set to spring   10
are letters that may compose themselves all wrong,
besieging sentences
from which there is no rescue.

In a drop of ink there's a goodly reserve
of huntsmen with eyes squinting to take aim,   15
ready to dash down the steep pen,
surround the doe and level their guns.

They forget that this is not real life.
Other laws, black on white, here hold sway.
The twinkling of an eye will last as long as I wish,   20
will consent to be divided into small eternities
full of bullets stopped in flight.
Forever, if I command it, nothing will happen here.
Against my will no leaf will fall
nor blade of grass bend under the full stop of a hoof.   25

Is there then such a world
over which I rule sole and absolute?

A time I bind with chains of signs?
An existence perpetuated at my command?

The joy of writing.   30
The power of preserving.
The revenge of a mortal hand.

Connections to Other Selections

1. Discuss the themes of "The Joy of Writing" and Emily Dickinson's "To make a
   prairie it takes a clover and one bee" (p. 832). What is the role of the poet's
   imagination in each poem?
2. Write an essay that considers Szymborska's view of the writer's imagination and
   John Keats's as expressed in "Keats on the Truth of the Imagination," the Perspective on page 817.

SHINKICHI TAKAHASHI (Japanese/1901–1987)

Born in the fishing village of Shikoku on the smallest of Japan's four
main islands, Shinkichi Takahashi dropped out of high school and moved to
Tokyo in search of a literary career, self-educating himself along the way. He
became a disciple of a Zen Master and wrote poetry as well as numerous
commentaries on Japanese culture. His major collections include *Afterimages*
(1970) and *Collected Poems*, which was awarded the Ministry of Education
Prize for Art.

Explosion   1973
TRANSLATED BY LUCIEN STRYK AND TAKASHI IKEMOTO

I'm an unthinking dog,
a good-for-nothing cat,
a fog over gutter,
a blossom-swiping rain.

I close my eyes, breathe —   5
radioactive air! A billion years
and I'll be shrunk to half,
pollution strikes my marrow.

So what — I'll whoop at what
remains. Yet scant blood left,
reduced to emptiness by nuclear   10
fission, I'm running very fast.

1. Discuss the views of nuclear weapons presented in "Explosion" and Denise Levertov's "Gathered at the River" (p. 1053).
2. How does the "So what" of line 9 in this poem compare in tone with Neruda's "Sweetness, Always" (p. 1033)?

TOMAS TRANSTROMER (Swedish/b. 1931)

Born in Stockholm, Sweden, Tomas Transtromer's work is translated more than any other contemporary Scandinavian poet's. He has worked as a psychologist with juvenile offenders and handicapped persons. His collections of poetry include *Night Vision* (1971), *Windows and Stones: Selected Poems* (1972), *Truth Barriers* (1978), and *Selected Poems* (1981). Among his awards are the Petrarch Prize (1981), and a lifetime subsidy from the government of Sweden.

April and Silence 1991
TRANSLATED BY ROBIN FULTON

Spring lies desolate.
The velvet-dark ditch
crawls by my side
without reflections.

The only thing that shines   5
is yellow flowers.

I am carried in my shadow
like a violin
in its black box.

The only thing I want to say   10
glitters out of reach
like the silver
in a pawnbroker's.

Connections to Other Selections

1. Discuss the description of spring in this poem and in W. D. Snodgrass's "April Inventory" (p. 1000).
2. In an essay explain how the dictions used in "April and Silence" and Edna St. Vincent Millay's "Never May the Fruit Be Plucked" (p. 635) contribute to the poems' meanings.

AMY CLAMPITT (b. 1920)

Born in New Providence, Iowa, Amy Clampitt graduated from Grinnell College and now is based primarily in New York City. Her collections of poems include *The Kingfisher* (1983), *What the Light Was Like* (1985), *Archaic Figure* (1987), and *Westward* (1990). She has been writer-in-residence at the College of William and Mary, Amherst College, and Washington University as well as a Phi Beta Kappa Poet at the Harvard Literary Exercises. Among her awards are fellowships from the Guggenheim Foundation and the American Academy of Poets.

Nothing Stays Put   1989

The strange and wonderful are too much with us.
The protea of the antipodes — a great,
globed, blazing honeybee of a bloom —
for sale in the supermarket! We are in
our decadence, we are not entitled.   5
What have we done to deserve
all the produce of the tropics —
this fiery trove, the largesse of it
heaped up like cannonballs, these pineapples, bossed
and crested, standing like troops at attention,   10
these tiers, these balconies of green, festoons
grown sumptuous with stoop labor?

The exotic is everywhere, it comes to us
before there is a yen or a need for it. The green-
grocers, uptown and down, are from South Korea.   15
Orchids, opulence by the pailful, just slightly
fatigued by the plane trip from Hawaii, are
disposed on the sidewalks; alstroemerias, freesias
flattened a bit in translation from overseas; gladioli
likewise estranged from their piercing ancestral crimson;   20
as well as, less altered from the original blue cornflower
of the roadsides and railway embankments of Europe, these
bachelor's buttons. But it isn't the railway embankments
their featherweight wheels of cobalt remind me of — it's
a row of them among prim colonnades of cosmos,   25
snapdragon, nasturtium, bloodsilk red poppies
in my grandmother's garden; a prairie childhood,
the grassland shorn, overlaid with a grid,
unsealed, furrowed, harrowed, and sown with immigrant grasses,
their massive corduroy, their wavering feltings embroidered   30

here and there by the scarlet shoulder patch of cannas
on a courthouse lawn, by a love knot, a cross-stitch
of living matter, sown and tended by women,
nurturers everywhere of the strange and wonderful,
beneath whose hands what had been alien begins,   35
as it alters, to grow as though it were indigenous.

But at this remove what I think of as
strange and wonderful — strolling the side streets of Manhattan
on an April afternoon, seeing hybrid pear trees in blossom,
a tossing, vertiginous colonnade of foam up above —   40
is the white petalfall, the warm snowdrift
of the indigenous wild plum of my childhood.
Nothing stays put. The world is a wheel.
All that we know, that we're
made of, is motion.   45

Connections to Other Selections

1. Clampitt's opening line echoes Wordsworth's "The World Is Too Much with Us"
   (p. 756) and therefore invites comparison. How does Clampitt's theme relate to
   Wordsworth's? Are their complaints similar or different?
2. Write an essay comparing the speakers' tones in this poem and in Ginsberg's "A
   Supermarket in California" (p. 779). Explain whether Ginsberg's poem might also
   be aptly titled "Nothing Stays Put."

ROBERT CREELEY (b. 1926)

Born in Arlington, Massachusetts, Robert Creely attended Harvard University, which he left in 1944 to serve as an ambulance driver in India and
Burma during World War II. After living in France and Spain in the early
1950s, he returned to the United States and taught at Black Mountain College
in North Carolina (where he founded the *Black Mountain Review*) and at
various colleges and universities throughout the United States and Canada.
His recent publications include *The Collected Poems of Robert Creeley, 1945–
1975* (1983), *Collected Essays* (1989), and his edition of *The Essential Burns*
(1989).

Fathers   1986

Scattered, aslant
faded faces a column
a rise of the packed

peculiar place to a
modest height makes   5
a view of common lots
in winter then, a ground
of battered snow crusted
at the edges under
it all, there under   10
my fathers their
faded women, friends,
the family all echoed,
names trees more tangible
physical place more tangible   15
the air of this place the road
going past to Watertown
or down to my mother's
grave, my father's grave, not
now this resonance of   20
each other one was his, his
survival only, his curious
reticence, his dead state,
his emptiness, his acerbic
edge cuts the hands to   25
hold him, hold on, wants
the ground, *wants* this frozen ground.

Connections to Other Selections

1. Compare the speaker's tone in this poem with that in Hall's "My Son, My Executioner" (p. 955).
2. Write an essay comparing the structures of this poem and Thomas's "Do not go
   gentle into that good night" (p. 760). How does the form of each poem contribute
   to its effects?

RITA DOVE (b. 1952)

Born and raised in Akron, Ohio, Rita Dove was educated at Miami
University of Ohio and the University of Iowa. In 1987 she was awarded the
Pulitzer Prize in poetry for *Thomas and Beulah* (1986). Her other volumes
of poetry include *The Yellow House on the Corner* (1980), *Museum* (1983),
and *Grace Notes* (1989). A collection of short stories, *Fifth Sunday*, was
published in 1985 and a novel, *Through the Ivory Gate*, appeared in 1991.
Dove has taught at Arizona State University and the University of Virginia.
She has received fellowships from Fulbright/Hays, the National Endowment
for the Arts, and the Guggenheim Foundation, and in 1993 she was appointed
to the position of Poet Laureate.

The Satisfaction Coal Company

1986

1.
What to do with a day.
Leaf through *Jet*. Watch T.V.
Freezing on the porch
but he goes anyhow, snow too high
for a walk, the ice treacherous.   5
Inside, the gas heater takes care of itself;
he doesn't even notice being warm.

Everyone says he looks great.
Across the street a drunk stands smiling
at something carved in a tree.   10
The new neighbor with the floating hips
scoots out to get the mail
and waves once, brightly,
storm door clipping her heel on the way in.

2.
Twice a week he had taken the bus down Glendale hill   15
to the corner of Market. Slipped through
the alley by the canal and let himself in.
Started to sweep
with terrible care, like a woman
brushing shine into her hair,   20
same motion, same lullaby.
No curtains — the cop on the beat
stopped outside once in the hour
to swing his billy club and glare.

It was better on Saturdays   25
when the children came along:
he mopped while they emptied
ashtrays, clang of glass on metal
then a dry scutter. Next they counted
nailheads studding the leather cushions.   30
Thirty-four! they shouted,
that was the year and
they found it mighty amusing.

But during the week he noticed more —
lights when they gushed or dimmed   35
at the Portage Hotel, the 10:32
picking up speed past the B & O switchyard,
floorboards trembling and the explosive
kachook kachook kachook kachook
and the oiled rails ticking underneath.   40

3.
They were poor then but everyone had been poor.
He hadn't minded the sweeping,

just the thought of it — like now
when people ask him what he's thinking
and he says *I'm listening*.   45

Those nights walking home alone,
the bucket of coal scraps banging his knee,
he'd hear a roaring furnace
with its dry, familiar heat. Now the nights
take care of themselves — as for the days,   50
there is the canary's sweet curdled song,
the wino smiling through his dribble.
Past the hill, past the gorge
choked with wild sumac in summer,
the corner has been upgraded.   55
Still, he'd like to go down there someday
to stand for a while, and get warm.

Connections to Other Selections

1. Discuss the use of images in this poem and William Blake's "London" (p. 652). How do the images establish the tone of each poem?
2. Write an essay on the treatment of poverty in Dove's poem and in Toni Cade Bambara's short story, "The Lesson" (p. 143).

LOUISE ERDRICH (b. 1954)

A biographical note on Louise Erdrich appears on page 132, before her short story "I'm a Mad Dog Biting Myself for Sympathy."

Captivity   1984

He (my captor) gave me a bisquit, which I put in my pocket, and not daring to eat it, buried it under a log, fearing he had put something in it to make me love him.
            –from the narrative of the captivity of Mrs. Mary Rowlandson,°
                    who was taken prisoner by the Wampanoag when Lancaster,
                            Massachusetts, was destroyed, in the year 1676.

The stream was swift, and so cold
I thought I would be sliced in two.
But he dragged me from the flood

Mrs. Mary Rowlandson (1637?–1711?): Held captive for three months by a Native-American tribe during the King Philip's War, Rowlandson recounted her experiences in her *Narrative* (1682).

by the ends of my hair.
I had grown to recognize his face.   5
I could distinguish it from the others.
There were times I feared I understood
his language, which was not human,
and I knelt to pray for strength.

We were pursued! By God's agents   10
or pitch devils I did not know.
Only that we must march.
Their guns were loaded with swan shot.
I could not suckle and my child's wail
put them in danger.   15
He had a woman
with teeth black and glittering.
She fed the child milk of acorns.
The forest closed, the light deepened.

I told myself that I would starve   20
before I took food from his hands
but I did not starve.
One night
he killed a deer with a young one in her
and gave me to eat of the fawn.   25
It was so tender,
the bones like the stems of flowers,
that I followed where he took me.
The night was thick. He cut the cord
that bound me to the tree.   30

After that the birds mocked.
Shadows gaped and roared
and the trees flung down
their sharpened lashes.
He did not notice God's wrath.   35
God blasted fire from half-buried stumps.
I hid my face in my dress, fearing He would burn us all
but this, too, passed.

Rescued, I see no truth in things.
My husband drives a thick wedge   40
through the earth, still it shuts
to him year after year.
My child is fed of the first wheat.
I lay myself to sleep
on a Holland-laced pillowbeer.°   *pillowcase*   45
I lay to sleep.
And in the dark I see myself
as I was outside their circle.

They knelt on deerskins, some with sticks,
and he led his company in the noise   50

until I could no longer bear
the thought of how I was.
I stripped a branch
and struck the earth,
in time, begging it to open   55
to admit me
as he was
and feed me honey from the rock.

Connections to Other Selections

1. Discuss the themes of Erdrich's poem and Paula Gunn Allen's "Pocahontas to Her
   English Husband, John Rolfe" (p. 920).
2. Write an essay comparing the narrative voice in "Captivity" with that in "Ruby Tells
   All" (p. 749) by Miller Williams.

DEBORAH GARRISON (b. 1965)

Raised in Ann Arbor, Michigan, Deborah Garrison graduated from
Brown University and currently lives in New York City, where she works on
the editorial staff of *The New Yorker*. She has not published a collection of
poems to date, but her poetry appears regularly in *The New Yorker*.

She Was Waiting to Be Told   1990

For you she learned to wear a short black slip
and red lipstick,
how to order a glass of red wine
and finish it. She learned to reach out
as if to touch your arm and then not   5
touch it, changing the subject.
Didn't you think, she'd begin, or
Weren't you sorry. . . .

To call your best friends
by their schoolboy names   10
and give them kisses good-bye,
to turn her head away when they say
Your wife! So your confidence grows.
She doesn't ask what you want
because she knows.   15

Isn't that what you think?

When actually she was only waiting
to be told *Take off your dress* —
to be stunned, and then do this,
never rehearsed, but perfectly obvious: 20
in one motion up, over, and gone,
the X of her arms crossing and uncrossing,
her face flashing away from you in the fabric
so that you couldn't say if she was
appearing or disappearing.   25

Connections to Other Selections

1. Write an essay comparing the woman in "She Was Waiting to Be Told" and John
   Keats's "La Belle Dame sans Merci" (p. 807).
2. Discuss the relationship between the man and woman in Garrison's poem and in
   Richard Wilbur's "A Late Aubade" (p. 634).

MARK HALLIDAY (b. 1949)

Born in Ann Arbor, Michigan, Mark Halliday earned a B.A. and an M.A.
from Brown University, and a Ph.D. from Brandeis University. A teacher at
the University of Pennsylvania, his poems have appeared in a variety of
periodicals, including *The Massachusetts Review*, *Michigan Quarterly Review*,
and *The New Republic*. His collection of poems *Little Star* was selected by
The National Poetry Series for publication in 1987. He has also written a
critical study on poet Wallace Stevens titled *Stevens and the Interpersonal*
(1991).

On the whole this is quite successful work:
your main argument about the poet's ambivalence —
how he loves the very things he attacks —
is mostly persuasive and always engaging.
At the same time,   5

           there are spots
where your thinking becomes, for me,
alarmingly opaque, and your syntax seems to jump
backwards through unnecessary hoops,
as on p. 2 where you speak of "precognitive awareness   10
not yet disestablished by the shell that encrusts
each thing that a person actually says"
or at the top of p. 5 where your discussion of
"subverbal undertow miming the subversion of self-belief
woven counter to desire's outreach"   15
leaves me groping for firmer footholds.
(I'd have said it differently,
or rather, said something else.)
And when you say that women "could not fulfill themselves" (p. 6)
"in that era" (only forty years ago, after all!)   20
are you so sure that the situation is so different today?
Also, how does Whitman bluff his way into
your penultimate paragraph? He is the *last* poet
I would have quoted in this context!
What plausible way of behaving   25
does the passage you quote represent? Don't you think
literature should ultimately reveal possibilities for *action*?

Please notice how I've repaired your use of semicolons.

And yet, despite what may seem my cranky response,
I do admire the freshness of   30
your thinking and your style; there is
a vitality here; your sentences thrust themselves forward
with a confidence as impressive as it is cheeky. . . .
You are not
        me, finally,   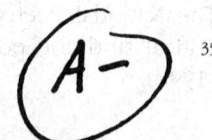 35
and though this is an awkward problem, involving
the inescapable fact that you are so young, so young
it is also a delightful provocation.

Connections to Other Selections

1. Compare the ways in which Halliday reveals the speaker's character in this poem with the strategies used by Robert Browning in "My Last Duchess" (p. 702).
2. Write an essay on the professor in this poem and in Fay Weldon's short story "IND AFF, or Out of Love in Sarajevo" (p. 562). What are the significant similarities and differences between them?

JUDY PAGE HEITZMAN (b. 1952)

Judy Page Heitzman lives in Marshfield, Massachusetts, and teaches English at Duxbury High School. She has not published a collection of poems to date, but her poetry has appeared in *The New Yorker*, *Yankee Magazine*, *Wind*, *Yarro*, and *Three Rivers Poetry Journal*.

The Schoolroom on the Second Floor of the Knitting Mill

ominous threatening

1991

While most of us copied letters out of books,
Mrs. Lawrence carved and cleaned her nails.
Now the red and buff cardinals at my back-room window
make me miss her, her room, her hallway,
even the chimney outside   5
that broke up the sky.

In my memory it is afternoon.
Sun streams in through the door
next to the fire escape where we are lined up
getting our coats on to go out to the playground,   10
the tether ball, its towering height, the swings.
She tells me to make sure the line
does not move up over the threshold.
That would be dangerous.
So I stand guard at the door.   15
Somehow it happens
the way things seem to happen when we're not really looking,
or we are looking, just not the right way.
Kids crush up like cattle, pushing me over the line.

Judy is not a good leader is all Mrs. Lawrence says.   20
She says it quietly. Still, everybody hears.
Her arms hang down like sausages. ← NEGATIVE
I hear her every time I fail. ← CLIMAX

1. Compare the representations and meanings of being a schoolchild in this poem and in Emily Dickinson's "From all the Jails the Boys and Girls" (p. 852).
2. Discuss how the past impinges on the present in Heitzman's poem and in Margaret Atwood's short story "Death by Landscape" (p. 529).

GALWAY KINNELL (b. 1927)

   Born in Providence, Rhode Island, Galway Kinnell earned degrees from Princeton University and the University of Rochester. He has taught at a number of universities in the United States and abroad and currently teaches in the creative writing program at New York University. He has been awarded fellowships from the Guggenheim, MacArthur, and Rockefeller foundations as well as a Pulitzer Prize and a National Institute of Arts and Letters award. His volumes of poetry include *The Avenue Bearing the Initial of Christ into the New World: Poems 1946–64* (1974); *Mortal Acts, Mortal Words* (1980); *Selected Poems* (1982); *The Past* (1985); and *When One Has Lived a Long Time Alone* (1990).

After Making Love We Hear Footsteps   1980

For I can snore like a bullhorn
or play loud music
or sit up talking with any reasonably sober Irishman
and Fergus will only sink deeper
into his dreamless sleep, which goes by all in one flash,   5
but let there be that heavy breathing
or a stifled come-cry anywhere in the house
and he will wrench himself awake
and make for it on the run — as now, we lie together,
after making love, quiet, touching along the length of our bodies,   10
familiar touch of the long-married,
and he appears — in his baseball pajamas, it happens,
the neck opening so small
he has to screw them on, which one day may make him wonder
about the mental capacity of baseball players —   15
and says, "Are you loving and snuggling? May I join?"
He flops down between us and hugs us and snuggles himself to sleep,
his face gleaming with satisfaction at being this very child.

In the half darkness we look at each other
and smile   20

and touch arms across his little, startlingly muscled body —
this one whom habit of memory propels to the ground of his making,
sleeper only the mortal sounds can sing awake,
this blessing love gives again into our arms.

Connections to Other Selections

1. Discuss how this poem helps to bring into focus the sense of loss Frost evokes in "Home Burial" (p. 876).
2. Write an essay comparing the tone and theme of this poem and those of Hall's "My Son, My Executioner" (p. 955), paying particular attention to the treatment of the child in each poem.

YUSEF KOMUNYAKAA (b. 1947)

Yusef Komunyakaa, born in Bogalusa, Louisiana, a Vietnam veteran, earned an M.F.A. from the University of California and now teaches creative writing and African-American studies at Indiana University. Among his awards is a National Endowment for the Arts fellowship. His volumes of poetry include *Copacetic* (1984), *I Apologize for the Eyes in My Head* (1986), and *Dien Cai Dau* (1989).

Facing It   1988

My black face fades,
hiding inside the black granite.
I said I wouldn't,
dammit: No tears.
I'm stone. I'm flesh.   5
My clouded reflection eyes me
like a bird of prey, the profile of night
slanted against morning. I turn
this way — the stone lets me go.
I turn that way — I'm inside   10
the Vietnam Veterans Memorial
again, depending on the light
to make a difference.
I go down the 58,022 names,
half-expecting to find   15
my own in letters like smoke.
I touch the name Andrew Johnson;
I see the booby trap's white flash.
Names shimmer on a woman's blouse
but when she walks away   20

the names stay on the wall.
Brushstrokes flash, a red bird's
wings cutting across my stare.
The sky. A plane in the sky.
A white vet's image floats   25
closer to me, then his pale eyes
look through mine. I'm a window.
He's lost his right arm
inside the stone. In the black mirror
a woman's trying to erase names: 30
No, she's brushing a boy's hair.

Connections to Other Selections

1. Discuss the speakers' attitudes toward war in "Facing It" and e. e. cummings's "next to of course god america i" (p. 691).
2. In an essay compare the treatment of memory and sorrow in "Facing It" and Tim O'Brien's "How to Tell a True War Story" (p. 552).

DENISE LEVERTOV (b. 1923)

Born in Essex, England, Denise Levertov was educated at home, served as a nurse during World War II, and in 1948 emigrated to the United States. Levertov has taught at Vassar, Drew, City College of New York, MIT, Tufts, Stanford, and Brandeis and has received awards from the Guggenheim Foundation, the National Institute of Arts and Letters, and the National Endowment for the Arts. Much of her poetry reflects her continuing political activism, which began in the 1960s. Her collections of poems include *Collected Earlier Poems 1940–1960* (1979), *Denise Levertov: Poems 1960–1967* (1983), *Denise Levertov: Poems 1968–1972* (1987), and *A Door in the Hive* (1989).

Gathered at the River   1983

For Beatrice Hawley and John Jagel

As if the trees were not indifferent . . .

A breeze flutters the candles but the trees give off
a sense of listening, of hush.

The dust of August on their leaves.
But it grows dark. Their dark green   5
is something known about, not seen.

But summer twilight takes away
only color, not form. The tree-forms,
massive trunks and the great domed heads,
leaning in towards us, are visible,   10

a half-circle of attention.

They listen because the war
we speak of, the human war with ourselves,

the war against earth,
against nature,   15
is a war against them.

The words are spoken
of those who survived a while,
living shadowgraphs, eyes fixed forever
on witnessed horror,   20
who survived to give
testimony, that no-one
may plead ignorance.
Contra naturam.° The trees,   *Against nature (Latin)*
the trees are not indifferent.   25

We intone together, *Never again,*

we stand in a circle,
singing, speaking, making vows,

remembering the dead
of Hiroshima,   30
of Nagasaki.

We are holding candles: we kneel to set them
afloat on the dark river
as they do
there in Hiroshima. We are invoking   35

saints and prophets,
heroes and heroines of justice and peace,
to be with us, to help us
stop the torment of our evil dreams . . .

Windthreatened flames bob on the current . . .   40

They don't get far from shore. But none capsizes
even in the swell of a boat's wake.

The waxy paper cups sheltering them
catch fire. But still the candles
sail their gold downstream.   45

And still the trees ponder our strange doings, as if
well aware that if we fail,
we fail for them:
if our resolves and prayers are weak and fail

there will be nothing left of their slow and innocent wisdom,   50

no roots,
no bole nor branch,

no memory
of shade,
of leaf,   55

no pollen.

Connections to Other Selections

1. In her comments on "Gathered at the River" (p. 1073), Levertov affirms her
   "underlying belief in a great design, a potential harmony which can be violated
   or be sustained." How does Frost's "Design" (p. 887) comment on Levertov's
   beliefs? Explain whether you agree with Levertov or not.
2. Levertov also expresses a concern in her essay for the necessity of having "a sense
   of the sacredness of the earthly creation" and mentions that Gerard Manley
   Hopkins has always been one of her favorite poets. Write an essay comparing
   "Gathered at the River" and Hopkins's "God's Grandeur" (p. 720) or "Pied Beauty"
   (p. 962). What significant similarities do you find?

PETER MEINKE (b. 1932)

Peter Meinke, born in Brooklyn, New York, earned a B.A. at Hamilton
College, an M.A. at the University of Michigan, and a Ph.D. at the University
of Minnesota. In addition to teaching at Eckerd College, he has served as a
visiting professor at many colleges and universities and received a number
of grants, including National Endowment for the Arts fellowships in 1974
and 1989. Among his poetry collections are *The Rat Poems* (1978), *Trying
to Surprise God* (1981), *Night Watch on the Chesapeake* (1986), and *Far from
Home* (1988).

Air seeps through alleys and our diaphragms
balloon blackly with this mix of
carbon monoxide and the thousand corrosives a city
doles out free to its constituents;
everyone's jogging through Edgemont Park,   5
frightened by death and fatty tissue,
gasping at the maximal heart rate,
hoping to outlive all the others streaming
in the lanes like lemmings lurching toward their last
jump. I join in despair   10
knowing my arteries jammed with
lint and tobacco, lard and bourbon — my
medical history a noxious marsh:
newts and moles slink through the sodden veins,
owls hoot in the lungs' dark branches;   15
probably I shall keel off the john like
queer Uncle George and lie on the bathroom floor
raging about Shirley Clark, my true love in
seventh grade, God bless her wherever she lives
tied to that turkey who hugely   20
undervalues the beauty of her tiny earlobes, one
view of which (either one: they are both perfect)
would add years to my life and I could skip these
x-rays, turn in my insurance card, and trade
yoga and treadmills and jogging and zen and   25
zucchini for drinking and dreaming of her, breathing hard.

Connections to Other Selections

1. Write an essay comparing the way Sharon Olds connects sex and exercise in "Sex
   without Love" (p. 1056) with Meinke's treatment here.
2. Compare the voices in this poem and in Kinnell's "After Making Love We Hear
   Footsteps" (p. 1050). Which do you find more appealing? Why?

SHARON OLDS (b. 1942)

Born in San Francisco and educated at Stanford and Columbia, Sharon
Olds has received the Lamont award from the Academy of American Poets
as well as fellowships from the National Endowment for the Arts and the
Guggenheim Foundation. She has taught creative writing at New York Uni-
versity and at Goldwater Hospital for the physically disabled on Roosevelt
Island, New York. Her volumes of poems include *Satan Says* (1980), *The
Dead and the Living* (1984), and *The Gold Cell* (1987).

How do they do it, the ones who make love
without love? Beautiful as dancers,
gliding over each other like ice skaters
over the ice, fingers hooked
inside each other's bodies, faces   5
red as steak, wine, wet as the
children at birth whose mothers are going to
give them away. How do they come to the
come to the   come to the   God   come to the
still waters, and not love   10
the one who came there with them, light
rising slowly as steam off their joined
skin? These are the true religious,
the purists, the pros, the ones who will not
accept a false Messiah, love the   15
priest instead of the God. They do not
mistake the lover for their own pleasure,
they are like great runners: they know they are alone
with the road surface, the cold, the wind,
the fit of their shoes, their over-all cardio-   20
vascular health — just factors, like the partner
in the bed, and not the truth, which is the
single body alone in the universe
against its own best time.

Connections to Other Selections

1. How does the treatment of sex and love in Olds's poem compare with that in
   e. e. cummings's "she being Brand" (p. 623)?
2. Just as Olds describes sex without love, she implies a definition of love in this
   poem. Consider whether the lovers in Wilbur's "A Late Aubade" (p. 634) fall within
   Olds's definition.

CATHY SONG (b. 1955)

Born in Hawaii and educated at Wellesley College and Boston University,
Cathy Song teaches at the University of Hawaii at Manōa. Her collections of
poems include *Picture Bride* (1983), winner of the Yale Series of Younger
Poets Award and nominated for a National Book Critics Circle Award, and
Frameless Windows, Squares of Light (1988).

The White Porch

1983

I wrap the blue towel
after washing,
around the damp
weight of hair, bulky
as a sleeping cat,   5
and sit out on the porch.
Still dripping water,
it'll be dry by supper,
by the time the dust
settles off your shoes,   10
though it's only five
past noon. Think
of the luxury: how to use
the afternoon like the stretch
of lawn spread before me.   15
There's the laundry,
sun-warm clothes at twilight,
and the mountain of beans
in my lap. Each one,
I'll break and snap   20
thoughtfully in half.

But there is this slow arousal.
The small buttons
of my cotton blouse
are pulling away from my body.   25
I feel the strain of threads,
the swollen magnolias
heavy as a flock of birds
in the tree. Already,
the orange sponge cake   30
is rising in the oven.
I know you'll say it makes
your mouth dry
and I'll watch you
drench your slice of it   35
in canned peaches
and lick the plate clean.

So much hair, my mother
used to say, grabbing
the thick braided rope   40
in her hands while we washed
the breakfast dishes, discussing
dresses and pastries.
My mind often elsewhere

as we did the morning chores together.   45
Sometimes, a few strands
would catch in her gold ring.
I worked hard then,
anticipating the hour
when I would let the rope down   50
at night, strips of sheets,
knotted and tied,
while she slept in tight blankets.
My hair, freshly washed
like a measure of wealth,   55
like a bridal veil.
Crouching in the grass,
you would wait for the signal,
for the movement of curtains
before releasing yourself   60
from the shadow of moths.
Cloth, hair and hands,
smuggling you in.

Connections to Other Selections

1. Compare the images used to describe the speaker's "slow arousal" in this poem
   with Croft's images in "Home-Baked Bread" (p. 660). What similarities do you see?
   What makes each description so effective?
2. Write an essay comparing images of sensuality in this poem and Li Ho's "A Beautiful
   Girl Combs Her Hair" (p. 616). Which poem seems more erotic to you? Why?

STEPHEN STEPANCHEV (b. 1915)

Born in New York, Stephen Stepanchev was a professor of English at
Queens College, City University of New York, from 1949 to 1985. His works
include literary criticism and history as well as poetry: *American Poetry Since
1945: A Critical Survey* (1965); *A Man Running in the Rain* (1969); *The Mad
Bomber* (1972); *Mining the Darkness* (1975); *Medusa and Others* (1975); and
Descent (1988).

Cornered on the Corner   1991

An oil rose: gold and pink petals flare on the asphalt.
Oil spurts from a sizzling wok. A hot light spits
On the sidewalk. A pigeon struts out of the way
Of a starling. It pecks at a shining black bag.

A blond woman in green jeans, swinging   5
A green purse, cruises past the gang on the corner.
They are watching the girls and the days go by. "Fresh meat,"
Bud says, spitting at the front page of the *News*.

Charley whittles a stick with a machete and grunts,
"Jailbait." Raymond combs his flattop and laughs   10
At his cool image in a plate-glass window.
Sal puts out his hand for an imaginary feel of butt.

A *Watchtower* lady hands out prophetic books.
"The end is near," she says, but the boys can't read.

The sun has dried the oil rose in the street.   15
A Cadillac whistles as its master nears.

Connections to Other Selections

1. Discuss the use of imagery in Stepanchev's poem and Alberto Ríos's "Seniors"
   (p. 610). How do the images contribute to the themes of these poems?
2. Write an essay on the treatment of masculinity in "Cornered on the Corner" and
   Sharon Olds's "Rite of Passage" (p. 783).

C. K. WILLIAMS (b. 1936)

Born in Newark, New Jersey, and educated at Bucknell University and
the University of Pennsylvania, C. K. Williams has worked as a therapist,
editor, and writer and has taught creative writing at a number of schools,
including Boston, Columbia, Drexel, and George Mason universities. He has
received a Guggenheim Fellowship, the National Book Critics Circle Award,
and *The Paris Review*'s Connor Prize. His collections of poetry include *Poems
1963–1988*, and *Flesh and Blood* (1988).

The Mirror   1991

The way these days she dresses with more attention to go out to pass the
    afternoon alone,
shopping or just taking walks, she says, than when they go together to a restau-
    rant or party:
it's such a subtle thing, how even speak of it, how imagine he'd be able to
    explain it to her?
The way she looks for such long moments in the mirror as she gets ready,
    putting on her makeup;
the way she looks so deeply at herself, gazes at her eyes, her mouth, down
    along her breasts: 5

what is he to say, that she's looking at herself in ways he's never seen before,
  more *carnally*?
She would tell him he was mad, or say something else he doesn't want no
  matter what to hear.
The way she puts her jacket on with a flourish, the way she gaily smiles going
  out the door,
the door, the way the door clicks shut, the way its latch clicks shut behind her
  so emphatically.
What is he to think? What is he to say, to whom? The mirror, jacket, latch, the
  awful door?   10
He can't touch the door, he's afraid he'll break the frightening covenant he's
  made with it.
He can't look into the mirror, either, the dark, malicious void: who knows
  what he might see?

Connections to Other Selections

1. Discuss how mirrors reflect more than mere images in this poem and in Sylvia
   Plath's "Mirror" (p. 674).
2. When this poem was originally published in *The New Yorker,* the wider format of
   the magazine page allowed the lines of the poem to be printed without turns
   (that is, the words "afternoon alone" were printed as part of line 1, and so forth).
   This format gave the poem the look of a block of prose. Consider Williams's poem
   as it was originally printed and compare it with George Starbuck's "Japanese Fish"
   (p. 778). What makes these works poetry rather than prose?

25. Perspectives on Poetry

A variety of observations about poetry is presented in this chapter. The pieces offer a wide range of topics related to reading and writing poetry. The perspectives include William Wordsworth on the nature of poetry, Matthew Arnold on classic and popular literature, Ezra Pound on free verse, Dylan Thomas on the words used in poetry, and Denise Levertov on the background and form of one of her poems. In addition, there are poems about poetry by Walt Whitman, Archibald MacLeish, and Robert Francis. These relatively short pieces provide materials to explore some of the topics and issues that readers and writers of poetry have found perennially interesting and challenging.

WILLIAM WORDSWORTH (1770–1850)
On the Nature of Poets and Poetry   1802

Taking up the subject, then, upon general grounds, I ask what is meant by the word "poet"? What is a poet? To whom does he address himself? And what language is to be expected from him? He is a man speaking to men: a man, it is true, endued with more lively sensibility, more enthusiasm and tenderness, who has a greater knowledge of human nature, and a more comprehensive soul, than are supposed to be common among mankind; a man pleased with his own passions and volitions, and who rejoices more than other men in the spirit of life that is in him; delighting to contemplate similar volitions and passions as manifested in the goings-on of the universe, and habitually impelled to create them where he does not find them. To these qualities he has added a disposition to be affected more than other men by absent things as if they were present; an ability of conjuring up in himself passions, which are indeed far from being the same as those produced by real events, yet (especially in those parts of the general sympathy which are pleasing and delightful) do more nearly resemble the passions produced by real events, than anything which, from the motions of their own minds merely, other men are accustomed to feel in themselves; whence, and from practice, he has acquired a greater readiness and power in expressing what he thinks and feels, and especially those thoughts and feelings which, by his own choice, or from the structure of his own mind, arise in him without immediate external excitement. . . .

I have said that poetry is the spontaneous overflow of powerful feelings: it takes its origin from emotion recollected in tranquility: the emotion is contemplated till by a species of reaction the tranquility gradually disappears, and an emotion, kindred to that which was before the subject of contemplation, is gradually produced, and does itself actually exist in the mind. In this mood successful composition generally begins, and in a mood similar to this it is carried on; but the emotion, of whatever kind and in whatever degree, from various causes is qualified by various pleasures, so that in describing any passions whatsoever, which are voluntarily described, the mind will upon the whole be in a state of enjoyment. Now, if nature be thus cautious in preserving in a state of enjoyment a being thus employed, the poet ought to profit by the lesson thus held forth to him, and ought especially to take care, that whatever passions he communicates to his reader, those passions, if his reader's mind be sound and vigorous, should always be accompanied with an overbalance of pleasure. Now the music of harmonious metrical language, the sense of difficulty overcome, and the blind association of pleasure which has been previously received from works of rhyme or meter of the same or similar construction, an indistinct perception perpetually renewed of language closely resembling that of real life, and yet, in the circumstance of meter, differing from it so widely, all these imperceptibly make up a complex feeling of delight, which is of the most important use in tempering the painful feeling which will always be found intermingled with powerful descriptions of the deeper passions. This effect is always produced in pathetic and impassioned poetry; while, in lighter compositions, the ease and gracefulness with which the poet manages his numbers are themselves confessedly a principal source of the gratification of the reader. I might perhaps include all which it is *necessary* to say upon this subject by affirming, what few persons will deny, that, of two descriptions, either of passions, manners, or characters, each of them equally well executed, the one in prose and the other in verse, the verse will be read a hundred times where the prose is read once.

From *Preface to Lyrical Ballads, with Pastoral and Other Poems*

Considerations for Critical Thinking and Writing

1. Discuss Wordsworth's description of a poet's sensibility and "ability of conjuring up in himself passions." What characteristics do you associate with a poetic temperament?
2. Explain why a writer's emotions are (or are not) so much more important in poetry than in prose.
3. Given that Wordsworth describes poetry as "the spontaneous overflow of powerful feelings," why can't his poems be characterized as formless bursts of raw emotion? Consider, for example, "London, 1802" (p. 675), "My Heart Leaps Up" (p. 738), or "The World Is Too Much with Us" (p. 756) to illustrate your response.

PERCY BYSSHE SHELLEY (1792–1822)
On Poets as "Unacknowledged Legislators" 1821

The most unfailing herald, companion, and follower of the awakening of a great people to work a beneficial change in opinion or institution, is poetry. At such periods there is an accumulation of the power of communicating and receiving intense and impassioned conceptions respecting man and nature. The persons in whom this power resides, may often, as far as regards many portions of their nature, have little apparent correspondence with that spirit of good of which they are the ministers. But even whilst they deny and abjure, they are yet compelled to serve, the power which is seated upon the throne of their own soul. It is impossible to read the compositions of the most celebrated writers of the present day without being startled with the electric life which burns within their words. They measure the circumference and sound the depths of human nature with a comprehensive and all-penetrating spirit, and they are themselves perhaps the most sincerely astonished at its manifestations, for it is less their spirit than the spirit of the age. Poets are the hierophants° of an unapprehended inspiration, the mirrors of the gigantic shadows which futurity casts upon the present, the words which express what they understand not; the trumpets which sing to battle, and feel not what they inspire: the influence which is moved not, but moves. Poets are the unacknowledged legislators of the world.

From *A Defense of Poetry*

hierophants: Interpreters of sacred mysteries.

Considerations for Critical Thinking and Writing

1. What kinds of powers does Shelley attribute to poets?
2. Compare Shelley's view of the poet with Karl Shapiro's (p. 1067).

WALT WHITMAN (1819–1892)
When I Heard the Learned Astronomer 1865

When I heard the learned astronomer,
When the proofs, the figures, were ranged in columns before me,
When I was shown the charts and diagrams, to add, divide, and measure them,
When I sitting heard the astronomer where he lectured with much applause in the lecture-room,
How soon unaccountable I became tired and sick,

Till rising and gliding out I wandered off by myself,
In the mystical moist night-air, and from time to time,
Looked up in perfect silence at the stars.

Considerations for Critical Thinking and Writing

1. How does this poem illustrate the differences between poetry and science?
2. Many people today — rightly or wrongly — continue to regard science and poetry as antithetical. What do you think of their view? Write an essay about the methods and purposes of science and poetry in which you explore the differences and/or similarities between them. Use specific poems as evidence for your argument.

MATTHEW ARNOLD (1822–1888)
On Classic and Popular Literature   1888

The benefit of being able clearly to feel and deeply to enjoy the best, the truly classic, in poetry, — is an end . . . of supreme importance. We are often told that an era is opening in which we are to see multitudes of a common sort of readers, and masses of a common sort of literature; that such readers do not want and could not relish anything better than such literature, and that to provide it is becoming a vast and profitable industry. Even if good literature entirely lost currency with the world, it would still be abundantly worth while to continue to enjoy it by oneself. But it never will lose currency with the world, in spite of momentary appearances; it never will lose supremacy. Currency and supremacy are insured to it, not indeed by the world's deliberate and conscious choice, but by something far deeper, — by the instinct of self-preservation in humanity.

From "The Study of Poetry"

Considerations for Critical Thinking and Writing

1. What, in your opinion, makes a work of literature "truly classic"?
2. What kinds of assumptions does Arnold implicitly make about readers of classics and the "multitudes of a common sort"? Do you agree with his categorizations and assessment of these two kinds of readers? Why or why not?
3. Take a stroll through your local bookstore to get a sense of the amount of space allocated to "classics," science fiction, romances, fantasy, mysteries, cookbooks, health books, and so on. Pay particular attention to the poetry section. Also, check to see what books are on the current best-seller lists (they're usually posted by the cash register). Then write a two-part report: in the first part write up your findings as you think Arnold would describe such a "vast and profitable industry"; in the second explain why you agree or disagree with Arnold's perspective.

EZRA POUND (1885–1972)
On Free Verse
1912

I think one should write vers libre [free verse] when one "must," that is to say, only when the "thing" builds up a rhythm more beautiful than that of set meters, or more real, more a part of the emotion of the "thing," more germane, intimate, interpretative than the measure of regular accentual verse; a rhythm which discontents one with set iambic or set anapestic.

From "Prolegomena," *Poetry Review*

Considerations for Critical Thinking and Writing

1. What implications are there in Pound's statement concerning the relation of a poem's form to its content?
2. Compare this view with Whitman's (p. 1063).
3. Select a free verse poem from the text and apply Pound's criteria to it. How are the poem's lines arranged to be "a part of the emotion of the 'thing' "?

ARCHIBALD MacLEISH (1892–1982)
Ars Poetica
1926

A poem should be palpable and mute
As a globed fruit,

Dumb
As old medallions to the thumb,

Silent as the sleeve-worn stone   5
Of casement ledges where the moss has grown —

A poem should be wordless
As the flight of birds.

A poem should be motionless in time
As the moon climbs,   10

Leaving, as the moon releases
Twig by twig the night-entangled trees,

Leaving, as the moon behind the winter leaves,
Memory by memory the mind —

A poem should be motionless in time   15
As the moon climbs.

A poem should be equal to:
Not true.

For all the history of grief
An empty doorway and a maple leaf.   20

For love
The leaning grasses and two lights above the sea —

A poem should not mean
But be.

Considerations for Critical Thinking and Writing

1. The Latin title of this poem is translated as "The Art of Poetry." What is MacLeish's view of good poetry? In what sense can a poem be "wordless"? How do lines 19–20 illustrate that?
2. Explain the final two lines. Does the poem contradict its own announced values?
3. How does MacLeish's attitude toward poetry compare with Robert Francis's view in "Glass" (below)?

ROBERT FRANCIS (1901–1987)
Glass   1949

Words of a poem should be glass
But glass so simple-subtle its shape
Is nothing but the shape of what it holds.

A glass spun for itself is empty,
Brittle, at best Venetian trinket.   5
Embossed glass hides the poem or its absence

Words should be looked through, should be windows.
The best word were invisible.
The poem is the thing the poet thinks.

If the impossible were not   10
And if the glass, only the glass,
Could be removed, the poem would remain.

Considerations for Critical Thinking and Writing

1. How is the form of a poem ideally like glass, according to Francis? Why is that not an achievable ideal?
2. Compare what Francis has to say about the words of a poem with what Dylan Thomas says (p. 1068). Although each approaches the topic from a different perspective, do you think they are in basic agreement or disagreement?

e. e. cummings (1894–1962)
On the Artist's Responsibility

1953

So far as I am concerned, poetry and every other art was and is and forever will be strictly and distinctly a question of individuality . . . . poetry is being, not doing. If you wish to follow, even at a distance, the poet's calling (and here, as always, I speak from my own totally biased and entirely personal point of view) you've got to come out of the measurable doing universe into the immeasurable house of being. . . . Nobody else can be alive for you; nor can you be alive for anybody else. Toms can be Dicks and Dicks can be Harrys, but none of them can ever be you. There's the artist's responsibility; and the most awful responsibility on earth. If you can take it, take it — and be. If you can't, cheer up and go about other people's business; and do (or undo) till you drop.

From *i: Six Nonlectures*

Considerations for Critical Thinking and Writing

1. What does cummings mean when he says "poetry is being, not doing"? How does this compare with MacLeish's view in "Ars Poetica" (p. 1065)?
2. How is cummings's insistence upon individuality reflected in the style of "l(a" (p. 600) and the theme of "next to of course god america i" (p. 691)?

KARL SHAPIRO (b. 1913)
On the Poet's Vision

1960

The poet really does see the world differently, and everything in it. He does not deliberately go into training to sharpen his senses; he is a poet because his senses are naturally open and vitally sensitive. But what the poet sees with his always new vision is not what is "imaginary"; he sees what others have forgotten how to see. The poet is always inadvertently stripping away the veils and showing us his reality. Many poets, as we know, go mad because they cannot bear the worlds of illusion and falsehood in which most human beings spend their lives.

From *In Defense of Ignorance*

Considerations for Critical Thinking and Writing

1. Select a poem from this book that illustrates Shapiro's statement that poets see "what others have forgotten how to see." What "reality" does the poem offer that you had forgotten, overlooked, or hadn't previously apprehended?
2. Do you agree that "most human beings spend their lives" in "worlds of illusion and falsehood"? Why or why not?

DYLAN THOMAS (1914–1953)

On the Words in Poetry 1961

You want to know why and how I just began to write poetry. . . .

To answer . . . this question, I should say I wanted to write poetry in the beginning because I had fallen in love with words. The first poems I knew were nursery rhymes, and before I could read them for myself I had come to love just the words of them, the words alone. What the words stood for, symbolized, or meant, was of very secondary importance. What mattered was the *sound* of them as I heard them for the first time on the lips of the remote and incomprehensible grown-ups who seemed, for some reason, to be living in my world. And these words were, to me, as the notes of bells, the sounds of musical instruments, the noises of wind, sea, and rain, the rattle of milkcarts, the clopping of hooves on cobbles, the fingering of branches on a window pane, might be to someone, deaf from birth, who has miraculously found his hearing. I did not care what the words said, overmuch, not what happened to Jack and Jill and the Mother Goose rest of them; I cared for the shapes of sound that their names, and the words describing their actions, made in my ears; I cared for the colors the words cast on my eyes. I realize that I may be, as I think back all that way, romanticizing my reactions to the simple and beautiful words of those pure poems; but that is all I can honestly remember, however much time might have falsified my memory. I fell in love — that is the only expression I can think of — at once, and am still at the mercy of words, though sometimes now, knowing a little of their behavior very well, I think I can influence them slightly and have even learned to beat them now and then, which they appear to enjoy. I tumbled for words at once. And, when I began to read the nursery rhymes for myself, and, later, to read other verses and ballads, I knew that I had discovered the most important things, to me, that could be ever. There they were, seemingly lifeless, made only of black and white, but out of them, out of their own being, came love and terror and pity and pain and wonder and all the other vague abstractions that make our ephemeral lives dangerous, great, and bearable. Out of them came the gusts and grunts and hiccups and heehaws of the common fun of the earth; and though what the words meant was, in its own way, often deliciously funny enough, so much funnier seemed to me, at that almost forgotten time, the shape and shade and size and noise of the words as they hummed, strummed, jugged, and galloped along. That was the time of innocence; words burst upon me, unencumbered by trivial or portentous association; words were their springlike selves, fresh with Eden's dew, as they flew out of the air. They made their own original associations as they sprang and shone. The words, "Ride a cock-horse to Banbury Cross," were as haunting to me, who did not know then what a cock-horse was nor cared a damn where Banbury Cross might be, as, much later, were such lines as John Donne's, "Go and catch a falling star, Get with child a mandrake root," which also I could not understand when I first read them. And as I read more and more, and it was not all verse, by any means, my love for the real life of words increased until I knew that I must live *with* them and *in* them always. I knew, in fact, that I must be a writer of words, and nothing else. The first thing was to feel and know their sound and substance;

what I was going to do with those words, what use I was going to make of them, what I was going to *say* through them, would come later. I knew I had to know them most intimately in all their forms and moods, their ups and downs, their chops and changes, their needs and demands. (Here, I am afraid, I am beginning to talk too vaguely. I do not like writing *about* words, because then I often use bad and wrong and stale and wooly words. What I like to do is treat words as a craftsman does his wood or stone or what-have-you, to hew, carve, mold, coil, polish, and plane them into patterns, sequences, sculptures, fugues of sound expressing some lyrical impulse, some spiritual doubt or conviction, some dimly-realized truth I must try to reach and realize.)

From *Early Prose Writings*

Considerations for Critical Thinking and Writing

1. Why does Thomas value nursery rhymes so highly? What nursery rhyme was your favorite as a child? Why were you enchanted by it?
2. Explain what you think Thomas would have to say about Carroll's "Jabberwocky" (p. 722) or Swenson's "A Nosty Fright" (p. 711).
3. Consider Thomas's comparison at the end of this passage, in which he likens a poet's work to a craftsman's. In what sense is making poetry similar to sculpting, painting, or composing music? What are some of the significant differences?

SYLVIA PLATH (1932–1963)
On "Headline Poetry"   1962

The issues of our time which preoccupy me at the moment are the incalculable genetic effects of fallout and a documentary article on the terrifying, mad, omnipotent marriage of big business and the military in America. . . . Does this influence the kind of poetry I write? Yes, but in a sidelong fashion. I am not gifted with the tongue of Jeremiah,° though I may be sleepless enough before my vision of the apocalypse. My poems do not turn out to be about Hiroshima, but about a child forming itself finger by finger in the dark. They are not about the terrors of mass extinction, but about the bleakness of the moon over a yew tree in a neighboring graveyard. Not about the testaments of tortured Algerians, but about the night thoughts of a tired surgeon.

In a sense, these poems are deflections. I do not think they are an escape. For me, the real issues of our time are the issues of every time — the hurt and wonder of loving; making in all its forms, children, loaves of bread, paintings, building; and the conservation of life of all people in all places, the jeopardizing of which no abstract doubletalk of "peace" or "implacable foes" can excuse.

I do not think a "headline poetry" would interest more people any more profoundly than the headlines. And unless the up-to-the-minute poem grows out of something closer to the bone than a general, shifting philanthropy and

Jeremiah: (c. 650–585 B.C.) One of the greatest Old Testament prophets.

is, indeed, that unicorn-thing — a real poem — it is in danger of being screwed up as rapidly as the news sheet itself.

From "Context," London Magazine, February 1962

Considerations for Critical Thinking and Writing

1. Why does Plath refuse to write "headline poetry"? What kind of poetry does she prefer? Read the Plath poems included in this anthology (see the index) and discuss whether the issues they address "are the issues of every time."
2. Do you agree that the poetry Plath prefers is not "an escape" from contemporary issues? Explain why or why not.
3. Compare Plath's view of poetry with Audre Lorde's perspective (below). Write an essay about the significant similarities and differences you find between the two.

AUDRE LORDE (1934–1992)
Poems Are Not Luxuries   1977

For each of us as women, there is a dark place within where hidden and growing our true spirit rises, "Beautiful and tough as chestnut / Stanchions against our nightmare of weakness" and of impotence. These places of possibility within ourselves are dark because they are ancient and hidden; they have survived and grown strong through darkness. Within these deep places, each one of us holds an incredible reserve of creativity and power, storehouse of unexamined and unrecorded emotion and feeling. The woman's place of power within each of us is neither white nor surface; it is dark, it is ancient, and it is deep.

When we view living, in the european mode, only as a problem to be solved, we rely solely upon our ideas to make us free, for these were what the white fathers told us were precious. But as we become more in touch with our own ancient, black, noneuropean view of living as a situation to be experienced and interacted with, we learn more and more to cherish our feelings, to respect those hidden sources of our power from where true knowledge and therefore lasting action comes. At this point in time, I believe that women carry within ourselves the possibility for fusion of these two approaches as a keystone for survival, and we come closest to this combination in our poetry. I speak here of poetry as the revelation or distillation of experience, not the sterile word play that, too often, the white fathers distorted the word *poetry* to mean — in order to cover their desperate wish for imagination without insight.

For women, then, poetry is not a luxury. It is a vital necessity of our existence. It forms the quality of the light within which we predicate our hopes and dreams toward survival and change, first made into language, then into idea, then into more tangible action. Poetry is the way we help give name to the nameless so it can be thought. The farthest external horizons of our hopes and fears are cobbled by our poems, carved from the rock experiences of our daily lives.

As they become known and accepted to ourselves, our feelings, and the honest exploration of them, become sanctuaries and fortresses and spawning grounds for the most radical and daring of ideas, the house of difference so necessary to change and the conceptualization of any meaningful action. Right now, I could name at least ten ideas I would once have found intolerable or incomprehensible and frightening, except as they came after dreams and poems. This is not idle fantasy, but the true meaning of "It feels right to me." We can train ourselves to respect our feelings and to discipline (transpose) them into a language that catches those feelings so they can be shared. And where that language does not yet exist, it is our poetry which helps to fashion it. Poetry is not only dream or vision, it is the skeleton architecture of our lives.

From "Poems Are Not Luxuries," in *Claims for Poetry*,
edited by Donald Hall

Considerations for Critical Thinking and Writing

1. What distinctions does Lorde make between black culture and "european" culture? How does she describe their different approaches to poetry? Do you agree or disagree with Lorde's assessment?
2. According to Lorde, why can't poetry be regarded as a luxury?
3. Read Lorde's poem "Hanging Fire" (p. 974) and discuss whether you think it fulfills her description of what poetry can do.

MARK STRAND (b. 1934)
On the Audience for Poetry
1977

Interviewer: Are you disturbed by a sense of coterie in recent poetry, by the fact that the audience is so small and ingrown?

Strand: The impression is a little deceptive. The audience for poetry is actually growing bigger, and it constantly changes. A lot of people are interested in poetry for a while, then fall behind and lose interest and get intrigued by other things. But new people are always coming along. The smallness of the audience doesn't bother me. I don't believe poetry is for everyone any more than I believe roast pork is for everyone. Poetry is demanding. It takes a certain amount of getting used to, a period of initiation. Only those people who are willing to spend *time* with it really get anything out of it. No, the lack of audience doesn't bother me. Some poets have 100,000 readers, but I don't believe that many really read poetry. I think if I had that many readers I'd begin to feel that something was *wrong* in my poems.

From an interview by Richard Vine and Robert von Hallberg
in *Chicago Review*, Spring 1977

Considerations for Critical Thinking and Writing

1. What is your impression about the size of audiences for poetry? Are they growing larger or smaller? Explain why.
2. Write an essay in which you agree or disagree with Strand's statement "I don't believe poetry is for everyone any more than I believe roast pork is for everyone."
3. Do you think that if a poet is very popular, there might be something *"wrong"* with his or her poems? Explain why or why not.

GALWAY KINNELL (b. 1927)
The Female and Male Principles of Poetry 1989

If poetry could be divided into two parts, knowing and making, then I would give to knowing the name *the female principle,* and to making I would give the name *the male principle.* Another poet might reverse those names, because these things are myths that just accumulate and we can use them as flexibly as we want. In my own case, you see, I had an Irish mother who brooded and thought and meditated a lot on things and was very articulate. I thought of her as a knower; she really wanted to know. She'd always ask me really hard questions, "Do you really think there's a heaven?" and she would mean it. She wasn't trying to educate me, she wanted to know if there was a heaven. My father, on the other hand, was a maker, he was a carpenter. I spent many hours at his side making things that were solid, had good structure, that wouldn't fall apart, that would last forever.

When I'm writing and I'm doing that beam work and that kind of construction, I always feel that what I'm doing owes a lot to my father, but when I have these moments when I think I know something, which is the most essential thing in poetry, I think that my mother is talking through me. That's why it's worked out that way in my mythology. But I can see how it might be completely different for somebody else.

From "Being with Reality: An Interview with Galway Kinnell,"
Columbia Magazine

Considerations for Critical Thinking and Writing

1. Read Kinnell's "Blackberry Eating" (p. 714) and discuss the poem in terms of Kinnell's ideas about the female principle of knowing and the male principle of making. Can you see evidence of the two principles at work in this poem?
2. One can talk about these principles in relation to reading poetry as well as writing it. Choose three or four poems from Chapter 24 and decide which aspects of the poems you simply know (either by intuition or by a sudden apprehension) and which aspects you must work at to understand. Would you use Kinnell's distinction between female knowing and male making to describe your experience of the poems?

DENISE LEVERTOV (b. 1923)

On "Gathered at the River"

1985

This is the prose of it: Each year on August 6 (and sometimes on August 9 as well) some kind of memorial observance of the bombing of Hiroshima and Nagasaki is held in the Boston/Cambridge area, as in so many other locations. Some years this has consisted of a silent vigil held near Faneuil Hall and other monuments of the American Revolution. Participants stand in a circle facing outward to display signs explaining the theme of the vigil, or pace slowly round, sometimes accompanied by the drums and chanting of attendant Buddhist monks. People stay for varying periods — there may be a constant presence for three days and nights. In 1982 the poet Suzanne Belote (of the Catholic radical peace group Ailanthus) and some others created a variation on this event. Participants (with the usual age range — babes in arms to white-haired old men and women) came to the Cambridge Friends' Meeting House for a brief preparatory assembly, then filed out to receive a candle apiece — thick Jahrzeit candles nailed to pieces of wood and shielded by paper cups — and proceeded to walk in a hushed column along Memorial Drive, beside the Charles River. The sun was low; a long summer day was ending. When we got to the wide grassy area near the Lars Anderson Bridge, where our ceremony was to take place, it was twilight. Shielding flickering flames from the evening breeze, we formed a large circle, into the center of which stepped successive readers of portions from the descriptions recorded (as in the book *Unforgettable Fire*) by survivors of the atomic bombings. A period of silence followed. And then "saints and prophets, heroes and heroines of justice and peace" — including Gandhi, Martin Luther King, A. J. Muste, Emma Goldman, Archbishop Romero, Eugene Debs, Pope John XXIII, Dorothy Day, Saint Francis of Assisi, Saint Thomas More, Prince Kropotkin, Ammon Hennacy, the Prophet Isaiah, and many others I can't remember — were invoked. A form of ritual — an ecumenical liturgy — had been devised for the occasion, and as each such name was uttered by some member of the circle, the rest responded with a phrase that said essentially, "Be with us, great spirits, in this time of great need." The persons conducting the continuum of the liturgy turned slowly as they read the survivors' testimony, or statements of dedication to the cause of peace, so that all could hear at least part of each passage: for we had no microphones, preferring to depend on the unaided human voice for an occasion which had a personal, intimate character for each participant rather than being a PR event. Some music was interspersed among the verbal antiphonies, and the human atmosphere was solemn, harmonious, truly dedicated: from within it I began to feel the strong presence of the trees which half encircled us. Cars passed along Memorial Drive — slowed as drivers craned to see what was happening — passed on. A few blinked their lights in a friendly way, guessing from the date, I suppose, why we were there.

While we earnestly committed — or recommitted — ourselves to do all in our power to prevent nuclear war from ever taking place, it was growing dark. In the soft summer darkness details stood out: hands cupping wicks, small children's gold-illumined faces gazing up in wonder at the crouch and leap of flames, adults' heads bent close to one another as they clustered in twos and threes to relight candles blown out. And now the first part of the ritual was over and it was time to set our candles afloat, as they are set on the river in Hiroshima each year, that river where many drowned in the vain attempt to escape the burning of their own flesh.

People scrambled and helped each other down the short slope of the riverbank to launch the little candle-boats. Oblivious, a motorboat or two sped upriver, and minutes after a big slow wave would reach the shore. The water was black; the candle-boats seemed so fragile, and so tenacious. And all the time the large plane trees (saved from a road-widening project years before, incidentally, by citizens who chained themselves to their trunks in protest), and the other trees and bushes near them, were intensely, watchfully present. I have been asked if I really believe trees can listen. I've always thought our scientific knowledge has made us very arrogant in our assumptions. Wiser and older individuals and cultures have believed other kinds of consciousness and feeling could and did exist alongside of ours; I see no reason to disagree. It is not that I don't know trees have no "gray matter." It is possible that there are other routes to sentience than those with which we consider ourselves familiar.

The form of the poem: The title came from the literal sense of our being gathered there on the shore of the Charles, and also with the cognizance of the Quaker sense of gathering—a *"gathered meeting"* being, to my understanding, one which has not merely acquired the full complement of those who are going to attend it but which has attained a certain level, or quality, of attunement. Then, too, I had a vague memory of the song or hymn from which James Wright took the title of one of his books, and which I presumed must refer to the river of Jordan—"one more river, one more river to cross," as another song says. And though the symbolism there is of heaven lying upon the far shore, yet there is also, in the implication of *lastness,* of a final ordeal, the clear sense of a catastrophic alternative to attaining that shore. (No doubt *Pilgrim's Progress* was in the back of my mind too.) The analogy is obviously not a very close one, since survival of life on earth is a more modest goal than eternal bliss. Yet, relative to the hell proposed by our twentieth-century compound of the ancient vices of greed and love of power with nuclear and other "advanced" technology, mere survival would be a kind of heaven—especially since survival is not a static condition but offers the opportunity, and therefore the hope, of positive change. (For if one hopes for the survival of life on earth, one must logically hope and *intend* also the reshaping of those forces and factors which, unchanged, will only continue to threaten annihilation by one means or another.)

The structure of the poem stems as directly as the title from my experience of the event. The first line stands alone because that perception of the trees as animate and not uninterested presences—witnesses—was the discrete first in a series of heightened perceptions, most of which came in clusters. The following two-line stanza expands the first, more tentative observation, and places the trees' air of attention in the context of a breeze (which does not seem to distract them) and of the fluttering candles, which are thus introduced right at the start. Looking more closely at the trees, I see their late-summer color, but then recognize I am no longer seeing it, for dusk is falling—literally, but also metaphorically. The next stanza notes the largeness (and implied gravity, in both senses) of the trees, which it is not too dark to see, then again in a single line reasserts with more assurance the focus of my own attention: the trees' attentiveness. Following that comes the recognition of why, and for what, they are listening. The Latin words introduced here (echoing Pound's use of them) express the idea that "sin" occurs when humans violate the well-being of their own species and other living things, denying the natural law, the interdependence of all. (That usury belongs in this category, as Pound reemphasized, is not irrelevant to the subject of this poem, recalling the economic underpinning of the arms race and of war itself.)

My underlying belief in a great design, a potential harmony which can be violated or be sustained, probably strikes some people as quaint; but I would be dishonest, as person and artist, if I disowned it. I don't at this stage of my life feel ready for a public discussion of my religious concepts: but I think it must be clear from my writings that I have never been an atheist, and that — given my background and the fact that all my life George Herbert, Henry Vaughan, Thomas Traherne, and Gerard Manley Hopkins have been on my "short list" of favorite poets — whatever degree of belief I might attain would have a Christian context. This in turn implies a concern with the osmosis of "faith and works" and a sense of the sacredness of the earthly creation. That sense, not exclusive to Christianity, and deeply experienced and expressed by, for instance, Native Americans, is linked for Christians to the mystery of the Incarnation. To violate ourselves and our world is to violate the Divine.

The trees' concern, proposed with a tentative "as if" at the beginning, and then as an impression they "give off," is now asserted unequivocally. Once more comes a single line, "We intone together, *Never again*," focused on the purpose of our gathering; and the words "never again" bring together the thought of the Nazi Holocaust with that of the crime committed by the U.S. against Japanese civilians, a crime advocates of the arms race prepare to commit again on a scale vaster than that of any massacre in all of history. This association might carry with it, I would hope, the sense that those who vow to work for prevention of war also are dedicated to political, economic, and racial justice, and understand something of the connections between long-standing oppression, major and "minor" massacres, and the giant shadow of global war and annihilation.

The narration continues, up to the launching of the candle-boats; pauses — a pause indicated by the asterisk — as we hold our breath to watch them go; and continues as they "bob on the current" and, though close to shore, begin to move downstream. Like ourselves, they are few and pitifully small. But at least they don't sink. Like all candles lit for the dead or in prayer, they combine remembrance with aspiration.

Finally the poem returns its regard to the trees, with the feeling that they know what we know — a knowledge those lines state and which it would be silly to paraphrase. The single lines again center on the primary realizations. Indeed, I see that a kind of précis of the entire poem could be extracted by reading the isolated lines alone:

As if the trees were not indifferent . . .
. . . .
a half-circle of attention.
. . . .

We intone together, *Never again*.

Windthreatened flames bob on the current . . .

there will be nothing left of their slow and innocent wisdom,

no pollen,

except that one absolutely essential bone would be missing from that skeleton: the "if" of "if we fail." The poem, like the ceremony it narrates, and which gives it its slow, serious *pace* and, I hope, tone, is about interconnection, about dread, and about hope; that word, *if,* is its core.

> " 'Gathered at the River': Background and Form" in *Singular Voices: American Poetry Today,* edited by Stephen Berg (Levertov's essay was written in response to a request from Berg.)

Considerations for Critical Thinking and Writing

1. In this essay, Levertov describes why and how she wrote "Gathered at the River" (p. 1053). Does her account of the memorial observance help you to appreciate the poem more? Why or why not? Is the background information to the poem ("the prose of it") essential for an understanding of it?
2. Why is the word *if* essential to the poem's meaning?
3. Does Levertov exhaust the possibilities for discussing the poem? What can you add to her comments?
4. Poets are usually extremely reluctant to comment on their own poetry. Why do you think they frequently refuse to talk about the background and form of their poems?

ALICE FULTON (b. 1952)
On the Validity of Free Verse   1987

Until recently, I believed that Pound (along with Blake and Whitman, among others) had managed to establish beyond all argument the value of *vers libre* as a poetic medium. I thought that questions concerning the validity of free verse could be filed along with such antique quarrels as "Is photography Art?" and "Is abstract art Art?" In the past few years, however, I've heard many people — professors, poets, readers — speak of free verse as a failed experiment. To these disgruntled souls, free verse apparently describes an amorphous prosaic spouting, distinguished chiefly by its neglect of meter or rhyme, pattern or plan. Perhaps the word *free* contributes to the misconception. It's easy to interpret *free* as "free from all constraints of form," which lead to "free-for-all." However, any poet struggling with the obdurate qualities of language can testify that the above connotations of "free" do not apply to verse.

Since it's impossible to write unaccented English, free verse has meter. Of course, rather than striving for regularity, the measure of free verse may change from line to line, just as the tempo of twentieth-century music may change from bar to bar. As for allegations about formlessness, it seems to me that only an irregular structure with no beginning or end could be described as formless. (If the structure were regular, we could deduce the whole from a part. If irregular and therefore unpredictable, we'd need to see the whole in order to grasp its shape.) By this definition, there are fairly few examples of formless phenomena: certain concepts of God or of the expanding universe come to mind. However, unlike the accidental forms of nature, free verse is characterized by the poet's conscious shaping of content and language: the poet's choices at each step of the creative process give rise to form. Rather than relying on regular meter or rhyme as a means of ordering, the structures of free verse may be based upon registers of diction, irregular meter, sound as analogue for content, syllabics, accentuals, the interplay of chance with chosen elements, theories of lineation, recurring words, or whatever design delights the imagination and intellect. I suspect that the relation between content and form can be important or arbitrary in both metered and free verse. In regard to conventional forms, it's often assumed that decisions concerning content follow decisions concerning form (the add-subject-and-stir approach). However, poets consciously choose different subjects for sonnets than for ballads, thus exemplifying the interdependency of content and form. The reverse assumption is made about free verse: that the subject supersedes or, at best, dictates the form. But this is not necessarily the case. The poet can decide to utilize a structural device, such as the ones suggested previously, and then proceed to devise the content.

When we read a sestina, the form is clearly discernible. This is partly because we've read so many sestinas (familiarity breeds recognition) and partly because it's easy to perceive a highly repetitive pattern. More complex designs, however, often appear to be random until scrutinized closely. Much of what we call free verse tries to create a structure suitable only to itself — a pattern that has never appeared before, perhaps. As in serious modern music or jazz, the repetitions, if they do exist, may be so widely spaced that it takes several readings to discern them. Or the poems' unifying elements may be new to the reader, who must become a creative and active participant in order to appreciate the overall scheme. This is not meant to be a dismissal of the time-honored poetic forms. I admire and enjoy poets who breathe new life into seemingly dead conventions or structures. And I'm intrigued by poetry that borrows its shape from the models around us: poems in the form of TV listings, letters, recipes, and so forth. But I also value the analysis required and the discovery inherent in reading work that invents a form peculiar to itself. I like the idea of varying the meter from line to line so that nuances of tone can find their rhythmic correlative (or antithesis).

From *Ecstatic Occasions, Expedient Forms,* edited by David Lehman

Considerations for Critical Thinking and Writing

1. How does Fulton defend free verse against "allegations about formlessness"?
2. Compare Fulton's comments on the relationship of a poem's form to its content with Whitman's views (p. 1063).
3. Browse through Chapter 24 and choose a poem "that invents a form peculiar to itself." Now analyze that poem.

ROBERT J. FOGELIN (b. 1932)

A Case against Metaphors
1988

    Recent writers on metaphor often insist, sometimes in extravagant terms, on the power of metaphors. They also complain about the prejudice against metaphor that springs, they suggest, from a narrow, literalist (positivist) conception of language. The fact of the matter is that the vast majority of metaphors are routine and uninteresting. Many metaphors are lame, misleading, overblown, inaccurate, et cetera. Metaphors, in indicating that one thing is like another, so far say very little. Their strength, which they share with comparisons in general, is that their near-emptiness makes them adaptable for use in a wide variety of contexts. On the reverse side, the near-emptiness of metaphors also makes them serviceable for those occasions when we want to avoid saying, and perhaps thinking, what we really mean. Euphemisms are typically couched in metaphors. Metaphors can be evasions — including poetic evasions.

From *Figuratively Speaking*

Considerations for Critical Thinking and Writing

1. Why does Fogelin object to many uses of metaphors? Explain why you agree or disagree with his assessment.
2. Choose a poem from this anthology and write an essay that either supports or refutes Fogelin's assertions.

DRAMA

DRAMA

26. Reading Drama

READING DRAMA RESPONSIVELY

The publication of a short story, novel, or poem represents for most writers the final step in a long creative process that might have begun with an idea, issue, emotion, or question that demanded expression. *Playwrights* — writers who make plays — may begin a work in the same way as other writers, but rarely are they satisfied with only its publication, because most dramatic literature — what we call *plays* — is written to be performed by actors on a stage before an audience. Playwrights typically create a play keeping in mind not only readers but also actors, producers, directors, costumers, designers, technicians, and a theater full of other support staff who have a hand in presenting the play to a live audience.

Drama is literature equipped with arms, legs, tears, laughs, whispers, shouts, and gestures that are alive and immediate. Indeed, the word *drama* derives from the Greek word *dran,* meaning "to do" or "to perform." The text of many plays — the *script* — may come to life fully only when the written words are transformed into a performance. Although there are plays that do not invite production, they are relatively few. Such plays, written to be read rather than performed, are called *closet dramas.* In this kind of work (primarily associated with nineteenth-century English literature), literary art outweighs all other considerations. The majority of playwrights, however, view the written word as the beginning of a larger creation and hope that a producer will deem their scripts worthy of production.

Given that most playwrights intend their works to be performed, it might be argued that reading a play is a poor substitute for seeing it acted on a stage — perhaps something like reading a recipe without having access to the ingredients and a kitchen. This analogy is tempting, but it overlooks the literary dimensions of a script; the words we hear on a stage were written first. Read from a page, these words can feed an imagination in ways that a recipe cannot satisfy a hungry cook. We can fill in a play's missing faces, voices, actions, and settings in much the same way that we imagine these elements in a short story or novel. Like any play director, we are free to include as many ingredients as we have an appetite for.

This imaginative collaboration with the playwright creates a mental world that can be nearly as real and vivid as a live performance. Sometimes readers find that they prefer their own reading of a play to a director's interpretation. Shakespeare's Hamlet, for instance, has been presented as a whining son, but you may read him as a strong prince. Rich plays often accommodate a wide range of imaginative responses to their texts. Reading, then, is an excellent way to appreciate and evaluate a production of a play. Moreover, reading is valuable in its own right, because it allows us to enter the playwright's created world even when a theatrical production is unavailable.

Reading a play, however, requires more creative imagining than sitting in an audience watching actors on a stage presenting lines and actions before you. As a reader you become the play's director; you construct an interpretation based on the playwright's use of language, development of character, arrangement of incidents, description of settings, and directions for staging. Keeping track of the playwright's handling of these elements will help you to organize your response to the play. You may experience suspense, fear, horror, sympathy, or humor, but whatever experience a play evokes, ask yourself why you respond to it as you do. You may discover that your assessment of Hamlet's character is different from someone else's, but whether you find him heroic, indecisive, neurotic, or a complex of competing qualities, you'll be better equipped to articulate your interpretation of him if you pay attention to your responses and ask yourself questions as you read. Consider, for example, how his reactions might be similar to or different from your own. How does his language reveal his character? Does his behavior seem justified? How would you play the role yourself? What actor do you think might best play the Hamlet that you have created in your imagination? Why would he or she (women have also played Hamlet onstage) fill the role best?

These kinds of questions (see Questions for Responsive Reading, p. 1110) can help you to think and talk about your responses to a play. Happily, such questions needn't — and often can't — be fully answered as you read the play. Frequently you must experience the entire play before you can determine how its elements work together. That's why reading a play can be such a satisfying experience. You wouldn't think of asking a live actor onstage to repeat her lines because you didn't quite comprehend their significance, but you can certainly reread a page in a book. Rereading allows you to replay language, characters, and incidents carefully and thoroughly to your own satisfaction.

TRIFLES

In the following play, Susan Glaspell skillfully draws on many dramatic elements and creates an intense story that is as effective on the page as it is in the theater. Glaspell wrote *Trifles* in 1916 for the Provincetown Players on Cape Cod, in Massachusetts. Their performance of the work helped her develop a reputation as a writer sensitive to feminist issues. The year after *Trifles* was produced, Glaspell transformed the play into a short story titled "A Jury of Her Peers." (A passage from the story appears on p. 1976 for comparison.)

Glaspell's life in the Midwest provided her with the setting for *Trifles*. Born and raised in Davenport, Iowa, she graduated from Drake University in 1899 and then worked for a short time as a reporter on the *Des Moines News,* until her short stories were accepted in magazines such as *Harper's* and *Ladies' Home Journal.* Glaspell moved to the Northeast when she was in her early thirties to continue writing fiction and drama. She published some twenty plays, novels, and more than forty short stories. *Alison's House,* based on Emily Dickinson's life, earned her a Pulitzer Prize for drama in 1931. *Trifles* and "A Jury of Her Peers" remain, however, Glaspell's best-known works.

Glaspell wrote *Trifles* to complete a bill that was to feature several one-act plays by Eugene O'Neill. In *The Road to the Temple* (1926) she recalls how the play came to her as she sat in the theater looking at a bare stage. First, "the stage became a kitchen. . . . Then the door at the back opened, and people all bundled up came in — two or three men. I wasn't sure which, but sure enough about the two women, who hung back, reluctant to enter that kitchen. When I was a newspaper reporter out in Iowa, I was sent downstate to do a murder trial, and I never forgot going to the kitchen of a woman who had been locked up in town."

Trifles is about a murder committed in a midwestern farmhouse, but the play goes beyond the kinds of questions raised by most whodunit stories. The murder is the occasion instead of the focus. The play's major concerns are the moral, social, and psychological aspects of the assumptions and perceptions of the men and women who search for the murderer's motive. Glaspell is finally more interested in the meaning of Mrs. Wright's life than in the details of Mr. Wright's death.

As you read the play keep track of your responses to the characters and note in the margin the moments when Glaspell reveals how men and women respond differently to the evidence before them. What do those moments suggest about the kinds of assumptions these men and women make about themselves and each other? How do their assumptions compare with your own?

SUSAN GLASPELL (1882–1948)

Trifles   1916

Characters

George Henderson, county attorney
Henry Peters, sheriff
Lewis Hale, a neighboring farmer
Mrs. Peters
Mrs. Hale

SCENE: *The kitchen in the now abandoned farmhouse of John Wright, a gloomy kitchen, and left without having been put in order — the walls covered with a faded wall paper. Down right is a door leading to the parlor. On the right wall above this door is a built-in kitchen cupboard with shelves in the upper portion and drawers below. In the rear wall at right, up two steps is a door opening onto stairs leading to the second floor. In the rear wall at left is a door to the shed and from there to the outside. Between these two doors is an old-fashioned black iron stove. Running along the left wall from the shed door is an old iron sink and sink shelf, in which is set a hand pump. Downstage of the sink is an uncurtained window. Near the window is an old wooden rocker. Center stage is an unpainted wooden kitchen table with straight chairs on either side. There is a small chair down right. Unwashed pans under the sink, a loaf of bread outside the breadbox, a dish towel on the table — other signs of incompleted work. At the rear the shed door opens and the Sheriff comes in followed by the County Attorney and Hale. The Sheriff and Hale are men in middle life, the County Attorney is a young man; all are much bundled up and go at once to the stove. They are followed by the two women — the Sheriff's wife, Mrs. Peters, first; she is a slight wiry woman, a thin nervous face. Mrs. Hale is larger and would ordinarily be called more comfortable looking, but she is disturbed now and looks fearfully about as she enters. The women have come in slowly, and stand close together near the door.*

County Attorney (at stove rubbing his hands): This feels good. Come up to the fire, ladies.

Mrs. Peters (after taking a step forward): I'm not — cold.

Sheriff (unbuttoning his overcoat and stepping away from the stove to right of table as if to mark the beginning of official business): Now, Mr. Hale, before we move things about, you explain to Mr. Henderson just what you saw when you came here yesterday morning.

County Attorney (crossing down to left of the table): By the way, has anything been moved? Are things just as you left them yesterday?

Sheriff (looking about): It's just about the same. When it dropped below zero last night I thought I'd better send Frank out this morning to make a fire for us — *(sits right of center table)* no use getting pneumonia with a big case on, but I told him not to touch anything except the stove — and you know Frank.

County Attorney: Somebody should have been left here yesterday.

Sheriff: Oh — yesterday. When I had to send Frank to Morris Center for that man who went crazy — I want you to know I had my hands full yesterday. I knew you could get back from Omaha by today and as long as I went over everything here myself———

County Attorney: Well, Mr. Hale, tell just what happened when you came here yesterday morning.

Hale (crossing down to above table): Harry and I had started to town with a load of potatoes. We came along the road from my place and as I got here I said, "I'm going to see if I can't get John Wright to go in with me on a party telephone." I spoke to Wright about it once before and he put me off, saying folks talked too much anyway, and all he asked was peace and quiet — I guess you know about how much he talked himself; but I thought maybe if I went to the house and talked about it before his wife, though I said to Harry that I didn't know as what his wife wanted made much difference to John———

County Attorney: Let's talk about that later, Mr. Hale. I do want to talk about that, but tell now just what happened when you got to the house.

Hale: I didn't hear or see anything; I knocked at the door, and still it was all quiet inside. I knew they must be up, it was past eight o'clock. So I knocked again, and I thought I heard somebody say, "Come in." I wasn't sure, I'm not sure yet, but I opened the door — this door (indicating the door by which the two women are still standing) and there in that rocker — (pointing to it) sat Mrs. Wright. (They all look at the rocker down left.)

County Attorney: What — was she doing?

Hale: She was rockin' back and forth. She had her apron in her hand and was kind of — pleating it.

County Attorney: And how did she — look?

Hale: Well, she looked queer.

County Attorney: How do you mean — queer?

Hale: Well, as if she didn't know what she was going to do next. And kind of done up.

County Attorney (takes out notebook and pencil and sits left of center table): How did she seem to feel about your coming?

Hale: Why, I don't think she minded — one way or other. She didn't pay much attention. I said, "How do, Mrs. Wright, it's cold, ain't it?" And she said, "Is it?" — and went on kind of pleating at her apron. Well, I was surprised; she didn't ask me to come up to the stove, or to set down, but just sat there, not even looking at me, so I said, "I want to see John." And then she — laughed. I guess you would call it a laugh. I thought of Harry and the team outside, so I said a little sharp: "Can't I see John?" "No," she says, kind o' dull like. "Ain't he home?" says I. "Yes," says she, "he's home." "Then why can't I see him?" I asked her, out of patience. " 'Cause he's dead," says she. "Dead?" says I. She just nodded her head, not getting a bit excited, but rockin' back and forth. "Why — where is he?" says I, not knowing what to say. She just pointed upstairs — like that. (Himself pointing to the room above.) I started for the stairs, with the idea of going up there. I walked from there to here — then I says, "Why, what did he die of?" "He died of a rope round his neck," says she, and just went on pleatin' at her apron. Well, I went out and called Harry. I thought I might — need help. We went upstairs and there he was lyin'———

County Attorney: I think I'd rather have you go into that upstairs, where you can point it all out. Just go on now with the rest of the story.

Hale: Well, my first thought was to get that rope off. It looked . . . *(stops; his face twitches)* . . . but Harry, he went up to him, and he said, "No, he's dead all right, and we'd better not touch anything." So we went back downstairs. She was still sitting that same way. "Has anybody been notified?" I asked. "No," says she, unconcerned. "Who did this, Mrs. Wright?" said Harry. He said it businesslike — and she stopped pleatin' of her apron. "I don't know," she says. "You don't *know?*" says Harry. "No," says she. "Weren't you sleepin' in the bed with him?" says Harry. "Yes," says she, "but I was on the inside." "Somebody slipped a rope round his neck and strangled him and you didn't wake up?" says Harry. "I didn't wake up," she said after him. We must 'a' looked as if we didn't see how that could be, for after a minute she said, "I sleep sound." Harry was going to ask her more questions but I said maybe we ought to let her tell her story first to the coroner, or the sheriff, so Harry went fast as he could to Rivers' place, where there's a telephone.

County Attorney: And what did Mrs. Wright do when she knew that you had gone for the coroner?

Hale: She moved from the rocker to that chair over there *(pointing to a small chair in the down right corner)* and just sat there with her hands held together and looking down. I got a feeling that I ought to make some conversation, so I said I had come in to see if John wanted to put in a telephone, and at that she started to laugh, and then she stopped and looked at me — scared. *(The County Attorney, who has had his notebook out, makes a note.)* I dunno, maybe it wasn't scared. I wouldn't like to say it was. Soon Harry got back, and then Dr. Lloyd came and you, Mr. Peters, and so I guess that's all I know that you don't.

County Attorney (rising and looking around): I guess we'll go upstairs first — and then out to the barn and around there. *(To the Sheriff.)* You're convinced that there was nothing important here — nothing that would point to any motive?

Sheriff: Nothing here but kitchen things. *(The County Attorney, after again looking around the kitchen, opens the door of a cupboard closet in right wall. He brings a small chair from right — gets on it and looks on a shelf. Pulls his hand away, sticky.)*

County Attorney: Here's a nice mess. *(The women drew nearer up center.)*

Mrs. Peters (to the other woman): Oh, her fruit; it did freeze. *(To the Lawyer.)* She worried about that when it turned so cold. She said the fire'd go out and her jars would break.

Sheriff (rises): Well, can you beat the women! Held for murder and worryin' about her preserves.

County Attorney (getting down from chair): I guess before we're through she may have something more serious than preserves to worry about. *(Crosses down right center.)*

Hale: Well, women are used to worrying over trifles. *(The two women move a little closer together.)*

County Attorney (with the gallantry of a young politician): And yet, for all their worries, what would we do without the ladies? *(The women do not unbend.*

He goes below the center table to the sink, takes a dipperful of water from the pail, and pouring it into a basin, washes his hands. While he is doing this the Sheriff and Hale cross to cupboard, which they inspect. The County Attorney starts to wipe his hands on the roller towel, turns it for a cleaner place.) Dirty towels! *(Kicks his foot against the pans under the sink.)* Not much of a housekeeper, would you say, ladies?

Mrs. Hale (stiffly): There's a great deal of work to be done on a farm.

County Attorney: To be sure. And yet *(with a little bow to her)* I know there are some Dickson County farmhouses which do not have such roller towels. *(He gives it a pull to expose its full length again.)*

Mrs. Hale: Those towels get dirty awful quick. Men's hands aren't always as clean as they might be.

County Attorney: Ah, loyal to your sex, I see. But you and Mrs. Wright were neighbors. I suppose you were friends, too.

Mrs. Hale (shaking her head): I've not seen much of her of late years. I've not been in this house — it's more than a year.

County Attorney (crossing to women up center): And why was that? You didn't like her?

Mrs. Hale: I liked her all well enough. Farmers' wives have their hands full, Mr. Henderson. And then ——

County Attorney: Yes ——?

Mrs. Hale (looking about): It never seemed a very cheerful place.

County Attorney: No — it's not cheerful. I shouldn't say she had the homemaking instinct.

Mrs. Hale: Well, I don't know as Wright had, either.

County Attorney: You mean that they didn't get on very well?

Mrs. Hale: No, I don't mean anything. But I don't think a place'd be any cheerfuller for John Wright's being in it.

County Attorney: I'd like to talk more of that a little later. I want to get the lay of things upstairs now. *(He goes past the women to up right where steps lead to a stair door.)*

Sheriff: I suppose anything Mrs. Peters does'll be all right. She was to take in some clothes for her, you know, and a few little things. We left in such a hurry yesterday.

County Attorney: Yes, but I would like to see what you take, Mrs. Peters, and keep an eye out for anything that might be of use to us.

Mrs. Peters: Yes, Mr. Henderson. *(The men leave by up right door to stairs. The women listen to the men's steps on the stairs, then look about the kitchen.)*

Mrs. Hale (crossing left to sink): I'd hate to have men coming into my kitchen, snooping around and criticizing. *(She arranges the pans under sink which the Lawyer had shoved out of place.)*

Mrs. Peters: Of course it's no more than their duty. *(Crosses to cupboard up right.)*

Mrs. Hale: Duty's all right, but I guess that deputy sheriff that came out to make the fire might have got a little of this on. *(Gives the roller towel a pull.)* Wish I'd thought of that sooner. Seems mean to talk about her for not having things slicked up when she had to come away in such a hurry. *(Crosses right to Mrs. Peters at cupboard.)*

Mrs. Peters (who has been looking through cupboard, lifts one end of towel that covers a pan): She had bread set. *(Stands still.)*

Mrs. Hale (eyes fixed on a loaf of bread beside the breadbox, which is on a low shelf of the cupboard): She was going to put this in there. *(Picks up loaf, abruptly drops it. In a manner of returning to familiar things.)* It's a shame about her fruit. I wonder if it's all gone. *(Gets up on the chair and looks.)* I think there's some here that's all right, Mrs. Peters. Yes — here; *(holding it toward the window)* this is cherries, too. *(Looking again.)* I declare I believe that's the only one. *(Gets down, jar in her hand. Goes to the sink and wipes it off on the outside.)* She'll feel awful bad after all her hard work in the hot weather. I remember the afternoon I put up my cherries last summer. *(She puts the jar on the big kitchen table, center of the room. With a sigh, is about to sit down in the rocking chair. Before she is seated realizes what chair it is; with a slow look at it, steps back. The chair which she has touched rocks back and forth. Mrs. Peters moves to center table and they both watch the chair rock for a moment or two.)*

Mrs. Peters (shaking off the mood which the empty rocking chair has evoked. Now in a businesslike manner she speaks): Well I must get those things from the front room closet. *(She goes to the door at the right but, after looking into the other room, steps back.)* You coming with me, Mrs. Hale? You could help me carry them. *(They go in the other room; reappear, Mrs. Peters carrying a dress, petticoat, and skirt, Mrs. Hale following with a pair of shoes.)* My, it's cold in there. *(She puts the clothes on the big table and hurries to the stove.)*

Mrs. Hale (right of center table examining the skirt): Wright was close. I think maybe that's why she kept so much to herself. She didn't even belong to the Ladies' Aid. I suppose she felt she couldn't do her part, and then you don't enjoy things when you feel shabby. I heard she used to wear pretty clothes and be lively, when she was Minnie Foster, one of the town girls singing in the choir. But that — oh, that was thirty years ago. This all you want to take in?

Mrs. Peters: She said she wanted an apron. Funny thing to want, for there isn't much to get you dirty in jail, goodness knows. But I suppose just to make her feel more natural. *(Crosses to cupboard.)* She said they was in the top drawer in this cupboard. Yes, here. And then her little shawl that always hung behind the door. *(Opens stair door and looks.)* Yes, here it is. *(Quickly shuts door leading upstairs.)*

Mrs. Hale (abruptly moving toward her): Mrs. Peters?

Mrs. Peters: Yes, Mrs. Hale? *(At up right door.)*

Mrs. Hale: Do you think she did it?

Mrs. Peters (in a frightened voice): Oh, I don't know.

Mrs. Hale: Well, I don't think she did. Asking for an apron and her little shawl. Worrying about her fruit.

Mrs. Peters (starts to speak, glances up, where footsteps are heard in the room above. In a low voice): Mr. Peters says it looks bad for her. Mr. Henderson is awful sarcastic in a speech and he'll make fun of her sayin' she didn't wake up.

Mrs. Hale: Well, I guess John Wright didn't wake when they was slipping that rope under his neck.

Mrs. Peters (crossing slowly to table and placing shawl and apron on table with other clothing): No, it's strange. It must have been done awful crafty and still. They say it was such a — funny way to kill a man, rigging it all up like that.

Mrs. Hale (crossing to left of Mrs. Peters at table): That's just what Mr. Hale said. There was a gun in the house. He says that's what he can't understand.

Mrs. Peters: Mr. Henderson said coming out that what was needed for the case was a motive; something to show anger, or — sudden feeling.

Mrs. Hale (who is standing by the table): Well, I don't see any signs of anger around here. *(She puts her hand on the dish towel, which lies on the table, stands looking down at table, one-half of which is clean, the other half messy.)* It's wiped to here. *(Makes a move as if to finish work, then turns and looks at loaf of bread outside the breadbox. Drops towel. In that voice of coming back to familiar things.)* Wonder how they are finding things upstairs. *(Crossing below table to down right.)* I hope she had it a little more red-up up there. You know, it seems kind of *sneaking.* Locking her up in town and then coming out here and trying to get her own house to turn against her!

Mrs. Peters: But, Mrs. Hale, the law is the law.

Mrs. Hale: I s'pose 'tis. *(Unbuttoning her coat.)* Better loosen up your things, Mrs. Peters. You won't feel them when you go out. *(Mrs. Peters takes off her fur tippet, goes to hang it on chair back left of table, stands looking at the work basket on floor near down left window.)*

Mrs. Peters: She was piecing a quilt. *(She brings the large sewing basket to the center table and they look at the bright pieces, Mrs. Hale above the table and Mrs. Peters left of it.)*

Mrs. Hale: It's a log cabin pattern. Pretty, isn't it? I wonder if she was goin' to quilt it or just knot it? *(Footsteps have been heard coming down the stairs. The Sheriff enters followed by Hale and the County Attorney.)*

Sheriff: They wonder if she was going to quilt it or just knot it! *(The men laugh, the women look abashed.)*

County Attorney (rubbing his hands over the stove): Frank's fire didn't do much up there, did it? Well, let's go out to the barn and get that cleared up. *(The men go outside by up left door.)*

Mrs. Hale (resentfully): I don't know as there's anything so strange, our takin' up our time with little things while we're waiting for them to get the evidence. *(She sits in chair right of table smoothing out a block with decision.)* I don't see as it's anything to laugh about.

Mrs. Peters (apologetically): Of course they've got awful important things on their minds. *(Pulls up a chair and joins Mrs. Hale at the left of the table.)*

Mrs. Hale (examining another block): Mrs. Peters, look at this one. Here, this is the one she was working on, and look at the sewing! All the rest of it has been so nice and even. And look at this! It's all over the place! Why, it looks as if she didn't know what she was about! *(After she has said this they look at each other, then start to glance back at the door. After an instant Mrs. Hale has pulled at a knot and ripped the sewing.)*

Mrs. Peters: Oh, what are you doing, Mrs. Hale?

Mrs. Hale (mildly): Just pulling out a stitch or two that's not sewed very good. *(Threading a needle.)* Bad sewing always made me fidgety.

Mrs. Peters (with a glance at door, nervously): I don't think we ought to touch things.

Mrs. Hale: I'll just finish up this end. *(Suddenly stopping and leaning forward.)* Mrs. Peters?

Mrs. Peters: Yes, Mrs. Hale?

Mrs. Hale: What do you suppose she was so nervous about?

Mrs. Peters: Oh — I don't know. I don't know as she was nervous. I sometimes sew awful queer when I'm just tired. *(Mrs. Hale starts to say something, looks at Mrs. Peters, then goes on sewing.)* Well, I must get these things wrapped up. They may be through sooner than we think. *(Putting apron and other things together.)* I wonder where I can find a piece of paper, and string. *(Rises.)*

Mrs. Hale: In that cupboard, maybe.

Mrs. Peters (crosses right looking in cupboard): Why, here's a bird-cage. *(Holds it up)*. Did she have a bird, Mrs. Hale?

Mrs. Hale: Why, I don't know whether she did or not — I've not been here for so long. There was a man around last year selling canaries cheap, but I don't know as she took one; maybe she did. She used to sing real pretty herself.

Mrs. Peters (glancing around): Seems funny to think of a bird here. But she must have had one, or why would she have a cage? I wonder what happened to it?

Mrs. Hale: I s'pose maybe the cat got it.

Mrs. Peters: No, she didn't have a cat. She's got that feeling some people have about cats — being afraid of them. My cat got in her room and she was real upset and asked me to take it out.

Mrs. Hale: My sister Bessie was like that. Queer, ain't it?

Mrs. Peters (examining the cage): Why, look at this door. It's broke. One hinge is pulled apart. *(Takes a step down to Mrs. Hale's right.)*

Mrs. Hale (looking too): Looks as if someone must have been rough with it.

Mrs. Peters: Why, yes. *(She brings the cage forward and puts it on the table.)*

Mrs. Hale (glancing toward up left door): I wish if they're going to find any evidence they'd be about it. I don't like this place.

Mrs. Peters: But I'm awful glad you came with me, Mrs. Hale. It would be lonesome for me sitting here alone.

Mrs. Hale: It would, wouldn't it? *(Dropping her sewing.)* But I tell you what I do wish, Mrs. Peters. I wish I had come over sometimes when *she* was here. I — *(looking around the room)* — wish I had.

Mrs. Peters: But of course you were awful busy, Mrs. Hale — your house and your children.

Mrs. Hale (rises and crosses left): I could've come. I stayed away because it weren't cheerful — and that's why I ought to have come. I — *(looking out left window)* — I've never liked this place. Maybe because it's down in a hollow and you don't see the road. I dunno what it is, but it's a lonesome place and always was. I wish I had come over to see Minnie Foster sometimes. I can see now — *(Shakes her head.)*

Mrs. Peters (left of table and above it): Well, you mustn't reproach yourself, Mrs. Hale. Somehow we just don't see how it is with other folks until — something turns up.

Mrs. Hale: Not having children makes less work — but it makes a quiet house, and Wright out to work all day, and no company when he did come in. *(Turning from window.)* Did you know John Wright, Mrs. Peters?

Mrs. Peters: Not to know him; I've seen him in town. They say he was a good man.

Mrs. Hale: Yes — good; he didn't drink, and kept his word as well as most, I guess, and paid his debts. But he was a hard man, Mrs. Peters. Just to pass the time of day with him — *(Shivers.)* Like a raw wind that gets to the bone. *(Pauses, her eye falling on the cage.)* I should think she would 'a' wanted a bird. But what do you suppose went with it?

Mrs. Peters: I don't know, unless it got sick and died. *(She reaches over and swings the broken door, swings it again, both women watch it.)*

Mrs. Hale: You weren't raised round here, were you? *(Mrs. Peters shakes her head.)* You didn't know — her?

Mrs. Peters: Not till they brought her yesterday.

Mrs. Hale: She — come to think of it, she was kind of like a bird herself — real sweet and pretty, but kind of timid and — fluttery. How — she — did — change. *(Silence: then as if struck by a happy thought and relieved to get back to everyday things. Crosses right above Mrs. Peters to cupboard, replaces small chair used to stand on to its original place down right.)* Tell you what, Mrs. Peters, why don't you take the quilt in with you? It might take up her mind.

Mrs. Peters: Why, I think that's a real nice idea, Mrs. Hale. There couldn't possibly be any objection to it could there? Now, just what would I take? I wonder if her patches are in here — and her things. *(They look in the sewing basket.)*

Mrs. Hale (crosses to right of table): Here's some red. I expect this has got sewing things in it. *(Brings out a fancy box.)* What a pretty box. Looks like something somebody would give you. Maybe her scissors are in here. *(Opens box. Suddenly puts her hand to her nose.)* Why ——— *(Mrs. Peters bends nearer, then turns her face away.)* There's something wrapped up in this piece of silk.

Mrs. Peters: Why, this isn't her scissors.

Mrs. Hale (lifting the silk): Oh, Mrs. Peters — it's ——— *(Mrs. Peters bends closer.)*

Mrs. Peters: It's the bird.

Mrs. Hale: But, Mrs. Peters — look at it! Its neck! Look at its neck! It's all — other side *to.*

Mrs. Peters: Somebody — wrung — its — neck. *(Their eyes meet. A look of growing comprehension, of horror. Steps are heard outside. Mrs. Hale slips box under quilt pieces, and sinks into her chair. Enter Sheriff and County Attorney. Mrs. Peters steps down left and stands looking out of window.)*

County Attorney (as one turning from serious things to little pleasantries): Well, ladies, have you decided whether she was going to quilt it or knot it? *(Crosses to center above table.)*

Mrs. Peters: We think she was going to — knot it. *(Sheriff crosses to right of stove, lifts stove lid, and glances at fire, then stands warming hands at stove.)*

County Attorney: Well, that's interesting, I'm sure. *(Seeing the bird-cage.)* Has the bird flown?

Mrs. Hale (putting more quilt pieces over the box): We think the — cat got it.

County Attorney *(preoccupied):* Is there a cat? *(Mrs. Hale glances in a quick covert way at Mrs. Peters.)*

Mrs. Peters *(turning from window takes a step in):* Well, not *now.* They're superstitious, you know. They leave.

County Attorney *(to Sheriff Peters, continuing an interrupted conversation):* No sign at all of anyone having come from the outside. Their own rope. Now let's go up again and go over it piece by piece. *(They start upstairs.)* It would have to have been someone who knew just the ———— *(Mrs. Peters sits down left of table. The two women sit there not looking at one another, but as if peering into something and at the same time holding back. When they talk now it is in the manner of feeling their way over strange ground, as if afraid of what they are saying, but as if they cannot help saying it.)*

Mrs. Hale *(hesitatively and in hushed voice):* She liked the bird. She was going to bury it in that pretty box.

Mrs. Peters *(in a whisper):* When I was a girl — my kitten — there was a boy took a hatchet, and before my eyes — and before I could get there ———— *(Covers her face an instant.)* If they hadn't held me back I would have — *(catches herself, looks upstairs where steps are heard, falters weakly)* — hurt him.

Mrs. Hale *(with a slow look around her):* I wonder how it would seem never to have had any children around. *(Pause.)* No, Wright wouldn't like the bird — a thing that sang. She used to sing. He killed that, too.

Mrs. Peters *(moving uneasily):* We don't know who killed the bird.

Mrs. Hale: I knew John Wright.

Mrs. Peters: It was an awful thing was done in this house that night, Mrs. Hale. Killing a man while he slept, slipping a rope around his neck that choked the life out of him.

Mrs. Hale: His neck. Choked the life out of him. *(Her hand goes out and rests on the bird-cage.)*

Mrs. Peters *(with rising voice):* We don't know who killed him. We don't *know.*

Mrs. Hale *(her own feeling not interrupted):* If there'd been years and years of nothing, then a bird to sing to you, it would be awful — still, after the bird was still.

Mrs. Peters *(something within her speaking):* I know what stillness is. When we homesteaded in Dakota, and my first baby died — after he was two years old, and me with no other then ————

Mrs. Hale *(moving):* How soon do you suppose they'll be through looking for the evidence?

Mrs. Peters: I know what stillness is. *(Pulling herself back.)* The law has got to punish crime, Mrs. Hale.

Mrs. Hale *(not as if answering that):* I wish you'd seen Minnie Foster when she wore a white dress with blue ribbons and stood up there in the choir and sang. *(A look around the room.)* Oh, I *wish* I'd come over here once in a while! That was a crime! That was a crime! Who's going to punish that?

Mrs. Peters *(looking upstairs):* We mustn't — take on.

Mrs. Hale: I might have known she needed help! I know how things can be — for women. I tell you, it's queer, Mrs. Peters. We live close together and we live far apart. We all go through the same things — it's all just a different kind of the same thing. *(Brushes her eyes, noticing the jar of fruit, reaches out for it.)* If I was you I wouldn't tell her her fruit was gone. Tell her it *ain't.* Tell her it's all right. Take this in to prove it to her. She — she may never know whether it was broke or not.

Mrs. Peters (takes the jar, looks about for something to wrap it in; takes petticoat from the clothes brought from the other room, very nervously begins winding this around the jar. In a false voice): My, it's a good thing the men couldn't hear us. Wouldn't they just laugh! Getting all stirred up over a little thing like a — dead canary. As if that could have anything to do with — with — wouldn't they *laugh! (The men are heard coming downstairs.)*

Mrs. Hale (under her breath): Maybe they would — maybe they wouldn't.

County Attorney: No, Peters, it's all perfectly clear except a reason for doing it. But you know juries when it comes to women. If there was some definite thing. *(Crosses slowly to above table. Sheriff crosses down right. Mrs. Hale and Mrs. Peters remain seated at either side of table.)* Something to show — something to make a story about — a thing that would connect up with this strange way of doing it ———— *(The women's eyes meet for an instant. Enter Hale from outer door.)*

Hale (remaining by door): Well, I've got the team around. Pretty cold out there.

County Attorney: I'm going to stay awhile by myself. *(To the Sheriff.)* You can send Frank out for me, can't you? I want to go over everything. I'm not satisfied that we can't do better.

Sheriff: Do you want to see what Mrs. Peters is going to take in? *(The Lawyer picks up the apron, laughs.)*

County Attorney: Oh, I guess they're not very dangerous things the ladies have picked out. *(Moves a few things about, disturbing the quilt pieces which cover the box. Steps back.)* No, Mrs. Peters doesn't need supervising. For that matter a sheriff's wife is married to the law. Ever think of it that way, Mrs. Peters?

Mrs. Peters: Not — just that way.

Sheriff (chuckling): Married to the law. *(Moves to down right door to the other room.)* I just want you to come in here a minute, George. We ought to take a look at these windows.

County Attorney (scoffingly): Oh, windows!

Sheriff: We'll be right out, Mr. Hale. *(Hale goes outside. The Sheriff follows the County Attorney into the room. Then Mrs. Hale rises, hands tight together, looking intensely at Mrs. Peters, whose eyes make a slow turn, finally meeting Mrs. Hale's. A moment Mrs. Hale holds her, then her own eyes point the way to where the box is concealed. Suddenly Mrs. Peters throws back quilt pieces and tries to put the box in the bag she is carrying. It is too big. She opens box, starts to take bird out, cannot touch it, goes to pieces, stands there helpless. Sound of a knob turning in the other room. Mrs. Hale snatches the box and puts it in the pocket of her big coat. Enter County Attorney and Sheriff, who remains down right.)*

County Attorney (crosses to up left door facetiously): Well, Henry, at least we found out that she was not going to quilt it. She was going to — what is it you call it, ladies?

Mrs. Hale (standing center below table facing front, her hand against her pocket): We call it — knot it, Mr. Henderson.

Curtain.

Considerations for Critical Thinking and Writing

1. Describe the setting of this play. What kind of atmosphere is established by the details in the opening scene?
2. Where are Mrs. Hale and Mrs. Peters while Mr. Hale explains to the county attorney how the murder was discovered? How does their location suggest the relationship between the men and the women in the play?
3. What kind of person was Minnie Foster before she married? How do you think her marriage affected her?
4. Characterize John Wright. Why did his wife kill him?
5. Why do the men fail to see the clues that Mrs. Hale and Mrs. Peters discover?
6. What is the significance of the bird cage and the dead bird? Why do Mrs. Hale and Mrs. Peters respond so strongly to them? How do you respond?
7. Why don't Mrs. Hale and Mrs. Peters reveal the evidence they have uncovered? What would you have done?
8. How do the men's conversations and actions reveal their attitudes toward women?
9. Why do you think Glaspell allows us only to hear about Mr. and Mrs. Wright? What is the effect of their never appearing on stage?
10. Does your impression of Mrs. Wright change in the course of the play? If so, what changes it?
11. What is the significance of the play's last line, spoken by Mrs. Hale: "We call it — knot it, Mr. Henderson"? Explain what you think the tone of Mrs. Hale's voice is when she says this line. What is she feeling? What are you feeling?
12. Several times the characters say things that they don't mean, and this creates a discrepancy between what appears to be and what is actually true. Point to instances of irony in the play and explain how they contribute to its effects and meanings. (For discussions of irony elsewhere in this book, see the Index of Terms.)
13. Explain the significance of the play's title. Do you think *Trifles* or "A Jury of Her Peers," Glaspell's title for the short story version of the play, is more appropriate? Can you think of other titles that capture the play's central concerns?
14. If possible, find a copy of "A Jury of Her Peers" in the library (reprinted in *The Best Short Stories of 1917*, ed. E. J. O'Brien [Boston: Small, Maynard 1918], pp. 256–82), and write an essay that explores the differences between the play and the short story. (An alternative is to work with the excerpt in Chapter 34, p. 1976.)

Connections to Other Selections

1. Compare and contrast how Glaspell provides background information in *Trifles* with how Sophocles does so in *Oedipus the King* (p. 1120).
2. Write an essay comparing the views of marriage in *Trifles* and in Chopin's short story "The Story of an Hour" (p. 12). What similarities do you find in the themes of these two works? Are there any significant differences between the works?
3. In an essay compare Mrs. Wright's motivation for committing murder with that of Matt Fowler, the central character from Andre Dubus's short story "Killings" (p. 57). To what extent do you think they are responsible for and guilty of these crimes?

ELEMENTS OF DRAMA

Trifles is a **one-act play;** in other words, the entire play takes place in a single location and unfolds as one continuous action. As in a short story, the characters in a one-act play are presented economically, and the action is sharply focused. In contrast, full-length plays can include many characters as well as different settings in place and time. The main divisions of a full-length play are typically **acts;** their ends are indicated by lowering a curtain or turning up the houselights. Playwrights frequently employ acts to accommodate changes in time, setting, characters on stage, or mood. In many full-length plays, such as Shakespeare's *Hamlet,* acts are further divided into **scenes;** according to tradition a scene changes when the location of the action changes or a when a new character enters. Acts and scenes are **conventions** that are understood and accepted by audiences because they have come, through usage and time, to be recognized as familiar techniques. The major convention of a one-act play is that it typically consists of only a single scene; nevertheless, one-act plays contain many of the elements of drama that characterize their full-length counterparts.

One-act plays create their effects through compression. They especially lend themselves to modestly budgeted productions with limited stage facilities, such as those put on by little theater groups. However, the potential of a one-act play to move audiences and readers is not related to its length. As *Trifles* shows, one-acts represent a powerful form of dramatic literature.

The single location that comprises the **setting** for *Trifles* is described at the very beginning of the play; it establishes an atmosphere that will later influence our judgment of Mrs. Wright. The kitchen, "gloomy" and with walls "covered with a faded wall paper," is disordered, bare, and sparsely equipped with a stove, sink, and rocker — each of them "old" — an unpainted table, some chairs, three doors, and an uncurtained window. The only color mentioned is, appropriately, black. These details are just enough to allow us to imagine the stark, uninviting place where Mrs. Wright spent most of her time. Moreover, "signs of incompleted work," coupled with the presence of the sheriff and county attorney, create an immediate tension by suggesting that something is terribly wrong. Before a single word is spoken, **suspense** is created as the characters enter. This suspenseful situation causes an anxious uncertainty about what will happen next.

The setting is further developed through the use of **exposition,** a device that provides the necessary background information about the characters and their circumstances. For example, we immediately learn through **dialogue** — the verbal exchanges between characters — that Mr. Henderson, the county attorney, is just back from Omaha. This establishes the setting as somewhere in the Midwest, where winters can be brutally cold and barren. We also find out that John Wright has been murdered and that his wife has been arrested for the crime.

Even more important, Glaspell deftly characterizes the Wrights through exposition alone. Mr. Hale's conversation with Mr. Henderson explains how Mr. Wright's body was discovered, but it also reveals that Wright was a noncommunicative man, who refused to share a "party telephone" and who did not consider "what his wife wanted." Later Mrs. Hale adds to this characterization when she tells Mrs. Peters that though Mr. Wright was an honest, good man who paid his bills and did not drink, he was a "hard man" and "Like a raw wind that gets to the bone." Mr. Hale's description of Mrs. Wright sitting in the kitchen dazed and disoriented gives us a picture of a shattered, exhausted woman. But it is Mrs. Hale who again offers further insights when she describes how Minnie Foster, a sweet, pretty, timid young woman who sang in the choir, was changed by her marriage to Mr. Wright and by her childless, isolated life on the farm.

This information about Mr. and Mrs. Wright is worked into the dialogue throughout the play in order to suggest the nature of the *conflict* or struggle between them, a motive, and, ultimately, a justification for the murder. In the hands of a skillful playwright, exposition is not merely a mechanical device, it can provide important information while simultaneously developing characterizations and moving the action forward.

The action is shaped by the *plot,* the author's arrangement of incidents in the play that gives the story a particular focus and emphasis. Plot involves more than simply what happens; it involves how and why things happen. Glaspell begins with a discussion of the murder. Why? She could have begun with the murder itself: the distraught Mrs. Wright looping the rope around her husband's neck. The moment would be dramatic and horribly vivid. We neither see the body nor hear very much about it. When Mr. Hale describes finding Mr. Wright's body, Glaspell has the county attorney cut him off by saying, "I think I'd rather have you go into that upstairs, where you can point it all out. Just go on now with the rest of the story." It is precisely the "rest of the story" that interests Glaspell. Her arrangement of incidents prevents us from sympathizing with Mr. Wright. We are, finally, invited to see Mrs. Wright instead of her husband as the victim.

Mr. Henderson's efforts to discover a motive for the murder appear initially to be the play's focus, but the real conflicts are explored in what seems to be a *subplot,* a secondary action that reinforces or contrasts with the main plot. The discussions between Mrs. Hale and Mrs. Peters and the tensions between the men and the women turn out to be the main plot because they address the issues that Glaspell chooses to explore. Those issues are not about murder but about marriage and how men and women relate to each other.

The *protagonist* of *Trifles,* the central character with whom we tend to identify, is Mrs. Hale. The *antagonist,* the character who is in some kind of opposition to the central character, is the county attorney, Mr. Henderson. These two characters embody the major conflicts presented in the play because each speaks for a different set of characters who represent disparate values. Mrs. Hale and Mr. Henderson are developed less individually than as representative types.

Mrs. Hale articulates a sensitivity to Mrs. Wright's miserable life as well as an awareness of how women are repressed in general by men; she also helps Mrs. Peters to arrive at a similar understanding. When Mrs. Hale defends Mrs. Wright's soiled towels from Mr. Henderson's criticism, Glaspell has her say more than the county attorney is capable of hearing. The *stage directions,* the playwright's instructions about how the actors are to move and behave, indicate that Mrs. Hale responds "stiffly" to Mr. Henderson's disparagements: "Men's hands aren't always as clean as they might be." Mrs. Hale eventually comes to see that the men are, in a sense, complicit because it was insensitivity like theirs that drove Mrs. Wright to murder.

Mr. Henderson, on the other hand, represents the law in a patriarchal, conventional society that blithely places a minimal value on the concerns of women. In his attempt to gather evidence against Mrs. Wright, he implicitly defends men's severe dominance over women. He also patronizes Mrs. Hale and Mrs. Peters. Like Sheriff Peters and Mr. Hale, he regards the women's world as nothing more than "kitchen things" and "trifles." Glaspell, however, patterns the plot so that the women see more about Mrs. Wright's motives than the men do and shows that the women have a deeper understanding of justice.

Many plays are plotted in what has come to be called a *pyramidal pattern,* because the plot is divided into three essential parts. Such plays begin with a *rising action,* in which complication creates conflict for the protagonist. The resulting tension builds to the second major division, known as the *climax,* when the action reaches a final *crisis,* a turning point that has a powerful effect on the protagonist. The third part consists of *falling action;* here the tensions are diminished in the *resolution* of the plot's conflicts and complications (the resolution is also referred to as the *conclusion* or *dénouement,* a French word meaning "unknotting"). These divisions may occur at different times. There are many variations to this pattern. The terms are helpful for identifying various moments and movements within a given plot, but they are less useful if seen as a means of reducing dramatic art to a formula.

Because *Trifles* is a one-act play, this pyramidal pattern is less elaborately worked out than it might be in a full-length play, but the basic elements of the pattern can still be discerned. The complication consists mostly of Mrs. Hale's refusal to assign moral or legal guilt to Mrs. Wright's murder of her husband. Mrs. Hale is able to discover the motive in the domestic details that are beneath the men's consideration. The men fail to see the significance of the fruit jars, messy kitchen, and badly sewn quilt.

At first Mrs. Peters seems to voice the attitudes associated with the men. Unlike Mrs. Hale, who is "more comfortable looking," Mrs. Peters is "a slight wiry woman" with "a thin nervous face" who sounds like her husband, the sheriff, when she insists, "the law is the law." She also defends the men's patronizing attitudes, because "they've got awful important things on their minds." But Mrs. Peters is a *foil* — a character whose behavior and values contrast with the protagonist's — only up to a point. When the most telling clue is discovered, Mrs. Peters suddenly understands, along with Mrs. Hale, the motive for the killing. Mrs. Wright's caged life was no longer tolerable to her after her husband had killed the bird (which was the one bright spot in her life and which represents her early life as the young Minnie Foster). This revelation brings about the climax, when the two women must decide whether to tell the men what they have discovered. Both women empathize with Mrs. Wright as they confront this crisis, and their sense of common experience leads them to withhold the evidence.

This resolution ends the play's immediate conflicts and complications. Presumably, without a motive the county attorney will have difficulty prosecuting Mrs. Wright — at least to the fullest extent of the law. However, the larger issues related to the *theme,* the central idea or meaning of the play, are left unresolved. The men have both missed the clues and failed to perceive the suffering that acquits Mrs. Wright in the minds of the two women. The play ends with Mrs. Hale's ironic answer to Mr. Henderson's question about quilting. When she says "knot it," she gives him part of the evidence he needs to connect Mrs. Wright's quilting with the knot used to strangle her husband. Mrs. Hale knows — and we know — that Mr. Henderson will miss the clue she offers because he is blinded by his own self-importance and assumptions.

Though brief, *Trifles* is a masterful representation of dramatic elements working together to keep both audiences and readers absorbed in its characters and situations.

DRAMA IN POPULAR FORMS

Audiences for live performances of plays have been thinned by high ticket prices but perhaps even more significantly by the impact of motion pictures and television. Motion pictures, the original threat to live theater, have in turn been superseded by television (along with videocassettes), now the most popular form of entertainment in America. Television audiences are measured in the millions. Probably more people have seen a single weekly episode of a top-rated prime-time program such as *Murphy Brown* in one evening than have viewed a live performance of *Hamlet* in nearly four hundred years.

Though most of us are seated more often before a television than before live actors, our limited experience with the theater presents relatively few obstacles to appreciation, because many of the basic elements of drama are similar whether the performance is on videotape or on a stage. Television has undoubtedly seduced audiences that otherwise might have been attracted to the theater, but television obviously satisfies some aspects of our desire for drama and can be seen as a potential introduction to live theater rather than as its irresistible rival.

Significant differences do, of course, exist between television and theater productions. Most obviously, television's special camera effects can capture phenomena such as earthquakes, raging fires, car chases, and space travel that cannot be realistically rendered on a live stage. The presentation of characters and the plotting of action are also handled differently owing to both the possibilities and limitations of television and the theater. Television's multiple camera angles and close-ups provide a degree of intimacy that cannot be duplicated by actors on stage, yet this intimacy does not achieve the immediacy that live actors create. On commercial television the plot must accommodate itself to breaks in the action so that advertisements can be aired at regular intervals. Beyond these and many other differences, however, there are enough important similarities that the experience of watching television shows can enhance our understanding of a theater production.

NORTHERN EXPOSURE

Northern Exposure, which airs on CBS, was first produced for television in the summer of 1990 during a season of reruns. No one expected this hour-long comedy series to become so popular, but it quickly found a vast audience due to favorable reviews and word-of-mouth praise. Because no episodes were ready for the fall season, there was a hiatus until the spring of 1991, when new shows attracted an even larger audience and more widespread acclaim in response to the program's unconventional, remote setting, the unpredictable characters, and the unusual plots.

The setting is the tiny town of Cicely, Alaska. With a population of 839, this dinky town sits quietly amid beautiful, snow-peaked mountains. From the first moments when the credits roll, and we see an ungainly moose wandering the deserted main street of Cicely in the early morning, there is a sense of incongruity. This town is filled with totem poles, pickup trucks, and bleak store fronts, and whatever the moose is sniffing out seems worth investigating. For despite its stark barrenness, it appears almost enchanted; it cries out for explanation: Who lives here? What do they do here? Why did they come here?

The people who populate this town are a remarkable assortment of eccentric but believable characters. Among the loggers, trappers, fishermen, Native Americans, and rugged individualists are a number of fascinating characters who lend their strange charm to the seemingly unpromising town. Maurice Minnifield, for example, is a former astronaut who heads the chamber of commerce and owns the newspaper, radio station, and fifteen thousand "acres of opportunity." His ambitious entrepreneurial vision of the surrounding wilderness is to transform it into fast-food franchises, malls, and resorts. Contrasting with Minnifield is the modest, relaxed tavern owner Holling Vincoeur, an affable man in his early sixties who is comfortable with the pool table, dart board, and the good company who pass the time at his Western-style bar. (Notice how the last name suggests the nature of each character; "Vincoeur" means "wine heart" in French.) Holling lives with Shelly Tambo, a beautiful twenty-year-old winner of the Miss Northwest Passage pageant. Their winter-summer relationship provides some amusing generational issues and tensions. For romance there is also Maggie O'Connell, a bush pilot in her late twenties who fled her status as the rich daughter of a Grosse Point, Michigan, automotive executive. And in the background we hear the voice of Chris ("In the Morning") Stevens, a disc jockey for KBHR radio, also in his late twenties, who speculates about the lives of the townsfolk and who is as familiar with the great philosophers of the East and West as he is with literature, blues, classics, and top forty.

The central character of the show, however, is Joel Fleishman, a Jewish doctor from Columbia University medical school who received a $125,000 scholarship from the state of Alaska on the condition that he practice in the state for four years. Incredulous that he actually has to fulfill this legal obligation, Fleishman resents his "indentured servitude"; he could be making a fortune in New York City and ordering bagels at kosher delis rather than practicing Band-Aid medicine in Cicely and eating mooseburgers. Instead of being surrounded by sophisticated colleagues, Fleishman works with Marilyn Whirlwind, his sole assistant, an enigmatic, laconic Native American who insists on calling patients by a number rather than a name. While Fleishman always maintains his New York edge, he is both astonished and at times appreciative of the odd — even weird — characters and situations he encounters. Though *Northern Exposure* uses Fleishman's savvy and skepticism to frame the eccentricities of the residents of Cicely, the show also evokes with affection the independence and open-endedness of the rural Northwest.

The plots in this series are often offbeat, irreverent, or even absurd. We're as likely to see a ghost walk down the main street as a moose. Somehow it works that Maggie O'Connell's boyfriends all meet untimely deaths; there was Dave, for example, who died when he took a nap on a glacier, and Rick, who was killed by a falling satellite. However bizarre, events seem credible in this land of possibility. They also seem benign rather than threatening or tragic because this is, after all, a comedy based on Fleishman's having to adjust to Cicely's raw, quirky, often inexplicable world unbound by the conventional expectations that inform life in the lower forty-eight states.

The following scenes from *Northern Exposure* are from a script titled "Get Real." They trace a subplot involving Holling Vincoeur and his companion Shelly Tambo. As brief as these scenes are, they contain some of the dramatic elements found in a play.

DIANE FROLOV AND ANDREW SCHNEIDER
Northern Exposure

1991

"GET REAL"

[The following scenes do not appear one after the other in the original script but are interspersed as a subplot around several other lines of action, all of which relate to this episode's central theme concerning the difficulties and mysterious irrationalities that accompany the joys of love.]

[SCENE ONE.] *Int[erior] Radio Station — Day*

Entering, Chris finds Holling waiting for him.

Holling: Chris.

Chris: Hey, Holling.

Holling: I need to talk to a man of experience. (*Beat.*) With women.

Chris: I'm your guy.

Holling: A significant thing happened to me yesterday . . . I saw Shelly's feet for the first time.

Chris: You never saw her feet before?

Holling: Of course, I have. Many times. I've held them, I've caressed them, I've kissed them.

Chris: Yeah. . . ?

Holling: I used to gaze at Shelly's feet and see angels. I'd see flowers — swans . . .

Chris: Children playing.

Holling: That, too. (*Beat.*) The point is, yesterday when I looked at Shelly's feet, all I saw were feet. Tired feet. Truth is — I found them unattractive — unattractive and very large.

Chris: Interesting.

Holling looks questioningly at him.

Chris: People notice things about their significant others they don't like all the time. The way they chew their food, or clip their toenails — It's a necessary part of having a real relationship. Personally, I'm not into that, but lots of folks seem to get over the hump and keep fueling the domestic fires. (*Considers.*) On the other hand, for me, when I begin to see flaws, chinks in the romantic armor, it's a foreshadowing, a sure sign.

Holling: Of what?

Chris: You know, that love's about to skip out the back door. Adios. Finito Benito.

Holling (flinches): Oh.

Chris: Hopefully, in your case, that isn't it. (*Considers.*) Big feet, huh?

Holling: Inordinately large.

Chris: Wow. Who'd've guessed. (*Considers.*) Maybe 'cause she's tall, you don't really notice. It's a proportion thing.

Holling (swallows): Well, thank you, Chris. You've been a great help.

Chris: Cool.

Resolute, Holling exits.

[SCENE TWO.] *Int[erior] Holling's Living Room — Night*

Shelly, using a small electric razorlike gadget, shaves lint balls from a sweater. Holling, grim and determined, enters. He talks over the gadget's buzz.

Shelly (not looking up): I found this thing in the Lillian Vernon catalogue — it takes fuzz balls off clothes.

Holling: Shelly, we have to talk.

Shelly: It's like giving your sweater a haircut.

Holling (approaching her): Shelly . . . (*Wincing at the buzz.*) Could you please turn that off?

Shelly (off his expression): Sure. (*Turns it off.*) What do you want to yack about, babe?

Holling (steeling himself): Well, there's something on my mind — something that has to do with you and me.

Shelly: Yeah . . . ?

Holling: I've thought long and hard about this, and I decided there's no point beating around the bush, no sense trying to pretend that what was is, and what is, will be, so . . .

Shelly: Spit it out, babe.

Shelly watches as Holling gets down on one knee and takes her hand.

Holling: Will you marry me, Shelly?

Shelly: Huh?

Holling: Will you marry me?

She pulls back.

Shelly: Why?

Holling: Why what?

Shelly: Why do you want to marry me all of a sudden?

Holling: Well, it's the right thing to do and . . . it'll make you happy.

Shelly (pulling away): I *am* happy. What gives, Holling?

Holling: Nothing.

Shelly (stands): A year ago, you dumped me at the altar. You were totally freaked about getting hitched.

Holling (gets up): Well, that was then — this is now.

Shelly: That's a crock. (*Pointing an accusatory finger.*) Something's really wrong if you want to marry me, Holling Vincouer. What gives?!

Holling (beat): Well, it's not that important — it's a trivial thing . . . I just happened to notice that your feet. . . .

Shelly: My feet?

Holling: Well, yes — they're. . . .

Shelly: What?!

Holling: Big.

Shelly is surprised and hurt.

Shelly: God . . . (*Beat; stunned.*) I can't believe it! I can't believe you said that! You actually said that!

Holling: Well, you asked and I thought that —

Shelly: You think I don't know my feet are big?! I know I have big feet! But I'd rather have big feet than a little mean heart any day.

Holling: Shelly —

Shelly (hurt): How could you, Holling? How could you say that to me?!

Holling (entreating): Shell. . . .

Shelly: No! You've said what you had to say, Holling, and that's more than enough. I don't want to hear any more.

She exits. Holling stares after her — what have I done?

FADE IN

[SCENE THREE.] *Int[erior] Maggie's Dining Room — Night*

A miserable Shelly, her eyes bloodshot from crying, sits at the table. Maggie brings her a comforting cup of hot chocolate.

Maggie: Here, drink this cocoa.

Shelly (sniffs): Thanks.

Shelly takes a sip.

Maggie: How could he say that to you? It's not even true. You don't have big feet.

Shelly: Yes, I do.

Maggie: Oh, come on. You do not. What size shoe do you wear?

Shelly (sniffs): Eleven.

Maggie (surprised): Eleven?

Shelly: See.

Maggie: I never noticed. (*Looking at Shelly's foot.*) Men's eleven?

Shelly (defensive): No! Women's.

Maggie: Even if your feet are extremely large, he shouldn't've said it to your face. (*Beat.*) You know, Shelly, if you think about it, maybe it's good this happened now.

Shelly: Why?!

Maggie: Because you're young. I'm almost thirty, and I'm just beginning to realize that the whole idea of male-female relationships is inherently flawed — that it can't work.

Shelly: It can.

Maggie: No, I think we're kidding ourselves. You can't have a pure, honest relationship with a man. Either you're lovers, or you want to be lovers, or you're trying not to be lovers so you can be friends. In any case, sex is always there — looming — like a shadow, like an undertow.

Shelly: I like sex.

Maggie: Of course, you like sex. I like sex. But is it worth it? Look what you're going through. (*As Shelly considers.*) Think how unfettered life would be if we didn't have to worry about men. Think how unfettered we'd feel. We wouldn't have to waste time making ourselves attractive to the opposite sex — we could wear what we wanted — we could get fat — we could stop shaving our legs.

Shelly (makes an "ick" face): Why?

Maggie: Just an example. Look at me — I haven't had a legitimate date since Rick died. And I feel great.

Shelly (horrified): You haven't had a date since then?

Maggie (defensive): I've had offers — the guys just didn't interest me. The point is, celibacy has given me an entirely new perspective.

Shelly (recoiling): It has?

Maggie: Shelly, when you stop the cat-and-mouse seduction games — the mating rituals — you can really focus on what's important.

Shelly: Like what?

Maggie: Like what? Like . . . like yourself. Like . . . food. (*Convincing herself as much as Shelly.*) You know, we have this idea that celibacy is bad — that it's some kind of deprivation. We shouldn't look at it like that — no — we should look at it as an opportunity — an opportunity to be strong and self-reliant.

Shelly just stares at her.

Maggie: There've been lots of women who didn't toe the traditional male-female line. And they had great lives. Satisfying lives. Amelia Earhart — Queen Victoria — Dian Fossey.

Shelly: Who?

Maggie: Gorillas in the Mist. She didn't need men — no — she lived alone in the jungle. She found purpose — total fulfillment — with nothing but a group of apes.

Shelly stares at Maggie in numb horror.

[SCENE FOUR.] *Int[erior] Holling's Living Room — Day*

The shades are drawn; the room is dark. Holling, in his bathrobe, sits numbly in a chair, holding one of Shelly's sweaters, smelling it. He is unshaven, disheveled. Shelly enters, carrying a bag. Surprised to see her, Holling stands and adjusts his robe.

Holling: Shelly . . .

Shelly: I just came to get some things.

Holling: Oh.

Shelly (beat): Holling, it's two o'clock in the afternoon (*Off his blank look.*) Why aren't you dressed?

Holling: I don't know.

Shelly: Get some light in here.

She opens the blinds. Holling blinks at the brightness.

Shelly: There.

She looks at him, then exits to the bedroom. Holling, not knowing how to appeal to Shelly, rubs his forehead. After a beat, Shelly reappears.

Shelly: Holling.

Holling (hopeful): Yes, Shelly?

Shelly (pointing): Where's my blue sweater?

Holling (realizing): Oh. (*Extending it.*) Here.

Taking the sweater, Shelly begins folding it. Beat.

Holling: Shelly, I'd just like to say —
Shelly: I don't want to talk about it.
Holling: No. Of course not.
Shelly (hurt): You know, some things — when you say them — you can never unsay them. You can't take them back.
Holling: I know, Shelly.
Shelly (packing the sweater): And some things — when you say them — they change everything.
Holling: I know.
Shelly: Then why did you do it?

He shakes his head, "I don't know." She zips her bag closed.

Holling: Shelly, I keep imagining I can turn back the hands of the clock — it's yesterday — the moment just before I said what I said — and when you ask me what's wrong — I say, "Nothing. Nothing at all. Everything's perfect." I don't ask you to marry me and I never say what I said.
Shelly: Yeah. But you'd still be thinking it. (*Off Holling's pained look.*) And that's the problem. When you look at me, Holling, I'll always think you're thinking about my feet — those two big feet.
Holling: Shelly, if I've learned anything in the last couple days, it's that you are more to me than your feet — much, much more.

She looks at him, torn.

Shelly: I gotta go.

Grabbing her bag, she exits. . . .

FADE IN

[Scene Five.] *Int[erior] Maggie's Cabin — Day*

Maggie enters carrying a bag of groceries.

Maggie (calls): Shelly. . . ?
Shelly (off-stage; from the bathroom): Just a sec.
Maggie (unloading the groceries): Ruth-Anne had a special on leg of lamb. I usually don't make it 'cause it's just me. But I thought with the two of us. . . .

Shelly enters, carrying her overnight bag. Seeing her, Maggie indicates the leg of lamb.

Maggie: I'll rub it with garlic and rosemary — make some cous cous. (*Pulling out a bottle of wine.*) I thought a Merlot would be good.
Shelly: I'm sorry, Maggie — but I'm not going to be here for dinner.

Maggie looks at her, taking in the clothes and bag.

Shelly: I changed my mind. I'm going back. (*Off Maggie's look.*) To Holling.
Maggie: Oh.
Shelly: He was so sad and bummed out, sitting there in the dark, smelling my funky blue sweater. (*Beat.*) He loves me.

Maggie: Oh. Well, that's good — that's wonderful. (*Beat.*) But what about, you know — the foot thing.

Shelly: Oh, I'm not totally forgiving him — I'm still real p.o.'d. But he's sorry and I still love him and I wanna be with him. (*Sighs.*) So. . . .

Maggie: Wow . . .

Shelly: Yeah.

Maggie: I'm impressed. I don't think I could do that — forgive him. I mean, men hurt me — I wanna kill 'em.

Shelly (shrugs): To tell you the truth, there's some stuff about Holling that really bugs me. He doesn't rinse the sink out after he shaves and I'm sick of all those little hairs and gunk. And lots of times before bed he eats a banana — I hate the smell of bananas — it's a real turn-off. (*Beat.*) Anyway, now I can tell him. (*Grabbing her stuff.*) We'll have dinner some other time — you know, like chicks' night out.

Maggie: Sure. (*Beat.*) Look, why don't you take the wine — you know — celebrate.

Shelly: That's okay. I don't like wine in cork-type bottles — it's usually too sour. We'll just have a couple beers. Thanks.

Maggie nods as Shelly exits.

[SCENE SIX.] *Int[erior] Holling's Bar Kitchen — Day*

Shelly is busy, alternately flipping burgers and dicing lettuce. Holling enters.

Holling (cautious): Excuse me, Shelly, table four needs a tuna sandwich, whole wheat.

Shelly (slapping on the mayonnaise): Tuna, wheat.

Holling (pointing): And Maurice wants a toasted bun on his patty melt.

Shelly (popping a bun in the toaster): Toast.

Holling: Is there anything I can do to help you back here?

She looks at him. She wants to make up as much as he.

Shelly: You could slice some pickles.

Holling: Yes, I'd like that. Thank you.

Picking up a knife, he begins slicing pickles. They both work silently. Beat. Holling glances at her. Shelly glances back. Holling sets his knife down.

Holling: Shelly. . . .

Shelly: I know.

Dropping her spatula, she moves into his arms.

Holling (holding her): I'm so sorry I hurt you.

Pulling back, he looks her in the eye.

Holling: I'd love you if your feet were big as logs.

They kiss.

Considerations for Critical Thinking and Writing

1. Why is it important to Holling that he suddenly notices that Shelly's feet are big? How had he thought about them before?
2. Do you think reactions resembling Holling's negative response to Shelly's feet are typical of most relationships after a period of time?
3. Why does Holling ask Shelly to marry him?
4. Compare the advice offered by Chris to Holling and by Maggie to Shelly. Which advice do you think is more helpful?
5. Explain how humor is worked into each scene. What other emotions are evoked? Describe the overall tone of the excerpted scenes.
6. View an episode of *Northern Exposure*. How does reading a script compare with watching the show? Which do you prefer? Why?

Connections to Other Selections

1. Compare the script's treatment of Shelly's physical imperfection with Nathaniel Hawthorne's treatment of Georgianna's imperfection in his short story "The Birthmark" (p. 261). How does a comic perspective on the issue lead to very different results from those produced by Hawthorne's approach?
2. In an essay compare the ideas about love expressed in the script with views of love in Helen Farries's poem "Magic of Love" (p. 606) and John Frederick Nims's "Love Poem" (p. 606). Which poem's treatment of love is more like the script's? Why?

Like those of many plays, the settings for these scenes are not detailed. The radio station is not described at all and the only detail offered for Maggie's dining room is that it contains a table. The second time we see Holling's living room we are told that the "shades are drawn; the room is dark," but that's all. Even without a set designer's version of these scenes, we readily create a mental picture of these places that provides a background for the characters. In the final tavern scene, Shelly flips the burgers and dices the lettuce, but we supply the grill and the countertop. For the television show realistic sets were used that replicated the details a viewer would observe in a cluttered funky radio station, a simple and functionally decorated Alaskan home, or a tightly packed tavern kitchen. If the scenes were presented on stage, however, a set designer might use minimal sets and props to suggest rather than duplicate these locations. The director of such a production would rely on the viewers' imaginations to create the details of the setting.

Similarly, the stage directions are spare; little information is provided about how the characters move or how they are dressed (notice the exception — and importance — of Holling's bathrobe as an indication of his emotional despair over Shelly's leaving). The details are left to the director or the reader. In sum, the fact that a stage is relatively bare doesn't mean the audience has to perceive it that way. A combination of convincing dialogue and compelling acting can build a world. So can imaginative readers.

As brief as they are, these scenes include exposition to provide the necessary background about the characters and their circumstances. We learn through dialogue, for example, that Holling's proposal of marriage upsets Shelly because only the year before he left her standing at the altar; as Shelly puts it, he was "totally freaked about getting hitched." Similarly, we learn from Maggie's defense of celibacy that she hasn't had a date since her boyfriend Rick died. These bits of information help to characterize Holling and Maggie and allow an audience to place their attitudes and comments in a larger context that also will be useful for understanding how other characters read them. Rather than dramatizing background information, the scriptwriter arranges incidents to create a particular focus and effect while working in the necessary exposition through the characters' dialogue.

The plot in these scenes shapes the conflicts to emphasize humor. As in any good play, incidents are carefully arranged to achieve a particular effect. In the opening scene we are confronted with the humorous irony of a sixty-three-year-old man asking advice from a "man of experience" who is only twenty-eight. The dialogue between Holling and Chris quickly establishes the conflict: Holling, the protagonist, has suddenly recognized that when he looks at Shelly's feet, they no longer evoke ideal images of angels, flowers, or swans; instead, he sees only tired, unattractive, very large feet (here's the complication of the pyramidal plot pattern discussed in Elements of Drama, p. 1097). This complication sets up a conflict between Holling's idealization of Shelly and who she really is.

Afraid and guilty that he might be falling out of love with Shelly, Holling unexpectedly asks Shelly to marry him in the second scene. This further complicates matters because Shelly's earlier experience of being dumped at the altar by Holling alerts her that something must be very wrong. When she finally learns what is troubling Holling, she is so stunned and hurt that she seeks comfort and advice from Maggie in the third scene. But Maggie's manufactured tough-mindedness about the joys of being a woman free of any entanglements with men is unintentionally comic for the audience and horrifies Shelly. Now she has as many conflicts as Holling.

The climax occurs in the fourth scene when Holling, disheveled and depressed over the likelihood of losing Shelly, reaches a crisis, a turning point that causes him to realize that "if I've learned anything in the last couple of days, it's that you are more to me than your feet." As it turns out, Chris's offhand advice in the first scene about how becoming aware of a partner's flaws is a "necessary part of having a real relationship" is correct. This is the important lesson Holling must learn, and it echoes the significance of the title, "Get Real."

In the fifth scene the falling action takes place in Maggie's cabin as the conflicts, complications, and tensions are resolved when Shelly tells Maggie that despite her hurt and anger, she still loves Holling. Moreover, in another comic turn, Shelly explains that now she'll feel justified to tell him about his flaws, such as leaving his whiskers in the sink or eating a banana just before bed (the latter habit comically and subtly suggesting that perhaps Shelly has more in common with Dian Fossey than she knows).

The final resolution is played out in the last scene when a cautious Holling and a tentative Shelly are working in the kitchen and glance at each other. Responding instinctively and openly, they move into each other's arms and kiss. As familiar as this pyramidal love story pattern is, the plot is nonetheless satisfying because the characters are deftly individualized and there are numerous surprises along the way — as well as the harmonious union that so typically ends comedy.

The scenes that make up this subplot are carefully interwoven into the theme of the main story, which involves a small troupe of circus performers whose old school bus — painted with surreal images of floating cows and dancing dogs — breaks down and is towed into Cicely for repairs. The head of the troupe, a Ph.D. in physics from Berkeley, has left behind the objective, rational world of quantum physics to be a magician and tour with a palm-reader, a "Flying Man," and Chinese acrobats. Their presence in town helps to renew a sense of magic in its citizens (in an earlier draft of "Get Real" the title was "Magic"). For example, Joel Fleishman gives up intensive studying to become board certified in internal medicine in favor of juggling more complicated personal elements of his life, while Maggie abandons her fantasies of a life without Joel and decides to pursue a complicated relationship with him. In contrast to these plot lines, however, is the poignantly sad story of Joel's stoic assistant, Marilyn, who almost runs off with the "Flying Man" but decides she cannot because she realizes there would be no real life for her in a circus troupe.

Each of the characters, in short, gets real in one way or another. Chris announces the script's theme over the radio when, as the repaired circus bus pulls out of town, he reflects upon and reaffirms the value of magic by equating it with love — "the stuff not ruled by 'rational' law." The entire episode has a dreamlike quality to it (the "Flying Man" really does fly) that is reminiscent of Shakespeare's *A Midsummer Night's Dream* (see p. 1224), another comedy that revolves around lovers in complicated ways and explores the relationship between dream and reality.

PERSPECTIVE

CARL SAUTTER (b. 1949)
On the Principles of Screenwriting 1988

A key principle of any form of screenwriting is that *a script is not linear.* An interesting TV movie or screenplay does not move from one obvious step to the next. Instead, a good script surprises us by skipping the boring steps we don't need to see and letting information come out where it is most interesting, not necessarily where it is most logical. This is a direct contradiction to the fundamentals of expository writing we all learned in Senior English: the lead paragraph introduces the most important information; each paragraph starts with a topic sentence, etc. Not in a screenplay. If the most important information is in the first scene of a movie, the movie has no plot. If each scene begins with a lead sentence, there's no reason to see the rest of the scene. The emphasis in expository writing is on making a point clearly. The emphasis in screenwriting is on making the point in the most interesting way possible.

All of which leads to [another] important basic of the screenwriting craft — *avoid anything that is OTN* ("On the nose"). This pejorative acronym is used widely (and excessively) by story editors, producers, and critics. OTN means that the writer has made an obvious choice. A plot twist may be OTN because it's exactly the twist the reader expected (which means it wasn't a twist at all). A character may be OTN because he or she is a cliché: the prostitute with the heart of gold, the villain with a missing finger, the smart-aleck maid. Dialogue may be OTN when characters say exactly what they are feeling or what they have learned. When a character is facing a gun and says "I've got to get out of here," *that's* OTN. When the crisis is resolved and the hero kisses the heroine and proclaims "I'm so happy," *that's* OTN. The audience should realize these feelings and lessons from the story they're seeing, not from what the characters say about themselves. To avoid being OTN, the writer must try to find subtle and surprising ways to advance the story and the characters. . . .

Finally, one of the hardest basic lessons to learn is that *screenwriting is visual writing*. It is always better to show something than to talk about it. The less characters talk about the plot, the better . . . the story should move through visuals — reactions from the characters, physical action, anything the audience can see. Surprisingly, the rule holds true even for radio drama, where there is no picture whatsoever. The best radio scripts create a picture of the story through dialogue and stage directions, allowing the listener to see what's happening even though there are no pictures. This is the gift of the great radio storytellers — Garrison Keillor, Orson Welles. We've never seen Lake Wobegon, but we all have a good idea what it looks like.

From *How to Sell Your Screenplay:*
The Real Rules of Film and Television

Considerations for Critical Thinking and Writing

1. A successful screenwriter who includes among his credits award-winning scripts for *Moonlighting*, Sautter makes a crucial distinction between screenwriting and expository writing. Describe this distinction and explain why you agree or disagree with it.
2. Using a scene from *Northern Exposure* as a model, and keeping in mind Sautter's principles for screenwriting, try writing a scene for one of the short stories in this anthology that captures an important moment in the plot.

QUESTIONS FOR RESPONSIVE READING

The remaining plays in this anthology are rich with possibilities for both reading and production. The questions in this section can help you consider important elements that reveal a play's effects and meanings. These questions are general and will not, therefore, always be relevant to a particular play. Many of them, however, should prove useful for thinking, talking, and writing about drama. If you are uncertain about the meaning of a term used in a question, consult the Index of Terms for pages that discuss the term. Some of these terms are defined in the fiction and poetry sections, because they are relevant for fiction and poetry as well as drama.

1. Did you enjoy the play? What, specifically, pleased or displeased you about what was expressed and how it was expressed?

2. What is the significance of the play's title? How does it suggest the author's overall emphasis?

3. What information do the stage directions provide about the characters, action, and setting? Are these directions primarily descriptive, or are they also interpretive?

4. How is the exposition presented? What does it reveal? How does the playwright's choice *not* to dramatize certain events on stage help to determine what the focus of the play is?

5. In what ways is the setting important? Would the play be altered significantly if the setting were changed?

6. Are foreshadowings used to suggest what is to come? Are flashbacks used to dramatize what has already happened?

7. What is the major conflict the protagonist faces? What complications constitute the rising action? Where is the climax? Is the conflict resolved?

8. Are one or more subplots used to qualify or complicate the main plot? Is the plot unified so that each incident somehow has a function that relates it to some other element in the play?

9. Does the author purposely avoid a pyramidal plot structure of rising action, climax, and falling action? Is the plot experimental? Is the plot logically and chronologically organized, or is it fantastical or absurd? What effects are produced by the plot? How does it reflect the author's view of life?

10. Who is the protagonist? Who (or what) is the antagonist?

11. By what means does the playwright reveal character? What do the characters' names, physical qualities, actions, and words convey about them? What do the characters reveal about each other?

12. What is the purpose of the minor characters? Are they individualized, or do they primarily represent ideas or attitudes? Are any character foils used?

13. Do the characters all use the same kind of language, or is their speech differentiated? Is it formal or informal? How do the characters' diction and manner of speaking serve to characterize them?

14. Does your response to the characters change in the course of the play? What causes the change?

15. Are words and images repeated in the play so that they take on special meanings? Which speeches seem particularly important? Why?

16. How does the playwright's use of language contribute to the tone of the play? Is the dialogue, for example, predominantly light, humorous, relaxed, sentimental, sad, angry, intense, or violent?

17. Are any symbols used in the play? Which actions, characters, settings, objects, or words convey more than their literal meanings?

18. Are any unfamiliar theatrical conventions used that present problems in understanding the play? How does knowing more about the nature of the theater from which the play originated help to resolve these problems?

19. Is the theme stated directly, or is it developed implicitly through the plot, characters, or some other element? Does the theme confirm or challenge most people's values?

20. How does the play reflect the values of the society in which it is set and in which it was written?

21. How does the play reflect or challenge your own values?

22. Is there a recording, film, or videocassette of the play available in your library or media center? How does this version compare with your own reading?

23. How would you produce the play on a stage? Consider scenery, costumes, casting, and characterizations. What would you emphasize most in your production?

24. Is there a particular critical approach that seems especially appropriate for this play (see the discussion "Critical Strategies for Reading" beginning on p. 1995)?

25. How might biographical information about the author help the reader to grasp the central concerns of the play?

26. How might historical information about the play provide a useful context for interpretation?

27. To what extent do your own experiences, values, beliefs, and assumptions inform your interpretation?

28. What kinds of evidence from the play are you focusing on to support your interpretation? Does your interpretation leave out any important elements that might undercut or qualify your interpretation?

29. Given that there are a variety of ways to interpret the play, which one seems the most useful to you?

27. A Study of Sophocles

Sophocles lived a long, productive life (496?–406 B.C.) in Athens. During his life Athens became a dominant political and cultural power after the Persian Wars, but before he died Sophocles witnessed the decline of Athens as a result of the Peloponnesian Wars and the city's subsequent surrender to Sparta. He saw Athenian culture reach remarkable heights as well as collapse under enormous pressures.

Sophocles embodied much of the best of Athenian culture; he enjoyed success as a statesman, general, treasurer, priest, and, of course, prize-winning dramatist. Although surviving fragments indicate that he wrote over 120 plays, only a handful remain intact. Those that survive consist of the three plays he wrote about Oedipus and his children — *Oedipus the King, Oedipus at Colonus,* and *Antigone* — and four additional tragedies: *Philoctetes, Ajax, Maidens of Trachis,* and *Electra.*

His plays won numerous prizes at festival competitions because of his careful, subtle plotting and the sense of inevitability with which their action is charged. Moreover, his development of character is richly complex. Instead of relying on the extreme situations and exaggerated actions that earlier tragedians used, Sophocles created powerfully motivated characters who even today fascinate audiences with their psychological depth.

In addition to crafting sophisticated tragedies for the Greek theater, Sophocles introduced several important innovations to the stage. Most important, he broke the tradition of using only two actors; adding a third resulted in more complicated relationships and intricate dialogue among characters. As individual actors took center stage more often, Sophocles reduced the role of the chorus (discussed on p. 1115). This shift placed even more emphasis on the actors, although the chorus remained important as a means of commenting on the action and establishing its tone. Sophocles was also the first dramatist to write plays with specific actors in mind, a development that many later playwrights, including Shakespeare, exploited usefully. But without question Sophocles' greatest contribution to drama was

Oedipus the King, which, it has been argued, is the most influential drama ever written.

Chronology

c. 496 B.C. Born at Colonus.

480   Athenian victory over the Persians at Salamis. (Sophocles participates as a musician in the victory celebration.)

468   Sophocles' first triumph (over Aeschylus) in the drama competition at the Festival of Dionysus.

443–42 Serves as one of the treasurers of the league against Persia.

c. 441 Writes *Antigone.*

431   The Peloponnesian War begins. This conflict among the Greek states (including Athens and Sparta) lasts nearly thirty years.

c. 430 Writes *Oedipus the King.*

413   Athenian force defeated in Sicily. Sophocles is chosen as one of the leaders to deal with the Sicilian crisis.

406   Sophocles dies.

404   Athens capitulates to Sparta.

401   *Oedipus at Colonus* produced posthumously.

THEATRICAL CONVENTIONS OF GREEK DRAMA

More than twenty-four hundred years have passed since 430 B.C., when Sophocles' *Oedipus the King* was probably first produced on a Greek stage. We inhabit a vastly different planet than Sophocles' audience did, yet concerns about what it means to be human in a world that frequently runs counter to our desires and aspirations have remained relatively constant. The ancient Greeks continue to speak to us. But inexperienced readers or viewers may have some initial difficulty understanding the theatrical conventions used in classical Greek tragedies such as *Oedipus the King* and *Antigone.* If Sophocles were alive today, he would very likely need some sort of assistance with the conventions of an Arthur Miller play or a television production of *Northern Exposure.*

Classical Greek drama developed from religious festivals that paid homage to Dionysus, the god of wine and fertility. Most of the details of these festivals have been lost, but we do know that they included dancing and singing that celebrated legends about Dionysus. From these choral songs developed stories of both Dionysus and mortal culture-heroes. These heroes became the subject of playwrights whose works were produced in contests at the festivals. The Dionysian festivals lasted more than five hundred years, but relatively few of their plays have survived. Among the works of the three great writers of tragedy, only seven plays each by Sophocles and Aeschylus (525?–456 B.C.) and nineteen plays by Euripides (480?–406 B.C.) survive.

Plays were such important events in Greek society that they were partially funded by the state. The Greeks associated drama with religious and community values as well as entertainment. In a sense, their plays celebrate their civilization; in approving the plays, audiences applauded their own culture. The enormous popularity of the plays is indicated by the size of surviving amphitheaters. Although information about these theaters is sketchy, we do know that most of them shared a common form. They were built into hillsides with rising rows of seats accommodating more than fourteen thousand people. These seats partially encircled an *orchestra* or "dancing place," where the *chorus* of a dozen or so men chanted lines and danced.

Tradition credits the Greek poet Thespis with adding an actor who was separate from the choral singing and dancing of early performances. A second actor was subsequently included by Aeschylus and a third, as noted earlier, by Sophocles. These additions made possible the conflicts and complicated relationships that evolved into the dramatic art we know today. The two or three male actors who played all the roles appeared behind the orchestra in front of the *skene,* a stage building that served as dressing rooms. As Greek theater evolved, a wall of the skene came to be painted to suggest a palace or some other setting, and the roof was employed to indicate, for instance, a mountain location. Sometimes gods were lowered from the roof by mechanical devices to set matters right among the mortals below. This method of rescuing characters from complications beyond their abilities to resolve was known in Latin as *deus ex machina* ("god from the machine"), a term now used to describe any improbable means by which an author provides a too-easy resolution for a story.

Inevitably, the conventions of the Greek theaters affected how plays were presented. Few if any scene changes occurred, because the amphitheater stage was set primarily for one location. If an important event happened somewhere else, it was reported by a minor character, such as a messenger. The chorus also provided necessary background information. In *Oedipus the King* and *Antigone,* the choruses, acting as townspeople, also assess the characters' strengths and weaknesses, praising them for their virtues, chiding them for their rashness, and giving them advice. The reactions of the chorus provide a connection between the actors and audience because the chorus is at once a participant in and an observer of the action. In addition, the chorus helps structure the action by indicating changes in scene or mood. Thus the chorus could be used in a variety of ways to shape the audience's response to the play's action and characters.

Actors in classical Greek amphitheaters faced considerable challenges. An intimate relationship with the audience was impossible because many spectators would have been too far away to see a facial expression or subtle gesture. Indeed, some in the audience would have had difficulty even hearing the voices of individual actors. To compensate for these disadvantages, actors wore large masks that extravagantly expressed the major characters' emotions or identified the roles of minor characters. The masks also allowed the two or three actors in a performance to play all the characters without confusing the audience. Each mask was fitted so that the mouthpiece amplified the actor's voice. The actors were further equipped with padded costumes and elevated shoes *(cothurni* or *buskins)* that made them appear larger than life.

As a result of these adaptive conventions, Greek plays tend to emphasize words — formal, impassioned speeches — more than physical action. We are invited to ponder actions and events rather than to see all of them enacted. Although the stark simplicity of Greek theater does not offer an audience realistic detail, the classical tragedies that have survived present characters in dramatic situations that transcend theatrical conventions. Tragedy, it seems, has always been compelling for human beings, regardless of the theatrical forms it has taken.

A Greek tragedy is typically divided into five parts: prologue, parodos,

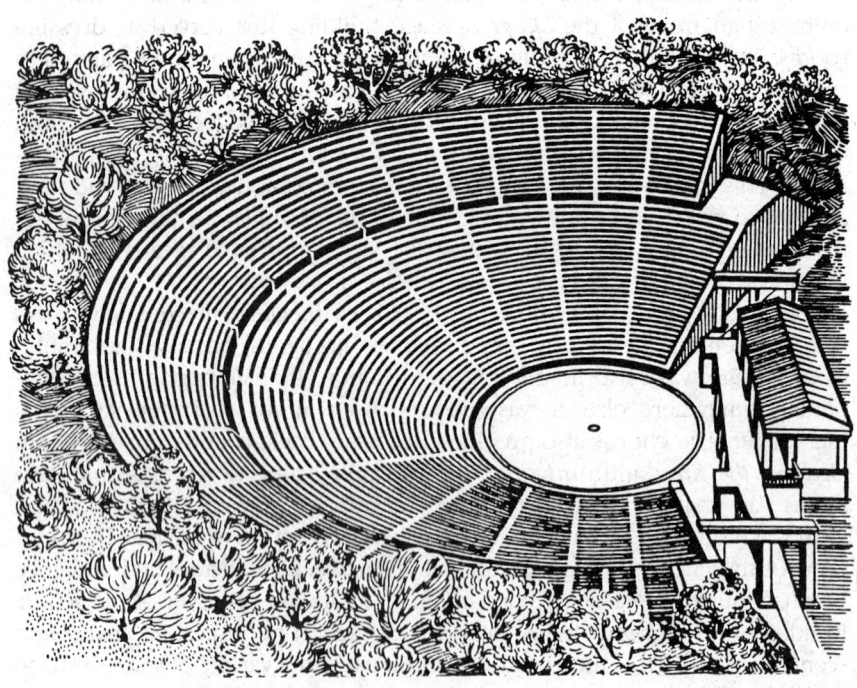

Based on scholarly sources, this drawing represents the features typical of classical Greek theater. (Drawing by Gerda Becker. From Kenneth Macgowan and William Melnitz, *The Living Stage,* © 1990 by Prentice Hall/A Division of Simon & Schuster.)

episodia, stasimon, and exodus. In some translations these terms appear as headings, but in more recent translations, as those by Robert Fagles included here, the headings do not appear. Still, understanding these terms provides a sense of the overall rhythm of a Greek play. The opening speech or dialogue is known as the *prologue* and usually gives the exposition necessary to follow the subsequent action. In the *parodos* the chorus makes its first entrance and gives its perspective on what the audience has learned in the prologue. Several *episodia*, or episodes, follow, in which characters engage in dialogue that frequently consists of heated debates dramatizing the play's conflicts. Following each episode is a choral ode or *stasimon*, in which the chorus responds to and interprets the preceding dialogue. The *exodus*, or last scene, follows the final episode and stasimon; in it the resolution occurs and the characters leave the stage.

The effect of alternating dialogues and choral odes has sometimes been likened to that of opera. Greek tragedies were written in verse, and the stasima were chanted or sung as the chorus moved rhythmically, so the plays have a strong musical element that is not always apparent on the printed page. If we remember their musical qualities we are less likely to forget that no matter how terrifying or horrific the conflicts they describe, these plays are stately, measured, and dignified works that reflect a classical Greek sense of order and proportion.

TRAGEDY

Newspapers are filled with daily reports of "tragedies": a child is struck and crippled by a car; an airplane plunges into a suburban neighborhood; a volcano erupts and kills tens of thousands. These unexpected instances of suffering are commonly and accurately described as "tragic," but they are not tragedies in the literary sense of the term. A literary *tragedy* presents courageous individuals who confront powerful forces within or outside themselves with a dignity that reveals the breadth and depth of the human spirit in the face of failure, defeat, and even death.

Aristotle (384–322 B.C.), in his *Poetics,* defined *tragedy* on the basis of the plays contemporary to him. His definition has generated countless variations, qualifications, and interpretations, but we still derive our literary understanding of this term from Aristotle.

The protagonist of a Greek tragedy is someone regarded as extraordinary rather than typical: a great man or woman brought from happiness to agony. The character's stature is important because it makes his or her fall all the more terrifying. The protagonist also carries mythic significance for the audience. Oedipus and Antigone, for example, are not only human beings but legendary figures from a distant, revered past. Although the gods do not appear onstage in either *Oedipus the King* or *Antigone,* their power is ever-present as the characters invoke their help or attempt to defy them. In addition, Greek tragedy tends to be public rather than private. The fate of the community — the state — is often linked with that of the protagonist, as when Thebes suffers a plague as a result of Oedipus's mistaken actions.

The protagonists of classical Greek tragedies (and of those of Shakespeare) are often rulers of noble birth who represent the monarchical values of their periods, but in modern tragedies the protagonists are more likely to reflect democratic values that make it possible for anyone to be a suitable subject. What is finally important is not so much the protagonist's social stature as a greatness of character that steadfastly confronts suffering, whether it comes from supernatural, social, or psychological forces. Although Greek tragic heroes were aristocrats, the nobility of their characters was more significant than their inherited titles and privileges.

The protagonist's eminence and determination to complete some task or goal make him or her admirable in Greek tragedy, but that does not free the protagonist from what Aristotle described as "some error or frailty" that brings about his or her misfortune. The term Aristotle used for this weakness is *hamartia*. This word has frequently been interpreted to mean that the protagonist's fall is the result of an internal *tragic flaw*, such as an excess of pride, ambition, passion, or some other character trait that leads directly to disaster.

Sometimes, however, misfortunes are not the result of a character flaw but of misunderstood events that overtake and thwart the protagonist's best intentions. Thus, virtue can lead to tragedy too. *Hamartia* has also been interpreted to mean "wrong act" — a mistake based not on a personal failure but on circumstances outside the protagonist's personality and control. Many readers find that a combination of these two interpretations sheds the most light on the causes of the tragic protagonist's fall. Both internal and external forces can lead to downfall, because the protagonist's personality may determine crucial judgments that result in mistaken actions.

However the idea of tragic flaw is understood, it is best not to use it as a means of reducing the qualities of a complex character to an adjective or two that labels Oedipus as guilty of "overweening pride" (the Greek term for which is *hubris* or *hybris*) or Antigone as "fated." The protagonists of tragedies require more careful characterization than a simplistic label can provide.

Whatever the causes of the tragic protagonist's downfall, he or she accepts responsibility for it. Hence, even in his or her encounter with failure (and possibly death) the tragic protagonist displays greatness of character. Perhaps it is the witnessing of this greatness, which seems both to accept and to transcend human limitations, that makes audiences feel relief rather than hopelessness at the end of a tragedy. Aristotle described this response as a *catharsis*, or purgation of the emotions of "pity and fear." We are faced with the protagonist's misfortune, which often seems out of proportion to his or her actions, and so we are likely to feel compassionate pity. Simultaneously, we may experience fear, because the failure of the protagonist, who is so great in stature and power, is a frightening reminder of our own vulnerabilities. Ultimately, however, both these negative emotions are purged, because the tragic protagonist's suffering is an affirmation of human values — even if they are not always triumphant — rather than a despairing denial of them.

Nevertheless, tragedies are disturbing. Instead of coming away with the reassurance of a happy ending, we must take solace in the insight produced by the hero's suffering. And just as our expectations are changed, so are the protagonist's. Aristotle described the moment in the plot when this change occurs as a *reversal* (*peripeteia*), the point when the hero's fortunes turn in an unexpected direction. He more specifically defined this term as meaning an action performed by a character that has the opposite of its intended effect. An example cited by Aristotle is the messenger's attempts to relieve Oedipus's anxieties about his relationship to his father and mother. Instead, the messenger reveals previously unknown information that eventually results in a *recognition* (*anagnorisis*); Oedipus discovers the terrible truth that he has killed his father and married his mother.

Tragedy is typically filled with ironies, because there are so many moments in the plot when what seems to be turns out to be radically different from what actually is. Because of this, a particular form of irony called *dramatic irony* is also known as *tragic irony*. In dramatic irony, the meaning of a character's words or actions is understood by the audience but not by the character. Audiences of Greek tragedy shared with the playwrights a knowledge of the stories on which many tragic plots were based. Consequently, they frequently were aware of what was going to happen before the characters were. When Oedipus declares that he will seek out the person responsible for the plague that ravishes his city, the audience already knows that the person Oedipus pursues is himself.

OEDIPUS THE KING

A familiarity with the Oedipus legend allows modern readers to appreciate the series of ironies that unfolds in Sophocles' *Oedipus the King*. In the opening scene, Oedipus appears with a "telltale limp." As an infant, he had been abandoned by his parents, Laius and Jocasta, the king and queen of Thebes, because a prophecy warned that their son would kill his father and marry his mother. They instructed a servant to leave him on a mountain to die. The infant's feet were pierced and pinned together, but he was not left on the mountain; instead the servant, out of pity, gave him to a shepherd, who in turn presented him to the king and queen of Corinth. They named him Oedipus (for "swollen foot") and raised him as their own son.

Upon reaching manhood, Oedipus learned from an oracle that he would kill his father and marry his mother; to avoid this horrendous fate, he left Corinth forever. In his travels, Oedipus found his way blocked by a chariot at a crossroads; in a fit of anger, he killed the servants and their passenger. That passenger, unknown to Oedipus, was his real father. In Thebes, Oedipus successfully answered the riddle of the Sphinx, a winged lion with a woman's head. The reward for defeating this dreaded monster was both the crown and the dead king's wife. Oedipus and Jocasta had four children and prospered. But when the play begins, Oedipus's rule is troubled by a plague that threatens to destroy Thebes, and he is determined to find the cause of the plague in order to save the city again.

Oedipus the King is widely recognized as the greatest of the surviving Greek tragedies. Numerous translations are available (Robert Fagles's recent highly regarded translations of Oedipus the King and Antigone, the choice here, are especially accessible to modern readers. For an excerpt from another version of Oedipus the King, see Perspectives on Sophocles, p. 1204). The play has absorbed readers for centuries because Oedipus's character — his intelligence, confidence, rashness, and suffering — represents powers and limitations that are both exhilarating and chastening. Although no reader or viewer is likely to identify with Oedipus's extreme circumstances, anyone can appreciate his heroic efforts to find the truth about himself. In that sense, he is one of us — at our best.

SOPHOCLES (496?–406 B.C.)

Oedipus the King   c. 430 B.C.

TRANSLATED BY ROBERT FAGLES

Characters

Oedipus, King of Thebes
A *Priest* of Zeus
Creon, brother of Jocasta
A *Chorus* of Theban citizens and their *Leader*
Tiresias, a blind prophet
Jocasta, the queen, wife of Oedipus
A *Messenger* from Corinth
A *Shepherd*
A *Messenger* from inside the palace
Antigone, Ismene, daughters of Oedipus and Jocasta
Guards and attendants
Priests of Thebes

TIME AND SCENE: *The royal house of Thebes. Double doors dominate the facade; a stone altar stands at the center of the stage.*

Many years have passed since Oedipus solved the riddle of the Sphinx and ascended the throne of Thebes, and now a plague has struck the city. A procession of priests enters; suppliants, broken and despondent, they carry branches wound in wool and lay them on the altar.

The doors open. Guards assemble. Oedipus comes forward, majestic but for a telltale limp, and slowly views the condition of his people.

Oedipus: Oh my children, the new blood of ancient Thebes,
    why are you here? Huddling at my altar,
    praying before me, your branches wound in wool.°
    Our city reeks with the smoke of burning incense,
    rings with cries for the Healer and wailing for the dead.   5
    I thought it wrong, my children, to hear the truth
    from others, messengers. Here I am myself —
    you all know me, the world knows my fame:
    I am Oedipus.

Helping a Priest to his feet.

                        Speak up, old man. Your years,
    your dignity — you should speak for the others.   10
    Why here and kneeling, what preys upon you so?
    Some sudden fear? some strong desire?
    You can trust me; I am ready to help,
    I'll do anything. I would be blind to misery
    not to pity my people kneeling at my feet.   15
Priest: Oh Oedipus, king of the land, our greatest power!
    You see us before you, men of all ages
    clinging to your altars. Here are boys,
    still too weak to fly from the nest,
    and here the old, bowed down with the years,   20
    the holy ones — a priest of Zeus° myself — and here
    the picked, unmarried men, the young hope of Thebes.
    And all the rest, your great family gathers now,
    branches wreathed, massing in the squares,
    kneeling before the two temples of queen Athena°   25
    or the river-shrine where the embers glow and die
    and Apollo sees the future in the ashes.
                                        Our city —
    look around you, see with your own eyes —
    our ship pitches wildly, cannot lift her head
    from the depths, the red waves of death . . .   30
    Thebes is dying. A blight on the fresh crops
    and the rich pastures, cattle sicken and die,
    and the women die in labor, children stillborn,
    and the plague, the fiery god of fever hurls down
    on the city, his lightning slashing through us —   35
    raging plague in all its vengeance, devastating
    the house of Cadmus!° And Black Death luxuriates
    in the raw, wailing miseries of Thebes.

    Now we pray to you. You cannot equal the gods,
    your children know that, bending at your altar.   40
    But we do rate you first of men,

---

3 *wool:* Wool was used in offerings to Apollo, god of poetry, sun, prophecy, and healing.
21 *Zeus:* The highest Olympian deity and father of Apollo.   25 *Athena:* Goddess of wisdom and
protector of Greek cities.   37 *Cadmus:* The legendary founder of Thebes.

both in the common crises of our lives
and face-to-face encounters with the gods.
You freed us from the Sphinx; you came to Thebes
and cut us loose from the bloody tribute we had paid   45
that harsh, brutal singer. We taught you nothing,
no skill, no extra knowledge, still you triumphed.
A god was with you, so they say, and we believe it —
you lifted up our lives.

So now again,
Oedipus, king, we bend to you, your power —   50
we implore you, all of us on our knees:
find us strength, rescue! Perhaps you've heard
the voice of a god or something from other men,
Oedipus . . . what do you know?
The man of experience — you see it every day —   55
his plans will work in a crisis, his first of all.

Act now — we beg you, best of men, raise up our city!
Act, defend yourself, your former glory!
Your country calls you savior now
for your zeal, your action years ago.   60
Never let us remember of your reign:
you helped us stand, only to fall once more.
Oh raise up our city, set us on our feet.
The omens were good that day you brought us joy —
be the same man today!   65
Rule our land, you know you have the power,
but rule a land of the living, not a wasteland.
Ship and towered city are nothing, stripped of men
alive within it, living all as one.

Oedipus:

My children,
I pity you. I see — how could I fail to see   70
what longings bring you here? Well I know
you are sick to death, all of you,
but sick as you are, not one is sick as I.
Your pain strikes each of you alone, each
in the confines of himself, no other. But my spirit   75
grieves for the city, for myself and all of you.
I wasn't asleep, dreaming. You haven't wakened me —
I've wept through the nights, you must know that,
groping, laboring over many paths of thought.
After a painful search I found one cure: 80
I acted at once. I sent Creon,
my wife's own brother, to Delphi ° —
Apollo the Prophet's oracle — to learn

82 *Delphi:* The shrine where the oracle of Apollo held forth.

what I might do or say to save our city.

Today's the day. When I count the days gone by   85
it torments me . . . what is he doing?
Strange, he's late, he's gone too long.
But once he returns, then, then I'll be a traitor
if I do not do all the god makes clear.
Priest: Timely words. The men over there   90
are signaling — Creon's just arriving.
Oedipus:

Sighting Creon, then turning to the altar.

                  Lord Apollo,
let him come with a lucky word of rescue,
shining like his eyes!
Priest: Welcome news, I think — he's crowned, look,
and the laurel wreath is bright with berries.   95
Oedipus: We'll soon see. He's close enough to hear —

Enter Creon from the side; his face is shaded with a wreath.

Creon, prince, my kinsman, what do you bring us?
What message from the god?
Creon: Good news.
    I tell you even the hardest things to bear,
if they should turn out well, all would be well.   100
Oedipus: Of course, but what were the god's *words?* There's no hope
and nothing to fear in what you've said so far.
Creon: If you want my report in the presence of these . . .

Pointing to the priests while drawing Oedipus toward the palace.

I'm ready now, or we might go inside.
Oedipus: Speak out,
speak to us all. I grieve for these, my people,   105
far more than I fear for my own life.
Creon: Very well,
I will tell you what I heard from the god.
Apollo commands us — he was quite clear —
"Drive the corruption from the land,
don't harbor it any longer, past all cure,   110
don't nurse it in your soil — root it out!"
Oedipus: How can we cleanse ourselves — what rites?
What's the source of the trouble?
Creon: Banish the man, or pay back blood with blood.
Murder sets the plague-storm on the city.
Oedipus: Whose murder?   115
    Whose fate does Apollo bring to light?
Creon: Our leader,
my lord, was once a man named Laius,
before you came and put us straight on course.

Oedipus: I know —
    or so I've heard. I never saw the man myself.
Creon: Well, he was killed, and Apollo commands us now —   120
    he could not be more clear,
    "Pay the killers back — whoever is responsible."
Oedipus: Where on earth are they? Where to find it now,
    the trail of the ancient guilt so hard to trace?
Creon: "Here in Thebes," he said.   125
    Whatever is sought for can be caught, you know,
    whatever is neglected slips away.
Oedipus: But where,
    in the palace, the fields or foreign soil,
    where did Laius meet his bloody death?
Creon: He went to consult an oracle, he said,   130
    and he set out and never came home again.
Oedipus: No messenger, no fellow-traveler saw what happened?
    Someone to cross-examine?
Creon: No,
    they were all killed but one. He escaped,
    terrified, he could tell us nothing clearly,   135
    nothing of what he saw — just one thing.
Oedipus: What's that?
    One thing could hold the key to it all,
    a small beginning gives us grounds for hope.
Creon: He said thieves attacked them — a whole band,
    not single-handed, cut King Laius down.
Oedipus: A thief,   140
    so daring, wild, he'd kill a king? Impossible,
    unless conspirators paid him off in Thebes.
Creon: We suspected as much. But with Laius dead
    no leader appeared to help us in our troubles.
Oedipus: Trouble? Your *king* was murdered — royal blood!   145
    What stopped you from tracking down the killer
    then and there?
Creon: The singing, riddling Sphinx.
    She . . . persuaded us to let the mystery go
    and concentrate on what lay at our feet.
Oedipus: No,
    I'll start again — I'll bring it all to light myself!   150
    Apollo is right, and so are you, Creon,
    to turn our attention back to the murdered man.
    Now you have *me* to fight for you, you'll see:
    I am the land's avenger by all rights
    and Apollo's champion too.   155
    But not to assist some distant kinsman, no,
    for my own sake I'll rid us of this corruption.
    Whoever killed the king may decide to kill me too,
    with the same violent hand — by avenging Laius
    I defend myself.

To the priests.

　　　　　　　　　　Quickly, my children.　　　　　　　　160
　　Up from the steps, take up your branches now.

To the guards.

　　One of you summon the city here before us,
　　tell them I'll do everything. God help us,
　　we will see our triumph — or our fall.

Oedipus and Creon enter the palace, followed by the guards.

Priest: Rise, my sons. The kindness we came for　　　　　165
　　Oedipus volunteers himself.
　　Apollo has sent his word, his oracle —
　　Come down, Apollo, save us, stop the plague.

The priests rise, remove their branches, and exit to the side. Enter a Chorus, the citizens of Thebes, who have not heard the news that Creon brings. They march around the altar, chanting.

Chorus:　　　　　　　　　　　　　　　Zeus!
　　Great welcome voice of Zeus, what do you bring?
　　What word from the gold vaults of Delphi　　　　　170
　　comes to brilliant Thebes? I'm racked with terror —
　　　　　　　　　　terror shakes my heart
　　and I cry your wild cries, Apollo, Healer of Delos°
　　I worship you in dread . . . what now, what is your price?
　　some new sacrifice? some ancient rite from the past　　175
　　come round again each spring? —
　　　　　　　　what will you bring to birth?
　　Tell me, child of golden Hope
　　　　　　warm voice that never dies!
　　You are the first I call, daughter of Zeus　　　　　180
　　deathless Athena — I call your sister Artemis,°
　　heart of the market place enthroned in glory,
　　　　　　　　　　guardian of our earth —
　　I call Apollo astride the thunderheads of heaven —
　　O triple shield against death, shine before me now!　　185
　　If ever, once in the past, you stopped some ruin
　　launched against our walls
　　　　　　　　you hurled the flame of pain
　　far, far from Thebes — you gods
　　　　　　come now, come down once more!

　　　　　　　　　　　　No, no　　　　　　190
　　the miseries numberless, grief on grief, no end —
　　too much to bear, we are all dying
　　O my people . . .

173 *Delos:* Apollo was born on this sacred island.　　181 *Artemis:* Apollo's sister, goddess of hunting, the moon, and chastity.

Thebes like a great army dying
and there is no sword of thought to save us, no   195
and the fruits of our famous earth, they will not ripen
no and the women cannot scream their pangs to birth —
screams for the Healer, children dead in the womb
       and life on life goes down
                 you can watch them go   200
   like seabirds winging west, outracing the day's fire
down the horizon, irresistibly
      streaking on to the shores of Evening
                       Death
so many deaths, numberless deaths on deaths, no end —
Thebes is dying, look, her children   205
stripped of pity . . .
   generations strewn on the ground
unburied, unwept, the dead spreading death
and the young wives and gray-haired mothers with them
cling to the altars, trailing in from all over the city —   210
Thebes, city of death, one long cortege
     and the suffering rises
            wails for mercy rise
   and the wild hymn for the Healer blazes out
clashing with our sobs our cries of mourning —   215
     O golden daughter of god, send rescue
     radiant as the kindness in your eyes!

Drive him back! — the fever, the god of death
                   that raging god of war
not armored in bronze, not shielded now, he burns me,   220
battle cries in the onslaught burning on —
O rout him from our borders!
Sail him, blast him out to the Sea-queen's chamber
            the black Atlantic gulfs
   or the northern harbor, death to all   225
where the Thracian surf comes crashing.
Now what the night spares he comes by day and kills —
the god of death.

        O lord of the stormcloud,
you who twirl the lightning, Zeus, Father,
thunder Death to nothing!   230

Apollo, lord of the light, I beg you —
      whip your longbow's golden cord
showering arrows on our enemies — shafts of power
champions strong before us rushing on!

Artemis, Huntress,   235
torches flaring over the eastern ridges —
            ride Death down in pain!

God of the headdress gleaming gold, I cry to you —

your name and ours are one, Dionysus° —
>come with your face aflame with wine
>>your raving women's cries°
>your army on the march! Come with the lightning
come with torches blazing, eyes ablaze with glory!
Burn that god of death that all gods hate!

Oedipus enters from the palace to address the Chorus, as if addressing the entire city of Thebes.

Oedipus: You pray to the gods? Let me grant your prayers.   245
>Come, listen to me — do what the plague demands:
>you'll find relief and lift your head from the depths.

>I will speak out now as a stranger to the story,
>a stranger to the crime. If I'd been present then,
>there would have been no mystery, no long hunt   250
>without a clue in hand. So now, counted
>a native Theban years after the murder,
>to all of Thebes I make this proclamation:
>if any one of you knows who murdered Laius,
>the son of Labdacus, I order him to reveal   255
>the whole truth to me. Nothing to fear,
>even if he must denounce himself,
>let him speak up
>and so escape the brunt of the charge —
>he will suffer no unbearable punishment,   260
>nothing worse than exile, totally unharmed.

Oedipus pauses, waiting for a reply.

>>Next,
>if anyone knows the murderer is a stranger,
>a man from alien soil, come, speak up.
>I will give him a handsome reward, and lay up
>gratitude in my heart for him besides.   265

Silence again, no reply.

>But if you keep silent, if anyone panicking,
>trying to shield himself or friend or kin,
>rejects my offer, then hear what I will do.
>I order you, every citizen of the state
>where I hold throne and power: banish this man —   270
>whoever he may be — never shelter him, never
>speak a word to him, never make him partner
>to your prayers, your victims burned to the gods.
>Never let the holy water touch his hands.
>Drive him out, each of you, from every home.   275
>*He* is the plague, the heart of our corruption,

239 *Dionysus:* God of fertility and wine.   241 *Your . . . cries:* Dionysus was attended by female celebrants.

as Apollo's oracle has revealed to me
just now. So I honor my obligations:
I fight for the god and for the murdered man.

Now my curse on the murderer. Whoever he is,   280
a lone man unknown in his crime
or one among many, let that man drag out
his life in agony, step by painful step —
I curse myself as well . . . if by any chance
he proves to be an intimate of our house,   285
here at my hearth, with my full knowledge,
may the curse I just called down on him strike me!

These are your orders: perform them to the last.
I command you, for my sake, for Apollo's, for this country
blasted root and branch by the angry heavens.   290
Even if god had never urged you on to act,
how could you leave the crime uncleansed so long?
A man so noble — your king, brought down in blood —
you should have searched. But I am the king now,
I hold the throne that he held then, possess his bed   295
and a wife who shares our seed . . . why, our seed
might be the same, children born of the same mother
might have created blood-bonds between us
if his hope of offspring hadn't met disaster —
but fate swooped at his head and cut him short.   300
So I will fight for him as if he were my father,
stop at nothing, search the world
to lay my hands on the man who shed his blood,
the son of Labdacus descended of Polydorus,
Cadmus of old and Agenor, founder of the line: 305
their power and mine are one.
                                    Oh dear gods,
my curse on those who disobey these orders!
Let no crops grow out of the earth for them —
shrivel their women, kill their sons,
burn them to nothing in this plague   310
that hits us now, or something even worse.
But you, loyal men of Thebes who approve my actions,
may our champion, Justice, may all the gods
be with us, fight beside us to the end!
Leader: In the grip of your curse, my king, I swear   315
I'm not the murderer, cannot point him out.
As for the search, Apollo pressed it on us —
he should name the killer.
Oedipus: Quite right,
but to force the gods to act against their will —
no man has the power.
Leader: Then if I might mention   320

the next best thing . . .

Oedipus: The third best too —
don't hold back, say it.

Leader: I still believe . . .
Lord Tiresias sees with the eyes of Lord Apollo.
Anyone searching for the truth, my king,
might learn it from the prophet, clear as day.   325

Oedipus: I've not been slow with that. On Creon's cue
I sent the escorts, twice, within the hour.
I'm surprised he isn't here.

Leader: We need him —
without him we have nothing but old, useless rumors.

Oedipus: Which rumors? I'll search out every word.   330

Leader: Laius was killed, they say, by certain travelers.

Oedipus: I know — but no one can find the murderer.

Leader: If the man has a trace of fear in him
he won't stay silent long,
not with your curses ringing in his ears.   335

Oedipus: He didn't flinch at murder,
he'll never flinch at words.

Enter Tiresias, the blind prophet, led by a boy with escorts in attendance. He remains at a distance.

Leader: Here is the one who will convict him, look,
they bring him on at last, the seer, the man of god.
The truth lives inside him, him alone.

Oedipus: O Tiresias,   340
master of all the mysteries of our life,
all you teach and all you dare not tell,
signs in the heavens, signs that walk the earth!
Blind as you are, you can feel all the more
what sickness haunts our city. You, my lord,   345
are the one shield, the one savior we can find.

We asked Apollo — perhaps the messengers
haven't told you — he sent his answer back:
"Relief from the plague can only come one way.
Uncover the murderers of Laius,   350
put them to death or drive them into exile."
So I beg you, grudge us nothing now, no voice,
no message plucked from the birds, the embers
or the other mantic ways within your grasp.
Rescue yourself, your city, rescue me —   355
rescue everything infected by the dead.
We are in your hands. For a man to help others
with all his gifts and native strength:
that is the noblest work.

Tiresias: How terrible — to see the truth

when the truth is only pain to him who sees!   360
I knew it well, but I put it from my mind,
else I never would have come.
Oedipus: What's this? Why so grim, so dire?
Tiresias: Just send me home. You bear your burdens,
I'll bear mine. It's better that way,   365
please believe me.
Oedipus: Strange response — unlawful,
unfriendly too to the state that bred and raised you;
you're withholding the word of god.
Tiresias: I fail to see
that your own words are so well-timed.
I'd rather not have the same thing said of me . . .   370
Oedipus: For the love of god, don't turn away,
not if you know something. We beg you,
all of us on our knees.
Tiresias: None of you knows —
and I will never reveal my dreadful secrets,
not to say your own.   375
Oedipus: What? You know and you won't tell?
You're bent on betraying us, destroying Thebes?
Tiresias: I'd rather not cause pain for you or me.
So why this . . . useless interrogation?
You'll get nothing from me.
Oedipus: Nothing! You,   380
you scum of the earth, you'd enrage a heart of stone!
You won't talk? Nothing moves you?
Out with it, once and for all!
Tiresias: You criticize my temper . . . unaware
of the one *you* live with, you revile me.   385
Oedipus: Who could restrain his anger hearing you?
What outrage — you spurn the city!
Tiresias: What will come will come.
Even if I shroud it all in silence.
Oedipus: What will come? You're bound to *tell* me that.   390
Tiresias: I'll say no more. Do as you like, build your anger
to whatever pitch you please, rage your worst —
Oedipus: Oh I'll let loose, I have such fury in me —
now I see it all. You helped hatch the plot,
you did the work, yes, short of killing him   395
with your own hands — and given eyes I'd say
you did the killing single-handed!
Tiresias: Is that so!
I charge you, then, submit to that decree
you just laid down: from this day onward
speak to no one, not these citizens, not myself.   400
You are the curse, the corruption of the land!
Oedipus: You, shameless —
aren't you appalled to start up such a story?

You think you can get away with this?

Tiresias: I have already.

The truth with all its power lives inside me.   405

Oedipus: Who primed you for this? Not your prophet's trade.

Tiresias: You did, you forced me, twisted it out of me.

Oedipus: What? Say it again — I'll understand it better.

Tiresias: Didn't you understand, just now?

Or are you tempting me to talk?   410

Oedipus: No, I can't say I grasped your meaning.

Out with it, again!

Tiresias: I say you are the murderer you hunt.

Oedipus: That obscenity, twice — by god, you'll pay.

Tiresias: Shall I say more, so you can really rage?   415

Oedipus: Much as you want. Your words are nothing —
futile.

Tiresias: You cannot imagine . . . I tell you,
you and your loved ones live together in infamy,
you cannot see how far you've gone in guilt.

Oedipus: You think you can keep this up and never suffer?   420

Tiresias: Indeed, if the truth has any power.

Oedipus: It does

but not for you, old man. You've lost your power,
stone-blind, stone-deaf — senses, eyes blind as stone!

Tiresias: I pity you, flinging at me the very insults
each man here will fling at you so soon.

Oedipus: Blind,   425

lost in the night, endless night that nursed you!
You can't hurt me or anyone else who sees the light —
you can never touch me.

Tiresias: True, it is not your fate

to fall at my hands. Apollo is quite enough,
and he will take some pains to work this out.   430

Oedipus: Creon! Is this conspiracy his or yours?

Tiresias: Creon is not your downfall, no, you are your own.

Oedipus: O power —

wealth and empire, skill outstripping skill
in the heady rivalries of life,
what envy lurks inside you! Just for this,   435
the crown the city gave me — I never sought it,
they laid it in my hands — for this alone, Creon,
the soul of trust, my loyal friend from the start
steals against me . . . so hungry to overthrow me
he sets this wizard on me, this scheming quack,   440
this fortune-teller peddling lies, eyes peeled
for his own profit — seer blind in his craft!

Come here, you pious fraud. Tell me,
when did you ever prove yourself a prophet?
When the Sphinx, that chanting Fury kept her deathwatch here,   445

why silent then, not a word to set our people free?
There was a riddle, not for some passer-by to solve —
it cried out for a prophet. Where were you?
Did you rise to the crisis? Not a word,
you and your birds, your gods — nothing.   450
No, but I came by, Oedipus the ignorant,
I stopped the Sphinx! With no help from the birds,
the flight of my own intelligence hit the mark.

And this is the man you'd try to overthrow?
You think you'll stand by Creon when he's king?   455
You and the great mastermind —
you'll pay in tears, I promise you, for this,
this witch-hunt. If you didn't look so senile
the lash would teach you what your scheming means!
Leader: I'd suggest his words were spoken in anger,   460
    Oedipus . . . yours too, and it isn't what we need.
    The best solution to the oracle, the riddle
    posed by god — we should look for that.
Tiresias: You are the king no doubt, but in one respect,
    at least, I am your equal: the right to reply.   465
    I claim that privilege too.
    I am not your slave. I serve Apollo.
    I don't need Creon to speak for me in public.
                                                        So,
you mock my blindness? Let me tell you this.
You with your precious eyes,   470
you're blind to the corruption of your life,
to the house you live in, those you live with —
who are your parents? Do you know? All unknowing
you are the scourge of your own flesh and blood,
the dead below the earth and the living here above,   475
and the double lash of your mother and your father's curse
will whip you from this land one day, their footfall
treading you down in terror, darkness shrouding
your eyes that now can see the light!
                                    Soon, soon
you'll scream aloud — what haven won't reverberate?   480
What rock of Cithaeron° won't scream back in echo?
That day you learn the truth about your marriage,
the wedding-march that sang you into your halls,
the lusty voyage home to the fatal harbor!
And a load of other horrors you'd never dream   485
will level you with yourself and all your children.

There. Now smear us with insults — Creon, myself
and every word I've said. No man will ever
be rooted from the earth as brutally as you.

481 *Cithaeron:* The mountains where Oedipus was abandoned as an infant.

Oedipus: Enough! Such filth from him? Insufferable — 490
    what, still alive? Get out —
    faster, back where you came from — vanish!
Tiresias: I'd never have come if you hadn't called me here.
Oedipus: If I thought you'd blurt out such absurdities,
    you'd have died waiting before I'd had you summoned. 495
Tiresias: Absurd, am I? To you, not to your parents:
    the ones who bore you found me sane enough.
Oedipus: Parents — who? Wait . . . who is my father?
Tiresias: This day will bring your birth and your destruction.
Oedipus: Riddles — all you can say are riddles, murk and darkness. 500
Tiresias: Ah, but aren't you the best man alive at solving riddles?
Oedipus: Mock me for that, go on, and you'll reveal my greatness.
Tiresias: Your great good fortune, true, it was your ruin.
Oedipus: Not if I saved the city — what do I care?
Tiresias: Well then, I'll be going.

To his attendant.

                      Take me home, boy. 505
Oedipus: Yes, take him away. You're a nuisance here.
    Out of the way, the irritation's gone.

Turning his back on Tiresias, moving toward the palace.

Tiresias: I will go,
    once I have said what I came here to say.
    I'll never shrink from the anger in your eyes —
    you can't destroy me. Listen to me closely: 510
    the man you've sought so long, proclaiming,
    cursing up and down, the murderer of Laius —
    he is here. A stranger,
    you may think, who lives among you,
    he soon will be revealed a native Theban 515
    but he will take no joy in the revelation.
    Blind who now has eyes, beggar who now is rich,
    he will grope his way toward a foreign soil,
    a stick tapping before him step by step.

Oedipus enters the palace.

    Revealed at last, brother and father both 520
    to the children he embraces, to his mother
    son and husband both — he sowed the loins
    his father sowed, he spilled his father's blood!

    Go in and reflect on that, solve that.
    And if you find I've lied 525
    from this day onward call the prophet blind.

Tiresias and the boy exit to the side.

Chorus: Who —
    who is the man the voice of god denounces

resounding out of the rocky gorge of Delphi?
        The horror too dark to tell,
whose ruthless bloody hands have done the work?   530
His time has come to fly
        to outrace the stallions of the storm
                        his feet a streak of speed —
Cased in armor, Apollo son of the Father
lunges on him, lightning-bolts afire!   535
And the grim unerring Furies°
                closing for the kill.

                        Look,
the word of god has just come blazing
flashing off Parnassus'° snowy heights!
        That man who left no trace —   540
after him, hunt him down with all our strength!
Now under bristling timber
        up through rocks and caves he stalks
                        like the wild mountain bull —
cut off from men, each step an agony, frenzied, racing blind   545
but he cannot outrace the dread voices of Delphi
ringing out of the heart of Earth,
        the dark wings beating around him shrieking doom
                the doom that never dies, the terror —

The skilled prophet scans the birds and shatters me with terror! 550
I can't accept him, can't deny him, don't know what to say,
I'm lost, and the wings of dark foreboding beating —
I cannot see what's come, what's still to come . . .
and what could breed a blood feud between
        Laius' house and the son of Polybus?°   555
I know of nothing, not in the past and not now,
no charge to bring against our king, no cause
to attack his fame that rings throughout Thebes —
        not without proof — not for the ghost of Laius,
        not to avenge a murder gone without a trace.   560

Zeus and Apollo know, they know, the great masters
        of all the dark and depth of human life.
But whether a mere man can know the truth,
whether a seer can fathom more than I —
there is no test, no certain proof   565
        though matching skill for skill
a man can outstrip a rival. No, not till I see
these charges proved will I side with his accusers.
We saw him then, when the she-hawk° swept against him,
saw with our own eyes his skill, his brilliant triumph —   570

---

536 *Furies:* Three spirits who avenged evildoers.   539 *Parnassus:* A mountain in Greece associated
with Apollo.   555 *Polybus:* The King of Corinth, who is thought to be Oedipus's father.   569 *she-hawk:* The Sphinx.

there was the test — he was the joy of Thebes!
Never will I convict my king, never in my heart.

Enter Creon from the side.

Creon: My fellow-citizens, I hear King Oedipus
    levels terrible charges at me. I had to come.
    I resent it deeply. If, in the present crisis,   575
    he thinks he suffers any abuse from me,
    anything I've done or said that offers him
    the slightest injury, why, I've no desire
    to linger out this life, my reputation a shambles.
    The damage I'd face from such an accusation   580
    is nothing simple. No, there's nothing worse:
    branded a traitor in the city, a traitor
    to all of you and my good friends.
Leader: True,
    but a slur might have been forced out of him,
    by anger perhaps, not any firm conviction.   585
Creon: The charge was made in public, wasn't it?
    I put the prophet up to spreading lies?
Leader: Such things were said . . .
    I don't know with what intent, if any.
Creon: Was his glance steady, his mind right   590
    when the charge was brought against me?
Leader: I really couldn't say. I never look
    to judge the ones in power.

The doors open. Oedipus enters.

                          Wait,
    here's Oedipus now.
Oedipus: You — here? You have the gall
    to show your face before the palace gates?   595
    You, plotting to kill me, kill the king —
    I see it all, the marauding thief himself
    scheming to steal my crown and power!
                       Tell me,
    in god's name, what did you take me for,
    coward or fool, when you spun out your plot?   600
    Your treachery — you think I'd never detect it
    creeping against me in the dark? Or sensing it,
    not defend myself? Aren't you the fool,
    you and your high adventure. Lacking numbers,
    powerful friends, out for the big game of empire —   605
    you need riches, armies to bring that quarry down!
Creon: Are you quite finished? It's your turn to listen
    for just as long as you've . . . instructed me.
    Hear me out, then judge me on the facts.
Oedipus: You've a wicked way with words, Creon,   610

but I'll be slow to learn — from you.
I find you a menace, a great burden to me.

Creon: Just one thing, hear me out in this.

Oedipus: Just one thing,
don't tell me you're not the enemy, the traitor.

Creon: Look, if you think crude, mindless stubbornness   615
such a gift, you've lost your sense of balance.

Oedipus: If you think you can abuse a kinsman,
then escape the penalty, you're insane.

Creon: Fair enough, I grant you. But this injury
you say I've done you, what is it?   620

Oedipus: Did you induce me, yes or no,
to send for that sanctimonious prophet?

Creon: I did. And I'd do the same again.

Oedipus: All right then, tell me, how long is it now
since Laius . . .

Creon: Laius — what did *he* do?

Oedipus: Vanished,   625
swept from sight, murdered in his tracks.

Creon: The count of the years would run you far back . . .

Oedipus: And that far back, was the prophet at his trade?

Creon: Skilled as he is today, and just as honored.

Oedipus: Did he ever refer to me then, at that time?

Creon: No,   630
never, at least, when I was in his presence.

Oedipus: But you did investigate the murder, didn't you?

Creon: We did our best, of course, discovered nothing.

Oedipus: But the great seer never accused me then — why not?

Creon: I don't know. And when I don't, *I* keep quiet.   635

Oedipus: You do know this, you'd tell it too —
if you had a shred of decency.

Creon: What?
If I know, I won't hold back.

Oedipus: Simply this:
if the two of you had never put heads together,
we'd never have heard about *my* killing Laius.   640

Creon: If that's what he says . . . well, you know best.
But now I have a right to learn from you
as you just learned from me.

Oedipus: Learn your fill,
you never will convict me of the murder.

Creon: Tell me, you're married to my sister, aren't you?   645

Oedipus: A genuine discovery — there's no denying that.

Creon: And you rule the land with her, with equal power?

Oedipus: She receives from me whatever she desires.

Creon: And I am the third, all of us are equals?

Oedipus: Yes, and it's there you show your stripes —   650
you betray a kinsman.

Creon: Not at all.
Not if you see things calmly, rationally,
as I do. Look at it this way first:
who in his right mind would rather rule
and live in anxiety than sleep in peace?   655
Particularly if he enjoys the same authority.
Not I, I'm not the man to yearn for kingship,
not with a king's power in my hands. Who would?
No one with any sense of self-control.
Now, as it is, you offer me all I need,   660
not a fear in the world. But if I wore the crown . . .
there'd be many painful duties to perform,
hardly to my taste.
                         How could kingship
please me more than influence, power
without a qualm? I'm not that deluded yet,   665
to reach for anything but privilege outright,
profit free and clear.
Now all men sing my praises, all salute me,
now all who request your favors curry mine.
I'm their best hope: success rests in me.   670
Why give up that, I ask you, and borrow trouble?
A man of sense, someone who sees things clearly
would never resort to treason.
No, I've no lust for conspiracy in me,
nor could I ever suffer one who does.   675

Do you want proof? Go to Delphi yourself,
examine the oracle and see if I've reported
the message word-for-word. This too:
if you detect that I and the clairvoyant
have plotted anything in common, arrest me,   680
execute me. Not on the strength of one vote,
two in this case, mine as well as yours.
But don't convict me on sheer unverified surmise.

How wrong it is to take the good for bad,
purely at random, or take the bad for good.   685
But reject a friend, a kinsman? I would as soon
tear out the life within us, priceless life itself.
You'll learn this well, without fail, in time.
Time alone can bring the just man to light;
the criminal you can spot in one short day.
Leader: Good advice,   690
my lord, for anyone who wants to avoid disaster.
Those who jump to conclusions may be wrong.
Oedipus: When my enemy moves against me quickly,
plots in secret, I move quickly too, I must,
I plot and pay him back. Relax my guard a moment,   695

waiting his next move — he wins his objective,
I lose mine.
Creon: What do you want?
You want me banished?
Oedipus: No, I want you dead.
Creon: Just to show how ugly a grudge can . . .
Oedipus: So,
still stubborn? you don't think I'm serious?   700
Creon: I think you're insane.
Oedipus: Quite sane — in my behalf.
Creon: Not just as much in mine?
Oedipus: You — my mortal enemy?
Creon: What if you're wholly wrong?
Oedipus: No matter — I must rule.
Creon: Not if you rule unjustly.
Oedipus: Hear him, Thebes, my city!
Creon: My city too, not yours alone!   705
Leader: Please, my lords.

Enter Jocasta from the palace.

                        Look, Jocasta's coming,
and just in time too. With her help
you must put this fighting of yours to rest.
Jocasta: Have you no sense? Poor misguided men,
such shouting — why this public outburst?   710
Aren't you ashamed, with the land so sick,
to stir up private quarrels?

To Oedipus.

Into the palace now. And Creon, you go home.
Why make such a furor over nothing?
Creon: My sister, it's dreadful . . . Oedipus, your husband,   715
he's bent on a choice of punishments for me,
banishment from the fatherland or death.
Oedipus: Precisely. I caught him in the act, Jocasta,
plotting, about to stab me in the back.
Creon: Never — curse me, let me die and be damned   720
if I've done you any wrong you charge me with.
Jocasta: Oh god, believe it, Oedipus,
honor the solemn oath he swears to heaven.
Do it for me, for the sake of all your people.

The Chorus begins to chant.

Chorus: Believe it, be sensible   725
give way, my king, I beg you!
Oedipus: What do you want from me, concessions?
Chorus: Respect him — he's been no fool in the past
and now he's strong with the oath he swears to god.
Oedipus: You know what you're asking?

Chorus: I do.

Oedipus: Then out with it!   730

Chorus: The man's your friend, your kin, he's under oath —
     don't cast him out, disgraced
     branded with guilt on the strength of hearsay only.

Oedipus: Know full well, if that's what you want
     you want me dead or banished from the land.

Chorus: Never —   735
     no, by the blazing Sun, first god of the heavens!
        Stripped of the gods, stripped of loved ones,
     let me die by inches if that ever crossed my mind.
     But the heart inside me sickens, dies as the land dies
     and now on top of the old griefs you pile this,   740
     your fury — both of you!

Oedipus: Then let him go,
     even if it does lead to my ruin, my death
     or my disgrace, driven from Thebes for life.
     It's you, not him I pity — your words move me.
     He, wherever he goes, my hate goes with him.   745

Creon: Look at you, sullen in yielding, brutal in your rage —
     you'll go too far. It's perfect justice:
     natures like yours are hardest on themselves.

Oedipus: Then leave me alone — get out!

Creon: I'm going.
     You're wrong, so wrong. These men know I'm right.   750

Exit to the side. The Chorus turns to Jocasta.

Chorus: Why do you hesitate, my lady
        why not help him in?

Jocasta: Tell me what's happened first.

Chorus: Loose, ignorant talk started dark suspicions
     and a sense of injustice cut deeply too.   755

Jocasta: On both sides?

Chorus: Oh yes.

Jocasta: What did they say?

Chorus: Enough, please, enough! The land's so racked already
     or so it seems to me . . .
     End the trouble here, just where they left it.

Oedipus: You see what comes of your good intentions now?   760
     And all because you tried to blunt my anger.

Chorus: My king,
     I've said it once, I'll say it time and again —
        I'd be insane, you know it,
     senseless, ever to turn my back on you.
     You who set our beloved land — storm-tossed, shattered —   765
     straight on course. Now again, good helmsman,
     steer us through the storm!

The Chorus draws away, leaving Oedipus and Jocasta side by side.

Jocasta: For the love of god,
    Oedipus, tell me too, what is it?
    Why this rage? You're so unbending.
Oedipus: I will tell you. I respect you, Jocasta,   770
    much more than these . . .

Glancing at the Chorus.

    Creon's to blame, Creon schemes against me.
Jocasta: Tell me clearly, how did the quarrel start?
Oedipus: He says *I* murdered Laius — I am guilty.
Jocasta: How does he know? Some secret knowledge   775
    or simple hearsay?
Oedipus: Oh, he sent his prophet in
    to do his dirty work. You know Creon,
    Creon keeps his own lips clean.
Jocasta: A prophet?
    Well then, free yourself of every charge!
    Listen to me and learn some peace of mind: 780
    no skill in the world,
    nothing human can penetrate the future.
    Here is proof, quick and to the point.
    An oracle came to Laius one fine day
    (I won't say from Apollo himself   785
    but his underlings, his priests) and it said
    that doom would strike him down at the hands of a son,
    our son, to be born of our own flesh and blood. But Laius,
    so the report goes at least, was killed by strangers,
    thieves, at a place where three roads meet . . . my son —   790
    he wasn't three days old and the boy's father
    fastened his ankles, had a henchman fling him away
    on a barren, trackless mountain.
                      There, you see?
    Apollo brought neither thing to pass. My baby
    no more murdered his father than Laius suffered —   795
    his wildest fear — death at his own son's hands.
    That's how the seers and their revelations
    mapped out the future. Brush them from your mind.
    Whatever the god needs and seeks
    he'll bring to light himself, with ease.
Oedipus: Strange,   800
    hearing you just now . . . my mind wandered,
    my thoughts racing back and forth.
Jocasta: What do you mean? Why so anxious, startled?
Oedipus: I thought I heard you say that Laius
    was cut down at a place where three roads meet.   805
Jocasta: That was the story. It hasn't died out yet.
Oedipus: Where did this thing happen? Be precise.
Jocasta: A place called Phocis, where two branching roads,

one from Daulia, one from Delphi,
come together — a crossroads. 810
Oedipus: When? How long ago?
Jocasta: The heralds no sooner reported Laius dead
than you appeared and they hailed you king of Thebes.
Oedipus: My god, my god — what have you planned to do to me?
Jocasta: What, Oedipus? What haunts you so?
Oedipus: Not yet. 815
Laius — how did he look? Describe him.
Had he reached his prime?
Jocasta: He was swarthy,
and the gray had just begun to streak his temples,
and his build . . . wasn't far from yours.
Oedipus: Oh no no,
I think I've just called down a dreadful curse 820
upon myself — I simply didn't know!
Jocasta: What are you saying? I shudder to look at you.
Oedipus: I have a terrible fear the blind seer can see.
I'll know in a moment. One thing more —
Jocasta: Anything,
afraid as I am — ask, I'll answer, all I can. 825
Oedipus: Did he go with a light or heavy escort,
several men-at-arms, like a lord, a king?
Jocasta: There were five in the party, a herald among them,
and a single wagon carrying Laius.
Oedipus: Ai —
now I can see it all, clear as day. 830
Who told you all this at the time, Jocasta?
Jocasta: A servant who reached home, the lone survivor.
Oedipus: So, could he still be in the palace — even now?
Jocasta: No indeed. Soon as he returned from the scene
and saw you on the throne with Laius dead and gone, 835
he knelt and clutched my hand, pleading with me
to send him into the hinterlands, to pasture,
far as possible, out of sight of Thebes.
I sent him away. Slave though he was,
he'd earned that favor — and much more. 840
Oedipus: Can we bring him back, quickly?
Jocasta: Easily. Why do you want him so?
Oedipus: I'm afraid,
Jocasta, I have said too much already.
That man — I've got to see him.
Jocasta: Then he'll come.
But even I have a right, I'd like to think, 845
to know what's torturing you, my lord.
Oedipus: And so you shall — I can hold nothing back from you,
now I've reached this pitch of dark foreboding.
Who means more to me than you? Tell me,

whom would I turn toward but you   850
as I go through all this?

My father was Polybus, king of Corinth.
My mother, a Dorian, Merope. And I was held
the prince of the realm among the people there,
till something struck me out of nowhere,   855
something strange . . . worth remarking perhaps,
hardly worth the anxiety I gave it.
Some man at a banquet who had drunk too much
shouted out — he was far gone, mind you —
that I am not my father's son. Fighting words!   860
I barely restrained myself that day
but early the next I went to mother and father,
questioned them closely, and they were enraged
at the accusation and the fool who let it fly.
So as for my parents I was satisfied,   865
but still this thing kept gnawing at me,
the slander spread — I had to make my move.
                                              And so,
unknown to mother and father I set out for Delphi,
and the god Apollo spurned me, sent me away
denied the facts I came for,   870
but first he flashed before my eyes a future
great with pain, terror, disaster — I can hear him cry,
"You are fated to couple with your mother, you will bring
a breed of children into the light no man can bear to see —
you will kill your father, the one who gave you life!"   875
I heard all that and ran. I abandoned Corinth,
from that day on I gauged its landfall only
by the stars, running, always running
toward some place where I would never see
the shame of all those oracles come true.   880
And as I fled I reached that very spot
where the great king, you say, met his death.
Now, Jocasta, I will tell you all.
Making my way toward this triple crossroad
I began to see a herald, then a brace of colts   885
drawing a wagon, and mounted on the bench . . . a man,
just as you've described him, coming face-to-face,
and the one in the lead and the old man himself
were about to thrust me off the road — brute force —
and the one shouldering me aside, the driver,   890
I strike him in anger! — and the old man, watching me
coming up along his wheels — he brings down
his prod, two prongs straight at my head!
I paid him back with interest!
Short work, by god — with one blow of the staff   895
in this right hand I knock him out of his high seat,

roll him out of the wagon, sprawling headlong —
I killed them all — every mother's son!

Oh, but if there is any blood-tie
between Laius and this stranger . . .   900
what man alive more miserable than I?
More hated by the gods? *I* am the man
no alien, no citizen welcomes to his house,
law forbids it — not a word to me in public,
driven out of every hearth and home.   905
And all these curses I — no one but I
brought down these piling curses on myself!
And you, his wife, I've touched your body with these,
the hands that killed your husband cover you with blood.

Wasn't I born for torment? Look me in the eyes!   910
I am abomination — heart and soul!
I must be exiled, and even in exile
never see my parents, never set foot
on native earth again. Else I'm doomed
to couple with my mother and cut my father down . . .   915
Polybus who reared me, gave me life.

                                                        But why, why?
Wouldn't a man of judgment say — and wouldn't he be right —
some savage power has brought this down upon my head?

Oh no, not that, you pure and awesome gods,
never let me see that day! Let me slip   920
from the world of men, vanish without a trace
before I see myself stained with such corruption,
stained to the heart.
Leader: My lord, you fill our hearts with fear.
But at least until you question the witness,   925
do take hope.
Oedipus: Exactly. He is my last hope —
I'm waiting for the shepherd. He is crucial.
Jocasta: And once he appears, what then? Why so urgent?
Oedipus: I'll tell you. If it turns out that his story
matches yours, I've escaped the worst.   930
Jocasta: What did I say? What struck you so?
Oedipus: You said *thieves* —
he told you a whole band of them murdered Laius.
So, if he still holds to the same number,
I cannot be the killer. One can't equal many.
But if he refers to one man, one alone,   935
clearly the scales come down on me:
I am guilty.
Jocasta: Impossible. Trust me,
I told you precisely what he said,
and he can't retract it now;
the whole city heard it, not just I.   940

And even if he should vary his first report
by one man more or less, still, my lord,
he could never make the murder of Laius
truly fit the prophecy. Apollo was explicit:
my son was doomed to kill my husband . . . my son,   945
poor defenseless thing, he never had a chance
to kill his father. They destroyed him first.

So much for prophecy. It's neither here nor there.
From this day on, I wouldn't look right or left.
Oedipus: True, true. Still, that shepherd,   950
someone fetch him — now!
Jocasta: I'll send at once. But do let's go inside.
I'd never displease you, least of all in this.

Oedipus and Jocasta enter the palace.

Chorus: Destiny guide me always
Destiny find me filled with reverence   955
     pure in word and deed.
Great laws tower above us, reared on high
born for the brilliant vault of heaven —
     Olympian sky their only father,
nothing mortal, no man gave them birth,   960
their memory deathless, never lost in sleep:
within them lives a mighty god, the god does not grow old.

Pride breeds the tyrant
violent pride, gorging, crammed to bursting
     with all that is overripe and rich with ruin —   965
clawing up to the heights, headlong pride
crashes down the abyss — sheer doom!
     No footing helps, all foothold lost and gone,
But the healthy strife that makes the city strong —
I pray that god will never end that wrestling: 970
god, my champion, I will never let you go.

But if any man comes striding, high and mighty
     in all he says and does,
no fear of justice, no reverence
for the temples of the gods —   975
     let a rough doom tear him down,
repay his pride, breakneck, ruinous pride!
If he cannot reap his profits fairly
     cannot restrain himself from outrage —
mad, laying hands on the holy things untouchable!   980

     Can such a man, so desperate, still boast
     he can save his life from the flashing bolts of god?
          If all such violence goes with honor now
               why join the sacred dance?

Never again will I go reverent to Delphi,   985
    the inviolate heart of Earth
or Apollo's ancient oracle at Abae
or Olympia of the fires —
    unless these prophecies all come true
for all mankind to point toward in wonder.   990
King of kings, if you deserve your titles
    Zeus, remember, never forget!
You and your deathless, everlasting reign.

        They are dying, the old oracles sent to Laius,
            now our masters strike them off the rolls.   995
                Nowhere Apollo's golden glory now —
                    the gods, the gods go down.

Enter Jocasta from the palace, carrying a suppliant's branch wound in wool.

Jocasta: Lords of the realm, it occurred to me,
    just now, to visit the temples of the gods,
    so I have my branch in hand and incense too.   1000

    Oedipus is beside himself. Racked with anguish,
    no longer a man of sense, he won't admit
    the latest prophecies are hollow as the old —
    he's at the mercy of every passing voice
    if the voice tells of terror.   1005
    I urge him gently, nothing seems to help,
    so I turn to you, Apollo, you are nearest.

Placing her branch on the altar, while an old herdsman enters from the side, not the one just summoned by the king but an unexpected messenger from Corinth.

    I come with prayers and offerings . . . I beg you,
    cleanse us, set us free of defilement!
    Look at us, passengers in the grip of fear,   1010
    watching the pilot of the vessel go to pieces.
Messenger:

Approaching Jocasta and the Chorus.

    Strangers, please, I wonder if you could lead us
    to the palace of the king . . . I think it's Oedipus.
    Better, the man himself — you know where he is?
Leader: This is his palace, stranger. He's inside.   1015
    But here is his queen, his wife and mother
    of his children.
Messenger: Blessings on you, noble queen,
    queen of Oedipus crowned with all your family —
    blessings on you always!
Jocasta: And the same to you, stranger, you deserve it . . .   1020
    such a greeting. But what have you come for?
    Have you brought us news?

Messenger: Wonderful news —
    for the house, my lady, for your husband too.
Jocasta: Really, what? Who sent you?
Messenger: Corinth.
    I'll give you the message in a moment.   1025
    You'll be glad of it — how could you help it? —
    though it costs a little sorrow in the bargain.
Jocasta: What can it be, with such a double edge?
Messenger: The people there, they want to make your Oedipus
    king of Corinth, so they're saying now.   1030
Jocasta: Why? Isn't old Polybus still in power?
Messenger: No more. Death has got him in the tomb.
Jocasta: What are you saying? Polybus, dead? — dead?
Messenger: If not,
    if I'm not telling the truth, strike me dead too.
Jocasta:

To a servant.

    Quickly, go to your master, tell him this!   1035

    You prophecies of the gods, where are you now?
    This is the man that Oedipus feared for years,
    he fled him, not to kill him — and now he's dead,
    quite by chance, a normal, natural death,
    not murdered by his son.
Oedipus:

Emerging from the palace.

                    Dearest,   1040
    what now? Why call me from the palace?
Jocasta:

Bringing the Messenger closer.

    Listen to *him,* see for yourself what all
    those awful prophecies of god have come to.
Oedipus: And who is he? What can he have for me?
Jocasta: He's from Corinth, he's come to tell you   1045
    your father is no more — Polybus — he's dead!
Oedipus:

Wheeling on the Messenger.

    What? Let me have it from your lips.
Messenger: Well,
    if that's what you want first, then here it is:
    make no mistake, Polybus is dead and gone.
Oedipus: How — murder? sickness? — what? what killed him?   1050
Messenger: A light tip of the scales can put old bones to rest.
Oedipus: Sickness then — poor man, it wore him down.
Messenger: That,
    and the long count of years he'd measured out.

Oedipus: So!
    Jocasta, why, why look to the Prophet's hearth,
    the fires of the future? Why scan the birds   1055
    that scream above our heads? They winged me on
    to the murder of my father, did they? That was my doom?
    Well look, he's dead and buried, hidden under the earth,
    and here I am in Thebes, I never put hand to sword —
    unless some longing for me wasted him away,   1060
    then in a sense you'd say I caused his death.
    But now, all those prophecies I feared — Polybus
    packs them off to sleep with him in hell!
    They're nothing, worthless.
Jocasta: There.
    Didn't I tell you from the start?   1065
Oedipus: So you did. I was lost in fear.
Jocasta: No more, sweep it from your mind forever.
Oedipus: But my mother's bed, surely I must fear —
Jocasta: Fear?
    What should a man fear? It's all chance,
    chance rules our lives. Not a man on earth   1070
    can see a day ahead, groping through the dark.
    Better to live at random, best we can.
    And as for this marriage with your mother —
    have no fear. Many a man before you,
    in his dreams, has shared his mother's bed.   1075
    Take such things for shadows, nothing at all —
    Live, Oedipus,
    as if there's no tomorrow!
Oedipus: Brave words,
    and you'd persuade me if mother weren't alive.
    But mother lives, so for all your reassurances   1080
    I live in fear, I must.
Jocasta: But your father's death,
    that, at least, is a great blessing, joy to the eyes!
Oedipus: Great, I know . . . but I fear *her* — she's still alive.
Messenger: Wait, who is this woman, makes you so afraid?
Oedipus: Merope, old man. The wife of Polybus.   1085
Messenger: The queen? What's there to fear in her?
Oedipus: A dreadful prophecy, stranger, sent by the gods.
Messenger: Tell me, could you? Unless it's forbidden
    other ears to hear.
Oedipus: Not at all.
    Apollo told me once — it is my fate —   1090
    I must make love with my own mother,
    shed my father's blood with my own hands.
    So for years I've given Corinth a wide berth,
    and it's been my good fortune too. But still,
    to see one's parents and look into their eyes   1095
    is the greatest joy I know.

Messenger: You're afraid of that?
   That kept you out of Corinth?
Oedipus: My *father,* old man —
   so I wouldn't kill my father.
Messenger: So that's it.
   Well then, seeing I came with such good will, my king,
   why don't I rid you of that old worry now?   1100
Oedipus: What a rich reward you'd have for that.
Messenger: What do you think I came for, majesty?
   So you'd come home and I'd be better off.
Oedipus: Never, I will never go near my parents.
Messenger: My boy, it's clear, you don't know what you're doing.   1105
Oedipus: What do you mean, old man? For god's sake, explain.
Messenger: If you ran from *them,* always dodging home . . .
Oedipus: Always, terrified Apollo's oracle might come true —
Messenger: And you'd be covered with guilt, from both your parents.
Oedipus: That's right, old man, that fear is always with me.   1110
Messenger: Don't you know? You've really nothing to fear.
Oedipus: But why? If I'm their son — Merope, Polybus?
Messenger: Polybus was nothing to you, that's why, not in blood.
Oedipus: What are you saying — Polybus was not my father?
Messenger: No more than I am. He and I are equals.
Oedipus: My father —   1115
   how can my father equal nothing? You're nothing to me!
Messenger: Neither was he, no more your father than I am.
Oedipus: Then why did he call me his son?
Messenger: You were a gift,
   years ago — know for a fact he took you
   from my hands.
Oedipus: No, from another's hands?   1120
   Then how could he love me so? He loved me, deeply . . .
Messenger: True, and his early years without a child
   made him love you all the more.
Oedipus: And you, did you . . .
   buy me? find me by accident?
Messenger: I stumbled on you,
   down the woody flanks of Mount Cithaeron.
Oedipus: So close,   1125
   what were you doing here, just passing through?
Messenger: Watching over my flocks, grazing them on the slopes.
Oedipus: A herdsman, were you? A vagabond, scraping for wages?
Messenger: Your savior too, my son, in your worst hour.
Oedipus: Oh —
   when you picked me up, was I in pain? What exactly?   1130
Messenger: Your ankles . . . they tell the story. Look at them.
Oedipus: Why remind me of that, that old affliction?
Messenger: Your ankles were pinned together; I set you free.
Oedipus: That dreadful mark — I've had it from the cradle.

Messenger: And you got your name from that misfortune too,   1135
  the name's still with you.
Oedipus: Dear god, who did it? —
  mother? father? Tell me.
Messenger: I don't know.
  The one who gave you to me, he'd know more.
Oedipus: What? You took me from someone else?
  You didn't find me yourself?
Messenger: No sir,   1140
  another shepherd passed you on to me.
Oedipus: Who? Do you know? Describe him.
Messenger: He called himself a servant of . . .
  if I remember rightly — Laius.

Jocasta turns sharply.

Oedipus: The king of the land who ruled here long ago?   1145
Messenger: That's the one. That herdsman was *his* man.
Oedipus: Is he still alive? Can I see him?
Messenger: They'd know best, the people of these parts.

Oedipus and the Messenger turn to the Chorus.

Oedipus: Does anyone know that herdsman,
  the one he mentioned? Anyone seen him   1150
  in the fields, in town? Out with it!
  The time has come to reveal this once for all.
Leader: I think he's the very shepherd you wanted to see,
  a moment ago. But the queen, Jocasta,
  she's the one to say.
Oedipus: Jocasta,   1155
  you remember the man we just sent for?
  Is *that* the one he means?
Jocasta: That man . . .
  why ask? Old shepherd, talk, empty nonsense,
  don't give it another thought, don't even think —
Oedipus: What — give up now, with a clue like this?   1160
  Fail to solve the mystery of my birth?
  Not for all the world!
Jocasta: Stop — in the name of god,
  if you love your own life, call off this search!
  My suffering is enough.
Oedipus: Courage!
  Even if my mother turns out to be a slave,   1165
  and I a slave, three generations back,
  you would not seem common.
Jocasta: Oh no,
  listen to me, I beg you, don't do this.
Oedipus: Listen to you? No more. I must know it all,
  see the truth at last.

Jocasta: No, please —   1170
    for your sake — I want the best for you!
Oedipus: Your best is more than I can bear.
Jocasta: You're doomed —
    may you never fathom who you are!
Oedipus:

To a servant.

    Hurry, fetch me the herdsman, now!
    Leave her to glory in her royal birth.   1175
Jocasta: Aieeeeee —
             man of agony —
    that is the only name I have for you,
    that, no other — ever, ever, ever!

Flinging through the palace doors. A long, tense silence follows.

Leader: Where's she gone, Oedipus?
    Rushing off, such wild grief . . .   1180
    I'm afraid that from this silence
    something monstrous may come bursting forth.
Oedipus: Let it burst! Whatever will, whatever must!
    I must know my birth, no matter how common
    it may be — must see my origins face-to-face.   1185
    She perhaps, she with her woman's pride
    may well be mortified by my birth,
    but I, I count myself the son of Chance,
    the great goddess, giver of all good things —
    I'll never see myself disgraced. She is my mother!   1190
    And the moons have marked me out, my blood-brothers,
    one moon on the wane, the next moon great with power.
    That is my blood, my nature — I will never betray it,
    never fail to search and learn my birth!
Chorus: Yes — if I am a true prophet   1195
        if I can grasp the truth,
     by the boundless skies of Olympus,
    at the full moon of tomorrow, Mount Cithaeron
    you will know how Oedipus glories in you —
    you, his birthplace, nurse, his mountain-mother!   1200
    And we will sing you, dancing out your praise —
    you lift our monarch's heart!
      Apollo, Apollo, god of the wild cry
         may our dancing please you!
                       Oedipus —
        son, dear child, who bore you?   1205
    Who of the nymphs who seem to live forever
    mated with Pan,° the mountain-striding Father?

1207 *Pan:* God of shepherds, who was, like Hermes and Dionysus, associated with the wilderness.

Who was your mother? who, some bride of Apollo
the god who loves the pastures spreading toward the sun?
    Or was it Hermes, king of the lightning ridges?   1210
Or Dionysus, lord of frenzy, lord of the barren peaks —
did he seize you in his hands, dearest of all his lucky finds? —
    found by the nymphs, their warm eyes dancing, gift
to the lord who loves them dancing out his joy!

Oedipus strains to see a figure coming from the distance. Attended by palace
guards, an old Shepherd enters slowly, reluctant to approach the king.

Oedipus: I never met the man, my friends . . . still,   1215
    if I had to guess, I'd say that's the shepherd,
    the very one we've looked for all along.
    Brothers in old age, two of a kind,
    he and our guest here. At any rate
    the ones who bring him in are my own men,   1220
    I recognize them.

Turning to the leader.

                         But you know more than I,
    you should, you've seen the man before.
Leader: I know him, definitely. One of Laius' men,
    a trusty shepherd, if there ever was one.
Oedipus: You, I ask you first, stranger,   1225
    you from Corinth — is this the one you mean?
Messenger: You're looking at him. He's your man.
Oedipus:

To the Shepherd.

    You, old man, come over here —
    look at me. Answer all my questions.
    Did you ever serve King Laius?
Shepherd: So I did . . .   1230
    a slave, not bought on the block though,
    born and reared in the palace.
Oedipus: Your duties, your kind of work?
Shepherd: Herding the flocks, the better part of my life.
Oedipus: Where, mostly? Where did you do your grazing?
Shepherd: Well,   1235
    Cithaeron sometimes, or the foothills round about.
Oedipus: This man — you know him? ever see him there?
Shepherd:

Confused, glancing from the Messenger to the King.

    Doing what — what man do you mean?
Oedipus:

Pointing to the Messenger.

    This one here — ever have dealings with him?
Shepherd: Not so I could say, but give me a chance,   1240

my memory's bad . . .

Messenger: No wonder he doesn't know me, master.
But let me refresh his memory for him.
I'm sure he recalls old times we had
on the slopes of Mount Cithaeron;   1245
he and I, grazing our flocks, he with two
and I with one — we both struck up together,
three whole seasons, six months at a stretch
from spring to the rising of Arcturus° in the fall,
then with winter coming on I'd drive my herds   1250
to my own pens, and back he'd go with his
to Laius' folds.

To the Shepherd.

                              Now that's how it was,
wasn't it — yes or no?

Shepherd: Yes, I suppose . . .
it's all so long ago.

Messenger: Come, tell me,
you gave me a child back then, a boy, remember?   1255
A little fellow to rear, my very own.

Shepherd: What? Why rake up that again?

Messenger: Look, here he is, my fine old friend —
the same man who was just a baby then.

Shepherd: Damn you, shut your mouth — quiet!   1260

Oedipus: Don't lash out at him, old man —
you need lashing more than he does.

Shepherd: Why,
master, majesty — what have I done wrong?

Oedipus: You won't answer his question about the boy.

Shepherd: He's talking nonsense, wasting his breath.   1265

Oedipus: So, you won't talk willingly —
then you'll talk with pain.

The guards seize the Shepherd.

Shepherd: No, dear god, don't torture an old man!

Oedipus: Twist his arms back, quickly!

Shepherd: God help us, why? —
what more do you need to know?   1270

Oedipus: Did you give him that child? He's asking.

Shepherd: I did . . . I wish to god I'd died that day.

Oedipus: You've got your wish if you don't tell the truth.

Shepherd: The more I tell, the worse the death I'll die.

Oedipus: Our friend here wants to stretch things out, does he?   1275

Motioning to his men for torture.

Shepherd: No, no, I gave it to him — I just said so.

1249 *Arcturus:* A star whose rising marked the end of summer.

Oedipus: Where did you get it? Your house? Someone else's?
Shepherd: It wasn't mine, no, I got it from . . . someone.
Oedipus: Which one of them?

Looking at the citizens.

                            Whose house?
Shepherd: No —
    god's sake, master, no more questions!   1280
Oedipus: You're a dead man if I have to ask again.
Shepherd: Then — the child came from the house . . .
    of Laius.
Oedipus: A slave? or born of his own blood?
Shepherd: Oh no,
    I'm right at the edge, the horrible truth — I've got to say it!
Oedipus: And I'm at the edge of hearing horrors, yes, but I must hear!   1285
Shepherd: All right! His son, they said it was — his son!
    But the one inside, your wife,
    she'd tell it best.
Oedipus: My wife —
    she gave it to you?   1290
Shepherd: Yes, yes, my king.
Oedipus: Why, what for?
Shepherd: To kill it.
Oedipus: Her own child,
    how could she?   1295
Shepherd: She was afraid —
    frightening prophecies.
Oedipus: What?
Shepherd: They said —
    he'd kill his parents.
Oedipus: But you gave him to this old man — why?   1300
Shepherd: I pitied the little baby, master,
    hoped he'd take him off to his own country,
    far away, but he saved him for this, this fate.
    If you are the man he says you are, believe me,
    you were born for pain.
Oedipus: O god —   1305
    all come true, all burst to light!
    O light — now let me look my last on you!
    I stand revealed at last —
    cursed in my birth, cursed in marriage,
    cursed in the lives I cut down with these hands!   1310

Rushing through the doors with a great cry. The Corinthian Messenger, the Shepherd, and attendants exit slowly to the side.

Chorus: O the generations of men
    the dying generations — adding the total
    of all your lives I find they come to nothing . . .

does there exist, is there a man on earth
who seizes more joy than just a dream, a vision?   1315
And the vision no sooner dawns than dies
blazing into oblivion.

You are my great example, you, your life,
your destiny, Oedipus, man of misery —
I count no man blest.

              You outranged all men!   1320
        Bending your bow to the breaking-point
you captured priceless glory, O dear god,
and the Sphinx came crashing down,
            the virgin, claws hooked
like a bird of omen singing, shrieking death —   1325
like a fortress reared in the face of death
you rose and saved our land.

From that day on we called you king
we crowned you with honors, Oedipus, towering over all —
mighty king of the seven gates of Thebes.   1330

But now to hear your story — is there a man more agonized?
More wed to pain and frenzy? Not a man on earth,
the joy of your life ground down to nothing
O Oedipus, name for the ages —
        one and the same wide harbor served you   1335
                son and father both
son and father came to rest in the same bridal chamber.
How, how could the furrows your father plowed
bear you, your agony, harrowing on
in silence O so long?

             But now for all your power   1340
Time, all-seeing Time has dragged you to the light,
judged your marriage monstrous from the start —
the son and the father tangling, both one —
O child of Laius, would to god
        I'd never seen you, never never!   1345
        Now I weep like a man who wails the dead
and the dirge comes pouring forth with all my heart!
I tell you the truth, you gave me life
my breath leapt up in you
and now you bring down night upon my eyes.   1350

Enter a Messenger from the palace.

Messenger: Men of Thebes, always the first in honor,
what horrors you will hear, what you will see,
what a heavy weight of sorrow you will shoulder . . .
if you are true to your birth, if you still have
some feeling for the royal house of Thebes.   1355
I tell you neither the waters of the Danube

nor the Nile can wash this palace clean.
Such things it hides, it soon will bring to light —
terrible things, and none done blindly now,
all done with a will. The pains   1360
we inflict upon ourselves hurt most of all.
Leader: God knows we have pains enough already.
    What can you add to them?
Messenger: The queen is dead.
Leader: Poor lady — how?
Messenger: By her own hand. But you are spared the worst,   1365
    you never had to watch . . . I saw it all,
    and with all the memory that's in me
    you will learn what that poor woman suffered.

Once she'd broken in through the gates,
dashing past us, frantic, whipped to fury,   1370
ripping her hair out with both hands —
straight to her rooms she rushed, flinging herself
across the bridal-bed, doors slamming behind her —
once inside, she wailed for Laius, dead so long,
remembering how she bore his child long ago,   1375
the life that rose up to destroy him, leaving
its mother to mother living creatures
with the very son she'd borne.
Oh how she wept, mourning the marriage-bed
where she let loose that double brood — monsters —   1380
husband by her husband, children by her child.
                                            And then —
but how she died is more than I can say. Suddenly
Oedipus burst in, screaming, he stunned us so
we couldn't watch her agony to the end,
our eyes were fixed on him. Circling   1385
like a maddened beast, stalking, here, there
crying out to us —
                    Give him a sword! His wife,
no wife, his mother, where can he find the mother earth
that cropped two crops at once, himself and all his children?
He was raging — one of the dark powers pointing the way,   1390
none of us mortals crowding around him, no,
with a great shattering cry — someone, something leading him on —
he hurled at the twin doors and bending the bolts back
out of their sockets, crashed through the chamber.
And there we saw the woman hanging by the neck,   1395
cradled high in a woven noose, spinning,
swinging back and forth. And when he saw her,
giving a low, wrenching sob that broke our hearts,
slipping the halter from her throat, he eased her down,
in a slow embrace he laid her down, poor thing . . .   1400
then, what came next, what horror we beheld!

He rips off her brooches, the long gold pins
holding her robes — and lifting them high,
looking straight up into the points,
he digs them down the sockets of his eyes, crying, "You,   1405
you'll see no more the pain I suffered, all the pain I caused!
Too long you looked on the ones you never should have seen,
blind to the ones you longed to see, to know! Blind
from this hour on! Blind in the darkness — blind!"
His voice like a dirge, rising, over and over   1410
raising the pins, raking them down his eyes.
And at each stroke blood spurts from the roots,
splashing his beard, a swirl of it, nerves and clots —
black hail of blood pulsing, gushing down.

These are the griefs that burst upon them both,   1415
coupling man and woman. The joy they had so lately,
the fortune of their old ancestral house
was deep joy indeed. Now, in this one day,
wailing, madness and doom, death, disgrace,
all the griefs in the world that you can name,   1420
all are theirs forever.
Leader: Oh poor man, the misery —
has he any rest from pain now?

A voice within, in torment.

Messenger: He's shouting,
"Loose the bolts, someone, show me to all of Thebes!
My father's murderer, my mother's — "
No, I can't repeat it, it's unholy.   1425
Now he'll tear himself from his native earth,
not linger, curse the house with his own curse.
But he needs strength, and a guide to lead him on.
This is sickness more than he can bear.

The palace doors open.

                                 Look,
he'll show you himself. The great doors are opening —   1430
you are about to see a sight, a horror
even his mortal enemy would pity.

*Enter Oedipus, blinded, led by a boy. He stands at the palace steps, as if surveying
his people once again.*

Chorus: O the terror —
the suffering, for all the world to see,
the worst terror that ever met my eyes.
What madness swept over you? What god,   1435
what dark power leapt beyond all bounds,
beyond belief, to crush your wretched life? —
godforsaken, cursed by the gods!

I pity you but I can't bear to look.
I've much to ask, so much to learn,   1440
so much fascinates my eyes,
but you . . . I shudder at the sight.
Oedipus: Oh, Ohhh —
the agony! I am agony —
where am I going? where on earth?
where does all this agony hurl me?   1445
where's my voice? —
winging, swept away on a dark tide —
My destiny, my dark power, what a leap you made!
Chorus: To the depths of terror, too dark to hear, to see.
Oedipus: Dark, horror of darkness   1450
my darkness, drowning, swirling around me
crashing wave on wave — unspeakable, irresistible
headwind, fatal harbor! Oh again,
the misery, all at once, over and over
the stabbing daggers, stab of memory   1455
raking me insane.
Chorus: No wonder you suffer
twice over, the pain of your wounds,
the lasting grief of pain.
Oedipus: Dear friend, still here?
Standing by me, still with a care for me,
the blind man? Such compassion,   1460
loyal to the last. Oh it's you,
I know you're here, dark as it is
I'd know you anywhere, your voice —
it's yours, clearly yours.
Chorus: Dreadful, what you've done . . .
how could you bear it, gouging out your eyes?   1465
What superhuman power drove you on?
Oedipus: Apollo, friends, Apollo —
he ordained my agonies — these, my pains on pains!
But the hand that struck my eyes was mine,
mine alone — no one else —   1470
I did it all myself!
What good were eyes to me?
Nothing I could see could bring me joy.
Chorus: No, no, exactly as you say.
Oedipus: What can I ever see?
What love, what call of the heart   1475
can touch my ears with joy? Nothing, friends.
Take me away, far, far from Thebes,
quickly, cast me away, my friends —
this great murderous ruin, this man cursed to heaven,
the man the deathless gods hate most of all!   1480
Chorus: Pitiful, you suffer so, you understand so much . . .
I wish you'd never known.

Oedipus: Die, die —
    whoever he was that day in the wilds
    who cut my ankles free of the ruthless pins,
      he pulled me clear of death, he saved my life   1485
      for this, this kindness —
              Curse him, kill him!
    If I'd died then, I'd never have dragged myself,
    my loved ones through such hell.
Chorus: Oh if only . . . would to god.
Oedipus: I'd never have come to this,   1490
    my father's murderer — never been branded
  mother's husband, all men see me now! Now,
    loathed by the gods, son of the mother I defiled
    coupling in my father's bed, spawning lives in the loins
  that spawned my wretched life. What grief can crown this grief?   1495
    It's mine alone, my destiny — I am Oedipus!
Chorus: How can I say you've chosen for the best?
  Better to die than be alive and blind.
Oedipus: What I did was best — don't lecture me,
  no more advice. I, with *my* eyes,   1500
  how could I look my father in the eyes
  when I go down to death? Or mother, so abused . . .
  I've done such things to the two of them,
  crimes too huge for hanging.
             Worse yet,
  the sight of my children, born as they were born,   1505
  how could I long to look into their eyes?
  No, not with these eyes of mine, never.
  Not this city either, her high towers,
  the sacred glittering images of her gods —
  I am misery! I, her best son, reared   1510
  as no other son of Thebes was ever reared,
  I've stripped myself, I gave the command myself.
  All men must cast away the great blasphemer,
  the curse now brought to light by the gods,
  the son of Laius — I, my father's son!   1515

Now I've exposed my guilt, horrendous guilt,
could I train a level glance on you, my countrymen?
Impossible! No, if I could just block off my ears,
the springs of hearing, I would stop at nothing —
I'd wall up my loathsome body like a prison,   1520
blind to the sound of life, not just the sight.
Oblivion — what a blessing . . .
for the mind to dwell a world away from pain.

O Cithaeron, why did you give me shelter?
Why didn't you take me, crush my life out on the spot?   1525
I'd never have revealed my birth to all mankind.

O Polybus, Corinth, the old house of my fathers,

so I believed — what a handsome prince you raised —
under the skin, what sickness to the core.
Look at me! Born of outrage, outrage to the core.   1530

O triple roads — it all comes back, the secret,
dark ravine, and the oaks closing in
where the three roads join . . .
You drank my father's blood, my own blood
spilled by my own hands — you still remember me?   1535
What things you saw me do? Then I came here
and did them all once more!
                                    Marriages! O marriage,
you gave me birth, and once you brought me into the world
you brought my sperm rising back, springing to light
fathers, brothers, sons — one deadly breed —   1540
brides, wives, mothers. The blackest things
a man can do, I have done them all!

                                    No more —
it's wrong to name what's wrong to do. Quickly,
for the love of god, hide me somewhere,
kill me, hurl me into the sea   1545
where you can never look on me again.

Beckoning to the Chorus as they shrink away.

                                    Closer,
it's all right. Touch the man of sorrow.
Do. Don't be afraid. My troubles are mine
and I am the only man alive who can sustain them.

Enter Creon from the palace, attended by palace guards.

Leader: Put your requests to Creon. Here he is,   1550
    just when we need him. He'll have a plan, he'll act.
    Now that he's the sole defense of the country
    in your place.
Oedipus: Oh no, what can I say to him?
    How can I ever hope to win his trust?
    I wronged him so, just now, in every way.   1555
    You must see that — I was so wrong, so wrong.
Creon: I haven't come to mock you, Oedipus,
    or to criticize your former failings.

Turning to the guards.

                                    You there,
    have you lost all respect for human feeling?
    At least revere the Sun, the holy fire   1560
    that keeps us all alive. Never expose a thing
    of guilt and holy dread so great it appalls
    the earth, the rain from heaven, the light of day!
    Get him into the halls — quickly as you can.

Piety demands no less. Kindred alone   1565
    should see a kinsman's shame. This is obscene.
Oedipus: Please, in god's name . . . you wipe my fears away,
    coming so generously to me, the worst of men.
    Do one thing more, for your sake, not mine.
Creon: What do you want? Why so insistent?   1570
Oedipus: Drive me out of the land at once, far from sight,
    where I can never hear a human voice.
Creon: I'd have done that already, I promise you.
    First I wanted the god to clarify my duties.
Oedipus: The god? His command was clear, every word: 1575
    death for the father-killer, the curse —
    he said destroy me!
Creon: So he did. Still, in such a crisis
    it's better to ask precisely what to do.
Oedipus: You'd ask the oracle about a man like me?   1580
Creon: By all means. And this time, I assume,
    even you will obey the god's decrees.
Oedipus: I will,
    I will. And you, I command you — I beg you . . .
    the woman inside, bury her as you see fit.
    It's the only decent thing,   1585
    to give your own the last rites. As for me,
    never condemn the city of my fathers
    to house my body, not while I'm alive, no,
    let me live on the mountains, on Cithaeron,
    my favorite haunt, I have made it famous.   1590
    Mother and father marked out that rock
    to be my everlasting tomb — buried alive.
    Let me die there, where they tried to kill me.
    Oh but this I know: no sickness can destroy me,
    nothing can. I would never have been saved   1595
    from death — I have been saved
    for something great and terrible, something strange.
    Well let my destiny come and take me on its way!

    About my children, Creon, the boys at least,
    don't burden yourself. They're men;   1600
    wherever they go, they'll find the means to live.
    But my two daughters, my poor helpless girls,
    clustering at our table, never without me
    hovering near them . . . whatever I touched,
    they always had their share. Take care of them,   1605
    I beg you. Wait, better — permit me, would you?
    Just to touch them with my hands and take
    our fill of tears. Please . . . my king.
    Grant it, with all your noble heart.
    If I could hold them, just once, I'd think   1610

I had them with me, like the early days
when I could see their eyes.

Antigone and Ismene, two small children, are led in from the palace by a nurse.

What's that?
O god! Do I really hear you sobbing? —
my two children. Creon, you've pitied me?
Sent me my darling girls, my own flesh and blood!   1615
Am I right?

Creon: Yes, it's my doing.
I know the joy they gave you all these years,
the joy you must feel now.

Oedipus: Bless you, Creon!
May god watch over you for this kindness,
better than he ever guarded me.

                    Children, where are you?   1620
Here, come quickly —

Groping for Antigone and Ismene, who approach their father cautiously, then embrace him.

                    Come to these hands of mine,
your brother's hands, your own father's hands
that served his once bright eyes so well —
that made them blind. Seeing nothing, children,
knowing nothing, I became your father,   1625
I fathered you in the soil that gave me life.

How I weep for you — I cannot see you now . . .
just thinking of all your days to come, the bitterness,
the life that rough mankind will thrust upon you.
Where are the public gatherings you can join,   1630
the banquets of the clans? Home you'll come,
in tears, cut off from the sight of it all,
the brilliant rites unfinished.
And when you reach perfection, ripe for marriage,
who will he be, my dear ones? Risking all   1635
to shoulder the curse that weighs down my parents,
yes and you too — that wounds us all together.
What more misery could you want?
Your father killed his father, sowed his mother,
one, one and the selfsame womb sprang you —   1640
he cropped the very roots of his existence.

Such disgrace, and you must bear it all!
Who will marry you then? Not a man on earth.
Your doom is clear: you'll wither away to nothing,
single, without a child.

Turning to Creon.

                    Oh Creon,   1645
you are the only father they have now . . .

we who brought them into the world
are gone, both gone at a stroke —
Don't let them go begging, abandoned,
women without men. Your own flesh and blood!   1650
Never bring them down to the level of my pains.
Pity them. Look at them, so young, so vulnerable,
shorn of everything — you're their only hope.
Promise me, noble Creon, touch my hand.

Reaching toward Creon, who draws back.

You, little ones, if you were old enough   1655
to understand, there is much I'd tell you.
Now, as it is, I'd have you say a prayer.
Pray for life, my children,
live where you are free to grow and season.
Pray god you find a better life than mine,   1660
the father who begot you.
Creon: Enough.
You've wept enough. Into the palace now.
Oedipus: I must, but I find it very hard.
Creon: Time is the great healer, you will see.
Oedipus: I am going — you know on what condition?   1665
Creon: Tell me. I'm listening.
Oedipus: Drive me out of Thebes, in exile.
Creon: Not I. Only the gods can give you that.
Oedipus: Surely the gods hate me so much —
Creon: You'll get your wish at once.
Oedipus: You consent?   1670
Creon: I try to say what I mean; it's my habit.
Oedipus: Then take me away. It's time.
Creon: Come along, let go of the children.
Oedipus: No —
don't take them away from me, not now! No no no!

*Clutching his daughters as the guards wrench them loose and take them through
the palace doors.*

Creon: Still the king, the master of all things?   1675
No more: here your power ends.
None of your power follows you through life.

*Exit Oedipus and Creon to the palace. The Chorus comes forward to address the
audience directly.*

Chorus: People of Thebes, my countrymen, look on Oedipus.
He solved the famous riddle with his brilliance,
he rose to power, a man beyond all power.   1680
Who could behold his greatness without envy?
Now what a black sea of terror has overwhelmed him.

Now as we keep our watch and wait the final day,
count no man happy till he dies, free of pain at last.

Exit in procession.

Considerations for Critical Thinking and Writing

1. In the opening scene what does the priest's speech reveal about how Oedipus has been regarded as a ruler of Thebes?
2. What do Oedipus's confrontations with Tiresias and Creon indicate about his character?
3. Aristotle defined a tragic flaw as consisting of "error and frailties." What errors does Oedipus make? What are his frailties?
4. What causes Oedipus's downfall? Is he simply a pawn in a predetermined game played by the gods? Can he be regarded as responsible for the suffering and death in the play?
5. Locate instances of dramatic irony in the play. How do they serve as foreshadowings?
6. Describe the function of the Chorus. How does the Chorus's view of life and the gods differ from Jocasta's?
7. Trace the images of vision and blindness throughout the play. How are they related to the theme? Why does Oedipus blind himself instead of joining Jocasta in suicide?
8. "What goes on four feet in the morning, two at noon, and three in the evening?" This was the riddle posed by the Sphinx. Oedipus answered the question correctly: "Man," because babies crawl, adults walk erect, and in old age people use canes. How is this riddle related to the other questions Oedipus seeks to answer?
9. What is your assessment of Oedipus at the end of the play? Was he foolish? heroic? fated? To what extent can your emotions concerning him be described as "pity and fear"?
10. Is it possible for a twentieth-century reader to identify with Oedipus's plight? What philosophic issues does he confront?
11. *Oedipus complex* is a well-known term used in psychoanalysis. What does it mean? Does the concept offer any insights into the conflicts dramatized in the play?

Connections to Other Selections

1. Consider the endings of *Oedipus the King* and Shakespeare's *Hamlet* (p. 1281). What feelings do you have about these endings? Are they irredeemably unhappy? Is there anything that suggests hope for the future at the ends of these plays?
2. Sophocles does not include violence in his plays; any bloodshed occurs offstage. Compare and contrast the effects of this strategy with the use of violence in either *Hamlet* (p. 1281) or *The Tempest* (p. 1381).
3. Write an essay explaining why *Oedipus the King* cannot be considered a realistic play in the way that Henrik Ibsen's *A Doll House* (p. 1517) can be.

ANTIGONE

Antigone was actually written before Sophocles' other two plays about Oedipus and his family. *Oedipus the King* ends with Oedipus, the king of Thebes, blinding himself because he has unknowingly murdered his father and married his mother, Jocasta. Creon, his brother-in-law, becomes the ruler of Thebes and is entrusted with caring for Oedipus's two daughters, Antigone and Ismene. *Oedipus at Colonus* continues the story some twenty years later. Oedipus has been rejected by his two sons, Polynices and Eteocles, and wanders in exile, cared for by Antigone. Meanwhile, his sons struggle for power in Thebes. Polynices travels to Argos to gather a force to attack his brother as Oedipus arrives in Colonus, near Athens. There Oedipus curses his sons for their ruthless selfishness and predicts their violent deaths. Oedipus, however, dies in peace, with dignity, and bestows a blessing on Athens.

Antigone begins after the two brothers have killed each other in battle. The throne of Thebes subsequently returns to Creon, who decrees that Polynices was traitorous and therefore must not be buried. As the play opens, Antigone tells her sister that she will defy Creon's ruling, even though the penalty for disobedience is death.

Antigone's insistence on obeying the law of the gods instead of civil laws dramatizes a conflict that continues to move audiences and readers who ponder the relation of the individual's conscience to the demands of the state. One manifestation of this concern in the twentieth century is Jean Anouilh's 1944 production of *Antigone* in Paris, when that city was occupied by German troops during World War II. Anouilh's Antigone reflects the French resistance movement, and his Creon is a representative of German authority who must preserve order in the face of unyielding opposition. (A brief excerpt of this play appears on p. 1207.) Sophocles' play — as does Anouilh's — presents an agonizing dilemma. Neither Antigone nor Creon is wholly virtuous or blameless, so the complexities they embody remain a moral and intellectual challenge.

SOPHOCLES (496?–406 B.C.)

Antigone   c. 441 B.C.

TRANSLATED BY ROBERT FAGLES

Characters

Antigone, daughter of Oedipus and Jocasta
Ismene, sister of Antigone
A *Chorus* of old Theban citizens and their *Leader*
Creon, king of Thebes, uncle of Antigone and Ismene
A *Sentry*
Haemon, son of Creon and Eurydice
Tiresias, a blind prophet
A *Messenger*
Eurydice, wife of Creon
Guards, attendants, and a boy

TIME AND SCENE. *The royal house of Thebes. It is still night, and the invading armies of Argos have just been driven from the city. Fighting on opposite sides, the sons of Oedipus, Eteocles and Polynices, have killed each other in combat. Their uncle, Creon, is now king of Thebes.*

Enter Antigone, slipping through the central doors of the palace. She motions to her sister, Ismene, who follows her cautiously toward an altar at the center of the stage.

Antigone: My own flesh and blood — dear sister, dear Ismene,
 how many griefs our father Oedipus handed down!
 Do you know one, I ask you, one grief
 that Zeus° will not perfect for the two of us
 while we still live and breathe? There's nothing,   5
 no pain — our lives are pain — no private shame,
 no public disgrace, nothing I haven't seen
 in your griefs and mine. And now this:
 an emergency decree, they say, the Commander
 has just declared for all of Thebes.   10
 What, haven't you heard? Don't you see?
 The doom reserved for enemies
 marches on the ones we love the most.
Ismene: Not I, I haven't heard a word, Antigone.
 Nothing of loved ones,   15
 no joy or pain has come my way, not since
 the two of us were robbed of our two brothers,
 both gone in a day, a double blow —
 not since the armies of Argos vanished,
 just this very night. I know nothing more,   20
 whether our luck's improved or ruin's still to come.
Antigone: I thought so. That's why I brought you out here,
 past the gates, so you could hear in private.
Ismene: What's the matter? Trouble, clearly . . .
 you sound so dark, so grim.   25
Antigone: Why not? Our own brothers' burial!
 Hasn't Creon graced one with all the rites,
 disgraced the other? Eteocles, they say,
 has been given full military honors,
 rightly so — Creon's laid him in the earth   30
 and he goes with glory down among the dead.
 But the body of Polynices, who died miserably —
 why, a city-wide proclamation, rumor has it,
 forbids anyone to bury him, even mourn him.
 He's to be left unwept, unburied, a lovely treasure   35
 for birds that scan the field and feast to their heart's content.

 Such, I hear, is the martial law our good Creon
 lays down for you and me — yes, me, I tell you —

_____

4 *Zeus:* The highest Olympian deity.

and he's coming here to alert the uninformed
in no uncertain terms,   40
and he won't treat the matter lightly. Whoever
disobeys in the least will die, his doom is sealed:
stoning to death inside the city walls!

There you have it. You'll soon show what you are,
worth your breeding, Ismene, or a coward —   45
for all your royal blood.
Ismene: My poor sister, if things have come to this,
who am I to make or mend them, tell me,
what good am I to you?
Antigone: Decide.
Will you share the labor, share the work?   50
Ismene: What work, what's the risk? What do you mean?
Antigone:

Raising her hands.

Will you lift up his body with these bare hands
and lower it with me?
Ismene: What? You'd bury him —
when a law forbids the city?
Antigone: Yes!
He is my brother and — deny it as you will —   55
your brother too.
No one will ever convict me for a traitor.
Ismene: So desperate, and Creon has expressly —
Antigone: No,
he has no right to keep me from my own.
Ismene: Oh my sister, think —   60
think how our own father died, hated,
his reputation in ruins, driven on
by the crimes he brought to light himself
to gouge out his eyes with his own hands —
then mother . . . his mother and wife, both in one,   65
mutilating her life in the twisted noose —
and last, our two brothers dead in a single day,
both shedding their own blood, poor suffering boys,
battling out their common destiny hand-to-hand.

Now look at the two of us, left so alone . . .   70
think what a death we'll die, the worst of all
if we violate the laws and override
the fixed decree of the throne, its power —
we must be sensible. Remember we are women,
we're not born to contend with men. Then too,   75
we're underlings, ruled by much stronger hands,
so we must submit in this, and things still worse.

I, for one, I'll beg the dead to forgive me —

I'm forced, I have no choice — I must obey
the ones who stand in power. Why rush to extremes?   80
    It's madness, madness.
Antigone: I won't insist,
    no, even if you should have a change of heart,
    I'd never welcome you in the labor, not with me.
    So, do as you like, whatever suits you best —
    I'll bury him myself.   85
    And even if I die in the act, that death will be a glory.
    I'll lie with the one I love and loved by him —
    an outrage sacred to the gods! I have longer
    to please the dead than please the living here:
    in the kingdom down below I'll lie forever.   90
    Do as you like, dishonor the laws
    the gods hold in honor.
Ismene: I'd do them no dishonor . . .
    but defy the city? I have no strength for that.
Antigone: You have your excuses. I am on my way,
    I'll raise a mound for him, for my dear brother.   95
Ismene: Oh Antigone, you're so rash — I'm so afraid for you!
Antigone: Don't fear for me. Set your own life in order.
Ismene: Then don't, at least, blurt this out to anyone.
    Keep it a secret. I'll join you in that, I promise.
Antigone: Dear god, shout it from the rooftops. I'll hate you   100
    all the more for silence — tell the world!
Ismene: So fiery — and it ought to chill your heart.
Antigone: I know I please where I must please the most.
Ismene: Yes, if you can, but you're in love with impossibility.
Antigone: Very well then, once my strength gives out   105
    I will be done at last.
Ismene: You're wrong from the start,
    you're off on a hopeless quest.
Antigone: If you say so, you will make me hate you,
    and the hatred of the dead, by all rights,
    will haunt you night and day.   110
    But leave me to my own absurdity, leave me
    to suffer this — dreadful thing. I'll suffer
    nothing as great as death without glory.

Exit to the side.

Ismene: Then go if you must, but rest assured,
    wild, irrational as you are, my sister,   115
    you are truly dear to the ones who love you.

*Withdrawing to the palace. Enter a Chorus, the old citizens of Thebes, chanting
as the sun begins to rise.*

Chorus: Glory! — great beam of sun, brightest of all

that ever rose on the seven gates of Thebes,
        you burn through night at last!
                Great eye of the golden day,   120
mounting the Dirce's° banks you throw him back —
the enemy out of Argos, the white shield, the man of bronze —
he's flying headlong now
        the bridle of fate stampeding him with pain!

        And he had driven against our borders,   125
        launched by the warring claims of Polynices —
        like an eagle screaming, winging havoc
        over the land, wings of armor
        shielded white as snow,
        a huge army massing,   130
        crested helmets bristling for assault.

He hovered above our roofs, his vast maw gaping
closing down around our seven gates,
        his spears thirsting for the kill
                        but now he's gone, look,   135
before he could glut his jaws with Theban blood
or the god of fire put our crown of towers to the torch.
He grappled the Dragon none can master — Thebes —
        the clang of our arms like thunder at his back!

        Zeus hates with a vengeance all bravado,   140
        the mighty boasts of men. He watched them
        coming on in a rising flood, the pride
        of their golden armor ringing shrill —
        and brandishing his lightning
        blasted the fighter just at the goal,   145
        rushing to shout his triumph from our walls.

Down from the heights he crashed, pounding down on the earth!
And a moment ago, blazing torch in hand —
        mad for attack, ecstatic
he breathed his rage, the storm   150
        of his fury hurling at our heads!
But now his high hopes have laid him low
and down the enemy ranks the iron god of war
        deals his rewards, his stunning blows — Ares°
        rapture of battle, our right arm in the crisis.   155

        Seven captains marshaled at seven gates
        seven against their equals, gave
        their brazen trophies up to Zeus,
        god of the breaking rout of battle,
        all but two: those blood brothers,   160

---

121 *the Dirce:* A river near Thebes.   154 *Ares:* God of war.

one father, one mother — matched in rage,
spears matched for the twin conquest —
clashed and won the common prize of death.

But now for Victory! Glorious in the morning,
joy in her eyes to meet our joy   165
     she is winging down to Thebes,
our fleets of chariots wheeling in her wake —
    Now let us win oblivion from the wars,
thronging the temples of the gods
in singing, dancing choirs through the night!   170
    Lord Dionysus,° god of the dance
    that shakes the land of Thebes, now lead the way!

Enter Creon from the palace, attended by his guard.

    But look, the king of the realm is coming,
    Creon, the new man for the new day,
    whatever the gods are sending now . . .   175
    what new plan will he launch?
    Why this, this special session?
    Why this sudden call to the old men
    summoned at one command?

Creon: My countrymen,
the ship of state is safe. The gods who rocked her,   180
after a long, merciless pounding in the storm,
have righted her once more.
                 Out of the whole city
I have called you here alone. Well I know,
first, your undeviating respect
for the throne and royal power of King Laius.   185
Next, while Oedipus steered the land of Thebes,
and even after he died, your loyalty was unshakable,
you still stood by their children. Now then,
since the two sons are dead — two blows of fate
in the same day, cut down by each other's hands,   190
both killers, both brothers stained with blood —
as I am next in kin to the dead,
I now possess the throne and all its powers.

Of course you cannot know a man completely,
his character, his principles, sense of judgment,   195
not till he's shown his colors, ruling the people,
making laws. Experience, there's the test.
As I see it, whoever assumes the task,
the awesome task of setting the city's course,
and refuses to adopt the soundest policies   200
but fearing someone, keeps his lips locked tight,
he's utterly worthless. So I rate him now,

---

171 Dionysus: God of fertility and wine.

I always have. And whoever places a friend
above the good of his own country, he is nothing:
I have no use for him. Zeus my witness,   205
Zeus who sees all things, always —
I could never stand by silent, watching destruction
march against our city, putting safety to rout,
nor could I ever make that man a friend of mine
who menaces our country. Remember this: 210
our country *is* our safety.
Only while she voyages true on course
can we establish friendships, truer than blood itself.
Such are my standards. They make our city great.

Closely akin to them I have proclaimed,   215
just now, the following decree to our people
concerning the two sons of Oedipus.
Eteocles, who died fighting for Thebes,
excelling all in arms: he shall be buried,
crowned with a hero's honors, the cups we pour   220
to soak the earth and reach the famous dead.

But as for his blood brother, Polynices,
who returned from exile, home to his father-city
and the gods of his race, consumed with one desire —
to burn them roof to roots — who thirsted to drink   225
his kinsmen's blood and sell the rest to slavery:
that man — a proclamation has forbidden the city
to dignify him with burial, mourn him at all.
No, he must be left unburied, his corpse
carrion for the birds and dogs to tear,   230
an obscenity for the citizens to behold!

These are my principles. Never at my hands
will the traitor be honored above the patriot.
But whoever proves his loyalty to the state:
I'll prize that man in death as well as life.   235
Leader: If this is your pleasure, Creon, treating
our city's enemy and our friend this way . . .
The power is yours, I suppose, to enforce it
with the laws, both for the dead and all of us,
the living.
Creon: Follow my orders closely then,   240
be on your guard.
Leader: We're too old.
Lay that burden on younger shoulders.
Creon: No, no,
I don't mean the body — I've posted guards already.
Leader: What commands for us then? What other service?
Creon: See that you never side with those who break my orders.   245

Leader: Never. Only a fool could be in love with death.
Creon: Death is the price — you're right. But all too often
   the mere hope of money has ruined many men.

A Sentry enters from the side.

Sentry: My lord,
   I can't say I'm winded from running, or set out
   with any spring in my legs either — no sir,   250
   I was lost in thought, and it made me stop, often,
   dead in my tracks, wheeling, turning back,
   and all the time a voice inside me muttering,
   "Idiot, why? You're going straight to your death."
   Then muttering, "Stopped again, poor fool?   255
   If somebody gets the news to Creon first,
   what's to save your neck?"
                          And so,
   mulling it over, on I trudged, dragging my feet,
   you can make a short road take forever . . .
   but at last, look, common sense won out,   260
   I'm here, and I'm all yours,
   and even though I come empty-handed
   I'll tell my story just the same, because
   I've come with a good grip on one hope,
   what will come will come, whatever fate —   265
Creon: Come to the point!
   What's wrong — why so afraid?
Sentry: First, myself, I've got to tell you,
   I didn't do it, didn't see who did —
   Be fair, don't take it out on me.   270
Creon: You're playing it safe, soldier,
   barricading yourself from any trouble.
   It's obvious, you've something strange to tell.
Sentry: Dangerous too, and danger makes you delay
   for all you're worth.   275
Creon: Out with it — then dismiss!
Sentry: All right, here it comes. The body —
   someone's just buried it, then run off . . .
   sprinkled some dry dust on the flesh,
   given it proper rites.
Creon: What?   280
   What man alive would dare —
Sentry: I've no idea, I swear it.
   There was no mark of a spade, no pickaxe there,
   no earth turned up, the ground packed hard and dry,
   unbroken, no tracks, no wheelruts, nothing,
   the workman left no trace. Just at sunup   285
   the first watch of the day points it out —
   it was a wonder! We were stunned . . .

a terrific burden too, for all of us, listen:
you can't see the corpse, not that it's buried,
really, just a light cover of road-dust on it,   290
as if someone meant to lay the dead to rest
and keep from getting cursed.
Not a sign in sight that dogs or wild beasts
had worried the body, even torn the skin.

But what came next! Rough talk flew thick and fast,   295
guard grilling guard—we'd have come to blows
at last, nothing to stop it; each man for himself
and each the culprit, no one caught red-handed,
all of us pleading ignorance, dodging the charges,
ready to take up red-hot iron in our fists,   300
go through fire, swear oaths to the gods —
"I didn't do it, I had no hand in it either,
not in the plotting, not in the work itself!"

Finally, after all this wrangling came to nothing,
one man spoke out and made us stare at the ground,   305
hanging our heads in fear. No way to counter him,
no way to take his advice and come through
safe and sound. Here's what he said:
"Look, we've got to report the facts to Creon,
we can't keep this hidden." Well, that won out,   310
and the lot fell on me, condemned me,
unlucky as ever, I got the prize. So here I am,
against my will and yours too, well I know —
no one wants the man who brings bad news.

Leader: My king,
ever since he began I've been debating in my mind,   315
could this possibly be the work of the gods?
Creon: Stop —
before you make me choke with anger—the gods!
You, you're senile, must you be insane?
You say—why it's intolerable—say the gods
could have the slightest concern for that corpse?   320
Tell me, was it for meritorious service
they proceeded to bury him, prized him so? The hero
who came to burn their temples ringed with pillars,
their golden treasures—scorch their hallowed earth
and fling their laws to the winds.   325
Exactly when did you last see the gods
celebrating traitors? Inconceivable!

No, from the first there were certain citizens
who could hardly stand the spirit of my regime,
grumbling against me in the dark, heads together,   330
tossing wildly, never keeping their necks beneath
the yoke, loyally submitting to their king.
These are the instigators, I'm convinced —

they've perverted my own guard, bribed them
to do their work.
Money! Nothing worse   335
in our lives, so current, rampant, so corrupting.
Money — you demolish cities, root men from their homes,
you train and twist good minds and set them on
to the most atrocious schemes. No limit,
you make them adept at every kind of outrage,   340
every godless crime — money!
Everyone —
the whole crew bribed to commit this crime,
they've made one thing sure at least:
sooner or later they will pay the price.

Wheeling on the Sentry.

You —
I swear to Zeus as I still believe in Zeus,   345
if you don't find the man who buried that corpse,
the very man, and produce him before my eyes,
simple death won't be enough for you,
not till we string you up alive
and wring the immorality out of you.   350
Then you can steal the rest of your days,
better informed about where to make a killing.
You'll have learned, at last, it doesn't pay
to itch for rewards from every hand that beckons.
Filthy profits wreck most men, you'll see —   355
they'll never save your life.
Sentry: Please,
may I say a word or two, or just turn and go?
Creon: Can't you tell? Everything you say offends me.
Sentry: Where does it hurt you, in the ears or in the heart?
Creon: And who are you to pinpoint my displeasure?   360
Sentry: The culprit grates on your feelings,
I just annoy your ears.
Creon: Still talking?
You talk too much! A born nuisance —
Sentry: Maybe so,
but I never did this thing, so help me!
Creon: Yes you did —
what's more, you squandered your life for silver!   365
Sentry: Oh it's terrible when the one who does the judging
judges things all wrong.
Creon: Well now,
you just be clever about your judgments —
if you fail to produce the criminals for me,
you'll swear your dirty money brought you pain.   370

Turning sharply, reentering the palace.

Sophocles / Antigone 1173

Sentry: I hope he's found. Best thing by far.
    But caught or not, that's in the lap of fortune;
    I'll never come back, you've seen the last of me.
    I'm saved, even now, and I never thought,
    I never hoped —   375
    dear gods, I owe you all my thanks!

Rushing out.

Chorus: Numberless wonders
    terrible wonders walk the world but none the match for man —
    that great wonder crossing the heaving gray sea,
                driven on by the blasts of winter
    on through breakers crashing left and right,   380
        holds his steady course
    and the oldest of the gods he wears away —
    the Earth, the immortal, the inexhaustible —
    as his plows go back and forth, year in, year out
        with the breed of stallions turning up the furrows.   385

    And the blithe, lightheaded race of birds he snares,
    the tribes of savage beasts, the life that swarms the depths —
                with one fling of his nets
    woven and coiled tight, he takes them all,
        man the skilled, the brilliant!   390
    He conquers all, taming with his techniques
    the prey that roams the cliffs and wild lairs,
    training the stallion, clamping the yoke across
        his shaggy neck, and the tireless mountain bull.

    And speech and thought, quick as the wind   395
    and the mood and mind for law that rules the city —
        all these he has taught himself
    and shelter from the arrows of the frost
    when there's rough lodging under the cold clear sky
    and the shafts of lashing rain —   400
        ready, resourceful man!
                Never without resources
    never an impasse as he marches on the future —
    only Death, from Death alone he will find no rescue
    but from desperate plagues he has plotted his escapes.   405

    Man the master, ingenious past all measure
    past all dreams, the skills within his grasp —
        he forges on, now to destruction
    now again to greatness. When he weaves in
    the laws of the land, and the justice of the gods   410
    that binds his oaths together
        he and his city rise high —
            but the city casts out

that man who weds himself to inhumanity
thanks to reckless daring. Never share my hearth   415
never think my thoughts, whoever does such things.

Enter Antigone from the side, accompanied by the Sentry.

Here is a dark sign from the gods —
what to make of this? I know her,
how can I deny it? That young girl's Antigone!
Wretched, child of a wretched father,   420
Oedipus. Look, is it possible?
They bring you in like a prisoner —
why? did you break the king's laws?
Did they take you in some act of mad defiance?
Sentry: She's the one, she did it single-handed —   425
we caught her burying the body. Where's Creon?

Enter Creon from the palace.

Leader: Back again, just in time when you need him.
Creon: In time for what? What is it?
Sentry: My king,
there's nothing you can swear you'll never do —
second thoughts make liars of us all.   430
I could have sworn I wouldn't hurry back
(what with your threats, the buffeting I just took),
but a stroke of luck beyond our wildest hopes,
what a joy, there's nothing like it. So,
back I've come, breaking my oath, who cares?   435
I'm bringing in our prisoner — this young girl —
we took her giving the dead the last rites.
But no casting lots this time; this is *my* luck,
my prize, no one else's.
                        Now, my lord,
here she is. Take her, question her,   440
cross-examine her to your heart's content.
But set me free, it's only right —
I'm rid of this dreadful business once for all.
Creon: Prisoner! Her? You took her — where, doing what?
Sentry: Burying the man. That's the whole story.
Creon: What?   445
You mean what you say, you're telling me the truth?
Sentry: She's the one. With my own eyes I saw her
bury the body, just what you've forbidden.
There. Is that plain and clear?
Creon: What did you see? Did you catch her in the act?   450
Sentry: Here's what happened. We went back to our post,
those threats of yours breathing down our necks —
we brushed the corpse clean of the dust that covered it,

stripped it bare . . . it was slimy, going soft,
and we took to high ground, backs to the wind   455
so the stink of him couldn't hit us;
jostling, baiting each other to keep awake,
shouting back and forth — no napping on the job,
not this time. And so the hours dragged by
until the sun stood dead above our heads,   460
a huge white ball in the noon sky, beating,
blazing down, and then it happened —
suddenly, a whirlwind!
Twisting a great dust-storm up from the earth,
a black plague of the heavens, filling the plain,   465
ripping the leaves off every tree in sight,
choking the air and sky. We squinted hard
and took our whipping from the gods.

And after the storm passed — it seemed endless —
there, we saw the girl!   470
And she cried out a sharp, piercing cry,
like a bird come back to an empty nest,
peering into its bed, and all the babies gone . . .
Just so, when she sees the corpse bare
she bursts into a long, shattering wail   475
and calls down withering curses on the heads
of all who did the work. And she scoops up dry dust,
handfuls, quickly, and lifting a fine bronze urn,
lifting it high and pouring, she crowns the dead
with three full libations.

                      Soon as we saw   480
we rushed her, closed on the kill like hunters,
and she, she didn't flinch. We interrogated her,
charging her with offenses past and present —
she stood up to it all, denied nothing. I tell you,
it made me ache and laugh in the same breath.   485
It's pure joy to escape the worst yourself,
it hurts a man to bring down his friends.
But all that, I'm afraid, means less to me
than my own skin. That's the way I'm made.
Creon:

Wheeling on Antigone.

                                You,
with your eyes fixed on the ground — speak up.   490
Do you deny you did this, yes or no?
Antigone: I did it. I don't deny a thing.
Creon:

To the sentry.

You, get out, wherever you please —
you're clear of a very heavy charge.

He leaves; Creon turns back to Antigone.

You, tell me briefly, no long speeches — 495
were you aware a decree had forbidden this?
Antigone: Well aware. How could I avoid it? It was public.
Creon: And still you had the gall to break this law?
Antigone: Of course I did. It wasn't Zeus, not in the least,
who made this proclamation — not to me. 500
Nor did that Justice, dwelling with the gods
beneath the earth, ordain such laws for men.
Nor did I think your edict had such force
that you, a mere mortal, could override the gods,
the great unwritten, unshakable traditions. 505
They are alive, not just today or yesterday:
they live forever, from the first of time,
and no one knows when they first saw the light.

These laws — I was not about to break them,
not out of fear of some man's wounded pride, 510
and face the retribution of the gods.
Die I must, I've known it all my life —
how could I keep from knowing? — even without
your death-sentence ringing in my ears.
And if I am to die before my time 515
I consider that a gain. Who on earth,
alive in the midst of so much grief as I,
could fail to find his death a rich reward?
So for me, at least, to meet this doom of yours
is precious little pain. But if I had allowed 520
my own mother's son to rot, an unburied corpse —
that would have been an agony! This is nothing.
And if my present actions strike you as foolish,
let's just say I've been accused of folly
by a fool.
Leader: Like father like daughter, 525
passionate, wild . . .
she hasn't learned to bend before adversity.
Creon: No? Believe me, the stiffest stubborn wills
fall the hardest; the toughest iron,
tempered strong in the white-hot fire, 530
you'll see it crack and shatter first of all.
And I've known spirited horses you can break
with a light bit — proud, rebellious horses.
There's no room for pride, not in a slave,
not with the lord and master standing by. 535

This girl was an old hand at insolence
when she overrode the edicts we made public.

But once she'd done it — the insolence,
twice over — to glory in it, laughing,
mocking us to our face with what she'd done. 540
I'm not the man, not now: she is the man
if this victory goes to her and she goes free.

Never! Sister's child or closer in blood
than all my family clustered at my altar
worshiping Guardian Zeus — she'll never escape, 545
she and her blood sister, the most barbaric death.
Yes, I accuse her sister of an equal part
in scheming this, this burial.

To his attendants.

                                        Bring her here!
I just saw her inside, hysterical, gone to pieces.
It never fails: the mind convicts itself 550
in advance, when scoundrels are up to no good,
plotting in the dark. Oh but I hate it more
when a traitor, caught red-handed,
tries to glorify his crimes.
Antigone: Creon, what more do you want 555
    than my arrest and execution?
Creon: Nothing. Then I have it all.
Antigone: Then why delay? Your moralizing repels me,
    every word you say — pray god it always will.
    So naturally all I say repels you too.
                                        Enough. 560
Give me glory! What greater glory could I win
than to give my own brother decent burial?
These citizens here would all agree,

To the Chorus.

    they'd praise me too
    if their lips weren't locked in fear. 565

Pointing to Creon.

    Lucky tyrants — the perquisites of power!
    Ruthless power to do and say whatever pleases *them.*
Creon: You alone, of all the people in Thebes,
    see things that way.
Antigone: They see it just that way
    but defer to you and keep their tongues in leash. 570
Creon: And you, aren't you ashamed to differ so from them?
    So disloyal!
Antigone: Not ashamed for a moment,
    not to honor my brother, my own flesh and blood.
Creon: Wasn't Eteocles a brother too — cut down, facing him?
Antigone: Brother, yes, by the same mother, the same father. 575

Creon: Then how can you render his enemy such honors,
   such impieties in his eyes?
Antigone: He'll never testify to that,
   Eteocles dead and buried.
Creon: He will —
   if you honor the traitor just as much as him.   580
Antigone: But it was his brother, not some slave that died —
Creon: Ravaging our country! —
   but Eteocles died fighting in our behalf.
Antigone: No matter — Death longs for the same rites for all.
Creon: Never the same for the patriot and the traitor.   585
Antigone: Who, Creon, who on earth can say the ones below
   don't find this pure and uncorrupt?
Creon: Never. Once an enemy, never a friend,
   not even after death.
Antigone: I was born to join in love, not hate —   590
   that is my nature.
Creon: Go down below and love,
   if love you must — love the dead! While I'm alive,
   no woman is going to lord it over me.

Enter Ismene from the palace, under guard.

Chorus: Look,
   Ismene's coming, weeping a sister's tears,
   loving sister, under a cloud . . .   595
   her face is flushed, her cheeks streaming.
   Sorrow puts her lovely radiance in the dark.
Creon: You —
   in my house, you viper, slinking undetected,
   sucking my life-blood! I never knew
   I was breeding twin disasters, the two of you   600
   rising up against my throne. Come, tell me,
   will you confess your part in the crime or not?
   Answer me. Swear to me.
Ismene: I did it, yes —
   if only she consents — I share the guilt,
   the consequences too.
Antigone: No,   605
   Justice will never suffer that — not you,
   you were unwilling. I never brought you in.
Ismene: But now you face such dangers . . . I'm not ashamed
   to sail through trouble with you,
   make your troubles mine.
Antigone: Who did the work?   610
   Let the dead and the god of death bear witness!
   I've no love for a friend who loves in words alone.
Ismene: Oh no, my sister, don't reject me, please,
   let me die beside you, consecrating
   the dead together.

Antigone: Never share my dying,   615
    don't lay claim to what you never touched.
    My death will be enough.
Ismene: What do I care for life, cut off from you?
Antigone: Ask Creon. Your concern is all for him.
Ismene: Why abuse me so? It doesn't help you now.
Antigone: You're right —   620
    if I mock you, I get no pleasure from it,
    only pain.
Ismene: Tell me, dear one,
    what can I do to help you, even now?
Antigone: Save yourself. I don't grudge you your survival.
Ismene: Oh no, no, denied my portion in your death?   625
Antigone: You chose to live, I chose to die.
Ismene: Not, at least,
    without every kind of caution I could voice.
Antigone: Your wisdom appealed to one world — mine, another.
Ismene: But look, we're both guilty, both condemned to death.
Antigone: Courage! Live your life. I gave myself to death,   630
    long ago, so I might serve the dead.
Creon: They're both mad, I tell you, the two of them.
    One's just shown it, the other's been that way
    since she was born.
Ismene: True, my king,
    the sense we were born with cannot last forever . . .   635
    commit cruelty on a person long enough
    and the mind begins to go.
Creon: Yours did,
    when you chose to commit your crimes with her.
Ismene: How can I live alone, without her?
Creon: Her?
    Don't even mention her — she no longer exists.   640
Ismene: What? You'd kill your own son's bride?
Creon: Absolutely:
    there are other fields for him to plow.
Ismene: Perhaps,
    but never as true, as close a bond as theirs.
Creon: A worthless woman for my son? It repels me.
Ismene: Dearest Haemon, your father wrongs you so!   645
Creon: Enough, enough — you and your talk of marriage!
Ismene: Creon — you're really going to rob your son of Antigone?
Creon: Death will do it for me — break their marriage off.
Leader: So, it's settled then? Antigone must die?
Creon: Settled, yes — we both know that.   650

To the guards.

    Stop wasting time. Take them in.
    From now on they'll act like women.
    Tie them up, no more running loose;

even the bravest will cut and run,
once they see Death coming for their lives.   655

*The guards escort Antigone and Ismene into the palace. Creon remains while
the old citizens form their chorus.*

Chorus: Blest, they are the truly blest who all their lives
    have never tasted devastation. For others, once
    the gods have rocked a house to its foundations
       the ruin will never cease, cresting on and on
    from one generation on throughout the race —   660
    like a great mounting tide
    driven on by savage northern gales,
       surging over the dead black depths
    roiling up from the bottom dark heaves of sand
    and the headlands, taking the storm's onslaught full-force,   665
    roar, and the low moaning
              echoes on and on

                  and now
    as in ancient times I see the sorrows of the house,
    the living heirs of the old ancestral kings,
    piling on the sorrows of the dead
       and one generation cannot free the next —   670
    some god will bring them crashing down,
    the race finds no release.
    And now the light, the hope
       springing up from the late last root
    in the house of Oedipus, that hope's cut down in turn   675
    by the long, bloody knife swung by the gods of death
    by a senseless word
           by fury at the heart.

                    Zeus,
    yours is the power, Zeus, what man on earth
    can override it, who can hold it back?
    Power that neither Sleep, the all-ensnaring   680
       no, nor the tireless months of heaven
    can ever overmaster — young through all time,
    mighty lord of power, you hold fast
       the dazzling crystal mansions of Olympus.
    And throughout the future, late and soon   685
    as through the past, your law prevails:
    no towering form of greatness
       enters into the lives of mortals
           free and clear of ruin.

                    True,
    our dreams, our high hopes voyaging far and wide   690
    bring sheer delight to many, to many others
       delusion, blithe, mindless lusts
    and the fraud steals on one slowly . . . unaware

till he trips and puts his foot into the fire.
> He was a wise old man who coined   695
the famous saying: "Sooner or later
foul is fair, fair is foul
to the man the gods will ruin" —
> He goes his way for a moment only
> > free of blinding ruin.   700

Enter Haemon from the palace.

> Here's Haemon now, the last of all your sons.
Does he come in tears for his bride,
his doomed bride, Antigone —
bitter at being cheated of their marriage?

Creon: We'll soon know, better than seers could tell us.   705

Turning to Haemon.

> Son, you've heard the final verdict on your bride?
Are you coming now, raving against your father?
Or do you love me, no matter what I do?

Haemon: Father, I'm your *son* . . . you in your wisdom
set my bearings for me — I obey you.   710
No marriage could ever mean more to me than you,
whatever good direction you may offer.

Creon: Fine, Haemon.
That's how you ought to feel within your heart,
subordinate to your father's will in every way.
That's what a man prays for: to produce good sons —   715
households full of them, dutiful and attentive,
so they can pay his enemy back with interest
and match the respect their father shows his friend.
But the man who rears a brood of useless children,
what has he brought into the world, I ask you?   720
Nothing but trouble for himself, and mockery
from his enemies laughing in his face.
> > > > > Oh Haemon,
never lose your sense of judgment over a woman.
The warmth, the rush of pleasure, it all goes cold
in your arms, I warn you . . . a worthless woman   725
in your house, a misery in your bed.
What wound cuts deeper than a loved one
turned against you? Spit her out,
like a mortal enemy — let the girl go.
Let her find a husband down among the dead.   730

Imagine it: I caught her in naked rebellion,
the traitor, the only one in the whole city.
I'm not about to prove myself a liar,
not to my people, no, I'm going to kill her!
That's right — so let her cry for mercy, sing her hymns   735
to Zeus who defends all bonds of kindred blood.

Why, if I bring up my own kin to be rebels,
think what I'd suffer from the world at large.
Show me the man who rules his household well:
I'll show you someone fit to rule the state.   740
That good man, my son,
I have every confidence he and he alone
can give commands and take them too. Staunch
in the storm of spears he'll stand his ground,
a loyal, unflinching comrade at your side.   745

But whoever steps out of line, violates the laws
or presumes to hand out orders to his superiors,
he'll win no praise from me. But that man
the city places in authority, his orders
must be obeyed, large and small,   750
right and wrong.
                      Anarchy —
show me a greater crime in all the earth!
She, she destroys cities, rips up houses,
breaks the ranks of spearmen into headlong rout.
But the ones who last it out, the great mass of them   755
owe their lives to discipline. Therefore
we must defend the men who live by law,
never let some woman triumph over us.
Better to fall from power, if fall we must,
at the hands of a man — never be rated   760
inferior to a woman, never.
Leader: To us,
unless old age has robbed us of our wits,
you seem to say what you have to say with sense.
Haemon: Father, only the gods endow a man with reason,
the finest of all their gifts, a treasure.   765
Far be it from me — I haven't the skill,
and certainly no desire, to tell you when,
if ever, you make a slip in speech . . . though
someone else might have a good suggestion.

Of course it's not for you,   770
in the normal run of things, to watch
whatever men say or do, or find to criticize.
The man in the street, you know, dreads your glance,
he'd never say anything displeasing to your face.
But it's for me to catch the murmurs in the dark,   775
the way the city mourns for this young girl.
"No woman," they say, "ever deserved death less,
and such a brutal death for such a glorious action.
She, with her own dear brother lying in his blood —
she couldn't bear to leave him dead, unburied,   780
food for the wild dogs or wheeling vultures.
Death? She deserves a glowing crown of gold!"

Sophocles / Antigone 1183

So they say, and the rumor spreads in secret,
darkly . . .
                    I rejoice in your success, father —
nothing more precious to me in the world.   785
What medal of honor brighter to his children
than a father's growing glory? Or a child's
to his proud father? Now don't, please,
be quite so single-minded, self-involved,
or assume the world is wrong and you are right.   790
Whoever thinks that he alone possesses intelligence,
the gift of eloquence, he and no one else,
and character too . . . such men, I tell you,
spread them open — you will find them empty.

                                                No,
it's no disgrace for a man, even a wise man,   795
to learn many things and not to be too rigid.
You've seen trees by a raging winter torrent,
how many sway with the flood and salvage every twig,
but not the stubborn — they're ripped out, roots and all.
Bend or break. The same when a man is sailing: 800
haul your sheets too taut, never give an inch,
you'll capsize, go the rest of the voyage
keel up and the rowing-benches under.

Oh give way. Relax your anger — change!
I'm young, I know, but let me offer this: 805
it would be best by far, I admit,
if a man were born infallible, right by nature.
If not — and things don't often go that way,
it's best to learn from those with good advice.
Leader: You'd do well, my lord, if he's speaking to the point, 810
        to learn from him,

Turning to Haemon.

                    and you, my boy, from him.
        You both are talking sense.
Creon: So,
        men our age, we're to be lectured, are we? —
        schooled by a boy his age?
Haemon: Only in what is right. But if I seem young,   815
        look less to my years and more to what I do.
Creon: Do? Is admiring rebels an achievement?
Haemon: I'd never suggest that you admire treason.
Creon: Oh? —
        isn't that just the sickness that's attacked her?
Haemon: The whole city of Thebes denies it, to a man.   820
Creon: And is Thebes about to tell me how to rule?
Haemon: Now, you see? Who's talking like a child?
Creon: Am I to rule this land for others — or myself?

Haemon: It's no city at all, owned by one man alone.
Creon: What? The city *is* the king's — that's the law! 825
Haemon: What a splendid king you'd make of a desert island —
    you and you alone.
Creon:

To the Chorus.

                                This boy, I do believe,
    is fighting on her side, the woman's side.
Haemon: If you are a woman, yes;
    my concern is all for you. 830
Creon: Why, you degenerate — bandying accusations,
    threatening me with justice, your own father!
Haemon: I see my father offending justice — wrong.
Creon: Wrong?
    To protect my royal rights?
Haemon: Protect your rights?
    When you trample down the honors of the gods? 835
Creon: You, you soul of corruption, rotten through —
    woman's accomplice!
Haemon: That may be,
    but you'll never find me accomplice to a criminal.
Creon: That's what *she* is,
    and every word you say is a blatant appeal for her — 840
Haemon: And you, and me, and the gods beneath the earth.
Creon: You'll never marry her, not while she's alive.
Haemon: Then she'll die . . . but her death will kill another.
Creon: What, brazen threats? You go too far!
Haemon: What threat?
    Combating your empty, mindless judgments with a word? 845
Creon: You'll suffer for your sermons, you and your empty wisdom!
Haemon: If you weren't my father, I'd say you were insane.
Creon: Don't flatter me with Father — you woman's slave!
Haemon: You really expect to fling abuse at me
    and not receive the same?
Creon: Is that so! 850
    Now, by heaven, I promise you, you'll pay —
    taunting, insulting me! Bring her out,
    that hateful — she'll die now, here,
    in front of his eyes, beside her groom!
Haemon: No, no, she will never die beside me — 855
    don't delude yourself. And you will never
    see me, never set eyes on my face again.
    Rage your heart out, rage with friends
    who can stand the sight of you.

Rushing out.

Leader: Gone, my king, in a burst of anger. 860

Sophocles / Antigone 1185

A temper young as his . . . hurt him once,
he may do something violent.
Creon: Let him do —
dream up something desperate, past all human limit!
Good riddance. Rest assured,
he'll never save those two young girls from death.   865
Leader: Both of them, you really intend to kill them both?
Creon: No, not her, the one whose hands are clean;
you're quite right.
Leader: But Antigone —
what sort of death do you have in mind for her?
Creon: I'll take her down some wild, desolate path   870
never trod by men, and wall her up alive
in a rocky vault, and set out short rations,
just a gesture of piety
to keep the entire city free of defilement.
There let her pray to the one god she worships: 875
Death — who knows? — may just reprieve her from death.
Or she may learn at last, better late than never,
what a waste of breath it is to worship Death.

Exit to the palace.

Chorus: Love, never conquered in battle
Love the plunderer laying waste the rich!
Love standing the night-watch   880
                              guarding a girl's soft cheek,
you range the seas, the shepherds' steadings off in the wilds —
not even the deathless gods can flee your onset,
nothing human born for a day —   885
whoever feels your grip is driven mad.
                                                          Love
you wrench the minds of the righteous into outrage,
swerve them to their ruin — you have ignited this,
this kindred strife, father and son at war
                              and Love alone the victor —   890
warm glance of the bride triumphant, burning with desire!
Throned in power, side-by-side with the mighty laws!
Irresistible Aphrodite,° never conquered —
Love, you mock us for your sport.

Antigone is brought from the palace under guard.

But now, even I'd rebel against the king,   895
I'd break all bounds when I see this —
I fill with tears, can't hold them back,
not any more . . . I see Antigone make her way
to the bridal vault where all are laid to rest.
Antigone: Look at me, men of my fatherland,   900

893 *Aphrodite:* Goddess of love.

        setting out on the last road
    looking into the last light of day
    the last I'll ever see . . .
    the god of death who puts us all to bed
    takes me down to the banks of Acheron° alive —   905
        denied my part in the wedding-songs,
    no wedding-song in the dusk has crowned my marriage —
    I go to wed the lord of the dark waters.
Chorus: Not crowned with glory, crowned with a dirge,
    you leave for the deep pit of the dead.   910
    No withering illness laid you low,
    no strokes of the sword — a law to yourself,
    alone, no mortal like you, ever, you go down
    to the halls of Death alive and breathing.
Antigone: But think of Niobe° — well I know her story —   915
        think what a living death she died,
    Tantalus' daughter, stranger queen from the east:
    there on the mountain heights, growing stone
    binding as ivy, slowly walled her round
    and the rains will never cease, the legends say   920
    the snows will never leave her . . .
            wasting away, under her brows the tears
    showering down her breasting ridge and slopes —
    a rocky death like hers puts me to sleep.
Chorus: But she was a god, born of gods,   925
    and we are only mortals born to die.
    And yet, of course, it's a great thing
    for a dying girl to hear, just hear
    she shares a destiny equal to the gods,
    during life and later, once she's dead.
Antigone: O you mock me!   930
    Why, in the name of all my fathers' gods
    why can't you wait till I am gone —
        must you abuse me to my face?
    O my city, all your fine rich sons!
    And you, you springs of the Dirce,   935
    holy grove of Thebes where the chariots gather,
            you at least, you'll bear me witness, look,
    unmourned by friends and forced by such crude laws
    I go to my rockbound prison, strange new tomb —
        always a stranger, O dear god,   940
    I have no home on earth and none below,
        not with the living, not with the breathless dead.
Chorus: You went too far, the last limits of daring —
    smashing against the high throne of Justice!

---

905 *Acheron:* A river in the underworld, to which the dead go.   915 *Niobe:* A queen of Thebes who was punished by the gods for her pride and was turned into stone.

Your life's in ruins, child — I wonder . . .   945
    do you pay for your father's terrible ordeal?
Antigone: There — at last you've touched it, the worst pain
    the worst anguish! Raking up the grief for father
        three times over, for all the doom
    that's struck us down, the brilliant house of Laius.   950
    O mother, your marriage-bed
    the coiling horrors, the coupling there —
        you with your own son, my father — doomstruck mother!
    Such, such were my parents, and I their wretched child.
    I go to them now, cursed, unwed, to share their home —   955
        I am a stranger! O dear brother, doomed
        in your marriage — your marriage murders mine,
            your dying drags me down to death alive!

Enter Creon.

Chorus: Reverence asks some reverence in return —
    but attacks on power never go unchecked,   960
        not by the man who holds the reins of power.
    Your own blind will, your passion has destroyed you.
Antigone: No one to weep for me, my friends,
    no wedding-song — they take me away
    in all my pain . . . the road lies open, waiting.   965
    Never again, the law forbids me to see
    the sacred eye of day. I am agony!
    No tears for the destiny that's mine,
    no loved one mourns my death.
Creon: Can't you see?
    If a man could wail his own dirge *before* he dies,   970
    he'd never finish.

To the guards.

                        Take her away, quickly!
    Wall her up in the tomb, you have your orders.
    Abandon her there, alone, and let her choose —
    death or a buried life with a good roof for shelter.
    As for myself, my hands are clean. This young girl —   975
    dead or alive, she will be stripped of her rights,
    her stranger's rights, here in the world above.
Antigone: O tomb, my bridal-bed — my house, my prison
    cut in the hollow rock, my everlasting watch!
    I'll soon be there, soon embrace my own,   980
    the great growing family of our dead
    Persephone° has received among her ghosts.
                                    I,
    the last of them all, the most reviled by far,

982 *Persephone:* Queen of the underworld.

go down before my destined time's run out.
But still I go, cherishing one good hope: 985
my arrival may be dear to father,
dear to you, my mother,
dear to you, my loving brother, Eteocles —
When you died I washed you with my hands,
I dressed you all, I poured the cups 990
across your tombs. But now, Polynices,
because I laid your body out as well,
this, this is my reward. Nevertheless
I honored you — the decent will admit it —
well and wisely too.

                       Never, I tell you, 995
if I had been the mother of children
or if my husband died, exposed and rotting —
I'd never have taken this ordeal upon myself,
never defied our people's will. What law,
you ask, do I satisfy with what I say? 1000
A husband dead, there might have been another.
A child by another too, if I had lost the first.
But mother and father both lost in the halls of Death,
no brother could ever spring to light again.

For this law alone I held you first in honor. 1005
For this, Creon, the king, judges me a criminal
guilty of dreadful outrage, my dear brother!
And now he leads me off, a captive in his hands,
with no part in the bridal-song, the bridal-bed,
denied all joy of marriage, raising children — 1010
deserted so by loved ones, struck by fate,
I descend alive to the caverns of the dead.

What law of the mighty gods have I transgressed?
Why look to the heavens any more, tormented as I am?
Whom to call, what comrades now? Just think, 1015
my reverence only brands me for irreverence!
Very well: if this is the pleasure of the gods,
once I suffer I will know that I was wrong.
But if these men are wrong, let them suffer
nothing worse than they mete out to me — 1020
these masters of injustice!
Leader: Still the same rough winds, the wild passion
    raging through the girl.
Creon:

To the guards.

                      Take her away.
    You're wasting time — you'll pay for it too.
Antigone: Oh god, the voice of death. It's come, it's here. 1025
Creon: True. Not a word of hope — your doom is sealed.

Antigone: Land of Thebes, city of all my fathers —
    O you gods, the first gods of the race!
    They drag me away, now, no more delay.
    Look on me, you noble sons of Thebes —   1030
    the last of a great line of kings,
    I alone, see what I suffer now
    at the hands of what breed of men —
    all for reverence, my reverence for the gods!

She leaves under guard; the Chorus gathers.

Chorus: Danaë, Danaë° —   1035
    even she endured a fate like yours,
        in all her lovely strength she traded
    the light of day for the bolted brazen vault —
    buried within her tomb, her bridal-chamber,
    wed to the yoke and broken.   1040
        But she was of glorious birth
                  my child, my child
    and treasured the seed of Zeus within her womb,
    the cloudburst streaming gold!
        The power of fate is a wonder,   1045
        dark, terrible wonder —
        neither wealth nor armies
        towered walls nor ships
        black hulls lashed by the salt
        can save us from that force.   1050

    The yoke tamed him too
        young Lycurgus° flaming in anger
    king of Edonia, all for his mad taunts
    Dionysus clamped him down, encased
    in the chain-mail of rock   1055
        and there his rage
              his terrible flowering rage burst —
    sobbing, dying away . . . at last that madman
    came to know his god —
        the power he mocked, the power   1060
        he taunted in all his frenzy
        trying to stamp out
        the women strong with the god —
        the torch, the raving sacred cries —
        enraging the Muses° who adore the flute.   1065

    And far north where the Black Rocks
        cut the sea in half
    and murderous straits

1035 *Danaë:* Locked in a cell by her father because it was prophesied that her son would kill him, but visited by Zeus in the form of a shower of gold. Their son was Perseus.   1052 *Lycurgus:* Punished by Dionysus because he would not worship him.   1065 *Muses:* Goddesses of the arts.

split the coast of Thrace
   a forbidding city stands
where once, hard by the walls
the savage Ares thrilled to watch
a king's new queen, a Fury rearing in rage
   against his two royal sons —
      her bloody hands, her dagger-shuttle
stabbing out their eyes — cursed, blinding wounds —
their eyes blind sockets screaming for revenge!

They wailed in agony, cries echoing cries
   the princes doomed at birth . . .
and their mother doomed to chains,
walled off in a tomb of stone —
   but she traced her own birth back
to a proud Athenian line and the high gods
and off in caverns half the world away,
born of the wild North Wind
   she sprang on her father's gales,
      racing stallions up the leaping cliffs —
child of the heavens. But even on her the Fates
the gray everlasting Fates rode hard
my child, my child.

Enter Tiresias, the blind prophet, led by a boy.

Tiresias: Lords of Thebes,
   I and the boy have come together,
hand in hand. Two see with the eyes of one . . .
   so the blind must go, with a guide to lead the way.
Creon: What is it, old Tiresias? What news now?
Tiresias: I will teach you. And you obey the seer.
Creon: I will,
   I've never wavered from your advice before.
Tiresias: And so you kept the city straight on course.
Creon: I owe you a great deal, I swear to that.
Tiresias: Then reflect, my son: you are poised,
   once more, on the razor-edge of fate.
Creon: What is it? I shudder to hear you.
Tiresias: You will learn
   when you listen to the warnings of my craft.
As I sat on the ancient seat of augury,°
   in the sanctuary where every bird I know
will hover at my hands — suddenly I heard it,
a strange voice in the wingbeats, unintelligible,
barbaric, a mad scream! Talons flashing, ripping,
they were killing each other — that much I knew —

1103 *seat of augury:* Where Tiresias looked for omens among birds.

the murderous fury whirring in those wings
made that much clear!
                              I was afraid,   1110
I turned quickly, tested the burnt-sacrifice,
ignited the altar at all points — but no fire,
the god in the fire never blazed.
Not from those offerings . . . over the embers
slid a heavy ooze from the long thighbones,   1115
smoking, sputtering out, and the bladder
puffed and burst — spraying gall into the air —
and the fat wrapping the bones slithered off
and left them glistening white. No fire!
The rites failed that might have blazed the future   1120
with a sign. So I learned from the boy here;
he is my guide, as I am guide to others.
                              And it's you —
your high resolve that sets this plague on Thebes.
The public altars and sacred hearths are fouled,
one and all, by the birds and dogs with carrion   1125
torn from the corpse, the doomstruck son of Oedipus!
And so the gods are deaf to our prayers, they spurn
the offerings in our hands, the flame of holy flesh.
No birds cry out an omen clear and true —
they're gorged with the murdered victim's blood and fat.   1130
Take these things to heart, my son, I warn you.
All men make mistakes, it is only human.
But once the wrong is done, a man
can turn his back on folly, misfortune too,
if he tries to make amends, however low he's fallen,   1135
and stops his bullnecked ways. Stubbornness
brands you for stupidity — pride is a crime.
No, yield to the dead!
Never stab the fighter when he's down.
Where's the glory, killing the dead twice over?   1140

I mean you well. I give you sound advice.
It's best to learn from a good adviser
when he speaks for your own good:
it's pure gain.
Creon: Old man — all of you! So,
you shoot your arrows at my head like archers at the target —   1145
I even have *him* loosed on me, this fortune-teller.
Oh his ilk has tried to sell me short
and ship me off for years. Well,
drive your bargains, traffic — much as you like —
in the gold of India, silver-gold of Sardis.   1150
You'll never bury that body in the grave,
not even if Zeus's eagles rip the corpse

and wing their rotten pickings off to the throne of god!
Never, not even in fear of such defilement
will I tolerate his burial, that traitor.   1155
Well I know, we can't defile the gods —
no mortal has the power.
                                                No,
reverend old Tiresias, all men fall,
it's only human, but the wisest fall obscenely
when they glorify obscene advice with rhetoric —   1160
all for their own gain.
Tiresias: Oh god, is there a man alive
who knows, who actually believes . . .
Creon: What now?
What earth-shattering truth are you about to utter?
Tiresias: . . . just how much a sense of judgment, wisdom   1165
is the greatest gift we have?
Creon: Just as much, I'd say,
as a twisted mind is the worst affliction going.
Tiresias: You are the one who's sick, Creon, sick to death.
Creon: I am in no mood to trade insults with a seer.
Tiresias: You have already, calling my prophecies a lie.
Creon: Why not?   1170
You and the whole breed of seers are mad for money!
Tiresias: And the whole race of tyrants lusts to rake it in.
Creon: This slander of yours —
are you aware you're speaking to the king?
Tiresias: Well aware. Who helped you save the city?
Creon: You —   1175
you have your skills, old seer, but you lust for injustice!
Tiresias: You will drive me to utter the dreadful secret in my heart.
Creon: Spit it out! Just don't speak it out for profit.
Tiresias: Profit? No, not a bit of profit, not for you.
Creon: Know full well, you'll never buy off my resolve.   1180
Tiresias: Then know this too, learn this by heart!
The chariot of the sun will not race through
so many circuits more, before you have surrendered
one born of your own loins, your own flesh and blood,
a corpse for corpses given in return, since you have thrust   1185
to the world below a child sprung for the world above,
ruthlessly lodged a living soul within the grave —
then you've robbed the gods below the earth,
keeping a dead body here in the bright air,
unburied, unsung, unhallowed by the rites.   1190

You, you have no business with the dead,
nor do the gods above — this is violence
you have forced upon the heavens.
And so the avengers, the dark destroyers late

but true to the mark, now lie in wait for you,   1195
the Furies sent by the gods and the god of death
to strike you down with the pains that you perfected!

There. Reflect on that, tell me I've been bribed.
The day comes soon, no long test of time, not now,
that wakes the wails for men and women in your halls.   1200
Great hatred rises against you —
cities in tumult, all whose mutilated sons
the dogs have graced with burial, or the wild beasts,
some wheeling crow that wings the ungodly stench of carrion
back to each city, each warrior's hearth and home.   1205

These arrows for your heart! Since you've raked me
I loose them like an archer in my anger,
arrows deadly true. You'll never escape
their burning, searing force.

Motioning to his escort.

Come, boy, take me home.   1210
So he can vent his rage on younger men,
and learn to keep a gentler tongue in his head
and better sense than what he carries now.

Exit to the side.

Leader: The old man's gone, my king —
terrible prophecies. Well I know,   1215
since the hair on this old head went gray,
he's never lied to Thebes.
Creon: I know it myself — I'm shaken, torn.
It's a dreadful thing to yield . . . but resist now?
Lay my pride bare to the blows of ruin?   1220
That's dreadful too.
Leader: But good advice,
Creon, take it now, you must.
Creon: What should I do? Tell me . . . I'll obey.
Leader: Go! Free the girl from the rocky vault
and raise a mound for the body you exposed.   1225
Creon: That's your advice? You think I should give in?
Leader: Yes, my king, quickly. Disasters sent by the gods
cut short our follies in a flash.
Creon: Oh it's hard.
giving up the heart's desire . . . but I will do it —
no more fighting a losing battle with necessity.   1230
Leader: Do it now, go, don't leave it to others.
Creon: Now — I'm on my way! Come, each of you,
take up axes, make for the high ground,
over there, quickly! I and my better judgment

have come round to this — I shackled her,   1235
I'll set her free myself. I am afraid . . .
it's best to keep the established laws
to the very day we die.

Rushing out, followed by his entourage. The Chorus clusters around the altar.

Chorus: God of a hundred names!
                              Great Dionysus —
          Son and glory of Semele! Pride of Thebes —   1240
Child of Zeus whose thunder rocks the clouds —
Lord of the famous lands of evening —
King of the Mysteries!
                              King of Eleusis, Demeter's plain°
her breasting hills that welcome in the world —
Great Dionysus!
                              Bacchus,° living in Thebes   1245
the mother-city of all your frenzied women —
                                                  Bacchus
          living along the Ismenus'° rippling waters
standing over the field sown with the Dragon's teeth!

You — we have seen you through the flaring smoky fires,
          your torches blazing over the twin peaks   1250
where nymphs of the hallowed cave climb onward
                              fired with you, your sacred rage —
we have seen you at Castalia's running spring°
and down from the heights of Nysa° crowned with ivy
the greening shore rioting vines and grapes   1255
                    down you come in your storm of wild women
                              ecstatic, mystic cries —
                                             Dionysus —
down to watch and ward the roads of Thebes!

First of all cities, Thebes you honor first
you and your mother, bride of the lightning —   1260
come, Dionysus! now your people lie
in the iron grip of plague,
come in your racing, healing stride
                    down Parnassus'° slopes
or across the moaning straits.
                              Lord of the dancing —   1265
dance, dance the constellations breathing fire!
Great master of the voices of the night!

1243 *Demeter's plain:* The goddess of grain was worshiped at Eleusis, near Athens.   1245 *Bacchus:*
Another name for Dionysus.   1247 *Ismenus:* A river near Thebes where the founders of the
city were said to have sprung from a dragon's teeth.   1253 *Castalia's running spring:* The sacred
spring of Apollo's oracle at Delphi.   1254 *Nysa:* A mountain where Dionysus was worshiped.
1264 *Parnassus:* A mountain in Greece that was sacred to Dionysus as well as other gods and
goddesses.

Sophocles / Antigone **1195**

Child of Zeus, God's offspring, come, come forth!
Lord, king, dance with your nymphs, swirling, raving
arm-in-arm in frenzy through the night   1270
    they dance you, Iacchus° —
                       Dance, Dionysus
giver of all good things!

Enter a Messenger from the side.

Messenger: Neighbors,
friends of the house of Cadmus° and the kings,
there's not a thing in this life of ours
I'd praise or blame as settled once for all.   1275
Fortune lifts and Fortune fells the lucky
and unlucky every day. No prophet on earth
can tell a man his fate. Take Creon:
there was a man to rouse your envy once,
as I see it. He saved the realm from enemies;   1280
taking power, he alone, the lord of the fatherland,
he set us true on course — flourished like a tree
with the noble line of sons he bred and reared . . . .
and now it's lost, all gone.
                      Believe me,
when a man has squandered his true joys,   1285
he's good as dead, I tell you, a living corpse.
Pile up riches in your house, as much as you like —
live like a king with a huge show of pomp,
but if real delight is missing from the lot,
I wouldn't give you a wisp of smoke for it,   1290
not compared with joy.
Leader: What now?
What new grief do you bring the house of kings?
Messenger: Dead, dead — and the living are guilty of their death!
Leader: Who's the murderer? Who is dead? Tell us.
Messenger: Haemon's gone, his blood spilled by the very hand —   1295
Leader: His father's or his own?
Messenger: His own . . .
raging mad with his father for the death —
Leader: Oh great seer,
you saw it all, you brought your word to birth!
Messenger: Those are the facts. Deal with them as you will.

As he turns to go, Eurydice enters from the palace.

Leader: Look, Eurydice. Poor woman, Creon's wife,   1300
    so close at hand. By chance perhaps,
    unless she's heard the news about her son.
Eurydice: My countrymen,
    all of you — I caught the sound of your words

1271 *Iacchus:* Dionysus.   1273 *Cadmus:* The legendary founder of Thebes.

as I was leaving to do my part,
to appeal to queen Athena° with my prayers.   1305
I was just loosing the bolts, opening the doors,
when a voice filled with sorrow, family sorrow,
struck my ears, and I fell back, terrified,
into the women's arms — everything went black.
Tell me the news, again, whatever it is . . .   1310
sorrow and I are hardly strangers;
I can bear the worst.
Messenger: I — dear lady,
    I'll speak as an eye-witness. I was there.
And I won't pass over one word of the truth.
Why should I try to soothe you with a story,   1315
only to prove a liar in a moment?
Truth is always best.
                            So,
I escorted your lord, I guided him
to the edge of the plain where the body lay,
Polynices, torn by the dogs and still unmourned.   1320
And saying a prayer to Hecate of the Crossroads,
Pluto° too, to hold their anger and be kind,
we washed the dead in a bath of holy water
and plucking some fresh branches, gathering . . .
what was left of him, we burned them all together   1325
and raised a high mound of native earth, and then
we turned and made for that rocky vault of hers,
the hollow, empty bed of the bride of Death.
And far off, one of us heard a voice,
a long wail rising, echoing   1330
out of that unhallowed wedding-chamber;
he ran to alert the master and Creon pressed on,
closer — the strange, inscrutable cry came sharper,
throbbing around him now, and he let loose
a cry of his own, enough to wrench the heart,   1335
"Oh god, am I the prophet now? going down
the darkest road I've ever gone? My son —
it's *his* dear voice, he greets me! Go, men,
closer, quickly! Go through the gap,
the rocks are dragged back —   1340
right to the tomb's very mouth — and look,
see if it's Haemon's voice I think I hear,
or the gods have robbed me of my senses."

The king was shattered. We took his orders,
went and searched, and there in the deepest,   1345
dark recesses of the tomb we found her . . .

1305 *Athena:* Goddess of wisdom and protector of Greek cities.   1321–22 *Hecate, Pluto:* Gods of
the underworld.

hanged by the neck in a fine linen noose,
strangled in her veils — and the boy,
his arms flung around her waist,
clinging to her, wailing for his bride,   1350
dead and down below, for his father's crimes
and the bed of his marriage blighted by misfortune.
When Creon saw him, he gave a deep sob,
he ran in, shouting, crying out to him,
"Oh my child — what have you done? what seized you,   1355
what insanity? what disaster drove you mad?
Come out, my son! I beg you on my knees!"
But the boy gave him a wild burning glance,
spat in his face, not a word in reply,
he drew his sword — his father rushed out,   1360
running as Haemon lunged and missed! —
and then, doomed, desperate with himself,
suddenly leaning his full weight on the blade,
he buried it in his body, halfway to the hilt.
And still in his senses, pouring his arms around her,   1365
he embraced the girl and breathing hard,
released a quick rush of blood,
bright red on her cheek glistening white.
And there he lies, body enfolding body . . .
he has won his bride at last, poor boy,   1370
not here but in the houses of the dead.

Creon shows the world that of all the ills
afflicting men the worst is lack of judgment.

Eurydice turns and reenters the palace.

Leader: What do you make of that? The lady's gone,
without a word, good or bad.
Messenger: I'm alarmed too   1375
but here's my hope — faced with her son's death,
she finds it unbecoming to mourn in public.
Inside, under her roof, she'll set her women
to the task and wail the sorrow of the house.
She's too discreet. She won't do something rash.   1380
Leader: I'm not so sure. To me, at least,
a long heavy silence promises danger,
just as much as a lot of empty outcries.
Messenger: We'll see if she's holding something back,
hiding some passion in her heart.   1385
I'm going in. You may be right — who knows?
Even too much silence has its dangers.

*Exit to the palace. Enter Creon from the side, escorted by attendants carrying
Haemon's body on a bier.*

Leader: The king himself! Coming toward us,

look, holding the boy's head in his hands.
Clear, damning proof, if it's right to say so —   1390
proof of his own madness, no one else's,
    no, his own blind wrongs.
Creon: Ohhh,
so senseless, so insane . . . my crimes,
my stubborn, deadly —
Look at us, the killer, the killed,   1395
father and son, the same blood — the misery!
My plans, my mad fanatic heart,
my son, cut off so young!
Ai, dead, lost to the world,
not through your stupidity, no, my own.
Leader: Too late,   1400
too late, you see what justice means.
Creon: Oh I've learned
through blood and tears! Then, it was then,
when the god came down and struck me — a great weight
shattering, driving me down that wild savage path,
ruining, trampling down my joy. Oh the agony,   1405
    the heartbreaking agonies of our lives.

Enter the Messenger from the palace.

Messenger: Master,
what a hoard of grief you have, and you'll have more.
The grief that lies to hand you've brought yourself —

Pointing to Haemon's body.

the rest, in the house, you'll see it all too soon.
Creon: What now? What's worse than this?
Messenger: The queen is dead.   1410
The mother of this dead boy . . . mother to the end —
poor thing, her wounds are fresh.
Creon: No, no,
harbor of Death, so choked, so hard to cleanse! —
why me? why are you killing me?
Herald of pain, more words, more grief?   1415
I died once, you kill me again and again!
What's the report, boy . . . some news for me?
My wife dead? O dear god!
Slaughter heaped on slaughter?

The doors open; the body of Eurydice is brought out on her bier.

Messenger: See for yourself:
now they bring her body from the palace.
Creon: Oh no,   1420
another, a second loss to break the heart.
What next, what fate still waits for me?

I just held my son in my arms and now,
        look, a new corpse rising before my eyes —
            wretched, helpless mother — O my son!   1425
Messenger: She stabbed herself at the altar,
        then her eyes went dark, after she'd raised
        a cry for the noble fate of Megareus,° the hero
        killed in the first assault, then for Haemon,
        then with her dying breath she called down   1430
        torments on your head — you killed her sons.
Creon: Oh the dread,
        I shudder with dread! Why not kill me too? —
        run me through with a good sharp sword?
        Oh god, the misery, anguish —
        I, I'm churning with it, going under.   1435
Messenger: Yes, and the dead, the woman lying there,
        piles the guilt of all their deaths on you.
Creon: How did she end her life, what bloody stroke?
Messenger: She drove home to the heart with her own hand,
        once she learned her son was dead . . . that agony.   1440
Creon: And the guilt is all mine —
        can never be fixed on another man,
        no escape for me. I killed you,
        I, god help me, I admit it all!

To his attendants.

        Take me away, quickly, out of sight.   1445
        I don't even exist — I'm no one. Nothing.
Leader: Good advice, if there's any good in suffering.
        Quickest is best when troubles block the way.
Creon:

Kneeling in prayer.

        Come, let it come! — that best of fates for me
        that brings the final day, best fate of all.   1450
        Oh quickly, now —
        so I never have to see another sunrise.
Leader: That will come when it comes;
        we must deal with all that lies before us.
        The future rests with the ones who tend the future.   1455
Creon: That prayer — I poured my heart into that prayer!
Leader: No more prayers now. For mortal men
        there is no escape from the doom we must endure.
Creon: Take me away, I beg you, out of sight.
        A rash, indiscriminate fool!   1460
        I murdered you, my son, against my will —
        you too, my wife . . .
                            Wailing wreck of a man,
        whom to look to? where to lean for support?

1428 *Megareus:* A son of Creon and Eurydice; he died when Thebes was attacked.

1200 A Study of Sophocles

Desperately turning from Haemon to Eurydice on their biers.

> Whatever I touch goes wrong — once more
> a crushing fate's come down upon my head.   1465

The Messenger and attendants lead Creon into the palace.

Chorus: Wisdom is by far the greatest part of joy,
> and reverence toward the gods must be safeguarded.
> The mighty words of the proud are paid in full
> with mighty blows of fate, and at long last
>   those blows will teach us wisdom.   1470

The old citizens exit to the side.

Considerations for Critical Thinking and Writing

1. What are Creon's reasons for issuing the decree forbidding Polynices' burial? What are Antigone's reasons for rejecting Creon's order? Whose arguments are more convincing?
2. What is the Chorus's position on Creon's decree? Does the Chorus see the conflict between Antigone and Creon as simply a collision between two strong-willed individuals, or does it see a larger issue at stake?
3. Despite the title, it is sometimes argued that the protagonist of the play is Creon rather than Antigone, because he undergoes a significant change, while she has already died offstage. Whose story is it?
4. How does Ismene serve as a foil to Antigone? Does Ismene seem weak, or is she reasonable? Why does Antigone reject her sister's offer to martyr herself?
5. How does Haemon serve as a foil to Creon? Is Haemon's decision to commit suicide plausible?
6. What is Creon's attitude toward women? How does this affect his reaction to Antigone's disobedience to the state?
7. Who is responsible for what happens? Does Sophocles suggest that the tragedy could have been avoided if Creon or Antigone had behaved differently? Do Creon and Antigone share any similar characteristics?
8. Describe what you think Sophocles' attitudes were concerning the competing claims for the authority of the state over the individual. Explain how those views are indicated in the play and whether you agree or disagree with them.
9. How might the emphasis of the play have been changed if Sophocles had included the scene in the tomb between Haemon and Antigone? Why do you think he left out such a potentially affecting scene?
10. If you were to stage this play in a contemporary setting, describe what kinds of sets you would use and how you would costume the players.

Connections to Other Selections

1. How is Creon's reaction to Haemon's and Tiresias's pleas that he rescind the decree similar to Oedipus's reaction to Creon and Tiresias in *Oedipus the King?*
2. What similarities and differences are there in Sophocles' characterization of Creon in *Antigone* and in *Oedipus the King?*
3. Consider this assessment of Antigone by the leader of the Chorus (lines 525–27):

> Like father like daughter,
> passionate, wild . . .
> she hasn't learned to bend before adversity.

Does this accurately characterize Antigone? What similarities are there between Oedipus and his daughter? Could these lines also be used to describe Haemon and Ismene?

PERSPECTIVES ON SOPHOCLES

ARISTOTLE (384–322 B.C.)
On Tragic Character c. 340 B.C.

Now since in the finest kind of tragedy the structure should be complex and not simple, and since it should also be a representation of terrible and piteous events (that being the special mark of this type of imitation), in the first place, it is evident that good men ought not to be shown passing from happiness to misfortune, for this does not inspire either pity or fear, but only revulsion; nor evil men rising from ill fortune to prosperity, for this is the most untragic plot of all — it lacks every requirement, in that it neither elicts human sympathy nor stirs pity or fear. And again, neither should an extremely wicked man be seen falling from prosperity into misfortune, for a plot so constructed might indeed call forth human sympathy, but would not excite pity or fear, since the first is felt for a person whose misfortune is undeserved and the second for someone like ourselves — pity for the man suffering undeservedly, fear for the man like ourselves — and hence neither pity nor fear would be aroused in this case. We are left with the man whose place is between these extremes. Such is the man who on the one hand is not pre-eminent in virtue and justice, and yet on the other hand does not fall into misfortune through vice or depravity, but falls because of some mistake; one among the number of the highly renowned and prosperous, such as Oedipus . . . and other famous men from families like [his].

It follows that the plot which achieves excellence will necessarily be single in outcome and not, as some say, double, and will consist in a change of fortune, not to prosperity from misfortune, but the opposite, from prosperity to misfortune, occasioned not by depravity, but by some great mistake on the part of one who is either such as I have described or better than this rather than worse. What actually has taken place has confirmed this; for though at first the poets accepted whatever myths came to hand, today the finest tragedies are founded upon the stories of only a few houses . . . and such . . . as have chanced to suffer terrible things or to do them. So then, tragedy having this construction is the finest kind of tragedy from an artistic point of view. And consequently those persons fall into the same error who bring it as a charge against Euripides° that this is what he does in his tragedies and that most of his plays have unhappy endings. For this is in fact the right procedure, as I have said; and the best proof is that on the stage and in the dramatic contests, plays of this kind seem the most tragic, provided they are successfully worked out, and Euripides, even if in everything else his management is faulty, seems at any rate to be the most tragic of the poets.

Euripides: Fifth century B.C. Greek playwright whose tragedies include *Electra, Medea,* and *Alcestis.*

Second to this is the kind of plot that some persons place first, that which like the *Odyssey*° has a double structure and ends in opposite ways for the better characters and the worse. If it seems to be first, that is attributable to the weakness of the audience, since the poets only follow their lead and compose the kind of plays the spectators want. The pleasure it gives, however, is not that which comes from tragedy, but is rather the pleasure proper to comedy; for in comedy those who in the legend are the worst of enemies . . . end by leaving the scene as friends, and nobody is killed by anybody. . . .

With regard to the Characters there are four things to aim at. First and foremost is that the characters be good. The personages will have character if, as aforesaid, they reveal in speech or in action what their moral choices are, and a good character will be one whose choices are good. It is possible to portray goodness in every class of persons; a woman may be good and a slave may be good, though perhaps as a class women are inferior and slaves utterly base. The second requisite is to make the character appropriate. Thus it is possible to portray any character as manly, but inappropriate for a female character to be manly or formidable in the way I mean. Third is to make the characters lifelike, which is something different from making them good and appropriate as described above. Fourth is to make them consistent. Even if the person being imitated is inconsistent and this is what the character is supposed to be, he should nevertheless be portrayed as consistently inconsistent. . . .

In the characters and in the plot-construction alike, one must strive for that which is either necessary or probable, so that whatever a character of any kind says or does may be the sort of thing such a character will inevitably or probably say or do and the events of the plot may follow one after another either inevitably or with probability. (Obviously, then, the *denouement* of the plot should arise from the plot itself and not be brought about "from the machine." . . . The machine is to be used for matters lying outside the drama, either antecedents of the action which a human being cannot know, or things subsequent to the action that have to be prophesied and announced; for we accept it that the gods see everything. Within the events of the plot itself, however, there should be nothing unreasonable, or if there is, it should be kept outside the play proper as is done in the *Oedipus* of Sophocles.)

Inasmuch as tragedy is an imitation of persons who are better than the average, the example of good portrait-painters should be followed. These, while reproducing the distinctive appearance of their subjects in a recognizable likeness, make them° handsomer in the picture than they are in reality. Similarly the poet when he comes to imitate men who are irascible or easygoing or have other defects of character should depict them as such and yet as good men at the same time.

From *Poetics,* translated by James Hutton

Odyssey: The epic by the ancient Greek poet Homer that chronicles the voyage home from the Trojan War of Odysseus (also known as Ulysses).

Considerations for Critical Thinking and Writing

1. Why does Aristotle insist that both virtuous and depraved characters are unsuitable as tragic figures? What kind of person constitutes a tragic character according to him?
2. Aristotle argues that it is "inappropriate for a female character to be manly or formidable." Do you think Antigone fits this negative description? Does she seem "inferior" to the men in the play?
3. Aristotle says that characters should be "lifelike," but he also points out that characters should be made "handsomer . . . than they are in reality." Is this a contradiction? Explain why or why not.

SOPHOCLES (496?–406 B.C.)
Another Translation of a
Scene from Oedipus the King   1920

Enter Oedipus, blind.

Chorus: O sight for all the world to see
           Most terrible! O suffering
       Of all mine eyes have seen most terrible!
           Alas! What Fury came on thee?
           What evil Spirit, from afar,
           O Oedipus! O Wretched!
               Leapt on thee, to destroy?
           I cannot even Alas! look
           Upon thy face, though much I have
       To ask of thee, and much to hear,
           Aye, and to see — I cannot!
           Such terror is in thee!
Oedipus: Alas! O Wretched! Whither go
           My steps? My voice? It seems to float
               Far, far away from me.
           Alas! Curse of my Life, how far
               Thy leap hath carried thee!
Chorus: To sorrows none can bear to see or hear.
Oedipus: Ah! The cloud!
       Visitor unspeakable! Darkness upon me horrible!
       Unconquerable! Cloud that may not ever pass away!
                       Alas!
       And yet again, alas! How deep they stab —
       These throbbing pains, and all those memories.
Chorus: Where such afflictions are, I marvel not,
       If soul and body made one doubled woe.

Oedipus: Ah! My friend!
Still remains thy friendship. Still thine is the help that comforts me,
And kindness, that can look upon these dreadful eyes unchanged.
                    Ah me!
My friend, I feel thy presence. Though mine eyes
Be darkened, yet I hear thy voice, and know.
Chorus: Oh, dreadful deed! How wert thou steeled to quench
Thy vision thus? What Spirit came on thee?
Oedipus: Apollo! 'Twas Apollo, friends,
Willed the evil, willed, and brought the agony to pass!
            And yet the hand that struck was mine, mine only, wretched.
            Why should I see, whose eyes
Had no more any good to look upon?
Chorus: 'Twas even as thou sayest.
Oedipus: Aye. For me . . . Nothing is left for sight.
                    Nor anything to love:
Nor shall the sound of greetings any more
            Fall pleasant on my ear.
Away! Away! Out of the land, away!
        Banishment, Banishment! Fatal am I, accursed,
        And the hate on me, as on no man else, of the gods!
Chorus: Unhappy in thy fortune and the wit
That shows it thee. Would thou hadst never known.
Oedipus: A curse upon the hand that loosed
In the wilderness the cruel fetters of my feet,
        Rescued me, gave me life! Ah! Cruel was his pity,
            Since, had I died, so much
I had not harmed myself and all I love.
Chorus: Aye, even so 'twere better.
Oedipus: Aye, for life never had led me then
                To shed my father's blood;
            Men had not called me husband of the wife
                That bore me in the womb.
But now — but now — Godless am I, the son
        Born of impurity, mate of my father's bed,
            And if worse there be, I am Oedipus! It is mine!
Chorus: In this I know not how to call thee wise,
For better wert thou dead than living — blind.
Oedipus: Nay, give me no more counsel. Bid me not
    Believe my deed, thus done, is not well done.
I know 'tis well. When I had passed the grave,
How could those eyes have met my father's gaze,
Or my unhappy mother's — since on both
I have done wrongs beyond all other wrong?
Or live and see my children? — Children born
As they were born! What pleasure in that sight?
None for these eyes of mine, for ever, none.
Nor in the sight of Thebes, her castles, shrines

And images of the gods, whereof, alas!
I robbed myself — myself, I spoke that word,
I that she bred and nurtured, I her prince,
And bade her thrust the sinner out, the man
Proved of the gods polluted — Laïus' son.
When such a stain by my own evidence
Was on me, could I raise my eyes to them?
No! Had I means to stop my ears, and choke
The wells of sound, I had not held my hand,
But closed my body like a prison-house
To hearing as to sight. Sweet for the mind
To dwell withdrawn, where troubles could not come.
    Cithaeron! Ah, why didst thou welcome me?
Why, when thou hadst me there, didst thou not kill,
Never to show the world myself — my birth!
    O Polybus, and Corinth, and the home
Men called my father's ancient house, what sores
Festered beneath that beauty that ye reared,
Discovered now, sin out of sin begot.
    O ye three roads, O secret mountain-glen,
Trees, and a pathway narrowed to the place
Where met the three, do you remember me?
I gave you blood to drink, my father's blood,
And so my own! Do you remember that?
The deed I wrought for you? Then, how I passed
Hither to other deeds?
           O Marriage-bed
That gave me birth, and, having borne me, gave
Fresh children to your seed, and showed the world
Father, son, brother, mingled and confused,
Bride, mother, wife in one, and all the shame
Of deeds the foulest ever known to man.
    No. Silence for a deed so ill to do
Is better. Therefore lead me hence, away!
To hide me or to kill. Or to the sea
Cast me, where you shall look on me no more.
Come! Deign to touch me, though I am a man
Accurséd. Yield! Fear nothing! Mine are woes
That no man else, but I alone, must bear.

Translated by J. T. Sheppard

Considerations for Critical Thinking and Writing

1. This excerpt from Sheppard's translation corresponds to lines 1433–1549 in Robert Fagles's translation (pp. 1156–1159). Examine both versions of the scene and describe the diction and tone of each. If you find one of the translations more effective than the other, indicate why.
2. Explain whether the different translations affect your understanding or interpretation of the scene.

MURIEL RUKEYSER (1913–1980)
On Oedipus the King

MYTH

Long afterward, Oedipus, old and blinded, walked the
roads.   He smelled a familiar smell.   It was
the Sphinx.   Oedipus said, "I want to ask one question.
Why didn't I recognize my mother?"   "You gave the
wrong answer," said the Sphinx.   "But that was what   5
made everything possible," said Oedipus.   "No," she said.
"When I asked, What walks on four legs in the morning,
two at noon, and three in the evening, you answered,
Man.   You didn't say anything about woman."
"When you say Man," said Oedipus, "you include women   10
too. Everyone knows that."   She said, "That's what
you think."

Considerations for Critical Thinking and Writing

1. What elements of the Oedipus story does Rukeyser allude to in the poem?
2. To what does the title refer? How does the word *myth* carry more than one meaning?
3. This poem is amusing, but its ironic ending points to a serious theme. What is it? Does Sophocles' play address any of the issues raised in the poem?

JEAN ANOUILH (1910–1987)
A Scene from Antigone

Creon: I shall save you yet. (*He goes below the table to the chair at end of table, takes off his coat, and places it on the chair.*) God knows, I have things enough to do today without wasting my time on an insect like you. There's plenty to do, I assure you, when you've just put down a revolution. But urgent things can wait. I am not going to let politics be the cause of your death. For it is a fact that this whole business is nothing but politics: the mournful shade of Polynices, the decomposing corpse, the sentimental weeping, and the hysteria that you mistake for heroism — nothing but politics.

Look here. I may not be soft, but I'm fastidious. I like things clean, shipshape, well scrubbed. Don't think that I am not just as offended as you are by the thought of that meat rotting in the sun. In the evening, when the breeze comes in off the sea, you can smell it in the palace, and it nauseates me. But I refuse even to shut my window. It's vile; and I can tell you what I wouldn't tell anybody else: it's stupid, monstrously stupid. But the people of Thebes have got to have their noses rubbed into it a little longer. My God! If it was up to me, I should have had them bury your brother long ago as a mere matter of public hygiene. I admit that what I am doing is childish. But if the featherheaded rabble I govern are to understand what's what, that stench has got to fill the town for a month!

Antigone (turns to him): You are a loathsome man!

Creon: I agree. My trade forces me to be. We could argue whether I ought or ought not to follow my trade; but once I take on the job, I must do it properly.

Antigone: Why do you do it at all?

Creon: My dear, I woke up one morning and found myself King of Thebes. God knows, there were other things I loved in life more than power.

Antigone: Then you should have said no.

Creon: Yes, I could have done that. Only, I felt that it would have been cowardly. I should have been like a workman who turns down a job that has to be done. So I said yes.

Antigone: So much the worse for you, then. I didn't say yes. I can say no to anything I think vile, and I don't have to count the cost. But because you said yes, all that you can do, for all your crown and your trappings, and your guards — all that you can do is to have me killed.

Creon: Listen to me.

Antigone: If I want to. I don't have to listen to you if I don't want to. You've said your *yes*. There is nothing more you can tell me that I don't know. You stand there, drinking in my words. *(She moves behind chair.)* Why is it that you don't call your guards? I'll tell you why. You want to hear me out to the end; that's why.

Creon: You amuse me.

Antigone: Oh, no, I don't. I frighten you. That is why you talk about saving me. Everything would be so much easier if you had a docile, tongue-tied little Antigone living in the palace. I'll tell you something, Uncle Creon: I'll give you back one of your own words. You are too fastidious to make a good tyrant. But you are going to have to put me to death today, and you know it. And that's what frightens you. God! Is there anything uglier than a frightened man!

Creon: Very well. I am afraid, then. Does that satisfy you? I am afraid that if you insist upon it, I shall have to have you killed. And I don't want to.

Antigone: I don't have to do things that I think are wrong. If it comes to that, you didn't really want to leave my brother's body unburied, did you? Say it! Admit that you didn't.

Creon: I have said it already.

Antigone: But you did it just the same. And now, though you don't want to do it, you are going to have me killed. And you call that being a king!

Creon: Yes, I call that being a king.

Antigone: Poor Creon! My nails are broken, my fingers are bleeding, my arms are covered with the welts left by the paws of your guards — but I am a queen!

Creon: Then why not have pity on me, and live? Isn't your brother's corpse, rotting there under my windows, payment enough for peace and order in Thebes? My son loves you. Don't make me add your life to the payment. I've paid enough.

Antigone: No, Creon! You said yes, and made yourself king. Now you will never stop paying.

Creon: But God in heaven! Won't you try to understand me! I'm trying hard enough to understand you! There had to be one man who said yes. Somebody had to agree to captain the ship. She had sprung a hundred leaks; she was loaded to the water line with crime, ignorance, poverty. The wheel was swinging with the wind. The crew refused to work and were looting the cargo. The officers were building a raft, ready to slip overboard and desert the ship. The mast was splitting, the wind was howling, the sails were beginning to rip. Every man jack on board was about to drown — and only because the only thing they thought of was their own skins and their cheap little day-to-day traffic. Was that a time, do you think, for playing with words like yes and no? Was that a time for a man to be weighing the pros and cons, wondering if he wasn't going to pay too dearly later on; if he wasn't going to lose his life, or his family, or his touch with other men? You grab the wheel, you right the ship in the face of a mountain of water. You shout an order, and if one man refuses to obey, you shoot straight into the mob. Into the mob, I say! The beast as nameless as the wave that crashes down upon your deck; as nameless as the whipping wind. The thing that drops when you shoot may be someone who poured you a drink the night before; but it has no name. And you, braced at the wheel, you have no name, either. Nothing has a name — except the ship, and the storm. *(A pause as he looks at her.)* Now do you understand?

Antigone: I am not here to understand. That's all very well for you. I am here to say no to you, and die.

Creon: It is easy to say no.

Antigone: Not always.

Creon: It is easy to say no. To say yes, you have to sweat and roll up your sleeves and plunge both hands into life up to the elbows. It is easy to say no, even if saying no means death. All you have to do is to sit still and wait. Wait to go on living; wait to be killed. That is the coward's part. *No* is one of your man-made words. Can you imagine a world in which trees say *no* to the sap? In which beasts say *no* to hunger or to propagation? Animals are good, simple, tough. They move in droves, nudging one another onwards, all traveling the same road. Some of them keel over, but the rest go on; and no matter how many may fall by the wayside, there are always those few left that go on bringing their young into the world, traveling the same road with the same obstinate will, unchanged from those who went before.

Antigone: Animals, eh, Creon! What a king you could be if only men were animals!

Translated by Lewis Galantière

Considerations for Critical Thinking and Writing

1. What are Creon's reasons for not burying Polynices? How does he defend his actions as a ruler?
2. In what sense is Antigone correct when she describes Creon as "too fastidious to make a good tyrant"?
3. Do you agree with Creon that Antigone takes "the coward's part" by saying no rather than yes? With which character do you sympathize more? How might Creon's

position be related to the fact that France was occupied by German troops during World War II, when Anouilh wrote this play?

4. How does Anouilh's treatment of Creon compare with Sophocles'?

MAURICE SAGOFF

A Humorous Distillation of Antigone   1980

Tyrant Creon's stern advice is
"Do not bury Polynices!
Thebes' defenders had to squash him —
Now we'll let the buzzards nosh him!"
But Antigone, the brave,   5
Dared to dig her brother's grave:
"Man-made laws my soul defies —
Live by laws divine!" she cries.

Creon locks her up, the demon!
Though she's pledged to marry Haemon   10
(That's his son). Now comes a seer
Prophesying woes severe:
If her brother's not entombed
And she dies, then Haemon's doomed!

Creon seeing things go screwy,   15
Wilts, and tries to bang a U-ee,
But the Gods who drive the hearse
Seldom shove it in reverse . . .
Carnage follows, sure as Fate;
Here's the body-count to date —   20
1. Antigone 2. her brother
3. young Haemon 4. his mother
(If more bodies fail to fall,
It's because the cast is small).

Strung-out Creon takes the blame.   25
Exits, croaking "Rotten shame!"

From Shrinklits: Seventy of the World's Towering Classics Cut Down to Size

Considerations for Critical Thinking and Writing

1. Sagoff writes in his tongue-in-cheek introduction to *Shrinklits* that "inside every fat book is a skinny book trying to get out, struggling to cut through the mummylike wrappings of long-winded descriptions, superfluous characters, endless conversations, and turgid style." How successful is this poem in summarizing the plot of *Antigone*? What is left out of Sagoff's account?

2. Using Sagoff's version of *Antigone* as your inspiration, choose another play in the text and try writing a shrinklit that does it humorous justice.

R. G. A. BUXTON (b. 1948)
The Major Critical Issue in Antigone   1984

It seems agreed that the main critical issue is: how do we evaluate the respective moral positions of Antigone and Creon. Provided this is not asked in order to achieve "that nice apportionment of blame to which critics are so much more prone than dramatists,"[1] but rather with the aim of teasing out just what is at stake between the two principal figures, the question is worthwhile.

Defenders of Creon appear from time to time. There is no doubt that some of the sentiments he expresses, particularly in his opening programmatic speech, are laudable in themselves; nor should there be any doubt that Creon receives some measure of sympathy as he carries his son's body on stage at the end. But is his original proclamation (it is not a law) morally acceptable? Tiresias' dire warnings strongly suggest it is not. There has been much argument about how Creon's edict related to Athenian law, but certain points are clear: although there was apparently nothing abnormal in the denial of burial in his homeland to a traitor, not only was there a custom, specifically associated with Athens, according to which one should not pass a corpse by without placing some dust upon it, but also, in forbidding Polynices burial *anywhere,* in actively ensuring that his body be torn apart by dogs and birds, Creon plainly went too far.

Most critics accept the moral impropriety of Creon's proclamation and disagree only in the degree (or absence) of qualification which they allow in their approval of Antigone. For some the approval is absolute; others, believing gray to be a more interesting color than black and white, stress problematic aspects of her behavior — harshness towards Ismene, relentless concern with honor, etc. A beneficial corollary of the latter approach is that, by emphasizing the particularity of Antigone's character, it makes us less likely to reduce the play to an opposition between principles — city *versus* kin-bond, state *versus* individual, or whatever. Neither Creon nor Antigone is the vehicle for a simple idea: "the theme of . . . *Antigone* . . . [is] the tragedy of two human downfalls, separate in nature, . . . following one another as contrasting patterns."[2]

From *Sophocles*

Considerations for Critical Thinking and Writing

1. How do you think "the particularity of Antigone's character . . . makes us less likely to reduce the play to an opposition between principles"? How does Sophocles' characterization of her make the play more complex?
2. Write an essay in which you agree or disagree that the theme of *Antigone* is "the tragedy of two human downfalls, separate in nature . . . following one another as

[1] R. P. Winnington-Ingram, *Sophocles: An Interpretation* (Cambridge, England: Cambridge UP, 1980), 75.
[2] K. Reinhardt, *Sophocles* (Oxford, England: Oxford UP, 1979), 65. For *Antigone* as comprising two interdependent and equally important downfalls, see J. C. Hogan, "The Protagonists of the *Antigone*," *Arethusa* 5(1972), 93–100.

contrasting patterns." Do you think this theme is a means of resolving critical debate about the play or a way to evade having to choose between Antigone and Creon?

CYNTHIA P. GARDINER (b. 1942)
The Function of the Chorus in Antigone   1987

[*Antigone* is] concerned with the topic of political morality, with philosophies of governance and the conflict of religion and law. Yet despite the immensity of these abstractions, the immediate dramatic intent of the poet is not the subject of critical dispute, in that critics do not tend to hold violently contradictory opinions about the poet's own views. Nearly everyone agrees that Sophocles intended to portray Antigone's burial of Polynices as "right" — sanctioned by the gods according to Tiresias' revelations — and Creon's opposition to the burial as "wrong," insofar as his opposition arises from tyrannical behavior. It then becomes merely a question of the degree to which one condemns Creon or approves Antigone; the latter course usually involves an appraisal of Antigone's motives and of her behavior as a woman.

The lengthy and frequent lyrics have exerted considerable influence upon the interpretation of the play's symbolism and judgment. Some of the odes are apparently so loosely connected to the action that they can be readily lifted out of context to function as independent poems. Or, when left in the play, they seem sometimes so ambiguous that their relevance to the plot is perceptible only through the most detailed and subtle analysis. It is generally agreed nowadays that the most productive approach to interpreting the choral lyrics is to assume that they arise from a distinct and consistent persona. This being accepted, it is again a question of the degree to which one believes that the chorus support either Creon or Antigone. Some say that the chorus are utterly devoted to Creon throughout the play, or right up to the last possible moment at line 1272; some, that they begin by supporting the king but change their minds at one earlier point or another during the action. Others see the chorus as vacillating between viewpoints until a decision is forced upon them by Tiresias; still others see them as Antigone's partisans, though necessarily secret ones, from the very beginning.

From *The Sophoclean Chorus: A Study of Character and Function*

Considerations for Critical Thinking and Writing

1. Do you agree with Gardiner that Antigone was "right" and Creon "wrong"? Explain why. How is this issue made complicated by Antigone's character?
2. Of the various interpretations Gardiner summarizes concerning the chorus's loyalty to Creon or Antigone, which do you think is more accurate? In an essay explain why.

28. A Study of William Shakespeare

Although relatively little is known about William Shakespeare's life, his writings reveal him to have been an extraordinary man. His vitality, compassion, and insights are evident in his broad range of characters, who have fascinated generations of audiences, and his powerful use of the English language, which has been celebrated since his death nearly four centuries ago. His contemporary Ben Jonson rightly claimed that "he was not of an age, but for all time!" Shakespeare's plays have been produced so often and his writings read so widely that quotations from them have woven their way into our everyday conversations. If you have ever experienced "fear and trembling" because there was "something in the wind" or discovered that it was "a foregone conclusion" that you would "make a virtue of necessity," then it wouldn't be quite accurate for you to say that Shakespeare "was Greek to me," because these phrases come, respectively, from his plays *Much Ado about Nothing, Comedy of Errors, Othello, The Two Gentlemen of Verona,* and *Julius Caesar.* Many more examples could be cited, but it is enough to say that Shakespeare's art endures. His words may give us only an oblique glimpse of his life, but they continue to give us back the experience of our own lives.

Shakespeare was born in Stratford-on-Avon on or about April 23, 1564. His father, an important citizen who held several town offices, married a woman from a prominent family; however, when their son was only a teenager, the family's financial situation became precarious. Shakespeare probably attended the Stratford grammar school, but no records of either his schooling or his early youth exist. As limited as his education was, it is clear that he was for his time a learned man. At the age of eighteen, he struck out on his own and married the twenty-six-year-old Anne Hathaway, who bore him a daughter in 1583 and twins, a boy and a girl, in 1585. Before he was twenty-one, Shakespeare had a wife and three children to support.

What his life was like for the next seven years is not known, but there is firm evidence that by 1592 he was in London enjoying some success as both an actor and a playwright. By 1594 he had also established himself as a poet with two lengthy poems, *Venus and Adonis* and *The Rape of Lucrece*. But it was in the theater that he made his living and his strongest reputation. He was well connected with a successful troupe first known as the Lord Chamberlain's Men; they built the famous Globe Theatre in 1599. Later this company, because of the patronage of King James, came to be known as the King's Men. Writing plays for this company throughout his career, Shakespeare also became one of its principal shareholders, an arrangement that allowed him to prosper in London as well as in his native Stratford, where in 1597 he bought a fine house called New Place. About 1611 he retired there with his family, although he continued writing plays. He died on April 23, 1616, and was buried at Holy Trinity Church in Stratford.

The documented details of Shakespeare's life provide barely enough information for a newspaper obituary. But if his activities remain largely unknown, his writings — among them thirty-seven plays and one hundred and fifty-four sonnets — more than compensate for that loss. Plenty of authors have produced more work, but no writer has created so much literature that has been so universally admired. Within twenty-five years Shakespeare's dramatic works included *Hamlet, Macbeth, King Lear, Othello, Julius Caesar, Richard III, 1 Henry IV, Romeo and Juliet, Love's Labour's Lost, A Midsummer Night's Dream, The Tempest, Twelfth Night,* and *Measure for Measure*. These plays represent a broad range of characters and actions conveyed in poetic language that reveals human nature as well as the author's genius.

Chronology

1564   Born in April in Stratford-on-Avon. Shakespeare's birthday is traditionally observed on April 23.

1568   Shakespeare's father becomes bailiff (comparable to mayor).

1582   Marries Anne Hathaway.

1583   Daughter Susanna is born.

1585   Twins, Hamnet and Judith, are born.

1585–92 The "lost years" — there are many myths about how Shakespeare spent this time before he became known as a playwright in London, but none can be proven and nothing definite is known.

1592   Works as an actor and playwright in London.

1592–93 Writes *Richard III,* among other plays.

1593   Narrative poem *Venus and Adonis* is published.

1594   Works as actor and playwright with the Lord Chamberlain's Company of players, a company that performs at the Globe Theatre.

c. 1594– Writes *Romeo and Juliet, Richard II,* and *A Midsummer Night's*
96   *Dream,* among other plays.

1596   Hamnet (Shakespeare's son) dies.

1596–98 Writes *1 Henry IV* and *2 Henry IV.*

1599   Writes *Julius Caesar.*

c. 1600 Writes *Hamlet.*

1601   Shakespeare's father dies.

1603   Queen Elizabeth I of England dies.

1603–04 Writes *Othello.*

1604   King James I of England is coronated. (James patronizes
        Shakespeare's company, so they become known as the King's Men.)

1605–07 Writes *King Lear, Macbeth,* and *Antony and Cleopatra.*

c. 1610– Writes *The Tempest.*
11

1616   Dies on April 23.

1623   First Folio edition of Shakespeare's plays is published.

SHAKESPEARE'S THEATER

Drama languished in Europe after the fall of Rome during the fifth and sixth centuries. From about A.D. 400 to 900 almost no record of dramatic productions exists except for those of minstrels and other entertainers, such as acrobats and jugglers, who traveled through the countryside. The Catholic church was instrumental in suppressing drama because the theater — represented by the excesses of Roman productions — was seen as subversive. No state-sponsored festivals brought people together in huge theaters the way they had in Greek and Roman times.

In the tenth century, however, the church helped revive theater by incorporating dialogues into the Mass as a means of dramatizing portions of the Gospels. These brief dialogues developed into more elaborate mystery plays, miracle plays, and morality plays, anonymous works that were created primarily to inculcate religious principles rather than to entertain. But these works also marked the reemergence of relatively large dramatic productions.

Mystery plays dramatize stories from the Bible, such as the Creation, the Fall of Adam and Eve, or the Crucifixion. The most highly regarded surviving example is *The Second Shepherd's Play* (c. 1400), which dramatizes Christ's nativity. *Miracle plays* are based on the lives of saints. An extant play of the late fifteenth century, for example, is titled *Saint Mary Magdalene.* *Morality plays* present allegorical stories in which virtues and vices are personified to teach humanity how to achieve salvation. *Everyman* (c. 1500), the most famous example, has as its central conflict every person's struggle to avoid the sins that lead to Hell and practice the virtues that are rewarded in Heaven.

The clergy who performed these plays gave way to trade guilds that presented them outside the church on stages featuring scenery and costumed characters. The plays' didactic content was gradually abandoned in favor of broad humor and worldly concerns. Thus by the sixteenth century religious drama had been replaced largely by secular drama.

Because theatrical productions were no longer sponsored and financed by the church or trade guilds during Shakespeare's lifetime, playwrights had to figure out ways to draw audiences willing to pay for entertainment. This necessitated some simple but important changes. Somehow, people had to be prevented from seeing a production unless they paid. Hence an enclosed space with controlled access was created. In addition, the plays had to change frequently enough to keep audiences returning, and this resulted in more experienced actors and playwrights sensitive to their audiences' tastes and interests. Plays compelling enough to attract audiences had to employ powerful writing brought to life by convincing actors in entertaining productions. Shakespeare always wrote his dramas for the stage — for audiences who would see and hear his characters. The conventions of the theater for which he wrote are important, then, for appreciating and understanding his plays. Detailed information about Elizabethan theater (theater during the reign of Elizabeth I, from 1558 to 1603) is less than abundant, but historians have been able to piece together a good sense of what the theaters were like from sources such as drawings, building contracts, and stage directions.

Early performances of various kinds took place in the courtyards of inns and taverns. These secular entertainments attracted people of all classes. To the dismay of London officials, such gatherings were also settings for the illegal activities of brawlers, thieves, and prostitutes. To avoid licensing regulations, some theaters were constructed outside the city's limits. The Globe, for instance, built by the Lord Chamberlain's company with which Shakespeare was closely associated, was located on the south bank of the Thames River. Regardless of the play, an Elizabethan theatergoer was likely to have an exciting time. Playwrights understood the varied nature of their audiences, so the plays appealed to a broad range of sensibilities and tastes. Philosophy and poetry rubbed shoulders with violence and sexual jokes, and somehow all were made compatible.

Physically, Elizabethan theaters resembled the courtyards where they originated, but the theaters could accommodate more people — perhaps as many as twenty-five hundred. The exterior of a theater building was many-sided or round and enclosed a yard that was only partially roofed over, to take advantage of natural light. The interior walls consisted of three galleries

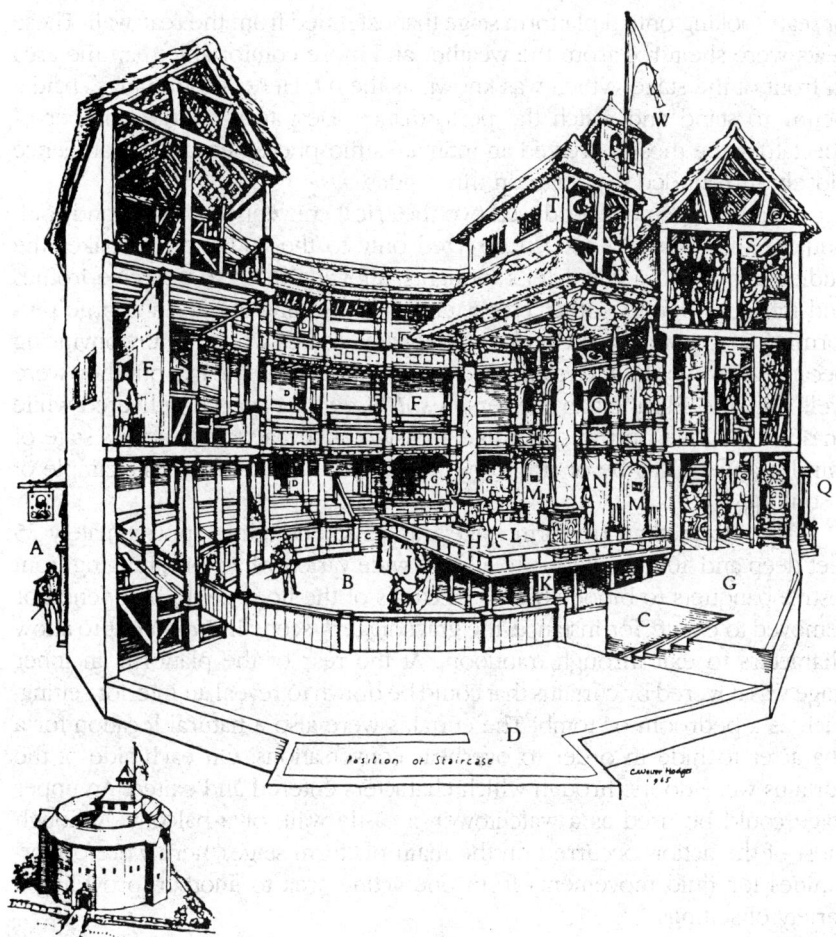

A	Main Entrance
B	The Yard
C	Entrances to lowest gallery
D	Position of entrances to staircase and upper galleries
E	Corridor serving the different sections of the middle gallery
F	Middle gallery ("Twopenny Rooms")
G	Position of "Gentlemen's Rooms" or "Lords Rooms"
H	The stage
J	The hanging being put up round the stage
K	The "Hell" under the stage
L	The stage trap leading down to the Hell

M	Stage doors
N	Curtained "place behind the stage"
O	Gallery above the stage, used as required sometimes by musicians, sometimes by spectators, and often as part of the play
P	Backstage area (the tiring-house)
Q	Tiring-house door
R	Dressing-rooms
S	Wardrobe and storage
T	The hut housing the machine for lowering enthroned gods, etc., to the stage
U	The "Heavens"
W	Hoisting the playhouse flag

A conjectural reconstruction of the Globe Theatre, 1599–1613. (Drawing by C. Walter Hodges from his *The Globe Restored,* published by Oxford University Press. © 1968 C. Walter Hodges. Reprinted by permission of Oxford University Press.)

of seats looking onto a platform stage that extended from the rear wall. These seats were sheltered from the weather and more comfortable than the area in front of the stage, which was known as the *pit.* Here "groundlings" paid a penny to stand and watch the performance. Despite the large number of spectators, the theater created an intimate atmosphere because the audience closely surrounded the stage on three sides.

This arrangement produced two theatrical conventions: asides and soliloquies. An *aside* is a speech directed only to the audience. It makes the audience privy to a character's thoughts, allowing them to perceive ironies and intrigues that the other characters know nothing about. In a large performing space, such as a Greek amphitheater, asides would be unconvincing because they would have to be declaimed loudly to be heard, but they were well suited to Elizabethan theaters. A *soliloquy* is a speech delivered while an actor is alone on the stage; like an aside, it reveals a character's state of mind. Hamlet's "To be or not to be" speech is the most famous example of a soliloquy.

The Elizabethan platform stage was large enough — approximately 25 feet deep and 40 feet wide — to allow a wide variety of actions, ranging from festive banquets to bloody battles. Sections of the floor could be opened or removed to create, for instance, the gravediggers' scene in *Hamlet* or to allow characters to exit through trapdoors. At the rear of the platform an inner stage was covered by curtains that could be drawn to reveal an interior setting, such as a bedroom or tomb. The curtains were also a natural location for a character to hide in order to overhear conversations. On each side of the curtains were doors through which characters entered and exited. An upper stage could be used as a watchtower, a castle wall, or a balcony. Although most of the action occurred on the main platform stage, there were opportunities for fluid movements from one acting area to another, providing a variety of settings.

These settings were not, however, elaborately indicated by scenery or props. A scene might change when one group of characters left the stage and another entered. A table and some chairs could be carried on quickly to suggest a tavern. But the action was not interrupted for set changes. Instead, the characters' speeches often identify the location of a scene. (In modern editions of Shakespeare's plays, editors indicate in brackets the scene breaks, settings, and movements of actors not identified in the original manuscripts to help readers keep track of things.) Today's performances of the plays frequently use more elaborate settings and props. But Shakespeare's need to paint his scenery with words resulted in many poetic descriptions. Here is one of moonlight from *Merchant of Venice:*

> How sweet the moonlight sleeps upon this bank!
> Here will we sit and let the sounds of music
> Creep in our ears. Soft stillness and the night
> Become the touches of sweet harmony.

Although the settings were scant and the props mostly limited to what an actor carried onto the stage (a sword, a document, a shovel), Elizabethan costuming was an elaborate visual treat that identified the characters. Moreover, because women were not permitted to act in the theater, their roles were played by young boys dressed in female costumes. In addition, elaborate sound effects were used to create atmosphere. A flourish of trumpets might accompany the entrance of a king; small cannons might be heard during a battle; thunder might punctuate a storm. In short, Elizabethan theater was alive with sights and sounds, but at the center of the stage was the playwright's language; that's where the magic began.

THE RANGE OF SHAKESPEARE'S DRAMA: HISTORY, COMEDY, AND TRAGEDY

Shakespeare's plays fall into three basic categories: histories, comedies, and tragedies. Broadly speaking, a history play is any drama based on historical materials. In this sense, Shakespeare's *Antony and Cleopatra* and *Julius Caesar* would fit the definition, since they feature historical figures. More specifically, though, a *history play* is a British play based primarily on Raphael Holinshed's *Chronicles of England, Scotland, and Ireland* (1578). This account of British history was popular toward the end of the sixteenth century because of the patriotic pride that was produced by the British defeat of the Spanish Armada in 1588, and it was an important source for a series of plays Shakespeare wrote treating the reigns of British kings from Richard II to Henry VIII. The political subject matter of these plays both entertained audiences and instructed them in the virtues and vices involved in England's past efforts to overcome civil war and disorder. Ambition, deception, and treason were of more than historical interest. Shakespeare's audiences saw these plays about the fifteenth century as ways of sorting through the meanings of both the calamities of the past and the uncertainties of the present.

Although Shakespeare used Holinshed's *Chronicles* as a source, he did not hesitate to make changes for dramatic purposes. In *1 Henry IV,* for example, he ages Henry IV to contrast him with the youthful Prince Hal, and he makes Hotspur younger than he actually was to have him serve as a foil to the prince. The serious theme of Hal's growth into the kind of man who would make an ideal king is counterweighted by Shakespeare's comic creation of Falstaff, that good-humored "huge hill of flesh" filled with delightful contradictions. Falstaff had historic antecedents, but the true source of his identity is the imagination of Shakespeare, a writer who was, after all, a dramatist first.

Comedy is a strong element in *1 Henry IV,* but the play's overall tone is serious. Falstaff's riotous behavior ultimately gives way to the measured march of English history. While Shakespeare encourages us to laugh at some of the participants, we are not invited to laugh at the history of English monarchies. Comedy even appears in Shakespeare's tragedies, as in Hamlet's jests with the gravediggers, or in Emilia's biting remarks in *Othello*. This use of comedy is called *comic relief,* a humorous scene or incident that alleviates tension in an otherwise serious work. In many instances these moments enhance the thematic significance of the story in addition to providing laughter. When Hamlet jokes with the gravediggers we laugh, but something hauntingly serious about the humor also intensifies our more serious emotions.

A true comedy, however, lacks a tragedy's sense that some great disaster will finally descend on the protagonist. There are conflicts and obstacles that must be confronted, but in comedy the characters delight us by overcoming whatever initially thwarts them. We can laugh at their misfortunes because we are confident that everything will turn out fine in the end. Shakespearean comedy tends to follow this general principle; it begins with problems and ends with their resolution.

Shakespeare's comedies are called *romantic comedies* because they typically involve lovers whose hearts are set on each other but whose lives are complicated by disapproving parents, deceptions, jealousies, illusions, confused identities, disguises, or other misunderstandings. Conflicts are present, but they are more amusing than threatening. This lightness is apparent in some of the comedies' titles: the conflict in a play such as *A Midsummer Night's Dream* is, in a sense, *Much Ado about Nothing — As You Like It* in a comedy. Shakespeare orchestrates the problems and confusion that typify the initial plotting of a romantic comedy into harmonious wedding arrangements in the final scenes. In these comedies life is a celebration, a feast that always satisfies, because the generosity of the humor leaves us with a revived appetite for life's surprising possibilities. Discord and misunderstanding give way to concord and love. Marriage symbolizes a pledge that life itself is renewable, so we are left with a sense of new beginnings.

Although a celebration of life, comedy is also frequently used as a vehicle for criticizing human affairs. *Satire* casts a critical eye on vices and follies by holding them up to ridicule — usually to point out an absurdity so that it can be avoided or corrected. In *Twelfth Night* Malvolio is satirized for his priggishness and pomposity. He thinks himself better than almost everyone around him, but Shakespeare reveals him to be comic as well as pathetic. We come to understand what Malvolio will apparently never comprehend: that no one can take him as seriously as he takes himself. Polonius is subjected to a similar kind of scrutiny in *Hamlet*.

Malvolio's ambitious efforts to attract Olivia's affections are rendered absurd by Shakespeare's use of both high and low comedy. *High comedy* consists of verbal wit, while *low comedy* is generally associated with physical action and is less intellectual. Through puns and witty exchanges, Shakespeare's high comedy displays Malvolio's inconsistencies of character. His self-importance is deflated by low comedy. We are treated to a *farce,* a form of humor based on exaggerated, improbable incongruities, when the staid Malvolio is tricked into wearing bizarre clothing and behaving like a fool to win Olivia. Our laughter is Malvolio's pain, but though he has been "notoriously abus'd" and he vows in the final scene to be "reveng'd on the whole pack" of laughing conspirators who have tricked him, the play ends on a light note. Indeed, it concludes with a song, the last line of which reminds us of the predominant tone of the play as well as the nature of comedy: "And we'll strive to please you every day."

Tragedy, in contrast, does not promise peace and contentment. The basic characteristics of tragedy have already been outlined in the context of Greek drama (see Chapter 27). Like Greek tragic heroes, Shakespeare's protagonists are exceptional human beings whose stature makes their misfortune all the more dramatic. These characters pay a high price for their actions. Oedipus's search for the killer of Laius, Antigone's and Creon's refusal to compromise their principles, Hamlet's agonized conviction that "The time is out of joint," and Othello's willingness to doubt his wife's fidelity all lead to irreversible results. Comic plots are largely free of this sense of inevitability. Instead of the festive mood that prevails once the characters in a comedy recognize their true connection to each other, tragedy gives us dark reflections that emanate from suffering. The laughter of comedy is a shared experience, a recognition of human likeness, but suffering estranges tragic heroes from the world around them.

Some of the wrenching differences between comedy and tragedy can be experienced in *Othello*. Although this play is a tragedy, Shakespeare includes in its plot many of the ingredients associated with comedy. For a time it seems possible that Othello and Desdemona will overcome the complications of a disapproving father, along with the seemingly minor deceptions, awkward misperceptions, and tender illusions that hover around them. But in *Othello* marriage is not a sign of concord displacing discord; instead, love and marriage mark the beginning of the tragic action.

Another important difference between tragedy and comedy is the way characters are presented. The tragic protagonist is portrayed as a remarkable individual whose unique qualities compel us with their power and complexity. Macbeth is not simply a murderer nor is Othello merely a jealous husband. But despite their extreme passions, behavior, and even crimes, we identify with tragic heroes in ways that we do not with comic characters. We can laugh at pretentious fools, smug hypocrites, clumsy oafs, and thwarted lovers because we see them from a distance. They are amusing precisely because their problems are not ours; we recognize them as types instead of as ourselves (or so we think). No reader of *Twelfth Night* worries about Sir Toby Belch's excessive drinking; he is a cheerful "sot" whose passion for ale is cause for celebration rather than concern. Shakespeare's comedy is sometimes disturbing — Malvolio's character certainly is — but it is never devastating. Tragic heroes do confront devastation; they command our respect and compassion because they act in spite of terrifying risks. Their triumph is not measured by the attainment of what they seek but by the wisdom that defeat imposes on them.

A NOTE ON READING SHAKESPEARE

Readers who have had no previous experience with Shakespeare's language may find it initially daunting. They might well ask whether people ever talked the way, for example, Hamlet does in his most famous soliloquy:

> To be, or not to be: that is the question:
> Whether 'tis nobler in the mind to suffer
> The slings and arrows of outrageous fortune,
> Or to take arms against a sea of troubles,
> And by opposing end them?

People did not talk like this in Elizabethan times. Hamlet speaks poetry. Shakespeare might have had him say something like this: "The most important issue one must confront is whether the pain that life inevitably creates should be passively accepted or resisted." But Shakespeare chose poetry to reveal the depth and complexity of Hamlet's experience. This heightened language is used to clarify rather than obscure his characters' thoughts. Shakespeare has Hamlet, as well as many other characters, speak in prose too, but in general his plays are written in poetry. If you keep in mind that Shakespeare's dialogue is not typically intended to imitate everyday speech, it should be easier to understand that his language is more than simply a vehicle for expressing the action of the play.

Here are a few practical suggestions to enhance your understanding of and pleasure in reading Shakespeare's plays.

1. Keep track of the characters by referring to the *dramatis personae* (characters) listed and briefly described at the beginning of each play.
2. Remember that poetic language deserves to be read slowly and carefully. A difficult passage can sometimes be better understood if it's read aloud. Don't worry if every line isn't absolutely clear to you.
3. Pay attention to the annotations, which explain unfamiliar words, phrases, and allusions in the text. These can be distracting, but they are sometimes necessary to determine the basic meaning of a passage.
4. As you read each scene, try to imagine how it would be played on a stage.
5. If you find the reading especially difficult, try listening to a recording of the play. (Most college libraries have records and tapes of Shakespeare's plays.) Allowing professional actors to do the reading aloud for you can enrich your imaginative reconstruction of the action and characters. Hearing a play can help you with subsequent readings of it.

6. After reading the play, view a film or videocassette recording of a performance. It is important to view the performance *after* your reading, though, so that your own mental re-creation of the play is not short-circuited by a director's production.

And finally, to quote Hamlet, "Be not too tame . . . let your own discretion be your tutor." Read Shakespeare's work as best you can; it warrants such careful attention not because the language and characters are difficult to understand, but because they offer so much to enjoy.

A MIDSUMMER NIGHT'S DREAM

A Midsummer Night's Dream, one of Shakespeare's most popular plays with readers and audiences, is a romantic comedy about the complex nature of love and marriage. Though some serious points about law and social order are made along the way, the action is propelled by the powers of youth, romance, love, passion, and the hilarious pursuits of characters turned about by fairies, illusions, and their own misunderstandings.

Shakespeare uses several sets of couples to dramatize love's tribulations and triumphs. The play opens with Theseus, Duke of Athens, making arrangements to wed Hippolyta, queen of the Amazons. Once enemies, they now seek love and peace in the harmony of marriage. Their union represents the happy necessity of order in the state and suggests a model of behavior that the other characters struggle to achieve.

In contrast to the serene plans for the royal wedding is the conflict produced by four Athenian youths who are thwarted in love: Helena loves Demetrius, but Demetrius loves Hermia, who wants to marry Lysander. This collision of passions is further complicated by Hermia's father, who insists in the Duke's presence that if she doesn't marry Demetrius, she must die or spend her life in a nunnery. Much of the play's conflict concerns how these two young couples align their love for one another so that each desires and is desired by the right person. When Hermia defies her father and refuses to marry Demetrius, she flees to the woods, followed by Lysander and Demetrius as well as Helena, who is in pursuit of Demetrius.

Once in the woods, the lovers find themselves in a supernatural world, the unpredictable kingdom of Oberon and Titania, the king and queen of the fairies. This fourth couple creates even more confusion through Oberon's impatience with Titania. Their quarrel results in Oberon ordering his servant, Puck, to cast magical spells on the lovers as well as on Titania. This gives Puck the license to reveal their foolishness while eventually saving them from their own confused passions. Their reconciliations and reunions are not achieved, however, until Puck puts them through a series of comic encounters based on their illusions and vulnerabilities.

The final act includes the play within the play, "the most lamentable comedy" of two more lovers, Pyramus and Thisbe, who misunderstand one another. This travesty of a tragedy is put on by Athenian craftsmen — who are clearly better laborers than they are actors — at the Duke's request for a wedding entertainment. This play within the play reinforces the larger play's concerns about the nature of love and, indeed, of reality itself, because it raises questions about the fluid, complex relationship between art and reality. Ultimately, however, questions, issues, and conflicts give way to a generous sense of everything working out for the best as the play ends with Puck's warm assurances to the audience and his gentle urging to "Give me your hands."

WILLIAM SHAKESPEARE (1564–1616)

A Midsummer Night's Dream   c. 1595

[Dramatis Personae

Theseus, Duke of Athens
Hippolyta, Queen of the Amazons, betrothed to Theseus
Philostrate, Master of the Revels
Egeus, father of Hermia

Hermia, daughter of Egeus, in love with Lysander
Lysander, in love with Hermia
Demetrius, in love with Hermia and favored by Egeus
Helena, in love with Demetrius

Oberon, King of the Fairies
Titania, Queen of the Fairies
Puck, or Robin Goodfellow
Peaseblossom, ⎫
Cobweb,   ⎬ fairies attending Titania
Mote,   ⎪
Mustardseed, ⎭
Other Fairies attending

Peter Quince, a carpenter,   ⎫   Prologue
Nick Bottom, a weaver,   ⎪   Pyramus
Francis Flute, a bellows mender,   ⎬ representing   Thisbe
Tom Snout, a tinker,   ⎪   Wall
Snug, a joiner,   ⎪   Lion
Robin Starveling, a tailor,   ⎭   Moonshine
Lords and Attendants on Theseus and Hippolyta

SCENE: Athens, and a wood near it.]

Scene I: *Athens. Theseus' court.*]

Enter Theseus, Hippolyta, [and Philostrate,] with others.

Theseus: Now, fair Hippolyta, our nuptial hour
    Draws on apace. Four happy days bring in
    Another moon; but, O, methinks, how slow
    This old moon wanes! She lingers° my desires,
    Like to a stepdame° or a dowager°   5
    Long withering out° a young man's revenue.
Hippolyta: Four days will quickly steep themselves° in night;
    Four nights will quickly dream away the time;
    And then the moon, like to a silver bow
    New bent in heaven, shall behold the night   10
    Of our solemnities.°
Theseus: Go, Philostrate,
    Stir up the Athenian youth to merriments.
    Awake the pert and nimble spirit of mirth.
    Turn melancholy forth to funerals;
    The pale companion° is not for our pomp.°   *[Exit Philostrate.]*   15
    Hippolyta, I wooed thee with my sword°
    And won thy love doing thee injuries;
    But I will wed thee in another key,
    With pomp, with triumph,° and with reveling.

Enter Egeus and his daughter Hermia, and Lysander, and Demetrius.

Egeus: Happy be Theseus, our renownèd duke!   20
Theseus: Thanks, good Egeus. What's the news with thee?
Egeus: Full of vexation come I, with complaint
    Against my child, my daughter Hermia. —
    Stand forth, Demetrius. — My noble lord,
    This man hath my consent to marry her. —   25
    Stand forth, Lysander. — And, my gracious Duke,
    This man hath bewitched the bosom of my child.
    Thou, thou Lysander, thou hast given her rhymes
    And interchanged love tokens with my child.
    Thou hast by moonlight at her window sung   30
    With feigning° voice verses of feigning° love,
    And stol'n the impression of her fantasy°

Act I, Scene I.   4 *lingers:* Postpones, delays the fulfillment of.   5 *stepdame:* Stepmother; *a dowager:*
I.e., a widow (whose right of inheritance from her dead husband is eating into her son's estate).
6 *withering out:* Causing to dwindle.   7 *steep themselves:* Saturate themselves, be absorbed in.
11 *solemnities:* Festive ceremonies of marriage.   15 *companion:* Fellow; *pomp:* Ceremonial
magnificence.   16 *with my sword:* I.e., in a military engagement against the Amazons, when Hippolyta
was taken captive.   19 *triumph:* Public festivity.   31 *feigning:* (1) Counterfeiting (2) faining, desirous.   32 *And . . . fantasy:* And made her fall in love with you (imprinting your image on her
imagination) by stealthy and dishonest means.

With bracelets of thy hair, rings, gauds,° conceits,°
Knacks,° trifles, nosegays, sweetmeats — messengers
Of strong prevailment in° unhardened youth.   35
With cunning hast thou filched my daughter's heart,
Turned her obedience, which is due to me,
To stubborn harshness. And, my gracious Duke,
Be it so° she will not here before Your Grace
Consent to marry with Demetrius,   40
I beg the ancient privilege of Athens:
As she is mine, I may dispose of her,
Which shall be either to this gentleman
Or to her death, according to our law
Immediately° provided in that case.   45
Theseus: What say you, Hermia? Be advised, fair maid.
  To you your father should be as a god —
  One that composed your beauties, yea, and one
  To whom you are but as a form in wax
  By him imprinted, and within his power   50
  To leave° the figure or disfigure° it.
  Demetrius is a worthy gentleman.
Hermia: So is Lysander.
Theseus: In himself he is;
  But in this kind,° wanting° your father's voice,°
  The other must be held the worthier.   55
Hermia: I would my father looked but with my eyes.
Theseus: Rather your eyes must with his judgment look.
Hermia: I do entreat Your Grace to pardon me.
  I know not by what power I am made bold,
  Nor how it may concern° my modesty   60
  In such a presence here to plead my thoughts;
  But I beseech Your Grace that I may know
  The worst that may befall me in this case
  If I refuse to wed Demetrius.
Theseus: Either to die the death° or to abjure   65
  Forever the society of men.
  Therefore, fair Hermia, question your desires,
  Know of your youth, examine well your blood,°
  Whether, if you yield not to your father's choice,
  You can endure the livery° of a nun,   70
  For aye° to be in shady cloister mewed,°
  To live a barren sister all your life,
  Chanting faint hymns to the cold fruitless moon.
  Thrice blessèd they that master so their blood
  To undergo such maiden pilgrimage;   75

33 *gauds:* Playthings; *conceits:* Fanciful trifles. 34 *Knacks:* Knickknacks. 35 *prevailment in:* Influence on. 39 *Be it so:* If. 45 *Immediately:* Directly, with nothing intervening. 51 *leave:* I.e., leave unaltered; *disfigure:* Obliterate. 54 *kind:* Respect; *wanting:* Lacking; *voice:* Approval. 60 *concern:* Befit. 65 *die the death:* Be executed by legal process. 68 *blood:* Passions. 70 *livery:* Habit, costume. 71 *aye:* Ever; *mewed:* Shut in (said of a hawk, poultry, etc.).

But earthlier happy° is the rose distilled°
Than that which, withering on the virgin thorn,
Grows, lives, and dies in single blessedness.
Hermia: So will I grow, so live, so die, my lord,
Ere I will yield my virgin patent° up   80
Unto his lordship, whose unwishèd yoke
My soul consents not to give sovereignty.
Theseus: Take time to pause, and by the next new moon —
The sealing day betwixt my love and me
For everlasting bond of fellowship —   85
Upon that day either prepare to die
For disobedience to your father's will,
Or° else to wed Demetrius, as he would,
Or on Diana's altar to protest°
For aye austerity and single life.   90
Demetrius: Relent, sweet Hermia, and, Lysander, yield
Thy crazèd° title to my certain right.
Lysander: You have her father's love, Demetrius;
Let me have Hermia's. Do you marry him.
Egeus: Scornful Lysander! True, he hath my love,   95
And what is mine my love shall render him.
And she is mine, and all my right of her
I do estate unto° Demetrius.
Lysander: I am, my lord, as well derived° as he,
As well possessed;° my love is more than his;   100
My fortunes every way as fairly° ranked,
If not with vantage,° as Demetrius';
And, which is more than all these boasts can be,
I am beloved of beauteous Hermia.
Why should not I then prosecute my right?   105
Demetrius, I'll avouch it to his head,°
Made love to Nedar's daughter, Helena,
And won her soul; and she, sweet lady, dotes,
Devoutly dotes, dotes in idolatry
Upon this spotted° and inconstant man.   110
Theseus: I must confess that I have heard so much,
And with Demetrius thought to have spoke thereof;
But, being overfull of self-affairs,°
My mind did lose it. But, Demetrius, come,
And come, Egeus, you shall go with me;   115
I have some private schooling° for you both.
For you, fair Hermia, look you arm yourself°
To fit your fancies° to your father's will,

---

76 *earthlier happy:* Happier as respects this world; *distilled:* I.e., to make perfume.   80 *patent:*
Privilege.   88 *Or:* Either.   89 *protest:* Vow.   92 *crazèd:* Cracked, unsound.   98 *estate unto:*
Settle or bestow upon.   99 *as well derived:* As well born and descended.   100 *possessed:* Endowed
with wealth.   101 *fairly:* Handsomely.   102 *vantage:* Superiority.   106 *head:* I.e., face.
110 *spotted:* I.e., morally stained.   113 *self-affairs:* My own concerns.   116 *schooling:* Admonition.
117 *look you arm:* Take care you prepare.   118 *fancies:* Likings, thoughts of love.

Or else the law of Athens yields you up—
Which by no means we may extenuate°—   120
To death or to a vow of single life.
Come, my Hippolyta. What cheer, my love?
Demetrius and Egeus, go° along.
I must employ you in some business
Against° our nuptial, and confer with you   125
Of something nearly that° concerns yourselves.
Egeus: With duty and desire we follow you.

Exeunt [all but Lysander and Hermia].

Lysander: How now, my love, why is your cheek so pale?
How chance the roses there do fade so fast?
Hermia: Belike° for want of rain, which I could well   130
Beteem° them from the tempest of my eyes.
Lysander: Ay me! For aught that I could ever read,
Could ever hear by tale or history,
The course of true love never did run smooth;
But either it was different in blood°—   135
Hermia: O cross!° Too high to be enthralled to low.
Lysander: Or else misgrafted° in respect of years—
Hermia: O spite! Too old to be engaged to young.
Lysander: Or else it stood upon the choice of friends°—
Hermia: O hell, to choose love by another's eyes!   140
Lysander: Or if there were a sympathy° in choice,
War, death, or sickness did lay siege to it,
Making it momentany° as a sound,
Swift as a shadow, short as any dream,
Brief as the lightning in the collied° night   145
That in a spleen° unfolds° both heaven and earth,
And ere a man hath power to say "Behold!"
The jaws of darkness do devour it up.
So quick° bright things come to confusion.°
Hermia: If then true lovers have been ever crossed,°   150
It stands as an edict in destiny.
Then let us teach our trial patience,°
Because it is a customary cross,
As due to love as thoughts, and dreams, and sighs,
Wishes, and tears, poor fancy's° followers.   155
Lysander: A good persuasion.° Therefore, hear me, Hermia:
I have a widow aunt, a dowager
Of great revenue, and she hath no child.
From Athens is her house remote seven leagues;

120 *extenuate:* Mitigate, relax.   123 *go:* I.e., come.   125 *Against:* In preparation for.   126 *nearly that:* That closely.   130 *Belike:* Very likely.   131 *Beteem:* Grant, afford.   135 *blood:* Hereditary station.   136 *cross:* Vexation.   137 *misgrafted:* Ill grafted, badly matched.   139 *friends:* Relatives.   141 *sympathy:* Agreement.   143 *momentany:* Lasting but a moment.   145 *collied:* Blackened (as with coal dust), darkened.   146 *in a spleen:* In a swift impulse, in a violent flash; *unfolds:* Reveals.   149 *quick:* Quickly; also, living, alive; *confusion:* Ruin.   150 *ever crossed:* Always thwarted.   152 *teach . . . patience:* I.e., teach ourselves patience in this trial.   155 *fancy's:* Amorous passion's.   156 *persuasion:* Doctrine.

And she respects° me as her only son.   160
There, gentle Hermia, may I marry thee,
And to that place the sharp Athenian law
Cannot pursue us. If thou lovest me, then,
Steal forth thy father's house tomorrow night;
And in the wood, a league without° the town,   165
Where I did meet thee once with Helena
To do observance to a morn of May,°
There will I stay for thee.
Hermia: My good Lysander!
I swear to thee, by Cupid's strongest bow,
By his best arrow° with the golden head,   170
By the simplicity° of Venus' doves,°
By that which knitteth souls and prospers loves,
And by that fire which burned the Carthage queen°
When the false Trojan° under sail was seen,
By all the vows that ever men have broke,   175
In number more than ever women spoke,
In that same place thou hast appointed me
Tomorrow truly will I meet with thee.
Lysander: Keep promise, love. Look, here comes Helena.

Enter Helena.

Hermia: God speed, fair° Helena! Whither away?   180
Helena: Call you me fair? That "fair" again unsay.
Demetrius loves your fair.° O happy fair!°
Your eyes are lodestars,° and your tongue's sweet air°
More tunable° than lark to shepherd's ear
When wheat is green, when hawthorn buds appear.   185
Sickness is catching. O, were favor° so,
Yours would I catch, fair Hermia, ere I go;
My ear should catch your voice, my eye your eye,
My tongue should catch your tongue's sweet melody.
Were the world mine, Demetrius being bated,°   190
The rest I'd give to be to you translated.°
O, teach me how you look and with what art
You sway° the motion° of Demetrius' heart.
Hermia: I frown upon him, yet he loves me still.
Helena: O, that your frowns would teach my smiles such skill!   195
Hermia: I give him curses, yet he gives me love.

---

160 *respects:* Regards.   165 *without:* Outside.   167 *do . . . May:* Perform the ceremonies of May
Day.   170 *best arrow:* (Cupid's best gold-pointed arrows were supposed to induce love; his blunt
leaden arrows, aversion.)   171 *simplicity:* Innocence; *doves:* I.e., those that drew Venus' chariot.
173, 174 *Carthage queen, false Trojan:* (Dido, Queen of Carthage, immolated herself on a funeral pyre
after having been deserted by the Trojan hero Aeneas.)   180 *fair:* Fair-complexioned (generally
regarded by the Elizabethans as more beautiful than a dark complexion).   182 *your fair:* Your beauty
(even though Hermia is dark complexioned); *happy fair:* Lucky fair one.   183 *lodestars:* Guiding
stars; *air:* Music.   184 *tunable:* Tuneful, melodious.   186 *favor:* Appearance, looks.   190 *bated:*
Excepted.   191 *translated:* Transformed.   193 *sway:* Control; *motion:* Impulse.

Helena: O, that my prayers could such affection° move!°
Hermia: The more I hate, the more he follows me.
Helena: The more I love, the more he hateth me.
Hermia: His folly, Helena, is no fault of mine.   200
Helena: None, but your beauty. Would that fault were mine!
Hermia: Take comfort. He no more shall see my face.
　　Lysander and myself will fly this place.
　　Before the time I did Lysander see
　　Seemed Athens as a paradise to me.°   205
　　O, then, what graces in my love do dwell,
　　That he hath turned a heaven unto a hell?
Lysander: Helen, to you our minds we will unfold.
　　Tomorrow night, when Phoebe° doth behold
　　Her silver visage in the watery glass,°   210
　　Decking with liquid pearl the bladed grass,
　　A time that lovers' flights doth still° conceal,
　　Through Athens' gates have we devised to steal.
Hermia: And in the wood, where often you and I
　　Upon faint° primrose beds were wont to lie,   215
　　Emptying our bosoms of their counsel° sweet,
　　There my Lysander and myself shall meet,
　　And thence from Athens turn away our eyes
　　To seek new friends and stranger companies.°
　　Farewell, sweet playfellow. Pray thou for us,   220
　　And good luck grant thee thy Demetrius!
　　Keep word, Lysander. We must starve our sight
　　From lovers' food till morrow deep midnight.
Lysander: I will, my Hermia. *(Exit Hermia.)* Helena, adieu.
　　As you on him, Demetrius dote on you!　　　　　　　　　　　　*Exit Lysander.*　225
Helena: How happy some o'er other some can be!°
　　Through Athens I am thought as fair as she.
　　But what of that? Demetrius thinks not so;
　　He will not know what all but he do know.
　　And as he errs, doting on Hermia's eyes,   230
　　So I, admiring of° his qualities.
　　Things base and vile, holding no quantity,°
　　Love can transpose to form and dignity.
　　Love looks not with the eyes, but with the mind,
　　And therefore is winged Cupid painted blind.   235
　　Nor hath Love's mind of any judgment taste;°
　　Wings and no eyes figure° unheedy haste.

197 *affection:* Passion; *move:* Arouse.　　204–205 *Before . . . to me:* (Hermia seemingly means that love has led to complications and jealousies, making Athens hell for her.)　　209 *Phoebe:* Diana, the moon.　　210 *glass:* Mirror.　　212 *still:* Always.　　215 *faint:* Pale.　　216 *counsel:* Secret thought.　　219 *stranger companies:* The company of strangers.　　226 *o'er . . . can be:* Can be in comparison to some others.　　231 *admiring of:* Wondering at.　　232 *holding no quantity:* I.e., unsubstantial, unshapely.　　236 *Nor . . . taste:* I.e., nor has Love, which dwells in the fancy or imagination, any *taste* or least bit of judgment or reason.　　237 *figure:* Are a symbol of.

And therefore is Love said to be a child,
Because in choice° he is so oft beguiled.°
As waggish° boys in game° themselves forswear,   240
So the boy Love is perjured everywhere.
For ere Demetrius looked on Hermia's eyne,°
He hailed down oaths that he was only mine;
And when this hail some heat from Hermia felt,
So he dissolved, and showers of oaths did melt.   245
I will go tell him of fair Hermia's flight.
Then to the wood will he tomorrow night
Pursue her; and for this intelligence°
If I have thanks, it is a dear° expense.°
But herein mean I to enrich my pain,   250
To have his sight thither and back again.   *Exit.*

[SCENE II: *Athens.*]

*Enter Quince the carpenter, and Snug the joiner, and Bottom the weaver, and
Flute the bellows mender, and Snout the tinker, and Starveling the tailor.*

Quince: Is all our company here?
Bottom: You were best to call them generally,° man by man, according to
    the scrip.°
Quince: Here is the scroll of every man's name which is thought fit, through
    all Athens, to play in our interlude° before the Duke and the Duchess on   5
    his wedding day at night.
Bottom: First, good Peter Quince, say what the play treats on, then read the
    names of the actors, and so grow to° a point.
Quince: Marry,° our play is "The most lamentable comedy and most cruel
    death of Pyramus and Thisbe."   10
Bottom: A very good piece of work, I assure you, and a merry. Now, good
    Peter Quince, call forth your actors by the scroll. Masters, spread your-
    selves.
Quince: Answer as I call you. Nick Bottom,° the weaver.
Bottom: Ready. Name what part I am for, and proceed.   15
Quince: You, Nick Bottom, are set down for Pyramus.
Bottom: What is Pyramus? A lover or a tyrant?
Quince: A lover, that kills himself most gallant for love.
Bottom: That will ask some tears in the true performing of it. If I do it, let
    the audience look to their eyes. I will move storms; I will condole° in   20

239 *in choice:* In choosing; *beguiled:* Self-deluded, making unaccountable choices.   240 *waggish:*
Playful, mischievous; *game:* Sport, jest.   242 *eyne:* Eyes (old form of plural).   248 *intelligence:*
Information.   249 *a dear expense:* I.e., a trouble worth taking on my part, or a begrudging effort on
his part; *dear:* Costly.   SCENE II.   2 *generally:* (Bottom's blunder for "individually.")   3 *scrip:*
Scrap (Bottom's error for "script,").   5 *interlude:* Play.   8 *grow to:* Come to.   9 *Marry:* (A mild
oath; originally the name of the Virgin Mary.)   14 *Bottom:* (As a weaver's term, a *bottom* was an
object around which thread was wound.)   20 *condole:* Lament, arouse pity.

some measure. To the rest — yet my chief humor° is for a tyrant. I could
play Ercles° rarely, or a part to tear a cat° in, to make all split.°
> "The raging rocks
> And shivering shocks
> Shall break the locks   25
>   Of prison gates;
> And Phibbus' car°
> Shall shine from far
> And make and mar
>   The foolish Fates."   30

This was lofty! Now name the rest of the players. This is Ercles' vein, a
tyrant's vein. A lover is more condoling.

Quince: Francis Flute, the bellows mender.

Flute: Here, Peter Quince.

Quince: Flute, you must take Thisbe on you.   35

Flute: What is Thisbe? A wandering knight?

Quince: It is the lady that Pyramus must love.

Flute: Nay, faith, let not me play a woman. I have a beard coming.

Quince: That's all one.° You shall play it in a mask, and you may speak as
small° as you will.   40

Bottom: An° I may hide my face, let me play Thisbe too. I'll speak in a
monstrous little voice: "Thisne, Thisne!" "Ah, Pyramus, my lover dear! Thy
Thisbe dear, and lady dear!"

Quince: No, no, you must play Pyramus, and Flute, you Thisbe.

Bottom: Well, proceed.   45

Quince: Robin Starveling, the tailor.

Starveling: Here, Peter Quince.

Quince: Robin Starveling, you must play Thisbe's mother. Tom Snout, the
tinker.

Snout: Here, Peter Quince.   50

Quince: You, Pyramus' father; myself, Thisbe's father; Snug, the joiner, you,
the lion's part; and I hope here is a play fitted.

Snug: Have you the lion's part written? Pray you, if it be, give it me, for I am
slow of study.

Quince: You may do it extempore, for it is nothing but roaring.   55

Bottom: Let me play the lion too. I will roar that I will do any man's heart
good to hear me. I will roar that I will make the Duke say, "Let him roar
again, let him roar again."

Quince: An you should do it too terribly, you would fright the Duchess and
the ladies, that they would shriek; and that were enough to hang us all. 60

All: That would hang us, every mother's son.

Bottom: I grant you, friends, if you should fright the ladies out of their wits,
they would have no more discretion but to hang us; but I will aggravate°

---

21 *humor:* Inclination, whim.   22 *Ercles:* Hercules (the tradition of ranting came from Seneca's
Hercules Furens); *tear a cat:* I.e., rant; *make all split:* I.e., cause a stir, bring the house down.
27 *Phibbus' car:* Phoebus', the sun god's, chariot.   39 *That's all one:* It makes no difference.
40 *small:* High-pitched.   41 *An:* If (also at line 59).   63 *aggravate:* (Bottom's blunder for "moderate.")

my voice so that I will roar you° as gently as any sucking dove;° I will
roar you an 'twere° any nightingale.   65

Quince: You can play no part but Pyramus; for Pyramus is a sweet-faced man,
    a proper° man as one shall see in a summer's day, a most lovely gentle-
    manlike man. Therefore you must needs play Pyramus.

Bottom: Well, I will undertake it. What beard were I best to play it in?

Quince: Why, what you will.   70

Bottom: I will discharge° it in either your° straw-color beard, your orange-
    tawny beard, your purple-in-grain° beard, or your French-crown-color°
    beard, your perfect yellow.

Quince: Some of your French crowns° have no hair at all, and then you will
    play barefaced. But, masters, here are your parts. [*He distributes parts.*] 75
    And I am to entreat you, request you, and desire you to con° them by
    tomorrow night, and meet me in the palace wood, a mile without the
    town, by moonlight. There will we rehearse; for if we meet in the city,
    we shall be dogged with company, and our devices° known. In the
    meantime I will draw a bill° of properties, such as our play wants. I pray   80
    you, fail me not.

Bottom: We will meet, and there we may rehearse most obscenely° and
    courageously. Take pains, be perfect.° Adieu.

Quince: At the Duke's oak we meet.

Bottom: Enough. Hold, or cut bowstrings.°   *Exeunt.*   85

[ACT II

Scene I: *A wood near Athens.*]

Enter a Fairy at one door, and Robin Goodfellow [Puck] at another.

Puck: How now, spirit, whither wander you?

Fairy: Over hill, over dale,
        Thorough° bush, thorough brier,
    Over park, over pale,°
        Thorough flood, thorough fire,   5
    I do wander everywhere,
        Swifter than the moon's sphere;°
    And I serve the Fairy Queen,
        To dew° her orbs° upon the green.

64 *roar you:* I.e., roar for you; *sucking dove:* (Bottom conflates *sitting dove* and *sucking lamb,* two
proverbial images of innocence.)   65 *an 'twere:* As if it were.   67 *proper:* Handsome.   71 *dis-*
charge: Perform; *your:* I.e., you know the kind I mean.   72 *purple-in-grain:* Dyed a very deep red
(from *grain,* the name applied to the dried insect used to make the dye);   72 *French-crown-color:*
I.e., color of a French crown, a gold coin.   74 *crowns:* Heads bald from syphilis, the "French disease."
76 *con:* Learn by heart.   79 *devices:* Plans.   80 *draw a bill:* Draw up a list.   82 *obscenely:* (An
unintentionally funny blunder, whatever Bottom meant to say.)   83 *perfect:* I.e., letter-perfect in
memorizing your parts.   85 *Hold . . . bowstrings:* (An archers' expression, not definitely explained,
but probably meaning here "keep your promises, or give up the play.")   Act II. Scene I.   3 *Thor-*
ough: Through.   4 *pale:* Enclosure.   7 *sphere:* Orbit.   9 *dew:* Sprinkle with dew; *orbs:* Circles,
i.e., fairy rings (circular bands of grass, darker than the surrounding area, caused by fungi enriching
the soil).

The cowslips tall her pensioners° be.   10
In their gold coats spots you see;
Those be rubies, fairy favors;°
    In those freckles live their savors.°
I must go seek some dewdrops here
And hang a pearl in every cowslip's ear.   15
Farewell, thou lob° of spirits; I'll be gone.
Our Queen and all her elves come here anon.°
Puck: The King doth keep his revels here tonight.
Take heed the Queen come not within his sight.
For Oberon is passing fell° and wrath,°   20
Because that she as her attendant hath
A lovely boy, stolen from an Indian king;
She ne'er had so sweet a changeling.°
And jealous Oberon would have the child
Knight of his train, to trace° the forests wild.   25
But she perforce° withholds the lovèd boy,
Crowns him with flowers, and makes him all her joy.
And now they never meet in grove or green,
By fountain° clear, or spangled starlight sheen,°
But they do square,° that all their elves for fear   30
Creep into acorn cups and hide them there.
Fairy: Either I mistake your shape and making quite,
Or else you are that shrewd° and knavish sprite°
Called Robin Goodfellow. Are not you he
That frights the maidens of the villagery,°   35
Skim milk,° and sometimes labor in the quern,°
And bootless° make the breathless huswife° churn,
And sometimes make the drink to bear no barm,°
Mislead night wanderers,° laughing at their harm?
Those that "Hobgoblin" call you, and "Sweet Puck,"°   40
You do their work, and they shall have good luck.
Are you not he?
Puck: Thou speakest aright;
I am that merry wanderer of the night.
I jest to Oberon and make him smile
When I a fat and bean-fed° horse beguile,   45
Neighing in likeness of a filly foal;

---

10 *pensioners:* Retainers, members of the royal bodyguard.   12 *favors:* Love tokens.   13 *savors:*
Sweet smells.   16 *lob:* Country bumpkin.   17 *anon:* At once.   20 *passing fell:* Exceedingly angry;
wrath: Wrathful.   23 *changeling:* Child exchanged for another by the fairies.   25 *trace:* Range
through.   26 *perforce:* Forcibly.   29 *fountain:* Spring; *starlight sheen:* Shining starlight.
30 *square:* Quarrel.   33 *shrewd:* Mischievous; *sprite:* Spirit.   35 *villagery:* Village population.
36 *Skim milk:* I.e., steal the cream; *quern:* Hand mill (where Puck presumably hampers the grinding
of grain).   37 *bootless:* In vain (Puck prevents the cream from turning to butter); *huswife:* Housewife.
38 *barm:* Head on the ale (Puck prevents the barm or yeast from producing fermentation).   39 *Mislead night wanderers:* I.e., mislead with false fire those who walk abroad at night (hence earning Puck
his other names of Jack o' Lantern and Will o' the Wisp).   40 *Those . . . Puck:* I.e., those who call you
by the names you favor rather than those denoting the mischief you do.   45 *bean-fed:* Well fed on
field beans.

And sometimes lurk I in a gossip's° bowl
In very likeness of a roasted crab,°
And when she drinks, against her lips I bob
And on her withered dewlap° pour the ale.   50
The wisest aunt,° telling the saddest° tale,
Sometimes for three-foot stool mistaketh me;
Then slip I from her bum, down topples she,
And "Tailor"° cries, and falls into a cough;
And then the whole choir° hold their hips and laugh,   55
And waxen° in their mirth, and neeze,° and swear
A merrier hour was never wasted° there.
But, room,° fairy! Here comes Oberon.
Fairy: And here my mistress. Would that he were gone!

Enter [Oberon] the King of Fairies at one door, with his train, and [Titania] the Queen at another, with hers.

Oberon: Ill met by moonlight, proud Titania.   60
Titania: What, jealous Oberon? Fairies, skip hence.
    I have forsworn his bed and company.
Oberon: Tarry, rash wanton.° Am not I thy lord?
Titania: Then I must be thy lady; but I know
    When thou hast stolen away from Fairyland   65
    And in the shape of Corin° sat all day,
    Playing on the pipes of corn° and versing love
    To amorous Phillida.° Why art thou here
    Come from the farthest step° of India,
    But that, forsooth, the bouncing Amazon,   70
    Your buskined° mistress and your warrior love,
    To Theseus must be wedded, and you come
    To give their bed joy and prosperity.
Oberon: How canst thou thus for shame, Titania,
    Glance at my credit with Hippolyta,°   75
    Knowing I know thy love to Theseus?
    Didst not thou lead him through the glimmering night
    From Perigenia,° whom he ravishèd?
    And make him with fair Aegles° break his faith,
    With Ariadne° and Antiopa?°   80
Titania: These are the forgeries of jealousy;

---

47 *gossip's:* Old woman's.   48 *crab:* Crab apple.   50 *dewlap:* Loose skin on neck.   51 *aunt:* Old woman; *saddest:* Most serious.   54 *Tailor:* (Possibly because she ends up sitting cross-legged on the floor, looking like a tailor, or else referring to the *tail* or buttocks).   55 *choir:* Company. 56 *waxen:* Increase; *neeze:* Sneeze.   57 *wasted:* Spent.   58 *room:* Stand aside, make room. 63 *wanton:* Headstrong creature.   66, 68 *Corin, Phillida:* (Conventional names of pastoral lovers). 67 *corn:* (Here, oat stalks).   69 *step:* Farthest limit of travel, or, perhaps, *steep,* "mountain range." 71 *buskined:* Wearing half-boots called buskins.   75 *Glance . . . Hippolyta:* Make insinuations about my favored relationship with Hippolyta.   78 *Perigenia:* I.e., Perigouna, one of Theseus' conquests. (This and the following women are named in Thomas North's translation of Plutarch's "Life of Theseus.")   79 *Aegles:* I.e., Aegle, for whom Theseus deserted Ariadne according to some accounts. 80 *Ariadne:* The daughter of Minos, King of Crete, who helped Theseus to escape the labyrinth after killing the Minotaur; later she was abandoned by Theseus; *Antiopa:* Queen of the Amazons and wife of Theseus; elsewhere identified with Hippolyta, but here thought of as a separate woman.

And never, since the middle summer's spring,°
Met we on hill, in dale, forest, or mead,°
By pavèd° fountain or by rushy° brook,
Or in° the beachèd margent° of the sea,   85
To dance our ringlets° to° the whistling wind,
But with thy brawls thou hast disturbed our sport.
Therefore the winds, piping to us in vain,
As in revenge, have sucked up from the sea
Contagious° fogs which, falling in the land,   90
Hath every pelting° river made so proud
That they have overborne their continents.°
The ox hath therefore stretched his yoke° in vain,
The plowman lost his sweat, and the green corn°
Hath rotted ere his youth attained a beard;   95
The fold° stands empty in the drownèd field,
And crows are fatted with the murrain° flock;
The nine-men's morris° is filled up with mud,
And the quaint mazes° in the wanton° green
For lack of tread are undistinguishable.   100
The human mortals want° their winter° here;
No night is now with hymn or carol blessed.
Therefore° the moon, the governess of floods,
Pale in her anger, washes° all the air,
That rheumatic diseases° do abound.   105
And thorough this distemperature° we see
The seasons alter: hoary-headed frosts
Fall in the fresh lap of the crimson rose,
And on old Hiems° thin and icy crown
An odorous chaplet of sweet summer buds   110
Is, as in mockery, set. The spring, the summer,
The childing° autumn, angry winter, change
Their wonted liveries,° and the mazèd° world
By their increase° now knows not which is which.
And this same progeny of evils comes   115
From our debate,° from our dissension.
We are their parents and original.°
Oberon: Do you amend it, then. It lies in you.

82 *middle summer's spring:* Beginning of midsummer.   83 *mead:* Meadow.   84 *pavèd:* With pebbled bottom; *rushy:* Bordered with rushes.   85 *in:* On; *margent:* Edge, border.   86 *ringlets:* Dances in a ring (see *orbs* in line 9); *to:* To the sound of.   90 *Contagious:* Noxious.   91 *pelting:* Paltry. 92 *continents:* Banks that contain them.   93 *stretched his yoke:* I.e., pulled at his yoke in plowing. 94 *corn:* Grain of any kind.   96 *fold:* Pen for sheep or cattle.   97 *murrain:* Having died of the plague.   98 *nine-men's morris:* I.e., portion of the village green marked out in a square for a game played with nine pebbles or pegs.   99 *quaint mazes:* I.e., intricate paths marked out on the village green to be followed rapidly on foot as a kind of contest; *wanton:* Luxuriant.   101 *want:* Lack; *winter:* I.e., regular winter season; or, proper observances of winter, such as the *hymn* or *carol* in the next line (?).   103 *Therefore:* I.e., as a result of our quarrel.   104 *washes:* Saturates with moisture. 105 *rheumatic diseases:* Colds, flu, and other respiratory infections.   106 *distemperature:* Disturbance in nature.   109 *Hiems':* The winter god's.   112 *childing:* Fruitful, pregnant.   113 *wonted liveries:* Usual apparel; *mazèd:* Bewildered.   114 *their increase:* Their yield, what they produce. 116 *debate:* Quarrel.   117 *original:* Origin.

Why should Titania cross her Oberon?
I do but beg a little changeling boy   120
To be my henchman.°
Titania: Set your heart at rest.
The fairy land buys not the child of me.
His mother was a vot'ress of my order,°
And in the spicèd Indian air by night
Full often hath she gossiped by my side   125
And sat with me on Neptune's yellow sands,
Marking th' embarkèd traders° on the flood,°
When we have laughed to see the sails conceive
And grow big-bellied with the wanton° wind;
Which she, with pretty and with swimming° gait,   130
Following — her womb then rich with my young squire —
Would imitate, and sail upon the land
To fetch me trifles, and return again
As from a voyage, rich with merchandise.
But she, being mortal, of that boy did die;   135
And for her sake do I rear up her boy,
And for her sake I will not part with him.
Oberon: How long within this wood intend you stay?
Titania: Perchance till after Theseus' wedding day.
If you will patiently dance in our round°   140
And see our moonlight revels, go with us;
If not, shun me, and I will spare° your haunts.
Oberon: Give me that boy, and I will go with thee.
Titania: Not for thy fairy kingdom. Fairies, away!
We shall chide downright, if I longer stay.   145

                              Exeunt [Titania with her train].

Oberon: Well, go thy way. Thou shalt not from° this grove
Till I torment thee for this injury.
My gentle Puck, come hither. Thou rememb'rest
Since° once I sat upon a promontory,
And heard a mermaid on a dolphin's back   150
Uttering such dulcet° and harmonious breath°
That the rude° sea grew civil at her song,
And certain stars shot madly from their spheres
To hear the sea-maid's music?
Puck: I remember.
Oberon: That very time I saw, but thou couldst not,   155
Flying between the cold moon and the earth
Cupid, all° armed. A certain° aim he took
At a fair vestal° thronèd by° the west,

121 *henchman:* Attendant, page.   123 *was . . . order:* Had taken a vow to serve me.   127 *traders:*
Trading vessels; *flood:* Flood tide.   129 *wanton:* (1) Playful (2) amorous.   130 *swimming:* Smooth,
gliding.   140 *round:* Circular dance.   142 *spare:* Shun.   146 *from:* Go from.   149 *Since:*
When.   151 *dulcet:* Sweet; *breath:* Voice, song.   152 *rude:* Rough.   157 *all:* Fully; *certain;* Sure.
158 *vestal:* Vestal virgin (contains a complimentary allusion to Queen Elizabeth as a votaress of Diana
and probably refers to an actual entertainment in her honor at Elvetham in 1591); *by:* In the region of.

And loosed° his love shaft smartly from his bow
As° it should pierce a hundred thousand hearts;   160
But I might° see young Cupid's fiery shaft
Quenched in the chaste beams of the watery moon,
And the imperial vot'ress passèd on,
In maiden meditation, fancy-free.°
Yet marked I where the bolt° of Cupid fell: 165
It fell upon a little western flower,
Before milk-white, now purple with love's wound,
And maidens call it love-in-idleness.°
Fetch me that flower; the herb I showed thee once.
The juice of it on sleeping eyelids laid   170
Will make or man or° woman madly dote
Upon the next live creature that it sees.
Fetch me this herb, and be thou here again
Ere the leviathan° can swim a league.

Puck: I'll put a girdle round about the earth   175
In forty° minutes.   *[Exit.]*

Oberon: Having once this juice,
I'll watch Titania when she is asleep
And drop the liquor of it in her eyes.
The next thing then she waking looks upon,
Be it on lion, bear, or wolf, or bull,   180
On meddling monkey, or on busy ape,
She shall pursue it with the soul of love.
And ere I take this charm from off her sight,
As I can take it with another herb,
I'll make her render up her page to me.   185
But who comes here? I am invisible,
And I will overhear their conference.

Enter Demetrius, Helena following him.

Demetrius: I love thee not; therefore pursue me not.
Where is Lysander and fair Hermia?
The one I'll slay; the other slayeth me.
Thou toldst me they were stol'n unto this wood;   190
And here am I, and wood° within this wood
Because I cannot meet my Hermia.
Hence, get thee gone, and follow me no more.
Helena: You draw me, you hardhearted adamant!°
But yet you draw not iron, for my heart   195
Is true as steel. Leave you° your power to draw,
And I shall have no power to follow you.

---

159 *loosed:* Released.   160 *As:* As if.   161 *might:* Could.   164 *fancy-free:* Free of love's spell.
165 *bolt:* Arrow.   168 *love-in-idleness:* Pansy, heartsease.   171 *or . . . or:* Either . . . or.   174 *le-viathan:* Sea monster, whale.   176 *forty:* (Used indefinitely).   192 *and wood:* And mad, frantic (with an obvious wordplay on *wood,* meaning "woods").   195 *adamant:* Lodestone, magnet (with pun on *hardhearted,* since adamant was also thought to be the hardest of all stones and was confused with the diamond).   197 *Leave you:* Give up.

Demetrius: Do I entice you? Do I speak you fair?°
    Or rather do I not in plainest truth   200
    Tell you I do not nor I cannot love you?
Helena: And even for that do I love you the more.
    I am your spaniel; and, Demetrius,
    The more you beat me I will fawn on you.
    Use me but as your spaniel, spurn me, strike me,   205
    Neglect me, lose me; only give me leave,
    Unworthy as I am, to follow you.
    What worser place can I beg in your love —
    And yet a place of high respect with me —
    Than to be usèd as you use your dog?   210
Demetrius: Tempt not too much the hatred of my spirit,
    For I am sick when I do look on thee.
Helena: And I am sick when I look not on you.
Demetrius: You do impeach° your modesty too much
    To leave° the city and commit yourself   215
    Into the hands of one that loves you not,
    To trust the opportunity of night
    And the ill counsel of a desert° place
    With the rich worth of your virginity.
Helena: Your virtue° is my privilege.° For that°   220
    It is not night when I do see your face,
    Therefore I think I am not in the night;
    Nor doth this wood lack worlds of company,
    For you, in my respect,° are all the world.
    Then how can it be said I am alone   225
    When all the world is here to look on me?
Demetrius: I'll run from thee and hide me in the brakes,°
    And leave thee to the mercy of wild beasts.
Helena: The wildest hath not such a heart as you.
    Run when you will. The story shall be changed: 230
    Apollo flies and Daphne holds the chase,°
    The dove pursues the griffin,° the mild hind°
    Makes speed to catch the tiger — bootless° speed,
    When cowardice pursues and valor flies!
Demetrius: I will not stay° thy questions.° Let me go!   235
    Or if thou follow me, do not believe
    But I shall do thee mischief in the wood.
Helena: Ay, in the temple, in the town, the field,
    You do me mischief. Fie, Demetrius!

199 *speak you fair:* Speak courteously to you.   214 *impeach:* Call into question.   215 *To leave:* By leaving.   218 *desert:* Deserted.   220 *virtue:* Goodness or power to attract; *privilege:* Safeguard, warrant; *For that:* Because.   224 *in my respect:* As far as I am concerned, in my esteem.   227 *brakes:* Thickets.   231 *Apollo . . . chase:* (In the ancient myth, Daphne fled from Apollo and was saved from rape by being transformed into a laurel tree; here it is the female who *holds the chase,* or pursues, instead of the male.)   232 *griffin:* A fabulous monster with the head and wings of an eagle and the body of a lion; *hind:* Female deer.   233 *bootless:* Fruitless.   235 *stay:* Wait for, put up with; *questions:* Talk or argument.

Your wrongs do set a scandal on my sex.°   240
We cannot fight for love, as men may do;
We should be wooed and were not made to woo.   *[Exit Demetrius.]*
I'll follow thee and make a heaven of hell,
To die upon° the hand I love so well.   *[Exit.]*
Oberon: Fare thee well, nymph. Ere he do leave this grove   245
Thou shalt fly him, and he shall seek thy love.

Enter Puck.

Has thou the flower there? Welcome, wanderer.
Puck: Ay, there it is.   *[He offers the flower.]*
Oberon: I pray thee, give it me.
I know a bank where the wild thyme blows,°
Where oxlips° and the nodding violet grows,   250
Quite overcanopied with luscious woodbine,°
With sweet muskroses° and with eglantine.°
There sleeps Titania sometime of° the night,
Lulled in these flowers with dances and delight;
And there the snake throws° her enameled skin,   255
Weed° wide enough to wrap a fairy in.
And with the juice of this I'll streak° her eyes
And make her full of hateful fantasies.
Take thou some of it, and seek through this grove.
                      [He gives some love juice.]
A sweet Athenian lady is in love   260
With a disdainful youth. Anoint his eyes,
But do it when the next thing he espies
May be the lady. Thou shalt know the man
By the Athenian garments he hath on.
Effect it with some care, that he may prove   265
More fond on° her than she upon her love;
And look thou meet me ere the first cock crow.
Puck: Fear not, my lord, your servant shall do so.   *Exeunt [separately].*

[SCENE II: *The wood.*]

Enter Titania, Queen of Fairies, with her train.

Titania: Come, now a roundel° and a fairy song;
   Then, for the third part of a minute,° hence —
   Some to kill cankers° in the muskrose buds,
   Some war with reremice° for their leathern wings

---

240 *Your . . . sex:* I.e., the wrongs that you do me cause me to act in a manner that disgraces my sex.
244 *upon:* By.   249 *blows:* Blooms.   250 *oxlips:* Flowers resembling cowslip and primrose.
251 *woodbine:* Honeysuckle.   252 *muskroses:* A kind of large, sweet-scented rose; *eglantine:* Sweet-
brier, another kind of rose.   253 *sometime of:* For part of.   255 *throws:* Sloughs off, sheds.
256 *Weed:* Garment.   257 *streak:* Anoint, touch gently.   266 *fond on:* Doting on.   SCENE II.
1 *roundel:* Dance in a ring.   2 *the third . . . minute:* (Indicative of the fairies' quickness).   3 *cankers:* Cankerworms (i.e., caterpillars or grubs).   4 *reremice:* Bats.

To make my small elves coats, and some keep back   5
The clamorous owl, that nightly hoots and wonders
At our quaint° spirits. Sing me now asleep.
Then to your offices, and let me rest.

Fairies sing.

First Fairy: You spotted snakes with double° tongue,
    Thorny hedgehogs, be not seen;   10
    Newts° and blindworms, do no wrong;
    Come not near our Fairy Queen.
Chorus [dancing]: Philomel,° with melody
    Sing in our sweet lullaby;
    Lulla, lulla, lullaby, lulla, lulla, lullaby.   15
    Never harm
    Nor spell nor charm
    Come our lovely lady nigh.
    So good night, with lullaby.
First Fairy: Weaving spiders, come not here;   20
    Hence, you long-legged spinners, hence!
    Beetles black, approach not near;
    Worm nor snail, do no offense.°
Chorus [dancing]: Philomel, with melody
    Sing in our sweet lullaby;   25
    Lulla, lulla, lullaby, lulla, lulla, lullaby.
    Never harm
    Nor spell nor charm
    Come our lovely lady nigh.
    So good night, with lullaby.   30
                           [Titania sleeps.]
Second Fairy: Hence, away! Now all is well.
    One aloof stand sentinel.°   *[Exeunt Fairies, leaving one sentinel.]*

Enter Oberon [and squeezes the flower on Titania's eyelids].

Oberon: What thou seest when thou dost wake,
    Do it for thy true love take;
    Love and languish for his sake.   35
    Be it ounce,° or cat, or bear,
    Pard,° or boar with bristled hair,
    In thy eye that shall appear

---

7 *quaint:* Dainty.   9 *double:* Forked.   11 *Newts:* Water lizards (considered poisonous, as were *blindworms*—small snakes with tiny eyes—and spiders).   13 *Philomel:* The nightingale. (Philomela, daughter of King Pandion, was transformed into a nightingale, according to Ovid's *Metamorphoses* 6, after she had been raped by her sister Procne's husband, Tereus.)   23 *offense:* Harm.   32 *sentinel:* (Presumably Oberon is able to outwit or intimidate this guard.)   36 *ounce:* Lynx.   37 *Pard:* Leopard.

When thou wak'st, it is thy dear.
Wake when some vile thing is near. *[Exit.]* 40

Enter Lysander and Hermia.

Lysander: Fair love, you faint with wandering in the wood;
    And to speak truth, I have forgot our way.
  We'll rest us, Hermia, if you think it good,
    And tarry for the comfort of the day.
Hermia: Be it so, Lysander. Find you out a bed, 45
  For I upon this bank will rest my head.
Lysander: One turf shall serve as pillow for us both;
  One heart, one bed, two bosoms, and one troth.°
Hermia: Nay, good Lysander, for my sake, my dear,
  Lie further off yet. Do not lie so near. 50
Lysander: O, take the sense, sweet, of my innocence!°
  Love takes the meaning in love's conference.°
  I mean that my heart unto yours is knit,
  So that but one heart we can make of it;
  Two bosoms interchainèd with an oath— 55
  So then two bosoms and a single troth.
  Then by your side no bed-room me deny,
  For lying so, Hermia, I do not lie.°
Hermia: Lysander riddles very prettily.
  Now much beshrew° my manners and my pride 60
  If Hermia meant to say Lysander lied.
  But, gentle friend, for love and courtesy
  Lie further off, in human° modesty.
  Such separation as may well be said
  Becomes a virtuous bachelor and a maid, 65
  So far be distant; and, good night, sweet friend.
  Thy love ne'er alter till thy sweet life end!
Lysander: Amen, amen, to that fair prayer, say I,
  And then end life when I end loyalty!
  Here is my bed. Sleep give thee all his rest! 70
Hermia: With half that wish the wisher's eyes be pressed!°
        [They sleep, separated by a short distance.]

Enter Puck.

Puck: Through the forest have I gone,
    But Athenian found I none
    On whose eyes I might approve°
    This flower's force in stirring love. 75

---

48 *troth:* Faith, trothplight.   51 *take . . . innocence:* I.e., interpret my intention as innocent.
52 *Love . . . conference:* I.e., when lovers confer, love teaches each lover to interpret the other's
meaning lovingly.   58 *lie:* Tell a falsehood (with a riddling pun on *lie,* "recline").   60 *beshrew:*
Curse (but mildly meant).   63 *human:* Courteous (and perhaps suggesting "humane,").   71 *With
. . . pressed:* I.e., may we share your wish, so that your eyes too are *pressed,* closed, in sleep.   74 *approve:* Test.

Night and silence. — Who is here?
Weeds of Athens he doth wear.
This is he, my master said,
Despisèd the Athenian maid;
And here the maiden, sleeping sound,   80
On the dank and dirty ground.
Pretty soul, she durst not lie
Near this lack-love, this kill-courtesy.
Churl, upon thy eyes I throw
All the power this charm doth owe.°   *[He applies the love juice.]*   85
When thou wak'st, let love forbid
Sleep his seat on thy eyelid.
So awake when I am gone,
For I must now to Oberon.   *Exit.*

Enter Demetrius and Helena, running.

Helena: Stay, though thou kill me, sweet Demetrius!   90
Demetrius: I charge thee, hence, and do not haunt me thus.
Helena: O, wilt thou darkling° leave me? Do not so.
Demetrius: Stay, on thy peril!° I alone will go.   *[Exit.]*
Helena: O, I am out of breath in this fond° chase!
The more my prayer, the lesser is my grace.°   95
Happy is Hermia, wheresoe'er she lies,°
For she hath blessèd and attractive eyes.
How came her eyes so bright? Not with salt tears;
If so, my eyes are oftener washed than hers.
No, no, I am as ugly as a bear,   100
For beasts that meet me run away for fear.
Therefore no marvel though Demetrius
Do, as a monster, fly my presence thus.°
What wicked and dissembling glass of mine
Made me compare° with Hermia's sphery eyne?°   105
But who is here? Lysander, on the ground?
Dead, or asleep? I see no blood, no wound.
Lysander, if you live, good sir, awake.
Lysander [awaking]: And run through fire I will for thy sweet sake.
Transparent° Helena! Nature shows art,°   110
That through thy bosom makes me see thy heart.
Where is Demetrius? O, how fit a word
Is that vile name to perish on my sword!
Helena: Do not say so, Lysander; say not so.
What though he love your Hermia? Lord, what though?   115
Yet Hermia still loves you. Then be content.

---

85 *owe:* Own.   92 *darkling:* In the dark.   93 *on thy peril:* I.e., on pain of danger to you if you
don't obey me and stay.   94 *fond:* Doting.   95 *my grace:* The favor I obtain.   96 *lies:* Dwells.
102–103 *no marvel . . . thus:* I.e., no wonder that Demetrius flies from me as from a monster.
105 *compare:* Vie; *sphery eyne:* Eyes as bright as stars in their spheres.   110 *Transparent:* (1) Radiant
(2) able to be seen through, lacking in deceit; *art:* Skill, magic power.

Lysander: Content with Hermia? No! I do repent
 The tedious minutes I with her have spent.
 Not Hermia but Helena I love.
 Who will not change a raven for a dove?   120
 The will° of man is by his reason swayed,
 And reason says you are the worthier maid.
 Things growing are not ripe until their season;
 So I, being young, till now ripe not° to reason.
 And, touching° now the point° of human skill,°   125
 Reason becomes the marshal to my will
 And leads me to your eyes, where I o'erlook°
 Love's stories written in love's richest book.
Helena: Wherefore° was I to this keen mockery born?
 When at your hands did I deserve this scorn?   130
 Is't not enough, is't not enough, young man,
 That I did never — no, nor never can —
 Deserve a sweet look from Demetrius' eye,
 But you must flout my insufficiency?
 Good troth,° you do me wrong, good sooth,° you do,   135
 In such disdainful manner me to woo.
 But fare you well. Perforce I must confess
 I thought you lord of° more true gentleness.°
 O, that a lady, of° one man refused,
 Should of another therefore be abused!°   *Exit.* 140
Lysander: She sees not Hermia. Hermia, sleep thou there,
 And never mayst thou come Lysander near!
 For as a surfeit of the sweetest things
 The deepest loathing to the stomach brings,
 Or as the heresies that men do leave   145
 Are hated most of those they did deceive,°
 So thou, my surfeit and my heresy,
 Of all be hated, but the most of° me!
 And, all my powers, address° your love and might
 To honor Helen and to be her knight!   *Exit.* 150
Hermia [awaking]: Help me, Lysander, help me! Do thy best
 To pluck this crawling serpent from my breast!
 Ay me, for pity! What a dream was here!
 Lysander, look how I do quake with fear.
 Methought a serpent ate my heart away,   155
 And you sat smiling at his cruel prey.°
 Lysander! What, removed? Lysander! Lord!
 What, out of hearing? Gone? No sound, no word?
 Alack, where are you? Speak, an if° you hear;

---

121 *will:* Desire. 124 *ripe not:* (Am) not ripened. 125 *touching:* Reaching; *point:* Summit; *skill:* Judgment. 127 *o'erlook:* Read. 129 *Wherefore:* Why. 135 *Good troth, good sooth:* I.e., indeed, truly. 138 *lord of:* I.e., possessor of; *gentleness:* courtesy. 139 *of:* By. 140 *abused:* Ill treated. 145–146 *as . . . deceive:* As renounced heresies are hated most by those persons who formerly were deceived by them. 148 *Of . . . of:* By . . . by. 149 *address:* Direct, apply. 156 *prey:* Act of preying. 159 *an if:* If.

Speak, of all loves!° I swoon almost with fear.   160
No? Then I well perceive you are not nigh.
Either death, or you, I'll find immediately.

Exit. [The sleeping Titania remains.]

[ACT III

SCENE I: *The wood.*]

Enter the clowns° [Quince, Snug, Bottom, Flute, Snout, and Starveling].

Bottom: Are we all met?
Quince: Pat, pat,° and here's a marvelous convenient place for our rehearsal.
    This green plot shall be our stage, this hawthorn brake° our tiring-house,°
    and we will do it in action as we will do it before the Duke.
Bottom: Peter Quince?   5
Quince: What sayest thou, bully° Bottom?
Bottom: There are things in this comedy of Pyramus and Thisbe that will
    never please. First, Pyramus must draw a sword to kill himself, which the
    ladies cannot abide. How answer you that?
Snout: By'r lakin,° a parlous fear.   10
Starveling: I believe we must leave the killing out, when all is done.°
Bottom: Not a whit. I have a device to make all well. Write me° a prologue,
    and let the prologue seem to say, we will do no harm with our swords,
    and that Pyramus is not killed indeed; and for the more better assurance,
    tell them that I, Pyramus, am not Pyramus but Bottom the weaver. This   15
    will put them out of fear.
Quince: Well, we will have such a prologue, and it shall be written in eight
    and six.°
Bottom: No, make it two more: let it be written in eight and eight.
Snout: Will not the ladies be afeard of the lion?   20
Starveling: I fear it, I promise you.
Bottom: Masters, you ought to consider with yourself, to bring in — God
    shield us! — a lion among ladies° is a most dreadful thing. For there is
    not a more fearful° wildfowl than your lion living, and we ought to look
    to 't.   25
Snout: Therefore another prologue must tell he is not a lion.
Bottom: Nay, you must name his name, and half his face must be seen
    through the lion's neck, and he himself must speak through, saying thus
    or to the same defect:° "Ladies," or "Fair ladies, I would wish you," or "I

160 *of all loves:* For love's sake.   ACT III. SCENE I.   *clowns:* Rustics.   2 *Pat:* On the dot, punctually.
3 *brake:* Thicket; *tiring-house:* Attiring area, hence backstage.   6 *bully:* I.e., worthy, jolly, fine fellow.
10 *By 'r lakin:* By our ladykin, i.e., the Virgin Mary; *parlous:* Perilous, alarming.   11 *when all is done:*
I.e., when all is said and done.   12 *Write me:* I.e., write at my suggestion (*me* is used colloquially).
18 *eight and six:* Alternate lines of eight and six syllables, a common ballad measure.   23 *lion among
ladies:* (A contemporary pamphlet tells how, at the christening in 1594 of Prince Henry, eldest son of
King James VI of Scotland, later James I of England, a "blackamoor" instead of a lion drew the triumphal
chariot, since the lion's presence might have "brought some fear to the nearest.")   24 *fearful:*
Fear-inspiring.   29 *defect:* (Bottom's blunder for "effect.")

would request you," or "I would entreat you, not to fear, not to tremble; 30
my life for yours.° If you think I come hither as a lion, it were pity of my
life.° No, I am no such thing; I am a man as other men are." And there
indeed let him name his name, and tell them plainly he is Snug the joiner.

Quince: Well, it shall be so. But there is two hard things: that is, to bring the
moonlight into a chamber; for, you know, Pyramus and Thisbe meet by 35
moonlight.

Snout: Doth the moon shine that night we play our play?

Bottom: A calendar, a calendar! Look in the almanac. Find out moonshine,
find out moonshine.   *[They consult an almanac.]*

Quince: Yes, it doth shine that night. 40

Bottom: Why then may you leave a casement of the great chamber window
where we play open, and the moon may shine in at the casement.

Quince: Ay; or else one must come in with a bush of thorns° and a lantern
and say he comes to disfigure,° or to present,° the person of Moonshine.
Then there is another thing: we must have a wall in the great chamber; 45
for Pyramus and Thisbe, says the story, did talk through the chink of a
wall.

Snout: You can never bring in a wall. What say you, Bottom?

Bottom: Some man or other must present Wall. And let him have some
plaster, or some loam, or some roughcast° about him, to signify wall; or 50
let him hold his fingers thus, and through that cranny shall Pyramus and
Thisbe whisper.

Quince: If that may be, then all is well. Come, sit down, every mother's son,
and rehearse your parts. Pyramus, you begin. When you have spoken
your speech, enter into that brake, and so everyone according to his cue. 55

Enter Robin [Puck].

Puck [aside]: What hempen homespuns° have we swaggering here
So near the cradle° of the Fairy Queen?
What, a play toward?° I'll be an auditor;
An actor, too, perhaps, if I see cause.

Quince: Speak, Pyramus. Thisbe, stand forth. 60

Bottom [as Pyramus]: "Thisbe, the flowers of odious savors sweet — "

Quince: Odors, odors.

Bottom: " — Odors savors sweet;
So hath thy breath, my dearest Thisbe dear.
But hark, a voice! Stay thou but here awhile, 65
And by and by I will to thee appear."   *Exit.*

Puck: A stranger Pyramus than e'er played here.°   *[Exit.]*

---

31 *my life for yours:* I.e., I pledge my life to make your lives safe.   31–32 *it were . . . life:* I.e., I should
be sorry, by my life; or, my life would be endangered.   43 *bush of thorns:* Bundle of thornbush fagots
(part of the accoutrements of the man in the moon, according to the popular notions of the time, along
with his lantern and his dog).   44 *disfigure:* (Quince's blunder for "figure");   44 *present:* Represent.   50 *roughcast:* A mixture of lime and gravel used to plaster the outside of buildings.
56 *hempen homespuns:* I.e., rustics dressed in clothes woven of coarse, homespun fabric made from
hemp.   57 *cradle:* I.e., Titania's bower.   58 *toward:* About to take place.   67 *A stranger . . . here:*
(Either Puck refers to an earlier dramatic version played in the same theater, or he has conceived of
a plan to present a "stranger" Pyramus than ever seen before.)

Flute: Must I speak now?

Quince: Ay, marry, must you; for you must understand he goes but to see a
noise that he heard, and is to come again.   70

Flute [as Thisbe]: "Most radiant Pyramus, most lily-white of hue,
Of color like the red rose on triumphant° brier,
Most brisky juvenal° and eke° most lovely Jew,°
As true as truest horse that yet would never tire.
I'll meet thee, Pyramus, at Ninny's tomb."   75

Quince: "Ninus'° tomb," man. Why, you must not speak that yet. That you
answer to Pyramus. You speak all your part° at once, cues and all.
Pyramus, enter. Your cue is past; it is "never tire."

Flute: O — "As true as truest horse, that yet would never tire."

[Enter Puck, and Bottom as Pyramus with the ass head.°]

Bottom: "If I were fair,° Thisbe, I were° only thine."   80

Quince: O, monstrous! O, strange! We are haunted. Pray, masters! Fly, masters! Help!

[Exeunt Quince, Snug, Flute, Snout, and Starveling.]

Puck: I'll follow you, I'll lead you about a round,°
Thorough bog, thorough bush, thorough brake, thorough brier.
Sometimes a horse I'll be, sometimes a hound,   85
A hog, a headless bear, sometimes a fire;°
And neigh, and bark, and grunt, and roar, and burn,
Like horse, hound, hog, bear, fire, at every turn.   *Exit.*

Bottom: Why do they run away? This is a knavery of them to make me
afeard.   90

Enter Snout.

Snout: O Bottom, thou art changed! What do I see on thee?

Bottom: What do you see? You see an ass head of your own, do you?

[Exit Snout.]

Enter Quince.

Quince: Bless thee, Bottom, bless thee! Thou art translated.°   *Exit.*

Bottom: I see their knavery. This is to make an ass of me, to fright me, if
they could. But I will not stir from this place, do what they can. I will   95
walk up and down here, and will sing, that they shall hear I am not afraid.

[He sings.]

The ouzel cock° so black of hue,
With orange-tawny bill,

---

72 *triumphant:* Magnificent.   73 *brisky juvenal:* Lively youth; *eke:* Also; *Jew:* (An absurd repetition of
the first syllable of *juvenal* and an indication of how desperately Quince searches for his rhymes.)
76 *Ninus':* Mythical founder of Nineveh (whose wife, Semiramis, was supposed to have built the walls
of Babylon where the story of Pyramus and Thisbe takes place).   77 *part:* (An actor's *part* was a script
consisting only of his speeches and their cues.)   *with the ass head:* (This stage direction . . . presumably refers to a standard stage property.)   80 *fair:* Handsome; *were:* Would be.   83 *about a round:*
Roundabout.   86 *fire:* Will-o'-the-wisp.   93 *translated:* Transformed.   97 *ouzel cock:* Male blackbird.

The throstle° with his note so true,
        The wren with little quill°—   100
Titania [awaking]: What angel wakes me from my flowery bed?
Bottom [sings]
        The finch, the sparrow, and the lark,
        The plainsong° cuckoo gray,
        Whose note full many a man doth mark,
        And dares not answer nay°—   105
For indeed, who would set his wit to° so foolish a bird? Who would give
a bird the lie,° though he cry "cuckoo" never so?°
Titania: I pray thee, gentle mortal, sing again.
Mine ear is much enamored of thy note;
So is mine eye enthrallèd to thy shape;   110
And thy fair virtue's force° perforce doth move me
On the first view to say, to swear, I love thee.
Bottom: Methinks, mistress, you should have little reason for that. And yet,
to say the truth, reason and love keep little company together nowadays
—the more the pity that some honest neighbors will not make them   115
friends. Nay, I can gleek° upon occasion.
Titania: Thou art as wise as thou art beautiful.
Bottom: Not so, neither. But if I had wit enough to get out of this wood, I
have enough to serve mine own turn.°
Titania: Out of this wood do not desire to go.   120
Thou shalt remain here, whether thou wilt or no.
I am a spirit of no common rate.°
The summer still doth tend upon my state,°
And I do love thee. Therefore, go with me.
I'll give thee fairies to attend on thee,   125
And they shall fetch thee jewels from the deep,
And sing while thou on pressèd flowers dost sleep.
And I will purge thy mortal grossness° so
That thou shalt like an airy spirit go.
Peaseblossom, Cobweb, Mote,° and Mustardseed!   130

Enter four Fairies [Peaseblossom, Cobweb, Mote, and Mustardseed].

Peaseblossom: Ready.
Cobweb: And I.
Mote: And I.
Mustardseed: And I.
All: Where shall we go?
Titania: Be kind and courteous to this gentleman.

99 *throstle:* Song thrush.   100 *quill:* (Literally, a reed pipe; hence, the bird's piping song.)
103 *plainsong:* Singing a melody without variations.   105 *dares . . . nay:* I.e., cannot deny that he is
a cuckold.   106 *set his wit to:* Employ his intelligence to answer.   107 *give . . . lie:* Call the bird a
liar; *never so:* Ever so much.   111 *thy . . . force:* The power of your unblemished excellence.
116 *gleek:* Jest.   119 *serve . . . turn:* Answer my purpose.   122 *rate:* Rank, value.   123 *still . . .
state:* Always waits upon me as a part of my royal retinue.   128 *mortal grossness:* Materiality (i.e., the
corporal nature of a mortal being).   130 *Mote:* I.e., speck. (The two words *moth* and *mote* were
pronounced alike, and both meanings may be present.)

Hop in his walks and gambol in his eyes;°
Feed him with apricots and dewberries,°   135
With purple grapes, green figs, and mulberries;
The honey bags steal from the humble-bees,
And for night tapers crop their waxen thighs
And light them at the fiery glowworms' eyes,
To have my love to bed and to arise;   140
And pluck the wings from painted butterflies
To fan the moonbeams from his sleeping eyes.
Nod to him, elves, and do him courtesies.

Peaseblossom: Hail, mortal!

Cobweb: Hail!   145

Mote: Hail!

Mustardseed: Hail!

Bottom: I cry your worships mercy,° heartily. I beseech your worship's name.

Cobweb: Cobweb.

Bottom: I shall desire you of more acquaintance,° good Master Cobweb. If I   150
cut my finger, I shall make bold with you.° — Your name, honest gentleman?

Peaseblossom: Peaseblossom.

Bottom: I pray you, commend me to Mistress Squash,° your mother, and to
Master Peascod,° your father. Good Master Peaseblossom, I shall desire   155
you of more acquaintance too. — Your name, I beseech you, sir?

Mustardseed: Mustardseed.

Bottom: Good Master Mustardseed, I know your patience° well. That same
cowardly, giantlike ox-beef hath devoured many a gentleman of your
house. I promise you, your kindred hath made my eyes water° ere now.   160
I desire you of more acquaintance, good Master Mustardseed.

Titania: Come wait upon him; lead him to my bower.
The moon methinks looks with a watery eye;
And when she weeps,° weeps every little flower,
Lamenting some enforcèd° chastity.   165
Tie up my lover's tongue;° bring him silently.   *Exeunt.*

[Scene II: *The wood.*]

Enter [Oberon,] King of Fairies.

Oberon: I wonder if Titania be awaked;
Then, what it was that next came in her eye,
Which she must dote on in extremity.

[Enter] Robin Goodfellow [Puck].

134 *in his eyes:* In his sight (i.e., before him).   135 *dewberries:* Blackberries.   148 *I cry . . . mercy:*
I beg pardon of your worships (for presuming to ask a question).   150 *I . . . acquaintance:* I crave
to be better acquainted with you.   151 *If . . . you:* (Cobwebs were used to stanch bleeding.)
154 *Squash:* Unripe pea pod.   155 *Peascod:* Ripe pea pod.   158 *your patience:* What you have
endured (mustard is eaten with beef).   160 *water:* (1) Weep for sympathy (2) smart, sting.   164 *she
weeps:* I.e., she causes dew.   165 *enforcèd:* Forced, violated; or, possibly, constrained (since Titania
at this moment is hardly concerned about chastity).   166 *Tie . . . tongue:* (Presumably Bottom is
braying like an ass.)

Here comes my messenger. How now, mad spirit?
What night-rule° now about this haunted° grove?   5
Puck: My mistress with a monster is in love.
Near to her close° and consecrated bower,
While she was in her dull° and sleeping hour,
A crew of patches,° rude mechanicals,°
That work for bread upon Athenian stalls,°   10
Were met together to rehearse a play
Intended for great Theseus' nuptial day.
The shallowest thickskin of that barren sort,°
Who Pyramus presented,° in their sport
Forsook his scene° and entered in a brake.   15
When I did him at this advantage take,
An ass's noll° I fixèd on his head.
Anon his Thisbe must be answerèd,
And forth my mimic° comes. When they him spy,
As wild geese that the creeping fowler° eye,   20
Or russet-pated choughs,° many in sort,°
Rising and cawing at the gun's report,
Sever° themselves and madly sweep the sky,
So, at his sight, away his fellows fly;
And, at our stamp, here o'er and o'er one falls;   25
He "Murder!" cries and help from Athens calls.
Their sense thus weak, lost with their fears thus strong,
Made senseless things begin to do them wrong,
For briers and thorns at their apparel snatch;
Some, sleeves — some, hats; from yielders all things catch.°   30
I led them on in this distracted fear
And left sweet Pyramus translated there,
When in that moment, so it came to pass,
Titania waked and straightway loved an ass.
Oberon: This falls out better than I could devise.   35
But hast thou yet latched° the Athenian's eyes
With the love juice, as I did bid thee do?
Puck: I took him sleeping — that is finished too —
And the Athenian woman by his side,
That, when he waked, of force° she must be eyed.   40

Enter Demetrius and Hermia.

Oberon: Stand close. This is the same Athenian.
Puck: This is the woman, but not this the man.   *[They stand aside.]*

Scene II.   5 *night-rule:* Diversion or misrule for the night; *haunted:* Much frequented.   7 *close:*
Secret, private.   8 *dull:* Drowsy.   9 *patches:* Clowns, fools; *rude mechanicals:* Ignorant artisans.
10 *stalls:* Market booths.   13 *barren sort:* Stupid company or crew.   14 *presented:* Acted.
15 *scene:* Playing area.   17 *noll:* Noddle, head.   19 *mimic:* Burlesque actors.   20 *fowler:* Hunter
of game birds.   21 *russet-pated choughs:* Reddish brown or gray-headed jackdaws; *in sort:* In a flock.
23 *Sever:* I.e., scatter.   30 *from . . . catch:* I.e., everything preys on those who yield to fear.
36 *latched:* Fastened, snared.   40 *of force:* Perforce.

Demetrius: O, why rebuke you him that loves you so?
Lay breath so bitter on your bitter foe.
Hermia: Now I but chide; but I should use thee worse,   45
For thou, I fear, hast given me cause to curse.
If thou hast slain Lysander in his sleep,
Being o'er shoes° in blood, plunge in the deep,
And kill me too.
The sun was not so true unto the day   50
As he to me. Would he have stolen away
From sleeping Hermia? I'll believe as soon
This whole° earth may be bored, and that the moon
May through the center creep, and so displease
Her brother's° noontide with th' Antipodes.°   55
It cannot be but thou hast murdered him;
So should a murderer look, so dead,° so grim.
Demetrius: So should the murdered look, and so should I,
Pierced through the heart with your stern cruelty.
Yet you, the murderer, look as bright, as clear   60
As yonder Venus in her glimmering sphere.
Hermia: What's this to° my Lysander? Where is he?
Ah, good Demetrius, wilt thou give him me?
Demetrius: I had rather give his carcass to my hounds.
Hermia: Out, dog! Out, cur! Thou driv'st me past the bounds   65
Of maiden's patience. Hast thou slain him, then?
Henceforth be never numbered among men.
O, once° tell true, tell true, even for my sake:
Durst thou have looked upon him being awake?
And hast thou killed him sleeping? O brave touch!°   70
Could not a worm,° an adder, do so much?
An adder did it; for with doubler° tongue
Than thine, thou serpent, never adder stung.
Demetrius: You spend your passion° on a misprised mood.°
I am not guilty of Lysander's blood,   75
Nor is he dead, for aught that I can tell.
Hermia: I pray thee, tell me then that he is well.
Demetrius: And if I could, what should I get therefor?°
Hermia: A privilege never to see me more.
And from thy hated presence part I so.   80
See me no more, whether he be dead or no.   *Exit.*
Demetrius: There is no following her in this fierce vein.
Here therefore for a while I will remain.
So sorrow's heaviness doth heavier° grow

---

48 *Being oe'er shoes:* Having waded in so far.   53 *whole:* Solid.   55 *Her brother's:* I.e., the sun's;
th' Antipodes: The people on the opposite side of the earth (where the moon is imagined bringing
night to noontime).   57 *dead:* Deadly, or deathly pale.   62 *to:* To do with.   68 *once:* Once and
for all.   70 *brave touch!:* Fine stroke! (said ironically).   71 *worm:* Serpent.   72 *doubler:* (1) More
forked (2) more deceitful.   74 *passion:* Violent feelings; *misprised mood:* Anger based on misconception.   78 *therefor:* In return for that.   84 *heavier:* (1) Harder to bear (2) more drowsy.

For debt that bankrupt° sleep doth sorrow owe,   85
Which now in some slight measure it will pay,
If for his tender here I make some stay.°   *[He] lie[s] down [and sleeps].*
Oberon: What hast thou done? Thou hast mistaken quite
And laid the love juice on some true love's sight.
Of thy misprision° must perforce ensue   90
Some true love turned, and not a false turned true.
Puck: Then fate o'errules, that, one man holding troth,°
A million fail, confounding oath° on oath.
Oberon: About the wood go swifter than the wind,
And Helena of Athens look° thou find.   95
All fancy-sick° she is and pale of cheer°
With sighs of love, that cost the fresh blood° dear.
By some illusion see thou bring her here.
I'll charm his eyes against she do appear.°
Puck: I go, I go, look how I go,   100
Swifter than arrow from the Tartar's bow.°   *[Exit.]*
Oberon [applying love juice to Demetrius' eyes]:   Flower of this purple dye,
    Hit with Cupid's archery,
    Sink in apple° of his eye.
    When his love he doth espy,   105
    Let her shine as gloriously
    As the Venus of the sky.
    When thou wak'st, if she be by,
    Beg of her for remedy.

Enter Puck.

Puck: Captain of our fairy band,   110
    Helena is here at hand,
    And the youth, mistook by me,
    Pleading for a lover's fee.°
    Shall we their fond pageant° see?
    Lord, what fools these mortals be!   115
Oberon: Stand aside. The noise they make
    Will cause Demetrius to awake.
Puck: Then will two at once woo one;
    That must needs be sport alone.°

85 *bankrupt:* (Demetrius is saying that his sleepiness adds to the weariness caused by sorrow.)
86–87 *Which . . . stay:* I.e., to a small extent, I will be able to "pay back" and hence find some relief
from sorrow, if I pause here awhile (*make some stay*) while sleep "tenders" or offers itself by way of
paying the debt owed to sorrow.   90 *misprision:* Mistake.   92 *that . . . troth:* In that, for each man
keeping true faith in love.   93 *confounding . . . oath:* I.e., breaking oath after oath.   95 *look:* I.e.,
be sure.   96 *fancy-sick:* Lovesick; *cheer:* Face.   97 *sighs . . . blood:* (An allusion to the physiological
theory that each sigh costs the heart a drop of blood.)   99 *against . . . appear:* In anticipation of her
coming.   101 *Tartar's bow:* (Tartars were famed for their skill with the bow.)   104 *apple:* Pupil.
113 *fee:* Privilege, reward.   114 *fond pageant:* Foolish spectacle.   119 *alone:* Unequaled.

And those things do best please me   120
    That befall preposterously.°   *[They stand aside.]*

Enter Lysander and Helena.

Lysander: Why should you think that I should woo in scorn?
    Scorn and derision never come in tears.
    Look when° I vow, I weep; and vows so born,
        In their nativity all truth appears.°   125
    How can these things in me seem scorn to you,
    Bearing the badge° of faith to prove them true?
Helena: You do advance° your cunning more and more.
        When truth kills truth,° O, devilish-holy fray!
    These vows are Hermia's. Will you give her o'er?   130
        Weigh oath with oath, and you will nothing weigh.
    Your vows to her and me, put in two scales,
        Will even weigh, and both as light as tales.°
Lysander: I had no judgment when to her I swore.
Helena: Nor none, in my mind, now you give her o'er.   135
Lysander: Demetrius loves her, and he loves not you.
Demetrius [awaking]: O Helen, goddess, nymph, perfect, divine!
    To what, my love, shall I compare thine eyne?
    Crystal is muddy. O, how ripe in show°
    Thy lips, those kissing cherries, tempting grow!   140
    That pure congealèd white, high Taurus'° snow,
    Fanned with the eastern wind, turns to a crow°
    When thou hold'st up thy hand. O, let me kiss
    This princess of pure white, this seal° of bliss!
Helena: O spite! O hell! I see you all are bent   145
    To set against° me for your merriment.
    If you were civil and knew courtesy,
    You would not do me thus much injury.
    Can you not hate me, as I know you do,
    But you must join in souls° to mock me too?   150
    If you were men, as men you are in show,
    You would not use a gentle lady so —
    To vow, and swear, and superpraise° my parts,°
    When I am sure you hate me with your hearts.
    You both are rivals, and love Hermia,   155
    And now both rivals to mock Helena.
    A trim° exploit, a manly enterprise,
    To conjure tears up in a poor maid's eyes

---

121 *preposterously:* Out of the natural order.   124 *Look when:* Whenever.   124–125 *vows . . .*
appears: I.e., vows made by one who is weeping give evidence thereby of their sincerety.   127 *badge:*
Identifying device such as that worn on servants' livery (here, his tears).   128 *advance:* Carry forward,
display.   129 *truth kills truth:* I.e., one of Lysander's vows must invalidate the other.   133 *tales:* Lies.
139 *show:* Appearance.   141 *Taurus:* A lofty mountain range in Asia Minor.   142 *turns to a crow:*
I.e., seems black by contrast.   144 *seal:* Pledge.   146 *set against:* Attack.   150 *in souls:* I.e., heart
and soul.   153 *superpraise:* Overpraise; *parts:* Qualities.   157 *trim:* Pretty, fine (said ironically).

With your derision! None of noble sort°
Would so offend a virgin and extort° 160
A poor soul's patience, all to make you sport.
Lysander: You are unkind, Demetrius. Be not so.
For you love Hermia; this you know I know.
And here, with all good will, with all my heart,
In Hermia's love I yield you up my part; 165
And yours of Helena to me bequeath,
Whom I do love, and will do till my death.
Helena: Never did mockers waste more idle breath.
Demetrius: Lysander, keep thy Hermia; I will none.°
If e'er I loved her, all that love is gone. 170
My heart to her but as guestwise sojourned,°
And now to Helen is it home returned,
There to remain.
Lysander: Helen, it is not so.
Demetrius: Disparage not the faith thou dost not know,
Lest, to thy peril, thou aby° it dear. 175
Look where thy love comes; yonder is thy dear.

Enter Hermia.

Hermia: Dark night, that from the eye his° function takes,
The ear more quick of apprehension makes;
Wherein it doth impair the seeing sense,
It pays the hearing double recompense. 180
Thou art not by mine eye, Lysander, found;
Mine ear, I thank it, brought me to thy sound.
But why unkindly didst thou leave me so?
Lysander: Why should he stay, whom love doth press to go?
Hermia: What love could press Lysander from my side? 185
Lysander: Lysander's love, that would not let him bide —
Fair Helena, who more engilds° the night
Than all yon fiery oes° and eyes of light.
Why seek'st thou me? Could not this make thee know
The hate I bear thee made me leave thee so? 190
Hermia: You speak not as you think. It cannot be.
Helena: Lo, she is one of this confederacy!
Now I perceive they have conjoined all three
To fashion this false sport, in spite of me.°
Injurious Hermia, most ungrateful maid! 195
Have you conspired, have you with these contrived°
To bait° me with this foul derision?
Is all the counsel° that we two have shared —
The sisters' vows, the hours that we have spent

159 *sort:* Character, quality.   160 *extort:* Twist, torture.   169 *will none:* I.e., want no part of her.
171 *to . . . sojourned:* Only visited with her.   175 *aby:* Pay for.   177 *his:* Its.   187 *engilds:* Gilds,
brightens with a golden light.   188 *oes:* Spangles (here, stars).   194 *in spite of me:* To vex me.
196 *contrived:* Plotted.   197 *bait:* Torment, as one sets on dogs to bait a bear.   198 *counsel:*
Confidential talk.

When we have chid the hasty-footed time   200
For parting us — O, is all forgot?
All schooldays' friendship, childhood innocence?
We, Hermia, like two artificial° gods
Have with our needles created both one flower,
Both on one sampler, sitting on one cushion,   205
Both warbling of one song, both in one key,
As if our hands, our sides, voices, and minds
Had been incorporate.° So we grew together,
Like to a double cherry, seeming parted,
But yet an union in partition,   210
Two lovely° berries molded on one stem;
So, with two seeming bodies but one heart,
Two of the first, like coats in heraldry,
Due but to one and crownèd with one crest.°
And will you rend our ancient love asunder,   215
To join with men in scorning your poor friend?
It is not friendly, 'tis not maidenly.
Our sex, as well as I, may chide you for it,
Though I alone do feel the injury.
Hermia: I am amazèd at your passionate words.   220
  I scorn you not. It seems that you scorn me.
Helena: Have you not set Lysander, as in scorn,
  To follow me and praise my eyes and face?
  And made your other love, Demetrius,
  Who even but now did spurn me with his foot,   225
  To call me goddess, nymph, divine, and rare,
  Precious, celestial? Wherefore speaks he this
  To her he hates? And wherefore doth Lysander
  Deny your love, so rich within his soul,
  And tender° me, forsooth, affection,   230
  But by your setting on, by your consent?
  What though I be not so in grace° as you,
  So hung upon with love, so fortunate,
  But miserable most, to love unloved?
  This you should pity rather than despise.   235
Hermia: I understand not what you mean by this.
Helena: Ay, do! Persever, counterfeit sad° looks,
  Make mouths° upon° me when I turn my back,
  Wink each at other, hold the sweet jest up.°
  This sport, well carried,° shall be chronicled.   240
  If you have any pity, grace, or manners,
  You would not make me such an argument.°

---

203 *artificial:* Skilled in art or creation.   208 *incorporate:* Of one body.   211 *lovely:* Loving.
213–214 *Two . . . crest:* I.e., we have two separate bodies, just as a coat of arms in heraldry can be
represented twice on a shield but surmounted by a single crest.   230 *tender:* Offer.   232 *grace:*
Favor.   237 *sad:* Grave, serious.   238 *mouths:* I.e., mows, faces, grimaces; *upon:* At.   239 *hold
. . . up:* Keep up the joke.   240 *carried:* Managed.   242 *argument:* Subject for a jest.

But fare ye well. 'Tis partly my own fault,
Which death, or absence, soon shall remedy.
Lysander: Stay, gentle Helena; hear my excuse,   245
My love, my life, my soul, fair Helena!
Helena: O excellent!
Hermia [to Lysander]: Sweet, do not scorn her so.
Demetrius [to Lysander]: If she cannot entreat,° I can compel.
Lysander: Thou canst compel no more than she entreat.   250
Thy threats have no more strength than her weak prayers.
Helen, I love thee, by my life, I do!
I swear by that which I will lose for thee,
To prove him false that says I love thee not.
Demetrius [to Helena]: I say I love thee more than he can do.   255
Lysander: If thou say so, withdraw, and prove it too.°
Demetrius: Quick, come!
Hermia: Lysander, whereto tends all this?
Lysander: Away, you Ethiope!°   *[He tries to break away from Hermia.]*
Demetrius: No, no; he'll
Seem to break loose; take on as° you would follow,
But yet come not. You are a tame man. Go!   260
Lysander [to Hermia]: Hang off,° thou cat, thou burr! Vile thing, let loose,
Or I will shake thee from me like a serpent!
Hermia: Why are you grown so rude? What change is this,
Sweet love?
Lysander: Thy love? Out, tawny Tartar, out!
Out, loathèd med'cine!° O hated potion, hence!   265
Hermia: Do you not jest?
Helena: Yes, sooth,° and so do you.
Lysander: Demetrius, I will keep my word with thee.
Demetrius: I would I had your bond, for I perceive
A weak bond° holds you. I'll not trust your word.
Lysander: What, should I hurt her, strike her, kill her dead?   270
Although I hate her, I'll not harm her so.
Hermia: What, can you do me greater harm than hate?
Hate me? Wherefore? O me, what news,° my love?
Am not I Hermia? Are not you Lysander?
I am as fair now as I was erewhile.°   275
Since night you loved me; yet since night you left me.
Why, then you left me — O, the gods forbid! —
In earnest, shall I say?
Lysander: Ay, by my life!
And never did desire to see thee more.
Therefore be out of hope, of question, of doubt;   280

---

249 *entreat:* I.e., succeed by entreaty.   256 *withdraw . . . too:* I.e., withdraw with me and prove your
claim in a duel (the two gentlemen are armed).   258 *Ethiope:* (Referring to Hermia's relatively dark
hair and complexion; see also *tawny Tartar* six lines later.)   259 *take on as:* Act as if, make a fuss
as if.   261 *Hang off:* Let go.   265 *med'cine:* I.e., poison.   266 *sooth:* Truly.   269 *weak bond:*
I.e., Hermia's arm (with a pun on *bond,* "oath," in the previous line).   273 *what news:* What is the
matter.   275 *erewhile:* Just now.

Be certain, nothing truer. 'Tis no jest
That I do hate thee and love Helena.
Hermia [to Helena]: O me! You juggler! You cankerblossom!°
You thief of love! What, have you come by night
And stol'n my love's heart from him?
Helena: Fine, i' faith!   285
Have you no modesty, no maiden shame,
No touch of bashfulness? What, will you tear
Impatient answers from my gentle tongue?
Fie, fie! You counterfeit, you puppet,° you!
Hermia: "Puppet"? Why, so!° Ay, that way goes the game.   290
Now I perceive that she hath made compare
Between our statures; she hath urged her height,
And with her personage, her tall personage,
Her height, forsooth, she hath prevailed with him.
And are you grown so high in his esteem   295
Because I am so dwarfish and so low?
How low am I, thou painted maypole? Speak!
How low am I? I am not yet so low
But that my nails can reach unto thine eyes.

                    [She flails at Helena but is restrained.]

Helena: I pray you, though you mock me, gentlemen,   300
Let her not hurt me. I was never curst;°
I have no gift at all in shrewishness;
I am a right° maid for my cowardice.
Let her not strike me. You perhaps may think,
Because she is something° lower than myself,   305
That I can match her.
Hermia: Lower? Hark, again!
Helena: Good Hermia, do not be so bitter with me.
I evermore did love you, Hermia,
Did ever keep your counsels, never wronged you,
Save that, in love unto Demetrius,   310
I told him of your stealth° unto this wood.
He followed you; for love I followed him.
But he hath chid me hence° and threatened me
To strike me, spurn me, nay, to kill me too.
And now, so° you will let me quiet go,   315
To Athens will I bear my folly back
And follow you no further. Let me go.
You see how simple and how fond° I am.
Hermia: Why, get you gone. Who is't that hinders you?
Helena: A foolish heart, that I leave here behind.   320

---

283 *cankerblossom:* Worm that destroys the flower bud, or wild rose.   289 *puppet:* (1) Counterfeit
(2) dwarfish woman (in reference to Hermia's smaller stature).   290 *Why, so:* I.e., Oh, so that's how
it is.   301 *curst:* Shrewish.   303 *right:* True.   305 *something:* Somewhat.   311 *stealth:* Stealing
away.   313 *chid me hence:* Driven me away with his scolding.   315 *so:* If only.   318 *fond:* Foolish.

Hermia: What, with Lysander?

Helena: With Demetrius.

Lysander: Be not afraid; she shall not harm thee, Helena.

Demetrius: No, sir, she shall not, though you take her part.

Helena: O, when she is angry, she is keen° and shrewd.°   325
  She was a vixen when she went to school;
  And though she be but little, she is fierce.

Hermia: "Little" again? Nothing but "low" and "little"?
  Why will you suffer her to flout me thus?
  Let me come to her.

Lysander: Get you gone, you dwarf!
  You minimus,° of hindering knotgrass° made!   330
  You bead, you acorn!

Demetrius: You are too officious
  In her behalf that scorns your services.
  Let her alone. Speak not of Helena;
  Take not her part. For, if thou dost intend°
  Never so little show of love to her,   335
  Thou shalt aby° it.

Lysander: Now she holds me not.
  Now follow, if thou dar'st, to try whose right,
  Of thine or mine, is most in Helena.   *[Exit.]*

Demetrius: Follow? Nay, I'll go with thee, cheek by jowl.°

                                        [Exit, following Lysander.]

Hermia: You, mistress, all this coil° is 'long of° you.   340
  Nay, go not back.°

Helena: I will not trust you, I,
  Nor longer stay in your curst company.
  Your hands than mine are quicker for a fray;
  My legs are longer, though, to run away.   *[Exit.]*

Hermia: I am amazed and know not what to say.   *Exit.*   345

[Oberon and Puck come forward.]

Oberon: This is thy negligence. Still thou mistak'st,
  Or else committ'st thy knaveries willfully.

Puck: Believe me, king of shadows, I mistook.
  Did not you tell me I should know the man
  By the Athenian garments he had on?   350
  And so far blameless proves my enterprise
  That I have 'nointed an Athenian's eyes;
  And so far° am I glad it so did sort,°
  As° this their jangling I esteem a sport.

Oberon: Thou seest these lovers seek a place to fight.   355
  Hie° therefore, Robin, overcast the night;

---

324 *keen:* Fierce, cruel; *shrewd:* Shrewish.   330 *minimus:* Diminutive creature; *knotgrass:* A weed, an infusion of which was thought to stunt the growth.   334 *intend:* Give sign of.   336 *aby:* Pay for. 339 *cheek by jowl:* I.e., side by side.   340 *coil:* Turmoil, dissension; *'long of:* On account of. 341 *go not back:* I.e., don't retreat (Hermia is again proposing a flight).   353 *so far:* At least to this extent; *sort:* Turn out.   354 *As:* In that.   356 *Hie:* Hasten.

The starry welkin° cover thou anon
With drooping fog as black as Acheron,°
And lead these testy rivals so astray
As° one come not within another's way.   360
Like to Lysander sometimes frame thy tongue,
Then stir Demetrius up with bitter wrong;°
And sometimes rail thou like Demetrius.
And from each other look thou lead them thus,
Till o'er their brows death-counterfeiting sleep   365
With leaden legs and batty° wings doth creep.
Then crush this herb° into Lysander's eye,   [giving herb]
Whose liquor hath this virtuous° property,
To take from thence all error with his° might
And make his eyeballs roll with wonted° sight.   370
When they next wake, all this derision°
Shall seem a dream and fruitless vision,
And back to Athens shall the lovers wend
With league whose date° till death shall never end.
Whiles I in this affair do thee employ,   375
I'll to my queen and beg her Indian boy;
And then I will her charmèd eye release
From monster's view, and all things shall be peace.
Puck: My fairy lord, this must be done with haste,
For night's swift dragons° cut the clouds full fast,   380
And yonder shines Aurora's harbinger,°
At whose approach ghosts, wand'ring here and there,
Troop home to churchyards. Damnèd spirits all,
That in crossways and floods have burial,°
Already to their wormy beds are gone.   385
For fear lest day should look their shames upon,
They willfully themselves exile from light
And must for aye° consort with black-browed night.
Oberon: But we are spirits of another sort.
I with the Morning's love° have oft made sport,   390
And, like a forester,° the groves may tread
Even till the eastern gate, all fiery red,
Opening on Neptune with fair blessèd beams,
Turns into yellow gold his salt green streams.
But notwithstanding, haste, make no delay.   395
We may effect this business yet ere day.   [Exit.]

357 *welkin:* Sky.   358 *Acheron:* River of Hades (here representing Hades itself).   360 *As:* That.
362 *wrong:* Insults.   366 *batty:* Batlike.   367 *this herb:* I.e., the antidote (mentioned in II.i.184) to
love-in-idleness.   368 *virtuous:* Efficacious.   369 *his:* Its.   370 *wonted:* Accustomed.   371 *derision:* Laughable business.   374 *date:* Term of existence.   380 *dragons:* (Supposed by Shakespeare
to be yoked to the car of the goddess of night or the moon.)   381 *Aurora's harbinger:* The morning
star, precursor of dawn.   384 *crossways . . . burial:* (Those who had committed suicide were buried
at crossways, with a stake driven through them; those who intentionally or accidentally drowned [in
floods or deep water] would be condemned to wander disconsolately for lack of burial rights.)
388 *for aye:* Forever.   390 *the Morning's love:* Cephalus, a beautiful youth beloved by Aurora; or
perhaps the goddess of the dawn herself.   391 *forester:* Keeper of a royal forest.

Puck: Up and down, up and down,
    I will lead them up and down.
    I am feared in field and town.
    Goblin,° lead them up and down.   400
Here comes one.

Enter Lysander.

Lysander: Where art thou, proud Demetrius? Speak thou now.
Puck [mimicking Demetrius]: Here, villain, drawn° and ready. Where art
    thou?
Lysander: I will be with thee straight.°
Puck: Follow me, then,
    To plainer° ground.   *[Lysander wanders about,° following the voice.]*

Enter Demetrius.

Demetrius: Lysander! Speak again!   405
    Thou runaway, thou coward, art thou fled?
    Speak! In some bush? Where dost thou hide thy head?
Puck [mimicking Lysander]: Thou coward, art thou bragging to the stars,
    Telling the bushes that thou look'st for wars,
    And wilt not come? Come, recreant;° come, thou child,   410
    I'll whip thee with a rod. He is defiled
    That draws a sword on thee.
Demetrius: Yea, art thou there?
Puck: Follow my voice. We'll try° no manhood here.   *Exeunt.*

[Lysander returns.]

Lysander: He goes before me and still dares me on.
    When I come where he calls, then he is gone.   415
    The villain is much lighter-heeled than I.
    I followed fast, but faster he did fly,
    That fallen am I in dark uneven way,
    And here will rest me. *[He lies down.]* Come, thou gentle day!
    For if but once thou show me thy gray light,   420
    I'll find Demetrius and revenge this spite. *[He sleeps.]*

[Enter] Robin [Puck] and Demetrius.

Puck: Ho, ho, ho! Coward, why com'st thou not?
Demetrius: Abide° me, if thou dar'st; for well I wot°
    Thou runn'st before me, shifting every place,
    And dar'st not stand nor look me in the face.   425
    Where art thou now?
Puck: Come hither. I am here.

---

400 *Goblin:* Hobgoblin (Puck refers to himself.).   403 *drawn:* With drawn sword.   404 *straight:*
Immediately.   405 *plainer:* More open.   *Lysander wanders about:* (Lysander may exit here, but
perhaps not; neither exit nor reentrance is indicated in the early texts.)   410 *recreant:* Cowardly
wretch.   413 *try:* Test.   423 *Abide:* Confront, face; *wot:* know.

Demetrius: Nay, then, thou mock'st me. Thou shalt buy° this dear,°
    If ever I thy face by daylight see.
    Now go thy way. Faintness constraineth me
    To measure out my length on this cold bed.   430
    By day's approach look to be visited.   *[He lies down and sleeps.]*

Enter Helena.

Helena: O weary night, O long and tedious night,
      Abate° thy hours! Shine comforts from the east,
    That I may back to Athens by daylight
      From these that my poor company detest;   435
    And sleep, that sometimes shuts up sorrow's eye,
    Steal me awhile from mine own company. *[She lies down and] sleep[s].*
Puck: Yet but three? Come one more;
      Two of both kinds makes up four.
      Here she comes, curst° and sad.   440
      Cupid is a knavish lad,
      Thus to make poor females mad.

[Enter Hermia.]

Hermia: Never so weary, never so in woe,
      Bedabbled with the dew and torn with briers,
    I can no further crawl, no further go;   445
      My legs can keep no pace with my desires.
    Here will I rest me till the break of day.
    Heavens shield Lysander, if they mean a fray!
                      [She lies down and sleeps.]
Puck: On the ground
      Sleep sound.   450
      I'll apply
      To your eye,
    Gentle lover, remedy.   *[He squeezes the juice on Lysander's eyes.]*
      When thou wak'st,
      Thou tak'st   455
      True delight
      In the sight
    Of thy former lady's eye;
    And the country proverb known,
    That every man should take his own,   460
    In your waking shall be shown:
      Jack shall have Jill;°
      Naught shall go ill;
    The man shall have his mare again, and all shall be well.
                  [Exit. The four sleeping lovers remain.]

---

427 *buy:* Aby, pay for; *dear:* Dearly.   433 *Abate:* Lessen, shorten.   440 *curst:* Ill-tempered.
462 *Jack shall have Jill:* (Proverbial for "boy gets girl.")

[ACT IV

Scene I: *The wood. The lovers are still asleep onstage.*]

Enter [Titania,] Queen of Fairies, and [Bottom the] clown, and Fairies; and [Oberon,] the King, behind them.

Titania: Come, sit thee down upon this flowery bed,
    While I thy amiable° cheeks do coy,°
And stick muskroses in thy sleek smooth head,
    And kiss thy fair large ears, my gentle joy.   *[They recline.]*   5

Bottom: Where's Peaseblossom?

Peaseblossom: Ready.

Bottom: Scratch my head, Peaseblossom. Where's Monsieur Cobweb?

Cobweb: Ready.

Bottom: Monsieur Cobweb, good monsieur, get you your weapons in your hand, and kill me a red-hipped humble-bee on the top of a thistle; and,   10 good monsieur, bring me the honey bag. Do not fret yourself too much in the action, monsieur; and, good monsieur, have a care the honey bag break not. I would be loath to have you overflown with a honey bag, signor. *[Exit Cobweb.]* Where's Monsieur Mustardseed?

Mustardseed: Ready.   15

Bottom: Give me your neaf,° Monsieur Mustardseed. Pray you, leave your courtesy,° good monsieur.

Mustardseed: What's your will?

Bottom: Nothing, good monsieur, but to help Cavalery° Cobweb° to scratch. I must to the barber's, monsieur, for methinks I am marvelous hairy about   20 the face; and I am such a tender ass, if my hair do but tickle me I must scratch.

Titania: What, wilt thou hear some music, my sweet love?

Bottom: I have a reasonable good ear in music. Let's have the tongs and the bones.°   *[Music: tongs, rural music.°]*   25

Titania: Or say, sweet love, what thou desirest to eat.

Bottom: Truly, a peck of provender.° I could munch your good dry oats. Methinks I have a great desire to a bottle° of hay. Good hay, sweet hay, hath no fellow.°

Titania: I have a venturous fairy that shall seek   30
    The squirrel's hoard, and fetch thee new nuts.

Bottom: I had rather have a handful or two of dried peas. But, I pray you, let none of your people stir° me. I have an exposition° of sleep come upon me.

Act IV. Scene I.   2 *amiable:* Lovely; *coy:* Caress.   16 *neaf:* Fist.   17 *leave your courtesy:* I.e., stop bowing, or put on your hat.   19 *Cavalery:* Cavalier (form of address for a gentleman); *Cobweb:* (Seemingly an error, since Cobweb has been sent to bring honey, while Peaseblossom has been asked to scratch.)   25 *tongs . . . bones:* Instruments for rustic music (the tongs were played like a triangle, whereas the bones were held between the fingers and used as clappers).   *Music . . . music:* (This stage direction is added from the Folio.)   27 *peck of provender:* One-quarter bushel of grain.   28 *bottle:* Bundle.   29 *fellow:* Equal.   33 *stir:* Disturb; *exposition of:* (Bottom's phrase for "disposition to.")

Titania: Sleep thou, and I will wind thee in my arms.   35
  Fairies, begone, and be all ways° away.   *[Exeunt Fairies.]*
  So doth the woodbine° the sweet honeysuckle
  Gently entwist; the female ivy so
  Enrings the barky fingers of the elm.
  O, how I love thee! How I dote on thee!   *[They sleep.]* 40

Enter Robin Goodfellow [Puck].

Oberon [coming forward]: Welcome, good Robin. Seest thou this sweet
  sight?
  Her dotage now I do begin to pity.
  For, meeting her of late behind the wood
  Seeking sweet favors° for this hateful fool,
  I did upbraid her and fall out with her.   45
  For she his hairy temples then had rounded
  With coronet of fresh and fragrant flowers;
  And that same dew, which sometime° on the buds
  Was wont to swell like round and orient pearls,°
  Stood now within the pretty flowerets' eyes   50
  Like tears that did their own disgrace bewail.
  When I had at my pleasure taunted her,
  And she in mild terms begged my patience,
  I then did ask of her her changeling child,
  Which straight she gave me, and her fairy sent   55
  To bear him to my bower in Fairyland.
  And, now I have the boy, I will undo
  This hateful imperfection of her eyes.
  And, gentle Puck, take this transformèd scalp
  From off the head of this Athenian swain,   60
  That he, awaking when the other° do,
  May all to Athens back again repair,°
  And think no more of this night's accidents
  But as the fierce vexation of a dream.
  But first I will release the Fairy Queen.   65
                          [He squeezes an herb on her eyes.]
    Be as thou wast wont to be;
    See as thou wast wont to see.
    Dian's bud° o'er Cupid's flower
    Hath such force and blessèd power.
  Now, my Titania, wake you, my sweet queen.   70
Titania [awaking]: My Oberon! What visions have I seen!
  Methought I was enamored of an ass.

36 *all ways:* In all directions.   37 *woodbine:* Bindweed, a climbing plant that twines in the opposite
direction from that of honeysuckle.   44 *favors:* I.e., gifts of flowers.   48 *sometime:* Formerly.
49 *orient pearls:* I.e., the most beautiful of all pearls, those coming from the Orient.   61 *other:* Others.
62 *repair:* Return.   68 *Dian's bud:* (Perhaps the flower of the *agnus castus* or chaste-tree, supposed
to preserve chastity; or perhaps referring simply to Oberon's herb by which he can undo the effects
of "Cupid's flower," the love-in-idleness of II.i.166–168.)

Oberon: There lies your love.

Titania: How came these things to pass?

    O, how mine eyes do loathe his visage now!

Oberon: Silence awhile. Robin, take off this head.   75

    Titania, music call, and strike more dead

    Than common sleep of all these five° the sense.

Titania: Music, ho! Music, such as charmeth° sleep!   *[Music.]*

Puck [removing the ass head]: Now, when thou wak'st, with thine own fool's

    eyes peep.

Oberon: Sound, music! Come, my queen, take hands with me,   80

    And rock the ground whereon these sleepers be.   *[They dance.]*

    Now thou and I are new in amity,

    And will tomorrow midnight solemnly°

    Dance in Duke Theseus' house triumphantly,

    And bless it to all fair prosperity.   85

    There shall the pairs of faithful lovers be

    Wedded, with Theseus, all in jollity.

Puck: Fairy King, attend, and mark:

    I do hear the morning lark.

Oberon: Then, my queen, in silence sad,°   90

    Trip we after night's shade.

    We the globe can compass soon,

    Swifter than the wandering moon.

Titania: Come, my lord, and in our flight

    Tell me how it came this night   95

    That I sleeping here was found

    With these mortals on the ground.

            Exeunt [Oberon, Titania, and Puck]. Wind horn [within].

Enter Theseus and all his train; [Hippolyta, Egeus].

Theseus: Go, one of you, find out the forester,

    For now our observation° is performed;

    And since we have the vaward° of the day,   100

    My love shall hear the music of my hounds.

    Uncouple° in the western valley; let them go.

    Dispatch, I say, and find the forester.   *[Exit an Attendant.]*

    We will, fair queen, up to the mountain's top

    And mark the musical confusion   105

    Of hounds and echo in conjunction.

Hippolyta: I was with Hercules and Cadmus° once

    When in a wood of Crete they bayed° the bear

---

77 *these five:* I.e., the four lovers and Bottom.   78 *charmeth:* Brings about, as though by a charm.
83 *solemnly:* Ceremoniously.   90 *sad:* Sober.   99 *observation:* I.e., observance to a morn of May
(I.i.167).   100 *vaward:* Vanguard, i.e., earliest part.   102 *Uncouple:* Set free for the hunt.
107 *Cadmus:* Mythical founder of Thebes. (This story about him is unknown.)   108 *bayed:* Brought
to bay.

With hounds of Sparta.° Never did I hear
Such gallant chiding;° for, besides the groves,   110
The skies, the fountains, every region near
Seemed all one mutual cry. I never heard
So musical a discord, such sweet thunder.
Theseus: My hounds are bred out of the Spartan kind,°
So flewed,° so sanded;° and their heads are hung   115
With ears that sweep away the morning dew;
Crook-kneed, and dewlapped° like Thessalian bulls;
Slow in pursuit, but matched in mouth like bells,
Each under each.° A cry° more tunable°
Was never holloed to nor cheered° with horn   120
In Crete, in Sparta, nor in Thessaly.
Judge when you hear. *[He sees the sleepers.]* But soft!° What nymphs are
    these?
Egeus: My lord, this is my daughter here asleep,
And this Lysander; this Demetrius is;
This Helena, old Nedar's Helena.   125
I wonder of° their being here together.
Theseus: No doubt they rose up early to observe
The rite of May, and hearing our intent,
Came here in grace of our solemnity.°
But speak, Egeus. Is not this the day   130
That Hermia should give answer of her choice?
Egeus: It is, my lord.
Theseus: Go bid the huntsmen wake them with their horns.

                                                    [Exit an Attendant.]

Shout within. Wind horns. They all start up.

Good morrow, friends. Saint Valentine° is past.
Begin these woodbirds but to couple now?   135
Lysander: Pardon, my lord.   *[They kneel.]*
Theseus: I pray you all, stand up.   *[They stand.]*
I know you two are rival enemies;
How comes this gentle concord in the world,
That hatred is so far from jealousy°
To sleep by hate and fear no enmity?   140
Lysander: My lord, I shall reply amazedly,
Half sleep, half waking; but as yet, I swear,
I cannot truly say how I came here.
But, as I think — for truly would I speak,
And now I do bethink me, so it is —   145

109 *hounds of Sparta:* (A breed famous in antiquity for their hunting skill.)   110 *chiding:* I.e., yelping.
114 *kind:* Strain, breed.   115 *So flewed:* Similarly having large hanging chaps or fleshy covering of
the jaw; *sanded:* Of sandy color.   117 *dewlapped:* Having pendulous folds of skin under the neck.
118–119 *matched . . . each:* I.e., harmoniously matched in their various cries like a set of bells, from
treble down to bass.   119 *cry:* Pack of hounds; *tunable:* Well tuned, melodious.   120 *cheered:*
Encouraged.   122 *soft:* I.e., gently, wait a minute.   126 *wonder of:* Wonder at.   129 *in . . . solemnity:* In honor of our wedding ceremony.   134 *Saint Valentine:* (Birds were supposed to choose
their mates on Saint Valentine's Day.)   139 *jealousy:* Suspicion.

I came with Hermia hither. Our intent
Was to be gone from Athens, where° we might,
Without° the peril of the Athenian law—

Egeus: Enough, enough, my lord; you have enough.
   I beg the law, the law, upon his head.   150
   They would have stol'n away; they would, Demetrius,
   Thereby to have defeated° you and me,
   You of your wife and me of my consent,
   Of my consent that she should be your wife.

Demetrius: My lord, fair Helen told me of their stealth,   155
   Of this their purpose hither° to this wood,
   And I in fury hither followed them,
   Fair Helena in fancy° following me.
   But, my good lord, I wot not by what power—
   But by some power it is—my love to Hermia,   160
   Melted as the snow, seems to me now
   As the remembrance of an idle gaud°
   Which in my childhood I did dote upon;
   And all the faith, the virtue of my heart,
   The object and the pleasure of mine eye,   165
   Is only Helena. To her, my lord,
   Was I betrothed ere I saw Hermia,
   But like a sickness did I loathe this food;
   But, as in health, come to my natural taste,
   Now I do wish it, love it, long for it,   170
   And will forevermore be true to it.

Theseus: Fair lovers, you are fortunately met.
   Of this discourse we more will hear anon.
   Egeus, I will overbear your will;
   For in the temple, by and by, with us   175
   These couples shall eternally be knit.
   And, for° the morning now is something° worn,
   Our purposed hunting shall be set aside.
   Away with us to Athens. Three and three,
   We'll hold a feast in great solemnity.°   180
   Come Hippolyta.   *[Exeunt Theseus, Hippolyta, Egeus, and train.]*

Demetrius: These things seem small and undistinguishable,
   Like far-off mountains turnèd into clouds.

Hermia: Methinks I see these things with parted° eye,
   When everything seems double.

Helena: So methinks;   185
   And I have found Demetrius like a jewel,
   Mine own, and not mine own.°

Demetrius: Are you sure

---

147 *where:* Wherever; or, to where.   148 *Without:* Outside of, beyond.   152 *defeated:* Defrauded.
156 *hither:* In coming hither.   158 *in fancy:* Driven by love.   162 *idle gaud:* Worthless trinket.
177 *for:* Since; *something:* Somewhat.   180 *in great solemnity:* With great ceremony.   184 *parted:*
I.e., improperly focused.   186–187 *like . . . mine own:* I.e., like a jewel that one finds by chance and
therefore possesses but cannot certainly consider one's own property.

That we are awake? It seems to me
That yet we sleep, we dream. Do not you think
The Duke was here, and bid us follow him?   190
Hermia: Yea, and my father.
Helena: And Hippolyta.
Lysander: And he did bid us follow to the temple.
Demetrius: Why, then, we are awake. Let's follow him,
And by the way let us recount our dreams.   *[Exeunt the lovers.]*
Bottom [awaking]: When my cue comes, call me, and I will answer. My next   195
    is "Most fair Pyramus." Heigh-ho! Peter Quince! Flute, the bellows
    mender! Snout, the tinker! Starveling! God's° my life, stolen hence and
    left me asleep! I have had a most rare vision. I have had a dream, past
    the wit of man to say what dream it was. Man is but an ass if he go about°
    to expound this dream. Methought I was — there is no man can tell what.   200
    Methought I was — and methought I had — but man is but a patched°
    fool if he will offer° to say what methought I had. The eye of man hath
    not heard, the ear of man hath not seen, man's hand is not able to taste,
    his tongue to conceive, nor his heart to report° what my dream was. I
    will get Peter Quince to write a ballad° of this dream. It shall be called   205
    "Bottom's Dream," because it hath no bottom;° and I will sing it in the
    latter end of a play, before the Duke. Peradventure, to make it the more
    gracious, I shall sing it at her° death.   *[Exit.]*

[Scene II: *Athens.*]

Enter Quince, Flute, [Snout, and Starveling].

Quince: Have you sent to Bottom's house? Is he come home yet?
Starveling: He cannot be heard of. Out of doubt he is transported.°
Flute: If he come not, then the play is marred. It goes not forward. Doth it?
Quince: It is not possible. You have not a man in all Athens able to discharge°
    Pyramus but he.   5
Flute: No, he hath simply the best wit° of any handicraft man in Athens.
Quince: Yea, and the best person° too, and he is a very paramour for a sweet
    voice.
Flute: You must say "paragon." A paramour is, God bless us, a thing of
    naught.°   10

Enter Snug the joiner.

Snug: Masters, the Duke is coming from the temple, and there is two or
    three lords and ladies more married. If our sport had gone forward, we
    had all been made men.°

---

197 *God's:* May God save.   199 *go about:* Attempt.   201 *patched:* Wearing motley, i.e., a dress of
various colors.   202 *offer:* Venture.   202–204 *The eye . . . report:* (Bottom garbles the terms of
1 Corinthians 2:9.)   205 *ballad:* (The proper medium for relating sensational stories and preposterous events.)   206 *hath no bottom:* Is unfathomable.   208 *her:* Thisbe's (?)   Scene II.   2 *transported:* Carried off by fairies; or, possibly, transformed.   4 *discharge:* Perform.   6 *wit:* Intellect
7 *person:* Appearance.   9–10 *a . . . naught:* A shameful thing.   12–13 *we . . . men:* I.e., we would
have had our fortunes made.

Flute: O sweet bully Bottom! Thus hath he lost sixpence a day° during his life; he could not have scaped sixpence a day. An the Duke had not given him sixpence a day for playing Pyramus, I'll be hanged. He would have deserved it. Sixpence a day in Pyramus, or nothing. 15

Enter Bottom.

Bottom: Where are these lads? Where are these hearts?°
Quince: Bottom! O most courageous day! O most happy hour!
Bottom: Masters, I am to discourse wonders.° But ask me not what; for if I tell you, I am no true Athenian. I will tell you everything, right as it fell out. 20
Quince: Let us hear, sweet Bottom.
Bottom: Not a word of° me. All that I will tell you is that the Duke hath dined. Get your apparel together, good strings° to your beards, new ribbons to your pumps;° meet presently° at the palace; every man look o'er his part; for the short and the long is, our play is preferred.° In any case, let Thisbe have clean linen; and let not him that plays the lion pare his nails, for they shall hang out for the lion's claws. And, most dear actors, eat no onions nor garlic, for we are to utter sweet breath; and I do not doubt but to hear them say it is a sweet comedy. No more words. Away! Go, away! 25 30

[Exeunt.]

[ACT V

Enter Theseus, Hippolyta, and Philostrate, [lords, and attendants].

Hippolyta: 'Tis strange, my Theseus, that° these lovers speak of.
Theseus: More strange than true. I never may° believe
These antique° fables nor these fairy toys.°
Lovers and madmen have such seething brains,
Such shaping fantasies,° that apprehend° 5
More than cool reason ever comprehends.°
The lunatic, the lover, and the poet
Are of imagination all compact.°
One sees more devils than vast hell can hold;
That is the madman. The lover, all as frantic, 10
Sees Helen's° beauty in a brow of Egypt.°
The poet's eye, in a fine frenzy rolling,

14 *sixpence a day:* I.e., as a royal pension.   18 *hearts:* Good fellows.   20 *am . . . wonders:* Have wonders to relate.   24 *of:* Out of.   25 *strings:* (To attach the beards).   26 *pumps:* Light shoes or slippers; *presently:* Immediately.   27 *preferred:* Selected for consideration.   Act V. Scene I.
1 *that:* That which.   2 *may:* Can.   3 *antique:* Old-fashioned (punning, too, on *antic*, "strange," "grotesque"); *fairy toys:* Trifling stories about fairies.   5 *fantasies:* Imaginations; *apprehend:* Conceive, imagine.   6 *comprehends:* Understands.   8 *compact:* Formed, composed.   11 *Helen's:* I.e., of Helen of Troy, pattern of beauty; *brow of Egypt:* I.e., face of a gypsy.

Doth glance from heaven to earth, from earth to heaven;
And as imagination bodies forth
The forms of things unknown, the poet's pen   15
Turns them to shapes and gives to airy nothing
A local habitation and a name.
Such tricks hath strong imagination
That, if it would but apprehend some joy,
It comprehends some bringer° of that joy;   20
Or in the night, imagining some fear,°
How easy is a bush supposed a bear!
Hippolyta: But all the story of the night told over,
And all their minds transfigured so together,
More witnesseth than fancy's images°   25
And grows to something of great constancy;°
But, howsoever,° strange and admirable.°

Enter lovers: Lysander, Demetrius, Hermia, and Helena.

Theseus: Here come the lovers, full of joy and mirth.
Joy, gentle friends! Joy and fresh days of love
Accompany your hearts!
Lysander: More than to us   30
Wait in your royal walks, your board, your bed!
Theseus: Come now, what masques,° what dances shall we have,
To wear away this long age of three hours
Between our after-supper and bedtime?
Where is our usual manager of mirth?   35
What revels are in hand? Is there no play
To ease the anguish of a torturing hour?
Call Philostrate.
Philostrate: Here, mighty Theseus.
Theseus: Say, what abridgment° have you for this evening?
What masque? What music? How shall we beguile   40
The lazy time, if not with some delight?
Philostrate [giving him a paper]: There is a brief° how many sports are ripe.
Make choice of which Your Highness will see first.
Thesus [reads]: "The battle with the Centaurs,° to be sung
By an Athenian eunuch to the harp"?   45
We'll none of that. That have I told my love,
In glory of my kinsman° Hercules.
[He reads] "The riot of the tipsy Bacchanals,
Tearing the Thracian singer in their rage"?°

20 *bringer:* I.e., source.   21 *fear:* Object of fear.   25 *More . . . images:* Testifies to something more
substantial than mere imaginings.   26 *constancy:* Certainty.   27 *howsoever:* In any case; *admirable:*
A source of wonder.   32 *masques:* Courtly entertainments.   39 *abridgment:* Pastime (to abridge
or shorten the evening).   42 *brief:* Short written statement, summary.   44 *battle . . . Centaurs:*
(Probably refers to the battle of the Centaurs and the Lapithae, when the Centaurs attempted to carry
off Hippodamia, bride of Theseus' friend Pirothous. The story is told in Ovid's *Metamorphoses* 12.)
47 *kinsman:* (Plutarch's "Life of Theseus" states that Hercules and Theseus were near kinsmen. Theseus
is referring to a version of the battle of the Centaurs in which Hercules was said to be present.)
48–49 *The riot . . . rage:* (This was the story of the death of Orpheus, as told in *Metamorphoses* 11.)

That is an old device;° and it was played   50
When I from Thebes came last a conqueror.
[He reads.] "The thrice three Muses mourning for the death
Of Learning, late deceased in beggary"?°
That is some satire, keen and critical,
Not sorting with° a nuptial ceremony.   55
[He reads.] "A tedious brief scene of young Pyramus
And his love Thisbe; very tragical mirth"?
Merry and tragical? Tedious and brief?
That is, hot ice and wondrous strange° snow.
How shall we find the concord of this discord?   60
Philostrate: A play there is, my lord, some ten words long,
    Which is as brief as I have known a play;
    But by ten words, my lord, it is too long,
    Which makes it tedious. For in all the play
    There is not one word apt, one player fitted.   65
    And tragical, my noble lord, it is,
    For Pyramus therein doth kill himself.
    Which, when I saw rehearsed, I must confess,
    Made mine eyes water; but more merry tears
    The passion of loud laughter never shed.   70
Theseus: What are they that do play it?
Philostrate: Hardhanded men that work in Athens here,
    Which never labored in their minds till now,
    And now have toiled° their unbreathed° memories
    With this same play, against° your nuptial.   75
Theseus: And we will hear it.
Philostrate: No, my noble lord,
    It is not for you. I have heard it over,
    And it is nothing, nothing in the world;
    Unless you can find sport in their intents,
    Extremely stretched° and conned° with cruel pain   80
    To do you service.
Theseus: I will hear that play;
    For never anything can be amiss
    When simpleness° and duty tender it.
    Go, bring them in; and take your places, ladies.
                    [Philostrate goes to summon the players.]
Hippolyta: I love not to see wretchedness o'ercharged,°   85
    And duty in his service° perishing.
Theseus: Why, gentle sweet, you shall see no such thing.

---

50 *device:* Show, performance.   52–53 *The thrice . . . beggary:* (Possibly an allusion to Spenser's *Teares of the Muses,* 1591, though "satires" deploring the neglect of learning and the creative arts were commonplace.)   55 *sorting with:* Befitting.   59 *strange:* (Sometimes emended to an adjective that would contrast with *snow,* just as *hot* contrasts with *ice.*)   74 *toiled:* Taxed; *unbreathed:* Unexercised. 75 *against:* In preparation for.   80 *stretched:* Strained; *conned:* Memorized.   83 *simpleness:* Simplicity.   85 *wretchedness o'ercharged:* Social or intellectual inferiors overburdened.   86 *his service:* Its attempt to serve.

Hippolyta: He says they can do nothing in this kind.°
Theseus: The kinder we, to give them thanks for nothing.
    Our sport shall be to take what they mistake;   90
    And what poor duty cannot do, noble respect°
    Takes it in might, not merit.°
    Where I have come, great clerks° have purposèd
    To greet me with premeditated welcomes;
    Where I have seen them shiver and look pale,   95
    Make periods in the midst of sentences,
    Throttle their practiced accent° in their fears,
    And in conclusion dumbly have broke off,
    Not paying me a welcome. Trust me, sweet,
    Out of this silence yet I picked a welcome;   100
    And in the modesty of fearful duty
    I read as much as from the rattling tongue
    Of saucy and audacious eloquence.
    Love, therefore, and tongue-tied simplicity
    In least° speak most, to my capacity.°   105

[Philostrate returns.]

Philostrate: So please Your Grace, the Prologue° is addressed.°
Thesus: Let him approach.   *[A flourish of trumpets.]*

Enter the Prologue [Quince].

Prologue: If we offend, it is with our good will.
    That you should think, we come not to offend,
    But with good will. To show our simple skill,   110
    That is the true beginning of our end.
    Consider, then, we come but in despite.
    We do not come, as minding° to content you,
    Our true intent is. All for your delight
    We are not here, That you should here repent you,   115
    The actors are at hand; and, by their show,
    You shall know all that you are like to know.
Theseus: This fellow doth not stand upon points.°
Lysander: He hath rid° his prologue like a rough° colt; he knows not the
    stop.° A good moral, my lord: it is not enough to speak, but to speak true. 120
Hippolyta: Indeed, he hath played on his prologue like a child on a re-
    corder:° a sound, but not in government.°
Theseus: His speech was like a tangled chain: nothing° impaired, but all
    disordered. Who is next?

88 *kind:* Kind of thing.   91 *respect:* Evaluation, consideration.   92 *Takes . . . merit:* Values it for
the effort made rather than for the excellence achieved.   93 *clerks:* Learned men.   97 *practiced*
accent: I.e., rehearsed speech; or, usual way of speaking.   105 *least:* I.e., saying least; *to my capacity:*
In my judgment and understanding.   106 *Prologue:* Speaker of the prologue; *addressed:* Ready.
113 *minding:* Intending.   118 *stand upon points:* (1) Heed niceties or small points (2) pay attention
to punctuation in his reading. (The humor of Quince's speech is in the blunders of its punctuation.)
119 *rid:* Ridden; *rough:* unbroken.   120 *stop:* (1) Stopping of a colt by reining it in (2) punctuation
mark.   121–122 *recorder:* Wind instrument like a flute.   122 *government:* Control.   123 *noth-*
ing: Not at all.

Enter Pyramus [Bottom], and Thisbe [Flute], and Wall [Snout], and Moonshine [Starveling], and Lion [Snug].

Prologue: Gentles, perchance you wonder at this show;   125
   But wonder on, till truth make all things plain.
This man is Pyramus, if you would know;
   This beauteous lady Thisbe is, certain.
This man with lime and roughcast doth present
   Wall, that vile wall which did these lovers sunder;   130
And through Wall's chink, poor souls, they are content
   To whisper. At the which let no man wonder.
This man, with lantern, dog, and bush of thorn,
   Presenteth Moonshine; for, if you will know,
By moonshine did these lovers think no scorn°   135
   To meet at Ninus' tomb, there, there to woo.
This grisly beast, which Lion hight° by name,
The trusty Thisbe coming first by night
Did scare away, or rather did affright;
And as she fled, her mantle she did fall,°   140
   Which Lion vile with bloody mouth did stain.
Anon comes Pyramus, sweet youth and tall,°
   And finds his trusty Thisbe's mantle slain;
Whereat, with blade, with bloody, blameful blade,
   He bravely broached° his boiling bloody breast.   145
And Thisbe, tarrying in mulberry shade,
   His dagger drew, and died. For all the rest,
Let Lion, Moonshine, Wall, and lovers twain
At large° discourse, while here they do remain.
                    Exeunt Lion, Thisbe, and Moonshine.

Theseus: I wonder if the lion be to speak.   150
Demetrius: No wonder, my lord. One lion may, when many asses do.
Wall: In this same interlude° it doth befall
   That I, one Snout by name, present a wall;
   And such a wall as I would have you think
   That had in it a crannied hole or chink,   155
   Through which the lovers, Pyramus and Thisbe,
   Did whisper often, very secretly.
   This loam, this roughcast, and this stone doth show
   That I am that same wall; the truth is so.
   And this the cranny is, right and sinister,°   160
   Through which the fearful lovers are to whisper.
Theseus: Would you desire lime and hair to speak better?
Demetrius: It is the wittiest partition° that ever I heard discourse,
   my lord.

---

135 *think no scorn:* Think it no disgraceful matter.   137 *hight:* Is called.   140 *fall:* Let fall.
142 *tall:* Courageous.   145 *broached:* Stabbed.   149 *At large:* In full, at length.   152 *interlude:*
Play.   160 *right and sinister:* I.e., the right side of it and the left; or, running from right to left,
horizontally.   163 *partition:* (1) Wall (2) section of a learned treatise or oration.

[Pyramus comes forward.]

Theseus: Pyramus draws near the wall. Silence! 165
Pyramus: O grim-looked° night! O night with hue so black!
   O night, which ever art when day is not!
   O night, O night! Alack, alack, alack,
     I fear my Thisbe's promise is forgot.
   And thou, O wall, O sweet, O lovely wall, 170
     That stand'st between her father's ground and mine,
   Thou wall, O wall, O sweet and lovely wall,
     Show me thy chink, to blink through with mine eyne.
                      [Wall makes a chink with his fingers.]
   Thanks, courteous wall. Jove shield thee well for this.
   But what see I? No Thisbe do I see. 175
   O wicked wall, through whom I see no bliss!
   Cursed be thy stones for thus deceiving me!
Theseus: The wall, methinks, being sensible,° should curse again.°
Pyramus: No, in truth, sir, he should not. "Deceiving me" is Thisbe's cue:
   she is to enter now, and I am to spy her through the wall. You shall see, 180
   it will fall pat° as I told you. Yonder she comes.

Enter Thisbe.

Thisbe: O wall, full often hast thou heard my moans
     For parting my fair Pyramus and me.
   My cherry lips have often kissed thy stones,
     Thy stones with lime and hair knit up in thee. 185
Pyramus: I see a voice. Now will I to the chink,
     To spy an° I can hear my Thisbe's face.
   Thisbe!
Thisbe: My love! Thou art my love, I think.
Pyramus: Think what thou wilt, I am thy lover's grace,° 190
   And like Limander° am I trusty still.
Thisbe: And I like Helen,° till the Fates me kill.
Pyramus: Not Shafalus to Procrus° was so true.
Thisbe: As Shafalus to Procrus, I to you.
Pyramus: O, kiss me through the hole of this vile wall! 195
Thisbe: I kiss the wall's hole, not your lips at all.
Pyramus: Wilt thou at Ninny's tomb meet me straightway?
Thisbe: 'Tide life, 'tide° death, I come without delay.
                      [Exeunt Pyramus and Thisbe.]
Wall: Thus have I, Wall, my part dischargèd so;
   And, being done, thus Wall away doth go.   *[Exit.]* 200
Theseus: Now is the mural down between the two neighbors.
Demetrius: No remedy, my lord, when walls are so willful° to hear without
   warning.°

166 *grim-looked:* Grim-looking.   178 *sensible:* Capable of feeling; *again:* In return.   181 *pat:* Exactly.   187 *an:* If.   190 *lover's grace:* I.e., gracious lover.   191–192 *Limander, Helen:* (Blunders for "Leander" and "Hero").   193 *Shafalus, Procrus:* (Blunders for "Cephalus" and "Procris," also famous lovers).   198 *Tide:* Betide, come.   202–203 *willful:* Willing. *without warning:* I.e., without warning the parents. (Demetrius makes a joke on the proverb "Walls have ears.")

Hippolyta: This is the silliest stuff that ever I heard.

Theseus: The best in this kind° are but shadows,° and the worst are no worse,   205
if imagination amend them.

Hippolyta: It must be your imagination then, and not theirs.

Theseus: If we imagine no worse of them than they of themselves, they may
pass for excellent men. Here come two noble beasts in, a man and a lion.

Enter Lion and Moonshine.

Lion: You, ladies, you, whose gentle hearts do fear   210
    The smallest monstrous mouse that creeps on floor,
May now perchance both quake and tremble here,
    When lion rough in wildest rage doth roar.
Then know that I, as Snug the joiner, am
A lion fell,° nor else no lion's dam;   215
For, if I should as lion come in strife
Into this place, 'twere pity on my life.

Theseus: A very gentle beast, and of a good conscience.

Demetrius: The very best at a beast, my lord, that e'er I saw.

Lysander: This lion is a very fox for his valor.°   220

Theseus: True; and a goose for his discretion.°

Demetrius: Not so, my lord, for his valor cannot carry his discretion, and the
fox carries the goose.

Theseus: His discretion, I am sure, cannot carry his valor; for the goose
carries not the fox. It is well. Leave it to his discretion, and let us listen   225
to the moon.

Moon: This lanthorn° doth the hornèd moon present —

Demetrius: He should have worn the horns on his head.°

Theseus: He is no crescent,° and his horns are invisible within the circumference.   230

Moon: This lanthorn doth the hornèd moon present;
Myself the man i' the moon do seem to be.

Theseus: This is the greatest error of all the rest. The man should be put into
the lanthorn. How is it else the man i' the moon?

Demetrius: He dares not come there for° the candle, for you see it is already   235
in snuff.°

Hippolyta: I am weary of this moon. Would he would change!

Theseus: It appears, by his small light of discretion, that he is in the wane;
but yet, in courtesy, in all reason, we must stay the time.

---

205 *in this kind:* Of this sort; *shadows:* Likenesses, representations.   215 *lion fell:* Fierce lion (with
a play on the idea of "lion skin").   220 *is . . . valor:* I.e., his valor consists of craftiness and discretion.
221 *a goose . . . discretion:* I.e., as discreet as a goose, that is, more foolish than discreet.   227 *lanthorn:* (This original spelling, *lanthorn,* may suggest a play on the *horn* of which lanterns were made
and also on a cuckold's horns; however, the spelling *lanthorn* is not used consistently for comic effect
in this play or elsewhere. At Act V, Scene 1, line 133, for example, the word is *lantern* in the original.)
228 *on his head:* (As a sign of cuckoldry).   229 *crescent:* A waxing moon.   235 *for:* Because of, for
fear of.   236 *in snuff:* (1) Offended (2) in need of snuffing or trimming.

Lysander: Proceed, Moon.   240

Moon: All that I have to say is to tell you that the lanthorn is the moon, I,
  the man i' the moon, this thornbush my thornbush, and this dog my dog.

Demetrius: Why, all these should be in the lanthorn, for all these are in the
  moon. But silence! Here comes Thisbe.

Enter Thisbe.

Thisbe: This is old Ninny's tomb. Where is my love?   245

Lion [roaring]: O!

Demetrius: Well roared, Lion.   *[Thisbe runs off, dropping her mantle.]*

Theseus: Well run, Thisbe.

Hippolyta: Well shone, Moon. Truly, the moon shines with a good grace.
                                           [The Lion worries Thisbe's mantle.]

Theseus: Well moused,° Lion.   250

[Enter Pyramus; exit Lion.]

Demetrius: And then came Pyramus.

Lysander: And so the lion vanished.

Pyramus: Sweet Moon, I thank thee for thy sunny beams;
  I thank thee, Moon, for shining now so bright;
  For, by thy gracious, golden, glittering gleams,   255
  I trust to take of truest Thisbe sight.
      But stay, O spite!
      But mark, poor knight,
  What dreadful dole° is here?
      Eyes, do you see?   260
      How can it be?
  O dainty duck! O dear!
      Thy mantle good,
      What, stained with blood?
  Approach, ye Furies° fell!°   265
      O Fates,° come, come,
      Cut thread and thrum;°
  Quail,° crush, conclude, and quell!°

Theseus: This passion, and the death of a dear friend, would go near to make
  a man look sad.°   270

Hippolyta: Beshrew my heart, but I pity the man.

Pyramus: O, wherefore, Nature, didst thou lions frame?
  Since lion vile hath here deflowered my dear,
  Which is — no, no, which was — the fairest dame
  That lived, that loved, that liked, that looked with cheer.°   275
      Come, tears, confound,

---

250 *moused:* Shaken, torn, bitten.   259 *dole:* Grievous event.   265 *Furies:* Avenging goddesses of
Greek myth; *fell:* Fierce.   266 *Fates:* The three goddesses (Clotho, Lachesis, Atropos) of Greek myth
who spun, drew, and cut the thread of human life.   267 *thread and thrum:* I.e., everything—the good
and bad alike; literally, the warp in weaving and the loose end of the warp.   268 *Quail:* Overpower;
quell: Kill, destroy.   269–270 *This . . . sad:* I.e., if one had other reason to grieve, one might be sad,
but not from this absurd portrayal of passion.   275 *cheer:* Countenance.

        Out, sword, and wound
    The pap° of Pyramus;
        Ay, that left pap,
        Where heart doth hop.   *[He stabs himself.]*   280
    Thus die I, thus, thus, thus.
        Now am I dead,
        Now am I fled;
    My soul is in the sky.
        Tongue, lose thy light;   285
        Moon, take thy flight.   *[Exit Moonshine.]*
    Now die, die, die, die, die.   *[Pyramus dies.]*

Demetrius: No die, but an ace,° for him; for he is but one.°
Lysander: Less than an ace, man; for he is dead, he is nothing.
Theseus: With the help of a surgeon he might yet recover, and yet prove an   290
    ass.°
Hippolyta: How chance Moonshine is gone before Thisbe comes back and
    finds her lover?
Theseus: She will find him by starlight.

[Enter Thisbe.]

    Here she comes; and her passion ends the play.   295
Hippolyta: Methinks she should not use a long one for such a Pyramus. I
    hope she will be brief.
Demetrius: A mote° will turn the balance, which Pyramus, which° Thisbe, is
    the better: he for a man, God warrant us; she for a woman, God bless
    us.   300
Lysander: She hath spied him already with those sweet eyes.
Demetrius: And thus she means,° videlicet:°
Thisbe: Asleep, my love?
        What, dead, my dove?
        O Pyramus, arise!   305
        Speak, speak. Quite dumb?
        Dead, dead? A tomb
    Must cover thy sweet eyes.
        These lily lips,
        This cherry nose,   310
    These yellow cowslip cheeks,
        Are gone, are gone!
        Lovers, make moan.
    His eyes were green as leeks.
        O Sisters Three,°   315
        Come, come to me,

---

278 *pap:* Breast.   288 *ace:* The side of the die featuring the single pip, or spot (the pun is on *die* as
a singular of *dice;* Bottom's performance is not worth a whole *die* but rather one single face of it, one
small portion); *one:* (1) An individual person, (2) unique.   291 *ass:* (With a pun on *ace*).
298 *mote:* Small particle; *which . . . which:* Whether . . . or.   302 *means:* Moans, laments (with a pun
on the meaning, "lodge a formal complaint"); *videlicet:* To wit.   315 *Sisters Three:* The Fates.

With hands as pale as milk;
   Lay them in gore,
   Since you have shore°
With shears his thread of silk.   320
   Tongue, not a word.
   Come, trusty sword,
   Come, blade, my breast imbrue!°   *[She stabs herself.]*
   And farewell, friends.
   Thus Thisbe ends.   325
   Adieu, adieu, adieu.   *[She dies.]*

Theseus: Moonshine and Lion are left to bury the dead.
Demetrius: Ay, and Wall too.
Bottom [starting up, as Flute does also]: No, I assure you, the wall is down
   that parted their fathers. Will it please you to see the epilogue, or to hear 330
   a Bergomask dance° between two of our company?

[The other players enter.]

Theseus: No epilogue, I pray you; for your play needs no excuse. Never
   excuse; for when the players are all dead, there need none to be blamed.
   Marry, if he that writ it had played Pyramus and hanged himself in
   Thisbe's garter, it would have been a fine tragedy; and so it is, truly, and
   very notably discharged. But, come, your Bergomask. Let your epilogue
   alone.   *[A dance.]* 335
The iron tongue° of midnight hath told° twelve.
Lovers, to bed, 'tis almost fairy time.
I fear we shall outsleep the coming morn   340
As much as we this night have overwatched.°
This palpable-gross° play hath well beguiled
The heavy° gait of night. Sweet friends, to bed.
A fortnight hold we this solemnity,
In nightly revels and new jollity.   *Exeunt.* 345

Enter Puck [carrying a broom].

Puck: Now the hungry lion roars,
   And the wolf behowls the moon,
   Whilst the heavy° plowman snores,
     All with weary task fordone.°
   Now the wasted brands° do glow,   350
     Whilst the screech owl, screeching loud,
   Puts the wretch that lies in woe
     In remembrance of a shroud.
   Now it is the time of night
     That the graves, all gaping wide,   355

319 *shore:* Shorn.   323 *imbrue:* Stain with blood.   331 *Bergomask dance:* A rustic dance named
from Bergamo, a province in the state of Venice.   338 *iron tongue:* I.e., of a bell; *told:* Counted,
struck ("tolled").   341 *overwatched:* Stayed up too late.   342 *palpable-gross:* Palpably gross, obviously crude.   343 *heavy:* Drowsy, dull.   348 *heavy:* Tired.   349 *fordone:* Exhausted.
350 *wasted brands:* Burned-out logs.

Every one lets forth his sprite,°
   In the church-way paths to glide.
And we fairies, that do run
   By the triple Hecate's° team.
From the presence of the sun,   360
   Following darkness like a dream,
Now are frolic.° Not a mouse
   Shall disturb this hallowed house.
I am sent with broom before,
To sweep the dust behind° the door.   365

Enter [Oberon and Titania,] King and Queen of Fairies, with all their train.

Oberon: Through the house give glimmering light,
   By the dead and drowsy fire;
Every elf and fairy sprite
   Hop as light as bird from brier;
And this ditty, after me,   370
   Sing, and dance it trippingly.
Titania: First, rehearse° your song by rote,
   To each word a warbling note.
Hand in hand, with fairy grace,
Will we sing, and bless this place.   *[Song and dance.]* 375
Oberon: Now, until the break of day,
   Through this house each fairy stray.
To the best bride-bed will we,
   Which by us shall blessèd be;
And the issue there create°   380
   Ever shall be fortunate.
So shall all the couples three
   Ever true in loving be;
And the blots of Nature's hand
   Shall not in their issue stand;   385
Never mole, harelip, nor scar,
   Nor mark prodigious,° such as are
Despisèd in nativity,
   Shall upon their children be.
With this field dew consecrate,°   390
   Every fairy take his gait,°
And each several° chamber bless,
   Through this palace, with sweet peace;

---

356 *Every . . . sprite:* Every grave lets forth its ghost.   359 *triple Hecate's:* (Hecate ruled in three capacities: as Luna or Cynthia in heaven, as Diana on earth, and as Proserpina in hell.)   362 *frolic:* Merry.   365 *behind:* From behind, or else like sweeping the dirt under the carpet (Robin Goodfellow was a household spirit who helped good housemaids and punished lazy ones, but he could, of course, be mischievous.).   372 *rehearse:* Recite.   380 *create:* Created.   387 *prodigious:* Monstrous, unnatural.   390 *consecrate:* Consecrated.   391 *take his gait:* Go his way.   392 *several:* Separate.

And the owner of it blest
Ever shall in safety rest.   395
Trip away; make no stay;
Meet me all by break of day.

                                   Exeunt [Oberon, Titania, and train].

Puck [to the audience]: If we shadows have offended,
Think but this, and all is mended,
That you have but slumbered here°   400
While these visions did appear.
And this weak and idle theme,
No more yielding but° a dream,
Gentles, do not reprehend.
If you pardon, we will mend.°   405
And, as I am an honest Puck,
If we have unearnèd luck
Now to scape the serpent's tongue,°
We will make amends ere long;
Else the Puck a liar call.   410
So, good night unto you all.
Give me your hands,° if we be friends,
And Robin shall restore amends.°   *[Exit.]*

---

400 *That . . . here:* I.e., that it is a "midsummer night's dream."   403 *No . . . but:* Yielding no more
than.   405 *mend:* Improve.   408 *serpent's tongue:* I.e., hissing.   412 *Give . . . hands:* Applaud.
413 *restore amends:* Give satisfaction in return.

Considerations for Critical Thinking and Writing

1. Describe how the two settings, Athens and the nearby woods, reflect different
   social and psychological environments as well as different types of behavior
   among the characters.
2. Discuss the significance of the play's title. What expectations does it create for
   you?
3. What is the symbolic function of the marriage of Theseus and Hippolyta? How is
   that function revealed in the scenes in which they appear?
4. Characterize the four young lovers. How individualized are their personalities?
   How does the extent of their characterizations suggest their function in the play?
5. What makes Bottom such a comic figure? How does his behavior shed light on
   the behavior of the other characters?
6. Consider how women — Hippolyta, Titania, Hermia, and Helena — are presented
   in the play. What characteristics do they have in common? How do they relate to
   the men in their lives?
7. Why does Puck describe "mortals" as "fools"? To what degree does this description
   fit the fairies as well?
8. How might Puck be regarded as the play's director as well as a central character?
9. How does the plot bring together the four groups of characters — Theseus and
   Hippolyta, the four lovers, the craftsmen, and the fairies — into a unified whole?
   Write a plot summary of the play that connects these four groups of characters.
   How does this summary resemble popular situation comedies that you've seen
   on television?

10. Choose a scene that you find particularly funny and analyze how the humor is created. Describe how the scene contributes to the rest of the play.
11. What is the relationship between the play-within-the play, "Pyramus and Thisbe," and *A Midsummer Night's Dream*? How do the plot and theme of each serve as commentaries on each other?
12. Despite its comic scenes and happy ending, at various moments this play does raise the specter of potential tragedy. How seriously do you think we are meant to worry about the characters? What are your emotions about the young lovers as they struggle to sort things out in the woods? Discuss how this play might be transformed into a tragedy.

Connections to Other Selections

1. Write an essay concerning the problematic nature of love in *A Midsummer Night's Dream* and David Henry Hwang's *M. Butterfly* (p. 1921). How is the depiction of love in each play used to create conflict?
2. Discuss Shakespeare's use of the play-within-the play in *A Midsummer Night's Dream* and in *Hamlet* (p. 1281). What emotions does each produce? What conflicts and themes do they emphasize? What attitudes do they suggest about the nature of drama?
3. In an essay discuss the significance of marriage in *A Midsummer Night's Dream* and Henrik Ibsen's *A Doll House* (p. 1517).
4. Write an essay that explores the difficulty of distinguishing between reality and illusion in *A Midsummer Night's Dream* and a very different work, Tim O'Brien's short story "How to Tell a True War Story" (p. 552). What are the similarities and differences in their perspectives on the actual and imaginary?

HAMLET, PRINCE OF DENMARK

Hamlet, the most famous play in English literature, continues to fascinate and challenge both readers and audiences. Interpretations of Hamlet's character and actions abound, because the play has produced so many intense and varied responses. No small indication of the tragedy's power is that actors long to play its title role.

A brief summary can suggest the movement of the plot but not the depth of Hamlet's character. After learning of his father's death, Prince Hamlet returns to the Danish court from his university studies to find Claudius, the dead king's brother, ruling Denmark and married to Hamlet's mother, Gertrude. Her remarriage within two months of his father's death has left Hamlet disillusioned, confused, and suspicious of Claudius. When his father's ghost appears before Hamlet to reveal that Claudius murdered the king, Hamlet is confronted with having to avenge his father's death.

Hamlet's efforts to carry out this obligation would have been a familiar kind of plot to Elizabethan audiences. *Revenge tragedy* was a well established type of drama that traced its antecedents to Greek and Roman plays, particularly through the Roman playwright Seneca (c. 3 B.C.–A.D. 65), whose plays were translated and produced in English in the late sixteenth century. Shakespeare's audiences knew its conventions, particularly from Thomas

Kyd's popular *Spanish Tragedy* (c. 1587). Basically, this type of play consists of a murder that has to be avenged by a relative of the victim. Typically, the victim's ghost appears to demand revenge, and invariably madness of some sort is worked into subsequent events, which ultimately result in the deaths of the murderer, the avenger, and a number of other characters. Crime, madness, ghostly anguish, poison, overheard conversations, conspiracies, and a final scene littered with corpses: *Hamlet* subscribes to the basic ingredients of the formula, but it also transcends the conventions of revenge tragedy because Hamlet contemplates not merely revenge but suicide and the meaning of life itself.

Hamlet must face not only a diseased social order but also conflicts within himself when his indecisiveness becomes as agonizing as the corruption surrounding him. However, Hamlet is also a forceful and attractive character. His intelligence is repeatedly revealed in his penetrating use of language; through images and metaphors he creates a perspective on his world that is at once satiric and profoundly painful. His astonishing and sometimes shocking wit is leveled at his mother, his beloved Ophelia, and Claudius as well as himself. Nothing escapes his critical eye and divided imagination. Hamlet, no less than the people around him, is perplexed by his alienation from life.

Hamlet's limitations as well as his virtues make him one of Shakespeare's most complex characters. His keen self-awareness is both agonizing and liberating. Although he struggles throughout the play with painful issues ranging from family loyalties to matters of state, he retains his dignity as a tragic hero, a hero whom generations of audiences have found compelling.

WILLIAM SHAKESPEARE (1564–1616)
Hamlet, Prince of Denmark 1600

[Dramatis Personae

Claudius, King of Denmark
Hamlet, son to the late and nephew to the present king
Polonius, lord chamberlain
Horatio, friend to Hamlet
Laertes, son to Polonius
Voltimand
Cornelius
Rosencrantz
Guildenstern } courtiers
Osric
A Gentleman
A Priest
Marcellus } officers
Bernardo

Francisco, a soldier
Reynaldo, servant to Polonius
Players
Two Clowns, grave-diggers
Fortinbras, Prince of Norway
A Captain
English Ambassadors
Gertrude, Queen of Denmark, and mother to *Hamlet*
Ophelia, daughter to Polonius
Lords, Ladies, Officers, Soldiers, Sailors, Messengers, and other Attendants
Ghost of Hamlet's Father

SCENE: *Denmark.*]

[ACT I

SCENE I: *Elsinore. A platform° before the castle.*]

Enter Bernardo and Francisco, two sentinels.

Bernardo: Who's there?
Francisco: Nay, answer me:° stand, and unfold yourself.
Bernardo: Long live the king!°
Francisco: Bernardo?
Bernardo: He.
Francisco: You come most carefully upon your hour.   5
Bernardo: 'Tis now struck twelve; get thee to bed, Francisco.
Francisco: For this relief much thanks: 'tis bitter cold,
 And I am sick at heart.
Bernardo: Have you had quiet guard?
Francisco: Not a mouse stirring.   10
Bernardo: Well, good night.
 If you do meet Horatio and Marcellus,
 The rivals° of my watch, bid them make haste.

Enter Horatio and Marcellus.

Francisco: I think I hear them. Stand, ho! Who is there?
Horatio: Friends to this ground.
Marcellus: And liegemen to the Dane.   15
Francisco: Give you° good night.
Marcellus: O, farewell, honest soldier:
 Who hath reliev'd you?
Francisco: Bernardo hath my place.
 Give you good night.   *Exit Francisco.*
Marcellus: Holla! Bernardo!

ACT I. SCENE I.   *platform:* A level space on the battlements of the royal castle at Elsinore, a Danish
seaport; now Helsingör.   2 *me:* This is emphatic, since Francisco is the sentry.   3 *Long live the
king:* Either a password or greeting; Horatio and Marcellus use a different one in line 15.   13 *rivals:*
Partners.   16 *Give you:* God give you.

Bernardo: Say,
 What, is Horatio there?
Horatio: A piece of him.
Bernardo: Welcome, Horatio: welcome, good Marcellus.   20
Marcellus: What, has this thing appear'd again to-night?
Bernardo: I have seen nothing.
Marcellus: Horatio says 'tis but our fantasy,
 And will not let belief take hold of him
 Touching this dreaded sight, twice seen of us: 25
 Therefore I have entreated him along
 With us to watch the minutes of this night;
 That if again this apparition come,
 He may approve° our eyes and speak to it.
Horatio: Tush, tush, 'twill not appear.
Bernardo: Sit down awhile;   30
 And let us once again assail your ears,
 That are so fortified against our story
 What we have two nights seen.
Horatio: Well, sit we down,
 And let us hear Bernardo speak of this.
Bernardo: Last night of all,   35
 When yond same star that's westward from the pole°
 Had made his course t' illume that part of heaven
 Where now it burns, Marcellus and myself,
 The bell then beating one, —

Enter Ghost.

Marcellus: Peace, break thee off; look, where it comes again!   40
Bernardo: In the same figure, like the king that's dead.
Marcellus: Thou art a scholar;° speak to it, Horatio.
Bernardo: Looks 'a not like the king? mark it, Horatio.
Horatio: Most like: it harrows° me with fear and wonder.
Bernardo: It would be spoke to.°
Marcellus: Speak to it, Horatio.   45
Horatio: What art thou that usurp'st this time of night,
 Together with that fair and warlike form
 In which the majesty of buried Denmark°
 Did sometimes march? by heaven I charge thee, speak!
Marcellus: It is offended.
Bernardo: See it stalks away!   50
Horatio: Stay! speak, speak! I charge thee, speak!   *Exit Ghost.*
Marcellus: 'Tis gone, and will not answer.
Bernardo: How now, Horatio! you tremble and look pale:
 Is not this something more than fantasy?
 What think you on 't?   55

29 *approve:* Corroborate.   36 *pole:* Polestar.   42 *scholar:* Exorcisms were performed in Latin, which Horatio as an educated man would be able to speak.   44 *harrows:* Lacerates the feelings. 45 *It . . . to:* A ghost could not speak until spoken to.   48 *buried Denmark:* The buried king of Denmark.

Horatio: Before my God, I might not this believe
    Without the sensible and true avouch
    Of mine own eyes.
Marcellus: Is it not like the king?
Horatio: As thou art to thyself:
    Such was the very armour he had on   60
    When he the ambitious Norway combated;
    So frown'd he once, when, in an angry parle,
    He smote° the sledded Polacks° on the ice.
    'Tis strange.
Marcellus: Thus twice before, and jump° at this dead hour,   65
    With martial stalk hath he gone by our watch.
Horatio: In what particular thought to work I know not;
    But in the gross and scope° of my opinion,
    This bodes some strange eruption to our state.
Marcellus: Good now,° sit down, and tell me, he that knows,   70
    Why this same strict and most observant watch
    So nightly toils° the subject° of the land,
    And why such daily cast° of brazen cannon,
    And foreign mart° for implements of war;
    Why such impress° of shipwrights, whose sore task   75
    Does not divide the Sunday from the week;
    What might be toward, that this sweaty haste
    Doth make the night joint-labourer with the day:
    Who is't that can inform me?
Horatio: That can I;
    At least, the whisper goes so. Our last king,   80
    Whose image even but now appear'd to us,
    Was, as you know, by Fortinbras of Norway,
    Thereto prick'd on° by a most emulate° pride,
    Dar'd to the combat; in which our valiant Hamlet—
    For so this side of our known world esteem'd him—   85
    Did slay this Fortinbras; who, by a seal'd compact,
    Well ratified by law and heraldry,°
    Did forfeit, with his life, all those his lands
    Which he stood seiz'd° of, to the conqueror:
    Against the which, a moiety competent°   90
    Was gaged by our king; which had return'd
    To the inheritance of Fortinbras,
    Had he been vanquisher; as, by the same comart,°
    And carriage° of the article design'd,
    His fell to Hamlet. Now, sir, young Fortinbras,   95
    Of unimproved° mettle hot and full,°

63 *smote:* Defeated; *sledded Polacks:* Polanders using sledges.   65 *jump:* Exactly.   68 *gross and scope:* General drift.   70 *Good now:* An expression denoting entreaty or expostulation.   72 *toils:* Causes or makes to toil; *subject:* people, subjects.   73 *cast:* Casting, founding.   74 *mart:* Buying and selling, traffic.   75 *impress:* Impressment.   83 *prick'd on:* Incited; *emulate:* Rivaling.   87 *law and heraldry:* Heraldic law, governing combat.   89 *seiz'd:* Possessed.   90 *moiety competent:* Adequate or sufficient portion.   93 *comart:* Joint bargain.   94 *carriage:* Import, bearing.   96 *unimproved:* Not turned to account; *hot and full:* Full of fight.

Hath in the skirts of Norway here and there
Shark'd up° a list of lawless resolutes,°
For food and diet,° to some enterprise
That hath a stomach in't; which is no other —   100
As it doth well appear unto our state —
But to recover of us, by strong hand
And terms compulsatory, those foresaid lands
So by his father lost: and this, I take it,
Is the main motive of our preparations,   105
The source of this our watch and the chief head
Of this post-haste and romage° in the land.

Bernardo: I think it be no other but e'en so:
Well may it sort° that this portentous figure
Comes armed through our watch; so like the king   110
That was and is the question of these wars.

Horatio: A mote° it is to trouble the mind's eye.
In the most high and palmy state° of Rome,
A little ere the mightiest Julius fell,
The graves stood tenantless and the sheeted dead   115
Did squeak and gibber in the Roman streets:
As stars with trains of fire° and dews of blood,
Disasters° in the sun; and the moist star°
Upon whose influence Neptune's empire° stands
Was sick almost to doomsday with eclipse: 120
And even the like precurse° of fear'd events,
As harbingers preceding still the fates
And prologue to the omen coming on,
Have heaven and earth together demonstrated
Unto our climatures and countrymen. —   125

Enter Ghost.

But soft, behold! lo, where it comes again!
I'll cross° it, though it blast me. Stay, illusion!
If thou hast any sound, or use of voice,
Speak to me!   *It° spreads his arms.*
If there be any good thing to be done,   130
That may to thee do ease and grace to me,
Speak to me!
If thou art privy to thy country's fate,
Which, happily, foreknowing may avoid,
O, speak!   135

---

98 *Shark'd up:* Got together in haphazard fashion; *resolutes:* Desperadoes.   99 *food and diet:* No pay but their keep.   107 *romage:* Bustle, commotion.   109 *sort:* Suit.   112 *mote:* Speck of dust. 113 *palmy state:* Triumphant sovereignty.   117 *stars . . . fire:* I.e., comets.   118 *Disasters:* Unfavorable aspects; *moist star:* The moon, governing tides.   119 *Neptune's empire:* The sea.   121 *precurse:* Heralding.   127 *cross:* Meet, face; thus bringing down the evil influence on the person who crosses it.   129 *It:* The Ghost, or perhaps Horatio.

Or if thou hast uphoarded in thy life
Extorted treasure in the womb of earth,
For which, they say, you spirits oft walk in death,   *The cock crows.*
Speak of it:° stay, and speak! Stop it, Marcellus.
Marcellus: Shall I strike at it with my partisan?°   140
Horatio: Do, if it will not stand.
Bernardo: 'Tis here!
Horatio: 'Tis here!
Marcellus: 'Tis gone!   *[Exit Ghost.]*
We do it wrong, being so majestical,
To offer it the show of violence;
For it is, as the air, invulnerable,   145
And our vain blows malicious mockery.
Bernardo: It was about to speak, when the cock crew.°
Horatio: And then it started like a guilty thing
Upon a fearful summons. I have heard,
The cock, that is the trumpet to the morn,   150
Doth with his lofty and shrill-sounding throat
Awake the god of day; and, at his warning,
Whether in sea or fire, in earth or air,
Th' extravagant and erring° spirit hies
To his confine:° and of the truth herein   155
This present object made probation.°
Marcellus: It faded on the crowing of the cock.
Some say that ever 'gainst° that season comes
Wherein our Saviour's birth is celebrated,
The bird of dawning singeth all night long: 160
And then, they say, no spirit dare stir abroad;
The nights are wholesome; then no planets strike,°
No fairy takes, nor witch hath power to charm,
So hallow'd and so gracious° is that time.
Horatio: So have I heard and do in part believe it.   165
But, look, the morn, in russet mantle clad,
Walks o'er the dew of yon high eastward hill:
Break we our watch up; and by my advice,
Let us impart what we have seen to-night
Unto young Hamlet; for, upon my life,   170
This spirit, dumb to us, will speak to him.
Do you consent we shall acquaint him with it,
As needful in our loves, fitting our duty?
Marcellus: Let's do 't, I pray; and I this morning know
Where we shall find him most conveniently.   *Exeunt.* 175

133–139 *If . . . it:* Horatio recites the traditional reasons why ghosts might walk.   140 *partisan:*
Long-handled spear with a blade having lateral projections.   147 *cock crew:* According to traditional
ghost lore, spirits returned to their confines at cockcrow. 154 *extravagant and erring:* Wandering.
Both words mean the same thing.   155 *confine:* Place of confinement.   156 *probation:* Proof, trial.
158 *'gainst:* Just before.   162 *planets strike:* It was thought that planets were malignant and might
strike travelers by night.   164 *gracious:* Full of goodness.

[SCENE II: *A room of state in the castle.*]

Flourish. Enter Claudius, King of Denmark, Gertrude the Queen, Councilors, Polonius and his Son Laertes, Hamlet, cum aliis° [including Voltimand and Cornelius].

King: Though yet of Hamlet our dear brother's death
    The memory be green, and that it us befitted
    To bear our hearts in grief and our whole kingdom
    To be contracted in one brow of woe,
    Yet so far hath discretion fought with nature   5
    That we with wisest sorrow think on him,
    Together with remembrance of ourselves.
    Therefore our sometime sister, now our queen,
    Th' imperial jointress° to this warlike state,
    Have we, as 'twere with a defeated joy, —   10
    With an auspicious and a dropping eye,
    With mirth in funeral and with dirge in marriage,
    In equal scale weighing delight and dole, —
    Taken to wife: nor have we herein barr'd
    Your better wisdoms, which have freely gone   15
    With this affair along. For all, our thanks.
    Now follows, that° you know, young Fortinbras,
    Holding a weak supposal° of our worth,
    Or thinking by our late dear brother's death
    Our state to be disjoint° and out of frame,°   20
    Colleagued° with this dream of his advantage,°
    He hath not fail'd to pester us with message,
    Importing° the surrender of those lands
    Lost by his father, with all bands of law,
    To our most valiant brother. So much for him.   25
    Now for ourself and for this time of meeting:
    Thus much the business is: we have here writ
    To Norway, uncle of young Fortinbras, —
    Who, impotent and bed-rid, scarcely hears
    Of this his nephew's purpose, — to suppress   30
    His further gait° herein; in that the levies,
    The lists and full proportions, are all made
    Out of his subject:° and we here dispatch
    You, good Cornelius, and you, Voltimand,
    For bearers of this greeting to old Norway;   35
    Giving to you no further personal power
    To business with the king, more than the scope
    Of these delated° articles allow.

SCENE II.   *cum aliis:* With others.   9 *jointress:* Woman possessed of a jointure, or, joint tenancy of an estate.   17 *that:* That which.   18 *weak supposal:* Low estimate.   20 *disjoint:* Distracted, out of joint; *frame:* Order.   21 *Colleagued:* added to; *dream ... advantage:* Visionary hope of success. 23 *Importing:* Purporting, pertaining to.   31 *gait:* Proceeding.   33 *Out of his subject:* At the expense of Norway's subjects (collectively).   38 *delated:* Expressly stated.

Farewell, and let your haste commend your duty.

Cornelius: ⎤
Voltimand: ⎦ In that and all things will we show our duty.   40

King: We doubt it nothing: heartily farewell.

          [Exeunt Voltimand and Cornelius.]

 And now, Laertes, what's the news with you?
 You told us of some suit; what is't, Laertes?
 You cannot speak of reason to the Dane,°
 And lose your voice:° what wouldst thou beg, Laertes,   45
 That shall not be my offer, not thy asking?
 The head is not more native° to the heart,
 The hand more instrumental° to the mouth,
 Than is the throne of Denmark to thy father.
 What wouldst thou have, Laertes?

Laertes: My dread lord,   50
 Your leave and favour to return to France;
 From whence though willingly I came to Denmark,
 To show my duty in your coronation,
 Yet now, I must confess, that duty done,
 My thoughts and wishes bend again toward France   55
 And bow them to your gracious leave and pardon.°

King: Have you your father's leave? What says Polonius?

Polonius: He hath, my lord, wrung from me my slow leave
 By laboursome petition, and at last
 Upon his will I seal'd my hard consent: 60
 I do beseech you, give him leave to go.

King: Take thy fair hour, Laertes; time be thine,
 And thy best graces spend it at thy will!
 But now, my cousin° Hamlet, and my son,—

Hamlet [aside]: A little more than kin, and less than kind!°   65

King: How is it that the clouds still hang on you?

Hamlet: Not so, my lord; I am too much in the sun.°

Queen: Good Hamlet, cast thy nighted colour off,
 And let thine eye look like a friend on Denmark.
 Do not for ever with thy vailed lids   70
 Seek for thy noble father in the dust:
 Thou know'st 'tis common; all that lives must die,
 Passing through nature to eternity.

Hamlet: Ay, madam, it is common.°

Queen: If it be,
 Why seems it so particular with thee?   75

Hamlet: Seems, madam! nay, it is; I know not "seems."

44 *the Dane:* Danish king. 45 *lose your voice:* Speak in vain. 47 *native:* Closely connected, related. 48 *instrumental:* Serviceable. 56 *leave and pardon:* Permission to depart. 64 *cousin:* Any kin not of the immediate family. 65 *A little . . . kind:* My relation to you has become more than kinship warrants; it has also become unnatural. 67 *I am . . . sun:* The senses seem to be: I am too much out of doors, I am too much in the sun of your grace (ironical), I am too much of a son to you. Possibly an allusion to the proverb "Out of heaven's blessing into the warm sun"; i.e., Hamlet is out of house and home in being deprived of the kingship. 74 *Ay . . . common:* It is common, but it hurts nevertheless; possibly a reference to the commonplace quality of the queen's remark.

'Tis not alone my inky cloak, good mother,
Nor customary suits° of solemn black,
Nor windy suspiration° of forc'd breath,
No, nor the fruitful river in the eye,   80
Nor the dejected 'haviour of the visage,
Together with all forms, moods, shapes of grief,
That can denote me truly: these indeed seem,
For they are actions that a man might play:
But I have that within which passeth show;   85
These but the trappings and the suits of woe.

King: 'Tis sweet and commendable in your nature, Hamlet,
To give these mourning duties to your father:
But, you must know, your father lost a father;
That father lost, lost his, and the survivor bound   90
In filial obligation for some term
To do obsequious° sorrow: but to persever
In obstinate condolement° is a course
Of impious stubbornness; 'tis unmanly grief;
It shows a will most incorrect° to heaven,   95
A heart unfortified, a mind impatient,
An understanding simple and unschool'd:
For what we know must be and is as common
As any the most vulgar thing° to sense,
Why should we in our peevish opposition   100
Take it to heart? Fie! 'tis a fault to heaven,
A fault against the dead, a fault to nature,
To reason most absurd; whose common theme
Is death of fathers, and who still hath cried,
From the first corse till he that died to-day,   105
"This must be so." We pray you, throw to earth
This unprevailing° woe, and think of us
As of a father: for let the world take note,
You are the most immediate° to our throne;
And with no less nobility° of love   110
Than that which dearest father bears his son,
Do I impart° toward you. For your intent
In going back to school in Wittenberg,°
It is most retrograde° to our desire:
And we beseech you, bend you° to remain   115
Here, in the cheer and comfort of our eye,
Our chiefest courtier, cousin, and our son.

Queen: Let not thy mother lose her prayers, Hamlet:
I pray thee, stay with us; go not to Wittenberg.

---

78 *customary suits:* Suits prescribed by custom for mourning.   79 *windy suspiration:* Heavy sighing.
92 *obsequious:* Dutiful.   93 *condolement:* Sorrowing.   95 *incorrect:* Untrained, uncorrected.
99 *vulgar thing:* Common experience.   107 *unprevailing:* Unavailing.   109 *most immediate:* Next
in succession.   110 *nobility:* High degree.   112 *impart:* The object is apparently *love* (l. 110).
113 *Wittenberg:* Famous German university founded in 1502.   114 *retrograde:* Contrary.
115 *bend you:* Incline yourself; imperative.

Hamlet: I shall in all my best obey you, madam.   120
King: Why, 'tis a loving and a fair reply:
    Be as ourself in Denmark. Madam, come;
    This gentle and unforc'd accord of Hamlet
    Sits smiling to my heart: in grace whereof,
    No jocund health that Denmark drinks to-day,   125
    But the great cannon to the clouds shall tell,
    And the king's rouse° the heaven shall bruit again,°
    Re-speaking earthly thunder. Come away.

                       Flourish. Exeunt all but Hamlet.

Hamlet: O, that this too too sullied flesh would melt,
    Thaw and resolve itself into a dew!   130
    Or that the Everlasting had not fix'd
    His canon 'gainst self-slaughter! O God! God!
    How weary, stale, flat and unprofitable,
    Seem to me all the uses of this world!
    Fie on't! ah fie! 'tis an unweeded garden,   135
    That grows to seed; things rank and gross in nature
    Possess it merely.° That it should come to this!
    But two months dead: nay, not so much, not two:
    So excellent a king; that was, to this,
    Hyperion° to a satyr; so loving to my mother   140
    That he might not beteem° the winds of heaven
    Visit her face too roughly. Heaven and earth!
    Must I remember? why, she would hang on him,
    As if increase of appetite had grown
    By what it fed on: and yet, within a month —   145
    Let me not think on't — Frailty, thy name is woman! —
    A little month, or ere those shoes were old
    With which she followed my poor father's body,
    Like Niobe,° all tears: — why she, even she —
    O God! a beast, that wants discourse of reason,°   150
    Would have mourn'd longer — married with my uncle,
    My father's brother, but no more like my father
    Than I to Hercules: within a month:
    Ere yet the salt of most unrighteous tears
    Had left the flushing in her galled° eyes,   155
    She married. O, most wicked speed, to post
    With such dexterity° to incestuous sheets!
    It is not nor it cannot come to good:
    But break, my heart; for I must hold my tongue.

Enter Horatio, Marcellus, and Bernardo.

Horatio: Hail to your lordship!

---

127 *rouse:* Draft of liquor; *bruit again:* Echo.   137 *merely:* Completely, entirely.   140 *Hyperion:* God of the sun in the older regime of ancient gods.   141 *beteem:* Allow.   149 *Niobe:* Tantalus's daughter, who boasted that she had more sons and daughters than Leto; for this Apollo and Artemis slew her children. She was turned into stone by Zeus on Mount Sipylus.   150 *discourse of reason:* Process or faculty of reason.   155 *galled:* Irritated.   157 *dexterity:* Facility.

Hamlet: I am glad to see you well: 160
    Horatio!—or I do forget myself.
Horatio: The same, my lord, and your poor servant ever.
Hamlet: Sir, my good friend; I'll change that name with you:°
    And what make you from Wittenberg, Horatio?
    Marcellus?   165
Marcellus: My good lord—
Hamlet: I am very glad to see you. Good even, sir.
    But what, in faith, make you from Wittenberg?
Horatio: A truant disposition, good my lord.
Hamlet: I would not hear your enemy say so,   170
    Nor shall you do my ear that violence,
    To make it truster of your own report
    Against yourself: I know you are no truant.
    But what is your affair in Elsinore?
    We'll teach you to drink deep ere you depart.   175
Horatio: My lord, I came to see your father's funeral.
Hamlet: I prithee, do not mock me, fellow-student;
    I think it was to see my mother's wedding.
Horatio: Indeed, my lord, it follow'd hard° upon.
Hamlet: Thrift, thrift, Horatio! the funeral bak'd meats°   180
    Did coldly furnish forth the marriage tables.
    Would I had met my dearest° foe in heaven
    Or ever I had seen that day, Horatio!
    My father!—methinks I see my father.
Horatio: Where, my lord!
Hamlet: In my mind's eye, Horatio.   185
Horatio: I saw him once; 'a° was a goodly king.
Hamlet: 'A was a man, take him for all in all,
    I shall not look upon his like again.
Horatio: My lord, I think I saw him yesternight.
Hamlet: Saw? who?   190
Horatio: My lord, the king your father.
Hamlet: The king my father!
Horatio: Season your admiration° for a while
    With an attent ear, till I may deliver,
    Upon the witness of these gentlemen,
    This marvel to you.
Hamlet: For God's love, let me hear.   195
Horatio: Two nights together had these gentlemen,
    Marcellus and Bernardo, on their watch,
    In the dead waste and middle of the night,
    Been thus encount'red. A figure like your father,
    Armed at point exactly, cap-a-pe,°   200

163 *I'll . . . you:* I'll be your servant, you shall be my friend; also explained as "I'll exchange the name
of friend with you."   179 *hard:* Close.   180 *bak'd meats:* Meat pies.   182 *dearest:* Direst. The
adjective *dear* in Shakespeare has two different origins: O.E. *deore,* "beloved," and O.E. *deor,* "fierce."
Dearest is the superlative of the second.   186 *'a:* He.   192 *Season your admiration:* Restrain your
astonishment.   200 *cap-a-pe:* From head to foot.

Appears before them, and with solemn march
Goes slow and stately by them: thrice he walk'd
By their oppress'd° and fear-surprised eyes,
Within his truncheon's° length; whilst they, distill'd°
Almost to jelly with the act° of fear,   205
Stand dumb and speak not to him. This to me
In dreadful secrecy impart they did;
And I with them the third night kept the watch:
Where, as they had deliver'd, both in time,
Form of the thing, each word made true and good,   210
The apparition comes: I knew your father;
These hands are not more like.
Hamlet: But where was this?
Marcellus: My lord, upon the platform where we watch'd.
Hamlet: Did you not speak to it?
Horatio: My lord, I did;
But answer made it none: yet once methought   215
It lifted up it° head and did address
Itself to motion, like as it would speak;
But even then the morning cock crew loud,
And at the sound it shrunk in haste away,
And vanish'd from our sight.
Hamlet: 'Tis very strange.   220
Horatio: As I do live, my honour'd lord, 'tis true;
And we did think it writ down in our duty
To let you know of it.
Hamlet: Indeed, indeed, sirs, but this troubles me.
Hold you the watch to-night?
Marcellus: ⎫
Bernardo: ⎬ We do, my lord.   225
Hamlet: Arm'd, say you?
Marcellus: ⎫
Bernardo: ⎬ Arm'd, my lord.
Hamlet: From top to toe?
Marcellus: ⎫
Bernardo: ⎬ My lord, from head to foot.
Hamlet: Then saw you not his face?
Horatio: O, yes, my lord; he wore his beaver° up.   230
Hamlet: What, look'd he frowningly?
Horatio: A countenance more in sorrow than in anger.
Hamlet: Pale or red?
Horatio: Nay, very pale.
Hamlet: And fix'd his eyes upon you?
Horatio: Most constantly.
Hamlet: I would I had been there.   235
Horatio: It would have much amaz'd you.

203 *oppress'd*: Distressed.   204 *truncheon*: Officer's staff; *distill'd*: Softened, weakened.   205 *act*:
Action.   216 *it*: Its.   230 *beaver*: Visor on the helmet.

Hamlet: Very like, very like. Stay'd it long?

Horatio: While one with moderate haste might tell a hundred.

Marcellus: ⎫
Bernardo: ⎬ Longer, longer.

Horatio: Not when I saw't.

Hamlet: His beard was grizzled, — no?   240

Horatio: It was, as I have seen it in his life,
    A sable° silver'd.

Hamlet: I will watch to-night;
    Perchance 'twill walk again.

Horatio: I warr'nt it will.

Hamlet: If it assume my noble father's person,
    I'll speak to it, though hell itself should gape   245
    And bid me hold my peace. I pray you all,
    If you have hitherto conceal'd this sight,
    Let it be tenable in your silence still;
    And whatsoever else shall hap to-night,
    Give it an understanding, but no tongue: 250
    I will requite your loves. So, fare you well:
    Upon the platform, 'twixt eleven and twelve,
    I'll visit you.

All: Our duty to your honour.

Hamlet: Your loves, as mine to you: farewell.

                          Exeunt [all but Hamlet].

    My father's spirit in arms! all is not well;   255
    I doubt° some foul play: would the night were come!
    Till then sit still, my soul: foul deeds will rise,
    Though all the earth o'erwhelm them, to men's eyes.   *Exit.*

[SCENE III: *A room in Polonius's house.*]

Enter Laertes and Ophelia, his Sister.

Laertes: My necessaries are embark'd: farewell:
    And, sister, as the winds give benefit
    And convoy is assistant,° do not sleep,
    But let me hear from you.

Ophelia: Do you doubt that?

Laertes: For Hamlet and the trifling of his favour,   5
    Hold it a fashion° and a toy in blood,°
    A violet in the youth of primy° nature,
    Forward,° not permanent, sweet, not lasting,
    The perfume and suppliance of a minute;°
    No more.

Ophelia: No more but so?

---

242 *sable:* Black color.   256 *doubt:* Fear.   SCENE III.   3 *convoy is assistant:* Means of conveyance are available.   6 *fashion:* Custom, prevailing usage; *toy in blood:* Passing amorous fancy.   7 *primy:* In its prime.   8 *Forward:* Precocious.   9 *suppliance of a minute:* Diversion to fill up a minute.

Laertes: Think it no more: 10
    For nature, crescent,° does not grow alone
    In thews° and bulk, but, as this temple° waxes,
    The inward service of the mind and soul
    Grows wide withal. Perhaps he loves you now,
    And now no soil° nor cautel° doth besmirch   15
    The virtue of his will: but you must fear,
    His greatness weigh'd,° his will is not his own;
    For he himself is subject to his birth:
    He may not, as unvalued persons do,
    Carve for himself; for on his choice depends   20
    The safety and health of this whole state;
    And therefore must his choice be circumscrib'd
    Unto the voice and yielding° of that body
    Whereof he is the head. Then if he says he loves you,
    It fits your wisdom so far to believe it   25
    As he in his particular act and place
    May give his saying deed;° which is no further
    Than the main voice of Denmark goes withal.
    Then weigh what loss your honour may sustain,
    If with too credent° ear you list his songs,   30
    Or lose your heart, or your chaste treasure open
    To his unmast'red° importunity.
    Fear it, Ophelia, fear it, my dear sister,
    And keep you in the rear of your affection,
    Out of the shot and danger of desire.   35
    The chariest° maid is prodigal enough,
    If she unmask her beauty to the moon:
    Virtue itself 'scapes not calumnious strokes:
    The canker galls the infants of the spring,°
    Too oft before their buttons° be disclos'd,°   40
    And in the morn and liquid dew° of youth
    Contagious blastments° are most imminent.
    Be wary then; best safety lies in fear:
    Youth to itself rebels, though none else near.
Ophelia: I shall the effect of this good lesson keep,   45
    As watchman to my heart. But, good my brother,
    Do not, as some ungracious° pastors do,
    Show me the steep and thorny way to heaven;
    Whiles, like a puff'd° and reckless libertine,
    Himself the primrose path of dalliance treads,   50
    And recks° not his own rede.°

11 _crescent:_ Growing, waxing.   12 _thews:_ Bodily strength; _temple:_ Body.   15 _soil:_ blemish; _cautel:_
Crafty device.   17 _greatness weigh'd:_ High position considered.   23 _voice and yielding:_ Assent,
approval.   27 _deed:_ Effect.   30 _credent:_ Credulous.   32 _unmast'red:_ Unrestrained.   36 _chari-
est:_ Most scrupulously modest.   39 _The canker . . . spring:_ The cankerworm destroys the young plants
of spring.   40 _buttons:_ buds; _disclos'd:_ opened.   41 _liquid dew:_ I.e., time when dew is fresh.
42 _blastments:_ Blights.   47 _ungracious:_ Graceless.   49 _puff'd:_ Bloated.   51 _recks:_ Heeds, _rede:_
Counsel.

Enter Polonius.

Laertes: O, fear me not.
     I stay too long: but here my father comes.
     A double° blessing is a double grace;
     Occasion° smiles upon a second leave.
Polonius: Yet here, Laertes? aboard, aboard, for shame!   55
     The wind sits in the shoulder of your sail,
     And you are stay'd for. There; my blessing with thee!
     And these few precepts° in thy memory
     Look thou character.° Give thy thoughts no tongue,
     Nor any unproportion'd° thought his act.   60
     Be thou familiar, but by no means vulgar.°
     Those friends thou hast, and their adoption tried,
     Grapple them to thy soul with hoops of steel;
     But do not dull thy palm with entertainment
     Of each new-hatch'd, unfledg'd° comrade. Beware   65
     Of entrance to a quarrel, but being in,
     Bear't that th' opposed may beware of thee.
     Give every man thy ear, but few thy voice;
     Take each man's censure, but reserve thy judgement.
     Costly thy habit as thy purse can buy,   70
     But not express'd in fancy;° rich, not gaudy;
     For the apparel oft proclaims the man,
     And they in France of the best rank and station
     Are of a most select and generous chief in that.°
     Neither a borrower nor a lender be;   75
     For loan oft loses both itself and friend,
     And borrowing dulleth edge of husbandry.°
     This above all: to thine own self be true,
     And it must follow, as the night the day,
     Thou canst not then be false to any man.   80
     Farewell: my blessing season° this in thee!
Laertes: Most humbly do I take my leave, my lord.
Polonius: The time invites you; go; your servants tend.
Laertes: Farewell, Ophelia; and remember well
     What I have said to you.
Ophelia: 'Tis in my memory lock'd,   85
     And you yourself shall keep the key of it.
Laertes: Farewell.   *Exit Laertes.*
Polonius: What is 't, Ophelia, he hath said to you?
Ophelia: So please you, something touching the Lord Hamlet.
Polonius: Marry, well bethought: 90
     'Tis told me, he hath very oft of late

---

53 *double:* I.e., Laertes has already bade his father good-by.   54 *Occasion:* Opportunity.   58 *precepts:* Many parallels have been found to the series of maxims which follows, one of the closer being that in Lyly's *Euphues.*   59 *character:* Inscribe.   60 *unproportion'd:* Inordinate.   61 *vulgar:* Common.   65 *unfledg'd:* Immature.   71 *express'd in fancy:* Fantastical in design.   74 *Are ... that: Chief* is usually taken as a substantive meaning "head," "eminence."   77 *husbandry:* Thrift. 81 *season:* Mature.

Given private time to you; and you yourself
Have of your audience been most free and bounteous:
If it be so, as so't is put on° me,
And that in way of caution, I must tell you,   95
You do not understand yourself so clearly
As it behooves my daughter and your honour.
What is between you? give me up the truth.
Ophelia: He hath, my lord, of late made many tenders°
    Of his affection to me.   100
Polonius: Affection! pooh! you speak like a green girl,
    Unsifted° in such perilous circumstance.
    Do you believe his tenders, as you call them?
Ophelia: I do not know, my lord, what I should think.
Polonius: Marry, I will teach you: think yourself a baby;   105
    That you have ta'en these tenders° for true pay,
    Which are not sterling.° Tender° yourself more dearly;
    Or — not to crack the wind° of the poor phrase,
    Running it thus — you'll tender me a fool.°
Ophelia: My lord, he hath importun'd me with love   110
    In honourable fashion.
Polonius: Ay, fashion° you may call it; go to, go to.
Ophelia: And hath given countenance° to his speech, my lord,
    With almost all the holy vows of heaven.
Polonius: Ay, springes° to catch woodcocks.° I do know,   115
    When the blood burns, how prodigal the soul
    Lends the tongue vows: these blazes, daughter,
    Giving more light than heat, extinct in both,
    Even in their promise, as it is a-making,
    You must not take for fire. From this time   120
    Be somewhat scanter of your maiden presence;
    Set your entreatments° at a higher rate
    Than a command to parley.° For Lord Hamlet,
    Believe so much in him,° that he is young,
    And with a larger tether may he walk   125
    Than may be given you: in few,° Ophelia,
    Do not believe his vows; for they are brokers;°
    Not of that dye° which their investments° show,
    But mere implorators of° unholy suits,
    Breathing° like sanctified and pious bawds,   130
    The better to beguile. This is for all:
    I would not, in plain terms, from this time forth,
    Have you so slander° any moment leisure,

94 *put on:* Impressed on.   99, 103 *tenders:* Offers.   102 *Unsifted:* Untried.   106 *tenders:* Promises to pay.   107 *sterling:* Legal currency; *Tender:* Hold.   108 *crack the wind:* I.e., run it until it is
broken-winded.   109 *tender ... fool:* Show me a fool (for a daughter).   112 *fashion:* Mere form,
pretense.   113 *countenance:* Credit, support.   115 *springes:* Snares; *woodcocks:* Birds easily
caught, type of stupidity.   122 *entreatments:* Conversations, interviews.   123 *command to parley:*
Mere invitation to talk.   124 *so ... him:* This much concerning him.   126 *in few:* Briefly.
127 *brokers:* Go-betweens, procurers.   128 *dye:* Color or sort; *investments:* Clothes.   129 *implor-
ators of:* Solicitors of.   130 *Breathing:* Speaking.   133 *slander:* Bring disgrace or reproach upon.

As to give words or talk with the Lord Hamlet.
Look to 't, I charge you: come your ways.   135
Ophelia: I shall obey, my lord.
                                                                                        Exeunt.

[SCENE IV: *The platform.*]

Enter Hamlet, Horatio, and Marcellus.

Hamlet: The air bites shrewdly; it is very cold.
Horatio: It is a nipping and an eager air.
Hamlet: What hour now?
Horatio: I think it lacks of twelve.
Marcellus: No, it is struck.
Horatio: Indeed? I heard it not: then it draws near the season   5
  Wherein the spirit held his wont to walk.

A flourish of trumpets, and two pieces go off.

  What does this mean, my lord?
Hamlet: The king doth wake° to-night and takes his rouse,°
  Keeps wassail,° and the swagg'ring up-spring° reels;°
  And, as he drains his draughts of Rhenish° down,   10
  The kettle-drum and trumpet thus bray out
  The triumph of his pledge.°
Horatio: Is it a custom?
Hamlet: Ay, marry, is 't:
  But to my mind, though I am native here
  And to the manner born,° it is a custom   15
  More honour'd in the breach than the observance.
  This heavy-headed revel east and west
  Makes us traduc'd and tax'd of other nations:
  They clepe° us drunkards, and with swinish phrase°
  Soil our addition;° and indeed it takes   20
  From our achievements, though perform'd at height,
  The pith and marrow of our attribute.°
  So, oft it chances in particular men,
  That for some vicious mole of nature° in them,
  As, in their birth—wherein they are not guilty,   25
  Since nature cannot choose his origin—
  By the o'ergrowth of some complexion,
  Oft breaking down the pales° and forts of reason,
  Or by some habit that too much o'er-leavens°
  The form of plausive° manners, that these men,   30
  Carrying, I say, the stamp of one defect,

SCENE IV.   8 *wake:* Stay awake, hold revel; *rouse:* Carouse, drinking bout.   9 *wassail:* Carousal;
up-spring: Last and wildest dance at German merry-makings. *reels:* Reels through.   10 *Rhenish:* Rhine
wine.   12 *triumph . . . pledge:* His glorious achievement as a drinker.   15 *to . . . born:* Destined by
birth to be subject to the custom in question.   19 *clepe:* Call; *with swinish phrase:* By calling us swine.
20 *addition:* Reputation.   22 *attribute:* Reputation.   24 *mole of nature:* Natural blemish in one's
constitution.   28 *pales:* Palings (as of a fortification).   29 *o'er-leavens:* Induces a change throughout
(as yeast works in bread).   30 *plausive:* Pleasing.

Being nature's livery,° or fortune's star,° —
Their virtues else — be they as pure as grace,
As infinite as man may undergo —
Shall in the general censure take corruption   35
From that particular fault: the dram of eale°
Doth all the nobel substance of a doubt
To his own scandal.°

Enter Ghost.

Horatio: Look, my lord, it comes!
Hamlet: Angels and ministers of grace° defend us!
  Be thou a spirit of health or goblin damn'd,   40
  Bring with thee airs from heaven or blasts from hell,
  Be thy intents wicked or charitable,
  Thou com'st in such a questionable° shape
  That I will speak to thee: I'll call thee Hamlet,
  King, father, royal Dane: O, answer me!   45
  Let me not burst in ignorance; but tell
  Why thy canoniz'd° bones, hearsed° in death,
  Have burst their cerements;° why the sepulchre,
  Wherein we saw thee quietly interr'd,
  Hath op'd his ponderous and marble jaws,   50
  To cast thee up again. What may this mean,
  That thou, dead corse, again in complete steel
  Revisits thus the glimpses of the moon,°
  Making night hideous; and we fools of nature°
  So horridly to shake our disposition   55
  With thoughts beyond the reaches of our souls?
  Say, why is this? wherefore? what should we do?

[Ghost] beckons [Hamlet].

Horatio: It beckons you to go away with it,
  As if it some impartment° did desire
  To you alone.
Marcellus: Look, with what courteous action   60
  It waves you to a more removed° ground:
  But do not go with it.
Horatio: No, by no means.
Hamlet: It will not speak; then I will follow it.
Horatio: Do not, my lord!
Hamlet: Why, what should be the fear?
  I do not set my life at a pin's fee;   65

32 *nature's livery:* Endowment from nature; *fortune's star:* The position in which one is placed
by fortune, a reference to astrology. The two phrases are aspects of the same thing.   36–38 *the dram*
... *scandal:* A famous crux: *dram of eale* has had various interpretations, the preferred one being
probably, "a dram of evil."   39 *ministers of grace:* Messengers of God.   43 *questionable:* Inviting
question or conversation.   47 *canoniz'd:* Buried according to the canons of the church; *hearsed:*
Coffined.   48 *cerements:* Grave-clothes.   53 *glimpses of the moon:* The earth by night.   54 *fools
of nature:* Mere men, limited to natural knowledge.   59 *impartment:* Communication.   61 *removed:* Remote.

And for my soul, what can it do to that,
Being a thing immortal as itself?
It waves me forth again: I'll follow it.
Horatio: What if it tempt you toward the flood, my lord,
Or to the dreadful summit of the cliff   70
That beetles o'er° his base into the sea,
And there assume some other horrible form,
Which might deprive your sovereignty of reason°
And draw you into madness? think of it:
The very place puts toys of desperation,°   75
Without more motive, into every brain
That looks so many fathoms to the sea
And hears it roar beneath.
Hamlet: It waves me still.
Go on; I'll follow thee.
Marcellus: You shall not go, my lord.
Hamlet: Hold off your hands!   80
Horatio: Be rul'd; you shall not go.
Hamlet: My fate cries out,
And makes each petty artere° in this body
As hardy as the Nemean lion's° nerve.°
Still am I call'd. Unhand me, gentlemen.
By heaven, I'll make a ghost of him that lets° me!   85
I say, away! Go on; I'll follow thee.   *Exeunt Ghost and Hamlet.*
Horatio: He waxes desperate with imagination.
Marcellus: Let's follow; 'tis not fit thus to obey him.
Horatio: Have after. To what issue° will this come?
Marcellus: Something is rotten in the state of Denmark.   90
Horatio: Heaven will direct it.°
Marcellus: Nay, let's follow him.   *Exeunt.*

[SCENE V: *Another part of the platform.*]

Enter Ghost and Hamlet.

Hamlet: Whither wilt thou lead me? speak; I'll go no further.
Ghost: Mark me.
Hamlet: I will.
Ghost: My hour is almost come,
When I to sulphurous and tormenting flames
Must render up myself.
Hamlet: Alas, poor ghost!   5

71 *beetles o'er:* Overhangs threateningly.   73 *deprive ... reason:* Take away the sovereignty of your
reason. It was thought that evil spirits would sometimes assume the form of departed spirits in order
to work madness in a human creature.   75 *toys of desperation:* Freakish notions of suicide.
82 *artere:* Artery.   83 *Nemean lion's:* The Nemean lion was one of the monsters slain by Hercules;
nerve: Sinew, tendon. The point is that the arteries which were carrying the spirits out into the body
were functioning and were as stiff and hard as the sinews of the lion.   85 *lets:* Hinders.   89 *issue:*
Outcome.   91 *it:* I.e., the outcome.

Ghost: Pity me not, but lend thy serious hearing
    To what I shall unfold.
Hamlet: Speak; I am bound to hear.
Ghost: So art thou to revenge, when thou shalt hear.
Hamlet: What?
Ghost: I am thy father's spirit,   10
    Doom'd for a certain term to walk the night,
    And for the day confin'd to fast° in fires,
    Till the foul crimes done in my days of nature
    Are burnt and purg'd away. But that I am forbid
    To tell the secrets of my prison-house,   15
    I could a tale unfold whose lightest word
    Would harrow up thy soul, freeze thy young blood,
    Make thy two eyes, like stars, start from their spheres,°
    Thy knotted° and combined° locks to part
    And each particular hair to stand an end,   20
    Like quills upon the fretful porpentine:°
    But this eternal blazon° must not be
    To ears of flesh and blood. List, list, O, list!
    If thou didst ever thy dear father love —
Hamlet: O God!   25
Ghost: Revenge his foul and most unnatural° murder.
Hamlet: Murder!
Ghost: Murder most foul, as in the best it is;
    But this most foul, strange and unnatural.
Hamlet: Haste me to know't, that I, with wings as swift   30
    As meditation or the thoughts of love,
    May sweep to my revenge.
Ghost: I find thee apt;
    And duller shouldst thou be than the fat weed°
    That roots itself in ease on Lethe wharf,°
    Wouldst thou not stir in this. Now, Hamlet, hear: 35
    'Tis given out that, sleeping in my orchard,
    A serpent stung me; so the whole ear of Denmark
    Is by a forged process of my death
    Rankly abus'd: but know, thou noble youth,
    The serpent that did sting thy father's life   40
    Now wears his crown.
Hamlet: O my prophetic soul!
    My uncle!
Ghost: Ay, that incestuous, that adulterate° beast,
    With witchcraft of his wit, with traitorous gifts, —

SCENE V.   12 *fast:* Probably, do without food. It has been sometimes taken in the sense of doing general penance.   18 *spheres:* Orbits.   19 *knotted:* Perhaps intricately arranged; *combined:* Tied, bound.   21 *porpentine:* Porcupine.   22 *eternal blazon:* Promulgation or proclamation of eternity, revelation of the hereafter.   26 *unnatural:* I.e., pertaining to fratricide.   33 *fat weed:* Many suggestions have been offered as to the particular plant intended, including asphodel; probably a general figure for plants growing along rotting wharves and piles.   34 *Lethe wharf:* Bank of the river of forgetfulness in Hades.   43 *adulterate:* Adulterous.

O wicked wit and gifts, that have the power 45
So to seduce!—won to his shameful lust
The will of my most seeming-virtuous queen:
O Hamlet, what a falling-off was there!
From me, whose love was of that dignity
That it went hand in hand even with the vow 50
I made to her in marriage, and to decline
Upon a wretch whose natural gifts were poor
To those of mine!
But virtue, as it never will be moved,
Though lewdness court it in a shape of heaven, 55
So lust, though to a radiant angel link'd,
Will sate itself in a celestial bed,
And prey on garbage.
But, soft! methinks I scent the morning air;
Brief let me be. Sleeping within my orchard, 60
My custom always of the afternoon,
Upon my secure° hour thy uncle stole,
With juice of cursed hebona° in a vial,
And in the porches of my ears did pour
The leperous° distilment; whose effect 65
Holds such an enmity with blood of man
That swift as quicksilver it courses through
The natural gates and alleys of the body,
And with a sudden vigour it doth posset°
And curd, like eager° droppings into milk, 70
The thin and wholesome blood: so did it mine;
And a most instant tetter bark'd about,
Most lazar-like,° with vile and loathsome crust,
All my smooth body.
Thus was I, sleeping, by a brother's hand 75
Of life, of crown, of queen, at once dispatch'd:°
Cut off even in the blossoms of my sin,
Unhous'led,° disappointed,° unanel'd,°
No reck'ning made, but sent to my account
With all my imperfections on my head: 80
O, horrible! O, horrible! most horrible!°
If thou hast nature in thee, bear it not;
Let not the royal bed of Denmark be
A couch for luxury° and damned incest.
But, howsomever thou pursues this act, 85
Taint not thy mind,° nor let thy soul contrive

---

62 *secure:* Confident, unsuspicious.   63 *hebona:* Generally supposed to mean henbane, conjectured *hemlock; ebenus,* meaning "yew."   65 *leperous:* Causing leprosy.   69 *posset:* Coagulate, curdle. 70 *eager:* Sour, acid.   73 *lazar-like:* Leperlike.   76 *dispatch'd:* Suddenly bereft.   78 *Unhous'led:* Without having received the sacrament; *disappointed:* Unready, without equipment for the last journey; *unanel'd:* Without having received extreme unction.   81 *O . . . horrible:* Many editors give this line to Hamlet; Garrick and Sir Henry Irving spoke it in that part.   84 *luxury:* Lechery.   86 *Taint . . . mind:* Probably, deprave not thy character, do nothing except in the pursuit of a natural revenge.

Against thy mother aught: leave her to heaven
And to those thorns that in her bosom lodge,
To prick and sting her. Fare thee well at once!
The glow-worm shows the matin° to be near,   90
And 'gins to pale his uneffectual fire:°
Adieu, adieu, adieu! remember me.   *[Exit.]*
Hamlet: O all you host of heaven! O earth! what else?
And shall I couple° hell? O, fie! Hold, hold, my heart;
And you, my sinews, grow not instant old,   95
But bear me stiffly up. Remember thee!
Ay, thou poor ghost, whiles memory holds a seat
In this distracted globe.° Remember thee!
Yea, from the table of my memory
I'll wipe away all trivial fond records,   100
All saws° of books, all forms, all pressures° past,
That youth and observation copied there;
And thy commandment all alone shall live
Within the book and volume of my brain,
Unmix'd with baser matter: yes, by heaven!   105
O most pernicious woman!
O villain, villain, smiling, damned villain!
My tables,° — meet it is I set it down,
That one may smile, and smile, and be a villain;
At least I am sure it may be so in Denmark: *[Writing.]*   110
So, uncle, there you are. Now to my word;°
It is "Adieu, adieu! remember me,"
I have sworn't.

Enter Horatio and Marcellus.

Horatio: My lord, my lord —
Marcellus: ⎱   Lord Hamlet, —
Horatio: ⎰   Heavens secure him!
Hamlet: So be it!   115
Marcellus: Hillo, ho, ho,° my lord!
Hamlet: Hillo, ho, ho, boy! come, bird, come.
Marcellus: How is't, my noble lord?
Horatio: What news, my lord?
Hamlet: O, wonderful!
Horatio: Good my lord, tell it.
Hamlet: No; you will reveal it.   120
Horatio: Not I, my lord, by heaven.
Marcellus: Nor I, my lord.
Hamlet: How say you, then; would heart of man once think it?
    But you'll be secret?

90 *matin:* Morning. 91 *uneffectual fire:* Cold light. 94 *couple:* Add. 98 *distracted globe:* Confused head. 101 *saws:* Wise sayings; *pressures:* Impressions stamped. 108 *tables:* Probably a small portable writing-tablet carried at the belt. 111 *word:* Watchword. 116 *Hillo, ho, ho:* A falconer's call to a hawk in air.

Horatio: ⎱
Marcellus: ⎰ Ay, by heaven, my lord.

Hamlet: There's ne'er a villain dwelling in all Denmark
　　But he's an arrant° knave. 125

Horatio: There needs no ghost, my lord, come from the grave
　　To tell us this.

Hamlet: 　　　　　Why, right; you are in the right;
　　And so, without more circumstance at all,
　　I hold it fit that we shake hands and part:
　　You, as your business and desire shall point you; 130
　　For every man has business and desire,
　　Such as it is; and for my own poor part,
　　Look you, I'll go pray.

Horatio: These are but wild and whirling words, my lord.

Hamlet: I am sorry they offend you, heartily; 135
　　Yes, 'faith, heartily.

Horatio: 　　　　　There's no offence, my lord.

Hamlet: Yes, by Saint Patrick,° but there is, Horatio,
　　And much offence too. Touching this vision here,
　　It is an honest° ghost, that let me tell you:
　　For your desire to know what is between us, 140
　　O'ermaster 't as you may. And now, good friends,
　　As you are friends, scholars and soldiers,
　　Give me one poor request.

Horatio: What is 't, my lord? we will.

Hamlet: Never make known what you have seen to-night.

Horatio: ⎱
Marcellus: ⎰ My lord, we will not.

Hamlet: 　　　　　Nay, but swear 't.

Horatio: 　　　　　　　　In faith, 145
　　My lord, not I.

Marcellus: 　　　　　Nor I, my lord, in faith.

Hamlet: Upon my sword.°

Marcellus: 　　　　We have sworn, my lord, already.

Hamlet: Indeed, upon my sword, indeed. 　　*Ghost cries under the stage.*

Ghost: Swear.

Hamlet: Ah, ha, boy! say'st thou so? art thou there, truepenny?° 150
　　Come on — you hear this fellow in the cellarage —
　　Consent to swear.

Horatio: 　　　　Propose the oath, my lord.

Hamlet: Never to speak of this that you have seen,
　　Swear by my sword.

Ghost [beneath]: Swear. 155

Hamlet: Hic et ubique?° then we'll shift our ground.
　　Come hither, gentlemen,

---

125 *arrant:* Thoroughgoing. 　137 *Saint Patrick:* St. Patrick was keeper of Purgatory and patron saint of all blunders and confusion. 　139 *honest:* I.e., a real ghost and not an evil spirit. 　147 *sword:* I.e., the hilt in the form of a cross. 　150 *truepenny:* Good old boy, or the like. 　156 *Hic et ubique?:* Here and everywhere?

And lay your hands again upon my sword:
   Swear by my sword,
   Never to speak of this that you have heard.   160
Ghost [beneath]: Swear by his sword.
Hamlet: Well said, old mole! canst work i' th' earth so fast?
   A worthy pioner!° Once more remove, good friends.
Horatio: O day and night, but this is wondrous strange!
Hamlet: And therefore as a stranger give it welcome.   165
   There are more things in heaven and earth, Horatio,
   Than are dreamt of in your philosophy.
   But come;
   Here, as before, never, so help you mercy,
   How strange or odd soe'er I bear myself,   170
   As I perchance hereafter shall think meet
   To put an antic° disposition on,
   That you, at such times seeing me, never shall,
   With arms encumb'red° thus, or this head-shake,
   Or by pronouncing of some doubtful phrase,   175
   As "Well, well, we know," or "We could, an if we would,"
   Or "If we list to speak," or "There be, an if they might,"
   Or such ambiguous giving out,° to note°
   That you know aught of me: this not to do,
   So grace and mercy at your most need help you,   180
   Swear.
Ghost [beneath]: Swear.
Hamlet: Rest, rest, perturbed spirit! *[They swear.]* So, gentlemen,
   With all my love I do commend me to you:
   And what so poor a man as Hamlet is   185
   May do, t' express his love and friending° to you,
   God willing, shall not lack. Let us go in together;
   And still your fingers on your lips, I pray.
   The time is out of joint: O cursed spite,
   That ever I was born to set it right!   190
   Nay, come, let's go together.   *Exeunt.*

[ACT II

Scene I: *A room in Polonius's house.*]

Enter old Polonius with his man [Reynaldo].

Polonius: Give him this money and these notes, Reynaldo.
Reynaldo: I will, my lord.
Polonius: You shall do marvellous wisely, good Reynaldo,

---

163 *pioner:* Digger, miner.   172 *antic:* Fantastic.   174 *encumb'red:* Folded or entwined.
178 *giving out:* Profession of knowledge; *to note:* To give a sign.   186 *friending:* Friendliness.

Before you visit him, to make inquire
Of his behaviour.
Reynaldo: My lord, I did intend it.   5
Polonius: Marry, well said; very well said. Look you, sir,
 Inquire me first what Danskers° are in Paris;
 And how, and who, what means, and where they keep,°
 What company, at what expense; and finding
 By this encompassment° and drift° of question   10
 That they do know my son, come you more nearer
 Than your particular demands will touch it:°
 Take° you, as 'twere, some distant knowledge of him;
 As thus, "I know his father and his friends,
 And in part him": do you mark this, Reynaldo?   15
Reynaldo: Ay, very well, my lord.
Polonius: "And in part him; but" you may say "not well:
 But, if 't be he I mean, he's very wild;
 Addicted so and so": and there put on° him
 What forgeries° you please; marry, none so rank   20
 As may dishonour him; take heed of that;
 But, sir, such wanton,° wild and usual slips
 As are companions noted and most known
 To youth and liberty.
Reynaldo: As gaming, my lord.
Polonius: Ay, or drinking, fencing,° swearing, quarrelling,   25
 Drabbing;° you may go so far.
Reynaldo: My lord, that would dishonour him.
Polonius: 'Faith, no; as you may season it in the charge.
 You must not put another scandal on him,
 That he is open to incontinency;°   30
 That's not my meaning: but breathe his faults so quaintly°
 That they may seem the taints of liberty,°
 The flash and outbreak of a fiery mind,
 A savageness in unreclaimed° blood,
 Of general assault.°
Reynaldo: But, my good lord, —   35
Polonius: Wherefore should you do this?
Reynaldo: Ay, my lord,
 I would know that.
Polonius: Marry, sir, here's my drift;
 And, I believe, it is a fetch of wit:°
 You laying these slight sullies on my son,

ACT II. SCENE I.   7 *Danskers:* Danke was a common variant for "Denmark"; hence "Dane."   8 *keep:*
Dwell.   10 *encompassment:* Roundabout talking; *drift:* Gradual approach or course.   11–12 *come
. . . it:* I.e., you will find out more this way than by asking pointed questions.   13 *Take:* Assume,
pretend.   19 *put on:* Impute to.   20 *forgeries:* Invented tales.   22 *wanton:* Sportive, unrestrained.   25 *fencing:* Indicative of the ill repute of professional fencers and fencing schools in
Elizabethan times.   26 *Drabbing:* Associating with immoral women.   30 *incontinency:* Habitual
loose behavior.   31 *quaintly:* Delicately, ingeniously.   32 *taints of liberty:* Blemishes due to freedom.   34 *unreclaimed:* Untamed.   35 *general assault:* Tendency that assails all untrained youth.
38 *fetch of wit:* Clever trick.

As 'twere a thing a little soil'd i' th' working,   40
Mark you,
Your party in converse, him you would sound,
Having ever° seen in the prenominate° crimes
The youth you breathe of guilty, be assur'd
He closes with you in this consequence;°   45
"Good sir," or so, or "friend," or "gentleman,"
According to the phrase or the addition
Of man and country.
Reynaldo: Very good, my lord.
Polonius: And then, sir, does 'a this — 'a does — what was I about to say? By
the mass, I was about to say something: where did I leave?   50
Reynaldo: At "closes in the consequence," at "friend or so," and "gentle-
man."
Polonius: At "closes in the consequence," ay, marry;
He closes thus: "I know the gentleman;
I saw him yesterday, or t' other day,   55
Or then, or then; with such, or such; and, as you say,
There was 'a gaming; there o'ertook in 's rouse;°
There falling out at tennis": or perchance,
"I saw him enter such a house of sale,"
Videlicet,° a brothel, or so forth.   60
See you now;
Your bait of falsehood takes this carp of truth:
And thus do we of wisdom and of reach,°
With windlasses° and with assays of bias,°
By indirections° find directions° out: 65
So by my former lecture° and advice,
Shall you my son. You have me, have you not?
Reynaldo: My lord, I have.
Polonius: God bye ye;° fare ye well.
Reynaldo: Good my lord!
Polonius: Observe his inclination in yourself.°   70
Reynaldo: I shall, my lord.
Polonius: And let him ply his music.°
Reynaldo: Well, my lord.
Polonius: Farewell!   *Exit Reynaldo.*

Enter Ophelia.

          How now, Ophelia! what's the matter?
Ophelia: O, my lord, my lord, I have been so affrighted!
Polonius: With what, i' th' name of God?   75

43 *ever:* At any time; *prenominate:* Before-mentioned.   45 *closes ... consequence:* Agrees with you
in this conclusion.   57 *o'ertook in 's rouse:* Overcome by drink.   60 *Videlicet:* Namely.
63 *reach:* Capacity, ability.   64 *windlasses:* I.e., circuitous paths; *assays of bias:* Attempts that resemble
the course of the bowl, which, being weighted on one side, has a curving motion.   65 *indirections:*
Devious courses; *directions:* Straight courses, i.e., the truth.   66 *lecture:* Admonition.   68 *bye ye:*
Be with you.   70 *Observe ... yourself:* In your own person, not by spies; or conform your own
conduct to his inclination; or test him by studying yourself.   72 *ply his music:* Probably to be taken
literally.

Ophelia: My lord, as I was sewing in my closet,°
　　　Lord Hamlet, with his doublet° all unbrac'd;°
　　　No hat upon his head; his stockings foul'd,
　　　Ungart'red, and down-gyved° to his ankle;
　　　Pale as his shirt; his knees knocking each other;　　　　　　　80
　　　And with a look so piteous in purport
　　　As if he had been loosed out of hell
　　　To speak of horrors, — he comes before me.
Polonius: Mad for thy love?
Ophelia:　　　　　My lord, I do not know;
　　　But truly, I do fear it.
Polonius:　　　　　What said he?　　　　　　　　　　　　　　85
Ophelia: He took me by the wrist and held me hard;
　　　Then goes he to the length of all his arm;
　　　And, with his other hand thus o'er his brow,
　　　He falls to such perusal of my face
　　　As 'a would draw it. Long stay'd he so;　　　　　　　　　　90
　　　At last, a little shaking of mine arm
　　　And thrice his head thus waving up and down,
　　　He rais'd a sigh so piteous and profound
　　　As it did seem to shatter all his bulk°
　　　And end his being: that done, he lets me go:　　　　　　　95
　　　And, with his head over his shoulder turn'd,
　　　He seem'd to find his way without his eyes;
　　　For out o' doors he went without their helps,
　　　And, to the last, bended their light on me.
Polonius: Come, go with me: I will go seek the king.　　　　　100
　　　This is the very ecstasy of love,
　　　Whose violent property° fordoes° itself
　　　And leads the will to desperate undertakings
　　　As oft as any passion under heaven
　　　That does afflict our natures. I am sorry.　　　　　　　　105
　　　What, have you given him any hard words of late?
Ophelia: No, my good lord, but, as you did command,
　　　I did repel his letters and denied
　　　His access to me.
Polonius:　　　　　That hath made him mad.
　　　I am sorry that with better heed and judgement　　　　　110
　　　I had not quoted° him: I fear'd he did but trifle,
　　　And meant to wrack thee; but, beshrew my jealousy!°
　　　By heaven, it is as proper to our age
　　　To cast beyond° ourselves in our opinions
　　　As it is common for the younger sort　　　　　　　　　　115
　　　To lack discretion. Come, go we to the king:

76 *closet:* Private chamber.　　77 *doublet:* Close-fitting coat; *unbrac'd:* Unfastened.　　79 *down-gyved:*
Fallen to the ankles (like gyves or fetters).　　94 *bulk:* Body.　　102 *property:* Nature; *fordoes:* Destroys.
111 *quoted:* Observed.　　112 *beshrew my jealousy:* Curse my suspicions.　　114 *cast beyond:* Over-
shoot, miscalculate.

This must be known; which, being kept close, might move
More grief to hide than hate to utter love.°
Come.   *Exeunt.*

[SCENE II: *A room in the castle.*]

Flourish. Enter King and Queen, Rosencrantz, and Guildenstern [with others].

King: Welcome, dear Rosencrantz and Guildenstern!
　　Moreover that° we much did long to see you,
　　The need we have to use you did provoke
　　Our hasty sending. Something have you heard
　　Of Hamlet's transformation; so call it,   5
　　Sith° nor th' exterior nor the inward man
　　Resembles that it was. What it should be,
　　More than his father's death, that thus hath put him
　　So much from th' understanding of himself,
　　I cannot dream of: I entreat you both,   10
　　That, being of so young days° brought up with him,
　　And sith so neighbour'd to his youth and haviour,
　　That you vouchsafe your rest° here in our court
　　Some little time: so by your companies
　　To draw him on to pleasures, and to gather,   15
　　So much as from occasion you may glean,
　　Whether aught, to us unknown, afflicts him thus,
　　That, open'd, lies within our remedy.
Queen: Good gentlemen, he hath much talk'd of you;
　　And sure I am two men there are not living   20
　　To whom he more adheres. If it will please you
　　To show us so much gentry° and good will
　　As to expend your time with us awhile,
　　For the supply and profit° of our hope,
　　Your visitation shall receive such thanks   25
　　As fits a king's remembrance.
Rosencrantz:　　　　　　　Both your majesties
　　Might, by the sovereign power you have of us,
　　Put your dread pleasures more into command
　　Than to entreaty.
Guildenstern:　　　　　　But we both obey,
　　And here give up ourselves, in the full bent°   30
　　To lay our service freely at your feet,
　　To be commanded.
King: Thanks, Rosencrantz and gentle Guildenstern.
Queen: Thanks, Guildenstern and gentle Rosencrantz:

117–118 *might . . . love:* I.e., I might cause more grief to others by hiding the knowledge of Hamlet's
love to Ophelia than hatred to me and mine by telling of it.　SCENE II.　2 *Moreover that:* Besides
the fact that.　6 *Sith:* Since.　11 *of . . . days:* From such early youth.　13 *vouchsafe your rest:*
Please to stay.　22 *gentry:* Courtesy.　24 *supply and profit:* Aid and successful outcome.　30 *in
. . . bent:* To the utmost degree of our mental capacity.

And I beseech you instantly to visit   35
My too much changed son. Go, some of you,
And bring these gentlemen where Hamlet is.
Guildenstern: Heavens make our presence and our practices
    Pleasant and helpful to him!
Queen: Ay, amen!
            Exeunt Rosencrantz and Guildenstern [with some Attendants].

Enter Polonius.

Polonius: Th' ambassadors from Norway, my good lord,   40
    Are joyfully return'd.
King: Thou still hast been the father of good news.
Polonius: Have I, my lord? I assure my good liege,
    I hold my duty, as I hold my soul,
    Both to my God and to my gracious king: 45
    And I do think, or else this brain of mine
    Hunts not the trail of policy so sure
    As it hath us'd to do, that I have found
    The very cause of Hamlet's lunacy.
King: O, speak of that; that do I long to hear.   50
Polonius: Give first admittance to th' ambassadors;
    My news shall be the fruit to that great feast.
King: Thyself do grace to them, and bring them in.   *[Exit Polonius.]*
    He tells me, my dear Gertrude, he hath found
    The head and source of all your son's distemper.   55
Queen: I doubt° it is no other but the main;°
    His father's death, and our o'erhasty marriage.
King: Well, we shall sift him.

Enter Ambassadors [Voltimand and Cornelius, with Polonius.]

            Welcome, my good friends!
    Say, Voltimand, what from our brother Norway?
Voltimand: Most fair return of greetings and desires.   60
    Upon our first, he sent out to suppress
    His nephew's levies; which to him appear'd
    To be a preparation 'gainst the Polack;
    But, better look'd into, he truly found
    It was against your highness: whereat griev'd,   65
    That so his sickness, age and impotence
    Was falsely borne in hand,° sends out arrests
    On Fortinbras; which he, in brief, obeys;
    Receives rebuke from Norway, and in fine°
    Makes vow before his uncle never more   70
    To give th' assay° of arms against your majesty.
    Whereon old Norway, overcome with joy,
    Gives him three score thousand crowns in annual fee,
    And his commission to employ those soldiers,

56 *doubt:* Fear; *main:* Chief point, principal concern.   67 *borne in hand:* Deluded.   69 *in fine:* In
the end.   71 *assay:* Assault, trial (of arms).

So levied as before, against the Polack: 75
With an entreaty, herein further shown, *[giving a paper.]*
That it might please you to give quiet pass
Through your dominions for this enterprise,
On such regards of safety and allowance°
As therein are set down.
King: It likes° us well;   80
And at our more consider'd° time we'll read,
Answer, and think upon this business.
Meantime we thank you for your well-took labour:
Go to your rest; at night we'll feast together:
Most welcome home!   *Exeunt Ambassadors.*
Polonius: This business is well ended.   85
My liege, and madam, to expostulate
What majesty should be, what duty is,
Why day is day, night night, and time is time,
Were nothing but to waste night, day and time.
Therefore, since brevity is the soul of wit,°   90
And tediousness the limbs and outward flourishes,°
I will be brief: your noble son is mad:
Mad call I it; for, to define true madness
What is 't but to be nothing else but mad?
But let that go.
Queen: More matter, with less art.   95
Polonius: Madam, I swear I use no art at all.
That he is mad, 'tis true: 'tis true 'tis pity;
And pity 'tis 'tis true: a foolish figure;°
But farewell it, for I will use no art.
Mad let us grant him, then: and now remains   100
That we find out the cause of this effect,
Or rather say, the cause of this defect,
For this effect defective comes by cause:
Thus it remains, and the remainder thus.
Perpend.°   105
I have a daughter — have while she is mine —
Who, in her duty and obedience, mark,
Hath given me this: now gather, and surmise. *[Reads the letter]* "To the
celestial and my soul's idol,
the most beautified Ophelia," —   110
That's an ill phrase, a vile phrase; "beautified" is a vile phrase: but you
shall hear. Thus: *[Reads.]*
"In her excellent white bosom, these, & c."
Queen: Came this from Hamlet to her?
Polonius: Good madam, stay awhile; I will be faithful.   *[Reads.]* 115
          "Doubt thou the stars are fire;

79 *safety and allowance:* Pledges of safety to the country and terms of permission for the troops to
pass.   80 *likes:* Pleases.   81 *consider'd:* Suitable for deliberation.   90 *wit:* Sound sense or judgment. 91 *flourishes:* Ostentation, embellishments.   98 *figure:* Figure of speech.   105 *Perpend:*
Consider.

<pre>
          Doubt that the sun doth move;
       Doubt truth to be a liar;
          But never doubt I love.
</pre>
     "O dear Ophelia, I am ill at these numbers;° I have not art to   120
reckon° my groans: but that I love thee best, O most best, believe it.
Adieu.
          "Thine evermore, most dear lady, whilst this machine° is to him,
                                                         HAMLET."

     This, in obedience, hath my daughter shown me,   125
     And more above,° hath his solicitings,
     As they fell out° by time, by means° and place,
     All given to mine ear.
King: But how hath she
     Receiv'd his love?
Polonius: What do you think of me?
King: As of a man faithful and honourable.   130
Polonius: I would fain prove so. But what might you think,
     When I had seen this hot love on the wing —
     As I perceiv'd it, I must tell you that,
     Before my daughter told me — what might you,
     Or my dear majesty your queen here, think,   135
     If I had play'd the desk or table-book,°
     Or given my heart a winking,° mute and dumb,
     Or look'd upon this love with idle sight;
     What might you think? No, I went round to work,
     And my young mistress thus I did bespeak:°   140
     "Lord Hamlet is a prince, out of thy star;°
     This must not be": and then I prescripts gave her,
     That she should lock herself from his resort,
     Admit no messengers, receive no tokens.
     Which done, she took the fruits of my advice;   145
     And he, repelled — a short tale to make —
     Fell into a sadness, then into a fast,
     Thence to a watch,° thence into a weakness,
     Thence to a lightness,° and, by this declension,°
     Into the madness wherein now he raves,   150
     And all we mourn for.
King: Do you think 'tis this?
Queen: It may be, very like.
Polonius: Hath there been such a time — I would fain know that —
     That I have positively said " 'Tis so,"
     When it prov'd otherwise?
King: Not that I know.   155

---

120 *ill ... numbers:* Unskilled at writing verses.   121 *reckon:* Number metrically, scan.   123 *ma-chine:* Bodily frame.   126 *more above:* Moreover.   127 *fell out:* Occurred; *means:* Opportunities (of access).   136 *play'd ... table-book:* I.e., remained shut up, concealed this information. 137 *given ... winking:* Given my heart a signal to keep silent.   140 *bespeak:* Address.   141 *out ... star:* Above thee in position.   148 *watch:* State of sleeplessness.   149 *lightness:* Lightheadedness; *declension:* Decline, deterioration.

Shakespeare / Hamlet: Act II, Scene II **1311**

Polonius [pointing to his head and shoulder]: Take this from this, if this be
    otherwise:
    If circumstances lead me, I will find
    Where truth is hid, though it were hid indeed
    Within the centre.°
King: How may we try it further?   160
Polonius: You know, sometimes he walks four hours together
    Here in the lobby.
Queen: So he does indeed.
Polonius: At such a time I'll loose my daughter to him:
    Be you and I behind an arras° then;
    Mark the encounter: if he love her not   165
    And be not from his reason fall'n thereon,°
    Let me be no assistant for a state,
    But keep a farm and carters.
King: We will try it.

Enter Hamlet [reading on a book].

Queen: But, look, where sadly the poor wretch comes reading.
Polonius: Away, I do beseech you both, away: 170
                  Exeunt King and Queen [with Attendants].
    I'll board° him presently. O, give me leave.
    How does my good Lord Hamlet?
Hamlet: Well, God-a-mercy.
Polonius: Do you know me, my lord?
Hamlet: Excellent well; you are a fishmonger.°   175
Polonius: Not I, my lord.
Hamlet: Then I would you were so honest a man.
Polonius: Honest, my lord!
Hamlet: Ay, sir; to be honest, as this world goes, is to be one man picked
    out of ten thousand.   180
Polonius: That's very true, my lord.
Hamlet: For if the sun breed maggots in a dead dog, being a good kissing
    carrion,° — Have you a daughter?
Polonius: I have, my lord.
Hamlet: Let her not walk i' the sun:° conception° is a blessing: but as your   185
    daughter may conceive — Friend, look to 't.
Polonius [aside]: How say you by° that? Still harping on my daughter: yet he
    knew me not at first; 'a said I was a fishmonger: 'a is far gone, far gone:
    and truly in my youth I suffered much extremity for love; very near this.
    I'll speak to him again. What do you read, my lord?   190
Hamlet: Words, words, words.
Polonius: What is the matter,° my lord?

160 *centre:* Middle point of the earth.   164 *arras:* Hanging, tapestry.   166 *thereon:* On that account.   171 *board:* Accost.   175 *fishmonger:* An opprobrious expression meaning "bawd," "pro-
curer."   183 *good kissing carrion:* I.e., a good piece of flesh for kissing (?).   185 *i' the sun:* In the
sunshine of princely favors; *conception:* Quibble on "understanding" and "pregnancy."   187 *by:*
Concerning.   192 *matter:* Substance.

Hamlet: Between who?°

Polonius: I mean, the matter that you read, my lord.

Hamlet: Slanders, sir: for the satirical rogue says here that old men have   195
grey beards, that their faces are wrinkled, their eyes purging° thick amber and plum-tree gum and that they have a plentiful lack of wit, together with most weak hams: all which, sir, though I most powerfully
and potently believe, yet I hold it not honesty° to have it thus set down,
for yourself, sir, should be old as I am, if like a crab you could go   200
backward.

Polonius [aside]: Though this be madness, yet there is method in 't. — Will
you walk out of the air, my lord?

Hamlet: Into my grave.

Polonius: Indeed, that's out of the air. *(Aside.)* How pregnant sometimes   205
his replies are! a happiness° that often madness hits on, which reason
and sanity could not so prosperously° be delivered of. I will leave him,
and suddenly contrive the means of meeting between him and my
daughter. — My honourable lord, I will most humbly take my leave of
you.   210

Hamlet: You cannot, sir, take from me any thing that I will more willingly
part withal: except my life, except my life, except my life.

Enter Guildenstern and Rosencrantz.

Polonius: Fare you well, my lord.

Hamlet: These tedious old fools!

Polonius: You go to seek the Lord Hamlet; there he is.   215

Rosencrantz [to Polonius]: God save you, sir!   *[Exit Polonius.]*

Guildenstern: My honoured lord!

Rosencrantz: My most dear lord!

Hamlet: My excellent good friends! How dost thou, Guildenstern? Ah,
Rosencrantz! Good lads, how do ye both?   220

Rosencrantz: As the indifferent° children of the earth.

Guildenstern: Happy, in that we are not over-happy;
On Fortune's cap we are not the very button.

Hamlet: Nor the soles of her shoe?

Rosencrantz: Neither, my lord.   225

Hamlet: Then you live about her waist, or in the middle of her favours?

Guildenstern: 'Faith, her privates° we.

Hamlet: In the secret parts of Fortune? O, most true; she is a strumpet. What's
the news?

Rosencrantz: None, my lord, but that the world's grown honest.   230

Hamlet: Then is doomsday near: but your news is not true. Let me question
more in particular: what have you, my good friends, deserved at the hands
of Fortune, that she sends you to prison hither?

Guildenstern: Prison, my lord!

Hamlet: Denmark's a prison.   235

Rosencrantz: Then is the world one.

193 *Between who:* Hamlet deliberately takes *matter* as meaning "basis of dispute."   196 *purging:* dis-
charging.   199 *honesty:* Decency.   206 *happiness:* Felicity of expression.   207 *prosperously:* Successfully.   221 *indifferent:* Ordinary.   227 *privates:* I.e., ordinary men (sexual pun on *private parts*).

Hamlet: A goodly one; in which there are many confines,° wards and dun-
geons, Denmark being one o' the worst.

Rosencrantz: We think not so, my lord.

Hamlet: Why, then, 'tis none to you; for there is nothing either good or bad,   240
but thinking makes it so: to me it is a prison.

Rosencrantz: Why then, your ambition makes it one; 'tis too narrow for your
mind.

Hamlet: O God, I could be bounded in a nutshell and count myself a king
of infinite space, were it not that I have bad dreams.   245

Guildenstern: Which dreams indeed are ambition, for the very substance of
the ambitious° is merely the shadow of a dream.

Hamlet: A dream itself is but a shadow.

Rosencrantz: Truly, and I hold ambition of so airy and light a quality that it
is but a shadow's shadow.   250

Hamlet: Then are our beggars bodies, and our monarchs and outstretched
heroes the beggars' shadows. Shall we to the court? for, by my fay,° I
cannot reason.°

Rosencrantz:
Guildenstern: We'll wait upon° you.

Hamlet: No such matter: I will not sort° you with the rest of my servants, for,
to speak to you like an honest man, I am most dreadfully attended.° But,   255
in the beaten way of friendship,° what make you at Elsinore?

Rosencrantz: To visit you, my lord: no other occasion.

Hamlet: Beggar that I am, I am ever poor in thanks; but I thank you: and
sure, dear friends, my thanks are too dear a° halfpenny. Were you not
sent for? Is it your own inclining? Is it a free visitation? Come, come, deal   260
justly with me: come, come; nay, speak.

Guildenstern: What should we say, my lord?

Hamlet: Why, any thing, but to the purpose. You were sent for; and there
is a kind of confession in your looks which your modesties have not
craft enough to colour: I know the good king and queen have sent for   265
you.

Rosencrantz: To what end, my lord?

Hamlet: That you must teach me. But let me conjure° you, by the rights of
our fellowship, by the consonancy of our youth,° by the obligation of our
ever-preserved love, and by what more dear a better proposer° could   270
charge you withal, be even and direct with me, whether you were sent
for, or no?

Rosencrantz [aside to Guildenstern]: What say you?

Hamlet [aside]: Nay, then, I have an eye of you. — If you love me, hold not
off.   275

Guildenstern: My lord, we were sent for.

Hamlet: I will tell you why; so shall my anticipation prevent your discovery,° and your secrecy to the king and queen moult no feather. I have

---

237 *confines:* Places of confinement.   246–247 *very . . . ambitious:* That seemingly most substantial
thing which the ambitious pursue.   252 *fay:* Faith.   253 *reason:* Argue; *wait upon:* Accompany.
254 *sort:* Class.   255 *dreadfully attended:* Poorly provided with servants.   256 *in the . . . friendship:*
As a matter of course among friends.   259 *a:* I.e., at a.   268 *conjure:* Adjure, entreat.   269 *consonancy of our youth:* The fact that we are of the same age.   270 *better proposer:* One more skillful
in finding proposals.   278 *prevent your discovery:* Forestall your disclosure.

of late — but wherefore I know not — lost all my mirth, forgone all custom of exercises; and indeed it goes so heavily with my disposition 280 that this goodly frame, the earth, seems to me a sterile promontory, this most excellent canopy, the air, look you, this brave o'erhanging firmament, this majestical roof fretted° with golden fire, why, it appeareth nothing to me but a foul and pestilent congregation of vapours. What a piece of work is a man! how noble in reason! how infinite in faculties!° 285 in form and moving how express° and admirable! in action how like an angel! in apprehension° how like a god! the beauty of the world! the paragon of animals! And yet, to me, what is this quintessence° of dust? man delights not me: no, nor woman neither, though by your smiling you seem to say so. 290

Rosencrantz: My lord, there was no such stuff in my thoughts.

Hamlet: Why did you laugh then, when I said "man delights not me"?

Rosencrantz: To think, my lord, if you delight not in man, what lenten° entertainment the players shall receive from you: we coted° them on the way; and hither are they coming, to offer you service. 295

Hamlet: He that plays the king shall be welcome; his majesty shall have tribute of me; the adventurous knight shall use his foil and target;° the lover shall not sigh gratis; the humorous man° shall end his part in peace; the clown shall make those laugh whose lungs are tickle o' the sere;° and the lady shall say her mind freely, or the blank verse shall 300 halt for 't.° What players are they?

Rosencrantz: Even those you were wont to take delight in, the tragedians of the city.

Hamlet: How chances it they travel? their residence,° both in reputation and profit, was better both ways. 305

Rosencrantz: I think their inhibition° comes by the means of the late innovation.°

Hamlet: Do they hold the same estimation they did when I was in the city? are they so followed?

Rosencrantz: No, indeed, are they not. 310

Hamlet: How comes it? do they grow rusty?

Rosencrantz: Nay, their endeavour keeps in the wonted pace: but there is, sir, an aery° of children, little eyases,° that cry out on the top of question,° and are most tyrannically° clapped for 't: these are now the fashion, and so berattle° the common stages° — so they call them — that 315

283 *fretted:* Adorned.   285 *faculties:* Capacity.   286 *express:* Well-framed (?), exact (?).   287 *apprehension:* Understanding.   288 *quintessence:* The fifth essence of ancient philosophy, supposed to be the substance of the heavenly bodies and to be latent in all things.   293 *lenten:* Meager.   294 *coted:* Overtook and passed beyond.   297 *foil and target:* Sword and shield.   298 *humorous man:* Actor who takes the part of the humor characters.   299–300 *tickle o' the sere:* Easy on the trigger.   300–301 *the lady ... for 't:* The lady (fond of talking) shall have opportunity to talk, blank verse or no blank verse.   304 *residence:* Remaining in one place.   306 *inhibition:* Formal prohibition (from acting plays in the city or, possibly, at court).   307 *innovation:* The new fashion in satirical plays performed by boy actors in the "private" theaters.   311–331 *How ... load too:* The passage is the famous one dealing with the War of the Theatres (1599–1602); namely, the rivalry between the children's companies and the adult actors.   313 *aery:* Nest; *eyases:* Young hawks.   313–314 *cry ... question:* Speak in a high key dominating conversation; clamor forth the height of controversy; probably "excel" (cf. l. 459); perhaps intended to decry leaders of the dramatic profession.   314 *tyrannically:* Outrageously.   315 *berattle:* Berate; *common stages:* Public theaters.

many wearing rapiers° are afraid of goose-quills° and dare scarce come
thither.

Hamlet: What, are they children? who maintains 'em? how are they escoted?° Will they pursue the quality° no longer than they can sing?°
will they not say afterwards, if they should grow themselves to com- 320
mon° players — as it is most like, if their means are no better — their
writers do them wrong, to make them exclaim against their own succession?°

Rosencrantz: 'Faith, there has been much to do on both sides; and the nation
holds it no sin to tarre° them to controversy: there was, for a while, no 325
money bid for argument,° unless the poet and the player went to cuffs°
in the question.°

Hamlet: Is't possible?

Guildenstern: O, there has been much throwing about of brains.

Hamlet: Do the boys carry it away?° 330

Rosencrantz: Ay, that they do, my lord; Hercules and his load° too.

Hamlet: It is not very strange; for my uncle is king of Denmark, and those
that would make mows° at him while my father lived, give twenty, forty,
fifty, a hundred ducats° a-piece for his picture in little.° 'Sblood, there is
something in this more than natural, if philosophy could find it out. 335

A flourish [of trumpets within].

Guildenstern: There are the players.

Hamlet: Gentlemen, you are welcome to Elsinore. Your hands, come then:
the appurtenance of welcome is fashion and ceremony: let me comply°
with you in this garb,° lest my extent° to the players, which, I tell you,
must show fairly outwards, should more appear like entertainment than 340
yours. You are welcome: but my uncle-father and aunt-mother are deceived.

Guildenstern: In what, my dear lord?

Hamlet: I am but mad north-north-west:° when the wind is southerly I know
a hawk from a handsaw.° 345

Enter Polonius.

Polonius: Well be with you, gentlemen!

Hamlet: Hark you, Guildenstern; and you too: at each ear a hearer: that great
baby you see there is not yet out of his swaddling-clouts.°

Rosencrantz: Happily he is the second time come to them; for they say an
old man is twice a child. 350

316 *many wearing rapiers:* Many men of fashion, who were afraid to patronize the common players
for fear of being satirized by the poets who wrote for the children; *goose-quills:* I.e., pens of satirists.
319 *escoted:* Maintained.   *quality:* Acting profession; *no longer . . . sing:* I.e., until their voices change.
321 *common:* Regular, adult.   323 *succession:* future careers.   325 *tarre:* Set on (as dogs).
326 *argument:* Probably, plot for a play; *went to cuffs:* Came to blows.   327 *question:* Controversy.
330 *carry it away:* Win the day.   331 *Hercules . . . load:* Regarded as an allusion to the sign of the
Globe Theatre, which was Hercules bearing the world on his shoulder.   333 *mows:* Grimaces.
334 *ducats:* Gold coins worth 9s. 4d; *in little:* In miniature.   338 *comply:* Observe the formalities of
courtesy.   339 *garb:* Manner; *extent:* Showing of kindness.   344 *I am . . . north-north-west:* I am
only partly mad, i.e., in only one point of the compass.   345 *handsaw:* A proposed reading of
hernshaw would mean "heron"; *handsaw* may be an early corruption of *hernshaw*. Another view
regards *hawk* as the variant of *hack*, a tool of the pickax type, and *handsaw* as a saw operated by hand.
348 *swaddling-clouts:* Cloths in which to wrap a newborn baby.

Hamlet: I will prophesy he comes to tell me of the players; mark it. — You
  say right, sir: o' Monday morning;° 'twas then indeed.
Polonius: My lord, I have news to tell you.
Hamlet: My lord, I have news to tell you. When Roscius° was an actor in
  Rome, —   355
Polonius: The actors are come hither, my lord.
Hamlet: Buz, buz!°
Polonius: Upon my honour, —
Hamlet: Then came each actor on his ass, —
Polonius: The best actors in the world, either for tragedy, comedy, history, 360
  pastoral, pastoral-comical, historical-pastoral, tragical-historical, tragical-
  comical-historical-pastoral, scene individable,° or poem unlimited:° Se-
  neca° cannot be too heavy, nor Plautus° too light. For the law of writ and
  the liberty,° these are the only men.
Hamlet: O Jephthah, judge of Israel,° what a treasure hadst thou!   365
Polonius: What a treasure had he, my lord?
Hamlet: Why,
  "One fair daughter, and no more,
     The which he loved passing well."
Polonius [aside]: Still on my daughter.   370
Hamlet: Am I not i' the right, old Jephthah?
Polonius: If you call me Jephthah, my lord, I have a daughter that I love
  passing° well.
Hamlet: Nay, that follows not.
Polonius: What follows, then, my lord?   375
Hamlet: Why,
        "As by lot, God wot,"
  and then, you know,
  "It came to pass, as most like° it was," —
  the first row° of the pious chanson° will show you more; for look, where
  my abridgement comes.°   380

Enter the Players.

  You are welcome, masters; welcome, all. I am glad to see thee well.
  Welcome, good friends. O, old friend! why, thy face is valanced° since I
  saw thee last: comest thou to beard me in Denmark? What, my young
  lady and mistress! By'r lady, your ladyship is nearer to heaven than when
  I saw you last, by the altitude of a chopine.° Pray God, your voice, like a 385
  piece of uncurrent° gold, be not cracked within the ring.° Masters, you

352 *o' Monday morning:* Said to mislead Polonius.   354 *Roscius:* A famous Roman actor.
357 *Buz, buz:* An interjection used at Oxford to denote stale news.   362 *scene individable:* A play
observing the unity of place; *poem unlimited:* A play disregarding the unities of time and place.
363 *Seneca:* Writer of Latin tragedies, model of early Elizabethan writers of tragedy.   *Plautus:* Writer
of Latin comedy.   363–364 *law ... liberty:* Pieces written according to rules and without rules, i.e.,
"classical" and "romantic" dramas.   365 *Jephthah ... Israel:* Jephthah had to sacrifice his daughter;
see Judges 11.   373 *Passing:* Surpassingly.   378 *like:* Probable.   379 *row:* Stanza; *chanson:* Ballad.   380 *abridgement comes:* Opportunity comes for cutting short the conversation.   382 *va-
lanced:* Fringed (with a beard).   385 *chopine:* Kind of shoe raised by the thickness of the heel; worn
in Italy, particularly at Venice.   386 *uncurrent:* Not passable as lawful coinage; *cracked within the
ring:* In the center of coins were rings enclosing the sovereign's head; if the coin was cracked within
this ring, it was unfit for currency.

are all welcome. We'll e'en to 't like French falconers, fly at any thing we see: we'll have a speech straight: come, give us a taste of your quality; come, a passionate speech.   390

First Player: What speech, my good lord?

Hamlet: I heard thee speak me a speech once, but it was never acted; or, if it was, not above once; for the play, I remember, pleased not the million; 'twas caviary to the general:° but it was — as I received it, and others, whose judgements in such matters cried in the top of° mine — an excellent play, well digested in the scenes, set down with as much mod-   395 esty as cunning.° I remember, one said there were no sallets° in the lines to make the matter savoury, nor no matter in the phrase that might indict° the author of affectation; but called it an honest method, as wholesome as sweet, and by very much more handsome than fine.° One speech in 't I chiefly loved: 'twas Æneas' tale to Dido;° and thereabout of   400 it especially, where he speaks of Priam's slaughter: if it live in your memory, begin at this line: let me see, let me see —
"The rugged Pyrrhus,° like th' Hyrcanian beast,°" —
'tis not so: — it begins with Pyrrhus: —
"The rugged Pyrrhus, he whose sable arms,   405
Black as his purpose, did the night resemble
When he lay couched in the ominous horse,°
Hath now this dread and black complexion smear'd
With heraldry more dismal; head to foot
Now is he total gules;° horridly trick'd°   410
With blood of fathers, mothers, daughters, sons,
Bak'd and impasted° with the parching streets,
That lend a tyrannous and a damned light
To their lord's murder: roasted in wrath and fire,
And thus o'er-sized° with coagulate gore,   415
With eyes like carbuncles, the hellish Pyrrhus
Old grandsire Priam seeks."
So, proceed you.

Polonius: 'Fore God, my lord, well spoken, with good accent and good discretion.

First Player: "Anon he finds him   420
Striking too short at Greeks; his antique sword,
Rebellious to his arm, lies where it falls,
Repugnant° to command: unequal match'd,
Pyrrhus at Priam drives; in rage strikes wide;
But with the whiff and wind of his fell sword   425

---

393 *caviary to the general:* Not relished by the multitude.   394 *cried in the top of:* Spoke with greater authority than.   396 *cunning:* Skill; *sallets:* Salads: here, spicy improprieties.   398 *indict:* Convict. 399 *as wholesome ... fine:* Its beauty was not that of elaborate ornament, but that of order and proportion.   400 *Æneas' tale to Dido:* The lines recited by the player are imitated from Marlowe and Nashe's *Dido Queen of Carthage* (II. i. 214 ff.). They are written in such a way that the conventionality of the play within a play is raised above that of ordinary drama.   403 *Pyrrhus:* A Greek hero in the Trojan War; *Hyrcanian beast:* The tiger; see Virgil, *Aeneid,* IV. 266.   407 *ominous horse:* Trojan horse. 410 *gules:* Red, a heraldic term; *trick'd:* Spotted, smeared.   412 *impasted:* Made into a paste. 415 *o'er-sized:* Covered as with size or glue.   423 *Repugnant:* Disobedient.

Th' unnerved father falls. Then senseless Ilium,°
Seeming to feel this blow, with flaming top
Stoops to his base, and with a hideous crash
Takes prisoner Pyrrhus' ear: for, lo! his sword
Which was declining on the milky head   430
Of reverend Priam, seem'd i' th' air to stick:
So, as a painted tyrant,° Pyrrhus stood,
And like a neutral to his will and matter,°
Did nothing.
But, as we often see, against° some storm,   435
A silence in the heavens, the rack° stand still,
The bold winds speechless and the orb below
As hush as death, anon the dreadful thunder
Doth rend the region,° so, after Pyrrhus' pause,
Aroused vengeance sets him new a-work;   440
And never did the Cyclops' hammers fall
On Mars's armour forg'd for proof eterne°
With less remorse than Pyrrhus' bleeding sword
Now falls on Priam.
Out, out, thou strumpet, Fortune! All you gods,   445
In general synod,° take away her power;
Break all the spokes and fellies° from her wheel,
And bowl the round nave° down the hill of heaven,
As low as to the fiends!"
Polonius: This is too long.   450
Hamlet: It shall to the barber's, with your beard. Prithee, say on: he's for a
    jig° or a tale of bawdry,° or he sleeps: say on: come to Hecuba.°
First Player: "But who, ah woe! had seen the mobled° queen — "
Hamlet: "The mobled queen?"
Polonius: That's good; "mobled queen" is good.   455
First Player: "Run barefoot up and down, threat'ning the flames
    With bisson rheum;° a clout° upon that head
    Where late the diadem stood, and for a robe,
    About her lank and all o'er-teemed° loins,
    A blanket, in the alarm of fear caught up;   460
    Who this had seen, with tongue in venom steep'd,
    'Gainst Fortune's state would treason have pronounc'd:°
    But if the gods themselves did see her then
    When she saw Pyrrhus make malicious sport
    In mincing with his sword her husband's limbs,   465
    The instant burst of clamour that she made,
    Unless things mortal move them not at all,

426 *Then senseless Ilium:* Insensate Troy.   432 *painted tyrant:* Tyrant in a picture.   433 *matter:*
Task.   435 *against:* Before.   436 *rack:* Mass of clouds.   439 *region:* Assembly.   442 *proof
eterne:* External resistance to assault.   446 *synod:* Assembly.   447 *fellies:* Pieces of wood forming
the rim of a wheel.   448 *nave:* Hub.   452 *jig:* Comic performance given at the end or in an interval
of a play; *bawdry:* Indecency; *Hecuba:* Wife of Priam, king of Troy.   453 *mobled:* Muffled.   457 *bis-
son rheum:* Blinding tears; *clout:* Piece of cloth.   459 *o'er-teemed:* Worn out with bearing children.
462 *pronounc'd:* Proclaimed.

Would have made milch° the burning eyes of heaven,
And passion in the gods."

Polonius: Look, whe'r he has not turned° his colour and has tears in 's eyes. 470
Prithee, no more.

Hamlet: 'Tis well; I'll have thee speak out the rest soon. Good my lord, will
you see the players well bestowed? Do you hear, let them be well used;
for they are the abstract° and brief chronicles of the time: after your
death you were better have a bad epitaph than their ill report while you 475
live.

Polonius: My lord, I will use them according to their desert.

Hamlet: God's bodykins,° man, much better: use every man after his desert,
and who shall 'scape whipping? Use them after your own honour and
dignity: the less they deserve, the more merit is in your bounty. Take 480
them in.

Polonius: Come, sirs.

Hamlet: Follow him, friends: we'll hear a play tomorrow. *[Aside to First
Player.]* Dost thou hear me, old friend; can you play the Murder of
Gonzago? 485

First Player: Ay, my lord.

Hamlet: We'll ha 't to-morrow night. You could, for a need, study a speech
of some dozen or sixteen lines,° which I would set down and insert in 't,
could you not?

First Player: Ay, my lord. 490

Hamlet: Very well. Follow that lord; and look you mock him not. — My good
friends, I'll leave you till night: you are welcome to Elsinore.

                          Exeunt Polonius and Players.

Rosencrantz: Good my lord!   *Exeunt [Rosencrantz and Guildenstern.]*

Hamlet: Ay, so, God bye to you. — Now I am alone.
O, what a rogue and peasant° slave am I! 495
Is it not monstrous that this player here,
But in a fiction, in a dream of passion,
Could force his soul so to his own conceit
That from her working all his visage wann'd,°
Tears in his eyes, distraction in 's aspect, 500
A broken voice, and his whole function suiting
With forms to his conceit?° and all for nothing!
For Hecuba!
What's Hecuba to him, or he to Hecuba,
That he should weep for her? What would he do, 505
Had he the motive and the cue for passion
That I have? He would drown the stage with tears
And cleave the general ear with horrid speech,
Make mad the guilty and appall the free,
Confound the ignorant, and amaze indeed 510

---

468 *milch:* Moist with tears.   470 *turned:* Changed.   474 *abstract:* Summary account.
478 *bodykins:* Diminutive form of the oath "by God's body."   488 *dozen or sixteen lines:* Critics have
amused themselves by trying to locate Hamlet's lines. Lucianus's speech III. ii. 226–231 is the best guess.
495 *peasant:* Base.   499 *wann'd:* Grew pale.   501–502 *his whole ... conceit:* His whole being
responded with forms to suit his thought.

The very faculties of eyes and ears.
Yet I,
A dull and muddy-mettled° rascal, peak,°
Like John-a-dreams,° unpregnant of° my cause,
And can say nothing; no, not for a king.   515
Upon whose property° and most dear life
A damn'd defeat was made. Am I a coward?
Who calls me villain? breaks my pate across?
Plucks off my beard, and blows it in my face?
Tweaks me by the nose? gives me the lie i' th' throat,   520
As deep as to the lungs? who does me this?
Ha!
'Swounds, I should take it: for it cannot be
But I am pigeon-liver'd° and lack gall
To make oppression bitter, or ere this   525
I should have fatted all the region kites°
With this slave's offal: bloody, bawdy villain!
Remorseless, treacherous, lecherous, kindless° villain!
O, vengeance!
Why, what an ass am I! This is most brave,   530
That I, the son of a dear father murder'd,
Prompted to my revenge by heaven and hell,
Must, like a whore, unpack my heart with words,
And fall a-cursing, like a very drab,°
A stallion!°   535
Fie upon 't! foh! About,° my brains! Hum, I have heard
That guilty creatures sitting at a play
Have by the very cunning of the scene
Been struck so to the soul that presently
They have proclaim'd their malefactions;   540
For murder, though it have no tongue, will speak
With most miraculous organ. I'll have these players
Play something like the murder of my father
Before mine uncle: I'll observe his looks:
I'll tent° him to the quick: if 'a do blench,°   545
I know my course. The spirit that I have seen
May be the devil:° and the devil hath power
T' assume a pleasing shape; yea, and perhaps
Out of my weakness and my melancholy,
As he is very potent with such spirits,°   550
Abuses me to damn me: I'll have grounds

---

513 *muddy-mettled:* Dull-spirited; *peak:* Mope, pine.   514 *John-a-dreams:* An expression occurring
elsewhere in Elizabethan literature to indicate a dreamer; *unpregnant of:* Not quickened by.
516 *property:* Proprietorship (of crown and life).   524 *pigeon-liver'd:* The pigeon was supposed to
secrete no gall; if Hamlet, so he says, had had gall, he would have felt the bitterness of oppression,
and avenged it.   526 *region kites:* Kites of the air.   528 *kindless:* Unnatural.   534 *drab:* Prostitute.
535 *stallion:* Prostitute (male or female).   536 *About:* About it, or turn thou right about.   545 *tent:*
Probe; *blench:* Quail, flinch.   547 *May be the devil:* Hamlet's suspicion is properly grounded in the
belief of the time.   550 *spirits:* Humors.

More relative° than this:° the play's the thing
Wherein I'll catch the conscience of the king.   *Exit.*

[ACT III

Scene I: *A room in the castle.*]

Enter King, Queen, Polonius, Ophelia, Rosencrantz, Guildenstern, Lords.

King: And can you, by no drift of conference,°
  Get from him why he puts on this confusion,
  Grating so harshly all his days of quiet
  With turbulent and dangerous lunacy?
Rosencrantz: He does confess he feels himself distracted;   5
  But from what cause 'a will by no means speak.
Guildenstern: Nor do we find him forward° to be sounded,
  But, with a crafty madness, keeps aloof,
  When we would bring him on to some confession
  Of his true state.
Queen: Did he receive you well?   10
Rosencrantz: Most like a gentleman.
Guildenstern: But with much forcing of his disposition.°
Rosencrantz: Niggard of question;° but, of our demands,
  Most free in his reply.
Queen: Did you assay° him
  To any pastime?   15
Rosencrantz: Madam, it so fell out, that certain players
  We o'er-raught° on the way: of these we told him;
  And there did seem in him a kind of joy
  To hear of it: they are here about the court,
  And, as I think, they have already order   20
  This night to play before him.
Polonius: 'Tis most true:
  And he beseech'd me to entreat your majesties
  To hear and see the matter.
King: With all my heart; and it doth much content me
  To hear him so inclin'd.   25
  Good gentlemen, give him a further edge,°
  And drive his purpose into these delights.
Rosencrantz: We shall, my lord.   *Exeunt Rosencrantz and Guildenstern.*
King: Sweet Gertrude, leave us too;
  For we have closely° sent for Hamlet hither,
  That he, as 'twere by accident, may here   30
  Affront° Ophelia:

552 *relative:* Closely related, definite; *this:* I.e., the ghost's story.   Act III. Scene I.   1 *drift of conference:* Device of conversation.   7 *forward:* Willing.   12 *forcing of his disposition:* I.e., against his
will.   13 *Niggard of question:* Sparing of conversation.   14 *assay:* Try to win.   17 *o'er-raught:*
Overtook.   26 *edge:* Incitement.   29 *closely:* Secretly.   31 *Affront:* Confront.

Her father and myself, lawful espials,°
Will so bestow ourselves that, seeing, unseen,
We may of their encounter frankly judge,
And gather by him, as he is behav'd,   35
If 't be th' affliction of his love or no
That thus he suffers for.
Queen: I shall obey you.
And for your part, Ophelia, I do wish
That your good beauties be the happy cause
Of Hamlet's wildness:° so shall I hope your virtues   40
Will bring him to his wonted way again,
To both your honours.
Ophelia: Madam, I wish it may.   [Exit Queen.]
Polonius: Ophelia, walk you here. Gracious,° so please you,
We will bestow ourselves. [To Ophelia.] Read on this book;
That show of such an exercise° may colour°   45
Your loneliness. We are oft to blame in this, —
'Tis too much prov'd — that with devotion's visage
And pious action we do sugar o'er
The devil himself.
King: [aside] O, 'tis too true!
How smart a lash that speech doth give my conscience!   50
The harlot's cheek, beautied with plast'ring art,
Is not more ugly to° the thing° that helps it
Than is my deed to my most painted word:
O heavy burthen!
Polonius: I hear him coming: let's withdraw, my lord.   55
                          [Exeunt King and Polonius.]

Enter Hamlet.

Hamlet: To be, or not to be: that is the question:
Whether 'tis nobler in the mind to suffer
The slings and arrows of outrageous fortune,
Or to take arms against a sea° of troubles,
And by opposing end them? To die: to sleep;   60
No more; and by a sleep to say we end
The heart-ache and the thousand natural shocks
That flesh is heir to, 'tis a consummation
Devoutly to be wish'd. To die, to sleep;
To sleep: perchance to dream: ay, there's the rub;   65
For in that sleep of death what dreams may come
When we have shuffled° off this mortal coil,°
Must give us pause: there's the respect°

32 *lawful espials:* Legitimate spies.   40 *wildness:* Madness.   43 *Gracious:* Your grace (addressed
to the king).   45 *exercise:* Act of devotion (the book she reads is one of devotion); *colour:* Give a
plausible appearance to.   52 *to:* Compared to; *thing:* I.e., the cosmetic.   59 *sea:* The mixed metaphor of this speech has often been commented on; a later emendation *siege* has sometimes been
spoken on the stage.   67 *shuffled:* Sloughed, cast; *coil:* Usually means "turmoil"; here, possibly "body"
(conceived of as wound about the soul like rope); *clay, soil, veil,* have been suggested as emendations.
68 *respect:* Consideration.

That makes calamity of so long life;°
For who would bear the whips and scorns of time,° 70
Th' oppressor's wrong, the proud man's contumely,
The pangs of despis'd° love, the law's delay,
The insolence of office° and the spurns°
That patient merit of th' unworthy takes,
When he himself might his quietus° make 75
With a bare bodkin?° who would fardels° bear,
To grunt and sweat under a weary life,
But that the dread of something after death,
The undiscover'd country from whose bourn°
No traveller returns, puzzles the will 80
And makes us rather bear those ills we have
Than fly to others that we know not of?
Thus conscience° does make cowards of us all;
And thus the native hue° of resolution
Is sicklied o'er° with the pale cast° of thought, 85
And enterprises of great pitch° and moment°
With this regard° their currents° turn awry,
And lose the name of action — Soft you now!
The fair Ophelia! Nymph, in thy orisons°
Be all my sins rememb'red.
Ophelia: Good my lord, 90
How does your honour for this many a day?
Hamlet: I humbly thank you; well, well, well.
Ophelia: My lord, I have remembrances of yours,
That I have longed long to re-deliver;
I pray you, now receive them.
Hamlet: No, not I; 95
I never gave you aught.
Ophelia: My honour'd lord, you know right well you did;
And, with them, words of so sweet breath compos'd
As made the things more rich: their perfume lost,
Take these again; for to the noble mind 100
Rich gifts wax poor when givers prove unkind.
There, my lord.
Hamlet: Ha, ha! are you honest?
Ophelia: My lord?
Hamlet: Are you fair? 105
Ophelia: What means your lordship?

---

69 *of . . . life:* So long-lived. 70 *time:* The world. 72 *despis'd:* Rejected. 73 *office:* Office-hold-
ers; *spurns:* Insults. 75 *quietus:* Acquittance; here, death. 76 *bare bodkin:* Mere dagger; *bare* is
sometimes understood as "unsheathed;" *fardels:* Burdens. 79 *bourn:* Boundary. 83 *conscience:*
Probably, inhibition by the faculty of reason restraining the will from doing wrong. 84 *native hue:*
Natural color; metaphor derived from the color of the face. 85 *sicklied o'er,* Given a sickly tinge;
cast: Shade of color. 86 *pitch:* Height (as of a falcon's flight); *moment:* Importance. 87 *regard:*
Respect, consideration; *currents:* Courses. 89 *orisons:* Prayers. 103–8 *are you . . . beauty: Honest*
meaning "truthful" and "chaste" and *fair* meaning "just, honorable" (l. 107) and "beautiful" (l. 108) are
not mere quibbles; the speech has the irony of a *double entendre.*

Hamlet: That if you be honest and fair, your honesty° should admit no discourse to° your beauty.

Ophelia: Could beauty, my lord, have better commerce° than with honesty?

Hamlet: Ay, truly; for the power of beauty will sooner transform honesty from 110 what it is to a bawd than the force of honesty can translate beauty into his likeness: this was sometime a paradox, but now the time° gives it proof. I did love you once.

Ophelia: Indeed, my lord, you made me believe so.

Hamlet: You should not have believed me; for virtue cannot so inoculate° 115 our old stock but we shall relish of it:° I loved you not.

Ophelia: I was the more deceived.

Hamlet: Get thee to a nunnery: why wouldst thou be a breeder of sinners? I am myself indifferent honest;° but yet I could accuse me of such things that it were better my mother had not borne me: I am very proud, 120 revengeful, ambitious, with more offences at my beck° than I have thoughts to put them in, imagination to give them shape, or time to act them in. What should such fellows as I do crawling between earth and heaven? We are arrant knaves, all; believe none of us. Go thy ways to a nunnery. Where's your father? 125

Ophelia: At home, my lord.

Hamlet: Let the doors be shut upon him, that he may play the fool no where but in 's own house. Farewell.

Ophelia: O, help him, you sweet heavens!

Hamlet: If thou dost marry, I'll give thee this plague for thy dowry: be thou 130 as chaste as ice, as pure as snow, thou shalt not escape calumny. Get thee to a nunnery, go: farewell. Or, if thou wilt needs marry, marry a fool; for wise men know well enough what monsters° you make of them. To a nunnery, go, and quickly too. Farewell.

Ophelia: O heavenly powers, restore him! 135

Hamlet: I have heard of your° paintings too, well enough; God hath given you one face, and you make yourselves another: you jig,° you amble, and you lisp; you nick-name God's creatures, and make your wantonness your ignorance.° Go to, I'll no more on 't; it hath made me mad. I say, we will have no moe marriage: those that are married already, all but one,° shall 140 live; the rest shall keep as they are. To a nunnery, go.

Exit.

Ophelia: O, what a noble mind is here o'er-thrown!
The courtier's, soldier's, scholar's, eye, tongue, sword;
Th' expectancy and rose° of the fair state,
The glass of fashion and the mould of form,° 145
Th' observ'd of all observers,° quite, quite down!

107 *your honesty:* Your chastity. 108 *discourse to:* Familiar intercourse with. 109 *commerce:* Intercourse. 112 *the time:* The present age. 115 *inoculate:* Graft (metaphorical). 116 *but . . . it:* I.e., that we do not still have about us a taste of the old stock; I.e., retain our sinfulness. 119 *indifferent honest:* Moderately virtuous. 121 *beck:* Command. 133 *monsters:* An allusion to the horns of a cuckold. 136 *your:* Indefinite use. 137 *jig:* Move with jerky motion; probably allusion to the *jig,* or song and dance, of the current stage. 138–139 *make . . . ignorance:* I.e., excuse your wantonness on the ground of your ignorance. 140 *one:* i.e., The king. 144 *expectancy and rose:* Source of hope. 145 *The glass . . . form:* The mirror of fashion and the pattern of courtly behavior. 146 *observ'd . . . observers:* I.e., the center of attention in the court.

And I, of ladies most deject and wretched,
That suck'd the honey of his music vows,
Now see that noble and most sovereign reason,
Like sweet bells jangled, out of time and harsh;   150
That unmatch'd form and feature of blown° youth
Blasted with ecstasy:° O, woe is me,
T' have seen what I have seen, see what I see!

Enter King and Polonius.

King: Love! his affections do not that way tend;
Nor what he spake, though it lack'd form a little,   155
Was not like madness. There's something in his soul,
O'er which his melancholy sits on brood;
And I do doubt° the hatch and the disclose°
Will be some danger: which for to prevent,
I have in quick determination   160
Thus set it down: he shall with speed to England,
For the demand of our neglected tribute:
Haply the seas and countries different
With variable° objects shall expel
This something-settled° matter in his heart,   165
Whereon his brains still beating puts him thus
From fashion of himself.° What think you on 't?
Polonius: It shall do well: but yet do I believe
The origin and commencement of his grief
Sprung from neglected love. How now, Ophelia!   170
You need not tell us what Lord Hamlet said;
We heard it all. My lord, do as you please;
But, if you hold it fit, after the play
Let his queen mother all alone entreat him
To show his grief: let her be round° with him;   175
And I'll be plac'd, so please you, in the ear
Of all their conference. If she find him not,
To England send him, or confine him where
Your wisdom best shall think.
King: It shall be so:
Madness in great ones must not unwatch'd go.   *Exeunt.*   180

[Scene II: *A hall in the castle.*]

Enter Hamlet and three of the Players.

Hamlet: Speak the speech, I pray you, as I pronounced it to you, trippingly
on the tongue: but if you mouth it, as many of your° players do, I had as
lief the town-crier spoke my lines. Nor do not saw the air too much with
your hand, thus, but use all gently; for in the very torrent, tempest, and,

151 *blown:* Blooming. 152 *ecstasy:* Madness. 158 *doubt:* Fear; *disclose:* Disclosure or revelation
(by chipping of the shell). 164 *variable:* Various. 165 *something-settled:* Somewhat settled.
167 *From ... himself:* Out of his natural manner. 175 *round:* Blunt. Scene II. 2 *your:* Indefinite use.

as I may say, whirlwind of your passion, you must acquire and beget a   5
temperance that may give it smoothness. O, it offends me to the soul to
hear a robustious° periwig-pated° fellow tear a passion to tatters, to very
rags, to split the ears of the groundlings,° who for the most part are
capable of° nothing but inexplicable° dumb-shows and noise: I would
have such a fellow whipped for o'er-doing Termagant;° it out-herods   10
Herod:° pray you, avoid it.

First Player: I warrant your honour.

Hamlet: Be not too tame neither, but let your own discretion be your tutor:
suit the action to the word, the word to the action; with this special
observance, that you o'er-step not the modesty of nature: for any thing   15
so overdone is from the purpose of playing, whose end, both at the first
and now, was and is, to hold, as 't were, the mirror up to nature; to show
virtue her own feature, scorn her own image, and the very age and body
of the time his form and pressure.° Now this overdone, or come tardy
off,° though it make the unskilful laugh, cannot but make the judicious   20
grieve; the censure of the which one° must in your allowance o'erweigh
a whole theatre of others. O, there be players that I have seen play, and
heard others praise, and that highly, not to speak it profanely, that, neither
having the accent of Christians nor the gait of Christian, pagan, nor man,
have so strutted and bellowed that I have thought some of nature's   25
journeymen° had made men and not made them well, they imitated
humanity so abominably.

First Player: I hope we have reformed that indifferently° with us, sir.

Hamlet: O, reform it altogether. And let those that play your clowns speak
no more than is set down for them; for there be of° them that will   30
themselves laugh, to set on some quantity of barren° spectators to laugh
too; though, in the mean time, some necessary question of the play be
then to be considered: that's villanous, and shows a most pitiful ambition in the fool that uses it. Go, make you ready.

[Exeunt Players.]

Enter Polonius, Guildenstern, and Rosencrantz.

How now, my lord! will the king hear this piece of work?   35

Polonius: And the queen too, and that presently.

Hamlet: Bid the players make haste.   *[Exit Polonius.]*

Will you two help to hasten them?

Rosencrantz: }
Guildenstern: } We will, my lord.   *Exeunt they two.*

Hamlet: What ho! Horatio!

Enter Horatio.

7 *robustious:* Violent, boisterous; *periwig-pated:* Wearing a wig.   8 *groundlings:* Those who stood in
the yard of the theater.   9 *capable of:* Susceptible of being influenced by; *inexplicable:* Of no
significance worth explaining.   10 *Termagant:* A god of the Saracens; a character in the St. Nicholas
play, where one of his worshipers, leaving him in charge of goods, returns to find them stolen;
whereupon he beats the god (or idol), which howls vociferously.   11 *Herod:* Herod of Jewry; a
character in *The Slaughter of the Innocents* and other cycle plays. The part was played with great noise
and fury.   19 *pressure:* Stamp, impressed character.   19–20 *come tardy off:* Inadequately done.
21 *the censure ... one:* The judgment of even one of whom.   26 *journeymen:* Laborers not yet
masters in their trade.   28 *indifferently:* Fairly, tolerably.   30 *of:* i.e., Some among them.   31 *barren:* I.e., of wit.

Horatio: Here, sweet lord, at your service.   40

Hamlet: Horatio, thou art e'en as just° a man
    As e'er my conversation cop'd withal.

Horatio: O, my dear lord, —

Hamlet: Nay, do not think I flatter;
    For what advancement may I hope from thee
    That no revenue hast but thy good spirits,   45
    To feed and clothe thee? Why should the poor be flatter'd?
    No, let the candied tongue lick absurd pomp,
    And crook the pregnant° hinges of the knee
    Where thrift° may follow fawning. Dost thou hear?
    Since my dear soul was mistress of her choice   50
    And could of men distinguish her election,
    S' hath seal'd thee for herself; for thou hast been
    As one, in suff'ring all, that suffers nothing,
    A man that fortune's buffets and rewards
    Hast ta'en with equal thanks: and blest are those   55
    Whose blood and judgement are so well commeddled,
    That they are not a pipe for fortune's finger
    To sound what stop° she please. Give me that man
    That is not passion's slave, and I will wear him
    In my heart's core, ay, in my heart of heart,   60
    As I do thee. — Something too much of this. —
    There is a play to-night before the king;
    One scene of it comes near the circumstance
    Which I have told thee of my father's death:
    I prithee, when thou seest that act afoot,   65
    Even with the very comment of thy soul°
    Observe my uncle: if his occulted° guilt
    Do not itself unkennel in one speech,
    It is a damned° ghost that we have seen,
    And my imaginations are as foul   70
    As Vulcan's stithy.° Give him heedful note;
    For I mine eyes will rivet to his face,
    And after we will both our judgements join
    In censure of his seeming.°

Horatio: Well, my lord:
    If 'a steal aught the whilst this play is playing,   75
    And 'scape detecting, I will pay the theft.

Enter trumpets and kettledrums, King, Queen, Polonius, Ophelia, [Rosencrantz, Guildenstern, and others].

Hamlet: They are coming to the play; I must be idle:° Get you a place.

King: How fares our cousin Hamlet?

41 *just:* Honest, honorable.   48 *pregnant:* Pliant.   49 *thrift:* profit.   58 *stop:* Hole in a wind instrument for controlling the sound.   66 *very . . . soul:* Inward and sagacious criticism.   67 *occulted:* Hidden.   69 *damned:* In league with Satan.   71 *stithy:* Smithy, place of *stiths* (anvils).   74 *censure . . . seeming:* Judgment of his appearance or behavior.   77 *idle:* Crazy, or not attending to anything serious.

Hamlet: Excellent, i' faith; of the chameleon's dish:° I eat the air, promise-crammed: you cannot feed capons so.   80

King: I have nothing with° this answer, Hamlet; these words are not mine.°

Hamlet: No, nor mine now. *[To Polonius.]* My lord, you played once i' the university, you say?

Polonius: That did I, my lord; and was accounted a good actor.

Hamlet: What did you enact?   85

Polonius: I did enact Julius Cæsar: I was killed i' the Capitol; Brutus killed me.

Hamlet: It was a brute part of him to kill so capital a calf there. Be the players ready?

Rosencrantz: Ay, my lord; they stay upon your patience.   90

Queen: Come hither, my dear Hamlet, sit by me.

Hamlet: No, good mother, here's metal more attractive.

Polonius [to the king]: O, ho! do you mark that?

Hamlet: Lady, shall I lie in your lap?

                            [Lying down at Ophelia's feet.]

Ophelia: No, my lord.   95

Hamlet: I mean, my head upon your lap?

Ophelia: Ay, my lord.

Hamlet: Do you think I meant country° matters?

Ophelia: I think nothing, my lord.

Hamlet: That's a fair thought to lie between maids' legs.   100

Ophelia: What is, my lord?

Hamlet: Nothing.

Ophelia: You are merry, my lord.

Hamlet: Who, I?

Ophelia: Ay, my lord.   105

Hamlet: O God, your only° jig-maker.° What should a man do but be merry? for, look you, how cheerfully my mother looks, and my father died within's two hours.

Ophelia: Nay, 'tis twice two months, my lord.

Hamlet: So long? Nay then, let the devil wear black, for I'll have a suit of   110 sables.° O heavens! die two months ago, and not forgotten yet? Then there's hope a great man's memory may outlive his life half a year: but, by 'r lady, 'a must build churches, then; or else shall 'a suffer not thinking on,° with the hobbyhorse, whose epitaph is "For, O, for, O, the hobby-horse is forgot."°   115

The trumpets sound. Dumb show follows.
    Enter a King and a Queen [very lovingly]; the Queen embracing him, and he her. [She kneels, and makes show of protestation unto him.] He takes her up, and

---

79 *chameleon's dish:* Chameleons were supposed to feed on air. (Hamlet deliberately misinterprets the king's "fares" as "feeds.")   81 *have ... with:* Make nothing of; *are not mine:* Do not respond to what I asked.   98 *country:* With a bawdy pun.   106 *your only:* Only your; *jig-maker:* Composer of jigs (song and dance).   110–111 *suit of sables:* Garments trimmed with the fur of the sable, with a quibble on *sable* meaning "black."   113–114 *suffer ... on:* Undergo oblivion.   114–115 "*For ... forgot*": Verse of a song occurring also in *Love's Labour's Lost,* III. i. 30. The hobbyhorse was a character in the Morris Dance.

declines his head upon her neck: he lies him down upon a bank of flowers: she, seeing him asleep, leaves him. Anon comes in another man, takes off his crown, kisses it, pours poison in the sleeper's ears, and leaves him. The Queen returns; finds the King dead, makes passionate action. The Poisoner, with some three or four come in again, seem to condole with her. The dead body is carried away. The Poisoner wooes the Queen with gifts: she seems harsh awhile, but in the end accepts love. [Exeunt.]

Ophelia: What means this, my lord?
Hamlet: Marry, this is miching mallecho;° it means mischief.
Ophelia: Belike this show imports the argument of the play.

Enter Prologue.

Hamlet: We shall know by this fellow: the players cannot keep counsel; they'll
    tell all.   120
Ophelia: Will 'a tell us what this show meant?
Hamlet: Ay, or any show that you'll show him: be not you ashamed to show,
    he'll not shame to tell you what it means.
Ophelia: You are naught, you are naught:° I'll mark the play.
Prologue: For us, and for our tragedy,   125
    Here stooping° to your clemency,
    We beg your hearing patiently.   *[Exit.]*
Hamlet: Is this a prologue, or the posy° of a ring?
Ophelia: 'Tis brief, my lord.
Hamlet: As woman's love.   130

Enter [two Players as] King and Queen.

Player King: Full thirty times hath Phoebus' cart gone round
    Neptune's salt wash° and Tellus'° orbed ground,
    And thirty dozen moons with borrowed° sheen
    About the world have times twelve thirties been,
    Since love our hearts and Hymen° did our hands   135
    Unite commutual° in most sacred bands.
Player Queen: So many journeys may the sun and moon
    Make us again count o'er ere love be done!
    But, woe is me, you are so sick of late,
    So far from cheer and from your former state,   140
    That I distrust° you. Yet, though I distrust,
    Discomfort you, my lord, it nothing must:
    For women's fear and love holds quantity;°
    In neither aught, or in extremity.
    Now, what my love is, proof hath made you know;   145
    And as my love is siz'd, my fear is so:
    Where love is great, the littlest doubts are fear;
    Where little fears grow great, great love grows there.
Player King: 'Faith, I must leave thee, love, and shortly too;

117 *miching mallecho:* Sneaking mischief.   124 *naught:* Indecent.   126 *stooping:* Bowing.
128 *posy:* Motto.   132 *salt wash:* The sea; *Tellus:* Goddess of the earth *(orbed ground).*   133 *borrowed:* I.e., reflected.   135 *Hymen:* God of matrimony.   136 *commutual:* Mutually.   141 *distrust:* Am anxious about.   143 *holds quantity:* Keeps proportion between.

My operant° powers their functions leave° to do: 150
And thou shalt live in this fair world behind,
Honour'd, belov'd; and haply one as kind
For husband shalt thou —
Player Queen: O, confound the rest!
Such love must needs be treason in my breast:
In second husband let me be accurst!   155
None wed the second but who kill'd the first.
Hamlet (aside): Wormwood, wormwood.
Player Queen: The instances that second marriage move
Are base respects of thrift, but none of love:
A second time I kill my husband dead,   160
When second husband kisses me in bed.
Player King: I do believe you think what now you speak;
But what we do determine oft we break.
Purpose is but the slave to memory,
Of violent birth, but poor validity: 165
Which now, like fruit unripe, sticks on the tree;
But fall, unshaken, when they mellow be.
Most necessary 'tis that we forget
To pay ourselves what to ourselves is debt:
What to ourselves in passion we propose,   170
The passion ending, doth the purpose lose.
The violence of either grief or joy
Their own enactures° with themselves destroy:
Where joy most revels, grief doth most lament;
Grief joys, joy grieves, on slender accident.   175
This world is not for aye,° nor 'tis not strange
That even our loves should with our fortunes change;
For 'tis a question left us yet to prove,
Whether love lead fortune, or else fortune love.
The great man down, you mark his favourite flies;   180
The poor advanc'd makes friends of enemies.
And hitherto doth love on fortune tend;
For who° not needs shall never lack a friend,
And who in want a hollow friend doth try,
Directly seasons° him his enemy.   185
But, orderly to end where I begun,
Our wills and fates do so contrary run
That our devices still are overthrown;
Our thoughts are ours, their ends° none of our own:
So think thou wilt no second husband wed;   190
But die thy thoughts when thy first lord is dead.
Player Queen: Nor earth to me give food, nor heaven light!
Sport and repose lock from me day and night!
To desperation turn my trust and hope!

---

150 *operant:* Active; *leave:* Cease.   173 *enactures:* Fulfillments.   176 *aye:* Ever.   183 *who:* Whoever.   185 *seasons:* Matures, ripens.   189 *ends:* Results.

An anchor's° cheer° in prison be my scope!   195
Each opposite° that blanks° the face of joy
Meet what I would have well and it destroy!
Both here and hence pursue me lasting strife,
If, once a widow, ever I be wife!
Hamlet: If she should break it now!   200
Player King: 'Tis deeply sworn. Sweet, leave me here awhile;
My spirits grow dull, and fain I would beguile
The tedious day with sleep.   *[Sleeps.]*
Player Queen: Sleep rock thy brain;
And never come mischance between us twain!   *Exit.*
Hamlet: Madam, how like you this play?   205
Queen: The lady doth protest too much, methinks.
Hamlet: O, but she'll keep her word.
King: Have you heard the argument? Is there no offence in 't?
Hamlet: No, no, they do but jest, poison in jest; no offence i' the world.
King: What do you call the play?   210
Hamlet: The Mouse-trap. Marry, how? Tropically.° This play is the image of
a murder done in Vienna: Gonzago° is the duke's name; his wife, Baptista:
you shall see anon; 't is a knavish piece of work: but what o' that? your
majesty and we that have free souls, it touches us not: let the galled jade°
winch,° our withers° are unwrung.°   215

Enter Lucianus.

This is one Lucianus, nephew to the king.
Ophelia: You are as good as a chorus,° my lord.
Hamlet: I could interpret between you and your love, if I could see the
puppets dallying.°
Ophelia: You are keen, my lord, you are keen.   220
Hamlet: It would cost you a groaning to take off my edge.
Ophelia: Still better, and worse.°
Hamlet: So you mistake° your husbands. Begin, murderer; pox,° leave thy
damnable faces, and begin. Come: the croaking raven doth bellow for
revenge.   225
Lucianus: Thoughts black, hands apt, drugs fit, and time agreeing;
Confederate° season, else no creature seeing;
Thou mixture rank, of midnight weeds collected,
With Hecate's° ban° thrice blasted, thrice infected,

---

195 *An anchor's:* An anchorite's; *cheer:* Fare; sometimes printed as *chair.*   196 *opposite:* Adverse
thing; *blanks:* Causes to *blanch* or grow pale.   211 *Tropically:* Figuratively, *trapically* suggests a pun
on *trap* in *Mouse-trap* (1. 211).   212 *Gonzago:* In 1538 Luigi Gonzago murdered the Duke of Urbano
by pouring poisoned lotion in his ears.   214 *galled jade:* Horse whose hide is rubbed by saddle or
harness.   215 *winch:* Wince; *withers:* The part between the horse's shoulder blades; *unwrung:* Not
wrung or twisted.   217 *chorus:* In many Elizabethan plays the action was explained by an actor known
as the "chorus"; at a puppet show the actor who explained the action was known as an "interpreter,"
as indicated by the lines following.   219 *dallying:* With sexual suggestion, continued in *keen* (sexually
aroused), *groaning* (i.e., in pregnancy), and *edge* (i.e., sexual desire or impetuosity).   222 *Still ...*
worse: More keen, less decorous.   223 *mistake:* Err in taking; *pox:* An imprecation.   227 *Confed-*
erate: Conspiring (to assist the murderer).   229 *Hecate:* The goddess of witchcraft; *ban:* Curse.

Thy natural magic and dire property, 230
On wholesome life usurp immediately.

[Pours the poison into the sleeper's ears.]

Hamlet: 'A poisons him i' the garden for his estate. His name's Gonzago: the
story is extant, and written in very choice Italian: you shall see anon how
the murderer gets the love of Gonzago's wife.

Ophelia: The king rises. 235
Hamlet: What, frighted with false fire!°
Queen: How fares my lord?
Polonius: Give o'er the play.
King: Give me some light: away!
Polonius: Lights, lights, lights!   *Exeunt all but Hamlet and Horatio.* 240
Hamlet: Why, let the strucken deer go weep,
    The hart ungalled play;
For some must watch, while some must sleep:
    Thus runs the world away.°
Would not this,° sir, and a forest of feathers° — if the rest of my fortunes 245
turn Turk with° me — with two Provincial roses° on my razed° shoes, get
me a fellowship in a cry° of players,° sir?
Horatio: Half a share.°
Hamlet: A whole one, I.
    For thou dost know, O Damon dear, 250
    This realm dismantled° was
    Of Jove himself; and now reigns here
       A very, very° — pajock.°
Horatio: You might have rhymed.
Hamlet: O good Horatio, I'll take the ghost's word for a thousand pound. 255
Didst perceive?
Horatio: Very well, my lord.
Hamlet: Upon the talk of the poisoning?
Horatio: I did very well note him.
Hamlet: Ah, ha! Come, some music! come, the recorders!° 260
    For if the king like not the comedy,
    Why then, belike, he likes it not, perdy.°
    Come, some music!

Enter Rosencrantz and Guildenstern.

Guildenstern: Good my lord, vouchsafe me a word with you.

---

236 *false fire:* Fireworks, or a blank discharge.   241–244 *Why . . . away:* Probably from an old ballad,
with allusion to the popular belief that a wounded deer retires to weep and die. Cf. *As You Like It,* II.
i. 66.   245 *this:* I.e., the play; *feathers:* Allusion to the plumes which Elizabethan actors were fond of
wearing.   246 *turn Turk with:* Go back on; *two Provincial roses:* Rosettes of ribbon like the roses of
Provins near Paris, or else the roses of Provence; *razed:* Cut, slashed (by way of ornament).   247 *fellowship . . . players:* Partnership in a theatrical company; *cry:* Pack (as of hounds).   248 *Half a share:*
Allusion to the custom in dramatic companies of dividing the ownership into a number of shares among
the householders.   250–253 *For . . . very:* Probably from an old ballad having to do with Damon and
Pythias.   251 *dismantled:* Stripped, divested.   253 *pajock:* Peacock (a bird with a bad reputation).
Possibly the word was *patchock,* diminutive of *patch,* clown.   260 *recorders:* Wind instruments of the
flute kind.   262 *perdy:* Corruption of *par dieu.*

Hamlet: Sir, a whole history. 265
Guildenstern: The king, sir,—
Hamlet: Ay, sir, what of him?
Guildenstern: Is in his retirement marvellous distempered.
Hamlet: With drink, sir?
Guildenstern: No, my lord, rather with choler.° 270
Hamlet: Your wisdom should show itself more richer to signify this to his
doctor; for, for me to put him to his purgation would perhaps plunge
him into far more choler.
Guildenstern: Good my lord, put your discourse into some frame° and start
not so wildly from my affair. 275
Hamlet: I am tame, sir: pronounce.
Guildenstern: The queen, your mother, in most great affliction of spirit, hath
sent me to you.
Hamlet: You are welcome.
Guildenstern: Nay, good my lord, this courtesy is not of the right breed. If it 280
shall please you to make me a wholesome° answer, I will do your
mother's commandment; if not, your pardon and my return shall be the
end of my business.
Hamlet: Sir, I cannot.
Guildenstern: What, my lord? 285
Hamlet: Make you a wholesome answer; my wit's diseased: but, sir, such
answer as I can make, you shall command; or, rather, as you say, my
mother: therefore no more, but to the matter:° my mother, you say,—
Rosencrantz: Then thus she says; your behaviour hath struck her into amaze-
ment and admiration. 290
Hamlet: O wonderful son, that can so 'stonish a mother! But is there no
sequel at the heels of this mother's admiration? Impart.
Rosencrantz: She desires to speak with you in her closet, ere you go to
bed.
Hamlet: We shall obey, were she ten times our mother. Have you any further 295
trade with us?
Rosencrantz: My lord, you once did love me.
Hamlet: And do still, by these pickers and stealers.°
Rosencrantz: Good my lord, what is your cause of distemper? you do, surely,
bar the door upon your own liberty, if you deny your griefs to your 300
friend.
Hamlet: Sir, I lack advancement.
Rosencrantz: How can that be, when you have the voice° of the king himself
for your succession in Denmark?
Hamlet: Ay, sir, but "While the grass grows,"°—the proverb is something 305
musty.

Enter the Players with recorders.

270 *choler:* Bilious disorder, with quibble on the sense "anger." 274 *frame:* Order. 281 *wholesome:* Sensible. 288 *matter:* Matter in hand. 298 *pickers and stealers:* Hands, so called from the
catechism "to keep my hands from picking and stealing." 303 *voice:* Support. 305 *"While . . .
grows":* The rest of the proverb is "the silly horse starves." Hamlet may be destroyed while he is waiting
for the succession to the kingdom.

O, the recorders! let me see one. To withdraw° with you: — why do you go
about to recover the wind° of me, as if you would drive me into a toil?°
Guildenstern: O, my lord, if my duty be too bold, my love is too unman-
nerly.°   310
Hamlet: I do not well understand that. Will you play upon this pipe?
Guildenstern: My lord, I cannot.
Hamlet: I pray you.
Guildenstern: Believe me, I cannot.
Hamlet: I beseech you.   315
Guildenstern: I know no touch of it, my lord.
Hamlet: 'Tis as easy as lying: govern these ventages° with your fingers and
thumb, give it breath with your mouth, and it will discourse most elo-
quent music. Look you, these are the stops.
Guildenstern: But these cannot I command to any utterance of harmony; I   320
have not the skill.
Hamlet: Why, look you now, how unworthy a thing you make of me! You
would play upon me; you would seem to know my stops; you would
pluck out the heart of my mystery; you would sound me from my lowest
note to the top of my compass:° and there is much music, excellent voice,   325
in this little organ;° yet cannot you make it speak. 'Sblood, do you think
I am easier to be played on than a pipe? Call me what instrument you
will, though you can fret° me, you cannot play upon me.

Enter Polonius.

God bless you, sir!
Polonius: My lord, the queen would speak with you, and presently.   330
Hamlet: Do you see yonder cloud that 's almost in shape of a camel?
Polonius: By the mass, and 'tis like a camel, indeed.
Hamlet: Methinks it is like a weasel.
Polonius: It is backed like a weasel.
Hamlet: Or like a whale?   335
Polonius: Very like a whale.
Hamlet: Then I will come to my mother by and by. *[Aside.]* They fool me to
the top of my bent.° — I will come by and by.°
Polonius: I will say so.   *[Exit.]*
Hamlet: By and by is easily said.   340
Leave me, friends.   *[Exeunt all but Hamlet.]*
'Tis now the very witching time° of night,
When churchyards yawn and hell itself breathes out
Contagion to this world: now could I drink hot blood,
And do such bitter business as the day   345
Would quake to look on. Soft! now to my mother.
O heart, lose not thy nature; let not ever

307 *withdraw:* Speak in private.   308 *recover the wind:* Get to the windward side; *toil:* Snare.
309–310 *if . . . unmannerly:* If I am using an unmannerly boldness, it is my love which occasions it.
317 *ventages:* Stops of the recorders.   325 *compass:* Range of voice.   326 *organ:* Musical instrument, i.e., the pipe.   328 *fret:* Quibble on meaning "irritate" and the piece of wood, gut, or metal
which regulates the fingering.   338 *top of my bent:* Limit of endurance, i.e., extent to which a bow
may be bent; *by and by:* Immediately.   342 *witching time:* I.e., time when spells are cast.

The soul of Nero° enter this firm bosom:
Let me be cruel, not unnatural:
I will speak daggers to her, but use none;   350
My tongue and soul in this be hypocrites;
How in my words somever she be shent,°
To give them seals° never, my soul, consent!   *Exit.*

[SCENE III: *A room in the castle.*]

Enter King, Rosencrantz, and Guildenstern.

King: I like him not, nor stands it safe with us
     To let his madness range. Therefore prepare you;
     I your commission will forthwith dispatch,°
     And he to England shall along with you:
     The terms° of our estate° may not endure   5
     Hazard so near us as doth hourly grow
     Out of his brows.°
Guildenstern: We will ourselves provide:
     Most holy and religious fear it is
     To keep those many many bodies safe
     That live and feed upon your majesty.   10
Rosencrantz: The single and peculiar° life is bound,
     With all the strength and armour of the mind,
     To keep itself from noyance;° but much more
     That spirit upon whose weal depend and rest
     The lives of many. The cess° of majesty   15
     Dies not alone; but, like a gulf,° doth draw
     What's near it with it: it is a massy wheel,
     Fix'd on the summit of the highest mount,
     To whose huge spokes ten thousand lesser things
     Are mortis'd and adjoin'd; which, when it falls,   20
     Each small annexment, petty consequence,
     Attends° the boist'rous ruin. Never alone
     Did the king sigh, but with a general groan.
King: Arm° you, I pray you, to this speedy voyage;
     For we will fetters put about this fear,   25
     Which now goes too free-footed.
Rosencrantz: We will haste us.
                    Exeunt Gentlemen [Rosencrantz and Guildenstern].

Enter Polonius.

Polonius: My lord, he's going to his mother's closet:
     Behind the arras° I'll convey° myself,

348 *Nero:* Murderer of his mother, Agrippina.   352 *shent:* Rebuked.   353 *give them seals:* Confirm
with deeds.   SCENE III.   3 *dispatch:* Prepare.   5 *terms:* Condition, circumstances; *estate:* State.
7 *brows:* Effronteries.   11 *single and peculiar:* Individual and private.   13 *noyance:* Harm.
15 *cess:* Decease.   16 *gulf:* Whirlpool.   22 *Attends:* Participates in.   24 *Arm:* Prepare.
28 *arras:* Screen of tapestry placed around the walls of household apartments; *convey:* Implication of
secrecy, *convey* was often used to mean "steal."

To hear the process;° I'll warrant she'll tax him home:°
And, as you said, and wisely was it said,   30
'Tis meet that some more audience than a mother,
Since nature makes them partial, should o'erhear
The speech, of vantage.° Fare you well, my liege:
I'll call upon you ere you go to bed,
And tell you what I know.

King: Thanks, dear my lord.   35

                                              Exit [Polonius].

O, my offence is rank, it smells to heaven;
It hath the primal eldest curse° upon't,
A brother's murder. Pray can I not,
Though inclination be as sharp as will:°
My stronger guilt defeats my strong intent;   40
And, like a man to double business bound,
I stand in pause where I shall first begin,
And both neglect. What if this cursed hand
Were thicker than itself with brother's blood,
Is there not rain enough in the sweet heavens   45
To wash it white as snow? Whereto serves mercy
But to confront° the visage of offence?
And what's in prayer but this two-fold force,
To be forestalled° ere we come to fall,
Or pardon'd being down? Then I'll look up;   50
My fault is past. But, O, what form of prayer
Can serve my turn? "Forgive me my foul murder"?
That cannot be: since I am still possess'd
Of those effects for which I did the murder,
My crown, mine own ambition° and my queen.   55
May one be pardon'd and retain th' offence?°
In the corrupted currents° of this world
Offence's gilded hand° may shove by justice,
And oft 'tis seen the wicked prize° itself
Buys out the law: but 'tis not so above;   60
There is no shuffling,° there the action lies°
In his true nature; and we ourselves compell'd,
Even to the teeth and forehead° of our faults,
To give in evidence. What then? what rests?°
Try what repentance can: what can it not?   65
Yet what can it when one can not repent?
O wretched state! O bosom black as death!
O limed° soul, that, struggling to be free,

---

29 *process:* Proceedings; *tax him home:* Reprove him severely.   33 *of vantage:* From an advantageous place.   37 *primal eldest curse:* The curse of Cain, the first to kill his brother.   39 *sharp as will:* I.e., his desire is as strong as his determination.   47 *confront:* Oppose directly.   49 *forestalled:* Prevented.   55 *ambition:* I.e., realization of ambition.   56 *offence:* Benefit accruing from offense. 57 *currents:* Courses.   58 *gilded hand:* Hand offering gold as a bribe.   59 *wicked prize:* Prize won by wickedness.   61 *shuffling:* Escape by trickery; *lies:* Is sustainable.   63 *teeth and forehead:* Very face.   64 *rests:* Remains.   68 *limed:* Caught as with birdlime.

Art more engag'd!° Help, angels! Make assay!°
Bow, stubborn knees; and, heart with strings of steel,   70
Be soft as sinews of the new-born babe!
All may be well.   *[He kneels.]*

Enter Hamlet.

Hamlet: Now might I do it pat,° now he is praying;
And now I'll do't. And so 'a goes to heaven;
And so am I reveng'd. That would be scann'd:°   75
A villain kills my father; and for that,
I, his sole son, do this same villain send
To heaven.
Why, this is hire and salary, not revenge.
'A took my father grossly, full of bread;°   80
With all his crimes broad blown,° as flush° as May;
And how his audit stands who knows save heaven?
But in our circumstance and course° of thought,
'Tis heavy with him: and am I then reveng'd,
To take him in the purging of his soul,   85
When he is fit and season'd for his passage?°
No!
Up, sword; and know thou a more horrid hent:°
When he is drunk asleep,° or in his rage,
Or in th' incestuous pleasure of his bed;   90
At game, a-swearing, or about some act
That has no relish of salvation in't;
Then trip him, that his heels may kick at heaven,
And that his soul may be as damn'd and black
As hell, whereto it goes. My mother stays: 95
This physic° but prolongs thy sickly days.   *Exit.*
King: [Rising] My words fly up, my thoughts remain below:
Words without thoughts never to heaven go.   *Exit.*

[SCENE IV: *The Queen's closet.*]

Enter [Queen] Gertrude and Polonius.

Polonius: 'A will come straight. Look you lay° home to him:
Tell him his pranks have been too broad° to bear with,
And that your grace hath screen'd and stood between
Much heat° and him. I'll sconce° me even here.
Pray you, be round° with him.   5
Hamlet (within): Mother, mother, mother!

---

69 *engag'd:* Embedded; *assay:* Trial.   73 *pat:* Opportunely.   75 *would be scann'd:* Needs to be
looked into.   80 *full of bread:* Enjoying his worldly pleasures (see Ezekiel 16:49).   81 *broad
blown:* In full bloom; *flush:* Lusty.   83 *in . . . course:* As we see it in our mortal situation.   86 *fit
. . . passage:* I.e., reconciled to heaven by forgiveness of his sins.   88 *hent:* Seizing; or more probably,
occasion of seizure.   89 *drunk asleep:* In a drunken sleep.   96 *physic:* Purging (by prayer).   SCENE
IV.   1 *lay:* Thrust.   2 *broad:* Unrestrained.   4 *Much heat:* I.e., the king's anger; *sconce:* Hide.
5 *round:* Blunt.

Queen: I'll warrant you,
  Fear me not: withdraw, I hear him coming.
                                [Polonius hides behind the arras.]

Enter Hamlet.

Hamlet: Now, mother, what's the matter?
Queen: Hamlet, thou hast thy father much offended.
Hamlet: Mother, you have my father° much offended.   10
Queen: Come, come, you answer with an idle tongue.
Hamlet: Go, go, you question with a wicked tongue.
Queen: Why, how now, Hamlet!
Hamlet: What's the matter now?
Queen: Have you forgot me?
Hamlet: No, by the rood,° not so:
  You are the queen, your husband's brother's wife;   15
  And — would it were not so! — you are my mother.
Queen: Nay, then, I'll set those to you that can speak.
Hamlet: Come, come, and sit you down; you shall not budge;
  You go not till I set you up a glass
  Where you may see the inmost part of you.   20
Queen: What wilt thou do? thou wilt not murder me?
  Help, help, ho!
Polonius [behind]: What, ho! help, help; help!
Hamlet [drawing]: How now! a rat? Dead, for a ducat, dead!
                                [Makes a pass through the arras.]
Polonius [behind]: O, I am slain!   *[Falls and dies.]* 25
Queen: O me, what hast thou done?
Hamlet: Nay, I know not:
  Is it the king?
Queen: O, what a rash and bloody deed is this!
Hamlet: A bloody deed! almost as bad, good mother,
  As kill a king, and marry with his brother.   30
Queen: As kill a king!
Hamlet: Ay, lady, it was my word.
                    [Lifts up the arras and discovers Polonius.]
  Thou wretched, rash, intruding fool, farewell!
  I took thee for thy better: take thy fortune;
  Thou find'st to be too busy is some danger.
  Leave wringing of your hands: peace! sit you down,   35
  And let me wring your heart; for so I shall,
  If it be made of penetrable stuff,
  If damned custom have not braz'd° it so
  That it be proof and bulwark against sense.
Queen: What have I done, that thou dar'st wag thy tongue   40
  In noise so rude against me?
Hamlet: Such an act
  That blurs the grace and blush of modesty,

9–10 *thy father, my father:* I.e., Claudius, the elder Hamlet.   14 *rood:* Cross.   38 *braz'd:* Brazened,
hardened.

Calls virtue hypocrite, takes off the rose
From the fair forehead of an innocent love
And sets a blister° there, makes marriage-vows   45
As false as dicers' oaths: O, such a deed
As from the body of contraction° plucks
The very soul, and sweet religion° makes
A rhapsody° of words: heaven's face does glow
O'er this solidity and compound mass   50
With heated visage, as against the doom
Is thought-sick at the act.°

Queen: Ay me, what act,
That roars so loud, and thunders in the index?°

Hamlet: Look here, upon this picture, and on this.
The counterfeit presentment° of two brothers.   55
See, what a grace was seated on this brow;
Hyperion's° curls; the front° of Jove himself;
An eye like Mars, to threaten and command;
A station° like the herald Mercury
New-lighted on a heaven-kissing hill;   60
A combination and a form indeed,
Where every god did seem to set his seal,
To give the world assurance° of a man:
This was your husband. Look you now, what follows:
Here is your husband; like a mildew'd ear,°   65
Blasting his wholesome brother. Have you eyes?
Could you on this fair mountain leave to feed,
And batten° on this moor?° Ha! have you eyes?
You cannot call it love; for at your age
The hey-day° in the blood is tame, it's humble,   70
And waits upon the judgement: and what judgement
Would step from this to this? Sense, sure, you have,
Else could you not have motion;° but sure, that sense
Is apoplex'd;° for madness would not err,
Nor sense to ecstasy was ne'er so thrall'd°   75
But it reserv'd some quantity of choice,°
To serve in such a difference. What devil was't
That thus hath cozen'd° you at hoodman-blind?°
Eyes without feeling, feeling without sight,

---

45 *sets a blister:* Brands as a harlot.   47 *contraction:* The marriage contract.   48 *religion:* Religious
vows.   49 *rhapsody:* Senseless string.   49–52 *heaven's . . . act:* Heaven's face blushes to look down
upon this world, compounded of the four elements, with hot face as though the day of doom were
near, and thought-sick at the deed (i.e., Gertrude's marriage).   53 *index:* Prelude or preface.
55 *counterfeit presentment:* Portrayed representation.   57 *Hyperion's:* The sun god's; *front:* Brow.
59 *station:* Manner of standing.   63 *assurance:* Pledge, guarantee.   65 *mildew'd ear:* See Genesis
41:5–7.   68 *batten:* Grow fat; *moor:* Barren upland.   70 *hey-day:* State of excitement.   72–
73 *Sense . . . motion:* Sense and motion are functions of the middle or sensible soul, the possession of
sense being the basis of motion.   74 *apoplex'd:* Paralyzed. Mental derangement was thus of three
sorts: apoplexy, ecstasy, and diabolic possession.   75 *thrall'd:* Enslaved.   76 *quantity of choice:*
Fragment of the power to choose.   78 *cozen'd:* Tricked, cheated; *hoodman-blind:* Blindman's buff.

Ears without hands or eyes, smelling sans° all,   80
Or but a sickly part of one true sense
Could not so mope.°
O shame! where is thy blush? Rebellious hell,
If thou canst mutine° in a matron's bones,
To flaming youth let virtue be as wax,   85
And melt in her own fire: proclaim no shame
When the compulsive ardour gives the charge,°
Since frost itself as actively doth burn
And reason pandars will.°
Queen: O Hamlet, speak no more:
Thou turn'st mine eyes into my very soul;   90
And there I see such black and grained° spots
As will not leave their tinct.
Hamlet: Nay, but to live
In the rank sweat of an enseamed° bed,
Stew'd in corruption, honeying and making love
Over the nasty sty, —
Queen: O, speak to me no more;   95
These words, like daggers, enter in mine ears;
No more, sweet Hamlet!
Hamlet: A murderer and a villain;
A slave that is not twentieth part the tithe
Of your precedent lord;° a vice of kings;°
A cutpurse of the empire and the rule,   100
That from a shelf the precious diadem stole,
And put it in his pocket!
Queen: No more!

Enter Ghost.

Hamlet: A king of shreds and patches,° —
Save me, and hover o'er me with your wings,
You heavenly guards! What would your gracious figure?   105
Queen: Alas, he's mad!
Hamlet: Do you not come your tardy son to chide,
That, laps'd in time and passion,° lets go by
Th' important° acting of your dread command?
O, say!   110

---

80 *sans:* Without.   82 *mope:* Be in a depressed, spirtless state, act aimlessly.   84 *mutine:* Mutiny,
rebel.   87 *gives the charge:* Delivers the attack.   89 *reason pandars will:* The normal and proper
situation was one in which reason guided the will in the direction of good; here, reason is perverted
and leads in the direction of evil.   91 *grained:* Dyed in grain.   93 *enseamed:* Loaded with grease,
greased.   99 *precedent lord:* I.e., the elder Hamlet; *vice of kings:* Buffoon of kings; a reference to
the Vice, or clown, of the morality plays and interludes.   103 *shreds and patches:* I.e., motley, the
traditional costume of the Vice.   108 *laps'd ... passion:* Having suffered time to slip and passion to
cool; also explained as "engrossed in casual events and lapsed into mere fruitless passion, so that he
no longer entertains a rational purpose."   109 *important:* Urgent.

Ghost: Do not forget: this visitation
    Is but to whet thy almost blunted purpose.
    But, look, amazement° on thy mother sits:
    O, step between her and her fighting soul:
    Conceit in weakest bodies strongest works: 115
    Speak to her, Hamlet.
Hamlet: How is it with you, lady?
Queen: Alas, how is 't with you,
    That you do bend your eye on vacancy
    And with th' incorporal° air do hold discourse?
    Forth at your eyes your spirits wildly peep;   120
    And, as the sleeping soldiers in th' alarm,
    Your bedded° hair, like life in excrements,°
    Start up, and stand an° end. O gentle son,
    Upon the heat and flame of thy distemper
    Sprinkle cool patience. Whereon do you look?   125
Hamlet: On him, on him! Look you, how pale he glares!
    His form and cause conjoin'd,° preaching to stones,
    Would make them capable. — Do not look upon me;
    Lest with this piteous action you convert
    My stern effects:° then what I have to do   130
    Will want true colour;° tears perchance for blood.
Queen: To whom do you speak this?
Hamlet: Do you see nothing there?
Queen: Nothing at all; yet all that is I see.
Hamlet: Nor did you nothing hear?
Queen: No, nothing but ourselves.
Hamlet: Why, look you there! look, how it steals away!   135
    My father, in his habit as he liv'd!
    Look, where he goes, even now, out at the portal!   *Exit Ghost.*
Queen: This is the very coinage of your brain:
    This bodiless creation ecstasy
    Is very cunning in.
Hamlet: Ecstasy!   140
    My pulse, as yours, doth temperately keep time,
    And makes as healthful music: it is not madness
    That I have utt'red: bring me to the test,
    And I the matter will re-word,° which madness
    Would gambol° from. Mother, for love of grace,   145
    Lay not that flattering unction° to your soul,
    That not your trespass, but my madness speaks:
    It will but skin and film the ulcerous place,

---

113 *amazement:* Frenzy, distraction.   119 *incorporal:* Immaterial.   122 *bedded:* Laid in smooth layers; *excrements:* The hair was considered an excrement or voided part of the body.   123 *an:* On. 127 *conjoin'd:* United.   129–130 *convert ... effects:* Divert me from my stern duty. For *effects,* possibly *affects* (affections of the mind).   131 *want true colour:* Lack good reason so that (with a play on the normal sense of *colour*) I shall shed tears instead of blood.   144 *re-word:* Repeat in words.   145 *gambol:* Skip away.   146 *unction:* Ointment used medicinally or as a rite; suggestion that forgiveness for sin may not be so easily achieved.

Whiles rank corruption, mining° all within,
Infects unseen. Confess yourself to heaven;   150
Repent what's past; avoid what is to come;°
And do not spread the compost° on the weeds,
To make them ranker. Forgive me this my virtue;°
For in the fatness° of these pursy° times
Virtue itself of vice must pardon beg,   155
Yea, curb° and woo for leave to do him good.
Queen: O Hamlet, thou hast cleft my heart in twain.
Hamlet: O, throw away the worser part of it,
And live the purer with the other half.
Good night: but go not to my uncle's bed;   160
Assume a virtue, if you have it not.
That monster, custom, who all sense doth eat,
Of habits devil, is angel yet in this,
That to the use of actions fair and good
He likewise gives a frock or livery,   165
That aptly is put on. Refrain to-night,
And that shall lend a kind of easiness
To the next abstinence: the next more easy;
For use almost can change the stamp of nature,
And either ... the devil, or throw him out°   170
With wondrous potency. Once more, good night:
And when you are desirous to be bless'd,°
I'll blessing beg of you. For this same lord,   *[Pointing to Polonius.]*
I do repent: but heaven hath pleas'd it so,
To punish me with this and this with me,   175
That I must be their scourge and minister.
I will bestow him, and will answer well
The death I gave him. So, again, good night.
I must be cruel, only to be kind:
Thus bad begins and worse remains behind.   180
One word more, good lady.
Queen: What shall I do?
Hamlet: Not this, by no means, that I bid you do:
Let the bloat° king tempt you again to bed;
Pinch wanton on your cheek; call you his mouse;
And let him, for a pair of reechy° kisses,   185
Or paddling in your neck with his damn'd fingers,
Make you to ravel all this matter out,
That I essentially° am not in madness,
But mad in craft. 'Twere good you let him know;
For who, that's but a queen, fair, sober, wise,   190

---

149 *mining:* Working under the surface.   151 *what is to come:* I.e., the sins of the future.
152 *compost:* Manure.   153 *this my virtue:* My virtuous talk in reproving you.   154 *fatness:* Grossness; *pursy:* Short-winded, corpulent.   156 *curb:* Bow, bend the knee.   170 Defective line usually
emended by inserting *master* after *either.*   172 *be bless'd:* Become blessed, i.e., repentant.
183 *bloat:* Bloated.   185 *reechy:* Dirty, filthy.   188 *essentially:* In my essential nature.

Would from a paddock,° from a bat, a gib,°
Such dear concernings° hide? who would do so?
No, in despite of sense and secrecy,
Unpeg the basket on the house's top,
Let the birds fly, and, like the famous ape,°   195
To try conclusions,° in the basket creep,
And break your own neck down.
Queen: Be thou assur'd, if words be made of breath,
    And breath of life, I have no life to breathe
    What thou hast said to me.   200
Hamlet: I must to England; you know that?
Queen: Alack,
    I had forgot: 'tis so concluded on.
Hamlet: There's letters seal'd: and my two schoolfellows,
    Whom I will trust as I will adders fang'd,
    They bear the mandate; they must sweep my way,°   205
    And marshal me to knavery. Let it work;
    For 'tis the sport to have the enginer°
    Hoist° with his own petar:° and 't shall go hard
    But I will delve one yard below their mines,
    And blow them at the moon: O, 'tis most sweet,   210
    When in one line two crafts° directly meet.
    This man shall set me packing:°
    I'll lug the guts into the neighbour room.
    Mother, good night. Indeed this counsellor
    Is now most still, most secret and most grave,   215
    Who was in life a foolish prating knave.
    Come, sir, to draw° toward an end with you.
    Good night, mother.
                    Exeunt [severally; Hamlet dragging in Polonius.]

[ACT IV

SCENE I: *A room in the castle.*]

Enter King and Queen, with Rosencrantz and Guildenstern.

King: There's matter in these sighs, these profound heaves:

---

191 *paddock:* Toad; *gib:* Tomcat.   192 *dear concernings:* Important affairs.   195 *the famous ape:*
A letter from Sir John Suckling seems to supply other details of the story, otherwise not identified: "It
is the story of the jackanapes and the partridges; thou starest after a beauty till it be lost to thee, then
let'st out another, and starest after that till it is gone too."   196 *conclusions:* Experiments.
205 *sweep my way:* Clear my path.   207 *enginer:* Constructor of military works, or possibly, artillery-
man.   208 *Hoist:* Blown up; *petar:* Defined as a small engine of war used to blow in a door or make
a breach, and as a case filled with explosive materials.   211 *two crafts:* Two acts of guile, with quibble
on the sense of "two ships."   212 *set me packing:* Set me to making schemes, and set me to lugging
(him), and, also, send me off in a hurry.   217 *draw:* Come, with quibble on literal sense.

You must translate: 'tis fit we understand them.
Where is your son?
Queen: Bestow this place on us a little while.

[Exeunt Rosencrantz and Guildenstern.]

Ah, mine own lord, what have I seen to-night!   5
King: What, Gertrude? How does Hamlet?
Queen: Mad as the sea and wind, when both contend
Which is the mightier: in his lawless fit,
Behind the arras hearing something stir,
Whips out his rapier, cries, "A rat, a rat!"   10
And, in this brainish° apprehension,° kills
The unseen good old man.
King: O heavy dead!
It had been so with us, had we been there:
His liberty is full of threats to all;
To you yourself, to us, to every one.   15
Alas, how shall this bloody deed be answer'd?
It will be laid to us, whose providence°
Should have kept short,° restrain'd and out of haunt,°
This mad young man: but so much was our love,
We would not understand what was most fit;   20
But, like the owner of a foul disease,
To keep it from divulging,° let it feed
Even on the pith of life. Where is he gone?
Queen: To draw apart the body he hath kill'd:
O'er whom his very madness, like some ore   25
Among a mineral° of metals base,
Shows itself pure; 'a weeps for what is done.
King: O Gertrude, come away!
The sun no sooner shall the mountains touch,
But we will ship him hence: and this vile deed   30
We must, with all our majesty and skill,
Both countenance and excuse. Ho, Guildenstern!

Enter Rosencrantz and Guildenstern.

Friends both, go join you with some further aid:
Hamlet in madness hath Polonius slain,
And from his mother's closet hath he dragg'd him: 35
Go seek him out; speak fair, and bring the body
Into the chapel. I pray you, haste in this.

[Exeunt Rosencrantz and Guildenstern.]

Come, Gertrude, we'll call up our wisest friends;
And let them know, both what we mean to do,
And what's untimely done . . .°   40

ACT IV. SCENE I.   11 *brainish:* Headstrong, passionate; *apprehension:* Conception, imagination.
17 *providence:* Foresight.   18 *short:* I.e., on a short tether; *out of haunt:* Secluded.   22 *divulging:*
Becoming evident.   26 *mineral:* Mine.   40 Defective line; some editors add: *so, haply, slander;*
others add: *for, haply, slander;* other conjectures.

Whose whisper o'er the world's diameter,°
As level° as the cannon to his blank,°
Transports his pois'ned shot, may miss our name,
And hit the woundless° air. O, come away!
My soul is full of discord and dismay.   *Exeunt.*   45

[SCENE II: *Another room in the castle.*]

Enter Hamlet.

Hamlet: Safely stowed.
Rosencrantz: ⎫
Guildenstern: ⎭ (*within*) Hamlet! Lord Hamlet!
Hamlet: But soft, what noise? who calls on Hamlet? O, here they come.

Enter Rosencrantz and Guildenstern.

Rosencrantz: What have you done, my lord, with the dead body?
Hamlet: Compounded it with dust, whereto 'tis kin.
Rosencrantz: Tell us where 'tis, that we may take it thence   5
    And bear it to the chapel.
Hamlet: Do not believe it.
Rosencrantz: Believe what?
Hamlet: That I can keep your counsel° and not mine own. Besides, to be
    demanded of a sponge! what replication° should be made by the son of   10
    a king?
Rosencrantz: Take you me for a sponge, my lord?
Hamlet: Ay, sir, that soaks up the king's countenance, his rewards, his author-
    ities.° But such officers do the king best service in the end: he keeps
    them, like an ape an apple, in the corner of his jaw; first mouthed, to be   15
    last swallowed: when he needs what you have gleaned, it is but squeezing
    you, and, sponge, you shall be dry again.
Rosencrantz: I understand you not, my lord.
Hamlet: I am glad of it: a knavish speech sleeps in a foolish ear.
Rosencrantz: My lord, you must tell us where the body is, and go with us to   20
    the king.
Hamlet: The body is with the king, but the king is not with the body.° The
    king is a thing —
Guildenstern: A thing, my lord!
Hamlet: Of nothing: bring me to him. Hide fox, and all after.°   *Exeunt.*   25

41 *diameter:* Extent from side to side.   42 *level:* Straight; *blank:* White spot in the center of a target.
44 *woundless:* Invulnerable.   SCENE II.   9 *keep your counsel:* Hamlet is aware of their treachery
but says nothing about it.   10 *replication:* Reply.   14 *authorities:* Authoritative backing.   22 *The
body* ... *body:* There are many interpretations; possibly, "The body lies in death with the king, my
father; but my father walks disembodied"; or "Claudius has the bodily possession of kingship, but
kingliness, or justice of inheritance, is not with him."   25 *Hide* ... *after:* An old signal cry in the game
of hide-and-seek.

[SCENE III: *Another room in the castle.*]

Enter King, and two or three.

King: I have sent to seek him, and to find the body.
How dangerous is it that this man goes loose!
Yet must not we put the strong law on him:
He's lov'd of the distracted° multitude,
Who like not in their judgement, but their eyes;   5
And where 'tis so, th' offender's scourge° is weigh'd,°
But never the offence. To bear all smooth and even,
This sudden sending him away must seem
Deliberate pause:° diseases desperate grown
By desperate appliance are reliev'd,   10
Or not at all.

Enter Rosencrantz, [Guildenstern,] and all the rest.

              How now! what hath befall'n?
Rosencrantz: Where the dead body is bestow'd, my lord,
We cannot get from him.
King: But where is he?
Rosencrantz: Without, my lord; guarded, to know your pleasure.
King: Bring him before us.   15
Rosencrantz: Ho! bring in the lord.

They enter [with Hamlet].

King: Now, Hamlet, where's Polonius?
Hamlet: At supper.
King: At supper! where?
Hamlet: Not where he eats, but where 'a is eaten: a certain convocation of   20
politic° worms° are e'en at him. Your worm is your only emperor for
diet: we fat all creatures else to fat us, and we fat ourselves for maggots:
your fat king and your lean beggar is but variable service,° two dishes,
but to one table: that's the end.
King: Alas, alas!   25
Hamlet: A man may fish with the worm that hath eat of a king, and eat of
the fish that hath fed of that worm.
King: What dost thou mean by this?
Hamlet: Nothing but to show you how a king may go a progress° through
the guts of a beggar.   30
King: Where is Polonius?
Hamlet: In heaven; send thither to see: if your messenger find him not
there, seek him i' the other place yourself. But if indeed you find him
not within this month, you shall nose him as you go up the stairs into
the lobby.   35

SCENE III.   4 *distracted:* I.e., without power of forming logical judgments.   6 *scourge:* Punishment;
weigh'd: Taken into consideration.   9 *Deliberate pause:* Considered action.   20–21 *convocation
. . . worms:* Allusion to the Diet of Worms (1521); *politic:* Crafty.   23 *variable service:* A variety of
dishes.   29 *progress:* Royal journey of state.

King [to some Attendants]: Go seek him there.

Hamlet: 'A will stay till you come.   [Exeunt Attendants.]

King: Hamlet, this deed, for thine especial safety, —
    Which we do tender,° as we dearly grieve
    For that which thou hast done, — must send thee hence   40
    With fiery quickness: therefore prepare thyself;
    The bark is ready, and the wind at help,
    Th' associates tend, and everything is bent
    For England.

Hamlet: For England!

King: Ay, Hamlet.

Hamlet: Good.

King: So is it, if thou knew'st our purposes.   45

Hamlet: I see a cherub° that sees them. But, come; for England! Farewell,
    dear mother.

King: Thy loving father, Hamlet.

Hamlet: My mother: father and mother is man and wife; man and wife is one
    flesh; and so, my mother. Come, for England!   *Exit.*   50

King: Follow him at foot;° tempt him with speed aboard;
    Delay it not; I'll have him hence to-night:
    Away! for every thing is seal'd and done
    That else leans on th' affair: pray you, make haste.
                                  [*Exeunt all but the King.*]
    And, England, if my love thou hold'st at aught —   55
    As my great power thereof may give thee sense,
    Since yet thy cicatrice° looks raw and red
    After the Danish sword, and thy free awe°
    Pays homage to us — thou mayst not coldly set
    Our sovereign process; which imports at full,   60
    By letters congruing to that effect,
    The present death of Hamlet. Do it, England;
    For like the hectic° in my blood he rages,
    And thou must cure me: till I know 'tis done,
    Howe'er my haps,° my joys were ne'er begun.   *Exit.*   65

[SCENE IV: *A plain in Demark.*]

Enter Fortinbras with his Army over the stage.

Fortinbras: Go, captain, from me greet the Danish king;
    Tell him that, by his license,° Fortinbras
    Craves the conveyance° of a promis'd march
    Over his kingdom. You know the rendezvous.
    If that his majesty would aught with us,   5
    We shall express our duty in his eye;°

39 *tender:* Regard, hold dear.   46 *cherub:* Cherubim are angels of knowledge.   51 *at foot:* Close
behind, at heel.   57 *cicatrice:* Scar.   58 *free awe:* Voluntary show of respect.   63 *hectic:* Fever.
65 *haps:* Fortunes.   SCENE IV.   2 *license:* Leave.   3 *conveyance:* Escort, convoy.   6 *in his eye:*
In his presence.

And let him know so.

Captain: I will do't, my lord.

Fortinbras: Go softly° on.   *[Exeunt all but Captain.]*

Enter Hamlet, Rosencrantz, [Guildenstern,] &c.

Hamlet: Good sir, whose powers are these?

Captain: They are of Norway, sir.   10

Hamlet: How purpos'd, sir, I pray you?

Captain: Against some part of Poland.

Hamlet: Who commands them, sir?

Captain: The nephew to old Norway, Fortinbras.

Hamlet: Goes it against the main° of Poland, sir,   15
 Or for some frontier?

Captain: Truly to speak, and with no addition,
 We go to gain a little patch of ground
 That hath in it no profit but the name.
 To pay five ducats, five, I would not farm it;°   20
 Nor will it yield to Norway or the Pole
 A ranker rate, should it be sold in fee.°

Hamlet: Why, then the Polack never will defend it.

Captain: Yes, it is already garrison'd.

Hamlet: Two thousand souls and twenty thousand ducats   25
 Will not debate the question of this straw:°
 This is th' imposthume° of much wealth and peace,
 That inward breaks, and shows no cause without
 Why the man dies. I humbly thank you, sir.

Captain: God be wi' you, sir.   *[Exit.]*

Rosencrantz: Will 't please you go, my lord?   30

Hamlet: I'll be with you straight. Go a little before.

          [Exeunt all except Hamlet.]

 How all occasions° do inform against° me,
 And spur my dull revenge! What is a man,
 If his chief good and market of his time°
 Be but to sleep and feed? a beast, no more.   35
 Sure, he that made us with such large discourse,
 Looking before and after, gave us not
 That capability and god-like reason
 To fust° in us unus'd. Now, whether it be
 Bestial oblivion, or some craven scruple   40
 Of thinking too precisely on th' event,
 A thought which, quarter'd, hath but one part wisdom
 And ever three parts coward, I do not know
 Why yet I live to say "This thing 's to do";
 Sith I have cause and will and strength and means   45

---

8 *softly:* Slowly. 15 *main:* Country itself. 20 *farm it:* Take a lease of it. 22 *fee:* Fee simple.
26 *debate ... straw:* Settle this trifling matter. 27 *imposthume:* Purulent abscess or swelling.
32 *occasions:* Incidents, events; *inform against:* generally defined as "show," "betray" (i.e., his tardiness); more probably *inform* means "take shape," as in *Macbeth,* II. i. 48. 34 *market of his time:* The
best use he makes of his time, or, that for which he sells his time. 39 *fust:* Grow moldy.

To do 't. Examples gross as earth exhort me:
Witness this army of such mass and charge
Led by a delicate and tender prince,
Whose spirit with divine ambition puff'd
Makes mouths at the invisible event,   50
Exposing what is mortal and unsure
To all that fortune, death and danger dare,
Even for an egg-shell. Rightly to be great
Is not to stir without great argument,
But greatly to find quarrel in a straw   55
When honour's at the stake. How stand I then,
That have a father kill'd, a mother stain'd,
Excitements of° my reason and my blood,
And let all sleep? while, to my shame, I see
The imminent death of twenty thousand men,   60
That, for a fantasy and trick° of fame,
Go to their graves like beds, fight for a plot°
Whereon the numbers cannot try the cause,
Which is not tomb enough and continent
To hide the slain? O, from this time forth,   65
My thoughts be bloody, or be nothing worth!   *Exit.*

[SCENE V: *Elsinore. A room in the castle.*]

Enter Horatio, [Queen] Gertrude, and a Gentleman.

Queen: I will not speak with her.
Gentleman: She is importunate, indeed distract:
  Her mood will needs be pitied.
Queen: What would she have?
Gentleman: She speaks much of her father; says she hears
  There's tricks° i' th' world; and hems, and beats her heart;°   5
  Spurns enviously at straws;° speaks things in doubt,
  That carry but half sense: her speech is nothing,
  Yet the unshaped° use of it doth move
  The hearers to collection;° they yawn° at it,
  And botch° the words up fit to their own thoughts;   10
  Which, as her winks, and nods, and gestures yield° them,
  Indeed would make one think there might be thought,
  Though nothing sure, yet much unhappily.°
Horatio: 'Twere good she were spoken with: for she may strew
  Dangerous conjectures in ill-breeding minds.°   15
Queen: Let her come in.   *[Exit Gentleman.]*
  [Aside.] To my sick soul, as sin's true nature is,

58 *Excitements of:* Incentives to.   61 *trick:* Toy, trifle.   62 *plot:* I.e., of ground.   SCENE V.
5 *tricks:* Deceptions; *heart:* I.e., breast.   6 *Spurns . . . straws:* Kicks spitefully at small objects in her
path.   8 *unshaped:* Unformed, artless.   9 *collection:* Inference, a guess at some sort of meaning;
yawn: Wonder.   10 *botch:* Patch.   11 *yield:* Deliver, bring forth (her words).   13 *much unhap-*
pily: Expressive of much unhappiness.   15 *ill-breeding minds:* Minds bent on mischief.

Each toy seems prologue to some great amiss:°
So full of artless jealousy is guilt,
It spills itself in fearing to be spilt.°   20

Enter Ophelia [distracted].

Ophelia: Where is the beauteous majesty of Denmark?
Queen: How now, Ophelia!
Ophelia (she sings): How should I your true love know
        From another one?
    By his cockle hat° and staff,   25
        And his sandal shoon.°
Queen: Alas, sweet lady, what imports this song?
Ophelia: Say you? nay, pray you mark.
    (Song) He is dead and gone, lady,
        He is dead and gone;   30
    At his head a grass-green turf,
        At his heels a stone.
    O, ho!
Queen: Nay, but, Ophelia —
Ophelia: Pray you, mark   35
    [Sings.] White his shroud as the mountain snow, —

Enter King.

Queen: Alas, look here, my lord.
Ophelia (Song): Larded° all with flowers;
    Which bewept to the grave did not go
        With true-love showers.   40
King: How do you, pretty lady?
Ophelia: Well, God 'ild° you! They say the owl° was a baker's daughter. Lord,
    we know what we are, but know not what we may be. God be at your
    table!
King: Conceit upon her father.   45
Ophelia: Pray let's have no words of this; but when they ask you what it
    means, say you this:
    (Song) To-morrow is Saint Valentine's day,
        All in the morning betime,
    And I a maid at your window,   50
        To be your Valentine.°
    Then up he rose, and donn'd his clothes,
        And dupp'd° the chamber-door;
    Let in the maid, that out a maid
        Never departed more.   55
King: Pretty Ophelia!

18 *great amiss:* Calamity, disaster.   19–20 *So . . . spilt:* Guilt is so full of suspicion that it unskillfully
betrays itself in fearing to be betrayed.   25 *cockle hat:* Hat with cockleshell stuck in it as a sign that
the wearer has been a pilgrim to the shrine of St. James of Compostella. The pilgrim's garb was a
conventional disguise for lovers.   26 *shoon:* Shoes.   38 *Larded:* Decorated.   42 *God 'ild:* God
yield or reward; *owl:* Reference to a monkish legend that a baker's daughter was turned into an owl
for refusing bread to the Saviour.   51 *Valentine:* This song alludes to the belief that the first girl seen
by a man on the morning of this day was his valentine or true love.   53 *dupp'd:* Opened.

Ophelia: Indeed, la, without an oath, I'll make an end on 't:
　　[Sings.] By Gis° and by Saint Charity,
　　　　Alack, and fie for shame!
　　Young men will do 't, if they come to 't;　　　　　　　　　　60
　　　　By cock,° they are to blame.
　　Quoth she, before you tumbled me,
　　　　You promis'd me to wed.
　　So would I ha' done, by yonder sun,
　　　　An thou hadst not come to my bed.　　　　　　　　　　65
King: How long hath she been thus?
Ophelia: I hope all will be well. We must be patient: but I cannot choose
　　but weep, to think they would lay him i' the cold ground. My brother
　　shall know of it: and so I thank you for your good counsel. Come, my
　　coach! Good night, ladies; good night, sweet ladies; good night, good　　70
　　night.　　　　　　　　　　　　　　　　　　　　　　*[Exit.]*
King: Follow her close; give her good watch, I pray you.　　*[Exit Horatio.]*
　　O, this is the poison of deep grief; it springs
　　All from her father's death. O Gertrude, Gertrude,
　　When sorrows come, they come not single spies,　　　　　　75
　　But in battalions. First, her father slain:
　　Next your son gone; and he most violent author
　　Of his own just remove: the people muddied,
　　Thick and unwholesome in their thoughts and whispers,
　　For good Polonius' death; and we have done but greenly,°　　80
　　In hugger-mugger° to inter him: poor Ophelia
　　Divided from herself and her fair judgement,
　　Without the which we are pictures, or mere beasts:
　　Last, and as much containing as all these,
　　Her brother is in secret come from France;　　　　　　　85
　　Feeds on his wonder, keeps himself in clouds,°
　　And wants not buzzers° to infect his ear
　　With pestilent speeches of his father's death;
　　Wherein necessity, of matter beggar'd,°
　　Will nothing stick° our person to arraign　　　　　　　　90
　　In ear and ear.° O my dear Gertrude, this,
　　Like to a murd'ring-piece,° in many places
　　Gives me superfluous death.　　　　　　　　　　*A noise within.*
Queen:　　　　　　Alack, what noise is this?
King: Where are my Switzers?° Let them guard the door.

Enter a Messenger.

　　What is the matter?
Messenger:　　　　　Save yourself, my lord:　　　　　　　95

---

58 *Gis:* Jesus.　　61 *cock:* Perversion of "God" in oaths.　　80 *greenly:* Foolishly.　　81 *hugger-mug-ger:* Secret haste.　　86 *in clouds:* Invisible.　　87 *buzzers:* Gossipers.　　89 *of matter beggar'd:* Un-provided with facts.　　90 *nothing stick:* Not hesitate.　　91 *In ear and ear:* In everybody's ears.　　92 *murd'ring-piece:* Small cannon or mortar; suggestion of numerous missiles fired.　　94 *Switzers:* Swiss guards, mercenaries.

The ocean, overpeering° of his list,°
Eats not the flats with more impiteous haste
Than young Laertes, in a riotous head,
O'erbears your officers. The rabble call him lord;
And, as the world were now but to begin,   100
Antiquity forgot, custom not known,
The ratifiers and props of every word,°
They cry "Choose we: Laertes shall be king":
Caps, hands, and tongues, applaud it to the clouds:
"Laertes shall be king, Laertes king!"   *A noise within.*   105
Queen: How cheerfully on the false trail they cry!
    O, this is counter,° you false Danish dogs!
King: The doors are broke.

Enter Laertes with others.

Laertes: Where is this king? Sirs, stand you all without.
Danes: No, let's come in.
Laertes: I pray you, give me leave.   110
Danes: We will, we will.   *[They retire without the door.]*
Laertes: I thank you: keep the door. O thou vile king,
    Give me my father!
Queen: Calmly, good Laertes.
Laertes: That drop of blood that's calm proclaims me bastard,
    Cries cuckold to my father, brands the harlot   115
    Even here, between the chaste unsmirched brow
    Of my true mother.
King: What is the cause, Laertes,
    That thy rebellion looks so giant-like?
    Let him go, Gertrude; do not fear our person:
    There's such divinity doth hedge a king,   120
    That treason can but peep to° what it would,°
    Acts little of his will. Tell me, Laertes,
    Why thou art thus incens'd. Let him go, Gertrude.
    Speak, man.
Laertes: Where is my father?
King: Dead.
Queen: But not by him.   125
King: Let him demand his fill.
Laertes: How came he dead? I'll not be juggled with:
    To hell, allegiance! vows, to the blackest devil!
    Conscience and grace, to the profoundest pit!
    I dare damnation. To this point I stand,   130
    That both the worlds I give to negligence,°
    Let come what comes; only I'll be reveng'd

96 *overpeering:* Overflowing; *list:* Shore.   102 *word:* Promise.   107 *counter:* A hunting term meaning to follow the trail in a direction opposite to that which the game has taken.   121 *peep to:* I.e., look at from afar off; *would:* Wishes to do.   131 *give to negligence:* He despises both the here and the hereafter.

Most throughly° for my father.

King: Who shall stay you?

Laertes: My will,° not all the world's:
And for my means, I'll husband them so well,   135
They shall go far with little.

King: Good Laertes,
If you desire to know the certainty
Of your dear father, is 't writ in your revenge,
That, swoopstake,° you will draw both friend and foe,
Winner and loser?   140

Laertes: None but his enemies.

King: Will you know them then?

Laertes: To his good friends thus wide I'll ope my arms;
And like the kind life-rend'ring pelican,°
Repast° them with my blood.

King: Why, now you speak
Like a good child and a true gentleman.   145
That I am guiltless of your father's death,
And am most sensibly in grief for it,
It shall as level to your judgement 'pear
As day does to your eye.

                    A noise within: "Let her come in."

Laertes: How now! what noise is that?   150

Enter Ophelia.

O heat,° dry up my brains! tears seven times salt,
Burn out the sense and virtue of mine eye!
By heaven, thy madness shall be paid with weight,
Till our scale turn the beam. O rose of May!
Dear maid, kind sister, sweet Ophelia!   155
O heavens! is 't possible, a young maid's wits
Should be as mortal as an old man's life?
Nature is fine in love, and where 'tis fine,
It sends some precious instance of itself
After the thing it loves.   160

Ophelia (Song): They bore him barefac'd on the bier;
Hey non nonny, nonny, hey nonny;
And in his grave rain'd many a tear: —
Fare you well, my dove!

Laertes: Hadst thou thy wits, and didst persuade revenge,   165
It could not move thus.

Ophelia [sings]: You must sing a-down a-down,
An you call him a-down-a.
O, how the wheel° becomes it! It is the false steward,°

---

133 *throughly:* Thoroughly.   134 *My will:* He will not be stopped except by his own will.
139 *swoopstake:* Literally, drawing the whole stake at once, i.e., indiscriminately.   143 *pelican:* Reference to the belief that the pelican feeds its young with its own blood.   144 *Repast:* Feed.
151 *heat:* Probably the heat generated by the passion of grief.   169 *wheel:* Spinning wheel as accompaniment to the song refrain; *false steward:* The story is unknown.

that stole his master's daughter. 170

Laertes: This nothing's more than matter.

Ophelia: There's rosemary,° that's for remembrance; pray you, love, remember: and there is pansies,° that's for thoughts.

Laertes: A document° in madness, thoughts and remembrance fitted.

Ophelia: There's fennel° for you, and columbines:° there's rue° for you; and 175
here's some for me: we may call it herb of grace o' Sundays: O, you must wear your rue with a difference. There's a daisy:° I would give you some violets,° but they withered all when my father died: they say 'a made a good end, —

[*Sings.*] For bonny sweet Robin is all my joy.° 180

Laertes: Thought° and affliction, passion, hell itself,
She turns to favour and to prettiness.

Ophelia (Song): And will 'a not come again?°
And will 'a not come again?
No, no, he is dead: 185
Go to thy death-bed:
He never will come again.

His beard was as white as snow,
All flaxen was his poll:°
He is gone, he is gone, 190
And we cast away° moan:
God ha' mercy on his soul!

And of all Christian souls, I pray God. God be wi' you.   [*Exit.*]

Laertes: Do you see this, O God?

King: Laertes, I must commune with your grief, 195
Or you deny me right.° Go but apart,
Make choice of whom your wisest friends you will,
And they shall hear and judge 'twixt you and me:
If by direct or by collateral° hand
They find us touch'd,° we will our kingdom give, 200
Our crown, our life, and all that we call ours,
To you in satisfaction; but if not,
Be you content to lend your patience to us,
And we shall jointly labour with your soul
To give it due content.

Laertes: Let this be so; 205
His means of death, his obscure funeral —
No trophy, sword, nor hatchment° o'er his bones,

---

172 *rosemary:* Used as a symbol of remembrance both at weddings and at funerals.   173 *pansies:* Emblems of love and courtship. Cf. French *pensées.*   174 *document:* Piece of instruction or lesson. 175 *fennel:* Emblem of flattery; *columbines:* Emblem of unchastity (?) or ingratitude (?); *rue:* Emblem of repentance. It was usually mingled with holy water and then known as *herb of grace.* Ophelia is probably playing on the two meanings of *rue,* "repentant" and "even for ruth (pity)"; the former signification is for the queen, the latter for herself.   177 *daisy:* Emblem of dissembling, faithlessness. 178 *violets:* Emblems of faithfulness.   180 *For . . . joy:* Probably a line from a Robin Hood ballad. 181 *Thought:* Melancholy thought.   183 *And . . . again:* This song appeared in the songbooks as "The Merry Milkmaids' Dumps."   189 *poll:* Head.   191 *cast away:* Shipwrecked.   196 *right:* My rights. 199 *collateral:* Indirect.   200 *touch'd:* Implicated.   207 *hatchment:* Tablet displaying the armorial bearings of a deceased person.

No noble rite nor formal ostentation —
Cry to be heard, as 'twere from heaven to earth,
That I must call 't in question.
King: So you shall;   210
And where th' offence is let the great axe fall.
I pray you, go with me.   *Exeunt.*

[SCENE VI: *Another room in the castle.*]

Enter Horatio and others.

Horatio: What are they that would speak with me?
Gentleman: Sea-faring men, sir: they say they have letters for you.
Horatio: Let them come in.   *[Exit Gentleman]*
   I do not know from what part of the world
   I should be greeted, if not from lord Hamlet.   5

Enter Sailors.

First Sailor: God bless you, sir.
Horatio: Let him bless thee too.
First Sailor: 'A shall sir, an 't please him. There's a letter for you, sir; it comes
   from the ambassador that was bound for England; if your name be
   Horatio, as I am let to know it is.   10
Horatio [Reads]: "Horatio, when thou shalt have overlooked this, give these
   fellows some means° to the king: they have letters for him. Ere we were
   two days old at sea, a pirate of very warlike appointment gave us chase.
   Finding ourselves too slow of sail, we put on a compelled valour, and in
   the grapple I boarded them: on the instant they got clear of our ship;   15
   so I alone became their prisoner. They have dealt with me like thieves
   of mercy:° but they knew what they did; I am to do a good turn for them.
   Let the king have the letters I have sent; and repair thou to me with as
   much speed as thou wouldest fly death. I have words to speak in thine
   ear will make thee dumb; yet are they much too light for the bore° of   20
   the matter. These good fellows will bring thee where I am. Rosencrantz
   and Guildenstern hold their course for England: of them I have much to
   tell thee. Farewell.
                           "He that thou knowest thine, HAMLET."
                   Come, I will give you way for these your letters;   25
   And do 't the speedier, that you may direct me
   To him from whom you brought them.   *Exeunt.*

[SCENE VII: *Another room in the castle.*]

Enter King and Laertes.

King: Now must your conscience° my acquittance seal,
   And you must put me in your heart for friend,

SCENE VI.   12 *means:* Means of access.   16–17 *thieves of mercy:* Merciful thieves.   20 *bore:* Caliber, importance.   SCENE VII.   1 *conscience:* Knowledge that this is true.

Sith you have heard, and with a knowing ear,
That he which hath your noble father slain
Pursued my life.
Laertes: It well appears: but tell me   5
Why you proceeded not against these feats,
So criminal and so capital° in nature,
As by your safety, wisdom, all things else,
You mainly° were stirr'd up.
King: O, for two special reasons;
Which may to you, perhaps, seem much unsinew'd,°   10
But yet to me th' are strong. The queen his mother
Lives almost by his looks; and for myself —
My virtue or my plague, be it either which —
She's so conjunctive° to my life and soul,
That, as the star moves not but in his sphere,°   15
I could not but by her. The other motive,
Why to a public count° I might not go,
Is the great love the general gender° bear him;
Who, dipping all his faults in their affection,
Would, like the spring° that turneth wood to stone,   20
Convert his gyves° to graces; so that my arrows,
Too slightly timber'd° for so loud° a wind,
Would have reverted to my bow again,
And not where I had aim'd them.
Laertes: And so have I a noble father lost;   25
A sister driven into desp'rate terms,°
Whose worth, if praises may go back° again,
Stood challenger on mount° of all the age°
For her perfections: but my revenge will come.
King: Break not your sleeps for that: you must not think   30
That we are made of stuff so flat and dull
That we can let our beard be shook with danger
And think it pastime. You shortly shall hear more:
I lov'd your father, and we love ourself;
And that, I hope, will teach you to imagine —   35

Enter a Messenger with letters.

How now! what news?
Messenger: Letters, my lord, from Hamlet:
These to your majesty; this to the queen.°
King: From Hamlet! who brought them?
Messenger: Sailors, my lord, they say; I saw them not:

7 *capital:* Punishable by death.   9 *mainly:* Greatly.   10 *unsinew'd:* Weak.   14 *conjunctive:* Com-
formable (the next line suggesting planetary conjunction).   15 *sphere:* The hollow sphere in which,
according to Ptolemaic astronomy, the planets were supposed to move.   17 *count:* Account, reckoning.   18 *general gender:* Common people.   20 *spring:* I.e., one heavily charged with lime.
21 *gyves:* Fetters; here, faults, or possibly, punishments inflicted (on him).   22 *slightly timber'd:* Light;
loud: Strong.   26 *terms:* State, condition.   27 *go back:* I.e., to Ophelia's former virtues.   28 *on
mount:* Set up on high, *mounted* (on horseback); *of all the age:* Qualifies *challenger* and not *mount.*
37 *to the queen:* One hears no more of the letter to the queen.

They were given me by Claudio;° he receiv'd them   40
Of him that brought them.

King: Laertes, you shall hear them.
Leave us.   *[Exit Messenger.]*
[Reads.] "High and mighty, You shall know I am set naked° on your
kingdom. To-morrow shall I beg leave to see your kingly eyes: when I
shall, first asking your pardon thereunto, recount the occasion of my   45
sudden and more strange return.   "HAMLET."
What should this mean? Are all the rest come back?
Or is it some abuse, and no such thing?

Laertes: Know you the hand?

King: 'Tis Hamlet's character. "Naked!"
And in a postscript here, he says "alone."   50
Can you devise° me?

Laertes: I'm lost in it, my lord. But let him come;
It warms the very sickness in my heart,
That I shall live and tell him to his teeth,
"Thus didst thou."

King: If it be so, Laertes —   55
As how should it be so? how otherwise?° —
Will you be rul'd by me?

Laertes: Ay, my lord;
So you will not o'errule me to a peace.

King: To thine own peace. If he be now return'd,
As checking at° his voyage, and that he means   60
No more to undertake it, I will work him
To an exploit, now ripe in my device,
Under the which he shall not choose but fall:
And for his death no wind of blame shall breathe,
But even his mother shall uncharge the practice°   65
And call it accident.

Laertes: My lord, I will be rul'd;
The rather, if you could devise it so
That I might be the organ.°

King: It falls right.
You have been talk'd of since your travel much,
And that in Hamlet's hearing, for a quality   70
Wherein, they say, you shine: your sum of parts
Did not together pluck such envy from him
As did that one, and that, in my regard,
Of the unworthiest siege.°

Laertes: What part is that, my lord?

King: A very riband in the cap of youth,   75

---

40 *Claudio:* This character does not appear in the play.   43 *naked:* Unprovided (with retinue).
51 *devise:* Explain to.   56 *As ... otherwise?* How can this (Hamlet's return) be true? (yet) how
otherwise than true (since we have the evidence of his letter)? Some editors read *How should it not
be so,* etc., making the words refer to Laertes's desire to meet with Hamlet.   60 *checking at:* Used in
falconry of a hawk's leaving the quarry to fly at a chance bird, turn aside.   65 *uncharge the practice:*
Acquit the stratagem of being a plot.   68 *organ:* Agent, instrument.   74 *siege:* Rank.

Yet needful too; for youth no less becomes
The light and careless livery that it wears
Than settled age his sables° and his weeds,
Importing health and graveness. Two months since,
Here was a gentleman of Normandy: —   80
I have seen myself, and serv'd against, the French,
And they can well° on horseback: but this gallant
Had witchcraft in 't; he grew unto his seat;
And to such wondrous doing brought his horse,
As had he been incorps'd and demi-natur'd°   85
With the brave beast: so far he topp'd° my thought,
That I, in forgery° of shapes and tricks,
Come short of what he did.
Laertes: A Norman was 't?
King: A Norman.
Laertes: Upon my life, Lamord.°
King: The very same.   90
Laertes: I know him well: he is the brooch indeed
  And gem of all the nation.
King: He made confession° of you,
  And gave you such a masterly report
  For art and exercise° in your defence°   95
  And for your rapier most especial,
  That he cried out, 'twould be a sight indeed,
  If one could match you: the scrimers° of their nation,
  He swore, had neither motion, guard, nor eye,
  If you oppos'd them. Sir, this report of his   100
  Did Hamlet so envenom with his envy
  That he could nothing do but wish and beg
  Your sudden coming o'er, to play° with you.
  Now, out of this, —
Laertes: What out of this, my lord?
King: Laertes, was your father dear to you?   105
  Or are you like the painting of a sorrow,
  A face without a heart?
Laertes: Why ask you this?
King: Not that I think you did not love your father;
  But that I know love is begun by time;
  And that I see, in passages of proof,°   110
  Time qualifies the spark and fire of it.
  There lives within the very flame of love
  A kind of wick or snuff that will abate it;
  And nothing is at a like goodness still;

78 *sables:* Rich garments.   82 *can well:* Are skilled.   85 *incorps'd and demi-natur'd:* Of one body
and nearly of one nature (like the centaur).   86 *topp'd:* Surpassed.   87 *forgery:* Invention.
90 *Lamord:* This refers possibly to Pietro Monte, instructor to Louis XII's master of the horse.
93 *confession:* Grudging admission of superiority.   95 *art and exercise:* Skillful exercise; *defence:*
Science of defense in sword practice.   98 *scrimers:* Fencers.   103 *play:* Fence.   110 *passages of
proof:* Proved instances.

For goodness, growing to a plurisy,° 115
Dies in his own too much:° that we would do,
We should do when we would; for this "would" changes
And hath abatements° and delays as many
As there are tongues, are hands, are accidents;°
And then this "should" is like a spendthrift° sigh, 120
That hurts by easing. But, to the quick o' th' ulcer:°—
Hamlet comes back: what would you undertake,
To show yourself your father's son in deed
More than in words?

Laertes: To cut his throat i' th' church.

King: No place, indeed, should murder sanctuarize;° 125
Revenge should have no bounds. But, good Laertes,
Will you do this, keep close within your chamber.
Hamlet return'd shall know you are come home:
We'll put on those shall praise your excellence
And set a double varnish on the fame 130
The Frenchman gave you, bring you in fine together
And wager on your heads: he, being remiss,
Most generous and free from all contriving,
Will not peruse the foils; so that, with ease,
Or with a little shuffling, you may choose 135
A sword unbated,° and in a pass of practice°
Requite him for your father.

Laertes: I will do 't:
And, for that purpose, I'll anoint my sword.
I bought an unction of a mountebank,°
So mortal that, but dip a knife in it, 140
Where it draws blood no cataplasm° so rare,
Collected from all simples° that have virtue
Under the moon,° can save the thing from death
That is but scratch'd withal: I'll touch my point
With this contagion, that, if I gall° him slightly, 145
It may be death.

King: Let's further think of this;
Weigh what convenience both of time and means
May fit us to our shape:° if this should fail,
And that our drift look through our bad performance,°
'Twere better not assay'd: therefore this project 150
Should have a back or second, that might hold,
If this should blast in proof.° Soft! let me see:

---

115 *plurisy:* Excess, plethora.   116 *in his own too much:* Of its own excess.   118 *abatements:* Diminutions.   119 *accidents:* Occurrences, incidents.   120 *spendthrift:* An allusion to the belief that each sigh cost the heart a drop of blood.   121 *quick o' th' ulcer:* Heart of the difficulty.   125 *sanctuarize:* Protect from punishment; allusion to the right of sanctuary with which certain religious places were invested.   136 *unbated:* Not blunted, having no button; *pass of practice:* Treacherous thrust. 139 *mountebank:* Quack doctor.   141 *cataplasm:* Plaster or poultice.   142 *simples:* Herbs. 143 *Under the moon:* I.e., when collected by moonlight to add to their medicinal value.   145 *gall:* Graze, wound.   148 *shape:* Part we propose to act.   149 *drift ... performance:* Intention be disclosed by our bungling.   152 *blast in proof:* Burst in the test (like a cannon).

We'll make a solemn wager on your cunnings:°
I ha 't:
When in your motion you are hot and dry —   155
As make your bouts more violent to that end —
And that he calls for drink, I'll have prepar'd him
A chalice° for the nonce, whereon but sipping,
If he by chance escape your venom'd stuck,°
Our purpose may hold there. But stay, what noise?   160

Enter Queen.

Queen: One woe doth tread upon another's heel,
    So fast they follow: your sister's drown'd, Laertes.
Laertes: Drown'd! O, where?
Queen: There is a willow° grows askant° the brook,
    That shows his hoar° leaves in the glassy stream;   165
    There with fantastic garlands did she make
    Of crow-flowers,° nettles, daisies, and long purples°
    That liberal° shepherds give a grosser name,
    But our cold maids do dead men's fingers call them:
    There, on the pendent boughs her crownet° weeds   170
    Clamb'ring to hang, an envious sliver° broke;
    When down her weedy° trophies and herself
    Fell in the weeping brook. Her clothes spread wide;
    And, mermaid-like, awhile they bore her up:
    Which time she chanted snatches of old lauds;°   175
    As one incapable° of her own distress,
    Or like a creature native and indued°
    Upon that element: but long it could not be
    Till that her garments, heavy with their drink,
    Pull'd the poor wretch from her melodious lay   180
    To muddy death.
Laertes: Alas, then, she is drown'd?
Queen: Drown'd, drown'd.
Laertes: Too much of water hast thou, poor Ophelia,
    And therefore I forbid my tears: but yet
    It is our trick;° nature her custom holds,   185
    Let shame say what it will: when these are gone,
    The woman will be out.° Adieu, my lord:
    I have a speech of fire, that fain would blaze,
    But that this folly drowns it.   *Exit.*
King: Let's follow, Gertrude:
    How much I had to do to calm his rage!   190

153 *cunnings:* Skills.   158 *chalice:* Cup.   159 *stuck:* Thrust (from *stoccado*).   164 *willow:* For
its significance of forsaken love; *askant:* Aslant.   165 *hoar:* White (i.e., on the underside).
167 *crow-flowers:* Buttercups; *long purples:* Early purple orchis.   168 *liberal:* Probably, free-spoken.
170 *crownet:* Coronet; made into a chaplet.   171 *sliver:* Branch.   172 *weedy:* I.e., of plants.
175 *lauds:* Hymns.   176 *incapable:* Lacking capacity to apprehend.   177 *indued:* Endowed with
qualities fitting her for living in water.   185 *trick:* Way.   186–187 *when . . . out:* When my tears are
all shed, the woman in me will be satisfied.

Now fear I this will give it start again;
Therefore let 's follow. *Exeunt.*

[ACT V

<small>SCENE I:</small> *A churchyard.*]

Enter two Clowns° [with spades, &c.].

First Clown: Is she to be buried in Christian burial when she wilfully seeks
    her own salvation?
Second Clown: I tell thee she is; therefore make her grave straight:° the
    crowner° hath sat on her, and finds it Christian burial.
First Clown: How can that be, unless she drowned herself in her own   5
    defence?
Second Clown: Why, 'tis found so.
First Clown: It must be "se offendendo";° it cannot be else. For here lies the
    point: if I drown myself wittingly,° it argues an act: and an act hath three
    branches;° it is, to act, to do, and to perform: argal,° she drowned herself   10
    wittingly.
Second Clown: Nay, but hear you, goodman delver,° —
First Clown: Give me leave. Here lies the water; good: here stands the man;
    good: if the man go to this water, and drown himself, it is, will he, nill
    he, he goes, — mark you that; but if the water come to him and drown   15
    him, he drowns not himself: argal, he that is not guilty of his own death
    shortens not his own life.
Second Clown: But is this law?
First Clown: Ay, marry, is 't; crowner's quest° law.
Second Clown: Will you ha' the truth on 't? If this had not been a gentle-   20
    woman, she should have been buried out o' Christian burial.
First Clown: Why, there thou say'st:° and the more pity that great folk should
    have countenance° in this world to drown or hang themselves, more than
    their even° Christian. Come, my spade. There is no ancient gentlemen
    but gardeners, ditchers, and grave-makers: they hold up° Adam's profes-   25
    sion.
Second Clown: Was he a gentleman?
First Clown: 'A was the first that ever bore arms.
Second Clown: Why, he had none.
First Clown: What, art a heathen? How dost thou understand the Scripture?   30
    The Scripture says "Adam digged": could he dig without arms? I'll put

<small>ACT V. SCENE I.</small>   *Clowns:* The word *clown* was used to denote peasants as well as humorous characters;
here applied to the rustic type of clown.   3 *straight:* Straightway, immediately; some interpret "from
east to west in a direct line, parallel with the church."   4 *crowner:* Coroner.   8 *"se offendendo:"*
For *se defendendo,* term used in verdicts of justifiable homicide.   9 *wittingly:* Intentionally.
10 *three branches:* Parody of legal phraseology; *argal:* Corruption of *ergo,* therefore.   12 *delver:*
Digger.   19 *quest:* Inquest.   22 *there thou say'st:* That's right.   23 *countenance:* Privilege.
24 *even:* Fellow.   25 *hold up:* Maintain, continue.

another question to thee: if thou answerest me not to the purpose, confess thyself° —

Second Clown: Go to.°

First Clown: What is he that builds stronger than either the mason, the 35
shipwright, or the carpenter?

Second Clown: The gallows-maker; for that frame outlives a thousand tenants.

First Clown: I like thy wit well, in good faith: the gallows does well; but how
does it well? it does well to those that do ill: now thou dost ill to say the 40
gallows is built stronger than the church: argal, the gallows may do well
to thee. To 't again, come.

Second Clown: "Who builds stronger than a mason, a shipwright, or a
carpenter?"

First Clown: Ay, tell me that, and unyoke.° 45

Second Clown: Marry, now I can tell.

First Clown: To 't.

Second Clown: Mass,° I cannot tell.

Enter Hamlet and Horatio [at a distance].

First Clown: Cudgel thy brains no more about it, for your dull ass will not
mend his pace with beating; and, when you are asked this question next, 50
say "a grave-maker": the houses he makes lasts till doomsday. Go, get
thee in, and fetch me a stoup° of liquor.

       [Exit Second Clown.] Song. [He digs.]
In youth, when I did love, did love,
 Methought it was very sweet,
To contract — O — the time, for — a — my behove,° 55
 O, methought, there — a — was nothing — a — meet.

Hamlet: Has this fellow no feeling of his business, that 'a sings at gravemaking?

Horatio: Custom hath made it in him a property of easiness.°

Hamlet: 'Tis e'en so: the hand of little employment hath the daintier sense. 60

First Clown: (*Song.*) But age, with his stealing steps,
 Hath claw'd me in his clutch,
And hath shipped me into the land
 As if I had never been such.   *[Throws up a skull.]*

Hamlet: That skull had a tongue in it, and could sing once: how the knave 65
jowls° it to the ground, as if 'twere Cain's jaw-bone,° that did the first
murder! This might be the pate of a politician,° which this ass now
o'er-reaches;° one that would circumvent God, might it not?

Horatio: It might, my lord.

Hamlet: Or of a courtier; which could say "Good morrow, sweet lord! How 70

---

33 *confess thyself:* "And be hanged" completes the proverb. 34 *Go to:* Perhaps, "begin," or some
other form of concession. 45 *unyoke:* After this great effort you may unharness the team of your
wits. 48 *Mass:* By the Mass. 52 *stoup:* Two-quart measure. 55 *behove:* Benefit. 59 *property
of easiness:* A peculiarity that now is easy. 66 *jowls:* Dashes; *Cain's jaw-bone:* Allusion to the old
tradition that Cain slew Abel with the jawbone of an ass. 67 *politician:* Schemer, plotter; *o'er-reaches:*
Quibble on the literal sense and the sense "circumvent."

dost thou, sweet lord?" This might be my lord such-a-one, that praised my lord such-a-one's horse, when he meant to beg it; might it not?

Horatio: Ay, my lord.

Hamlet: Why, e'en so: and now my Lady Worm's; chapless,° and knocked about the mazzard° with a sexton's spade: here's fine revolution, an we 75 had the trick to see 't. Did these bones cost no more the breeding, but to play at loggats° with 'em? mine ache to think on 't.

First Clown: (Song.) A pick-axe, and a spade, a spade,
　　　For and° a shrouding sheet:
　　　O, a pit of clay for to be made 80
　　　For such a guest is meet.　　　　　　*[Throws up another skull.]*

Hamlet: There 's another: why may not that be the skull of a lawyer? Where be his quiddities° now, his quillities,° his cases, his tenures,° and his tricks? why does he suffer this mad knave now to knock him about the sconce° with a dirty shovel, and will not tell him of his action of battery? 85 Hum! This fellow might be in 's time a great buyer of land, with his statutes, his recognizances,° his fines, his double vouchers,° his recoveries:° is this the fine° of his fines, and the recovery of his recoveries, to have his fine pate full of fine dirt? will his vouchers vouch him no more of his purchases, and double ones too, than the length and breadth of a 90 pair of indentures?° The very conveyances of his lands will scarcely lie in this box; and must the inheritor° himself have no more, ha?

Horatio: Not a jot more, my lord.

Hamlet: Is not parchment made of sheep-skins?

Horatio: Ay, my lord, and of calf-skins° too. 95

Hamlet: They are sheep and calves which seek out assurance in that.° I will speak to this fellow. Whose grave's this, sirrah?

First Clown: Mine, sir.
　　　[Sings.] O, a pit of clay for to be made
　　　For such a guest is meet. 100

Hamlet: I think it be thine, indeed; for thou liest in 't.

First Clown: You lie out on 't, sir, and therefore 't is not yours: for my part, I do not lie in 't, yet it is mine.

Hamlet: Thou dost lie in 't, to be in 't and say it is thine: 'tis for the dead, not for the quick; therefore thou liest. 105

First Clown: 'Tis a quick lie, sir; 'twill away again, from me to you.

Hamlet: What man dost thou dig it for?

First Clown: For no man, sir.

Hamlet: What woman, then?

First Clown: For none, neither. 110

Hamlet: Who is to be buried in 't?

---

74 *chapless:* Having no lower jaw.　75 *mazzard:* Head.　77 *loggats:* A game in which six sticks are thrown to lie as near as possible to a stake fixed in the ground, or block of wood on a floor.　79 *For and:* And moreover.　83 *quiddities:* Subtleties, quibbles; *quillities:* Verbal niceties, subtle distinctions; *tenures:* The holding of a piece of property or office or the conditions or period of such holding. 85 *sconce:* Head.　87 *statutes, recognizances:* Legal terms connected with the transfer of land; *vouchers:* Persons called on to warrant a tenant's title; *recoveries:* Process for transfer of entailed estate. 88 *fine:* The four uses of this word are as follows: (1) end, (2) legal process, (3) elegant, (4) small. 91 *indentures:* Conveyances or contracts.　92 *inheritor:* Possessor, owner.　95 *calfskins:* Parchments.　96 *assurance in that:* Safety in legal parchments.

First Clown: One that was a woman, sir; but, rest her soul, she's dead.

Hamlet: How absolute° the knave is! we must speak by the card,° or equiv-
ocation° will undo us. By the Lord, Horatio, these three years I have taken
note of it; the age is grown so picked° that the toe of the peasant comes   115
so near the heel of the courtier, he galls° his kibe.° How long hast thou
been a grave-maker?

First Clown: Of all the day i' the year, I came to 't that day that our last king
Hamlet overcame Fortinbras.

Hamlet: How long is that since?   120

First Clown: Cannot you tell that? every fool can tell that: it was the very day
that young Hamlet was born; he that is mad, and sent into England.

Hamlet: Ay, marry, why was he sent into England?

First Clown: Why, because 'a was mad: 'a shall recover his wits there; or, if
'a do not, 'tis no great matter there.   125

Hamlet: Why?

First Clown: 'Twill not be seen in him there; there the men are as mad as
he.

Hamlet: How came he mad?

First Clown: Very strangely, they say.   130

Hamlet: How strangely?

First Clown: Faith, e'en with losing his wits.

Hamlet: Upon what ground?

First Clown: Why, here in Denmark: I have been sexton here, man and boy,
thirty years.°   135

Hamlet: How long will a man lie i' the earth ere he rot?

First Clown: Faith, if 'a be not rotten before 'a die — as we have many pocky°
corses now-a-days, that will scarce hold the laying in — 'a will last you
some eight year or nine year: a tanner will last you nine year.

Hamlet: Why he more than another?   140

First Clown: Why, sir, his hide is so tanned with his trade, that 'a will keep
out water a great while; and your water is a sore decayer of your
whoreson dead body. Here's a skull now hath lain you i' th' earth three
and twenty years.

Hamlet: Whose was it?   145

First Clown: A whoreson mad fellow's it was: whose do you think it was?

Hamlet: Nay, I know not.

First Clown: A pestilence on him for a mad rogue! 'a poured a flagon of
Rhenish on my head once. This same skull, sir, was Yorick's skull, the
king's jester.   150

Hamlet: This?

First Clown: E'en that.

Hamlet: Let me see. *[Takes the skull.]* Alas, poor Yorick! I knew him, Horatio: a fellow of infinite jest, of most excellent fancy: he hath borne me
on his back a thousand times; and now, how abhorred in my imagination it is! my gorge rises at it. Here hung those lips that I have kissed I

---

113 *absolute:* Positive, decided; *by the card:* With precision, i.e., by the mariner's card on which the
points of the compass were marked; *equivocation:* Ambiguity in the use of terms.   115 *picked:*
Refined, fastidious.   116 *galls:* Chafes; *kibe:* Chilblain.   135 *thirty years:* This statement with that in
line 122 shows Hamlet's age to be thirty years.   137 *pocky:* Rotten, diseased.

know not how oft. Where be your gibes now? your gambols? your
songs? your flashes of merriment, that were wont to set the table on a
roar? Not one now, to mock your own grinning? quite chap-fallen? Now
get you to my lady's chamber, and tell her, let her paint an inch thick,   160
to this favour she must come; make her laugh at that. Prithee, Horatio,
tell me one thing.

Horatio: What's that, my lord?

Hamlet: Dost thou think Alexander looked o' this fashion i' the earth?

Horatio: E'en so.   165

Hamlet: And smelt so? pah!   *[Puts down the skull.]*

Horatio: E'en so, my lord.

Hamlet: To what base uses we may return, Horatio! Why may not imagination
trace the noble dust of Alexander, till 'a find it stopping a bung   170
hole?

Horatio: 'Twere to consider too curiously,° to consider so.

Hamlet: No, faith, not a jot; but to follow him thither with modesty enough,
and likelihood to lead it: as thus: Alexander died, Alexander was buried,
Alexander returneth into dust; the dust is earth; of earth we make loam;°
and why of that loam, whereto he was converted, might they not stop a   175
beer-barrel?

> Imperious° Cæsar, dead and turn'd to clay,
> Might stop a hole to keep the wind away:
> O, that that earth, which kept the world in awe,
> Should patch a wall t'expel the winter's flaw!°   180

But soft! but soft awhile! here comes the king,

*Enter King, Queen, Laertes, and the Corse of [Ophelia, in procession, with
Priest, Lords, etc.].*

> The queen, the courtiers: who is this they follow?
> And with such maimed rites? This doth betoken
> The corse they follow did with desp'rate hand
> Fordo° it° own life: 'twas of some estate.   185
> Couch° we awhile, and mark.   *[Retiring with Horatio.]*

Laertes: What ceremony else?

Hamlet: That is Laertes,
> A very noble youth: mark.

Laertes: What ceremony else?

First Priest: Her obsequies have been as far enlarg'd°   190
> As we have warranty: her death was doubtful;
> And, but that great command o'ersways the order,
> She should in ground unsanctified have lodg'd
> Till the last trumpet; for charitable prayers,
> Shards,° flints and pebbles should be thrown on her: 195
> Yet here she is allow'd her virgin crants,°

171 *curiously:* Minutely.   174 *loam:* Clay paste for brickmaking.   177 *Imperious:* Imperial.
180 *flaw:* Gust of wind.   185 *Fordo:* Destroy; *it:* Its.   186 *Couch:* Hide, lurk.   190 *enlarg'd:*
Extended, referring to the fact that suicides are not given full burial rites.   195 *Shards:* Broken bits
of pottery.   196 *crants:* Garlands customarily hung upon the biers of unmarried women.

Her maiden strewments° and the bringing home
Of bell and burial.°
Laertes: Must there no more be done?
First Priest: No more be done:
We should profane the service of the dead   200
To sing a requiem and such rest to her
As to peace-parted° souls.
Laertes: Lay her i' th' earth:
And from her fair and unpolluted flesh
May violets spring! I tell thee, churlish priest,
A minist'ring angel shall my sister be,   205
When thou liest howling.°
Hamlet: What, the fair Ophelia!
Queen: Sweets to the sweet: farewell!

                                                            [Scattering flowers.]

I hop'd thou shouldst have been my Hamlet's wife;
I thought thy bride-bed to have deck'd, sweet maid,
And not have strew'd thy grave.
Laertes: O, treble woe   210
Fall ten times treble on that cursed head,
Whose wicked deed thy most ingenious sense°
Depriv'd thee of! Hold off the earth awhile,
Till I have caught her once more in mine arms:

                                                            [Leaps into the grave.]

Now pile your dust upon the quick and dead,   215
Till of this flat a mountain you have made,
T' o'ertop old Pelion,° or the skyish head
Of blue Olympus.
Hamlet: *[Advancing]* What is he whose grief
Bears such an emphasis? whose phrase of sorrow
Conjures the wand'ring stars,° and makes them stand   220
Like wonder-wounded hearers? This is I,
Hamlet the Dane.   *[Leaps into the grave.]*
Laertes: The devil take thy soul!   *[Grappling with him.]*
Hamlet: Thou pray'st not well.
I prithee, take thy fingers from my throat;
For, though I am not splenitive° and rash,   225
Yet have I in me something dangerous,
Which let thy wisdom fear: hold off thy hand.
King: Pluck them asunder.
Queen: Hamlet, Hamlet!
All: Gentlemen, —
Horatio: Good my lord, be quiet.

197 *strewments:* Traditional strewing of flowers. 197–198 *bringing . . . burial:* The laying to rest of
the body, to the sound of the bell. 202 *peace-parted:* Allusion to the text "Lord, now lettest thou thy
servant depart in peace." 206 *howling:* I.e., in hell. 212 *ingenious sense:* Mind endowed with
finest qualities. 217 *Pelion:* Olympus, Pelion, and Ossa are mountains in the north of Thessaly.
220 *wand'ring stars:* Planets. 225 *splenitive:* Quick-tempered.

[The Attendants part them, and they come out of the grave.]

Hamlet: Why, I will fight with him upon this theme   230
     Until my eyelids will no longer wag.°
Queen: O my son, what theme?
Hamlet: I lov'd Ophelia: forty thousand brothers
     Could not, with all their quantity° of love,
     Make up my sum. What wilt thou do for her?   235
King: O, he is mad, Laertes.
Queen: For love of God, forbear° him.
Hamlet: 'Swounds,° show me what thou 'lt do:
     Woo't° weep? woo't fight? woo't fast? woo't tear thyself?
     Woo't drink up eisel?° eat a crocodile?   240
     I'll do 't. Dost thou come here to whine?
     To outface me with leaping in her grave?
     Be buried quick with her, and so will I:
     And, if thou prate of mountains, let them throw
     Millions of acres on us, till our ground,   245
     Singeing his pate against the burning zone,°
     Make Ossa like a wart! Nay, an thou 'lt mouth,
     I'll rant as well as thou.
Queen: This is mere madness:
     And thus awhile the fit will work on him;
     Anon, as patient as the female dove.   250
     When that her golden couplets° are disclos'd,
     His silence will sit drooping.
Hamlet: Hear you, sir;
     What is the reason that you use me thus?
     I lov'd you ever: but it is no matter;
     Let Hercules himself do what he may,   255
     The cat will mew and dog will have his day.
King: I pray thee, good Horatio, wait upon him.

                              Exit Hamlet and Horatio.

[To Laertes.] Strengthen your patience in° our last night's speech;
     We'll put the matter to the present push.°
     Good Gertrude, set some watch over your son.   260
     This grave shall have a living° monument:
     An hour of quiet shortly shall we see;
     Till then, in patience our proceeding be.   *Exeunt.*

---

231 *wag:* Move (not used ludicrously).   234 *quantity:* Some suggest that the word is used in a deprecatory sense (little bits, fragments).   237 *forbear:* Leave alone.   238 *'Swounds:* Oath, "God's wounds."   239 *Woo 't:* Wilt thou.   240 *eisel:* Vinegar. Some editors have taken this to be the name of a river, such as the Yssel, the Weissel, and the Nile.   246 *burning zone:* Sun's orbit.   251 *golden couplets:* The pigeon lays two eggs; the young when hatched are covered with golden down.   258 *in:* By recalling.   259 *present push:* Immediate test.   261 *living:* Lasting; also refers (for Laertes's benefit) to the plot against Hamlet.

[Scene II: *A hall in the castle.*]

Enter Hamlet and Horatio.

Hamlet: So much for this, sir: now shall you see the other;
    You do remember all the circumstance?
Horatio: Remember it, my lord!
Hamlet: Sir, in my heart there was a kind of fighting,
    That would not let me sleep: methought I lay   5
    Worse than the mutines° in the bilboes.° Rashly,°
    And prais'd be rashness for it, let us know,
    Our indiscretion sometime serves us well,
    When our deep plots do pall:° and that should learn us
    There's a divinity that shapes our ends,   10 ·
    Rough-hew° them how we will, —
Horatio: That is most certain.
Hamlet: Up from my cabin,
    My sea-gown° scarf'd about me, in the dark
    Grop'd I to find out them; had my desire,
    Finger'd° their packet, and in fine° withdrew   15
    To mine own room again; making so bold,
    My fears forgetting manners, to unseal
    Their grand commission; where I found, Horatio, —
    O royal knavery! — an exact command,
    Larded° with many several sorts of reasons   20
    Importing Denmark's health and England's too,
    With, ho! such bugs° and goblins in my life,°
    That, on the supervise,° no leisure bated,°
    No, not to stay the grinding of the axe,
    My head should be struck off.
Horatio: Is 't possible?   25
Hamlet: Here's the commission: read it at more leisure.
    But wilt thou hear me how I did proceed?
Horatio: I beseech you.
Hamlet: Being thus be-netted round with villanies, —
    Ere I could make a prologue to my brains,   30
    They had begun the play° — I sat me down,
    Devis'd a new commission, wrote it fair:
    I once did hold it, as our statists° do,
    A baseness to write fair° and labour'd much
    How to forget that learning, but, sir, now   35
    It did me yeoman's° service: wilt thou know

SCENE II.   6 *mutines:* Mutineers; *bilboes:* Shackles; *Rashly:* Goes with line 12.   9 *pall:* Fail.
11 *Rough-hew:* Shape roughly; it may mean "bungle."   13 *sea-gown:* "A sea-gown, or a coarse,
high-collered, and short-sleeved gowne, reaching down to the mid-leg, and used most by seamen and
saylors" (Cotgrave, quoted by Singer).   15 *Finger'd:* Pilfered, filched; *in fine:* Finally.   20 *Larded:*
Enriched.   22 *such ... life:* Such imaginary dangers if I were allowed to live; *bugs:* Bugbears.
23 *supervise:* Perusal; *leisure bated:* Delay allowed.   30–31 *prologue ... play:* I.e., before I could
begin to think, my mind had made its decision.   33 *statists:* Statesmen.   34 *fair:* In a clear hand.
36 *yeoman's:* I.e., faithful.

Th' effect of what I wrote?

Horatio: Ay, good my lord.

Hamlet: An earnest conjuration from the king,
    As England was his faithful tributary,
    As love between them like the palm might flourish,   40
    As peace should still her wheaten garland° wear
    And stand a comma° 'tween their amities,
    And many such-like 'As'es° of great charge,°
    That, on the view and knowing of these contents,
    Without debatement further, more or less,   45
    He should the bearers put to sudden death,
    Not shriving-time° allow'd.

Horatio: How was this seal'd?

Hamlet: Why, even in that was heaven ordinant.°
    I had my father's signet in my purse,
    Which was the model of that Danish seal;   50
    Folded the writ up in the form of th' other,
    Subscrib'd it, gave 't th' impression, plac'd it safely,
    The changeling never known. Now, the next day
    Was our sea-fight; and what to this was sequent°
    Thou know'st already.   55

Horatio: So Guildenstern and Rosencrantz go to 't.

Hamlet: Why, man, they did make love to this employment;
    They are not near my conscience; their defeat
    Does by their own insinuation° grow:
    'Tis dangerous when the baser nature comes   60
    Between the pass° and fell incensed° points
    Of mighty opposites.

Horatio: Why, what a king is this!

Hamlet: Does it not, think thee, stand° me now upon —
    He that hath kill'd my king and whor'd my mother,
    Popp'd in between th' election° and my hopes,   65
    Thrown out his angle° for my proper life,
    And with such coz'nage° — is 't not perfect conscience,
    To quit° him with this arm? and is 't not to be damn'd,
    To let this canker° of our nature come
    In further evil?   70

Horatio: It must be shortly known to him from England
    What is the issue of the business there.

Hamlet: It will be short: the interim is mine;
    And a man's life's no more than to say "One."
    But I am very sorry, good Horatio,   75

---

41 *wheaten garland:* Symbol of peace.   42 *comma:* Smallest break or separation. Here *amity* begins and *amity* ends the period, and *peace* stands between like a dependent clause. The comma indicates continuity, link.   43 *'As'es:* The "whereases" of a formal document, with play on the word *ass; charge:* Import, and burden.   47 *shriving-time:* Time for absolution.   48 *ordinant:* Directing.   54 *sequent:* Subsequent.   59 *insinuation:* Interference.   61 *pass:* Thrust; *fell incensed:* Fiercely angered. 63 *stand:* Become incumbent.   65 *election:* The Danish throne was filled by election.   66 *angle:* Fishing line.   67 *coz'nage:* Trickery.   68 *quit:* Repay.   69 *canker:* Ulcer, or possibly the worm which destroys buds and leaves.

That to Laertes I forgot myself;
For, by the image of my cause, I see
The portraiture of his: I'll court his favours:
But, sure, the bravery° of his grief did put me
Into a tow'ring passion.

Horatio: Peace! who comes here?   80

Enter a Courtier [Osric].

Osric: Your lordship is right welcome back to Denmark.

Hamlet: I humbly thank you, sir. *[To Horatio.]* Dost know this water-fly?°

Horatio: No, my good lord.

Hamlet: Thy state is the more gracious; for 'tis a vice to know him. He hath
much land, and fertile: let a beast be lord of beasts,° and his crib shall 85
stand at the king's mess:° 'tis a chough;° but, as I say, spacious in the
possession of dirt.

Osric: Sweet lord, if your lordship were at leisure, I should impart a thing
to you from his majesty.

Hamlet: I will receive it, sir, with all diligence of spirit. Put your bonnet to 90
his right use; 'tis for the head.

Osric: I thank you lordship, it is very hot.

Hamlet: No, believe me, 'tis very cold; the wind is northerly.

Osric: It is indifferent° cold, my lord, indeed.

Hamlet: But yet methinks it is very sultry and hot for my complexion.   95

Osric: Exceedingly, my lord; it is very sultry, — as 'twere, — I cannot tell how.
But, my lord, his majesty bade me signify to you that 'a has laid a great
wager on your head: sir, this is the matter, —

Hamlet: I beseech you, remember° —

                        [Hamlet moves him to put on his hat.]

Osric: Nay, good my lord; for mine ease,° in good faith. Sir, here is newly 100
come to court Laertes; believe me, an absolute gentleman, full of most
excellent differences, of very soft° society and great showing:° indeed, to
speak feelingly° of him, he is the card° or calendar of gentry,° for you
shall find in him the continent of what part a gentleman would see.

Hamlet: Sir, his definement° suffers no perdition° in you; though, I know, 105
to divide him inventorially° would dozy° the arithmetic of memory, and
yet but yaw° neither, in respect of his quick sail. But, in the verity of
extolment, I take him to be a soul of great article;° and his infusion° of
such dearth and rareness,° as, to make true diction of him, his sem-

---

79 *bravery:* Bravado.   82 *water-fly:* Vain or busily idle person.   85 *lord of beasts:* Cf. Genesis 1:26,
28; *his crib . . . mess:* He shall eat at the king's table, i.e., be one of the group of persons (usually four)
constituting a *mess* at a banquet.   86 *chough:* Probably, chattering jackdaw; also explained as *chuff,*
provincial boor or churl.   94 *indifferent:* Somewhat.   99 *remember:* I.e., remember thy courtesy;
conventional phrase for "Be covered."   100 *mine ease:* Conventional reply declining the invitation
of "Remember thy courtesy."   102 *soft:* Gentle; *showing:* Distinguished appearance.   103 *feelingly:*
With just perception; *card:* Chart, map; *gentry:* Good breeding.   105 *definement:* Definition; *perdition:* Loss, diminution.   106 *divide him inventorially:* I.e., enumerate his graces; *dozy:* Dizzy.
107 *yaw:* To move unsteadily (of a ship).   108 *article:* Moment or importance; *infusion:* Infused
temperament, character imparted by nature.   109 *dearth and rareness:* Rarity.

blable° is his mirror; and who else would trace° him, his umbrage,°   110
   nothing more.
Osric: Your lordship speaks most infallibly of him.
Hamlet: The concernancy,° sir? why do we wrap the gentleman in our more
   rawer breath?°
Osric: Sir?   115
Horatio [aside to Hamlet]: Is 't not possible to understand in another
   tongue?° You will do 't, sir, really.
Hamlet: What imports the nomination° of this gentleman?
Osric: Of Laertes?
Horatio [aside to Hamlet]: His purse is empty already; all 's golden words   120
   are spent.
Hamlet: Of him, sir.
Osric: I know you are not ignorant —
Hamlet: I would you did, sir; yet, in faith, if you did, it would not much
   approve° me. Well, sir?   125
Osric: You are not ignorant of what excellence Laertes is —
Hamlet: I dare not confess that, lest I should compare with him in excellence;
   but, to know a man well, were to know himself.°
Osric: I mean, sir, for his weapon; but in the imputation° laid on him by
   them, in his meed° he's unfellowed.   130
Hamlet: What's his weapon?
Osric: Rapier and dagger.
Hamlet: That's two of his weapons: but, well.
Osric: The king, sir, hath wagered with him six Barbary horses: against the
   which he has impawned,° as I take it, six French rapiers and poniards,   135
   with their assigns, as girdle, hangers,° and so: three of the carriages, in
   faith, are very dear to fancy,° very responsive° to the hilts, most delicate°
   carriages, and of very liberal conceit.°
Hamlet: What call you the carriages?
Horatio [aside to Hamlet]: I knew you must be edified by the margent° ere   140
   you had done.
Osric: The carriages, sir, are the hangers.
Hamlet: The phrase would be more german° to the matter, if we could carry
   cannon by our sides: I would it might be hangers till then. But, on: six
   Barbary horses against six French swords, their assigns, and three liberal-   145
   conceited carriages; that's the French bet against the Danish. Why is this
   "impawned," as you call it?
Osric: The king, sir, hath laid, that in a dozen passes between yourself and
   him, he shall not exceed you three hits: he hath laid on twelve for nine;
   and it would come to immediate trial, if your lordship would vouchsafe   150
   the answer.

110 *semblable:* True likeness; *trace:* Follow; *umbrage:* Shadow.   113 *concernancy:* Import.
114 *breath:* Speech.   116 *Is 't . . . tongue?:* I.e., can one converse with Osric only in this outlandish jargon?   118 *nomination:* Naming.   125 *approve:* Command.   128 *but . . . himself:* But to
know a man as excellent were to know Laertes.   129 *imputation:* Reputation.   130 *meed:* Merit.
135 *he has impawned:* He has wagered.   136 *hangers:* Straps on the sword belt from which the
sword hung.   137 *dear to fancy:* Fancifully made; *responsive:* Probably, well balanced, corresponding
closely; *delicate:* I.e., in workmanship.   138 *liberal conceit:* Elaborate design.   140 *margent:* Margin of a book, place for explanatory notes.   143 *german:* Germain, appropriate.

Hamlet: How if I answer "no"?

Osric: I mean, my lord, the opposition of your person in trial.

Hamlet: Sir, I will walk here in the hall: if it please his majesty, it is the breathing time° of day with me; let the foils be brought, the gentleman willing, and the king hold his purpose, I will win for him as I can; if not, I will gain nothing but my shame and the odd hits. 155

Osric: Shall I re-deliver you e'en so?

Hamlet: To this effect, sir; after what flourish your nature will.

Osric: I commend my duty to your lordship. 160

Hamlet: Yours, yours. *[Exit Osric.]* He does well to commend it himself; there are no tongues else for 's turn.

Horatio: This lapwing° runs away with the shell on his head.

Hamlet: 'A did comply, sir, with his dug,° before 'a sucked it. Thus has he — and many more of the same breed that I know the drossy° age dotes on — only got the tune° of the time and out of an habit of encounter;° a kind of yesty° collection, which carries them through and through the most fann'd and winnowed° opinions; and do but blow them to their trial, the bubbles are out.° 165

Enter a Lord.

Lord: My lord, his majesty commended him to you by young Osric, who brings back to him, that you attend him in the hall: he sends to know if your pleasure hold to play with Laertes, or that you will take longer time. 170

Hamlet: I am constant to my purposes; they follow the king's pleasure: if his fitness speaks, mine is ready; now or whensoever, provided I be so able as now. 175

Lord: The king and queen and all are coming down.

Hamlet: In happy time.°

Lord: The queen desires you to use some gentle entertainment to Laertes before you fall to play. 180

Hamlet: She well instructs me. *[Exit Lord.]*

Horatio: You will lose this wager, my lord.

Hamlet: I do not think so; since he went into France, I have been in continual practice; I shall win at the odds. But thou wouldst not think how ill all 's here about my heart: but it is no matter. 185

Horatio: Nay, good my lord, —

Hamlet: It is but foolery; but it is such a kind of gain-giving,° as would perhaps trouble a woman.

Horatio: If your mind dislike any thing, obey it: I will forestall their repair hither, and say you are not fit. 190

Hamlet: Not a whit, we defy augury: there's a special providence in the fall of a sparrow. If it be now, 'tis not to come; if it be not to come, it will

155 *breathing time:* Exercise period.   163 *lapwing:* Peewit; noted for its wiliness in drawing a visitor away from its nest and its supposed habit of running about when newly hatched with its head in the shell; possibly an allusion to Osric's hat.   164 *did comply . . . dug:* Paid compliments to his mother's breast.   165 *drossy:* Frivolous.   166 *tune:* Temper, mood.   166–167 *habit of encounter:* Demeanor of social intercourse; *yesty:* Frothy.   168 *fann'd and winnowed:* Select and refined.   168–169 *blow . . . out:* I.e., put them to the test, and their ignorance is exposed.   178 *In happy time:* A phrase of courtesy.   187 *gain-giving:* Misgiving.

be now; if it be not now, yet it will come: the readiness is all:° since no
man of aught he leaves knows, what is 't to leave betimes? Let be.

*A table prepared. [Enter] Trumpets, Drums, and Officers with cushions; King,
Queen, [Osric,] and all the State; foils, daggers, [and wine borne in;] and Laertes.*

King: Come, Hamlet, come, and take this hand from me.   195

[The King puts Laertes's hand into Hamlet's.]

Hamlet: Give me your pardon, sir: I have done you wrong;
    But pardon 't as you are a gentleman.
    This presence° knows,
    And you must needs have heard, how I am punish'd
    With a sore distraction. What I have done,   200
    That might your nature, honour and exception°
    Roughly awake, I here proclaim was madness.
    Was 't Hamlet wrong'd Laertes? Never Hamlet:
    If Hamlet from himself be ta'en away,
    And when he's not himself does wrong Laertes,   205
    Then Hamlet does it not, Hamlet denies it.
    Who does it, then? His madness: if 't be so,
    Hamlet is of the faction that is wrong'd;
    His madness is poor Hamlet's enemy.
    Sir, in this audience,   210
    Let my disclaiming from a purpos'd evil
    Free me so far in your most generous thoughts,
    That I have shot mine arrow o'er the house,
    And hurt my brother.
Laertes: I am satisfied in nature,°
    Whose motive, in this case, should stir me most   215
    To my revenge: but in my terms of honour
    I stand aloof; and will no reconcilement,
    Till by some elder masters, of known honour,
    I have a voice° and precedent of peace,
    To keep my name ungor'd. But till that time,   220
    I do receive your offer'd love like love,
    And will not wrong it.
Hamlet: I embrace it freely;
    And will this brother's wager frankly play.
    Give us the foils. Come on.
Laertes: Come, one for me.
Hamlet: I'll be your foil,° Laertes: in mine ignorance   225
    Your skill shall, like a star i' th' darkest night,
    Stick fiery off° indeed.
Laertes: You mock me, sir.
Hamlet: No, by this hand.

---

193 *all:* All that matters.   198 *presence:* Royal assembly.   201 *exception:* Disapproval.   214 *nature:* I.e., he is personally satisfied, but his honor must be satisfied by the rules of the code of honor.
219 *voice:* Authoritative pronouncement.   225 *foil:* Quibble on the two senses: "background which
sets something off," and "blunted rapier for fencing."   227 *Stick fiery off:* Stand out brilliantly.

King: Give them the foils, young Osric. Cousin Hamlet,
   You know the wager?
Hamlet: Very well, my lord;   230
   Your grace has laid the odds o' th' weaker side.
King: I do not fear it; I have seen you both:
   But since he is better'd, we have therefore odds.
Laertes: This is too heavy, let me see another.
Hamlet: This likes me well. These foils have all a length?   235

[They prepare to play.]

Osric: Ay, my good lord.
King: Set me the stoups of wine upon that table.
   If Hamlet give the first or second hit,
   Or quit in answer of the third exchange,
   Let all the battlements their ordnance fire;   240
   The king shall drink to Hamlet's better breath;
   And in the cup an union° shall he throw,
   Richer than that which four successive kings
   In Denmark's crown have worn. Give me the cups;
   And let the kettle° to the trumpet speak,   245
   The trumpet to the cannoneer without,
   The cannons to the heavens, the heavens to earth,
   "Now the king drinks to Hamlet." Come begin: *Trumpets the while.*
   And you, the judges, bear a wary eye.
Hamlet: Come on, sir.
Laertes: Come, my lord.   *[They play.]*
Hamlet: One.
Laertes: No.
Hamlet: Judgement.   250
Osric: A hit, a very palpable hit.

Drum, trumpets, and shot. Flourish. A piece goes off.

Laertes: Well; again.
King: Stay; give me drink. Hamlet, this pearl° is thine;
   Here's to thy health. Give him the cup.
Hamlet: I'll play this bout first; set it by awhile.
   Come. *[They play.]* Another hit; what say you?   255
Laertes: A touch, a touch, I do confess 't.
King: Our son shall win.
Queen: He's fat,° and scant of breath.
   Here, Hamlet, take my napkin, rub thy brows:
   The queen carouses° to thy fortune, Hamlet.
Hamlet: Good madam!
King: Gertrude, do not drink.   260
Queen: I will, my lord; I pray you, pardon me. *[Drinks.]*

242 *union:* Pearl.   245 *kettle:* Kettledrum.   252 *pearl:* I.e., the poison.   257 *fat:* Not physically
fit, out of training. Some earlier editors speculated that the term applied to the corpulence of Richard
Burbage, who originally played the part, but the allusion now appears unlikely. *Fat* may also suggest
"sweaty."   259 *carouses:* Drinks a toast.

King [aside]: It is the poison'd cup: it is too late.
Hamlet: I dare not drink yet, madam; by and by.
Queen: Come, let me wipe thy face.
Laertes: My lord, I'll hit him now.
King: I do not think 't.   265
Laertes [aside]: And yet 'tis almost 'gainst my conscience.
Hamlet: Come, for the third, Laertes: you but dally;
     I pray you, pass with your best violence;
     I am afeard you make a wanton° of me.
Laertes: Say you so? come on.   *[They play.]*   270
Osric: Nothing, neither way.
Laertes: Have at you now!

[Laertes wounds Hamlet; then, in scuffling, they change rapiers,° and Hamlet wounds Laertes.]

King: Part them; they are incens'd.
Hamlet: Nay, come again.   *[The Queen falls.]*
Osric: Look to the queen there, ho!
Horatio: They bleed on both sides. How is it, my lord?
Osric: How is 't, Laertes?   275
Laertes: Why, as a woodcock° to mine own springe,° Osric;
     I am justly kill'd with mine own treachery.
Hamlet: How does the queen?
King: She swounds° to see them bleed.
Queen: No, no, the drink, the drink, — O my dear Hamlet, —
     The drink, the drink! I am poison'd.   *[Dies.]*   280
Hamlet: O villany! Ho! let the door be lock'd:
     Treachery! Seek it out.   *[Laertes falls.]*
Laertes: It is here, Hamlet: Hamlet, thou art slain;
     No med'cine in the world can do thee good;
     In thee there is not half an hour of life;   285
     The treacherous instrument is in thy hand,
     Unbated° and envenom'd: the foul practice
     Hath turn'd itself on me; lo, here I lie,
     Never to rise again: thy mother's poison'd:
     I can no more: the king, the king's to blame.   290
Hamlet: The point envenom'd too!
     Then, venom, to thy work.   *[Stabs the King.]*
All: Treason! treason!
King: O, yet defend me, friends; I am but hurt.
Hamlet: Here, thou incestuous, murd'rous, damned Dane,
     Drink off this potion. Is thy union here?   295
     Follow my mother.   *[King dies.]*
Laertes: He is justly serv'd;
     It is a poison temper'd° by himself.

---

269 *wanton:* Spoiled child.   272 *in scuffling, they change rapiers:* According to a widespread stage tradition, Hamlet receives a scratch, realizes that Laertes's sword is unbated, and accordingly forces an exchange.   276 *woodcock:* As type of stupidity or as decoy; *springe:* Trap, snare.   278 *swounds:* Swoons.   287 *Unbated:* Not blunted with a button.   298 *temper'd:* Mixed.

Exchange forgiveness with me, noble Hamlet:
Mine and my father's death come not upon thee,   300
Nor thine on me!   *[Dies.]*
Hamlet: Heaven make thee free of it! I follow thee.
I am dead, Horatio. Wretched queen, adieu!
You that look pale and tremble at this chance,
That are but mutes° or audience to this act,
Had I but time — as this fell sergeant,° Death,   305

Is strict in his arrest — O, I could tell you —
But let it be. Horatio, I am dead;
Thou livest; report me and my cause aright
To the unsatisfied.
Horatio: Never believe it:
I am more an antique Roman° than a Dane: 310
Here 's yet some liquor left.
Hamlet: As th' art a man,
Give me the cup: let go, by heaven, I'll ha 't.
O God! Horatio, what a wounded name,
Things standing thus unknown, shall live behind me!   315
If thou didst ever hold me in thy heart,
Absent thee from felicity awhile,
And in this harsh world draw thy breath in pain,
To tell my story.   *A march afar off.*
        What warlike noise is this?
Osric: Young Fortinbras, with conquest come from Poland,   320
To the ambassadors of England gives
This warlike volley.
Hamlet: O, I die, Horatio;
The potent poison quite o'er-crows° my spirit:
I cannot live to hear the news from England;
But I do prophesy th' election lights   325
On Fortinbras: he has my dying voice;
So tell him, with th' occurrents,° more and less,
Which have solicited.° The rest is silence.   *[Dies.]*
Horatio: Now cracks a noble heart. Good night, sweet prince;
And flights of angels sing thee to thy rest!   330
Why does the drum come hither?   *[March within.]*

Enter Fortinbras, with the [English] Ambassadors [and others].

Fortinbras: Where is this sight?
Horatio: What is it you would see?
If aught of woe or wonder, cease your search.
Fortinbras: This quarry° cries on havoc.° O proud Death,
What feast is toward in thine eternal cell,   335

---

305 *mutes:* Performers in a play who speak no words.   306 *sergeant:* Sheriff's officer.   311 *Roman:*
It was the Roman custom to follow masters in death.   323 *o'er-crows:* Triumphs over.   327 *occur-
rents:* Events, incidents.   328 *solicited:* Moved, urged.   334 *quarry:* Heap of dead; *cries on havoc:*
Proclaims a general slaughter.

That thou so many princes at a shot
So bloodily hast struck?
First Ambassador: The sight is dismal;
    And our affairs from England come too late:
    The ears are senseless that should give us hearing,
    To tell him his commandment is fulfill'd,   340
    That Rosencrantz and Guildenstern are dead:
    Where should we have our thanks?
Horatio: Not from his mouth,°
    Had it th' ability of life to thank you:
    He never gave commandment for their death.
    But since, so jump° upon this bloody question,°   345
    You from the Polack wars, and you from England,
    Are here arriv'd, give order that these bodies
    High on a stage° be placed to the view;
    And let me speak to th' yet unknowing world
    How these things came about: so shall you hear   350
    Of carnal, bloody, and unnatural acts,
    Of accidental judgements, casual slaughters,
    Of deaths put on by cunning and forc'd cause,
    And, in this upshot, purposes mistook
    Fall'n on th' inventors' heads: all this can I   355
    Truly deliver.
Fortinbras: Let us haste to hear it,
    And call the noblest to the audience.
    For me, with sorrow I embrace my fortune:
    I have some rights of memory° in this kingdom,
    Which now to claim my vantage doth invite me.   360
Horatio: Of that I shall have also cause to speak,
    And from his mouth whose voice will draw on more:°
    But let this same be presently perform'd,
    Even while men's minds are wild; lest more mischance,
    On° plots and errors, happen.
Fortinbras: Let four captains   365
    Bear Hamlet, like a soldier, to the stage;
    For he was likely, had he been put on,
    To have prov'd most royal: and, for his passage,°
    The soldiers' music and the rites of war
    Speak loudly for him.   370
    Take up the bodies: such a sight as this
    Becomes the field,° but here shows much amiss.
    Go, bid the soldiers shoot.

Exeunt [marching, bearing off the dead bodies; after which a peal of ordnance is shot off].

342 *his mouth:* I.e., the king's.   345 *jump:* Precisely; *question:* Dispute.   348 *stage:* Platform.
359 *of memory:* Traditional, remembered.   362 *voice ... more:* Vote will influence still others.
365 *On:* On account of, or possibly, on top of, in addition to.   358 *passage:* Death.   372 *field:* I.e.,
of battle.

Considerations for Critical Thinking and Writing

1. Claudius urges Hamlet to leave behind his "obstinate condolement" and give up grieving for his dead father because it represents "impious stubbornness" (I.ii.93–94). Consider Claudius's advice in this speech (lines 87–117). Is it sensible? Why won't Hamlet heed this advice?
2. Are Polonius's admonitions to Laertes and Ophelia in Act I, Scene iii good advice? What does his advice suggest about life at court, given that he is the chief counselor to the king?
3. When the ghost tells Hamlet that Claudius murdered him, Hamlet cries out, "O my prophetic soul!" (I.v.41). Why? What does the ghost demand of Hamlet?
4. What is known about the kind of person Hamlet was before his father's death? Does he have the stature of a tragic hero such as Oedipus? How does news of the murder and his mother's remarriage affect his behavior and view of life? Is he mad, as Polonius assumes, or is he pretending to be mad? Is there a "method in 't" (II.ii.202)? What do we learn from Hamlet's soliloquies?
5. Why does Hamlet find avenging his father's death so difficult? Why doesn't he take decisive action as soon as he seems convinced of Claudius's guilt?
6. What is the purpose of the play within the play? How does it provide a commentary on the action of the larger play?
7. Is Ophelia connected in any way with the crime Hamlet seeks to avenge? Why is he so brutal to Ophelia in Act III, Scene i? Why does she go mad?
8. Does Hamlet think Gertrude is as guilty as Claudius? Why is Hamlet so thoroughly disgusted by her in Act III, Scene iv?
9. Why doesn't Hamlet kill Claudius as he prays (III.iii)? Do you feel any sympathy for Claudius in this scene, or is he presented as a callous murderer?
10. If Hamlet had killed Claudius in Act III and the play had ended there, what would be missing in Hamlet's perceptions of himself and the world? How does his character develop in Acts IV and V? What softens our realization that Hamlet is in various degrees responsible for the deaths of Polonius, Ophelia, Laertes, Rosencrantz, Guildenstern, Claudius, and Gertrude?
11. What purpose does Fortinbras serve in the action? Would anything be lost if he were edited out of the play?
12. Despite its tragic dimensions, *Hamlet* includes humorous scenes and many witty lines delivered by the title character himself. Locate those scenes and lines, and then determine the tone and purpose of the play's humor.

Connections to Other Selections

1. Compare and contrast the humor in *Hamlet* with the humor in Molière's *Tartuffe* (p. 1458). How do you account for the tonal differences in their humor?
2. What kind of a king is Claudius? How does he compare with Creon in Sophocles' *Antigone* (p. 1164)? How are matters of state and the political atmosphere in the world of each play affected by the rules of Claudius and Creon?
3. Here's a long reach but a potentially interesting one: write an essay that considers Gertrude as a wife and mother alongside Nora in Henrik Ibsen's *A Doll House* (p. 1517). How responsible are they to themselves and to others? Can they be discussed in the same breath, or are they from such different worlds that nothing useful can be said about comparing them? Either way, explain your response.

THE TEMPEST

The Tempest, one of Shakespeare's last plays, is usually associated with his three other romances — *The Winters' Tale, Cymbeline,* and *Pericles* — which are concerned with an affirmation of life by characters who endure loss but are reconciled to the good that can come from misfortune. Unlike the violent and dark world of tragedy, romance ends peacefully with the plot bringing us a sense of new beginnings and possibilities.

The play is set on an imaginary enchanted island that evoked for Shakespeare's contemporaries all the exotic strangeness and infinite possibility that explorers attested to in their travel narratives of the newly discovered world of America. This new world became an ambiguous theater for the European imagination: the dream was that paradise might be regained in unspoiled nature free of corrupt histories and sin, but the nightmare was that civilization could be lost in the base, unformed primitivism of unredeemed nature. Shakespeare explores both the powerful attractions and terrifying anxieties his contemporaries experienced concerning this "brave new world."

Twelve years before the action of the play begins, Prospero, a magician and the deposed Duke of Milan, is stranded on a nearly deserted tropical island with his young daughter, Miranda. They had been betrayed by Prospero's brother, Antonio, who usurped the dukedom with the help of Alonso, King of Naples. As the play opens, Prospero, owing to his magical powers, knows that his enemies are sailing near the island, and with the help of his supernatural servant, Ariel, he creates a tempest that forces them to abandon ship and seek refuge on the island.

Ariel divides the refugees into three groups consisting of Prince Ferdinand, the gallant son of Alonso; King Alonso and those attending him, including Sebastion, his treacherous brother, and Antonio, who betrayed Prospero; and Stephano and Trinculo, a pair of comic figures who conspire against Prospero. Shakespeare — through Prospero's magic — plots the action around these three groups as each undergoes a series of ordeals. At the center of the play's energy is Caliban, the aboriginal inhabitant of the island. A deformed savage enslaved by Prospero, Caliban is the product of a sexual union between a witch (who practiced black magic, in contrast to Prospero's white magic) and a devil. Caliban's primitivism seems at once debased and innocent, but however he is perceived, he serves as a means of measuring the characters from the civilized world who stumble onto the island. In his dealings with the other characters Caliban indirectly indicates the significance and value of civilization while simultaneously suggesting its abuses and corruptions.

In the face of usurpation, murderous conspiracies, lust, and depravity, Prospero uses magic to impose discipline and order on his island refugees, and he does so in a spirit of tolerance and forgiveness. What might have become a tragic story of revenge upon those who would destroy Prospero is instead a romantic comedy. Romance ends with reconciliation and love rather than horror and death; *The Tempest* concludes with the serene anticipation of Ferdinand and Miranda's marriage, as vengeance gives merciful way to harmony. In the Epilogue, Prospero steps partially out of character and urges upon his audience a prayer for mercy in all things: "As you from

crimes would pardoned be, / Let your indulgence set me free." The play
makes clear that more than applause is at stake here, since forgiveness is so
crucial to weathering tempests in the real world off the magical island and
off the stage.

WILLIAM SHAKESPEARE (1564–1616)
The Tempest

c. 1611

Names of the Actors

Alonso, King of Naples
Sebastian, his brother
Prospero, the right Duke of Milan
Antonio, his brother, the usurping Duke of Milan
Ferdinand, son to the King of Naples
Gonzalo, an honest old councillor
Adrain and ⎱ lords
Francisco, ⎰
Caliban, a savage and deformed slave
Trinculo, a jester
Stephano, a drunken butler
Master of a ship
Boatswain
Mariners

Miranda, daughter to Prospero

Ariel, an airy spirit
Iris,   ⎫
Ceres,   ⎪
Juno,   ⎬ [presented by] spirits
Nymphs, ⎪
Reapers, ⎭
[*Other Spirits attending on Prospero*]

THE SCENE: *An uninhabited island*

[ACT I

SCENE I: *On board ship, off the island's coast.*]

*A tempestuous noise of thunder and lightning heard. Enter a Shipmaster and
a Boatswain.*

Master: Boatswain!
Boatswain: Here, Master. What cheer?

Master: Good,° speak to the mariners. Fall to 't yarely,° or we run ourselves aground. Bestir, bestir! *Exit.*

Enter Mariners.

Boatswain: Heigh, my hearts! Cheerly, cheerly, my hearts! Yare, yare! Take 5 in the topsail. Tend° to the Master's whistle. — Blow° till thou burst thy wind, if room enough!°

Enter Alonso, Sebastian, Antonio, Ferdinand, Gonzalo, and others.

Alonso: Good Boatswain, have care. Where's the Master? Play the men.°
Boatswain: I pray now, keep below.
Antonio: Where is the Master, Boatswain? 10
Boatswain: Do you not hear him? You mar our labor. Keep° your cabins! You do assist the storm.
Gonzalo: Nay, good,° be patient.
Boatswain: When the sea is. Hence! What cares these roarers° for the name of king? To cabin! Silence! Trouble us not. 15
Gonzalo: Good, yet remember whom thou hast aboard.
Boatswain: None that I more love than myself. You are a councillor; if you can command these elements to silence and work the peace of the present,° we will not hand° a rope more. Use your authority. If you cannot, give thanks you have lived so long and make yourself ready in 20 your cabin for the mischance of the hours, if it so hap° — Cheerly, good hearts! — Out of our way, I say. *Exit.*
Gonzalo: I have great comfort from this fellow. Methinks he hath no drowning mark upon him; his complexion is perfect gallows.° Stand fast, good Fate, to his hanging! Make the rope of his destiny our cable, for our own 25 doth little advantage.° If he be not born to be hanged, our case is miserable.° *Exeunt [courtiers].*

Enter Boatswain.

Boatswain: Down with the topmast! Yare! Lower, lower! Bring her to try wi' the main course.° *(A cry within.)* A plague upon this howling! They are louder than the weather or our office.° 30

Enter Sebastian, Antonio, and Gonzalo.

Yet again? What do you hear? Shall we give o'er° and drown? Have you a mind to sink?
Sebastian: A pox o' your throat, you bawling, blasphemous, incharitable dog!
Boatswain: Work you, then.

Act I. Scene I. 3 *Good:* I.e., it's good you've come, or, my good fellow; *yarely:* Nimbly. 6 *Tend:* Attend; *Blow:* (Addressed to the wind). 7 *if room enough:* As long as we have sea room enough. 8 *Play the men:* Act like men (?) ply, urge the men to exert themselves (?). 11 *Keep:* Remain in. 13 *good:* Good fellow. 14 *roarers:* Waves or winds, or both; spoken to as though they were "bullies" or "blusterers." 18–19 *work . . . present:* Bring calm to our present circumstances. 19 *hand:* Handle. 21 *hap:* Happen. 24 *complexion . . . gallows:* Appearance shows he was born to be hanged (and therefore, according to the proverb, in no danger of drowning). 25–26 *our . . . advantage:* Our own cable is of little benefit. 26–27 *case is miserable:* Circumstances are desperate. 28–29 *Bring . . . course:* Sail her close to the wind by means of the mainsail. 30 *our office:* I.e., the noise we make at our work. 31 *give o'er:* Give up.

Antonio: Hang, cur! Hang, you whoreson, insolent noisemaker! We are less   35
   afraid to be drowned than thou art.
Gonzalo: I'll warrant him for drowning,° though the ship were no stronger
   than a nutshell and as leaky as an unstanched° wench.
Boatswain: Lay her ahold, ahold!° Set her two courses.° Off to sea again! Lay
   her off!   40

Enter Mariners, wet.

Mariners: All lost! To prayers, to prayers! All lost!
            [The Mariners run about in confusion, exiting at random.]
Boatswain: What, must our mouths be cold?°
Gonzalo: The King and Prince at prayers! Let's assist them,
   For our case is as theirs.
Sebastian: I am out of patience.
Antonio: We are merely° cheated of our lives by drunkards.   45
   This wide-chapped° rascal! Would thou mightst lie drowning
   The washing of ten tides!°
Gonzalo: He'll be hanged yet,
   Though every drop of water swear against it
   And gape at wid'st° to glut° him.
   (A confused noise within:)   "Mercy on us!" —
   "We split, we split!"° — "Farewell my wife and children!" —   50
   "Farewell, brother!" — "We split, we split, we split!"   *[Exit Boatswain.]*
Antonio: Let's all sink wi' the King.
Sebastian: Let's take leave of him.   *Exit [with Antonio].*
Gonzalo: Now would I give a thousand furlongs of sea for an acre of barren
   ground: long heath,° brown furze,° anything. The wills above be done!   55
   But I would fain° die a dry death.   *Exit.*

[SCENE II: *The island, near Prospero's cell. On the Elizabethan stage, this cell
is implicitly at hand throughout the play, although in some scenes the convention of flexible distance allows us to imagine characters in other parts
of the island.*]

Enter Prospero [in his magic cloak] and Miranda.

Miranda: If by your art,° my dearest father, you have
   Put the wild waters in this roar, allay° them.
   The sky, it seems, would pour down stinking pitch,
   But that the sea, mounting to th' welkin's cheek,°
   Dashes the fire out. O, I have suffered   5

---

37 *warrant him for drowning:* Guarantee that he will never be drowned.   38 *unstanched:* Insatiable,
loose, unrestrained (suggesting also "incontinent" and "menstrual").   39 *ahold:* Ahull, close to the
wind; *courses:* Sails, i.e., foresail as well as mainsail, set in an attempt to get the ship back out into open
water.   42 *must . . . cold:* I.e., must we drown in the cold sea, or, let us heat up our mouths with
liquor.   45 *merely:* Utterly.   46 *wide-chapped:* With mouth wide open.   47 *lie . . . tides:* (Pirates
were hanged on the shore and left until three tides had come in.)   49 *at wid'st:* Wide open; *glut:*
Swallow.   50 *split:* Break apart.   55 *heath:* Heather; *furze:* Gorse, a weed growing on wasteland.
56 *fain:* Rather.   SCENE II.   1 *art:* Magic.   2 *allay:* Pacify.   4 *welkin's cheek:* Sky's face.

With those that I saw suffer! A brave° vessel,
Who had, no doubt, some noble creature in her,
Dashed all to pieces. O, the cry did knock
Against my very heart! Poor souls, they perished.
Had I been any god of power, I would   10
Have sunk the sea within the earth or ere°
It should the good ship so have swallowed and
The freighting° souls within her.

Prospero: Be collected.°
No more amazement.° Tell your piteous° heart
There's no harm done.

Miranda: O, woe the day!

Prospero: No harm.   15
I have done nothing but° in care of thee,
Of thee, my dear one, thee, my daughter, who
Art ignorant of what thou art, naught knowing
Of whence I am, nor that I am more better°
Than Prospero, master of a full° poor cell,   20
And thy no greater father.

Miranda: More to know.
Did never meddle° with my thoughts.

Prospero: 'Tis time
I should inform thee farther. Lend thy hand
And pluck my magic garment from me. So,

                     [laying down his magic cloak and staff]
Lie there, my art. —Wipe thou thine eyes. Have comfort.   25
The direful spectacle of the wreck,° which touched
The very virtue° of compassion in thee,
I have with such provision° in mine art
So safely ordered that there is no soul—
No, not so much perdition° as an hair   30
Betid° to any creature in the vessel
Which° thou heard'st cry, which thou saw'st sink. Sit down,
For thou must now know farther.

Miranda [sitting]:   You have often
Begun to tell me what I am, but stopped
And left me to a bootless inquisition,°   35
Concluding, "Stay, not yet."

Prospero: The hour's now come;
The very minute bids thee ope thine ear.
Obey, and be attentive. Canst thou remember
A time before we came unto this cell?
I do not think thou canst, for then thou wast not   40
Out° three years old.

---

6 *brave:* Gallant, splendid.   11 *or ere:* Before.   13 *freighting:* Forming the cargo; *collected:* Calm,
composed.   14 *amazement:* Consternation; *piteous:* Pitying.   16 *but:* Except.   19 *more better:* Of
higher rank.   20 *full:* Very.   22 *meddle:* Mingle.   26 *wreck:* Shipwreck.   27 *virtue:* Essence.
28 *provision:* Foresight.   30 *perdition:* Loss.   31 *Betid:* Happened.   32 *Which:* Whom.
35 *bootless inquisition:* Profitless inquiry.   41 *Out:* Fully.

Miranda: Certainly, sir, I can.

Prospero: By what? By any other house or person?
    Of anything the image, tell me, that
    Hath kept with thy remembrance.

Miranda: 'Tis far off,
    And rather like a dream than an assurance   45
    That my remembrance warrants.° Had I not
    Four or five women once that tended me?

Prospero: Thou hadst, and more, Miranda. But how is it
    That this lives in thy mind? What seest thou else
    In the dark backward and abysm of time?°   50
    If thou rememberest aught° ere thou cam'st here,
    How thou cam'st here thou mayst.

Miranda: But that I do not.

Prospero: Twelve year since, Miranda, twelve year since,
    Thy father was the Duke of Milan and
    A prince of power.

Miranda: Sir, are not you my father?   55

Prospero: Thy mother was a piece° of virtue, and
    She said thou wast my daughter; and thy father
    Was Duke of Milan, and his only heir
    And princess no worse issued.°

Miranda: O the heavens!
    What foul play had we, that we came from thence?   60
    Or blessèd was't we did?

Prospero: Both, both, my girl.
    By foul play, as thou sayst, were we heaved thence,
    But blessedly holp° hither.

Miranda: O, my heart bleeds
    To think o' the teen that I have turned you to,°
    Which is from° my remembrance! Please you, farther.   65

Prospero: My brother and thy uncle, called Antonio —
    I pray thee mark me — that a brother should
    Be so perfidious! — he whom next° thyself
    Of all the world I loved, and to him put
    The manage° of my state, as at that time   70
    Through all the seigniories° it was the first,
    And Prospero the prime° duke, being so reputed
    In dignity, and for the liberal arts
    Without a parallel; those being all my study,
    The government I cast upon my brother   75
    And to my state grew stranger,° being transported°

45–46 *assurance . . . warrants:* Certainty that my memory guarantees.   50 *backward . . . time:* Abyss
of the past.   51 *aught:* Anything.   56 *piece:* Masterpiece, exemplar.   59 *no worse issued:* No less
nobly born, descended.   63 *holp:* Helped.   64 *teen . . . to:* Trouble I've caused you to remember
or put you to.   65 *from:* Out of.   68 *next:* Next to.   70 *manage:* Management, administration.
71 *seigniories:* I.e., city-states of northern Italy.   72 *prime:* First in rank and importance.   76 *to . . .*
stranger: I.e., withdrew from my responsibilities as duke; *transported:* Carried away.

And rapt in secret studies. Thy false uncle —
Dost thou attend me?

Miranda: Sir, most heedfully.

Prospero: Being once perfected° how to grant suits,
How to deny them, who t' advance and who   80
To trash° for overtopping,° new created
The creatures° that were mine, I say, or changed 'em,
Or else new formed 'em;° having both the key°
Of officer and office, set all hearts i' the state
To what tune pleased his ear, that° now he was   85
The ivy which had hid my princely trunk
And sucked my verdure° out on 't.° Thou attend'st not.

Miranda: O, good sir, I do.

Prospero: I pray thee, mark me.
I, thus neglecting worldly ends, all dedicated
To closeness° and the bettering of my mind   90
With that which, but by being so retired,
O'erprized all popular rate,° in my false brother
Awaked an evil nature; and my trust,
Like a good parent,° did beget of° him
A falsehood in its contrary as great   95
As my trust was, which had indeed no limit,
A confidence sans° bound. He being thus lorded°
Not only with what my revenue yielded
But what my power might else° exact, like one
Who, having into° truth by telling of it,   100
Made such a sinner of his memory
To° credit his own lie,° he did believe
He was indeed the Duke, out o'° the substitution
And executing th' outward face of royalty°
With all prerogative. Hence his ambition growing —   105
Dost thou hear?

Miranda: Your tale, sir, would cure deafness.

Prospero: To have no screen between this part he played

---

79 *perfected:* Grown skillful.   81 *trash:* Check a hound by tying a cord or weight to its neck;
overtopping: Running too far ahead of the pack; surmounting, exceeding one's authority.   82 *creatures:* Dependents.   82–83 *or changed . . . formed 'em:* I.e., either changed their loyalties and duties
or else created new ones.   83 *key:* (1) Key for unlocking (2) tool for tuning stringed instruments.
85 *that:* So that.   87 *verdure:* Vitality; *on 't:* Of it.   90 *closeness:* Retirement, seclusion.   91–
92 *but . . . rate:* I.e., were it not that its private nature caused me to neglect my public responsibilities,
had a value far beyond what public opinion could appreciate, or, simply because it was done in such
seclusion, had a value not appreciated by popular opinion.   94 *good parent:* (Alludes to the proverb
that good parents often bear bad children; see also line 120); *of:* In.   97 *sans:* Without; *lorded:* Raised
to lordship, with power and wealth.   99 *else:* Otherwise, additionally.   100–102 *Who . . . lie:* I.e.,
who, by repeatedly telling the lie (that he was indeed Duke of Milan), made his memory such a
confirmed sinner against truth that he began to believe his own lie; *into:* Unto, against; *To:* So as to.
103 *out o':* As a result of.   104 *And . . . royalty:* And (as a result of) his carrying out all the visible
functions of royalty.   107–108 *To have . . . it for:* To have no separation or barrier between his role
and himself. (Antonio wanted to act in his own person, not as substitute.)

And him he played it for,° he needs will be°
Absolute Milan.° Me, poor man, my library   110
Was dukedom large enough. Of temporal royalties°
He thinks me now incapable; confederates° —
So dry° he was for sway° — wi' the King of Naples
To give him annual tribute, do him° homage,
Subject his coronet to his° crown, and bend°
The dukedom yet° unbowed — alas, poor Milan! —   115
To most ignoble stooping.
Miranda: O the heavens!
Prospero: Mark his condition° and th' event,° then tell me
  If this might be a brother.
Miranda: I should sin
  To think but° nobly of my grandmother.
  Good wombs have borne bad sons.
Prospero: Now the condition.   120
  This King of Naples, being an enemy
  To me inveterate, hearkens° my brother's suit,
  Which was that he,° in lieu o' the premises°
  Of homage and I know not how much tribute,
  Should presently extirpate° me and mine   125
  Out of the dukedom and confer fair Milan,
  With all the honors, on my brother. Whereon,
  A treacherous army levied, one midnight
  Fated to th' purpose did Antonio open
  The gates of Milan, and, i' the dead of darkness,   130
  The ministers for the purpose° hurried thence
  Me and thy crying self.
Miranda: Alack, for pity!
  I, not remembering how I cried out then,
  Will cry it o'er again. It is a hint°
  That wrings° mine eyes to 't.
Prospero: Hear a little further,   135
  And then I'll bring thee to the present business
  Which now's upon's, without the which this story
  Were most impertinent.°
Miranda: Wherefore° did they not
  That hour destroy us?
Prospero: Well demanded,° wench.°
  My tale provokes that question. Dear, they durst not,   140

---

108 *needs will be:* Insisted on becoming.   109 *Absolute Milan:* Unconditional Duke of Milan.
110 *temporal royalties:* Practical prerogatives and responsibilities of a sovereign.   111 *confederates:*
Conspires, allies himself.   112 *dry:* Thirsty; *sway:* Power.   113 *him:* I.e., the King of Naples.
114 *his . . . his:* Antonio's . . . the King of Naples'; *bend:* Make bow down.   115 *yet:* Hitherto.
117 *condition:* Pact; *event:* Outcome.   119 *but:* Other than.   122 *hearkens:* Listens to.   123 *he:*
The King of Naples; *in . . . premises:* In return for the stipulation.   125 *presently extirpate:* At once
remove.   131 *ministers . . . purpose:* Agents employed to do this; *thence:* From there.   134 *hint:*
Occasion.   135 *wrings:* (1) Constrains (2) wrings tears from.   138 *impertinent:* Irrelevant; *Wherefore:* Why.   139 *demanded:* Asked; *wench:* (Here a term of endearment.)

So dear the love my people bore me, nor set
A mark so bloody° on the business, but
With colors fairer° painted their foul ends.
In few,° they hurried us aboard a bark,°
Bore us some leagues to sea, where they prepared   145
A rotten carcass of a butt,° not rigged,
Nor tackle,° sail, nor mast; the very rats
Instinctively have quit° it. There they hoist us,
To cry to th' sea that roared to us, to sigh
To th' winds whose pity, sighing back again,   150
Did us but loving wrong.°

Miranda: Alack, what trouble
Was I then to you!

Prospero: O, a cherubin
Thou wast that did preserve me. Thou didst smile,
Infusèd with a fortitude from heaven,
When I have decked° the sea with drops full salt,   155
Under my burden groaned, which° raised in me
An undergoing stomach,° to bear up
Against what should ensue.

Miranda: How came we ashore?

Prospero: By Providence divine.   160
Some food we had, and some fresh water, that
A noble Neapolitan, Gonzalo,
Out of his charity, who being then appointed
Master of this design, did give us, with
Rich garments, linens, stuffs,° and necessaries,   165
Which since have steaded much.° So, of° his gentleness,
Knowing I loved my books, he furnished me
From mine own library with volumes that
I prize above my dukedom.

Miranda: Would° I might
But ever° see that man!

Prospero: Now I arise.   *[He puts on his magic cloak.]*   170
Sit still, and hear the last of our sea sorrow.°
Here in this island we arrived; and here
Have I, thy schoolmaster, made thee more profit°
Than other princess'° can, that have more time
For vainer° hours and tutors not so careful.   175

Miranda: Heavens thank you for 't! And now, I pray you, sir—

141–142 *set . . . bloody:* I.e., make obvious their murderous intent (from the practice of marking with the blood of the prey those who have participated in a successful hunt.)   143 *fairer:* Apparently more attractive.   144 *few:* Few words; *bark:* Ship.   146 *butt:* Cask, tub.   147 *Nor tackle:* Neither rigging.   148 *quit:* Abandoned.   151 *Did . . . wrong:* (I.e., the winds pitied Prospero and Miranda, though of necessity they blew them from shore.)   155 *decked:* Covered (with salt tears); adorned.   156 *which:* I.e., the smile.   157 *undergoing stomach:* Courage to go on.   165 *stuffs:* Supplies.   166 *steaded much:* Been of much use; *So, of:* Similarly, out of.   169 *Would:* I wish.   170 *But ever:* I.e., someday.   171 *sea sorrow:* Sorrowful adventure at sea.   173 *more profit:* Profit more.   174 *princess':* Princesses (or the word may be *princes,* referring to royal children both male and female).   175 *vainer:* More foolishly spent.

For still 'tis beating in my mind — your reason
For raising this sea storm?
Prospero: Know thus far forth:
By accident most strange, bountiful Fortune,
Now my dear lady,° hath mine enemies   180
Brought to this shore; and by my prescience
I find my zenith° doth depend upon
A most auspicious star, whose influence°
If now I court not, but omit,° my fortunes
Will ever after droop. Here cease more questions.   185
Thou art inclined to sleep. 'Tis a good dullness,°
And give it way.° I know thou canst not choose.   [Miranda sleeps.]
Come away,° servant, come! I am ready now.
Approach, my Ariel, come.

Enter Ariel.

Ariel: All hail, great master, grave sir, hail! I come   190
To answer thy best pleasure; be 't to fly,
To swim, to dive into the fire, to ride
On the curled clouds, to thy strong bidding task°
Ariel and all his quality.°
Prospero: Hast thou, spirit,
Performed to point° the tempest that I bade thee?   195
Ariel: To every article.
I boarded the King's ship. Now on the beak,°
Now in the waist,° the deck,° in every cabin,
I flamed amazement.° Sometimes I'd divide
And burn in many places; on the topmast,   200
The yards, and bowsprit would I flame distinctly,°
Then meet and join. Jove's lightning, the precursors
O' the dreadful thunderclaps, more momentary
And sight-outrunning° were not.° The fire and cracks
Of sulfurous roaring the most mighty Neptune°   205
Seem to besiege and make his bold waves tremble,
Yea, his dread trident shake.
Prospero: My brave spirit!
Who was so firm, so constant, that this coil°
Would not infect his reason?
Ariel: Not a soul
But felt a fever of the mad° and played   210
Some tricks of desperation. All but mariners
Plunged in the foaming brine and quit the vessel,

180 *my dear lady:* (Refers to Fortune, not Miranda.)   182 *zenith:* Height of fortune (astrological
term).   183 *influence:* Astrological power.   184 *omit:* Ignore.   186 *dullness:* Drowsiness.
187 *give it way:* Let it happen (i.e., don't fight it).   188 *Come away:* Come.   193 *task:* Make
demands upon.   194 *quality:* (1) Fellow spirits (2) abilities.   195 *to point:* To the smallest detail.
197 *beak:* Prow.   198 *waist:* Midships; *deck:* Poop deck at the stern.   199 *flamed amazement:*
Struck terror in the guise of fire, i.e., Saint Elmo's fire.   201 *distinctly:* In different places.
204 *sight-outrunning:* Swifter than sight; *were not:* Could not have been.   205 *Neptune:* Roman god
of the sea.   208 *coil:* Tumult.   210 *of the mad:* I.e., such as madmen feel.

Then all afire with me. The King's son, Ferdinand,
With hair up-staring° — then like reeds, not hair —
Was the first man that leapt; cried, "Hell is empty,   215
And all the devils are here!"
Prospero: Why, that's my spirit!
But was not this nigh shore?
Ariel: Close by, my master.
Prospero: But are they, Ariel, safe?
Ariel: Not a hair perished.
On their sustaining garments° not a blemish,
But fresher than before; and, as thou bad'st° me,   220
In troops° I have dispersed them, 'bout the isle.
The King's son have I landed by himself,
Whom I left cooling° of the air with sighs
In an odd angle° of the isle, and sitting,
His arms in this sad knot.°   *[He folds his arms.]*
Prospero: Of the King's ship,   225
The mariners, say how thou hast disposed,
And all the rest o' the fleet.
Ariel: Safely in harbor
Is the King's ship; in the deep nook,° where once
Thou called'st me up at midnight to fetch dew°
From the still-vexed Bermudas,° there she's hid;   230
The mariners all under hatches stowed,
Who, with a charm joined to their suffered labor,°
I have left asleep. And for the rest o' the fleet,
Which I dispersed, they all have met again
And are upon the Mediterranean float°   235
Bound sadly home for Naples,
Supposing that they saw the King's ship wrecked
And his great person perish.
Prospero: Ariel, thy charge
Exactly is performed. But there's more work.
What is the time o' the day?
Ariel: Past the mid season.°   240
Prospero: At least two glasses.° The time twixt six and now
Must by us both be spent most preciously.
Ariel: Is there more toil? Since thou dost give me pains,°
Let me remember° thee what thou hast promised,
Which is not yet performed me.
Prospero: How now? Moody?   245
What is 't thou canst demand?
Ariel: My liberty.

214 *up-staring:* Standing on end.   219 *sustaining garments:* Garments that buoyed them up in the
sea.   220 *bad'st:* Ordered.   221 *troops:* groups.   223 *cooling of:* Cooling.   224 *angle:* Corner.
225 *sad knot:* (Folded arms are indicative of melancholy.)   228 *nook:* Bay.   229 *dew:* (Collected
at midnight for magical purposes; compare with line 325.)   230 *still-vexed Bermudas:* Ever
stormy Bermudas. . . .   232 *with . . . labor:* By means of a spell added to all the labor they have
undergone.   235 *float:* Sea.   240 *mid season:* Noon.   241 *glasses:* Hourglasses.   243 *pains:* Labors.   244 *remember:* Remind.

Prospero: Before the time be out? No more!

Ariel: I prithee,
    Remember I have done thee worthy service,
    Told thee no lies, made thee no mistakings, served
    Without or grudge or grumblings. Thou did promise   250
    To bate° me a full year.

Prospero: Dost thou forget
    From what a torment I did free thee?

Ariel: No.

Prospero: Thou dost, and think'st it much to tread the ooze
    Of the salt deep,
    To run upon the sharp wind of the north,   255
    To do me° business in the veins° o' the earth
    When it is baked° with frost.

Ariel: I do not, sir.

Prospero: Thou liest, malignant thing! Hast thou forgot
    The foul witch Sycorax, who with age and envy°
    Was grown into a hoop?° Hast thou forgot her?   260

Ariel: No, sir.

Prospero: Thou hast. Where was she born? Speak. Tell me.

Ariel: Sir, in Argier.°

Prospero: O, was she so? I must
    Once in a month recount what thou hast been,
    Which thou forgett'st. This damned witch Sycorax,   265
    For mischiefs manifold and sorceries terrible
    To enter human hearing, from Argier,
    Thou know'st, was banished. For one thing she did°
    They would not take her life. Is not this true?

Ariel: Ay, sir.   270

Prospero: This blue-eyed° hag was hither brought with child°
    And here was left by the sailors. Thou, my slave,
    As thou report'st thyself, was then her servant;
    And, for° thou wast a spirit too delicate
    To act her earthy and abhorred commands,   275
    Refusing her grand hests,° she did confine thee,
    By help of her more potent ministers
    And in her most unmitigable rage,
    Into a cloven pine, within which rift
    Imprisoned thou didst painfully remain   280
    A dozen years; within which space she died
    And left thee there, where thou didst vent thy groans
    As fast as mill wheels strike.° Then was this island—

251 *bate:* Remit, deduct.   256 *do me:* Do for me; *veins:* Veins of minerals, or, underground streams, thought to be analogous to the veins of the human body.   257 *baked:* Hardened.   259 *envy:* Malice. 260 *grown into a hoop:* I.e., so bent over with age as to resemble a hoop.   263 *Argier:* Algiers. 268 *one . . . did:* (Perhaps a reference to her pregnancy, for which her life would be spared.) 271 *blue-eyed:* With dark circles under the eyes or with blue eyelids, implying pregnancy; *with child:* Pregnant.   274 *for:* Because.   276 *hests:* Commands.   283 *as mill wheels strike:* As the blades of a mill wheel strike the water.

Save° for the son that she did litter° here,
A freckled whelp,° hag-born° — not honored with   285
A human shape.
Ariel: Yes, Caliban her son.°
Prospero: Dull thing, I say so:° he, that Caliban
  Whom now I keep in service. Thou best know'st
  What torment I did find thee in. Thy groans
  Did make wolves howl, and penetrate the breasts   290
  Of ever-angry bears. It was a torment
  To lay upon the damned, which Sycorax
  Could not gain undo. It was mine art,
  When I arrived and heard thee, that made gape°
  The pine and let thee out.
Ariel: I thank thee, master.   295
Prospero: If thou more murmur'st, I will rend an oak
  And peg thee in his° knotty entrails till
  Thou hast howled away twelve winters.
Ariel: Pardon, master.
  I will be correspondent° to command
  And do my spriting° gently.°   300
Prospero: Do so, and after two days
  I will discharge thee.
Ariel: That's my noble master!
  What shall I do? Say what? What shall I do?
Prospero: Go make thyself like a nymph o' the sea. Be subject
  To no sight but thine and mine, invisible   305
  To every eyeball else. Go take this shape
  And hither come in 't. Go, hence with diligence!   *Exit [Ariel].*
  Awake, dear heart, awake! Thou hast slept well.
  Awake!
Miranda: The strangeness of your story put   310
  Heaviness° in me.
Prospero: Shake it off. Come on,
  We'll visit Caliban, my slave, who never
  Yields us kind answer.
Miranda: 'Tis a villain, sir,
  I do not love to look on.
Prospero: But, as 'tis,
  We cannot miss° him. He does make our fire,   315
  Fetch in our wood, and serves in offices°
  That profit us. — What ho! Slave! Caliban!
  Thou earth, thou! Speak.
Caliban (within):   There's wood enough within.

---

284 *Save:* Except; *litter:* Give birth to.   285 *whelp:* Offspring (used of animals); *hag-born:* Born of a
female demon.   286 *Yes . . . son:* (Ariel is probably concurring with Prospero's comment about a
"freckled whelp," not contradicting the point about "A human shape.")   287 *Dull . . . so:* I.e., exactly,
that's what I said, you dullard.   294 *gape:* Open wide.   297 *his:* Its.   299 *correspondent:* Responsive, submissive.   300 *spriting:* Duties as a spirit; *gently:* Willingly, ungrudgingly.   311 *Heaviness:*
Drowsiness.   315 *miss:* Do without.   316 *offices:* Functions, duties.

Prospero: Come forth, I say! There's other business for thee.
 Come, thou tortoise! When?° 320

Enter Ariel like a water nymph.

 Fine apparition! My quaint° Ariel,
 Hark in thine ear. *[He whispers.]*
Ariel: My lord, it shall be done. *Exit.*
Prospero: Thou poisonous slave, got° by the devil himself
 Upon thy wicked dam,° come forth!

Enter Caliban.

Caliban: As wicked° dew as e'er my mother brushed 325
 With raven's feather from unwholesome fen°
 Drop on you both! A southwest° blow on ye
 And blister you all o'er!
Prospero: For this, be sure, tonight thou shalt have cramps,
 Side-stitches that shall pen thy breath up. Urchins° 330
 Shall forth at vast° of night that they may work
 All exercise on thee. Thou shalt be pinched
 As thick as honeycomb,° each pinch more stinging
 Than bees that made 'em.°
Caliban: I must eat my dinner.
 This island's mine, by Sycorax my mother, 335
 Which thou tak'st from me. When thou cam'st first,
 Thou strok'st me and made much of me, wouldst give me
 Water with berries in 't, and teach me how
 To name the bigger light, and how the less,°
 That burn by day and night. And then I loved thee 340
 And showed thee all the qualities o' th' isle,
 The fresh springs, brine pits, barren place and fertile.
 Cursed be I that did so! All the charms°
 Of Sycorax, toads, beetles, bats, light on you!
 For I am all the subjects that you have, 345
 Which first was mine own king; and here you sty° me
 In this hard rock, whiles you do keep from me
 The rest o' th' island.
Prospero: Thou most lying slave,
 Whom stripes° may move, not kindness! I have used thee,
 Filth as thou art, with humane° care, and lodged thee 350
 In mine own cell, till thou didst seek to violate
 The honor of my child.

---

320 *When:* (An exclamation of impatience). 321 *quaint:* Ingenious. 323 *got:* Begotten, sired.
324 *dam:* Mother (used of animals). 325 *wicked:* Mischievous, harmful. 326 *fen:* Marsh, bog.
327 *southwest:* I.e., wind thought to bring disease. 330 *Urchins:* Hedgehogs; here, suggesting goblins
in the guise of hedgehogs. 331 *vast:* Lengthy, desolate time. (Malignant spirits were thought to be
restricted to the hours of darkness.) 333 *As thick as honeycomb:* I.e., all over, with as many pinches
as a honeycomb has cells. 334 *'em:* I.e., the honeycomb. 339 *the bigger . . . less:* I.e., the sun and
the moon (see Genesis 1:16: "God then made two great lights: the greater light to rule the day, and
the less light to rule the night"). 343 *charms:* Spells. 346 *sty:* Confine as in a sty. 349 *stripes:*
Lashes. 350 *humane:* (Not distinguished as word from *human*.)

Caliban: Oho, oho! Would 't had been done!
Thou didst prevent me; I had peopled else°
This isle with Calibans.
Miranda: Abhorrèd slave,   355
Which any print° of goodness wilt not take,
Being capable of all ill! I pitied thee,
Took pains to make thee speak, taught thee each hour
One thing or other. When thou didst not, savage,
Know thine own meaning, but wouldst gabble like   360
A thing most brutish, I endowed thy purposes°
With words that made them known. But thy vile race,°
Though thou didst learn, had that in 't which good natures
Could not abide to be with; therefore wast thou
Deservedly confined into this rock,   365
Who hadst deserved more than a prison.°
Caliban: You taught me language, and my prifit on 't
Is I know how to curse. The red plague° rid° you
For learning° me your language!
Prospero: Hagseed,° hence!
Fetch us in fuel, and be quick, thou'rt best,°   370
To answer other business.° Shrugg'st thou, malice?
If thou neglect'st or dost unwillingly
What I command, I'll rack thee with old° cramps,
Fill all thy bones with aches,° make thee roar
That beasts shall tremble at thy din.
Caliban: No, pray thee.   375
[Aside.] I must obey. His art is of such power
It would control my dam's god, Setebos,°
And make a vassal of him.
Prospero: So, slave, hence!   *Exit Caliban.*

*Enter Ferdinand; and Ariel, invisible,° playing and singing. [Ferdinand does
not see Prospero and Miranda.]*

Ariel's Song.

Ariel: Come unto these yellow sands,
And then take hands;   380
Curtsied when you have,° and kissed
The wild waves whist,°

354 *peopled else:* Otherwise populated.   355–366 *Abhorrèd . . . prison:* (Sometimes assigned by
editors to Prospero).   356 *print:* Imprint, impression.   361 *purposes:* Meanings, desires.
362 *race:* Natural disposition; species, nature.   368 *red plague:* Plague characterized by red sores
and evacuation of blood; *rid:* Destroy.   369 *learning:* Teaching; *Hagseed:* Offspring of a female
demon.   370 *thou'rt best:* You'd be well advised.   371 *answer other business:* Perform other tasks.
373 *old:* Such as old people suffer, or, plenty of.   374 *aches:* (Pronounced "aitches").   376 *Setebos:*
(A god of the Patagonians, named in Robert Eden's *History of Travel,* 1577).   377 *Ariel, invisible:*
(Ariel wears a garment that by convention indicates he is invisible to the other characters.)   381 *Curtsied . . . have:* When you have curtsied.   381–382 *kissed . . . whist:* Kissed the waves into silence, or,
kissed while the waves are being hushed.

Foot it featly° here and there,
And, sweet sprites,° bear
The burden.° Hark, hark!

Burden, dispersedly° [within]. Bow-wow.   385
The watchdogs bark.

[Burden, dispersedly within.] Bow-wow.
Hark, hark! I hear
The strain of strutting chanticleer
Cry Cock-a-diddle-dow.

Ferdinand: Where should this music be? I' th' air or th' earth?   390
It sounds no more; and sure it waits upon°
Some god o' th' island. Sitting on a bank,°
Weeping again the King my father's wreck,
This music crept by me upon the waters,
Allaying both their fury and my passion°   395
With its sweet air. Thence° I have followed it,
Or it hath drawn me rather. But 'tis gone.
No, it begins again.

Ariel's Song.

Ariel: Full fathom five thy father lies.
Of his bones are coral made.   400
Those are pearls that were his eyes.
Nothing of him that doth fade
But doth suffer a sea change
Into something rich and strange.
Sea nymphs hourly ring his knell.°

Burden [within]. Ding dong.   405
Hark, now I hear them, ding dong bell.

Ferdinand: The ditty does remember° my drowned father.
This is no mortal business, nor no sound
That the earth owes.° I hear it now above me.

Prospero [to Miranda]: The fringèd curtains of thine eye advance°   410
And say what thou seest yond.

Miranda: What is 't? A spirit?
Lord, how it looks about! Believe me, sir,
It carries a brave° form. But 'tis a spirit.

Prospero: No, wench, it eats and sleeps and hath such senses
As we have, such. This gallant which thou seest   415
Was in the wreck; and, but° he's something stained°
With grief, that's beauty's canker,° thou mightst call him

---

383 *Foot it featly:* Dance nimbly.   384 *sprites:* Spirits.   385 *burden:* Refrain, undersong.
385 *dispersedly:* I.e., from all directions, not in unison.   391 *waits upon:* Serves, attends.
392 *bank:* Sandbank.   395 *passion:* Grief.   396 *Thence:* I.e., from the bank on which I sat.
405 *knell:* Announcement of a death by the tolling of a bell.   407 *remember:* Commemorate.
409 *owes:* Owns.   410 *advance:* Raise.   413 *brave:* Excellent.   416 *but:* Except that; *something
stained:* Somewhat disfigured.   417 *canker:* Cankerworm (feeding on buds and leaves).

A goodly person. He hath lost his fellows
And strays about to find 'em.

Miranda: I might call him
A thing divine, for nothing natural   420
I ever saw so noble.

Prospero [aside]:   It goes on,° I see,
As my soul prompts it. — Spirit, fine spirit, I'll free thee
Within two days for this.

Ferdinand [seeing Miranda]: Most sure, the goddess
On whom these airs° attend! — Vouchsafe° my prayer   425
May know° if you remain° upon this island,
And that you will some good instruction give
How I may bear me° here. My prime° request,
Which I do last pronounce, is — O you wonder!° —
If you be maid or no?°

Miranda: No wonder, sir,   430
But certainly a maid.

Ferdinand: My language? Heavens!
I am the best° of them that speak this speech,
Were I but where 'tis spoken.

Prospero [coming forward]:   How? The best?
What wert thou if the King of Naples heard thee?

Ferdinand: A single° thing, as I am now, that wonders   435
To hear thee speak of Naples.° He does hear me,°
And that he does I weep.° Myself am Naples,°
Who with mine eyes, never since at ebb,° beheld
The King my father wrecked.

Miranda: Alack, for mercy!

Ferdinand: Yes, faith, and all his lords, the Duke of Milan   440
And his brave son° being twain.

Prospero [aside]:   The Duke of Milan
And his more braver° daughter could control° thee,
If now 'twere fit to do 't. At the first sight
They have changed eyes.° — Delicate Ariel,
I'll set thee free for this. *[To Ferdinand.]* A word, good sir.   445
I fear you have done yourself some wrong.° A word!

Miranda [aside]: Why speaks my father so urgently? This
Is the third man that e'er I saw, the first
That e'er I sighed for. Pity move my father
To be inclined my way!

---

421 *It goes on:* I.e., my plan works.   425 *airs:* Songs; *Vouchsafe:* Grant.   426 *May know:* I.e., that
I may know; *remain:* Dwell.   428 *bear me:* Conduct myself; *prime:* Chief.   429 *wonder:* (Miranda's
name means "to be wondered at.")   430 *maid or no:* I.e., a human maiden as opposed to a goddess
or married woman.   432 *best:* I.e., in birth.   435 *single:* (1) Solitary, being at once King of Naples
and myself (2) feeble.   436, 437 *Naples:* The King of Naples.   436 *He does bear me:* I.e., the King
of Naples does hear my words, for I am King of Naples.   437 *And . . . weep:* I.e., and I weep at this
reminder that my father is seemingly dead, leaving me heir.   438 *at ebb:* I.e., dry, not weeping.
441 *son:* (The only reference in the play to a son of Antonio.)   442 *more braver:* More splendid;
control: Refute.   444 *changed eyes:* Exchanged amorous glances.   446 *done . . . wrong:* I.e., spoken falsely.

Ferdinand: O, if a virgin,   450
And your affection not gone forth, I'll make you
The Queen of Naples.
Prospero: Soft, sir! One word more.
[Aside.] They are both in either's° power's; but this swift business
I must uneasy° make, lest too light winning
Make the prize light.° *[To Ferdinand.]* One word more: I charge thee   455
That thou attend° me. Thou dost here usurp
The name thou ow'st° not, and hast put thyself
Upon this island as a spy, to win it
From me, the lord on 't.°
Ferdinand: No, as I am a man.
Miranda: There's nothing ill can dwell in such a temple.   460
If the ill spirit have so fair a house,
Good things will strive to dwell with 't.°
Prospero: Follow me. —
Speak not you for him; he's a traitor. — Come,
I'll manacle thy neck and feet together.
Seawater shalt thou drink; thy food shall be   465
The fresh-brook mussels, withered roots, and husks
Wherein the acorn cradled. Follow.
Ferdinand: No!
I will resist such entertainment° till
Mine enemy has more power.

             He draws, and is charmed° from moving.
Miranda: O dear father,
Make not too rash° a trial of him, for   470
He's gentle,° and not fearful.°
Prospero: What, I say,
My foot° my tutor? — Put thy sword up, traitor,
Who mak'st a show but dar'st not strike, thy conscience
Is so possessed with guilt. Come, from thy ward,°
For I can here disarm thee with this stick   475
And make thy weapon drop. *[He brandishes his staff.]*
Miranda [trying to hinder him]: Beseech you, father!
Prospero: Hence! Hang not on my garments.
Miranda: Sir, have pity!
I'll be his surety.°
Prospero: Silence! One word more
Shall make me chide thee, if not hate thee. What,   480
An advocate for an impostor? Hush!
Thou think'st there is no more such shapes as he,
Having seen but him and Caliban. Foolish wench,

453 *both in either's:* Each in the other's.   454 *uneasy:* Difficult.   454–455 *light . . . light:* Easy . . .
cheap.   456 *attend:* Follow, obey.   457 *ow'st:* Ownest.   459 *on 't:* Of it.   462 *strive . . . with 't:*
I.e., expel the evil and occupy the *temple,* the body.   468 *entertainment:* Treatment.   470 *charmed:*
Magically prevented.   470 *rash:* Harsh.   471 *gentle:* Wellborn; *fearful:* Frightening, dangerous, or
perhaps, cowardly.   472 *foot:* Subordinate (Miranda, the foot, presumes to instruct Prospero, the
head.).   474 *ward:* Defensive posture (in fencing).   479 *surety:* Guarantee.

To° the most of men this is a Caliban,
    And they to him are angels.
Miranda: My affections   485
    Are then most humble; I have no ambition
    To see a goodlier man.
Prospero [to Ferdinand]:   Come on, obey.
    Thy nerves° are in their infancy again
    And have no vigor in them.
Ferdinand: So they are.
    My spirits,° as in a dream, are all bound up.   490
    My father's loss, the weakness which I feel,
    The wreck of all my friends, nor this man's threats
    To whom I am subdued, are but light° to me,
    Might I but through my prison once a day
    Behold this maid. All corners else° o' th' earth   495
    Let liberty make use of; space enough
    Have I in such a prison.
Prospero [aside]: It works. [To Ferdinand.] Come on. —[To Ariel]
    Thou hast done well, fine Ariel! [To Ferdinand.] Follow me.
    [To Ariel.] Hark what thou else shalt do me.°
Miranda [to Ferdinand]:   Be of comfort.   500
    My father's of a better nature, sir,
    Than he appears by speech. This is unwonted°
    Which now came from him.
Prospero [to Ariel]:   Thou shalt be as free
    As mountain winds; but then° exactly do
    All points of my command.
Ariel: To th' syllable.   505
Prospero [to Ferdinand]: Come, follow. [To Miranda.] Speak not for him.
                                                              Exeunt.

[ACT II

Scene I: Another part of the island.]

Enter Alonso, Sebastian, Antonio, Gonzalo, Adrian, Francisco, and others.

Gonzalo [to Alonso]: Beseech you, sir, be merry. You have cause,
    So have we all, of joy, for our escape
    Is much beyond our loss. Our hint° of woe
    Is common; every day some sailor's wife,
    The masters of some merchant, and the merchant,°   5
    Have just our theme of woe. But for the miracle,

484 To: Compared to.   488 nerves: Sinews.   490 spirits: Vital powers.   493 light: Unimportant.
495 corners else: Other corners, regions.   500 me: For me.   502 unwonted: Unusual.   504 then:
Until then, or, if that is to be so.   Act II. Scene I.   3 hint: Occasion.   5 masters . . . the merchant:
Officers of some merchant vessel and the merchant himself, the owner.

I mean our preservation, few in millions
Can speak like us. Then wisely, good sir, weigh
Our sorrow with° our comfort.
Alonso: Prithee, peace.
Sebastian [aside to Antonio]: He receives comfort like cold porridge.°   10
Antonio [aside to Sebastian]: The visitor° will not give him o'er° so.
Sebastian: Look, he's winding up the watch of his wit; by and by it will strike.
Gonzalo [to Alonso]: Sir —
Sebastian [aside to Antonio]: One. Tell.°
Gonzalo: When every grief is entertained   15
   That's offered, comes to th' entertainer° —
Sebastian: A dollar.°
Gonzalo: Dolor comes to him, indeed. You have spoken truer than you
   purposed.
Sebastian: You have taken it wiselier than I meant you should.   20
Gonzalo [to Alonso]: Therefore, my lord —
Antonio: Fie, what a spendthrift is he of his tongue!
Alonso [to Gonzalo]: I prithee, spare.°
Gonzalo: Well, I have done. But yet —
Sebastian [aside to Antonio]: He will be talking.   25
Antonio [aside to Sebastian]: Which, of he or Adrian, for a good wager, first
   begins to crow?°
Sebastian: The old cock.°
Antonio: The cockerel.°
Sebastian: Done. The wager?   30
Antonio: A laughter.°
Sebastian: A match!°
Adrian: Though this island seem to be desert° —
Antonio: Ha, ha, ha!
Sebastian: So, you're paid.°   35
Adrian: Uninhabitable and almost inaccessible —
Sebastian: Yet —
Adrian: Yet —
Antonio: He could not miss 't.°
Adrian: It must needs be° of subtle, tender, and delicate   40
   temperance.°

---

9 *with:* Against.   10 *porridge:* (Punningly suggested by *peace,* i.e., "peas" or "pease," a common
ingredeint of porridge).   11 *visitor:* One taking nourishment and comfort to the sick, as Gonzalo is
doing; *give him o'er:* Abandon him.   14 *Tell:* Keep count.   15–16 *When . . . entertainer:* When
every sorrow that presents itself is accepted without resistance, there comes to the recipient.   17 *dollar:* Widely circulated coin, the German thaler and the Spanish piece of eight (Sebastian puns on
entertainer in the sense of innkeeper; to Gonzalo, *dollar* suggests "dolor," grief).   23 *spare:* Forbear,
cease.   26–27 *Which . . . crow:* Which of the two, Gonzalo or Adrian, do you bet will speak (crow)
first?   28 *old cock:* I.e., Gonzalo.   29 *cockerel:* I.e., Adrian.   31 *laughter:* (1) Burst of laughter
(2) sitting of eggs. (When Adrian, the *cockerel,* begins to speak two lines later, Sebastian loses the
bet. . . .)   32 *A match:* A bargain; agreed.   33 *desert:* Uninhabited.   35 *you're paid:* I.e., you've
had your laugh.   39 *miss 't:* (1) Avoid saying "Yet" (2) miss the island.   40 *must needs be:* Has to
be.   41 *temperance:* Mildness of climate.

Antonio: Temperance° was a delicate° wench.

Sebastian: Ay, and a subtle,° as he most learnedly delivered.°

Adrian: The air breathes upon us here most sweetly.

Sebastian: As if it had lungs, and rotten ones.   45

Antonio: Or as 'twere perfumed by a fen.

Gonzalo: Here is everything advantageous to life.

Antonio: True, save° means to live.

Sebastian: Of that there's none, or little.

Gonzalo: How lush and lusty° the grass looks! How green!   50

Antonio: The ground indeed is tawny.°

Sebastian: With an eye° of green in 't.

Antonio: He misses not much.

Sebastian: No. He doth but° mistake the truth totally.

Gonzalo: But the rarity of it is — which is indeed almost beyond credit — 55

Sebastian: As many vouched rarities° are.

Gonzalo: That our garments, being, as they were, drenched in the sea, hold
notwithstanding their freshness and glosses, being rather new-dyed than
stained with salt water.

Antonio: If but one of his pockets° could speak, would it not say he lies?   60

Sebastian: Ay, or very falsely pocket up° his report.°

Gonzalo: Methinks our garments are now as fresh as when we put them on
first in Afric, at the marriage of the King's fair daughter Claribel to the
King of Tunis.

Sebastian: 'Twas a sweet marriage, and we prosper well in our return.   65

Adrian: Tunis was never graced before with such a paragon to° their queen.

Gonzalo: Not since widow Dido's° time.

Antonio [aside to Sebastian]: Widow? A pox o' that! How came that "widow"
in? Widow Dido!

Sebastian: What if he had said "widower Aeneas" too? Good Lord, how you 70
take° it!

Adrian [to Gonzalo]: "Widow Dido" said you? You make me study of° that.
She was of Carthage, not of Tunis.

Gonzalo: This Tunis, sir, was Carthage.

Adrian: Carthage?   75

Gonzalo: I assure you, Carthage.

---

42 *Temperance:* A girl's name; *delicate:* (Here it means "given to pleasure, voluptuous"; in line 40,
"pleasant." Antonio is evidently suggesting that *tender, and delicate temperance* sounds like a Puritan
phrase, which Antonio then mocks by applying the words to a woman rather than an island. He began
this bawdy comparison with a double entendre on *inaccessible,* line 36.)   43 *subtle:* (Here it means
"tricky, sexually crafty"; in line 40, "delicate."); *delivered:* Uttered. (Sebastian joins Antonio in baiting
the Puritans with his use of the pious cant phrase *learnedly delivered.*)   48 *save:* Except.   50 *lusty:*
Healty.   51 *tawny:* dull brown, yellowish.   52 *eye:* Tinge, or spot (perhaps with reference to
Gonzalo's eye or judgment).   54 *but:* Merely.   56 *vouched rarities:* Allegedly real though strange
sights.   60 *pockets:* I.e., because they are muddy.   61 *pocket up:* I.e., conceal, suppress; often used
in the sense of "receive unprotestingly, fail to respond to a challenge"; *his report:* (Sebastian's jest is
that the evidence of Gonzalo's soggy and sea-stained pockets would confute Gonzalo's speech and his
reputation for truth telling.)   66 *to:* For.   67 *widow Dido:* Queen of Carthage, deserted by Aeneas.
(She was, in fact, a widow when Aeneas, a widower, met her, but Antonio may be amused at Gonzalo's
prudish use of the term "widow" to describe a woman deserted by her lover.)   71 *take:* Understand,
respond to, interpret.   72 *study of:* Think about.

Antonio: His word is more than the miraculous harp.°
Sebastian: He hath raised the wall, and houses too.
Antonio: What impossible matter will he make easy next?
Sebastian: I think he will carry this island home in his pocket and give it his   80
    son for an apple.
Antonio: And, sowing the kernels° of it in the sea, bring forth more islands.
Gonzalo: Ay.°
Antonio: Why, in good time.°
Gonzalo [to Alonso]: Sir, we were talking° that our garments seem now as   85
    fresh as when we were at Tunis at the marriage of your daughter, who
    is now queen.
Antonio: And the rarest° that e'er came there.
Sebastian: Bate,° I beseech you, widow Dido.
Antonio: O, widow Dido! Ay, widow Dido.   90
Gonzalo: Is not, sir, my doublet° as fresh as the first day I wore it? I mean,
    in a sort.°
Antonio: That "sort"° was well wished for.
Gonzalo: When I wore it at your daugher's marriage.
Alonso: You cram these words into mine ears against   95
    The stomach of my sense.° Would I had never
    Married° my daughter there! For, coming thence,
    My son is lost and, in my rate,° she too,
    Who is so far from Italy removed
    I ne'er again shall see her. O thou mine heir   100
    Of Naples and of Milan, what strange fish
    Hath made his meal on thee?
Francisco: Sir, he may live.
    I saw him beat the surges° under him
    And ride upon their backs. He trod the water,
    Whose enmity he flung aside, and breasted   105
    The surge most swoll'n that met him. His bold head
    'Bove the contentious waves he kept, and oared
    Himself with his good arms in lusty° stroke
    To th' shore, that o'er his° wave-worn basis bowed,°
    As° stooping to relieve him. I not doubt   110
    He came alive to land.
Alonso: No, no, he's gone.

---

77 *miraculous harp:* (Alludes to Amphion's harp, with which he raised the walls of Thebes; Gonzalo has exceeded that deed by recreating ancient Carthage — *wall and houses* — mistakenly on the site of modern-day Tunis. Some Renaissance commentators believed, like Gonzalo, that the two sites were near each other.)   82 *kernels:* Seeds.   83 *Ay:* (Gonzalo may be reasserting his point about Carthage, or he may be responding ironically to Antonio, who, in turn, answers sarcastically.)   84 *in good time:* (An expression of ironical acquiescence or amazement, i.e., "sure, right away.")   85 *talking:* Saying.   88 *rarest:* Most remarkable, beautiful.   89 *Bate:* Abate, except, leave out (Sebastian says sardonically, surely you should allow widow Dido to be an exception).   91 *doublet:* Close-fitting jacket.   92 *in a sort:* In a way.   93 *sort:* (Antonio plays on the idea of drawing lots and on "fishing" for something to say.)   96 *The stomach . . . sense:* My appetite for hearing them.   97 *Married:* Given in marriage.   98 *rate:* Estimation, opinion.   103 *surges:* Waves.   108 *lusty:* Vigorous. 109 *that . . . bowed:* I.e., that projected out over the base of the cliff that had been eroded by the surf, thus seeming to bend down toward the sea; *his:* Its.   110 *As:* As if.

Sebastian [to Alonso]: Sir, you may thank yourself for this great loss,
That° would not bless our Europe with your daughter,
But rather° loose° her to an African,
Where she at least is banished from your eye,°   115
Who hath cause to wet the grief on 't.°
Alonso: Prithee, peace.
Sebastian: You were kneeled to and importuned° otherwise
By all of us, and the fair soul herself
Weighed between loathness and obedience at
Which end o' the beam should bow.° We have lost your son,   120
I fear, forever. Milan and Naples have
More widows in them of this business' making°
Than we bring men to comfort them.
The fault's your own.
Alonso: So is the dear'st° o' the loss.   125
Gonzalo: My lord Sebastian,
The truth you speak doth lack some gentleness
And time° to speak it in. You rub the sore
When you should bring the plaster.°
Sebastian: Very well.
Antonio: And most chirurgeonly.°   130
Gonzalo [to Alonso]: It is foul weather in us all, good sir,
When you are cloudy.
Sebastian [to Antonio]:   Fowl° weather?
Antonio [to Sebastian]:   Very foul.
Gonzalo: Had I plantation° of this isle, my lord —
Antonio [to Sebastian]: He'd sow 't with nettle seed.
Sebastian: Or docks, or mallows.° 135
Gonzalo: And were the king on 't, what would I do?
Sebastian: Scape° being drunk for want° of wine.
Gonzalo: I' the commonwealth I would by contraries°
Execute all things; for no kind of traffic,°
Would I admit; no name of magistrate;   140
Letters° should not be known; riches, poverty,
And use of service,° none; contract, succession,°

---

113 *That:* You who.   114 *rather:* Would rather; *loose:* (1) Release, let loose (2) lose.   115 *is banished from your eye:* Is not constantly before your eye to serve as a reproachful reminder of what you have done.   116 *Who . . . on 't:* I.e., your eye, which has good reason to weep because of this, or, Claribel, who has good reason to weep for it.   117 *importuned:* Urged, implored.   118–120 *the fair . . . bow:* Claribel herself was poised uncertainly between unwillingness to marry and obedience to her father as to which end of the scales should sink, which should prevail.   122 *of . . . making:* On account of this marriage and subsequent shipwreck.   125 *dear'st:* Heaviest, most costly.   128 *time:* Appropriate time.   129 *plaster:* (A medical application).   130 *chirurgeonly:* Like a skilled surgeon. (Antonio mocks Gonzalo's medical analogy of a *plaster* aplied curatively to a wound.)   132 *Fowl:* (With a pun on *foul,* returning to the imagery of lines 26–29).   134 *plantation:* Colonization (with subsequent wordplay on the literal meaning, "planting").   135 *docks, mallows:* (Weeds used as antidotes for nettle stings).   137 *Scape:* Escape; *want:* Lack. (Sebastian jokes sarcastically that this hypothetical ruler would be saved from dissipation only by the barrenness of the island.)   138 *by contraries:* By what is directly opposite to usual custom.   139 *traffic:* Trade.   141 *Letters:* Learning. 142 *use of service:* Custom of employing servants; *succession:* Holding of property by right of inheritance.

Bourn, bound of land, tilth,° vineyard, none;
No use of metal, corn,° or wine, or oil;
No occupation; all men idle, all,   145
And women too, but innocent and pure;
No sovereignty—
Sebastian: Yet he would be king on 't.
Antonio: The latter end of his commonwealth forgets the beginning.
Gonzalo: All things in common nature should produce
Without sweat or endeavor. Treason, felony,   150
Sword, pike,° knife, gun, or need of any engine°
Would I not have; but nature should bring forth,
Of its own kind, all foison,° all abundance,
To feed my innocent people.
Sebastian: No marrying 'mong his subjects?   155
Antonio: None, man, all idle—whores and knaves.
Gonzalo: I would with such perfection govern, sir,
T' excel the Golden Age.°
Sebastian: 'Save° His Majesty!
Antonio: Long live Gonzalo!
Gonzalo: And—do you mark me, sir?
Alonso: Prithee, no more. Thou dost talk nothing to me.   160
Gonzalo: I do well believe Your Highness, and did it to minister occasion°
    to these gentlemen, who are of such sensible° and nimble lungs that they
    always use° to laugh at nothing.
Antonio: 'Twas you we laughed at.
Gonzalo: Who in this kind of merry fooling am nothing to you; so you may   165
    continue, and laugh at nothing still.
Antonio: What a blow was there given!
Sebastian: An° it had not fallen flat-long.°
Gonzalo: You are gentlemen of brave mettle;° you would lift the moon out
    of her sphere° if she would continue in it five weeks without changing.   170

Enter Ariel [invisible] playing solemn music.

Sebastian: We would so, and then go a-batfowling.°
Antonio: Nay, good my lord, be not angry.
Gonzalo: No, I warrant you, I will not adventure my discretion so weakly.°
    Will you laugh me asleep? For I am very heavy.°
Antonio: Go sleep, and hear us.°   175

---

143 *Bourn . . . tilth:* Boundaries, property limits, tillage of soil.   144 *corn:* Grain.   151 *pike:* Lance;
engine: Instrument of warfare.   153 *foison:* Plenty.   158 *the Golden Age:* The age, according to
Hesiod, when Cronus, or Saturn, ruled the world; an age of innocence and abundance; *'Save:* God save.
161 *minister occasion:* Furnish opportunity.   162 *sensible:* Sensitive.   163 *use:* Are accustomed.
168 *An:* If; *flat-long:* With the flat of the sword, i.e., ineffectually (Compare with "fallen flat.").
169 *mettle:* Temperament, courage.   (The sense of *metal,* indistinguishable as a form from *mettle,*
continues the metaphor of the sword.)   170 *sphere:* Orbit (literally, one of the concentric zones
occupied by planets in Ptolemaic astronomy).   171 *a-batfowling:* Hunting birds at night with lantern
and *bat,* or "stick"; also, gulling a simpleton (Gonzalo is the simpleton, or fowl, and Sebastian will use
the moon as his lantern).   173 *adventure . . . weakly:* Risk my reputation for discretion for so trivial
a cause (by getting angry at these sarcastic fellows).   174 *heavy:* Sleepy.   175 *Go . . . us:* I.e., get
ready for sleep, and we'll do our part by laughing.

[All sleep except Alonso, Sebastian, and Antonio.]

Alonso: What, all so soon asleep? I wish mine eyes
    Would, with themselves, shut up my thoughts.° I find
    They are inclined to do so.
Sebastian: Please you, sir,
    Do not omit° the heavy° offer of it.
    It seldom visits sorrow; when it doth,   180
    It is a comforter.
Antonio: We two, my lord,
    Will guard your person while you take your rest,
    And watch your safety.
Alonso: Thank you. Wondrous heavy.

                                     [Alonso sleeps. Exit Ariel.]
Sebastian: What a strange drowsiness possesses them!
Antonio: It is the quality o' the climate.
Sebastian: Why   185
    Doth it not then our eyelids sink? I find not
    Myself disposed to sleep.
Antonio: Nor I. My spirits are nimble.
    They° fell together all, as by consent;°
    They dropped, as by a thunderstroke. What might,
    Worthy Sebastian, O, what might — ? No more.   190
    And yet methinks I see it in thy face,
    What thou shouldst be. Th' occasion speaks thee,° and
    My strong imagination sees a crown
    Dropping upon thy head.
Sebastian: What, art thou waking?
Antonio: Do you not hear me speak?
Sebastian: I do, and surely   195
    It is a sleepy° language, and thou speak'st
    Out of thy sleep. What is it thou didst say?
    This is a strange repose, to be asleep
    With eyes wide open — standing, speaking, moving —
    And yet so fast asleep.
Antonio: Noble Sebastian,   200
    Thou lett'st thy fortune sleep — die, rather; wink'st°
    Whiles thou art waking.
Sebastian: Thou dost snore distinctly;°
    There's meaning in thy snores.
Antonio: I am more serious than my custom. You
    Must be so too if heed° me, which to do   205
    Trebles thee o'er.°
Sebastian: Well, I am standing water.°

177 *Would . . . thoughts:* Would shut off my melancholy brooding when they close themselves in sleep.
179 *omit:* Neglect; *heavy:* Drowsy.   188 *They:* The sleepers; *consent:* Common agreement.
192 *occasion speaks thee:* Opportunity of the moment calls upon you, i.e., proclaims you usurper of
Alonso's crown.   196 *sleepy:* Dreamlike, fantastic.   201 *wink'st:* (You) shut your eyes.   202 *distinctly:* Articulately.   205 *if heed:* If you heed.   206 *Trebles thee o'er:* Makes you three times as great
and rich; *standing water:* Water that neither ebbs nor flows, at a standstill.

Antonio: I'll teach you how to flow.

Sebastian: Do so. To ebb°
    Hereditary sloth° instructs me.

Antonio: O,
    If you but knew how you the purpose cherish
    Whiles thus you mock it!° How, in stripping it,   210
    You more invest° it!° Ebbing men, indeed,
    Most often do so near the bottom° run
    By their own fear or sloth.

Sebastian: Prithee, say on.
    The setting° of thine eye and cheek proclaim
    A matter° from thee, and a birth indeed   215
    Which throes° thee much to yield.°

Antonio: Thus, sir:
    Although this lord° of weak remembrance,° this
    Who shall be of as little memory
    When he is earthed,° hath here almost persuaded —
    For he's a spirit of persuasion, only   220
    Professes to persuade° — the King his son's alive,
    'Tis as impossible that he's undrowned
    As he that sleeps here swims.

Sebastian: I have no hope
    That he's undrowned.

Antonio: O, out of that "no hope"
    What great hope have you! No hope that way° is   225
    Another way so high a hope that even
    Ambition cannot pierce a wink° beyond,
    But doubt discovery there.° Will you grant with me
    That Ferdinand is drowned?

Sebastian: He's gone.

Antonio: Then tell me,
    Who's the next heir of Naples?

Sebastian: Claribel.   230

Antonio: She that is Queen of Tunis; she that dwells
    Ten leagues beyond man's life;° she that from Naples
    Can have no note,° unless the sun were post° —

207 *ebb:* Recede, decline.   208 *Hereditary sloth:* Natural laziness and the position of younger brother, one who cannot inherit.   209–210 *If . . . mock it:* If you only knew how much you really enhance the value of ambition even while your words mock your purpose.   210–211 *How . . . invest it:* I.e., how the more you speak flippantly of ambition, the more you, in effect, affirm it; *invest:* Clothe (Antonio's paradox is that, by skeptically stripping away illusions, Sebastian can see the essence of a situation and the opportunity it presents or that, by disclaiming and deriding his purpose, Sebastian shows how valuable it really is).   112 *the bottom:* I.e., on which unadventurous men may go aground and miss the tide of fortune.   214 *setting:* Set expression (of earnestness).   215 *matter:* Matter of importance.   216 *throes:* Causes pain, as in giving birth; *yield:* Give forth, speak about.   217 *this lord:* I.e., Gonzalo. *remembrance:* (1) Power of remembering (2) being remembered after his death.   219 *earthed:* Buried.   220–221 *only . . . persuade:* Whose whole function (as a privy councillor) is to persuade.   225 *that way:* I.e., in regard to Ferdinand's being saved.   227–228 *Ambition . . . there:* Ambition itself cannot see any further than that hope (of the crown), is unsure of finding anything to achieve beyond it or even there.   227 *wink:* Glimpse.   232 *Ten . . . life:* I.e., further than the journey of a lifetime.   233 *note:* News, intimation; *post:* Messenger.

The Man i' the Moon's too slow — till newborn chins
Be rough and razorable;° she that from° whom   235
We all were sea-swallowed, though some cast° again,
And by that destiny to perform an act
Whereof what's past is prologue, what to come
In yours and my discharge.°
Sebastian: What stuff is this? How say you?   240
  'Tis true my brother's daughter's Queen of Tunis,
  So is she heir of Naples, twixt which regions
  There is some space.
Antonio: A space whose every cubit°
  Seems to cry out, "How shall that Claribel
  Measure us° back to Naples? Keep° in Tunis,   245
  And let Sebastian wake."° Say this were death
  That now hath seized them, why, they were no worse
  Than now they are. There be° that can rule Naples
  As well as he that sleeps, lords that can prate°
  As amply and unnecessarily   250
  As this Gonzalo. I myself could make
  A chough of as deep chat.° O, that you bore
  The mind that I do! What a sleep were this
  For your advancement! Do you understand me?
Sebastian: Methinks I do.
Antonio: And how does your content°   255
  Tender° your own good fortune?
Sebastian: I remember
  You did supplant your brother Prospero.
Antonio: True.
  And look how well my garments sit upon me,
  Much feater° than before. My brother's servants
  Were then my fellows. Now they are my men.   260
Sebastian: But, for your conscience?
Antonio: Ay, sir, where lies that? If 'twere a kibe,°
  'Twould put me to° my slipper; but I feel not
  This deity in my bosom. Twenty consciences
  That stand twixt me and Milan,° candied° be they°   265
  And melt ere they molest!° Here lies your brother,
  No better than the earth he lies upon,
  If he were that which now he's like — that's dead,
  Whom I, with this obedient steel, three inches of it,

---

235 *razorable:* Ready for shaving; *from:* On our voyage from.   236 *cast:* Were disgorged (with a pun on *casting* of parts for a play).   239 *discharge:* Performance.   243 *cubit:* Ancient measure of length of about twenty inches.   245 *Measure us:* I.e., traverse the cubits, find her way; *Keep:* Stay (addressed to Clairbel).   246 *wake:* I.e., to his good fortune.   248 *There be:* There are those.   249 *prate:* Speak foolishly.   251–252 *I . . . chat:* I could teach a jackdaw to talk as wisely, or, be such a garrulous talker myself.   255 *content:* Desire, inclination.   256 *Tender:* Regard, look after.   259 *feater:* More becomingly, fittingly.   262 *kibe:* Chillblain, here a sore on the heel.   263 *put me to:* Oblige me to wear.   265 *Milan:* The dukedom of Milan; *candied:* Frozen, congealed in crystalline form; *be they:* May they be.   266 *molest:* Interfere.

Can lay to bed forever; whiles you, doing thus,° 270
To the perpetual wink° for aye° might put
This ancient morsel, this Sir Prudence, who
Should not° upbraid our course. For all the rest,
They'll take suggestion° as a cat laps milk;
They'll tell the clock° to any business that 275
We say befits the hour.
Sebastian: Thy case, dear friend,
Shall be my precedent. As thou gott'st Milan,
I'll come by Naples. Draw thy sword. One stroke
Shall free thee from the tribute° which thou payest,
And I the king shall love thee.
Antonio: Draw together; 280
And when I rear my hand, do you the like
To fall it° on Gonzalo.   *[They draw.]*
Sebastian: O, but one word.   *[They talk apart.]*

Enter Ariel [invisible], with music and song.

Ariel [to Gonzalo]: My master through his art foresees the danger
That you, his friend, are in, and sends me forth —
For else his project dies — to keep them living. 285
                                        Sings in Gonzalo's ear.
    While you here do snoring lie,
    Open-eyed conspiracy
        His time° doth take.
    If of life you keep a care,
    Shake off slumber, and beware. 290
        Awake, awake!
Antonio: Then let us both be sudden.°
Gonzalo [waking]: Now, good angels preserve the King!
                                        [The others wake.]
Alonso: Why, how now, ho, awake? Why are you drawn?
    Wherefore this ghastly looking?
Gonzalo: What's the matter? 295
Sebastian: Whiles we stood here securing° your repose,
    Even now, we heard a hollow burst of bellowing
    Like bulls, or rather lions. Did 't not wake you?
    It struck mine ear most terribly.
Alonso: I heard nothing.
Antonio: O, 'twas a din to fright a monster's ear, 300
    To make an earthquake! Sure it was the roar
    Of a whole herd of lions.
Alonso: Heard you this, Gonzalo?
Gonzalo: Upon mine honor, sir. I heard a humming,

270 *thus:* Similarly. (The actor makes a stabbing gesture.)   271 *wink:* Sleep, closing of eyes; *aye:*
Ever.   273 *Should not:* Would not then be able to.   274 *take suggestion:* Respond to prompting.
275 *tell the clock:* I.e., agree, answer appropriately, chime.   279 *tribute:* (See I.ii.113–124.)
282 *fall it:* Let it fall.   288 *time:* Opportunity.   292 *sudden:* Quick.   296 *securing:* Standing
guard over.

And that a strange one too, which did awake me.   305
I shaked you, sir, and cried.° As mine eyes opened,
I saw their weapons drawn. There was a noise,
That's verily.° 'Tis best we stand upon our guard,
Or that we quit this place. Let's draw our weapons.
Alonso: Lead off this ground, and let's make further search   310
For my poor son.
Gonzalo: Heavens keep him from these beasts!
For he is, sure, i' th' island.
Alonso: Lead away.
Ariel [aside]: Prospero my lord shall know what I have done.
So, King, go safely on to seek thy son.   Exeunt [separately].

[Scene II: Another part of the island.]

Enter Caliban with a burden of wood. A noise of thunder heard.

Caliban: All the infections that the sun sucks up
From bogs, fens, flats,° on Prosper fall, and make him
By inchmeal° a disease! His spirits hear me,
And yet I needs must° curse. But they'll nor° pinch,
Fright me with urchin shows,° pitch me i' the mire,   5
Nor lead me, like a firebrand,° in the dark
Out of my way, unless he bid 'em. But
For every trifle are they set upon me,
Sometimes like apes, that mow° and chatter at me
And after bite me; then like hedgehogs, which   10
Lie tumbling in my barefoot way and mount
Their pricks at my footfall. Sometimes am I
All wound with° adders, who with cloven tongues
Do hiss me into madness.

Enter Trinculo.
                              Lo, now, lo!
Here comes a spirit of his, and to torment me   15
For bringing wood in slowly. I'll fall flat.
Perchance he will not mind° me.   [He lies down.]
Trinculo: Here's neither bush nor shrub to bear off° any weather at all. And
another storm brewing; I hear it sing i' the wind. Yond same black cloud,
yond huge one, looks like a foul bombard° that would shed his° liquor.   20
If it should thunder as it did before, I know not where to hide my head.
Yond same cloud cannot choose but fall by pailfuls. [Seeing Caliban.]
What have we here, a man or a fish? Dead or alive? A fish, he smells like
a fish; a very ancient and fishlike smell; a kind of not-of-the-newest Poor
John.° A strange fish! Were I in England now, as once I was, and had but   25

---

306 *cried:* Called out.   308 *verily:* True.   Scene II.   2 *flats:* Swamps.   3 *By inchmeal:* Inch by
inch.   4 *needs must:* Have to; *nor:* Neither.   5 *urchin shows:* Elvish apparitions shaped like hedgehogs.   6 *like a firebrand:* They in the guise of a will-o'-the-wisp.   9 *mow:* Make faces.
13 *wound with:* Entwined by.   17 *mind:* Notice.   18 *bear off:* Keep off.   20 *foul bombard:* Dirty
leather jug; *his:* Its.   25 *Poor John:* Salted fish, type of poor fare.

this fish painted,° not a holiday fool there but would give a piece of silver. There would this monster make a man.° Any strange beast there makes a man. When they will not give a doit° to relieve a lame beggar, they will lay out ten to see a dead Indian. Legged like a man, and his fins like arms! Warm, o' my troth!° I do now let loose my opinion, hold it° no longer: this is no fish, but an islander, that hath lately suffered° by a thunderbolt. *[Thunder.]* Alas, the storm is come again! My best way is to creep under his gaberdine.° There is no other shelter hereabout. Misery acquaints a man with strange bedfellows. I will here shroud° till the dregs° of the storm be past. 30

35

[He creeps under Caliban's garment.]

Enter Stephano, singing, [a bottle in his hand].

Stephano: I shall no more to sea, to sea,
        Here shall I die ashore — "
This is a very scurvy tune to sing at a man's funeral.
Well, here's my comfort. *Drinks.*
    (*Sings.*)
        "The master, the swabber,° the boatswain, and I, 40
            The gunner and his mate,
        Loved Mall, Meg, and Marian, and Margery,
            But none of us cared for Kate.
                For she had a tongue with a tang,°
                Would cry to a sailor. 'Go hang!' 45
        She loved not the savor of tar nor of pitch,
        Yet a tailor might scratch her where'er she did itch.°
            Then to sea, boys, and let her go hang!"
This is a scurvy tune too. But here's my comfort. *Drinks.*
Caliban: Do not torment me!° O! 50
Stephano: What's the matter?° Have we devils here? Do you put tricks upon 's° with savages and men of Ind,° ha? I have not scaped drowning to be afeard now of your four legs. For it hath been said, "As proper° a man as ever went on four legs° cannot make him give ground"; and it shall be said so again while Stephano breathes at'° nostrils. 55
Caliban: This spirit torments me! O!
Stephano: This is some monster of the isle with four legs, who hath got, as I take it, an ague.° Where the devil should he learn° our language? I will

---

26 *painted:* I.e., painted on a sign set up outside a booth or tent at a fair.   27 *make a man:* (1) make one's fortune (2) be indistinguishable from an Englishman.   28 *doit:* Small coin.   30 *o' my troth:* By my faith; *hold it:* Hold it in.   31 *suffered:* I.e., died.   33 *gaberdine:* Cloak, loose upper garment. 34 *shroud:* Take shelter.   35 *dregs:* I.e., last remains (as in a *bombard* or jug, line 20).   40 *swabber:* Crew member whose job is to wash the decks.   44 *tang:* Sting.   47 *tailor . . . itch:* (A dig at tailors for their supposed effeminacy and a bawdy suggestion of satisfying a sexual craving.)   50 *Do . . . me:* (Caliban assumes that one of Prospero's spirits has come to punish him.)   51 *What's the matter:* What's going on here?   51–52 *put tricks upon 's:* Trick us with conjuring shows. *Ind:* India. 53 *proper:* Handsome.   54 *four legs:* (The conventional phrase would supply *two* legs, but the creature Stephano thinks he sees has four.)   55 *at':* At the.   58 *ague:* Fever. (Probably both Caliban and Trinculo are quaking; see lines 68 and 94.)   58 *should he learn:* Could he have learned.

give him some relief, if it be but for that.° If I can recover° him and keep
him tame and get to Naples with him, he's a present for any emperor   60
that ever trod on neat's leather.°

Caliban: Do not torment me, prithee. I'll bring my wood home faster.

Stephano: He's in his fit now and does not talk after the wisest.° He shall
taste of my bottle. If he have never drunk wine afore,° it will go near to°
remove his fit. If I can recover° him and keep him tame, I will not take   65
too much° for him. He shall pay for him that hath° him,° and that soundly.

Caliban: Thou dost me yet but little hurt; thou wilt anon,° I know it by thy
trembling. Now Prosper works upon thee.

Stephano: Come on your ways. Open your mouth. Here is that which will
give language to you, cat. Open your mouth.° This will shake your   70
shaking. I can tell you, and that soundly. *[Giving Caliban a drink.]* You
cannot tell who's your friend. Open your chaps° again.

Trinculo: I should know that voice. It should be — but he is drowned, and
these are devils. O, defend me!

Stephano: Four legs and two voices — a most delicate° monster! His forward   75
voice now is to speak well of his friend; his backward voice° is to utter
foul speeches and to detract. If all the wine in my bottle will recover
him,° I will help° his ague. Come. *[Giving a drink.]* Amen! I will pour
some in thy other mouth.

Trinculo: Stephano!   80

Stephano: Doth thy other mouth call me?° Mercy, mercy! This is a devil, and
no monster. I will leave him. I have no long spoon.°

Trinculo: Stephano! If thou beest Stephano, touch me and speak to me, for
I am Trinculo — be not afeard — thy good friend Trinculo.

Stephano: If thou beest Trinculo, come forth. I'll pull thee by the lesser legs.   85
If any be Trinculo's legs, these are they. *[Pulling him out.]* Thou art very
Trinculo indeed! How cam'st thou to be the siege° of this mooncalf?° Can
he vent° Trinculos?

Trinculo: I took him to be killed with a thunderstroke. But art thou not
drowned, Stephano? I hope now thou art not drowned. Is the storm   90
overblown?° I hid me under the dead mooncalf's gaberdine for fear of
the storm. And art thou living, Stephano? O Stephano, two Neapolitans
scaped!   *[He capers with Stephano.]*

Stephano: Prithee, do not turn me about. My stomach is not constant.°

Caliban: These be fine things, an if° they be not spirits.   95

---

59 *for that:* I.e., for knowing our language; *recover:* Restore.   61 *neat's leather:* Cowhide.   63 *after
the wisest:* in the wisest fashion.   64 *afore:* Before; *go near to:* Be in a fair way to.   65 *recover:*
Restore.   65–66 *I will . . . much:* I.e., no sum can be too much.   66 *He shall . . . hath him:* I.e.,
anyone who wants him will have to pay dearly for him; *hath:* Possesses, receives.   67 *anon:* Presently.
70 *cat . . . mouth:* (Allusion to the proverb "Good liquor will make a cat speak.")   72 *chaps:* Jaws.
75 *delicate:* Ingenious.   76 *backward voice:* (Trinculo and Caliban are facing in opposite directions.
Stephano supposes the monster to have a rear end that can emit *foul speeches* or foul-smelling wind
at the monster's *other mouth,* line 81.)   77–78 *If . . . him:* Even if it takes all the wine in my bottle
to cure him.   78 *help:* Cure.   81 *call me:* I.e., call me by name, know supernaturally who I am.
82 *long spoon:* (Allusion to the proverb "He that sups with the devil has need of a long spoon.")
87 *siege:* Excrement; *mooncalf:* Monstrous or misshapen creature (whose deformity is caused by the
malignant influence of the moon).   88 *vent:* Excrete, defecate.   91 *overblown:* Blown over.
94 *not constant:* Unsteady.   95 *an if:* If.

That's a brave° god, and bears° celestial liquor.
I will kneel to him.

Stephano: How didst thou scape? How cam'st thou hither? Swear by this
bottle how thou cam'st hither. I escaped upon a butt of sack° which the
sailors heaved o'erboard — by this bottle,° which I made of the bark of   100
a tree with mine own hands since° I was cast ashore.

Caliban [kneeling]: I'll swear upon that bottle to be thy true subject, for the
liquor is not earthly.

Stephano: Here. Swear then how thou escapedst.

Trinculo: Swum ashore, man, like a duck. I can swim like a duck, I'll be   105
sworn.

Stephano: Here, kiss the book.° Though thou canst swim like a duck, thou
art made like a goose.

                                                [Giving him a drink.]

Trinculo: O Stephano, hast any more of this?

Stephano: The whole butt, man. My cellar is in a rock by the seaside, where   110
my wine is hid. — How now, mooncalf? How does thine ague?

Caliban: Hast thou not dropped from heaven?

Stephano: Out o' the moon, I do assure thee. I was the Man i' the Moon
when time was.°

Caliban: I have seen thee in her, and I do adore thee.   115
My mistress showed me thee, and thy dog, and thy bush.°

Stephano: Come, swear to that. Kiss the book. I will furnish it anon with new
contents. Swear.   *[Giving him a drink.]*

Trinculo: By this good light,° this is a very shallow monster! I afeard of him?
A very weak monster! The Man i' the Moon? A most poor credulous   120
monster! Well drawn,° monster, in good sooth!°

Caliban [to Stephano]: I'll show thee every fertile inch o' th' island,
And I will kiss thy foot. I prithee, be my god.

Trinculo: By this light, a most perfidious and drunken monster! When 's
god's asleep, he'll rob his bottle.°   125

Caliban: I'll kiss thy foot. I'll swear myself thy subject.

Stephano: Come on then. Down, and swear.   *[Caliban kneels.]*

Trinculo: I shall laugh myself to death at this puppy-headed monster. A most
scurvy monster! I could find in my heart to beat him —

Stephano: Come, kiss.   130

Trinculo: But that the poor monster's in drink.° An abominable monster!

Caliban: I'll show thee the best springs. I'll pluck thee berries.
I'll fish for thee and get thee wood enough.
A plague upon the tyrant that I serve!
I'll bear him no more sticks, but follow thee,   135
Thou wondrous man.

96 *brave:* Fine, magnificent; *bears:* He carries.   99 *butt of sack:* Barrel of Canary wine.   100 *by this
bottle:* I.e., I swear by this bottle.   101 *since:* After.   107 *book:* I.e., bottle (but with ironic reference
to the practice of kissing the Bible in swearing an oath; see *I'll be sworn* in line 105–106).   114 *when
time was:* Once upon a time.   116 *dog . . . bush:* (The Man in the Moon was popularly imagined to
have with him a dog and a bush of thorn.)   119 *By . . . light:* By God's light, by this good light from
heaven.   121 *Well drawn:* Well pulled (on the bottle); *in good sooth:* Truly, indeed.   124–
125 *When . . . bottle:* I.e., Caliban wouldn't even stop at robbing his god of his bottle if he could catch
him asleep.   131 *in drink:* Drunk.

Trinculo: A most ridiculous monster, to make a
  wonder of a poor drunkard!
Caliban: I prithee, let me bring thee where crabs° grow,
  And I with my long nails will dig thee pignuts,°   140
  Show thee a jay's nest, and instruct thee how
  To snare the nimble marmoset.° I'll bring thee
  To clustering filberts, and sometimes I'll get thee
  Young scamels° from the rock. Wilt thou go with me?
Stephano: I prithee now, lead the way without any more talking. — Trinculo,   145
  the King and all our company else° being drowned, we will inherit°
  here. — Here, bear my bottle. — Fellow Trinculo, we'll fill him by and
  by again.
Caliban (sings drunkenly): Farewell, master, farewell, farewell!
Trinculo: A howling monster; a drunken monster!   150
Caliban: No more dams I'll make for fish,
      Nor fetch in firing°
        At requiring,
    Nor scrape trenchering,° nor wash dish.
      'Ban, 'Ban, Ca–Caliban   155
        Has a new master. Get a new man!°
  Freedom, high-day! High-day,° freedom! Freedom, high-day, freedom!
Stephano: O brave monster! Lead the way.   *Exeunt.*

[ACT III

Scene I: *Before Prospero's cell.*]

Enter Ferdinand, bearing a log.

Ferdinand: There be some sports are painful, and their labor
  Delight in them sets off.° Some kinds of baseness°
  Are nobly undergone,° and most poor° matters
  Point to rich ends. This my mean° task
  Would be as heavy to me as odious, but°   5
  The mistress which I serve quickens° what's dead
  And makes my labors pleasures. O, she is

139 *crabs:* Crab apples, or perhaps crabs.   140 *pignuts:* Earthnuts, edible tuberous roots.
142 *marmoset:* Small monkey.   144 *scamels:* (Possibly *seamews,* mentioned in Strachey's letter, or
shellfish, or perhaps from *squamelle,* "furnished with little scales." Contemporary French and Italian
travel accounts report that the natives of Patagonia in South America ate small fish described as *fort
scameux* and *squame.*)   146 *else:* In addition, besides ourselves; *inherit:* Take possession.
152 *firing:* Firewood.   154 *trenchering:* Trenchers, wooden plates.   156 *Get a new man:* (Addressed to Prospero.)   157 *high-day:* Holiday.   Act III. Scene I.   1–2 *There . . . sets off:* Some
pastimes are laborious, but the pleasure we get from them compensates for the effort. (Pleasure is *set
off* by labor as a jewel is set off by its foil.)   2 *baseness:* Menial activity.   3 *undergone:* Undertaken;
most poor: Poorest.   4 *mean:* Lowly.   5 *but:* Were it not that.   6 *quickens:* Gives life to.

Ten times more gentle than her father's crabbed,
And he's composed of harshness. I must remove
Some thousands of these logs and pile them up,   10
Upon a sore injunction.° My sweet mistress
Weeps when she sees me work and says such baseness
Had never like executor.° I forget;°
But these sweet thoughts do even refresh my labors,
Most busy lest when I do it.°

Enter Miranda; and Prospero [at a distance, unseen].

Miranda: Alas now, pray you,   15
Work not so hard. I would the lightning had
Burnt up those logs that you are enjoined° to pile!
Pray, set it down and rest you. When this° burns,
'Twill weep° for having wearied you. My father
Is hard at study. Pray now, rest yourself.   20
He's safe for these° three hours.
Ferdinand: O most dear mistress,
The sun will set before I shall discharge°
What I must strive to do.
Miranda: If you'll sit down,
I'll bear your logs the while. Pray, give me that.
I'll carry it to the pile.
Ferdinand: No, precious creature,   25
I had rather crack my sinews, break my back,
Than you should such dishonor undergo
While I sit lazy by.
Miranda: It would become me
As well as it does you; and I should do it
With much more ease, for my good will is to it,   30
And yours it is against.
Prospero [aside]:   Poor worm, thou art infected!
This visitation° shows it.
Miranda: You look wearily.
Ferdinand: No, noble mistress, 'tis fresh morning with me
When you are by° at night. I do beseech you —
Chiefly that I might set it in my prayers —   35
What is your name?
Miranda: Miranda. — O my father,
I have broke your hest° to say so.
Ferdinand: Admired Miranda!°
Indeed the top of admiration, worth

---

11 *sore injunction:* Severe command.   13 *Had . . . executor:* I.e., was never before undertaken by
so noble a being; *I forget:* I.e., I forget that I'm supposed to be working, or, I forget my happiness,
oppressed by my labor.   15 *Most . . . it:* I.e., busy at my labor but with my mind on other things (?)
(the line may be in need of emendation).   17 *enjoined:* Commanded.   18 *this:* I.e., the log.
19 *weep:* I.e., exude resin.   21 *these:* The next.   22 *discharge:* Complete.   32 *visitation:* (1)
Miranda's visit to Ferdinand (2) visitation of the plague, i.e., infection of love.   34 *by:* Nearby.
37 *hest:* Command; *Admired Miranda:* (Her name means "to be admired or wondered at.")

What's dearest° to the world! Full many a lady
I have eyed with best regard,° and many a time   40
The harmony of their tongues hath into bondage
Brought my too diligent° ear. For several° virtues
Have I liked several women, never any
With so full soul but some defect in her
Did quarrel with the noblest grace she owed°   45
And put it to the foil.° But you, O you,
So perfect and so peerless, are created
Of° every creature's best!
Miranda: I do not know
One of my sex; no woman's face remember,
Save, from my glass, mine own. Nor have I seen   50
More that I may call men than you, good friend,
And my dear father. How features are abroad°
I am skilless° of; but, by my modesty,°
The jewel in my dower, I would not wish
Any companion in the world but you;   55
Nor can imagination form a shape,
Besides yourself, to like of.° But I prattle
Something° too wildly, and my father's precepts
I therein do forget.
Ferdinand: I am in my condition°
A prince, Miranda; I do think, a king —   60
I would, not so! — and would° no more endure
This wooden slavery° than to suffer
The flesh-fly° blow° my mouth. Hear my soul speak:
The very instant that I saw you did
My heart fly to your service, there resides   65
To make me slave to it, and for your sake
Am I this patient long-man.
Miranda: Do you love me?
Ferdinand: O heaven, O earth, bear witness to this sound,
And crown what I profess with kind event°
If I speak true! If hollowly,° invert°   70
What best is boded° me to mischief!° I
Beyond all limit of what° else i' the world
Do love, prize, honor you.
Miranda [weeping]:   I am a fool
To weep at what I am glad of.
Prospero [aside]:   Fair encounter

---

39 *dearest:* Most treasured.   40 *best regard:* Thoughtful and approving attention.   42 *diligent:* Attentive; *several:* Various (also on line 43).   45 *owed:* Owned.   46 *put . . . foil:* (1) Overthrew it (as in wrestling) (2) served as a *foil,* or "contrast," to set it off.   48 *Of:* Out of.   52 *How . . . abroad:* What people look like in other places.   53 *skilless:* Ignorant; *modesty:* Virginity.   57 *like of:* Be pleased with, be fond of.   58 *Something:* Somewhat.   59 *condition:* Rank.   61 *would:* Wish (it were).   62 *wooden slavery:* Being compelled to carry wood.   63 *flesh-fly:* Insect that deposits its eggs in dead flesh; *blow:* Befoul with fly eggs.   69 *kind event:* Favorable outcome.   70 *hollowly:* Insincerely, falsely; *invert:* Turn.   71 *boded:* In store for; *mischief:* Harm.   72 *what:* Whatever.

Of two most rare affections! Heavens rain grace　　　　　　　　　75
On that which breeds between 'em!

Ferdinand:　　　　　　　　　　　　　　　Wherefore weep you?

Miranda: At mine unworthiness, that dare not offer
What I desire to give, and much less take
What I shall die° to want.° But this is trifling,
And all the more it seeks to hide itself　　　　　　　　　　　　80
The bigger bulk it shows. Hence, bashful cunning,°
And prompt me, plain and holy innocence!
I am your wife, if you will marry me;
If not, I'll die your maid.° To be your fellow°
You may deny me, but I'll be your servant　　　　　　　　　　85
Whether you will° or no.

Ferdinand:　　　　　　　　　　My mistress,° dearest,
And I thus humble ever.

Miranda: My husband, then?

Ferdinand: Ay, with a heart as willling°
As bondage e'er of freedom. Here's my hand.　　　　　　　　90

Miranda [clasping his hand]: And mine, with my heart in 't. And now farewell
Till half an hour hence.

Ferdinand:　　　　　　　　　　A thousand thousand!°

　　　　　　　　　　　Exeunt [Ferdinand and Miranda, separately].

Prospero: So glad of this as they I cannot be,
Who are surprised with all;° but my rejoicing
At nothing can be more. I'll to my book,　　　　　　　　　　95
For yet ere suppertime must I perform
Much business appertaining.°　　　　　　　　　　　　　*Exit.*

[Scene II: *Another part of the island.*]

Enter Caliban, Stephano, and Trinculo.

Stephano: Tell not me. When the butt is out,° we will drink water, not a drop
　　before. Therefore bear up and board 'em.° Servant monster, drink to me.

Trinculo: Servant monster? The folly of° this island! They say there's but five
　　upon this isle. We are three of them; if th' other two be brained° like us,
　　the state totters.　　　　　　　　　　　　　　　　　　　　　　　　5

Stephano: Drink, servant monster, when I bid thee. Thy eyes are almost set°
　　in thy head.　　　　　　　　　　　　　　　　　　　*[Giving a drink.]*

Trinculo: Where should they be set° else? He were a brave° monster indeed
　　if they were set in his tail.

79 *die:* (Probably with an unconscious sexual meaning that underlies all of lines 77–81.) *to want:* Through lacking.　81 *bashful cunning:* Coyness.　84 *maid:* Handmaiden, servant; *fellow:* mate, equal.　86 *will:* Desire it; *My mistress:* I.e., the woman I adore and serve (not an illicet sexual partner).　89 *willing:* Desirous.　92 *A thousand thousand:* I.e., a thousand thousand farewells.　94 *with all:* By everything that has happened, or, *withal,* "with it."　97 *appertaining:* Related to this.　Act III. Scene II.　1 *out:* Empty.　2 *bear . . . 'em:* (Stephano uses the terminology of maneuvering at sea and boarding a vessel under attack as a way of urging an assault on the liquor supply.)　3 *folly of:* I.e., stupidity found on.　5 *be brained:* Are endowed with intelligence.　6 *set:* Fixed in a drunken stare, or, sunk, like the sun.　8 *set:* Placed; *brave:* Fine, splendid.

Stephano: My man-monster hath drowned his tongue in sack. For my part, 10
the sea cannot drown me. I swam, ere I could recover° the shore, five
and thirty leagues° off and on.° By this light,° thou shalt be my lieutenant,
monster, or my standard.°

Trinculo: Your lieutenant, if you list;° he's no standard.

Stephano: We'll not run,° Monsieur Monster. 15

Trinculo: Nor go° neither, but you'll lie° like dogs and yet say nothing
neither.

Stephano: Mooncalf, speak once in thy life, if thou beest a good mooncalf.

Caliban: How does thy honor? Let me lick thy shoe.
I'll not serve him. He is not valiant. 20

Trinculo: Thou liest, most ignorant monster, I am in case to jostle a constable.° Why, thou debauched° fish, thou, was there ever man a coward that
hath drunk so much sack° as I today? Wilt thou tell a monstrous lie, being
but half a fish and half a monster?

Caliban: Lo, how he mocks me! Wilt thou let him, my lord? 25

Trinculo: "Lord," quoth he? That a monster should be such a natural!°

Caliban: Lo, lo, again! Bite him to death, I prithee.

Stephano: Trinculo, keep a good tongue in your head. If you prove a muti-
neer — the next tree!° The poor monster's my subject, and he shall not
suffer indignity. 30

Caliban: I thank my noble lord. Wilt thou be pleased
To hearken once again to the suit I made to thee?

Stephano: Marry,° will I. Kneel and repeat it. I will stand, and so shall
Trinculo.   *[Caliban kneels.]*

Enter Ariel, invisible.°

Caliban: As I told thee before, I am subject to a tyrant, 35
A sorcerer, that by his cunning hath
Cheated me of the island.

Ariel [mimicking Trinculo]: Thou liest.

Caliban: Thou liest, thou jesting monkey, thou!
I would my valiant master would destroy thee.
I do not lie. 40

Stephano: Trinculo, if you trouble him any more in 's tale, by this hand, I
will supplant° some of your teeth.

Trinculo: Why, I said nothing.

Stephano: Mum, then, and no more. — Proceed.

Caliban: I say by sorcery he got this isle; 45

---

11 *recover:* Gain, reach.   12 *leagues:* Units of distance, each equaling about three miles; *off and on:*
Intermittently; *By this light:* (An oath: by the light of the sun.)   13 *standard:* Standard-bearer, ensign
(as distinguished from *lieutenant,* lines 12, 14).   14 *list:* Prefer; *no standard:* I.e., not able to stand
up.   15 *run:* (1) Retreat (2) urinate (taking Trinculo's *standard,* line 13, in the old sense of "conduit").
16 *go:* Walk; *lie:* (1) Tell lies (2) lie prostrate (3) excrete.   21–22 *in case . . . constable:* I.e., in fit
condition, made valiant by drink, to taunt or challenge the police.   22 *debauched:* (1) Seduced away
from proper service and allegiance (2) depraved.   23 *sack:* Spanish white wine.   26 *natural:* (1)
Idiot (2) natural as opposed to unnatural, monsterlike.   29 *the next tree:* I.e., you'll hang.
32 *Marry:* I.e., indeed (originally an oath, "by the Virgin Mary").   34 *invisible:* I.e., wearing a garment
to connote invisibility, as at I.ii.378.   42 *supplant:* Uproot, displace.

From me he got it. If thy greatness will
Revenge it on him — for I know thou dar'st,
But this thing° dare not —

Stephano: That's most certain.

Caliban: Thou shalt be lord of it, and I'll serve thee.   50

Stephano: How now shall this be compassed?° Canst thou bring me to the
party?

Caliban: Yea, yea, my lord. I'll yield him thee asleep,
Where thou mayst knock a nail into his head.

Ariel: Thou liest; thou canst not.   55

Caliban: What a pied ninny's° this! Thou scurvy patch!° —
I do beseech thy greatness, give him blows
And take his bottle from him. When that's gone
He shall drink naught but brine, for I'll not show him
Where the quick freshes° are.   60

Stephano: Trinculo, run into no further danger. Interrupt the monster one
word further° and, by this hand, I'll turn my mercy out o' doors° and
make a stockfish° of thee.

Trinculo: Why, what did I? I did nothing. I'll go farther off.°

Stephano: Didst thou not say he lied?   65

Ariel: Thou liest.

Stephano: Do I so? Take thou that. *[He beats Trinculo.]* As you like this, give
me the lie° another time.

Trinculo: I did not give the lie. Out o' your wits and hearing too? A pox o'
your bottle! This can sack and drinking do. A murrain° on your monster,   70
and the devil take your fingers!

Caliban: Ha, ha, ha!

Stephano: Now, forward with your tale. *[To Trinculo.]* Prithee, stand further
off.

Caliban: Beat him enough. After a little time   75
I'll beat him too.

Stephano: Stand farther. — Come, proceed.

Caliban: Why, as I told thee, 'tis a custom with him
I' th' afternoon to sleep. There thou mayst brain him,
Having first seized his books; or with a log   80
Batter his skull, or paunch° him with a stake,
Or cut his weasand° with thy knife. Remember
First to possess his books, for without them
He's but a sot,° as I am, nor hath not
One spirit to command. They all do hate him   85
As rootedly as I. Burn but his books.
He has brave utensils° — for so he calls them —
Which, when he has a house, he'll deck withal.°

48 *this thing:* I.e., Trinculo.   51 *compassed:* Achieved.   56 *pied ninny:* Fool in motley; *patch:* Fool.
60 *quick freshes:* Running springs.   61–62 *one word further:* I.e., one more time.   62 *turn . . .
doors:* I.e., forget about being merciful.   63 *stockfish:* Dried cod beaten before cooking.   64 *off:*
Away.   67–68 *give me the lie:* Call me a liar to my face.   70 *murrain:* Plague (literally, a cattle
disease).   81 *paunch:* Stab in the belly.   82 *weasand:* Windpipe.   84 *sot:* Fool.   87 *brave
utensils:* Fine furnishings.   88 *deck withal:* Furnish it with.

And that most deeply to consider is
The beauty of his daughter. He himself   90
Calls her a nonpareil. I never saw a woman
But only Sycorax my dam and she;
But she as far surpasseth Sycorax
As great'st does least.

Stephano: Is it so brave° a lass?   95

Caliban: Ay, lord. She will become° thy bed, I warrant,
And bring thee forth brave brood.

Stephano: Monster, I will kill this man. His daughter and I will be king and
queen — save Our Graces! — and Trinculo and thyself shall be viceroys.
Dost thou like the plot, Trinculo?   100

Trinculo: Excellent.

Stephano: Give me thy hand. I am sorry I beat thee; but, while thou liv'st,
keep a good tongue in thy head.

Caliban: Within this half hour will he be asleep.
Wilt thou destroy him then?   105

Stephano: Ay, on mine honor.

Ariel [aside]: This will I tell my master.

Caliban: Thou mak'st me merry; I am full of pleasure.
Let us be jocund.° Will you troll the catch°
You taught me but whilere?°   110

Stephano: At thy request, monster, I will do reason, any reason.° — Come on,
Trinculo, let us sing.   *Sings.*
    "Flout° 'em and scout° 'em
    And scout 'em and flout em!
        Thought is free."   115

Caliban: That's not the tune.

                        Ariel plays the tune on a tabor° and pipe.

Stephano: What is this same?

Trinculo: This is the tune of our catch, played by the picture of Nobody.°

Stephano: If thou beest a man, show thyself in thy likeness. If thou beest a
devil, take 't° as thou list.   120

Trinculo: O, forgive me my sins!

Stephano: He that dies pays all debts.° I defy thee. Mercy upon us!

Caliban: Art thou afeard?

Stephano: No, monster, not I.

Caliban: Be not afeard. The isle is full of noises,   125
Sounds, and sweet airs, that give delight and hurt not.
Sometimes a thousand twangling instruments
Will hum about mine ears, and sometimes voices
That, if I then had waked after long sleep,
Will make me sleep again; and then, in dreaming,   130

---

95 *brave:* Splendid, attractive.   96 *become:* Suit (sexually).   109 *jocund:* Jovial, merry; *troll the
catch:* Sing the round.   110 *but whilere:* Only a short time ago.   111 *reason, any reason:* Anything
reasonable.   113 *Flout:* Scoff at; *scout:* Deride.   116 s.d. *tabor:* Small drum.   118 *picture of
Nobody:* (Refers to a familiar figure with head, arms, and legs but no trunk.)   120 *take 't . . . list:* I.e.,
take my defiance as you please, as best you can.   122 *He . . . debts:* I.e., if I have to die, at least that
will be the end of all my woes and obligations.

The clouds methought would open and show riches
Ready to drop upon me, that when I waked
I cried to dream° again.
Stephano: This will prove a brave kingdom to me, where I shall have my
music for nothing.   135
Caliban: When Prospero is destroyed.
Stephano: That shall be by and by.° I remember the story.
Trinculo: The sound is going away. Let's follow it, and after do our work.
Stephano: Lead, monster; we'll follow. I would I could see this taborer! He
lays it on.°   140
Trinculo: Wilt come? I'll follow, Stephano.

Exeunt [following Ariel's music].

[SCENE III: *Another part of the island.*]

Enter Alonso, Sebastian, Antonio, Gonzalo, Adrian, Francisco, etc.

Gonzalo: By 'r lakin,° I can go no further, sir.
My old bones aches. Here's a maze trod indeed
Through forthrights and meanders!° By your patience,
I needs must° rest me.
Alonso: Old lord, I cannot blame thee,
Who am myself attached° with weariness,   5
To th' dulling of my spirits.° Sit down and rest.
Even here I will put off my hope, and keep it
No longer for° my flatterer. He is drowned
Whom thus we stray to find, and the sea mocks
Our frustrate° search on land. Well, let him go.   10

[Alonso and Gonzalo sit.]

Antonio [aside to Sebastian]: I am right° glad that he's so out of hope.
Do not, for° one repulse, forgo the purpose
That you resolved t' effect.
Sebastian [to Antonio]:   The next advantage
Will we take throughly.°
Antonio [to Sebastian]:   Let it be tonight,
For, now° they are oppressed with travel,° they   15
Will not, nor cannot, use° such vigilance
As when they are fresh.
Sebastian [to Antonio]:   I say tonight. No more.

Solemn and strange music; and Prospero on the top,° invisible.

Alonso: What harmony is this? My good friends, hark!
Gonzalo: Marvelous sweet music!

133 *to dream:* Desirous of dreaming.   137 *by and by:* Very soon.   140 *lays it on:* I.e., plays the
drum vigorously.   SCENE III.   1 *By 'r lakin:* By our Ladykin, by our Lady.   3 *forthrights and
meanders:* Paths straight and crooked.   4 *needs must:* Have to.   5 *attached:* Seized.   6 *To . . .
spirits:* To the point of being dull-spirited.   8 *for:* As.   10 *frustrate:* Frustrated.   11 *right:* Very.
12 *for:* Because of.   14 *throughly:* Thoroughly.   15 *now:* Now that; *travel:* . . . Carrying the sense
of labor as well as traveling.   16 *use:* Apply.   17 *on the top:* At some high point of the tiring-house
or the theater, on a third level above the gallery.

Shakespeare / The Tempest: Act III, Scene III   1419

Enter several strange shapes, bringing in a banquet, and dance about it with gentle actions of salutations; and, inviting the King, etc., to eat, they depart.

Alonso: Give us kind keepers,° heavens! What were these?   20
Sebastian: A living° drollery.° Now I will believe
    That there are unicorns; that in Arabia
    There is one tree, the phoenix' throne, one phoenix°
    At this hour reigning there.
Antonio: I'll believe both;
    And what does else want credit,° come to me   25
    And I'll be sworn 'tis true. Travelers ne'er did lie,
    Though fools at home condemn 'em.
Gonzalo: If in Naples
    I should report this now, would they believe me
    If I should say I saw such islanders?
    For, certes,° these are people of the island,   30
    Who, though they are of monstrous° shape, yet note,
    Their manners are more gentle, kind, than of
    Our human generation you shall find
    Many, nay, almost any.
Prospero [aside]:   Honest lord,
    Thou hast said well, for some of you there present   35
    Are worse than devils.
Alonso: I cannot too much muse°
    Such shapes, such gesture, and such sound, expressing —
    Although they want° the use of tongue — a kind
    Of excellent dumb discourse.
Prospero [aside]:   Praise in departing.°
Francisco: They vanished strangely.
Sebastian: No matter, since   40
    They have left their viands° behind, for we have stomachs.°
    Will 't please you taste of what is here?
Alonso: Not I.
Gonzalo: Faith, sir, you need not fear. When we were boys,
    Who would believe that there were mountaineers°
    Dewlapped° like bulls, whose throats had hanging at 'em   45
    Wallets° of flesh? Or that there were such men
    Whose heads stood in their breasts? Which now we find
    Each putter-out of five for one° will bring us
    Good warrant° of.

---

20 *kind keepers:* Guardian angels.   21 *living:* With live actors; *drollery:* Comic entertainment, caricature, puppet show.   23 *phoenix:* Mythical bird consumed to ashes every five hundred to six hundred years, only to be renewed into another cycle.   25 *want credit:* Lack credence.   30 *certes:* Certainly. 31 *monstrous:* Unnatural.   36 *muse:* Wonder at.   38 *want:* Lack.   39 *Praise in departing:* I.e., save your praise until the end of the performance (proverbial).   41 *viands:* Provisions; *stomachs:* Appetites.   44 *mountaineers:* Mountain dwellers.   45 *Dewlapped:* Having a dewlap, or fold of skin hanging from the neck, like cattle.   46 *Wallets:* Pendent folds of skin, wattles. . . .   48 *putter-out . . . one:* One who invests money or gambles on the risks of travel on the condition that the traveler who returns safely is to receive five times the amount deposited; hence, any traveler.   49 *Good warrant:* Assurance; *stand to:* Fall to; take the risk.

Alonso: I will stand to° and feed,
　　Although my last° — no matter, since I feel
　　The best° is past. Brother, my lord the Duke,   50
　　Stand to, and do as we.   *[They approach the table.]*

Thunder and lightning. Enter Ariel, like a harpy,° claps his wings upon the
table, and with a quaint device° the banquet vanishes.°

Ariel: You are three men of sin, whom Destiny —
　　That hath to instrument this lower world
　　And what is in 't — the never-surfeited sea   55
　　Hath caused to belch up you,° and on this island
　　Where man doth not inhabit, you 'mongst men
　　Being most unfit to life. I have made you mad;
　　And even with suchlike valor° men hang and drown
　　Their proper° selves.
　　　　　　[Alonso, Sebastian, and Antonio draw their swords.]
　　　　　　　　You fools! I and my fellows   60
　　Are ministers of Fate. The elements
　　Of whom° your swords are tempered° may as well
　　Wound the loud winds, or with bemocked-at° stabs
　　Kill the still-closing° waters, as diminish
　　One dowl° that's in my plume. My fellow ministers   65
　　Are like° invulnerable. If° you could hurt,
　　Your swords are now too massy° for your strengths
　　And will not be uplifted. But remember —
　　For that's my business to you — that you three
　　From Milan did supplant good Prospero;   70
　　Exposed unto the sea, which hath requit° it,
　　Him and his innocent child; for which foul deed
　　The powers, delaying, not forgetting, have
　　Incensed the seas and shores, yea, all the creatures,
　　Against your peace. Thee of thy son, Alonso,   75
　　They have bereft; and do pronounce by me
　　Ling'ring perdition,° worse than any death
　　Can be at once, shall step by step attend
　　You and your ways; whose° wraths to guard you from —
　　Which here, in this most desolate isle, else° falls   80
　　Upon your heads — is nothing° but heart's sorrow
　　And a clear° life ensuing.

---

50 *Although my last:* Even if this were to be my last meal.   51 *best:* Best part of life.   52 *harpy:* A
fabulous monster with a woman's face and breasts and a vulture's body, supposed to be a minister of
divine vengeance; *quaint device:* Ingenious stage contrivance; *the banquet vanishes:* I.e., the food
vanishes; the table remains until line 82.   53–56 *whom . . . up you:* You whom Destiny, controller
of the sublunary world as its instrument, has caused the ever hungry sea to belch up.   59 *suchlike*
valor: I.e., the reckless valor derived from madness.   60 *proper:* Own.   62 *whom:* Which; *tempered:*
Composed and hardened.   63 *bemocked-at:* Scorned.   64 *still-closing:* Always closing again when
parted.   65 *dowl:* Soft, fine feather.   66 *like:* Likewise, similarly; *If:* Even if.   67 *massy:* Heavy.
71 *requit:* Requited, avenged.   77 *perdition:* Ruin, destruction.   79 *whose:* (Refers to the heavenly
powers.)   80 *else:* Otherwise.   81 *is nothing:* There is no way.   82 *clear:* Unspotted, innocent.

He vanishes in thunder; then, to soft music, enter the shapes again, and dance, with mocks and mows,° and carrying out the table.

Prospero: Bravely° the figure of this harpy hast thou
    Performed, my Ariel; a grace it had devouring.°
    Of my instruction hast thou nothing bated°   85
    In what thou hadst to say. So,° with good life°
    And observation strange,° my meaner° ministers
    Their several kinds° have done. My high charms work,
    And these mine enemies are all knit up
    In their distractions.° They now are in my power;   90
    And in these fits I leave them, while I visit
    Young Ferdinand, whom they suppose is drowned,
    And his and mine loved darling.   *[Exit above.]*
Gonzalo: I' the name of something holy, sir, why° stand you
    In this strange stare?
Alonso: O, it° is monstrous, monstrous!   95
    Methought the billows° spoke and told me of it;
    The winds did sing it to me, and the thunder,
    That deep and dreadful organ pipe, pronounced
    The name of Prosper; it did bass my trespass.°
    Therefor° my son i' th' ooze is bedded; and   100
    I'll seek him deeper than e'er plummet° sounded,°
    And with him there lie mudded.   *Exit.*
Sebastian: But one fiend at a time,
    I'll fight their legions o'er.°
Antonio: I'll be thy second.
                    Exeunt [Sebastian and Antonio].
Gonzalo: All three of them are desperate.° Their great guilt,   105
    Like poison given to work a great time after,
    Now 'gins to bite the spirits.° I do beseech you,
    That are of suppler joints, follow them swiftly
    And hinder them from what this ecstasy°
    May now provoke them to.
Adrian: Follow, I pray you.   110
                      Exeunt omnes.

---

mocks and mows: Mocking gestures and grimaces.   83 *Bravely:* Finely, dashingly.   84 *a grace . . . devouring:* I.e., you gracefully caused the banquet to disappear as if you had consumed it (with puns on *grace,* meaning "gracefulness" and "a blessing on the meal," and on *devouring,* meaning "a literal eating" and "an all-consuming or ravishing grace").   85 *bated:* Abated, omitted.   86 *So:* In the same fashion; *good life:* Faithful reproduction.   87 *observation strange:* Exceptional attention to detail; *meaner:* I.e., subordinate to Ariel.   88 *several kinds:* Individual parts.   90 *distractions:* Trancelike state.   94 *why:* (Gonzalo was not addressed in Ariel's speech to the *three men of sin,* line 53, and is not, as they are, in a maddened state; see lines 105–107.)   95 *it:* I.e., my sin (also in line 96).   96 *billows:* Waves.   99 *bass my trespass:* Proclaim my trespass like a bass note in music.   100 *Therefor:* In consequence of that.   101 *plummet:* A lead weight attached to a line for testing depth; *sounded:* Probed, tested the depth of.   104 *o'er:* One after another.   105 *desperate:* Despairing and reckless.   107 *bite the spirits:* Sap their vital powers through anguish.   109 *ecstasy:* Mad frenzy.

[ACT IV

SCENE I: *Before Prospero's cell.*]

Enter Prospero, Ferdinand, and Miranda.

Prospero: If I have too austerely punished you,
Your companion makes amends, for I
Have given you here a third° of mine own life,
Or that for which I live; who once again
I tender° to thy hand. All thy vexations   5
Were but my trials of thy love, and thou
Hast strangely° stood the test. Here, afore heaven,
I ratify this my rich gift. O Ferdinand,
Do not smile at me that I boast her off,°
For thou shalt find she will outstrip all praise   10
And make it halt° behind her.
Ferdinand: I do believe it.
Against an oracle.°
Prospero: Then, as my gift and thine own acquisition
Worthily purchased, take my daughter. But
If thou dost break her virgin-knot before   15
All sanctimonious° ceremonies may
With full and holy rite be ministered,
No sweet aspersion° shall the heavens let fall
To make this contract grow; but barren hate,
Sour-eyed disdain, and discord shall bestrew   20
The union of your bed with weeds° so loathly
That you shall hate it both. Therefore take heed,
As Hymen's lamps shall light you.°
Ferdinand: As I hope
For quiet days, fair issue,° and long life,
With such love as 'tis now, the murkiest den,   25
The most opportune place, the strong'st suggestion°
Our worser genius° can,° shall never melt
Mine honor into lust, to° take away
The edge° of that day's celebration

ACT IV. SCENE I.   3 *a third:* I.e., Miranda, into whose education Prospero has put a third of his life (?) or who represents a large part of what he cares about, along with his dukedom and his learned study (?).   5 *tender:* Offer.   7 *strangely:* Extraordinarily.   9 *boast her off:* I.e., praise her so, or, perhaps an error for "boast of her." . . .   11 *halt:* Limp.   12 *Against an oracle:* Even if an oracle should declare otherwise.   16 *sanctimonious:* Sacred.   18 *aspersion:* Dew, shower.   21 *weeds:* (In place of the flowers customarily strewn on the marriage bed).   23 *As . . . you:* I.e., as you long for happiness and concord in your marriage. (Hymen was the Greek and Roman god of marriage; his symbolic torches, the wedding torches, were supposed to burn brightly for a happy marriage and smokily for a troubled one.)   24 *issue:* Offspring.   26 *suggestion:* Temptation.   27 *worser genius:* Evil genius, or, evil attendant spirit; *can:* Is capable of.   28 *to:* So as to.   29 *edge:* Keen enjoyment, sexual ardor.

When I shall think or° Phoebus' steeds are foundered°   30
Or Night kept chained below.
Prospero: Fairly spoke.
Sit then and talk with her. She is thine own.

                    [Ferdinand and Miranda sit and talk together.]
What,° Ariel! My industrious servant, Ariel!

Enter Ariel.

Ariel: What would my potent master? Here I am.
Prospero: Thou and thy meaner fellows° your last service   35
Did worthily perform, and I must use you
In such another trick.° Go bring the rabble,°
O'er whom I give thee power, here to this place.
Incite them to quick motion, for I must
Bestow upon the eyes of this young couple   40
Some vanity° of mine art. It is my promise,
And they expect it from me.
Ariel: Presently?°
Prospero: Ay, with a twink.°
Ariel: Before you can say "Come" and "Go,"
And breathe twice, and cry "So, so,"   45
Each one, tripping on his toe,
Will be here with mop and mow.°
Do you love me, master? No?
Prospero: Dearly, my delicate Ariel. Do not approach
Till thou dost hear me call.
Ariel: Well; I conceive.°   *Exit.*   50
Prospero: Look thou be true;° do not give dalliance
Too much the rein. The strongest oaths are straw
To the fire i' the blood. Be more abstemious,
Or else good night° your vow!
Ferdinand: I warrant° you, sir,
The white cold virgin snow upon my heart°   55
Abates the ardor of my liver.°
Prospero: Well.
Now come, my Ariel! Bring a corollary,°
Rather than want° a spirit. Appear, and pertly!°—
No tongue!° All eyes! Be silent.   *Soft music.*

Enter Iris.°

30 *or:* Either; *foundered:* Broken down, made lame. (Ferdinand will wait impatiently for the bridal night.) 33 *What:* Now then. 35 *meaner fellows:* Subordinates. 37 *trick:* Device; *rabble:* Band, i.e., the *meaner fellows* of line 35. 41 *vanity:* (1) Illusion (2) trifle (3) desire for admiration, conceit. 42 *Presently:* Immediately. 43 *with a twink:* In the twinkling of an eye. 47 *mop and mow:* Gestures and grimaces. 50 *conceive:* Understand. 51 *true:* True to your promise. 54 *good night:* I.e., say good-bye to; *warrant:* Guarantee. 55 *The white . . . heart:* I.e., the ideal of chastity and consciousness of Miranda's chaste innocence enshrined in my heart. 56 *liver:* (As the presumed seat of the passions). 57 *corollary:* Surplus, extra supply. 58 *want:* Lack; *pertly:* Briskly. 59 *No tongue:* All the beholders are to be silent (lest the spirits vanish); *Iris:* Goddess of the rainbow and Juno's messenger.

Iris: Ceres,° most bounteous lady, thy rich leas°   60
    Of wheat, rye, barley, vetches,° oats, and peas;
    Thy turfy mountains, where live nibbling sheep,
    And flat meads° thatched with stover,° them to keep;
    Thy banks with pionèd and twillèd° brims,
    Which spongy° April at thy hest° betrims   65
    To make cold nymphs chaste crowns; and thy broom groves,°
    Whose shadow the dismissèd bachelor° loves,
    Being lass-lorn; thy poll-clipped° vineyard;
    And thy sea marge,° sterile and rocky hard,
    Where thou thyself dost air:° the queen o' the sky,°   70
    Whose watery arch° and messenger am I,
    Bids thee leave these, and with her sovereign grace,

                        Juno descends° [slowly in her car].

    Here on this grass plot, in this very place,
    To come and sport. Her peacocks° fly amain.°
    Approach, rich Ceres, her to entertain.°   75

Enter Ceres.

Ceres: Hail, many-colored messenger, that ne'er
    Dost disobey the wife of Jupiter,
    Who with thy saffron° wings upon my flowers
    Diffusest honeydrops, refreshing showers,
    And with each end of thy blue bow° dost crown   80
    My bosky° acres and my unshrubbed down,°
    Rich scarf° to my proud earth. Why hath thy queen
    Summoned me hither to this short-grassed green?
Iris: A contract of true love to celebrate,
    And some donation freely to estate°   85
    On the blest lovers.
Ceres: Tell me, heavenly bow,
    If Venus or her son,° as° thou dost know,
    Do now attend the Queen? Since they did plot
    The means that° dusky° Dis my daughter got,°
    Her° and her blind boy's scandaled° company   90
    I have forsworn.
Iris: Of her society°

60 *Ceres:* Goddess of the generative power of nature; *leas:* Meadows.   61 *vetches:* Plants for forage, fodder.   63 *meads:* Meadows; *stover:* Winter fodder for cattle.   64 *pionèd and twillèd:* Undercut by the swift current and protected by roots and branches that tangle to form a barricade.   65 *spongy:* Wet; *hest:* Command.   66 *broom groves:* Clumps of broom, gorse, yellow-flowered shrub. 67 *dismissèd bachelor:* Rejected male lover.   68 *poll-clipped:* Pruned, lopped at the top, or *pole-clipped,* "hedged in with poles."   69 *sea marge:* Shore.   70 *thou . . . air:* You take the air, go for walks; *queen o' the sky:* I.e., Juno.   71 *watery arch:* Rainbow.   72 *Juno descends:* I.e., starts her descent from the "heavens" above the stage (?).   74 *peacocks:* Birds sacred to Juno and used to pull her chariot; *amain:* With full speed.   75 *entertain:* Receive.   78 *saffron:* Yellow.   80 *bow:* I.e., rainbow.   81 *bosky:* wooded; *unshrubbed down:* Open upland.   82 *scarf:* (The rainbow is like a colored silk band adorning the earth.)   85 *estate:* Bestow.   87 *son:* I.e., cupid; *as:* As far as. 89 *that:* Whereby; *dusky:* Dark; *Dis . . . got:* (Pluto, or *Dis,* god of the infernal regions, carried off Proserpina, daughter of Ceres, to be his bride in Hades.)   90 *her:* I.e., Venus'; *scandaled:* Scandalous. 91 *society:* Company.

Be not afraid. I met her deity°
Cutting the clouds towards Paphos,° and her son
Dove-drawn° with her. Here thought they to have done°
Some wanton charm° upon this man and maid,   95
Whose vows are that no bed-right shall be paid
Till Hymen's torch be lighted; but in vain.
Mars's hot minion° is returned° again;
Her waspish-headed° son has broke his arrows,
Swears he will shoot no more, but play with sparrows°   100
And be a boy right out.°

[Juno alights.]

Ceres: Highest Queen of state,°
     Great Juno, comes; I know her by her gait.°
Juno: How does my bounteous sister?° Go with me
     To bless this twain, that they may prosperous be,
     And honored in their issue.°   *They sing:* 105
Juno: Honor, riches, marriage blessing,
     Long continuance, and increasing,
     Hourly joys be still° upon you!
     Juno sings her blessings on you.
Ceres: Earth's increase, foison plenty,°   110
     Barns and garners° never empty,
     Vines with clustering bunches growing,
     Plants with goodly burden bowing;

     Spring come to you at the farthest
     In the very end of harvest!°   115
     Scarcity and want shall shun you;
     Ceres' blessing so is on you.
Ferdinand: This is a most majestic vision, and
     Harmonious charmingly.° May I be bold
     To think these spirits?
Prospero: Spirits, which by mine art   120
     I have from their confines called to enact
     My present fancies.
Ferdinand: Let me live here ever!
     So rare a wondered° father and a wife
     Makes this place Paradise.
               Juno and Ceres whisper, and send Iris on employment.

---

92 *her deity:* I.e., Her Highness.   93 *Paphos:* Place on the island of Cyprus, sacred to Venus.
94 *Dove-drawn:* (Venus' chariot was drawn by doves); *done:* Placed.   95 *wanton charm:* Lustful
spell.   98 *Mars's hot minion:* I.e., Venus, the beloved of Mars; *returned:* I.e., returned to Paphos.
99 *waspish-headed:* Hotheaded, peevish.   100 *sparrows:* (Supposed lustful, and sacred to Venus.)
101 *right out:* Outright; *Highest . . . state:* Most majestic Queen.   102 *gait:* I.e., majestic bearing.
103 *sister:* I.e., fellow goddess (?).   105 *issue:* Offspring.   108 *still:* Always.   110 *foison plenty:*
Plentiful harvest.   111 *garners:* Granaries.   115 *In . . . harvest:* I.e., with no winter in between.
119 *charmingly:* Enchantingly.   123 *wondered:* Wonder-performing, wondrous.

Prospero: Sweet now, silence!
　　Juno and Ceres whisper seriously;   125
　　There's something else to do. Hush and be mute,
　　Or else our spell is marred.
Iris [calling offstage]: You nymphs, called naiads,° of the windring° brooks,
　　With your sedged° crowns and ever-harmless° looks,
　　Leave your crisp° channels, and on this green land   130
　　Answer your summons; Juno does command.
　　Come, temperate° nymphs, and help to celebrate
　　A contract of true love. Be not too late.

Enter certain nymphs.

　　You sunburned sicklemen,° of August weary,°
　　Come hither from the furrow° and be merry.   135
　　Make holiday; your rye-straw hats put on,
　　And these fresh nymphs encounter° every one
　　In country footing.°

Enter certain reapers, properly° habited. They join with the nymphs in a grace-
ful dance, towards the end whereof Prospero starts suddenly, and speaks; after
which, to a strange, hollow, and confused noise, they heavily° vanish.

Prospero [aside]: I had forgot that foul conspiracy
　　Of the beast Caliban and his confederates   140
　　Against my life. The minute of their plot
　　Is almost come. *[To the Spirits.]* Well done! Avoid;° no more!
Ferdinand [to Miranda]: This is strange. Your father's in some passion
　　That works° him strongly.
Miranda: Never till this day
　　Saw I him touched with anger so distempered.   145
Prospero: You do look, my son, in a moved sort,°
　　As if you were dismayed. Be cheerful, sir.
　　Our revels° now are ended. These our actors,
　　As I foretold you, were all spirits and
　　Are melted into air, into thin air;   150
　　And, like the baseless fabric° of this vision,
　　The cloud-capped towers, the gorgeous palaces,
　　The solemn temples, the great globe° itself,
　　Yea, all which it inherit,° shall dissolve,
　　And, like this insubstantial pageant faded,   155
　　Leave not a rack° behind. We are such stuff
　　As dreams are made on,° and our little life

128 *naiads:* Nymphs of springs, rivers, or lakes; *windring:* Wandering, winding (?).　129 *sedged:*
Made of reeds; *ever-harmless:* Ever innocent.　130 *crisp:* Curled, rippled.　132 *temperate:* Chaste.
134 *sicklemen:* Harvesters, field workers who cut down grain and grass; *of August weary:* I.e., weary
of the hard work of the harvest.　135 *furrow:* I.e., plowed fields.　137 *encounter:* Join.
138 *country footing:* Country dancing; *properly:* Suitably; *heavily:* Slowly, dejectedly.　142 *Avoid:*
Withdraw.　144 *works:* Affects, agitates.　146 *moved sort:* Troubled state, condition.　148 *revels:*
Entertainment, pageant.　151 *baseless fabric:* Unsubstantial theatrical edifice or contrivance.
153 *great globe:* (With a glance at the Globe Theatre).　154 *which it inherit:* Who subsequently
occupy it.　156 *rack:* Wisp of cloud.　157 *on:* Of.

Is rounded° with a sleep. Sir, I am vexed.
Bear with my weakness. My old brain is troubled.
Be not disturbed with° my infirmity.   160
If you be pleased, retire° into my cell
And there repose. A turn or two I'll walk
To still my beating° mind.

Ferdinand, Miranda: We wish your peace.

Exeunt [Ferdinand and Miranda].

Prospero: Come with a thought!° I thank thee, Ariel. Come.

Enter Ariel.

Ariel: Thy thoughts I cleave° to. What's thy pleasure?
Prospero: Spirit,   165
We must prepare to meet with Caliban.
Ariel: Ay, my commander. When I presented° Ceres,
I thought to have told thee of it, but I feared
Lest I might anger thee.
Prospero: Say again, where didst thou leave these varlets?   170
Ariel: I told you, sir, they were red-hot with drinking;
So full of valor that they smote the air
For breathing in their faces, beat the ground
For kissing of their feet; yet always bending°
Towards their project. Then I beat my tabor,   175
At which, like unbacked° colts, they pricked their ears,
Advanced° their eyelids, lifted up their noses
As° they smelt music. So I charmed their ears
That calflike they my lowing° followed through
Toothed briers, sharp furzes, pricking gorse,° and thorns,   180
Which entered their frail shins. At last I left them
I' the filthy-mantled° pool beyond your cell,
There dancing up to the chins, that the foul lake
O'erstunk° their feet.
Prospero: This was well done, my bird.
Thy shape invisible retain thou still.   185
The trumpery° in my house, go bring it hither,
For stale° to catch these thieves.
Ariel: I go, I go.   *Exit.*
Prospero: A devil, a born devil, on whose nature
Nurture can never stick; on whom my pains,
Humanely taken, all, all lost, quite lost!   190

158 *rounded:* Surrounded (before birth and after death), or crowned, rounded off.   160 *with:* By.
161 *retire:* Withdraw, go.   163 *beating:* Agitated.   164 *with a thought:* I.e., on the instant, or,
summoned by my thought, no sooner thought of than here.   165 *cleave:* Cling, adhere.   167 *presented:* Acted the part of, or, introduced.   174 *bending:* Aiming.   176 *unbacked:* Unbroken, un-
ridden.   177 *Advanced:* Lifted up.   178 *As:* As if.   179 *lowing:* Mooing.   180 *furzes, gorse:*
Prickly shrubs.   182 *filthy-mantled:* Covered with a slimy coating.   184 *O'erstunk:* Smelled worse
than, or, caused to stink terribly.   186 *trumpery:* Cheap goods, the *glistering apparel* mentioned in
the following stage direction.   187 *stale:* (1) Decoy (2) out-of-fashion garments (with possible further
suggestions of "horse piss," as in line 198, and "steal," pronounced like *stale*). *For stale* could also mean
"fit for a prostitute."

And as with age his body uglier grows,
So his mind cankers.° I will plague them all,
Even to roaring.

Enter Ariel, loaden with glistering apparel, etc.

Come, hang them on this line.°

*[Ariel hangs up the showy finery; Prospero and Ariel remain,° invisible.] Enter
Caliban, Stephano, and Trinculo, all wet.*

Caliban: Pray you, tread softly, that the blind mole may
Not hear a foot fall. We now are near his cell.   195
Stephano: Monster, your fairy, which you say is a harmless fairy, has done
little better than played the jack° with us.
Trinculo: Monster, I do smell all horse piss, at which my nose is in great
indignation.
Stephano: So is mine. Do you hear, monster? If I should take a displeasure   200
against you, look you —
Trinculo: Thou wert but a lost monster.
Caliban: Good my lord, give me thy favor still.
Be patient, for the prize I'll bring thee to
Shall hoodwink this mischance.° Therefore speak softly.   205
All's hushed as midnight yet.
Trinculo: Ay, but to lose our bottles in the pool —
Stephano: There is not only disgrace and dishonor in that, monster, but an
infinite loss.
Trinculo: That's more to me than my wetting. Yet this is your harmless fairy,   210
monster!
Stephano: I will fetch off my bottle, though I be o'er ears° for my labor.
Caliban: Prithee, my king, be quiet. Seest thou here,
This is the mouth o' the cell. No noise, and enter.
Do that good mischief which may make this island   215
Thine own forever, and I thy Caliban
For aye thy footlicker.
Stephano: Give me thy hand. I do begin to have bloody thoughts.
Trinculo [seeing the finery]: O King Stephano! O peer!° O worthy Stephano!
Look what a wardrobe here is for thee!   220
Caliban: Let it alone, thou fool, it is but trash.
Trinculo: Oho, monster! We know what belongs to a frippery.° O King
Stephano!   *[He puts on a gown.]*
Stephano: Put off° that gown, Trinculo. By this hand, I'll have that gown.
Trinculo: Thy Grace shall have it.   225
Caliban: The dropsy° drown this fool! What do you mean

192 *cankers:* Festers, grows malignant.   193 *line:* Lime tree or linden. s.d. *Prospero and Ariel remain:*
(The staging is uncertain. They may instead exit here and return with the spirits at line 247.)
197 *jack:* (1) knave (2) will-o'-the-wisp.   205 *hoodwink this mischance:* (Misfortune is to be prevented from doing further harm by being hooded like a hawk and also put out of remembrance.)
212 *o'er ears:* I.e., totally submerged and perhaps drowned.   219 *King . . . peer:* (Alludes to the old
ballad beginning, "King Stephen was a worthy peer.")   222 *frippery:* Place where cast-off clothes are
sold.   224 *Put off:* Put down, or, take off.   226 *dropsy:* Disease characterized by the accumulation
of fluid in the connective tissue of the body.

To dote thus on such luggage?° Let 't alone
And do the murder first. If he awake,
From toe to crown° he'll fill our skins with pinches,
Make us strange stuff.   230

Stephano: Be you quiet, monster. — Mistress line,° is not this my jerkin?° *[He
takes it down.]* Now is the jerkin under the line.° Now, jerkin, you are
like° to lose your hair and prove a bald° jerkin.

Trinculo: Do, do!° We steal by line and level,° an 't like° Your Grace.

Stephano: I thank thee for that jest. Here's a garment for 't. *[He gives a*   235
garment.] Wit shall not go unrewarded while I am king of this country.
"Steal by line and level" is an excellent pass of pate.° There's another
garment for 't.

Trinculo: Monster, come, put some lime° upon your fingers, and away with
the rest.   240

Caliban: I will have none on 't. We shall lose our time,
And all be turned to barnacles,° or to apes
With foreheads villainous° low.

Stephano: Monster, lay to° your fingers. Help to bear this° away where my
hogshead° of wine is, or I'll turn you out of my kingdom. Go to,° carry   245
this.

Trinculo: And this.

Stephano: Ay, and this.

> *[They load Caliban with more and more garments.]*

*A noise of hunters heard. Enter divers spirits, in shape of dogs and hounds,
hunting them about, Prospero and Ariel setting them on.*

Prospero: Hey, Mountain, hey!

Ariel: Silver! There it goes, Silver!   250

Prospero: Fury, Fury! There, Tyrant, there! Hark! Hark!

> *[Caliban, Stephano, and Trinculo are driven out.]*

Go, charge my goblins that they grind their joints
With dry° convulsions,° shorten up their sinews
With agèd° cramps, and more pinch-spotted make them
Than pard° or cat o' mountain.°

Ariel: Hark, they roar!   255

---

227 *luggage:* Cumbersome trash.   229 *crown:* Head.   231 *Mistress line:* (Addressed to the linden
or lime tree upon which, at line 193, Ariel hung the *glistering apparel*); *jerkin:* Jacket made of leather.
232 *under the line:* Under the lime tree (with punning sense of being south of the equinoctial line or
equator; sailors on long voyages to the southern regions were popularly supposed to lose their hair
from scurvy or other diseases. Stephano also quibbles bawdily on losing hair through syphilis, and in
Mistress and *jerkin*).   233 *like:* Likely; *bald:* (1) Hairless, napless (2) meager.   234 *Do, do:* I.e.,
bravo (said in response to the jesting or to the taking of the jerkin, or both); *by line and level:* I.e., by
means of plumb line and carpenter's level, methodically (with pun on *line*, "lime tree," line 232, and
steal, pronounced like *stale,* i.e., prostitute, continuing Stephano's bawdy quibble); *an't like:* If it please.
237 *pass of pate:* Sally of wit. (The metaphor is from fencing.)   239 *lime:* Birdlime, sticky substance
(to give Caliban sticky fingers).   242 *barnacles:* Barnacle geese, formerly supposed to be hatched
from barnacles attached to trees or to rotting timber; here, evidently used, like *apes,* as types of
simpletons.   243 *villainous:* Miserably.   244 *lay to:* Start using; *this:* I.e., the *glistering apparel.*
245 *hogshead:* Large cask; *Go to:* (An expression of exhortation or remonstrance.)   253 *dry:* Associated with age, arthritic (?); *convulsions:* Cramps.   254 *agèd:* Characteristic of old age.   255 *pard:*
Panther or leopard; *cat o' mountain:* Wildcat.

Prospero: Let them be hunted soundly.° At this hour
    Lies at my mercy all mine enemies.
    Shortly shall all my labors end, and thou
    Shalt have the air at freedom. For a little°
    Follow, and do me service.   *Exeunt.*   260

[ACT V

Sᴄᴇɴᴇ I: *Before Prospero's cell.*]

Enter Prospero in his magic robes, [with his staff,] and Ariel.

Prospero: Now does my project gather to a head.
    My charms crack° not, my spirits obey, and Time
    Goes upright with his carriage.° How's the day?
Ariel: On° the sixth hour, at which time, my lord,
    You said our work should cease.
Prospero: I did say so,   5
    When first I raised the tempest. Say, my spirit,
    How fares the King and 's followers?
Ariel: Confined together
    In the same fashion as you gave in charge,
    Just as you left them; all prisoners, sir,
    In the line grove° which weather-fends° your cell.   10
    They cannot budge till your release.° The King,
    His brother, and yours abide all three distracted,°
    And the remainder mourning over them,
    Brim full of sorrow and dismay; but chiefly
    Him that you termed, sir, the good old lord, Gonzalo.   15
    His tears runs down his beard like winter's drops
    From eaves of reeds.° Your charm so strongly works 'em
    That if you now beheld them your affections°
    Would become tender.
Prospero: Dost thou think so, spirit?
Ariel: Mine would, sir, were I human.°
Prospero: And mine shall.   20
    Hast thou, which art but air, a touch,° a feeling
    Of their afflictions, and shall not myself,
    One of their kind, that relish all as sharply
    Passion as they,° be kindlier° moved than thou art?

256 *soundly:* Thoroughly (and suggesting the sounds of the hunt).   259 *little:* Little while longer.
Aᴄᴛ V. Sᴄᴇɴᴇ I.   2 *crack:* Collapse, fail. (The metaphor is probably alchemical, as in *project* and *gather to a head,* line 1.)   3 *his carriage:* Its burden (time is no longer heavily burdened and so can go *upright,* "standing straight and unimpeded").   4 *On:* Approaching.   10 *line grove:* Grove of lime trees; *weather-fends:* Protects from the weather.   11 *your release:* You release them.   12 *distracted:* Out of their wits.   17 *eaves of reeds:* Thatched roofs.   18 *affections:* Disposition, feelings.   20 *human: Humane* [as well as human.]   21 *touch:* Sense, apprehension.   23–24 *that . . . they:* I who experience human passions as acutely as they.   24 *kindlier:* (1) More sympathetically (2) more naturally, humanly.

Though with their high wrongs I am struck to the quick,   25
Yet with my nobler reason 'gainst my fury
Do I take part. The rarer° action is
In virtue than in vengeance. They being penitent,
The sole drift of my purpose doth extend
Not a frown further. Go release them, Ariel.   30
My charms I'll break, their senses I'll restore,
And they shall be themselves.
Ariel: I'll fetch them, sir.

Exit.
[Prospero traces a charmed circle with his staff.]
Prospero: Ye elves of hills, brooks, standing lakes, and groves,
And ye that on the sands with printless foot
Do chase the ebbing Neptune, and do fly him   35
When he comes back; you demi-puppets° that
By moonshine do the green sour ringlets° make,
Whereof the ewe not bites; and you whose pastime
Is to make midnight mushrooms,° that rejoice
To hear the solemn curfew;° by whose aid,   40
Weak masters° though ye be, I have bedimmed
The noontide sun, called forth the mutinous winds,
And twixt the green sea and the azured vault°
Set roaring war; to the dread rattling thunder
Have I given fire,° and rifted° Jove's stout oak°   45
With his own bolt;° the strong-based promontory
Have I made shake, and by the spurs° plucked up
The pine and cedar; graves at my command
Have waked their sleepers, oped, and let 'em forth
By my so potent art.° But this rough° magic   50
I here abjure, and when I have required°
Some heavenly music — which even now I do —
To work mine end upon their senses that°
This airy charm° is for, I'll break my staff,
Bury it certain fathoms in the earth,   55
And deeper than did ever plummet sound
I'll drown my book.   *Solemn music.*

*Here enters Ariel before; then Alonso, with a frantic gesture, attended by
Gonzalo; Sebastian and Antonio in like manner, attended by Adrian and
Francisco. They all enter the circle which Prospero had made, and there stand
charmed; which Prospero observing, speaks:*

27 *rarer:* Nobler.   33–50 *Ye . . . art:* (This famous passage is an embellished paraphrase of Golding's
translation of Ovid's *Metamorphoses,* Book VII, lines 197–219.)   36 *demi-puppets:* Puppets of half size,
i.e., elves and fairies.   37 *green sour ringlets:* Fairy rings, circles in grass (actually produced by
mushrooms).   39 *midnight mushrooms:* Mushrooms appearing overnight.   40 *curfew:* Evening
bell, usually rung at nine o'clock, ushering in the time when spirits are abroad.   41 *Weak masters:*
I.e., subordinate spirits, as in IV.i.35 (?).   43 *the azured vault:* I.e., the sky.   44–45 *to . . . fire:* I
have discharged the dread rattling thunderbolt.   45 *rifted:* Riven, split; *oak:* A tree that was sacred to
Jove.   46 *bolt:* Lightning bolt.   47 *spurs:* Roots.   50 *rough:* Violent.   51 *required:* Requested.
53 *their senses that:* The senses of those whom.   54 *airy charm:* I.e., music.

1432 A Study of William Shakespeare

[To Alonso.] A solemn air,° and° the best comforter
To an unsettled fancy,° cure thy brains,
Now useless, boiled° within thy skull! *[To Sebastian and Antonio.]*
There stand,   60
For you are spell-stopped. —
Holy Gonzalo, honorable man,
Mine eyes, e'en sociable° to the show° of thine,
Fall° fellowly drops. *[Aside.]* The charm dissolves apace,
And as the morning steals upon the night,   65
Melting the darkness, so their rising senses
Begin to chase the ignorant fumes° that mantle°
Their clearer° reason. — O good Gonzalo,
My true preserver, and a loyal sir
To him thou follow'st! I will pay thy graces°   70
Home° both in word and deed. — Most cruelly
Didst thou, Alonso, use me and my daughter.
Thy brother was a furtherer° in the act. —
Thou art pinched° for 't now, Sebastian. *[To Antonio.]* Flesh and blood,
You, brother mine, that entertained ambition,   75
Expelled remorse° and nature,° whom,° with Sebastian,
Whose inward pinches therefore are most strong,
Would here have killed your king, I do forgive thee,
Unnatural though thou art. — Their understanding
Begins to swell, and the approaching tide   80
Will shortly fill the reasonable shore°
That now lies foul and muddy. Not one of them
That yet looks on me, or would know me. — Ariel,
Fetch me the hat and rapier in my cell.
             [Ariel goes to the cell and returns immediately.]
I will discase° me and myself present   85
As I was sometime Milan.° Quickly, spirit!
Thou shalt ere long be free.   *Ariel sings and helps to attire him.*
Ariel: Where the bee sucks, there suck I.
     In a cowslip's bell I lie;
     There I couch° when owls do cry.   90
     On the bat's back I do fly
     After° summer merrily.
     Merrily, merrily shall I live now
     Under the blossom that hangs on the bough.
Prospero: Why, that's my dainty Ariel! I shall miss thee,   95

---

58 *air:* Song; *and:* I.e., which is.   59 *fancy:* Imagination.   60 *boiled:* I.e., extremely agitated.
63 *sociable:* Sympathetic; *show:* Appearance.   64 *Fall:* Let fall.   67 *ignorant fumes:* Fumes that
render them incapable of comprehension; *mantle:* Envelop.   68 *clearer:* Growing clearer.   70 *pay
thy graces:* Requite your favors and virtues.   71 *Home:* Fully.   73 *furtherer:* Accomplice.
74 *pinched:* Punished, afflicted.   76 *remorse:* Pity; *nature:* Natural feeling; *whom:* I.e., who.
81 *reasonable shore:* Shores of reason, i.e., minds (their reason returns, like the incoming tide).
85 *discase:* Disrobe.   86 *As . . . Milan:* In my former appearance as Duke of Milan.   90 *couch:* Lie.
92 *After:* I.e., pursuing.

But yet thou shalt have freedom. So, so, so.°
To the King's ship, invisible as thou art!
There shalt thou find the mariners asleep
Under the hatches. The Master and the Boatswain
Being awake, enforce them to this place,   100
And presently,° I prithee.
Ariel: I drink the air before me and return
Or ere° your pulse twice beat.   *Exit.*
Gonzalo: All torment, trouble, wonder, and amazement
Inhabits here. Some heavenly power guide us   105
Out of this fearful° country!
Prospero: Behold, sir King,
The wrongèd Duke of Milan, Prospero.
For more assurance that a living prince
Does now speak to thee, I embrace thy body;
And to thee and thy company I bid   110
A hearty welcome.   *[Embracing him.]*
Alonso: Whe'er thou be'st he or no,
Or some enchanted trifle° to abuse° me,
As late° I have been, I not know. Thy pulse
Beats as of flesh and blood; and, since I saw thee,
Th' affliction of my mind amends, with which   115
I fear a madness held me. This must crave°—
An if this be at all°—a most strange story.°
Thy dukedom I resign,° and do entreat
Thou pardon me my wrongs.° But how should Prospero
Be living, and be here?
Prospero [to Gonzalo]:   First, noble friend,   120
Let me embrace thine age,° whose honor cannot
Be measured or confined.   *[Embracing him.]*
Gonzalo: Whether this be
Or be not, I'll not swear.
Prospero: You do yet taste
Some subtleties° o' th' isle, that will not let you
Believe things certain. Welcome, my friends all!   125
[Aside to Sebastian and Antonio.] But you, my brace° of lords, were I so
    minded,
I here could pluck His Highness' frown upon you
And justify you° traitors. At this time
I will tell no tales.
Sebastian: The devil speaks in him.
Prospero: No.

---

96 *So, so, so:* (Expresses approval of Ariel's help as valet.)   101 *presently:* Immediately.   103 *Or ere:* Before.   106 *fearful:* Frightening.   112 *trifle:* Trick of magic; *abuse:* Deceive.   113 *late:* Lately.   116 *crave:* Require.   117 *An . . . all:* If this is actually happening; *story:* I.e., explanation.   118 *Thy . . . resign:* (Alonso made arrangements with Antonio at the time of Prospero's banishment for Milan to pay tribute to Naples; see I.ii.113–127.)   119 *wrongs:* Wrongdoings.   121 *thine age:* Your venerable self.   124 *subtleties:* Illusions, magical powers (playing on the idea of "pastries, concoctions").   126 *brace:* Pair.   128 *justify you:* Prove you to be.

[To Antonio.] For you, most wicked sir, whom to call brother   130
    Would even infect my mouth, I do forgive
    Thy rankest fault — all of them; and require
    My dukedom of thee, which perforce° I know
    Thou must restore.
Alonso: If thou be'st Prospero,
    Give us particulars of thy preservation,   135
    How thou hast met us here, whom° three hours since
    Were wrecked upon this shore; where I have lost —
    How sharp the point of this remembrance is! —
    My dear son Ferdinand.
Prospero: I am woe° for 't, sir.
Alonso: Irreparable is the loss, and Patience   140
    Says it is past her cure.
Prospero: I rather think
    You have not sought her help, of whose soft grace°
    For the like loss I have her sovereign° aid
    And rest myself content.
Alonso: You the like loss?
Prospero: As great to me as late,° and supportable   145
    To make the dear loss, have I° means much weaker
    Than you may call to comfort you; for I
    Have lost my daughter.
Alonso: A daughter?
    O heavens, that they were living both in Naples,   150
    The king and queen there! That° they were, I wish
    Myself were mudded° in that oozy bed
    Where my son lies. When did you lose your daughter?
Prospero: In this last tempest. I perceive these lords
    At this encounter do so much admire°   155
    That they devour their reason° and scarce think
    Their eyes do offices of truth, their words
    Are natural breath.° But, howsoever you have
    Been jostled from your senses, know for certain
    That I am Prospero and that very duke   160
    Which was thrust forth of° Milan, who most strangely
    Upon this shore, where you were wrecked, was landed
    To be the lord on 't. No more yet of this,
    For 'tis a chronicle of day by day,°
    Not a relation for a breakfast nor   165
    Befitting this first meeting. Welcome, sir.
    This cell's my court. Here have I few attendants,

---

133 *perforce:* Necessarily.   136 *whom:* I.e., who.   139 *woe:* Sorry.   142 *of . . . grace:* By whose
mercy.   143 *sovereign:* Efficacious.   145 *late:* Recent.   145–146 *supportable . . . have I:* To make
the deeply felt loss bearable, I have.   151 *That:* So that.   152 *mudded:* Buried in the mud.
155 *admire:* Wonder.   156 *devour their reason:* I.e., are openmouthed, dumbfounded.   156–
158 *scarce . . . breath:* Scarcely believe that their eyes inform them accurately as to what they see or
that their words are naturally spoken.   161 *of:* From.   164 *of day by day:* Requiring days to tell.

And subjects none abroad.° Pray you, look in.
My dukedom since you have given me again,
I will requite° you with as good a thing,   170
At least bring forth a wonder to content ye
As much as me my dukedom.

Here Prospero discovers° Ferdinand and Miranda, playing at chess.

Miranda: Sweet lord, you play me false.°
Ferdinand: No, my dearest love,
I would not for the world.   175
Miranda: Yes, for a score of kingdoms you should wrangle,
And I would call it fair play.°
Alonso: If this prove
A vision° of the island, one dear son
Shall I twice lose.
Sebastian: A most high miracle!
Ferdinand [approaching his father]:
Though the seas threaten, they are merciful;   180
I have cursed them without cause.   *[He kneels.]*
Alonso: Now all the blessings
Of a glad father compass° thee about!
Arise, and say how thou cam'st here.

                                                        [Ferdinand rises.]

Miranda: O, wonder!
How many goodly creatures are there here!
How beauteous mankind is! O brave° new world   185
That has such people in 't!
Prospero: 'Tis new to thee.
Alonso: What is this maid with whom thou wast at play?
Your eld'st° acquaintance cannot be three hours.
Is she the goddess that hath severed us,
And brought us thus together?
Ferdinand: Sir, she is mortal;   190
But by immortal Providence she's mine.
I chose her when I could not ask my father
For his advice, nor thought I had one. She
Is daughter to this famous Duke of Milan,
Of whom so often I have heard renown,   195
But never saw before; of whom I have
Received a second life; and second father
This lady makes him to me.
Alonso: I am hers.

168 *abroad:* Away from here, anywhere else.   170 *requite:* Repay.   172 *discovers:* I.e., by opening
a curtain, presumably rearstage.   173 *play me false:* I.e., press your advantage.   176–177 *Yes . . .
play:* I.e., yes, even if we were playing for twenty kingdoms, something less than the whole world, you
would still press your advantage against me, and I would lovingly let you do it as though it were fair
play, or, if you were to play not just for stakes but literally for kingdoms, my complaint would be out
of order in that your "wrangling" would be proper.   178 *vision:* Illusion.   182 *compass:* Encom-
pass, embrace.   185 *brave:* Splendid, gorgeously appareled, handsome.   188 *eld'st:* Longest.

But O, how oddly will it sound that I
    Must ask my child forgiveness!
Prospero: There, sir, stop.   200
    Let us not burden our remembrances with
    A heaviness° that's gone.
Gonzalo: I have inly° wept,
    Or should have spoke ere this. Look down, you gods,
    And on this couple drop a blessèd crown!
    For it is you that have chalked forth the way°   205
    Which brought us hither.
Alonso: I say amen, Gonzalo!
Gonzalo: Was Milan° thrust from Milan, that his issue
    Should become kings of Naples? O, rejoice
    Beyond a common joy, and set it down
    With gold on lasting pillars: In one voyage   210
    Did Claribel her husband find at Tunis,
    And Ferdinand, her brother, found a wife
    Where he himself was lost; Prospero his dukedom
    In a poor isle; and all of us ourselves
    When no man was his own.°
Alonso [to Ferdinand and Miranda]: Give me your hands.   215
    Let grief and sorrow still° embrace his° heart
    That° doth not wish you joy!
Gonzalo: Be it so! Amen!

Enter Ariel, with the Master and Boatswain amazedly following.

    O, look, sir, look, sir! Here is more of us.
    I prophesied, if a gallows were on land,
    This fellow could not drown. — Now, blasphemy,°   220
    That swear'st grace o'erboard,° not an oath° on shore?
    Hast thou no mouth by land? What is the news?
Boatswain: The best news is that we have safely found
    Our King and company; the next, our ship —
    Which, but three glasses° since, we gave out° split —   225
    Is tight and yare° and bravely° rigged as when
    We first put out to sea.
Ariel [aside to Prospero]:   Sir, all this service
    Have I done since I went.
Prospero [aside to Ariel]:   My tricksy° spirit!
Alonso: These are not natural events; they strengthen°
    From strange to stranger. Say, how came you hither?   230

---

202 *heaviness:* Sadness; *inly:* Inwardly.   205 *chalked . . . way:* Marked as with a piece of chalk the pathway.   207 *Was Milan:* Was the Duke of Milan.   214–215 *all . . . own:* All of us have found ourselves and our sanity when we all had lost our senses.   216 *still:* Always; *his:* That person's. 217 *That:* Who.   220 *blasphemy:* I.e., blasphemer.   221 *That swear'st grace o'erboard:* I.e., you who banish heavenly grace from the ship by your blasphemies; *not an oath:* Aren't you going to swear an oath.   225 *glasses:* I.e., hours; *gave out:* Reported, professed to be.   226 *yare:* Ready; *bravely:* Splendidly.   228 *tricksy:* Ingenious, sportive.   229 *strengthen:* Increase.

Boatswain: If I did think, sir, I were well awake,
    I'd strive to tell you. We were dead of sleep,°
    And — how we know not — all clapped under hatches,
    Where but even now, with strange and several° noises
    Of roaring, shrieking, howling, jingling chains,   235
    And more diversity of sounds, all horrible,
    We were awaked; straightway at liberty;
    Where we, in all her trim, freshly beheld
    Our royal, good, and gallant ship, our Master
    Cap'ring° to eye her. On a trice,° so please you,   240
    Even in a dream, were we divided from them°
    And were brought moping° hither.
Ariel [aside to Prospero]:   Was 't well done?
Prospero [aside to Ariel]: Bravely, my diligence. Thou shalt be free.
Alonso: This is as strange a maze as e'er men trod,
    And there is in this business more than nature   245
    Was ever conduct° of. Some oracle
    Must rectify our knowledge.
Prospero: Sir, my liege,
    Do not infest° your mind with beating on°
    The strangeness of this business. At picked° leisure,
    Which shall be shortly, single° I'll resolve° you,   250
    Which to you shall seem probable,° of every
    These° happened accidents;° till when, be cheerful
    And think of each thing well.° *[Aside to Ariel.]* Come hither, spirit.
    Set Caliban and his companions free.
    Untie the spell. *[Exit Ariel.]* How fares my gracious sir?   255
    There are yet missing of your company
    Some few odd° lads that you remember not.

Enter Ariel, driving in Caliban, Stephano, and Trinculo, in their stolen apparel.

Stephano: Every man shift° for all the rest,° and let no man take care for
    himself; for all is but fortune. Coragio,° bully monster,° coragio! 260
Trinculo: If these be true spies° which I wear in my head, here's a goodly
    sight.
Caliban: O Setebos, these be brave° spirits indeed!
    How fine° my master is! I am afraid
    He will chastise me.   265
Sebastian: Ha, ha!
    What things are these, my lord Antonio?
    Will money buy 'em?

232 *dead of sleep:* Deep in sleep.   234 *several:* Diverse.   240 *Cap'ring to eye:* Dancing for joy to
see; *On a trice:* In an instant.   241 *them:* I.e.,the other crew members.   242 *moping:* In a daze.
246 *conduct:* Guide.   248 *infest:* Harass, disturb; *beating on:* Worrying about.   249 *picked:* Chosen, convenient.   250 *single:* Privately, by my own human powers; *resolve:* Satisfy, explain to.
251 *probable:* Plausible.   251–252 *of every These:* About every one of these.   252 *accidents:* Occurrences.   253 *well:* Favorably.   257 *odd:* Unaccounted for.   259 *shift:* Provide; *for all the rest:*
(Stephano drunkenly gets wrong the saying "Every man for himself.")   260 *Coragio:* Courage; *bully
monster:* Gallant monster (ironical).   261 *true spies:* Accurate observers (i.e., sharp eyes).
263 *brave:* Handsome.   264 *fine:* Splendidly attired.

Antonio: Very like. One of them
    Is a plain fish, and no doubt marketable.
Prospero: Mark but the badges° of these men, my lords,   270
    Then say if they be true.° This misshapen knave,
    His mother was a witch, and one so strong
    That could control the moon, make flows and ebbs,
    And deal in her command without her power.°
    These three have robbed me, and this demidevil —   275
    For he's a bastard° one — had plotted with them
    To take my life. Two of these fellows you
    Must know and own.° This thing of darkness I
    Acknowledge mine.
Caliban: I shall be pinched to death.
Alonso: Is not this Stephano, my drunken butler?   280
Sebastian: He is drunk now. Where had he wine?
Alonso: And Trinculo is reeling ripe.° Where should they
    Find this grand liquor that hath gilded° em?
    [To Trinculo.] How cam'st thou in this pickle?°
Trinculo: I have been in such a pickle since I saw you last that, I fear me,   285
    will never out of my bones. I shall not fear flyblowing.°
Sebastian: Why, how now, Stephano?
Stephano: O, touch me not! I am not Stephano, but a cramp.
Prospero: You'd be king o' the isle, sirrah?°
Stephano: I should have been a sore° one, then.   290
Alonso [pointing to Caliban]: This is a strange thing as e'er I looked on.
Prospero: He is as disproportioned in his manners
    As in his shape. — Go, sirrah, to my cell.
    Take with you your companions. As you look
    To have my pardon, trim° it handsomely.   295
Caliban: Ay, that I will; and I'll be wise hereafter
    And seek for grace.° What a thrice-double ass
    Was I to take this drunkard for a god
    And worship this dull fool!
Prospero: Go to. Away!
Alonso: Hence, and bestow your luggage where you found it.   300
Sebastian: Or stole it, rather.
                    [Exeunt Caliban, Stephano, and Trinculo.]
Prospero: Sir, I invite Your Highness and your train
    To my poor cell, where you shall take your rest
    For this one night; which, part of it, I'll waste°

270 *badges:* Emblems of cloth or silver worn by retainers to indicate whom they serve. (Prospero refers here to the stolen clothes as emblems of their villainy.)   271 *true:* Honest.   274 *deal . . . power:* Wield the moon's power, either without her authority or beyond her influence, or, even though to do so was beyond Sycorax's own power.   276 *bastard:* Counterfeit.   278 *own:* Recognize, admit as belonging to you.   282 *reeling ripe:* Stumblingly drunk.   283 *gilded:* (1) Flushed, made drunk (2) covered with gilt (suggesting the horse urine).   284 *pickle:* (1) Fix, predicament (2) pickling brine (in this case, horse urine).   286 *flyblowing:* I.e., being fouled by fly eggs (from which he is saved by being pickled).   289 *sirrah:* (Standard form of address to an inferior, here expressing reprimand.)   290 *sore:* (1) Tyrannical (2) sorry, inept (3) wracked by pain.   295 *trim:* Prepare, decorate.   297 *grace:* Pardon, favor.   304 *waste:* Spend.

With such discourse as, I not doubt, shall make it   305
Go quick away: the story of my life,
And the particular accidents° gone by
Since I came to this isle. And in the morn
I'll bring you to your ship, and so to Naples,
Where I have hope to see the nuptial   310
Of these our dear-belovèd solemnized;
And thence retire me° to my Milan, where
Every third thought shall be my grave.
Alonso: I long
To hear the story of your life, which must
Take° the ear strangely.
Prospero: I'll deliver° all;   315
And promise you calm seas, auspicious gales,
And sail so expeditious that shall catch
Your royal fleet far off.° *[Aside to Ariel.]* My Ariel, chick,
That is thy charge. Then to the elements
Be free, and fare thou well! — Please you, draw near.°   320

                            Exeunt omnes [except Prospero.]

EPILOGUE

Spoken by Prospero.

Now my charms are all o'erthrown,
And what strength I have 's mine own,
Which is most faint. Now, 'tis true,
I must be here confined by you
Or sent to Naples. Let me not,   5
Since I have my dukedom got
And pardoned the deceiver, dwell
In this bare island by your spell,
But release me from my bands°
With the help of your good hands.°   10
Gentle breath° of yours my sails
Must fill, or else my project fails,
Which was to please. Now I want°
Spirits to enforce,° art to enchant,
And my ending is despair,   15
Unless I be relieved by prayer,°
Which pierces so that it assaults°

---

307 *accidents:* Occurrences.   312 *retire me:* Return.   315 *Take:* Take effect upon, enchant; *deliver:*
Declare, relate.   317–318 *catch . . . far off:* Enable you to catch up with the main part of your royal
fleet, now afar off enroute to Naples (see I.ii.235–236).   320 *draw near:* I.e., enter my cell.   Epilogue.
9 *bands:* Bonds.   10 *hands:* I.e., applause (the noise of which would break the spell of silence).
11 *Gentle breath:* Favorable breeze (produced by hands clapping or favorable comment).   13 *want:*
Lack.   14 *enforce:* Control.   16 *prayer:* I.e., Prospero's petition to the audience.   17 *assaults:*
Rightfully gains the attention of.

Mercy itself, and frees° all faults.
As you from crimes° would pardoned be,
Let your indulgence° set me free.   *Exit.*   20

18 *frees:* Obtains forgiveness for.   19 *crimes:* Sins.   20 *indulgence:* (1) Humoring, lenient approval
(2) remission of punishment for sin.

Considerations for Critical Thinking and Writing

1. Explain how Ariel and Caliban serve as character foils for each other. Consider their physical appearances and their roles as servants to Prospero.
2. Though Caliban is presented as a depraved savage, does he have any dignity or redeeming features? Why isn't he merely a flat character?
3. Describe Miranda. How is she a product of "nurture" rather than nature? What values does she represent in the play?
4. Why does Prospero initially want to make difficult the relationship between Miranda and Ferdinand? How does this complicate the plot?
5. How does Ferdinand's love for Miranda differ from Caliban's attraction to her? How do their responses to her reveal the character of each?
6. Describe how Sebastian and Antonio's plan to kill King Alonso parallels the plan of Caliban, Stephano, and Trinculo to kill Prospero. How do these parallel plots serve as commentaries on each other?
7. Prospero has been criticized by some readers as an overbearing patriarchal figure, a colonist, and even a racist. Consider these assertions and determine through your own perspective on him whether you agree or disagree with these charges.
8. According to Gonzalo, what constitutes an ideal commonwealth (II.i.138–157)? How does Gonzalo's vision of a ruler's power compare with Prospero's? How does it compare with Sebastian's and Stephano's ambitions for power?
9. Stephano, King Alonso's drunken butler, says to Caliban "You cannot tell who's your friend" (II.ii.71–72). How does this warning represent an important element in the plot of the play?
10. Discuss Prospero's comparison of life to the stage (IV.i.148–158). How is the theme of reality and illusion made an issue throughout the play?
11. How does Prospero's magic differ from that of Sycorax? Why do you think Prospero gives up his magic (V.i.50–57)?
12. Describe the natural world depicted on the island. Is it innocent or corrupt? Is it redeemed by contact with civilization or corrupted by it?

Connections to Other Selections

1. In an essay compare *The Tempest*'s island setting with the forest in *A Midsummer Night's Dream* (p. 1224). Describe each setting and explain how it represents a state of mind as well as a physical location.
2. Compare Prospero's attitudes about revenge against those who conspire against him with Hamlet's attitudes. Why can't Hamlet agree with Prospero's conviction that "The rarer action is/In virtue than in vengeance" (V.i.27–28)?
3. Write an essay on the function of illusion in *The Tempest* and *The Glass Menagerie* (p. 1666). How do the characters' illusions indicate the thematic concerns of each play?

4. Discuss in an essay the father-daughter relationships in *The Tempest* and in Nathaniel Hawthorne's short story "Rappaccini's Daughter" (p. 273). In particular consider the degree to which Miranda and Beatrice are protected, victimized, or both by their fathers.

PERSPECTIVES ON SHAKESPEARE

Objections to the Elizabethan Theater by the Mayor of London

1597

The inconueniences that grow by Stage playes abowt the Citie of London.

1. They are a speaciall cause of corrupting their Youth, conteninge nothinge but vnchast matters, lascivious devices, shiftes of Coozenage, & other lewd & vngodly practizes, being so as that they impresse the very qualitie & corruption of manners which they represent, Contrary to the rules & art prescribed for the makinge of Comedies eaven amonge the Heathen, who vsed them seldom & at certen sett tymes, and not all the year longe as our manner is. Whearby such as frequent them, beinge of the base & refuze sort of people or such young gentlemen as haue small regard of credit or conscience, drawe the same into imitacion and not to the avoidinge the like vices which they represent.

2. They are the ordinary places for vagrant persons, Maisterles men, thieves, horse stealers, whoremongers, Coozeners, Conycatchers, contrivers of treason, and other idele and daungerous persons to meet together & to make theire matches to the great displeasure of Almightie God & the hurt & annoyance of her Maiesties people, which cannot be prevented nor discovered by the Gouernours of the Citie for that they are owt of the Citiees iurisdiction.

3. They maintaine idlenes in such persons as haue no vocation & draw apprentices and other seruantes from theire ordinary workes and all sortes of people from the resort vnto sermons and other Christian exercises, to the great hinderance of traides & prophanation of religion established by her highnes within this Realm.

4. In the time of sickness it is fownd by experience, that many hauing sores and yet not hart sicke take occasion hearby to walk abroad & to recreat themselves by heareinge a play Whearby others are infected, and them selves also many things miscarry.

From Edmund K. Chambers, The Elizabethan Stage

Considerations for Critical Thinking and Writing

1. Summarize the mayor's objections to the theater. Do any of his reasons for protesting theatrical productions seem reasonable to you? Why or why not?
2. Are any of these concerns reflected in attitudes about the theater today? Why or why not?
3. How would you defend *Hamlet* or *The Tempest* against charges that they draw some people into "imitacion and not to the avoidinge the like vices which they represent"?

SAMUEL JOHNSON (1709–1784)
On Shakespeare's Characters

1765

Shakespeare is above all writers, at least above all modern writers, the poet of nature: the poet that holds up to his readers a faithful mirror of manners and life. His characters are not modified by the customs of particular places, unpracticed by the rest of the world; by the peculiarities of studies or professions, which can operate but upon small numbers; or by the accidents of transient fashions or temporary opinions: they are the genuine progeny of common humanity, such as the world will always supply, and observation will always find. His persons act and speak by the influence of those general passions and principles by which all minds are agitated, and the whole system of life is continued in motion. In the writings of other poets a character is too often an individual; in those of Shakespeare it is commonly a species.

From the Preface to Johnson's Edition of Shakespeare.

Considerations for Critical Thinking and Writing

1. Johnson made this famous assessment of Shakespeare's ability to portray "common humanity" in the eighteenth century. As a twentieth-century reader, explain why you agree or disagree with Johnson's view that Shakespeare's characters have universal appeal.
2. Write an essay discussing whether you think it is desirable or necessary for characters to be "a faithful mirror of manners and life." Along the way consider whether you encountered any characters in *Hamlet* or *The Tempest* that do not provide what you consider to be an accurate mirror of human life.

SIGMUND FREUD (1856–1939)
On Repression in Hamlet

1900

Another of the great creations of tragic poetry, Shakespeare's *Hamlet,* has its roots in the same soil as *Oedipus Rex.* But the changed treatment of the same material reveals the whole difference in the mental life of these two widely separated epochs of civilization: the secular advance of repression in the emotional life of mankind. In the *Oedipus* the child's wishful fantasy that underlies it is brought into the open and realized as it would be in a dream. In *Hamlet* it remains repressed; and — just as in the case of a neurosis — we only learn of its existence from its inhibiting consequences. Strangely enough, the overwhelming effect produced by the more modern tragedy has turned out to be compatible with the fact that people have remained completely in the dark as to the hero's character. The play is built up on Hamlet's hesitations over fulfilling the task of revenge that is assigned to him; but its text offers no reasons or motives for these hesitations and an immense variety of attempts at interpreting them have failed to produce a result. According to the view which was originated by Goethe and is still the prevailing one today, Hamlet represents the type of man whose power of direct action is paralyzed by an excessive development of his intellect. (He is "sicklied o'er with the pale cast of thought.") According to another view, the dramatist has tried to portray a pathologically irresolute character which might be classed as neurasthenic. The plot of the drama shows us, however, that Hamlet is far from being represented as a person incapable of taking any action. We see him doing so on two occasions: first in a sudden outburst of temper, when he runs his sword through the eavesdropper behind the arras, and secondly in a premeditated and even crafty fashion, when, with all the callousness of a Renaissance prince, he sends the two courtiers to the death that had been planned for himself. What is it, then, that inhibits him in fulfilling the task set him by his father's ghost? The answer, once again, is that it is the peculiar nature of the task. Hamlet is able to do anything — except take vengeance on the man who did away with his father and took that father's place with his mother, the man who shows him the repressed wishes of his own childhood realized. Thus the loathing which should drive him on to revenge is replaced in him by self-reproaches, by scruples of conscience, which remind him that he himself is literally no better than the sinner whom he is to punish. Here I have translated into conscious terms what was bound to remain unconscious in Hamlet's mind; and if anyone is inclined to call him a hysteric, I can only accept the fact as one that is implied by my interpretation. The distaste for sexuality expressed by Hamlet in his conversation with Ophelia fits in very well with this: the same distaste which was destined to take possession of the poet's mind more and more during the years that followed, and which reached its extreme expression in *Timon of Athens*. For it can of course only be the poet's own mind which confronts us in Hamlet. I observe in a book on Shakespeare by Georg Brandes (1896) a statement that *Hamlet* was written immediately after the death of Shakespeare's father (in 1601), that is, under the immediate impact of his bereavement and, as we may well assume, while his childhood feelings about his father had been freshly revived. It is known, too, that Shakespeare's own son who died at an early age bore the name of "Hamnet," which is identical with "Hamlet." Just as *Hamlet* deals with the relation of a son to his parents, so *Macbeth* (written at approximately the same period) is concerned with the subject of childlessness. But just as all neurotic symptoms are, and, for that matter, dreams, are capable of being "overinterpreted" and indeed need to be, if they are to be fully understood, so all genuinely creative writings are the product of more than a single motive and more than a single impulse in the poet's mind, and are open to more than a single interpretation. In what I have written I have only attempted to interpret the deepest layer of impulses in the mind of the creative writer.

From *The Interpretation of Dreams*

Considerations for Critical Thinking and Writing

1. What reason does Freud offer for Hamlet's inability to avenge his father's death? Explain whether you find Freud's reasoning convincing.
2. Read the section on psychological criticism (p. 2004) in Chapter 35, "Critical Strategies for Reading," and then discuss Freud's assertion that "it can of course only be the poet's mind which confronts us in Hamlet." Explain why you agree or disagree.
3. Write an essay discussing whether you think Freud's approach to *Hamlet* opens up perspectives on the play or narrowly limits them.

JAN KOTT (b. 1914)
On Producing Hamlet
1964

No Dane of flesh and blood has been written about so extensively as Hamlet. Shakespeare's prince is certainly the best known representative of his nation. Innumerable glossaries and commentaries have grown round Hamlet, and he is one of the few literary heroes who live apart from the text, apart from the theater. His name means something even to those who have never seen or read Shakespeare's play. In this respect he is rather like Leonardo's Mona Lisa. We know she is smiling even before we have seen the picture, as it were. It contains not only what Leonardo expressed in it but also everything that has been written about it. Too many people — girls, women, poets, painters — have tried to solve the mystery of that smile. It is not just Mona Lisa that is smiling at us now, but all those who have tried to analyze, or imitate, that smile.

This is also the case with *Hamlet,* or rather — with *Hamlet* in the theater. For we have been separated from the text not only by Hamlet's "independent life" in our culture, but simply by the size of the play. *Hamlet* cannot be performed in its entirety, because the performance would last nearly six hours. One has to select, curtail, and cut. One can perform only one of several *Hamlets* potentially existing in this arch-play. It will always be a poorer *Hamlet* than Shakespeare's *Hamlet* is; but it may also be a *Hamlet* enriched by being of our time. It may, but I would rather say — it must be so.

For *Hamlet* cannot be played simply. This may be the reason why it is so tempting to producers and actors. Many generations have seen their own reflections in this play. The genius of *Hamlet* consists, perhaps, in the fact that the play can serve as a mirror. An ideal *Hamlet* would be one most true to Shakespeare and most modern at the same time. Is this possible? I do not know. But we can only appraise any Shakespearean production by asking how much there is of Shakespeare in it, and how much of us.

What I have in mind is not a forced topicality, a *Hamlet* that would be set in a cellar of young existentialists. *Hamlet* has been performed for that matter in evening dress and in circus tights; in medieval armor and in Renaissance costume. Costumes do not matter. What matters is that through Shakespeare's text we ought to get at our modern experience, anxiety, and sensibility.

There are many subjects in *Hamlet.* There is politics, force opposed to morality; there is discussion of the divergence between theory and practice, of the ultimate purpose of life; there is tragedy of love, as well as family drama; political, eschatological, and metaphysical problems are considered. There is everything you want, including deep psychological analysis, a bloody story, a duel, and general slaughter. One can select at will. But one must know what one selects, and why.

From *"Hamlet* of the Mid-Century" in *Shakespeare Our Contemporary,*
translated by Boleslaw Taborski

Considerations for Critical Thinking and Writing

1. "Many generations have seen their own reflections in this play." Use this statement as a basis for researching productions of *Hamlet*. How have events contemporary to the play's performances influenced the ways it has been presented?

2. Explain why you think it is good or bad for a producer to interpret a play in light of events contemporary to it.
3. If you were to produce *Hamlet* today, what would you emphasize? Consider how you would handle the setting, costuming, casting, and theme.
4. What do you think a reader-response critic would have to say about Kott's comments on producing *Hamlet?* Base your answer on the discussion of reader-response criticism in Chapter 35, "Critical Strategies for Reading," p. 2012.

KAREN S. HENRY (b. 1954)
The Play Within the Play in Hamlet   1989

Imprisoned in a world of spies, Hamlet imagines the theater to be the ultimate watcher — the spy set on spies. Lionel Abel describes the perverted interaction between the characters in Elsinore as projection or dramatization: "What has not been noticed . . . is that there is hardly a scene in the whole work in which some character is not trying to dramatize another" (*Metatheatre* 45). Abel's comment highlights the theatricalization of all experience that is rampant in this play. Hamlet, one of the many directors in the play, turns to the theater to mirror Claudius's crime back to him and thus expose him. The theater, however, becomes more than Hamlet's means of seeing through and exposing corruption; the play within the play exposes Hamlet to Claudius just as it reveals Claudius to Hamlet, setting off a series of events that lead to the inevitable and fatal conflict between these characters.

Hamlet intends his play to reestablish the ground for judgment and decision: "I'll have grounds/ More relative than this. The play's the thing/ Wherein I'll catch the conscience of the King." But Hamlet never lets the play do its work; he never trusts that it can have a strong enough effect. Like the bad actors he warns the players against imitating, he saws the air too much and "in the very torrent, tempest, and whirlwind" of his passion he deforms his play. As he becomes more and more impassioned, his interpretations of the dramatic action usurp it entirely, becoming the central action in the scene. We see Hamlet as the director who cannot step out of the show. His interruptions are a way of manipulating Ophelia, Gertrude, and ultimately Claudius, but they are also nearly out of his control, and so they make him vulnerable to his enemies. He hurts and embarrasses Ophelia and forces a reaction out of Gertrude that merely frustrates him further. With these two, the interruptions remain part of the theatrical scene as the play within the play continues. With Claudius, however, theater breaks into life at Elsinore when the King stops the play within the play.

Before that moment, the *Mousetrap* advances the larger plot by interacting dynamically with it. The play within the play proceeds as Claudius asks questions of Hamlet, giving the Prince an opportunity to twist the knife a bit further with each answer:

King: Have you heard the argument? Is there no offence in't?
Hamlet: No, no, they do but jest, poison in jest; no offence i' the world.
King: What do you call the play?

Hamlet: The Mouse-trap. . . . 'tis a knavish piece of work: but what o' that?
Your majesty, and we that have free souls, it touches us not: let the galled
jade winch, our withers are unwrung.

(III. ii. 208–211, 213–215)

Hamlet's thinly veiled irony complicates the larger plot. Once Claudius is certain that Hamlet is baiting him, he cannot let the nephew escape.

In his excess, Hamlet subverts his own contrivance. Instead of detaching himself from the action to watch Claudius's response to the mirror image of his crime, Hamlet enters wildly and makes himself conspicuous as the antagonist of the King. Any objective perception of Claudius is therefore marred. Who in the court, except Horatio, would be willing to say that the King suffers from a guilty conscience and not from anger against his mad nephew who seems to threaten him with assassination. By manipulating the play, Hamlet provokes and warns Claudius — the nephew knows the uncle's secret. Hamlet threatens to expose Claudius with the exposition about the poisoning: " 'A poisons him i' the garden for his estate. . . . You shall see anon how the murderer gets the love of Gonzago's wife" (III. ii. 232–234). And Claudius responds by calling for lights, thus stopping Hamlet's game. Hamlet and Horatio interpret Claudius's act as a confession of guilt, but only the theater audience (watchers watching watchers) can confirm this interpretation.

From "The Shattering of Resemblance:
The Mirror in Shakespeare"

Considerations for Critical Thinking and Writing

1. Explain in detail how the play within the play creates the crisis in *Hamlet.*
2. In what sense is Hamlet "one of the many directors in the play"? What other characters also function as directors? How do their actions warrant such a description?
3. In an essay explore the significance of Henry's provocative phrase describing the theater audience as "watchers watching watchers." How might this phrase also be used to describe other scenes in the play? What does it suggest about the nature of Hamlet's world?

LINDA BAMBER (b. 1945)
Feminine Rebellion and Masculine Authority
in A Midsummer Night's Dream   1981

In the comedies, the feminine challenges the status quo either overtly or through its command of socially subversive forces like sexuality, romantic passion, household revels, and so forth.

The best example of the relationship between male dominance and the status quo comes in *A Midsummer Night's Dream,* which begins with a rebellion of the feminine against the power of masculine authority. Hermia refuses the man both Aegeus and Theseus order her to marry; her refusal sends us off into the forest, beyond the power of the father and the masculine state. Once in the forest, of course, we find the social situation metaphorically repeated in this world of imagination and nature. The fairy king, Oberon, rules the forest. His rule, too, is troubled by the rebellion of the feminine. Titania has refused to give him her page, the child of a human friend who died in childbirth. But by the end of the story Titania is conquered, the child relinquished, and order restored. Even here the comic upheavals, whether we see them as May games or bad dreams, are associated with an uprising of women. David P. Young has pointed out how firmly this play connects order with masculine dominance and the disruption of order with the rebellion of the feminine:

> It is appropriate that Theseus, as representative of daylight and right reason, should have subdued his bride-to-be to the rule of his masculine will. That is the natural order of things. It is equally appropriate that Oberon, as king of darkness and fantasy, should have lost control of his wife, and that the corresponding natural disorder described by Titania should ensue.[1]

The natural order, the status quo, is for men to rule women. When they fail to do so, we have the exceptional situation, the festive, disruptive, disorderly moment of comedy.

A *Midsummer Night's Dream* is actually an anomaly among the festive comedies. It is unusual for the forces of the green world to be directed, as they are here, by a masculine figure. Because the green world here is a partial reproduction of the social world, the feminine is reduced to a kind of first cause of the action while a masculine power directs it. In the other festive comedies the feminine Other presides. She does not *command* the forces of the alternative world, as Oberon does, but since she acts in harmony with these forces her will and desire often prevail.

Where are we to bestow our sympathies? On the forces that make for the disruption of the status quo and therefore for the plot? Or on the force that asserts itself against the disruption and reestablishes a workable social order? Of course we cannot choose. We can only say that in comedy we owe our holiday to such forces as the tendency of the feminine to rebel, whereas to the successful reassertion of masculine power we owe our everyday order. Shakespearean comedy endorses both sides. Holiday is, of course, the subject and the analogue of each play; but the plays always end in a return to everyday life. The optimistic reading of Shakespearean comedy says that everyday life is clarified and enriched by our holiday from it; according to the pessimistic reading the temporary subversion of the social order has revealed how much that order excludes, how high a price we pay for it. But whether our return to everyday life is a comfortable one or not, the return itself is the inevitable conclusion to the journey out.

From *Comic Women, Tragic Men:*
A Study of Gender and Genre in Shakespeare

---

[1] David P. Young, *Something of Great Constancy* (New Haven, CT: Yale UP, 1966), 183.

Considerations for Critical Thinking and Writing

1. What distinctions does Bamber make between the "optimistic" and "pessimistic" readings of Shakespearean comedy? In an essay explain how you would categorize your own reading of *A Midsummer Night's Dream*.
2. Compare Bamber's view of the "disruptive, disorderly moment of comedy" with James Kincaid's view of comedy in the following perspective. How do Bamber and Kincaid define the comic?

JAMES KINCAID (b. 1937)
On the Value of Comedy in the Face of Tragedy 1991

[O]ur current hierarchical arrangement (tragedy high — comedy low) betrays an acquiescence in the most smothering of political conservatisms. Put another way, by coupling tragedy with the sublime, the ineffable, the metaphysical and by aligning comedy with the mundane, the quotidian, and the material we manage to muffle, even to erase, the most powerful narratives of illumination and liberation we have. . . .

The point is comic relief, the *concept* of comic relief and who it relieves. Now we usually refer to comic relief in the same tone we use for academic deans, other people's children, Melanie Griffith, the new criticism, jogging, Big Macs, the *New York Times Book Review,* leisure suits, people who go on cruises, realtors, and the MLA: bemused contempt. (Which is what we think about comic relief.) Comedy is that which attends on, offers relaxation from, prepares us for more of — something else, something serious and demanding. Comedy is not demanding — it does not demand or take, it gives. And we know that any agency which gives cannot be worth much. Tragedy's seriousness is guaranteed by its bullying greed, its insistence on having things its own way and pulling from us not only our tears, which we value little, but our attention, which we hate to give. Comedy, on the other hand, doesn't care if we attend closely. Tragedy is sleek and single-minded, comedy rumpled and hospitable to any idea or agency. Tragedy stares us out of countenance; comedy winks and leers and drools. Tragedy is all dressed up; comedy is always taking things off, mooning us. We find it inevitable that we associate tragedy with the high, comedy with the low. What is at issue here is the nature of that inevitability, our willingness to conspire in a discourse which pays homage to tragic grandeur and reduces comedy to release, authorized license, periodic relief — like a sneeze or yawn or belch. By allowing such discourse to flow through us, we add our bit of cement to the cultural edifice that sits on top of comedy, mashes it down into a mere adjunct to tragedy, its reverse and inferior half, its silly little carnival. By cooperating in this move, we relieve orthodox and conservative power structures of any pressure that might be exercised against them. Comic relief relieves the status quo, in other words, contains the power of comedy. . . .

Let's put it this way, comedy is not a mode that stands in opposition to tragedy. Comedy is the *whole* story, the narrative which refuses to leave things out. Tragedy insists on a formal structure that is unified and coherent, formally balanced and elegantly tight. Only that which is coordinate is allowed to adorn the tragic body. With comedy, nothing is sacrificed, nothing lost; the discoordinate and the discontinuous are especially welcome. Tragedy protects itself by its linearity, its tight conclusiveness; comedy's generosity and ability never to end make it gloriously vulnerable. Pitting tragedy against comedy is running up algebra against recess. . . .

> From a paper read at the 1991 meeting of the Modern Language Association,
> "Who Is Relieved by the Idea of Comic Relief?"

Considerations for Critical Thinking and Writing

1. What distinctions does Kincaid make between comedy and tragedy? How does his description of tragedy compare with Aristotle's (see p. 1202)?
2. How does Kincaid's description of comedy fit *A Midsummer Night's Dream*?
3. According to Kincaid, why is the denigration of comedy a conservative impulse? In an essay explain why you agree or disagree with the argument.

TWO COMPLEMENTARY CRITICAL READINGS

G. WILSON KNIGHT (1897–1985)
Prospero's Civilizing Influence   1947

The Tempest at no point contradicts the essence of English history, widely viewed; and can, very generally, be considered as reflecting the destiny of Shakespeare's land, then young.

The background action is, as usual with Shakespeare, political. This strong political reference distinguishes the Shakespearian statement from our other examples of visionary literature, whilst also enabling it to reflect the wider history of Great Britain, itself so largely concerned with the attempt to fuse Christianity and politics. Prospero is Plato's philosopher-king betrayed by a Machiavellian "policy"; and Ariel's denunciation of his betrayers is an indictment of the second-rate, or third-rate, in government, so criminally opposed against the first-rate, arduous, idealism. Prospero himself, against whose magic swords are futile, is now at least no impractical dreamer. He curtly dismisses his masque to meet Caliban's revolution; which, though it seem trivial, is yet, its implications understood, far otherwise, symbolizing that bestial retrogression and drunken worship of a Stephano as "wondrous man" (II.ii.136) in place of a Prospero, that utter miscarriage of all true valuation, which lurks within every denial of highest sovereignty. Prospero's story is set between an impractical idealism on the one side and political villainy and lust on the other; while dramatizing the attainment of a practical idealism negatively pointed by the satire on Gonzalo's Utopian dream. *The Tempest* accordingly falls into alignment with Shakespeare's massed statements elsewhere in definition of true sovereignty and, directly or indirectly, of British destiny; the "liberal arts" (I.ii.73) of Renaissance Europe are here shaped firmly into an Elizabethan mold; while Britain has, since Shakespeare's day, labored with varying success towards the middle course suggested.

The inclusiveness of Prospero's art illustrates a British tendency. The building up of our island population by continental invasion produced a blend of unbending integrity and wide catholicity properly reflected in Prospero. Since Shakespeare's day the drawing to our island of other peoples has, as was prophesied in Queen Elizabeth's prayer before the Armada, more than once characterized our history. The implied equation of Prospero's island with Great Britain remains, however, a momentary analogy that could bear no stress.

Prospero's magic is largely a sea-magic; his island story is sea-rooted . . . and ends with a voyage home; in the interim, he has been gradually mastering the sea-powers. Similarly Great Britain has labored at ocean-mastery; the "ocean" being both the actual ocean and those oceanic instincts, or forces, within man which it so consistently throughout the ages symbolizes. British colonization from the start went hand in hand with Puritanism; the early colonizers, not unlike Prospero, being impelled by political or religious tyrannies to follow their soul-cravings across the sea and there work out the controlled magic of personal integration.

Suppose that Britain's contribution were being assessed some ten thousand years hence by an enlightened historian. He would probably point to (1) her in-ruling severe, yet inclusive and tolerant, religious and political instincts, of which her first colonial adventures and the Puritan revolution were active examples; (2) her inventive and poetic genius variously concerned with the tapping and use of natural energy; and (3) her colonizing, especially her will to raise savage peoples from superstition and blood-sacrifice, taboos and witchcraft and the attendant fears and slaveries, to a more enlightened existence. Little ingenuity is needed to find correspondences with Prospero, Ariel, and Caliban. Especially we may equate the king who is yet no tyrant, the student-prince un-at-home with forceful action, who yet, under pressure of his island existence, gains power to control armed opposition, with the dimly apprehended pacifism inspiring Great Britain's history and the implied liberalism of her constitutional monarchy; only gestures as yet, but gestures that speak "an excellent dumb discourse." As for Miranda, what of her? Without her, perhaps, our ten-thousand-years-hence historian would not have been born; or, at least, been in no position to write his book.

It is, perhaps, inevitable that Shakespeare, whose work . . . is so saturated with the spirit of his land, should, in such a summation of that work in *The Tempest,* have outlined, among much else, a myth of the national soul.

From *The Crown of Life: Essays in Interpretation of Shakespeare's Final Plays*

Considerations for Critical Thinking and Writing

1. How does Knight describe Prospero as a ruler? Explain why you agree or disagree.
2. What connections does Knight make between the play and the history of Great Britain? How is Britain's history of colonization regarded by Knight? What assumptions does he make about civilization and "savage peoples?"
3. Compare the views expressed about colonization here with the issues raised in the perspective that follows by Alden T. Vaughan.

ALDEN T. VAUGHAN (b. 1929)
Caliban as a Sociopolitical Symbol 1988

For nearly four centuries, writers, speakers, and casual commentators have ransacked Shakespeare's works for useful metaphors. Often the purpose has been less literary than ideological — to signify a social or political position by invoking a familiar Shakespearean phrase or character. During the past century, probably the most frequent and malleable Shakespearean sociopolitical symbol has been *The Tempest's* Caliban, for the "savage and deformed slave" has played varied metaphoric roles in response to changing national and international ideologies. This essay explores Caliban's adoption by late nineteenth- and twentieth-century writers, especially in Latin America and Africa, as a potent symbol of either Western imperialism or imperialism's victims.

Beginning in the 1890s, and especially since 1950, many writers from Third World nations have contended that *The Tempest* embodies heretofore neglected meanings for their societies and that Caliban conveys a very different message than traditional scholarship has allowed. Such authors — few are Shakespearean scholars but many are distinguished in other fields — argue that Caliban is no mere fish or monster or even, as has often been argued, a North American Indian. His true significance lies instead in emblematic identifications with modern men and women, especially Latin Americans and Africans, no matter how anachronistic those identifications may seem to *Tempest* specialists.

Authors who invoke Caliban as an image of Latin Americans or Africans agree that he is a palpable and poignant symbol, but they disagree, sometimes vehemently, about who or what he symbolizes. Diametrical opposites are proposed: Caliban as exemplar of imperialist oppressors (the prevalent view in the late nineteenth and early twentieth centuries) or Caliban as emblem of oppressed natives (prevalent in recent decades). Advocates of the first approach find Shakespeare's monster a handy image for everything gross and vicious in a domineering nation or social class — Yankee imperialism, for example, or European racism. The second and now more widespread view stresses Caliban's implicit virtues — his innate sensitivity, rough dignity, articulateness, and intelligence — rather than his cruder characteristics. Thus recast, Caliban stands for the countless victims of European imperialism and colonization. Like Caliban (so the argument goes), colonized peoples are disinherited, exploited, and subjugated. Like he, they learned a conqueror's language and perhaps his values. Like he, they endured enslavement and contempt by European usurpers and eventually rebelled. . . .

Either approach — Caliban as oppressor or Caliban as oppressed — differs fundamentally from traditional interpretive modes. Whereas traditional scholarship is at least partly concerned with the probable prototypes for Shakespeare's characters, most Third-World authors who borrow emblems from *The Tempest* ignore, as irrelevant, Shakespeare's sources and intentions. The Third World interpretation of Caliban is symbolic, not historic; it adopts Caliban for what he represents to the observer, not for what Shakespeare may have had in mind. Few Third World authors who apply *Tempest* images contend that Shakespeare expected his audience to see Caliban as a black African, brown mestizo, or white American; instead, they want modern readers to accept Shakespeare's dramatic symbols because, retrospectively, they fit. New situations give the play's characters new meanings. As one exponent of Caliban metaphors explains, "*The Tempest* is a Masque, an art form strongly dependent on symbolism. It presents figures that are suggestive, evocative, and allusive; and it often relies on mythopoetic references for full effect. If we accept this, . . . we may . . . come out with applications appropriate for a present cultural dilemma."

From *Massachusetts Review,* Summer 1988

Considerations for Critical Thinking and Writing

1. According to Vaughan, how has Caliban been read as a sociopolitical symbol? How have these readings conflicted?
2. What do you think of appropriating a literary character for the purpose of clarifying "a present cultural dilemma"?
3. Explain in an essay how G. Wilson Knight's approach to Prospero (in the preceding perspective) is similar to the uses to which Caliban has been put by the Third World interpretations described by Vaughan.

29. Neoclassical Drama

The French *neoclassical drama* of the seventeenth century developed from the Renaissance revival of classical Greek and Roman literature (*neo-* means new). During the reign of Louis XIV, the absolute monarch known as the Sun King, drama in France grew vigorously, as it had about a half century earlier in Elizabethan England. The arts were part of the elegant luxury that Louis XIV surrounded himself with in his palace at Versailles. Though he was fiercely jealous of power and characterized his relationship to his subjects with the declaration "I am the state," he was also a generous patron of the theater, who encouraged and supported a variety of playwrights. The two most successful tragedians of French neoclassical theater were Pierre Corneille (1606–1684) and Jean Racine (1639–1699), while the unrivaled writer of comedy was Molière (1622–1673).

Molière (whose real name was Jean-Baptiste Poquelin) was the son of a prosperous Paris furniture maker who was also an official upholsterer to the king. The young Poquelin studied the classics, philosophy, and law. With his fine education and family connections, he could have lived a secure, respectable life as a lawyer or as the successor to his father's post, but instead he devoted his entire adult life to drama. The career he chose was neither easy nor highly regarded; the theater was then widely perceived as corruptive and disreputable. Indeed, Molière may have taken his stage name to avoid embarrassing his family. In 1643 he joined a dramatic troupe called The Illustrious Theater, which soon went bankrupt and landed him in debtor's prison for a short while.

Since there was little chance of success in Paris, the troupe toured the provinces for more than a dozen years, during which Molière developed his acting and writing skills. In 1658 the troupe was invited to perform before the court of Louis XIV. Favorably impressed with the performance, the king gave the troupe official recognition and a theater in Paris. This royal favor provided Molière with the opportunity to write, direct, and act for the rest of his life. From among the roughly thirty plays he wrote, the best known and most important comedies, in addition to *Tartuffe* (1669), include *The*

School for Wives (1662), *The Misanthrope* (1666), *The Doctor in Spite of Himself* (1666), *The Miser* (1668), and *The Would-Be Gentleman* (1670). Molière's death came only a few hours after he had acted the leading role in his last play, ironically titled *The Imaginary Invalid* (1673).

THEATRICAL CONVENTIONS
OF NEOCLASSICAL DRAMA

Like Shakespeare, Molière was both an actor and a playwright; he knew intimately the theater for which he wrote. French neoclassical theater differed from Shakespeare's because Molière's contemporaries placed heavy emphasis on the *classical unities* of time, place, and action. Neoclassical scholars and critics, deriving their principles from Renaissance interpretations of Aristotle's *Poetics,* insisted that a play must confine itself to a twenty-four-hour period, restrict its setting to one location, and develop only one line of action, without digressions or elaborate subplots. Unity of action also means that comedy and tragedy must be kept entirely separate; there was to be no mixing of comic scenes with the high seriousness of tragedy and no blending of permanent pain and suffering with laughter. It was assumed that a play had to observe these unities to be a great work of art; plays that violated these standards were often judged badly made or crude.

Molière respects the classical unities in *Tartuffe* with no strain: the consistent action — comic throughout despite its teetering on several dangerous, almost disastrous precipices — occurs within a single day in a setting restricted to a room of Orgon's house. Viewed from a historical perspective, these unities reflect neoclassical ideals of order and restraint, but as critical standards they represent theatrical fashions rather than irrefutable principles. *Hamlet,* to name only one example, ignores all three classical unities. Molière himself dispensed with them when they did not suit his purposes.

Neoclassical theater derived its physical structure from Italian Renaissance stages and eventually developed into the kind of theater familiar to modern playgoers. In contrast to classical Greek or Elizabethan performing areas, the theater in Molière's time was enclosed by a roof that protected an auditorium as elegantly appointed as the aristocrats and well-to-do merchants who attended the performances. The stage was at one end of a long rectangle so that the audience viewed the action either from seats in front of the stage or from galleries along the sides of the auditorium. The *proscenium arch* separated the actors from the audience and formed a *picture-frame stage,* which, when the curtain that hung from the proscenium arch was drawn, created the effect of looking into a room that had one of its walls removed.

The stage and auditorium were lighted by hundreds of candles in chandeliers. Although the dim lighting could not be focused exclusively on the stage, the audience could see the painted scenery that served as background to the action. The scenes typically portrayed a room, a courtyard, or a street; they were usually neither elaborate nor realistic. No attempt would have been made in a seventeenth-century production of *Tartuffe,* for example, to detail the room in which the action occurs; a painted background and a table for a prop would have sufficed.

Costuming, however, was more elaborate, because actors wore contemporary dress that reflected their characters' social position. Paris became known as the center of fashion during the reign of Louis XIV. Earlier, boys had been used to act women's roles, but women were permitted on stage in neoclassical theater. Thus, both actors and actresses could convincingly re-create in their dress and manners the social milieu of the majority of their affluent audience.

Molière's plays were considerably less physical than those of the Elizabethan stage, in which sword play and brawls might result in more characters being dead than alive by the end of the final scene. Neoclassical comedies relied more on wit and sophisticated manners for their drama. The classical unities influenced the nature of the action onstage by creating a sense of proportion and decorum, while offstage the restraint and moderation of the social environment determined that conflicts would be resolved through reasoned, witty dialogue rather than violence.

SATIRE

Molière's reputation rests on his brilliant satires of the fashions, conventions, and morals of middle- and upper-class society. This kind of satire, known as a *comedy of manners,* uses characters that tend to be more types than individualized personalities. These types developed from stock characterizations popular in sixteenth-century Italian *commedia dell'arte,* a form of farce that also featured gags and improvisational acting. Young lovers, a shrewd servant, a bumbling fool, a rich tyrannical father, or a convincing hypocrite appear in various forms in Molière's comedies and in the work of many subsequent comic writers. In *Tartuffe,* Orgon and Dorine are more interesting and developed than stock characters, but their origins can be traced to the characterizations of the foolish father and clever, faithful maid that developed in *commedia dell'arte.*

Unlike a romantic comedy, such as Shakespeare's *Midsummer Night's Dream,* a comedy of manners plays down complicated plots (usually involving lovers) and emphasizes clever, refined dialogue, whose humor is pointed and whose purpose is reform as well as entertainment. Satire is directed against human follies and any behavior that fails to measure up to the standards of moderate, rational, responsible conduct. In *Tartuffe,* Valère and Mariane correspond to the type of young lovers so familiar in genial romantic comedies, but the predominant tone is critical instead of celebratory. In spite of the many laughs Molière's satire provides, his criticism of human faults represents a serious impulse.

In his preface to *Tartuffe,* Molière makes clear that this satiric comedy is calculated to expose vices that might otherwise be overlooked, tolerated, or even mistakenly revered.

> If the function of comedy is to correct men's vices, I do not see why any should be exempt. Such a condition in our society would be much more dangerous than the thing itself; and we have seen that the theater is admirably suited to provide correction. The most forceful lines of a serious moral statement are usually less powerful than those of satire; and nothing will reform most men better than the depiction of their faults. It is a vigorous blow to vices to expose them to public laughter. Criticism is taken lightly, but men will not tolerate satire. They are quite willing to be mean, but they never like to be ridiculed.

Tartuffe is a satire of religious hypocrisy and the gullibility of those who accept the fraudulent piety of rapacious liars.

Molière found that his audiences of aristocrats and rising middle-class hopefuls offered plenty to satirize; affected ladies, quacks, misers, wicked noblemen, and other eccentrics all merited exposure. If he sometimes made his audiences uncomfortable, it was because they felt the sting of his ridicule. Molière believed his job was to reveal the absurdities of his time and "make respectable people laugh" at those who took themselves too seriously and were therefore ridiculous, dangerous, or both.

TARTUFFE

Although *Tartuffe*'s ending befits a comedy, the play's beginnings on the stage were anything but happy. Molière's first version of the play was presented before Louis XIV at Versailles in 1664. The king liked the play, but the church pressured him to ban it, because it was perceived as a wholesale attack on the clergy. One critic described Molière as "a demon in the flesh . . . who should be burned alive." To defuse this criticism and make clear that he was attacking only false piety, Molière revised the play and changed the title to *The Impostor* in 1667, when it was again produced. His critics, however, descended on the play once more and succeeded in persuading the king to ban it. Not until 1669 was Molière allowed to produce the play as it now exists. Since then *Tartuffe* has been popular with readers and viewers who enjoy seeing self-serving hypocrites exposed and blind zealots restored to sight.

But finally the play is compelling less for the justice meted out to Tartuffe than for his character. He is a first-class villain. Even if the play's ending is not convincing, Tartuffe's evil is because he so thoroughly preys on Orgon and his family. Tartuffe is not content to gain Orgon's and his mother's confidence; he would also appropriate Orgon's wife, daughter, and all his wealth.

But Orgon is also a threat to the family's happiness. He is hopelessly blind to the hypocrite's deceptions. Indeed, were it not for the rest of his family we might be tempted to leave him to Tartuffe's manipulations; he very nearly deserves to be victimized for his stupidity. In contrast to Orgon are Cléante, Dorine, and Elmire, who see through Tartuffe's assumed piety. These characters represent Molière's own values of moderation and deep suspicion of irrational extremes. They see clearly and help Orgon to discover his delusion. We are invited to judge Orgon as well as Tartuffe.

Molière wrote in tightly balanced rhyming couplets that create a concise, light, playful effect. In French these couplets are in iambic hexameter, a form known as **alexandrines**. The following English translation by Richard Wilbur, however, uses iambic pentameter rhymed couplets, because they capture Molière's elegant language while avoiding the too-obvious rhythms created by six-foot English lines. With pentameter lines Wilbur re-creates the nimble wit of the original French.

MOLIÈRE
[JEAN-BAPTISTE POQUELIN] (1622–1673)
Tartuffe   1669

TRANSLATED BY RICHARD WILBUR

Characters

Madame Pernelle, Orgon's mother
Orgon, Elmire's husband
Elmire, Orgon's wife
Damis, Orgon's son, Elmire's stepson
Mariane, Orgon's daughter, Elmire's stepdaughter, in love with Valère
Valère, in love with Mariane
Cléante, Orgon's brother-in-law
Tartuffe, a hypocrite
Dorine, Mariane's lady's-maid
M. Loyal, a bailiff
A Police Officer
Flipote, Mme Pernelle's maid

THE SCENE THROUGHOUT: *Orgon's house in Paris*

ACT I

SCENE I

Madame Pernelle and Flipote, her maid; Elmire, Dorine, Cléante, Mariane, Damis

Madame Pernelle: Come, come, Flipote; it's time I left this place.
Elmire: I can't keep up, you walk at such a pace.

Madame Pernelle: Don't trouble, child; no need to show me out.
It's not your manners I'm concerned about.
Elmire: We merely pay you the respect we owe.   5
But, Mother, why this hurry? Must you go?
Madame Pernelle: I must. This house appalls me. No one in it
Will pay attention for a single minute.
Children, I take my leave much vexed in spirit.
I offer good advice, but you won't hear it.   10
You all break in and chatter on and on.
It's like a madhouse with the keeper gone.
Dorine: If . . .
Madame Pernelle: Girl, you talk too much, and I'm afraid
You're far too saucy for a lady's-maid.
You push in everywhere and have your say.   15
Damis: But . . .
Madame Pernelle: You, boy, grow more foolish every day.
To think my grandson should be such a dunce!
I've said a hundred times, if I've said it once,
That if you keep the course on which you've started,
You'll leave your worthy father broken-hearted.   20
Mariane: I think . . .
Madame Pernelle: And you, his sister, seems so pure,
So shy, so innocent, and so demure.
But you know what they say about still waters.
I pity parents with secretive daughters.
Elmire: Now, Mother . . .
Madame Pernelle: And as for you, child, let me add   25
That your behavior is extremely bad,
And a poor example for these children, too.
Their dear, dead mother did far better than you.
You're much too free with money, and I'm distressed
To see you so elaborately dressed.   30
When it's one's husband that one aims to please,
One has no need of costly fripperies.
Cléante: Oh, Madam, really . . .
Madame Pernelle: You are her brother, Sir,
And I respect and love you; yet if I were
My son, this lady's good and pious spouse,   35
I wouldn't make you welcome in my house.
You're full of worldly counsels which, I fear,
Aren't suitable for decent folk to hear.
I've spoken bluntly, Sir; but it behooves us
Not to mince words when righteous fervor moves us.   40
Damis: Your man Tartuffe is full of holy speeches . . .
Madame Pernelle: And practises precisely what he preaches.
He's a fine man, and should be listened to.
I will not hear him mocked by fools like you.
Damis: Good God! Do you expect me to submit   45

To the tyranny of that carping hypocrite?
Must we forgo all joys and satisfactions
Because that bigot censures all our actions?
Dorine: To hear him talk — and he talks all the time —
There's nothing one can do that's not a crime. 50
He rails at everything, your dear Tartuffe.
Madame Pernelle: Whatever he reproves deserves reproof.
He's out to save your souls, and all of you
Must love him, as my son would have you do.
Damis: Ah no, Grandmother, I could never take 55
To such a rascal, even for my father's sake.
That's how I feel, and I shall not dissemble.
His every action makes me seethe and tremble
With helpless anger, and I have no doubt
That he and I will shortly have it out. 60
Dorine: Surely it is a shame and a disgrace
To see this man usurp the master's place —
To see this beggar who, when first he came,
Had not a shoe or shoestring to his name
So far forget himself that he behaves 65
As if the house were his, and we his slaves.
Madame Pernelle: Well, mark my words, your souls would fare far better
If you obeyed his precepts to the letter.
Dorine: You see him as a saint. I'm far less awed;
In fact, I see right through him. He's a fraud. 70
Madame Pernelle: Nonsense!
Dorine: His man Laurent's the same, or worse;
I'd not trust either with a penny purse.
Madame Pernelle: I can't say what his servant's morals may be;
His own great goodness I can guarantee.
You all regard him with distaste and fear 75
Because he tells you what you're loath to hear,
Condemns your sins, points out your moral flaws,
And humbly strives to further Heaven's cause.
Dorine: If sin is all that bothers him, why is it
He's so upset when folk drop in to visit? 80
Is Heaven so outraged by a social call
That he must prophesy against us all?
I'll tell you what I think: if you ask me,
He's jealous of my mistress' company.
Madame Pernelle: Rubbish! *(To Elmire.)* He's not alone, child, in
complaining 85
Of all your promiscuous entertaining.
Why, the whole neighborhood's upset, I know,
By all these carriages that come and go,
With crowds of guests parading in and out
And noisy servants loitering about. 90
In all of this, I'm sure there's nothing vicious;

But why give people cause to be suspicious?
Cléante: They need no cause; they'll talk in any case.
　　Madam, this world would be a joyless place
　　If, fearing what malicious tongues might say,　　　　　　　95
　　We locked our doors and turned our friends away.
　　And even if one did so dreary a thing,
　　D'you think those tongues would cease their chattering?
　　One can't fight slander; it's a losing battle;
　　Let us instead ignore their tittle-tattle.　　　　　　　　100
　　Let's strive to live by conscience' clear decrees,
　　And let the gossips gossip as they please.
Dorine: If there is talk against us, I know the source:
　　It's Daphne and her little husband, of course.
　　Those who have greatest cause for guilt and shame　　105
　　Are quickest to besmirch a neighbor's name.
　　When there's a chance for libel, they never miss it;
　　When something can be made to seem illicit
　　They're off at once to spread the joyous news,
　　Adding to fact what fantasies they choose.　　　　　　　110
　　By talking up their neighbor's indiscretions
　　They seek to camouflage their own transgressions,
　　Hoping that other's innocent affairs
　　Will lend a hue of innocence to theirs,
　　Or that their own black guilt will come to seem　　　　115
　　Part of a general shady color-scheme.
Madame Pernelle: All that is quite irrelevant. I doubt
　　That anyone's more virtuous and devout
　　Than dear Orante; and I'm informed that she
　　Condemns your mode of life most vehemently.　　　　　120
Dorine: Oh, yes, she's strict, devout, and has no taint
　　Of worldliness; in short, she seems a saint.
　　But it was time which taught her that disguise;
　　She's thus because she can't be otherwise.
　　So long as her attractions could enthrall,　　　　　　　125
　　She flounced and flirted and enjoyed it all,
　　But now that they're no longer what they were
　　She quits a world which fast is quitting her,
　　And wears a veil of virtue to conceal
　　Her bankrupt beauty and her lost appeal.　　　　　　　130
　　That's what becomes of old coquettes today:
　　Distressed when all their lovers fall away,
　　They see no recourse but to play the prude,
　　And so confer a style on solitude.
　　Thereafter, they're severe with everyone,　　　　　　　135
　　Condemning all our actions, pardoning none,
　　And claiming to be pure, austere, and zealous
　　When, if the truth were known, they're merely jealous.
　　And cannot bear to see another know

The pleasures time has forced them to forgo.   140
Madame Pernelle (initially to Elmire): That sort of talk is what you like to
    hear;
  Therefore you'd have us all keep still, my dear,
  While Madam rattles on the livelong day,
  Nevertheless, I mean to have my say.
  I tell you that you're blest to have Tartuffe   145
  Dwelling, as my son's guest, beneath this roof;
  That Heaven has sent him to forestall its wrath
  By leading you, once more, to the true path;
  That all he reprehends is reprehensible,
  And that you'd better heed him, and be sensible.   150
  These visits, balls, and parties in which you revel
  Are nothing but inventions of the Devil.
  One never hears a word that's edifying:
  Nothing but chaff and foolishness and lying,
  As well as vicious gossip in which one's neighbor   155
  Is cut to bits with epee, foil, and saber.
  People of sense are driven half-insane
  At such affairs, where noise and folly reign
  And reputations perish thick and fast.
  As a wise preacher said on Sunday last,   160
  Parties are Towers of Babylon, because
  The guests all babble on with never a pause;
  And then he told a story which, I think . . .
  (To Cléante.) I heard that laugh, Sir, and I saw that wink!
  Go find your silly friends and laugh some more!   165
  Enough; I'm going; don't show me to the door.
  I leave this household much dismayed and vexed;
  I cannot say when I shall see you next.
  (Slapping Flipote.) Wake up, don't stand there gaping into space!
  I'll slap some sense into that stupid face.   170
  Move, move, you slut.

SCENE II

Cléante, Dorine

Cléante: I think I'll stay behind;
  I want no further pieces of her mind.
  How that old lady . . .
Dorine: Oh, what wouldn't she say
  If she could hear you speak of her that way!
  She'd thank you for the *lady,* but I'm sure   5
  She'd find the *old* a little premature.
Cléante: My, what a scene she made, and what a din!
  And how this man Tartuffe has taken her in!
Dorine: Yes, but her son is even worse deceived;
  His folly must be seen to be believed.   10

In the late troubles, he played an able part
And served his king with wise and loyal heart,
But he's quite lost his senses since he fell
Beneath Tartuffe's infatuating spell.
He calls him brother, and loves him as his life,   15
Preferring him to mother, child, or wife.
In him and him alone will he confide;
He's made him his confessor and his guide;
He pets and pampers him with love more tender
Than any pretty mistress could engender,   20
Gives him the place of honor when they dine,
Delights to see him gorging like a swine,
Stuffs him with dainties till his guts distend,
And when he belches, cries "God bless you, friend!"
In short, he's mad; he worships him; he dotes;   25
His deeds he marvels at, his words he quotes,
Thinking each act a miracle, each word
Oracular as those that Moses heard.
Tartuffe, much pleased to find so easy a victim,
Has in a hundred ways beguiled and tricked him,   30
Milked him of money, and with his permission
Established here a sort of Inquisition.
Even Laurent, his lackey, dares to give
Us arrogant advice on how to live;
He sermonizes us in thundering tones   35
And confiscates our ribbons and colognes.
Last week he tore a kerchief into pieces
Because he found it pressed in a *Life of Jesus:*
He said it was a sin to juxtapose
Unholy vanities and holy prose.   40

SCENE III

Elmire, Damis, Dorine, Mariane, Cléante

Elmire (to Cléante): You did well not to follow; she stood in the door
    And said *verbatim* all she'd said before.
    I saw my husband coming. I think I'd best
    Go upstairs now, and take a little rest.
Cléante: I'll wait and greet him here; then I must go.   5
    I've really only time to say hello.
Damis: Sound him about my sister's wedding, please.
    I think Tartuffe's against it, and that he's
    Been urging Father to withdraw his blessing.
    As you well know, I'd find that most distressing.   10
    Unless my sister and Valère can marry,
    My hopes to wed *his* sister will miscarry,
    And I'm determined . . .
Dorine: He's coming.

Orgon, Cléante, Dorine

Orgon: Ah, Brother, good-day.
Cléante: Well, welcome back. I'm sorry I can't stay.
    How was the country? Blooming, I trust, and green?
Orgon: Excuse me, Brother; just one moment.
    (To Dorine.)   Dorine . . .
    (To Cléante.) To put my mind at rest, I always learn   5
    The household news the moment I return.
    (To Dorine.) Has all been well, these two days I've been gone?
    How are the family? What's been going on?
Dorine: Your wife, two days ago, had a bad fever,
    And a fierce headache which refused to leave her.   10
Orgon: Ah. And Tartuffe?
Dorine: Tartuffe? Why, he's round and red,
    Bursting with health, and excellently fed.
Orgon: Poor fellow!
Dorine: That night, the mistress was unable
    To take a single bite at the dinner-table.
    Her headache-pains, she said, were simply hellish.   15
Orgon: Ah. And Tartuffe?
Dorine: He ate his meal with relish,
    And zealously devoured in her presence
    A leg of mutton and a brace of pheasants.
Orgon: Poor fellow!
Dorine: Well, the pains continued strong,
    And so she tossed and tossed the whole night long,   20
    Now icy-cold, now burning like a flame.
    We sat beside her bed till morning came.
Orgon: Ah. And Tartuffe?
Dorine: Why, having eaten, he rose
    And sought his room, already in a doze,
    Got into his warm bed, and snored away   25
    In perfect peace until the break of day.
Orgon: Poor fellow!
Dorine: After much ado, we talked her
    Into dispatching someone for the doctor.
    He bled her, and the fever quickly fell.
Orgon: Ah. And Tartuffe?
Dorine: He bore it very well.   30
    To keep his cheerfulness at any cost,
    And make up for the blood *Madame* had lost,
    He drank, at lunch, four beakers full of port.
Orgon: Poor fellow!
Dorine: Both are doing well, in short.
    I'll go and tell *Madame* that you've expressed   35
    Keen sympathy and anxious interest.

Orgon, Cléante

Cléante: That girl was laughing in your face, and though
    I've no wish to offend you, even so
    I'm bound to say that she had some excuse.
    How can you possibly be such a goose?
    Are you so dazed by this man's hocus-pocus   5
    That all the world, save him, is out of focus?
    You've given him clothing, shelter, food, and care;
    Why must you also . . .
Orgon: Brother, stop right there.
    You do not know the man of whom you speak.
Cléante: I grant you that. But my judgment's not so weak   10
    That I can't tell, by his effect on others . . .
Orgon: Ah, when you meet him, you two will be like brothers!
    There's been no loftier soul since time began.
    He is a man who . . . a man who . . . an excellent man.
    To keep his precepts is to be reborn,   15
    And view this dunghill of a world with scorn.
    Yes, thanks to him I'm a changed man indeed.
    Under his tutelage my soul's been freed
    From earthly loves, and every human tie:
    My mother, children, brother, and wife could die,   20
    And I'd not feel a single moment's pain.
Cléante: That's a fine sentiment, Brother; most humane.
Orgon: Oh, had you seen Tartuffe as I first knew him,
    Your heart, like mine, would have surrendered to him.
    He used to come into our church each day   25
    And humbly kneel nearby, and start to pray.
    He'd draw the eyes of everybody there
    By the deep fervor of his heartfelt prayer;
    He'd sigh and weep, and sometimes with a sound
    Of rapture he would bend and kiss the ground;   30
    And when I rose to go, he'd run before
    To offer me holy-water at the door.
    His serving-man, no less devout than he,
    Informed me of his master's poverty;
    I gave him gifts, but in his humbleness   35
    He'd beg me every time to give him less.
    "Oh, that's too much," he'd cry, "too much by twice!
    I don't deserve it. The half, Sir, would suffice."
    And when I wouldn't take it back, he'd share
    Half of it with the poor, right then and there.   40
    At length, Heaven prompted me to take him in
    To dwell with us, and free our souls from sin.
    He guides our lives, and to protect my honor
    Stays by my wife, and keeps an eye upon her;
    He tells me whom she sees, and all she does,   45

And seems more jealous than I ever was!
And how austere he is! Why, he can detect
A mortal sin where you would least suspect;
In smallest trifles, he's extremely strict.
Last week, his conscience was severely pricked   50
Because, while praying, he had caught a flea
And killed it, so he felt, too wrathfully.

Cléante: Good God, man! Have you lost your common sense —
Or is this all some joke at my expense?
How can you stand there and in all sobriety . . .   55

Orgon: Brother, your language savors of impiety.
Too much free-thinking's made your faith unsteady,
And as I've warned you many times already,
'Twill get you into trouble before you're through.

Cléante: So I've been told before by dupes like you: 60
Being blind, you'd have all others blind as well;
The clear-eyed man you call an infidel,
And he who sees through humbug and pretense
Is charged, by you, with want of reverence.
Spare me your warnings, Brother; I have no fear   65
Of speaking out, for you and Heaven to hear,
Against affected zeal and pious knavery.
There's true and false in piety, as in bravery,
And just as those whose courage shines the most
In battle, are the least inclined to boast,   70
So those whose hearts are truly pure and lowly
Don't make a flashy show of being holy.
There's a vast difference, so it seems to me,
Between true piety and hypocrisy:
How do you fail to see it, may I ask?   75
Is not a face quite different from a mask?
Cannot sincerity and cunning art,
Reality and semblance, be told apart?
Are scarecrows just like men, and do you hold
That a false coin is just as good as gold?   80
Ah, Brother, man's a strangely fashioned creature
Who seldom is content to follow Nature,
But recklessly pursues his inclination
Beyond the narrow bounds of moderation,
And often, by transgressing Reason's laws,   85
Perverts a lofty aim or noble cause.
A passing observation, but it applies.

Orgon: I see, dear Brother, that you're profoundly wise;
You harbor all the insight of the age.
You are our one clear mind, our only sage,   90
The era's oracle, its Cato° too,
And all mankind are fools compared to you.

91 *Cato:* (234–149 B.C.) Roman statesman who upheld high morals and the simple life.

Cléante: Brother, I don't pretend to be a sage,
Nor have I all the wisdom of the age.
There's just one insight I would dare to claim: 95
I know that true and false are not the same;
And just as there is nothing I more revere
Than a soul whose faith is steadfast and sincere,
Nothing that I more cherish and admire
Than honest zeal and true religious fire,   100
So there is nothing that I find more base
Than specious piety's dishonest face —
Than these bold mountebanks, these histrios
Whose impious mummeries and hollow shows
Exploit our love of Heaven, and make a jest   105
Of all that men think holiest and best;
These calculating souls who offer prayers
Not to their Maker, but as public wares,
And seek to buy respect and reputation
With lifted eyes and sighs of exaltation;   110
These charlatans, I say, whose pilgrim souls
Proceed, by way of Heaven, toward earthly goals,
Who weep and pray and swindle and extort,
Who preach the monkish life, but haunt the court,
Who make their zeal the partner of their vice —   115
Such men are vengeful, sly, and cold as ice,
And when there is an enemy to defame
They cloak their spite in fair religion's name,
Their private spleen and malice being made
To seem a high and virtuous crusade,   · 120
Until, to mankind's reverent applause,
They crucify their foe in Heaven's cause.
Such knaves are all too common; yet, for the wise,
True piety isn't hard to recognize,
And, happily, these present times provide us   125
With bright examples to instruct and guide us.
Consider Ariston and Périandre;
Look at Oronte, Alcidamas, Clitandre;°
Their virtue is acknowledged; who could doubt it?
But you won't hear them beat the drum about it.   130
They're never ostentatious, never vain,
And their religion's moderate and humane;
It's not their way to criticize and chide:
They think censoriousness a mark of pride,
And therefore, letting others preach and rave,   135
They show, by deeds, how Christians should behave.
They think no evil of their fellow man,
But judge of him as kindly as they can.
They don't intrigue and wangle and conspire;

127–128 *Consider . . . Clitandre:* Made-up classical-sounding names; not real people.

To lead a good life is their one desire; 140
The sinner wakes no rancorous hate in them;
It is the sin alone which they condemn;
Nor do they try to show a fiercer zeal
For Heaven's cause than Heaven itself could feel.
These men I honor, these men I advocate 145
As models for us all to emulate.
Your man is not their sort at all, I fear:
And, while your praise of him is quite sincere,
I think that you've been dreadfully deluded.
Orgon: Now then, dear Brother, is your speech concluded? 150
Cléante: Why, yes.
Orgon:　　　　　Your servant, Sir. *(He turns to go.)*
Cléante:　　　　　No, Brother; wait.
There's one more matter. You agreed of late
That young Valère might have your daughter's hand.
Orgon: I did.
Cléante: And set the date, I understand.
Orgon: Quite so.
Cléante:　　　You've now postponed it; is that true? 155
Orgon: No doubt.
Cléante:　　　The match no longer pleases you?
Orgon: Who knows?
Cléante:　　　　D'you mean to go back on your word?
Orgon: I won't say that.
Cléante:　　　　　Has anything occurred
Which might entitle you to break your pledge?
Orgon: Perhaps.
Cléante:　　　Why must you hem, and haw, and hedge? 160
The boy asked me to sound you in this affair . . .
Orgon: It's been a pleasure.
Cléante:　　　　　But what shall I tell Valère?
Orgon: Whatever you like.
Cléante:　　　　But what have you decided?
What are your plans?
Orgon:　　　　I plan, Sir, to be guided
By Heaven's will.
Cléante:　　　Come, Brother, don't talk rot. 165
You've given Valère your word; will you keep it, or not?
Orgon: Good day.
Cléante:　　　This looks like poor Valère's undoing;
I'll go and warn him that there's trouble brewing.

ACT II

Orgon, Mariane

Orgon: Mariane.
Mariane: Yes, Father?
Orgon: A word with you; come here.
Mariane: What are you looking for?
Orgon (peering into a small closet): Eavesdroppers, dear.
I'm making sure we shan't be overheard.
Someone in there could catch our every word.
Ah, good, we're safe. Now, Mariane, my child, 5
  You're a sweet girl who's tractable and mild,
  Whom I hold dear, and think most highly of.
Mariane: I'm deeply grateful, Father, for your love.
Orgon: That's well said, Daughter; and you can repay me
  If, in all things, you'll cheerfully obey me. 10
Mariane: To please you, Sir, is what delights me best
Orgon: Good, good. Now, what d'you think of Tartuffe, our guest?
Mariane: I, Sir?
Orgon. Yes. Weigh your answer; think it through.
Mariane: Oh, dear. I'll say whatever you wish me to.
Orgon: That's wisely said, my Daughter. Say of him, then, 15
  That he's the very worthiest of men,
  And that you're fond of him, and would rejoice
  In being his wife, if that should be my choice.
  Well?
Mariane: What?
Orgon: What's that?
Mariane: I . . .
Orgon: Well?
Mariane: Forgive me, pray.
Orgon: Did you not hear me?
Mariane: Of *whom,* Sir, must I say 20
  That I am fond of him, and would rejoice
  In being his wife, if that should be your choice?
Orgon: Why, of Tartuffe.
Mariane: But, Father, that's false, you know.
  Why would you have me say what isn't so?
Orgon: Because I am resolved it shall be true. 25
  That it's my wish should be enough for you.
Mariane: You can't mean, Father . . .
Orgon: Yes, Tartuffe shall be
  Allied by marriage to this family,
  And he's to be your husband, is that clear?
  It's a father's privilege . . . 30

Dorine, Orgon, Mariane

Orgon (to Dorine):　　　　　What are you doing in here?
　　Is curiosity so fierce a passion
　　With you, that you must eavesdrop in this fashion?
Dorine: There's lately been a rumor going about —
　　Based on some hunch or chance remark, no doubt —　　　　5
　　That you mean Mariane to wed Tartuffe.
　　I've laughed it off, of course, as just a spoof.
Orgon: You find it so incredible?
Dorine:　　　　　　　　　Yes, I do.
　　I won't accept that story, even from you.
Orgon: Well, you'll believe it when the thing is done.　　　　10
Dorine: Yes, yes, of course. Go on and have your fun.
Orgon: I've never been more serious in my life.
Dorine: Ha!
Orgon:　　Daughter, I mean it; you're to be his wife.
Dorine: No, don't believe your father; it's all a hoax.
Orgon: See here, young woman . . .
Dorine:　　　　　　　　　　Come, Sir, no more jokes;　　15
　　You can't fool us.
Orgon:　　　　　　How dare you talk that way?
Dorine: All right, then: we believe you, sad to say.
　　But how a man like you, who looks so wise
　　And wears a moustache of such splendid size,
　　Can be so foolish as to . . .
Orgon:　　　　　　　　Silence, please!　　　　20
　　My girl, you take too many liberties.
　　I'm master here, as you must not forget.
Dorine: Do let's discuss this calmly; don't be upset.
　　You can't be serious, Sir, about this plan.
　　What should that bigot want with Mariane?　　　　25
　　Praying and fasting ought to keep him busy.
　　And then, in terms of wealth and rank, what is he?
　　Why should a man of property like you
　　Pick out a beggar son-in-law?
Orgon:　　　　　　　　That will do.
　　Speak of his poverty with reverence.　　　　30
　　His is a pure and saintly indigence
　　Which far transcends all worldly pride and pelf.
　　He lost his fortune, as he says himself,
　　Because he cared for Heaven alone, and so
　　Was careless of his interests here below.　　　　35
　　I mean to get him out of his present straits
　　And help him to recover his estates —
　　Which, in his part of the world, have no small fame.
　　Poor though he is, he's a gentleman just the same.

Dorine: Yes, so he tells us; and, Sir, it seems to me   40
    Such pride goes very ill with piety.
    A man whose spirit spurns this dungy earth
    Ought not to brag of lands and noble birth;
    Such worldly arrogance will hardly square
    With meek devotion and the life of prayer.   45
    . . . But this approach, I see, has drawn a blank;
    Let's speak, then, of his person, not his rank.
    Doesn't it seem to you a trifle grim
    To give a girl like her to a man like him?
    When two are so ill-suited, can't you see   50
    What the sad consequence is bound to be?
    A young girl's virtue is imperilled, Sir,
    When such a marriage is imposed on her;
    For if one's bridegroom isn't to one's taste,
    It's hardly an inducement to be chaste,   55
    And many a man with horns upon his brow
    Has made his wife the thing that she is now.
    It's hard to be a faithful wife, in short,
    To certain husbands of a certain sort,
    And he who gives his daughter to a man she hates   60
    Must answer for her sins at Heaven's gates.
    Think, Sir, before you play so risky a role.
Orgon: This servant-girl presumes to save my soul!
Dorine: You would do well to ponder what I've said.
Orgon: Daughter, we'll disregard this dunderhead.   65
    Just trust your father's judgment. Oh, I'm aware
    That I once promised you to young Valère;
    But now I hear he gambles, which greatly shocks me;
    What's more, I've doubts about his orthodoxy.
    His visits to church, I note, are very few.   70
Dorine: Would you have him go at the same hours as you,
    And kneel nearby, to be sure of being seen?
Orgon: I can dispense with such remarks, Dorine.
    (To Mariane.) Tartuffe, however, is sure of Heaven's blessing,
    And that's the only treasure worth possessing.   75
    This match will bring you joys beyond all measure;
    Your cup will overflow with every pleasure;
    You two will interchange your faithful loves
    Like two sweet cherubs, or two turtle-doves.
    No harsh word shall be heard, no frown be seen.   80
    And he shall make you happy as a queen.
Dorine: And she'll make him a cuckold, just wait and see.
Orgon: What language!
Dorine: Oh, he's a man of destiny;
    He's *made* for horns, and what the stars demand
    Your daughter's virtue surely can't withstand.   85
Orgon: Don't interrupt me further. Why can't you learn
    That certain things are none of your concern?

Dorine: It's for your own sake that I interfere.

She repeatedly interrupts Orgon just as he is turning to speak to his daughter.

Orgon: Most kind of you. Now, hold your tongue, d'you hear?

Dorine: If I didn't love you . . .

Orgon: Spare me your affection.   90

Dorine: I love you, Sir, in spite of your objection.

Orgon: Blast!

Dorine: I can't bear, Sir, for your honor's sake,
   To let you make this ludicrous mistake.

Orgon: You mean to go on talking?

Dorine: If I didn't protest
   This sinful marriage, my conscience couldn't rest.   95

Orgon: If you don't hold your tongue, you little shrew . . .

Dorine: What, lost your temper? A pious man like you?

Orgon: Yes! Yes! You talk and talk. I'm maddened by it.
   Once and for all, I tell you to be quiet.

Dorine: Well, I'll be quiet. But I'll be thinking hard.   100

Orgon: Think all you like, but you had better guard
   That saucy tongue of yours, or I'll . . .

(Turning back to Mariane.)   Now, child,
   I've weighed this matter fully.

Dorine (aside):   It drives me wild
   That I can't speak.

Orgon turns his head, and she is silent.

Orgon: Tartuffe is no young dandy,
   But, still, his person . . .

Dorine (aside):   Is as sweet as candy.   105

Orgon: Is such that, even if you shouldn't care
   For his other merits . . .

He turns and stands facing Dorine, arms crossed.

Dorine (aside):   They'll make a lovely pair.
   If I were she, no man would marry me
   Against my inclination, and go scot-free.
   He'd learn, before the wedding-day was over,   110
   How readily a wife can find a lover.

Orgon (to Dorine): It seems you treat my orders as a joke.

Dorine: Why, what's the matter? 'Twas not to you I spoke.

Orgon: What *were* you doing?

Dorine: Talking to myself, that's all.

Orgon: Ah! *(Aside.)* One more bit of impudence and gall,   115
   And I shall give her a good slap in the face.

He puts himself in position to slap her; Dorine, whenever he glances at her, stands immobile and silent.

   Daughter, you shall accept, and with good grace,
   The husband I've selected . . . Your wedding-day . . .
   (To Dorine.) Why don't you talk to yourself?

Dorine: I've nothing to say.
Orgon: Come, just one word.
Dorine: No thank you, Sir. I pass.   120
Orgon: Come, speak; I'm waiting.
Dorine: I'd not be such an ass.
Orgon (turning to Mariane): In short, dear Daughter, I mean to be obeyed,
     And you must bow to the sound choice I've made.
Dorine (moving away): I'd not wed such a monster, even in jest.

Orgon attempts to slap her, but misses.

Orgon: Daughter, that maid of yours is a thorough pest;   125
     She makes me sinfully annoyed and nettled.
     I can't speak further; my nerves are too unsettled.
     She's so upset me by her insolent talk,
     I'll calm myself by going for a walk.

SCENE III

Dorine, Mariane

Dorine (returning): Well, have you lost your tongue, girl? Must I play
     Your part, and say the lines you ought to say?
     Faced with a fate so hideous and absurd,
     Can you not utter one dissenting word?
Mariane: What good would it do? A father's power is great.   5
Dorine: Resist him now, or it will be too late.
Mariane: But . . .
Dorine: Tell him one cannot love at a father's whim;
     That you shall marry for yourself, not him;
     That since it's you who are to be the bride,
     It's you, not he, who must be satisfied;   10
     And that if his Tartuffe is so sublime,
     He's free to marry him at any time.
Mariane: I've bowed so long to Father's strict control,
     I couldn't oppose him now, to save my soul.
Dorine: Come, come, Mariane. Do listen to reason, won't you?   15
     Valère has asked your hand. Do you love him, or don't you?
Mariane: Oh, how unjust of you! What can you mean
     By asking such a question, dear Dorine?
     You know the depth of my affection for him;
     I've told you a hundred times how I adore him.   20
Dorine: I don't believe in everything I hear;
     Who knows if your professions were sincere?
Mariane: They were, Dorine, and you do me wrong to doubt it;
     Heaven knows that I've been all too frank about it.
Dorine: You love him, then?
Mariane: Oh, more than I can express.   25
Dorine: And he, I take it, cares for you no less?

Mariane: I think so.

Dorine: And you both, with equal fire,
   Burn to be married?

Mariane: That is our one desire.

Dorine: What of Tartuffe, then? What of your father's plan?

Mariane: I'll kill myself, if I'm forced to wed that man.   30

Dorine: I hadn't thought of that recourse. How splendid!
   Just die, and all your troubles will be ended!
   A fine solution. Oh, it maddens me
   To hear you talk in that self-pitying key.

Mariane: Dorine, how harsh you are! It's most unfair.   35
   You have no sympathy for my despair.

Dorine: I've none at all for people who talk drivel
   And, faced with difficulties, whine and snivel.

Mariane: No doubt I'm timid, but it would be wrong . . .

Dorine: True love requires a heart that's firm and strong.   40

Mariane: I'm strong in my affection for Valère,
   But coping with my father is his affair.

Dorine: But if your father's brain has grown so cracked
   Over his dear Tartuffe that he can retract
   His blessing, though your wedding-day was named,   45
   It's surely not Valère who's to be blamed.

Mariane: If I defied my father, as you suggest,
   Would it not seem unmaidenly, at best?
   Shall I defend my love at the expense
   Of brazenness and disobedience?   50
   Shall I parade my heart's desires, and flaunt . . .

Dorine: No, I ask nothing of you. Clearly you want
   To be Madame Tartuffe, and I feel bound
   Not to oppose a wish so very sound.
   What right have I to criticize the match?   55
   Indeed, my dear, the man's a brilliant catch.
   Monsieur Tartuffe! Now, there's a man of weight!
   Yes, yes, Monsieur Tartuffe, I'm bound to state,
   Is quite a person; that's not to be denied;
   'Twill be no little thing to be his bride.   60
   The world already rings with his renown;
   He's a great noble — in his native town;
   His ears are red, he has a pink complexion,
   And all in all, he'll suit you to perfection.

Mariane: Dear God!

Dorine: Oh, how triumphant you will feel   65
   At having caught a husband so ideal!

Mariane: Oh, do stop teasing, and use your cleverness
   To get me out of this appalling mess.
   Advise me, and I'll do whatever you say.

Dorine: Ah no, a dutiful daughter must obey   70
   Her father, even if he weds her to an ape.

You've a bright future; why struggle to escape?
Tartuffe will take you back where his family lives,
To a small town aswarm with relatives —
Uncles and cousins whom you'll be charmed to meet.   75
You'll be received at once by the elite,
Calling upon the bailiff's wife, no less —
Even, perhaps, upon the mayoress,
Who'll sit you down in the *best* kitchen chair.
Then, once a year, you'll dance at the village fair   80
To the drone of bagpipes — two of them, in fact —
And see a puppet-show, or an animal act.
Your husband . . .
Mariane: Oh, you turn my blood to ice!
Stop torturing me, and give me your advice.
Dorine (threatening to go): Your servant, Madam.
Mariane: Dorine, I beg of you . . .   85
Dorine: No, you deserve it; this marriage must go through.
Mariane: Dorine!
Dorine: No.
Mariane: Not Tartuffe! You know I think him . . .
Dorine: Tartuffe's your cup of tea, and you shall drink him.
Mariane: I've always told you everything, and relied . . .
Dorine: No. You deserve to be tartuffified.   90
Mariane: Well, since you mock me and refuse to care,
    I'll henceforth seek my solace in despair:
    Despair shall be my counsellor and friend,
    And help me bring my sorrows to an end.

She starts to leave.

Dorine: There now, come back; my anger has subsided.   95
    You do deserve some pity, I've decided.
Mariane: Dorine, if Father makes me undergo
    This dreadful martyrdom, I'll die, I know.
Dorine: Don't fret; it won't be difficult to discover
    Some plan of action . . . But here's Valère, your lover.   100

SCENE IV

Valère, Mariane, Dorine

Valère: Madam, I've just received some wondrous news
    Regarding which I'd like to hear your views.
Mariane: What news?
Valère: You're marrying Tartuffe.
Mariane: I find
    That Father does have such a match in mind.
Valère: Your father, Madam . . .
Mariane: . . . has just this minute said   5

That it's Tartuffe he wishes me to wed.
Valère: Can he be serious?
Mariane: Oh, indeed he can;
He's clearly set his heart upon the plan.
Valère: And what position do you propose to take, Madam?
Mariane: Why — I don't know.
Valère: For heaven's sake —   10
You don't know?
Mariane: No.
Valère: Well, well!
Mariane: Advise me, do.
Valère: Marry the man. That's my advice to you.
Mariane: That's your advice?
Valère: Yes.
Mariane: Truly?
Valère: Oh, absolutely.
You couldn't choose more wisely, more astutely.
Mariane: Thanks for this counsel; I'll follow it, of course.   15
Valère: Do, do; I'm sure 'twill cost you no remorse.
Mariane: To give it didn't cause your heart to break.
Valère: I gave it, Madam, only for your sake.
Mariane: And it's for your sake that I take it, Sir.
Dorine (withdrawing to the rear of the stage): Let's see which fool will prove
   the stubborner.   20
Valère: So! I am nothing to you, and it was flat
   Deception when you . . .
Mariane: Please, enough of that.
You've told me plainly that I should agree
To wed the man my father's chosen for me,
And since you've designed to counsel me so wisely,   25
I promise, Sir, to do as you advise me.
Valère: Ah, no, 'twas not by me that you were swayed.
No, your decision was already made;
Though now, to save appearances, you protest
That you're betraying me at my behest.   30
Mariane: Just as you say.
Valère: Quite so. And I now see
That you were never truly in love with me.
Mariane: Alas, you're free to think so if you choose.
Valère: I choose to think so, and here's a bit of news:
You've spurned my hand, but I know where to turn   35
For kinder treatment, as you shall quickly learn.
Mariane: I'm sure you do. Your noble qualities
Inspire affection . . .
Valère: Forget my qualities, please.
They don't inspire you overmuch, I find.
But there's another lady I have in mind   40
Whose sweet and generous nature will not scorn
To compensate me for the loss I've borne.

Mariane: I'm no great loss, and I'm sure that you'll transfer
    Your heart quite painlessly from me to her.
Valère: I'll do my best to take it in my stride.   45
    The pain I feel at being cast aside
    Time and forgetfulness may put an end to.
    Or if I can't forget, I shall pretend to.
    No self-respecting person is expected
    To go on loving once he's been rejected.   50
Mariane: Now, that's a fine, high-minded sentiment.
Valère: One to which any sane man would assent.
    Would you prefer it if I pined away
    In hopeless passion till my dying day?
    Am I to yield you to a rival's arms   55
    And not console myself with other charms?
Mariane: Go then: console yourself; don't hesitate.
    I wish you to; indeed, I cannot wait.
Valère: You wish me to?
Mariane: Yes.
Valère: That's the final straw.
    Madam, farewell. Your wish shall be my law.   60

He starts to leave, and then returns: this repeatedly.

Mariane: Splendid.
Valère (coming back again):
               This breach, remember, is of your making;
    It's you who've driven me to the step I'm taking.
Mariane: Of course.
Valère (coming back again):
               Remember, too, that I am merely
    Following your example.
Mariane: I see that clearly.
Valère: Enough. I'll go and do your bidding, then.   65
Mariane: Good.
Valère (coming back again):
               You shall never see my face again.
Mariane: Excellent.
Valère (walking to the door, then turning about):
               Yes?
Mariane: What?
Valère: What's that? What did you say?
Mariane: Nothing. You're dreaming.
Valère: Ah. Well, I'm on my way.
    Farewell, *Madame.*

He moves slowly away.

Mariane: Farewell.
Dorine (to Mariane):   If you ask me,
    Both of you are as mad as mad can be.   70
    Do stop this nonsense, now. I've only let you

Squabble so long to see where it would get you.
Whoa there, Monsieur Valère!

She goes and seizes Valère by the arm; he makes a great show of resistance.

Valère: What's this, Dorine?
Dorine: Come here.
Valère: No, no, my heart's too full of spleen.
Don't hold me back; her wish must be obeyed.   75
Dorine: Stop!
Valère: It's too late now; my decision's made.
Dorine: Oh, pooh!
Mariane (aside): He hates the sight of me, that's plain.
I'll go, and so deliver him from pain.
Dorine (leaving Valère, running after Mariane):
And now *you* run away! Come back.
Mariane: No, no.
Nothing you say will keep me here. Let go!   80
Valère (aside): She cannot bear my presence, I perceive.
To spare her further torment, I shall leave.
Dorine (leaving Mariane, running after Valère): Again! You'll not escape,
Sir; don't you try it.
Come here, you two. Stop fussing, and be quiet.

She takes Valère by the hand, then Mariane, and draws them together.

Valère (to Dorine): What do you want of me?
Mariane (to Dorine):   What is the point of this?   85
Dorine: We're going to have a little armistice.
    (To Valère.) Now weren't you silly to get so overheated?
Valère: Didn't you see how badly I was treated?
Dorine (to Mariane): Aren't you a simpleton, to have lost your head?
Mariane: Didn't you hear the hateful things he said?   90
Dorine (to Valère): You're both great fools. Her sole desire, Valère,
Is to be yours in marriage. To that I'll swear.
    (To Mariane.) He loves you only, and he wants no wife
But you, Mariane. On that I'll stake my life.
Mariane (to Valère): Then why you advised me so, I cannot see.   95
Valère (to Mariane): On such a question, why ask advice of *me?*
Dorine: Oh, you're impossible. Give me your hands, you two.
    (To Valère.)   Yours first.
Valère (giving Dorine his hand): But why?
Dorine (to Mariane):   And now a hand from you.
Mariane (also giving Dorine her hand):
What are you doing?
Dorine: There: a perfect fit.
You suit each other better than you'll admit.   100

Valère and Mariane hold hands for some time without looking at each other.

Valère (turning toward Mariane): Ah, come, don't be so haughty. Give a man
    A look of kindness, won't you, Mariane?

Mariane turns toward Valère and smiles.

Dorine: I tell you, lovers are completely mad!
Valère (to Mariane): Now come, confess that you were very bad
    To hurt my feelings as you did just now.   105
    I have a just complaint, you must allow.
Mariane: *You* must allow that you were most unpleasant . . .
Dorine: Let's table that discussion for the present;
    Your father has a plan which must be stopped.
Mariane: Advise us, then: what means must we adopt?   110
Dorine: We'll use all manner of means, and all at once.
    (To Mariane.) Your father's addled; he's acting like a dunce.
    Therefore you'd better humor the old fossil.
    Pretend to yield to him, be sweet and docile,
    And then postpone, as often as necessary,   115
    The day on which you have agreed to marry.
    You'll thus gain time, and time will turn the trick.
    Sometimes, for instance, you'll be taken sick,
    And that will seem good reason for delay;
    Or some bad omen will make you change the day —   120
    You'll dream of muddy water, or you'll pass
    A dead man's hearse, or break a looking-glass.
    If all else fails, no man can marry you
    Unless you take his ring and say "I do."
    But now, let's separate. If they should find   125
    Us talking here, our plot might be divined.
    (To Valère.) Go to your friends, and tell them what's occurred,
    And have them urge her father to keep his word.
    Meanwhile, we'll stir her brother into action,
    And get Elmire, as well, to join our faction.   130
    Good-bye.
Valère (to Mariane):
          Though each of us will do his best,
    It's your true heart on which my hopes shall rest.
Mariane (to Valère): Regardless of what Father may decide,
    None but Valère shall claim me as his bride.
Valère: Oh, how those words content me! Come what will . . .   135
Dorine: Oh, lovers, lovers! Their tongues are never still.
    Be off, now.
Valère (turning to go, then turning back):
          One last word . . .
Dorine: No time to chat:
    You leave by this door; and *you* leave by that.

(Dorine pushes them, by the shoulders, toward opposing doors.)

ACT III

Damis, Dorine

Damis: May lightning strike me even as I speak,
 May all men call me cowardly and weak,
 If any fear or scruple holds me back
 From settling things, at once, with that great quack!
Dorine: Now, don't give way to violent emotion.   5
 Your father's merely talked about this notion,
 And words and deeds are far from being one.
 Much that is talked about is left undone.
Damis: No, I must stop that scoundrel's machinations;
 I'll go and tell him off; I'm out of patience.   10
Dorine: Do calm down and be practical. I had rather
 My mistress dealt with him — and with your father.
 She has some influence with Tartuffe, I've noted.
 He hangs upon her words, seems most devoted,
 And may, indeed, be smitten by her charm.   15
 Pray Heaven it's true! 'Twould do our cause no harm.
 She sent for him, just now, to sound him out
 On this affair you're so incensed about;
 She'll find out where he stands, and tell him, too,
 What dreadful strife and trouble will ensue   20
 If he lends countenance to your father's plan.
 I couldn't get in to see him, but his man
 Says that he's almost finished with his prayers.
 Go, now. I'll catch him when he comes downstairs.
Damis: I want to hear this conference, and I will.   25
Dorine: No, they must be alone.
Damis: Oh, I'll keep still.
Dorine: Not you. I know your temper. You'd start a brawl,
 And shout and stamp your foot and spoil it all.
 Go on.
Damis: I won't; I have a perfect right . . .
Dorine: Lord, you're a nuisance! He's coming; get out of sight.   30

Damis conceals himself in a closet at the rear of the stage.

Tartuffe, Dorine

Tartuffe (observing Dorine, and calling to his manservant offstage):
 Hang up my hair-shirt, put my scourge in place,
 And pray, Laurent, for Heaven's perpetual grace.
 I'm going to the prison now, to share
 My last few coins with the poor wretches there.

Dorine (aside): Dear God, what affectation! What a fake!   5
Tartuffe: You wished to see me?
Dorine: Yes . . .
Tartuffe (taking a handkerchief from his pocket):
                                        For mercy's sake,
    Please take this handkerchief, before you speak.
Dorine: What?
Tartuffe: Cover that bosom, girl. The flesh is weak,
    And unclean thoughts are difficult to control.
    Such sights as that can undermine the soul.   10
Dorine: Your soul, it seems, has very poor defenses,
    And flesh makes quite an impact on your senses.
    It's strange that you're so easily excited;
    My own desires are not so soon ignited,
    And if I saw you naked as a beast,   15
    Not all your hide would tempt me in the least.
Tartuffe: Girl, speak more modestly; unless you do,
    I shall be forced to take my leave of you.
Dorine: Oh, no, it's I who must be on my way;
    I've just one little message to convey.   20
    Madame is coming down, and begs you, Sir,
    To wait and have a word or two with her.
Tartuffe: Gladly.
Dorine (aside): That had a softening effect!
    I think my guess about him was correct.
Tartuffe: Will she be long?
Dorine: No: that's her step I hear.   25
    Ah, here she is, and I shall disappear.

Scene III

Elmire, Tartuffe

Tartuffe: May Heaven, whose infinite goodness we adore,
    Preserve your body and soul forevermore,
    And bless your days, and answer thus the plea
    Of one who is its humblest votary.
Elmire: I thank you for that pious wish. But please   5
    Do take a chair and let's be more at ease.

They sit down.

Tartuffe: I trust that you are once more well and strong?
Elmire: Oh, yes: the fever didn't last for long.
Tartuffe: My prayers are too unworthy, I am sure,
    To have gained from Heaven this most gracious cure;   10
    But lately, Madam, my every supplication
    Has had for object your recuperation.
Elmire: You shouldn't have troubled so. I don't deserve it.
Tartuffe: Your health is priceless, Madam, and to preserve it

I'd gladly give my own, in all sincerity.   15
Elmire: Sir, you outdo us all in Christian charity.
    You've been most kind. I count myself your debtor.
Tartuffe: 'Twas nothing, Madam. I long to serve you better.
Elmire: There's a private matter I'm anxious to discuss.
    I'm glad there's no one here to hinder us.   20
Tartuffe: I too am glad; it floods my heart with bliss
    To find myself alone with you like this.
    For just this chance I've prayed with all my power —
    But prayed in vain, until this happy hour.
Elmire: This won't take long, Sir, and I hope you'll be   25
    Entirely frank and unconstrained with me.
Tartuffe: Indeed, there's nothing I had rather do
    Than bare my inmost heart and soul to you.
    First, let me say that what remarks I've made
    About the constant visits you are paid   30
    Were prompted not by any mean emotion,
    But rather by a pure and deep devotion,
    A fervent zeal . . .
Elmire: No need for explanation.
    Your sole concern, I'm sure, was my salvation.
Tartuffe (taking Elmire's hand and pressing her fingertips): Quite so; and
    such great fervor do I feel . . .   35
Elmire: Ooh! Please! You're pinching!
Tartuffe: 'Twas from excess of zeal.
    I never meant to cause you pain, I swear.
    I'd rather . . .

He places his hand on Elmire's knee.

Elmire: What can your hand be doing there?
Tartuffe: Feeling your gown; what soft, fine-woven stuff!
Elmire: Please, I'm extremely ticklish. That's enough.   40

She draws her chair away; Tartuffe pulls his after her.

Tartuffe (fondling the lace collar of her gown): My, my, what lovely lace-
    work on your dress!
    The workmanship's miraculous, no less.
    I've not seen anything to equal it.
Elmire: Yes, quite. But let's talk business for a bit.
    They say my husband means to break his word   45
    And give his daughter to you, Sir. Had you heard?
Tartuffe: He did once mention it. But I confess
    I dream of quite a different happiness.
    It's elsewhere, Madam, that my eyes discern
    The promise of that bliss for which I yearn.   50
Elmire: I see: you care for nothing here below.
Tartuffe: Ah, well — my heart's not made of stone, you know.

Elmire: All your desires mount heavenward, I'm sure,
    In scorn of all that's earthly and impure.
Tartuffe: A love of heavenly beauty does not preclude   55
    A proper love for earthly pulchritude;
    Our senses are quite rightly captivated
    By perfect works our Maker has created.
    Some glory clings to all that Heaven has made;
    In you, all Heaven's marvels are displayed.   60
    On that fair face, such beauties have been lavished,
    The eyes are dazzled and the heart is ravished;
    How could I look on you, O flawless creature,
    And not adore the Author of all Nature,
    Feeling a love both passionate and pure   65
    For you, his triumph of self-portraiture?
    At first, I trembled lest that love should be
    A subtle snare that Hell had laid for me;
    I vowed to flee the sight of you, eschewing
    A rapture that might prove my soul's undoing;   70
    But soon, fair being, I became aware
    That my deep passion could be made to square
    With rectitude, and with my bounden duty.
    I thereupon surrendered to your beauty.
    It is, I know, presumptuous on my part   75
    To bring you this poor offering of my heart,
    And it is not my merit, Heaven knows,
    But your compassion on which my hopes repose.
    You are my peace, my solace, my salvation;
    On you depends my bliss — or desolation;   80
    I bide your judgment and, as you think best,
    I shall be either miserable or blest.
Elmire: Your declaration is most gallant, Sir,
    But don't you think it's out of character?
    You'd have done better to restrain your passion   85
    And think before you spoke in such a fashion.
    It ill becomes a pious man like you . . .
Tartuffe: I may be pious, but I'm human too:
    With your celestial charms before his eyes,
    A man has not the power to be wise.   90
    I know such words sound strangely, coming from me,
    But I'm no angel, nor was meant to be,
    And if you blame my passion, you must needs
    Reproach as well the charms on which it feeds.
    Your loveliness I had no sooner seen   95
    Than you became my soul's unrivalled queen;
    Before your seraph glance, divinely sweet,
    My heart's defenses crumbled in defeat,
    And nothing fasting, prayer, or tears might do
    Could stay my spirit from adoring you.   100

My eyes, my sighs have told you in the past
What now my lips make bold to say at last,
And if, in your great goodness, you will deign
To look upon your slave, and ease his pain, —
If, in compassion for my soul's distress,   105
You'll stoop to comfort my unworthiness,
I'll raise to you, in thanks for that sweet manna,
An endless hymn, an infinite hosanna.
With me, of course, there need be no anxiety,
No fear of scandal or of notoriety.   110
These young court gallants, whom all the ladies fancy,
Are vain in speech, in action rash and chancy;
When they succeed in love, the world soon knows it;
No favor's granted them but they disclose it
And by the looseness of their tongues profane   115
The very altar where their hearts have lain.
Men of my sort, however, love discreetly,
And one may trust our reticence completely.
My keen concern for my good name insures
The absolute security of yours;   120
In short, I offer you, my dear Elmire,
Love without scandal, pleasure without fear.
Elmire: I've heard your well-turned speeches to the end.
And what you urge I clearly apprehend.
Aren't you afraid that I may take a notion   125
To tell my husband of your warm devotion,
And that, supposing he were duly told,
His feelings toward you might grow rather cold?
Tartuffe: I know, dear lady, that your exceeding charity
Will lead your heart to pardon my temerity;   130
That you'll excuse my violent affection
As human weakness, human imperfection;
And that — O fairest! — you will bear in mind
That I'm but flesh and blood, and am not blind.
Elmire: Some women might do otherwise, perhaps,   135
But I shall be discreet about your lapse;
I'll tell my husband nothing of what's occurred
If, in return, you'll give your solemn word
To advocate as forcefully as you can
The marriage of Valère and Mariane,   140
Renouncing all desire to dispossess
Another of his rightful happiness,
And . . .

SCENE IV

Damis, Elmire, Tartuffe

Damis (emerging from the closet where he has been hiding):
          No! We'll not hush up this vile affair;

I heard it all inside that closet there,
Where Heaven, in order to confound the pride
Of this great rascal, prompted me to hide.
Ah, now I have my long-awaited chance   5
To punish his deceit and arrogance,
And give my father clear and shocking proof
Of the black character of his dear Tartuffe.

Elmire: Ah no, Damis; I'll be content if he
Will study to deserve my leniency.   10
I've promised silence — don't make me break my word;
To make a scandal would be too absurd.
Good wives laugh off such trifles, and forget them;
Why should they tell their husbands, and upset them?

Damis: You have your reasons for taking such a course,   15
And I have reasons, too, of equal force.
To spare him now would be insanely wrong.
I've swallowed my just wrath for far too long
And watched this insolent bigot bringing strife
And bitterness into our family life.   20
Too long he's meddled in my father's affairs,
Thwarting my marriage-hopes, and poor Valère's.
It's high time that my father was undeceived,
And now I've proof that can't be disbelieved —
Proof that was furnished me by Heaven above.   25
It's too good not to take advantage of.
This is my chance, and I deserve to lose it
If, for one moment, I hesitate to use it.

Elmire: Damis . . .

Damis: No, I must do what I think right.
Madam, my heart is bursting with delight,   30
And, say whatever you will, I'll not consent
To lose the sweet revenge on which I'm bent.
I'll settle matters without more ado;
And here, most opportunely, is my cue.

SCENE V

Orgon, Tartuffe, Damis, Elmire

Damis: Father, I'm glad you've joined us. Let us advise you
Of some fresh news which doubtless will surprise you.
You've just now been repaid with interest
For all your loving-kindness to our guest.
He's proved his warm and grateful feelings toward you;   5
It's with a pair of horns he would reward you.
Yes, I surprised him with your wife, and heard
His whole adulterous offer, every word.
She, with her all too gentle disposition,
Would not have told you of his proposition;   10

But I shall not make terms with brazen lechery,
And feel that not to tell you would be treachery.
Elmire: And I hold that one's husband's peace of mind
Should not be spoilt by tattle of this kind.
One's honor doesn't require it: to be proficient   15
In keeping men at bay is quite sufficient.
These are my sentiments, and I wish, Damis,
That you had heeded me and held your peace.

SCENE VI

Orgon, Damis, Tartuffe

Orgon: Can it be true, this dreadful thing I hear?
Tartuffe: Yes, Brother, I'm a wicked man, I fear:
A wretched sinner, all depraved and twisted,
The greatest villain that has ever existed.
My life's one heap of crimes, which grows each minute;   5
There's naught but foulness and corruption in it;
And I perceive that Heaven, outraged by me,
Has chosen this occasion to mortify me.
Charge me with any deed you wish to name;
I'll not defend myself, but take the blame.   10
Believe what you are told, and drive Tartuffe
Like some base criminal from beneath your roof;
Yes, drive me hence, and with a parting curse:
I shan't protest, for I deserve far worse.
Orgon (to Damis): Ah, you deceitful boy, how dare you try   15
To stain his purity with so foul a lie?
Damis: What! Are you taken in by such a bluff?
Did you not hear . . . ?
Orgon: Enough, you rogue, enough!
Tartuffe: Ah, Brother, let him speak; you're being unjust.
Believe his story; the boy deserves your trust.   20
Why, after all, should you have faith in me?
How can you know what I might do, or be?
Is it on my good actions that you base
Your favor? Do you trust my pious face?
Ah, no, don't be deceived by hollow shows;   25
I'm far, alas, from being what men suppose;
Though the world takes me for a man of worth,
I'm truly the most worthless man on earth.
(To Damis.) Yes, my dear son, speak out now: call me the chief
Of sinners, a wretch, a murderer, a thief;   30
Load me with all the names men most abhor;
I'll not complain; I've earned them all, and more;
I'll kneel here while you pour them on my head
As a just punishment for the life I've led.

Orgon (to Tartuffe): This is too much, dear Brother.

   (To Damis.)   Have you no heart?   35

Damis: Are you so hoodwinked by this rascal's art . . . ?

Orgon: Be still, you monster.

   (To Tartuffe.)   Brother, I pray you, rise.

   (To Damis.) Villain!

Damis: But . . .

Orgon: Silence!

Damis: Can't you realize . . . ?

Orgon: Just one word more, and I'll tear you limb from limb.

Tartuffe: In God's name, Brother, don't be harsh with him.   40

   I'd rather far be tortured at the stake

   Than see him bear one scratch for my poor sake.

Orgon (to Damis): Ingrate!

Tartuffe: If I must beg you, on bended knee,

   To pardon him . . .

Orgon (falling to his knees, addressing Tartuffe):

              Such goodness cannot be!

   (To Damis.) Now, *there's* true charity!

Damis: What, you . . . ?

Orgon: Villain, be still!   45

   I know your motives; I know you wish him ill:

   Yes, all of you — wife, children, servants, all —

   Conspire against him and desire his fall,

   Employing every shameful trick you can

   To alienate me from this saintly man.   50

   Ah, but the more you seek to drive him away,

   The more I'll do to keep him. Without delay,

   I'll spite this household and confound its pride

   By giving him my daughter as his bride.

Damis: You're going to force her to accept his hand?   55

Orgon: Yes, and this very night, d'you understand?

   I shall defy you all, and make it clear

   That I'm the one who gives the orders here.

   Come, wretch, kneel down and clasp his blessed feet,

   And ask his pardon for your black deceit.   60

Damis: I ask that swindler's pardon? Why, I'd rather . . .

Orgon: So! You insult him, and defy your father!

   A stick! A stick! *(To Tartuffe.)* No, no — release me, do.

   (To Damis.) Out of my house this minute! Be off with you,

   And never dare set foot in it again.   65

Damis: Well, I shall go, but . . .

Orgon: Well, go quickly, then.

   I disinherit you; an empty purse

   Is all you'll get from me — except my curse!

Orgon, Tartuffe

Orgon: How he blasphemed your goodness! What a son!

Tartuffe: Forgive him, Lord, as I've already done.

    (To Orgon.) You can't know how it hurts when someone tries

    To blacken me in my dear Brother's eyes.

Orgon: Ahh!

Tartuffe: The mere thought of such ingratitude   5

    Plunges my soul into so dark a mood . . .

    Such horror grips my heart . . . I gasp for breath,

    And cannot speak, and feel myself near death.

Orgon: (He runs, in tears, to the door through which he has just driven his

    son.) You blackguard! Why did I spare you? Why did I not

    Break you in little pieces on the spot?   10

    Compose yourself, and don't be hurt, dear friend.

Tartuffe: These scenes, these dreadful quarrels, have got to end.

    I've much upset your household, and I perceive

    That the best thing will be for me to leave.

Orgon: What are you saying!

Tartuffe: They're all against me here;   15

    They'd have you think me false and insincere.

Orgon: Ah, what of that? Have I ceased believing in you?

Tartuffe: Their adverse talk will certainly continue,

    And charges which you now repudiate

    You may find credible at a later date.   20

Orgon: No, Brother, never.

Tartuffe: Brother, a wife can sway

    Her husband's mind in many a subtle way.

Orgon: No, no.

Tartuffe: To leave at once is the solution;

    Thus only can I end their persecution.

Orgon: No, no, I'll not allow it; you shall remain.   25

Tartuffe: Ah well; 'twill mean much martyrdom and pain,

    But if you wish it . . .

Orgon: Ah!

Tartuffe: Enough; so be it.

    But one thing must be settled, as I see it.

    For your dear honor, and for our friendship's sake,

    There's one precaution I feel bound to take.   30

    I shall avoid your wife, and keep away . . .

Orgon: No, you shall not, whatever they may say.

    It pleases me to vex them, and for spite

    I'd have them see you with her day and night.

    What's more, I'm going to drive them to despair   35

    By making you my only son and heir;

    This very day, I'll give to you alone

Clear deed and title to everything I own.
A dear, good friend and son-in-law-to-be
Is more than wife, or child, or kin to me.   40
Will you accept my offer, dearest son?
Tartuffe: In all things, let the will of Heaven be done.
Orgon: Poor fellow! Come, we'll go draw up the deed.
Then let them burst with disappointed greed!

ACT IV

Scene I

Cléante, Tartuffe

Cléante: Yes, all the town's discussing it, and truly,
Their comments do not flatter you unduly.
I'm glad we've met, Sir, and I'll give my view
Of this sad matter in a word or two.
As for who's guilty, that I shan't discuss;   5
Let's say it was Damis who caused the fuss;
Assuming, then, that you have been ill-used
By young Damis, and groundlessly accused,
Ought not a Christian to forgive, and ought
He not to stifle every vengeful thought?   10
Should you stand by and watch a father make
His only son an exile for your sake?
Again I tell you frankly, be advised:
The whole town, high and low, is scandalized;
This quarrel must be mended, and my advice is   15
Not to push matters to a further crisis.
No, sacrifice your wrath to God above,
And help Damis regain his father's love.
Tartuffe: Alas, for my part I should take great joy
In doing so. I've nothing against the boy.   20
I pardon all, I harbor no resentment;
To serve him would afford me much contentment.
But Heaven's interest will not have it so:
If he comes back, then I shall have to go.
After his conduct — so extreme, so vicious —   25
Our further intercourse would look suspicious.
God knows what people would think! Why, they'd describe
My goodness to him as a sort of bribe;
They'd say that out of guilt I made pretense
Of loving-kindness and benevolence —   30
That, fearing my accuser's tongue, I strove
To buy his silence with a show of love.
Cléante: Your reasoning is badly warped and stretched,

And these excuses, Sir, are most far-fetched.
Why put yourself in charge of Heaven's cause?   35
Does Heaven need our help to enforce its laws?
Leave vengeance to the Lord, Sir; while we live,
Our duty's not to punish, but forgive;
And what the Lord commands, we should obey
Without regard to what the world may say.   40
What! Shall the fear of being misunderstood
Prevent our doing what is right and good?
No, no; let's simply do what Heaven ordains,
And let no other thoughts perplex our brains.

Tartuffe: Again, Sir, let me say that I've forgiven   45
Damis, and thus obeyed the laws of Heaven;
But I am not commanded by the Bible
To live with one who smears my name with libel.

Cléante: Were you commanded, Sir, to indulge the whim
Of poor Orgon, and to encourage him   50
In suddenly transferring to your name
A large estate to which you have no claim?

Tartuffe: 'Twould never occur to those who know me best
To think I acted from self-interest.
The treasures of this world I quite despise;   55
Their specious glitter does not charm my eyes;
And if I have resigned myself to taking
The gift which my dear Brother insists on making,
I do so only, as he well understands,
Lest so much wealth fall into wicked hands,   60
Lest those to whom it might descend in time
Turn it to purposes of sin and crime,
And not, as I shall do, make use of it
For Heaven's glory and mankind's benefit.

Cléante: Forget these trumped-up fears. Your argument   65
Is one the rightful heir might well resent;
It *is* a moral burden to inherit
Such wealth, but give Damis a chance to bear it.
And would it not be worse to be accused
Of swindling, than to see that wealth misused?   70
I'm shocked that you allowed Orgon to broach
This matter, and that you feel no self-reproach;
Does true religion teach that lawful heirs
May freely be deprived of what is theirs?
And if the Lord has told you in your heart   75
That you and young Damis must dwell apart,
Would it not be the decent thing to beat
A generous and honorable retreat,
Rather than let the son of the house be sent,
For your convenience, into banishment?   80
Sir, if you wish to prove the honesty
Of your intentions . . .

Tartuffe: Sir, it is half-past three.
　　I've certain pious duties to attend to,
　　And hope my prompt departure won't offend you.
Cléante (alone): Damn.

Scene II

Elmire, Cléante, Mariane, Dorine

Dorine: Stay, Sir, and help Mariane, for Heaven's sake!
　　She's suffering so, I fear her heart will break.
　　Her father's plan to marry her off tonight
　　Has put the poor child in a desperate plight.
　　I hear him coming. Let's stand together, now,   5
　　And see if we can't change his mind, somehow,
　　About this match we all deplore and fear.

Scene III

Orgon, Mariane, Dorine, Elmire, Cléante

Orgon: Hah! Glad to find you all assembled here.
　　(To Mariane.) This contract, child, contains your happiness,
　　And what it says I think your heart can guess.
Mariane (falling to her knees): Sir, by that Heaven which sees me here distressed,
　　And by whatever else can move your breast,   5
　　Do not employ a father's power, I pray you,
　　To crush my heart and force it to obey you,
　　Nor by your harsh commands oppress me so
　　That I'll begrudge the duty which I owe —
　　And do not so embitter and enslave me   10
　　That I shall hate the very life you gave me.
　　If my sweet hopes must perish, if you refuse
　　To give me to the one I've dared to choose,
　　Spare me at least — I beg you, I implore —
　　The pain of wedding one whom I abhor;   15
　　And do not, by a heartless use of force,
　　Drive me to contemplate some desperate course.
Orgon (feeling himself touched by her): Be firm, my soul. No human weakness, now.
Mariane: I don't resent your love for him. Allow
　　Your heart free rein, Sir; give him your property,   20
　　And if that's not enough, take mine from me;
　　He's welcome to my money; take it, do,
　　But don't, I pray, include my person too.
　　Spare me, I beg you; and let me end the tale
　　Of my sad days behind a convent veil.   25
Orgon: A convent! Hah! When crossed in their amours,

All lovesick girls have the same thought as yours.
Get up! The more you loathe the man, and dread him,
The more ennobling it will be to wed him.
Marry Tartuffe, and mortify your flesh!   30
Enough; don't start that whimpering afresh.
Dorine: But why . . . ?
Orgon: Be still, there. Speak when you're spoken to.
Not one more bit of impudence out of you.
Cléante: If I may offer a word of counsel here . . .
Orgon: Brother, in counseling you have no peer;   35
All your advice is forceful, sound, and clever;
I don't propose to follow it, however.
Elmire (to Orgon): I am amazed, and don't know what to say;
Your blindness simply takes my breath away.
You are indeed bewitched, to take no warning   40
From our account of what occurred this morning.
Orgon: Madam, I know a few plain facts, and one
Is that you're partial to my rascal son;
Hence, when he sought to make Tartuffe the victim
Of a base lie, you dared not contradict him.   45
Ah, but you underplayed your part, my pet;
You should have looked more angry, more upset.
Elmire: When men make overtures, must we reply
With righteous anger and a battle-cry?
Must we turn back their amorous advances   50
With sharp reproaches and with fiery glances?
Myself, I find such offers merely amusing,
And make no scenes and fusses in refusing;
My taste is for good-natured rectitude,
And I dislike the savage sort of prude   55
Who guards her virtue with her teeth and claws,
And tears men's eyes out for the slightest cause:
The Lord preserve me from such honor as that,
Which bites and scratches like an alley-cat!
I've found that a polite and cool rebuff   60
Discourages a lover quite enough.
Orgon: I know the facts, and I shall not be shaken.
Elmire: I marvel at your power to be mistaken.
Would it, I wonder, carry weight with you
If I could *show* you that our tale was true?   65
Orgon: Show me?
Elmire: Yes.
Orgon: Rot.
Elmire: Come, what if I found a way
To make you see the facts as plain as day?
Orgon: Nonsense.
Elmire: Do answer me; don't be absurd.
I'm not now asking you to trust our word.

Suppose that from some hiding-place in here   70
You learned the whole sad truth by eye and ear —
What would you say of your good friend, after that?
Orgon: Why, I'd say . . . nothing. By Jehoshaphat!
   It can't be true.
Elmire: You've been too long deceived.
   And I'm quite tired of being disbelieved.   75
   Come now: let's put my statements to the test,
   And you shall see the truth made manifest.
Orgon: I'll take that challenge. Now do your uttermost.
   We'll see how you make good your empty boast.
Elmire (to Dorine): Send him to me.
Dorine: He's crafty; it may be hard   80
   To catch the cunning scoundrel off his guard.
Elmire: No, amorous men are gullible. Their conceit
   So blinds them that they're never hard to cheat.
   Have him come down. *(To Cléante and Mariane.)* Please leave us, for
      a bit.

SCENE IV

Elmire, Orgon

Elmire: Pull up this table, and get under it.
Orgon: What?
Elmire: It's essential that you be well-hidden.
Orgon: Why there?
Elmire: Oh, Heavens! Just do as you are bidden.
   I have my plans; we'll soon see how they fare.
   Under the table, now; and once you're there,   5
   Take care that you are neither seen nor heard.
Orgon: Well, I'll indulge you, since I gave my word
   To see you through this infantile charade.
Elmire: Once it is over, you'll be glad we played.
   (To her husband, who is now under the table.) I'm going to act quite
      strangely, now, and you   10
   Must not be shocked at anything I do.
   Whatever I may say, you must excuse
   As part of that deceit I'm forced to use.
   I shall employ sweet speeches in the task
   Of making that impostor drop his mask;   15
   I'll give encouragement to his bold desires,
   And furnish fuel to his amorous fires.
   Since it's for your sake, and for his destruction,
   That I shall seem to yield to his seduction,
   I'll gladly stop whenever you decide   20
   That all your doubts are fully satisfied.

I'll count on you, as soon as you have seen
What sort of man he is, to intervene,
And not expose me to his odious lust
One moment longer than you feel you must.   25
Remember: you're to save me from my plight
Whenever . . . He's coming! Hush! Keep out of sight!

SCENE V

Tartuffe, Elmire, Orgon

Tartuffe: You wish to have a word with me, I'm told.
Elmire: Yes. I've a little secret to unfold.
  Before I speak, however, it would be wise
  To close that door, and look about for spies.

Tartuffe goes to the door, closes it, and returns.

  The very last thing that must happen now   5
  Is a repetition of this morning's row.
  I've never been so badly caught off guard.
  Oh, how I feared for you! You saw how hard
  I tried to make that troublesome Damis
  Control his dreadful temper, and hold his peace.   10
  In my confusion, I didn't have the sense
  Simply to contradict his evidence;
  But as it happened, that was for the best,
  And all has worked out in our interest.
  This storm has only bettered your position;   15
  My husband doesn't have the least suspicion,
  And now, in mockery of those who do,
  He bids me be continually with you.
  And that is why, quite fearless of reproof,
  I now can be alone with my Tartuffe,   20
  And why my heart — perhaps too quick to yield —
  Feels free to let its passion be revealed.
Tartuffe: Madam, your words confuse me. Not long ago,
  You spoke in quite a different style, you know.
Elmire: Ah, Sir, if that refusal made you smart,   25
  It's little that you know of woman's heart,
  Or what that heart is trying to convey
  When it resists in such a feeble way!
  Always, at first, our modesty prevents
  The frank avowal of tender sentiments;   30
  However high the passion which inflames us,
  Still, to confess its power somehow shames us.
  Thus we reluct, at first, yet in a tone
  Which tells you that our heart is overthrown,
  That what our lips deny, our pulse confesses,   35

And that, in time, all noes will turn to yesses.
I fear my words are all too frank and free,
And a poor proof of woman's modesty;
But since I'm started, tell me, if you will —
Would I have tried to make Damis be still,   40
Would I have listened, calm and unoffended,
Until your lengthy offer of love was ended,
And been so very mild in my reaction,
Had your sweet words not given me satisfaction?
And when I tried to force you to undo   45
The marriage-plans my husband has in view,
What did my urgent pleading signify
If not that I admired you, and that I
Deplored the thought that someone else might own
Part of a heart I wished for mine alone?   50
Tartuffe: Madam, no happiness is so complete
As when, from lips we love, come words so sweet;
Their nectar floods my every sense, and drains
In honeyed rivulets through all my veins.
To please you is my joy, my only goal;   55
Your love is the restorer of my soul;
And yet I must beg leave, now, to confess
Some lingering doubts as to my happiness.
Might this not be a trick? Might not the catch
Be that you wish me to break off the match   60
With Mariane, and so have feigned to love me?
I shan't quite trust your fond opinion of me
Until the feelings you've expressed so sweetly
Are demonstrated somewhat more concretely,
And you have shown, by certain kind concessions,   65
That I may put my faith in your professions.
Elmire (she coughs, to warn her husband): Why be in such a hurry? Must
          my heart
Exhaust its bounty at the very start?
To make that sweet admission cost me dear,
But you'll not be content, it would appear,   70
Unless my store of favors is disbursed
To the last farthing, and at the very first.
Tartuffe: The less we merit, the less we dare to hope,
And with our doubts, mere words can never cope.
We trust no promised bliss till we receive it;   75
Not till a joy is ours can we believe it.
I, who so little merit your esteem,
Can't credit this fulfillment of my dream,
And shan't believe it, Madam, until I savor
Some palpable assurance of your favor.   80
Elmire: My, how tyrannical your love can be,
And how it flusters and perplexes me!

How furiously you take one's heart in hand,
And make your every wish a fierce command!
Come, must you hound and harry me to death?   85
Will you not give me time to catch my breath?
Can it be right to press me with such force,
Give me no quarter, show me no remorse,
And take advantage, by your stern insistence,
Of the fond feelings which weaken my resistance?   90

Tartuffe: Well, if you look with favor upon my love,
Why, then, begrudge me some clear proof thereof?

Elmire: But how can I consent without offense
To Heaven, toward which you feel such reverence?

Tartuffe: If Heaven is all that holds you back, don't worry.   95
I can remove that hindrance in a hurry.
Nothing of that sort need obstruct our path.

Elmire: Must one not be afraid of Heaven's wrath?

Tartuffe: Madam, forget such fears, and be my pupil,
And I shall teach you how to conquer scruple.   100
Some joys, it's true, are wrong in Heaven's eyes;
Yet Heaven is not averse to compromise;
There is a science, lately formulated,
Whereby one's conscience may be liberated,
And any wrongful act you care to mention   105
May be redeemed by purity of intention.
I'll teach you, Madam, the secrets of that science;
Meanwhile, just place on me your full reliance.
Assuage my keen desires, and feel no dread:
The sin, if any, shall be on my head.   110

Elmire coughs, this time more loudly.

You've a bad cough.

Elmire: Yes, yes. It's bad indeed.

Tartuffe (producing a little paper bag): A bit of licorice may be what you
      need.

Elmire: No, I've a stubborn cold, it seems. I'm sure it
Will take much more than licorice to cure it.

Tartuffe: How aggravating.

Elmire: Oh, more than I can say.   115

Tartuffe: If you're still troubled, think of things this way:
No one shall know our joys, save us alone,
And there's no evil till the act is known;
It's scandal, Madam, which makes it an offense,
And it's no sin to sin in confidence.   120

Elmire (having coughed once more): Well, clearly I must do as you require,
And yield to your importunate desire.
It is apparent, now, that nothing less
Will satisfy you, and so I acquiesce.
To go so far is much against my will;   125
I'm vexed that it should come to this; but still,

Since you are so determined on it, since you
Will not allow mere language to convince you,
And since you ask for concrete evidence, I
See nothing for it, now, but to comply.   130
If this is sinful, if I'm wrong to do it,
So much the worse for him who drove me to it.
The fault can surely not be charged to me.
Tartuffe: Madam, the fault is mine, if fault there be,
And . . .
Elmire: Open the door a little, and peek out;   135
I wouldn't want my husband poking about.
Tartuffe: Why worry about the man? Each day he grows
More gullible; one can lead him by the nose.
To find us here would fill him with delight,
And if he saw the worst, he'd doubt his sight.   140
Elmire: Nevertheless, do step out for a minute
Into the hall, and see that no one's in it.

SCENE VI

Orgon, Elmire

Orgon (coming out from under the table): That man's a perfect monster, I
     must admit!
I'm simply stunned. I can't get over it.
Elmire: What, coming out so soon? How premature!
Get back in hiding, and wait until you're sure.
Stay till the end, and be convinced completely;   5
We mustn't stop till things are proved concretely.
Orgon: Hell never harbored anything so vicious!
Elmire: Tut, don't be hasty. Try to be judicious.
Wait, and be certain that there's no mistake.
No jumping to conclusions, for Heaven's sake!   10

She places Orgon behind her, as Tartuffe re-enters.

SCENE VII

Tartuffe, Elmire, Orgon

Tartuffe (not seeing Orgon): Madam, all things have worked out to
     perfection;
I've given the neighboring rooms a full inspection;
No one's about; and now I may at last . . .
Orgon (intercepting him): Hold on, my passionate fellow, not so fast!
I should advise a little more restraint.   5
Well, so you thought you'd fool me, my dear saint!
How soon you wearied of the saintly life —
Wedding my daughter, and coveting my wife!
I've long suspected you, and had a feeling

That soon I'd catch you at your double-dealing. 10
Just now, you've given me evidence galore;
It's quite enough; I have no wish for more.
Elmire (to Tartuffe): I'm sorry to have treated you so slyly,
But circumstances forced me to be wily.
Tartuffe: Brother, you can't think . . .
Orgon: No more talk from you; 15
Just leave this household, without more ado.
Tartuffe: What I intended . . .
Orgon: That seems fairly clear.
Spare me your falsehoods and get out of here.
Tartuffe: No, I'm the master, and you're the one to go!
This house belongs to me, I'll have you know, 20
And I shall show you that you can't hurt *me*
By this contemptible conspiracy,
That those who cross me know not what they do,
And that I've means to expose and punish you,
Avenge offended Heaven, and make you grieve 25
That ever you dared order me to leave.

Scene VIII

Elmire, Orgon

Elmire: What was the point of all that angry chatter?
Orgon: Dear God, I'm worried. This is no laughing matter.
Elmire: How so?
Orgon: I fear I understood his drift.
I'm much disturbed about that deed of gift.
Elmire: You gave him . . . ?
Orgon: Yes, it's all been drawn and signed. 5
But one thing more is weighing on my mind.
Elmire: What's that?
Orgon: I'll tell you; but first let's see if there's
A certain strong-box in his room upstairs.

ACT V

Scene I

Orgon, Cléante

Cléante: Where are you going so fast?
Orgon: God knows!
Cléante: Then wait;
Let's have a conference, and deliberate
On how this situation's to be met.
Orgon: That strong-box has me utterly upset;

      This is the worst of many, many shocks.   5

Cléante: Is there some fearful mystery in that box?

Orgon: My poor friend Argas brought that box to me

    With his own hands, in utmost secrecy;

    'Twas on the very morning of his flight.

    It's full of papers which, if they came to light,   10

    Would ruin him — or such is my impression.

Cléante: Then why did you let it out of your possession?

Orgon: Those papers vexed my conscience, and it seemed best

    To ask the counsel of my pious guest.

    The cunning scoundrel got me to agree   15

    To leave the strong-box in his custody,

    So that, in case of an investigation,

    I could employ a slight equivocation,

    And swear I didn't have it, and thereby,

    At no expense to conscience, tell a lie.   20

Cléante: It looks to me as if you're out on a limb.

    Trusting him with that box, and offering him

    That deed of gift, were actions of a kind

    Which scarcely indicate a prudent mind.

    With two such weapons, he has the upper hand,   25

    And since you're vulnerable, as matters stand,

    You erred once more in bringing him to bay.

    You should have acted in some subtler way.

Orgon: Just think of it: behind that fervent face,

    A heart so wicked, and a soul so base!   30

    I took him in, a hungry beggar, and then . . .

    Enough, by God! I'm through with pious men:

    Henceforth I'll hate the whole false brotherhood,

    And persecute them worse than Satan could.

Cléante: Ah, there you go — extravagant as ever!   35

    Why can you not be rational? You never

    Manage to take the middle course, it seems,

    But jump, instead, between absurd extremes.

    You've recognized your recent grave mistake

    In falling victim to a pious fake;   40

    Now, to correct that error, must you embrace

    An even greater error in its place,

    And judge our worthy neighbors as a whole

    By what you've learned of one corrupted soul?

    Come, just because one rascal made you swallow   45

    A show of zeal which turned out to be hollow,

    Shall you conclude that all men are deceivers,

    And that, today, there are no true believers?

    Let atheists make that foolish inference;

    Learn to distinguish virtue from pretense,   50

    Be cautious in bestowing admiration,

    And cultivate a sober moderation.

Don't humor fraud, but also don't asperse
True piety; the latter fault is worse,
And it is best to err, if err one must,   55
As you have done, upon the side of trust.

Scene II

Damis, Orgon, Cléante

Damis: Father, I hear that scoundrel's uttered threats
Against you; that he pridefully forgets
How, in his need, he was befriended by you,
And means to use your gifts to crucify you.
Orgon: It's true, my boy. I'm too distressed for tears.   5
Damis: Leave it to me, Sir; let me trim his ears.
Faced with such insolence, we must not waver.
I shall rejoice in doing you the favor
Of cutting short his life, and your distress.
Cléante: What a display of young hotheadedness!   10
Do learn to moderate your fits of rage.
In this just kingdom, this enlightened age,
One does not settle things by violence.

Scene III

Madame Pernelle, Dorine, Orgon, Mariane, Damis, Cléante, Elmire

Madame Pernelle: I hear strange tales of very strange events.
Orgon: Yes, strange events which these two eyes beheld.
The man's ingratitude is unparalleled.
I save a wretched pauper from starvation,
House him, and treat him like a blood relation,   5
Shower him every day with my largesse,
Give him my daughter, and all that I possess;
And meanwhile the unconscionable knave
Tries to induce my wife to misbehave;
And not content with such extreme rascality,   10
Now threatens me with my own liberality,
And aims, by taking base advantage of
The gifts I gave him out of Christian love,
To drive me from my house, a ruined man,
And make me end a pauper, as he began.   15
Dorine: Poor fellow!
Madame Pernelle: No, my son, I'll never bring
Myself to think him guilty of such a thing.
Orgon: How's that?
Madame Pernelle: The righteous always were maligned.
Orgon: Speak clearly, Mother. Say what's on your mind.
Madame Pernelle: I mean that I can smell a rat, my dear.   20
You know how everybody hates him, here.

Orgon: That has no bearing on the case at all.

Madame Pernelle: I told you a hundred times, when you were small,
That virtue in this world is hated ever;
Malicious men may die, but malice never. 25

Orgon: No doubt that's true, but how does it apply?

Madame Pernelle: They've turned you against him by a clever lie.

Orgon: I've told you, I was there and saw it done.

Madame Pernelle: Ah, slanderers will stop at nothing, Son.

Orgon: Mother, I'll lose my temper . . . For the last time, 30
I tell you I was witness to the crime.

Madame Pernelle: The tongues of spite are busy night and noon,
And to their venom no man is immune.

Orgon: You're talking nonsense. Can't you realize
I saw it; saw it; saw it with my eyes? 35
Saw, do you understand me? Must I shout it
Into your ears before you'll cease to doubt it?

Madame Pernelle: Appearances can deceive, my son. Dear me,
We cannot always judge by what we see.

Orgon: Drat! Drat!

Madame Pernelle: One often interprets things awry; 40
Good can seem evil to a suspicious eye.

Orgon: Was I to see his pawing at Elmire
As an act of charity?

Madame Pernelle: Till his guilt is clear,
A man deserves the benefit of the doubt.
You should have waited, to see how things turned out. 45

Orgon: Great God in Heaven, what more proof did I need?
Was I to sit there, watching, until he'd . . .
You drive me to the brink of impropriety.

Madame Pernelle: No, no, a man of such surpassing piety
Could not do such a thing. You cannot shake me. 50
I don't believe it, and you shall not make me.

Orgon: You vex me so that, if you weren't my mother,
I'd say to you . . . some dreadful thing or other.

Dorine: It's your turn now, Sir, not to be listened to;
You'd not trust us, and now she won't trust you. 55

Cléante: My friends, we're wasting time which should be spent
In facing up to our predicament.
I fear that scoundrel's threats weren't made in sport.

Damis: Do you think he'd have the nerve to go to court?

Elmire: I'm sure he won't: they'd find it all too crude 60
A case of swindling and ingratitude.

Cléante: Don't be too sure. He won't be at a loss
To give his claims a high and righteous gloss;
And clever rogues with far less valid cause
Have trapped their victims in a web of laws. 65
I say again that to antagonize
A man so strongly armed was most unwise.

Orgon: I know it; but the man's appalling cheek

Outraged me so, I couldn't control my pique.

Cléante: I wish to Heaven that we could devise   70
Some truce between you, or some compromise.

Elmire: If I had known what cards he held, I'd not
Have roused his anger by my little plot.

Orgon (to Dorine, as M. Loyal enters): What is that fellow looking for? Who
is he?
Go talk to him — and tell him that I'm busy.   75

SCENE IV

*Monsieur Loyal, Damis, Elmire, Madame Pernelle, Mariane, Cléante, Orgon,
Dorine*

Monsieur Loyal: Good day, dear sister. Kindly let me see
Your master.

Dorine: He's involved with company,
And cannot be disturbed just now, I fear.

Monsieur Loyal: I hate to intrude; but what has brought me here
Will not disturb your master, in any event.   5
Indeed, my news will make him most content.

Dorine: Your name?

Monsieur Loyal: Just say that I bring greetings from
Monsieur Tartuffe, on whose behalf I've come.

Dorine (to Orgon): Sir, he's a very gracious man, and bears
A message from Tartuffe, which he declares,   10
Will make you most content.

Cléante: Upon my word,
I think this man had best be seen, and heard.

Orgon: Perhaps he has some settlement to suggest.
How shall I treat him? What manner would be best?

Cléante: Control your anger, and if he should mention   15
Some fair adjustment, give him your full attention.

Monsieur Loyal: Good health to you, good Sir. May Heaven confound
Your enemies, and may your joys abound.

Orgon (aside, to Cléante): A gentle salutation: it confirms
My guess that he is here to offer terms.   20

Monsieur Loyal: I've always held your family most dear;
I served your father, Sir, for many a year.

Orgon: Sir, I must ask your pardon; to my shame,
I cannot now recall your face or name.

Monsieur Loyal: Loyal's my name; I come from Normandy,   25
And I'm a bailiff, in all modesty.
For forty years, praise God, it's been my boast
To serve with honor in that vital post,
And I am here, Sir, if you will permit
The liberty, to serve you with this writ . . .   30

Orgon: To — *what?*

Monsieur Loyal: Now, please, Sir, let us have no friction:
    It's nothing but an order of eviction.
    You are to move your goods and family out
    And make way for new occupants, without
    Deferment or delay, and give the keys . . .   35

Orgon: I? Leave this house?

Monsieur Loyal: Why yes, Sir, if you please.
    This house, Sir, from the cellar to the roof,
    Belongs now to the good Monsieur Tartuffe,
    And he is lord and master of your estate
    By virtue of a deed of present date,   40
    Drawn in due form, with clearest legal phrasing . . .

Damis: Your insolence is utterly amazing!

Monsieur Loyal: Young man, my business here is not with you,
    But with your wise and temperate father, who,
    Like every worthy citizen, stands in awe   45
    Of justice, and would never obstruct the law.

Orgon: But . . .

Monsieur Loyal: Not for a million, Sir, would you rebel
    Against authority; I know that well.
    You'll not make trouble, Sir, or interfere
    With the execution of my duties here.   50

Damis: Someone may execute a smart tattoo
    On that black jacket of yours, before you're through.

Monsieur Loyal: Sir, bid your son be silent. I'd much regret
    Having to mention such a nasty threat
    Of violence, in writing my report.   55

Dorine (aside): This man Loyal's a most disloyal sort!

Monsieur Loyal: I love all men of upright character,
    And when I agreed to serve these papers, Sir,
    It was your feelings that I had in mind.
    I couldn't bear to see the case assigned   60
    To someone else, who might esteem you less
    And so subject you to unpleasantness.

Orgon: What's more unpleasant than telling a man to leave
    His house and home?

Monsieur Loyal: You'd like a short reprieve?
    If you desire it, Sir, I shall not press you,   65
    But wait until tomorrow to dispossess you.
    Splendid. I'll come and spend the night here, then,
    Most quietly, with half a score of men.
    For form's sake, you might bring me, just before
    You go to bed, the keys to the front door.   70
    My men, I promise, will be on their best
    Behavior, and will not disturb your rest.
    But bright and early, Sir, you must be quick
    And move out all your furniture, every stick:

The men I've chosen are both young and strong,   75
And with their help it shouldn't take you long.
In short, I'll make things pleasant and convenient,
And since I'm being so extremely lenient,
Please show me, Sir, a like consideration,
And give me your entire cooperation.   80
Orgon (aside): I may be all but bankrupt, but I vow
I'd give a hundred louis, here and now,
Just for the pleasure of landing one good clout
Right on the end of that complacent snout.
Cléante: Careful; don't make things worse.
Damis: My bootsole itches   85
To give that beggar a good kick in the breeches.
Dorine: Monsieur Loyal, I'd love to hear the whack
Of a stout stick across your fine broad back.
Monsieur Loyal: Take care: a woman too may go to jail if
She uses threatening language to a bailiff.   90
Cléante: Enough, enough, Sir. This must not go on.
Give me that paper, please, and then begone.
Monsieur Loyal: Well, *au revoir.* God give you all good cheer!
Orgon: May God confound you, and him who sent you here!

Scene V

Orgon, Elmire, Dorine, Cléante, Madame Pernelle, Damis, Mariane

Orgon: Now, Mother, was I right or not? This writ
Should change your notion of Tartuffe a bit.
Do you perceive his villainy at last?
Madame Pernelle: I'm thunderstruck. I'm utterly aghast.
Dorine: Oh, come, be fair. You mustn't take offense   5
At this new proof of his benevolence.
He's acting out of selfless love, I know.
Material things enslave the soul, and so
He kindly has arranged your liberation
From all that might endanger your salvation.   10
Orgon: Will you not ever hold your tongue, you dunce?
Cléante: Come, you must take some action, and at once.
Elmire: Go tell the world of the low trick he's tried.
The deed of gift is surely nullified
By such behavior, and public rage will not   15
Permit the wretch to carry out his plot.

Scene VI

Valère, Elmire, Damis, Orgon, Mariane, Dorine, Cléante, Madame Pernelle

Valère: Sir, though I hate to bring you more bad news,
Such is the danger that I cannot choose.
A friend who is extremely close to me

And knows my interest in your family
Has, for my sake, presumed to violate   5
The secrecy that's due to things of state,
And sends me word that you are in a plight
From which your one salvation lies in flight.
That scoundrel who's imposed upon you so
Denounced you to the King an hour ago   10
And, as supporting evidence, displayed
The strong-box of a certain renegade
Whose secret papers, so he testified,
You had disloyally agreed to hide.
I don't know just what charges may be pressed,   15
But there's a warrant out for your arrest;
Tartuffe has been instructed, furthermore,
To guide the arresting officer to your door.
Cléante: He's clearly done this to facilitate
His seizure of your house and your estate.   20
Orgon: That man, I must say, is a vicious beast!
Valère: Quick, Sir; you mustn't tarry in the least.
My carriage is outside, to take you hence;
This thousand louis should cover all expense
Let's lose no time, or you shall be undone;   25
The sole defense, in this case, is to run.
I shall go with you all the way, and place you
In a safe refuge to which they'll never trace you.
Orgon: Alas, dear boy, I wish that I could show you
My gratitude for everything I owe you.   30
But now is not the time; I pray the Lord
That I may live to give you your reward.
Farewell, my dears; be careful . . .
Cléante: Brother, hurry.
We shall take care of things; you needn't worry.

SCENE VII

The Officer, Elmire, Dorine, Tartuffe, Mariane, Cléante, Valère, Madame Pernelle, Damis, Orgon

Tartuffe: Gently, Sir, gently; stay right where you are.
No need for haste; your lodging isn't far.
You're off to prison, by order of the Prince.
Orgon: This is the crowning blow, you wretch; and since
It means my total ruin and defeat,   5
Your villainy is now at last complete.
Tartuffe: You needn't try to provoke me; it's no use.
Those who serve Heaven must expect abuse.
Cléante: You are indeed most patient, sweet, and blameless.
Dorine: How he exploits the name of Heaven! It's shameless.   10

Molière / Tartuffe: Act V, Scene VII **1505**

Tartuffe: Your taunts and mockeries are all for naught;
    To do my duty is my only thought.
Mariane: Your love of duty is most meritorious,
    And what you've done is little short of glorious.
Tartuffe: All deeds are glorious, Madam, which obey   15
    The sovereign prince who sent me here today.
Orgon: I rescued you when you were destitute;
    Have you forgotten that, you thankless brute?
Tartuffe: No, no, I well remember everything;
    But my first duty is to serve my King.   20
    That obligation is so paramount
    That other claims, beside it, do not count;
    And for it I would sacrifice my wife,
    My family, my friend, or my own life.
Elmire: Hypocrite!
Dorine: All that we most revere, he uses   25
    To cloak his plots and camouflage his ruses.
Cléante: If it is true that you are animated
    By pure and loyal zeal, as you have stated,
    Why was this zeal not roused until you'd sought
    To make Orgon a cuckold, and been caught?   30
    Why weren't you moved to give your evidence
    Until your outraged host had driven you hence?
    I shan't say that the gift of all his treasure
    Ought to have damped your zeal in any measure;
    But if he is a traitor, as you declare,   35
    How could you condescend to be his heir?
Tartuffe (to the officer): Sir, spare me all this clamor; it's growing shrill.
    Please carry out your orders, if you will.
Officer: Yes, I've delayed too long, Sir. Thank you kindly.
    You're just the proper person to remind me.   40
    Come, you are off to join the other boarders
    In the King's prison, according to his orders.
Tartuffe: Who? I, Sir?
Officer: Yes.
Tartuffe: To prison? This can't be true!
Officer: I owe an explanation, but not to you.
    (To Orgon.) Sir, all is well; rest easy, and be grateful   45
    We serve a Prince to whom all sham is hateful,
    A Prince who sees into our inmost hearts,
    And can't be fooled by any trickster's arts.
    His royal soul, though generous and human,
    Views all things with discernment and acumen;   50
    His sovereign reason is not lightly swayed,
    And all his judgments are discreetly weighed.
    He honors righteous men of every kind,
    And yet his zeal for virtue is not blind,
    Nor does his love of piety numb his wits   55
    And make him tolerant of hypocrites.

'Twas hardly likely that this man could cozen
A King who's foiled such liars by the dozen.
With one keen glance, the King perceived the whole
Perverseness and corruption of his soul,   60
And thus high Heaven's justice was displayed:
Betraying you, the rogue stood self-betrayed.
The King soon recognized Tartuffe as one
Notorious by another name, who'd done
So many vicious crimes that one could fill   65
Ten volumes with them, and be writing still.
But to be brief: our sovereign was appalled
By this man's treachery toward you, which he called
The last, worst villainy of a vile career,
And bade me follow the impostor here   70
To see how gross his impudence could be,
And force him to restore your property.
Your private papers, by the King's command,
I hereby seize and give into your hand.
The King, by royal order, invalidates   75
The deed which gave this rascal your estates,
And pardons, furthermore, your grave offense
In harboring an exile's documents.
By these decrees, our Prince rewards you for
Your loyal deeds in the late civil war,   80
And shows how heartfelt is his satisfaction
In recompensing any worthy action,
How much he prizes merit, and how he makes
More of men's virtues than of their mistakes.

Dorine: Heaven be praised!

Madame Pernelle: I breathe again, at last.   85

Elmire: We're safe.

Mariane: I can't believe the danger's past.

Orgon (to Tartuffe): Well, traitor, now you see . . .

Cléante: Ah, Brother, please,
    Let's not descend to such indignities.
    Leave the poor wretch to his unhappy fate,
    And don't say anything to aggravate   90
    His present woes; but rather hope that he
    Will soon embrace an honest piety,
    And mend his ways, and by a true repentance
    Move our just King to moderate his sentence.
    Meanwhile, go kneel before your sovereign's throne   95
    And thank him for the mercies he has shown.

Orgon: Well said: let's go at once and, gladly kneeling,
    Express the gratitude which all are feeling.
    Then, when that first great duty has been done,
    We'll turn with pleasure to a second one,   100
    And give Valère, whose love has proven so true,
    The wedded happiness which is his due.

Considerations for Critical Thinking and Writing

1. In what ways is Orgon like his mother, Madame Pernelle?
2. Although Tartuffe does not appear in Acts I and II, he is characterized through the use of exposition. How do Madame Pernelle's and Orgon's views of Tartuffe differ from those of the other characters, especially Cléante and Dorine? Which perspective is more convincing? Explain why.
3. What effect does Tartuffe have on Orgon? Pay particular attention to Orgon's speech claiming he is a "changed man" (I.v.12–21).
4. How does Cléante distinguish between those who are "true and false in piety" (I.v.68–149)?
5. What reasons does Dorine give in Act II, Scene ii for Mariane not to marry Tartuffe? Are they sound reasons? How are Dorine and Mariane used as character foils?
6. Describe Dorine's sense of humor. How is it appropriate to her station in life as a companion (not merely a maid) to Mariane?
7. What is the effect of Tartuffe's entrance in Act III, Scene ii? How do you respond to him? Although he is a rogue, he commands interest. Why?
8. How does Tartuffe stay in Orgon's favor in Act III, Scene vi even though he has been accused of coveting Orgon's wife?
9. In Act IV Tartuffe tells Elmire that "there's no evil till the act is known" (IV.v.118). Explain how this assertion constitutes an example of dramatic irony.
10. In Act V, Scene i, line 35, why does Cléante accuse Orgon of being "extravagant as ever"? What is Cléante's advice to Orgon?
11. What is the effect of Madame Pernelle's refusal to believe Orgon when he describes Tartuffe as an "unconscionable knave" (V.iii.8)?
12. What values does Cléante represent? Why is it significant that Molière does not at any time treat him comically, as he does most of the other characters?
13. How do you respond to the use of the deus ex machina at the play's conclusion, when Molière introduces the king's officer to save Orgon and his family from imprisonment and poverty? Can the ending be justified, or is it too obviously a tribute to Molière's patron?
14. Is it accurate to describe the play as an attack on religion? Why or why not?
15. Choose a scene that is particularly comic and describe how you would stage it. Consider the setting, the costumes, the actors' gestures, and the manner in which they deliver their lines.

Connections to Other Selections

1. Explain how Sophocles or Shakespeare might have changed the ending of *Tartuffe* to transform it into a tragedy. What revisions in the plot do you think one or the other would make? Explain your proposed changes.
2. Write an essay exploring religion in *Tartuffe* and *Antigone* (p. 1164).
3. Choose a brief but interesting incident from Glaspell's *Trifles* (p. 1084), Henrik Ibsen's *A Doll House* (p. 1517), or Anton Chekhov's *The Cherry Orchard* (p. 1569) and rewrite it as you think Molière would if he were to subject the moment you choose to his satiric wit.

MOLIÈRE (1622–1673)
Defense of Tartuffe   1664

Here is a comedy that has excited a good deal of discussion and that has been under attack for a long time; and the persons who are mocked by it have made it plain that they are more powerful in France than all whom my plays have satirized up to this time. Noblemen, ladies of fashion, cuckolds, and doctors all kindly consented to their presentation, which they themselves seemed to enjoy along with everyone else; but hypocrites do not understand banter: they became angry at once, and found it strange that I was bold enough to represent their actions and to care to describe a profession shared by so many good men. This is a crime for which they cannot forgive me, and they have taken up arms against my comedy in a terrible rage. They were careful not to attack it at the point that had wounded them: they are too crafty for that and too clever to reveal their true character. In keeping with their lofty custom, they have used the cause of God to mask their private interests; and *Tartuffe,* they say, is a play that offends piety: it is filled with abominations from beginning to end, and nowhere is there a line that does not deserve to be burned. Every syllable is wicked, the very gestures are criminal, and the slightest glance, turn of the head, or step from right to left conceals mysteries that they are able to explain to my disadvantage. In vain did I submit the play to the criticism of my friends and the scrutiny of the public: all the corrections I could make, the judgment of the king and queen who saw the play, the approval of great princes and ministers of state who honored it with their presence, the opinion of good men who found it worthwhile, all this did not help. They will not let go of their prey, and every day of the week they have pious zealots abusing me in public and damning me out of charity.

I would care very little about all they might say except that their devices make enemies of men whom I respect and gain the support of genuinely good men, whose faith they know and who, because of the warmth of their piety, readily accept the impressions that others present to them. And it is this which forces me to defend myself. Especially to the truly devout do I wish to vindicate my play, and I beg of them with all my heart not to condemn it before seeing it, to rid themselves of preconceptions, and not aid the cause of men dishonored by their actions.

If one takes the trouble to examine my comedy in good faith, he will surely see that my intentions are innocent throughout, and tend in no way to make fun of what men revere; that I have presented the subject with all the precautions that its delicacy imposes; and that I have used all the art and skill that I could to distinguish clearly the character of the hypocrite from that of the truly devout man. For that purpose I used two whole acts to prepare the appearance of my scoundrel. Never is there a moment's doubt about his character; he is known at once from the qualities I have given him; and from one end of the play to the other, he does not say a word, he does not perform an action which does not depict to the audience the character of a wicked man, and which does not bring out in sharp relief the character of the truly good man which I oppose to it.

From the preface to *Tartuffe,* translated by Richard Wilbur.

Considerations for Critical Thinking and Writing

1. How does Molière use in *Tartuffe* "art and skill . . . to distinguish clearly the character of the hypocrite from that of the truly devout man"?
2. Molière urges his audience not to "condemn" his play "before seeing it, [and] to rid themselves of preconceptions." To what extent do you think censors have preconceptions about the works — whether they are plays, novels, films, music, or magazines — they would suppress?
3. Use library sources to investigate the reception of the early productions of *Tartuffe,* and describe the major issues associated with the play. Explain why you find Molière's defense convincing or not.

RICHARD WILBUR (b. 1921)
Is Tartuffe *a Satire on Religious Hypocrisy?* 1963

There may be people who deny comedy the right to be serious, and think it improper for any but trivial themes to consort with laughter. It would take people of that kind to find in *Tartuffe* anything offensive to religion. The warped characters of the play express an obviously warped religious attitude, which is corrected by the reasonable orthodoxy of Cléante, the wholesomeness of Dorine, and the entire testimony of the action. The play is not a satire on religion, as those held who kept it off the boards for five years. Is it, then, a satire on religious hypocrisy, as Molière claimed in his polemical preface of 1669?

The play speaks often of religious hypocrisy, displays it in action, and sometimes seems to be gesturing toward its practitioners in seventeenth-century French society. Tartuffe is made to recommend, more than once, those Jesuitical techniques for easing the conscience which Pascal attacked in the *Provincial Letters.* Cléante makes a long speech against people who feign piety for the sake of preferment or political advantage. And yet no one in the play can be said to be a religious hypocrite in any representative sense. Tartuffe may at times suggest or symbolize the slippery casuist, or the sort of hypocrite denounced by Cléante, but he is not himself such a person. He is a versatile parasite or confidence man, with a very long criminal record, and to pose as a holy man is not his only *modus operandi:* we see him, in the last act, shifting easily from the role of saint to that of hundred-percenter. As for the other major characters who might qualify, Madame Pernelle is simply a nasty bigot, while the religious attitudes of her son Orgon are, for all their underlying corruption, quite sincere.

Tartuffe is only incidentally satiric; what we experience in reading or seeing it, as several modern critics have argued, is not a satire but a "deep" comedy in which (1) a knave tries to control life by cold chicanery, (2) a fool tries to oppress life by unconscious misuse of the highest values, and (3) life, happily, will not have it.

From the Introduction to *Tartuffe*

Considerations for Critical Thinking and Writing

1. According to Wilbur what kind of person would be offended by the treatment of religion in *Tartuffe*? Why is being offended an inappropriate response?
2. Explain why you agree or disagree that Tartuffe is not a religious hypocrite.
3. In an essay compare Wilbur's view of religious hypocrisy in *Tartuffe* with Molière's own position in his preface. Explain why you agree with Wilbur's or Molière's position.

30. Modern Drama

REALISM

Realism is a literary technique that attempts to create the appearance of life as it is actually experienced. Characters in modern realistic plays (written during and after the last quarter of the nineteenth century) speak dialogue that we might hear in our daily lives. These characters are not larger than life but representative of it; they seem to speak the way we do rather than in highly poetic language, formal declarations, asides, or soliloquies. It is impossible to imagine a heroic figure such as Oedipus inhabiting a comfortably furnished living room and chatting about his wife's household budget the way Torvald Helmer does in Henrik Ibsen's *A Doll House*. Realism brings into focus commonplace, everyday life rather than the extraordinary kinds of events that make up Sophocles' *Oedipus the King* or Shakespeare's *Hamlet*.

Realistic characters can certainly be heroic, but like Nora Helmer, they find that their strength and courage are tested in the context of events ordinary people might experience. Work, love, marriage, children, and death are often the focus of realistic dramas. These subjects can also constitute much of the material in nonrealistic plays, but modern realistic dramas present such material in the realm of the probable. Conflicts in realistic plays are likely to reflect problems in our own lives. Hence, making ends meet takes precedence over saving a kingdom; middle- and lower-class individuals take center stage as primary characters in main plots rather than being secondary characters in subplots. Thus we can see why the nineteenth-century movement toward realism paralleled the rise of a middle class eagerly seeking representations of its concerns in the theater.

Before the end of the nineteenth century, however, few attempts were made in the theater to present life as it is actually lived. The chorus's role in Sophocles' *Oedipus the King*, the allegorical figures in morality plays, the remarkable mistaken identities in Shakespeare's comedies, or the rhymed couplets spoken in Molière's *Tartuffe* represent theatrical conventions rather than life. Theatergoers have understood and appreciated these conventions for centuries — and still do — but in the nineteenth century social, political, and industrial revolutions helped create an atmosphere in which some playwrights found it necessary to create works that more directly reflected their audiences' lives.

Playwrights such as Henrik Ibsen and Anton Chekhov refused to join the ranks of their romantic contemporaries, who they felt falsely idealized life. The most popular plays immediately preceding the works of these realistic writers consisted primarily of love stories and action-packed plots. Such *melodramas* offer audiences thrills and chills as well as happy endings. They typically include a virtuous individual struggling under the tyranny of a wicked oppressor, who is defeated only at the last moment. Suspense is reinforced by a series of pursuits, captures, and escapes that move the plot quickly and deemphasize character or theme. These representations of extreme conflicts enjoyed wide popularity in the nineteenth century — indeed, they still do — because their formula was varied enough to be entertaining yet their outcomes were always comforting to the audience's sense of justice. But from the realists' perspective, melodramas were merely escape fantasies that distorted life by refusing to examine the real world closely and objectively.

Realists attempted to open their audiences' eyes; to their minds, the only genuine comfort was in knowing the truth. Many of their plays concern controversial issues of the day and focus on people who fall prey to indifferent societal institutions. English dramatist John Galsworthy (1867–1933) examined social values in *Strife* (1909) and *Justice* (1910), two plays whose titles broadly suggest the nature of his concerns. British playwright George Bernard Shaw (1856–1950) often used comedy and irony as means of awakening his audiences to contemporary problems: *Arms and the Man* (1894) satirizes romantic attitudes toward war, and *Mrs. Warren's Profession* (1898) indicts a social and economic system that drives a woman to prostitution. Chekhov's plays are populated by characters frustrated by their social situations and their own sensibilities; they are ordinary people who long for happiness but become entangled in everyday circumstances that limit their lives. Ibsen also took a close look at his characters' daily lives. His plays attack societal conventions and challenge popular attitudes toward marriage; he stunned audiences by dramatizing the suffering of a man dying of syphilis.

With these kinds of materials, Ibsen and his contemporaries popularized the *problem play*, a drama that represents a social issue in order to awaken the audience to it. These plays usually reject romantic plots in favor of holding up a mirror that reflects not simply what audiences want to see but what the playwright sees in them. Nineteenth-century realistic theater was no refuge from the social, economic, and psychological problems that melodrama ignored or sentimentalized.

NATURALISM

Related to realism is another movement, called ***naturalism***. Essentially more of a philosophical attitude than a literary technique, naturalism derives its name from the idea that human beings are part of nature and subject to its laws. According to naturalists, heredity and environment shape and control people's lives; their behavior is determined more by instinct than by reason. This deterministic view argues that human beings have no transcendent identity, because there is no soul or spiritual world that ultimately distinguishes humanity from any other form of life. Characters in naturalistic plays are generally portrayed as victims overwhelmed by internal and external forces. Thus literary naturalism tends to include not only the commonplace but the sordid, destructive, and chaotic aspects of life. Naturalism, then, is an extreme form of realism.

The earliest and most articulate voice of naturalism was that of French author Émile Zola (1840–1902), who urged artists to draw their characters from life and present their histories as faithfully as scientists report laboratory findings. Zola's best-known naturalistic play, *Thérèse Raquin* (1873), is a dramatization of an earlier novel involving a woman whose passion causes her to take a lover and plot with him to kill her husband. In his preface to the novel, Zola explains that his purpose is to take "a strong man and unsatisfied woman," "throw them into a violent drama and note scrupulously the sensations and acts of these creatures." The diction of Zola's statement reveals his nearly clinical approach, which becomes even more explicit when Zola likens his method of revealing character to that of an autopsy: "I have simply done on two living bodies the work which surgeons do on corpses."

Although some naturalistic plays have been successfully produced and admired (notably Maxim Gorky's *The Lower Depths* [1902], set in a grim boardinghouse occupied by characters who suffer poverty, crime, betrayal, disease, and suicide), few important dramatists fully subscribed to naturalism's extreme methods and values. Nevertheless, the movement significantly influenced playwrights. Because of its insistence on the necessity of closely observing characters' environment, playwrights placed a new emphasis on detailed settings and natural acting. This verisimilitude became a significant feature of realistic drama.

THEATRICAL CONVENTIONS OF MODERN DRAMA

The picture-frame stage that is often used for realistic plays typically reproduces the setting of a room in some detail. Within the stage, framed by a proscenium arch (from which the curtain hangs), scenery and props are used to create an illusion of reality. Whether the "small bookcase with leather-bound books" described in the opening scene of Ibsen's *A Doll*

House is only painted scenery or an actual case with books, it will probably look real to the audience. Removing the fourth wall of a room so that an audience can look in fosters the illusion that the actions onstage are real events happening before unseen spectators. The texture of Nora's life is communicated by the set as well as by what she says and does. That doesn't happen in a play like Sophocles' *Antigone*. Technical effects can make us believe there is wood burning in a fireplace or snow falling outside a window. Outdoor settings are made similarly realistic by props and painted sets. In Chekhov's *The Cherry Orchard,* for example, the second act opens in a meadow with the faint outline of a city on the horizon.

In addition to lifelike sets, a particular method of acting is used to create a realistic atmosphere. Actors address each other instead of directing formal speeches toward the audience; they act within the setting, not merely before it. At the beginning of the twentieth century Konstantin Stanislavsky (1863–1938), a Russian director, teacher, and actor, developed a system of acting that was an important influence in realistic theater. He trained actors to identify with the inner emotions of the characters they played. They were encouraged to recall from their own lives emotional responses similar to those they were portraying. The goal was to present a role truthfully by first feeling and then projecting the character's situation. Among Stanislavsky's early successes in this method were the plays of Chekhov.

There are, however, degrees of realism on the stage. Tennessee Williams's *The Glass Menagerie* (p. 1666), for example, is a partially realistic portrayal of characters whose fragile lives are founded on illusions. Williams's dialogue rings true, and individual scenes resemble the kind of real-life action we would imagine such vulnerable characters engaging in, but other elements of the play are nonrealistic. For instance, Williams uses Tom as a major character in the play as well as a narrator and a stage manager. Here is part of Williams's stage directions: "The narrator is an undisguised convention of the play. He takes whatever license with dramatic convention as is convenient to his purposes." Although this play can be accurately described as including realistic elements, Williams, like many other contemporary playwrights, does not attempt an absolute fidelity to reality. He uses flashbacks — as does Arthur Miller in *Death of a Salesman* (p. 1712) — to present incidents that occurred before the opening scene because the past impinges so heavily on the present. Most playwrights don't attempt to duplicate reality, since that can now be done so well by motion pictures.

Realism needn't lock a playwright into a futile attempt to make everything appear as it is in life. There is no way to avoid theatrical conventions: actors impersonate characters in a setting that is, after all, a stage. Indeed, even the dialogue in a realistic play is quite different from the pauses, sentence fragments, repetitions, silences, and incoherencies that characterize the way people usually speak. Realistic dialogue may seem like ordinary speech, but it, like Shakespeare's poetic language, is constructed. If we remember that realistic drama represents only the appearance of reality and that what we read on a page or see and hear onstage is the result of careful selecting, editing, and even distortion, then we are more likely to appreciate the playwright's art.

A DOLL HOUSE

Henrik Ibsen was born in Skien, Norway, to wealthy parents, who lost their money while he was a young boy. His early experiences with small-town life and genteel poverty sensitized him to the problems that he subsequently dramatized in a number of his plays. At age sixteen he was apprenticed to a druggist; he later thought about studying medicine, but by his early twenties he was earning a living writing and directing plays in various Norwegian cities. By the time of his death he enjoyed an international reputation for his treatment of social issues related to middle-class life.

Ibsen's earliest dramatic works were historical and romantic plays, some in verse. His first truly realistic work was *The Pillars of Society* (1877), whose title ironically hints at the corruption and hypocrisy exposed in it. The realistic social-problem plays for which he is best known followed. These dramas at once fascinated and shocked international audiences. Among his most produced and admired works are *A Doll House* (1879), *Ghosts* (1881), *An Enemy of the People* (1882), *The Wild Duck* (1884), and *Hedda Gabler* (1890). The common denominator in many of Ibsen's dramas is his interest in individuals struggling for an authentic identity in the face of tyrannical social conventions. This conflict often results in his characters being divided between a sense of duty to themselves and their responsibility to others.

Ibsen used such external and internal conflicts to propel his plays' action. Like many of his contemporaries who wrote realistic plays, he adopted the form of the well-made play. A dramatic structure popularized in France by Eugène Scribe (1791–1861) and Victorien Sardou (1831–1908), the **well-made play** employs conventions including plenty of suspense created by meticulous plotting. Extensive exposition explains past events that ultimately lead to an inevitable climax. Tension is released when a secret that reverses the protagonist's fortunes is revealed. Ibsen, having directed a number of Scribe's plays in Norway, knew their cause-to-effect plot arrangements and used them for his own purposes in his problem plays.

A Doll House dramatizes the tensions of a nineteenth-century middle-class marriage in which a wife struggles to step beyond the limited identity imposed on her by her husband and society. Although the Helmers' pleasant apartment seems an unlikely setting for the fierce conflicts that develop, the issues raised in the play are unmistakably real. *A Doll House* affirms the necessity to reject hypocrisy, complacency, cowardice, and stifling conventions if life is to have dignity and meaning. Several critical approaches to the play can be found in Chapter 31, "Critical Case Study: Henrik Ibsen's *A Doll House.*"

HENRIK IBSEN (1828–1906)

A Doll House   1879

TRANSLATED BY ROLF FJELDE

The Characters

Torvald Helmer, a lawyer
Nora, his wife
Dr. Rank
Mrs. Linde
Nils Krogstad, a bank clerk
The Helmers' three small children
Anne-Marie, their nurse
Helene, a maid
A Delivery Boy

SCENE: *The action takes place in Helmer's residence.*

ACT I

A comfortable room, tastefully but not expensively furnished. A door to the right in the back wall leads to the entryway; another to the left leads to HELMER'S *study. Between these doors, a piano. Midway in the left-hand wall a door, and further back a window. Near the window a round table with an armchair and a small sofa. In the right-hand wall, toward the rear, a door, and nearer the foreground a porcelain stove with two armchairs and a rocking chair beside it. Between the stove and the side door, a small table. Engravings on the walls. An etagère with china figures and other small art objects; a small bookcase with richly bound books; the floor carpeted; a fire burning in the stove. It is a winter day.*

A bell rings in the entryway; shortly after we hear the door being unlocked. Nora *comes into the room, humming happily to herself; she is wearing street clothes and carries an armload of packages, which she puts down on the table to the right. She has left the hall door open; and through it a* Delivery Boy *is seen, holding a Christmas tree and a basket, which he gives to the* Maid *who let them in.*

Nora: Hide the tree well, Helene. The children mustn't get a glimpse of it till this evening, after it's trimmed. (*To the Delivery Boy, taking out her purse.*) How much?
Delivery Boy: Fifty, ma'am.

Nora: There's a crown. No, keep the change. (*The* Boy *thanks her and leaves. Nora shuts the door. She laughs softly to herself while taking off her street things. Drawing a bag of macaroons from her pocket, she eats a couple, then steals over and listens at her husband's study door.*) Yes, he's home. (*Hums again as she moves to the table right.*)

Helmer (from the study): Is that my little lark twittering out there?

Nora (busy opening some packages): Yes, it is.

Helmer: Is that my squirrel rummaging around?

Nora: Yes!

Helmer: When did my squirrel get in?

Nora: Just now. (*Putting the macaroon bag in her pocket and wiping her mouth.*) Do come in, Torvald, and see what I've bought.

Helmer: Can't be disturbed. (*After a moment he opens the door and peers in, pen in hand.*) Bought, you say? All that there? Has the little spendthrift been out throwing money around again?

Nora: Oh, but Torvald, this year we really should let ourselves go a bit. It's the first Christmas we haven't had to economize.

Helmer: But you know we can't go squandering.

Nora: Oh yes, Torvald, we can squander a little now. Can't we? Just a tiny, wee bit. Now that you've got a big salary and are going to make piles and piles of money.

Helmer: Yes — starting New Year's. But then it's a full three months till the raise comes through.

Nora: Pooh! We can borrow that long.

Helmer: Nora! (*Goes over and playfully takes her by the ear.*) Are your scatter-brains off again? What if today I borrowed a thousand crowns, and you squandered them over Christmas week, and then on New Year's Eve a roof tile fell on my head and I lay there —

Nora (putting her hand on his mouth): Oh! Don't say such things!

Helmer: Yes, but what if it happened — then what?

Nora: If anything so awful happened, then it just wouldn't matter if I had debts or not.

Helmer: Well, but the people I'd borrowed from?

Nora: Them? Who cares about them! They're strangers.

Helmer: Nora, Nora, how like a woman! No, but seriously, Nora, you know what I think about that. No debts! Never borrow! Something of freedom's lost — and something of beauty, too — from a home that's founded on borrowing and debt. We've made a brave stand up to now, the two of us; and we'll go right on like that the little while we have to.

Nora (going toward the stove): Yes, whatever you say, Torvald.

Helmer (following her): Now, now, the little lark's wings mustn't droop. Come on, don't be a sulky squirrel. (*Taking out his wallet.*) Nora, guess what I have here.

Nora (turning quickly): Money!

Helmer: There, see. (*Hands her some notes.*) Good grief, I know how costs go up in a house at Christmastime.

Nora: Ten — twenty — thirty — forty. Oh, thank you, Torvald; I can manage no end on this.

Helmer: You really will have to.

Nora: Oh yes, I promise I will! But come here so I can show you everything I bought. And so cheap! Look, new clothes for Ivar here — and a sword. Here a horse and a trumpet for Bob. And a doll and a doll's bed here for Emmy; they're nothing much, but she'll tear them to bits in no time anyway. And here I have dress material and handkerchiefs for the maids. Old Anne-Marie really deserves something more.

Helmer: And what's in that package there?

Nora (with a cry): Torvald, no! You can't see that till tonight!

Helmer: I see. But tell me now, you little prodigal, what have you thought of for yourself?

Nora: For myself? Oh, I don't want anything at all.

Helmer: Of course you do. Tell me just what — within reason — you'd most like to have.

Nora: I honestly don't know. Oh, listen, Torvald —

Helmer: Well?

Nora (fumbling at his coat buttons, without looking at him): If you want to give me something, then maybe you could — you could —

Helmer: Come on, out with it.

Nora (hurriedly): You could give me money, Torvald. No more than you think you can spare; then one of these days I'll buy something with it.

Helmer: But Nora —

Nora: Oh please, Torvald darling, do that! I beg you, please. Then I could hang the bills in pretty gilt paper on the Christmas tree. Wouldn't that be fun?

Helmer: What are those little birds called that always fly through their fortunes?

Nora: Oh yes, spendthrifts; I know all that. But let's do as I say, Torvald; then I'll have time to decide what I really need most. That's very sensible, isn't it?

Helmer (smiling): Yes, very — that is, if you actually hung onto the money I give you, and you actually used it to buy yourself something. But it goes for the house and for all sorts of foolish things, and then I only have to lay out some more.

Nora: Oh, but Torvald —

Helmer: Don't deny it, my dear little Nora. (*Putting his arm around her waist.*) Spendthrifts are sweet, but they use up a frightful amount of money. It's incredible what it costs a man to feed such birds.

Nora: Oh, how can you say that! Really, I save everything I can.

Helmer (laughing): Yes, that's the truth. Everything you can. But that's nothing at all.

Nora (humming, with a smile of quiet satisfaction): Hm, if you only knew what expenses we larks and squirrels have, Torvald.

Helmer: You're an odd little one. Exactly the way your father was. You're never at a loss for scaring up money; but the moment you have it, it runs right out through your fingers; you never know what you've done with it. Well, one takes you as you are. It's deep in your blood. Yes, these things are hereditary, Nora.

Nora: Ah, I could wish I'd inherited many of Papa's qualities.

Helmer: And I couldn't wish you anything but just what you are, my sweet little lark. But wait; it seems to me you have a very — what should I call it? — a very suspicious look today —

Nora: I do?

Helmer: You certainly do. Look me straight in the eye.

Nora (looking at him): Well?

Helmer (shaking an admonitory finger): Surely my sweet tooth hasn't been running riot in town today, has she?

Nora: No. Why do you imagine that?

Helmer: My sweet tooth really didn't make a little detour through the confectioner's?

Nora: No, I assure you, Torvald—

Helmer: Hasn't nibbled some pastry?

Nora: No, not at all.

Helmer: Not even munched a macaroon or two?

Nora: No, Torvald, I assure you, really—

Helmer: There, there now. Of course I'm only joking.

Nora (going to the table, right): You know I could never think of going against you.

Helmer: No, I understand that; and you *have* given me your word. (*Going over to her.*) Well, you keep your little Christmas secrets to yourself, Nora darling. I expect they'll come to light this evening, when the tree is lit.

Nora: Did you remember to ask Dr. Rank?

Helmer: No. But there's no need for that; it's assumed he'll be dining with us. All the same, I'll ask him when he stops by here this morning. I've ordered some fine wine. Nora, you can't imagine how I'm looking forward to this evening.

Nora: So am I. And what fun for the children, Torvald!

Helmer: Ah, it's so gratifying to know that one's gotten a safe, secure job, and with a comfortable salary. It's a great satisfaction, isn't it?

Nora: Oh, it's wonderful!

Helmer: Remember last Christmas? Three whole weeks before, you shut yourself in every evening till long after midnight, making flowers for the Christmas tree, and all the other decorations to surprise us. Ugh, that was the dullest time I've ever lived through.

Nora: It wasn't at all dull for me.

Helmer (smiling): But the outcome *was* pretty sorry, Nora.

Nora: Oh, don't tease me with that again. How could I help it that the cat came in and tore everything to shreds.

Helmer: No, poor thing, you certainly couldn't. You wanted so much to please us all, and that's what counts. But it's just as well that the hard times are past.

Nora: Yes, it's really wonderful.

Helmer: Now I don't have to sit here alone, boring myself, and you don't have to tire your precious eyes and your fair little delicate hands—

Nora (clapping her hands): No, is it really true, Torvald, I don't have to? Oh, how wonderfully lovely to hear! (*Taking his arm.*) Now I'll tell you just how I've thought we should plan things. Right after Christmas—(*The doorbell rings.*) Oh, the bell. (*Straightening the room up a bit.*) Somebody would have to come. What a bore!

Helmer: I'm not home to visitors, don't forget.

Maid (from the hall doorway): Ma'am, a lady to see you—

Nora: All right, let her come in.

Maid (to Helmer): And the doctor's just come too.

Helmer: Did he go right to my study?

Maid: Yes, he did.

Helmer goes into his room. The Maid shows in Mrs. Linde, dressed in traveling clothes, and shuts the door after her.

Mrs. Linde (in a dispirited and somewhat hesitant voice): Hello, Nora.

Nora (uncertain): Hello —

Mrs. Linde: You don't recognize me.

Nora: No, I don't know — but wait, I think — (*Exclaiming.*) What! Kristine! Is it really you?

Mrs. Linde: Yes, it's me.

Nora: Kristine! To think I didn't recognize you. But then, how could I? (*More quietly.*) How you've changed, Kristine!

Mrs. Linde: Yes, no doubt I have. In nine — ten long years.

Nora: Is it so long since we met! Yes, it's all of that. Oh, these last eight years have been a happy time, believe me. And so now you've come in to town, too. Made the long trip in the winter. That took courage.

Mrs. Linde: I just got here by ship this morning.

Nora: To enjoy yourself over Christmas, of course. Oh, how lovely! Yes, enjoy ourselves, we'll do that. But take your coat off. You're not still cold? (*Helping her.*) There now, let's get cozy here by the stove. No, the easy chair there! I'll take the rocker here. (*Seizing her hands.*) Yes, now you have your old look again; it was only in that first moment. You're a bit more pale, Kristine — and maybe a bit thinner.

Mrs. Linde: And much, much older, Nora.

Nora: Yes, perhaps a bit older; a tiny, tiny bit; not much at all. (*Stopping short; suddenly serious.*) Oh, but thoughtless me, to sit here, chattering away. Sweet, good Kristine, can you forgive me?

Mrs. Linde: What do you mean, Nora?

Nora (softly): Poor Kristine, you've become a widow.

Mrs. Linde: Yes, three years ago.

Nora: Oh, I knew it, of course; I read it in the papers. Oh, Kristine, you must believe me; I often thought of writing you then, but I kept postponing it, and something always interfered.

Mrs. Linde: Nora dear, I understand completely.

Nora: No, it was awful of me, Kristine. You poor thing, how much you must have gone through. And he left you nothing?

Mrs. Linde: No.

Nora: And no children?

Mrs. Linde: No.

Nora: Nothing at all, then?

Mrs. Linde: Not even a sense of loss to feed on.

Nora (looking incredulously at her): But Kristine, how could that be?

Mrs. Linde (smiling wearily and smoothing her hair): Oh, sometimes it happens, Nora.

Nora: So completely alone. How terribly hard that must be for you. I have three lovely children. You can't see them now; they're out with the maid. But now you must tell me everything —

Mrs. Linde: No, no, no, tell me about yourself.

Nora: No, you begin. Today I don't want to be selfish. I want to think only of
you today. But there *is* something I must tell you. Did you hear of the
wonderful luck we had recently?

Mrs. Linde: No, what's that?

Nora: My husband's been made manager in the bank, just think!

Mrs. Linde: Your husband? How marvelous!

Nora: Isn't it? Being a lawyer is such an uncertain living, you know, especially
if one won't touch any cases that aren't clean and decent. And of course
Torvald would never do that, and I'm with him completely there. Oh, we're
simply delighted, believe me! He'll join the bank right after New Year's and
start getting a huge salary and lots of commissions. From now on we can
live quite differently — just as we want. Oh, Kristine, I feel so light and happy!
Won't it be lovely to have stacks of money and not a care in the world?

Mrs. Linde: Well, anyway, it would be lovely to have enough for necessities.

Nora: No, not just for necessities, but stacks and stacks of money!

Mrs. Linde (smiling): Nora, Nora, aren't you sensible yet? Back in school you
were such a free spender.

Nora (with a quiet laugh): Yes, that's what Torvald still says. (*Shaking her finger.*)
But "Nora, Nora" isn't as silly as you all think. Really, we've been in no
position for me to go squandering. We've had to work, both of us.

Mrs. Linde: You too?

Nora: Yes, at odd jobs — needlework, crocheting, embroidery, and such — (*Casually.*) and other things too. You remember that Torvald left the department
when we were married? There was no chance of promotion in his office,
and of course he needed to earn more money. But that first year he drove
himself terribly. He took on all kinds of extra work that kept him going
morning and night. It wore him down, and then he fell deathly ill. The
doctors said it was essential for him to travel south.

Mrs. Linde: Yes, didn't you spend a whole year in Italy?

Nora: That's right. It wasn't easy to get away, you know. Ivar had just been born.
But of course we had to go. Oh, that was a beautiful trip, and it saved
Torvald's life. But it cost a frightful sum, Kristine.

Mrs. Linde: I can well imagine.

Nora: Four thousand, eight hundred crowns it cost That's really a lot of money.

Mrs. Linde: But it's lucky you had it when you needed it.

Nora: Well, as it was, we got it from Papa.

Mrs. Linde: I see. It was just about the time your father died.

Nora: Yes, just about then. And, you know, I couldn't make that trip out to nurse
him. I had to stay here, expecting Ivar any moment, and with my poor sick
Torvald to care for. Dearest Papa, I never saw him again, Kristine. Oh, that
was the worst time I've known in all my marriage.

Mrs. Linde: I know how you loved him. And then you went off to Italy?

Nora: Yes. We had the means now, and the doctors urged us. So we left a month
after.

Mrs. Linde: And your husband came back completely cured?

Nora: Sound as a drum!

Mrs. Linde: But — the doctor?

Nora: Who?

Mrs. Linde: I thought the maid said he was a doctor, the man who came in with me.

Nora: Yes, that was Dr. Rank — but he's not making a sick call. He's our closest friend, and he stops by at least once a day. No, Torvald hasn't had a sick moment since, and the children are fit and strong, and I am, too. (*Jumping up and clapping her hands.*) Oh, dear God, Kristine, what a lovely thing to live and be happy! But how disgusting of me — I'm talking of nothing but my own affairs. (*Sits on a stool close by Kristine, arms resting across her knees.*) Oh, don't be angry with me! Tell me, is it really true that you weren't in love with your husband? Why did you marry him, then?

Mrs. Linde: My mother was still alive, but bedridden and helpless — and I had my two younger brothers to look after. In all conscience, I didn't think I could turn him down.

Nora: No, you were right there. But was he rich at the time?

Mrs. Linde: He was very well off, I'd say. But the business was shaky, Nora. When he died, it all fell apart, and nothing was left.

Nora: And then — ?

Mrs. Linde: Yes, so I had to scrape up a living with a little shop and a little teaching and whatever else I could find. The last three years have been like one endless workday without a rest for me. Now it's over, Nora. My poor mother doesn't need me, for she's passed on. Nor the boys, either; they're working now and can take care of themselves.

Nora: How free you must feel —

Mrs. Linde: No — only unspeakably empty. Nothing to live for now. (*Standing up anxiously.*) That's why I couldn't take it any longer out in that desolate hole. Maybe here it'll be easier to find something to do and keep my mind occupied. If I could only be lucky enough to get a steady job, some office work —

Nora: Oh, but Kristine, that's so dreadfully tiring, and you already look so tired. It would be much better for you if you could go off to a bathing resort.

Mrs. Linde (going toward the window): I have no father to give me travel money, Nora.

Nora (rising): Oh, don't be angry with me.

Mrs. Linde (going to her): Nora dear, don't you be angry with me. The worst of my kind of situation is all the bitterness that's stored away. No one to work for, and yet you're always having to snap up your opportunities. You have to live; and so you grow selfish. When you told me the happy change in your lot, do you know I was delighted less for your sakes than for mine?

Nora: How so? Oh, I see. You think maybe Torvald could do something for you.

Mrs. Linde: Yes, that's what I thought.

Nora: And he will, Kristine! Just leave it to me; I'll bring it up so delicately — find something attractive to humor him with. Oh, I'm so eager to help you.

Mrs. Linde: How very kind of you, Nora, to be so concerned over me — doubly kind, considering you really know so little of life's burdens yourself.

Nora: I — ? I know so little — ?

Mrs. Linde (smiling): Well, my heavens — a little needlework and such — Nora, you're just a child.

Nora (tossing her head and pacing the floor): You don't have to act so superior.

Mrs. Linde: Oh?

Nora: You're just like the others. You all think I'm incapable of anything serious —

Mrs. Linde: Come now —

Nora: That I've never had to face the raw world.

Mrs. Linde: Nora dear, you've just been telling me all your troubles.

Nora: Hm! Trivia! (*Quietly.*) I haven't told you the big thing.

Mrs. Linde: Big thing? What do you mean?

Nora: You look down on me so, Kristine, but you shouldn't. You're proud that you worked so long and hard for your mother.

Mrs. Linde: I don't look down on a soul. But it *is* true: I'm proud — and happy, too — to think it was given to me to make my mother's last days almost free of care.

Nora: And you're also proud thinking of what you've done for your brothers.

Mrs. Linde: I feel I've a right to be.

Nora: I agree. But listen to this, Kristine — I've also got something to be proud and happy for.

Mrs. Linde: I don't doubt it. But whatever do you mean?

Nora: Not so loud. What if Torvald heard! He mustn't, not for anything in the world. Nobody must know, Kristine. No one but you.

Mrs. Linde: But what is it, then?

Nora: Come here. (*Drawing her down beside her on the sofa.*) It's true — I've also got something to be proud and happy for. I'm the one who saved Torvald's life.

Mrs. Linde: Saved — ? Saved how?

Nora: I told you about the trip to Italy. Torvald never would have lived if he hadn't gone south —

Mrs. Linde: Of course; your father gave you the means —

Nora (smiling): That's what Torvald and all the rest think, but —

Mrs. Linde: But — ?

Nora: Papa didn't give us a pin. I was the one who raised the money.

Mrs. Linde: You? That whole amount?

Nora: Four thousand, eight hundred crowns. What do you say to that?

Mrs. Linde: But Nora, how was it possible? Did you win the lottery?

Nora (disdainfully): The lottery? Pooh! No art to that.

Mrs. Linde: But where did you get it from then?

Nora (humming, with a mysterious smile): Hmm, tra-la-la-la.

Mrs. Linde: Because you couldn't have borrowed it.

Nora: No? Why not?

Mrs. Linde: A wife can't borrow without her husband's consent.

Nora (tossing her head): Oh, but a wife with a little business sense, a wife who knows how to manage —

Mrs. Linde: Nora, I simply don't understand —

Nora: You don't have to. Whoever said I *borrowed* the money? I could have gotten it other ways. (*Throwing herself back on the sofa.*) I could have gotten it from some admirer or other. After all, a girl with my ravishing appeal —

Mrs. Linde: You lunatic.

Nora: I'll bet you're eaten up with curiosity, Kristine.

Mrs. Linde: Now listen here, Nora — you haven't done something indiscreet?

Nora (sitting up again): Is it indiscreet to save your husband's life?

Mrs. Linde: I think it's indiscreet that without his knowledge you —

Nora: But that's the point: he mustn't know! My Lord, can't you understand? He mustn't ever know the close call he had. It was to *me* the doctors came to say his life was in danger — that nothing could save him but a stay in the south. Didn't I try strategy then! I began talking about how lovely it would be for me to travel abroad like other young wives; I begged and I cried; I told him please to remember my condition, to be kind and indulge me; and then I dropped a hint that he could easily take out a loan. But at that, Kristine, he nearly exploded. He said I was frivolous, and it was his duty as man of the house not to indulge me in whims and fancies — as I think he called them. Aha, I thought, now you'll just have to be saved — and that's when I saw my chance.

Mrs. Linde: And your father never told Torvald the money wasn't from him?

Nora: No, never. Papa died right about then. I'd considered bringing him into my secret and begging him never to tell. But he was too sick at the time — and then, sadly, it didn't matter.

Mrs. Linde: And you've never confided in your husband since?

Nora: For heaven's sake, no! Are you serious? He's so strict on that subject. Besides — Torvald, with all his masculine pride — how painfully humiliating for him if he ever found out he was in debt to me. That would just ruin our relationship. Our beautiful, happy home would never be the same.

Mrs. Linde: Won't you ever tell him?

Nora (thoughtfully, half smiling): Yes — maybe sometime, years from now, when I'm no longer so attractive. Don't laugh! I only mean when Torvald loves me less than now, when he stops enjoying my dancing and dressing up and reciting for him. Then it might be wise to have something in reserve — (*Breaking off.*) How ridiculous! That'll never happen — Well, Kristine, what do you think of my big secret? I'm capable of something too, hm? You can imagine, of course, how this thing hangs over me. It really hasn't been easy meeting the payments on time. In the business world there's what they call quarterly interest and what they call amortization, and these are always so terribly hard to manage. I've had to skimp a little here and there, wherever I could, you know. I could hardly spare anything from my house allowance, because Torvald has to live well. I couldn't let the children go poorly dressed; whatever I got for them, I felt I had to use up completely — the darlings!

Mrs. Linde: Poor Nora, so it had to come out of your own budget, then?

Nora: Yes, of course. But I was the one most responsible, too. Every time Torvald gave me money for new clothes and such, I never used more than half; always bought the simplest, cheapest outfits. It was a godsend that everything looks so well on me that Torvald never noticed. But it did weigh me down at times, Kristine. It *is* such a joy to wear fine things. You understand.

Mrs. Linde: Oh, of course.

Nora: And then I found other ways of making money. Last winter I was lucky enough to get a lot of copying to do. I locked myself in and sat writing every evening till late in the night. Ah, I was tired so often, dead tired. But still it was wonderful fun, sitting and working like that, earning money. It was almost like being a man.

Mrs. Linde: But how much have you paid off this way so far?

Nora: That's hard to say, exactly. These accounts, you know, aren't easy to figure. I only know that I've paid out all I could scrape together. Time and again I haven't known where to turn (*Smiling.*) Then I'd sit here dreaming of a rich old gentleman who had fallen in love with me —

Mrs. Linde: What! Who is he?

Nora: Oh, really! And that he'd died, and when his will was opened, there in big letters it said, "All my fortune shall be paid over in cash, immediately, to that enchanting Mrs. Nora Helmer."

Mrs. Linde: But Nora dear — who *was* this gentleman?

Nora: Good grief, can't you understand? The old man never existed; that was only something I'd dream up time and again whenever I was at my wits' end for money. But it makes no difference now; the old fossil can go where he pleases for all I care; I don't need him or his will — because now I'm free. (*Jumping up.*) Oh, how lovely to think of that, Kristine! Carefree! To know you're carefree, utterly carefree; to be able to romp and play with the children, and to keep up a beautiful, charming home — everything just the way Torvald likes it! And think, spring is coming, with big blue skies. Maybe we can travel a little then. Maybe I'll see the ocean again. Oh yes, it *is* so marvelous to live and be happy!

The front doorbell rings.

Mrs. Linde (rising): There's the bell. It's probably best that I go.

Nora: No, stay. No one's expected. It must be for Torvald.

Maid (from the hall doorway): Excuse me, ma'am — there's a gentleman here to see Mr. Helmer, but I didn't know — since the doctor's with him —

Nora: Who is the gentleman?

Krogstad (from the doorway): It's me, Mrs. Helmer.

Mrs. Linde starts and turns away toward the window.

Nora (stepping toward him, tense, her voice a whisper): You? What is it? Why do you want to speak to my husband?

Krogstad: Bank business — after a fashion. I have a small job in the investment bank, and I hear now your husband is going to be our chief —

Nora: In other words, its —

Krogstad: Just dry business, Mrs. Helmer. Nothing but that.

Nora: Yes, then please be good enough to step into the study. (*She nods indifferently as she sees him out by the hall door, then returns and begins stirring up the stove.*)

Mrs. Linde: Nora — who was that man?

Nora: That was a Mr. Krogstad — a lawyer.

Mrs. Linde: Then it really was him.

Nora: Do you know that person?

Mrs. Linde: I did once — many years ago. For a time he was a law clerk in our town.

Nora: Yes, he's been that.

Mrs. Linde: How he's changed.

Nora: I understand he had a very unhappy marriage.

Mrs. Linde: He's a widower now.

Nora: With a number of children. There now, it's burning. (*She closes the stove door and moves the rocker a bit to one side.*)

Mrs. Linde: They say he has a hand in all kinds of business.

Nora: Oh? That may be true; I wouldn't know. But let's not think about business. It's so dull.

Dr. Rank enters from Helmer's study.

Rank (still in the doorway): No, no really — I don't want to intrude, I'd just as soon talk a little while with your wife. (*Shuts the door, then notices Mrs. Linde.*) Oh, beg pardon. I'm intruding here too.

Nora: No, not at all. (*Introducing him.*) Dr. Rank, Mrs. Linde.

Rank: Well now, that's a name much heard in this house. I believe I passed the lady on the stairs as I came.

Mrs. Linde: Yes, I take the stairs very slowly. They're rather hard on me.

Rank: Uh-hm, some touch of internal weakness?

Mrs. Linde: More overexertion, I'd say.

Rank: Nothing else? Then you're probably here in town to rest up in a round of parties?

Mrs. Linde: I'm here to look for work.

Rank: Is that the best cure for overexertion?

Mrs. Linde: One has to live, Doctor.

Rank: Yes, there's a common prejudice to that effect.

Nora: Oh, come on, Dr. Rank — you really do want to live yourself.

Rank: Yes, I really do. Wretched as I am, I'll gladly prolong my torment indefinitely. All my patients feel like that. And it's quite the same, too, with the morally sick. Right at this moment there's one of those moral invalids in there with Helmer —

Mrs. Linde (softly): Ah!

Nora: Who do you mean?

Rank: Oh, it's a lawyer, Krogstad, a type you wouldn't know. His character is rotten to the root — but even he began chattering all-importantly about how he had to *live.*

Nora: Oh? What did he want to talk to Torvald about?

Rank: I really don't know. I only heard something about the bank.

Nora: I didn't know that Krog — that this man Krogstad had anything to do with the bank.

Rank: Yes, he's gotten some kind of berth down there. (*To Mrs. Linde.*) I don't know if you also have, in your neck of the woods, a type of person who scuttles about breathlessly, sniffing out hints of moral corruption, and then maneuvers his victim into some sort of key position where he can keep an eye on him. It's the healthy these days that are out in the cold.

Mrs. Linde: All the same, it's the sick who most need to be taken in.

Rank (with a shrug): Yes, there we have it. That's the concept that's turning society into a sanatorium.

Nora, lost in her thoughts, breaks out into quiet laughter and claps her hands.

Rank: Why do you laugh at that? Do you have any real idea of what society is?

Nora: What do I care about dreary old society? I was laughing at something quite different — something terribly funny. Tell me, Doctor — is everyone who works in the bank dependent now on Torvald?

Rank: Is that what you find so terribly funny?

Nora (smiling and humming): Never mind, never mind! (*Pacing the floor.*) Yes, that's really immensely amusing: that we — that Torvald has so much power now over all those people. (*Taking the bag out of her pocket.*) Dr. Rank, a little macaroon on that?

Rank: See here, macaroons! I thought they were contraband here.

Nora: Yes, but these are some that Kristine gave me.

Mrs. Linde: What? I — ?

Nora: Now, now, don't be afraid. You couldn't possibly know that Torvald had forbidden them. You see, he's worried they'll ruin my teeth. But hmp! Just this once! Isn't that so, Dr. Rank? Help yourself! (*Puts a macaroon in his mouth.*) And you too, Kristine. And I'll also have one, only a little one — or two, at the most. (*Walking about again.*) Now I'm really tremendously happy. Now there's just one last thing in the world that I have an enormous desire to do.

Rank: Well! And what's that?

Nora: It's something I have such a consuming desire to say so Torvald could hear.

Rank: And why can't you say it?

Nora: I don't dare. It's quite shocking.

Mrs. Linde: Shocking?

Rank: Well, then it isn't advisable. But in front of us you certainly can. What do you have such a desire to say so Torvald could hear?

Nora: I have such a huge desire to say — to hell and be damned!

Rank: Are you crazy?

Mrs. Linde: My goodness, Nora!

Rank: Go on, say it. Here he is.

Nora (hiding the macaroon bag): Shh, shh, shh!

Helmer comes in from his study, hat in hand, overcoat over his arm.

Nora (going toward him): Well, Torvald dear, are you through with him?

Helmer: Yes, he just left.

Nora: Let me introduce you — this is Kristine, who's arrived here in town.

Helmer: Kristine — ? I'm sorry, but I don't know —

Nora: Mrs. Linde, Torvald dear. Mrs. Kristine Linde.

Helmer: Of course. A childhood friend of my wife's, no doubt?

Mrs. Linde: Yes, we knew each other in those days.

Nora: And just think, she made the long trip down here in order to talk with you.

Helmer: What's this?

Mrs. Linde: Well, not exactly —

Nora: You see, Kristine is remarkably clever in office work, and so she's terribly eager to come under a capable man's supervision and add more to what she already knows —

Helmer: Very wise, Mrs. Linde.

Nora: And then when she heard that you'd become a bank manager — the story was wired out to the papers — then she came in as fast as she could and — Really, Torvald, for my sake you can do a little something for Kristine, can't you?

Helmer: Yes, it's not at all impossible. Mrs. Linde, I suppose you're a widow?

Mrs. Linde: Yes.

Helmer: Any experience in office work?

Mrs. Linde: Yes, a good deal.

Helmer: Well, it's quite likely that I can make an opening for you —

Nora (clapping her hands): You see, you see!

Helmer: You've come at a lucky moment, Mrs. Linde.

Mrs. Linde: Oh, how can I thank you?

Helmer: Not necessary. (*Putting his overcoat on.*) But today you'll have to excuse me —

Rank: Wait, I'll go with you. (*He fetches his coat from the hall and warms it at the stove.*)

Nora: Don't stay out long, dear.

Helmer: An hour; no more.

Nora: Are you going too, Kristine?

Mrs. Linde (putting on her winter garments): Yes, I have to see about a room now.

Helmer: Then perhaps we can all walk together.

Nora (helping her): What a shame we're so cramped here, but it's quite impossible for us to —

Mrs. Linde: Oh, don't even think of it! Good-bye, Nora dear, and thanks for everything.

Nora: Good-bye for now. Of course you'll be back this evening. And you too, Dr. Rank. What? If you're well enough? Oh, you've got to be! Wrap up tight now.

In a ripple of small talk the company moves out into the hall; children's voices are heard outside on the steps.

Nora: There they are! There they are! (*She runs to open the door. The children come in with their nurse, Anne-Marie.*) Come in, come in! (*Bends down and kisses them.*) Oh, you darlings — ! Look at them, Kristine. Aren't they lovely!

Rank: No loitering in the draft here.

Helmer: Come, Mrs. Linde — this place is unbearable now for anyone but mothers.

Dr. Rank, Helmer, and Mrs. Linde go down the stairs. Anne-Marie goes into the living room with the children. Nora follows, after closing the hall door.

Nora: How fresh and strong you look. Oh, such red cheeks you have! Like apples and roses. (*The children interrupt her throughout the following.*) And it was so much fun? That's wonderful. Really? You pulled both Emmy and Bob on the sled? Imagine, all together! Yes, you're a clever boy, Ivar. Oh, let me hold her a bit, Anne-Marie. My sweet little doll baby! (*Takes the smallest from the nurse and dances with her.*) Yes, yes, Mama will dance with Bob as well. What? Did you throw snowballs? Oh, if I'd only been there! No, don't bother, Anne-Marie — I'll undress them myself. Oh yes, let me. It's such fun. Go in and rest; you look half frozen. There's hot coffee waiting for you on the stove. (*The nurse goes into the room to the left. Nora takes the children's winter things off, throwing them about, while the children talk to her all at once.*) Is that so? A big dog chased you? But it didn't bite? No, dogs never bite little, lovely doll babies. Don't peek in the packages, Ivar! What is it? Yes, wouldn't you like to know. No, no, it's an ugly something. Well? Shall we play? What shall we play? Hide-and-seek? Yes, let's play hide-and-seek. Bob must hide first. I must? Yes, let me hide first. (*Laughing and shouting, she and the children play in and out of the living room and the adjoining room to the right. At last Nora hides under the table. The children come storming in, search, but cannot find her, then hear her muffled laughter, dash over to the table, lift the cloth up and find her. Wild shouting. She creeps forward as if to scare them. More shouts. Meanwhile, a knock at the hall door; no one has noticed it. Now the door half opens, and Krogstad appears. He waits a moment; the game goes on.*)

Krogstad: Beg pardon, Mrs. Helmer —

Nora (with a strangled cry, turning and scrambling to her knees: Oh! What do you want?

Krogstad: Excuse me. The outer door was ajar; it must be someone forgot to shut it —

Nora (rising): My husband isn't home, Mr. Krogstad.

Krogstad: I know that.

Nora: Yes — then what do you want here?

Krogstad: A word with you.

Nora: With — ? (*To the children, quietly.*) Go in to Anne-Marie. What? No, the strange man won't hurt Mama. When he's gone, we'll play some more. (*She leads the children into the room to the left and shuts the door after them. Then, tense and nervous:*) You want to speak to me?

Krogstad: Yes, I want to.

Nora: Today? But it's not yet the first of the month —

Krogstad: No, it's Christmas Eve. It's going to be up to you how merry a Christmas you have.

Nora: What is it you want? Today I absolutely can't —

Krogstad: We won't talk about that till later. This is something else. You do have a moment to spare, I suppose?

Nora: Oh yes, of course — I do, except —

Krogstad: Good. I was sitting over at Olsen's Restaurant when I saw your husband go down the street —

Nora: Yes?

Krogstad: With a lady.

Nora: Yes. So?

Krogstad: If you'll pardon my asking: wasn't that lady a Mrs. Linde?

Nora: Yes.

Krogstad: Just now come into town?

Nora: Yes, today.

Krogstad: She's a good friend of yours?

Nora: Yes, she is. But I don't see —

Krogstad: I also knew her once.

Nora: I'm aware of that.

Krogstad: Oh? You know all about it. I thought so. Well, then let me ask you short and sweet: is Mrs. Linde getting a job in the bank?

Nora: What makes you think you can cross-examine me, Mr. Krogstad — you, one of my husband's employees? But since you ask, you might as well know — yes, Mrs. Linde's going to be taken on at the bank. And I'm the one who spoke for her, Mr. Krogstad. Now you know.

Krogstad: So I guessed right.

Nora (pacing up and down): Oh, one does have a tiny bit of influence, I should hope. Just because I am a woman, don't think it means that — When one has a subordinate position, Mr. Krogstad, one really ought to be careful about pushing somebody who — hm —

Krogstad: Who has influence?

Nora: That's right.

Krogstad (in a different tone): Mrs. Helmer, would you be good enough to use your influence on my behalf?

Nora: What? What do you mean?

Krogstad: Would you please make sure that I keep my subordinate position in the bank?

Nora: What does that mean? Who's thinking of taking away your position?

Krogstad: Oh, don't play the innocent with me. I'm quite aware that your friend would hardly relish the chance of running into me again; and I'm also aware now whom I can thank for being turned out.

Nora: But I promise you —

Krogstad: Yes, yes, yes, to the point: there's still time, and I'm advising you to use your influence to prevent it.

Nora: But Mr. Krogstad, I have absolutely no influence.

Krogstad: You haven't? I thought you were just saying —

Nora: You shouldn't take me so literally. I! How can you believe that I have any such influence over my husband?

Krogstad: Oh, I've known your husband from our student days. I don't think the great bank manager's more steadfast than any other married man.

Nora: You speak insolently about my husband, and I'll show you the door.

Krogstad: The lady has spirit.

Nora: I'm not afraid of you any longer. After New Year's, I'll soon be done with the whole business.

Krogstad (restraining himself): Now listen to me, Mrs. Helmer. If necessary, I'll fight for my little job in the bank as if it were life itself.

Nora: Yes, so it seems.

Krogstad: It's not just a matter of income; that's the least of it. It's something else — All right, out with it! Look, this is the thing. You know, just like all the others, of course, that once, a good many years ago, I did something rather rash.

Nora: I've heard rumors to that effect.

Krogstad: The case never got into court; but all the same, every door was closed in my face from then on. So I took up those various activities you know about. I had to grab hold somewhere; and I dare say I haven't been among the worst. But now I want to drop all that. My boys are growing up. For their sakes, I'll have to win back as much respect as possible here in town. That job in the bank was like the first rung in my ladder. And now your husband wants to kick me right back down in the mud again.

Nora: But for heaven's sake, Mr. Krogstad, it's simply not in my power to help you.

Krogstad: That's because you haven't the will to — but I have the means to make you.

Nora: You certainly won't tell my husband that I owe you money?

Krogstad: Hm — what if I told him that?

Nora: That would be shameful of you. (*Nearly in tears.*) This secret — my joy and my pride — that he should learn it in such a crude and disgusting way — learn it from you. You'd expose me to the most horrible unpleasantness —

Krogstad: Only unpleasantness?

Nora (vehemently): But go on and try. It'll turn out the worse for you, because then my husband will really see what a crook you are, and then you'll *never* be able to hold your job.

Krogstad: I asked if it was just domestic unpleasantness you were afraid of?

Nora: If my husband finds out, then of course he'll pay what I owe at once, and then we'd be through with you for good.

Krogstad (a step closer): Listen, Mrs. Helmer — you've either got a very bad memory, or else no head at all for business. I'd better put you a little more in touch with the facts.

Nora: What do you mean?

Krogstad: When your husband was sick, you came to me for a loan of four thousand, eight hundred crowns.

Nora: Where else could I go?

Krogstad: I promised to get you that sum —

Nora: And you got it.

Krogstad: I promised to get you that sum, on certain conditions. You were so involved in your husband's illness, and so eager to finance your trip, that I guess you didn't think out all the details. It might just be a good idea to remind you. I promised you the money on the strength of a note I drew up.

Nora: Yes, and that I signed.

Krogstad: Right. But at the bottom I added some lines for your father to guarantee the loan. He was supposed to sign down there.

Nora: Supposed to? He did sign.

Krogstad: I left the date blank. In other words, your father would have dated his signature himself. Do you remember that?

Nora: Yes, I think —

Krogstad: Then I gave you the note for you to mail to your father. Isn't that so?

Nora: Yes.

Krogstad: And naturally you sent it at once — because only some five, six days later you brought me the note, properly signed. And with that, the money was yours.

Nora: Well, then; I've made my payments regularly, haven't I?

Krogstad: More or less. But — getting back to the point — those were hard times for you then, Mrs. Helmer.

Nora: Yes, they were.

Krogstad: Your father was very ill, I believe.

Nora: He was near the end.

Krogstad: He died soon after?

Nora: Yes.

Krogstad: Tell me, Mrs. Helmer, do you happen to recall the date of your father's death? The day of the month, I mean.

Nora: Papa died the twenty-ninth of September.

Krogstad: That's quite correct; I've already looked into that. And now we come to a curious thing — (*Taking out a paper.*) which I simply cannot comprehend.

Nora: Curious thing? I don't know —

Krogstad: This is the curious thing: that your father co-signed the note for your loan three days after his death.

Nora: How — ? I don't understand.

Krogstad: Your father died the twenty-ninth of September. But look. Here your father dated his signature October second. Isn't that curious, Mrs. Helmer? (*Nora is silent.*) Can you explain it to me? (*Nora remains silent.*) It's also remarkable that the words "October second" and the year aren't written in your father's hand, but rather in one that I think I know. Well, it's easy to understand. Your father forgot perhaps to date his signature, and then someone or other added it, a bit sloppily, before anyone knew of his death. There's nothing wrong in that. It all comes down to the signature. And there's no question about *that,* Mrs. Helmer. It really *was* your father who signed his own name here, wasn't it?

Nora (after a short silence, throwing her head back and looking squarely at him): No, it wasn't. *I* signed Papa's name.

Krogstad: Wait, now — are you fully aware that this is a dangerous confession?

Nora: Why? You'll soon get your money.

Krogstad: Let me ask you a question — why didn't you send the paper to your father?

Nora: That was impossible. Papa was so sick. If I'd asked him for his signature, I also would have had to tell him what the money was for. But I couldn't tell him, sick as he was, that my husband's life was in danger. That was just impossible.

Krogstad: Then it would have been better if you'd given up the trip abroad.

Nora: I couldn't possibly. The trip was to save my husband's life. I couldn't give that up.

Krogstad: But didn't you ever consider that this was a fraud against me?

Nora: I couldn't let myself be bothered by that. You weren't any concern of mine. I couldn't stand you, with all those cold complications you made, even though you knew how badly off my husband was.

Krogstad: Mrs. Helmer, obviously you haven't the vaguest idea of what you've involved yourself in. But I can tell you this: it was nothing more and nothing worse that I once did — and it wrecked my whole reputation.

Nora: You? Do you expect me to believe that you ever acted bravely to save your wife's life?

Krogstad: Laws don't inquire into motives.

Nora: Then they must be very poor laws.

Krogstad: Poor or not — if I introduce this paper in court, you'll be judged according to law.

Nora: This I refuse to believe. A daughter hasn't a right to protect her dying father from anxiety and care? A wife hasn't a right to save her husband's life? I don't know much about laws, but I'm sure that somewhere in the books these things are allowed. And you don't know anything about it — you who practice the law? You must be an awful lawyer, Mr. Krogstad.

Krogstad: Could be. But business — the kind of business we two are mixed up in — don't you think I know about that? All right. Do what you want now. But I'm telling you *this*: if I get shoved down a second time, you're going to keep me company. (*He bows and goes out through the hall.*)

Nora (pensive for a moment, then tossing her head): Oh, really! Trying to frighten me! I'm not so silly as all that. (*Begins gathering up the children's clothes, but soon stops.*) But — ? No, but that's impossible! I did it out of love.

The Children (in the doorway, left): Mama, that strange man's gone out the door.

Nora: Yes, yes, I know it. But don't tell anyone about the strange man. Do you hear? Not even Papa!

The Children: No, Mama. But now will you play again?

Nora: No, not now.

The Children: Oh, but Mama, you promised.

Nora: Yes, but I can't now. Go inside; I have too much to do. Go in, go in, my sweet darlings. (*She herds them gently back in the room and shuts the door after them. Settling on the sofa, she takes up a piece of embroidery and makes some stitches, but soon stops abruptly.*) No! (*Throws the work aside, rises, goes to the hall door and calls out.*) Helene! Let me have the tree in here. (*Goes to the table, left, opens the table drawer, and stops again.*) No, but that's utterly impossible!

Maid (with the Christmas tree): Where should I put it, ma'am?

Nora: There. The middle of the floor.

Maid: Should I bring anything else?

Nora: No, thanks. I have what I need.

The Maid, who has set the tree down, goes out.

Nora (absorbed in trimming the tree): Candles here — and flowers here. That terrible creature! Talk, talk, talk! There's nothing to it at all. The tree's going to be lovely. I'll do anything to please you, Torvald. I'll sing for you, dance for you —

Helmer comes in from the hall, with a sheaf of papers under his arm.

Nora: Oh! You're back so soon?

Helmer: Yes, Has anyone been here?

Nora: Here? No.

Helmer: That's odd. I saw Krogstad leaving the front door.

Nora: So? Oh yes, that's true. Krogstad was here a moment.

Helmer: Nora, I can see by your face that he's been here, begging you to put in a good word for him.

Nora: Yes.

Helmer: And it was supposed to seem like your own idea? You were to hide it from me that he'd been here. He asked you that, too, didn't he?

Nora: Yes, Torvald, but —

Helmer: Nora, Nora, and you could fall for that? Talk with that sort of person and promise him anything? And then in the bargain, tell me an untruth.

Nora: An untruth — ?

Helmer: Didn't you say that no one had been here? (*Wagging his finger.*) My little songbird must never do that again. A songbird needs a clean beak to warble with. No false notes. (*Putting his arm about her waist.*) That's the way it should be, isn't it? Yes, I'm sure of it. (*Releasing her.*) And so, enough of that. (*Sitting by the stove.*) Ah, how snug and cozy it is here. (*Leafing among his papers.*)

Nora (busy with the tree, after a short pause): Torvald!

Helmer: Yes.

Nora: I'm so much looking forward to the Stenborgs' costume party, day after tomorrow.

Helmer: And I can't wait to see what you'll surprise me with.

Nora: Oh, that stupid business!

Helmer: What?

Nora: I can't find anything that's right. Everything seems so ridiculous, so inane.

Helmer: So my little Nora's come to *that* recognition?

Nora (going behind his chair, her arms resting on its back): Are you very busy, Torvald?

Helmer: Oh —

Nora: What papers are those?

Helmer: Bank matters.

Nora: Already?

Helmer: I've gotten full authority from the retiring management to make all necessary changes in personnel and procedure. I'll need Christmas week for that. I want to have everything in order by New Year's.

Nora: So that was the reason this poor Krogstad —

Helmer: Hm.

Nora (still leaning on the chair and slowly stroking the nape of his neck): If you weren't so very busy, I would have asked you an enormous favor, Torvald.

Helmer: Let's hear. What is it?

Nora: You know, there isn't anyone who has your good taste — and I want so much to look well at the costume party. Torvald, couldn't you take over and decide what I should be and plan my costume?

Helmer: Ah, is my stubborn little creature calling for a lifeguard?

Nora: Yes, Torvald, I can't get anywhere without your help.

Helmer: All right — I'll think it over. We'll hit on something.

Nora: Oh, how sweet of you. (*Goes to the tree again. Pause.*) Aren't the red flowers pretty — ? But tell me, was it really such a crime that this Krogstad committed?

Helmer: Forgery. Do you have any idea what that means?

Nora: Couldn't he have done it out of need?

Helmer: Yes, or thoughtlessness, like so many others. I'm not so heartless that I'd condemn a man categorically for just one mistake.

Nora: No, of course not, Torvald!

Helmer: Plenty of men have redeemed themselves by openly confessing their crimes and taking their punishment.

Nora: Punishment — ?

Helmer: But now Krogstad didn't go that way. He got himself out by sharp practices, and that's the real cause of his moral breakdown.

Nora: Do you really think that would — ?

Helmer: Just imagine how a man with that sort of guilt in him has to lie and cheat and deceive on all sides, has to wear a mask even with the nearest and dearest he has, even with his own wife and children. And with the children, Nora — that's where it's most horrible.

Nora: Why?

Helmer: Because that kind of atmosphere of lies infects the whole life of a home. Every breath the children take in is filled with the germs of something degenerate.

Nora (coming closer behind him): Are you sure of that?

Helmer: Oh, I've seen it often enough as a lawyer. Almost everyone who goes bad early in life has a mother who's a chronic liar.

Nora: Why just — the mother?

Helmer: It's usually the mother's influence that's dominant, but the father's works in the same way, of course. Every lawyer is quite familiar with it. And still this Krogstad's been going home year in, year out, poisoning his own children with lies and pretense; that's why I call him morally lost. (*Reaching his hands out toward her.*) So my sweet little Nora must promise me never to plead his cause. Your hand on it. Come, come, what's this? Give me your hand. There, now. All settled. I can tell you it'd be impossible for me to work alongside of him. I literally ~~fell~~ *feel* physically revolted when I'm anywhere near such a person.

Nora (withdraws her hand and goes to the other side of the Christmas tree): How hot it is here! And I've got so much to do.

Helmer (getting up and gathering his papers): Yes, and I have to think about getting some of these read through before dinner. I'll think about your costume, too. And something to hang on the tree in gilt paper, I may even see about that. (*Putting his hand on her head.*) Oh you, my darling little songbird. (*He goes into his study and closes the door after him.*)

Nora (softly, after a silence): Oh, really! it isn't so. It's impossible. It must be impossible.

Anne-Marie (in the doorway, left): The children are begging so hard to come in to Mama.

Nora: No, no, no, don't let them in to me! You stay with them, Anne-Marie.

Anne-Marie: Of course, ma'am. (*Closes the door.*)

Nora (pale with terror): Hurt my children — ! Poison my home? (*A moment's pause; then she tosses her head.*) That's not true. Never. Never in all the world.

ACT II

Same room. Beside the piano the Christmas tree now stands stripped of ornament, burned-down candle stubs on its ragged branches. Nora's street clothes lie on the sofa. Nora, alone in the room, moves restlessly about; at last she stops at the sofa and picks up her coat.

Nora (dropping the coat again): Someone's coming! (*Goes toward the door, listens.*) No — there's no one. Of course — nobody's coming today, Christmas Day — or tomorrow, either. But maybe — (*Opens the door and looks out.*) No, nothing in the mailbox. Quite empty. (*Coming forward.*) What nonsense! He won't do anything serious. Nothing terrible could happen. It's impossible. Why, I have three small children.

Anne-Marie, with a large carton, comes in from the room to the left.

Anne-Marie: Well, at last I found the box with the masquerade clothes.
Nora: Thanks. Put it on the table.
Anne-Marie (does so): But they're all pretty much of a mess.
Nora: Ahh! I'd love to rip them in a million pieces!
Anne-Marie: Oh, mercy, they can be fixed right up. Just a little patience.
Nora: Yes, I'll go get Mrs. Linde to help me.
Anne-Marie: Out again now? In this nasty weather? Miss Nora will catch cold — get sick.
Nora: Oh, worse things could happen. How are the children?
Anne-Marie: The poor mites are playing with their Christmas presents, but —
Nora: Do they ask for me much?
Anne-Marie: They're so used to having Mama around, you know.
Nora: Yes, but Anne-Marie, I *can't* be together with them as much as I was.
Anne-Marie: Well, small children get used to anything.
Nora: You think so? Do you think they'd forget their mother if she was gone for good?
Anne-Marie: Oh, mercy — gone for good!
Nora: Wait, tell me, Anne-Marie — I've wondered so often — how could you ever have the heart to give your child over to strangers?
Anne-Marie: But I had to, you know, to become little Nora's nurse.
Nora: Yes, but how could you *do* it?
Anne-Marie: When I could get such a good place? A girl who's poor and who's gotten in trouble is glad enough for that. Because that slippery fish, he didn't do a thing for me, you know.
Nora: But your daughter's surely forgotten you.
Anne-Marie: Oh, she certainly has not. She's written to me, both when she was confirmed and when she was married.
Nora (clasping her about the neck): You old Anne-Marie, you were a good mother for me when I was little.
Anne-Marie: Poor little Nora, with no other mother but me.
Nora: And if the babies didn't have one, then I know that you'd — What silly talk! (*Opening the carton.*) Go in to them. Now I'll have to — Tomorrow you can see how lovely I'll look.

Anne-Marie: Oh, there won't be anyone at the party as lovely as Miss Nora. (*She goes off into the room, left.*)

Nora (begins unpacking the box, but soon throws it aside): Oh, if I dared to go out. If only nobody would come. If only nothing would happen here while I'm out. What craziness — nobody's coming. Just don't think. This muff — needs a brushing. Beautiful gloves, beautiful gloves. Let it go. Let it go! One, two, three, four, five, six — (*With a cry.*) Oh, there they are! (*Poises to move toward the door, but remains irresolutely standing. Mrs. Linde enters from the hall, where she has removed her street clothes.*)

Nora: Oh, it's you, Kristine. There's no one else out there? How good that you've come.

Mrs. Linde: I hear you were up asking for me.

Nora: Yes, I just stopped by. There's something you really can help me with. Let's get settled on the sofa. Look, there's going to be a costume party tomorrow evening at the Stenborgs' right above us, and now Torvald wants me to go as a Neapolitan peasant girl and dance the tarantella that I learned in Capri.

Mrs. Linde: Really, are you giving a whole performance?

Nora: Torvald says yes, I should. See, here's the dress. Torvald had it made for me down there; but now it's all so tattered that I just don't know —

Mrs. Linde: Oh, we'll fix that up in no time. It's nothing more than the trimmings — they're a bit loose here and there. Needle and thread? Good, now we have what we need.

Nora: Oh, how sweet of you!

Mrs. Linde (sewing): So you'll be in disguise tomorrow, Nora. You know what? I'll stop by then for a moment and have a look at you all dressed up. But listen, I've absolutely forgotten to thank you for that pleasant evening yesterday.

Nora (getting up and walking about): I don't think it was as pleasant as usual yesterday. You should have come to town a bit sooner, Kristine — Yes, Torvald really knows how to give a home elegance and charm.

Mrs. Linde: And you do, too, if you ask me. You're not your father's daughter for nothing. But tell me, is Dr. Rank always so down in the mouth as yesterday?

Nora: No, that was quite an exception. But he goes around critically ill all the time — tuberculosis of the spine, poor man. You know, his father was a disgusting thing who kept mistresses and so on — and that's why the son's been sickly from birth.

Mrs. Linde (lets her sewing fall to her lap): But my dearest Nora, how do you know about such things?

Nora (walking more jauntily): Hmp! When you've had three children, then you've had a few visits from — from women who know something of medicine, and they tell you this and that.

Mrs. Linde (resumes sewing; a short pause): Does Dr. Rank come here every day?

Nora: Every blessed day. He's Torvald's best friend from childhood, and *my* good friend, too. Dr. Rank almost belongs to this house.

Mrs. Linde: But tell me — is he quite sincere? I mean, doesn't he rather enjoy flattering people?

Nora: Just the opposite. Why do you think that?

Mrs. Linde: When you introduced us yesterday, he was proclaiming that he'd often heard my name in this house; but later I noticed that your husband hadn't the slightest idea who I really was. So how could Dr. Rank — ?

Nora: But it's all true, Kristine. You see, Torvald loves me beyond words, and, as he puts it, he'd like to keep me all to himself. For a long time he'd almost be jealous if I even mentioned any of my old friends back home. So of course I dropped that. But with Dr. Rank I talk a lot about such things, because he likes hearing about them.

Mrs. Linde: Now listen, Nora; in many ways you're still like a child. I'm a good deal older than you, with a little more experience. I'll tell you something: you ought to put an end to all this with Dr. Rank.

Nora: What should I put an end to?

Mrs. Linde: Both parts of it, I think. Yesterday you said something about a rich admirer who'd provide you with money —

Nora: Yes, one who doesn't exist — worse luck. So?

Mrs. Linde: Is Dr. Rank well off?

Nora: Yes, he is.

Mrs. Linde: With no dependents?

Nora: No, no one. But —

Mrs. Linde: And he's over here every day?

Nora: Yes, I told you that.

Mrs. Linde: How can a man of such refinement be so grasping?

Nora: I don't follow you at all.

Mrs. Linde: Now don't try to hide it, Nora. You think I can't guess who loaned you the forty-eight hundred crowns?

Nora: Are you out of your mind? How could you think such a thing! A friend of ours, who comes here every single day. What an intolerable situation that would have been!

Mrs. Linde: Then it really wasn't him.

Nora: No, absolutely not. It never even crossed my mind for a moment — And he had nothing to lend in those days; his inheritance came later.

Mrs. Linde: Well, I think that was a stroke of luck for you, Nora dear.

Nora: No, it never would have occurred to me to ask Dr. Rank — Still, I'm quite sure that if I had asked him —

Mrs. Linde: Which you won't, of course.

Nora: No, of course not. I can't see that I'd ever need to. But I'm quite positive that if I talked to Dr. Rank —

Mrs. Linde: Behind your husband's back?

Nora: I've got to clear up this other thing; *that's* also behind his back. I've *got* to clear it all up.

Mrs. Linde: Yes, I was saying that yesterday, but —

Nora (pacing up and down): A man handles these problems so much better than a woman —

Mrs. Linde: One's husband does, yes.

Nora: Nonsense. (*Stopping.*) When you pay everything you owe, then you get your note back, right?

Mrs. Linde: Yes, naturally.

Nora: And can rip it into a million pieces and burn it up — that filthy scrap of paper!

Mrs. Linde (looking hard at her, laying her sewing aside, and rising slowly): Nora, you're hiding something from me.

Nora: You can see it in my face?

Mrs. Linde: Something's happened to you since yesterday morning. Nora, what is it?

Nora (hurrying toward her): Kristine! (*Listening.*) Shh! Torvald's home. Look, go in with the children a while. Torvald can't bear all this snipping and stitching. Let Anne-Marie help you.

Mrs. Linde (gathering up some of the things): All right, but I'm not leaving here until we've talked this out. (*She disappears into the room, left, as Torvald enters from the hall.*)

Nora: Oh, how I've been waiting for you, Torvald dear.

Helmer: Was that the dressmaker?

Nora: No, that was Kristine. She's helping me fix up my costume. You know, it's going to be quite attractive.

Helmer: Yes, wasn't that a bright idea I had?

Nora: Brilliant! But then wasn't I good as well to give in to you?

Helmer: Good — because you give in to your husband's judgment? All right, you little goose, I know you didn't mean it like that. But I won't disturb you. You'll want to have a fitting, I suppose.

Nora: And you'll be working?

Helmer: Yes. (*Indicating a bundle of papers.*) See. I've been down to the bank. (*Starts toward his study.*)

Nora: Torvald.

Helmer (stops): Yes.

Nora: If your little squirrel begged you, with all her heart and soul, for something — ?

Helmer: What's that?

Nora: Then would you do it?

Helmer: First, naturally, I'd have to know what it was.

Nora: Your squirrel would scamper about and do tricks, if you'd only be sweet and give in.

Helmer: Out with it.

Nora: Your lark would be singing high and low in every room —

Helmer: Come on, she does that anyway.

Nora: I'd be a wood nymph and dance for you in the moonlight.

Helmer: Nora — don't tell me it's that same business from this morning?

Nora (coming closer): Yes, Torvald, I beg you, please!

Helmer: And you actually have the nerve to drag that up again?

Nora: Yes, yes, you've got to give in to me; you *have* to let Krogstad keep his job in the bank.

Helmer: My dear Nora, I've slated his job for Mrs. Linde.

Nora: That's awfully kind of you. But you could just fire another clerk instead of Krogstad.

Helmer: This is the most incredible stubbornness! Because you go and give an impulsive promise to speak up for him, I'm expected to —

Nora: That's not the reason, Torvald. It's for your own sake. That man does writing for the worst papers; you said it yourself. He could do you any amount of harm. I'm scared to death of him —

Helmer: Ah, I understand. It's the old memories haunting you.

Nora: What do you mean by that?

Helmer: Of course, you're thinking about your father.

Nora: Yes, all right. Just remember how those nasty gossips wrote in the papers about Papa and slandered him so cruelly. I think they'd have had him dismissed if the department hadn't sent you up to investigate, and if you hadn't been so kind and open-minded toward him.

Helmer: My dear Nora, there's a notable difference between your father and me. Your father's official career was hardly above reproach. But mine is; and I hope it'll stay that way as long as I hold my position.

Nora: Oh, who can ever tell what vicious minds can invent? We could be so snug and happy now in our quiet, carefree home — you and I and the children, Torvald! That's why I'm pleading with you so —

Helmer: And just by pleading for him you make it impossible for me to keep him on. It's already known at the bank that I'm firing Krogstad. What if it's rumored around now that the new bank manager was vetoed by his wife —

Nora: Yes, what then — ?

Helmer: Oh yes — as long as our little bundle of stubbornness gets her way — ! I should go and make myself ridiculous in front of the whole office — give people the idea I can be swayed by all kinds of outside pressure. Oh, you can bet I'd feel the effects of that soon enough! Besides — there's something that rules Krogstad right out at the bank as long as I'm the manager.

Nora: What's that?

Helmer: His moral failings I could maybe overlook if I had to —

Nora: Yes, Torvald, why not?

Helmer: And I hear he's quite efficient on the job. But he was a crony of mine back in my teens — one of those rash friendships that crop up again and again to embarrass you later in life. Well, I might as well say it straight out: we're on a first-name basis. And that tactless fool makes no effort at all to hide it in front of others. Quite the contrary — he thinks that entitles him to take a familiar air around me, and so every other second he comes booming out with his "Yes, Torvald!" and "Sure thing, Torvald!" I tell you, it's been excruciating for me. He's out to make my place in the bank un-bearable.

Nora: Torvald, you can't be serious about all this.

Helmer: Oh no? Why not?

Nora: Because these are such petty considerations.

Helmer: What are saying? Petty? You think I'm petty!

Nora: No, just the opposite, Torvald dear. That's exactly why —

Helmer: Never mind. You call my motives petty; then I might as well be just that. Petty! All right! We'll put a stop to this for good. (*Goes to the hall door and calls.*) Helene!

Nora: What do you want?

Helmer (searching among his papers): A decision. (*The maid comes in.*) Look here; take this letter; go out with it at once. Get hold of a messenger and have him deliver it. Quick now. It's already addressed. Wait, here's some money.

Maid: Yes, sir. (*She leaves with the letter.*)

Helmer (straightening his papers): There, now, little Miss Willful.

Nora (breathlessly): Torvald, what was that letter?

Helmer: Krogstad's notice.

Nora: Call it back, Torvald! There's still time. Oh, Torvald, call it back! Do it for my sake — for your sake, for the children's sake! Do you hear, Torvald; do it! You don't know how this can harm us.

Helmer: Too late.

Nora: Yes, too late.

Helmer: Nora dear, I can forgive you this panic, even though basically you're insulting me. Yes, you are! Or isn't it an insult to think that *I* should be afraid of a courtroom hack's revenge? But I forgive you anyway, because this shows so beautifully how much you love me. (*Takes her in his arms.*) This is the way it should be, my darling Nora. Whatever comes, you'll see; when it really counts, I have strength and courage enough as a man to take on the whole weight myself.

Nora (terrified): What do you mean by that?

Helmer: The whole weight, I said.

Nora (resolutely): No, never in all the world.

Helmer: Good. So we'll share it, Nora, as man and wife. That's as it should be. (*Fondling her.*) Are you happy now? There, there, there — not these frightened dove's eyes. It's nothing at all but empty fantasies — Now you should run through your tarantella and practice your tambourine. I'll go to the inner office and shut both doors, so I won't hear a thing; you can make all the noise you like. (*Turning in the doorway.*) And when Rank comes, just tell him where he can find me. (*He nods to her and goes with his papers into the study, closing the door.*)

Nora (standing as though rooted, dazed with fright, in a whisper): He really could do it. He will do it. He'll do it in spite of everything. No, not that, never, never! Anything but that! Escape! A way out — (*The doorbell rings.*) Dr. Rank! Anything but that! *Anything,* whatever it is! (*Her hands pass over her face, smoothing it; she pulls herself together, goes over and opens the hall door. Dr. Rank stands outside, hanging his fur coat up. During the following scene, it begins getting dark.*)

Nora: Hello, Dr. Rank. I recognized your ring. But you mustn't go in to Torvald yet; I believe he's working.

Rank: And you?

Nora: For you, I always have an hour to spare — you know that. (*He has entered, and she shuts the door after him.*)

Rank: Many thanks. I'll make use of these hours while I can.

Nora: What do you mean by that? While you can?

Rank: Does that disturb you?

Nora: Well, it's such an odd phrase. Is anything going to happen?

Rank: What's going to happen is what I've been expecting so long — but I honestly didn't think it would come so soon.

Nora (gripping his arm): What is it you've found out? Dr. Rank, you have to tell me!

Rank (sitting by the stove): It's all over for me. There's nothing to be done about it.

Nora (breathing easier): Is it you — then — ?

Rank: Who else? There's no point in lying to one's self. I'm the most miserable of all my patients, Mrs. Helmer. These past few days I've been auditing my internal accounts. Bankrupt! Within a month I'll probably be laid out and rotting in the churchyard.

Nora: Oh, what a horrible thing to say.

Rank: The thing itself is horrible. But the worst of it is all the other horror before it's over. There's only one final examination left; when I'm finished with that, I'll know about when my disintegration will begin. There's something I want to say. Helmer with his sensitivity has such a sharp distaste for anything ugly. I don't want him near my sickroom.

Nora: Oh, but Dr. Rank —

Rank: I won't have him in there. Under no condition. I'll lock my door to him — As soon as I'm completely sure of the worst, I'll send you my calling card marked with a black cross, and you'll know then the wreck has started to come apart.

Nora: No, today you're completely unreasonable. And I wanted you so much to be in a really good humor.

Rank: With death up my sleeve? And then to suffer this way for somebody else's sins. Is there any justice in that? And in every single family, in some way or another, this inevitable retribution of nature goes on —

Nora (her hands pressed over her ears): Oh, stuff! Cheer up! Please — be gay!

Rank: Yes, I'd just as soon laugh at it all. My poor, innocent spine, serving time for my father's gay army days.

Nora (by the table, left): He was so infatuated with asparagus tips and pâté de foie gras, wasn't that it?

Rank: Yes — and with truffles.

Nora: Truffles, yes. And then with oysters, I suppose?

Rank: Yes, tons of oysters, naturally.

Nora: And then the port and champagne to go with it. It's so sad that all these delectable things have to strike at our bones.

Rank: Especially when they strike at the unhappy bones that never shared in the fun.

Nora: Ah, that's the saddest of all.

Rank (looks searchingly at her): Hm.

Nora (after a moment): Why did you smile?

Rank: No, it was you who laughed.

Nora: No, it was you who smiled, Dr. Rank!

Rank (getting up): You're even a bigger tease than I'd thought.

Nora: I'm full of wild ideas today.

Rank: That's obvious.

Nora (putting both hands on his shoulders): Dear, dear Dr. Rank, you'll never die for Torvald and me.

Rank: Oh, that loss you'll easily get over. Those who go away are soon forgotten.

Nora (looks fearfully at him): You believe that?

Rank: One makes new connections, and then —

Nora: Who makes new connections?

Rank: Both you and Torvald will when I'm gone. I'd say you're well under way already. What was that Mrs. Linde doing here last evening?

Nora: Oh, come — you can't be jealous of poor Kristine?

Rank: Oh yes, I am. She'll be my successor here in the house. When I'm down under, that woman will probably —

Nora: Shh! Not so loud. She's right in there.

Rank: Today as well. So you see.

Nora: Only to sew on my dress. Good gracious, how unreasonable you are. (*Sitting on the sofa.*) Be nice now, Dr. Rank. Tomorrow you'll see how beautifully I'll dance; and you can imagine then that I'm dancing only for you — yes, and of course for Torvald, too — that's understood. (*Takes various items out of the carton.*) Dr. Rank, sit over here and I'll show you something.

Rank (sitting): What's that?

Nora: Look here. Look.

Rank: Silk Stockings.

Nora: Flesh-colored. Aren't they lovely? Now it's so dark here, but tomorrow — No, no, no, just look at the feet. Oh well, you might as well look at the rest.

Rank: Hm —

Nora: Why do you look so critical? Don't you believe they'll fit?

Rank: I've never had any chance to form an opinion on that.

Nora (glancing at him a moment): Shame on you. (*Hits him lightly on the ear with the stockings.*) That's for you. (*Puts them away again.*)

Rank: And what other splendors am I going to see now?

Nora: Not the least bit more, because you've been naughty. (*She hums a little and rummages among her things.*)

Rank (after a short silence): When I sit here together with you like this, completely easy and open, then I don't know — I simply can't imagine — whatever would have become of me if I'd never come into this house.

Nora (smiling): Yes, I really think you feel completely at ease with us.

Rank (more quietly, staring straight ahead): And then to have to go away from it all —

Nora: Nonsense, you're not going away.

Rank (his voice unchanged): — and not even be able to leave some poor show of gratitude behind, scarcely a fleeting regret — no more than a vacant place that anyone can fill.

Nora: And if I asked you now for —? No —

Rank: For what?

Nora: For a great proof of your friendship —

Rank: Yes, yes?

Nora: No, I mean — for an exceptionally big favor —

Rank: Would you really, for once, make me so happy?

Nora: Oh, you haven't the vaguest idea what it is.

Rank: All right, then tell me.

Nora: No, but I can't, Dr. Rank — it's all out of reason. It's advice and help, too — and a favor —

Rank: So much the better. I can't fathom what you're hinting at. Just speak out. Don't you trust me?

Nora: Of course. More than anyone else. You're my best and truest friend, I'm sure. That's why I want to talk to you. All right, then, Dr. Rank: there's something you can help me prevent. You know how deeply, how inexpressibly dearly Torvald loves me; he'd never hesitate a second to give up his life for me.

Rank (leaning close to her): Nora — do you think he's the only one —

Nora (with a slight start): Who — ?

Rank: Who'd gladly give up his life for you.

Nora (heavily): I see.

Rank: I swore to myself you should know this before I'm gone. I'll never find a better chance. Yes, Nora, now you know. And also you know now that you can trust me beyond anyone else.

Nora (rising, natural and calm): Let me by.

Rank (making room for her, but still sitting): Nora —

Nora (in the hall doorway): Helene, bring the lamp in. (*Goes over to the stove.*) Ah, dear Dr. Rank, that was really mean of you.

Rank (getting up): That I've loved you just as deeply as somebody else? Was *that* mean?

Nora: No, but that you came out and told me. That was quite unnecessary —

Rank: What do you mean? Have you known — ?

The Maid comes in with the lamp, sets it on the table, and goes out again.

Rank: Nora — Mrs. Helmer — I'm asking you: have you known about it?

Nora: Oh, how can I tell what I know or don't know? Really, I don't know what to say — Why did you have to be so clumsy, Dr. Rank! Everything was so good.

Rank: Well, in any case, you now have the knowledge that my body and soul are at your command. So won't you speak out?

Nora (looking at him): After that?

Rank: Please, just let me know what it is.

Nora: You can't know anything now.

Rank: I have to. You mustn't punish me like this. Give me the chance to do whatever is humanly possible for you.

Nora: Now there's nothing you can do for me. Besides, actually, I don't need any help. You'll see — it's only my fantasies. That's what it is. Of course! (*Sits in the rocker, looks at him, and smiles.*) What a nice one you are, Dr. Rank. Aren't you a little bit ashamed, now that the lamp is here?

Rank: No, not exactly. But perhaps I'd better go — for good?

Nora: No, you certainly can't do that. You must come here just as you always have. You know Torvald can't do without you.

Rank: Yes, but *you*?

Nora: You know how much I enjoy it when you're here.

Rank: That's precisely what threw me off. You're a mystery to me. So many times I've felt you'd almost rather be with me than with Helmer.

Nora: Yes — you see, there are some people that one loves most and other people that one would almost prefer being with.

Rank: Yes, there's something to that.

Nora: When I was back home, of course I loved Papa most. But I always thought it was so much fun when I could sneak down to the maids' quarters, because they never tried to improve me, and it was always so amusing, the way they talked to each other.

Rank: Aha, so it's *their* place that I've filled.

Nora (jumping up and going to him): Oh, dear, sweet Dr. Rank, that's not what I meant at all. But you can understand that with Torvald it's just the same as with Papa —

The Maid enters from the hall.

Maid: Ma'am — please! (*She whispers to Nora and hands her a calling card.*)

Nora (glancing at the card): Ah! (*Slips it into her pocket.*)

Rank: Anything wrong?

Nora: No, no, not at all. It's only some — it's my new dress —

Rank: Really? But — there's your dress.

Nora: Oh, that. But this is another one — I ordered it — Torvald mustn't know —

Rank: Ah, now we have the big secret.

Nora: That's right. Just go in with him — he's back in the inner study. Keep him there as long as —

Rank: Don't worry. He won't get away. (*Goes into the study.*)

Nora (to the Maid): And he's standing waiting in the kitchen?

Maid: Yes, he came up by the back stairs.

Nora: But didn't you tell him somebody was here?

Maid: Yes, but that didn't do any good.

Nora: He won't leave?

Maid: No, he won't go till he's talked with you, ma'am.

Nora: Let him come in, then — but quietly. Helene, don't breathe a word about this. It's a surprise for my husband.

Maid: Yes, yes, I understand — (*Goes out.*)

Nora: This horror — it's going to happen. No, no, no, it can't happen, it mustn't. (*She goes and bolts Helmer's door. The Maid opens the hall door for Krogstad and shuts it behind him. He is dressed for travel in a fur coat, boots, and a fur cap.*)

Nora (going toward him): Talk softly. My husband's home.

Krogstad: Well, good for him.

Nora: What do you want?

Krogstad: Some information.

Nora: Hurry up, then. What is it?

Krogstad: You know, of course, that I got my notice.

Nora: I couldn't prevent it, Mr. Krogstad. I fought for you to the bitter end, but nothing worked.

Krogstad: Does your husband's love for you run so thin? He knows everything I can expose you to, and all the same he dares to —

Nora: How can you imagine he knows anything about this?

Krogstad: Ah, no — I can't imagine it either, now. It's not at all like my fine Torvald Helmer to have so much guts —

Nora: Mr. Krogstad, I demand respect for my husband!

Krogstad: Why, of course — all due respect. But since the lady's keeping it so carefully hidden, may I presume to ask if you're also a bit better informed than yesterday about what you've actually done?

Nora: More than you could ever teach me.

Krogstad: Yes, I *am* such an awful lawyer.

Nora: What is it you want from me?

Krogstad: Just a glimpse of how you are, Mrs. Helmer. I've been thinking about you all day long. A cashier, a night-court scribbler, a — well, a type like me also has a little of what they call a heart, you know.

Nora: Then show it. Think of my children.

Krogstad: Did you or your husband ever think of mine? But never mind. I simply wanted to tell you that you don't need to take this thing too seriously. For the present, I'm not proceeding with any action.

Nora: Oh no, really! Well — I knew that.

Krogstad: Everything can be settled in a friendly spirit. It doesn't have to get around town at all; it can stay just among us three.

Nora: My husband must never know anything of this.

Krogstad: How can you manage that? Perhaps you can pay me the balance?

Nora: No, not right now.

Krogstad: Or you know some way of raising the money in a day or two?

Nora: No way that I'm willing to use.

Krogstad: Well, it wouldn't have done you any good, anyway. If you stood in front of me with a fistful of bills, you still couldn't buy your signature back.

Nora: Then tell me what you're going to do with it.

Krogstad: I'll just hold onto it — keep it on file. There's no outsider who'll even get wind of it. So if you've been thinking of taking some desperate step —

Nora: I have.

Krogstad: Been thinking of running away from home —

Nora: I have!

Krogstad: Or even of something worse —

Nora: How could you guess that?

Krogstad: You can drop those thoughts.

Nora: How could you guess I was thinking of *that*?

Krogstad: Most of us think about *that* at first. I thought about it too, but I discovered I hadn't the courage —

Nora (lifelessly): I don't either.

Krogstad (relieved): That's true, you haven't the courage? You too?

Nora: I don't have it — I don't have it.

Krogstad: It would be terribly stupid, anyway. After that first storm at home blows out, why, then — I have here in my pocket a letter for your husband —

Nora: Telling everything?

Krogstad: As charitably as possible.

Nora (quickly): He mustn't ever get that letter. Tear it up. I'll find some way to get money.

Krogstad: Beg pardon, Mrs. Helmer, but I think I just told you —

Nora: Oh, I don't mean the money I owe you. Let me know how much you want from my husband, and I'll manage it.

Krogstad: I don't want money from your husband.

Nora: What do you want, then?

Krogstad: I'll tell you what. I want to recoup, Mrs. Helmer; I want to get on in the world — and there's where your husband can help me. For a year and a half I've kept myself clean of anything disreputable — all that time strug-

gling with the worst conditions; but I was satisfied, working my way up step
by step. Now I've been written right off, and I'm just not in the mood to
come crawling back. I tell you, I want to move on. I want to get back in the
bank — in a better position. Your husband can set up a job for me —

Nora: He'll never do that!

Krogstad: He'll do it. I know him. He won't dare breathe a word of protest. And
once I'm in there together with him, you just wait and see! Inside of a year,
I'll be the manager's right-hand man. It'll be Nils Krogstad, not Torvald
Helmer, who runs the bank.

Nora: You'll never see the day!

Krogstad: Maybe you think you can —

Nora: I have the courage now — for *that*.

Krogstad: Oh, you don't scare me. A smart, spoiled lady like you —

Nora: You'll see; you'll see!

Krogstad: Under the ice, maybe? Down in the freezing coal-black water? There,
till you float up in the spring, ugly, unrecognizable, with your hair falling
out —

Nora: You don't frighten me.

Krogstad: Nor do you frighten me. One doesn't do these things, Mrs. Helmer.
Besides, what good would it be? I'd still have him safe in my pocket.

Nora: Afterwards? When I'm no longer — ?

Krogstad: Are you forgetting that *I'll* be in control then over your final reputation? (*Nora stands speechless, staring at him.*) Good; now I've warned you.
Don't do anything stupid. When Helmer's read my letter, I'll be waiting for
his reply. And bear in mind that it's your husband himself who's forced me
back to my old ways. I'll never forgive him for that. Good-bye, Mrs. Helmer.
(*He goes out through the hall.*)

Nora (goes to the hall door, opens it a crack, and listens): He's gone. Didn't
leave the letter. Oh no, no, that's impossible too! (*Opening the door more
and more.*) What's that? He's standing outside — not going downstairs. He's
thinking it over? Maybe he'll — ? (*A letter falls in the mailbox; then Krogstad's
footsteps are heard, dying away down a flight of stairs. Nora gives a muffled
cry and runs over toward the sofa table. A short pause.*) In the mailbox.
(*Slips warily over to the hall door.*) It's lying there. Torvald, Torvald — now
we're lost!

Mrs. Linde (entering with costume from the room, left): There now, I can't see
anything else to mend. Perhaps you'd like to try —

Nora (in a hoarse whisper): Kristine, come here.

Mrs. Linde (tossing the dress on the sofa): What's wrong? You look upset.

Nora: Come here. See that letter? *There!* Look — through the glass in the mailbox.

Mrs. Linde: Yes, yes, I see it.

Nora: That letter's from Krogstad —

Mrs. Linde: Nora — it's Krogstad who loaned you the money!

Nora: Yes, and now Torvald will find out everything.

Mrs. Linde: Believe me, Nora, it's best for both of you.

Nora: There's more you don't know. I forged a name.

Mrs. Linde: But for heaven's sake — ?

Nora: I only want to tell you that, Kristine, so that you can be my witness.

Mrs. Linde: Witness? Why should I — ?

Nora: If I should go out of my mind — it could easily happen —

Mrs. Linde: Nora!

Nora: Or anything else occurred — so I couldn't be present here —

Mrs. Linde: Nora, Nora, you aren't yourself at all!

Nora: And someone should try to take on the whole weight, all of the guilt, you follow me —

Mrs. Linde: Yes, of course, but why do you think — ?

Nora: Then you're the witness that it isn't true, Kristine. I'm very much myself; my mind right now is perfectly clear; and I'm telling you: nobody else has known about this; I alone did everything. Remember that.

Mrs. Linde: I will. But I don't understand all this.

Nora: Oh, how could you ever understand it? It's the miracle now that's going to take place.

Mrs. Linde: The miracle?

Nora: Yes, the miracle. But it's so awful, Kristine. It mustn't take place, not for anything in the world.

Mrs. Linde: I'm going right over and talk with Krogstad.

Nora: Don't go near him; he'll do you some terrible harm!

Mrs. Linde: There was a time once when he'd gladly have done anything for me.

Nora: He?

Mrs. Linde: Where does he live?

Nora: Oh, how do I know? Yes. (*Searches in her pocket.*) Here's his card. But the letter, the letter — !

Helmer (from the study, knocking on the door): Nora!

Nora (with a cry of fear): Oh! What is it? What do you want?

Helmer: Now, now, don't be so frightened. We're not coming in. You locked the door — are you trying on the dress?

Nora: Yes, I'm trying it. I'll look just beautiful, Torvald.

Mrs. Linde (who has read the card): He's living right around the corner.

Nora: Yes, but what's the use? We're lost. The letter's in the box.

Mrs. Linde: And your husband has the key?

Nora: Yes, always.

Mrs. Linde: Krogstad can ask for his letter back unread; he can find some excuse —

Nora: But it's just this time that Torvald usually —

Mrs. Linde: Stall him. Keep him in there. I'll be back as quick as I can. (*She hurries out through the hall entrance.*)

Nora (goes to Helmer's door, opens it, and peers in): Torvald!

Helmer (from the inner study): Well — does one dare set foot in one's own living room at last? Come on, Rank, now we'll get a look — (*In the doorway.*) But what's this?

Nora: What, Torvald dear?

Helmer: Rank had me expecting some grand masquerade.

Rank (in the doorway): That was my impression, but I must have been wrong.

Nora: No one can admire me in my splendor — not till tomorrow.

Helmer: But Nora dear, you look so exhausted. Have you practiced too hard?

Nora: No, I haven't practiced at all yet.

Helmer: You know, it's necessary —

Nora: Oh, it's absolutely necessary, Torvald. But I can't get anywhere without your help. I've forgotten the whole thing completely.

Helmer: Ah, we'll soon take care of that.

Nora: Yes, take care of me, Torvald, please! Promise me that? Oh, I'm so nervous. That big party — You must give up everything this evening for me. No business — don't even touch your pen. Yes? Dear Torvald, promise?

Helmer: It's a promise. Tonight I'm totally at your service — you little helpless thing. Hm — but first there's one thing I want to — (*Goes toward the hall door.*)

Nora: What are you looking for?

Helmer: Just to see if there's any mail.

Nora: No, no, don't do that, Torvald!

Helmer: Now what?

Nora: Torvald, please. There isn't any.

Helmer: Let me look, though. (*Starts out. Nora, at the piano, strikes the first notes of the tarantella. Helmer, at the door, stops.*) Aha!

Nora: I can't dance tomorrow if I don't practice with you.

Helmer (going over to her): Nora dear, are you really so frightened?

Nora: Yes, so terribly frightened. Let me practice right now; there's still time before dinner. Oh, sit down and play for me, Torvald. Direct me. Teach me, the way you always have.

Helmer: Gladly, if it's what you want. (*Sits at the piano.*)

Nora (snatches the tambourine up from the box, then a long, varicolored shawl, which she throws around herself, whereupon she springs forward and cries out): Play for me now! Now I'll dance!

Helmer plays and Nora dances. Rank stands behind Helmer at the piano and looks on.

Helmer (as he plays): Slower. Slow down.

Nora: Can't change it.

Helmer: Not so violent, Nora!

Nora: Has to be just like this.

Helmer (stopping): No, no, that won't do at all.

Nora (laughing and swinging her tambourine): Isn't that what I told you?

Rank: Let me play for her.

Helmer (getting up): Yes, go on. I can teach her more easily then.

Rank sits at the piano and plays; Nora dances more and more wildly. Helmer has stationed himself by the stove and repeatedly gives her directions; she seems not to hear them; her hair loosens and falls over her shoulders; she does not notice, but goes on dancing. Mrs. Linde enters.

Mrs. Linde (standing dumbfounded at the door): Ah — !

Nora (still dancing): See what fun, Kristine!

Helmer: But Nora darling, you dance as if your life were at stake.

Nora: And it is.

Helmer: Rank, stop! This is pure madness. Stop it, I say!

Rank breaks off playing, and Nora halts abruptly.

Helmer (going over to her): I never would have believed it. You've forgotten everything I taught you.

Nora (throwing away the tambourine): You see for yourself.

Helmer: Well, there's certainly room for instruction here.

Nora: Yes, you see how important it is. You've got to teach me to the very last minute. Promise me that, Torvald?

Helmer: You can bet on it.

Nora: You mustn't, either today or tomorrow, think about anything else but me; you mustn't open any letters — or the mailbox —

Helmer: Ah, it's still the fear of that man —

Nora: Oh yes, yes, that too.

Helmer: Nora, it's written all over you — there's already a letter from him out there.

Nora: I don't know. I guess so. But you mustn't read such things now; there mustn't be anything ugly between us before it's all over.

Rank (quietly to Helmer): You shouldn't deny her.

Helmer (putting his arms around her): The child can have her way. But tomorrow night, after you've danced —

Nora: Then you'll be free.

Maid (in the doorway, right): Ma'am, dinner is served.

Nora: We'll be wanting champagne, Helene.

Maid: Very good, ma'am. (*Goes out.*)

Helmer: So — a regular banquet, hm?

Nora: Yes, a banquet — champagne till daybreak! (*Calling out.*) And some macaroons, Helene. Heaps of them — just this once.

Helmer (taking her hands): Now, now, now — no hysterics. Be my own little lark again.

Nora: Oh, I will soon enough. But go on in — and you, Dr. Rank. Kristine, help me put up my hair.

Rank (whispering, as they go): There's nothing wrong — really wrong, is there?

Helmer: Oh, of course not. It's nothing more than this childish anxiety I was telling you about. (*They go out, right.*)

Nora: Well?

Mrs. Linde: Left town.

Nora: I could see by your face.

Mrs. Linde: He'll be home tomorrow evening. I wrote him a note.

Nora: You shouldn't have. Don't try to stop anything now. After all, it's a wonderful joy, this waiting here for the miracle.

Mrs. Linde: What is it you're waiting for?

Nora: Oh, you can't understand that. Go in to them; I'll be along in a moment.

Mrs. Linde goes into the dining room. Nora stands a short while as if composing herself; then she looks as her watch.)

Nora: Five. Seven hours to midnight. Twenty-four hours to the midnight after, and then the tarentella's done. Seven and twenty-four? Thirty-one hours to live.

Helmer (in the doorway, right): What's become of the little lark?

Nora (going toward him with open arms): Here's your lark!

ACT III

Helmer is patriarchal

Same scene. The table, with chairs around it, has been moved to the center of the room. A lamp on the table is lit. The hall door stands open. Dance music drifts down from the floor above. Mrs. Linde sits at the table, absently paging through a book, trying to read, but apparently unable to focus her thoughts. Once or twice she pauses, tensely listening for a sound at the outer entrance.

Mrs. Linde (glancing at her watch): Not yet — and there's hardly any time left. If only he's not — (*Listening again.*) Ah, there he is. (*She goes out in the hall and cautiously opens the outer door. Quiet footsteps are heard on the stairs. She whispers:*) Come in. Nobody's here.

Krogstad (in the doorway): I found a note from you at home. What's back of all this?

Mrs. Linde: I just *had* to talk to you.

Krogstad: Oh? And it just *had* to be here in this house?

Mrs. Linde: At my place it was impossible; my room hasn't a private entrance. Come in; we're all alone. The maid's asleep, and the Helmers are at the dance upstairs.

Krogstad (entering the room): Well, well, the Helmers are dancing tonight? Really?

Mrs. Linde: Yes, why not?

Krogstad: How true — why not?

Mrs. Linde: All right, Krogstad, let's talk.

Krogstad: Do we two have anything more to talk about?

Mrs. Linde: We have a great deal to talk about.

Krogstad: I wouldn't have thought so.

Mrs. Linde: No, because you've never understood me, really.

Krogstad: Was there anything more to understand — except what's all too common in life? A calculating woman throws over a man the moment a better catch comes by.

Mrs. Linde: You think I'm so thoroughly calculating? You think I broke it off lightly?

Krogstad: Didn't you?

Mrs. Linde: Nils — is that what you really thought?

Krogstad: If you cared, then why did you write me the way you did?

Mrs. Linde: What else could I do? If I had to break off with you, then it was my job as well to root out everything you felt for me.

Krogstad (wringing his hands): So that was it. And this — all this, simply for money!

Mrs. Linde: Don't forget I had a helpless mother and two small brothers. We couldn't wait for you, Nils; you had such a long road ahead of you then.

Krogstad: That may be; but you still hadn't the right to abandon me for somebody else's sake.

Mrs. Linde: Yes — I don't know. So many, many times I've asked myself if I did have that right.

Krogstad (more softly): When I lost you, it was as if all the solid ground dissolved from under my feet. Look at me; I'm a half-drowned man now, hanging onto a wreck.

Mrs. Linde: Help may be near.

Krogstad: It was near — but then you came and blocked it off.

Mrs. Linde: Without my knowing it, Nils. Today for the first time I learned that it's you I'm replacing at the bank.

Krogstad: All right — I believe you. But now that you know, will you step aside?

Mrs. Linde: No, because that wouldn't benefit you in the slightest.

Krogstad: Not "benefit" me, hm! I'd step aside anyway.

Mrs. Linde: I've learned to be realistic. Life and hard, bitter necessity have taught me that.

Krogstad: And life's taught me never to trust fine phrases.

Mrs. Linde: Then life's taught you a very sound thing. But you do have to trust in actions, don't you?

Krogstad: What does that mean?

Mrs. Linde: You said you were hanging on like a half-drowned man to a wreck.

Krogstad: I've good reason to say that.

Mrs. Linde: I'm also like a half-drowned woman on a wreck. No one to suffer with; no one to care for.

Krogstad: You made your choice.

Mrs. Linde: There wasn't any choice then.

Krogstad: So — what of it?

Mrs. Linde: Nils, if only we two shipwrecked people could reach across to each other.

Krogstad: What are you saying?

Mrs. Linde: Two on one wreck are at least better off than each on his own.

Krogstad: Kristine!

Mrs. Linde: Why do you think I came into town?

Krogstad: Did you really have some thought of me?

Mrs. Linde: I have to work to go on living. All my born days, as long as I can remember, I've worked, and it's been my best and my only joy. But now I'm completely alone in the world; it frightens me to be so empty and lost. To work for yourself — there's no joy in that. Nils, give me something — someone to work for.

Krogstad: I don't believe all this. It's just some hysterical feminine urge to go out and make a noble sacrifice.

Mrs. Linde: Have you ever found me to be hysterical?

Krogstad: Can you honestly mean this? Tell me — do you know everything about my past?

Mrs. Linde: Yes.

Krogstad: And you know what they think I'm worth around here.

Mrs. Linde: From what you were saying before, it would seem that with me you could have been another person.

Krogstad: I'm positive of that.

Mrs. Linde: Couldn't it happen still?

Krogstad: Kristine — you're saying this in all seriousness? Yes, you are! I can see it in you. And do you really have the courage, then —?

Mrs. Linde: I need to have someone to care for; and your children need a mother. We both need each other. Nils, I have faith that you're good at heart — I'll risk everything together with you.

Krogstad (gripping her hands): Kristine, thank you, thank you — Now I know I can win back a place in their eyes. Yes — but I forgot —

Mrs. Linde (listening): Shh! The tarantella. Go now! Go on!

Krogstad: Why? What is it?

Mrs. Linde: Hear the dance up there? When that's over, they'll be coming down.

Krogstad: Oh, then I'll go. But — it's all pointless. Of course, you don't know the move I made against the Helmers.

Mrs. Linde: Yes, Nils, I know.

Krogstad: And all the same, you have the courage to — ?

Mrs. Linde: I know how far despair can drive a man like you.

Krogstad: Oh, if I only could take it all back.

Mrs. Linde: You easily could — your letter's still lying in the mailbox.

Krogstad: Are you sure of that?

Mrs. Linde: Positive. But —

Krogstad (looks at her searchingly): Is that the meaning of it, then? You'll save your friend at any price. Tell me straight out. Is that it?

Mrs. Linde: Nils — anyone who's sold herself for somebody else once isn't going to do it again.

Krogstad: I'll demand my letter back.

Mrs. Linde: No, no.

Krogstad: Yes, of course. I'll stay here till Helmer comes down; I'll tell him to give me my letter again — that it only involves my dismissal — that he shouldn't read it —

Mrs. Linde: No, Nils, don't call the letter back.

Krogstad: But wasn't that exactly why you wrote me to come here?

Mrs. Linde: Yes, in that first panic. But it's been a whole day and night since then, and in that time I've seen such incredible things in this house. Helmer's got to learn everything; this dreadful secret has to be aired; those two have to come to a full understanding; all these lies and evasions can't go on.

Krogstad: Well, then, if you want to chance it. But at least there's one thing I can do, and do right away —

Mrs. Linde (listening): Go now, go quick! The dance is over. We're not safe another second.

Krogstad: I'll wait for you downstairs.

Mrs. Linde: Yes, please do; take me home.

Krogstad: I can't believe it; I've never been so happy. (*He leaves by way of the outer door; the door between the room and the hall stays open.*)

Mrs. Linde (straightening up a bit and getting together her street clothes): How different now! How different! Someone to work for, to live for — a home to build. Well, it is worth the try! Oh, if they'd only come! (*Listening.*) Ah, there they are. Bundle up. (*She picks up her hat and coat. Nora's and Helmer's voice can be heard outside; a key turns in the lock, and Helmer brings Nora into the hall almost by force. She is wearing the Italian costume with a large black shawl about her; he has on evening dress, with a black domino open over it.*)

Nora (struggling in the doorway): No, no, no, not inside! I'm going up again. I don't want to leave so soon.

Helmer: But Nora dear —

Nora: Oh, I beg you, please, Torvald. From the bottom of my heart, *please* — only an hour more!

Helmer: Not a single minute, Nora darling. You know our agreement. Come on, in we go; you'll catch cold out here. (*In spite of her resistance, he gently draws her into the room.*)

Mrs. Linde: Good evening.

Nora: Kristine!

Helmer: Why, Mrs. Linde — are you here so late?

Mrs. Linde: Yes, I'm sorry, but I did want to see Nora in costume.

Nora: Have you been sitting here, waiting for me?

Mrs. Linde: Yes. I didn't come early enough; you were all upstairs; and then I thought I really couldn't leave without seeing you.

Helmer (removing Nora's shawl): Yes, take a good look. She's worth looking at, I can tell you that, Mrs. Linde. Isn't she lovely?

Mrs. Linde: Yes, I should say —

Helmer: A dream of loveliness, isn't she? That's what everyone thought at the party, too. But she's horribly stubborn — this sweet little thing. What's to be done with her? Can you imagine, I almost had to use force to pry her away.

Nora: Oh, Torvald, you're going to regret you didn't indulge me, even for just a half hour more.

Helmer: There, you see. She danced her tarantella and got a tumultuous hand — which was well earned, although the performance may have been a bit too naturalistic — I mean it rather overstepped the proprieties of art. But never mind — what's important is, she made a success, an overwhelming success. You think I could let her stay on after that and spoil the effect? Oh no; I took my lovely little Capri girl — my capricious little Capri girl, I should say — took her under my arm; one quick tour of the ballroom, a curtsy to every side, and then — as they say in novels — the beautiful vision disappeared. An exit should always be effective, Mrs. Linde, but that's what I can't get Nora to grasp. Phew, it's hot in here. (*Flings the domino on a chair and opens the door to his room.*) Why's it dark in here? Oh yes, of course. Excuse me. (*He goes in and lights a couple of candles.*)

Nora (in a sharp, breathless whisper): So?

Mrs. Linde (quietly): I talked with him.

Nora: And — ?

Mrs. Linde: Nora — you must tell your husband everything.

Nora (dully): I knew it.

Mrs. Linde: You've got nothing to fear from Krogstad, but you have to speak out.

Nora: I won't tell.

Mrs. Linde: Then the letter will.

Nora: Thanks, Kristine. I know now what's to be done. Shh!

Helmer (reentering): Well, then, Mrs. Linde — have you admired her?

Mrs. Linde: Yes, and now I'll say good night.

Helmer: Oh, come, so soon? Is this yours, this knitting?

Mrs. Linde: Yes, thanks. I nearly forgot it.

Helmer: Do you knit, then?

Mrs. Linde: Oh yes.

Helmer: You know what? You should embroider instead.

Mrs. Linde: Really? Why?

Helmer: Yes, because it's a lot prettier. See here, one holds the embroidery so, in the left hand, and then one guides the needle with the right — so — in an easy, sweeping curve — right?

Mrs. Linde: Yes, I guess that's —

Helmer: But, on the other hand, knitting — it can never be anything but ugly. Look, see here, the arms tucked in, the knitting needles going up and down — there's something Chinese about it. Ah, that was really a glorious champagne they served.

Mrs. Linde: Yes, good night, Nora, and don't be stubborn anymore.

Helmer: Well put, Mrs. Linde!

Mrs. Linde: Good night, Mr. Helmer.

Helmer (accompanying her to the door): Good night, good night. I hope you get home all right. I'd be very happy to — but you don't have far to go. Good night, good night. (*She leaves. He shuts the door after her and returns.*) There, now, at last we got her out the door. She's a deadly bore, that creature.

Nora: Aren't you pretty tired, Torvald?

Helmer: No, not a bit.

Nora: You're not sleepy?

Helmer: Not at all. On the contrary, I'm feeling quite exhilarated. But you? Yes, you really look tired and sleepy.

Nora: Yes, I'm very tired. Soon now I'll sleep.

Helmer: See! You see! I was right all along that we shouldn't stay longer.

Nora: Whatever you do is always right.

Helmer (kissing her brow): Now my little lark talks sense. Say, did you notice what a time Rank was having tonight?

Nora: Oh, was he? I didn't get to speak with him.

Helmer: I scarcely did either, but it's a long time since I've seen him in such high spirits. (*Gazes at her a moment, then comes nearer her.*) Hm — it's marvelous, though, to be back home again — to be completely alone with you. Oh, you bewitchingly lovely young woman!

Nora: Torvald, don't look at me like that!

Helmer: Can't I look at my richest treasure? At all that beauty that's mine, mine alone — completely and utterly.

Nora (moving around to the other side of the table): You mustn't talk to me that way tonight.

Helmer (following her): The tarantella is still in your blood, I can see — and it makes you even more enticing. Listen. The guests are beginning to go. (*Dropping his voice.*) Nora — it'll soon be quiet through this whole house.

Nora: Yes, I hope so.

Helmer: You do, don't you, my love? Do you realize — when I'm out at a party like this with you — do you know why I talk to you so little, and keep such a distance away; just send you a stolen look now and then — you know why I do it? It's because I'm imagining then that you're my secret darling, my secret bride-to-be, and that no one suspects there's anything between us.

Nora: Yes, yes; oh, yes, I know you're always thinking of me.

Helmer: And then when we leave and I place the shawl over those fine young rounded shoulders — over that wonderful curving neck — then I pretend that you're my young bride, that we're just coming from the wedding, that for the first time I'm bringing you into my house — that for the first time I'm alone with you — completely alone with you, your trembling young beauty! All this evening I've longed for nothing but you. When I saw you turn and sway in the tarantella — my blood was pounding till I couldn't stand it — that's why I brought you down here so early —

Nora: Go away, Torvald! Leave me alone. I don't want all this.

Helmer: What do you mean? Nora, you're teasing me. You will, won't you? Aren't I your husband — ?

A knock at the outside door.

Nora (startled): What's that?

Helmer (going toward the hall): Who is it?

Rank (outside): It's me. May I come in a moment?

Helmer (with quiet irritation): Oh, what does he want now? (*Aloud.*) Hold on. (*Goes and opens the door.*) Oh, how nice that you didn't just pass us by!

Rank: I thought I heard your voice, and then I wanted so badly to have a look in. (*Lightly glancing about.*) Ah, me, these old familiar haunts. You have it snug and cozy in here, you two.

Helmer: You seemed to be having it pretty cozy upstairs, too.

Rank: Absolutely. Why shouldn't I? Why not take in everything in life? As much as you can, anyway, and as long as you can. The wine was superb —

Helmer: The champagne especially.

Rank: You noticed that too? It's amazing how much I could guzzle down.

Nora: Torvald also drank a lot of champagne this evening.

Rank: Oh?

Nora: Yes, and that always makes him so entertaining.

Rank: Well, why shouldn't one have a pleasant evening after a well-spent day?

Helmer: Well spent? I'm afraid I can't claim that.

Rank (slapping him on the back): But I can, you see!

Nora: Dr. Rank, you must have done some scientific research today.

Rank: Quite so.

Helmer: Come now — little Nora talking about scientific research!

Nora: And can I congratulate you on the results?

Rank: Indeed you may.

Nora: Then they were good?

Rank: The best possible for both doctor and patient — certainty.

Nora (quickly and searchingly): Certainty?

Rank: Complete certainty. So don't I owe myself a gay evening afterwards?

Nora: Yes, you're right, Dr. Rank.

Helmer: I'm with you — just so long as you don't have to suffer for it in the morning.

Rank: Well, one never gets something for nothing in life.

Nora: Dr. Rank — are you very fond of masquerade parties?

Rank: Yes, if there's a good array of odd disguises —

Nora: Tell me, what should we two go as at the next masquerade?

Helmer: You little featherhead — already thinking of the next!

Rank: We two? I'll tell you what: you must go as Charmed Life —

Helmer: Yes, but find a costume for *that*!

Rank: Your wife can appear just as she looks every day.

Helmer: That was nicely put. But don't you know what you're going to be?

Rank: Yes, Helmer, I've made up my mind.

Helmer: Well?

Rank: At the next masquerade I'm going to be invisible.

Helmer: That's a funny idea.

Rank: They say there's a hat — black, huge — have you never heard of the hat that makes you invisible? You put it on, and then no one on earth can see you.

Helmer (suppressing a smile): Ah, of course.

Rank: But I'm quite forgetting what I came for. Helmer, give me a cigar, one of the dark Havanas.

Helmer: With the greatest pleasure. (*Holds out his case.*)

Rank: Thanks. (*Takes one and cuts off the tip.*)

Nora (striking a match): Let me give you a light.

Rank: Thank you. (*She holds the match for him; he lights the cigar.*) And now good-bye.

Helmer: Good-bye, good-bye, old friend.

Nora: Sleep well, Doctor.

Rank: Thanks for that wish.

Nora: Wish me the same.

Rank: You? All right, if you like — Sleep well. And thanks for the light. (*He nods to them both and leaves.*)

Helmer (his voice subdued): He's been drinking heavily.

Nora (absently): Could be. (*Helmer takes his keys from his pocket and goes out in the hall.*) Torvald — what are you after?

Helmer: Got to empty the mailbox; it's nearly full. There won't be room for the morning papers.

Nora: Are you working tonight?

Helmer: You know I'm not. Why — what's this? Someone's been at the lock.

Nora: At the lock — ?

Helmer: Yes, I'm positive. What do you suppose — ? I can't imagine one of the maids — ? Here's a broken hairpin. Nora, it's yours —

Nora (quickly): Then it must be the children —

Helmer: You'd better break them of that. Hm, hm — well, opened it after all. (*Takes the contents out and calls into the kitchen.*) Helene! Helene, would you put out the lamp in the hall. (*He returns to the room shutting the hall door, then displays the handful of mail.*) Look how it's piled up. (*Sorting through them.*) Now what's this?

Nora (at the window): The letter! Oh, Torvald, no!

Helmer: Two calling cards — from Rank.

Nora: From Dr. Rank?

Helmer (examining them): "Dr. Rank, Consulting Physician." They were on top. He must have dropped them in as he left.

Nora: Is there anything on them?

Helmer: There's a black cross over the name. See? That's a gruesome notion. He could almost be announcing his own death.

Nora: That's just what he's doing.

Helmer: What! You've heard something? Something he's told you?

Nora: Yes. That when those cards came, he'd be taking his leave of us. He'll shut himself in now and die.

Helmer: Ah, my poor friend! Of course I knew he wouldn't be here much longer. But so soon — And then to hide himself away like a wounded animal.

Nora: If it has to happen, then it's best it happens in silence — don't you think so, Torvald?

Helmer (pacing up and down): He'd grown right into our lives. I simply can't imagine him gone. He with his suffering and loneliness — like a dark cloud setting off our sunlit happiness. Well, maybe it's best this way. For him, at least. (*Standing still.*) And maybe for us too, Nora. Now we're thrown back on each other, completely. (*Embracing her.*) Oh you, my darling wife, how can I hold you close enough? You know what, Nora — time and again I've wished you were in some terrible danger, just so I could stake my life and soul and everything, for your sake.

Nora (tearing herself away, her voice firm and decisive): Now you must read your mail, Torvald.

Helmer: No, no, not tonight. I want to stay with you, dearest.

Nora: With a dying friend on your mind?

Helmer: You're right. We've both had a shock. There's ugliness between us — these thoughts of death and corruption. We'll have to get free of them first. Until then — we'll stay apart.

Nora (clinging about his neck): Torvald — good night! Good night!

Helmer (kissing her on the cheek): Good night, little songbird. Sleep well, Nora. I'll be reading my mail now. (*He takes the letters into his room and shuts the door after him.*)

Nora (with bewildered glances, groping about, seizing Helmer's domino, throwing it around her, and speaking in short, hoarse, broken whispers): Never see him again. Never, never. (*Putting her shawl over her head.*) Never see the children either — them, too. Never, never. Oh, the freezing black water! The depths — down — Oh, I wish it were over — He has it now; he's reading it — now. Oh no, no, not yet. Torvald, good-bye, you and the children — (*She starts for the hall; as she does, Helmer throws open his door and stands with an open letter in his hand.*)

Helmer: Nora!

Nora (screams): Oh — !

Helmer: What is this? You know what's in this letter?

Nora: Yes, I know. Let me go! Let me out!

Helmer (holding her back): Where are you going?

Nora (struggling to break loose): You can't save me, Torvald!

Helmer (slumping back): True! Then it's true what he writes? How horrible? No, no, it's impossible — it can't be true.

Nora: It *is* true. I've loved you more than all this world.

Helmer: Ah, none of your slippery tricks.

Nora (taking one step toward him): Torvald — !

Helmer: What *is* this you've blundered into!

Nora: Just let me loose. You're not going to suffer for my sake. You're not going to take on my guilt.

Helmer: No more play-acting. (*Locks the hall door.*) You stay right here and give me a reckoning. You understand what you've done? Answer! You understand?

Nora (looking squarely at him, her face hardening): Yes. I'm beginning to understand everything now.

Helmer (striding about): Oh, what an awful awakening! In all these eight years — she who was my pride and joy — a hypocrite, a liar — worse, worse — a criminal! How infinitely disgusting it all is! The shame! (*Nora says nothing and goes on looking straight at him. He stops in front of her.*) I should have suspected something of the kind. I should have known. All your father's flimsy values — Be still! All your father's flimsy values have come out in you. No religion, no morals, no sense of duty — Oh, how I'm punished for letting him off! I did it for your sake, and you repay me like this.

Nora: Yes, like this.

Helmer: Now you've wrecked all my happiness — ruined my whole future. Oh, it's awful to think of. I'm in a cheap little grafter's hands; he can do anything he wants with me, ask for anything, play with me like a puppet — and I can't breathe a word. I'll be swept down miserably into the depths on account of a featherbrained woman.

Nora: When I'm gone from this world, you'll be free.

Helmer: Oh, quit posing. Your father had a mess of those speeches too. What good would that ever do me if you were gone from this world, as you say? Not the slightest. He can still make the whole thing known; and if he does, I could be falsely suspected as your accomplice. They might even think that I was behind it — that I put you up to it. And all that I can thank you for — you that I've coddled the whole of our marriage. Can you see now what you've done to me?

Nora (icily calm): Yes.

Helmer: It's so incredible, I just can't grasp it. But we'll have to patch up whatever we can. Take off the shawl. I said, take if off! I've got to appease him somehow or other. The thing has to be hushed up at any cost. And as for you and me, it's got to seem like everything between us is just as it was — to the outside world, that is. You'll go right on living in this house, of course. But you can't be allowed to bring up the children; I don't dare trust you with them — Oh, to have to say this to someone I've loved so much! Well, that's done with. From now on happiness doesn't matter; all that matters is saving the bits and pieces, the appearance — (*The doorbell rings. Helmer starts.*) What's that? And so late. Maybe the worst — ? You think he'd — ? Hide, Nora! Say you're sick. (*Nora remains standing motionless. Helmer goes and opens the door.*)

Maid (half dressed, in the hall): A letter for Mrs. Helmer.

Helmer: I'll take it. (*Snatches the letter and shuts the door.*) Yes, it's from him. You don't get it; I'm reading it myself.

Nora: Then read it.

Helmer (by the lamp): I hardly dare. We may be ruined, you and I. But — I've got to know. (*Rips open the letter, skims through a few lines, glances at an enclosure, then cries out joyfully.*) Nora! (*Nora looks inquiringly at him.*) Nora! Wait — better check it again — Yes, yes, it's true. I'm saved. Nora, I'm saved!

Nora: And I?

Helmer: You too, of course. We're both saved, both of us. Look. He's sent back your note. He says he's sorry and ashamed — that a happy development in his life — oh, who cares what he says! Nora, we're saved! No one can hurt you. Oh, Nora, Nora — but first, this ugliness all has to go. Let me see — (*Takes a look at the note.*) No, I don't want to see it; I want the whole thing to fade like a dream. (*Tears the note and both letters to pieces, throws them into the stove and watches them burn.*) There — now there's nothing left — He wrote that since Christmas Eve you — Oh, they must have been three terrible days for you, Nora.

Nora: I fought a hard fight.

Helmer: And suffered pain and saw no escape but — No, we're not going to dwell on anything unpleasant. We'll just be grateful and keep on repeating: it's over now, it's over! You hear me, Nora? You don't seem to realize — it's over. What's it mean — that frozen look? Oh, poor little Nora, I understand. You can't believe I've forgiven you. But I have, Nora; I swear I have. I know that what you did, you did out of love for me.

Nora: That's true.

Helmer: You loved me the way a wife ought to love her husband. It's simply the means that you couldn't judge. But you think I love you any the less for not knowing how to handle your affairs? No, no — just lean on me; I'll guide you and teach you. I wouldn't be a man if this feminine helplessness didn't make you twice as attractive to me. You mustn't mind those sharp words I said — that was all in the first confusion of thinking my world had collapsed. I've forgiven you, Nora; I swear I've forgiven you.

Nora: My thanks for your forgiveness. (*She goes out through the door, right.*)

Helmer: No, wait — (*Peers in.*) What are you doing in there?

Nora (inside): Getting out of my costume.

Helmer (by the open door): Yes, do that. Try to calm yourself and collect your thoughts again, my frightened little songbird. You can rest easy now; I've got wide wings to shelter you with. (*Walking about close by the door.*) How snug and nice our home is, Nora. You're safe here; I'll keep you like a hunted dove I've rescued out of a hawk's claws. I'll bring peace to your poor, shuddering heart. Gradually it'll happen, Nora; you'll see. Tomorrow all this will look different to you; then everything will be as it was. I won't have to go on repeating I forgive you; you'll feel it for yourself. How can you imagine I'd ever conceivably want to disown you — or even blame you in any way? Ah, you don't know a man's heart, Nora. For a man there's something indescribably sweet and satisfying in knowing he's forgiven his wife — and forgiven her out of a full and open heart. It's as if she belongs to him in two ways now: in a sense he's given her fresh into the world again, and she's become his wife and his child as well. From now on that's what you'll be to me — you little, bewildered, helpless thing. Don't be afraid of anything, Nora; just open your heart to me, and I'll be conscience and will to you both — (*Nora enters in her regular clothes.*) What's this? Not in bed? You've changed your dress?

Nora: Yes, Torvald, I've changed my dress.

Helmer: But why now, so late?

Nora: Tonight I'm not sleeping.

Helmer: But Nora dear —

Nora (looking at her watch): It's still not so very late. Sit down, Torvald; we have a lot to talk over. (*She sits at one side of the table.*)

Helmer: Nora — what is this? That hard expression —

Nora: Sit down. This'll take some time. I have a lot to say.

Helmer (sitting at the table directly opposite her): You worry me, Nora. And I don't understand you.

Nora: No, that's exactly it. You don't understand me. And I've never understood you either — until tonight. No, don't interrupt. You can just listen to what I say. We're closing out accounts, Torvald.

Helmer: How do you mean that?

Nora (after a short pause): Doesn't anything strike you about our sitting here like this?

Helmer: What's that?

Nora: We've been married now eight years. Doesn't it occur to you that this is the first time we two, you and I, man and wife, have ever talked seriously together?

Helmer: What do you mean — seriously?

Nora: In eight whole years — longer even — right from our first acquaintance, we've never exchanged a serious word on any serious thing.

Helmer: You mean I should constantly go and involve you in problems you couldn't possibly help me with?

Nora: I'm not talking of problems. I'm saying that we've never sat down seriously together and tried to get to the bottom of anything.

Helmer: But dearest, what good would that ever do you?

Nora: That's the point right there: you've never understood me. I've been wronged greatly, Torvald — first by Papa, and then by you.

Helmer: What! By us — the two people who've loved you more than anyone else?

Nora (shaking her head): You never loved me. You've thought it fun to be in love with me, that's all.

Helmer: Nora, what a thing to say!

Nora: Yes, it's true now, Torvald. When I lived at home with Papa, he told me all his opinions, so I had the same ones too; or if they were different I hid them, since he wouldn't have cared for that. He used to call me his doll-child, and he played with me the way I played with my dolls. Then I came into your house —

Helmer: How can you speak of our marriage like that?

Nora (unperturbed): I mean, then I went from Papa's hands into yours. You arranged everything to your own taste, and so I got the same taste as you — or I pretended to; I can't remember. I guess a little of both, first one, then the other. Now when I look back, it seems as if I'd lived here like a beggar — just from hand to mouth. I've lived by doing tricks for you, Torvald. But that's the way you wanted it. It's a great sin what you and Papa did to me. You're to blame that nothing's become of me.

Helmer: Nora, how unfair and ungrateful you are! Haven't you been happy here?

Nora: No, never. I thought so — but I never have.

Helmer: Not — not happy!

Nora: No, only lighthearted. And you've always been so kind to me. But our home's been nothing but a playpen. I've been your doll-wife here, just as at home I was Papa's doll-child. And in turn the children have been my dolls. I thought it was fun when you played with me, just as they thought it fun when I played with them. That's been our marriage, Torvald.

Helmer: There's some truth in what you're saying — under all the raving exaggeration. But it'll all be different after this. Playtime's over; now for the schooling.

Nora: Whose schooling — mine or the children's?

Helmer: Both yours and the children's, dearest.

Nora: Oh, Torvald, you're not the man to teach me to be a good wife to you.

Helmer: And you can say that?

Nora: And I — how am I equipped to bring up children?

Helmer: Nora!

Nora: Didn't you say a moment ago that that was no job to trust me with?

Helmer: In a flare of temper! Why fasten on that?

Nora: Yes, but you were so very right. I'm not up to the job. There's another job I have to do first. I have to try to educate myself. You can't help me with that. I've got to do it alone. And that's why I'm leaving you now.

Helmer (jumping up): What's that?

Nora: I have to stand completely alone, if I'm ever going to discover myself and the world out there. So I can't go on living with you.

Helmer: Nora, Nora!

Nora: I want to leave right away. Kristine should put me up for the night —

Helmer: You're insane! You've no right! I forbid you!

Nora: From here on, there's no use forbidding me anything. I'll take with me whatever is mine. I don't want a thing from you, either now or later.

Helmer: What kind of madness is this!

Nora: Tomorrow I'm going home — I mean, home where I came from. It'll be easier up there to find something to do.

Helmer: Oh, you blind, incompetent child!

Nora: I must learn to be competent, Torvald.

Helmer: Abandon your home, your husband, your children! And you're not even thinking what people will say.

Nora: I can't be concerned about that. I only know how essential this is.

Helmer: Oh, it's outrageous. So you'll run out like this on your most sacred vows.

Nora: What do you think are my most sacred vows?

Helmer: And I have to tell you that! Aren't they your duties to your husband and children?

Nora: I have other duties equally sacred.

Helmer: That isn't true. What duties are they?

Nora: Duties to myself.

Helmer: Before all else, you're a wife and mother.

Nora: I don't believe in that anymore. I believe that, before all else, I'm a human being, no less than you — or anyway, I ought to try to become one. I know the majority thinks you're right, Torvald, and plenty of books agree with you, too. But I can't go on believing what the majority says, or what's written in books. I have to think over these things myself and try to understand them.

Helmer: Why can't you understand your place in your own home? On a point like that, isn't there one everlasting guide you can turn to? Where's your religion?

Nora: Oh, Torvald, I'm really not sure what religion is.

Helmer: What — ?

Nora: I only know what the minister said when I was confirmed. He told me religion was this thing and that. When I get clear and away by myself, I'll go into that problem too. I'll see if what the minister said was right, or, in any case, if it's right for me.

Helmer: A young woman your age shouldn't talk like that. If religion can't move you, I can try to rouse your conscience. You do have some moral feeling? Or, tell me — has that gone too?

Nora: It's not easy to answer that, Torvald. I simply don't know. I'm all confused about these things. I just know I see them so differently from you. I find out, for one thing, that the law's not at all what I'd thought — but I can't get it through my head that the law is fair. A woman hasn't a right to protect her dying father or save her husband's life! I can't believe that.

Helmer: You talk like a child. You don't know anything of the world you live in.

Nora: No, I don't. But now I'll begin to learn for myself. I'll try to discover who's right, the world or I.

Helmer: Nora, you're sick; you've got a fever. I almost think you're out of your head.

Nora: I've never felt more clearheaded and sure in my life.

Helmer: And — clearheaded and sure — you're leaving your husband and children?

Nora: Yes.

Helmer: Then there's only one possible reason.

Nora: What?

Helmer: You no longer love me.

Nora: No. That's exactly it.

Helmer: Nora! You can't be serious!

Nora: Oh, this is so hard, Torvald — you've been so kind to me always. But I can't help it. I don't love you anymore.

Helmer (struggling for composure): Are you also clearheaded and sure about that?

Nora: Yes, completely. That's why I can't go on staying here.

Helmer: Can you tell me what I did to lose your love?

Nora: Yes, I can tell you. It was this evening when the miraculous thing didn't come — then I knew you weren't the man I'd imagined.

Helmer: Be more explicit; I don't follow you.

Nora: I've waited now so patiently eight long years — for, my Lord, I know miracles don't come every day. Then this crisis broke over me, and such a certainty filled me: *now* the miraculous event would occur. While Krogstad's letter was lying out there, I never for an instant dreamed that you could give in to his terms. I was so utterly sure you'd say to him: go on, tell your tale to the whole wide world. And when he'd done that —

Helmer: Yes, what then? When I'd delivered my own wife into shame and disgrace—

Nora: When he'd done that, I was so utterly sure that you'd step forward, take the blame on yourself and say: I am the guilty one.

Helmer: Nora—!

Nora: You're thinking I'd never accept such a sacrifice from you? No, of course not. But what good would my protests be against you? That was the miracle I was waiting for, in terror and hope. And to stave that off, I would have taken my life.

Helmer: I'd gladly work for you day and night, Nora—and take on pain and deprivation. But there's no one who gives up honor for love.

Nora: Millions of women have done just that.

Helmer: Oh, you think and talk like a silly child.

Nora: Perhaps. But you neither think nor talk like the man I could join myself to. When your big fright was over—and it wasn't from any threat against me, only for what might damage you—when all the danger was past, for you it was just as if nothing had happened. I was exactly the same, your little lark, your doll, that you'd have to handle with double care now that I'd turned out so brittle and frail. (*Gets up.*) Torvald—in that instant it dawned on me that for eight years I've been living here with a stranger, and that I've even conceived three children—oh, I can't stand the thought of it! I could tear myself to bits.

Helmer (heavily): I see. There a gulf that's opened between us—that's clear. Oh, but Nora, can't we bridge it somehow?

Nora: The way I am now, I'm no wife for you.

Helmer: I have the strength to make myself over.

Nora: Maybe—if your doll gets taken away.

Helmer: But to part! To part from you! No, Nora no—I can't imagine it.

Nora (going out, right): All the more reason why it has to be. (*She reenters with her coat and a small overnight bag, which she puts on a chair by the table.*)

Helmer: Nora, Nora, not now! Wait till tomorrow.

Nora: I can't spend the night in a strange man's room.

Helmer: But couldn't we live here like brother and sister—

Nora: You know very well how long that would last. (*Throws her shawl about her.*) Good-bye, Torvald. I won't look in on the children. I know they're in better hands than mine. The way I am now, I'm no use to them.

Helmer: But someday, Nora—someday—?

Nora: How can I tell? I haven't the least idea what'll become of me.

Helmer: But you're my wife, now and wherever you go.

Nora: Listen, Torvald—I've heard that when a wife deserts her husband's house just as I'm doing, then the law frees him from all responsibility. In any case, I'm freeing you from being responsible. Don't feel yourself bound, any more than I will. There has to be absolute freedom for us both. Here, take your ring back. Give me mine.

Helmer: That too?

Nora: That too.

Helmer: There it is.

Nora: Good. Well, now it's all over. I'm putting the keys here. The maids know all about keeping up the house — better than I do. Tomorrow, after I've left town, Kristine will stop by to pack up everything that's mine from home. I'd like those things shipped up to me.

Helmer: Over! All over! Nora, won't you ever think about me?

Nora: I'm sure I'll think of you often, and about the children and the house here.

Helmer: May I write you?

Nora: No — never. You're not to do that.

Helmer: Oh, but let me send you —

Nora: Nothing. Nothing.

Helmer: Or help you if you need it.

Nora: No. I accept nothing from strangers.

Helmer: Nora — can I never be more than a stranger to you?

Nora (picking up her overnight bag): Ah, Torvald — it would take the greatest miracle of all —

Helmer: Tell me the greatest miracle!

Nora: You and I both would have to transform ourselves to the point that — Oh, Torvald, I've stopped believing in miracles.

Helmer: But I'll believe. Tell me! Transform ourselves to the point that — ?

Nora: That our living together could be a true marriage. (*She goes out down the hall.*)

Helmer (sinks down on a chair by the door, face buried in his hands): Nora! Nora! (*Looking about and rising.*) Empty. She's gone. (*A sudden hope leaps in him.*) The greatest miracle — ?

From below, the sound of a door slamming shut.

Considerations for Critical Thinking and Writing

1. Nora lies several times during the play. What kind of lies are they? Do her lies indicate that she is not to be trusted, or are they a sign of something else about her personality?
2. What kind of wife does Helmer want Nora to be? He affectionately calls her names such as "lark" and "squirrel." What does this reveal about his attitude toward her?
3. Why is Nora "pale with terror" at the end of Act I? What is the significance of the description of the Christmas tree now "stripped of ornament, [with] burned-down candle stubs on its ragged branches" that opens Act II? What other symbols are used in the play?
4. What is Dr. Rank's purpose in the play?
5. How does the relationship between Krogstad and Mrs. Linde serve to emphasize certain qualities in the Helmers' marriage?
6. Is Krogstad's decision not to expose Nora's secret convincing? Does his shift from villainy to generosity seem adequately motivated?
7. Why does Nora reject Helmer's efforts to smooth things over between them and start again? Do you have any sympathy for Helmer?
8. What is the significance of the play's title?
9. Would you describe the ending as essentially happy or unhappy? Is the play more like a comedy or a tragedy?
10. Ibsen once wrote a different ending for the play to head off producers who might have been tempted to change the final scene to placate the public's sense of morality. In the second conclusion, Helmer forces Nora to look in on their

sleeping children. This causes her to realize that she cannot leave her family even though it means sacrificing herself. Ibsen called this version of the ending a "barbaric outrage" and didn't use it. Which ending do you prefer? Why?

11. Ibsen believed that a "dramatist's business is not to answer questions, but only to ask them." What questions are raised in the play? Does Ibsen propose any specific answers?

12. What makes this play a work of realism? Are there any elements that seem not to be realistic?

Connections to Other Selections

1. What does Nora have in common with the protagonist in Godwin's "A Sorrowful Woman" (p. 30)? What significant differences are there between them?

2. Explain how Torvald's attitude toward Nora is similar to the men's attitudes toward women in Glaspell's *Trifles* (p. 1084). Write an essay exploring how the assumptions the men make about women in both plays contribute to the plays' conflicts.

3. Write an essay that compares and contrasts Nora's response to the social and legal expectations of her society with Antigone's in Sophocles' play (p. 1164). To what values does each character pledge her allegiance?

PERSPECTIVE

HENRIK IBSEN (1828–1906)
Notes for A Doll House   1878

There are two kinds of spiritual law, two kinds of conscience, one in man and another, altogether different, in woman. They do not understand each other; but in practical life the woman is judged by man's law, as though she were not a woman but a man.

The wife in the play ends by having no idea of what is right or wrong; natural feeling on the one hand and belief in authority on the other have altogether bewildered her.

A woman cannot be herself in the society of the present day, which is an exclusively masculine society, with laws framed by men and with a judicial system that judges feminine conduct from a masculine point of view.

She has committed forgery, and she is proud of it; for she did it out of love for her husband, to save his life. But this husband with his commonplace principles of honor is on the side of the law and looks at the question from the masculine point of view.

Spiritual conflicts. Oppressed and bewildered by the belief in authority, she loses faith in her moral right and ability to bring up her children. Bitterness. A mother in modern society, like certain insects who go away and die when she has done her duty in the propagation of the race. Love of life, of home, of husband and children and family. Now and then a womanly shaking off of her thoughts. Sudden return of anxiety and terror. She must bear it all alone. The catastrophe approaches, inexorably, inevitably. Despair, conflict, and destruction.

From *From Ibsen's Workshop,* translated by A. G. Chater

Considerations for Critical Thinking and Writing

1. Given the ending of *A Doll House,* what do you think of Ibsen's early view in his notes that "the wife in the play ends by having no idea of what is right or wrong"? Would you describe Nora as "altogether bewildered"? Why or why not?
2. "A woman cannot be herself in the society of the present day, which is an exclusively masculine society." Why is this statement true of Nora? Explain why you agree or disagree that this observation is accurate today.
3. How does oppressive "authority" loom large for Nora? What kind of authority creates "spiritual conflicts" for her?

More perspectives appear in the next chapter, "Critical Case Study: Henrik Ibsen's *A Doll House,*" p. 1613.

THE CHERRY ORCHARD

Anton Chekhov, grandson of a serf and son of an unsuccessful grocer, was born in Taganrog, a small town in southern Russia. He studied medicine at Moscow University and began practicing in 1884. During his medical training, he wrote short stories to support himself and his family (one of them, "The Lady with the Pet Dog," appears on p. 150). Within a few years Chekhov had published two well-received collections of short stories and decided to give up his medical career to be a writer. He did, however, continue to treat his poor neighbors without charge. His compassion and generosity are also reflected in his ability to create sympathetic, convincing characters in his literary works.

Chekhov's first significant success in the theater was *The Seagull* (1896), which was produced by the Moscow Art Theater under the direction of Konstantin Stanislavsky, a champion of realistic methods of acting. *The Seagull* and Chekhov's three other major plays, *Uncle Vanya* (1899), *The Three Sisters* (1901), and *The Cherry Orchard* (1903), are studies of the changing texture of Russian life at the turn of the century. His characters come from a cross section of society, ranging from valiant but ineffectual aristocrats to noble peasants. The future seems bleak for everyone because there is no energy or direction: civil government is merely officious, intellectuals are too self-absorbed, and the church has retreated to backward-looking tradition.

In contrast to Ibsen's plays, little appears to happen in Chekhov's dramas. They lack the sense of inevitable direction intrinsic to the well-made play. Although Ibsen's characters are typically riddled with uncertainties, they take decisive actions or are forcefully acted upon. But in a Chekhov play changes, if any, are measured in small, seemingly inconsequential actions. He creates a slice of life onstage, in which characters frequently talk around issues or past each other so that direct confrontations — the makings of dramatic moments — are relatively rare. Therefore, we must listen carefully to the characters' small talk if we are to follow their deepest concerns. Chekhov uses this method intentionally to mirror the circumstances of most people's lives. He avoids heroics and extreme actions in favor of daily lives; however, his characters' routine activities are typically puncutated by a pistol shot when conflicts break through the polite, trivial veneer. Chekhov does incorporate some melodramatic elements in his plays, but they occur offstage and are subordinated to his interest in subtleties of character.

The Cherry Orchard focuses on a Russian family whose life is rudely and inexorably changed by an urban industrial order that threatens to transform a country estate into subdivided building lots. Chekhov does not definitively choose sides in this shift in power from landed aristocrats to a new class of capitalists; he simply presents his characters amid historic circumstances, which seem to offer opportunities for some but to bewilder and frustrate others.

ANTON CHEKHOV (1860–1904)
The Cherry Orchard   1903

TRANSLATED BY ANN DUNNIGAN

Characters in the Play

Ranevskaya, Lyubov Andreyevna, a landowner
Anya, her daughter, seventeen years old
Varya, her adopted daughter, twenty-four years old
Gayev, Leonid Andreyevich, Madame Ranevskaya's brother
Lopakhin, Yermolai Alekseyevich, a merchant
Trofimov, Pyotr Sergeyevich, a student
Semyonov-Pishchik, Boris Borisovich, a landowner
Charlotta Ivanovna, a governess
Yepikhodov, Semyon Panteleyevich, a clerk
Dunyasha, a maid
Firs, an old valet, eighty-seven years old
Yasha, a young footman
A Stranger
The Stationmaster
A Post-Office Clerk
Guests, Servants

SCENE: *The action takes place on Madame Ranevskaya's estate.*

ACT I

A room that is still called the nursery. One of the doors leads into Anya's room. Dawn; the sun will soon rise. It is May, the cherry trees are in bloom, but it is cold in the orchard; there is a morning frost. The windows in the room are closed. Enter Dunyasha with a candle, and Lopakhin with a book in his hand.

Lopakhin: The train is in, thank God. What time is it?

Dunyasha: Nearly two. (*Blows out the candle.*) It's already light.

Lopakhin: How late is the train, anyway? A couple of hours at least. (*Yawns and stretches.*) I'm a fine one! What a fool I've made of myself! Came here on purpose to meet them at the station, and then overslept. . . . Fell asleep in the chair. It's annoying. . . . You might have waked me.

Dunyasha: I thought you had gone. (*Listens.*) They're coming now, I think!

Lopakhin (listens): No . . . they've got to get the luggage and one thing and another. (*Pause.*) Lyubov Andreyevna has lived abroad for five years, I don't know what she's like now. . . . She's a fine person. Sweet-tempered, simple. I remember when I was a boy of fifteen, my late father — he had a shop in the village then — gave me a punch in the face and made my nose bleed. . . . We had come into the yard here for some reason or other, and he'd had a drop too much. Lyubov Andreyevna — I remember as if it were yesterday — still young, and so slender, led me to the washstand in this very room, the nursery. "Don't cry, little peasant," she said, "it will heal in time for your wedding. . . . " (*Pause.*) Little peasant . . . my father was a peasant, it's true, and here I am in a white waistcoat and tan shoes. Like a pig in a pastry shop. . . . I may be rich, I've made a lot of money, but if you think about it, analyze it, I'm a peasant through and through. (*Turning pages of the book.*) Here I've been reading this book, and I didn't understand a thing. Fell asleep over it. (*Pause.*)

Dunyasha: The dogs didn't sleep all night: they can tell that their masters are coming.

Lopakhin: What's the matter with you, Dunyasha, you're so . . .

Dunyasha: My hands are trembling. I'm going to faint.

Lopakhin: You're much too delicate, Dunyasha. You dress like a lady, and do your hair like one, too. It's not right. You should know your place.

Enter Yepikhodov with a bouquet; he wears a jacket and highly polished boots that squeak loudly. He drops the flowers as he comes in.

Yepikhodov (picking up the flowers): Here, the gardener sent these. He says you're to put them in the dining room. (*Hands the bouquet to Dunyasha.*)

Lopakhin: And bring me some kvas.

Dunyasha: Yes, sir. (*Goes out.*)

Yepikhodov: There's a frost this morning — three degrees — and the cherry trees are in bloom. I cannot approve of our climate. (*Sighs.*) I cannot. Our climate is not exactly conducive. And now, Yermolai Alekseyevich, permit me to append: the day before yesterday I bought myself a pair of boots, which, I venture to assure you, squeak so that it's quite infeasible. What should I grease them with?

Lopakhin: Leave me alone. You make me tired.

Yepikhodov: Every day some misfortune happens to me. But I don't complain, I'm used to it, I even smile.

Dunyasha enters, serves Lopakhin the kvas.

Yepikhodov: I'm going. (*Stumbles over a chair and upsets it.*) There! (*As if in triumph.*) Now you see, excuse the expression . . . the sort of circumstance, incidentally. . . . It's really quite remarkable! (*Goes out.*)

Dunyasha: You know, Yermolai Alekseyich, I have to confess that Yepikhodov has proposed to me.

Lopakhin: Ah!

Dunyasha: And I simply don't know. . . . He's a quiet man, but sometimes, when he starts talking, you can't understand a thing he says. It's nice, and full of feeling, only it doesn't make sense. I sort of like him. He's madly in love with me. But he's an unlucky fellow: every day something happens to him. They tease him about it around here; they call him Two-and-twenty Troubles.

Lopakhin (listening): I think I hear them coming . . .

Dunyasha: They're coming! What's the matter with me? I'm cold all over.

Lopakhin: They're really coming. Let's go and meet them. Will she recognize me? It's five years since we've seen each other.

Dunyasha (agitated): I'll faint this very minute . . . Oh, I'm going to faint!

Two carriages are heard driving up to the house. Lopakhin and Dunyasha go out quickly. The stage is empty. There is a hubbub in the adjoining rooms. Firs hurriedly crosses the stage leaning on a stick. He has been to meet Lyubov Andreyevna and wears old-fashioned livery and a high hat. He mutters something to himself, not a word of which can be understood. The noise offstage grows louder and louder. A voice: "Let's go through here. . . ." Enter Lyubov Andreyevna, Anya, Charlotta Ivanovna with a little dog on a chain, all in traveling dress; Varya wearing a coat and kerchief; Gayev, Semyonov-Pishchik, Lopakhin, Dunyasha with a bundle and parasol; servants with luggage — all walk through the room.

Anya: Let's go this way. Do you remember, Mama, what room this is?

Lyubov Andreyevna (joyfully, through tears): The nursery!

Varya: How cold it is! My hands are numb. (*To Lyubov Andreyevna.*) Your rooms, both the white one and the violet one, are just as you left them, Mama.

Lyubov Andreyevna: The nursery . . . my dear, lovely nursery. . . . I used to sleep here when I was little. . . . (*Weeps.*) And now, like a child, I . . .(*Kisses her brother, Varya, then her brother again.*) Varya hasn't changed; she still looks like a nun. And I recognized Dunyasha. . . . (*Kisses Dunyasha.*)

Gayev: The train was two hours late. How's that? What kind of management is that?

Charlotta (to Pishchik): My dog even eats nuts.

Pishchik (amazed): Think of that now!

They all go out except Anya and Dunyasha.

Dunyasha: We've been waiting and waiting for you. . . . (*Takes off Anya's coat and hat.*)

Anya: I didn't sleep for four nights on the road . . . now I feel cold.

Dunyasha: It was Lent when you went away, there was snow and frost then, but now? My darling! (*Laughs and kisses her.*) I've waited so long for you, my joy, my precious . . . I must tell you at once, I can't wait another minute. . . .

Anya (listlessly): What now?

Dunyasha: The clerk, Yepikhodov, proposed to me just after Easter.

Anya: You always talk about the same thing. . . . (*Straightening her hair.*) I've lost all my hairpins. . . . (*She is so exhausted she can hardly stand.*)

Dunyasha: I really don't know what to think. He loves me — he loves me so!

Anya (looking through the door into her room, tenderly): My room, my windows . . . it's just as though I'd never been away. I am home! Tomorrow morning I'll get up and run into the orchard. . . . Oh, if I could only sleep! I didn't sleep during the entire journey, I was so tormented by anxiety.

Dunyasha: Pyotr Sergeich arrived the day before yesterday.

Anya (joyfully): Petya!

Dunyasha: He's asleep in the bathhouse, he's staying there. "I'm afraid of being in the way," he said. (*Looks at her pocket watch.*) I ought to wake him up, but Varvara Mikhailovna told me not to. "Don't you wake him," she said.

Enter Varya with a bunch of keys at her waist.

Varya: Dunyasha, coffee, quickly . . . Mama's asking for coffee.

Dunyasha: This very minute. (*Goes out.*)

Varya: Thank God, you've come! You're home again. (*Caressing her.*) My little darling has come back! My pretty one is here!

Anya: I've been through so much.

Varya: I can imagine!

Anya: I left in Holy Week, it was cold then. Charlotta never stopped talking and doing her conjuring tricks the entire journey. Why did you saddle me with Charlotta?

Varya: You couldn't have traveled alone, darling. At seventeen!

Anya: When we arrived in Paris, it was cold, snowing. My French is awful. . . . Mama was living on the fifth floor, and when I got there, she had all sorts of Frenchmen and ladies with her, and an old priest with a little book, and it was full of smoke, dismal. Suddenly I felt sorry for Mama, so sorry. I took her head in my arms and held her close and couldn't let her go. Afterward she kept hugging me and crying. . . .

Varya (through her tears): Don't talk about it, don't talk about it. . . .

Anya: She had already sold her villa near Mentone, and she had nothing left, nothing. And I hadn't so much as a kopeck left, we barely managed to get there. But Mama doesn't understand! When we had dinner in a station restaurant, she always ordered the most expensive dishes and tipped each of the waiters a ruble. Charlotta is the same. And Yasha also ordered a dinner, it was simply awful. You know, Yasha is Mama's footman; we brought him with us.

Varya: I saw the rogue.

Anya: Well, how are things? Have you paid the interest?

Varya: How could we?

Anya: Oh, my God, my God!

Varya: In August the estate will be put up for sale.

Anya: My God!

Lopakhin peeps in at the door and moo's like a cow.

Lopakhin: Moo-o-o! (*Disappears.*)

Varya (through her tears): What I couldn't do to him! (*Shakes her fist.*)

Anya (embracing Varya, softly): Varya, has he proposed to you? (*Varya shakes her head.*) But he loves you. . . . Why don't you come to an understanding, what are you waiting for?

Varya: I don't think anything will ever come of it. He's too busy, he has no time for me . . . he doesn't even notice me. I've washed my hands of him, it makes me miserable to see him. . . . Everyone talks of our wedding, they all congratulate me, and actually there's nothing to it — it's all like a dream. . . . (*In a different tone.*) You have a brooch like a bee.

Anya (sadly): Mama bought it. (*Goes into her own room; speaks gaily, like a child.*) In Paris I went up in a balloon!

Varya: My darling is home! My pretty one has come back!

Dunyasha has come in with the coffeepot and prepares coffee.

Varya (stands at the door of Anya's room): You know, darling, all day long I'm busy looking after the house, but I keep dreaming. If we could marry you to a rich man I'd be at peace. I could go into a hermitage, then to Kiev, to Moscow, and from one holy place to another. . . . I'd go on and on. What a blessing!

Anya: The birds are singing in the orchard. What time is it?

Varya: It must be after two. Time you were asleep, darling. (*Goes into Anya's room.*) What a blessing!

Yasha enters with a lap robe and a traveling bag.

Yasha (crosses the stage mincingly): May one go through here?

Dunyasha: A person would hardly recognize you, Yasha. Your stay abroad has done wonders for you.

Yasha: Hm. . . . And who are you?

Dunyasha: When you left here I was only that high — (*Indicating with her hand.*) I'm Dunyasha, Fyodor Kozoyedov's daughter. You don't remember!

Yasha: Hm. . . . A little cucumber! (*Looks around, then embraces her; she cries out and drops a saucer. He quickly goes out.*)

Varya (in a tone of annoyance, from the doorway): What's going on here?

Dunyasha (tearfully): I broke a saucer.

Varya: That's good luck.

Anya: We ought to prepare Mama: Petya is here. . . .

Varya: I gave orders not to wake him.

Anya (pensively): Six years ago Father died, and a month later brother Grisha drowned in the river . . . a pretty little seven-year-old boy. Mama couldn't bear it and went away . . . went without looking back. . . . (*Shudders.*) How I understand her, if she only knew! (*Pause.*) And Petya Trofimov was Grisha's tutor, he may remind her. . . .

Enter Firs wearing a jacket and a white waistcoat.

Firs (goes to the coffeepot, anxiously): The mistress will have her coffee here. (*Puts on white gloves.*) Is the coffee ready? (*To Dunyasha, sternly.*) You! Where's the cream?

Dunyasha: Oh, my goodness! (*Quickly goes out.*)

Firs (fussing over the coffeepot): Ah, what an addlepate! (*Mutters to himself.*) They've come back from Paris. . . . The master used to go to Paris . . . by carriage. . . . (*Laughs.*)

Varya: What is it, Firs?

Firs: If you please? (*Joyfully*) My mistress has come home! At last! Now I can die. . . . (*Weeps with joy.*)

Enter Lyubov Andreyevna, Gayev, and Semyonov-Pishchik, the last wearing a sleeveless peasant coat of fine cloth and full trousers. Gayev, as he comes in, goes through the motions of playing billiards.

Lyubov Andreyevna: How does it go? Let's see if I can remember . . . cue ball into the corner! Double the rail to center table.

Gayev: Cut shot into the corner! There was a time, sister, when you and I used to sleep here in this very room, and now I'm fifty-one, strange as it may seem. . . .

Lopakhin: Yes, time passes.

Gayev: How's that?

Lopakhin: Time, I say, passes.

Gayev: It smells of patchouli here.

Anya: I'm going to bed. Good night, Mama. (*Kisses her mother.*)

Lyubov Andreyevna: My precious child. (*Kisses her hands.*) Are you glad to be home? I still feel dazed.

Anya: Good night, Uncle.

Gayev (kisses her face and hands): God bless you. How like your mother you are! (*To his sister.*) At her age you were exactly like her, Lyuba.

Anya shakes hands with Lopakhin and Pishchik and goes out, closing the door after her.

Lyubov Andreyevna: She's exhausted.

Pishchik: Must have been a long journey.

Varya: Well, gentlemen? It's after two, high time you were going.

Lyubov Andreyevna (laughs): You haven't changed, Varya. (*Draws Varya to her and kisses her.*) I'll just drink my coffee and then we'll all go. (*Firs places a cushion under her feet.*) Thank you, my dear. I've got used to coffee. I drink it day and night. Thanks, dear old man. (*Kisses him.*)

Varya: I'd better see if all the luggage has been brought in.

Lyubov Andreyevna: Is this really me sitting here? (*Laughs.*) I feel like jumping about and waving my arms. (*Buries her face in her hands.*) What if it's only a dream! God knows I love my country, love it dearly. I couldn't look out the train window, I was crying so! (*Through tears.*) But I must drink my coffee. Thank you, Firs, thank you, my dear old friend. I'm so glad you're still alive.

Firs: The day before yesterday.

Gayev: He's hard of hearing.

Lopakhin: I must go now, I'm leaving for Kharkov about five o'clock. It's so annoying! I wanted to have a good look at you, and have a talk. You're as splendid as ever.

Pishchik (breathing heavily): Even more beautiful. . . . Dressed like a Parisienne. . . . There goes my wagon, all four wheels!

Lopakhin: Your brother here, Leonid Andreich, says I'm a boor, a moneygrubber, but I don't mind. Let him talk. All I want is that you should trust me as you used to, and that your wonderful, touching eyes should look at me as they did then. Merciful God! My father was one of your father's serfs, and your grandfather's, but you yourself did so much for me once, that I've forgotten all that and love you as if you were my own kin — more than my kin.

Lyubov Andreyevna: I can't sit still, I simply cannot. (*Jumps up and walks about the room in great excitement.*) I cannot bear this joy. . . . Laugh at me, I'm silly. . . . My dear little bookcase . . . (*Kisses bookcase.*) my little table . . .

Gayev: Nurse died while you were away.

Lyubov Andreyevna (sits down and drinks coffee): Yes, God rest her soul. They wrote me.

Gayev: And Anastasy is dead. Petrushka Kosoi left me and is now with the police inspector in town. (*Takes a box of hard candies from his pocket and begins to suck one.*)

Pishchik: My daughter, Dashenka . . . sends her regards . . .

Lopakhin: I wish I could tell you something very pleasant and cheering. (*Glances at his watch.*) I must go directly, there's no time to talk, but . . . well, I'll say it in a couple of words. As you know, the cherry orchard is to be sold to pay your debts. The auction is set for August twenty-second, but you need not worry, my dear, you can sleep in peace, there is a way out. This is my plan. Now, please listen! Your estate is only twenty versts from town, the railway runs close by, and if the cherry orchard and the land along the river were cut up into lots and leased for summer cottages, you'd have, at the very least, an income of twenty-five thousand a year.

Gayev: Excuse me, what nonsense!

Lyubov Andreyevna: I don't quite understand you, Yermolai Alekseich.

Lopakhin: You will get, at the very least, twenty-five rubles a year for a two-and-a-half-acre lot, and if you advertise now, I guarantee you won't have a single plot of ground left by autumn, everything will be snapped up. In short, I congratulate you, you are saved. The site is splendid, the river is deep. Only, of course, the ground must be cleared . . . you must tear down all the old outbuildings, for instance, and this house, which is worthless, cut down the old cherry orchard —

Lyubov Andreyevna: Cut it down? Forgive me, my dear, but you don't know what you are talking about. If there is one thing in the whole province that is interesting, not to say remarkable, it's our cherry orchard.

Lopakhin: The only remarkable thing about this orchard is that it is very big. There's a crop of cherries every other year, and then you can't get rid of them, nobody buys them.

Gayev: This orchard is even mentioned in the *Encyclopedia.*

Lopakhin (glancing at his watch): If we don't think of something and come to a decision, on the twenty-second of August the cherry orchard, and the entire estate, will be sold at auction. Make up your minds! There is no other way out, I swear to you. None whatsoever.

Firs: In the old days, forty or fifty years ago, the cherries were dried, soaked, marinated, and made into jam, and they used to —

Gayev: Be quiet, Firs.

Firs: And they used to send cartloads of dried cherries to Moscow and Kharkov. And that brought in money! The dried cherries were soft and juicy in those days, sweet, fragrant. . . . They had a method then . . .

Lyubov Andreyevna: And what has become of that method now?

Firs: Forgotten. Nobody remembers. . . .

Pishchik: How was it in Paris? What's it like there? Did you eat frogs?

Lyubov Andreyevna: I ate crocodiles.

Pishchik: Think of that now!

Lopakhin: There used to be only the gentry and the peasants living in the country, but now these summer people have appeared. All the towns, even the smallest ones, are surrounded by summer cottages. And it is safe to say that in another twenty years these people will multiply enormously. Now the summer resident only drinks tea on his porch, but it may well be that he'll take to cultivating his acre, and then your cherry orchard will be a happy, rich, luxuriant —

Gayev (indignantly): What nonsense!

Enter Varya and Yasha.

Varya: There are two telegrams for you, Mama. (*Picks out a key and with a jingling sound opens an old-fashioned bookcase.*) Here they are.

Lyubov Andreyevna: From Paris. (*Tears up the telegrams without reading them.*) That's all over. . . .

Gayev: Do you know, Lyuba, how old this bookcase is? A week ago I pulled out the bottom drawer, and what do I see? Some figures burnt into it. The bookcase was made exactly a hundred years ago. What do you think of that? Eh? We could have celebrated its jubilee. It's an inanimate object, but nevertheless, for all that, it's a bookcase.

Pishchik: A hundred years . . . think of that now!

Gayev: Yes . . . that is something. . . . (*Feeling the bookcase.*) Dear, honored bookcase, I salute thy existence, which for over one hundred years has served the glorious ideals of goodness and justice; thy silent appeal to fruitful endeavor, unflagging in the course of a hundred years, tearfully sustaining through generations of our family, courage and faith in a better future, and fostering in us ideals of goodness and social consciousness. . . .

A pause.

Lopakhin: Yes . . .

Lyubov Andreyevna: You are the same as ever, Lyonya.

Gayev (somewhat embarrassed): Carom into the corner, cut shot to center table.

Lopakhin (looks at this watch): Well, time for me to go.

Yasha (hands medicine to Lyubov Andreyevna): Perhaps you will take your pills now.

Pishchik: Don't take medicaments, dearest lady, they do neither harm nor good. Let me have them, honored lady. (*Takes the pill box, shakes the pills into his hand, blows on them, puts them into his mouth, and washes them down with kvas.*) There!

Lyubov Andreyevna (alarmed): Why, you must be mad!

Pishchik: I've taken all the pills.

Lopakhin: What a glutton!

Everyone laughs.

Firs: The gentleman stayed with us during Holy Week . . . ate half a bucket of pickles. . . . (*Mumbles.*)

Lyubov Andreyevna: What is he saying?

Varya: He's been muttering like that for three years now. We've grown used to it.

Yasha: He's in his dotage.

Charlotta Ivanovna, very thin, tightly laced, in a white dress with a lorgnette at her belt, crosses the stage.

Lopakhin: Forgive me, Charlotta Ivanovna, I haven't had a chance to say how do you do to you. (*Tries to kiss her hand.*)

Charlotta (pulls her hand away): If I permit you to kiss my hand you'll be wanting to kiss my elbow next, then my shoulder.

Lopakhin: I have no luck today. (*Everyone laughs.*) Charlotta Ivanovna, show us a trick!

Lyubov Andreyevna: Charlotta, show us a trick!

Charlotta: No. I want to sleep. (*Goes out.*)

Lopakhin: In three weeks we'll meet again. (*Kisses Lyubov Andreyevna's hand.*) Good-bye till then. Time to go. (*To Gayev.*) Good-bye. (*Kisses Pishchik.*) Good-bye. (*Shakes hands with Varya, then with Firs and Yasha.*) I don't feel like going. (*To Lyubov Andreyevna.*) If you make up your mind about the summer cottages and come to a decision, let me know; I'll get you a loan of fifty thousand or so. Think it over seriously.

Varya (angrily): Oh, why don't you go!

Lopakhin: I'm going, I'm going. (*Goes out.*)

Gayev: Boor. Oh, pardon. Varya's going to marry him, he's Varya's young man.

Varya: Uncle dear, you talk too much.

Lyubov Andreyevna: Well, Varya, I shall be very glad. He's a good man.

Pishchik: A man, I must truly say . . . most worthy . . . And my Dashenka . . . says, too, that . . . says all sorts of things. (*Snores but wakes up at once.*) In any case, honored lady, oblige me . . . a loan of two hundred and forty rubles . . . tomorrow the interest on my mortgage is due . . .

Varya (in alarm): We have nothing, nothing at all!

Lyubov Andreyevna: I really haven't any money.

Pishchik: It'll turn up. (*Laughs.*) I never lose hope. Just when I thought everything was lost, that I was done for, lo and behold — the railway ran through my land . . . and they paid me for it. And before you know it, something else will turn up, if not today — tomorrow. . . . Dashenka will win two hundred thousand . . . she's got a lottery ticket.

Lyubov Andreyevna: The coffee is finished, we can go to bed.

Firs (brushing Gayev's clothes, admonishingly): You've put on the wrong trousers again. What am I to do with you?

Varya (softly): Anya's asleep. (*Quietly opens the window.*) The sun has risen, it's no longer cold. Look, Mama dear, what wonderful trees! Oh, Lord, the air! The starlings are singing!

Gayev (opens another window): The orchard is all white. You havn't forgotten, Lyuba? That long avenue there that runs straight — straight as a stretched-out strap; it gleams on moonlight nights. Remember? You've not forgotten?

Lyubov Andreyevna (looking out the window at the orchard): Oh, my childhood, my innocence! I used to sleep in this nursery, I looked out from here into the orchard, happiness awoke with me each morning, it was just as it is now, nothing has changed. (*Laughing with joy*) All, all white! Oh, my orchard! After the dark, rainy autumn and the cold winter, you are young again, full of happiness, the heavenly angels have not forsaken you. . . . If I could cast off this heavy stone weighing on my breast and shoulders, if I could forget my past!

Gayev: Yes, and the orchard will be sold for our debts, strange as it may seem. . . .

Lyubov Andreyevna: Look, our dead mother walks in the orchard . . . in a white dress! (*Laughs with joy.*) It is she!

Gayev: Where?

Varya: God be with you, Mama dear.

Lyubov Andreyevna: There's no one out there, I just imagined it. To the right, as you turn to the summerhouse, a slender white sapling is bent over . . . it looks like a woman.

Enter Trofimov wearing a shabby student's uniform and spectacles.

Lyubov Andreyevna: What a wonderful orchard! The white masses of blossoms, the blue sky —

Trofimov: Lyubov Andreyevna! (*She looks around at him.*) I only want to pay my respects, then I'll go at once. (*Kisses her hand ardently.*) I was told to wait until morning, but I hadn't the patience.

Lyubov Andreyevna looks at him, puzzled.

Varya (through tears): This is Petya Trofimov.

Trofimov: Petya Trofimov, I was Grisha's tutor. . . . Can I have changed so much?

Lyubov Andreyevna embraces him, quietly weeping.

Gayev (embarrassed): There, there, Lyuba.

Varya (crying): Didn't I tell you, Petya, to wait til tomorrow?

Lyubov Andreyevna: My Grisha . . . my little boy . . . Grisha . . . my son . . .

Varya: What can we do, Mama dear? It's God's will.

Trofimov (gently, through tears): Don't don't. . . .

Lyubov Andreyevna (quietly weeping): My little boy dead, drowned. . . . Why? Why, my friend? (*In a lower voice.*) Anya is sleeping in there, and I'm talking loudly . . . making all this noise. . . . But Petya, why do you look so bad? Why have you grown so old?

Trofimov: A peasant woman in the train called me a mangy gentleman.

Lyubov Andreyevna: You were just a boy then, a charming little student, and now your hair is thin — and spectacles! Is it possible you are still a student? (*Goes toward the door.*)

Trofimov: I shall probably be an eternal student.

Lyubov Andreyevna (kisses her brother, then Varya): Now, go to bed. . . . You've grown older too, Leonid.

Pishchik (follows her): Well, seems to be time to sleep. . . . Oh, my gout! I'm staying the night. Lyubov Andreyevna, my soul, tomorrow morning . . . two hundred and forty rubles. . . .

Gayev: He keeps at it.

Pishchik: Two hundred and forty rubles . . . to pay the interest on my mortgage.

Lyubov Andreyevna: I have no money, my friend.

Pishchik: My dear, I'll pay it back. . . . It's a trifling sum.

Lyubov Andreyevna: Well, all right, Leonid will give it to you . . . Give it to him, Leonid.

Gayev: Me give it to him! . . . Hold out your pocket!

Lyubov Andreyevna: It can't be helped, give it to him . . . He needs it. . . . He'll pay it back.

Lyubov Andreyevna, Trofimov, Pishchik and Firs go out. Gayev, Varya, and Yasha remain.

Gayev: My sister hasn't yet lost her habit of squandering money. (*To Yasha.*) Go away, my good fellow, you smell of the henhouse.

Yasha (with a smirk): And you, Leonid Andreyevich, are just the same as ever.

Gayev: How's that? (*To Varya.*) What did he say?

Varya: Your mother has come from the village; she's been sitting in the servants' room since yesterday, waiting to see you. . . .

Yasha: Let her wait, for God's sake!

Varya: Aren't you ashamed?

Yasha: A lot I need her! She could have come tomorrow. (*Goes out.*)

Varya: Mama's the same as ever, she hasn't changed a bit. She'd give away everything, if she could.

Gayev: Yes. . . . (*A pause.*) If a great many remedies are suggested for a disease, it means that the disease is incurable. I keep thinking, racking my brains, I have many remedies, a great many, and that means, in effect, that I have none. It would be good to receive a legacy from someone, good to marry our Anya to a very rich man, good to go to Yaroslav and try our luck with our aunt, the Countess. She is very, very rich, you know.

Varya (crying): If only God would help us!

Gayev: Stop bawling. Auntie's very rich, but she doesn't like us. In the first place, sister married a lawyer, not a nobleman . . . (*Anya appears in the doorway.*) She married beneath her, and it cannot be said that she has conducted herself very virtuously. She is good, kind, charming, and I love her dearly, but no matter how much you allow for extenuating circumstances, you must admit she leads a sinful life. You feel it in her slightest movement.

Varya (in a whisper): Anya is standing in the doorway.

Gayev: What? (*Pause.*) Funny, something got into my right eye . . . I can't see very well. And Thursday, when I was in the district court . . .

Anya enters.

Varya: Why aren't you asleep, Anya?

Anya: I can't get to sleep. I just can't.

Gayev: My little one! (*Kisses Anya's face and hands.*) My child . . . (*Through tears.*) You are not my niece, you are my angel, you are everything to me. Believe me, believe . . .

Anya: I believe you, Uncle. Everyone loves you and respects you, but, Uncle dear, you must keep quiet, just keep quiet. What were you saying just now about my mother, about your own sister? What made you say that?

Gayev: Yes, yes. . . . (*Covers his face with her hand.*) Really, it's awful! My God!

God help me! And today I made a speech to the bookcase . . . so stupid! And it was only when I had finished that I realized it was stupid.

Varya: It's true, Uncle dear, you ought to keep quiet. Just don't talk, that's all.

Anya: If you could keep from talking, it would make things easier for you, too.

Gayev: I'll be quiet. (*Kisses Anya's and Varya's hands.*) I'll be quiet. Only this is about business. On Thursday I was in the district court, well, a group of us gathered together and began talking about one thing and another, this and that, and it seems it might be possible to arrange a loan on a promissory note to pay the interest at the bank.

Varya: If only God would help us!

Gayev: On Tuesday I'll go and talk it over again. (*To Varya.*) Stop bawling. (*To Anya.*) Your mama will talk to Lopakhin; he, of course, will not refuse her. . . . And as soon as you've rested, you will go to Yaroslav to the Countess, your great-aunt. In that way we shall be working from three directions — and our business is in the hat. We'll pay the interest, I'm certain of it. . . . (*Puts a candy in his mouth.*) On my honor, I'll swear by anything you like, the estate shall not be sold. (*Excitedly.*) By my happiness, I swear it! Here's my hand on it, call me a worthless, dishonorable man if I let it come to auction! I swear by my whole being!

Anya (a calm mood returns to her, she is happy): How good you are, Uncle, how clever! (*Embraces him.*) Now I am at peace! I'm at peace! I'm happy!

Enter Firs.

Firs (reproachfully): Leonid Andreich, have you no fear of God? When are you going to bed?

Gayev: Presently, presently. Go away, Firs. I'll . . . all right, I'll undress myself. Well, children, bye-bye. . . . Details tomorrow, and now go to sleep. (*Kisses Anya and Varya.*) I am a man of the eighties. . . . They don't think much of that period today, nevertheless, I can say that in the course of my life I have suffered not a little for my convictions. It is not for nothing that the peasant loves me. You have to know the peasant! You have to know from what —

Anya: There you go again, Uncle!

Varya: Uncle dear, do be quiet.

Firs (angrily): Leonid Andreich!

Gayev: I'm coming, I'm coming. . . . Go to bed. A clean double rail shot to center table. . . . (*Goes out; Firs hobbles after him.*)

Anya: I'm at peace now. I would rather not go to Yaroslav, I don't like my great-aunt, but still, I'm at peace, thanks to Uncle. (*She sits down.*)

Varya: We must get some sleep. I'm going now. Oh, something unpleasant happened while you were away. In the old servants' quarters, as you know, there are only the old people: Yefimushka, Polya, Yevstignei, and, of course, Karp. They began letting in all sorts of rogues to spend the night — I didn't say anything. But then I heard they'd been spreading a rumor that I'd given an order for them to be fed nothing but dried peas. Out of stinginess, you see. . . . It was all Yevstignei's doing. . . . Very well, I think, if that's how it is, you just wait. I send for Yevstignei . . . *Yawning.*) he comes. . . . "How is it, Yevstignei," I say, "that you could be such a fool. . . ." (*Looks at Anya.*) She's fallen asleep. (*Takes her by the arm.*) Come to your little bed. . . . Come along. (*Leading her.*) My little darling fell asleep. Come. . . . (*They go.*)

In the distance, beyond the orchard, a shepherd is playing on a reed pipe. Trofimov crosses the stage, and, seeing Varya and Anya, stops.

Varya: Sh! She's asleep . . . asleep. . . . Come along, darling.

Anya (softly, half-asleep): I'm so tired. . . . Those bells . . . Uncle . . . dear . . . Mama and Uncle . . .

Varya: Come, darling, come along. (*They go into Anya's room.*)

Trofimov (deeply moved): My sunshine! My spring!

ACT II

A meadow. An old, lopsided, long-abandoned little chapel; near it a well, large stones that apparently were once tombstones, and an old bench. A road to the Gayev manor house can be seen. On one side, where the cherry orchard begins, tall poplars loom. In the distance a row of telegraph poles, and far, far away, on the horizon, the faint outline of a large town, which is visible only in very fine, clear weather. The sun will soon set. Charlotta, Yasha, and Dunyasha are sitting on the bench; Yepikhodov stands near playing something sad on the guitar. They are all lost in thought. Charlotta wears an old forage cap; she has taken a gun from her shoulder and is adjusting the buckle on the sling.

Charlotta (reflectively): I haven't got a real passport, I don't know how old I am, but it always seems to me that I'm quite young. When I was a little girl, my father and mother used to travel from one fair to another giving performances — very good ones. And I did the *salto mortale°* and all sorts of tricks. Then when Papa and Mama died, a German lady took me to live with her and began teaching me. Good. I grew up and became a governess. But where I came from and who I am — I do not know. . . . Who my parents were — perhaps they weren't even married — I don't know. (*Takes a cucumber out of her pocket and eats it.*) I don't know anything. (*Pause.*) One wants so much to talk, but there isn't anyone to talk to . . . I have no one.

Yepikhodov (plays the guitar and sings): "What care I for the clamorous world, what's friend or foe to me?" . . . How pleasant it is to play a mandolin!

Dunyasha: That's a guitar, not a mandolin. (*Looks at herself in a hand mirror and powders her face.*)

Yepikhodov: To a madman, in love, it is a mandolin. . . . (*Sings.*) "Would that the heart were warmed by the flame of requited love . . ."

Yasha joins in.

Charlotta: How horribly these people sing! . . . Pfui! Like jackals!

Dunyasha (to Yasha): Really, how fortunate to have been abroad!

Yasha: Yes, to be sure. I cannot but agree with you there. (*Yawns, then lights a cigar.*)

Yepikhodov: It stands to reason. Abroad everything has long since been fully constituted.

Yasha: Obviously.

Yepikhodov: I am a cultivated man, I read all sorts of remarkable books, but I

---

salto mortale: A standing somersault.

am in no way able to make out my own inclinations, what it is I really want, whether, strictly speaking, to live or to shoot myself; nevertheless, I always carry a revolver on me. Here it is. (*Shows revolver.*)

Charlotta: Finished. Now I'm going. (*Slings the gun over her shoulder.*) You're a very clever man, Yepikhodov, and quite terrifying; women must be mad about you. Brrr! (*Starts to go.*) These clever people are all so stupid, there's no one for me to talk to. . . . Alone, always alone, I have no one . . . and who I am, and why I am, nobody knows. . . . (*Goes out unhurriedly.*)

Yepikhodov: Strictly speaking, all else aside, I must state regarding myself, that fate treats me unmercifully, as a storm does a small ship. If, let us assume, I am mistaken, then why, to mention a single instance, do I wake up this morning, and there on my chest see a spider of terrifying magnitude? . . . Like that. (*Indicates with both hands.*) And likewise, I take up some kvas to quench my thirst, and there see something in the highest degree unseemly, like a cockroach. (*Pause.*) Have you read Buckle?° (*Pause.*) If I may trouble you, Avdotya Fedorovna, I should like to have a word or two with you.

Dunyasha: Go ahead.

Yepikhodov: I prefer to speak with you alone. . . . (*Sighs.*)

Dunyasha (embarrassed): Very well . . . only first bring me my little cape . . . you'll find it by the cupboard. . . . It's rather damp here. . . .

Yepikhodov: Certainly, ma'am . . . I'll fetch it, ma'am. . . . Now I know what to do with my revolver. . . . (*Takes the guitar and goes off playing it.*)

Yasha: Two-and-twenty Troubles! Between ourselves, a stupid fellow. (*Yawns.*)

Dunyasha: God forbid that he should shoot himself (*Pause.*) I've grown so anxious, I'm always worried. I was only a little girl when I was taken into the master's house, and now I'm quite unused to the simple life, and my hands are white as can be, just like a lady's. I've become so delicate, so tender and ladylike, I'm afraid of everything. . . . Frightfully so. And, Yasha, if you deceive me, I just don't know what will become of my nerves.

Yasha (kisses her): You little cucumber! Of course, a girl should never forget herself. What I dislike above everything is when a girl doesn't conduct herself properly.

Dunyasha: I'm passionately in love with you; you're educated, you can discuss anything. (*Pause.*)

Yasha (yawns): Yes. . . . As I see it, it's like this: if a girl loves somebody, that means she's immoral. (*Pause.*) Very pleasant smoking a cigar in the open air. . . . (*Listens.*) Someone's coming this way. . . . It's the masters. (*Dunyasha impulsively embraces him.*) You go home, as if you'd been to the river to bathe; take that path, otherwise they'll see you and suspect me of having a rendezvous with you. I can't endure that sort of thing.

Dunyasha (with a little cough): My head is beginning to ache from your cigar. . . . (*Goes out.*)

Yasha remains, sitting near the chapel. Lyubov Andreyevna, Gayev, and Lopakhin enter.

Buckle: Henry Thomas Buckle (1821–1862), a radical historian who formulated a scientific basis for history emphasizing the interrelationship of climate, food production, population, and wealth.

Lopakhin: You must make up your mind once and for all — time won't stand still. The question, after all, is quite simple. Do you agree to lease the land for summer cottages or not? Answer in one word: yes or no? Only one word!

Lyubov Andreyevna: Who is it that smokes those disgusting cigars out here? (*Sits down.*)

Gayev: Now that the railway line is so near, it's made things convenient. (*Sits down.*) We went to town and had lunch . . . cue ball to the center! I feel like going to the house first and playing a game.

Lyubov Andreyevna: Later.

Lopakhin: Just one word! (*Imploringly.*) Do give me an answer!

Gayev (yawning): How's that?

Lyubov Andreyevna (looks into her purse): Yesterday I had a lot of money, and today there's hardly any left. My poor Varya tries to economize by feeding everyone milk soup, and in the kitchen the old people get nothing but dried peas, while I squander money foolishly. . . . (*Drops the purse, scattering gold coins.*) There they go. . . . (*Vexed.*)

Yasha: Allow me, I'll pick them up in an instant. (*Picks up the money.*)

Lyubov Andreyevna: Please do, Yasha. And why did I go to town for lunch? . . . That miserable restaurant of yours with its music, and tablecloths smelling of soap. . . . Why drink so much, Lyonya? Why eat so much? Why talk so much? Today in the restaurant again you talked too much, and it was all so pointless. About the seventies, about the decadents. And to whom? Talking to waiters about the decadents!

Lopakhin: Yes.

Gayev (waving his hand): I'm incorrigible, that's evident. . . . (*Irritably to Yasha.*) Why do you keep twirling about in front of me?

Yasha (laughs): I can't help laughing when I hear your voice.

Gayev (to his sister): Either he or I —

Lyubov Andreyevna: Go away, Yasha, run along.

Yasha (hands Lyubov Andreyevna her purse): I'm going, right away. (*Hardly able to contain his laughter.*) This very instant. . . . (*Goes out.*)

Lopakhin: That rich man, Deriganov, is prepared to buy the estate. They say he's coming to the auction himself.

Lyubov Andreyevna: Where did you hear that?

Lopakhin: That's what they're saying in town.

Lyubov Andreyevna: Our aunt in Yaroslav promised to send us something, but when and how much, no one knows.

Lopakhin: How much do you think she'll send? A hundred thousand? Two hundred?

Lyubov Andreyevna: Oh . . . ten or fifteen thousand, and we'll be thankful for that.

Lopakhin: Forgive me, but I have never seen such frivolous, such queer, unbusinesslike people as you, my friends. You are told in plain language that your estate is to be sold, and it's as though you don't understand it.

Lyubov Andreyevna: But what are we to do? Tell us what to do.

Lopakhin: I tell you every day. Every day I say the same thing. Both the cherry orchard and the land must be leased for summer cottages, and it must be done now, as quickly as possible — the auction is close at hand. Try to understand! Once you definitely decide on the cottages, you can raise as much money as you like, and then you are saved.

Lyubov Andreyevna: Cottages, summer people — forgive me, but it's so vulgar.

Gayev: I agree with you, absolutely.

Lopakhin: **I'll either burst into tears, start shouting, or fall into a faint! I can't** stand it! You've worn me out! (*To Gayev.*) You're an old woman!

Gayev: How's that?

Lopakhin: An old woman! (*Starts to go.*)

Lyubov Andreyevna (alarmed): No, don't go, stay, my dear. I beg you. Perhaps we'll think of something!

Lopakhin: What is there to think of?

Lyubov Andreyevna: Don't go away, please. With you here it's more cheerful somehow. . . . (*Pause.*) I keep expecting something to happen, like the house caving in on us.

Gayev (in deep thought): Double rail shot into the corner. . . . Cross table to the center. . . .

Lyubov Andreyevna: We have sinned so much. . . .

Lopakhin: What sins could you have —

Gayev (puts a candy into his mouth): They say I've eaten up my entire fortune in candies. . . . (*Laughs.*)

Lyubov Andreyevna: Oh, my sins. . . . I've always squandered money recklessly, like a madwoman, and I married a man who did nothing but amass debts. My husband died from champagne — he drank terribly — then, to my sorrow, I fell in love with another man, lived with him, and just at that time — that was my first punishment, a blow on the head — my little boy was drowned . . . here in a river. And I went abroad, went away for good, never to return, never to see this river. . . . I closed my eyes and ran, beside myself, and *he* after me . . . callously, without pity. I bought a villa near Mentone, because he fell ill there, and for three years I had no rest, day or night. The sick man wore me out, my soul dried up. Then last year, when the villa was sold to pay my debts, I went to Paris, and there he stripped me of everything, and left me for another woman; I tried to poison myself. . . . So stupid, so shameful. . . . And suddenly I felt a longing for Russia, for my own country, for my little girl. . . . (*Wipes away her tears.*) Lord, Lord, be merciful, forgive my sins! Don't punish me any more! (*Takes a telegram out of her pocket.*) This came today from Paris. . . . He asks my forgiveness, begs me to return. . . . (*Tears up telegram.*) Do I hear music? (*Listens.*)

Gayev: That's our famous Jewish band. You remember, four violins, a flute and double bass.

Lyubov Andreyevna: It's still in existence? We ought to send for them some time and give a party.

Lopakhin (listens): I don't hear anything. . . . (*Sings softly.*) "The Germans, for pay, will turn Russians into Frenchmen, they say." (*Laughs.*) What a play I saw yesterday at the theater — very funny!

Lyubov Andreyevna: There was probably nothing funny about it. Instead of going to see plays you ought to look at yourselves a little more often. How drab your lives are, how full of futile talk!

Lopakhin: That's true. I must say, this life of ours is stupid. . . . (*Pause.*) My father was a peasant, an idiot; he understood nothing, taught me nothing; all he did was beat me when he was drunk, and always with a stick. As a matter of fact, I'm as big a blockhead and idiot as he was. I never learned anything, my handwriting's disgusting, I write like a pig — I'm ashamed to have people see it.

Lyubov Andreyevna: You ought to get married, my friend.

Lopakhin: Yes . . . that's true.

Lyubov Andreyevna: To our Varya. She's a nice girl.

Lopakhin: Yes.

Lyubov Andreyevna: She's a girl who comes from simple people, works all day long, but the main thing is she loves you. Besides, you've liked her for a long time now.

Lopakhin: Well? I've nothing against it. . . . She's a good girl. (*Pause.*)

Gayev: I've been offered a place in the bank. Six thousand a year. . . . Have you heard?

Lyubov Andreyevna: How could you! You stay where you are. . . .

Firs enters carrying an overcoat.

Firs (To Gayev): If you please, sir, put this on, it's damp.

Gayev (puts on the overcoat): You're a pest, old man.

Firs: Never mind. . . . You went off this morning without telling me. (*Looks him over.*)

Lyubov Andreyevna: How you have aged, Firs!

Firs: What do you wish, madam?

Lopakhin: She says you've grown very old!

Firs: I've lived a long time. They were arranging a marriage for me before your papa was born. . . . (*Laughs.*) I was already head footman when the Emancipation came.° At that time I wouldn't consent to my freedom, I stayed with the masters. . . . (*Pause.*) I remember, everyone was happy, but what they were happy about, they themselves didn't know.

Lopakhin: It was better in the old days. At least they flogged them.

Firs (not hearing): Of course. The peasants kept to the masters, the masters kept to the peasants; but now they have all gone their own ways, you can't tell about anything.

Gayev: Be quiet, Firs. Tomorrow I must go to town. I've been promised an introduction to a certain general who might let us have a loan.

Lopakhin: Nothing will come of it. And you can rest assured, you won't even pay the interest.

Lyubov Andreyevna: He's raving. There is no such general.

Enter Trofimov, Anya, and Varya.

Gayev: Here come our young people.

Anya: There's Mama.

Lyubov Andreyevna (tenderly): Come, come along, my darlings. (*Embraces Anya and Varya.*) If you only knew how I love you both! Sit here beside me — there, like that.

when the Emancipation came: Serfs were freed in 1861.

They all sit down.

Lopakhin: Our eternal student is always with the young ladies.

Trofimov: That's none of your business.

Lopakhin: He'll soon be fifty, but he's still a student.

Trofimov: Drop your stupid jokes.

Lopakhin: What are you so angry about, you queer fellow?

Trofimov: Just leave me alone.

Lopakhin (laughs): Let me ask you something: what do you make of me?

Trofimov: My idea of you, Yermolai Alekseich, is this: you're a rich man, you will soon be a millionaire. Just as the beast of prey, which devours everything that crosses its path, is necessary in the metabolic process, so are you necessary.

Everyone laughs.

Varya: Petya, you'd better tell us something about the planets.

Lyubov Andreyevna: No, let's go on with yesterday's conversation.

Trofimov: What was it about?

Gayev: About the proud man.

Trofimov: We talked a long time yesterday, but we didn't get anywhere. In the proud man, in your sense of the word, there's something mystical. And you may be right from your point of view, but if you look at it simply, without being abstruse, why even talk about pride? Is there any sense in it if, physiologically, man is poorly constructed, if, in the vast majority of cases, he is coarse, ignorant, and profoundly unhappy? We should stop admiring ourselves. We should just work, and that's all.

Gayev: You die, anyway.

Trofimov: Who knows? And what does it mean — to die? It may be that man has a hundred senses, and at his death only the five that are known to us perish, and the other ninety-five go on living.

Lyubov Andreyevna: How clever you are, Petya!

Lopakhin (ironically): Terribly clever!

Trofimov: Mankind goes forward, perfecting its powers. Everything that is now unattainable will some day be comprehensible and within our grasp, only we must work, and help with all our might those who are seeking the truth. So far, among us here in Russia, only a very few work. The great majority of the intelligentsia that I know seek nothing, do nothing, and as yet are incapable of work. They call themselves the intelligentsia, yet they belittle their servants, treat the peasants like animals, are wretched students, never read anything serious, and do absolutely nothing; they only talk about science and know very little about art. They all look serious, have grim expressions, speak of weighty matters, and philosophize; and meanwhile anyone can see that the workers eat abominably, sleep without pillows, thirty or forty to a room, and everywhere there are bedbugs, stench, dampness, and immorality. . . . It's obvious that all our fine talk is merely to delude ourselves and others. Show me the day nurseries they are always talking about — and where are the reading rooms? They only write about them in novels, but in reality they don't exist. There is nothing but filth, vulgarity, asiaticism.° . . . I'm afraid of

---

asiaticism: Associated with backwardness and apathy.

those very serious countenances, I don't like them, I'm afraid of serious conversations. We'd do better to remain silent.

Lopakhin: You know, I get up before five in the morning, and I work from morning to night; now, I'm always handling money, my own and other people's, and I see what people around me are like. You have only to start doing something to find out how few honest, decent people there are. Sometimes, when I can't sleep, I think: "Lord, Thou gavest us vast forests, boundless fields, broad horizons, and living in their midst we ourselves ought truly to be giants. . . ."

Lyubov Andreyevna: Now you want giants! They're good only in fairy tales, otherwise they're frightening.

Yepikhodov crosses at the rear of the stage, playing the guitar.

Lyubov Andreyevna (pensively): There goes Yepikhodov . . .

Anya (pensively): There goes Yepikhodov . . .

Gayev: The sun has set, ladies and gentlemen.

Trofimov: Yes.

Gayev (in a low voice, as though reciting): Oh, Nature, wondrous Nature, you shine with eternal radiance, beautiful and indifferent; you, whom we call mother, unite within yourself both life and death, giving life and taking it away. . . .

Varya (beseechingly): Uncle dear!

Anya: Uncle, you're doing it again!

Trofimov: You'd better cue the ball into the center.

Gayev: I'll be silent, silent.

All sit lost in thought. The silence is broken only by the subdued muttering of Firs. Suddenly a distant sound is heard, as if from the sky, like the sound of a snapped string mournfully dying away.

Lyubov Andreyevna: What was that?

Lopakhin: I don't know. Somewhere far off in a mine shaft a bucket's broken loose. But somewhere very far away.

Gayev: It might be a bird of some sort . . . like a heron.

Trofimov: Or an owl . . .

Lyubov Andreyevna (shudders): It's unpleasant somehow. . . . (*Pause.*)

Firs: The same thing happened before the troubles: an owl hooted and the samovar hissed continually.

Gayev: Before what troubles?

Firs: Before the Emancipation.

Lyubov Andreyevna: Come along, my friends, let us go, evening is falling. (*To Anya.*) There are tears in your eyes — what is it, my little one?

Embraces her.

Anya: It's all right, Mama. It's nothing.

Trofimov: Someone is coming.

A stranger appears wearing a shabby white forage cap and an overcoat. He is slightly drunk.

Stranger: Permit me to inquire, can I go straight through here to the station?

Gayev: You can. Follow the road.

Stranger: I am deeply grateful to you. (*Coughs.*) Splendid weather. . . . (*Reciting.*) "My brother, my suffering brother . . . come to the Volga, whose groans" . . . (*To Varya.*) Mademoiselle, will you oblige a hungry Russian with thirty kopecks?

Varya, frightened, cries out.

Lopakhin (angrily): There's a limit to everything.

Lyubov Andreyevna (panic-stricken): Here you are — take this. . . . (*Fumbles in her purse.*) I have no silver. . . . Never mind, here's a gold piece for you. . . .

Stranger: I am deeply grateful to you. (*Goes off.*)

Laughter.

Varya (frightened): I'm leaving . . . I'm leaving. . . . Oh, Mama, dear, there's nothing in the house for the servants to eat, and you give him a gold piece!

Lyubov Andreyevna: What's to be done with such a silly creature? When we get home I'll give you all I've got. Yermolai Alekseyevich, you'll lend me some more!

Lopakhin: At your service.

Lyubov Andreyevna: Come, my friends, it's time to go. Oh, Varya, we have definitely made a match for you. Congratulations!

Varya (through tears): Mama, that's not something to joke about.

Lopakhin: "Aurelia, get thee to a nunnery . . ."°

Gayev: Look, my hands are trembling: it's a long time since I've played a game of billiards.

Lopakhin: "Aurelia, O Nymph, in thy orisons, be all my sins remember'd!"°

Lyubov Andreyevna: Let us go, my friends, it will soon be suppertime.

Varya: He frightened me. My heart is simply pounding.

Lopakhin: Let me remind you, ladies and gentlemen: on the twenty-second of August the cherry orchard is to be sold. Think about that — Think!

All go out except Trofimov and Anya.

Anya (laughs): My thanks to the stranger for frightening Varya, now we are alone.

Trofimov: Varya is so afraid we might suddenly fall in love with each other that she hasn't left us alone for days. With her narrow mind she can't understand that we are above love. To avoid the petty and the illusory, which prevent our being free and happy — that is the aim and meaning of life. Forward! We are moving irresistibly toward the bright star that burns in the distance! Forward! Do not fall behind, friends!

Anya (clasping her hands): How well you talk! (*Pause.*) It's marvelous here today!

Trofimov: Yes, the weather is wonderful.

Anya: What have you done to me, Petya, that I no longer love the cherry orchard as I used to? I loved it so tenderly, it seemed to me there was no better place on earth than our orchard.

"*Aurelia . . . nunnery*": Lopakhin incorrectly substitutes Aurelia for "Ophelia," an allusion to Shakespeare's *Hamlet* (III. i. 136), when Hamlet rejects Ophelia.
"*Aurelia . . . remember'd!*": The end of Hamlet's "To be or not to be" soliloquy (III. i. 89–90).

Trofimov: All Russia is our orchard. It is a great and beautiful land, and there are many wonderful places in it. (*Pause.*) Just think, Anya: your grandfather, your great-grandfather, and all your ancestors were serf-owners, possessors of living souls. Don't you see that from every cherry tree, from every leaf and trunk, human beings are peering out at you? Don't you hear their voices? To possess living souls—that has corrupted all of you, those who lived before and you who are living now, so that your mother, you, your uncle, no longer perceive that you are living in debt, at someone else's expense, at the expense of those whom you wouldn't allow to cross your threshold. . . . We are at least two hundred years behind the times, we have as yet absolutely nothing, we have no definite attitude toward the past, we only philosophize, complain of boredom, or drink vodka. Yet it's quite clear that to begin to live we must first atone for the past, be done with it, and we can atone for it only by suffering, only by extraordinary, unceasing labor. Understand this, Anya.

Anya: The house we live in hasn't really been ours for a long time, and I shall leave it, I give you my word.

Trofimov: If you have the keys of the household, throw them into the well and go. Be as free as the wind.

Anya (in ecstasy): How well you put that!

Trofimov: Believe me, Anya, believe me! I am not yet thirty, I am young, still a student, but I have already been through so much! As soon as winter comes, I am hungry, sick, worried, poor as a beggar, and—where has not fate driven me! Where have I not been? And yet always, every minute of the day and night, my soul was filled with inexplicable premonitions. I have a premonition of happiness, Anya, I can see it . . .

Anya: The moon is rising.

Yepikhodov is heard playing the same melancholy song on the guitar. The moon rises. Somewhere near the poplars Varya is looking for Anya and calling: "Anya, where are you?"

Trofimov: Yes, the moon is rising. (*Pause.*) There it is—happiness . . . it's coming, nearer and nearer, I can hear its footsteps. And if we do not see it, if we do not recognize it, what does it matter? Others will see it.

Varya's Voice: Anya! Where are you?

Trofimov: That Varya again! (*Angrily.*) It's revolting!

Anya: Well? Let's go down to the river. It's lovely there.

Trofimov: Come on. (*They go.*)

Varya's Voice: Anya! Anya!

ACT III

The drawing room, separated by an arch from the ballroom. The chandelier is lighted. The Jewish band that was mentioned in Act II is heard playing in the hall. It is evening. In the ballroom they are dancing a grand rond. The voice of Semyonov-Pishchik: "Promenade à une paire!"° They all enter the drawing room:

"Promenade à une paire!": "Walk in pairs" (French).

Pishchik and Charlotta Ivanovna are the first couple. Trofimov and Lyubov Andreyevna the second, Anya and the Post-Office Clerk the third, Varya and the Stationmaster the fourth, etc. Varya, quietly weeping, dries her tears as she dances. Dunyasha is in the last couple. As they cross the drawing room Pishchik calls: "Grand rond, balancez!" and "Les cavaliers à genoux et remercier vos dames!"° Firs, wearing a dress coat, brings in a tray with seltzer water. Pishchik and Trofimov come into the drawing room.

Pishchik: I'm a full-blooded man, I've already had two strokes, and dancing's hard work for me, but as they say, "If you run with the pack, you can bark or not, but at least wag your tail." At that, I'm as strong as a horse. My late father — quite a joker he was, God rest his soul — used to say, talking about our origins, that the ancient line of Semyonov-Pishchik was descended from the very horse that Caligula had seated in the Senate.° . . . (*Sits down.*) But the trouble is — no money! A hungry dog believes in nothing but meat. . . . (*Snores but wakes up at once.*) It's the same with me — I can think of nothing but money. . . .

Trofimov: You know, there really is something equine about your figure.

Pishchik: Well, a horse is a fine animal. . . . You can sell a horse.

There is the sound of a billiard game in the next room. Varya appears in the archway.

Trofimov (teasing her): Madame Lopakhina! Madame Lopakhina!

Varya (angrily): Mangy gentleman!

Trofimov: Yes, I am a mangy gentleman, and proud of it!

Varya (reflecting bitterly): Here we've hired musicians, and what are we going to pay them with? (*Goes out.*)

Trofimov (to Pishchik): If the energy you have expended in the course of your life trying to find money to pay interest had gone into something else, ultimately, you might very well have turned the world upside down.

Pishchik: Nietzsche° . . . the philosopher . . . the greatest, most renowned . . . a man of tremendous intellect . . . says in his works that it is possible to forge banknotes.

Trofimov: And have you read Nietzsche?

Pishchik: Well . . . Dashenka told me. I'm in such a state now that I'm just about ready for forging. . . . The day after tomorrow I have to pay three hundred and ten rubles . . . I've got a hundred and thirty. . . . (*Feels in his pocket, grows alarmed.*) The money is gone! I've lost the money! (*Tearfully.*) Where is my money? (*Joyfully.*) Here it is, inside the lining. . . . I'm all in a sweat. . . .

Lyubov Andreyevna and Charlotta Ivanovna come in.

Lyubov Andreyevna (humming a Lezginka°): Why does Leonid take so long?

"Grand rond . . . dames": Instructions in the dance: "Large circle, . . . men, kneel down and thank your ladies!"
Caligula . . . Senate: Caligula (A.D. 12–41) was a Roman emperor (A.D. 37–41).
Nietzsche: Friedrich Nietzsche (1844–1900), German philosopher and poet who developed the idea of the superman, beyond traditional morality
Lezginka: A popular, lively Russian dance.

What is he doing in town? (*To Dunyasha.*) Dunyasha, offer the musicians some tea.

Trofimov: In all probability, the auction didn't take place.

Lyubov Andreyevna: It was the wrong time to have the musicians, the wrong time to give a dance. . . . Well, never mind. . . . (*Sits down and hums softly.*)

Charlotta (gives Pishchik a deck of cards): Here's a deck of cards for you. Think of a card.

Pishchik: I've thought of one.

Charlotta: Now shuffle the pack. Very good. And now, my dear Mr. Pishchik, hand it to me. *Ein, zwei, drei!°* Now look for it — it's in your side pocket.

Pishchik (takes the card out of his side pocket): The eight of spades — absolutely right! (*Amazed.*) Think of that, now!

Charlotta (holding the deck of cards in the palm of her hand, to Trofimov): Quickly, tell me, which card is on top?

Trofimov: What? Well, the queen of spades.

Charlotta: Right! (*To Pishchik.*) Now which card is on top?

Pishchik: The ace of hearts.

Charlotta: Right! (*Claps her hands and the deck of cards disappears.*) What lovely weather we're having today! (*A mysterious feminine voice, which seems to come from under the floor, answers her: "Oh, yes, splendid weather, madam."*) You are so nice, you're my ideal. . . . (*The voice: "And I'm very fond of you, too, madam."*)

Stationmaster (applauding): Bravo, Madame Ventriloquist!

Pishchik (amazed): Think of that, now! Most enchanting Charlotta Ivanovna . . . I am simply in love with you. . . .

Charlotta: In love? (*Shrugs her shoulders.*) Is it possible that you can love? *Guter Mensch, aber schlechter Musikant.°*

Trofimov (claps Pishchik on the shoulder): You old horse, you!

Charlotta: Attention, please! One more trick. (*Takes a lap robe from a chair.*) Here's a very fine lap robe; I should like to sell it. (*Shakes it out.*) Doesn't anyone want to buy it?

Pishchik (amazed): Think of that, now!

Charlotta: Ein, zwei, drei! (*Quickly raises the lap robe; behind it stands Anya, who curtseys, runs to her mother, embraces her, and runs back into the ballroom amid the general enthusiasm.*)

Lyubov Andreyevna (applauding): Bravo, bravo!

Charlotta: Once again! *Ein, zwei, drei.* (*Raises the lap robe; behind it stands Varya, who bows.*)

Pishchik (amazed): Think of that, now!

Charlotta: The end! (*Throws the robe at Pishchik, makes a curtsey, and runs out of the room.*)

Pishchik (hurries after her): The minx! . . . What a woman! What a woman! (*Goes out.*)

Lyubov Andreyevna: And Leonid still not here. What he is doing in town so long, I do not understand! It must be all over by now. Either the estate is

---

Ein, zwei, drei!: "One, two, three" (German).
Guter Mensch, aber schlecter Musikant: "Good man, but poor musician" (German).

sold, or the auction didn't take place — but why keep us in suspense so long!

Varya (trying to comfort her): Uncle has bought it, I am certain of that.

Trofimov (mockingly): Yes.

Varya: Great-aunt sent him power of attorney to buy it in her name and transfer the debt. She's doing it for Anya's sake. And I am sure, with God's help, Uncle will buy it.

Lyubov Andreyevna: Our great-aunt in Yaroslavl sent fifteen thousand to buy the estate in her name — she doesn't trust us — but that's not even enough to pay the interest. (*Covers her face with her hands.*) Today my fate will be decided, my fate . . .

Trofimov (teasing Varya): Madame Lopakhina!

Varya (angrily): Eternal student! Twice already you've been expelled from the university.

Lyubov Andreyevna: Why are you so cross, Varya? If he teases you about Lopakhin, what of it? Go ahead and marry Lopakhin if you want to. He's a nice man, he's interesting. And if you don't want to, don't. Nobody's forcing you, my pet.

Varya: To be frank, Mama dear, I regard this matter seriously. He is a good man, I like him.

Lyubov Andreyevna: Then marry him. I don't know what you're waiting for!

Varya: Mama, I can't propose to him myself. For the last two years everyone's been talking to me about him; everyone talks, but he is either silent or he jokes. I understand. He's getting rich, he's absorbed in business, he has no time for me. If I had some money, no matter how little, if it were only a hundred rubles, I'd drop everything and go far away. I'd go into a nunnery.

Trofimov: A blessing!

Varya (to Trofimov): A student ought to be intelligent! (*In a gentle tone, tearfully.*) How homely you have grown, Petya, how old! (*To Lyubov Andreyevna, no longer crying.*) It's just that I cannot live without work, Mama. I must be doing something every minute.

Yasha enters.

Yasha (barely able to suppress his laughter): Yepikhodov has broken a billiard cue! (*Goes out.*)

Varya: But why is Yepikhodov here? Who gave him permission to play billiards? I don't understand these people. . . . (*Goes out.*)

Lyubov Andreyevna: Don't tease her, Petya. You can see she's unhappy enough without that.

Trofimov: She's much too zealous, always meddling in other people's affairs. All summer long she's given Anya and me no peace — afraid a romance might develop. What business is it of hers? Besides, I've given no occasion for it, I am far removed from such banality. We are above love!

Lyubov Andreyevna: And I suppose I am beneath love. (*In great agitation.*) Why isn't Leonid here? If only I knew whether the estate had been sold or not! The disaster seems to me so incredible that I don't even know what to think, I'm lost. . . . I could scream this very instant . . . I could do something foolish. Save me, Petya. Talk to me, say something. . . .

Trofimov: Whether or not the estate is sold today — does it really matter? That's all done with long ago; there's no turning back, the path is overgrown. Be calm, my dear. One must not deceive oneself; at least once in one's life one ought to look the truth straight in the eye.

Lyubov Andreyevna: What truth? You can see where there is truth and where there isn't, but I seem to have lost my sight, I see nothing. You boldly settle all the important problems, but tell me, my dear boy, isn't it because you are young and have not yet had to suffer for a single one of your problems? You boldly look ahead, but isn't it because you neither see nor expect anything dreadful, since life is still hidden from your young eyes? You're bolder, more honest, deeper than we are, but think about it, be just a little bit magnanimous, and spare me. You see, I was born here, my mother and father lived here, and my grandfather. I love this house, without the cherry orchard my life has no meaning for me, and if it must be sold, then sell me with the orchard. . . . (*Embraces Trofimov and kisses him on the forehead.*) And my son was drowned here. . . . (*Weeps.*) Have pity on me, you good, kind man.

Trofimov: You know I feel for you with all my heart.

Lyubov Andreyevna: But that should have been said differently, quite differently. . . . (*Takes out her handkerchief and a telegram falls to the floor.*) My heart is heavy today, you can't imagine. It's so noisy here, my soul quivers at every sound, I tremble all over, and yet I can't go to my room. When I am alone the silence frightens me. Don't condemn me, Petya . . . I love you as if you were my own. I would gladly let you marry Anya, I swear it, only you must study, my dear, you must get your degree. You do nothing, fate simply tosses you from place to place — it's so strange. . . . Isn't that true? Isn't it? And you must do something about your beard, to make it grow somehow. . . . (*Laughs.*) You're so funny!

Trofimov (picks up the telegram): I have no desire to be an Adonis.

Lyubov Andreyevna: That's a telegram from Paris. I get them every day. One yesterday, one today. That wild man has fallen ill again, he's in trouble again. . . . He begs my forgiveness, implores me to come, and really, I ought to go to Paris to be near him. Your face is stern, Petya, but what can one do, my dear? What am I to do? He is ill, he's alone and unhappy, and who will look after him there, who will keep him from making mistakes, who will give him his medicine on time? And why hide it or keep silent, I love him, that's clear. I love him, love him. . . . It's a millstone round my neck, I'm sinking to the bottom with it, but I love that stone, I cannot live without it. (*Presses Trofimov's hand.*) Don't think badly of me, Petya, and don't say anything to me, don't say anything. . . .

Trofimov (through tears): For God's sake, forgive my frankness: you know that he robbed you!

Lyubov Andreyevna: No, no, no, you mustn't say such things! (*Covers her ears.*)

Trofimov: But he's a scoundrel! You're the only one who doesn't know it! He's a petty scoundrel, a nonentity —

Lyubov Andreyevna (angry, but controlling herself): You are twenty-six or twenty-seven years old, but you're still a schoolboy.

Trofimov: That may be!

Lyubov Andreyevna: You should be a man, at your age you ought to understand those who love. And you ought to be in love yourself. (*Angrily.*) Yes, yes! It's not purity with you, it's simply prudery, you're a ridiculous crank, a freak —

Trofimov (horrified): What is she saying!

Lyubov Andreyevna: "I am above love!" You're not above love, you're just an addlepate, as Firs would say. Not to have a mistress at your age!

Trofimov (in horror): This is awful! What is she saying! . . . (*Goes quickly toward the ballroom.*) This is awful . . . I can't . . . I won't stay here. . . . (*Goes out, but immediately returns.*) All is over between us! (*Goes out to the hall.*)

Lyubov Andreyevna (calls after him): Petya, wait! You absurd creature, I was joking! Petya!

In the hall there is the sound of someone running quickly downstairs and suddenly falling with a crash. Anya and Varya scream, but a moment later laughter is heard.

Lyubov Andreyevna: What was that?

Anya runs in.

Anya (laughing): Petya fell down the stairs! (*Runs out.*)

Lyubov Andreyevna: What a funny boy that Petya is!

The stationmaster stands in the middle of the ballroom and recites A. Tolstoy's "The Sinner."° Everyone listens to him, but he has no sooner spoken a few lines than the sound of a waltz is heard from the hall and the recitation is broken off. They all dance. Trofimov, Anya, Varya, and Lyubov Andreyevna come in from the hall.

Lyubov Andreyevna: Come, Petya . . . come, you pure soul . . . please, forgive me. . . . Let's dance. . . . (*They dance.*)

Anya and Varya dance. Firs comes in, puts his stick by the side door. Yasha also comes into the drawing room and watches the dancers.

Yasha: What is it, grandpa?

Firs: I don't feel well. In the old days we used to have generals, barons, admirals, dancing at our balls, but now we send for the post-office clerk and the stationmaster, and even they are none too eager to come. Somehow I've grown weak. The late master, their grandfather, dosed everyone with sealing wax, no matter what ailed them. I've been taking sealing wax every day for twenty years or more; maybe that's what's kept me alive.

Yasha: You bore me, grandpa. (*Yawns.*) High time you croaked.

Firs: Ah, you . . . addlepate! (*Mumbles.*)

Trofimov and Lyubov Andreyevna dance from the ballroom into the drawing room.

Lyubov Andreyevna: Merci. I'll sit down a while. (*Sits.*) I'm tired.

A. Tolstoy's "The Sinner": Alexey Konstantinovich Tolstoy (1817–1875), Russian novelist (*Prince Serebryany,* 1863), dramatist (*The Death of Ivan the Terrible,* 1866), and poet. "The Sinner" is a poem contemporary with this play in which Christ appears at a society banquet.

Anya comes in.

Anya (excitedly): There was man in the kitchen just now saying that the cherry orchard was sold today.

Lyubov Andreyevna: Sold to whom?

Anya: He didn't say. He's gone. (*Dances with Trofimov; they go into the ballroom.*)

Yasha: That was just some old man babbling. A stranger.

Firs: Leonid Andreich is not back yet, still hasn't come. And he's wearing the light, between-seasons overcoat; like enough he'll catch cold. Ah, when they're young they're green.

Lyubov Andreyevna: This is killing me. Yasha, go and find out who it was sold to.

Yasha: But that old man left long ago. (*Laughs.*)

Lyubov Andreyevna (slightly annoyed): Well, what are you laughing at? What are you so happy about?

Yasha: That Yepikhodov is very funny! Hopeless! Two-and-twenty Troubles.

Lyubov Andreyevna: Firs, if the estate is sold, where will you go?

Firs: Wherever you tell me to go, I'll go.

Lyubov Andreyevna: Why do you look like that? Aren't you well? You ought to go to bed.

Firs: Yes . . . (*With a smirk.*) Go to bed, and without me who will serve, who will see to things? I'm the only one in the whole house.

Yasha (to Lyubov Andreyevna): Lyubov Andreyevna! Permit me to make a request, be so kind! If you go back to Paris again, do me the favor of taking me with you. It is positively impossible for me to stay here. (*Looking around, then in a low voice.*) There's no need to say it, you can see for yourself, it's an uncivilized country, the people have no morals, and the boredom! The food they give us in the kitchen is unmentionable, and besides, there's this Firs who keeps walking about mumbling all sorts of inappropriate things. Take me with you, be so kind!

Enter Pishchik.

Pishchik: May I have the pleasure of a waltz with you, fairest lady? (*Lyubov Andreyevna goes with him.*) I really must borrow a hundred and eighty rubles from you, my charmer . . . I really must. . . . (*Dancing.*) Just a hundred and eighty rubles. . . . (*They pass into the ballroom.*)

Yasha (softly sings): "Wilt thou know my soul's unrest . . ."

In the ballroom a figure in a gray top hat and checked trousers is jumping about, waving its arms; there are shouts of "Bravo, Charlotta Ivanovna!"

Dunyasha (stopping to powder her face): The young mistress told me to dance — there are lots of gentlemen and not enough ladies — but dancing makes me dizzy, and my heart begins to thump. Firs Nikolayevich, the post-office clerk just said something to me that took my breath away.

The music grows more subdued.

Firs: What did he say to you?

Dunyasha: "You," he said, "are like a flower."

Yasha (yawns): What ignorance. . . . (*Goes out.*)

Dunyasha: Like a flower. . . . I'm such a delicate girl, I just adore tender words.
Firs: You'll get your head turned.

Enter Yepikhodov.

Yepikhodov: Avdotya Fyodorovna, you are not desirous of seeing me . . . I might almost be some sort of insect. (*Sighs.*) Ah, life!
Dunyasha: What is it you want?
Yepikhodov: Indubitably, you may be right. (*Sighs.*) But, of course, if one looks at it from a point of view, then, if I may so express myself, and you will forgive my frankness, you have completely reduced me to a state of mind. I know my fate, every day some misfortune befalls me, but I have long since grown accustomed to that; I look upon my fate with a smile. But you gave me your word, and although I —
Dunyasha: Please, we'll talk about it later, but leave me in peace now. Just now I'm dreaming. . . . (*Plays with her fan.*)
Yepikhodov: Every day a misfortune, and yet, if I may so express myself, I merely smile, I even laugh.

Varya enters from the ballroom.

Varya: Are you still here, Semyon? What a disrespectful man you are, really! (*To Dunyasha.*) Run along, Dunyasha. (*To Yepikhodov.*) First you play billiards and break a cue, then you wander about the drawing room as though you were a guest.
Yepikhodov: You cannot, if I may so express myself, penalize me.
Varya: I am not penalizing you. I'm telling you. You do nothing but wander from one place to another, and you don't do your work. We keep a clerk, but for what, I don't know.
Yepikhodov (offended): Whether I work, or wander about, or eat, or play billiards, these are matters to be discussed only by persons of discernment, and my elders.
Varya: You dare say that to me! (*Flaring up.*) You dare? You mean to say I have no discernment? Get out of here! This instant!
Yepikhodov (intimidated): I beg you to express yourself in a more delicate manner.
Varya (beside herself): Get out, this very instant! Get out! (*He goes to the door, she follows him.*) Two-and-twenty Troubles! Don't let me set eyes on you again!
Yepikhodov (goes out, his voice is heard behind the door): I shall lodge a complaint against you!
Varya: Oh, you're coming back? (*Seizes the stick left near the door by Firs.*) Come, come on. . . . Come, I'll show you. . . . Ah, so you're coming, are you? Then take that — (*Swings the stick just as Lopakhin enters.*)
Lopakhin: Thank you kindly.
Varya (angrily and mockingly): I beg your pardon.
Lopakhin: Not at all. I humbly thank you for your charming reception.
Varya: Don't mention it. (*Walks away, then looks back and gently asks.*) I didn't hurt you, did I?
Lopakhin: No, it's nothing. A huge bump coming up, that's all.

Voices in the ballroom: "Lopakhin has come! Yermolai Alekseich!" Pishchik enters.

Pishchik: As I live and breathe! (*Kisses Lopakhin.*) There is a whiff of cognac about you, dear soul. And we've been making merry here, too.

Enter Lyubov Andreyevna.

Lyubov Andreyevna: Is that you, Yermolai Alekseich? What kept you so long? Where's Leonid?

Lopakhin: Leonid Andreich arrived with me, he's coming . . .

Lyubov Andreyevna (agitated): Well, what happened? Did the sale take place? Tell me!

Lopakhin (embarrassed, fearing to reveal his joy): The auction was over by four o'clock. . . . We missed the train, had to wait till half past nine. (*Sighing heavily.*) Ugh! My head is swimming. . . .

Enter Gayev; he carries his purchases in one hand and wipes away his tears with the other.

Lyubov Andreyevna: Lyonya, what happened? Well, Lyonya? (*Impatiently, through tears.*) Be quick, for God's sake!

Gayev (not answering her, simply waves his hand. To Firs, weeping): Here, take these. . . . There's anchovies, Kerch herrings. . . . I haven't eaten anything all day. . . . What I have been through! (*The click of billiard balls is heard through the open door to the billiard room, and Yasha's voice: "Seven and eighteen!" Gayev's expression changes, he is no longer weeping.*) I'm terribly tired. Firs, help me change. (*Goes through the ballroom to his own room, followed by Firs.*)

Pishchik: What happened at the auction? Come on, tell us!

Lyubov Andreyevna: Is the cherry orchard sold?

Lopakhin: It's sold.

Lyubov Andreyevna: Who bought it?

Lopakhin: I bought it. (*Pause.*)

Lyubov Andreyevna is overcome; she would fall to the floor if it were not for the chair and table near which she stands. Varya takes the keys from her belt and throws them on the floor in the middle of the drawing room and goes out.

Lopakhin: I bought it! Kindly wait a moment, ladies and gentlemen, my head is swimming, I can't talk. . . . (*Laughs.*) We arrived at the auction, Deriganov was already there. Leonid Andreich had only fifteen thousand, and straight off Deriganov bid thirty thousand over and above the mortgage. I saw how the land lay, so I got into the fight and bid forty. He bid forty-five. I bid fifty-five. In other words, he kept raising it by five thousand, and I by ten. Well, it finally came to an end. I bid ninety thousand above the mortgage, and it was knocked down to me. The cherry orchard is now mine! Mine! (*Laughs uproariously.*) Lord! God in heaven! The cherry orchard is mine! Tell me I'm drunk, out of my mind, that I imagine it. . . . (*Stamps his feet.*) Don't laugh at me! If my father and my grandfather could only rise from their graves and see all that has happened, how their Yermolai, their beaten, half-literate Yermolai, who used to run about barefoot in winter, how that same Yermolai has bought an estate, the most beautiful estate in the whole world! I bought the estate where my father and grandfather were slaves, where they weren't even allowed in the kitchen. I'm asleep, this is just some dream of mine, it only seems to be. . . . It's the fruit of your imagination, hidden in the darkness of uncertainty. . . . (*Picks up the keys, smiling tenderly.*) She threw down the keys, wants to show that she's not mistress here any more. . . . (*Jingles the keys.*) Well, no matter. (*The orchestra is heard tuning up.*) Hey, musicians, play, I want to hear you! Come on, everybody, and see how Yermolai Lopakhin will lay the ax to the cherry orchard, how the trees will fall to the ground! We're going to build summer cottages, and our grandsons and great-grandsons will see a new life here. . . . Music! Strike up!

The orchestra plays. Lyubov Andreyevna sinks into a chair and weeps bitterly.

Lopakhin (*reproachfully*): Why didn't you listen to me, why? My poor friend, there's no turning back now. (*With tears.*) Oh, if only all this could be over quickly, if somehow our discordant, unhappy life could be changed!

Pishchik (*takes him by the arm; speaks in an undertone*): She's crying. Let's go into the ballroom, let her be alone. . . . Come on. . . . (*Leads him into the ballroom.*)

Lopakhin: What's happened? Musicians, play so I can hear you! Let everything be as I want it! (*Ironically.*) Here comes the new master, owner of the cherry orchard! (*Accidentally bumps into a little table, almost upsetting the candelabrum.*) I can pay for everything! (*Goes out with Pishchik.*)

There is no one left in either the drawing room or the ballroom except Lyubov Andreyevna, who sits huddled up and weeping bitterly. The music plays softly. Anya and Trofimov enter hurriedly. Anya goes to her mother and kneels before her. Trofimov remains in the doorway of the ballroom.

Anya: Mama! . . . Mama, you're crying! Dear, kind, good Mama, my beautiful one, I love you . . . I bless you. The cherry orchard is sold, it's gone, that's true, true, but don't cry, Mama, life is still before you, you still have your good, pure soul. . . . Come with me, come, darling, we'll go away from here! . . . We'll plant a new orchard, more luxuriant than this one. You will see it and understand; and joy, quiet, deep joy, will sink into your soul, like the evening sun, and you will smile, Mama! Come, darling, let us go. . . .

ACT IV

The scene is the same as Act I. There are neither curtains on the windows nor pictures on the walls, and only a little furniture piled up in one corner, as if for sale. There is a sense of emptiness. Near the outer door, at the rear of the stage, suitcases, traveling bags, etc., are piled up. Through the open door on the left the voices of Varya and Anya can be heard. Lopakhin stands waiting. Yasha is holding a tray with little glasses of champagne. In the hall, Yepikhodov is tying up a box. Off stage, at the rear, there is a hum of voices. It is the peasants who have come to say good-bye. Gayev's voice: "Thanks, brothers, thank you."

Yasha: The peasants have come to say good-bye. In my opinion, Yermolai Alekseich, peasants are good-natured, but they don't know much.

The hum subsides. Lyubov Andreyevna enters from the hall with Gayev. She is not crying, but she is pale, her face twitches, and she cannot speak.

Gayev: You gave them your purse, Lyuba. That won't do! That won't do!

Lyubov Andreyevna: I couldn't help it! I couldn't help it! (*They both go out.*)

Lopakhin (in the doorway, calls after them): Please, do me the honor of having a little glass at parting. I didn't think of bringing champagne from town, and at the station I found only one bottle. Please! What's the matter, friends, don't you want any? (*Walks away from the door.*) If I'd known that, I wouldn't have bought it. Well, then I won't drink any either. (*Yasha carefully sets the tray down on a chair.*) At least you have a glass, Yasha.

Yasha: To those who are departing! Good luck! (*Drinks.*) This champagne is not the real stuff, I can assure you.

Lopakhin: Eight rubles a bottle. (*Pause.*) It's devilish cold in here.

Yasha: They didn't light the stoves today; it doesn't matter, since we're leaving. (*Laughs.*)

Lopakhin: Why are you laughing?

Yasha: Because I'm pleased.

Lopakhin: It's October, yet it's sunny and still outside, like summer. Good for building. (*Looks at his watch, then calls through the door.*) Bear in mind, ladies and gentlemen, only forty-six minutes till train time! That means leaving for the station in twenty minutes. Better hurry up!

Trofimov enters from outside wearing an overcoat.

Trofimov: Seems to me it's time to start. The carriages are at the door. What the devil has become of my rubbers? They're lost. (*Calls through the door.*) Anya, my rubbers are not here. I can't find them.

Lopakhin: I've got to go to Kharkov. I'm taking the same train you are. I'm going to spend the winter in Kharkov. I've been hanging around here with you, and I'm sick and tired of loafing. I can't live without work, I don't know what to do with my hands; they dangle in some strange way, as if they didn't belong to me.

Trofimov: We'll soon be gone, then you can take up your useful labors again.

Lopakhin: Here, have a little drink.

Trofimov: No, I don't want any.

Lopakhin: So you're off for Moscow?

Trofimov: Yes, I'll see them into town, and tomorrow I'll go to Moscow.

Lopakhin: Yes. . . . Well, I expect the professors haven't been giving any lectures: they're waiting for you to come!

Trofimov: That's none of your business.

Lopakhin: How many years is it you've been studying at the university?

Trofimov: Can't you think of something new? That's stale and flat. (*Looks for his rubbers.*) You know, we'll probably never see each other again, so allow me to give you one piece of advice at parting: don't wave your arms about! Get out of that habit — of arm-waving. And another thing, building cottages and counting on the summer residents in time becoming independent farmers — that's just another form of arm-waving. Well, when all's said and done, I'm fond of you anyway. You have fine, delicate fingers, like an artist; you have a fine delicate soul.

Lopakhin (embraces him): Good-bye, my dear fellow. Thank you for everything. Let me give you some money for the journey, if you need it.

Trofimov: What for? I don't need it.

Lopakhin: But you haven't any!

Trofimov: I have. Thank you. I got some money for a translation. Here it is in my pocket. (*Anxiously.*) But where are my rubbers?

Varya (from the next room): Here, take the nasty things! (*Flings a pair of rubbers onto the stage.*)

Trofimov: What are you so cross about, Varya? Hm. . . . But these are not my rubbers.

Lopakhin: In the spring I sowed three thousand acres of poppies, and now I've made forty thousand rubles clear. And when my poppies were in bloom, what a picture it was! So, I'm telling you, I've made forty thousand, which means I'm offering you a loan because I can afford to. Why turn up your nose? I'm a peasant — I speak bluntly.

Trofimov: Your father was a peasant, mine was a pharmacist — which proves absolutely nothing. (*Lopakhin takes out his wallet.*) No, don't — even if you gave me two hundred thousand I wouldn't take it. I'm a free man. And everything that is valued so highly and held so dear by all of you, rich and poor alike, has not the slightest power over me — it's like a feather floating in the air. I can get along without you, I can pass you by, I'm strong and proud. Mankind is advancing toward the highest truth, the highest happiness attainable on earth, and I am in the front ranks!

Lopakhin: Will you get there?

Trofimov: I'll get there. (*Pause.*) I'll either get there or I'll show others the way to get there.

The sound of axes chopping down trees is heard in the distance.

Lopakhin: Well, good-bye, my dear fellow. It's time to go. We turn up our noses at one another, but life goes on just the same. When I work for a long time without stopping, my mind is easier, and it seems to me that I, too, know why I exist. But how many there are in Russia, brother, who exist nobody knows why. Well, it doesn't matter, that's not what makes the wheels go round. They say Leonid Andreich has taken a position in the bank, six thousand a year. . . . Only, of course, he won't stick it out, he's too lazy. . . .

Anya (in the doorway): Mama asks you not to start cutting down the cherry orchard until she's gone.

Trofimov: Yes, really, not to have had the tact . . . (*Goes out through the hall.*)

Lopakhin: Right away, right away. . . . Ach, what people. . . . (*Follows Trofimov out.*)

Anya: Has Firs been taken to the hospital?

Yasha: I told them this morning. They must have taken him.

Anya (to Yepikhodov, who is crossing the room): Semyon Panteleich, please find out if Firs has been taken to the hospital.

Yasha (offended): I told Yegor this morning. Why ask a dozen times?

Yepikhodov: It is my conclusive opinion that the venerable Firs is beyond repair; it's time he was gathered to his fathers. And I can only envy him. (*Puts a suitcase down on a hatbox and crushes it.*) There you are! Of course! I knew it! (*Goes out.*)

Yasha (mockingly): Two-and-twenty Troubles!

Varya (through the door): Has Firs been taken to the hospital?

Anya: Yes, he has.

Varya: Then why didn't they take the letter to the doctor?

Anya: We must send it on after them. . . . (*Goes out.*)

Varya (from the adjoining room): Where is Yasha? Tell him his mother has come to say good-bye to him.

Yasha (waves his hand): They really try my patience.

Dunyasha has been fussing with the luggage; now that Yasha is alone she goes up to him.

Dunyasha: You might give me one little look, Yasha. You're going away . . . leaving me. . . . (*Cries and throws herself on his neck.*)

Yasha: What's there to cry about? (*Drinks champagne.*) In six days I'll be in Paris again. Tomorrow we'll take the express, off we go, and that's the last you'll see of us. I can hardly believe it. *Vive la France!* This place is not for me, I can't live here. . . . It can't be helped. I've had enough of this ignorance — I'm fed up with it. (*Drinks champagne.*) What are you crying for? Behave yourself properly, then you won't cry.

Dunyasha (looks into a small mirror and powders her face): Send me a letter from Paris. You know, I loved you, Yasha, how I loved you! I'm such a tender creature, Yasha!

Yasha: Here they come. (*Busies himself with the luggage, humming softly.*)

Enter Lyubov Andreyevna, Gayev, Charlotta Ivanovna.

Gayev: We ought to be leaving. There's not much time now. (*Looks at Yasha.*) Who smells of herring?

Lyubov Andreyevna: In about ten minutes we should be getting into the carriages. (*Glances around the room.*) Good-bye, dear house, old grandfather. Winter will pass, spring will come, and you will no longer be here, they will tear you down. How much these walls have seen! (*Kisses her daughter warmly.*) My treasure, you are radiant, your eyes are sparkling like two diamonds. Are you glad? Very?

Anya: Very! A new life is beginning, Mama!

Gayev (cheerfully): Yes, indeed, everything is all right now. Before the cherry orchard was sold we were all worried and miserable, but afterward, when the question was finally settled once and for all, everybody calmed down and felt quite cheerful. . . . I'm in a bank now, a financier . . . cue ball into the center . . . and you, Lyuba, say what you like, you look better, no doubt about it.

Lyubov Andreyevna: Yes. My nerves are better, that's true. (*Her hat and coat are handed to her.*) I sleep well. Carry out my things, Yasha, it's time. (*To Anya.*) My little girl, we shall see each other soon. . . . I shall go to Paris and live there on the money your great-aunt sent to buy the estate — long live Auntie! — but that money won't last long.

Anya: You'll come back soon, Mama, soon . . . won't you? I'll study hard and pass my high-school examinations, and then I can work and help you. We'll read all sorts of books together, Mama. . . . Won't we? (*Kisses her mother's hand.*) We'll read in the autumn evenings, we'll read lots of books, and a new and wonderful world will open up before us. . . . (*Dreaming.*) Mama, come back. . . .

Lyubov Andreyevna: I'll come, my precious. (*Embraces her.*)

Enter Lopakhin, Charlotta Ivanovna is softly humming a song.

Gayev: Happy Charlotta: she's singing!

Charlotta (picks up a bundle and holds it like a baby in swaddling clothes): Bye, baby, bye. . . . (*A baby's crying is heard, "Wah! Wah!"*) Be quiet, my darling, my dear little boy. (*"Wah! Wah!"*) I'm so sorry for you! (*Throws the bundle down.*) You will find me a position, won't you? I can't go on like this.

Lopakhin: We'll find something, Charlotta Ivanovna, don't worry.

Gayev: Everyone is leaving us, Varya's going away . . . all of a sudden nobody needs us.

Charlotta: I have nowhere to go in town. I must go away. (*Hums.*) It doesn't matter . . .

Enter Pishchik.

Lopakhin: Nature's wonder!

Pishchik (panting): Ugh! Let me catch my breath. . . . I'm exhausted. . . . My esteemed friends. . . . Give me some water. . . .

Gayev: After money, I suppose? Excuse me, I'm fleeing from temptation. . . . (*Goes out.*)

Pishchik: It's a long time since I've been to see you . . . fairest lady. . . . (*To Lopakhin.*) So you're here. . . . Glad to see you, you intellectual giant. . . . Here . . . take it . . . four hundred rubles . . . I still owe you eight hundred and forty . . .

Lopakhin (shrugs his shoulders in bewilderment): I must be dreaming. . . . Where did you get it?

Pishchik: Wait . . . I'm hot. . . . A most extraordinary event. Some Englishmen came to my place and discovered some kind of white clay on my land. (*To Lyubov Andreyevna.*) And four hundred for you . . . fairest, most wonderful lady. . . . (*Hands her the money.*) The rest later. (*Takes a drink of water.*) Just now a young man in the train was saying that a certain . . . great philosopher recommends jumping off roofs. . . . "Jump!" he says, and therein lies the whole problem. (*In amazement.*) Think of that, now! . . . Water!

Lopakhin: Who were those Englishmen?

Pishchik: I leased them the tract of land with the clay on it for twenty-four years. . . . And now, excuse me, I have no time . . . I must be trotting along . . . I'm going to Znoikov's . . . to Kardamanov's . . . I owe everybody. (*Drinks.*) Keep well . . . I'll drop in on Thursday . . .

Lyubov Andreyevna: We're just moving into town, and tomorrow I go abroad . . .

Pishchik: What? (*Alarmed.*) Why into town? That's why I see the furniture . . . suitcases. . . . Well, never mind. . . . (*Through tears.*) Never mind. . . . Men of the greatest intellect, those Englishmen. . . . Never mind. . . . Be happy . . . God will help you. . . . Never mind. . . . Everything in this world comes to an end. . . . (*Kisses Lyubov Andreyevna's hand.*) And should the news reach you that my end has come, just remember this old horse, and say: "There once lived a certain Semyonov-Pishchik, God rest his soul." . . . Splendid weather. . . . Yes. . . . (*Goes out greatly disconcerted, but immediately returns and speaks from the doorway.*) Dashenka sends her regards. (*Goes out.*)

Lyubov Andreyevna: Now we can go. I am leaving with two things on my mind.

First — that Firs is sick. (*Looks at her watch.*) We still have about five minutes. . . .

Anya: Mama, Firs has already been taken to the hospital. Yasha sent him there this morning.

Lyubov Andreyevna: My second concern is Varya. She's used to getting up early and working, and now, with no work to do, she's like a fish out of water. She's grown pale and thin, and cries all the time, poor girl. . . . (*Pause.*) You know very well, Yemolai Alekseich, that I dreamed of marrying her to you, and everything pointed to your getting married. (*Whispers to Anya, who nods to Charlotta, and they both go out.*) She loves you, you are fond of her, and I don't know — I don't know why it is you seem to avoid each other. I can't understand it!

Lopakhin: To tell you the truth, I don't understand it myself. The whole thing is strange, somehow. . . . If there's still time, I'm ready right now. . . . Let's finish it up — and *basta,*° but without you I feel I'll never be able to propose to her.

Lyubov Andreyevna: Splendid! After all, it only takes a minute. I'll call her in at once. . . .

Lopakhin: And we even have the champagne. (*Looks at the glasses.*) Empty! Somebody's already drunk it. (*Yasha coughs.*) That's what you call lapping it up.

Lyubov Andreyevna (animatedly): Splendid! We'll leave you. . . . Yasha, *allez!*° I'll call her. . . . (*At the door.*) Varya, leave everything and come here. Come! (*Goes out with Yasha.*)

Lopakhin (looking at his watch): Yes. . . . (*Pause.*)

Behind the door there is smothered laughter and whispering; finally Varya enters.

Varya (looking over the luggage for a long time): Strange, I can't seem to find it . . .

Lopakhin: What are you looking for?

Varya: I packed it myself, and I can't remember . . . (*Pause.*)

Lopakhin: Where are you going now, Varya Mikhailovna?

Varya: I? To the Ragulins'. . . . I've agreed to go there to look after the house . . . as a sort of housekeeper.

Lopakhin: At Yashnevo? That would be about seventy versts from here. (*Pause.*) Well, life in this house has come to an end. . . .

Varya (examining the luggage): Where can it be? . . . Perhaps I put it in the trunk. . . . Yes, life in this house has come to an end . . . there'll be no more . . .

Lopakhin: And I'm off for Kharkov . . . by the next train. I have a lot to do. I'm leaving Yepikhodov here . . . I've taken him on.

Varya: Really!

Lopakhin: Last year at this time it was already snowing, if you remember, but now it's still and sunny. It's cold though. . . . About three degrees of frost.

basta: "Enough" (Italian).
allez: "Go" (French).

Varya: I haven't looked. (*Pause.*) And besides, our thermometer's broken. (*Pause.*)

A voice from the yard calls: "Yermolai Alekseich!"

Lopakhin (as if he had been waiting for a long time for the call): Coming! (*Goes out quickly.*)

Varya sits on the floor, lays her head on a bundle of clothes, and quietly sobs. The door opens and Lyubov Andreyevna enters cautiously.

Lyubov Andreyevna: Well? (*Pause.*) We must be going.

Varya (no longer crying, dries her eyes): Yes, it's time, Mama dear. I can get to the Ragulins' today, if only we don't miss the train.

Lyubov Andreyevna (in the doorway): Anya, put your things on!

Enter Anya, then Gayev and Charlotta Ivanovna. Gayev wears a warm overcoat with a hood. The servants and coachmen come in. Yepikhodov bustles about the luggage.

Lyubov Andreyevna: Now we can be on our way.

Anya (joyfully): On our way!

Gayev: My friends, my dear, cherished friends! Leaving this house forever, can I pass over in silence, can I refrain from giving utterance, as we say farewell, to those feelings that now fill my whole being —

Anya (imploringly): Uncle!

Varya: Uncle dear, don't!

Gayev (forlornly): Double the rail off the white to center table . . . yellow into the side pocket. . . . I'll be quiet. . . .

Enter Trofimov, then Lopakhin.

Trofimov: Well, ladies and gentlemen, it's time to go!

Lopakhin: Yepikhodov, my coat!

Lyubov Andreyevna: I'll sit here just one more minute. It's as though I had never before seen what the walls of this house were like, what the ceiling were like, and now I look at them hungrily, with such tender love . . .

Gayev: I remember when I was six years old, sitting on this window sill on Whitsunday, watching my father going to church . . .

Lyubov Andreyevna: Have they taken all the things?

Lopakhin: Everything, I think. (*Puts on his overcoat.*) Yepikhodov, see that everything is in order.

Yepikhodov (in a hoarse voice): Rest assured, Yermolai Alekseich!

Lopakhin: What's the matter with your voice?

Yepikhodov: Just drank some water . . . must have swallowed something.

Yasha (contemptuously): What ignorance!

Lyubov Andreyevna: When we go — there won't be a soul left here. . . .

Lopakhin: Till spring.

Varya (pulls an umbrella out of a bundle as though she were going to hit someone; Lopakhin pretends to be frightened): Why are you — I never thought of such a thing!

Trofimov: Ladies and gentlemen, let's get into the carriages — it's time now! The train will soon be in!

Varya: Petya there they are — your rubbers, by the suitcase. (*Tearfully.*) And what dirty old things they are!

Trofimov (putting on his rubbers): Let's go, ladies and gentlemen!

Gayev (extremely upset, afraid of bursting into tears): The train . . . the station. . . . Cross table to the center, double the rail . . . on the white into the corner.°

Lyubov Andreyevna: Let us go!

Gayev: Are we all here? No one in there? (*Locks the side door on the left.*) There are some things stored in there, we must lock up. Let's go!

Anya: Good-bye, house! Good-bye, old life!

Trofimkov: Hail to the new life! (*Goes out with Anya.*)

Varya looks around the room and slowly goes out. Yasha and Charlotta with her dog go out.

Lopakhin: And so, till spring. Come along, my friends. . . . Till we meet! (*Goes out.*)

Lyubov Andreyevna and Gayev are left alone. As though they had been waiting for this, they fall onto each other's necks and break into quiet, restrained sobs, afraid of being heard.

Gayev (in despair): My sister, my sister. . . .

Lyubov Andreyevna: Oh, my dear, sweet, lovely orchard! . . . My life, my youth, my happiness, good-bye! . . . Good-bye!

Anya's Voice (gaily calling): Mama!

Trofimov's Voice (gay and excited): Aa-oo!

Lyubov Andreyevna: One last look at these walls, these windows. . . . Mother loved to walk about in this room. . . .

Gayev: My sister, my sister!

Anya's voice: Mama!

Trofimov's Voice: Aa-oo!

Lyubov Andreyevna: We're coming! (*They go out.*)

The stage is empty. There is the sound of doors being locked, then of the carriages driving away. It grows quiet. In the stillness there is the dull thud of an ax on a tree, a forlorn, melancholy sound. Footsteps are heard. From the door on the right Firs appears. He is dressed as always in a jacket and white waistcoat, and wears slippers. He is ill.

Firs (goes to the door and tries the handle): Locked. They have gone. . . . (*Sits down on the sofa.*) They've forgotten me. . . . Never mind . . . I'll sit here awhile. . . . I expect Leonid Andreich hasn't put on his fur coat and has gone off in his overcoat. (*Sighs anxiously.*) And I didn't see to it. . . . When they're young, they're green! (*Mumbles something which cannot be understood.*) I'll lie down awhile. . . . There's no strength left in you, nothing's left, nothing. . . . Ach, you . . . addlepate! (*Lies motionless.*)

A distant sound is heard that seems to come from the sky, the sound of a snapped string mournfully dying away. A stillness falls, and nothing is heard but the thud of the ax on a tree far away in the orchard.

Cross . . . corner: Billiards terminology.

Considerations for Critical Thinking and Writing

1. How well do the characters in the play cope with the details of everyday life? How do their outward conversations and actions suggest their inner lives?
2. Many of the play's characters philosophize about the meaning of life. What conclusions do they reach? What do they want from life? What do they get?
3. Why do you think Chekhov uses a cherry orchard rather than simply uncultivated woods as the center of the play's controversy? How does the cherry orchard reveal aspects of its owners?
4. How is life outside the cherry orchard depicted? How does it differ from life in the family's world?
5. Which characters embody the coming "new order"? Describe how Chekhov uses them as foils to those characters associated with the agrarian values of the "old order"?
6. Discuss Chekhov's use of time in the play. How do particular characters relate to the past, present, and future?
7. Comment on the appropriateness of the play's title.
8. Why do you think the play ends with the sound of the ax? What kinds of social changes are represented by the destruction of the orchard?
9. Explain whether you think the play ends on a hopeful or a pessimistic note. Do you think things are likely to get better or worse?
10. Chekhov objected to solemn, melancholy productions of *The Cherry Orchard*. He insisted that the play is not a "heavy drama" or tragedy "but a comedy, in parts even a farce." In contrast, Konstantin Stanislavsky, the director of the play's first production, believed, "It is definitely not a comedy . . . but a tragedy." What is your own view of the play's depiction of Russian life? Explain why you think it is more like a comedy or a tragedy.

Connections to Other Selections

1. How do the love relationships in Ibsen's *A Doll House* (p. 1517) and *The Cherry Orchard* reflect larger social issues in each play?
2. Compare and contrast the way characters try to insulate themselves from the outside world in *The Cherry Orchard* and in Tennessee Williams's *The Glass Menagerie* (p. 1666).
3. Read the section on Marxist criticism (p. 2008) in Chapter 35, "Critical Strategies for Reading." Write an essay discussing how you think a Marxist critic would approach *The Cherry Orchard*.

PERSPECTIVES ON CHEKHOV

ANTON CHEKHOV (1860–1904)
On What Artists Do Best 1888

In conversation with my literary colleagues I always insist that it is not the artist's business to solve problems that require a specialist's knowledge. It is a bad thing if a writer tackles a subject he does not understand. We have specialists for dealing with special questions: it is their business to judge of the commune, of the future, of capitalism, of the evils of drunkenness, of boots, of the diseases of women. An artist must judge only of what he understands, his field is just as limited as that of any other specialist — I repeat this and insist on it always. That in his sphere there are no questions, but only answers, can be maintained only by those who have never written and have had no experience of thinking in images. An artist observes, selects, guesses, combines — and this in itself pre-supposes a problem: unless he had set himself a problem from the very first there would be nothing to conjecture and nothing to select. To put it briefly, I will end by using the language of psychiatry: if one denies that creative work involves problems and purposes, one must admit that an artist creates without premeditation or intention, in a state of abberation; therefore, if an author boasted to me of having written a novel without a preconceived design, under a sudden inspiration, I should call him mad.

You are right in demanding that an artist should take an intelligent attitude to his work, but you confuse two things: *solving a problem and stating a problem correctly.* It is only the second that is obligatory for the artist. . . . It is the business of the judge to put the right questions, but the answers must be given by the jury according to their own lights.

From a letter to A. S. Souvorin, October 27, 1888,
in *Letters of Anton Tchekhov to His Family and Friends,*
translated by Constance Garnett

Considerations for Critical Thinking and Writing

1. Explain whether you agree with Chekhov that an artist's "field is just as limited as that of any other specialist." Write an essay on Chekhov's assertion that "it is not the artist's business to solve problems."
2. How does *The Cherry Orchard* reflect Chekhov's insistence that his job is to "put the right questions" rather than to answer them?

DAVID MAMET (b. 1947)
Notes on The Cherry Orchard   1985

When playing poker it is a good idea to determine what cards your opponents might be playing. There are two ways to do this. One involves watching their idiosyncrasies — the way they hold their cards when bluffing as opposed to the way they hold them when they have a strong hand; their unconscious self-revelatory gestures; the way they play with their chips when unsure. This method of gathering information is called looking for "tells."

The other way to gather information is to analyze your opponent's hand according to what he *bets.*

These two methods are analogous — in the theater — to a concern with *characterization,* and a concern with *action;* or, to put it a bit differently: a concern with the *way* a character does something and, on the other hand, the actual *thing that he does.*

I recently worked on an adaptation of *The Cherry Orchard.*

My newfound intimacy with the play led me to look past the quiddities of the characters and examine what it is that they are actually doing. I saw this:

The title is a flag of convenience. Nobody in the play gives a damn about the cherry orchard.

In the first act Lyubov returns. We are informed that her beloved Estate is going to be sold unless someone acts quickly to avert this catastrophe.

She is told this by the rich Lopahin. He then immediately tells her that he has a plan: cut down the cherry orchard, raze the house, and build tract housing for the summer people.

This solution would save (although alter) the estate.
Lopahin keeps reiterating his offer throughout the play. Lyubov will not accept. Lopahin finally buys the estate.

"Well," one might say, "one cannot save one's beloved cherry orchard by cutting it down." That, of course, is true. But, in the text, other alternatives are offered.

Reference is made to the Rich Aunt in Yaroslavl ("Who is so very rich"), and who adores Lyubov's daughter, Anya. A flying mendicant mission is proposed but never materializes. The point here is not that this mission is viewed as a good bet, it isn't, but that, if the action of the protagonist (supposedly Lyubov) were to save the cherry orchard, she would grasp *any* possibility of help.

The more likely hope of salvation is fortuitous marriage. Gaev, Lyubov's brother, in enumerating the alternatives lists: inheriting money, begging from the rich aunt, marrying Anya off to a rich man.

The first is idle wishing, and we've struck off the second, but what about the third alternative?

There's nobody much around for Anya. But what about her stepsister, Varya?

Varya, Lyubov's adopted daughter, is not only nubile, she is *in love*. With whom is she in love? She is in love with Lopahin.

Why, *Hell*. If I wanted to save *my* cherry orchard, and *my* adopted daughter was in love (and we are told that her affections are by no means abhorrent to their recipient) with the richest man in town, what would *I* do? What would *you* do? It's the easy way out, the play ends in a half-hour and everybody gets to go home early.

But Lyubov does *not* press this point, though she makes reference to it in every act. She does *not* press on to a happy marriage between Varya and Lopahin. Nor, curiously, is this match ever mentioned as a solution for the problem of the cherry orchard. The problem of the botched courtship of Varya and Lopahin exists only as one of a number of supposed subplots. (More on this later.)

In the penultimate scene of the play Lyubov, who is leaving the now-sold estate to return to Paris, attempts to tie up loose ends. She exhorts Lopahin to propose to Varya, and he says he will. Left alone, Lopahin loses his nerve and does not propose. Why does Lyubov, on learning this, not press her case? Why did she not do so sooner?

Even now, at the end of the play, if Lyubov *really* cared about the cherry orchard, she could easily *force* Lopahin to propose to Varya, and then get the bright idea that all of them could live on the estate as one happy family. And Lopahin would not refuse her.

But she does not do so. Is this from lack of inventiveness? No. It is from lack of concern. The cherry orchard is not her concern.

What about Lopahin? Why is *he* cutting down the cherry orchard? He has been, from youth, infatuated with Lyubov. She is a goddess to him, her estate is a fairyland to him, and his great desire in the play is to please her. (In fact, if one were to lapse into a psychological overview of the play at this point one might say that the reason Lopahin can't propose to Varya is that he is in love with Lyubov.)

Lopahin buys the estate. For ninety-thousand rubles, which means nothing to him. He then proceeds to cut down the trees, which he knows will upset his goddess, Lyubov; and to raze the manor house. His parents were slaves in that house. Lyubov grew up in the house, he doesn't need the money, why is he cutting down the trees? (Yes, yes, yes; we encounter half-hearted addenda in re: future generations being won back to the land. But it doesn't wash. Why? If Lopahin wanted to build a summer colony he could build it anywhere. He could have built it without Lyubov's land and without her permission. If his objective were the building of summer homes and he were faced with two tracts, one where he had to cut down his idol's home, and one where he did not, which would he pick? Well, he has an infinite number of tracts. He can build anywhere he wants. Why cut down the trees and sadden his beloved idol? Having bought the estate he could easily let it sit, and, should the spirit move him subsequently, build his resort elsewhere.)

What, in effect, is going on here?

Nothing that has to do with trees.

The play is a series of scenes about sexuality, and, particularly, frustrated sexuality.

The play was inspired, most probably, by the scene in *Anna Karenina*° between Kitty's friend, Mlle. Varenka, and her gentleman companion, Mr. Koznyshez. The two of them, lonely, nice people, are brought together through the office of mutual friends. Each should marry, they are a perfect match. In one of the finest scenes in the book we are told that each knew the time had arrived, that it was Now or Never. They go for a walk, Mr. Koznyshez is about to propose when a question about mushrooms comes to his mind, the mood is broken, and so the two nice people are doomed to loneliness.

If this description sounds familiar it should. Chekhov, pregnant of his theme, lifted it shamelessly (and probably unconsciously) from Tolstoy and gave it to Lopahin and Varya.

Not only do *they* play out the scene, EVERYBODY IN THE PLAY PLAYS OUT THE SAME SCENE.

Anya is in love with Pyotr Trofimov, the tutor of her late brother. Trofimov is in love with *her*, but is too repressed to make the first move. He, in fact, declares that he is above love, while, in a soliloquy, refers to Anya as "My springtime, my dear morning sun."

Epihodov, the estate bookkeeper, is in love with Dunyasha, the chambermaid. He keeps trying to propose, but she thinks him a boor and will not hear him out. *She* is in love with Yasha, Lyubov's footman. Yasha seduces and abandons her as he is in love with himself.

Lyubov herself is in love. She gave her fortune to her paramour and nursed him through three years of his sickness. He deserted her for a younger woman.

Now: *this* is the reason she has returned to the estate. It is purely coincidental that she returns just prior to the auction of the orchard. *Why* is it coincidental?

Anna Karenina: Epic novel by the Russian writer Leo Tolstoy (1828–1910).

Because, as we have seen, she doesn't come back to *save* it. If she wanted to she could. *Why* does she come back? What is the event that prompts her to return again to Paris? The continual telegrams of her roué lover begging forgiveness.

Why did Lyubov come home? To lick her wounds, to play for time, to figure out a new course for her life.

Now: none of these is a theatrically compelling action. (The last comes closest, but it could be done in seclusion and does not need other characters. As, indeed, *Lyubov* is, essentially a monologue — there's nothing she *wants* from anyone onstage.)

If Lyubov is doing nothing but these solitary, reflective acts, why is she the protagonist of the play? She *isn't.*

The play has no protagonist. It has a couple of squad leaders. The reason it has no protagonist is that it has no through-action. It has one scene repeated by various couples.

To continue: Lyubov's brother is Gaev. He is a perennial bachelor, and is referred to several times in the text as an old lady. What does *he* want? Not much of anything. Yes, he cries at the end when the orchard is cut down. But he appears to be just as happy going to work in the bank and playing caroms as he is lounging around the morning room and playing caroms.

The other odd characters are Firs, the ancient butler, who is happy the mistress has returned, and Semyonov Pishtchik, a poor neighbor, who is always looking on the bright side.

He, Firs, and Gaev are local color. They are all celibate, and seen as somewhat doddering in different degrees. And they are all happy. Because they are not troubled by Sex. They are not involved in the play's one and oft-repeated action: to consummate, clarify, or rectify an unhappy sexual situation.

The cherry orchard and its imminent destruction is nothing other than an effective dramatic device.

The play is not "If you don't pay the mortgage I'll take your cow." It is "Kiss me quick because I'm dying of cancer."

The *obstacle* in the play does not grow out of, and does not even *refer* to the actions of the characters. The play works because it is a compilation of brilliant scenes.

I would guess — judging from its similarity to many of his short stories — that he wrote the scenes between the servant girl Dunyasha and Epihodov first. That perhaps sparked the idea of a scene between Dunyasha and the man *she* loves, Yasha, a footman just returned from Paris. Who did this fine footman return with? The mistress. *Et ensuite.*°

To continue this conceit: what did Chekhov do when he had two hours worth of scenes and thirteen characters running around a country house? He had, as any playwright has, three choices.

He could shelve the material as brilliant sketches; he could *examine* the material and attempt to discern any intrinsically dramatic through-action, and extrapolate the play out of *that.* . . .

To return: Chekhov has thirteen people stuck in a summer house. He has a lot of brilliant scenes. His third alternative is to come up with a pretext which will keep them in the same place and *talking* to each other for a while. This is

Et ensuite: And so on (French).

one of the alternatives and dilemmas of the modern dramatist: "Gosh, this material is *fantastic*. What can I do to just keep the people in the house?"

One can have a piece of jewelry stolen, one can have a murder committed, one can have a snowstorm, one can have the car break down, one can have The Olde Estate due to be sold for debts in three weeks unless someone comes up with a good solution.

I picture Chekhov coming up with this pretext and saying, "Naaaa, they'll never go for it." I picture him watching rehearsals and *wincing* every time Lopahin says (as he says frequently): "Just remember, you have only three (two, one) weeks until the cherry orchard is to be sold." "Fine," he must have thought. "That's real playwriting. One doesn't see Horatio coming out every five minutes and saying, 'Don't forget, Hamlet, your uncle killed your dad and now he's sleeping with your Ma!' "

"Oh no," he must have thought, "I'll never get away with it." But he did, and left us a play we cherish.

Why do we cherish the play? Because it is about the struggle between the Old Values of the Russian Aristocracy and their loosening grasp on power? I think not. For, finally, a play is about — and is *only* about — the actions of its characters. We, as audience, understand a play not in terms of the superficial idiosyncrasies or social *states* of its characters (they, finally, *separate* us from the play), but only in terms of the *action* the characters are trying to accomplish. (Set *Hamlet* in Waukegan and it's still a great play.)

The enduring draw of *The Cherry Orchard* is not that it is set in a dying Czarist Russia or that it has rich folks and poor folks. We are drawn to the play because it speaks to our *subconscious* — which is what a play should do. And we subconsciously perceive and enjoy the reiterated action of this reiterated scene: two people at odds — each trying to fulfill his or her frustrated sexuality.

From an adaptation of *The Cherry Orchard*
by David Mamet

Considerations for Critical Thinking and Writing

1. How convincing do you find Mamet's argument that "Nobody in the play gives a damn about the cherry orchard"?
2. Read the discussion on psychological strategies for approaching literature (p. 2004) and write an essay that agrees or disagrees with Mamet's assertion that what the play is really about is "frustrated sexuality."

PETER BROOK (b. 1925)
On Chekhov's "Hypervital" Characters   1987

In Chekhov's work, each character has its own existence: not one of them resembles another, particularly in *The Cherry Orchard,* which presents a microcosm of the political tendencies of the time. There are those who believe in social transformations, others attached to a disappearing past. None of them can achieve satisfaction or plenitude, and seen from outside, their existences might well appear empty, senseless. But they all burn with intense desires. They are not disillusioned, quite the contrary: in their own ways, they are all searching for a better quality of life, emotionally and socially. Their drama is that society — the outside world — blocks their energy. The complexity of their behavior is not indicated in the words, it emerges from the mosaic construction of an infinite number of details. What is essential is to see that these are not plays about lethargic people. They are hypervital people in a lethargic world, forced to dramatize the minutest happening out of a passionate desire to live. They have not given up.

From The Shifting Point

Considerations for Critical Thinking and Writing

1. Choose a character from *The Cherry Orchard* and test Brook's assertion that Chekhov's characters are not "lethargic people" but "hypervital people." How is the "complexity" of the character you discuss revealed in "the mosaic construction of an infinite number of details" associated with the character?
2. Write an essay either supporting or refuting Brook's view that the characters in *The Cherry Orchard* "have not given up."

31. Critical Case Study: Henrik Ibsen's *A Doll House*

This chapter provides several critical approaches to Henrik Ibsen's *A Doll House,* which appears in Chapter 30, p. 1517. There have been numerous critical approaches to this play because it raises so many issues relating to matters such as relationships between men and women, history, and biography, as well as imagery, symbolism, and irony. The following critical excerpts offer a small and partial sample of the possible formalist, biographical, historical, mythological, psychological, sociological, and other perspectives that have attempted to shed light on the play (see Chapter 35, "Critical Strategies for Reading," for a discussion of a variety of critical methods). They should help you to enjoy the play more by raising questions, providing insights, and inviting you further into the text.

The following letter offers a revealing vignette of the historical contexts for *A Doll House.* Professor Richard Panofsky of Southeastern Massachusetts University has provided the letter and this background information: "The translated letter was written in 1844 by Marcus (1807–1865) to his wife Ulrike (1816–1888), after six children had been born. This upper-middle-class Jewish family lived in Hamburg, Germany, where Marcus was a doctor. As the letter implies, Ulrike had left home and children: the letter establishes conditions for her to return. A woman in upper-class society of the time had few choices in an unhappy marriage. Divorce or separation meant ostracism; as Marcus writes, 'your husband, children, and the entire city threaten indifference or even contempt.' And she could not take a job, as she would have no profession to step into. In any case, Ulrike did return home. Between 1846 and 1857 the marriage produced eight more children. Beyond what the letter shows, we do not know the reasons for the separation or what the later marriage relationship was like."

A Nineteenth-Century Husband's Letter to His Wife   1844

Dear Wife,   June 23, 1844

You have sinned greatly — and maybe I too; but this much is certain: Adam sinned after Eve had already sinned. So it is with us; you, alone, carry the guilt of all the misfortune which, however, I helped to enlarge later by my behavior. Listen now, since I still believe certain things to be necessary in order that we may have a peaceful life. If we want not only to be content for a day but forever, you will have to follow my wishes. So examine yourself and determine if you are strong enough to conquer your false ambitions and your stubbornness to submit to all the conditions, the fulfillment of which I cannot ignore. Every sensible person will tell you that all I ask of you is what is easily understood. If you insist on remaining stubborn, then do not return to my house, for you will never be happy with me; your husband, children, and the entire city threaten indifference or even contempt.

But if you decide to act *sensibly* and *correctly,* that is *justly* and *kindly,* then be certain that many in the world will envy you.

I am including here the paper which I read to you in front of the rabbi; ask anyone in your residence if the wishes expressed by me are not quite reasonable, and are of a kind to which every wife can agree for the welfare of domestic happiness. In any case, act in a way you think best.

When you decide to return, write to tell me on which day and hour you depart from Berlin and give me your itinerary whether by way of Kuestrin and Pinne or by way of Wollstein. I will then meet you at Wollstein or Pinne. I expect you will bring Solomon with you.

Don't travel unprepared. If you need money, ask your father.

May God enlighten your heart and mind

I remain your so far unhappy,   [Marcus]

Greetings to my parents, brothers, and sisters; also your brother. Show them what you wish, this letter, the enclosure, whatever you want. The children are fortunately healthy.

If you want to return with joy and peace, write me by return mail. In that case, I would rather send you a carriage. Maybe Madam Fraenkel will come along. . . .

(Enclosure)

My wife promises — for which every wife is obligated to her husband — to follow my wishes in everything and to strictly obey my orders. It is already self-evident that our marital relations have often been disturbed by the fact that my wife does not follow my wishes but believes herself to be entitled to act on her own, even if this is totally against my orders. In order not to have to remind my wife every second what my wishes are regarding homemaking and public conduct — wishes which I have often expressed — I want to make here a few rules which shall serve as a code of conduct. A home is best run if the work for each hour is planned ahead of time, if possible.

Servants get up no later than 5:00 A.M. in summer and 6:00 A.M. in winter, the children an hour later. The cook prepares breakfast. The nursemaid puts out clothes for every child, prepares water and sponge, cleans the combs, etc. The cook should stay in the kitchen unless there is time to clean the rooms. At least once a week the rooms should be cleaned whenever possible, but not all on the same day.

Every Wednesday, the people in the house should do a laundry. Every last

Wednesday in the month, there shall be a large laundry with an outside washer woman. At least every Monday, the seamstress shall come into the house to fix what is necessary.

Every Thursday or Friday, bread is baked for the week; I think it is best to buy grain and have it ground, but to knead it at home.

Every Friday special bread (Barches) should be bought for the evening meal.

The kitchen list will be prepared and discussed every Thursday evening, jointly, by me and my wife; but my wish is to be decisive.

After this, provisions are to be bought every Friday at the market. For this purpose, my wife, herself, will go to the market on Fridays, accompanied by a servant; she can substitute a special woman who does errands (Faktorfrau) if she wishes, but not a servant.

All expenditures have to be written down daily and punctually.

The children receive a bath every Thursday evening. The children's clothes must be kept in a specially appointed chest, with a separate compartment for each child with the child's name upon it. The boys' suits and girls' dresses are to be kept separately. To keep used laundry, there must be a hamper easily accessible. Equally important is the food storage box in which provisions are kept in order, locked and safe from vermin.

The kitchen should be kept in order. Once a week all woodwork and copper must be scoured. The lights and lamps have to be cleaned daily. Toward servants, one has to be strict and just. Therefore, one should not call them names which aren't suitable for a decent wife. One should give them enough nourishing food. Disobedience and obstinacy are to be referred to me.

My wife will never make visits in my absence. However, she should visit the synagogue every Saturday — at least once a month; also she should go for a walk with the children at least once a week.

Considerations for Critical Thinking and Writing

1. Describe the tone of Marcus's letter to his wife. To what extent does he accept responsibility for their separation? What significant similarities and differences do you find between Marcus and Torvald Helmer?
2. Read the discussion on historical criticism in Chapter 35, "Critical Strategies for Reading" (p. 2005). How do you think a new historicist would use this letter to shed light on *A Doll House*?
3. Write a response to the letter from what you imagine the wife's point of view to be.
4. No information is available about this couple's marriage after Ulrike returned home. In an essay, speculate upon what you think their relationship was like later in their marriage.

ERROL DURBACH (b. 1941)

Durbach provides a close formalist reading of the tree to reveal how it reinforces the play's action and themes of transformation.

The Function of the Christmas Tree in A Doll's House°   1941

The most striking visual metonymy of the multiple processes of transformation occurring in the house . . . is the Christmas tree. Nora enters *A Doll's House* blithely happy and humming, laden with gifts for the children, a doll and a doll's cot for the girl, a sword and horse and trumpet for her little boys — gifts that innocuously reveal the stereotypes to which she gives her consent and the extent to which her values are shaped by the social expectations of her world. (She has also surreptitiously smuggled in a packet of macaroons, which she nibbles, like a child among children, only when out of sight of Torvald.) But the grand treat is only momentarily glimpsed, for she instructs the maid to hide away the tree immediately, lest the children see it before it is decorated. The tree is brought onstage again toward the end of Act I, and conspicuously placed in the center of the room as the focal point of Nora's vision of Christmas. By the time the tree is dragged out of concealment, however, Nora's world has already been transformed by the intrusion of a threatening reality in the person of Krogstad. There is something pathetically defensive about her placement of the tree — as if it were a gesture of blatant denial that her Eden is crumbling about her and a desperate attempt to deny that truth by fabricating a sort of talisman against disaster. At one level, the tree functions as a channel of Nora's emotions — not a symbol, but a barometer of feeling. At another level, the tree reveals the woman's psychological strategy of evasion, an attempt to perpetuate an image of family solidarity and happiness against all evidence to the contrary. She transforms the tree fantastically, tinselling and prinking it until it begins to radiate an appalling sense of false and misleading gaiety, becoming an emblem of the deceptive values generated in the dolls' house, ostensibly for the delight of the children. And as she distracts herself with the act of prettifying the tree, so her thoughts turn to the fancy dress ball at the Stenborgs and what she will wear. Masquerade, decoration, dressing up, duplicity — the line between innocuous partying and a damaging denial of reality is difficult to locate, but the tinkering with the tree is clearly emblematic of Nora's assumption of a disguise in a manic attempt to shore up a house on the verge of collapse.

The curtain rises on Act II to reveal the next stage in the Christmas tree's transformation: it stands tucked away in a corner, . . . "wrecked and disheveled," with stumps of burnt-out candles, no longer a talismanic protection against the encroachment of external forces on Nora's once secure domain. Again, the tree

---

A Doll's House: Rolf Fjelde's translation, used in this anthology, translates the title as *A Doll House* in order to emphasize that the whole household, including Torvald as well as Nora, lives an unreal, doll-like existence.

functions as a conductor of emotional atmosphere. A depressive melancholy has settled over a world bereft of illusions and infects every attempt to resuscitate them with a sense of vanity. The devastated tree now presides over the slow process of self-discovery in which Nora comes to recognize the enemy not as some outside invader of her macaroon-filled paradise, but as the deeply lodged habits of mind and the unconscious responses of a lifetime of dolls' house conditioning. Its transformation into a burnt-out, stripped-down repository of false illusions and evasionary tactics provides a striking visual counterpart to the transformative shocks that will change a doll into a woman through an alteration in moral consciousness.

From *A Doll's House: Ibsen's Myth of Transformation*

Considerations for Critical Thinking and Writing

1. According to Durbach, what is the function of the Christmas tree in the play?
2. How does Durbach connect the tree to Nora's emotional life?
3. In an essay write a close reading of the function of Nora's wild dance at the end of Act II. How does this dance relate to the play's action and themes?

CAROL STRONGIN TUFTS
A Psychoanalytic Reading of Nora (1986)

> I am not a member of the Women's Rights League. Whatever I have written has been without any conscious thought of making propaganda. I have been more the poet and less the social philosopher than people generally seem inclined to believe. . . . To me it has seemed a problem of mankind in general. And if you read my books carefully you will understand this. . . . My task has been the *description of humanity*. To be sure, whenever such a description is felt to be reasonably true, the reader will read his own feelings and sentiments into the work of the poet. These are then attributed to the poet; but incorrectly so. Every reader remolds the work beautifully and neatly, each according to his own personality. Not only those who write but also those who read are poets. They are collaborators.[1]

To look again at Ibsen's famous and often-quoted words — his assertion that *A Doll House* was not intended as propaganda to promote the cause of women's rights — is to realize the sarcasm aimed by the playwright at those nineteenth-century "collaborators" who insisted on viewing his play as a treatise and Nora, his heroine, as the romantic standard-bearer for the feminist cause. Yet there is also a certain irony implicit in such a realization, for directors, actors, audiences, and critics turning to this play a little over one hundred years after its first performance bring with them the historical, cultural, and psychological experience which itself places them in the role of Ibsen's collaborators. Because

[1]Speech delivered at the Banquet of the Norwegian League for Women's Rights, Christiania, 26 May 1898, in *Ibsen: Letters and Speeches,* ed. Evert Sprinchorn (New York: Hill and Wang, 1964), p. 337.

it is a theatrical inevitability that each dramatic work which survives its time and place of first performance does so to be recast in productions mounted in succeeding times and different places, A Doll House can never so much be simply reproduced as it must always be re-envisioned. And if the spectacle of a woman walking out on her husband and children in order to fulfill her "duties to (her)self" is no longer the shock for us today that it was for audiences at the end of the nineteenth century, a production of A Doll House which resonates with as much immediacy and power for us as it did for its first audiences may do so through the discovery within Ibsen's text of something of our own time and place. For in A Doll House, as Rolf Fjelde has written, "(i)t is the entire house . . . which is on trial, the total complex of relationships, including husband, wife, children, servants, upstairs and downstairs, that is tested by the visitors that come and go, embodying aspects of the inescapable reality outside."[2] And a production which approaches that reality through the experience of Western culture in the last quarter of the twentieth century may not only discover how uneasy was Ibsen's relationship to certain aspects of the forces of Romanticism at work in his own society, but, in so doing, may also come to fashion a Doll House which shifts emphasis away from the celebration of the Romantic belief in the sovereignty of the individual to the revelation of an isolating narcissism — a narcissism that has become all too familiar to us today.[3]

The characters of A Doll House are, to be sure, not alone in dramatic literature in being self-preoccupied, for self-preoccupation is a quality shared by characters from Oedipus to Hamlet and on into modern drama. Yet if a contemporary production is to suggest the narcissistic self-absorption of Ibsen's characters, it must do so in such a way as to imply motivations for their actions and delineate their relationships with one another. Thus it is important to establish a conceptual framework which will provide a degree of precision for the use of the term 'narcissism' in this discussion so as to distinguish it from the kind of self-absorption which is an inherent quality necessarily shared by all dramatic characters. For that purpose, it is useful to turn to the criteria established by the Task Force on Nomenclature and Statistics of the American Psychiatric Association for diagnosing the narcissistic personality:

A. Grandiose sense of self-importance and uniqueness, e.g., exaggerates achievements and talents, focuses on how special one's problems are.
B. Preoccupation with fantasies of unlimited success, power, brilliance, beauty, or ideal love.
C. Exhibitionistic: requires constant attention and admiration.
D. Responds to criticism, indifference of others, or defeat with either cool indifference, or with marked feelings of rage, inferiority, shame, humiliation, or emptiness.

[2]Rolf Fjelde, Introduction to A Doll House, in Henrik Ibsen, The Complete Major Prose Plays (New York: Farrar, Straus, Giroux, 1978), p. 121.
[3]For studies of the prevalence of the narcissistic personality disorder in contemporary psychoanalytic literature, see Otto F. Kernberg, Borderline Conditions and Pathological Narcissism (New York: J. Aronson, 1975); Heinz Kohut, The Analysis of the Self (New York: International Universities Press, 1971); and Peter L. Giovachinni, Psychoanalysis of Character Disorders (New York: J. Aronson, 1975). See also Christopher Lasch, The Culture of Narcissism (New York: Norton, 1979), for a discussion of narcissism as the defining characteristic of contemporary American society.

E. At least two of the following are characteristics of disturbances in interpersonal relationships:
   1. Lack of empathy: inability to recognize how others feel, e.g., unable
   to appreciate the distress of someone who is seriously ill.
   2. Entitlement: expectation of special favors without assuming recipro-
   cal responsibilities, e.g., surprise and anger that people won't do
   what he wants.
   3. Interpersonal exploitiveness: takes advantage of others to indulge
   own desires for self-aggrandizement, with disregard for the personal
   integrity and rights of others.
   4. Relationships characteristically vacillate between the extremes of
   over-idealization and devaluation.[4]

These criteria, as they provide a background against which to consider Nora's
relationship with both Kristine Linde and Dr. Rank, will serve to illuminate
not only those relationships themselves, but also the relationship of Nora
and her husband which is at the center of the play. Moreover, if these criteria
are viewed as outlines for characterization — but not as reductive psychoanalytic constructs leading to "case studies" — it becomes possible to discover a Nora of greater complexity than the totally sympathetic victim turned
romantic heroine who has inhabited most productions of the play. And, most
important of all, as Nora and her relationships within the walls of her "doll
house" come to imply a paradigm of the dilemma of all human relationships
in the greater society outside, the famous sound of the slamming door may
come to resonate even more loudly for us than it did for the audiences of
the nineteenth century with a profound and immediate sense of irony and
ambiguity, an irony and ambiguity which could not have escaped Ibsen
himself.

From "Recasting *A Doll House:* Narcissism As Character Motivation
in Ibsen's Play," *Comparative Drama,* Summer 1986

Considerations for Critical Thinking and Writing

1. What is Tufts's purpose in arguing that Nora be seen as narcissistic?
2. Using the criteria of the American Psychiatric Association, consider Nora's personality. Write an essay either refuting the assertion that she has a narcissistic personality or supporting it.
3. How does Tufts's reading compare with Joan Templeton's feminist reading of Nora
   in the perspective on p. 1620? Which do you find more convincing? Why?

[4]Task Force on Nomenclature and Statistics, American Psychiatric Association, *DSM-III: Diagnostic
Criteria Draft* (New York, 1978), pp. 103–04.

JOAN TEMPLETON (b. 1940)

This feminist perspective summarizes the arguments against reading the play as dramatization of a feminist heroine.

Is A Doll House *a Feminist Text?*   1989

A Doll House *is no more about women's rights than Shakespeare's* Richard II *is about the divine right of kings, or* Ghosts *about syphilis. . . . Its theme is the need of every individual to find out the kind of person he or she is and to strive to become that person.*[1]

Ibsen has been resoundingly saved from feminism, or, as it was called in his day, "the woman question." His rescuers customarily cite a statement the dramatist made on 26 May 1898 at a seventieth-birthday banquet given in his honor by the Norwegian Women's Rights League:

> I thank you for the toast, but must disclaim the honor of having consciously worked for the women's rights movement. . . . True enough, it is desirable to solve the woman problem, along with all the others; but that has not been the whole purpose. My task has been the description of humanity.[2]

Ibsen's champions like to take this disavowal as a precise reference to his purpose in writing *A Doll House* twenty years earlier, his "original intention," according to Maurice Valency.[3] Ibsen's biographer Michael Meyer urges all reviewers of *Doll House* revivals to learn Ibsen's speech by heart,[4] and James McFarlane, editor of *The Oxford Ibsen,* includes it in his explanatory material on *A Doll House,* under "Some Pronouncements of the Author," as though Ibsen had been speaking of the play.[5] Whatever propaganda feminists may have made of *A Doll House,* Ibsen, it is argued, never meant to write a play about the highly topical subject of women's rights; Nora's conflict represents something other than, or something more than, woman's. In an article commemorating the half century of Ibsen's death, R. M. Adams explains, "*A Doll House* represents a woman imbued with the idea of becoming a person, but it proposes nothing categorical about women becoming people; in fact, its real theme has nothing to do with the sexes."[6] Over twenty years later, after feminism had resurfaced as an international movement, Einar Haugen, the doyen of American Scandinavian studies, insisted that "Ibsen's Nora is not just a woman arguing for female liberation; she

[1]Michael Meyer, *Ibsen* (Garden City: Doubleday, 1971), 457. (This is not the Michael Meyer who is editor of *The Bedford Introduction to Literature.*)
[2]Henrik Ibsen, *Letters and Speeches,* ed. and trans. Evert Sprinchorn (New York: Hill, 1964), 337.
[3]Maurice Valency, *The Flower and the Castle: An Introduction to Modern Drama* (New York: Schocken, 1982), 151.
[4]Meyer, 774.
[5]James McFarlane, "*A Doll's House:* Commentary" in *The Oxford Ibsen,* ed. McFarlane (Oxford UP, 1961), V, 456.
[6]R. M. Adams, "The Fifty-First Anniversary," *Hudson Review* 10 (1957), 416.

is much more. She embodies the comedy as well as the tragedy of modern life."[7]
In the Modern Language Association's *Approaches to Teaching* A Doll House, the editor speaks disparagingly of "reductionist views of (*A Doll House*) as a feminist drama." Summarizing a "major theme" in the volume as "the need for a broad view of the play and a condemnation of a static approach," she warns that discussions of the play's "connection with feminism" have value only if they are monitored, "properly channeled and kept firmly linked to Ibsen's text."[8]

Removing the woman question from *A Doll House* is presented as part of a corrective effort to free Ibsen from his erroneous reputation as a writer of thesis plays, a wrongheaded notion usually blamed on Shaw, who, it is claimed, mistakenly saw Ibsen as the nineteenth century's greatest iconoclast and offered that misreading to the public as *The Quintessence of Ibsenism*. Ibsen, it is now de rigueur to explain, did not stoop to "issues." He was a poet of the truth of the human soul. That Nora's exit from her dollhouse has long been the principal international symbol for women's issues, including many that far exceed the confines of her small world, is irrelevant to the essential meaning of *A Doll House*, a play, in Richard Gilman's phrase, "pitched beyond sexual difference."[9] Ibsen, explains Robert Brustein, "was completely indifferent to (the woman question) except as a metaphor for individual freedom."[10] Discussing the relation of *A Doll House* to feminism, Halvdan Koht, author of the definitive Norwegian Ibsen life, says in summary, "Little by little the topical controversy died away; what remained was the work of art, with its demand for truth in every human relation."[11]

Thus, it turns out, the *Uncle Tom's Cabin* of the women's rights movement is not really about women at all. "Fiddle-faddle," pronounced R. M. Adams, dismissing feminist claims for the play.[12] Like angels, Nora has no sex. Ibsen meant her to be Everyman.

From "The *Doll House* Backlash: Criticism, Feminism, and Ibsen,"
PMLA, January, 1989.

Considerations for Critical Thinking and Writing

1. What kinds of arguments are used to reject *A Doll House* as a feminist text?
2. From the tone of the summaries provided, what would you say is Templeton's attitude toward these arguments?
3. Read the section on feminist criticism in "Critical Strategies for Reading," p. 2008, and write an essay addressing the summarized arguments as you think a feminist critic might respond.

[7]Einar Haugen, Ibsen's Drama: *Author to Audience* (Minneapolis: U of Minnesota P, 1979), vii.
[8]Yvonne Shafer, ed., *Approaches to Teaching Ibsen's* A Doll House (New York: MLA, 1985), 32.
[9]Richard Gilman, *The Making of Modern Drama* (New York: Farrar, 1972), 65.
[10]Robert Brustein, *The Theatre of Revolt* (New York: Little, 1962), 105.
[11]Halvdau Koht, *Life of Ibsen* (New York: Blom, 1971), 323.
[12]Adams, 416.

32. Experimental Trends in Drama

BEYOND REALISM

Realistic drama has remained popular throughout the twentieth century, but from its beginnings it has been continually challenged by nonrealistic modes of theater. By the end of the nineteenth century, playwrights reacting against realism began to develop a variety of new approaches to setting, action, and character. Instead of creating a slice of life onstage, modern experimental playwrights drew on purely theatrical devices, ranging from stark sets and ritualistic actions to symbolic characterizations and audience participation. In general, such devices were designed to jar audiences' expectations and to heighten their awareness that what appeared before them was indeed a theatrical production. A glimpse of some of the nonrealistic movements in drama suggests how the possibilities for affecting audiences have been broadened by experimental theater.

Symbolist drama rejected the realists' assumption that life can be understood objectively and scientifically. The symbolists emphasized a subjective, emotional response to life because they believed that ultimate realities can only be recognized intuitively. Since absolute truth cannot be directly perceived, symbolists such as the Belgian playwright Maurice Maeterlinck (1862–1949) sought to express spiritual truth through settings, characters, and actions that suggest a transcendent reality. Maeterlinck's most famous symbolist play, *Pelléas and Mélisande* (1892), is a story of love and vengeance that includes mysterious forebodings, symbolic objects, and unexplained powerful forces. The elements of the play make no attempt to create the texture of ordinary life.

Other playwrights — such as William Butler Yeats (1865–1939) in Ireland, Paul Claudel (1868–1955) in France, Leonid Andreyev (1871–1919) in Russia, and Federico García Lorca (1898–1936) in Spain — also used some of the techniques associated with symbolist plays, but the movement never enjoyed wide popularity because audiences often found the plays' action too vague and their language too cryptic. Nevertheless, symbolist drama had an important influence on the work of subsequent playwrights, such as Tennessee Williams's *The Glass Menagerie* (p. 1666) and Arthur Miller's *Death of a Salesman* (p. 1712); these dramatists effectively used symbols in plays that contain both realistic and nonrealistic qualities.

Another nonrealistic movement, known as *expressionism,* was popular from the end of World War I until the mid-1920s. Expressionist playwrights emphasized the internal lives of their characters and deliberately distorted reality by creating an outward manifestation of an inner state of being. The late plays of Swedish dramatist August Strindberg (1849–1912) anticipate expressionistic techniques. Strindberg's preface to *A Dream Play* (1902) reflects the impact that Freudian psychology would eventually have on the theater.

> The author has tried to imitate the disconnected but seemingly logical form of the dream. Anything may happen; everything is possible and probable. Time and space do not exist. On an insignificant background of reality, imagination designs and embroiders novel patterns: a medley of memories, experiences, free fancies, absurdities, and improvisations.

In such nonrealistic drama the action does not have to proceed chronologically because the playwright dramatizes the emotional life of the characters, which blends the past with the present rather than moving in a fixed linear way. This fluidity of development can be seen in the *flashbacks* of Williams's *The Glass Menagerie* and Miller's *Death of a Salesman.*

The *epic theater* of Bertolt Brecht is, like symbolism and expressionism, a long way from the realistic elements in Ibsen's *A Doll House.* Brecht kept a distance between his characters and the audience. This strategy of alienation was designed to alert audiences to important social problems that might be overlooked if an individual's struggles became too emotionally absorbing. Brecht's drama, by casting new light on chronic human problems such as poverty, injustice, and war, was a means to convey hope and evidence that society could be changed for the better. Brecht called his drama "epic" to distinguish it from Aristotle's notion of drama. The episodic structure was designed to prevent the audience from being swept up in the action or losing themselves in an inevitable tragedy. Instead, Brecht wanted the audience to analyze the action and realize that certain consequences weren't inevitable but could be avoided. This distancing, the dramatization of societal issues, and the use of loosely connected scenes sometimes narrated by a kind of stage manager are the hallmarks of "epic" drama.

Epic theater revels in stylized theatricality. The major action in *The Caucasian Chalk Circle,* for example, consists of a play within a play. Brecht's dramas use suggestive rather than detailed settings, and their scenery and props are frequently changed as the audience watches. His actors make clear that they are pretending to be characters. They may speak or sing in verse, address the audience, or comment on issues with other characters who are not participants in the immediate action. In brief, Brecht's theater is keenly conscious of itself as theater.

In contrast to this didactic theater, the *theater of the absurd* was a response to the twentieth century's loss of faith in reason, religion, and life itself. These doubts produced an approach to drama that emphasizes chaotic, irrational forces and portrays human beings as more the victims than the makers of their world.

Absurdists such as Samuel Beckett (1906–1989), French dramatist Eugène Ionesco (b. 1912), English playwright Harold Pinter (b. 1930), and American writer Edward Albee (b. 1928) employ a variety of approaches to drama, but they share some assumptions about what subjects are important. Absurdism challenges the belief that life is ordered and meaningful. Instead of positing traditional values that give human beings a sense of purpose in life, absurdists dramatize our inability to comprehend fully our identities and destinies. Unlike heroic characters such as Oedipus or Hamlet, who retain their dignity despite their defeats, the characters in absurdist dramas frequently seem pathetically comic as they drift from one destructive moment to the next. These *antiheroes* are often bewildered, ineffectual, deluded, and lost. If they learn anything, it is that the world isolates them in an existence devoid of God and absolute values.

The basic premise of absurdism — that life is meaningless — is often presented in a nonrealistic manner to disrupt our expectations. In a realistic play such as Ibsen's *A Doll House,* characters act pretty much the way we believe people behave. The motivation of these characters and the plausibility of their actions are comprehensible, but in an absurdist drama we are confronted with characters who appear in a series of disconnected incidents that lead to deeper confusion. What would we make of Nora if Ibsen had her appear in the final act costumed as a doll? This would be not only bizarre but unacceptable in a realistic play. However, it could make dramatic sense in an absurdist adaptation that sought to dramatize Nora's loss of identity and dehumanization as a result of her marriage.

Nora's appearance as a doll would, of course, be laughably inconsistent with what we judge to be real or reasonable. And yet we might find ourselves sympathizing with her situation. Suppose that instead of slamming the door and leaving her husband in the final scene, Nora moved stiffly about the room costumed as a doll while Helmer complacently sipped sherry and read the evening paper. Such an ending would suggest that she had been defeated by the circumstances in her life. Her condition — being nothing more than someone's toy — would be both absurd and pathetic. If we laughed at this scene, we would do so because Nora's situation is grotesquely humorous, a parody of her assumptions, hopes, and expectations. This is the world of *tragicomedy,* where laughter and pain coexist and where there is neither the happy resolution that typifies comic plots nor the transformational suffering that brings clarification to the tragic hero. It is the world dramatized, for example, in the opening scene of Harold Pinter's *The Dumb Waiter* when Ben tells Gus about an item he's read in the paper.

Ben: A man of eighty-seven wanted to cross the road. But there was a lot of traffic, see? He couldn't see how he was going to squeeze through. So he crawled under a lorry [truck].
Gus: He what?
Ben: He crawled under a lorry. A stationary lorry.
Gus: No?
Ben: The lorry started and ran over him.
Gus: Go on!
Ben: That's what it says here.
Gus: Get away.
Ben: It's enough to make you want to puke, isn't it?
Gus: Who advised him to do a thing like that?
Ben: A man of eighty-seven crawling under a lorry!
Gus: It's unbelievable.
Ben: It's down here in black and white.
Gus: Incredible.

As much as Gus finds the story difficult to believe and Ben is sickened by it, it is a fact that the old man was crushed under ridiculous circumstances. His death is unexpected, accidental, incomprehensible, and meaningless — except that what happened to the old man is, from an absurdist's perspective, really no different from what life has in store for all of us one way or the other.

An absurdist playwright may, as Pinter does, employ realistic settings and speech, but he or she goes beyond realistic conventions to challenge the rational assumptions we make about our lives. Pinter insists that "a play is not an essay." Background information, character motivation, action — nothing presented on an absurdist's stage is governed by the conventions of realism. The absurdists typically refuse to create the illusion of reality because there is, finally, no reality to imitate. If conversations in their plays are sometimes fragmented and seemingly inconsequential, the reason is that absurdists dramatize people's combined inability and unwillingness to communicate with one another. Indeed, Samuel Beckett's *Act without Words* contains no dialogue, and in his *Krapp's Last Tape* a single character addresses only his own tape-recorded voice. To some extent we must suspend common sense and logic if we are to appreciate the visions and voices in an absurdist play.

Although many other nonrealistic movements developed in the twentieth century, these four — symbolism, expressionism, epic theater, and the theater of the absurd — embrace the major differences between nonrealistic and realistic drama. The theater continually tests its own possibilities. In the 1960s and 1970s, for example, some acting companies in New York completely collapsed the usual distinctions between audience and actors. The Living Theater went even further by moving into the streets, where the actors and audiences engaged in dramatic political statements aimed at raising the social consciousness of people wherever they were. Some critics argued that this was not really theater but merely an exuberant kind of political rally. However, proponents of these productions — known as *guerrilla theater* — argued that protest drama is both politically and artistically valid. In any case, although today's playwrights seem considerably less inclined to take to the streets, there is a tolerance for a wide range of possible relationships between actors and audiences. Audiences (and readers) can expect symbolic characters, expressionistic settings, poetic language, monologues, and extreme actions in productions that also contain realistic elements. In *Route 1 & 9* (1981), a piece created by an experimental theater company called The Wooster Group, for example, audiences found themselves confronted with passages from Thornton Wilder's idealized version of America in *Our Town* that were coupled with a pornographic film and a black vaudeville act. This unlikely combination was used to comment on Wilder's conception of America in which issues of sex and race are largely ignored. Increasingly, experimental theater has cultivated an eclectic approach to drama, using a variety of media, cultures, playwrights, and even languages to enrich an audience's experience. Parts of Robert Wilson's *CIVIL warS* (1984) — a work never staged in its entirety in any one place — were performed in several countries, including France, Italy, and the United States, and drew upon different languages as well as cultures to evoke a wide range of experiences from history, literature, myths, and even dreams. The Album of Contemporary Plays in Chapter 33 attests to the traditions and innovations that contemporary dramatists have incorporated into their dramatic art.

KRAPP'S LAST TAPE

Samuel Beckett was born near Dublin to a middle-class Irish-Protestant family. After graduating from Trinity College, Dublin, in 1927, he studied in Paris, where he met James Joyce and was influenced by Joyce's innovative use of language. There Beckett began his own experiments in poetry and fiction. He returned to Ireland to teach at Trinity College and earned an M.A. in 1931, but he left teaching the following year to travel in Europe. He permanently settled in Paris in the late 1930s. During this period his publications included two volumes of poetry, *Whoroscope* (1930) and *Echo's Bones* (1935), a collection of stories, *More Pricks Than Kicks* (1934), and a novel, *Murphy* (1938).

During World War II, Beckett's work for the French resistance made it necessary for him to flee German-occupied France, but he returned to Paris at the end of the war and began writing the works that would earn him the Nobel Prize for literature in 1969. Writing mostly in French and translating his work into English later, Beckett produced both novels — *Molloy* (1951) *Malone Dies* (1951), *Watt* (1953), *The Unnamable* (1953), and *How It Is*

(1961) — and plays — *Waiting for Godot* (1952), *Endgame* (1957), *Krapp's Last Tape* (1958, first written in English), and *Happy Days* (1961).

These works are populated by characters who live meager, isolated existences that sometimes seem barely human. Yet their aspirations and desires are expressed in simple activities that are attempts to transcend the endless meaningless routines that make up their lives. In an illogical and absurdly comic world stripped of any lasting meaning, these characters appear in minimal settings, having little to say and even less to do.

Waiting for Godot, Beckett's most famous play, brought absurdist principles to popular audiences. Its seemingly pointless dialogue is spoken by two clownish vagabonds while they wait for a mysterious Mr. Godot, who never appears. The play has no clearly identifiable conflict; instead, the action tends to be random and repetitive. Nothing much happens, but there is tension nonetheless among strange characters who hope in an apparently hopeless world.

In *Krapp's Last Tape,* Beckett uses only one character onstage. The play is more than a monologue, however, because the protagonist engages in a kind of conversation with his own tape-recorded voice. Every year on his birthday Krapp has recorded his impressions of that year's events and methodically cataloged and indexed them. Krapp observes his sixty-ninth birthday by listening to portions of a tape he recorded thirty years earlier. Hence, there are two Krapps in the play: an elderly man and his younger self on tape. This device allows Beckett to present Krapp's relation to his past in an intriguing, complex manner; we witness a character thinking aloud with a part of himself he no longer knows. If the older Krapp appears strange to us, we should not overlook the fact that he is even stranger to himself.

SAMUEL BECKETT (1906–1989)
Krapp's Last Tape   1958

A PLAY IN ONE ACT

SCENE: *A late evening in the future.*

Krapp's den. Front center a small table, the two drawers of which open towards audience. Sitting at the table, facing front, i.e. across from the drawers, a wearish old man: Krapp.

   Rusty black narrow trousers too short for him. Rusty black sleeveless waistcoat, four capacious pockets. Heavy silver watch and chain. Grimy white shirt open at neck, no collar. Surprising pair of dirty white boots, size ten at least, very narrow and pointed.

   White face. Purple nose. Disordered gray hair. Unshaven.

   Very near-sighted (but unspectacled). Hard of hearing.

   Cracked voice. Distinctive intonation.

   Laborious walk.

On the table a tape-recorder with microphone and a number of cardboard boxes containing reels of recorded tapes.

Table and immediately adjacent area in strong white light. Rest of stage in darkness.

Krapp remains a moment motionless, heaves a great sigh, looks at his watch, fumbles in his pockets, takes out an envelope, puts it back, fumbles, takes out a small bunch of keys, raises it to his eyes, chooses a key, gets up and moves to front of table. He stoops, unlocks first drawer, peers into it, takes out a reel of tape, peers at it, puts it back, locks drawer, unlocks second drawer, peers into it, feels about inside it, takes out a large banana, peers at it, locks drawer, puts keys back in his pocket. He turns, advances to edge of stage, halts, strokes banana, peels it, drops skin at his feet, puts end of banana in his mouth and remains motionless, staring vacuously before him. Finally he bites off the end, turns aside, and begins pacing to and fro at edge of stage, in the light, i.e. not more than four or five paces either way, meditatively eating banana. He treads on skin, slips, nearly falls, recovers himself, stoops and peers at skin and finally pushes it, still stooping, with his foot over the edge of stage into pit. He resumes his pacing, finishes banana, returns to table, sits down, remains a moment motionless, heaves a great sigh, takes keys from his pockets, raises them to his eyes, chooses key, gets up and moves to front of table, unlocks second drawer, takes out a second large banana, peers at it, locks drawer, puts back keys in his pocket, turns, advances to edge of stage, halts, strokes banana, peels it, tosses skin into pit, puts end of banana in his mouth, and remains motionless, staring vacuously before him. Finally he has an idea, puts banana in his waistcoat pocket, the end emerging, and goes with all the speed he can muster backstage into darkness. Ten seconds. Loud pop of cork. Fifteen seconds. He comes back into light carrying an old ledger and sits down at table. He lays ledger on table, wipes his mouth, wipes his hands on the front of his waistcoat, brings them smartly together and rubs them.

Krapp *(briskly):* Ah! *(He bends over ledger, turns the pages, finds the entry he wants, reads.)* Box . . . thrree . . . spool . . . five. *(He raises his head and stares front. With relish.)* Spool! *(Pause.)* Spooool! *(Happy smile. Pause. He bends over table, starts peering and poking at the boxes.)* Box . . . thrree . . . thrree . . . four . . . two . . . *(with surprise)* nine! good God! . . . seven . . . ah! the little rascal! *(He takes up box, peers at it.)* Box thrree. *(He lays it on table, opens it, and peers at spools inside.)* Spool . . . *(he peers at ledger)* . . . five *(he peers at spools)* . . . five . . . five! . . . ah! the little scoundrel! *(He takes out a spool, peers at it.)* Spool five. *(He lays it on table, closes box three, puts it back with the others, takes up the spool.)* Box thrree, spool five. *(He bends over the machine, looks up. With relish.)* Spooool! *(Happy smile. He bends, loads spool on machine, rubs his hands.)* Ah! *(He peers at ledger, reads entry at foot of page.)* Mother at rest at last . . . Hm . . . The black ball . . . *(He raises his head, stares blankly front. Puzzled.)* Black ball? . . . *(He peers again at ledger, reads.)* The dark nurse . . . *(He raises his head, broods, peers again at ledger, reads.)* Slight improvement in bowel condition . . . Hm . . . Memorable . . . what? *(He peers closer.)* Equinox, memorable equinox. *(He raises his head, stares blankly front. Puzzled.)* Memorable equinox? . . . *(Pause. He shrugs his shoulders, peers again at ledger, reads.)* Farewell to — *(he turns the page)* — love.

He raises his head, broods, bends over machine, switches on, and assumes listening posture; i.e. leaning forward, elbows on table, hand cupping ear towards machine, face front.

Tape (strong voice, rather pompous, clearly Krapp's at a much earlier time):
Thirty-nine today, sound as a — *(Settling himself more comfortably he knocks one of the boxes off the table, curses, switches off, sweeps boxes and ledger violently to the ground, winds tape back to beginning, switches on, resumes posture.)* Thirty-nine today, sound as a bell, apart from my old weakness, and intellectually I have now every reason to suspect at the . . . *(hesitates)* . . . crest of the wave — or thereabouts. Celebrated the awful occasion, as in recent years, quietly at the Winehouse. Not a soul. Sat before the fire with closed eyes, separating the grain from the husks. Jotted down a few notes, on the back of an envelope. Good to be back in my den, in my old rags. Have just eaten I regret to say three bananas and only with difficulty refrained from a fourth. Fatal things for a man with my condition. *(Vehemently.)* Cut 'em out! *(Pause.)* The new light above my table is a great improvement. With all this darkness round me I feel less alone. *(Pause.)* In a way. *(Pause.)* I love to get up and move about in it, then back here to . . . *(hesitates)* . . . me. *(Pause.)* Krapp.

Pause.

The grain, now what I wonder do I mean by that, I mean . . . *(hesitates)* . . . I suppose I mean those things worth having when all the dust has — when all *my* dust has settled. I close my eyes and try and imagine them.

Pause. Krapp closes his eyes briefly.

Extraordinary silence this evening, I strain my ears and do not hear a sound. Old Miss McGlome always sings at this hour. But not tonight. Songs of her girlhood, she says. Hard to think of her as a girl. Wonderful woman though. Connaught, I fancy. *(Pause.)* Shall I sing when I am her age, if I ever am? No. *(Pause.)* Did I sing as a boy? No. *(Pause.)* Did I ever sing? No.

Pause.

Just been listening to an old year, passages at random. I did not check in the book, but it must be at least ten or twelve years ago. At that time I think I was still living on and off with Bianca in Kedar Street. Well out of that, Jesus yes! Hopeless business. *(Pause.)* Not much about her, apart from a tribute to her eyes. Very warm. I suddenly saw them again. *(Pause.)* Incomparable! *(Pause.)* Ah well . . . *(Pause.)* These old P.M.s are gruesome, but I often find them — *(Krapp switches off, broods, switches on)* — a help before embarking on a new . . . *(hesitates)* . . . retrospect. Hard to believe I was ever that young whelp. The voice! Jesus! And the aspirations! *(Brief laugh in which Krapp joins.)* And the resolutions! *(Brief laugh in which Krapp joins.)* To drink less, in particular. *(Brief laugh of Krapp alone.)* Statistics. Seventeen hundred hours, out of the preceding eight thousand odd, consumed on licensed premises alone. More than 20%, say 40% of his waking life. *(Pause.)* Plans for a less . . . *(hesitates)* . . . engrossing sexual life. Last illness of his father. Flagging pursuit of happiness. Unattainable laxation. Sneers at what he calls his youth and thanks to God that it's over. *(Pause.)* False ring there. *(Pause.)* Shadows of the opus . . . magnum. Closing with a — *(brief laugh)* — yelp to Providence. *(Prolonged laugh in which Krapp joins.)* What remains of all that misery? A girl in a shabby green coat, on a railway-station platform? No?

Pause.

When I look —

Krapp switches off, broods, looks at his watch, gets up, goes backstage into darkness. Ten seconds. Pop of cork. Ten seconds. Second cork. Ten seconds. Third cork. Ten seconds. Brief burst of quavering song.

Krapp *(sings):* Now the day is over,
    Night is drawing nigh-igh,
    Shadows — °

Fit of coughing. He comes back into light, sits down, wipes his mouth, switches on, resumes his listening posture.

Tape: — back on the year that is gone, with what I hope is perhaps a glint of the old eye to come, there is of course the house on the canal where mother lay a-dying, in the late autumn, after her long viduity° *(Krapp gives a start),* and the — *(Krapp switches off, winds back tape a little, bends his ear closer to machine, switches on)* — a — dying, after her long viduity, and the —

Krapp switches off, raises his head, stares blankly before him. His lips move in the syllables of "viduity." No sound. He gets up, goes backstage into darkness, comes back with an enormous dictionary, lays it on table, sits down and looks up the word.

Krapp *(reading from dictionary):* State — or condition of being — or remaining — a widow — or widower. *(Looks up. Puzzled.)* Being — or remaining? . . . *(Pause. He peers again at dictionary. Reading.)* "Deep weeds of viduity" . . . Also of an animal, especially a bird . . . the vidua or weaver-bird . . . Black plumage of male . . . *(He looks up. With relish.)* The vidua-bird!

Pause. He closes dictionary, switches on, resumes listening posture.

Tape: — bench by the weir from where I could see her window. There I sat, in the biting wind, wishing she were gone. *(Pause.)* Hardly a soul, just a few regulars, nursemaids, infants, old men, dogs. I got to know them quite well — oh by appearance of course I mean! One dark young beauty I recollect particularly, all white and starch, incomparable bosom, with a big black hooded perambulator, most funereal thing. Whenever I looked in her direction she had her eyes on me. And yet when I was bold enough to speak to her — not having been introduced — she threatened to call a policeman. As if I had designs on her virtue! *(Laugh. Pause.)* The face she had! The eyes! Like . . . *(hesitates)* . . . chrysolite! *(Pause.)* Ah well . . . *(Pause.)* I was there when — *(Krapp switches off, broods, switches on again)* — the blind went down, one of those dirty brown roller affairs, throwing a ball for a little white dog, as chance would have it. I happened to look up and there it was. All over and done with, at last. I sat on for a few moments with the ball in

---

Now . . . Shadows: From the hymn "Now the Day Is Over" by Sabine Baring-Gould (1834–1924), author of "Onward, Christian Soldiers."
viduity: Widowhood.

my hand and the dog yelping and pawing at me. *(Pause.)* Moments. Her moments, my moments. *(Pause.)* The dog's moments. *(Pause.)* In the end I held it out to him and he took it in his mouth, gently, gently. A small, old, black, hard, solid rubber ball. *(Pause.)* I shall feel it, in my hand, until my dying day. *(Pause.)* I might have kept it. *(Pause.)* But I gave it to the dog.

Pause.

Ah well . . .

Pause.

Spiritually a year of profound gloom and indigence until that memorable night in March, at the end of the jetty, in the howling wind, never to be forgotten, when suddenly I saw the whole thing. The vision, at last. This I fancy is what I have chiefly to record this evening, against the day when my work will be done and perhaps no place left in my memory, warm or cold, for the miracle that . . . *(hesitates)* . . . for the fire that set it alight. What I suddenly saw then was this, that the belief I had been going on all my life, namely — *(Krapp switches off impatiently, winds tape forward, switches on again)* — great granite rocks the foam flying up in the light of the lighthouse and the wind-gauge spinning like a propellor, clear to me at last that the dark I have always struggled to keep under is in reality my most — *(Krapp curses, switches off, winds tape forward, switches on again)* — unshatterable association until my dissolution of storm and night with the light of the understanding and the fire — *(Krapp curses louder, switches off, winds tape forward, switches on again)* — my face in her breasts and my hand on her. We lay there without moving. But under us all moved, and moved us, gently, up and down, and from side to side.

Pause.

Past midnight. Never knew such silence. The earth might be uninhabited.

Pause.

Here I end —

Krapp switches off, winds tape back, switches on again.

— upper lake, with the punt, bathed off the bank, then pushed out into the stream and drifted. She lay stretched out on the floorboards with her hands under her head and her eyes closed. Sun blazing down, bit of a breeze, water nice and lively. I noticed a scratch on her thigh and asked her how she came by it. Picking gooseberries, she said. I said again I thought it was hopeless and no good going on, and she agreed, without opening her eyes. *(Pause.)* I asked her to look at me and after a few moments — *(pause)* — after a few moments she did, but the eyes just slits, because of the glare. I bent over her to get them in the shadow and they opened. *(Pause. Low.)* Let me in. *(Pause.)* We drifted in among the flags and stuck. The way they went down, sighing, before the stem! *(Pause.)* I lay down across her with my face in her breasts and my hand on her. We lay there without moving. But under us all moved, and moved us, gently, up and down, and from side to side.

Pause.

Past midnight. Never knew —

Krapp switches off, broods. Finally he fumbles in his pockets, encounters the banana, takes it out, peers at it, puts it back, fumbles, brings out the envelope, fumbles, puts back envelope, looks at his watch, gets up and goes backstage into darkness. Ten seconds. Sound of bottle against glass, then brief siphon. Ten seconds. Bottle against glass alone. Ten seconds. He comes back a little unsteadily into light, goes to front of table, takes out keys, raises them to his eyes, chooses key, unlocks first drawer, peers into it, feels about inside, takes out reel, peers at it, locks drawer, puts keys back in his pocket, goes and sits down, takes reel off machine, lays it on dictionary, loads virgin reel on machine, takes envelope from his pocket, consults back of it, lays it on table, switches on, clears his throat, and begins to record.

Krapp: Just been listening to that stupid bastard I took myself for thirty years ago, hard to believe I was ever as bad as that. Thank God that's all done with anyway. *(Pause.)* The eyes she had! *(Broods, realizes he is recording silence, switches off, broods. Finally.)* Everything there, everything, all the — *(Realizes this is not being recorded, switches on.)* Everything there, everything on this old muckball, all the light and dark and famine and feasting of . . . *(hesitates)* . . . the ages! *(In a shout.)* Yes! *(Pause.)* Let that go! Jesus! Take his mind off his homework! Jesus! *(Pause. Weary.)* Ah well, maybe he was right. *(Pause.)* Maybe he was right. *(Broods. Realizes. Switches off. Consults envelope.)* Pah! *(Crumples it and throws it away. Broods. Switches on.)* Nothing to say, not a squeak. What's a year now? The sour cud and the iron stool. *(Pause.)* Revelled in the word spool. *(With relish.)* Spooool! Happiest moment of the past half million. *(Pause.)* Seventeen copies sold, of which eleven at trade price to free circulating libraries beyond the seas. Getting known. *(Pause.)* One pound six and something, eight I have little doubt. *(Pause.)* Crawled out once or twice, before the summer was cold. Sat shivering in the park, drowned in dreams and burning to be gone. Not a soul. *(Pause.)* Last fancies. *(Vehemently.)* Keep 'em under! *(Pause.)* Scalded the eyes out of me reading *Effie* again, a page a day, with tears again. Effie . . . *(Pause.)* Could have been happy with her, up there on the Baltic, and the pines, and the dunes. *(Pause.)* Could I? *(Pause.)* And she? *(Pause.)* Pah! *(Pause.)* Fanny came in a couple of times. Bony old ghost of a whore. Couldn't do much, but I suppose better than a kick in the crutch. The last time wasn't so bad. How do you manage it, she said, at your age? I told her I'd been saving up for her all my life. *(Pause.)* Went to Vespers once, like when I was in short trousers. *(Pause. Sings.)*

Now the day is over.
Night is drawing nigh-igh,
Shadows — *(coughing, then almost inaudible)* — of the evening
Steal across the sky.

(Gasping.) Went to sleep and fell off the pew. *(Pause.)* Sometimes wondered in the night if a last effort mightn't — *(Pause.)* Ah finish your booze now and get to your bed. Go on with this drivel in the morning. Or leave it at that. *(Pause.)* Leave it at that. *(Pause.)* Lie propped up in the dark — and wander.

Be again in the dingle on a Christmas Eve, gathering holly, the red-berried. *(Pause.)* Be again on Croghan on a Sunday morning, in the haze, with the bitch, stop and listen to the bells. *(Pause.)* And so on. *(Pause.)* Be again, be again. *(Pause.)* All that old misery. *(Pause.)* Once wasn't enough for you. *(Pause.)* Lie down across her.

Long pause. He suddenly bends over machine, switches off, wrenches off tape, throws it away, puts on the other, winds it forward to the passage he wants, switches on, listens staring front.

Tape: — gooseberries, she said. I said again I thought it was hopeless and no good going on, and she agreed, without opening her eyes. *(Pause.)* I asked her to look at me and after a few moments — *(pause)* — after a few moments she did, but the eyes just slits, because of the glare. I bent over her to get them in the shadow and they opened. *(Pause. Low.)* Let me in. *(Pause.)* We drifted in among the flags and stuck. The way they went down, sighing, before the stem! *(Pause.)* I lay down across her with my face in her breasts and my hand on her. We lay there without moving. But under us all moved, and moved us, gently, up and down, and from side to side.

Pause. Krapp's lips move. No sound.

Past midnight. Never knew such silence. The earth might be uninhabited.

Pause.

Here I end this reel. Box — *(pause)* — three, spool — *(pause)* — five. *(Pause.)* Perhaps my best years are gone. When there was a chance of happiness. But I wouldn't want them back. Not with the fire in me now. No, I wouldn't want them back.

Krapp motionless staring before him. The tape runs on in silence.

Curtain

Considerations for Critical Thinking and Writing

1. Why do you think the play is set in "a late evening in the future" rather than the present?
2. What does Krapp's physical description reveal about him?
3. Why does Krapp make tape recordings? How does he use them?
4. What is the effect of the many pauses in the play?
5. What are Krapp's attitudes toward his earlier perceptions about life? Compare and contrast the sixty-nine-year-old Krapp with the thirty-nine-year-old on the tape.
6. What career hopes did the younger Krapp have? How do you know whether he was successful?
7. How does Krapp, in retrospect, seem to feel about his life?
8. Although Krapp is obviously not a conventional dramatic hero, is there anything heroic about what he says or does? How do you respond to him?
9. What do you make of the play's title? A student once suggested that if the play were to have a subtitle, Beckett could have used the heading of one of Krapp's ledger entries: "Farewell to love." Explain whether this proposed subtitle reflects the play's major concerns.

10. Do you think the sixty-nine-year-old Krapp changes or develops during the play? In the final scene, how does he act differently from the way he behaved in the opening scene?

Connections to Other Selections

1. Write an essay in which you explore some important similarities or differences between Krapp and Willy Loman in Arthur Miller's *Death of a Salesman* (p. 1712) or the narrator in Robert Frost's "The Road Not Taken" (p. 871).
2. Compare and contrast the use of tape recorders in *Krapp's Last Tape* and David Henry Hwang's *M. Butterfly* (p. 1921). Do you think the tape recorders heighten or lessen the dramatic effects of each play?
3. Discuss this assessment of Chekhov and Beckett by Peter Brook *(The Shifting Point):* "With Chekhov, periods, commas, points of suspension, are all of a fundamental importance, as fundamental as the 'pauses' precisely indicated by Beckett. If one fails to observe them, one loses the rhythm and tensions of the play."

PERSPECTIVE

MARTIN ESSLIN (b. 1918)
On the Theater of the Absurd 1961

Concerned as it is with the ultimate realities of the human condition, the relatively few fundamental problems of life and death, isolation and communication, the Theater of the Absurd, however grotesque, frivolous, and irreverent it may appear, represents a return to the original, religious function of the theater — the confrontation of man with the spheres of myth and religious reality. Like ancient Greek tragedy and the medieval mystery plays and baroque allegories, the Theater of the Absurd is intent on making its audience aware of man's precarious and mysterious position in the universe.

The difference is merely that in ancient Greek tragedy — and comedy — as well as in the medieval mystery play and the baroque *auto sacramental,* the ultimate realities concerned were generally known and universally accepted metaphysical systems, while the Theater of the Absurd expresses the absence of any such generally accepted cosmic system of values. Hence, much more modestly, the Theater of the Absurd makes no pretense at explaining the ways of God to man. It can merely present, in anxiety or with derision, an individual human being's intuition of the ultimate realities as he experiences them; the fruits of one man's descent into the depths of his personality, his dreams, fantasies, and nightmares.

While former attempts at confronting man with the ultimate realities of his condition projected a coherent and generally recognized version of the truth, the Theater of the Absurd merely communicates one poet's most intimate and personal intuition of the human situation, his own *sense of being,* his individual vision of the world. This is the *subject matter* of the Theater of the Absurd, and it determines its *form,* which must, of necessity, represent a convention of the stage basically different from the "realistic" theater of our time.

As the Theater of the Absurd is not concerned with conveying information or presenting the problems or destinies of characters that exist outside the author's inner world, as it does not expound a thesis or debate ideological propositions, it is not concerned with the representation of events, the narration of the fate or the adventures of characters, but instead with the presentation of one individual's basic situation. It is a theater of situation as against a theater of events in sequence, and therefore it uses a language based on patterns of concrete images rather than argument and discursive speech. And since it is trying to present a sense of being, it can neither investigate nor solve problems of conduct or morals.

From *The Theatre of the Absurd*

Considerations for Critical Thinking and Writing

1. What does Esslin see as the essential difference between the theater of the absurd and Greek or medieval theaters in terms of their treatment of "ultimate realities"?
2. To what extent does Esslin's description of the theater of the absurd apply to *Krapp's Last Tape*?
3. Here's one to stretch your imagination: Take Krapp's "situation" and write a summary of how you think Sophocles, Shakespeare, or Ibsen might have developed it into a play. Consider, for example, what the focus of the conflict would be and how the story would end.

THE DUMB WAITER

Harold Pinter, one of Britain's most important contemporary playwrights, was born in East London to working-class parents. After studying briefly at the Royal Academy of Dramatic Art, he acted in a touring repertory company from 1949 to 1957. He wrote his first play, *The Room,* in 1957, the same year he wrote *The Birthday Party* and *The Dumb Waiter* (not produced until 1959). Pinter's first commercial success was *The Caretaker* (1960). He has acted, directed, and written for radio, television, film, and the stage. His numerous plays include *A Slight Ache* (1959), *A Night Out* (1960), *The Dwarfs* (1960), *The Homecoming* (1965), *No Man's Land* (1975), *Betrayal* (1978), *One for the Road* (1984), and *Mountain Language* (1988). His successes have been marked by many theater, television, and film awards.

Although Pinter's plays seem realistic on the surface, they typically turn out to be mysteriously ambiguous and even bizarre. His characters speak and act naturally — the way Ibsen's or Chekhov's might — but their behavior often seems unmotivated as they express deep emotions in highly charged domestic settings that usually consist of a single room.

For example, in *The Homecoming,* one of Pinter's most highly regarded plays, the action is set in a rundown house in London where an all-male family consisting of Max, the father of Lenny, a pimp, and Joey, a demolition worker by day and boxer by night, live together with Max's brother. These characters continually argue and viciously insult each other. Soon a third brother, Teddy, a philosophy professor in America who had left years before, returns with his wife Ruth for a surprise visit. When Max greets Teddy, he shouts, "Who asked you to bring tarts in here?" Ruth is not only verbally assaulted but also subjected to Lenny's attempts to dominate and seduce her. Finally Ruth is seen lying on the sofa with Joey as her philosophical husband looks on. The family proposes that she stay on at the house after Teddy returns to America; she will earn her keep through prostitution when she is not busy with the family. The play ends with Teddy departing and Ruth remaining behind to service the multiple needs of the family.

Characters in Pinter's plays frequently defy rational explanations; their identities shift, their obscure pasts somehow intrude on the present, and they engage in alternately humorous and terrifying conversations filled with troubled meanings. His plays appear direct and simple, but beneath their realistic texture are subtle designs that disrupt conventional expectations.

In *The Dumb Waiter,* while two men wait in a basement room for instructions from their boss, they engage in what sounds like aimless, disconnected conversation about topics ranging from newspaper items to a broken toilet. Suddenly, a service elevator in the wall, a dumb waiter, clatters down with orders that are as surprising as they are mysteriously menacing.

HAROLD PINTER (b. 1930)
The Dumb Waiter 1957

SCENE: *A basement room. Two beds, flat against the back wall. A serving hatch, closed, between the beds. A door to the kitchen and lavatory, left. A door to a passage, right.*

Ben is lying on a bed, left, reading a paper. Gus is sitting on a bed, right, tying his shoelaces, with difficulty. Both are dressed in shirts, trousers, and braces.
   Silence.
   Gus ties his laces, rises, yawns, and begins to walk slowly to the door, left. He stops, looks down, and shakes his foot.
   Ben lowers his paper and watches him. Gus kneels and unties his shoelace and slowly takes off the shoe. He looks inside it and brings out a flattened matchbox. He shakes it and examines it. Their eyes meet. Ben rattles his paper and reads. Gus puts the matchbox in his pocket and bends down to put on his shoe. He ties his lace, with difficulty. Ben lowers his paper and watches him. Gus walks to the door, left, stops, and shakes the other foot. He kneels, unties his shoelace, and slowly takes off the shoe. He looks inside it and brings out a flattened cigarette packet. He shakes it and examines it. Their eyes meet. Ben rattles his paper and reads. Gus puts the packet in his pocket, bends down, puts on his shoe, and ties the lace.
   He wanders off, left.
   Ben slams the paper down on the bed and glares after him. He picks up the paper and lies on his back, reading.
   Silence.
   A lavatory chain is pulled twice, off left, but the lavatory does not flush.
   Silence.
   Gus re-enters, left, and halts at the door, scratching his head.

Ben slams down the paper.

Ben: Kaw!

He picks up the paper.

What about this? Listen to this!

He refers to the paper.

A man of eighty-seven wanted to cross the road. But there was a lot of traffic, see? He couldn't see how he was going to squeeze through. So he crawled under a lorry.

Gus: He what?

Ben: He crawled under a lorry.° A stationary lorry.

Gus: No?

Ben: The lorry started and ran over him.

Gus: Go on!

Ben: That's what it says here.

Gus: Get away.

Ben: It's enough to make you want to puke, isn't it?

Gus: Who advised him to do a thing like that?

Ben: A man of eighty-seven crawling under a lorry!

Gus: It's unbelievable.

Ben: It's down here in black and white.

Gus: Incredible.

Silence.
Gus shakes his head and exits. Ben lies back and reads.
The lavatory chain is pulled once off left, but the lavatory does not flush.
Ben whistles at an item in the paper.
Gus re-enters.

I want to ask you something.

Ben: What are you doing out there?

Gus: Well, I was just —

Ben: What about the tea?

Gus: I'm just going to make it.

Ben: Well, go on, make it.

Gus: Yes, I will. *(He sits in a chair. Ruminatively.)* He's laid on some very nice crockery this time, I'll say that. It's sort of striped. There's a white stripe.

Ben reads.

It's very nice. I'll say that.

Ben turns the page.

You know, sort of round the cup. Round the rim. All the rest of it's black, you see. Then the saucer's black, except for right in the middle, where the cup goes, where it's white.

Ben reads.

lorry: Truck.

Then the plates are the same, you see. Only they've got a black stripe — the plates — right across the middle. Yes, I'm quite taken with the crockery.

Ben (still reading): What do you want plates for? You're not going to eat.

Gus: I've brought a few biscuits.

Ben: Well, you'd better eat them quick.

Gus: I always bring a few biscuits. Or a pie. You know I can't drink tea without anything to eat.

Ben: Well, make the tea then, will you? Time's getting on.

Gus brings out the flattened cigarette packet and examines it.

Gus: You got any cigarettes? I think I've run out.

He throws the packet high up and leans forward to catch it.

I hope it won't be a long job, this one.

Aiming carefully, he flips the packet under his bed.

Oh, I wanted to ask you something.

Ben (slamming his paper down): Kaw!

Gus: What's that?

Ben: A child of eight killed a cat!

Gus: Get away.

Ben: It's a fact. What about that, eh? A child of eight killing a cat!

Gus: How did he do it?

Ben: It was a girl.

Gus: How did she do it?

Ben: She —

He picks up the paper and studies it.

It doesn't say.

Gus: Why not?

Ben: Wait a minute. It just says — Her brother, aged eleven, viewed the incident from the toolshed.

Gus: Go on!

Ben: That's bloody ridiculous.

Pause.

Gus: I bet he did it.

Ben: Who?

Gus: The brother.

Ben: I think you're right.

Pause.

(Slamming down the paper.) What about that, eh? A kid of eleven killing a cat and blaming it on his little sister of eight! It's enough to —

He breaks off in disgust and seizes the paper. Gus rises.

Gus: What time is he getting in touch?

Ben reads.

What time is he getting in touch?

Ben: What's the matter with you? It could be any time. Any time.

Gus (moves to the foot of Ben's bed): Well, I was going to ask you something.

Ben: What?

Gus: Have you noticed the time that tank takes to fill?

Ben: What tank?

Gus: In the lavatory.

Ben: No. Does it?

Gus: Terrible.

Ben: Well, what about it?

Gus: What do you think's the matter with it?

Ben: Nothing.

Gus: Nothing?

Ben: It's got a deficient ballcock, that's all.

Gus: A deficient what?

Ben: Ballcock.

Gus: No? Really?

Ben: That's what I should say.

Gus: Go on! That didn't occur to me.

Gus wanders to his bed and presses the mattress.

I didn't have a very restful sleep today, did you? It's not much of a bed. I could have done with another blanket too. *(He catches sight of a picture on the wall.)* Hello, what's this? *(Peering at it.)* "The First Eleven."° Cricketers. You seen this, Ben?

Ben (reading): What?

Gus: The first eleven.

Ben: What?

Gus: There's a photo here of the first eleven.

Ben: What first eleven?

Gus (studying the photo): It doesn't say.

Ben: What about that tea?

Gus: They all look a bit old to me.

Gus wanders downstage, looks out front, then all about the room.

I wouldn't like to live in this dump. I wouldn't mind if you had a window, you could see what it looked like outside.

Ben: What do you want a window for?

Gus: Well, I like to have a bit of a view, Ben. It wiles away the time.

He walks about the room.

I mean, you come into a place when it's still dark, you come into a room you've never seen before, you sleep all day, you do your job, and then you go away in the night again.

Pause.

I like to get a look at the scenery. You never get the chance in this job.

Ben: You get your holidays, don't you?

"*The First Eleven*": A cricket team.

Gus: Only a fortnight.

Ben (lowering the paper): You kill me. Anyone would think you're working every day. How often do we do a job? Once a week? What are you complaining about?

Gus: Yes, but we've got to be on tap though, haven't we? You can't move out of the house in case a call comes.

Ben: You know what your trouble is?

Gus: What?

Ben: You haven't got any interests.

Gus: I've got interests.

Ben: What? Tell me one of your interests.

Pause.

Gus: I've got interests.

Ben: Look at me. What have I got?

Gus: I don't know. What?

Ben: I've got my woodwork. I've got my model boats. Have you ever seen me idle? I'm never idle. I know how to occupy my time, to its best advantage. Then when a call comes, I'm ready.

Gus: Don't you ever get a bit fed up?

Ben: Fed up? What with?

Silence.

Ben reads. Gus feels in the pocket of his jacket, which hangs on the bed.

Gus: You got any cigarettes? I've run out.

The lavatory flushes off left.

There she goes.

Gus sits on his bed.

No, I mean, I say the crockery's good. It is. It's very nice. But that's about all I can say for this place. It's worse than the last one. Remember that last place we were in? Last time, where was it? At least there was a wireless there. No, honest. He doesn't seem to bother much about our comfort these days.

Ben: When are you going to stop jabbering?

Gus: You'd get rheumatism in a place like this, if you stay long.

Ben: We're not staying long. Make the tea, will you? We'll be on the job in a minute.

Gus picks up a small bag by his bed and brings out a packet of tea. He examines it and looks up.

Gus: Eh, I've been meaning to ask you.

Ben: What the hell is it now?

Gus: Why did you stop the car this morning, in the middle of that road?

Ben (lowering the paper): I thought you were asleep.

Gus: I was, but I woke up when you stopped. You did stop, didn't you?

Pause.

In the middle of that road. It was still dark, don't you remember? I looked out. It was all misty. I thought perhaps you wanted to kip,° but you were sitting up dead straight, like you were waiting for something.

Ben: I wasn't waiting for anything.

Gus: I must have fallen asleep again. What was all that about then? Why did you stop?

Ben (picking up the paper): We were too early.

Gus: Early? *(He rises.)* What do you mean? We got the call, didn't we, saying we were to start right away. We did. We shoved out on the dot. So how could we be too early?

Ben (quietly): Who took the call, me or you?

Gus: You.

Ben: We were too early.

Gus: Too early for what?

Pause.

You mean someone had to get out before we got in?

He examines the bedclothes.

I thought these sheets didn't look too bright. I thought they ponged° a bit. I was too tired to notice when I got in this morning. Eh, that's taking a bit of a liberty, isn't it? I don't want to share my bed-sheets. I told you things were going down the drain. I mean, we've always had clean sheets laid on up till now. I've noticed it.

Ben: How do you know those sheets weren't clean?

Gus: What do you mean?

Ben: How do you know they weren't clean? You've spent the whole day in them, haven't you?

Gus: What, you mean it might be my pong? *(He sniffs sheets.)* Yes. *(He sits slowly on bed.)* It could be my pong, I suppose. It's difficult to tell. I don't really know what I pong like, that's the trouble.

Ben (referring to the paper): Kaw!

Gus: Eh, Ben.

Ben: Kaw!

Gus: Ben.

Ben: What?

Gus: What town are we in? I've forgotten.

Ben: I've told you. Birmingham.

Gus: Go on!

He looks with interest about the room.

That's in the Midlands. The second biggest city in Great Britain. I'd never have guessed.

He snaps his fingers.

Eh, it's Friday today, isn't it? It'll be Saturday tomorrow.

Ben: What about it?

Kip: Nap.
ponged: Smelled.

Gus (excited): We could go and watch the Villa.°

Ben: They're playing away.

Gus: No, are they? Caarr! What a pity.

Ben: Anyway, there's no time. We've got to get straight back.

Gus: Well, we have done in the past, haven't we? Stayed over and watched a game, haven't we? For a bit of relaxation.

Ben: Things have tightened up, mate. They've tightened up.

Gus chuckles to himself.

Gus: I saw the Villa get beat in a cup tie once. Who was it against now? White shirts. It was one-all at half-time. I'll never forget it. Their opponents won by a penalty. Talk about drama. Yes, it was a disputed penalty. Disputed. They got beat two-one, anyway, because of it. You were there yourself.

Ben: Not me.

Gus: Yes, you were there. Don't you remember that disputed penalty?

Ben: No.

Gus: He went down just inside the area. Then they said he was just acting. I didn't think the other bloke touched him myself. But the referee had the ball on the spot.

Ben: Didn't touch him! What are you talking about? He laid him out flat!

Gus: Not the Villa. The Villa don't play that sort of game.

Ben: Get out of it.

Pause.

Gus: Eh, that must have been here, in Birmingham.

Ben: What must?

Gus: The Villa. That must have been here.

Ben: They were playing away.

Gus: Because you know who the other team was? It was the Spurs. It was Tottenham Hotspur.

Ben: Well, what about it?

Gus: We've never done a job in Tottenham.

Ben: How do you know?

Gus: I'd remember Tottenham.

Ben turns on his bed to look at him.

Ben: Don't make me laugh, will you?

Ben turns back and reads. Gus yawns and speaks through his yawn.

Gus: When's he going to get in touch?

Pause.

Yes, I'd like to see another football match. I've always been an ardent football fan. Here, what about coming to see the Spurs tomorrow?

Ben (tonelessly): They're playing away.

Gus: Who are?

Ben: The Spurs.

Villa: A soccer team.

Gus: Then they might be playing here.

Ben: Don't be silly.

Gus: If they're playing away they might be playing here. They might be playing the Villa.

Ben (tonelessly): But the Villa are playing away.

Pause. An envelope slides under the door, right. Gus sees it. He stands, looking at it.

Gus: Ben.

Ben: Away. They're all playing away.

Gus: Ben, look here.

Ben: What?

Gus: Look.

Ben turns his head and sees the envelope. He stands.

Ben: What's that?

Gus: I don't know.

Ben: Where did it come from?

Gus: Under the door.

Ben: Well, what is it?

Gus: I don't know.

They stare at it.

Ben: Pick it up.

Gus: What do you mean?

Ben: Pick it up!

Gus slowly moves towards it, bends and picks it up.

What is it?

Gus: An envelope.

Ben: Is there anything on it?

Gus: No.

Ben: Is it sealed?

Gus: Yes.

Ben: Open it.

Gus: What?

Ben: Open it!

Gus opens it and looks inside.

What's in it?

Gus empties twelve matches into his hand.

Gus: Matches.

Ben: Matches?

Gus: Yes.

Ben: Show it to me.

Gus passes the envelope. Ben examines it.

Nothing on it. Not a word.

Gus: That's funny, isn't it?

Ben: It came under the door?
Gus: Must have done.
Ben: Well, go on.
Gus: Go on where?
Ben: Open the door and see if you can catch anyone outside.
Gus: Who, me?
Ben: Go on!

Gus stares at him; puts the matches in his pocket, goes to his bed, and brings a revolver from under the pillow. He goes to the door, opens it, looks out, and shuts it.

Gus: No one.

He replaces the revolver.

Ben: What did you see?
Gus: Nothing.
Ben: They must have been pretty quick.

Gus takes the matches from pocket and looks at them.

Gus: Well, they'll come in handy.
Ben: Yes.
Gus: Won't they?
Ben: Yes, you're always running out, aren't you?
Gus: All the time.
Ben: Well, they'll come in handy then.
Gus: Yes.
Ben: Won't they?
Gus: Yes, I could do with them. I could do with them too.
Ben: You could, eh?
Gus: Yes.
Ben: Why?
Gus: We haven't got any.
Ben: Well, you've got some now, haven't you?
Gus: I can light the kettle now.
Ben: Yes, you're always cadging° matches. How many have you got there?
Gus: About a dozen.
Ben: Well, don't lose them. Red too. You don't even need a box.

Gus probes his ear with a match.

    (Slapping his hand.) Don't waste them! Go on, go and light it.
Gus: Eh?
Ben: Go and light it.
Gus: Light what?
Ben: The kettle.
Gus: You mean the gas.
Ben: Who does?
Gus: You do.

---

cadging: Begging.

Ben (his eyes narrowing): What do you mean, I mean the gas?

Gus: Well, that's what you mean, don't you? The gas.

Ben (powerfully): If I say go and light the kettle I mean go and light the kettle.

Gus: How can you light a kettle?

Ben: It's a figure of speech! Light the kettle. It's a figure of speech!

Gus: I've never heard it.

Ben: Light the kettle! It's common usage!

Gus: I think you've got it wrong.

Ben (menacing): What do you mean?

Gus: They say put on the kettle.

Ben (taut): Who says?

They stare at each other, breathing hard.

   (Deliberately.) I have never in all my life heard anyone say put on the kettle.

Gus: I bet my mother used to say it.

Ben: Your mother? When did you last see your mother?

Gus: I don't know, about —

Ben: Well, what are you talking about your mother for?

They stare.

   Gus, I'm not trying to be unreasonable. I'm just trying to point out something to you.

Gus: Yes, but —

Ben: Who's the senior partner here, me or you?

Gus: You.

Ben: I'm only looking after your interests, Gus. You've got to learn, mate.

Gus: Yes, but I've never heard —

Ben (vehemently): Nobody says light the gas! What does the gas light?

Gus: What does the gas — ?

Ben (grabbing him with two hands by the throat, at arm's length): THE KETTLE, YOU FOOL!

Gus takes the hands from his throat.

Gus: All right, all right.

Pause.

Ben: Well, what are you waiting for?

Gus: I want to see if they light.

Ben: What?

Gus: The matches.

He takes out the flattened box and tries to strike.

   No.

He throws the box under the bed.

Ben stares at him.

Gus raises his foot.

   Shall I try it on here?

Ben stares. Gus strikes a match on his shoe. It lights.

   Here we are.

Ben (wearily): Put on the bloody kettle, for Christ's sake.

Ben goes to his bed, but, realising what he has said, stops and half turns. They look at each other. Gus slowly exits, left. Ben slams his paper down on the bed and sits on it, head in hands.

Gus (entering): It's going.
Ben: What?
Gus: The stove.

Gus goes to his bed and sits.

I wonder who it'll be tonight.

Silence.

Eh, I've been wanting to ask you something.
Ben (putting his legs on the bed): Oh, for Christ's sake.
Gus: No. I was going to ask you something.

He rises and sits on Ben's bed.

Ben: What are you sitting on my bed for?

Gus sits.

What's the matter with you? You're always asking me questions. What's the matter with you?
Gus: Nothing.
Ben: You never used to ask me so many damn questions. What's come over you?
Gus: No, I was just wondering.
Ben: Stop wondering. You've got a job to do. Why don't you just do it and shut up?
Gus: That's what I was wondering about.
Ben: What?
Gus: The job.
Ben: What job?
Gus (tentatively): I thought perhaps you might know something.

Ben looks at him.

I thought perhaps you — I mean — have you got any idea — who it's going to be tonight?
Ben: Who what's going to be?

They look at each other.

Gus (at length): Who it's going to be.

Silence.

Ben: Are you feeling all right?
Gus: Sure.
Ben: Go and make the tea.
Gus: Yes, sure.

Gus exits, left, Ben looks after him. He then takes his revolver from under the pillow and checks it for ammunition. Gus re-enters.

The gas has gone out.

Ben: Well, what about it?

Gus: There's a meter.

Ben: I haven't got any money.

Gus: Nor have I.

Ben: You'll have to wait.

Gus: What for?

Ben: For Wilson.

Gus: He might not come. He might just send a message. He doesn't always come.

Ben: Well, you'll have to do without it, won't you?

Gus: Blimey.

Ben: You'll have a cup of tea afterwards. What's the matter with you?

Gus: I like to have one before.

Ben holds the revolver up to the light and polishes it.

Ben: You'd better get ready anyway.

Gus: Well, I don't know, that's a bit much, you know, for my money.

He picks up a packet of tea from the bed and throws it into the bag.

I hope he's got a shilling, anyway, if he comes. He's entitled to have. After all, it's his place, he could have seen there was enough gas for a cup of tea.

Ben: What do you mean, it's his place?

Gus: Well, isn't it?

Ben: He's probably only rented it. It doesn't have to be his place.

Gus: I know it's his place. I bet the whole house is. He's not even laying on any gas now either.

Gus sits on his bed.

It's his place all right. Look at all the other places. You go to this address, there's a key there, there's a teapot, there's never a soul in sight — *(He pauses.)* Eh, nobody ever hears a thing, have you ever thought of that? We never get any complaints, do we, too much noise or anything like that? You never see a soul, do you? — except the bloke who comes. You ever noticed that? I wonder if the walls are soundproof. *(He touches the wall above his bed.)* Can't tell. All you do is wait, eh? Half the time he doesn't even bother to put in an appearance, Wilson.

Ben: Why should he? He's a busy man.

Gus (thoughtfully): I find him hard to talk to, Wilson. Do you know that, Ben?

Ben: Scrub round it, will you?

Pause.

Gus: There are a number of things I want to ask him. But I can never get round to it, when I see him.

Pause.

I've been thinking about the last one.

Ben: What last one?

Gus: That girl.

Ben grabs the paper, which he reads.

(Rising, looking down at Ben.) How many times have you read that paper?

Ben slams the paper down and rises.

Ben (angrily): What do you mean?

Gus: I was just wondering how many times you'd —

Ben: What are you doing, criticizing me?

Gus: No, I was just —

Ben: You'll get a swipe round your earhole if you don't watch your step.

Gus: Now look here, Ben —

Ben: I'm not looking anywhere! *(He addresses the room.)* How many times have
  I — ! A bloody liberty!

Gus: I didn't mean that.

Ben: You just get on with it, mate. Get on with it, that's all.

Ben gets back on the bed.

Gus: I was just thinking about that girl, that's all.

Gus sits on his bed.

She wasn't much to look at, I know, but still. It was a mess though, wasn't
it? What a mess. Honest, I can't remember a mess like that one. They don't
seem to hold together like men, women. A looser texture, like. Didn't she
spread, eh? She didn't half spread. Kaw! But I've been meaning to ask you.

Ben sits up and clenches his eyes.

Who clears up after we've gone? I'm curious about that. Who does the clearing up? Maybe they don't clear up. Maybe they just leave them there, eh?
What do you think? How many jobs have we done? Blimey, I can't count
them. What if they never clear anything up after we've gone.

Ben (pityingly): You mutt. Do you think we're the only branch of this organization? Have a bit of common. They got departments for everything.

Gus: What cleaners and all?

Ben: You birk!°

Gus: No, it was that girl made me start to think —

*There is a loud clatter and racket in the bulge of wall between the beds, of
something descending. They grab their revolvers, jump up, and face the wall.
The noise comes to a stop. Silence. They look at each other. Ben gestures sharply
towards the wall. Gus approaches the wall slowly. He bangs it with his revolver.
It is hollow. Ben moves to the head of his bed, his revolver cocked. Gus puts his
revolver on his bed and pats along the bottom of the center panel. He finds a
rim. He lifts the panel. Disclosed is a serving-hatch, a "dumb waiter." A wide box
is held by pulleys. Gus peers into the box. He brings out a piece of paper.*

Ben: What is it?

Gus: You have a look at it.

Ben: Read it.

Gus (reading): Two braised steak and chips. Two sago puddings. Two teas
  without sugar.

---

birk: Fool.

Ben: Let me see that. *(He takes the paper.)*
Gus (to himself): Two teas without sugar.
Ben: Mmnn.
Gus: What do you think of that?
Ben: Well —

The box goes up. Ben levels his revolver.

Gus: Give us a chance? They're in a hurry, aren't they?

Ben rereads the note. Gus looks over his shoulder.

That's a bit — that's a bit funny, isn't it?
Ben (quickly): No. It's not funny. It probably used to be a café here, that's all. Upstairs. These places change hands very quickly.
Gus: A café?
Ben: Yes.
Gus: What, you mean this was the kitchen, down here?
Ben: Yes, they change hands overnight, these places. Go into liquidation. The people who run it, you know, they don't find it a going concern, they move out.
Gus: You mean the people who ran this place didn't find it a going concern and moved out?
Gus: Sure.
Gus: WELL, WHO'S GOT IT NOW?

Silence.

Ben: What do you mean, who's got it now?
Gus: Who's got it now? If they moved out, who moved in?
Ben: Well, that all depends —

The box descends with a clatter and bang. Ben levels his revolver. Gus goes to the box and brings out a piece of paper.

Gus (reading): Soup of the day. Liver and onions. Jam tart.

A pause. Gus looks at Ben. Ben takes the note and reads it. He walks slowly to the hatch. Gus follows. Ben looks into the hatch but not up it. Gus puts his hand on Ben's shoulder. Ben throws it off. Gus puts his finger to his mouth. He leans on the hatch and swiftly looks up it. Ben flings him away in alarm. Ben looks at the note. He throws his revolver on the bed and speaks with decision.

Ben: We'd better send something up.
Gus: Eh?
Ben: We'd better send something up.
Gus: Oh! Yes. Yes. Maybe you're right.

They are both relieved at the decision.

Ben (purposefully): Quick! What have you got in that bag?
Gus: Not much.

Gus goes to the hatch and shouts up it.

Wait a minute!
Ben: Don't do that!

Gus examines the contents of the bag and brings them out, one by one.

Gus: Biscuits. A bar of chocolate. Half a pint of milk.
Ben: That all?
Gus: Packet of tea.
Ben: Good.
Gus: We can't send the tea. That's all the tea we've got.
Ben: Well, there's no gas. You can't do anything with it, can you?
Gus: Maybe they can send us down a bob.°
Ben: What else is there?
Gus (reaching into bag): One Eccles cake.°
Ben: One Eccles cake?
Gus: Yes.
Ben: You never told me you had an Eccles cake.
Gus: Didn't I?
Ben: Why only one? Didn't you bring one for me?
Gus: I didn't think you'd be keen.
Ben: Well, you can't send up one Eccles cake, anyway.
Gus: Why not?
Ben: Fetch one of those plates.
Gus: All right

Gus goes towards the door, left, and stops.

    Do you mean I can keep the Eccles cake then?
Ben: Keep it?
Gus: Well, they don't know we've got it, do they?
Ben: That's not the point.
Gus: Can't I keep it?
Ben: No, you can't. Get the plate.

Gus exits, left. Ben looks in the bag. He brings out a packet of crisps.° Enter Gus with a plate.

    (Accusingly, holding up the crisps.) Where did these come from?
Gus: What?
Ben: Where did these crisps come from?
Gus: Where did you find them?
Ben (hitting him on the shoulder): You're playing a dirty game, my lad!
Gus: I only eat those with beer!
Ben: Well, where were you going to get the beer?
Gus: I was saving them till I did.
Ben: I'll remember this. Put everything on the plate.

They pile everything on to the plate. The box goes up without the plate.

    Wait a minute!

They stand.

---

bob: A shilling for the gas meter.
Eccles cake: A sugared pastry.
crisps: Potato chips.

Gus: It's gone up.
Ben: It's all your stupid fault, playing about!
Gus: What do we do now?
Ben: We'll have to wait till it comes down.

Ben puts the plate on the bed, puts on his shoulder holster, and starts to put on his tie.

You'd better get ready.

Gus goes to his bed, puts on his tie, and starts to fix his holster.

Gus: Hey, Ben.
Ben: What?
Gus: What's going on here?

Pause.

Ben: What do you mean?
Gus: How can this be a café?
Ben: It used to be a café.
Gus: Have you seen the gas stove?
Ben: What about it?
Gus: It's only got three rings.
Ben: So what?
Gus: Well, you couldn't cook much on three rings, not for a busy place like this.
Ben (irritably): That's why the service is slow!

Ben puts on his waistcoat.

Gus: Yes, but what happens when we're not here? What do they do then? All these menus coming down and nothing going up. It might have been going on like this for years.

Ben brushes his jacket.

What happens when we go?

Ben puts on his jacket.

They can't do much business.

The box descends. They turn about. Gus goes to the hatch and brings out a note.

Gus (reading): Macaroni Pastitsio. Ormitha Macarounada.
Ben: What was that?
Gus: Macaroni Pastitsio. Ormitha Macarounada.
Ben: Greek dishes.
Gus: No.
Ben: That's right.
Gus: That's pretty high class.
Ben: Quick before it goes up.

Gus puts the plate in the box.

Gus (calling up the hatch): Three McVitie and Price! One Lyons Red Label! One Smith's Crisps! One Eccles cake! One Fruit and Nut!
Ben: Cadbury's.

Gus (up the hatch): Cadbury's!

Ben (handing the milk): One bottle of milk.

Gus (up the hatch): One bottle of milk! Half a pint! *(He looks at the label.)* Express Dairy! *(He puts the bottle in the box.)*

The box goes up.

Just did it.

Ben: You shouldn't shout like that.

Gus: Why not?

Ben: It isn't done.

Ben goes to his bed.

Well, that should be all right, anyway, for the time being.

Gus: You think so, eh?

Ben: Get dressed, will you? It'll be any minute now.

Gus puts on his waistcoat. Ben lies down and looks up at the ceiling.

Gus: This is some place. No tea and no biscuits.

Ben: Eating makes you lazy, mate. You're getting lazy, you know that? You don't want to get slack on your job.

Gus: Who me?

Ben: Slack, mate, slack.

Gus: Who me? Slack?

Ben: Have you checked your gun? You haven't even checked your gun. It looks disgraceful, anyway. Why don't you ever polish it?

Gus rubs his revolver on the sheet. Ben takes out a pocket mirror and straightens his tie.

Gus: I wonder where the cook is. They must have had a few, to cope with that. Maybe they had a few more gas stoves. Eh! Maybe there's another kitchen along the passage.

Ben: Of course there is! Do you know what it takes to make an Ormitha Macarounada?

Gus: No, what?

Ben: An Ormitha — ! Buck your ideas up,° will you?

Gus: Takes a few cooks, eh?

Gus puts his revolver in its holster.

The sooner we're out of this place the better.

He puts on his jacket.

Why doesn't he get in touch? I feel like I've been here years. *(He takes his revolver out of its holster to check the ammunition.)* We've never let him down though, have we? We've never let him down. I was thinking only the other day, Ben. We're reliable, aren't we?

He puts his revolver back in its holster.

Buck . . . up: Be quiet.

Still, I'll be glad when it's over tonight.

He brushes his jacket.

I hope the bloke's not going to get excited tonight, or anything. I'm feeling a bit off. I've got a splitting headache.

Silence.
The box descends. Ben jumps up.
Gus collects the note.

(*Reading.*) One Bamboo Shoots, Water Chestnuts and Chicken. One Char Siu and Beansprouts.
Ben: Beansprouts?
Gus: Yes.
Ben: Blimey.
Gus: I wouldn't know where to begin.

He looks back at the box. The packet of tea is inside it. He picks it up.

They've sent back the tea.
Ben (anxious): What'd they do that for?
Gus: Maybe it isn't tea-time.

The box goes up. Silence.

Ben (throwing the tea on the bed, and speaking urgently): Look here. We'd better tell them.
Gus: Tell them what?
Ben: That we can't do it, we haven't got it.
Gus: All right then.
Ben: Lend us your pencil. We'll write a note.

Gus, turning for a pencil, suddenly discovers the speaking-tube, which hangs on the right wall of the hatch facing his bed.

Gus: What's this?
Ben: What?
Gus: This.
Ben (examining it): This? It's a speaking-tube.
Gus: How long has that been there?
Ben: Just the job. We should have used it before, instead of shouting up there.
Gus: Funny I never noticed it before.
Ben: Well, come on.
Gus: What do you do?
Ben: See that? That's a whistle.
Gus: What, this?
Ben: Yes, take it out. Pull it out.

Gus does so.

That's it.
Gus: What do we do now?
Ben: Blow into it.
Gus: Blow?
Ben: It whistles up there if you blow. Then they know you want to speak. Blow.

Gus blows. Silence.

Gus (tube at mouth): I can't hear a thing.
Ben: Now you speak! Speak into it!

Gus looks at Ben, then speaks into the tube.

Gus: The larder's bare!
Ben: Give me that!

He grabs the tube and puts it to his mouth.

> (*Speaking with great deference.*) Good evening. I'm sorry to — bother you, but we just thought we'd better let you know that we haven't got anything left. We sent up all we had. There's no more food down here.

He brings the tube slowly to his ear.

> What?

To mouth.

> What?

To ear. He listens. To mouth.

> No, all we had we sent up.

To ear. He listens. To mouth.

> Oh, I'm very sorry to hear that.

To ear. He listens. To Gus.

> The Eccles cake was stale.

He listens. To Gus.

> The chocolate was melted.

He listens. To Gus.

> The milk was sour.

Gus: What about the crisps?
Ben (listening): The biscuits were mouldy.

He glares at Gus. Tube to mouth.

> Well, we're very sorry about that.

Tube to ear.

> What?

To mouth.

> What?

To ear.

> Yes. Yes.

To mouth.

> Yes certainly. Certainly. Right away.

To ear. The voice has ceased. He hangs up the tube.

(*Excitedly.*) Did you hear that?

Gus: What?

Ben: You know what he said? Light the kettle! Not put on the kettle! Not light the gas! But light the kettle!

Gus: How can we light the kettle?

Ben: What do you mean?

Gus: There's no gas.

Ben (clapping hand to head): Now what do we do?

Gus: What did he want us to light the kettle for?

Ben: For tea. He wanted a cup of tea.

Gus: He wanted a cup of tea! What about me? I've been wanting a cup of tea all night!

Ben (despairingly): What do we do now?

Gus: What are we supposed to drink?

Ben sits on his bed, staring.

What about us?

Ben sits.

I'm thirsty too. I'm starving. And he wants a cup of tea. That beats the band, that does.

Ben lets his head sink on to his chest.

I could do with a bit of sustenance myself. What about you? You look as if you could do with something too.

Gus sits on his bed.

We send him up all we've got and he's not satisfied. No, honest, it's enough to make the cat laugh. Why did you send him up all that stuff? (*Thoughtfully.*) Why did I send it up?

Pause.

Who knows what he's got upstairs? He's probably got a salad bowl. They must have something up there. They won't get much from down here. You notice they didn't ask for any salads? They've probably got a salad bowl up there. Cold meat, radishes, cucumbers. Watercress. Roll mops.

Pause.

Hardboiled eggs.

Pause.

The lot. They've probably got a crate of beer too. Probably eating my crisps with a pint of beer now. Didn't have anything to say about those crisps, did he? They do all right, don't worry about that. You don't think they're just going to sit there and wait for stuff to come up from down here, do you? That'll get them nowhere.

Pause.

They do all right.

Pause.

And he wants a cup of tea.

Pause.

That's past a joke, in my opinion.

He looks over at Ben, rises, and goes to him.

What's the matter with you? You don't look too bright. I feel like an Alka-Seltzer myself.

Ben sits up.

Ben (in a low voice): Time's getting on.
Gus: I know. I don't like doing a job on an empty stomach.
Ben (wearily): Be quiet a minute. Let me give you your instructions.
Gus: What for? We always do it the same way, don't we?
Ben: Let me give you your instructions.

Gus sighs and sits next to Ben on the bed. The instructions are stated and repeated automatically.

When we get the call, you go over and stand behind the door.
Gus: Stand behind the door.
Ben: If there's a knock on the door you don't answer it.
Gus: If there's a knock on the door I don't answer it.
Ben: But there won't be a knock on the door.
Gus: So I won't answer it.
Ben: When the bloke comes in —
Gus: When the bloke comes in —
Ben: Shut the door behind him.
Gus: Shut the door behind him.
Ben: Without divulging your presence.
Gus: Without divulging my presence.
Ben: He'll see me and come towards me.
Gus: He'll see you and come towards you.
Ben: He won't see you.
Gus (absently): Eh?
Ben: He won't see you.
Gus: He won't see me.
Ben: But he'll see me.
Gus: He'll see you.
Ben: He won't know you're there.
Gus: He won't know you're there.
Ben: He won't know *you're* there.
Gus: He won't know I'm there.
Ben: I take out my gun.
Gus: You take out your gun.
Ben: He stops in his tracks.
Gus: He stops in his tracks.
Ben: If he turns round —
Gus: If he turns round —

Ben: You're there.
Gus: I'm here.

Ben frowns and presses his forehead.

You've missed something out.
Ben: I know. What?
Gus: I haven't taken my gun out, according to you.
Ben: You take your gun out —
Gus: After I've closed the door.
Ben: After you've closed the door.
Gus: You've never missed that out before, you know that?
Ben: When he sees you behind him —
Gus: Me behind him —
Ben: And me in front of him —
Gus: And you in front of him —
Ben: He'll feel uncertain —
Gus: Uneasy.
Ben: He won't know what to do.
Gus: So what will he do?
Ben: He'll look at me and he'll look at you.
Gus: We won't say a word.
Ben: We'll look at him.
Gus: He won't say a word.
Ben: He'll look at us.
Gus: And we'll look at him.
Ben: Nobody says a word.

Pause.

Gus: What do we do if it's a girl?
Ben: We do the same.
Gus: Exactly the same?
Ben: Exactly.

Pause.

Gus: We don't do anything different?
Ben: We do exactly the same.
Gus: Oh.

Gus rises, and shivers.

Excuse me.

He exits through the door on the left. Ben remains sitting on the bed, still.
The lavatory chain is pulled once off left, but the lavatory does not flush.
Silence.
Gus re-enters and stops inside the door, deep in thought. He looks at Ben, then
walks slowly across to his own bed. He is troubled. He stands, thinking. He turns
and looks at Ben. He moves a few paces towards him.

(*Slowly in a low, tense voice.*) Why did he send us matches if he knew there
was no gas?

Silence.

Ben stares in front of him. Gus crosses to the left side of Ben, to the foot of his bed, to get to his other ear.

Ben. Why did he send us matches if he knew there was no gas?

Ben looks up.

Why did he do that?

Ben: Who?

Gus: Who sent us those matches?

Ben: What are you talking about?

Gus stares down at him.

Gus (thickly): Who is it upstairs?

Ben (nervously): What's one thing to do with another?

Gus: Who is it, though?

Ben: What's one thing to do with another?

Ben fumbles for his paper on the bed.

Gus: I asked you a question.

Ben: Enough!

Gus (with growing agitation): I asked you before. Who moved in? I asked you. You said the people who had it before moved out. Well, who moved in?

Ben (hunched): Shut up.

Gus: I told you, didn't I?

Ben (standing): Shut up!

Gus (feverishly): I told you before who owned this place, didn't I? I told you.

Ben hits him viciously on the shoulder.

I told you who ran this place, didn't I?

Ben hits him viciously on the shoulder.

(*Violently.*) Well, what's he playing all these games for? That's what I want to know. What's he doing it for?

Ben: What games?

Gus (passionately, advancing): What's he doing it for? We've been through our tests, haven't we? We got right through our tests, years ago, didn't we? We took them together, don't you remember, didn't we? We've proved ourselves before now, haven't we? We've always done our job. What's he doing all this for? What's the idea? What's he playing these games for?

The box in the shaft comes down behind them. The noise is this time accompanied by a shrill whistle, as it falls. Gus rushes to the hatch and seizes the note.

(*Reading.*) Scampi!

He crumples the note, picks up the tube, takes out the whistle, blows, and speaks.

WE'VE GOT NOTHING LEFT! NOTHING! DO YOU UNDERSTAND?

Ben seizes the tube and flings Gus away. He follows Gus and slaps him hard, back-handed, across the chest.

Ben: Stop it! You maniac!

Gus: But you heard!

Ben (savagely): That's enough! I'm warning you!

Silence.
Ben hangs the tube. He goes to his bed and lies down. He picks up his paper and reads.
Silence.
The box goes up.
They turn quickly, their eyes meet. Ben turns to his paper.
Slowly Gus goes back to his bed, and sits.
Silence.
The hatch falls back into place.
They turn quickly, their eyes meet. Ben turns back to his paper.
Silence.
Ben throws his paper down.

Ben: Kaw!

He picks up the paper and looks at it.

Listen to this!

Pause.

What about that, eh?

Pause.

Kaw!

Pause.

Have you ever heard such a thing?
Gus (dully): Go on!
Ben: It's true.
Gus: Get away.
Ben: It's down here in black and white.
Gus (very low): Is that a fact?
Ben: Can you imagine it.
Gus: It's unbelievable.
Ben: It's enough to make you want to puke, isn't it?
Gus (almost inaudible): Incredible.

Ben shakes his head. He puts the paper down and rises. He fixes the revolver in his holster.
Gus stands up. He goes towards the door on the left.

Ben: Where are you going?
Gus: I'm going to have a glass of water.

He exits. Ben brushes dust off his clothes and shoes. The whistle in the speaking-tube blows. He goes to it, takes the whistle out, and puts the tube to his ear. He listens. He puts it to his mouth.

Ben: Yes.

To ear. He listens. To mouth.

Straight away. Right.

To ear. He listens. To mouth.

Sure we're ready.

To ear. He listens. To mouth.

Understood. Repeat. He has arrived and will be coming in straight away. The normal method to be employed. Understood.

To ear. He listens. To mouth.

Sure we're ready.

To ear. He listens. To mouth.

Right.

He hangs the tube up.

Gus!

He takes out a comb and combs his hair, adjusts his jacket to diminish the bulge of the revolver. The lavatory flushes off left. Ben goes quickly to the door, left.

Gus!

The door right opens sharply. Ben turns, his revolver levelled at the door.
Gus stumbles in.
He is stripped of his jacket, waistcoat, tie, holster, and revolver.
He stops, body stooping, his arms at his sides.
He raises his head and looks at Ben.
A long silence.
They stare at each other.

Curtain

Considerations for Critical Thinking and Writing

1. At what point do you realize that Ben and Gus are not ordinary workers but hired killers? Why isn't the nature of the "job" made clear at the beginning of the play?
2. How are Ben and Gus different from the typical gangsters that appear in stories about professional killers?
3. Contrast Gus's personality and sensibilities with Ben's. Which character is smarter and more competent? Which do you find more sympathetic?
4. Why has the organization ordered Gus's execution? Are there any foreshadowings to suggest that he will be the next victim?
5. Do you think Ben will shoot Gus in the final scene? Why do you suppose Pinter doesn't dramatize the shooting?
6. Many silences and pauses punctuate the play's dialogue. How do they affect your response to the verbal exchanges between Ben and Gus? How do they help create the tone of the play?
7. Does the comedy seem appropriate to the overall tone of the play? What, for instance, is the purpose of their efforts to fill the orders for exotic foods that come from the dumb waiter?
8. Consider this statement by Pinter: "Communication itself between people is so frightening that rather than do that there is a continual cross-talk, a continual talking about other things rather than what is at the root of their relationship." How does dialogue in *The Dumb Waiter* dramatize Pinter's view of the way people communicate with one another?

9. What is the meaning of the play's title? Is there a pun on "dumb waiter"? Does the dumb waiter carry any symbolic meaning?

10. The surface of this play is realistic. The setting is a furnished basement room and the two lower-class criminals speak as we might expect two impatient hired killers to pass the time while awaiting orders. What is it, then, that makes this an absurdist play?

Connections to Other Selections

1. Compare the endings of *The Dumb Waiter* and *A Doll House* (p. 1517). What kinds of questions about what happens next does the ending of each play produce? What emotions does each ending create for you?

2. Write an essay comparing the humor in *The Dumb Waiter* and *Krapp's Last Tape* (p. 1627).

3. Compare Pinter's use of violence with the violence in one of the short stories by Flannery O'Connor in this anthology. To get started, read Claire Kahane's "The Function of Violence in O'Connor's Fiction" (p. 427). What important similarities and differences do you find in their treatment of violence?

RODEO

Jane Martin is a pseudonym. The author's identity is known only to a handful of administrators at the Actors Theatre of Louisville who handle permissions for productions and reprints of the play. *Rodeo* is one of eleven monologues in *Talking With.* . . . Martin has also published other plays including *Coup/Clucks* (1982), *What Mama Don't Know* (1988), and *Cementville* (1991).

Although only one character appears in *Rodeo,* the monologue is surprisingly moving as she describes what the rodeo once was, how it has changed, and what it means to her. At first glance the subject matter may not seem very promising for drama, but the character's energy, forthrightness, and colorful language transform seemingly trivial details into significant meanings.

JANE MARTIN
Rodeo   1981

A young woman in her late twenties sits working on a piece of tack. Beside her is a Lone Star beer in the can. As the lights come up we hear the last verse of a Tanya Tucker song or some other female country-western vocalist. She is wearing old worn jeans and boots plus a long-sleeved workshirt with the sleeves rolled up. She works until the song is over and then speaks.

Big Eight: Shoot — Rodeo's just goin' to hell in a handbasket. Rodeo used to be somethin'. I loved it. I did. Once Daddy an' a bunch of 'em was foolin' around with some old bronc over to our place and this ol' red nose named

Cinch got bucked off and my Daddy hooted and said he had him a nine-year-old girl, namely me, wouldn't have no damn trouble cowboyin' that horse. Well, he put me on up there, stuck that ridin' rein in my hand, gimme a kiss, and said, "Now there's only one thing t' remember Honey Love, if ya fall off you jest don't come home." Well I stayed up. You gotta stay on a bronc eight seconds. Otherwise the ride don't count. So from that day on my daddy called me Big Eight. Heck! That's all the name I got anymore . . . Big Eight.

Used to be fer cowboys, the rodeo did. Do it in some open field, folks would pull their cars and pick-ups round it, sit on the hoods, some ranch hand'd bulldog him some rank steer and everybody'd wave their hats and call him by name. Ride us some buckin' stock, rope a few calves, git throwed off a bull, and then we'd jest git us to a bar and tell each other lies about how good we were.

Used to be a family thing. Wooly Billy Tilson and Tammy Lee had them five kids on the circuit. Three boys, two girls and Wooly and Tammy. Wasn't no two-beer rodeo in Oklahoma didn't have a Tilson entered. Used to call the oldest girl Tits. Tits Tilson. Never seen a girl that top-heavy could ride so well. Said she only fell off when the gravity got her. Cowboys used to say if she landed face down you could plant two young trees in the holes she'd leave. Ha! Tits Tilson.

Used to be people came to a rodeo had a horse of their own back home. Farm people, ranch people — lord, they *knew* what they were lookin' at. Knew a good ride from a bad ride, knew hard from easy. You broke some bones er spent the day eatin' dirt, at least ya got appreciated.

Now they bought the rodeo. Them. Coca-Cola, Pepsi Cola, Marlboro damn cigarettes. You know the ones I mean. Them. Hire some New York faggot t' sit on some ol' stuffed horse in front of a sagebrush photo n' smoke that junk. Hell, tobacco wasn't made to smoke, honey, it was made to chew. Lord wanted ya filled up with smoke he would've set ya on fire. Damn it gets me!

There's some guy in a banker's suit runs the rodeo now. Got him a pinky ring and a digital watch, honey. Told us we oughta have a watchamacallit, choriographus or somethin', some ol' ballbuster used to be with the Ice damn Capades. Wants us to ride around dressed up like Mickey Mouse, Pluto, crap like that. Told me I had to haul my butt through the barrel race done up like Minnie damn Mouse in a tu-tu. Huh uh, honey! Them people is so screwed-up they probably eat what they run over in the road.

Listen, they got the clowns wearin' Astronaut suits! I ain't lyin'. You know what a rodeo clown does! You go down, fall off whatever — the clown runs in front of the bull so's ya don't git stomped. Pin-stripes, he got 'em in space suits tellin' jokes on a microphone. First horse see 'em, done up like the Star Wars went crazy. Best buckin' horse on the circuit, name of Piss 'N' Vinegar, took one look at them clowns, had him a heart attack and died. Cowboy was ridin' him got hisself squashed. Twelve hundred pounds of coronary arrest jes fell right through 'em. Blam! Vio con dios. Crowd thought that was funnier than the astronauts. I swear it won't be long before they're strappin' ice-skates on the ponies. Big crowds now. Ain't hardly no ranch people, no farm people, nobody I know. Buncha disco babies and dee-vorce lawyers — designer jeans and day-glo Stetsons. Hell, the whole bunch of 'em wears French perfume. Oh it smells like money now! Got it on the cable T and V — hey, you know what, when ya rodeo yer just bound to kick yerself up some dust — well now, seems like that fogs up the ol' TV camera, so they told us a while back that from now on we was gonna ride on some new stuff called Astro-dirt. Dust free. Artificial damn dirt, honey. Lord have mercy.

Banker Suit called me in the other day said "Lurlene . . ." "Hold it," I said, "Who's this Lurlene? Round here they call me Big Eight." "Well, Big Eight," he said, "My name's Wallace." "Well that's a real surprise t' me," I said, "Cause aroun' here everybody jes calls you Dumb-ass." My, he laughed real big, slapped his big ol' desk, an' then he said I wasn't suitable for the rodeo no more. Said they was lookin' fer another type, somethin' a little more in the showgirl line, like the Dallas Cowgirls maybe. Said the ridin' and ropin' wasn't the thing no more. Talked on about floats, costumes, dancin' chor-eog-aphy. If I was a man I woulda pissed on his shoe. Said he'd give me a lifetime pass though. Said I could come to his rodeo any time I wanted.

Rodeo used to be people ridin' horses for the pleasure of people who rode horses — made you feel good about what you could do. Rodeo wasn't worth no money to nobody. Money didn't have nothing to do with it! Used to be seven Tilsons riding in the rodeo. Wouldn't none of 'em dress up like Donald damn Duck so they quit. That there's the law of gravity!

There's a bunch of assholes in this country sneak around until they see ya havin' fun and then they buy the fun and start in sellin' it. See, they figure if ya love it, they can sell it. Well you look out, honey! They want to make them a dollar out of what you love. Dress *you* up like Minnie Mouse. Sell your rodeo. Turn *yer* pleasure into Ice damn Capades. You hear what I'm sayin'? You're jus' merchandise to them, sweetie. You're jus' merchandise to them.

Blackout.

Considerations for Critical Thinking and Writing

1. Big Eight is presented as an old-fashioned rodeo type. What associations or stereotypes do you have about such people? What assumptions do you make about them? How does the author use those expectations to heighten your understanding of Big Eight's character?
2. How has the rodeo changed from how it "used to be"? How do you account for those changes?
3. Comment on Big Eight's use of language. Why is it appropriate for her character?
4. How would you describe Big Eight's brand of humor? How does it affect your understanding of her?
5. How do your feelings about Big Eight develop during the course of the monologue?
6. What does the rodeo mean to Big Eight?

Connections to Other Selections

1. Compare and contrast a Shakespeare monologue from either *Hamlet* (p. 1281) or *A Midsummer Night's Dream* (p. 1224) with the style and content of *Rodeo*.

2. In an essay discuss the nostalgic tone in *Rodeo* and Stephen Crane's short story "The Bride Comes to Yellow Sky" (p. 203). In your response consider each work's treatment of the West.
3. Compare the attitudes expressed about merchandising in *Rodeo* with those expressed in Arthur Miller's *Death of a Salesman* (p. 1712).

33. A Collection of Plays

THE GLASS MENAGERIE

Thomas Lanier Williams, who kept his college nickname, Tennessee, was born in Columbus, Mississippi, the son of a traveling salesman. In 1918 the family moved to St. Louis, Missouri, where his father became the sales manager of a shoe company. Williams's mother, the daughter of an Episcopal clergyman, was withdrawn and genteel in contrast to his aggressive father, who contemptuously called him "Miss Nancy" as a way of mocking his weak physical condition and his literary pursuits. This family atmosphere of repression and anger makes its way into many of Williams's works through characterizations of domineering men and psychologically vulnerable women.

Williams began writing in high school and at the age of seventeen published his first short story in *Weird Tales*. His education at the University of Missouri was interrupted when he had to go to work in a shoe factory. This "living death," as he put it, led to a nervous breakdown, but he eventually resumed his studies at Washington University and finally graduated from the University of Iowa in 1938. During his college years, Williams wrote one-act plays; in 1940 his first full-length play, *Battle of Angels,* opened in Boston, but none of these early plays achieved commercial success. In 1945, however, *The Glass Menagerie* won large, enthusiastic audiences as well as the Drama Critics' Circle Award, which marked the beginning of a series of theatrical triumphs for Williams including *Streetcar Named Desire* (1947), *The Rose Tattoo* (1950), *Cat on a Hot Tin Roof* (1955), *Suddenly Last Summer* (1958), and *The Night of the Iguana* (1961).

The Glass Menagerie reflects Williams's fascination with characters who face lonely struggles in emotionally and financially starved environments. Although Williams's use of colloquial southern speech is realistic, the play also employs nonrealistic techniques, such as shifts in time, projections on screens, music, and lighting effects, to express his characters' thoughts and inner lives. (Williams describes these devices in his production notes to the play; see p. 1979.) As much as these techniques are unconventional, Wil-

1665

liams believed that they represented "a more penetrating and vivid expression of things as they are." The lasting popularity of *The Glass Menagerie* indicates that his assessment was correct.

TENNESSEE WILLIAMS (1911–1983)
The Glass Menagerie 1945

> *nobody,not even the rain,has such small hands*
> – e. e. cummings

List of Characters

Amanda Wingfield, the mother. A little woman of great but confused vitality clinging frantically to another time and place. Her characterization must be carefully created, not copied from type. She is not paranoiac, but her life is paranoia. There is much to admire in Amanda, and as much to love and pity as there is to laugh at. Certainly she has endurance and a kind of heroism, and though her foolishness makes her unwittingly cruel at times, there is tenderness in her slight person.

Laura Wingfield, her daughter. Amanda, having failed to establish contact with reality, continues to live vitally in her illusions, but Laura's situation is even graver. A childhood illness has left her crippled, one leg slightly shorter than the other, and held in a brace. This defect need not be more than suggested on the stage. Stemming from this, Laura's separation increases till she is like a piece of her own glass collection, too exquisitely fragile to move from the shelf.

Tom Wingfield, her son. And the narrator of the play. A poet with a job in a warehouse. His nature is not remorseless, but to escape from a trap he has to act without pity.

Jim O'Connor, the gentleman caller. A nice, ordinary, young man.

SCENE: *An alley in St. Louis.*
PART I: *Preparation for a Gentleman Caller.*
PART II: *The Gentleman Calls.*
TIME: *Now and the Past.*

SCENE I

The Wingfield apartment is in the rear of the building, one of those vast hivelike conglomerations of cellular living-units that flower as warty growths in overcrowded urban centers of lower middle-class population and are symptomatic of the impulse of this largest and fundamentally enslaved section of American society to avoid fluidity and differentiation and to exist and function as one interfused mass of automatism.

The apartment faces an alley and is entered by a fire-escape, a structure whose name is a touch of accidental poetic truth, for all of these huge buildings are always burning with the slow and implacable fires of human desperation. The fire-escape is included in the set — that is, the landing of it and steps descending from it.

The scene is memory and is therefore nonrealistic. Memory takes a lot of poetic license. It omits some details; others are exaggerated, according to the emotional value of the articles it touches, for memory is seated predominantly in the heart. The interior is therefore rather dim and poetic.

At the rise of the curtain, the audience is faced with the dark, grim rear wall of the Wingfield tenement. This building, which runs parallel to the footlights, is flanked on both sides by dark, narrow alleys which run into murky canyons of tangled clotheslines, garbage cans, and the sinister latticework of neighboring fire-escapes. It is up and down these side alleys that exterior entrances and exits are made, during the play. At the end of Tom's opening commentary, the dark tenement wall slowly reveals (by means of a transparency) the interior of the ground floor Wingfield apartment.

Downstage is the living room, which also serves as a sleeping room for Laura, the sofa unfolding to make her bed. Upstage, center, and divided by a wide arch or second proscenium with transparent faded portieres (or second curtain), is the dining room. In an old-fashioned what-not in the living room are seen scores of transparent glass animals. A blown-up photograph of the father hangs on the wall of the living room, facing the audience, to the left of the archway. It is the face of a very handsome young man in a doughboy's First World War cap. He is gallantly smiling, ineluctably smiling, as if to say, "I will be smiling forever."

The audience hears and sees the opening scene in the dining room through both the transparent fourth wall of the building and the transparent gauze portieres of the dining-room arch. It is during this revealing scene that the fourth wall slowly ascends, out of sight. This transparent exterior wall is not brought down again until the very end of the play, during Tom's final speech.

The narrator is an undisguised convention of the play. He takes whatever license with dramatic convention as is convenient to his purposes.

Tom enters dressed as a merchant sailor from alley, stage left, and strolls across the front of the stage to the fire-escape. There he stops and lights a cigarette. He addresses the audience.

Tom: Yes, I have tricks in my pocket, I have things up my sleeve. But I am the opposite of a stage magician. He gives you illusion that has the appearance of truth. I give you truth in the pleasant disguise of illusion. To begin with, I turn back time. I reverse it to that quaint period, the thirties, when the huge middle class of America was matriculating in a school for the blind. Their eyes had failed them, or they had failed their eyes, and so they were having their fingers pressed forcibly down on the fiery Braille alphabet of a dissolving economy. In Spain there was revolution. Here there was only shouting and confusion. In Spain there was Guernica.° Here there were disturbances of labor, sometimes pretty violent, in otherwise peaceful cities such as Chicago, Cleveland, Saint Louis. . . . This is the social background of the play.

(Music.)

The play is memory. Being a memory play, it is dimly lighted, it is sentimental,

Guernica: A town in northern Spain destroyed by German bombers in 1937 during the Spanish Civil War.

it is not realistic. In memory everything seems to happen to music. That explains the fiddle in the wings. I am the narrator of the play, and also a character in it. The other characters are my mother, Amanda, my sister, Laura, and a gentleman caller who appears in the final scenes. He is the most realistic character in the play, being an emissary from a world of reality that we were somehow set apart from. But since I have a poet's weakness for symbols, I am using this character also as a symbol; he is the long delayed but always expected something that we live for. There is a fifth character in the play who doesn't appear except in this larger-than-life photograph over the mantel. This is our father who left us a long time ago. He was a telephone man who fell in love with long distances; he gave up his job with the telephone company and skipped the light fantastic out of town. . . . The last we heard of him was a picture post-card from Mazatlán, on the Pacific coast of Mexico, containing a message of two words — "Hello — Good-bye!" and no address. I think the rest of the play will explain itself. . . .

Amanda's voice becomes audible through the portieres.

> (*Legend on screen: "Où sont les neiges."°*)
> *He divides the portieres and enters the upstage area.*
> *Amanda and Laura are seated at a drop-leaf table. Eating is indicated by gestures without food or utensils. Amanda faces the audience.*
> *Tom and Laura are seated in profile.*
> *The interior has lit up softly and through the scrim we see Amanda and Laura seated at the table in the upstage area.*

Amanda (calling): Tom?

Tom: Yes, Mother.

Amanda: We can't say grace until you come to the table!

Tom: Coming, Mother. (*He bows slightly and withdraws, reappearing a few moments later in his place at the table.*)

Amanda (to her son): Honey, don't *push* with your *fingers.* If you have to push with something, the thing to push with is a crust of bread. And chew — chew! Animals have sections in their stomachs which enable them to digest food without mastication, but human beings are supposed to chew their food before they swallow it down. Eat food leisurely, son, and really enjoy it. A well-cooked meal has lots of delicate flavors that have to be held in the mouth for appreciation. So chew your food and give your salivary glands a chance to function!

Tom deliberately lays his imaginary fork down and pushes his chair back from the table.

Tom: I haven't enjoyed one bite of this dinner because of your constant directions on how to eat it. It's you that makes me rush through meals with your hawklike attention to every bite I take. Sickening — spoils my appetite — all this discussion of animals' secretion — salivary glands — mastication!

Amanda (lightly): Temperament like a Metropolitan star! (*He rises and crosses downstage.*) You're not excused from the table.

Où sont les neiges: Part of a line from a poem by the French medieval writer François Villon; the full line translates, "But where are the snows of Yesteryear?"

Tom: I am getting a cigarette.

Amanda: You smoke too much.

Laura rises.

Laura: I'll bring in the blanc mange.

He remains standing with his cigarette by the portieres during the following.

Amanda (rising): No, sister, no, sister — you be the lady this time and I'll be the darky.

Laura: I'm already up.

Amanda: Resume your seat, little sister — I want you to stay fresh and pretty — for gentlemen callers!

Laura: I'm not expecting any gentlemen callers.

Amanda (crossing out to kitchenette. Airily): Sometimes they come when they are least expected! Why, I remember one Sunday afternoon in Blue Mountain — *(Enters kitchenette.)*

Tom: I know what's coming!

Laura: Yes. But let her tell it.

Tom: Again?

Laura: She loves to tell it.

Amanda returns with bowl of dessert.

Amanda: One Sunday afternoon in Blue Mountain — your mother received — *seventeen!* — gentlemen callers! Why, sometimes there weren't chairs enough to accommodate them all. We had to send the nigger over to bring in folding chairs from the parish house.

Tom (remaining at portieres): How did you entertain those gentlemen callers?

Amanda: I understood the art of conversation!

Tom: I bet you could talk.

Amanda: Girls in those days *knew* how to talk, I can tell you.

Tom: Yes?

(Image: Amanda as a girl on a porch greeting callers.)

Amanda: They knew how to entertain their gentlemen callers. It wasn't enough for a girl to be possessed of a pretty face and a graceful figure — although I wasn't slighted in either respect. She also needed to have a nimble wit and a tongue to meet all occasions.

Tom: What did you talk about?

Amanda: Things of importance going on in the world! Never anything coarse or common or vulgar. *(She addresses Tom as though he were seated in the vacant chair at the table though he remains by portieres. He plays this scene as though he held the book.)* My callers were gentlemen — all! Among my callers were some of the most prominent young planters of the Mississippi Delta — planters and sons of planters!

Tom motions for music and a spot of light on Amanda.
Her eyes lift, her face glows, her voice becomes rich and elegiac.
(Screen legend: "Où sont les neiges.")

There was young Champ Laughlin who later became vice-president of the Delta Planters Bank. Hadley Stevenson who was drowned in Moon Lake and left his widow one hundred and fifty thousand in Government bonds. There were the Cutrere brothers, Wesley and Bates. Bates was one of my bright particular beaux! He got in a quarrel with that wild Wainright boy. They shot it out on the floor of Moon Lake Casino. Bates was shot through the stomach. Died in the ambulance on his way to Memphis. His widow was also well-provided for, came into eight or ten thousand acres, that's all. She married him on the rebound — never loved her — carried my picture on him the night he died! And there was that boy that every girl in the Delta had set her cap for! That beautiful, brilliant young Fitzhugh boy from Green County!

Tom: What did he leave his widow?

Amanda: He never married! Gracious, you talk as though all of my old admirers had turned up their toes to the daisies!

Tom: Isn't this the first you mentioned that still survives?

Amanda: That Fitzhugh boy went North and made a fortune — came to be known as the Wolf of Wall Street! He had the Midas touch, whatever he touched turned to gold! And I could have been Mrs. Duncan J. Fitzhugh, mind you! But — I picked your *father!*

Laura (rising): Mother, let me clear the table.

Amanda: No dear, you go in front and study your typewriter chart. Or practice your shorthand a little. Stay fresh and pretty! — It's almost time for our gentlemen callers to start arriving. *(She flounces girlishly toward the kitchenette.)* How many do you suppose we're going to entertain this afternoon?

Tom throws down the paper and jumps up with a groan.

Laura (alone in the dining room): I don't believe we're going to receive any, Mother.

Amanda (reappearing, airily): What? No one — not one? You must be joking! *(Laura nervously echoes her laugh. She slips in a fugitive manner through the half-open portieres and draws them gently behind her. A shaft of very clear light is thrown on her face against the faded tapestry of the curtains.) (Music: "The Glass Menagerie" under faintly.) (Lightly.)* Not one gentleman caller? It can't be true! There must be a flood, there must have been a tornado!

Laura: It isn't a flood, it's not a tornado, Mother. I'm just not popular like you were in Blue Mountain. . . . *(Tom utters another groan. Laura glances at him with a faint, apologetic smile. Her voice catching a little.)* Mother's afraid I'm going to be an old maid.

(The scene dims out with "Glass Menagerie" music.)

SCENE II

"Laura, Haven't You Ever Liked Some Boy?"

On the dark stage the screen is lighted with the image of blue roses.
  Gradually Laura's figure becomes apparent and the screen goes out.
  The music subsides.
  Laura is seated in the delicate ivory chair at the small clawfoot table.

She wears a dress of soft violet material for a kimono — her hair tied back from her forehead with a ribbon.

She is washing and polishing her collection of glass.

Amanda appears on the fire-escape steps. At the sound of her ascent, Laura catches her breath, thrusts the bowl of ornaments away and seats herself stiffly before the diagram of the typewriter keyboard as though it held her spellbound. Something has happened to Amanda. It is written in her face as she climbs to the landing: a look that is grim and hopeless and a little absurd.

She has on one of those cheap or imitation velvety-looking cloth coats with imitation fur collar. Her hat is five or six years old, one of those dreadful cloche hats that were worn in the late twenties, and she is clasping an enormous black patent-leather pocketbook with nickel clasp and initials. This is her full-dress outfit, the one she usually wears to the D.A.R.°

Before entering she looks through the door.

She purses her lips, opens her eyes wide, rolls them upward, and shakes her head.

Then she slowly lets herself in the door. Seeing her mother's expression Laura touches her lips with a nervous gesture.

Laura: Hello, Mother, I was — *(She makes a nervous gesture toward the chart on the wall. Amanda leans against the shut door and stares at Laura with a martyred look.)*

Amanda: Deception? Deception? *(She slowly removes her hat and gloves, continuing the swift suffering stare. She lets the hat and gloves fall on the floor — a bit of acting.)*

Laura (shakily): How was the D.A.R. meeting? *(Amanda slowly opens her purse and removes a dainty white handkerchief, which she shakes out delicately and delicately touches to her lips and nostrils.)* Didn't you go to the D.A.R. meeting, Mother?

Amanda (faintly, almost inaudibly): — No. — No. *(Then more forcibly.)* I did not have the strength — to go to the D.A.R. In fact, I did not have the courage! I wanted to find a hole in the ground and hide myself in it forever! *(She crosses slowly to the wall and removes the diagram of the typewriter keyboard. She holds it in front of her for a second, staring at it sweetly and sorrowfully — then bites her lips and tears it in two pieces.)*

Laura (faintly): Why did you do that, Mother? *(Amanda repeats the same procedure with the chart of the Gregg Alphabet.°)* Why are you —

Amanda: Why? Why? How old are you, Laura?

Laura: Mother, you know my age.

Amanda: I thought that you were an adult; it seems that I was mistaken. *(She crosses slowly to the sofa and sinks down and stares at Laura.)*

Laura: Please don't stare at me, Mother.

Amanda closes her eyes and lowers her head. Count ten.

Amanda: What are we going to do, what is going to become of us, what is the future?

D.A.R.: Daughters of the American Revolution; members must document that they have ancestors who served the patriots' cause in the Revolutionary War.
Gregg Alphabet: System of shorthand symbols invented by John Robert Gregg.

Count ten.

Laura: Has something happened, Mother? *(Amanda draws a long breath and takes out the handkerchief again. Dabbing process.)* Mother, has — something happened?

Amanda: I'll be all right in a minute. I'm just bewildered — *(count five)* — by life. . . .

Laura: Mother, I wish that you would tell me what's happened.

Amanda: As you know, I was supposed to be inducted into my office at the D.A.R. this afternoon. *(Image: A swarm of typewriters.)* But I stopped off at Rubicam's Business College to speak to your teachers about your having a cold and ask them what progress they thought you were making down there.

Laura: Oh. . . .

Amanda: I went to the typing instructor and introduced myself as your mother. She didn't know who you were. Wingfield, she said. We don't have any such student enrolled at the school! I assured her she did, that you had been going to classes since early in January. "I wonder," she said, "if you could be talking about that terribly shy little girl who dropped out of school after only a few days' attendance?" "No," I said, "Laura, my daughter, has been going to school every day for the past six weeks!" "Excuse me," she said. She took the attendance book out and there was your name, unmistakably printed, and all the dates you were absent until they decided that you had dropped out of school. I still said, "No, there must have been some mistake! There must have been some mix-up in the records!" And she said, "No — I remember her perfectly now. Her hand shook so that she couldn't hit the right keys! The first time we gave a speed-test, she broke down completely — was sick at the stomach and almost had to be carried into the wash-room! After that morning she never showed up any more. We phoned the house but never got any answer" — while I was working at Famous and Barr, I suppose, demonstrating those — Oh! I felt so weak I could barely keep on my feet. I had to sit down while they got me a glass of water! Fifty dollars' tuition, all of our plans — my hopes and ambitions for you — just gone up the spout, just gone up the spout like that. *(Laura draws a long breath and gets awkwardly to her feet. She crosses to the Victrola, and winds it up.)* What are you doing?

Laura: Oh! *(She releases the handle and returns to her seat.)*

Amanda: Laura, where have you been going when you've gone out pretending that you were going to business college?

Laura: I've just been going out walking.

Amanda: That's not true.

Laura: It is. I just went walking.

Amanda: Walking? Walking? In winter? Deliberately courting pneumonia in that light coat? Where did you walk to, Laura?

Laura: It was the lesser of two evils, Mother. *(Image: Winter scene in park.)* I couldn't go back up. I — threw up — on the floor!

Amanda: From half past seven till after five every day you mean to tell me you walked around in the park, because you wanted to make me think that you were still going to Rubicam's Business College?

Laura: It wasn't as bad as it sounds. I went inside places to get warmed up.

Amanda: Inside where?

Laura: I went in the art museum and the bird-houses at the Zoo. I visited the penguins every day! Sometimes I did without lunch and went to the movies. Lately I've been spending most of my afternoons in the Jewel-box, that big glass house where they raise the tropical flowers.

Amanda: You did all this to deceive me, just for the deception? *(Laura looks down.)* Why?

Laura: Mother, when you're disappointed, you get that awful suffering look on your face, like the picture of Jesus' mother in the museum!

Amanda: Hush!

Laura: I couldn't face it.

Pause. A whisper of strings.
(Legend: "The Crust of Humility.")

Amanda (hopelessly fingering the huge pocketbook): So what are we going to do the rest of our lives? Stay home and watch the parades go by? Amuse ourselves with the glass menagerie, darling? Eternally play those worn-out phonograph records your father left as a painful reminder of him? We won't have a business career — we've given that up because it gave us nervous indigestion! *(Laughs wearily.)* What is there left but dependency all our lives? I know so well what becomes of unmarried women who aren't prepared to occupy a position. I've seen such pitiful cases in the South — barely tolerated spinsters living upon the grudging patronage of sister's husband or brother's wife! — stuck away in some little mousetrap of a room — encouraged by one in-law to visit another — little birdlike women without any nest — eating the crust of humility all their life! Is that the future that we've mapped out for ourselves? I swear it's the only alternative I can think of! It isn't a very pleasant alternative, is it? Of course — some girls *do marry.* *(Laura twists her hands nervously.)* Haven't you ever liked some boy?

Laura: Yes. I liked one once. *(Rises.)* I came across his picture a while ago.

Amanda (with some interest): He gave you his picture?

Laura: No, it's in the year-book.

Amanda (disappointed): Oh — a high-school boy.

(Screen image: Jim as a high-school hero bearing a silver cup.)

Laura: Yes. His name was Jim. *(Laura lifts the heavy annual from the clawfoot table.)* Here he is in *The Pirates of Penzance.*

Amanda (absently): The what?

Laura: The operetta the senior class put on. He had a wonderful voice and we sat across the aisle from each other Mondays, Wednesdays, and Fridays in the Aud. Here he is with the silver cup for debating! See his grin?

Amanda (absently): He must have had a jolly disposition.

Laura: He used to call me — Blue Roses.

(Image: Blue roses.)

Amanda: Why did he call you such a name as that?

Laura: When I had that attack of pleurosis — he asked me what was the matter when I came back. I said pleurosis — he thought that I said Blue Roses! So that's what he always called me after that. Whenever he saw me, he'd holler,

"Hello, Blue Roses!" I didn't care for the girl that he went out with. Emily Meisenbach. Emily was the best-dressed girl at Soldan. She never struck me, though, as being sincere. . . . It says in the Personal Section — they're engaged. That's — six years ago! They must be married by now.

Amanda: Girls that aren't cut out for business careers usually wind up married to some nice man. *(Gets up with a spark of revival.)* Sister, that's what you'll do!

Laura utters a startled, doubtful laugh. She reaches quickly for a piece of glass.

Laura: But, Mother —

Amanda: Yes? *(Crossing to photograph.)*

Laura (in a tone of frightened apology): I'm — crippled!

(Image: Screen.)

Amanda: Nonsense! Laura, I've told you never, never to use that word. Why, you're not crippled, you just have a little defect — hardly noticeable, even! When people have some slight disadvantage like that, they cultivate other things to make up for it — develop charm — and vivacity — and — *charm!* That's all you have to do! *(She turns again to the photograph.)* One thing your father had *plenty of* — was *charm!*

Tom motions to the fiddle in the wings.
(The scene fades out with music.)

SCENE III

(Legend on the screen: "After the Fiasco — ")
Tom speaks from the fire-escape landing.

Tom: After the fiasco at Rubicam's Business College, the idea of getting a gentleman caller for Laura began to play a more important part in Mother's calculations. It became an obsession. Like some archetype of the universal unconscious, the image of the gentleman caller haunted our small apartment. . . . *(Image: Young man at door with flowers.)* An evening at home rarely passed without some allusion to this image, this specter, this hope. . . . Even when he wasn't mentioned, his presence hung in Mother's preoccupied look and in my sister's frightened, apologetic manner — hung like a sentence passed upon the Wingfields! Mother was a woman of action as well as words. She began to take logical steps in the planned direction. Late that winter and in the early spring — realizing that extra money would be needed to properly feather the nest and plume the bird — she conducted a vigorous campaign on the telephone, roping in subscribers to one of those magazines for matrons called *The Home-maker's Companion,* the type of journal that features the serialized sublimations of ladies of letters who think in terms of delicate cuplike breasts, slim, tapering waists, rich, creamy thighs, eyes like wood-smoke in autumn, fingers that soothe and caress like strains of music, bodies as powerful as Etruscan sculpture.

(Screen image: Glamour magazine cover.)
Amanda enters with phone on long extension cord. She is spotted in the dim stage.

Amanda: Ida Scott? This is Amanda Wingfield! We *missed* you at the D.A.R. last Monday! I said to myself: She's probably suffering with that sinus condition! How is that sinus condition? Horrors! Heaven have mercy! — You're a Christian martyr, yes, that's what you are, a Christian martyr! Well, I just now happened to notice that your subscription to the *Companion*'s about to expire! Yes, it expires with the next issue, honey! — just when that wonderful new serial by Bessie Mae Hopper is getting off to such an exciting start. Oh, honey, it's something that you can't miss! You remember how *Gone with the Wind* took everybody by storm? You simply couldn't go out if you hadn't read it. All everybody *talked* was Scarlett O'Hara. Well, this is a book that critics already compare to *Gone with the Wind*. It's the *Gone with the Wind* of the post–World War generation! — What? — Burning? — Oh, honey, don't let them burn, go take a look in the oven and I'll hold the wire! Heavens — I think she's hung up!

(Dim out.)

(Legend on screen: "You think I'm in love with Continental Shoemakers?")

Before the stage is lighted, the violent voices of Tom and Amanda are heard. They are quarreling behind the portieres. In front of them stands Laura with clenched hands and panicky expression.

A clear pool of light on her figure throughout this scene.

Tom: What in Christ's name am I —
Amanda (shrilly): Don't you use that —
Tom: Supposed to do!
Amanda: Expression! Not in my —
Tom: Ohhh!
Amanda: Presence! Have you gone out of your senses?
Tom: I have, that's true, *driven* out!
Amanda: What is the matter with you, you — big — big — IDIOT!
Tom: Look — I've got *no thing,* no single thing —
Amanda: Lower your voice!
Tom: In my life here that I can call my own! Everything is —
Amanda: Stop that shouting!
Tom: Yesterday you confiscated my books! You had the nerve to —
Amanda: I took that horrible novel back to the library — yes! That hideous book by that insane Mr. Lawrence.° *(Tom laughs wildly.)* I cannot control the output of diseased minds or people who cater to them — *(Tom laughs still more wildly.)* BUT I WON'T ALLOW SUCH FILTH BROUGHT INTO MY HOUSE! No, no, no, no, no!
Tom: House, house! Who pays rent on it, who makes a slave of himself to —
Amanda (fairly screeching): Don't you DARE to —
Tom: No, no, *I* mustn't say things! *I've* got to just —
Amanda: Let me tell you —
Tom: I don't want to hear any more! *(He tears the portieres open. The upstage area is lit with a turgid smoky red glow.)*

Amanda's hair is in metal curlers and she wears a very old bathrobe, much too large for her slight figure, a relic of the faithless Mr. Wingfield.

Mr. Lawrence: D. H. Lawrence (1885–1930), English poet and novelist who advocated sexual freedom.

An upright typewriter and a wild disarray of manuscripts are on the drop-leaf table. The quarrel was probably precipitated by Amanda's interruption of his creative labor. A chair lying overthrown on the floor.

Their gesticulating shadows are cast on the ceiling by the fiery glow.

Amanda: You *will* hear more, you —

Tom: No, I won't hear more, I'm going out!

Amanda: You come right back in —

Tom: Out, out, out! Because I'm —

Amanda: Come back here, Tom Wingfield! I'm not through talking to you!

Tom: Oh, go —

Laura (desperately): Tom!

Amanda: You're going to listen, and no more insolence from you! I'm at the end of my patience! *(He comes back toward her.)*

Tom: What do you think I'm at? Aren't I supposed to have any patience to reach the end of, Mother? I know, I know. It seems unimportant to you, what I'm *doing* — what I *want* to do — having a little *difference* between them! You don't think that —

Amanda: I think you've been doing things that you're ashamed of. That's why you act like this. I don't believe that you go every night to the movies. Nobody goes to the movies night after night. Nobody in their right minds goes to the movies as often as you pretend to. People don't go to the movies at nearly midnight, and movies don't let out at two A.M. Come in stumbling. Muttering to yourself like a maniac! You get three hours' sleep and then go to work. Oh, I can picture the way you're doing down there. Moping, doping, because you're in no condition.

Tom (wildly): No, I'm in no condition!

Amanda: What right have you got to jeopardize your job? Jeopardize the security of us all? How do you think we'd manage if you were —

Tom: Listen! You think I'm crazy *about* the *warehouse!* *(He bends fiercely toward her slight figure.)* You think I'm in love with the Continental Shoemakers? You think I want to spend fifty-five *years* down there in that — *celotex interior!* with — *fluorescent* — *tubes!* Look! I'd rather somebody picked up a crowbar and battered out my brains — than go back mornings! I *go!* Every time you come in yelling that God damn *"Rise and Shine!" "Rise and Shine!"* I say to myself "How *lucky dead* people are!" But I get up. I *go!* For sixty-five dollars a month I give up all that I dream of doing and being *ever!* And you say self — *self's* all I ever think of. Why, listen, if self is what I thought of, Mother, I'd be where he is — ! *(Pointing to father's picture.)* As far as the system of transportation reaches! *(He starts past her. She grabs his arm.)* Don't grab at me, Mother!

Amanda: Where are you going?

Tom: I'm going to the *movies!*

Amanda: I don't believe that lie!

Tom (crouching toward her, overtowering her tiny figure. She backs away, gasping): I'm going to opium dens! Yes, opium dens, dens of vice and criminals' hang-outs, Mother. I've joined the Hogan gang, I'm a hired assassin, I carry a tommy-gun in a violin case! I run a string of cat-houses in the Valley!

They call me Killer, Killer Wingfield, I'm leading a double-life, a simple, honest warehouse worker by day, by night a dynamic *czar* of the *underworld, Mother.* I go to gambling casinos, I spin away fortunes on the roulette table! I wear a patch over one eye and a false mustache, sometimes I put on green whiskers. On those occasions they call me — *El Diablo!°* Oh, I could tell you things to make you sleepless! My enemies plan to dynamite this place. They're going to blow us all sky-high some night! I'll be glad, very happy, and so will you! You'll go up, up on a broomstick, over Blue Mountain with seventeen gentlemen callers! You ugly — babbling old — *witch.* . . . *(He goes through a series of violent, clumsy movements, seizing his overcoat, lunging to the door, pulling it fiercely open. The women watch him, aghast. His arm catches in the sleeve of the coat as he struggles to pull it on. For a moment he is pinioned by the bulky garment. With an outraged groan he tears the coat off again, splitting the shoulders of it, and hurls it across the room. It strikes against the shelf of Laura's glass collection, there is a tinkle of shattering glass. Laura cries out as if wounded.)*

(Music legend: "The Glass Menagerie.")

Laura *(shrilly):* My glass! — menagerie. . . . *(She covers her face and turns away.)*

But Amanda is still stunned and stupefied by the "ugly witch" so that she barely notices this occurrence. Now she recovers her speech.

Amanda *(in an awful voice):* I won't speak to you — until you apologize! *(She crosses through portieres and draws them together behind her. Tom is left with Laura. Laura clings weakly to the mantel with her face averted. Tom stares at her stupidly for a moment. Then he crosses to shelf. Drops awkwardly to his knees to collect the fallen glass, glancing at Laura as if he would speak but couldn't.)*

"The Glass Menagerie" steals in as
(The scene dims out.)

SCENE IV

The interior is dark. Faint light in the alley.
*   A deep-voiced bell in a church is tolling the hour of five as the scene commences.*
*   Tom appears at the top of the alley. After each solemn boom of the bell in the tower, he shakes a little noise-maker or rattle as if to express the tiny spasm of man in contrast to the sustained power and dignity of the Almighty. This and the unsteadiness of his advance make it evident that he has been drinking.*
*   As he climbs the few steps to the fire-escape landing light steals up inside. Laura appears in night-dress, observing Tom's empty bed in the front room.*
*   Tom fishes in his pockets for the door-key, removing a motley assortment of*

El Diablo: The devil (Spanish).

articles in the search, including a perfect shower of movie-ticket stubs and an empty bottle. At last he finds the key, but just as he is about to insert it, it slips from his fingers. He strikes a match and crouches below the door.

Tom (bitterly): One crack — and it falls through!

Laura opens the door.

Laura: Tom! Tom, what are you doing?
Tom: Looking for a door-key.
Laura: Where have you been all this time?
Tom: I have been to the movies.
Laura: All this time at the movies?
Tom: There was a very long program. There was a Garbo picture and a Mickey Mouse and a travelogue and a newsreel and a preview of coming attractions. And there was an organ solo and a collection for the milk-fund — simultaneously — which ended up in a terrible fight between a fat lady and an usher!
Laura (innocently): Did you have to stay through everything?
Tom: Of course! And, oh, I forgot! There was a big stage show! The headliner on this stage show was Malvolio the Magician. He performed wonderful tricks, many of them, such as pouring water back and forth between pitchers. First it turned to wine and then it turned to beer and then it turned to whiskey. I know it was whiskey it finally turned into because he needed somebody to come up out of the audience to help him, and I came up — both shows! It was Kentucky Straight Bourbon. A very generous fellow, he gave souvenirs. (He pulls from his back pocket a shimmering rainbow-colored scarf.) He gave me this. This is his magic scarf. You can have it, Laura. You wave it over a canary cage and you get a bowl of gold-fish. You wave it over the gold-fish bowl and they fly away canaries. . . . But the wonderfullest trick of all was the coffin trick. We nailed him into a coffin and he got out of the coffin without removing one nail. (He has come inside.) There is a trick that would come in handy for me — get me out of this 2 by 4 situation! (Flops onto bed and starts removing shoes.)
Laura: Tom — Shhh!
Tom: What you shushing me for?
Laura: You'll wake up Mother.
Tom: Goody, goody! Pay 'er back for all those "Rise an' Shines." (Lies down, groaning.) You know it don't take much intelligence to get yourself into a nailed-up coffin, Laura. But who in hell ever got himself out of one without removing one nail?

As if in answer, the father's grinning photograph lights up.
(Scene dims out.)
Immediately following: The church bell is heard striking six. At the sixth stroke the alarm clock goes off in Amanda's room, and after a few moments we hear her calling: "Rise and Shine! Rise and Shine! Laura, go tell your brother to rise and shine!"

Tom (sitting up slowly): I'll rise — but I won't shine.

The light increases.

Amanda: Laura, tell your brother his coffee is ready.

Laura slips into front room.

Laura: Tom! it's nearly seven. Don't make Mother nervous. *(He stares at her stupidly. Beseechingly.)* Tom, speak to Mother this morning. Make up with her, apologize, speak to her!

Tom: She won't to me. It's her that started not speaking.

Laura: If you just say you're sorry she'll start speaking.

Tom: Her not speaking — is that such a tragedy?

Laura: Please — please!

Amanda (calling from kitchenette): Laura, are you going to do what I asked you to do, or do I have to get dressed and go out myself?

Laura: Going, going — soon as I get on my coat! *(She pulls on a shapeless felt hat with nervous, jerky movement, pleadingly glancing at Tom. Rushes awkwardly for coat. The coat is one of Amanda's, inaccurately made-over, the sleeves too short for Laura.)* Butter and what else?

Amanda (entering upstage): Just butter. Tell them to charge it.

Laura: Mother, they make such faces when I do that.

Amanda: Sticks and stones may break my bones, but the expression on Mr. Garfinkel's face won't harm us! Tell your brother his coffee is getting cold.

Laura (at door): Do what I asked you, will you, will you, Tom?

He looks sullenly away.

Amanda: Laura, go now or just don't go at all!

Laura (rushing out): Going — going! *(A second later she cries out. Tom springs up and crosses to the door. Amanda rushes anxiously in. Tom opens the door.)*

Tom: Laura?

Laura: I'm all right. I slipped, but I'm all right.

Amanda (peering anxiously after her): If anyone breaks a leg on those fire-escape steps, the landlord ought to be sued for every cent he possesses! *(She shuts door. Remembers she isn't speaking and returns to other room.)*

As Tom enters listlessly for his coffee, she turns her back to him and stands rigidly facing the window on the gloomy gray vault of the areaway. Its light on her face with its aged but childish features is cruelly sharp, satirical as a Daumier° print. (Music under: "Ave Maria.")

Tom glances sheepishly but sullenly at her averted figure and slumps at the table. The coffee is scalding hot; he sips it and gasps and spits it back in the cup. At his gasp, Amanda catches her breath and half turns. Then catches herself and turns back to window.

Tom blows on his coffee, glancing sidewise at his mother. She clears her throat. Tom clears his. He starts to rise. Sinks back down again, scratches his head, clears his throat again. Amanda coughs. Tom raises his cup in both hands to blow on it, his eyes staring over the rim of it at his mother for several moments. Then he slowly sets the cup down and awkwardly and hesitantly rises from the chair.

Daumier: Honoré Daumier (1808–1879), French caricaturist, lithographer, and painter who mercilessly satirized bourgeois society.

Tom (hoarsely): Mother. I — I apologize. Mother. *(Amanda draws a quick, shuddering breath. Her face works grotesquely. She breaks into childlike tears.)* I'm sorry for what I said, for everything that I said, I didn't mean it.

Amanda (sobbingly): My devotion has made me a witch and so I make myself hateful to my children!

Tom: No, you *don't.*

Amanda: I worry so much, don't sleep, it makes me nervous!

Tom (gently): I understand that.

Amanda: I've had to put up a solitary battle all these years. But you're my right-hand bower! Don't fall down, don't fail!

Tom (gently): I try, Mother.

Amanda (with great enthusiasm): Try and you will SUCCEED! *(The notion makes her breathless.)* Why, you — you're just *full* of natural endowments! Both of my children — they're *unusual* children! Don't you think I know it? I'm so — *proud!* Happy and — feel I've — so much to be thankful for but — Promise me one thing, son!

Tom: What, Mother?

Amanda: Promise, son, you'll — never be a drunkard!

Tom (turns to her grinning): I will never be a drunkard, Mother.

Amanda: That's what frightened me so, that you'd be drinking! Eat a bowl of Purina!

Tom: Just coffee, Mother.

Amanda: Shredded wheat biscuit?

Tom: No. No, Mother, just coffee.

Amanda: You can't put in a day's work on an empty stomach. You've got ten minutes — don't gulp! Drinking too-hot liquids makes cancer of the stomach. . . . Put cream in.

Tom: No, thank you.

Amanda: To cool it.

Tom: No! No, thank you, I want it black.

Amanda: I know, but it's not good for you. We have to do all that we can to build ourselves up. In these trying times we live in, all that we have to cling to is — each other. . . . That's why it's so important to — Tom, I — I sent out your sister so I could discuss something with you. If you hadn't spoken I would have spoken to you. *(Sits down.)*

Tom (gently): What is it, Mother, that you want to discuss?

Amanda: Laura!

Tom puts his cup down slowly.
(Legend on screen: "Laura.")
(Music: "The Glass Menagerie.")

Tom: — Oh. — Laura . . .

Amanda (touching his sleeve): You know how Laura is. So quiet but — still water runs deep! She notices things and I think she — broods about them. *(Tom looks up.)* A few days ago I came in and she was crying.

Tom: What about?

Amanda: You.

Tom: Me?

Amanda: She has an idea that you're not happy here.

Tom: What gave her that idea?

Amanda: What gives her any idea? However, you do act strangely. I — I'm not criticizing, understand *that!* I know your ambitions do not lie in the warehouse, that like everybody in the whole wide world — you've had to — make sacrifices, but — Tom — Tom — life's not easy, it calls for — Spartan endurance! There's so many things in my heart that I cannot describe to you! I've never told you but I — *loved* your father. . . .

Tom (gently): I know that, Mother.

Amanda: And you — when I see you taking after his ways! Staying out late — and — well, you *had* been drinking the night you were in that — terrifying condition! Laura says that you hate the apartment and that you go out nights to get away from it! Is that true, Tom?

Tom: No. You say there's so much in your heart that you can't describe to me. That's true of me, too. There's so much in my heart that I can't describe to *you!* So let's respect each other's —

Amanda: But, why — *why,* Tom — are you always so *restless?* Where do you go to, nights?

Tom: I — go to the movies.

Amanda: Why do you go to the movies so much, Tom?

Tom: I go to the movies because — I like adventure. Adventure is something I don't have much of at work, so I go to the movies.

Amanda: But, Tom, you go to the movies *entirely too much!*

Tom: I like a lot of adventure.

Amanda looks baffled, then hurt. As the familiar inquisition resumes he becomes hard and impatient again. Amanda slips back into her querulous attitude toward him.

(Image on screen: Sailing vessel with Jolly Roger.)

Amanda: Most young men find adventure in their careers.

Tom: Then most young men are not employed in a warehouse.

Amanda: The world is full of young men employed in warehouses and offices and factories.

Tom: Do all of them find adventure in their careers?

Amanda: They do or they do without it! Not everybody has a craze for adventure.

Tom: Man is by instinct a lover, a hunter, a fighter, and none of those instincts are given much play at the warehouse!

Amanda: Man is by instinct! Don't quote instinct to me! Instinct is something that people have got away from! It belongs to animals! Christian adults don't want it!

Tom: What do Christian adults want, then, Mother?

Amanda: Superior things! Things of the mind and the spirit! Only animals have to satisfy instincts! Surely your aims are somewhat higher than theirs! Than monkeys — pigs —

Tom: I reckon they're not.

Amanda: You're joking. However, that isn't what I wanted to discuss.

Tom (rising): I haven't much time.

Amanda (pushing his shoulders): Sit down.

Tom: You want me to punch in red° at the warehouse, Mother?

Amanda: You have five minutes. I want to talk about Laura.

(Legend: "Plans and provisions.")

Tom: All right! What about Laura?

Amanda: We have to be making plans and provisions for her. She's older than you, two years, and nothing has happened. She just drifts along doing nothing. It frightens me terribly how she just drifts along.

Tom: I guess she's the type that people call home girls.

Amanda: There's no such type, and if there is, it's a pity! That is unless the home is hers, with a husband!

Tom: What?

Amanda: Oh, I can see the handwriting on the wall as plain as I see the nose in front of my face! It's terrifying! More and more you remind me of your father! He was out all hours without explanation — Then *left! Goodbye!* And me with the bag to hold. I saw that letter you got from the Merchant Marine. I know what you're dreaming of. I'm not standing here blindfolded. Very well, then. Then *do* it! But not till there's somebody to take your place.

Tom: What do you mean?

Amanda: I mean that as soon as Laura has got somebody to take care of her, married, a home of her own, independent — why, then you'll be free to go wherever you please, on land, on sea, whichever way the wind blows! But until that time you've got to look out for your sister. I don't say me because I'm old and don't matter! I say for your sister because she's young and dependent. I put her in business college — a dismal failure! Frightened her so it made her sick to her stomach. I took her over to the Young People's League at the church. Another fiasco. She spoke to nobody, nobody spoke to her. Now all she does is fool with those pieces of glass and play those worn-out records. What kind of a life is that for a girl to lead!

Tom: What can I do about it?

Amanda: Overcome selfishness! Self, self, self is all that you ever think of! *(Tom springs up and crosses to get his coat. It is ugly and bulky. He pulls on a cap with earmuffs.)* Where is your muffler? Put your wool muffler on! *(He snatches it angrily from the closet and tosses it around his neck and pulls both ends tight.)* Tom! I haven't said what I had in mind to ask you.

Tom: I'm too late to —

Amanda (catching his arms — very importunately. Then shyly.) Down at the warehouse, aren't there some — nice young men?

Tom: No!

Amanda: There *must* be — *some.*

Tom: Mother —

Gesture.

Amanda: Find out one that's clean-living — doesn't drink and — ask him out for sister!

Tom: What?

Amanda: For *sister!* To *meet!* Get *acquainted!*

---

punch in red: Be late for work.

Tom (stamping to door): Oh, my go-osh!

Amanda: Will you? *(He opens door. Imploringly.)* Will you? *(He starts down.)* Will you? *Will* you, dear?

Tom (calling back): YES!

Amanda closes the door hesitantly and with a troubled but faintly hopeful expression.

(Screen image: Glamour *magazine cover.)*

Spot Amanda at phone.

Amanda: Ella Cartwright? This is Amanda Wingfield! How are you, honey? How is that kidney condition? *(Count five.)* Horrors! *(Count five.)* You're a Christian martyr, yes, honey, that's what you are, a Christian martyr! Well, I just happened to notice in my little red book that your subscription to the *Companion* has just run out! I knew that you wouldn't want to miss out on the wonderful serial starting in this new issue. It's by Bessie Mae Hopper, the first thing she's written since *Honeymoon for Three.* Wasn't that a strange and interesting story? Well, this one is even lovelier, I believe. It has a sophisticated society background. It's all about the horsey set on Long Island!

(Fade out.)

SCENE V

(Legend on screen: "Annunciation.") Fade with music.

It is early dusk of a spring evening. Supper has just been finished in the Wingfield apartment. Amanda and Laura in light colored dresses are removing dishes from the table, in the upstage area, which is shadowy, their movements formalized almost as a dance or ritual, their moving forms as pale and silent as moths.

Tom, in white shirt and trousers, rises from the table and crosses toward the fire-escape.

Amanda (as he passes her): Son, will you do me a favor?

Tom: What?

Amanda: Comb your hair! You look so pretty when your hair is combed! *(Tom slouches on sofa with evening paper. Enormous caption "Franco Triumphs."*⁹*)* There is only one respect in which I would like you to emulate your father.

Tom: What respect is that?

Amanda: The care he always took of his appearance. He never allowed himself to look untidy. *(He throws down the paper and crosses to fire-escape.)* Where are you going?

Tom: I'm going out to smoke.

Amanda: You smoke too much. A pack a day at fifteen cents a pack. How much would that amount to in a month? Thirty times fifteen is how much, Tom? Figure it out and you will be astounded at what you could save. Enough to

---

"Franco Triumphs": In January 1939 the Republican forces of Francisco Franco (1892–1975) defeated the Loyalists, ending the Spanish Civil War.

give you a night-school course in accounting at Washington U! Just think what a wonderful thing that would be for you, son!

Tom is unmoved by the thought.

Tom: I'd rather smoke. *(He steps out on landing, letting the screen door slam.)*
Amanda (sharply): I know! That's the tragedy of it. . . . *(Alone, she turns to look at her husband's picture.)*

(Dance music: "All the World Is Waiting for the Sunrise!")

Tom (to the audience): Across the alley from us was the Paradise Dance Hall. On evenings in spring the windows and doors were open and the music came outdoors. Sometimes the lights were turned out except for a large glass sphere that hung from the ceiling. It would turn slowly about and filter the dusk with delicate rainbow colors. Then the orchestra played a waltz or a tango, something that had a slow and sensuous rhythm. Couples would come outside, to the relative privacy of the alley. You could see them kissing behind ash-pits and telephone poles. This was the compensation for lives that passed like mine, without any change or adventure. Adventure and change were imminent in this year. They were waiting around the corner for all these kids. Suspended in the mist over the Berchtesgaden,° caught in the folds of Chamberlain's° umbrella — In Spain there was Guernica! But here there was only hot swing music and liquor, dance halls, bars, and movies, and sex that hung in the gloom like a chandelier and flooded the world with brief, deceptive rainbows. . . . All the world was waiting for bombardments!

Amanda turns from the picture and comes outside.

Amanda (sighing): A fire-escape landing's a poor excuse for a porch. *(She spreads a newspaper on a step and sits down, gracefully and demurely as if she were settling into a swing on a Mississippi veranda.)* What are you looking at?
Tom: The moon.
Amanda: Is there a moon this evening?
Tom: It's rising over Garfinkel's Delicatessen.
Amanda: So it is! A little silver slipper of a moon. Have you made a wish on it yet?
Tom: Um-hum.
Amanda: What did you wish for?
Tom: That's a secret.
Amanda: A secret, huh? Well, I won't tell mine either. I will be just as mysterious as you.
Tom: I bet I can guess what yours is.
Amanda: Is my head so transparent?
Tom: You're not a sphinx.
Amanda: No, I don't have secrets. I'll tell you what I wished for on the moon. Success and happiness for my precious children! I wish for that whenever there's a moon, and when there isn't a moon, I wish for it, too.

Berchtesgaden: A resort in the German Alps where Adolf Hitler had a heavily protected villa.
Chamberlain: Neville Chamberlain (1869–1940); British prime minister who sought to avoid war with Hitler through a policy of appeasement.

Tom: I thought perhaps you wished for a gentleman caller.

Amanda: Why do you say that?

Tom: Don't you remember asking me to fetch one?

Amanda: I remember suggesting that it would be nice for your sister if you brought home some nice young man from the warehouse. I think I've made that suggestion more than once.

Tom: Yes, you have made it repeatedly.

Amanda: Well?

Tom: We are going to have one.

Amanda: What?

Tom: A gentleman caller!

(The Annunciation is celebrated with music.)
Amanda rises.
(Image on screen: Caller with bouquet.)

Amanda: You mean you have asked some nice young man to come over?

Tom: Yep. I've asked him to dinner.

Amanda: You really did?

Tom: I did!

Amanda: You did, and did he — *accept?*

Tom: He did!

Amanda: Well, well — well, well! That's — lovely!

Tom: I thought that you would be pleased.

Amanda: It's definite, then?

Tom: Very definite.

Amanda: Soon?

Tom: Very soon.

Amanda: For heaven's sake, stop putting on and tell me some things, will you?

Tom: What things do you want me to tell you?

Amanda: Naturally I would like to know when he's *coming!*

Tom: He's coming tomorrow.

Amanda: Tomorrow?

Tom: Yep. Tomorrow.

Amanda: But, Tom!

Tom: Yes, Mother?

Amanda: Tomorrow gives me no time!

Tom: Time for what?

Amanda: Preparations! Why didn't you phone me at once, as soon as you asked him, the minute that he accepted? Then, don't you see, I could have been getting ready!

Tom: You don't have to make any fuss.

Amanda: Oh, Tom, Tom, Tom, of course I have to make a fuss! I want things nice, not sloppy! Not thrown together. I'll certainly have to do some fast thinking, won't I?

Tom: I don't see why you have to think at all.

Amanda: You just don't know. We can't have a gentleman caller in a pig-sty! All my wedding silver has to be polished, the monogrammed table linen ought to be laundered! The windows have to be washed and fresh curtains put up. And how about clothes? We have to *wear* something, don't we?

Tom: Mother, this boy is no one to make a fuss over!

Amanda: Do you realize he's the first young man we've introduced to your sister? It's terrible, dreadful, disgraceful that poor little sister has never received a single gentleman caller! Tom, come inside! *(She opens the screen door.)*

Tom: What for?

Amanda: I want to ask you some things.

Tom: If you're going to make such a fuss, I'll call it off, I'll tell him not to come.

Amanda: You certainly won't do anything of the kind. Nothing offends people worse than broken engagements. It simply means I'll have to work like a Turk! We won't be brilliant, but we'll pass inspection. Come on inside. *(Tom follows, groaning.)* Sit down.

Tom: Any particular place you would like me to sit?

Amanda: Thank heavens I've got that new sofa! I'm also making payments on a floor lamp I'll have sent out! And put the chintz covers on, they'll brighten things up! Of course I'd hoped to have these walls re-papered. . . . What is the young man's name?

Tom: His name is O'Connor.

Amanda: That, of course, means fish — tomorrow is Friday! I'll have that salmon loaf — with Durkee's dressing! What does he do? He works at the warehouse?

Tom: Of course! How else would I —

Amanda: Tom, he — doesn't drink?

Tom: Why do you ask me that?

Amanda: Your father *did!*

Tom: Don't get started on that!

Amanda: He *does* drink, then?

Tom: Not that I know of!

Amanda: Make sure, be certain! The last thing I want for my daughter's a boy who drinks!

Tom: Aren't you being a little premature? Mr. O'Connor has not yet appeared on the scene!

Amanda: But will tomorrow. To meet your sister, and what do I know about his character? Nothing! Old maids are better off than wives of drunkards!

Tom: Oh, my God!

Amanda: Be still!

Tom (leaning forward to whisper): Lots of fellows meet girls whom they don't marry!

Amanda: Oh, talk sensibly, Tom — and don't be sarcastic! *(She has gotten a hairbrush.)*

Tom: What are you doing?

Amanda: I'm brushing that cow-lick down! What is this young man's position at the warehouse?

Tom (submitting grimly to the brush and the interrogation): This young man's position is that of a shipping clerk, Mother.

Amanda: Sounds to me like a fairly responsible job, the sort of a job *you* would be in if you just had more *get-up*. What is his salary? Have you got any idea?

Tom: I would judge it to be approximately eighty-five dollars a month.

Amanda: Well — not princely, but —

Tom: Twenty more than I make.

Amanda: Yes, how well I know! But for a family man, eighty-five dollars a month is not much more than you can just get by on. . . .

Tom: Yes, but Mr. O'Connor is not a family man.

Amanda: He might be, mightn't he? Some time in the future?

Tom: I see. Plans and provisions.

Amanda: You are the only young man that I know of who ignores the fact that the future becomes the present, the present the past, and the past turns into everlasting regret if you don't plan for it!

Tom: I will think that over and see what I can make of it.

Amanda: Don't be supercilious with your mother! Tell me some more about this — what do you call him?

Tom: James D. O'Connor. The D. is for Delaney.

Amanda: Irish on *both* sides! *Gracious!* And doesn't drink?

Tom: Shall I call him up and ask him right this minute?

Amanda: The only way to find out about those things is to make discreet inquiries at the proper moment. When I was a girl in Blue Mountain and it was suspected that a young man drank, the girl whose attentions he had been receiving, if any girl *was,* would sometimes speak to the minister of his church, or rather her father would if her father was living, and sort of feel him out on the young man's character. That is the way such things are discreetly handled to keep a young woman from making a tragic mistake!

Tom: Then how did you happen to make a tragic mistake?

Amanda: That innocent look of your father's had everyone fooled! He *smiled* — the world was *enchanted!* No girl can do worse than put herself at the mercy of a handsome appearance! I hope that Mr. O'Connor is not too good-looking.

Tom: No, he's not too good-looking. He's covered with freckles and hasn't too much of a nose.

Amanda: He's not right-down homely, though?

Tom: Not right-down homely. Just medium homely, I'd say.

Amanda: Character's what to look for in a man.

Tom: That's what I've always said, Mother.

Amanda: You've never said anything of the kind and I suspect you would never give it a thought.

Tom: Don't be suspicious of me.

Amanda: At least I hope he's the type that's up and coming.

Tom: I think he really goes in for self-improvement.

Amanda: What reason have you to think so?

Tom: He goes to night school.

Amanda (beaming): Splendid! What does he do, I mean study?

Tom: Radio engineering and public speaking!

Amanda: Then he has visions of being advanced in the world! Any young man who studies public speaking is aiming to have an executive job some day! And radio engineering? A thing for the future! Both of these facts are very illuminating. Those are the sort of things that a mother should know concerning any young man who comes to call on her daughter. Seriously or — not.

Tom: One little warning. He doesn't know about Laura. I didn't let on that we had dark ulterior motives. I just said, why don't you come have dinner with us? He said okay and that was the whole conversation.

Amanda: I bet it was! You're eloquent as an oyster. However, he'll know about Laura when he gets here. When he sees how lovely and sweet and pretty she is, he'll thank his lucky stars he was asked to dinner.

Tom: Mother, you mustn't expect too much of Laura.

Amanda: What do you mean?

Tom: Laura seems all those things to you and me because she's ours and we love her. We don't even notice she's crippled any more.

Amanda: Don't say crippled! You know that I never allow that word to be used!

Tom: But face facts, Mother. She is and — that's not all —

Amanda: What do you mean "not all"?

Tom: Laura is very different from other girls.

Amanda: I think the difference is all to her advantage.

Tom: Not quite all — in the eyes of others — strangers — she's terribly shy and lives in a world of her own and those things make her seem a little peculiar to people outside the house.

Amanda: Don't say peculiar.

Tom: Face the facts. She is.

(The dance-hall music changes to a tango that has a minor and somewhat ominous tone.)

Amanda: In what way is she peculiar — may I ask?

Tom (gently): She lives in a world of her own — a world of — little glass ornaments, Mother. . . . *(Gets up. Amanda remains holding brush, looking at him, troubled.)* She plays old phonograph records and — that's about all — *(He glances at himself in the mirror and crosses to door.)*

Amanda (sharply): Where are you going?

Tom: I'm going to the movies. *(Out screen door.)*

Amanda: Not to the movies, every night to the movies! *(Follows quickly to screen door.)* I don't believe you always go to the movies! *(He is gone. Amanda looks worriedly after him for a moment. Then vitality and optimism return and she turns from the door. Crossing to portieres.)* Laura! Laura! *(Laura answers from kitchenette.)*

Laura: Yes, Mother.

Amanda: Let those dishes go and come in front! *(Laura appears with dish towel. Gaily.)* Laura, come here and make a wish on the moon!

Laura (entering): Moon — moon?

Amanda: A little silver slipper of a moon. Look over your left shoulder, Laura, and make a wish! *(Laura looks faintly puzzled as if called out of sleep. Amanda seizes her shoulders and turns her at angle by the door.)* Now! Now, darling, *wish!*

Laura: What shall I wish for, Mother?

Amanda (her voice trembling and her eyes suddenly filling with tears): Happiness! Good Fortune!

The violin rises and the stage dims out.

SCENE VI

(Image: High school hero.)

Tom: And so the following evening I brought Jim home to dinner. I had known Jim slightly in high school. In high school Jim was a hero. He had tremendous Irish good nature and vitality with the scrubbed and polished look of white chinaware. He seemed to move in a continual spotlight. He was a star in basketball, captain of the debating club, president of the senior class and the glee club and he sang the male lead in the annual light operas. He was always running or bounding, never just walking. He seemed always at the point of defeating the law of gravity. He was shooting with such velocity through his adolescence that you would logically expect him to arrive at nothing short of the White House by the time he was thirty. But Jim apparently ran into more interference after his graduation from Soldan. His speed had definitely slowed. Six years after he left high school he was holding a job that wasn't much better than mine.

(Image: Clerk.)

He was the only one at the warehouse with whom I was on friendly terms. I was valuable to him as someone who could remember his former glory, who had seen him win basketball games and the silver cup in debating. He knew of my secret practice of retiring to a cabinet of the washroom to work on poems when business was slack in the warehouse. He called me Shakespeare. And while the other boys in the warehouse regarded me with suspicious hostility, Jim took a humorous attitude toward me. Gradually his attitude affected the others, their hostility wore off, and they also began to smile at me as people smile at an oddly fashioned dog who trots across their paths at some distance.

I knew that Jim and Laura had known each other at Soldan, and I had heard Laura speak admiringly of his voice. I didn't know if Jim remembered her or not. In high school Laura had been as unobtrusive as Jim had been astonishing. If he did remember Laura, it was not as my sister, for when I asked him to dinner, he grinned and said, "You know, Shakespeare, I never thought of you as having folks!"

He was about to discover that I did. . . .

(Light up stage.)
(Legend on screen: "The Accent of a Coming Foot.")
Friday evening. It is about five o'clock of a late spring evening which comes "scattering poems in the sky."
A delicate lemony light is in the Wingfield apartment.
Amanda has worked like a Turk in preparation for the gentleman caller. The results are astonishing. The new floor lamp with its rose-silk shade is in place, a colored paper lantern conceals the broken light fixture in the ceiling, new billowing white curtains are at the windows, chintz covers are on chairs and sofa, a pair of new sofa pillows make their initial appearance.
Open boxes and tissue paper are scattered on the floor.
Laura stands in the middle with lifted arms while Amanda crouches before her, adjusting the hem of the new dress, devout and ritualistic. The dress is

*colored and designed by memory. The arrangement of Laura's hair is changed;
it is softer and more becoming. A fragile, unearthly prettiness has come out in
Laura: she is like a piece of translucent glass touched by light, given a momentary
radiance, not actual, not lasting.*

Amanda (impatiently): Why are you trembling?

Laura: Mother, you've made me so nervous!

Amanda: How have I made you nervous?

Laura: By all this fuss! You make it seem so important!

Amanda: I don't understand you, Laura. You couldn't be satisfied with just sitting
    home, and yet whenever I try to arrange something for you, you seem to
    resist it. *(She gets up.)* Now take a look at yourself. No, wait! Wait just a
    moment — I have an idea!

Laura: What is it now?

*Amanda produces two powder puffs which she wraps in handkerchiefs and stuffs
in Laura's bosom.*

Laura: Mother, what are you doing?

Amanda: They call them "Gay Deceivers"!

Laura: I won't wear them!

Amanda: You will!

Laura: Why should I?

Amanda: Because, to be painfully honest, your chest is flat.

Laura: You make it seem like we were setting a trap.

Amanda: All pretty girls are a trap, a pretty trap, and men expect them to be.
    (Legend: "A Pretty Trap.") Now look at yourself, young lady. This is the
    prettiest you will ever be! I've got to fix myself now! You're going to be
    surprised by your mother's appearance! *(She crosses through portieres, hum-
    ming gaily.)*

Laura moves slowly to the long mirror and stares solemnly at herself.

   *A wind blows the white curtains inward in a slow, graceful motion and with
a faint, sorrowful sighing.*

Amanda (off stage): It isn't dark enough yet. *(She turns slowly before the mirror
    with a troubled look).*

(Legend on screen: "This Is My Sister: Celebrate Her with Strings!" Music.)

Amanda (laughing, off): I'm going to show you something. I'm going to make
    a spectacular appearance!

Laura: What is it, Mother?

Amanda: Possess your soul in patience — you will see! Something I've resur-
    rected from that old trunk! Styles haven't changed so terribly much after all.
    . . . *(She parts the portieres.)* Now just look at your mother! *(She wears a
    girlish frock of yellowed voile with a blue silk sash. She carries a bunch of
    jonquils — the legend of her youth is nearly revived. Feverishly.)* This is the
    dress in which I led the cotillion. Won the cakewalk twice at Sunset Hill,
    wore one spring to the Governor's ball in Jackson! See how I sashayed
    around the ballroom, Laura? *(She raises her skirt and does a mincing step
    around the room.)* I wore it on Sundays for my gentlemen callers! I had it
    on the day I met your father — I had malaria fever all that spring. The change

of climate from East Tennessee to the Delta — weakened resistance — I had a little temperature all the time — not enough to be serious — just enough to make me restless and giddy! Invitations poured in — parties all over the Delta! — "Stay in bed," said Mother, "you have fever!" — but I just wouldn't. — I took quinine but kept on going, going! — Evenings, dances! — Afternoons, long, long rides! Picnics — lovely! — So lovely, that country in May. — All lacy with dogwood, literally flooded with jonquils! — That was the spring I had the craze for jonquils. Jonquils became an absolute obsession. Mother said, "Honey, there's no more room for jonquils." And still I kept bringing in more jonquils. Whenever, wherever I saw them, I'd say, "Stop! Stop! I see jonquils!" I made the young men help me gather the jonquils! It was a joke, Amanda and her jonquils! Finally there were no more vases to hold them, every available space was filled with jonquils. No vases to hold them? All right, I'll hold them myself! And then I — *(She stops in front of the picture.) (Music.)* met your father! Malaria fever and jonquils and then — this — boy. . . . *(She switches on the rose-colored lamp.)* I hope they get here before it starts to rain. *(She crosses upstage and places the jonquils in bowl on table.)* I gave your brother a little extra change so he and Mr. O'Connor could take the service car home.

Laura (with altered look): What did you say his name was?
Amanda: O'Connor.
Laura: What is his first name?
Amanda: I don't remember. Oh, yes, I do. It was — Jim!

Laura sways slightly and catches hold of a chair.
(Legend on screen: "Not Jim!")

Laura (faintly): Not — Jim!
Amanda: Yes, that was it, it was Jim! I've never known a Jim that wasn't nice!

(Music: Ominous.)

Laura: Are you sure his name is Jim O'Connor?
Amanda: Yes. Why?
Laura: Is he the one that Tom used to know in high school?
Amanda: He didn't say so. I think he just got to know him at the warehouse.
Laura: There was a Jim O'Connor we both knew in high school — *(Then, with effort.)* If that is the one that Tom is bringing to dinner — you'll have to excuse me, I won't come to the table.
Amanda: What sort of nonsense is this?
Laura: You asked me once if I'd ever liked a boy. Don't you remember I showed you this boy's picture?
Amanda: You mean the boy you showed me in the year book?
Laura: Yes, that boy.
Amanda: Laura, Laura, were you in love with that boy?
Laura: I don't know, Mother. All I know is I couldn't sit at the table if it was him!
Amanda: It won't be him! It isn't the least bit likely. But whether it is or not, you will come to the table. You will not be excused.
Laura: I'll have to be, Mother.
Amanda: I don't intend to humor your silliness, Laura. I've had too much from

you and your brother, both! So just sit down and compose yourself till they
come. Tom has forgotten his key so you'll have to let them in, when they
arrive.

Laura (panicky): Oh, Mother — *you* answer the door!

Amanda (lightly): I'll be in the kitchen — busy!

Laura: Oh, Mother, please answer the door, don't make me do it!

Amanda (crossing into kitchenette): I've got to fix the dressing for the salmon.
Fuss, fuss — silliness! — over a gentleman caller!

Door swings shut. Laura is left alone
   (Legend: "Terror!")
   *She utters a low moan and turns off the lamp — sits stiffly on the edge of the
sofa, knotting her fingers together.*
   (Legend on screen: "The Opening of a Door!")
   *Tom and Jim appear on the fire-escape steps and climb to landing. Hearing
their approach, Laura rises with a panicky gesture. She retreats to the portieres.
The doorbell. Laura catches her breath and touches her throat. Low drums.*

Amanda (calling): Laura, sweetheart! The door!

Laura stares at it without moving.

Jim: I think we just beat the rain.

Tom: Uh-huh. *(He rings again, nervously. Jim whistles and fishes for a cigarette.)*

Amanda (very, very gaily): Laura, that is your brother and Mr. O'Connor! Will
you let them in, darling?

Laura crosses toward kitchenette door.

Laura (breathlessly): Mother — you go to the door!

*Amanda steps out of kitchenette and stares furiously at Laura. She points impe-
riously at the door.*

Laura: Please, please!

Amanda (in a fierce whisper): What is the matter with you, you silly thing?

Laura (desperately): Please, you answer it, *please!*

Amanda: I told you I wasn't going to humor you, Laura. Why have you chosen
this moment to lose your mind?

Laura: Please, please, please, you go!

Amanda: You'll have to go to the door because I can't!

Laura (despairingly): I can't either!

Amanda: Why?

Laura: I'm *sick!*

Amanda: I'm sick, too — of your nonsense! Why can't you and your brother be
normal people? Fantastic whims and behavior! *(Tom gives a long ring.)*
Preposterous goings on! Can you give me one reason — *(Calls out lyrically.)*
— why should you be afraid to open a door? Now you answer it, Laura!

Laura: Oh, oh, oh . . . *(She returns through the portieres. Darts to the Victrola
and winds it frantically and turns it on.)*

Amanda: Laura Wingfield, you march right to that door!

Laura: Yes — yes, Mother!

A faraway, scratchy rendition of "Dardanella" softens the air and gives her strength to move through it. She slips to the door and draws it cautiously open. Tom enters with the caller, Jim O'Connor.

Tom: Laura, this is Jim. Jim, this is my sister, Laura.
Jim (stepping inside): I didn't know that Shakespeare had a sister!
Laura (retreating stiff and trembling from the door): How — how do you do?
Jim (heartily extending his hand): Okay!

Laura touches it hesitantly with hers.

Jim: Your hand's *cold,* Laura!
Laura: Yes, well — I've been playing the Victrola . . .
Jim: Must have been playing classical music on it! You ought to play a little hot swing music to warm you up!
Laura: Excuse me — I haven't finished playing the Victrola . . .

She turns awkwardly and hurries into the front room. She pauses a second by the Victrola. Then catches her breath and darts through the portieres like a frightened deer.

Jim (grinning): What was the matter?
Tom: Oh — with Laura? Laura is — terribly shy.
Jim: Shy, huh? It's unusual to meet a shy girl nowadays. I don't believe you ever mentioned you had a sister.
Tom: Well, now you know. I have one. Here is the *Post Dispatch.* You want a piece of it?
Jim: Uh-huh.
Tom: What piece? The comics?
Jim: Sports! *(Glances at it.)* Ole Dizzy Dean is on his bad behavior.
Tom (disinterest): Yeah? *(Lights cigarette and crosses back to fire-escape door.)*
Jim: Where are *you* going?
Tom: I'm going out on the terrace.
Jim (goes after him): You know, Shakespeare — I'm going to sell you a bill of goods!
Tom: What goods?
Jim: A course I'm taking.
Tom: Huh?
Jim: In public speaking! You and me, we're not the warehouse type.
Tom: Thanks — that's good news. But what has public speaking got to do with it?
Jim: It fits you for — executive positions!
Tom: Awww.
Jim: I tell you it's done a helluva lot for me.

(Image: Executive at desk.)

Tom: In what respect?
Jim: In every! Ask yourself what is the difference between you an' me and men in the office down front? Brains? — No! — Ability? — No! Then what? Just one little thing —
Tom: What is that one little thing?

Jim: Primarily it amounts to — social poise! Being able to square up to people and hold your own on any social level!

Amanda (off stage): Tom?

Tom: Yes, Mother?

Amanda: Is that you and Mr. O'Connor?

Tom: Yes, Mother.

Amanda: Well, you just make yourselves comfortable in there.

Tom: Yes, Mother.

Amanda: Ask Mr. O'Connor if he would like to wash his hands.

Jim: Aw — no — no — thank you — I took care of that at the warehouse. Tom —

Tom: Yes?

Jim: Mr. Mendoza was speaking to me about you.

Tom: Favorably?

Jim: What do you think?

Tom: Well —

Jim: You're going to be out of a job if you don't wake up.

Tom: I am waking up —

Jim: You show no signs.

Tom: The signs are interior.

(Image on screen: The sailing vessel with Jolly Roger again.)

Tom: I'm planning to change. (*He leans over the rail speaking with quiet exhilaration. The incandescent marquees and signs of the first-run movie houses light his face from across the alley. He looks like a voyager.*) I'm right at the point of committing myself to a future that doesn't include the warehouse and Mr. Mendoza or even a night-school course in public speaking.

Jim: What are you gassing about?

Tom: I'm tired of the movies.

Jim: Movies!

Tom: Yes, movies! Look at them — (*A wave toward the marvels of Grand Avenue.*) All of those glamorous people — having adventures — hogging it all, gobbling the whole thing up! You know what happens? People go to the *movies* instead of *moving!* Hollywood characters are supposed to have all the adventures for everybody in America, while everybody in America sits in a dark room and watches them have them! Yes, until there's a war. That's when adventure becomes available to the masses! *Everyone's* dish, not only Gable's! Then the people in the dark room come out of the dark room to have some adventures themselves — Goody, goody — It's our turn now, to go to the South Sea Island — to make a safari — to be exotic, far-off — But I'm not patient. I don't want to wait till then. I'm tired of the *movies* and I am *about* to *move!*

Jim (incredulously): Move?

Tom: Yes.

Jim: When?

Tom: Soon!

Jim: Where? Where?

(Theme three: Music seems to answer the question, while Tom thinks it over. He searches among his pockets.)

Tom: I'm starting to boil inside. I know I seem dreamy, but inside — well, I'm boiling! Whenever I pick up a shoe, I shudder a little thinking how short life is and what I am doing! — Whatever that means. I know it doesn't mean shoes — except as something to wear on a traveler's feet! *(Finds paper.)* Look —

Jim: What?

Tom: I'm a member.

Jim (reading): The Union of Merchant Seamen.

Tom: I paid my dues this month, instead of the light bill.

Jim: You will regret it when they turn the lights off.

Tom: I won't be here.

Jim: How about your mother?

Tom: I'm like my father. The bastard son of a bastard! See how he grins? And he's been absent going on sixteen years!

Jim: You're just talking, you drip. How does your mother feel about it?

Tom: Shhh — Here comes Mother! Mother is not acquainted with my plans!

Amanda (enters portieres): Where are you all?

Tom: On the terrace, Mother.

They start inside. She advances to them. Tom is distinctly shocked at her appearance. Even Jim blinks a little. He is making his first contact with girlish Southern vivacity and in spite of the night-school course in public speaking is somewhat thrown off the beam by the unexpected outlay of social charm.

Certain responses are attempted by Jim but are swept aside by Amanda's gay laughter and chatter. Tom is embarrassed but after the first shock Jim reacts very warmly. Grins and chuckles, is altogether won over.

(Image: Amanda as a girl.)

Amanda (coyly smiling, shaking her girlish ringlets): Well, well, well, so this is Mr. O'Connor. Introductions entirely unnecessary. I've heard so much about you from my boy. I finally said to him, Tom — good gracious! — why don't you bring this paragon to supper? I'd like to meet this nice young man at the warehouse! — Instead of just hearing him sing your praises so much! I don't know why my son is so stand-offish — that's not Southern behavior! Let's sit down and — I think we could stand a little more air in here! Tom, leave the door open. I felt a nice fresh breeze a moment ago. Where has it gone? Mmm, so warm already! And not quite summer, even. We're going to burn up when summer really gets started. However, we're having — we're having a very light supper. I think light things are better fo' this time of year. The same as light clothes are. Light clothes an' light food are what warm weather calls fo'. You know our blood gets so thick during th' winter — it takes a while fo' us to *adjust* ou'selves! — when the season changes. . . . It's come so quick this year. I wasn't prepared. All of a sudden — heavens! Already summer! — I ran to the trunk an' pulled out this light dress — Terribly old! Historical almost! But feels so good — so good an' co-ol, y'know. . . .

Tom: Mother —

Amanda: Yes, honey?

Tom: How about — supper?

Amanda: Honey, you go ask Sister if supper is ready! You know that Sister is in full charge of supper! Tell her you hungry boys are waiting for it. *(To Jim.)* Have you met Laura?

Jim: She —

Amanda: Let you in? Oh, good, you've met already! It's rare for a girl as sweet an' pretty as Laura to be domestic! But Laura is, thank heavens, not only pretty but also very domestic. I'm not at all. I never was a bit. I never could make a thing but angel-food cake. Well, in the South we had so many servants. Gone, gone, gone. All vestiges of gracious living! Gone completely! I wasn't prepared for what the future brought me. All of my gentlemen callers were sons of planters and so of course I assumed that I would be married to one and raise my family on a large piece of land with plenty of servants. But man proposes — and woman accepts the proposal! — To vary that old, old saying a little bit — I married no planter! I married a man who worked for the telephone company! — that gallantly smiling gentleman over there! *(Points to the picture.)* A telephone man who — fell in love with long distance! — Now he travels and I don't even know where! — But what am I going on for about my — tribulations! Tell me yours — I hope you don't have any! Tom?

Tom (returning): Yes, Mother?

Amanda: Is supper nearly ready?

Tom: It looks to me like supper is on the table.

Amanda: Let me look — *(She rises prettily and looks through portieres.)* Oh, lovely — But where is Sister?

Tom: Laura is not feeling well and she says that she thinks she'd better not come to the table.

Amanda: What? — Nonsense! — Laura? Oh, Laura!

Laura (off stage, faintly): Yes, Mother.

Amanda: You really must come to the table. We won't be seated until you come to the table! Come in, Mr. O'Connor. You sit over there and I'll — Laura? Laura Wingfield! You're keeping us waiting, honey! We can't say grace until you come to the table!

The back door is pushed weakly open and Laura comes in. She is obviously quite faint, her lips trembling, her eyes wide and staring. She moves unsteadily toward the table.

(Legend: "Terror!")

Outside a summer storm is coming abruptly. The white curtains billow inward at the windows and there is a sorrowful murmur and deep blue dusk.

Laura suddenly stumbles — She catches at a chair with a faint moan.

Tom: Laura!

Amanda: Laura! *(There is a clap of thunder.) (Legend: "Ah!") (Despairingly.)* Why, Laura, you *are* sick, darling! Tom, help your sister into the living room, dear! Sit in the living room, Laura — rest on the sofa. Well! *(To the gentleman caller.)* Standing over the hot stove made her ill! — I told her that it was just too warm this evening, but — *(Tom comes back in. Laura is on the sofa.)* Is Laura all right now?

Tom: Yes.

Amanda: What *is* that? Rain? A nice cool rain has come up! *(She gives the gentleman caller a frightened look.)* I think we may — have grace — now . . . *(Tom looks at her stupidly.)* Tom, honey — you say grace!

Tom: Oh . . . "For these and all thy mercies —" *(They bow their heads, Amanda stealing a nervous glance at Jim. In the living room Laura, stretched on the sofa, clenches her hand to her lips, to hold back a shuddering sob.)* God's Holy Name be praised —

(The scene dims out.)

SCENE VII

A Souvenir

Half an hour later. Dinner is just being finished in the upstage area, which is concealed by the drawn portieres.
    As the curtain rises Laura is still huddled upon the sofa, her feet drawn under her, her head resting on a pale blue pillow, her eyes wide and mysteriously watchful. The new floor lamp with its shade of rose-colored silk gives a soft, becoming light to her face, bringing out the fragile, unearthly prettiness which usually escapes attention. There is a steady murmur of rain, but it is slackening and stops soon after the scene begins; the air outside becomes pale and luminous as the moon breaks out.
    A moment after the curtain rises, the lights in both rooms flicker and go out.

Jim: Hey, there, Mr. Light Bulb!

Amanda laughs nervously.
(Legend: "Suspension of a Public Service.")

Amanda: Where was Moses when the lights went out? Ha-ha. Do you know the answer to that one, Mr. O'Connor?
Jim: No, Ma'am, what's the answer?
Amanda: In the dark! *(Jim laughs appreciatively.)* Everybody sit still. I'll light the candles. Isn't it lucky we have them on the table? Where's a match? Which of you gentlemen can provide a match?
Jim: Here.
Amanda: Thank you, sir.
Jim: Not at all, Ma'am!
Amanda: I guess the fuse has burnt out. Mr. O'Connor, can you tell a burnt-out fuse? I know I can't and Tom is a total loss when it comes to mechanics. *(Sound: Getting up: Voices recede a little to kitchenette.)* Oh, be careful you don't bump into something. We don't want our gentleman caller to break his neck. Now wouldn't that be a fine howdy-do?
Jim: Ha-ha! Where is the fuse-box?
Amanda: Right here next to the stove. Can you see anything?
Jim: Just a minute.
Amanda: Isn't electricity a mysterious thing? Wasn't it Benjamin Franklin who tied a key to a kite? We live in such a mysterious universe, don't we? Some people say that science clears up all the mysteries for us. In my opinion it only creates more! Have you found it yet?
Jim: No, Ma'am. All these fuses look okay to me.
Amanda: Tom!
Tom: Yes, Mother?

Amanda: That light bill I gave you several days ago. The one I told you we got the notices about?
Tom: Oh. — Yeah.

(Legend: "Ha!")

Amanda: You didn't neglect to pay it by any chance?
Tom: Why, I —
Amanda: Didn't! I might have known it!
Jim: Shakespeare probably wrote a poem on that light bill, Mrs. Wingfield.
Amanda: I might have known better than to trust him with it! There's such a high price for negligence in this world!
Jim: Maybe the poem will win a ten-dollar prize.
Amanda: We'll just have to spend the remainder of the evening in the nineteenth century, before Mr. Edison made the Mazda lamp!
Jim: Candlelight is my favorite kind of light.
Amanda: That shows you're romantic! But that's no excuse for Tom. Well, we got through dinner. Very considerate of them to let us get through dinner before they plunged us into everlasting darkness, wasn't it, Mr. O'Connor?
Jim: Ha-ha!
Amanda: Tom, as a penalty for your carelessness you can help me with the dishes.
Jim: Let me give you a hand.
Amanda: Indeed you will not!
Jim: I ought to be good for something.
Amanda: Good for something? *(Her tone is rhapsodic.) You?* Why, Mr. O'Connor, nobody, *nobody's* given me this much entertainment in years — as you have!
Jim: Aw, now, Mrs. Wingfield!
Amanda: I'm not exaggerating, not one bit! But Sister is all by her lonesome. You go keep her company in the parlor! I'll give you this lovely old candelabrum that used to be on the altar at the church of the Heavenly Rest. It was melted a little out of shape when the church burnt down. Lightning struck it one spring. Gypsy Jones was holding a revival at the time and he intimated that the church was destroyed because the Episcopalians gave card parties.
Jim: Ha-ha.
Amanda: And how about coaxing Sister to drink a little wine? I think it would be good for her! Can you carry both at once?
Jim: Sure. I'm Superman!
Amanda: Now, Thomas, get into this apron!

The door of kitchenette swings closed on Amanda's gay laughter; the flickering light approaches the portieres.

Laura sits up nervously as he enters. Her speech at first is low and breathless from the almost intolerable strain of being alone with a stranger.

(Legend: "I Don't Suppose You Remember Me at All!")

In her first speeches in this scene, before Jim's warmth overcomes her paralyzing shyness, Laura's voice is thin and breathless as though she has run up a steep flight of stairs.

Jim's attitude is gently humorous. In playing this scene it should be stressed that while the incident is apparently unimportant, it is to Laura the climax of her secret life.

Jim: Hello, there, Laura.
Laura (faintly): Hello. *(She clears her throat.)*
Jim: How are you feeling now? Better?
Laura: Yes. Yes, thank you.
Jim: This is for you. A little dandelion wine. *(He extends it toward her with extravagant gallantry.)*
Laura: Thank you.
Jim: Drink it — but don't get drunk! *(He laughs heartily. Laura takes the glass uncertainly; laughs shyly.)* Where shall I set the candles?
Laura: Oh — oh, anywhere . . .
Jim: How about here on the floor? Any objections?
Laura: No.
Jim: I'll spread a newspaper under to catch the drippings. I like to sit on the floor. Mind if I do?
Laura: Oh, no.
Jim: Give me a pillow?
Laura: What?
Jim: A pillow!
Laura: Oh . . . *(Hands him one quickly.)*
Jim: How about you? Don't you like to sit on the floor?
Laura: Oh — yes.
Jim: Why don't you, then?
Laura: I — will.
Jim: Take a pillow! *(Laura does. Sits on the other side of the candelabrum. Jim crosses his legs and smiles engagingly at her.)* I can't hardly see you sitting way over there.
Laura: I can — see you.
Jim: I know, but that's not fair, I'm in the limelight. *(Laura moves her pillow closer.)* Good! Now I can see you! Comfortable?
Laura: Yes.
Jim: So am I. Comfortable as a cow. Will you have some gum?
Laura: No, thank you.
Jim: I think that I will indulge, with your permission. *(Musingly unwraps it and holds it up.)* Think of the fortune made by the guy that invented the first piece of chewing gum. Amazing, huh? The Wrigley Building is one of the sights of Chicago. — I saw it summer before last when I went up to the Century of Progress. Did you take in the Century of Progress?
Laura: No, I didn't.
Jim: Well, it was quite a wonderful exposition. What impressed me most was the Hall of Science. Gives you an idea of what the future will be in America, even more wonderful than the present time is! *(Pause. Smiling at her.)* Your brother tells me you're shy. Is that right, Laura?
Laura: I — don't know.
Jim: I judge you to be an old-fashioned type of girl. Well, I think that's a pretty good type to be. Hope you don't think I'm being too personal — do you?
Laura (hastily, out of embarrassment): I believe I *will* take a piece of gum, if

you — don't mind. *(Clearing her throat.)* Mr. O'Connor, have you — kept up with your singing?

Jim: Singing? Me?

Laura: Yes. I remember what a beautiful voice you had.

Jim: When did you hear me sing?

(Voice offstage in the pause.)

Voice (offstage): O blow, ye winds, heigh-ho,
            A-roving I will go!
            I'm off to my love
            With a boxing glove —
            Ten thousand miles away!

Jim: You say you've heard me sing?

Laura: Oh, yes! Yes, very often . . . I — don't suppose you remember me — at all?

Jim (smiling doubtfully): You know I have an idea I've seen you before. I had that idea soon as you opened the door. It seemed almost like I was about to remember your name. But the name that I started to call you — wasn't a name! And so I stopped myself before I said it.

Laura: Wasn't it — Blue Roses?

Jim (springs up, grinning): Blue Roses! My gosh, yes — Blue Roses! That's what I had on my tongue when you opened the door! Isn't it funny what tricks your memory plays? I didn't connect you with the high school somehow or other. But that's where it was; it was high school. I didn't even know you were Shakespeare's sister! Gosh, I'm sorry.

Laura: I didn't expect you to. You — barely knew me!

Jim: But we did have a speaking acquaintance, huh?

Laura: Yes, we — spoke to each other.

Jim: When did you recognize me?

Laura: Oh, right away!

Jim: Soon as I came in the door?

Laura: When I heard your name I thought it was probably you. I knew that Tom used to know you a little in high school. So when you came in the door — Well, then I was — sure.

Jim: Why didn't you *say* something, then?

Laura (breathlessly): I didn't know what to say, I was — too surprised!

Jim: For goodness' sakes! You know, this sure is funny!

Laura: Yes! Yes, isn't it, though . . .

Jim: Didn't we have a class in something together?

Laura: Yes, we did.

Jim: What class was that?

Laura: It was — singing — Chorus!

Jim: Aw!

Laura: I sat across the aisle from you in the Aud.

Jim: Aw.

Laura: Mondays, Wednesdays, and Fridays.

Jim: Now I remember — you always came in late.

Laura: Yes, it was so hard for me, getting upstairs. I had that brace on my leg — it clumped so loud!

Jim: I never heard any clumping.

Laura (wincing in the recollection): To me it sounded like — thunder!

Jim: Well, well, well. I never even noticed.

Laura: And everybody was seated before I came in. I had to walk in front of all those people. My seat was in the back row. I had to go clumping all the way up the aisle with everyone watching!

Jim: You shouldn't have been self-conscious.

Laura: I know, but I was. It was always such a relief when the singing started.

Jim: Aw, yes, I've placed you now! I used to call you Blue Roses. How was it that I got started calling you that?

Laura: I was out of school a little while with pleurosis. When I came back you asked me what was the matter. I said I had pleurosis — you thought I said Blue Roses. That's what you always called me after that!

Jim: I hope you didn't mind.

Laura: Oh, no — I liked it. You see, I wasn't acquainted with many — people. . . .

Jim: As I remember you sort of stuck by yourself.

Laura: I — I — never had much luck at — making friends.

Jim: I don't see why you wouldn't.

Laura: Well, I — started out badly.

Jim: You mean being —

Laura: Yes, it sort of — stood between me —

Jim: You shouldn't have let it!

Laura: I know, but it did, and —

Jim: You were shy with people!

Laura: I tried not to be but never could —

Jim: Overcome it?

Laura: No, I — I never could!

Jim: I guess being shy is something you have to work out of kind of gradually.

Laura (sorrowfully): Yes — I guess it —

Jim: Takes time!

Laura: Yes —

Jim: People are not so dreadful when you know them. That's what you have to remember! And everybody has problems, not just you, but practically everybody has got some problems. You think of yourself as having the only problems, as being the only one who is disappointed. But just look around you and you will see lots of people as disappointed as you are. For instance, I hoped when I was going to high school that I would be further along at this time, six years later, than I am now — You remember that wonderful write-up I had in *The Torch?*

Laura: Yes! *(She rises and crosses to table.)*

Jim: It said I was bound to succeed in anything I went into! *(Laura returns with the annual.)* Holy Jeez! *The Torch!* (*He accepts it reverently. They smile across it with mutual wonder. Laura crouches beside him and they begin to turn through it. Laura's shyness is dissolving in his warmth.)*

Laura: Here you are in *Pirates of Penzance!*

Jim (wistfully): I sang the baritone lead in that operetta.

Laura (rapidly): So — *beautifully!*

Jim (protesting): Aw —

Laura: Yes, yes — beautifully — beautifully!

Jim: You heard me?

Laura: All three times!

Jim: No!

Laura: Yes!

Jim: All three performances?

Laura (looking down): Yes.

Jim: Why?

Laura: I — wanted to ask you to — autograph my program.

Jim: Why didn't you ask me to?

Laura: You were always surrounded by your own friends so much that I never had a chance to.

Jim: You should have just —

Laura: Well, I — thought you might think I was —

Jim: Thought I might think you was — what?

Laura: Oh —

Jim (with reflective relish): I was beleaguered by females in those days.

Laura: You were terribly popular!

Jim: Yeah —

Laura: You had such a — friendly way —

Jim: I was spoiled in high school.

Laura: Everybody — liked you!

Jim: Including you?

Laura: I — yes, I — I did, too — *(She gently closes the book in her lap.)*

Jim: Well, well, well! — Give me that program, Laura. *(She hands it to him. He signs it with a flourish.)* There you are — better late than never!

Laura: Oh, I — what a — surprise!

Jim: My signature isn't worth very much right now. But some day — maybe — it will increase in value! Being disappointed is one thing and being discouraged is something else. I am disappointed but I'm not discouraged. I'm twenty-three years old. How old are you?

Laura: I'll be twenty-four in June.

Jim: That's not old age.

Laura: No, but —

Jim: You finished high school?

Laura (with difficulty): I didn't go back.

Jim: You mean you dropped out?

Laura: I made bad grades in my final examinations. *(She rises and replaces the book and the program. Her voice strained.)* How is — Emily Meisenbach getting along?

Jim: Oh, that kraut-head!

Laura: Why do you call her that?

Jim: That's what she was.

Laura: You're not still — going with her?

Jim: I never see her.

Laura: It said in the Personal Section that you were — engaged!

Jim: I know, but I wasn't impressed by that — propaganda!

Laura: It wasn't — the truth?

Jim: Only in Emily's optimistic opinion!
Laura: Oh —

(Legend: "What Have You Done since High School?")
   Jim lights a cigarette and leans indolently back on his elbows smiling at Laura with a warmth and charm which light her inwardly with altar candles. She remains by the table and turns in her hands a piece of glass to cover her tumult.

Jim (after several reflective puffs on a cigarette): What have you done since high school? *(She seems not to hear him.)* Huh? *(Laura looks up.)* I said what have you done since high school, Laura?
Laura: Nothing much.
Jim: You must have been doing something these six long years.
Laura: Yes.
Jim: Well, then, such as what?
Laura: I took a business course at business college —
Jim: How did that work out?
Laura: Well, not very — well — I had to drop out, it gave me — indigestion —

Jim laughs gently.

Jim: What are you doing now?
Laura: I don't do anything — much. Oh, please don't think I sit around doing nothing! My glass collection takes up a good deal of my time. Glass is something you have to take good care of.
Jim: What did you say — about glass?
Laura: Collection I said — I have one — *(She clears her throat and turns away again, acutely shy.)*
Jim (abruptly): You know what I judge to be the trouble with you? Inferiority complex! Know what that is? That's what they call it when someone low-rates himself! I understand it because I had it, too. Although my case was not so aggravated as yours seems to be. I had it until I took up public speaking, developed my voice, and learned that I had an aptitude for science. Before that time I never thought of myself as being outstanding in any way whatsoever! Now I've never made a regular study of it, but I have a friend who says I can analyze people better than doctors that make a profession of it. I don't claim that to be necessarily true, but I can sure guess a person's psychology, Laura! *(Takes out his gum.)* Excuse me, Laura. I always take it out when the flavor is gone. I'll use this scrap of paper to wrap it in. I know how it is to get it stuck on a shoe. Yep — that's what I judge to be your principal trouble. A lack of confidence in yourself as a person. You don't have the proper amount of faith in yourself. I'm basing that fact on a number of your remarks and also on certain observations I've made. For instance that clumping you thought was so awful in high school. You say that you even dreaded to walk into class. You see what you did? You dropped out of school, you gave up an education because of a clump, which as far as I know was practically nonexistent! A little physical defect is what you have. Hardly noticeable even! Magnified thousands of times by imagination! You know what my strong advice to you is? Think of yourself as *superior* in some way!

Laura: In what way would I think?

Jim: Why, man alive, Laura! Just look about you a little. What do you see? A world full of common people! All of 'em born and all of 'em going to die! Which of them has one-tenth of your good points! Or mine! Or anyone else's, as far as that goes — Gosh! Everybody excels in some one thing. Some in many! *(Unconsciously glances at himself in the mirror.)* All you've got to do is discover in *what!* Take me, for instance. *(He adjusts his tie at the mirror.)* My interest happened to lie in electrodynamics. I'm taking a course in radio engineering at night school, Laura, on top of a fairly responsible job at the warehouse. I'm taking that course and studying public speaking.

Laura: Ohhhh.

Jim: Because I believe in the future of television! *(Turning back to her.)* I wish to be ready to go up right along with it. Therefore I'm planning to get in on the ground floor. In fact, I've already made the right connections and all that remains is for the industry itself to get under way! Full steam — *(His eyes are starry.)* Knowledge — Zzzzzp! *Money* — Zzzzzzp! — *Power!* That's the cycle democracy is built on! *(His attitude is convincingly dynamic. Laura stares at him, even her shyness eclipsed in her absolute wonder. He suddenly grins.)* I guess you think I think a lot of myself!

Laura: No — o-o-o, I —

Jim: Now how about you? Isn't there something you take more interest in than anything else?

Laura: Well, I do — as I said — have my — glass collection —

A peal of girlish laughter from the kitchen.

Jim: I'm not right sure I know what you're talking about. What kind of glass is it?

Laura: Little articles of it, they're ornaments mostly! Most of them are little animals made out of glass, the tiniest little animals in the world. Mother calls them a glass menagerie! Here's an example of one, if you'd like to see it! This one is one of the oldest. It's nearly thirteen. *(He stretches out his hand.)* *(Music: "The Glass Menagerie.")* Oh, be careful — if you breathe, it breaks!

Jim: I'd better not take it. I'm pretty clumsy with things.

Laura: Go on, I trust you with him! *(Places it in his palm.)* There now — you're holding him gently! Hold him over the light, he loves the light! You see how the light shines through him?

Jim: It sure does shine!

Laura: I shouldn't be partial, but he is my favorite one.

Jim: What kind of thing is this one supposed to be?

Laura: Haven't you noticed the single horn on his forehead?

Jim: A unicorn, huh?

Laura: Mmm-hmmm!

Jim: Unicorns, aren't they extinct in the modern world?

Laura: I know!

Jim: Poor little fellow, he must feel sort of lonesome.

Laura (smiling): Well, if he does he doesn't complain about it. He stays on a shelf with some horses that don't have horns and all of them seem to get along nicely together.

Jim: How do you know?

Laura (lightly): I haven't heard any arguments among them!

Jim (grinning): No arguments, huh? Well, that's a pretty good sign! Where shall I set him?

Laura: Put him on the table. They all like a change of scenery once in a while!

Jim (stretching): Well, well, well, well — Look how big my shadow is when I stretch!

Laura: Oh, oh, yes — it stretches across the ceiling!

Jim (crossing to door): I think it's stopped raining. *(Opens fire-escape door.)* Where does the music come from?

Laura: From the Paradise Dance Hall across the alley.

Jim: How about cutting the rug a little, Miss Wingfield?

Laura: Oh, I —

Jim: Or is your program filled up? Let me have a look at it. *(Grasps imaginary card.)* Why, every dance is taken! I'll have to scratch some out. *(Waltz music: "La Golondrina.")* Ahhh, a waltz! *(He executes some sweeping turns by himself then holds his arms toward Laura.)*

Laura (breathlessly): I — can't dance!

Jim: There you go, that inferiority stuff!

Laura: I've never danced in my life!

Jim: Come on, try!

Laura: Oh, but I'd step on you!

Jim: I'm not made out of glass.

Laura: How — how — how do we start?

Jim: Just leave it to me. You hold your arms out a little.

Laura: Like this?

Jim: A little bit higher. Right. Now don't tighten up, that's the main thing about it — relax.

Laura (laughing breathlessly): It's hard not to.

Jim: Okay.

Laura: I'm afraid you can't budge me.

Jim: What do you bet I can't? *(He swings her into motion.)*

Laura: Goodness, yes, you can!

Jim: Let yourself go, now, Laura, just let yourself go.

Laura: I'm —

Jim: Come on!

Laura: Trying.

Jim: Not so stiff — Easy does it!

Laura: I know but I'm —

Jim: Loosen th' backbone! There now, that's a lot better.

Laura: Am I?

Jim: Lots, lots better! *(He moves her about the room in a clumsy waltz.)*

Laura: Oh, my!

Jim: Ha-ha!

Laura: Goodness, yes you can!

Jim: Ha-ha-ha! *(They suddenly bump into the table. Jim stops.)* What did we hit on?

Laura: Table.

Jim: Did something fall off it? I think —

Laura: Yes.

Jim: I hope it wasn't the little glass horse with the horn!

Laura: Yes.

Jim: Aw, aw, aw. Is it broken?

Laura: Now it is just like all the other horses.

Jim: It's lost its —

Laura: Horn! It doesn't matter. Maybe it's a blessing in disguise.

Jim: You'll never forgive me. I bet that that was your favorite piece of glass.

Laura: I don't have favorites much. It's no tragedy, Freckles. Glass breaks so easily. No matter how careful you are. The traffic jars the shelves and things fall off them.

Jim: Still I'm awfully sorry that I was the cause.

Laura (smiling): I'll just imagine he had an operation. The horn was removed to make him feel less — freakish! *(They both laugh.)* Now he will feel more at home with the other horses, the ones that don't have horns . . .

Jim: Ha-ha, that's very funny! *(Suddenly serious.)* I'm glad to see that you have a sense of humor. You know — you're — well — very different! Surprisingly different from anyone else I know! *(His voice becomes soft and hesitant with a genuine feeling.)* Do you mind me telling you that? *(Laura is abashed beyond speech.)* You make me feel sort of — I don't know how to put it! I'm usually pretty good at expressing things, but — This is something that I don't know how to say! *(Laura touches her throat and clears it — turns the broken unicorn in her hands.) (Even softer.)* Has anyone ever told you that you were pretty?

Pause: Music.

(Laura looks up slowly, with wonder, and shakes her head.) Well, you are! In a very different way from anyone else. And all the nicer because of the difference, too. *(His voice becomes low and husky. Laura turns away, nearly faint with the novelty of her emotions.)* I wish that you were my sister. I'd teach you to have some confidence in yourself. The different people are not like other people, but being different is nothing to be ashamed of. Because other people are not such wonderful people. They're one hundred times one thousand. You're one times one! They walk all over the earth. You just stay here. They're common as — weeds, but — you — well, you're — *Blue Roses!*

(Image on screen: Blue Roses.)
(Music changes.)

Laura: But blue is wrong for — roses . . .

Jim: It's right for you — You're — pretty!

Laura: In what respect am I pretty?

Jim: In all respects — believe me! Your eyes — your hair — are pretty! Your hands are pretty! *(He catches hold of her hand.)* You think I'm making this up because I'm invited to dinner and have to be nice. Oh, I could do that! I could put on an act for you, Laura, and say lots of things without being very sincere. But this time I am. I'm talking to you sincerely. I happened to notice you had this inferiority complex that keeps you from feeling comfortable with people. Somebody needs to build your confidence up and make you proud instead of shy and turning away and — blushing — Somebody ought to — ought to — *kiss* you, Laura! *(His hand slips slowly up her arm to her shoulder.) (Music swells tumultuously.) (He suddenly turns her about and kisses her on the lips. When he releases her Laura sinks on the sofa with a bright, dazed look. Jim backs away and fishes in his pocket for a cigarette.) (Legend on screen: "Souvenir.")* Stumble-john! *(He lights the cigarette, avoiding her look. There is a peal of girlish laughter from Amanda in the kitchen. Laura slowly raises and opens her hand. It still contains the little broken glass animal. She looks at it with a tender, bewildered expression.)* Stumble-john! I shouldn't have done that — That was way off the beam. You don't smoke, do you? *(She looks up, smiling, not hearing the question. He sits beside her a little gingerly. She looks at him speechlessly — waiting. He coughs decorously and moves a little farther aside as he considers the situation and senses her feelings, dimly, with perturbation. Gently.)* Would you — care for a — mint? *(She doesn't seem to hear him but her look grows brighter even.)* Peppermint — Life Saver? My pocket's a regular drug store — wherever I go . . . *(He pops a mint in his mouth. Then gulps and decides to make a clean breast of it. He speaks slowly and gingerly.)* Laura, you know, if I had a sister like you, I'd do the same thing as Tom. I'd bring out fellows — introduce her to them. The right type of boys of a type to — appreciate her. Only — well — he made a mistake about me. Maybe I've got no call to be saying this. That may not have been the idea in having me over. But what if it was? There's nothing wrong about that. The only trouble is that in my case — I'm not in a situation to — do the right thing. I can't take down your number and say I'll phone. I can't call up next week and — ask for a date. I thought I had better explain the situation in case you misunderstood it and — hurt your feelings. . . . *(Pause. Slowly, very slowly, Laura's look changes, her eyes returning slowly from his to the ornament in her palm.)*

Amanda utters another gay laugh in the kitchen.

Laura (faintly): You — won't — call again?

Jim: No, Laura, I can't. *(He rises from the sofa.)* As I was just explaining, I've — got strings on me, Laura, I've — been going steady! I go out all the time with a girl named Betty. She's a home-girl like you, and Catholic, and Irish, and in a great many ways we — get along fine. I met her last summer on a moonlight boat trip up the river to Alton, on the *Majestic.* Well — right away from the start it was — love! *(Legend: Love!) (Laura sways slightly forward and grips the arm of the sofa. He fails to notice, now enrapt in his own comfortable being.)* Being in love has made a new man of me! *(Leaning stiffly forward, clutching the arm of the sofa, Laura struggles visibly with her storm. But Jim is oblivious, she is a long way off.)* The power of love is really pretty tremendous! Love is something that — changes the whole world, Laura! *(The storm abates a little and Laura leans back. He notices her again.)* It happened that Betty's aunt took sick, she got a wire and had to go to Centralia. So Tom — when he asked me to dinner — I naturally just accepted the invitation, not knowing that you — that he — that I — *(He stops awkwardly.)* Huh — I'm a stumble-john! *(He flops back on the sofa. The holy candles in the altar of Laura's face have been snuffed out! There is a look of almost*

infinite desolation. Jim glances at her uneasily.) I wish that you would —
say something. *(She bites her lip which was trembling and then bravely smiles.
She opens her hand again on the broken glass ornament. Then she gently
takes his hand and raises it level with her own. She carefully places the
unicorn in the palm of his hand, then pushes his fingers closed upon it.)*
What are you — doing that for? You want me to have him? — Laura? *(She
nods.)* What for?

Laura: A — souvenir . . .

She rises unsteadily and crouches beside the Victrola to wind it up.
  (Legend on screen: "Things Have a Way of Turning Out So Badly.")
  (Or image: "Gentleman caller waving good-bye! — Gaily.")
  *At this moment Amanda rushes brightly back in the front room. She bears a
pitcher of fruit punch in an old-fashioned cut-glass pitcher and a plate of
macaroons. The plate has a gold border and poppies painted on it.*

Amanda: Well, well, well! Isn't the air delightful after the shower? I've made you
  children a little liquid refreshment. *(Turns gaily to the gentleman caller.)*
  Jim, do you know that song about lemonade?

  "Lemonade, lemonade
  Made in the shade and stirred with a spade —
  Good enough for any old maid!"

Jim (uneasily): Ha-ha! No — I never heard it.
Amanda: Why, Laura! You look so serious!
Jim: We were having a serious conversation.
Amanda: Good! Now you're better acquainted!
Jim (uncertainly): Ha-ha! Yes.
Amanda: You modern young people are much more serious-minded than my
  generation. I was so gay as a girl!
Jim: You haven't changed, Mrs. Wingfield.
Amanda: Tonight I'm rejuvenated! The gaiety of the occasion, Mr. O'Connor!
  (She tosses her head with a peal of laughter. Spills lemonade.) Oooo! I'm
  baptizing myself!
Jim: Here — let me —
Amanda (setting the pitcher down): There now. I discovered we had some
  maraschino cherries. I dumped them in, juice and all!
Jim: You shouldn't have gone to that trouble, Mrs. Wingfield.
Amanda: Trouble, trouble? Why it was loads of fun! Didn't you hear me cutting
  up in the kitchen? I bet your ears were burning! I told Tom how outdone
  with him I was for keeping you to himself so long a time! He should have
  brought you over much, much sooner! Well, now that you've found your
  way, I want you to be a very frequent caller! Not just occasional but all the
  time. Oh, we're going to have a lot of gay times together! I see them coming!
  Mmm, just breathe that air! So fresh, and the moon's so pretty! I'll skip back
  out — I know where my place is when young folks are having a — serious
  conversation!
Jim: Oh, don't go out, Mrs. Wingfield. The fact of the matter is I've got to be
  going.

Amanda: Going, now? You're joking! Why, it's only the shank of the evening, Mr. O'Connor!

Jim: Well, you know how it is.

Amanda: You mean you're a young workingman and have to keep workingmen's hours. We'll let you off early tonight. But only on the condition that next time you stay later. What's the best night for you? Isn't Saturday night the best night for you workingmen?

Jim: I have a couple of time-clocks to punch, Mrs. Wingfield. One at morning, another one at night!

Amanda: My, but you *are* ambitious! You work at night, too?

Jim: No, Ma'am, not work but — Betty! *(He crosses deliberately to pick up his hat. The band at the Paradise Dance Hall goes into a tender waltz.)*

Amanda: Betty? Betty? Who's — Betty! *(There is an ominous cracking sound in the sky.)*

Jim: Oh, just a girl. The girl I go steady with! *(He smiles charmingly. The sky falls.)*

(Legend: "The Sky Falls.")

Amanda (a long-drawn exhalation): Ohhhh . . . Is it a serious romance, Mr. O'Connor?

Jim: We're going to be married the second Sunday in June.

Amanda: Ohhhh — how nice! Tom didn't mention that you were engaged to be married.

Jim: The cat's not out of the bag at the warehouse yet. You know how they are. They call you Romeo and stuff like that. *(He stops at the oval mirror to put on his hat. He carefully shapes the brim and the crown to give a discreetly dashing effect.)* It's been a wonderful evening, Mrs. Wingfield. I guess this is what they mean by Southern hospitality.

Amanda: It really wasn't anything at all.

Jim: I hope it don't seem like I'm rushing off. But I promised Betty I'd pick her up at the Wabash depot, an' by the time I get my jalopy down there her train'll be in. Some women are pretty upset if you keep 'em waiting.

Amanda: Yes, I know — The tyranny of women! *(Extends her hand.)* Good-bye, Mr. O'Connor. I wish you luck — and happiness — and success! All three of them, and so does Laura — Don't you, Laura?

Laura: Yes!

Jim (taking her hand): Good-bye, Laura. I'm certainly going to treasure that souvenir. And don't you forget the good advice I gave you. *(Raises his voice to a cheery shout.)* So long, Shakespeare! Thanks again, ladies — Good night!

He grins and ducks jauntily out.

Still bravely grimacing, Amanda closes the door on the gentleman caller. Then she turns back to the room with a puzzled expression. She and Laura don't dare to face each other. Laura crouches beside the Victrola to wind it.

Amanda (faintly): Things have a way of turning out so badly. I don't believe that I would play the Victrola. Well, well — well — Our gentleman caller was engaged to be married! Tom!

Tom (from back): Yes, Mother?

Amanda: Come in here a minute. I want to tell you something awfully funny.

Tom (enters with macaroon and a glass of the lemonade): Has the gentleman caller gotten away already?

Amanda: The gentleman caller has made an early departure. What a wonderful joke you played on us!

Tom: How do you mean?

Amanda: You didn't mention that he was engaged to be married.

Tom: Jim? Engaged?

Amanda: That's what he just informed us.

Tom: I'll be jiggered! I didn't know about that.

Amanda: That seems very peculiar.

Tom: What's peculiar about it?

Amanda: Didn't you call him your best friend down at the warehouse?

Tom: He is, but how did I know?

Amanda: It seems extremely peculiar that you wouldn't know your best friend was going to be married!

Tom: The warehouse is where I work, not where I know things about people!

Amanda: You don't know things anywhere! You live in a dream; you manufacture illusions! *(He crosses to door.)* Where are you going?

Tom: I'm going to the movies.

Amanda: That's right, now that you've had us make such fools of ourselves. The effort, the preparations, all the expense! The new floor lamp, the rug, the clothes for Laura! All for what? To entertain some other girl's fiancé! Go to the movies, go! Don't think about us, a mother deserted, an unmarried sister who's crippled and has no job! Don't let anything interfere with your selfish pleasure! Just go, go, go — to the movies!

Tom: All right, I will! The more you shout about my selfishness to me the quicker I'll go, and I won't go to the movies!

Amanda: Go, then! Then go to the moon — you selfish dreamer!

Tom smashes his glass on the floor. He plunges out on the fire-escape, slamming the door. Laura screams — cut by door.

Dance-hall music up. Tom goes to the rail and grips it desperately, lifting his face in the chill white moonlight penetrating the narrow abyss of the alley.

(Legend on screen: "And So Good-Bye . . .")

Tom's closing speech is timed with the interior pantomime. The interior scene is played as though viewed through sound-proof glass. Amanda appears to be making a comforting speech to Laura who is huddled upon the sofa. Now that we cannot hear the mother's speech, her silliness is gone and she has dignity and tragic beauty. Laura's dark hair hides her face until at the end of the speech she lifts it to smile at her mother. Amanda's gestures are slow and graceful, almost dancelike, as she comforts the daughter. At the end of her speech she glances a moment at the father's picture — then withdraws through the portieres. At close of Tom's speech, Laura blows out the candles, ending the play.

Tom: I didn't go to the moon, I went much further — for time is the longest distance between two places — Not long after that I was fired for writing a poem on the lid of a shoe-box. I left Saint Louis. I descended the steps of this fire-escape for a last time and followed, from then on, in my father's footsteps, attempting to find in motion what was lost in space — I traveled around a great deal. The cities swept about me like dead leaves, leaves that were brightly colored but torn away from the branches. I would have stopped, but I was pursued by something. It always came upon me unawares, taking me altogether by surprise. Perhaps it was a familiar bit of music. Perhaps it was only a piece of transparent glass — Perhaps I am walking along a street at night, in some strange city, before I have found companions. I pass the lighted window of a shop where perfume is sold. The window is filled with pieces of colored glass, tiny transparent bottles in delicate colors, like bits of a shattered rainbow. Then all at once my sister touches my shoulder. I turn around and look into her eyes. . . . Oh, Laura, Laura, I tried to leave you behind me, but I am more faithful than I intended to be! I reach for a cigarette, I cross the street, I run into the movies or a bar, I buy a drink, I speak to the nearest stranger — anything that can blow your candles out! *(Laura bends over the candles)* — for nowadays the world is lit by lightning! Blow out your candles, Laura — and so good-bye . . .

She blows the candles out.
(The Scene Dissolves.)

Connections to Other Selections

1. Discuss the symbolic significance of the glass menagerie in Williams's play and the cherry orchard in Chekhov's play (p. 1569). How do the objects' symbolic values contribute to the theme of each play?
2. Compare and contrast the nonrealistic techniques that Williams uses with those used by Arthur Miller in *Death of a Salesman* (p. 1712).
3. Write an essay that explores Tom's narrative function in *The Glass Menagerie* with that of the Chorus in Sophocles' *Oedipus the King* (p. 1120) and *Antigone* (p. 1164).

DEATH OF A SALESMAN

Arthur Miller was born in New York City to middle-class Jewish parents. His mother was a teacher and his father a clothing manufacturer. In 1938 he graduated from the University of Michigan, where he had begun writing plays. Six years later his first Broadway play, *The Man Who Had All the Luck,* closed after only a few performances, but *All My Sons* (1947) earned the admiration of both critics and audiences. This drama of family life launched his career, and his next play was even more successful. *Death of a Salesman* (1949) won a Pulitzer Prize and established his international reputation so that Miller, along with Tennessee Williams, became one of the most successful American playwrights of the 1940s and 1950s. During this period, his plays included an adaptation of Henrik Ibsen's *Enemy of the People* (1951), *The Crucible* (1953), and *A View from the Bridge* (1955). Among his later works are *The Misfits* (1961, a screenplay), *After the Fall* (1964), *Incident at Vichy* (1964), *The Price* (1968), *The Creation of the World and Other Business* (1972), *The Archbishop's Ceiling* (1976), *The American Clock* (1980), *Time Bends* (1987, essays), and *The Ride Down Mt. Morgan* (1991).

In *Death of a Salesman* Miller's concerns and techniques are similar to those of social realism. His characters' dialogue sounds much like ordinary speech and deals with recognizable family problems ranging from feelings about one another to personal aspirations. Like Ibsen and Chekhov, Miller places his characters in a social context so that their behavior within the family suggests larger implications: the death of this salesman raises issues concerning the significance and value of the American dream of success.

Although such qualities resemble some of the techniques and concerns of realistic drama, Miller also uses other techniques to express Willy Loman's thoughts. In a sense, the play allows the audience to observe what goes on inside the protagonist's head. (At one point Miller was going to title the play *The Inside of His Head.*) When Willy thinks of the past, we see those events reenacted on stage in the midst of present events. This reenactment is achieved through the use of symbolic nonrealistic sets that appear or disappear as the stage lighting changes to reveal Willy's state of mind.

Willy Loman is in many ways an ordinary human being — indeed, painfully so. He is neither brilliant nor heroic, and his life is made up of unfulfilled dreams and self-deceptions. Yet Miller conceived of him as a tragic figure because, as he wrote in "Tragedy and the Common Man" (see p. 1981), "the common man is as apt a subject for tragedy . . . as kings." Willy's circumstances are radically different from those of Oedipus or Hamlet, but Miller manages to create a character whose human dignity evokes tragic feelings for many readers and viewers.

ARTHUR MILLER (b. 1915)
Death of a Salesman 1949

CERTAIN PRIVATE CONVERSATIONS IN TWO ACTS AND A REQUIEM
Cast

Willy Loman	Happy
Linda	Bernard
Biff	The Woman
Charley	Stanley
Uncle Ben	Miss Forsythe
Howard Wagner	Letta
Jenny	

SCENE: *The action takes place in Willy Loman's house and yard and in various places he visits in the New York and Boston of today.*

Throughout the play, in the stage directions, left and right mean stage left and stage right.

ACT I

A melody is heard, played upon a flute. It is small and fine, telling of grass and trees and the horizon. The curtain rises.

Before us is the Salesman's house. We are aware of towering, angular shapes behind it, surrounding it on all sides. Only the blue light of the sky falls upon the house and forestage; the surrounding area shows an angry glow of orange. As more light appears, we see a solid vault of apartment houses around the small, fragile-seeming home. An air of the dream clings to the place, a dream rising out of reality. The kitchen at center seems actual enough, for there is a kitchen table with three chairs, and a refrigerator. But no other fixtures are seen. At the back of the kitchen there is a draped entrance, which leads to the living-room. To the right of the kitchen, on a level raised two feet, is a bedroom furnished only with a brass bedstead and a straight chair. On a shelf over the bed a silver athletic trophy stands. A window opens onto the apartment house at the side.

Behind the kitchen, on a level raised six and a half feet, is the boys' bedroom, at present barely visible. Two beds are dimly seen, and at the back of the room a dormer window. (This bedroom is above the unseen living-room.) At the left a stairway curves up to it from the kitchen.

The entire setting is wholly or, in some places, partially transparent. The roof-line of the house is one-dimensional; under and over it we see the apartment buildings. Before the house lies an apron, curving beyond the forestage into the orchestra. This forward area serves as the back yard as well as the locale of all Willy's imaginings and of his city scenes. Whenever the action is in the present the actors observe the imaginary wall-lines, entering the house only through its door at the left. But in the scenes of the past these boundaries are broken, and characters enter or leave a room by stepping "through" a wall onto the forestage.

From the right, Willy Loman, the Salesman, enters, carrying two large sample cases. The flute plays on. He hears but is not aware of it. He is past sixty years of age, dressed quietly. Even as he crosses the stage to the doorway of the house, his exhaustion is apparent. He unlocks the door, comes into the kitchen, and thankfully lets his burden down, feeling the soreness of his palms. A word-sigh escapes his lips — it might be "Oh, boy, oh, boy." He closes the door, then carries his cases out into the living-room, through the draped kitchen doorway.

Linda, his wife, has stirred in her bed at the right. She gets out and puts on a robe, listening. Most often jovial, she has developed an iron repression of her exceptions to Willy's behavior — she more than loves him, she admires him, as though his mercurial nature, his temper, his massive dreams and little cruelties, served her only as sharp reminders of the turbulent longings within him, longings which she shares but lacks the temperament to utter and follow to their end.

Linda (hearing Willy outside the bedroom, calls with some trepidation): Willy!
Willy: It's all right. I came back.
Linda: Why? What happened? *(Slight pause.)* Did something happen, Willy?
Willy: No, nothing happened.
Linda: You didn't smash the car, did you?

Willy (with casual irritation): I said nothing happened. Didn't you hear me?

Linda: Don't you feel well?

Willy: I'm tired to the death. *(The flute has faded away. He sits on the bed beside her, a little numb.)* I couldn't make it. I just couldn't make it, Linda.

Linda (very carefully, delicately): Where were you all day? You look terrible.

Willy: I got as far as a little above Yonkers. I stopped for a cup of coffee. Maybe it was the coffee.

Linda: What?

Willy (after a pause): I suddenly couldn't drive any more. The car kept going off onto the shoulder, y'know?

Linda (helpfully): Oh. Maybe it was the steering again. I don't think Angelo knows the Studebaker.

Willy: No, it's me, it's me. Suddenly I realize I'm goin' sixty miles an hour and I don't remember the last five minutes. I'm — I can't seem to — keep my mind to it.

Linda: Maybe it's your glasses. You never went for your new glasses.

Willy: No, I see everything. I came back ten miles an hour. It took me nearly four hours from Yonkers.

Linda (resigned): Well, you'll just have to take a rest, Willy, you can't continue this way.

Willy: I just got back from Florida.

Linda: But you didn't rest your mind. Your mind is overactive, and the mind is what counts, dear.

Willy: I'll start out in the morning. Maybe I'll feel better in the morning. *(She is taking off his shoes.)* These goddam arch supports are killing me.

Linda: Take an aspirin. Should I get you an aspirin? It'll soothe you.

Willy (with wonder): I was driving along, you understand? And I was fine. I was even observing the scenery. You can imagine, me looking at scenery, on the road every week of my life. But it's so beautiful up there, Linda, the trees are so thick, and the sun is warm. I opened the windshield and just let the warm air bathe over me. And then all of a sudden I'm goin' off the road! I'm tellin' ya, I absolutely forgot I was driving. If I'd've gone the other way over the white line I might've killed somebody. So I went on again — and five minutes later I'm dreamin' again, and I nearly — *(He presses two fingers against his eyes.)* I have such thoughts, I have such strange thoughts.

Linda: Willy, dear. Talk to them again. There's no reason why you can't work in New York.

Willy: They don't need me in New York. I'm the New England man. I'm vital in New England.

Linda: But you're sixty years old. They can't expect you to keep traveling every week.

Willy: I'll have to send a wire to Portland. I'm supposed to see Brown and Morrison tomorrow morning at ten o'clock to show the line. Goddammit, I could sell them! *(He starts putting on his jacket.)*

Linda (taking the jacket from him): Why don't you go down to the place tomorrow and tell Howard you've simply got to work in New York? You're too accommodating, dear.

Willy: If old man Wagner was alive I'd a been in charge of New York now! That man was a prince, he was a masterful man. But that boy of his, that Howard, he don't appreciate. When I went north the first time, the Wagner Company didn't know where New England was!

Linda: Why don't you tell those things to Howard, dear?

Willy (encouraged): I will, I definitely will. Is there any cheese?

Linda: I'll make you a sandwich.

Willy: No, go to sleep. I'll take some milk. I'll be up right away. The boys in?

Linda: They're sleeping. Happy took Biff on a date tonight.

Willy (interested): That so?

Linda: It was so nice to see them shaving together, one behind the other, in the bathroom. And going out together. You notice? The whole house smells of shaving lotion.

Willy: Figure it out. Work a lifetime to pay off a house. You finally own it, and there's nobody to live in it.

Linda: Well, dear, life is a casting off. It's always that way.

Willy: No, no, some people — some people accomplish something. Did Biff say anything after I went this morning?

Linda: You shouldn't have criticized him, Willy, especially after he just got off the train. You mustn't lose your temper with him.

Willy: When the hell did I lose my temper? I simply asked him if he was making any money. Is that a criticism?

Linda: But, dear, how could he make any money?

Willy (worried and angered): There's such an undercurrent in him. He became a moody man. Did he apologize when I left this morning?

Linda: He was crestfallen, Willy. You know how he admires you. I think if he finds himself, then you'll both be happier and not fight any more.

Willy: How can he find himself on a farm? Is that a life? A farmhand? In the beginning, when he was young, I thought, well, a young man, it's good for him to tramp around, take a lot of different jobs. But it's more than ten years now and he has yet to make thirty-five dollars a week!

Linda: He's finding himself, Willy.

Willy: Not finding yourself at the age of thirty-four is a disgrace!

Linda: Shh!

Willy: The trouble is he's lazy, goddammit!

Linda: Willy, please!

Willy: Biff is a lazy bum!

Linda: They're sleeping. Get something to eat. Go on down.

Willy: Why did he come home? I would like to know what brought him home.

Linda: I don't know. I think he's still lost, Willy. I think he's very lost.

Willy: Biff Loman is lost. In the greatest country in the world a young man with such — personal attractiveness, gets lost. And such a hard worker. There's one thing about Biff — he's not lazy.

Linda: Never.

Willy (with pity and resolve): I'll see him in the morning; I'll have a nice talk with him. I'll get him a job selling. He could be big in no time. My God! Remember how they used to follow him around in high school? When he smiled at one of them their faces lit up. When he walked down the street . . . *(He loses himself in reminiscences.)*

Linda (trying to bring him out of it): Willy, dear, I got a new kind of American-type cheese today. It's whipped.

Willy: Why do you get American when I like Swiss?

Linda: I just thought you'd like a change —

Willy: I don't want a change! I want Swiss cheese. Why am I always being contradicted?

Linda (with a covering laugh): I thought it would be a surprise.

Willy: Why don't you open a window in here, for God's sake?

Linda (with infinite patience): They're all open, dear.

Willy: The way they boxed us in here. Bricks and windows, windows and bricks.

Linda: We should've bought the land next door.

Willy: The street is lined with cars. There's not a breath of fresh air in the neighborhood. The grass don't grow any more, you can't raise a carrot in the back yard. They should've had a law against apartment houses. Remember those two beautiful elm trees out there? When I and Biff hung the swing between them?

Linda: Yeah, like being a million miles from the city.

Willy: They should've arrested the builder for cutting those down. They massacred the neighborhood. *(Lost.)* More and more I think of those days, Linda. This time of year it was lilac and wisteria. And then the peonies would come out, and the daffodils. What fragrance in this room!

Linda: Well, after all, people had to move somewhere.

Willy: No, there's more people now.

Linda: I don't think there's more people. I think —

Willy: There's more people! That's what's ruining this country! Population is getting out of control. The competition is maddening! Smell the stink from that apartment house! And another one on the other side . . . . How can they whip cheese?

On Willy's last line, Biff and Happy raise themselves up in their beds, listening.

Linda: Go down, try it. And be quiet.

Willy (turning to Linda, guiltily): You're not worried about me, are you, sweetheart?

Biff: What's the matter?

Happy: Listen!

Linda: You've got too much on the ball to worry about.

Willy: You're my foundation and my support, Linda.

Linda: Just try to relax, dear. You make mountains out of molehills.

Willy: I won't fight with him any more. If he wants to go back to Texas, let him go.

Linda: He'll find his way.

Willy: Sure. Certain men just don't get started till later in life. Like Thomas Edison, I think. Or B. F. Goodrich. One of them was deaf. *(He starts for the bedroom doorway.)* I'll put my money on Biff.

Linda: And Willy — if it's warm Sunday we'll drive in the country. And we'll open the windshield, and take lunch.

Willy: No, the windshields don't open on the new cars.

Linda: But you opened it today.

Willy: Me? I didn't. *(He stops.)* Now isn't that peculiar! Isn't that a remarkable — *(He breaks off in amazement and fright as the flute is heard distantly.)*

Linda: What, darling?

Willy: That is the most remarkable thing.

Linda: What, dear?

Willy: I was thinking of the Chevy. *(Slight pause.)* Nineteen twenty-eight . . . when I had that red Chevy — *(Breaks off.)* That funny? I coulda sworn I was driving that Chevy today.

Linda: Well, that's nothing. Something must've reminded you.

Willy: Remarkable. Ts. Remember those days? The way Biff used to simonize that car? The dealer refused to believe there was eighty thousand miles on it. *(He shakes his head.)* Heh! *(To Linda.)* Close your eyes, I'll be right up. *(He walks out of the bedroom.)*

Happy (to Biff): Jesus, maybe he smashed up the car again!

Linda (calling after Willy): Be careful on the stairs, dear! The cheese is on the middle shelf! *(She turns, goes over to the bed, takes his jacket, and goes out of the bedroom.)*

Light has risen on the boys' room. Unseen, Willy is heard talking to himself, "Eighty thousand miles," and a little laugh. Biff gets out of bed, comes downstage a bit, and stands attentively. Biff is two years older than his brother Happy, well built, but in these days bears a worn air and seems less self-assured. He has succeeded less, and his dreams are stronger and less acceptable than Happy's. Happy is tall, powerfully made. Sexuality is like a visible color on him, or a scent that many women have discovered. He, like his brother, is lost, but in a different way, for he has never allowed himself to turn his face toward defeat and is thus more confused and hard-skinned, although seemingly more content.

Happy (getting out of bed): He's going to get his license taken away if he keeps that up. I'm getting nervous about him, y'know, Biff?

Biff: His eyes are going.

Happy: No, I've driven with him. He sees all right. He just doesn't keep his mind on it. I drove into the city with him last week. He stops at a green light and then it turns red and he goes. *(He laughs.)*

Biff: Maybe he's color-blind.

Happy: Pop? Why he's got the finest eye for color in the business. You know that.

Biff (sitting down on his bed): I'm going to sleep.

Happy: You're not still sour on Dad, are you, Biff?

Biff: He's all right, I guess.

Willy (underneath them, in the living-room): Yes, sir, eighty thousand miles — eighty-two thousand!

Biff: You smoking?

Happy (holding out a pack of cigarettes): Want one?

Biff (taking a cigarette): I can never sleep when I smell it.

Willy: What a simonizing job, heh!

Happy (with deep sentiment): Funny, Biff, y'know? Us sleeping in here again? The old beds. *(He pats his bed affectionately.)* All the talk that went across those two beds, huh? Our whole lives.

Biff: Yeah. Lotta dreams and plans.

Happy (with a deep and masculine laugh): About five hundred women would like to know what was said in this room.

They share a soft laugh.

Biff: Remember that big Betsy something — what the hell was her name — over on Bushwick Avenue?

Happy (combing his hair): With the collie dog!

Biff: That's the one. I got you in there, remember?

Happy: Yeah, that was my first time — I think. Boy, there was a pig! *(They laugh, almost crudely.)* You taught me everything I know about women. Don't forget that.

Biff: I bet you forgot how bashful you used to be. Especially with girls.

Happy: Oh, I still am, Biff.

Biff: Oh, go on.

Happy: I just control it, that's all. I think I got less bashful and you got more so. What happened, Biff? Where's the old humor, the old confidence? *(He shakes Biff's knee. Biff gets up and moves restlessly about the room.)* What's the matter?

Biff: Why does Dad mock me all the time?

Happy: He's not mocking you, he —

Biff: Everything I say there's a twist of mockery on his face. I can't get near him.

Happy: He just wants you to make good, that's all. I wanted to talk to you about Dad for a long time, Biff. Something's — happening to him. He — talks to himself.

Biff: I noticed that this morning. But he always mumbled.

Happy: But not so noticeable. It got so embarrassing I sent him to Florida. And you know something? Most of the time he's talking to you.

Biff: What's he say about me?

Happy: I can't make it out.

Biff: What's he say about me?

Happy: I think the fact that you're not settled, that you're still kind of up in the air . . .

Biff: There's one or two other things depressing him, Happy.

Happy: What do you mean?

Biff: Never mind. Just don't lay it all to me.

Happy: But I think if you just got started — I mean — is there any future for you out there?

Biff: I tell ya, Hap, I don't know what the future is. I don't know — what I'm supposed to want.

Happy: What do you mean?

Biff: Well, I spent six or seven years after high school trying to work myself up. Shipping clerk, salesman, business of one kind or another. And it's a measly manner of existence. To get on that subway on the hot mornings in summer. To devote your whole life to keeping stock, or making phone calls, or selling or buying. To suffer fifty weeks of the year for the sake of a two-week vacation, when all you really desire is to be outdoors, with your shirt off. And always to have to get ahead of the next fella. And still — that's how you build a future.

Happy: Well, you really enjoy it on a farm? Are you content out there?

Biff (with rising agitation): Hap, I've had twenty or thirty different kinds of jobs since I left home before the war, and it always turns out the same. I just realized it lately. In Nebraska when I herded cattle, and the Dakotas, and Arizona, and now in Texas. It's why I came home now, I guess, because I realized it. This farm I work on, it's spring there now, see? And they've got about fifteen new colts. There's nothing more inspiring or — beautiful than the sight of a mare and a new colt. And it's cool there now, see? Texas is cool now, and it's spring. And whenever spring comes to where I am, I suddenly get the feeling, my God, I'm not gettin' anywhere! What the hell am I doing, playing around with horses, twenty-eight dollars a week! I'm thirty-four years old, I oughta be makin' my future. That's when I come running home. And now, I get here, and I don't know what to do with myself. *(After a pause.)* I've always made a point of not wasting my life, and everytime I come back here I know that all I've done is to waste my life.

Happy: You're a poet, you know that, Biff? You're a — you're an idealist!

Biff: No, I'm mixed up very bad. Maybe I oughta get married. Maybe I oughta get stuck into something. Maybe that's my trouble. I'm like a boy. I'm not married. I'm not in business, I just — I'm like a boy. Are you content, Hap? You're a success, aren't you? Are you content?

Happy: Hell, no!

Biff: Why? You're making money, aren't you?

Happy (moving about with energy, expressiveness): All I can do now is wait for the merchandise manager to die. And suppose I get to be merchandise manager? He's a good friend of mine, and he just built a terrific estate on Long Island. And he lived there about two months and sold it, and now he's building another one. He can't enjoy it once it's finished. And I know that's just what I would do. I don't know what the hell I'm workin' for. Sometimes I sit in my apartment — all alone. And I think of the rent I'm paying. And it's crazy. But then, it's what I always wanted. My own apartment, a car, and plenty of women. And still, goddammit, I'm lonely.

Biff (with enthusiasm): Listen, why don't you come out West with me?

Happy: You and I, heh?

Biff: Sure, maybe we could buy a ranch. Raise cattle, use our muscles. Men built like we are should be working out in the open.

Happy (avidly): The Loman Brothers, heh?

Biff (with vast affection): Sure, we'd be known all over the counties!

Happy (enthralled): That's what I dream about, Biff. Sometimes I want to just rip my clothes off in the middle of the store and outbox that goddam merchandise manager. I mean I can outbox, outrun, and outlift anybody in that store, and I have to take orders from those common, petty sons-of-bitches till I can't stand it any more.

Biff: I'm tellin' you, kid, if you were with me I'd be happy out there.

Happy (enthused): See, Biff, everybody around me is so false that I'm constantly lowering my ideals . . .

Biff: Baby, together we'd stand up for one another, we'd have someone to trust.

Happy: If I were around you —

Biff: Hap, the trouble is we weren't brought up to grub for money. I don't know how to do it.

Happy: Neither can I!

Biff: Then let's go!

Happy: The only thing is — what can you make out there?

Biff: But look at your friend. Builds an estate and then hasn't the peace of mind to live in it.

Happy: Yeah, but when he walks into the store the waves part in front of him. That's fifty-two thousand dollars a year coming through the revolving door, and I got more in my pinky finger than he's got in his head.

Biff: Yeah, but you just said —

Happy: I gotta show some of those pompous, self-important executives over there that Hap Loman can make the grade. I want to walk into the store the way he walks in. Then I'll go with you, Biff. We'll be together yet, I swear. But take those two we had tonight. Now weren't they gorgeous creatures?

Biff: Yeah, yeah, most gorgeous I've had in years.

Happy: I get that any time I want, Biff. Whenever I feel disgusted. The trouble is, it gets like bowling or something. I just keep knockin' them over and it doesn't mean anything. You still run around a lot?

Biff: Naa. I'd like to find a girl — steady, somebody with substance.

Happy: That's what I long for.

Biff: Go on! You'd never come home.

Happy: I would! Somebody with character, with resistance! Like Mom, y'know? You're gonna call me a bastard when I tell you this. That girl Charlotte I was with tonight is engaged to be married in five weeks. *(He tries on his new hat.)*

Biff: No kiddin'!

Happy: Sure, the guy's in line for the vice-presidency of the store. I don't know what gets into me, maybe I just have an overdeveloped sense of competition or something, but I went and ruined her, and furthermore I can't get rid of her. And he's the third executive I've done that to. Isn't that a crummy characteristic? And to top it all, I go to their weddings! *(Indignantly, but laughing.)* Like I'm not supposed to take bribes. Manufacturers offer me a hundred-dollar bill now and then to throw an order their way. You know how honest I am, but it's like this girl, see. I hate myself for it. Because I don't want the girl, and, still, I take it and — I love it!

Biff: Let's to to sleep.

Happy: I guess we didn't settle anything, heh?

Biff: I just got one idea that I think I'm going to try.

Happy: What's that?

Biff: Remember Bill Oliver?

Happy: Sure, Oliver is very big now. You want to work for him again?

Biff: No, but when I quit he said something to me. He put his arm on my shoulder, and he said, "Biff, if you ever need anything, come to me."

Happy: I remember that. That sounds good.

Biff: I think I'll go to see him. If I could get ten thousand or even seven or eight thousand dollars I could buy a beautiful ranch.

Happy: I bet he'd back you. 'Cause he thought highly of you, Biff. I mean, they all do. You're well liked, Biff. That's why I say to come back here, and we both have the apartment. And I'm tellin' you, Biff, any babe you want . . .

Biff: No, with a ranch I could do the work I like and still be something. I just wonder though. I wonder if Oliver still thinks I stole that carton of basketballs.

Happy: Oh, he probably forgot that long ago. It's almost ten years. You're too sensitive. Anyway, he didn't really fire you.

Biff: Well, I think he was going to. I think that's why I quit. I was never sure whether he knew or not. I know he thought the world of me, though. I was the only one he'd let lock up the place.

Willy (below): You gonna wash the engine, Biff?

Happy: Shh!

Biff looks at Happy, who is gazing down, listening. Willy is mumbling in the parlor.

Happy: You hear that?

They listen. Willy laughs warmly.

Biff (growing angry): Doesn't he know Mom can hear that?

Willy: Don't get your sweater dirty, Biff!

A look of pain crosses Biff's face.

Happy: Isn't that terrible? Don't leave again, will you? You'll find a job here. You gotta stick around. I don't know what to do about him, it's getting embarrassing.

Willy: What a simonizing job!

Biff: Mom's hearing that!

Willy: No kiddin', Biff, you got a date? Wonderful!

Happy: Go on to sleep. But talk to him in the morning, will you?

Biff (reluctantly getting into bed): With her in the house. Brother!

Happy (getting into bed): I wish you'd have a good talk with him.

The light on their room begins to fade.

Biff (to himself in bed): That selfish, stupid . . .

Happy: Sh . . . Sleep, Biff.

Their light is out. Well before they have finished speaking, Willy's form is dimly seen below in the darkened kitchen. He opens the refrigerator, searches in there, and takes out a bottle of milk. The apartment houses are fading out, and the entire house and surroundings become covered with leaves. Music insinuates itself as the leaves appear.

Willy: Just wanna be careful with those girls, Biff, that's all. Don't make any promises. No promises of any kind. Because a girl, y'know, they always believe what you tell 'em, and you're very young, Biff, you're too young to be talking seriously to girls.

Light rises on the kitchen. Willy, talking, shuts the refrigerator door and comes downstage to the kitchen table. He pours milk into a glass. He is totally immersed in himself, smiling faintly.

Willy: Too young entirely, Biff. You want to watch your schooling first. Then when you're all set, there'll be plenty of girls for a boy like you. *(He smiles broadly at a kitchen chair.*) That so? The girls pay for you? (*He laughs.*) Boy, you must really be makin' a hit.

Willy is gradually addressing — physically — a point offstage, speaking through the wall of the kitchen, and his voice has been rising in volume to that of a normal conversation.

Willy: I been wondering why you polish the car so careful. Ha! Don't leave the hubcaps, boys. Get the chamois to the hubcaps. Happy, use newspaper on the windows, it's the easiest thing. Show him how to do it, Biff! You see, Happy? Pad it up, use it like a pad. That's it, that's it, good work. You're doin' all right, Hap. (*He pauses, then nods in approbation for a few seconds, then looks upward.*) Biff, first thing we gotta do when we get time is clip that big branch over the house. Afraid it's gonna fall in a storm and hit the roof. Tell you what. We get a rope and sling her around, and then we climb up there with a couple of saws and take her down. Soon as you finish the car, boys, I wanna see ya. I got a surprise for you, boys.
Biff (offstage): Whatta ya got, Dad?
Willy: No, you finish first. Never leave a job till you're finished — remember that. (*Looking toward the "big trees."*) Biff, up in Albany I saw a beautiful hammock. I think I'll buy it next trip, and we'll hang it right between those two elms. Wouldn't that be something? Just swingin' there under those branches. Boy, that would be . . .

Young Biff and Young Happy appear from the direction Willy was addressing. Happy carries rags and a pail of water. Biff, wearing a sweater with a block "S," carries a football.

Biff (pointing in the direction of the car offstage): How's that, Pop, professional?
Willy: Terrific. Terrific job, boys. Good work, Biff.
Happy: Where's the surprise, Pop?
Willy: In the back seat of the car.
Happy: Boy! (*He runs off.*)
Biff: What is it, Dad? Tell me, what'd you buy?
Willy (laughing, cuffs him): Never mind, something I want you to have.
Biff (turns and starts off): What is it, Hap?
Happy (offstage): It's a punching bag!
Biff: Oh, Pop!
Willy: It's got Gene Tunney's signature on it!

Happy runs onstage with a punching bag.

Biff: Gee, how'd you know we wanted a punching bag?
Willy: Well, it's the finest thing for the timing.
Happy (lies down on his back and pedals with his feet): I'm losing weight, you notice, Pop?
Willy (to Happy): Jumping rope is good too.
Biff: Did you see the new football I got?
Willy (examining the ball): Where'd you get a new ball?
Biff: The coach told me to practice my passing.
Willy: That so? And he gave you the ball, heh?
Biff: Well, I borrowed it from the locker room. (*He laughs confidentially.*)

Willy (laughing with him at the theft): I want you to return that.

Happy: I told you he wouldn't like it!

Biff (angrily): Well, I'm bringing it back!

Willy (stopping the incipient argument, to Happy): Sure, he's gotta practice with a regulation ball, doesn't he? *(To Biff.)* Coach'll probably congratulate you on your initiative!

Biff: Oh, he keeps congratulating my initiative all the time, Pop.

Willy: That's because he likes you. If somebody else took that ball there'd be an uproar. So what's the report, boys, what's the report?

Biff: Where'd you go this time, Dad? Gee we were lonesome for you.

Willy (pleased, puts an arm around each boy and they come down to the apron): Lonesome, heh?

Biff: Missed you every minute.

Willy: Don't say? Tell you a secret, boys. Don't breathe it to a soul. Someday I'll have my own business, and I'll never have to leave home any more.

Happy: Like Uncle Charley, heh?

Willy: Bigger than Uncle Charley! Because Charley is not — liked. He's liked, but he's not — well liked.

Biff: Where'd you go this time, Dad?

Willy: Well, I got on the road, and I went north to Providence. Met the Mayor.

Biff: The Mayor of Providence!

Willy: He was sitting in the hotel lobby.

Biff: What'd he say?

Willy: He said, "Morning!" And I said, "You got a fine city here, Mayor." And then he had coffee with me. And then I went to Waterbury. Waterbury is a fine city. Big clock city, the famous Waterbury clock. Sold a nice bill there. And then Boston — Boston is the cradle of the Revolution. A fine city. And a couple of other towns in Mass., and on to Portland and Bangor and straight home!

Biff: Gee, I'd love to go with you sometime, Dad.

Willy: Soon as summer comes.

Happy: Promise?

Willy: You and Hap and I, and I'll show you all the towns. America is full of beautiful towns and fine, upstanding people. And they know me, boys, they know me up and down New England. The finest people. And when I bring you fellas up, there'll be open sesame for all of us, 'cause one thing, boys: I have friends. I can park my car in any street in New England, and the cops protect it like their own. This summer, heh?

Biff and Happy (together): Yeah! You bet!

Willy: We'll take our bathing suits.

Happy: We'll carry your bags, Pop!

Willy: Oh, won't that be something! Me comin' into the Boston stores with you boys carryin' my bags. What a sensation!

Biff is prancing around, practicing passing the ball.

Willy: You nervous, Biff, about the game?

Biff: Not if you're gonna be there.

Willy: What do they say about you in school, now that they made you captain?

Happy: There's a crowd of girls behind him everytime the classes change.

Biff (taking Willy's hand): This Saturday, Pop, this Saturday — just for you, I'm going to break through for a touchdown.

Happy: You're supposed to pass.

Biff: I'm takin' one play for Pop. You watch me, Pop, and when I take off my helmet, that means I'm breakin' out. Then you watch me crash through that line!

Willy (kisses Biff): Oh, wait'll I tell this in Boston!

Bernard enters in knickers. He is younger than Biff, earnest and loyal, a worried boy.

Bernard: Biff, where are you? You're supposed to study with me today.

Willy: Hey, looka Bernard. What're you lookin' so anemic about, Bernard?

Bernard: He's gotta study, Uncle Willy. He's got Regents next week.

Happy (tauntingly, spinning Bernard around): Let's box, Bernard!

Bernard: Biff! (He gets away from Happy.) Listen, Biff, I heard Mr. Birnbaum say that if you don't start studyin' math, he's gonna flunk you, and you won't graduate. I heard him!

Willy: You better study with him, Biff. Go ahead now.

Bernard: I heard him!

Biff: Oh, Pop, you didn't see my sneakers! (He holds up a foot for Willy to look at.)

Willy: Hey, that's a beautiful job of printing!

Bernard (wiping his glasses): Just because he printed University of Virginia on his sneakers doesn't mean they've got to graduate him, Uncle Willy!

Willy (angrily): What're you talking about? With scholarships to three universities they're gonna flunk him?

Bernard: But I heard Mr. Birnbaum say —

Willy: Don't be a pest, Bernard! (To his boys.) What an anemic!

Bernard: Okay, I'm waiting for you in my house, Biff.

Bernard goes off. The Lomans laugh.

Willy: Bernard is not well liked, is he?

Biff: He's liked, but he's not well liked.

Happy: That's right, Pop.

Willy: That's just what I mean. Bernard can get the best marks in school, y'understand, but when he gets out in the business world, y'understand, you are going to be five times ahead of him. That's why I thank Almighty God you're both built like Adonises.° Because the man who makes an appearance in the business world, the man who creates personal interest, is the man who gets ahead. Be liked and you will never want. You take me, for instance. I never have to wait in line to see a buyer. "Willy Loman is here!" That's all they have to know, and I go right through.

Biff: Did you knock them dead, Pop?

Willy: Knocked 'em cold in Providence, slaughtered 'em in Boston.

Happy (on his back, pedaling again): I'm losing weight, you notice, Pop?

Linda enters, as of old, a ribbon in her hair, carrying a basket of washing.

Adonis: In Greek mythology a young man known for his good looks and favored by Aphrodite, goddess of love and beauty.

Linda (with youthful energy): Hello, dear!

Willy: Sweetheart!

Linda: How'd the Chevy run?

Willy: Chevrolet, Linda, is the greatest car ever built. *(To the boys.)* Since when do you let your mother carry wash up the stairs?

Biff: Grab hold there, boy!

Happy: Where to, Mom?

Linda: Hang them up on the line. And you better go down to your friends, Biff. The cellar is full of boys. They don't know what to do with themselves.

Biff: Ah, when Pop comes home they can wait!

Willy (laughs appreciatively): You better go down and tell them what to do, Biff.

Biff: I think I'll have them sweep out the furnace room.

Willy: Good work, Biff.

Biff (goes through wall-line of kitchen to doorway at back and calls down): Fellas! Everybody sweep out the furnace room! I'll be right down!

Voices: All right! Okay, Biff.

Biff: George and Sam and Frank, come out back! We're hangin' up the wash! Come on, Hap, on the double! *(He and Happy carry out the basket.)*

Linda: The way they obey him!

Willy: Well, that's training, the training. I'm tellin' you, I was sellin' thousands and thousands, but I had to come home.

Linda: Oh, the whole block'll be at that game. Did you sell anything?

Willy: I did five hundred gross in Providence and seven hundred gross in Boston.

Linda: No! Wait a minute, I've got a pencil. *(She pulls pencil and paper out of her apron pocket.)* That makes your commission . . . Two hundred — my God! Two hundred and twelve dollars!

Willy: Well, I didn't figure it yet, but . . .

Linda: How much did you do?

Willy: Well, I — I did — about a hundred and eighty gross in Providence. Well, no — it came to — roughly two hundred gross on the whole trip.

Linda (without hesitation): Two hundred gross. That's . . . *(She figures.)*

Willy: The trouble was that three of the stores were half closed for inventory in Boston. Otherwise I woulda broke records.

Linda: Well, it makes seventy dollars and some pennies. That's very good.

Willy: What do we owe?

Linda: Well, on the first there's sixteen dollars on the refrigerator —

Willy: Why sixteen?

Linda: Well, the fan belt broke, so it was a dollar eighty.

Willy: But it's brand new.

Linda: Well, the man said that's the way it is. Till they work themselves in, y'know.

They move through the wall-line into the kitchen.

Willy: I hope we didn't get stuck on that machine.

Linda: They got the biggest ads of any of them!

Willy: I know, it's a fine machine. What else?

Linda: Well, there's nine-sixty for the washing machine. And for the vacuum cleaner there's three and a half due on the fifteenth. Then the roof, you got twenty-one dollars remaining.

Willy: It don't leak, does it?

Linda: No, they did a wonderful job. Then you owe Frank for the carburetor.

Willy: I'm not going to pay that man! That goddam Chevrolet, they ought to prohibit the manufacture of that car!

Linda: Well, you owe him three and a half. And odds and ends, comes to around a hundred and twenty dollars by the fifteenth.

Willy: A hundred and twenty dollars! My God, if business don't pick up I don't know what I'm gonna do!

Linda: Well, next week you'll do better.

Willy: Oh, I'll knock 'em dead next week. I'll go to Hartford. I'm very well liked in Hartford. You know, the trouble is, Linda, people don't seem to take to me.

They move onto the forestage.

Linda: Oh, don't be foolish.

Willy: I know it when I walk in. They seem to laugh at me.

Linda: Why? Why would they laugh at you? Don't talk that way, Willy.

Willy moves to the edge of the stage. Linda goes into the kitchen and starts to darn stockings.

Willy: I don't know the reason for it, but they just pass me by. I'm not noticed.

Linda: But you're doing wonderful, dear. You're making seventy to a hundred dollars a week.

Willy: But I gotta be at it ten, twelve hours a day. Other men — I don't know — they do it easier. I don't know why — I can't stop myself — I talk too much. A man oughta come in with a few words. One thing about Charley. He's a man of few words, and they respect him.

Linda: You don't talk too much, you're just lively.

Willy (smiling): Well, I figure, what the hell, life is short, a couple of jokes. *(To himself.)* I joke too much! *(The smile goes.)*

Linda: Why? You're —

Willy: I'm fat. I'm very — foolish to look at, Linda. I didn't tell you, but Christmas time I happened to be calling on F. H. Stewarts, and a salesman I know, as I was going in to see the buyer I heard him say something about — walrus. And I — I cracked him right across the face. I won't take that. I simply will not take that. But they do laugh at me. I know that.

Linda: Darling . . .

Willy: I gotta overcome it. I know I gotta overcome it. I'm not dressing to advantage, maybe.

Linda: Willy, darling, you're the handsomest man in the world —

Willy: Oh, no, Linda.

Linda: To me you are. *(Slight pause.)* The handsomest.

From the darkness is heard the laughter of a woman. Willy doesn't turn to it, but it continues through Linda's lines.

Linda: And the boys, Willy. Few men are idolized by their children the way you are.

Music is heard as behind a scrim, to the left of the house, The Woman, dimly seen, is dressing.

Willy (with great feeling): You're the best there is, Linda, you're a pal, you know that? On the road — on the road I want to grab you sometimes and just kiss the life outa you.

The laughter is loud now, and he moves into a brightening area at the left, where The Woman has come from behind the scrim and is standing, putting on her hat, looking into a "mirror" and laughing.

Willy: 'Cause I get so lonely — especially when business is bad and there's nobody to talk to. I get the feeling that I'll never sell anything again, that I won't make a living for you, or a business, a business for the boys. *(He talks through The Woman's subsiding laughter; The Woman primps at the "mirror.")* There's so much I want to make for —

The Woman: Me? You didn't make me, Willy. I picked you.

Willy (pleased): You picked me?

The Woman (who is quite proper-looking, Willy's age): I did. I've been sitting at that desk watching all the salesmen go by, day in, day out. But you've got such a sense of humor, and we do have such a good time together, don't we?

Willy: Sure, sure. *(He takes her in his arms.)* Why do you have to go now?

The Woman: It's two o'clock . . .

Willy: No, come on in! *(He pulls her.)*

The Woman: . . . my sisters'll be scandalized. When'll you be back?

Willy: Oh, two weeks about. Will you come up again?

The Woman: Sure thing. You do make me laugh. It's good for me. *(She squeezes his arm, kisses him.)* And I think you're a wonderful man.

Willy: You picked me, heh?

The Woman: Sure. Because you're so sweet. And such a kidder.

Willy: Well, I'll see you next time I'm in Boston.

The Woman: I'll put you right through to the buyers.

Willy (slapping her bottom): Right. Well, bottoms up!

The Woman (slaps him gently and laughs): You just kill me, Willy. *(He suddenly grabs her and kisses her roughly.)* You kill me. And thanks for the stockings. I love a lot of stockings. Well, good night.

Willy: Good night. And keep your pores open!

The Woman: Oh, Willy!

The Woman bursts out laughing, and Linda's laughter blends in. The Woman disappears into the dark. Now the area at the kitchen table brightens. Linda is sitting where she was at the kitchen table, but now is mending a pair of her silk stockings.

Linda: You are, Willy. The handsomest man. You've got no reason to feel that —

Willy (coming out of The Woman's dimming area and going over to Linda): I'll make it all up to you, Linda, I'll —

Linda: There's nothing to make up, dear. You're doing fine, better than —

Willy (noticing her mending): What's that?

Linda: Just mending my stockings. They're so expensive —

Willy (angrily, taking them from her): I won't have you mending stockings in this house! Now throw them out!

Linda puts the stockings in her pocket.

Bernard (entering on the run): Where is he? If he doesn't study!

Willy (moving to the forestage, with great agitation): You'll give him the answers!

Bernard: I do, but I can't on a Regents! That's a state exam! They're liable to arrest me!

Willy: Where is he? I'll whip him, I'll whip him!

Linda: And he'd better give back that football, Willy, it's not nice.

Willy: Biff! Where is he? Why is he taking everything?

Linda: He's too rough with the girls, Willy. All the mothers are afraid of him!

Willy: I'll whip him!

Bernard: He's driving the car without a license!

The Woman's laugh is heard.

Willy: Shut up!

Linda: All the mothers —

Willy: Shut up!

Bernard (backing quietly away and out): Mr. Birnbaum says he's stuck up.

Willy: Get outa here!

Bernard: If he doesn't buckle down he'll flunk math! *(He goes off.)*

Linda: He's right, Willy, you've gotta —

Willy (exploding at her): There's nothing the matter with him! You want him to be a worm like Bernard? He's got spirit, personality . . .

As he speaks, Linda, almost in tears, exits into the living-room. Willy is alone in the kitchen, wilting and staring. The leaves are gone. It is night again, and the apartment houses look down from behind.

Willy: Loaded with it. Loaded! What is he stealing? He's giving it back, isn't he? Why is he stealing? What did I tell him? I never in my life told him anything but decent things.

Happy in pajamas has come down the stairs; Willy suddenly becomes aware of Happy's presence.

Happy: Let's go now, come on.

Willy (sitting down at the kitchen table): Huh! Why did she have to wax the floors herself? Everytime she waxes the floors she keels over. She knows that!

Happy: Shh! Take it easy. What brought you back tonight?

Willy: I got an awful scare. Nearly hit a kid in Yonkers. God! Why didn't I go to Alaska with my brother Ben that time! Ben! That man was a genius, that man was success incarnate! What a mistake! He begged me to go.

Happy: Well, there's no use in —

Willy: You guys! There was a man started with the clothes on his back and ended up with diamond mines!

Happy: Boy, someday I'd like to know how he did it.

Willy: What's the mystery? The man knew what he wanted and went out and got it! Walked into a jungle, and comes out, the age of twenty-one, and he's rich! The world is an oyster, but you don't crack it open on a mattress!

Happy: Pop, I told you I'm gonna retire you for life.

Willy: You'll retire me for life on seventy goddam dollars a week? And your women and your car and your apartment, and you'll retire me for life! Christ's sake, I couldn't get past Yonkers today! Where are you guys, where are you? The woods are burning! I can't drive a car!

Charley has appeared in the doorway. He is a large man, slow of speech, laconic, immovable. In all he says, despite what he says, there is pity, and, now, trepidation. He has a robe over pajamas, slippers on his feet. He enters the kitchen.

Charley: Everything all right?

Happy: Yeah, Charley, everything's . . .

Willy: What's the matter?

Charley: I heard some noise. I thought something happened. Can't we do something about the walls? You sneeze in here, and in my house hats blow off.

Happy: Let's go to bed, Dad. Come on.

Charley signals to Happy to go.

Willy: You go ahead, I'm not tired at the moment.

Happy (to Willy): Take it easy, huh? *(He exits.)*

Willy: What're you doin' up?

Charley (sitting down at the kitchen table opposite Willy): Couldn't sleep good. I had a heartburn.

Willy: Well, you don't know how to eat.

Charley: I eat with my mouth.

Willy: No, you're ignorant. You gotta know about vitamins and things like that.

Charley: Come on, let's shoot. Tire you out a little.

Willy (hesitantly): All right. You got cards?

Charley (taking a deck from his pocket): Yeah, I got them. Someplace. What is it with those vitamins?

Willy (dealing): They build up your bones. Chemistry.

Charley: Yeah, but there's no bones in a heartburn.

Willy: What are you talkin' about? Do you know the first thing about it?

Charley: Don't get insulted.

Willy: Don't talk about something you don't know anything about.

They are playing. Pause.

Charley: What're you doin' home?

Willy: A little trouble with the car.

Charley: Oh. *(Pause.)* I'd like to take a trip to California.

Willy: Don't say.

Charley: You want a job?

Willy: I got a job, I told you that. *(After a slight pause.)* What the hell are you offering me a job for?

Charley: Don't get insulted.

Willy: Don't insult me.

Charley: I don't see no sense in it. You don't have to go on this way.

Willy: I got a good job. *(Slight pause.)* What do you keep comin' in here for?

Charley: You want me to go?

Willy (after a pause, withering): I can't understand it. He's going back to Texas again. What the hell is that?

Charley: Let him go.

Willy: I got nothin' to give him, Charley, I'm clean, I'm clean.

Charley: He won't starve. None a them starve. Forget about him.

Willy: Then what have I got to remember?

Charley: You take it too hard. To hell with it. When a deposit bottle is broken you don't get your nickel back.

Willy: That's easy enough for you to say.

Charley: That ain't easy for me to say.

Willy: Did you see the ceiling I put up in the living-room?

Charley: Yeah, that's a piece of work. To put up a ceiling is a mystery to me. How do you do it?

Willy: What's the difference?

Charley: Well, talk about it.

Willy: You gonna put up a ceiling?

Charley: How could I put up a ceiling?

Willy: Then what the hell are you bothering me for?

Charley: You're insulted again.

Willy: A man who can't handle tools is not a man. You're disgusting.

Charley: Don't call me disgusting, Willy.

Uncle Ben, carrying a valise and an umbrella, enters the forestage from around the right corner of the house. He is a stolid man, in his sixties, with a mustache and an authoritative air. He is utterly certain of his destiny, and there is an aura of far places about him. He enters exactly as Willy speaks.

Willy: I'm getting awfully tired, Ben.

Ben's music is heard. Ben looks around at everything.

Charley: Good, keep playing; you'll sleep better. Did you call me Ben?

Ben looks at his watch.

Willy: That's funny. For a second there you reminded me of my brother Ben.

Ben: I only have a few minutes. *(He strolls, inspecting the place. Willy and Charley continue playing.)*

Charley: You never heard from him again, heh? Since that time?

Willy: Didn't Linda tell you? Couple of weeks ago we got a letter from his wife in Africa. He died.

Charley: That so.

Ben (chuckling): So this is Brooklyn, eh?

Charley: Maybe you're in for some of his money.

Willy: Naa, he had seven sons. There's just one opportunity I had with that man . . .

Ben: I must make a train, William. There are several properties I'm looking at in Alaska.

Willy: Sure, sure! If I'd gone with him to Alaska that time, everything would've been totally different.

Charley: Go on, you'd froze to death up there.

Willy: What're you talking about?

Ben: Opportunity is tremendous in Alaska, William. Surprised you're not up there.

Willy: Sure, tremendous.

Charley: Heh?

Willy: There was the only man I ever met who knew the answers.

Charley: Who?

Ben: How are you all?

Willy (taking a pot, smiling): Fine, fine.

Charley: Pretty sharp tonight.

Ben: Is mother living with you?

Willy: No, she died a long time ago.

Charley: Who?

Ben: That's too bad. Fine specimen of a lady, Mother.

Willy (to Charley): Heh?

Ben: I'd hoped to see the old girl.

Charley: Who died?

Ben: Heard anything from Father, have you?

Willy (unnerved): What do you mean, who died?

Charley (taking a pot): What're you talkin' about?

Ben (looking at his watch): William, it's half-past eight!

Willy (as though to dispel his confusion he angrily stops Charley's hand): That's my build!

Charley: I put the ace —

Willy: If you don't know how to play the game I'm not gonna throw my money away on you!

Charley (rising): It was my ace, for God's sake!

Willy: I'm through, I'm through!

Ben: When did Mother die?

Willy: Long ago. Since the beginning you never knew how to play cards.

Charley (picks up the cards and goes to the door): All right! Next time I'll bring a deck with five aces.

Willy: I don't play that kind of game!

Charley (turning to him): You ought to be ashamed of yourself!

Willy: Yeah?

Charley: Yeah! *(He goes out.)*

Willy (slamming the door after him): Ignoramus!

Ben (as Willy comes toward him through the wall-line of the kitchen): So you're William.

Willy (shaking Ben's hand): Ben! I've been waiting for you so long! What's the answer? How did you do it?

Ben: Oh, there's a story in that.

Linda enters the forestage, as of old, carrying the wash basket.

Linda: Is this Ben?

Ben (gallantly): How do you do, my dear.

Linda: Where've you been all these years? Willy's always wondered why you —

Willy (pulling Ben away from her impatiently): Where is Dad? Didn't you follow him? How did you get started?

Ben: Well, I don't know how much you remember.

Willy: Well, I was just a baby, of course, only three or four years old —

Ben: Three years and eleven months.

Willy: What a memory, Ben!

Ben: I have many enterprises, William, and I have never kept books.

Willy: I remember I was sitting under the wagon in — was it Nebraska?

Ben: It was South Dakota, and I gave you a bunch of wild flowers.

Willy: I remember you walking away down some open road.

Ben (laughing): I was going to find Father in Alaska.

Willy: Where is he?

Ben: At that age I had a very faulty view of geography, William. I discovered after a few days that I was heading due south, so instead of Alaska, I ended up in Africa.

Linda: Africa!

Willy: The Gold Coast!

Ben: Principally diamond mines.

Linda: Diamond mines!

Ben: Yes, my dear. But I've only a few minutes —

Willy: No! Boys! Boys! *(Young Biff and Happy appear.)* Listen to this. This is your Uncle Ben, a great man! Tell my boys, Ben!

Ben: Why, boys, when I was seventeen I walked into the jungle, and when I was twenty-one I walked out. *(He laughs.)* And by God I was rich.

Willy (to the boys): You see what I been talking about? The greatest things can happen!

Ben (glancing at his watch): I have an appointment in Ketchikan Tuesday week.

Willy: No, Ben! Please tell about Dad. I want my boys to hear. I want them to know the kind of stock they spring from. All I remember is a man with a big beard, and I was in Mamma's lap, sitting around a fire, and some kind of high music.

Ben: His flute. He played the flute.

Willy: Sure, the flute, that's right!

New music is heard, a high, rollicking tune.

Ben: Father was a very great and a very wild-hearted man. We would start in Boston, and he'd toss the whole family into the wagon, and then he'd drive the team right across the country; through Ohio, and Indiana, Michigan, Illinois, and all the Western states. And we'd stop in the towns and sell the flutes that he'd made on the way. Great inventor, Father. With one gadget he made more in a week than a man like you could make in a lifetime.

Willy: That's just the way I'm bringing them up, Ben — rugged, well liked, all-around.

Ben: Yeah? *(To Biff.)* Hit that, boy — hard as you can. *(He pounds his stomach.)*

Biff: Oh, no, sir!

Ben (taking boxing stance): Come on, get to me. *(He laughs.)*

Willy: Go to it, Biff! Go ahead, show him!

Biff: Okay! *(He cocks his fists and starts in.)*

Linda (to Willy): Why must he fight, dear?

Ben (sparring with Biff): Good boy! Good boy!

Willy: How's that, Ben, heh?

Happy: Give him the left, Biff!

Linda: Why are you fighting?

Ben: Good boy! *(Suddenly comes in, trips Biff, and stands over him, the point of his umbrella poised over Biff's eye.)*

Linda: Look out, Biff!

Biff: Gee!

Ben (patting Biff's knee): Never fight fair with a stranger, boy. You'll never get out of the jungle that way. *(Taking Linda's hand and bowing):* It was an honor and a pleasure to meet you, Linda.

Linda (withdrawing her hand coldly, frightened): Have a nice — trip.

Ben (to Willy): And good luck with your — what do you do?

Willy: Selling.

Ben: Yes. Well . . . *(He raises his hand in farewell to all.)*

Willy: No, Ben, I don't want you to think . . . *(He takes Ben's arm to show him.)* It's Brooklyn, I know, but we hunt too.

Ben: Really, now.

Willy: Oh, sure, there's snakes and rabbits and — that's why I moved out here. Why, Biff can fell any one of these trees in no time! Boys! Go right over to where they're building the apartment house and get some sand. We're gonna rebuild the entire front stoop now! Watch this, Ben!

Biff: Yes, sir! On the double, Hap!

Happy (as he and Biff run off): I lost weight, Pop, you notice?

Charley enters in knickers, even before the boys are gone.

Charley: Listen, if they steal any more from that building the watchman'll put the cops on them!

Linda (to Willy): Don't let Biff . . .

Ben laughs lustily.

Willy: You shoulda seen the lumber they brought home last week. At least a dozen six-by-tens worth all kinds a money.

Charley: Listen, if that watchman —

Willy: I gave them hell, understand. But I got a couple of fearless characters there.

Charley: Willy, the jails are full of fearless characters.

Ben (clapping Willy on the back, with a laugh at Charley): And the stock exchange, friend!

Willy (joining in Ben's laughter): Where are the rest of your pants?

Charley: My wife bought them.

Willy: Now all you need is a golf club and you can go upstairs and go to sleep. *(To Ben).* Great athlete! Between him and his son Bernard they can't hammer a nail!

Bernard (rushing in): The watchman's chasing Biff!

Willy (angrily): Shut up! He's not stealing anything!

Linda (alarmed, hurrying off left): Where is he? Biff, dear! *(She exits.)*

Willy (moving toward the left, away from Ben): There's nothing wrong. What's the matter with you?

Ben: Nervy boy. Good!

Willy (laughing): Oh, nerves of iron, that Biff!

Charley: Don't know what it is. My New England man comes back and he's bleedin', they murdered him up there.

Willy: It's contacts, Charley, I got important contacts!

Charley (sarcastically): Glad to hear it, Willy. Come in later, we'll shoot a little casino. I'll take some of your Portland money. *(He laughs at Willy and exits.)*

Willy (turning to Ben): Business is bad, it's murderous. But not for me, of course.

Ben: I'll stop by on my way back to Africa.

Willy (longingly): Can't you stay a few days? You're just what I need, Ben, because I — I have a fine position here, but I — well, Dad left when I was such a baby and I never had a chance to talk to him and I still feel — kind of temporary about myself.

Ben: I'll be late for my train.

They are at opposite ends of the stage.

Willy: Ben, my boys — can't we talk? They'd go into the jaws of hell for me, see, but I —

Ben: William, you're being first-rate with your boys. Outstanding, manly chaps!

Willy (hanging on to his words): Oh, Ben, that's good to hear! Because sometimes I'm afraid that I'm not teaching them the right kind of — Ben, how should I teach them?

Ben (giving great weight to each word, and with a certain vicious audacity): William, when I walked into the jungle, I was seventeen. When I walked out I was twenty-one. And, by God, I was rich! *(He goes off into darkness around the right corner of the house.)*

Willy: . . . was rich! That's just the spirit I want to imbue them with! To walk into a jungle! I was right! I was right! I was right!

Ben is gone, but Willy is still speaking to him as Linda, in nightgown and robe, enters the kitchen, glances around for Willy, then goes to the door of the house, looks out, and sees him. Comes down to his left. He looks at her.

Linda: Willy, dear? Willy?

Willy: I was right!

Linda: Did you have some cheese? *(He can't answer.)* It's very late, darling. Come to bed, heh?

Willy (looking straight up): Gotta break your neck to see a star in this yard.

Linda: You coming in?

Willy: Whatever happened to that diamond watch fob? Remember? When Ben came from Africa that time? Didn't he give me a watch fob with a diamond in it?

Linda: You pawned it, dear. Twelve, thirteen years ago. For Biff's radio correspondence course.

Willy: Gee, that was a beautiful thing. I'll take a walk.

Linda: But you're in your slippers.

Willy (starting to go around the house at the left): I was right! I was! *(Half to Linda, as he goes, shaking his head.)* What a man! There was a man worth talking to. I was right!

Linda (calling after Willy): But in your slippers, Willy!

Willy is almost gone when Biff, in his pajamas, comes down the stairs and enters the kitchen.

Biff: What is he doing out there?

Linda: Sh!

Biff: God Almighty, Mom, how long has he been doing this?

Linda: Don't, he'll hear you.

Biff: What the hell is the matter with him?

Linda: It'll pass by morning.

Biff: Shouldn't we do anything?

Linda: Oh, my dear, you should do a lot of things, but there's nothing to do, so go to sleep.

Happy comes down the stairs and sits on the steps.

Happy: I never heard him so loud, Mom.

Linda: Well, come around more often; you'll hear him. *(She sits down at the table and mends the lining of Willy's jacket.)*

Biff: Why didn't you ever write me about this, Mom?

Linda: How would I write to you? For over three months you had no address.

Biff: I was on the move. But you know I thought of you all the time. You know that, don't you, pal?

Linda: I know, dear, I know. But he likes to have a letter. Just to know that there's still a possibility for better things.

Biff: He's not like this all the time, is he?

Linda: It's when you come home he's always the worst.

Biff: When I come home?

Linda: When you write you're coming, he's all smiles, and talks about the future, and — he's just wonderful. And then the closer you seem to come, the more shaky he gets, and then, by the time you get here, he's arguing, and he seems angry at you. I think it's just that maybe he can't bring himself to — to open up to you. Why are you so hateful to each other? Why is that?

Biff (evasively): I'm not hateful, Mom.

Linda: But you no sooner come in the door than you're fighting!

Biff: I don't know why. I mean to change. I'm tryin', Mom, you understand?

Linda: Are you home to stay now?

Biff: I don't know. I want to look around, see what's doin'.

Linda: Biff, you can't look around all your life, can you?

Biff: I just can't take hold, Mom. I can't take hold of some kind of a life.

Linda: Biff, a man is not a bird, to come and go with the springtime.

Biff: Your hair . . . *(He touches her hair.)* Your hair got so gray.

Linda: Oh, it's been gray since you were in high school. I just stopped dyeing it, that's all.

Biff: Dye it again, will ya? I don't want my pal looking old. *(He smiles.)*

Linda: You're such a boy! You think you can go away for a year and . . . You've got to get it into your head now that one day you'll knock on this door and there'll be strange people here —

Biff: What are you talking about? You're not even sixty, Mom.

Linda: But what about your father?

Biff (lamely): Well, I meant him too.

Happy: He admires Pop.

Linda: Biff, dear, if you don't have any feeling for him, then you can't have any feeling for me.

Biff: Sure I can, Mom.

Linda: No. You can't just come to see me, because I love him. *(With a threat, but only a threat, of tears.)* He's the dearest man in the world to me, and I won't have anyone making him feel unwanted and low and blue. You've got to make up your mind now, darling, there's no leeway any more. Either he's your father and you pay him that respect, or else you're not to come here. I know he's not easy to get along with — nobody knows that better than me — but . . . .

Willy (from the left, with a laugh): Hey, hey, Biffo!

Biff (starting to go out after Willy): What the hell is the matter with him? *(Happy stops him.)*

Linda: Don't — don't go near him!

Biff: Stop making excuses for him! He always, always wiped the floor with you. Never had an ounce of respect for you.

Happy: He's always had respect for —

Biff: What the hell do you know about it?

Happy (surlily): Just don't call him crazy!

Biff: He's got no character — Charley wouldn't do this. Not in his own house — spewing out that vomit from his mind.

Happy: Charley never had to cope with what he's got to.

Biff: People are worse off than Willy Loman. Believe me, I've seen them!

Linda: Then make Charley your father, Biff. You can't do that, can you? I don't say he's a great man. Willy Loman never made a lot of money. His name was never in the paper. He's not the finest character that ever lived. But he's a human being, and a terrible thing is happening to him. So attention must be paid. He's not to be allowed to fall into his grave like an old dog. Attention, attention must be finally paid to such a person. You called him crazy —

Biff: I didn't mean —

Linda: No, a lot of people think he's lost his — balance. But you don't have to be very smart to know what his trouble is. The man is exhausted.

Happy: Sure!

Linda: A small man can be just as exhausted as a great man. He works for a company thirty-six years this March, opens up unheard-of territories to their trademark, and now in his old age they take his salary away.

Happy (indignantly): I didn't know that, Mom.

Linda: You never asked, my dear! Now that you get your spending money someplace else you don't trouble your mind with him.

Happy: But I gave you money last —

Linda: Christmas time, fifty dollars! To fix the hot water it cost ninety-seven fifty! For five weeks he's been on straight commission, like a beginner, an unknown!

Biff: Those ungrateful bastards!

Linda: Are they any worse than his sons? When he brought them business, when he was young, they were glad to see him. But now his old friends, the old buyers that loved him so and always found some order to hand him in a pinch — they're all dead, retired. He used to be able to make six, seven calls a day in Boston. Now he takes his valises out of the car and puts them back and takes them out again and he's exhausted. Instead of walking he talks now. He drives seven hundred miles, and when he gets there no one knows him any more, no one welcomes him. And what goes through a man's mind, driving seven hundred miles home without having earned a cent? Why shouldn't he talk to himself? Why? When he has to go to Charley and borrow fifty dollars a week and pretend to me that it's his pay? How long can that go on? How long? You see what I'm sitting here and waiting for? And you tell me he has no character? The man who never worked a day but for your benefit? When does he get the medal for that? Is this his reward — to turn around at the age of sixty-three and find his sons, who he loved better than his life, one a philandering bum —

Happy: Mom!

Linda: That's all you are, my baby! *(To Biff.)* And you! What happened to the love you had for him? You were such pals! How you used to talk to him on the phone every night! How lonely he was till he could come home to you!

Biff: All right, Mom. I'll live here in my room, and I'll get a job. I'll keep away from him, that's all.

Linda: No, Biff. You can't stay here and fight all the time.

Biff: He threw me out of this house, remember that.

Linda: Why did he do that? I never knew why.

Biff: Because I know he's a fake and he doesn't like anybody around who knows!

Linda: Why a fake? In what way? What do you mean?

Biff: Just don't lay it all at my feet. It's between me and him — that's all I have to say. I'll chip in from now on. He'll settle for half my pay check. He'll be all right. I'm going to bed. *(He starts for the stairs.)*

Linda: He won't be all right.

Biff (turning on the stairs, furiously): I hate this city and I'll stay here. Now what do you want?

Linda: He's dying, Biff.

Happy turns quickly to her, shocked.

Biff (after a pause): Why is he dying?

Linda: He's been trying to kill himself.

Biff (with great horror): How?

Linda: I live from day to day.

Biff: What're you talking about?

Linda: Remember I wrote you that he smashed up the car again? In February?

Biff: Well?

Linda: The insurance inspector came. He said that they have evidence. That all these accidents in the last year — weren't — weren't — accidents.

Happy: How can they tell that? That's a lie.

Linda: It seems there's a woman . . . *(She takes a breath as):*

　⎰*Biff (sharply but contained):* What woman?

　⎱*Linda (simultaneously):* . . . and this woman . . .

Linda: What?

Biff: Nothing. Go ahead.

Linda: What did you say?

Biff: Nothing. I just said what woman?

Happy: What about her?

Linda: Well, it seems she was walking down the road and saw his car. She says that he wasn't driving fast at all, and that he didn't skid. She says he came to that little bridge, and then deliberately smashed into the railing, and it was only the shallowness of the water that saved him.

Biff: Oh, no, he probably just fell asleep again.

Linda: I don't think he fell asleep.

Biff: Why not?

Linda: Last month . . . *(With great difficulty.)* Oh, boys, it's so hard to say a thing like this! He's just a big stupid man to you, but I tell you there's more good in him than in many other people. *(She chokes, wipes her eyes.)* I was looking for a fuse. The lights blew out, and I went down the cellar. And behind the fuse box — it happened to fall out — was a length of rubber pipe — just short.

Happy: No kidding?

Linda: There's a little attachment on the end of it. I knew right away. And sure enough, on the bottom of the water heater there's a new little nipple on the gas pipe.

Happy (angrily): That — jerk.

Biff: Did you have it taken off?

Linda: I'm — I'm ashamed to. How can I mention it to him? Every day I go down and take away that little rubber pipe. But, when he comes home, I put it back where it was. How can I insult him that way? I don't know what to do. I live from day to day, boys. I tell you, I know every thought in his mind. It sounds so old-fashioned and silly, but I tell you he put his whole life into you and you've turned your backs on him. *(She is bent over in chair, weeping, her face in her hands.)* Biff, I swear to God! Biff, his life is in your hands!

Happy (to Biff): How do you like that damned fool!

Biff (kissing her): All right, pal, all right. It's all settled now. I've been remiss. I know that, Mom. But now I'll stay, and I swear to you, I'll apply myself. *(Kneeling in front of her, in a fever of self-reproach.)* It's just — you see, Mom, I don't fit in business. Not that I won't try. I'll try, and I'll make good.

Happy: Sure you will. The trouble with you in business was you never tried to please people.

Biff: I know, I —

Happy: Like when you worked for Harrison's. Bob Harrison said you were tops, and then you go and do some damn fool thing like whistling whole songs in the elevator like a comedian.

Biff (against Happy): So what? I like to whistle sometimes.

Happy: You don't raise a guy to a responsible job who whistles in the elevator!

Linda: Well, don't argue about it now.

Happy: Like when you'd go off and swim in the middle of the day instead of taking the line around.

Biff (his resentment rising): Well, don't you run off? You take off sometimes, don't you? On a nice summer day?

Happy: Yeah, but I cover myself!

Linda: Boys!

Happy: If I'm going to take a fade the boss can call any number where I'm supposed to be and they'll swear to him that I just left. I'll tell you something that I hate to say, Biff, but in the business world some of them think you're crazy.

Biff (angered): Screw the business world!

Happy: All right, screw it! Great, but cover yourself!

Linda: Hap, Hap!

Biff: I don't care what they think! They've laughed at Dad for years, and you know why? Because we don't belong in this nuthouse of a city! We should be mixing cement on some open plain, or — or carpenters. A carpenter is allowed to whistle!

Willy walks in from the entrance of the house, at left.

Willy: Even your grandfather was better than a carpenter. *(Pause. They watch him.)* You never grew up. Bernard does not whistle in the elevator, I assure you.

Biff (as though to laugh Willy out of it): Yeah, but you do, Pop.

Willy: I never in my life whistled in an elevator! And who in the business world thinks I'm crazy?

Biff: I didn't mean it like that, Pop. Now don't make a whole thing out of it, will ya?

Willy: Go back to the West! Be a carpenter, a cowboy, enjoy yourself!

Linda: Willy, he was just saying —

Willy: I heard what he said!

Happy (trying to quiet Willy): Hey, Pop, come on now . . .

Willy (continuing over Happy's line): They laugh at me, heh? Go to Filene's, go to the Hub, go to Slattery's, Boston. Call out the name Willy Loman and see what happens! Big shot!

Biff: All right, Pop.

Willy: Big!

Biff: All right!

Willy: Why do you always insult me?

Biff: I didn't say a word. *(To Linda.)* Did I say a word?

Linda: He didn't say anything, Willy.

Willy (going to the doorway of the living-room): All right, good night, good night.

Linda: Willy, dear, he just decided . . .

Willy (to Biff): If you get tired hanging around tomorrow, paint the ceiling I put up in the living-room.

Biff: I'm leaving early tomorrow.

Happy: He's going to see Bill Oliver, Pop.

Willy (interestedly): Oliver? For what?

Biff (with reserve, but trying, trying): He always said he'd stake me. I'd like to go into business, so maybe I can take him up on it.

Linda: Isn't that wonderful?

Willy: Don't interrupt. What's wonderful about it? There's fifty men in the City of New York who'd stake him. *(To Biff.)* Sporting goods?

Biff: I guess so. I know something about it and —

Willy: He knows something about it! You know sporting goods better than Spalding, for God's sake! How much is he giving you?

Biff: I don't know, I didn't even see him yet, but —

Willy: Then what're you talkin' about?

Biff (getting angry): Well, all I said was I'm gonna see him, that's all!

Willy (turning away): Ah, you're counting your chickens again.

Biff (starting left for the stairs): Oh, Jesus, I'm going to sleep!

Willy (calling after him): Don't curse in this house!

Biff (turning): Since when did you get so clean?

Happy (trying to stop them): Wait a . . .

Willy: Don't use that language to me! I won't have it!

Happy (grabbing Biff, shouts): Wait a minute! I got an idea. I got a feasible idea. Come here, Biff, let's talk this over now, let's talk some sense here. When I was down in Florida last time, I thought of a great idea to sell sporting goods. It just came back to me. You and I, Biff — we have a line, the Loman Line. We train a couple of weeks, and put on a couple of exhibitions, see?

Willy: That's an idea!

Happy: Wait! We form two basketball teams, see? Two water-polo teams. We play each other. It's a million dollars' worth of publicity. Two brothers, see? The Loman Brothers. Displays in the Royal Palms — all the hotels. And banners over the ring and the basketball court: "Loman Brothers." Baby, we could sell sporting goods!

Willy: That is a one-million-dollar idea!

Linda: Marvelous!

Biff: I'm in great shape as far as that's concerned.

Happy: And the beauty of it is, Biff, it wouldn't be like a business. We'd be out playin' ball again . . .

Biff (enthused): Yeah, that's . . .

Willy: Million-dollar . . .

Happy: And you wouldn't get fed up with it, Biff. It'd be the family again. There'd be the old honor, and comradeship, and if you wanted to go off for a swim or somethin' — well, you'd do it! Without some smart cooky gettin' up ahead of you!

Willy: Lick the world! You guys together could absolutely lick the civilized world.

Biff: I'll see Oliver tomorrow. Hap, if we could work that out . . .

Linda: Maybe things are beginning to —

Willy (wildly enthused, to Linda): Stop interrupting! *(To Biff.)* But don't wear sport jacket and slacks when you see Oliver.

Biff: No, I'll —

Willy: A business suit, and talk as little as possible, and don't crack any jokes.

Biff: He did like me. Always liked me.

Linda: He loved you!

Willy (to Linda): Will you stop! *(To Biff.)* Walk in very serious. You are not applying for a boy's job. Money is to pass. Be quiet, fine, and serious. Everybody likes a kidder, but nobody lends him money.

Happy: I'll try to get some myself, Biff. I'm sure I can.

Willy: I see great things for you kids, I think your troubles are over. But remember, start big and you'll end big. Ask for fifteen. How much you gonna ask for?

Biff: Gee, I don't know —

Willy: And don't say "Gee." "Gee" is a boy's word. A man walking in for fifteen thousand dollars does not say "Gee!"

Biff: Ten, I think, would be top though.

Willy: Don't be so modest. You always started too low. Walk in with a big laugh. Don't look worried. Start off with a couple of your good stories to lighten things up. It's not what you say, it's how you say it — because personality always wins the day.

Linda: Oliver always thought the highest of him —

Willy: Will you let me talk?

Biff: Don't yell at her, Pop, will ya?

Willy (angrily): I was talking, wasn't I?

Biff: I don't like you yelling at her all the time, and I'm tellin' you, that's all.

Willy: What're you, takin' over this house?

Linda: Willy —

Willy (turning on her): Don't take his side all the time, goddammit!

Biff (furiously): Stop yelling at her!

Willy (suddenly pulling on his cheek, beaten down, guilt ridden): Give my best to Bill Oliver — he may remember me. *(He exits through the living-room doorway.)*

Linda (her voice subdued): What'd you have to start that for? *(Biff turns away.)* You see how sweet he was as soon as you talked hopefully? *(She goes over to Biff.)* Come up and say good night to him. Don't let him go to bed that way.

Happy: Come on, Biff, let's buck him up.

Linda: Please, dear. Just say good night. It takes so little to make him happy. Come. *(She goes through the living-room doorway, calling upstairs from within the living-room.)* Your pajamas are hanging in the bathroom, Willy!

Happy (looking toward where Linda went out): What a woman! They broke the mold when they made her. You know that, Biff?

Biff: He's off salary. My God, working on commission!

Happy: Well, let's face it: he's no hot-shot selling man. Except that sometimes, you have to admit, he's a sweet personality.

Biff (deciding): Lend me ten bucks, will ya? I want to buy some new ties.

Happy: I'll take you to a place I know. Beautiful stuff. Wear one of my striped shirts tomorrow.

Biff: She got gray. Mom got awful old. Gee, I'm gonna go in to Oliver tomorrow and knock him for a —

Happy: Come on up. Tell that to Dad. Let's give him a whirl. Come on.

Biff (steamed up): You know, with ten thousand bucks, boy!

Happy (as they go into the living-room): That's the talk, Biff, that's the first time I've heard the old confidence out of you! *(From within the living-room, fading off.)* You're gonna live with me, kid, and any babe you want just say the word . . . (The last lines are hardly heard. They are mounting the stairs to their parents' bedroom.)*

Linda (entering her bedroom and addressing Willy, who is in the bathroom. She is straightening the bed for him): Can you do anything about the shower? It drips.

Willy (from the bathroom): All of a sudden everything falls to pieces! Goddam plumbing, oughta be sued, those people. I hardly finished putting it in and the thing . . . *(His words rumble off.)*

Linda: I'm just wondering if Oliver will remember him. You think he might?

Willy (coming out of the bathroom in his pajamas): Remember him? What's the matter with you, you crazy? If he'd've stayed with Oliver he'd be on top by now! Wait'll Oliver gets a look at him. You don't know the average caliber any more. The average young man today — *(he is getting into bed)* — is got a caliber of zero. Greatest thing in the world for him was to bum around.

Biff and Happy enter the bedroom. Slight pause.

Willy (stops short, looking at Biff): Glad to hear it, boy.
Happy: He wanted to say good night to you, sport.
Willy (to Biff): Yeah. Knock him dead, boy. What'd you want to tell me?
Biff: Just take it easy, Pop. Good night. *(He turns to go.)*
Willy (unable to resist): And if anything falls off the desk while you're talking to him — like a package or something — don't you pick it up. They have office boys for that.
Linda: I'll make a big breakfast —
Willy: Will you let me finish? *(To Biff.)* Tell him you were in the business in the West. Not farm work.
Biff: All right, Dad.
Linda: I think everything —
Willy (going right through her speech): And don't undersell yourself. No less than fifteen thousand dollars.
Biff (unable to bear him): Okay. Good night, Mom. *(He starts moving.)*
Willy: Because you got a greatness in you, Biff, remember that. You got all kinds a greatness . . . *(He lies back, exhausted. Biff walks out.)*
Linda (calling after Biff): Sleep well, darling!
Happy: I'm gonna get married, Mom. I wanted to tell you.
Linda: Go to sleep, dear.
Happy (going): I just wanted to tell you.
Willy: Keep up the good work. *(Happy exits.)* God . . . remember that Ebbets Field game? The championship of the city?
Linda: Just rest. Should I sing to you?
Willy: Yeah. Sing to me. *(Linda hums a soft lullaby.)* When that team came out — he was the tallest, remember?
Linda: Oh, yes. And in gold.

Biff enters the darkened kitchen, takes a cigarette, and leaves the house. He comes downstage into a golden pool of light. He smokes, staring at the night.

Willy: Like a young god. Hercules — something like that. And the sun, the sun all around him. Remember how he waved to me? Right up from the field, with the representatives of three colleges standing by? And the buyers I brought, and the cheers when he came out — Loman, Loman, Loman! God Almighty, he'll be great yet. A star like that, magnificent, can never really fade away!

The light on Willy is fading. The gas heater begins to glow through the kitchen wall, near the stairs, a blue flame beneath red coils.

Linda (timidly): Willy dear, what has he got against you?
Willy: I'm so tired. Don't talk any more.

Biff slowly returns to the kitchen. He stops, stares toward the heater.

Linda: Will you ask Howard to let you work in New York?
Willy: First thing in the morning. Everything'll be all right.

Biff reaches behind the heater and draws out a length of rubber tubing. He is horrified and turns his head toward Willy's room, still dimly lit, from which the strains of Linda's desperate but monotonous humming rise.

Willy (*staring through the window into the moonlight*): Gee, look at the moon moving between the buildings!

Biff wraps the tubing around his hand and quickly goes up the stairs.

Curtain

ACT II

Music is heard, gay and bright. The curtain rises as the music fades away. Willy, in shirt sleeves, is sitting at the kitchen table, sipping coffee, his hat in his lap. Linda is filling his cup when she can.

Willy: Wonderful coffee. Meal in itself.

Linda: Can I make you some eggs?

Willy: No. Take a breath.

Linda: You look so rested, dear.

Willy: I slept like a dead one. First time in months. Imagine, sleeping till ten on a Tuesday morning. Boys left nice and early, heh?

Linda: They were out of here by eight o'clock.

Willy: Good work!

Linda: It was so thrilling to see them leaving together. I can't get over the shaving lotion in this house!

Willy (*smiling*): Mmm —

Linda: Biff was very changed this morning. His whole attitude seemed to be hopeful. He couldn't wait to get downtown to see Oliver.

Willy: He's heading for a change. There's no question, there simply are certain men that take longer to get — solidified. How did he dress?

Linda: His blue suit. He's so handsome in that suit. He could be a — anything in that suit!

Willy gets up from the table. Linda holds his jacket for him.

Willy: There's no question, no question at all. Gee, on the way home tonight I'd like to buy some seeds.

Linda (*laughing*): That'd be wonderful. But not enough sun gets back there. Nothing'll grow any more.

Willy: You wait, kid, before it's all over we're gonna get a little place out in the country, and I'll raise some vegetables, a couple of chickens . . .

Linda: You'll do it yet, dear.

Willy walks out of his jacket. Linda follows him.

Willy: And they'll get married, and come for a weekend. I'd build a little guest house. 'Cause I got so many fine tools, all I'd need would be a little lumber and some peace of mind.

Linda (*joyfully*): I sewed the lining . . .

Willy: I could build two guest houses, so they'd both come. Did he decide how much he's going to ask Oliver for?

Linda (getting him into the jacket): He didn't mention it, but I imagine ten or fifteen thousand. You going to talk to Howard today?

Willy: Yeah. I'll put it to him straight and simple. He'll just have to take me off the road.

Linda: And Willy, don't forget to ask for a little advance, because we've got the insurance premium. It's the grace period now.

Willy: That's a hundred . . . ?

Linda: A hundred and eight, sixty-eight. Because we're a little short again.

Willy: Why are we short?

Linda: Well, you had the motor job on the car . . .

Willy: That goddam Studebaker!

Linda: And you got one more payment on the refrigerator . . .

Willy: But it just broke again!

Linda: Well, it's old, dear.

Willy: I told you we should've bought a well-advertised machine. Charley bought a General Electric and it's twenty years old and it's still good, that son-of-a-bitch.

Linda: But, Willy —

Willy: Whoever heard of a Hastings refrigerator? Once in my life I would like to own something outright before it's broken! I'm always in a race with the junkyard! I just finished paying for the car and it's on its last legs. The refrigerator consumes belts like a goddam maniac. They time those things. They time them so when you finally paid for them, they're used up.

Linda (buttoning up his jacket as he unbuttons it): All told, about two hundred dollars would carry us, dear. But that includes the last payment on the mortgage. After this payment, Willy, the house belongs to us.

Willy: It's twenty-five years!

Linda: Biff was nine years old when we bought it.

Willy: Well, that's a great thing. To weather a twenty-five year mortgage is —

Linda: It's an accomplishment.

Willy: All the cement, the lumber, the reconstruction I put in this house! There ain't a crack to be found in it any more.

Linda: Well, it served its purpose.

Willy: What purpose? Some stranger'll come along, move in, and that's that. If only Biff would take this house, and raise a family . . . *(He starts to go.)* Good-by, I'm late.

Linda (suddenly remembering): Oh, I forgot! You're supposed to meet them for dinner.

Willy: Me?

Linda: At Frank's Chop House on Forty-eighth near Sixth Avenue.

Willy: Is that so! How about you?

Linda: No, just the three of you. They're gonna blow you to a big meal!

Willy: Don't say! Who thought of that?

Linda: Biff came to me this morning, Willy, and he said, "Tell Dad, we want to blow him to a big meal." Be there six o'clock. You and your two boys are going to have dinner.

Willy: Gee whiz! That's really somethin'. I'm gonna knock Howard for a loop, kid. I'll get an advance, and I'll come home with a New York job. Goddammit, now I'm gonna do it!

Linda: Oh, that's the spirit, Willy!

Willy: I will never get behind a wheel the rest of my life!

Linda: It's changing, Willy, I can feel it changing!

Willy: Beyond a question. G'by, I'm late. *(He starts to go again.)*

Linda (calling after him as she runs to the kitchen table for a handkerchief): You got your glasses?

Willy: (feels for them, then comes back in): Yeah, yeah, got my glasses.

Linda (giving him the handkerchief): And a handkerchief.

Willy: Yeah, handkerchief.

Linda: And your saccharine?

Willy: Yeah, my saccharine.

Linda: Be careful on the subway stairs.

She kisses him, and a silk stocking is seen hanging from her hand. Willy notices it.

Willy: Will you stop mending stockings? At least while I'm in the house. It gets me nervous. I can't tell you. Please.

Linda hides the stocking in her hand as she follows Willy across the forestage in front of the house.

Linda: Remember, Frank's Chop House.

Willy (passing the apron): Maybe beets would grow out there.

Linda (laughing): But you tried so many times.

Willy: Yeah. Well, don't work hard today. *(He disappears around the right corner of the house.)*

Linda: Be careful!

As Willy vanishes, Linda waves to him. Suddenly the phone rings. She runs across the stage and into the kitchen and lifts it.

Linda: Hello? Oh, Biff! I'm so glad you called, I just . . . Yes, sure, I just told him. Yes, he'll be there for dinner at six o'clock, I didn't forget. Listen, I was just dying to tell you. You know that little rubber pipe I told you about? That he connected to the gas heater? I finally decided to go down the cellar this morning and take it away and destroy it. But it's gone! Imagine? He took it away himself, it isn't there! *(She listens.)* When? Oh, then you took it. Oh — nothing, it's just that I'd hoped he'd taken it away himself. Oh, I'm not worried, darling, because this morning he left in such high spirits, it was like the old days! I'm not afraid any more. Did Mr. Oliver see you? . . . Well, you wait there then. And make a nice impression on him, darling. Just don't perspire too much before you see him. And have a nice time with Dad. He may have big news too! . . . That's right, a New York job. And be sweet to him tonight, dear. Be loving to him. Because he's only a little boat looking for a harbor. *(She is trembling with sorrow and joy.)* Oh, that's wonderful, Biff, you'll save his life. Thanks, darling. Just put your arm around him when he comes into the restaurant. Give him a smile. That's the boy . . . Good-bye, dear. . . . You got your comb? . . . That's fine. Good-bye, Biff dear.

In the middle of her speech, Howard Wagner, thirty-six, wheels in a small type-writer table on which is a wire-recording machine and proceeds to plug it in. This is on the left forestage. Light slowly fades on Linda as it rises on Howard.

Howard is intent on threading the machine and only glances over his shoulder as Willy appears.

Willy: Pst! Pst!

Howard: Hello, Willy, come in.

Willy: Like to have a little talk with you, Howard.

Howard: Sorry to keep you waiting. I'll be with you in a minute.

Willy: What's that, Howard?

Howard: Didn't you ever see one of these? Wire recorder.

Willy: Oh. Can we talk a minute?

Howard: Records things. Just got delivery yesterday. Been driving me crazy, the most terrific machine I ever saw in my life. I was up all night with it.

Willy: What do you do with it?

Howard: I bought it for dictation, but you can do anything with it. Listen to this. I had it home last night. Listen to what I picked up. The first one is my daughter. Get this. *(He flicks the switch and "Roll Out the Barrel" is heard being whistled.)* Listen to that kid whistle.

Willy: That is lifelike, isn't it?

Howard: Seven years old. Get that tone.

Willy: Ts, ts. Like to ask a little favor if you . . .

The whistling breaks off, and the voice of Howard's daughter is heard.

His Daughter: "Now you, Daddy."

Howard: She's crazy for me! *(Again the same song is whistled.)* That's me! Ha! *(He winks.)*

Willy: You're very good!

The whistling breaks off again. The machine runs silent for a moment.

Howard: Sh! Get this now, this is my son.

His Son: "The capital of Alabama is Montgomery; the capital of Arizona is Phoenix; the capital of Arkansas is Little Rock; the capital of California is Sacramento . . ." *(and on, and on).*

Howard (holding up five fingers): Five years old, Willy!

Willy: He'll make an announcer some day!

His Son (continuing): "The capital . . ."

Howard: Get that — alphabetical order! *(The machine breaks off suddenly.)* Wait a minute. The maid kicked the plug out.

Willy: It certainly is a —

Howard: Sh, for God's sake!

His Son: "It's nine o'clock, Bulova watch time. So I have to go to sleep."

Willy: That really is —

Howard: Wait a minute! The next is my wife.

They wait.

Howard's Voice: "Go on, say something." *(Pause.)* "Well, you gonna talk?"

His Wife: "I can't think of anything."

Howard's Voice: "Well, talk — it's turning."

His Wife (shyly, beaten): "Hello." *(Silence.)* "Oh, Howard, I can't talk into this . . ."

Howard (snapping the machine off): That was my wife.

Willy: That is a wonderful machine. Can we —

Howard: I tell you, Willy, I'm gonna take my camera, and my bandsaw, and all my hobbies, and out they go. This is the most fascinating relaxation I ever found.

Willy: I think I'll get one myself.

Howard: Sure, they're only a hundred and a half. You can't do without it. Supposing you wanna hear Jack Benny, see? But you can't be at home at that hour. So you tell the maid to turn the radio on when Jack Benny comes on, and this automatically goes on with the radio . . .

Willy: And when you come home you . . .

Howard: You can come home twelve o'clock, one o'clock, any time you like, and you get yourself a Coke and sit yourself down, throw the switch, and there's Jack Benny's program in the middle of the night!

Willy: I'm definitely going to get one. Because lots of time I'm on the road, and I think to myself, what I must be missing on the radio!

Howard: Don't you have a radio in the car?

Willy: Well, yeah, but who ever thinks of turning it on?

Howard: Say, aren't you supposed to be in Boston?

Willy: That's what I want to talk to you about, Howard. You got a minute? *(He draws a chair in from the wing.)*

Howard: What happened? What're you doing here?

Willy: Well . . .

Howard: You didn't crack up again, did you?

Willy: Oh, no. No . . .

Howard: Geez, you had me worried there for a minute. What's the trouble?

Willy: Well, tell you the truth, Howard. I've come to the decision that I'd rather not travel any more.

Howard: Not travel! Well, what'll you do?

Willy: Remember, Christmas time, when you had the party here? You said you'd try to think of some spot for me here in town.

Howard: With us?

Willy: Well, sure.

Howard: Oh, yeah, yeah. I remember. Well, I couldn't think of anything for you, Willy.

Willy: I tell ya, Howard. The kids are all grown up, y'know. I don't need much any more. If I could take home — well, sixty-five dollars a week, I could swing it.

Howard: Yeah, but Willy, see I —

Willy: I tell ya why, Howard. Speaking frankly and between the two of us, y'know — I'm just a little tired.

Howard: Oh, I could understand that, Willy. But you're a road man, Willy, and we do a road business. We've only got a half-dozen salesmen on the floor here.

Willy: God knows, Howard, I never asked a favor of any man. But I was with the firm when your father used to carry you in here in his arms.

Howard: I know that, Willy, but —

Willy: Your father came to me the day you were born and asked me what I thought of the name of Howard, may he rest in peace.

Howard: I appreciate that, Willy, but there just is no spot here for you. If I had a spot I'd slam you right in, but I just don't have a single solitary spot.

He looks for his lighter. Willy has picked it up and gives it to him. Pause.

Willy (with increasing anger): Howard, all I need to set my table is fifty dollars a week.

Howard: But where am I going to put you, kid?

Willy: Look, it isn't a question of whether I can sell merchandise, is it?

Howard: No, but it's a business, kid, and everybody's gotta pull his own weight.

Willy (desperately): Just let me tell you a story, Howard —

Howard: 'Cause you gotta admit, business is business.

Willy (angrily): Business is definitely business, but just listen for a minute. You don't understand this. When I was a boy — eighteen, nineteen — I was already on the road. And there was a question in my mind as to whether selling had a future for me. Because in those days I had a yearning to go to Alaska. See, there were three gold strikes in one month in Alaska, and I felt like going out. Just for the ride, you might say.

Howard (barely interested): Don't say.

Willy: Oh, yeah, my father lived many years in Alaska. He was an adventurous man. We've got quite a little streak of self-reliance in our family. I thought I'd go out with my older brother and try to locate him, and maybe settle in the North with the old man. And I was almost decided to go, when I met a salesman in the Parker House. His name was Dave Singleman. And he was eighty-four years old, and he'd drummed merchandise in thirty-one states. And old Dave, he'd go up to his room, y'understand, put on his green velvet slippers — I'll never forget — and pick up his phone and call the buyers, and without ever leaving his room, at the age of eighty-four, he made his living. And when I saw that, I realized that selling was the greatest career a man could want. 'Cause what could be more satisfying than to be able to go, at the age of eighty-four, into twenty or thirty different cities, and pick up a phone, and be remembered and loved and helped by so many different people? Do you know? when he died — and by the way he died the death of a salesman, in his green velvet slippers in the smoker of the New York, New Haven, and Hartford, going into Boston — when he died, hundreds of salesmen and buyers were at his funeral. Things were sad on a lotta trains for months after that. *(He stands up. Howard has not looked at him.)* In those days there was personality in it, Howard. There was respect, and comradeship, and gratitude in it. Today, it's all cut and dried, and there's no chance for bringing friendship to bear — or personality. You see what I mean? They don't know me any more.

Howard (moving away, to the right): That's just the thing, Willy.

Willy: If I had forty dollars a week — that's all I'd need. Forty dollars, Howard.

Howard: Kid, I can't take blood from a stone, I —

Willy (desperation is on him now): Howard, the year Al Smith° was nominated, your father came to me and —

Howard (starting to go off): I've got to see some people, kid.

Al Smith: Democratic candidate for president of the United States in 1928; lost the election to Herbert Hoover.

Willy (stopping him): I'm talking about your father! There were promises made across this desk! You mustn't tell me you've got people to see — I put thirty-four years into this firm, Howard, and now I can't pay my insurance! You can't eat the orange and throw the peel away — a man is not a piece of fruit! *(After a pause.)* Now pay attention. Your father — in 1928 I had a big year. I averaged a hundred and seventy dollars a week in commissions.

Howard (impatiently): Now, Willy, you never averaged —

Willy (banging his hand on the desk): I averaged a hundred and seventy dollars a week in the year of 1928! And your father came to me — or rather, I was in the office here — it was right over this desk — and he put his hand on my shoulder —

Howard (getting up): You'll have to excuse me, Willy, I gotta see some people. Pull yourself together. *(Going out.)* I'll be back in a little while.

On Howard's exit, the light on his chair grows very bright and strange.

Willy: Pull myself together! What the hell did I say to him? My God, I was yelling at him! How could I! *(Willy breaks off, staring at the light, which occupies the chair, animating it. He approaches this chair, standing across the desk from it.)* Frank, Frank, don't you remember what you told me that time? How you put your hand on my shoulder, and Frank . . . *(He leans on the desk and as he speaks the dead man's name he accidentally switches on the recorder, and instantly:)*

Howard's Son: ". . . of New York is Albany. The capital of Ohio is Cincinnati, the capital of Rhode Island is . . ." *(The recitation continues.)*

Willy (leaping away with fright, shouting): Ha! Howard! Howard! Howard!

Howard (rushing in): What happened?

Willy (pointing at the machine, which continues nasally, childishly, with the capital cities): Shut it off! Shut it off!

Howard (pulling the plug out): Look, Willy . . .

Willy (pressing his hands to his eyes): I gotta get myself some coffee. I'll get some coffee . . .

Willy starts to walk out. Howard stops him.

Howard (rolling up the cord): Willy, look . . .

Willy: I'll go to Boston.

Howard: Willy, you can't go to Boston for us.

Willy: Why can't I go?

Howard: I don't want you to represent us. I've been meaning to tell you for a long time now.

Willy: Howard, are you firing me?

Howard: I think you need a good long rest, Willy.

Willy: Howard —

Howard: And when you feel better, come back, and we'll see if we can work something out.

Willy: But I gotta earn money, Howard. I'm in no position to —

Howard: Where are your sons? Why don't your sons give you a hand?

Willy: They're working on a very big deal.

Howard: This is no time for false pride, Willy. You go to your sons and you tell them that you're tired. You've got two great boys, haven't you?

Willy: Oh, no question, no question, but in the meantime . . .

Howard: Then that's that, heh?

Willy: All right, I'll go to Boston tomorrow.

Howard: No, no.

Willy: I can't throw myself on my sons. I'm not a cripple!

Howard: Look, kid, I'm busy this morning.

Willy (grasping Howard's arm): Howard, you've got to let me go to Boston!

Howard (hard, keeping himself under control): I've got a line of people to see this morning. Sit down, take five minutes, and pull yourself together, and then go home, will ya? I need the office, Willy. *(He starts to go, turns, remembering the recorder, starts to push off the table holding the recorder.)* Oh, yeah. Whenever you can this week, stop by and drop off the samples. You'll feel better, Willy, and then come back and we'll talk. Pull yourself together, kid, there's people outside.

Howard exits, pushing the table off left. Willy stares into space, exhausted. Now the music is heard — Ben's music — first distantly, then closer, closer. As Willy speaks, Ben enters from the right. He carries valise and umbrella.

Willy: Oh, Ben, how did you do it? What is the answer? Did you wind up the Alaska deal already?

Ben: Doesn't take much time if you know what you're doing. Just a short business trip. Boarding ship in an hour. Wanted to say good-by.

Willy: Ben, I've got to talk to you.

Ben (glancing at his watch): Haven't the time, William.

Willy (crossing the apron to Ben): Ben, nothing's working out. I don't know what to do.

Ben: Now, look here, William. I've bought timberland in Alaska and I need a man to look after things for me.

Willy: God, timberland! Me and my boys in those grand outdoors!

Ben: You've a new continent at your doorstep, William. Get out of these cities, they're full of talk and time payments and courts of law. Screw on your fists and you can fight for a fortune up there.

Willy: Yes, yes! Linda, Linda!

Linda enters as of old, with the wash.

Linda: Oh, you're back?

Ben: I haven't much time.

Willy: No, wait! Linda, he's got a proposition for me in Alaska.

Linda: But you've got — *(To Ben.)* He's got a beautiful job here.

Willy: But in Alaska, kid, I could —

Linda: You're doing well enough, Willy!

Ben (to Linda): Enough for what, my dear?

Linda (frightened of Ben and angry at him): Don't say those things to him! Enough to be happy right here, right now. *(To Willy, while Ben laughs.)* Why must everybody conquer the world? You're well liked, and the boys love you, and someday — *(to Ben)* — why, old man Wagner told him just the other day that if he keeps it up he'll be a member of the firm, didn't he, Willy?

Willy: Sure, sure. I am building something with this firm, Ben, and if a man is building something he must be on the right track, mustn't he?

Ben: What are you building? Lay your hand on it. Where is it?

Willy (hesitantly): That's true, Linda, there's nothing.

Linda: Why? *(To Ben.)* There's a man eighty-four years old —

Willy: That's right, Ben, that's right. When I look at that man I say, what is there to worry about?

Ben: Bah!

Willy: It's true, Ben. All he has to do is go into any city, pick up the phone, and he's making his living and you know why?

Ben (picking up his valise): I've got to go.

Willy (holding Ben back): Look at this boy!

Biff, in his high school sweater, enters carrying suitcase. Happy carries Biff's shoulder guards, gold helmet, and football pants.

Willy: Without a penny to his name, three great universities are begging for him, and from there the sky's the limit, because it's not what you do, Ben. It's who you know and the smile on your face! It's contacts, Ben, contacts! The whole wealth of Alaska passes over the lunch table at the Commodore Hotel, and that's the wonder, the wonder of this country, that a man can end with diamonds here on the basis of being liked! *(He turns to Biff.)* And that's why when you get out on that field today it's important. Because thousands of people will be rooting for you and loving you. *(To Ben, who has again begun to leave.)* And Ben! when he walks into a business office his name will sound out like a bell and all the doors will open to him! I've seen it, Ben, I've seen it a thousand times! You can't feel it with your hand like timber, but it's there!

Ben: Good-by, William.

Willy: Ben, am I right? Don't you think I'm right? I value your advice.

Ben: There's a new continent at your doorstep, William. You could walk out rich. Rich! *(He is gone.)*

Willy: We'll do it here, Ben! You hear me? We're gonna do it here!

Young Bernard rushes in. The gay music of the Boys is heard.

Bernard: Oh, gee, I was afraid you left already!

Willy: Why? What time is it?

Bernard: It's half-past one!

Willy: Well, come on, everybody! Ebbets Field next stop! Where's the pennants? *(He rushes through the wall-line of the kitchen and out into the living-room.)*

Linda (to Biff): Did you pack fresh underwear?

Biff (who has been limbering up): I want to go!

Bernard: Biff, I'm carrying your helmet, ain't I?

Happy: I'm carrying the helmet.

Bernard: How am I going to get in the locker room?

Linda: Let him carry the shoulder guards. *(She puts her coat and hat on in the kitchen.)*

Bernard: Can I, Biff? 'Cause I told everybody I'm going to be in the locker room.

Happy: In Ebbets Field it's the clubhouse.

Bernard: I meant the clubhouse. Biff!

Happy: Biff!

Biff (grandly, after a slight pause): Let him carry the shoulder guards.

Happy (as he gives Bernard the shoulder guards): Stay close to us now.

Willy rushes in with the pennants.

Willy (handing them out): Everybody wave when Biff comes out on the field. *(Happy and Bernard run off.)* You set now, boy?

The music has died away.

Biff: Ready to go, Pop. Every muscle is ready.

Willy (at the edge of the apron): You realize what this means?

Biff: That's right, Pop.

Willy (feeling Biff's muscles): You're comin' home this afternoon captain of the All-Scholastic Championship Team of the City of New York.

Biff: I got it, Pop. And remember, pal, when I take off my helmet, that touchdown is for you.

Willy: Let's go! *(He is starting out, with his arm around Biff, when Charley enters, as of old, in knickers.)* I got no room for you, Charley.

Charley: Room? For what?

Willy: In the car.

Charley: You goin' for a ride? I wanted to shoot some casino.

Willy (furiously): Casino! *(Incredulously.)* Don't you realize what today is?

Linda: Oh, he knows, Willy. He's just kidding you.

Willy: That's nothing to kid about!

Charley: No, Linda, what's goin' on?

Linda: He's playing in Ebbets Field.

Charley: Baseball in this weather?

Willy: Don't talk to him. Come on, come on! *(He is pushing them out.)*

Charley: Wait a minute, didn't you hear the news?

Willy: What?

Charley: Don't you listen to the radio? Ebbets Field just blew up.

Willy: You go to hell! *(Charley laughs. Pushing them out.)* Come on, come on! We're late.

Charley (as they go): Knock a homer, Biff, knock a homer!

Willy (the last to leave, turning to Charley): I don't think that was funny, Charley. This is the greatest day of his life.

Charley: Willy, when are you going to grow up?

Willy: Yeah, heh? When this game is over, Charley, you'll be laughing out of the other side of your face. They'll be calling him another Red Grange. Twenty-five thousand a year.

Charley (kidding): Is that so?

Willy: Yeah, that's so.

Charley: Well, then, I'm sorry, Willy. But tell me something.

Willy: What?

Charley: Who is Red Grange?

Willy: Put up your hands. Goddam you, put up your hands!

Charley, chuckling, shakes his head and walks away, around the left corner of the stage. Willy follows him. The music rises to a mocking frenzy.

Willy: Who the hell do you think you are, better than everybody else? You don't know everything, you big, ignorant, stupid . . . Put up your hands!

Light rises, on the right side of the forestage, on a small table in the reception room of Charley's office. Traffic sounds are heard. Bernard, now mature, sits whistling to himself. A pair of tennis rackets and an overnight bag are on the floor beside him.

Willy (offstage): What are you walking away for? Don't walk away! If you're going to say something say it to my face! I know you laugh at me behind my back. You'll laugh out of the other side of your goddam face after this game. Touchdown! Touchdown! Eighty thousand people! Touchdown! Right between the goal posts.

Bernard is a quiet, earnest, but self-assured young man. Willy's voice is coming from right upstage now. Bernard lowers his feet off the table and listens. Jenny, his father's secretary, enters.

Jenny (distressed): Say, Bernard, will you go out in the hall?

Bernard: What is that noise? Who is it?

Jenny: Mr. Loman. He just got off the elevator.

Bernard (getting up): Who's he arguing with?

Jenny: Nobody. There's nobody with him. I can't deal with him any more, and your father gets all upset everytime he comes. I've got a lot of typing to do, and your father's waiting to sign it. Will you see him?

Willy (entering): Touchdown! Touch — *(He sees Jenny.)* Jenny, Jenny, good to see you. How're ya? Workin'? Or still honest?

Jenny: Fine. How've you been feeling?

Willy: Not much any more, Jenny. Ha, ha! *(He is surprised to see the rackets.)*

Bernard: Hello, Uncle Willy.

Willy (almost shocked): Bernard! Well, look who's here! *(He comes quickly, guiltily, to Bernard and warmly shakes his hand.)*

Bernard: How are you? Good to see you.

Willy: What are you doing here?

Bernard: Oh, just stopped by to see Pop. Get off my feet till my train leaves. I'm going to Washington in a few minutes.

Willy: Is he in?

Bernard: Yes, he's in his office with the accountant. Sit down.

Willy (sitting down): What're you going to do in Washington?

Bernard: Oh, just a case I've got there, Willy.

Willy: That so? *(Indicating the rackets.)* You going to play tennis there?

Bernard: I'm staying with a friend who's got a court.

Willy: Don't say. His own tennis court. Must be fine people, I bet.

Bernard: They are, very nice. Dad tells me Biff's in town.

Willy (with a big smile): Yeah, Biff's in. Working on a very big deal, Bernard.

Bernard: What's Biff doing?

Willy: Well, he's been doing very big things in the West. But he decided to establish himself here. Very big. We're having dinner. Did I hear your wife had a boy?

Bernard: That's right. Our second.

Willy: Two boys! What do you know!

Bernard: What kind of a deal has Biff got?

Willy: Well, Bill Oliver — very big sporting-goods man — he wants Biff very badly. Called him in from the West. Long distance, carte blanche, special deliveries. Your friends have their own private tennis court?

Bernard: You still with the old firm, Willy?

Willy (after a pause): I'm — I'm overjoyed to see how you made the grade, Bernard, overjoyed. It's an encouraging thing to see a young man really — really — Looks very good for Biff — very — *(He breaks off, then.)* Bernard — *(He is so full of emotion, he breaks off again.)*

Bernard: What is it, Willy?

Willy (small and alone): What — what's the secret?

Bernard: What secret?

Willy: How — how did you? Why didn't he ever catch on?

Bernard: I wouldn't know that, Willy.

Willy (confidentially, desperately): You were his friend, his boyhood friend. There's something I don't understand about it. His life ended after that Ebbets Field game. From the age of seventeen nothing good ever happened to him.

Bernard: He never trained himself for anything.

Willy: But he did, he did. After high school he took so many correspondence courses. Radio mechanics; television; God knows what, and never made the slightest mark.

Bernard (taking off his glasses): Willy, do you want to talk candidly?

Willy (rising, faces Bernard): I regard you as a very brilliant man, Bernard. I value your advice.

Bernard: Oh, the hell with the advice, Willy. I couldn't advise you. There's just one thing I've always wanted to ask you. When he was supposed to graduate, and the math teacher flunked him —

Willy: Oh, that son-of-a-bitch ruined his life.

Bernard: Yeah, but, Willy, all he had to do was go to summer school and make up that subject.

Willy: That's right, that's right.

Bernard: Did you tell him not to go to summer school?

Willy: Me? I begged him to go. I ordered him to go!

Bernard: Then why wouldn't he go?

Willy: Why? Why! Bernard, that question has been trailing me like a ghost for the last fifteen years. He flunked the subject, and laid down and died like a hammer hit him!

Bernard: Take it easy, kid.

Willy: Let me talk to you — I got nobody to talk to. Bernard, Bernard, was it my fault? Y'see? It keeps going around in my mind, maybe I did something to him. I got nothing to give him.

Bernard: Don't take it so hard.

Willy: Why did he lay down? What is the story there? You were his friend!

Bernard: Willy, I remember, it was June, and our grades came out. And he'd flunked math.

Willy: That son-of-a-bitch!

Bernard: No, it wasn't right then. Biff just got very angry, I remember, and he was ready to enroll in summer school.

Willy (surprised): He was?

Bernard: He wasn't beaten by it at all. But then, Willy, he disappeared from the block for almost a month. And I got the idea that he'd gone up to New England to see you. Did he have a talk with you then?

Willy stares in silence.

Bernard: Willy?

Willy (with a strong edge of resentment in his voice): Yeah, he came to Boston. What about it?

Bernard: Well, just that when he came back — I'll never forget this, it always mystifies me. Because I'd thought so well of Biff, even though he'd always taken advantage of me. I loved him, Willy, y'know? And he came back after that month and took his sneakers — remember those sneakers with "University of Virginia" printed on them? He was so proud of those, wore them every day. And he took them down in the cellar, and burned them up in the furnace. We had a fist fight. It lasted at least half an hour. Just the two of us, punching each other down the cellar, and crying right through it. I've often thought of how strange it was that I knew he'd given up his life. What happened in Boston, Willy?

Willy looks at him as at an intruder.

Bernard: I just bring it up because you asked me.

Willy (angrily): Nothing. What do you mean, "What happened?" What's that got to do with anything?

Bernard: Well, don't get sore.

Willy: What are you trying to do, blame it on me? If a boy lays down is that my fault?

Bernard: Now, Willy, don't get —

Willy: Well, don't — don't talk to me that way! What does that mean, "What happened?"

Charley enters. He is in his vest, and he carries a bottle of bourbon.

Charley: Hey, you're going to miss that train. (He waves the bottle.)

Bernard: Yeah, I'm going. (He takes the bottle.) Thanks, Pop. (He picks up his rackets and bag.) Good-by, Willy, and don't worry about it. You know. "If at first you don't succeed . . ."

Willy: Yes, I believe in that.

Bernard: But sometimes, Willy, it's better for a man just to walk away.

Willy: Walk away?

Bernard: That's right.

Willy: But if you can't walk away?

Bernard (after a slight pause): I guess that's when it's tough. (Extending his hand.) Good-by, Willy.

Willy (shaking Bernard's hand): Good-by, boy.

Charley (an arm on Bernard's shoulder): How do you like this kid? Gonna argue a case in front of the Supreme Court.

Bernard (protesting): Pop!

Willy (genuinely shocked, pained, and happy): No! The Supreme Court!

Bernard: I gotta run. 'By, Dad!

Charley: Knock 'em dead, Bernard!

Bernard goes off.

Willy (as Charley takes out his wallet): The Supreme Court! And he didn't even mention it!

Charley (counting out money on the desk): He don't have to — he's gonna do it.

Willy: And you never told him what to do, did you? You never took any interest in him.

Charley: My salvation is that I never took any interest in any thing. There's some money — fifty dollars. I got an accountant inside.

Willy: Charley, look . . . *(With difficulty.)* I got my insurance to pay. If you can manage it — I need a hundred and ten dollars.

Charley doesn't reply for a moment; merely stops moving.

Willy: I'd draw it from my bank but Linda would know, and I . . .

Charley: Sit down, Willy.

Willy (moving toward the chair): I'm keeping an account of everything, remember. I'll pay every penny back. *(He sits.)*

Charley: Now listen to me, Willy.

Willy: I want you to know I appreciate . . .

Charley (sitting down on the table): Willy, what're you doin'? What the hell is goin' on in your head?

Willy: Why? I'm simply . . .

Charley: I offered you a job. You can make fifty dollars a week. And I won't send you on the road.

Willy: I've got a job.

Charley: Without pay? What kind of a job is a job without pay? *(He rises.)* Now, look, kid, enough is enough. I'm no genius but I know when I'm being insulted.

Willy: Insulted!

Charley: Why don't you want to work for me?

Willy: What's the matter with you? I've got a job.

Charley: Then what're you walkin' in here every week for?

Willy (getting up): Well, if you don't want me to walk in here —

Charley: I am offering you a job.

Willy: I don't want your goddam job!

Charley: When the hell are you going to grow up?

Willy (furiously): You big ignoramus, if you say that to me again I'll rap you one! I don't care how big you are! *(He's ready to fight.)*

Pause.

Charley (kindly, going to him): How much do you need, Willy?

Willy: Charley, I'm strapped. I'm strapped. I don't know what to do. I was just fired.

Charley: Howard fired you?

Willy: That snotnose. Imagine that? I named him. I named him Howard.

Charley: Willy, when're you gonna realize that them things don't mean anything? You named him Howard, but you can't sell that. The only thing you got in this world is what you can sell. And the funny thing is that you're a salesman, and you don't know that.

Willy: I've always tried to think otherwise, I guess. I always felt that if a man was impressive, and well liked, that nothing —

Charley: Why must everybody like you? Who liked J. P. Morgan? Was he impressive? In a Turkish bath he'd look like a butcher. But with his pockets on he was very well liked. Now listen, Willy, I know you don't like me, and nobody can say I'm in love with you, but I'll give you a job because — just for the hell of it, put it that way. Now what do you say?

Willy: I — I just can't work for you, Charley.

Charley: What're you, jealous of me?

Willy: I can't work for you, that's all, don't ask me why.

Charley (angered, takes out more bills): You been jealous of me all your life, you damned fool! Here, pay your insurance. *(He puts the money in Willy's hand.)*

Willy: I'm keeping strict accounts.

Charley: I've got some work to do. Take care of yourself. And pay your insurance.

Willy (moving to the right): Funny, y'know? After all the highways, and the trains, and the appointments, and the years, you end up worth more dead than alive.

Charley: Willy, nobody's worth nothin' dead. *(After a slight pause.)* Did you hear what I said?

Willy stands still, dreaming.

Charley: Willy!

Willy: Apologize to Bernard for me when you see him. I didn't mean to argue with him. He's a fine boy. They're all fine boys, and they'll end up big — all of them. Someday they'll all play tennis together. Wish me luck, Charley. He saw Bill Oliver today.

Charley: Good luck.

Willy (on the verge of tears): Charley, you're the only friend I got. Isn't that a remarkable thing? *(He goes out.)*

Charley: Jesus!

Charley stares after him a moment and follows. All light blacks out. Suddenly raucous music is heard, and a red glow rises behind the screen at right. Stanley, a young waiter, appears, carrying a table, followed by Happy, who is carrying two chairs.

Stanley (putting the table down): That's all right, Mr. Loman, I can handle it myself. *(He turns and takes the chairs from Happy and places them at the table.)*

Happy (glancing around): Oh, this is better.

Stanley: Sure, in the front there you're in the middle of all kinds a noise. Whenever you got a party, Mr. Loman, you just tell me and I'll put you back here. Y'know, there's a lotta people they don't like it private, because when they go out they like to see a lotta action around them because they're sick and tired to stay in the house by theirself. But I know you, you ain't from Hackensack. You know what I mean?

Happy (sitting down): So how's it coming, Stanley?

Stanley: Ah, it's a dog's life. I only wish during the war they'd a took me in the Army. I coulda been dead by now.

Happy: My brother's back, Stanley.

Stanley: Oh, he come back, heh? From the Far West.

Happy: Yeah, big cattle man, my brother, so treat him right. And my father's coming too.

Stanley: Oh, your father too!

Happy: You got a couple of nice lobsters?

Stanley: Hundred per cent, big.

Happy: I want them with the claws.

Stanley: Don't worry, I don't give you no mice. *(Happy laughs.)* How about some wine? It'll put a head on the meal.

Happy: No. You remember, Stanley, that recipe I brought you from overseas? With the champagne in it?

Stanley: Oh, yeah, sure. I still got it tacked up yet in the kitchen. But that'll have to cost a buck apiece anyways.

Happy: That's all right.

Stanley: What'd you, hit a number or somethin'?

Happy: No, it's a little celebration. My brother is — I think he pulled off a big deal today. I think we're going into business together.

Stanley: Great! That's the best for you. Because a family business, you know what I mean? — that's the best.

Happy: That's what I think.

Stanley: 'Cause what's the difference? Somebody steals? It's in the family. Know what I mean? *(Sotto voce.°)* Like this bartender here. The boss is goin' crazy what kinda leak he's got in the cash register. You put it in but it don't come out.

Happy (raising his head): Sh!

Stanley: What?

Happy: You notice I wasn't lookin' right or left, was I?

Stanley: No.

Happy: And my eyes are closed.

Stanley: So what's the — ?

Happy: Strudel's comin'.

Stanley (catching on, looks around): Ah, no, there's no —

He breaks off as a furred, lavishly dressed girl enters and sits at the next table. Both follow her with their eyes.

Stanley: Geez, how'd ya know?

Happy: I got radar or something. *(Staring directly at her profile.)* Oooooooo . . . Stanley.

Stanley: I think that's for you, Mr. Loman.

Happy: Look at that mouth. Oh, God. And the binoculars.

Stanley: Geez, you got a life, Mr. Loman.

Happy: Wait on her.

Stanley (going to the girl's table): Would you like a menu, ma'am?

Girl: I'm expecting someone, but I'd like a —

Sotto voce: Softly, "under the breath" (Italian).

Happy: Why don't you bring her — excuse me, miss, do you mind? I sell champagne, and I'd like you to try my brand. Bring her a champagne, Stanley.

Girl: That's awfully nice of you.

Happy: Don't mention it. It's all company money. *(He laughs.)*

Girl: That's a charming product to be selling, isn't it?

Happy: Oh, gets to be like everything else. Selling is selling, y'know.

Girl: I suppose.

Happy: You don't happen to sell, do you?

Girl: No, I don't sell.

Happy: Would you object to a compliment from a stranger? You ought to be on a magazine cover.

Girl (looking at him a little archly): I have been.

Stanley comes in with a glass of champagne.

Happy: What'd I say before, Stanley? You see? She's a cover girl.

Stanley: Oh, I could see, I could see.

Happy (to the Girl): What magazine?

Girl: Oh, a lot of them. *(She takes the drink.)* Thank you.

Happy: You know what they say in France, don't you? "Champagne is the drink of the complexion" — Hya, Biff!

Biff has entered and sits with Happy.

Biff: Hello, kid. Sorry I'm late.

Happy: I just got here. Uh, Miss — ?

Girl: Forsythe.

Happy: Miss Forsythe, this is my brother.

Biff: Is Dad here?

Happy: His name is Biff. You might've heard of him. Great football player.

Girl: Really? What team?

Happy: Are you familiar with football?

Girl: No, I'm afraid I'm not.

Happy: Biff is quarterback with the New York Giants.

Girl: Well, that is nice, isn't it? *(She drinks.)*

Happy: Good health.

Girl: I'm happy to meet you.

Happy: That's my name. Hap. It's really Harold, but at West Point they called me Happy.

Girl (now really impressed): Oh, I see. How do you do? *(She turns her profile.)*

Biff: Isn't Dad coming?

Happy: You want her?

Biff: Oh, I could never make that.

Happy: I remember the time that idea would never come into your head. Where's the old confidence, Biff?

Biff: I just saw Oliver —

Happy: Wait a minute. I've got to see that old confidence again. Do you want her? She's on call.

Biff: Oh, no. *(He turns to look at the Girl.)*

Happy: I'm telling you. Watch this. *(Turning to the Girl.)* Honey? *(She turns to him.)* Are you busy?

Girl: Well, I am . . . but I could make a phone call.

Happy: Do that, will you, honey? And see if you can get a friend. We'll be here for a while. Biff is one of the greatest football players in the country.

Girl (standing up): Well, I'm certainly happy to meet you.

Happy: Come back soon.

Girl: I'll try.

Happy: Don't try, honey, try hard.

The Girl exits. Stanley follows, shaking his head in bewildered admiration.

Happy: Isn't that a shame now? A beautiful girl like that? That's why I can't get married. There's not a good woman in a thousand. New York is loaded with them, kid!

Biff: Hap, look —

Happy: I told you she was on call!

Biff (strangely unnerved): Cut it out, will ya? I want to say something to you.

Happy: Did you see Oliver?

Biff: I saw him all right. Now look, I want to tell Dad a couple of things and I want you to help me.

Happy: What? Is he going to back you?

Biff: Are you crazy? You're out of your goddam head, you know that?

Happy: Why? What happened?

Biff (breathlessly): I did a terrible thing today, Hap. It's been the strangest day I ever went through. I'm all numb, I swear.

Happy: You mean he wouldn't see you?

Biff: Well, I waited six hours for him, see? All day. Kept sending my name in. Even tried to date his secretary so she'd get me to him, but no soap.

Happy: Because you're not showin' the old confidence, Biff. He remembered you, didn't he?

Biff (stopping Happy with a gesture): Finally, about five o'clock, he comes out. Didn't remember who I was or anything. I felt like such an idiot, Hap.

Happy: Did you tell him my Florida idea?

Biff: He walked away. I saw him for one minute. I got so mad I could've torn the walls down! How the hell did I ever get the idea I was a salesman there? I even believed myself that I'd been a salesman for him! And then he gave me one look and — I realized what a ridiculous lie my whole life has been! We've been talking in a dream for fifteen years. I was a shipping clerk.

Happy: What'd you do?

Biff (with great tension and wonder): Well, he left, see. And the secretary went out. I was all alone in the waiting-room. I don't know what came over me, Hap. The next thing I know I'm in his office — paneled walls, everything. I can't explain it. I — Hap, I took his fountain pen.

Happy: Geez, did he catch you?

Biff: I ran out. I ran down all eleven flights. I ran and ran and ran.

Happy: That was an awful dumb — what'd you do that for?

Biff (agonized): I don't know, I just — wanted to take something, I don't know. You gotta help me, Hap, I'm gonna tell Pop.

Happy: You crazy? What for?

Biff: Hap, he's got to understand that I'm not the man somebody lends that kind of money to. He thinks I've been spiting him all these years and it's eating him up.

Happy: That's just it. You tell him something nice.

Biff: I can't.

Happy: Say you got a lunch date with Oliver tomorrow.

Biff: So what do I do tomorrow?

Happy: You leave the house tomorrow and come back at night and say Oliver is thinking it over. And he thinks it over for a couple of weeks, and gradually it fades away and nobody's the worse.

Biff: But it'll go on forever!

Happy: Dad is never so happy as when he's looking forward to something!

Willy enters.

Happy: Hello, scout!

Willy: Gee, I haven't been here in years!

Stanley has followed Willy in and sets a chair for him. Stanley starts off but Happy stops him.

Happy: Stanley!

Stanley stands by, waiting for an order.

Biff (going to Willy with guilt, as to an invalid): Sit down, Pop. You want a drink?

Willy: Sure, I don't mind.

Biff: Let's get a load on.

Willy: You look worried.

Biff: N-no. *(To Stanley.)* Scotch all around. Make it doubles.

Stanley: Doubles, right. *(He goes.)*

Willy: You had a couple already, didn't you?

Biff: Just a couple, yeah.

Willy: Well, what happened, boy? *(Nodding affirmatively, with a smile.)* Everything go all right?

Biff (takes a breath, then reaches out and grasps Willy's hand.) Pal . . . *(He is smiling bravely, and Willy is smiling too.)* I had an experience today.

Happy: Terrific, Pop.

Willy: That so? What happened?

Biff (high, slightly alcoholic, above the earth): I'm going to tell you everything from first to last. It's been a strange day. *(Silence. He looks around, composes himself as best he can, but his breath keeps breaking the rhythm of his voice.)* I had to wait quite a while for him, and —

Willy: Oliver.

Biff: Yeah, Oliver. All day, as a matter of cold fact. And a lot of — instances — facts, Pop, facts about my life came back to me. Who was it, Pop? Who ever said I was a salesman with Oliver?

Willy: Well, you were.

Biff: No, Dad, I was a shipping clerk.

Willy: But you were practically —

Biff (with determination): Dad, I don't know who said it first, but I was never a salesman for Bill Oliver.

Willy: What're you talking about?

Biff: Let's hold on to the facts tonight, Pop. We're not going to get anywhere bullin' around. I was a shipping clerk.

Willy (angrily): All right, now listen to me —

Biff: Why don't you let me finish?

Willy: I'm not interested in stories about the past or any crap of that kind because the woods are burning, boys, you understand? There's a big blaze going on all around. I was fired today.

Biff (shocked): How could you be?

Willy: I was fired, and I'm looking for a little good news to tell your mother, because the woman has waited and the woman has suffered. The gist of it is that I haven't got a story left in my head, Biff. So don't give me a lecture about facts and aspects. I am not interested. Now what've you got to say to me?

Stanley enters with three drinks. They wait until he leaves.

Willy: Did you see Oliver?

Biff: Jesus, Dad!

Willy: You mean you didn't go up there?

Happy: Sure he went up there.

Biff: I did. I — saw him. How could they fire you?

Willy (on the edge of his chair): What kind of a welcome did he give you?

Biff: He won't even let you work on commission?

Willy: I'm out! *(Driving.)* So tell me, he gave you a warm welcome?

Happy: Sure, Pop, sure!

Biff (driven): Well, it was kind of —

Willy: I was wondering if he'd remember you. *(To Happy.)* Imagine, man doesn't see him for ten, twelve years and gives him that kind of a welcome!

Happy: Damn right!

Biff (trying to return to the offensive): Pop, look —

Willy: You know why he remembered you, don't you? Because you impressed him in those days.

Biff: Let's talk quietly and get this down to the facts, huh?

Willy (as though Biff had been interrupting): Well, what happened? It's great news, Biff. Did he take you into his office or'd you talk in the waiting-room?

Biff: Well, he came in, see, and —

Willy (with a big smile): What'd he say? Betcha he threw his arm around you.

Biff: Well, he kinda —

Willy: He's a fine man. *(To Happy.)* Very hard man to see, y'know.

Happy (agreeing): Oh, I know.

Willy (to Biff): Is that where you had the drinks?

Biff: Yeah, he gave me a couple of — no, no!

Happy (cutting in): He told him my Florida idea.

Willy: Don't interrupt. *(To Biff.)* How'd he react to the Florida idea?

Biff: Dad, will you give me a minute to explain?

Willy: I've been waiting for you to explain since I sat down here! What happened? He took you into his office and what?

Biff: Well — I talked. And — and he listened, see.

Willy: Famous for the way he listens, y'know. What was his answer?

Biff: His answer was — *(He breaks off, suddenly angry.)* Dad, you're not letting me tell you what I want to tell you!

Willy (accusing, angered): You didn't see him, did you?

Biff: I did see him!

Willy: What'd you insult him or something? You insulted him, didn't you?

Biff: Listen, will you let me out of it, will you just let me out of it!

Happy: What the hell!

Willy: Tell me what happened!

Biff (to Happy): I can't talk to him!

A single trumpet note jars the ear. The light of green leaves stains the house, which holds the air of night and a dream. Young Bernard enters and knocks on the door of the house.

Young Bernard (frantically): Mrs. Loman, Mrs. Loman!

Happy: Tell him what happened!

Biff (to Happy): Shut up and leave me alone!

Willy: No, no! You had to go and flunk math!

Biff: What math? What're you talking about?

Young Bernard: Mrs. Loman, Mrs. Loman!

Linda appears in the house, as of old.

Willy (wildly): Math, math, math!

Biff: Take it easy, Pop!

Young Bernard: Mrs. Loman!

Willy (furiously): If you hadn't flunked you'd've been set by now!

Biff: Now, look, I'm gonna tell you what happened, and you're going to listen to me.

Young Bernard: Mrs. Loman!

Biff: I waited six hours —

Happy: What the hell are you saying?

Biff: I kept sending in my name but he wouldn't see me. So finally he . . . *(He continues unheard as light fades low on the restaurant.)*

Young Bernard: Biff flunked math!

Linda: No!

Young Bernard: Birnbaum flunked him! They won't graduate him!

Linda: But they have to. He's gotta go to the university. Where is he? Biff! Biff!

Young Bernard: No, he left. He went to Grand Central.

Linda: Grand — You mean he went to Boston!

Young Bernard: Is Uncle Willy in Boston?

Linda: Oh, maybe Willy can talk to the teacher. Oh, the poor, poor boy!

Light on house area snaps out.

Biff (at the table, now audible, holding up a gold fountain pen): . . . so I'm washed up with Oliver, you understand? Are you listening to me?

Willy (at a loss): Yeah, sure. If you hadn't flunked —

Biff: Flunked what? What're you talking about?

Willy: Don't blame everything on me! I didn't flunk math — you did! What pen?

Happy: That was awful dumb, Biff, a pen like that is worth —

Willy (seeing the pen for the first time): You took Oliver's pen?

Biff (weakening): Dad, I just explained it to you.

Willy: You stole Bill Oliver's fountain pen!

Biff: I didn't exactly steal it! That's just what I've been explaining to you!

Happy: He had it in his hand and just then Oliver walked in, so he got nervous and stuck it in his pocket!

Willy: My God, Biff!

Biff: I never intended to do it, Dad!

Operator's Voice: Standish Arms, good evening!

Willy (shouting): I'm not in my room!

Biff (frightened): Dad, what's the matter? *(He and Happy stand up.)*

Operator: Ringing Mr. Loman for you!

Willy: I'm not there, stop it!

Biff (horrified, gets down on one knee before Willy): Dad, I'll make good, I'll make good. *(Willy tries to get to his feet. Biff holds him down.)* Sit down now.

Willy: No, you're no good, you're no good for anything.

Biff: I am, Dad, I'll find something else, you understand? Now don't worry about anything. *(He holds up Willy's face.)* Talk to me, Dad.

Operator: Mr. Loman does not answer. Shall I page him?

Willy (attempting to stand, as though to rush and silence the Operator): No, no, no!

Happy: He'll strike something, Pop.

Willy: No, no . . .

Biff (desperately, standing over Willy): Pop, listen! Listen to me! I'm telling you something good. Oliver talked to his partner about the Florida idea. You listening? He — he talked to his partner, and he came to me . . . I'm going to be all right, you hear? Dad, listen to me, he said it was just a question of the amount!

Willy: Then you . . . got it?

Happy: He's gonna be terrific, Pop!

Willy (trying to stand): Then you got it, haven't you? You got it! You got it!

Biff (agonized, holds Willy down): No, no. Look, Pop. I'm supposed to have lunch with them tomorrow. I'm just telling you this so you'll know that I can still make an impression, Pop. And I'll make good somewhere, but I can't go tomorrow, see?

Willy: Why not? You simply —

Biff: But the pen, Pop!

Willy: You give it to him and tell him it was an oversight!

Happy: Sure, have lunch tomorrow!

Biff: I can't say that —

Willy: You were doing a crossword puzzle and accidentally used his pen!

Biff: Listen, kid, I took those balls years ago, now I walk in with his fountain pen? That clinches it, don't you see? I can't face him like that! I'll try elsewhere.

Page's Voice: Paging Mr. Loman!

Willy: Don't you want to be anything?

Biff: Pop, how can I go back?

Willy: You don't want to be anything, is that what's behind it?

Biff (now angry at Willy for not crediting his sympathy): Don't take it that way!

You think it was easy walking into that office after what I'd done to him? A team of horses couldn't have dragged me back to Bill Oliver!

Willy: Then why'd you go?

Biff: Why did I go? Why did I go! Look at you! Look at what's become of you!

Off left, The Woman laughs.

Willy: Biff, you're going to lunch tomorrow, or —

Biff: I can't go. I've got no appointment!

Happy: Biff, for . . . !

Willy: Are you spiting me?

Biff: Don't take it that way! Goddammit!

Willy (strikes Biff and falters away from the table): You rotten little louse! Are you spiting me?

The Woman: Someone's at the door, Willy!

Biff: I'm no good, can't you see what I am?

Happy (separating them): Hey, you're in a restaurant! Now cut it out, both of you! *(The girls enter.)* Hello, girls, sit down.

The Woman laughs, off left.

Miss Forsythe: I guess we might as well. This is Letta.

The Woman: Willy, are you going to wake up?

Biff (ignoring Willy): How're ya, miss, sit down. What do you drink?

Miss Forsythe: Letta might not be able to stay long.

Letta: I gotta get up very early tomorrow. I got jury duty. I'm so excited! Were you fellows ever on a jury?

Biff: No, but I been in front of them! *(The girls laugh.)* This is my father.

Letta: Isn't he cute? Sit down with us, Pop.

Happy: Sit him down, Biff!

Biff (going to him): Come on, slugger, drink us under the table. To hell with it! Come on, sit down, pal.

On Biff's last insistence, Willy is about to sit.

The Woman (now urgently): Willy, are you going to answer the door!

The Woman's call pulls Willy back. He starts right, befuddled.

Biff: Hey, where are you going?

Willy: Open the door.

Biff: The door?

Willy: The washroom . . . the door . . . where's the door?

Biff (leading Willy to the left): Just go straight down.

Willy moves left.

The Woman: Willy, Willy, are you going to get up, get up, get up, get up?

Willy exits left.

Letta: I think it's sweet you bring your daddy along.

Miss Forsythe: Oh, he isn't really your father!

Biff (at left, turning to her resentfully): Miss Forsythe, you've just seen a prince walk by. A fine, troubled prince. A hard-working, unappreciated prince. A pal, you understand? A good companion. Always for his boys.

Letta: That's so sweet.

Happy: Well, girls, what's the program? We're wasting time. Come on, Biff. Gather round. Where would you like to go?

Biff: Why don't you do something for him?

Happy: Me!

Biff: Don't you give a damn for him, Hap?

Happy: What're you talking about? I'm the one who —

Biff: I sense it, you don't give a good goddamn about him. *(He takes the rolled-up hose from his pocket and puts it on the table in front of Happy.)* Look what I found in the cellar, for Christ's sake. How can you bear to let it go on?

Happy: Me? Who goes away? Who runs off and —

Biff: Yeah, but he doesn't mean anything to you. You could help him — I can't! Don't you understand what I'm talking about? He's going to kill himself, don't you know that?

Happy: Don't I know it! Me!

Biff: Hap, help him! Jesus . . . help him . . . Help me, help me, I can't bear to look at his face! *(Ready to weep, he hurries out, up right.)*

Happy (starting after him): Where are you going?

Miss Forsythe: What's he so mad about?

Happy: Come on, girls, we'll catch up with him.

Miss Forsythe (as Happy pushes her out): Say, I don't like that temper of his!

Happy: He's just a little overstrung, he'll be all right!

Willy (off left, as The Woman laughs): Don't answer! Don't answer!

Letta: Don't you want to tell your father —

Happy: No, that's not my father. He's just a guy. Come on, we'll catch Biff, and, honey, we're going to paint this town! Stanley, where's the check! Hey, Stanley!

They exit. Stanley looks toward left.

Stanley (calling to Happy indignantly): Mr. Loman! Mr. Loman!

Stanley picks up a chair and follows them off. Knocking is heard off left. The Woman enters, laughing. Willy follows her. She is in a black slip; he is buttoning his shirt. Raw, sensuous music accompanies their speech.

Willy: Will you stop laughing? Will you stop?

The Woman: Aren't you going to answer the door? He'll wake the whole hotel.

Willy: I'm not expecting anybody.

The Woman: Whyn't you have another drink, honey, and stop being so damn self-centered?

Willy: I'm so lonely.

The Woman: You know you ruined me, Willy? From now on, whenever you come to the office, I'll see that you go right through to the buyers. No waiting at my desk any more, Willy. You ruined me.

Willy: That's nice of you to say that.

The Woman: Gee, you are self-centered! Why so sad? You are the saddest, self-centeredest soul I ever did see-saw. *(She laughs. He kisses her.)* Come on inside, drummer boy. It's silly to be dressing in the middle of the night. *(As knocking is heard.)* Aren't you going to answer the door?

Willy: They're knocking on the wrong door.

The Woman: But I felt the knocking. And he heard us talking in here. Maybe the hotel's on fire!

Willy (his terror rising): It's a mistake.

The Woman: Then tell him to go away!

Willy: There's nobody there.

The Woman: It's getting on my nerves, Willy. There's somebody standing out there and it's getting on my nerves!

Willy (pushing her away from him): All right, stay in the bathroom here, and don't come out. I think there's a law in Massachusetts about it, so don't come out. It may be that new room clerk. He looked very mean. So don't come out. It's a mistake, there's no fire.

The knocking is heard again. He takes a few steps away from her, and she vanishes into the wing. The light follows him, and now he is facing Young Biff, who carries a suitcase. Biff steps toward him. The music is gone.

Biff: Why didn't you answer?

Willy: Biff! What are you doing in Boston?

Biff: Why didn't you answer? I've been knocking for five minutes, I called you on the phone —

Willy: I just heard you. I was in the bathroom and had the door shut. Did anything happen home?

Biff: Dad — I let you down.

Willy: What do you mean?

Biff: Dad . . .

Willy: Biffo, what's this about? *(Putting his arm around Biff.)* Come on, let's go downstairs and get you a malted.

Biff: Dad, I flunked math.

Willy: Not for the term?

Biff: The term. I haven't got enough credits to graduate.

Willy: You mean to say Bernard wouldn't give you the answers?

Biff: He did, he tried, but I only got a sixty-one.

Willy: And they wouldn't give you four points?

Biff: Birnbaum refused absolutely. I begged him, Pop, but he won't give me those points. You gotta talk to him before they close the school. Because if he saw the kind of man you are, and you just talked to him in your way, I'm sure he'd come through for me. The class came right before practice, see, and I didn't go enough. Would you talk to him? He'd like you, Pop. You know the way you could talk.

Willy: You're on. We'll drive right back.

Biff: Oh, Dad, good work! I'm sure he'll change it for you!

Willy: Go downstairs and tell the clerk I'm checkin' out. Go right down.

Biff: Yes, sir! See, the reason he hates me, Pop — one day he was late for class so I got up at the blackboard and imitated him. I crossed my eyes and talked with a lithp.

Willy (laughing): You did? The kids like it?

Biff: They nearly died laughing!

Willy: Yeah: What'd you do?

Biff: The thquare root of thixthty twee is . . . *(Willy bursts out laughing; Biff joins him.)* And in the middle of it he walked in!

Willy laughs and The Woman joins in offstage.

Willy (without hesitation): Hurry downstairs and —
Biff: Somebody in there?
Willy: No, that was next door.

The Woman laughs offstage.

Biff: Somebody got in your bathroom!
Willy: No, it's the next room, there's a party —
The Woman (enters, laughing. She lisps this:) Can I come in? There's something in the bathtub, Willy, and it's moving!

Willy looks at Biff, who is staring open-mouthed and horrified at The Woman.

Willy: Ah — you better go back to your room. They must be finished painting by now. They're painting her room so I let her take a shower here. Go back, go back . . . *(He pushes her.)*
The Woman (resisting): But I've got to get dressed, Willy, I can't —
Willy: Get out of here! Go back, go back . . . *(Suddenly striving for the ordinary):* This is Miss Francis, Biff, she's a buyer. They're painting her room. Go back, Miss Francis, go back . . .
The Woman: But my clothes, I can't go out naked in the hall!
Willy (pushing her offstage): Get outa here! Go back, go back!

Biff slowly sits down on his suitcase as the argument continues offstage.

The Woman: Where's my stockings? You promised me stockings, Willy!
Willy: I have no stockings here!
The Woman: You had two boxes of size nine sheers for me, and I want them!
Willy: Here, for God's sake, will you get outa here!
The Woman (enters holding a box of stockings): I just hope there's nobody in the hall. That's all I hope. *(To Biff.)* Are you football or baseball?
Biff: Football.
The Woman (angry, humiliated): That's me too. G'night. *(She snatches her clothes from Willy, and walks out.)*
Willy (after a pause): Well, better get going. I want to get to the school first thing in the morning. Get my suits out of the closet. I'll get my valise. *(Biff doesn't move.)* What's the matter? *(Biff remains motionless, tears falling.)* She's a buyer. Buys for J. H. Simmons. She lives down the hall — they're painting. You don't imagine — *(He breaks off. After a pause.)* Now listen, pal, she's just a buyer. She sees merchandise in her room and they have to keep it looking just so . . . *(Pause. Assuming command.)* All right, get my suits. *(Biff doesn't move.)* Now stop crying and do as I say. I gave you an order. Biff, I gave you an order! Is that what you do when I give you an order? How dare you cry! *(Putting his arm around Biff.)* Now look, Biff, when you grow up you'll understand about these things. You mustn't — you mustn't overemphasize a thing like this. I'll see Birnbaum first thing in the morning.
Biff: Never mind.

Willy (getting down beside Biff): Never mind! He's going to give you those points. I'll see to it.

Biff: He wouldn't listen to you.

Willy: He certainly will listen to me. You need those points for the U. of Virginia.

Biff: I'm not going there.

Willy: Heh? If I can't get him to change that mark you'll make it up in summer school. You've got all summer to —

Biff (his weeping breaking from him): Dad . . .

Willy (infected by it): Oh, my boy . . .

Biff: Dad . . .

Willy: She's nothing to me, Biff. I was lonely, I was terribly lonely.

Biff: You — you gave her Mama's stockings! *(His tears break through and he rises to go.)*

Willy (grabbing for Biff): I gave you an order!

Biff: Don't touch me, you — liar!

Willy: Apologize for that!

Biff: You fake! You phony little fake! You fake! *(Overcome, he turns quickly and weeping fully goes out with his suitcase. Willy is left on the floor on his knees.)*

Willy: I gave you an order! Biff, come back here or I'll beat you! Come back here! I'll whip you!

Stanley comes quickly in from the right and stands in front of Willy.

Willy (shouts at Stanley): I gave you an order . . .

Stanley: Hey, let's pick it up, pick it up, Mr. Loman. *(He helps Willy to his feet.)* Your boys left with the chippies. They said they'll see you home.

A second waiter watches some distance away.

Willy: But we were supposed to have dinner together.

Music is heard, Willy's theme.

Stanley: Can you make it?

Willy: I'll — sure, I can make it. *(Suddenly concerned about his clothes.)* Do I — I look all right?

Stanley: Sure, you look all right. *(He flicks a speck off Willy's lapel.)*

Willy: Here — here's a dollar.

Stanley: Oh, your son paid me. It's all right.

Willy (putting it in Stanley's hand): No, take it. You're a good boy.

Stanley: Oh, no, you don't have to . . .

Willy: Here — here's some more, I don't need it any more. *(After a slight pause.)* Tell me — is there a seed store in the neighborhood?

Stanley: Seeds? You mean like to plant?

As Willy turns, Stanley slips the money back into his jacket pocket.

Willy: Yes. Carrots, peas . . .

Stanley: Well, there's hardware stores on Sixth Avenue, but it may be too late now.

Willy (anxiously): Oh, I'd better hurry. I've got to get some seeds. *(He starts off to the right.)* I've got to get some seeds, right away. Nothing's planted. I don't have a thing in the ground.

Willy hurries out as the light goes down. Stanley moves over to the right after him, watches him off. The other waiter has been staring at Willy.

Stanley (to the waiter): Well, whatta you looking at?

The waiter picks up the chairs and moves off right. Stanley takes the table and follows him. The light fades on this area. There is a long pause, the sound of the flute coming over. The light gradually rises on the kitchen, which is empty. Happy appears at the door of the house, followed by Biff. Happy is carrying a large bunch of long-stemmed roses. He enters the kitchen, looks around for Linda. Not seeing her, he turns to Biff, who is just outside the house door, and makes a gesture with his hands, indicating "Not here, I guess." He looks into the living-room and freezes. Inside, Linda, unseen, is seated, Willy's coat on her lap. She rises ominously and quietly and moves toward Happy, who backs up into the kitchen, afraid.

Happy: Hey, what're you doing up? *(Linda says nothing but moves toward him implacably.)* Where's Pop? *(He keeps backing to the right, and now Linda is in full view in the doorway to the living-room.)* Is he sleeping?

Linda: Where were you?

Happy (trying to laugh it off): We met two girls, Mom, very fine types. Here, we brought you some flowers. *(Offering them to her.)* Put them in your room, Ma.

She knocks them to the floor at Biff's feet. He has now come inside and closed the door behind him. She stares at Biff, silent.

Happy: Now what'd you do that for? Mom, I want you to have some flowers —

Linda (cutting Happy off, violently to Biff): Don't you care whether he lives or dies?

Happy (going to the stairs): Come upstairs, Biff.

Biff (with a flare of disgust, to Happy): Go away from me! *(To Linda.)* What do you mean, lives or dies? Nobody's dying around here, pal.

Linda: Get out of my sight! Get out of here!

Biff: I wanna see the boss.

Linda: You're not going near him!

Biff: Where is he? *(He moves into the living-room and Linda follows.)*

Linda (shouting after Biff): You invite him for dinner. He looks forward to it all day — *(Biff appears in his parents' bedroom, looks around, and exits.)* — and then you desert him there. There's no stranger you'd do that to!

Happy: Why? He had a swell time with us. Listen, when I — *(Linda comes back into the kitchen)* — desert him I hope I don't outlive the day!

Linda: Get out of here!

Happy: Now look, Mom . . .

Linda: Did you have to go to women tonight? You and your lousy rotten whores!

Biff re-enters the kitchen.

Happy: Mom, all we did was follow Biff around trying to cheer him up! *(To Biff.)* Boy, what a night you gave me!

Linda: Get out of here, both of you, and don't come back! I don't want you tormenting him any more. Go on now, get your things together! *(To Biff.)* You can sleep in his apartment. *(She starts to pick up the flowers and stops herself.)* Pick up this stuff, I'm not your maid any more. Pick it up, you bum, you!

Happy turns his back to her in refusal. Biff slowly moves over and gets down on his knees, picking up the flowers.

Linda: You're a pair of animals! Not one, not another living soul would have had the cruelty to walk out on that man in a restaurant!

Biff (not looking at her): Is that what he said?

Linda: He didn't have to say anything. He was so humiliated he nearly limped when he came in.

Happy: But, Mom, he had a great time with us —

Biff (cutting him off violently): Shut up!

Without another word, Happy goes upstairs.

Linda: You! You didn't even go in to see if he was all right!

Biff (still on the floor in front of Linda, the flowers in his hand; with self-loathing): No. Didn't. Didn't do a damned thing. How do you like that, heh? Left him babbling in a toilet.

Linda: You louse. You . . .

Biff: Now you hit it on the nose! *(He gets up, throws the flowers in the waste-basket.)* The scum of the earth, and you're looking at him!

Linda: Get out of here!

Biff: I gotta talk to the boss, Mom. Where is he?

Linda: You're not going near him. Get out of this house!

Biff (with absolute assurance, determination): No. We're gonna have an abrupt conversation, him and me.

Linda: You're not talking to him!

Hammering is heard from outside the house, off right. Biff turns toward the noise.

Linda (suddenly pleading): Will you please leave him alone?

Biff: What's he doing out there?

Linda: He's planting the garden!

Biff (quietly): Now? Oh, my God!

Biff moves outside, Linda following. The light dies down on them and comes up on the center of the apron as Willy walks into it. He is carrying a flashlight, a hoe, and handful of seed packets. He raps the top of the hoe sharply to fix it firmly, and then moves to the left, measuring off the distance with his foot. He holds the flashlight to look at the seed packets, reading off the instructions. He is in the blue of night.

Willy: Carrots . . . quarter-inch apart. Rows . . . one-foot rows. *(He measures it off.)* One foot. *(He puts down a package and measures off.)* Beets. *(He puts down another package and measures again.)* Lettuce. *(He reads the package, puts it down.)* One foot — *(He breaks off as Ben appears at the right and moves slowly down to him.)* What a proposition, ts, ts. Terrific, terrific. 'Cause she's suffered, Ben, the woman has suffered. You understand me? A man can't go out the way he came in, Ben, a man has got to add up to something. You can't, you can't — *(Ben moves toward him as though to interrupt.)* You gotta consider, now. Don't answer so quick. Remember, it's a guaranteed twenty-thousand-dollar proposition. Now look, Ben, I want you to go through the ins and outs of this thing with me. I've got nobody to talk to, Ben, and the woman has suffered, you hear me?

Ben (standing still, considering): What's the proposition?

Willy: It's twenty thousand dollars on the barrelhead. Guaranteed, gilt-edged, you understand?

Ben: You don't want to make a fool of yourself. They might not honor the policy.

Willy: How can they dare refuse? Didn't I work like a coolie to meet every premium on the nose? And now they don't pay off? Impossible!

Ben: It's called a cowardly thing, William.

Willy: Why? Does it take more guts to stand here the rest of my life ringing up a zero?

Ben (yielding): That's a point, William. *(He moves, thinking, turns.)* And twenty thousand — that *is* something one can feel with the hand, it is there.

Willy (now assured, with rising power): Oh, Ben, that's the whole beauty of it! I see it like a diamond, shining in the dark, hard and rough, that I can pick up and touch in my hand. Not like — like an appointment! This would not be another damned-fool appointment, Ben, and it changes all the aspects. Because he thinks I'm nothing, see, and so he spites me. But the funeral — *(Straightening up.)* Ben, that funeral will be massive! They'll come from Maine, Massachusetts, Vermont, New Hampshire! All the old-timers with the strange license plates — that boy will be thunder-struck, Ben, because he never realized — I am known! Rhode Island, New York, New Jersey — I am known, Ben, and he'll see it with his eyes once and for all. He'll see what I am, Ben! He's in for a shock, that boy!

Ben (coming to the edge of the garden): He'll call you a coward.

Willy (suddenly fearful): No, that would be terrible.

Ben: Yes. And a damned fool.

Willy: No, no, he mustn't, I won't have that! *(He is broken and desperate.)*

Ben: He'll hate you, William.

The gay music of the Boys is heard.

Willy: Oh, Ben, how do we get back to all the great times? Used to be so full of light, and comradeship, the sleigh-riding in winter, and the ruddiness on his cheeks. And always some kind of good news coming up, always something nice coming up ahead. And never even let me carry the valises in the house, and simonizing, simonizing that little red car! Why, why can't I give him something and not have him hate me?

Ben: Let me think about it. *(He glances at his watch.)* I still have a little time. Remarkable proposition, but you've got to be sure you're not making a fool of yourself.

Ben drifts off upstage and goes out of sight. Biff comes down from the left.

Willy (suddenly conscious of Biff, turns and looks up at him, then begins picking up the packages of seeds in confusion): Where the hell is that seed? *(Indignantly.)* You can't see nothing out here! They boxed in the whole goddamn neighborhood!

Biff: There are people all around here. Don't you realize that?

Willy: I'm busy. Don't bother me.

Biff (taking the hoe from Willy): I'm saying good-by to you, Pop. *(Willy looks at him, silent, unable to move.)* I'm not coming back any more.

Willy: You're not going to see Oliver tomorrow?

Biff: I've got no appointment, Dad.

Willy: He put his arm around you, and you've got no appointment?

Biff: Pop, get this now, will you? Everytime I've left it's been a fight that sent me out of here. Today I realized something about myself and I tried to explain it to you and I — I think I'm just not smart enough to make any sense out of it for you. To hell with whose fault it is or anything like that. *(He takes Willy's arm.)* Let's just wrap it up, heh? Come on in, we'll tell Mom. *(He gently tries to pull Willy to left.)*

Willy (frozen, immobile, with guilt in his voice): No, I don't want to see her.

Biff: Come on! *(He pulls again, and Willy tries to pull away.)*

Willy (highly nervous): No, no, I don't want to see her.

Biff (tries to look into Willy's face, as if to find the answer there): Why don't you want to see her?

Willy (more harshly now): Don't bother me, will you?

Biff: What do you mean, you don't want to see her? You don't want them calling you yellow, do you? This isn't your fault; it's me, I'm a bum. Now come inside! *(Willy strains to get away.)* Did you hear what I said to you?

Willy pulls away and quickly goes by himself into the house. Biff follows.

Linda (to Willy): Did you plant, dear?

Biff (at the door, to Linda): All right, we had it out. I'm going and I'm not writing any more.

Linda (going to Willy in the kitchen): I think that's the best way, dear. 'Cause there's no use drawing it out, you'll just never get along.

Willy doesn't respond.

Biff: People ask where I am and what I'm doing, you don't know, and you don't care. That way it'll be off your mind and you can start brightening up again. All right? That clears it, doesn't it? *(Willy is silent, and Biff goes to him.)* You gonna wish me luck, scout? *(He extends his hand.)* What do you say?

Linda: Shake his hand, Willy.

Willy (turning to her, seething with hurt): There's no necessity to mention the pen at all, y'know.

Biff (gently): I've got no appointment, Dad.

Willy (erupting fiercely): He put his arm around . . . ?

Biff: Dad, you're never going to see what I am, so what's the use of arguing? If I strike oil I'll send you a check. Meantime forget I'm alive.

Willy (to Linda): Spite, see?

Biff: Shake hands, Dad.

Willy: Not my hand.

Biff: I was hoping not to go this way.

Willy: Well, this is the way you're going. Good-by.

Biff looks at him a moment, then turns sharply and goes to the stairs.

Willy (stops him with): May you rot in hell if you leave this house!

Biff (turning): Exactly what is it that you want from me?

Willy: I want you to know, on the train, in the mountains, in the valleys, wherever you go, that you cut down your life for spite!

Biff: No, no.

Willy: Spite, spite, is the word of your undoing! And when you're down and out, remember what did it. When you're rotting somewhere beside the railroad tracks, remember, and don't you dare blame it on me!

Biff: I'm not blaming it on you!

Willy: I won't take the rap for this, you hear?

Happy comes down the stairs and stands on the bottom step, watching.

Biff: That's just what I'm telling you!

Willy (sinking into a chair at the table, with full accusation): You're trying to put a knife in me — don't think I don't know what you're doing!

Biff: All right, phony! Then let's lay it on the line. *(He whips the rubber tube out of his pocket and puts it on the table.)*

Happy: You crazy —

Linda: Biff! *(She moves to grab the hose, but Biff holds it down with his hand.)*

Biff: Leave it there! Don't move it!

Willy (not looking at it): What is that?

Biff: You know goddam well what that is.

Willy (caged, wanting to escape): I never saw that.

Biff: You saw it. The mice didn't bring it into the cellar! What is this supposed to do, make a hero out of you? This supposed to make me sorry for you?

Willy: Never heard of it.

Biff: There'll be no pity for you, you hear it? No pity!

Willy (to Linda:) You hear the spite!

Biff: No, you're going to hear the truth — what you are and what I am!

Linda: Stop it!

Willy: Spite!

Happy (coming down toward Biff): You cut it now!

Biff (to Happy): The man don't know who we are! The man is gonna know! *(To Willy.)* We never told the truth for ten minutes in this house!

Happy: We always told the truth!

Biff (turning on him): You big blow, are you the assistant buyer? You're one of the two assistants to the assistant, aren't you?

Happy: Well, I'm practically —

Biff: You're practically full of it! We all are! And I'm through with it. *(To Willy.)* Now hear this, Willy, this is me.

Willy: I know you!

Biff: You know why I had no address for three months? I stole a suit in Kansas City and I was in jail. *(To Linda, who is sobbing.)* Stop crying. I'm through with it.

Linda turns away from them, her hands covering her face.

Willy: I suppose that's my fault!

Biff: I stole myself out of every good job since high school!

Willy: And whose fault is that?

Biff: And I never got anywhere because you blew me so full of hot air I could never stand taking orders from anybody! That's whose fault it is!

Willy: I hear that!

Linda: Don't, Biff!

Biff: It's goddam time you heard that! I had to be boss big shot in two weeks, and I'm through with it!

Willy: Then hang yourself! For spite, hang yourself!

Biff: No! Nobody's hanging himself, Willy! I ran down eleven flights with a pen in my hand today. And suddenly I stopped, you hear me? And in the middle of that office building, do you hear this? I stopped in the middle of that building and I saw — the sky. I saw the things that I love in this world. The work and the food and time to sit and smoke. And I looked at the pen and said to myself, what the hell am I grabbing this for? Why am I trying to become what I don't want to be? What am I doing in an office, making a contemptuous, begging fool of myself, when all I want is out there, waiting for me the minute I say I know who I am! Why can't I say that, Willy? *(He tries to make Willy face him, but Willy pulls away and moves to the left.)*

Willy: (with hatred, threateningly): The door of your life is wide open!

Biff: Pop! I'm a dime a dozen, and so are you!

Willy (turning on him now in an uncontrolled outburst): I am not a dime a dozen! I am Willy Loman, and you are Biff Loman!

Biff starts for Willy, but is blocked by Happy. In his fury, Biff seems on the verge of attacking his father.

Biff: I am not a leader of men, Willy, and neither are you. You were never anything but a hard-working drummer who landed in the ash can like all the rest of them! I'm one dollar an hour, Willy! I tried seven states and couldn't raise it. A buck an hour! Do you gather my meaning? I'm not bringing home any prizes any more, and you're going to stop waiting for me to bring them home!

Willy (directly to Biff): You vengeful, spiteful mut!

Biff breaks from Happy. Willy, in fright, starts up the stairs. Biff grabs him.

Biff (at the peak of his fury): Pop, I'm nothing! I'm nothing, Pop. Can't you understand that? There's no spite in it any more. I'm just what I am, that's all.

Biff's fury has spent itself, and he breaks down, sobbing, holding on to Willy, who dumbly fumbles for Biff's face.

Willy (astonished): What're you doing? What're you doing? *(To Linda.)* Why is he crying?

Biff (crying, broken): Will you let me go, for Christ's sake? Will you take that phony dream and burn it before something happens? *(Struggling to contain himself, he pulls away and moves to the stairs.)* I'll go in the morning. Put him — put him to bed. *(Exhausted, Biff moves up the stairs to his room.)*

Willy (after a long pause, astonished, elevated): Isn't that — isn't that remarkable? Biff — he likes me!

Linda: He loves you, Willy!

Happy (deeply moved): Always did, Pop.

Willy: Oh, Biff! *(Staring wildly.)* He cried! Cried to me. *(He is choking with his love, and now cries out his promise.)* That boy — that boy is going to be magnificent!

Ben appears in the light just outside the kitchen.

Ben: Yes, outstanding, with twenty thousand behind him.

Linda (sensing the racing of his mind, fearfully, carefully): Now come to bed, Willy. It's all settled now.

Willy (finding it difficult not to rush out of the house): Yes, we'll sleep. Come on. Go to sleep, Hap.

Ben: And it does take a great kind of a man to crack the jungle.

In accents of dread, Ben's idyllic music starts up.

Happy (his arm around Linda): I'm getting married, Pop, don't forget it. I'm changing everything. I'm gonna run that department before the year is up. You'll see, Mom. *(He kisses her.)*

Ben: The jungle is dark but full of diamonds, Willy.

Willy turns, moves, listening to Ben.

Linda: Be good. You're both good boys, just act that way, that's all.

Happy: 'Night, Pop. *(He goes upstairs.)*

Linda (to Willy): Come, dear.

Ben (with greater force): One must go in to fetch a diamond out.

Willy (to Linda, as he moves slowly along the edge of the kitchen, toward the door): I just want to get settled down, Linda. Let me sit alone for a little.

Linda (almost uttering her fear): I want you upstairs.

Willy (taking her in his arms): In a few minutes, Linda. I couldn't sleep right now. Go on, you look awful tired. *(He kisses her.)*

Ben: Not like an appointment at all. A diamond is rough and hard to the touch.

Willy: Go on now. I'll be right up.

Linda: I think this is the only way, Willy.

Willy: Sure, it's the best thing.

Ben: Best thing!

Willy: The only way. Everything is gonna be — go on, kid, get to bed. You look so tired.

Linda: Come right up.

Willy: Two minutes.

Linda goes into the living-room, then reappears in her bedroom. Willy moves just outside the kitchen door.

Willy: Loves me. *(Wonderingly.)* Always loved me. Isn't that a remarkable thing? Ben, he'll worship me for it!

Ben (with promise): It's dark there, but full of diamonds.

Willy: Can you imagine that magnificence with twenty thousand dollars in his pocket?

Linda (calling from her room): Willy! Come up!

Willy (calling into the kitchen): Yes! Yes. Coming! It's very smart, you realize that, don't you, sweetheart? Even Ben sees it. I gotta go, baby. 'By! 'By! *(Going over to Ben, almost dancing.)* Imagine? When the mail comes he'll be ahead of Bernard again!

Ben: A perfect proposition all around.

Willy: Did you see how he cried to me? Oh, if I could kiss him, Ben!

Ben: Time, William, time!

Willy: Oh, Ben, I always knew one way or another we were gonna make it, Biff and I!

Ben (looking at his watch): The boat. We'll be late. *(He moves slowly off into the darkness.)*

Willy (elegiacally, turning to the house): Now when you kick off, boy, I want a seventy-yard boot, and get right down the field under the ball, and when you hit, hit low and hit hard, because it's important, boy. *(He swings around and faces the audience.)* There's all kinds of important people in the stands, and the first thing you know . . . *(Suddenly realizing he is alone.)* Ben! Ben, where do I . . . ? *(He makes a sudden movement of search.)* Ben, how do I . . . ?

Linda (calling): Willy, you coming up?

Willy (uttering a gasp of fear, whirling about as if to quiet her): Sh! *(He turns around as if to find his way; sounds, faces, voices, seem to be swarming in upon him and he flicks at them, crying.)* Sh! Sh! *(Suddenly music, faint and high, stops him. It rises in intensity, almost to an unbearable scream. He goes up and down on his toes, and rushes off around the house.)* Shhh!

Linda: Willy?

There is no answer. Linda waits. Biff gets up off his bed. He is still in his clothes. Happy sits up. Biff stands listening.

Linda (with real fear): Willy, answer me! Willy!

There is the sound of a car starting and moving away at full speed.

Linda: No!

Biff (rushing down the stairs): Pop!

As the car speeds off, the music crashes down in a frenzy of sound, which becomes the soft pulsation of a single cello string. Biff slowly returns to his bedroom. He and Happy gravely don their jackets. Linda slowly walks out of her room. The music has developed into a dead march. The leaves of day are appearing over everything. Charley and Bernard, somberly dressed, appear and knock on the kitchen door. Biff and Happy slowly descend the stairs to the kitchen as Charley and Bernard enter. All stop a moment when Linda, in clothes of mourning, bearing a little bunch of roses, comes through the draped doorway into the kitchen. She goes to Charley and takes his arm. Now all move toward the audience, through the wall-line of the kitchen. At the limit of the apron, Linda lays down the flowers, kneels, and sits back on her heels. All stare down at the grave.

REQUIEM

Charley: It's getting dark, Linda.

Linda doesn't react. She stares at the grave.

Biff: How about it, Mom? Better get some rest, heh? They'll be closing the gate soon.

Linda makes no move. Pause.

Happy (deeply angered): He had no right to do that. There was no necessity for it. We would've helped him.

Charley (grunting): Hmmm.

Biff: Come along, Mom.

Linda: Why didn't anybody come?

Charley: It was a very nice funeral.

Linda: But where are all the people he knew? Maybe they blame him.

Charley: Naa. It's a rough world, Linda. They wouldn't blame him.

Linda: I can't understand it. At this time especially. First time in thirty-five years we were just about free and clear. He only needed a little salary. He was even finished with the dentist.

Charley: No man only needs a little salary.

Linda: I can't understand it.

Biff: There were a lot of nice days. When he'd come home from a trip; or on Sundays, making the stoop; finishing the cellar; putting on the new porch; when he built the extra bathroom; and put up the garage. You know something, Charley, there's more of him in that front stoop than in all the sales he ever made.

Charley: Yeah. He was a happy man with a batch of cement.

Linda: He was so wonderful with his hands.

Biff: He had the wrong dreams. All, all, wrong.

Happy (almost ready to fight Biff): Don't say that!

Biff: He never knew who he was.

Charley (stopping Happy's movement and reply. To Biff): Nobody dast blame this man. You don't understand: Willy was a salesman. And for a salesman, there is no rock bottom to the life. He don't put a bolt to a nut, he don't tell you the law or give you medicine. He's a man way out there in the blue, riding on a smile and a shoeshine. And when they start not smiling back — that's an earthquake. And then you get yourself a couple of spots on your hat, and you're finished. Nobody dast blame this man. A salesman is got to dream, boy. It comes with the territory.

Biff: Charley, the man didn't know who he was.

Happy (infuriated): Don't say that!

Biff: Why don't you come with me, Happy?

Happy: I'm not licked that easily. I'm staying right in this city, and I'm gonna beat this racket! *(He looks at Biff, his chin set.)* The Loman Brothers!

Biff: I know who I am, kid.

Happy: All right, boy. I'm gonna show you and everybody else that Willy Loman did not die in vain. He had a good dream. It's the only dream you can have — to come out number-one man. He fought it out here, and this is where I'm gonna win it for him.

Biff (with a hopeless glance at Happy, bends toward his mother): Let's go, Mom.

Linda: I'll be with you in a minute. Go on, Charley. *(He hesitates.)* I want to, just for a minute. I never had a chance to say good-by.

Charley moves away, followed by Happy. Biff remains a slight distance up and left of Linda. She sits there, summoning herself. The flute begins, not far away, playing behind her speech.

Linda: Forgive me, dear. I can't cry. I don't know what it is, but I can't cry. I don't understand it. Why did you ever do that? Help me, Willy, I can't cry. It seems to me that you're just on another trip. I keep expecting you. Willy, dear, I can't cry. Why did you do it? I search and search and I search, and I can't understand it, Willy. I made the last payment on the house today. Today, dear. And there'll be nobody home. *(A sob rises in her throat.)* We're free and clear. *(Sobbing more fully, released.)* We're free. *(Biff comes slowly toward her.)* We're free . . . We're free . . .

Biff lifts her to her feet and moves out up right with her in his arms. Linda sobs quietly. Bernard and Charley come together and follow them, followed by Happy. Only the music of the flute is left on the darkening stage as over the house the hard towers of the apartment buildings rise into sharp focus, and

The Curtain Falls

Connections to Other Selections

1. Compare and contrast Willy Loman with Polonius in Shakespeare's *Hamlet* (p. 1281). To what extent is each character wise, foolish, deluded, and hypocritical? Explain why Loman can be seen as a tragic character while Polonius cannot be.
2. Read Allen Ginsberg's poem "America" (p. 952), and compare its treatment of the American dream with the one in *Death of a Salesman*. How do the tones of the two works differ?
3. What similarities do you find between the endings of *Death of a Salesman* and Chekhov's *The Cherry Orchard* (p. 1569)? Are the endings happy? unhappy? or something else?

A RAISIN IN THE SUN

Lorraine Hansberry, the youngest of four children raised by African-American parents who migrated from the South, was born in Chicago, Illinois. Her father was a successful businessman who provided the family with a comfortable middle-class home where distinguished blacks such as W. E. B. DuBois, Langston Hughes, Duke Ellington, and Paul Robeson visited. Her mother was politically active and served as a ward commissioner for the Republican Party. When Hansberry was eight years old, the family bought a house in a white neighborhood, challenging segregationist real estate practices that excluded blacks. The Hansberrys endured violent hostility while fighting a lower court eviction, and with the support from the National Association for the Advancement of Colored People won a victory in the Supreme Court.

After graduating from the segregated public schools of Chicago, Hansberry studied at the University of Wisconsin for two years, but in 1950 moved to New York City. There she attended classes at the New School for Social Research and wrote for *Freedom*, a radical Harlem periodical published by Paul Robeson. During the course of her brief career, ended by cancer when she was only thirty-four years old, Hansberry remained a committed civil rights activist.

She began writing *A Raisin in the Sun* in 1956. Eventually it was produced on Broadway in 1959, bringing her international recognition. At the age of twenty-eight, Hansberry was the first black female playwright to be produced on Broadway, and the play was awarded the New York Drama Critics Circle Award for Best Play of the Year in competition with such successful dramatists as Eugene O'Neill and Tennessee Williams. *A Raisin in the Sun* has been translated into more than thirty languages and produced around the world. Among Hansberry's other writings are *The Movement: Documentary of a Struggle for Equality* (1964); *The Sign in Sidney Brustein's Window* (1965), a play in production at the time of her death; *To Be Young, Gifted and Black* (1969), a play published posthumously; and *Lorraine Hansberry: The Collected Last Plays* (1983).

In *A Raisin in the Sun,* Hansberry does not flinch from the tough realities that confronted African-Americans contemporary to her. Racism, segregation, and a lack of economic opportunities seem brutally to mock the aspirations of her characters. Yet Hansberry sustained a sense of optimism owing to the growing activism of the civil rights movement during the 1950s. The play explores the difficulties of a black working-class family's struggle to overcome the racism and poverty in their lives and makes a connection between their efforts and the struggles of African countries to become free from colonialism. Her characters retain their humanity and dignity in the face of fierce social pressures and individual crises. Her realistic portrayal of racial issues, family conflicts, and relations between men and women presents a hostile world but also one that is capable of change. Her work, she once wrote, was about "not only what *is* but what is *possible.*"

The following poem by Langston Hughes (1902–1967) is the source for the play's title and serves as a fitting introduction to many of the issues dramatized in *A Raisin in the Sun.*

Harlem (A Dream Deferred)

What happens to a dream deferred?

    Does it dry up
    Like a raisin in the sun?
    Or fester like a sore —
    And then run?
    Does it stink like rotten meat?
    Or crust and sugar over —
    Like a syrupy sweet?

Maybe it just sags
Like a heavy load.
Or does it explode?

–Langston Hughes

LORRAINE HANSBERRY (1930–1965)
A Raisin in the Sun   1959

Characters (in order of appearance)

Ruth Younger
Travis Younger
Walter Lee Younger, brother
Beneatha Younger
Lena Younger, Mama
Joseph Asagai
George Murchison
Mrs. Johnson
Karl Lindner
Bobo
Moving Men

*The action of the play is set in Chicago's Southside, sometime between World War II
and the present.*

ACT I

SCENE I. *[Friday morning.]*

   *The Younger living room would be a comfortable and well-ordered room
if it were not for a number of indestructible contradictions to this state of being.
Its furnishings are typical and undistinguished and their primary feature now
is that they have clearly had to accommodate the living of too many people for
too many years — and they are tired. Still, we can see that at some time, a time
probably no longer remembered by the family (except perhaps for Mama), the
furnishings of this room were actually selected with care and love and even
hope — and brought to this apartment and arranged with taste and pride.*
   *That was a long time ago. Now the once loved pattern of the couch
upholstery has to fight to show itself from under acres of crocheted doilies and
couch covers which have themselves finally come to be more important than the
upholstery. And here a table or a chair has been moved to disguise the worn
places in the carpet; but the carpet has fought back by showing its weariness,
with depressing uniformity, elsewhere on its surface.*
   Weariness has, in fact, won in this room. Everything has been polished,

washed, sat on, used, scrubbed too often. *All pretenses but living itself have long since vanished from the very atmosphere of this room.*

Moreover, a section of this room, for it is not really a room unto itself, though the landlord's lease would make it seem so, slopes backward to provide a small kitchen area, where the family prepares the meals that are eaten in the living room proper, which must also serve as dining room. The single window that has been provided for these "two" rooms is located in this kitchen area. The sole natural light the family may enjoy in the course of a day is only that which fights its way through this little window.

At left, a door leads to a bedroom which is shared by Mama and her daughter, Beneatha. At right, opposite, is a second room (which in the beginning of the life of this apartment was probably a breakfast room) which serves as a bedroom for Walter and his wife, Ruth.

Time: Sometime between World War II and the present.

Place: Chicago's Southside.

At Rise: It is morning dark in the living room. Travis is asleep on the make-down bed at center. An alarm clock sounds from within the bedroom at right, and presently Ruth enters from that room and closes the door behind her. She crosses sleepily toward the window. As she passes her sleeping son she reaches down and shakes him a little. At the window she raises the shade and a dusky Southside morning light comes in feebly. She fills a pot with water and puts it on to boil. She calls to the boy, between yawns, in a slightly muffled voice.

Ruth is about thirty. We can see that she was a pretty girl, even exceptionally so, but now it is apparent that life has been little that she expected, and disappointment has already begun to hang in her face. In a few years, before thirty-five even, she will be known among her people as a "settled woman."

She crosses to her son and gives him a good, final, rousing shake.

Ruth: Come on now, boy, it's seven thirty! (*Her son sits up at last, in a stupor of sleepiness.*) I say hurry up, Travis! You ain't the only person in the world got to use a bathroom! (*The child, a sturdy, handsome little boy of ten or eleven, drags himself out of the bed and almost blindly takes his towels and "today's clothes" from drawers and a closet and goes out to the bathroom, which is in an outside hall and which is shared by another family or families on the same floor. Ruth crosses to the bedroom door at right and opens it and calls in to her husband.*) Walter Lee! . . . It's after seven thirty! Lemme see you do some waking up in there now! (*She waits.*) You better get up from there, man! It's after seven thirty I tell you. (*She waits again.*) All right, you just go ahead and lay there and next thing you know Travis be finished and Mr. Johnson'll be in there and you'll be fussing and cussing round here like a madman! And be late too! (*She waits, at the end of patience.*) Walter Lee — it's time for you to GET UP!

She waits another second and then starts to go into the bedroom, but is apparently satisfied that her husband has begun to get up. She stops, pulls the door to, and returns to the kitchen area. She wipes her face with a moist cloth and runs her fingers through her sleep-disheveled hair in a vain effort and ties an apron around her housecoat. The bedroom door at right opens and her husband stands in the doorway in his pajamas, which are rumpled and mismated. He is a lean, intense young man in his middle thirties, inclined to quick nervous movements and erratic speech habits—and always in his voice there is a quality of indictment.

Walter: Is he out yet?

Ruth: What you mean *out?* He ain't hardly got in there good yet.

Walter (wandering in, still more oriented to sleep than to a new day): Well, what was you doing all that yelling for if I can't even get in there yet? (*Stopping and thinking.*) Check coming today?

Ruth: They *said* Saturday and this is just Friday and I hopes to God you ain't going to get up here first thing this morning and start talking to me 'bout no money—'cause I 'bout don't want to hear it.

Walter: Something the matter with you this morning?

Ruth: No—I'm just sleepy as the devil. What kind of eggs you want?

Walter: Not scrambled. (*Ruth starts to scramble eggs.*) Paper come? (*Ruth points impatiently to the rolled up* Tribune *on the table, and he gets it and spreads it out and vaguely reads the front page.*) Set off another bomb yesterday.

Ruth (maximum indifference): Did they?

Walter (looking up): What's the matter with you?

Ruth: Ain't nothing the matter with me. And don't keep asking me that this morning.

Walter: Ain't nobody bothering you. (*Reading the news of the day absently again.*) Say Colonel McCormick is sick.

Ruth (affecting tea-party interest): Is he now? Poor thing.

Walter (sighing and looking at his watch): Oh, me. (*He waits.*) Now what is that boy doing in that bathroom all this time? He just going to have to start getting up earlier. I can't be being late to work on account of him fooling around in there.

Ruth (turning on him): Oh, no he ain't going to be getting up no earlier no such thing! It ain't his fault that he can't get to bed no earlier nights 'cause he got a bunch of crazy good-for-nothing clowns sitting up running their mouths in what is supposed to be his bedroom after ten o'clock at night . . .

Walter: That's what you mad about, ain't it? The things I want to talk about with my friends just couldn't be important in your mind, could they?

He rises and finds a cigarette in her handbag on the table and crosses to the little window and looks out, smoking and deeply enjoying this first one.

Ruth (almost matter of factly, a complaint too automatic to deserve emphasis): Why you always got to smoke before you eat in the morning?

Walter (at the window): Just look at 'em down there . . . Running and racing to work . . . (*He turns and faces his wife and watches her a moment at the stove, and then, suddenly.*) You look young this morning, baby.

Ruth (indifferently): Yeah?

Walter: Just for a second—stirring them eggs. Just for a second it was—you looked real young again. (*He reaches for her; she crosses away. Then, drily.*) It's gone now—you look like yourself again!

Ruth: Man, if you don't shut up and leave me alone.

Walter (looking out to the street again): First thing a man ought to learn in life is not to make love to no colored woman first thing in the morning. You all some eeeevil people at eight o'clock in the morning.

Travis appears in the hall doorway, almost fully dressed and quite wide awake now, his towels and pajamas across his shoulders. He opens the door and signals for his father to make the bathroom in a hurry.

Travis (watching the bathroom): Daddy, come on!

Walter gets his bathroom utensils and flies out to the bathroom.

Ruth: Sit down and have your breakfast, Travis.
Travis: Mama, this is Friday. (*Gleefully.*) Check coming tomorrow, huh?
Ruth: You get your mind off money and eat your breakfast.
Travis (eating): This is the morning we supposed to bring the fifty cents to school.
Ruth: Well, I ain't got no fifty cents this morning.
Travis: Teacher say we have to.
Ruth: I don't care what teacher say. I ain't got it. Eat your breakfast, Travis.
Travis: I *am* eating.
Ruth: Hush up now and just eat!

The boy gives her an exasperated look for her lack of understanding, and eats grudgingly.

Travis: You think Grandmama would have it?
Ruth: No! And I want you to stop asking your grandmother for money, you hear me?
Travis (outraged): Gaaaleee! I don't ask her, she just gimme it sometimes!
Ruth: Travis Willard Younger — I got too much on me this morning to be —
Travis: Maybe Daddy —
Ruth: Travis!

The boy hushes abruptly. They are both quiet and tense for several seconds.

Travis (presently): Could I maybe go carry some groceries in front of the super-market for a little while after school then?
Ruth: Just hush, I said. (*Travis jabs his spoon into his cereal bowl viciously, and rests his head in anger upon his fists.*) If you through eating, you can get over there and make up your bed.

The boy obeys stiffly and crosses the room, almost mechanically, to the bed and more or less folds the bedding into a heap, then angrily gets his books and cap.

Travis (sulking and standing apart from her unnaturally): I'm gone.
Ruth (looking up from the stove to inspect him automatically): Come here. (*He crosses to her and she studies his head.*) If you don't take this comb and fix this here head, you better! (*Travis puts down his books with a great sigh of oppression, and crosses to the mirror. His mother mutters under her breath about his "slubbornness."*) 'Bout to march out of here with that head looking just like chickens slept in it! I just don't know where you get your slubborn ways . . . And get your jacket, too. Looks chilly out this morning.
Travis (with conspicuously brushed hair and jacket): I'm gone.
Ruth: Get carfare and milk money — (*Waving one finger.*) — and not a single penny for no caps, you hear me?
Travis (with sullen politeness): Yes'm.

He turns in outrage to leave. His mother watches after him as in his frustration he approaches the door almost comically. When she speaks to him, her voice has become a very gentle tease.

Ruth (mocking; as she thinks he would say it): Oh, Mama makes me so mad sometimes, I don't know what to do! (*She waits and continues to his back as he stands stock-still in front of the door.*) I wouldn't kiss that woman good-bye for nothing in this world this morning! (*The boy finally turns around and rolls his eyes at her, knowing the mood has changed and he is vindicated; he does not, however, move toward her yet.*) Not for nothing in this world! (*She finally laughs aloud at him and holds out her arms to him and we see that it is a way between them, very old and practiced. He crosses to her and allows her to embrace him warmly but keeps his face fixed with masculine rigidity. She holds him back from her presently and looks at him and runs her fingers over the features of his face. With utter gentleness —.*) Now — whose little old angry man are you?

Travis (the masculinity and gruffness start to fade at last): Aw gaalee — Mama . . .

Ruth (mimicking): Aw — gaaaaalleeeee, Mama! (*She pushes him, with rough playfulness and finality, toward the door.*) Get on out of here or you going to be late.

Travis (in the face of love, new aggressiveness): Mama, could I *please* go carry groceries?

Ruth: Honey, it's starting to get so cold evenings.

Walter (coming in from the bathroom and drawing a make-believe gun from a make-believe holster and shooting at his son): What is it he wants to do?

Ruth: Go carry groceries after school at the supermarket.

Walter: Well, let him go . . .

Travis (quickly, to the ally): I *have* to — she won't gimme the fifty cents . . .

Walter (to his wife only): Why not?

Ruth (simply, and with flavor): "Cause we don't have it.

Walter (to Ruth only): What you tell the boy things like that for? (*Reaching down into his pants with a rather important gesture.*) Here, son —

He hands the boy the coin, but his eyes are directed to his wife's. Travis takes the money happily.

Travis: Thanks, Daddy.

He starts out. Ruth watches both of them with murder in her eyes. Walter stands and stares back at her with defiance, and suddenly reaches into his pocket again on an afterthought.

Walter (without even looking at his son, still staring hard at his wife): In fact, here's another fifty cents . . . Buy yourself some fruit today — or take a taxicab to school or something!

Travis: Whoopee —

He leaps up and clasps his father around the middle with his legs, and they face each other in mutual appreciation; slowly Walter Lee peeks around the boy to catch the violent rays from his wife's eyes and draws his head back as if shot.

Walter: You better get down now — and get to school, man.

Travis (at the door): O.K. Good-bye.

He exits.

Walter (after him, pointing with pride): That's *my* boy. (*She looks at him in disgust and turns back to her work.*) You know what I was thinking 'bout in the bathroom this morning?

Ruth: No.

Walter: How come you always try to be so pleasant!

Ruth: What is there to be pleasant 'bout!

Walter: You want to know what I was thinking 'bout in the bathroom or not!

Ruth: I know what you thinking 'bout.

Walter (ignoring her): 'Bout what me and Willy Harris was talking about last night.

Ruth (immediately — a refrain): Willy Harris is a good-for-nothing loudmouth.

Walter: Anybody who talks to me has got to be a good-for-nothing loudmouth, ain't he? And what you know about who is just a good-for-nothing loudmouth? Charlie Atkins was just a "good-for-nothing loudmouth" too, wasn't he! When he wanted me to go in the dry-cleaning business with him. And now — he's grossing a hundred thousand a year. A hundred thousand dollars a year! You still call *him* a loudmouth!

Ruth (bitterly): Oh, Walter Lee . . .

She folds her head on her arms over the table.

Walter (rising and coming to her and standing over her): You tired, ain't you? Tired of everything. Me, the boy, the way we live — this beat-up hole — everything. Ain't you? (*She doesn't look up, doesn't answer.*) So tired — moaning and groaning all the time, but you wouldn't do nothing to help, would you? You couldn't be on my side that long for nothing, could you?

Ruth: Walter, please leave me alone.

Walter: A man needs for a woman to back him up . . .

Ruth: Walter —

Walter: Mama would listen to you. You know she listen to you more than she do me and Bennie. She think more of you. All you have to do is just sit down with her when you drinking your coffee one morning and talking 'bout things like you do and — (*He sits down beside her and demonstrates graphically what he thinks her methods and tone should be.*) — you just sip your coffee, see, and say easy like that you been thinking 'bout that deal Walter Lee is so interested in, 'bout the store and all, and sip some more coffee, like what you saying ain't really that important to you — And the next thing you know, she be listening good and asking you questions and when I come home — I can tell her the details. This ain't no fly-by-night proposition, baby. I mean we figured it out, me and Willy and Bobo.

Ruth (with a frown): Bobo?

Walter: Yeah. You see, this little liquor store we got in mind cost seventy-five thousand and we figured the initial investment on the place be 'bout thirty thousand, see. That be ten thousand each. Course, there's a couple of hundred you got to pay so's you don't spend your life just waiting for them clowns to let your license get approved —

Ruth: You mean graft?

Walter (frowning impatiently): Don't call it that. See there, that just goes to show you what women understand about the world. Baby, don't *nothing* happen for you in the world 'less you pay *somebody* off!

Ruth: Walter, leave me alone! (*She raises her head and stares at him vigorously — then says, more quietly.*) *Eat* your eggs, they gonna be cold.

Walter (straightening up from her and looking off): That's it. There you are. Man say to his woman: I got me a dream. His woman say: Eat your eggs. (*Sadly, but gaining in power.*) Man say: I got to take hold of this here world, baby! And a woman will say: Eat your eggs and go to work. (*Passionately now.*) Man say: I got to change my life, I'm choking to death, baby! And his woman say — (*In utter anguish as he brings his fists down on his thighs.*) — Your eggs is getting cold!

Ruth (softly): Walter, that ain't none of our money.

Walter (not listening at all or even looking at her): This morning, I was lookin' in the mirror and thinking about it . . . I'm thirty-five years old; I been married eleven years and I got a boy who sleeps in the living room — (*Very, very quietly.*) — and all I got to give him is stories about how rich white people live . . .

Ruth: Eat your eggs, Walter.

Walter (slams the table and jumps up): — DAMN MY EGGS — DAMN ALL THE EGGS THAT EVER WAS!

Ruth: Then go to work.

Walter (looking up at her): See — I'm trying to talk to you 'bout myself — (*Shaking his head with the repetition.*) — and all you can say is eat them eggs and go to work.

Ruth (wearily): Honey, you never say nothing new. I listen to you every day, every night and every morning, and you never say nothing new. (*Shrugging.*) So you would rather *be* Mr. Arnold than be his chauffeur. So — I would *rather* be living in Buckingham Palace.

Walter: That is just what is wrong with the colored woman in this world . . . Don't understand about building their men up and making 'em feel like they somebody. Like they can do something.

Ruth (drily, but to hurt): There *are* colored men who do things.

Walter: No thanks to the colored woman.

Ruth: Well, being a colored woman, I guess I can't help myself none.

She rises and gets the ironing board and sets it up and attacks a huge pile of rough-dried clothes, sprinkling them in preparation for the ironing and then rolling them into tight fat balls.

Walter (mumbling): We one group of men tied to a race of women with small minds!

His sister Beneatha enters. She is about twenty, as slim and intense as her brother. She is not as pretty as her sister-in-law, but her lean, almost intellectual face has a handsomeness of its own. She wears a bright-red flannel nightie, and her thick hair stands wildly about her head. Her speech is a mixture of many things; it is different from the rest of the family's insofar as education has permeated her sense of English — and perhaps the Midwest rather than the South has finally — at last — won out in her inflection; but not altogether, because over all of it is a soft slurring and transformed use of vowels which is the decided influence of the Southside. She passes through the room without looking at either Ruth or

Walter and goes to the outside door and looks, a little blindly, out to the bathroom. She sees that it has been lost to the Johnsons. She closes the door with a sleepy vengeance and crosses to the table and sits down a little defeated.

Beneatha: I am going to start timing those people.

Walter: You should get up earlier.

Beneatha (her face in her hands. She is still fighting the urge to go back to bed): Really — would you suggest dawn? Where's the paper?

Walter (pushing the paper across the table to her as he studies her almost clinically, as though he has never seen her before): You a horrible-looking chick at this hour.

Beneatha (drily): Good morning, everybody.

Walter (senselessly): How is school coming?

Beneatha (in the same spirit): Lovely. Lovely. And you know, biology is the greatest. *(Looking up at him.)* I dissected something that looked just like you yesterday.

Walter: I just wondered if you've made up your mind and everything.

Beneatha (gaining in sharpness and impatience): And what did I answer yesterday morning — and the day before that?

Ruth (from the ironing board, like someone disinterested and old): Don't be so nasty, Bennie.

Beneatha (still to her brother): And the day before that and the day before that!

Walter (defensively): I'm interested in you. Something wrong with that? Ain't many girls who decide —

Walter and Beneatha (in unison): — "to be a doctor."

Silence.

Walter: Have we figured out yet just exactly how much medical school is going to cost?

Ruth: Walter Lee, why don't you leave that girl alone and get out of here to work?

Beneatha (exits to the bathroom and bangs on the door): Come on out of there, please!

She comes back into the room.

Walter (looking at his sister intently): You know the check is coming tomorrow.

Beneatha (turning on him with a sharpness all her own): That money belongs to Mama, Walter, and it's for her to decide how she wants to use it. I don't care if she wants to buy a house or a rocket ship or just nail it up somewhere and look at it. It's hers. Not ours — *hers.*

Walter (bitterly): Now ain't that fine! You just got your mother's interest at heart, ain't you, girl? You such a nice girl — but if Mama got that money she can always take a few thousand and help you through school too — can't she?

Beneatha: I have never asked anyone around here to do anything for me!

Walter: No! And the line between asking and just accepting when the time comes is big and wide — ain't it!

Beneatha (with fury): What do you want from me, Brother — that I quit school or just drop dead, which!

Walter: I don't want nothing but for you to stop acting holy 'round here. Me and Ruth done made some sacrifices for you — why can't you do something for the family?

Ruth: Walter, don't be dragging me in it.

Walter: You are in it — Don't you get up and go work in somebody's kitchen for the last three years to help put clothes on her back?

Ruth: Oh, Walter — that's not fair . . .

Walter: It ain't that nobody expects you to get on your knees and say thank you, Brother; thank you, Ruth; thank you, Mama — and thank you, Travis, for wearing the same pair of shoes for two semesters —

Beneatha (dropping to her knees): Well — I *do* — all right? — thank everybody! And forgive me for ever wanting to be anything at all! (*Pursuing him on her knees across the floor.*) FORGIVE ME, FORGIVE ME, FORGIVE ME!

Ruth: Please stop it! Your mama'll hear you.

Walter: Who the hell told you you had to be a doctor? If you so crazy 'bout messing 'round with sick people — then go be a nurse like other women — or just get married and be quiet . . .

Beneatha: Well — you finally got it said . . . It took you three years but you finally got it said. Walter, give up; leave me alone — it's Mama's money.

Walter: He was my father, too!

Beneatha: So what? He was mine, too — and Travis' grandfather — but the insurance money belongs to Mama. Picking on me is not going to make her give it to you to invest in any liquor stores — (*Underbreath, dropping into a chair.*) — and I for one say, God bless Mama for that!

Walter (to Ruth): See — did you hear? Did you hear!

Ruth: Honey, please go to work.

Walter: Nobody in this house is ever going to understand me.

Beneatha: Because you're a nut.

Walter: Who's a nut?

Beneatha: You — you are a nut. Thee is mad, boy.

Walter (looking at his wife and his sister from the door, very sadly): The world's most backward race of people, and that's a fact.

Beneatha (turning slowly in her chair): And then there are all those prophets who would lead us out of the wilderness — (*Walter slams out of the house.*) — into the swamps!

Ruth: Bennie, why you always gotta be pickin' on your brother? Can't you be a little sweeter sometimes? (*Door opens. Walter walks in. He fumbles with his cap, starts to speak, clears throat, looks everywhere but at Ruth. Finally:*)

Walter (to Ruth): I need some money for carfare.

Ruth (looks at him, then warms; teasing, but tenderly): Fifty cents? (*She goes to her bag and gets money.*) Here — take a taxi!

Walter exits. Mama enters. She is a woman in her early sixties, full-bodied and strong. She is one of those women of a certain grace and beauty who wear it so unobtrusively that it takes a while to notice. Her dark-brown face is surrounded by the total whiteness of her hair, and, being a woman who has adjusted to many things in life and overcome many more, her face is full of strength. She has, we can see, wit and faith of a kind that keep her eyes lit and full of interest and expectancy. She is, in a word, a beautiful woman. Her bearing is perhaps most like the noble bearing of the women of the Hereros of Southwest Africa —

rather as if she imagines that as she walks she still bears a basket or a vessel upon her head. Her speech, on the other hand, is as careless as her carriage is precise — she is inclined to slur everything — but her voice is perhaps not so much quiet as simply soft.

Mama: Who that 'round here slamming doors at this hour?

She crosses through the room, goes to the window, opens it, and brings in a feeble little plant growing doggedly in a small pot on the window sill. She feels the dirt and puts it back out.

Ruth: That was Walter Lee. He and Bennie was at it again.

Mama: My children and they tempers. Lord, if this little old plant don't get more sun than it's been getting it ain't never going to see spring again. (*She turns from the window.*) What's the matter with you this morning, Ruth? You looks right peaked. You aiming to iron all them things? Leave some for me. I'll get to 'em this afternoon. Bennie honey, it's too drafty for you to be sitting 'round half dressed. Where's your robe?

Beneatha: In the cleaners.

Mama: Well, go get mine and put it on.

Beneatha: I'm not cold, Mama, honest.

Mama: I know — but you so thin . . .

Beneatha (irritably): Mama, I'm not cold.

Mama (seeing the make-down bed as Travis has left it): Lord have mercy, look at that poor bed. Bless his heart — he tries, don't he?

She moves to the bed Travis has sloppily made up.

Ruth: No — he don't half try at all 'cause he knows you going to come along behind him and fix everything. That's just how come he don't know how to do nothing right now — you done spoiled that boy so.

Mama (folding bedding): Well — he's a little boy. Ain't supposed to know 'bout housekeeping. My baby, that's what he is. What you fix for his breakfast this morning?

Ruth (angrily): I feed my son, Lena!

Mama: I ain't meddling — (*Underbreath; busy-bodyish.*) I just noticed all last week he had cold cereal, and when it starts getting this chilly in the fall a child ought to have some hot grits or something when he goes out in the cold —

Ruth (furious): I gave him hot oats — is that all right!

Mama: I ain't meddling. (*Pause.*) Put a lot of nice butter on it? (*Ruth shoots her an angry look and does not reply.*) He likes lots of butter.

Ruth (exasperated): Lena —

Mama (to Beneatha. Mama is inclined to wander conversationally some-times): What was you and your brother fussing 'bout this morning?

Beneatha: It's not important, Mama.

She gets up and goes to look out at the bathroom, which is apparently free, and she picks up her towels and rushes out.

Mama: What was they fighting about?

Ruth: Now you know as well as I do.

Mama (shaking her head): Brother still worrying hisself sick about that money?

Ruth: You know he is.

Mama: You had breakfast?

Ruth: Some coffee.

Mama: Girl, you better start eating and looking after yourself better. You almost thin as Travis.

Ruth: Lena —

Mama: Un-hunh?

Ruth: What are you going to do with it?

Mama: Now don't you start, child. It's too early in the morning to be talking about money. It ain't Christian.

Ruth: It's just that he got his heart set on that store —

Mama: You mean that liquor store that Willy Harris want him to invest in?

Ruth: Yes —

Mama: We ain't no business people, Ruth. We just plain working folks.

Ruth: Ain't nobody business people till they go into business. Walter Lee say colored people ain't never going to start getting ahead till they start gambling on some different kinds of things in the world — investments and things.

Mama: What done got into you, girl? Walter Lee done finally sold you on investing.

Ruth: No, Mama, something is happening between Walter and me. I don't know what it is — but he needs something — something I can't give him any more. He needs this chance, Lena.

Mama (frowning deeply): But liquor, honey —

Ruth: Well — like Walter say — I spec people going to always be drinking themselves some liquor.

Mama: Well — whether they drinks it or not ain't none of my business. But whether I go into business selling it to 'em *is,* and I don't want that on my ledger this late in life. (*Stopping suddenly and studying her daughter-in-law.*) Ruth Younger, what's the matter with you today? You look like you could fall over right there.

Ruth: I'm tired.

Mama: Then you better stay home from work today.

Ruth: I can't stay home. She'd be calling up the agency and screaming at them, "My girl didn't come in today — send me somebody! My girl didn't come in!" Oh, she just have a fit . . .

Mama: Well, let her have it. I'll just call her up and say you got the flu —

Ruth (laughing): Why the flu?

Mama: 'Cause it sounds respectable to 'em. Something white people get, too. They know 'bout the flu. Otherwise they think you been cut up or something when you tell 'em you sick.

Ruth: I got to go in. We need the money.

Mama: Somebody would of thought my children done all but starved to death the way they talk about money here late. Child, we got a great big old check coming tomorrow.

Ruth (sincerely, but also self-righteously): Now that's your money. It ain't got nothing to do with me. We all feel like that — Walter and Bennie and me — even Travis.

Mama (thoughtfully, and suddenly very far away): Ten thousand dollars —
Ruth: Sure is wonderful.
Mama: Ten thousand dollars.
Ruth: You know what you should do, Miss Lena? You should take yourself a trip
somewhere. To Europe or South America or someplace —
Mama (throwing up her hands at the thought): Oh, child!
Ruth: I'm serious. Just pack up and leave! Go on away and enjoy yourself some.
Forget about the family and have yourself a ball for once in your life —
Mama (drily): You sound like I'm just about ready to die. Who'd go with me?
What I look like wandering 'round Europe by myself?
Ruth: Shoot — these here rich white women do it all the time. They don't think
nothing of packing up they suitcases and piling on one of them big steam-
ships and — swoosh! — they gone, child.
Mama: Something always told me I wasn't no rich white woman.
Ruth: Well — what are you going to do with it then?
Mama: I ain't rightly decided. (*Thinking. She speaks now with emphasis.*) Some
of it got to be put away for Beneatha and her schoolin' — and ain't nothing
going to touch that part of it. Nothing. (*She waits several seconds, trying to
make up her mind about something, and looks at Ruth a little tentatively
before going on.*) Been thinking that we maybe could meet the notes on a
little old two-story somewhere, with a yard where Travis could play in the
summertime, if we use part of the insurance for a down payment and
everybody kind of pitch in. I could maybe take on a little day work again,
few days a week —
*Ruth (studying her mother-in-law furtively and concentrating on her ironing,
anxious to encourage without seeming to):* Well, Lord knows, we've put
enough rent into this here rat trap to pay for four houses by now . . .
*Mama (looking up at the words "rat trap" and then looking around and leaning
back and sighing — in a suddenly reflective mood —):* "Rat trap" — yes,
that's all it is. (*Smiling.*) I remember just as well the day me and Big Walter
moved in here. Hadn't been married but two weeks and wasn't planning on
living here no more than a year. (*She shakes her head at the dissolved dream.*)
We was going to set away, little by little, don't you know, and buy a little
place out in Morgan Park. We had even picked out the house. (*Chuckling a
little.*) Looks right dumpy today. But Lord, child, you should know all the
dreams I had 'bout buying that house and fixing it up and making me a little
garden in the back — (*She waits and stops smiling.*) And didn't none of it
happen.

Dropping her hands in a futile gesture.

Ruth (keeps her head down, ironing): Yes, life can be a barrel of disappointments,
sometimes.
Mama: Honey, Big Walter would come in here some nights back then and slump
down on that couch there and just look at the rug, and look at me and look
at the rug and then back at me — and I'd know he was down then . . . really
down. (*After a second very long and thoughtful pause; she is seeing back to
times that only she can see.*) And then, Lord, when I lost that baby — little
Claude — I almost thought I was going to lose Big Walter too. Oh, that man
grieved hisself! He was one man to love his children.

Ruth: Ain't nothin' can tear at you like losin' your baby.

Mama: I guess that's how come that man finally worked hisself to death like he done. Like he was fighting his own war with this here world that took his baby from him.

Ruth: He sure was a fine man, all right. I always liked Mr. Younger.

Mama: Crazy 'bout his children! God knows there was plenty wrong with Walter Younger — hard-headed, mean, kind of wild with women — plenty wrong with him. But he sure loved his children. Always wanted them to have something — be something. That's where Brother gets all these notions, I reckon. Big Walter used to say, he'd get right wet in the eyes sometimes, lean his head back with the water standing in his eyes and say, "Seem like God didn't see fit to give the black man nothing but dreams — but He did give us children to make them dreams seem worthwhile." (*She smiles.*) He could talk like that, don't you know.

Ruth: Yes, he sure could. He was a good man, Mr. Younger.

Mama: Yes, a fine man — just couldn't never catch up with his dreams, that's all.

Beneatha comes in, brushing her hair and looking up to the ceiling, where the sound of a vacuum cleaner has started up.

Beneatha: What could be so dirty on that woman's rugs that she has to vacuum them every single day?

Ruth: I wish certain young women 'round here who I could name would take inspiration about certain rugs in a certain apartment I could also mention.

Beneatha (shrugging): How much cleaning can a house need, for Christ's sakes.

Mama (not liking the Lord's name used thus): Bennie!

Ruth: Just listen to her — just listen!

Beneatha: Oh, God!

Mama: If you use the Lord's name just one more time —

Beneatha (a bit of a whine): Oh, Mama —

Ruth: Fresh — just fresh as salt, this girl!

Beneatha (drily): Well — if the salt loses its savor —

Mama: Now that will do. I just ain't going to have you 'round here reciting the scriptures in vain — you hear me?

Beneatha: How did I manage to get on everybody's wrong side by just walking into a room?

Ruth: If you weren't so fresh —

Beneatha: Ruth, I'm twenty years old.

Mama: What time you be home from school today?

Beneatha: Kind of late. (*With enthusiasm.*) Madeline is going to start my guitar lessons today.

Mama and Ruth look up with the same expression.

Mama: Your *what* kind of lessons?

Beneatha: Guitar.

Ruth: Oh, Father!

Mama: How come you done taken it in your mind to learn to play the guitar?

Beneatha: I just want to, that's all.

Mama (smiling): Lord, child, don't you know what to do with yourself? How long it going to be before you get tired of this now — like you got tired of that little play-acting group you joined last year? (*Looking at Ruth.*) And what was it the year before that?

Ruth: The horseback-riding club for which she bought that fifty-five-dollar riding habit that's been hanging in the closet ever since!

Mama (to Beneatha): Why you got to flit so from one thing to another, baby?

Beneatha (sharply): I just want to learn to play the guitar. Is there anything wrong with that?

Mama: Ain't nobody trying to stop you. I just wonders sometimes why you has to flit so from one thing to another all the time. You ain't never done nothing with all that camera equipment you brought home —

Beneatha: I don't flit! I — I experiment with different forms of expression —

Ruth: Like riding a horse?

Beneatha: — People have to express themselves one way or another.

Mama: What is it you want to express?

Beneatha (angrily): Me! (*Mama and Ruth look at each other and burst into raucous laughter.*) Don't worry — I don't expect you to understand.

Mama (to change the subject): Who you going out with tomorrow night?

Beneatha (with displeasure): George Murchison again.

Mama (pleased): Oh — you getting a little sweet on him?

Ruth: You ask me, this child ain't sweet on nobody but herself — (*Under breath.*) Express herself!

They laugh.

Beneatha: Oh — I like George all right, Mama. I mean I like him enough to go out with him and stuff, but —

Ruth (for devilment): What does *and stuff* mean?

Beneatha: Mind your own business.

Mama: Stop picking at her now, Ruth. (*She chuckles — then a suspicious sudden look at her daughter as she turns in her chair for emphasis.*) What DOES it mean?

Beneatha (wearily): Oh, I just mean I couldn't ever really be serious about George. He's — he's so shallow.

Ruth: Shallow — what do you mean he's shallow? He's *Rich!*

Mama: Hush, Ruth.

Beneatha: I know he's rich. He knows he's rich, too.

Ruth: Well — what other qualities a man got to have to satisfy you, little girl?

Beneatha: You wouldn't even begin to understand. Anybody who married Walter could not possibly understand.

Mama (outraged): What kind of way is that to talk about your brother?

Beneatha: Brother is a flip — let's face it.

Mama (to Ruth, helplessly): What's a flip?

Ruth (glad to add kindling): She's saying he's crazy.

Beneatha: Not crazy. Brother isn't really crazy yet — he — he's an elaborate neurotic.

Mama: Hush your mouth!

Beneatha: As for George. Well. George looks good — he's got a beautiful car and he takes me to nice places and, as my sister-in-law says, he is probably the richest boy I will ever get to know and I even like him sometimes —

but if the Youngers are sitting around waiting to see if their little Bennie is going to tie up the family with the Murchisons, they are wasting their time.

Ruth: You mean you wouldn't marry George Murchison if he asked you some-day? That pretty, rich thing? Honey, I knew you was odd —

Beneatha: No I would not marry him if all I felt for him was what I feel now. Besides, George's family wouldn't really like it.

Mama: Why not?

Beneatha: Oh, Mama — The Murchisons are honest-to-God-real-*live*-rich colored people, and the only people in the world who are more snobbish than rich white people are rich colored people. I thought everybody knew that. I've met Mrs. Murchison. She's a scene!

Mama: You must not dislike people 'cause they well off, honey.

Beneatha: Why not? It makes just as much sense as disliking people 'cause they are poor, and lots of people do that.

Ruth (a wisdom-of-the-ages manner. To Mama): Well, she'll get over some of this —

Beneatha: Get over it? What are you talking about, Ruth? Listen, I'm going to be a doctor. I'm not worried about who I'm going to marry yet — if I ever get married.

Mama and Ruth: If!

Mama: Now, Bennie —

Beneatha: Oh, I probably will . . . but first I'm going to be a doctor, and George, for one, still thinks that's pretty funny. I couldn't be bothered with that. I am going to be a doctor and everybody around here better understand that!

Mama (kindly): 'Course you going to be a doctor, honey, God willing.

Beneatha (drily): God hasn't got a thing to do with it.

Mama: Beneatha — that just wasn't necessary.

Beneatha: Well — neither is God. I get sick of hearing about God.

Mama: Beneatha!

Beneatha: I mean it! I'm just tired of hearing about God all the time. What has He got to do with anything? Does He pay tuition?

Mama: You 'bout to get your fresh little jaw slapped!

Ruth: That's just what she needs, all right!

Beneatha: Why? Why can't I say what I want to around here, like everybody else?

Mama: It don't sound nice for a young girl to say things like that — you wasn't brought up that way. Me and your father went to trouble to get you and Brother to church every Sunday.

Beneatha: Mama, you don't understand. It's all a matter of ideas, and God is just one idea I don't accept. It's not important. I am not going out and be immoral or commit crimes because I don't believe in God. I don't even think about it. It's just that I get tired of Him getting credit for all the things the human race achieves through its own stubborn effort. There simply is no blasted God — there is only man and it is *He* who makes miracles!

Mama absorbs this speech, studies her daughter and rises slowly and crosses to Beneatha and slaps her powerfully across the face. After, there is only silence and the daughter drops her eyes from her mother's face, and Mama is very tall before her.

Mama: Now — you say after me, in my mother's house there is still God. (*There is a long pause and Beneatha stares at the floor wordlessly. Mama repeats the phrase with precision and cool emotion.*) In my mother's house there is still God.

Beneatha: In my mother's house there is still God.

A long pause.

Mama (walking away from Beneatha, too disturbed for triumphant posture. Stopping and turning back to her daughter): There are some ideas we ain't going to have in this house. Not long as I am at the head of this family.

Beneatha: Yes, ma'am.

Mama walks out of the room.

Ruth (almost gently, with profound understanding): You think you a woman, Bennie — but you still a little girl. What you did was childish — so you got treated like a child.

Beneatha: I see. (*quietly.*) I also see that everybody thinks it's all right for Mama to be a tyrant. But all the tyranny in the world will never put a God in the heavens!

She picks up her books and goes out. Pause.

Ruth (goes to Mama's door): She said she was sorry.

Mama (coming out, going to her plant): They frightens me, Ruth. My children.

Ruth: You got good children, Lena. They just a little off sometimes — but they're good.

Mama: No — there's something come down between me and them that don't let us understand each other and I don't know what it is. One done almost lost his mind thinking 'bout money all the time and the other done commence to talk about things I can't seem to understand in no form or fashion. What is it that's changing, Ruth.

Ruth (soothingly, older than her years): Now . . . you taking it all too seriously. You just got strong-willed children and it takes a strong woman like you to keep 'em in hand.

Mama (looking at her plant and sprinkling a little water on it): They spirited all right, my children. Got to admit they got spirit — Bennie and Walter. Like this little old plant that ain't never had enough sunshine or nothing — and look at it . . .

She has her back to Ruth, who has had to stop ironing and lean against something and put the back of her hand to her forehead.

Ruth (trying to keep Mama from noticing): You . . . sure . . . loves that little old thing, don't you? . . .

Mama: Well, I always wanted me a garden like I used to see sometimes at the back of the houses down home. This plant is close as I ever got to having one. (*She looks out of the window as she replaces the plant.*) Lord, ain't nothing as dreary as the view from this window on a dreary day, is there? Why ain't you singing this morning, Ruth? Sing that "No Ways Tired." That song always lifts me up so — (*She turns at last to see that Ruth has slipped*

quietly to the floor, in a state of semiconsciousness.) Ruth! Ruth honey—
what's the matter with you . . . Ruth!

Curtain.

SCENE II. [*The following morning.*]

*It is the following morning; a Saturday morning, and house cleaning is in
progress at the Youngers. Furniture has been shoved hither and yon and Mama
is giving the kitchen-area walls a washing down. Beneatha, in dungarees, with
a handkerchief tied around her face, is spraying insecticide into the cracks in
the walls. As they work, the radio is on and a Southside disk-jockey program is
inappropriately filling the house with a rather exotic saxophone blues. Travis,
the sole idle one, is leaning on his arms, looking out of the window.*

Travis: Grandmama, that stuff Bennie is using smells awful. Can I go downstairs,
please?
Mama: Did you get all them chores done already? I ain't seen you doing much.
Travis: Yes'm — finished early. Where did Mama go this morning?
Mama (looking at Beneatha): She had to go on a little errand.

*The phone rings. Beneatha runs to answer it and reaches it before Walter, who
has entered from bedroom.*

Travis: Where?
Mama: To tend to her business.
Beneatha: Haylo . . . (*Disappointed.*) Yes, he is. (*She tosses the phone to Walter,
who barely catches it.*) It's Willie Harris again.
Walter (as privately as possible under Mama's gaze): Hello, Willie. Did you get
the papers from the lawyer? . . . No, not yet. I told you the mailman doesn't
get here till ten-thirty . . . No, I'll come there . . . Yeah! Right away. (*He hangs
up and goes for his coat.*)
Beneatha: Brother, where did Ruth go?
Walter (as he exits): How should I know!
Travis: Aw come on, Grandma. Can I go outside?
Mama: Oh, I guess so. You stay right in front of the house, though, and keep a
good lookout for the postman.
Travis: Yes'm. (*He darts into bedroom for stickball and bat, reenters, and sees
Beneatha on her knees spraying under sofa with behind upraised. He edges
closer to the target, takes aim, and lets her have it. She screams.*) Leave them
poor little cockroaches alone, they ain't bothering you none! (*He runs as
she swings the spraygun at him viciously and playfully.*) Grandma! Grandma!
Mama: Look out there, girl, before you be spilling some of that stuff on that
child!
Travis (safely behind the bastion of Mama): That's right — look out, now! (*He
exits.*)
Beneatha (drily): I can't imagine that it would hurt him — it has never hurt the
roaches.
Mama: Well, little boys' hides ain't as tough as Southside roaches. You better
get over there behind the bureau. I seen one marching out of there like
Napoleon yesterday.

Beneatha: There's really only one way to get rid of them, Mama —

Mama: How?

Beneatha: Set fire to this building! Mama, where did Ruth go?

Mama (looking at her with meaning): To the doctor, I think.

Beneatha: The doctor? What's the matter? (*They exchange glances.*) You don't think —

Mama (with her sense of drama): Now I ain't saying what I think. But I ain't never been wrong 'bout a woman neither.

The phone rings.

Beneatha (at the phone): Hay-lo . . . (*Pause, and a moment of recognition.*) Well — when did you get back! . . . And how was it? . . . Of course I've missed you — in my way . . . This morning? No . . . house cleaning and all that and Mama hates it if I let people come over when the house is like this . . . You *have?* Well, that's different . . . What is it — Oh, what the hell, come on over . . . Right, see you then. *Arrividerci.*

She hangs up.

Mama (who has listened vigorously, as is her habit): Who is that you inviting over here with this house looking like this? You ain't got the pride you was born with!

Beneatha: Asagai doesn't care how houses look, Mama — he's an intellectual.

Mama: Who?

Beneatha: Asagai — Joseph Asagai. He's an African boy I met on campus. He's been studying in Canada all summer.

Mama: What's his name?

Beneatha: Asagai, Joseph. Ah-sah-guy . . . He's from Nigeria.

Mama: Oh, that's the little country that was founded by slaves way back . . .

Beneatha: No, Mama — that's Liberia.

Mama: I don't think I never met no African before.

Beneatha: Well, do me a favor and don't ask him a whole lot of ignorant questions about Africans. I mean, do they wear clothes and all that —

Mama: Well, now, I guess if you think we so ignorant 'round here maybe you shouldn't bring your friends here —

Beneatha: It's just that people ask such crazy things. All anyone seems to know about when it comes to Africa is Tarzan —

Mama (indignantly): Why should I know anything about Africa?

Beneatha: Why do you give money at church for the missionary work?

Mama: Well, that's to help save people.

Beneatha: You mean save them from *heathenism* —

Mama (innocently): Yes.

Beneatha: I'm afraid they need more salvation from the British and the French.

Ruth comes in forlornly and pulls off her coat with dejection. They both turn to look at her.

Ruth (dispiritedly): Well, I guess from all the happy faces — everybody knows.

Beneatha: You pregnant?

Mama: Lord have mercy, I sure hope it's a little old girl. Travis ought to have sister.

Beneatha and Ruth give her a hopeless look for this grandmotherly enthusiasm.

Beneatha: How far along are you?

Ruth: Two months.

Beneatha: Did you mean to? I mean did you plan it or was it an accident?

Mama: What do you know about planning or not planning?

Beneatha: Oh, Mama.

Ruth (wearily): She's twenty years old, Lena.

Beneatha: Did you plan it, Ruth?

Ruth: Mind your own business.

Beneatha: It is my business — where is he going to live, on the *roof?* (*There is silence following the remark as the three women react to the sense of it.*) Gee — I didn't mean that, Ruth, honest. Gee, I don't feel like that at all. I — I think it is wonderful.

Ruth (dully): Wonderful.

Beneatha: Yes — really.

Mama (looking at Ruth, worried): Doctor say everything going to be all right?

Ruth (far away): Yes — she says everything is going to be fine . . .

Mama (immediately suspicious): "She" — What doctor you went to?

Ruth folds over, near hysteria.

Mama (worriedly hovering over Ruth): Ruth honey — what's the matter with you — you sick?

Ruth has her fists clenched on her thighs and is fighting hard to suppress a scream that seems to be rising in her.

Beneatha: What's the matter with her, Mama?

Mama (working her fingers in Ruth's shoulders to relax her): She be all right. Women gets right depressed sometimes when they get her way. (*Speaking softly, expertly, rapidly.*) Now you just relax. That's right . . . just lean back, don't think 'bout nothing at all . . . nothing at all —

Ruth: I'm all right . . .

The glassy-eyed look melts and then she collapses into a fit of heavy sobbing. The bell rings.

Beneatha: Oh, my God — that must be Asagai.

Mama (to Ruth): Come on now, honey. You need to lie down and rest awhile . . . then have some nice hot food.

They exit, Ruth's weight on her mother-in-law. Beneatha, herself profoundly disturbed, opens the door to admit a rather dramatic-looking young man with a large package.

Asagai: Hello, Alaiyo —

Beneatha (holding the door open and regarding him with pleasure): Hello . . . (*Long pause.*) Well — come in. And please excuse everything. My mother was very upset about my letting anyone come here with the place like this.

Asagai (coming into the room): You look disturbed too . . . Is something wrong?

Beneatha (still at the door, absently): Yes . . . we've all got acute ghetto-itus. (*She smiles and comes toward him, finding a cigarette and sitting.*) So — sit down!

No! Wait! (*She whips the spraygun off sofa where she had left it and puts the cushions back. At last perches on arm of sofa. He sits.*) So, how was Canada?

Asagai (a sophisticate): Canadian.

Beneatha (looking at him): Asagai, I'm very glad you are back.

Asagai (looking back at her in turn): Are you really?

Beneatha: Yes — very.

Asagai: Why? — you were quite glad when I went away. What happened?

Beneatha: You went away.

Asagai: Ahhhhhhhh.

Beneatha: Before — you wanted to be so serious before there was time.

Asagai: How much time must there be before one knows what one feels?

Beneatha (stalling this particular conversation. Her hands pressed together, in a deliberately childish gesture): What did you bring me?

Asagai (handing her the package): Open it and see.

Beneatha (eagerly opening the package and drawing out some records and the colorful robes of a Nigerian woman): Oh Asagai! . . . You got them for me! . . . How beautiful . . . and the records too! (*She lifts out the robes and runs to the mirror with them and holds the drapery up in front of herself.*)

Asagai (coming to her at the mirror): I shall have to teach you how to drape it properly. (*He flings the material about her for the moment and stands back to look at her.*) Ah — Oh-pay-gay-day, oh-gbah-mu-shay. (*A Yoruba exclamation for admiration.*) You wear it well . . . very well . . . mutilated hair and all.

Beneatha (turning suddenly): My hair — what's wrong with my hair?

Asagai (shrugging): Were you born with it like that?

Beneatha (reaching up to touch it): No . . . of course not.

She looks back to the mirror, disturbed.

Asagai (smiling): How then?

Beneatha: You know perfectly well how . . . as crinkly as yours . . . that's how.

Asagai: And it is ugly to you that way?

Beneatha (quickly): Oh, no — not ugly . . . (*More slowly, apologetically.*) But it's so hard to manage when it's, well — raw.

Asagai: And so to accommodate that — you mutilate it every week?

Beneatha: It's not mutilation!

Asagai (laughing aloud at her seriousness): Oh . . . please! I am only teasing you because you are so very serious about these things. (*He stands back from her and folds his arms across his chest as he watches her pulling at her hair and frowning in the mirror.*) Do you remember the first time you met me at school? . . . (*He laughs.*) You came up to me and you said — and I thought you were the most serious little thing I had ever seen — you said: (*He imitates her.*) "Mr. Asagai — I want very much to talk with you. About Africa. You see, Mr. Asagai, I am looking for my *identity!*"

He laughs.

Beneatha (turning to him, not laughing): Yes —

Her face is quizzical, profoundly disturbed.

Asagai (still teasing and reaching out and taking her face in his hands and turning her profile to him): Well . . . it is true that this is not so much a profile of a Hollywood queen as perhaps a queen of the Nile — (*A mock dismissal of the importance of the question.*) But what does it matter? Assimilationism is so popular in your country.

Beneatha (wheeling, passionately, sharply): I am not an assimilationist!

Asagai (the protest hangs in the room for a moment and Asagai studies her, his laughter fading): Such a serious one. (*There is a pause.*) So — you like the robes? You must take excellent care of them — they are from my sister's personal wardrobe.

Beneatha (with incredulity): You — you sent all the way home — for me?

Asagai (with charm): For you — I would do much more . . . Well, that is what I came for. I must go.

Beneatha: Will you call me Monday?

Asagai: Yes . . . We have a great deal to talk about. I mean about identity and time and all that.

Beneatha: Time?

Asagai: Yes. About how much time one needs to know what one feels.

Beneatha: You see! You never understood that there is more than one kind of feeling which can exist between a man and a woman — or, at least, there should be.

Asagai (shaking his head negatively but gently): No. Between a man and a woman there need be only one kind of feeling. I have that for you . . . Now even . . . right this moment . . .

Beneatha: I know — and by itself — it won't do. I can find that anywhere.

Asagai: For a woman it should be enough.

Beneatha: I know — because that's what it says in all the novels that men write. But it isn't. Go ahead and laugh — but I'm not interested in being someone's little episode in America or — (*With feminine vengeance.*) — one of them! (*Asagai has burst into laughter again.*) That's funny as hell, huh!

Asagai: It's just that every American girl I have known has said that to me. White — black — in this you are all the same. And the same speech, too!

Beneatha (angrily): Yuk, yuk, yuk!

Asagai: It's how you can be sure that the world's most liberated women are not liberated at all. You all talk about it too much!

Mama enters and is immediately all social charm because of the presence of a guest.

Beneatha: Oh — Mama — this is Mr. Asagai.

Mama: How do you do?

Asagai (total politeness to an elder): How do you do, Mrs. Younger. Please forgive me for coming at such an outrageous hour on a Saturday.

Mama: Well, you are quite welcome. I just hope you understand that our house don't always look like this. (*Chatterish.*) You must come again. I would love to hear all about — (*Not sure of the name.*) — your country. I think it's so sad the way our American Negroes don't know nothing about Africa 'cept Tarzan and all that. And all that money they pour into these churches when they ought to be helping you people over there drive out them French and Englishmen done taken away your land.

The mother flashes a slightly superior look at her daughter upon completion of the recitation.

Asagai (taken aback by this sudden and acutely unrelated expression of sympathy): Yes . . . yes . . .

Mama (smiling at him suddenly and relaxing and looking him over): How many miles is it from here to where you come from?

Asagai: Many thousands.

Mama (looking at him as she would Walter): I bet you don't half look after yourself, being away from your mama either. I spec you better come 'round here from time to time to get yourself some decent homecooked meals . . .

Asagai (moved): Thank you. Thank you very much. *(They are all quiet, then —)* Well . . . I must go. I will call you Monday, Alaiyo.

Mama: What's that he call you?

Asagai: Oh — "Alaiyo." I hope you don't mind. It is what you would call a nickname, I think. It is a Yoruba word. I am a Yoruba.

Mama (looking at Beneatha): I — I thought he was from — *(Uncertain.)*

Asagai (understanding): Nigeria is my country. Yoruba is my tribal origin —

Beneatha: You didn't tell us what Alaiyo means . . . for all I know, you might be calling me Little Idiot or something . . .

Asagai: Well . . . let me see . . . I do not know how just to explain it . . . The sense of a thing can be so different when it changes languages.

Beneatha: You're evading.

Asagai: No — really it is difficult . . . *(Thinking.)* It means . . . it means One for Whom Bread — Food — Is Not Enough. *(He looks at her.)* Is that all right?

Beneatha (understanding, softly): Thank you.

Mama (looking from one to the other and not understanding any of it): Well . . . that's nice . . . You must come see us again — Mr. —

Asagai: Ah-sah-guy . . .

Mama: Yes . . . Do come again.

Asagai: Good-bye.

He exits.

Mama (after him): Lord, that's a pretty thing just went out here! *(Insinuatingly, to her daughter.)* Yes, I guess I see why we done commence to get so interested in Africa 'round here. Missionaries my aunt Jenny!

She exits.

Beneatha: Oh, Mama! . . .

She picks up the Nigerian dress and holds it up to her in front of the mirror again. She sets the headdress on haphazardly and then notices her hair again and clutches at it and then replaces the headdress and frowns at herself. Then she starts to wriggle in front of the mirror as she thinks a Nigerian woman might. Travis enters and stands regarding her.

Travis: What's the matter, girl, you cracking up?

Beneatha: Shut up.

She pulls the headdress off and looks at herself in the mirror and clutches at her hair again and squinches her eyes as if trying to imagine something. Then, suddenly, she gets her raincoat and kerchief and hurriedly prepares for going out.

Mama *(coming back into the room):* She's resting now. Travis, baby, run next door and ask Miss Johnson to please let me have a little kitchen cleanser. This here can is empty as Jacob's kettle.

Travis: I just came in.

Mama: Do as you told. (*He exits and she looks at her daughter.*) Where you going?

Beneatha *(halting at the door):* To become a queen of the Nile!

She exits in a breathless blaze of glory. Ruth appears in the bedroom doorway.

Mama: Who told you to get up?

Ruth: Ain't nothing wrong with me to be lying in no bed for. Where did Bennie go?

Mama *(drumming her fingers):* Far as I could make out — to Egypt. (*Ruth just looks at her.*) What time is it getting to?

Ruth: Ten twenty. And the mailman going to ring that bell this morning just like he done every morning for the last umpteen years.

Travis comes in with the cleanser can.

Travis: She say to tell you that she don't have much.

Mama *(angrily):* Lord, some people I could name sure is tight-fisted! (*Directing her grandson.*) Mark two cans of cleanser on the list there. If she that hard up for kitchen cleanser, I sure don't want to forget to get her none!

Ruth: Lena — maybe the woman is just short on cleanser —

Mama *(not listening):* — Much baking powder as she done borrowed from me all these years, she could of done gone into the baking business!

The bell sounds suddenly and sharply and all three are stunned — serious and silent — midspeech. In spite of all the other conversations and distractions of the morning, this is what they have been waiting for, even Travis, who looks helplessly from his mother to his grandmother. Ruth is the first to come to life again.

Ruth *(to Travis):* Get down them steps, boy!

Travis snaps to life and flies out to get the mail.

Mama *(her eyes wide, her hand to her breast):* You mean it done really come?

Ruth *(excited):* Oh, Miss Lena!

Mama *(collecting herself):* Well . . . I don't know what we all so excited about 'round here for. We known it was coming for months.

Ruth: That's a whole lot different from having it come and being able to hold it in your hands . . . a piece of paper worth ten thousand dollars . . . (*Travis bursts back into the room. He holds the envelope high above his head, like a little dancer, his face is radiant and he is breathless. He moves to his grandmother with sudden slow ceremony and puts the envelope into her hands. She accepts it, and then merely holds it and looks at it.*) Come on! Open it . . . Lord have mercy, I wish Walter Lee was here!

Travis: Open it, Grandmama!

Mama *(staring at it):* Now you all be quiet. It's just a check.

Ruth: Open it . . .

Mama (still staring at it): Now don't act silly . . . We ain't never been no people to act silly 'bout no money —

Ruth (swiftly): We ain't never had none before — OPEN IT!

Mama finally makes a good strong tear and pulls out the thin blue slice of paper and inspects it closely. The boy and his mother study it raptly over Mama's shoulders.

Mama: Travis! (*She is counting off with doubt.*) Is that the right number of zeros.

Travis: Yes'm . . . ten thousand dollars. Gaalee, grandmama, you rich.

Mama (She holds the check away from her, still looking at it. Slowly her face sobers into a mask of unhappiness): Ten thousand dollars. (*She hands it to Ruth.*) Put it away somewhere, Ruth. (*She does not look at Ruth; her eyes seem to be seeing something somewhere very far off.*) Ten thousand dollars they give you. Ten thousand dollars.

Travis (to his mother, sincerely): What's the matter with Grandmama — don't she want to be rich?

Ruth (distractedly): You go on out and play now, baby. (*Travis exits. Mama starts wiping dishes absently, humming intently to herself. Ruth turns to her, with kind exasperation.*) You've gone and got yourself upset.

Mama (not looking at her): I spec if it wasn't for you all . . . I would just put that money away or give it to the church or something.

Ruth: Now what kind of talk is that. Mr. Younger would just be plain mad if he could hear you talking foolish like that.

Mama (stopping and staring off): Yes . . . he sure would. (*Sighing.*) We got enough to do with that money, all right. (*She halts then, and turns and looks at her daughter-in-law hard; Ruth avoids her eyes and Mama wipes her hands with finality and starts to speak firmly to Ruth.*) Where did you go today, girl?

Ruth: To the doctor.

Mama (impatiently): Now, Ruth . . . you know better than that. Old Doctor Jones is strange enough in his way but there ain't nothing 'bout him make somebody slip and call him "she" — like you done this morning.

Ruth: Well, that's what happened — my tongue slipped.

Mama: You went to see that woman, didn't you?

Ruth (defensively, giving herself away): What woman you talking about?

Mama (angrily): That woman who —

Walter enters in great excitement.

Walter: Did it come?

Mama (quietly): Can't you give people a Christian greeting before you start asking about money?

Walter (to Ruth): Did it come? (*Ruth unfolds the check and lays it quietly before him, watching him intently with thoughts of her own. Walter sits down and grasps it close and counts off the zeros.*) Ten thousand dollars — (*He turns suddenly, frantically to his mother and draws some papers out of his breast pocket.*) Mama — look. Old Willy Harris put everything on paper —

Mama: Son — I think you ought to talk to your wife . . . I'll go on out and leave you alone if you want —

Walter: I can talk to her later — Mama, look —

Mama: Son —

Walter: WILL SOMEBODY PLEASE LISTEN TO ME TODAY!

Mama (quietly): I don't 'low no yellin' in this house, Walter Lee, and you know it — (*Walter stares at them in frustration and starts to speak several times.*) And there ain't going to be no investing in no liquor stores.

Walter: But, Mama, you ain't even looked at it.

Mama: I don't aim to have to speak on that again.

A long pause.

Walter: You ain't looked at it and you don't aim to have to speak on that again? You ain't even looked at it and *you* have decided — (*Crumpling his papers.*) Well, *you* tell that to my boy tonight when you put him to sleep on the living-room couch . . . (*Turning to Mama and speaking directly to her.*) Yeah — and tell it to my wife, Mama, tomorrow when she has to go out of here to look after somebody else's kids. And tell it to *me*, Mama, every time we need a new pair of curtains and I have to watch *you* go out and work in somebody's kitchen. Yeah, you tell me then!

Walter starts out.

Ruth: Where you going?

Walter: I'm going out!

Ruth: Where?

Walter: Just out of this house somewhere —

Ruth (getting her coat): I'll come too.

Walter: I don't want you to come!

Ruth: I got something to talk to you about, Walter.

Walter: That's too bad.

Mama (still quietly): Walter Lee — (*She waits and he finally turns and looks at her.*) Sit down.

Walter: I'm a grown man, Mama.

Mama: Ain't nobody said you wasn't grown. But you still in my house and my presence. And as long as you are — you'll talk to your wife civil. Now sit down.

Ruth (suddenly): Oh, let him go on out and drink himself to death! He makes me sick to my stomach! (*She flings her coat against him and exits to bedroom.*)

Walter (violently flinging the coat after her): And you turn mine too, baby! (*The door slams behind her.*) That was my biggest mistake —

Mama (still quietly): Walter, what is the matter with you?

Walter: Matter with me? Ain't nothing the matter with *me*!

Mama: Yes there is. Something eating you up like a crazy man. Something more than me not giving you this money. The past few years I been watching it happen to you. You get all nervous acting and kind of wild in the eyes — (*Walter jumps up impatiently at her words.*) I said sit there now, I'm talking to you!

Walter: Mama — I don't need no nagging at me today.

Mama: Seem like you getting to a place where you always tied up in some kind of knot about something. But if anybody ask you 'bout it you just yell at 'em and bust out the house and go out and drink somewheres. Walter Lee, people can't live with that. Ruth's a good, patient girl in her way — but you getting to be too much. Boy, don't make the mistake of driving that girl away from you.

Walter: Why — what she do for me?

Mama: She loves you.

Walter: Mama — I'm going out. I want to go off somewhere and be by myself for a while.

Mama: I'm sorry 'bout your liquor store, son. It just wasn't the thing for us to do. That's what I want to tell you about —

Walter: I got to go out, Mama —

He rises.

Mama: It's dangerous, son.

Walter: What's dangerous?

Mama: When a man goes outside his home to look for peace.

Walter (beseechingly): Then why can't there never be no peace in this house then?

Mama: You done found it in some other house?

Walter: No — there ain't no woman! Why do women always think there's a woman somewhere when a man gets restless. (*Picks up the check.*) Do you know what this money means to me? Do you know what this money can do for us? (*Puts it back.*) Mama — Mama — I want so many things . . .

Mama: Yes, son —

Walter: I want so many things that they are driving me kind of crazy . . . Mama — look at me.

Mama: I'm looking at you. You a good-looking boy. You got a job, a nice wife, a fine boy, and —

Walter: A job. (*Looks at her.*) Mama, a job? I open and close car doors all day long. I drive a man around in his limousine and I say, "Yes, sir; no, sir; very good, sir; shall I take the Drive, sir?" Mama, that ain't no kind of job . . . that ain't nothing at all. (*Very quietly.*) Mama, I don't know if I can make you understand.

Mama: Understand what, baby?

Walter (quietly): Sometimes it's like I can see the future stretched out in front of me — just plain as day. The future, Mama. Hanging over there at the edge of my days. Just waiting for me — a big, looming blank space — full of *nothing.* Just waiting for *me.* But it don't have to be. (*Pause. Kneeling beside her chair.*) Mama — sometimes when I'm downtown and I pass them cool, quiet-looking restaurants where them white boys are sitting back and talking 'bout things . . . sitting there turning deals worth millions of dollars . . . sometimes I see guys don't look much older than me —

Mama: Son — how come you talk so much 'bout money?

Walter (with immense passion): Because it is life, Mama!

Mama (quietly): Oh — (*Very quietly.*) So now it's life. Money is life. Once upon a time freedom used to be life — now it's money. I guess the world really do change . . .

Walter: No — it was always money, Mama. We just didn't know about it.

Mama: No . . . something has changed. (*She looks at him.*) You something new, boy. In my time we was worried about not being lynched and getting to the North if we could and how to stay alive and still have a pinch of dignity too . . . Now here come you and Beneatha — talking 'bout things we ain't never even thought about hardly, me and your daddy. You ain't satisfied or proud of nothing we done. I mean that you had a home; that we kept you out of trouble till you was grown; that you don't have to ride to work on the back of nobody's streetcar — You my children — but how different we done become.

Walter (a long beat. He pats her hand and gets up): You just don't understand, Mama, you just don't understand.

Mama: Son — do you know your wife is expecting another baby? (*Walter stands, stunned, and absorbs what his mother has said.*) That's what she wanted to talk to you about. (*Walter sinks down into a chair.*) This ain't for me to be telling — but you ought to know. (*She waits.*) I think Ruth is thinking 'bout getting rid of that child.

Walter (slowly understanding): — No — no — Ruth wouldn't do that.

Mama: When the world gets ugly enough — a woman will do anything for her family. *The part that's already living.*

Walter: You don't know Ruth, Mama, if you think she would do that.

Ruth opens the bedroom door and stands there a little limp.

Ruth (beaten): Yes I would too, Walter. (*Pause.*) I gave her a five-dollar down payment.

There is total silence as the man stares at his wife and the mother stares at her son.

Mama (presently): Well — (*Tightly.*) Well — son, I'm waiting to hear you say something . . . (*She waits.*) I'm waiting to hear how you be your father's son. Be the man he was . . . (*Pause. The silence shouts.*) Your wife say she going to destroy your child. And I'm waiting to hear you talk like him and say we a people who give children life, not who destroys them — (*She rises.*) I'm waiting to see you stand up and look like your daddy and say we done give up one baby to poverty and that we ain't going to give up nary another one . . . I'm waiting.

Walter: Ruth — (*He can say nothing.*)

Mama: If you a son of mine, tell her! (*Walter picks up his keys and his coat and walks out. She continues, bitterly.*) You . . . you are a disgrace to your father's memory. Somebody get me my hat!

Curtain.

ACT II

Scene I

   Time: Later the same day.
   At rise: Ruth is ironing again. She has the radio going. Presently Beneatha's bedroom door opens and Ruth's mouth falls and she puts down the iron in fascination.

Ruth: What have we got on tonight!

Beneatha (emerging grandly from the doorway so that we can see her thoroughly robed in the costume Asagai brought): You are looking at what a well-dressed Nigerian woman wears — (*She parades for Ruth, her hair completely hidden by the headdress; she is coquettishly fanning herself with an ornate oriental fan, mistakenly more like Butterfly than any Nigerian that ever was.*) Isn't it beautiful? (*She promenades to the radio and, with an arrogant flourish, turns off the good loud blues that is playing.*) Enough of this assimilationist junk! (*Ruth follows her with her eyes as she goes to the phonograph and puts on a record and turns and waits ceremoniously for the music to come up. Then, with a shout —*) OCOMOGOSIAY!

Ruth jumps. The music comes up, a lovely Nigerian melody. Beneatha listens, enraptured, her eyes far way — "back to the past." She begins to dance. Ruth is dumfounded.

Ruth: What kind of dance is that?

Beneatha: A folk dance.

Ruth (Pearl Bailey): What kind of folks do that, honey?

Beneatha: It's from Nigeria. It's a dance of welcome.

Ruth: Who you welcoming?

Beneatha: The men back to the village.

Ruth: Where they been?

Beneatha: How should I know — out hunting or something. Anyway, they are coming back now . . .

Ruth: Well, that's good.

Beneatha (with the record):

> *Alundi, alundi / Alundi alunya / Jop pu a jeepua / Ang gu sooooooooooo
> Ai yai yae . . . / Ayehaye — alundi . . .*

Walter comes in during this performance; he has obviously been drinking. He leans against the door heavily and watches his sister, at first with distaste. Then his eyes look off — "back to the past" — as he lifts both his fists to the roof, screaming.

Walter: YEAH . . . AND ETHIOPIA STRETCH FORTH HER HANDS AGAIN! . . .

Ruth (drily, looking at him): Yes — and Africa sure is claiming her own tonight. (*She gives them both up and starts ironing again.*)

Walter (all in a drunken, dramatic shout): Shut up! . . . I'm diggin them drums . . . them drums move me! . . . (*He makes his weaving way to his wife's face and leans in close to her.*) In my *heart of hearts* — (*He thumps his chest.*) — I am much warrior!

Ruth (without even looking up): In your heart of hearts you are much drunkard.

Walter (coming away from her and starting to wander around the room, shouting): Me and Jomo . . . (*Intently, in his sister's face. She has stopped dancing to watch him in this unknown mood.*) That's my man, Kenyatta. (*Shouting and thumping his chest.*) FLAMING SPEAR! HOT DAMN! (*He is suddenly in possession of an imaginary spear and actively spearing enemies all over the room.*) OCOMOGOSIAY . . .

Beneatha (to encourage Walter, thoroughly caught up with this side of him): OCOMOGOSIAY, FLAMING SPEAR!

Walter: THE LION IS WAKING . . . OWIMOWEH!

He pulls his shirt open and leaps up on the table and gestures with his spear.

Beneatha: OWIMOWEH!

Walter (On the table, very far gone, his eyes pure glass sheets. He sees what we cannot, that he is a leader of his people, a great chief, a descendant of Chaka, and that the hour to march has come): Listen, my black brothers —

Beneatha: OCOMOGOSIAY!

Walter: — Do you hear the waters rushing against the shores of the coast-lands —

Beneatha: OCOMOGOSIAY!

Walter: — Do you hear the screeching of the cocks in yonder hills beyond where the chiefs meet in council for the coming of the mighty war —

Beneatha: OCOMOGOSIAY!

And now the lighting shifts subtly to suggest the world of Walter's imagination, and the mood shifts from pure comedy. It is the inner Walter speaking: the Southside chauffeur has assumed an unexpected majesty.

Walter: — Do you hear the beating of the wings of the birds flying low over the mountains and the low places of our land —

Beneatha: OCOMOGOSIAY!

Walter: — Do you hear the singing of the women, singing the war songs of our fathers to the babies in the great houses? Singing the sweet war songs! (*The doorbell rings.*) OH, DO YOU HEAR, MY *BLACK* BROTHERS!

Beneatha (completely gone): We hear you, Flaming Spear —

Ruth shuts off the phonograph and opens the door. George Murchison enters.

Walter: Telling us to prepare for the GREATNESS OF THE TIME! (*Lights back to normal. He turns and sees George.*) Black Brother!

He extends his hand for the fraternal clasp.

George: Black Brother, hell!

Ruth (having had enough, and embarrassed for the family): Beneatha, you got company — what's the matter with you? Walter Lee Younger, get down off that table and stop acting like a fool . . .

Walter comes down off the table suddenly and makes a quick exit to the bathroom.

Ruth: He's had a little to drink . . . I don't know what her excuse is.

George (to Beneatha): Look honey, we're going to the theater — we're not going to be *in* it . . . so go change, huh?

Beneatha looks at him and slowly, ceremoniously, lifts her hands and pulls off the headdress. Her hair is close-cropped and unstraightened. George freezes mid-sentence and Ruth's eyes all but fall out of her head.

George: What in the name of —

Ruth (touching Beneatha's hair): Girl, you done lost your natural mind? Look at your head!

George: What have you done to your head — I mean your hair!

Beneatha: Nothing — except cut it off.

Ruth: Now that's the truth — it's what ain't been done to it! You expect this boy to go out with you with your head all nappy like that?

Beneatha (looking at George): That's up to George. It he's ashamed of his heritage —

George: Oh, don't be so proud of yourself, Bennie — just because you look eccentric.

Beneatha: How can something that's natural be eccentric?

George: That's what being eccentric means — being natural. Get dressed.

Beneatha: I don't like that, George.

Ruth: Why must you and your brother make an argument out of everything people say?

Beneatha: Because I hate assimilationist Negroes!

Ruth: Will somebody please tell me what assimila-whoever means!

George: Oh, it's just a college girl's way of calling people Uncle Toms — but that isn't what it means at all.

Ruth: Well, what does it mean?

Beneatha (cutting George off and staring at him as she replies to Ruth): It means someone who is willing to give up his own culture and submerge himself completely in the dominant, and in this case *oppressive* culture!

George: Oh, dear, dear, dear! Here we go! A lecture on the African past! On our Great West African Heritage! In one second we will hear all about the great Ashanti empires; the great Songhay civilizations; and the great sculpture of Bénin — and then some poetry in the Bantu — and the whole monologue will end with the word *heritage!* (*Nastily.*) Let's face it, baby, your heritage is nothing but a bunch of raggedy-assed spirituals and some grass huts!

Beneatha: GRASS HUTS! (*Ruth crosses to her and forcibly pushes her toward the bedroom.*) See there . . . you are standing there in your splendid ignorance talking about people who were the first to smelt iron on the face of the earth! (*Ruth is pushing her through the door.*) The Ashanti were performing surgical operations when the English — (*Ruth pulls the door to, with Beneatha on the other side, and smiles graciously at George. Beneatha opens the door and shouts the end of the sentence defiantly at George.*) — were still tatooing themselves with blue dragons! (*She goes back inside.*)

Ruth: Have a seat, George. (*They both sit. Ruth folds her hands rather primly on her lap, determined to demonstrate the civilization of the family.*) Warm, ain't it? I mean for September. (*Pause.*) Just like they always say about Chicago weather: if it's too hot or cold for you, just wait a minute and it'll change. (*She smiles happily at this cliché of clichés.*) Everybody say it's got to do with them bombs and things they keep setting off. (*Pause.*) Would you like a nice cold beer?

George: No, thank you. I don't care for beer. (*He looks at his watch.*) I hope she hurries up.

Ruth: What time is the show?

George: It's an eight-thirty curtain. That's just Chicago, though. In New York standard curtain time is eight forty.

He is rather proud of this knowledge.

Ruth (properly appreciating it): You get to New York a lot?

George (offhand): Few times a year.

Ruth: Oh — that's nice. I've never been to New York.

Walter enters. We feel he has relieved himself, but the edge of unreality is still with him.

Walter: New York ain't got nothing Chicago ain't. Just a bunch of hustling people all squeezed up together — being "Eastern."

He turns his face into a screw of displeasure.

George: Oh — you've been?
Walter: *Plenty* of times.
Ruth (shocked at the lie): Walter Lee Younger!
Walter (staring her down): Plenty! (*Pause.*) What we got to drink in this house? Why don't you offer this man some refreshment. (*To George.*) They don't know how to entertain people in this house, man.
George: Thank you — I don't really care for anything.
Walter (feeling his head; sobriety coming): Where's Mama?
Ruth: She ain't come back yet.
Walter (looking Murchison over from head to toe, scrutinizing his carefully casual tweed sports jacket over cashmere V-neck sweater over soft eyelet shirt and tie, and soft slacks, finished off with white buckskin shoes): Why all you college boys wear them faggoty-looking white shoes?
Ruth: Walter Lee!

George Murchison ignores the remark.

Walter (to Ruth): Well, they look crazy as hell — white shoes, cold as it is.
Ruth (crushed): You have to excuse him —
Walter: No he don't! Excuse me for what? What you always excusing me for! I'll excuse myself when I needs to be excused! (*A pause.*) They look as funny as them black knee socks Beneatha wears out of here all the time.
Ruth: It's the college *style*, Walter.
Walter: Style, hell. She looks like she got burnt legs or something!
Ruth: Oh, Walter —
Walter (an irritable mimic): Oh, Walter! Oh, Walter! (*To Murchison.*) How's your old man making out? I understand you all going to buy that big hotel on the Drive? (*He finds a beer in the refrigerator, wanders over to Murchison, sipping and wiping his lips with the back of his hand, and straddling a chair backwards to talk to the other man.*) Shrewd move. Your old man is all right, man. (*Tapping his head and half winking for emphasis.*) I mean he knows how to operate. I mean he thinks *big,* you know what I mean, I mean for a *home,* you know? But I think he's kind of running out of ideas now. I'd like to talk to him. Listen, man, I got some plans that could turn this city upside down. I mean think like he does. *Big.* Invest big, gamble big, hell, lose *big* if you have to, you know what I mean. It's hard to find a man on this whole Southside who understands my kind of thinking — you dig? (*He scrutinizes Murchison again, drinks his beer, squints his eyes and leans in close, confidential, man to man.*) Me and you ought to sit down and talk sometimes, man. Man, I got me some ideas . . .
Murchison (with boredom): Yeah — sometimes we'll have to do that, Walter.

Walter (understanding the indifference, and offended): Yeah — well, when you get the time, man. I know you a busy little boy.

Ruth: Walter, please —

Walter (bitterly, hurt): I know ain't nothing in this world as busy as you colored college boys with your fraternity pins and white shoes . . .

Ruth (covering her face with humiliation): Oh, Walter Lee —

Walter: I see you all all the time — with the books tucked under your arms — going to your (*British A — a mimic.*) "clahsses." And for what! What the hell you learning over there? Filling up your heads — (*Counting off on his fingers.*) — with the sociology and the psychology — but they teaching you how to be a man? How to take over and run the world? They teaching you how to run a rubber plantation or a steel mill? Naw — just to talk proper and read books and wear them faggoty-looking white shoes . . .

George (looking at him with distaste, a little above it all): You're all wacked up with bitterness, man.

Walter (intently, almost quietly, between the teeth, glaring at the boy): And you — ain't you bitter, man? Ain't you just about had it yet? Don't you see no stars gleaming that you can't reach out and grab? You happy? — You contented son-of-a-bitch — you happy? You got it made? Bitter? Man, I'm a volcano. Bitter? Here I am a giant — surrounded by ants! Ants who can't even understand what it is the giant is talking about.

Ruth (passionately and suddenly): Oh, Walter — ain't you with nobody!

Walter (violently): No! 'Cause ain't nobody with me! Not even my own mother!

Ruth: Walter, that's a terrible thing to say!

Beneatha enters, dressed for the evening in a cocktail dress and earrings, hair natural.

George: Well — hey — (*Crosses to Beneatha; thoughtful, with emphasis, since this is a reversal.*) You look great!

Walter (seeing his sister's hair for the first time): What's the matter with your head?

Beneatha (tired of the jokes now): I cut it off, Brother.

Walter (coming close to inspect it and walking around her): Well, I'll be damned. So that's what they mean by the African bush . . .

Beneatha: Ha ha. Let's go, George.

George (looking at her): You know something? I like it. It's sharp. I mean it really is. (*Helps her into her wrap.*)

Ruth: Yes — I think so, too. (*She goes to the mirror and starts to clutch at her hair.*)

Walter: Oh no! You leave yours alone, baby. You might turn out to have a pin-shaped head or something!

Beneatha: See you all later.

Ruth: Have a nice time.

George: Thanks. Good night. (*Half out the door, he reopens it. To Walter.*) Good night, Prometheus!

Beneatha and George exit.

Walter (to Ruth): Who is Prometheus?

Ruth: I don't know. Don't worry about it.

Walter (in fury, pointing after George): See there — they get to a point where they can't insult you man to man — they got to go talk about something ain't nobody never heard of!

Ruth: How do you know it was an insult? (*To humor him.*) Maybe Prometheus is a nice fellow.

Walter: Prometheus! I bet there ain't even no such thing! I bet that simple-minded clown —

Ruth: Walter —

She stops what she is doing and looks at him.

Walter (yelling): Don't start!

Ruth: Start what?

Walter: Your nagging! Where was I? Who was I with? How much money did I spend?

Ruth (plaintively): Walter Lee — why don't we just try to talk about it . . .

Walter (not listening): I been out talking with people who understand me. People who care about the things I got on my mind.

Ruth (wearily): I guess that means people like Willy Harris.

Walter: Yes, people like Willy Harris.

Ruth (with a sudden flash of impatience): Why don't you all just hurry up and go into the banking business and stop talking about it!

Walter: Why? You want to know why? 'Cause we all tied up in a race of people that don't know how to do nothing but moan, pray and have babies!

The line is too bitter even for him and he looks at her and sits down.

Ruth: Oh, Walter . . . (*Softly.*) Honey, why can't you stop fighting me?

Walter (without thinking): Who's fighting you? Who even cares about you?

This line begins the retardation of his mood.

Ruth: Well — (*She waits a long time, and then with resignation starts to put away her things.*) I guess I might as well go on to bed . . . (*More or less to herself.*) I don't know where we lost it . . . but we have . . . (*Then, to him.*) I — I'm sorry about this new baby, Walter. I guess maybe I better go on and do what I started . . . I guess I just didn't realize how bad things was with us . . . I guess I just didn't really realize — (*She starts out to the bedroom and stops.*) You want some hot milk?

Walter: Hot milk?

Ruth: Yes — hot milk.

Walter: Why hot milk?

Ruth: 'Cause after all that liquor you come home with you ought to have something hot in your stomach.

Walter: I don't want no milk.

Ruth: You want some coffee then?

Walter: No, I don't want no coffee. I don't want nothing hot to drink. (*Almost plaintively.*) Why you always trying to give me something to eat?

Ruth (standing and looking at him helplessly): What *else* can I give you, Walter Lee Younger?

She stands and looks at him and presently turns to go out again. He lifts his head and watches her going away from him in a new mood which began to emerge when he asked her "Who cares about you?"

Walter: It's been rough, ain't it, baby? (*She hears and stops but does not turn around and he continues to her back.*) I guess between two people there ain't never as much understood as folks generally thinks there is. I mean like between me and you — (*She turns to face him.*) How we gets to the place where we scared to talk softness to each other. (*He waits, thinking hard himself.*) Why you think it got to be like that? (*He is thoughtful, almost as a child would be.*) Ruth, what is it gets into people ought to be close?

Ruth: I don't know, honey. I think about it a lot.

Walter: On account of you and me, you mean? The way things are with us. The way something done come down between us.

Ruth: There ain't so much between us, Walter . . . Not when you come to me and try to talk to me. Try to be with me . . . a little even.

Walter (total honesty): Sometimes . . . sometimes . . . I don't even know how to try.

Ruth: Walter —

Walter: Yes?

Ruth (coming to him, gently and with misgiving, but coming to him): Honey . . . life don't have to be like this. I mean sometimes people can do things so that things are better . . . You remember how we used to talk when Travis was born . . . about the way we were going to live . . . the kind of house . . . (*She is stroking his head.*) Well, it's all starting to slip away from us . . .

He turns her to him and they look at each other and kiss, tenderly and hungrily. The door opens and Mama enters — Walter breaks away and jumps up. A beat.

Walter: Mama, where have you been?

Mama: My — them steps is longer than they used to be. Whew! (*She sits down and ignores him.*) How you feeling this evening, Ruth?

Ruth shrugs, disturbed at having been interrupted and watching her husband knowingly.

Walter: Mama, where have you been all day?

Mama (still ignoring him and leaning on the table and changing to more comfortable shoes): Where's Travis?

Ruth: I let him go out earlier and he ain't come back yet. Boy, is he going to get it!

Walter: Mama!

Mama (as if she has heard him for the first time): Yes, son?

Walter: Where did you go this afternoon?

Mama: I went downtown to tend to some business that I had to tend to.

Walter: What kind of business?

Mama: You know better than to question me like a child, Brother.

Walter (rising and bending over the table): Where were you, Mama? (*Bringing his fists down and shouting.*) Mama, you didn't go do something with that insurance money, something crazy?

The front door opens slowly, interrupting him, and Travis peeks his head in, less than hopefully.

Travis (to his mother): Mama, I —

Ruth: "Mama I" nothing! You're going to get it, boy! Get on in that bedroom and get yourself ready!

Travis: But I —

Mama: Why don't you all never let the child explain hisself.

Ruth: Keep out of it now, Lena.

Mama clamps her lips together, and Ruth advances toward her son menacingly.

Ruth: A thousand times I have told you not to go off like that —

Mama (holding out her arms to her grandson): Well — at least let me tell him something. I want him to be the first one to hear . . . Come here, Travis *(The boy obeys, gladly.)* Travis — *(She takes him by the shoulder and looks into his face.)* — you know that money we got in the mail this morning?

Travis: Yes'm —

Mama: Well — what you think your grandmama gone and done with that money?

Travis: I don't know, Grandmama.

Mama (putting her finger on his nose for emphasis): She went out and she bought you a house! *(The explosion comes from Walter at the end of the revelation and he jumps up and turns away from all of them in a fury. Mama continues, to Travis.)* You glad about the house? It's going to be yours when you get to be a man.

Travis: Yeah — I always wanted to live in a house.

Mama: All right, gimme some sugar then — *(Travis puts his arms around her neck as she watches her son over the boy's shoulder. Then, to Travis, after the embrace.)* Now when you say your prayers tonight, you thank God and your grandfather — 'cause it was him who give you the house — in his way.

Ruth (taking the boy from Mama and pushing him toward the bedroom): Now you get out of here and get ready for your beating.

Travis: Aw, Mama —

Ruth: Get on in there — *(Closing the door behind him and turning radiantly to her mother-in-law.)* So you went and did it!

Mama (quietly, looking at her son with pain): Yes, I did.

Ruth (raising both arms classically): PRAISE GOD! *(Looks at Walter a moment, who says nothing. She crosses rapidly to her husband.)* Please, honey — let me be glad . . . you be glad too. *(She has laid her hands on his shoulders, but he shakes himself free of her roughly, without turning to face her.)* Oh, Walter . . . a home . . . *a home. (She comes back to Mama.)* Well — where is it? How big is it? How much it going to cost?

Mama: Well —

Ruth: When we moving?

Mama (smiling at her): First of the month.

Ruth (throwing back her head with jubilance): Praise God!

Mama (tentatively, still looking at her son's back turned against her and Ruth): It's — it's a nice house too . . . *(She cannot help speaking directly to him. An imploring quality in her voice, her manner, makes her almost like a girl now.)* Three bedrooms — nice big one for you and Ruth . . . Me and Beneatha still have to share our room, but Travis have one of his own — and *(With difficulty.)* I figure if the — new baby — is a boy, we could get one of them double-decker outfits . . . And there's a yard with a little patch of dirt where I could maybe get to grow me a few flowers . . . And a nice big basement . . .

Ruth: Walter honey, be glad —

Mama (still to his back, fingering things on the table): 'Course I don't want to make it sound fancier than it is . . . It's just a plain little old house — but it's made good and solid — and it will be *ours.* Walter Lee — it makes a difference in a man when he can walk on floors that belong to *him* . . .

Ruth: Where is it?

Mama (frightened at this telling): Well — well — it's out there in Clybourne Park —

Ruth's radiance fades abruptly, and Walter finally turns slowly to face his mother with incredulity and hostility.

Ruth: Where?

Mama (matter-of-factly): Four o six Clybourne Street, Clybourne Park.

Ruth: Clybourne Park? Mama, there ain't no colored people living in Clybourne Park.

Mama (almost idiotically): Well, I guess there's going to be some now.

Walter (bitterly): So that's the peace and comfort you went out and bought for us today!

Mama (raising her eyes to meet his finally): Son — I just tried to find the nicest place for the least amount of money for my family.

Ruth (trying to recover from the shock): Well — well — 'course I ain't one never been 'fraid of no crackers, mind you — but — well, wasn't there no other houses nowhere?

Mama: Them houses they put up for colored in them areas way out all seem to cost twice as much as other houses. I did the best I could.

Ruth (struck senseless with the news, in its various degrees of goodness and trouble, she sits a moment, her fists propping her chin in thought, and then she starts to rise, bringing her fists down with vigor, the radiance spreading from cheek to cheek again): Well — well — All I can say is — if this is my time in life — MY TIME — to say good-bye — (*And she builds with momentum as she starts to circle the room with an exuberant, almost tearfully happy release.*) — to these Goddamned cracking walls! — (*She pounds the walls.*) — and these marching roaches! — (*She wipes at an imaginary army of marching roaches.*) — and this cramped little closet which ain't now or never was no kitchen! . . . then I say it loud and good, HALLELUJAH! AND GOOD-BYE MISERY . . . I DON'T NEVER WANT TO SEE YOUR UGLY FACE AGAIN! (*She laughs joyously, having practically destroyed the apartment, and flings her arms up and lets them come down happily, slowly, reflectively, over her abdomen, aware for the first time perhaps that the life therein pulses with happiness and not despair.*) Lena?

Mama (moved, watching her happiness): Yes, honey?

Ruth (looking off): Is there — is there a whole lot of sunlight?

Mama (understanding): Yes, child, there's a whole lot of sunlight.

Long pause.

Ruth (collecting herself and going to the door of the room Travis is in): Well —

I guess I better see 'bout Travis. (*To Mama.*) Lord, I sure don't feel like whipping nobody today!

She exits.

Mama (*The mother and son are left alone now and the mother waits a long time, considering deeply, before she speaks*): Son — you — you understand what I done, don't you? (*Walter is silent and sullen.*) I — I just seen my family falling apart today . . . just falling to pieces in front of my eyes . . . We couldn't of gone on like we was today. We was going backwards 'stead of forwards — talking 'bout killing babies and wishing each other was dead . . . When it gets like that in life — you just got to do something different, push on out and do something bigger . . . (*She waits.*) I wish you say something, son . . . I wish you'd say how deep inside you you think I done the right thing —

Walter (*crossing slowly to his bedroom door and finally turning there and speaking measuredly*): What you need me to say you done right for? *You* the head of this family. You run our lives like you want to. It was your money and you did what you wanted with it. So what you need for me to say it was all right for? (*Bitterly, to hurt her as deeply as he knows is possible.*) So you butchered up a dream of mine — you — who always talking 'bout your children's dreams . . .

Mama: Walter Lee —

He just closes the door behind him. Mama sits alone, thinking heavily.

Curtain.

SCENE II

Time: *Friday night, a few weeks later.*
At rise: *Packing crates mark the intention of the family to move. Beneatha and George come in, presumably from an evening out again.*

George: O.K. . . . O.K., whatever you say . . . (*They both sit on the couch. He tries to kiss her. She moves away.*) Look, we've had a nice evening; let's not spoil it, huh? . . .

He again turns her head and tries to nuzzle in and she turns away from him, not with distaste but with momentary lack of interest; in a mood to pursue what they were talking about.

Beneatha: I'm *trying* to talk to you.
George: We always talk.
Beneatha: Yes — and I love to talk.
George (*exasperated; rising*): I know it and I don't mind it sometimes . . . I want you to cut it out, see — The moody stuff, I mean. I don't like it. You're a nice-looking girl . . . all over. That's all you need, honey, forget the atmosphere. Guys aren't going to go for the atmosphere — they're going to go for what they see. Be glad for that. Drop the Garbo routine. It doesn't go with you. As for myself, I want a nice — (*Groping.*) — simple (*Thoughtfully.*) — sophisticated girl . . . not a poet — O.K.?

He starts to kiss her, she rebuffs him again and he jumps up.

Beneatha: Why are you angry, George?

George: Because this is stupid! I don't go out with you to discuss the nature of "quiet desperation" or to hear all about your thoughts — because the world will go on thinking what it thinks regardless —

Beneatha: Then why read books? Why go to school?

George (with artificial patience, counting on his fingers): It's simple. You read books — to learn facts — to get grades — to pass the course — to get a degree. That's all — it has nothing to do with thoughts.

A long pause.

Beneatha: I see. (*He starts to sit.*) Good night, George.

George looks at her a little oddly, and starts to exit. He meets Mama coming in.

George: Oh — hello, Mrs. Younger.

Mama: Hello, George, how you feeling?

George: Fine — fine, how are you?

Mama: Oh, a little tired. You know them steps can get you after a day's work. You all have a nice time tonight?

George: Yes — a fine time. A fine time.

Mama: Well, good night.

George: Good night. (*He exits. Mama closes the door behind her.*) Hello, honey. What you sitting like that for?

Beneatha: I'm just sitting.

Mama: Didn't you have a nice time?

Beneatha: No.

Mama: No? What's the matter?

Beneatha: Mama, George is a fool — honest. (*She rises.*)

Mama (hustling around unloading the packages she has entered with. She stops): Is he, baby?

Beneatha: Yes.

Beneatha makes up Travis's bed as she talks.

Mama: You sure?

Beneatha: Yes.

Mama: Well — I guess you better not waste your time with no fools.

Beneatha looks up at her mother, watching her put groceries in the refrigerator. Finally she gathers up her things and starts into the bedroom. At the door she stops and looks back at her mother.

Beneatha: Mama —

Mama: Yes, baby —

Beneatha: Thank you.

Mama: For what?

Beneatha: For understanding me this time.

She exits quickly and the mother stands, smiling a little, looking at the place where Beneatha just stood. Ruth enters.

Ruth: Now don't you fool with any of this stuff, Lena —

Mama: Oh, I just thought I'd sort a few things out. Is Brother here?

Ruth: Yes.
Mama (with concern): Is he —
Ruth (reading her eyes): Yes.

Mama is silent and someone knocks on the door. Mama and Ruth exchange weary and knowing glances and Ruth opens it to admit the neighbor, Mrs. Johnson,[1] who is a rather squeaky wide-eyed lady of no particular age, with a newspaper under her arm.

Mama (changing her expression to acute delight and a ringing cheerful greeting): Oh — hello there, Johnson.
Johnson (this is a woman who decided long ago to be enthusiastic about EVERYTHING in life and she is inclined to wave her wrist vigorously at the height of her exclamatory comments): Hello there, yourself! H'you this evening, Ruth?
Ruth (not much of a deceptive type): Fine, Mis' Johnson, h'you?
Johnson: Fine. (*Reaching out quickly, playfully, and patting Ruth's stomach.*) Ain't you starting to poke out none yet! (*She mugs with delight at the over-familiar remark and her eyes dart around looking at the crates and packing preparation; Mama's face is a cold sheet of endurance.*) Oh, ain't we getting ready round here, though! Yessir! Lookathere! I'm telling you the Youngers is really getting ready to "move on up a little higher!" — Bless God!
Mama (a little drily, doubting the total sincerity of the Blesser): Bless God.
Johnson: He's good, ain't He?
Mama: Oh yes, He's good.
Johnson: I mean sometimes He works in mysterious ways . . . but He works, don't He!
Mama (the same): Yes, he does.
Johnson: I'm just soooooo happy for y'all. And this here child — (*About Ruth.*) looks like she could just pop open with happiness, don't she. Where's all the rest of the family?
Mama: Bennie's gone to bed —
Johnson: Ain't no . . . (*The implication is pregnancy.*) sickness done hit you — I hope . . . ?
Mama: No — she just tired. She was out this evening.
Johnson (all is a coo, an emphatic coo): Aw — ain't that lovely. She still going out with the little Murchison boy?
Mama (drily): Ummmm huh.
Johnson: That's lovely. You sure got lovely children, Younger. Me and Isaiah talks all the time 'bout what fine children you was blessed with. We sure do.
Mama: Ruth, give Mis' Johnson a piece of sweet potato pie and some milk.
Johnson: Oh honey, I can't stay hardly a minute — I just dropped in to see if there was anything I could do. (*Accepting the food easily.*) I guess y'all seen the news what's all over the colored paper this week . . .
Mama: No — didn't get mine yet this week.
Johnson (lifting her head and blinking with the spirit of catastrophe): You mean

---

[1]This character and the scene of her visit were cut from the original production and early editions of the play.

you ain't read 'bout them colored people that was bombed out their place out there?

Ruth straightens with concern and takes the paper and reads it. Johnson notices her and feeds commentary.

Johnson: Ain't it something how bad these here white folks is getting here in Chicago! Lord, getting so you think you right down in Mississippi! (*With a tremendous and rather insincere sense of melodrama.*) 'Course I thinks it's wonderful how our folk keeps on pushing out. You hear some of these Negroes round here talking 'bout how they don't go where they ain't wanted and all that — but not me, honey! (*This is a lie.*) Wilhemenia Othella Johnson goes anywhere, any time she feels like it! (*With head movement for emphasis.*) Yes I do! Why if we left it up to these here crackers, the poor niggers wouldn't have nothing — (*She clasps her hand over her mouth.*) Oh, I always forgets you don't 'low that word in your house.

Mama (quietly, looking at her): No — I don't 'low it.

Johnson (vigorously again): Me neither! I was just telling Isaiah yesterday when he come using it in front of me — I said, "Isaiah, it's just like Mis' Younger says all the time — "

Mama: Don't you want some more pie?

Johnson: No — no thank you; this was lovely. I got to get on over home and have my midnight coffee. I hear some people say it don't let them sleep but I finds I can't close my eyes right lessen I done had that laaaast cup of coffee . . . (*She waits. A beat. Undaunted.*) My Goodnight coffee, I calls it!

Mama (with much eye-rolling and communication between herself and Ruth): Ruth, why don't you give Mis' Johnson some coffee.

Ruth gives Mama an unpleasant look for her kindness.

Johnson (accepting the coffee): Where's Brother tonight?

Mama: He's lying down.

Johnson: MMmmmmmm, he sure gets his beauty rest, don't he? Good-looking man. Sure is a good-looking man! (*Reaching out to pat Ruth's stomach again.*) I guess that's how come we keep on having babies around here. (*She winks at Mama.*) One thing 'bout Brother, he always know how to have a *good* time. And soooooo ambitious! I bet it was his idea y'all moving out to Clybourne Park. Lord — I bet this time next month y'all's names will have been in the papers plenty — (*Holding up her hands to mark off each word of the headline she can see in front of her.*) "NEGROES INVADE CLYBOURNE PARK — BOMBED!"

Mama (she and Ruth look at the woman in amazement): We ain't exactly moving out there to get bombed.

Johnson: Oh honey — you know I'm praying to God every day that don't nothing like that happen! But you have to think of life like it is — and these here Chicago peckerwoods is some baaaad peckerwoods.

Mama (wearily): We done thought about all that Mis' Johnson.

Beneatha comes out of the bedroom in her robe and passes through to the bathroom. Mrs. Johnson turns.

Johnson: Hello there, Bennie!

Beneatha (crisply): Hello, Mrs. Johnson.

Johnson: How is school?

Beneatha (crisply): Fine, thank you. (*She goes out.*)

Johnson (insulted): Getting so she don't have much to say to nobody.

Mama: The child was on her way to the bathroom.

Johnson: I know — but sometimes she act like ain't got time to pass the time of day with nobody ain't been to college. Oh — I ain't criticizing her none. It's just — you know how some of our young people gets when they get a little education. (*Mama and Ruth say nothing, just look at her.*) Yes — well. Well, I guess I better get on home. (*Unmoving.*) 'Course I can understand how she must be proud and everything — being the only one in the family to make something of herself. I know just being a chauffeur ain't never satisfied Brother none. He shouldn't feel like that, though. Ain't nothing wrong with being a chauffeur.

Mama: There's plenty wrong with it.

Johnson: What?

Mama: Plenty. My husband always said being any kind of a servant wasn't a fit thing for a man to have to be. He always said a man's hands was made to make things, or to turn the earth with — not to drive nobody's car for 'em — or — (*She looks at her own hands.*) carry they slop jars. And my boy is just like him — he wasn't meant to wait on nobody.

Johnson (rising, somewhat offended): Mmmmmmmmmm. The Youngers is too much for me! (*She looks around.*) You sure one proud-acting bunch of colored folks. Well — I always thinks like Booker T. Washington said that time — "Education has spoiled many a good plow hand" —

Mama: Is that what old Booker T. said?

Johnson: He sure did.

Mama: Well, it sounds just like him. The fool.

Johnson (indignantly): Well — he was one of our great men.

Mama: Who said so?

Johnson (nonplussed): You know, me and you ain't never agreed about some things, Lena Younger. I guess I better be going —

Ruth (quickly): Good night.

Johnson: Good night. Oh — (*Thrusting it at her.*) You can keep the paper! (*With a trill.*) 'Night.

Mama: Good night, Mis' Johnson.

Mrs. Johnson exits.

Ruth: If ignorance was gold . . .

Mama: Shush. Don't talk about folks behind their backs.

Ruth: You do.

Mama: I'm old and corrupted. (*Beneatha enters.*) You was rude to Mis' Johnson, Beneatha, and I don't like it at all.

Beneatha (at her door): Mama, if there are two things we, as a people, have got to overcome, one is the Klu Klux Klan — and the other is Mrs. Johnson. (*She exits.*)

Mama: Smart aleck.

The phone rings.

Ruth: I'll get it.

Mama: Lord, ain't this a popular place tonight.

Ruth (at the phone): Hello — Just a minute. (*Goes to door.*) Walter, it's Mrs. Arnold. (*Waits. Goes back to the phone. Tense.*) Hello. Yes, this is his wife speaking . . . He's lying down now. Yes . . . well, he'll be in tomorrow. He's been very sick. Yes — I know we should have called, but we were so sure he'd be able to come in today. Yes — yes, I'm very sorry. Yes . . . Thank you very much. (*She hangs up. Walter is standing in the doorway of the bedroom behind her.*) That was Mrs. Arnold.

Walter (indifferently): Was it?

Ruth: She said if you don't come in tomorrow that they are getting a new man . . .

Walter: Ain't that sad — ain't that crying sad.

Ruth: She said Mr. Arnold has had to take a cab for three days . . . Walter, you ain't been to work for three days! (*This is a revelation to her.*) Where you been, Walter Lee Younger? (*Walter looks at her and starts to laugh.*) You're going to lose your job.

Walter: That's right . . . (*He turns on the radio.*)

Ruth: Oh, Walter, and with your mother working like a dog every day —

A steamy, deep blues pours into the room.

Walter: That's sad too — Everything is sad.

Mama: What you been doing for these three days, son?

Walter: Mama — you don't know all the things a man what got leisure can find to do in this city . . . What's this — Friday night? Well — Wednesday I borrowed Willy Harris' car and I went for a drive . . . just me and myself and I drove and drove . . . Way out . . . way past South Chicago, and I parked the car and I sat and looked at the steel mills all day long. I just sat in the car and looked at them big black chimneys for hours. Then I drove back and I went to the Green Hat. (*Pause.*) And Thursday — Thursday I borrowed the car again and I got in it and I pointed it the other way and I drove the other way — for hours — way, way up to Wisconsin, and I looked at the farms. I just drove and looked at the farms. Then I drove back and I went to the Green Hat. (*Pause.*) And today — today I didn't get the car. Today I just walked. All over the Southside. And I looked at the Negroes and they looked at me and finally I just sat down on the curb at Thirty-ninth and South Parkway and I just sat there and watched the Negroes go by. And then I went to the Green Hat. You all sad? You all depressed? And you know where I am going right now —

Ruth goes out quietly.

Mama: Oh, Big Walter, is this the harvest of our days?

Walter: You know what I like about the Green Hat? I like this little cat they got there who blows a sax . . . He blows. He talks to me. He ain't but 'bout five feet tall and he's got a conked head and his eyes is always closed and he's all music —

Mama (rising and getting some papers out of her handbag): Walter —

Walter: And there's this other guy who plays the piano . . . and they got a sound. I mean they can work on some music . . . They got the best little combo in the world in the Green Hat . . . You can just sit there and drink and listen to them three men play and you realize that don't nothing matter worth a damn, but just being there —

Mama: I've helped do it to you, haven't I, son? Walter I been wrong.

Walter: Naw — you ain't never been wrong about nothing, Mama.

Mama: Listen to me, now. I say I been wrong, son. That I been doing to you what the rest of the world been doing to you. (*She turns off the radio.*) Walter — (*She stops and he looks up slowly at her and she meets his eyes pleadingly.*) What you ain't never understood is that I ain't got nothing, don't own nothing, ain't never really wanted nothing that wasn't for you. There ain't nothing as precious to me . . . There ain't nothing worth holding on to, money, dreams, nothing else — if it means — if it means it's going to destroy my boy. (*She takes an envelope out of her handbag and puts it in front of him and he watches her without speaking or moving.*) I paid the man thirty-five hundred dollars down on the house. That leaves sixty-five hundred dollars. Monday morning I want you to take this money and take three thousand dollars and put it in a savings account for Beneatha's medical schooling. The rest you put in a checking account — with your name on it. And from now on any penny that come out of it or that go in it is for you to look after. For you to decide. (*She drops her hands a little helplessly.*) It ain't much, but it's all I got in the world and I'm putting it in your hands. I'm telling you to be the head of this family from now on like you supposed to be.

Walter (stares at the money): You trust me like that, Mama?

Mama: I ain't never stop trusting you. Like I ain't never stop loving you.

She goes out, and Walter sits looking at the money on the table. Finally, in a decisive gesture, he gets up, and, in mingled joy and desperation, picks up the money. At the same moment, Travis enters for bed.

Travis: What's the matter, Daddy? You drunk?

Walter (sweetly, more sweetly than we have ever known him): No, Daddy ain't drunk. Daddy ain't going to never be drunk again . . .

Travis: Well, good night, Daddy.

The father has come from behind the couch and leans over, embracing his son.

Walter: Son, I feel like talking to you tonight.

Travis: About what?

Walter: Oh, about a lot of things. About you and what kind of man you going to be when you grow up . . . Son — son, what do you want to be when you grow up?

Travis: A bus driver.

Walter (laughing a little): A what? Man, that ain't nothing to want to be!

Travis: Why not?

Walter: 'Cause, man — it ain't big enough — you know what I mean.

Travis: I don't know then. I can't make up my mind. Sometimes Mama asks me that too. And sometimes when I tell her I just want to be like you — she says she don't want me to be like that and sometimes she says she does. . . .

Walter (gathering him up in his arms): You know what, Travis? In seven years you going to be seventeen years old. And things is going to be very different

with us in seven years, Travis. . . . One day when you are seventeen I'll come
   home — home from my office downtown somewhere —

Travis: You don't work in no office, Daddy.

Walter: No — but after tonight. After what your daddy gonna do tonight, there's
   going to be offices — a whole lot of offices. . . .

Travis: What you gonna do tonight, Daddy?

Walter: You wouldn't understand yet, son, but your daddy's gonna make a
   transaction . . . a business transaction that's going to change our lives. . . .
   That's how come one day when you 'bout seventeen years old I'll come
   home and I'll be pretty tired, you know what I mean, after a day of conferences and secretaries getting things wrong the way they do . . . 'cause an
   executive's life is hell, man — (*The more he talks the farther away he gets.*)
   And I'll pull the car up on the driveway . . . just a plain black Chrysler, I
   think, with white walls — no — black tires. More elegant. Rich people don't
   have to be flashy . . . though I'll have to get something a little sportier for
   Ruth — maybe a Cadillac convertible to do her shopping in. . . . And I'll
   come up the steps to the house and the gardener will be clipping away at
   the hedges and he'll say, "Good evening, Mr. Younger." And I'll say, "Hello,
   Jefferson, how are you this evening?" And I'll go inside and Ruth will come
   downstairs and meet me at the door and we'll kiss each other and she'll take
   my arm and we'll go up to your room to see you sitting on the floor with
   the catalogues of all the great schools in America around you. . . . All the
   great schools in the world! And — and I'll say, all right son — it's your
   seventeenth birthday, what is it you've decided? . . . Just tell me where you
   want to go to school and you'll *go.* Just tell me, what it is you want to be —
   and you'll *be* it. . . . Whatever you want to be — Yessir! (*He holds his arms
   open for Travis.*) You just name it, son . . . (*Travis leaps into them.*) and I
   hand you the world!

*Walter's voice has risen in pitch and hysterical promise and on the last line he
lifts Travis high.*

Blackout.

SCENE III

   Time: *Saturday, moving day, one week later.*
   Before the curtain rises, Ruth's voice, a strident, dramatic church alto, cuts
through the silence.
   It is, in the darkness, a triumphant surge, a penetrating statement of expec-
tation: "Oh, Lord, I don't feel no ways tired! Children, oh, glory hallelujah!"
   As the curtain rises we see that Ruth is alone in the living room, finishing
up the family's packing. It is moving day. She is nailing crates and tying cartons.
Beneatha enters, carrying a guitar case, and watches her exuberant sister-in-law.

Ruth: Hey!

Beneatha (putting away the case): Hi.

Ruth (pointing at a package): Honey — look in that package there and see what
   I found on sale this morning at the South Center. (*Ruth gets up and moves*

to the package and draws out some curtains.) Lookahere — hand-turned hems!

Beneatha: How do you know the window size out there?

Ruth (who hadn't thought of that): Oh — Well, they bound to fit something in the whole house. Anyhow, they was too good a bargain to pass up. (*Ruth slaps her head, suddenly remembering something.*) Oh, Bennie — I meant to put a special note on that carton over there. That's your mama's good china and she wants 'em to be very careful with it.

Beneatha: I'll do it.

Beneatha finds a piece of paper and starts to draw large letters on it.

Ruth: You know what I'm going to do soon as I get in that new house?

Beneatha: What?

Ruth: Honey — I'm going to run me a tub of water up to here . . . (*With her fingers practically up to her nostrils.*) And I'm going to get in it — and I am going to sit . . . and sit . . . and sit in that hot water and the first person who knocks to tell *me* to hurry up and come out —

Beneatha: Gets shot at sunrise.

Ruth (laughing happily): You said it, sister! (*Noticing how large Beneatha is absent-mindedly making the note*): Honey, they ain't going to read that from no airplane.

Beneatha (laughing herself): I guess I always think things have more emphasis if they are big, somehow.

Ruth (looking up at her and smiling): You and your brother seem to have that as a philosophy of life. Lord, that man — done changed so 'round here. You know — you know what we did last night? Me and Walter Lee?

Beneatha: What?

Ruth (smiling to herself): We went to the movies. (*Looking at Beneatha to see if she understands.*) We went to the movies. You know the last time me and Walter went to the movies together?

Beneatha: No.

Ruth: Me neither. That's how long it been. (*Smiling again.*) But we went last night. The picture wasn't much good, but that didn't seem to matter. We went — and we held hands.

Beneatha: Oh, Lord!

Ruth: We held hands — and you know what?

Beneatha: What?

Ruth: When we come out of the show it was late and dark and all the stores and things was closed up . . . and it was kind of chilly and there wasn't many people on the streets . . . and we was still holding hands, me and Walter.

Beneatha: You're killing me.

Walter enters with a large package. His happiness is deep in him; he cannot keep still with his newfound exuberance. He is singing and wiggling and snapping his fingers. He puts his package in a corner and puts a phonograph record, which he has brought in with him, on the record player. As the music, soulful and sensuous, comes up he dances over to Ruth and tries to get her to dance with him. She gives in at last to his raunchiness and in a fit of giggling allows herself to be drawn into his mood. They dip and she melts into his arms in a classic, body-melting "slow drag."

Beneatha (regarding them a long time as they dance, then drawing in her breath for a deeply exaggerated comment which she does not particularly mean): Talk about — olddddddddddd-fashionedddddddd — Negroes!

Walter (stopping momentarily): What kind of Negroes?

He says this in fun. He is not angry with her today, nor with anyone. He starts to dance with his wife again.

Beneatha: Old-fashioned.

Walter (as he dances with Ruth): You know, when these *New Negroes* have their convention — *(Pointing at his sister.)* — that is going to be the chairman of the Committee on Unending Agitation. *(He goes on dancing, then stops.)* Race, race, race! . . . Girl, I do believe you are the first person in the history of the entire human race to successfully brainwash yourself. *(Beneatha breaks up and he goes on dancing. He stops again, enjoying his tease.)* Damn, even the N double A C P takes a holiday sometimes! *(Beneatha and Ruth laugh. He dances with Ruth some more and starts to laugh and stops and pantomimes someone over an operating table.)* I can just see that chick someday looking down at some poor cat on an operating table and before she starts to slice him, she says . . . *(Pulling his sleeves back maliciously.)* "By the way, what are your views on civil rights down there? . . ."

He laughs at her again and starts to dance happily. The bell sounds.

Beneatha: Sticks and stones may break my bones but . . . words will never hurt me!

Beneatha goes to the door and opens it as Walter and Ruth go on with the clowning. Beneatha is somewhat surprised to see a quiet-looking middle-aged white man in a business suit holding his hat and a briefcase in his hand and consulting a small piece of paper.

Man: Uh — how do you do, miss. I am looking for a Mrs. — *(He looks at the slip of paper.)* Mrs. Lena Younger? *(He stops short, struck dumb at the sight of the oblivious Walter and Ruth.)*

Beneatha (smoothing her hair with slight embarrassment): Oh — yes, that's my mother. Excuse me. *(She closes the door and turns to quiet the other two.)* Ruth! Brother! *(Enunciating precisely but soundlessly: "There's a white man at the door!" They stop dancing, Ruth cuts off the phonograph, Beneatha opens the door. The man casts a curious quick glance at all of them.)* Uh — come in please.

Man (coming in): Thank you.

Beneatha: My mother isn't here just now. Is it business?

Man: Yes . . . well, of a sort.

Walter (freely, the Man of the House): Have a seat. I'm Mrs. Younger's son. I look after most of her business matters.

Ruth and Beneatha exchange amused glances.

Man (regarding Walter, and sitting): Well — My name is Karl Lindner . . .

Walter (stretching out his hand): Walter Younger. This is my wife — *(Ruth nods politely.)* — and my sister.

Lindner: How do you do.

Walter (amiably, as he sits himself easily on a chair, leaning forward on his knees with interest and looking expectantly into the newcomer's face): What can we do for you, Mr. Lindner!

Lindner (some minor shuffling of the hat and briefcase on his knees): Well — I am a representative of the Clybourne Park Improvement Association —

Walter (pointing): Why don't you sit your things on the floor?

Lindner: Oh — yes. Thank you. (*He slides the briefcase and hat under the chair.*) And as I was saying — I am from the Clybourne Park Improvement Association and we have had it brought to our attention at the last meeting that you people — or at least your mother — has bought a piece of residential property at — (*He digs for the slip of paper again.*) — four o six Clybourne Street . . .

Walter: That's right. Care for something to drink? Ruth, get Mr. Lindner a beer.

Lindner (upset for some reason): Oh — no, really. I mean thank you very much, but no thank you.

Ruth (innocently): Some coffee?

Lindner: Thank you, nothing at all.

Beneatha is watching the man carefully.

Lindner: Well, I don't know how much you folks know about our organization. (*He is a gentle man; thoughtful and somewhat labored in his manner.*) It is one of these community organizations set up to look after — oh, you know, things like block upkeep and special projects and we also have what we call our New Neighbors Orientation Committee . . .

Beneatha (drily): Yes — and what do they do?

Lindner (turning a little to her and then returning the main force to Walter): Well — it's what you might call a sort of welcoming committee, I guess. I mean they, we — I'm the chairman of the committee — go around and see the new people who move into the neighborhood and sort of give them the lowdown on the way we do things out in Clybourne Park.

Beneatha (with appreciation of the two meanings, which escape Ruth and Walter): Un-huh.

Lindner: And we also have the category of what the association calls — (*He looks elsewhere.*) — uh — special community problems . . .

Beneatha: Yes — and what are some of those?

Walter: Girl, let the man talk.

Lindner (with understated relief): Thank you. I would sort of like to explain this thing in my own way. I mean I want to explain to you in a certain way.

Walter: Go ahead.

Lindner: Yes. Well. I'm going to try to get right to the point. I'm sure we'll all appreciate that in the long run.

Beneatha: Yes.

Walter: Be still now!

Lindner: Well —

Ruth (still innocently): Would you like another chair — you don't look comfortable.

Lindner (more frustrated than annoyed): No, thank you very much. Please. Well — to get right to the point, I — (*A great breath, and he is off at last.*) I am sure you people must be aware of some of the incidents which have happened in various parts of the city when colored people have moved into certain areas — (*Beneatha exhales heavily and starts tossing a piece of fruit up and down in the air.*) Well — because we have what I think is going to be a unique type of organization in American community life — not only do we deplore that kind of thing — but we are trying to do something about it. (*Beneatha stops tossing and turns with a new and quizzical interest to the man.*) We feel — (*gaining confidence in his mission because of the interest in the faces of the people he is talking to.*) — we feel that most of the trouble in this world, when you come right down to it — (*He hits his knee for emphasis.*) — most of the trouble exists because people just don't sit down and talk to each other.

Ruth (*nodding as she might in church, pleased with the remark*): You can say that again, mister.

Lindner (*more encouraged by such affirmation*): That we don't try hard enough in this world to understand the other fellow's problem. The other guy's point of view.

Ruth: Now that's right.

Beneatha and Walter merely watch and listen with genuine interest.

Lindner: Yes — that's the way we feel out in Clybourne Park. And that's why I was elected to come here this afternoon and talk to you people. Friendly like, you know, the way people should talk to each other and see if we couldn't find some way to work this thing out. As I say, the whole business is a matter of *caring* about the other fellow. Anybody can see that you are a nice family of folks, hard working and honest I'm sure. (*Beneatha frowns slightly, quizzically, her head tilted regarding him.*) Today everybody knows what it means to be on the outside of *something.* And of course, there is always somebody who is out to take advantage of people who don't always understand.

Walter: What do you mean?

Lindner: Well — you see our community is made up of people who've worked hard as the dickens for years to build up that little community. They're not rich and fancy people; just hard-working, honest people who don't really have much but those little homes and a dream of the kind of community they want to raise their children in. Now, I don't say we are perfect and there is a lot wrong in some of the things they want. But you've got to admit that a man, right or wrong, has the right to want to have the neighborhood he lives in a certain kind of way. And at the moment the overwhelming majority of our people out there feel that people get along better, take more of a common interest in the life of the community, when they share a common background. I want you to believe me when I tell you that race prejudice simply doesn't enter into it. It is a matter of the people of Clybourne Park believing, rightly or wrongly, as I say, that for the happiness of all concerned that our Negro families are happier when they live in their *own* communities.

Beneatha (*with a grand and bitter gesture*): This, friends, is the Welcoming Committee!

Walter (*dumfounded, looking at Lindner*): Is this what you came marching all the way over here to tell us?

Lindner: Well, now we've been having a fine conversation. I hope you'll hear me all the way through.

Walter (tightly): Go ahead, man.

Lindner: You see — in the face of all the things I have said, we are prepared to make your family a very generous offer . . .

Beneatha: Thirty pieces and not a coin less!

Walter: Yeah?

Lindner (putting on his glasses drawing a form out of the briefcase): Our association is prepared, through the collective effort of our people, to buy the house from you at a financial gain to your family.

Ruth: Lord have mercy, ain't this the living gall!

Walter: All right, you through?

Lindner: Well, I want to give you the exact terms of the financial arrangement —

Walter: We don't want to hear no exact terms of no arrangements. I want to know if you got any more to tell us 'bout getting together?

Lindner (taking off his glasses): Well — I don't suppose that you feel . . .

Walter: Never mind how I feel — you got any more to say 'bout how people ought to sit down and talk to each other? . . . Get out of my house, man.

He turns his back and walks to the door.

Lindner (looking around at the hostile faces and reaching and assembling his hat and briefcase): Well — I don't understand why you people are reacting this way. What do you think you are going to gain by moving into a neighborhood where you just aren't wanted and where some elements — well — people can get awful worked up when they feel that their whole way of life and everything they've ever worked for is threatened.

Walter: Get out.

Lindner (at the door, holding a small card): Well — I'm sorry it went like this.

Walter: Get out.

Lindner (almost sadly regarding Walter): You just can't force people to change their hearts, son.

He turns and put his card on a table and exits. Walter pushes the door to with stinging hatred, and stands looking at it. Ruth just sits and Beneatha just stands. They say nothing. Mama and Travis enter.

Mama: Well — this all the packing got done since I left out of here this morning. I testify before God that my children got all the energy of the *dead!* What time the moving men due?

Beneatha: Four o'clock. You had a caller, Mama.

She is smiling, teasingly.

Mama: Sure enough — who?

Beneatha (her arms folded saucily): The Welcoming Committee.

Walter and Ruth giggle.

Mama (innocently): Who?

Beneatha: The Welcoming Committee. They said they're sure going to be glad to see you when you get there.

Walter (devilishly): Yeah, they said they can't hardly wait to see your face.

Laughter.

Mama (sensing their facetiousness): What's the matter with you all?

Walter: Ain't nothing the matter with us. We just telling you 'bout the gentleman who came to see you this afternoon. From the Clybourne Park Improvement Association.

Mama: What he want?

Ruth (in the same mood as Beneatha and Walter): To welcome you, honey.

Walter: He said they can't hardly wait. He said the one thing they don't have, that they just *dying* to have out there is a fine family of fine colored people! (*To Ruth and Beneatha.*) Ain't that right!

Ruth (mockingly): Yeah! He left his card —

Beneatha (handing card to Mama): In case.

Mama reads and throws it on the floor — understanding and looking off as she draws her chair up to the table on which she has put her plant and some sticks and some cord.

Mama: Father, give us strength. (*Knowingly — and without fun.*) Did he threaten us?

Beneatha: Oh — Mama — they don't do it like that any more. He talked Brotherhood. He said everybody ought to learn how to sit down and hate each other with good Christian fellowship.

She and Walter shake hands to ridicule the remark.

Mama (sadly): Lord, protect us . . .

Ruth: You should hear the money those folks raised to buy the house from us. All we paid and then some.

Beneatha: What they think we going to do — eat 'em?

Ruth: No, honey, marry 'em.

Mama (shaking her head): Lord, Lord, Lord . . .

Ruth: Well — that's the way the crackers crumble. (*A beat.*) Joke.

Beneatha (laughingly noticing what her mother is doing): Mama, what are you doing?

Mama: Fixing my plant so it won't get hurt none on the way . . .

Beneatha: Mama, you going to take *that* to the new house?

Mama: Un-huh —

Beneatha: That raggedy-looking old thing?

Mama (stopping and looking at her): It expresses ME!

Ruth (with delight, to Beneatha): So there, Miss Thing!

Walter comes to Mama suddenly and bends down behind her and squeezes her in his arms with all his strength. She is overwhelmed by the suddenness of it and, though delighted, her manner is like that of Ruth and Travis.

Mama: Look out now, boy! You make me mess up my thing here!

Walter (his face lit, he slips down on his knees beside her, his arms still about her): Mama . . . you know what it means to climb up in the chariot?

Mama (gruffly, very happy): Get on away from me now . . .

Ruth (near the gift-wrapped package, trying to catch Walter's eye): Psst —

Walter: What the old song say, Mama . . .

Ruth: Walter — Now?

She is pointing at the package.

Walter (speaking the lines, sweetly, playfully, in his mother's face):

I got wings . . . you got wings . . .
All God's Children got wings . . .

Mama: Boy — get out of my face and do some work . . .

Walter:

When I get to heaven gonna put on my wings,
Gonna fly all over God's heaven . . .

Beneatha (teasingly, from across the room): Everybody talking 'bout heaven ain't going there!

Walter (to Ruth, who is carrying the box across to them): I don't know, you think we ought to give her that . . . Seems to me she ain't been very appreciative around here.

Mama (eying the box, which is obviously a gift): What is that?

Walter (taking it from Ruth and putting it on the table in front of Mama): Well — what you all think? Should we give it to her?

Ruth: Oh — she was pretty good today.

Mama: I'll good you —

She turns her eyes to the box again.

Beneatha: Open it, Mama.

She stands up, looks at it, turns and looks at all of them, and then presses her hands together and does not open the package.

Walter (sweetly): Open it, Mama. It's for you. (*Mama looks in his eyes. It is the first present in her life without its being Christmas. Slowly she opens her package and lifts out, one by one, a brand-new sparkling set of gardening tools. Walter continues, prodding.*) Ruth made up the note — read it . . .

Mama (picking up the card and adjusting her glasses): "To our own Mrs. Miniver — Love from Brother, Ruth and Beneatha." Ain't that lovely . . .

Travis (tugging at his father's sleeve): Daddy, can I give her mine now?

Walter: All right, son. (*Travis flies to get his gift.*)

Mama: Now I don't have to use my knives and forks no more . . .

Walter: Travis didn't want to go in with the rest of us, Mama. He got his own. (*Somewhat amused.*) We don't know what it is . . .

Travis (racing back in the room with a large hatbox and putting it in front of his grandmother): Here!

Mama: Lord have mercy, baby. You done gone and bought your grandmother a hat?

Travis (very proud): Open it!

She does and lifts out an elaborate, but very elaborate, wide gardening hat, and all the adults break up at the sight of it.

Ruth: Travis, honey, what is that?

Travis (who thinks it is beautiful and appropriate): It's a gardening hat! Like the ladies always have on in the magazines when they work in their gardens.

Beneatha (giggling fiercely): Travis — we were trying to make Mama Mrs. Miniver — not Scarlett O'Hara!

Mama (indignantly): What's the matter with you all! This here is a beautiful hat! (*Absurdly.*) I always wanted me one just like it!

She pops it on her head to prove it to her grandson, and the hat is ludicrous and considerably oversized.

Ruth: Hot dog! Go, Mama!
Walter (doubled over with laughter): I'm sorry, Mama — but you look like you ready to go out and chop you some cotton sure enough!

They all laugh except Mama, out of deference to Travis's feelings.

Mama (gathering the boy up to her): Bless your heart — this is the prettiest hat I ever owned — (*Walter, Ruth, and Beneatha chime in — noisily, festively, and insincerely congratulating Travis on his gift.*) What are we all standing around here for? We ain't finished packin' yet. Bennie, you ain't packed one book.

The bell rings.

Beneatha: That couldn't be the movers . . . it's not hardly two good yet —

Beneatha goes into her room. Mama starts for door.

Walter (turning, stiffening): Wait — wait — I'll get it.

He stands and looks at the door.

Mama: You expecting company, son?
Walter (just looking at the door): Yeah — yeah . . .

Mama looks at Ruth, and they exchange innocent and unfrightened glances.

Mama (not understanding): Well, let them in, son.
Beneatha (from her room): We need some more string.
Mama: Travis — you run to the hardware and get me some string cord.

Mama goes out and Walter turns and looks at Ruth. Travis goes to a dish for money.

Ruth: Why don't you answer the door, man?
Walter (suddenly bounding across the floor to embrace her): 'Cause sometimes it hard to let the future begin! (*Stooping down in her face.*)

> *I got wings! You got wings!*
> *All God's children got wings!*

He crosses to the door and throws it open. Standing there is a very slight little man in a not-too-prosperous business suit and with haunted frightened eyes and a hat pulled down tightly, brim up, around his forehead. Travis passes between the men and exits. Walter leans deep in the man's face, still in his jubilance.

> *When I get to heaven gonna put on my wings,*
> *Gonna fly all over God's heaven . . .*

The little man just stares at him.

> *Heaven —*

Suddenly he stops and looks past the little man into the empty hallway.

Where's Willy, man?

Bobo: He ain't with me.

Walter (not disturbed): Oh — come on in. You know my wife.

Bobo (dumbly, taking off his hat): Yes — h'you, Miss Ruth.

Ruth (quietly, a mood apart from her husband already, seeing Bobo): Hello, Bobo.

Walter: You right on time today . . . Right on time. That's the way! (*He slaps Bobo on his back.*) Sit down . . . lemme hear.

Ruth stands stiffly and quietly in back of them, as though somehow she senses death, her eyes fixed on her husband.

Bobo (his frightened eyes on the floor, his hat in his hands): Could I please get a drink of water, before I tell you about it, Walter Lee?

Walter does not take his eyes off the man. Ruth goes blindly to the tap and gets a glass of water and brings it to Bobo.

Walter: There ain't nothing wrong, is there?

Bobo: Lemme tell you —

Walter: Man — didn't nothing go wrong?

Bobo: Lemme tell you — Walter Lee. (*Looking at Ruth and talking to her more than to Walter.*) You know how it was. I got to tell you how it was. I mean first I got to tell you how it was all the way . . . I mean about the money I put in, Walter Lee . . .

Walter (with taut agitation now): What about the money you put in?

Bobo: Well — it wasn't much as we told you — me and Willy — (*He stops.*) I'm sorry, Walter. I got a bad feeling about it. I got a real bad feeling about it . . .

Walter: Man, what you telling me about all this for? . . . Tell me what happened in Springfield . . .

Bobo: Springfield.

Ruth (like a dead woman): What was supposed to happen in Springfield?

Bobo (to her): This deal that me and Walter went into with Willy — Me and Willy was going to go down to Springfield and spread some money 'round so's we wouldn't have to wait so long for the liquor license . . . That's what we were going to do. Everybody said that was the way you had to do, you understand, Miss Ruth?

Walter: Man — what happened down there?

Bobo (a pitiful man, near tears): I'm trying to tell you, Walter.

Walter (screaming at him suddenly): THEN TELL ME, GODDAMMIT . . . WHAT'S THE MATTER WITH YOU?

Bobo: Man . . . I didn't go to no Springfield, yesterday.

Walter (halted, life hanging in the moment): Why not?

Bobo (the long way, the hard way to tell): 'Cause I didn't have no reasons to . . .

Walter: Man, what are you talking about!

Bobo: I'm talking about the fact that when I got to the train station yesterday morning — eight o'clock like we planned . . . Man — *Willy didn't never show up.*

Walter: Why . . . where was he . . . where is he?

Bobo: That's what I'm trying to tell you . . . I don't know . . . I waited six hours . . . I called his house . . . and I waited . . . six hours . . . I waited in that train station six hours . . . (*Breaking into tears.*) That was all the extra money I had in the world . . . (*Looking up at Walter with the tears running down his face.*) Man, *Willy is gone.*

Walter: Gone, what you mean Willy is gone? Gone where? You mean he went by himself. You mean he went off to Springfield by himself—to take care of getting the license—(*Turns and looks anxiously at Ruth.*) You mean maybe he didn't want too many people in on the business down there? (*Looks to Ruth again, as before.*) You know Willy got his own ways. (*Looks back to Bobo.*) Maybe you was late yesterday and he just went on down there without you. Maybe—maybe—he's been callin' you at home tryin' to tell you what happened or something. Maybe—maybe—he just got sick. He's somewhere—he's got to be somewhere. We just got to find him—me and you got to find him. (*Grabs Bobo senselessly by the collar and starts to shake him.*) We got to!

Bobo (in sudden angry, frightened agony): What's the matter with you, Walter! When a cat take off with your money he don't leave you no road maps!

Walter (turning madly, as though he is looking for Willy in the very room): Willy! . . . Willy . . . don't do it . . . Please don't do it . . . Man, not with that money . . . Man, please, not with that money . . . Oh, God . . . Don't let it be true . . . (*He is wandering around, crying out for Willy and looking for him or perhaps for help from God.*) Man . . . I trusted you . . . Man, I put my life in your hands . . . (*He starts to crumple down on the floor as Ruth just covers her face in horror. Mama opens the door and comes into the room, with Beneatha behind her.*) Man . . . (*He starts to pound the floor with his fists, sobbing wildly.*) THAT MONEY IS MADE OUT OF MY FATHER'S FLESH—

Bobo (standing over him helplessly): I'm sorry, Walter . . . (*only Walter's sobs reply. Bobo puts on his hat.*) I had my life staked on this deal, too . . .

He exits.

Mama (to Walter): Son—(*She goes to him, bends down to him, talks to his bent head.*) Son . . . Is it gone? Son, I gave you sixty-five hundred dollars. Is it gone? All of it? Beneatha's money too?

Walter (lifting his head slowly): Mama . . . I never . . . went to the bank at all . . .

Mama (not wanting to believe him): You mean . . . your sister's school money . . . you used that too . . . Walter? . . .

Walter: Yessss! All of it . . . It's all gone . . .

There is total silence. Ruth stands with her face covered with her hands; Beneatha leans forlornly against a wall, fingering a piece of red ribbon from the mother's gift. Mama stops and looks at her son without recognition and then, quite without thinking about it, starts to beat him senselessly in the face. Beneatha goes to them and stops it.

Beneatha: Mama!

Mama stops and looks at both of her children and rises slowly and wanders vaguely, aimlessly away from them.

Mama: I seen . . . him . . . night after night . . . come in . . . and look at that rug

. . . and then look at me . . . the red showing in his eyes . . . the veins moving in his head . . . I seen him grow thin and old before he was forty . . . working and working and working like somebody's old horse . . . killing himself . . . and you — you give it all away in a day — (*She raises her arms to strike him again.*)

Beneatha: Mama —

Mama: Oh, God . . . (*She looks up to Him.*) Look down here — and show me the strength.

Beneatha: Mama —

Mama (folding over): Strength . . .

Beneatha (plaintively): Mama . . .

Mama: Strength!

Curtain.

ACT III

Time: An hour later.

At curtain, there is a sullen light of gloom in the living room, gray light not unlike that which began the first scene of Act I. At left we can see Walter within his room, alone with himself. He is stretched out on the bed, his shirt out and open, his arms under his head. He does not smoke, he does not cry out, he merely lies there, looking up at the ceiling, much as if he were alone in the world.

In the living room Beneatha sits at the table, still surrounded by the now almost ominous packing crates. She sits looking off. We feel that this is a mood struck perhaps an hour before, and it lingers now, full of the empty sound of profound disappointment. We see on a line from her brother's bedroom the sameness of their attitudes. Presently the bell rings and Beneatha rises without ambition or interest in answering. It is Asagai, smiling broadly, striding into the room with energy and happy expectation and conversation.

Asagai: I came over . . . I had some free time. I thought I might help with the packing. Ah, I like the look of packing crates! A household in preparation for a journey! It depresses some people . . . but for me . . . it is another feeling. Something full of the flow of life, do you understand? Movement, progress . . . It makes me think of Africa.

Beneatha: Africa!

Asagai: What kind of a mood is this? Have I told you how deeply you move me?

Beneatha: He gave away the money, Asagai . . .

Asagai: Who gave away what money?

Beneatha: The insurance money. My brother gave it away.

Asagai: Gave it away?

Beneatha: He made an investment! With a man even Travis wouldn't have trusted with his most worn-out marbles.

Asagai: And it's gone?

Beneatha: Gone!

Asagai: I'm very sorry . . . And you, now?

Beneatha: Me? . . . Me? . . . Me, I'm nothing . . . Me. When I was very small . . . we used to take our sleds out in the wintertime and the only hills we had were the ice-covered stone steps of some houses down the street. And we used to fill them in with snow and make them smooth and slide down them all day . . . and it was very dangerous, you know . . . far too steep . . . and sure enough one day a kid named Rufus came down too fast and hit the sidewalk and we saw his face just split open right there in front of us . . . And I remember standing there looking at his bloody open face thinking that was the end of Rufus. But the ambulance came and they took him to the hospital and they fixed the broken bones and they sewed it all up . . . and the next time I saw Rufus he just had a little line down the middle of his face . . . I never got over that . . .

Asagai: What?

Beneatha: That that was what one person could do for another, fix him up — sew up the problem, make him all right again. That was the most marvelous thing in the world . . . I wanted to do that. I always thought it was the one concrete thing in the world that a human being could do. Fix up the sick, you know — and make them whole again. This was truly being God . . .

Asagai: You wanted to be God?

Beneatha: No — I wanted to cure. It used to be so important to me. I wanted to cure. It used to matter. I used to care. I mean about people and how their bodies hurt . . .

Asagai: And you've stopped caring?

Beneatha: Yes — I think so.

Asagai: Why?

Beneatha (bitterly): Because it doesn't seem deep enough, close enough to what ails mankind! It was a child's way of seeing things — or an idealist's.

Asagai: Children see things very well sometimes — and idealists even better.

Beneatha: I know that's what you think. Because you are still where I left off. You with all your talk and dreams about Africa! You still think you can patch up the world. Cure the Great Sore of Colonialism — (*Loftily, mocking it.*) with the Penicillin of Independence —!

Asagai: Yes!

Beneatha: Independance *and then what?* What about all the crooks and thieves and just plain idiots who will come into power and steal and plunder the same as before — only now they will be black and do it in the name of the new Independence — WHAT ABOUT THEM?!

Asagai: That will be the problem for another time. First we must get there.

Beneatha: And where does it end?

Asagai: End? Who even spoke of an end? To life? To living?

Beneatha: An end to misery! To stupidity! Don't you see there isn't any real progress, Asagai, there is only one large circle that we march in, around and around, each of us with our own little picture in front of us — our own little mirage that we think is the future.

Asagai: That is the mistake.

Beneatha: What?

Asagai: What you just said — about the circle. It isn't a circle — it is simply a long line — as in geometry, you know, one that reaches into infinity. And because we cannot see the end — we also cannot see how it changes. And it is very odd but those who see the changes — who dream, who will not give up — are called idealists . . . and those who see only the circle — we call *them* the "realists"!

Beneatha: Asagai, while I was sleeping in that bed in there, people went out and took the future right out of my hands! And nobody asked me, nobody consulted me — they just went out and changed my life!

Asagai: Was it your money?

Beneatha: What?

Asagai: Was it your money he gave away?

Beneatha: It belonged to all of us.

Asagai: But did you earn it? Would you have had it at all if your father had not died?

Beneatha: No.

Asagai: Then isn't there something wrong in a house — in a world — where all dreams, good or bad, must depend on the death of a man? I never thought to see *you* like this, Alaiyo. You! Your brother made a mistake and you are grateful to him so that now you can give up the ailing human race on account of it! You talk about what good is struggle, what good is anything! Where are we all going and why are we bothering!

Beneatha: AND YOU CANNOT ANSWER IT!

Asagai (shouting over her): I LIVE THE ANSWER! (Pause.) In my village at home it is the exceptional man who can even read a newspaper . . . or who ever sees a book at all. I will go home and much of what I will have to say will seem strange to the people of my village. But I will teach and work and things will happen, slowly and swiftly. At times it will seem that nothing changes at all . . . and then again the sudden dramatic events which make history leap into the future. And then quiet again. Retrogression even. Guns, murder, revolution. And I even will have moments when I wonder if the quiet was not better than all that death and hatred. But I will look about my village at the illiteracy and disease and ignorance and I will not wonder long. And perhaps . . . perhaps I will be a great man . . . I mean perhaps I will hold on to the substance of truth and find my way always with the right course . . . and perhaps for it I will be butchered in my bed some night by the servants of empire . . .

Beneatha: The martyr!

Asagai (he smiles): . . . or perhaps I shall live to be a very old man, respected and esteemed in my new nation . . . And perhaps I shall hold office and this is what I'm trying to tell you, Alaiyo: perhaps the things I believe now for my country will be wrong and outmoded, and I will not understand and do terrible things to have things my way or merely to keep my power. Don't you see that there will be young men and women — not British soldiers then, but my own black countrymen — to step out of the shadows some evening and slit my then useless throat? Don't you see they have always been there . . . that they always will be. And that such a thing as my own death will be an advance? They who might kill me even . . . actually replenish all that I was.

Beneatha: Oh, Asagai, I know all that.

Asagai: Good! Then stop moaning and groaning and tell me what you plan to do.

Beneatha: Do?

Asagai: I have a bit of a suggestion.

Beneatha: What?

Asagai (rather quietly for him): That when it is all over — that you come home with me —

Beneatha (staring at him and crossing away with exasperation): Oh — Asagai — at this moment you decide to be romantic!

Asagai (quickly understanding the misunderstanding): My dear, young creature of the New World — I do not mean across the city — I mean across the ocean: home — to Africa.

Beneatha (slowly understanding and turning to him with murmured amazement): To Africa?

Asagai: Yes! . . . (*smiling and lifting his arms playfully.*) Three hundred years later the African Prince rose up out of the seas and swept the maiden back across the middle passage over which her ancestors had come —

Beneatha (unable to play): To — to Nigeria?

Asagai: Nigeria. Home. (*Coming to her with genuine romantic flippancy.*) I will show you our mountains and our stars; and give you cool drinks from gourds and teach you the old songs and the ways of our people — and, in time, we will pretend that — (*Very softly.*) — you have only been away for a day. Say that you'll come — (*He swings her around and takes her full in his arms in a kiss which proceeds to passion.*)

Beneatha (pulling away suddenly): You're getting me all mixed up —

Asagai: Why?

Beneatha: Too many things — too many things have happened today. I must sit down and think. I don't know what I feel about anything right this minute.

She promptly sits down and props her chin on her fist.

Asagai (charmed): All right, I shall leave you. No — don't get up. (*Touching her, gently, sweetly.*) Just sit awhile and think . . . Never be afraid to sit awhile and think. (*He goes to door and looks at her.*) How often I have looked at you and said, "Ah — so this is what the New World hath finally wrought . . ."

He exits. Beneatha sits on alone. Presently Walter enters from his room and starts to rummage through things, feverishly looking for something. She looks up and turns in her seat.

Beneatha (hissingly): Yes — just look at what the New World hath wrought! . . . Just look! (*She gestures with bitter disgust.*) There he is! *Monsieur le petit bourgeois noir* — himself! There he is — Symbol of a Rising Class! Entrepreneur! Titan of the system! (*Walter ignores her completely and continues frantically and destructively looking for something and hurling things to floor and tearing things out of their place in his search. Beneatha ignores the eccentricity of his actions and goes on with the monologue of insult.*) Did you dream of yachts on Lake Michigan, Brother? Did you see yourself on that Great Day sitting down at the Conference Table, surrounded by all the mighty bald-headed men in America? All halted, waiting, breathless, waiting for your pronouncements on industry? Waiting for you — Chairman of the Board! (*Walter finds what he is looking for — a small piece of white paper — and pushes it in his pocket and puts on his coat and rushes out*

without ever having looked at her. She shouts after him.) I look at you and I
see the final triumph of stupidity in the world!

*The door slams and she returns to just sitting again. Ruth comes quickly out of
Mama's room.*

Ruth: Who was that?
Beneatha: Your husband.
Ruth: Where did he go?
Beneatha: Who knows — maybe he has an appointment at U.S. Steel.
Ruth (anxiously, with frightened eyes): You didn't say nothing bad to him, did
    you?
Beneatha: Bad? Say anything bad to him? No — I told him he was a sweet boy
    and full of dreams and everything is strictly peachy keen, as the ofay kids
    say!

*Mama enters from her bedroom. She is lost, vague, trying to catch hold, to make
some sense of her former command of the world, but it still eludes her. A sense
of waste overwhelms her gait; a measure of apology rides on her shoulders. She
goes to her plant, which has remained on the table, looks at it, picks it up and
takes it to the window sill and sits it outside, and she stands and looks at it a
long moment. Then she closes the window, straightens her body with effort and
turns around to her children.*

Mama: Well — ain't it a mess in here, though? (*A false cheerfulness, a beginning
    of something.*) I guess we all better stop moping around and get some work
    done. All this unpacking and everything we got to do. (*Ruth raises her head
    slowly in response to the sense of the line; and Beneatha in similar manner
    turns very slowly to look at her mother.*) One of you all better call the moving
    people and tell 'em not to come.
Ruth: Tell 'em not to come?
Mama: Of course, baby. Ain't no need in 'em coming all the way here and
    having to go back. They charges for that too. (*She sits down, fingers to her
    brow, thinking.*) Lord, ever since I was a little girl, I always remembers
    people saying, "Lena — Lena Eggleston, you aims too high all the time. You
    needs to slow down and see life a little more like it is. Just slow down some."
    That's what they always used to say down home — "Lord, that Lena Eggleston
    is a high-minded thing. She'll get her due one day!"
Ruth: No, Lena . . .
Mama: Me and Big Walter just didn't never learn right.
Ruth: Lena, no! We gotta go. Bennie — tell her . . .

*She rises and crosses to Beneatha with her arms outstretched. Beneatha doesn't
respond.*

    Tell her we can still move . . . the notes ain't but a hundred and twenty-five
    a month. We got four grown people in this house — we can work . . .
Mama (to herself): Just aimed too high all the time —
*Ruth (turning and going to Mama fast — the words pouring out with urgency
    and desperation):* Lena — I'll work . . . I'll work twenty hours a day in all
    the kitchens in Chicago . . . I'll strap my baby on my back if I have to and

scrub all the floors in America and wash all the sheets in America if I have to — but we got to MOVE! We got to get OUT OF HERE!!

Mama reaches out absently and pats Ruth's hand.

Mama: No — I sees things differently now. Been thinking 'bout some of the things we could do to fix this place up some. I seen a second-hand bureau over on Maxwell Street just the other day that could fit right there. (*She points to where the new furniture might go. Ruth wanders away from her.*) Would need some new handles on it and then a little varnish and it look like something brand-new. And — we can put up them new curtains in the kitchen . . . Why this place be looking fine. Cheer us all up so that we forget trouble ever come . . . (*To Ruth.*) And you could get some nice screens to put up in your room round the baby's bassinet . . . (*She looks at both of them pleadingly.*) Sometimes you just got to know when to give up some things . . . and hold on to what you got . . .

Walter enters from the outside, looking spent and leaning against the door, his coat hanging from him.

Mama: Where you been, son?
Walter (breathing hard): Made a call.
Mama: To who, son?
Walter: To The Man. (*He heads for his room.*)
Mama: What man, baby?
Walter (stops in the door): The Man, Mama. Don't you know who The Man is?
Ruth: Walter Lee?
Walter: *The Man.* Like the guys in the streets say — The Man. Captain Boss — Mistuh Charley . . . Old Cap'n Please Mr. Bossman . . .
Beneatha (suddenly): Lindner!
Walter: That's right! That's good. I told him to come right over.
Beneatha (fiercely, understanding): For what? What do you want to see him for!
Walter (looking at his sister): We going to do business with him.
Mama: What you talking 'bout, son?
Walter: Talking 'bout life, Mama. You all always telling me to see life like it is. Well — I laid in there on my back today . . . and I figured it out. Life just like it is. Who gets and who don't get. (*He sits down with his coat on and laughs.*) Mama, you know it's all divided up. Life is. Sure enough. Between the takers and the "tooken." (*He laughs.*) I've figured it out finally. (*He looks around at them.*) Yeah. Some of us always getting "tooken." (*He laughs.*) People like Willy Harris, they don't never get "tooken." And you know why the rest of us do? 'Cause we all mixed up. Mixed up bad. We get to looking 'round for the right and the wrong; and we worry about it and cry about it and stay up nights trying to figure out 'bout the wrong and the right of things all the time . . . And all the time, man, them takers is out there operating, just taking and taking. Willy Harris? Shoot — Willy Harris don't even count. He don't even count in the big scheme of things. But I'll say one thing for old Willy Harris . . . he's taught me something. He's taught me to keep my eye on what counts in this world. Yeah — (*Shouting out a little.*) Thanks, Willy!
Ruth: What did you call that man for, Walter Lee?

Walter: Called him to tell him to come on over to the show. Gonna put on a show for the man. Just what he wants to see. You see, Mama, the man came here today and he told us that them people out there where you want us to move — well they so upset they willing to pay us *not* to move! (*He laughs again.*) And — and oh, Mama — you would of been proud of the way me and Ruth and Bennie acted. We told him to get out . . . Lord have mercy! We told the man to get out! Oh, we was some proud folks this afternoon, yeah. (*He lights a cigarette.*) We were still full of that old-time stuff . . .

Ruth (coming toward him slowly): You talking 'bout taking them people's money to keep us from moving in that house?

Walter: I ain't just talking 'bout it, baby — I'm telling you that's what's going to happen!

Beneatha: Oh, God! Where is the bottom! Where is the real honest-to-God bottom so he can't go any farther!

Walter: See — that's the old stuff. You and that boy that was here today. You all want everybody to carry a flag and a spear and sing some marching songs, huh? You wanna spend your life looking into things and trying to find the right and the wrong part, huh? Yeah. You know what's going to happen to that boy someday — he'll find himself sitting in a dungeon, locked in forever — and the takers will have the key! Forget it, baby! There ain't no causes — there ain't nothing but taking in this world, and he who takes most is smartest — and it don't make a damn bit of difference *how.*

Mama: You making something inside me cry, son. Some awful pain inside me.

Walter: Don't cry, Mama. Understand. That white man is going to walk in that door able to write checks for more money than we ever had. It's important to him and I'm going to help him . . . I'm going to put on the show, Mama.

Mama: Son — I come from five generations of people who was slaves and sharecroppers — but ain't nobody in my family never let nobody pay 'em no money that was a way of telling us we wasn't fit to walk the earth. We ain't never been that poor. (*Raising her eyes and looking at him.*) We ain't never been that — dead inside.

Beneatha: Well — we are dead now. All the talk about dreams and sunlight that goes on in this house. It's all dead now.

Walter: What's the matter with you all! I didn't make this world! It was give to me this way! Hell, yes, I want me some yachts someday! Yes, I want to hang some real pearls 'round my wife's neck. Ain't she supposed to wear no pearls? Somebody tell me — tell me, who decides which women is suppose to wear pearls in this world. I tell you I am a *man* — and I think my wife should wear some pearls in this world!

This last line hangs a good while and Walter begins to move about the room. The word "Man" has penetrated his consciousness; he mumbles it to himself repeatedly between strange agitated pauses as he moves about.

Mama: Baby, how you going to feel on the inside?

Walter: Fine! . . . Going to feel fine . . . a man . . .

Mama: You won't have nothing left then, Walter Lee.

Walter (coming to her): I'm going to feel fine, Mama. I'm going to look that son-of-a-bitch in the eyes and say — (*He falters.*) — and say, "All right, Mr. Lindner — (*He falters even more.*) — that's *your* neighborhood out there! You got the right to keep it like you want! You got the right to have it like you want! Just write the check and — the house is yours." And — and I am going to say — (*His voice almost breaks.*) "And you — you people just put the money in my hand and you won't have to live next to this bunch of stinking niggers! . . ." (*He straightens up and moves away from his mother, walking around the room.*) And maybe — maybe I'll just get down on my black knees . . . (*He does so; Ruth and Bennie and Mama watch him in frozen horror.*) "Captain, Mistuh, Bossman — (*Groveling and grinning and wringing his hands in profoundly anguished imitation of the slow-witted movie stereotype.*) A-hee-hee-hee! Oh, yassuh boss! Yasssssuh! Great white — (*Voice breaking, he forces himself to go on.*) — Father, just gi' ussen de money, fo' God's sake, and we's — we's ain't gwine come out deh and dirty up yo' white folks neighborhood . . ." (*He breaks down completely.*) And I'll feel fine! Fine! FINE! (*He gets up and goes into the bedroom.*)

Beneatha: That is not a man. That is nothing but a toothless rat.

Mama: Yes — death done come in this here house. (*She is nodding, slowly, reflectively.*) Done come walking in my house on the lips of my children. You what supposed to be my beginning again. You — what supposed to be my harvest. (*To Beneatha.*) You — you mourning your brother?

Beneatha: He's no brother of mine.

Mama: What you say?

Beneatha: I said that that individual in that room is no brother of mine.

Mama: That's what I thought you said. You feeling like you better than he is today? (*Beneatha does not answer.*) Yes? What you tell him a minute ago? That he wasn't a man? Yes? You give him up for me? You done wrote his epitaph too — like the rest of the world? Well, who give you the privilege?

Beneatha: Be on my side for once! You saw what he just did, Mama! You saw him — down on his knees. Wasn't it you who taught me to despise any man who would do that? Do what he's going to do?

Mama: Yes — I taught you that. Me and your daddy. But I thought I taught you something else too . . . I thought I taught you to love him.

Beneatha: Love him? There is nothing left to love.

Mama: There is *always* something left to love. And if you ain't learned that, you ain't learned nothing. (*Looking at her.*) Have you cried for that boy today? I don't mean for yourself and for the family 'cause we lost the money. I mean for him: what he been through and what it done to him. Child, when do you think is the time to love somebody the most? When they done good and made things easy for everybody? Well then, you ain't through learning — because that ain't the time at all. It's when he's at his lowest and can't believe in hisself 'cause the world done whipped him so! When you starts measuring somebody, measure him right, child, measure him right. Make sure you done taken into account what hills and valleys he come through before he got to wherever he is.

Travis bursts into the room at the end of the speech, leaving the door open.

Travis: Grandmama — the moving men are downstairs! The truck just pulled up.

Mama (turning and looking at him): Are they, baby? They downstairs?

She sighs and sits. Lindner appears in the doorway. He peers in and knocks lightly, to gain attention, and comes in. All turn to look at him.

Lindner (hat and briefcase in hand): Uh — hello . . .

Ruth crosses mechanically to the bedroom door and opens it and lets it swing open freely and slowly as the lights come up on Walter within, still in his coat, sitting at the far corner of the room. He looks up and out through the room to Lindner.

Ruth: He's here.

A long minute passes and Walter slowly gets up.

Lindner (coming to the table with efficiency, putting his briefcase on the table and starting to unfold papers and unscrew fountain pens): Well, I certainly was glad to hear from you people. (*Walter has begun the trek out of the room, slowly and awkwardly, rather like a small boy, passing the back of his sleeve across his mouth from time to time.*) Life can really be so much simpler than people let it be most of the time. Well — with whom do I negotiate? You, Mrs. Younger, or your son here? (*Mama sits with her hands folded on her lap and her eyes closed as Walter advances. Travis goes closer to Lindner and looks at the papers curiously.*) Just some official papers, sonny.

Ruth: Travis, you go downstairs —

Mama (opening her eyes and looking into Walter's): No. Travis, you stay right here. And you make him understand what you doing, Walter Lee. You teach him good. Like Willy Harris taught you. You show where our five generations done come to. (*Walter looks from her to the boy, who grins at him innocently.*) Go ahead, son — (*She folds her hands and closes her eyes.*) Go ahead.

Walter (at last crosses to Lindner, who is reviewing the contract): Well, Mr. Lindner. (*Beneatha turns away.*) We called you — (*There is a profound, simple groping quality in his speech.*) — because, well, me and my family (*He looks around and shifts from one foot to the other.*) Well — we are very plain people . . .

Lindner: Yes —

Walter: I mean — I have worked as a chauffeur most of my life — and my wife here, she does domestic work in people's kitchens. So does my mother. I mean — we are plain people . . .

Lindner: Yes, Mr. Younger —

Walter (really like a small boy, looking down at his shoes and then up at the man): And — uh — well, my father, well, he was a laborer most of his life. . . .

Lindner (absolutely confused): Uh, yes — yes, I understand. (*He turns back to the contract.*)

Walter (a beat; staring at him): And my father — (*With sudden intensity.*) My father almost *beat a man to death* once because this man called him a bad name or something, you know what I mean?

Lindner (looking up, frozen): No, no, I'm afraid I don't —

Walter (a beat. The tension hangs; then Walter steps back from it): Yeah. Well — what I mean is that we come from people who had a lot of *pride.* I mean — we are very proud people. And that's my sister over there and she's going to be a doctor — and we are very proud —

Lindner: Well — I am sure that is very nice, but —

Walter: What I am telling you is that we called you over here to tell you that we are very proud and that this — (*Signaling to Travis.*) Travis, come here. (*Travis crosses and Walter draws him before him facing the man.*) This is my son, and he makes the sixth generation our family in this country. And we have all thought about your offer —

Lindner: Well, good . . . good —

Walter: And we have decided to move into our house because my father — my father — he earned it for us brick by brick. (*Mama has her eyes closed and is rocking back and forth as though she were in church, with her head nodding the Amen yes.*) We don't want to make no trouble for nobody or fight no causes, and we will try to be good neighbors. And that's *all* we got to say about that. (*He looks the man absolutely in the eyes.*) We don't want your money. (*He turns and walks away.*)

Lindner (looking around at all of them): I take it then — that you have decided to occupy . . .

Beneatha: That's what the man said.

Lindner (to Mama in her reverie): Then I would like to appeal to you, Mrs. Younger. You are older and wiser and understand things better I am sure . . .

Mama: I am afraid you don't understand. My son said we was going to move and there ain't nothing left for me to say. (*Briskly.*) You know how these young folks is nowadays, mister. Can't do a thing with 'em! (*As he opens his mouth, she rises.*) Good-bye.

Lindner (folding up his materials): Well — if you are that final about it . . . there is nothing left for me to say. (*He finishes, almost ignored by the family, who are concentrating on Walter Lee. At the door Lindner halts and looks around.*) I sure hope you people know what you're getting into.

He shakes his head and exits.

Ruth (looking around and coming to life): Well, for God's sake — if the moving men are here — LET'S GET THE HELL OUT OF HERE!

Mama (into action): Ain't it the truth! Look at all this here mess. Ruth, put Travis' good jacket on him . . . Walter Lee, fix your tie and tuck your shirt in, you look like somebody's hoodlum! Lord have mercy, where is my plant? (*She flies to get it amid the general bustling of the family, who are deliberately trying to ignore the nobility of the past moment.*) You all start on down . . . Travis child, don't go empty-handed . . . Ruth, where did I put that box with my skillets in it? I want to be in charge of it myself . . . I'm going to make us the biggest dinner we ever ate tonight . . . Beneatha, what's the matter with them stockings? Pull them things up, girl . . .

The family starts to file out as two moving men appear and begin to carry out the heavier pieces of furniture, bumping into the family as they move about.

Beneatha: Mama, Asagai asked me to marry him today and go to Africa —

Mama (in the middle of her getting-ready activity): He did? You ain't old enough to marry nobody — (*Seeing the moving men lifting one of her chairs precariously.*) Darling, that ain't no bale of cotton, please handle it so we can sit in it again! I had that chair twenty-five years . . .

The movers sigh with exasperation and go on with their work.

Beneatha (girlishly and unreasonably trying to pursue the conversation): To go to Africa, Mama — be a doctor in Africa . . .

Mama (distracted): Yes, baby —

Walter: Africa! What he want you to go to Africa for?

Beneatha: To practice there . . .

Walter: Girl, if you don't get all them silly ideas out your head! You better marry yourself a man with some loot . . .

Beneatha (angrily, precisely as in the first scene of the play): What have you got to do with who I marry!

Walter: Plenty. Now I think George Murchison —

Beneatha: George Murchison! I wouldn't marry him if he was Adam and I was Eve!

Walter and Beneatha go out yelling at each other vigorously and the anger is loud and real till their voices diminish. Ruth stands at the door and turns to Mama and smiles knowingly.

Mama (fixing her hat at last): Yeah — they something all right, my children . . .

Ruth: Yeah — they're something. Let's go, Lena.

Mama (stalling, starting to look around at the house): Yes — I'm coming. Ruth —

Ruth: Yes?

Mama (quietly, woman to woman): He finally come into his manhood today, didn't he? Kind of like a rainbow after the rain . . .

Ruth (biting her lip lest her own pride explode in front of Mama): Yes, Lena.

Walter's voice calls for them raucously.

Walter (off stage): Y'all come on! These people charges by the hour, you know!

Mama (waving Ruth out vaguely): All right, honey — go on down. I be down directly.

Ruth hesitates, then exits. Mama stands, at last alone in the living room, her plant on the table before her as the lights start to come down. She looks around at all the walls and ceilings and suddenly, despite herself, while the children call below, a great heaving thing rises in her and she puts her fist to her mouth to stifle it, takes a final desperate look, pulls her coat about her, pats her hat, and goes out. The lights dim down. The door opens and she comes back in, grabs her plant, and goes out for the last time.

Curtain.

Connections to Other Selections

1. The play's title is a line from the Langston Hughes poem that introduces the play (p. 1780). Explain how the context of the entire poem helps to explain the play's title and its major concerns.
2. Consider Lena Younger's role as a mother in *A Raisin in the Sun.* Explain why you think she is nurturing or overbearing. Compare her character with Amanda Wingfield's in Tennessee Williams's *The Glass Menagerie* (p. 1666).
3. Write an essay that compares the dreams the Youngers struggle to realize with those of the Lomans in Arthur Miller's *Death of a Salesman* (p. 1712). What

similarities and differences about the nature of each family's dreams do you find in the plays?

4. In an essay compare the economic, social, and moral pressures on the families in *A Raisin in the Sun* and August Wilson's *Fences* (p. 1872). How does each family cope with these pressures? Discuss which family you think is more successful in confronting them.

AN ALBUM OF WORLD LITERATURE

THE STRONG BREED

Born Oluwole Akinwande Soyinka in the western Nigerian town of Akinwande, Wole Soyinka has embodied in his life and art the contradictions and tensions that can often seem inevitable for the European-educated, English-speaking, African writer. "Selective eclecticism," he once said, is "the right of every productive being." Although he has written and published novels and poetry, Soyinka is most renowned as a playwright whose work often focuses on the tragic consequences of a clash between colonial and tribal values. Educated at Leeds University in England, he subsequently began an active career as a playwright as well as a political reformer and social critic. His autobiography *The Man Died* (1973) records his experiences as a political prisoner in Nigeria.

Soyinka's many plays include *The Swamp Dwellers* (1958), *The Invention* (1959), *The Lion and the Jewel* (1959), *A Dance of Forests* (1960), *The Strong Breed* (1963), *Madmen and Specialists* (1970), and *Death and the King's Horseman* (1976). He has also written two novels and three volumes of poetry. In 1986 he was awarded the Nobel Prize for literature.

Like nearly all of Soyinka's writing, *The Strong Breed* is steeped in African tribal culture and tradition, but the play's abiding concern for human suffering and social justice invites all readers to step into the small village in which one "night's work" changes the lives of its inhabitants.

WOLE SOYINKA (Nigerian/b. 1934)
The Strong Breed   1963

Characters

Eman, a stranger
Sunma, Jaguna's daughter
Ifada, an idiot
A Girl
Jaguna
Oroge
Attendant Stalwarts, the villagers

From Eman's past —
Old Man, his father
Omae, his betrothed
Tutor
Priest
Attendants, the villagers

The scenes are described briefly, but very often a darkened stage with lit area will not only suffice but is necessary. Except for the one indicated place, there can be no break in the action. A distracting scene-change would be ruinous. A mud house, with space in front of it. Eman, in light buba and trousers, stands at the window, looking out. Inside, Sunma is clearing the table of what looks like a modest clinic, putting the things away in a cupboard. Another rough table in the room is piled with exercise books, two or three worn textbooks, etc. Sunma appears agitated. Outside, just below the window, crouches Ifada. He looks up with a shy smile from time to time, waiting for Eman to notice him.

Sunma (hesitant): You will have to make up your mind soon, Eman. The lorry leaves very shortly.

As Eman does not answer, Sunma continues her work, more nervously. Two villagers, obvious travelers, pass hurriedly in front of the house, the man has a small raffia sack, the woman a cloth-covered basket, the man enters first, turns, and urges the woman who is just emerging to hurry.

Sunma (seeing them, her tone is more intense): Eman, are we going or aren't we? You will leave it till too late.
Eman (quietly): There is still time — if you want to go.
Sunma: If I want to go . . . and you?

Eman makes no reply.

Sunma (bitterly): You don't really want to leave here. You never want to go away — even for a minute.

Ifada continues his antics. Eman eventually pats him on the head and the boy grins happily. Leaps up suddenly and returns with a basket of oranges, which he offers Eman.

Eman: My gift for today's festival enh?

Ifada nods, grinning.

Eman: They look ripe — that's a change.
Sunma (she has gone inside the room. Looks round the door): Did you call me?
Eman: No. *(She goes back.)* And what will you do tonight, Ifada? Will you take part in the dancing? Or perhaps you will mount your own masquerade?

Ifada shakes his head, regretfully.

Eman: You won't? So you haven't any? But you would like to own one.

Ifada nods eagerly.

Eman: Then why don't you make your own?

Ifada stares, puzzled by this idea.

Eman: Sunma will let you have some cloth you know. And bits of wool . . .

Sunma (coming out): Who are you talking to, Eman?

Eman: Ifada. I am trying to persuade him to join the young maskers.

Sunma (losing control): What does he want here? Why is he hanging round us?

Eman (amazed): What . . . ? I said Ifada, Ifada.

Sunma: Just tell him to go away. Let him go and play somewhere else!

Eman: What is this? Hasn't he always played here?

Sunma: I don't want him here. *(Rushes to the window.)* Get away, idiot. Don't bring your foolish face here any more, do you hear? Go on, go away from here . . .

Eman (restraining her): Control yourself, Sunma. What on earth has got into you?

Ifada, hurt and bewildered, backs slowly away.

Sunma: He comes crawling round here like some horrible insect. I never want to lay my eyes on him again.

Eman: I don't understand. It *is* Ifada you know, Ifada! The unfortunate one who runs errands for you and doesn't hurt a soul.

Sunma: I cannot bear the sight of him.

Eman: You can't do what? It can't be two days since he last fetched water for you.

Sunma: What else can he do except that? He is useless. Just because we have been kind to him. . . . Others would have put him in an asylum.

Eman: You are not making sense. He is not a madman, he is just a little more unlucky than other children. *(Looks keenly at her.)* But what is the matter?

Sunma: It's nothing. I only wish we had sent him off to one of those places for creatures like him.

Eman: He is quite happy here. He doesn't bother anyone and he makes himself useful.

Sunma: Useful! Is that one of any use to anybody? Boys of his age are already earning a living but all he can do is hang around and drool at the mouth.

Eman: But he does work. You know he does a lot for you.

Sunma: Does he? And what about the farm you started for him! Does he ever work on it? Or have you forgotten that it was really for Ifada you cleared that brush. Now you have to go and work it yourself. You spend all your time on it and you have no room for anything else.

Eman: That wasn't his fault. I should first have asked him if he was fond of farming.

Sunma: Oh, so he can choose? As if he shouldn't be thankful for being allowed to live.

Eman: Sunma!

Sunma: He does not like farming but he knows how to feast his dumb mouth on the fruits.

Eman: But I want him to. I encourage him.

Sunma: Well keep him. I don't want to see him any more.

Eman (after some moments): But why? You cannot be telling all the truth. What has he done?

Sunma: The sight of him fills me with revulsion.

Eman (goes to her and holds her): What really is it? *(Sunma avoids his eyes.)* It is almost as if you are forcing yourself to hate him. Why?

Sunma: That is not true. Why should I?

Eman: Then what is the secret? You've even played with him before.

Sunma: I have always merely tolerated him. But I cannot any more. Suddenly my disgust won't take him any more. Perhaps . . . perhaps it is the new year. Yes, yes, it must be the new year.

Eman: I don't believe that.

Sunma: It must be. I am a woman, and these things matter. I don't want a misshape near me. Surely for one day in the year, I may demand some wholesomeness.

Eman: I do not understand you.

Sunma is silent.

It was cruel of you. And to Ifada who is so helpless and alone. We are the only friends he has.

Sunma: No, just you. I have told you, with me it has always been only an act of kindness. And now I haven't any pity left for him.

Eman: No. He is not a wholesome being.

He turns back to looking through the window.

Sunma (half-pleading): Ifada can rouse your pity. And yet if anything, I need more kindness from you. Every time my weakness betrays me, you close your mind against me . . . Eman . . . Eman . . .

A Girl comes in view, dragging an effigy by a rope attached to one of its legs. She stands for a while gazing at Eman. Ifada, who has crept back shyly to his accustomed position, becomes somewhat excited when he sees the effigy. The Girl is unsmiling. She possesses, in fact, a kind of inscrutability which does not make her hard but is unsettling.

Girl: Is the teacher in?

Eman (smiling): No.

Girl: Where is he gone?

Eman: I don't really know. Shall I ask?

Girl: Yes, do.

Eman (turning slightly): Sunma, a girl outside wants to know . . .

Sunma turns away, goes into the inside room.

Eman: Oh. (*Returns to the girl, but his slight gaiety is lost.*) There is no one at home who can tell me.

Girl: Why are you not in?

Eman: I don't really know. Maybe I went somewhere.

Girl: All right. I will wait until you get back.

She pulls the effigy to her, sits down.

Eman (slowly regaining his amusement): So you are ready for the new year.

Girl (without turning round): I am not going to the festival.

Eman: Then why have you got that?

Girl: Do you mean my carrier? I am unwell you know. My mother says it will take away my sickness with the old year.

Eman: Won't you share the carrier with your playmates?

Girl: Oh, no. Don't you know I play alone? The other children won't come near me. Their mothers would beat them.

Eman: But I have never seen you here. Why don't you come to the clinic?

Girl: My mother said No.

Gets up, begins to move off.

Eman: You are not going away?

Girl: I must not stay talking to you. If my mother caught me . . .

Eman: All right, tell me what you want before you go.

Girl (stops. For some moments she remains silent): I must have some clothes for my carrier.

Eman: Is that all? You wait a moment.

Sunma comes out as he takes down a buba from the wall. She goes to the window and glares almost with hatred at the Girl. The Girl retreats hastily, still impassive.

By the way, Sunma, do you know who that girl is?

Sunma: I hope you don't really mean to give her that.

Eman: Why not? I hardly ever use it.

Sunma: Just the same don't give it to her. She is not a child. She is as evil as the rest of them.

Eman: What has got into you today?

Sunma: All right, all right. Do what you wish.

She withdraws. Baffled, Eman returns to the window.

Eman: Here . . . will this do? Come and look at it.

Girl: Throw it.

Eman: What is the matter? I am not going to eat you.

Girl: No one lets me come near them.

Eman: But I am not afraid of catching your disease.

Girl: Throw it.

Eman shrugs and tosses the buba. She takes it without a word and slips it on the effigy, completely absorbed in the task. Eman watches for a while, then joins Sunma in the inner room.

Girl (after a long, cool survey of Ifada): You have a head like a spider's egg, and your mouth dribbles like a roof. But there is no one else. Would you like to play?

Ifada nods eagerly, quite excited.

Girl: You will have to get a stick.

Ifada rushes around, finds a big stick, and whirls it aloft, bearing down on the carrier.

Girl: Wait. I don't want you to spoil it. If it gets torn I shall drive you away. Now, let me see how you are going to beat it.

Ifada hits it gently.

Girl: You may hit harder than that. As long as there is something left to hang at the end.

She appraises him up and down.

You are not very tall . . . will you be able to hang it from a tree?

Ifada nods, grinning happily.

Girl: You will hang it up and I will set fire to it. *(Then, with surprising venom.)* But just because you are helping me, don't think it is going to cure you. I am the one who will get well at midnight, do you understand? It is my carrier and it is for me alone. *(She pulls at the rope to make sure that it is well attached to the leg.)* Well don't stand there drooling. Let's go.

She begins to walk off, dragging the effigy in the dust. Ifada remains where he is for some moments, seemingly puzzled. Then his face breaks into a large grin and he leaps after the procession, belaboring the effigy with all his strength. The stage remains empty for some moments. Then the horn of a lorry is sounded and Sunma rushes out. The hooting continues for some time with a rhythmic pattern. Eman comes out.

Eman: I am going to the village . . . I shan't be back before nightfall.
Sunma (blankly): Yes.
Eman (hesitates): Well what do you want me to do?
Sunma: The lorry was hooting just now.
Eman: I didn't hear it.
Sunma: It will leave in a few minutes. And you did promise we could go away.
Eman: I promised nothing. Will you go home by yourself or shall I come back for you?
Sunma: You don't even want me here?
Eman: But you have to go home, haven't you?
Sunma: I had hoped we would watch the new year together — in some other place.
Eman: Why do you continue to distress yourself?
Sunma: Because you will not listen to me. Why do you continue to stay where nobody wants you?
Eman: That is not true.
Sunma: It is. You are wasting your life on people who really want you out of their way.
Eman: You don't know what you are saying.
Sunma: You think they love you? Do you think they care at all for what you — or I — do for them?
Eman: Them? These are your own people. Sometimes you talk as if you were a stranger too.
Sunma: I wonder if I really sprang from here. I know they are evil and I am not. From the oldest to the smallest child, they are nourished in evil and unwholesomeness in which I have no part.
Eman: You knew this when you returned?
Sunma: You reproach me then for trying at all?
Eman: I reproach you with nothing? But you must leave me out of your plans. I can have no part in them.
Sunma (nearly pleading): Once I could have run away. I would have gone and never looked back.
Eman: I cannot listen when you talk like that.

Sunma: I swear to you, I do not mind what happens afterwards. But you must help me tear myself away from here. I can no longer do it by myself. . . . It is only a little thing. And we have worked so hard this past year . . . surely we can go away for a week . . . even a few days would be enough.

Eman: I have told you, Sunma . . .

Sunma (desperately): Two days, Eman. Only two days.

Eman (distressed): But I tell you I have no wish to go.

Sunma (suddenly angry): Are you so afraid then?

Eman: Me? Afraid of what?

Sunma: You think you will not want to come back.

Eman (pitying): You cannot dare me that way.

Sunma: Then why won't you leave here, even for an hour? If you are so sure that your life is settled here, why are you afraid to do this thing for me? What is so wrong that you will not go into the next town for a day or two?

Eman: I don't want to. I do not have to persuade you, or myself about anything. I simply have no desire to go away.

Sunma (his quiet confidence appears to incense her): You are afraid. You accuse me of losing my sense of mission, but you are afraid to put yours to the test.

Eman: You are wrong, Sunma. I have no sense of mission. But I have found peace here and I am content with that.

Sunma: I haven't. For a while I thought that too, but I found there could be no peace in the midst of so much cruelty. Eman, tonight at least, the last night of the old year . . .

Eman: No, Sunma. I find this too distressing; you should go home now.

Sunma: It is the time for making changes in one's life, Eman. Let's breathe in the new year away from here.

Eman: You are hurting yourself.

Sunma: Tonight. Only tonight. We will come back tomorrow, as early as you like. But let us go away for this one night. Don't let another year break on me in this place . . . you don't know how important it is to me, but I will tell you, I will tell you on the way . . . but we must not be here today, Eman, do this one thing for me.

Eman (sadly): I cannot.

Sunma (suddenly calm): I was a fool to think it would be otherwise. The whole village may use you as they will but for me there is nothing. Sometimes I think you believe that doing anything for me makes you unfaithful to some part of your life. If it was a woman then I pity her for what she must have suffered.

Eman winces and hardens slowly. Sunma notices nothing.

Keeping faith with so much is slowly making you inhuman. *(Seeing the change in Eman.)* Eman. Eman. What is it?

As she goes towards him, Eman goes into the house.

Sunma (apprehensive, follows him): What did I say? Eman, forgive me, forgive me please.

Eman remains facing into the slow darkness of the room. Sunma, distressed, cannot decide what to do.

I swear I didn't know. . . . . I would not have said it for all the world.

A lorry is heard taking off somewhere nearby. The sound comes up and slowly fades away into the distance. Sunma starts visibly, goes slowly to the window.

Sunma (as the sound dies off, to herself): What happens now?
Eman (joining her at the window): What did you say?
Sunma: Nothing.
Eman: Was that not the lorry going off?
Sunma: It was.
Eman: I am sorry I couldn't help you.

Sunma, about to speak, changes her mind.

Eman: I think you ought to go home now.
Sunma: No, don't send me away. It's the least you can do for me. Let me stay here until all the noise is over.
Eman: But are you not needed at home? You have a part in the festival.
Sunma: I have renounced it; I am Jaguna's eldest daughter only in name.
Eman: Renouncing one's self is not so easy — surely you know that.
Sunma: I don't want to talk about it. Will you at least let us be together tonight?
Eman: But . . . .
Sunma: Unless you are afraid my father will accuse you of harboring me.
Eman: All right, we will go out together.
Sunma: Go out? I want us to stay here.
Eman: When there is so much going on outside?
Sunma: Some day you will wish that you went away when I tried to make you.
Eman: Are we going back to that?
Sunma: No. I promise you I will not recall it again. But you must know that it was also for your sake that I tried to get us away.
Eman: For me? How?
Sunma: By yourself you can do nothing here. Have you not noticed how tightly we shut out strangers? Even if you lived here for a lifetime, you would remain a stranger.
Eman: Perhaps that is what I like. There is peace in being a stranger.
Sunma: For a while perhaps. But they would reject you in the end. I tell you it is only I who stand between you and contempt. And because of this you have earned their hatred. I don't know why I say this now, except that somehow, I feel that it no longer matters. It is only I who have stood between you and much humiliation.
Eman: Think carefully before you say any more. I am incapable of feeling indebted to you. This will make no difference at all.
Sunma: I ask for nothing. But you must know it all the same. It is true I hadn't the strength to go by myself. And I must confess this now, if you had come with me, I would have done everything to keep you from returning.
Eman: I know that.
Sunma: You see, I bare myself to you. For days I had thought it over, this was to be a new beginning for us. And I placed my fate wholly in your hands. Now the thought will not leave me, I have a feeling which will not be shaken off, that in some way, you have tonight totally destroyed my life.
Eman: You are depressed, you don't know what you are saying.

Sunma: Don't think I am accusing you. I say all this only because I cannot help it.

Eman: We must not remain shut up here. Let us go and be part of the living.

Sunma: No. Leave them alone.

Eman: Surely you don't want to stay indoors when the whole town is alive with rejoicing.

Sunma: Rejoicing! Is that what it seems to you? No, let us remain here. Whatever happens I must not go out until all this is over.

There is silence. It has grown much darker.

Eman: I shall light the lamp.

Sunma (eager to do something): No, let me do it.

She goes into the inner room. Eman paces the room, stops by a shelf, and toys with the seeds in an "ayo" board, takes down the whole board and places it on a table, playing by himself.

The Girl is now seen coming back, still dragging her "carrier." Ifada brings up the rear as before. As he comes round the corner of the house two men emerge from the shadows. A sack is thrown over Ifada's head, the rope is pulled tight rendering him instantly helpless. The Girl has reached the front of the house before she turns round at the sound of scuffle. She is in time to see Ifada thrown over the shoulders and borne away. Her face betraying no emotion at all, the Girl backs slowly away, turns, and flees, leaving the "carrier" behind. Sunma enters, carrying two kerosene lamps. She hangs one up from the wall.

Eman: One is enough.

Sunma: I want to leave one outside.

She goes out, hangs the lamp from a nail just above the door. As she turns she sees the effigy and gasps. Eman rushes out.

Eman: What is it? Oh, is that what frightened you?

Sunma: I thought . . . I didn't really see it properly.

Eman goes towards the object, stoops to pick it up.

Eman: It must belong to that sick girl.

Sunma: Don't touch it.

Eman: Let's keep it for her.

Sunma: Leave it alone. Don't touch it, Eman.

Eman (shrugs and goes back): You are very nervous.

Sunma: Let's go in.

Eman: Wait. (*He detains her by the door, under the lamp.*) I know there is something more than you've told me. What are you afraid of tonight?

Sunma: I was only scared by that thing. There is nothing else.

Eman: I am not blind, Sunma. It is true I would not run away when you wanted me to, but that doesn't mean I do not feel things. What does tonight really mean that it makes you so helpless?

Sunma: It is only a mood. And your indifference to me . . . let's go in.

Eman moves aside and she enters; he remains there for a moment and then follows. She fiddles with the lamp, looks vaguely round the room, then goes and shuts the door, bolting it. When she turns, it is to meet Eman's eyes, questioning.

Sunma: There is a cold wind coming in.

Eman keeps his gaze on her.

Sunma: It *was* getting cold.

She moves guiltily to the table and stands by the ayo board, rearranging the seeds. Eman remains where he is a few moments, then brings a stool and sits opposite her. She sits down also and they begin to play in silence.

Sunma: What brought you here at all, Eman? And what makes you stay?

There is another silence.

Sunma: I am not trying to share your life. I know you too well by now. But at least we have worked together since you came. Is there nothing at all I deserve to know?

Eman: Let me continue a stranger — especially to you. Those who have much to give fulfill themselves only in total loneliness.

Sunma: Then there is no love in what you do.

Eman: There is. Love comes to me more easily with strangers.

Sunma: That is unnatural.

Eman: Not for me. I know I find consummation only when I have spent myself for a total stranger.

Sunma: It seems unnatural to me. But then I am a woman. I have a woman's longings and weaknesses. And the ties of blood are very strong in me.

Eman (smiling): You think I have cut loose from all these — ties of blood.

Sunma: Sometimes you are so inhuman.

Eman: I don't know what that means. But I am very much my father's son.

They play in silence. Suddenly Eman pauses, listening.

Eman: Did you hear that?

Sunma (quickly): I heard nothing . . . it's your turn.

Eman: Perhaps some of the mummers are coming this way.

Eman, about to play, leaps up suddenly.

Sunma: What is it? Don't you want to play any more?

Eman moves to the door.

Sunma: No. Don't go out, Eman.

Eman: If it's the dancers I want to ask them to stay. At least we won't have to miss everything.

Sunma: No, no. Don't open the door. Let us keep out everyone tonight.

A terrified and disordered figure bursts suddenly round the corner, past the window and begins hammering at the door. It is Ifada. Desperate with terror, he pounds madly at the door, dumb-moaning all the while.

Eman: Isn't that Ifada?

Sunma: They are only fooling about. Don't pay any attention.

Eman (looks round the window): That is Ifada. *(Begins to unbolt the door.)*

Sunma (pulling at his hands): It is only a trick they are playing on you. Don't take any notice, Eman.

Eman: What are you saying? The boy is out of his senses with fear.

Sunma: No, no. Don't interfere, Eman. For God's sake don't interfere.

Eman: Do you know something of this then?

Sunma: You are a stranger here, Eman. Just leave us alone and go your own way. There is nothing you can do.

Eman (he tries to push her out of the way but she clings fiercely to him): Have you gone mad? I tell you the boy must come in.

Sunma: Why won't you listen to me, Eman? I tell you it's none of your business. For your own sake do as I say.

Eman pushes her off, unbolts the door. Ifada rushes in, clasps Eman round the knees, dumb-moaning against his legs.

Eman (manages to rebolt the door): What is it, Ifada? What is the matter?

Shouts and voices are heard coming nearer the house.

Sunma: Before it's too late, let him go. For once, Eman, believe what I tell you. Don't harbor him or you will regret it all your life.

Eman tries to calm Ifada, who becomes more and more abject as the outside voices get nearer.

Eman: What have they done to him? At least tell me that. What is going on, Sunma?

Sunma (with sudden venom): Monster! Could you not take yourself somewhere else?

Eman: Stop talking like that.

Sunma: He could have run into the bush couldn't he? Toad! Why must he follow us with his own disasters!

Voices outside: It's here. . . . Round the back. . . . Spread, spread . . . this way . . . no, head him off . . . use the bush path and head him off . . . get some more lights . . .

Eman listens. Lifts Ifada bodily and carries him into the inner room. Returns at once, shutting the door behind him.

Sunma (slumps into a chair, resigned): You always follow your own way.

Jaguna (comes round the corner followed by Oroge and three men, one bearing a torch): I knew he would come here.

Oroge: I hope our friend won't make trouble.

Jaguna: He had better not. You, recall all the men and tell them to surround the house.

Oroge: But he may not be in the house after all.

Jaguna: I know he is here . . . *(To the men.)* . . . go on, do as I say.

He bangs on the door.

Teacher, open your door . . . you two stay by the door. If I need you I will call you.

Eman opens the door.

Jaguna (speaks as he enters): We know he is here.

Eman: Who?

Jaguna: Don't let us waste time. We are grown men, teacher. You understand me and I understand you. But we must take back the boy.

Eman: This is my house.

Jaguna: Daughter, you'd better tell your friend. I don't think he quite knows our ways. Tell him why he must give up the boy.

Sunma: Father, I . . .

Jaguna: Are you going to tell him or aren't you?

Sunma: Father, I beg you, leave us alone tonight . . .

Jaguna: I thought you might be a hindrance. Go home then if you will not use your sense.

Sunma: But there are other ways . . .

Jaguna (turning to the men): See that she gets home. I no longer trust her. If she gives trouble carry her. And see that the women stay with her until all this is over.

Sunma departs, accompanied by one of the men.

Jaguna: Now, teacher . . .

Oroge (restrains him): You see, Mister Eman, it is like this. Right now, nobody knows that Ifada has taken refuge here. No one except us and our men — and they know how to keep their mouths shut. We don't want to have to burn down the house, you see, but if the word gets around, we would have no choice.

Jaguna: In fact, it may be too late already. A carrier should end up in the bush, not in a house. Anyone who doesn't guard his door when the carrier goes by has himself to blame. A contaminated house should be burnt down.

Oroge: But we are willing to let it pass. Only, you must bring him out quickly.

Eman: All right. But at least you will let me ask you something.

Jaguna: What is there to ask? Don't you understand what we have told you?

Eman: Yes. But why did you pick on a helpless boy? Obviously he is not willing.

Jaguna: What is the man talking about? Ifada is a godsend. Does he have to be willing?

Eman: In my home, we believe that a man should be willing.

Oroge: Mister Eman, I don't think you quite understand. This is not a simple matter at all. I don't know what you do, but here, it is not a cheap task for anybody. No one in his senses would do such a job. Why do you think we give refuge to idiots like him? We don't know where he came from. One morning, he is simply there, just like that. From nowhere at all. You see, there is a purpose in that.

Jaguna: We only waste time.

Oroge: Jaguna, be patient. After all, the man has been with us for some time now and deserves to know. The evil of the old year is no light thing to load on any man's head.

Eman: I know something about that.

Oroge: You do? *(Turns to Jaguna, who snorts impatiently.)* You see I told you so, didn't I? From the moment you came I saw you were one of the knowing ones.

Jaguna: Then let him behave like a man and give back the boy.

Eman: It is you who are not behaving like men.

Jaguna (advances aggressively): That is a quick mouth you have . . .

Oroge: Patience, Jaguna . . . if you want the new year to cushion the land there must be no deeds of anger. What did you mean, my friend?

Eman: It is a simple thing. A village which cannot produce its own carrier contains no men.

Jaguna: Enough. Let there be no more talk or this business will be ruined by some rashness. You . . . come inside. Bring the boy out, he must be in the room there.

Eman: Wait.

The men hesitate.

Jaguna (hitting the nearer one and propelling him forward): Go on. Have you changed masters now that you listen to what he says?

Oroge (sadly): I am sorry you would not understand, Mister Eman. But you ought to know that no carrier may return to the village. If he does, the people will stone him to death. It has happened before. Surely it is too much to ask a man to give up his own soil.

Eman: I know others who have done more.

Ifada is brought out, abjectly dumb-moaning.

Eman: You can see him with your own eyes. Does it really have meaning to use one as unwilling as that?

Oroge (smiling): He shall be willing. Not only willing but actually joyous. I am the one who prepares them all, and I have seen worse. This one escaped before I began to prepare him for the event. But you will see him later tonight, the most joyous creature in the festival. Then perhaps you will understand.

Eman: Then it is only a deceit. Do you believe the spirit of a new year is so easily fooled?

Jaguna: Take him out. *(The men carry out Ifada.)* You see, it is so easy to talk. You say there are no men in this village because they cannot provide a willing carrier. And yet I heard Oroge tell you we only use strangers. There is only one other stranger in the village, but I have not heard him offer himself. *(Spits.)* It is so easy to talk is it not?

He turns his back on him. They go off, taking Ifada with them, limp and silent. The only sign of life is that he strains his neck to keep his eyes on Eman till the very moment that he disappears from sight. Eman remains where they left him, staring after the group.

A blackout lasting no more than a minute. The lights come up slowly, and Ifada is seen returning to the house. He stops at the window and looks in. Seeing no one, he bangs on the sill. Appears surprised that there is no response. He slithers down on his favorite spot, then sees the effigy still lying where the Girl had dropped it in her flight. After some hesitation, he goes towards it, begins to strip it of the clothing. Just then the Girl comes in.

Girl: Hey, leave that alone. You know it's mine.

Ifada pauses, then speeds up his action.

Girl: I said it is mine. Leave it where you found it. *(She rushes at him and begins to struggle for possession of the carrier.)* Thief! Thief! Let it go, it is mine. Let it go. You animal, just because I let you play with it. Idiot! Idiot!

The struggle becomes quite violent. The Girl is hanging to the effigy and Ifada lifts her with it, flinging her all about. The Girl hangs on grimly.

Girl: You are spoiling it . . . why don't you get your own? Thief! Let it go, you thief!

Sunma comes in walking very fast, throwing apprehensive glances over her shoulder. Seeing the two children, she becomes immediately angry. Advances on them.

Sunma: So you've made this place your playground. Get away, you untrained pigs. Get out of here.

Ifada flees at once, the Girl retreats also, retaining possession of the carrier.
      Sunma goes to the door. She has her hand on the door when the significance of Ifada's presence strikes her for the first time. She stands rooted to the spot, then turns slowly round.

Sunma: Ifada! What are you doing here?

Ifada is bewildered. Sunma turns suddenly and rushes into the house, flying into the inner room and out again.

      Eman! Eman! Eman!

She rushes outside.

      Where did he go? Where did they take him?

Ifada distressed, points. Sunma seizes him by the arm, drags him off.

      Take me there at once. God help you if we are too late. You loathsome thing, if you have let him suffer . . .

Her voice fades into other shouts, running footsteps, banged tins, bells, dogs, etc., rising in volume.

      It is a narrow passageway between two mudhouses. At the far end one man after another is seen running across the entry, the noise dying off gradually.
      About halfway down the passage, Eman is crouching against the wall, tense with apprehension. As the noise dies off, he seems to relax, but the alert, hunted look is still in his eyes, which are ringed in a reddish color. The rest of his body has been whitened with a floury substance. He is naked down to the waist, wears a baggy pair of trousers, calf-length, and around both feet are bangles.

Eman: I will simply stay here till dawn. I have done enough.

A window is thrown open and a woman empties some slop from a pail. With a startled cry Eman leaps aside to avoid it and the woman puts out her head.

Woman: Oh, my head. What have I done! Forgive me, neighbor . . . Eh, it's the carrier! *(Very rapidly she clears her throat and spits on him, flings the pail at him and runs off, shouting.)* He's here. The carrier is hiding in the passage. Quickly, I have found the carrier!

The cry is taken up and Eman flees down the passage. Shortly afterwards his pursuers come pouring down the passage in full cry. After the last of them come Jaguna and Oroge.

Oroge: Wait, wait. I cannot go so fast.

Jaguna: We will rest a little then. We can do nothing anyway.

Oroge: If only he had let me prepare him.

Jaguna: They are the ones who break first, these fools who think they were born to carry suffering like a hat. What are we to do now?

Oroge: When they catch him I must prepare him.

Jaguna: He? It will be impossible now. There can be no joy left in that one.

Oroge: Still, it took him by surprise. He was not expecting what he met.

Jaguna: Why then did he refuse to listen? Did he think he was coming to sit down to a feast? He had not even gone through one compound before he bolted. Did he think he was taken round the people to be blessed? A woman, that is all he is.

Oroge: No, no. He took the beating well enough. I think he is the kind who would let himself be beaten from night till dawn and not utter a sound. He would let himself be stoned until he dropped dead.

Jaguna: Then what made him run like a coward?

Oroge: I don't know. I don't really know. It is a night of curses, Jaguna. It is not many unprepared minds will remain unhinged under the load.

Jaguna: We must find him. It is a poor beginning for a year when our own curses remain hovering over our homes because the carrier refused to take them.

They go. The scene changes. Eman is crouching beside some shrubs, torn and bleeding.

Eman: They are even guarding my house . . . as if I would go there, but I need water . . . they could at least grant me that . . . I can be thirsty too . . . *(He pricks his ears.)* . . . there must be a stream nearby . . . *(As he looks round him, his eyes widen at a scene he encounters.)*

An Old Man, short and vigorous looking, is seated on a stool. He also is wearing calf-length baggy trousers, white. On his head, a white cap. An attendant is engaged in rubbing his body with oil. Round his eyes, two white rings have already been marked.

Old Man: Have they prepared the boat?

Attendant: They are making the last sacrifice.

Old Man: Good. Did you send for my son?

Attendant: He's on his way.

Old Man: I have never met the carrying of the boat with such a heavy heart. I hope nothing comes of it.

Attendant: The gods will not desert us on that account.

Old Man: A man should be at his strongest when he takes the boat, my friend. To be weighed down inside and out is not a wise thing. I hope when the moment comes I shall have found my strength.

Enter Eman, a wrapper round his waist and a danski° over it.

Old Man: I meant to wait until after my journey to the river, but my mind is so burdened with my own grief and yours I could not delay it. You know I

---

danski: A garment.

must have all my strength. But I sit here, feeling it all eaten slowly away by my unspoken grief. It helps to say it out. It even helps to cry sometimes.

He signals to the attendant to leave them.

Come nearer . . . we will never meet again, son. Not on this side of the flesh. What I do not know is whether you will return to take my place.

Eman: I will never come back.

Old Man: Do you know what you are saying? Ours is a strong breed, my son. It is only a strong breed that can take this boat to the river year after year and wax stronger on it. I have taken down each year's evils for over twenty years. I hoped you would follow me.

Eman: My life here died with Omae.

Old Man: Omae died giving birth to your child and you think the world is ended. Eman, my pain did not begin when Omae died. Since you sent her to stay with me, son, I lived with the burden of knowing that this child would die bearing your son.

Eman: Father . . .

Old Man: Don't you know it was the same with you? And me? No woman survives the bearing of the strong ones. Son, it is not the mouth of the boaster that says he belongs to the strong breed. It is the tongue that is red with pain and black with sorrow. Twelve years you were away, my son, and for those twelve years I knew the love of an old man for his daughter and the pain of a man helplessly awaiting his loss.

Eman: I wish I had stayed away. I wish I never came back to meet her.

Old Man: It had to be. But you know now what slowly ate away my strength. I awaited your return with love and fear. Forgive me then if I say that your grief is light. It will pass. This grief may drive you now from home. But you must return.

Eman: You do not understand. It is not grief alone.

Old Man: What is it then? Tell me, I can still learn.

Eman: I was away twelve years. I changed much in that time.

Old Man: I am listening.

Eman: I am unfitted for your work, father. I wish to say no more. But I am totally unfitted for your call.

Old Man: It is only time you need, son. Stay longer and you will answer the urge of your blood.

Eman: That I stayed at all was because of Omae. I did not expect to find her waiting. I would have taken her away, but hard as you claim to be, it would have killed you. And I was a tired man. I needed peace. Because Omae was peace, I stayed. Now nothing holds me here.

Old Man: Other men would rot and die doing this task year after year. It is strong medicine which only we can take. Our blood is strong like no other. Anything you do in life must be less than this, son.

Eman: That is not true, father.

Old Man: I tell you it is true. Your own blood will betray you, son, because you cannot hold it back. If you make it do less than this, it will rush to your head and burst it open. I say what I know, my son.

Eman: There are other tasks in life, father. This one is not for me. There are even greater things you know nothing of.

Old Man: I am very sad. You only go to give to others what rightly belongs to us. You will use your strength among thieves. They are thieves because they take what is ours, they have no claim of blood to it. They will even lack the knowledge to use it wisely. Truth is my companion at this moment, my son. I know everything I say will surely bring the sadness of truth.

Eman: I am going, father.

Old Man: Call my attendant. And be with me in your strength for this last journey. A-ah, did you hear that? It came out without my knowing it; this is indeed my last journey. But I am not afraid.

Eman goes out. A few moments later, the attendant enters.

Attendant: The boat is ready.

Old Man: So am I.

He sits perfectly still for several moments. Drumming begins somewhere in the distance, and the Old Man sways his head almost imperceptibly. Two men come in bearing a miniature boat, containing an indefinable mound. They rush it in and set it briskly down near the Old Man, and stand well back. The Old Man gets up slowly, the attendant watching him keenly. He signs to the men, who lift the boat quickly onto the Old Man's head. As soon as it touches his head, he holds it down with both hands and runs off, the men give him a start, then follow at a trot. As the last man disappears Oroge limps in and comes face to face with Eman — as carrier — who is now seen still standing beside the shrubs, staring into the scene he has just witnessed. Oroge, struck by the look on Eman's face, looks anxiously behind him to see what has engaged Eman's attention. Eman notices him then, and the pair stare at each other. Jaguna enters, sees him and shouts, "Here he is," rushes at Eman, who is whipped back to the immediate and flees, Jaguna in pursuit. Three or four others enter and follow them. Oroge remains where he is, thoughtful.

Jaguna (re-enters): They have closed in on him now, we'll get him this time.

Oroge: It is nearly midnight.

Jaguna: You were standing there looking at him as if he was some strange spirit. Why didn't you shout?

Oroge: You shouted didn't you? Did that catch him?

Jaguna: Don't worry. We have him now. But things have taken a bad turn. It is no longer enough to drive him past every house. There is too much contamination about already.

Oroge (not listening): He saw something. Why may I not know what it was?

Jaguna: What are you talking about?

Oroge: Hm. What is it?

Jaguna: I said there is too much harm done already. The year will demand more from this carrier than we thought.

Oroge: What do you mean?

Jaguna: Do we have to talk with the full mouth?

Oroge: S-sh . . . look!

Jaguna turns just in time to see Sunma fly at him, clawing at his face like a crazed tigress.

Sunma: Murderer! What are you doing to him. Murderer! Murderer!

Jaguna finds himself struggling really hard to keep off his daughter, he succeeds in pushing her off and striking her so hard on the face that she falls to her knees. He moves on her to hit her again.

Oroge (comes between): Think what you are doing, Jaguna, she is your daughter.
Jaguna: My daughter! Does this one look like my daughter? Let me cripple the harlot for life.
Oroge: That is a wicked thought, Jaguna.
Jaguna: Don't come between me and her.
Oroge: Nothing in anger — do you forget what tonight is?
Jaguna: Can you blame me for forgetting?

Draws his hand across his cheek — it is covered with blood.

Oroge: This is an unhappy night for us all. I fear what is to come of it.
Jaguna: Let's go. I cannot restrain myself in this creature's presence. My own daughter . . . and for a stranger . . .

They go off. Ifada, who came in with Sunma and had stood apart, horror-stricken, comes shyly forward. He helps Sunma up. They go off, he holding Sunma bent and sobbing.
    Enter Eman — as carrier. He is physically present in the bounds of this next scene, a side of a round thatched hut. A young girl, about fourteen, runs in, stops beside the hut. She looks carefully to see that she is not observed, puts her mouth to a little hole in the wall.

Omae: Eman . . . Eman . . .

Eman — as carrier — responds, as he does throughout the scene, but they are unaware of him.

Eman (from inside): Who is it?
Omae: It is me, Omae.
Eman: How dare you come here!

Two hands appear at the hole and, pushing outwards, create a much larger hole through which Eman puts out his head. It is Eman as a boy, the same age as the girl.

    Go away at once. Are you trying to get me into trouble!
Omae: What is the matter?
Eman: You. Go away.
Omae: But I came to see you.
Eman: Are you deaf? I say I don't want to see you. Now go before my tutor catches you.
Omae: All right. Come out.
Eman: Do what!
Omae: Come out.
Eman: You must be mad.
Omae (sits on the ground): All right, if you don't come out I shall simply stay here until your tutor arrives.
Eman (about to explode, thinks better of it and the head disappears. A moment later he emerges from behind the hut): What sort of a devil has got into you?
Omae: None. I just wanted to see you.
Eman (his mimicry is nearly hysterical): "None. I just wanted to see you." Do

you think this place is the stream where you can go and molest innocent
people?

Omae (coyly): Aren't you glad to see me?

Eman: I am not.

Omae: Why?

Eman: Why? Do you really ask me why? Because you are a woman and a most
troublesome woman. Don't you know anything about this at all? We are not
meant to see any woman. So go away before more harm is done.

Omae (flirtatious): What is so secret about it anyway? What do they teach you?

Eman: Nothing any woman can understand.

Omae: Ha ha. You think we don't know eh? You've all come to be circumcised.

Eman: Shut up. You don't know anything.

Omae: Just think, all this time you haven't been circumcised, and you dared
make eyes at us women.

Eman: Thank you — woman. Now go.

Omae: Do they give you enough to eat?

Eman (testily): No. We are so hungry that when silly girls like you turn up, we
eat them.

Omae (feigning tears): Oh, oh, oh, he's abusing me. He's abusing me.

Eman (alarmed): Don't try that here. Go quickly if you are going to cry.

Omae: All right, I won't cry.

Eman: Cry or no cry, go away and leave me alone. What do you think will
happen if my tutor turns up now?

Omae: He won't.

Eman (mimicking): "He won't." I suppose you are his wife and he tells you
where he goes. In fact this is just the time he comes round to our huts. He
could be at the next hut this very moment.

Omae: Ha-ha. You're lying. I left him by the stream, pinching the girls' bottoms.
Is that the sort of thing he teaches you?

Eman: Don't say anything against him or I shall beat you. Isn't it you loose girls
who tease him, wiggling your bottoms under his nose?

Omae (going tearful again): A-ah, so I am one of the loose girls eh?

Eman: Now don't start accusing me of things I didn't say.

Omae: But you said it. You said it.

Eman: I didn't. Look, Omae, someone will hear you and I'll be in disgrace. Why
don't you go before anything happens.

Omae: It's all right. My friends have promised to hold your old rascal tutor till
I get back.

Eman: Then go back right now. I have work to do. *(Going in.)*

Omae (runs after and tries to hold him. Eman leaps back, genuinely scared):
What is the matter? I was not going to bite you.

Eman: Do you know what you nearly did? You almost touched me!

Omae: Well?

Eman: Well! Isn't it enough that you let me set my eyes on you? Must you now
totally pollute me with your touch? Don't you understand anything?

Omae: Oh, that.

Eman (nearly screaming): It is not "oh that." Do you think this is only a joke
or a little visit like spending the night with your grandmother? This is an

important period of my life. Look, these huts, we built them with our own hands. Every boy builds his own. We learn things, do you understand? And we spend much time just thinking. At least, I do. It is the first time I have had nothing to do except think. Don't you see, I am becoming a man. For the first time, I understand that I have a life to fulfill. Has that thought ever worried you?

Omae: You are frightening me.

Eman: There. That is all you can say. And what use will that be when a man finds himself alone — like that? *(Points to the hut.)* A man must go on his own, go where no one can help him, and test his strength. Because he may find himself one day sitting alone in a wall as round as that. In there, my mind could hold no other thought. I may never have such moments again to myself. Don't dare to come and steal any more of it.

Omae (this time, genuinely tearful): Oh, I know you hate me. You only want to drive me away.

Eman (impatiently): Yes, yes, I know I hate you — but go.

Omae (going, all tears. Wipes her eyes, suddenly all mischief): Eman.

Eman: What now?

Omae: I only want to ask one thing . . . do you promise to tell me?

Eman: Well, what is it?

Omae (gleefully): Does it hurt?

She turns instantly and flees, landing straight into the arms of the returning tutor.

Tutor: Te-he-he . . . what have we here? What little mouse leaps straight into the beak of the wise old owl eh?

Omae struggles to free herself, flies to the opposite side, grimacing with distaste.

Tutor: I suppose you merely came to pick some fruits eh? You did not sneak here to see any of my children.

Omae: Yes, I came to steal your fruits.

Tutor: Te-he-he . . . I thought so. And that dutiful son of mine over there. He saw you and came to chase you off my fruit trees didn't he? Te-he-he . . . I'm sure he did, isn't that so, my young Eman?

Eman: I was talking to her.

Tutor: Indeed you were. Now be good enough to go into your hut until I decide your punishment. *(Eman withdraws.)* Te-he-he . . . now now, my little daughter, you need not be afraid of me.

Omae (spiritedly): I am not.

Tutor: Good. Very good. We ought to be friendly. *(His voice becomes leering.)* Now this is nothing to worry you, my daughter . . . a very small thing indeed. Although of course if I were to let it slip that your young Eman had broken a strong taboo, it might go hard on him, you know. I am sure you would not like that to happen, would you?

Omae: No.

Tutor: Good. You are sensible, my girl. Can you wash clothes?

Omae: Yes.

Tutor: Good. If you will come with me now to my hut, I shall give you some clothes to wash, and then we will forget all about this matter eh? Well, come on.

Omae: I shall wait here. You go and bring the clothes.

Tutor: Eh? What is that? Now now, don't make me angry. You should know better than to talk back at your elders. Come now.

He takes her by the arm, and tries to drag her off.

Omae: No no, I won't come to your hut. Leave me. Leave me alone, you shameless old man.

Tutor: If you don't come I shall disgrace the whole family of Eman, and yours too.

Eman reenters with a small bundle.

Eman: Leave her alone. Let us go, Omae.

Tutor: And where do you think you are going?

Eman: Home.

Tutor: Te-he-he . . . As easy as that eh? You think you can leave here any time you please? Get right back inside that hut!

Eman takes Omae by the arm and begins to walk off.

Tutor: Come back at once.

He goes after him and raises his stick. Eman catches it, wrenches it from him, and throws it away.

Omae (hopping delightedly): Kill him. Beat him to death.

Tutor: Help! Help! He is killing me! Help!

Alarmed, Eman clamps his hand over his mouth.

Eman: Old tutor, I don't mean you any harm, but you mustn't try to harm me either. *(He removes his hand.)*

Tutor: You think you can get away with your crime. My report shall reach the elders before you ever get into town.

Eman: You are afraid of what I will say about you? Don't worry. Only if you try to shame me, then I will speak. I am not going back to the village anyway. Just tell them I have gone, no more. If you say one word more than that I shall hear of it the same day and I shall come back.

Tutor: You are telling me what to do? But don't think to come back next year because I will drive you away. Don't think to come back here even ten years from now. And don't send your children. *(Goes off with threatening gestures.)*

Eman: I won't come back.

Omae: Smoked vulture! But Eman, he says you cannot return next year. What will you do?

Eman: It is a small thing one can do in the big towns.

Omae: I thought you were going to beat him that time. Why didn't you crack his dirty hide?

Eman: Listen carefully, Omae . . . I am going on a journey.

Omae: Come on. Tell me about it on the way.

Eman: No, I go that way. I cannot return to the village.

Omae: Because of that wretched man? Anyway you will first talk to your father.

Eman: Go and see him for me. Tell him I have gone away for some time. I think he will know.

Omae: But, Eman . . .

Eman: I haven't finished. You will go and live with him till I get back. I have spoken to him about you. Look after him!

Omae: But what is this journey? When will you come back?

Eman: I don't know. But this is a good moment to go. Nothing ties me down.

Omae: But, Eman, you want to leave me.

Eman: Don't forget all I said. I don't know how long I will be. Stay in my father's house as long as you remember me. When you become tired of waiting, you must do as you please. You understand? You must do as you please.

Omae: I cannot understand anything, Eman. I don't know where you are going or why. Suppose you never came back! Don't go, Eman. Don't leave me by myself.

Eman: I must go. Now let me see you on your way.

Omae: I shall come with you.

Eman: Come with me! And who will look after you? Me? You will only be in my way, you know that! You will hold me back and I shall desert you in a strange place. Go home and do as I say. Take care of my father and let him take care of you. *(He starts going but Omae clings to him.)*

Omae: But, Eman, stay the night at least. You will only lose your way. Your father, Eman, what will he say? I won't remember what you said . . . come back to the village . . . I cannot return alone, Eman . . . come with me as far as the crossroads.

His face set, Eman strides off and Omae loses balance as he increases his pace. Falling, she quickly wraps her arms around his ankle, but Eman continues unchecked, dragging her along.

Omae: Don't go, Eman . . . Eman, don't leave me, don't leave me . . . don't leave your Omae . . . don't go, Eman . . . don't leave your Omae . . .

Eman — as carrier — makes a nervous move as if he intends to go after the vanished pair. He stops but continues to stare at the point where he last saw them. There is stillness for a while. Then the Girl enters from the same place and remains looking at Eman. Startled, Eman looks apprehensively round him. The Girl goes nearer but keeps beyond arm's length.

Girl: Are you the carrier?

Eman: Yes, I am Eman.

Girl: Why are you hiding?

Eman: I really came for a drink of water . . . er . . . is there anyone in front of the house?

Girl: No.

Eman: But there might be people in the house. Did you hear voices?

Girl: There is no one here.

Eman: Good. Thank you. *(He is about to go, stops suddenly.)* Er . . . would you . . . you will find a cup on the table. Could you bring me the water out here? The water pot is in a corner.

The Girl goes. She enters the house, then, watching Eman carefully, slips out and runs off.

Eman (sitting): Perhaps they have all gone home. It will be good to rest. *(He hears voices and listens hard.)* Too late. *(Moves cautiously nearer the house.)* Quickly, girl, I can hear people coming. Hurry up. *(Looks through the window.)* Where are you? Where is she? *(The truth dawns on him suddenly and he moves off, sadly.)*

Enter Jaguna and Oroge, led by the Girl.

Girl (pointing): He was there.

Jaguna: Ay, he's gone now. He is a sly one is your friend. But it won't save him forever.

Oroge: What was he doing when you saw him?

Girl: He asked me for a drink of water.

Jaguna ⎱
Oroge ⎰ : Ah! *(They look at each other.)*

Oroge: We should have thought of that.

Jaguna: He is surely finished now. If only we had thought of it earlier.

Oroge: It is not too late. There is still an hour before midnight.

Jaguna: We must call back all the men. Now we need only wait for him — in the right place.

Oroge: Everyone must be told. We don't want anyone heading him off again.

Jaguna: And it works so well. This is surely the help of the gods themselves, Oroge. Don't you know at once what is on the path to the stream?

Oroge: The sacred trees.

Jaguna: I tell you it is the very hand of the gods. Let us go.

An overgrown part of the village. Eman wanders in, aimlessly, seemingly uncaring of discovery. Beyond him, an area lights up, revealing a group of people clustered round a spot, all the heads are bowed. One figure stands away and separate from them. Even as Eman looks, the group breaks up and the people disperse, coming down and past him. Only three people are left, a man (Eman) whose back is turned, the village Priest, and the isolated one. They stand on opposite sides of the grave, the man on the mound of earth. The Priest walks round to the man's side and lays a hand on his shoulder.

Priest: Come.

Eman: I will. Give me a few moments here alone.

Priest: Be comforted.

They fall silent.

Eman: I was gone twelve years but she waited. She whom I thought had too much of the laughing child in her. Twelve years I was a pilgrim, seeking the vain shrine of secret strength. And all the time, strange knowledge, this silent strength of my child-woman.

Priest: We all saw it. It was a lesson to us; we did not know that such goodness could be found among us.

Eman: Then why? Why the wasted years if she had to perish giving birth to my child? *(They are both silent.)* I do not really know for what great meaning I searched. When I returned, I could not be certain I had found it. Until I reached my home and I found her a full-grown woman, still a child at heart. When I grew to believe it, I thought, this, after all, is what I sought. It was here all the time. And I threw away my new-gained knowledge. I buried the part of me that was formed in strange places. I made a home in my birthplace.

Priest: That was as it should be.

Eman: Any truth of that was killed in the cruelty of her brief happiness.

Priest (looks up and sees the figure standing away from them, the child in his arms. He is totally still): Your father — he is over there.

Eman: I knew he would come. Has he my son with him?

Priest: Yes.

Eman: He will let no one take the child. Go and comfort him, priest. He loved Omae like a daughter, and you all know how well she looked after him. You see how strong we really are. In his heart of hearts the old man's love really awaited a daughter. Go and comfort him. His grief is more than mine.

The Priest goes. The Old Man has stood well away from the burial group. His face is hard and his gaze unswerving from the grave. The Priest goes to him, pauses, but sees that he can make no dent in the man's grief. Bowed, he goes on his way.

Eman, as carrier, walks towards the graveside, the other Eman having gone. His feet sink into the mound and he breaks slowly on to his knees, scooping up the sand in his hands and pouring it on his head. The scene blacks out slowly.

Enter Jaguna and Oroge.

Oroge: We have only a little time.

Jaguna: He will come. All the wells are guarded. There is only the stream left him. The animal must come to drink.

Oroge: You are sure it will not fail — the trap, I mean.

Jaguna: When Jaguna sets the trap, even elephants pay homage — their trunks downwards and one leg up in the sky. When the carrier steps on the fallen twigs, it is up in the sacred trees with him.

Oroge: I shall breathe again when this long night is over.

They go out.

Enter Eman — as carrier — from the same direction as the last two entered. In front of him is a still figure, the Old Man as he was, carrying the dwarf boat.

Eman (joyfully): Father.

The figure does not turn round.

Eman: It is your son. Eman. *(He moves nearer.)* Don't you want to look at me? It is I, Eman. *(He moves nearer still.)*

Old Man: You are coming too close. Don't you know what I carry on my head?

Eman: But, father, I am your son.

Old Man: Then go back. We cannot give the two of us.

Eman: Tell me first where you are going.

Old Man: Do *you* ask that? Where else but to the river?

Eman (visibly relieved): I only wanted to be sure. My throat is burning. I have been looking for the stream all night.

Old Man: It is the other way.

Eman: But you said . . .

Old Man: I take the longer way, you know how I must do this. It is quicker if you take the other way. Go now.

Eman: No, I will only get lost again. I shall go with you.

Old Man: Go back, my son. Go back.

Eman: Why? Won't you even look at me?

Old Man: Listen to your father. Go back.

Eman: But, father!

He makes to hold him. Instantly the Old Man breaks into a rapid trot. Eman hesitates, then follows, his strength nearly gone.

Eman: Wait, father. I am coming with you . . . wait . . . wait for me, father . . .

There is a sound of twigs breaking, of a sudden trembling in the branches. Then silence.

The front of Eman's house. The effigy is hanging from the sheaves. Enter Sunma. Still supported by Ifada, she stands transfixed as she sees the hanging figure. Ifada appears to go mad, rushes at the object, and tears it down. Sunma, her last bit of will gone, crumbles against the wall. Some distance away from them, partly hidden, stands the Girl, impassively watching. Ifada hugs the effigy to him, stands above Sunma. The Girl remains where she is, observing. Almost at once, the villagers begin to return, subdued and guilty. They walk across the front, skirting the house as widely as they can. No word is exchanged. Jaguna and Oroge eventually appear. Jaguna, who is leading, sees Sunma as soon as he comes in view. He stops at once, retreating slightly.

Oroge (almost whispering): What is it?

Jaguna: The viper.

Oroge looks cautiously at the woman.

Oroge: I don't think she will even see you.

Jaguna: Are you sure? I am in no frame of mind for another meeting with her.

Oroge: Let's go home.

Jaguna: I am sick to the heart of the cowardice I have seen tonight.

Oroge: That is the nature of men.

Jaguna: Then it is a sorry world to live in. We did it for them. It was all for their own common good. What did it benefit me whether the man lived or died? But did you see them? One and all they looked up at the man and words died in their throats.

Oroge: It was no common sight.

Jaguna: Women could not have behaved so shamefully. One by one they crept off like sick dogs. Not one could raise a curse.

Oroge: It was not only him they fled. Do you see how unattended we are?

Jaguna: There are those who will pay for this night's work!

Oroge: Ay, let us go home.

They go off. Sunma, Ifada, and the Girl remain as they are, the light fading slowly on them.

Connections to Other Selections

1. Compare and contrast Eman's role as a scapegoat with that of Oedipus in Sophocles' *Oedipus the King* (p. 1120).
2. How does the use of flashbacks provide essential information about the two protagonists in *The Strong Breed* and in Miller's *Death of a Salesman* (p. 1712)?
3. Read the discussion of mythological criticism (p. 2010) in Chapter 35, "Critical Strategies for Reading." Explain what you think a mythological critic would have to say about *The Strong Breed*.

PERSPECTIVE

JAMES GIBB
Ritual Sacrifice in The Strong Breed   1986

The Strong Breed is a serious play of considerable substance, it shows a moment of spiritual growth in a community and provides excellent theater. Eman brings the growth, for when faced by moral choices he rises to the occasion and sacrifices himself for his convictions. He insults the men of the village and ridicules the practice of using a vulnerable and unwilling carrier. He argues that "the spirit of a new year [will not be] fooled" by an unwilling carrier. Challenged to be "a man" himself and discovering that Jaguna has captured Ifada, he offers himself: he becomes a willing sacrifice. In this there are deliberate parallels to the self-sacrifice of Christ and of the Yoruba deity Obatala, and the drama takes on the qualities of a passion play. From the reaction of the villagers it is clear that Eman's sacrificial death has an impact on the community. The final mood indicates that a climax has been reached and passed, those who have been part of it will never be the same again. This new year provides opportunities for a new beginning in Jaguna's village.

From *Wole Soyinka*

Considerations for Critical Thinking and Writing

1. What parallels can you find between the self-sacrifice of Eman and that of Christ?
2. Use the library to learn about the Yoruba deity Obatala. How does this story figure in the action of *The Strong Breed*?
3. Write an essay on the impact of Eman's death on the community.
4. Do you agree with Gibb's interpretation of the ending? Are there "opportunities for a new beginning in Jaguna's village"? Explain why or why not.

AN ALBUM OF CONTEMPORARY PLAYS

FENCES

August Wilson, who, as a young poet "wanted to be Dylan Thomas," has become in the past decade a major force in the American theater. He has projected a sequence of ten plays that will chronicle the black experience in the United States in each decade of the twentieth century. *Ma Rainey's Black Bottom,* the first of these to be completed, premiered at the Yale Repertory Theatre in 1984, went to Broadway shortly thereafter, and eventually won the New York Drama Critics' Circle Award. The plays that have so far followed are *Fences* (1985), *Joe Turner's Come and Gone* (1986), *The Piano Lesson* (1987), and *Two Trains Running* (1989).

Born in Pittsburgh, Pennsylvania, Wilson grew up in the Hill, a black neighborhood to which his mother had come from North Carolina. His white father never lived with the family. Wilson quit school at sixteen and worked in a variety of menial jobs, meanwhile submitting poetry to a number of local publications. He didn't begin to find his writing voice, however, until he moved to Minneapolis–St. Paul, where he founded the Black Horizons Theatre Company in 1968 and later started the Playwrights Center. He supported himself during part of this time by writing skits for the Science Museum of Minnesota.

Fences offers a complex look at the internal and external pressures on a black tenement family living in Pittsburgh during the 1950s.

AUGUST WILSON (b. 1945)
Fences 1985

Characters

Troy Maxson
Jim Bono, Troy's friend
Rose, Troy's wife
Lyons, Troy's oldest son by previous marriage
Gabriel, Troy's brother
Cory, Troy and Rose's son
Raynell, Troy's daughter

SETTING: *The setting is the yard which fronts the only entrance to the Maxson household, an ancient two-story brick house set back off a small alley in a big-city neighborhood. The entrance to the house is gained by two or three steps leading to a wooden porch badly in need of paint.*

A relatively recent addition to the house and running its full width, the porch lacks congruence. It is a sturdy porch with a flat roof. One or two chairs of dubious value sit at one end where the kitchen window opens onto the porch. An old-fashioned icebox stands silent guard at the opposite end.

The yard is a small dirt yard, partially fenced, except for the last scene, with a wooden sawhorse, a pile of lumber, and other fence-building equipment set off to the side. Opposite is a tree from which hangs a ball made of rags. A baseball bat leans against the tree. Two oil drums serve as garbage receptacles and sit near the house at right to complete the setting.

THE PLAY: *Near the turn of the century, the destitute of Europe sprang on the city with tenacious claws and an honest and solid dream. The city devoured them. They swelled its belly until it burst into a thousand furnaces and sewing machines, a thousand butcher shops and bakers' ovens, a thousand churches and hospitals and funeral parlors and money-lenders. The city grew. It nourished itself and offered each man a partnership limited only by his talent, his guile, and his willingness and capacity for hard work. For the immigrants of Europe, a dream dared and won true.*

The descendants of African slaves were offered no such welcome or participation. They came from places called the Carolinas and the Virginias, Georgia, Alabama, Mississippi, and Tennessee. They came strong, eager, searching. The city rejected them and they fled and settled along the riverbanks and under bridges in shallow, ramshackle houses made of sticks and tarpaper. They collected rags and wood. They sold the use of their muscles and their bodies. They cleaned houses and washed clothes, they shined shoes, and in quiet desperation and vengeful pride, they stole, and lived in pursuit of their own dream. That they could breathe free, finally, and stand to meet life with the force of dignity and whatever eloquence the heart could call upon.

By 1957, the hard-won victories of the European immigrants had solidified the industrial might of America. War had been confronted and won with new energies that used loyalty and patriotism as its fuel. Life was rich, full, and flourishing. The Milwaukee Braves won the World Series, and the hot winds of change that would make the sixties a turbulent, racing, dangerous, and provocative decade had not yet begun to blow full.

ACT I

SCENE I

It is 1957. Troy and Bono enter the yard, engaged in conversation. Troy is fifty-three years old, a large man with thick, heavy hands; it is this largeness that he strives to fill out and make an accommodation with. Together with his blackness, his largeness informs his sensibilities and the choices he has made in his life.

Of the two men, Bono is obviously the follower. His commitment to their friendship of thirty-odd years is rooted in his admiration of Troy's honesty, capacity for hard work, and his strength, which Bono seeks to emulate.

It is Friday night, payday, and the one night of the week the two men engage in a ritual of talk and drink. Troy is usually the most talkative and at times he can be crude and almost vulgar, though he is capable of rising to profound heights of expression. The men carry lunch buckets and wear or carry burlap aprons and are dressed in clothes suitable to their jobs as garbage collectors.

Bono: Troy, you ought to stop that lying!
Troy: I ain't lying! The nigger had a watermelon this big. *(He indicates with his hands.)* Talking about . . . "What watermelon, Mr. Rand?" I liked to fell out! "What watermelon, Mr. Rand?" . . . And it sitting there big as life.
Bono: What did Mr. Rand say?
Troy: Ain't said nothing. Figure if the nigger too dumb to know he carrying a watermelon, he wasn't gonna get much sense out of him. Trying to hide that great big old watermelon under his coat. Afraid to let the white man see him carry it home.

Bono: I'm like you . . . I ain't got no time for them kind of people.

Troy: Now what he look like getting mad cause he see the man from the union talking to Mr. Rand?

Bono: He come to me talking about . . . "Maxson gonna get us fired." I told him to get away from me with that. He walked away from me calling you a troublemaker. What Mr. Rand say?

Troy: Ain't said nothing. He told me to go down the Commissioner's office next Friday. They called me down there to see them.

Bono: Well, as long as you got your complaint filed, they can't fire you. That's what one of them white fellows tell me.

Troy: I ain't worried about them firing me. They gonna fire me cause I asked a question? That's all I did. I went to Mr. Rand and asked him, "Why? Why you got the white mens driving and the colored lifting?" Told him, "what's the matter, don't I count? You think only white fellows got sense enough to drive a truck. That ain't no paper job! Hell, anybody can drive a truck. How come you got all whites driving and the colored lifting?" He told me "take it to the union." Well, hell, that's what I done! Now they wanna come up with this pack of lies.

Bono: I told Brownie if the man come and ask him any questions . . . just tell the truth! It ain't nothing but something they done trumped up on you cause you filed a complaint on them.

Troy: Brownie don't understand nothing. All I want them to do is change the job description. Give everybody a chance to drive the truck. Brownie can't see that. He ain't got that much sense.

Bono: How you figure he be making out with that gal be up at Taylors' all the time . . . that Alberta gal?

Troy: Same as you and me. Getting just as much as we is. Which is to say nothing.

Bono: It is, huh? I figure you doing a little better than me . . . and I ain't saying what I'm doing.

Troy: Aw, nigger, look here . . . I know you. If you had got anywhere near that gal, twenty minutes later you be looking to tell somebody. And the first one you gonna tell . . . that you gonna want to brag to . . . is me.

Bono: I ain't saying that. I see where you be eyeing her.

Troy: I eye all the women. I don't miss nothing. Don't never let nobody tell you Troy Maxson don't eye the women.

Bono: You been doing more than eyeing her. You done bought her a drink or two.

Troy: Hell yeah, I bought her a drink! What that mean? I bought you one, too. What that mean cause I buy her a drink? I'm just being polite.

Bono: It's all right to buy her one drink. That's what you call being polite. But when you wanna be buying two or three . . . that's what you call eyeing her.

Troy: Look here, as long as you known me . . . you ever known me to chase after women?

Bono: Hell yeah! Long as I done known you. You forgetting I knew you when.

Troy: Naw, I'm talking about since I been married to Rose?

Bono: Oh, not since you been married to Rose. Now, that's the truth, there. I can say that.

Troy: All right then! Case closed.

Bono: I see you be walking up around Alberta's house. You supposed to be at Taylors' and you be walking up around there.

Troy: What you watching where I'm walking for? I ain't watching after you.

Bono: I seen you walking around there more than once.

Troy: Hell, you liable to see me walking anywhere! That don't mean nothing cause you see me walking around there.

Bono: Where she come from anyway? She just kinda showed up one day.

Troy: Tallahassee. You can look at her and tell she one of them Florida gals. They got some big healthy women down there. Grow them right up out the ground. Got a little bit of Indian in her. Most of them niggers down in Florida got some Indian in them.

Bono: I don't know about that Indian part. But she damn sure big and healthy. Woman wear some big stockings. Got them great big old legs and hips as wide as the Mississippi River.

Troy: Legs don't mean nothing. You don't do nothing but push them out of the way. But them hips cushion the ride!

Bono: Troy, you ain't got no sense.

Troy: It's the truth! Like you riding on Goodyears!

Rose enters from the house. She is ten years younger than Troy, her devotion to him stems from her recognition of the possibilities of her life without him: a succession of abusive men and their babies, a life of partying and running the streets, the Church, or aloneness with its attendant pain and frustration. She recognizes Troy's spirit as a fine and illuminating one and she either ignores or forgives his faults, only some of which she recognizes. Though she doesn't drink, her presence is an integral part of the Friday night rituals. She alternates between the porch and the kitchen, where supper preparations are under way.

Rose: What you all out here getting into?

Troy: What you worried about what we getting into for? This is men talk, woman.

Rose: What I care what you all talking about? Bono, you gonna stay for supper?

Bono: No, I thank you, Rose. But Lucille say she cooking up a pot of pigfeet.

Troy: Pigfeet! Hell, I'm going home with you! Might even stay the night if you got some pigfeet. You got something in there to top them pigfeet, Rose?

Rose: I'm cooking up some chicken. I got some chicken and collard greens.

Troy: Well, go on back in the house and let me and Bono finish what we was talking about. This is men talk. I got some talk for you later. You know what kind of talk I mean. You go on and powder it up.

Rose: Troy Maxson, don't you start that now!

Troy (puts his arm around her): Aw, woman . . . come here. Look here, Bono . . . when I met this woman . . . I got out that place, say, "Hitch up my pony, saddle up my mare . . . there's a woman out there for me somewhere. I looked here. Looked there. Saw Rose and latched on to her." I latched on to her and told her — I'm gonna tell you the truth — I told her, "Baby, I don't wanna marry, I just wanna be your man." Rose told me . . . tell him what you told me, Rose.

Rose: I told him if he wasn't the marrying kind, then move out the way so the marrying kind could find me.

Troy: That's what she told me. "Nigger, you in my way. You blocking the view! Move out the way so I can find me a husband." I thought it over two or three days. Come back —

Rose: Ain't no two or three days nothing. You was back the same night.

Troy: Come back, told her . . . "Okay, baby . . . but I'm gonna buy me a banty rooster and put him out there in the backyard . . . and when he see a stranger come, he'll flap his wings and crow . . ." Look here, Bono, I could watch the front door by myself . . . it was that back door I was worried about.

Rose: Troy, you ought not talk like that. Troy ain't doing nothing but telling a lie.

Troy: Only thing is . . . when we first got married . . . forget the rooster . . . we ain't had no yard!

Bono: I hear you tell it. Me and Lucille was staying down there on Logan Street. Had two rooms with the outhouse in the back. I ain't mind the outhouse none. But when that goddamn wind blow through there in the winter . . . that's what I'm talking about! To this day I wonder why in the hell I ever stayed down there for six long years. But see, I didn't know I could do no better. I thought only white folks had inside toilets and things.

Rose: There's a lot of people don't know they can do no better than they doing now. That's just something you got to learn. A lot of folks still shop at Bella's.

Troy: Ain't nothing wrong with shopping at Bella's. She got fresh food.

Rose: I ain't said nothing about if she got fresh food. I'm talking about what she charge. She charge ten cents more than the A&P.

Troy: The A&P ain't never done nothing for me. I spends my money where I'm treated right. I go down to Bella, say, "I need a loaf of bread, I'll pay you Friday." She give it to me. What sense that make when I got money to go and spend it somewhere else and ignore the person who done right by me? That ain't in the Bible.

Rose: We ain't talking about what's in the Bible. What sense it make to shop there when she overcharge?

Troy: You shop where you want to. I'll do my shopping where the people been good to me.

Rose: Well, I don't think it's right for her to overcharge. That's all I was saying.

Bono: Look here . . . I got to get on. Lucille going be raising all kind of hell.

Troy: Where you going, nigger? We ain't finished this pint. Come here, finish this pint.

Bono: Well, hell, I am . . . if you ever turn the bottle loose.

Troy (hands him the bottle): The only thing I say about the A&P is I'm glad Cory got that job down there. Help him take care of his school clothes and things. Gabe done moved out and things getting tight around here. He got that job. . . . He can start to look out for himself.

Rose: Cory done went and got recruited by a college football team.

Troy: I told that boy about that football stuff. The white man ain't gonna let him get nowhere with that football. I told him when he first come to me with it. Now you come telling me he done went and got more tied up in it. He ought to go and get recruited in how to fix cars or something where he can make a living.

Rose: He ain't talking about making no living playing football. It's just something the boys in school do. They gonna send a recruiter by to talk to you. He'll tell you he ain't talking about making no living playing football. It's a honor to be recruited.

Troy: It ain't gonna get him nowhere. Bono'll tell you that.

Bono: If he be like you in the sports . . . he's gonna be all right. Ain't but two men ever played baseball as good as you. That's Babe Ruth° and Josh Gibson.° Them's the only two men ever hit more home runs than you.

Troy: What it ever get me? Ain't got a pot to piss in or a window to throw it out of.

Rose: Times have changed since you was playing baseball, Troy. That was before the war. Times have changed a lot since then.

Troy: How in hell they done changed?

Rose: They got lots of colored boys playing ball now. Baseball and football.

Bono: You right about that, Rose. Times have changed, Troy. You just come along too early.

Troy: There ought not never have been no time called too early! Now you take that fellow . . . what's that fellow they had playing right field for the Yankees back then? You know who I'm talking about, Bono. Used to play right field for the Yankees.

Rose: Selkirk?

Troy: Selkirk! That's it! Man batting .269, understand? .269. What kind of sense that make? I was hitting .432 with thirty-seven home runs! Man batting .269 and playing right field for the Yankees! I saw Josh Gibson's daughter yesterday. She walking around with raggedy shoes on her feet. Now I bet you Selkirk's daughter ain't walking around with raggedy shoes on her feet! I bet you that!

Rose: They got a lot of colored baseball players now. Jackie Robinson° was the first. Folks had to wait for Jackie Robinson.

Troy: I done seen a hundred niggers play baseball better than Jackie Robinson. Hell, I know some teams Jackie Robinson couldn't even make! What you talking about Jackie Robinson. Jackie Robinson wasn't nobody. I'm talking about if you could play ball then they ought to have let you play. Don't care what color you were. Come telling me I come along too early. If you could play . . . then they ought to have let you play.

Troy takes a long drink from the bottle.

Rose: You gonna drink yourself to death. You don't need to be drinking like that.

Troy: Death ain't nothing. I done seen him. Done wrassled with him. You can't tell me nothing about death. Death ain't nothing but a fastball on the outside corner. And you know what I'll do to that! Lookee here, Bono . . . am I lying? You get one of them fastballs, about waist high, over the outside corner

Babe Ruth (1895--1948): One of the greatest American baseball players.
Josh Gibson (1911–1947): Powerful baseball player known in the 1930s as the Babe Ruth of the Negro leagues.
Jackie Robinson (1919–1972): The first black baseball player in the major leagues (1947).

of the plate where you can get the meat of the bat on it . . . and good god! You can kiss it goodbye. Now, am I lying?

Bono: Naw, you telling the truth there. I seen you do it.

Troy: If I'm lying . . . that 450 feet worth of lying! *(Pause.)* That's all death is to me. A fastball on the outside corner.

Rose: I don't know why you want to get on talking about death.

Troy: Ain't nothing wrong with talking about death. That's part of life. Everybody gonna die. You gonna die, I'm gonna die. Bono's gonna die. Hell, we all gonna die.

Rose: But you ain't got to talk about it. I don't like to talk about it.

Troy: You the one brought it up. Me and Bono was talking about baseball . . . you tell me I'm gonna drink myself to death. Ain't that right, Bono? You know I don't drink this but one night out of the week. That's Friday night. I'm gonna drink just enough to where I can handle it. Then I cuts it loose. I leave it alone. So don't you worry about me drinking myself to death. 'Cause I ain't worried about Death. I done seen him. I done wrestled with him.

Look here, Bono . . . I looked up one day and Death was marching straight at me. Like Soldiers on Parade! The Army of Death was marching straight at me. The middle of July, 1941. It got real cold just like it be winter. It seem like Death himself reached out and touched me on the shoulder. He touch me just like I touch you. I got cold as ice and Death standing there grinning at me.

Rose: Troy, why don't you hush that talk.

Troy: I say . . . what you want, Mr. Death? You be wanting me? You done brought your army to be getting me? I looked him dead in the eye. I wasn't fearing nothing. I was ready to tangle. Just like I'm ready to tangle now. The Bible say be ever vigilant. That's why I don't get but so drunk. I got to keep watch.

Rose: Troy was right down there in Mercy Hospital. You remember he had pneumonia? Laying there with a fever talking plumb out of his head.

Troy: Death standing there staring at me . . . carrying that sickle in his hand. Finally he say, "You want bound over for another year?" See, just like that . . . "You want bound over for another year?" I told him, "Bound over hell! Let's settle this now!"

It seem like he kinda fell back when I said that, and all the cold went out of me. I reached down and grabbed that sickle and threw it just as far as I could throw it . . . and me and him commenced to wrestling.

We wrestled for three days and three nights. I can't say where I found the strength from. Every time it seemed like he was gonna get the best of me, I'd reach way down deep inside myself and find the strength to do him one better.

Rose: Every time Troy tell that story he find different ways to tell it. Different things to make up about it.

Troy: I ain't making up nothing. I'm telling you the facts of what happened. I wrestled with Death for three days and three nights and I'm standing here to tell you about it. *(Pause.)* All right. At the end of the third night we done weakened each other to where we can't hardly move. Death stood up, throwed on his robe . . . had him a white robe with a hood on it. He

throwed on that robe and went off to look for his sickle. Say, "I'll be back."
Just like that. "I'll be back." I told him, say, "Yeah, but . . . you gonna have
to find me!" I wasn't no fool. I wan't going looking for him. Death ain't
nothing to play with. And I know he's gonna get me. I know I got to join
his army . . . his camp followers. But as long as I keep my strength and see
him coming . . . as long as I keep up my vigilance . . . he's gonna have to
fight to get me. I ain't going easy.

Bono: Well, look here, since you got to keep up your vigilance . . . let me have
the bottle.

Troy: Aw hell, I shouldn't have told you that part. I should have left out that
part.

Rose: Troy be talking that stuff and half the time don't even know what he be
talking about.

Troy: Bono know me better than that.

Bono: That's right. I know you. I know you got some Uncle Remus° in your
blood. You got more stories than the devil got sinners.

Troy: Aw hell, I done seen him too! Done talked with the devil.

Rose: Troy, don't nobody wanna be hearing all that stuff.

*Lyons enters the yard from the street. Thirty-four years old, Troy's son by a
previous marriage, he sports a neatly trimmed goatee, sport coat, white shirt,
tieless and buttoned at the collar. Though he fancies himself a musician, he is
more caught up in the rituals and "idea" of being a musician than in the actual
practice of the music. He has come to borrow money from Troy, and while he
knows he will be successful, he is uncertain as to what extent his lifestyle will be
held up to scrutiny and ridicule.*

Lyons: Hey, Pop.

Troy: What you come "Hey, Popping" me for?

Lyons: How you doing, Rose? (He kisses her.) Mr. Bono. How you doing?

Bono: Hey, Lyons . . . how you been?

Troy: He must have been doing all right. I ain't seen him around here last week.

Rose: Troy, leave your boy alone. He come by to see you and you wanna start
all that nonsense.

Troy: I ain't bothering Lyons. (Offers him the bottle.) Here . . . get you a drink.
We got an understanding. I know why he come by to see me and he know
I know.

Lyons: Come on, Pop . . . I just stopped by to say hi . . . see how you was
doing.

Troy: You ain't stopped by yesterday.

Rose: You gonna stay for supper, Lyons? I got some chicken cooking in the oven.

Lyons: No, Rose . . . thanks. I was just in the neighborhood and thought I'd stop
by for a minute.

Troy: You was in the neighborhood all right, nigger. You telling the truth there.
You was in the neighborhood cause it's my payday.

Lyons: Well, hell, since you mentioned it . . . let me have ten dollars.

Uncle Remus: Black storyteller who recounts traditional black tales in the book by Joel Chandler
Harris.

Troy: I'll be damned! I'll die and go to hell and play blackjack with the devil before I give you ten dollars.

Bono: That's what I wanna know about . . . that devil you done seen.

Lyons: What . . . Pop done seen the devil? You too much, Pops.

Troy: Yeah, I done seen him. Talked to him too!

Rose: You ain't seen no devil. I done told you that man ain't had nothing to do with the devil. Anything you can't understand, you want to call it the devil.

Troy: Look here, Bono . . . I went down to see Hertzberger about some furniture. Got three rooms for two-ninety-eight. That what it say on the radio. "Three rooms . . . two-ninety-eight." Even made up a little song about it. Go down there . . . man tell me I can't get no credit. I'm working every day and can't get no credit. What to do? I got an empty house with some raggedy furniture in it. Cory ain't got no bed. He's sleeping on a pile of rags on the floor. Working every day and can't get no credit. Come back here — Rose'll tell you — madder than hell. Sit down . . . try to figure what I'm gonna do. Come a knock on the door. Ain't been living here but three days. Who know I'm here? Open the door . . . devil standing there bigger than life. White fellow . . . white fellow . . . got on good clothes and everything. Standing there with a clipboard in his hand. I ain't had to say nothing. First words come out of his mouth was . . . "I understand you need some furniture and can't get no credit." I liked to fell over. He say, "I'll give you all the credit you want, but you got to pay the interest on it." I told him, "Give me three rooms worth and charge whatever you want." Next day a truck pulled up here and two men unloaded them three rooms. Man what drove the truck give me a book. Say send ten dollars, first of every month to the address in the book and everything will be all right. Say if I miss a payment the devil was coming back and it'll be hell to pay. That was fifteen years ago. To this day . . . the first of the month I send my ten dollars, Rose'll tell you.

Rose: Troy lying.

Troy: I ain't never seen that man since. Now you tell me who else that could have been but the devil? I ain't sold my soul or nothing like that, you understand. Naw, I wouldn't have truck with the devil about nothing like that. I got my furniture and pays my ten dollars the first of the month just like clockwork.

Bono: How long you say you been paying this ten dollars a month?

Troy: Fifteen years!

Bono: Hell, ain't you finished paying for it yet? How much the man done charged you?

Troy: Ah hell, I done paid for it. I done paid for it ten times over! The fact is I'm scared to stop paying it.

Rose: Troy lying. We got that furniture from Mr. Glickman. He ain't paying no ten dollars a month to nobody.

Troy: Aw hell, woman. Bono know I ain't that big a fool.

Lyons: I was just getting ready to say . . . I know where there's a bridge for sale.

Troy: Look here, I'll tell you this . . . it don't matter to me if he was the devil. It don't matter if the devil give credit. Somebody has got to give it.

Rose: It ought to matter. You going around talking about having truck with the devil . . . God's the one you gonna have to answer to. He's the one gonna be at the Judgment.

Lyons: Yeah, well, look here, Pop . . . let me have that ten dollars. I'll give it back to you. Bonnie got a job working at the hospital.

Troy: What I tell you, Bono? The only time I see this nigger is when he wants something. That's the only time I see him.

Lyons: Come on, Pop, Mr. Bono don't want to hear all that. Let me have the ten dollars. I told you Bonnie working.

Troy: What that mean to me? "Bonnie working." I don't care if she working. Go ask her for the ten dollars if she working. Talking about "Bonnie working." Why ain't you working?

Lyons: Aw, Pop, you know I can't find no decent job. Where am I gonna get a job at? You know I can't get no job.

Troy: I told you I know some people down there. I can get you on the rubbish if you want to work. I told you that the last time you came by here asking me for something.

Lyons: Naw, Pop . . . thanks. That ain't for me. I don't wanna be carrying nobody's rubbish. I don't wanna be punching nobody's time clock.

Troy: What's the matter, you too good to carry people's rubbish? Where you think that ten dollars you talking about come from? I'm just supposed to haul people's rubbish and give my money to you cause you too lazy to work. You too lazy to work and wanna know why you ain't got what I got.

Rose: What hospital Bonnie working at? Mercy?

Lyons: She's down at Passavant working in the laundry.

Troy: I ain't got nothing as it is. I give you that ten dollars and I got to eat beans the rest of the week. Naw . . . you ain't getting no ten dollars here.

Lyons: You ain't got to be eating no beans. I don't know why you wanna say that.

Troy: I ain't got no extra money. Gabe done moved over to Miss Pearl's paying her the rent and things done got tight around here. I can't afford to be giving you every payday.

Lyons: I ain't asked you to give me nothing. I asked you to loan me ten dollars. I know you got ten dollars.

Troy: Yeah, I got it. You know why I got it? Cause I don't throw my money away out there in the streets. You living the fast life . . . wanna be a musician . . . running around in them clubs and things . . . then, you learn to take care of yourself. You ain't gonna find me going and asking nobody for nothing. I done spent too many years without.

Lyons: You and me is two different people, Pop.

Troy: I done learned my mistake and learned to do what's right by it. You still trying to get something for nothing. Life don't owe you nothing. You owe it to yourself. Ask Bono. He'll tell you I'm right.

Lyons: You got your way of dealing with the world . . . I got mine. The only thing that matters to me is the music.

Troy: Yeah, I can see that! It don't matter how you gonna eat . . . where your next dollar is coming from. You telling the truth there.

Lyons: I know I got to eat. But I got to live too. I need something that gonna help me to get out of the bed in the morning. Make me feel like I belong in the world. I don't bother nobody. I just stay with the music cause that's the only way I can find to live in the world. Otherwise there ain't no telling what I might do. Now I don't come criticizing you and how you live. I just come by to ask you for ten dollars. I don't wanna hear all that about how I live.

Troy: Boy, your mamma did a hell of a job raising you.

Lyons: You can't change me, Pop. I'm thirty-four years old. If you wanted to change me, you should have been there when I was growing up. I come by to see you . . . ask for ten dollars and you want to talk about how I was raised. You don't know nothing about how I was raised.

Rose: Let the boy have ten dollars, Troy.

Troy (to Lyons): What the hell you looking at me for? I ain't got no ten dollars. You know what I do with my money. *(To Rose.)* Give him ten dollars if you want him to have it.

Rose: I will. Just as soon as you turn it loose.

Troy (handing Rose the money): There it is. Seventy-six dollars and forty-two cents. You see this, Bono? Now, I ain't gonna get but six of that back.

Rose: You ought to stop telling that lie. Here, Lyons. *(She hands him the money.)*

Lyons: Thanks, Rose. Look . . . I got to run . . . I'll see you later.

Troy: Wait a minute. You gonna say, "thanks, Rose" and ain't gonna look to see where she got that ten dollars from? See how they do me, Bono?

Lyons: I know she got it from you, Pop. Thanks. I'll give it back to you.

Troy: There he go telling another lie. Time I see that ten dollars . . . he'll be owing me thirty more.

Lyons: See you, Mr. Bono.

Bono: Take care, Lyons!

Lyons: Thanks, Pop. I'll see you again.

Lyons exits the yard.

Troy: I don't know why he don't go and get him a decent job and take care of that woman he got.

Bono: He'll be all right, Troy. The boy is still young.

Troy: The *boy* is thirty-four years old.

Rose: Let's not get off into all that.

Bono: Look here . . . I got to be going. I got to be getting on. Lucille gonna be waiting.

Troy (puts his arm around Rose): See this woman, Bono? I love this woman. I love this woman so much it hurts. I love her so much . . . I done run out of ways of loving her. So I got to go back to basics. Don't you come by my house Monday morning talking about time to go to work . . . 'cause I'm still gonna be stroking!

Rose: Troy! Stop it now!

Bono: I ain't paying him no mind, Rose. That ain't nothing but gin-talk. Go on, Troy. I'll see you Monday.

Troy: Don't you come by my house, nigger! I done told you what I'm gonna be doing.

The lights go down to black.

The lights come up on Rose hanging up clothes. She hums and sings softly to herself. It is the following morning.

Rose (sings): Jesus, be a fence all around me every day
  Jesus, I want you to protect me as I travel on my way.
  Jesus, be a fence all around me every day.

Troy enters from the house.

  Jesus, I want you to protect me
  As I travel on my way.
  (To Troy.) 'Morning, You ready for breakfast? I can fix it soon as I finish
  hanging up these clothes?
Troy: I got the coffee on. That'll be all right. I'll just drink some of that this
  morning.
Rose: That 651 hit yesterday. That's the second time this month. Miss Pearl hit
  for a dollar . . . seem like those that need the least always get lucky. Poor
  folks can't get nothing.
Troy: Them numbers don't know nobody. I don't know why you fool with them.
  You and Lyons both.
Rose: It's something to do.
Troy: You ain't doing nothing but throwing your money away.
Rose: Troy, you know I don't play foolishly. I just play a nickel here and a nickel
  there.
Troy: That's two nickels you done thrown away.
Rose: Now I hit sometimes . . . that makes up for it. It always comes in handy
  when I do hit. I don't hear you complaining then.
Troy: I ain't complaining now. I just say it's foolish. Trying to guess out of six
  hundred ways which way the number gonna come. If I had all the money
  niggers, these Negroes, throw away on numbers for one week — just one
  week — I'd be a rich man.
Rose: Well, you wishing and calling it foolish ain't gonna stop folks from playing
  numbers. That's one thing for sure. Besides . . . some good things come
  from playing numbers. Look where Pope done bought him that restaurant
  off of numbers.
Troy: I can't stand niggers like that. Man ain't had two dimes to rub together.
  He walking around with his shoes all run over bumming money for cigarettes. All right. Got lucky there and hit the numbers . . .
Rose: Troy, I know all about it.
Troy: Had good sense, I'll say that for him. He ain't throwed his money away. I
  seen niggers hit the numbers and go through two thousand dollars in four
  days. Man bought him that restaurant down there . . . fixed it up real nice
  . . . and then didn't want nobody to come in it! A Negro go in there and
  can't get no kind of service. I seen a white fellow come in there and order
  a bowl of stew. Pope picked all the meat out the pot for him. Man ain't had
  nothing but a bowl of meat! Negro come behind him and ain't got nothing
  but the potatoes and carrots. Talking about what numbers do for people,

you picked a wrong example. Ain't done nothing but make a worser fool out of him than he was before.

Rose: Troy, you ought to stop worrying about what happened at work yesterday.

Troy: I ain't worried. Just told me to be down there at the Commissioner's office on Friday. Everybody think they gonna fire me. I ain't worried about them firing me. You ain't got to worry about that. *(Pause.)* Where's Cory? Cory in the house? *(Calls.)* Cory?

Rose: He gone out.

Troy: Out, huh? He gone out 'cause he know I want him to help me with this fence. I know how he is. That boy scared of work.

Gabriel enters. He comes halfway down the alley and, hearing Troy's voice, stops.

Troy (continues): He ain't done a lick of work in his life.

Rose: He had to go to football practice. Coach wanted them to get in a little extra practice before the season start.

Troy: I got his practice . . . running out of here before he get his chores done.

Rose: Troy, what is wrong with you this morning? Don't nothing set right with you. Go on back in there and go to bed . . . get up on the other side.

Troy: Why something got to be wrong with me? I ain't said nothing wrong with me.

Rose: You got something to say about everything. First it's the numbers . . . then it's the way the man runs his restaurant . . . then you done got on Cory. What's it gonna be next? Take a look up there and see if the weather suits you . . . or is it gonna be how you gonna put up the fence with the clothes hanging in the yard.

Troy: You hit the nail on the head then.

Rose: I know you like I know the back of my hand. Go on in there and get you some coffee . . . see if that straighten you up. 'Cause you ain't right this morning.

Troy starts into the house and sees Gabriel. Gabriel starts singing. Troy's brother, he is seven years younger than Troy. Injured in World War II, he has a metal plate in his head. He carries an old trumpet tied around his waist and believes with every fiber of his being that he is the Archangel Gabriel.° He carries a chipped basket with an assortment of discarded fruits and vegetables he has picked up in the strip district and which he attempts to sell.

Gabriel (singing): Yes, ma'am, I got plums
You ask me how I sell them
Oh ten cents apiece
Three for a quarter
Come and buy now
'Cause I'm here today
And tomorrow I'll be gone

Gabriel enters.

Hey, Rose!

Rose: How you doing, Gabe?

°*Archangel Gabriel:* Considered one of God's primary messengers in the Old and New Testaments.

Gabriel: There's Troy . . . Hey, Troy!

Troy: Hey, Gabe.

Exit into kitchen.

Rose (to Gabriel): What you got there?

Gabriel: You know what I got, Rose. I got fruits and vegetables.

Rose (looking in basket): Where's all these plums you talking about?

Gabriel: I ain't got no plums today, Rose. I was just singing that. Have some tomorrow. Put me in a big order for plums. Have enough plums tomorrow for St. Peter and everybody.

Troy reenters from kitchen, crosses to steps.

   (*To Rose.*) Troy's mad at me.

Troy: I ain't mad at you. What I got to be mad at you about? You ain't done nothing to me.

Gabriel: I just moved over to Miss Pearl's to keep out from in your way. I ain't mean no harm by it.

Troy: Who said anything about that? I ain't said anything about that.

Gabriel: You ain't mad at me, is you?

Troy: Naw . . . I ain't mad at you, Gabe. If I was mad at you I'd tell you about it.

Gabriel: Got me two rooms. In the basement. Got my own door too. Wanna see my key? (*He holds up a key.*) That's my own key! Ain't nobody else got a key like that. That's my key! My two rooms!

Troy: Well, that's good, Gabe. You got your own key . . . that's good.

Rose: You hungry, Gabe? I was just fixing to cook Troy his breakfast.

Gabriel: I'll take some biscuits. You got some biscuits? Did you know when I was in heaven . . . every morning me and St. Peter° would sit down by the gate and eat some big fat biscuits? Oh, yeah! We had us a good time. We'd sit there and eat us them biscuits and then St. Peter would go off to sleep and tell me to wake him up when it's time to open the gates for the judgment.

Rose: Well, come on . . . I'll make up a batch of biscuits.

Rose exits into the house.

Gabriel: Troy . . . St. Peter got your name in the book. I seen it. It say . . . Troy Maxson. I say . . . I know him! He got the same name like what I got. That's my brother!

Troy: How many times you gonna tell me that, Gabe?

Gabriel: Ain't got my name in the book. Don't have to have my name. I done died and went to heaven. He got your name though. One morning St. Peter was looking at his book . . . marking it up for the judgment . . . and he let me see your name. Got it in there under M. Got Rose's name . . . I ain't seen it like I seen yours . . . but I know it's in there. He got a great big book. Got everybody's name what was ever been born. That's what he told me. But I seen your name. Seen it with my own eyes.

Troy: Go on in the house there. Rose going to fix you something to eat.

Gabriel: Oh, I ain't hungry. I done had breakfast with Aunt Jemimah. She come

St. Peter: One of Jesus's disciples, believed to be the keeper of the gates to Heaven.

by and cooked me up a whole mess of flapjacks. Remember how we used to eat them flapjacks?

Troy: Go on in the house and get you something to eat now.

Gabriel: I got to sell my plums. I done sold some tomatoes. Got me two quarters. Wanna see? *(He shows Troy his quarters.)* I'm gonna save them and buy me a new horn so St. Peter can hear me when it's time to open the gates. *(Gabriel stops suddenly. Listens.)* Hear that? That's the hellhounds. I got to chase them out of here. Go on get out of here! Get out!

Gabriel exits singing.

> Better get ready for the judgment
> Better get ready for the judgment
> My Lord is coming down

Rose enters from the house.

Troy: He's gone off somewhere.

Gabriel (offstage): Better get ready for the judgment
> Better get ready for the judgment morning
> Better get ready for the judgment
> My God is coming down

Rose: He ain't eating right. Miss Pearl say she can't get him to eat nothing.

Troy: What you want me to do about it, Rose? I done did everything I can for the man. I can't make him get well. Man got half his head blown away . . . what you expect?

Rose: Seem like something ought to be done to help him.

Troy: Man don't bother nobody. He just mixed up from that metal plate he got in his head. Ain't no sense for him to go back into the hospital.

Rose: Least he be eating right. They can help him take care of himself.

Troy: Don't nobody wanna be locked up, Rose. What you wanna lock him up for? Man go over there and fight the war . . . messin' around with them Japs, get half his head blown off . . . and they give him a lousy three thousand dollars. And I had to swoop down on that.

Rose: Is you fixing to go into that again?

Troy: That's the only way I got a roof over my head . . . cause of that metal plate.

Rose: Ain't no sense you blaming yourself for nothing. Gabe wasn't in no condition to manage that money. You done what was right by him. Can't nobody say you ain't done what was right by him. Look how long you took care of him . . . till he wanted to have his own place and moved over there with Miss Pearl.

Troy: That ain't what I'm saying, woman! I'm just stating the facts. If my brother didn't have that metal plate in his head . . . I wouldn't have a pot to piss in or a window to throw it out of. And I'm fifty-three years old. Now see if you can understand that!

Troy gets up from the porch and starts to exit the yard.

Rose: Where you going off to? You been running out of here every Saturday for weeks. I thought you was gonna work on this fence?

Troy: I'm gonna walk down to Taylors'. Listen to the ball game. I'll be back in a bit. I'll work on it when I get back.

He exits the yard. The lights go to black.

SCENE III

The lights come up on the yard. It is four hours later. Rose is taking down the clothes from the line. Cory enters carrying his football equipment.

Rose: Your daddy like to had a fit with you running out of here this morning without doing your chores.

Cory: I told you I had to go to practice.

Rose: He say you were supposed to help him with this fence.

Cory: He been saying that the last four or five Saturdays, and then he don't never do nothing, but go down to Taylors. Did you tell him about the recruiter?

Rose: Yeah, I told him.

Cory: What he say?

Rose: He ain't said nothing too much. You get in there and get started on your chores before he gets back. Go on and scrub down them steps before he gets back here hollering and carrying on.

Cory: I'm hungry. What you got to eat, Mama?

Rose: Go on and get started on your chores. I got some meat loaf in there. Go on and make you a sandwich . . . and don't leave no mess in there.

Cory exits into the house. Rose continues to take down the clothes. Troy enters the yard and sneaks up and grabs her from behind.

Troy! Go on, now. You liked to scared me to death. What was the score of the game? Lucille had me on the phone and I couldn't keep up with it.

Troy: What I care about the game? Come here, woman. *(He tries to kiss her.)*

Rose: I thought you went down Taylors' to listen to the game. Go on, Troy! You supposed to be putting up this fence.

Troy (attempting to kiss her again): I'll put it up when I finish with what is at hand.

Rose: Go on, Troy. I ain't studying you.

Troy (chasing after her): I'm studying you . . . fixing to do my homework!

Rose: Troy, you better leave me alone.

Troy: Where's Cory? That boy brought his butt home yet?

Rose: He's in the house doing his chores.

Troy (calling): Cory! Get your butt out here, boy!

Rose exits into the house with the laundry. Troy goes over to the pile of wood, picks up a board, and starts sawing. Cory enters from the house.

Troy: You just now coming in here from leaving this morning?

Cory: Yeah, I had to go to football practice.

Troy: Yeah, what?

Cory: Yessir.

Troy: I ain't but two seconds off you noway. The garbage sitting in there overflowing . . . you ain't done none of your chores . . . and you come in here talking about "Yeah."

Cory: I was just getting ready to do my chores now, Pop . . .

Troy: Your first chore is to help me with this fence on Saturday. Everything else come after that. Now get that saw and cut them boards.

Cory takes the saw and begins cutting the boards. Troy continues working. There is a long pause.

Cory: Hey, Pop . . . why don't you buy a TV?

Troy: What I want with a TV? What I want one of them for?

Cory: Everybody got one. Earl, Ba Bra . . . Jesse!

Troy: I ain't asked you who had one. I say what I want with one?

Cory: So you can watch it. They got lots of things on TV. Baseball games and everything. We could watch the World Series.

Troy: Yeah . . . and how much this TV cost?

Cory: I don't know. They got them on sale for around two hundred dollars.

Troy: Two hundred dollars, huh?

Cory: That ain't that much, Pop.

Troy: Naw, it's just two hundred dollars. See that roof you got over your head at night? Let me tell you something about that roof. It's been over ten years since that roof was last tarred. See now . . . the snow come this winter and sit up there on that roof like it is . . . and it's gonna seep inside. It's just gonna be a little bit . . . ain't gonna hardly notice it. Then the next thing you know, it's gonna be leaking all over the house. Then the wood rot from all that water and you gonna need a whole new roof. Now, how much you think it cost to get that roof tarred?

Cory: I don't know.

Troy: Two hundred and sixty-four dollars . . . cash money. While you thinking about a TV, I got to be thinking about the roof . . . and whatever else go wrong here. Now if you had two hundred dollars, what would you do . . . fix the roof or buy a TV?

Cory: I'd buy a TV. Then when the roof started to leak . . . when it needed fixing . . . I'd fix it.

Troy: Where you gonna get the money from? You done spent it for a TV. You gonna sit up and watch the water run all over your brand new TV.

Cory: Aw, Pop. You got money. I know you do.

Troy: Where I got it at, huh?

Cory: You got it in the bank.

Troy: You wanna see my bankbook? You wanna see that seventy-three dollars and twenty-two cents I got sitting up in there.

Cory: You ain't got to pay for it all at one time. You can put a down payment on it and carry it on home with you.

Troy: Not me. I ain't gonna owe nobody nothing if I can help it. Miss a payment and they come and snatch it right out your house. Then what you got? Now, soon as I get two hundred dollars clear, then I'll buy a TV. Right now, as soon as I get two hundred and sixty-four dollars, I'm gonna have this roof tarred.

Cory: Aw . . . Pop!

Troy: You go on and get you two hundred dollars and buy one if ya want it. I got better things to do with my money.

Cory: I can't get no two hundred dollars. I ain't never seen two hundred dollars.

Troy: I'll tell you what . . . you get you a hundred dollars and I'll put the other hundred with it.

Cory: All right, I'm gonna show you.

Troy: You gonna show me how you can cut them boards right now.

Cory begins to cut the boards. There is a long pause.

Cory: The Pirates won today. That makes five in a row.

Troy: I ain't thinking about the Pirates. Got an all-white team. Got that boy . . . that Puerto Rican boy . . . Clemente. Don't even half-play him. That boy could be something if they give him a chance. Play him one day and sit him on the bench the next.

Cory: He gets a lot of chances to play.

Troy: I'm talking about playing regular. Playing every day so you can get your timing. That's what I'm talking about.

Cory: They got some white guys on the team that don't play every day. You can't play everybody at the same time.

Troy: If they got a white fellow sitting on the bench . . . you can bet your last dollar he can't play! The colored guy got to be twice as good before he get on the team. That's why I don't want you to get all tied up in them sports. Man on the team and what it get him? They got colored on the team and don't use them. Same as not having them. All them teams the same.

Cory: The Braves got Hank Aaron and Wes Covington. Hank Aaron hit two home runs today. That makes forty-three.

Troy: Hank Aaron ain't nobody. That what you supposed to do. That's how you supposed to play the game. Ain't nothing to it. It's just a matter of timing . . . getting the right follow-through. Hell, I can hit forty-three home runs right now!

Cory: Not off no major-league pitching, you couldn't.

Troy: We had better pitching in the Negro leagues. I hit seven home runs off of Satchel Paige.° You can't get no better than that!

Cory: Sandy Koufax. He's leading the league in strikeouts.

Troy: I ain't thinking of no Sandy Koufax.

Cory: You got Warren Spahn and Lew Burdette. I bet you couldn't hit no home runs off of Warren Spahn.

Troy: I'm through with it now. You go on and cut them boards. *(Pause.)* Your mama tell me you done got recruited by a college football team? Is that right?

Cory: Yeah. Coach Zellman say the recruiter gonna be coming by to talk to you. Get you to sign the permission papers.

Troy: I thought you supposed to be working down there at the A&P. Ain't you suppose to be working down there after school?

Cory: Mr. Stawicki say he gonna hold my job for me until after the football season. Say starting next week I can work weekends.

Satchel Paige (1906?–1982): Legendary black pitcher in the Negro leagues.

Troy: I thought we had an understanding about this football stuff? You suppose to keep up with your chores and hold that job down at the A&P. Ain't been around here all day on a Saturday. Ain't none of your chores done . . . and now you telling me you done quit your job.

Cory: I'm going to be working weekends.

Troy: You damn right you are! And ain't no need for nobody coming around here to talk to me about signing nothing.

Cory: Hey, Pop . . . you can't do that. He's coming all the way from North Carolina.

Troy: I don't care where he coming from. The white man ain't gonna let you get nowhere with that football noway. You go on and get your book-learning so you can work yourself up in that A&P or learn how to fix cars or build houses or something, get you a trade. That way you have something can't nobody take away from you. You go on and learn how to put your hands to some good use. Besides hauling people's garbage.

Cory: I get good grades, Pop. That's why the recruiter wants to talk with you. You got to keep up your grades to get recruited. This way I'll be going to college. I'll get a chance . . .

Troy: First you gonna get your butt down there to the A&P and get your job back.

Cory: Mr. Stawicki done already hired somebody else 'cause I told him I was playing football.

Troy: You a bigger fool than I thought . . . to let somebody take away your job so you can play some football. Where you gonna get your money to take out your girlfriend and whatnot? What kind of foolishness is that to let somebody take away your job?

Cory: I'm still gonna be working weekends.

Troy: Naw . . . naw. You getting your butt out of here and finding you another job.

Cory: Come on, Pop! I got to practice. I can't work after school and play football too. The team needs me. That's what Coach Zellman say . . .

Troy: I don't care what nobody else say. I'm the boss . . . you understand? I'm the boss around here. I do the only saying what counts.

Cory: Come on, Pop!

Troy: I asked you . . . did you understand?

Cory: Yeah . . .

Troy: What?!

Cory: Yessir.

Troy: You go on down there to that A&P and see if you can get your job back. If you can't do both . . . then you quit the football team. You've got to take the crookeds with the straights.

Cory: Yessir. *(Pause.)* Can I ask you a question?

Troy: What the hell you wanna ask me? Mr. Stawicki the one you got the questions for.

Cory: How come you ain't never liked me?

Troy: Liked you? Who the hell say I got to like you? What law is there say I got to like you? Wanna stand up in my face and ask a damn fool-ass question like that. Talking about liking somebody. Come here, boy, when I talk to you.

Cory comes over to where Troy is working. He stands slouched over and Troy shoves him on his shoulder.

Straighten up, goddammit! I asked you a question . . . what law is there say I got to like you?

Cory: None.

Troy: Well, all right then! Don't you eat every day? *(Pause.)* Answer me when I talk to you! Don't you eat every day?

Cory: Yeah.

Troy: Nigger, as long as you in my house, you put that sir on the end of it when you talk to me!

Cory: Yes . . . sir.

Troy: You eat every day.

Cory: Yessir!

Troy: Got a roof over your head.

Cory: Yessir!

Troy: Got clothes on your back.

Cory: Yessir.

Troy: Why you think that is?

Cory: Cause of you.

Troy: Ah, hell I know it's cause of me . . . but why do you think that is?

Cory (hesitant): Cause you like me.

Troy: Like you? I go out of here every morning . . . bust my butt . . . putting up with them crackers° every day . . . cause I like you? You are the biggest fool I ever saw. *(Pause.)* It's my job. It's my responsibility! You understand that? A man got to take care of his family. You live in my house . . . sleep you behind on my bedclothes . . . fill you belly up with my food . . . cause you my son. You my flesh and blood. Not cause I like you! Cause it's my duty to take care of you. I owe a responsibility to you! Let's get this straight right here . . . before it go along any further . . . I ain't got to like you. Mr. Rand don't give me my money come payday cause he likes me. He give me cause he owe me. I done give you everything I had to give you. I gave you your life! Me and your mama worked that out between us. And liking your black ass wasn't part of the bargain. Don't you try and go through life worrying about if somebody like you or not. You best be making sure they doing right by you. You understand what I'm saying, boy?

Cory: Yessir.

Troy: Then get the hell out of my face, and get on down to that A&P.

Rose has been standing behind the screen door for much of the scene. She enters as Cory exits.

Rose: Why don't you let the boy go ahead and play football, Troy? Ain't no harm in that. He's just trying to be like you with the sports.

Troy: I don't want him to be like me! I want him to move as far away from my life as he can get. You the only decent thing that ever happened to me. I wish him that. But I don't wish him a thing else from my life. I decided seventeen years ago that boy wasn't getting involved in no sports. Not after what they did to me in the sports.

---

crackers: White people, often used to refer disparagingly to poor whites.

Rose: Troy, why don't you admit you was too old to play in the major leagues? For once . . . why don't you admit that?

Troy: What do you mean too old? Don't come telling me I was too old. I just wasn't the right color. Hell, I'm fifty-three years old and can do better than Selkirk's .269 right now!

Rose: How's was you gonna play ball when you were over forty? Sometimes I can't get no sense out of you.

Troy: I got good sense, woman. I got sense enough not to let my boy get hurt over playing no sports. You been mothering that boy too much. Worried about if people like him.

Rose: Everything that boy do . . . he do for you. He wants you to say "Good job, son." That's all.

Troy: Rose, I ain't got time for that. He's alive. He's healthy. He's got to make his own way. I made mine. Ain't nobody gonna hold his hand when he get out there in that world.

Rose: Times have changed from when you was young, Troy. People change. The world's changing around you and you can't even see it.

Troy (slow, methodical): Woman . . . I do the best I can do. I come in here every Friday. I carry a sack of potatoes and a bucket of lard. You all line up at the door with your hands out. I give you the lint from my pockets. I give you my sweat and my blood. I ain't got no tears. I done spent them. We go upstairs in that room at night . . . and I fall down on you and try to blast a hole into forever. I get up Monday morning . . . find my lunch on the table. I go out. Make my way. Find my strength to carry me through to the next Friday. *(Pause.)* That's all I got, Rose. That's all I got to give. I can't give nothing else.

Troy exits into the house. The lights go down to black.

SCENE IV

It is Friday. Two weeks later. Cory starts out of the house with his football equipment. The phone rings.

Cory (calling): I got it! *(He answers the phone and stands in the screen door talking.)* Hello? Hey, Jesse. Naw . . . I was just getting ready to leave now.

Rose (calling): Cory!

Cory: I told you, man, them spikes is all tore up. You can use them if you want, but they ain't no good. Earl got some spikes.

Rose (calling): Cory!

Cory (calling to Rose): Mam? I'm talking to Jesse. *(Into phone.)* When she say that? *(Pause.)* Aw, you lying, man. I'm gonna tell her you said that.

Rose (calling): Cory, don't you go nowhere!

Cory: I got to go to the game, Ma! *(Into the phone.)* Yeah, hey, look, I'll talk to you later. Yeah, I'll meet you over Earl's house. Later. Bye, Ma.

Cory exits the house and starts out the yard.

Rose: Cory, where you going off to? You got that stuff all pulled out and thrown all over your room.

Cory (in the yard): I was looking for my spikes. Jesse wanted to borrow my spikes.

Rose: Get up there and get that cleaned up before your daddy get back in here.

Cory: I got to go to the game! I'll clean it up *when I get back.*

Cory exits.

Rose: That's all he need to do is see that room all messed up.

Rose exits into the house. Troy and Bono enter the yard. Troy is dressed in clothes other than his work clothes.

Bono: He told him the same thing he told you. Take it to the union.

Troy: Brownie ain't got that much sense. Man wasn't thinking about nothing. He wait until I confront them on it . . . then he wanna come crying seniority. *(Calls.)* Hey, Rose!

Bono: I wish I could have seen Mr. Rand's face when he told you.

Troy: He couldn't get it out of his mouth! Liked to bit his tongue! When they called me down there to the Commissioner's office . . . he thought they was gonna fire me. Like everybody else.

Bono: I didn't think they was gonna fire you. I thought they was gonna put you on the warning paper.

Troy: Hey, Rose! *(To Bono.)* Yeah, Mr. Rand like to bit his tongue.

Troy breaks the seal on the bottle, takes a drink, and hands it to Bono.

Bono: I see you run right down to Taylors' and told that Alberta gal.

Troy (calling): Hey Rose! *(To Bono.)* I told everybody. Hey, Rose! I went down there to cash my check.

Rose (entering from the house): Hush all that hollering, man! I know you out here. What they say down there at the Commissioner's office?

Troy: You supposed to come when I call you, woman. Bono'll tell you that. *(To Bono.)* Don't Lucille come when you call her?

Rose: Man, hush your mouth. I ain't no dog . . . talk about "come when you call me."

Troy (puts his arm around Rose): You hear this, Bono? I had me an old dog used to get uppity like that. You say, "C'mere, Blue!" . . . and he just lay there and look at you. End up getting a stick and chasing him away trying to make him come.

Rose: I ain't studying you and your dog. I remember you used to sing that old song.

Troy (he sings): Hear it ring! Hear it ring! I had a dog his name was Blue.

Rose: Don't nobody wanna hear you sing that old song.

Troy (sings): You know Blue was mighty true.

Rose: Used to have Cory running around here singing that song.

Bono: Hell, I remember that song myself.

Troy (sings): You know Blue was a good old dog.
   Blue treed a possum in a hollow log.
   That was my daddy's song. My daddy made up that song.

Rose: I don't care who made it up. Don't nobody wanna hear you sing it.

Troy (makes a song like calling a dog): Come here, woman.

Rose: You come in here carrying on, I reckon they ain't fired you. What they say down there at the Commissioner's office?

Troy: Look here, Rose . . . Mr. Rand called me into his office today when I got back from talking to them people down there . . . it come from up top . . . he called me in and told me they was making me a driver.

Rose: Troy, you kidding!

Troy: No I ain't. Ask Bono.

Rose: Well, that's great, Troy. Now you don't have to hassle them people no more.

Lyons enters from the street.

Troy: Aw hell, I wasn't looking to see you today. I thought you was in jail. Got it all over the front page of the *Courier* about them raiding Sefus's place . . . where you be hanging out with all them thugs.

Lyons: Hey, Pop . . . that ain't got nothing to do with me. I don't go down there gambling. I go down there to sit in with the band. I ain't got nothing to do with the gambling part. They got some good music down there.

Troy: They got some rogues . . . is what they got.

Lyons: How you been, Mr. Bono? Hi, Rose.

Bono: I see where you playing down at the Crawford Grill tonight.

Rose: How come you ain't brought Bonnie like I told you? You should have brought Bonnie with you, she ain't been over in a month of Sundays.

Lyons: I was just in the neighborhood . . . thought I'd stop by.

Troy: Here he come . . .

Bono: Your daddy got a promotion on the rubbish. He's gonna be the first colored driver. Ain't got to do nothing but sit up there and read the paper like them white fellows.

Lyons: Hey, Pop . . . if you knew how to read you'd be all right.

Bono: Naw . . . naw . . . you mean if the nigger knew how to *drive* he'd be all right. Been fighting with them people about driving and ain't even got a license. Mr. Rand know you ain't got no driver's license?

Troy: Driving ain't nothing. All you do is point the truck where you want it to go. Driving ain't nothing.

Bono: Do Mr. Rand know you ain't got no driver's license? That's what I'm talking about. I ain't asked if driving was easy. I asked if Mr. Rand know you ain't got no driver's license.

Troy: He ain't got to know. The man ain't got to know my business. Time he find out, I have two or three driver's licenses.

Lyons (going into his pocket): Say, look here, Pop . . .

Troy: I knew it was coming. Didn't I tell you, Bono? I know what kind of "Look here, Pop" that was. The nigger fixing to ask me for some money. It's Friday night. It's my payday. All them rogues down there on the avenue . . . the ones that ain't in jail . . . and Lyons is hopping in his shoes to get down there with them.

Lyons: See, Pop . . . if you give somebody else a chance to talk sometimes, you'd see that I was fixing to pay you back your ten dollars like I told you. Here . . . I told you I'd pay you when Bonnie got paid.

Troy: Naw . . . you go ahead and keep that ten dollars. Put it in the bank. The

next time you feel like you wanna come by here and ask me for something
. . . you go on down there and get that.

Lyons: Here's your ten dollars, Pop. I told you I don't want you to give me nothing. I just wanted to borrow ten dollars.

Troy: Naw . . . you go on and keep that for the next time you want to ask me.

Lyons: Come on, Pop . . . here go your ten dollars.

Rose: Why don't you go on and let the boy pay you back, Troy?

Lyons: Here you go, Rose. If you don't take it I'm gonna have to hear about it for the next six months. *(He hands her the money.)*

Rose: You can hand yours over here too, Troy.

Troy: You see this, Bono. You see how they do me.

Bono: Yeah, Lucille do me the same way.

Gabriel is heard singing offstage. He enters.

Gabriel: Better get ready for the Judgment! Better get ready for . . . Hey! . . . Hey! . . . There's Troy's boy!

Lyons: How are you doing, Uncle Gabe?

Gabriel: Lyons . . . The King of the Jungle! Rose . . . hey, Rose. Got a flower for you. *(He takes a rose from his pocket.)* Picked it myself. That's the same rose like you is!

Rose: That's right nice of you, Gabe.

Lyons: What you been doing, Uncle Gabe?

Gabriel: Oh, I been chasing hellhounds and waiting on the time to tell St. Peter to open the gates.

Lyons: You been chasing hellhounds, huh? Well . . . you doing the right thing, Uncle Gabe. Somebody got to chase them.

Gabriel: Oh, yeah . . . I know it. The devil's strong. The devil ain't no pushover. Hellhounds snipping at everybody's heels. But I got my trumpet waiting on the judgment time.

Lyons: Waiting on the Battle of Armageddon, huh?

Gabriel: Ain't gonna be too much of a battle when God get to waving that Judgment sword. But the people's gonna have a hell of a time trying to get into heaven if them gates ain't open.

Lyons (putting his arm around Gabriel): You hear this, Pop. Uncle Gabe, you all right!

Gabriel (laughing with Lyons): Lyons! King of the Jungle.

Rose: You gonna stay for supper, Gabe? Want me to fix you a plate?

Gabriel: I'll take a sandwich, Rose. Don't want no plate. Just wanna eat with my hands. I'll take a sandwich.

Rose: How about you, Lyons? You staying? Got some short ribs cooking.

Lyons: Naw, I won't eat nothing till after we finished playing. *(Pause.)* You ought to come down and listen to me play, Pop.

Troy: I don't like that Chinese music. All that noise.

Rose: Go on in the house and wash up, Gabe . . . I'll fix you a sandwich.

Gabriel (to Lyons, as he exits): Troy's mad at me.

Lyons: What you mad at Uncle Gabe for, Pop?

Rose: He thinks Troy's mad at him cause he moved over to Miss Pearl's.

Troy: I ain't mad at the man. He can live where he want to live at.

Lyons: What he move over there for? Miss Pearl don't like nobody.

Rose: She don't mind him none. She treats him real nice. She just don't allow all that singing.

Troy: She don't mind that rent he be paying . . . that's what she don't mind.

Rose: Troy, I ain't going through that with you no more. He's over there cause he want to have his own place. He can come and go as he please.

Troy: Hell, he could come and go as he please here. I wasn't stopping him. I ain't put no rules on him.

Rose: It ain't the same thing, Troy. And you know it.

Gabriel comes to the door.

Now, that's the last I wanna hear about that. I don't wanna hear nothing else about Gabe and Miss Pearl. And next week . . .

Gabriel: I'm ready for my sandwich, Rose.

Rose: And next week . . . when that recruiter come from that school . . . I want you to sign that paper and go on and let Cory play football. Then that'll be the last I have to hear about that.

Troy (to Rose as she exits into the house): I ain't thinking about Cory nothing.

Lyons: What . . . Cory got recruited? What school he going to?

Troy: That boy walking around here smelling his piss . . . thinking he's grown. Thinking he's gonna do what he want, irrespective of what I say. Look here, Bono . . . I left the Commissioner's office and went down to the A&P . . . that boy ain't working down there. He lying to me. Telling me he got his job back . . . telling me he working weekends . . . telling me he working after school . . . Mr. Stawicki tell me he ain't working down there at all!

Lyons: Cory just growing up. He's just busting at the seams trying to fill out your shoes.

Troy: I don't care what he's doing. When he get to the point where he wanna disobey me . . . then it's time for him to move on. Bono'll tell you that. I bet he ain't never disobeyed his daddy without paying the consequences.

Bono: I ain't never had a chance. My daddy came on through . . . but I ain't never knew him to see him . . . or what he had on his mind or where he went. Just moving on through. Searching out the New Land. That's what the old folks used to call it. See a fellow moving around from place to place . . . woman to woman . . . called it searching out the New Land. I can't say if he ever found it. I come along, didn't want no kids. Didn't know if I was gonna be in one place long enough to fix on them right as their daddy. I figured I was going searching too. As it turned out I been hooked up with Lucille near about as long as your daddy been with Rose. Going on sixteen years.

Troy: Sometimes I wish I hadn't known my daddy. He ain't cared nothing about no kids. A kid to him wasn't nothing. All he wanted was for you to learn how to walk so he could start you to working. When it come time for eating . . . he ate first. If there was anything left over, that's what you got. Man would sit down and eat two chickens and give you the wing.

Lyons: You ought to stop that, Pop. Everybody feed their kids. No matter how hard times is . . . everybody care about their kids. Make sure they have something to eat.

Troy: The only thing my daddy cared about was getting them bales of cotton in to Mr. Lubin. That's the only thing that mattered to him. Sometimes I used to wonder why he was living. Wonder why the devil hadn't come and got him. "Get them bales of cotton in to Mr. Lubin" and find out he owe him money . . .

Lyons: He should have just went on and left when he saw he couldn't get nowhere. That's what I would have done.

Troy: How he gonna leave with eleven kids? And where he gonna go? He ain't knew how to do nothing but farm. No, he was trapped and I think he knew it. But I'll say this for him . . . he felt a responsibility toward us. Maybe he ain't treated us the way I felt he should have . . . but without that responsibility he could have walked off and left us . . . made his own way.

Bono: A lot of them did. Back in those days what you talking about . . . they walk out their front door and just take on down one road or another and keep on walking.

Lyons: There you go! That's what I'm talking about.

Bono: Just keep on walking till you come to something else. Ain't you never heard of nobody having the walking blues? Well, that's what you call it when you just take off like that.

Troy: My daddy ain't had them walking blues! What you talking about? He stayed right there with his family. But he was just as evil as he could be. My mama couldn't stand him. Couldn't stand that evilness. She run off when I was about eight. She sneaked off one night after he had gone to sleep. Told me she was coming back for me. I ain't never seen her no more. All his women run off and left him. He wasn't good for nobody.

When my turn come to head out, I was fourteen and got to sniffing around Joe Canewell's daughter. Had us an old mule we called Greyboy. My daddy sent me out to do some plowing and I tied up Greyboy and went to fooling around with Joe Canewell's daughter. We done found us a nice little spot, got real cozy with each other. She about thirteen and we done figured we was grown anyway . . . so we down there enjoying ourselves . . . ain't thinking about nothing. We didn't know Greyboy had got loose and wandered back to the house and my daddy was looking for me. We down there by the creek enjoying ourselves when my daddy come up on us. Surprised us. He had them leather straps off the mule and commenced to whupping me like there was no tomorrow. I jumped up, mad and embarrassed. I was scared of my daddy. When he commenced to whupping on me . . . quite naturally I run to get out of the way. *(Pause.)* Now I thought he was mad cause I ain't done my work. But I see where he was chasing me off so he could have the gal for himself. When I see what the matter of it was, I lost all fear of my daddy. Right there is where I become a man . . . at fourteen years of age. *(Pause.)* Now it was my turn to run him off. I picked up them same reins that he had used on me. I picked up them reins and commenced to whupping on him. The gal jumped up and run off . . . and when my daddy turned to face me, I could see why the devil had never come to get him . . . cause he was the devil himself. I don't know what happened. When I woke up, I was laying right there by the creek, and Blue . . . this old dog we had . . . was licking my face. I thought I was blind. I couldn't see nothing. Both my eyes were swollen shut. I laid there and cried. I didn't know what I was gonna do. The only thing I knew was the time had come for me to leave my daddy's house. And right there the world suddenly got big. And it was a long time before I could cut it down to where I could handle it.

Part of that cutting down was when I got to the place where I could feel him kicking in my blood and knew that the only thing that separated us was the matter of a few years.

Gabriel enters from the house with a sandwich.

Lyons: What you got there, Uncle Gabe?

Gabriel: Got me a ham sandwich. Rose gave me a ham sandwich.

Troy: I don't know what happened to him. I done lost touch with everybody except Gabriel. But I hope he's dead. I hope he found some peace.

Lyons: That's a heavy story, Pop. I didn't know you left home when you was fourteen.

Troy: And didn't know nothing. The only part of the world I knew was the forty-two acres of Mr. Lubin's land. That's all I knew about life.

Lyons: Fourteen's kinda young to be out on your own. *(Phone rings.)* I don't even think I was ready to be out on my own at fourteen. I don't know what I would have done.

Troy: I got up from the creek and walked on down to Mobile. I was through with farming. Figured I could do better in the city. So I walked the two hundred miles to Mobile.

Lyons: Wait a minute . . . you ain't walked no two hundred miles, Pop. Ain't nobody gonna walk no two hundred miles. You talking about some walking there.

Bono: That's the only way you got anywhere back in them days.

Lyons: Shhh. Damn if I wouldn't have hitched a ride with somebody!

Troy: Who you gonna hitch it with? They ain't had no cars and things like they got now. We talking about 1918.

Rose (entering): What you all out here getting into?

Troy (to Rose): I'm telling Lyons how good he got it. He don't know nothing about this I'm talking.

Rose: Lyons, that was Bonnie on the phone. She say you supposed to pick her up.

Lyons: Yeah, okay, Rose.

Troy: I walked on down to Mobile and hitched up with some of them fellows that was heading this way. Got up here and found out . . . not only couldn't you get a job . . . you couldn't find no place to live. I thought I was in freedom. Shhh. Colored folks living down there on the riverbanks in whatever kind of shelter they could find for themselves. Right down there under the Brady Street Bridge. Living in shacks made of sticks and tarpaper. Messed around there and went from bad to worse. Started stealing. First it was food. Then I figured, hell, if I steal money I can buy me some food. Buy me some shoes too! One thing led to another. Met your mama. I was young and anxious to be a man. Met your mama and had you. What I do that for? Now I got to worry about feeding you and her. Got to steal three times as much. Went out one day looking for somebody to rob . . . that's what I was, a robber. I'll tell you the truth. I'm ashamed of it today. But it's the truth. Went to rob this fellow . . . pulled out my knife . . . and he pulled out a gun. Shot me in the chest. I felt just like somebody had taken a hot branding iron and laid it on me. When he shot me I jumped at him with my knife. They told me I killed him and they put me in the penitentiary and locked me up for fifteen years. That's where I met Bono. That's where I learned how to play baseball. Got out that place and your mama had taken you and went on to make life without me. Fifteen years was a long time for her to wait. But that fifteen years cured me of that robbing stuff. Rose'll tell you. She asked me when I met her if I had gotten all that foolishness out of my system. And I told her, "Baby, it's you and baseball all what count with me." You hear me, Bono? I meant it too. She say, "Which one comes first?" I told her, "Baby, ain't no doubt it's baseball . . . but you stick and get old with me and we'll both outlive this baseball." Am I right, Rose? And it's true.

Rose: Man, hush your mouth. You ain't said no such thing. Talking about, "Baby, you know you'll always be number one with me." That's what you was talking.

Troy: You hear that, Bono. That's why I love her.

Bono: Rose'll keep you straight. You get off the track, she'll straighten you up.

Rose: Lyons, you better get on up and get Bonnie. She waiting on you.

Lyons (gets up to go): Hey, Pop, why don't you come on down to the Grill and hear me play?

Troy: I ain't going down there. I'm too old to be sitting around in them clubs.

Bono: You got to be good to play down at the Grill.

Lyons: Come on, Pop . . .

Troy: I got to get up in the morning.

Lyons: You ain't got to stay long.

Troy: Naw, I'm gonna get my supper and go on to bed.

Lyons: Well, I got to go. I'll see you again.

Troy: Don't you come around my house on my payday.

Rose: Pick up the phone and let somebody know you coming. And bring Bonnie with you. You know I'm always glad to see her.

Lyons: Yeah, I'll do that, Rose. You take care now. See you, Pop. See you, Mr. Bono. See you, Uncle Gabe.

Gabriel: Lyons! King of the Jungle!

Lyons exits.

Troy: Is supper ready, woman? Me and you got some business to take care of. I'm gonna tear it up too.

Rose: Troy, I done told you now!

Troy (puts his arm around Bono): Aw hell, woman . . . this is Bono. Bono like family. I done known this nigger since . . . how long I done know you?

Bono: It's been a long time.

Troy: I done know this nigger since Skippy was a pup. Me and him done been through some times.

Bono: You sure right about that.

Troy: Hell, I done know him longer than I known you. And we still standing shoulder to shoulder. Hey, look here, Bono . . . a man can't ask for no more than that. (Drinks to him.) I love you, nigger.

Bono: Hell, I love you too . . . I got to get home see my woman. You got yours in hand. I got to go get mine.

Bono starts to exit as Cory enters the yard, dressed in his football uniform. He gives Troy a hard, uncompromising look.

Cory: What you do that for, Pop?

He throws his helmet down in the direction of Troy.

Rose: What's the matter? Cory . . . what's the matter?

Cory: Papa done went up to the school and told Coach Zellman I can't play football no more. Wouldn't even let me play the game. Told him to tell the recruiter not to come.

Rose: Troy . . .

Troy: What you Troying me for. Yeah, I did it. And the boy know why I did it.

Cory: Why you wanna do that to me? That was the one chance I had.

Rose: Ain't nothing wrong with Cory playing football, Troy.

Troy: The boy lied to me. I told the nigger if he wanna play football . . . to keep up his chores and hold down that job at the A&P. That was the conditions. Stopped down there to see Mr. Stawicki . . .

Cory: I can't work after school during the football season, Pop! I tried to tell you that Mr. Stawicki's holding my job for me. You don't never want to listen to nobody. And then you wanna go and do this to me!

Troy: I ain't done nothing to you. You done it to yourself.

Cory: Just cause you didn't have a chance! You just scared I'm gonna be better than you, that's all.

Troy: Come here.

Rose: Troy . . .

Cory reluctantly crosses over to Troy.

Troy: All right! See. You done made a mistake.

Cory: I didn't even do nothing!

Troy: I'm gonna tell you what your mistake was. See . . . you swung at the ball and didn't hit it. That's strike one. See, you in the batter's box now. You swung and you missed. That's strike one. Don't you strike out!

Lights fade to black.

ACT II

SCENE I

The following morning. Cory is at the tree hitting the ball with the bat. He tries to mimic Troy, but his swing is awkward, less sure. Rose enters from the house.

Rose: Cory, I want you to help me with this cupboard.

Cory: I ain't quitting the team. I don't care what Poppa say.

Rose: I'll talk to him when he gets back. He had to go see about your Uncle Gabe. The police done arrested him. Say he was disturbing the peace. He'll be back directly. Come on in here and help me clean out the top of this cupboard.

Cory exits into the house. Rose sees Troy and Bono coming down the alley.

Troy . . . what they say down there?

Troy: Ain't said nothing. I give them fifty **dollars and** they let him go. I'll talk to you about it. Where's Cory?

Rose: He's in there helping me clean out these cupboards.

Troy: Tell him to get his butt out here.

Troy and Bono go over to the pile of wood. Bono picks up the saw and begins sawing.

Troy (to Bono): All they want is the money. That makes six or seven times I done went down there and got him. See me coming they stick out their *hands.*

Bono: Yeah. I know what you mean. That's all they care about . . . that money. They don't care about what's right. *(Pause.)* Nigger, why you got to go and get some hard wood? You ain't doing nothing but building a little old fence. Get you some soft pine wood. That's all you need.

Troy: I know what I'm doing. This is outside wood. You put pine wood inside the house. Pine wood is inside wood. This here is outside wood. Now you tell me where the fence is gonna be?

Bono: You don't need this wood. You can put it up with pine wood and it'll stand as long as you gonna be here looking at it.

Troy: How you know how long I'm gonna be here, nigger? Hell, I might just live forever. Live longer than old man Horsely.

Bono: That's what Magee used to say.

Troy: Magee's a damn fool. Now you tell me who you ever heard of gonna pull their own teeth with a pair of rusty pliers.

Bono: The old folks . . . my granddaddy used to pull his teeth with pliers. They ain't had no dentists for the colored folks back then.

Troy: Get clean pliers! You understand? Clean pliers! Sterilize them! Besides we ain't living back then. All Magee had to do was walk over to Doc Goldblum's.

Bono: I see where you and that Tallahassee gal . . . that Alberta . . . I see where you all done got tight.

Troy: What you mean "got tight"?

Bono: I see where you be laughing and joking with her all the time.

Troy: I laughs and jokes with all of them, Bono. You know me.

Bono: That ain't the kind of laughing and joking I'm talking about.

Cory enters from the house.

Cory: How you doing, Mr. Bono?

Troy: Cory? Get that saw from Bono and cut some wood. He talking about the wood's too hard to cut. Stand back there, Jim, and let that young boy show you how it's done.

Bono: He's sure welcome to it.

Cory takes the saw and begins to cut the wood.

Whew-e-e! Look at that. Big old strong boy. Look like Joe Louis.° Hell, must be getting old the way I'm watching that boy whip through that wood.

Cory: I don't see why Mama want a fence around the yard noways.

Joe Louis (1914–1981): Black American boxer who held the world heavyweight championship title.

Troy: Damn if I know either. What the hell she keeping out with it? She ain't got nothing nobody want.

Bono: Some people build fences to keep people out . . . and other people build fences to keep people in. Rose wants to hold on to you all. She loves you.

Troy: Hell, nigger, I don't need nobody to tell me my wife loves me. Cory . . . go on in the house and see if you can find that other saw.

Cory: Where's it at?

Troy: I said find it! Look for it till you find it!

Cory exits into the house.

What's that supposed to mean? Wanna keep us in?

Bono: Troy . . . I done known you seem like damn near my whole life. You and Rose both. I done know both of you all for a long time. I remember when you met Rose. When you was hitting them baseball out the park. A lot of them old gals was after you then. You had the pick of the litter. When you picked Rose, I was happy for you. That was the first time I knew you had any sense. I said . . . My man Troy knows what he's doing . . . I'm gonna follow this nigger . . . he might take me somewhere. I been following you too. I done learned a whole heap of things about life watching you. I done learned how to tell where the shit lies. How to tell it from the alfalfa. You done learned me a lot of things. You showed me how to not make the same mistakes . . . to take life as it comes along and keep putting one foot in front of the other. *(Pause.)* Rose a good woman, Troy.

Troy: Hell, nigger, I know she a good woman. I been married to her for eighteen years. What you got on your mind, Bono?

Bono: I just say she a good woman. Just like I say anything. I ain't got to have nothing on my mind.

Troy: You just gonna say she a good woman and leave it hanging out there like that? Why you telling me she a good woman?

Bono: She loves you, Troy. Rose loves you.

Troy: You saying I don't measure up. That's what you trying to say. I don't measure up cause I'm seeing this other gal. I know what you trying to say.

Bono: I know what Rose means to you, Troy. I'm just trying to say I don't want to see you mess up.

Troy: Yeah, I appreciate that, Bono. If you was messing around on Lucille I'd be telling you the same thing.

Bono: Well, that's all I got to say. I just say that because I love you both.

Troy: Hell, you know me . . . I wasn't out there looking for nothing. You can't find a better woman than Rose. I know that. But seems like this woman just stuck onto me where I can't shake her loose. I done wrestled with it, tried to throw her off me . . . but she just stuck on tighter. Now she's stuck on for good.

Bono: You's in control . . . that's what you tell me all the time. You responsible for what you do.

Troy: I ain't ducking the responsibility of it. As long as it sets right in my heart . . . then I'm okay. Cause that's all I listen to. It'll tell me right from wrong every time. And I ain't talking about doing Rose no bad turn. I love Rose. She done carried me a long ways and I love and respect her for that.

Bono: I know you do. That's why I don't want to see you hurt her. But what you gonna do when she find out? What you got then? If you try and juggle both of them . . . sooner or later you gonna drop one of them. That's common sense.

Troy: Yeah, I hear what you saying, Bono. I been trying to figure a way to work it out.

Bono: Work it out right, Troy. I don't want to be getting all up between you and Rose's business . . . but work it so it come out right.

Troy: Ah hell, I get all up between you and Lucille's business. When you gonna get that woman that refrigerator she been wanting? Don't tell me you ain't got no money now. I know who your banker is. Mellon don't need that money bad as Lucille want that refrigerator. I'll tell you that.

Bono: Tell you what I'll do . . . when you finish building this fence for Rose . . . I'll buy Lucille that refrigerator.

Troy: You done stuck your foot in your mouth now!

Troy grabs up a board and begins to saw. Bono starts to walk out the yard.

Hey, nigger . . . where you going?

Bono: I'm going home. I know you don't expect me to help you now. I'm protecting my money. I wanna see you put that fence up by yourself. That's what I want to see. You'll be here another six months without me.

Troy: Nigger, you ain't right.

Bono: When it comes to my money . . . I'm right as fireworks on the Fourth of July.

Troy: All right, we gonna see now. You better get out your bankbook.

Bono exits, and Troy continues to work. Rose enters from the house.

Rose: What they say down there? What's happening with Gabe?

Troy: I went down there and got him out. Cost me fifty dollars. Say he was disturbing the peace. Judge set up a hearing for him in three weeks. Say to show cause why he shouldn't be recommitted.

Rose: What was he doing that cause them to arrest him?

Troy: Some kids was teasing him and he run them off home. Say he was howling and carrying on. Some folks seen him and called the police. That's all it was.

Rose: Well, what's you say? What'd you tell the judge?

Troy: Told him I'd look after him. It didn't make no sense to recommit the man. He stuck out his big greasy palm and told me to give him fifty dollars and take him on home.

Rose: Where's he at now? Where'd he go off to?

Troy: He's gone about his business. He don't need nobody to hold his hand.

Rose: Well, I don't know. Seem like that would be the best place for him if they did put him into the hospital. I know what you're gonna say. But that's what I think would be best.

Troy: The man done had his life ruined fighting for what? And they wanna take and lock him up. Let him be free. He don't bother nobody.

Rose: Well, everybody got their own way of looking at it I guess. Come on and get your lunch. I got a bowl of lima beans and some cornbread in the oven. Come and get something to eat. Ain't no sense you fretting over Gabe.

Rose turns to go into the house.

Troy: Rose . . . got something to tell you.

Rose: Well, come on . . . wait till I get this food on the table.

Troy: Rose!

She stops and turns around.

> I don't know how to say this. *(Pause.)* I can't explain it none. It just sort of grows on you till it gets out of hand. It starts out like a little bush . . . and the next thing you know it's a whole forest.

Rose: Troy . . . what is you talking about?

Troy: I'm talking, woman, let me talk. I'm trying to find a way to tell you . . . I'm gonna be a daddy. I'm gonna be somebody's daddy.

Rose: Troy . . . you're not telling me this? You're gonna be . . . . what?

Troy: Rose . . . now . . . see . . .

Rose: You telling me you gonna be somebody's daddy? You telling your *wife* this?

Gabriel enters from the street. He carries a rose in his hand.

Gabriel: Hey, Troy! Hey, Rose!

Rose: I have to wait eighteen years to hear something like this.

Gabriel: Hey, Rose . . . I got a flower for you. *(He hands it to her.)* That's a rose. Same rose like you is.

Rose: Thanks, Gabe.

Gabriel: Troy, you ain't mad at me is you? Them bad mens come and put me away. You ain't mad at me is you?

Troy: Naw, Gabe, I ain't mad at you.

Rose: Eighteen years and you wanna come with this.

Gabriel (takes a quarter out of his pocket): See what I got? Got a brand new quarter.

Troy: Rose . . . it's just . . .

Rose: Ain't nothing you can say, Troy. Ain't no way of explaining that.

Gabriel: Fellow that give me this quarter had a whole mess of them. I'm gonna keep this quarter till it stop shining.

Rose: Gabe, go on in the house there. I got some watermelon in the Frigidaire. Go on and get you a piece.

Gabriel: Say, Rose . . . you know I was chasing hellhounds and them bad mens come and get me and take me away. Troy helped me. He come down there and told them they better let me go before he beat them up. Yeah, he did!

Rose: You go on and get you a piece of watermelon, Gabe. Them bad mens is gone now.

Gabriel: Okay, Rose . . . gonna get me some watermelon. The kind with the stripes on it.

Gabriel exits into the house.

Rose: Why, Troy? Why? After all these years to come dragging this in to me now. It don't make no sense at your age. I could have expected this ten or fifteen years ago, but not now.

Troy: Age ain't got nothing to do with it, Rose.

Rose: I done tried to be everything a wife should be. Everything a wife could
be. Been married eighteen years and I got to live to see the day you tell me
you been seeing another woman and done fathered a child by her. And you
know I ain't never wanted no half nothing in my family. My whole family is
half. Everybody got different fathers and mothers . . . my two sisters and my
brother. Can't hardly tell who's who. Can't never sit down and talk about
Papa and Mama. It's your papa and your mama and my papa and my
mama . . .

Troy: Rose . . . stop it now.

Rose: I ain't never wanted that for none of my children. And now you wanna
drag your behind in here and tell me something like this.

Troy: You ought to know. It's time for you to know.

Rose: Well, I don't want to know, goddamn it!

Troy: I can't just make it go away. It's done now. I can't wish the circumstance
of the thing away.

Rose: And you don't want to either. Maybe you want to wish me and my boy
away. Maybe that's what you want? Well, you can't wish us away. I've got
eighteen years of my life invested in you. You ought to have stayed upstairs
in my bed where you belong.

Troy: Rose . . . now listen to me . . . we can get a handle on this thing. We can
talk this out . . . come to an understanding.

Rose: All of a sudden it's "we." Where was "we" at when you was down there
rolling around with some godforsaken woman? "We" should have come to
an understanding before you started making a damn fool of yourself. You're
a day late and a dollar short when it comes to an understanding with me.

Troy: It's just . . . She gives me a different idea . . . a different understanding
about myself. I can step out of this house and get away from the pressures
and problems . . . be a different man. I ain't got to wonder how I'm gonna
pay the bills or get the roof fixed. I can just be a part of myself that I ain't
never been.

Rose: What I want to know . . . is do you plan to continue seeing her. That's all
you can say to me.

Troy: I can sit up in her house and laugh. Do you understand what I'm saying.
I can laugh out loud . . . and it feels good. It reaches all the way down to
the bottom of my shoes. *(Pause.)* Rose, I can't give that up.

Rose: Maybe you ought to go on and stay down there with her . . . if she's a
better woman than me.

Troy: It ain't about nobody being a better woman or nothing. Rose, you ain't
the blame. A man couldn't ask for no woman to be a better wife than you've
been. I'm responsible for it. I done locked myself into a pattern trying to
take care of you all that I forgot about myself.

Rose: What the hell was I there for? That was my job, not somebody else's.

Troy: Rose, I done tried all my life to live decent . . . to live a clean . . . hard
. . . useful life. I tried to be a good husband to you. In every way I knew
how. Maybe I come into the world backwards, I don't know. But . . . you
born with two strikes on you before you come to the plate. You got to guard
it closely . . . always looking for the curve ball on the inside corner. You
can't afford to let none get past you. You can't afford a call strike. If you

going down . . . you going down swinging. Everything lined up against you. What you gonna do. I fooled them, Rose. I bunted. When I found you and Cory and a halfway decent job . . . I was safe. Couldn't nothing touch me. I wasn't gonna strike out no more. I wasn't going back to the penitentiary. I wasn't gonna lay in the streets with a bottle of wine. I was safe. I had me a family. A job. I wasn't gonna get that last strike. I was on first looking for one of them boys to knock me in. To get me home.

Rose: You should have stayed in my bed, Troy.

Troy: Then when I saw that gal . . . she firmed up my backbone. And I got to thinking that if I tried . . . I just might be able to steal second. Do you understand after eighteen years I wanted to steal second.

Rose: You should have held me tight. You should have grabbed me and held on.

Troy: I stood on first base for eighteen years and I thought . . . well, goddamn it . . . go on for it!

Rose: We're not talking about baseball! We're talking about you going off to lay in bed with another woman . . . and then bring it home to me. That's what we're talking about. We ain't talking about no baseball.

Troy: Rose, you're not listening to me. I'm trying the best I can to explain it to you. It's not easy for me to admit that I been standing in the same place for eighteen years.

Rose: I been standing with you! I been right here with you, Troy. I got a life too. I gave eighteen years of my life to stand in the same spot with you. Don't you think I ever wanted other things? Don't you think I had dreams and hopes? What about my life? What about me. Don't you think it ever crossed my mind to want to know other men? That I wanted to lay up somewhere and forget about my responsibilities? That I wanted someone to make me laugh so I could feel good? You not the only one who's got wants and needs. But I held on to you, Troy. I took all my feelings, my wants and needs, my dreams . . . and I buried them inside you. I planted a seed and watched and prayed over it. I planted myself inside you and waited to bloom. And it didn't take me no eighteen years to find out the soil was hard and rocky and it wasn't never gonna bloom.

But I held on to you, Troy. I held you tighter. You was my husband. I owed you everything I had. Every part of me I could find to give you. And upstairs in that room . . . with the darkness falling in on me . . . . I gave everything I had to try and erase the doubt that you wasn't the finest man in the world. And wherever you was going . . . I wanted to be there with you. Cause you was my husband. Cause that's the only way I was gonna survive as your wife. You always talking about what you give . . . . and what you don't have to give. But you take too. You take . . . . and don't even know nobody's giving!

Rose turns to exit into the house; Troy grabs her arm.

Troy: You say I take and don't give!

Rose: Troy! You're hurting me!

Troy: You say I take and don't give!

Rose: Troy . . . . you're hurting my arm! Let go!

Troy: I done give you everything I got. Don't you tell that lie on me.

Rose: Troy!
Troy: Don't you tell that lie on me!

Cory enters from the house.

Cory: Mama!
Rose: Troy. You're hurting me.
Troy: Don't you tell me about no taking and giving.

Cory comes up behind Troy and grabs him. Troy, surprised, is thrown off balance just as Cory throws a glancing blow that catches him on the chest and knocks him down. Troy is stunned, as is Cory.

Rose: Troy. Troy. No!

Troy gets to his feet and starts at Cory.

> Troy . . . no. Please! Troy!

Rose pulls on Troy to hold him back. Troy stops himself.

Troy (to Cory): All right. That's strike two. You stay away from around me, boy. Don't you strike out. You living with a full count. Don't you strike out.

Troy exits out the yard as the lights go down.

Scene II

It is six months later, early afternoon. Troy enters from the house and starts to exit the yard. Rose enters from the house.

Rose: Troy, I want to talk to you.
Troy: All of a sudden, after all this time, you want to talk to me, huh? You ain't wanted to talk to me for months. You ain't wanted to talk to me last night. You ain't wanted no part of me then. What you wanna talk to me about now?
Rose: Tomorrow's Friday.
Troy: I know what day tomorrow is. You think I don't know tomorrow's Friday? My whole life I ain't done nothing but look to see Friday coming and you got to tell me it's Friday.
Rose: I want to know if you're coming home.
Troy: I always come home, Rose. You know that. There ain't never been a night I ain't come home.
Rose: That ain't what I mean . . . and you know it. I want to know if you're coming straight home after work.
Troy: I figure I'd cash my check . . . hang out at Taylors' with the boys . . . maybe play a game of checkers . . .
Rose: Troy, I can't live like this. I won't live like this. You livin' on borrowed time with me. It's been going on six months now you ain't been coming home.
Troy: I be here every night. Every night of the year. That's 365 days.
Rose: I want you to come home tomorrow after work.
Troy: Rose . . . I don't mess up my pay. You know that now. I take my pay and I give it to you. I don't have no money but what you give me back. I just want to have a little time to myself . . . a little time to enjoy life.
Rose: What about me? When's my time to enjoy life?

Troy: I don't know what to tell you, Rose. I'm doing the best I can.

Rose: You ain't been home from work but time enough to change your clothes and run out . . . and you wanna call that the best you can do?

Troy: I'm going over to the hospital to see Alberta. She went into the hospital this afternoon. Look like she might have the baby early. I won't be gone long.

Rose: Well, you ought to know. They went over to Miss Pearl's and got Gabe today. She said you told them to go ahead and lock him up.

Troy: I ain't said no such thing. Whoever told you that is telling a lie. Pearl ain't doing nothing but telling a big fat lie.

Rose: She ain't had to tell me. I read it on the papers.

Troy: I ain't told them nothing of the kind.

Rose: I saw it right there on the papers.

Troy: What it say, huh?

Rose: It said you told them to take him.

Troy: Then they screwed that up, just the way they screw up everything. I ain't worried about what they got on the paper.

Rose: Say the government send part of his check to the hospital and the other part to you.

Troy: I ain't got nothing to do with that if that's the way it works. I ain't made up the rules about how it work.

Rose: You did Gabe just like you did Cory. You wouldn't sign the paper for Cory . . . but you signed for Gabe. You signed that paper.

The telephone is heard ringing inside the house.

Troy: I told you I ain't signed nothing, woman! The only thing I signed was the release form. Hell, I can't read, I don't know what they had on that paper! I ain't signed nothing about sending Gabe away.

Rose: I said send him to the hospital . . . you said let him be free . . . now you done went down there and signed him to the hospital for half his money. You went back on yourself, Troy. You gonna have to answer for that.

Troy: See now . . . you been over there talking to Miss Pearl. She done got mad cause she ain't getting Gabe's rent money. That's all it is. She's liable to say anything.

Rose: Troy, I seen where you signed the paper.

Troy: You ain't seen nothing I signed. What she doing got papers on my brother anyway? Miss Pearl telling a big fat lie. And I'm gonna tell her about it too! You ain't seen nothing I signed. Say . . . you ain't seen nothing I signed.

Rose exits into the house to answer the telephone. Presently she returns.

Rose: Troy . . . that was the hospital. Alberta had the baby.

Troy: What she have? What is it?

Rose: It's a girl.

Troy: I better get on down to the hospital to see her.

Rose: Troy . . .

Troy: Rose . . . I got to go see her now. That's only right . . . what's the matter . . . the baby's all right, ain't it?

Rose: Alberta died having the baby.

Troy: Died . . . you say she's dead? Alberta's dead?

Rose: They said they done all they could. They couldn't do nothing for her.

Troy: The baby? How's the baby?

Rose: They say it's healthy. I wonder who's gonna bury her.

Troy: She had family, Rose. She wasn't living in the world by herself.

Rose: I know she wasn't living in the world by herself.

Troy: Next thing you gonna want to know if she had any insurance.

Rose: Troy, you ain't got to talk like that.

Troy: That's the first thing that jumped out your mouth. "Who's gonna bury her?" Like I'm fixing to take on that task for myself.

Rose: I am your wife. Don't push me away.

Troy: I ain't pushing nobody away. Just give me some space. That's all. Just give me some room to breathe.

Rose exits into the house. Troy walks about the yard.

Troy (with a quiet rage that threatens to consume him): All right . . . Mr. Death. See now . . . I'm gonna tell you what I'm gonna do. I'm gonna take and build me a fence around this yard. See? I'm gonna build me a fence around what belongs to me. And then I want you to stay on the other side. See? You stay over there until you're ready for me. Then you come on. Bring your army. Bring your sickle. Bring your wrestling clothes. I ain't gonna fall down on my vigilance this time. You ain't gonna sneak up on me no more. When you ready for me . . . when the top of your list say Troy Maxson . . . that's when you come around here. You come up and knock on the front door. Ain't nobody else got nothing to do with this. This is between you and me. Man to man. You stay on the other side of that fence until you ready for me. Then you come up and knock on the front door. Anytime you want. I'll be ready for you.

The lights go down to black.

SCENE III

The lights come up on the porch. It is late evening three days later. Rose sits listening to the ball game waiting for Troy. The final out of the game is made and Rose switches off the radio. Troy enters the yard carrying an infant wrapped in blankets. He stands back from the house and calls.

Rose enters and stands on the porch. There is a long, awkward silence, the weight of which grows heavier with each passing second.

Troy: Rose . . . I'm standing here with my daughter in my arms. She ain't but a wee bittie little old thing. She don't know nothing about grownups' business. She innocent . . . and she ain't got no mama.

Rose: What you telling me for, Troy?

She turns and exits into the house.

Troy: Well . . . I guess we'll just sit out here on the porch.

He sits down on the porch. There is an awkward indelicateness about the way he handles the baby. His largeness engulfs and seems to swallow it. He speaks loud enough for Rose to hear.

A man's got to do what's right for him. I ain't sorry for nothing I done. It felt right in my heart. *(To the baby.)* What you smiling at? Your daddy's a big man. Got these great big old hands. But sometimes he's scared. And right now your daddy's scared cause we sitting out here and ain't got no home. Oh, I been homeless before. I ain't had no little baby with me. But I been homeless. You just be out on the road by your lonesome and you see one of them trains coming and you just kinda go like this . . .

He sings as a lullaby.

Please, Mr. Engineer let a man ride the line
Please, Mr. Engineer let a man ride the line
I ain't got no ticket please let me ride the blinds

Rose enters from the house. Troy, hearing her steps behind him, stands and faces her.

She's my daughter, Rose. My own flesh and blood. I can't deny her no more than I can deny them boys. *(Pause.)* You and them boys is my family. You and them and this child is all I got in the world. So I guess what I'm saying is . . . I'd appreciate it if you'd help me take care of her.

Rose: Okay, Troy . . . you're right. I'll take care of your baby for you . . . cause . . . like you say . . . she's innocent . . . and you can't visit the sins of the father upon the child. A motherless child has got a hard time. *(She takes the baby from him.)* From right now . . . this child got a mother. But you a womanless man.

Rose turns and exits into the house with the baby. Lights go down to black.

SCENE IV

It is two months later. Lyons enters from the street. He knocks on the door and calls.

Lyons: Hey, Rose! *(Pause.)* Rose!

Rose (from inside the house): Stop that yelling. You gonna wake up Raynell. I just got her to sleep.

Lyons: I just stopped by to pay Papa this twenty dollars I owe him. Where's Papa at?

Rose: He should be here in a minute. I'm getting ready to go down to the church. Sit down and wait on him.

Lyons: I got to go pick up Bonnie over her mother's house.

Rose: Well, sit it down there on the table. He'll get it.

Lyons (enters the house and sets the money on the table): Tell Papa I said thanks. I'll see you again.

Rose: All right, Lyons. We'll see you.

Lyons starts to exit as Cory enters.

Cory: Hey, Lyons.

Lyons: What's happening, Cory? Say man, I'm sorry I missed your graduation. You know I had a gig and couldn't get away. Otherwise, I would have been there, man. So what you doing?

Cory: I'm trying to find a job.

Lyons: Yeah I know how that go, man. It's rough out here. Jobs are scarce.

Cory: Yeah, I know.

Lyons: Look here, I got to run. Talk to Papa . . . he know some people. He'll be able to help get you a job. Talk to him . . . see what he say.

Cory: Yeah . . . all right, Lyons.

Lyons: You take care. I'll talk to you soon. We'll find some time to talk.

Lyons exits the yard. Cory wanders over to the tree, picks up the bat, and assumes a batting stance. He studies an imaginary pitcher and swings. Dissatisfied with the result, he tries again. Troy enters. They eye each other for a beat. Cory puts the bat down and exits the yard. Troy starts into the house as Rose exits with Raynell. She is carrying a cake.

Troy: I'm coming in and everybody's going out.

Rose: I'm taking this cake down to the church for the bake sale. Lyons was by to see you. He stopped by to pay you your twenty dollars. It's laying in there on the table.

Troy (going into his pocket): Well . . . here go this money.

Rose: Put it in there on the table, Troy. I'll get it.

Troy: What time you coming back?

Rose: Ain't no use in you studying me. It don't matter what time I come back.

Troy: I just asked you a question, woman. What's the matter . . . can't I ask you a question?

Rose: Troy, I don't want to go into it. Your dinner's in there on the stove. All you got to do is heat it up. And don't you be eating the rest of them cakes in there. I'm coming back for them. We having a bake sale at the church tomorrow.

Rose exits the yard. Troy sits down on the steps, takes a pint bottle from his pocket, opens it, and drinks. He begins to sing.

Troy: Hear it ring! Hear it ring!
    Had an old dog his name was Blue
    You know Blue was mighty true
    You know Blue was a good old dog
    Blue trees a possum in a hollow log
    You know from that he was a good old dog

Bono enters the yard.

Bono: Hey, Troy.

Troy: Hey, what's happening, Bono?

Bono: I just thought I'd stop by to see you.

Troy: What you stop by and see me for? You ain't stopped by in a month of Sundays. Hell, I must owe you money or something.

Bono: Since you got your promotion I can't keep up with you. Used to see you every day. Now I don't even know what route you working.

Troy: They keep switching me around. Got me out in Greentree now . . . . hauling white folks' garbage.

Bono: Greentree, huh? You lucky, at least you ain't got to be lifting them barrels. Damn if they ain't getting heavier. I'm gonna put in my two years and call it quits.

Troy: I'm thinking about retiring myself.

Bono: You got it easy. You can *drive* for another five years.

Troy: It ain't the same, Bono. It ain't like working the back of the truck. Ain't got nobody to talk to . . . feel like you working by yourself. Naw, I'm thinking about retiring. How's Lucille?

Bono: She all right. Her arthritis get to acting up on her sometime. Saw Rose on my way in. She going down to the church, huh?

Troy: Yeah, she took up going down there. All them preachers looking for somebody to fatten their pockets. *(Pause.)* Got some gin here.

Bono: Naw, thanks. I just stopped by to say hello.

Troy: Hell, nigger . . . you can take a drink. I ain't never known you to say no to a drink. You ain't got to work tomorrow.

Bono: I just stopped by. I'm fixing to go over to Skinner's. We got us a domino game going over his house every Friday.

Troy: Nigger, you can't play no dominoes. I used to whup you four games out of five.

Bono: Well, that learned me. I'm getting better.

Troy: Yeah? Well, that's all right.

Bono: Look here . . . I got to be getting on. Stop by sometime, huh?

Troy: Yeah, I'll do that, Bono. Lucille told Rose you bought her a new refrigerator.

Bono: Yeah, Rose told Lucille you had finally built your fence . . . so I figured we'd call it even.

Troy: I knew you would.

Bono: Yeah . . . okay. I'll be talking to you.

Troy: Yeah, take care, Bono. Good to see you. I'm gonna stop over.

Bono: Yeah. Okay, Troy.

Bono exits. Troy drinks from the bottle.

Troy: Old Blue died and I dig his grave
Let him down with a golden chain
Every night when I hear old Blue bark
I know Blue treed a possum in Noah's Ark.
Hear it ring! Hear it ring!

Cory enters the yard. They eye each other for a beat. Troy is sitting in the middle of the steps. Cory walks over.

Cory: I got to get by.

Troy: Say what? What's you say?

Cory: You in my way. I got to get by.

Troy: You got to get by where? This is my house. Bought and paid for. In full. Took me fifteen years. And if you wanna go in my house and I'm sitting on the steps . . . you say excuse me. Like your mama taught you.

Cory: Come on, Pop . . . I got to get by.

Cory starts to maneuver his way past Troy. Troy grabs his leg and shoves him back.

Troy: You just gonna walk over top of me?

Cory: I live here too!

Troy (advancing toward him): You just gonna walk over top of me in my own house?

Cory: I ain't scared of you.

Troy: I ain't asked if you was scared of me. I asked you if you was fixing to walk over top of me in my own house? That's the question. You ain't gonna say excuse me? You just gonna walk over top of me?

Cory: If you wanna put it like that.

Troy: How else am I gonna put it?

Cory: I was walking by you to go into the house cause you sitting on the steps drunk, singing to yourself. You can put it like that.

Troy: Without saying excuse me???

Cory doesn't respond.

I asked you a question. Without saying excuse me???

Cory: I ain't got to say excuse me to you. You don't count around here no more.

Troy: Oh, I see . . . I don't count around here no more. You ain't got to say excuse me to your daddy. All of a sudden you done got so grown that your daddy don't count around here no more . . . Around here in his own house and yard that he done paid for with the sweat of his brow. You done got so grown to where you gonna take over. You gonna take over my house. Is that right? You gonna wear my pants. You gonna go in there and stretch out on my bed. You ain't got to say excuse me cause I don't count around here no more. Is that right?

Cory: That's right. You always talking this dumb stuff. Now, why don't you just get out my way?

Troy: I guess you got someplace to sleep and something to put in your belly. You got that, huh? You got that? That's what you need. You got that, huh?

Cory: You don't know what I got. You ain't got to worry about what I got.

Troy: You right! You one hundred percent right! I done spent the last seventeen years worrying about what you got. Now it's your turn, see? I'll tell you what to do. You grown . . . we done established that. You a man. Now, let's see you act like one. Turn your behind around and walk out this yard. And when you get out there in the alley . . . you can forget about this house. See? Cause this is my house. You go on and be a man and get your own house. You can forget about this. Cause this is mine. You go on and get yours cause I'm through with doing for you.

Cory: You talking about what you did for me . . . what'd you ever give me?

Troy: Them feet and bones! That pumping heart, nigger! I give you more than anybody else is ever gonna give you.

Cory: You ain't never gave me nothing! You ain't never done nothing but hold me back. Afraid I was gonna be better than you. All you ever did was try and make me scared of you. I used to tremble every time you called my name. Every time I heard your footsteps in the house. Wondering all the time . . . what's Papa gonna say if I do this? . . . What's he gonna say if I do that? . . . What's Papa gonna say if I turn on the radio? And Mama, too . . . she tries . . . but she's scared of you.

Troy: You leave your mama out of this. She ain't got nothing to do with this.

Cory: I don't know how she stand you . . . after what you did to her.

Troy: I told you to leave your mama out of this!

He advances toward Cory.

Cory: What you gonna do . . . give me a whupping? You can't whup me no more. You're too old. You just an old man.

Troy (shoves him on his shoulder): Nigger! That's what you are. You just another nigger on the street to me!

Cory: You crazy! You know that?

Troy: Go on now! You got the devil in you. Get on away from me!

Cory: You just a crazy old man . . . talking about I got the devil in me.

Troy: Yeah, I'm crazy! If you don't get on the other side of that yard . . . I'm gonna show you how crazy I am! Go on . . . get the hell out of my yard.

Cory: It ain't your yard. You took Uncle Gabe's money he got from the army to buy this house and then you put him out.

Troy (advances on Cory): Get your black ass out of my yard!

Troy's advance backs Cory up against the tree. Cory grabs up the bat.

Cory: I ain't going nowhere! Come on . . . put me out! I ain't scared of you.

Troy: That's my bat!

Cory: Come on!

Troy: Put my bat down!

Cory: Come on, put me out.

Cory swings at Troy, who backs across the yard.

What's the matter? You so bad . . . put me out!

Troy advances toward Cory.

Cory (backing up): Come on! Come on!

Troy: You're gonna have to use it! You wanna draw that bat back on me . . . you're gonna have to use it.

Cory: Come on! . . . Come on!

Cory swings the bat at Troy a second time. He misses. Troy continues to advance toward him.

Troy: You're gonna have to kill me! You wanna draw that bat back on me. You're gonna have to kill me.

Cory, backed up against the tree, can go no farther. Troy taunts him. He sticks out his head and offers him a target.

Come on! Come on!

Cory is unable to swing the bat. Troy grabs it.

Troy: Then I'll show you.

Cory and Troy struggle over the bat. The struggle is fierce and fully engaged. Troy ultimately is the stronger and takes the bat from Cory and stands over him ready to swing. He stops himself.

Go on and get away from around my house.

Cory, stung by his defeat, picks himself up, walks slowly out of the yard and up the alley.

Cory: Tell Mama I'll be back for my things.

Troy: They'll be on the other side of that fence.

Cory exits.

Troy: I can't taste nothing. Helluljah! I can't taste nothing no more. *(Troy assumes a batting posture and begins to taunt Death, the fastball on the outside corner.)* Come on! It's between you and me now! Come on! Anytime you want! Come on! I be ready for you . . . but I ain't gonna be easy.

The lights go down on the scene.

SCENE V

The time is 1965. The lights come up in the yard. It is the morning of Troy's funeral. A funeral plaque with a light hangs beside the door. There is a small garden plot off to the side. There is noise and activity in the house as Rose, Gabriel, and Bono have gathered. The door opens and Raynell, seven years old, enters dressed in a flannel nightgown. She crosses to the garden and pokes around with a stick. Rose calls from the house.

Rose: Raynell!
Raynell: Mam?
Rose: What you doing out there?
Raynell: Nothing.

Rose comes to the door.

Rose: Girl, get in here and get dressed. What you doing?
Raynell: Seeing if my garden growed.
Rose: I told you it ain't gonna grow overnight. You got to wait.
Raynell: It don't look like it never gonna grow. Dag!
Rose: I told you a watched pot never boils. Get in here and get dressed.
Raynell: This ain't even no pot, Mama.
Rose: You just have to give it a chance. It'll grow. Now you come on and do what I told you. We got to be getting ready. This ain't no morning to be playing around. You hear me?
Raynell: Yes, mam.

Rose exits into the house. Raynell continues to poke at her garden with a stick. Cory enters. He is dressed in a Marine corporal's uniform, and carries a duffel bag. His posture is that of a military man, and his speech has a clipped sternness.

Cory (to Raynell): Hi. *(Pause.)* I bet your name is Raynell.
Raynell: Uh huh.
Cory: Is your mama home?

Raynell runs up on the porch and calls through the screen door.

Raynell: Mama . . . there's some man out here. Mama?

Rose comes to the door.
Rose: Cory? Lord have mercy! Look here, you all!

Rose and Cory embrace in a tearful reunion as Bono and Lyons enter from the house dressed in funeral clothes.

Bono: Aw, looka here . . .

Rose: Done got all grown up!

Cory: Don't cry, Mama. What you crying about?

Rose: I'm just so glad you made it.

Cory: Hey Lyons. How you doing, Mr. Bono.

Lyons goes to embrace Cory.

Lyons: Look at you, man. Look at you. Don't he look good, Rose. Got them Corporal stripes.

Rose: What took you so long?

Cory: You know how the Marines are, Mama. They got to get all their paperwork straight before they let you do anything.

Rose: Well, I'm sure glad you made it. They let Lyons come. Your Uncle Gabe's still in the hospital. They don't know if they gonna let him out or not. I just talked to them a little while ago.

Lyons: A Corporal in the United States Marines.

Bono: Your daddy knew you had it in you. He used to tell me all the time.

Lyons: Don't he look good, Mr. Bono?

Bono: Yeah, he remind me of Troy when I first met him. *(Pause.)* Say, Rose, Lucille's down at the church with the choir. I'm gonna go down and get the pallbearers lined up. I'll be back to get you all.

Rose: Thanks, Jim.

Cory: See you, Mr. Bono.

Lyons (with his arm around Raynell): Cory . . . look at Raynell. Ain't she precious? She gonna break a whole lot of hearts.

Rose: Raynell, come and say hello to your brother. This is your brother, Cory. You remember Cory.

Raynell: No, Mam.

Cory: She don't remember me, Mama.

Rose: Well, we talk about you. She heard us talk about you. *(To Raynell.)* This is your brother, Cory. Come on and say hello.

Raynell: Hi.

Cory: Hi. So you're Raynell. Mama told me a lot about you.

Rose: You all come on into the house and let me fix you some breakfast. Keep up your strength.

Cory: I ain't hungry, Mama.

Lyons: You can fix me something, Rose. I'll be in there in a minute.

Rose: Cory, you sure you don't want nothing? I know they ain't feeding you right.

Cory: No, Mama . . . thanks. I don't feel like eating. I'll get something later.

Rose: Raynell . . . get on upstairs and get that dress on like I told you.

Rose and Raynell exit into the house.

Lyons: So . . . I hear you thinking about getting married.

Cory: Yeah, I done found the right one, Lyons. It's about time.

Lyons: Me and Bonnie been split up about four years now. About the time Papa retired. I guess she just got tired of all them changes I was putting her through. *(Pause.)* I always knew you was gonna make something out yourself. Your head was always in the right direction. So . . . you gonna stay in . . . make it a career . . . put in your twenty years?

Cory: I don't know. I got six already, I think that's enough.

Lyons: Stick with Uncle Sam and retire early. Ain't nothing out here. I guess Rose told you what happened with me. They got me down the workhouse. I thought I was being slick cashing other people's checks.

Cory: How much time you doing?

Lyons: They give me three years. I got that beat now. I ain't got but nine more months. It ain't so bad. You learn to deal with it like anything else. You got to take the crookeds with the straights. That's what Papa used to say. He used to say that when he struck out. I seen him strike out three times in a row . . . and the next time up he hit the ball over the grandstand. Right out there in Homestead Field. He wasn't satisfied hitting in the seats . . . he want to hit it over everything! After the game he had two hundred people standing around waiting to shake his hand. You got to take the crookeds with the straights. Yeah, Papa was something else.

Cory: You still playing?

Lyons: Cory . . . you know I'm gonna do that. There's some fellows down there we got us a band . . . we gonna try and stay together when we get out . . . but yeah, I'm still playing. It still helps me to get out of bed in the morning. As long as it do that I'm gonna be right there playing and trying to make some sense out of it.

Rose (calling): Lyons, I got these eggs in the pan.

Lyons: Let me go on and get these eggs, man. Get ready to go bury Papa. *(Pause.)* How you doing? You doing all right?

Cory nods. Lyons touches him on the shoulder and they share a moment of silent grief. Lyons exits into the house. Cory wanders about the yard. Raynell enters.

Raynell: Hi.

Cory: Hi.

Raynell: Did you used to sleep in my room?

Cory: Yeah . . . that used to be my room.

Raynell: That's what Papa call it. "Cory's room." It got your football in the closet.

Rose comes to the door.

Rose: Raynell, get in there and get them good shoes on.

Raynell: Mama, can't I wear these? Them other one hurt my feet.

Rose: Well, they just gonna have to hurt your feet for a while. You ain't said they hurt your feet when you went down to the store and got them.

Raynell: They didn't hurt then. My feet done got bigger.

Rose: Don't you give me no backtalk now. You get in there and get them shoes on.

Raynell exits into the house.

Ain't too much changed. He still got that piece of rag tied to that tree. He was out here swinging that bat. I was just ready to go back in the house. He swung that bat and then he just fell over. Seem like he swung it and stood there with this grin on his face . . . and then he just fell over. They carried him on down to the hospital, but I knew there wasn't no need . . . why don't you come on in the house?

Cory: Mama . . . I got something to tell you. I don't know how to tell you this . . . but I've got to tell you . . . I'm not going to Papa's funeral.

Rose: Boy, hush your mouth. That's your daddy you talking about. I don't want hear that kind of talk this morning. I done raised you to come to this? You standing there all healthy and grown talking about you ain't going to your daddy's funeral?

Cory: Mama . . . listen . . .

Rose: I don't want to hear it, Cory. You just get that thought out of your head.

Cory: I can't drag Papa with me everywhere I go. I've got to say no to him. One time in my life I've got to say no.

Rose: Don't nobody have to listen to nothing like that. I know you and your daddy ain't seen eye to eye, but I ain't got to listen to that kind of talk this morning. Whatever was between you and your daddy . . . the time has come to put it aside. Just take it and set it over there on the shelf and forget about it. Disrespecting your daddy ain't gonna make you a man, Cory. You got to find a way to come to that on your own. Not going to your daddy's funeral ain't gonna make you a man.

Cory: The whole time I was growing up . . . living in his house . . . Papa was like a shadow that followed you everywhere. It weighed on you and sunk into your flesh. It would wrap around you and lay there until you couldn't tell which one was you anymore. That shadow digging in your flesh. Trying to crawl in. Trying to live through you. Everywhere I looked, Troy Maxson was staring back at me . . . hiding under the bed . . . in the closet. I'm just saying I've got to find a way to get rid of that shadow, Mama.

Rose: You just like him. You got him in you good.

Cory: Don't tell me that, Mama.

Rose: You Troy Maxson all over again.

Cory: I don't want to be Troy Maxson. I want to be me.

Rose: You can't be nobody but who you are, Cory. That shadow wasn't nothing but you growing into yourself. You either got to grow into it or cut it down to fit you. But that's all you got to make life with. That's all you got to measure yourself against that world out there. Your daddy wanted you to be everything he wasn't . . . and at the same time he tried to make you into everything he was. I don't know if he was right or wrong . . . but I do know he meant to do more good than he meant to do harm. He wasn't always right. Sometimes when he touched he bruised. And sometimes when he took me in his arms he cut.

When I first met your daddy I thought . . . Here is a man I can lay down with and make a baby. That's the first thing I thought when I seen him. I was thirty years old and had done seen my share of men. But when he walked up to me and said, "I can dance a waltz that'll make you dizzy," I thought, Rose Lee, here is a man that you can open yourself up to and be filled to bursting. Here is a man that can fill all them empty spaces you been tipping around the edges of. One of them empty spaces was being somebody's mother.

I married your daddy and settled down to cooking his supper and keeping clean sheets on the bed. When your daddy walked through the house he was so big he filled it up. That was my first mistake. Not to make him leave some room for me. For my part in the matter. But at that time I wanted that. I wanted a house that I could sing in. And that's what your daddy gave me. I didn't know to keep up his strength I had to give up little pieces of mine. I did that. I took on his life as mine and mixed up the pieces so that you couldn't hardly tell which was which anymore. It was my choice. It was my life and I didn't have to live it like that. But that's what life offered me in the way of being a woman and I took it. I grabbed hold of it with both hands.

By the time Raynell came into the house, me and your daddy had done lost touch with one another. I didn't want to make my blessing off of nobody's misfortune . . . but I took on to Raynell like she was all them babies I had wanted and never had.

The phone rings.

Like I'd been blessed to relive a part of my life. And if the Lord see fit to keep up my strength . . . I'm gonna do her just like your daddy did you . . . I'm gonna give her the best of what's in me.

Raynell (entering, still with her old shoes): Mama . . . Reverend Tollivier on the phone.

Rose exits into the house.

Raynell: Hi.
Cory: Hi.
Raynell: You in the Army or the Marines?
Cory: Marines.
Raynell: Papa said it was the Army. Did you know Blue?
Cory: Blue? Who's Blue?
Raynell: Papa's dog what he sing about all the time.
Cory (singing): Hear it ring! Hear it ring!
  I had a dog his name was Blue
  You know Blue was mighty true
  You know Blue was a good old dog
  Blue treed a possum in a hollow log
  You know from that he was a good old dog.
  Hear it ring! Hear it ring!

Raynell joins in singing.

Cory and Raynell: Blue treed a possum out on a limb
  Blue looked at me and I looked at him
  Grabbed that possum and put him in a sack
  Blue stayed there till I came back
  Old Blue's feets was big and round
  Never allowed a possum to touch the ground.

  Old Blue died and I dug his grave
  I dug his grave with a silver spade
  Let him down with a golden chain
  And every night I call his name
  Go on Blue, you good dog you
  Go on Blue, you good dog you

Raynell: Blue laid down and died like a man
　　Blue laid down and died . . .
Both: Blue laid down and died like a man
　　Now he's treeing possums in the Promised Land
　　I'm gonna tell you this to let you know
　　Blue's gone where the good dogs go
　　When I hear old Blue bark
　　When I hear old Blue bark
　　Blue treed a possum in Noah's Ark
　　Blue treed a possum in Noah's Ark.

Rose comes to the screen door.

Rose: Cory, we gonna be ready to go in a minute.
Cory (to Raynell): You go on in the house and change them shoes like Mama
　　told you so we can go to Papa's funeral.
Raynell: Okay, I'll be back.

*Raynell exits into the house. Cory gets up and crosses over to the tree. Rose stands
in the screen door watching him. Gabriel enters from the alley.*

Gabriel (calling): Hey, Rose!
Rose: Gabe?
Gabriel: I'm here, Rose. Hey Rose, I'm here!

Rose enters from the house.

Rose: Lord . . . Look here, Lyons!
Lyons: See, I told you, Rose . . . I told you they'd let him come.
Cory: How you doing, Uncle Gabe?
Lyons: How you doing, Uncle Gabe?
Gabriel: Hey, Rose. It's time. It's time to tell St. Peter to open the gates. Troy,
　　you ready? You ready, Troy. I'm gonna tell St. Peter to open the gates. You
　　get ready now.

*Gabriel, with great fanfare, braces himself to blow. The trumpet is without a
mouthpiece. He puts the end of it into his mouth and blows with great force, like
a man who has been waiting some twenty-odd years for this single moment. No
sound comes out of the trumpet. He braces himself and blows again with the
same result. A third time he blows. There is a weight of impossible description
that falls away and leaves him bare and exposed to a frightful realization. It is
a trauma that a sane and normal mind would be unable to withstand. He
begins to dance. A slow, strange dance, eerie and life-giving. A dance of atavistic
signature and ritual. Lyons attempts to embrace him. Gabriel pushes Lyons away.
He begins to howl in what is an attempt at song, or perhaps a song turning
back into itself in an attempt at speech. He finishes his dance and the gates of
heaven stand open as wide as God's closet.*

　　That's the way that go!

Connections to Other Selections

1. Compare and contrast Troy Maxson with Willy Loman in Miller's *Death of a Salesman* (p. 1712). How do these protagonists relate to their sons?
2. How might the narrator's experiences in Ralph Ellison's short story "Battle Royal" (p. 187) be used to shed light on Troy's conflicts in *Fences*?
3. Consider how the titles for Soyinka's *The Strong Breed* (p. 1846) and Wilson's *Fences* might be used interchangeably.

M. BUTTERFLY

David Henry Hwang is the son of immigrant Chinese-American parents. Educated at Stanford University, he had his first play, *FOB,* produced there in his senior year and subsequently staged at the New York Shakespeare Festival's Public Theater; it won an Obie Award in 1981. His other plays include *The Dance and the Railroad* (1981), *Family Devotions* (1981), and two one-act plays, *The House of Sleeping Beauties* (1983) and *The Sound of a Voice* (1983), all of which were produced at the Public Theater. *Broken Promises* (1983) is a collection of four of his plays.

M. Butterfly premiered in 1988 and quickly claimed several major prizes: the Outer Critics Circle Award for best Broadway play, the Drama Desk Award for best new play, the John Gassner Award for best American play, and the Tony Award for best play of the year. Hwang is already regarded as one of the most interesting and talented young playwrights in the United States, and *M. Butterfly,* based on a fascinating story of espionage and astonishing sexual misidentification, dazzles both audiences and readers with its remarkable eroticism, insights, and beauty.

DAVID HENRY HWANG (b. 1957)
M. Butterfly   1988

The Characters

Rene Gallimard
Song Liling
Marc/Man No. 2/Consul Sharpless
Renee/Woman at Party/Pinup Girl
Comrade Chin/Suzuki/Shu-Fang
Helga
Toulon/Man No. 1/Judge
Dancers

Time and Place

The action of the play takes place in a Paris prison in the present, and, in recall, during the decade 1960–1970 in Beijing, and from 1966 to the present in Paris.

Playwright's Notes

A former French diplomat and a Chinese opera singer have been sentenced to six years in jail for spying for China after a two-day trial that traced a story of clandestine love and mistaken sexual identity. . . .

Mr. Bouriscot was accused of passing information to China after he fell in love with Mr. Shi, whom he believed for twenty years to be a woman.

– The New York Times, May 11, 1986

This play was suggested by international newspaper accounts of a recent espionage trial. For purposes of dramatization, names have been changed, characters created, and incidents devised or altered, and this play does not purport to be a factual record of real events or real people.

I could escape this feeling
With my China girl . . . .

– David Bowie & Iggy Pop

ACT I

SCENE I

M. Gallimard's prison cell. Paris. 1988.

Lights fade up to reveal Rene Gallimard, sixty-five, in a prison cell. He wears a comfortable bathrobe, and looks old and tired. The sparsely furnished cell contains a wooden crate, upon which sits a hot plate with a kettle, and a portable tape recorder. Gallimard sits on the crate staring at the recorder, a sad smile on his face.

Upstage Song, who appears as a beautiful woman in traditional Chinese garb, dances a traditional piece from the Peking Opera, surrounded by the percussive clatter of Chinese music.

Then, slowly, lights and sound cross-fade; the Chinese opera music dissolves into a Western opera, the "Love Duet" from Puccini's Madame Butterfly. *Song continues dancing, now to the Western accompaniment. Though her movements are the same, the difference in music now gives them a balletic quality.*

Gallimard rises, and turns upstage towards the figure of Song, who dances without acknowledging him.

Gallimard: Butterfly, Butterfly . . .

He forces himself to turn away, as the image of Song fades out, and talks to us.

Gallimard: The limits of my cell are as such: four-and-a-half meters by five. There's one window against the far wall; a door, very strong, to protect me from autograph hounds. I'm responsible for the tape recorder, the hot plate, and this charming coffee table.

When I want to eat, I'm marched off to the dining room — hot, steaming slop appears on my plate. When I want to sleep, the light bulb turns itself off — the work of fairies. It's an enchanted space I occupy. The French — we know how to run a prison.

But, to be honest, I'm not treated like an ordinary prisoner. Why? Because I'm a celebrity. You see, I make people laugh.

I never dreamed this day would arrive. I've never been considered witty or clever. In fact, as a young boy, in an informal poll among my grammar school classmates, I was voted "least likely to be invited to a party." It's a title I managed to hold on to for many years. Despite some stiff competition.

But now, how the tables turn! Look at me: the life of every social function in Paris. Paris? Why be modest: My fame has spread to Amsterdam, London, New York. Listen to them! In the world's smartest parlors. I'm the one who lifts their spirits!

With a flourish, Gallimard directs our attention to another part of the stage.

SCENE II

A party. 1988.
    Lights go up on a chic-looking parlor, where a well-dressed trio, two men and one woman, make conversation. Gallimard also remains lit; he observes them from his cell.

Woman: And what of Gallimard?
Man 1: Gallimard?
Man 2: Gallimard!
Gallimard (to us): You see? They're all determined to say my name, as if it were some new dance.
Woman: He still claims not to believe the truth.
Man 1: What? Still? Even since the trial?
Woman: Yes. Isn't it mad?
Man 2 (laughing): He says . . . it was dark . . . and she was very modest!

The trio break into laughter.

Man 1: So — what? He never touched her with his hands?
Man 2: Perhaps he did, and simply misidentified the equipment. A compelling case for sex education in the schools.
Woman: To protect the National Security — the Church can't argue with that.
Man 1: That's impossible! How could he not know?
Man 2: Simple ignorance.
Man 1: For twenty years?
Man 2: Time flies when you're being stupid.
Woman: Well, I thought the French were ladies' men.
Man 2: It seems Monsieur Gallimard was overly anxious to live up to his national reputation.
Woman: Well, he's not very good-looking.
Man 1: No, he's not.
Man 2: Certainly not.
Woman: Actually, I feel sorry for him.
Man 2: A toast! To Monsieur Gallimard!

Woman: Yes! To Gallimard!
Man 1: To Gallimard!
Man 2: Vive la différence!

They toast, laughing. Lights down on them.

SCENE III

M. Gallimard's cell.

Gallimard (smiling): You see? They toast me. I've become a patron saint of the socially inept. Can they really be so foolish? Men like that — they should be scratching at my door, begging to learn my secrets! For I, Rene Gallimard, you see, I have known, and been loved by . . . the Perfect Woman.

Alone in this cell, I sit night after night, watching our story play through my head, always searching for a new ending, one which redeems my honor, where she returns at last to my arms. And I imagine you — my ideal audience — who come to understand and even, perhaps just a little, to envy me.

He turns on his tape recorder. Over the house speakers, we hear the opening phrases of Madame Butterfly.

Gallimard: In order for you to understand what I did and why, I must introduce you to my favorite opera: *Madame Butterfly.* By Giacomo Puccini. First produced at La Scala, Milan, in 1904, it is now beloved throughout the Western world.

As Gallimard describes the opera, the tape segues in and out to sections he may be describing.

Gallimard: And why not? Its heroine, Cio-Cio-San, also known as Butterfly, is a feminine ideal, beautiful and brave. And its hero, the man for whom she gives up everything, is — *(He pulls out a naval officer's cap from under his crate, pops it on his head, and struts about.)* — not very good-looking, not too bright, and pretty much a wimp: Benjamin Franklin Pinkerton of the U.S. Navy. As the curtain rises, he's just closed on two great bargains: one on a house, the other on a woman — call it a package deal.

Pinkerton purchased the rights to Butterfly for one hundred yen — in modern currency, equivalent to about . . . sixty-six cents. So, he's feeling pretty pleased with himself as Sharpless, the American consul, arrives to witness the marriage.

Marc, wearing an official cap to designate Sharpless, enters and plays the character.

Sharpless/Marc: Pinkerton!

Pinkerton/Gallimard: Sharpless! How's it hangin'? It's a great day, just great. Between my house, my wife, and the rickshaw ride in from town, I've saved nineteen cents just this morning.

Sharpless: Wonderful. I can see the inscription on your tombstone already: "I saved a dollar, here I lie." *(He looks around.)* Nice house.

Pinkerton: It's artistic. Artistic, don't you think? Like the way the shoji screens slide open to reveal the wet bar and disco mirror ball? Classy, huh? Great for impressing the chicks.

Sharpless: "Chicks"? Pinkerton, you're going to be a married man!

Pinkerton: Well, sort of.

Sharpless: What do you mean?

Pinkerton: This country — Sharpless, it is okay. You got all these geisha girls running around —

Sharpless: I know! I live here!

Pinkerton: Then, you know the marriage laws, right? I split for one month, it's annulled!

Sharpless: Leave it to you to read the fine print. Who's the lucky girl?

Pinkerton: Cio-Cio-San. Her friends call her Butterfly. Sharpless, she eats out of my hand!

Sharpless: She's probably very hungry.

Pinkerton: Not like American girls. It's true what they say about Oriental girls. They want to be treated bad!

Sharpless: Oh, please!

Pinkerton: It's true!

Sharpless: Are you serious about this girl?

Pinkerton: I'm marrying her, aren't I?

Sharpless: Yes — with generous trade-in terms.

Pinkerton: When I leave, she'll know what it's like to have loved a real man. And I'll even buy her a few nylons.

Sharpless: You aren't planning to take her with you?

Pinkerton: Huh? Where?

Sharpless: Home!

Pinkerton: You mean, America? Are you crazy? Can you see her trying to buy rice in St. Louis?

Sharpless: So, you're not serious.

Pause

Pinkerton/Gallimard (as Pinkerton): Consul, I am a sailor in port. *(as Gallimard.)* They then proceed to sing the famous duet, "The Whole World Over."

The duet plays on the speakers. Gallimard, as Pinkerton, lip-syncs his lines from the opera.

Gallimard: To give a rough translation: "The whole world over, the Yankee travels, casting his anchor wherever he wants. Life's not worth living unless he can win the hearts of the fairest maidens, then hotfoot it off the premises ASAP." *(He turns towards Marc.)* In the preceding scene, I played Pinkerton, the womanizing cad, and my friend Marc from school . . . *(Marc bows grandly for our benefit.)* played Sharpless, the sensitive soul of reason. In life, however, our positions were usually — no, always — reversed.

Scene IV

École Nationale.° Aix-en-Provence. 1947.

Gallimard: No, Marc, I think I'd rather stay home.

Marc: Are you crazy?! We are going to Dad's condo in Marseilles! You know what happened last time?

Gallimard: Of course I do.

Marc: Of course you don't! You never know. . . . They stripped, Rene!

Gallimard: Who stripped?

Marc: The girls!

Gallimard: Girls? Who said anything about girls?

Marc: Rene, we're a buncha university guys goin' up to the woods. What are we gonna do — talk philosophy?

Gallimard: What girls? Where do you get them?

Marc: Who cares? The point is, they come. On trucks. Packed in like sardines. The back flips open, babes hop out, we're ready to roll.

Gallimard: You mean, they just — ?

Marc: Before you know it, every last one of them — they're stripped and splashing around my pool. There's no moon out, they can't see what's going on, their boobs are flapping, right? You close your eyes, reach out — it's grab bag, get it? Doesn't matter whose ass is between whose legs, whose teeth are sinking into who. You're just in there, going at it, eyes closed, on and on for as long as you can stand. *(Pause.)* Some fun, huh?

Gallimard: What happens in the morning?

Marc: In the morning, you're ready to talk some philosophy. *(Beat.)* So how 'bout it?

Gallimard: Marc, I can't . . . I'm afraid they'll say no — the girls. So I never ask.

Marc: You don't have to ask! That's the beauty — don't you see? They don't have to say yes. It's perfect for a guy like you, really.

Gallimard: You go ahead . . . I may come later.

Marc: Hey, Rene — it doesn't matter that you're clumsy and got zits — they're not looking!

Gallimard: Thank you very much.

Marc: Wimp.

Marc walks over to the other side of the stage, and starts waving and smiling at women in the audience.

Gallimard (to us): We now return to my version of *Madame Butterfly* and the events leading to my recent conviction for treason.

Gallimard notices Marc making lewd gestures.

Gallimard: Marc, what are you doing?

Marc: Huh? *(Sotto voce.)* Rene, there're a lotta great babes out there. They're probably lookin' at me and thinking, "What a dangerous guy."

École Nationale: National School.

Gallimard: Yes — how could they help but be impressed by your cool sophistication?

Gallimard pops the Sharpless cap on Marc's head, and points him offstage. Marc exits, leering.

Scene V

M. Gallimard's cell.

Gallimard: Next, Butterfly makes her entrance. We learn her age — fifteen . . . but very mature for her years.

Lights come up on the area where we saw Song dancing at the top of the play. She appears there again, now dressed as Madame Butterfly, moving to the "Love Duet." Gallimard turns upstage slightly to watch, transfixed.

Gallimard: But as she glides past him, beautiful, laughing softly behind her fan, don't we who are men sigh with hope? We, who are not handsome, nor brave, nor powerful, yet somehow believe, like Pinkerton, that we deserve a Butterfly. She arrives with all her possessions in the folds of her sleeves, lays them all out, for her man to do with as he pleases. Even her life itself — she bows her head as she whispers that she's not even worth the hundred yen he paid for her. He's already given too much, when we know he's really had to give nothing at all.

Music and lights on Song out. Gallimard sits at his crate.

Gallimard: In real life, women who put their total worth at less than sixty-six cents are quite hard to find. The closest we come is in the pages of these magazines. *(He reaches into his crate, pulls out a stack of girlie magazines, and begins flipping through them.)* Quite a necessity in prison. For three or four dollars, you get seven or eight women.

    I first discovered these magazines at my uncle's house. One day, as a boy of twelve. The first time I saw them in his closet . . . all lined up — my body shook. Not with lust — no, with power. Here were women — a shelf-ful — who would do exactly as I wanted.

The "Love Duet" creeps in over the speakers. Special comes up, revealing, not Song this time, but a pinup girl in a sexy negligee, her back to us. Gallimard turns upstage and looks at her.

Girl: I know you're watching me.
Gallimard: My throat . . . it's dry.
Girl: I leave my blinds open every night before I go to bed.
Gallimard: I can't move.
Girl: I leave my blinds open and the lights on.
Gallimard: I'm shaking. My skin is hot, but my penis is soft. Why?
Girl: I stand in front of the window.
Gallimard: What is she going to do?
Girl: I toss my hair, and I let my lips part . . . barely.
Gallimard: I shouldn't be seeing this. It's so dirty. I'm so bad.
Girl: Then, slowly, I lift off my nightdress.
Gallimard: Oh, god. I can't believe it. I can't —

Girl: I toss it to the ground.

Gallimard: Now, she's going to walk away. She's going to —

Girl: I stand there, in the light, displaying myself.

Gallimard: No. She's — why is she naked?

Girl: To you.

Gallimard: In front of a window? This is wrong. No —

Girl: Without shame.

Gallimard: No, she must . . . like it.

Girl: I like it.

Gallimard: She . . . she wants me to see.

Girl: I want you to see.

Gallimard: I can't believe it! She's getting excited!

Girl: I can't see you. You can do whatever you want.

Gallimard: I can't do a thing. Why?

Girl: What would you like me to do . . . next?

Lights go down on her. Music off. Silence, as Gallimard puts away his magazines. Then he resumes talking to us.

Gallimard: Act Two begins with Butterfly staring at the ocean. Pinkerton's been called back to the U.S., and he's given his wife a detailed schedule of his plans. In the column marked "return date," he's written "when the robins nest." This failed to ignite her suspicions. Now, three years have passed without a peep from him. Which brings a response from her faithful servant, Suzuki.

Comrade Chin enters, playing Suzuki.

Suzuki: Girl, he's a loser. What'd he ever give you? Nineteen cents and those ugly Day-Glo stockings? Look, it's finished! Kaput! Done! And you should be glad! I mean, the guy was a woofer! He tried before, you know — before he met you, he went down to geisha central and plunked down his spare change in front of the usual candidates — everyone else gagged! These are hungry prostitutes, and they were not interested, get the picture? Now, stop slathering when an American ship sails in, and let's make some bucks — I mean, yen! We are broke!

Now, what about Yamadori? Hey, hey — don't look away — the man is a prince — figuratively, and, what's even better, literally. He's rich, he's handsome, he says he'll die if you don't marry him — and he's even willing to overlook the little fact that you've been deflowered all over the place by a foreign devil. What do you mean, "But he's Japanese?" What do you think you are? You think you've been touched by the whitey god? He was a sailor with dirty hands!

Suzuki stalks offstage.

Gallimard: She's also visited by Consul Sharpless, sent by Pinkerton on a minor errand.

Marc enters, as Sharpless.

Sharpless: I hate this job.

Gallimard: This Pinkerton — he doesn't show up personally to tell his wife he's abandoning her. No, he sends a government diplomat . . . at taxpayers' expense.

Sharpless: Butterfly? Butterfly? I have some bad — I'm going to be ill. Butterfly, I came to tell you —

Gallimard: Butterfly says she knows he'll return and if he doesn't she'll kill herself rather than go back to her own people. *(Beat.)* This causes a lull in the conversation.

Sharpless: Let's put it this way . . .

Gallimard: Butterfly runs into the next room, and returns holding —

Sound cue: a baby crying. Sharpless, "seeing" this, backs away.

Sharpless: Well, good. Happy to see things going so well. I suppose I'll be going now. Ta ta. Ciao. *(He turns away. Sound cue out.)* I hate this job. *(He exits.)*

Gallimard: At that moment, Butterfly spots in the harbor an American ship — the *Abramo Lincoln!*

Music cue: "The Flower Duet." Song, still dressed as Butterfly, changes into a wedding kimono, moving to the music.

Gallimard: This is the moment that redeems her years of waiting. With Suzuki's help, they cover the room with flowers —

Chin, as Suzuki, trudges onstage and drops a lone flower without much enthusiasm.

Gallimard: — and she changes into her wedding dress to prepare for Pinkerton's arrival.

Suzuki helps Butterfly change. Helga enters, and helps Gallimard change into a tuxedo.

Gallimard: I married a woman older than myself — Helga.

Helga: My father was ambassador to Australia. I grew up among criminals and kangaroos.

Gallimard: Hearing that brought me to the altar —

Helga exits.

Gallimard: — where I took a vow renouncing love. No fantasy woman would ever want me, so, yes, I would settle for a quick leap up the career ladder. Passion, I banish, and in its place — practicality!

But my vows had long since lost their charm by the time we arrived in China. The sad truth is that all men want a beautiful woman, and the uglier the man, the greater the want.

Suzuki makes final adjustments of Butterfly's costume, as does Gallimard of his tuxedo.

Gallimard: I married late, at age thirty-one. I was faithful to my marriage for eight years. Until the day when, as a junior-level diplomat in puritanical Peking, in a parlor at the German ambassador's house, during the "Reign of a Hundred Flowers,"° I first saw her . . . singing the death scene from *Madame Butterfly.*

Suzuki runs offstage.

SCENE VI

German ambassador's house. Beijing. 1960.
    The upstage special area now becomes a stage. Several chairs face upstage, representing seating for some twenty guests in the parlor. A few "diplomats" — Renee, Marc, Toulon — in formal dress enter and take seats.
    Gallimard also sits down, but turns towards us and continues to talk. Orchestral accompaniment on the tape is now replaced by a simple piano. Song picks up the death scene from the point where Butterfly uncovers the hara-kiri knife.

Gallimard: The ending is pitiful. Pinkerton, in an act of great courage, stays home and sends his American wife to pick up Butterfly's child. The truth, long deferred, has come up to her door.

Song, playing Butterfly, sings the lines from the opera in her own voice — which, though not classical, should be decent.

Song: "Con onor muore / chi non puo serbar / vita con onore."
Gallimard (simultaneously): "Death with honor / Is better than life / Life with dishonor."

The stage is illuminated; we are now completely within an elegant diplomat's residence. Song proceeds to play out an abbreviated death scene. Everyone in the room applauds. Song, shyly, takes her bows. Others in the room rush to congratulate her. Gallimard remains with us.

Gallimard: They say in opera the voice is everything. That's probably why I'd never before enjoyed opera. Here . . . here was a Butterfly with little or no voice — but she had the grace, the delicacy . . . I believed this girl. I believed her suffering. I wanted to take her in my arms — so delicate, even I could protect her, take her home, pamper her until she smiled.

Over the course of the preceding speech, Song has broken from the upstage crowd and moved directly upstage of Gallimard.

Song: Excuse me. Monsieur . . . ?

Gallimard turns upstage, shocked.

Gallimard: Oh! Gallimard. Mademoiselle . . . ? A beautiful . . .
Song: Song Liling.
Gallimard: A beautiful performance.
Song: Oh, please.
Gallimard: I usually —
Song: You make me blush. I'm no opera singer at all.

"Reign of a Hundred Flowers": A brief period in 1957 when freedom of expression was allowed in China.

Gallimard: I usually don't like *Butterfly.*

Song: I can't blame you in the least.

Gallimard: I mean, the story —

Song: Ridiculous.

Gallimard: I like the story, but . . . what?

Song: Oh, you like it?

Gallimard: I . . . what I mean is, I've always seen it played by huge women in so much bad makeup.

Song: Bad makeup is not unique to the West.

Gallimard: But, who can believe them?

Song: And you believe me?

Gallimard: Absolutely. You were utterly convincing. It's the first time —

Song: Convincing? As a Japanese woman? The Japanese used hundreds of our people for medical experiments during the war, you know. But I gather such an irony is lost on you.

Gallimard: No! I was about to say, it's the first time I've seen the beauty of the story.

Song: Really?

Gallimard: Of her death. It's a . . . a pure sacrifice. He's unworthy, but what can she do? She loves him . . . so much. It's a very beautiful story.

Song: Well, yes, to a Westerner.

Gallimard: Excuse me?

Song: It's one of your favorite fantasies, isn't it? The submissive Oriental woman and the cruel white man.

Gallimard: Well, I didn't quite mean . . .

Song: Consider it this way: what would you say if a blonde homecoming queen fell in love with a short Japanese businessman? He treats her cruelly, then goes home for three years, during which time she prays to his picture and turns down marriage from a young Kennedy. Then, when she learns he has remarried, she kills herself. Now, I believe you would consider this girl to be a deranged idiot, correct? But because it's an Oriental who kills herself for a Westerner — ah! — you find it beautiful.

Silence.

Gallimard: Yes . . . well . . . I see your point . . .

Song: I will never do Butterfly again, Monsieur Gallimard. If you wish to see some real theater, come to the Peking Opera sometime. Expand your mind.

Song walks offstage. Other guests exit with her.

Gallimard (to us): So much for protecting her in my big Western arms.

SCENE VII

M. Gallimard's apartment. Beijing. 1960.
    Gallimard changes from his tux into a casual suit. Helga enters.

Gallimard: The Chinese are an incredibly arrogant people.

Helga: They warned us about that in Paris, remember?

Gallimard: Even Parisians consider them arrogant. That's a switch.

Helga: What is it that Madame Su says? "We are a very old civilization." I never know if she's talking about her country or herself.

Gallimard: I walk around here, all I hear every day, everywhere is how *old* this culture is. The fact that "old" may be synonymous with "senile" doesn't occur to them.

Helga: You're not going to change them. "East is east, west is west, and . . ." whatever that guy said.

Gallimard: It's just that — silly. I met . . . at Ambassador Koening's tonight — you should've been there.

Helga: Koening? Oh god, no. Did he enchant you all again with the history of Bavaria?

Gallimard: No. I met, I suppose, the Chinese equivalent of a diva. She's a singer in the Chinese opera.

Helga: They have an opera, too? Do they sing in Chinese? Or maybe — in Italian?

Gallimard: Tonight, she did sing in Italian.

Helga: How'd she manage that?

Gallimard: She must've been educated in the West before the Revolution. Her French is very good also. Anyway, she sang the death scene from *Madame Butterfly.*

Helga: Madame Butterfly! Then I should have come. *(She begins humming, floating around the room as if dragging long kimono sleeves.)* Did she have a nice costume? I think it's a classic piece of music.

Gallimard: That's what *I* thought, too. Don't let her hear you say that.

Helga: What's wrong?

Gallimard: Evidently the Chinese hate it.

Helga: She hated it, but she performed it anyway? Is she perverse?

Gallimard: They hate it because the white man gets the girl. Sour grapes if you ask me.

Helga: Politics again? Why can't they just hear it as a piece of beautiful music? So, what's in their opera?

Gallimard: I don't know. But, whatever it is, I'm sure it must be *old.*

Helga exits.

Scene VIII

Chinese opera house and the streets of Beijing. 1960.
The sound of gongs clanging fills the stage.

Gallimard: My wife's innocent question kept ringing in my ears. I asked around, but no one knew anything about the Chinese opera. It took four weeks, but my curiosity overcame my cowardice. This Chinese diva — this unwilling Butterfly — what did she do to make her so proud?

  The room was hot, and full of smoke. Wrinkled faces, old women, teeth missing — a man with a growth on his neck, like a human toad. All smiling, pipes falling from their mouths, cracking nuts between their teeth, a live chicken pecking at my foot — all looking, screaming, gawking . . . at her.

The upstage area is suddenly hit with a harsh white light. It has become the stage for the Chinese opera performance. Two dancers enter, along with Song. Galli-

mard stands apart, watching. Song glides gracefully amidst the two dancers. Drums suddenly slam to a halt. Song strikes a pose, looking straight at Gallimard. Dancers exit. Light change. Pause, then Song walks right off the stage and straight up to Gallimard.

Song: Yes. You. White man. I'm looking straight at you.
Gallimard: Me?
Song: You see any other white men? It was too easy to spot you. How often does a man in my audience come in a tie?

Song starts to remove her costume. Underneath, she wears simple baggy clothes. They are now backstage. The show is over.

Song: So, you are an adventurous imperialist?
Gallimard: I . . . thought it would further my education.
Song: It took you four weeks. Why?
Gallimard: I've been busy.
Song: Well, education has always been undervalued in the West, hasn't it?
Gallimard (laughing): I don't think that's true.
Song: No, you wouldn't. You're a Westerner. How can you objectively judge your own values?
Gallimard: I think it's possible to achieve some distance.
Song: Do you? *(Pause.)* It stinks in here. Let's go.
Gallimard: These are the smells of your loyal fans.
Song: I love them for being my fans, I hate the smell they leave behind. I too can distance myself from my people. *(She looks around, then whispers in his ear.)* "Art for the masses" is a shitty excuse to keep artists poor. *(She pops a cigarette in her mouth.)* Be a gentleman, will you? And light my cigarette.

Gallimard fumbles for a match.

Gallimard: I don't . . . smoke.
Song (lighting her own): Your loss. Had you lit my cigarette, I might have blown a puff of smoke right between your eyes. Come.

They start to walk about the stage. It is a summer night on the Beijing streets. Sounds of the city play on the house speakers.

Song: How I wish there were even a tiny café to sit in. With cappuccinos, and men in tuxedos and bad expatriate jazz.
Gallimard: If my history serves me correctly, you weren't even allowed into the clubs in Shanghai before the Revolution.
Song: Your history serves you poorly, Monsieur Gallimard. True, there were signs reading "No dogs and Chinamen." But a woman, especially a delicate Oriental woman — we always go where we please. Could you imagine it otherwise? Clubs in China filled with pasty, big-thighed white women, while thousands of slender lotus blossoms wait just outside the door? Never. The clubs would be empty. *(Beat.)* We have always held a certain fascination for you Caucasian men, have we not?
Gallimard: But . . . that fascination is imperialist, or so you tell me.
Song: Do you believe everything I tell you? Yes. It is always imperialist. But sometimes . . . sometimes, it is also mutual. Oh — this is my flat.
Gallimard: I didn't even —

Song: Thank you. Come another time and we will further expand your mind.

Song exits. Gallimard continues roaming the streets as he speaks to us.

Gallimard: What was that? What did she mean, "Sometimes . . . it is mutual"? Women do not flirt with me. And I normally can't talk to them. But tonight, I held up my end of the conversation.

SCENE IX

Gallimard's bedroom. Beijing. 1960.
  Helga enters.

Helga: You didn't tell me you'd be home late.
Gallimard: I didn't intend to. Something came up.
Helga: Oh? Like what?
Gallimard: I went to the . . . to the Dutch ambassador's home.
Helga: Again?
Gallimard: There was a reception for a visiting scholar. He's writing a six-volume treatise on the Chinese revolution. We all gathered that meant he'd have to live here long enough to actually write six volumes, and we all expressed our deepest sympathies.
Helga: Well, I had a good night too. I went with the ladies to a martial arts demonstration. Some of those men — when they break those thick boards — *(she mimes fanning herself.)* whoo-whoo!

Helga exits. Lights dim.

Gallimard: I lied to my wife. Why? I've never had any reason to lie before. But what reason did I have tonight? I didn't do anything wrong. That night, I had a dream. Other people, I've been told, have dreams when angels appear. Or dragons, or Sophia Loren in a towel. In my dream, Marc from school appeared.

Marc enters, in a nightshirt and cap.

Marc: Rene! You met a girl!

Gallimard and Marc stumble down the Beijing streets. Night sounds over the speakers.

Gallimard: It's not that amazing, thank you.
Marc: No! It's so monumental, I heard about it halfway around the world in my sleep!
Gallimard: I've met girls before, you know.
Marc: Name one. I've come across time and space to congratulate you. *(He hands Gallimard a bottle of wine.)*
Gallimard: Marc, this is expensive.
Marc: On those rare occasions when you become a formless spirit, why not steal the best?

Marc pops open the bottle, begins to share it with Gallimard.

Gallimard: You embarrass me. She . . . there's no reason to think she likes me.
Marc: "Sometimes, it is mutual"?

Gallimard: Oh.

Marc: "Mutual"? "Mutual"? What does that mean?

Gallimard: You heard?

Marc: It means the money is in the bank, you only have to write the check!

Gallimard: I am a married man!

Marc: And an excellent one too. I cheated after . . . six months. Then again and again, until now — three hundred girls in twelve years.

Gallimard: I don't think we should hold that up as a model.

Marc: Of course not! My life — it is disgusting! Phooey! Phooey! But, you — you are the model husband.

Gallimard: Anyway, it's impossible. I'm a foreigner.

Marc: Ah, yes. She cannot love you, it is taboo, but something deep inside her heart . . . she cannot help herself . . . she must surrender to you. It is her destiny.

Gallimard: How do you imagine all this?

Marc: The same way you do. It's an old story. It's in our blood. They fear us, Rene. Their women fear us. And their men — their men hate us. And, you know something? They are all correct.

They spot a light in a window.

Marc: There! There, Rene!

Gallimard: It's her window.

Marc: Late at night — it burns. The light — it burns for you.

Gallimard: I won't look. It's not respectful.

Marc: We don't have to be respectful. We're foreign devils.

Enter Song, in a sheer robe, her face completely swathed in black cloth. The "One Fine Day" aria creeps in over the speakers. With her back to us, Song mimes attending to her toilette. Her robe comes loose, revealing her white shoulders.

Marc: All your life you've waited for a beautiful girl who would lay down for you. All your life you've smiled like a saint when it's happened to every other man you know. And you see them in magazines and you see them in movies. And you wonder, what's wrong with me? Will anyone beautiful ever want me? As the years pass, your hair thins and you struggle to hold on to even your hopes. Stop struggling, Rene. The wait is over. *(He exits.)*

Gallimard: Marc? Marc?

At that moment, Song, her back still towards us, drops her robe. A second of her naked back, then a sound cue: a phone ringing, very loud. Blackout, followed in the next beat by a special up on the bedroom area, where a phone now sits. Gallimard stumbles across the stage and picks up the phone. Sound cue out. Over the course of his conversation, area lights fill in the vicinity of his bed. It is the following morning.

Gallimard: Yes? Hello?

Song (offstage): Is it very early?

Gallimard: Why, yes.

Song (offstage): How early?

Gallimard: It's . . . it's 5:30. Why are you — ?

Song (offstage): But it's light outside. Already.

Gallimard: It is. The sun must be in confusion today.

Over the course of Song's next speech, her upstage special comes up again. She sits in a chair, legs crossed, in a robe, telephone to her ear.

Song: I waited until I saw the sun. That was as much discipline as I could manage for one night. Do you forgive me?
Gallimard: Of course . . . for what?
Song: Then I'll ask you quickly. Are you really interested in the opera?
Gallimard: Why, yes. Yes I am.
Song: Then come again next Thursday. I am playing *The Drunken Beauty.* May I count on you?
Gallimard: Yes. You may.
Song: Perfect. Well, I must be getting to bed. I'm exhausted. It's been a very long night for me.

Song hangs up; special on her goes off. Gallimard begins to dress for work.

SCENE X

Song Liling's apartment. Beijing. 1960.

Gallimard: I returned to the opera that next week, and the week after that . . . she keeps our meetings so short — perhaps fifteen, twenty minutes at most. So I am left each week with a thirst which is intensified. In this way, fifteen weeks have gone by. I am starting to doubt the words of my friend Marc. But no, not really. In my heart, I know she has . . . an interest in me. I suspect this is her way. She is outwardly bold and outspoken, yet her heart is shy and afraid. It is the Oriental in her at war with her Western education.
Song (offstage): I will be out in an instant. Ask the servant for anything you want.
Gallimard: Tonight, I have finally been invited to enter her apartment. Though the idea is almost beyond belief, I believe she is afraid of me.

Gallimard looks around the room. He picks up a picture in a frame, studies it. Without his noticing, Song enters, dressed elegantly in a black gown from the twenties. She stands in the doorway looking like Anna May Wong.°

Song: That is my father.
Gallimard (surprised): Mademoiselle Song . . .

She glides up to him, snatches away the picture.

Song: It is very good that he did not live to see the Revolution. They would, no doubt, have made him kneel on broken glass. Not that he didn't deserve such a punishment. But he is my father. I would've hated to see it happen.
Gallimard: I'm very honored that you've allowed me to visit your home.

Song curtseys.

Song: Thank you. Oh! Haven't you been poured any tea?
Gallimard: I'm really not —

Anna May Wong (1905–1961): Chinese-American actress known for her exotic beauty but most often cast as a villain.

Song (to her offstage servant): Shu-Fang! Cha! Kwai-lah! *(To Gallimard.)* I'm sorry.
   You want everything to be perfect —
Gallimard: Please.
Song: — and before the evening even begins —
Gallimard: I'm really not thirsty.
Song: — it's ruined.
Gallimard (sharply): Mademoiselle Song!

Song sits down.

Song: I'm sorry.
Gallimard: What are you apologizing for now?

Pause; Song starts to giggle.

Song: I don't know!

Gallimard laughs.

Gallimard: Exactly my point.
Song: Oh, I am silly. Light-headed. I promise not to apologize for anything else
   tonight, do you hear me?
Gallimard: That's a good girl.

Shu-Fang, a servant girl, comes out with a tea tray and starts to pour.

Song (to Shu-Fang): No! I'll pour myself for the gentleman!

Shu-Fang, staring at Gallimard, exits.

Gallimard: You have a beautiful home.
Song: No, I . . . I don't even know why I invited you up.
Gallimard: Well, I'm glad you did.

Song looks around the room.

Song: There is an element of danger to your presence.
Gallimard: Oh?
Song: You must know.
Gallimard: It doesn't concern me. We both know why I'm here.
Song: It doesn't concern me either. No . . . well perhaps . . .
Gallimard: What?
Song: Perhaps I am slightly afraid of scandal.
Gallimard: What are we doing?
Song: I'm entertaining you. In my parlor.
Gallimard: In France, that would hardly —
Song: France. France is a country living in the modern era. Perhaps even ahead
   of it. China is a nation whose soul is firmly rooted two thousand years in
   the past. What I do, even pouring the tea for you now . . . it has . . .
   implications. The walls and windows say so. Even my own heart, strapped
   inside this Western dress . . . even it says things — things I don't care to
   hear.

*Song hands Gallimard a cup of tea. Gallimard puts his hand over both the teacup
and Song's hand.*

Gallimard: This is a beautiful dress.

Song: Don't.

Gallimard: What?

Song: I don't even know if it looks right on me.

Gallimard: Believe me —

Song: You are from France. You see so many beautiful women.

Gallimard: France? Since when are the European women —?

Song: Oh! What am I trying to do, anyway?!

Song runs to the door, composes herself, then turns towards Gallimard.

Song: Monsieur Gallimard, perhaps you should go.

Gallimard: But . . . why?

Song: There's something wrong about this.

Gallimard: I don't see what.

Song: I feel . . . I am not myself.

Gallimard: No. You're nervous.

Song: Please. Hard as I try to be modern, to speak like a man, to hold a Western woman's strong face up to my own . . . in the end, I fail. A small, frightened heart beats too quickly and gives me away. Monsieur Gallimard, I'm a Chinese girl. I've never . . . never invited a man up to my flat before. The forwardness of my actions makes my skin burn.

Gallimard: What are you afraid of? Certainly not me, I hope.

Song: I'm a modest girl.

Gallimard: I know. And very beautiful. *(He touches her hair.)*

Song: Please — go now. The next time you see me, I shall again be myself.

Gallimard: I like you the way you are right now.

Song: You are a cad.

Gallimard: What do you expect? I'm a foreign devil.

Gallimard walks downstage. Song exits.

Gallimard (to us): Did you hear the way she talked about Western women? Much differently than the first night. She does — she feels inferior to them — and to me.

Scene XI

The French embassy. Beijing. 1960.
   Gallimard moves towards a desk.

Gallimard: I determined to try an experiment. In *Madame Butterfly,* Cio-Cio-San fears that the Western man who catches a butterfly will pierce its heart with a needle, then leave it to perish. I began to wonder: had I, too, caught a butterfly who would writhe on a needle?

Marc enters, dressed as a bureaucrat, holding a stack of papers. As Gallimard speaks, Marc hands papers to him. He peruses, then signs, stamps, or rejects them.

Gallimard: Over the next five weeks, I worked like a dynamo. I stopped going to the opera, I didn't phone or write her. I knew this little flower was waiting for me to call, and, as I wickedly refused to do so, I felt for the first time that rush of power — the absolute power of a man.

Marc continues acting as the bureaucrat, but he now speaks as himself.

Marc: Rene! It's me.

Gallimard: Marc — I hear your voice everywhere now. Even in the midst of work.

Marc: That's because I'm watching you — all the time.

Gallimard: You were always the most popular guy in school.

Marc: Well, there's no guarantee of failure in life like happiness in high school. Somehow I knew I'd end up in the suburbs working for Renault and you'd be in the Orient picking exotic women off the trees. And they say there's no justice.

Gallimard: That's why you were my friend?

Marc: I gave you a little of my life, so that now you can give me some of yours. *(Pause.)* Remember Isabelle?

Gallimard: Of course I remember! She was my first experience.

Marc: We all wanted to ball her. But she only wanted me.

Gallimard: I had her.

Marc: Right. You balled her.

Gallimard: You were the only one who ever believed me.

Marc: Well, there's a good reason for that. *(Beat.)* C'mon. You must've guessed.

Gallimard: You told me to wait in the bushes by the cafeteria that night. The next thing I knew, she was on me. Dress up in the air.

Marc: She never wore underwear.

Gallimard: My arms were pinned to the dirt.

Marc: She loved the superior position. A girl ahead of her time.

Gallimard: I looked up, and there was this woman . . . bouncing up and down on my loins.

Marc: Screaming, right?

Gallimard: Screaming, and breaking off the branches all around me, and pounding my butt up and down into the dirt.

Marc: Huffing and puffing like a locomotive.

Gallimard: And in the middle of all this, the leaves were getting into my mouth, my legs were losing circulation, I thought, "God. So this is *it?*"

Marc: You thought that?

Gallimard: Well, I was worried about my legs falling off.

Marc: You didn't have a good time?

Gallimard: No, that's not what I — I had a great time!

Marc: You're sure?

Gallimard: Yeah. Really.

Marc: 'Cuz I wanted you to have a good time.

Gallimard: I did.

Pause.

Marc: Shit. *(Pause.)* When all is said and done, she was kind of a lousy lay, wasn't she? I mean, there was a lot of energy there, but you never knew what she was doing with it. Like when she yelled "I'm coming!" — hell, it was so loud, you wanted to go, "Look, it's not that big a deal."

Gallimard: I got scared. I thought she meant someone was actually coming. *(Pause.)* But, Marc?

Marc: What?

Gallimard: Thanks.

Marc: Oh, don't mention it.
Gallimard: It was my first experience.
Marc: Yeah. You got her.
Gallimard: I got her.
Marc: Wait! Look at that letter again!

Gallimard picks up one of the papers he's been stamping, and rereads it.

Gallimard (to us): After six weeks, they began to arrive. The letters.

Upstage special on Song, as Madame Butterfly. The scene is underscored by the "Love Duet."

Song: Did we fight? I do not know. Is the opera no longer of interest to you? Please come — my audiences miss the white devil in their midst.

Gallimard looks up from the letter, towards us.

Gallimard (to us): A concession, but much too dignified. *(Beat; he discards the letter.)* I skipped the opera again that week to complete a position paper on trade.

The bureaucrat hands him another letter.

Song: Six weeks have passed since last we met. Is this your practice — to leave friends in the lurch? Sometimes I hate you, sometimes I hate myself, but always I miss you.
Gallimard (to us): Better, but I don't like the way she calls me "friend." When a woman calls a man her "friend," she's calling him a eunuch or a homosexual. *(Beat; he discards the letter.)* I was absent from the opera for the seventh week, feeling a sudden urge to clean out my files.

Bureaucrat hands him another letter.

Song: Your rudeness is beyond belief. I don't deserve this cruelty. Don't bother to call. I'll have you turned away at the door.
Gallimard (to us): I didn't. *(He discards the letter; bureaucrat hands him another.)* And then finally, the letter that concluded my experiment.
Song: I am out of words. I can hide behind dignity no longer. What do you want? I have already given you my shame.

Gallimard gives the letter back to Marc, slowly. Special on Song fades out.

Gallimard (to us): Reading it, I became suddenly ashamed. Yes, my experiment had been a success. She was turning on my needle. But the victory seemed hollow.
Marc: Hollow?! Are you crazy?
Gallimard: Nothing, Marc. Please go away.
Marc (exiting, with papers): Haven't I taught you anything?
Gallimard: "I have already given you my shame." I had to attend a reception that evening. On the way, I felt sick. If there is a God, surely he would punish me now. I had finally gained power over a beautiful woman, only to abuse it cruelly. There must be justice in the world. I had the strange feeling that the ax would fall this very evening.

Ambassador Toulon's residence. Beijing. 1960.
    Sound cue: party noises. Light change. We are now in a spacious residence.
Toulon, the French ambassador, enters and taps Gallimard on the shoulder.

Toulon: Gallimard? Can I have a word? Over here.

Gallimard (to us): Manuel Toulon. French ambassador to China. He likes to
    think of us all as his children. Rather like God.

Toulon: Look, Gallimard, there's not much to say. I've liked you. From the day
    you walked in. You were no leader, but you were tidy and efficient.

Gallimard: Thank you, sir.

Toulon: Don't jump the gun. Okay, our needs in China are changing. It's em-
    barrassing that we lost Indochina. Someone just wasn't on the ball there. I
    don't mean you personally, of course.

Gallimard: Thank you, sir.

Toulon: We're going to be doing a lot more information-gathering in the future.
    The nature of our work here is changing. Some people are just going to
    have to go. It's nothing personal.

Gallimard: Oh.

Toulon: Want to know a secret? Vice-Consul LeBon is being transferred.

Gallimard (to us): My immediate superior!

Toulon: And most of his department.

Gallimard (to us): Just as I feared! God has seen my evil heart —

Toulon: But not you.

Gallimard (to us): — and he's taking her away just as . . . *(To Toulon.)* Excuse
    me, sir?

Toulon: Scare you? I think I did. Cheer up, Gallimard. I want you to replace
    LeBon as vice-consul.

Gallimard: You — ? Yes, well, thank you, sir.

Toulon: Anytime.

Gallimard: I . . . accept with great humility.

Toulon: Humility won't be part of the job. You're going to coordinate the
    revamped intelligence division. Want to know a secret? A year ago, you
    would've been out. But the past few months, I don't know how it happened,
    you've become this new aggressive confident . . . thing. And they also tell
    me you get along with the Chinese. So I think you're a lucky man, Gallimard.
    Congratulations.

*They shake hands. Toulon exits. Party noises out. Gallimard stumbles across a
darkened stage.*

Gallimard: Vice-consul? Impossible! As I stumbled out of the party, I saw it
    written across the sky: There is no God. Or, no — say that there is a God.
    But that God . . . understands. Of course! God who creates Eve to serve
    Adam, who blesses Solomon with his harem but ties Jezebel to a burning
    bed° — that God is a man. And he understands! At age thirty-nine, I was
    suddenly initiated into the way of the world.

God who creates Eve . . . burning bed: Eve, Adam, Solomon, and Jezebel are biblical characters. See
Gen. 2:18–25; I Kings 11:1–8; and II Kings 9:11–37.

Song Liling's apartment. Beijing. 1960.
Song enters, in a sheer dressing gown.

Song: Are you crazy?
Gallimard: Mademoiselle Song —
Song: To come here — at this hour? After . . . after eight weeks?
Gallimard: It's the most amazing —
Song: You bang on my door? Scare my servants, scandalize the neighbors?
Gallimard: I've been promoted. To vice-consul.

Pause.

Song: And what is that supposed to mean to me?
Gallimard: Are you my Butterfly?
Song: What are you saying?
Gallimard: I've come tonight for an answer: are you my Butterfly?
Song: Don't you know already?
Gallimard: I want you to say it.
Song: I don't want to say it.
Gallimard: So, that is your answer?
Song: You know how I feel about —
Gallimard: I do remember one thing.
Song: What?
Gallimard: In the letter I received today.
Song: Don't.
Gallimard: "I have already given you my shame."
Song: It's enough that I even wrote it.
Gallimard: Well, then —
Song: I shouldn't have it splashed across my face.
Gallimard: — if that's all true —
Song: Stop!
Gallimard: Then what is one more short answer?
Song: I don't want to!
Gallimard: Are you my Butterfly? *(Silence; he crosses the room and begins to touch her hair.)* I want from you honesty. There should be nothing false between us. No false pride.

Pause.

Song: Yes, I am. I am your Butterfly.
Gallimard: Then let me be honest with you. It is because of you that I was promoted tonight. You have changed my life forever. My little Butterfly, there should be no more secrets: I love you.

He starts to kiss her roughly. She resists slightly.

Song: No . . . no . . . gently . . . please, I've never . . .
Gallimard: No?
Song: I've tried to appear experienced, but . . . the truth is . . . no.
Gallimard: Are you cold?
Song: Yes. Cold.

Gallimard: Then we will go very, very slowly.

He starts to caress her; her gown begins to open.

Song: No . . . let me . . . keep my clothes . . .
Gallimard: But . . .
Song: Please . . . it all frightens me. I'm a modest Chinese girl.
Gallimard: My poor little treasure.
Song: I am your treasure. Though inexperienced, I am not . . . ignorant. They
    teach us things, our mothers, about pleasing a man.
Gallimard: Yes?
Song: I'll do my best to make you happy. Turn off the lights.

*Gallimard gets up and heads for a lamp. Song, propped up on one elbow, tosses
her hair back and smiles.*

Song: Monsieur Gallimard?
Gallimard: Yes, Butterfly?
Song: "Vieni, vieni!"
Gallimard: "Come, darling."
Song: "Ah! Dolce notte!"
Gallimard: "Beautiful night."
Song: "Tutto estatico d'amor ride il ciel!"
Gallimard: "All ecstatic with love, the heavens are filled with laughter."

He turns off the lamp. Blackout.

ACT II

Scene I

M. Gallimard's cell. Paris. 1988.
    Lights up on Gallimard. He sits in his cell, reading from a leaflet.

Gallimard: This, from a contemporary critic's commentary on *Madame Butterfly:*
    "Pinkerton suffers from . . . being an obnoxious bounder whom every man
    in the audience itches to kick." Bully for us men in the audience! Then, in
    the same note: "Butterfly is the most irresistibly appealing of Puccini's 'Little
    Women.' Watching the succession of her humiliations is like watching a child
    under torture." *(He tosses the pamphlet over his shoulder.)* I suggest that,
    while we men may all want to kick Pinkerton, very few of us would pass up
    the opportunity to *be* Pinkerton.

Gallimard moves out of his cell.

Scene II

Gallimard and Butterfly's flat. Beijing. 1960.
    *We are in a simple but well-decorated parlor. Gallimard moves to sit on a
sofa, while Song, dressed in a chong sam,° enters and curls up at his feet.*

chong sam: A tight-fitting dress with side slits in the skirt.

Gallimard (to us): We secured a flat on the outskirts of Peking. Butterfly, as I was calling her now, decorated our "home" with Western furniture and Chinese antiques. And there, on a few stolen afternoons or evenings each week, Butterfly commenced her education.

Song: The Chinese men — they keep us down.

Gallimard: Even in the "New Society"?

Song: In the "New Society," we are all kept ignorant equally. That's one of the exciting things about loving a Western man. I know you are not threatened by a woman's education.

Gallimard: I'm no saint, Butterfly.

Song: But you come from a progressive society.

Gallimard: We're not always reminding each other how "old" we are, if that's what you mean.

Song: Exactly. We Chinese — once, I suppose, it is true, we ruled the world. But so what? How much more exciting to be part of the society ruling the world today. Tell me — what's happening in Vietnam?

Gallimard: Oh, Butterfly — you want me to bring my work home?

Song: I want to know what you know. To be impressed by my man. It's not the particulars so much as the fact that you're making decisions which change the shape of the world.

Gallimard: Not the world. At best, a small corner.

Toulon enters, and sits at a desk upstage.

SCENE III

French embassy. Beijing. 1961.
   Gallimard moves downstage, to Toulon's desk. Song remains upstage, watching.

Toulon: And a more troublesome corner is hard to imagine.

Gallimard: So, the Americans plan to begin bombing?

Toulon: This is very secret, Gallimard: yes. The Americans don't have an embassy here. They're asking us to be their eyes and ears. Say Jack Kennedy signed an order to bomb North Vietnam, Laos. How would the Chinese react?

Gallimard: I think the Chinese will squawk —

Toulon: Uh-huh.

Gallimard: — but, in their hearts, they don't even like Ho Chi Minh.°

Pause.

Toulon: What a bunch of jerks. Vietnam was *our* colony. Not only didn't the Americans help us fight to keep them, but now, seven years later, they've come back to grab the territory for themselves. It's very irritating.

Gallimard: With all due respect, sir, why should the Americans have won our war for us back in fifty-four if we didn't have the will to win it ourselves?

Toulon: You're kidding, aren't you?

Pause.

Ho Chi Minh (1890–1969): President of North Vietnam (1945–1969).

Gallimard: The Orientals simply want to be associated with whoever shows the most strength and power. You live with the Chinese, sir. Do you think they like Communism?

Toulon: I live in China. Not with the Chinese.

Gallimard: Well, I —

Toulon: You live with the Chinese.

Gallimard: Excuse me?

Toulon: I can't keep a secret.

Gallimard: What are you saying?

Toulon: Only that I'm not immune to gossip. So, you're keeping a native mistress? Don't answer. It's none of my business. *(Pause.)* I'm sure she must be gorgeous.

Gallimard: Well . . .

Toulon: I'm impressed. You had the stamina to go out into the streets and hunt one down. Some of us have to be content with the wives of the expatriate community.

Gallimard: I do feel . . . fortunate.

Toulon: So, Gallimard, you've got the inside knowledge — what *do* the Chinese think?

Gallimard: Deep down, they miss the old days. You know, cappuccinos, men in tuxedos —

Toulon: So what do we tell the Americans about Vietnam?

Gallimard: Tell them there's a natural affinity between the West and the Orient.

Toulon: And that you speak from experience?

Gallimard: The Orientals are people too. They want the good things we can give them. If the Americans demonstrate the will to win, the Vietnamese will welcome them into a mutually beneficial union.

Toulon: I don't see how the Vietnamese can stand up to American firepower.

Gallimard: Orientals will always submit to a greater force.

Toulon: I'll note your opinions in my report. The Americans always love to hear how "welcome" they'll be. *(He starts to exit.)*

Gallimard: Sir?

Toulon: Mmmm?

Gallimard: This . . . rumor you've heard.

Toulon: Uh-huh?

Gallimard: How . . . widespread do you think it is?

Toulon: It's only widespread within this embassy. Where nobody talks because everybody is guilty. We were worried about you, Gallimard. We thought you were the only one here without a secret. Now you go and find a lotus blossom . . . and top us all. *(He exits.)*

Gallimard (to us): Toulon knows! And he approves! I was learning the benefits of being a man. We form our own clubs, sit behind thick doors, smoke — and celebrate the fact that we're still boys. *(He starts to move downstage, towards Song.)* So, over the —

Suddenly Comrade Chin enters. Gallimard backs away.

Gallimard (to Song): No! Why does she have to come in?

Song: Rene, be sensible. How can they understand the story without her? Now, don't embarrass yourself.

Gallimard moves down center.

Gallimard (to us): Now, you will see why my story is so amusing to so many people. Why they snicker at parties in disbelief. Please — try to understand it from my point of view. We are all prisoners of our time and place. *(He exits.)*

SCENE IV

Gallimard and Butterfly's flat. Beijing. 1961.

Song (to us): 1961. The flat Monsieur Gallimard rented for us. An evening after he has gone.

Chin: Okay, see if you can find out when the Americans plan to start bombing Vietnam. If you can find out what cities, even better.

Song: I'll do my best, but I don't want to arouse his suspicions.

Chin: Yeah, sure, of course. So, what else?

Song: The Americans will increase troops in Vietnam to 170,000 soldiers with 120,000 militia and 11,000 American advisors.

Chin (writing): Wait, wait, 120,000 militia and —

Song: — 11,000 American —

Chin: — American advisors. *(Beat.)* How do you remember so much?

Song: I'm an actor.

Chin: Yeah. *(Beat.)* Is that how come you dress like that?

Song: Like what, Miss Chin?

Chin: Like that dress! You're wearing a dress. And every time I come here, you're wearing a dress. Is that because you're an actor? Or what?

Song: It's a . . . disguise, Miss Chin.

Chin: Actors, I think they're all weirdos. My mother tells me actors are like gamblers or prostitutes or —

Song: It helps me in my assignment.

Pause.

Chin: You're not gathering information in any way that violates Communist Party principles, are you?

Song: Why would I do that?

Chin: Just checking. Remember: when working for the Great Proletarian State, you represent our Chairman Mao in every position you take.

Song: I'll try to imagine the Chairman taking my positions.

Chin: We all think of him this way. Good-bye, comrade. *(She starts to exit.)* Comrade?

Song: Yes?

Chin: Don't forget: there is no homosexuality in China!

Song: Yes, I've heard.

Chin: Just checking. *(She exits.)*

Song (to us): What passes for a woman in modern China.

Gallimard sticks his head out from the wings.

Gallimard: Is she gone?

Song: Yes, Rene. Please continue in your own fashion.

Beijing. 1961–1963.
  Gallimard moves to the couch where Song still sits. He lies down in her lap, and she strokes his forehead.

Gallimard (to us): And so, over the years 1961, '62, '63, we settled into our routine, Butterfly and I. She would always have prepared a light snack and then, ever so delicately, and only if I agreed, she would start to pleasure me. With her hands, her mouth . . . too many ways to explain, and too sad, given my present situation. But mostly we would talk. About my life. Perhaps there is nothing more rare than to find a woman who passionately listens.

Song remains upstage, listening, as Helga enters and plays a scene downstage with Gallimard.

Helga: Rene, I visited Dr. Bolleart this morning.
Gallimard: Why? Are you ill?
Helga: No, no. You see, I wanted to ask him . . . that question we've been discussing.
Gallimard: And I told you, it's only a matter of time. Why did you bring a doctor into this? We just have to keep trying — like a crapshoot, actually.
Helga: I went, I'm sorry. But listen: he says there's nothing wrong with me.
Gallimard: You see? Now, will you stop — ?
Helga: Rene, he says he'd like you to go in and take some tests.
Gallimard: Why? So he can find there's nothing wrong with both of us?
Helga: Rene, I don't ask for much. One trip! One visit! And then, whatever you want to do about it — you decide.
Gallimard: You're assuming he'll find something defective!
Helga: No! Of course not! Whatever he finds — if he finds nothing, we decide what to do about nothing! But go!
Gallimard: If he finds nothing, we keep trying. Just like we do now.
Helga: But at least we'll know! *(Pause.)* I'm sorry. *(She starts to exit.)*
Gallimard: Do you really want me to see Dr. Bolleart?
Helga: Only if you want a child, Rene. We have to face the fact that time is running out. Only if you want a child. *(She exits.)*
Gallimard (to Song): I'm a modern man, Butterfly. And yet, I don't want to go. It's the same old voodoo. I feel like God himself is laughing at me if I can't produce a child.
Song: You men of the West — you're obsessed by your odd desire for equality. Your wife can't give you a child, and *you're* going to the doctor?
Gallimard: Well, you see, she's already gone.
Song: And because this incompetent can't find the defect, you now have to subject yourself to him? It's unnatural.
Gallimard: Well, what is the "natural" solution?
Song: In Imperial China, when a man found that one wife was inadequate, he turned to another — to give him his son.
Gallimard: What do you — ? I can't . . . marry you, yet.
Song: Please. I'm not asking you to be my husband. But I am already your wife.
Gallimard: Do you want to . . . have my child?

Song: I thought you'd never ask.

Gallimard: But, your career . . . your —

Song: Phooey on my career! That's your Western mind, twisting itself into strange shapes again. Of course I love my career. But what would I love most of all? To feel something inside me — day and night — something I know is yours. *(Pause.)* Promise me . . . you won't go to this doctor. Who is this Western quack to set himself as judge over the man I love? I know who is a man, and who is not. *(She exits.)*

Gallimard (to us): Dr. Bolleart? Of course I didn't go. What man would?

Scene VI

Beijing. 1963.

   Party noises over the house speakers. Renee enters, wearing a revealing gown.

Gallimard: 1963. A party at the Austrian embassy. None of us could remember the Austrian ambassador's name, which seemed somehow appropriate. *(To Renee.)* So, I tell the Americans, Diem° must go. The U.S. wants to be respected by the Vietnamese, and yet they're propping up this nobody seminarian as her president. A man whose claim to fame is his sister-in-law imposing fanatic "moral order" campaigns? Oriental women — when they're good, they're very good, but when they're bad, they're Christians.

Renee: Yeah.

Gallimard: And what do you do?

Renee: I'm a student. My father exports a lot of useless stuff to the Third World.

Gallimard: How useless?

Renee: You know. Squirt guns, confectioner's sugar, Hula Hoops . . .

Gallimard: I'm sure they appreciate the sugar.

Renee: I'm here for two years to study Chinese.

Gallimard: Two years!

Renee: That's what everybody says.

Gallimard: When did you arrive?

Renee: Three weeks ago.

Gallimard: And?

Renee: I like it. It's primitive, but . . . well, this is the place to learn Chinese, so here I am.

Gallimard: Why Chinese?

Renee: I think it'll be important someday.

Gallimard: You do?

Renee: Don't ask me when, but . . . that's what I think.

Gallimard: Well, I agree with you. One hundred percent. That's very farsighted.

Renee: Yeah. Well of course, my father thinks I'm a complete weirdo.

Gallimard: He'll thank you someday.

Renee: Like when the Chinese start buying Hula Hoops?

Gallimard: There're a billion bellies out there.

Diem: Ngo Dinh Diem (1901–1963), president of South Vietnam (1955–1963), assassinated in a coup d'etat supported by the United States.

Renee: And if they end up taking over the world — well, then I'll be lucky to know Chinese too, right?

Pause.

Gallimard: At this point, I don't see how the Chinese can possibly take —
Renee: You know what I *don't* like about China?
Gallimard: Excuse me? No — what?
Renee: Nothing to do at night.
Gallimard: You come to parties at embassies like everyone else.
Renee: Yeah, but they get out at ten. And then what?
Gallimard: I'm afraid the Chinese idea of a dance hall is a dirt floor and a man with a flute.
Renee: Are you married?
Gallimard: Yes. Why?
Renee: You wanna . . . fool around?

Pause.

Gallimard: Sure.
Renee: I'll wait for you outside. What's your name?
Gallimard: Gallimard. Rene.
Renee: Weird. I'm Renee too. *(She exits.)*
Gallimard (to us): And so, I embarked on my first extra-extramarital affair. Renee was picture perfect. With a body like those girls in the magazines. If I put a tissue paper over my eyes, I wouldn't have been able to tell the difference. And it was exciting to be with someone who wasn't afraid to be seen completely naked. But is it possible for a woman to be *too* uninhibited, *too* willing, so as to seem almost too . . . masculine?

Chuck Berry° blares from the house speakers, then comes down in volume as Renee enters, toweling her hair.

Renee: You have a nice weenie.
Gallimard: What?
Renee: Penis. You have a nice penis.
Gallimard: Oh. Well, thank you. That's very . . .
Renee: What — can't take a compliment?
Gallimard: No, it's very . . . reassuring.
Renee: But most girls don't come out and say it, huh?
Gallimard: And also . . . what did you call it?
Renee: Oh. Most girls don't call it a "weenie," huh?
Gallimard: It sounds very —
Renee: Small, I know.
Gallimard: I was going to say, "young."
Renee: Yeah. Young, small, same thing. Most guys are pretty, uh, sensitive about that. Like, you know, I had a boyfriend back home in Denmark. I got mad at him once and called him a little weeniehead. He got so mad! He said at least I should call him a great big weeniehead.
Gallimard: I suppose I just say "penis."

Chuck Berry: Influential American rock 'n' roll musician whose first recording came out in 1955.

Renee: Yeah. That's pretty clinical. There's "cock," but that sounds like a chicken. And "prick" is painful, and "dick" is like you're talking about someone who's not in the room.

Gallimard: Yes. It's a . . . bigger problem than I imagined.

Renee: I — I think maybe it's because I really don't know what to do with them — that's why I call them "weenies."

Gallimard: Well, you did quite well with . . . mine.

Renee: Thanks, but I mean, really *do* with them. Like, okay, have you ever looked at one? I mean, really?

Gallimard: No, I suppose when it's part of you, you sort of take it for granted.

Renee: I guess. But, like, it just hangs there. This little . . . flap of flesh. And there's so much fuss that we make about it. Like, I think the reason we fight wars is because we wear clothes. Because no one knows — between the men, I mean — who has the biggest . . . weenie. So, if I'm a guy with a small one, I'm going to build a really big building or take over a really big piece of land or write a really long book so the other men don't know, right? But, see, it never really works, that's the problem. I mean, you conquer the country, or whatever, but you're still wearing clothes, so there's no way to prove absolutely whose is bigger or smaller. And that's what we call a civilized society. The whole world run by a bunch of men with pricks the size of pins. *(She exits.)*

Gallimard (to us): This was simply not acceptable.

A high-pitched chime rings through the air. Song, dressed as Butterfly, appears in the upstage special. She is obviously distressed. Her body swoons as she attempts to clip the stems of flowers she's arranging in a vase.

Gallimard: But I kept up our affair, wildly, for several months. Why? I believe because of Butterfly. She knew the secret I was trying to hide. But, unlike a Western woman, she didn't confront me, threaten, even pout. I remembered the words of Puccini's *Butterfly:*

Song: "Noi siamo gente avvezza / alle piccole cose / umili e silenziose."

Gallimard: "I come from a people / Who are accustomed to little / Humble and silent." I saw Pinkerton and Butterfly, and what she would say if he were unfaithful . . . nothing. She would cry, alone, into those wildly soft sleeves, once full of possessions, now empty to collect her tears. It was her tears and her silence that excited me, every time I visited Renee.

Toulon (offstage): Gallimard!

Toulon enters. Gallimard turns towards him. During the next section, Song, up center, begins to dance with the flowers. It is a drunken, reckless dance, where she breaks small pieces off the stems.

Toulon: They're killing him.

Gallimard: Who? I'm sorry? What?

Toulon: Bother you to come over at this late hour?

Gallimard: No . . . of course not.

Toulon: Not after you hear my secret. Champagne?

Gallimard: Um . . . thank you.

Toulon: You're surprised. There's something that you've wanted, Gallimard. No, not a promotion. Next time. Something in the world. You're not aware of this, but there's an informal gossip circle among intelligence agents. And some of ours heard from some of the Americans —

Gallimard: Yes?

Toulon: That the U.S. will allow the Vietnamese generals to stage a coup . . . and assassinate President Diem.

The chime rings again. Toulon freezes. Gallimard turns upstage and looks at Butterfly, who slowly and deliberately clips a flower off its stem. Gallimard turns back towards Toulon.

Gallimard: I think . . . that's a very wise move!

Toulon unfreezes.

Toulon: It's what you've been advocating. A toast?

Gallimard: Sure. I consider this a vindication.

Toulon: Not exactly. "To the test. Let's hope you pass."

They drink. The chime rings again. Toulon freezes. Gallimard turns upstage, and Song clips another flower.

Gallimard (to Toulon): The test?

Toulon (unfreezing): It's a test of everything you've been saying. I personally think the generals probably will stop the Communists. And you'll be a hero. But if anything goes wrong, then your opinions won't be worth a pig's ear. I'm sure that won't happen. But sometimes it's easier when they don't listen to you.

Gallimard: They're your opinions too, aren't they?

Toulon: Personally, yes.

Gallimard: So we agree.

Toulon: But my opinions aren't on that report. Yours are. Cheers.

Toulon turns away from Gallimard and raises his glass. At that instant Song picks up the vase and hurls it to the ground. It shatters. Song sinks down amidst the shards of the vase, in a calm, childlike trance. She sings softly, as if reciting a child's nursery rhyme.

Song (repeat as necessary): "The whole world over, the white man travels, setting anchor, wherever he likes. Life's not worth living, unless he finds, the finest maidens, of every land . . ."

Gallimard turns downstage towards us. Song continues singing.

Gallimard: I shook as I left his house. That coward! That worm! To put the burden for his decisions on my shoulders!

I started for Renee's. But no, that was all I needed. A schoolgirl who would question the role of the penis in modern society. What I wanted was revenge. A vessel to contain my humiliation. Though I hadn't seen her in several weeks, I headed for Butterfly's.

Gallimard enters Song's apartment.

Song: Oh! Rene . . . I was dreaming!

Gallimard: You've been drinking?

Song: If I can't sleep, then yes, I drink. But then, it gives me these dreams which — Rene, it's been almost three weeks since you visited me last.

Gallimard: I know. There's been a lot going on in the world.

Song: Fortunately I am drunk. So I can speak freely. It's not the world, it's you and me. And an old problem. Even the softest skin becomes like leather to a man who's touched it too often. I confess I don't know how to stop it. I don't know how to become another woman.

Gallimard: I have a request.

Song: Is this a solution? Or are you ready to give up the flat?

Gallimard: It may be a solution. But I'm sure you won't like it.

Song: Oh well, that's very important. "Like it?" Do you think I "like" lying here alone, waiting, always waiting for your return? Please — don't worry about what I may not "like."

Gallimard: I want to see you . . . naked.

Silence.

Song: I thought you understood my modesty. So you want me to — what — strip? Like a big cowboy girl? Shiny pasties on my breasts? Shall I fling my kimono over my head and yell "ya-hoo" in the process? I thought you respected my shame!

Gallimard: I believe you gave me your shame many years ago.

Song: Yes — and it is just like a white devil to use it against me. I can't believe it. I thought myself so repulsed by the passive Oriental and the cruel white man. Now I see — we are always most revolted by the things hidden within us.

Gallimard: I just mean —

Song: Yes?

Gallimard: — that it will remove the only barrier left between us.

Song: No, Rene. Don't couch your request in sweet words. Be yourself — a cad — and know that my love is enough, that I submit — submit to the worst you can give me. *(Pause.)* Well, come. Strip me. Whatever happens, know that you have willed it. Our love, in your hands. I'm helpless before my man.

Gallimard starts to cross the room.

Gallimard: Did I not undress her because I knew, somewhere deep down, what I would find? Perhaps. Happiness is so rare that our mind can turn somersaults to protect it.

 At the time, I only knew that I was seeing Pinkerton stalking towards his Butterfly, ready to reward her love with his lecherous hands. The image sickened me, pulled me to my knees, so I was crawling towards her like a worm. By the time I reached her, Pinkerton . . . had vanished from my heart. To be replaced by something new, something unnatural, that flew in the face of all I'd learned in the world — something very close to love.

He grabs her around the waist; she strokes his hair.

Gallimard: Butterfly, forgive me.

Song: Rene . . .

Gallimard: For everything. From the start.

Song: I'm . . .

Gallimard: I want to —

Song: I'm pregnant. *(Beat.)* I'm pregnant. *(Beat.)* I'm pregnant.

Beat.

Gallimard: I want to marry you!

SCENE VII

Gallimard and Butterfly's flat. Beijing. 1963.

  Downstage, Song paces as Comrade Chin reads from her notepad. Upstage, Gallimard is still kneeling. He remains on his knees throughout the scene, watching it.

Song: I need a baby.
Chin (from pad): He's been spotted going to a dorm.
Song: I need a baby.
Chin: At the Foreign Language Institute.
Song: I need a baby.
Chin: The room of a Danish girl. . . . What do you mean, you need a baby?!
Song: Tell Comrade Kang — last night, the entire mission, it could've ended.
Chin: What do you mean?
Song: Tell Kang — he told me to strip.
Chin: Strip?!
Song: Write!
Chin: I tell you, I don't understand nothing about this case anymore. Nothing.
Song: He told me to strip, and I took a chance. Oh, we Chinese, we know how to gamble.
Chin (writing): ". . . told him to strip."
Song: My palms were wet, I had to make a split-second decision.
Chin: Hey! Can you slow down?!

Pause.

Song: You write faster, I'm the artist here. Suddenly, it hit me — "All he wants is for her to submit. Once a woman submits, a man is always ready to become 'generous.'"
Chin: You're just gonna end up with rough notes.
Song: And it worked! He gave in! Now, if I can just present him with a baby. A Chinese baby with blond hair — he'll be mine for life!
Chin: Kang will never agree! The trading of babies has to be a counterrevolutionary act!
Song: Sometimes, a counterrevolutionary act is necessary to counter a counterrevolutionary act.

Pause.

Chin: Wait.
Song: I need one . . . in seven months. Make sure it's a boy.
Chin: This doesn't sound like something the Chairman would do. Maybe you'd better talk to Comrade Kang yourself.
Song: Good. I will.

Chin gets up to leave.

Song: Miss Chin? Why, in the Peking Opera, are women's roles played by men?

Chin: I don't know. Maybe, a reactionary remnant of male —

Song: No. *(Beat.)* Because only a man knows how a woman is supposed to act.

Chin exits. Song turns upstage, towards Gallimard.

Gallimard (calling after Chin): Good riddance! *(To Song.)* I could forget all that betrayal in an instant, you know. If you'd just come back and become Butterfly again.

Song: Fat chance. You're here in prison, rotting in a cell. And I'm on a plane, winging my way back to China. Your President pardoned me of our treason, you know.

Gallimard: Yes, I read about that.

Song: Must make you feel . . . lower than shit.

Gallimard: But don't you, even a little bit, wish you were here with me?

Song: I'm an artist, Rene. You were my greatest . . . acting challenge. *(She laughs.)* It doesn't matter how rotten I answer, does it? You still adore me. That's why I love you, Rene. *(She points to us.)* So — you were telling your audience about the night I announced I was pregnant.

Gallimard puts his arms around Song's waist. He and Song are in the positions they were in at the end of Scene VI.

SCENE VIII

Same.

Gallimard: I'll divorce my wife. We'll live together here, and then later in France.

Song: I feel so . . . ashamed.

Gallimard: Why?

Song: I had begun to lose faith. And now, you shame me with your generosity.

Gallimard: Generosity? No, I'm proposing for very selfish reasons.

Song: Your apologies only make me feel more ashamed. My outburst a moment ago!

Gallimard: Your outburst? What about my request?!

Song: You've been very patient dealing with my . . . eccentricities. A Western man, used to women freer with their bodies —

Gallimard: It was sick! Don't make excuses for me.

Song: I have to. You don't seem willing to make them for yourself.

Pause.

Gallimard: You're crazy.

Song: I'm happy. Which often looks like crazy.

Gallimard: Then make me crazy. Marry me.

Pause.

Song: No.

Gallimard: What?

Song: Do I sound silly, a slave, if I say I'm not worthy?

Gallimard: Yes. In fact you do. No one has loved me like you.

Song: Thank you. And no one ever will. I'll see to that.

Gallimard: So what is the problem?

Song: Rene, we Chinese are realists. We understand rice, gold, and guns. You are a diplomat. Your career is skyrocketing. Now, what would happen if you divorced your wife to marry a Communist Chinese actress?

Gallimard: That's not being realistic. That's defeating yourself before you begin.

Song: We conserve our strength for the battles we can win.

Gallimard: That sounds like a fortune cookie!

Song: Where do you think fortune cookies come from!

Gallimard: I don't care.

Song: You do. So do I. And we should. That is why I say I'm not worthy. I'm worthy to love and even to be loved by you. But I am not worthy to end the career of one of the West's most promising diplomats.

Gallimard: It's not that great a career! I made it sound like more than it is!

Song: Modesty will get you nowhere. Flatter yourself, and you flatter me. I'm flattered to decline your offer. *(She exits.)*

Gallimard (to us): Butterfly and I argued all night. And, in the end, I left, knowing I would never be her husband. She went away for several months — to the countryside, like a small animal. Until the night I received her call.

A baby's cry from offstage. Song enters, carrying a child.

Song: He looks like you.

Gallimard: Oh! *(Beat; he approaches the baby.)* Well, babies are never very attractive at birth.

Song: Stop!

Gallimard: I'm sure he'll grow more beautiful with age. More like his mother.

Song: "*Chi vide mai / a bimbo del Giappon . . .*"

Gallimard: "What baby, I wonder, was ever born in Japan" — or China, for that matter —

Song: ". . . *occhi azzurrini?*"

Gallimard: "With azure eyes" — they're actually sort of brown, wouldn't you say?

Song: "*E il labbro.*"

Gallimard: "And such lips!" *(He kisses Song.)* And such lips.

Song: "*E i ricciolini d'oro schietto?*"

Gallimard: "And such a head of golden" — if slightly patchy — "curls?"

Song: I'm going to call him "Peepee."

Gallimard: Darling, could you repeat that because I'm sure a rickshaw just flew by overhead.

Song: You heard me.

Gallimard: "Song Peepee"? May I suggest Michael, or Stephan, or Adolph?

Song: You may, but I won't listen.

Gallimard: You can't be serious. Can you imagine the time this child will have in school?

Song: In the West, yes.

Gallimard: It's worse than naming him Ping Pong or Long Dong or —

Song: But he's never going to live in the West, is he?

Pause.

Gallimard: That wasn't my choice.

Song: It is mine. And this is my promise to you: I will raise him, he will be our child, but he will never burden you outside of China.

Gallimard: Why do you make these promises? I want to be burdened! I want a scandal to cover the papers!

Song (to us): Prophetic.

Gallimard: I'm serious.

Song: So am I. His name is as I registered it. And he will never live in the West.

Song exits with the child.

Gallimard (to us): Is it possible that her stubbornness only made me want her more. That drawing back at the moment of my capitulation was the most brilliant strategy she could have chosen. It is possible. But it is also possible that by this point she could have said, could have done . . . anything, and I would have adored her still.

SCENE IX

Beijing. 1966.
A driving rhythm of Chinese percussion fills the stage.

Gallimard: And then, China began to change. Mao became very old, and his cult became very strong. And, like many old men, he entered his second childhood. So he handed over the reins of state to those with minds like his own. And children ruled the Middle Kingdom° with complete caprice. The doctrine of the Cultural Revolution° implied continuous anarchy. Contact between Chinese and foreigners became impossible. Our flat was confiscated. Her fame and my money now counted against us.

Two dancers in Mao suits and red-starred caps enter, and begin crudely mimicking revolutionary violence, in an agitprop fashion.

Gallimard: And somehow the American war went wrong too. Four hundred thousand dollars were being spent for every Viet Cong° killed; so General Westmoreland's° remark that the Oriental does not value life the way Americans do was oddly accurate. Why weren't the Vietnamese people giving in? Why were they content instead to die and die and die again?

Toulon enters. Percussion and dancers continue upstage.

Toulon: Congratulations, Gallimard.

Gallimard: Excuse me, sir?

Toulon: Not a promotion. That was last time. You're going home.

Gallimard: What?

Toulon: Don't say I didn't warn you.

Gallimard: I'm being transferred . . . because I was wrong about the American war?

Toulon: Of course not. We don't care about the Americans. We care about your

---

Middle Kingdom: The royal domain of China during its feudal period.
Cultural Revolution: The reactionary campaign of 1965–1967 against opponents of the ideas of China's leader, Mao Tse-tung.
Viet Cong: Member of the Vietnamese Communist movement, against which U.S. forces were fighting.
General Westmoreland: William Westmoreland (b. 1914), commander of American troops in Vietnam from 1964 to 1968.

mind. The quality of your analysis. In general, everything you've predicted here in the Orient . . . just hasn't happened.

Gallimard: I think that's premature.

Toulon: Don't force me to be blunt. Okay, you said China was ready to open to Western trade. The only thing they're trading out there are Western heads. And, yes, you said the Americans would succeed in Indochina. You were kidding, right?

Gallimard: I think the end is in sight.

Toulon: Don't be pathetic. And don't take this personally. You were wrong. It's not your fault.

Gallimard: But I'm going home.

Toulon: Right. Could I have the number of your mistress? *(Beat.)* Joke! Joke! Eat a croissant for me.

Toulon exits. Song, wearing a Mao suit, is dragged in from the wings as part of the upstage dance. They "beat" her, then lampoon the acrobatics of the Chinese opera, as she is made to kneel onstage.

Gallimard (simultaneously): I don't care to recall how Butterfly and I said our hurried farewell. Perhaps it was better to end our affair before it killed her.

Gallimard exits. Percussion rises in volume. The lampooning becomes faster, more frenetic. At its height, Comrade Chin walks across the stage with a banner reading: "The Actor Renounces His Decadent Profession!" She reaches the kneeling Song. At the moment Chin touches Song's chin, percussion stops with a thud. Dancers strike poses.

Chin: Actor-oppressor, for years you have lived above the common people and looked down on their labor. While the farmer ate millet—

Song: I ate pastries from France and sweetmeats from silver trays.

Chin: And how did you come to live in such an exalted position?

Song: I was a plaything for the imperialists!

Chin: What did you do?

Song: I shamed China by allowing myself to be corrupted by a foreigner . . .

Chin: What does this mean? The People demand a full confession!

Song: I engaged in the lowest perversions with China's enemies!

Chin: What perversions? Be more clear!

Song: I let him put it up my ass!

Dancers look over, disgusted.

Chin: Aaaa-ya! How can you use such sickening language?!

Song: My language . . . is only as foul as the crimes I committed . . .

Chin: Yeah. That's better. So—what do you want to do . . . now?

Song: I want to serve the people

Percussion starts up, with Chinese strings.

Chin: What?

Song: I want to serve the people!

Dancers regain their revolutionary smiles, and begin a dance of victory.

Chin: What?!

Song: I want to serve the people!!

Dancers unveil a banner: "The Actor Is Re-Habilitated!" Song remains kneeling before Chin, as the dancers bounce around them, then exit. Music out.

SCENE X

A commune. Hunan Province. 1970

Chin: How you planning to do that?
Song: I've already worked four years in the fields of Hunan, Comrade Chin.
Chin: So? Farmers work all their lives. Let me see your hands.

Song holds them out for her inspection.

Chin: Goddamn! Still so smooth! How long does it take to turn you actors into good anythings? Hunh. You've just spent too many years in luxury to be any good to the Revolution.
Song: I served the Revolution.
Chin: Serve the Revolution? Bullshit! You wore dresses! Don't tell me — I was there. I saw you! You and your white vice-consul! Stuck up there in your flat, living off the People's Treasury! Yeah, I knew what was going on! You two . . . homos! Homos! Homos! *(Pause; she composes herself.)* Ah! Well . . . you will serve the people, all right. But not with the Revolution's money. This time, you use your own money.
Song: I have no money.
Chin: Shut up! And you won't stink up China anymore with your pervert stuff. You'll pollute the place where pollution begins — the West.
Song: What do you mean?
Chin: Shut up! You're going to France. Without a cent in your pocket. You find your consul's house, you make him pay your expenses —
Song: No.
Chin: And you give us weekly reports! Useful information!
Song: That's crazy. It's been four years.
Chin: Either that, or back to rehabilitation center!
Song: Comrade Chin, he's not going to support me! Not in France! He's a white man! I was just his plaything —
Chin: Oh yuck! Again with the sickening language? Where's my stick?
Song: You don't understand the mind of a man.

Pause.

Chin: Oh no? No I don't? Then how come I'm married, huh? How come I got a man? Five, six years ago, you always tell me those kind of things, I felt very bad. But not now! Because what does the Chairman say? He tells us *I'm* now the smart one, you're now the nincompoop! *You're* the blockhead, the harebrain, the nitwit! You think you're so smart? You understand "The Mind of a Man"? Good! Then *you* go to France and be a pervert for Chairman Mao!

Chin and Song exit in opposite directions.

Paris. 1968–1970.
  Gallimard enters.

Gallimard: And what was waiting for me back in Paris? Well, better Chinese food than I'd eaten in China. Friends and relatives. A little accounting, regular schedule, keeping track of traffic violations in the suburbs. . . . And the indignity of students shouting the slogans of Chairman Mao at me — in French.

Helga: Rene? Rene? *(She enters, soaking wet.)* I've had a . . . problem. *(She sneezes.)*

Gallimard: You're wet.

Helga: Yes, I . . . coming back from the grocer's. A group of students, waving red flags, they —

Gallimard fetches a towel.

Helga: — they ran by, I was caught up along with them. Before I knew what was happening —

Gallimard gives her the towel.

Helga: Thank you. The police started firing water cannons at us. I tried to shout, to tell them I was the wife of a diplomat, but — you know how it is . . . *(Pause.)* Needless to say, I lost the groceries. Rene, what's happening to France?

Gallimard: What's — ? Well, nothing, really.

Helga: Nothing?! The storefronts are in flames, there's glass in the streets, buildings are toppling — and I'm wet!

Gallimard: Nothing! . . . that I care to think about.

Helga: And is that why you stay in this room?

Gallimard: Yes, in fact.

Helga: With the incense burning? You know something? I hate incense. It smells so sickly sweet.

Gallimard: Well, I hate the French. Who just smell — period!

Helga: And the Chinese were better?

Gallimard: Please — don't start.

Helga: When we left, this exact same thing, the riots —

Gallimard: No, no . . .

Helga: Students screaming slogans, smashing down doors —

Gallimard: Helga —

Helga: It was all going on in China, too. Don't you remember?!

Gallimard: Helga! Please! *(Pause.)* You have never understood China, have you? You walk in here with these ridiculous ideas, that the West is falling apart, that China was spitting in our faces. You come in, dripping of the streets, and you leave water all over my floor. *(He grabs Helga's towel, begins mopping up the floor.)*

Helga: But it's the truth!

Gallimard: Helga, I want a divorce.

Pause; Gallimard continues mopping the floor.

Helga: I take it back. China is . . . beautiful. Incense, I like incense.

Gallimard: I've had a mistress.

Helga: So?

Gallimard: For eight years.

Helga: I knew you would. I knew you would the day I married you. And now what? You want to marry her?

Gallimard: I can't. She's in China.

Helga: I see. You know that no one else is ever going to marry me, right?

Gallimard: I'm sorry.

Helga: And you want to leave. For someone who's not here, is that right?

Gallimard: That's right.

Helga: You can't live with her, but still you don't want to live with me.

Gallimard: That's right.

Pause.

Helga: Shit. How terrible that I can figure that out. *(Pause.)* I never thought I'd say it. But, in China, I was happy. I knew, in my own way, I knew that you were not everything you pretended to be. But the pretense — going on your arm to the embassy ball, visiting your office and the guards saying, "Good morning, good morning, Madame Gallimard" — the pretense . . . was very good indeed. *(Pause.)* I hope everyone is mean to you for the rest of your life. *(She exits.)*

Gallimard (to us): Prophetic.

Marc enters with two drinks.

Gallimard (to Marc): In China, I was different from all other men.

Marc: Sure. You were white. Here's your drink.

Gallimard: I felt . . . touched.

Marc: In the head? Rene, I don't want to hear about the Oriental love goddess. Okay? One night — can we just drink and throw up without a lot of conversation?

Gallimard: You still don't believe me, do you?

Marc: Sure I do. She was the most beautiful, et cetera, et cetera, blasé, blasé.

Pause.

Gallimard: My life in the West has been such a disappointment.

Marc: Life in the West is like that. You'll get used to it. Look, you're driving me away. I'm leaving. Happy, now? *(He exits, then returns.)* Look, I have a date tomorrow night. You wanna come? I can fix you up with —

Gallimard: Of course. I would love to come.

Pause.

Marc: Uh — on second thought, no. You'd better get ahold of yourself first.

He exits; Gallimard nurses his drink.

Gallimard (to us): This is the ultimate cruelty, isn't it? That I can talk and talk and to anyone listening, it's only air — too rich a diet to be swallowed by a mundane world. Why can't anyone understand? That in China, I once loved, and was loved by, very simply, the Perfect Woman.

Song enters, dressed as Butterfly in wedding dress.

Gallimard (to Song): Not again. My imagination is hell. Am I asleep this time? Or did I drink too much?

Song: Rene!

Gallimard: God, it's too painful! That you speak?

Song: What are you talking about? Rene — touch me.

Gallimard: Why?

Song: I'm real. Take my hand.

Gallimard: Why? So you can disappear again and leave me clutching at the air? For the entertainment of my neighbors who — ?

Song touches Gallimard.

Song: Rene?

Gallimard takes Song's hand. Silence.

Gallimard: Butterfly? I never doubted you'd return.

Song: You hadn't . . . forgotten — ?

Gallimard: Yes, actually, I've forgotten everything. My mind, you see — there wasn't enough room in this hard head — not for the world *and* for you. No, there was only room for one. *(Beat.)* Come, look. See? Your bed has been waiting, with the Klimt° poster you like, and — see? The *xiang lu*° you gave me?

Song: I . . . I don't know what to say.

Gallimard: There's nothing to say. Not at the end of a long trip. Can I make you some tea?

Song: But where's your wife?

Gallimard: She's by my side. She's by my side at last.

Gallimard reaches to embrace Song. Song sidesteps, dodging him.

Gallimard: Why?!

Song (to us): So I did return to Rene in Paris. Where I found —

Gallimard: Why do you run away? Can't we show them how we embraced that evening?

Song: Please. I'm talking.

Gallimard: You have to do what I say! I'm conjuring you up in *my* mind!

Song: Rene, I've never done what you've said. Why should it be any different in your mind? Now split — the story moves on, and I must change.

Gallimard: I welcomed you into my home! I didn't have to, you know! I could've left you penniless on the streets of Paris! But I took you in!

Song: Thank you.

Gallimard: So . . . please . . . don't change.

Song: You know I have to. You know I will. And anyway, what difference does it make? No matter what your eyes tell you, you can't ignore the truth. You already know too much.

Gallimard exits. Song turns to us.

Song: The change I'm going to make requires about five minutes. So I thought

---

Klimt: Gustav Klimt (1863–1918), painter of the Austrian Secession style.
xiang lu: Incense burner.

you might want to take this opportunity to stretch your legs, enjoy a drink, or listen to the musicians. I'll be here, when you return, right where you left me.

Song goes to a mirror in front of which is a wash basin of water. She starts to remove her makeup as stagelights go to half and houselights come up.

ACT III

Scene I

A courthouse in Paris. 1986.

    As he promised, Song has completed the bulk of his transformation onstage by the time the houselights go down and the stagelights come up full. As he speaks to us, he removes his wig and kimono, leaving them on the floor. Underneath, he wears a well-cut suit.

Song: So I'd done my job better than I had a right to expect. Well, give him some credit, too. He's right — I was in a fix when I arrived in Paris. I walked from the airport into town, then I located, by blind groping, the Chinatown district. Let me make one thing clear: whatever else may be said about the Chinese, they are stingy! I slept in doorways three days until I could find a tailor who would make me this kimono on credit. As it turns out, maybe I didn't even need it. Maybe he would've been happy to see me in a simple shift and mascara. But . . . better safe than sorry.

    That was 1970, when I arrived in Paris. For the next fifteen years, yes, I lived a very comfy life. Some relief, believe me, after four years on a fucking commune in Nowheresville, China. Rene supported the boy and me, and I did some demonstrations around the country as part of my "cultural exchange" cover. And then there was the spying.

Song moves upstage, to a chair. Toulon enters as a judge, wearing the appropriate wig and robes. He sits near Song. It's 1986, and Song is testifying in a courtroom.

Song: Not much at first. Rene had lost all his high-level contacts. Comrade Chin wasn't very interested in parking-ticket statistics. But finally, at my urging, Rene got a job as a courier, handling sensitive documents. He'd photograph them for me, and I'd pass them on to the Chinese embassy.

Judge: Did he understand the extent of his activity?

Song: He didn't ask. He knew that I needed those documents, and that was enough.

Judge: But he must've known he was passing classified information.

Song: I can't say.

Judge: He never asked what you were going to do with them?

Song: Nope.

Pause.

Judge: There is one thing that the court — indeed, that all of France — would like to know.

Song: Fire away.

Judge: Did Monsieur Gallimard know you were a man?

Song: Well, he never saw me completely naked. Ever.

Judge: But surely, he must've . . . how can I put this?

Song: Put it however you like. I'm not shy. He must've felt around?

Judge: Mmmmm.

Song: Not really. I did all the work. He just laid back. Of course we did enjoy more . . . complete union, and I suppose he *might* have wondered why I was always on my stomach, but. . . . But what you're thinking is, "Of course a wrist must've brushed . . . a hand hit . . . over twenty years!" Yeah. Well, Your Honor, it was my job to make him think I was a woman. And chew on this: it wasn't all that hard. See, my mother was a prostitute along the Bundt before the Revolution. And, uh, I think it's fair to say she learned a few things about Western men. So I borrowed her knowledge. In service to my country.

Judge: Would you care to enlighten the court with this secret knowledge? I'm sure we're all very curious.

Song: I'm sure you are. *(Pause.)* Okay, Rule One is: Men always believe what they want to hear. So a girl can tell the most obnoxious lies and the guys will believe them every time — "This is my first time" — "That's the biggest I've ever seen" — or *both,* which, if you really think about it, is not possible in a single lifetime. You've maybe heard those phrases a few times in your own life, yes, Your Honor?

Judge: It's not my life, Monsieur Song, which is on trial today.

Song: Okay, okay, just trying to lighten up the proceedings. Tough room.

Judge: Go on.

Song: Rule Two: As soon as a Western man comes into contact with the East — he's already confused. The West has sort of an international rape mentality towards the East. Do you know rape mentality?

Judge: Give us your definition, please.

Song: Basically, "Her mouth says no, but her eyes say yes."

   The West thinks of itself as masculine — big guns, big industry, big money — so the East is feminine — weak, delicate, poor . . . but good at art, and full of inscrutable wisdom — the feminine mystique.

   Her mouth says no, but her eyes say yes. The West believes the East, deep down, *wants* to be dominated — because a woman can't think for herself.

Judge: What does this have to do with my question?

Song: You expect Oriental countries to submit to your guns, and you expect Oriental women to be submissive to your men. That's why you say they make the best wives.

Judge: But why would that make it possible for you to fool Monsieur Gallimard? Please — get to the point.

Song: One, because when he finally met his fantasy woman, he wanted more than anything to believe that she was, in fact, a woman. And second, I am an Oriental. And being an Oriental, I could never be completely a man.

Pause.

Judge: Your armchair political theory is tenuous, Monsieur Song.

Song: You think so? That's why you'll lose in all your dealings with the East.

Judge: Just answer my question: did he know you were a man?

Pause.

Song: You know, Your Honor, I never asked.

SCENE II

Same.
    Music from the "Death Scene" from Butterfly *blares over the house speakers. It is the loudest thing we've heard in this play.*
    Gallimard enters, crawling towards Song's wig and kimono.

Gallimard: Butterfly? Butterfly?

Song remains a man, in the witness box, delivering a testimony we do not hear.

Gallimard (to us): In my moment of greatest shame, here, in this courtroom —
with that . . . person up there, telling the world. . . . What strikes me
especially is how shallow he is, how glib and obsequious . . . completely
. . . without substance! The type that prowls around discos with a gold
medallion stinking of garlic. So little like my Butterfly.
    Yet even in this moment my mind remains agile, flip-flopping like a
man on a trampoline. Even now, my picture dissolves, and I see that . . .
witness . . . talking to me.

Song suddenly stands straight up in his witness box, and looks at Gallimard.

Song: Yes. You. White man.

Song steps out of the witness box, and moves downstage towards Gallimard. Light change.

Gallimard (to Song): Who? Me?
Song: Do you see any other white men?
Gallimard: Yes. There're white men all around. This is a French courtroom.
Song: So you are an adventurous imperialist. Tell me, why did it take you so
long? To come back to this place?
Gallimard: What place?
Song: This theater in China. Where we met many years ago.
Gallimard (to us): And once again, against my will, I am transported.

Chinese opera music comes up on the speakers. Song begins to do opera moves, as he did the night they met.

Song: Do you remember? The night you gave your heart?
Gallimard: It was a long time ago.
Song: Not long enough. A night that turned your world upside down.
Gallimard: Perhaps.
Song: Oh, be honest with me. What's another bit of flattery when you've already
given me twenty years' worth? It's a wonder my head hasn't swollen to the
size of China.
Gallimard: Who's to say it hasn't?
Song: Who's to say? And what's the shame? In pride? You think I could've pulled
this off if I wasn't already full of pride when we met? No, not just pride.

Arrogance. It takes arrogance, really — to believe you can will, with your eyes and your lips, the destiny of another. *(He dances.)* C'mon. Admit it. You still want me. Even in slacks and a button-down collar.

Gallimard: I don't see what the point of —

Song: You don't? Well maybe, Rene, just maybe — I want you.

Gallimard: You do?

Song: Then again, maybe I'm just playing with you. How can you tell? *(Reprising his feminine character, he sidles up to Gallimard.)* "How I wish there were even a small café to sit in. With men in tuxedos, and cappuccinos, and bad expatriate jazz." Now you want to kiss me, don't you?

Gallimard (pulling away): What makes you — ?

Song: — so sure? See? I take the words from your mouth. Then I wait for you to come and retrieve them. *(He reclines on the floor.)*

Gallimard: Why?! Why do you treat me so cruelly?

Song: Perhaps I *was* treating you cruelly. But now — I'm being nice. Come here, my little one.

Gallimard: I'm not your little one!

Song: My mistake. It's I who am *your* little one, right?

Gallimard: Yes, I —

Song: So come get your little one. If you like, I may even let you strip me.

Gallimard: I mean, you were! Before . . . but not like this!

Song: I was? Then perhaps I still am. If you look hard enough. *(He starts to remove his clothes.)*

Gallimard: What — what are you doing?

Song: Helping you to see through my act.

Gallimard: Stop that! I don't want to! I don't —

Song: Oh, but you asked me to strip, remember?

Gallimard: What? That was years ago! And I took it back!

Song: No. You postponed it. Postponed the inevitable. Today, the inevitable has come calling.

From the speakers, cacophony: Butterfly mixed in with Chinese gongs.

Gallimard: No! Stop! I don't want to see!

Song: Then look away.

Gallimard: You're only in my mind! All this is in my mind! I order you! To stop!

Song: To what? To strip? That's just what I'm —

Gallimard: No! Stop! I want you — !

Song: You want me?

Gallimard: To stop!

Song: You know something, Rene? Your mouth says no, but your eyes say yes. Turn them away. I dare you.

Gallimard: I don't have to! Every night, you say you're going to strip, but then I beg you and you stop!

Song: I guess tonight is different.

Gallimard: Why? Why should that be?

Song: Maybe I've become frustrated. Maybe I'm saying "Look at me, you fool!" Or maybe I'm just feeling . . . sexy. *(He is down to his briefs.)*

Gallimard: Please. This is unnecessary. I know what you are.

Song: You do? What am I?

Gallimard: A — a man.

Song: You don't really believe that.

Gallimard: Yes I do! I knew all the time somewhere that my happiness was temporary, my love a deception. But my mind kept the knowledge at bay. To make the wait bearable.

Song: Monsieur Gallimard — the wait is over.

Song drops his briefs. He is naked. Sound cue out. Slowly, we and Song come to the realization that what we had thought to be Gallimard's sobbing is actually his laughter.

Gallimard: Oh god! What an idiot! Of course!

Song: Rene — what?

Gallimard: Look at you! You're a man! (He bursts into laughter again.)

Song: I fail to see what's so funny!

Gallimard: "You fail to see —!" I mean, you never did have much of a sense of humor, did you? I just think it's ridiculously funny that I've wasted so much time on just a man!

Song: Wait. I'm not "just a man."

Gallimard: No? Isn't that what you've been trying to convince me of?

Song: Yes, but what I mean —

Gallimard: And now, I finally believe you, and you tell me it's not true? I think you must have some kind of identity problem.

Song: Will you listen to me?

Gallimard: Why?! I've been listening to you for twenty years. Don't I deserve a vacation?

Song: I'm not just any man!

Gallimard: Then, what exactly are you?

Song: Rene, how can you ask — ? Okay, what about this?

He picks up Butterfly's robes, starts to dance around. No music.

Gallimard: Yes, that's very nice. I have to admit.

Song holds out his arm to Gallimard.

Song: It's the same skin you've worshipped for years. Touch it.

Gallimard: Yes, it does feel the same.

Song: Now — close your eyes.

Song covers Gallimard's eyes with one hand. With the other, Song draws Gallimard's hand up to his face. Gallimard, like a blind man, lets his hands run over Song's face.

Gallimard: This skin, I remember. The curve of her face, the softness of her cheek, her hair against the back of my hand . . .

Song: I'm your Butterfly. Under the robes, beneath everything, it was always me. Now, open your eyes and admit it — you adore me. (He removes his hand from Gallimard's eyes.)

Gallimard: You, who knew every inch of my desires — how could you, of all people, have made such a mistake?

Song: What?

Gallimard: You showed me your true self. When all I loved was the lie. A perfect lie, which you let fall to the ground — and now, it's old and soiled.

Song: So — you never really loved me? Only when I was playing a part?

Gallimard: I'm a man who loved a woman created by a man. Everything else — simply falls short.

Pause.

Song: What am I supposed to do now?

Gallimard: You were a fine spy, Monsieur Song, with an even finer accomplice. But now I believe you should go. Get out of my life!

Song: Go where? Rene, you can't live without me. Not after twenty years.

Gallimard: I certainly can't live with you — not after twenty years of betrayal.

Song: Don't be stubborn! Where will you go?

Gallimard: I have a date . . . with my Butterfly.

Song: So, throw away your pride. And come . . .

Gallimard: Get away from me! Tonight, I've finally learned to tell fantasy from reality. And, knowing the difference, I choose fantasy.

Song: I'm your fantasy!

Gallimard: You? You're as real as hamburger. Now get out! I have a date with my Butterfly and I don't want your body polluting the room! *(He tosses Song's suit at him.)* Look at these — you dress like a pimp.

Song: Hey! These are Armani slacks and — ! *(He puts on his briefs and slacks.)* Let's just say . . . I'm disappointed in you, Rene. In the crush of your adoration, I thought you'd become something more. More like . . . a woman.

But no. Men. You're like the rest of them. It's all in the way we dress, and make up our faces, and bat our eyelashes. You really have so little imagination!

Gallimard: You, Monsieur Song? Accuse me of too little imagination? You, if anyone, should know — I am pure imagination. And in imagination I will remain. Now get out!

Gallimard bodily removes Song from the stage, taking his kimono.

Song: Rene! I'll never put on those robes again! You'll be sorry!

Gallimard (to Song): I'm already sorry! *(Looking at the kimono in his hands.)* Exactly as sorry . . . as a Butterfly.

SCENE III

M. Gallimard's prison cell. Paris. 1988.

Gallimard: I've played out the events of my life night after night, always searching for a new ending to my story, one where I leave this cell and return forever to my Butterfly's arms.

Tonight I realize my search is over. That I've looked all along in the wrong place. And now, to you, I will prove that my love was not in vain — by returning to the world of fantasy where I first met her.

He picks up the kimono; dancers enter.

Gallimard: There is a vision of the Orient that I have. Of slender women in chong sams and kimonos who die for the love of unworthy foreign devils. Who are born and raised to be the perfect women. Who take whatever punishment we give them, and bounce back, strengthened by love, unconditionally. It is a vision that has become my life.

Dancers bring the washbasin to him and help him make up his face.

Gallimard: In public, I have continued to deny that Song Liling is a man. This brings me headlines, and is a source of great embarrassment to my French colleagues, who can now be sent into a coughing fit by the mere mention of Chinese food. But alone, in my cell, I have long since faced the truth.

And the truth demands a sacrifice. For mistakes made over the course of a lifetime. My mistakes were simple and absolute — the man I loved was a cad, a bounder. He deserved nothing but a kick in the behind, and instead I gave him . . . all my love.

Yes — love. Why not admit it all? That was my undoing, wasn't it? Love warped my judgment, blinded my eyes, rearranged the very lines on my face . . . until I could look in the mirror and see nothing but . . . a woman.

Dancers help him put on the Butterfly wig.

Gallimard: I have a vision. Of the Orient. That, deep within its almond eyes, there are still women. Women willing to sacrifice themselves for the love of a man. Even a man whose love is completely without worth.

Dancers assist Gallimard in donning the kimono. They hand him a knife.

Gallimard: Death with honor is better than life . . . life with dishonor. *(He sets himself center stage, in a seppuku position.)* The love of a Butterfly can withstand many things — unfaithfulness, loss, even abandonment. But how can it face the one sin that implies all others? The devastating knowledge that, underneath it all, the object of her love was nothing more, nothing less than . . . a man. *(He sets the tip of the knife against his body.)* It is 1988. And I have found her at last. In a prison on the outskirts of Paris. My name is Rene Gallimard — also known as Madame Butterfly.

Gallimard turns upstage and plunges the knife into his body, as music from the "Love Duet" blares over the speakers. He collapses into the arms of the dancers, who lay him reverently on the floor. The image holds for several beats. Then a tight special up on Song, who stands as a man, staring at the dead Gallimard. He smokes a cigarette; the smoke filters up through the lights. Two words leave his lips.

Song: Butterfly? Butterfly?

Smoke rises as lights fade slowly to black.

Connections to Other Selections

1. At first glance Rene Gallimard and Sophocles' Oedipus in *Oedipus the King* (p. 1120) are very different kinds of characters, but how might their situations — particularly their discoveries about themselves — be compared? What significant similarities do you find in these two characters? Explain whether you think Gallimard can be seen as a tragic character.
2. Compare the function of Puccini's *Madame Butterfly* in *M. Butterfly* with that of the play within the play in Shakespeare's *Hamlet* (p. 1281). How are these internal

dramatic actions used to comment on the events of each larger play? How is role playing relevant to the theme of each play?

3. Compare and contrast the way women are represented in *M. Butterfly* and Yukio Mishima's short story "Patriotism" (p. 506).

4. Write an essay comparing Gallimard's illusions with those of Amanda in Tennessee Williams's *The Glass Menagerie* (p. 1666).

TENDER OFFER

Born in Brooklyn, New York, in 1950, Wendy Wasserstein has studied at Mount Holyoke College, City College of New York, and the Yale School of Drama. A resident of Greenwich Village, she is also a resident playwright at New York's Playwrights Horizon Theatre off-Broadway, where many of her plays have been performed before audiences receptive to Wasserstein's humorous treatment of feminist issues. Among her plays are *Uncommon Women* (1977), *Isn't It Romantic* (1980), and the enormously successful *The Heidi Chronicles* (1988), which won numerous honors including a Tony Award, a Pulitzer Prize, and the New York Drama Critics Circle Award. In 1990 her book of essays, *Bachelor Girl,* was published. She has received National Endowment for the Arts and Guggenheim grants in support of her work.

Tender Offer, which appeared in a special issue of one-act plays in the spring 1991 *Antaeus,* is a brief but absorbing treatment of the tentative relationship between a father and daughter. Characteristic of Wasserstein's work, this play uses humor deftly to present a serious moment that requires a "good deal" to resolve it.

WENDY WASSERSTEIN (b. 1950)
Tender Offer   1991

A girl of around nine is alone in a dance studio. She is dressed in traditional leotards and tights. She begins singing to herself, "Nothing Could be Finer Than to Be in Carolina." She maps out a dance routine, including parts for the chorus. She builds to a finale. A man, Paul, around thirty-five, walks in. He has a sweet, though distant, demeanor. As he walks in, Lisa notices him and stops.

Paul: You don't have to stop, sweetheart.
Lisa: That's okay.
Paul: Looked very good.
Lisa: Thanks.
Paul: Don't I get a kiss hello?
Lisa: Sure.
Paul (embraces her): Hi, Tiger.
Lisa: Hi, Dad.

Paul: I'm sorry I'm late.

Lisa: That's okay.

Paul: How'd it go?

Lisa: Good.

Paul: Just good?

Lisa: Pretty good.

Paul: "Pretty good." You mean you got a lot of applause or "pretty good" you could have done better?

Lisa: Well, Courtney Palumbo's mother thought I was pretty good. But you know the part in the middle when everybody's supposed to freeze and the big girl comes out. Well, I think I moved a little bit.

Paul: I thought what you were doing looked very good.

Lisa: Daddy, that's not what I was doing. That was tap-dancing. I made that up.

Paul: Oh. Well it looked good. Kind of sexy.

Lisa: Yuch!

Paul: What do you mean "yuch"?

Lisa: Just yuch!

Paul: You don't want to be sexy?

Lisa: I don't care.

Paul: Let's go, Tiger. I promised your mother I'd get you home in time for dinner.

Lisa: I can't find my leg warmers.

Paul: You can't find your what?

Lisa: Leg warmers. I can't go home till I find my leg warmers.

Paul: I don't see you looking for them.

Lisa: I was waiting for you.

Paul: Oh.

Lisa: Daddy.

Paul: What?

Lisa: Nothing.

Paul: Where do you think you left them?

Lisa: Somewhere around here. I can't remember.

Paul: Well, try to remember, Lisa. We don't have all night.

Lisa: I told you. I think somewhere around here.

Paul: I don't see them. Let's go home now. You'll call the dancing school tomorrow.

Lisa: Daddy, I can't go home till I find them. Miss Judy says it's not professional to leave things.

Paul: Who's Miss Judy?

Lisa: She's my ballet teacher. She once danced the lead in *Swan Lake,* and she was a June Taylor dancer.

Paul: Well, then, I'm sure she'll understand about the leg warmers.

Lisa: Daddy, Miss Judy wanted to know why you were late today.

Paul: Hmmmmmmmmm?

Lisa: Why were you late?

Paul: I was in a meeting. Business. I'm sorry.

Lisa: Why did you tell Mommy you'd come instead of her if you knew you had business?

Paul: Honey, something just came up. I thought I'd be able to be here. I was looking forward to it.

Lisa: I wish you wouldn't make appointments to see me.

Paul: Hmmmmmmmm.

Lisa: You shouldn't make appointments to see me unless you know you're going to come.

Paul: Of course I'm going to come.

Lisa: No, you're not. Talia Robbins told me she's much happier living without her father in the house. Her father used to come home late and go to sleep early.

Paul: Lisa, stop it. Let's go.

Lisa: I can't find my leg warmers.

Paul: Forget your leg warmers.

Lisa: Daddy.

Paul: What is it?

Lisa: I saw this show on television, I think it was WPIX Channel 11. Well, the father was crying about his daughter.

Paul: Why was he crying? Was she sick?

Lisa: No. She was at school. And he was at business. And he just missed her, so he started to cry.

Paul: What was the name of this show?

Lisa: I don't know. I came in in the middle.

Paul: Well, Lisa, I certainly would cry if you were sick or far away, but I know that you're well and you're home. So no reason to get maudlin.

Lisa: What's maudlin?

Paul: Sentimental, soppy. Frequently used by children who make things up to get attention.

Lisa: I am sick! I am sick! I have Hodgkin's disease and a bad itch on my leg.

Paul: What do you mean you have Hodgkin's disease? Don't say things like that.

Lisa: Swoosie Kurtz, she had Hodgkin's disease on a TV movie last year, but she got better and now she's on *Love Sidney*.

Paul: Who is Swoosie Kurtz?

Lisa: She's an actress named after an airplane. I saw her on *Live at Five*.

Paul: You watch too much television; you should do your homework. Now, put your coat on.

Lisa: Daddy, I really do have a bad itch on my leg. Would you scratch it?

Paul: Lisa, you're procrastinating.

Lisa: Why do you use words I don't understand? I hate it. You're like Daria Feldman's mother. She always talks in Yiddish to her husband so Daria won't understand.

Paul: Procrastinating is not Yiddish.

Lisa: Well, I don't know what it is.

Paul: Procrastinating means you don't want to go about your business.

Lisa: I don't go to business. I go to school.

Paul: What I mean is you want to hang around here until you and I are late for dinner and your mother's angry and it's too late for you to do your homework.

Lisa: I do not.

Paul: Well, it sure looks that way. Now put your coat on and let's go.

Lisa: Daddy.

Paul: Honey, I'm tired. Really, later.

Lisa: Why don't you want to talk to me?

Paul: I do want to talk to you. I promise when we get home we'll have a nice talk.

Lisa: No, we won't. You'll read the paper and fall asleep in front of the news.

Paul: Honey, we'll talk on the weekend, I promise. Aren't I taking you to the theater this weekend? Let me look. (*He takes out appointment book.*) Yes. Sunday. *Joseph and the Amazing Technicolor Raincoat* with Lisa. Okay, Tiger?

Lisa: Sure. It's Dreamcoat.

Paul: What?

Lisa: Nothing. I think I see my leg warmers. (*She goes to pick them up, and an odd-looking trophy.*)

Paul: What's that?

Lisa: It's stupid. I was second best at the dance recital, so they gave me this thing. It's stupid.

Paul: Lisa.

Lisa: What?

Paul: What did you want to talk about?

Lisa: Nothing.

Paul: Was it about my missing your recital? I'm really sorry, Tiger. I would have liked to have been here.

Lisa: That's okay.

Paul: Honest?

Lisa: Daddy, you're prostrastinating.

Paul: I'm procrastinating. Sit down. Let's talk. So. How's school?

Lisa: Fine.

Paul: You like it?

Lisa: Yup.

Paul: You looking forward to camp this summer?

Lisa: Yup.

Paul: Is Daria Feldman going back?

Lisa: Nope.

Paul: Why not?

Lisa: I don't know. We can go home now. Honest, my foot doesn't itch anymore.

Paul: Lisa, you know what you do in business when it seems like there's nothing left to say? That's when you really start talking. Put a bid on the table.

Lisa: What's a bid?

Paul: You tell me what you want and I'll tell you what I've got to offer. Like Monopoly. You want Boardwalk, but I'm only willing to give you the Rail-roads. Now, because you are my daughter I'd throw in Water Works and Electricity. Understand, Tiger?

Lisa: No. I don't like board games. You know, Daddy, we could get Space Invaders for our home for thirty-five dollars. In fact, we could get an Osborne System for two thousand. Daria Feldman's parents . . .

Paul: Daria Feldman's parents refuse to talk to Daria, so they bought a computer to keep Daria busy so they won't have to speak in Yiddish. Daria will probably grow up to be a homicidal maniac lesbian prostitute.

Lisa: I know what that word prostitute means.

Paul: Good. (*Pause.*) You still haven't told me about school. Do you still like your teacher?

Lisa: She's okay.

Paul: Lisa, if we're talking try to answer me.

Lisa: I am answering you. Can we go home now, please?

Paul: Damn it, Lisa, if you want to talk to me . . . Talk to me!

Lisa: I can't wait till I'm old enough so I can make my own money and never have to see you again. Maybe I'll become a prostitute.

Paul: Young lady, that's enough.

Lisa: I hate you, Daddy! I hate you! (*She throws her trophy into the trash bin.*)

Paul: What'd you do that for?

Lisa: It's stupid.

Paul: Maybe I wanted it.

Lisa: What for?

Paul: Maybe I wanted to put it where I keep your dinosaur and the picture you made of Mrs. Kimbel with the chicken pox.

Lisa: You got mad at me when I made that picture. You told me I had to respect Mrs. Kimbel because she was my teacher.

Paul: That's true. But she wasn't my teacher. I liked her better with the chicken pox. (*Pause.*) Lisa, I'm sorry. I was very wrong to miss your recital, and you don't have to become a prostitute. That's not the type of profession Miss Judy has in mind for you.

Lisa (mumbles): No.

Paul: No. (*Pause.*) So Talia Robbins is really happy her father moved out?

Lisa: Talia Robbins picks open the eighth-grade lockers during gym period. But she did that before her father moved out.

Paul: You can't always judge someone by what they do or what they don't do. Sometimes you come home from dancing school and run upstairs and shut the door, and when I finally get to talk to you, everything is "okay" or "fine." Yup or nope?

Lisa: Yup.

Paul: Sometimes, a lot of times, I come home and fall asleep in front of the television. So you and I spend a lot of time being a little scared of each other. Maybe?

Lisa: Maybe.

Paul: Tell you what. I'll make you a tender offer.

Lisa: What?

Paul: I'll make you a tender offer. That's when one company publishes in the newspaper that they want to buy another company. And the company that publishes is called the Black Knight because they want to gobble up the poor little company. So the poor little company needs to be rescued. And then a White Knight comes along and makes a bigger and better offer so the shareholders won't have to tender shares to the Big Black Knight. You with me?

Lisa: Sort of.

Paul: I'll make you a tender offer like the White Knight. But I don't want to own you. I just want to make a much better offer. Okay?

Lisa (sort of understanding): Okay. (*Pause. They sit for a moment.*) Sort of,

Daddy, what do you think about? I mean, like when you're quiet what do you think about?

Paul: Oh, business usually. If I think I made a mistake or if I think I'm doing okay. Sometimes I think about what I'll be doing five years from now and if it's what I hoped it would be five years ago. Sometimes I think about what your life will be like, if Mount Saint Helens will erupt again. What you'll become if you'll study penmanship or word processing. If you speak kindly of me to your psychiatrist when you are in graduate school. And how the hell I'll pay for your graduate school. And sometimes I try and think what it was I thought about when I was your age.

Lisa: Do you ever look out your window at the clouds and try to see which kinds of shapes they are? Like one time, honest, I saw the head of Walter Cronkite in a flower vase. Really! Like look don't those kinda look like if you turn it upside down, two big elbows or two elephant trunks dancing?

Paul: Actually still looks like Walter Cronkite in a flower vase to me. But look up a little. See the one that's still moving? That sorta looks like a whale on a thimble.

Lisa: Where?

Paul: Look up. To your right.

Lisa: I don't see it. Where?

Paul: The other way.

Lisa: Oh, yeah! There's the head and there's the stomach. Yeah! (*Lisa picks up her trophy.*) Hey, Daddy.

Paul: Hey, Lisa.

Lisa: You can have this thing if you want it. But you have to put it like this, because if you put it like that it is gross.

Paul: You know what I'd like? So I can tell people who come into my office why I have this gross stupid thing on my shelf, I'd like it if you could show me your dance recital.

Lisa: Now?

Paul: We've got time. Mother said she won't be home till late.

Lisa: Well, Daddy, during a lot of it I freeze and the big girl in front dances.

Paul: Well, how 'bout the number you were doing when I walked in?

Lisa: Well, see, I have parts for a lot of people in that one, too.

Paul: I'll dance the other parts.

Lisa: You can't dance.

Paul: Young lady, I played Yvette Mimimeux in a *Hasty Pudding Show.*

Lisa: Who's Yvette Mimimeux?

Paul: Watch more television. You'll find out. (*Paul stands up.*) So I'm ready. (*He begins singing.*) "Nothing could be finer than to be in Carolina."

Lisa: Now I go. In the morning. And now you go. Dum-da.

Paul (obviously not a tap dancer): Da-da-dum.

Lisa (whines): Daddy!

Paul (mimics her): Lisa! Nothing could be finer . . .

Lisa: That looks dumb.

Paul: Oh, yeah? You think they do this better in *The Amazing Minkcoat?* No way! Now you go — da da da dum.

Lisa: Da da da dum.

Paul: If I had Aladdin's lamp for only a day, I'd make a wish. . . .

Lisa: Daddy, that's maudlin!

Paul: I know it's maudlin. And here's what I'd say:

Lisa and Paul: I'd say that "nothing could be finer than to be in Carolina in the mooooooooooornin'."

Connections to Other Selections

1. Compare the fathers in *Tender Offer* and Bharati Mukherjee's short story "Fathering" (p. 77). Which father do you prefer? Explain why.
2. *Tender Offer* and Jane Martin's *Rodeo* (p. 1661) are extremely brief dramatic works that present conflicts in which business serves as an antagonist. Write an essay on the nature of the conflicts in each play and how business is the source of those conflicts.

34. Perspectives on Drama

Among the selections in this chapter are commentaries that focus on individual plays as well as drama in general. Included are the opening scene from Susan Glaspell's short story version of *Trifles,* Tennessee Williams's production notes to *The Glass Menagerie,* Arthur Miller on tragedy in the twentieth century, Eric Bentley on drama as literature and performance, a student essay on *Death of a Salesman,* and interviews with August Wilson and David Henry Hwang. These and several other miscellaneous items should stimulate responses to both particular plays and broad issues associated with dramatic literature and performances.

SUSAN GLASPELL (1882–1948)
From the Short Story Version of Trifles   1917

When Martha Hale opened the storm-door and got a cut of the north wind, she ran back for her big woolen scarf. As she hurriedly wound that round her head her eye made a scandalized sweep of her kitchen. It was no ordinary thing that called her away — it was probably farther from ordinary than anything that had ever happened in Dickson County. But what her eye took in was that her kitchen was in no shape for leaving: her bread all ready for mixing, half the flour sifted and half unsifted.

She hated to see things half done; but she had been at that when the team from town stopped to get Mr. Hale, and then the sheriff came running in to say his wife wished Mrs. Hale would come too — adding, with a grin, that he guessed she was getting scarey and wanted another woman along. So she had dropped everything right where it was.

"Martha!" now came her husband's impatient voice. "Don't keep folks waiting out here in the cold."

She again opened the storm-door, and this time joined the three men and the one woman waiting for her in the big two-seated buggy.

After she had the robes tucked around her she took another look at the woman who sat beside her on the back seat. She had met Mrs. Peters the year before at the county fair, and the thing she remembered about her was that she didn't seem like a sheriff's wife. She was small and thin and didn't have a strong voice. Mrs. Gorman, sheriff's wife before Gorman went out and Peters came in, had a voice that somehow seemed to be backing up the law with every word. But if Mrs. Peters didn't look like a sheriff's wife, Peters made it up in looking like a sheriff. He was to a dot the kind of man who could get himself elected sheriff — a heavy man with a big voice, who was particularly genial with the law-abiding, as if to make it plain that he knew the difference between criminals and noncriminals. And right there it came into Mrs. Hale's mind, with a stab, that this man who was so pleasant and lively with all of them was going to the Wrights' now as a sheriff.

"The country's not very pleasant this time of year," Mrs. Peters at last ventured, as if she felt they ought to be talking as well as the men.

Mrs. Hale scarcely finished her reply, for they had gone up a little hill and could see the Wright place now, and seeing it did not make her feel like talking. It looked very lonesome this cold March morning. It had always been a lonesome-looking place. It was down in a hollow, and the poplar trees around it were lonesome-looking trees. The men were looking at it and talking about what had happened. The county attorney was bending to one side of the buggy, and kept looking steadily at the place as they drew up to it.

"I'm glad you came with me," Mrs. Peters said nervously, as the two women were about to follow the men in through the kitchen door.

Even after she had her foot on the door-step, her hand on the knob, Martha Hale had a moment of feeling she could not cross that threshold. And the reason it seemed she couldn't cross it now was simply because she hadn't crossed it before. Time and time again it had been in her mind, "I ought to go over and see Minnie Foster" — she still thought of her as Minnie Foster, though for twenty years she had been Mrs. Wright. And then there was always something to do and Minnie Foster would go from her mind. But *now* she could come.

The men went over to the stove. The women stood close together by the door. Young Henderson, the county attorney, turned around and said, "Come up to the fire, ladies."

Mrs. Peters took a step forward, then stopped. "I'm not — cold," she said.

And so the two women stood by the door, at first not even so much as looking around the kitchen.

The men talked for a minute about what a good thing it was the sheriff had sent his deputy out that morning to make a fire for them, and then Sheriff Peters stepped back from the stove, unbuttoned his outer coat, and leaned his hands on the kitchen table in a way that seemed to mark the beginning of official business. "Now, Mr. Hale," he said in a sort of semiofficial voice, "before we move things about, you tell Mr. Henderson just what it was you saw when you came here yesterday morning."

The county attorney was looking around the kitchen.

"By the way," he said, "has anything been moved?" He turned to the sheriff. "Are things just as you left them yesterday?"

Peters looked from cupboard to sink; from that to a small worn rocker a little to one side of the kitchen table.

"It's just the same."

"Somebody should have been left here yesterday," said the county attorney.

"Oh — yesterday," returned the sheriff, with a little gesture as if yesterday having been more than he could bear to think of. "When I had to send Frank to Morris Center for that man who went crazy — let me tell you, I had my hands full *yesterday*. I knew you could get back from Omaha by to-day, George, and as long as I went over everything here myself — "

"Well, Mr. Hale," said the county attorney, in a way of letting what was past and gone go, "tell just what happened when you came here yesterday morning."

Mrs. Hale, still leaning against the door, had that sinking feeling of the mother whose child is about to speak a piece. Lewis often wandered along and got things mixed up in a story. She hoped he would tell this straight and plain, and not say unnecessary things that would just make things harder for Minnie Foster. He didn't begin at once, and she noticed that he looked queer — as if standing in that kitchen and having to tell what he had seen there yesterday morning made him almost sick.

"Yes, Mr. Hale?" the county attorney reminded.

"Harry and I had started to town with a load of potatoes," Mrs. Hale's husband began.

Harry was Mrs. Hale's oldest boy. He wasn't with them now, for the very good reason that those potatoes never got to town yesterday and he was taking them this morning, so he hadn't been home when the sheriff stopped to say he wanted Mr. Hale to come over to the Wright place and tell the county attorney his story there, where he could point it all out. With all Mrs. Hale's other emotions came the fear that maybe Harry wasn't dressed warm enough — they hadn't any of them realized how that north wind did bite.

"We come along this road," Hale was going on, with a motion of his hand to the road over which they had just come, "and as we got in sight of the house I says to Harry, 'I'm goin' to see if I can't get John Wright to take a telephone.' You see," he explained to Henderson, "unless I can get somebody to go in with me they won't come out this branch road except for a price *I* can't pay. I'd spoke to Wright about it once before; but he put me off, saying folks talked too much anyway, and all he asked was peace and quiet — guess you know about how much he talked himself. But I thought maybe if I went to the house and talked about it before his wife, and said all the women-folks liked the telephones, and that in this lonesome stretch of road it would be a good thing — well, I said to Harry that that was what I was going to say — though I said at the same time that I didn't know as what his wife wanted made much difference to John — "

Now, there he was! — saying things he didn't need to say. Mrs. Hale tried to catch her husband's eye, but fortunately the county attorney interrupted with:

"Let's talk about that a little later, Mr. Hale. I do want to talk about that, but I'm anxious now to get along to just what happened when you got here."

From "A Jury of Her Peers"

Considerations for Critical Thinking and Writing

1. In this opening scene from the story, how is the setting established differently from the way it is in the play (p. 1084)?
2. What kind of information is provided in the opening paragraphs of the story that

is missing from the play's initial scene? What is emphasized early in the story but not in the play?

3. Which version brings us into more intimate contact with the characters? How is that achieved?
4. Does the short story title, "A Jury of Her Peers," suggest any shift in emphasis from the play's title, *Trifles?*
5. Explain why you prefer one version over another.

TENNESSEE WILLIAMS (1911–1983)
Production Notes to The Glass Menagerie   1945

Being a "memory play," *The Glass Menagerie* can be presented with unusual freedom of convention. Because of its considerably delicate or tenuous material, atmospheric touches and subtleties of direction play a particularly important part. Expressionism and all other unconventional techniques in drama have only one valid aim, and that is a closer approach to truth. When a play employs unconventional techniques, it is not, or certainly shouldn't be, trying to escape its responsibility of dealing with reality, or interpreting experience, but is actually or should be attempting to find a closer approach, a more penetrating and vivid expression of things as they are. The straight realistic play with its genuine Frigidaire and authentic ice cubes, its characters that speak exactly as its audience speaks, corresponds to the academic landscape and has the same virtue of a photographic likeness. Everyone should know nowadays the unimportance of the photographic in art: that truth, life, or reality is an organic thing which the poetic imagination can represent or suggest, in essence, only through transformation, through changing into other forms than those which were merely present in appearance.

These remarks are not meant as a preface only to this particular play. They have to do with a conception of a new, plastic theater which must take the place of the exhausted theater of realistic conventions if the theater is to resume vitality as a part of our culture.

The Screen Device. There is *only one important difference between the original and acting version of the play* and that is the *omission* in the latter of the device which I tentatively included in my *original* script. This device was the use of a screen on which were projected magic-lantern slides bearing images or titles. I do not regret the omission of this device from the present Broadway production. The extraordinary power of Miss Taylor's° performance made it suitable to have the utmost simplicity in the physical production. But I think it may be interesting to some readers to see how this device was conceived. So I am putting it into the published manuscript. These images and legends, projected from behind, were cast on a section of wall between the front-room and dining-room areas, which should be indistinguishable from the rest when not in use.

Miss Taylor's: Laurette Taylor (1884–1946) played the role of Amanda in the original Broadway production.

The purpose of this will probably be apparent. It is to give accent to certain values in each scene. Each scene contains a particular point (or several) which is structurally the most important. In an episodic play, such as this, the basic structure or narrative line may be obscured from the audience; the effect may seem fragmentary rather than architectural. This may not be the fault of the play so much as a lack of attention in the audience. The legend or image upon the screen will strengthen the effect of what is merely allusion in the writing and allow the primary point to be made more simply and lightly than if the entire responsibility were on the spoken lines. Aside from this structural value, I think the screen will have a definite emotional appeal, less definable but just as important. An imaginative producer or director may invent many other uses for this device than those indicated in the present script. In fact the possibilities of the device seem much larger to me than the instance of this play can possibly utilize.

The Music. Another extra-literary accent in this play is provided by the use of music. A single recurring tune, "The Glass Menagerie," is used to give emotional emphasis to suitable passages. This tune is like circus music, not when you are on the grounds or in the immediate vicinity of the parade, but when you are at some distance and very likely thinking of something else. It seems under those circumstances to continue almost interminably and it weaves in and out of your preoccupied consciousness; then it is the lightest, most delicate music in the world and perhaps the saddest. It expresses the surface vivacity of life with the underlying strain of immutable and inexpressible sorrow. When you look at a piece of delicately spun glass you think of two things: how beautiful it is and how easily it can be broken. Both of those ideas should be woven into the recurring tune, which dips in and out of the play as if it were carried on a wind that changes. It serves as a thread of connection and allusion between the narrator with his separate point in time and space and the subject of his story. Between each episode it returns as reference to the emotion, nostalgia, which is the first condition of the play. It is primarily Laura's music and therefore comes out most clearly when the play focuses upon her and the lovely fragility of glass which is her image.

The Lighting. The lighting in the play is not realistic. In keeping with the atmosphere of memory, the stage is dim. Shafts of light are focused on selected areas or actors, sometimes in contradistinction to what is the apparent center. For instance, in the quarrel scene between Tom and Amanda, in which Laura has no active part, the clearest pool of light is on her figure. This is also true of the supper scene, when her silent figure on the sofa should remain the visual center. The light upon Laura should be distinct from the others, having a peculiar pristine clarity such as light used in early religious portraits of female saints or madonnas. A certain correspondence to light in religious paintings, such as El Greco's,° where the figures are radiant in atmosphere that is relatively dusky, could be effectively used throughout the play. (It will also permit a more effective use of the screen.) A free, imaginative use of light can be of enormous value in giving a mobile, plastic quality to plays of a more or less static nature.

El Greco (1541–1614): Greek painter who worked primarily in Spain and is known for the unearthly lighting in his large canvases.

Considerations for Critical Thinking and Writing

1. What was your response to the screen device as you read the play? Do you think the device would enhance a production of the play or prove to be a distraction?
2. How does Williams's description of music and lighting serve as a summary of the play's tone? Does this tone come through in your reading of the play or is it dependent upon the music and lighting? Explain your answer.
3. Explain whether you agree with Williams's assertion that "theater of realistic conventions" is "exhausted."

TENNESSEE WILLIAMS (1911–1983)
On Theme   1948

For a writer who is not intentionally obscure, and never, in his opinion, obscure at all, I do get asked a hell of a lot of questions which I can't answer. I have never been able to say what was the theme of my play and I don't think I've ever been conscious of writing with a theme in mind. I am always surprised when, after a play has opened, I read in the papers what the play is about. . . . I am thankful for these highly condensed and stimulating analyses, but it would never have occurred to me that that was the story I was trying to tell. Usually when asked about a theme, I look vague and say, "It is a play about life. . . ."

From *Where I Live: Selected Essays,* edited by Christine R. Day

Considerations for Critical Thinking and Writing

1. Williams's disclaimer invites the inevitable question: What is the theme of *The Glass Menagerie*? Write an essay that answers this question.
2. Discuss whether you think it is likely (or possible) to write a play without "a theme in mind."
3. How do Williams's comments on theme compare with Thomas McCormack's in "On the Problem of Teaching Theme" (p. 581)?

ARTHUR MILLER (b. 1915)
Tragedy and the Common Man   1949

In this age few tragedies are written. It has often been held that the lack is due to a paucity of heroes among us, or else that modern man has had the blood drawn out of his organs of belief by the skepticism of science, and the heroic attack on life cannot feed on an attitude of reserve and circumspection. For one reason or another, we are often held to be below tragedy — or tragedy above us. The inevitable conclusion is, of course, that the tragic mode is archaic, fit only for the very highly placed, the kings or the kingly, and where this admission is not made in so many words it is most often implied.

I believe that the common man is as apt a subject for tragedy in its highest sense as kings were. On the face of it this ought to be obvious in the light of modern psychiatry, which bases its analysis upon classic formulations, such as the Oedipus and Orestes complexes, for instance, which were enacted by royal beings, but which apply to everyone in similar emotional situations.

More simply, when the question of tragedy in art is not at issue, we never hesitate to attribute to the well-placed and the exalted the very same mental processes as the lowly. And finally, if the exaltation of tragic action were truly a property of the high-bred character alone, it is inconceivable that the mass of mankind should cherish tragedy above all other forms, let alone be capable of understanding it.

As a general rule, to which there may be exceptions unknown to me, I think the tragic feeling is evoked in us when we are in the presence of a character who is ready to lay down his life, if need be, to secure one thing — his sense of personal dignity. From Orestes to Hamlet, Medea to Macbeth, the underlying struggle is that of the individual attempting to gain his "rightful" position in his society.

Sometimes he is one who has been displaced from it, sometimes one who seeks to attain it for the first time, but the fateful wound from which the inevitable events spiral is the wound of indignity, and its dominant force is indignation. Tragedy, then, is the consequence of a man's total compulsion to evaluate himself justly.

In the sense of having been initiated by the hero himself, the tale always reveals what has been called his "tragic flaw," a failing that is not peculiar to grand or elevated characters. Nor is it necessarily a weakness. The flaw, or crack in the character, is really nothing — and need be nothing — but his inherent unwillingness to remain passive in the face of what he conceives to be a challenge to his dignity, his image of his rightful status. Only the passive, only those who accept their lot without active retaliation, are "flawless." Most of us are in that category.

But there are among us today, as there always have been, those who act against the scheme of things that degrades them, and in the process of action, everything we have accepted out of fear or insensitivity or ignorance is shaken before us and examined, and from this total onslaught by an individual against the seemingly stable cosmos surrounding us — from this total examination of the "unchangeable" environment — comes the terror and the fear that is classically associated with tragedy.

More important, from this total questioning of what has been previously unquestioned, we learn. And such a process is not beyond the common man. In revolutions around the world, these past thirty years, he has demonstrated again and again this inner dynamic of all tragedy.

Insistence upon the rank of the tragic hero, or the so-called nobility of his character, is really but a clinging to the outward forms of tragedy. If rank or nobility of character was indispensable, then it would follow that the problems of those with rank were the particular problems of tragedy. But surely the right of one monarch to capture the domain from another no longer raises our passions, nor are our concepts of justice what they were to the mind of an Elizabethan king.

The quality in such plays that does shake us, however, derives from the underlying fear of being displaced, the disaster inherent in being torn away from our chosen image of what and who we are in this world. Among us today this fear is as strong, and perhaps stronger, than it ever was. In fact, it is the common man who knows this fear best.

Now, if it is true that tragedy is the consequence of a man's total compulsion to evaluate himself justly, his destruction in the attempt posits a wrong or an evil in his environment. And this is precisely the morality of tragedy and its lesson. The discovery of the moral law, which is what the enlightenment of tragedy consists of, is not the discovery of some abstract or metaphysical quantity.

The tragic right is a condition of life, a condition in which the human personality is able to flower and realize itself. The wrong is the condition which suppresses man, perverts the flowing out of his love and creative instinct. Tragedy enlightens — and it must, in that it points the heroic finger at the enemy of man's freedom. The thrust for freedom is the quality in tragedy which exalts. The revolutionary questioning of the stable environment is what terrifies. In no way is the common man debarred from such thoughts or such actions.

Seen in this light, our lack of tragedy may be partially accounted for by the turn which modern literature has taken toward the purely psychiatric view of life, or the purely sociological. If all our miseries, our indignities, are born and bred within our minds, then all action, let alone the heroic action, is obviously impossible.

And if society alone is responsible for the cramping of our lives, then the protagonist must needs be so pure and faultless as to force us to deny his validity as a character. From neither of these views can tragedy derive, simply because neither represents a balanced concept of life. Above all else, tragedy requires the finest appreciation by the writer of cause and effect.

No tragedy can therefore come about when its author fears to question absolutely everything, when he regards any institution, habit, or custom as being either everlasting, immutable, or inevitable. In the tragic view the need of man to wholly realize himself is the only fixed star, and whatever it is that hedges his nature and lowers it is ripe for attack and examination. Which is not to say that tragedy must preach revolution.

The Greeks could probe the very heavenly origin of their ways and return to confirm the rightness of laws. And Job could face God in anger, demanding his right, and end in submission. But for a moment everything is in suspension, nothing is accepted, and in this stretching and tearing apart of the cosmos, in the very action of so doing, the character gains "size," the tragic stature which is spuriously attached to the royal or the high born in our minds. The commonest of men may take on that stature to the extent of his willingness to throw all he has into the contest, the battle to secure his rightful place in his world.

There is a misconception of tragedy with which I have been struck in review after review, and in many conversations with writers and readers alike. It is the idea that tragedy is of necessity allied to pessimism. Even the dictionary says nothing more about the word than that it means a story with a sad or unhappy ending. This impression is so firmly fixed that I almost hesitate to claim that in truth tragedy implies more optimism in its author than does comedy, and that its final result ought to be the reinforcement of the onlooker's brightest opinions of the human animal.

For, if it is true to say that in essence the tragic hero is intent upon claiming his whole due as a personality, and if this struggle must be total and without reservation, then it automatically demonstrates the indestructible will of man to achieve his humanity.

The possibility of victory must be there in tragedy. Where pathos rules, where pathos is finally derived, a character has fought a battle he could not possibly have won. The pathetic is achieved when the protagonist is, by virtue of his witlessness, his insensitivity, or the very air he gives off, incapable of grappling with a much superior force.

Pathos truly is the mode for the pessimist. But tragedy requires a nicer balance between what is possible and what is impossible. And it is curious, although edifying, that the plays we revere, century after century, are the tragedies. In them, and in them alone, lies the belief — optimistic, if you will — in the perfectibility of man.

It is time, I think, that we who are without kings, took up this bright thread of our history and followed it to the only place it can possibly lead in our time — the heart and spirit of the average man.

From Theater Essays of Arthur Miller

Considerations for Critical Thinking and Writing

1. According to Miller, why is there a "lack" of tragedy in modern literature? Why do psychological and sociological accounts of human behavior limit the possibilities for tragedy?
2. Why is the "common man" a suitable subject for tragedy? How does Miller's view of tragedy compare with Aristotle's (p. 1202)?
3. What distinction does Miller make between tragedy and pathos? Which term best characterizes Willy Loman in *Death of a Salesman?* Explain why.

ARTHUR MILLER (b. 1915)
On Biff and Willy Loman 1950

A serious theme is entertaining to the extent that it is not trifled with, not cleverly angled, but met in head-on collision. [The audience] will not consent to suffer while the creators stand by with tongue in cheek. They have a way of knowing. Nobody can blame them.

And there have been certain disappointments, one above all. I am sorry the self-realization of the older son, Biff, is not a weightier counterbalance to Willy's disaster in the audience's mind.

And certain things are more clearly known, or so it seems now. We want to give of ourselves, and yet all we train for is to take, as though nothing less will keep the world at a safe distance. Every day we contradict our will to create, which is to give. The end of man is not security, but without security we are without the elementary condition of humaneness.

To me the tragedy of Willy Loman is that he gave his life, or sold it, in order to justify the waste of it. It is the tragedy of a man who did believe that he alone was not meeting the qualifications laid down for mankind by those clean-shaven frontiersmen who inhabit the peaks of broadcasting and advertising offices. From those forests of canned goods high up near the sky, he heard the thundering command to succeed as it ricocheted down the newspaper-lined canyons of his city, heard not a human voice, but a wind of a voice to which no human can reply in kind, except to stare into the mirror at a failure.

From the *New York Times,* February 5, 1950

Considerations for Critical Thinking and Writing

1. Discuss what you think Miller has in mind when he refers to Biff's "self-realization."
2. According to Miller, what influences Willy to make him feel like a failure?
3. How is Miller's description of "the tragedy of Willy Loman" dramatized in the play?

ERIC BENTLEY (b. 1916)
On Drama as Literature and Performance   1964

Is a play complete without performance? The question has been answered with equal vehemence in both the affirmative and the negative. The choice goes by temperamental preference: "literary" persons believe in the unaided script; "theatrical" persons believe in performance. Both are right. A good play leads a double existence, and is a complete "personality" in both its lives. When a theatrical person says a play has been misinterpreted in performance, he is certainly implying that a play is *there* and has its integrity before the interpreters touch it. As for literary persons, their concession that a play does have another life as well as that of the book is to be found, if nowhere else, in their dismissal of bits they don't like as "merely theatrical." In other words, their position really is not that the theatrical dimension doesn't exist but that they wish it didn't.

Each group is trying to make a virtue of its own *déformation profession-nelle.*° Theatrical people have their limitations as interpreters of literature. Literary people have theirs as interpreters of theater. If we can avoid the blindnesses of both parties, the only real problem lies in understanding the *difference* between script-alone and script-as-performed, for any given passage may have a different import in the two different contexts. Finally, one is not forced into any choice between literature and theater, and to know *Hamlet,* or any great play, should be to know it from stage and study, both. A fine performance will never fail to throw light on at least an aspect of the play, while even the best reading in the study will fall far short of embracing all its aspects.

The question whether one should prefer to read or to see a play is best answered pragmatically. If one can read well to oneself, one will hardly prefer to go and see a mediocre performance. But, for anyone capable of relishing theater — and that includes more people than know it — even though the written

déformation professionnelle: Professional bias.

script has its own completeness, there is no pleasure to top that of seeing a dramatic masterpiece masterfully performed. What is added means so much in such an immediate, sensuous way. If plot, characterization, and dialogue give body to the theme, and transform thought into wisdom, and a view into a vision, adequate performance helps them to do so in various ways but above all by adding that final and conclusive concretion, the living actor.

From "Enactment" in The Life of the Drama

Considerations for Critical Thinking and Writing

1. How does Bentley resolve the competing claims of "literary" and "theatrical" people who argue over whether a play can be "complete without performance"?
2. Explain why you prefer to read or see a play. If you do both, which do you prefer first — the reading or the performance? Why?

JOHN WAGNER (b. 1967)
A *Student Essay on* Death of a Salesman   1986

They Used to Tell Me I Was Building a Dream

In the requiem to *Death of a Salesman* Charley says that a salesman is "a man out there in the blue, riding on a smile and a shoeshine." Through Charley's short speech Arthur Miller drives home his reason for making Willy Loman a salesman, and not a lawyer, a teacher, or a writer. A person in sales builds a life on the intangible, the unreal. He or she markets a personal attractiveness that comes from confidence, the ability to make a buyer believe the catchy slogans even though they are rarely the truth. Sales is a business built on bombast, on bull. (Wear these stockings, madam, and the men will follow you all around town!) If products sold according to their worth, there would be no need for salespeople. A person in sales does not sell a product so much as an idea, a persona, an image.

When Willy Loman decided to become a salesman, the career held promise, like a brightly colored orange hanging from a tree. He pictured himself growing old like Dave Singleman, the eighty-year-old salesman who made his living phoning buyers from his hotel room. Instead, with age Willy's personal attractiveness has grown as stale as his jokes and as weak as his smile, thin and empty as the guarantee on a broken refrigerator. Now that the shine has become dull and there is no color, no flavor left to the man, Willy shouts, "You can't eat the orange and throw the peel away!" But isn't that the sensible thing to do? What good is the peel, once the fruit is gone? Willy has made the comparison himself — he has as little to offer as a withered orange peel, as a cracked and faded shell with no life left to protect.

No one forces Willy to declare himself worthless. No one drives him off the road. No one told him what to do with his life. His brother Ben invited him to go to Alaska and Africa, where the rewards are concrete, but Willy believed in the life he was building as a young man and he believes in it right up to the end. When Ben comes back to ask "What are you building? Lay your hand on it.

Where is it?" Willy insists that what he is building cannot be felt with the hand, but that it is there all the same.

Willy never loses sight of the future he has bargained for. Hopefully he borrows his last dollars to make his insurance payments, trading in the last of his credibility on a gamble. He happily sells his life for a possible twenty thousand dollars, for a dream. And when the salesman dies, he leaves no railroad, no tower to the sun. Once has has made his last sale, nothing remains.

Considerations for Critical Thinking and Writing

1. Wagner asserts that "a person in sales does not sell a product so much as an idea, a persona, an image." Discuss this idea along with Miller's comment in his introduction to the play that "when asked what Willy was selling, what was in his bags, I could only reply, 'Himself.'"
2. Does Wagner seem sympathetic to Willy? Are you? Specifically, what is unheroic about Willy's behavior? What, if anything, do you find heroic about him?
3. How is Willy's dream representative of the American dream of success? Do you think his story is relevant only to American culture?

DAVID SAVRAN (b. 1950)
An Interview with August Wilson   1987

Savran: In reading *Fences,* I came to view Troy more and more critically as the play progressed, sharing Rose's point of view. We see that Troy has been crippled by his father. That's being replayed in Troy's relationship with Cory. Do you think there's a way out of that cycle?

Wilson: Surely. First of all, we're all like our parents. The things we are taught early in life, how to respond to the world, our sense of morality — everything, we get from them. Now you can take that legacy and do with it anything you want to do. It's in your hands. Cory is Troy's son. How can he be Troy's son without sharing Troy's values? I was trying to get at why Troy made the choices he made, how they have influenced his values, and how he attempts to pass those along to his son. Each generation gives the succeeding generation what they think they need. One question in the play is "Are the tools we are given sufficient to compete in a world that is different from the one our parents knew?" I think they are — it's just that we have to do different things with the tools. That's all Troy has to give. Troy's flaw is that he does not recognize that the world was changing. That's because he spent fifteen years in a penitentiary.

As African-Americans, we should demand to participate in society as Africans. That's the way out of the vicious cycle of poverty and neglect that exists in 1987 in America, where you have a huge percentage of blacks living in the equivalent of South African townships, in housing projects. No one is inviting these people to participate in society. Look at the poverty levels — $8,500 for a family of four, if you have $8,501 you're not counted. Those statistics would go up enormously if we had an honest assessment of the cost of living in America. I don't know how anybody can support a family of four on $8,500. What I'm saying is that 85 or 90 percent of blacks in America are living in abject poverty and, for the most part, are crowded into what amount to concentration camps. The situation for blacks in America is worse than it was forty years ago. Some sociologists will tell you about the tremendous progress we've made. They didn't put me out when I walked in the door. And you can always point to someone who works on Wall Street, or is a doctor. But they don't count in the larger scheme of things.

Savran: Do you have any idea how these political changes could take place?

Wilson: I'm not sure. I know that blacks must be allowed their cultural differences. I think the process of assimilation to white American society was a big mistake. We don't want to be like you. Blacks living in housing projects are isolated from the society, for the most part — living as they choose, as Africans. Only they don't realize the value in what they're doing because they have accepted their victimization. They've marked themselves as victims. Once they recognize that, they can begin to move through society in a different manner, from a stronger position, and claim what is theirs.

Savran: A project of yours is to point up what happens when oppression is internalized.

Wilson: Yes, transfer of aggression to the wrong target. I think it's interesting that the two roads open to blacks for "full participation" are entertainment and sports. *Ma Rainey* and *Fences,* and I didn't plan it that way. I don't think that they're the correct roads. I think Troy's right. Now with the benefit of historical perspective, I can say that the athletic scholarship was actually a way of exploiting. Now you've got two million kids who think they're going to play in the NBA. In the sixties the universities made a lot of money off of athletics. You had kids playing for free who, by and large, were not getting educated, were taking courses in basketweaving. Some of them could barely read.

Savran: Troy may be right about that issue, but it seems that he has passed on certain destructive traits in spite of himself. Take the hostility between father and son.

Wilson: I think every generation says to the previous generation: you're in my way, I've got to get by. The father-son conflict is actually a normal generational conflict that happens all the time.

Savran: So it's a healthy and a good thing?

Wilson: Oh, sure. Troy is seeing this boy walk around, smelling his piss. Two men cannot live in the same household. Troy would have been tremendously disappointed if Cory had not challenged him. Troy knows that this boy has to go out and do battle with that world: "So I had best prepare him because I know that's a harsh, cruel place out there. But that's going to be easy compared to what he's getting here. Ain't nobody gonna whip your ass like I'm gonna whip it." He has a tremendous love for the kid. But he's not going to say, "I love you," he's going to demonstrate it. He's carrying garbage for seventeen years just for the kid. The only world Troy knows is the one that he made. Cory's going to go on to find another one, he's going to arrive at the same place as Troy. I think one of the most important lines in the play is when Troy is talking about his father: "I got to the place where I could feel him kicking in my blood and knew that the only thing that separated us was the matter of a few years."

Hopefully, Cory will do things a bit differently with his son. For Troy, sports was not the way to go, the white man wouldn't let him get away with that. "Get you a job, with your hands, something that nobody can take away from you." The idea of school — he doesn't know what that is. That's for white folks. Very few blacks had paperwork jobs. But if you knew how to fix cars, you could always make some money. That's what Troy wants for Cory. There aren't many people who ever jumped up in Troy's face. So he's proud of the kid at the same time that he expresses a hurt that all men feel. You got to cut your kid loose at some point. There's that sense of loss and separation. You find out how Troy left his father's house and you see how Cory leaves his house. I suspect with Cory it will repeat with some differences and maybe, after five or six generations, they'll find a different way to do it.

Savran: Where Cory ends up is very ambiguous, as a marine in 1965.

Wilson: Yes. For the average black kid on the street, that was an alternative. You went into the army because you could learn how to do something. I can remember my parents talking about the son of some friends: "He's in the navy. He *did* something" — as opposed to standing on the street corner, shooting drugs, drinking wine, and robbing stores. Lyons says to Cory, "I always knew you were going to make something out of yourself." It really wounds me. He's a corporal in the marines. For blacks, that is a sense of accomplishment. Therein lies one of the tragedies of blacks in America. Cory says, "I don't know. I put in six years. That's enough." Anyone who goes into the army and makes a career out of it is a loser. They sit there and are nurtured by the army and they don't have to confront life. Then they get out of the army and find there's nothing to do. They didn't learn any skills. And if they did, they can't find a job. Four months later, they're shooting dope. In the sixties a whole bunch of blacks went over, fought, and died in the Vietnam War. The survivors came back to the same street corners and found out nothing had changed. They still couldn't get a job.

At the end of *Fences* every person, with the exception of Raynell, is institutionalized. Rose is in a church. Lyons is in a penitentiary. Gabriel's in a mental hospital, and Cory's in the marines. The only free person is the girl, Troy's daughter, the hope for the future. That was conscious on my part because in '57 that's what I saw. Blacks have relied on institutions which are really foreign — except for the black church, which has been our saving grace. I have some problems with it but I recognize it as a central social organization and sometimes an economic organization for the black community. I would like to see blacks develop their own institutions that respond to their needs.

From *In Their Own Voices*

Considerations for Critical Thinking and Writing

1. Wilson describes Troy's "flaw" as an inability to "recognize that the world was changing." Discuss how completely this assessment describes Troy.
2. Write an essay discussing how Wilson uses the hostility between father and son in *Fences* as a means of treating larger social issues for blacks in America.
3. Read the section on historical criticism (p. 2005) in Chapter 35, "Critical Strategies for Reading." Discuss how useful and accurate you think *Fences* is in depicting black life in America for the past several decades.

RICHARD BERNSTEIN (b. 1944)

The News Source for M. Butterfly

1986

FRANCE JAILS TWO IN ODD CASE OF ESPIONAGE

Paris, May 10. A former French diplomat and a Chinese opera singer have been sentenced to six years in jail for spying for China after a two-day trial that traced a story of clandestine love and mistaken sexual identity.

A member of the French counterespionage service said at the trial, which ended Tuesday, that the operation to collect information on France was carried out by a Chinese Communist Party intelligence unit that no longer exists.

The Chinese government has denied any involvement in the case.

The case has been the talk of Paris lately, not so much because of the charge of spying itself as because of the circumstances. The case centered on a love affair between a young French diplomat, Bernard Boursicot, now forty-one years old, who was stationed in Peking two decades ago, and a popular Chinese opera singer, Shi Peipu, forty-six.

Mr. Boursicot was accused of passing information to China after he fell in love with Mr. Shi, whom he believed for twenty years to be a woman.

Testimony in the trial indicated that the affair began in 1964 when Mr. Boursicot, then twenty years old, was posted at the French Embassy in Peking as an accountant. There he met Mr. Shi, a celebrated singer at the Peking Opera, where female roles have, according to tradition, often been played by men.

Mr. Shi was a well-known cultural figure in Peking and one of the few individuals allowed by the Chinese authorities to have contacts with foreigners.

According to testimony, Mr. Shi told Mr. Boursicot at a reception in the French Embassy in Peking that he was actually a woman.

A love affair between the two ensued to the point where, after several months, Mr. Shi told Mr. Boursicot that he was pregnant; later he announced to the apparently credulous Mr. Boursicot that he had had a son, Shi Dudu, that the diplomat had fathered.

Asked by the trial judge how he could have been so completely taken in, Mr. Boursicot said: "I was shattered to learn that he is a man, but my conviction remains unshakable that for me at that time he was really a woman and was the first love of my life. And then, there was the child that I saw, Shi Dudu. He looked like me."

Further explaining his sexual misidentification of Mr. Shi, Mr. Boursicot said their meetings had been hasty affairs that always took place in the dark.

"He was very shy," Mr. Boursicot said. "I thought it was a Chinese custom."

Mr. Boursicot's espionage activities began in 1969, when he returned to Peking after a three-year absence. By then, China was at the height of the Cultural Revolution, and it was virtually impossible for foreigners to have personal relations with Chinese citizens.

Mr. Boursicot testified that a member of the Chinese secret service, whom he said he knew only as "Kang," approached him and said he could continue to see Mr. Shi if he provided intelligence information from the French Embassy.

Mr. Boursicot apparently believed that if he refused to comply, Mr. Shi would be persecuted.

Mr. Boursicot was accused of having turned over some 150 documents to Shi Peipu, who passed them on to "Kang." Mr. Boursicot said at the trial that the materials were generally not sensitive and were publicly available.

Later, from 1977 to 1979, Mr. Boursicot was posted at the French Embassy in Ulan Bator in Mongolia, where one of his duties was to make a weekly trip to Peking with the diplomatic pouch. He said he made photocopies of the documents in the diplomatic pouch and turned them over to Mr. Shi.

The case was uncovered in 1983 when Mr. Shi, accompanied by his putative son, Shi Dudu, was allowed to leave China. He lived in Paris with Mr. Boursicot, who said he continued to believe that Mr. Shi was a woman.

The arrival of a Chinese citizen in the home of a former French diplomat attracted the attention of the French counterespionage service. When the French police questioned Mr. Boursicot about his relations with Mr. Shi, he disclosed his spying activities.

From the *New York Times,* May 11, 1986

Considerations for Critical Thinking and Writing

1. What details of the news story does Hwang use? Which does he ignore?
2. Explain whether your knowledge of its source has any effect on your understanding or enjoyment of *M. Butterfly.*
3. Write a response to this explanation of the relationship: Mr. Shi "was very shy," Mr. Boursicot said. "I thought it was a Chinese custom."

DAVID SAVRAN (b. 1950)
An Interview with David Henry Hwang   1988

Savran: You strongly historicize the personal story [in *M. Butterfly*], comparing various imperialist ventures, like Vietnam, with Bouriscot's sexual imperialism.

Hwang: What I was trying to do in *Butterfly* — I didn't really know this except in retrospect — was to link imperialism, racism, and sexism. It necessitates a certain historical perspective.

Savran: And a look at the mythologies created to justify them.

Hwang: Particularly Puccini's *Madame Butterfly.*

Savran: So the play is really focused on two systems of domination, the cultural and the sexual.

Hwang: Cultural superiority is essentially economic. Whatever country dominates the world economically determines what culture is, for a while. There's a lag, because the country gets to determine the culture even after somebody else takes over economically. It still has the mystique of being the old culture, whether it's Britain or the United States. Probably the next world power is going to be

Japan. You can't deal with cultural mystique unless you deal with political mystique, political power.

Savran: I was interested in how you handled the fact that Bouriscot's mistress, Shi Peipu, is really a man. That makes for the reversal at the end, the fact that Shi turns out to be Pinkerton.

Hwang: That's the axis on which the play turns. Insofar as this is possible, I would like to seduce the audience during the first act into believing that Shi is a woman. We're so conditioned to think in certain ways about Oriental women and the relationship of the West to the East, that I think it would be fun to get into the audience's head in the first act, in a very reactionary way, and then blow it out later. I don't know to what degree that's possible because anyone who goes to see this play, especially if it runs any length of time, will probably know what it's about. But I still think it can work on some level.

Savran: So you want Shi played by a man?

Hwang: Definitely. You have to create the illusion for the audience, you have to trick them. It's dirty pool if you give them a woman and say, this is a woman, and later, when he appears as a man, you give them a man. You have to play by the rules. If you're saying that Bouriscot was seduced by a man, then you have to seduce the audience with a man. *Butterfly* runs the risk of indulging the sin it condemns, like violent movies that are supposedly antiviolence. If you cast a woman in that role, you'd condemn the oppression of women by oppressing a woman in a very attractive way on the stage. If you oppress a woman who actually is a man, it's much more interesting.

From In Their Own Voices

Considerations for Critical Thinking and Writing

1. Why does Hwang think it is essential that Shi/Song be played by a man? Discuss whether you agree or disagree with his assessment of who should play the role.
2. Consider your response to Song as you read the play. How does knowing that Song is actually a man rather than a woman affect your response to him and to Gallimard?
3. Write an essay that discusses the ways in which Hwang weaves his concerns about imperialism, racism, and sexism into the play.

CRITICAL THINKING AND WRITING

35. Critical Strategies for Reading

CRITICAL THINKING

Maybe this has happened to you: the assignment is to write an analysis of some aspect of a work, let's say Nathaniel Hawthorne's *The Scarlet Letter,* that interests you and takes into account critical sources that comment on and interpret the work. You cheerfully begin research in the library but quickly find yourself bewildered by several seemingly unrelated articles. The first traces the thematic significance of images of light and darkness in the novel; the second makes a case for Hester Prynne as a liberated woman; the third argues that Arthur Dimmesdale's guilt is a projection of Hawthorne's own emotions; and the fourth analyzes the introduction, "The Custom House," as an attack on bourgeois values. These disparate treatments may seem random and capricious — a confirmation of your worst suspicions that interpretations of literature are hit-or-miss excursions into areas that you know little about or didn't know even existed. But if you understand that the articles are written from different perspectives — formalist, feminist, psychological, and Marxist — and that the purpose of each is to enhance your understanding of the novel by discussing a particular element of it, then you can see that their varying strategies represent potentially interesting ways of opening up the text that might otherwise never have occurred to you. There are many ways to approach a text, and a useful first step is to develop a sense of direction, an understanding of how a perspective — your own or a critic's — shapes a discussion of a text.

This chapter offers an introduction to critical approaches to literature by outlining a variety of strategies for reading fiction, poetry, or drama. These strategies include approaches that have long been practiced by readers who have used, for example, the insights gleaned from biography and history to illuminate literary works as well as more recent approaches, such as those used by feminist, reader-response, and deconstructionist critics. Each of these perspectives is sensitive to point of view, symbol, tone, irony, and other literary elements that you have been studying, but each also casts those elements in a special light. The formalist approach emphasizes how the elements within a work achieve their effects, whereas biographical and psychological approaches lead outward from the work to consider the author's life and other writings. Even broader approaches, such as historical and sociological perspectives, connect the work to historic, social, and economic forces. Mythological readings represent the broadest approach, because they discuss the cultural and universal responses readers have to a work.

Any given strategy raises its own types of questions and issues while seeking particular kinds of evidence to support itself. An awareness of the assumptions and methods that inform an approach can help you to understand better the validity and value of a given critic's strategy for making sense of a work. More important, such an understanding can widen and deepen the responses of your own reading.

The critical thinking that goes into understanding a professional critic's approach to a work is not foreign to you because you have already used essentially the same kind of thinking to understand the work itself. The skills you have developed to produce a literary *analysis* that, for example, describes how a character, symbol, or rhyme scheme supports a theme are also useful for reading literary criticism, because such skills allow you to keep track of how the parts of a critical approach create a particular reading of a literary work. When you analyze a story, poem, or play by closely examining how its various elements relate to the whole, your *interpretation* — your articulation of what the work means to you as supported by an analysis of its elements — necessarily involves choosing what you focus upon in the work. The same is true of professional critics.

Critical readings presuppose choices in the kinds of material that are discussed. An analysis of the setting of John Updike's "A & P" (p. 485) would probably bring into focus the oppressive environment the protagonist associates with the store, rather than, say, the economic history of that supermarket chain. (For a student's analysis of the setting in "A & P" see p. 2059.) The economic history of a supermarket chain might be useful to a Marxist critic concerned with how class relations are revealed in "A & P," but for a formalist critic interested in identifying the unifying structures of the story such information would be irrelevant.

The Perspectives, Complementary Readings, and Critical Case Studies in this anthology offer opportunities to read critics using a wide variety of approaches to analyze and interpret texts. In the Critical Case Study on Ibsen's *A Doll House* (Chapter 31), for instance, Carol Strongin Tufts offers a psychoanalytic reading of Nora that characterizes her as a narcissistic personality rather than as a feminist heroine. The criteria she uses to evalaute Nora's behavior are drawn from the language used by the American Psychiatric Association. In contrast, Joan Templeton places Nora in the context of women's rights issues to argue that Nora must be read from a feminist perspective if the essential meaning of the play is to be understood. Each of these critics raises different questions, examines different evidence, and employs different assumptions to interpret Nora's character. Being aware of those differences — teasing them out so that you can see how they lead to competing conclusions — is a useful way to analyze the analysis itself. What is left out of an interpretation is sometimes as significant as what is included. As you read the critics, it's worth reminding yourself that your own critical thinking skills can help you to determine the usefulness of a particular approach.

The following overview is neither exhaustive in the types of critical approaches covered nor complete in its presentation of the complexities inherent in them, but it should help you to develop an appreciation of the intriguing possibilities that attend literary interpretation. The emphasis in this chapter is on ways of thinking about literature rather than on daunting lists of terms, names, and movements. Although a working knowledge of critical schools may be valuable and necessary for a fully informed use of a given critical approach, the aim here is more modest and practical. This chapter is no substitute for the shelves of literary criticism that can be found in your library, but it does suggest how readers using different perspectives organize their responses to texts.

The summaries of critical approaches that follow are descriptive, not evaluative. Each approach has its advantages and limitations, but those matters are best left to further study. Like literary artists, critics have their personal values, tastes, and styles. The appropriateness of a specific critical approach will depend, at least in part, on the nature of the literary work under discussion as well as on your own sensibilities and experience. However, any approach, if it is to enhance understanding, requires sensitivity, tact, and an awareness of the various literary elements of the text, including, of course, its use of language.

Successful critical approaches avoid eccentric decodings that reveal so-called hidden meanings which are not only hidden but totally absent from the text. For a parody of this sort of critical excess, see "A Reading of 'Stopping by Woods on a Snowy Evening'" (p. 899), in which Herbert R. Coursen, Jr., has some fun with a Robert Frost poem and Santa Claus while making a serious point about the dangers of overly ingenious readings. Literary criticism attempts, like any valid hypothesis, to account for phenomena — the text — without distorting or misrepresenting what it describes.

THE LITERARY CANON:
DIVERSITY AND CONTROVERSY

Before looking at the various critical approaches discussed in this chapter, it makes sense to consider first which literature has been traditionally considered worthy of such analysis. The discussion in the Introduction called The Changing Literary Canon (p. 7) may have already alerted you to the fact that in recent years many more works by women, minorities, and writers from around the world have been considered by scholars, critics, and teachers to merit serious study and inclusion in what is known as the literary canon. This increasing diversity has been celebrated by those who believe that multiculturalism taps new sources for the discovery of great literature while raising significant questions about language, culture, and society. At the same time, others have perceived this diversity as a threat to the established, traditional canon of Western culture.

The debates concerning who should be read, taught, and written about have sometimes been acrimonious as well as lively and challenging. Bitter arguments have been waged recently on campuses and in the press over what has come to be called "political correctness." Two camps — roughly — have formed around these debates: liberals and conservatives (the appropriateness of these terms is debatable but the oppositional positioning is unmistakable). The liberals are said to insist upon politically correct views from colleagues and students opening up the curriculum to multicultural texts from Asia, Africa, Latin America, and elsewhere, and to encourage more tolerant attitudes about race, class, gender, and sexual orientation. These revisionists, seeking a change in traditional attitudes, are sometimes accused of intimidating the opposition into silence and substituting ideological dogma for reason and truth. The conservatives are also portrayed as ideologues; in their efforts to preserve what they regard as the best from the past, they refuse to admit that Western classics, mostly written by white male Europeans, represent only a portion of human experience. These traditionalists are seen as advocating values that are neither universal nor eternal but merely privileged and entrenched. Conservatives are charged with refusing to acknowledge that their values also represent a political agenda, which is implicit in their preference for the works of canonical authors such as Homer, Virgil, Shakespeare, Milton, Tolstoy, and Faulkner. The reductive and contradictory nature of this national debate between liberals and conservatives has been neatly summed up by Katha Pollitt: "Read the conservatives' list and produce a nation of sexists and racists — or a nation of philosopher kings. Read the liberals' list and produce a nation of spiritual relativists — or a nation of open-minded world citizens" ("Canon to the Right of Me . . . ," *The Nation,* Sept. 23, 1991, p. 330).

These troubling and extreme alternatives can be avoided, of course, if the issues are not approached from such absolutist positions. Solutions to these issues cannot be suggested in this limited space, and, no doubt, solutions will evolve over time, but we can at least provide a perspective. Books — regardless of what list they are on — are not likely to unite a fragmented nation or to disunite a unified one. It is perhaps more useful and accurate to see issues of canonicity as reflecting political changes rather than being the primary causes of them. This is not to say that books don't have an impact on readers — that *Uncle Tom's Cabin,* for instance, did not galvanize antislavery sentiments in nineteenth-century America — but that book lists do not by themselves preserve or destroy the status quo.

It's worth noting that the curricula of American universities have always undergone significant and, some would say, wrenching changes. Only a little more than one hundred years ago there was strong opposition to teaching English, as well as other modern languages, alongside programs dominated by Greek and Latin. Only since the 1920s has American literature been made a part of the curriculum, and just five decades ago writers such as James Joyce, Virginia Woolf, Franz Kafka, and Ernest Hemingway were regarded with the same raised eyebrows that today might be raised about contemporary writers such as Gish Jen, Tim O'Brien, Rita Dove, or Fay Weldon. New voices do not drown out the past; they build on it, and eventually become part of the past as newer writers take their place alongside them. Neither resistance to change nor a denial of the past will have its way with the canon. Though both impulses are widespread, neither is likely to dominate the other, because there are too many reasonable, practical readers and teachers who instead of replacing Shakespeare, Melville, and other canonical writers have supplemented them with neglected writers from Western and other cultures. These readers experience the current debates about the canon not as a binary opposition but as an opportunity to explore important questions about continuity and change in our literature, culture, and society.

FORMALIST STRATEGIES

Formalist critics focus on the formal elements of a work — its language, structure, and tone. A formalist reads literature as an independent work of art rather than as a reflection of the author's state of mind or as a representation of a moment in history. Historic influences on a work, an author's intentions, or anything else outside the work are generally not treated by formalists (this is particularly true of the most famous modern formalists, known as the *New Critics,* who dominated American criticism from the 1940s through the 1960s). Instead, formalists offer intense examinations of the relationship between form and meaning within a work, emphasizing the subtle complexity of how a work is arranged. This kind of close reading pays special attention to what are often described as *intrinsic* matters in a literary work, such as diction, irony, paradox, metaphor, and symbol, as well as larger elements, such as plot, characterization, and narrative technique. Formalists examine how these elements work together to give a coherent shape to a work while contributing to its meaning. The answers to the questions formalists raise about how the shape and effect of a work are related come from the work itself. Other kinds of information that go beyond the text — biography, history, politics, economics, and so on — are typically regarded by formalists as *extrinsic* matters, which are considerably less important than what goes on within the autonomous text.

Poetry especially lends itself to close readings, because a poem's relative brevity allows for detailed analyses of nearly all its words and how they achieve their effects. For a student's formalist reading of how a pervasive sense of death is worked into a poem, see "A Reading of Dickinson's 'There's a certain Slant of light'" (p. 2054).

Formalist strategies are also useful for analyzing drama and fiction. In his well-known essay "The World of *Hamlet*," Maynard Mack explores Hamlet's character and predicament by paying close attention to the words and images that Shakespeare uses to build a world in which appearances mask reality and mystery is embedded in scene after scene. Mack points to recurring terms, such as *apparition, seems, assume,* and *put on,* as well as repeated images of acting, clothing, disease, and painting, to indicate the treacherous surface world Hamlet must penetrate to get to the truth. This pattern of deception provides an organizing principle around which Mack offers a reading of the entire play:

> Hamlet's problem, in its crudest form, is simply the problem of the avenger: he must carry out the injunction of the ghost and kill the king. But this problem . . . is presented in terms of a certain kind of world. The ghost's injunction to act becomes so inextricably bound up for Hamlet with the character of the world in which the action must be taken — its mysteriousness, its baffling appearances, its deep consciousness of infection, frailty, and loss — that he cannot come to terms with either without coming to terms with both.

Although Mack places *Hamlet* in the tradition of revenge tragedy, his reading of the play emphasizes Shakespeare's arrangement of language rather than literary history as a means of providing an interpretation that accounts for various elements of the play. Mack's formalist strategy explores how diction reveals meaning and how repeated words and images evoke and reinforce important thematic significances.

For an example of a work in which the shape of the plot serves as the major organizing principle, let's examine Kate Chopin's "The Story of an Hour" (p. 12), a two-page short story that takes only a few minutes to read. With the story fresh in your mind, consider how you might approach it from a formalist perspective. A first reading probably results in surprise at the story's ending: a grieving wife "afflicted with a heart trouble" suddenly dies of a heart attack, not because she's learned that her kind and loving husband has been killed in a terrible train accident but because she discovers that he is very much alive. Clearly, we are faced with an ironic situation since there is such a powerful incongruity between what is expected to happen and what actually happens. A likely formalist strategy for analyzing this story would be to raise questions about the ironic ending. Is this merely a trick ending, or is it a carefully wrought culmination of other elements in the story so that in addition to creating surprise the ending snaps the story shut on an interesting and challenging theme? Formalists value such complexities over simple surprise effects.

A second, closer reading indicates that Chopin's third-person narrator presents the story in a manner similar to Josephine's gentle attempts to break the news about Brently Mallard's death. The story is told in "veiled hints that [reveal] in half concealing." But unlike Josephine, who tries to protect her sister's fragile heart from stress, the narrator seeks to reveal Mrs. Mallard's complex heart. A formalist would look back over the story for signs of the ending in the imagery. Although Mrs. Mallard grieves immediately and unreservedly when she hears about the train disaster, she soon begins to feel a different emotion as she looks out the window at "the tops of trees . . . all aquiver with the new spring life." This symbolic evocation of renewal and rebirth — along with "the delicious breath of rain," the sounds of life in the street, and the birds singing — causes her to feel, in spite of her own efforts to repress her thoughts and emotions, "free, free, free!" She feels alive with a sense of possibility, with a "clear and exalted perception" that she "would live for herself" instead of for and through her husband.

It is ironic that this ecstatic "self-assertion" is interpreted by Josephine as grief, but the crowning irony for this "goddess of Victory" is the doctors' assumption that she dies of joy rather than of the shock of having to abandon her newly discovered self once she realizes her husband is still alive. In the course of an hour, Mrs. Mallard's life is irretrievably changed: her husband's assumed accidental death frees her, but the fact that he lives and all the expectations imposed on her by his continued life kill her. She does, indeed, die of a broken heart, but only Chopin's readers know the real ironic meaning of that explanation.

Although this brief discussion of some of the formal elements of Chopin's story does not describe all there is to say about how they produce an effect and create meaning, it does suggest the kinds of questions, issues, and evidence that a formalist strategy might raise in providing a close reading of the text itself.

BIOGRAPHICAL STRATEGIES

A knowledge of an author's life can help readers understand his or her work more fully. Events in a work might follow actual events in a writer's life just as characters might be based on people known by the author. Ernest Hemingway's "Soldier's Home" (p. 125) is a story about the difficulties of a World War I veteran named Krebs returning to his small hometown in Oklahoma, where he cannot adjust to the pious assumptions of his family and neighbors. He refuses to accept their innocent blindness to the horrors he has witnessed during the war. They have no sense of the brutality of modern life; instead they insist he resume his life as if nothing has happened.

There is plenty of biographical evidence to indicate that Krebs's unwillingness to lie about his war experiences reflects Hemingway's own responses upon his return to Oak Park, Illinois, in 1919. Krebs, like Hemingway, finds he has to leave the sentimentality, repressiveness, and smug complacency that threaten to render his experiences unreal: "the world they were in was not the world he was in."

An awareness of Hemingway's own war experiences and subsequent disillusionment with his hometown can be readily developed through available biographies, letters, and other works he wrote. Consider, for example, this passage from *By Force of Will: The Life and Art of Ernest Hemingway*, in which Scott Donaldson describes Hemingway's response to World War I:

> In poems, as in [*A Farewell to Arms*], Hemingway expressed his distaste for the first war. The men who had to fight the war did not die well:
>
> Soldiers pitch and cough and twitch —
>   All the world roars red and black;
> Soldiers smother in a ditch,
>   Choking through the whole attack.
>
> And what did they die for? They were "sucked in" by empty words and phrases —
>
> King and country,
> Christ Almighty,
> And the rest,
> Patriotism,
> Democracy,
> Honor —
>
> which spelled death. The bitterness of these outbursts derived from the distinction Hemingway drew between the men on the line and those who started the wars that others had to fight.

This kind of information can help to deepen our understanding of just how empathetically Krebs is presented in the story. Relevant facts about Hemingway's life will not make "Soldier's Home" a better written story than it is, but such information can make clearer the source of Hemingway's convictions and how his own experiences inform his major concerns as a storyteller.

Some formalist critics — some New Critics, for example — argue that interpretation should be based exclusively on internal evidence rather than on any biographical information outside the work. They argue that it is not possible to determine an author's intention and that the work must stand by itself. Although this is a useful caveat for keeping the work in focus, a reader who finds biography relevant would argue that biography can at the very least serve as a control on interpretation. A reader who, for example, finds Krebs at fault for not subscribing to the values of his hometown would be misreading the story, given both its tone and the biographical information available about the author. Although the narrator never *tells* the reader that Krebs is right or wrong for leaving town, the story's tone sides with his view of things. If, however, someone were to argue otherwise, insisting that the tone is not decisive and that Krebs's position is problematic, a reader familiar with Hemingway's own reactions could refute that argument with a powerful confirmation of Krebs's instincts to withdraw. Hence, many readers find biography useful for interpretation.

However, it is also worth noting that biographical information can complicate a work. Chopin's "Story of an Hour" presents a repressed wife's momentary discovery of what freedom from her husband might mean to her. She awakens to a new sense of herself when she learns of her husband's death, only to collapse of a heart attack when she sees that he is alive. Readers might be tempted to interpret this story as Chopin's fictionalized commentary about her own marriage, because her husband died twelve years before she wrote the story and seven years before she began writing fiction seriously. Biographers seem to agree, however, that Chopin's marriage was evidently satisfying to her and that she was not oppressed by her husband and did not feel oppressed.

Moreover, consider this diary entry from only one month after Chopin wrote the story (quoted by Per Seyersted in *Kate Chopin: A Critical Biography*):

> If it were possible for my husband and my mother to come back to earth, I feel that I would unhesitatingly give up everything that has come into my life since they left it and join my existence again with theirs. To do that, I would have to forget the past ten years of my growth — my real growth. But I would take back a little wisdom with me; it would be the spirit of perfect acquiescence.

This passage raises provocative questions instead of resolving them. How does that "spirit of perfect acquiescence" relate to Mrs. Mallard's insistence that she "would live for herself"? Why would Chopin be willing to "forget the past ten years of . . . growth" given her protagonist's desire for "self-assertion"? Although these and other questions raised by the diary entry cannot be answered here, this kind of biographical perspective certainly adds to the possibilities of interpretation.

Sometimes biographical information does not change our understanding so much as it enriches our appreciation of a work. It matters, for instance, that much of John Milton's poetry, so rich in visual imagery, was written after he became blind; and it is just as significant — to shift to a musical example — that a number of Ludwig van Beethoven's greatest works, including the Ninth Symphony, were composed after he succumbed to total deafness.

PSYCHOLOGICAL STRATEGIES

Given the enormous influence that Sigmund Freud's psychoanalytic theories have had on twentieth-century interpretations of human behavior, it is nearly inevitable that most people have some familiarity with his ideas concerning dreams, unconscious desires, and sexual repression, as well as his terms for different aspects of the psyche — the id, ego, and superego. Psychological approaches to literature draw upon Freud's theories and other psychoanalytic theories to understand more fully the text, the writer, and the reader. Critics use such approaches to explore the motivations of characters and the symbolic meanings of events, while biographers speculate about a writer's own motivations — conscious or unconscious — in a literary work. Psychological approaches are also used to describe and analyze the reader's personal responses to a text.

Although it is not feasible to explain psychoanalytic terms and concepts in so brief a space as this, it is possible to suggest the nature of a psychological approach. It is a strategy based heavily on the idea of the existence of a human unconscious — those impulses, desires, and feelings about which a person is unaware but which influence emotions and behavior.

Central to a number of psychoanalytic critical readings is Freud's concept of what he called the **Oedipus complex,** a term derived from Sophocles' tragedy *Oedipus the King* (p. 1120). This complex is predicated on a boy's unconscious rivalry with his father for his mother's love and his desire to eliminate his father in order to take his father's place with his mother. The female version of the psychological conflict is known as the **Electra complex,** a term used to describe a daughter's unconscious rivalry for her father. The name comes from a Greek legend about Electra who avenged the death of her father, Agamemnon, by killing her mother. In *The Interpretation of Dreams,* Freud explains why *Oedipus the King* "moves a modern audience no less than it did the contemporary Greek one." What unites their powerful attraction to the play is an unconscious response:

> There must be something which makes a voice within us ready to recognize the compelling force of destiny in the *Oedipus.* . . . . His destiny moves us only because it might have been ours — because the oracle laid the same curse upon us before our birth as upon him. It is the fate of all of us, perhaps, to direct our first sexual impulse towards our mother and our first hatred and our first murderous wish against our father. Our dreams convince us that this is so. King Oedipus, who slew his father Laius and married his mother Jocasta, merely shows us the fulfillment of our own childhood wishes . . . and we shrink back from him with the whole force of the repression by which those wishes have since that time been held down within us.

In this passage Freud interprets the unconscious motives of Sophocles in writing the play, Oedipus in acting within it, and the audience in responding to it.

A further application of the Oedipus complex can be observed in a classic interpretation of *Hamlet* by Ernest Jones, who used this concept to explain why Hamlet delays in avenging his father's death. This reading has been tightly summarized by Norman Holland, a recent psychoanalytic critic, in *The Shakespearean Imagination*. Holland shapes the issues into four major components:

> One, people over the centuries have been unable to say why Hamlet delays in killing the man who murdered his father and married his mother. Two, psychoanalytic experience shows that every child wants to do just exactly that. Three, Hamlet delays because he cannot punish Claudius for doing what he himself wished to do as a child and, unconsciously, still wishes to do: he would be punishing himself. Four, the fact that this wish is unconscious explains why people could not explain Hamlet's delay.

Although the Oedipus complex is, of course, not relevant to all psychological interpretations of literature, interpretations involving this complex do offer a useful example of how psychoanalytic critics tend to approach a text. (For Freud's discussion of *Hamlet,* see p. 1443.)

The situation in which Mrs. Mallard finds herself in Chopin's "The Story of an Hour" is not related to an Oedipus complex, but it is clear that news of her husband's death has released powerful unconscious desires for freedom that she had previously suppressed. As she grieved, "something" was "coming to her and she was waiting for it, fearfully." What comes to her is what she senses about the life outside her window; that's the stimulus, but the true source of what was to "possess her," which she strove to "beat . . . back with her [conscious] will" is her desperate desire for the autonomy and fulfillment she had been unable to admit did not exist in her marriage. A psychological approach to her story amounts to a case study in the destructive nature of self-repression. Moreover, the story might reflect Chopin's own views of her marriage — despite her conscious statements about her loving husband. And what about the reader's response? How might a psychological approach account for different responses in female and male readers to Mrs. Mallard's death? One needn't be versed in psychoanalytic terms to entertain this question.

HISTORICAL STRATEGIES

Historians sometimes use literature as a window onto the past, because literature frequently provides the nuances of an historic period that cannot be readily perceived through other sources. The characters in Harriet Beecher Stowe's *Uncle Tom's Cabin* (1852) display, for example, a complex set of white attitudes toward blacks in mid-nineteenth-century America that is absent from more traditional historic documents, such as census statistics or state laws. Another way of approaching the relationship between literature and history, however, is to use history as a means of understanding a literary work more clearly. The plot pattern of pursuit, escape, and capture in nineteenth-century slave narratives had a significant influence on Stowe's plotting of action in *Uncle Tom's Cabin*. This relationship demonstrates that the writing contemporary to an author is an important element of the history that helps to shape a work.

Literary historians shift the emphasis from the period to the work. Hence a literary historian might also examine mid-nineteenth-century abolitionist attitudes toward blacks to determine whether Stowe's novel is representative of those views or significantly to the right or left of them. Such a study might even indicate how closely the book reflects racial attitudes of twentieth-century readers. A work of literature may transcend time to the extent that it addresses the concerns of readers over a span of decades or centuries, but it remains for the literary historian a part of the past in which it was composed, a past that can reveal more fully a work's language, ideas, and purposes.

Literary historians move beyond both the facts of an author's personal life and the text itself to the social and intellectual currents in which the author composed the work. They place the work in the context of its time (as do many critical biographers, who write "life and times" studies), and sometimes they make connections with other literary works that may have influenced the author. The basic strategy of literary historians is to illuminate the historic background in order to shed light on some aspect of the work itself.

In Hemingway's "Soldier's Home" we learn that Krebs had been at Belleau Wood, Soissons, the Champagne, St. Mihiel, and the Argonne. Although nothing is said of these battles in the story, they were among the most bloody battles of the war; the wholesale butchery and staggering casualties incurred by both sides make credible the way Krebs's unstated but lingering memories have turned him into a psychological prisoner of war. Knowing something about the ferocity of those battles helps us account for Krebs's response in the story. Moreover, we can more fully appreciate Hemingway's refusal to have Krebs lie about the realities of war for the folks back home if we are aware of the numerous poems, stories, and plays published during World War I that presented war as a glorious, manly, transcendent sacrifice for God and country. Juxtaposing those works with "Soldier's Home" brings the differences into sharp focus.

Similarly, a reading of William Blake's poem "London" (p. 652) is less complete if we do not know of the horrific social conditions — the poverty, disease, exploitation, and hypocrisy — that characterized the city Blake laments in the late eighteenth century.

One last example: The repression expressed in the lines on Mrs. Mallard's face is more distinctly seen if Chopin's "The Story of an Hour" is placed in the context of "the women's question" as it continued to develop in the 1890s. Mrs. Mallard's impulse toward "self-assertion" runs parallel with a growing women's movement away from the role of long-suffering house-wife. This desire was widely regarded by traditionalists as a form of danger-ous selfishness that was considered as unnatural as it was immoral. It is no wonder that Chopin raises the question of whether Mrs. Mallard's sense of freedom owing to her husband's death isn't a selfish, "monstrous joy." Mrs. Mallard, however, dismisses this question as "trivial" in the face of her new perception of life, a dismissal that Chopin endorses by way of the story's ironic ending. The larger social context of this story would have been more apparent to Chopin's readers in 1894 than it is to readers in the 1990s. That is why an historical reconstruction of the limitations placed on married women helps to explain the pressures, tensions, and momentary — only momentary — release that Mrs. Mallard experiences.

Since the 1960s a development in historical approaches to literature known as *New Historicism* has emphasized the interaction between the historic context of a work and a modern reader's understanding and inter-pretation of the work. In contrast to many traditional literary historians, however, New Historicists attempt to describe the culture of a period by reading many different kinds of texts that traditional historians might have previously left for sociologists and anthropologists. New Historicists attempt to read a period in all its dimensions, including political, economic, social, and aesthetic concerns. These considerations could be used to explain the pressures that destroy Mrs. Mallard. A New Historicist might examine not only the story and the public attitudes toward women contemporary to "The Story of an Hour" but also documents such as suffragette tracts and medical diagnoses in order to explore how the same forces — expectations about how women are supposed to feel, think, and behave — shape different kinds of texts and how these texts influence each other. A New Historicist might, for example, examine medical records for evidence of "nervousness" and "hysteria" as common diagnoses for women who led lives regarded as too independent by their contemporaries.

Without an awareness of just how selfish and self-destructive Mrs. Mal-lard's impulses would have been in the eyes of her contemporaries, twentieth-century readers might miss the pervasive pressures embedded not only in her marriage but in the social fabric surrounding her. Her death is made more understandable by such an awareness. The doctors who diagnose her as suffering from "the joy that kills" are not merely insensitive or stupid; they represent a contrasting set of assumptions and values that are as historic and real as Mrs. Mallard's yearnings.

New Historicist criticism acknowledges more fully than traditional his-torical approaches the competing nature of readings of the past and thereby tends to offer new emphases and perspectives. New Historicism reminds us that there is not only one historic context for "The Story of an Hour." Those doctors reveal additional dimensions of late-nineteenth-century social atti-tudes that warrant our attention, whether we agree with them or not. By emphasizing that historical perceptions are governed, at least in part, by our own concerns and preoccupations, New Historicists sensitize us to the fact that the history on which we choose to focus is colored by being reconstructed from our own present moment. This reconstructed history affects our reading of texts.

SOCIOLOGICAL STRATEGIES, INCLUDING MARXIST AND FEMINIST STRATEGIES

Sociological approaches examine social groups, relationships, and values as they are manifested in literature. These approaches necessarily overlap historical analyses, but sociological approaches to a work emphasize more specifically the nature and effect of the social forces that shape power relationships between groups or classes of people. Such readings treat literature as either a document reflecting social conditions or a product of those conditions. The former view brings into focus the social milieu; the latter emphasizes the work. A sociological reading of Arthur Miller's *Death of a Salesman* (p. 1712) might, for instance, discuss how the characters' efforts to succeed reflect an increasingly competitive twentieth-century urban sensibility in America. Or it might emphasize how the "American Dream" of success shapes Willy Loman's aspirations and behavior. Clearly, there are numerous ways to talk about the societal aspects of a work. Two sociological strategies that have been especially influential are Marxist and feminist approaches.

Marxist Criticism

Marxist readings developed from the heightened interest in radical reform during the 1930s, when many critics looked to literature as a means of furthering proletarian social and economic goals, based largely on the writings of Karl Marx. *Marxist critics* focus on the ideological content of a work — its explicit and implicit assumptions and values about matters such as culture, race, class, and power. Marxist studies typically aim at not only revealing and clarifying ideological issues but also correcting social injustices. Some Marxist critics have used literature to describe the competing socioeconomic interests that too often advance capitalist money and power rather than socialist morality and justice. They argue that criticism, like literature, is essentially political because it either challenges or supports economic oppression. Even if criticism attempts to ignore class conflicts, it is politicized, according to Marxists, because it supports the status quo.

It is not surprising that Marxist critics pay more attention to the content and themes of literature than to its form. A Marxist critic would more likely be concerned with the exploitive economic forces that cause Willy Loman to feel trapped in Miller's *Death of a Salesman* than with the playwright's use of nonrealistic dramatic techniques to reveal Loman's inner thoughts. Similarly, a Marxist reading of Chopin's "The Story of an Hour" might draw on the evidence made available in a book published only a few years after the story by Charlotte Perkins Gilman titled *Women and Economics: A Study of the Economic Relation between Men and Women as a Factor in Social Evolution* (1898). An examination of this study could help explain how some of the "repression" Mrs. Mallard experiences was generated by the socioeconomic structure contemporary to her and how Chopin challenges the validity of that structure by having Mrs. Mallard resist it with her very life. A Marxist reading would see the protagonist's conflict as not only an individual issue but part of a larger class struggle.

Feminist Criticism

Feminist critics would also be interested in Gilman's study of *Women and Economics,* because they seek to correct or supplement what they regard as a predominantly male-dominated critical perspective with a feminist consciousness. Like other forms of sociological criticism, feminist criticism places literature in a social context, and, like those of Marxist criticism, its analyses often have sociopolitical purposes, purposes that might explain, for example, how images of women in literature reflect the patriarchal social forces that have impeded women's efforts to achieve full equality with men.

Feminists have analyzed literature by both men and women in an effort to understand literary representations of women as well as the writers and cultures that create them. Related to concerns about how gender affects the way men and women write about each other is an interest in whether women use language differently from the way men do. Consequently, feminist critics' approach to literature is characterized by the use of a broad range of disciplines, including history, sociology, psychology, and linguistics, to provide a perspective sensitive to feminist issues.

A feminist approach to Chopin's "The Story of an Hour" might explore the psychological stress created by the expectations that marriage imposes on Mrs. Mallard, expectations that literally and figuratively break her heart. Given that her husband is kind and loving, the issue is not her being married to Brently but her being married at all. Chopin presents marriage as an institution that creates in both men and women the assumed "right to impose a private will upon a fellow-creature." That "right," however, is seen, especially from a feminist perspective, as primarily imposed on women by men. A feminist critic might note, for instance, that the protagonist is introduced as "Mrs. Mallard" (we learn that her first name is Louise only later); she is defined by her marital status and her husband's name, a name whose origin from the Old French is related to the word *masle,* which means "male." The appropriateness of her name points up the fact that her emotions and the cause of her death are interpreted in male terms by the doctors. The value of a feminist perspective on this work can be readily discerned if a reader imagines Mrs. Mallard's story being told from the point of view of one of the doctors who diagnoses the cause of her death as a weak heart rather than as a fierce struggle.

MYTHOLOGICAL STRATEGIES

Mythological approaches to literature attempt to identify what in a work creates deep universal responses in readers. Whereas psychological critics interpret the symbolic meanings of characters and actions in order to understand more fully the unconscious dimensions of an author's mind, a character's motivation, or a reader's response, mythological critics (also frequently referred to as archetypal critics) interpret the hopes, fears, and expectations of entire cultures.

In this context myth is not to be understood simply as referring to stories about imaginary gods who perform astonishing feats in the causes of love, jealousy, or hatred. Nor are myths to be judged as merely erroneous, primitive accounts of how nature runs its course and humanity its affairs. Instead, literary critics use myths as a strategy for understanding how human beings try to account for their lives symbolically. Myths can be a window onto a culture's deepest perceptions about itself, because myths attempt to explain what otherwise seems unexplainable: a people's origin, purpose, and destiny.

All human beings have a need to make sense of their lives, whether they are concerned about their natural surroundings, the seasons, sexuality, birth, death, or the very meaning of existence. Myths help people organize their experiences; these systems of belief (less formally held than religious or political tenets but no less important) embody a culture's assumptions and values. What is important to the mythological critic is not the validity or truth of those assumptions and values; what matters is that they reveal common human concerns.

It is not surprising that although the details of mythic stories vary enormously, the essential patterns are often similar, because these myths attempt to explain universal experiences. There are, for example, numerous myths that redeem humanity from permanent death through a hero's resurrection and rebirth. The resurrection of Jesus for Christians symbolizes the ultimate defeat of death and coincides with the rebirth of nature's fertility in spring. Features of this rebirth parallel the Greek myths of Adonis and Hyacinth, who die but are subsequently transformed into living flowers; there are also similarities that connect these stories to the reincarnation of the Indian Buddha or the rebirth of the Egyptian Osiris. To be sure, important differences exist among these stories, but each reflects a basic human need to limit the power of death and to hope for eternal life.

Mythological critics look for underlying, recurrent patterns in literature that reveal universal meanings and basic human experiences for readers regardless of when or where they live. The characters, images, and themes that symbolically embody these meanings and experiences are called *archetypes*. This term designates universal symbols, which evoke deep and perhaps unconscious responses in a reader because archetypes bring with them the heft of our hopes and fears since the beginning of human time. Surely one of the most powerfully compelling archetypes is the death/rebirth theme that relates the human life cycle to the cycle of the seasons. Many others could be cited and would be exhausted only after all human concerns were catalogued, but a few examples can suggest some of the range of plots, images, and characters addressed.

Among the most common literary archetypes are stories of quests, initiations, scapegoats, meditative withdrawals, descents to the underworld, and heavenly ascents. These stories are often filled with archetypal images: bodies of water that may symbolize the unconscious or eternity or baptismal rebirth; rising suns, suggesting reawakening and enlightenment; setting suns, pointing toward death; colors such as green, evocative of growth and fertility, or black, indicating chaos, evil, and death. Along the way are earth mothers, fatal women, wise old men, desert places, and paradisal gardens. No doubt your own reading has introduced you to any number of archetypal plots, images, and characters.

Mythological critics attempt to explain how archetypes are embodied in literary works. Employing various disciplines, these critics articulate the power a literary work has over us. Some critics are deeply grounded in classical literature, whereas others are more conversant with philology, anthropology, psychology, or cultural history. Whatever their emphases, however, mythological critics examine the elements of a work in order to make larger connections that explain the work's lasting appeal.

A mythological reading of Sophocles' *Oedipus the King,* for example, might focus on the relationship between Oedipus's role as a scapegoat and the plague and drought that threaten to destroy Thebes. The city is saved and the fertility of its fields restored only after the corruption is located in Oedipus. His subsequent atonement symbolically provides a kind of rebirth for the city. Thus, the plot recapitulates ancient rites in which the well-being of a king was directly linked to the welfare of his people. If a leader were sick or corrupt, he had to be replaced in order to guarantee the health of the community.

A similar pattern can be seen in the rottenness that Shakespeare exposes in Hamlet's Denmark. *Hamlet* reveals an archetypal pattern similar to that of *Oedipus the King:* not until the hero sorts out the corruption in his world and in himself can vitality and health be restored in his world. Hamlet avenges his father's death and becomes a scapegoat in the process. When he fully accepts his responsibility to set things right, he is swept away along with the tide of intrigue and corruption that has polluted life in Denmark. The new order — established by Fortinbras at the play's end — is achieved precisely because Hamlet is willing and finally able to sacrifice himself in a necessary purgation of the diseased state.

These kinds of archetypal patterns exist potentially in any literary period. Consider how in Chopin's "The Story of an Hour" Mrs. Mallard's life parallels the end of winter and the earth's renewal in spring. When she feels a surge of new life after grieving over her husband's death, her own sensibilities are closely aligned with the "new spring life" that is "all aquiver" outside her window. Although she initially tries to resist that renewal by "beat[ing] it back with her will," she cannot control the life force that surges within her and all around her. When she finally gives herself to the energy and life she experiences, she feels triumphant — like a "goddess of Victory." But this victory is short-lived when she learns that her husband is still alive and with him all the obligations that made her marriage feel like a wasteland. Her death is an ironic version of a rebirth ritual. The coming of spring is an ironic contrast to her own discovery that she can no longer live a repressed, circumscribed life with her husband. Death turns out to be preferable to the living death that her marriage means to her. Although spring will go on, this "goddess of Victory" is defeated by a devastating social contract. The old, corrupt order continues, and that for Chopin is a cruel irony that mythological critics would see as an unnatural disruption of the nature of things.

READER-RESPONSE STRATEGIES

Reader-response criticism, as its name implies, focuses its attention on the reader rather than the work itself. This approach to literature describes what goes on in the reader's mind during the process of reading a text. In a sense, all critical approaches (especially psychological and mythological criticism) concern themselves with a reader's response to literature, but there is a stronger emphasis in reader-response criticism on the reader's active construction of the text. Although many critical theories inform reader-response criticism, all *reader-response critics* aim to describe the reader's experience of a work: in effect we get a reading of the reader, who comes to the work with certain expectations and assumptions, which are either met or not met. Hence the consciousness of the reader — produced by reading the work — is the subject matter of reader-response critics. Just as writing is a creative act, reading is, since it also produces a text.

Reader-response critics do not assume that a literary work is a finished product with fixed formal properties, as, for example, formalist critics do. Instead, the literary work is seen as an evolving creation of the reader's as he or she processes characters, plots, images, and other elements while reading. Some reader-response critics argue that this act of creative reading is, to a degree, controlled by the text, but it can produce many interpretations of the same text by different readers. There is no single definitive reading of a work, because the crucial assumption is that readers create rather than discover meanings in texts. Readers who have gone back to works they had read earlier in their lives often find that a later reading draws very different responses from them. What earlier seemed unimportant is now crucial; what at first seemed central is now barely worth noting. The reason, put simply, is that two different people have read the same text. Reader-response critics are not after the "correct" reading of the text or what the author presumably intended; instead they are interested in the reader's experience with the text.

These experiences change with readers; although the text remains the same, the readers do not. Social and cultural values influence readings, so that, for example, an avowed Marxist would be likely to come away from Miller's *Death of a Salesman* with a very different view of American capitalism than that of, say, a successful sales representative, who might attribute Willy Loman's fall more to his character than to the American economic system. Moreover, readers from different time periods respond differently to texts. An Elizabethan — concerned perhaps with the stability of monarchical rule — might respond differently to Hamlet's problems than would a twentieth-century reader well versed in psychology and concepts of what Freud called the Oedipus complex. This is not to say that anything goes, that Miller's play can be read as an amoral defense of cheating and rapacious business practices or that *Hamlet* is about the dangers of living away from home. The text does, after all, establish some limits that allow us to reject certain readings as erroneous. But reader-response critics do reject formalist approaches that describe a literary work as a self-contained object, the meaning of which can be determined without reference to any extrinsic matters, such as the social and cultural values assumed by either the author or the reader.

Reader-response criticism calls attention to how we read and what influences our readings. It does not attempt to define what a literary work means on the page but rather what it does to an informed reader, a reader who understands the language and conventions used in a given work. Reader-response criticism is not a rationale for mistaken or bizarre readings of works but an exploration of the possibilities for a plurality of readings shaped by the readers' experience with the text. This kind of strategy can help us understand how our responses are shaped by both the text and ourselves.

Chopin's "The Story of an Hour" illustrates how reader-response critical strategies read the reader. Chopin doesn't say that Mrs. Mallard's marriage is repressive; instead, that troubling fact dawns on the reader at the same time that the recognition forces its way into Mrs. Mallard's consciousness. Her surprise is also the reader's, because although she remains in the midst of intense grief, she is on the threshold of a startling discovery about the new possibilities life offers. How the reader responds to that discovery, however, is not entirely controlled by Chopin. One reader, perhaps someone who has recently lost a spouse, might find Mrs. Mallard's "joy" indeed "monstrous" and selfish. Certainly that's how Mrs. Mallard's doctors — the seemingly authoritative diagnosticians in the story — would very likely read her. But for other readers — especially late-twentieth-century readers steeped in feminist values — Mrs. Mallard's feelings require no justification. Such readers might find Chopin's ending to the story more ironic than she seems to have intended, because Mrs. Mallard's death could be read as Chopin's inability to envision a protagonist who has the strength of her convictions. In contrast, a reader in 1894 might have seen the ending as Mrs. Mallard's only escape from the repressive marriage her husband's assumed death suddenly allowed her to see. A late-twentieth-century reader probably would argue that it was the marriage that should have died rather than Mrs. Mallard, that she had other alternatives, not just obligations (as the doctors would have insisted), to consider.

By imagining different readers we can imagine a variety of responses to the story that are influenced by the readers' own impressions, memories, or experiences with marriage. Such imagining suggests the ways in which reader-response criticism opens up texts to a number of interpretations. As one final example, consider how readers' responses to "The Story of an Hour" would be affected if it were printed in two different magazines, read in the context of either *Ms.* or *Good Housekeeping.* What assumptions and beliefs would each magazine's readership be likely to bring to the story? How do you think the respective experiences and values of each magazine's readers would influence their readings?

DECONSTRUCTIONIST STRATEGIES

Deconstructionist critics insist that literary works do not yield fixed, single meanings. They argue that there can be no absolute knowledge about anything because language can never say what we intend it to mean. Anything we write conveys meanings we did not intend, so the deconstructionist argument goes. Language is not a precise instrument but a power whose meanings are caught in an endless web of possibilities that cannot be untangled. Accordingly, any idea or statement that insists on being understood separately can ultimately be "deconstructed" to reveal its relations and connections to contradictory and opposite meanings.

Unlike other forms of criticism, deconstructionism seeks to destabilize meanings instead of establishing them. In contrast to formalists such as the New Critics, who closely examine a work in order to call attention to how its various components interact to establish a unified whole, deconstructionists try to show how a close examination of the language in a text inevitably reveals conflicting, contradictory impulses that "deconstruct" or break down its apparent unity.

Although deconstructionists and New Critics both examine the language of a text closely, deconstructionists focus on the gaps and ambiguities that reveal a text's instability and indeterminacy, whereas New Critics look for patterns that explain how the text's fixed meaning is structured. Deconstructionists painstakingly examine the competing meanings within the text rather than attempting to resolve them into a unified whole.

The questions deconstructionists ask are aimed at discovering and describing how a variety of possible readings are generated by the elements of a text. In contrast to a New Critic's concerns about the ultimate meaning of a work, a deconstructionist is primarily interested in how the use of language — diction, tone, metaphor, symbol, and so on — yields only provisional, not definitive, meanings. Consider, for example, the following excerpt from an American Puritan poet, Anne Bradstreet. The excerpt is from "The Flesh and the Spirit" (1678), which consists of an allegorical debate between two sisters, the body and the soul. During the course of the debate, Flesh, a consummate materialist, insists that Spirit values ideas that do not exist and that her faith in idealism is both unwarranted and insubstantial in the face of the material values that earth has to offer — riches, fame, and physical pleasure. Spirit, however, rejects the materialistic worldly argument that the only ultimate reality is physical reality and pledges her faith in God:

> Mine eye doth pierce the heavens and see
> What is invisible to thee.
> My garments are not silk nor gold,
> Nor such like trash which earth doth hold,
> But royal robes I shall have on,
> More glorious than the glist'ring sun;
> My crown not diamonds, pearls, and gold,
> But such as angels' heads enfold
> The city where I hope to dwell,
> There's none on earth can parallel;
> The stately walls both high and strong,
> Are made of precious jasper stone;
> The gates of pearl, both rich and clear,
> And angels are for porters there;
> The streets thereof transparent gold,
> Such as no eye did e'er behold;
> A crystal river there doth run,
> Which doth proceed from the Lamb's throne.

A deconstructionist would point out that Spirit's language — her use of material images such as jasper stone, pearl, gold, and crystal — cancels the explicit meaning of the passage by offering a supermaterialistic reward to the spiritually faithful. Her language, in short, deconstructs her intended meaning by employing the same images that Flesh would use to describe the rewards of the physical world. A deconstructionist reading, then, reveals the impossibility of talking about the invisible and spiritual worlds without using materialistic (that is, metaphoric) language. Thus Spirit's very language demonstrates a contradiction and conflict in her conviction that the world of here and now must be rejected for the hereafter. Her language deconstructs her meaning.

Deconstructionists look for ways to question and extend the meanings of a text. A deconstructionist might find, for example, the ironic ending of Chopin's "The Story of an Hour" less tidy and conclusive than would a New Critic, who might attribute Mrs. Mallard's death to her sense of lost personal freedom. A deconstructionist might use the story's ending to suggest that the narrative shares the doctors' inability to imagine a life for Mrs. Mallard apart from her husband.

As difficult as it is controversial, deconstructionism is not easily summarized or paraphrased. For an example of deconstructionism in practice and how it differs from New Criticism, see Andrew P. Debicki's "New Criticism and Deconstructionism: Two Attitudes in Teaching Poetry" in Perspectives (p. 2025).

SELECTED BIBLIOGRAPHY

Canonical Issues

"The Changing Culture of the University." Special Issue. *Partisan Review* 58 (Spring 1991): 185–410.

Gates, Henry Louis, Jr. *The Signifying Monkey.* New York: Oxford UP, 1988.

Lauter, Paul. *Canons and Contexts.* New York: Oxford UP, 1991.

"The Politics of Liberal Education." Special Issue. *South Atlantic Quarterly* 89 (Winter 1990): 1–234.

Sykes, Charles J. *The Hollow Men: Politics and Corruption in Higher Education.* Washington, D.C.: Regnery Gateway, 1990.

Formalist Strategies

Brooks, Cleanth. *The Well Wrought Urn: Studies in the Structure of Poetry.* New York: Reynal and Hitchcock, 1947.

Crane, Ronald Salmon. *The Languages of Criticism and the Structure of Poetry.* Toronto: U of Toronto P, 1953.

Eliot, Thomas Stearns. *The Sacred Wood: Essays in Poetry and Criticism.* London: Methuen, 1920.

Fekete, John. *The Critical Twilight: Explorations in the Ideology of Anglo-American Literary Theory from Eliot to McLuhan.* London: Routledge, 1977.

Lemon, Lee T., and Marion J. Reis, eds. *Russian Formalist Criticism: Four Essays.* Lincoln: U of Nebraska P, 1965.

Ransom, John Crowe. *The New Criticism.* Norfolk, CT: New Directions, 1941.

Wellek, Rene, and Austin Warren. *Theory of Literature.* New York: Harcourt, Brace and World, 1949.

Biographical and Psychological Strategies

Bleich, David. *Subjective Criticism.* Baltimore: Johns Hopkins UP, 1978.

Bloom, Harold. *The Anxiety of Influence.* New York: Oxford UP, 1975.

Crews, Frederick. *The Sins of the Fathers: Hawthorne's Psychological Themes.* New York: Oxford UP, 1966.

Felman, Shoshana. *Writing and Madness (Literature/Philosophy/Psycho-analysis)*. Ithaca: Cornell UP, 1985.

Felman, Shoshana, ed. *Literature and Psychoanalysis: The Question of Reading: Otherwise*. Baltimore: Johns Hopkins UP, 1981.

Freud, Sigmund. *The Standard Edition of the Complete Psychological Works*. 24 vols. 1940–1968. London: Hogarth Press and the Institute of Psychoanalysis, 1953.

Holland, Norman. *The Dynamics of Literary Response*. New York: Oxford UP, 1968.

Jones, Ernest. *Hamlet and Oedipus*. New York: Doubleday, 1949.

Lesser, Simon O. *Fiction and the Unconscious*. Chicago: U of Chicago P, 1957.

Skura, Meredith Anne. *The Literary Use of the Psychoanalytic Process*. New Haven: Yale UP, 1981.

Weiss, Daniel. *The Critic Agonistes: Psychology, Myth, and the Art of Fiction*. Ed. Stephen Arkin and Eric Solomon. Seattle: U of Washington P, 1985.

Historical and New Historicist Strategies

Armstrong, Nancy. *Desire and Domestic Fiction*. New York: Oxford UP, 1987.

Dollimore, Jonathan. *Radical Tragedy: Religion, Ideology and Power in the Drama of Shakespeare and His Contemporaries*. Brighton, Eng.: Harvester Press, 1984.

Geertz, Clifford. *The Interpretation of Cultures: Selected Essays*. New York: Basic Books, 1973.

Greenblatt, Stephen. *Renaissance Self-Fashioning: From More to Shakespeare*. Chicago: U of Chicago P, 1980.

Lindenberger, Herbert. *Historical Drama: The Relation of Literature and Reality*. Chicago: U of Chicago P, 1975.

McGann, Jerome. *The Beauty of Inflections: Literary Investigations in Historical Method and Theory*. Oxford: Clarendon P, 1985.

Tennenhouse, Leonard. *Power on Display: The Politics of Shakespeare's Genres*. New York: Methuen, 1986.

White, Hayden. *Tropics of Discourse: Essays in Cultural Criticism*. Baltimore: Johns Hopkins UP, 1978.

Sociological Strategies (Including Marxist and Feminist Strategies)

Adorno, Theodor. *Prisms: Cultural Criticism and Society*. 1955. London: Neville Spearman, 1967.

Beauvoir, Simone de. *The Second Sex*. Trans. H. M. Parshley. New York: Knopf, 1972. Trans. of *Le deuxième sexe*. Paris: Gallimard, 1949.

Benjamin, Walter. *Illuminations*. New York: Harcourt, Brace and World, 1968.

Benstock, Shari, ed. *Feminist Issues and Literary Scholarship.* Bloomington: Indiana UP, 1987.

Cixous, Hélène, and Catherine Clément. *The Newly Born Woman.* Trans. Betsy Wing. Minneapolis: U of Minnesota P, 1986.

Eagleton, Terry. *Criticism and Ideology: A Study in Marxist Literary Theory.* London: New Left Books, 1976.

Fetterley, Judith. *The Resisting Reader: A Feminist Approach to American Fiction.* Bloomington: Indiana UP, 1978.

Frow, John. *Marxist and Literary History.* Cambridge: Harvard UP, 1986.

Gilbert, Sandra M., and Susan Gubar. *The Madwoman in the Attic: The Woman Writer and the Nineteenth-Century Literary Imagination.* New Haven: Yale UP, 1979.

Irigaray, Luce. *This Sex Which Is Not One.* Ithaca: Cornell UP, 1985. Trans. of *Ce sexe qui n'en est pas un.* Paris. Éditions de Minuit, 1977.

Jameson, Fredric. *The Political Unconscious: Studies in the Ideology of Form.* Ithaca: Cornell UP, 1979.

Kolodny, Annette. "Some Notes on Defining a 'Feminist Literary Criticism.'" *Critical Inquiry* 2 (1975): 75–92.

Lukács, Georg. *Realism in Our Time: Literature and the Class Struggle.* 1957. New York: Harper and Row, 1964.

Marx, Karl, and Fredrich Engels. *Marx and Engels on Literature and Art.* St. Louis: Telos Press, 1973.

Millet, Kate. *Sexual Politics.* New York: Avon Books, 1970.

Showalter, Elaine. *A Literature of Their Own: British Women Novelists from Brontë to Lessing.* Princeton: Princeton UP, 1977.

Smith, Barbara. *Toward a Black Feminist Criticism.* New York: Out and Out Books, 1977.

Trotsky, Leon. *Literature and the Revolution.* 1924. Ann Arbor: U of Michigan P, 1960.

Williams, Raymond. *Marxism and Literature.* Oxford: Oxford UP, 1977.

Mythological Strategies

Bodkin, Maud. *Archetypal Patterns in Poetry.* London: Oxford UP, 1934.

Frye, Northrop. *Anatomy of Criticism: Four Essays.* Princeton: Princeton UP, 1957.

Jung, Carl Gustav. *Complete Works.* Eds. Herbert Read, Michael Fordham, and Gerhard Adler. 17 vols. New York: Pantheon, 1953–.

Reader-Response Strategies

Booth, Wayne, C. *The Rhetoric of Fiction.* 2nd ed. Chicago: U of Chicago P, 1983.

Eco, Umberto. *The Role of the Reader: Explorations in the Semiotics of Texts.* Bloomington: Indiana UP, 1979.

Escarpit, Robert. *Sociology of Literature.* Painesville, Ohio: Lake Erie College P, 1965.

Fish, Stanley. *Is There a Text in This Class? The Authority of Interpretive Communities*. Cambridge: Harvard UP, 1980.

Freund, Elizabeth. *The Return of the Reader: Reader-Response Criticism*. London: Methuen, 1987.

Holland, Norman N. *5 Readers Reading*. New Haven: Yale UP, 1975.

Iser, Wolfgang. *The Implied Reader: Patterns of Communication in Prose Fiction from Bunyan to Beckett*. Baltimore: Johns Hopkins UP, 1974.

Jauss, Hans Robert. "Literary History as a Challenge to Literary Theory." *Toward an Aesthetics of Reception*. Trans. Timothy Bahti. Minneapolis: U of Minnesota P, 1982. pp. 3–46.

Rosenblatt, Louise. *Literature as Exploration*. 1938. New York: MLA, 1983.

Suleiman, Susan, and Inge Crosman, eds. *The Reader in the Text: Essays on Audience and Interpretation*. Princeton: Princeton UP, 1980.

Tompkins, Jane P., ed. *Reader-Response Criticism: From Formalism to Post-Structuralism*. Baltimore: Johns Hopkins UP, 1980.

Deconstructionist and Other Poststructuralist Strategies

Culler, Jonathan. *On Deconstruction: Theory and Criticism after Structuralism*. Ithaca: Cornell UP, 1982.

de Man, Paul. *Blindness and Insight*. New York: Oxford UP, 1971.

Derrida, Jacques. *Of Grammatology*. 1967. Baltimore: Johns Hopkins UP, 1976.

———. *Writing and Difference*. 1967. Chicago: U of Chicago P, 1978.

Foucault, Michel. *The Order of Things: An Archaeology of the Human Sciences*. 1966. London: Tavistock, 1970.

———. *Language, Counter-Memory, Practice*. Ithaca: Cornell UP, 1977.

Gasche, Rodolphe. "Deconstruction as Criticism." *Glyph* 6 (1979): 177–216.

Hartman, Geoffrey H. *Criticism in the Wilderness*. New Haven: Yale UP, 1980.

Johnson, Barbara. *The Critical Difference: Essays in the Contemporary Rhetoric of Reading*. Baltimore: Johns Hopkins UP, 1980.

Melville, Stephen W. *Philosophy Beside Itself: On Deconstruction and Modernism*. Theory and History of Literature 27. Minneapolis: U of Minnesota P, 1986.

Said, Edward W. *The World, the Text, and the Critic*. Cambridge: Harvard UP, 1983.

Smith, Barbara Hernstein. *On the Margins of Discourse: The Relation of Literature to Language*. Chicago: U of Chicago P, 1979.

SUSAN SONTAG (b. 1933)
Against Interpretation   1964

Like the fumes of the automobile and of heavy industry which befoul the urban atmosphere, the effusion of interpretations of art today poisons our sensibilities. In a culture whose already classical dilemma is the hypertrophy of the intellect at the expense of energy and sensual capability, interpretation is the revenge of the intellect upon art.

Even more. It is the revenge of the intellect upon the world. To interpret is to impoverish, to deplete the world — in order to set up a shadow world of "meanings." It is to turn *the* world into *this* world. ("This world"! As if there were any other.)

The world, our world, is depleted, impoverished enough. Away with all duplicates of it, until we again experience more immediately what we have. . . .

In most modern instances, interpretation amounts to the philistine refusal to leave the work of art alone. Real art has the capacity to make us nervous. By reducing the work of art to its content and then interpreting *that,* one tames the work of art. Interpretation makes art manageable, conformable.

This philistinism of interpretation is more rife in literature than in any other art. For decades now, literary critics have understood it to be their task to translate the elements of the poem or play or novel or story into something else.

From *Against Interpretation*

Considerations for Critical Thinking and Writing

1. What are Sontag's objections to "interpretation"? Explain whether you agree or disagree with them.
2. In what sense does interpretation make art "manageable" and "conformable"?
3. In an essay explore what you take to be both the dangers of interpretation and its contributions to your understanding of literature.

JUDITH FETTERLEY (b. 1938)
A Feminist Reading of "A Rose for Emily"   1978

"A Rose for Emily" is a story not of a conflict between the South and the North or between the old order and the new; it is a story of the patriarchy North and South, new and old, and of the sexual conflict within it. As Faulkner himself has implied, it is a story of a woman victimized and betrayed by the system of sexual politics, who nevertheless has discovered, within the structures that victimize her, sources of power for herself. . . . "A Rose for Emily" is the story of how to murder your gentleman caller and get away with it. Faulkner's story is an analysis of how men's attitudes toward women turn back upon themselves; it is a demonstration of the thesis that it is impossible to oppress without in turn being oppressed, it is impossible to kill without creating the conditions for your own murder. "A Rose for Emily" is the story of a *lady* and of her revenge for that grotesque identity. . . .

Not only is "A Rose for Emily" a supreme analysis of what men do to women by making them ladies; it is also an exposure of how this act in turn defines and recoils upon men. This is the significance of the dynamic that Faulkner establishes between Emily and Jefferson. And it is equally the point of the dynamic implied between the tableau of Emily and her father and the tableau which greets the men who break down the door of that room in the region above the stairs. When the would-be "suitors" finally get into her father's house, they discover the consequences of his oppression of her, for the violence contained in the rotted corpse of Homer Barron is the mirror image of the violence represented in the tableau, the back-flung front door flung back with a vengeance. Having been consumed by her father, Emily in turn feeds off Homer Barron, becoming, after his death, suspiciously fat. Or, to put it another way, it is as if, after her father's death, she has reversed his act of incorporating her by incorporating and becoming him, metamorphosed from the slender figure in white to the obese figure in black whose hair is "a vigorous iron-gray, like the hair of an active man." She has taken into herself the violence in him which thwarted her and has reenacted it upon Homer Barron.

That final encounter, however, is not simply an image of the reciprocity of violence. Its power of definition also derives from its grotesqueness, which makes finally explicit the grotesqueness that has been latent in the description of Emily throughout the story: "Her skeleton was small and spare; perhaps that was why what would have been merely plumpness in another was obesity in her. She looked bloated, like a body long submerged in motionless water, and of that pallid hue. Her eyes, lost in the fatty ridges of her face, looked like two small pieces of coal pressed into a lump of dough." The impact of this description depends on the contrast it establishes between Emily's reality as a fat, bloated figure in black and the conventional image of a lady — expectations that are fostered in the town by its emblematic memory of Emily as a slender figure in white and in us by the narrator's tone of romantic invocation and by the passage itself. Were she not expected to look so different, were her skeleton not small and spare, Emily would not be so grotesque. Thus, the focus is on the grotesqueness that results when stereotypes are imposed upon reality. And the implication of this focus is that the real grotesque is the stereotype itself. If Emily is both lady and grotesque, then the syllogism must be completed thus: the idea of a lady is grotesque. So Emily is metaphor and mirror for the town of Jefferson; and when, at the end, the town folk finally discover who and what she is, they have in fact encountered who and what they are.

From *The Resisting Reader: A Feminist Approach*
to American Fiction

Considerations for Critical Thinking and Writing

1. Discuss Fetterley's claim that Emily Grierson is a victim of a "system of sexual politics." What details of the story support this view?
2. What are the consequences of Emily's oppression by her father? How are the men in the story affected by it?
3. Write an essay that supports or refutes Fetterley's argument that "A Rose for Emily" is an implicitly feminist story about "the patriarchy North and South."

STANLEY FISH (b. 1938)
On What Makes an Interpretation Acceptable   1980

. . . After all, while "The Tyger" is obviously open to more than one interpretation, it is not open to an infinite number of interpretations. There may be disagreements as to whether the tiger is good or evil, or whether the speaker is Blake or a persona, and so on, but no one is suggesting that the poem is an allegory of the digestive processes or that it predicts the Second World War, and its limited plurality is simply a testimony to the capacity of a great work of art to generate multiple readings. The point is one that Wayne Booth makes when he asks, "Are we *right* to rule out at least some readings?" and then answers his own question with a resounding yes. It would be my answer too; but the real question is what gives us the right so to be right. A pluralist is committed to saying that there is something in the text which rules out some readings and allows others (even though no one reading can ever capture the text's "inexhaustible richness and complexity"). His best evidence is that in practice "we all in fact" do reject unacceptable readings and that more often than not we agree on the readings that are not rejected. . . . Booth concludes that there are justified limits to what we can legitimately do with a text, for "surely we could not go on disputing at all if a core of agreement did not exist." Again, I agree, but if, as I have argued, the text is always a function of interpretation, then the text cannot be the location of the core of agreement by means of which we reject interpretations. We seem to be at an impasse: on the one hand there would seem to be no basis for labeling an interpretation unacceptable, but on the other we do it all the time.

This, however, is an impasse only if one assumes that the activity of interpretation is itself unconstrained; but in fact the shape of that activity is determined by the literary institution which at any one time will authorize only a finite number of interpretative strategies. Thus, while there is no core of agreement *in* the text, there is a core of agreement (although one subject to change) concerning the ways of *producing* the text. Nowhere is this set of acceptable ways written down, but it is a part of everyone's knowledge of what it means to be operating within the literary institution as it is now constituted. A student of mine recently demonstrated this knowledge when, with an air of giving away a trade secret, she confided that she could go into any classroom, no matter what the subject of the course, and win approval for running one of a number of well-defined interpretive routines: she could view the assigned text as an instance of the tension between nature and culture; she could look in the text for evidence of large mythological oppositions; she could argue that the true subject of the text was its own composition, or that in the guise of fashioning a narrative the speaker was fragmenting and displacing his own anxieties and fears. She could not . . . argue that the text was a prophetic message inspired by the ghost of her Aunt Tilly.

My student's understanding of what she could and could not get away with, of the unwritten rules of the literary game, is shared by everyone who plays that game, by those who write and judge articles for publication in learned journals, by those who read and listen to papers at professional meetings, by those who seek and award tenure in innumerable departments of English and comparative literature, by the armies of graduate students for whom knowledge of the rules is the real mark of professional initiation. This does not mean that these rules and the practices they authorize are either monolithic or stable. Within the literary community there are subcommunities. . . . In a classroom whose authority figures include David Bleich and Norman Holland, a student might very well relate a text to her memories of a favorite aunt, while in other classrooms, dominated by the spirit of [Cleanth] Brooks and [Robert Penn] Warren, any such activity would immediately be dismissed as nonliterary, as something that isn't done.

The point is that while there is always a category of things that are not done (it is simply the reverse or flip side of the category of things that *are* done), the membership in that category is continually changing. It changes laterally as one moves from subcommunity to subcommunity, and it changes through time when once interdicted interpretive strategies are admitted into the ranks of the acceptable. Twenty years ago one of the things that literary critics didn't do was talk about the reader, at least in a way that made his experience the focus of the critical act. The prohibition on such talk was largely the result of [W. K.] Wimsatt's and [Monroe] Beardsley's famous essay "The Affective Fallacy," which argued that the variability of readers renders any investigation of their responses ad-hoc and relativistic: "The poem itself," the authors complained, "as an object of specifically critical judgment, tends to disappear." So influential was this essay that it was possible for a reviewer to dismiss a book merely by finding in it evidence that the affective fallacy had been committed. The use of a juridical terminology is not accidental; this was in a very real sense a *legal* finding of activity in violation of understood and institutionalized decorums. Today, however, the affective fallacy, no longer a fallacy but a methodology, is committed all the time, and its practitioners have behind them the full and authorizing weight of a fully articulated institutional apparatus. The "reader in literature" is regularly the subject of forums and workshops at the convention of the Modern Language Association; there is a reader newsletter which reports on the multitudinous labors of a reader industry; any list of currently active schools of literary criticism includes the school of "reader response," and two major university presses have published collections of essays designed both to display the variety of reader-centered criticism (the emergence of factions within a once interdicted activity is a sure sign of its having achieved the status of an orthodoxy) and to detail its history. None of this of course means that a reader-centered criticism is now invulnerable to challenge or attack, merely that it is now recognized as a competing literary strategy that cannot be dismissed simply by being named. It is acceptable not because everyone accepts it but because those who do not are now obliged to argue against it.

From Is There a Text in This Class?

Considerations for Critical Thinking and Writing

1. Why *can't* William Blake's "The Tyger" (see p. 746) be read as "an allegory of the digestive processes"? What principle does Fish use to rule out such a reading?
2. What kinds of strategies for reading have you encountered in your classroom experiences? Which have you found to be the most useful? Explain why.
3. Write an essay that describes what you "could and could not get away with" in the literature courses you have taken in high school and college.

ANNETTE KOLODNY (b. 1941)
On the Commitments of Feminist Criticism   1980

If feminist criticism calls anything into question, it must be that dog-eared myth of intellectual neutrality. For what I take to be the underlying spirit or message of any consciously ideologically premised criticism — that is, that ideas are important *because* they determine the ways we live, or want to live, in the world — is vitiated by confining those ideas to the study, the classroom, or the pages of our books. To write chapters decrying the sexual stereotyping of women in our literaure, while closing our eyes to the sexual harassment of our women students and colleagues; to display Katharine Hepburn and Rosalind Russell in our courses on "The Image of the Independent Career Women in Film," while managing not to notice the paucity of female administrators on our own campus; to study the women who helped make universal enfranchisement a political reality, while keeping silent about our activist colleagues who are denied promotion or tenure; to include segments on "Women in the Labor Movement" in our American studies or women's studies courses, while remaining willfully ignorant of the department secretary fired for efforts to organize a clerical workers' union; to glory in the delusions of "merit," "privilege," and "status" which accompany campus life in order to insulate ourselves from the millions of women who labor in poverty — all this is not merely hypocritical; it destroys both the spirit and the meaning of what we are about.

From "Dancing through the Minefield: Some Observations on the
Theory, Practice, and Politics of a Feminist Literary
Criticism," Feminist Studies, 6, 1980

Considerations for Critical Thinking and Writing

1. Why does Kolodny reject "intellectual neutrality" as a "myth"? Explain whether you agree or disagree with her point of view.
2. Kolodny argues that feminist criticism can be used as an instrument for social reform. Discuss the possibility and desirability of her position. Do you think other kinds of criticism can and should be used to create social change?

ANDREW P. DEBICKI (b. 1934)
New Criticism and Deconstructionism: Two Attitudes in Teaching Poetry   1985

[Let's] look at the ways in which a New Critic and a deconstructivist might handle a poem. My first example, untitled, is a work by Pedro Salinas, which I first analyzed many years ago and which I have recently taught to a group of students influenced by deconstruction:

> Sand: sleeping on the beach today
> and tomorrow caressed
> in the bosom of the sea:
> the sun's today, water's prize tomorrow.
> Softly you yield
> to the hand that presses you
> and go away with the first
> courting wind that appears.
> Pure and fickle sand,
> changing and clear beloved,
> I wanted you for my own,
> and held you against my chest and soul.
> But you escaped with the waves, the wind, the sun,
> and I remained without a beloved,
> my face turned to the wind which robbed her,
> and my eyes to the far-off sea in which she had
> green loves in a green shelter.

My original study of this poem, written very much in the New Critical tradition, focused on the unusual personification of sand and beloved and on the metaphorical pattern that it engendered. In the first part of the work, the physical elusiveness of sand (which slips through one's hand, flies with the wind, moves from shore to sea) evokes a coquettish woman, yielding to her lover and then escaping, running off with a personified wind, moving from one being to another. Watching these images, the reader gradually forgets that the poem is metaphorically describing sand and becomes taken up by the unusual correspondences with the figure of a flirting woman. When in the last part of the poem the speaker laments his loss, the reader is drawn into his lament for a fickle lover who has abandoned him.

Continuing a traditional analysis of this poem, we would conclude that its unusual personification/metaphor takes us beyond a literal level and leads us to a wider vision. The true subject of this poem is not sand, nor is it a flirt who tricks a man. The comparison between sand and woman, however, has made us feel the elusiveness of both, as well as the effect that this elusiveness has had on the speaker, who is left sadly contemplating it at the end of the poem. The poem has used its main image to embody a general vision of fleetingness and its effects.

My analysis, as developed thus far, is representative of a New Critical study. It focuses on the text and its central image, it describes a tension produced within the text, and it suggests a way in which this tension is resolved so as to move the poem beyond its literal level. In keeping with the tenets of traditional analytic criticism, it shows how the poem conveys a meaning that is far richer than its plot or any possible conceptual message. But while it is careful not to reduce the poem to a simple idea or to an equivalent of its prose summary, it does attempt to work all of its elements into a single interpretation which would satisfy every reader . . . : it makes all of the poem's meanings reside in its verbal structures, and it suggests that those meanings can be discovered and combined into a single cohesive vision as we systematically analyze those structures.

By attempting to find a pattern that will incorporate and resolve the poem's tensions, however, this reading leaves some loose ends, which I noticed even in my New Critical perspective — and which I found difficult to explain. To see the poem as the discovery of the theme of fleetingness by an insightful speaker, we have to ignore the fanciful nature of the comparison, the whimsical attitude to reality that it suggests, and the excessively serious lament of the speaker, which is difficult to take at face value — he laments the loss of *sand* with the excessive emotion of a romantic lover! The last lines, with their evocation of the beloved/ sand in an archetypal kingdom of the sea, ring a bit hollow. Once we notice all of this, we see the speaker as being somehow unreliable in his strong response to the situation. He tries too hard to equate the loss of sand with the loss of love, he paints himself as too much of a romantic, and he loses our assent when we realize that his rather cliché declarations are not very fitting. Once we become aware of the speaker's limitations, our perspective about the poem changes: we come to see its "meaning" as centered, not on the theme of fleetingness as such, but on a portrayal of the speaker's exaggerated efforts to embody this theme in the image of sand.

For the traditional New Critic, this would pose a dilemma. The reading of the poem as a serious embodiment of the theme of evanescence is undercut by an awareness of the speaker's unreliability. One can account for the conflict between readings, to some extent, by speaking of the poem's use of irony and by seeing a tension between the theme of evanescence and the speaker's excessive concern with an imaginary beloved (which blinds him to the larger issues presented by the poem). That still leaves unresolved, however, the poem's final meaning and effect. In class discussions, in fact, a debate between those students who asserted that the importance of the poem lay in its engendering the theme of fleetingness and those who noted the absurdity of the speaker often ended in an agreement that this was a "problem poem" which never resolved or integrated its "stresses" and its double vision. . . .

The deconstructive critic, however, would not be disturbed by a lack of resolution in the meanings of the poem and would use the conflict between interpretations as the starting point for further study. Noting that the view of evanescence produced by the poem's central metaphor is undercut by the speaker's unreliability, the deconstructive critic would explore the play of signification that the undercutting engenders. Calling into question the attempt to neatly define evanescence, on the one hand, and the speaker's excessive romanticism on the other, the poem would represent, for this critic, a creative confrontation of irresoluble visions. The image of the sand as woman, as well as the portrayal of the speaker, would represent a sort of "seam" in the text, an area of indeterminacy that would open the way to further readings. This image lets us see the speaker as a sentimental poet, attempting unsuccessfully to define evanescence by means of a novel metaphor but getting trapped in the theme of lost love, which he himself has engendered; it makes us think of the inadequacy of language, of the ways in which metaphorical expression and the clichés of a love lament can undercut each other.

Once we adopt such a deconstructivist perspective, we will find in the text details that will carry forward our reading. The speaker's statement that he held "her" against his "chest and his soul" underlines the conflict in his perspective: it juggles a literal perspective (he rubs sand against himself) and a metaphorical one (he reaches for his beloved), but it cannot fully combine them — "soul" is ludicrously inappropriate in reference to the former. The reader, noting the inappropriateness, has to pay attention to the inadequacy of language as used here. All in all, by engendering a conflict between various levels and perspectives, the poem makes us feel the incompleteness of any one reading, the way in which each one is a "misreading" (not because it is wrong, but because it is incomplete), and the creative lack of closure in the poem. By not being subject to closure, in fact, this text becomes all the more exciting: its view of the possibilities and limitations of metaphor, language, and perspective seems more valuable than any static portrayal of "evanescence."

The analyses I have offered of this poem exemplify the different classroom approaches that would be taken by a stereotypical New Critic, on the one hand, and a deconstructive critic on the other. Imbued with the desire to come to an overview of the literary work, the former will attempt to resolve its tensions (and probably remain unsatisfied with the poem). Skeptical of such a possibility and of the very existence of a definable "work," the latter will focus on the tensions that can be found in the text as vehicles for multiple readings. Given his or her attitude to the text, the deconstructive critic will not worry about going beyond its "limits" (which really do not exist). This will allow, of course, for more speculative readings; it will also lead to a discussion of ways in which the text can be extended and "cured" in successive readings, to the fact that it reflects on the process of its own creation, and to ways in which it will relate to other texts.

From *Writing and Reading DIFFERENTLY: Deconstruction
and the Teaching of Composition and Literature,*
edited by G. Douglas Atkins and Michael L. Johnson

Considerations for Critical Thinking and Writing

1. Explain how the New Critical and deconstructionist approaches to the Salinas poem differ. What kinds of questions are raised by each? What elements of the poem are focused on in each approach?

2. Write an essay explaining which reading of the poem you find more interesting. In your opening paragraph define what you mean by "interesting."
3. Choose one of the critical strategies for reading discussed in this chapter and discuss Salinas's poem from that perspective.

BROOK THOMAS (b. 1947)
A New Historical Approach to Keats's "Ode on a Grecian Urn"
1987

The traditional reception of the poem invites a discussion of its implied aesthetic. The poem's aesthetic is, however, intricately linked to its attitude to the past. The urn is, after all, Keats's "sylvan historian." To ask what sort of history a piece of art presents to us is, of course, to raise one of the central questions of historical criticism. It also opens up a variety of directions to take in historicizing the teaching of literature. . . .

To ask what history the urn relates to the reader easily leads to a discussion of how much our sense of the past depends upon art and the consequences of that dependency. These are important questions, because even if our students have little knowledge of the past or even interest in it, they do have an attitude toward it. A poem like Keats's "Ode" can help them reflect upon what that attitude is and on how it has been produced.

Such a discussion also offers a way to raise what critics have traditionally seen as the poem's central conflict: that between the temporal world of man and the atemporal world of art. The urn records two different visions of the past, both at odds with what we normally associate with historical accounts. On the one hand, it preserves a beauty that resists the destructive force of time. On the other, it records a quotidian scene populated by nameless people rather than the account of "famous" personages and "important" events our students often associate with traditional histories. Art, Keats seems to suggest, both keeps alive a sense of beauty in a world of change *and* gives us a sense of the felt life of the past. But in its search for a realm in which truth and beauty coexist, art risks freezing the "real" world and becoming a "cold pastoral," cut off from the very felt life it records. In dramatizing this conflict Keats's "Ode" allows students to see both art's power to keep the past alive and its tendency to distort it.

Chances are, however, that not all students share Keats's sense of the relationship between art and history. Rather than demonstrate their lack of "aesthetic appreciation," this difference can open up another direction to pursue in discussing the poem. To acknowledge a difference between our present attitude and the one embodied by Keats's poem is to call into question the conditions that have contributed to the changed attitude. Thus, if the first approach to the poem aims at having students reflect generally upon the influence art has on our attitude toward the past, this approach demands that we look at the specific historical conditions that help shape our general attitude toward both art and the past. In the case of the "Ode," this can lead to a discussion of the economic and political conditions of early nineteenth-century England that helped shape Keats's image of ancient Greece. On the one hand, there was England's self-image as the inheritor of ancient Greece's republican institutions and, on the other, a nostalgia for a harmonious pastoral world in contrast to the present state of industrialized, fragmented British society. Thus, the two versions of the past offered by Keats's sylvan historian — the aesthetic one in which harmony and beauty are preserved and the democratic one in which the life of everyday people is recorded — are related to specific historical conditions at the time Keats wrote. The challenge for our students — and for us — would be to speculate on how our attitudes towards art and history are shaped by our historical moment — how that moment is different from and similar to Keats's.

A third way to teach the poem historically is to concentrate on the urn itself as a historical as well as aesthetic object. "Where," we might ask our students, "would Keats have seen such an urn?" Most likely someone will respond, "A museum." If so, we are ready to discuss the phenomenon of the rise of the art museum in eighteenth- and nineteenth-century Europe, how cultural artifacts from the past were removed from their social setting and placed in museums to be contemplated as art. Seemingly taking us away from Keats's poem, such a discussion might be the best way to help our students understand Keats's aesthetic, for they will clearly see that in Keats's poem an urn that once had a practical social function now sparks aesthetic contemplation about the nature of truth, beauty, and the past. If we ask why the urn takes on this purely aesthetic function in a society that was increasingly practical, our students might start to glimpse how our modern notion of art has been defined in response to the social order.

To consider the urn a historical as well as an aesthetic object is also to raise political questions. For how, we might ask, did a Grecian urn (or the Elgin marbles, if we were to teach another Keats poem) end up in England in the first place? Such a question moves us from Keats's image of ancient Greece to a consideration of Greece in the early nineteenth century, and to how a number of Englishmen who sympathized with its struggle for liberation at the same time pillaged its cultural treasures and set them on display in London to advertise Britain's "advanced" cultural state. Thus, a very simple historical question about Keats's urn can force us to consider the political consequences of our cultural heritage. As Walter Benjamin warned, the cultural treasures that we so love have an origin we should not contemplate without horror: "They owe their existence not only to the efforts of the great minds and talents who have created them, but also to the anonymous toil of their contemporaries. There is no document of civilization which is not at the same time a document of barbarism" ("Theses on the Philosophy of History" in *Illuminations*, 256).

If we consider the task of historical scholarship to re-create the conditions of the past so that we can recover the author's original intention, the questions I have asked about Keats's "Ode" are not valid ones to ask. Clearly my questions are not primarily directed at recovering that intention. Instead, I am treating Keats's poem as social text, one that in telling us about the society that produced it also tells us about the society we inhabit today. This approach is not to say that we should completely abandon the effort to recover Keats's intention, but that, as in the case of formalist criticism, we need to go beyond the traditional historical scholar's efforts. We need to try both to reconstruct the author's intention — for instance, what Keats thought about art and history — and to read against the grain of his intention.

From "The Historical Necessities for — and Difficulties
with — New Historical Analysis in Introductory
Literature Courses," College English, September 1987

Considerations for Critical Thinking and Writing

1. Summarize the three historical approaches to "Ode on a Grecian Urn" (p. 813) Thomas describes. Which do you consider the most interesting? Explain why.
2. Write an essay that explores Thomas's claim that "a very simple historical question about the urn can force us to consider the political consequences of our cultural heritage."
3. Choose another poem from this anthology and treat it as a "social text." What kinds of questions can you ask about it that suggest the poem's historical significances?

HARRIET HAWKINS (b. 1939)
Should We Study King Kong *or* King Lear? 1988

There is nothing either good or bad, but thinking makes it so.
– Hamlet

Troilus: *What's aught but as 'tis valued?*
Hector: *But value dwells not in particular will:*
  It holds its estimate and dignity
  As well wherein 'tis precious of itself
  As in the prizer.
– Troilus and Cressida

    To what degree is great literature — or bad literature — an artificial category? Are there any good — or bad — reasons why most societies have given high status to certain works of art and not to others? Could Hamlet be right in concluding that there is *nothing* either good or bad but thinking — or criticial or ideological discourse — makes it so? Or are certain works of art so precious, so magnificent — or so trashy — that they obviously ought to be included in the canon or expelled from the classroom? So far as I know, there is not now any sign of a critical consensus on the correct answer to these questions either in England or in the United States.

    In England there are, on the one hand, eloquent cases for the defense of the value of traditional literary studies, like Dame Helen Gardner's last book, *In Defence of the Imagination.* On the other hand, there are critical arguments insisting that what really counts is not what you read, but the way that you read it. You might as well study *King Kong* as *King Lear,* because what matters is not the script involved, but the critical or ideological virtues manifested in your own "reading" of whatever it is that you are reading. Reviewing a controversial book entitled *Re-Reading English*, the poet Tom Paulin gives the following account of the issues involved in the debate:

> The contributors are collectively of the opinion that English literature is a dying subject and they argue that it can be revived by adopting a "socialist pedagogy" and introducing into the syllabus "other forms of writing and cultural production than the canon of literature" . . . it is now time to challenge "hierarchical" and "elitist" conceptions of literature and to demolish the bourgeois ideology which has been "naturalised" as literary value. . . . They wish to develop "a politics of reading" and to redefine the term "text" in order to admit newspaper reports, songs, and even mass demonstrations as subjects for tutorial discussion. Texts no longer have to be books: indeed, "it may be more democratic to study *Coronation Street* [England's most popular soap opera] than *Middlemarch*."

However one looks at these arguments, it seems indisputably true that the issues involved are of paramount critical, pedagogical, and social importance. There are, however, any number of different ways to look at the various arguments. So far as I am, professionally, concerned, they raise the central question, "Why should any of us still study, or teach, Shakespeare's plays (or *Paradise Lost* or *The Canterbury Tales*)?" After all, there are quite enough films, plays, novels, and poems being produced today (to say nothing of all those "other forms of writing," including literary criticism, that are clamoring for our attention) to satisfy anyone interested in high literature, or popular genres, or any form of "cultural production" whatsoever. They also raise the obviously reflexive question: "Assuming that all traditionally 'canonized' works were eliminated, overnight, from the syllabus of every English department in the world, would not comparable problems of priority, value, elitism, ideological pressure, authoritarianism, and arbitrariness almost(?) immediately arise with reference to *whatever* works — of whatsoever kind and nature — were substituted for them?"

If, say, the place on the syllabus currently assigned to *King Lear* were reassigned to *King Kong*, those of us currently debating the relative merits of the Quarto, the Folio, or a conflated version of *King Lear* would, *mutatis mutandis*,° have to decide whether to concentrate classroom attention on the "classic" version of *King Kong*, originally produced in 1933, or to focus on the 1974 remake (which by now has many ardent admirers of its own). Although classroom time might not allow the inclusion of both, a decision to exclude either version might well seem arbitrary or authoritarian and so give rise to grumbles about the "canon." Moreover, comparable questions of "canonization" might well arise with reference to other films excluded from a syllabus that included either version (or both versions) of *King Kong*. For example: why assign class time to *King Kong* and not to (say) *Slave Girls of the White Rhinoceros?* Who, if any, of us has the right to decide whether *King Lear* or *King Kong* or the *Slave Girls* should, or should not, be included on, or excluded from, the syllabus? And can the decision to include, or exclude, any one of them be made, by any one of us, on any grounds whatsoever that do *not* have to do with comparative merit, or comparative value judgments, or with special interests — that is, with the aes-

---

mutatis mutandis: Substituting different terms (Latin).

thetic or ideological priorities, preferences, and prejudices of the assigners of
positions on whatever syllabus there is? And insofar as most, if not all, of our
judgments and preferences are comparative, are they not, inevitably, hierarchical?

Is there, in fact, any form of endeavor or accomplishment known to the
human race — from sport to ballet to jazz to cooking — wherein comparative
standards of excellence comparable to certain "hierarchical" and "elitist" conceptions of literature are nonexistent? Even bad-film buffs find certain bad films
more gloriously bad than others. And, perhaps significantly given its comparatively short lifetime, the avant-garde cinema has, by now, produced snobs to rival
the most elitist literary critic who ever lived, such as the one who thus puts
down a friend who likes ordinary Hollywood films:

> Ah that's all right for you, I know the sort you are, but give me a private job
> that's shot on faded sepia sixteen millimetre stock with non-professional ac-
> tors . . . no story and dialogue in French *any day of the week*.

What is striking about this snob's assumption is how characteristic it is of a long
tradition of critical elitism that has consistently sneered at popular genres (e.g.,
romance fiction, soap operas, horror films, westerns, etc.) that are tainted by the
profit motive and so tend to "give the public what it wants" in the way of
sentimentality, sensationalism, sex, violence, romanticism, and the like.

From "*King Lear* to *King Kong* and Back: Shakespeare and Popular Modern
Genres" in "*Bad" Shakespeare: Revaluations of the Shakespeare Canon,*
edited by Maurice Charney.

Considerations for Critical Thinking and Writing

1. Do you agree or disagree that "great literature — or bad literature — [is] an artificial category"? Explain why.
2. Why would problems of "priority, value, elitism, ideological pressure, authoritarianism, and arbitrariness" probably become issues for evaluating any new works
   that replaced canonized works?
3. Write an essay in which you argue for (or against) studying popular arts (for
   example the *Northern Exposure* script on p. 1101) alongside the works of classic
   writers such as Shakespeare.

HENRY A. GIROUX (b. 1943)
The Canon and Liberal Arts Education   1990

In the current debate about the importance of constructing a particular
canon, the notion of naming and transmitting from one generation to the next
what can be defined as "cultural treasure" specifies what has become the central
argument for reforming the liberal arts. For that reason, perhaps, it appears as
though the debate were reducible to the question of the contents of course
syllabi. The notion of critical pedagogy for which I am arguing provides a
fundamental challenge to this position: it calls for an argument that transcends
the limited focus on the canon, that recognizes the crisis in liberal arts education
to be one of historical purpose and meaning, a crisis that challenges us to rethink

in a critical fashion the relationship between the role of the university and the imperatives of a democracy in a mass society.

Historically, education in the liberal arts was conceived of as the essential preparation for governing, for ruling — more specifically, the preparation and outfitting of the governing *elite*. The liberal arts curriculum, composed of the "best" that had been said or written, was intended, as Elizabeth Fox-Genovese has observed, "to provide selected individuals with a collective history, culture, and epistemology so that they could run the world effectively."[1] In this context the canon was considered to be a possession of the dominant classes or groups. Indeed, the canon was fashioned as a safeguard to insure that the cultural property of such groups was passed on from generation to generation along with the family estates. Thus, in these terms it seems most appropriate that the literary canon should be subject to revision — as it has been before in the course of the expansion of democracy — such that it might also incorporate and reflect the experience and aspirations of the women, minorities, and children of the working class who have been entering the academy.

Conceived of in this way, a radical vision of liberal arts education is to be found within its elite social origins and purpose. But this does not suggest that the most important questions confronting liberal arts reform lie in merely establishing the content of the liberal arts canon on the model of the elite universities. Instead, the most important questions become [those] of reformulating the meaning and purpose of higher education in ways that contribute to the cultivation and regeneration of an informed citizenry capable of actively participating in the shaping and governing of a democratic society. Within this discourse, the pedagogical becomes political and the notion of a liberal arts canon commands a more historically grounded and critical reading. The pedagogical becomes more political in that it proposes that the way in which students engage and examine knowledge is just as important an issue as the choosing of texts to be used in a class or program. That is, a democratic notion of liberal education rejects those views of the humanities which would treat texts as sacred and instruction as merely transmission. This notion of the canon undermines the possibility for dialogue, argument, and critical thinking; it treats knowledge as a form of cultural inheritance that is beyond considerations regarding how it might be implicated in social practices that exploit, infantilize, and oppress. The canons we have inherited, in their varied forms, cannot be dismissed as simply part of the ideology of privilege and domination. Instead, the privileged texts of the dominant or official canons should be explored with respect to the important role they have played in shaping, for better or worse, the major events of our time. But there are also forms of knowledge that have been marginalized by the official canons. There are noble traditions, histories, and narratives that speak to important struggles by women, blacks, minorities, and other subordinate groups that need to be heard so that such groups can lay claim to their own voices as part of a process of both affirmation and inquiry. At issue here is a notion of pedagogy as a form of cultural politics that rejects a facile restoration of the past, that rejects history as a monologue. A critical pedagogy recognizes that history is constituted in dialogue and that some of the voices that make up that dialogue

[1]Elizabeth Fox-Genovese, "The Claims of a Common Culture: Gender, Race, Class and the Canon," *Salmagundi* 72 (Fall 1986): 133.

have been eliminated. Such a pedagogy calls for a public debate regarding the dominant memories and repressed stories that constitute the historical narratives of a social order: in effect, canon formation becomes a matter of both rewriting and reinterpreting the past; canon formation embodies the ongoing "process of reconstructing the 'collective reflexivity' of lived cultural experience . . . which recognizes that the 'notions of the past and future are essentially notions of the present.'"[2] In this case, such notions are central to the politics of identity and power, and to the memories that structure how experience is individually and collectively authorized and experienced as a form of cultural identity. . . .

A critical pedagogy also rejects a discourse of value neutrality. Without subscribing to a language that polices behavior and desire, it aims at developing pedagogical practices informed by an ethical stance that contests racism, sexism, class exploitation, and other dehumanizing and exploitative social relations as ideologies and social practices that disrupt and devalue public life. This is a pedagogy that rejects detachment, though it does not silence in the name of its own ideological fervor or correctness. It acknowledges social injustices, but examines with care and in dialogue with itself and others how such injustices work through the discourses, experiences, and desires that constitute daily life and the subjectivities of the students who invest in them. It is a pedagogy guided by ethical principles that correspond to a radical practice rooted in historical experience. And it is a pedagogy that comprehends the historical consequences of what it means to take a moral and political position with respect to the horror and suffering of, for example, the Gulag, the Nazi Holocaust, or the Pol Pot regime. Such events not only summon up images of terror, domination, and resistance, but also provide a priori examples of what principles have to be both defended and fought against in the interest of freedom and life. Within this perspective, ethics becomes more than the discourse of moral relativism or a static transmission of reified history. Ethics becomes, instead, a continued engagement in which the social practices of everyday life are interrogated in relation to the principles of individual autonomy and democratic public life — not as a matter of received truth but as a constant engagement. This represents an ethical stance which provides the opportunity for individual capacities to be questioned and examined so that they can serve both to analyze and advance the possibilities inherent in all social forms. At issue is an ethical stance in which community, difference, remembrance, and historical consciousness become central categories as part of the language of public life.

From "Liberal Arts Education and the Struggle for Public Life: Dreaming about Democracy," *South Atlantic Quarterly*, 89, 1990.

Considerations for Critical Thinking and Writing

1. Why does Giroux take debates about canonical issues beyond course reading lists? Upon what historical conditions does he base his argument?
2. What kind of teaching — "critical pedagogy" — does Giroux call for? Why?

[2]Gail Guthrie Valaskakis, "The Chippewa and the Other: Living the Heritage of Lac Du Flambeau," *Cultural Studies* 2 (October 1988): 268.

3. According to Giroux, why should "value neutrality" be rejected by teachers and students?
4. Write an essay in which you agree or disagree that literature should be used to help create an "ethical stance" for its readers.

36. Reading and Writing

THE PURPOSE AND VALUE
OF WRITING ABOUT LITERATURE

Introductory literature courses typically include three components: reading, discussion, and writing. Students usually find the readings a pleasure, the class discussions a revelation, and the writing assignments — at least initially — a little intimidating. Writing an analysis of Melville's use of walls in "Bartleby, the Scrivener" (p. 83), for example, may seem considerably more daunting than making a case for animal rights or analyzing a campus newspaper editorial that calls for grade reforms. Like Bartleby, you might want to respond with "I would prefer not to." Literary topics are not, however, all that different from the kinds of papers assigned in English composition courses; many of the same skills are required for both. Regardless of the type of paper, you must develop a thesis and support it with evidence in language that is clear and persuasive.

Whether the subject matter is a marketing survey, a political issue, or a literary work, writing is a method of communicating information and perceptions. Writing teaches. But before writing becomes an instrument for informing the reader, it serves as a means of learning for the writer. An essay is a process of discovery as well as a record of what has been discovered. One of the chief benefits of writing is that we frequently realize what we want to say only after trying out ideas on a page and seeing our thoughts take shape in language.

More specifically, writing about a literary work encourages us to be better readers, because it requires a close examination of the elements of a short story, poem, or play. To determine how plot, character, setting, point of view, style, tone, irony, or any number of other literary elements function in a work, we must study them in relation to one another as well as separately. Speed-reading won't do. To read a text accurately and validly — neither ignoring nor distorting significant details — we must return to the work repeatedly to test our responses and interpretations. By paying attention to details and being sensitive to the author's use of language, we develop a clearer understanding of how the work conveys its effects and meanings.

Nevertheless, students sometimes ask why it is necessary or desirable to write about a literary work. Why not allow stories, poems, and plays to speak for themselves? Isn't it presumptuous to interpret Hemingway, Dickinson, or Shakespeare? These writers do, of course, speak for themselves, but they do so indirectly. Literary criticism does not seek to replace the text by explaining it but to enhance our readings of works by calling attention to elements that we might have overlooked or only vaguely sensed.

Another misunderstanding about the purpose of literary criticism is that it crankily restricts itself to finding faults in a work. Critical essays are sometimes mistakenly equated with newspaper and magazine reviews of recently published works. Reviews typically include summaries and evaluations to inform readers about a work's nature and quality, but critical essays assume that readers are already familiar with a work. Although a critical essay may point out limitations and flaws, most criticism — and certainly the kind of essay usually written in an introductory literature course — is designed to explain, analyze, and reveal the complexities of a work. Such sensitive consideration increases our appreciation of the writer's achievement and significantly adds to our enjoyment of a short story, poem, or play. In short, the purpose and value of writing about literature are that doing so leads to greater understanding and pleasure.

READING THE WORK CLOSELY

Know the piece of literature you are writing about before you begin your essay. Think about how the work makes you feel and how it is put together. The more familiar you are with how the various elements of the text convey effects and meanings, the more confident you will be explaining whatever perspective on it you ultimately choose. Do not insist that everything make sense on a first reading. Relax and enjoy yourself; you can be attentive and still allow the author's words to work their magic on you. With subsequent readings, however, go more slowly and analytically as you try to establish relations between characters, actions, images, or whatever else seems important. Ask yourself why you respond as you do. Think as you read, and notice how the parts of a work contribute to its overall nature. Whether the work is a short story, poem, or play, you will read relevant portions of it over and over, and you will very likely find more to discuss in each review if the work is rich.

It's best to avoid reading other critical discussions of a work before you are thoroughly familiar with it. There are several good reasons for following this advice. By reading interpretations before you know a work, you deny yourself the pleasure of discovery. That is a bit like starting with the last chapter in a mystery novel. But perhaps even more important than protecting the surprise and delight that a work might offer is that a premature reading of a critical discussion will probably short-circuit your own responses. You will see the work through the critic's eyes and have to struggle with someone else's perceptions and ideas before you can develop your own.

Reading criticism can be useful, but not until you have thought through your own impressions of the text. A guide should not be permitted to become a tyrant. This does not mean, however, that you should avoid background information about a work, for example, that Joyce Carol Oates's story "The Lady with the Pet Dog" was based on a similar story by Anton Chekhov. Knowing something about the author as well as historic and literary contexts can help to create expectations that enhance your reading.

TAKING NOTES

As you read, get in the habit of making marginal notations in your textbook. If you are working with a library book, use notecards and write down page or line numbers so that you can easily return to annotated passages. Use these cards to record reactions, raise questions, and make comments. They will freshen your memory and allow you to keep track of what goes on in the text.

Taking notes will preserve your initial reactions to the work. Many times first impressions are the best. Your response to a peculiar character in a story, a striking phrase in a poem, or a subtle bit of stage business in a play might lead to larger perceptions. The student paper on John Updike's "A & P" (p. 485), for example, began with the student writing "how come?" next to the story's title in her textbook. She thought it strange that the title didn't refer to a character or the story's conflict. That response eventually led her to examine the significance of the setting, which became the central idea of her paper.

You should take detailed notes only after you've read through the work. If you write too many notes during the first reading, you're likely to disrupt your response. Moreover, until you have a sense of the entire work, it will be difficult to determine how connections can be made among its various elements. In addition to recording your first impressions and noting significant passages, characters, actions, and so on, you should consult the Questions for Responsive Reading (fiction p. 457; poetry, p. 918; and drama, p. 1110). These questions can assist you in getting inside a work as well as organizing your notes.

Inevitably, you will take more notes than you finally use in the paper. Note taking is a form of thinking aloud, but because your ideas are on paper you don't have to worry about forgetting them. As you develop a better sense of a potential topic, your notes will become more focused and detailed.

CHOOSING A TOPIC

If your instructor assigns a topic or offers a choice from among an approved list of topics, some of your work is already completed. Instead of being asked to come up with a topic about *Antigone,* you may be assigned a three-page essay that specifically discusses "Antigone's Decision to Defy Creon." You also have the assurance that a specified topic will be manageable within the suggested number of pages. Unless you ask your instructor for permission to write on a different or related topic, be certain to address yourself to the assignment. An essay that does not discuss Antigone's decision but instead describes her relationship with her sister would be missing the point. Notice too that there is room even in an assigned topic to develop your own approach. One question that immediately comes to mind is whether Antigone is justified in defying Creon's authority. Assigned topics do not relieve you of thinking about an aspect of a work, but they do focus your thinking.

At some point during the course, you may have to begin an essay from scratch. You might, for example, be asked to write about a short story that somehow impressed you or that seemed particularly well written or filled with insights. Before you start considering a topic, you should have a sense of how long the paper will be, because the assigned length can help to determine the extent to which you should develop your topic. Ideally, the paper's length should be based on how much space you deem necessary to present your discussion clearly and convincingly, but if you have any doubts and no specific guidelines have been indicated, ask. The question is important; a topic that might be appropriate for a three-page paper could be too narrow for ten pages. Three pages would probably be adequate for a discussion of why Emily murders Homer in Faulkner's "A Rose for Emily." Conversely, it would be futile to try to summarize Faulkner's use of the South in his fiction in even ten pages; this would have to be narrowed to something like "Images of the South in 'A Rose for Emily.'" Be sure that the topic you choose can be adequately covered in the assigned number of pages.

Once you have a firm sense of how much you are expected to write, you can begin to decide on your topic. If you are to choose what work to write about, select one that genuinely interests you. Too often students pick a story, poem, or play because it is mercifully short or seems simple. Such works can certainly be the subjects of fine essays, but simplicity should not be the major reason for selecting them. Choose a work that has moved you so that you have something to say about it. The student who wrote about "A & P" was initially attracted to the story's title because she had once worked in a similar store. After reading the story, she became fascinated with its setting because Updike's descriptions seemed so accurate. Her paper then grew out of her curiosity about the setting's purpose. When a writer is engaged in a topic, the paper has a better chance of being interesting to a reader.

After you have settled on a particular work, your notes and annotations of the text should prove useful for generating a topic. The paper on "The A & P as a State of Mind" developed naturally from the notes (p. 2057) that the student jotted down about the setting and antagonist. If you think with a pen in your hand, you are likely to find when you review your notes that your thoughts have clustered into one or more topics. Perhaps there are patterns of imagery that seem to make a point about life. There may be scenes that are ironically paired or secondary characters who reveal certain qualities about the protagonist. Your notes and annotations on such aspects can lead you to a particular effect or impression. Having chuckled your way through Mark Twain's "The Story of the Bad Little Boy," you may discover that your notations about the story's humor point to a serious satire of society's values.

DEVELOPING A THESIS

When you are satisfied that you have something interesting to say about a work and that your notes have led you to a focused topic, you can formulate a *thesis*, the central idea of the paper. Whereas the topic indicates what the paper focuses on (the setting in "A & P"), the thesis explains what you have to say about the topic (because the intolerant setting of "A & P" is the antagonist in the story, it is crucial to our understanding of Sammy's decision to quit his job). The thesis should be a complete sentence (though sometimes it may require more than one sentence) that establishes your topic in clear, unambiguous language. The thesis may be revised as you get further into the topic and discover what you want to say about it, but once the thesis is firmly established it will serve as a guide for you and your reader, because all the information and observations in your essay should be related to the thesis.

One student on an initial reading of Andrew Marvell's "To His Coy Mistress" (p. 631) saw that the male speaker of the poem urges a woman to love now before time runs out for them. This reading gave him the impression that the poem is a simple celebration of the pleasures of the flesh, but on subsequent readings he underlined or noted these images: "Time's wingèd chariot hurrying near"; "Deserts of vast eternity"; "marble vault"; "worms"; "dust"; "ashes"; and these two lines: "The grave's a fine and private place, / But none, I think, do there embrace."

By listing these images associated with time and death, he established an inventory that could be separated from the rest of his notes on point of view, character, sounds, and other subjects. Inventorying notes allows patterns to emerge that you might have only vaguely perceived otherwise. Once these images are grouped, they call attention to something darker and more complex in Marvell's poem than a first impression might suggest.

These images may create a different feeling about the poem, but they still don't explain very much. One simple way to generate a thesis about a literary work is to ask the question "why?" Why do these images appear in the poem? Why does Hamlet hesitate to avenge his father's death? Why does Hemingway choose the Midwest as the setting of "Soldier's Home"? Your responses to these kinds of questions can lead to a thesis.

Writers sometimes use free writing to help themselves explore possible answers to such questions. It can be an effective way of generating ideas. Free writing is exactly that: the technique calls for nonstop writing without concern for mechanics or editing of any kind. Free writing for ten minutes or so on a question will result in fragments and repetitions, but it can also produce some ideas. Here's an example of a student's response to the question about the images in "To His Coy Mistress":

```
He wants her to make love.  Love poem.  There's little time.
Her crime.  He exaggerates.  Sincere?  Sly?  What's he want?
She says nothing--he says it all.  What about deserts, ashes,
graves, and worms?  Some love poem.  Sounds like an old Vin-
cent Price movie.  Full of sweetness but death creeps in.
Death--hurry hurry!  Tear pleasures.  What passion!  Where's
death in this?  How can a love poem be so ghoulish?  She does
nothing.  Maybe frightened?  Convinced?  Why death?  Love and
death--time--death.
```

This free writing contains several ideas; it begins by alluding to the poem's plot and speaker, but the central idea seems to be death. This emphasis led the student to four potential thesis statements for his essay about the poem:

1. "To His Coy Mistress" is a difficult poem.
2. Death in "To His Coy Mistress."
3. There are many images of death in "To His Coy Mistress."
4. On the surface, "To His Coy Mistress" is a celebration of the pleasures of the flesh, but this witty seduction is tempered by a chilling recognition of the reality of death.

The first statement is too vague to be useful. In what sense is the poem difficult? A more precise phrasing, indicating the nature of the difficulty, is needed. The second statement is a topic rather than a thesis. Because it is not a sentence, it does not express a complete idea about how the poem treats death. Although this could be an appropriate title, it is inadequate as a thesis statement. The third statement, like the first one, identifies the topic, but even though it is a sentence, it is not a complete idea that tells us anything significant beyond the fact it states. After these preliminary attempts to develop a thesis, the student remembered his first impression of the poem and incorporated it into his thesis statement. The fourth thesis is a useful approach to the poem because it limits the topic and indicates how it will be treated in the paper: the writer will begin with an initial impression of the poem and then go on to qualify it. An effective thesis, like this one, makes a clear statement about a manageable topic and provides a firm sense of direction for the paper.

Most writing assignments in a literature course require you to persuade readers that your thesis is reasonable and supported with evidence. Papers that report information without comment or evaluation are simply summaries. A plot summary of Shakespeare's *The Tempest,* for example, would have no thesis, but a paper that discussed how Prospero's oppression of Caliban represents European imperialism and colonialism would argue a thesis. Similarly, a paper that merely pointed out the death images in "To His Coy Mistress" would not contain a thesis, but a paper that attempted to make a case for the death imagery as a grim reminder of how vulnerable flesh is would involve persuasion. In developing a thesis, remember that you are expected not merely to present information but to argue a point.

ARGUING ABOUT LITERATURE

An argumentative essay is designed to make persuasive your interpretation of a work. Arguing about literature doesn't mean that you're engaged in an angry, antagonistic dispute (though controversial topics do sometimes engender heated debates; see for example Joan Templeton's comments in the Critical Case Study on Ibsen's *A Doll House* [p. 1620]). Instead, argumentation requires that you present your interpretation of a work (or a portion of it) by supporting your discussion with clearly defined terms, ample evidence, and a detailed analysis of relevant portions of the text.

If you have a choice, it's generally best to write about a topic that you feel strongly about. If you're not fascinated by Bartleby the Scrivener's haunting presence in Melville's short story, then perhaps you'll find chilling Emily Grierson's behavior in Faulkner's "A Rose for Emily," or maybe you can explain why Bartleby's character is so excruciatingly boring to you. If your essay is to be interesting and convincing, what is important is that it be written from a strong point of view that persuasively argues your evaluation, analysis, and interpretation of a work. It is not enough to say that you like or dislike a work; instead you must give your reader some ideas and evidence that can be accepted or rejected based on the quality of the answers to the questions you raise.

One way to come up with persuasive answers is to generate good questions that will lead you further into the text and to critical issues related to it. Notice how the Perspectives, Complementary Readings, and Critical Case Studies in this anthology raise significant questions and issues about texts from a variety of points of view. Moreover, the critical strategies for reading summarized in Chapter 35 can be a resource for raising questions that can be shaped into an argument. The following lists of questions for the critical approaches covered in Chapter 35 should be useful for discovering arguments you might make about a short story, poem, or play. The page number that follows each heading refers to the discussion in the anthology for that particular approach.

Formalist Questions (p. 1999)

1. How do various elements of the work — plot, character, point of view, setting, tone, diction, images, symbol, etc. — reinforce its meanings?
2. How are the elements related to the whole?
3. What is the work's major organizing principle? How is its structure unified?
4. What issues does the work raise? How does the work's structure resolve those issues?

Biographical Questions (p. 2001)

1. Are there facts about the writer's life relevant to your understanding of the work?
2. Are characters and incidents in the work versions of the writer's own experiences? Are they treated factually or imaginatively?
3. How do you think the writer's values are reflected in the work?

Psychological Questions (p. 2004)

1. How does the work reflect the author's personal psychology?
2. What do the characters' emotions and behavior reveal about their psychological states? What types of personalities are they?
3. Are psychological matters such as repression, dreams, and desire presented consciously or unconsciously by the author?

Historical Questions (p. 2005)

1. How does the work reflect the period in which it is written?
2. How does the work reflect the period it represents?
3. What literary or historical influences helped to shape the form and content of the work?
4. How important is the historical context (both the work's and your own) to interpreting the work?

Marxist Questions (p. 2008)

1. How are class differences presented in the work? Are characters

aware or unaware of the economic and social forces that affect their lives?

2. How do economic conditions determine the characters' lives?
3. What ideological values are explicit or implicit?

Feminist Questions (p. 2009)

1. How are women's lives portrayed in the work? Do the women in the work accept or reject these roles?
2. Is the form and content of the work influenced by the author's gender?
3. What are the relationships between men and women? Are these relationships sources of conflict? Do they provide resolutions to conflicts?

Mythological Questions (p. 2010)

1. How does the story resemble other stories in plot, character, setting, or use of symbols?
2. Are archetypes presented, such as quests, initiations, scapegoats, or withdrawals and returns?
3. Does the protagonist undergo any kind of transformation such as a movement from innocence to experience that seems archetypal?

Reader-Response Questions (p. 2012)

1. How do you respond to the work?
2. How do your own experiences and expectations affect your reading and interpretation?
3. What is the work's original or intended audience? To what extent are you similar to or different from that audience?

Deconstructionist Questions (p. 2014)

1. How are contradictory and opposing meanings expressed in the work?
2. How does meaning break down or deconstruct itself in the language of the text?
3. Would you say that ultimate definitive meanings are impossible to determine and establish in the text? Why? How does that affect your interpretation?

These questions will not apply to all texts; and they are not mutually exclusive. They can be combined to explore a text from several critical perspectives simultaneously. A feminist approach to Kate Chopin's "Story of an Hour" could also use Marxist concerns about class to make observations about the oppression of women's lives in the historical context of the nineteenth century. Your use of these questions should allow you to discover significant issues from which you can develop an argumentative essay that is organized around clearly defined terms, relevant evidence, and a persuasive analysis.

ORGANIZING A PAPER

After you have chosen a manageable topic and developed a thesis, a central idea about it, you can begin to organize your paper. Your thesis, even if it is still somewhat tentative, should help you decide what information will need to be included and provide you with a sense of direction.

Consider again the sample thesis in the section on developing a thesis:

On the surface, "To His Coy Mistress" is a celebration of the pleasures of the flesh, but this witty seduction is tempered by a chilling recognition of the reality of death.

This thesis indicates that the paper can be divided into two parts: the pleasures of the flesh and the reality of death. It also indicates an order: Because the central point is to show that the poem is more than a simple celebration, the pleasures of the flesh should be discussed first so that another, more complex, reading of the poem can follow. If the paper began with the reality of death, its point would be anticlimactic.

Having established such a broad and informal outline, you can draw upon your underlinings, margin notations, and notecards for the subheadings and evidence required to explain the major sections of your paper. This next level of detail would look like the following:

1. Pleasures of the flesh
   Part of the traditional tone of love poetry
2. Recognition of death
   Ironic treatment of love
      Diction
      Images
      Figures of speech
      Symbols
      Tone

This list was initially a jumble of terms, but the student arranged the items so that each of the two major sections leads to a discussion of tone. (The student also found it necessary to drop some biographical information from his notes because it was irrelevant to the thesis.) The list indicates that the first part of the paper will establish the traditional tone of love poetry that celebrates the pleasures of the flesh, while the second part will present a more detailed discussion about the ironic recognition of death. The emphasis is on the latter because that is the point to be argued in the paper. Hence, the thesis has helped to organize the parts of the paper, establish an order, and indicate the paper's proper proportions.

The next step is to fill in the subheadings with information from your notes. Many experienced writers find that making lists of information to be included under each subheading is an efficient way to develop paragraphs. For a longer paper (perhaps a research paper), you should be able to develop a paragraph or more on each subheading. On the other hand, a shorter paper may require that you combine several subheadings in a paragraph. You may also discover that while an informal list is adequate for a brief paper, a ten-page assignment could require a more detailed outline. Use the method that is most productive for you. Whatever the length of the essay, your presentation must be in a coherent and logical order that allows your reader to follow the argument and evaluate the evidence. The quality of your reading can be demonstrated only by the quality of your writing.

WRITING A DRAFT

The time for sharpening pencils, arranging your desk, and doing almost anything else instead of writing has ended. The first draft will appear on the page only if you stop avoiding the inevitable and sit, stand up, or lie down to write. It makes no difference how you write, just so you do. Now that you have developed a topic into a tentative thesis, you can assemble your notes and begin to flesh out whatever outline you have made.

Be flexible. Your outline should smoothly conduct you from one point to the next, but do not permit it to railroad you. If a relevant and important idea occurs to you now, work it into the draft. By using the first draft as a means of thinking about what you want to say, you will very likely discover more than your notes originally suggested. Plenty of good writers don't use outlines at all but discover ordering principles as they write. Do not attempt to compose a perfectly correct draft the first time around. Grammar, punctuation, and spelling can wait until you revise. Concentrate on what you are saying. Good writing most often occurs when you are in hot pursuit of an idea rather than in a nervous search for errors.

To make revising easier, leave wide margins and extra space between lines so that you can easily add words, sentences, and corrections. Write on only one side of the paper. Your pages will be easier to keep track of that way, and, if you have to clip a paragraph to place it elsewhere, you will not lose any writing on the other side.

If you are working on a word processor, you can take advantage of its capacity to make additions and deletions as well as move entire paragraphs by making just a few simple keyboard commands. Some software programs can also check spelling and certain grammatical elements in your writing. It's worth remembering, however, that though a clean copy fresh off a printer may look terrific, it will read only as well as the thinking and writing that have gone into it. Many writers prudently store their data on disks and print their pages each time they finish a draft to avoid loosing any material because of power failures or other problems. These printouts are also easier to read than the screen when you work on revisions.

Once you have a first draft on paper, you can delete material that is unrelated to your thesis and add material necessary to illustrate your points and make your paper convincing. The student who wrote "The A & P as a State of Mind" wisely dropped a paragraph that questioned whether Sammy displays chauvinistic attitudes toward women. Although this is an interesting issue, it has nothing to do with the thesis, which explains how the setting influences Sammy's decision to quit his job. Instead of including that paragraph, she added one that described Lengel's crabbed response to the girls so that she could lead up to the A & P "policy" he enforces.

Remember that your initial draft is only that. You should go through the paper many times — and then again — working to substantiate and clarify your ideas. You may even end up with several entire versions of the paper. Rewrite. The sentences within each paragraph should be related to a single topic. Transitions should connect one paragraph to the next so that there are no abrupt or confusing shifts. Awkward or wordy phrasing or unclear sentences and paragraphs should be mercilessly poked and prodded into shape.

Writing the Introduction and Conclusion

After you have clearly and adequately developed the body of your paper, pay particular attention to the introductory and concluding paragraphs. It's probably best to write the introduction — at least the final version of it — last, after you know precisely what you are introducing. Because this paragraph is crucial for generating interest in the topic, it should engage the reader and provide a sense of what the paper is about. There is no formula for writing effective introductory paragraphs, because each writing situation is different — depending on the audience, topic, and approach — but if you pay attention to the introductions of the essays you read, you will notice a variety of possibilities. The introductory paragraph to "The A & P as a State of Mind," for example, is a straightforward explanation of why the story's setting is important for understanding Updike's treatment of the antagonist. The rest of the paper then offers evidence to support this point.

Concluding paragraphs demand equal attention because they leave the reader with a final impression. The conclusion should provide a sense of closure instead of starting a new topic or ending abruptly. In the final paragraph about the significance of the setting in "A & P," the student brings together the reasons Sammy quit his job by referring to his refusal to accept Lengel's store policies. At the same time she makes this point, she also explains the significance of Sammy ringing up the "No Sale" mentioned in her introductory paragraph. Thus, we are brought back to where we began, but we now have a greater understanding of why Sammy quits his job. Of course, the body of your paper is the most important part of your presentation, but do remember that first and last impressions have a powerful impact on readers.

Using Quotations

Quotations can be a valuable means of marshaling evidence to illustrate and support your ideas. A judicious use of quoted material will make your points clearer and more convincing. Here are some guidelines that should help you use quotations effectively.

1. Brief quotations (four lines or fewer of prose or three lines or fewer of poetry) should be carefully introduced and integrated into the text of your paper with quotation marks around them.

> According to the narrator, Bertha "had a reputation for strictness." He tells us that she always "wore dark clothes, dressed her hair simply, and expected contrition and obedience from her pupils."

For brief poetry quotations, use a slash to indicate a division between lines.

> The concluding lines of Blake's "The Tyger" pose a disturbing question: "What immortal hand or eye / Dare frame thy fearful symmetry?"

Lengthy quotations should be separated from the text of your paper. More than three lines of poetry should be double spaced and centered on the page. More than four lines of prose should be double spaced and indented ten spaces from the left margin, with the right margin the same as for the text. Do *not* use quotation marks for the passage; the indentation indicates that the passage is a quotation. Lengthy quotations should not be used in place of your own writing. Use them only if they are absolutely necessary.

2. If any words are added to a quotation, use brackets to distinguish your addition from the original source.

> "He [Young Goodman Brown] is portrayed as self-righteous and disillusioned."

Any words inside quotation marks and not in brackets must be precisely those of the author. Brackets can also be used to change the grammatical structure of a quotation so that it fits into your sentence.

> Smith argues that Chekhov "present[s] the narrator in an ambivalent light."

If you drop any words from the source, use ellipses to indicate the omission.

> "Early to bed . . . makes a man healthy, wealthy, and wise."

Use ellipses following a period to indicate an omission at the end of a sentence.

> "Early to bed and early to rise makes a man healthy. . . ."

Use a single line of spaced periods to indicate the omission of a line or more of poetry or more than one paragraph of prose.

> Nothing would sleep in that cellar, dank as a ditch,
> Bulbs broke out of boxes hunting for chinks in the dark,
> . . . .
> Nothing would give up life:
> Even the dirt kept breathing a small breath.

3. You will be able to punctuate quoted material accurately and confidently if you observe these conventions.

Place commas and periods inside quotation marks.

> "Even the dirt," Roethke insists, "kept breathing a small breath."

Even though a comma does not appear after "dirt" in the original quotation, it is placed inside the quotation mark. The exception to this rule occurs when a parenthetical reference to a source follows the quotation.

> "Even the dirt," Roethke insists, "kept breathing a small breath" (11).

Punctuation marks other than commas or periods go outside the quotation marks unless they are part of the material quoted.

> What does Roethke mean when he writes that "the dirt kept breathing a small breath"?

> Yeats asked, "How can we know the dancer from the dance?"

REVISING AND EDITING

Put some distance — a day or so if you can — between yourself and each draft of your paper. The phrase that seemed just right on Wednesday may be revealed as all wrong on Friday. You'll have a better chance of detecting lumbering sentences and thin paragraphs if you plan ahead and give yourself the time to read your paper from a fresh perspective. Through the process of revision, you can transform a competent paper into an excellent one.

Begin by asking yourself if your approach to the topic requires any rethinking. Is the argument carefully thought out and logically presented? Are there any gaps in the presentation? How well is the paper organized? Do the paragraphs lead into one another? Does the body of the paper deliver what the thesis promises? Is the interpretation sound? Are any relevant and important elements of the work ignored or distorted to advance the thesis? Are the points supported with evidence? These large questions should be addressed before you focus on more detailed matters. If you uncover serious problems as a result of considering these questions, you'll probably have quite a lot of rewriting to do, but at least you will have the opportunity to correct the problems — even if doing so takes several drafts.

A useful technique for spotting awkward or unclear moments in the paper is to read it aloud. You might also try having a friend read it aloud to you. If your handwriting is legible, your friend's reading — perhaps accompanied by hesitations and puzzled expressions — could alert you to passages that need reworking. Having identified problems, you can readily correct them on a word processor or on the draft provided you've skipped lines and used wide margins. The final draft you hand in should be neat and carefully proofread for any inadvertent errors.

The following checklist offers questions to ask about your paper as you revise and edit it. Most of these questions will be familiar to you; however, if you need help with any of them, ask your instructor or review the appropriate section in a composition handbook.

Revision Checklist

1. Is the topic manageable? Is it too narrow or too broad?
2. Is the thesis clear? Is it based on a careful reading of the work?
3. Is the paper logically organized? Does it have a firm sense of direction?
4. Is your argument persuasive?
5. Should any material be deleted? Do any important points require further illustration or evidence?
6. Does the opening paragraph introduce the topic in an interesting manner?
7. Are the paragraphs developed, unified, and coherent? Are any too short or long?
8. Are there transitions linking the paragraphs?
9. Does the concluding paragraph provide a sense of closure?
10. Is the tone appropriate? Is it unduly flippant or pretentious?
11. Is the title engaging and suggestive?
12. Are the sentences clear, concise, and complete?
13. Are simple, complex, and compound sentences used for variety?
14. Have technical terms been used correctly? Are you certain of the meanings of all the words in the paper? Are they spelled correctly?
15. Have you documented any information borrowed from books, articles, or other sources? Have you quoted too much instead of summarizing or paraphrasing secondary material?
16. Have you used a standard format for citing sources (see p. 2075)?
17. Have you followed your instructor's guidelines for the manuscript format of the final draft?
18. Have you carefully proofread the final draft?

When you proofread your final draft, you may find a few typographical errors that must be corrected but do not warrant retyping an entire page. Provided there are not more than a handful of such errors throughout the page, they can be corrected as shown in the following passage. This example condenses a short paper's worth of errors; no single passage should be this shabby in your essay.

```
To add a letter or word, use a caret on the line where the ad-
         is
dition^needed.  To delete a word draw a single line through
through it.  Run-on words are separated by a vertical/line, and
inadvertent spaces are closed like t⌣his.  Transposed letters
are indicated this wⁿⁱ.  New paragraphs are noted with the
sign ¶ in front of where the next paragraph is to begin. ¶ Un-
less you . . .
```

These sorts of errors can be minimized by using correction fluids or tapes while you type. If you use a word processor, you can eliminate such errors completely by simply entering corrections as you proofread on the screen.

MANUSCRIPT FORM

The novelist and poet Peter De Vries once observed in his characteristically humorous way that he very much enjoyed writing but that he couldn't bear the "paper work." Behind this playful pun is a half-serious impatience with the mechanics of it all. You may feel some of that too, but this is not the time to allow a thoughtful, carefully revised paper to trip over minor details that can be easily accommodated. The final draft you hand in to your instructor should not only read well but look neat. If your instructor does not provide specific instructions concerning the format for the paper, follow these guidelines.

1. Papers (particularly long ones) should be typed on 8½ × 11-inch paper in double space. Avoid transparent paper such as onionskin; it is difficult to read and write comments on. The ribbon should be dark and the letters on the machine clear. If you compose on a word processor with a dot-matrix printer, be certain that the dots are close enough together to be legible. And don't forget to separate your pages and remove the strips of holes on each side of the pages if your printer uses a continuous paper feed. If your instructor accepts handwritten papers, write legibly in ink on only one side of a wide-lined page.

2. Use a one-inch margin at the top, bottom, and sides of each page. Unless you are instructed to include a separate title page, type your name, instructor's name, course number and section, and date on separate lines one inch below the upper-left corner of the first page. Double space between these lines and then center the title two spaces below the date. Do not underline or put quotation marks around your paper's title, but do use quotation marks around the titles of poems, short stories, or other brief works, and underline the titles of books and plays (for instance, Racial

Stereotypes in "Battle Royal" and <u>Fences</u>). Begin the text of your paper four spaces below the title. If you have used secondary sources, center the heading "Notes" or "Works Cited" one inch from the top of a separate page and then double space between it and the entries.

3. Number each page consecutively, beginning with page 2, a half inch from the top of the page in the upper-right corner.

4. Gather the pages with a paper clip rather than staples, folders, or some other device. That will make it easier for your instructor to handle the paper.

TYPES OF WRITING ASSIGNMENTS

The types of papers most frequently assigned in literature classes are explication, analysis, and comparison and contrast. Most writing about literature involves some combination of these skills. This section includes a sample explication, an analysis, and a comparison and contrast paper. (For a sample research paper that demonstrates a variety of strategies for documenting outside sources, see p. 2082.)

Explication

The purpose of this approach to a literary work is to make the implicit explicit. *Explication* is a detailed explanation of a passage of poetry or prose. Because explication is an intensive examination of a text line by line, it is mostly used to interpret a short poem in its entirety or a brief passage from a long poem, short story, or play. Explication can be used in any kind of paper when you want to be specific about how a writer achieves a certain effect. An explication pays careful attention to language: the connotations of words, allusions, figurative language, irony, symbol, rhythm, sound, and so on. These elements are examined in relation to one another and to the overall effect and meaning of the work.

The simplest way to organize an explication is to move through the passage line by line, explaining whatever seems significant. It is wise to avoid, however, an assembly-line approach that begins each sentence with "In line one. . . ." Instead, organize your paper in whatever way best serves your thesis. You might find that the right place to start is with the final lines, working your way back to the beginning of the poem or passage. The following sample explication on Dickinson's "There's a certain Slant of light" does just that. The student's opening paragraph refers to the final line of the poem in order to present her thesis. She explains that though the poem begins with an image of light, it is not a bright or cheery poem but one concerned with "the look of Death." Since the last line prompted her thesis, that is where she begins the explication.

You might also find it useful to structure a paper by discussing various elements of literature, so that you have a paragraph on connotative words followed by one on figurative language and so on. However your paper is organized, keep in mind that the aim of an explication is not simply to summarize the passage but to comment on the effects and meanings produced by the author's use of language in it. An effective explication (the Latin word *explicare* means "to unfold") displays a text to reveal how it works and what it signifies. Although writing an explication requires some patience and sensitivity, it is an excellent method for coming to understand and appreciate the elements and qualities that constitute literary art.

A STUDENT EXPLICATION

The sample paper by Bonnie Katz is the result of an assignment calling for an explication of about 750 words on any poem by Emily Dickinson. Katz selected "There's a certain Slant of light."

EMILY DICKINSON (1830–1886)
There's a certain Slant of light

c. 1861

There's a certain Slant of light,
Winter Afternoons —
That oppresses, like the Heft
Of Cathedral Tunes —

Heavenly Hurt, it gives us — 5
We can find no scar,
But internal difference,
Where the Meanings, are —

None may teach it — Any —
'Tis the Seal Despair — 10
An imperial affliction
Sent us of the Air —

When it comes, the Landscape listens —
Shadows — hold their breath —
When it goes, 'tis like the Distance 15
On the look of Death —

This essay comments on every line of the poem and provides a coherent reading that relates each line to the speaker's intense awareness of death. Although the essay discusses each stanza in the order that it appears, the introductory paragraph provides a brief overview explaining how the poem's images contribute to its total meaning. In addition, the student does not

(Text continues on page 2056.)

Bonnie Katz

Professor Quiello

English 109-2

October 26, 1992

A Reading of Dickinson's

"There's a certain Slant of light"

Because Emily Dickinson did not provide titles for her
poetry, editors follow the customary practice of using the
first line of a poem as its title. However, a more
appropriate title for "There's a certain Slant of light," one
that suggests what the speaker in the poem is most concerned
about, can be drawn from the poem's last line, which ends
with "the look of Death." Although the first line begins
with an image of light, nothing bright, carefree, or cheerful
appears in the poem. Instead, the predominant mood and
images are darkened by a sense of despair resulting from the
speaker's awareness of death.

In the first stanza, the "certain Slant of light" is
associated with "Winter Afternoons," a phrase that connotes
the end of a day, a season, and even life itself. Such light
is hardly warm or comforting. Not a ray or beam, this
slanting light suggests something unusual or distorted and
creates in the speaker a certain slant on life that is
consistent with the cold, dark mood that winter afternoons
can produce. Like the speaker, most of us have seen and felt
this sort of light: it "oppresses" and pervades our sense of
things when we encounter it. Dickinson uses the senses of
hearing and touch as well as sight to describe the
overwhelming oppressiveness that the speaker experiences.
The light is transformed into sound by a simile that tells us
it is "like the Heft / Of Cathedral Tunes." Moreover, the
"Heft" of that sound--the slow, solemn measures of tolling

church bells and organ music––weighs heavily on our spirits. Through the use of shifting imagery, Dickinson evokes a kind of spiritual numbness that we keenly feel and perceive through our senses.

By associating the winter light with "Cathedral Tunes," Dickinson lets us know that the speaker is concerned about more than the weather. Whatever it is that "oppresses" is related by connotation to faith, mortality, and God. The second and third stanzas offer several suggestions about this connection. The pain caused by the light is a "Heavenly Hurt." This "imperial affliction / Sent us of the Air" apparently comes from God above, and yet it seems to be part of the very nature of life. The oppressiveness we feel is in the air, and it can neither be specifically identified at this point in the poem nor be eliminated, for "None may teach it––Any." All we can know is that existence itself seems depressing under the weight of this "Seal [of] Despair." The impression left by this "Seal" is stamped within the mind or soul rather than externally. "We can find no scar," but once experienced this oppressiveness challenges our faith in life and its "Meanings."

The final stanza does not explain what those "Meanings" are, but it does make clear that the speaker is acutely aware of death. As the winter daylight fades, Dickinson projects the speaker's anxiety onto the surrounding landscape and shadows, which will soon be engulfed by the darkness that follows this light: "The Landscape listens–– / Shadows––hold their breath." This image firmly aligns the winter light in the first stanza with darkness. Paradoxically, the light in this poem illuminates the nature of darkness. Tension is released when the light is completely gone, but what remains is the despair that the "imperial affliction" has imprinted

on the speaker's sensibilities, for it is "like the Distance /
On the look of Death." There can be no relief from what that
"certain Slant of light" has revealed, because what has been
experienced is permanent--like the fixed stare in the eyes of
someone who is dead.

The speaker's awareness of death is conveyed in a
thoughtful, hushed tone. The lines are filled with fluid <u>l</u>
and smooth <u>s</u> sounds that are appropriate for the quiet,
meditative voice in the poem. The voice sounds tentative and
uncertain--perhaps a little frightened. This seems to be
reflected in the slightly irregular meter of the lines. The
stanzas are trochaic with the second and fourth lines of each
stanza having five syllables, but no stanza is identical
because each works a slight variation on the first stanza's
seven syllables in the first and third lines. The rhymes
also combine exact patterns with variations. The first and
third lines of each stanza are not exact rhymes, but the
second and fourth lines are exact so that the paired words
are more closely related: <u>Afternoons</u>, <u>Tunes</u>; <u>scar</u>, <u>are</u>;
<u>Despair</u>, <u>Air</u>; and <u>breath</u>, <u>Death</u>. There is a pattern to the
poem, but it is unobtrusively woven into the speaker's voice
in much the same way that "the look of Death" is subtly
present in the images and language of the poem.

hesitate to discuss a line out of sequence when it can be usefully connected to another phrase. This is especially apparent in the third paragraph, in her discussion of stanzas 2 and 3. The final paragraph describes some of the formal elements of the poem. It might be argued that this discussion could have been integrated into the previous paragraphs rather than placed at the end, but the student does make a connection in her concluding sentence between the pattern of language and its meaning.

Several other matters are worth noticing. The student works quotations into her own sentences to support her points. She quotes exactly as the words appear in the poem, even Dickinson's irregular use of capital letters. When something is added to a quotation to clarify it, it is enclosed in brackets so that the essayist's words will not be mistaken for the poet's: "Seal [of]

Despair." A slash is used to separate line divisions as in "imperial affliction/Sent us of the Air." And, finally, because the essay focuses on a short poem, it is not necessary to include line numbers, though they would be required in a study of a longer work.

Analysis

The preceding sample essay shows how an explication examines in detail the important elements in a work and relates them to the whole. An analysis, however, usually examines only a single element — such as plot, character, point of view, symbol, tone, or irony — and relates it to the entire work. An analytic topic separates the work into parts and focuses on a specific one; you might consider "Point of View in 'A Rose for Emily,' " "Patterns of Rhythm in Browning's 'My Last Duchess,' " or "The Significance of Fortinbras in *Hamlet.*" The specific element must be related to the work as a whole or it will appear irrelevant. It is not enough to point out that there are many death images in Marvell's "To His Coy Mistress"; the images must somehow be connected to the poem's overall effect.

Whether an analytic paper is just a few pages or many, it cannot attempt to discuss everything about the work it is considering. Only those elements that are relevant to the topic can be treated. This kind of focusing makes the topic manageable; this is why most papers that you write will probably be some form of analysis. Explications are useful for a short passage, but a line-by-line commentary on a story, play, or long poem simply isn't practical. Because analysis allows you to consider the central effect or meaning of an entire work by studying a single important element, it is a useful and common approach to longer works.

A STUDENT ANALYSIS

Nancy Lager's paper analyzes the setting in John Updike's "A & P" (the entire story appears on p. 485). The assignment simply asked for an essay of approximately 750 words on a short story written in the twentieth century. The approach was left to the student.

The idea for this essay began with Lager asking herself why Updike used "A & P" as the title. The initial answer to the question was that "the setting is important in this story." This answer was the rough beginning of a tentative thesis. What still had to be explained, though, was how the setting is important. To determine the significance of the setting, Lager jotted down some notes based on her underlinings and marginal notations.

> *A & P*
> "usual traffic"
> lights and tile
> "electric eye"

shoppers like "sheep," "houseslaves," "pigs"
"Alexandrov and Petrooshki" — Russia

New England Town
typical: bank, church, etc.
traditional
conservative
proper
near Salem — witch trials
puritanical
intolerant

Lengel
"manager"
"doesn't miss that much" (like lady shopper)
Sunday school
"It's our policy"
spokesman for A & P values

From these notes Lager saw that Lengel serves as the voice of the A & P. He is, in a sense, a personification of the intolerant atmosphere of the setting. This insight led to another version of her thesis statement: "The setting of 'A & P' is the antagonist of the story." That explained at least some of the setting's importance. By seeing Lengel as a spokesman for "A & P" policies, she could view him as a voice that articulates the morally smug atmosphere created by the setting. Finally, she considered why it is significant that the setting is the antagonist, and this generated her last thesis: "Because the intolerant setting of 'A & P' is the antagonist in the story, it is crucial to our understanding of Sammy's decision to quit his job." This thesis sentence does not appear precisely in these words in the essay, but it is the backbone of the introductory paragraph.

The remaining paragraphs consist of details that describe the A & P in the second paragraph, the New England town in the third, Lengel in the fourth, and Sammy's reasons for quitting in the concluding paragraph. Paragraphs 2, 3, and 4 are largely based on Lager's notes, which she used as an outline once her thesis was established. The essay is sharply focused, well organized, and generally well written. In addition, it suggests a number of useful guidelines for analytic papers.

1. Only those points related to the thesis are included. In another type of paper the role of the girls in the bathing suits, for example, might have been considerably more prominent.
2. The analysis keeps the setting in focus while at the same time indicating how it is significant in the major incident in the story — Sammy's quitting.
3. The title is a useful lead into the paper; it provides a sense of what the topic is. In addition, the title is drawn from a sentence (the final one of the first paragraph) that clearly explains its meaning.

(*Text continues on page 2061.*)

Nancy Lager

Professor Taylor

English 102-12

April 1, 1992

The A & P as a State of Mind

The setting of John Updike's "A & P" is crucial to our
understanding of Sammy's decision to quit his job. Although
Sammy is the central character in the story and we learn that
he is a principled, good-natured nineteen-year-old with a
sense of humor, Updike seems to invest as much effort in
describing the setting as he does in Sammy. The setting is
the antagonist and plays a role that is as important as
Sammy's. The title, after all, is not "Youthful Rebellion"
or "Sammy Quits" but "A & P." Even though Sammy knows that
his quitting will make life more difficult for him, he
instinctively insists upon rejecting what the A & P comes to
represent in the story. When he rings up a "No Sale" and
"saunter[s]" out of the store, he leaves behind not only a
job but the rigid state of mind associated with the A & P.

Sammy's descriptions of the A & P present a setting that
is ugly, monotonous, and rigidly regulated. The fluorescent
light is as blandly cool as the "checkerboard green-and-cream
rubber-tile floor." We can see the uniformity Sammy
describes because we have all been in chain stores. The
"usual traffic" moves in one direction (except for the
swimsuited girls, who move against it), and everything is
neatly ordered and categorized in tidy aisles. The
dehumanizing routine of this environment is suggested by
Sammy's offhanded references to the typical shoppers as
"sheep," "houseslaves," and "pigs." They seem to pace through
the store in a stupor; as Sammy tells us, not even dynamite
could move them.

The A & P is appropriately located "right in the middle" of a proper, conservative, traditional New England town north of Boston. This location, coupled with the fact that the town is only five miles from Salem, the site of the famous seventeenth-century witch trials, suggests a narrow, intolerant social atmosphere in which there is no room for stepping beyond the boundaries of what is regarded as normal and proper. The importance of this setting can be appreciated even more if we imagine the action taking place in, say, a mellow suburb of southern California. In this prim New England setting, the girls in their bathing suits are bound to offend somebody's sense of propriety.

As soon as Lengel sees the girls, the inevitable conflict begins. He embodies the dull conformity represented by the A & P. As "manager," he is both the guardian and enforcer of "policy." When he gives the girls "that sad Sunday-school-superintendent stare," we know we are in the presence of the A & P's version of a dreary bureaucrat who "doesn't miss that much." He is as unsympathetic and unpleasant as the woman "with rouge on her cheeks and no eyebrows" who pounces on Sammy for ringing up her "HiHo crackers" twice. Like the "electric eye" in the doorway, her vigilant eyes allow nothing to escape their notice. For Sammy the logical extension of Lengel's "policy" is the half-serious notion that one day the A & P might be known as the "Great Alexandrov and Petrooshki Tea Company." Sammy's connection between what he regards as mindless "policy" and Soviet oppression is obviously an exaggeration, but the reader is invited to entertain the similarities anyway.

The reason Sammy quits his job has less to do with defending the girls than with his own sense of what it means to be a decent human being. His decision is not an easy one.

He doesn't want to make trouble or disappoint his parents, and he knows his independence and self-reliance (the other side of New England tradition) will make life more complex for him. In spite of his own hesitations, he finds himself blurting out "Fiddle-de-doo" to Lengel's policies and in doing so knows that his grandmother "would have been pleased." Sammy's "No Sale" rejects the crabbed perspective on life that Lengel represents as manager of the A & P. This gesture is more than just negative, however, for as he punches in that last entry on the cash register, "the machine whirs 'pee-pul.'" His decision to quit his job at the A & P is an expression of his refusal to regard policies as more important than people.

4. The introductory paragraph is direct and clearly indicates the paper will argue that the setting serves as the antagonist of the story.

5. Brief quotations are deftly incorporated into the text of the paper to illustrate points. We are told what we need to know about the story as evidence is provided to support ideas. There is no unnecessary plot summary. Because "A & P" is only a few pages in length and is an assigned topic, page numbers are not included after quoted phrases. If the story were longer, page numbers would be helpful for the reader.

6. The paragraphs are well developed, unified, and coherent. They flow naturally from one to another. Notice, for example, the smooth transition worked into the final sentence of the third paragraph and the first sentence of the fourth paragraph.

7. Lager makes excellent use of her careful reading and notes by finding revealing connections among the details she has observed. The store's "electric eye," for instance, is related to the woman's and Lengel's watchfulness.

8. As events are described, the present tense is used. This avoids awkward tense shifts and lends an immediacy to the discussion.

9. The concluding paragraph establishes the significance of why the setting should be seen as the antagonist and provides a sense of closure by referring again to Sammy's "No Sale," which has been mentioned at the end of the first paragraph.

10. In short, Lager has demonstrated that she has read the work closely, has understood the relation of the setting to the major action, and has argued her thesis convincingly by using evidence from the story.

Comparison and Contrast

Another essay assignment in literature courses often combined with analytic topics is the type that requires you to write about similarities and differences between or within works. You might be asked to discuss "How Sounds Express Meanings in May Swenson's 'A Nosty Fright' and Lewis Carroll's 'Jabberwocky,'" or "Sammy's and Stokesie's Attitudes about Conformity in Updike's 'A & P.'" A *comparison* of either topic would emphasize their similarities, while a *contrast* would stress their differences. It is possible, of course, to include both perspectives in a paper if you find significant likenesses and differences. A comparison of Andrew Marvell's "To His Coy Mistress" and Richard Wilbur's "A Late Aubade" would, for example, yield similarities, because each poem describes a man urging his lover to make the most of their precious time together; however, important differences also exist in the tone and theme of each poem that would constitute a contrast. (You should, incidentally, be aware that the term *comparison* is sometimes used inclusively to refer to both similarities and differences. If you are assigned a comparison of two works, be sure that you understand what your instructor's expectations are; you may be required to include both approaches in the essay.)

When you choose your own topic, the paper will be more successful — more manageable — if you write on works that can be meaningfully related to each other. Although Robert Herrick's "To the Virgins, to Make Much of Time" and Shakespeare's *Hamlet* both have something to do with hesitation, the likelihood of anyone making a connection between the two that reveals something interesting and important is remote — though perhaps not impossible if the topic were conceived imaginatively and tactfully. That is not to say that comparisons of works from different genres should be avoided, but the relation between them should be strong, as would a treatment of black identity in M. Carl Holman's "Mr. Z" and August Wilson's *Fences*. Choose a topic that encourages you to ask significant questions about each work; the purpose of a comparison or contrast is to understand the works more clearly for having examined them together. Despite the obvious differences between Henrik Ibsen's *A Doll House* and Gail Godwin's "A Sorrowful Woman," the two are closely related if we ask why the wife in each work withdraws from her family.

Choose works to compare or contrast that intersect with each other in some significant way. They may, for example, be written by the same author, in the same genre, or about the same subject. Perhaps you can compare their use of some technique, such as irony or point of view. Regardless of the specific topic, be sure to have a thesis that allows you to organize your paper around a central idea that argues a point about the two works. If you merely draw up a list of similarities or differences without a thesis in mind, your paper will be little more than a series of observations with no apparent purpose. Keep in the foreground of your thinking what the comparison or contrast reveals about the works.

There is no single way to organize comparative papers since each topic is likely to have its own particular issues to resolve, but it is useful to be aware of two basic patterns that can be helpful with a comparison, a contrast, or a combination of both. One method that can be effective for relatively short papers consists of dividing the paper in half, first discussing one work and then the other. Here, for example, is a partial informal outline for a discussion of Sophocles' *Oedipus the King* and Shakespeare's *Hamlet;* the topic is a comparison and contrast: "Oedipus and Hamlet as Tragic Figures."

1. Oedipus
   a. The nature of the conflict
   b. Strengths and stature
   c. Weaknesses and mistakes
   d. What is learned
2. Hamlet
   a. The nature of the conflict
   b. Strengths and stature
   c. Weaknesses and mistakes
   d. What is learned

This organizational strategy can be effective provided that the second part of the paper combines the discussion of Hamlet with references to Oedipus so that the thesis is made clear and the paper unified without being repetitive. If the two characters were treated entirely separately, then the discussion would be merely parallel rather than integrated. In a lengthy paper, this organization probably would not work well because a reader would have difficulty remembering the points made in the first half as he or she reads on.

Thus for a longer paper it is usually better to create a more integrated structure that discusses both works as you take up each item in your outline. Here is the second basic pattern using the elements in partial outline just cited.

1. The nature of the conflict
   a. Oedipus
   b. Hamlet
2. Strengths and stature
   a. Oedipus
   b. Hamlet
3. Weaknesses and mistakes
   a. Oedipus
   b. Hamlet

4. What is learned
   a. Oedipus
   b. Hamlet

This pattern allows you to discuss any number of topics without requiring that your reader recall what you first said about the conflict Oedipus confronts before you discuss Hamlet's conflicts fifteen pages later. However you structure your comparison or contrast paper, make certain that a reader can follow its elements and keep track of its thesis.

A STUDENT COMPARISON

The following paper is in response to an assignment that required a comparison and contrast — about 750 words — of two assigned plays. The student chose to write an analysis of how the women in each play resist being defined by men.

Although these two plays are fairly lengthy, Monica Casis's brief analysis of them is satisfying because she specifically focuses on the women's struggle for self-definition. After introducing the topic in the first paragraph, she takes up *A Doll House* and *M. Butterfly* in a pattern similar to the first outline suggested for "Oedipus and Hamlet as Tragic Figures." Notice how Casis works in subsequent references to *A Doll House* as she discusses *M. Butterfly* so that her treatment is integrated and we are reminded why she is comparing and contrasting the two works. Though this brief paper cannot address all the complexities and subtleties of gender definition in the plays, her final paragraph sums up her points without being repetitive and reiterates the thesis with which she began.

Monica Casis

Professor Matthews

English 105—4

November 4, 1992

The Struggle for Women's Self—Definition in

A Doll House and M. Butterfly

Though Henrik Ibsen's A Doll House (1879) and David
Henry Hwang's M. Butterfly (1988) were written more than one
hundred years apart and portray radically different
characters in settings and circumstances that are strangely
foreign to one another, both plays raise similar questions
about the role of women and how they are defined in their
respective worlds. Each play presents a woman who initially
seems to be without a strong identity as she attempts to
conform to her partner's ideals of the perfect woman in an
effort to be accepted and loved. However, at the same time
Ibsen's Nora Helmer and Hwang's Song Liling are resourceful,
cunning, and manipulative. Though the plays seem to be about
the emergence of each woman's identity—-Nora's refusal to be
only a dutiful housewife and devoted mother and Song's
refusal to be a woman at all(!)—-these women are from the
beginning stronger and more autonomous than their partners
ever imagine them to be. Even so, that does not lead to
their ability to define themselves as either completely
autonomous or as women.

In A Doll House Nora is treated as her father's, then
her husband's, doll. She is called "squirrel," "spendthrift,"
and "lark" and is admonished for such things as eating sweets
or asking her husband to take her ideas into consideration.
Torvald's concept of the ideal woman is a showpiece who can
dress up, recite, and dance. As a mother she only plays with
her children, since she has Anne—Marie to take care of them.

As a housewife, she has no control over the household
finances and is given an allowance by her husband.

Although Nora externally conforms to her husband's
expectations, she has the strength and resourceful courage to
borrow money for a trip to Italy to save her husband's life
and does odd jobs in order to pay the debt that she has
committed forgery to secure. She is proud of her secret of
sacrificing for the family. She refers to herself as a
frivolous, helpless, dependent woman in order to coax her
husband into giving her money or to steer him away from the
mailbox carrying Krogstad's incriminating letter. Nora is
constantly lying in order to please her husband. So although
in one instance we see Nora as a woman trapped within her
husband's definition of her, the reader is also aware that
Nora uses his expectations to achieve her own goals. Once
Nora sees and understands her husband's superficiality and
selfishness--that Torvald is concerned with only what might
threaten him--she realizes she must abandon the confines of
his definitions of her.

In a similar manner Song plays upon the needs of
Gallimard. To Gallimard, the perfect woman is one who is
"beautiful" and "brave," but most important one whom he can
dominate and control. Song is Oriental which underlies the
cultural prejudice that she is expected to be subservient,
quiet, faithful, and obedient. When Gallimard refers to her
as Butterfly, she loses her individual identity as Nora had
lost hers within her pet names.

By the end of the play the reader is aware that Song is,
in fact, a man working as a spy to obtain important military
information from Gallimard. In order to keep hidden this
secret identity, Song acts as he believes men desire women to
be. As a woman Song refers to her "shame" or modesty so that

Gallimard will not undress her. She pretends that she has a
need to know everything he knows when in reality she is
appeasing his ego and passing on military information to his
enemies. Song tells Gallimard that she is trying to act
"modern" and "manly" but cannot. In actuality Song is an
actor who is acting the way a Chinese woman is assumed to
act. When Song observes that "Once a woman submits, a man is
always ready to become 'generous'" (p. 1953), she is actually
describing her method of control. Like Nora, the "woman"
Song appeals to her mate's egotistical needs in order to
fulfill her own personal goals, and in this case, the needs
of her political allegiances. Just as Nora is Torvald's doll
in need of care and protection, Song is Gallimard's doll,
beautiful and seemingly willing to accede to his every
desire.

The turning point in these plays occurs when Nora and
Song are faced with their dramatically changed relationships
with their mates. Nora becomes convinced that she will
corrupt her children and home with the guilt she bears--not
for borrowing the vacation money but for being with a man she
no longer knows. When Torvald learns of the truth from
Krogstad, he regards her as a liar, hypocrite, and criminal
and therefore repudiates her. Once Nora realizes the
selfishness of her husband, she also realizes she cannot go
on living the lie of being his ideal. Nora must leave her
husband and children in order to search for an identity
commensurate with her strengths. Song too gives up the lie
of her life and reveals herself to be a man. The controlling
roles are switched when Gallimard admits that he loves Song
and intends to marry her. It is when Song refuses marriage
and determines the future of the child that Gallimard openly
gives up control (which he never truly had). He supports

Song and the child, divorces Helga, and passes classified information to Song. Once Song has total control, she emerges as a man, free from any of Gallimard's efforts to define her.

   When Nora and Song come to terms with themselves, their situations are, however, no less problematic than when they falsely fulfilled the definitions imposed upon them. Nora leaves to pursue what may seem to some readers selfish desires, however necessary they are. In Ibsen's world, if a woman is not an obedient wife, mother, and nurturer, she defies definition. Similarly, Song's cruelty toward Gallimard and her revelation that <u>she</u> is not what <u>he</u> seems totally destroys Gallimard's image of Song as a woman, but we must understand that under the weight of that destruction Song's identity as a woman disappears, just as Nora does when she slams the door of the doll house she rejects. It seems that unless a man defines what a woman is in these two plays, the strong and resourceful woman must disappear rather than be allowed to redefine herself.

37. The Literary Research Paper

A close reading of a primary source such as a short story, poem, or play can give insights into a work's themes and effects, but sometimes you will want to know more. A published commentary by a critic who knows the work well and is familiar with the author's life and times can provide insights that otherwise may not be available. Such comments and interpretations — known as *secondary sources* — are, of course, not a substitute for the work itself, but they often can take you into a work further than if you made the journey by yourself.

After imagination, good sense, and energy, perhaps the next most important quality for writing a research paper is the ability to organize material. A research paper on a literary topic requires a writer to take account of quite a lot at once: the text, ideas, sources, and documentation techniques all make demands on one's efforts to present a topic clearly and convincingly.

The following list should give you a sense of what goes into creating a research paper. Although some steps on the list can be folded into one another, they offer an overview of the work that will involve you.

1. Choosing a topic
2. Finding sources
3. Evaluating sources
4. Taking notes
5. Developing a thesis
6. Organizing an outline
7. Writing drafts
8. Revising
9. Documenting sources
10. Preparing the final draft and proofreading

Even if you have never written a research paper, you most likely have already had experience choosing a topic, developing a thesis, organizing an outline, and writing a draft that you then revised, proofread, and handed in. Those skills represent six of the ten items on the list. This chapter briefly reviews some of these steps and focuses on the remaining tasks, unique to research paper assignments.

CHOOSING A TOPIC

Chapter 36 discussed the importance of reading a work closely and taking careful notes as a means of generating topics for writing about literature. If you know a work well and record your understanding of it in notes, you'll have impressions and ideas to choose from for potential topics. You may find it useful to review the information on pages 2037–2038 before reading the advice about putting together a research paper in this chapter.

The student author of the sample research paper "How the Narrator Cultivates a Rose for Emily" (p. 2082) was asked to write a five-page paper that demonstrated some familiarity with published critical perspectives on a Faulkner story of his choice. Before looking into critical discussions of the story, he read "A Rose for Emily" several times, taking notes and making comments in the margin of his textbook on each reading.

What prompted his choice of "A Rose for Emily" was a class discussion in which many of his classmates found the story's title inappropriate or misleading, because they could not understand how and why the story constituted a tribute to Emily given that she murdered a man and slept with his dead body over many years. The gruesome surprise ending revealing Emily as a murderer and necrophiliac hardly seemed to warrant a rose and a tribute for the central character. Why did Faulkner use such a title? Only after having thoroughly examined the story did the student go to the library to see what professional critics had to say about this question.

FINDING SOURCES

Whether your college library is large or small, its reference librarians can usually help you locate secondary sources about a particular work or author. Unless you choose a very recently published story, poem, or play about which little or nothing has been written, you should be able to find commentaries about a literary work efficiently and quickly. Here are some useful reference sources that can help you to establish both an overview of a potential topic and a list of relevant books and articles.

Annotated List of References

Baker, Nancy L. *A Research Guide for Undergraduate Students: English and American Literature*. 2nd ed. New York: MLA, 1985. Especially designed for students; a useful guide to reference sources.

Bryer, Jackson, ed. *Sixteen Modern American Authors: A Survey of Research and Criticism*. New York: Norton, 1973. Extensive bibliographic essays on Sherwood Anderson, Willa Cather, Hart Crane, Theodore Dreiser, T. S. Eliot, William Faulkner, F. Scott Fitzgerald, Robert Frost, Ernest Hemingway, Eugene O'Neill, Ezra Pound, Edwin Arlington Robinson, John Steinbeck, Wallace Stevens, William Carlos Williams, and Thomas Wolfe.

Corse, Larry B., and Sandra B. Corse. *Articles on American and British Literature: An Index to Selected Periodicals, 1950–1977*. Athens, OH: Swallow Press, 1981. Specifically designed for students using small college libraries.

Eddleman, Floyd E., ed. *American Drama Criticism: Interpretations, 1890–1977*. 2nd ed. Hamden, CT: Shoe String Press, 1979. Supplement 1984.

Elliot, Emory, et al. *Columbia Literary History of the United States*. New York: Columbia UP, 1988. This updates the discussions in Spiller (below) and reflects recent changes in the canon.

Harner, James L. *Literary Research Guide: A Guide to Reference Sources for the Study of Literature in English and Related Topics*. 2nd ed. New York: MLA, 1993. A selective but extensive annotated guide to important bibliographies, abstracts, data bases, histories, surveys, dictionaries, encyclopedias, and handbooks; an invaluable research tool with extensive, useful indexes.

Holman, C. Hugh, and William Harmon, *A Handbook to Literature*. 6th ed. New York: Macmillan, 1992. A thorough dictionary of literary terms that also provides brief, clear overviews of literary movements such as Romanticism.

Kuntz, Joseph M., and Nancy C. Martinez. *Poetry Explication: A Checklist of Interpretation since 1925 of British and American Poems Past and Present*. Boston: Hall, 1980.

MLA International Bibliography of Books and Articles on Modern Language and Literature. New York: MLA, 1921–. Compiled annually; a major source for articles and books.

The New Cambridge Bibliography of English Literature. 5 vols. Cambridge, Eng.: Cambridge University Press, 1967–77. An important source on the literature from A.D. 600 to 1950.

The Oxford History of English Literature. 13 vols. Oxford, Eng.: Oxford University Press, 1945–, in progress. The most comprehensive literary history.

The Penguin Companion to World Literature. 4 vols. New York: McGraw-Hill, 1969–71. Covers classical, Oriental, African, European, English, and American literature.

Preminger, Alex, and T. V. F. Brogan, eds. *The New Princeton Encyclopedia of Poetry and Poetics*. Princeton, NJ: Princeton University Press, 1993. Includes entries on technical terms and poetic movements.

Rees, Robert, and Earl N. Harbert. *Fifteen American Authors before 1900: Bibliographic Essays on Research and Criticism*. Madison: University of Wisconsin Press, 1971. Among the writers covered are Stephen Crane and Emily Dickinson.

Spiller, Robert E., et al. *Literary History of the United States*. 4th ed. 2 vols.

New York: Macmillan, 1974. Coverage of literary movements and individual writers from colonial times to the 1960s.

Walker, Warren S. *Twentieth-Century Short Story Explication*. 3rd ed. Hamden, CT: Shoe String Press, 1977. A bibliography of criticism on short stories written since 1800; supplements appear every few years.

These sources are available in the reference sections of most college libraries; ask a reference librarian to help you locate them.

Computer Searches

Researchers can locate materials in a variety of sources, including card catalogues, specialized encyclopedias, bibliographies, and indexes to periodicals. Many libraries now also provide computer searches that are linked to a data base of the libraries' holdings. This can be an efficient way to establish a bibliography on a specific topic. If your library has such a service, consult a reference librarian about how to use it and to determine if it is feasible for your topic. You may discover that the library charges a fee for such services. If a computer service is impractical, you can still collect the same information from printed sources.

EVALUATING SOURCES AND TAKING NOTES

Evaluate your sources for their reliability and the quality of their evidence. Check to see if an article or book has been superseded by later studies; try to use up-to-date sources. A popular magazine article will probably not be as authoritative as an article in a scholarly journal. Sources that are well documented with primary and secondary materials usually indicate that the author has done his or her homework. Books printed by university presses and established trade presses are preferable to books privately printed. But there are always exceptions. If you are uncertain about how to assess a book, try to find out something about the author. Are there any other books listed in the card catalogue that indicate the author's expertise? What do book reviews say about the work? Three valuable indexes to book reviews of literary studies are *Book Review Digest, Book Review Index,* and *Index to Book Reviews in the Humanities.* Your reference librarian can show you how to use these important tools for evaluating books. Reviews can be a quick means to get a broad perspective on writers and their works because reviewers often survey previous approaches to the topic under discussion.

As you prepare a list of reliable sources relevant to your topic, record the necessary bibliographic information so that it will be available when you make up the list of works cited for your paper. (See the illustration of a sample bibliography card.) For a book include the author, complete title, place of publication, publisher, and date. For an article include author, complete title, name of periodical, volume number, date of issue, and page numbers.

Sample Bibliography Card for a Book

Once you have assembled a tentative bibliography, you will need to take notes on your readings. If you are not using a word processor, use 3×5, 4×6, or 5×8-inch cards for note taking. They are easy to manipulate and can be readily sorted later on when you establish subheadings for your paper. Be sure to keep track of where the information comes from by writing the author's name and page number on each notecard. If you use more than one work by the same author include a brief title as well as the author's name. (See the illustration of the sample notecard.)

The sample notecard records the source of information (the complete publishing information is on the bibliography card) and provides a heading that will allow easy sorting later on. Notice that the information is summarized rather than quoted in large chunks. The student also includes a short

On the publication of "A Rose for Emily"   Minter 116

Minter describes "A Rose" as "one of Faulkner's finest short stories" yet it was rejected at _Scribner's_ when Faulkner submitted it.

[Can I work this in?]

Sample Notecard

note asking himself if this will be relevant to the topic — the meaning of the title of "A Rose for Emily." (As it turned out, this was not directly related to the topic, so it was dropped.)

Notecards can combine quotations, paraphrases, and summaries; you can also use them to cite your own ideas and give them headings so that you don't lose track of them. As you take notes try to record only points relevant to your topic. Although the sample card on Scribner's rejection of "A Rose for Emily" wasn't used in the paper, it might have been. At least that fact was an interesting possibility, even if it wasn't, finally, worth developing.

DEVELOPING A THESIS AND
ORGANIZING THE PAPER

As the notes on "A Rose for Emily" accumulated, the student sorted them into topics including

1. Publication history of the story
2. Faulkner on the title of "A Rose for Emily"
3. Is Emily simply insane?
4. The purpose of Emily's servant
5. The narrator
6. The townspeople's view of Emily
7. The surprise ending
8. Emily's admirable qualities
9. Homer's character

The student quickly saw that items 1, 4, and 9 were not directly related to his topic concerning the significance of the story's title. The remaining numbers (2, 3, 5, 6, 7, 8) are the topics taken up in the paper. The student had begun his reading of secondary sources with a tentative thesis that stemmed from his question about the appropriateness of the title. That "why" shaped itself into the expectation that he would have a thesis something like this: "The title justifies Emily's murder of Homer because . . . ."

The assumption was that he would find information that indicated some specific reason. But the more he read the more he discovered that it was possible only to speak about how the narrator prevents the reader from making a premature judgment about Emily rather than justifying her actions. Hence, he wisely changed his tentative thesis to this final thesis: "The narrator describes incidents and withholds information in such a way as to cause the reader to sympathize with Emily before her crime is revealed." This thesis helped the student explain why the title is accurate and useful rather than misleading.

Because the assignment was relatively brief, the student did not write up a formal outline but instead organized his stacks of usable notecards and proceeded to write the first draft from them.

REVISING

After writing your first draft, you should review the advice and revision checklist on pp. 2049–2051 so that you can read your paper with an objective eye. Two days after writing his next-to-last draft, the writer of "How the Narrator Cultivates a Rose for Emily" realized that he had allotted too much space for critical discussions of the narrator that were not directly related to his approach. He wanted to demonstrate a familiarity with these studies, but it was not essential that he summarize or discuss them. He corrected this by consolidating parenthetical references: "Though a number of studies discuss the story's narrator (see, for example, Kempton; Sullivan; and Watkins)." His earlier draft had included summaries of these studies that were tangential to his argument. The point is that he saw this himself after he took some time to approach the paper from a fresh perspective.

DOCUMENTING SOURCES

You must acknowledge the use of a source when you (1) quote someone's exact words, (2) summarize or borrow someone's opinions or ideas, or (3) use information and facts that are not considered to be common knowledge. The purpose of this documentation is to acknowledge your sources, to demonstrate that you are familiar with what others have thought about the topic, and to provide your reader access to the same sources. If your paper is not adequately documented, it will be vulnerable to a charge of *plagiarism* — the presentation of someone else's work as your own. Conscious plagiarism is easy to avoid; honesty takes care of that for most people. However, there is a more problematic form of plagiarism that is often inadvertent. Whether inadequate documentation is conscious or not, plagiarism is a serious matter and must be avoided. Papers can be evaluated only by what is on the page, not by their writers' intentions.

Let's look more closely at what constitutes plagiarism. Consider the following passage quoted from John Gassner's introduction to *Four Great Plays by Henrik Ibsen* (New York: Bantam, 1959), p. viii:

> Today it seems incredible that *A Doll's House*° should have created the furor it did. In exploding Victorian ideals of feminine dependency the play seemed revolutionary in 1879. When its heroine Nora left her home in search of self-development it seemed as if the sanctity of marriage had been flouted by a playwright treading the stage with cloven-feet.

Now read this plagiarized version:

> *A Doll's House* created a furor in 1879 by blowing up Victorian ideals about a woman's place in the world. Nora's search for self-fulfillment out-

---

Rolf Fjelde, whose translation is included in Chapter 30, renders the title as *A Doll House* in order to emphasize that the whole household, including Torvald as well as Nora, lives an unreal, doll-like existence.

side her home appeared to be an attack on the sanctity of marriage by a cloven-footed playwright.

Though the writer has shortened the passage and made some changes in the wording, this paragraph is basically the same as Gassner's. Indeed, several of his phrases are lifted almost intact. Even if a parenthetical reference had been included at the end of the passage and the source included in "Works Cited," the language of this passage would still be plagiarism because it is presented as the writer's own. Both language and ideas must be acknowledged.

Here is an adequately documented version of the passage:

> John Gassner has observed how difficult it is for today's readers to comprehend the intense reaction against *A Doll's House* in 1879. When Victorian audiences watched Nora walk out of her stifling marriage, they assumed that Ibsen was expressing a devilish contempt for the "sanctity of marriage" (viii).

This passage makes absolutely clear that the observation is Gassner's, and it is written in the student's own language with the exception of one quoted phrase. Had Gassner not been named in the passage, the parenthetical reference would have included his name: (Gassner viii).

Some mention should be made of the notion of common knowledge before we turn to the standard format for documenting sources. Observations and facts that are widely known and routinely included in many of your sources do not require documentation. It is not necessary to cite a source for the fact that Alfred, Lord Tennyson, was born in 1809 or that Ernest Hemingway loved to fish and hunt. Sometimes it will be difficult for you to determine what common knowledge is for a topic that you know little about. If you are in doubt, the best strategy is to supply a reference.

There are two basic ways to document sources. Traditionally, sources have been cited in footnotes at the bottom of each page or in endnotes grouped together at the end of the paper. Here is how a portion of the sample paper would look if footnotes were used instead of parenthetical documentation:

```
As Heller points out, before we learn of Emily's bizarre be-
havior we see her as a sympathetic--if antiquated--figure in
a town whose life and concerns have passed her by; hence, "we
are disposed to see Emily as victimized."[1]


      [1]Terry Heller, "The Telltale Hair: A Critical Study of
William Faulkner's 'A Rose for Emily,'" Arizona Quarterly 28
(1972): 306.
```

Unlike endnotes, which are double spaced throughout under the title of "Notes" on separate pages at the end of the paper, footnotes appear four spaces below the text. They are single spaced with double spaces between notes.

No doubt you will have encountered these documentation methods in your reading. A different style is recommended, however, in the third edition of the Modern Language Association's *MLA Handbook for Writers of Research Papers* (1988). The new style employs parenthetical references within the text of the paper; these are keyed to an alphabetical list of works cited at the end of the paper. This method is designed to be less distracting for the reader. Unless you are instructed to follow the footnote or endnote style for documentation, use the new parenthetical method explained in the next section.

The List of Works Cited

Items in the list of works cited are arranged alphabetically according to the author's last name and indented five spaces after the first line. This allows the reader to locate quickly the complete bibliographic information for the author's name cited within the parenthetical reference in the text. The following are common entries for literature papers and should be used as models. If some of your sources are of a different nature, consult Joseph Gibaldi and Walter S. Achtert, *MLA Handbook for Writers of Research Papers,* 3rd ed. (New York: MLA, 1988); many of the bibliographic possibilities you are likely to need are included in this source.

A Book by One Author

Hendrickson, Robert. <u>The Literary Life and Other Curiosities</u>.
      New York: Viking, 1981.

Notice that the author's name is in reverse order. This information, along with the full title, place of publication, publisher, and date should be taken from the title and copyright pages of the book. The title is underlined to indicate italics and is also followed by a period. If the city of publication is well known, it is unnecessary to include the state. Use the publication date on the title page; if none appears there use the copyright date (after ©) on the back of the title page.

A Book by Two Authors

Horton, Rod W., and Herbert W. Edwards. <u>Backgrounds of Ameri-</u>
      <u>can Literary Thought</u>. 3rd ed. Englewood Cliffs: Pren-
      tice, 1974.

Only the first author's name is given in reverse order. The edition number appears after the title.

A Book with More than Three Authors

```
Abrams, M. H., et al., eds.  The Norton Anthology of English
     Literature.  5th ed.  2 vols.  New York: Norton, 1986.
     Vol. 1.
```

The abbreviation *et al.* means "and others." It is used to avoid having to list all fourteen editors of this first volume of a two-volume work.

A Work in a Collection by the Same Author

```
O'Connor, Flannery.  "Greenleaf."  The Complete Stories.  By
     O'Connor.  New York: Farrar, 1971.  311-34.
```

Page numbers are given because the reference is to only a single story in the collection.

A Work in a Collection by Different Writers

```
Frost, Robert.  "Design."  The Bedford Introduction to Litera-
     ture.  Ed. Michael Meyer.  3rd ed.  Boston: Bedford-
     St. Martin's P, 1993.  887.
```

The hyphenated publisher's name indicates a publisher's imprint: Bedford Books of St. Martin's Press.

A Translated Book

```
Grass, Günter.  The Tin Drum.  Trans. Ralph Manheim.  New
     York: Vintage-Random, 1962.
```

An Introduction, Preface, Foreword, or Afterword

```
Johnson, Thomas H.  Introduction.  Final Harvest: Emily Dick-
     inson's Poems.  By Emily Dickinson.  Boston: Little,
     1961.  vii-xiv.
```

This cites the introduction by Johnson. Notice that a colon is used between the book's main title and subtitle. To cite a poem in this book use this method:

```
Dickinson, Emily.  "A Tooth upon Our Peace."  Final Harvest:
     Emily Dickinson's Poems.  Ed. Thomas H. Johnson.  Boston:
     Little, 1961.  110.
```

An Encyclopedia

```
"Wordsworth, William." The New Encyclopedia Britannica. 1984
    ed.
```

Because this encyclopedia is organized alphabetically, no page number or other information is given, only the edition number (if available) and date.

An Article in a Magazine

```
Morrow, Lance. "Scribble, Scribble, Eh, Mr. Toad." Time 24
    Feb. 1986: 84.
```

The citation for an unsigned article would begin with the title and be alphabetized by the first word of the title other than "a," "an," or "the."

An Article in a Scholarly Journal with Continuous Pagination beyond a Single Issue

```
Mahar, William J. "Black English in Early Blackface Min-
    strelsy: A New Interpretation of the Sources of Minstrel
    Show Dialect." American Quarterly 37 (1985): 260-85.
```

Because this journal uses continuous pagination instead of separate pagination for each issue, it is not necessary to include the month, season, or number of the issue. Only one of the quarterly issues will have pages numbered 260–85. If you are not certain whether a journal's pages are numbered continuously throughout a volume, supply the month, season, or issue number, as in the next entry.

An Article in a Scholarly Journal with Separate Pagination for Each Issue

```
Updike, John. "The Cultural Situation of the American
    Writer." American Studies International 15 (Spring
    1977): 19-28.
```

By noting the spring issue, the entry saves a reader looking through each issue of the 1977 volume for the correct article on pages 19–28.

An Article in a Newspaper

```
Ziegler, Philip. "The Lure of Gossip, the Rules of History."
    New York Times 23 Feb. 1986: sec. 7: 1+.
```

This citation indicates that the article appears on page 1 of section 7 and continues onto another page.

```
Stern, Milton.  "Melville's View of Law."  English 270 class
     lecture.  University of Connecticut, Storrs, 12 Mar.
     1992.
```

Parenthetical References

A list of works cited is not an adequate indication of how you have used sources in your paper. You must also provide the precise location of quotations and other information by using parenthetical references within the text of the paper. You do this by citing the author's name (or the source's title if the work is anonymous) and the page number.

> Collins points out that "Nabokov was misunderstood by early reviewers of his work" (28).

or

> Nabokov's first critics misinterpreted his stories (Collins 28).

Either way a reader will find the complete bibliographic entry in the list of works cited under Collins's name and know that the information cited in the paper appears on page 28. Notice that the end punctuation comes after the parentheses.

If you have listed more than one work by the same author, you would add a brief title to the parenthetical reference to distinguish between them. You could also include the full title in your text.

> Nabokov's first critics misinterpreted his stories (Collins "Early Reviews" 28).

or

> Collins points out in "Early Reviews of Nabokov's Fiction" that his early work was misinterpreted by reviewers (28).

There can be many variations on what is included in a parenthetical reference, depending on the nature of the entry in the list of works cited. But the general principle is simple enough: provide enough parenthetical information for a reader to find the work in "Works Cited." Examine the sample research paper for more examples of works cited and strategies for including parenthetical references. If you are puzzled by a given situation, ask your reference librarian to show you the *MLA Handbook*.

SAMPLE STUDENT RESEARCH PAPER

The following research paper by Tony Groulx follows the format described in the *MLA Handbook for Writers of Research Papers* (1988). This format is discussed in the preceding section on Documentation and in

Chapter 36, in the section "Manuscript Form" (pp. 2051–2052). Though the sample paper is short, it illustrates many of the techniques and strategies useful for writing an essay that includes secondary sources. (Faulkner's "A Rose for Emily" is reprinted on p. 47.)

Tony Groulx

Professor Hugo

English 109-3

December 3, 1992

How the Narrator Cultivates a Rose for Emily

William Faulkner's "A Rose for Emily" is an absorbing mystery story whose chilling ending contains a gruesome surprise. When we discover, along with the narrator and townspeople, what was left of Homer Barron's body, we may be surprised or not, depending upon how carefully we have been reading the story and keeping track of details such as Emily Grierson's purchase of rat poison and Homer's disappearance. Probably most readers anticipate finding Homer's body at the end of the story, because Faulkner carefully prepares the groundwork for the discovery as the townspeople force their way into that mysterious upstairs room where a "thin, acrid pall as of the tomb seemed to lie everywhere" (53). But very few readers, if any, are prepared for the story's final paragraph, when we realize that the strand of "iron-gray hair" (the last three words of the story) on the second pillow indicates that Emily has slept with Homer since she murdered him. This last paragraph produces the real horror in the story and an extraordinary revelation about Emily's character.

The final paragraph seems like the right place to begin a discussion of this story because the surprise ending not only creates a powerful emotional effect in us but also raises an important question about what we are to think of Emily. Is this isolated, eccentric woman simply mad? All the circumstantial evidence indicates that she is a murderer and necrophiliac, and yet Faulkner titles the story "A Rose for Emily," as if she is due some kind of tribute. The title

somehow qualifies the gasp of horror that the story leads up
to in the final paragraph. Why would anyone offer this woman
a "rose"? What's behind the title?

Faulkner was once directly asked the meaning of the
title and replied:

> Oh it's simply the poor woman had had no life at
> all. Her father had kept her more or less locked
> up and then she had a lover who was about to quit
> her, she had to murder him. It was just "A Rose
> for Emily"--that's all. (qtd. in Gwynn and Blotner
> 87-88)

This reply explains some of Emily's motivation for murdering
Homer but it doesn't actually address the purpose and meaning
of the title. If Emily killed Homer out of a kind of
emotional necessity--out of a fear of abandonment--how does
that explain the fact that the title seems to suggest that
the story is a way of paying respect to Emily? The question
remains.

Whatever respect the story creates for Emily cannot be
the result of her actions. Surely there can be no convincing
excuse made for murder and necrophilia; there is nothing to
praise about what she does. Instead, the tribute comes in
the form of how her story is told rather than what we are
told about her. To do this Faulkner uses a narrator who
tells Emily's story in such a way as to maximize our sympathy
for her. The grim information about Emily's "iron-gray hair"
on the pillow is withheld until the very end and not only to
produce a surprise but to permit the reader to develop a
sympathetic understanding of her before we are shocked and
disgusted by her necrophilia.

Significantly, the narrator begins the story with

Emily's death rather than Homer's. Though a number of studies discuss the story's narrator (see, for example, Kempton; Sullivan; and Watkins), Terry Heller's is one of the most comprehensive in its focus on the narrator's effects on the readers' response to Emily. As Heller points out, before we learn of Emily's bizarre behavior we see her as a sympathetic--if antiquated--figure in a town whose life and concerns have passed her by; hence, "we are disposed to see Emily as victimized" (306). Her refusal to pay her taxes is an index to her isolation and eccentricity, but this incident also suggests a degree of dignity and power lacking in the town officials who fail to collect her taxes. Her encounters with the officials of Jefferson--whether in the form of the sneaking aldermen who try to cover up the smell around her house or the druggist who unsuccessfully tries to get her to conform to the law when she buys arsenic--place her in an admirable light, because her willfulness is based upon her personal strength. Moreover, it is relatively easy to side with Emily when the townspeople are described as taking pleasure in her being reduced to poverty as a result of her father's death, because "now she too would know the old thrill and the old despair of a penny more or less" (50). The narrator's account of their pettiness, jealousy, and inability to make sense of Emily causes the reader to sympathize with Emily's eccentricities before we must judge her murderous behavior. We admire her for taking life on her own terms, and the narrator makes sure this response is in place prior to our realization that she also takes life.

We don't really know much about Emily because the narrator arranges the details of her life so that it's difficult to know what she's been up to. We learn, for example, about the smell around the house before she buys the

poison and Homer disappears, so that the cause and effect
relationship among these events is obscured. The narrator's
chronology of events is a bit slippery (for a detailed
reconstruction of the chronology see McGlynn and Nebecker's
revision of McGlynn's work), but the effect is to suspend
judgment of Emily. By the time we realize what she has done
we are already inclined to see her as outside community
values almost out of necessity. That's not to say that the
murdering of Homer is justified by the narrator, but it is to
say that her life maintains its private--though no longer
secret--dignity. Despite the final revelation, Emily remains
"dear, inescapable, impervious, tranquil, and perverse" (52).

     The narrator's "rose" to Emily is his recognition that
Emily is all these things--including "perverse." She evokes
"a sort of respectful affection for a fallen monument" (47).
She is, to be sure, "fallen," but she is also somehow
central--a "monument"--to the life of the community.
Faulkner does not offer a definitive reading of Emily but he
does have the narrator pay tribute to her by attempting to
provide a complex set of contexts for her actions--contexts
that include a repressive father, resistance to a changing
South and impinging North, the passage of time and its
influence on the present, and relations between men and women
as well as relations between generations. Robert Crosman
discusses the narrator's efforts to understand Emily:

          The narrator is himself a "reader" of Emily's
          story, trying to put together from fragments a
          complete picture, trying to find the meaning of her
          life in its impact upon an audience, the citizens
          of Jefferson, of which he is a member. (212)
The narrator refuses to dismiss Emily as simply mad or to
treat her life as merely a grotesque, sensational horror

story. Instead, his narrative method brings us into her life before we too hastily reject her, and in doing so it offers us a complex imaginative treatment of fierce determination and strength coupled with illusions and shocking eccentricities. The narrator's rose for Emily is paying her the tribute of placing that "long strand of iron-gray hair" in the context of her entire life.

Works Cited

Crosman, Robert. "How Readers Make Meaning." College Lit-
    erature 9 (1982): 207–15.

Faulkner, William. "A Rose for Emily." The Bedford Intro-
    duction to Literature. Ed. Michael Meyer. 3rd ed.
    Boston: Bedford–St. Martin's P, 1993. 47–53.

Gwynn, Frederick, and Joseph Blotner, eds. Faulkner in the
    University: Class Conferences at the University of Vir-
    ginia, 1957–58. Charlottesville: U of Virginia P, 1959.

Heller, Terry. "The Telltale Hair: A Critical Study of Wil-
    liam Faulkner's 'A Rose for Emily.'" Arizona Quarterly
    28 (1972): 301–18.

Kempton, K. P. The Short Story. Cambridge: Harvard UP,
    1954. 104–06.

McGlynn, Paul D. "The Chronology of 'A Rose for Emily.'"
    Studies in Short Fiction 6 (1969): 461–62.

Nebecker, Helen E. "Chronology Revised." Studies in Short
    Fiction 8 (1971): 471–73.

Sullivan, Ruth. "The Narrator in 'A Rose for Emily.'" The
    Journal of Narrative Technique 1 (1971): 159–78.

Watkins, F. C. "The Structure of 'A Rose for Emily.'" Mod-
    ern Language Notes 69 (1954): 508–10.

Epilogue

The end of a book is often the beginning of something for an engaged reader. The following prose poem by Karl Shapiro points you in a direction that can make you more familiar with the authors in *The Bedford Introduction to Literature,* as well as with the countless other writers waiting for you to discover them.

KARL SHAPIRO (b. 1913)
Libraries   1964

Libraries, where one takes on the smell of books, stale and attractive. Service with no motive, simple as U.S. mail. Fountains and palms, armchairs for smokers. Incredible library where ideas run for safety, place of rebirth of forgotten anthems, modern cathedral for lovers. Library, hotel lobby for the unemployed, the failure, the boy afraid to go home, penniless. Switchboards for questioners: what do you know about unicorns? How do you address a duchess? Palladian architecture of gleaming glass and redwood. Window displays of this week's twelve bestsellers. Magnificent quarters of the director, who dines with names of unknown fame. Lavatories, rendezvous of desperate homosexuals. In the periodical room the newspapers bound with a stick, carried like banners of surrender to pale oak tables. Library, asylum, platform for uninhibited leaps. In the genealogy room the delicate perspiration of effete brains. Room also of the secret catalogue, room of unlisted books, those sought by police, manuscript room with the door of black steel, manuscripts stolen in delicate professional theft from abroad, sealed for seventy-five years. Sutras on spools of film. And all this courtesy and all this trust, tons of trash and tons of greatness, burning in time with the slow cool burning, burning in the fires of poems that gut libraries, only to rebuild them, more grand and palladian, freer, more courteous, with cornerstones that say: Decide for yourself.

Acknowledgments *(continued from p. iv)*

John Cheever. "Reunion" from *The Stories of John Cheever.* Copyright © 1962 by John Cheever. Reprinted by permission of Alfred A. Knopf, Inc. "John Cheever Interview (On Morals in Fiction)" from *Writers at Work, Fifth Series* edited by George Plimpton. Intro. Francine du Plessix Gray. Copyright © 1981 by The Paris Review. Used by permission of Viking Penguin, a division of Penguin Books USA Inc.

Sandra Cisneros. "Barbie-Q" from *Woman Hollering Creek.* Copyright © 1991 by Sandra Cisneros. Published in the United States by Vintage Books, a division of Random House, Inc., New York, and simultaneously in Canada by Random House of Canada Limited, Toronto. Originally published in hardcover by Random House, Inc., New York, in 1991. Reprinted by permission of Susan Bergholz Literary Services, New York.

Colette. "The Hand" from *The Collected Stories of Colette.* Translation copyright © 1957, 1966, 1983 by Farrar, Straus & Giroux, Inc. Reprinted by permission of Farrar, Straus & Giroux, Inc.

A. R. Coulthard. "On the Visionary Ending of 'Revelation'" from "From Sermon to Parable: Four Conversion Stories by Flannery O'Connor," *American Literature* 55:1, March 1983, © Duke University Press. Reprinted by permission of the publisher.

e. e. cummings. "my sweet old etcetera," reprinted from *Is 5: poems* by e. e. cummings, edited by George James Firmage, by permission of Liveright Publishing Corporation. Copyright © 1985 by e. e. cummings Trust. Copyright 1926 by Horace Liveright. Copyright © 1954 by E. E. Cummings. Copyright © 1985 by George James Firmage.

Benjamin De Mott. "Abner Snopes as a Victim of Class" from *Close Imagining: An Introduction to Literature* by Benjamin De Mott, copyright © 1988. Reprinted with permission of St. Martin's Press, Inc.

Emily Dickinson. "A narrow Fellow in the Grass" reprinted by permission of the publishers and the Trustees of Amherst College from *The Poems of Emily Dickinson,* Thomas H. Johnson, ed., Cambridge, Mass.: The Belknap Press of Harvard University Press, Copyright © 1951, 1955, 1979, 1983 by the President and Fellows of Harvard College.

E. L. Doctorow. "The Importance of Fiction" from "The Ultimate Discourse," copyright © 1986 by E. L. Doctorow. First appeared in *Esquire.* Reprinted by permission of the author.

Andre Dubus. "Killings" from *Finding a Girl in America* by Andre Dubus. Copyright © 1980 by Andre Dubus. Reprinted by permission of David R. Godine, Publisher.

Ralph Ellison. "Battle Royal" from *Invisible Man* by Ralph Ellison. Copyright 1948 by Ralph Ellison. Reprinted by permission of Random House, Inc.

Louise Erdrich. "I'm a Mad Dog Biting Myself for Sympathy," copyright © 1990 by Louise Erdrich. Reprinted by permission of the author.

William Faulkner. "A Rose for Emily" from *The Collected Stories of William Faulkner* by William Faulkner. Copyright 1930 and renewed 1958 by William Faulkner. Reprinted by permission of Random House, Inc. "Barn Burning" from *The Collected Stories of William Faulkner* by William Faulkner. Copyright © 1950 by Random House, Inc. and renewed 1977 by Jill Faulkner Summers. "On 'A Rose for Emily,'" "On the Demands of Writing Short Stories" from *Faulkner in the University* by Gwynn and Blotner. Reprinted by permission of the University Press of Virginia.

James Ferguson. "Narrative Strategy in 'Barn Burning'" from *Faulkner's Short Stories* by James Ferguson, copyright © 1991. Reprinted by permission of the University of Tennessee Press.

Judith Fetterley. "A Feminist Reading of 'The Birthmark'" from *The Resisting Reader: A Feminist Approach to American Fiction.* Copyright © 1978. Reprinted by permission of Indiana University Press.

F. Scott Fitzgerald. "On the Continuity of a Writer's Works," excerpt from "One Hundred False Starts" by F. Scott Fitzgerald. Reprinted from the *Saturday Evening Post* © 1933 the Curtis Publishing Company.

Gabriel García Marquéz. "A Very Old Man with Enormous Wings" from *Collected Stories* by Gabriel García Marquéz. English Translation copyright © 1971 by Gabriel García Marquéz. Reprinted by permission of HarperCollins Publishers.

Marshall Bruce Gentry. "On the Revised Ending of 'Revelation'" from *Flannery O'Connor's Religion of the Grotesque,* pp. 42–43. Copyright © 1986. Reprinted by permission of the University of Mississippi Press.

Gail Godwin. "A Sorrowful Woman," copyright © 1971 by Gail Godwin, originally appeared in *Esquire* Magazine in 1971. Reprinted by permission of John Hawkins & Associates, Inc.

Bessie Head. "The Prisoner Who Wore Glasses" from *Tales of Tenderness and Power,* Heinemann International, 1990. Copyright © the Estate of Bessie Head. Reprinted by permission.

Ernest Hemingway. "Soldier's Home," from *In Our Time* by Ernest Hemingway, reprinted with permission of Charles Scribner's Sons, an imprint of Macmillan Publishing Company. Copyright 1925 by Charles Scribner's Sons; renewal copyright 1953 by Ernest Hemingway.

Jane Hiles. "Blood Ties in 'Barn Burning'" from "Kinship and Heredity in Faulkner's 'Barn Burning.'" Copyright © 1985. Reprinted by permission of *Mississippi Quarterly: The Journal of Southern Culture.*

Gish Jen. "In the American Society," copyright © 1986 by Gish Jen. First published in the *Southern Review.* Reprinted by permission of the author.

James Joyce. "Araby," "The Boarding House," "The Dead," "Eveline," from *Dubliners* by James Joyce. Copyright 1916 by B. W. Heubsch. Definitive text Copyright © 1967 by the Estate of James Joyce. Used by permission of Viking Penguin, a division of Penguin Books USA Inc.

Franz Kafka. "The Hunger Artist" from *The Penal Colony* by Franz Kafka, translated by Willa and Edwin Muir. Translation copyright 1948 and renewed 1976 by Schocken Books, Inc., published by Pantheon Books, a division of Random House, Inc.

Edward Kessler. "On O'Connor's Use of History" from *Flannery O'Connor and the Language of Apocalypse.* Copyright © 1986 by Princeton University Press. Reprinted by permission of Princeton University Press.

Jamaica Kincaid. "Girl" from *At the Bottom of the River* by Jamaica Kincaid. Copyright © 1978, 1979, 1981, 1982, 1983 by Jamaica Kincaid. Reprinted by permission of Farrar, Straus & Giroux, Inc.

D. H. Lawrence. "The Horse Dealer's Daughter," from *Complete Short Stories of D. H. Lawrence* by D. H. Lawrence. Copyright 1922 by Thomas B. Seltzer, Inc., renewed 1950 by Frieda Lawrence. Used by permission of Viking Penguin, a division of Penguin Books USA Inc.

Ursula K. Le Guin. "On Conflict in Fiction" adapted from "Conflict" from *Dancing at the Edge of the World: Thoughts on Words, Women, Places* by Ursula K. Le Guin. Copyright © 1987 by Ursula K. Le Guin. Used by permission of Grove Press, Inc.

Steven Mailloux. "Gauging the Reader's Response to Giovanni" reprinted from *Interpretive Conventions: The Reader in the Study of American Fiction.* Copyright © 1982 by Cornell University. Used by permission.

Katherine Mansfield. "Miss Brill" from *The Selected Short Stories of Katherine Mansfield* by Katherine Mansfield. Copyright 1922 by Alfred A. Knopf, Inc., and renewed 1950 by John Middleton Murry. Reprinted by permission of Alfred A. Knopf, Inc.

Mordecai Marcus. "What Is an Initiation Story?" from *The Journal of Aesthetics and Art Criticism* 19:2, pp. 222–23. Reprinted by permission of the publisher.

Dan McCall. "On the Lawyer's Character in 'Bartleby, the Scrivener'" reprinted from *The Silence of Bartleby* by Dan McCall. Copyright © 1989 by Cornell University. Used by permission.

Thomas McCormack. "On the Problem of Teaching Theme" from *The Fiction Editor* by Thomas McCormack. Copyright © 1988 by Daniel and Jessie McCormack. Reprinted with permission from St. Martin's Press, Inc.

Dorothy T. McFarland. "A Formalist Reading of 'Revelation'" from *Flannery O'Connor* by Dorothy T. McFarland. Copyright © 1976 by the Frederick Ungar Publishing Company. Reprinted by permission of the author.

Barbara McLean. "'The (Boar)ding House': Mrs. Mooney as Circe and Sow" excerpt from *James Joyce Quarterly* (Winter 1991, pp. 520–22). Copyright © 1991 by the University of Tulsa. Reprinted by permission.

Yukio Mishima. "Patriotism" from *Death In Midsummer.* Copyright © 1966 by New Directions Publishing Corp. Reprinted by permission of New Directions Publishing Corporation.

Tania Modleski. "The Popularity of Romance Novels" from *Loving with a Vengeance: Mass Produced Fantasies for Women.* Copyright © 1982. Reprinted by permission of Shoe String Press, Inc.

Bharati Mukherjee. "Fathering" from *The Middleman and Other Stories* by Bharati Mukherjee, copyright © 1988 by Bharati Mukherjee. Used by permission of Bharati Mukherjee and Grove Press, Inc.

Joyce Carol Oates. "The Lady with the Pet Dog" from *Marriages and Infidelities* by Joyce Carol Oates, copyright © 1972 by Joyce Carol Oates. Reprinted by permission of John Hawkins and Associates, Inc.

Tim O'Brien. "How to Tell a True War Story," copyright © 1987 by Tim O'Brien. Reprinted by permission of International Creative Management, Inc. First published in *Esquire* Magazine.

Flannery O'Connor. "Good Country People" from *A Good Man Is Hard to Find and Other Stories* by Flannery O'Connor. Copyright © 1955 Flannery O'Connor; renewed 1983 by Regina O'Connor. "A Good Man Is Hard to Find," copyright 1953 by Flannery O'Connor; renewed 1981 by Regina O'Connor. Reprinted from *A Good Man Is Hard to Find and Other Stories*. Both stories reprinted by permission of Harcourt Brace Jovanovich, Inc. "Parker's Back" and "Revelation" from *The Complete Stories* by Flannery O'Connor. Copyright © 1964, 1965 by the Estate of Mary Flannery O'Connor. Reprinted by permission of Farrar, Straus & Giroux, Inc.

Tillie Olsen. "I Stand Here Ironing" from *Tell Me a Riddle* by Tillie Olsen. Copyright © 1956, 1957, 1960, 1961 by Tillie Olsen. Used by permission of Delacorte Press/Seymour Lawrence, a division of Bantam Doubleday Dell Publishing Group, Inc.

Miles Orvell. "On the Humor in 'Good Country People'" from *Flannery O'Connor: An Introduction* by Miles Orvell, p. 141. Copyright © 1991. Reprinted by permission of the University of Mississippi Press.

Grace Paley. "Samuel" from *Enormous Changes at the Last Minute* by Grace Paley. Copyright © 1960, 1962, 1965, 1967, 1968, 1971, 1972, 1974 by Grace Paley. Reprinted by permission of Farrar, Straus & Giroux, Inc.

Patrick Parrinder. "On Self-Restraint in 'Eveline'" from *James Joyce* by Patrick Parrinder. Copyright © 1984 by Cambridge University Press. Reprinted by permission.

C. H. Peake. "On Fear in 'Eveline'" from *James Joyce: The Citizen and the Artist* by C. H. Deake, p. 22. Copyright © 1977. Reprinted by permission of Stanford University Press.

James Quinn and Ross Baldessarini. "A Psychological Reading of 'The Birthmark'" from "The Birthmark: a Deathmark," *University of Hartford Studies in Literature* 13 (1981). Reprinted by permission.

Fritz Senn. "'The Boarding House' Seen as a Tale of Misdirection" excerpt from *James Joyce Quarterly* 23, no. 4 (1986). Copyright © 1986 by the University of Tulsa. Reprinted by permission.

E. Earle Stibitz. "Irony in 'The Minister's Black Veil'" from "Ironic Unity in Hawthorne's Black Veil," *American Literature* 34:2, 1962, © Duke University Press. Reprinted by permission of the publisher.

Kent Thompson. "Unreeling" reprinted from *Leaping Up, Sliding Away* by Kent Thompson with the permission of Goose Lane Editions. Copyright © 1986 by Kent Thompson.

Tatiana Tolstaya. Excerpt from "On the Golden Porch" by Tatiana Tolstaya, trans. by Antonina Bouis. Copyright © 1989 by Tatiana Tolstaya. Reprinted by permission of Alfred A. Knopf, Inc.

Lionel Trilling. "On Personal Identity in 'The Dead'" from *The Experience of Literature,* edited by Lionel Trilling, copyright © 1967 by Holt, Rinehart and Winston, Inc., reprinted by permission of the publisher.

Michael Tritt. Excerpt from "'Young Goodman Brown' and the Psychology of Projection." *Studies in Short Fiction* 23 (1986): 113–17. Copyright © 1986 by Newberry College. Reprinted by permission of Newberry College.

John Updike. "A & P" from *Pigeon Feathers and Other Stories* by John Updike. Copyright © 1962 by John Updike. Reprinted by permission of Alfred A. Knopf, Inc. Originally appeared in *The New Yorker*. "Fiction's Subtlety" from "The Importance of Fiction" in *Odd Jobs* by John Updike. Copyright © 1991. Reprinted by permission of the author and Alfred A. Knopf, Inc. Originally appeared in *Esquire* Magazine.

Karen Van Der Zee. "A Secret Sorrow." Copyright © 1981 by Karen Van Der Zee. All rights reserved. Reproduction with the permission of the publisher, Harlequin Enterprises Limited, 225 Duncan Mill Road, Don Mills, Ontario, Canada M3B 3K9.

Gore Vidal. "The Popularity of the Tarzan Books," excerpt from "Tarzan Revisited," *Esquire* Magazine, December 1963. Reprinted by permission of the William Morris Agency, Inc., on behalf of the author. Copyright © 1963 by Gore Vidal.

Hyatt H. Waggoner. "Hawthorne's Style" from *Nathaniel Hawthorne* by Hyatt H. Waggoner. University of Minnesota Pamphlets on American Writers No. 23. Copyright © 1962 by the University of Minnesota, © 1990 by Louise Waggoner. Reprinted by permission of the University of Minnesota Press, Minneapolis.

Florence L. Walzl. "On the Ending of 'The Dead,'" excerpt from "Gabriel and Michael: The Conclusion of 'The Dead'" in *James Joyce Quarterly* (Fall 1986, pp. 17–31). Copyright © 1986 by the University of Tulsa. Reprinted by permission.

Fay Weldon. "IND AFF." Copyright © Fay Weldon 1988. First published in *The Observer* Magazine, 7th August 1988, reprinted by permission of Sheil Land Associates, Inc., 43 Doughty Street, London WC1N 2LF.

Eudora Welty. "Livvie" from *The Wide Net and Other Stories* by Eudora Welty. Copyright 1942, 1970 by Eudora Welty. Reprinted by permission of Harcourt Brace Jovanovich, Inc. "On the Plots of 'The Bride Comes to Yellow Sky' and 'Miss Brill'" from "The Reading and Writing of Short Stories" by Eudora Welty. Copyright © 1949 by Eudora Welty, renewed 1977 by Eudora Welty. Reprinted by permission of Russell & Volkening as agents for Eudora Welty.

Gayle Edward Wilson. "Conflict in 'Barn Burning'" from "Being Pulled in Two Ways." Copyright © 1971. Reprinted by permission of the *Mississippi Quarterly: The Journal of Southern Culture*.

Virginia Woolf. "Lappin and Lapinova" from *A Haunted House and Other Stories* by Virginia Woolf. Copyright © 1944 and renewed 1972 by Harcourt Brace Jovanovich. Reprinted by permission of the publisher, the Estate of Virginia Woolf, and the Hogarth Press.

POETRY

M. H. Abrams. "The Speakers in 'Ode on a Grecian Urn'" from *Literature and Belief: English Institute Essays* by M. H. Abrams. Copyright © 1958, Columbia University Press, New York. Reprinted by permission of the publishers.

Diane Ackerman. "A Fine, a Private Place" from *Lady Faustus* by Diane Ackerman. Copyright © 1983 by Diane Ackerman. Reprinted by permission of the author.

Claribel Alegría. "I Am Mirror" from *Sobrevito* by Claribel Alegría. Reprinted by permission of the author.

Paula Gunn Allen. "Pocahontas to Her English Husband, John Rolfe" from *Skin and Bones* by Paula Gunn Allen. West End Press, Inc. 1988. Reprinted by permission.

A. R. Ammons. "Coward" is reprinted from *Diversifications: Poems by A. R. Ammons* by A. R. Ammons. Reprinted by permission of W. W. Norton & Company, Inc. Copyright © 1975 by A. R. Ammons.

Charles R. Anderson. "Eroticism in 'Wild Nights — Wild Nights!'" from *Emily Dickinson's Poetry: Stairway of Surprise* by Charles R. Anderson. Copyright 1960 by Holt, Rinehart, and Winston. Reprinted by permission of the author.

Maya Angelou. "My Arkansas" from *And I Still Rise* by Maya Angelou. Copyright © 1978 by Maya Angelou. Reprinted by permission of Random House, Inc.

Richard Armour. "Going to Extremes" from *Light Armour* by Richard Armour. Reprinted by permission of Kathleen S. Armour.

John Ashbery. "Paradoxes and Oxymorons" from *The Shadow Train* by John Ashbery. Copyright © 1981 by John Ashbery. Reprinted by permission of Georges Borchardt, Inc.

Margaret Atwood. "You Fit Into Me" from *Power Politics* by Margaret Atwood (Toronto: House of Anansi Press, 1971). Reprinted by permission of Stoddart Publishing Co. Limited (Don Mills, Ontario) and Margaret Atwood, © 1980.

W. H. Auden. "The Unknown Citizen," "As I Walked Out One Evening," "Lay Your Sleeping Head, My Love," and "Musée des Beaux Arts" from *W. H. Auden: Collected Poems* by W. H. Auden, ed. Edward Mendelson. Copyright 1940 and renewed 1968 by W. H. Auden. Reprinted by permission of Random House, Inc. and Faber and Faber Ltd.

Regina Barreca. "Nighttime Fires" in *The Minnesota Review* (Fall 1986). Reprinted by permission of the author.

Matsuo Basho. "Under cherry trees" from *Japanese Haiku,* trans. by Peter Beilenson, Series I, © 1955–56, Peter Beilenson, Editor. Reprinted by permission of Peter Pauper Press, Inc.

Michael L. Baumann. "The 'Overwhelming Question' for Prufrock," excerpt from "Let Us Ask 'What Is It?'" in *Arizona Quarterly* 37 (Spring 1981) 47–58. Reprinted by permission.

John Berryman. "Dream Song 14" from *The Dream Songs* by John Berryman. Copyright © 1959, 1962, 1963, 1964, 1965, 1966, 1967, 1968, 1969 by John Berryman. Reprinted by permission of Farrar, Straus & Giroux, Inc.

Mei-Mei Berssenbrugge. "Jealousy" reprinted by permission of Station Hill Press.

Elizabeth Bishop. "Sonnet of Intimacy" by Vinícius de Moraes, "Manners," "The Shampoo," "The Fish," "Five Flights Up," and "Sestina" from *The Complete Poems: 1927–1979* by Elizabeth Bishop. Copyright © 1979, 1983 by Alice Helen Methfessel. Reprinted by permission of Farrar, Straus & Giroux, Inc.

Harold Bloom. "On 'Bright Star!'" from *The Visionary Company* by Harold Bloom. Copyright © 1971 by Harold Bloom. Reprinted by permission of the author.

Robert Bly. "Waking from Sleep" from *Silence in the Snowy Fields* by Robert Bly. Copyright © 1962 by Robert Bly. Reprinted by permission of the author.

Louise Bogan. "Single Sonnet" from *The Blue Estuaries* by Louise Bogan. Copyright © 1956 by Charles Scribner's Sons. Renewal Copyright © 1964 by Louise Bogan. Reprinted by permission of Farrar, Straus & Giroux, Inc.

Anne Bradstreet. "Before the Birth of One of Her Children" and "The Author to Her Book," reprinted by permission of the publishers from *The Works of Anne Bradstreet*, ed. by Jeannine Hensley, Cambridge, Mass.: Harvard University Press, Copyright © 1967 by the President and Fellows of Harvard College.

Cleanth Brooks. "History in 'Ode on a Grecian Urn'" first published in *The Sewanee Review*, vol. 52, no. 1 (Winter 1944). Reprinted with the permission of the author and the editor.

Gwendolyn Brooks. "The Bean Eaters," "We Real Cool," and "The Mother" from *Blacks* by Gwendolyn Brooks. Copyright © 1991 by Gwendolyn Brooks. Reprinted by permission of the author.

Reuben A. Brower. "On the 'Essence of Winter Sleep' in 'After Apple-Picking'" from *The Poetry of Robert Frost: Constellations of Intention* by Reuben A. Brower. Copyright © 1963 by Reuben A. Brower; renewed 1991 by Helen P. Brower. Reprinted by permission of Oxford University Press, Inc.

Michael Cadnum. "Cat Spy," copyright © by Michael Cadnum. First appeared in *Light Year '86*. Reprinted by permission of the author.

Tracy Chapman. "Fast Car" copyright © 1988 EMI April Music Inc. and Purple Rabbit Music. All rights controlled and administered by EMI April Music Inc. All rights reserved. International copyright secured. Used by permission.

Helen Chasin. "The Word *Plum*" from *Coming Close and Other Poems* by Helen Chasin. Copyright © 1968 by Yale University Press. Reprinted by permission.

John Ciardi. "Suburban" is reprinted from *For Instance* by John Ciardi, by permission of W. W. Norton & Company, Inc. Copyright © 1979 by John Ciardi.

Amy Clampitt. "Nothing Stays Put" from *Westward* by Amy Clampitt. Copyright © 1990 by Amy Clampitt. Reprinted by permission of Alfred A. Knopf, Inc.

Lucille Clifton. "For de Lawd" and "come home from the movies" from *good woman: poems and a memoir, 1969–1980* by Lucille Clifton. Copyright © 1987 by Lucille Clifton. Reprinted with the permission of BOA Editions, Ltd., 92 Park Avenue, Brockport, NY 14420.

Leonard Cohen. "Suzanne" copyright 1967 Leonard Cohen Stranger Music, Inc. Used by permission. All rights reserved.

Edmund Conti. "Pragmatist" from *Light Year '86*. Reprinted by permission of the author.

Robert G. Cook. "The Influence of Emerson's 'Self-Reliance' on Prufrock" from "Emerson's 'Self-Reliance,' Sweeney, and Prufrock," *American Literature* 42:2 (May 1970). Copyright © 1962 Duke University Press. Reprinted by permission of the publisher.

Herbert R. Coursen, Jr. "A Reading of 'Stopping by Woods on a Snowy Evening,'" excerpt from "The Ghost of Christmas Past: 'Stopping by the Woods on a Snowy Evening," *College English* (December 1962). Copyright © 1962 by the National Council of Teachers of English. Reprinted with permission.

Robert Creeley. "Fathers" from *Memory Gardens* by Robert Creeley. Copyright © 1986 by Robert Creeley. Reprinted by permission of New Directions Publishing Corporation.

Sally Croft. "Home-Baked Bread" from *Light Year '86*. Reprinted by permission of the author.

Countee Cullen. "For a Lady I Know" and "Saturday's Child" from *Color* by Countee Cullen. Copyright © 1925 by Harper & Brothers; copyright renewed 1953 by Ida M. Cullen. Reprinted by permission of GRM Associates, Inc., Agents for the Estate of Ida M. Cullen.

e. e. cummings. "in Just-" and "Buffalo Bill 's" reprinted from *tulips and chimneys* by e. e. cummings, Edited by George James Firmage, by permission of Liveright Publishing Corporation. Copyright 1923, 1925 and renewed 1951, 1953 by e. e. cummings. Copyright © 1973, 1976 by the Trustees for the e. e. cummings Trust. Copyright © 1973, 1976 by George James Firmage. "my sweet old etcetera," "since feeling is first," "she being Brand," and "next to of course god america i" reprinted from *is 5: poems* by e. e. cummings, edited by George James Firmage, by permission of Liveright Publishing Corporation. Copyright © 1985 by e. e. cummings Trust. Copyright 1926 by Horace Liveright. Copyright © 1954 by e. e. cummings. Copyright © 1985 by George James Firmage. "l(a" and "anyone lived in a pretty how town" are reprinted from *Complete Poems: 1913–1962*, by e. e. cummings, by permission of Liveright Publishing Corporation. Copyright © 1923, 1925, 1931, 1935, 1938, 1939, 1940, 1944, 1945, 1946, 1947, 1948, 1949, 1950, 1951, 1952, 1953, 1954, 1955, 1956, 1957, 1958, 1959, 1960, 1961, 1962 by the Trustees for the E. E. Cummings Trust. Copyright © 1961, 1963, 1968 by Marion Morehouse Cummings. "On the Artist's Responsibility" reprinted by permission of the publisher from *i: six nonlectures* by e. e. cummings, Cambridge, Mass.: Harvard University Press, Copyright © 1953 by e. e. cummings; © 1981 by E. E. Cummings Trust.

H. D. "Garden II" (Heat) from *Collected Poems 1912–1944*. Copyright © 1982 by the Estate of Hilda Doolittle. Reprinted by permission of New Directions Publishing Corporation.

Peter De Vries. "To His Importunate Mistress," copyright © 1986 by Peter De Vries. This poem first appeared in *The New Yorker*. Reprinted by permission of the author and the Watkins/Loomis Agency.

Emily Dickinson. "A Bird came down the Walk," "Success is counted sweetest," "Much Madness is divinest Sense," "The Brain — is wider than the Sky," "I heard a Fly buzz — when I died," "If I shouldn't be alive," "I taste a liquor never brewed — " "'Heaven' — is what I cannot reach!" "I'm Nobody! Who are you?" "The Robin's my Criterion for Tune," "The Soul Selects her own Society," "I dwell in possibility — " "After great pain, a formal feeling comes — " "Because I could not stop for Death — " "My Life had stood — a Loaded Gun — " "Tell all the Truth but tell it slant — " "From all the Jails the Boys and Girls," "I never saw a Moor — " "Shall I take thee, the Poet said," "There's a certain Slant of light" reprinted by permission of the publishers and the Trustees of Amherst College from *The Poems of Emily Dickinson*, Thomas H. Johnson, ed., Cambridge, Mass.: The Belknap Press of Harvard University Press, Copyright © 1951, 1955, 1979, 1983 by the President and Fellows of Harvard College. Also from *The Complete Poems of Emily Dickinson* edited by Thomas H. Johnson. Copyright 1929 by Martha Dickinson Bianchi; Copyright © renewed 1957 by Mary L. Hampson. By permission of Little, Brown and Company.

Rita Dove. "The Satisfaction Coal Company" reprinted from *Thouras and Beulah* by Rita Dove by permission of Carnegie Mellon University Press. © 1986 by Rita Dove.

Bernard Duyfhuizen. "'To His Coy Mistress': On How a Female Might Respond," excerpt from "Textual Harassment of Marvell's Coy Mistress: The Institutionalization of Masculine Criticism," *College English* (April 1988). Copyright © 1988 by the National Council of Teachers of English. Reprinted with permission.

Richard Eberhart. "The Groundhog" from *Collected Poems 1930–1986* by Richard Eberhart. Copyright © 1960, 1976, 1988 by Richard Eberhart. Reprinted by permission of Oxford University Press, Inc.

Jane Donahue Eberwein. "On Making Do with Dickinson" from "Doing Without: Dickinson as Yankee Woman Poet" by Jane Donahue Eberwein. Reprinted with permission of G. K. Hall, an imprint of Macmillan Publishing Company, from *Critical Essays on Emily Dickinson* by Paul J. Ferlazzo. Copyright © 1984 by Paul J. Ferlazzo.

T. S. Eliot. "Macavity: The Mystery Cat" from *Old Possum's Book of Practical Cats*, copyright 1939 by T. S. Eliot and renewed 1967 by Esme Valerie Eliot. Reprinted by permission of Harcourt Brace Jovanovich, Inc. and Faber and Faber Limited.

Louise Erdrich. "Captivity" from *Jacklight* by Louise Erdrich. Copyright © 1984 by Louise Erdrich. Reprinted by permission of Henry Holt and Company, Inc.

Martín Espada. "Tiburón" from *Trumpets from the Islands of Their Evictions* by Martín Espada. Copyright © 1987 by Bilingual Press/Editorial Bilingüe. Reprinted by permission of Bilingual Press/Editorial Bilingüe, Arizona State University, Tempe, AZ.

Elizabeth Eybers. "Emily Dickinson" from *Longman Anthology of World Literature by Women* edited by Marian Arkin and Barbara Shollar. Copyright © 1989 by Longman Publishing Group.

Ruth Fainlight. "Flower Feet" reprinted by permission; © 1989 Ruth Fainlight. Originally in *The New Yorker*.

Faiz Ahmed Faiz. "Prison Daybreak" from *The True Subject: Selected Poems of Faiz Ahmed Faiz*. Copyright © 1988 by Princeton University Press. Reprinted by permission of Princeton University Press.

Blanche Farley. "The Lover Not Taken" from *Light Year '85*. Reprinted by permission of the author.

Kenneth Fearing. "AD" from *New and Collected Poems* (Indiana University Press, 1956). Reprinted by permission of the Estate of Kenneth Fearing.

F. Scott Fitzgerald. "On the 'Extraordinary Genius' of Keats" from *The Crack-Up*. Copyright 1945 by New Directions Publishing Corp. Reprinted by permission of the New Directions Publishing Corporation.

Robert J. Fogelin. "A Case against Metaphors" from *Figuratively Speaking*, Yale University Press. Copyright © 1988. Reprinted by permission.

Carolyn Forché. "The Colonel" from *The Country Between Us* by Carolyn Forché. Copyright © 1980 by Carolyn Forché. Reprinted by permission of HarperCollins Publishers.

Robert Francis. "Excellence" and "Glass" reprinted from *Robert Francis: Collected Poems, 1936–1976* (Amherst: University of Massachusetts Press, 1976), copyright © 1941, 1949, 1972 by Robert Francis. Reprinted by permission of University of Massachusetts Press. "Catch" and "The Pitcher," copyright © 1950, 1953 by Robert Francis. Reprinted from *The Orb Weaver*, Wesleyan University Press by permission of the University Press of New England.

Robert Frost. "Acquainted with the Night," "Fire and Ice," "Stopping by Woods on a Snowy Evening," "Desert Places," "Design," "Neither Out Far nor In Deep," "Provide, Provide," "The Silken Tent," "The Gift Outright," "Nothing Gold Can Stay," "For Once, Then, Something," and "A Considerable Speck" from *The Poetry of Robert Frost* edited by Edward Connery Lathem. Copyright 1923, 1928, © 1964, 1969 by Holt, Rinehart and Winston. Copyright 1936, 1942, 1951, © 1956 by Robert Frost. Copyright © 1964, 1970 by Lesley Frost Ballantine. "Oven Bird," "The Road Not Taken," "The Pasture," "Mending Wall," "Home Burial," "After Apple-Picking," "Birches," and "Out, Out —" from *The Poetry of Robert Frost* edited by Edward Connery Lathem. Copyright 1916, 1930, 1939, © 1967, 1969 by Holt, Rinehart and Winston. Copyright 1944, © 1958 by Robert Frost. Copyright © 1967 by Lesley Frost Ballantine. Henry Holt and Company, Publisher. "In White" from *The Dimensions of Robert Frost* by Reginald L. Cook. Copyright © 1958 by Reginald L. Cook. Excerpt from "The Figure a Poem Makes" from *Selected Prose of Robert Frost* edited by Hyde Cox and Edward Connery Lathem. Copyright 1939, © 1967 by Holt, Rinehart and Winston. All of the above reprinted by permission of Henry Holt and Company, Inc. "On the Living Part of a Poem" reprinted by permission of New York University Press from *A Swinger of Birches: A Portrait of Robert Frost* by Sidney Cox. Copyright © 1957 by New York University Press, Inc. "On the Way to Read a Poem" from "Poetry and School" by Robert Frost in *The Atlantic Monthly*, June 1951. Reprinted by permission of Peter Gilbert.

Alice Fulton. "On the Validity of Free Verse" from *Ecstatic Occasions, Expedient Forms*, David Lehman, ed. Reprinted by permission of the author.

Tess Gallagher. "Black Silk" from *Amplitude* by Tess Gallagher. Copyright © 1987 by Tess Gallagher. Reprinted with the permission of Graywolf Press, Saint Paul, Minnesota.

Deborah Garrison. "She Was Waiting to Be Told" reprinted by permission. © 1990 Deborah Gottlieb Garrison. Originally in *The New Yorker*.

Diane Frolov and Andrew Schneider. Excerpt from "Get Real," script #77514, Episode 8 of *Northern Exposure*, aired on CBS. Copyright © 1991 by Universal City Studios, Inc. Reprinted by permission of Universal Studios, Inc.

Sandra M. Gilbert and Susan Gubar. "On Dickinson's White Dress" excerpted from *The Madwoman in the Attic* by Gilbert and Gubar. Yale University Press, 1979. Reprinted by permission.

Allen Ginsberg. "America" copyright © 1956 by Allen Ginsberg. "A Supermarket in California" copyright © 1955 by Allen Ginsberg. Both from *Collected Poems 1947–1980* by Allen Ginsberg. Reprinted by permission of HarperCollins Publishers.

Nikki Giovanni. "Nikki-Rosa" from *Black Feeling, Black Talk, Black Judgment* by Nikki Giovanni. Copyright © 1968, 1970 by Nikki Giovanni. "Poetry" from *The Women and the Men*. Copyright © 1968–1970 by Nikki Giovanni. Reprinted by permission of William Morrow & Company, Inc.

Judy Grahn. "She Who Bears It" from *The Work of the Common Woman*. Reprinted by permission of the Crossing Press.

Donald J. Greiner. "On What Comes 'After Apple-Picking'" from "The Indispensable Robert Frost" by Donald J. Greiner. Reprinted with permission of G. K. Hall, an imprint of Macmillan Publishing Company, from *Critical Essays on Robert Frost*, Philip L. Gerber, editor. Copyright © 1982 by Philip L. Gerber.

Eamon Grennan. "Bat" reprinted by permission; © 1991 Eamon Grennan. Originally in *The New Yorker*.

Donald Hall. "To a Waterfowl" from *The Town of Hill* by Donald Hall. Copyright © 1975 by Donald Hall. Reprinted by permission of David R. Godine, Publisher. "My Son, My Executioner" from *Old and New Poems* by Donald Hall. Copyright © 1990 by Donald Hall. Reprinted by permission of Ticknor & Fields, a Houghton Mifflin Co. imprint. All rights reserved.

Mark Halliday. "Graded Paper" from *Michigan Quarterly Review*. Reprinted by permission of the author.

William Hathaway. "Oh, Oh" from *Light Year '86*. This poem was originally published in the *Cincinnati Poetry Review*. Reprinted by permission of the author.

Robert Hayden. "Those Winter Sundays" is reprinted from *Angle of Ascent: New and Selected Poems*, by Robert Hayden, by permission of Liveright Publishing Corporation. Copyright © 1966, 1970, 1972, 1975 by Robert Hayden.

Seamus Heaney. "Digging" and "Mid-term Break" from *Poems: 1965–1975* by Seamus Heaney. Copyright © 1966, 1969, 1972, 1975, 1980 by Seamus Heaney. Reprinted by permission of Farrar, Straus & Giroux, Inc. and Faber and Faber Limited.

Anthony Hecht. "The Dover Bitch" from *Collected Earlier Poems* by Anthony Hecht. Copyright © 1990 by Anthony E. Hecht. Reprinted by permission of Alfred E. Knopf, Inc.

Judy Page Heitzman. "The Schoolroom on the Second Floor of the Knitting Mill" reprinted by permission. © 1991 Judy Page Heitzman. Originally in *The New Yorker*.

Thomas Wentworth Higginson. "On Meeting Dickinson for the First Time" reprinted by permission of the publishers from *The Letters of Emily Dickinson*, edited by Thomas H. Johnson, Cambridge, Mass.: The Belknap Press of Harvard University Press, Copyright © 1958, 1986 by the President and Fellows of Harvard College.

Conrad Hilberry. "The Frying Pan" first appeared in Field 19 (Fall 1978). Reprinted by permission of Oberlin College.

Edward Hirsch. "Fast Break" from *Wild Gratitude* by Edward Hirsch. Copyright © 1985 by Edward Hirsch. Reprinted by permission of Alfred A. Knopf, Inc.

Margaret Holley. "The Fireflies" copyright © 1991 Margaret Holley. Reprinted by permission of the author.

M. Carl Holman. "Mr. Z." Reprinted by permission of Mariella A. Holman.

A. E. Housman. "When I was one-and-twenty," "Loveliest of trees, the cherry now," "Terence, this is stupid stuff," "To an Athlete Dying Young," and "Is my team plowing" from *The Collected Poems of A. E. Housman*. Copyright 1939, 1940, © 1965 by Holt, Rinehart and Winston. Copyright © 1967, 1968 by Robert E. Symons. Reprinted by permission of Henry Holt and Company, Inc.

Langston Hughes. "Ballad of the Landlord" from *Montage of a Dream Deferred* by Langston Hughes. Copyright 1951 by Langston Hughes. Copyright renewed 1979 by George Houston Bass. Reprinted by permission of Harold Ober Associates Incorporated. "Harlem (A Dream Deferred)" from *The Panther and the Lash* by Langston Hughes. Copyright © 1951 by Langston Hughes. Reprinted by permission of Alfred A. Knopf, Inc.

Paul Humphrey. "Blow" from *Light Year '86*. Reprinted by permission of the author.

Mark Irwin. "Icicles" from *The Halls of Desire* by Mark Irwin. Copyright © 1987. Reprinted by permission of Galileo Press.

Bonnie Jacobson. "On Being Served Apples" from *Stopping for Time* by Bonnie Jacobson. Copyright © 1989. Reprinted by permission of GreenTower Press.

Randall Jarrell. "Next Day" © 1963, 1965 by Randall Jarrell from the book *The Lost World* published in *Randall Jarrell: the Complete Poems*, by Farrar, Straus, & Giroux. Permission by Rhoda Weyr Agency, NY. "The Death of the Ball Turrett Gunner" from *The Complete Poems* by Randall Jarrell. Copyright © 1945, renewal copyright © 1972 by Mrs. Randall Jarrell. Reprinted by permission of Farrar, Straus & Giroux, Inc.

Donald Justice. "Order In the Streets" from *Loser Weepers*. Reprinted by permission of the author. "The Snowfall" from *Summer Anniversaries*. Copyright © 1981 revised edition by Donald Justice. Wesleyan University Press by permission of University Press of New England.

Karl Keller. "Robert Frost on Dickinson" from *The Only Kangaroo Among the Beauty: Emily Dickinson in America*. Copyright © 1979. Reprinted by permission of Johns Hopkins University Press.

X. J. Kennedy. "First Confession" from *Nude Descending a Staircase* by X. J. Kennedy, copyright © 1961 by X. J. Kennedy. Reprinted by permission of Curtis Brown, Ltd. "In a Prominent Bar in Secaucus One Day" from *Cross Ties,* © 1985 by X. J. Kennedy. Reprinted by permission of the University of Georgia Press.

Galway Kinnell. "After Making Love, We Hear Footsteps" and "Blackberry Eating" from *Mortal Acts, Mortal Words* by Galway Kinnell. Copyright © 1980 by Galway Kinnell. Excerpt from "For Robert Frost" from *Flower Herding on Mount Monadnock* by Galway Kinnell. Copyright © 1964 by Galway Kinnell. All reprinted by permission of Houghton Mifflin Company. All rights reserved. "The Male and Female Principles of Poetry," from "Being with Reality: an Interview with Galway Kinnell," *Columbia Magazine of Poetry and Prose*, 14 (1989). Reprinted by permission of Galway Kinnell.

Carolyn Kizer. "Food for Love," reprinted from *Yin: New Poems* by Carolyn Kizer. Copyright © 1984 by Carolyn Kizer. Reprinted with the permission of BOA Editions, Ltd., 92 Park Ave., Brockport, NY 14420.

Etheridge Knight. "Eastern Guard Tower" from *Poems from Prison* by Etheridge Knight. Copyright © 1968 by Etheridge Knight (Broadside Press). "A Watts Mother Mourns While Boiling Beans" from *Belly Song and Other Poems* by Etheridge Knight. Copyright © 1973 (Broadside Press). Reprinted by permission of the author.

Yusef Komunyakaa. "Facing It" from *Dien Cai Dau*. Copyright © 1988 by Yusef Komunyakaa. Wesleyan University Press by permission of University Press of New England.

Ted Kooser. "The Blind Always Come as Such a Surprise" from *Heartland II: Poets of the Midwest*, edited by Lucien Stryk. Copyright © 1975. Reprinted by permission of Northern Illinois University Press. "Selecting a Reader" from *Sure Signs: New and Selected Poems*, by Ted Kooser, by permission of the University of Pittsburgh Press. Copyright © 1980 by Ted Kooser.

Maxine Kumin. "Woodchucks," copyright © 1971 by Maxine Kumin, "Morning Swim," copyright © 1965 by Maxine Kumin, from *Our Ground Time Here Will Be Brief* by Maxine Kumin. Used by permission of Viking Penguin, a division of Penguin Books USA Inc.

Philip Larkin. "Home Is So Sad" and "A Study of Reading Habits" from *The Whitsun Weddings* by Philip Larkin. Reprinted by permission of Faber and Faber Limited.

Richmond Lattimore. "The Crabs" from *Poems from Three Decades* (Scribner's). Reprinted by permission of Mrs. Richmond Lattimore.

Tato Laviera. "AmeRícan" reprinted from *AmeRícan* (Houston: Arte Publico Press–University of Houston, 1985) with permission of the publisher.

D. H. Lawrence. "Snake" from *The Complete Poems of D. H. Lawrence* by D. H. Lawrence. Copyright © 1964, 1971 by Angelo Ravagli and C. M. Weekley, Executors of the Estate of Frieda Lawrence Ravagli. Used by permission of Viking Penguin, a division of Penguin Books USA Inc.

David Lenson. "On the Contemporary Use of Rhyme" from *The Chronicle of Higher Education*, February 24, 1988. Reprinted by permission of the author.

Denise Levertov. "O Taste and See" from *Poems 1960–1967*. Copyright © 1964 by Denise Levertov. "Gathered at the River" from *Oblique Prayers*. Copyright © 1984 by Denise Levertov. "News Items" from *The Freeing of the Dust*. Copyright © 1975 by Denise Levertov. All of these reprinted by permission of New Directions Publishing Corporation. "On 'Gathered at the River'" from "'Gathered at the River': Background and Form" in *Singular Voices: American Poetry Today*, edited by Stephen Berg. Reprinted by permission of Denise Levertov.

Li Ho. "A Beautiful Girl Combs Her Hair" from *Four T'ang Poets: Field Translation Series #4*. Copyright © Oberlin College Press, 1980. Reprinted by permission.

Audre Lorde. "Hanging Fire" is reprinted from *The Black Unicorn: Poems by Audre Lorde*, by permission of W. W. Norton & Company, Inc. Copyright © 1978 by Audre Lorde. Permission to use "Poems Are Not Luxuries" is granted by Audre Lorde.

Robert Lowell. "Skunk Hour" from *Life Studies* by Robert Lowell. Copyright © 1956, 1959 by Robert Lowell. Renewal copyright © 1981, 1986, 1987 by Harriet W. Lowell, Caroline Lowell & Sheridan Lowell. Reprinted by permission of Farrar, Straus & Giroux, Inc.

Katharyn Howd Machan. "Hazel Tells LaVerne" from *Light Year '85*. Reprinted by permission of the author.

Archibald MacLeish. "Ars Poetica" from *Collected Poems 1917–1982* by Archibald MacLeish. Copyright © 1985 by the Estate of Archibald MacLeish. Reprinted by permission of Houghton Mifflin Company. All rights reserved.

Elaine Magarrell. "The Joy of Cooking" from *Sometime the Cow Kick Your Head, Light Year 88/89*. Reprinted by permission of the author.

Muhammad al-Maghut. "An Arab Traveler in a Space Ship" from *Modern Arabic Poetry: An Anthology*, edited by Salma Khadera Jayyusi. Copyright © 1987, Columbia University Press, New York. Reprinted by permission of the publisher.

Nazik al-Mála'ika. "I am" from *Issues of Contemporary in Women of the Fertile Crescent: Modern Poetry by Arab Women*, ed. Kamal Boullata. Reprinted by permission of Three Continents Press, Washington, D.C.

David McCord. "Epitaph on a Waiter" from *Odds without Ends*. Reprinted by permission of the author.

Michael McFee. "In Medias Res" from *Light Year '86*. Reprinted by permission of the author.

Claude McKay. "The Harlem Dancer" from *Selected Poems of Claude McKay*, published by Twayne Publishers, a division of G. K. Hall. Copyright © 1981. Reprinted by permission of the Estate of Claude McKay.

Peter Meinke. "The ABC of Aerobics" from *Night Watch on the Chesapeake*, by Peter Meinke, by permission of the University of Pittsburgh Press. Copyright © 1987 by Peter Meinke.

James Merrill. "Casual Wear" from *Selected Poems 1946–1985* by James Merrill. Copyright © 1992 by James Merrill. Reprinted by permission of Alfred A. Knopf.

Edna St. Vincent Millay. "Never May the Fruit Be Plucked," "I Too beneath Your Moon, Almighty Sex," and "I Will Put Chaos Into Fourteen Lines" copyright © 1923, 1939, 1951, 1967 by Edna St. Vincent Millay and Norma Millay Ellis. From *Collected Poems*, Harper & Row. Reprinted by permission of Elizabeth Barnett, literary executor.

Janice Townley Moore. "To A Wasp" from *Light Year '85*. Reprinted by permission of the author.

Marianne Moore. "The Fish" and "Poetry" reprinted with permission of Macmillan Publishing Company from *Collected Poems of Marianne Moore*. Copyright 1935 by Marianne Moore, renewed 1963 by Marianne Moore and T. S. Eliot.

Robert Morgan. "On the Shape of a poem" (*Epoch* Fall/Winter, 1983) reprinted by permission of the author. "Mountain Graveyard" from *Sigodlin*. Copyright © 1990 by Robert Morgan. Wesleyan University Press by permission of University Press of New England.

Jon Mukand. "Lullaby" from *Sutured Words: Contemporary Poems About Medicine*, ed. Jon Mukand. Aviva Press, 1987. Copyright © Jon Mukand.

Howard Nemerov. "Life Cycle of Common Man" from *The Collected Poems of Howard Nemerov* (University of Chicago Press, 1977) and "The Fourth of July." Both reprinted by permission of Margaret Nemerov, Trustee, the Howard Nemerov Trust.

Pablo Neruda. "Sweetness, always" from *Extravagaria* by Pablo Neruda. Translation copyright © 1969, 1970, 1972, 1974 by Alastair Reid. Originally published as *Estravagario,* copyright © 1958 by Editorial Losada, S.A., Buenos Aires. Reprinted by permission of Farrar, Straus & Giroux, Inc.

John Frederick Nims. "Love Poem" from *Selected Poems.* Copyright © 1982 by the University of Chicago. All rights reserved.

Frank O'Hara. "Ave Maria" from *The Collected Poems of Frank O'Hara.* Reprinted by permission.

Sharon Olds. "Rite of Passage" and "Sex Without Love" from *The Dead and the Living* by Sharon Olds. Copyright © 1975, 1978, 1979, 1980, 1981, 1982, 1983 by Sharon Olds. Reprinted by permission of Alfred A. Knopf, Inc.

Simon J. Ortiz. "My Father's Song" from *Going for the Rain* by Simon J. Ortiz. Copyright © 1976.

Wilfred Owen. "Dulce et Decorum Est" and "Anthem for Doomed Youth" from *The Collected Poems of Wilfred Owen.* Copyright © 1963 by Chatto & Windus, Ltd. Published by New Directions Publishing Company and The Hogarth Press. Reprinted by permission of New Directions Publishing Corporation, the Estate of Wilfred Owen, and Random Century Limited.

Dorothy Parker. "One Perfect Rose" from *The Portable Dorothy Parker* by Dorothy Parker, Introduction by Brendan Gill. Copyright 1928, renewed © 1956 by Dorothy Parker. Used by permission of Viking Penguin, a division of Penguin Books USA Inc.

Linda Pastan. "after minor surgery" is reprinted from *PM/AM: New and Selected Poems,* by Linda Pastan, by permission of W. W. Norton & Company, Inc. Copyright © 1982 by Linda Pastan. "Marks" is reprinted from *The Five Stages of Grief: Poems by Linda Pastan,* by permission of W. W. Norton & Company, Inc. Copyright © 1978 by Linda Pastan.

Octavio Paz. "The street" from *Early Poems 1935–1955.* Reprinted by permission of Indiana University Press.

Laurence Perrine. "The limerick's never averse" from *Light Year '86.* Reprinted by permission of the author.

John B. Pickard. "On 'I heard a Fly buzz — when I died'" from *Emily Dickinson: An Introduction and Interpretation* by John B. Pickard. Copyright © 1967 by Holt, Rinehart and Winston, Inc., reprinted by permission of the publisher.

Marge Piercy. "Barbie Doll," "The Secretary Chant," and "A Work of Artifice" from *Circles on the Water* by Marge Piercy. Copyright © 1969, 1971, 1973 by Marge Piercy. Reprinted by permission of Alfred A. Knopf, Inc.

Sylvia Plath. "Metaphors" copyright © 1960 by Ted Hughes. "Daddy" and "Mirror" copyright © 1963 by Ted Hughes. All from *The Collected Poems of Sylvia Plath,* ed. by Ted Hughes. Reprinted by permission of HarperCollins Publishers. "On 'Headline Poetry'" from "Context," *London Magazine,* February, 1962. Reprinted by permission.

Ruth Porritt. "Read this Poem from the Bottom Up" originally appeared in *The Laurel Review* and is reprinted by permission of the author.

Ezra Pound. "The Garden," "The River-Merchant's Wife: A Letter," and "In a Station of the Metro" from *Personae.* Copyright 1926 by Ezra Pound. Reprinted by permission of New Directions Publishing Corporation. "On Free Verse" from *The Literary Essays of Ezra Pound.* Copyright 1935 by Ezra Pound. Reprinted by permission of New Directions Publishing Corporation.

Dudley Randall. "Ballad of Birmingham" from *Poem Counter Poem* by Danner and Randall (Broadside Press).

Henry Reed. "Naming of Parts" from *A Map of Verona.* Reprinted by permission of the Estate of Henry Reed.

John Repp. "Cursing the Hole in the Screen, Wondering at the Romance Some Find In Summer." Reprinted by permission of the author.

David S. Reynolds. "Popular Literature and 'Wild Nights — Wild Nights!'" from *Beneath the American Renaissance* by David S. Reynolds. Copyright © 1988 by David S. Reynolds. Reprinted by permission of Alfred A. Knopf, Inc.

Adrienne Rich. "Living in Sin" is reprinted from *The Fact of a Doorframe: Poems Selected and New, 1950–1984,* by Adrienne Rich, by permission of W. W. Norton & Company, Inc. Copyright © 1984 by Adrienne Rich. Copyright © 1975, 1978 by W. W. Norton & Company, Inc. Copyright © 1981 by Adrienne Rich.

Rainer Maria Rilke. "The Panther" from *The Selected Poetry of Rainer Maria Rilke* by Rainer Maria Rilke, trans. by Stephen Mitchell. Copyright © 1982 by Stephen Mitchell. Reprinted by permission of Random House, Inc.

Alberto Ríos. "Seniors" from *Five Indiscretions.* Copyright © 1985 by Alberto Ríos. Reprinted by permission of the author.

Edwin Arlington Robinson. "Mr Flood's Party" reprinted with permission of Macmillan Publishing Company from *Collected Poems of Edwin Arlington Robinson.* Copyright 1921 by Edwin Arlington Robinson, renewed 1949 by Ruth Nivison.

Theodore Roethke. "I Knew A Woman," copyright 1954 by Theodore Roethke. "Root Cellar," copyright 1943 by Modern Poetry Association, Inc. "My Papa's Waltz," copyright 1942 by Hearst Magazines, Inc. from *The Collected Poems of Theodore Roethke* by Theodore Roethke. Used by permission of Doubleday, a division of Bantam Doubleday Dell Publishing Group, Inc.

Katerina Anghelaki-Rooke. "Tourism" from *Longman Anthology of World Literature by Women* edited by Marian Arkin and Barbara Shollar. Copyright © 1989 by Longman Publishing Group.

Frederick L. Rusch. "Society and Character in 'The Love Song of J. Alfred Prufrock'" from "Approaching Literature Through the Social Psychology of Erich Fromm" in *Psychological Perspectives on Literature: Freudian Dissidents and Non-Freudians,* ed. Joseph Natoli. Copyright © 1984. Reprinted by permission of Shoe String Press, Inc.

Sappho. "With his venom" from *Sappho: A New Translation,* trans./ed. Mary Barnard. © 1958, 1984 by Mary Barnard. Reprinted by permission of the University of California Press.

Elisabeth Schneider. "Hints of Eliot in Prufrock" from "Prufrock and After: The Theme of Change," *PMLA* 87 (1952): 1103–17. Reprinted by permission of the Modern Language Association of America.

John R. Searle. "Figuring Out Metaphors" from *Expression and Meaning.* Reprinted by permission of Cambridge University Press.

Anne Sexton. "Her Kind" from *To Bedlam and Part Way Back* by Anne Sexton. Copyright © 1960 by Anne Sexton. "Lobster" from *45 Mercy Street* by Anne Sexton. First published in *Antœus.* Copyright © 1976 by Linda Gray Sexton and Loring Conant, Jr., Executors of the Estate of Anne Sexton. Both reprinted by permission of Houghton Mifflin Company. All rights reserved.

Karl Shapiro. "Libraries" from *The Bourgeois Poet* by Karl Shapiro (Random House, 1964). Copyright © 1985 by Karl Shapiro. Reprinted by arrangement with Wieser & Wieser, Inc. 118 East 25th Street, New York, NY 10010.

Leslie Marmon Silko. "Where Mountain Lion Lay Down with Deer" copyright © 1981 by Leslie Marmon Silko. Reprinted from *Storyteller* by Leslie Marmon Silko, published by Seaver Books, New York, New York. Reprinted by permission of the publisher.

Louis Simpson. "American Poetry" from *At the End of the Open Road.* Copyright © 1963 by Louis Simpson. Wesleyan University Press by permission of University Press of New England.

David R. Slavitt. "Titanic" from *Big Nose* by David R. Slavitt. Copyright © 1983 by David R. Slavitt. Reprinted by permission of Louisiana State University Press.

Ernest Slyman. "Lightning Bugs" from *Sometime the Cow Kick Your Head, Light Year 88/89.* Reprinted by permission of the author.

Stevie Smith. "Valuable" from *Collected Poems.* Copyright © 1972 by Stevie Smith. Reprinted by permission of New Directions Publishing Corporation.

W. D. Snodgrass. "April Inventory" from *Heart's Needle* by W. D. Snodgrass. Copyright © 1957 by W. D. Snodgrass. Reprinted by permission of Alfred A. Knopf, Inc.

Gary Snyder. "After weeks of watching the roof leak" from "Hitch Hiking" in *The Back Country.* Copyright © 1967 by Gary Snyder. Reprinted by permission of New Directions Publishing Corporation.

Cathy Song. "The White Porch" from *Picture Bride.* Copyright © 1983 by Cathy Song. Copyright © 1983 by Yale University. Reprinted by permission.

Wole Soyinka. "Future Plans" from *A Shuttle in the Crypt* by Wole Soyinka. Copyright © 1972 by Wole Soyinka. Reprinted by permission of Hill & Wang, a division of Farrar, Straus & Giroux, Inc.

William Stafford. "Traveling through the Dark" from *Stories that Could Be True* by William Stafford. Copyright © 1960, 1977 by William Stafford. Reprinted by permission of the author.

George Starbuck. "Japanese Fish" from *Light Year '86.* Reprinted by permission of the author.

Timothy Steele. "Waiting for the Storm" from *Sapphics Against Anger and Other Poems.* Copyright © 1986 by Timothy Steele. Reprinted by permission of the author.

Stephen Stepanchev. "Cornered on the Corner" reprinted by permission; © 1991 Stephen Stepanchev. Originally in *The New Yorker.*

Jim Stevens. "Schizophrenia" first appeared in *Light: The Quarterly of Light Verse* (Spring, 1992). Copyright © 1992 by Jim Stevens. Reprinted by permission.

Wallace Stevens. "The Emperor of Ice-Cream," and "Sunday Morning" from *The Collected Poems of Wallace Stevens* by Wallace Stevens. Copyright 1923 and renewed 1951 by Wallace Stevens. Reprinted by permission of Alfred A. Knopf, Inc.

Jack Stillinger. "On 'The Eve of St. Agnes'" from "The Hoodwinking of Madeline: Skepticism in the Eve of St. Agnes," *Studies in Philology*, 58 (1961). Copyright © 1961 by the University of North Carolina Press. Reprinted by permission.

Mark Strand. "The Continuous Life" from *The Continuous Life* by Mark Strand. Copyright © 1990 by Mark Strand. Reprinted by permission of Alfred A. Knopf, Inc.

Robert H. Swennes. "Fear in 'Home Burial'" from "Man and Wife: the Dialogue of Contraries in Robert Frost's Poetry," *American Literature* 42:3, November 1970, © Duke University Press. Reprinted by permission of the publisher.

May Swenson. "A Nosty Fright" copyright © 1984 by May Swenson. "The Secret in the Cat" copyright © 1964 by May Swenson. Both used with permission of the Literary Estate of May Swenson.

Wislawa Szymborksa. "The Joy of Writing" from *Sounds, Feelings, Thoughts: Seventy Poems by Wislawa Szymborska*. Copyright © 1981 by Princeton University Press. Reprinted by permission of Princeton University Press.

Shinkichi Takahishi, "Explosion" from *The Penguin Book of Zen Poetry*, ed. and trans. Lucien Stryk and Takashi Ikemoto. Reprinted by permission of Lucien Stryk.

Dylan Thomas. "Do not go gentle into that good night," "Fern Hill," and "The Hand That Signed the Paper" from *Poems of Dylan Thomas*. Copyright 1939 by New Directions Publishing Corporation, 1945 by the Trustees for the Copyrights of Dylan Thomas, 1952 by Dylan Thomas. Reprinted by permission of New Directions Publishing Corporation and David Higham Associates. "On the Words in Poetry" from *Quite Early One Morning*. Copyright © 1964 by New Directions Publishing Corporation. Reprinted by permission of New Directions Publishing Corporation and David Higham Associates.

Mabel Loomis Todd. "The *Character* of Amherst" from *The Years and Hours of Emily Dickinson*, volume 2, by Jay Leda. Copyright © 1960. Reprinted by permission of Yale University Press.

Jean Toomer. "Reapers" is reprinted from *Cane* by Jean Toomer, by permission of Liveright Publishing Corporation. Copyright 1923 by Boni & Liveright. Copyright renewed 1951 by Jean Toomer.

Tomas Transtromer. "April and Silence" translated by Robin Fulton. First published in *The Kenyon Review* New Series, Summer 1991, vol. 13, no. 3. Copyright © 1991 by Kenyon College.

Lionel Trilling. "On Frost As a Terrifying Poet" from *Partisan Review*, Volume 26, Summer 1959. Reprinted by permission of Diana Trilling.

William Trowbridge. "Enter Dark Stranger" from *Enter Dark Stranger* by William Trowbridge. Copyright © 1989. Reprinted by permission of the University of Arkansas Press.

John Updike. "Dog's Death" from *Midpoint and Other Poems* by John Updike. Copyright © 1969 by John Updike. "Player Piano" from *The Carpentered Hen and Other Tame Creatures* by John Updike. Copyright © 1956 by John Updike. Both reprinted by permission of Alfred A. Knopf, Inc.

Alice Walker. "Revolutionary Petunias" from *Revolutionary Petunias and Other Poems*, copyright © 1972 by Alice Walker, reprinted by permission of Harcourt Brace Jovanovich, Inc.

Robert Wallace. "The Double-Play" copyright © 1961 by Robert Wallace from *Views of a Ferris Wheel*. Reprinted by permission of the author.

Robert Weisbuch. "On Dickinson's Use of Analogy" from *Emily Dickinson's Poetry* by Robert Weisbuch. Copyright © 1975. Reprinted by permission of The University of Chicago Press.

Richard Wilbur. "Year's End" from *Ceremony and Other Poems*, copyright 1949 and renewed 1977 by Richard Wilbur. "The Writer" from *The Mind Reader*, copyright © 1971 by Richard Wilbur. "Sleepless at Crown Point" from *The Mind Reader*, copyright © 1973 by Richard Wilbur. "Love Calls Us to the Things of This World" from *Things of This World*, copyright © 1956 and renewed 1984 by Richard Wilbur. "A Late Aubade" from *Walking to Sleep*, copyright © 1968 by Richard Wilbur. All reprinted by permission of Harcourt Brace Jovanovich, Inc.

C. K. Williams. "The Mirror" from *A Dream of Mind* by C. K. Williams. Copyright © 1992 by C. K. Williams. Reprinted by permission of Farrar, Straus & Giroux, Inc. First published in *The New Yorker*, October 21, 1991.

Miller Williams. "After a Bruebeck Concert" and "Ruby Tells All" from *Imperfect Love* Poems by Miller Williams. Copyright © 1983, 1984, 1985, 1986 by Miller Williams. Reprinted by Permission of Louisana State University Press.

William Carlos Williams. "Poem", "The Red Wheelbarrow," "Spring and All," and "This is Just to Say" from *The Collected Poems of William Carlos Williams, 1909–1939, vol. I*. Copyright 1938 by New Directions Publishing Corp. Reprinted by permission of New Directions Publishing Corporation.

Cynthia Griffin Wolff. "On the Many Voices in Dickinson's Poetry" from *Emily Dickinson* by Cynthia Griffin Wolff. Copyright © 1986 by Cynthia Griffin Wolff. Reprinted by permission of Alfred A. Knopf, Inc.

James Wright. "Lying in a Hammock at William Duffy's Farm in Pine Island, Minnesota" from *The Branch Will Not Break*. Copyright © 1961 by James Wright. Wesleyan University Press by permission of University Press of New England.

William Butler Yeats. "The Second Coming" reprinted with permission of Macmillan Publishing Company from *The Poems of W. B. Yeats: A New Edition*, edited by Richard J. Finneran. Copyright 1924 by Macmillan Publishing Company, renewed 1952 by Bertha Georgie Yeats. "Leda and the Swan" and "Sailing to Byzantium" reprinted with permission of Macmillan Publishing Company from *The Poems of W. B. Yeats: A New Edition*, edited by Richard J. Finneran. Copyright 1928 by Macmillan Publishing Company, renewed 1956 by Georgie Yeats. "Crazy Jane Talks with the Bishop" reprinted with permission of Macmillan Publishing Company from *The Poems of W. B. Yeats: A New Edition*, ed. by Richard J. Finneran. Copyright 1933 by Macmillan Publishing Company, renewed 1961 by Bertha Georgie Yeats.

DRAMA

Anonymous. "A Nineteenth-Century Husband's Letter to His Wife," trans. by Hans Panofsky. Original German text in the Archive of the Leo Baeck Institute, New York. Reprinted by permission of the Leo Baeck Institute and Nancy Panofsky.

Jean Anouilh. "A Scene from *Antigone*" from *Antigone* by Jean Anouilh, adapted and translated by Lewis Galantiere. Copyright 1946 by Random House, Inc. and renewed 1974 by Lewis Galantiere. Reprinted by permission of Random House, Inc.

Aristotle. "On Tragic Character" reprinted from *Aristotle's Poetics*, Trans. by James Hutton, by permission of W. W. Norton & Company, Inc. Copyright © 1982 by W. W. Norton & Company, Inc.

Linda Bamber. "Feminine Rebellion and Masculine Authority in *A Midsummer Night's Dream*." Reprinted from *Comic Women, Tragic Men: A Study of Gender and Genre in Shakespeare* by Linda Bamber with the permission of the publishers, Stanford University Press. © 1982 by the Board of Trustees of the Leland Stanford Junior University.

Samuel Beckett. *Krapp's Last Tape*, copyright © 1958 by Grove Press, Inc. Used permission of Grove Press, Inc.

Eric Bentley. "On Drama as Literature and Performance" reprinted by permission of Applause Books from *Life of the Drama* by Eric Bentley. Copyright © 1964 by Eric Bentley.

Richard Bernstein. "The News Source for *M. Butterfly*" from "France Jails 2 in Odd Case of Espionage" by Richard Bernstein, May 11, 1986. Copyright © 1950/86 by the New York Times Company. Reprinted by permission.

R. G. A. Buxton. "The Major Critical Issue in *Antigone*," excerpted from *Sophocles* by R. G. A. Buxton (Classical Association and The Joint Association of Classical Teachers). Copyright © 1984. Reprinted by permission of Oxford University Press.

Anton Chekhov. *The Cherry Orchard* from *The Major Plays of Anton Chekhov* by Anton Chekhov, trans. Ann Dunnigan. Translation copyright © 1964 by Ann Dunnigan. Used by permission of New American Library, a division of Penguin Books USA Inc.

Errol Durbach. "The Function of the Christmas Tree in *A Doll House*" reprinted with permission of Twayne Publishers, an imprint of Macmillan Publishing Company, from *A Doll's House: Ibsen's Myth of Transformation* by Errol Durbach. Copyright © 1991 by G. K. Hall & Co.

LITERARY THEORY

Anne Bradstreet. Excerpt from "The Flesh and the Spirit" reprinted by permission of the publishers from *The Works of Anne Bradstreet*, ed. Jeannine Hensley, Cambridge, Mass.: Harvard University Press, Copyright © 1967 by the President and Fellows of Harvard College.

Andrew P. Debicki. "New Criticism and Deconstructionism: Two Attitudes in Teaching Poetry" from *Writing and Reading Differently: Deconstruction and the Teaching of Composition and Literature,* edited by G. Douglas Atkins and Michael L. Johnson. Copyright © 1985 by the University Press of Kansas. Reprinted by permission.

Judith Fetterley. "A Feminist Reading of 'A Rose for Emily'" from *The Resisting Reader: A Feminist Approach to American Fiction* by Judith Fetterley. Copyright © 1978. Reprinted by permission of the Indiana University Press.

Henry A. Giroux. "The Canon and Liberal Arts Education," excerpted from "Liberal Arts Education and the Struggle for Public Life: Dreaming about Democracy" *South Atlantic Quarterly* 89:1 (1990) and Glenn and Herrnstein Smith *The Politics of Liberal Education* (1992), copyright Duke University Press. Reprinted with permission of the publisher.

Annette Kolodny. "On the Commitments of Feminist Criticism" from *Dancing Through the Minefield: Some Observations on the Theory, Practice and Politics of a Feminist Literary Criticism. Feminist Studies* 6, 1980. Excerpt reprinted with the permission of the author.

Pedro Salinas. "Presagios" from *The Complete Poems of Pedro Salinas.* Reprinted by permission of Mercedes Casanovas, Barcelona.

Susan Sontag. "Against Interpretation" from *Against Interpretation* by Susan Sontag. Copyright © 1964 by Susan Sontag. Reprinted by permission of Farrar, Straus and Giroux, Inc.

Brook Thomas. "A New Historical Approach to Keats 'Ode on a Grecian Urn,'" excerpt from "The Historical Necessities for — and Difficulties with — New Historical Analysis in Introductory Literature Courses," *College English,* September 1987. Copyright © 1987 by the National Council of Teachers of English. Reprinted with permission.

Index of First Lines

Index of Authors and Titles

Index of Terms